P9-CLR-925

REFERENCE

Best Books for Middle School and Junior High Readers

Grades 6-9

John T. Gillespie
Catherine Barr

Best Books for Middle School and Junior High Readers

Grades 6-9

John T. Gillespie

Catherine Barr

LIBRARIES
UNLIMITED
A Member of the Greenwood Publishing Group

Westport, Connecticut • London

Library of Congress Cataloging-in-Publication Data

Gillespie, John Thomas, 1928–
 Best books for middle school and junior high readers, grades 6–9 / by John T. Gillespie
and Catherine Barr.
  p. cm.
 Continuation of: Best Books for children.
 Includes bibliographical references and index.
 ISBN 1–59158–083–8
 1. Middle school students—Books and reading—United States. 2. Junior high school
students—Books and reading—United States. 3. Preteens—Books and reading—United
States. 4. Teenagers—Books and reading—United States. 5. Children's
literature—Bibliography. 6. Young adult literature—Bibliography. 7. Middle school
libraries—United States—Book lists. 8. Junior high school libraries—United States—Book
lists. I. Barr, Catherine, 1951– II. Gillespie, John Thomas, 1928– Best books for children.
III. Title.
 Z1037.G482 2004
 028.5'35—dc22   2004041798

British Library Cataloguing in Publication Data is available.

Library of Congress Catalog Card Number: 2004041798
ISBN: 1–59158–083–8

First published in 2004

Libraries Unlimited, 88 Post Road West, Westport, CT 06881
A Member of the Greenwood Publishing Group, Inc.
www.lu.com

Printed in the United States of America

The paper used in this book complies with the
Permanent Paper Standard issued by the National
Information Standards Organization (Z39.48–1984).

10 9 8 7 6 5 4 3 2

Contents

Literary History and Criticism

Language and Communication

Biography, Memoirs, Etc.

Philosophy and Religion

Society and the Individual

Guidance and Personal Development

Physical and Applied Sciences

Recreation and Sports

Major Subjects Arranged Alphabetically

Preface

At the present time, librarians and other specialists in children's literature have available, through both online and print sources, a large number of bibliographies that recommend books suitable for young people. Unfortunately, these sources vary widely in quality and usefulness. The Best Books series was created to furnish authoritative, reliable, and comprehensive bibliographies for use in libraries that collect material for readers from preschool through grade 12. The series now consists of three volumes: *Best Books for Children*, *Best Books for Middle and Junior High School Readers*, and *Best Books for High School Readers*.

Best Books for Middle and Junior High School Readers is a continuation of *Best Books for Children* (Libraries Unlimited, 7th edition, 2001) and its two-year supplement (Libraries Unlimited, 2003). *Best Books for Middle and Junior High School Readers* is intended to supply information on books recommended for readers in grades 6 through 9 or roughly ages 11 through 16. *Best Books for Children* contains books recommended for preschool through grade 6 readers and *Best Books for High School Readers* (Libraries Unlimited, 2004) covers grades 9 through 12.

As every librarian knows, reading levels are elastic. There is no such thing, for example, as a seventh-grade book. Instead there are only seventh-grade readers who, in their diversity, can represent a wide range of reading abilities and interests. This bibliography contains a liberal selection of entries that, one hopes, will accommodate readers in these grades and make allowance for their great range of tastes and reading competencies. By the ninth grade, a percentage of the books read should be at the adult level. Keeping this in mind, about one fifth of the entries in this volume are adult books suitable for young adult readers (they are designated by reading level grades of 6–12, 7–12, and 8–12 within the entries). At the other end of the spectrum, there are also many titles that are suitable for readers below the sixth grade (indicated by grade level designations such as 4–7, 4–8, 4–9,

5–7, and 5–8 within the entries). This has resulted in a slight duplication of titles in this book with those in *Best Books for Children*. Similarly, there is a slight overlap with *Best Books for High School Readers*.

In selecting books for inclusion, deciding on their arrangement, and collecting the information supplied on each, it was the editors' intention to reflect the current needs and interests of young readers while keeping in mind the latest trends and curricular emphases in today's schools.

General Scope and Criteria for Inclusion

Of the 14,196 titles listed in *Best Books for Middle and Junior High School Readers*, 13,523 are individually numbered entries and 673 are cited within the annotations as additional recommended titles by the same author (often these are titles that are part of an extensive series). If these titles do not have separate entries elsewhere in the volume, publication dates are generally given. However, some popular titles may have been published in several editions (and some may be out of print); in these cases the year of publication is not given. It should also be noted that some series are so extensive that, because of space limitations, only representative titles are included.

Excluded from this bibliography are general reference works, such as dictionaries and encyclopedias, except for a few single-volume works that are so heavily illustrated and attractive that they can also be used in the general circulation collection. Also excluded are professional books for librarians and teachers and mass market series books.

For most fiction and nonfiction, a minimum of two recommendations were required from the current reviewing sources consulted for a title to be considered for listing. However, there were a number of necessary exceptions. For example, in some reviewing journals only a few representative titles from extensive nonfiction series are reviewed even though others in the series will also be recommended. In such cases a single favorable review was enough for inclusion. This also held true for some of the adult titles suitable for young adult readers where, it has been found, reviewing journals tend to be less inclusive than with juvenile titles. Again, depending on the strength of the review, a single positive one was sufficient for inclusion. As well as favorable reviews, additional criteria such as availability, up-to-dateness, accuracy, usefulness, and relevance were considered. All titles were in print as of the end of February 2004.

Sources Used

A number of current and retrospective sources were used in compiling this bibliography. Of the retrospective sources, two were used extensively. They were *Best Books for Young Adult Readers* (Bowker, 1997) and *Best Books for Young Teen Readers* (Bowker, 2000). After out-of-print titles were removed, remaining entries in these bibliographies were evaluated for content, suitability, and currency before inclusion was recommended.

Book reviewing journals were consulted to obtain entries published after August 1999, when coverage in *Best Books for Young Teen Readers* ended. These current sources were *Booklist*, *Library Media Connection* (formerly *Book Report*), *School Library Journal*, and *VOYA (Voice of Youth Advocates)*. Other sources used include *Bulletin of the Center for Children's Books*, *Horn Book*, and *Horn Book Guide*. Reviews in issues of these journals were read and evaluated from September 1999 through January 2004, when this book's coverage ends.

Uses of This Book

Best Books for Middle and Junior High School Readers was designed to help librarians and media specialists with four vital tasks: (1) evaluating the adequacy of existing collections; (2) building new collections or strengthening existing holdings; (3) providing reading guidance to young adults; and (4) preparing bibliographies and reading lists. To increase the book's usefulness, particularly in preparation of bibliographies or suggested reading lists, titles are arranged under broad areas of interest or, in the case of nonfiction works, by curriculum-oriented subjects rather than the Dewey Decimal classification (suggested Dewey classification numbers are nevertheless provided within nonfiction entries). The subject arrangement corresponds roughly to the one used in *Best Books for Children*, minus its large section on picture books.

Some arbitrary decisions were made concerning placement of books under specific subjects. For example, books of experiments and projects in general science are placed under "Physical and Applied Sciences—Experiments and Projects," whereas books of experiments and projects on a specific branch of science (e.g., physics) appear under that branch. It is hoped that use of the many "see" and "see also" references in the Subject/Grade Level Index will help guide the user in this regard.

Arrangement

In the Table of Contents, subjects are arranged by the order in which they appear in the book. Following the Table of Contents is a listing of Major Subjects Arranged Alphabetically, which provides entry numbers as well as page numbers for easy access. Following the main body of the text, there are three indexes. The Author Index cites authors and editors, titles, and entry numbers (joint authors and editors are listed separately). The Title Index gives the book's entry number. Works of fiction in both of these indexes are indicated by (F) following the entry number. Finally, an extensive Subject/Grade Level Index lists entry numbers under hundreds of subject headings with specific grade-level suitability given for each entry. The following codes are used to identify general grade levels:

IJ   (Intermediate-Junior High) suitable for upper elementary and lower middle school

J   (Junior High) suitable for middle school and junior high

JS   (Junior-Senior High) suitable for junior high and senior high

Entries

A typical entry contains the following information where applicable: (1) author, joint author, or editor; (2) title and subtitle; (3) specific grade levels given in parentheses; (4) adapter or translator; (5) indication of illustrations; (6) publication date; (7) publisher and price of hardbound edition (LB = library binding); (8) International Standard Book Number (ISBN) of hardbound edition; (9) paperback publisher (paper) and price (if no publisher is listed it is the same as the hardbound edition); (10) ISBN of paperback edition; (11) annotation; (12) review citations; (13) Dewey Decimal classification number.

Review Citations

Review citations are given for books published and reviewed from 1985 through January 2004. These citations can be used to find more detailed information about each of the books listed. The periodical sources identified are:

Book Report (BR)
Booklist (BL)
Bulletin of the Center for Children's Books (BCCB)
Horn Book (HB)
Horn Book Guide (HBG)
Library Media Connection (LMC)
School Library Journal (SLJ)
VOYA (Voice of Youth Advocates) (VOYA)

Acknowledgments

With this volume, I am happy to announce a new coauthor/editor, Catherine Barr. Ms. Barr has been involved in the production of previous editions of the Best Books series, including the 2003 supplement to *Best Books for Children*, as well as many, many other publications. I welcome her expert- · ise in the field, as well as her fine organizational and administrative talents. Many other people should be thanked for helping in the preparation of this bibliography. In particular, let me single out our computer genius Julie Miller and our editor-in-chief, Barbara Ittner. Thank you all.

John Gillespie

Literary Forms

Fiction

Adventure and Survival Stories

1 Aaron, Chester. *Lackawanna* (6–9). 1986, Harper-Collins LB $11.89 (0-397-32058-2). In Depression New York, the youthful Lackawanna gang sets out to find a member who has been kidnapped. (Rev: BL 2/15/86; BR 9–10/86; SLJ 4/86; VOYA 6/86)

2 Aaron, Chester. *Out of Sight, Out of Mind* (6–9). 1985, HarperCollins LB $11.89 (0-397-32101-5). Twins with psychic powers are pursued by foreign agents who want their secret. (Rev: BR 3–4/86; VOYA 12/85)

3 Adams, W. Royce. *Me and Jay* (5–8). 2001, Rairarubia paper $10.99 (1-58832-021-9). Two 13-year-olds meet with trouble at every turn when they venture into forbidden territory in search of a hidden pond. (Rev: BL 1/1–15/02)

4 Aiken, Joan. *Dangerous Games* (4–7). Series: Wolves Chronicles. 1999, Delacorte $15.95 (0-385-32661-0). Dido Twite sets out on an adventurous quest to find Lord Herodsfoot, whose knowledge of clever games could help cheer the ailing King James. (Rev: BL 3/1/99; HB 1–2/99; HBG 10/99; SLJ 1/99)

5 Aiken, Joan. *Is Underground* (6–8). 1993, Dell paper $3.99 (0-440-41068-1). Is Twite seeks the whereabouts of Arun, her cousin, and Davy Suart, the king's son, who vanished in London under suspicious circumstances. Part of a long, entertaining series about the Twites. (Rev: BL 4/1/93)

6 Aiken, Joan. *Midnight Is a Place* (7–10). Series: Wolves Chronicles. 1974, Scholastic paper $2.95 (0 590 45406 X). In Victorian England, two young waifs are cast adrift in a hostile town when their guardian's house burns.

7 Aiken, Joan. *Midwinter Nightingale* (5–8). Series: Wolves Chronicles. 2003, Delacorte $15.95 (0-385-73081-0). Dido Twite and Simon, Duke of Battersea, continue their adventures in this eighth installment in the series, protecting a dying king, searching for a missing coronet, and defeating an evil baron. (Rev: BL 6/1–15/03; HBG 10/03; SLJ 6/03)

8 Alexander, Lloyd. *The Drackenberg Adventure* (5–8). 1988, Dell paper $3.99 (0-440-40296-4). This atypical heroine deals with villains and gypsies and attends the diamond jubilee of Maria-Sophia of Drackenberg. Part of series that includes *The Illyrian Adventure* (Bantam 1995); *The El Dorado Adventure* (Bantam 1990). (Rev: BCCB 6/88)

9 Alexander, Lloyd. *Gypsy Rizka* (4–7). 1999, Puffin paper $5.99 (0-14-130980-6). A delightful adventure story featuring Rizka, a young gypsy who lives alone in her wagon and becomes involved in a series of hilarious situations with the neighboring townspeople. (Rev: BL 3/15/99*; HB 3–4/99; HBG 10/99; SLJ 3/99)

10 Alexander, Lloyd. *The Illyrian Adventure* (6–9). 1986, Dell paper $3.99 (0-440-40297-2). Vesper Holly and her companion Brinnie get involved in an archaeological expedition and unforeseen adventure in this, the first of a recommended series. (Rev: BL 4/1/86; BR 11–12/86; SLJ 5/86; VOYA 12/86)

11 Alexander, Lloyd. *The Jedera Adventure* (5–8). 1989, Dell paper $4.50 (0-440-40295-6). Vesper decides to return a valuable library book borrowed by her late father, but the library is in the mythical kingdom of Jedera. (Rev: BL 6/1/89)

12 Alexander, Lloyd. *Westmark* (7–10). 1981, Dell paper $4.50 (0-440-99731-3). In this first of three volumes, Theo, in the imaginary kingdom of Westmark, joins revolutionaries intent on establishing a democracy. Also in this series *The Beggar Queen* (1984). (Rev: BL 12/15/89)

13 Anderson, Scott. *Unknown Rider* (6–9). 1995, Dennoch Pr. paper $12.50 (0-9644521-0-3). Combining fact and fiction, this is the story of fighter pilot Rick Wedon — his training, experiences in officer school, and his missions. (Rev: VOYA 8/96)

14 Asai, Carrie. *The Book of the Sword* (6–12). Series: Samurai Girl. 2003, Simon & Schuster paper $6.99 (0-689-85948-1). Heaven abandons her adoptive family when her brother is murdered in the middle of her arranged wedding and devotes herself to studying to be a samurai and avenging her brother. (Rev: SLJ 8/03)

15 Ashby, John. *Sea Gift* (6–8). 2003, Clarion $15.00 (0-395-77603-1). Lauchie and his friends set off on an exciting treasure hunt on the coast of Cape Breton Island after they discover a pistol and letter dating to 1632. (Rev: BL 9/15/03; SLJ 12/03)

16 Ashley, Bernard. *Break in the Sun* (6–9). Illus. 1980, Phillips $26.95 (0-87599-230-7). Patsy Bleigh runs away on a ship belonging to a theatrical company.

17 Ashley, Bernard. *A Kind of Wild Justice* (6–9). Illus. 1978, Phillips $26.95 (0-87599-229-3). Ronnie is threatened by the same gang that made his father a criminal.

18 Avi. *Captain Grey* (5–8). 1993, Morrow paper $4.95 (0-688-12234-5). In 1783, young Kevin is captured by pirates. A reissue.

19 Avi. *The Christmas Rat* (4–7). 2000, Simon & Schuster $16.00 (0-689-83842-5). Eric finds that he is on the side of the rat that is hiding in a basement storage area and is being hunted by a mysterious exterminator. (Rev: BCCB 10/00; BL 9/1/00; HB 11–12/00; HBG 3/01)

20 Avi. *Windcatcher* (4–7). 1991, Macmillan $16.95 (0-02-707761-6); Avon paper $4.99 (0-380-71805-7). Eleven-year-old Tony dreads a summer by the sea, but ends up finding a sailing adventure. (Rev: BCCB 5/91; BL 3/1/91; HB 5–6/91; SLJ 4/91)

21 Bacon, Katharine Jay. *Finn* (5–9). 1998, Simon & Schuster $16.00 (0-689-82216-2). After a traumatizing plane crash that killed his family, 15-year-old Finn refuses to talk until encounters with drug dealers force him to choose between remaining silent or saving his few remaining loved ones. (Rev: BCCB 11/98; BL 12/1/98; HBG 3/99; SLJ 11/98; VOYA 12/98)

22 Baillie, Allan. *Secrets of Walden Rising* (6–8). 1997, Viking $13.99 (0-670-87351-9). Murder and adventure mix in this story about two boys and their quest for gold in a part of Australia stricken by a severe drought. (Rev: BL 4/1/97; BR 1–2/98; HBG 3/98; SLJ 5/97)

23 Baird, Thomas. *Finding Fever* (6–8). 1982, HarperCollins $12.95 (0-06-020353-6). Kidnappers make off with Benny's sister's dog, and Benny sets out to investigate.

24 Bartholomew, Lois Thompson. *The White Dove* (5–8). 2000, Houghton $15.00 (0-618-00464-5). In this adventure story set in a mythical kingdom, Princess Tasha escapes from the evil Com and must undertake a dangerous mission to help overthrow the tyrant. (Rev: BL 3/1/00; HBG 10/00; SLJ 5/00)

25 Bawden, Nina. *Rebel on a Rock* (6–8). 1978, HarperCollins LB $13.89 (0-397-32140-6). Jo reluctantly believes that her stepfather is a spy for a cruel dictator.

26 Bernardo, Anilu. *Jumping Off to Freedom* (7–10). 1996, Arte Publico paper $9.95 (1-55885-088-0). The story of four refugees, including teenage David, on a harrowing voyage from Cuba to Florida on a raft. (Rev: BL 5/1/96; BR 9–10/96; SLJ 7/96; VOYA 6/96)

27 Blades, Ann. *A Boy of Tache* (6–9). 1995, Tundra paper $5.95 (0-88776-350-2). A Canadian novel of a boy's trek through the wilderness to save his grandfather's life.

28 Bodett, Tom. *Williwaw* (5–8). 1999, Random paper $5.50 (0-375-80687-3). The story of two youngsters — 13-year-old September Crane and her 12-year-old brother Ivan — and their life in the wilds of Alaska, where they are often left alone by their fisherman father. (Rev: BCCB 6/99; BL 4/1/99; HBG 10/99; SLJ 5/99)

29 Booth, Martin. *Panther* (4–7). 2001, Simon & Schuster $15.00 (0-689-82976-0). In this fast-moving plot set in England's West Country, Simon and Pati are convinced that there's a panther around and set out to track it. (Rev: BCCB 3/01; BL 2/1/01; HBG 10/01)

30 Brand, Max. *Dan Barry's Daughter* (7–12). 1976, Amereon LB $25.95 (0-88411-516-X). Harry is an accused murderer who, though innocent, is forced to hide. One of many recommended westerns by this prolific author.

31 Bunting, Eve. *The Hideout* (5–7). 1991, Harcourt $14.95 (0-15-233990-6). Andy decides to stage his own kidnapping so he can join his father in England. (Rev: BCCB 4/91; BL 4/1/91; SLJ 5/91)

32 Bunting, Eve. *Someone Is Hiding on Alcatraz Island* (5–8). 1986, Berkley paper $4.99 (0-425-10294-7). A boy and a young woman ranger are trapped by a gang of thugs on Alcatraz. (Rev: BL 7/88)

33 Bunting, Eve. *SOS Titanic* (6–9). 1996, Harcourt $13.00 (0-15-200271-5); paper $6.00 (0-15-201305-9). During his voyage on the *Titanic*, 15-year-old Barry O'Neill learns about the inequities of the class system and the true meaning of heroism. (Rev: BL 3/15/96; SLJ 4/96; VOYA 6/96)

34 Butler, Geoff. *The Hangashore* (6–8). Illus. 1998, Tundra $15.95 (0-88776-444-4). A picture book for older children about a stubborn, self-righteous magistrate from England who changes his mind about a slow-witted local boy and his own role in the Newfoundland community after the boy saves his life. (Rev: HBG 3/99; SLJ 2/99)

35 Butler, William. *The Butterfly Revolution* (7–12). 1961, Ballantine paper $6.50 (0-345-33182-6). A frightening story of problems in a boy's camp told in diary form by one of the campers.

36 Byars, Betsy. *Coast to Coast* (5–8). 1994, Dell paper $3.99 (0-440-40926-8). The adventures of Birch, 13, and her grandfather, who fly a Piper Cub from South Carolina to California. (Rev: BL 12/1/92; SLJ 1/93)

37 Cage, Elizabeth. *Spy Girls: License to Thrill* (6–9). Series: Spy Girls. 1998, Pocket Books paper $4.50 (0-671-02286-5). Three young women are recruited by the Tower, a part of the CIA, to find a document in the U.S. Embassy in London that lists the location of leftover Soviet nuclear warheads. (Rev: BL 3/1/99; SLJ 2/99)

38 Campbell, Eric. *The Place of Lions* (6–9). 1991, Harcourt $17.00 (0-15-262408-2). When their plane crashes over the Serengeti, Chris and his injured father must learn a lesson in survival while surrounded by poachers and a pride of lions. (Rev: BL 11/15/91; SLJ 11/91)

39 Campbell, Eric. *The Shark Callers* (7–10). 1994, Harcourt $10.95 (0-15-200007-0); paper $4.95 (0-15-200010-0). Parallel stories of two boys' survival in Papua New Guinea during a volcanic eruption and tidal wave. (Rev: BL 11/15/94; SLJ 9/94; VOYA 10/94)

40 Carey, D. L. *Twist of Fate* (5–9). Series: Distress Call 911. 1996, Archway paper $3.99 (0-671-55306-2). A light adventure story, the first in a series, about three teenagers who are involved in the emergency medical volunteer program at a local hospital. (Rev: VOYA 8/96)

41 Carter, Alden R. *Between a Rock and a Hard Place* (6–9). 1995, Scholastic paper $14.95 (0-590-48684-5). An exciting survival novel involving two boys on a 10-day canoe trip through the Minnesota lake country. (Rev: BL 1/1–15/96*; BR 3–4/96; SLJ 12/95; VOYA 4/96)

42 Casanova, Mary. *When Eagles Fall* (6–9). 2002, Hyperion $15.99 (0-7868-0665-6). Thirteen-year-old Alex, who isn't coping well with her brother's death and parents' divorce, is sent to help her father with eagle research and winds up stranded on a remote island with a wounded eaglet. (Rev: BL 6/1–15/02; HBG 10/02; SLJ 7/02; VOYA 2/03)

43 Cavanagh, Helen. *Panther Glade* (5–8). 1993, Simon & Schuster paper $16.00 (0-671-75617-6). Bill spends a summer in Florida with his great-aunt Cait. He's afraid of the Everglades and alligators, but he comes to appreciate Indian history and crafts. (Rev: BL 6/1–15/93; SLJ 6/93; VOYA 10/93)

44 Clark, Clara Gillow. *Willie and the Rattlesnake King* (5–7). 1997, Boyds Mills $14.95 (1-56397-654-4). When 13-year-old Willie joins a traveling medicine show he finds that life on the road isn't as glamorous as he expected. (Rev: BL 12/1/97; HBG 3/98; SLJ 11/97)

45 Coleman, Michael. *Weirdo's War* (5–8). 1998, Orchard paper $16.95 (0-531-30103-6). Noted for being the class misfit, Daniel is paired with Tozer, his nemesis, on a class excursion in this life-or-death survival story. (Rev: BCCB 11/98; BL 8/98; BR 5–6/99; HB 9–10/98*; HBG 3/99; SLJ 10/98; VOYA 4/99)

46 Cooney, Caroline B. *Flash Fire* (7–10). 1995, Scholastic paper $14.95 (0-590-25253-4). A girl's wish for a more exciting life comes true when a fire sweeps the wealthy Los Angeles neighborhood where she lives. (Rev: BL 11/1/95; SLJ 12/95; VOYA 12/95)

47 Cooney, Caroline B. *Flight No. 116 Is Down* (7–10). 1992, Scholastic paper $14.95 (0-590-44465-4). With a lightning pace, the author depicts the drama and human interest inherent in disaster. (Rev: BL 1/15/92; SLJ 2/92)

48 Cooney, Caroline B. *The Terrorist* (6–10). 1997, Scholastic paper $4.99 (0-590-22854-4). Teenage Laura devotes all her energies to finding the terrorist whose bomb was responsible for her young brother's death in London. (Rev: BL 7/97; BR 9–10/97; SLJ 9/97; VOYA 10/97)

49 Cormier, Robert. *After the First Death* (7–12). 1979, Pantheon $14.99 (0-394-94122-5). A busload of schoolchildren become the victims of a terrorist plot.

50 Creech, Sharon. *The Wanderer* (5–9). 2000, HarperCollins LB $16.89 (0-06-027731-9). In this Newbery Honor Book, 13-year-old Sophie, her two cousins, and three uncles sail across the Atlantic to England in a 45-foot yacht. (Rev: BCCB 4/00*; BL 4/1/00; HB 5–6/00; HBG 10/00; SLJ 4/00*)

51 Cunningham, Julia. *Dorp Dead* (6–8). Illus. 1993, Random paper $2.99 (0-679-84718-9). Gilly seeks freedom as an apprentice of Kobalt and finds instead that he's a prisoner.

52 Curry, Jane L. *The Big Smith Snatch* (5–7). 1989, Macmillan LB $16.00 (0-689-50478-0). The Smith children, fending for themselves in their parents' absence, discover that they have been kidnapped. (Rev: BL 9/1/89; SLJ 10/89)

53 Curry, Jane L. *The Great Smith House Hustle* (4–7). 1993, Macmillan $14.95 (0-689-50580-9). The Smith children uncover a real estate scam and help save their grandmother's house from being sold. (Rev: BL 5/1/93; SLJ 8/93)

54 Cussler, Clive. *Inca Gold* (5–9). 1998, Archway paper $4.99 (0-671-02056-0). In this successful adaption of the adult novel, Dirk Pitt and sidekick Al Giordino look for two scientists who disappeared in an Inca sacrificial well, and not only find them in an unexpected place but discover a new dead body and an old one as well. (Rev: VOYA 6/99)

55 Cussler, Clive. *Shock Wave* (5–9). 1999, Pocket Books paper $4.99 (0-671-02055-2). An abridgement for younger readers of Cussler's adult title about a plot to shatter the diamond market, and a mysterious plague that kills thousands of people and animals. (Rev: SLJ 4/99; VOYA 6/99)

56 DeFelice, Cynthia. *Lostman's River* (5–7). 1994, Macmillan LB $15.00 (0-02-726466-1). Tyler's trust is betrayed when he takes an eccentric scientist to a secret rookery in the Everglades and the man reveals himself to be an unscrupulous plume hunter. (Rev: BCCB 6/94; BL 5/15/94; HB 9–10/94; SLJ 7/94)

57 Demers, Barbara. *Willa's New World* (5–8). 2000, Coteau paper $6.95 (1-55050-150-X). An adventure story set in Canada around 1800 in which 15-year-old Willa is sent to a trading post on Hudson's Bay. (Rev: BL 9/15/00; SLJ 9/00)

58 Disher, Garry. *Ratface* (5–9). 1994, Ticknor $14.95 (0-395-69451-5). Kidnapped by a racist Australian cult known as the White League, Max, Christina, and Stefan escape captivity and are pursued by Ratface, a cult deputy. (Rev: BL 11/1/94; SLJ 12/94; VOYA 2/95)

59 Dowd, John. *Rare and Endangered: A Caribbean Island Eco-Adventure* (6–8). 2000, Peachtree paper $5.95 (1-56145-217-3). While tagging turtles on an exotic island, Jim and Julia must save themselves and their friend Miles from evil poachers. (Rev: SLJ 7/00; VOYA 6/00)

60 Doyon, Stephanie. *Leaving Home* (8–12). Series: On the Road. 1999, Simon & Schuster paper $4.50 (0-689-82107-7). High school graduate Miranda and friend Kirsten decide to postpone college for a year to travel cross-country. (Rev: BL 6/1–15/99; SLJ 9/99)

61 Duey, Kathleen, and Karen A. Bale. *Train Wreck: Kansas, 1892* (4–7). Series: Survival! 1999, Simon & Schuster paper $4.50 (0-689-82543-9). Two youngsters who are apprentices in a circus find themselves in a dangerous situation. (Rev: SLJ 6/99)

62 Dygard, Thomas J. *River Danger* (5–9). 1998, Morrow $15.99 (0-688-14852-2). An adventure story in which an older and younger brother happen on a car-theft ring while on a canoe trip in Arkansas. (Rev: BL 3/15/98; BR 11–12/98; HBG 10/98; SLJ 5/98)

63 Elmer, Robert. *Follow the Star* (5–8). Series: Young Underground. 1997, Bethany paper $5.99 (1-55661-660-0). In post–World War II Denmark, Henrik believes that his mother is being held captive by the Russians, who believe she is a spy. (Rev: SLJ 2/98)

64 Ewing, Lynne. *Drive-By* (5–8). 1996, Harper-Collins paper $4.99 (0-06-440649-0). When Tito's brother is killed in a gang-related shooting, he is bullied and threatened by the gang to reveal where his brother hid a cache of stolen money. (Rev: SLJ 8/96)

65 Fama, Elizabeth. *Overboard* (4–8). 2002, Cricket $15.95 (0-8126-2652-4). Fourteen-year-old Emily struggles to save her own life and that of a boy named Isman when a ferry sinks off the coast of Sumatra. (Rev: BCCB 6/02; BL 7/02; HBG 10/02; SLJ 7/02)

66 Ferris, Jean. *All That Glitters* (7–10). 1996, Farrar $16.00 (0-374-30204-9). In this adventure, Brian, 16, goes on a scuba-diving expedition with his father and an archaeologist investigating a shipwrecked Spanish galleon. (Rev: BL 2/15/96; SLJ 3/96; VOYA 6/96)

67 Ferris, Jean. *Song of the Sea* (7–9). Series: American Dreams. 1996, Avon paper $3.99 (0-380-78199-9). In the second title of this adventure series, set on the sea and in the Yucatan in 1814, privateer Raider Lyons lies near death as a result of wounds inflicted by the evil Captain Lawrence of the British navy and longs for the love of Rosie. (Rev: VOYA 10/96)

68 Fields, T. S. *Danger in the Desert* (5–7). 1997, Rising Moon $12.95 (0-87358-666-2); paper $6.95 (0-87358-664-6). A survival story about two boys who endure great hardships when they are left without food or supplies in the desert. (Rev: HBG 3/98; SLJ 11/97)

69 Fleck, Earl. *Chasing Bears: A Canoe-Country Adventure* (5–8). 1999, Holy Cow paper $12.95 (0-930100-90-5). An adventure story set near the Minnesota-Canada border that involves Danny, a 12-year-old who is on a canoe trip with his father and older brother. (Rev: SLJ 12/99)

70 Fleischman, Paul. *The Half-a-Moon Inn* (5–7). 1991, HarperCollins paper $4.99 (0-06-440364-5). A young mute boy sets out to find his mother in a violent snowstorm.

71 Fleischman, Sid. *The Ghost in the Noonday Sun* (5–7). 1989, Greenwillow $16.00 (0-688-08410-9); Scholastic paper $3.50 (0-590-43662-7). This pirate story features all the standard ingredients — a shanghaied boy, a villainous captain, and buried treasure. (Rev: VOYA 8/89)

72 Fleischman, Sid. *The Whipping Boy* (5–7). Illus. 1986, Greenwillow $16.99 (0-688-06216-4); Troll paper $4.95 (0-8167-1038-4). Prince Brat and his whipping boy, Jemmy, who takes the blame for all the bad things the prince does, find their roles reversed when they meet up with CutWater and Hold-Your-Nose Billy. Newbery Medal winner, 1987. (Rev: BCCB 3/86; BL 3/1/86; SLJ 5/86)

73 Freedman, Benedict, and Nancy Freedman. *Mrs. Mike* (7–12). 1968, Berkley paper $4.99 (0-425-10328-5). Based on a true story, this tells of Kathy, her love for her Mountie husband Mike, and her hard life in the Canadian Northwest.

74 Garland, Sherry. *The Silent Storm* (4–7). 1993, Harcourt $14.95 (0-15-274170-4). Alyssa, who has lost both of her parents in a violent storm and has become mute because of the trauma, hears that another hurricane is approaching. (Rev: BCCB 4/93; BL 6/1–15/93)

75 George, Jean Craighead. *Julie of the Wolves* (5–8). 1974, HarperCollins LB $16.89 (0-06-021944-0); paper $5.99 (0-06-440058-1). Julie (Inuit name, Miyax) begins a trek across frozen Alaska and is saved only by the friendship of a pack of wolves. Newbery Medal winner, 1973.

76 George, Jean Craighead. *Julie's Wolf Pack* (5–7). Illus. Series: Julie of the Wolves. 1997, HarperCollins LB $17.89 (0-06-027407-7). Kapu, leader of the pack, is captured by researchers in this continuing story of Julie and her wolf friends. (Rev: BL 9/1/97; BR 1–2/98; HBG 3/98; SLJ 9/97; VOYA 6/98)

77 George, Jean Craighead. *My Side of the Mountain* (6–9). 1959, Dutton $15.99 (0-525-44392-4). In this survival story, young Sam Gribley decides to spend a year alone in the Catskill Mountains. (Rev: BL 9/1/89)

78 George, Jean Craighead. *Shark Beneath the Reef* (7–9). 1989, HarperCollins $13.95 (0-06-021992-0); paper $4.95 (0-06-440308-4). The story of a young Mexican boy who is torn between becoming a shark fisherman like his father or going to college to be a marine biologist. (Rev: BL 6/1/89; BR 11–12/89; SLJ 6/89; VOYA 6/89)

79 George, Jean Craighead. *The Talking Earth* (6–8). 1983, HarperCollins LB $16.89 (0-06-021976-9); paper $5.99 (0-06-440212-6). A young Seminole girl spends three months in the Everglades alone. (Rev: BL 11/1/88)

80 George, Jean Craighead. *Tree Castle Island* (4–7). Illus. 2002, HarperCollins LB $16.89 (0-06-000255-7). A boy tests his survival skills in the Okefenokee Swamp, and meets the twin he never knew he had, in this tale rich in details about the setting. (Rev: BL 3/15/02; HBG 10/02; SLJ 5/02)

81 George, Jean Craighead. *Water Sky* (6–8). 1987, HarperCollins $16.89 (0-06-022199-2); paper $5.99

(0-06-440202-9). A boy is sent by his father to an Eskimo whaling camp to learn survival techniques. (Rev: BL 2/1/87; BR 9–10/87)

82 Glenn, Mel. *Foreign Exchange* (7–12). 1999, Morrow $16.99 (0-688-16472-2). Through free-verse reflections of teens and adults, the murder of a small-town girl is explored and, with it, the underlying prejudices, anger, and secrets of the town are revealed. (Rev: BL 4/15/99; SLJ 6/99; VOYA 12/99)

83 Glenn, Mel. *The Taking of Room 114* (8–12). 1997, Dutton $16.99 (0-525-67548-5). A story told in poetry form about a teacher, the villainous M. Wiedermayer, who held his history class hostage at gunpoint, and the backgrounds of the young people in his class. (Rev: BL 3/1/97; BR 11–12/97; SLJ 4/97; VOYA 2/98)

84 Golding, William. *Lord of the Flies* (8–12). 1999, Viking paper $14.00 (0-14-028333-1). When they are marooned on a deserted island, a group of English schoolboys soon lose their civilized ways.

85 Goodman, Joan Elizabeth. *Paradise* (7–12). 2002, Houghton $16.00 (0-618-11450-5). The fictionalized story of Marguerite de la Rocque, who in 1536, after being left on Canada's Isle of Demons by her explorer uncle, struggled to survive along with her maid and the young man she loves. (Rev: BL 11/15/02; HBG 3/03; SLJ 12/02; VOYA 12/02)

86 Gourley, Catherine, ed. *Read for Your Life: Tales of Survival from the Editors of Read Magazine* (5–8). Series: Best of Read. 1998, Millbrook paper $5.95 (0-7613-0344-8). This is a collection of excellent survival stories from 50 years of *Read*, a literary magazine for middle and high school students. (Rev: BL 8/98)

87 Hahn, Mary D. *The Spanish Kidnapping Disaster* (5–7). 1991, Houghton $16.00 (0-395-55696-1); Avon paper $4.50 (0-380-71712-3). Felix is tagging along on her mother's honeymoon in Spain and is not having a good time. (Rev: BCCB 5/91; BL 3/15/91; SLJ 5/91)

88 Harlow, Joan Hiatt. *Star in the Storm* (4–7). Illus. 2000, Simon & Schuster $16.00 (0-689-82905-1). This novel, set in Newfoundland in 1912, tells how a girl and her dog save a ship full of stranded passengers. (Rev: BCCB 3/00; BL 1/1–15/00; HB 3–4/00; HBG 10/00; SLJ 4/00)

89 Harper, Jo. *Delfino's Journey* (6–12). 2001, Texas Tech $15.95 (0-89672-437-9). Delfino and Salvador travel from Mexico to the United States in search of a new life but face many difficult challenges in this novel that interweaves Aztec folklore and information on illegal immigration. (Rev: BL 4/15/01; HBG 10/01)

90 Harrison, Michael. *It's My Life* (6–8). 1998, Holiday $15.95 (0-8234-1363-2). Martin's mother and her lover conspire to "kidnap" Martin to collect a ransom in this British thriller that is told alternately by Martin and his friend, Hannah. (Rev: BCCB 3/98; BL 3/1/98; HB 5–6/98; HBG 9/98; SLJ 4/98; VOYA 8/98)

91 Haugaard, Erik C. *Under the Black Flag* (5–7). 1994, Roberts Rinehart paper $8.95 (1-879373-63-7). Fourteen-year-old William is captured by the pirate Blackbeard and held for ransom in this 18th-century yarn. (Rev: BL 4/1/94; HB 9–10/94; SLJ 5/94)

92 Hausman, Gerald. *Castaways: Stories of Survival* (5–8). 2003, Greenwillow $15.99 (0-06-008598-3). True stories of shipwreck survivors inspired these six tales of endurance and good fortune. (Rev: BL 9/15/03; HBG 10/03; SLJ 6/03)

93 Hausman, Gerald. *Tom Cringle: Battle on the High Seas* (6–8). 2000, Simon & Schuster $16.95 (0-689-82810-1). This action novel set in the Caribbean in 1812 tells how an English boy becomes involved in battles, mutinies, an earthquake, and a shipwreck. (Rev: BCCB 7–8/00; BL 11/1/00; HBG 3/01; SLJ 11/00; VOYA 12/00)

94 Hausman, Gerald. *Tom Cringle: The Pirate and the Patriot* (6–8). 2001, Simon & Schuster $16.00 (0-689-82811-X). Tom Cringle, a 14-year-old lieutenant in the Royal Navy, fights pirates, braves storms, and conquers slave traders in this sequel to *Tom Cringle: Battle on the High Seas* (2000). (Rev: BL 9/15/01; HBG 3/02; SLJ 10/01)

95 Hawks, Robert. *The Richest Kid in the World* (4–8). 1992, Avon paper $2.99 (0-380-76241-2). Josh is kidnapped and taken to the estate of billionaire Grizzle Welch. (Rev: SLJ 5/92)

96 Hearne, Betsy. *Eli's Ghost* (5–7). 1987, Macmillan $13.95 (0-689-50420-9). Eli learns that his mother is not dead but has fled into the swamp, and he goes in search of her. (Rev: BCCB 3/87; BL 4/1/87; SLJ 4/87)

97 Helldorfer, M. C. *Spook House* (5–7). 1989, Pocket paper $2.99 (0-671-72326-X). Will and friends decide to give guided tours of an old abandoned house in their eastern shore Maryland town. (Rev: BL 10/1/89; HB 11–12/92; SLJ 10/89)

98 Heneghan, James. *Torn Away* (7–10). 1994, Viking $14.99 (0-670-85180-9). A teenager, forced to leave his home in Northern Ireland where he wants to stay and fight with the IRA, must join his uncle's family in Canada. (Rev: BL 2/15/94; SLJ 9/94; VOYA 4/94)

99 Hesse, Karen. *Stowaway* (5–8). Illus. 2000, Simon & Schuster $17.95 (0-689-83987-1). Told by an 11-year-old stowaway, this adventurous sea story tells of Captain Cook's two-and-a-half-year voyage around the world beginning in 1768. (Rev: BL 12/15/00; HB 1–2/01; HBG 3/01; SLJ 11/00; VOYA 4/01)

100 Hilgartner, Beth. *A Murder for Her Majesty* (5–8). 1986, Houghton paper $5.95 (0-395-61619-0). Alice disguises herself as a boy to escape her father's murderers. (Rev: BCCB 9/86; SLJ 10/86)

101 Hill, David. *Take It Easy* (7–10). 1997, Dutton $14.99 (0-525-45763-1). After an argument with his father, Rob Kennedy joins a hiking trip in a remote part of New Zealand that turns into a nightmare survival story. (Rev: BL 9/1/97; BR 1–2/98; SLJ 6/97; VOYA 10/97)

102 Hinton, S. E. *The Outsiders* (7–10). 1967, Viking $16.99 (0-670-53257-6). Two rival gangs — the "haves" and "have-nots" — fight it out on the streets of an Oklahoma city. (Rev: BL 11/15/97)

103 Hinton, S. E. *Rumble Fish* (7–10). 1975, Dell paper $5.99 (0-440-97534-4). Rusty-James loses everything he loves most including his brother.

104 Hinton, S. E. *Tex* (7–10). 1979, Dell paper $5.50 (0-440-97850-5). Tex and his 17-year-old older brother encounter problems with family, sex, and drugs.

105 Hinton, S. E. *That Was Then, This Is Now* (7–10). 1971, Viking $15.99 (0-670-69798-2). Bryon discovers that his "brother" Mark is a drug pusher.

106 Hobbs, Will. *The Big Wander* (7–10). 1992, Atheneum $17.00 (0-689-31767-0); Avon paper $5.95 (0-380-72140-6). Clay Lancaster, 14, and his brother Mike are on a "big waner," their last trip together before Mike goes away to college. (Rev: BL 10/15/92*; SLJ 11/92)

107 Hobbs, Will. *Down the Yukon* (5–8). 2001, HarperCollins LB $16.89 (0-06-029540-6). In this sequel to *Jason's Gold*, Jason decides to compete in a race to the new gold fields in Alaska. (Rev: BL 4/1/01; HBG 10/01; SLJ 5/01)

108 Hobbs, Will. *Far North* (7–12). 1996, Morrow $15.95 (0-688-14192-7). Fifteen-year old Gabe, his school roommate, and an elderly Native American are stranded in the Canadian wilderness. The boys survive even after the death of the wise old man. (Rev: BL 7/96; BR 9–10/96; SLJ 9/96; VOYA 2/97)

109 Hobbs, Will. *Ghost Canoe* (6–8). 1997, Morrow $15.95 (0-688-14193-5); Avon paper $5.99 (0-380-72537-1). Mystery, plenty of action, murder, Spanish treasure, and a dangerous villain are some of the elements in this historical adventure set on the northwest coast of Washington state. (Rev: BL 5/1/97; SLJ 4/97; VOYA 8/97)

110 Hobbs, Will. *Jackie's Wild Seattle* (5–8). 2003, HarperCollins $15.99 (0-688-17474-4). In the aftermath of September 11, 2001, Shannon, 14, and her younger brother spend an exciting and healing summer in Seattle with their animal rescuer uncle. (Rev: BL 6/1–15/03; SLJ 5/03; VOYA 8/03)

111 Hobbs, Will. *Jason's Gold* (5–9). 1999, Morrow $16.99 (0-688-15093-4). In this sharply realistic novel, 15-year-old Jason leaves Seattle in 1897 and, with a dog he has saved, heads for the Klondike and gold. (Rev: BL 8/99; HB 9–10/99; HBG 3/00; SLJ 11/99)

112 Hobbs, Will. *The Maze* (6–12). 1998, Morrow $15.95 (0-688-15092-6). After living in a series of foster homes and detention centers, Rick escapes to Canyonlands National Park in Utah where he is befriended by a loner who helps him find himself. (Rev: BL 9/1/98; HBG 3/99; SLJ 10/98; VOYA 2/99)

113 Hobbs, Will. *River Thunder* (8–12). 1997, Delacorte $15.95 (0-385-32316-6). In this sequel to *Downriver* (1996), Troy and his troubled teenage friends undertake an adventure-filled rafting trip through the Grand Canyon. (Rev: BL 9/1/97; BR 3–4/98; HBG 3/98; SLJ 9/97; VOYA 10/97)

114 Hobbs, Will. *Wild Man Island* (7–10). 2002, HarperCollins $15.95 (0-688-17473-6); HarperTrophy paper $5.99 (0-380-73310-2). An adventure story in which 14-year-old Andy becomes stranded on a remote Alaska island, faces many dangers, and tests his dead archaeologist father's theories about the earliest prehistoric immigrants to America. (Rev: BL 4/15/02; HB 7–8/02; HBG 10/02; SLJ 5/02; VOYA 6/02)

115 Holman, Felice. *Slake's Limbo* (5–9). 1974, Macmillan $16.00 (0-684-13926-X); paper $4.99 (0-689-71066-6). Thirteen-year-old Artemis Slake finds an ideal hideaway for four months in the labyrinth of the New York City subway. (Rev: BL 6/1/88)

116 Houston, James. *Frozen Fire* (6–8). 1977, Macmillan $17.95 (0-689-50083-1); paper $4.95 (0-689-71612-5). An Eskimo boy, Kayak, and his white friend set out to find Kayak's father, a prospector who has disappeared. A sequel is *Black Diamond*.

117 Hyde, Dayton O. *Mr. Beans* (5–7). 2000, Boyds Mills $14.95 (1-56397-866-0). In a small town in Oregon in the early 1940s, bully Mugsy wrongfully accuses a tame bear of attacking him, and timid Chirp frees the bear and takes off with him on a wilderness journey. (Rev: BL 11/15/00; HBG 10/01; SLJ 1/01; VOYA 4/01)

118 Hyland, Hilary. *The Wreck of the Ethie* (4–7). 1999, Peachtree paper $7.95 (1-56145-198-3). Told through the eyes of two youngsters, this is a novelization of a true incident in which a dog saved passengers after their ship sank off the coast of Newfoundland. (Rev: SLJ 4/00)

119 Ingold, Jeanette. *The Big Burn* (6–9). 2002, Harcourt $17.00 (0-15-216470-7). A giant forest fire that burned large areas of the Northwest in 1910 forms the backdrop for this adventure story. (Rev: BCCB 7–8/02; BL 6/1–15/02; HBG 3/03; SLJ 8/02; VOYA 8/02)

120 Johnson, Annabel, and Edgar Johnson. *The Grizzly* (5–7). 1964, HarperCollins paper $4.95 (0-06-440036-0). A perceptive story of a father-son relationship in which David, on a camping trip, saves his father's life when a grizzly bear attacks.

121 Karr, Kathleen. *Bone Dry* (5–8). 2002, Hyperion $15.99 (0-7868-0776-8). Young Matthew assists phrenologist Asa B. Cornwall in a hunt for the skull of Alexander the Great in this action-packed adventure story, a sequel to *Skullduggery* (2000). (Rev: BCCB 10/02; BL 9/15/02; HBG 10/03; SLJ 8/02; VOYA 8/02)

122 Kehret, Peg. *Don't Tell Anyone* (4–7). 2000, Dutton $15.99 (0-525-46388-7). After Megan sees a hit-and-run accident, she receives a threatening message in this adventure that also contains forgery, arson, and a kidnapping. (Rev: BCCB 5/00; BL 8/00; HBG 10/00; SLJ 4/00)

123 Kehret, Peg. *Earthquake Terror* (4–7). 1998, Puffin paper $4.99 (0-14-038343-3). A violent earthquake strikes the small island on which 12-year-old Jonathan is alone with his younger sister, Abby. (Rev: BCCB 3/96; BL 1/1–15/96; SLJ 2/96)

124 Kehret, Peg. *Night of Fear* (6–10). 1994, Dutton $14.99 (0-525-65136-5). This suspense novel for reluctant readers concerns the escape attempts of a boy who is abducted and taken on the road by a man who fits the description of a bank robber. (Rev: BL 2/15/94; SLJ 4/94; VOYA 2/94)

125 Kehret, Peg. *Searching for Candlestick Park* (5–8). 1997, Dutton $14.99 (0-525-65256-6). An adventure story about a boy who sets out from Seattle to find his father in San Francisco. (Rev: BL 8/97; BR 3–4/98; HBG 3/98; SLJ 9/97)

126 Klaveness, Jan O'Donnell. *Ghost Island* (7–10). 1987, Dell paper $2.95 (0-440-93097-9). Delia, her mother, and new stepfather encounter both family trauma and a murder involving poachers when they vacation on a remote Canadian lake. (Rev: BL 5/15/85; BR 11–12/85; SLJ 9/85; VOYA 2/86)

127 Konigsburg, E. L. *From the Mixed-Up Files of Mrs. Basil E. Frankweiler* (5–7). 1967, Macmillan $17.00 (0-689-20586-4); Dell paper $4.99 (0-440-43180-8). Adventure, suspense, detection, and humor are involved when 12-year-old Claudia and her younger brother elude the security guards and live for a week in New York's Metropolitan Museum of Art. Newbery Medal winner, 1968.

128 Lamensdorf, Len. *The Crouching Dragon* (6–9). 1999, Seascape $19.95 (0-9669741-5-8). In this novel set in a French coastal town in 1959, 14-year-old William and his friends secretly renovate a crumbling castle called the Crouching Dragon. (Rev: BL 9/1/99; VOYA 12/99)

129 L'Engle, Madeleine. *The Arm of the Starfish* (7–10). 1965, Farrar $18.00 (0-374-30396-7); Dell paper $4.99 (0-440-90183-9). A young scientist becomes involved in intrigue and the disappearance of Polly O'Keefe in this tale of danger.

130 L'Engle, Madeleine. *The Young Unicorns* (7–10). 1968, Farrar $16.00 (0-374-38778-8); Dell paper $5.50 (0-440-99919-7). In this novel set in New York City and involving the Austin family, a young gang threatens the lives of an ex-member and a blind musician.

131 Lester, Alison. *The Snow Pony* (6–12). 2003, Houghton $15.00 (0-618-25404-8). Fourteen-year-old Dusty's love for Snow Pony lightens the problems of her life in this novel set on an Australian cattle ranch. (Rev: BL 3/15/03; HBG 10/03; SLJ 4/03; VOYA 6/03)

132 Levin, Betty. *Fire in the Wind* (4–8). 1995, Greenwillow $15.00 (0-688-14299-0). Meg, a self-sufficient girl who cares for her younger brother and backward cousin, faces a crisis when a raging fire threatens her home. (Rev: BCCB 1/96; SLJ 10/95)

133 Little, Kimberly Griffiths. *Enchanted Runner* (5–7). 1999, Avon $15.00 (0-380-97623-4). Twelve-year-old Kendall, who is half Native American, hopes to excel in running as his ancestors did, and is given an unusual opportunity to test himself. (Rev: BCCB 9/99; BL 9/1/99; HBG 3/00; SLJ 12/99)

134 Lourie, Peter. *The Lost Treasure of Captain Kidd* (5–8). Illus. 1996, Shawangunk Pr. paper $10.95 (1-885482-03-5). Friends Killian and Alex set out to discover Captain Kidd's treasure buried on the banks of the Hudson River centuries ago. (Rev: BL 2/15/96; SLJ 6/96)

135 Macken, Walter. *Island of the Great Yellow Ox* (4–7). 1991, Simon & Schuster paper $14.00 (0-671-73800-3). An Irish boy and two American friends are shipwrecked on an uninhabited island, where they are held captive by ruthless archaeologists and must solve a mystery to survive. (Rev: BL 10/15/91; SLJ 10/91)

136 Marsden, John. *The Dead of Night* (6–10). Series: Tomorrow. 1997, Houghton $16.00 (0-395-83734-0). In this sequel to *Tomorrow, When the War Began* (1996), the teenage group continues its guerrilla activities against their enemy, a country that has invaded their homeland, Australia. (Rev: HBG 3/98; SLJ 11/97; VOYA 2/98)

137 Marsden, John. *A Killing Frost* (7–12). Series: Tomorrow. 1998, Houghton $16.00 (0-395-83735-9). In this third episode of an adventure series about a group of Australian teens who fight an enemy that has occupied their country, five young people carry out a plan to sink a container ship. (Rev: BCCB 4/98; BL 5/15/98; HB 7–8/98; HBG 9/98; SLJ 6/98; VOYA 6/98)

138 Marsden, John. *The Other Side of Dawn* (8–12). Series: Tomorrow. 2002, Houghton $16.00 (0-618-07028-1). Ellie's exploits are at the center of this action-packed seventh and final installment in the Tomorrow series, which leaves Ellie back home after peace has been declared, trying to adjust to postwar life. (Rev: BCCB 10/02; BL 10/15/02; HB 11/02; HBG 3/03; SLJ 10/02; VOYA 2/03)

139 Martin, Les. *X Marks the Spot* (6–9). 1995, HarperCollins paper $4.50 (0-06-440613-X). Based on an episode of the *X-Files*, two FBI agents investigate a series of mysterious deaths in Oregon. Also use *Darkness Falls* (1995). (Rev: VOYA 2/96)

140 Mazer, Harry. *The Island Keeper* (7–10). 1981, Dell paper $3.99 (0-440-94774-X). Feeling completely alone in this world, Cleo decides to run away to a desolate island that her father owns.

141 Mazer, Harry. *Snow Bound* (5–7). 1987, Dell $20.25 (0-8446-6240-2); paper $5.50 (0-440-96134-3). Tony and Cindy survive for several days after being trapped in a snow storm. (Rev: BL 9/1/89)

142 Mazer, Harry, and Norma Fox Mazer. *The Solid Gold Kid* (7–10). 1989, Bantam paper $4.50 (0-553-27851-7). A millionaire's son and four other teenagers are kidnapped.

143 Mikaelsen, Ben. *Red Midnight* (5–9). 2002, HarperCollins LB $15.89 (0-06-001228-5). After soldiers kill their family, a 12-year-old Guatemalan boy and his sister set off on a perilous journey to Florida in a canoe. (Rev: HBG 10/02; SLJ 5/02)

144 Miklowitz, Gloria D. *After the Bomb* (7–12). 1987, Scholastic paper $2.50 (0-590-40568-3). This novel describes the experiences of a group of young people after an atomic bomb falls on Los Angeles. (Rev: BL 6/15/86; SLJ 9/85; VOYA 8/85)

145 Miklowitz, Gloria D. *Camouflage* (8–10). 1998, Harcourt $16.00 (0-15-201467-5). When 14-year-old Kyle visits northern Michigan to spend a summer with his father, he becomes involved in a government-hating militia movement in which his father is a general. (Rev: BCCB 5/98; HBG 9/98; SLJ 4/98; VOYA 10/98)

146 Miller, Frances A. *The Truth Trap* (7–10). 1986, Fawcett paper $4.50 (0-449-70247-2). When Matt's parents are killed in a car accident, he leaves town only to be accused of a murder.

147 Mitchell, Nancy. *Global Warning: Attack on the Pacific Rim!* (5–8). Series: The Changing Earth Trilogy. 1999, Lightstream paper $5.95 (1-892713-02-0). A thrilling adventure story about Jenny Powers, a wheelchair-bound youngster, who must warn the authorities of an impending biological disaster at her school. (Rev: SLJ 10/99)

148 Morey, Walt. *Angry Waters* (6–9). 1990, Blue Heron paper $7.95 (0-936085-10-X). A hostile 15-year-old boy is unwillingly paroled to a family farm, where he comes to terms with himself. (Rev: VOYA 8/90)

149 Morey, Walt. *Death Walk* (6–10). 1991, Blue Heron $13.95 (0-936085-18-5). After being stranded in the Alaskan wilderness, a teenage boy must learn to survive in the harsh climate while on the run from killers. (Rev: BL 6/1/91; SLJ 6/91)

150 Morpurgo, Michael. *The Butterfly Lion* (4–8). 1997, Viking $14.99 (0-670-87461-2). A ghost narrates a touching adventure story about a boy in Africa and his pet lion, who are separated and, years later, reunited during World War I in France. (Rev: BL 6/1–15/97; SLJ 8/97)

151 Morpurgo, Michael. *Kensuke's Kingdom* (4–7). 2003, Scholastic paper $16.95 (0-439-38202-5). A boy washed onto a seemingly deserted island finds a friend in a Japanese solider who has lived there since World War II. (Rev: BL 2/15/03; HB 5–6/03; HBG 10/03; SLJ 3/03; VOYA 6/03)

152 Morrison, Dorothy Nafus. *Whisper Again* (6–8). 1987, Troll paper $2.95 (0-8167-1307-3). Stacey is unhappy when her family has to rent part of their ranch land to a summer camp. This is a sequel to *Whisper Goodbye* (1985). (Rev: BL 9/15/87; SLJ 12/87; VOYA 10/87)

153 Mowat, Farley. *Lost in the Barrens* (7–9). 1985, Bantam paper $5.50 (0-553-27525-9). Two boys lost in the wilderness of northern Canada must fight for survival.

154 Myers, Edward. *Hostage* (5–7). 1996, Hyperion $15.95 (0-7868-0115-8). During a hiking trip in Dinosaur National Monument, two youngsters are held hostage by a man who has stolen a dinosaur egg. (Rev: BCCB 2/96; BL 4/15/96; SLJ 4/96)

155 Myers, Edward. *Survival of the Fittest* (6–9). 2000, Montemayor paper $10.00 (0-9674477-2-0). Rus and his cousins survive a plane crash in the Peruvian rainforest and set off through the dangerous terrain in search of help. (Rev: SLJ 1/01)

156 Myers, Walter Dean. *The Mouse Trap* (6–8). 1990, HarperCollins LB $14.89 (0-06-024344-9). A group of boys in Harlem form a gang to explore a deserted building they believe contains hidden loot. (Rev: BL 4/15/90; SLJ 7/90; VOYA 6/90)

157 Napoli, Donna Jo. *Trouble on the Tracks* (5–7). 1997, Scholastic paper $14.95 (0-590-13447-7). Zach and his younger sister are embroiled in an Australian adventure involving smugglers and survival in a desert. (Rev: BCCB 3/97; BL 2/1/97; SLJ 3/97)

158 Naylor, Phyllis Reynolds. *The Fear Place* (5–7). 1994, Atheneum $16.95 (0-689-31866-9). When two brothers are left alone in a remote mountain camp for a few days, their mounting dislike of each other explodes in this gripping survival story. (Rev: BCCB 1/95; BL 12/15/94; SLJ 12/94)

159 Nolan, Peggy. *The Spy Who Came in from the Sea* (4–8). 1999, Pineapple $14.95 (1-56164-186-3). In this adventure story set in World War II Florida, 14-year-old Frank, who has a reputation for lying, is not believed when he claims to have seen a German sub off the coast. (Rev: HBG 3/00; SLJ 1/00)

160 O'Dell, Scott. *The Black Pearl* (7–9). 1967, Houghton $17.00 (0-395-06961-0). Young Ramon dives into a forbidden cave to collect a fabulous black pearl that in time seems to bring a curse to his family.

161 O'Dell, Scott. *Black Star, Bright Dawn* (5–8). 1988, Houghton $17.00 (0-395-47778-6); Fawcett paper $6.50 (0-449-70340-1). An Inuit girl decides to run the 1,197-mile sled dog race called the Iditarod. (Rev: BCCB 6/88; BL 4/1/88; BR 9–10/88; SLJ 5/88; VOYA 6/88)

162 O'Dell, Scott. *Island of the Blue Dolphins* (5–8). 1960, Houghton $16.00 (0-395-06962-9); Dell paper $6.50 (0-440-43988-4). An Indian girl spends 18 years alone on an island off the coast of California in the 1800s. Newbery Medal winner, 1961. A sequel is *Zia* (1976). (Rev: BL 3/1/88)

163 Olshan, Matthew. *Finn* (8–12). 2001, Bancrof $19.95 (1-890862-13-4); paper $14.95 (1-890862-14-2). Teenage Chloe, who has suffered an abusive childhood, and a pregnant Hispanic girl set off to find new lives in a Huck Finn-like adventure full of insight and social commentary. (Rev: BL 4/1/01; SLJ 4/01; VOYA 4/01)

164 Parkinson, Curtis. *Storm-Blast* (4–8). 2003, Tundra paper $7.95 (0-88776-630-7). On a sailing trip in the Caribbean, three teens become stranded in a small dinghy and must use their resources to survive. (Rev: SLJ 10/03; VOYA 8/03)

165 Patneaude, David. *The Last Man's Reward* (5–8). 1996, Albert Whitman LB $14.95 (0-8075-4370-5). In this adventure, a group of boys agree to a pact rewarding the last to leave the neighborhood. (Rev: BL 6/1–15/96; SLJ 7/96)

166 Paulsen, Gary. *Brian's Hunt* (6–9). 2003, Random $14.95 (0-385-74647-4). This story of Brian's return to the wilderness at the age of 16, his care for a wounded dog, and his distress over the fate of his Cree friends will please Hatchet fans. (Rev: BCCB 2/04; BL 1/1–15/04; SLJ 12/03)

167 Paulsen, Gary. *Brian's Winter* (5–9). 1996, Delacorte $15.95 (0-385-32198-8). In a reworking of the ending of *Hatchet*, in which Brian Robeson is rescued after surviving a plane crash, this novel tells what would have happened had Brian had to survive a harsh winter in the wilderness. (Rev: BL 12/15/95; BR 5–6/96; SLJ 2/96; VOYA 2/97)

168 Paulsen, Gary. *Canyons* (7–10). 1991, Dell paper $5.99 (0-440-21023-2). Brennan becomes obsessed with the story of a young Indian boy murdered by white men 100 years before. (Rev: SLJ 9/90)

169 Paulsen, Gary. *Dogsong* (8–10). 1985, Bradbury LB $16.00 (0-02-770180-8). An Eskimo youth faces hardship and danger when he ventures alone by dogsled into the wilderness. (Rev: BL 4/1/85; SLJ 4/85; VOYA 12/85)

170 Paulsen, Gary. *Hatchet* (6–9). 1987, Macmillan $16.95 (0-02-770130-1). Teenage Brian survives a plane crash in the Canadian wilderness but then must fend for himself. (Rev: BL 11/15/87; SLJ 12/87; VOYA 2/88)

171 Paulsen, Gary. *The Haymeadow* (6–9). Illus. 1992, Dell paper $4.99 (0-440-40923-3). A 14-year-old boy takes sheep out to pasture for the summer in this story about a boy who is trying to gain acceptance by his father. (Rev: BL 5/15/92*; SLJ 6/92)

172 Paulsen, Gary. *The River* (5–10). 1991, Delacorte $15.95 (0-385-30388-2). In this sequel to *Hatchet*, Paulsen takes the wilderness adventure beyond self-preservation and makes teen Brian responsible for saving someone else. (Rev: BL 5/15/91)

173 Paulsen, Gary. *The Voyage of the Frog* (6–8). 1989, Orchard $15.95 (0-531-05805-0); Dell paper $5.50 (0-440-40364-2). Alone on a 22-foot sailboat, a 14-year-old boy survives a 9-day sea ordeal. (Rev: BL 3/1/89; BR 9–10/89; SLJ 1/89; VOYA 2/89)

174 Paulsen, Gary. *The White Fox Chronicles: Escape, Return, Breakout* (6–9). 2000, Delacorte $8.95 (0-385-32254-2). Set in a violent future, this adventure story tells how teenager Cody Pierce, also known as White Fox, rescues a group of prisoners held in a concentration camp. (Rev: BL 8/00; HBG 9/00; SLJ 8/00; VOYA 12/00)

175 Peck, Richard. *Secrets of the Shopping Mall* (7–10). 1979, Dell paper $3.99 (0-440-98099-2). Two 8th-graders find they are not alone when they take up residence in a shopping mall.

176 Peck, Robert Newton. *Arly's Run* (6–9). 1991, Walker $16.95 (0-8027-8120-9). Orphaned Arly escapes from an early 19th-century Florida work farm and journeys to Moore Haven, where shelter has been arranged for him. (Rev: BL 12/15/91; SLJ 2/92)

177 Peck, Robert Newton. *The Cowboy Ghost* (5–9). 1999, HarperCollins LB $15.89 (0-06-028211-8). In order to prove his maturity to his overly critical father, 16-year-old Titus decides to help his brother in a grueling cattle drive across Florida. (Rev: BL 6/1–15/99; HBG 10/99; SLJ 3/99)

178 Peck, Robert Newton. *Nine Man Tree* (5–8). 1998, Random $18.99 (0-679-99257-X). Two children of a kind mother and an abusive father become involved in a hunt for a wild 500-pound boarhog in this novel set in the Florida wetlands. (Rev: BCCB 12/98; BL 8/98; SLJ 11/98)

179 Petersen, P. J. *Rising Water* (6–12). 2002, Simon & Schuster $16.00 (0-689-84148-5). Three teens take on rising floodwater and dangerous villains in a suspenseful story told in alternating voices. (Rev: BCCB 2/02; BL 3/1/02; HBG 10/02; SLJ 2/02)

180 Philbrick, Rodman. *Max the Mighty* (6–9). 1998, Scholastic $16.95 (0-590-18892-5); paper $4.99 (0-590-57964-9). Maxwell Kane and his new friend Worm, who is being abused by her stepfather, run away in a cross-country search for Worm's real father. (Rev: BL 6/1–15/98; BR 9–10/98; HB 7–8/98; HBG 9/98; SLJ 4/98; VOYA 6/98)

181 Phleger, Marjorie. *Pilot Down, Presumed Dead* (7–9). 1988, HarperCollins paper $5.95 (0-06-440067-0). A survival story involving a pilot whose plane crashes off the Baja California coast. A reissue.

182 Pilling, Ann. *The Year of the Worm* (5–7). 2000, Lion paper $7.50 (0-7459-4294-6). Lonely Peter Wrigley, who is mourning his father's death, gets his chance to become a hero when he uncovers a group of birds'-nest poachers in this English novel set in the Lake District. (Rev: SLJ 3/01)

183 Pullman, Philip. *The Tiger in the Well* (8–12). 1996, Demco $11.04 (0-606-09969-7). This conclusion of the rich historical trilogy that began with *The Ruby in the Smoke* (1987) and *The Shadow in the North* (1988) completes the adventures of Victorian heroine Sally Lockhart who, in this novel, encounters a man who wants passionately to destroy her. (Rev: BL 10/15/90)

184 Ransome, Arthur. *Swallows and Amazons* (4–7). 1985, Godine paper $14.95 (0-87923-573-X). These adventures of the four Walker children have been read for many years. A reissue. Others in the series *Swallowdale* (1985); *Peter Duck* (1987).

185 Ransome, Arthur. *Winter Holiday* (4–7). 1989, Godine paper $14.95 (0-87923-661-2). Further adventures of the Swallows and Amazons. A reissue. A sequel is *Coot Club*.

186 Rees, Celia. *Pirates!* (7–10). 2003, Bloomsbury $17.95 (1-58234-816-2). Horrified by the prospect of an arranged marriage to a plantation owner, teenage Nancy and a close slave friend run off and join a pirate crew in this swashbuckling adventure set in the 18th century. (Rev: BCCB 1/04; BL 12/15/03*; SLJ 10/03*)

187 Repp, Gloria. *Mik-Shrok* (4–8). Illus. 1998, Bob Jones Univ. paper $6.49 (1-57924-069-0). A married missionary couple journey to a remote Alaska village in 1950, where they begin their work and, in time, acquire a dog team led by Mik-Shrok. (Rev: BL 3/1/99)

188 Roberts, Willo Davis. *Megan's Island* (5–7). 1988, Macmillan LB $14.95 (0-689-31397-7). Eleven-year-old Megan and her brother are alarmed to discover that someone is following their family. (Rev: BCCB 4/88; BL 5/1/88; BR 9–10/88; SLJ 4/88; VOYA 6/88)

189 Roberts, Willo Davis. *What Could Go Wrong?* (6–9). 1989, Macmillan $15.00 (0-689-31438-8). A seemingly innocent plane trip from Seattle to San Francisco leads three cousins into danger and a confrontation with a gang of money launderers. (Rev: BL 4/15/89; SLJ 3/89; VOYA 8/89)

190 Rochman, Hazel, and Darlene Z. McCampbell, eds. *Leaving Home* (7–12). 1997, HarperCollins LB $16.89 (0-06-024874-2). These 16 stories by well-known writers describe various forms of leaving home, from immigration to a new country to running away or taking a trip. (Rev: BL 1/1–15/97; SLJ 3/97*)

191 Ruckman, Ivy. *Night of the Twisters* (6–8). 1984, HarperCollins paper $5.99 (0-06-440176-6). An account based on actual events about children who survive a devastating series of tornadoes.

192 Salisbury, Graham. *Shark Bait* (7–12). 1997, Bantam paper $4.50 (0-440-22803-4). Set in Hawaii, this novel deals with Eric Chock and his friends, one of whom is determined to kill a sailor like the one his mother ran away with. (Rev: BL 9/1/97; SLJ 9/97; VOYA 6/98)

193 Shahan, Sherry. *Frozen Stiff* (4–7). 1998, Delacorte $14.95 (0-385-32303-4). This exciting survival story set in Alaska involves two cousins, Cody and Derek, and their ill-fated kayak trip into the wilderness. (Rev: BCCB 5/98; BL 7/98; HBG 3/99; SLJ 8/98)

194 Shusterman, Neal. *Dissidents* (7–10). 1989, Little, Brown $13.95 (0-316-78904-6). A teenage boy joins his mother, the American ambassador in Moscow, and becomes involved in a spy caper. (Rev: BL 8/89; BR 11–12/89; SLJ 10/89)

195 Skurzynski, Gloria, and Alane Ferguson. *Cliff-Hanger* (4–7). 1999, National Geographic $15.95 (0-7922-7036-3). In Mesa Verde National Park, the Landon family encounters two problems — a foster care girl named Lucky, who is deceitful, and a rampaging cougar. (Rev: BL 4/15/99; HBG 10/99; SLJ 5/99)

196 Smith, Cotton. *Dark Trail to Dodge* (7–10). 1997, Walker $20.95 (0-8027-4158-4). Eighteen-year-old Tyrel Bannon faces unusual problems on his first cattle drive when rustlers attack and plan on taking no prisoners. (Rev: BL 6/1–15/97; VOYA 8/97)

197 Smith, Roland. *Jaguar* (5–8). 1997, Hyperion $16.49 (0-7868-2226-0). When Jake visits his zoologist father at a jaguar preserve in Brazil, he gets involved in a mystery and, at one point, must sur-

vive alone in the Amazon jungle. A sequel to *Thunder Cave*. (Rev: BL 5/15/97; BR 1–2/98; SLJ 6/97)

198 Smith, Roland. *Sasquatch* (4–7). 1998, Hyperion $15.95 (0-7868-0368-1). In this thrilling adventure story set on Mount St. Helens on the eve of its eruption, Dylan and his father set out to find a Sasquatch that has been sighted in the area. (Rev: BCCB 7–8/98; BL 4/15/98; HBG 10/98; SLJ 6/98; VOYA 10/98)

199 Soto, Gary. *Crazy Weekend* (4–7). 1994, Scholastic paper $13.95 (0-590-47814-1). Two boys are being pursued by some crooks in this fast-moving adventure story. (Rev: BCCB 7–8/94; SLJ 3/94)

200 Sperry, Armstrong. *Call It Courage* (5–8). 1968, Macmillan $16.95 (0-02-786030-2); paper $4.99 (0-689-71391-6). The "Crusoe" theme is interwoven with this story of a Polynesian boy's courage in facing the sea he feared. Newbery Medal winner, 1941.

201 Springer, Nancy. *Lionclaw* (5–8). Series: Tales of Rowan Hood. 2002, Putnam $16.99 (0-399-23716-X). Gentle, music-loving Lionel abandons his timidity when Rowan Hood is captured, but, despite his newfound courage, his father still refuses to accept him in this sequel to *Rowan Hood: Outlaw Girl of Sherwood Forest* (2001). (Rev: BL 10/1/02; HBG 10/03; SLJ 10/02; VOYA 12/02)

202 Springer, Nancy. *Outlaw Princess of Sherwood* (4–7). Series: Tales of Rowan Hood. 2003, Putnam $16.99 (0-399-23721-6). The third installment of this series features Princess Ettarde, whose father has hatched a dastardly plot to lure Etty away from Sherwood Forest. (Rev: BL 12/1/03; SLJ 9/03)

203 Springer, Nancy. *Rowan Hood: Outlaw Girl of Sherwood Forest* (4–7). Series: Tales of Rowan Hood. 2001, Putnam $16.99 (0-399-23368-7). A young girl finds adventure when she journeys to Sherwood Forest to find the father she doesn't know, Robin Hood. (Rev: BL 4/15/01; HBG 10/01; SLJ 7/01; VOYA 6/01)

204 Stewart, A. C. *Ossian House* (6–8). 1976, Phillips LB $26.95 (0-87599-219-6). An 11-year-old boy inherits a mansion in Scotland and sets out alone to live there for the summer.

205 Strasser, Todd. *Shark Bite* (5–8). Series: Against the Odds. 1998, Scholastic paper $3.99 (0-671-02309-8). After a freak storm in the Gulf of Mexico, 12-year-old Ian and friends must abandon their sinking sailboat. (Rev: BL 2/15/99; SLJ 12/98)

206 Strieber, Whitley. *Wolf of Shadows* (6–8). 1985, Knopf $9.99 (0-394-97224-4). A mother and daughter develop a relationship of trust with a pack of wolves after a nuclear war. (Rev: BL 1/1/86; SLJ 10/85; VOYA 4/86)

207 Sullivan, Paul. *The Unforgiving Land* (7–10). 1996, Royal Fireworks paper $9.99 (0-88092-256-7). A white trader gives guns and bullets to a group

13

of Inuit, causing a breakdown in the delicate harmony between nature and humankind and destruction of the Inuit way of life. (Rev: VOYA 8/96)

208 Swarthout, Glendon, and Kathryn Swarthout. *Whichaway* (7–10). 1997, Rising Moon paper $6.95 (0-87358-676-X). A reissue of an exciting story about a boy whose character is tested when he is trapped on top of a windmill with two broken legs in an isolated area of Texas. (Rev: BR 11–12/98; HBG 3/98; VOYA 2/98)

209 Tanaka, Shelley. *On Board the Titanic* (5–7). 1996, Hyperion $16.95 (0-7868-0283-9). Real-life characters are re-created in this story of 17-year-old Jack Thayer and his voyage on the *Titanic* with his parents. (Rev: BCCB 9/96; BL 9/1/96; SLJ 10/96)

210 Taylor, Theodore. *The Cay* (5–8). 1987, Doubleday $16.95 (0-385-07906-0); Avon paper $4.95 (0-380-00142-X). A blind boy and an old black sailor are shipwrecked on a coral island. (Rev: BL 9/1/89)

211 Taylor, Theodore. *The Odyssey of Ben O'Neal* (6–8). 1991, Avon paper $3.99 (0-380-71026-9). Action and humor are skillfully combined in this story of a trip by Ben and his friend Tee to England at the turn of the 20th century. Two others in the series *Teetoncey; Teetoncey and Ben O'Neal* (both 1981).

212 Taylor, Theodore. *Rogue Wave and Other Red-Blooded Sea Stories* (6–10). 1996, Harcourt $16.00 (0-15-201408-X). Eight compelling sea stories involve a range of characters and situations. (Rev: BL 11/1/96; BR 3–4/97; SLJ 4/97; VOYA 4/97)

213 Taylor, Theodore. *Timothy of the Cay: A Prequel-Sequel* (5–7). 1993, Harcourt $16.00 (0-15-288358-4). This tells what happened to the two main characters from the author's *The Cay* before their shipwreck on the Caribbean island and what happened after they were saved. (Rev: BCCB 11/93; BL 9/15/93; SLJ 10/93)

214 Thomas, Jane Resh. *Courage at Indian Deep* (5–7). 1984, Houghton paper $6.95 (0-395-55699-6). A young boy must help save a ship caught in a sudden storm.

215 Thomas, Rob. *Green Thumb* (6–8). 1999, Simon & Schuster $16.00 (0-689-81780-0). While trying to unmask an unscrupulous scientist in the Amazon rain forest, 13-year-old science genius Grady Jacobs becomes a target for murder. (Rev: BL 4/15/99; HBG 9/99; SLJ 6/99; VOYA 8/99)

216 Thompson, Julian. *Brothers* (7–12). 1998, Random $18.99 (0-679-99082-8). Chris trails his unstable brother to an eastern Montana militia camp, where there is a standoff between the zealots and local authorities. (Rev: BL 11/1/98; BR 5–6/99; HBG 3/99; SLJ 11/98; VOYA 10/98)

217 Thompson, Julian. *The Grounding of Group Six* (8–12). 1983, Avon paper $3.99 (0-380-83386-7). Five 16-year-olds think they are being sent to an exclusive school but actually they have been slated for murder.

218 Townsend, John Rowe. *The Islanders* (7–10). 1981, HarperCollins $11.95 (0-397-31940-1). Two strangers washed up on a remote island are regarded as enemies by the inhabitants.

219 Townsend, John Rowe. *Kate and the Revolution* (7–10). 1983, HarperCollins LB $12.89 (0-397-32016-7). A 17-year-old girl is attracted to a visiting prince and then the adventure begins.

220 Ullman, James R. *Banner in the Sky* (7–9). 1988, HarperCollins LB $12.89 (0-397-30264-9); paper $5.99 (0-06-447048-2). The thrilling story of a boy's determination to conquer a challenging Swiss mountain. (Rev: SLJ 2/88)

221 Vanasse, Deb. *Out of the Wilderness* (5–8). 1999, Clarion $15.00 (0-395-91421-3). Fifteen-year-old Josh, his father, and his older half-brother move to Willow Creek, Alaska, where they build a cabin and try to live off the land. (Rev: BL 3/15/99; HBG 10/99; SLJ 4/99; VOYA 8/99)

222 Voigt, Cynthia. *On Fortune's Wheel* (7–12). 1990, Macmillan $17.00 (0-689-31636-4). In this historical adventure, a young runaway couple are captured by pirates and sold into slavery. (Rev: BL 2/15/90; SLJ 3/90; VOYA 4/90)

223 Wallace, Bill. *Danger in Quicksand Swamp* (4–7). 1989, Holiday $16.95 (0-8234-0786-1). While searching for buried treasure, Ben and Jake become stranded on an island near Quicksand Swamp. (Rev: BL 1/1/90; SLJ 10/89)

224 Wallace, Bill. *Skinny-Dipping at Monster Lake* (5–8). 2003, Simon & Schuster $16.95 (0-689-85150-2). Kent helps solve the mystery of the Cedar Lake monster while on a fun-filled camping trip with his friends and father. (Rev: BL 5/15/03; SLJ 8/03)

225 Wallace, Bill. *Trapped in Death Cave* (5–8). 1984, Holiday $16.95 (0-8234-0516-8). Gary is convinced his grandpa was murdered to secure a map indicating where gold is buried.

226 Weaver, Will. *Memory Boy* (7–10). 2001, HarperCollins $15.95 (0-06-028811-6). In 2008, the global warming that follows a volcanic eruption forces Miles and his family to leave Minneapolis and seek refuge in their isolated vacation cabin. (Rev: BL 2/1/01; BR 11–12/01; HBG 10/01; SLJ 6/01; VOYA 8/01)

227 Whittaker, Dorothy Raymond. *Angels of the Swamp* (6–8). 1991, Walker $17.95 (0-8027-8129-2). Two teenage orphans who manage to survive on an island off the Florida coast discover they're not alone. (Rev: BL 1/15/92; SLJ 4/92)

228 Williams, Michael. *The Genuine Half-Moon Kid* (7–10). 1994, Dutton $15.99 (0-525-67479-5). Like questing Jason in Greek mythology, 18-year-old South African Jay Watson sets out with some friends to find a yellow wood box left him by his grandfather. (Rev: BL 6/1–15/94)

229 Wynne-Jones, Tim. *The Maestro* (6–8). 1996, Orchard LB $17.99 (0-531-08894-4). This moving novel describes a boy's maturation in the wilderness of northern Ontario and his friendship with a gifted musician. (Rev: BL 12/15/96*; SLJ 1/97; VOYA 4/97)

230 Yolen, Jane, and Bruce Coville. *Armageddon Summer* (7–12). 1998, Harcourt $17.00 (0-15-201767-4). When truckloads of artillery suddenly appear, events turn deadly for teenagers Marina and Jed, who are at a meeting of a millennial cult known as the Believers on a mountain in Massachusetts. (Rev: BCCB 9/98; BL 8/98; HBG 3/99; SLJ 10/98; VOYA 10/98)

231 Zindel, Paul. *Night of the Bat* (6–9). 2001, Hyperion $15.99 (0-7868-0340-1). Jake's exciting trip to join his father's research team in the Amazon turns into a horror story when a giant bat starts attacking the workers. (Rev: BCCB 7–8/01; BL 6/1–15/01; HBG 10/02; SLJ 9/01; VOYA 6/01)

232 Zindel, Paul. *Raptor* (5–9). 1998, Hyperion LB $15.49 (0-7868-2374-7). While on a paleontology dig, two friends discover a mysterious egg that hatches into a raptor; mayhem follows when its mother attempts to save her baby — and herself — from the mercenary director of the dig. (Rev: BL 9/1/98; HBG 3/99; SLJ 10/98; VOYA 8/99)

233 Zindel, Paul. *Reef of Death* (7–12). 1998, HarperCollins $15.95 (0-06-024728-2). A tale of terror about two teens, a monster creature that lives on an Australian reef, and a mad geologist who has a torture chamber on her freighter. (Rev: BL 3/1/98; HBG 9/98; SLJ 3/98; VOYA 4/98)

Animal Stories

234 Adler, C. S. *More Than a Horse* (5–7). 1997, Clarion $15.00 (0-395-79769-1). Leeann and her mother move to a dude ranch in Arizona, where the young girl develops a love of horses. (Rev: BCCB 3/97; BL 3/15/97; SLJ 4/97)

235 Adler, C. S. *One Unhappy Horse* (5–7). 2001, Clarion $15.00 (0-618-04912-6). Set on a small ranch near Tucson, this novel features 12-year-old Jan, her horse, Dove, an old lady in a retirement home, and Jan's new friend, Lisa. (Rev: BL 3/1/01; HBG 10/01; SLJ 4/01)

236 Adler, C. S. *That Horse Whiskey!* (6–8). 1996, Avon paper $3.99 (0-380-72601-7). Lainey, 13, disappointed that she didn't get a horse for her birthday, works at a stable training a stubborn horse and falls for a city boy. (Rev: BL 11/1/94; SLJ 11/94; VOYA 12/94)

237 Alter, Judith. *Callie Shaw, Stable Boy* (5–8). 1996, Eakin $16.95 (1-57168-092-6). During the Great Depression, Callie, disguised as a boy, works in a stable and uncovers a race-fixing racket. (Rev: BL 2/1/97; SLJ 8/97)

238 Alter, Judith. *Maggie and a Horse Named Devildust* (5–7). 1989, Ellen C. Temple paper $5.95 (0-936650-08-7). Maggie is determined to ride her spirited horse in the Wild West show in this historical horse story. (Rev: BL 4/15/89)

239 Alter, Judith. *Maggie and the Search for Devildust* (5–7). 1989, Ellen C. Temple paper $5.95 (0-936650-09-5). Maggie, a gorgeous girl of the Old West, sets out to find her horse, which has been stolen. (Rev: BL 10/1/89)

240 Arnosky, Jim. *Long Spikes* (4–7). Illus. 1992, Houghton $15.00 (0-395-58830-8). As spring turns to summer, a yearling buck and his twin sister travel together after the death of their mother. (Rev: BCCB 4/92; BL 5/1/92; SLJ 5/92)

241 Bagnold, Enid. *National Velvet* (5–8). 1985, Avon paper $4.99 (0-380-71235-0). The now-classic story of Heather Brown and her struggle to ride in the Grand National. A reissue. (Rev: BL 12/15/85)

242 Bastedo, Jamie. *Tracking Triple Seven* (5–7). 2001, Red Deer paper $9.95 (0-88995-238-8). Benji, a teenage boy grieving his mother's death, becomes involved with biologists tracking grizzly bears near his father's mine in Canada. (Rev: BL 2/1/02)

243 Bauer, Marion Dane. *Face to Face* (5–9). 1993, Dell paper $3.99 (0-440-40791-5). This novel of a troubled father-son relationship describes their reunion on a failed whitewater rafting trip and the painful aftermath when they separate again. (Rev: BL 9/15/91; SLJ 10/91)

244 Branford, Henrietta. *White Wolf* (7–12). 1999, Candlewick $16.99 (0-7636-0748-7). Kept as a pet, Snowy, a wolf cub, escapes, searches for a pack, and eventually has a family of its own in this tale set in the Pacific Northwest. (Rev: BL 8/99; HBG 9/99; SLJ 6/99; VOYA 10/99)

245 Brooke, Lauren. *Heartland: Coming Home* (4–7). 2000, Scholastic paper $4.50 (0-439-13020-4). When her mother dies, Amy works through her grief by helping horses with behavioral problems in this novel set on a Virginia horse farm. (Rev: BL 9/15/00)

246 Bryant, Bonnie. *The Long Ride* (6–9). Series: Pine Hollow. 1998, Bantam paper $4.50 (0-553-49242-X). A terrible accident revives the friendship of three horse-loving girls who have grown apart as they developed new interests in high school. (Rev: BL 11/15/98; SLJ 2/99)

247 Burgess, Melvin. *The Cry of the Wolf* (5–8). 1994, Morrow $17.99 (0-397-30693-8). Young Ben Tilley insists that wolves run past his farm in rural Surrey, even though they have supposedly been gone from England for 500 years. (Rev: BL 10/15/92; SLJ 9/92)

248 Burgess, Melvin. *Kite* (5–8). 2000, Farrar $16.00 (0-374-34228-8). In this novel set in rural England in 1964, Taylor's father, a games keeper on a large estate, must stand up to his employer who is cruel to animals and wants to eliminate some rare birds. (Rev: BCCB 6/00; BL 3/15/00; HBG 10/00; SLJ 4/00)

249 Campbell, Eric. *Papa Tembo* (7–12). 1998, Harcourt $16.00 (0-15-201727-5). This story set in Tanzania creates a fatal encounter between Papa Tembo, the father of elephants, and his arch enemy, Laurens Van Der Wel, the evil poacher. (Rev: BCCB 9/98; BL 8/98; HBG 9/99; SLJ 10/98; VOYA 10/98)

250 Carlson, Nolan. *Summer and Shiner* (5–8). 1992, Hearth paper $6.95 (0-9627947-4-0). In a small Kansas town in the 1940s, 12-year-old Carley adopts a raccoon called Shiner. (Rev: BL 9/15/92)

251 Casanova, Mary. *Stealing Thunder* (4–7). 1999, Hyperion LB $15.49 (0-7868-2268-6). A fast-paced adventure in which Libby plans to kidnap Thunder, a horse that is being abused by his owner. (Rev: HBG 10/99; SLJ 10/99)

252 Cavanna, Betty. *Going on Sixteen* (6–9). 1998, Morrow paper $5.95 (0-688-16324-6). This story of a shy girl's love for her dog has become a young adult classic. (Rev: BL 12/15/85; BR 1–2/86)

253 Cleary, Beverly. *Strider* (5–9). Illus. 1991, Morrow LB $16.89 (0-688-09901-7). In this sequel to the 1984 Newbery winner *Dear Mr. Henshaw,* Leigh Botts is beginning high school and still writing in his diary, with his beloved dog, Strider, by his side. (Rev: BCCB 10/91; BL 7/91*; HB 9–10/91; SLJ 9/91)

254 Corcoran, Barbara. *Wolf at the Door* (6–8). 1993, Atheneum $17.00 (0-689-31870-7). Lee, age 13, feels inferior to her beautiful sister until Lee rescues a young wolf and opposition from neighbors unites them. (Rev: BL 10/1/93; VOYA 12/93)

255 Crompton, Anne E. *The Snow Pony* (5–9). 1994, Simon & Schuster paper $3.99 (0-671-78507-9). New in town, a lonely 8th-grade girl is offered a job by her shy, misunderstood neighbor taming and grooming a pony for his grandson. (Rev: BL 9/15/91)

256 Curwood, James Oliver. *The Bear — A Novel* (8–12). 1989, Newmarket paper $6.95 (1-55704-053-2). A reissue of the 1916 novel about a grizzly bear and an orphaned black bear cub in the wilds of British Columbia. (Rev: VOYA 4/90)

257 Dann, Colin. *Nobody's Dog* (5–7). 2000, Hutchinson $22.95 (0-09-176900-0). After a series of adventures, an abandoned Border collie finds a permanent home with a loving master. (Rev: BCCB 9/98; SLJ 1/01)

258 DeJong, Meindert. *Along Came a Dog* (4–7). 1958, HarperCollins paper $5.99 (0-06-440114-6). The friendship of a timid, lonely dog and a toeless little red hen is the basis for a very moving story, full of suspense.

259 Eckert, Allan W. *Incident at Hawk's Hill* (6–8). 1995, Bantam paper $6.99 (0-316-20948-1). A 6-year-old boy wanders away from home and is nurtured and protected by a badger.

260 Farley, Steven. *The Black Stallion's Shadow* (5–7). 1996, Random $16.00 (0-679-85004-X). The Black Stallion develops a fear of shadows and trainer Alec Ramsay hopes for a cure. (Rev: BCCB 9/96; BL 9/15/96)

261 Farley, Walter. *The Black Stallion* (5–8). 1944, Random LB $11.99 (0-394-90601-2). A wild Arabian stallion and the boy who trained him star in this horse story first published in 1941. Other titles in the series are *The Black Stallion Returns* and *Son of the Black Stallion.*

262 Farley, Walter, and Steven Farley. *The Young Black Stallion* (5–9). 1989, Random $10.95 (0-394-84562-5). In this sequel to *The Black Stallion,* the reader learns about the early life of Shêtân. (Rev: BR 5–6/90; SLJ 12/89)

263 Gallico, Paul. *The Snow Goose* (7–12). Illus. 1941, Knopf $15.00 (0-394-44593-7); Tundra paper $9.99 (0-7710-3250-1). A hunchbacked artist and a young child nurse a wounded snow goose back to health, and it later returns to protect them in this large, illustrated 50th anniversary edition of the classic tale. (Rev: BL 9/15/92)

264 George, Jean Craighead. *The Cry of the Crow* (5–7). 1980, HarperCollins paper $5.99 (0-06-440131-6). Mandy finds a helpless baby crow in the woods and tames it.

265 George, Jean Craighead. *Frightful's Mountain* (5–8). 1999, Dutton $15.99 (0-525-46166-3). Frightful, the falcon in *My Side of the Mountain,* is the central character in this novel in which she has difficult and enjoyable adventures in the wild. (Rev: BL 9/1/99; HBG 3/00; SLJ 9/99; VOYA 6/00)

266 George, Jean Craighead. *Summer of the Falcon* (6–9). 1979, HarperCollins paper $4.95 (0-06-440095-6). June learns to take responsibility and accept discipline when she trains her own falcons.

267 Ghent, Natale. *Piper* (5–7). 2001, Orca paper $6.95 (1-55143-167-X). The love and attention young Wesley showers on a tiny Australian shepherd puppy helps her recover from the death of her father. (Rev: BL 3/1/01)

268 Gipson, Fred. *Old Yeller* (6–9). 1956, Harper-Collins $23.00 (0-06-011545-9); paper $5.99 (0-06-440382-3). A powerful story set in the Texas hill country about a 14-year-old boy and the ugly stray dog he comes to love. Also use *Savage Sam* (1976).

269 Graeber, Charlotte. *Grey Cloud* (6–8). Illus. 1979, Macmillan $8.95 (0-02-736690-2). Tom and Orville become friends when they train pigeons for a big race.

270 Greenberg, Martin H., and Charles G. Waugh, eds. *A Newbery Zoo: A Dozen Animal Stories by Newbery Award–Winning Authors* (4–7). 1995, Delacorte $16.95 (0-385-32263-1). Twelve animal stories by such Newbery winners as Beverly Cleary, Betsy Byars, and Jean Craighead George. (Rev: BL 1/15/95; SLJ 4/95)

271 Griffith, Helen V. *Foxy* (6–8). 1984, Greenwillow $15.00 (0-688-02567-6). Jeff doesn't like outdoor life but finding a homeless dog helps him fit in.

272 Hall, Elizabeth. *Child of the Wolves* (4–7). 1996, Houghton $16.00 (0-395-76502-1). Granite, a Siberian husky pup, must survive in the wilderness when he is separated from his family. (Rev: BCCB 3/96; BL 4/1/96; VOYA 6/96)

273 Hall, Lynn. *The Soul of the Silver Dog* (5–8). 1992, Harcourt $16.95 (0-15-277196-4). A handicapped dog bonds with his new teenage owner living in a troubled family. (Rev: BL 4/15/92; SLJ 6/92)

274 Hart, Alison. *Shadow Horse* (4–8). 1999, Random $15.00 (0-679-88642-7). When Jas begins caring for a neglected horse named Shadow, she uncovers suspicious facts about her old horse, which died a mysterious death. (Rev: BL 7/99; HBG 10/99; SLJ 10/99)

275 Hearne, Betsy. *The Canine Connection: Stories About Dogs and People* (5–8). 2003, Simon & Schuster $15.95 (0-689-85258-4). Twelve moving and arresting stories underline the close relationship between dogs and their human friends. (Rev: BL 4/15/03; HB 5–6/03*; HBG 10/03; SLJ 4/03)

276 Henkes, Kevin. *Protecting Marie* (5–7). 1995, Greenwillow $16.99 (0-688-13958-2). Fanny is afraid that she will lose her pet dog if her temperamental father decides the dog must go. (Rev: BCCB 3/95; BL 3/15/95; HB 7–8/95; SLJ 5/95*)

277 Henry, Marguerite. *King of the Wind* (5–8). 1990, Macmillan $17.95 (0-02-743629-2); Aladdin paper $4.99 (0-689-71486-6). The story of the famous stallion Godolphin Arabian, ancestor of Man O'War and founder of the Thoroughbred breed. Newbery Medal winner, 1949. Also use *Black Gold* and *Born to Trot* (both 1987).

278 Henry, Marguerite. *Misty of Chincoteague* (4–7). 1990, Simon & Schuster $17.95 (0-02-743622-5); paper $2.65 (0-689-82170-0). The classic story of wild island ponies. Two sequels are *Sea Star* and *Stormy, Misty's Foal* (both 1991).

279 Henry, Marguerite. *Mustang, Wild Spirit of the West* (6–8). 1992, Macmillan paper $4.99 (0-689-71601-X). An excellent horse story written by a master.

280 Hermes, Patricia. *Fly Away Home: The Novel and Story Behind the Film* (5–8). 1996, Newmarket paper $6.95 (1-55704-303-5). This is the true story of a girl and her father, who raise 16 geese and use an ultralight plane to teach them to migrate south. (Rev: VOYA 2/97)

281 High, Linda O. *Hound Heaven* (5–8). 1995, Holiday $15.95 (0-8234-1195-8). More than anything in the world, Silver Iris wants a dog, but her grandfather won't allow it. (Rev: BCCB 12/95; SLJ 11/95; VOYA 2/96)

282 Hobbs, Will. *Beardance* (7–12). 1993, Atheneum $17.00 (0-689-31867-7). Prospector Cloyd Atcity stays the winter in the Colorado mountains to ensure the survival of the last two grizzly cubs in the state after their mother and sibling die. (Rev: BL 11/15/93; SLJ 12/93; VOYA 12/93)

283 Holland, Isabelle. *Toby the Splendid* (6–8). 1987, Walker $13.95 (0-8027-6674-9). An intense argument arises between mother and daughter when young Janet buys a horse and wants to start riding. (Rev: BL 4/1/87; BR 9–10/87; SLJ 4/87; VOYA 8/89)

284 Hosler, Jay. *Clan Apis* (5–7). Illus. 2001, Active Synapse paper $15.00 (0-9677255-0-X). Nyuki, a honeybee, describes his hive's history and migration to a new location in a text presented in graphic-novel style that includes information about bees and their environment. (Rev: BL 7/01)

285 Howard, Jean G. *Half a Cage* (6–8). Illus. 1978, Tidal Pr. $5.50 (0-930954-07-6). Ann's pet monkey causes so many problems she wonders if she should give it away.

286 Jimenez, Juan Ramon. *Platero y Yo / Platero and I* (5–7). Trans. by Myra Cohn Livingston and Joseph F. Dominguez. 1994, Clarion $15.00 (0-395-62365-0). Using both Spanish and English texts, this book contains excerpts from the prose poem about a writer and his donkey. (Rev: BL 6/1–15/94) [863]

287 Jones, Adrienne. *The Hawks of Chelney* (7–9). Illus. 1978, HarperCollins $13.95 (0-06-023057-6). A young outcast and his girlfriend try to understand the hawks and their habits.

288 Katz, Welwyn W. *Whalesinger* (7–10). 1991, Macmillan paper $14.95 (0-689-50511-6). Two Vancouver teens spending their summer on the California coast encounter a corrupt research scientist, endangered whales, and natural disasters. (Rev: BL 2/1/91; SLJ 5/91)

289 Keehn, Sally M. *The First Horse I See* (5–9). 1999, Philomel $17.99 (0-399-23351-2). In this story filled with personal and family problems, the central issue involves Willo and the horse she has purchased in spite of its wild nature. (Rev: BCCB 9/99; BL 9/1/99; HBG 10/99; SLJ 7/99; VOYA 10/99)

290 Kennedy, Barbara. *The Boy Who Loved Alligators* (7–9). 1994, Atheneum $15.00 (0-689-31876-6). When young Jim's "friend," an alligator, eats the neighbor's dog, he's forced to face some hard truths. (Rev: BL 4/1/94; SLJ 6/94)

291 Kincaid, Beth. *Back in the Saddle* (5–9). Series: Silver Creek Riders. 1994, Berkley paper $3.99 (0-515-11480-4). This first book in the series focuses on four girls attending a summer riding camp and their relationships with each other and their horses. (Rev: BL 1/1/95; SLJ 12/94)

292 Kipling, Rudyard. *The Jungle Book: The Mowgli Stories* (4–7). 1995, Morrow $24.99 (0-688-09979-3). Eight stories about Mowgli are reprinted with 18 handsome watercolors. (Rev: BCCB 6/96; BL 10/15/95; SLJ 11/95)

293 Kjelgaard, James A. *Big Red* (6–9). 1956, Holiday $17.95 (0-8234-0007-7); Bantam paper $5.50 (0-553-15434-6). This is the perennial favorite about Danny and his Irish setter. Continued in *Irish Red* and *Outlaw Red*. (Rev: BL 9/1/89)

294 Kjelgaard, James A. *Snow Dog* (6–8). 1983, Bantam paper $4.99 (0-553-15560-1). In the wilderness, a snow dog fights for survival. A sequel is *Wild Trek*.

295 Kjelgaard, James A. *Stormy* (6–8). 1983, Bantam paper $5.50 (0-553-15468-0). Alan is helped to accept his father's being sent to prison through love for a retriever named Stormy.

296 Klass, David. *California Blue* (7–10). 1994, Scholastic paper $13.95 (0-590-46688-7). A 17-year-old California boy who cares about track and butterflies finds a chrysalis that turns out to be an unknown species. (Rev: BL 3/1/94; SLJ 4/94*; VOYA 6/94)

297 Knight, Eric. *Lassie Come Home* (6–9). 1978, Holt $16.95 (0-8050-0721-0). The classic story of how a faithful collie returns to the boy who was his first master.

298 Levin, Betty. *Away to Me, Moss* (5–7). 1994, Greenwillow $15.99 (0-688-13439-4). When his master has a stroke, Moss, a border collie, runs out of control. (Rev: BCCB 12/94; BL 10/1/94; SLJ 10/94)

299 Levin, Betty. *Look Back, Moss* (5–8). 1998, Greenwillow $15.00 (0-688-15696-7). Young Moss,

disturbed by his mother's lack of attention and his own weight problems, welcomes an injured sheepdog into the family. (Rev: BCCB 10/98; BL 8/98; HB 1–2/99; HBG 3/99; SLJ 11/98)

300 Lippincott, Joseph W. *Wilderness Champion* (7–9). 1944, HarperCollins $11.95 (0-397-30099-9). This novel, now almost 50 years old, tells about a most unusual hound dog.

301 Lowry, Lois. *Stay! Keeper's Story* (5–8). Illus. 1997, Houghton $15.00 (0-395-87048-8). A dog named Keeper narrates this story about his puppyhood and the three different masters he has had. (Rev: BL 11/1/97; HBG 3/98; SLJ 10/97)

302 Malterre, Elona. *The Last Wolf of Ireland* (5–7). 1990, Houghton $15.00 (0-395-54381-9). Devin and his friend Katey hide wolf pups when the pups are threatened. (Rev: BCCB 10/90; BL 9/15/90*; SLJ 10/90)

303 Maynard, Meredy. *Dreamcatcher* (5–7). 1995, Polestar paper $7.95 (1-896095-01-1). With the help of an American Indian girl, a 13-year-old boy secretly raises a baby raccoon that was abandoned in the woods. (Rev: SLJ 5/96)

304 Mazer, Harry. *The Dog in the Freezer* (6–9). 1997, Simon & Schuster paper $16.00 (0-689-80753-8). Three short novels about boys and dogs. In one, a dog changes places with his master, in another a fatherless boy finds love with his puppy, and in the title story, a boy wants to bury the dead dog of a neighbor. (Rev: BL 3/15/97; BR 9–10/97; HBG 3/98; SLJ 7/97)

305 Mikaelsen, Ben. *Rescue Josh McGuire* (6–9). 1991, Hyperion LB $14.89 (1-56282-100-8). Josh, 13, rescues an orphaned bear cub; when he is told it must be turned over to game authorities, he runs away into the mountains. (Rev: BL 12/15/91)

306 Mikaelsen, Ben. *Stranded* (6–8). 1995, Hyperion LB $16.49 (0-7868-2059-4). Koby, a 12-year-old girl who feels as isolated and stranded as the wounded pilot whales she helps rescue, learns about emotional barriers and reconciliation. (Rev: BL 8/95*; SLJ 6/95; VOYA 12/95)

307 Morey, Walt. *Gentle Ben* (5–8). Illus. 1991, Puffin paper $5.99 (0-14-036035-2). A warm story of deep trust and friendship between a boy and an Alaskan bear.

308 Morey, Walt. *Kavik the Wolf Dog* (7–9). 1977, Dutton $15.99 (0-525-33093-3). This is a story of survival and courage set in the Far North.

309 Morey, Walt. *Scrub Dog of Alaska* (4–8). 1989, Blue Heron paper $7.95 (0-936085-13-4). A pup, abandoned because of his small size, turns out to be a winner. Also use *Kavik the Wolf Dog* (1977, Dutton).

310 Morey, Walt. *Year of the Black Pony* (5–8). 1989, Blue Heron paper $6.95 (0-936085-14-2). A family story about a boy's love for his pony in rural Oregon at the turn of the 20th century.

311 Mowat, Farley. *The Dog Who Wouldn't Be* (4–7). 1957, Bantam paper $4.99 (0-553-27928-9). The humorous story of Mutt, a dog of character and personality, and his boy.

312 Mukerji, Dhan Gopal. *Gay-Neck: The Story of a Pigeon* (4–8). 1968, Dutton $15.99 (0-525-30400-2). A boy from India's brave carrier pigeon is selected to perform dangerous missions during World War I. Newbery Medal winner, 1928.

313 Myers, Anna. *Red-Dirt Jessie* (4–7). 1992, Walker $13.95 (0-8027-8172-1). In this tale of the Depression era in Oklahoma, 12-year-old Jessie helps keep her family together. (Rev: BCCB 10/92; BL 1/15/93; HB 1–2/93; SLJ 11/92*)

314 Naylor, Phyllis Reynolds. *Saving Shiloh* (4–7). 1997, Simon & Schuster $15.00 (0-689-81460-7). In this sequel to the Newbery Medal–winning *Shiloh* and *Shiloh Season*, Marty again encounters the evil Judd Travers, who has been accused of murder. (Rev: BL 9/1/97*; HB 9–10/97; HBG 3/98; SLJ 9/97)

315 Naylor, Phyllis Reynolds. *Shiloh* (4–8). 1991, Macmillan $16.00 (0-689-31614-3); Dell paper $5.50 (0-440-40752-4). When a beagle follows him home, Marty, from a West Virginia family with a strict code of honor, learns a painful lesson about right and wrong. Newbery Medal winner, 1992. (Rev: BCCB 10/91; BL 12/1/91*; HB 1–2/92; SLJ 9/91)

316 Naylor, Phyllis Reynolds. *Shiloh Season* (4–8). 1996, Simon & Schuster $15.00 (0-689-80647-7). The evil Judd Travers wants his dog back from the Prestons in this sequel to *Shiloh* (1991). (Rev: BCCB 12/96; BL 11/15/96*; BR 9–10/97; HB 11–12/96; SLJ 11/96)

317 O'Hara, Mary. *My Friend Flicka* (7–12). 1988, HarperCollins paper $6.00 (0-06-080902-7). This story about Ken McLaughlin and the filly named Flicka is continued in *Thunderhead, Son of Flicka*.

318 Parker, Cam. *A Horse in New York* (4–8). 1989, Avon paper $2.75 (0-380-75704-4). To save Blue, the horse she rode at summer camp, from destruction, Tiffin has to convince her parents to board him for the winter. (Rev: BL 12/15/89)

319 Peck, Robert Newton. *The Horse Hunters* (7–10). 1988, Random $15.95 (0-394-56980-6). A 15-year-old boy reaches manhood through capturing a white stallion in this novel set in Florida of the 1930s. (Rev: BL 2/15/89; BR 5–6/89; VOYA 6/89)

320 Pennac, Daniel. *Eye of the Wolf* (5–8). 2003, Candlewick $15.99 (0-7636-1896-9). A boy and a captive wolf, who have both suffered at the hands of humans, form a close connection. (Rev: BCCB

3/03; BL 3/1/03; HBG 10/03; SLJ 2/03, VOYA 6/03)

321 Pevsner, Stella. *Jon, Flora, and the Odd-Eyed Cat* (6–8). 1997, Pocket Books paper $3.99 (0-671-56105-7). Jon, 14, moves with his family to South Carolina, where he receives late-night visits from a cat. Soon he meets Flora, 12, the cat's crazy owner. (Rev: BL 11/1/94; SLJ 10/94; VOYA 12/94)

322 Peyton, K. M. *Blind Beauty* (6–10). 2001, Dutton $17.99 (0-525-46652-5). Twelve-year-old Tessa is angry at the world until she meets Buffoon, an unlikely racehorse that she trains to win the Grand National. (Rev: BCCB 2/01; BR 9–10/01; HBG 10/01; SLJ 3/01; VOYA 4/01)

323 Peyton, K. M. *The Team* (7–9). Illus. 1976, HarperCollins $12.95 (0-690-01083-4). Ruth is determined to own the special show pony that is for sale.

324 Platt, Chris. *Race the Wind!* (5–7). 2000, Random LB $16.99 (0-679-98657-X); paper $4.99 (0-679-88658-3). Kate wants to ride her horse, Willow King, in the Kentucky Derby but she is afraid that she will not get her license in time and rival Mark, a jockey, will ride instead. (Rev: HBG 3/01; SLJ 9/00)

325 Rawlings, Marjorie Kinnan. *The Yearling* (6–9). Illus. 1983, Macmillan paper $5.95 (0-02-044931-3). The classic story of Joss and the orphaned fawn he adopts. Illus. by N. C. Wyeth. (Rev: BL 9/1/89)

326 Rylant, Cynthia. *Every Living Thing* (6–9). Illus. 1985, Bradbury LB $14.00 (0-02-777200-4). In each of these 12 stories, the lives of humans change because of their relationship with animals. (Rev: HB 3–4/86; SLJ 12/85; VOYA 4/86)

327 Salten, Felix. *Bambi: A Life in the Woods* (5–8). 1926, Pocket paper $4.99 (0-671-66607-X). The growing to maturity of an Austrian deer.

328 Savage, Deborah. *To Race a Dream* (6–9). 1994, Houghton $16.00 (0-395-69252-0). In early 20th-century Minnesota, young Theodora dreams of being a harness-racing driver. She disguises herself as a boy and works as a stable hand. (Rev: BL 11/1/94*; SLJ 12/94; VOYA 10/94)

329 Sewell, Anna. *Black Beauty* (7–9). 1974, Airmont paper $1.50 (0-8049-0023-X). The classic sentimental story about the cruelty and kindness experienced by a horse in Victorian England.

330 Sherlock, Patti. *Four of a Kind* (5–9). 1991, Holiday $13.95 (0-8234-0913-9). Andy's grandfather agrees to lend him money to buy a pair of horses, and he sets his sights on winning the horse-pulling contest at a state fair. (Rev: BL 12/1/91; SLJ 10/91)

331 Snelling, Lauraine. *The Winner's Circle* (5–8). Series: Golden Filly. 1995, Bethany House paper $5.99 (1-55661-533-7). In this horse story, Trish Evanston, a high school senior who is also a jockey and Triple Crown winner, is being stalked by a mystery man who sends her threatening notes. (Rev: SLJ 10/95; VOYA 4/96)

332 Springer, Nancy. *The Boy on a Black Horse* (6–9). 1994, Atheneum $14.95 (0-689-31840-5). A story about a gypsy youth (a rom, as they prefer to be called) who has run off from his abusive father. (Rev: BL 4/15/94; SLJ 6/94; VOYA 6/94)

333 Springer, Nancy. *A Horse to Love* (4–8). 1987, HarperCollins $11.95 (0-06-025824-1). Erin's parents buy her a horse hoping that this will help cure her shyness. (Rev: BL 3/87; SLJ 3/87)

334 Sullivan, Paul. *Legend of the North* (7–12). 1995, Royal Fireworks paper $9.99 (0-88092-308-3). Set in northern Canada, this novel contains two narratives, the first about a young wolf's struggle for dominance within the pack, and the second about an elderly Inuit and his survival in the harsh tundra regions. (Rev: BL 1/1–15/96; VOYA 4/96)

335 Taylor, Theodore. *The Hostage* (5–8). 1988, Dell paper $3.99 (0-440-20923-4). Fourteen-year-old Jamie in Canada is stunned when his efforts to capture a trapped whale are misinterpreted. (Rev: BL 2/15/88; SLJ 3/88)

336 Taylor, Theodore. *The Trouble with Tuck* (5–8). 1989, Doubleday $16.95 (0-385-17774-7); Avon paper $4.95 (0-380-62711-6). The story of a golden Labrador retriever who becomes blind.

337 Taylor, Theodore. *Tuck Triumphant* (4–7). 1991, Avon paper $5.99 (0-380-71323-3). A 1950s novel about a blind dog in a loving family and the deaf Korean boy they adopt. (Rev: BL 2/1/91)

338 Taylor, William. *Agnes the Sheep* (5–7). 1991, Scholastic paper $13.95 (0-590-43365-2). A wild and woolly story about an ornery and ill-kempt sheep and the two middle-graders who must care for her. (Rev: BCCB 3/91*; BL 5/15/91*)

339 Terhune, Albert Payson. *Lad: A Dog* (7–9). 1993, Puffin paper $6.99 (0-14-036474-9). The classic story of a beautiful collie. The beginning of a lengthy series now all out of print.

340 Wilbur, Frances. *The Dog with Golden Eyes* (4–7). Illus. 1998, Milkweed $15.95 (1-57131-614-0); paper $6.95 (1-57131-615-9). Cassie befriends a white dog that turns out to be an arctic wolf, and she must find his owners before he becomes a target for the police or hunters. (Rev: BCCB 9/98; BL 9/1/98; BR 9–10/98; HBG 3/99; SLJ 7/98; VOYA 8/98)

341 Williams, Laura E. *The Ghost Stallion* (5–7). 1999, Holt $15.95 (0-8050-6193-2). On a horse ranch in rural Oregon in 1959, Mary Elizabeth participates in a hunt to capture a renegade stallion while still trying to adjust to the absence of her mother. (Rev: BCCB 1/00; BL 11/1/99; HBG 3/00; SLJ 11/99; VOYA 2/00)

Classics

Europe

GENERAL AND MISCELLANEOUS

342 Dumas, Alexandre. *The Count of Monte Cristo* (8–12). Illus. 1996, Random $25.95 (0-679-60199-6); NAL paper $6.95 (0-451-52195-1). The classic French novel about false imprisonment, escape, and revenge.

343 Dumas, Alexandre. *The Three Musketeers* (8–12). 1984, Dodd paper $5.95 (0-553-21337-7). A novel of daring and intrigue in France. Sequels are *The Man in the Iron Mask* and *Twenty Years After* (available in various editions).

344 Maupassant, Guy de. *The Best Short Stories of Guy de Maupassant* (7–12). 1968, Amereon $21.95 (0-88411-589-5). The French master is represented by 19 tales including "The Diamond Necklace."

345 Osborne, Mary P. *Favorite Medieval Tales* (4–9). Illus. 1997, Scholastic paper $17.95 (0-590-60042-7). This collection of tales about medieval heroes such as Beowulf, King Arthur, Roland, Robin Hood, and Gawain is also a good introduction to the art and literature of the Middle Ages and the development of the English language. (Rev: BL 5/1/98; HBG 9/98; SLJ 8/98)

346 Verne, Jules. *Around the World in Eighty Days* (5–8). Trans. by George Makepeace Towle. 1988, Morrow $24.99 (0-688-07508-8). Endpapers showing an 1829 world map highlight this handsome edition of the classic. (Rev: BL 2/15/89)

347 Verne, Jules. *Around the World in Eighty Days* (7–12). 1996, Puffin paper $4.99 (0-14-036711-X). Phileas Fogg and servant Passepartout leave on a world trip in this 1873 classic adventure. (Rev: SLJ 7/96)

348 Verne, Jules. *A Journey to the Center of the Earth* (7–12). Illus. 1984, Penguin paper $4.95 (0-14-002265-1). A group of adventurers enter the earth through a volcano in Iceland. First published in French in 1864.

349 Verne, Jules. *Twenty Thousand Leagues Under the Sea* (7–12). 1990, Viking paper $3.99 (0-14-036721-7). Evil Captain Nemo captures a group of underwater explorers. First published in 1869. A sequel is *The Mysterious Island* (1988 Macmillan).

350 Wyss, Johann D. *The Swiss Family Robinson* (6–9). 1999, Bantam paper $4.99 (0-440-41594-2). One of many editions of the classic survival story, first published in 1814, of a family marooned on a deserted island.

351 Wyss, Johann D. *Swiss Family Robinson* (4–6). 1949, Putnam $16.99 (0-448-06022-1). The classic story of a shipwrecked family is presented for a younger audience.

GREAT BRITAIN AND IRELAND

352 Barrie, J. M. *Peter Pan* (5–7). Illus. 2000, Chronicle $19.95 (0-8118-2297-4). Using illustrations from 15 different artists, this is an unusual, unabridged edition of Barrie's classic fantasy. (Rev: BL 11/1/00; HBG 3/01; SLJ 12/00)

353 Barrie, J. M. *Peter Pan* (5–8). Illus. 1995, Holt $19.95 (0-8050-0276-6); NAL paper $4.95 (0-451-52088-2). The classic tale of the boy who wouldn't grow up and of his adventures with the Darling children. (Rev: BL 12/15/87)

354 Brontë, Charlotte. *Jane Eyre* (6–12). Series: Illustrated Junior Library. 1983, Putnam $19.99 (0-448-06031-0); Bantam paper $4.95 (0-553-21140-4). The immortal love story of Jane and Mr. Rochester.

355 Burnett, Frances Hodgson. *The Secret Garden* (5–8). 1999, Scholastic paper $3.99 (0-439-09939-0). An easily read classic about a spoiled girl relocated to England and the unusual friendship she finds there.

356 Chaucer, Geoffrey. *Canterbury Tales* (4–8). Adapted by Barbara Cohen. 1988, Lothrop $21.99 (0-688-06201-6). Several of the popular stories are retold with handsome illustrations by Trina Schart Hyman. (Rev: BL 9/1/88; SLJ 8/88)

357 Defoe, Daniel. *Robinson Crusoe* (7–12). Illus. 1983, Macmillan $27.95 (0-684-17946-6); NAL paper $5.95 (0-451-52236-2). The classic survival story with illustrations by N. C. Wyeth.

358 Dickens, Charles. *A Christmas Carol* (7–12). Illus. Series: Whole Story. 2000, Viking paper $17.99 (0-670-88879-6). This volume contains the full text of the classic, with new illustrations, reproductions of period pictures, a biography of Dickens, and material on social conditions of the time. (Rev: BL 9/1/00; HBG 3/01)

359 Dickens, Charles. *A Christmas Carol* (7–12). 1983, Pocket Books paper $3.99 (0-671-47369-7). Scrooge discovers the true meaning of Christmas after some trying experiences.

360 Dickens, Charles. *A Christmas Carol* (6–8). 1983, Holiday $18.95 (0-8234-0486-2). A handsome edition of this classic illustrated by Trina S. Hyman.

361 Dickens, Charles. *A Christmas Carol* (4–8). 1995, Simon & Schuster paper $19.95 (0-689-80213-7). The classic Christmas story illustrated by Quentin Blake. (Rev: BL 10/15/95)

362 Dickens, Charles. *A Christmas Carol* (5–8). 1996, Morrow $18.00 (0-688-13606-0). An abridged version of Dickens's performance text, with excellent illustrations by Carter Goodrich. (Rev: BL 9/1/96; HB 1–2/96)

363 Dickens, Charles. *David Copperfield* (8–12). Illus. 1997, Viking paper $7.95 (0-14-043494-1).

Includes some little-known episodes that Dickens excerpted from his book for public readings, information about dramatic performance, and illustrations. (Rev: BL 12/15/95)

364 Dickens, Charles. *Great Expectations* (8–12). 1998, NAL paper $4.95 (0-451-52671-6). The story of Pip and his slow journey to maturity and fortune.

365 Dickens, Charles. *Oliver Twist* (7–12). 1961, NAL paper $4.95 (0-451-52351-2). In probably the most accessible of Dickens's works, readers meet such immortals as Fagin, Nancy, and Oliver himself.

366 Dickens, Charles. *A Tale of Two Cities* (7–12). 1960, NAL paper $3.95 (0-451-52441-1). The classic novel of sacrifice during the French Revolution. A reissue.

367 Doyle, Arthur Conan. *Adventures of Sherlock Holmes* (7–12). 1981, Avon paper $2.95 (0-380-78105-0). A collection of 12 of the most famous stories about this famous sleuth.

368 Doyle, Arthur Conan. *The Complete Sherlock Holmes: All 4 Novels and 56 Stories* (7–12). 1998, Bantam paper $13.90 (0-553-32825-5). In two volumes, all the stories and novels involving Holmes and foil Watson.

369 Doyle, Arthur Conan. *Sherlock Holmes: The Complete Novels and Stories* (8–12). 1986, Bantam paper $6.95 each (Vol. 1: 0-553-21241-9; Vol. 2: 0-553-21242-7). A handy collection in two volumes of all the writings about Holmes and Watson. (Rev: BL 3/15/87)

370 Eliot, George. *Silas Marner* (8–12). 1960, NAL paper $3.95 (0-451-52427-6). The love of an old man for a young child brings redemption in this classic English novel.

371 Kipling, Rudyard. *Captains Courageous* (7–10). 1964, Amereon LB $20.95 (0-88411-818-5). The story of a spoiled teenager who learns about life from common fishermen who save him when he falls overboard from an ocean liner.

372 Kipling, Rudyard. *The Jungle Book* (5–8). Illus. Series: The Whole Story. 1996, Viking $22.99 (0-670-86919-8). The original text of the adventures of Mowgli and his animal friends is reprinted in this handsome edition that includes background information on the India of Kipling's time, period illustrations, and newly commissioned paintings. (Rev: HB 1–2/96; SLJ 7/96)

373 Kipling, Rudyard. *The Jungle Books* (6–9). 1961, NAL paper $4.95 (0-451-52340-7). The complete 15 stories that make up the original two volumes of jungle books.

374 Stevenson, Robert Louis. *The Black Arrow* (7–12). 1998, Tor paper $3.99 (0-8125-6562-2). Set against the War of the Roses, this is an adventure story involving a young hero, Dick Shelton. First published in 1888.

375 Stevenson, Robert Louis. *Dr. Jekyll and Mr. Hyde* (7–12). 1990, Buccaneer LB $16.95 (0-89968-552-8). This 1886 horror classic involves a drug-induced change of personality. One of several editions.

376 Stevenson, Robert Louis. *Treasure Island* (6–10). Illus. Series: The Whole Story. 1996, Viking $23.99 (0-670-86920-1). This edition contains the complete text of this novel along with illustrations that are used to explain details of life during this period, particularly life at sea. (Rev: SLJ 7/96)

377 Swift, Jonathan. *Gulliver's Travels* (7–12). 1947, Putnam $17.99 (0-448-06010-8); NAL paper $3.95 (0-451-52219-2). The four fantastic voyages of Lemuel Gulliver. First published in 1726.

378 Wilde, Oscar. *The Picture of Dorian Gray* (6–12). Illus. 2001, Viking $25.99 (0-670-89494-X); paper $17.99 (0-670-89495-8). Informative sidebars and bright illustrations amplify many of the more esoteric aspects of Wilde's classic story about the young man who never ages. (Rev: BL 5/15/01; HBG 10/01; SLJ 8/01; VOYA 8/01)

United States

379 Alcott, Louisa May. *Little Women* (5–9). 1947, Putnam $19.99 (0-448-06019-1). One of the many fine editions of this enduring story. Two sequels are *Little Men* and *Jo's Boys*.

380 Cooper, James Fenimore. *The Last of the Mohicans* (8–12). 1986, Macmillan $28.00 (0-684-18711-6); paper $4.95 (0-553-21329-6). This is the second of the classic Leatherstocking Tales. The others are *The Pioneers, The Prairie, The Pathfinder,* and *The Deerslayer* (all available in various editions). (Rev: BL 1/87)

381 Crane, Stephen. *The Red Badge of Courage* (8–12). 1991, Random $9.99 (0-517-66844-0); Airmont paper $2.50 (0-8049-0003-5). The classic novel of a young man who explored the meanings of courage during the Civil War.

382 Eisner, Will. *Moby Dick* (6–12). Illus. 2001, NBM $15.95 (1-56163-293-7). A faithful retelling of the famous novel in full-color graphic-novel format. (Rev: BL 11/15/01; HBG 3/02; SLJ 1/02)

383 Henry, O. *The Gift of the Magi* (5–10). Illus. 1988, Simon & Schuster paper $14.00 (0-671-64706-7). A beautiful edition of this classic story of Christmas and true love, illustrated by Kevin King. (Rev: BL 12/15/88)

384 Henry, O. *The Gift of the Magi* (5–8). 1994, Ideals $14.95 (1-57102-003-9). The classic story of unselfish love at Christmas gets some handsome

illustrations. Another fine edition is illus. by Kevin King (1988, Simon & Schuster). (Rev: BL 8/94)

385 Irving, Washington. *The Legend of Sleepy Hollow and Other Selections* (7–12). 1963, Washington Square Pr. paper $3.99 (0-671-46211-3). The story of Ichabod Crane, the ill-fated schoolteacher, and his encounter with the headless horseman.

386 London, Jack. *The Call of the Wild* (5–10). Illus. 1996, Viking $21.99 (0-670-86918-X). Along with the full text of this novel about the heroic dog Buck, this edition supplies background material on the Klondike, the gold rush, sled dogs, and the author. (Rev: SLJ 7/96)

387 London, Jack. *The Sea-Wolf* (7–12). 1958, Macmillan $15.95 (0-02-574630-8). Wolf Larsen helps a ne'er-do-well and a female poet find their destinies in the classic that was originally published in 1904.

388 London, Jack. *White Fang* (6–8). Illus. 2000, Simon & Schuster $25.00 (0-689-82431-9). Excellent illustrations by Ed Young add to this edition of the classic story of a dog that sacrifices himself to save his master. First published in 1906. (Rev: BL 11/15/00; HBG 10/01)

389 Poe, Edgar Allan. *Tales of Edgar Allan Poe* (7–12). 1991, Morrow $24.99 (0-688-07509-6). Eerie watercolor paintings illustrate 14 of Poe's most unsettling stories. (Rev: BL 8/91)

390 Schmidt, Gary D. *Pilgrim's Progress* (4–7). 1994, Eerdmans $20.00 (0-8028-5080-4). A simple retelling of the classic in which Christian leaves his home to find the Celestial City. (Rev: BL 11/1/94; SLJ 12/94)

391 Twain, Mark. *Adventures of Huckleberry Finn* (7EN]12). 1993, Random $16.50 (0-679-42470-9). One of many editions.

392 Twain, Mark. *The Adventures of Tom Sawyer* (7–12). 1998, Oxford paper $5.95 (0-19-283389-8). The story of Tom, Aunt Polly, Becky Thatcher, and the villianous Injun Joe. First published in 1876.

393 Twain, Mark. *The Adventures of Tom Sawyer* (6–10). Illus. Series: The Whole Story. 1996, Viking $23.99 (0-670-86984-8). In addition to the full text of Twain's novel, captioned illustrations are used to portray life in the 1800s. One of many editions. (Rev: SLJ 1/97)

394 Twain, Mark. *A Connecticut Yankee in King Arthur's Court* (7–12). 1988, Morrow $24.99 (0-688-06346-2); Bantam paper $4.95 (0-553-21143-9). Through a time-travel fantasy, a swaggering Yankee is plummeted into the age of chivalry. First published in 1889. (Rev: BL 2/15/89)

395 Twain, Mark. *The Prince and the Pauper* (7–12). 1996, Andre Deutsch $9.95 (0-233-99081-1); Airmont paper $2.50 (0-8049-0032-9). A king and a poor boy switch places in 16th-century England. First published in 1881.

396 Twain, Mark. *Pudd'nhead Wilson* (7–12). 1966, Airmont paper $2.50 (0-8049-0124-4). In the Midwest of over 100 years ago, a black servant switches her baby with a white couple's child to ensure that he gets a fair chance at life.

397 Twain, Mark. *Tom Sawyer Abroad [and] Tom Sawyer, Detective* (7–12). 1981, Univ. of California Pr. $45.00 (0-520-04560-2); paper $13.95 (0-520-04561-0). Two sequels to *The Adventures of Tom Sawyer,* both involving Tom and Huck.

Contemporary Life and Problems

General and Miscellaneous

398 Abelove, Joan. *Saying It Out Loud* (8–12). 1999, Puffin paper $5.99 (0-14-131227-0). When Mindy's mother is dying of a brain tumor and her father provides little emotional support, Mindy turns to her friends. (Rev: BL 9/1/99; SLJ 9/99; VOYA 10/99)

399 Adler, C. S. *Always and Forever Friends* (5–7). 1990, Avon paper $3.99 (0-380-70687-3). Wendy, at 11, is having a painful struggle making new friends after Meg moves away until she meets Honor, who is African American and very hesitant about accepting Wendy. (Rev: BCCB 4/88; BL 4/1/88; SLJ 4/88)

400 Adler, C. S. *The Magic of the Glits* (5–7). 1987, Avon paper $2.50 (0-380-70403-X). Jeremy, age 12, takes care of 7-year-old Lynette for the summer. A reissue of the 1979 edition. Also use *Some Other Summer* (1988).

401 Adler, C. S. *Not Just a Summer Crush* (5–8). 1998, Houghton $15.00 (0-395-88532-9). When 12-year-old Hana Riley meets her former teacher during the family's summer vacation on Cape Cod, an innocent friendship develops to which Hana's parents object. (Rev: BCCB 10/98; BL 11/15/98; BR 5–6/99; HB 11–12/98; HBG 3/99; SLJ 11/98)

402 Agell, Charlotte. *Welcome Home or Someplace Like It* (5–8). 2003, Holt $16.95 (0-8050-7083-4). In her notebook (number 27), Aggie records her arrival with her brother at their grandfather's home in Maine and their experiences getting to know the town and its residents. (Rev: BCCB 1/04; BL 11/15/03; SLJ 11/03; VOYA 10/03)

403 Alcock, Vivien. *The Trial of Anna Cotman* (5–8). 1990, Houghton paper $6.95 (0-395-81649-1). Anna finds that the secret society to which she belongs is gradually becoming an instrument of terror. (Rev: SLJ 2/90)

404 Alcott, Louisa May. *The Quiet Little Woman: A Christmas Story* (4–7). 1999, Honor Bks. $14.99 (1-

56292-616-0). A collection of three sentimental Christmas stories in a small-format volume. (Rev: SLJ 10/99)

405 Angell, Judie. *The Buffalo Nickel Blues Band* (7–10). 1991, Macmillan paper $3.95 (0-689-71448-3). Five youngsters form a band and are sent on the road.

406 Armistead, John. *The $66 Summer* (5–9). 2000, Milkweed $15.95 (1-57131-626-4); paper $6.95 (1-57131-625-6). In 1955, 12-year-old George is spending a summer with his grandmother in Alabama where he makes friends with two African American boys and joins them in solving a mystery involving racism and tragedy. (Rev: BL 5/1/00; HBG 10/00; SLJ 5/00)

407 Atinsky, Steve. *Tyler on Prime Time* (5–7). 2002, Delacorte $14.95 (0-385-72917-0). Tyler has the time of his life when he auditions for a part in a TV show and learns about show business backstage and the problems involved. (Rev: BCCB 9/02; BL 5/1/02; HBG 10/02; SLJ 8/02)

408 Bauer, Joan. *Hope Was Here* (7–9). 2000, Putnam $16.99 (0-399-23142-0). When she and her aunt move to Wisconsin, 16-year-old Hope is pleasantly surprised and becomes involved in politics while working in a diner. (Rev: BL 9/15/00; HB 9–10/00; HBG 3/01; SLJ 11/00*; VOYA 2/01)

409 Bauer, Marion Dane. *On My Honor* (5–7). 1986, Houghton $15.00 (0-89919-439-7); Dell paper $4.99 (0-440-46633-4). A powerful story in which 12-year-old Joel faces telling his parents that his friend Tony has drowned in the river they promised never to swim. (Rev: BCCB 10/86; BL 9/1/86; SLJ 11/86)

410 Belton, Sandra. *Mysteries on Monroe Street* (4–7). Illus. 1998, Simon & Schuster $16.00 (0-689-81612-X). In this, the fourth book in the Ernestine and Amanda series set in the late 1950s (told in alternating chapters by each of these African American friends), the focus is on adolescent problems, family tensions, and racial integration. (Rev: BL 7/98; HBG 10/98; SLJ 6/98)

411 Bernard, Virginia. *Eliza Down Under: Going to Sydney* (5–8). Series: Going To. 2000, Four Corners paper $7.95 (1-893577-02-3). This novel deals with Eliza's adventures in Australia when she accompanies her mother to the 2000 Olympic Games in Sydney. (Rev: SLJ 3/00)

412 Björk, Christina. *Vendela in Venice* (4–7). Illus. 1999, R&S $18.00 (91-29-64559-X). Vendela travels to Venice with her father and falls in love with the enchanting city, describing its many attractions. (Rev: BL 11/15/99; HB 11–12/99; HBG 3/00; SLJ 1/00)

413 Blatchford, Claire H. *Nick's Secret* (5–7). 2000, Lerner LB $17.95 (0-8225-0743-9). When 13-year-old Nick, who is deaf, is summoned to a motel by

Darryl Smythe and his gang of vandals, the boy knows he is in for trouble. (Rev: BL 9/15/00; HBG 3/01; SLJ 12/00; VOYA 2/01)

414 Brashares, Ann. *The Second Summer of the Sisterhood* (8–12). 2003, Delacorte $15.95 (0-385-72934-0). Those traveling jeans continue to work their wonders for the four friends as they cope with romantic, family, and school challenges in this sequel that can be enjoyed without reading the earlier novel. (Rev: BL 4/15/03; HB 5–6/03; HBG 10/03; SLJ 5/03)

415 Brashares, Ann. *The Sisterhood of the Traveling Pants* (6–9). 2001, Delacorte $14.95 (0-385-72933-2). Four teenage girls who are spending the summer apart pin their hopes on a pair of jeans that seems to magically fit and flatter them all. (Rev: BCCB 12/01; BL 8/01; HB 11–12/01; HBG 3/02; SLJ 8/01*; VOYA 10/01)

416 Brinkerhoff, Shirley. *Second Choices* (6–8). Series: Nikki Sheridan. 2000, Bethany paper $5.99 (1-56179-880-0). Nikki Sheridan finds comfort in her Christian values as she faces her parents' divorce, telling the father of her child about his paternity, and an incident of school violence in this sixth and final installment in the series. (Rev: BL 3/1/01)

417 Brooks, Bruce. *Dolores: Seven Stories About Her* (8–12). 2002, HarperCollins $15.95 (0-06-027818-8). Dolores is kidnapped, gossiped about, and fought over — but always manages to come out all right — in these stories that take her from age 7 to 16. (Rev: BCCB 5/02; BL 5/15/02; HBG 10/02; SLJ 4/02; VOYA 6/02)

418 Brooks, Bruce. *Everywhere* (5–8). 1990, HarperCollins LB $16.89 (0-06-020729-9). Eleven-year-old Dooley, who is African American, helps a 10-year-old white boy live through the emotional trauma of waiting to see if his beloved grandfather will recover from a heart attack. (Rev: BCCB 10/90; BL 10/15/90*; SLJ 9/90*)

419 Burch, Robert. *Christmas with Ida Early* (5–7). 1985, Puffin paper $4.99 (0-14-031971-9). A preacher involves Ida in a Christmas pageant in this amusing story.

420 Butcher, Kristin. *The Runaways* (5–8). 1998, Kids Can $16.95 (1-55074-413-5). During an unsuccessful attempt to run away from home, young Nick Battle meets Luther, a homeless man, and through this friendship gains insights into poverty in America. (Rev: BL 4/15/98; HBG 10/98; SLJ 4/98)

421 Byars, Betsy. *The Animal, the Vegetable and John D. Jones* (5–8). 1983, Dell paper $3.99 (0-440-40356-1). Clara and Deanie must share their vacation with the brainy John D.

422 Byars, Betsy. *The Pinballs* (5–7). 1977, HarperCollins LB $16.89 (0-06-020918-6). Three misfits in a foster home band together to help lessen their problems.

423 Carlson, Ron. *The Speed of Light* (4–7). 2003, HarperTempest $15.99 (0-380-97837-7). Baseball, science experiments, and the mysteries of the universe occupy Larry and his two best friends during the summer before junior high. (Rev: BL 8/03; SLJ 7/03; VOYA 10/03)

424 Carlyle, Carolyn. *Mercy Hospital: Crisis!* (5–8). 1993, Avon paper $3.50 (0-380-76846-1). Three friends volunteer at a local hospital. (Rev: SLJ 7/93)

425 Carroll, Jenny. *Sanctuary* (7–12). Series: 1-800-WHERE-R-YOU. 2002, Simon & Schuster paper $5.99 (0-7434-1142-0). Jessica uses her psychic ability in an effort to rescue a boy being held by a white supremacist group. (Rev: SLJ 1/03)

426 Carroll, Jenny. *When Lightning Strikes* (6–12). Series: 1-800-Where-R-You. 2001, Pocket paper $5.99 (0-7434-1139-0). When 16-year-old Jessica is struck by lightning, she acquires psychic powers. In the sequel *Code Name Cassandra*, she tries unsuccessfully to live the life of a normal teen. (Rev: BL 5/15/01)

427 Casanova, Mary. *Riot* (5–8). 1996, Hyperion LB $14.49 (0-7868-2204-X). Young Bryan is caught up in his father's conflict concerning the hiring of nonunion workers at his workplace. (Rev: BCCB 1/97; BL 11/1/96; BR 3–4/97; SLJ 10/96)

428 Casanova, Mary. *Wolf Shadows* (5–7). 1997, Hyperion $15.49 (0-7868-2269-4). In this outdoor story, a sequel to *Moose Tracks*, Seth and his friend Matt quarrel about wolf-protection programs but are brought together when a severe blizzard occurs on the first day of hunting season. (Rev: BL 10/1/97; HBG 3/98; SLJ 10/97)

429 Cheripko, Jan. *Rat* (7–12). 2002, Boyds Mills $15.95 (1-59078-034-5). Fifteen-year-old Jeremy faces difficult choices in this novel that looks at moral questions against a backdrop of basketball. (Rev: HBG 10/03; SLJ 8/02)

430 Chocolate, Deborah M. *NEATE to the Rescue!* (4–7). 1992, Just Us paper $3.95 (0-940975-42-4). A 13-year-old African American girl and her friends help out when her mother's seat on the local council is put in doubt by a racist. (Rev: BCCB 3/93; BL 3/15/93)

431 Clark, Catherine. *Frozen Rodeo* (8–12). 2003, HarperCollins $15.99 (0-06-009070-7). What starts out as a dull summer has its high points for P.F. (Peggy Fleming) Farrell as she enjoys a teen romance, foils a robbery, and even finds time to help deliver her mother's baby. (Rev: BL 2/15/03; HBG 10/03; SLJ 3/03; VOYA 4/03)

432 Clements, Andrew. *The School Story* (4–7). Illus. 2001, Simon & Schuster $16.00 (0-689-82594-3). Two 12-year-old girls tackle the task of getting a book by a new author published. (Rev: BCCB 7–8/01; BL 6/1–15/01; HB 7–8/01; HBG 10/01; SLJ 6/01)

433 Clements, Andrew. *A Week in the Woods* (4–8). 2002, Simon & Schuster $16.95 (0-689-82596-X). Mark, a lonely 5th grader, and a forceful teacher test each other — and Mark's survival skills — on a weeklong camping trip. (Rev: BCCB 1/03; BL 10/1/02; HBG 3/03; SLJ 11/02)

434 Clinton, Cathryn. *The Calling* (6–10). 2001, Candlewick $15.99 (0-7636-1387-8). Twelve-year-old Esta Lea takes her healing powers on the road in this humorous story set in the South of the 1960s. (Rev: BCCB 12/01; BL 10/1/01; HBG 3/02; SLJ 8/01; VOYA 2/02)

435 Cobb, Katie. *Happenings* (6–10). 2002, Harper-Collins LB $15.89 (0-06-028928-7); paper $5.95 (0-06-447232-9). Kelsey and her classmates start a protest against their AP English teacher that spirals out of control, causing conflict between Kelsey and her guardian brother. (Rev: BL 3/1/02; HBG 10/02; SLJ 3/02; VOYA 2/02)

436 Coles, William E. *Compass in the Blood* (7–12). 2001, Simon & Schuster $16.00 (0-689-83181-1). A college student learns about betrayal while researching the story of a prison warden's wife who was accused of helping notorious villains to escape in 1902. (Rev: BL 5/1/01; HBG 10/01; SLJ 6/01; VOYA 8/01)

437 Colfer, Eoin. *Benny and Babe* (6–8). 2001, O'Brien paper $7.95 (0-86278-603-7). On a visit to his grandfather, Benny, 13, makes a new friend, and he and Babe have money-making and other, more dangerous adventures. (Rev: SLJ 3/02)

438 Colfer, Eoin. *Benny and Omar* (5–8). 2001, O'Brien paper $7.95 (0-86278-567-7). Benny, a young Irish lad, has trouble adjusting to his new life in Tunisia until he befriends Omar, a local orphan without a home, and the two have some exciting and amusing adventures. (Rev: BL 8/01; SLJ 12/01)

439 Coman, Carolyn. *Many Stones* (7–12). 2000, Front Street $15.95 (1-886910-55-3). A year after her sister was murdered there, Berry reluctantly travels with her father to South Africa to attend her memorial in this novel set during the proceedings of the Truth and Reconciliation Commission. (Rev: BL 11/1/00; BR 1–2/01; HB 1–2/01; HBG 3/01; SLJ 11/00*; VOYA 2/01)

440 Conrad, Pam. *Our House: The Stories of Levittown* (4–7). 1995, Scholastic paper $14.95 (0-590-46523-6). A series of fictional vignettes trace the history of the middle-class community of Levittown, New York. (Rev: BCCB 12/95; BL 1/1–15/96; HB 11–12/95; SLJ 11/95)

441 Cooley, Beth. *Ostrich Eye* (7–10). 2004, Delacorte $15.95 (0-385-73106-X). Ginger decides that the photographer who is following her and her

young sister is her long-lost father, with consequences that are nearly tragic. (Rev: BL 11/15/03)

442 Craven, Margaret. *I Heard the Owl Call My Name* (7–12). 1973, Dell paper $6.99 (0-440-34369-0). A terminally ill Anglican priest and his assignment in a coastal Indian community in British Columbia. The nonfiction story behind this book is told in *Again Calls the Owl*.

443 Creech, Sharon. *Granny Torrelli Makes Soup* (4–6). 2003, HarperCollins $15.99 (0-06-029290-3). Food, warmth, and wisdom blend as 12-year-old Rosie spends time with her grandmother and talks about her blind friend Bailey and other life experiences. (Rev: BL 9/1/03*; HB 11–12/03; SLJ 8/03*)

444 Crew, Linda. *Brides of Eden: A True Story Imagined* (7–12). 2001, HarperCollins $15.95 (0-06-028750-0). Teenage Eva Mae Hurt describes the influence that magnetic preacher Joshua Creffield has on a group of women, who renounce their families and their everyday lives to follow his lead in this book based on fact, set in early 20th-century Oregon. (Rev: BCCB 2/01; BL 12/15/00; HB 3–4/01; HBG 10/01; SLJ 2/01; VOYA 6/01)

445 Cruise, Robin. *Fiona's Private Pages* (5–7). 2000, Harcourt $15.00 (0-15-202210-4). In her journal Fiona explores the meaning of friendship, what makes a good friend, and how friends can help each other. (Rev: BL 5/15/00; HBG 10/00; SLJ 6/00)

446 Crutcher, Chris. *Whale Talk* (8–12). 2001, Greenwillow $15.95 (0-688-18019-1). T.J. Jones, a bright high school senior of mixed race who dislikes bullies and bigots, recounts his efforts to right some wrongs through recruiting unusual choices to his swim team. (Rev: BCCB 4/01; BL 4/1/01; HB 5–6/01; HBG 10/01; SLJ 5/01)

447 Dahl, Roald. *Matilda* (4–8). 1998, Puffin paper $6.99 (0-14-130106-6). Superbright 1st-grader Matilda deals with the evil school principal Miss Trunchbutt. (Rev: BCCB 10/88; HB 1–2/89; SLJ 10/88)

448 Danziger, Paula, and Ann M. Martin. *P. S. Longer Letter Later* (5–8). 1998, Scholastic paper $15.95 (0-590-21310-5). This novel consists of letters between two recently separated girlfriends — one who is adjusting well and the other who is facing family problems after her father loses his job and the family must change its lifestyle. (Rev: BL 6/1–15/98; BR 9–10/98; HBG 10/98; SLJ 5/98; VOYA 8/98)

449 Danziger, Paula, and Ann M. Martin. *Snail Mail No More* (5–7). 2000, Scholastic paper $16.95 (0-439-06335-3). Two 13-year-old friends correspond by e-mail and reveal funny, thought-provoking experiences that involve family and social problems. (Rev: BCCB 4/00; BL 3/15/00; HBG 10/00; SLJ 3/00; VOYA 4/00)

25

450 Deans, Sis. *Every Day and All the Time* (5–8). 2003, Holt $16.95 (0-8050-7337-X). Twelve-year-old Emily is still haunted by her brother's death and she resists the idea of selling the family house in which they all lived together. (Rev: BL 9/1/03; SLJ 12/03; VOYA 10/03)

451 DeFelice, Cynthia. *The Light on Hogback Hill* (4–8). 1993, Macmillan paper $15.00 (0-02-726453-X). When 11-year-olds Hadley and Josh discover that the Witch Woman of Hogback Hill is really a shy, deformed woman, they help her find the courage to return to town. (Rev: BCCB 12/93; BL 11/1/93; SLJ 11/93)

452 Dexter, Catherine. *Driving Lessons* (6–8). 2000, Candlewick $16.99 (0-7636-0515-8). Mattie's anger about being sent to South Dakota for the summer abates when she meets Lester. (Rev: BL 9/1/00; HB 11–12/00; HBG 3/01; SLJ 10/00; VOYA 4/01)

453 Donahue, John. *Till Tomorrow* (5–7). 2001, Farrar $16.00 (0-374-37580-1). When his family moves to a U.S. Army base in France in the early 1960s, Terry befriends an unpopular boy, with surprising results. (Rev: BCCB 11/01; BL 9/15/01; HBG 3/02; SLJ 9/01)

454 Dowell, Frances O'Roark. *Where I'd Like to Be* (5–8). 2003, Simon & Schuster $15.95 (0-689-84420-4). Maddie, a foster child living in a children's home, reveals her longing for a real home to a new friend. (Rev: BL 5/15/03; SLJ 4/03)

455 Doyon, Stephanie. *Taking Chances* (6–10). Series: On the Road. 1999, Simon & Schuster paper $4.50 (0-689-82109-3). Miranda and Kirsten compete for the same boy while on their way to California in this third book in the series. (Rev: SLJ 2/00)

456 Draper, Sharon. *Double Dutch* (7–10). 2002, Simon & Schuster $16.00 (0-689-84230-9). Eighth-graders Delia and Randy both have secrets — Delia can't read and Randy's father has disappeared, leaving him on his own. (Rev: BCCB 10/02; BL 9/1/02; HBG 10/02; SLJ 6/02; VOYA 8/02)

457 Draper, Sharon M. *The Battle of Jericho* (7–10). 2003, Simon & Schuster $16.95 (0-689-84232-5). Sixteen-year-old Jericho is initially thrilled when he's asked to pledge for membership in the Warriors of Distinction club, but subsequent events turn chilling. (Rev: BL 6/1–15/03; SLJ 6/03; VOYA 8/03)

458 Draper, Sharon M. *Darkness Before Dawn* (8–12). Series: Hazelwood High. 2001, Simon & Schuster $16.95 (0-689-83080-7). Keisha Montgomery copes with many issues — the suicide of her ex-boyfriend, a new relationship, date rape, and more in this novel set at Hazelwood High. (Rev: BCCB 3/01; BL 1/1–15/01; HBG 10/01; SLJ 2/01; VOYA 8/01)

459 Dunlop, Eileen. *Finn's Search* (4–7). 1994, Holiday $14.95 (0-8234-1099-4). Two Scottish boys try to save a gravel pit from local developers. (Rev: BCCB 12/94; BL 10/1/94; SLJ 10/94)

460 Ellerbee, Linda. *Girl Reporter Blows Lid Off Town!* (4–7). Series: Get Real. 2000, HarperCollins LB $14.89 (0-06-028245-2); paper $4.99 (0-06-440755-1). Casey Smith, a 6th-grade reporter, discovers the thrill of tracking down stories and getting at the truth in this lighthearted story set in a small town in the Berkshires. Also use *Girl Reporter Sinks School!* (Rev: BL 3/1/00; HBG 10/00; SLJ 6/00)

461 Ewing, Lynne. *Party Girl* (6–9). 1998, Random $17.99 (0-679-99285-5). A nightmarish look at Southern California gang culture is provided in this powerful novel about a girl who plots revenge when her closest friend is gunned down. (Rev: BL 8/98; HB 9–10/98; HBG 3/99; SLJ 9/98; VOYA 4/99)

462 Farrell, Mame. *And Sometimes Why* (6–9). 2001, Farrar $16.00 (0-374-32289-9). Thirteen-year-old Jack develops romantic feelings for long-time friend Chris, but his efforts to get together with her are stymied by misunderstandings and interference by others. (Rev: BCCB 4/01; BL 5/1/01; HB 5–6/01; HBG 10/01; SLJ 7/01; VOYA 6/01)

463 Ferris, Amy Schor. *A Greater Goode* (6–9). 2002, Houghton $15.00 (0-618-13154-X). Twelve-year-old Addie may be a little too warm-hearted when she takes in a pregnant young woman who has been abused. (Rev: BL 6/1–15/02; HBG 10/02; SLJ 4/02; VOYA 6/02)

464 Finch, Susan. *The Intimacy of Indiana* (8–12). 2001, Tudor $15.95 (0-936389-79-6). Readers follow three teens through the trials of their senior year in high school in small-town Indiana — SATs, college finance, romance, drugs, and of course parents. (Rev: BL 7/01)

465 Fine, Anne. *Up on Cloud Nine* (5–7). 2002, Delacorte LB $17.99 (0-385-90058-9). While Stolly lies unconscious in a hospital after an accident, his friend Ian remembers his unusual friend and his many strange but interesting habits. (Rev: BCCB 5/02; BL 6/1–15/02*; HB 7–8/02*; HBG 10/02; SLJ 6/02*)

466 Flake, Sharon. *The Skin I'm In* (5–9). 1998, Hyperion paper $15.49 (0-7868-2392-5). Maleeka Madison feels like an outsider in her new inner-city middle school, and she is led into delinquent behavior by bully Charlese. (Rev: BL 9/1/98; HBG 3/99)

467 Fleischman, Paul. *Seek* (7–12). 2001, Cricket $16.95 (0-8126-4900-1). For a school autobiography project, 17-year-old Rob makes a recording of important sounds in his life, including the voice of the father he never knew. (Rev: BCCB 11/01; BL 12/15/01; HB 11–12/01; HBG 3/02; SLJ 9/01*; VOYA 12/01)

468 Fletcher, Ralph. *Flying Solo* (5–8). 1998, Clarion $15.00 (0-395-87323-1). This novel answers the question, "What would a 6th-grade class do if their substitute teacher fails to appear and they are left alone for a whole day?" (Rev: BCCB 9/98; BL 8/98*; HB 11–12/98; HBG 3/99; SLJ 10/98)

469 Freymann-Weyr, Garret. *The Kings Are Already Here* (7–10). 2003, Houghton $15.00 (0-618-26363-2). Phebe's love of ballet dominates her life until she travels to Geneva to visit her father and meets Nikolai, a 16-year-old refugee who is obsessed with chess. (Rev: BL 2/15/03; HB 3–4/03; HBG 10/03; SLJ 4/03; VOYA 4/03)

470 Freymann-Weyr, Garret. *When I Was Older* (8–12). 2000, Houghton $15.00 (0-618-05545-2). The death of her younger brother precipitated the breakup of her parents' marriage, and Sophie has been careful to avoid new relationships until she meets Francis. (Rev: BL 11/1/00; HB 1–2/01; HBG 3/01; SLJ 10/00*)

471 Funke, Cornelia. *The Thief Lord* (6–9). 2002, Scholastic $16.95 (0-439-40437-1). Inspired by their dead mother's stories of the wonders of Venice, two boys run away from Hamburg and find an unusual home under the protection of a young Venetian thief. (Rev: BCCB 11/02; BL 10/15/02; HB 11–12/02; HBG 3/03; SLJ 10/02*; VOYA 4/03)

472 Gantos, Jack. *Heads or Tails: Stories from the Sixth Grade* (5–8). 1994, Farrar $16.00 (0-374-32909-5). A collection of eight unusual short stories about 6th-grader Jack, a born survivor who overcomes amazing obstacles in this book set in Fort Lauderdale. (Rev: BCCB 7–8/94; HB 7–8/94; SLJ 6/94*)

473 Gantos, Jack. *Jack on the Tracks: Four Seasons of Fifth Grade* (5–7). 1999, Farrar $16.00 (0-374-33665-2). An episodic novel (the fourth about Jack Henry) in which Jack, a preadolescent, has several innocent adventures while growing up. (Rev: BCCB 9/99; BL 9/1/99; HB 11–12/99; HBG 3/00; SLJ 10/99; VOYA 2/00)

474 Gantos, Jack. *Jack's Black Book* (5–8). 1997, Farrar $16.00 (0-374-33662-8). In this third semiautobiographical novel, Jack is living in Florida with his family, tries to build a coffin for his dead dog, hopes to improve his writing skills, and is sent to a vocational training school. (Rev: BL 10/15/97; BR 3–4/98; HBG 3/98; SLJ 10/97)

475 Garden, Nancy. *Meeting Melanie* (4–7). 2002, Farrar $16.00 (0-374-34943-6). Melanie's mother doesn't want Melanie to get friendly with the "natives" on the Maine island where they're spending the summer, but Melanie and Allie become fast allies nonetheless. (Rev: BCCB 1/03; BL 12/1/02; HBG 3/03; SLJ 9/02; VOYA 12/02)

476 Gilbert, Barbara Snow. *Paper Trail* (7–10). 2000, Front Street $15.95 (1-886910-44-8). A thought-provoking story of a boy torn between family loyalties and connections to a cult known as the Soldiers of God. (Rev: BL 7/00; HB 7–8/00; HBG 9/00; SLJ 8/00)

477 Gilson, Jamie. *Thirteen Ways to Sink a Sub* (4–7). 1982, Lothrop $15.95 (0-688-01304-X). The girls in Room 4A challenge the boys to see who can first make their substitute teacher cry. A sequel is *4B Goes Wild* (1983).

478 Goobie, Beth. *Before Wings* (7–10). 2001, Orca $16.95 (1-55143-161-0). An absorbing story that centers on the counselors at a summer camp and on 15-year-old Adrien's past illness and present mystical experiences. (Rev: BL 3/15/01; BR 11/01; HB 3–4/01; HBG 10/01; SLJ 4/01; VOYA 4/01)

479 Goobie, Beth. *The Lottery* (7–12). 2002, Orca $15.95 (1-55143-238-2). As the lottery winner, 15-year-old Sal must spend the year doing the bidding of a sinister student group, the Shadow Council. (Rev: BL 1/1–15/03; HBG 10/03; SLJ 3/03; VOYA 2/03)

480 Greene, Constance C. *A Girl Called Al* (5–7). 1991, Puffin paper $5.99 (0-14-034786-0). The friendship between two 7th graders and their apartment building superintendent is humorously and deftly recounted.

481 Gregory, Deborah. *Wishing on a Star* (5–8). Series: The Cheetah Girls. 1999, Hyperion paper $3.99 (0-7868-1384-9). A light novel about five girls in New York City who form a singing group, the Cheetah Girls, and are soon signed up for an important gig. (Rev: SLJ 1/00)

482 Grunwell, Jeanne Marie. *Mind Games* (5–8). 2003, Houghton $15.00 (0-618-17672-1). Six very different 7th graders get to know each other as they collaborate on a science fair project in this inventive novel sprinkled with press clippings and project notes. (Rev: BL 5/15/03; HB 5–6/03; HBG 10/03; LMC 10/03; SLJ 5/03)

483 Gutman, Dan. *The Million Dollar Kick* (5–8). 2001, Hyperion $16.49 (0-7868-2612-6). A 7th grader who hates soccer must face her shortcomings and deal with middle-school cliques when she is chosen to try to kick a $1 million goal. (Rev: BL 11/15/01; HBG 3/02; SLJ 12/01)

484 Haddix, Margaret P. *Leaving Fishers* (6–9). 1997, Simon & Schuster $17.00 (0-689-81125-X). High-schooler Dorrie becomes innocently involved in a religious cult called Fishers of Men and soon finds that getting out is difficult. (Rev: BL 12/15/97; BR 5–6/98; HBG 3/98; SLJ 10/97; VOYA 2/98)

485 Hahn, Mary D. *Daphne's Book* (6–8). 1983, Houghton $15.00 (0-89919-183-5); Avon paper $5.99 (0-380-72355-7). The story of a friendship between two very different girls.

486 Hall, Katy, and Lisa Eisenberg. *The Paxton Cheerleaders: Go for It, Patti!* (4–7). 1994, Simon & Schuster paper $3.50 (0-671-89490-X). Four 7th-grade girls from different backgrounds make the cheerleading team in their junior high school. (Rev: BL 2/1/95)

487 Hansen, Joyce. *The Gift-Giver* (4–7). 1980, Houghton paper $6.95 (0-89919-852-X). Doris forms a friendship with a quiet boy, Amir.

488 Henkes, Kevin. *Olive's Ocean* (5–8). 2003, Greenwillow $15.99 (0-06-053543-1). During a summer at the beach, Martha, an aspiring writer, wrestles with a classmate's sudden death, has her first whiff of romance, and gets to know her family and herself better. (Rev: BL 9/1/03*; HB 11–12/03*; SLJ 8/03*)

489 Hermes, Patricia. *I Hate Being Gifted* (5–8). 1992, Pocket paper $3.50 (0-671-74786-X). Everybody says it's an honor to be in the Learning Enrichment Activity Program, but KT thinks it can ruin her entire 6th-grade year. (Rev: BL 12/1/90)

490 Hill, Susan. *The Christmas Collection* (4–7). 1994, Candlewick $19.95 (1-56402-341-9). Four moving Christmas stories and a poem compose this holiday anthology. (Rev: BL 10/15/94)

491 Holt, Kimberly Willis. *When Zachary Beaver Came to Town* (5–9). 1999, Holt $16.95 (0-8050-6116-9). Thirteen-year-old Toby Wilson learns the value of love and friendship when he gets to know Zachary Beaver, a 643-pound teen who has been abandoned by his guardian. (Rev: BCCB 12/99; BL 9/15/99; HB 11–12/99; HBG 3/00; SLJ 11/99*; VOYA 12/99)

492 Holtwijk, Ineke. *Asphalt Angels* (8–12). Trans. by Wanda Boeke. 1999, Front Street $15.95 (1-886910-24-3). When a homeless boy in the slums of Rio de Janeiro joins a street gang, the Asphalt Angels, for protection from corrupt police officers, pedophiles, and other homeless people, he finds himself being drawn into a life of crime. (Rev: BL 8/99; HBG 4/00; SLJ 9/99; VOYA 12/99)

493 Holubitsky, Katherine. *Last Summer in Agatha* (6–10). 2001, Orca $16.95 (1-55143-188-2); paper $9.95 (1-55143-190-4). Rachel enjoys her summer in a small Canadian town but is distressed by her new friend Michael's continuing grief over his brother's death. (Rev: HBG 3/02; SLJ 12/01)

494 Honeycutt, Natalie. *Josie's Beau* (5–7). 1988, Avon paper $2.95 (0-380-70524-9). Beau's mother doesn't want him fighting, so Josie offers to say she's the one who fights — but the lie backfires. (Rev: BCCB 12/87; BL 12/1/87; SLJ 12/87)

495 Hossack, Sylvie. *Green Mango Magic* (4–7). 1999, Avon $14.00 (0-380-97613-7). Maile, who lives alone with her grandmother in Hawaii since her father abandoned her, finds a friend in Brooke, from Seattle, who is a recovering cancer patient. (Rev: BCCB 12/98; BL 5/1/99; HBG 10/99; SLJ 2/99; VOYA 8/99)

496 Howe, James. *The Misfits* (5–8). 2001, Simon & Schuster $16.00 (0-689-83955-3). A group of 7th-grade social misfits challenge the so-called norms at their school by running for student council and instituting a no-names-calling day. (Rev: BCCB 1/02; BL 11/15/01; HB 11–12/01; HBG 3/02; SLJ 11/01; VOYA 12/01)

497 Hudson, Wade. *Anthony's Big Surprise* (5–7). Series: NEATE. 1998, Just Us paper $3.95 (0-940975-42-6). Interracial tensions erupt in junior high school when some African American students are suspended and Anthony, who is also trying to cope with a family crisis, must deal with both problems. (Rev: SLJ 6/99)

498 Ingold, Jeanette. *Airfield* (7–10). 1999, Harcourt $17.00 (0-15-202053-5); Puffin paper $5.99 (0-14-131216-5). In the early days of aviation, Beatty, 15, spends time at the airport, making a good friend and hoping to see her pilot father and learn more from him about her dead mother. (Rev: BCCB 1/00; HBG 4/00; SLJ 10/99; VOYA 2/00)

499 Ingold, Jeanette. *Mountain Solo* (6–9). 2003, Harcourt $17.00 (0-15-202670-3). After an unsuccessful violin concert, 16-year-old Tess flees to her father's home in Montana where she meets Frederick, another violinist, and reviews her love of music, her past life, and her goals for the future. (Rev: BL 12/1/03; SLJ 11/03)

500 Jenkins, A. M. *Out of Order* (8–10). 2003, HarperCollins $15.99 (0-06-623968-0). Sophomore Colt relies on his good looks and athletic prowess to pull him through, but failing grades place him in the company of a brainy girl and his attitudes begin to change. (Rev: BL 9/1/03; HB 11–12/03; SLJ 9/03*; VOYA 10/03)

501 Jennings, Patrick. *The Beastly Arms* (5–7). 2001, Scholastic paper $16.95 (0-439-16589-X). A dreamy 6th grader who pictures animals in everything he sees, discovers a world of real beasts when he and his mother move to the Beastly Arms. (Rev: BCCB 10/01; BL 5/1/01; HB 7–8/01; HBG 10/01; SLJ 4/01)

502 Jennings, Richard W. *The Great Whale of Kansas* (5–9). 2001, Houghton $15.00 (0-618-10228-0). When a boy finds a prehistoric whale fossil in his backyard, the discovery brings unexpected consequences. (Rev: HB 9–10/01; HBG 3/02; SLJ 8/01; VOYA 2/02)

503 Johnson, Stephen T. *As the City Sleeps* (4–8). Illus. 2002, Viking $16.99 (0-670-88940-7). This picture book for older readers portrays a city at night, with eerie, enigmatic illustrations that include dreamlike creatures. (Rev: BL 12/1/02; HB 1–2/03; HBG 3/03; SLJ 1/03)

504 Jukes, Mavis. *Getting Even* (5–7). 1988, Knopf paper $4.50 (0-679-86570-5). Maggie seems unable to stop the nasty pranks of classmate Corky, and receives differing advice from her divorced parents. (Rev: BCCB 5/88; BL 4/1/88; SLJ 5/88)

505 Karr, Kathleen. *Gilbert and Sullivan Set Me Free* (6–10). 2003, Hyperion $15.99 (0-7868-1916-2). A production of Gilbert and Sullivan's "Pirates of Penzance" brings together the inmates of a women's prison in this story based on a true 1914 event. (Rev: BCCB 9/03; BL 5/15/03; HB 7–8/03; HBG 10/03; SLJ 7/03; VOYA 6/03)

506 Kherdian, David. *The Revelations of Alvin Tolliver* (5–7). 2001, Hampton Roads paper $7.95 (1-57174-255-7). Twelve-year-old Alvin is fascinated with nature and the great outdoors, and finds some unusual adult friends who introduce him to nature's charms. (Rev: BL 12/1/01; SLJ 3/02)

507 Kimmel, Elizabeth Cody. *Lily B. on the Brink of Cool* (4–8). 2003, HarperCollins $15.99 (0-06-000586-6). Lily Blennerhassett, 13 and an aspiring author who keeps a diary, has been spending a very boring summer and is easily seduced by the allure of the LeBlanc family and their active and sophisticated way of life. (Rev: BL 12/1/03; SLJ 10/03; VOYA 10/03)

508 Kline, Lisa Williams. *The Princesses of Atlantis* (5–7). 2002, Cricket $16.95 (0-8126-2855-1). Twelve-year-old Arlene experiences ups and downs in her friendship with Carly, with whom she is writing a novel about two princesses. (Rev: BL 4/15/02; HBG 10/02; SLJ 7/02)

509 Koertge, Ron. *The Heart of the City* (5–7). 1998, Orchard LB $16.99 (0-531-33078-8). Apprehensive about moving to the big city of Los Angeles, 10-year-old Joy soon finds a friend in a young African American girl and together they fight the takeover of an abandoned house by hoods. (Rev: BCCB 4/98; BL 4/1/98; HBG 10/98)

510 Konigsburg, E. L. *The Outcasts of 19 Schuyler Place* (4–8). 2004, Simon & Schuster $16.95 (0-689-86636-4). Rescued from summer camp by aging uncles, Margaret is dismayed to find that their prized garden sculptures are endangered in this absorbing, amusing, and thought-provoking novel. (Rev: BL 12/15/03*; SLJ 1/04*)

511 Konigsburg, E. L. *The View from Saturday* (5–7). 1996, Simon & Schuster $16.00 (0-689-80993-X). A complicated tale about four 6th-graders who are contestants in an Academic Bowl competition. Newbery Medal winner, 1997. (Rev: BCCB 11/96; BL 10/15/96; SLJ 9/96*)

512 Korman, Gordon. *No More Dead Dogs* (5–7). 2001, Hyperion LB $16.49 (0-7868-2462-X). Eighth-grade football player and truth-teller Wallace Wallace decides to add some fun to a boring play about a faithful dog in this complex and zany story. (Rev: BL 10/1/01; HBG 10/01)

513 Korman, Gordon. *The Twinkle Squad* (5–7). 1992, Scholastic paper $13.95 (0-590-45249-5). A

bossy, insecure 6th grader and a defender of weaker kids are sentenced to the school's Special Discussion Group. (Rev: BCCB 11/92; BL 9/15/92; SLJ 9/92)

514 Koss, Amy Goldman. *The Cheat* (5–8). 2003, Dial $16.99 (0-8037-2794-1). When three 8th-graders are caught cheating on a geography test, they have to make difficult decisions — do they reveal their source? (Rev: BCCB 2/03; BL 1/1–15/03; HBG 10/03; SLJ 1/03; VOYA 4/03)

515 Kropp, Paul. *The Countess and Me* (6–9). 2002, Fitzhenry & Whiteside $14.95 (1-55041-680-4). Young Jordan, eager to fit in at his new school, must decide whether to betray his eccentric neighbor to a group of delinquent boys. (Rev: BL 10/1/02; SLJ 11/02)

516 Lafaye, A. *Strawberry Hill* (5–8). 1999, Simon & Schuster $16.95 (0-689-82441-6). In this novel set in the 1970s, 12-year-old Raleia longs for a secure, old-fashioned life that her hippy parents don't provide. (Rev: BCCB 5/99; BL 8/99; HBG 10/99; SLJ 8/99; VOYA 10/99)

517 Lamm, Drew. *Bittersweet* (8–11). 2003, Clarion $15.00 (0-618-16443-X). When Taylor's grandmother, who has essentially raised her, falls ill, artist Taylor suddenly finds she lacks creativity and is unsure of her other relationships. (Rev: BCCB 2/04; BL 11/15/03; SLJ 12/03)

518 Lantz, Francess. *A Royal Kiss* (5–8). 2000, Simon & Schuster paper $3.99 (0-689-83422-5). In this light romance, 14-year-old Samantha Simms meets and falls in love with a real Prince who sweeps her off her feet. (Rev: SLJ 8/00)

519 Levy, Elizabeth. *Seventh Grade Tango* (5–7). 2000, Hyperion $16.49 (0-7868-2427-1). Seventh-grader Rebecca gets into a ballroom dancing program with her friend Scott, who is being chased by Samantha, much to Rebecca's annoyance. (Rev: BCCB 3/00; BL 3/1/00; HBG 10/00; SLJ 4/00)

520 Lewis, J. Patrick. *The Last Resort* (6–9). 2002, Creative Company $17.95 (1-56846-172-0). Noted poet J. Patrick Lewis uses word play and inventive characters to tell the story of an artist looking for inspiration, in this picture book for older readers full of thought-provoking images. (Rev: BL 2/1/03; HBG 3/03)

521 Lewis, Wendy. *Graveyard Girl* (7–10). 2000, Red Deer paper $7.95 (0-88995-202-7). While looking back at her high school yearbook, Ginger reminisces about her classmates and vignettes reveal their stories of marriage, achievement, and lost romance. (Rev: BL 1/1–15/01; SLJ 5/01; VOYA 6/01)

522 Lowry, Brigid. *Guitar Highway Rose* (8–12). 2003, Holiday $16.95 (0-8234-1790-5). Set in Australia, this story of two teens who run away from home presents the voices of various characters including teachers, family, and friends. (Rev: BL 2/15/04; SLJ 12/03)

523 Lubar, David. *Hidden Talents* (5–9). 1999, Tor $16.95 (0-312-86646-1). Five misfits, who are attending the last-resort Edgeview Alternative School, become friends and discover extrasensory talents they can use against the school bully. (Rev: BL 9/15/99; HBG 10/99; SLJ 11/99; VOYA 10/99)

524 Lubar, David. *Wizards of the Game* (6–8). 2003, Putnam $16.99 (0-399-23706-2). A role-playing game creates havoc when Mercer, who is in 8th grade, accidentally releases some supernatural monsters. (Rev: BL 2/15/03; SLJ 3/03; VOYA 4/03)

525 Lynch, L. M. *How I Wonder What You Are* (5–7). 2001, Knopf LB $17.99 (0-375-90663-0). A strange new family with an intriguing son moves into 6th-grader Laurel's neighborhood. (Rev: BCCB 11/01; BL 8/01; HBG 3/02; SLJ 7/01)

526 MacCullough, Carolyn. *Falling Through Darkness* (7–12). 2003, Roaring Brook $15.95 (0-7613-1934-4). After her boyfriend is killed, Ginny retreats into herself, reliving their time together and avoiding contact with others. (Rev: BL 11/15/03; HB 11–12/03; SLJ 11/03)

527 McDonald, Janet. *Twists and Turns* (7–12). 2003, Farrar $16.00 (0-374-39955-7). Sisters Keeba and Teesha, who have successfully navigated their way through high school, open a hair salon in the projects of Brooklyn Heights and face new challenges. (Rev: BL 7/03*; HB 9–10/03; SLJ 9/03)

528 McGuigan, Mary Ann. *Where You Belong* (5–8). 1997, Simon & Schuster $16.95 (0-689-81250-7). In 1963 in the Bronx, a lonely white girl growing up in poverty forms a friendship with an African American girl. (Rev: BCCB 5/97; BL 6/1–15/97; BR 11–12/97; SLJ 7/97; VOYA 8/97)

529 MacKall, Dandi Daley, and Terry K. Brown. *Portrait of Lies* (6–9). Series: TodaysGirls.com. 2000, Tommy Nelson paper $5.99 (0-8499-7561-1). Jamie wants to attend art camp and enters a contest despite her worries about her skills. (Rev: SLJ 11/00)

530 McKay, Hilary. *The Exiles in Love* (4–7). 1998, Simon & Schuster $16.00 (0-689-81752-5). Because of their grandmother's scheming, the four Conway sisters are able to spend their spring break on a farm in Brittany. (Rev: BCCB 4/98; BL 5/1/98*; HB 5–6/98*; HBG 10/98; SLJ 5/98)

531 McKenna, Colleen O'Shaughnessy. *Camp Murphy* (5–7). 1993, Scholastic paper $13.95 (0-590-45807-8). It's harder than it looks when Collette and friends decide to run a week-long day camp for the neighborhood kids. (Rev: BCCB 3/93; BL 3/15/93; SLJ 4/93)

532 Mazer, Norma Fox. *Mrs. Fish, Ape, and Me, the Dump Queen* (6–9). 1981, Avon paper $3.50 (0-380-69153-1). Joyce has been hurt by supposed friends but somehow she trusts the school custodian, Mrs. Fish.

533 Mikaelsen, Ben. *Touching Spirit Bear* (6–9). 2001, HarperCollins $15.99 (0-380-97744-3). Cole, an angry and violent 15-year-old, is sentenced according to Native American tradition to a year of solitude on an island in Alaska. (Rev: BCCB 5/01; BL 1/1–15/01; HBG 10/01; SLJ 2/01; VOYA 6/01)

534 Miller, Judi. *My Crazy Cousin Courtney* (5–7). 1993, Pocket paper $3.50 (0-671-73821-6). Cathy is shocked to discover how much she and her California cousin are alike. (Rev: BL 3/1/93)

535 Mills, Claudia. *Losers, Inc.* (5–7). 1997, Farrar $16.00 (0-374-34661-5). Ethan develops a crush on his new student teacher and tries every way possible to impress her. (Rev: BCCB 4/97; BL 3/1/97; SLJ 4/97)

536 Mills, Claudia. *Standing Up to Mr. O.* (4–7). 1998, Farrar $16.00 (0-374-34721-2). In spite of opposition from friends and teachers, Maggie McIntosh refuses to dissect specimens in biology class, even though she risks getting an F. (Rev: BCCB 10/98; BL 10/15/98; HB 9–10/98; HBG 3/99; SLJ 12/98)

537 Moeyaert, Bart. *Hornet's Nest* (8–10). Trans. from Dutch by David Colmer. 2000, Front Street $15.95 (1-886910-48-0). Translated from Dutch, this is a fablelike story of Susanna's efforts to solve some of the problems in her life and her village. (Rev: BL 9/15/00; HB 11–12/00; HBG 3/01; SLJ 11/00)

538 Moore, Martha. *Under the Mermaid Angel* (5–8). 1995, Delacorte $14.95 (0-385-32160-0). Thirteen-year-old Jesse is fascinated by her new neighbor, fast-talking, brash Roxanne. (Rev: BCCB 12/95; BL 8/95; SLJ 10/95; VOYA 12/95)

539 Moriarty, Jaclyn. *Feeling Sorry for Celia: A Novel* (7–12). 2001, St. Martin's $16.95 (0-312-26923-4). The teenage uncertainties and complex family and peer relationships of a 15-year-old Australian girl are revealed through a series of notes and letters. (Rev: BL 11/15/00; BR 5/01; SLJ 5/01; VOYA 4/01)

540 Morris, Deborah. *Teens 911: Snowbound, Helicopter Crash and Other True Survival Stories* (7–12). 2002, Health Communications paper $12.95 (0-7573-0039-1). Five stories that portray teens facing emergencies (being stranded, in helicopter crashes, rescuing residents of burning houses, and so forth) are followed by postscripts and survival quizzes. (Rev: SLJ 2/03; VOYA 2/03)

541 Myers, Anna. *When the Bough Breaks* (5–9). 2000, Walker $16.95 (0-8027-8725-8). The harrowing, suspenseful story of a foster child, her elderly neighbor, and the terrible secrets that each is hiding.

(Rev: BL 11/15/00; HB 1–2/01; HBG 3/01; SLJ 12/00; VOYA 4/01)

542 Naylor, Phyllis Reynolds. *Blizzard's Wake* (7–12). 2002, Simon & Schuster $16.95 (0-689-85220-7). In a blizzard in 1941, 15-year-old Kate comes face to face with the man who caused her mother's death. (Rev: BCCB 1/03; BL 10/15/02; HBG 3/03; SLJ 12/02)

543 Nolan, Han. *When We Were Saints* (7–10). 2003, Harcourt $17.00 (0-15-216371-9). After his grandfather's death, Archie, 14, is overwhelmed by a need to find God and, with his religious friend Clare, sets off on a pilgrimage to the Cloisters in New York. (Rev: BL 10/1/03; SLJ 11/03)

544 O'Brien, Judith. *Mary Jane* (7–10). 2003, Marvel $14.99 (0-7851-1308-8). Mary Jane has been fond of budding Spider-Man Peter Parker since they were both 9 years old and now, in high school, she has a definite crush. (Rev: SLJ 12/03)

545 O'Connor, Barbara. *Me and Rupert Goody* (5–7). 1999, Farrar $15.00 (0-374-34904-5). Set in Appalachia, this novel deals with the problems of young Jennalee, how she becomes friendly with the local store owner, and how this friendship is endangered when the owner's son moves into town. (Rev: BCCB 10/99; BL 11/1/99; HB 9–10/99; HBG 3/00; SLJ 10/99)

546 O'Keefe, Susan Heyboer. *My Life and Death by Alexandra Canarsie* (7–10). 2002, Peachtree $14.95 (1-56145-264-5). Allie, a lonely teenager, finds a friend and a mystery when she starts going to strangers' funerals. (Rev: HBG 10/02; SLJ 9/02; VOYA 4/02)

547 Paterson, Katherine. *Bridge to Terabithia* (6–8). 1977, HarperCollins LB $16.89 (0-690-04635-9); paper $5.99 (0-06-440184-7). Jess becomes a close friend of Leslie, a new girl in his school, and suffers agony after her accidental death. Newbery Medal winner, 1978. (Rev: SLJ 1/00)

548 Paulsen, Gary. *The Glass Cafe* (6–8). 2003, Random $12.95 (0-385-32499-5). Tony, 12, has an unusual mother who allows him to draw the women at the Kitty Kat Club, a situation that does not please social services. (Rev: BL 9/1/03; HBG 10/03; SLJ 6/03; VOYA 8/03)

549 Peck, Richard. *Amanda Miranda* (7–12). 1999, Dial $16.99 (0-8037-2489-6). An enthralling story of a servant and her lookalike mistress on board the *Titanic*, based on the 1979 adult novel. (Rev: BL 11/15/99; HBG 4/00)

550 Peck, Robert Newton. *Extra Innings* (7–12). 2001, HarperCollins $15.95 (0-06-028867-1). Aunt Vidalia reminisces about her early years and adventures with an African American baseball team during the Depression. (Rev: BCCB 3/01; BL 2/1/01; HBG 10/01; SLJ 3/01; VOYA 8/01)

551 Perkins, Lynne Rae. *All Alone in the Universe* (5–8). 1999, Greenwillow $15.95 (0-688-16881-7). Debbie is crushed when her friend of many years drops her for another, but she has the courage to adjust and reach out to others. (Rev: BCCB 10/99; BL 9/1/99*; HB 9–10/99; HBG 3/00; SLJ 10/99)

552 Powell, Randy. *Three Clams and an Oyster* (7–10). 2002, Farrar $16.00 (0-374-37526-7). Three teens who have played flag football together for years struggle to decide who should be their fourth man in this humorous and realistic novel. (Rev: BCCB 7–8/02; HB 7–8/02; HBG 10/02; SLJ 3/02; VOYA 8/02)

553 Qualey, Marsha. *One Night* (8–12). 2002, Dial $16.99 (0-8037-2602-3). Kelly, 19 and a former drug addict, meets an attractive Balkan prince and plots to feature him on her aunt's talk-radio show. (Rev: BCCB 3/02; BL 4/1/02; HBG 10/02; SLJ 6/02; VOYA 6/02)

554 Rallison, Janette. *Playing the Field* (5–7). 2002, Walker $16.95 (0-8027-8804-1). Thirteen-year-old McKay's friend Tony urges him to pursue pretty Serena, but McKay is more interested in friendship than romance. (Rev: BCCB 7–8/02; BL 5/15/02; HBG 10/02; SLJ 4/02; VOYA 6/02)

555 Randle, Kristen D. *Slumming* (8–11). 2003, HarperTempest $15.99 (0-06-001022-3). Three Mormon high school seniors decide to befriend the friendless and invite them to the school prom. (Rev: BCCB 9/03; BL 8/03; HB 7–8/03; SLJ 8/03; VOYA 8/03)

556 Reynolds, Marilyn. *Love Rules: True-to-Life Stories from Hamilton High* (8–12). Series: True-to-Life. 2001, Morning Glory $18.95 (1-885356-75-7); paper $9.95 (1-885356-76-5). Lynn, a white high school senior, learns about prejudice as she dates an African American football player and supports her lesbian friend Kit. (Rev: BL 8/01; HBG 3/02; SLJ 9/01; VOYA 10/01)

557 Romain, Trevor. *Under the Big Sky* (4–7). Illus. 2001, HarperCollins LB $14.89 (0-06-029495-7). Encouraged by his grandfather, a young boy searches far and wide for the secret of life. (Rev: BL 8/01; HBG 10/01; SLJ 8/01)

558 Rosen, Michael J. *Chaser: A Novel in E-mails* (6–9). 2002, Candlewick $15.99 (0-7636-1538-2). Fourteen-year-old Chase shares his dislike of his new rural home, and in particular his disdain for deer hunters, in e-mails to his sister and his friends back in Columbus, Ohio. (Rev: BL 6/1–15/02; HB 5–6/02; HBG 10/02; SLJ 5/02)

559 Rosen, Roger, and Patra McSharry, eds. *Border Crossings: Emigration and Exile* (8–12). Series: Icarus World Issues. 1992, Rosen LB $16.95 (0-8239-1364-3); paper $8.95 (0-8239-1365-1). Twelve fiction and nonfiction selections that illustrate the lives of those affected by geopolitical change. (Rev: BL 11/1/92)

560 Rylant, Cynthia. *God Went to Beauty School* (4–8). 2003, HarperCollins $15.99 (0-06-009433-8). God indulges in a lot of mortal activities, some fairly wacky, in this collection of thought-provoking poems. (Rev: BL 8/03; HB 7–8/03*; HBG 10/03; SLJ 6/03; VOYA 8/03)

561 Sachs, Marilyn. *The Bears' House* (4–7). 1987, Avon paper $2.99 (0-380-70582-6). A poor girl escapes from reality by living in a fantasy in her classroom. A reissue of the 1971 edition.

562 Schreiber, Ellen. *Vampire Kisses* (7–10). 2003, HarperCollins $15.99 (0-06-009334-X). When a new family moves into the town's old mansion, Raven, 16, imaginative, and a self-styled Goth, decides the handsome son could be a vampire. (Rev: BCCB 10/03; BL 11/15/03; SLJ 8/03)

563 Scott, Kieran. *Jingle Boy* (6–9). 2003, Delacorte $9.95 (0-385-73113-2). Christmas has always been Paul's favorite time, but this year calamities multiply — his mother loses her job, his father nearly electrocutes himself with the lights, his girlfriend says goodbye — and Paul decides he's had enough. (Rev: BL 10/15/03; SLJ 10/03)

564 Seidler, Tor. *The Dulcimer Boy* (4–8). 2003, HarperCollins/A Laura Geringer Bk. $15.99 (0-06-623609-6). A silver-stringed dulcimer plays a key role in this well-illustrated tale of twin brothers abandoned at a young age in early-20th-century New England. (Rev: HBG 10/03; SLJ 6/03)

565 Shura, Mary Francis. *The Josie Gambit* (5–7). 1986, Avon paper $2.50 (0-380-70497-8). Josie's friend Tory behaves in an inexplicable way to his new friend Greg. (Rev: BCCB 5/86; SLJ 9/86)

566 Skurzynski, Gloria. *Good-bye, Billy Radish* (5–7). Illus. 1992, Macmillan LB $15.00 (0-02-782921-9). Vignettes set against the backdrop of World War I Pennsylvania describe the friendship between two boys of different backgrounds. (Rev: BL 10/15/92; HB 11–12/92; SLJ 12/92*)

567 Smith, Carol, and Terry K. Brown. *Stranger Online* (6–9). Series: TodaysGirls.com. 2000, Tommy Nelson paper $5.99 (0-8499-7554-9). Amber receives threatening messages from someone who has entered the girls' private chat room. (Rev: SLJ 11/00)

568 Snyder, Zilpha Keatley. *The Egypt Game* (5–7). 1967, Macmillan $18.95 (0-689-30006-9); Dell paper $5.99 (0-440-42225-6). Humor and suspense mark an outstanding story of city children whose safety, while playing at an unsupervised re-creation of an Egyptian ritual, is threatened by a violent lunatic.

569 Springer, Nancy. *Blood Trail* (6–8). 2003, Holiday $16.95 (0-8234-1723-9). A suspenseful story about a boy afraid to reveal what he knows about his friend's murder. (Rev: BL 5/1/03; HBG 10/03; SLJ 5/03; VOYA 8/03)

570 Stark, Lynette. *Escape from Heart* (7–10). 2000, Harcourt $17.00 (0-15-202385-2). Sara Ruth's uncle is the autocratic and restrictive leader of the Mennonite community in which she lives. (Rev: BR 3–4/01; HBG 3/01; SLJ 10/00)

571 Stolz, Mary. *The Bully of Barkham Street* (4–8). 1963, HarperCollins paper $5.95 (0-06-440159-6). Eleven-year-old Martin goes through a typical phase of growing up — feeling misunderstood. Also use *A Dog on Barkham Street* (1960).

572 Tashjian, Janet. *The Gospel According to Larry* (7–10). 2001, Holt $16.95 (0-8050-6378-1). When Josh (a.k.a. "Larry") publishes his anticonsumerism worldview on the Web, he develops a cult following and discovers the dark side of fame. (Rev: BCCB 1/02; BL 11/1/01; HB 1–2/02*; HBG 3/02; SLJ 10/01; VOYA 12/01)

573 Thesman, Jean. *In the House of the Queen's Beasts* (6–8). 2001, Viking $15.99 (0-670-89288-2). Two diffident 14-year-old girls, Emily and Rowan, share their secrets and develop a tentative friendship in a secluded tree house. (Rev: BCCB 6/01; BL 2/15/01; BR 3–4/01; SLJ 3/01; VOYA 4/01)

574 Thomas, Rob. *Doing Time: Notes from the Undergrad* (8–10). 1997, Simon & Schuster $16.00 (0-689-80958-1). The 10 short stories in this fine collection deal with various aspects of volunteerism, why people participate, and their rewards. (Rev: BL 10/1/97; SLJ 11/97*; VOYA 12/97)

575 Tolan, Stephanie S. *Ordinary Miracles* (6–9). 1999, Morrow $15.95 (0-688-16269-X); HarperTrophy paper $5.95 (0-380-73322-6). Mark, the twin son of a preacher, suffers a crisis of faith and wonders if his future plans to enter the ministry are wise. (Rev: BCCB 10/99; BL 10/1/99; HBG 3/00; SLJ 10/99)

576 Vail, Rachel. *If You Only Knew* (4–7). Series: Friendship Ring. 1998, Scholastic paper $14.95 (0-590-03370-0). In this book shaped like a CD, Zoe Grandon, a 7th grader, gives up a boy she likes to pursue a friendship. (Rev: BCCB 10/98; BL 10/15/98; HBG 3/99; SLJ 10/98; VOYA 6/99)

577 Vail, Rachel. *Not That I Care* (4–7). Series: Friendship Ring. 1998, Scholastic paper $14.95 (0-590-03476-6). For a classroom presentation on 10 items that reveal who you are, Morgan Miller remembers crucial incidents in her life but, in her final report, glosses over the truth. (Rev: BCCB 12/98; BL 11/15/98; HBG 3/99; SLJ 12/98; VOYA 6/99)

578 Vail, Rachel. *Please, Please, Please* (4–7). Series: Friendship Ring. 1998, Scholastic paper $14.95 (0-590-00327-5). CJ Hurley has to overcome a controlling mother in order to hang out with her friends in this book shaped like a CD. (Rev: BCCB 10/98; BL 10/15/98; HBG 3/99; SLJ 12/98; VOYA 6/99)

579 Van Draanen, Wendelin. *Flipped* (5–8). 2001, Knopf $14.95 (0-375-81174-5). In 2nd grade Julianna was infatuated with Bryce, but now, six years later, the situation is reversed in this story told from each viewpoint in alternating chapters. (Rev: BCCB 1/02; BL 12/15/01; HBG 3/02; SLJ 11/01*; VOYA 12/01)

580 Van Draanen, Wendelin. *Swear to Howdy* (5–7). 2003, Knopf $15.95 (0-375-82505-3). Twelve-year-olds Rusty and Joey enjoy their inventive escapades until one of their pranks causes the death of Joey's sister and they must examine their pledge of silence. (Rev: BCCB 2/04; BL 10/1/03*; SLJ 11/03)

581 Vaupel, Robin. *My Contract with Henry* (5–8). 2003, Holiday $17.95 (0-8234-1701-8). An 8th-grade Thoreau project brings a group of outsider students together as they learn about the environment, the simple life, and each other. (Rev: BL 7/03; HBG 10/03; SLJ 7/03; VOYA 10/03)

582 Velasquez, Gloria. *Ankiza* (7–12). Series: Roosevelt High School. 2000, Piñata $16.95 (1-55885-308-1); paper $9.95 (1-55885-309-X). African American Ankiza learns about prejudice when she starts dating a white boy. (Rev: SLJ 4/01; VOYA 8/01)

583 Voigt, Cynthia. *Bad Girls in Love* (5–8). Series: Bad Girls. 2002, Simon & Schuster $15.95 (0-689-82471-8). Margalo falls in love with a popular boy and Michelle (Mikey) has a crush on a teacher in this fourth book of the series. (Rev: BCCB 10/02; BL 8/02; HB 9–10/02; HBG 3/03; SLJ 7/02)

584 Voigt, Cynthia. *It's Not Easy Being Bad* (5–7). 2000, Simon & Schuster $16.00 (0-689-82473-4). Seventh-graders Mikey and Margalo, who have reputations for being bad, come up with several plans for getting in with the popular set at school. (Rev: BCCB 12/00*; BL 11/15/00; HB 1–2/01; HBG 3/01; SLJ 11/00; VOYA 2/01)

585 Warner, Sally. *Bad Girl Blues* (5–8). 2001, HarperCollins LB $16.89 (0-06-028275-4). Sixth-grader Marguerite has been allowed to run wild, and when she is hurt in an accident, Quinney's parents invite her to stay, forcing Quinney and Marguerite to reassess their flagging friendship. (Rev: BL 7/01; HBG 10/01; SLJ 7/01; VOYA 10/01)

586 Waysman, Dvora. *Back of Beyond: A Bar Mitzvah Journey* (5–7). Illus. 1996, Pitspopany paper $4.95 (0-943706-54-8). On a trip to Australia, a 12-year-old Jewish boy becomes involved in the Aborigine culture and witnesses a ritual of manhood similar to a bar mitzvah. (Rev: SLJ 5/96)

587 Williams, Laura E. *Up a Creek* (7–10). 2001, Holt $15.95 (0-8050-6453-2). Thirteen-year-old Starshine Bott, daughter of a young, single-mother activist, wonders if her mother cares more for her social causes than she does for her. (Rev: BCCB 2/01; BL 1/1–15/01; HBG 10/01; SLJ 1/01; VOYA 4/01)

588 Withrow, Sarah. *Bat Summer* (4–7). 1999, Douglas & McIntyre $15.95 (0-88899-351-X). Lonely because his best friend is out of town, Terrence spends time with Lucy, a strange girl who wears a cape and pretends she is a bat. (Rev: BCCB 5/99; BL 7/99; SLJ 9/99; VOYA 8/99)

589 Wittlinger, Ellen. *Gracie's Girl* (4–7). 2000, Simon & Schuster $16.95 (0-689-82249-9). Bess and her best friend Ethan, both middle schoolers, get involved with a homeless old lady. (Rev: BCCB 2/01; BL 9/15/00; HBG 3/01; SLJ 11/00; VOYA 10/01)

590 Wittlinger, Ellen. *Razzle* (7–12). 2001, Simon & Schuster $17.00 (0-689-83565-5). New on Cape Cod, Kenyon becomes friends with an offbeat girl named Razzle — until he falls for beautiful Harley — in this mutilayered and appealing novel. (Rev: BCCB 10/01; BL 11/1/01; HB 11–12/01; HBG 3/02; SLJ 9/01; VOYA 10/01)

591 Wolff, Virginia Euwer. *True Believer* (7–12). 2001, Simon & Schuster $17.00 (0-689-82827-6). Poverty and violence are continuing forces in this sequel to *Make Lemonade*, in which LaVaughn fosters her college ambitions and finds romance. (Rev: BL 6/1–15/02; HB 1–2/01; HBG 10/01; SLJ 1/01; VOYA 4/01)

Ethnic Groups and Problems

592 Armstrong, William H. *Sounder* (6–10). Illus. 1969, HarperCollins LB $16.89 (0-06-020144-4); paper $5.99 (0-06-440020-4). The moving story of an African American sharecropper, his family, and his devoted coon dog, Sounder. Newbery Medal winner, 1970. A sequel is *Sour Land* (1971).

593 Asher, Sandy, ed. *With All My Heart, With All My Mind: Thirteen Stories About Growing Up Jewish* (5–9). 1999, Simon & Schuster $18.00 (0-689-82012-7). Thirteen contemporary young adult writers have contributed stories on the meaning of being Jewish in both the past and present. (Rev: BL 10/1/99; HBG 3/00; SLJ 11/99)

594 Balgassi, Haemi. *Tae's Sonata* (5–8). 1997, Clarion $15.00 (0-395-84314-6). When Tae, a Korean American, is given a school assignment on Korea she must come to terms with her native culture and the memories she has of her homeland. (Rev: BL 10/15/97; BR 5–6/98; HBG 3/98; SLJ 9/97)

595 Barrett, William E. *The Lilies of the Field* (8–12). Illus. 1988, Warner paper $5.99 (0-446-31500-1). A young black man, Homer Smith, helps a group of German nuns to achieve their dream.

596 Beake, Lesley. *Song of Be* (6–12). 1993, Penguin paper $3.99 (0-14-037498-1). The tragedy of Namibian natives who are caught in a changing world is told by the character Be, a 15-year-old girl working on a white man's ranch. (Rev: BL 12/1/93*; SLJ 3/94; VOYA 4/94)

597 Bell, William. *Zack* (7–12). 1999, Simon & Schuster $16.95 (0-689-82248-0). Zack Lane, a biracial teenager growing up in Ontario, travels to rural Mississippi to find his African American grandfather in this disturbing novel that explores bigotry and prejudice. (Rev: BL 5/15/99; HBG 4/00; SLJ 7/99; VOYA 8/99)

598 Bernardo, Anilu. *Fitting In* (6–8). 1996, Arte Publico paper $9.95 (1-55885-173-9). Five stories, each featuring an adolescent girl of Cuban background and a social concern about growing up Hispanic American. (Rev: BL 12/15/96; SLJ 11/96; VOYA 4/97)

599 Bernier-Grand, Carmen T. *In the Shade of the Nispero Tree* (4–7). 1999, Orchard LB $16.99 (0-531-33154-7). Prejudice and racism separate two friends in this story set in Ponce, Puerto Rico, during 1961. (Rev: BCCB 3/99; BL 4/1/99; HBG 10/99; SLJ 3/99)

600 Bertrand, Diane Gonzales. *Sweet Fifteen* (8–12). 1995, Arte Publico paper $9.95 (1-55885-133-X). While making a party dress for Stefanie Bonilla, age 14, Rita Navarro falls in love with her uncle and befriends her widowed mother, maturing in the process. (Rev: BL 6/1–15/95; SLJ 9/95)

601 Blume, Judy. *Iggie's House* (4–7). 1970, Macmillan LB $16.00 (0-02-711040-0); Dell paper $4.99 (0-440-44062-9). An African American family moves into Iggie's old house.

602 Bolden, Tonya, ed. *Rites of Passage: Stories About Growing Up by Black Writers from Around the World* (7–12). 1994, Hyperion $16.95 (1-56282-688-3). A collection of 17 stories that focus on growing up black in the United States, Africa, Australia, Great Britain, the Caribbean, and Central America. (Rev: BL 3/1/94; SLJ 6/94)

603 Bosse, Malcolm. *Ganesh* (7–9). 1981, HarperCollins LB $11.89 (0-690-04103-9). A young boy from India has difficulty fitting into the American Midwest and its ways.

604 Bruchac, Joseph. *The Heart of a Chief* (5–8). 1998, Dial $16.99 (0-8037-2276-1). Chris, an 11-year-old Penacook Indian, fights against three evils that beset his people: racial slurs, alcoholism, and gambling, in this novel about a boy trying to prove his identity. (Rev: BL 10/15/98; HBG 3/99; SLJ 12/98)

605 Bush, Lawrence. *Rooftop Secrets: And Other Stories of Anti-Semitism* (6–9). Illus. 1986, American Hebrew Cong. paper $9.95 (0-8074-0314-8). In each of these eight short stories, some form of anti-Semitism is encountered by a young person. (Rev: SLJ 11/86)

606 Buss, Fran L. *Journey of the Sparrows* (5–8). 1993, Dell paper $4.50 (0-440-40785-0). The plight of illegal aliens in the United States is the focus of this novel about three Salvadoran children. (Rev: BCCB 1/92; HB 11–12/91; SLJ 10/91)

607 Carlson, Lori M., ed. *American Eyes: New Asian-American Short Stories for Young Adults* (8–12). 1994, Holt $15.95 (0-8050-3544-3). These stories present widely varied answers to the question, What does it mean to Asian American adolescents to grow up in a country that views them as aliens? (Rev: BL 1/1/95; SLJ 1/95; VOYA 5/95)

608 Chambers, Veronica. *Quinceañera Means Sweet 15* (6–9). 2001, Hyperion LB $16.49 (0-7868-2426-3). Fourteen-year-old Brooklyn friends Marisol and Magdalena look ahead to their quinceanera coming-of-age parties with anticipation and some frustration. (Rev: BCCB 5/01; HBG 10/01; SLJ 6/01)

609 Childress, Alice. *A Hero Ain't Nothin' but a Sandwich* (7–10). 2000, Putnam paper $5.99 (0-698-11854-5). Benjie's life in Harlem, told from many viewpoints, involves drugs and rejection. (Rev: BL 10/15/88)

610 Childress, Alice. *Rainbow Jordan* (7–10). 1982, Avon paper $4.99 (0-380-58974-5). Rainbow is growing up alternately in a foster home and with a mother who is too preoccupied to care for her. (Rev: BL 10/15/88)

611 Cofer, Judith O. *An Island Like You* (7–12). 1995, Orchard LB $16.99 (0-531-08747-6). A collection of stories about Puerto Rican immigrant children experiencing tensions between two cultures. (Rev: BL 2/15/95*; SLJ 7/95)

612 Cooney, Caroline B. *Burning Up* (7–10). 1999, Delacorte $15.95 (0-385-32318-2). Macey uncovers shabby family secrets and learns about herself when she investigates the senseless murder of an African American teen and a long-ago incident in her town that nearly killed an African American teacher. (Rev: BL 12/1/98; BR 9–10/99; HBG 9/99; SLJ 2/99; VOYA 2/99)

613 Cruz, Maria Colleen. *Border Crossing* (4–8). 2003, Arte Publico paper $9.95 (1-55885-405-3). Ceci, 12, can't understand why her Mexican father won't speak Spanish or talk about his home, so she decides to go and investigate. (Rev: BL 11/15/03)

614 Curtis, Christopher Paul. *The Watsons Go to Birmingham — 1963* (4–8). 1995, Delacorte $16.95 (0-385-32175-9); Dell paper $6.50 (0-440-41412-1). An African American family returns to Alabama from Michigan to place their troubled son with his grandmother in this novel set in the 1960s. (Rev: BL 8/95; SLJ 10/95*; VOYA 12/95)

615 Danticat, Edwidge. *Behind the Mountains* (5–9). Series: First Person Fiction. 2002, Scholastic paper $16.95 (0-439-37299-2). Danticat skillfully introduces background information on Haitian history and politics into the journal of young Celiane Esperance, who leaves the island and moves to Brooklyn to join her much-missed father, a reunion that isn't as easy as she expected. (Rev: BCCB 2/03; BL 10/1/02; HBG 3/03; SLJ 10/02; VOYA 2/03)

616 Davis, Ossie. *Just Like Martin* (5–8). 1992, Simon & Schuster paper $15.00 (0-671-73202-1). A docunovel of 13-year-old Isaac's struggles with family problems and a vow of nonviolence during the 1960s civil rights movement. (Rev: BL 9/1/92; SLJ 10/92)

617 Doyle, Brian. *Uncle Ronald* (6–8). 1997, Groundwood $16.95 (0-88899-266-1). This novel, set in Ontario in 1895, tells about Mickey who, with his mother, flees an abusive alcoholic father to her family's farm run by her brother and twin sisters. (Rev: SLJ 5/97)

618 English, Karen. *Francie* (5–8). 1999, Farrar $17.00 (0-374-32456-5). Francie, a black girl growing up in segregated Alabama, places her family in danger when she helps a friend who is escaping a racist employer. (Rev: BCCB 10/99; BL 10/15/99; HB 9–10/99; HBG 3/00; SLJ 9/99; VOYA 2/00)

619 Fleischman, Paul. *Seedfolks* (4–8). Illus. 1997, HarperCollins LB $15.89 (0-06-027472-7). Thirteen people from many cultures explain why they have planted gardens in a vacant lot in Cleveland, Ohio. (Rev: BCCB 7–8/97; BL 5/15/97; BR 11–12/97; HB 5–6/97; SLJ 5/97*; VOYA 6/97)

620 Flores, Bettina R. *Chiquita's Diary* (6–9). Illus. 1995, Pepper Vine paper $13.50 (0-962-57777-4). Twelve-year-old Chiquita is determined to break out of the poverty that her widowed Mexican American mother endures, and she makes a start by becoming a mother's helper. (Rev: BL 2/15/96)

621 Fogelin, Adrian. *Crossing Jordan* (5–8). 2000, Peachtree $14.95 (1-56145-215-7). Set in contemporary Florida, this novel tells how 12-year-old Cass must keep her friendship with African American Jemmie a secret from her racist father. (Rev: BCCB 4/00; HBG 10/00; SLJ 6/00)

622 Gallo, Donald R., ed. *Join In: Multiethnic Short Stories by Outstanding Writers for Young Adults* (7–12). 1995, Bantam paper $5.99 (0-440-21957-4). Seventeen stories concerning the problems teenagers of other ethnic backgrounds have living in the United States. (Rev: BL 1/15/94; SLJ 11/93; VOYA 10/93)

623 Garland, Sherry. *Shadow of the Dragon* (6–12). 1993, Harcourt $10.95 (0-15-273330-5), paper $6.00 (0-15-273532-1). Danny Vo has grown up American since he emigrated from Vietnam as a child. Now traditional Vietnamese ways, the new American culture, and skinhead prejudice clash, resulting in his cousin's death. (Rev: BL 11/15/93*; SLJ 11/93; VOYA 12/93)

624 Gilmore, Rachna. *A Group of One* (7–10). 2001, Holt $16.95 (0-8050-6475-3). Fifteen-year-old Tara, a Canadian, learns to value her heritage when her grandmother arrives from India. (Rev: BCCB 9/01; BL 5/1/01; HB 9–10/01; HBG 3/02; SLJ 7/01; VOYA 8/01)

625 Gilson, Jamie. *Hello, My Name Is Scrambled Eggs* (5–7). 1985, Lothrop $15.95 (0-688-04095-0). Harvey looks forward to the arrival of a Vietnamese refugee family and their son, but runs into trouble with the prejudice of his American friend Quint. (Rev: BCCB 7/85; BL 4/14/85; SLJ 8/85)

626 Gordon, Sheila. *Waiting for the Rain: A Novel of South Africa* (7–12). 1996, Bantam paper $5.50 (0-440-22698-8). The story of the friendship between a black boy and a white boy in apartheid-ridden South Africa. (Rev: BL 8/87; SLJ 8/87; VOYA 12/87)

627 Green, Richard G. *Sing, like a Hermit Thrush* (6–9). 1995, Ricara paper $12.95 (0-911737-01-4). A young Native American teenager growing up on the Six Nations Reserve is confused by his gift of seeing events before they happen. (Rev: BL 4/15/96)

628 Grimes, Nikki. *Jazmin's Notebook* (6–10). 1998, Dial $15.99 (0-8037-2224-9). The journal of 14-year-old Jazmin, who writes about her tough, tender, and angry life in Harlem in the 1960s, living with her sister after her mother is hospitalized with a breakdown and her father has died. (Rev: BL 9/15/98; BR 1–2/99; HBG 9/98; SLJ 7/98; VOYA 10/98)

629 Grove, Vicki. *The Starplace* (6–8). 1999, Putnam $17.99 (0-399-23207-9). In this story set in 1961, 8th-grader Frannie defies the prejudice of her classmates and becomes friends with Celeste, the first black student in her junior high school. (Rev: BCCB 9/99; BL 6/1–15/99; HBG 9/99; SLJ 6/99; VOYA 12/99)

630 Hamilton, Virginia. *Arilla Sundown* (7–9). 1995, Scholastic paper $4.99 (0-590-22223-6). Arilla is part Indian and part black and growing up in a unique family situation.

631 Hamilton, Virginia. *A White Romance* (8–12). 1987, Scholastic paper $4.50 (0-590-13005-6). A formerly all-black high school becomes integrated and social values and relationships change. (Rev: SLJ 1/88; VOYA 2/88)

632 Hamilton, Virginia. *Zeely* (6–9). 1967, Macmillan $17.95 (0-02-742470-7). A beautiful, statuesque woman enters Geeder's life and he is convinced she is an African queen.

633 Hernandez, Irene B. *Across the Great River* (7–10). 1989, Arte Publico paper $9.95 (0-934770-

96-4). The harrowing story of a young Mexican girl and her family who illegally enter the United States. (Rev: BL 8/89; SLJ 8/89)

634 Hernandez, Jo Ann Y. *White Bread Competition* (7–12). 1997, Arte Publico paper $9.95 (1-55885-210-7). The effects of winning a spelling bee on Luz Rios and her Hispanic American family in San Antonio are explored in a series of vignettes. (Rev: BL 1/1–15/98; BR 9–10/98; SLJ 8/98; VOYA 4/98)

635 Hewett, Lorri. *Dancer* (7–10). 1999, Dutton $15.99 (0-525-45968-5). A 16-year-old African American ballet student faces several obstacles, including hostile classmates and a father who doesn't approve of her career choice. (Rev: BL 8/99; HB 9–10/99; HBG 4/00)

636 Hewett, Lorri. *Lives of Our Own* (6–9). 1998, Dutton $15.99 (0-525-45959-6). Shawna Riley, an African American teen new to her high school in Georgia, confronts the informal segregation she finds by writing an editorial in the school paper. (Rev: BL 2/15/98; HB 3–4/98; HBG 9/98; SLJ 4/98; VOYA 8/98)

637 Hewett, Lorri. *Soulfire* (7–12). Illus. 1996, Penguin paper $5.99 (0-14-038960-1). Todd Williams, 16, begins to take responsibility for his actions and seeks direction for his life in this coming-of-age novel set in the Denver projects. (Rev: BL 5/1/96; BR 9–10/96; SLJ 6/96*; VOYA 10/96)

638 Hobbs, Will. *Bearstone* (7–10). 1989, Macmillan $17.00 (0-689-31496-5). A hostile, resentful Indian teenager is sent to live with a rancher in Colorado. (Rev: BL 11/1/89; BR 3–4/90; SLJ 9/89; VOYA 12/89)

639 Hodge, Merle. *For the Life of Laetitia* (5–9). 1993, FSG paper $6.95 (0-374-42444-6). Rooted in Caribbean culture and language, this novel celebrates place and community as it confronts divisions of race, class, and gender. (Rev: BL 12/1/92; SLJ 1/93)

640 Hooks, William H. *Circle of Fire* (5–8). 1982, Macmillan $15.00 (0-689-50241-9). In rural North Carolina of 1936, three boys — one white and two African American — try to thwart an attack on Irish gypsies by the Ku Klux Klan. (Rev: BL 3/1/88)

641 Hyppolite, Joanne. *Ola Shakes It Up* (4–8). Illus. 1998, Delacorte $14.95 (0-385-32235-6). A spunky girl tries to prevent her parents from moving to a neighborhood where she will be the only African American in her school. (Rev: BL 2/15/98; HB 3–4/98; HBG 10/98; SLJ 2/98)

642 Irwin, Hadley. *Kim / Kimi* (7–10). 1987, Macmillan $16.00 (0-689-50428-4); Penguin paper $5.99 (0-14-032593-X). A half-Japanese teenager brought up in an all-white small town sets out to explore her Oriental roots. (Rev: BL 3/15/87; SLJ 5/87; VOYA 6/87)

643 Irwin, Hadley. *Sarah with an H* (6–8). 1996, Simon & Schuster $16.00 (0-689-80949-2). Newcomer Sarah, who is rich, bright, and pretty, is blocked from joining the "in" crowd partly because she is Jewish. (Rev: BL 9/1/96; SLJ 2/97; VOYA 12/96)

644 Jimenez, Francisco. *The Circuit: Stories from the Life of a Migrant Child* (5–10). 1997, Univ. of New Mexico Pr. paper $10.95 (0-8263-1797-9). Eleven moving stories about the lives, fears, hopes, and problems of children in Mexican migrant worker families. (Rev: BL 12/1/97)

645 Johnson, Angela. *Toning the Sweep* (7–12). 1993, Scholastic paper $5.99 (0-590-48142-8). This novel captures the innocence, vulnerability, and love of human interaction, as well as the melancholy, self-discovery, and introspection of an African American adolescent. (Rev: BL 4/1/93*; SLJ 4/93*)

646 Johnston, Tony. *Any Small Goodness: A Novel of the Barrio* (4–7). 2001, Scholastic paper $15.95 (0-439-18936-5). Eleven-year-old Arturo Rodriguez, whose Mexican family is new to Los Angeles, describes family life, school, celebrations, and dangers. (Rev: BL 9/15/01; HBG 3/02; SLJ 9/01; VOYA 10/01)

647 Jukes, Mavis. *Planning the Impossible* (6–8). 1999, Delacorte $14.95 (0-385-32243-7). In this companion to *Expecting the Unexpected*, 6th-grader River has problems with sex education, understanding adult behavior, her mother's pregnancy, and manipulative classmates trying to come between her and a boy she likes. (Rev: BL 6/1–15/99; HB 3–4/99; HBG 9/99; SLJ 4/99; VOYA 4/99)

648 Killingsworth, Monte. *Circle Within a Circle* (7–9). 1994, Macmillan paper $14.95 (0-689-50598-1). A runaway teenage boy and a Chinook Indian join a crusade to save a stretch of sacred land from commercial development. (Rev: BL 3/1/94; SLJ 6/94; VOYA 6/94)

649 Laird, Elizabeth. *Kiss the Dust* (6–10). 1992, Penguin $6.99 (0-14-036855-8). A docunovel about a refugee Kurdish teen caught up in the 1984 Iran-Iraq War. (Rev: BL 6/15/92)

650 Lee, Harper. *To Kill a Mockingbird* (8–12). 1977, HarperCollins $23.00 (0-397-00151-7). A lawyer in a small Southern town defends an African American man wrongfully accused of rape.

651 Lee, Lauren. *Stella: On the Edge of Popularity* (5–7). 1994, Polychrome $10.95 (1-879965-08-9). A Korean American girl has to choose between being popular and being loyal to her Korean culture. (Rev: BCCB 7–8/94; SLJ 9/94)

652 Lee, Marie G. *F Is for Fabuloso* (6–9). 1999, Avon $15.95 (0-380-97648-X). A sensitive story about Jin-Ha, a Korean girl, and the troubles she and her parents face in the United States. (Rev: BL 9/15/99; HBG 4/00)

653 Lee, Marie G. *Finding My Voice* (7–12). 1994, HarperCollins paper $5.99 (0-06-447245-0). Pressured by her strict Korean parents to get into Harvard, high-school senior Ellen Sung tries to find time for friendship, romance, and fun in her small Minnesota town. (Rev: BL 9/1/92; SLJ 10/92)

654 Lee, Marie G. *Necessary Roughness* (7–12). 1996, HarperCollins LB $14.89 (0-06-025130-1). Chan, a Korean American football enthusiast, and his twin sister, Young, encounter prejudice when their family moves to a small Minnesota community. (Rev: BL 1/1–15/97; BR 5–6/97; SLJ 1/97; VOYA 6/97)

655 Lehrman, Robert. *The Store That Mama Built* (4–7). 1992, Macmillan LB $13.95 (0-02-754632-2). The story of a Jewish immigrant family from Russia in Pennsylvania in 1917. (Rev: BCCB 5/92; BL 4/15/92; SLJ 7/92)

656 Lester, Julius. *Long Journey Home* (6–8). 1998, Viking paper $5.99 (0-14-038981-4). Six based-on-fact stories concerning slaves, ex-slaves, and their lives in a hostile America.

657 Lipsyte, Robert. *The Brave* (8–12). 1991, HarperCollins paper $5.99 (0-06-447079-2). A Native American heavyweight boxer is rescued from drugs, pimps, and hookers by a tough but tender ex-boxer/New York City cop. (Rev: BL 10/15/91; SLJ 10/91*)

658 Lipsyte, Robert. *The Chief* (7–10). 1995, HarperCollins paper $5.99 (0-06-447097-0). Sonny Bear can't decide whether to go back to the reservation, continue boxing, or become Hollywood's new Native American darling. Sequel to *The Brave*. (Rev: BL 6/1–15/93; VOYA 12/93)

659 Lipsyte, Robert. *Warrior Angel* (7–12). 2003, HarperCollins $15.99 (0-06-000496-7). In this fourth book about the young boxer, Sonny — first seen in *The Contender* (1967) — is the heavyweight champion, yet he still struggles to find his identity. (Rev: BCCB 2/03; BL 1/1–15/03; HB 3–4/03; HBG 10/03; SLJ 3/03; VOYA 4/03)

660 Lord, Bette Bao. *In the Year of the Boar and Jackie Robinson* (6–8). Illus. 1984, HarperCollins paper $5.99 (0-06-440175-8). A young Chinese girl finds that the world of baseball helps her adjust to her new home in America.

661 McLaren, Clemence. *Dance for the Land* (4–8). 1999, Simon & Schuster $16.00 (0-689-82393-2). A child of mixed parentage, moving back to Hawaii with her father, faces prejudice from relatives because of her light skin. (Rev: BL 2/15/99; HBG 10/99; SLJ 6/99)

662 Marino, Jan. *The Day That Elvis Came to Town* (7–10). 1993, Avon paper $3.50 (0-380-71672-0).

In this tale of southern blacks, Wanda is thrilled when a room in her parents' boarding house is rented to Mercedes, who makes her feel pretty and smart — and who once went to school with Elvis Presley. (Rev: BL 12/15/90*; SLJ 1/91*)

663 Markle, Sandra. *The Fledglings* (6–9). 1998, Boyds Mills paper $9.95 (1-56397-696-X). With her parents dead, Kate, 14, runs away to live with her Cherokee grandfather and immerses herself happily in his world. (Rev: BL 6/15/92)

664 Martinez, Victor. *Parrot in the Oven: Mi Vida* (7–10). 1996, HarperCollins LB $16.89 (0-06-026706-2). Through a series of vignettes, the story of Manuel, a teenage Mexican American, unfolds as he grows up in the city projects with an abusive father and a loving mother. (Rev: BL 10/15/96; SLJ 11/96)

665 Meriwether, Louise. *Daddy Was a Numbers Runner* (7–12). 1986, Feminist Pr. paper $16.59 (1-5586-1442-7). The story of Frances, a black girl, growing up in Harlem during the Depression.

666 Meyer, Carolyn. *Gideon's People* (5–7). 1996, Harcourt $12.00 (0-15-200303-7); paper $6.00 (0-15-200304-5). Similarities and differences in religious practices become apparent when an Orthodox Jewish boy spends time on an Amish farm in 1911. (Rev: BCCB 5/96; BL 5/1/96; SLJ 4/96; VOYA 6/96)

667 Meyer, Carolyn. *Jubilee Journey* (5–9). 1997, Harcourt $13.00 (0-15-201377-6); paper $6.00 (0-15-201591-4). This sequel to *White Lilacs* begins 75 years later and tells the story of Emily Rose, a biracial girl, who finds her spiritual identity when she visits her African American relatives in Texas. (Rev: BL 9/1/97; HBG 3/98; SLJ 1/98; VOYA 12/97)

668 Miklowitz, Gloria D. *The War Between the Classes* (7–10). 1986, Dell paper $4.99 (0-440-99406-3). A Japanese American girl finds that hidden prejudices and bigotry emerge when students in school are divided into four socioeconomic groups. (Rev: BL 4/15/85; SLJ 8/85; VOYA 6/85)

669 Mohr, Nicholasa. *El Bronx Remembered: A Novella and Stories* (7–9). 1993, HarperCollins paper $5.99 (0-06-447100-4). These 12 stories set in the Bronx reflect the general Puerto Rican experience in New York.

670 Mohr, Nicholasa. *Felita* (7–9). 1995, Bantam paper $4.50 (0-440-41295-1). Felita, a Puerto Rican girl, encounters problems when her family moves to a non-Spanish speaking neighborhood.

671 Mohr, Nicholasa. *Going Home* (6–8). 1986, Puffin paper $5.99 (0-14-130644-0). The young heroine finds a boyfriend and spends a summer in her family's home in Puerto Rico in this sequel to *Felita*. (Rev: BL 7/86; SLJ 8/86)

672 Mohr, Nicholasa. *Nilda* (7–9). 1986, Publico paper $11.95 (0-934770-61-1). The story of a 12-year-old Puerto Rican girl growing up in the New York barrio.

673 Moore, Yvette. *Freedom Songs* (6–12). 1991, Penguin paper $5.99 (0-14-036017-4). In 1968, Sheryl, 14, witnesses and then experiences acts of prejudice while visiting relatives in North Carolina. (Rev: BL 4/15/91; SLJ 3/91)

674 Murphy, Rita. *Black Angels* (5–7). 2001, Random paper $4.99 (0-440-22934-0). In this exciting novel set in Mystic, Georgia, in 1961, an 11-year-old girl is caught up in the struggle that pits the freedom riders and black leaders against racists including the Klan. (Rev: BCCB 3/01; BL 2/15/01)

675 Myers, Walter Dean. *The Dream Bearer* (5–8). 2003, HarperCollins $15.99 (0-06-029521-X). David, 12 and living in Harlem, gains valuable insights about his heritage and his ambitions when he gets to know an old man who calls himself a "dream bearer." (Rev: BL 7/03; SLJ 6/03; VOYA 6/03)

676 Myers, Walter Dean. *Fast Sam, Cool Clyde, and Stuff* (7–10). 1995, Peter Smith $20.25 (0-8446-6798-6); Puffin paper $5.99 (0-14-032613-8). Three male friends in Harlem join forces to found the 116th Street Good People.

677 Myers, Walter Dean. *The Glory Field* (7–10). 1994, Scholastic paper $14.95 (0-590-45897-3). This novel follows a family's 200-year history, from the capture of an African boy in the 1750s through the lives of his descendants on a small plot of South Carolina land called the Glory Field. (Rev: BL 10/1/94)

678 Myers, Walter Dean. *Motown and Didi: A Love Story* (7–9). 1984, Dell paper $4.99 (0-440-95762-1). In the midst of trouble and despair in Harlem, this is a tender love story.

679 Myers, Walter Dean. *145th Street: Stories* (5–9). 2000, Delacorte $15.95 (0-385-32137-6). A Harlem neighborhood is the setting for this collection of short stories dealing with a wide range of human emotions. (Rev: BL 12/15/99; HB 3–4/00; HBG 10/00; SLJ 4/00)

680 Myers, Walter Dean. *Scorpions* (7–9). 1988, HarperCollins LB $16.89 (0-06-024365-1). Gang warfare, death, and despair are the elements of this story set in present-day Harlem. (Rev: BL 9/1/88; BR 11–12/88; SLJ 9/88; VOYA 8/88)

681 Myers, Walter Dean. *Slam!* (8–12). 1996, Scholastic paper $15.95 (0-590-48667-5). Although Slam is successful on the school's basketball court, his personal life has problems caused by difficulties fitting into an all-white school, a very sick grandmother, and a friend who is involved in drugs. (Rev: BL 11/15/96; BR 11–12/96; SLJ 11/96; VOYA 2/97)

682 Myers, Walter Dean. *The Young Landlords* (7–10). 1979, Penguin paper $5.99 (0-14-034244-3). A group of African American teenagers take over a slum building in Harlem.

683 Namioka, Lensey. *April and the Dragon Lady* (7–12). 1994, Harcourt $10.95 (0-15-276644-8). A Chinese American high school junior must relinquish important activities to care for her ailing grandmother and struggles with the constraints of a traditional female role. (Rev: BL 3/1/94; SLJ 4/94; VOYA 6/94)

684 Namioka, Lensey. *Yang the Third and Her Impossible Family* (4–7). 1996, Bantam paper $4.50 (0-440-41231-5). Mary, part of a Chinese family newly arrived in Seattle, is embarrassed by her parents' old-country ways in this humorous story. (Rev: BCCB 5/95; BL 4/15/95; SLJ 8/95)

685 Neufeld, John. *Edgar Allan* (6–8). 1968, Phillips $26.95 (0-87599-149-1). Michael's family adopts a 3-year-old African American boy and the signs of bigotry begin.

686 Okimoto, Jean D. *Talent Night* (6–10). 1995, Scholastic paper $14.95 (0-590-47809-5). In this story, Rodney Suyama, 17, wants to be the first Japanese American rapper and to date beautiful Ivy Ramos. (Rev: BL 6/1–15/95; SLJ 5/95)

687 Osa, Nancy. *Cuba 15* (6–10). 2003, Delacorte $15.95 (0-385-72021-7). Violet Paz, who considers herself totally American, is surprised when her grandmother insists that she celebrate a traditional coming-of-age ceremony. (Rev: BL 7/03*)

688 Oughton, Jerrie. *Music from a Place Called Half Moon* (6–10). 1995, Houghton $16.00 (0-395-70737-4). Small-town bigotry and personal transformation in the 1950s figure in this novel about Native Americans. (Rev: BL 5/1/95; SLJ 4/95)

689 Pinkney, Andrea D. *Hold Fast to Dreams* (5–8). 1995, Morrow $16.00 (0-688-12832-7). A bright, resourceful African American girl faces problems when she finds she is the only black student in her new middle school. (Rev: BCCB 5/95; BL 2/15/95; HB 9–10/95; SLJ 4/95)

690 Pitts, Paul. *Racing the Sun* (5–7). 1988, Avon paper $5.99 (0-380-75496-7). Brandon begins to understand his Navajo heritage after his grandfather comes to live with him. (Rev: BL 9/15/88; SLJ 2/89)

691 Placide, Jaira. *Fresh Girl* (8–10). 2002, Random $15.95 (0-385-32753-6). Mardi, an immigrant from Haiti, has some difficulties adjusting to life in New York. (Rev: BCCB 3/02; BL 11/15/01; HB 3–4/02; HBG 10/02; SLJ 1/02*; VOYA 8/02)

692 Pullman, Philip. *The Broken Bridge* (8–12). 1992, Knopf $15.99 (0-679-91972-4). A biracial girl learns the truth about her heritage. (Rev: BL 2/15/92; SLJ 3/92*)

693 Qualey, Marsha. *Revolutions of the Heart* (7–12). 1993, Houghton $16.00 (0-395-64168-3). Cory lives in a small Wisconsin town that is torn by bigotry when Chippewa Indians reclaim their hunting and fishing rights. (Rev: BL 4/1/93; SLJ 5/93*)

694 Rana, Indi. *The Roller Birds of Rampur* (7–12). 1993, Ballantine paper $3.99 (0-449-70434-3). This coming-of-age story of a young woman caught between British and Indian cultures is a lively account of the immigration experience and of Indian culture. (Rev: BL 7/93; SLJ 5/93; VOYA 2/94)

695 Roseman, Kenneth. *The Other Side of the Hudson: A Jewish Immigrant Adventure* (5–8). Illus. Series: Do-It-Yourself Adventure. 1993, UAHC paper $8.95 (0-8074-0506-X). Using an interactive format, readers can choose various destinations for a young male Jewish immigrant after he arrives in New York City from Germany in 1851. (Rev: SLJ 6/94)

696 Rosen, Sybil. *Speed of Light* (5–9). 1999, Simon & Schuster $16.00 (0-689-82437-8). When Audrey's father, a Jewish worker in a small Virginia town in 1956, supports the appointment of the first African American police officer in town, it unleashes a flood of anti-Semitism. (Rev: BL 8/99; HBG 3/00; SLJ 8/99; VOYA 10/99)

697 Saldana, Rene, Jr. *The Jumping Tree: A Novel* (7–12). 2001, Delacorte $14.95 (0-385-32725-0). Rey, a Mexican American boy growing up in a poor family near the Mexican border, describes his life and his longing to become a man. (Rev: BL 5/15/01; HBG 10/01; SLJ 6/01)

698 Sebestyen, Ouida. *On Fire* (7–12). 1985, Little, Brown $12.95 (0-87113-010-6). Tater leaves home with his brother Sammy and takes a mining job where he confronts labor problems in this sequel to the author's powerful *Words by Heart*. (Rev: BL 5/15/85; SLJ 4/85; VOYA 8/85)

699 Sebestyen, Ouida. *Words by Heart* (5–7). 1979, Little, Brown $15.95 (0-316-77931-8). Race relations are explored when an African American family moves to an all-white community during the Reconstruction era. (Rev: BL 6/1/88)

700 Shalant, Phyllis. *When Pirates Came to Brooklyn* (4–7). 2002, Dutton $16.99 (0-525-46920-6). When Lee, who is Jewish, befriends Polly, who is Catholic, the two imaginative 11-year-olds learn a harsh lesson about prejudice in this tale set in 1960 Brooklyn. (Rev: BCCB 12/02; BL 10/15/02; HBG 3/03; SLJ 10/02)

701 Shea, Pegi Deitz. *Tangled Threads: A Hmong Girl's Story* (6–8). 2003, Clarion $15.00 (0-618-24748-3). Mai, a Hmong refugee newly arrived in the United States, is initially overwhelmed by her Americanized cousins and her new surroundings in this novel that conveys much information about Hmong culture. (Rev: BL 9/15/03; SLJ 11/03)

702 Sherman, Eileen B. *The Violin Players* (6–10). 1998, Jewish Publication Soc. $14.95 (0-8276-0595-1). When Melissa leaves New York City to spend part of her junior year in a small Missouri town, she encounters the ugliness of anti-Semitism for the first time. (Rev: BL 12/1/98; HBG 3/99; SLJ 3/99)

703 Singer, Isaac Bashevis. *The Power of Light: Eight Stories for Hanukkah* (7–10). Illus. 1980, Avon paper $2.50 (0-380-60103-6). Eight stories of the Festival of Lights that span centuries of Jewish history.

704 Smothers, Ethel Footman. *Down in the Piney Woods* (5–8). 1992, Random paper $4.99 (0-679-84714-6). The daily life of a strong African American sharecropper family in 1950s rural Georgia is described in a colloquial voice. (Rev: BL 12/15/91; SLJ 1/92)

705 Smothers, Ethel Footman. *Moriah's Pond* (4–7). 1995, Knopf $16.00 (0-679-84504-6). In this sequel to *Down in the Piney Woods* (1992), racial tensions surround African American youngsters growing up in rural Georgia in the 1950s. (Rev: BCCB 4/95; BL 1/15/95; SLJ 2/95)

706 Son, John. *Finding My Hat* (4–8). Series: First Person Fiction. 2003, Scholastic $16.95 (0-439-43538-2). Autobiography plays a large part in this frank, often funny novel about the son of Korean immigrants growing up in America in the 1970s and 1980s. (Rev: BL 11/15/03; LMC 11–12/03; SLJ 10/03)

707 Soto, Gary. *Local News* (4–7). 1993, Harcourt $14.00 (0-15-248117-6). This collection of 13 short stories deals with a number of Mexican American youngsters at home, school, and play. (Rev: BL 4/15/93; HB 7–8/93*)

708 Soto, Gary. *Petty Crimes* (5–8). 1998, Harcourt $17.00 (0-15-201658-9). Ten short stories about Mexican American teenagers in California's Central Valley deal with some humorous situations but more often with gangs, violence, and poverty. (Rev: BL 3/15/98; HBG 10/98; SLJ 5/98)

709 Soto, Gary. *Taking Sides* (6–9). 1991, Harcourt $17.00 (0-15-284076-1). Lincoln Mendoza moves from his inner-city San Francisco neighborhood to a middle-class suburb and must adjust to life in a new high school. (Rev: BL 12/1/91; SLJ 11/91)

710 Spinelli, Jerry. *Maniac Magee* (5–7). 1990, Little, Brown $15.95 (0-316-80722-2). This thought-provoking Newbery Medal winner (1991) tells the story of an amazing white boy who runs away from home and suddenly becomes aware of the racism in his town. (Rev: BL 6/1/90*; SLJ 6/90)

711 Sterling, Shirley. *My Name Is Seepeetza* (5–10). 1997, Douglas & McIntyre paper $5.95 (0-88899-165-7). Told in diary form, this autobiographical novel about a 6th-grade Native American girl tells of her heartbreak at the terrible conditions at her school where she is persecuted because of her race. (Rev: BL 3/1/97)

712 Talbert, Marc. *Star of Luis* (5–9). 1999, Houghton $15.00 (0-395-91423-X). Racial prejudice is the theme of this story, set in New Mexico during World War II, about a Hispanic American boy who discovers he is Jewish. (Rev: BCCB 5/99; BL 3/1/99; HBG 10/99; SLJ 5/99; VOYA 6/99)

713 Tan, Amy. *The Moon Lady* (5–8). Illus. 1992, Macmillan LB $16.95 (0-02-788830-4). An adaptation of "The Moon Lady" from Tan's adult bestseller *The Joy Luck Club,* which speaks to our common nightmares and secret wishes. (Rev: BL 9/1/92; SLJ 9/92)

714 Taylor, Mildred D. *The Road to Memphis* (7–12). 1990, Dial $16.99 (0-8037-0340-6). Set in 1941, this is a continuation of the story of the Logans, a poor black southern family who were previously featured in *Roll of Thunder, Hear My Cry* and *Let the Circle Be Unbroken.* (Rev: BL 5/15/90; SLJ 1/90; VOYA 8/90)

715 Uchida, Yoshiko. *The Happiest Ending* (6–8). 1985, Macmillan $15.00 (0-689-50326-1). There is a clash of cultures in this story of Japanese American families and an arranged marriage. By the author of *The Best Bad Thing.* (Rev: BL 11/1/85; SLJ 11/85)

716 Uchida, Yoshiko. *A Jar of Dreams* (4–7). 1981, Macmillan $16.95 (0-689-50210-9). In California of Depression days, a young Japanese girl encounters prejudice. A sequel is *The Best Bad Thing* (1983).

717 Uchida, Yoshiko. *Journey Home* (7–9). Illus. 1978, Macmillan $16.95 (0-689-50126-9); paper $4.99 (0-689-71641-9). A Japanese American family return to their ordinary life after being relocated during World War II.

718 Uchida, Yoshiko. *Journey to Topaz: A Story of the Japanese-American Evacuation* (4–7). 1985, Creative Arts paper $9.95 (0-916870-85-5). In this reissue of a 1971 title, 11-year-old Yuki and her family endure shameful treatment after Pearl Harbor.

719 Veciana-Suarez, Ana. *Flight to Freedom* (6–9). 2002, Scholastic $16.95 (0-439-38199-1). In her diary, Yara describes her old life in Cuba and her new life in 1960s Miami with all the attendant problems of new immigrants and teen development. (Rev: BCCB 2/03; BL 11/15/02; HB 1–2/03; HBG 3/03; SLJ 10/02; VOYA 2/03)

720 Velasquez, Gloria. *Maya's Divided World* (7–12). 1995, Arte Publico $12.95 (1-55885-126-7). A Chicana who seemingly leads a charmed life discovers that her parents are divorcing and her world falls apart. (Rev: BL 3/1/95; SLJ 4/95)

721 Vogiel, Eva. *Invisible Chains* (5–8). 2000, Judaica Pr. $19.95 (1-880582-57-0). In 1948, 14-year-old Frumie is sent with her crippled younger sister, Judy, to a boarding school for religiously observant Jewish girls. (Rev: BL 7/00; HBG 10/00)

722 Voigt, Cynthia. *Come a Stranger* (6–9). 1986, Simon & Schuster $15.95 (0-689-31289-X); Fawcett paper $3.95 (0-449-70246-4). Mina Smiths, a young African American girl introduced in *Dicey's Song,* has trouble achieving her identity as an individual and is helped by a young minister, Tamer Shipp (from *The Runner*). (Rev: BL 9/15/86; SLJ 10/86; VOYA 4/87)

723 Walters, Eric. *War of the Eagles* (5–7). 1998, Orca $14.00 (1-55143-118-1); paper $7.95 (1-55143-099-1). During the opening months of the war against Japan, a West Coast Canadian boy witnesses the growing prejudice against Japanese Canadians and also becomes aware of his own Indian heritage. (Rev: BL 12/15/98; BR 5–6/99; HBG 3/99; SLJ 12/98)

724 Woodson, Jacqueline. *The Dear One* (6–9). 1992, Dell paper $3.99 (0-440-21420-3). A pregnant African American teenager lives with the family of her mother's friend until the baby is born in this exploration of issues of women's sexuality. (Rev: BL 11/15/91)

725 Woodson, Jacqueline. *From the Notebooks of Melanin Sun May* (6–10). 1995, Scholastic paper $5.99 (0-590-45881-7). A 13-year-old African American boy's mother announces that she loves a fellow student, a white woman. (Rev: BL 4/15/95; SLJ 8/95)

726 Woodson, Jacqueline. *Maizon at Blue Hill* (5–8). 1992, Dell paper $3.99 (0-440-40899-7). Seventh-grader Maizon reluctantly leaves her Brooklyn home, her best friend, and her grandmother to attend a private boarding school for girls, where she must confront issues of race, class, prejudice, and identity. (Rev: BL 7/92; SLJ 11/92)

727 Wright, Richard. *Rite of Passage* (7–12). 1994, HarperCollins paper $5.99 (0-06-447111-X). This newly discovered novella, written in the 1940s, concerns a gifted 15-year-old who runs away from his loving Harlem home and survives on the streets with a violent gang. (Rev: BL 1/1/94; SLJ 2/94; VOYA 4/94)

728 Yep, Laurence, ed. *American Dragons: Twenty-Five Asian American Voices* (7–12). 1995, HarperCollins paper $6.99 (0-06-440603-2). Autobiographical stories, poems, and essays about children whose parents come from China, Japan, Korea, and Tibet, struggling to find "an identity that isn't generic." (Rev: BL 5/15/93; SLJ 7/93; VOYA 10/93)

729 Yep, Laurence. *Child of the Owl* (6–9). 1977, HarperCollins LB $16.89 (0-06-026743-7). A young girl goes to live with her grandmother in San Francisco's Chinatown.

730 Yep, Laurence. *Dragonwings* (7–9). 1975, HarperCollins LB $16.89 (0-06-026738-0); paper $6.99 (0-06-440085-9). At the turn of the 20th century, a young Chinese boy in San Francisco becomes an aviation pioneer. (Rev: BL 3/1/88)

731 Yep, Laurence. *Dream Soul* (5–8). 2000, HarperCollins LB $14.89 (0-06-028309-4). In this sequel to *Star Fisher* (1991), the Lees, a family of Chinese immigrants who live in Clarksburg, West Virginia, in 1927, face conflicts when the children want to celebrate Christmas. (Rev: BCCB 12/00; BL 12/1/00)

732 Yep, Laurence. *The Star Fisher* (6–10). 1991, Morrow $16.95 (0-688-09365-5). Drawing on his mother's childhood, Yep depicts a Chinese family's experiences when they arrive in West Virginia in 1927 to open a laundry. (Rev: BL 5/15/91; SLJ 5/91)

733 Yep, Laurence. *Thief of Hearts* (5–8). 1995, HarperTrophy paper $6.99 (0-06-440591-5). Stacy, who is half Chinese, goes back to San Francisco's Chinatown to trace her family roots. (Rev: BCCB 9/95; BL 7/95; SLJ 8/95)

734 Young, Ronder T. *Learning by Heart* (5–7). 1993, Houghton $14.95 (0-395-65369-X). Race relations and friendship become important to 10-year-old Rachel, who is growing up in a small southern town in the 1960s with the family's African American maid, whom she adores. (Rev: BCCB 12/93; BL 12/15/93; SLJ 10/93*)

Family Life and Problems

735 Adler, C. S. *Ghost Brother* (5–8). 1990, Houghton $15.00 (0-395-52592-6). After his older brother dies in an accident, 11-year-old Wally finds comfort in his ghost. (Rev: BCCB 5/90; BL 5/15/90; SLJ 5/90; VOYA 8/90)

736 Adler, C. S. *Her Blue Straw Hat* (4–7). 1997, Harcourt $16.00 (0-15-201466-7). Rachel has an opportunity to meet her stepfather's daughter during a summer vacation. (Rev: BL 9/1/97; HBG 3/98; SLJ 9/97)

737 Adler, C. S. *The Lump in the Middle* (6–10). 1991, Avon paper $3.50 (0-380-71176-1). Kelsey, the middle child, struggles for her identity after Dad loses his job. (Rev: BL 10/1/89; BR 1–2/90; SLJ 10/89; VOYA 2/90)

738 Adler, C. S. *The No Place Cat* (5–8). 2002, Clarion $15.00 (0-618-09644-2). Twelve-year-old Tess runs away from home only to find that life with her father and new stepfamily had its good side after all. (Rev: BCCB 4/02; HBG 10/02; SLJ 3/02)

739 Adler, C. S. *One Sister Too Many* (5–7). 1989, Macmillan paper $3.95 (0-689-71521-8). Casey and her reunited family are being driven crazy by the newest addition — a colicky baby. (Rev: BCCB 3/89; BL 3/15/89; SLJ 4/89)

740 Alcock, Vivien. *The Cuckoo Sister* (6–9). 1997, Houghton paper $4.95 (0-395-81651-3). A tough street waif appears at the Setons' door in London and claims to be the older daughter kidnapped many years before. (Rev: BL 8/86; SLJ 4/86; VOYA 8/86)

741 Alphin, Elaine Marie. *Counterfeit Son* (8–12). 2000, Harcourt $17.00 (0-15-202645-2). Reeling from his life with his now-dead murderer father, Cameron adopts the identity of one of the victims, hoping to find a family of his own. (Rev: BL 9/15/00; HBG 3/01; SLJ 12/00)

742 Alphin, Elaine Marie. *Picture Perfect* (6–9). 2003, Carolrhoda $15.95 (0-8225-0535-5). When his friend Teddy disappears, Ian, son of the principal, wonders if his father might be involved. (Rev: BL 8/03; SLJ 10/03)

743 Alvarez, Julia. *How Tia Lola Came to Visit Stay* (4–7). 2001, Knopf $15.95 (0-375-80215-0). Aunt Lola from the Dominican Republic comes to visit 10-year-old Miguel and his family in Vermont and everywhere she goes she spreads friendliness, enthusiasm, stories, and surprise parties. (Rev: BCCB 4/01; BL 2/15/01; HBG 10/01; SLJ 3/01)

744 Anderson, Janet S. *The Monkey Tree* (6–9). 1998, Dutton $15.99 (0-525-46032-2). Susanna's life seems to be coming apart, her grandmother has just died, the family has taken in reclusive Uncle Louie, her best friend has abandoned her, and her art teacher no longer thinks her work is good. (Rev: BCCB 12/98; BL 11/15/98; HBG 9/99; SLJ 11/98; VOYA 6/99)

745 Anfousse, Ginette. *A Terrible Secret* (7–12). Trans. from French by Jennifer Hutchison. 2001, Lorimer paper $4.99 (1-55028-704-4). A new neighbor, Ben, helps Maggie to recover from the death of her Down syndrome brother. (Rev: SLJ 9/01)

746 Arrington, Aileen. *Camp of the Angel* (5–8). 2003, Putnam $16.99 (0-399-23882-4). Despite the intervention of caring professionals, Jordan and her brother continue to suffer physical abuse from their alcoholic father until ultimately the care and love they give to a stray cat prompts Jordan to stand up to her father. (Rev: BL 3/1/03; HBG 10/03; SLJ 3/03)

747 Avi. *Sometimes I Think I Hear My Name* (6–9). 1995, Avon paper $5.99 (0-380-72424-3). A young boy disobeys his guardians to visit New York and find his parents.

748 Banks, Kate. *Walk Softly, Rachel* (7–10). 2003, Farrar $16.00 (0-374-38230-1). When Rachel, 14, reads her dead brother's diary she discovers that his life was not the ideal she had thought. (Rev: BL 10/15/03; SLJ 9/03*)

749 Banks, Lynne Reid. *Alice-by-Accident* (4–8). 2000, HarperCollins $14.95 (0-380-97865-2). Through school compositions and diaries, 9-year-old Alice describes her life, her mother — a lawyer and single parent, and her paternal grandmother. (Rev: BCCB 9/00; BL 6/1–15/00; HB 5–6/00; HBG 10/00; SLJ 6/00)

750 Barwin, Gary. *Seeing Stars* (6–12). 2002, Stoddart paper $7.95 (0-7737-6227-2). A quirky story about a boy who has been brought up in strange circumstances and who now wants the truth about his father and his family. (Rev: BL 7/02; SLJ 5/02)

751 Baskin, Nora Raleigh. *What Every Girl (Except Me) Knows* (5–8). 2001, Little, Brown $16.95 (0-316-07021-1). Young Gabby realizes that her family still hasn't come to terms with her mother's death. (Rev: BCCB 2/01; BL 6/1–15/01; HBG 10/01; SLJ 4/01; VOYA 6/01)

752 Bauer, Cat. *Harley, Like a Person* (7–10). 2000, Winslow $16.95 (1-890817-48-1); paper $6.95 (1-890817-49-X). Unhappy with her distant mother and an alcoholic father, Harley Columba becomes convinced that she is an adopted child. (Rev: BL 6/1–15/00; HB 5–6/00; HBG 9/00; SLJ 5/00)

753 Bauer, Joan. *Backwater* (7–10). 1999, Putnam $16.99 (0-399-23141-2). When 16-year-old Ivy Breedlove begins working on her family history, the trail leads to the New York State Adirondacks and eccentric, talented Aunt Jo. (Rev: BL 5/15/99; HB 7–8/99; HBG 9/99; SLJ 6/99; VOYA 8/99)

754 Bauer, Joan. *Rules of the Road* (6–10). 1998, Putnam $16.99 (0-399-23140-4). Jenna Boller is the confident, smart, and moral heroine of this novel that deals with the effects of alcoholism on a family and a girl's growing friendship with a wealthy, elderly woman. (Rev: BL 2/1/98; BR 1–2/99; HB 5–6/98; HBG 9/98; SLJ 3/98*; VOYA 6/98)

755 Bauer, Joan. *Stand Tall* (5–7). 2002, Putnam $16.99 (0-399-23473-X). Tree, a tall 7th grader, has a lot of challenges in this nonetheless humorous novel: his height, his lack of athletic ability, shuffling between his divorced parents' homes, and his veteran grandfather's ailments, to name just a few. (Rev: BCCB 10/02; BL 9/15/02; HB 11–12/02; HBG 3/03; SLJ 8/02)

756 Bawden, Nina. *Granny the Pag* (5–8). 1996, Clarion $15.00 (0-395-77604-X). Catriona is embarrassed by her grandmother's eccentric ways, such as riding motorbikes and wearing leather jackets, but that doesn't mean she wants to live with her parents instead. (Rev: BCCB 3/96; BL 4/1/96; BR 11–12/96; HB 9–10/96; SLJ 4/96*; VOYA 6/96)

757 Bawden, Nina. *The Outside Child* (6–8). 1994, Puffin paper $3.99 (0-14-036858-2). Jane discovers that her absent father remarried years ago and has a family she would like to meet. (Rev: BL 9/1/89; BR 3–4/90; SLJ 10/89; VOYA 12/89)

758 Bechard, Margaret. *My Mom Married the Principal* (5–8). 1998, Viking $14.99 (0-670-87394-2). For Jonah the 8th grade is the pits and having his stepfather as principal doesn't help. (Rev: BCCB 4/98; BL 3/1/98; HBG 10/98; SLJ 3/98; VOYA 2/98)

759 Berry, James. *A Thief in the Village and Other Stories* (7–12). 1988, Penguin paper $5.99 (0-14-034357-1). Nine stories about a teenager in Jamaica and everyday life on the Caribbean island. (Rev: BL 4/15/88; BR 9–10/88)

760 Betancourt, Jeanne. *Puppy Love* (5–6). Illus. 1986, Avon paper $2.50 (0-380-89958-2). Aviva is having trouble dealing with her divorced parents' new lives and her own crush on Bob Hanley. (Rev: BL 8/86; SLJ 12/86)

761 Birdseye, Tom. *Tucker* (5–8). 1990, Holiday $15.95 (0-8234-0813-2). A story set in rural Kentucky of a young boy reunited with his younger sister after seven years of separation caused by divorce. (Rev: BL 7/90; SLJ 6/90)

762 Block, Francesca L. *Witch Baby* (7–12). 1992, HarperCollins paper $5.99 (0-06-447065-2). This sequel to *Weetzie Bat* focuses on the foundling Witch Baby as she searches for her parents. (Rev: BL 8/91; SLJ 9/91*)

763 Blume, Judy. *It's Not the End of the World* (5–8). 1972, Bradbury LB $17.00 (0-02-711050-8); Dell paper $5.50 (0-440-44158-7). Twelve-year-old Karen's world seems to end when her parents are divorced and her older brother runs away.

764 Bond, Nancy. *Truth to Tell* (6–8). 1994, Macmillan $17.95 (0-689-50601-5). A 14-year-old girl finds herself on her way to New Zealand with her mother and not really understanding the reason for the relocation. (Rev: BL 4/15/94; SLJ 6/94; VOYA 8/94)

765 Boyd, Candy Dawson. *Charlie Pippin* (5–7). 1988, Puffin paper $5.99 (0-14-032587-5). A daughter tries to find out why her father is so embittered about his war experiences in Vietnam. (Rev: BCCB 5/87; BL 4/15/87; SLJ 4/87)

766 Boyd, Candy Dawson. *Chevrolet Saturdays* (5–10). 1993, Macmillan $16.00 (0-02-711765-0). After his parents divorce, Joey's mother marries Mr. Johnson, but Joey rejects and alienates his kindly stepfather. When Joey makes amends, new family ties are formed. (Rev: BL 5/15/93; SLJ 5/93)

767 Brady, Laurel. *Say You Are My Sister* (6–8). 2000, HarperCollins $15.95 (0-06-028307-6). During World War II, in a politically tense southern town, orphaned 12-year-old Mony and her older sister Georgie struggle to hold onto the family farm.

(Rev: BR 3–4/01; HBG 10/01; SLJ 10/00; VOYA 4/01)

768 Brandis, Marianne. *The Tinderbox* (6–8). 2003, Tundra paper $9.95 (0-88776-626-9). In Canada in 1830, 14-year-old Emma and her younger brother, recently orphaned in a fire, must decide whether to trust a woman who claims a family relationship. (Rev: BL 9/1/03)

769 Bridgers, Sue Ellen. *Home Before Dark* (7–10). 1998, Replica Books LB $29.95 (0-7351-0053-5). A migrant worker and his family settle down in a permanent home.

770 Bridgers, Sue Ellen. *Notes for Another Life* (7–12). 1981, Replica Books $24.95 (0-7351-0044-6). A brother and sister cope with a frequently absent mother and a mentally ill father. (Rev: BL 9/1/85; SLJ 10/85; VOYA 4/86)

771 Brisson, Pat. *Sky Memories* (4–7). Illus. 1999, Delacorte $14.95 (0-385-32606-8). Ten-year-old Emily and her mother share a special bond that cannot be broken, even when her mother has terminal cancer. (Rev: BCCB 7–8/99; BL 5/15/99; HBG 10/99; SLJ 8/99)

772 Brokaw, Nancy Steele. *Leaving Emma* (4–7). 1999, Clarion $15.00 (0-395-90699-7). When Emma's best friend moves away and her father is sent to work overseas, the young girl is left with a mother who suffers from bouts of depression. (Rev: BCCB 3/99; BL 3/1/99; HBG 10/99; SLJ 5/99)

773 Brooks, Bruce. *Midnight Hour Encores* (7–10). 1986, HarperCollins paper $6.99 (0-06-447021-0). Cello-playing Sib and her father Taxi take a transcontinental trip to meet Sib's mother, who left after her birth. (Rev: BL 9/15/86; SLJ 9/86; VOYA 12/86)

774 Brooks, Bruce. *What Hearts* (8–12). 1995, Demco $12.00 (0-606-08362-6). Four long stories about Asa, especially his relationship with his emotionally fragile mother and his hostile competition with his stepfather. (Rev: BL 9/1/92*; SLJ 11/92)

775 Brooks, Kevin. *Martyn Pig* (7–10). 2002, Scholastic $10.95 (0-439-29595-5). When Martyn's abusive father dies during a drunken argument, Martyn and a friend dispose of the body, setting off a complicated, suspenseful, and often amusing string of events. (Rev: BCCB 9/02; BL 5/1/02; HBG 10/02; SLJ 5/02*)

776 Brown, Susan M. *You're Dead, David Borelli* (5–7). 1995, Simon & Schuster $15.00 (0-689-31959-2). From a sheltered rich-kid life, David is suddenly thrown into a foster home in a rough neighborhood when his mother dies and his father disappears. (Rev: BL 6/1–15/95; SLJ 7/95)

777 Bunting, Eve. *Is Anybody There?* (4–7). 1990, HarperCollins paper $5.99 (0-06-440347-5). Marcus is both scared and angry after his latchkey disappears and things are stolen. (Rev: BCCB 10/88; BL 12/15/88; SLJ 12/88)

778 Bunting, Eve. *A Sudden Silence* (7–12). 1988, Fawcett paper $6.99 (0-449-70362-2). Jesse sets out to find the hit-and-run driver who killed his brother. (Rev: BL 4/15/88; SLJ 5/88)

779 Bunting, Eve. *Surrogate Sister* (7–10). 1984, HarperCollins LB $13.89 (0-397-32099-X). A 16-year-old girl copes with a pregnant mother who has offered to be a surrogate mother for a childless couple.

780 Burch, Robert. *Ida Early Comes over the Mountain* (4–8). 1990, Puffin paper $4.99 (0-14-034534-5). The four motherless Sutton children find a new and most unusual housekeeper in Ida.

781 Burtinshaw, Julie. *Adrift* (6–8). 2002, Raincoast paper $7.95 (1-55192-469-2). David, 14, and his younger sister Laura have exciting adventures when they rebel against the adults' plans for their future after their mother is hospitalized for depression. (Rev: SLJ 1/03; VOYA 12/02)

782 Byalick, Marcia. *It's a Matter of Trust* (7–9). 1995, Browndeer $11.00 (0-15-276660-X); paper $5.00 (0-15-200240-5). Erika's father confesses to a white-collar crime, and this novel traces the effects of this confession on the family, particularly on 16-year-old Erika and her relations with boyfriend Greg. (Rev: BR 1–2/96; SLJ 12/95; VOYA 2/96)

783 Byars, Betsy. *The Blossoms and the Green Phantom* (5–7). Illus. 1987, Dell paper $3.99 (0-440-40069-4). Junior is about to launch his greatest invention — a hot-air balloon that he hopes will be mistaken for a flying saucer. The three other books about the Blossoms are *The Blossoms Meet the Vulture Lady; The Not-Just-Anybody Family* (both Bantam, 1987); *A Blossom Promise* (Delacorte, 1987). (Rev: BCCB 4/87; BL 3/15/87; HB 3–4/87)

784 Byars, Betsy. *Cracker Jackson* (5–6). 1986, Puffin paper $5.99 (0-14-031881-X). Eleven-year-old Cracker proves a caring friend to his ex-baby-sitter when he suspects she is a victim of wife beating. (Rev: BL 4/1/85; HB 5–6/85; SLJ 5/85)

785 Byars, Betsy. *The Glory Girl* (6–8). 1985, Puffin paper $4.99 (0-14-031785-6). Anna, part of a family of gospel singers, teams up with an uncle fresh from prison to help in a family crisis.

786 Cadnum, Michael. *Zero at the Bone* (8–12). 1996, Viking $15.99 (0-670-86725-X). Anita, Cray's independent older sister, mysteriously disappears and, then, several months later, a body is found that meets her general description. (Rev: BL 8/96*; BR 1–2/97; SLJ 7/96*; VOYA 2/97)

787 Calvert, Patricia. *Glennis, Before and After* (5–8). 1996, Simon & Schuster $16.00 (0-689-80641-8). Glennis must face many harsh realities when her father is sent to prison for white-collar crime and her mother has a nervous breakdown. (Rev: BCCB 10/96; BL 9/1/96; BR 5–6/97; SLJ 9/96)

788 Carey, Janet Lee. *Wenny Has Wings* (5–7). 2002, Simon & Schuster $15.95 (0-689-84294-5). After young Will narrowly escapes death in an accident that killed his sister Wenny, he and his parents must work through their grief. (Rev: BCCB 7–8/02; BL 7/02; HBG 3/03; SLJ 7/02)

789 Caseley, Judith. *Losing Louisa* (8–12). 1999, Farrar $17.00 (0-374-34665-8). Lacey Levine, 16, who is living with her immature, profane mother, discovers that her older unmarried sister is pregnant. (Rev: BL 3/1/99; HBG 9/99; SLJ 3/99; VOYA 6/99)

790 Chambers, Veronica. *Marisol and Magdalena: The Sound of Our Sisterhood* (5–9). 1998, Hyperion LB $15.49 (0-7868-2385-8). Hispanic American Marisol is sent to live with her grandmother in Panama for a year, and hopes to track down her absent father. (Rev: BL 10/1/98; SLJ 12/98)

791 Choldenko, Gennifer. *Notes from a Liar and Her Dog* (5–8). 2001, Putnam $16.99 (0-399-23591-4). A teacher helps Ant, short for Antonia, get a job in a zoo with her friend Harrison, which boosts Ant's self-confidence somewhat, but she continues to find it difficult to relate to her mother. (Rev: BCCB 7–8/01; BL 4/15/01*; HBG 3/02; SLJ 4/01*; VOYA 8/01)

792 Christian, Mary Blount. *Growin' Pains* (6–8). 1985, Penguin paper $3.95 (0-317-63785-1). With the help of a disabled neighbor, Ginny Ruth continues to develop her writing talent in spite of her mother's objections. (Rev: BL 2/1/86; BR 5–6/86)

793 Christiansen, C. B. *I See the Moon* (5–7). 1994, Atheneum $14.95 (0-689-31928-2). Grown-up Bitte looks back at being 12, the year her unmarried older sister became pregnant. (Rev: BCCB 1/95; BL 2/1/95; SLJ 1/95)

794 Christiansen, C. B. *A Small Pleasure* (7–10). 1988, Macmillan $13.95 (0-689-31369-1). A young high school girl hides her grief over her father's fatal cancer by becoming the most popular girl in school. (Rev: BL 4/1/88; BR 9–10/88; SLJ 3/88; VOYA 6/88)

795 Cleary, Beverly. *Sister of the Bride* (6–9). 1963, Morrow $19.89 (0-688-31742-1); Avon paper $5.99 (0-380-72807-9). A young girl becomes too involved with the plans for her sister's wedding.

796 Cleaver, Vera. *Sweetly Sings the Donkey* (6–9). Illus. 1985, HarperCollins LB $12.89 (0-397-32157-0). Fourteen-year-old Lily Snow and her family hope that their inheritance in Florida will help them financially but this is not to be. (Rev: BL 10/1/85)

797 Cleaver, Vera. *Dust of the Earth* (7–9). 1975, HarperCollins $13.95 (0-397-31650-X). Fern and her family face problems when they move to a farm in South Dakota. (Rev: BL 3/1/89)

798 Cleaver, Vera, and Bill Cleaver. *Queen of Hearts* (7–9). 1978, HarperCollins $14.00 (0-397-31771-9). Wilma must take care of her grandmother whom she really dislikes.

799 Cleaver, Vera, and Bill Cleaver. *Where the Lilies Bloom* (6–10). Illus. 1969, HarperCollins $15.95 (0-397-31111-7). When her father dies, Mary Call must take care of her two siblings and keep the family together. A sequel is *Trial Valley*. (Rev: BL 2/1/89)

800 Cohn, Rachel. *The Steps* (4–7). 2003, Simon & Schuster $16.95 (0-689-84549-9). Annabel resents the complexity of her family life as she reluctantly sets out to visit her father and his new wife, baby, and stepchildren in Australia, but she gradually learns to accept the situation in this humorous portrayal. (Rev: BCCB 2/03; BL 1/1–15/03; HB 5–6/03; HBG 10/03; SLJ 2/03*)

801 Collier, James L. *Outside Looking In* (6–8). 1990, Avon paper $2.95 (0-380-70961-9). Fergie and his sister hate the nomadic life their parents lead and long to settle down. (Rev: BL 4/1/87; BR 9–10/87; SLJ 5/87; VOYA 10/87)

802 Colman, Hila. *Diary of a Frantic Kid Sister* (6–8). 1975, Archway paper $2.95 (0-671-61926-8). In diary format, Sarah tells of the frustrations of growing up in the shadow of a glamorous older sister.

803 Colman, Hila. *Rich and Famous Like My Mom* (6–9). 1988, Bantam paper $5.50 (0-440-22019-X). Cassandra is growing up in the shadow of her mother, a world-famous rock star. (Rev: BL 6/15/88)

804 Coman, Carolyn. *What Jamie Saw* (5–8). 1995, Front Street $13.95 (1-886910-02-2). In this novel seen through the eyes of a young boy, a mother and her family flee her physically abusive husband. (Rev: BCCB 12/95; BL 12/15/95*; SLJ 12/95*)

805 Connelly, Neil. *St. Michael's Scales* (6–10). 2002, Scholastic $16.95 (0-439-19445-8). Fifteen-year-old Keenan faces multiple problems — his mother is institutionalized, his older brother has run away, his father is distant, and Keenan is obsessed with the idea that his dead twin brother wants Keenan to kill himself. (Rev: BCCB 7–8/02; BL 3/15/02; HB 5–6/02; HBG 10/02; SLJ 6/02; VOYA 4/02)

806 Conrad, Pam. *Holding Me Here* (7–9). 1986, HarperCollins LB $12.89 (0-06-021339-6). Robin attempts to help a divorced woman who is hiding from her abusive former husband and fails tragically. (Rev: BL 3/15/86; BR 11–12/86; SLJ 3/86; VOYA 6/86)

807 Conrad, Pam. *My Daniel* (6–9). 1989, Harper-Collins LB $16.89 (0-06-021314-0). A grandmother's trip to a science museum unlocks memories of her own childhood. (Rev: BL 4/15/89; BR 11–12/89; SLJ 4/89; VOYA 6/89)

808 Cooney, Caroline B. *Tune in Anytime* (7–10). 1999, Delacorte $8.95 (0-385-32649-1). When her father files for divorce to marry his older daughter's college roommate and her mother is too self-involved to do anything it, Sophie's life seems to fly out of control. (Rev: HBG 4/00; SLJ 9/99; VOYA 12/99)

809 Cooney, Caroline B. *The Voice on the Radio* (7–10). 1996, Delacorte $15.95 (0-385-32213-5). In this sequel to *The Face on the Milk Carton* and *Whatever Happened to Janie?*, Janie realizes that her betrayer is actually her boyfriend, Reeve. (Rev: BL 10/1/96; BR 3–4/97; SLJ 9/96*; VOYA 12/96)

810 Cooney, Caroline B. *What Janie Found* (6–10). 2000, Delacorte $15.95 (0-385-32611-4). Janie, the heroine of previous books including *The Face on the Milk Carton,* finds closure for her family identity problems when she feels she must confront Hannah, her kidnapper and half-sister. (Rev: BL 2/15/00; HBG 3/01; SLJ 3/00; VOYA 4/00)

811 Cooney, Caroline B. *Whatever Happened to Janie?* (6–10). 1993, Delacorte $16.95 (0-385-31035-8); Dell paper $5.50 (0-440-21924-8). Janie, 15, after discovering she's a missing child on a milk carton, returns to her birth family, which has been searching for her since her kidnapping at age three. Sequel to *The Face on the Milk Carton.* (Rev: BL 6/1–15/93; SLJ 6/93; VOYA 8/93)

812 Corcoran, Barbara. *Family Secrets* (5–8). 1992, Macmillan LB $13.95 (0-689-31744-1). After a move to New England with her family, 13-year-old Tracy discovers she is adopted. (Rev: BL 3/1/92; SLJ 2/92)

813 Corcoran, Barbara. *I Am the Universe* (6–8). 1993, Harcourt paper $17.60 (0-15-300366-9). With an indifferent father at home and her mother seriously ill in the hospital, Katherine and her older brother take care of the house. (Rev: BL 10/1/86; SLJ 10/86; VOYA 12/86)

814 Corcoran, Barbara. *The Potato Kid* (5–8). 1993, Avon paper $3.50 (0-380-71213-X). In spite of her protests, Ellis must look after an underprivileged girl her mother takes in for the summer. (Rev: BCCB 11/89; BL 11/15/89; HB 1–2/90; SLJ 10/89; VOYA 2/90)

815 Couloumbis, Audrey. *Getting Near to Baby* (5–9). 1999, Putnam $17.99 (0-399-23389-X). When their baby sister dies and their mother sinks into a depression, 12 year old Willa Jo and Little Sister go to live with a bossy aunt in this story set in North Carolina. (Rev: BCCB 11/99; BL 11/1/99; HB 11–12/99; HBG 3/00; SLJ 10/99; VOYA 2/00)

816 Couloumbis, Audrey. *Say Yes* (6–9). 2002, Putnam $16.99 (0-399-23390-3). Alone after her stepmother disappears, 12-year-old Casey turns to crime in her effort to carry on with life in New York without resorting to welfare. (Rev: BCCB 7–8/02; BL 5/1/02; HB 7–8/02; HBG 10/02; SLJ 7/02; VOYA 4/02)

817 Creech, Sharon. *Ruby Holler* (4–7). 2002, HarperCollins LB $16.89 (0-06-027733-5). An elderly couple, Tiller and Sairy, invite 13-year-old troublesome twins Dallas and Florida to stay with them. (Rev: BCCB 7–8/02; BL 4/1/02; HB 5–6/02; HBG 10/02; SLJ 4/02)

818 Creech, Sharon. *Walk Two Moons* (7–9). 1994, HarperCollins LB $17.89 (0-06-023337-0). The story of Sal, 13, who goes to Idaho with her grandparents to be with her mother, who has been killed in a bus accident. (Rev: BL 11/15/94; SLJ 10/94*; VOYA 2/95)

819 Danziger, Paula. *The Divorce Express* (6–9). 1998, Putnam paper $5.99 (0-698-11685-2). A 14-year-old girl divides time between her divorced parents.

820 Danziger, Paula. *It's an Aardvark-Eat-Turtle World* (6–9). 1996, Bantam paper $3.99 (0-440-41399-0). When Rosie's father and the mother of her best friend move in together, complications begin. (Rev: BL 3/1/85; BR 9–10/85; SLJ 4/85; VOYA 6/85)

821 Danziger, Paula. *The Pistachio Prescription* (6–9). 1999, Putnam paper $5.99 (0-698-11690-9). Cassie, 13 years old, faces many family and personal problems including a compulsive need for pistachio nuts.

822 Darrow, Sharon. *The Painters of Lexieville* (7–10). 2003, Candlewick $16.99 (0-7636-1437-8). This story of poverty and violence features Pert, who yearns to go to Little Rock Beauty College and escape Lexieville and the unwelcome attentions of her Uncle Orris. (Rev: BCCB 1/04; BL 11/15/03)

823 Deans, Sis. *Racing the Past* (4–7). 2001, Holt $15.95 (0-8050-6635-7). Eleven-year-old Ricky, son of a recently deceased alcoholic father, finds that running provides him with comfort and growing self-esteem. (Rev: BCCB 6/01; BL 6/1–15/01; HB 7–8/01; HBG 10/01; SLJ 6/01*; VOYA 6/01)

824 Deaver, Julie Reece. *Chicago Blues* (6–10). 1995, HarperCollins $15.95 (0-06-024675-8). Two sisters are forced to make it on their own because of an alcoholic mother and experience struggle, success, and eventual forgiveness. (Rev: BL 9/1/95; SLJ 8/95; VOYA 12/95)

825 Deedy, Carmen A. *The Last Dance* (7–10). Illus. 1995, Peachtree $16.95 (1-56145-109-6). A picture book for young adults that tells of the abiding love through the years of husband and wife Ninny and Bessie. (Rev: BL 1/1–15/96; SLJ 1/96)

826 Deem, James M. *3 NBs of Julian Drew* (7–12). 1994, Houghton $16.00 (0-395-69453-1). Julian, 15, is emotionally and physically abused by his father and his demented stepmother. He finds strength by writing to his deceased mother in coded notebooks. (Rev: BL 10/15/94; SLJ 10/94*; VOYA 12/94)

827 de Guzman, Michael. *Melonhead* (4–7). 2002, Farrar $17.00 (0-374-34944-4). Sidney T. Mellon hops a bus to the East Coast to escape the cruelty of his mother and stepfamily in Seattle and the emotional detachment of his father in Los Angeles in a story rich with characterization and an emotionally satisfying ending. (Rev: BL 10/15/02; HBG 10/03; SLJ 9/02; VOYA 2/03)

828 Delacre, Lulu. *Salsa Stories* (4–7). Illus. 2000, Scholastic paper $15.95 (0-590-63118-7). After each of her relatives tells a childhood story about a favorite food, Carmen Teresa records them and supplies appropriate recipes. (Rev: BCCB 5/00; BL 5/1/00; HBG 10/00; SLJ 3/00; VOYA 6/00)

829 Derby, Pat. *Grams, Her Boyfriend, My Family and Me* (7–10). 1994, Farrar paper $7.95 (0-374-42790-9). A laid-back teenager finds himself becoming involved in family politics when his mother returns to work and his grandmother comes to live in their tiny house. (Rev: BL 3/15/94; SLJ 11/94*; VOYA 4/94)

830 Deuker, Carl. *High Heat* (5–8). 2003, Houghton $16.00 (0-618-31117-3). Even his baseball prowess seems to desert Shane when his father commits suicide and he must move to a tough new neighborhood and school. (Rev: BL 8/03; HBG 10/03; SLJ 7/03; VOYA 8/03)

831 Dewey, Jennifer O. *Navajo Summer* (5–8). Illus. 1998, Boyds Mills paper $14.95 (1-56397-248-4). When family life becomes intolerable for 12-year-old Janie, she runs away to spend time with the Wilsons, a close-knit Navajo family she met when horse-trading with her father. (Rev: BCCB 11/98; BL 10/1/98; HBG 3/99; SLJ 11/98)

832 Doherty, Berlie. *Holly Starcross* (6–10). 2002, HarperCollins $15.99 (0-06-001341-9). Holly is forced to choose between her mother's new family and her long-lost father in this dramatic British novel. (Rev: BCCB 12/02; BL 11/1/02; HB 9–10/02; HBG 3/03; SLJ 8/02)

833 Doody, Margaret Anne, et al., ed. *The Annotated Anne of Green Gables* (7–12). 1997, Oxford $39.95 (0-19-510428-5). A biography of Lucy Maud Montgomery and notes and annotations explaining references to the places, people, and settings add to this edition of Montgomery's novel. (Rev: SLJ 3/98; VOYA 6/98)

834 Dorris, Michael. *The Window* (6–9). 1997, Hyperion $16.95 (0-7868-0301-0). When her mother is placed in an alcohol rehab center, 11-year-old Rayona Taylor, half-black and half-Native American, must visit her father's relatives in Louisville. (Rev: BL 9/15/97; BR 3–4/98; HBG 3/98; SLJ 11/97)

835 Doucet, Sharon Arms. *Fiddle Fever* (4–7). 2000, Clarion $15.00 (0-618-04324-1). Felix disobeys his mother, who hates fiddle playing, and builds one out of a cigar box and practices in secret. (Rev: BL 9/1/00; HB 9–10/00; HBG 3/01; SLJ 10/00)

836 Dowell, Frances O'Roark. *Dovey Coe* (4–7). 2000, Simon & Schuster $16.00 (0-689-83174-9). The mountain country of North Carolina in 1928 is the setting of this story of a plucky girl who cares for her siblings and who gets involved in a murder trial. (Rev: BL 4/15/00; HBG 10/00; SLJ 5/00; VOYA 6/00)

837 Doyle, Eugenie. *Stray Voltage* (5–7). 2002, Front Street $16.95 (1-886910-86-3). The electrical problems in Ian's family barn reflect the flickering, unpredictable relationships at home, but a wise teacher helps Ian to cope with his circumstances. (Rev: BCCB 1/03; BL 1/1–15/03*; HBG 3/03; SLJ 10/02*; VOYA 2/03)

838 Draper, Sharon M. *Forged by Fire* (7–10). 1997, Simon & Schuster $16.95 (0-689-80699-X). Nine-year-old African American Gerald Nickelby must leave the comfort of his aunt's home to live with a neglectful mother, her daughter Angel, and husband Jordan, who is secretly sexually abusing young Angel. A companion volume to *Tears of a Tiger*. (Rev: BL 2/15/97; SLJ 3/97; VOYA 6/97)

839 Dreyer, Ann L. *After Elaine* (4–8). 2002, Cricket $16.95 (0-8126-2651-6). When her difficult older sister Elaine is killed in a car accident, Gina's grief manifests itself in destructive ways. (Rev: BCCB 5/02; BL 7/02; HBG 10/02; SLJ 7/02; VOYA 12/02)

840 Duffey, Betsy. *Coaster* (4–8). 1994, Viking $13.99 (0-670-85480-8). Hart, 12, misses his father since his parents' divorce and desperately hopes he will show up for their annual roller-coaster trip. (Rev: BCCB 10/94; BL 8/94; SLJ 9/94; VOYA 4/95)

841 Duncan, Lois. *A Gift of Magic* (5–8). 1990, Pocket paper $4.50 (0-671-72649-8). A young girl gifted with extrasensory perception adjusts to her parents' divorce.

842 Dunmore, Helen. *Brother Brother, Sister Sister* (5–8). 2000, Scholastic paper $4.50 (0-439-11322-9). Written in diary format, this is the story of Tanya, once an only child and now surrounded by babies after her mother has quadruplets. (Rev: SLJ 8/00)

843 Elliott, Laura Malone. *Flying South* (5–7). 2003, HarperCollins $15.99 (0-06-001214-5). In the turbulent political year of 1968, 10-year-old Alice describes her distant mother (who has marital ambitions) and the housekeeper and gardener who give Alice love and valuable advice. (Rev: BL 8/03; HBG 10/03; SLJ 5/03; VOYA 8/03)

844 Ellis, Sarah. *Out of the Blue* (5–7). Illus. 1995, Simon & Schuster paper $15.00 (0-689-80025-8). Twelve-year-old Megan discovers that she has a 24-year-old half-sister whom her mother gave up for adoption years ago. (Rev: BCCB 4/95; BL 5/1/95; HB 7–8/95; SLJ 5/95)

845 English, Karen. *Strawberry Moon* (5–8). Illus. 2001, Farrar $16.00 (0-374-47122-3). On the drive to Los Angeles to visit Auntie Dot, Junie tells her children about the time she herself spent as a child with Auntie Dot, a time made difficult by her parents' separation, and her daughter Imani wonders why Dad has stayed in Chicago. (Rev: BCCB 2/02; BL 12/15/01; HBG 3/02; SLJ 10/01)

846 Eulo, Elena Yates. *Mixed-Up Doubles* (8–11). 2003, Holiday $16.95 (0-8234-1706-9). In this poignant yet funny story of a tennis-playing family hit by divorce, middle child Hank, 14, narrates the effects on the children. (Rev: BCCB 7–8/03; BL 5/15/03; SLJ 7/03; VOYA 6/03)

847 Farmer, Penelope. *Penelope* (5–8). 1996, Simon & Schuster $16.00 (0-689-80121-1). Flora, who is being raised by her aunt's family in London, believes that she lived a previous life as Penelope, an 18th-century lord's daughter. (Rev: BL 4/1/96; SLJ 5/96; VOYA 8/96)

848 Fine, Anne. *The Book of the Banshee* (6–9). 1992, Little, Brown $13.95 (0-316-28315-0). English teenager Will Flowers's younger sister, Estelle, has become a banshee, and he decides his family life is like an account of World War I he is reading. (Rev: BL 12/1/91*)

849 Fitzhugh, Louise. *Nobody's Family Is Going to Change* (5–8). 1986, Farrar paper $5.95 (0-374-45523-6). There is considerable misunderstanding within a middle-class African American family but also much humor and warmth.

850 Flake, Sharon G. *Begging for Change* (7–12). 2003, Hyperion $15.99 (0-7868-0601-X). Raspberry resorts to stealing from a friend when her mother is hospitalized after being hit in the head and her addicted father reappears on the scene in this sequel to *Money Hungry* (2001). (Rev: BL 8/03*; SLJ 7/03; VOYA 6/03)

851 Flake, Sharon G. *Money Hungry* (7–10). 2001, Hyperion $15.99 (0-7868-0548-X). Raspberry Hill, 13, struggles to amass a sum of money that will keep her mother and herself safe from a life on the streets. (Rev: BL 6/1–15/01; HBG 10/01; SLJ 7/01)

852 Fleischman, Paul. *Rear View Mirrors* (7–10). 1986, HarperCollins $12.95 (0-06-021866-2). After her father's death, Olivia relives through memory a summer when she and her estranged father reconciled. (Rev: BL 3/1/86; BR 11–12/86; SLJ 5/86; VOYA 8/86)

853 Fleischman, Sid. *Bo and Mzzz Mad* (5–7). 2001, Greenwillow LB $15.89 (0-06-029398-5). When his father dies, 12-year-old Bo accepts an invitation from relatives despite a longstanding family feud. (Rev: BL 5/15/01*; HB 5–6/01; HBG 10/01; SLJ 5/01)

854 Fletcher, Ralph. *Fig Pudding* (5–7). 1995, Clarion $15.00 (0-395-71125-8). A year that brings both tragedy and hilarity in the life of a family of six children. (Rev: BCCB 5/95; BL 5/15/95; SLJ 7/95)

855 Fogelin, Adrian. *Anna Casey's Place in the World* (6–8). 2001, Peachtree $14.95 (1-56145-249-1). Twelve-year-old orphan Anna must adjust to her new foster home and begin to make friends. (Rev: BL 10/15/01; HBG 3/02; SLJ 12/01; VOYA 12/01)

856 Fogelin, Adrian. *My Brother's Hero* (5–8). 2002, Peachtree $14.95 (1-56145-274-2). When Ben and his family travel to Florida for a vacation, Ben meets a girl named Mica, whose life he finds exciting and mysterious. (Rev: BL 2/1/03; HBG 10/03; SLJ 2/03)

857 Fogelin, Adrian. *Sister Spider Knows All* (6–9). 2003, Peachtree $14.95 (1-56145-290-4). A sensitive and humorous novel narrated by Rox, 12, who is doing OK being brought up by her financially strapped grandmother and cousin John until John brings home a rich girlfriend who sees things differently. (Rev: BCCB 2/04; BL 12/15/03; SLJ 12/03)

858 Foggo, Cheryl. *One Thing That's True* (5–8). 1998, Kids Can $16.95 (1-55074-411-9). Roxanne is heartbroken when her older brother runs away after learning that he is adopted. (Rev: BCCB 5/98; BL 2/15/98; BR 11–12/98; HBG 10/98; SLJ 4/98)

859 Forbes, Kathryn. *Mama's Bank Account* (7–10). 1968, Harcourt paper $10.00 (0-15-656377-0). The story, told in vignettes, of a loving Norwegian family and of Mama's mythical bank account.

860 Fox, Paula. *The Eagle Kite* (6–10). 1995, Orchard LB $16.99 (0-531-08742-5). Liam goes through a tangle of denial, anger, shame, grief, and empathy after learning that his father is dying of AIDS. His mother says he got it from a blood transfusion, but Liam remembers seeing his father embrace a young man two years before. (Rev: BL 2/1/95*; SLJ 4/95*; VOYA 5/95)

861 Fox, Paula. *The Moonlight Man* (8–12). 1986, Bradbury LB $14.95 (0-02-735480-6). During a stay together in a house in Nova Scotia, teenager Catherine learns more about her adored alcoholic father than she wants to. (Rev: BL 4/15/86; SLJ 4/86; VOYA 8/86)

862 Fox, Paula. *One-Eyed Cat* (6–9). 1984, Bradbury $16.00 (0-02-735540-3); Dell paper $5.50 (0-440-46641-5). A boy growing up in upstate New

York during the 1930s confronts his own guilt when he secretly disobeys his father. (Rev: BL 6/1/88)

863 Fox, Paula. *The Village by the Sea* (5–8). 1988, Orchard $15.95 (0-531-05788-7); Dell paper $4.50 (0-440-40299-9). Emma is staying with an aunt and uncle while her father has heart surgery, and the three interact in complex ways. Also use the reissued *A Likely Place* (1997). (Rev: BCCB 7–8/88; BL 9/1/88; HB 9–10/88; SLJ 8/88; VOYA 10/88)

864 Frank, Lucy. *Just Ask Iris* (5–7). 2001, Simon & Schuster $17.00 (0-689-84406-9). In this book packed with memorable characters, a 12-year-old girl brings her stand-offish neighbors together while earning the money she needs to buy a bra. (Rev: BCCB 12/01; BL 11/15/01; HB 1–2/02; HBG 3/02; SLJ 12/01; VOYA 12/01)

865 Frank, Lucy. *Oy, Joy!* (6–9). 1999, Simon & Schuster paper $4.99 (0-689-84318-6). A funny and endearing story of the upheaval in 9th-grader Joy's life when her great-uncle Max moves in, takes over her room, and tries to engineer a match for her. (Rev: SLJ 9/99; VOYA 10/99)

866 Franklin, Kristine L. *Dove Song* (5–8). 1999, Candlewick $16.99 (0-7636-0409-7). After young Bobbie Lynn's father is declared missing in Vietnam, the girl's already-depressed mother retreats into a world where she sleeps all day. (Rev: BCCB 11/99; BL 10/15/99; HBG 3/00; SLJ 9/99; VOYA 2/00)

867 Franklin, Kristine L. *Eclipse* (6–9). 1995, Candlewick $14.99 (1-56402-544-6). A young girl feels confused and powerless when her father becomes ill and her family seems to fall apart. (Rev: BL 3/15/95; SLJ 4/95)

868 Franklin, Kristine L. *Lone Wolf* (4–7). 1997, Candlewick $17.99 (1-56402-935-2). Perry has problems with his father when the two move to the north woods of Minnesota and Perry faces a life of isolation. (Rev: BCCB 5/97; BL 7/97; SLJ 6/97*)

869 Frechette, Carole. *In the Key of Do* (6–9). 2003, Red Deer paper $9.95 (0-88995-254-X). Past and present are interwoven in this story of two girls in Montreal whose family circumstances bring them together. (Rev: BL 6/1–15/03; SLJ 6/03; VOYA 10/03)

870 Freeman, Suzanne. *The Cuckoo's Child* (5–8). 1996, Greenwillow $16.95 (0-688-14290-7). In 1962, Mia is leaving with her aunt in Tennessee and worrying about her missing parents. (Rev: BCCB 3/96; BL 3/15/96*; BR 9–10/96; HB 7–8/96; SLJ 4/96*)

871 French, Simon. *Change the Locks* (5–7). 1993, Scholastic paper $13.95 (0-590-45593-1). Steven wants to know about his past, but his single-parent mother remains silent on the topic. (Rev: BCCB 5–6/93; BL 5/1/93)

872 French, Simon. *Where in the World* (5–8). 2003, Peachtree $14.95 (1-56145-292-0). A move from Germany to Australia is difficult for Ari, a talented young violinist who spends time living in the past while trying to find ways to cope with the present. (Rev: BL 12/1/03; SLJ 12/03*)

873 Friesen, Gayle. *Janey's Girl* (6–9). 1998, Kids Can $16.95 (1-55074-461-5). When Claire and her mother visit her mother's hometown in rural British Columbia, the young girl meets her father for the first time and begins to find out truths about her family's past. (Rev: HBG 3/99; SLJ 11/98)

874 Friesen, Gayle. *Losing Forever* (7–10). 2002, Kids Can $16.95 (1-55337-031-7). As her mother prepares to remarry, 9th-grader Jes is still coping with her parents' divorce, her changing relationships with her friends, and her beautiful soon-to-be stepsister. (Rev: BCCB 11/02; BL 1/1–15/03; HBG 3/03; SLJ 11/02; VOYA 2/03)

875 Fritz, April Young. *Praying at the Sweetwater Motel* (4–7). 2003, Hyperion $15.99 (0-7868-1864-6). Sarah Jane, 12, describes her new life living in a motel with her mother and sister, and her hope that her parents will reunite despite her father's abusive behavior. (Rev: BCCB 11/03; BL 10/15/03; HB 11–12/03; SLJ 11/03)

876 Fritz, April Young. *Waiting to Disappear* (7–10). 2002, Hyperion $15.99 (0-7868-0790-3). Buddy must deal with her mother's mental illness just as high school begins in this story set in the 1950s. (Rev: BL 11/15/02; HBG 3/03; SLJ 10/02; VOYA 2/03)

877 Gantos, Jack. *Jack Adrift: Fourth Grade Without a Clue* (4–7). 2003, Farrar $16.00 (0-374-39987-5). In this prequel to the four previous books, Jack Henry is nine and has just moved to Cape Hatteras where he has comic experiences and more serious conversations with his dad. (Rev: BL 8/03; HB 11–12/03; SLJ 9/03)

878 Garland, Sherry. *Rainmaker's Dream* (6–9). 1997, Harcourt paper $6.00 (0-15-200652-4). After her family falls apart, 13-year-old Caroline runs away to a Wild West show where she discovers a secret about her mother's identity. (Rev: BL 4/1/97; SLJ 6/97; VOYA 8/97)

879 Gates, Doris. *Blue Willow* (5–8). 1940, Penguin paper $5.99 (0-14-030924-1). An easily read novel about a poor girl and the china plate that belonged to her mother. (Rev: BCCB 12/99)

880 Giff, Patricia Reilly. *The Gift of the Pirate Queen* (7–9). Illus. 1983, Dell paper $4.99 (0-440-43046-1). Grace's problems, which include taking care of a father and a diabetic sister, are reduced with the arrival of an Irish cousin.

881 Giff, Patricia Reilly. *Pictures of Hollis Woods* (5–7). 2002, Random $15.95 (0-385-32655-6). Twelve-year-old Hollis Woods has finally found a foster home where she feels safe, but when the artist who takes her in begins to suffer from dementia, Hollis finds herself in the position of caregiver. Newbery Honor Book, 2003. (Rev: BCCB 12/02; BL 10/15/02; HB 1–2/03; HBG 3/03; SLJ 9/02)

882 Gilliland, Hap, and William Walters. *Flint's Rock* (5–7). 1996, Roberts Rinehart paper $8.95 (1-879373-82-3). Flint, a young Cheyenne, faces problems when he moves with his parents from the reservation to Butte, Montana. (Rev: BCCB 5/96; BL 5/1/96)

883 Gilmore, Rachna. *Mina's Spring of Colors* (4–7). 2000, Fitzhenry & Whiteside $14.95 (1-55041-549-2); paper $8.95 (1-55041-534-4). Mina is happy when her grandfather comes from India, but with his arrival comes a culture clash that troubles the girl. (Rev: BL 6/1–15/00; SLJ 9/00; VOYA 12/00)

884 Gleitzman, Morris. *Puppy Fat* (5–7). 1996, Harcourt $11.00 (0-15-200047-X); paper $5.00 (0-15-200052-6). Beset by quarreling parents, Keith discovers that his father is attracted to his friend's mother. A sequel to *Misery Guts* and *Worry Worts* (both 1993). (Rev: BCCB 7–8/96; BL 6/1–15/96; SLJ 5/96; VOYA 8/96)

885 Golding, Theresa Martin. *The Secret Within* (5–8). 2002, Boyds Mills $16.95 (1-56397-995-0). Eighth-grader Carly's secret is that her father is abusive and a criminal; the neighbors in the family's new town help her and her mother to finally escape his grip. (Rev: BL 9/15/02; HBG 3/03; SLJ 8/02; VOYA 2/03)

886 Goobie, Beth. *Who Owns Kelly Paddik?* (7–10). Series: Orca Soundings. 2003, Orca paper $7.95 (1-55143-239-0). Kelly, 15, slowly comes to realize that she is not alone as she recovers from the sexual abuse inflicted by her father. (Rev: SLJ 11/03)

887 Goodman, Joan E. *Songs from Home* (5–7). Illus. 1994, Harcourt paper $4.95 (0-15-203591-5). Anna discovers the truth about her father, who has become a drifter in Italy singing for tips in restaurants. (Rev: BCCB 12/94; BL 9/1/94; SLJ 10/94)

888 Graff, Nancy Price. *A Long Way Home* (4–7). 2001, Clarion $15.00 (0-618-12042-4). Twelve-year-old Riley's mother has recently moved them to a small town, where her interest in an old boyfriend who refused to fight in Vietnam causes mixed feelings for the boy about courage, honor, and heroism. (Rev: BCCB 12/01; BL 11/15/01; HBG 3/02; SLJ 10/01; VOYA 10/01)

889 Graham, Rosemary. *My Not-So-Terrible Time at the Hippie Hotel* (6–10). 2003, Viking $15.99 (0-670-03611-0). Fourteen-year-old Tracy has not dealt well with her parents' divorce but finds a new friend and new confidence during a "Together Time" retreat on Cape Cod. (Rev: BL 8/03; HBG 10/03; SLJ 7/03)

890 Grant, Cynthia D. *Mary Wolf* (7–1?) 1995, Atheneum $16.00 (0-689-80007-X). A tale of a homeless family in which the only person who is logical and reasonable is the 16-year-old daughter. (Rev: BL 10/1/95; SLJ 10/95; VOYA 12/95)

891 Greene, Constance C. *Nora: Maybe a Ghost Story* (6–8). 1993, Harcourt $10.95 (0-15-277696-6); paper $4.95 (0-15-276895-5). When Nora and Patsy's father announces his intention to marry after three years of widowhood, they have to deal with resentment and their mother's ghostly presence. (Rev: BL 10/1/93; VOYA 12/93)

892 Greenfield, Eloise. *Sister* (5–7). 1974, Harper-Collins $15.99 (0-690-00497-4); paper $4.99 (0-06-440199-5). Four years in an African American girl's life, as revealed through scattered diary entries, during which she shows maturation, particularly in her attitude toward her sister.

893 Griffin, Adele. *Dive* (5–8). 1999, Hyperion LB $15.49 (0-7868-2389-5). A tangled family story in which 11-year-old Ben tries to become friends with his stepbrother, Dustin. (Rev: BCCB 6/99; BL 9/15/99; HB 11–12/99; HBG 3/00; VOYA 12/99)

894 Griffin, Adele. *Other Shepards* (5–8). 1998, Disney $14.95 (0-7868-0423-8). The two Shepard children live under the specter of the death of their three older siblings before they were born, but then Annie arrives in the household and gives them a new lease on life. (Rev: BCCB 11/98; BL 8/98; HBG 3/99; SLJ 9/98; VOYA 10/98)

895 Griffin, Adele. *Split Just Right* (5–8). 1997, Hyperion LB $15.49 (0-7868-2288-0); Disney paper $5.99 (0-7868-1295-8). Even though Danny's father has been gone as long as she can remember, she still wonders about him. (Rev: BL 6/1–15/97; HB 7–8/97; SLJ 6/97)

896 Griffin, Peni R. *The Music Thief* (5–7). 2002, Holt $16.95 (0-8050-7055-9). Alma must decide what to do when her brother and his friend burglarize a neighbor's house where she often trespasses to listen to music in this story set in San Antonio. (Rev: BCCB 1/03; BL 9/15/02; HBG 3/03; SLJ 12/02; VOYA 12/02)

897 Griffin, Peni R. *Vikki Vanishes* (6–9). 1995, Macmillan paper $15.00 (0-689-80028-2). A long-absent father shows up and enchants and steals away his 16-year-old daughter. (Rev: BL 5/15/95; SLJ 9/95)

898 Grover, Lorie Ann. *Loose Threads* (6–9). 2002, Simon & Schuster $16.95 (0-689-84419-0). Told in free verse by 7th-grade Kay, this is the story of a household of women struggling to cope with Kay's grandmother's breast cancer. (Rev: BL 11/15/02; HBG 3/03; SLJ 10/02)

899 Haas, Jessie. *Shaper* (5–7). 2002, HarperCollins LB $16.89 (0-06-000171-2). After 14-year-old Chad's dog dies, Chad's new neighbor helps him to train a new dog and to reconnect with his family. (Rev: BCCB 9/02; BL 7/02; HB 5–6/02*; HBG 10/02; SLJ 5/02)

900 Haddix, Margaret P. *Don't You Dare Read This, Mrs. Dunphrey* (7–10). 1996, Simon & Schuster $16.99 (0-689-80097-5). Tish keeps a journal for her sophomore English class in which she chronicles her many family problems culminating in her parents' abandonment of their children. (Rev: BL 10/15/96; SLJ 10/96; VOYA 12/96)

901 Haddix, Margaret Peterson. *Takeoffs and Landings* (6–10). 2001, Simon & Schuster $16.00 (0-689-83299-0). Popular 14-year-old Lori and her overweight older brother Chuck go on a lecture tour with their mother, and together the three finally start to talk about the guilt they feel over the death of the children's father. (Rev: BCCB 10/01; BL 11/15/01; HBG 3/02; SLJ 8/01; VOYA 10/01)

902 Hahn, Mary D. *As Ever, Gordy* (5–8). 1998, Houghton $15.00 (0-395-83627-1). After his grandmother's death, 13-year-old Gordy must move back to his hometown to live with his older brother, and there he finds himself in a downward spiral. A sequel to *Stepping on Cracks* and *Following My Own Footsteps.* (Rev: BCCB 6/98; BL 5/1/98; BR 11–12/98; HBG 10/98; SLJ 7/98; VOYA 4/99)

903 Hahn, Mary D. *The Jellyfish Season* (5–7). 1992, Avon paper $4.99 (0-380-71635-6). Kathleen must learn to cope with change: a move to Chesapeake Bay, a hostile cousin, her father's drinking, and her mother's pregnancy. (Rev: BCCB 2/86; BL 10/1/85; SLJ 10/85)

904 Hahn, Mary D. *Tallahassee Higgins* (5–7). 1987, Avon paper $4.99 (0-380-70500-1). With her mother gone to Hollywood with a boyfriend, 12-year-old Tallahassee is stuck in her mother's hometown, where she finds out a lot about her mother's childhood. (Rev: BCCB 4/87; BL 3/1/87; HB 5–6/87)

905 Hall, Barbara. *Dixie Storms* (7–12). 1990, Harcourt $15.95 (0-15-223825-5). Dutch's troubled relationships within her family worsen when cousin Norma comes to stay. (Rev: BL 5/1/90; SLJ 9/90)

906 Hall, Lynn. *Flying Changes* (7–12). 1991, Harcourt $13.95 (0-15-228790-6). An awkward Kansas teenager must give up her romantic dreams after her father is paralyzed and her mother, who abandoned her years before, returns home. (Rev: BL 6/15/91*)

907 Hamilton, Virginia. *M.C. Higgins, the Great* (6–10). 1974, Macmillan LB $17.00 (0-02-742480-4); paper $4.99 (0-02-043490-1). The Newbery Medal winner (1975) about a 13-year-old African American boy growing up in Appalachia as part of a loving family whose future is threatened by a possible mountain slide.

908 Hamilton, Virginia. *Plain City* (5–7). 1993, Scholastic paper $13.95 (0-590-47364-6). Buh-

laire's life changes dramatically when the father she believed to be dead unexpectedly arrives in town. (Rev: BCCB 11/93; BL 9/15/93*; SLJ 11/93*)

909 Hamilton, Virginia. *Second Cousins* (5–8). 1998, Scholastic paper $14.95 (0-590-47368-9). In this sequel to *Cousins,* 12-year-old Cammy learns a secret during a family reunion in her small Ohio town. (Rev: BCCB 11/98; BL 8/98; HB 1–2/99; HBG 3/99; SLJ 11/98; VOYA 2/99)

910 Hamilton, Virginia. *Time Pieces: The Book of Times* (5–8). 2002, Scholastic paper $16.95 (0-590-28881-4). A young girl living in rural Ohio hears stories about her great-grandfather's escape via the Underground Railroad in this semi-autobiographical novel. (Rev: BL 12/15/02; HBG 10/03; SLJ 12/02; VOYA 4/03)

911 Hansen, Joyce. *One True Friend* (4–7). 2001, Clarion $14.00 (0-395-84983-7). Amir's correspondence with his friend Doris comforts him as he tries to fulfill a deathbed promise to his mother to keep his family together. (Rev: BCCB 12/01; BL 12/15/01; HBG 3/02; SLJ 12/01; VOYA 10/01)

912 Harrar, George. *Parents Wanted* (6–9). 2001, Milkweed $17.95 (1-57131-632-9); paper $6.95 (1-57131-633-7). Andy Fleck, a foster child with ADD, sabotages his own adoption by accusing his prospective father of abuse. (Rev: BL 12/15/01; HBG 3/02; SLJ 11/01)

913 Harrison, Mette Ivie. *The Monster in Me* (5–8). 2003, Holiday $16.95 (0-8234-1713-1). A caring foster family and her growing enjoyment in running make Natalie, 13, more optimistic about life. (Rev: BL 4/1/03; HBG 10/03; SLJ 6/03; VOYA 10/03)

914 Harrison, Troon. *Goodbye to Atlantis* (7–10). 2002, Stoddart paper $7.95 (0-7737-6229-9). Stella, 14, whose mother died of cancer, initially resents being stuck with her father's girlfriend as a traveling companion. (Rev: BL 9/1/02; SLJ 4/02)

915 Hartnett, Sonya. *What the Birds See* (7–12). 2003, Candlewick $15.99 (0-7636-2092-0). A beautifully written complex story featuring three missing children and a lonely and fearful boy who is fascinated by three children who move in next door. (Rev: BCCB 3/03; BL 4/15/03; HB 5–6/03; HBG 10/03; SLJ 5/03; VOYA 6/03)

916 Hathorn, Libby. *Thunderwith* (7–10). 1991, Little, Brown $15.95 (0-316-35034-6). This story of an unhappy 15-year-old girl and a beautiful dingolike dog she finds is set in the Australian rain forest. (Rev: BL 9/1/91; SLJ 5/91*)

917 Hausman, Gerald. *Doctor Moledinky's Castle: A Hometown Tale* (5–8). 1995, Simon & Schuster paper $15.00 (0-689-80019-3). Twelve-year-old Andy and his best friend, Pauly, 11, spend the summer of 1957 getting involved in adventures and getting to know the different personalities in their hometown, Berkeley Bend, New Jersey. (Rev: BL 12/1/95; SLJ 10/95; VOYA 2/96)

918 Hausman, Gerald, and Uton Hinds. *The Jacob Ladder* (5–8). 2001, Orchard paper $15.95 (0-531-30331-4). This story of a young Jamaican who struggles valiantly to cope with poverty, a charismatic but neglectful father, and the problems of growing up is based on the youth of coauthor Uton Hinds. (Rev: BL 5/1/01; HBG 3/02; SLJ 4/01; VOYA 6/01)

919 Hehrlich, Gretel. *A Blizzard Year: Timmy's Almanac of the Seasons* (4–7). 1999, Hyperion LB $15.49 (0-7868-2309-7). Using a diary format, this novel covers a year in the life of 13-year-old Timmy, who is growing up with her family on a ranch in Wyoming. (Rev: HBG 3/00; SLJ 2/00)

920 Henkes, Kevin. *The Birthday Room* (5–7). 1999, Greenwillow $15.99 (0-688-16733-0). Ben travels to Oregon with his mother to visit Uncle Ian who was responsible for Ben's losing his little finger in an accident. (Rev: BCCB 9/99; BL 7/99; HB 9–10/99; HBG 3/00; SLJ 10/99)

921 Hermes, Patricia. *Heads, I Win* (4–7). Illus. 1988, Pocket paper $2.99 (0-671-67408-0). Bailey is foster-home smart; she always leaves before someone can dump her. (Rev: BL 6/15/88; SLJ 8/88)

922 Hermes, Patricia. *Sweet By and By* (4–8). 2002, HarperCollins LB $17.89 (0-06-029557-0). In this moving story that portrays the stages of grief, 11-year-old orphan Blessing is hit hard by the news that the grandmother with whom she lives is dying, and has difficulty accepting that she must live with another family. (Rev: BL 10/1/02; HBG 3/03; SLJ 10/02)

923 Hermes, Patricia. *You Shouldn't Have to Say Good-bye* (5–8). 1982, Scholastic paper $3.25 (0-590-43174-9). A moving novel about a girl whose mother is dying of cancer.

924 Hernandez, Irene B. *The Secret of Two Brothers* (7–10). 1995, Arte Publico paper $9.95 (1-55885-142-9). An action-packed story about two Mexican American boys who meet many challenges. Especially appealing to those whose first language is Spanish or for reluctant readers. (Rev: BL 10/1/95; SLJ 11/95)

925 Herschler, Mildred Barger. *The Darkest Corner* (5–9). 2000, Front Street $16.95 (1-886910-54-5). In this novel set in the Deep South of the 1960s, 10-year-old Teddy is shocked to discover that her beloved dad participated in the lynching of her best friend's father. (Rev: BL 1/1–15/01; HBG 3/01; SLJ 2/01; VOYA 2/01)

926 Hickman, Janet. *Jericho* (5–8). 1994. Greenwillow $15.00 (0-688-13398-3). When Angela takes care of her grandmother during her last illness, she learns about the many disappointments the old lady

faced during her life. (Rev: BCCB 11/94; BL 9/1/94; HB 11–12/94; SLJ 9/94)

927 Hicks, Betty. *Animal House and Iz* (4–7). 2003, Millbrook $15.95 (0-7613-1891-7). Elizabeth moves in with her father's new family and is surprised to find she enjoys her noisy stepbrothers and their lively life. (Rev: BL 4/15/03; HBG 10/03; SLJ 7/03; VOYA 8/03)

928 High, Linda O. *Maizie* (4–8). 1995, Holiday $14.95 (0-8234-1161-3). Maizie, a survivor, succeeds in spite of being abandoned by her mother and left with an alcoholic father. (Rev: BCCB 4/95; BL 4/15/95; HB 5–6/95; SLJ 4/95)

929 Hinton, S. E. *Taming the Star Runner* (7–12). 1989, Bantam paper $5.50 (0-440-20479-8). A tough delinquent is sent to his uncle's ranch to be straightened out and there he falls in love with Casey, who is trying to tame a wild horse named Star Runner. (Rev: BL 10/15/88; BR 11–12/88; SLJ 10/88; VOYA 12/88)

930 Hobbs, Valerie. *Carolina Crow Girl* (5–8). 2000, Puffin paper $5.99 (0-14-130976-8). Carolina, who lives in a school bus with her mother and baby sister, longs for a home like other 6th-graders have, but when she gets it, she realizes that there are more important things in life. (Rev: BCCB 6/99; BL 2/15/99; SLJ 4/99)

931 Hobbs, Valerie. *Charlie's Run* (4–7). 2000, Farrar $16.00 (0-374-34994-0). To escape his parents' impending separation, 11-year-old Joey hits the road and finds there are worse things in life than divorce. (Rev: BCCB 3/00; HB 3–4/00; HBG 10/00; SLJ 3/00; VOYA 12/00)

932 Hobbs, Valerie. *Tender* (8–12). 2001, Farrar $18.00 (0-374-37397-3). After her grandmother's death, Liv must adjust to a new life in California with a father she has never met. (Rev: BCCB 10/01; BL 8/01; HB 9–10/01; HBG 3/02; SLJ 9/01; VOYA 10/01)

933 Hoffman, Alice. *Green Angel* (6–12). 2003, Scholastic $16.95 (0-439-44384-9). Fifteen-year-old Green, so-called for her gardening skills, is the only member of her family to survive a major disaster. (Rev: BL 4/15/03; HB 3–4/03; HBG 10/03; SLJ 3/03*; VOYA 4/03)

934 Holcomb, Jerry Kimble. *The Chinquapin Tree* (5–9). 1998, Marshall Cavendish $14.95 (0-7614-5028-9). Faced with being sent back to their abusive mother, three youngsters head for the wilderness in this survival story set in Oregon. (Rev: BL 5/1/98; BR 1–2/99; HBG 10/98; SLJ 5/98)

935 Holeman, Linda. *Raspberry House Blues* (6–10). 2000, Tundra paper $6.95 (0-88776-493-2). Poppy's search for her birth mother looks hopeful for a while when she spends a summer in Winnipeg. (Rev: SLJ 12/00; VOYA 2/01)

936 Holt, Kimberly Willis. *Keeper of the Night* (6–10). 2003, Holt $16.95 (0-8050-6361-7). Isabel, a 13-year-old who lives on Guam, tells the story of her mother's suicide and the family's subsequent grief. (Rev: BL 4/15/03; HB 5–6/03; HBG 10/03; SLJ 5/03*; VOYA 6/03)

937 Holt, Kimberly Willis. *Dancing in Cadillac Light* (5–7). 2001, Putnam $16.99 (0-399-23402-0). A strong, tender story about 11-year-old Jaynell, a tomboy who is growing up in Moon, Texas, in 1968. (Rev: BCCB 3/01; BL 2/1/01; HB 3–4/01; HBG 10/01; SLJ 3/01; VOYA 4/01)

938 Holt, Kimberly Willis. *My Louisiana Sky* (6–9). 1998, Holt $16.95 (0-8050-5251-8). When Tiger Ann's caring grandmother dies, the young girl is tempted to leave her retarded parents and relocate to Baton Rouge to live with an aunt. (Rev: BCCB 6/98; BL 4/15/98; BR 11–12/98; HB 7–8/98*; HBG 9/98; SLJ 7/98; VOYA 8/98)

939 Holubitsky, Katherine. *Alone at Ninety Foot* (7–9). 1999, Orca $14.95 (1-55143-127-0); paper $5.95 (1-55143-129-7). Pamela can't get over the loss of her mother, who committed suicide by jumping from a bridge. (Rev: BCCB 12/99; HBG 4/00; SLJ 11/99)

940 Honeycutt, Natalie. *Twilight in Grace Falls* (5–9). 1997, Orchard LB $17.99 (0-531-33007-9). A moving novel about the closing of a lumber mill that brings unemployment to 11-year-old Dasie Jenson's father. (Rev: BCCB 6/97; BL 3/15/97*; BR 11–12/97; HB 7–8/97; SLJ 5/97; VOYA 8/97)

941 Horrocks, Anita. *What They Don't Know* (7–9). 1999, Stoddart paper $8.95 (0-7737-6001-6). After Hannah discovers a family secret that involves her identity, she heads down a path of self-destruction that her older sister tries to stop. (Rev: BL 11/1/99; SLJ 8/99; VOYA 10/99)

942 Horvath, Polly. *The Canning Season* (6–9). 2003, Farrar $16.00 (0-374-39956-5). Thirteen-year-old Ratchet is sent to live with twin great aunts in Maine in this complex and dark tale that includes some strong language and will appeal to readers interested in adult characters. (Rev: BL 4/1/03; HB 5–6/03*; HBG 10/03; SLJ 5/03*; VOYA 8/03)

943 Hughes, Dean. *Team Picture* (6–8). 1996, Simon & Schuster $16.00 (0-689-31924-X). In this sequel to *Family Pose* (1989), young David, a devoted baseball player, must confront his foster parent, Paul, because of his alcohol abuse. (Rev: BL 11/15/96*; SLJ 11/96*)

944 Hunter, Evan. *Me and Mr. Stenner* (5–8). 1976, HarperCollins $11.95 (0-397-31689-5). Abby's attitudes toward her new stepfather gradually change from resentment to love.

945 Hurwitz, Johanna. *DeDe Takes Charge!* (5–7). 1984, Morrow $15.95 (0-688-03853-0). DeDe's life is not the same A.D. (after divorce).

946 Jarrow, Gail. *If Phyllis Were Here* (5–7). 1989, Avon paper $2.75 (0-380-70634-2). Libby, age 11, has to learn to adjust to living without her best friend — her grandmother who moves to Florida. (Rev: BL 10/15/87; SLJ 9/87)

947 Jennings, Patrick. *Putnam and Pennyroyal* (4–7). 1999, Scholastic $15.95 (0-439-07965-9). Uncle Frank's colorful story about two birds serves as an allegory of the difficult relations in Cora's family. (Rev: BCCB 12/99; BL 11/15/99; HBG 3/00; SLJ 3/00)

948 Johnson, Angela. *Heaven* (6–10). 1998, Simon & Schuster $16.00 (0-689-82229-4). Marley, a 14-year-old African American girl, is devastated when she learns that she is adopted and that the couple she has regarded as her mother and father are really her aunt and uncle. (Rev: BCCB 12/98; BL 9/15/98; BR 5–6/99; HBG 3/99; SLJ 10/98; VOYA 2/99)

949 Johnson, Angela. *Looking for Red* (6–9). 2002, Simon & Schuster $16.00 (0-689-83253-2). Mystery, the supernatural, and family history are integral parts of this story about a middle-school girl trying to cope with the disappearance of her older brother. (Rev: BCCB 9/02; BL 4/15/02; HB 7–8/02; HBG 10/02; SLJ 7/02)

950 Johnson, Angela. *Songs of Faith* (5–8). 1998, Orchard LB $16.99 (0-531-33023-0). Doreen is a child of divorce who is particularly upset by her younger brother's problems adjusting after their father moves away. (Rev: BCCB 6/98; BL 2/15/98; HBG 10/98; SLJ 3/98; VOYA 6/98)

951 Johnston, Julie. *In Spite of Killer Bees* (7–10). 2001, Tundra $17.95 (0-88776-537-8). Aggie, 14, and her older sisters inherit a house from their grandfather and must endure suspicion on the part of their aunt and new neighbors before they succeed in forging new relationships. (Rev: BCCB 12/01; BL 1/1–15/02; HB 1–2/02; HBG 3/02; SLJ 12/01*; VOYA 12/01)

952 Johnston, Julie. *The Only Outcast* (6–10). 1998, Tundra $14.95 (0-88776-441-X). Based on fact, this is the story of the summer of 1904 when Fred Dickinson spent the summer with his grandparents in Ontario and found romance and a mystery. (Rev: BL 10/1/98; BR 1–2/99; HB 1–2/99; HBG 3/99; SLJ 1/99; VOYA 2/99)

953 Johnston, Lindsay Lee. *Soul Moon Soup* (5–7). 2002, Front Street $15.95 (1-886910-87-1). When homeless Phoebe and her mother hit bottom, Phoebe goes to live with her grandmother and slowly learns to value her own resources in this story told in verse. (Rev: BCCB 2/03; BL 11/15/02; HB 1–2/03; HBG 3/03; SLJ 11/02)

954 Johnston, Tim. *Never So Green* (6–10). 2002, Farrar $18.00 (0-374-35509-6). Twelve-year-old Tex, who has a growing interest in sex, is horrified to find that his stepsister is being sexually abused in this novel full of realistic characters and subplots. (Rev: BCCB 12/02; BL 9/1/02; HBG 3/03; SLJ 10/02)

955 Joosse, Barbara M. *Pieces of the Picture* (5–8). 1989, HarperCollins LB $12.89 (0-397-32343-3); paper $3.50 (0-06-440310-6). Emily is not happy when she and her mother move to Wisconsin after her father's death to earn a livelihood running an inn. (Rev: BL 6/1/89; BR 11–12/89; SLJ 4/89)

956 Karas, Phyllis. *Cry Baby* (5–9). 1996, Avon paper $4.50 (0-380-78513-7). Sam Sloan, 14, the youngest of four daughters, is horrified to learn that her 47-year-old mother is pregnant, begins failing tests at school, and secretly dates the boyfriend of her best friend, who is suffering from a severe eating disorder. (Rev: VOYA 4/97)

957 Kehret, Peg. *Sisters Long Ago* (5–8). 1992, Pocket paper $3.99 (0-671-78433-4). While surviving a near drowning, Willow has a glimpse of herself living another life in ancient Egypt. (Rev: SLJ 3/90)

958 Killingsworth, Monte. *Equinox* (5–8). Illus. 2001, Holt $16.95 (0-8050-6153-3). Fourteen-year-old Autumn has been happy living on her remote island, but changing relations between her parents threaten this idyll. (Rev: BL 8/01; HBG 3/02; SLJ 9/01; VOYA 10/01)

959 Kinsey-Warnock, Natalie. *As Long As There Are Mountains* (5–8). 1997, Dutton $14.99 (0-525-65236-1). When her father is injured, 13-year-old Iris wants to retain the family farm, but her older brother wants to sell it. (Rev: BL 8/97; BR 9–10/98; HBG 3/98; SLJ 8/97*; VOYA 4/98)

960 Klass, David. *You Don't Know Me* (6–9). 2001, Farrar $17.00 (0-374-38706-0). John, 14, retreats into his own world when faced with abuse from his mother's boyfriend. (Rev: BCCB 2/01; BL 3/1/01; HB 7–8/01; HBG 10/01; SLJ 3/01; VOYA 6/01)

961 Klein, Norma. *Breaking Up* (7–10). 1981, Avon paper $2.50 (0-380-55830-0). While visiting her divorced father in California, Alison falls in love with her best friend's brother.

962 Klein, Norma. *Mom, the Wolfman and Me* (5–8). 1972, Avon paper $3.50 (0-380-00791-6). Brett's mother is single but the Wolfman is becoming more than a steady boyfriend.

963 Klein, Robin. *The Sky in Silver Lace* (6–9). 1996, Viking $13.99 (0-670-86266-5). The four Melling sisters and their mother move to a large city in Australia to find better times in this sequel to *All in the Blue Unclouded Weather* (1992). (Rev: BCCB 2/96; BL 2/15/96; BR 9–10/96; HB 5–6/96; SLJ 2/96)

964 Koller, Jackie F. *A Place to Call Home* (7–10). 1995, Atheneum $16.00 (0-689-80024-X). Biracial Anna, 15, is a strong character in search of love and

roots following sexual abuse and rejection from her own family. (Rev: BL 10/15/95; SLJ 10/95; VOYA 2/96)

965 Koss, Amy Goldman. *The Ashwater Experiment* (5–8). 1999, Dial $16.99 (0-8037-2391-1). After spending nine months in Ashwater, California, Hillary doesn't want to leave when her nomadic, hippie parents decide to move on. (Rev: BCCB 6/99; BL 6/1–15/99; HB 7–8/99; HBG 10/99; SLJ 8/99; VOYA 10/99)

966 Koss, Amy Goldman. *Stolen Words* (5–7). 2001, Pleasant $14.95 (1-58485-377-8); paper $5.95 (1-58485-376-X). Robyn, 11, uses a diary to record her thoughts during her family's trip to Austria and her feelings about her Aunt Beth's death. (Rev: BL 9/15/01; HBG 3/02; VOYA 2/02)

967 Kurtz, Jane. *Jakarta Missing* (5–8). 2001, Greenwillow LB $16.89 (0-06-029402-7). Although Dakar has longed for her sister Jakarta to come from Kenya to their new home in North Dakota, Dakar's problems continue when Jakarta arrives. (Rev: BCCB 5/01; BL 5/15/01; HB 5–6/01; HBG 10/01; SLJ 5/01)

968 Lafaye, A. *Nissa's Place* (5–9). 1999, Simon & Schuster paper $4.99 (0-689-84250-3). Still unhappy about the arrival of a stepmother in her Louisiana home, Nissa, now 13, agrees to visit her mother in Chicago in this sequel to *The Year of the Sawdust Man* (1998). (Rev: BCCB 10/99; BL 10/15/99; HBG 3/00; SLJ 10/99)

969 Lafaye, A. *The Strength of Saints* (5–9). 2002, Simon & Schuster $16.95 (0-689-83200-1). Racial tensions and family problems plague 14-year-old Nissa, who is trying to run the local library in Harper, Louisiana, in this sequel to two earlier novels. (Rev: BL 6/1–15/02; HBG 10/02; SLJ 6/02; VOYA 8/02)

970 Lafaye, Alexandria. *The Year of the Sawdust Man* (5–8). 1998, Simon & Schuster $16.00 (0-689-81513-1). Set in a small Louisiana town in 1933, this novel tells of 11-year-old Nissa and her confusion and unhappiness when her mother leaves and her father shows a growing attachment to another woman. (Rev: BCCB 7–8/98; BL 6/1–15/98; HBG 9/98; SLJ 7/98)

971 Lantz, Francess. *Someone to Love* (7–10). 1997, Avon $14.00 (0-380-97477-0). Sara's secure family life changes when her parents decide to adopt the yet-unborn child of Iris, an unmarried teen. (Rev: BL 4/15/97; BR 9–10/97)

972 Lantz, Francess. *Stepsister from the Planet Weird* (5–8). 1997, Random $11.99 (0-679-97330-3); paper $3.99 (0-679-87330-9). Megan and her almost-stepsister Ariel, an alien from outer space, conspire to prevent Megan's mother and Ariel's father from marrying. (Rev: SLJ 2/98)

973 Lasky, Kathryn. *Memoirs of a Bookbat* (5–9). 1994, Harcourt $10.95 (0-15-215727-1). A free-thinking teen rejects the beliefs of her conservative, religious parents and hides her extensive reading habits. (Rev: BL 4/15/94; SLJ 7/94; VOYA 6/94)

974 Lelchuk, Alan. *On Home Ground* (7–10). Illus. 1987, Harcourt $9.95 (0-15-200560-9). Aaron seems to have nothing in common with his father, a Russian immigrant. (Rev: BL 1/1/88; SLJ 12/87; VOYA 4/88)

975 L'Engle, Madeleine. *Meet the Austins* (5–8). 1981, Dell paper $5.50 (0-440-95777-X). The Austin family — a tightly knit, loving group with four children — is disrupted when a young orphan girl comes to live with them.

976 L'Engle, Madeleine. *The Moon by Night* (7–10). 1963, Farrar $16.00 (0-374-35049-3); Dell paper $4.99 (0-440-95776-1). In this novel about the Austins, the family takes a cross-country camping trip and Vicki finds she is attracted to the wealthy, irresponsible Zachery Gray.

977 Levitin, Sonia. *The Singing Mountain* (7–12). 1998, Simon & Schuster $17.00 (0-689-80809-7). Family secrets are revealed when Carlie accompanies her aunt Vivian to Israel to convince Vivian's son to return to America. (Rev: BL 9/15/98; HB 11–12/98; HBG 3/99; SLJ 11/98; VOYA 2/99)

978 Levitin, Sonia. *Yesterday's Child* (7–10). 1997, Simon & Schuster $17.00 (0-689-80810-0). After her parent's death, Laura discovers some amazing family secrets when she goes through her mother's things. (Rev: BL 6/1–15/97; SLJ 6/97)

979 Levoy, Myron. *The Witch of Fourth Street and Other Stories* (4–7). Illus. 1991, Peter Smith $19.75 (0-8446-6450-2); HarperCollins paper $4.99 (0-06-440059-X). Eight stories about growing up poor on the Lower East Side of New York City.

980 Lewis, Beverly. *Whispers down the Lane* (5–8). Series: Summerhill Secrets. 1995, Bethany paper $5.99 (1-55661-476-4). An Amish girl agrees to hide Lissa, who has run away from her father's abusive treatment. (Rev: BL 9/1/95; SLJ 2/96)

981 Lindbergh, Anne. *The Worry Week* (5–7). 1985, Harcourt $12.95 (0-15-299675-3); Avon paper $2.95 (0-380-70394-7). Left alone with her sisters for a week in Maine, 11-year-old "Legs" spends most of her time tending to and worrying about her siblings. (Rev: BL 6/1/85; HB 9–10/85; SLJ 8/85)

982 Lisle, Janet Taylor. *The Crying Rocks* (6–9). 2003, Simon & Schuster $16.95 (0-689-85319-X). Joelle, who was adopted and is curious about her background, feels a strange connection with the Narragansett tribe she is researching. (Rev: BL 10/15/03; HB 11–12/03; SLJ 12/03)

983 Little, Jean. *Willow and Twig* (5–8). 2003, Viking $15.99 (0-670-88856-7). Two children who believe they are friendless as well as homeless are rescued by their grandmother and must remake their lives. (Rev: BCCB 3/03; BL 7/03; HBG 10/03; SLJ 8/03*)

984 Lowry, Lois. *Autumn Street* (7–9). 1980, Houghton $16.00 (0-395-27812-0); Dell paper $5.50 (0-440-40344-8). With her father away, Elizabeth and her mother and older sister move in with her grandmother. (Rev: BL 12/15/89)

985 Lowry, Lois. *Find a Stranger, Say Goodbye* (7–10). 1978, Houghton $17.00 (0-395-26459-6). A college-bound girl decides to find her natural mother.

986 Lowry, Lois. *Rabble Starkey* (6–9). 1987, Houghton $16.00 (0-395-43607-9); Dell paper $5.50 (0-440-40056-2). The story of a friendship between two girls (Rabble and Veronica), their 6th-grade year, and their many experiences with family and friends. (Rev: BL 3/15/87; BR 9–10/87; SLJ 4/87; VOYA 4/87)

987 Lowry, Lois. *Us and Uncle Fraud* (6–9). 1984, Houghton $16.00 (0-395-36633-X). Uncle Claude visits his sister and her four children and an experience in human relations begins.

988 Luger, Harriett. *Bye, Bye, Bali Kai* (5–7). 1996, Harcourt $11.00 (0-15-200862-4); paper $5.00 (0-15-200863-2). Suzie's family hits rock bottom when they are evicted and forced to live in an abandoned building. (Rev: BCCB 3/96; BL 6/1–15/96; SLJ 6/96; VOYA 6/96)

989 Lurie, April. *Dancing in the Streets of Brooklyn* (5–9). 2002, Delacorte $15.95 (0-385-72942-1). Judy, from a Norwegian immigrant family, is devastated to learn that the man she knows as "Pa" is not her birth father in this novel set in 1944. (Rev: BCCB 12/02; BL 11/15/02; HBG 3/03; SLJ 9/02)

990 Lynch, Chris. *Shadow Boxer* (6–10). 1993, HarperCollins LB $14.89 (0-06-023028-2). Their father's death leaves 14-year-old George and his hyperactive younger brother in a conflict that can only be resolved by dispelling their father's shadow. (Rev: BL 12/15/93; SLJ 9/93*; VOYA 12/93)

991 Lynn, Tracy. *Snow* (7–10). 2003, Simon & Schuster paper $5.99 (0-689-85556-7). The story of Snow White gets a new twist in this exciting novel set in Victorian England, in which Snow's growing beauty inflames her stepmother with jealousy and Snow flees from her father's castle to the dangers of the London streets. (Rev: BCCB 5/03; SLJ 8/03; VOYA 8/03)

992 McDonald, Janet. *Spellbound* (7–12). 2001, Farrar $16.00 (0-374-37140-7). Despite enormous obstacles, 16-year-old African American mother Raven decides to enter a spelling bee in hopes of going to college. (Rev: BCCB 10/01; BL 11/1/01; HB 1–2/02; HBG 3/02; SLJ 9/01; VOYA 10/01)

993 Mack, Tracy. *Birdland* (7–10). 2003, Scholastic $16.95 (0-439-53590-5). Jed's family has not recovered from the death of his brother Zeke, and Jed finds some comfort in videotaping their neighborhood and finding links to Zeke through the poems and journal he left. (Rev: BL 10/15/03*; SLJ 10/03)

994 Mack, Tracy. *Drawing Lessons* (5–8). 2000, Scholastic paper $15.95 (0-439-11202-8). Aurora, who adores her artist father, must adjust her expectations when she catches him in a compromising position with one of his models. (Rev: BCCB 3/00; BL 3/15/00; HBG 10/00; SLJ 3/00; VOYA 4/00)

995 McKay, Hilary. *The Exiles* (4–7). 1992, Macmillan $17.99 (0-689-50555-8). The four Conroe sisters are shipped off to Big Grandma's for the summer. She thinks they "read too much, answer back, and never do anything to help." (Rev: BCCB 11/92*; BL 1/1/93; HB 1–2/93*; SLJ 10/92)

996 McKay, Hilary. *The Exiles at Home* (4–7). 1994, Macmillan $15.95 (0-689-50610-4). In this sequel to *The Exiles*, the four Conway sisters sponsor the schooling of a young African boy and must find the money to pay for their generosity. (Rev: BCCB 1/95; BL 1/15/95*; SLJ 2/95)

997 McKay, Hilary. *Saffy's Angel* (4–7). 2002, Simon & Schuster $16.00 (0-689-84933-8). Saffron learns she was adopted into her artistic family and travels to Italy in search of her roots. (Rev: BCCB 5/02; BL 5/15/02; HB 7–8/02*; HBG 10/02; SLJ 5/02)

998 MacKinnon, Bernie. *Song for a Shadow* (8–12). 1991, Houghton $18.00 (0-395-55419-5). This novel concerns 18-year-old Aaron's attempts to sort out his relationships with his parents — his father has always seemed too wrapped up in his career, and his mother is emotionally troubled. (Rev: BL 3/15/91; SLJ 4/91)

999 MacLachlan, Patricia. *All the Place to Love* (5–8). Illus. 1994, HarperCollins LB $17.89 (0-06-021099-0). This picture book celebrates the love found in an extended rural family and the joy that a new arrival brings. (Rev: BCCB 7–8/94; BL 6/1–15/94*; SLJ 6/94)

1000 MacLachlan, Patricia. *Baby* (5–10). 1993, Delacorte $15.95 (0-385-31133-8). In this moving, beautifully written story, "Baby" refers to two youngsters: Larkin's brother (who died before the story begins) and Sophie, who's left in a basket on the driveway of Larkin's home. (Rev: BL 9/1/93; SLJ 11/93; VOYA 10/93)

1001 MacLachlan, Patricia. *Cassie Binegar* (4–7). 1982, HarperCollins LB $15.89 (0-06-024034-2); paper $4.95 (0-06-440195-2). Cassie is not happy with the disorder in her family situation.

1002 MacLachlan, Patricia. *Journey* (5–7). 1991, Delacorte $14.95 (0-385-30427-7). A boy named Journey and his sister Cat must make a new life for

themselves on their grandparents' farm. (Rev: BCCB 10/91; BL 9/15/91; HB 11–12/91*; SLJ 9/91)

1003 Mansfield, Creina. *Cherokee* (5–8). 2001, O'Brien paper $7.95 (0-86278-368-2). Gene's wonderful life with his jazz musician grandfather, Cherokee, comes to an end when his aunt decides he needs a home and an education. (Rev: SLJ 11/01)

1004 Marino, Jan. *For the Love of Pete* (5–8). 1994, Avon paper $3.50 (0-380-72281-X). Three devoted servants take Phoebe on a journey to find the father she has never met. (Rev: BCCB 7–8/93; BL 6/1–15/93; SLJ 5/93*)

1005 Marsden, John. *Letters from the Inside* (8–12). 1994, Houghton $16.00 (0-395-68985-6). Two teenage girls begin a correspondence, with their initial letters describing ideal fictitious lives. With time, they reveal that one has a violent brother and the other feels trapped within her family. (Rev: BL 10/15/94; SLJ 9/94*; VOYA 12/94)

1006 Martin, Ann M. *Ten Kids, No Pets* (4–7). 1988, Scholastic paper $3.50 (0-590-43620-1). The Rosso family — 12 strong — moves to New Jersey and a 100-year-old farmhouse. (Rev: BL 6/15/88; SLJ 5/88)

1007 Martin, Nora. *The Eagle's Shadow* (6–9). Illus. 1997, Scholastic paper $15.95 (0-590-36087-6). Twelve-year-old Clearie is sent to live with Tlingit relatives in Alaska and comes to accept the desertion by her mother. (Rev: BL 8/97; BR 11–12/97; HBG 3/98; SLJ 10/97; VOYA 4/98)

1008 Martin, Patricia A. *Memory Jug* (5–7). 1998, Hyperion LB $16.49 (0-7868-2368-2). Mack, who still misses her dead father, feels she is losing contact with the rest of her family when her mother finds a new boyfriend, her younger sister makes a new friend, and bossy Aunt Sydney moves in. (Rev: BCCB 11/98; BL 11/1/98; SLJ 11/98)

1009 Martin, Patricia A. *Travels with Rainie Marie* (5–7). 1997, Hyperion LB $16.49 (0-7868-2212-0). When there is no one to care for her and her five brothers and sisters, Rainie Marie is afraid that her bossy aunt will try to split up the family among various relatives. (Rev: BL 5/15/97; SLJ 7/97)

1010 Masterman-Smith, Virginia. *First Mate Tate* (7–9). 2000, Marshall Cavendish $14.95 (0-7614-5075-0). When her father's gambling brings the family close to financial ruin, First Mate Tate thinks up daring schemes to keep her family afloat. (Rev: BL 10/15/00; HBG 3/01; SLJ 9/00)

1011 Matas, Carol. *Sparks Fly Upward* (4–8). 2002, Clarion $15.00 (0-618-15964-9). Set in Manitoba in the early 20th century, this is the story of 12-year-old Rebecca, a Jewish girl, and her life with a Ukrainian foster family. (Rev: BCCB 7–8/02; BL 4/1/02; HBG 10/02; SLJ 3/02)

1012 Matthews, Kezi. *Flying Lessons* (5–7). 2002, Cricket $16.95 (0-8126-2671-0). A girl in a small southern town bonds with an eclectic bunch of adults after the airplane in which her mother was traveling disappears. (Rev: BL 12/15/02; HB 1–2/03; HBG 3/03; SLJ 12/02; VOYA 6/03)

1013 Matthews, Kezi. *John Riley's Daughter* (6–9). 2000, Front Street $15.95 (0-8126-2775-X). Memphis feels responsible when her mentally disabled aunt, Clover, runs off in this story of tangled family ties. (Rev: BCCB 6/00; HB 7–8/00; HBG 9/00; SLJ 7/00)

1014 Mazer, Harry. *Who Is Eddie Leonard?* (7–10). 1995, Demco $10.04 (0-606-08379-0). When his grandmother dies, Eddie sees a missing-child poster that convinces him he's really the kidnapped Jason Diaz. But the Diazes aren't the perfect family he imagined. (Rev: BL 11/15/93; SLJ 11/93; VOYA 4/94)

1015 Mazer, Norma Fox. *After the Rain* (7–10). 1987, Morrow $17.99 (0-688-06867-7); Avon paper $5.99 (0-380-75025-2). Rachel gradually develops a warm relationship with her terminally ill grandfather who is noted for his bad temper. (Rev: BL 5/1/87; BR 5–6/87; SLJ 5/87; VOYA 6/87)

1016 Mazer, Norma Fox. *D, My Name Is Danita* (6–8). 1991, Scholastic $13.95 (0-590-43655-4). The latest in this light series presents an interesting premise: Girl meets boy who turns out to be her older half-brother. (Rev: BL 4/1/91; SLJ 3/91)

1017 Mazer, Norma Fox. *Downtown* (7–10). 1984, Avon paper $4.95 (0-380-88534-4). Pete, 15, the son of anti-war demonstrators who are in hiding, faces problems when his mother reappears and wants to be part of his life.

1018 Mazer, Norma Fox. *Girlhearts* (5–9). 2001, HarperCollins LB $16.89 (0-688-06866-9). Thirteen-year-old Sarabeth faces many challenges and difficult choices when her single mother dies suddenly. (Rev: BCCB 4/01; BL 7/01; HBG 10/01; SLJ 5/01; VOYA 8/01)

1019 Mazer, Norma Fox. *Missing Pieces* (7–10). 1995, Morrow $16.00 (0-688-13349-5). A 14-year-old seeks a missing part of her life by looking for a father who abandoned her. (Rev: BL 4/1/95; SLJ 4/95*; VOYA 5/95)

1020 Mazer, Norma Fox. *Taking Terri Mueller* (7–10). 1983, Avon paper $5.99 (0-380-79004-1). Terri realizes that her beloved father has actually kidnapped her to keep her from her mother.

1021 Mead, Alice. *Junebug* (4–7). 1995, Farrar $16.00 (0-374-33964-3). Junebug, a young boy, realizes that the only hope for his family is to move from the city project where they live. (Rev: BCCB 12/95; BL 9/15/95; SLJ 11/95; VOYA 2/96)

1022 Mead, Alice. *Junebug in Trouble* (5–8). 2002, Farrar $16.00 (0-374-33969-4). Young Junebug and his mother move out of the housing projects, but Junebug continues to get into the trouble his mother was hoping to avoid. (Rev: BCCB 6/02; BL 4/15/02; HB 5–6/02; HBG 10/02; SLJ 3/02)

1023 Mead, Alice. *Soldier Mom* (5–7). 1999, Farrar $16.00 (0-374-37124-5). Jasmyn's life — including her basketball game — suffers when her mother, an army reservist, is called up during the Persian Gulf War and Jake, her mother's fiance, takes over managing the house. (Rev: BCCB 12/99; BL 9/1/99*; HB 9–10/99; HBG 3/00; SLJ 9/99)

1024 Mead, Alice. *Walking the Edge* (5–8). 1995, Albert Whitman LB $14.95 (0-8075-8649-8). Scott escapes the abuse of his drunken father by throwing himself into his 4-H science project. (Rev: SLJ 12/95)

1025 Metzger, Lois. *Barry's Sister* (5–8). 1992, Macmillan $15.95 (0-689-31521-X). When Ellen's new brother is born with cerebral palsy, she blames herself because she didn't want a baby brother. (Rev: BL 4/15/92; SLJ 6/92)

1026 Metzger, Lois. *Missing Girls* (5–8). 1999, Viking $15.99 (0-670-87777-8). Thirteen-year-old Carrie doesn't seem to fit in anywhere until she meets the seemingly ideal family of her friend Mona, but this, too, is revealed to be less than perfect. (Rev: BCCB 2/99; BL 2/1/99; BR 9–10/99; HB 5–6/99; HBG 10/99; SLJ 4/99; VOYA 6/99)

1027 Mikaelsen, Ben. *Countdown* (6–9). 1996, Hyperion LB $16.49 (0-7868-2207-1). Two 14-year-old boys (one who lives in a remote village in Kenya and the other whose home is at the Johnson Space Center) face similar personal problems, particularly the conflict each has with his father. (Rev: BL 1/1–15/97; BR 5–6/97; SLJ 3/97; VOYA 6/97)

1028 Miles, Betty. *Just the Beginning* (6–8). 1978, Avon paper $2.50 (0-380-01913-2). Being relatively poor in an upper-class neighborhood causes problems for 13-year-old Catherine Myers.

1029 Miller, Dorothy R. *Home Wars* (5–8). 1997, Simon & Schuster $16.00 (0-689-81411-9). Halley has misgivings when her father brings home three rifles, one for himself and the others for her two brothers. (Rev: BL 9/1/97; HBG 3/98; SLJ 10/97)

1030 Miller, Judi. *Purple Is My Game, Morgan Is My Name* (4–7). 1998, Pocket paper $3.99 (0-671-00280-5). In this humorous novel, young Morgan has two goals — to find a suitable career goal and to reunite her separated parents. (Rev: SLJ 11/98)

1031 Modiano, Patrick. *Catherine Certitude* (4–7). Trans. by William Rodarmor. 2001, Godine $17.95 (0-87923-959-X). An adult Catherine reminisces about her life as a youngster in Paris — living with her father, puzzling over his job, going to ballet classes, eating in restaurants — in this stylishly illustrated chapter book delivered in picture-book format. (Rev: BL 12/15/01; HBG 3/02; SLJ 2/02)

1032 Montgomery, L. M. *Anne of Green Gables* (7–9). 1995, Puffin paper $4.99 (0-14-036741-1). This is a reissue of the classic Canadian story of Anne and how she was gradually accepted in a foster home. Her story continued in *Anne of Avonlea, Anne of the Island, Anne of Windy Poplars, Anne's House of Dreams,* and *Anne of Ingleside.*

1033 Montgomery, L. M. *Christmas with Anne and Other Holiday Stories* (4–7). 1996, McClelland & Stewart Tundra Books $12.95 (0-7710-6204-4). A collection of 16 short pieces and stories (two from the Anne of Green Gables books) that deal with Christmas. (Rev: BL 9/1/96)

1034 Montgomery, L. M. *Emily of New Moon* (7–9). 1986, Bantam paper $4.99 (0-553-23370-X). Beginning when Emily is only 11, this trilogy continues in *Emily Climbs* and *Emily's Quest* and tells about the making of a writer. These are reissues.

1035 Moore, Ishbel. *Daughter* (6–12). 1999, Kids Can $14.95 (1-55074-535-2). Sylvie struggles to cope with her parents' divorce and her mother's Alzheimer's disease in this moving story. (Rev: BCCB 12/99; BL 11/15/99; HBG 4/00; SLJ 11/99)

1036 Moore, Martha. *Matchit* (4–7). 2002, Delacorte LB $17.99 (0-385-90023-6). When his father goes on vacation, 11-year-old Matchit must stay with an eccentric woman who runs a junkyard in this story about a child's hopes, fears, and self-esteem. (Rev: BCCB 6/02; BL 2/15/02; HBG 10/02; SLJ 4/02)

1037 Mori, Kyoko. *One Bird* (8–12). 1996, Fawcett paper $6.50 (0-449-70453-X). A coming-of-age story set in Japan about 15-year-old girl Megumi, who loses her mother yet finds people who understand and love her. (Rev: BL 10/15/95; SLJ 11/95; VOYA 2/96)

1038 Morpurgo, Michael. *Escape from Shangri-La* (5–7). 1998, Putnam $16.99 (0-399-23311-3). In this English novel, Cessie gradually forms a close relationship with an old boatman in a nursing home whom she believes to be her grandfather. (Rev: BCCB 12/98; BL 9/15/98; HBG 3/99; SLJ 11/98)

1039 Mosher, Richard. *The Taxi Navigator* (5–8). 1996, Philomel $15.95 (0-399-23104-8). As his parents head for divorce, 9-year-old Kyle shares many adventures with his taxi-driving Uncle Hank. (Rev: BL 9/15/96; SLJ 1/97)

1040 Myers, Anna. *Rosie's Tiger* (5–8). 1994, Walker $14.95 (0-8027-8305-8). When Rosie's brother returns from the Korean War, he brings a wife and son with him and Rosie becomes consumed by jealousy. (Rev: BL 9/15/94; SLJ 11/94)

1041 Myers, Walter Dean. *Somewhere in the Darkness* (7–12). 1992, Scholastic paper $14.95 (0-590-

42411-4). A father and son get to know each other after the father is released from prison. (Rev: BL 2/1/92*; SLJ 4/92*)

1042 Naylor, Phyllis Reynolds. *Being Danny's Dog* (4–7). 1995, Simon & Schuster $15.00 (0-689-31756-5). T.R.'s strong bond with his older brother, Danny, is tested when he discovers that Danny is involved in an unsavory plot. (Rev: BCCB 1/96; BL 10/1/95; SLJ 10/95)

1043 Naylor, Phyllis Reynolds. *Ice* (6–8). 1995, Atheneum $16.00 (0-689-80005-3). A 13-year-old girl learns about herself and relationships in her search for her father and her isolation from her mother. (Rev: BL 8/95; SLJ 10/95; VOYA 12/95)

1044 Naylor, Phyllis Reynolds. *Walker's Crossing* (6–12). 1999, Simon & Schuster $16.00 (0-689-82939-6). Shy Ryan Walker is beset with family problems — a sick father, a depressed mother, an older sister who wants to become Rodeo Queen, and a brother who has joined a militia group. (Rev: BCCB 11/99; BL 9/15/99; HBG 4/00; SLJ 11/99; VOYA 2/00)

1045 Nelson, Theresa. *Earthshine* (5–9). 1994, Orchard LB $17.99 (0-531-08717-4). "Slim" decides to live with her father and his lover, who is dying of AIDS. At a support group, she meets Isaiah, whose pregnant mother also has AIDS. (Rev: BL 9/1/94; SLJ 9/94*; VOYA 10/94)

1046 Nelson, Theresa. *Ruby Electric* (5–8). 2003, Simon & Schuster $16.95 (0-689-83852-2). The movie script she is writing brings 12-year-old Ruby needed relief from the realities of her life. (Rev: BL 7/03; HB 7–8/03; HBG 10/03; SLJ 6/03*; VOYA 10/03)

1047 Nixon, Joan Lowery. *Maggie Forevermore* (5–8). 1987, Harcourt $13.95 (0-15-250345-5). In this sequel to *Maggie, Too* and *And Maggie Makes Three* (both o.p.), 13-year-old Maggie resents spending Christmas with her father and his new wife in California. (Rev: BCCB 4/87; BL 3/1/87; SLJ 3/87)

1048 Nolan, Han. *A Face in Every Window* (7–10). 1999, Harcourt $16.00 (0-15-201915-4). Fourteen-year-old JP finds his life is coming undone when his grandmother dies and he is left with his impractical mother and retarded father. (Rev: BCCB 12/99; BL 11/1/99; HBG 4/00; SLJ 9/99; VOYA 12/99)

1049 Oates, Joyce Carol. *Freaky Green Eyes* (7–10). 2003, HarperCollins $16.99 (0-06-623759-9). Franky, 15, recounts the tensions between her artist mother and her abusive, controlling father and the buildup to her mother's eventual disappearance. (Rev: BL 12/1/03; HB 11–12/03; SLJ 10/03; VOYA 10/03)

1050 O'Connor, Barbara. *Moonpie and Ivy* (3–8). 2001, Farrar $16.00 (0-374-35059-0). Twelve-year-old Pearl is hurt and confused when her mother leaves her at Aunt Ivy's home and disappears. (Rev: BCCB 5/01; BL 5/1/01*; HB 5–6/01; HBG 10/01; SLJ 5/01; VOYA 6/01)

1051 Oughton, Jerrie. *Perfect Family* (6–9). 2000, Houghton $15.00 (0-395-98668-0). Set in a small town in North Carolina in the 1950s, this is the story of a girl named Welcome, an unwanted pregnancy, and the family that loves and supports her. (Rev: BL 4/15/00; HBG 9/00; SLJ 4/00; VOYA 6/00)

1052 Oughton, Jerrie. *The War in Georgia* (7–12). 1997, Bantam Doubleday Dell paper $4.50 (0-440-22752-6). During the last days of World War II in Atlanta, 13-year-old Shanta befriends a girl and her brain-injured brother and, through them, enters the nightmare world of child abuse. (Rev: BL 4/1/97; BR 9–10/97; SLJ 5/97)

1053 Park, Barbara. *The Graduation of Jake Moon* (5–8). 2000, Simon & Schuster $15.00 (0-689-83912-X). Jake Moon finds it impossible to cope with his grandfather's gradual disintegration from Alzheimer's disease. (Rev: BCCB 12/00; BL 6/1–15/00; HB 9–10/00; HBG 3/01; SLJ 9/00)

1054 Paterson, Katherine. *Come Sing, Jimmy Jo* (6–10). 1985, Avon paper $3.99 (0-380-70052-2). The family decides it's time to include James in their singing group. (Rev: BL 9/1/87; SLJ 4/85)

1055 Paterson, Katherine. *Jacob Have I Loved* (6–10). 1980, HarperCollins LB $16.89 (0-690-04079-2); paper $6.50 (0-06-440368-8). A story set in the Chesapeake Bay region about the rivalry between two sisters. Newbery Medal winner, 1981.

1056 Paterson, Katherine. *Park's Quest* (4–7). 1989, Puffin paper $5.99 (0-14-034262-1). A boy searches for the cause of his father's death in Vietnam. (Rev: BCCB 4/88; HB 7–8/88; SLJ 5/88)

1057 Paterson, Katherine. *The Same Stuff as Stars* (5–7). 2002, Clarion $15.00 (0-618-24744-0). An unhappy 11-year-old Angel and her younger brother Bernie are sent to live with their father's grandmother, where Angel finds comfort in a mysterious man who introduces her to astronomy. (Rev: BCCB 10/02; BL 9/15/02; HB 9–10/02; HBG 3/03; SLJ 8/02*)

1058 Patneaude, David. *Framed in Fire* (6–9). 1999, Albert Whitman LB $14.95 (0-8075-9098-3). Peter Larson, who lives with his mother and verbally abusive stepfather, discovers that his mother has lied to him about the death of his real father and sets out to find the truth. (Rev: BCCB 5/99; HBG 9/99; SLJ 4/99)

1059 Paulsen, Gary. *The Tent: A Parable in One Sitting* (6–10). 1995, Harcourt $15.00 (0-15-292879-0). A 14-year-old struggles to keep his values when his father fraudulently poses as an itinerant preacher. (Rev: BL 3/15/95; SLJ 5/95)

1060 Paulsen, Gary. *The Winter Room* (6–8). 1989, Watts LB $16.99 (0-531-08439-6). A quiet novel about an 11-year-old boy growing up on a farm in Minnesota. (Rev: BL 11/1/89; BR 5–6/90; SLJ 10/89; VOYA 12/89)

1061 Pearson, Kit. *A Handful of Time* (4–7). 1988, Puffin paper $5.99 (0-14-032268-X). Patricia is ill at ease staying with her aunt and cousins while her parents work out a divorce. (Rev: HB 7–8/88)

1062 Pearson, Mary E. *Scribbler of Dreams* (5–8). 2001, Harcourt $17.00 (0-15-202320-8). Bram, whose family feuds constantly with the Crutchfield clan, finds she has fallen in love with a Crutchfield boy and must keep her identity a secret from him. (Rev: BCCB 5/01; BL 4/15/01; HBG 10/01; SLJ 5/01; VOYA 6/01)

1063 Peck, Richard. *Father Figure* (7–10). 1996, Puffin paper $5.99 (0-14-037969-X). Jim and his younger brother are sent to live in Florida with a father they scarcely know.

1064 Peck, Richard. *Strays Like Us* (5–8). 1998, Dial $15.99 (0-8037-2291-5). Two unwanted youngsters, each living with relatives in a small Missouri town, together face family problems and the trauma of junior high school. (Rev: BCCB 4/98; BL 4/1/98*; BR 1–2/99; HB 5–6/98; HBG 10/98; SLJ 5/98)

1065 Peck, Robert Newton. *A Day No Pigs Would Die* (7–9). 1973, Knopf $25.00 (0-394-48235-2); Random paper $5.50 (0-679-85306-5). A Shaker farm boy in Vermont must give up his pet pig to help his family. (Rev: BL 3/1/89)

1066 Pendergraft, Patricia. *Miracle at Clement's Pond* (6–8). 1987, Putnam $13.95 (0-399-21438-0). Three children think they are doing a good deed when they deposit a baby they have found on a spinster's porch. (Rev: BL 8/87; SLJ 8/87; VOYA 8/87)

1067 Pevsner, Stella. *Would My Fortune Cookie Lie?* (5–8). 1996, Clarion $14.95 (0-395-73082-1). Thirteen-year-old Alexis, already upset by her father's desertion and a possible family move, becomes involved with a mysterious stranger and a devastating family secret. (Rev: BCCB 3/96; BL 2/15/96; BR 9–10/96; SLJ 4/96)

1068 Pfeffer, Susan Beth. *Devil's Den* (4–7). 1998, Walker $15.95 (0-8027-8650-2). Joey faces the pain of rejection when he seeks out his real father, discovers he is not wanted by him, and must accept living permanently with his mom and loving stepfather. (Rev: BCCB 5/98; BL 5/15/98; HBG 10/98; SLJ 6/98)

1069 Pfeffer, Susan Beth. *The Year Without Michael* (7–12). 1988, Demco $10.55 (0-606-03959-7). When Jody's brother Michael, a high school freshman, disappears, the solidarity of her family is shattered. (Rev: BL 10/1/87; BR 5–6/88; SLJ 11/87; VOYA 10/87)

1070 Polikoff, Barbara G. *Life's a Funny Proposition, Horatio* (4–7). 1992, Holt $14.95 (0-8050-1972-3). When his father dies, Horatio and his mother move to Wisconsin. (Rev: SLJ 8/92*)

1071 Porte, Barbara Ann. *Something Terrible Happened* (6–10). 1994, Orchard LB $17.99 (0-531-08719-0); Troll paper $4.50 (0-8167-3868-8). Part white, part West Indian, Gillian, 12, must adjust to living with her deceased father's "plain white" relatives when her mother contracts AIDS. (Rev: BL 9/15/94; SLJ 10/94; VOYA 10/94)

1072 Powell, Randy. *Run If You Dare* (7–10). 2001, Farrar $17.00 (0-374-39981-6). Gardner coasts through life until his father loses his job and then confides to Gardner that he is thinking about leaving home, causing Gardner to reassess both his father and himself. (Rev: BCCB 6/01; BL 8/01; HB 5–6/01*; HBG 10/01; SLJ 3/01*; VOYA 6/01)

1073 Powell, Randy. *Tribute to Another Dead Rock Star* (7–12). 1999, Farrar $17.00 (0-374-37748-0). Fifteen-year-old Gary returns to Seattle to speak at a concert honoring his deceased rock-star mother, who abused drugs and behaved irresponsibly, and must confront his mother's ex-boyfriend, the ex-boyfriend's new wife, and his mentally disabled stepbrother. (Rev: BL 3/1/99; HB 5–6/99; HBG 9/99; SLJ 5/99; VOYA 6/99)

1074 Pressler, Mirjam. *Halinka* (7–10). Trans. by Elizabeth D. Crawford. Illus. 1998, Holt $16.95 (0-8050-5861-3). The disturbing story of a 12-year-old Gypsy girl who lives with six other girls in a welfare home in Germany and of her many problems and her hope for a stable homelife. (Rev: BL 10/15/98; HB 1–2/99; HBG 3/99; SLJ 1/99; VOYA 4/99)

1075 Pringer, Nancy. *Toughing It* (7–10). 1994, Harcourt $10.95 (0-15-200008-9); paper $4.95 (0-15-200011-9). Tuff lives in a trailer with his alcoholic mother and her abusive boyfriend. When Tuff is murdered, Dillon, his younger brother, runs to the man who could be his father. (Rev: BL 9/1/94; SLJ 9/94; VOYA 8/94)

1076 Provoost, Anne. *My Aunt Is a Pilot Whale* (6–9). Trans. by Ria Bleumer. 1995, Women's Pr. paper $12.95 (0-88961-202-1). A story of family relationships and friendship but also of incest. (Rev: BL 3/1/95)

1077 Quarles, Heather. *A Door Near Here* (7–10). 1998, Doubleday $13.95 (0-385-32595-9). When her mother loses her job and retreats into alcoholism, 15-year-old Katherine must take care of herself and three younger siblings. (Rev: BL 9/1/98; HBG 3/99; VOYA 10/98)

1078 Quattlebaum, Mary. *Grover G. Graham and Me* (4–7). 2001, Delacorte $14.95 (0-385-32277-1). Eleven-year-old Ben reluctantly begins to care about the members of his new foster family, particu-

larly baby Grover. (Rev: BCCB 1/02; BL 9/15/01; HB 1–2/02; HBG 3/02; SLJ 10/01)

1079 Reynolds, Marilyn. *Baby Help: True-to-Life Series from Hamilton High* (8–12). Series: Hamilton High. 1998, Morning Glory $15.95 (1-885356-26-9); paper $8.95 (1-885356-27-7). Partner-abuse is explored in this novel about a teenage mother who is living with a difficult boyfriend and his unsympathetic mother. (Rev: BL 2/1/98; HBG 9/98; SLJ 3/98; VOYA 6/98)

1080 Rinn, Miriam. *The Saturday Secret* (4–7). Illus. 1998, Alef Design Group paper $7.95 (1-881283-26-7). Jason's resentment and anger at having to obey the strict rules imposed by his devout Orthodox Jewish stepfather are made more intense because of his grief at the death of his beloved father. (Rev: BL 10/1/98; SLJ 2/99)

1081 Roberts, Willo Davis. *What Are We Going to Do About David?* (5–8). 1993, Macmillan $16.00 (0-689-31793-X). Because his parents are considering divorce, David, 11, is sent to live with his grandmother, an understanding woman who helps him gain self-reliance and confidence. (Rev: BL 3/15/93; SLJ 4/93)

1082 Rodowsky, Colby. *Clay* (4–7). 2001, Farrar $16.00 (0-374-31338-5). Eleven-year-old Elsie and her autistic younger brother have been living a desperate life since her mother kidnapped them from their father four years before. (Rev: BCCB 3/01; BL 5/1/01; HBG 10/01; SLJ 4/01; VOYA 6/01)

1083 Rodowsky, Colby. *Not Quite a Stranger* (5–9). 2003, Farrar $16.00 (0-374-35548-7). In alternating chapters, 13-year-old Charlotte (Tottie) and 17-year-old Zach describe the upheaval in their lives when Zach's mother dies and he seeks a home with his and Tottie's father, who believed that Zach had been given up for adoption. (Rev: BCCB 8/03; BL 11/15/03; SLJ 9/03; VOYA 10/03)

1084 Rodowsky, Colby. *Spindrift* (5–8). 2000, Farrar $16.00 (0-374-37155-5). A realistic family story about 13-year-old Cassie who lives at Spindrift, a seaside bed-and-breakfast run by her grandmother, and who tries to reunite her sister and estranged husband. (Rev: BCCB 3/00; BL 2/15/00; HBG 10/00; SLJ 3/00)

1085 Ross, Ramon R. *The Dancing Tree* (5–7). 1995, Simon & Schuster $14.00 (0-689-80072-X). Zeenie's grandmother helps her cope with the sudden disappearance of her mother, who hopes to sort out her life. (Rev: BL 9/1/95; SLJ 2/96)

1086 Rottman, S. L. *Shadow of a Doubt* (7–10). Illus. 2003, Peachtree $14.95 (1-56145-291-2). Shadow is newly 15 and entering high school when his brother Daniel, who has been missing for years, reappears on the scene, suspected of murder. (Rev: BCCB 1/04; BL 11/15/03)

1087 Sachs, Marilyn. *Baby Sister* (7–10). 1986, Avon paper $3.50 (0-380-70358-0). Penny is torn between her admiration for her older sister and the realization that she is really selfish. (Rev: BL 2/15/86; BR 5–6/86; SLJ 8/86; VOYA 8/86)

1088 Sachs, Marilyn. *Ghosts in the Family* (5–8). 1995, Dutton $15.99 (0-525-45421-7). After her mother's death, Gabriella discovers disturbing information about her family and her absent father. (Rev: BL 1/1–15/96; SLJ 12/95; VOYA 4/96)

1089 Sachs, Marilyn. *Just Like a Friend* (6–9). 1990, Avon paper $2.95 (0-380-70964-3). The friendship between a mother and a daughter falls apart when father has a heart attack. (Rev: BL 10/15/89; BR 3–4/90; SLJ 12/89; VOYA 12/89)

1090 Sachs, Marilyn. *Surprise Party* (5–8). 1998, NAL $15.99 (0-525-45962-6). Sixth-grader Gen, who resents the fuss made over her attention-seeking younger brother, nevertheless works with him to plan a surprise anniversary party for their parents. (Rev: BL 6/1–15/98; HBG 10/98; SLJ 5/98)

1091 Sachs, Marilyn. *The Truth About Mary Rose* (6–8). 1995, Puffin paper $3.99 (0-14-037083-8). The first Mary Rose died at age 11 saving lives in a fire, but her modern counterpart learns the truth about her.

1092 Salisbury, Graham. *Lord of the Deep* (5–8). 2001, Delacorte $15.95 (0-385-72918-9). During his time working on his stepfather's deep-sea fishing boat, Mikey, 13, learns about financial problems, lying, unpleasant characters, and romance. (Rev: BCCB 7–8/01; BL 8/01; HB 9–10/01*; HBG 3/02; SLJ 8/01*; VOYA 8/01)

1093 Salmansohn, Karen. *Wherever I Go, There I Am* (4–7). Series: Alexandra Rambles On! 2002, Tricycle Pr. $12.95 (1-58246-079-5). Alexandra's journal reveals her angst about issues such as scary movies and becoming a teenager. (Rev: HBG 3/03; SLJ 2/03)

1094 Saroyan, William. *The Human Comedy* (7–12). 1973, Dell paper $6.50 (0-440-33933-2). Homer Macauley is growing up during World War II in America and becomes part of the everyday life that is the human comedy.

1095 Savage, Deborah. *Summer Hawk* (7–10). 1999, Houghton $16.00 (0-395-91163-X). In this coming-of-age story, 15-year-old Taylor has trouble relating to her mother and father, shuns the company of Rail Bogart, the other smart kid in her school, and showers her attention and affection on a young hawk she rescues. (Rev: BCCB 6/99; BL 3/1/99; HBG 9/99; SLJ 4/99; VOYA 4/99)

1096 Schmidt, Gary D. *The Sin Eater* (6–9). 1996, Dutton $15.99 (0-525-67541-8). When his father commits suicide, young Cole, who is living on a farm with his grandparents in New Hampshire, must

assume new responsibilities. (Rev: BL 11/1/96; BR 3–4/97; SLJ 1/97)

1097 Sebestyen, Ouida. *Far from Home* (7–10). 1980, Little, Brown $15.95 (0-316-77932-6); Dell paper $2.50 (0-440-92640-8). An orphaned boy is taken in by a couple who run a boardinghouse and there he uncovers secrets about his family's past.

1098 Seidler, Tor. *Brothers Below Zero* (5–8). 2002, HarperCollins LB $14.89 (0-06-029180-X). Artistic Tim, overwhelmed by his athletic younger brother, eventually runs away to the place he has felt most valued. (Rev: BCCB 3/02; BL 1/1–15/02; HBG 10/02; SLJ 4/02)

1099 Shange, Ntozake. *Daddy Says* (5–9). 2003, Simon & Schuster $15.95 (0-689-83081-5). Two sisters on a Texas ranch grapple with family problems at the same time that there is rodeo excitement. (Rev: BCCB 3/03; BL 3/15/03; HBG 10/03; SLJ 2/03; VOYA 2/03)

1100 Shearer, Alex. *The Great Blue Yonder* (5–8). 2002, Clarion $15.00 (0-618-21257-4). Twelve-year-old Harry, who has died in an accident, experiences afterlife on the Other Side and has the opportunity to review his relations with other family members. (Rev: BCCB 6/02; HBG 10/02; SLJ 4/02; VOYA 6/02)

1101 Shreve, Susan. *Goodbye, Amanda the Good* (4–7). 2000, Knopf LB $18.99 (0-679-99241-3). Between the 6th and 7th grades, Amanda, who has always been angelic, rebels, changes her ways, and becomes a hellion. (Rev: BCCB 2/00; BL 2/1/00; HBG 10/00; SLJ 3/00; VOYA 4/00)

1102 Shusterman, Neal. *What Daddy Did* (7–10). 1991, Little, Brown paper $15.95 (0-316-78906-2). A young boy recounts the story of how his father murdered his mother and how he ultimately comes to understand and forgive him. (Rev: BL 7/91; SLJ 6/91)

1103 Simmons, Michael. *Pool Boy* (7–10). 2003, Millbrook LB $22.90 (0-7613-2924-2). Spoiled teen Brett finds his life upended when his father is jailed for insider trading in this realistic first-person novel full of humor. (Rev: BL 4/1/03; HBG 10/03; SLJ 4/03*)

1104 Slate, Joseph. *Crossing the Trestle* (5–8). 1999, Marshall Cavendish $14.95 (0-7614-5053-X). Set in West Virginia in 1944, this novel centers on 11-year-old Petey and the problems he and his family face after their father is killed in an accident. (Rev: BCCB 12/99; BL 1/1–15/00; HBG 3/00; SLJ 10/99)

1105 Smith, Anne Warren. *Sister in the Shadow* (7–10). 1986, Avon paper $2.75 (0-380-70378-5). In competition with her successful younger sister, Sharon becomes a live-in baby-sitter with unhappy results. (Rev: BL 5/1/86; SLJ 5/86; VOYA 8/86)

1106 Smith, Doris Buchanan. *Return to Bitter Creek* (6–8). 1986, Penguin paper $5.99 (0-14-032223-X). In spite of Grandma's hostility, Lacey and her mother journey back home to North Carolina to rejoin mother's lover, David. (Rev: BL 7/86; SLJ 9/86)

1107 Smith, Roland. *Zach's Lie* (5–8). 2001, Hyperion $15.99 (0-7868-0617-6). Young Jack and Joanne have trouble adapting to their new roles as Zach and Wanda when they are taken into the witness protection program. (Rev: BL 5/15/01; HBG 10/01; SLJ 6/01; VOYA 6/01)

1108 Spinelli, Jerry. *Crash* (5–8). 1996, Knopf $16.00 (0-679-87957-9). Athlete Crash Coogan changes his bullying ways after his grandfather suffers a stroke. (Rev: BCCB 5/96; BL 6/1–15/96; HB 9–10/96; SLJ 6/96*)

1109 Springer, Nancy. *Separate Sisters* (5–7). 2001, Holiday $16.95 (0-8234-1544-9). Two teenage girls deal with the divorce of their parents in different ways. (Rev: BCCB 2/02; BL 2/1/02; HB 3–4/02; HBG 10/02; SLJ 2/02; VOYA 4/02)

1110 Stacey, Cherylyn. *How Do You Spell Abducted?* (4–8). 1996, Red Deer paper $7.95 (0-88995-148-9). When their divorced father abducts Deb, Paige, and Cory, the three youngsters must escape from his home in the U.S. and make their way back to their mother in Canada. (Rev: BR 3–4/97; SLJ 12/96)

1111 Stevenson, Laura C. *Happily After All* (4–7). 1990, Houghton $16.00 (0-395-50216-0). Becca goes to live with her mother, who she believes abandoned her when she was young. (Rev: BCCB 5/90; BL 4/15/90; HB 5–6/90; SLJ 6/90)

1112 Stone, Phoebe. *All the Blue Moons at the Wallace Hotel* (5–7). 2000, Little, Brown $15.95 (0-316-81645-0). This story about family love and problems centers around 11-year-old Fiona, her lively younger sister, their withdrawn mother, and the memories of the wealth the family once had. (Rev: BCCB 12/00; BL 12/1/00; HBG 3/01; SLJ 12/00; VOYA 2/01)

1113 Strasser, Todd. *Thief of Dreams* (6–8). 2003, Putnam $16.99 (0-399-23135-8). Martin is 13 when his parents leave him in the care of his long-lost uncle, who turns out to be a professional thief in this novel with a distinctive voice. (Rev: BCCB 3/03; HBG 10/03; SLJ 3/03; VOYA 8/03)

1114 Sweeney, Joyce. *The Spirit Window* (7–12). 1998, Delacorte $15.95 (0-385-32510-X). When 15-year-old Miranda journeys to Florida with her father, she falls in love with an older, part-Cherokee boy and becomes involved in environmental causes both of which bring her into conflict with her parent. (Rev: BL 2/15/98; BR 11–12/98; HBG 9/98; SLJ 3/98; VOYA 4/98)

1115 Talbert, Marc. *The Purple Heart* (5–8). 1992, HarperCollins $14.95 (0-06-020428-1); Avon paper $3.50 (0-380-71985-1). Luke's father has returned from Vietnam an anguished, brooding war hero, and Luke loses his father's Purple Heart, leading to confrontation and reconciliation. (Rev: BL 12/15/91*; SLJ 2/92)

1116 Talbert, Marc. *A Sunburned Prayer* (5–8). 1995, Simon & Schuster paper $4.50 (0-689-81326-0). Eloy walks 17 miles under the New Mexico sun to ask God for a miracle to save his grandmother's life. (Rev: BL 8/95; SLJ 7/95)

1117 Taylor, Mildred D. *Roll of Thunder, Hear My Cry* (6–8). 1976, Bantam paper $3.50 (0-553-25450-2). Set in rural Mississippi during the Depression, this Newbery Medal winner (1977) continues the story about African American Cassie Logan and her family. Begun in *Song of the Trees* (1975); continued in *Let the Circle Be Unbroken* (1981).

1118 Thesman, Jean. *The Last April Dancers* (7–10). 1987, Avon paper $2.75 (0-380-70614-8). Catherine tries to recover from the guilt caused by her father's suicide through friendship and love of a neighboring boy. (Rev: BL 9/15/87; SLJ 10/87; VOYA 10/87)

1119 Thesman, Jean. *The Tree of Bells* (7–10). 1999, Houghton $15.00 (0-395-90510-9). In this sequel to *The Ornament Tree*, the strong Deveraux women and their boarding house in Seattle are again featured, with the focus on Claire, now 16 and anxious for independence. (Rev: BCCB 7–8/99; BL 6/1–15/99; HBG 9/99; SLJ 7/99; VOYA 10/99)

1120 Thesman, Jean. *When the Road Ends* (5–8). 1992, Houghton $16.00 (0-395-59507-X). Mary tells how she and other foster children spend a summer in a remote cabin with a sick adult. (Rev: BCCB 4/92; HB 5–6/92; SLJ 4/92)

1121 Tomey, Ingrid. *The Queen of Dreamland* (6–9). 1996, Simon & Schuster $15.00 (0-689-80458-X). On her 14th birthday, Julie secretly discovers who her birth mother really is and begins living a double life by hiding this information from her step-parents. (Rev: BL 9/15/96; BR 5–6/97; SLJ 10/96; VOYA 4/97)

1122 Torres, Laura. *Crossing Montana* (7–10). 2002, Holiday $15.95 (0-8234-1643-7). Callie sets off on a journey across Montana in search of her missing grandfather, and in the process finds out the truth about her father's death. (Rev: BCCB 10/02; BL 8/02; HBG 10/02; SLJ 7/02; VOYA 8/02)

1123 Tullson, Diane. *Saving Jasey* (7–9). 2002, Orca paper $6.95 (1-55143-220-X). A dramatic story of two teens struggline to cope with problem-ridden families. (Rev: SLJ 4/02; VOYA 4/02)

1124 Valgardson, W. D. *Frances* (6–10). 2000, Groundwood $15.95 (0-88899-386-2); paper $5.95 (0-88899-397-8). Growing up in Manitoba, young

Frances probes into her Icelandic background and uncovers many family secrets, past and present. (Rev: BL 9/1/00; HBG 3/01; SLJ 9/00; VOYA 2/01)

1125 Vande Velde, Vivian. *Alison, Who Went Away* (6–8). 2001, Houghton $15.00 (0-618-04585-6). Fourteen-year-old Susan, who prefers to be called Sibyl, faces all the usual challenges of teen life, plus some less-usual family problems that include the disappearance of her older sister. (Rev: BCCB 4/01; BL 4/1/01; HBG 10/01; SLJ 4/01)

1126 Van Steenwyk, Elizabeth. *Three Dog Winter* (5–8). 1987, Walker $13.95 (0-8027-6718-4). A story of dog racing, this family tale tells of 12-year-old Scott and his Malamute, Kaylah. (Rev: BL 2/1/88; SLJ 12/87)

1127 Velasquez, Gloria. *Rina's Family Secret* (8–12). 1998, Arte Publico paper $9.95 (1-55885-233-6). Puerto Rican teenager Rina cannot endure life with her alcoholic stepfather, and so moves in with her grandmother. (Rev: BL 8/98; SLJ 10/98)

1128 Viglucci, Patricia C. *Sun Dance at Turtle Rock* (5–7). 1996, Patri paper $4.95 (0-9645914-9-9). The child of a racially mixed marriage feels uncomfortable when he visits his white grandfather. (Rev: BL 4/15/96)

1129 Voigt, Cynthia. *Dicey's Song* (5–9). 1982, Macmillan $17.95 (0-689-30944-9); Fawcett paper $5.99 (0-449-70276-6). This story of Dicey's life with her "Gram" in Maryland won a Newbery Medal (1983). Preceding it was *Homecoming* (1981) and a sequel is *A Solitary Blue* (1983). (Rev: BL 12/15/89)

1130 Voigt, Cynthia. *Seventeen Against the Dealer* (7–12). 1989, Macmillan $18.00 (0-689-31497-3). In this, the last of the Tillerman cycle, Dicey, now 21, decides to earn her living building boats. (Rev: BL 3/15/89; BR 9–10/89; SLJ 2/89; VOYA 4/89)

1131 Voigt, Cynthia. *A Solitary Blue* (7–9). 1983, Macmillan $18.00 (0-689-31008-0). Jeff is invited to spend a summer with his divorced mother.

1132 Voigt, Cynthia. *Sons from Afar* (6–10). 1987, Macmillan LB $15.95 (0-689-31349-7); Fawcett paper $4.50 (0-449-70293-6). In this part of the Tillerman family story, sons James and Sammy set out to see a father they have never known. (Rev: BL 9/15/87; SLJ 9/87; VOYA 10/87)

1133 Voigt, Cynthia. *Tree by Leaf* (6–8). 1988, Macmillan $15.95 (0-689-31403-5). Clothilde's father returns to Maine from World War I to find his family impoverished and himself a bitter, disfigured outcast. (Rev: BL 4/1/88; BR 9–10/88; SLJ 5/88; VOYA 8/88)

1134 Walker, Pamela. *Pray Hard* (5–8). 2001, Scholastic paper $15.95 (0-439-21586-2). After Amelia Forest's father dies in an airplane accident

for which she feels responsible, her life and that of her family fall apart. (Rev: BL 3/1/01; HBG 10/01; SLJ 7/01; VOYA 8/01)

1135 Wallace, Bill. *Beauty* (5–7). 1988, Holiday $16.95 (0-8234-0715-2). Luke finds the adjustment difficult when he and his mother go to live on his grandfather's Oklahoma farm. (Rev: BCCB 11/88; BL 2/1/89; SLJ 10/88)

1136 Wallace, Bill. *True Friends* (4–7). 1994, Holiday $15.95 (0-8234-1141-9). Everything in Courtney's life becomes a shambles and she must rely on her new friend Judy to help her. (Rev: BCCB 11/94; BL 10/15/94; SLJ 10/94)

1137 Warner, Sally. *How to Be a Real Person (in Just One Day)* (5–8). 2001, Random $15.95 (0-375-80434-X). Kara puts up a brave front when she is with her classmates but she is facing huge problems because her father has left and her mother has sunk into a depression. (Rev: BCCB 3/01; BL 2/15/01; HBG 10/01; SLJ 2/01; VOYA 8/01)

1138 Warner, Sally. *A Long Time Ago Today* (4–7). 2003, Viking $15.99 (0-670-03604-8). At the age of 12, Dilly wants to know what her mother, who died when Dilly was 6, was really like. (Rev: BL 11/1/03; SLJ 12/03)

1139 Wartski, Maureen C. *Dark Silence* (7–10). 1994, Ballantine paper $5.50 (0-449-70418-1). Teenager Randy must deal with her mother's recent death and the abuse of her neighbor, Delia. (Rev: BL 4/1/94; SLJ 7/94; VOYA 6/94)

1140 Weatherly, Lee. *Child X* (5–8). 2002, Knopf $15.95 (0-385-75009-9). Thirteen-year-old Jules (Juliet) faces many puzzles as her parents go through a high-profile and messy divorce that involves questions about Jules's parentage in this story from Britain. (Rev: BCCB 10/02; BL 7/02; HBG 10/02; SLJ 6/02; VOYA 8/02)

1141 Weaver, Will. *Claws* (7–10). 2003, HarperCollins $15.99 (0-06-009473-7). An e-mailed photograph brings an end to Jed's perfect life in this tense and sometimes melodramatic novel about parental adultery. (Rev: BL 4/15/03; HBG 10/03; SLJ 3/03; VOYA 6/03)

1142 Weeks, Sarah. *My Guy* (4–7). 2001, HarperCollins LB $14.89 (0-06-028370-X). Guy and Lana agree on only one thing — they don't want to become part of a blended family — and they set out to make sure it won't happen. (Rev: BCCB 6/01; BL 8/01; HB 7–8/01; HBG 10/01; SLJ 5/01)

1143 Weissenberg, Fran. *The Streets Are Paved with Gold* (7–9). 1990, Harbinger paper $6.95 (0-943173-51-5). Debbie is from a poor immigrant Jewish family and she is ashamed to bring her friends home. (Rev: BL 8/90; SLJ 8/90)

1144 White, Ellen E. *White House Autumn* (7–10). 1985, Avon paper $2.95 (0-380-89780-6). The daughter of the first female president of the United States feels her family is coming apart after an assassination attempt on her mother. (Rev: BL 11/1/85; SLJ 2/86; VOYA 4/86)

1145 White, Ruth. *Belle Prater's Boy* (5–9). 1996, Farrar $17.00 (0-374-30668-0). Set in Appalachia in the 1950s, this moving, often humorous story tells about Gypsy and her unusual cousin Woodrow, who hides a secret involving his mother's disappearance. (Rev: BL 4/15/96; BR 9–10/96; SLJ 4/96*)

1146 White, Ruth. *Tadpole* (5–8). 2003, Farrar $16.00 (0-374-31002-5). In this novel set in 1950s Appalachia, uncertain 10-year-old Carolina finds her own strengths when her 13-year-old cousin Tadpole arrives, running away from an abusive uncle. (Rev: BL 5/1/03; HB 5–6/03; HBG 10/03; SLJ 3/03*)

1147 Wiggin, Kate Douglas. *Rebecca of Sunnybrook Farm* (4–7). 1986, Dell paper $3.99 (0-440-47533-3). Rebecca is a spunky, curious girl living in a quiet Maine community of the 19th century. One of many editions.

1148 Wilder, Laura Ingalls. *Little House in the Big Woods* (4–7). 1953, HarperCollins LB $17.89 (0-06-026431-4); paper $6.99 (0-06-440001-8). Outstanding story of a log-cabin family in Wisconsin in the late 1800s. Also use *By the Shores of Silver Lake; Farmer Boy; Little House on the Prairie; Long Winter; On the Banks of Plum Creek; These Happy Golden Years* (all 1953); *Little Town on the Prairie* (1961); *The First Four Years* (1971).

1149 Wilhelm, Doug. *Raising the Shades* (6–8). 2001, Farrar $16.00 (0-374-36178-9). When his mother and sister leave home, Casey Butterfield, 13, tries to look after himself and his alcoholic father. (Rev: BCCB 5/01; BL 7/01; HBG 10/01; SLJ 5/01; VOYA 6/01)

1150 Willis, Patricia. *The Barn Burner* (5–8). 2000, Clarion $15.00 (0-395-98409-2). In 1933, 14-year-old Ross, a runaway, becomes involved with the Warfield family whose father is away looking for work. (Rev: BCCB 5/00; BL 4/15/00; HBG 10/00; SLJ 7/00)

1151 Wilson, Nancy H. *The Reason for Janey* (5–7). Illus. 1994, Macmillan $15.00 (0-02-793127-7). A mentally disabled woman helps Janey adjust to her parents' divorce and her father's departure. (Rev: BCCB 6/94; BL 4/15/94; HB 7–8/94; SLJ 5/94*)

1152 Wilson, Nancy Hope. *Mountain Pose* (5–7). 2001, Farrar $17.00 (0-374-35078-7). Ellie is surprised to inherit her grandmother's farm, but when she reads the diaries left for her she begins to understand more about her family. (Rev: BCCB 6/01; BL 8/01; HB 7–8/01; HBG 10/01; SLJ 4/01*; VOYA 6/01)

1153 Withrow, Sarah. *Box Girl* (6–9). 2001, Groundwood $15.95 (0-88899-407-9). Thirteen-year-old

Gwen is retreating into her own world, longing for a reunion with her absent mother, but a new friend who accepts Gwen's gay father and his partner succeeds in breaking through her reserve. (Rev: BCCB 12/01; BL 1/1–15/02; HB 1–2/02*; HBG 3/02; SLJ 12/01; VOYA 4/02)

1154 Wolff, Virginia E. *Make Lemonade* (7–12). 1993, Holt $17.95 (0-8050-2228-7); Scholastic paper $5.99 (0-590-48141-X). Rooted in the community of poverty, this story offers a penetrating view of the conditions that foster ignorance, destroy self-esteem, and challenge strength. (Rev: BL 6/1–15/93*; SLJ 7/93*; VOYA 10/93)

1155 Wood, June R. *A Share of Freedom* (6–8). 1994, Putnam $15.95 (0-399-22767-9). Freedom, an intelligent, independent 7th grader, has never met her father. Her mother's severe alcoholism lands Freedom and her brother in a foster home. (Rev: BL 9/1/94; SLJ 10/94*; VOYA 4/95)

1156 Wood, June R. *When Pigs Fly* (5–8). 1995, Putnam $16.95 (0-399-22911-6). A 13-year-old girl learns to cope with many problems, one of which is a younger sister with Down's syndrome. (Rev: BCCB 11/95; BL 12/1/95; SLJ 10/95; VOYA 12/95)

1157 Woodbury, Mary. *Brad's Universe* (5–8). 1998, Orca paper $7.95 (1-55143-120-3). In this novel set in a small Canadian town, Brad, at 14, is looking forward to being reunited with his absent father, but slowly comes to realize that the man has been convicted of child molesting. (Rev: SLJ 2/99; VOYA 4/99)

1158 Woodson, Jacqueline. *Hush* (5–9). 2002, Putnam $15.99 (0-399-23114-5). A girl and her family are relocated in the witness protection program after her father, a police officer, testifies against fellow cops in a case that involves racial prejudice. (Rev: BCCB 3/02; BL 1/1–15/02; HB 1–2/02; HBG 10/02; SLJ 2/02*; VOYA 2/02)

1159 Woodson, Jacqueline. *Lena* (6–9). 1999, Bantam Doubleday Dell $15.95 (0-385-32308-5). In this sequel to *I Hadn't Meant to Tell You This,* 13-year-old Lena and her young sister leave their abusive father after their mother's death and hit the road disguised as boys. (Rev: BL 2/1/99; HBG 9/99; SLJ 5/99; VOYA 2/99)

1160 Woodson, Jacqueline. *Miracle's Boys* (6–10). 2000, Putnam $15.99 (0-399-23113-7). Twelve-year-old African American LaFayette, growing up in a poor inner-city environment, is cared for by his oldest brother who is also responsible for the troubled middle brother, Charlie. (Rev: BL 2/15/00; HB 3–4/00; HBG 9/00; SLJ 5/00; VOYA 4/00)

1161 Wyeth, Sharon Dennis. *A Piece of Heaven* (5–8). 2001, Knopf $14.95 (0-679-88535-8). Haley's family is in crisis as her mother suffers a breakdown and her brother is taken to the juvenile detention center. (Rev: BCCB 3/01; BL 2/15/01; HBG 10/01; SLJ 2/01)

1162 Wynne-Jones, Tim. *Stephen Fair: A Novel* (7–10). 1998, HarperCollins paper $5.95 (0-06-447206-X). Long-hidden family secrets are revealed as 15-year-old Stephen Fair begins to experience nightmares that have deep meanings. (Rev: BL 6/1–15/98; BR 11–12/98; SLJ 5/98; VOYA 8/98)

Physical and Emotional Problems

1163 Arrick, Fran. *Steffie Can't Come Out to Play* (7–10). 1978, Simon & Schuster $8.95 (0-87888-135-2). Steffie runs away to New York City and is dragged into the nightmare world of prostitution.

1164 Atkins, Catherine. *Alt Ed* (8–10). 2003, Putnam $17.99 (0-399-23854-9). Susan, an unhappy sophomore, joins other outcast teens in an alternative education class designed to help them deal with differences. (Rev: BCCB 2/03; BL 1/1–15/03; HB 3–4/03; HBG 10/03; SLJ 3/03; VOYA 4/03)

1165 Banks, Sarah Harrell. *Under the Shadow of Wings* (5–9). 1997, Simon & Schuster $16.00 (0-689-81207-8). In this novel set in the South during World War II, Tattnall, age 11, has a special relationship with her older brain-damaged cousin. (Rev: BL 5/15/97; BR 11–12/97; SLJ 6/97)

1166 Baskin, Nora Raleigh. *Almost Home* (5–8). 2003, Little, Brown $16.95 (0-316-09313-0). Her friendship with Will helps 6th-grader Leah to gain confidence both at school and at her new home with her father and stepmother. (Rev: BL 5/1/03; HBG 10/03; SLJ 7/03; VOYA 8/03)

1167 Bauer, Marion Dane. *An Early Winter* (4–7). 1999, Clarion $15.00 (0-395-90372-6). When he convinces him to go on a camping trip, Tim doesn't realize that his Grandad is suffering from Alzheimer's disease. (Rev: BCCB 10/99; BL 12/1/99; HBG 3/00; SLJ 10/99)

1168 Bennett, Cherie. *Life in the Fat Lane* (6–9). 1998, Delacorte $15.95 (0-385-32274-7). Lara has everything — looks, a boyfriend, elected queen of the prom — but her life falls apart when she begins gaining weight and soon weighs over 200 pounds. (Rev: BL 1/1–15/98; BR 9–10/98; HBG 9/98; SLJ 3/98; VOYA 8/98)

1169 Bennett, Cherie. *Zink* (5–7). Illus. 1999, Random paper $4.99 (0-440-22810-7). The moving story of 10-year-old Becky, her struggle with a fatal case of leukemia, and her dreams of a herd of zebra and their heroic leader named Zink. (Rev: BCCB 11/99; BL 8/99; HBG 3/00; SLJ 2/00)

1170 Blume, Judy. *Deenie* (5–8). 1982, Macmillan $17.00 (0-02-711020-6); Dell paper $5.50 (0-440-93259-9). Instead of becoming a model, Deenie must cope with scoliosis and wearing a back brace.

1171 Brancato, Robin F. *Winning* (7–9). 1977, Bantam paper $2.95 (0-553-26597-0). A boy must adjust to paralysis resulting from a football accident. (Rev: BL 10/15/88)

1172 Brooks, Bruce. *Vanishing* (5–8). 1999, HarperCollins LB $14.89 (0-06-028237-1). A challenging novel about a hospitalized girl who gives up eating so she can't be sent home to her dysfunctional family, and the boy she meets who is in remission from a fatal disease. (Rev: BL 5/15/99; HB 5–6/99; HBG 10/99; SLJ 6/99; VOYA 10/99)

1173 Brown, Kay. *Willy's Summer Dream* (6–9). 1989, Harcourt $13.95 (0-15-200645-1). Willy lacks confidence because he is a slow learner. (Rev: BL 2/1/90; SLJ 12/89)

1174 Buchanan, Dawna Lisa. *The Falcon's Wing* (6–9). 1992, Orchard paper $16.99 (0-531-08586-4). A teenage girl learns to understand and defend her retarded cousin. (Rev: BL 2/1/92; SLJ 4/92)

1175 Butts, Nancy. *Cheshire Moon* (5–7). 1996, Front Street $14.95 (1-886910-08-1). A friendless deaf girl grieves for a cousin who has drowned at sea in this novel in an island setting. (Rev: BL 10/15/96; SLJ 11/96; VOYA 4/97)

1176 Byalick, Marcia. *Quit It* (4–7). 2002, Delacorte $15.95 (0-385-72997-9). Tourette's syndrome makes life difficult for 7th-grader Carrie but a lunchtime therapy group offers support, and new challenges. (Rev: BCCB 12/02; BL 10/1/02; HBG 3/03; SLJ 11/02)

1177 Byars, Betsy. *The Summer of the Swans* (5–7). 1970, Puffin paper $5.99 (0-14-031420-2). The story of a 14-year-old named Sara — moody, unpredictable, and on the brink of womanhood — and how her life changes when her younger, mentally retarded brother disappears. Newbery Medal winner, 1971.

1178 Cadnum, Michael. *Edge* (8–12). 1997, Puffin paper $5.99 (0-14-038714-5). Zachary, a confused high school dropout from a broken home, seeks revenge when his father is shot in the spine during a street robbery. (Rev: BL 6/1–15/97; SLJ 7/97; VOYA 12/97)

1179 Calvert, Patricia. *Picking Up the Pieces* (5–9). 1993, Scribners $15.00 (0-684-19558-5). A story of adjustments: Megan, 14, is wheelchair-bound for life after an accident and Julia, an aging actress, is trying to adjust to her declining career. (Rev: BL 5/1/93; SLJ 6/93; VOYA 8/93)

1180 Carter, Anne Laurel. *In the Clear* (4–7). 2001, Orca paper $6.95 (1-55143-192-0). A 12-year-old Canadian polio survivor in the 1950s works through her fears and struggles to recapture her lost childhood. (Rev: BL 11/15/01; SLJ 1/02)

1181 Cleaver, Vera, and Bill Cleaver. *Me Too* (7–9). 1973, HarperCollins $13.95 (0-397-31485-X); paper

$2.95 (0-06-440161-8). Linda is convinced that she can make her slightly retarded sister normal.

1182 Cole, Barbara. *Alex the Great* (8–12). 1989, Rosen LB $12.95 (0-8239-0941-7). The events leading up to Alex's drug overdose are told first by Alex and then by her friend, Deonna. (Rev: BR 9–10/89; VOYA 8/89)

1183 Cormier, Robert. *The Bumblebee Flies Anyway* (7–12). 1983, Dell paper $4.99 (0-440-90871-X). A terminally ill boy and his gradual realization of his situation.

1184 Crutcher, Chris. *Staying Fat for Sarah Byrnes* (7–12). 1993, Greenwillow $16.99 (0-688-11552-7). Overweight Eric's only friend is Sarah, whose face was severely burned as a child. Their attempt to escape her unbalanced father leads to an almost deadly climax. (Rev: BL 3/15/93; SLJ 3/93*; VOYA 8/93)

1185 Davis, Deborah. *My Brother Has AIDS* (6–9). 1994, Atheneum $15.00 (0-689-31922-3). In this realistic, accurate portrait of the caretaking families that love people with AIDS, Lacy, 13, is unprepared for the announcement that her beloved older brother is homosexual and dying of AIDS. (Rev: BL 11/15/94; SLJ 1/95; VOYA 5/95)

1186 Davis, Rebecca Fjelland. *Jake Riley: Irreparably Damaged* (7–10). 2003, HarperCollins $15.99 (0-06-051837-5). Lainey, a farm girl, struggles to cope with her friend Jake, a 15-year-old with frightening emotional problems. (Rev: BL 9/1/03; HBG 10/03; SLJ 7/03; VOYA 10/03)

1187 Denenberg, Barry. *Mirror, Mirror on the Wall: The Diary of Bess Brennan* (4–8). Series: Dear America. 2002, Scholastic paper $10.95 (0-439-19446-6). When she comes home at weekends, 12-year-old Bess, who has lost her sight, shares her new life and school experiences with her twin sister, in this novel set in the Depression that includes many details of how the blind cope. (Rev: BL 10/1/02; HBG 3/03; SLJ 10/02)

1188 Dewey, Jennifer Owlings. *Borderlands* (7–12). 2002, Marshall Cavendish $14.95 (0-7614-5114-5). When Jamie, an unhappy 17-year-old, is hospitalized after a suicide attempt she finds new friends and slowly comes to terms with her difficult relationship with her parents. (Rev: BL 9/1/02; HBG 10/02; SLJ 7/02)

1189 Diezeno, Patricia. *Why Me? The Story of Jenny* (7–10). 1976, Avon paper $3.50 (0-380-00563-8). A young rape victim doesn't know how to cope.

1190 Doyle, Malachy. *Georgie* (6–10). 2002, Bloomsbury $15.95 (1-58234-753-0). Georgie, 14, who has buried horrible memories under a cloak of isolation, slowly learns to trust his teacher and recovers his sanity. (Rev: BCCB 11/02; BL 9/1/02; SLJ 7/02)

1191 Draper, Sharon M. *Tears of a Tiger* (7–10), 1994, Atheneum $16.95 (0-689-31878-2). A star basketball player is killed in an accident after he and his friends drink and drive. The driver, who survives, is depressed and ultimately commits suicide. (Rev: BL 11/1/94; SLJ 2/95)

1192 Ellis, Ella Thorp. *The Year of My Indian Prince* (7–10). 2001, Delacorte $15.95 (0-385-32779-X). Sixteen-year-old April's battle with tuberculosis is eased by the attentions of a fellow patient, the son of an Indian maharajah, in this novel based on the author's own experiences. (Rev: BL 6/1–15/01; HBG 10/01; SLJ 6/01; VOYA 10/01)

1193 Ethridge, Kenneth E. *Toothpick* (7–10). 1985, Troll paper $2.50 (0-8167-1316-2). A friendship between Jamie, an outsider who is unsure of himself, and Janice, a terminally ill girl, gives him the confidence he needs. (Rev: BL 11/15/85; SLJ 12/85; VOYA 4/86)

1194 Farnes, Catherine. *Snow* (5–9). 1999, Bob Jones Univ. $6.49 (1-57924-199-9). A thoughtful novel about an albino girl's problems being accepted, even among students who profess to have Christian charity. (Rev: BL 7/99)

1195 Fields, Terri. *After the Death of Anna Gonzales* (7–12). 2002, Holt $16.95 (0-8050-7127-X). A collection of poems written by her friends reveal the terrible aftermath of a teenager's suicide. (Rev: BL 12/15/02; HBG 3/03; SLJ 11/02; VOYA 12/02)

1196 Fleischman, Paul. *Mind's Eye* (8–12). 1999, Holt $15.95 (0-8050-6314-5). The story of the relationship that develops among three people in a contemporary nursing home: Courtney, a 16-year-old girl paralyzed from an accident; May, who suffers from Alzheimer's disease; and Elva, a former high school English teacher, who tries to bring Courtney out of her bouts of sullenness and self-pity. (Rev: BL 9/1/99; HB 11–12/99; HBG 4/00; SLJ 8/99; VOYA 12/99)

1197 Gantos, Jack. *Joey Pigza Loses Control* (4–7). 2000, Farrar $16.00 (0-374-39989-1). Joey, a hyperactive kid, tries to please his father but goes haywire when his father destroys his medication in this Newbery Honor Book. (Rev: BCCB 9/00*; BL 9/1/00*; HB 9–10/00; HBG 3/01; SLJ 9/00; VOYA 2/01)

1198 Gantos, Jack. *Joey Pigza Swallowed the Key* (4–8). 1998, Farrar $16.00 (0-374-33664-4). Joey, who suffers from attention deficit disorder, causes so much trouble that he is sent to a special education center, where he learns to cope with his problem. (Rev: BCCB 11/98; BL 12/15/98; HB 11–12/98; HBG 3/99; SLJ 12/98*; VOYA 2/99)

1199 Gantos, Jack. *What Would Joey Do?* (5–8). 2002, Farrar $16.00 (0-374-39986-7). Hyperactive Joey is nearly overwhelmed by the antics of his parents, his dying grandmother, and the needs of his blind homeschool partner, but manages to cope in his own unusual way in this final installment in the Joey Pigza trilogy. (Rev: BCCB 11/02; BL 10/1/02*; HB 11–12/02; HBG 3/03; SLJ 9/02*; VOYA 12/02)

1200 Gavalda, Anna. *95 Pounds of Hope* (5–8). 2003, Viking $14.99 (0-670-03672-2). Grandpa encourages Gregory, 13 and still in 6th grade, to pursue his ambition of attending technical school and working with his hands. (Rev: BCCB 11/03; BL 11/15/03; SLJ 11/03)

1201 Gleitzman, Morris. *Blabber Mouth* (6–8). 1995, Harcourt $11.00 (0-15-200369-X); paper $5.00 (0-15-200370-3). A mute girl is anything but silent as she talks with her hands and inside her head. (Rev: BL 5/1/95; SLJ 6/95)

1202 Going, K. L. *Fat Kid Rules the World* (8–12). 2003, Putnam $17.99 (0-399-23990-1). An unlikely but beneficial friendship develops between suicidal, 300-pound Troy and dropout punk rock guitarist Curt. (Rev: BCCB 6/03*; BL 5/15/03*; HB 7–8/03; HBG 10/03; SLJ 5/03*; VOYA 6/03)

1203 Gould, Marilyn. *Golden Daffodils* (5–7). 1991, Allied Crafts paper $10.95 (0-9632305-1-4). Janis adjusts to her handicap resulting from cerebral palsy.

1204 Gould, Marilyn. *The Twelfth of June* (5–8). 1994, Allied Crafts LB $12.95 (0-9632305-4-9). Janis, who suffers from cerebral palsy, is suffering the first pangs of adolescence and is still fighting the battle to be treated like other girls her age, in this sequel to *Golden Daffodils* (1982). (Rev: SLJ 11/86; VOYA 12/86)

1205 Greene, Shep. *The Boy Who Drank Too Much* (7–9). 1979, Dell paper $5.50 (0-440-90493-5). At one time Buff's main concern was sports, now it's alcohol.

1206 Griffin, Adele. *Hannah, Divided* (4–7). 2002, Hyperion $15.99 (0-7868-0879-9). Hannah's amazing mathematic ability and obsessive-compulsive disorder make her different from everyone else, but with the help of her grandfather, a philanthropist, and a new friend, she perseveres in this novel set during the Depression. (Rev: BCCB 12/02; BL 10/1/02*; HB 11–12/02; HBG 3/03; SLJ 12/02; VOYA 12/02)

1207 Hall, Liza F. *Perk! The Story of a Teenager with Bulimia* (6–9). 1997, Gurze paper $10.95 (0-936077-27-1). The story of Priscilla, who binges on food then vomits, her disapproving parents, and her crush on an unsuitable boy. (Rev: BL 9/15/97; SLJ 4/98; VOYA 4/98)

1208 Hamilton, Virginia. *The Planet of Junior Brown* (7–9). 1971, Macmillan $18.00 (0-02-742510-X); paper $4.99 (0-02-043540-1). A 300-pound misfit is taken care of by his friends.

1209 Harrar, George. *Not as Crazy as I Seem* (7–10). 2003, Houghton $15.00 (0-618-26365-9).

Devon, 15, is frustrated by his obsessive-compulsive disorder and the different responses of his peers, his parents, and his doctor. (Rev: BL 2/15/03; HBG 10/03; SLJ 4/03; VOYA 6/03)

1210 Hautman, Pete. *Sweetblood* (8–12). 2003, Simon & Schuster $16.95 (0-689-85048-4). Sixteen-year-old Lucy, an insulin-dependent diabetic, links her condition with her interest in vampires. (Rev: BL 5/1/03*; HB 7–8/03; HBG 10/03; SLJ 7/03; VOYA 10/03)

1211 Helfman, Elizabeth. *On Being Sarah* (7–9). Illus. 1992, Albert Whitman LB $13.95 (0-8075-6068-5). Based on the life of a real person, this is the story of wheelchair-bound Sarah, 12, who has cerebral palsy, cannot vocalize, and communicates through Blissymbols. (Rev: BL 12/15/92; SLJ 1/93)

1212 Hesse, Karen. *The Music of Dolphins* (6–9). 1996, Scholastic paper $5.99 (0-590-89798-5). An intriguing novel about a young girl who has been raised by dolphins and, after being returned to the world of humans, longs for her life in the sea. (Rev: BL 10/15/96; BR 11–12/96; SLJ 11/96*; VOYA 2/97)

1213 Hesser, Terry S. *Kissing Doorknobs* (6–12). 1998, Delacorte $15.95 (0-385-32329-8). The funny, moving story of a girl afflicted with obsessive-compulsive disorder who even worries about her excessive worrying, and how she eventually gets help. (Rev: BL 6/1–15/98; BR 1–2/99; HBG 9/98; SLJ 6/98; VOYA 12/98)

1214 Hoekstra, Molly. *Upstream: A Novel* (7–12). 2001, Tudor paper $15.95 (0-936389-86-9). This story of a 16-year-old girl's struggle with anorexia gives a clear idea of the psychological problems associated with this illness. (Rev: SLJ 12/01)

1215 Howard, Ellen. *Edith, Herself* (5–7). 1987, Macmillan $15.00 (0-689-31314-4). In the 1890s, young Edith is sent to live with her married sister when their mother dies; there her life is complicated by epileptic seizures. (Rev: BCCB 5/87; BL 4/1/87; SLJ 4/87)

1216 Howe, James. *A Night Without Stars* (5–7). 1983, Macmillan $16.00 (0-689-30957-0); Avon paper $2.95 (0-380-69877-3). A novel about a young girl's hospitalization and serious operation.

1217 Howe, James. *The Watcher* (8–12). 1997, Simon & Schuster $16.00 (0-689-80186-6). The lives of three troubled teens converge in a horrific climax in this novel of child abuse. (Rev: BL 6/1–15/97; BR 11–12/97; SLJ 5/97; VOYA 8/97)

1218 Hughes, Monica. *Hunter in the Dark* (7–10). 1983, Avon paper $2.95 (0-380-67702-4). In spite of his leukemia, Mike goes on a secret hunting trip into a Canadian wilderness. (Rev: BL 11/1/88)

1219 Hurwin, Davida Wills. *A Time for Dancing* (7–12). 1995, Puffin paper $5.99 (0-14-038618-1).

A powerful story of two friends, one of whom is diagnosed with lymphoma. Their friendship becomes a story of saying good-bye and death. (Rev: BL 11/1/95*; SLJ 10/95; VOYA 12/95)

1220 Janover, Caroline. *Zipper: The Kid with ADHD* (4–7). Illus. 1997, Woodbine paper $11.95 (0-933149-95-6). Zipper Wilson suffers from attention deficit hyperactivity disorder and gradually learns to cope with it. (Rev: BL 2/1/98; SLJ 3/98)

1221 Johnson, Angela. *Humming Whispers* (8–12). 1995, Orchard LB $16.99 (0-531-08748-4). Sophy, 14, reveals the impact of her 24-year-old sister Nicole's schizophrenia on the lives of those who love her. (Rev: BL 2/15/95; SLJ 4/95; VOYA 5/95)

1222 Jung, Reinhardt. *Dreaming in Black and White* (5–8). Trans. from German by Anthea Bell. 2003, Penguin Putnam $15.99 (0-8037-2811-5). A boy with disabilities has waking dreams in which he travels back to Nazi Germany and suffers at the hands of his classmates, teachers, and eventually his father, in this compelling novel translated from German. (Rev: BCCB 9/03; BL 5/15/03; HB 9–10/03*; SLJ 8/03)

1223 Kachur, Wanda G. *The Nautilus* (5–7). 1997, Peytral paper $7.95 (0-9644271-5-X). A compassionate novel about a girl's rehabilitation after receiving spinal cord injuries in an automobile accident. (Rev: SLJ 9/97)

1224 Kent, Deborah. *Why Me? The Courage to Live* (6–9). 2001, Pocket paper $4.99 (0-7434-0031-3). Fifteen-year-old Chloe suffers various mystifying symptoms that interfere with her everyday life before she is diagnosed as having lupus. (Rev: BL 5/1/01)

1225 Klass, Sheila S. *Rhino* (7–10). 1993, Scholastic paper $13.95 (0-590-44250-3). Fourteen-year-old Annie suffers from a nose that is a family trait and looks too big for her face. (Rev: BL 1/15/94; SLJ 11/93; VOYA 12/93)

1226 Koertge, Ron. *Stoner and Spaz* (8–12). 2002, Candlewick $15.99 (0-7636-1608-&). An unlikely romance between a 16-year-old boy with cerebral palsy and a girl who is constantly stoned brings benefits to both of them. (Rev: BCCB 3/02; BL 5/1/02*)

1227 Koller, Jackie F. *The Falcon* (7–12). 1998, Simon & Schuster $17.00 (0-689-81294-9). In fulfilling a school journalism assignment, Luke explores his inner feelings and finds an emotional demon that has haunted him for years. (Rev: BL 4/15/98; BR 1–2/99; HBG 9/98; SLJ 5/98; VOYA 2/99)

1228 Lachtman, Ofelia Dumas. *Leticia's Secret* (5–8). 1997, Arte Publico $14.95 (1-55885-205-5); paper $7.95 (1-55885-209-3). Rosario, from a Mexican American family, shares many adventures with her cousin, the pretty Leticia, and is devastated to learn that she has a fatal disease. (Rev: SLJ 1/98)

1229 Lawrence, Iain. *Ghost Boy* (7–10). 2000, Delacorte $15.95 (0-385-32739-0). Set in America shortly after World War II, this is the story of shy, neglected, albino Harold Kline, who finds a warm home when he runs away to join a circus. (Rev: BCCB 10/00; BL 11/1/00; HBG 3/01; SLJ 9/00*; VOYA 12/00)

1230 Levoy, Myron. *Alan and Naomi* (7–9). 1977, HarperCollins paper $5.99 (0-06-440209-6). Alan tries to reach Naomi, whose mind has been warped by memories of the Holocaust. (Rev: BL 10/1/97)

1231 Lewis, Catherine, and Jane Yeomans. *Postcards to Father Abraham* (6–10). 2000, Simon & Schuster $17.95 (0-689-82852-7). Teenage Megan finds it difficult to make adjustments when she loses a leg to cancer. (Rev: BL 1/1–15/00; HBG 9/00; SLJ 5/00; VOYA 2/00)

1232 Lipsyte, Robert. *One Fat Summer* (7–12). 1991, HarperCollins paper $5.99 (0-06-447073-3). Bobby Marks is 14, fat, and unhappy in this first novel of three that traces Bobby's career through his first year of college. (Rev: BL 1/1–15/98)

1233 McBay, Bruce, and James Heneghan. *Waiting for Sarah* (7–10). 2003, Orca paper $7.95 (1-55143-270-6). Crippled in a car accident, Mike suffers from depression and withdrawal until he gets to know 8th-grader Sarah. (Rev: BL 9/15/03; SLJ 10/03)

1234 McCormick, Patricia. *Cut* (7–10). 2000, Front Street $16.95 (1-886910-61-8). In a hospital that treats teens with serious issues, including drugs and anorexia, Callie participates in group therapy and tries to face her own self-mutilation. (Rev: BL 1/1–15/01; HB 11–12/00; HBG 3/01; SLJ 12/00; VOYA 2/01)

1235 McDaniel, Lurlene. *How Do I Love Thee? Three Stories* (6–10). 2001, Bantam $9.95 (0-553-57154-0). Three dramatic stories combine young romance and critical illness with clever twists of plot. (Rev: BL 10/15/01; HBG 3/02; SLJ 11/01; VOYA 12/01)

1236 McDaniel, Lurlene. *Saving Jessica* (7–10). 1996, Bantam paper $4.99 (0-553-56721-7). When Jessica is stricken with kidney failure, her boyfriend, Jeremy, volunteers to donate one of his but his parents, fearful that he will die, refuse permission. (Rev: VOYA 4/96)

1237 McDaniel, Lurlene. *To Live Again* (5–9). 2001, Bantam paper $4.99 (0-553-57151-6). After three years of remission from leukemia, 16-year-old Dawn suffers a stroke that produces a terrible bout of depression. (Rev: BL 3/1/01)

1238 McDaniel, Lurlene. *Too Young to Die* (7–9). 1989, Bantam paper $4.99 (0-553-28008-2). Melissa discovers that she has leukemia and must learn to cope with this tragedy. Also use *Goodbye Doesn't*

Mean Forever (1989). (Rev: SLJ 8/89; VOYA 12/89)

1239 Maclean, John. *Mac* (8–12). 1987, Avon paper $2.95 (0-380-70700-4). A high school sophomore's life falls apart after he is sexually assaulted by a doctor during a physical exam. (Rev: BL 10/1/87; SLJ 11/87)

1240 Marino, Jan. *Eighty-Eight Steps to September* (5–7). 1989, Avon paper $2.95 (0-380-71001-3). Amy and Robbie have the usual sibling rivalry, until Robbie develops leukemia. (Rev: BCCB 5/89; BL 8/89)

1241 Marsden, John. *Checkers* (7–12). 1998, Houghton $15.00 (0-395-85754-6). A harrowing story, set in Australia, about a teenager who suffers a nervous breakdown after her prominent father is accused of unethical business practices, and about the love she and her dog, Checkers, share. (Rev: BCCB 10/98; BL 10/15/98; BR 5–6/99; HBG 3/99; SLJ 9/98; VOYA 12/98)

1242 Martin, Ann M. *A Corner of the Universe* (6–8). 2002, Scholastic paper $15.95 (0-439-38880-5). Hattie recalls the summer she became 12, when a mentally disabled uncle came to stay with her family. Newbery Honor Book, 2003. (Rev: BCCB 2/03; BL 12/1/02; HB 1–2/03*; HBG 3/03; SLJ 9/02*; VOYA 12/02)

1243 Mass, Wendy. *A Mango-Shaped Space* (6–10). 2003, Little, Brown $16.95 (0-316-52388-7). Mia, 13, eventually seeks help when she can no longer cope with her synesthesia, a sensory condition that produces color visions. (Rev: BL 4/1/03; HB 7–8/03; HBG 10/03; SLJ 3/03; VOYA 4/03)

1244 Mathis, Sharon. *Teacup Full of Roses* (7–12). 1987, Puffin paper $4.99 (0-14-032328-7). For mature teens, a novel about the devastating effects of drugs on an African American family.

1245 Mazer, Harry. *The Wild Kid* (4–8). 1998, Simon & Schuster $15.00 (0-689-80751-1). Sammy, a young boy with Down's syndrome, gets into all sorts of difficulties but finally makes a friend of a wild kid named Kevin who understands him and his problems. (Rev: BCCB 11/98; BL 8/98; HB 9–10/98*; HBG 3/99; SLJ 10/98; VOYA 2/99)

1246 Mazer, Norma Fox. *Silver* (6–9). 1988, Morrow $16.00 (0-688-06865-0). Sarabeth moves to a posh school and finds that her best friend there is being sexually abused. (Rev: BL 11/1/88; BR 11–12/88; SLJ 11/88; VOYA 2/89)

1247 Metzger, Lois. *Ellen's Case* (7–12). 1995, Atheneum $16.00 (0-689-31934-7). In this sequel to *Barry's Sister,* Ellen — now 16 and more understanding of her brother's cerebral palsy — is involved in an intense malpractice trial. (Rev: BL 8/95; SLJ 10/95; VOYA 12/95)

1248 Mikaelsen, Ben. *Petey* (6–9). 1998, Disney $15.95 (0-7868-0426-2). This is a touching story of an 8th-grade student, Trevor Ladd, and his friendship with Petey, an elderly man crippled from cerebral palsy, who was misdiagnosed as "an idiot" at the age of two and spent 68 years in an asylum, where he developed close relationships with his caretakers. (Rev: BCCB 10/98; BL 11/1/98; HBG 3/99; SLJ 11/98; VOYA 2/99)

1249 Miklowitz, Gloria D. *Past Forgiving* (8–10). 1995, Simon & Schuster $16.00 (0-671-88442-5). A teenage girl caught in an abusive relationship with her boyfriend. (Rev: BL 5/1/95; SLJ 6/95)

1250 Naylor, Phyllis Reynolds. *The Keeper* (6–10). 1986, Macmillan $16.00 (0-689-31204-0). Nick and his mother agonize over whether or not to have Nick's father institutionalized for the mentally ill. (Rev: BL 4/1/86; SLJ 5/86; VOYA 2/87)

1251 Neufeld, John. *Lisa, Bright and Dark* (7–9). 1969, Phillips $26.95 (0-87599-153-X). Her friend notices that Lisa is gradually sinking into mental illness but her parents seem indifferent.

1252 Nolan, Han. *Dancing on the Edge* (7–10). 1997, Harcourt $16.00 (0-15-201648-1). Beset by a series of personal and family crises, Miracle slowly descends into madness. (Rev: BL 10/1/97; HBG 3/98; SLJ 9/97*; VOYA 2/98)

1253 Oneal, Zibby. *The Language of Goldfish* (7–10). 1990, Puffin paper $5.99 (0-14-034540-X). Carrie appears to be slowly sinking into mental illness and seems unable to help herself.

1254 Orr, Wendy. *Peeling the Onion* (8–12). 1997, Holiday $16.95 (0-8234-1289-X); Bantam Doubleday Dell paper $4.99 (0-440-22773-9). An automobile accident leaves Anna with a broken back, debilitating pain, physical and mental handicaps, and questions about what to do with her life. (Rev: BL 4/1/97; SLJ 5/97*; VOYA 10/97)

1255 Paulsen, Gary. *The Monument* (6–9). 1991, Delacorte $15.00 (0-385-30518-4). A 13-year-old girl's friendship with an artist who is hired to create a monument in her small town transforms her. (Rev: BL 9/15/91; SLJ 10/91*)

1256 Peck, Richard. *Remembering the Good Times* (7–10). 1986, Delacorte $12.95 (0-385-29396-8); Bantam paper $5.50 (0-440-97339-2). A strong friendship between two boys and a girl is destroyed when one of them commits suicide. (Rev: BL 3/1/85; BR 9–10/85)

1257 Platt, Kin. *The Ape Inside Me* (6–8). 1979, HarperCollins LB $11.89 (0-397-31863-4). Eddie and Debbie work together to try and curb their terrible tempers.

1258 Riskind, Mary. *Apple Is My Sign* (5–6). 1995, Houghton paper $5.95 (0-395-65747-4). A deaf and mute boy is sent to a special school in the early 1900s.

1259 Roos, Stephen. *The Gypsies Never Came* (4–7). 2001, Simon & Schuster $15.00 (0-689-83147-1). Augie Knapp, who was born without a left hand, slowly develops confidence with the help of Lydie Rose, an eccentric outsider. (Rev: BCCB 5/01; BL 3/1/01; HB 5–6/01; HBG 10/01; SLJ 2/01; VOYA 12/01)

1260 Rubin, Susan G. *Emily Good As Gold* (6–8). 1993, Harcourt $10.95 (0-15-276632-4). Emily's parents see their developmentally disabled child as never being able to grow up, but Emily begins to do so on her own, especially sexually. (Rev: BL 11/1/93; SLJ 10/93)

1261 Ruckman, Ivy. *The Hunger Scream* (7–10). 1983, Walker $14.95 (0-8027-6514-9). Lily starves herself to become a popular member of the in-crowd.

1262 Scoppettone, Sandra. *Long Time Between Kisses* (7–10). 1982, HarperCollins $12.95 (0-06-025229-4). A 16-year-old brings together a victim of multiple sclerosis and his fiance.

1263 Seago, Kate. *Matthew Unstrung* (7–12). 1998, Dial $16.99 (0-8037-2230-3). Set in 1910, this novel portrays the descent into madness of a sensitive, teenage seminarian and his institutionalization after a nervous breakdown. (Rev: BL 5/1/98; HBG 9/98; SLJ 3/98; VOYA 2/98)

1264 Seidler, Tor. *The Silent Spillbills* (5–8). 1998, HarperCollins LB $14.89 (0-06-205181-4). Katrina faces problems trying to overcome her stuttering but stands up to her tyrannical grandfather to help save from extinction a rare bird known as the silent spillbill. (Rev: BCCB 1/99; BL 12/15/98; HBG 3/99; SLJ 4/99)

1265 Shaw, Susan. *Black-Eyed Suzie* (7–9). 2002, Boyds Mills $15.95 (1-56397-729-X); paper $4.95 (1-56397-701-X). In the pages of her diary and with the help of hospital staff, Suzie struggles to recover emotionally from her mother's physical abuse. (Rev: BCCB 9/02; BL 5/15/02; HBG 10/02; VOYA 8/02)

1266 Shreve, Susan. *Trout and Me* (5–7). 2002, Knopf LB $17.99 (0-375-91219-3). Two friends with ADD have very different family experiences. (Rev: BCCB 11/02; BL 8/02; HBG 3/03; SLJ 9/02)

1267 Shyer, Marlene Fanta. *Welcome Home, Jellybean* (5–8). 1978, Macmillan paper $4.99 (0-689-71213-8). Twelve-year-old Neil encounters a near-tragic situation when his older retarded sister comes home to stay.

1268 Sirof, Harriet. *Because She's My Friend* (7–10). 1993, Atheneum $16.00 (0-689-31844-8). Two girls of opposite temperament become friends when strong-willed Valerie's right leg is paralyzed after an accident and she meets well-behaved Terri. (Rev: BL 9/15/93; SLJ 10/93; VOYA 12/93)

1269 Slote, Alfred. *Hang Tough, Paul Mather* (4–7). 1973, HarperCollins paper $5.99 (0-06-440153-7). Paul recollects from his hospital bed the details of his struggle with leukemia. Told candidly and without sentimentality.

1270 Snyder, Zilpha Keatley. *The Witches of Worm* (5–8). 1972, Macmillan $17.95 (0-689-30066-2); Dell paper $5.50 (0-440-49727-2). A deeply disturbed girl believes that her selfish and destructive acts are caused by bewitchment.

1271 Sones, Sonya. *Stop Pretending: What Happened When My Big Sister Went Crazy* (6–9). 1999, HarperCollins $14.95 (0-06-028387-4). Thirteen-year-old Cookie's poems describe her older sister's painful struggle with mental illness in this novel based on the author's own experiences. (Rev: BCCB 10/99; BL 11/15/99*; HBG 4/00; SLJ 10/99)

1272 Strachan, Ian. *The Flawed Glass* (5–8). 1990, Little, Brown $14.95 (0-316-81813-5). Physically disabled Shona makes friends with an American boy on an island off the Scottish coast. (Rev: BCCB 11/90; BL 12/1/90; SLJ 1/91)

1273 Stratton, Allan. *Leslie's Journal* (8–12). 2000, Annick $19.95 (1-55037-665-9); paper $8.95 (1-55037-664-0). A new teacher reads Leslie's journal and learns about her boyfriend's abusive behavior. (Rev: HBG 10/01; SLJ 4/01; VOYA 2/01)

1274 Striegel, Jana. *Homeroom Exercise* (4–7). 2002, Holiday $16.95 (0-8234-1579-1). A 12-year-old who dreams of becoming a professional dancer is diagnosed with juvenile rheumatoid arthritis. (Rev: BL 3/1/02; HBG 10/02; SLJ 6/02; VOYA 8/02)

1275 Tan, Shaun. *The Red Tree* (6–12). Illus. 2003, Simply Read $15.95 (0-9688767-3-8). This arresting picture book for older readers portrays a girl searching for meaning in a frightening world, with a glimmer of hope that grows as the book reaches its conclusion. (Rev: BL 5/1/03)

1276 Tashjian, Janet. *Fault Line* (8–12). 2003, Holt $16.95 (0-8050-7200-4). Becky, 17, happy and enjoying doing comedy routines, finds her life changing when she falls for Kip, whose apparent self-confidence hides his abusive nature. (Rev: BL 9/1/03; HB 9–10/03; SLJ 10/03; VOYA 10/03)

1277 Tashjian, Janet. *Multiple Choice* (5–9). 1999, Holt $16.95 (0-8050-6086-3). Fourteen-year-old Monica realizes she needs outside help when her attempts to cope with her obsessive drive for perfection spin out of control with almost tragic consequences. (Rev: BL 6/1–15/99; HB 7–8/99; HBG 10/99; SLJ 9/99; VOYA 10/99)

1278 Tashjian, Janet. *Tru Confessions* (4–7). 1997, Holt $15.95 (0-8050-5254-2). Young Tru, an amateur filmmaker, begins a documentary about her developmentally delayed twin brother, Eddie, in this novel made up of Tru's diary entries, Internet conversations, and Eddie's computer graphics. (Rev: BL 1/1–15/98; HBG 3/98; SLJ 12/97; VOYA 12/97)

1279 Taylor, Michelle A. *The Angel of Barbican High* (7–12). 2002, Univ. of Queensland paper $15.95 (0-7022-3251-3). Jez feels responsible for the death of her boyfriend and pours out her guilt in her poems, which reveal that she is close to suicide. (Rev: SLJ 8/02)

1280 Thomas, Joyce C. *Marked by Fire* (8–12). 1982, Avon paper $4.50 (0-380-79327-X). After she is raped, a Southern black girl seems to lose her beautiful singing voice. A sequel is *Bright Shadow* (1984). (Rev: BL 7/88)

1281 Toten, Teresa. *The Game* (7–12). 2001, Red Deer paper $7.95 (0-88995-232-9). A dramatic story about Dani, a suicidal girl who finds friendship and succor at a clinic for troubled adolescents. (Rev: BL 2/15/02; VOYA 4/02)

1282 Trembath, Don. *Lefty Carmichael Has a Fit* (8–12). 2000, Orca paper $6.95 (1-55143-166-1). When 15-year-old Lefty discovers that he is an epileptic, he develops a fearful, cautious lifestyle that his friends and family try to change. (Rev: BL 1/1–15/00; SLJ 2/00; VOYA 4/00)

1283 Trueman, Terry. *Inside Out* (7–10). 2003, HarperCollins $15.99 (0-06-623962-1). An absorbing story about a schizophrenic teenager who is held hostage in a robbery attempt. (Rev: BL 9/1/03; SLJ 9/03; VOYA 10/03)

1284 Trueman, Terry. *Stuck in Neutral* (6–10). 2000, HarperCollins $14.95 (0-06-028519-2). Fourteen-year-old Shawn, whose severe cerebral palsy does not hamper his great intelligence, fears that his father may be planning to put him out of his misery. (Rev: BL 7/00; HB 5–6/00; HBG 10/00; SLJ 7/00; VOYA 12/00)

1285 Voigt, Cynthia. *Izzy, Willy-Nilly* (7–12). 1986, Macmillan $18.00 (0-689-31202-4). A 15-year-old girl's life changes dramatically when she has a leg amputated. (Rev: BL 5/1/86; SLJ 4/86; VOYA 12/86)

1286 Waite, Judy. *Shopaholic* (6–10). 2003, Simon & Schuster $16.95 (0-689-85138-3). Unhappy Taylor, a British 14-year-old, allows herself to fall in with glamorous Kat's plans despite her reservations. (Rev: BL 5/1/03; HBG 10/03; SLJ 7/03; VOYA 8/03)

1287 Warner, Sally. *Sort of Forever* (5–8). 1998, Knopf $17.99 (0-679-98648-0); Random paper $4.99 (0-375-80207-X). Twelve-year-old Cady discovers that her friend-for-life Nana has leukemia and has only a short time to live. (Rev: BCCB 5/98; BL 6/1–15/98; HBG 9/98; SLJ 7/98)

1288 Werlin, Nancy. *Are You Alone on Purpose?* (5–8). 1994, Houghton $16.00 (0-395-67350-X). Opposites attract when Alison, 13, hesitantly finds herself drawn to unruly Harry, who is confined to a wheelchair. (Rev: BCCB 12/94; BL 8/94; SLJ 9/94; VOYA 10/94)

1289 Wersba, Barbara. *Fat: A Love Story* (8–12). 1987, HarperCollins $11.95 (0-06-026400-4). Rita Formica, fat and unhappy, falls for rich, attractive Robert. (Rev: BL 6/1/87; SLJ 8/87; VOYA 6/87)

1290 White, Ruth. *Memories of Summer* (7–12). 2000, Farrar $16.00 (0-374-34945-2). Lyric is devastated when her older sister, Summer, must be hospitalized for her schizophrenia in this novel set in 1955. (Rev: BL 9/1/00; HB 9–10/00; HBG 3/01; SLJ 8/00*; VOYA 12/00)

1291 White, Ruth. *Weeping Willow* (7–10). 1992, Farrar paper $5.95 (0-374-48280-2). This uplifting novel conveying hill country life is about a girl who overcomes abuse to make her own way. (Rev: BL 6/15/92; SLJ 7/92)

1292 Wilson, Dawn. *Saint Jude* (8–12). 2001, Tudor $15.95 (0-936389-68-0). Taylor, who is bipolar, makes friends and learns to cope with her illness while in an outpatient program at St. Jude Hospital. (Rev: BL 11/1/01; SLJ 11/01)

1293 Wilson, Jacqueline. *Vicky Angel* (4–7). 2001, Delacorte $15.95 (0-385-72920-0). A girl conjures up the angel of her dead best friend in this book that examines loss, guilt, suicidal thoughts, and life after death. (Rev: BCCB 10/01; BL 11/15/01; HBG 3/02; SLJ 10/01; VOYA 12/01)

1294 Wilson, Nancy H. *Bringing Nettie Back* (5–7). 1992, Macmillan $15.00 (0-02-793075-0). The story of a friendship between two "opposites" and of Nettie's illness. (Rev: BL 1/1/93; SLJ 10/92)

1295 Wolff, Virginia E. *Probably Still Nick Swansen* (7–12). 1988, Holt $14.95 (0-8050-0701-6). Nick, a 16-year-old victim of slight brain dysfunction, tells his story of rejection and separation. (Rev: BL 11/15/88; BR 5–6/89; SLJ 12/88; VOYA 6/89)

1296 Woodruff, Joan L. *The Shiloh Renewal* (7–10). 1998, Black Heron $22.95 (0-930773-50-0). Sandy, who has been mentally and physically disabled since an automobile accident, tries to regain basic skills, recover from the brain trauma, and straighten out her life in this novel that takes place on a small farm near Shiloh National Park in Tennessee. (Rev: VOYA 12/98)

1297 Zephaniah, Benjamin. *Face* (6–9). 2002, Bloomsbury $15.95 (1-58234-774-3). After British teenager Martin's face is horribly burned in a car accident, he must learn to deal with rejection and prejudice. (Rev: BL 11/15/02; SLJ 12/02; VOYA 12/02)

Personal Problems and Growing into Maturity

1298 Adler, C. S. *Daddy's Climbing Tree* (5–7). 1993, Houghton $15.00 (0-395-63032-0). Jessica cannot adjust to the death of her father in a hit-and-run accident. (Rev: BCCB 7–8/93; BL 6/1–15/93; HB 7–8/93; SLJ 5/93)

1299 Adler, C. S. *What's to Be Scared Of, Suki?* (4–7). 1996, Clarion $13.95 (0-395-77600-7). A neighbor's handsome 13-year-old son helps Suki overcome her fears. (Rev: BL 11/1/96; SLJ 10/96)

1300 Adler, C. S. *Willie, the Frog Prince* (4–7). 1994, Clarion $15.00 (0-395-65615-X). Willie's inability to accept responsibility almost causes the loss of his dog, Booboo. (Rev: BL 4/15/94; SLJ 6/94)

1301 Aker, Don. *Stranger at Bay* (6–9). 1998, Stoddart paper $5.95 (0-7736-7468-3). Set in a town on the Bay of Fundy in Canada, this novel tells about Randy Forsythe's adjustment to a new home and stepmother while coping with a gang of bullies who want him to steal drugs from his father, who is a pharmaceutical salesman. (Rev: SLJ 7/98)

1302 Alphin, Elaine Marie. *Simon Says* (8–12). 2002, Harcourt $17.00 (0-15-216355-7). Charles, a brooding 16-year-old artist, is determined to remain nonconformist when he starts attending a boarding school for the arts in this thoughtful novel. (Rev: BCCB 6/02; BL 4/15/02; HBG 10/02; SLJ 6/02)

1303 Anderson, Laurie Halse. *Speak* (8–12). 1999, Farrar $16.00 (0-374-37152-0). A victim of rape, high school freshman Mellinda Sordino finds that her attacker is again threatening her. (Rev: BL 9/15/99; HB 9–10/99; HBG 4/00; SLJ 10/99; VOYA 12/99)

1304 Anderson, Mary. *Tune in Tomorrow* (7–9). 1985, Avon paper $2.50 (0-380-69870-6). Jo is fixated on two soap opera characters whom she later meets in real life.

1305 *Annie's Baby: The Diary of Anonymous, a Pregnant Teenager* (6–10). 1998, Demco $11.04 (0-606-13145-0); Avon paper $5.99 (0-380-79141-2). In diary format, this is the story of 14-year-old Annie, her love for an abusive rich boyfriend, and her rape and subsequent pregnancy. (Rev: SLJ 7/98; VOYA 6/98)

1306 Antle, Nancy. *Lost in the War* (6–10). 1998, Dial $15.99 (0-8037-2299-0). Lisa's father was killed during the Vietnam War and her mother was a nurse during the conflict, so her family is haunted by memories of a war that many people in their lives opposed. (Rev: BCCB 9/98; BL 8/98; HBG 9/98; SLJ 8/98; VOYA 8/98)

1307 Appelt, Kathi. *Kissing Tennessee: And Other Stories from the Stardust Dance* (5–9). 2000, Harcourt $15.00 (0-15-202249-X). Eight short stories follow several graduating 8th-graders on the night of their last junior high dance and explore the many adolescent problems they face. (Rev: BL 6/1–15/00; HBG 10/00; SLJ 9/00)

1308 Ashley, Bernard. *All My Men* (7–9). 1978, Phillips $26.95 (0-87599-228-5). In this English story, Paul pays a heavy price to be part of the "in" crowd.

1309 Ashley, Bernard. *Little Soldier* (8–12). 2002, Scholastic $16.95 (0-439-22424-1). Young Kaninda Bulumba is rescued from the incredible violence taking place in his native country only to find himself confronting gang violence in his new neighborhood in London. (Rev: BCCB 7–8/02; BL 5/1/02; HBG 10/02; SLJ 6/02*; VOYA 8/02)

1310 Ashley, Bernard. *Terry on the Fence* (6–8). Illus. 1977, Phillips $26.95 (0-87599-222-6). Unhappy at home, Terry unwillingly becomes a member of a street gang.

1311 Auch, Mary Jane. *Seven Long Years Until College* (4–7). 1991, Holiday $13.95 (0-8234-0901-5). Unhappy at home, Natalie runs away to join her older sister at college. (Rev: BCCB 1/92; SLJ 10/91)

1312 Avi. *Blue Heron* (5–8). 1992, Bradbury LB $17.00 (0-02-707751-9). A young girl with a troubled family life finds comfort in nature and a beautiful bird. (Rev: BL 1/15/92*; SLJ 4/92)

1313 Avi. *Nothing but the Truth: A Documentary Novel* (7–10). 1991, Orchard paper $17.99 (0-531-08559-7). A boy's expulsion from school is reported in a biased, inflammatory newspaper story and takes on patriotic and political overtones. (Rev: BL 9/15/91*; SLJ 9/91*)

1314 Avi. *A Place Called Ugly* (6–9). 1995, Avon paper $5.99 (0-380-72423-5). A 14-year-old boy protests the tearing down of a beach cottage to build a hotel.

1315 Avi. *What Do Fish Have to Do with Anything?* (5–8). Illus. 1997, Candlewick $16.99 (0-7636-0329-5); paper $6.99 (0-7636-0412-7). Seven excellent stories about youngsters facing the first pangs of adolescence. (Rev: BL 11/15/97; HB 11–12/97; HBG 3/98; SLJ 12/97*; VOYA 4/98)

1316 Bagdasarian, Adam. *First French Kiss and Other Traumas* (7–12). 2002, Farrar $16.00 (0-374-32338-0). A series of vignettes, based on the author's own experiences, relate comic, romantic, and sad "traumas" in Will's life from the ages of five to 20. (Rev: BL 8/02; HB 11–12/02; HBG 3/03; SLJ 10/02; VOYA 12/02)

1317 Baker, Jennifer. *Most Likely to Deceive* (6–10). Series: Class Secrets. 1995, Pocket Books paper $3.99 (0-671-51033-9). Newcomer Suzanne Willis discovers that even the most popular teens in the school have problems. (Rev: SLJ 2/96)

1318 Barnes, Joyce Annette. *Promise Me the Moon* (5–8). 1997, Dial $15.99 (0-8037-1798-9). Annie faces many problems in 8th grade, including being labeled an egghead, in this sequel to *The Baby Grand, the Moon in July, and Me* (1994). (Rev: BCCB 2/97; BL 11/15/96; BR 11–12/97; SLJ 2/97; VOYA 10/97)

1319 Bawden, Nina. *The Peppermint Pig* (6–8). 1975, HarperCollins LB $13.89 (0-397-31618-6). A brother and sister save a pig that they soon regard as a pet but they find something terrible is going to happen to it.

1320 Bechard, Margaret. *Hanging on to Max* (8–12). 2002, Millbrook $15.95 (0-7613-1579-9). Sam, a 17-year-old single father, faces difficult decisions as he juggles his father's demands and his own wish to go to college. (Rev: BCCB 5/02; BL 5/1/02; HB 5–6/02; HBG 10/02; SLJ 5/02*; VOYA 4/02)

1321 Beddard, Michael. *Stained Glass* (7–12). 2001, Tundra $17.95 (0-88776-552-1). When a stained glass window breaks and injures a young girl, Charles accompanies her on her search for her identity and begins to come to terms with his father's death. (Rev: BL 12/15/01; HB 1–2/02*; HBG 3/02; SLJ 1/02*; VOYA 12/01)

1322 Belton, Sandra. *McKendree* (5–8). 2000, Greenwillow $16.99 (0-688-15950-8). Tilara, the 14-year-old child of a mixed marriage, spends a summer in a West Virginia town where she does volunteer work in a home for the elderly and falls in love with a quiet, soft-spoken boy who is also a volunteer. (Rev: BL 8/00; HBG 10/00; SLJ 6/00; VOYA 2/01)

1323 Benjamin, Carol Lea. *The Wicked Stepdog* (4–7). 1982, Avon paper $2.50 (0-380-70089-1). Louise is in the midst of puberty problems and her father's remarriage.

1324 Bennett, Cherie, and Jeff Gottesfeld. *Stranger in the Mirror* (6–10). Series: Mirror Image. 1999, Pocket paper $4.99 (0-671-03630-0). Callie wants the popularity and good looks that her sister has, so she starts working out, losing weight, and changing her wardrobe. (Rev: BL 2/15/00; SLJ 3/00)

1325 Bennett, James W. *Plunking Reggie Jackson* (8–12). 2001, Simon & Schuster $16.00 (0-689-83137-4). High school senior Coley initially seems to have a lot going for him, but he faces an increasing number of challenges as an injury retires him to the bench, his girlfriend says she's pregnant, he struggles with family problems, and his grades drop. (Rev: BCCB 2/01; BL 4/1/01; HBG 10/01; SLJ 2/01; VOYA 4/01)

1326 Bertrand, Diane Gonzales. *Trino's Choice* (6–9). 1999, Arte Publico $16.95 (1-55885-279-4); paper $9.95 (1-55885-268-9). A Latino boy growing

up in a Texas trailer park succumbs to the offer of a hood who offers him chance at quick cash, but in time it leads to tragedy. (Rev: BL 6/1–15/99; VOYA 4/00)

1327 Bertrand, Diane Gonzales. *Trino's Time* (6–12). 2001, Arte Publico $14.95 (1-55885-316-2); paper $9.95 (1-55885-317-0). In this sequel to *Trino's Choice* (1999), things begin to look better for Trino's family as Trino gets a job and starts enjoying school. (Rev: BL 11/1/01; SLJ 7/01; VOYA 12/01)

1328 Betancourt, Jeanne. *Kate's Turn* (5–8). 1992, Scholastic $13.95 (0-590-43103-X). This story of the young ballerina Kate, who decides the price of fame is too high, shows the grueling, often painful life of a dancer. (Rev: BL 1/1/92; SLJ 2/92)

1329 Black, Jonah. *The Black Book (Diary of a Teenage Stud): Vol. 1: Girls, Girls, Girls* (8–12). 2001, Avon paper $4.99 (0-06-440798-5). Jonah, who has been expelled from a private school and is repeating his junior year at home, reveals the comic but touching details of his life and family as well as his private fantasies. Sequels are *Vol. 2: Stop, Don't Stop, Vol. 3: Run, Jonah, Run*, and *Vol. 4: Faster, Faster, Faster*. (Rev: BL 10/15/01; SLJ 8/01)

1330 Block, Francesca L. *Baby Be-Bop* (8–12). 1995, HarperCollins LB $13.89 (0-06-024880-7). Dirk is gay and struggles with self-loathing, among a number of debilitating emotions and experiences, until his grandmother shares her wisdom about loving and living. (Rev: BL 10/1/95*; SLJ 9/95)

1331 Block, Francesca L. *Echo* (8–12). 2001, HarperCollins $14.95 (0-06-028127-8). A series of interconnected stories set in glamorous Los Angeles follows the maturing of an unhappy young girl called Echo, who feels neglected by her talented parents and seeks attention where she can find it. (Rev: BCCB 10/01; BL 8/01; HB 9–10/01; HBG 3/02; SLJ 8/01; VOYA 10/01)

1332 Bloor, Edward. *Tangerine* (7–10). 1997, Harcourt $17.00 (0-15-201246-X); Scholastic paper $4.99 (0-590-43277-X). Although he wears thick glasses, Paul is able to see clearly the people around him, their problems and their mistakes, as he adjusts to his new home in Tangerine County, Florida. (Rev: BL 5/15/97; SLJ 4/97; VOYA 8/97)

1333 Blume, Judy. *Here's to You, Rachel Robinson* (6–8). 1993, Dell paper $5.50 (0-440-40946-2). This sequel to *Just As Long As We're Together* is full of multidimensional characters. (Rev: BL 9/1/93; SLJ 11/93; VOYA 12/93)

1334 Blume, Judy. *Just as Long as We're Together* (6–8). 1987, Dell paper $5.50 (0-440-40075-9). A student entering junior high faces problems involving weight, friendships, and a family that is disintegrating. (Rev: BL 8/87; BR 1–2/88; VOYA 2/88)

1335 Blume, Judy. *Then Again, Maybe I Won't* (5–8). 1971, Dell paper $4.99 (0-440-48659-9). Thirteen-year-old Tony faces many problems when his family relocates to suburban Long Island.

1336 Blume, Judy. *Tiger Eyes* (7–10). 1981, Dell paper $5.99 (0-440-98469-6). A girl struggles to cope with her father's violent death. (Rev: BL 7/88)

1337 Bohlmeijer, Arno. *Something Very Sorry* (5–8). 1996, Houghton $15.00 (0-395-74679-5). A terrible automobile accident in which Rose and her family are involved brings death into the family and changes her life forever. (Rev: BL 4/1/96; SLJ 7/96*)

1338 Boock, Paula. *Dare Truth or Promise* (8–12). 1999, Houghton $15.00 (0-395-97117-9). Two girls, Willa and Louise, attend a New Zealand high school and, though they are opposites in many ways, they fall in love. (Rev: BL 9/15/99; HB 9–10/99; HBG 4/00; SLJ 11/99; VOYA 10/99)

1339 Book, Rick. *Necking With Louise* (7–12). 1999, Red Deer paper $7.95 (0-88995-194-2). Set in Saskatchewan in 1965, this is a book of stories about Eric Anderson's 16th year, when he has his first date, plays in a championship hockey game, has a summer job, and reacts to his family and the land on which he lives. (Rev: BL 10/15/99; SLJ 3/00)

1340 Borntrager, Mary Christner. *Rebecca* (7–12). 1989, Herald Pr. paper $8.99 (0-8361-3500-8). A coming-of-age novel about an Amish girl and her attraction to a Mennonite young man. (Rev: SLJ 11/89)

1341 Bottner, Barbara. *Nothing in Common* (7–10). 1986, HarperCollins $12.95 (0-06-020604-7). When Mrs. Gregori dies, both her daughter and Melissa Warren, a teenager in the household where Mrs. Gregori worked, enter a period of grief. (Rev: VOYA 2/87)

1342 Bradley, Kimberly Brubaker. *Halfway to the Sky* (5–8). 2002, Delacorte LB $17.99 (0-385-90029-5). To escape her grief at the death of her brother and her parents' divorce, 12-year-old Dani decides to hike the Appalachian Trail from Georgia to Maine. (Rev: BCCB 5/02; BL 4/1/02; HBG 10/02; SLJ 4/02)

1343 Branscum, Robbie. *Johnny May Grows Up* (6–8). Illus. 1987, HarperCollins $11.95 (0-06-020606-3). Johnny May, a spunky mountain girl, has no money to continue her schooling after 8th grade. (Rev: BL 10/1/87; BR 3–4/88; SLJ 12/87)

1344 Bridgers, Sue Ellen. *Keeping Christina* (7–10). 1998, Replica Books LB $29.95 (0-7351-0042-X). Annie takes sad newcomer Christina under her wing, but she turns out to be a liar and troublemaker, which creates conflicts with Annie's family, friends, and boyfriend. (Rev: BL 7/93; SLJ 7/93)

1345 Bridgers, Sue Ellen. *Permanent Connections* (8–12). 1998, Replica Books LB $29.95 (0-7351-0043-8). When Rob's behavior gets out of control, the teenager is sent to his uncle's farm to cool off. (Rev: BL 2/15/87; BR 9–10/87; SLJ 3/87; VOYA 4/87)

1346 Brooks, Martha. *Being with Henry* (7–12). 2000, DK paper $17.99 (0-7894-2588-2). This coming-of-age story is about 16-year-old Laker who has been kicked out of his home, and his friendship with Henry, a 83-year-old widower. (Rev: BL 4/1/00; HB 5–6/00; HBG 9/00; SLJ 5/00; VOYA 6/00)

1347 Brooks, Martha. *Traveling On into the Light* (7–12). 1994, Orchard LB $16.99 (0-531-08713-1). Stories about runaways, suicide, and desertion, featuring romantic, sensitive, and smart teenage outsiders. (Rev: BL 8/94; SLJ 8/94*; VOYA 10/94)

1348 Bunting, Eve. *Blackwater* (5–8). 1999, HarperCollins LB $15.89 (0-06-027843-9). Brodie feels responsible for the drowning deaths of two young teenagers, but is unable to tell the truth and admit his guilt. (Rev: HBG 3/00; SLJ 8/99)

1349 Bunting, Eve. *Doll Baby* (5–10). 2000, Clarion $15.00 (0-395-93094-4). A simple, direct narrative in which 15-year-old Ellie explains how being pregnant and having a baby radically changed her life. (Rev: BL 11/1/00; HB 9–10/00; HBG 3/01; SLJ 10/00)

1350 Bunting, Eve. *If I Asked You, Would You Stay?* (8–10). 1984, HarperCollins LB $12.89 (0-397-32066-3). Two lonely people find comfort in love for each other.

1351 Bunting, Eve. *Jumping the Nail* (7–12). 1991, Harcourt $15.95 (0-15-241357-X). A dependent, unstable girl becomes unhinged when she is persuaded by her danger-seeking boyfriend to jump off a cliff with him. (Rev: BL 11/1/91; SLJ 12/91)

1352 Burch, Robert. *Queenie Peavy* (5–7). 1987, Penguin paper $5.99 (0-14-032305-8). Queenie, whose father is in prison, is growing up a defiant, disobedient girl in rural Georgia in the 1930s.

1353 Butler, Charles. *Timon's Tide* (6–12). 2000, Simon & Schuster $16.00 (0-689-82593-5). A surreal story about 17-year-old Daniel and how he gains control of his life through the intervention of his dead older brother. (Rev: BL 6/1–15/00; HBG 9/00; SLJ 6/00; VOYA 6/00)

1354 Byars, Betsy. *The Night Swimmers* (5–6). 1983, Bantam paper $4.50 (0-440-45857-9). An enterprising girl tries to be a housekeeper and to take care of her two brothers.

1355 Cadnum, Michael. *Breaking the Fall* (8–12). 1992, Viking $15.00 (0-670-84687-2). To help him forget that his parents are separating and he isn't playing baseball anymore, Stanley and Jared start housebreaking, taking token items to mark their daring. (Rev: BL 11/15/92; SLJ 9/92)

1356 Caldwell, V. M. *The Ocean Within* (5–7). 1999, Milkweed $15.95 (1-57131-623-X); paper $6.95 (1-57131-624-8). Elizabeth, who is on her third set of foster parents since she was orphaned five years before, has built walls of silence around herself that are impossible to penetrate. (Rev: BCCB 1/00; BL 9/1/99; HBG 3/00; SLJ 11/99; VOYA 4/00)

1357 Caldwell, V. M. *Tides* (5–7). Illus. 2001, Milkweed $16.95 (1-57131-628-0); paper $6.95 (1-57131-629-9). In this sequel to *The Ocean Within*, Elizabeth, age 12, has been adopted for a year but continues to find it difficult to fit into the family's way of life. (Rev: BCCB 7–8/01; BL 4/15/01; HBG 10/01; SLJ 8/01; VOYA 8/01)

1358 Caletti, Deb. *The Queen of Everything* (8–12). 2002, Simon & Schuster paper $5.99 (0-7434-3684-9). Jordan's life is turned upside-down by her grandmother's death, her father's new romance, and her own sexual experimentation. (Rev: BCCB 1/03; BL 11/15/02; SLJ 11/02; VOYA 2/03)

1359 Calvert, Patricia. *The Stone Pony* (7–9). 1983, NAL paper $2.99 (0-451-13729-9). In this touching novel, Jo Beth must adjust to the death of her older sister.

1360 Cameron, Ann. *Colibri* (5–8). 2003, Farrar $17.00 (0-374-31519-1). Twelve-year-old Rosa, who was kidnapped from her Mayan village when she was four, seeks to escape from the abusive "uncle" who is exploiting her. (Rev: BCCB 10/03; BL 10/1/03*; BR 9–10/03; HB 9–10/03; SLJ 10/03*)

1361 Cannon, A. E. *The Shadow Brothers* (7–12). 1992, Dell paper $3.99 (0-440-21167-0). Two foster brothers, one an American Indian, gradually grow apart under the strain of outside pressures. (Rev: BL 5/1/90; BR 5–6/90; SLJ 6/90)

1362 Capote, Truman. *The Thanksgiving Visitor* (5–7). 1996, Knopf $19.00 (0-679-83898-8). Buddy conquers his loneliness and fear of a bully, Odd Henderson, through his friendship with Miss Sook. (Rev: BL 10/15/96; SLJ 12/96)

1363 Cart, Michael. *My Father's Scar* (7–12). 1996, Simon & Schuster paper $16.00 (0-689-80749-X). Andy Logan, a college freshman, is about to have his first gay relationship and recalls growing up a lonely boy in a homophobic community. (Rev: BL 4/1/96; BR 3–4/97; SLJ 5/96; VOYA 8/96)

1364 Carter, Alden R. *Dogwolf* (7–10). 1994, Scholastic paper $13.95 (0-590-46741-7). In this coming-of-age novel, Pete realizes that a dogwolf that he's set free must be found and killed before it kills a human. (Rev: BL 1/1/95; SLJ 4/95; VOYA 2/95)

1365 Caseley, Judith. *Praying to A. L.* (5–8). 2000, Greenwillow $15.95 (0-688-15934-6). After her father dies, 12-year-old Sierra transfers all her love to a portrait of Abraham Lincoln given to her by her father. (Rev: BL 5/15/00; HBG 10/00; SLJ 6/00)

1366 Chan, Gillian. *Glory Days and Other Stories* (7–10). 1997, Kids Can $16.95 (1-55074-381-3). Five stories about young people at Elmwood High School, each of whom faces problems because of decisions that have been made. (Rev: BL 1/1–15/98; SLJ 10/97)

1367 Chan, Gillian. *Golden Girl and Other Stories* (7–10). 1997, Kids Can $14.95 (1-55074-385-6). Short stories about students in a high school, with details of their pleasures, pains, and concerns. (Rev: BL 9/15/97; SLJ 11/97)

1368 Choi, Sook N. *Gathering of Pearls* (7–10). 1994, Houghton $16.00 (0-395-67437-9). Sookan Bak leaves Korea in 1954 to attend a New York women's college, where she struggles to fit in. Second sequel to *The Year of Impossible Goodbyes*. (Rev: BL 9/1/94; SLJ 10/94; VOYA 10/94)

1369 Clarke, Judith. *Night Train* (8–11). 2000, Holt $16.95 (0-8050-6151-7). Luke Leman, an Australian teenager, finds that he is cracking under scholastic and family pressures and thinks he might be going insane. (Rev: BCCB 5/00; BL 6/1–15/00; HBG 9/00; SLJ 5/00)

1370 Cleary, Beverly. *Dear Mr. Henshaw* (4–7). 1983, Morrow LB $16.89 (0-688-02406-8); Dell paper $4.50 (0-440-41794-5). A Newbery Medal winner (1984) about a boy who pours out his problems in letters to a writer he greatly admires.

1371 Cleaver, Vera, and Bill Cleaver. *Ellen Grae* (6–8). 1967, HarperCollins LB $12.89 (0-397-30938-4). Ellen Grae, an imaginative girl, finds it impossible to assimilate the story of the death of her friend Ira's parents. Included in this volume is the sequel *Lady Ellen Grae*.

1372 Cleaver, Vera, and Bill Cleaver. *Grover* (6–9). 1987, HarperCollins $13.95 (0-397-31118-4). The death of his beloved mother seems more than Grover can handle. A reissue.

1373 Cleaver, Vera, and Bill Cleaver. *Hazel Rye* (6–9). 1983, HarperCollins LB $13.89 (0-397-31952-5); paper $3.95 (0-06-440156-1). Eleven-year-old Hazel rents the Poole family a small house in a citrus grove.

1374 Cohen, Miriam. *Robert and Dawn Marie 4Ever* (6–9). 1986, HarperCollins $11.95 (0-06-021396-5). Robert, a street waif, finds a new home and forms a friendship with Dawn Marie, a young girl whose mother disapproves of Robert. (Rev: BL 11/1/86; SLJ 12/86; VOYA 12/86)

1375 Cole, Brock. *The Goats* (6–9). 1987, Farrar paper $5.95 (0-374-42575-2). Two misfits at sum-mcr camp find inner strength and self knowledge when they are cruelly marooned on an island by fellow campers. (Rev: BL 11/15/87; SLJ 11/87; VOYA 4/88)

1376 Cole, Sheila. *What Kind of Love?* (8–10). 1995, Lothrop $15.00 (0-688-12848-3). A 15-year-old becomes pregnant and deals with hard decisions. (Rev: BL 3/15/95; SLJ 5/95)

1377 Collins, Pat L. *Signs and Wonders* (7–10). 1999, Houghton $15.00 (0-395-97119-5). Through letters to her grandmother, her father, and an imaginary guardian angel, a young girl in boarding school reveals her feelings of unhappiness, loneliness, and betrayal — and her belief that she has been chosen to bear the prophet of the next millennium. (Rev: BCCB 11/99; BL 10/1/99; HBG 4/00; SLJ 10/99; VOYA 10/99)

1378 Conford, Ellen. *Crush* (7–12). 1998, HarperCollins $15.95 (0-06-025414-9). In this collection of interrelated short stories, high school students face problems such as peer pressure, self-esteem, respect, alienation, greed, and heartbreak. (Rev: BCCB 3/98; BL 1/1–15/98; HB 3–4/98; HBG 9/98; SLJ 1/98; VOYA 6/98)

1379 Conford, Ellen. *Hail, Hail Camp Timberwood* (5–7). 1978, Little, Brown $14.95 (0-316-15291-9). Thirteen-year-old Melanie's first summer at camp.

1380 Conford, Ellen. *You Never Can Tell* (7–9). 1984, Little, Brown $14.95 (0-316-15267-6). Katie's soap opera heartthrob enters her high school.

1381 Conly, Jane L. *Crazy Lady!* (5–8). 1993, HarperCollins LB $16.89 (0-06-021360-4). In a city slum, Vernon forms a friendship with an eccentric woman and helps her care for her disabled teenage son. (Rev: BCCB 7–8/93; BL 5/15/93*; SLJ 4/93*)

1382 Conly, Jane L. *Trout Summer* (6–8). 1995, Holt $15.95 (0-8050-3933-3). During a summer spent in a rustic cabin with her mother and brother, 13-year-old Shana meets a crotchety neighbor and adjusts to her grandfather's death and father's desertion. (Rev: BL 1/1–15/96; BR 9–10/96; SLJ 12/95; VOYA 2/96)

1383 Conly, Jane L. *What Happened on Planet Kid* (4–8). 2000, Holt $16.95 (0-8050-6065-0). Twelve-year-old Dawn learns a lot about life, herself, and her dreams of becoming a major league pitcher during the summer she spends on a farm with her aunt and uncle. (Rev: BCCB 4/00; BL 5/15/00; HB 5–6/00; HBG 10/00; SLJ 5/00)

1384 Conly, Jane L. *When No One Was Watching* (5–8). 1995, Holt $16.95 (0-8050-3934-1). Three siblings face personal problems when they are forced to spend a summer with their Aunt Lulu in a squalid city row house. (Rev: BCCB 9/98; BL 5/15/98; HB 7–8/98*; HBG 10/98; SLJ 7/98)

1385 Cooney, Caroline B. *Driver's Ed* (7–12). 1994, Delacorte $16.95 (0-385-32087-6). Remy and Morgan are driving around town on an escapade ripping off street signs when they accidentally cause the death of an innocent pedestrian. (Rev: BL 6/1–15/94*; SLJ 8/94; VOYA 10/94)

1386 Cooney, Caroline B. *Summer Nights* (7–12). 1992, Scholastic paper $3.25 (0-590-45786-1). At a farewell party, five high school girls look back on their school years and their friendship. (Rev: SLJ 1/89)

1387 Cooney, Caroline B. *What Child Is This? A Christmas Story* (6–10). 1997, Delacorte $14.95 (0-385-32317-4). In a New England community, three teenagers and a child try to find what Christmas is all about. (Rev: BL 9/1/97; HBG 3/98; SLJ 10/97; VOYA 12/97)

1388 Cooper, Ilene. *Star-Spangled Summer* (5–8). Series: Holiday Five. 1996, Viking $14.99 (0-670-85655-X). Five 6th-grade girls struggle to make sure that their plans for summer camp are not spoiled. (Rev: BL 4/15/96; SLJ 5/96)

1389 Corcoran, Barbara. *You Put Up with Me, I'll Put Up with You* (6–8). 1989, Avon paper $2.50 (0-380-70558-3). A somewhat self-centered girl moves with her mother to a new community and has problems adjusting. (Rev: BL 3/15/87; BR 11–12/87; SLJ 3/87; VOYA 4/87)

1390 Cormier, Robert. *The Chocolate War* (7–12). 1993, Dell paper $3.99 (0-440-90032-8). A chocolate sale in a boys' private school creates power struggles. Followed by *Beyond the Chocolate War*.

1391 Cormier, Robert. *Frenchtown Summer* (6–10). 1999, Delacorte $16.95 (0-385-32704-8). A verse novel about a boy growing up in a small town in Massachusetts after World War I, the father he can't seem to reach, and the first pangs of adolescence. (Rev: BCCB 11/99; BL 9/15/99; HB 9–10/99; HBG 4/00; SLJ 9/99; VOYA 12/99)

1392 Cormier, Robert. *I Am the Cheese* (7–12). 1977, Pantheon $19.95 (0-394-83462-3). A multilevel novel about a boy's life after his parents are forced to go underground. (Rev: BL 6/1/88; HBG 3/98)

1393 Cormier, Robert. *The Rag and Bone Shop* (8–10). 2001, Delacorte $15.95 (0-385-72962-6). Shy, introverted 13-year-old Jason is a suspect in the murder of a 7-year-old girl in this dark and suspenseful story that features an ambitious and ruthless detective. (Rev: BCCB 12/01; BL 7/01; HB 11–12/01; HBG 3/02; SLJ 9/01; VOYA 10/01)

1394 Cormier, Robert. *Tunes for Bears to Dance To* (6–12). 1992, Dell paper $5.50 (0-440-21903-5). In a stark morality tale set in a Massachusetts town after World War II, Henry, 11, is tempted, corrupted, and redeemed. (Rev: BL 6/15/92; SLJ 9/92)

1395 Cormier, Robert. *We All Fall Down* (8–12). 1991, Dell paper $5.50 (0-440-21556-0). Random violence committed by four high school seniors is observed by the Avenger, who also witnesses the budding love affair of one of the victims of the attack. (Rev: BL 9/15/91*; SLJ 9/91*)

1396 Coryell, Susan. *Eaglebait* (6–9). 1989, Harcourt $14.95 (0-15-200442-4). An unpopular teenage nerd thinks he has found a friend in a new science teacher. (Rev: BL 11/1/89; SLJ 6/90)

1397 Cossi, Olga. *The Magic Box* (7–9). 1990, Pelican $12.95 (0-88289-748-9). Mara cannot seem to give up smoking until her mother, a former smoker, develops throat cancer. (Rev: BL 10/15/90; SLJ 8/90; VOYA 8/90)

1398 Cottonwood, Joe. *Babcock* (7–10). 1996, Scholastic paper $15.95 (0-590-22221-X). A teenager named Babcock recounts with humor and insight several months of his life in a town in the California Bay area, including everyday school experiences, falling in love, playing softball, and coping with an unexpected visit by an unwanted uncle. (Rev: BR 11–12/96; VOYA 6/97)

1399 Creech, Sharon. *Bloomability* (5–8). 1998, HarperCollins LB $16.89 (0-06-026994-4). In this amusing first-person narrative, middle-schooler Dinnie adjusts to her "second life" at a school in Switzerland as she makes friends from around the world and gains a sense of her own self-worth. (Rev: BCCB 10/98; BL 9/15/98; HB 9–10/98; HBG 3/99; SLJ 10/98; VOYA 2/99)

1400 Creech, Sharon. *Chasing Redbird* (6–9). 1997, HarperCollins LB $16.89 (0-06-026988-X). Thirteen-year-old Zinny, who lives in Appalachia, is trying to understand herself while adjusting to the death of her beloved Aunt Jessie. (Rev: BL 3/15/97; BR 9–10/97; HB 5–6/97; SLJ 4/97*)

1401 Creel, Ann Howard. *Nowhere, Now Here* (5–7). 2000, Pleasant $12.95 (1-58485-200-3). Twelve-year-old Laney is unhappy when she and her parents move from Florida to Colorado, where they plan to raise alpacas. (Rev: BL 9/15/00; HBG 10/01; SLJ 1/01)

1402 Cross, Gillian. *Tightrope* (7–12). 1999, Holiday $16.95 (0-8234-1512-0). To take her mind off the hours she spends caring for her invalid mother, Ashley begins to hang out with a local street gang. (Rev: BCCB 12/99; BL 9/15/99; HBG 4/00; SLJ 10/99; VOYA 4/00)

1403 Crowe, Carole. *Waiting for Dolphins* (6–12). 2000, Boyds Mills $16.95 (1-56397-847-4). Still recovering from her father's death in a boating incident, Molly must also adjust to her mother's new love interest. (Rev: BL 3/1/00; HBG 9/00; SLJ 4/00; VOYA 6/00)

1404 Cruise, Robin. *The Top-Secret Journal of Fiona Claire Jardin* (4–7). 1998, Harcourt $13.00 (0-15-201383-0). At the advice of her therapist, Fiona, age 11, keeps a journal about her problems, chiefly coping with her parents' divorce and living under a joint-custody agreement. (Rev: BL 4/15/98; HBG 10/98; SLJ 4/98)

1405 Crutcher, Chris. *Athletic Shorts: 6 Short Stories* (8–12). 1991, Greenwillow $16.95 (0-688-10816-4). These short stories focus on themes important to teens, such as sports, father-son friction, insecurity, and friendship. (Rev: BL 10/15/91; SLJ 9/91*)

1406 Cummings, Priscilla. *A Face First* (5–8). 2001, Dutton $16.99 (0-525-46522-7). After being severely burned in a car accident, Kelly sinks into a terrible depression particularly after she is told that she will have to wear a plastic face mask for two years. (Rev: BCCB 2/01; BL 2/1/01; HBG 10/01; SLJ 2/01; VOYA 2/01)

1407 Danziger, Paula. *Can You Sue Your Parents for Malpractice?* (6–9). 1998, Putnam paper $4.99 (0-698-11688-7). Lauren, 14 years old, faces a variety of problems both at home and at school.

1408 Danziger, Paula. *The Cat Ate My Gymsuit* (6–9). 1998, Demco paper $11.04 (0-606-13091-8). Marcy hates gym but finds in her school a supportive teacher. A sequel is *There's a Bat in Bunk Five* (1980).

1409 Danziger, Paula. *Remember Me to Harold Square* (6–9). Illus. 1999, Putnam paper $4.99 (0-698-11694-1). Kendra gets to know attractive Frank when they participate in scavenger hunts in New York City. (Rev: BL 10/1/87; BR 11–12/87; SLJ 11/87; VOYA 12/87)

1410 Deak, Erzsi, and Kristin Embry Litchman, eds. *Period Pieces: Stories for Girls* (4–8). 2003, HarperCollins LB $16.89 (0-06-623797-1). A collection of 13 stories about girls' experiences with their first periods, featuring a variety of characters and settings. (Rev: BCCB 3/03; BL 3/15/03; HBG 10/03; SLJ 3/03)

1411 Dean, Carolee. *Comfort* (7–10). 2002, Houghton $15.00 (0-618-13846-3). Fourteen-year-old Kenny persists in his dreams of making something of himself in spite of his mother's conflicting desires. (Rev: HBG 10/02; SLJ 3/02*; VOYA 4/02)

1412 Dessen, Sarah. *Dreamland* (8–10). 2000, Viking $15.99 (0-670-89122-3). After her sister runs away, Caitlin's life comes apart and she descends into drugs and sex. (Rev: BL 11/1/00; HB 9–10/00; HBG 3/01; SLJ 9/00)

1413 Dessen, Sarah. *Keeping the Moon* (6–10). 1999, Viking $15.99 (0-670-88549-5). Colie, a 15-year-old girl with little self-esteem, spends a summer with an eccentric aunt and finds a kind of salvation in a friendship with two waitresses and the love of a shy teenage artist. (Rev: BL 9/1/99; HBG 4/00; SLJ 9/99; VOYA 12/99)

1414 Dessen, Sarah. *Someone Like You* (7–12). 1998, Viking $16.99 (0-670-87778-6). Young Halley discovers that her best friend Scarlett is pregnant and Scarlett's boyfriend has been killed in an accident. (Rev: BL 5/15/98; HB 7–8/98; HBG 9/98; SLJ 6/98; VOYA 8/98)

1415 Dessen, Sarah. *That Summer* (7–12). 1996, Orchard LB $17.99 (0-531-08888-X). Haven is 15 and 5 feet 11, and to make matters worse, she has to be bridesmaid at her picture-perfect sister's wedding. (Rev: BL 10/15/96*; BR 3–4/97; SLJ 10/96; VOYA 12/96)

1416 De Vries, Anke. *Bruises* (6–10). Trans. by Stacey Knecht. 1996, Front Street $15.95 (1-886910-03-0); Dell paper $4.50 (0-440-22694-5). This novel, set in Holland, tells of the friendship between a sympathetic boy, Michael, and Judith, a disturbed, abused young girl. (Rev: BL 4/1/96; SLJ 6/96; VOYA 6/96)

1417 Dines, Carol. *Talk to Me: Stories and a Novella* (8–12). 1997, Bantam $15.95 (0-385-32271-2). Teenage problems like romance, family relations, jobs, and school troubles are the subjects of these six stories and a novella. (Rev: BL 7/97; BR 9–10/97; SLJ 7/97; VOYA 8/97)

1418 Doherty, Berlie. *Dear Nobody* (7–12). 1992, Morrow paper $5.95 (0-688-12764-9). This complex novel explores the consequences of a teenager's pregnancy and the resulting tensions with her boyfriend. (Rev: BL 10/1/92*; SLJ 10/92*)

1419 Doyle, Malachy. *Who Is Jesse Flood?* (6–9). 2002, Bloomsbury $14.95 (1-58234-776-X). Unhappy 14-year-old Jesse struggles to cope with his parents and his loneliness in his Northern Ireland hometown. (Rev: BCCB 12/02; BL 10/1/02; SLJ 10/02*)

1420 Draper, Sharon M. *Romiette and Julio* (6–10). 1999, Simon & Schuster $16.00 (0-689-82180-8). An updated version of Romeo and Juliet set in contemporary Cincinnati involving a Hispanic American boy, an African American girl, street gangs, and, in this case, a happy ending. (Rev: BL 9/15/99; HBG 4/00; SLJ 9/99; VOYA 12/99)

1421 Dreyer, Ellen. *Speechless in New York: Going to New York* (5–8). Series: Going To. 2000, Four Corners paper $7.95 (1-893577-01-5). Jessie is beset with personal problems when she flies to New York from Minnesota with the Prairie Youth Chorale. (Rev: SLJ 3/00)

1422 Duncan, Lois. *Trapped! Cages of the Mind and Body* (7–12). 1998, Simon & Schuster $16.00 (0-689-81335-X). Limitations caused by the mind and/or the body are explored in 13 stories, each by a different YA writer. (Rev: BL 7/98; HBG 3/99; SLJ 6/98; VOYA 8/98)

1423 Elish, Dan. *Born Too Short: Confessions of an Eighth-Grade Basket Case* (6–8). 2002, Simon & Schuster $16.00 (0-689-84386-0). Thirteen-year-old Matt details his jealousy of his successful, good-looking friend Keith and his anxiety about love in this humorous first-person narrative. (Rev: BL 2/1/02; HBG 10/02; SLJ 2/02)

1424 Ellis, Deborah. *Looking for X* (6–9). 2000, Douglas & McIntyre $15.95 (0-88899-378-1); paper $7.95 (0-88899-382-X). Khyber, a waif who is considered a loner by her classmates, is wrongfully accused of vandalism. (Rev: BCCB 9/00; BL 5/15/00; HB 7–8/00; HBG 9/00; SLJ 7/00)

1425 Ellis, Sarah. *Pick-Up Sticks* (5–8). 1992, Macmillan LB $15.00 (0-689-50550-7). A disgruntled teen learns a lesson in life after being sent to live with relatives. (Rev: BL 1/15/92; SLJ 3/92*)

1426 Evans, Douglas. *So What Do You Do?* (5–8). 1997, Front Street $14.95 (1-886910-20-0). Two middle-schoolers help their beloved former teacher who has become a homeless drunk. (Rev: BCCB 3/98; BL 11/1/97; BR 3–4/98; HBG 3/98; SLJ 1/98; VOYA 2/98)

1427 Eyerly, Jeannette. *Someone to Love Me* (7–10). 1987, HarperCollins LB $11.89 (0-397-32206-2). An unpopular high school girl is seduced by the school's glamor boy and decides, when she finds she is pregnant, to keep the child. (Rev: BL 2/1/87; BR 9–10/87; SLJ 4/87; VOYA 4/87)

1428 Facklam, Margery. *The Trouble with Mothers* (6–8). 1991, Avon paper $2.95 (0-380-71139-7). Troy is angered when the town censors target his mother's historical novel. (Rev: BL 3/1/89; SLJ 5/89; VOYA 6/89)

1429 Farish, Terry. *Talking in Animal* (7–9). 1996, Greenwillow $15.00 (0-688-14671-6). Siobhan lives partly in a fantasy world that revolves around training her beloved dog, Tree, to win competitions, but she moves toward reality when Tree becomes more and more sick and must be put down. (Rev: BR 11–12/96; SLJ 11/96; VOYA 4/97)

1430 Ferris, Jean. *Bad* (7–10). 1998, Farrar paper $4.95 (0-374-40475-5). Dallas gains self knowledge when she is sent to a women's correctional center for six months and meets gang members, drug dealers, a 14-year-old prostitute, and other unfortunates. (Rev: BL 10/1/98; SLJ 12/98; VOYA 2/99)

1431 Ferris, Jean. *Eight Seconds* (6–12). 2000, Harcourt $17.00 (0-15-202367-4). At rodeo camp, 18-year-old Ritchie discovers that his new rodeo friend is gay. (Rev: BL 10/1/00; HBG 3/01; SLJ 1/01)

1432 Ferris, Jean. *Of Sound Mind* (6–9). 2001, Farrar $16.00 (0-374-35580-0). High school senior Theo, who is the only hearing member of his demanding family, finds support and romance when he meets Ivy, who also can both hear and sign. (Rev: BCCB 10/01; BL 9/15/01; HB 11–12/01; HBG 3/02; SLJ 9/01; VOYA 10/01)

1433 Ferry, Charles. *A Fresh Start* (7–10). 1996, Proctor paper $8.95 (1-882792-18-1). This novel explores the problems of troubled teens in a summer-school program for young alcoholics. (Rev: SLJ 5/96; VOYA 10/96)

1434 Fienberg, Anna. *Borrowed Light* (8–10). 2000, Delacorte $14.95 (0-385-32758-7). Using many astrological images, the author of this novel tells about Callisto's pregnancy, her abortion, and her other family and personal problems. (Rev: BL 6/1–15/00; HB 7–8/00; HBG 9/00; SLJ 6/00)

1435 Filichia, Peter. *What's in a Name?* (7–12). 1988, Avon paper $2.75 (0-380-75536-X). Rose is so unhappy with her foreign-sounding last name that she decides to change it. (Rev: BL 3/1/89; VOYA 4/89)

1436 Fitzhugh, Louise. *Harriet the Spy* (6–8). 2001, Random paper $5.99 (0-440-41679-5). The story of a girl whose passion for honesty gets her into trouble. Followed by *The Long Secret*.

1437 Flake, Sharon G. *A Freak Like Me* (5–9). 1999, Hyperion paper $5.99 (0-7868-1307-5). In her inner-city middle school, Maleeka Madison is picked on by classmates because she is poorly dressed, darker than the others, and gets good grades. (Rev: BL 9/1/98; SLJ 11/98)

1438 Fleischman, Paul. *Whirligig* (7–10). 1998, Holt $16.95 (0-8050-5582-7). As penance for killing a teenager in an automobile accident, Brent must fashion four whirligigs and place them in the four corners of the United States. (Rev: BL 4/1/98; HB 7–8/98; HBG 9/98; SLJ 4/98; VOYA 6/98)

1439 Fletcher, Ralph J. *Spider Boy* (5–8). 1997, Houghton $15.00 (0-395-77606-6). Bobby — nicknamed Spider Boy because he knows so much about spiders — has trouble adjusting to his new life in the town of New Paltz, New York. (Rev: BCCB 4/97; BL 6/1–15/97; HB 7–8/97; SLJ 7/97)

1440 Flinn, Alex. *Breaking Point* (7–10). 2002, HarperCollins $15.95 (0-06-623847-1). Paul is so desperate to be accepted at his new school that he allows himself to be lured into increasingly perilous situations. (Rev: BL 9/1/02; HBG 10/02; SLJ 5/02; VOYA 6/02)

1441 Foon, Dennis. *Double or Nothing* (6–12). 2000, Annick $17.95 (1-55037-627-6); paper $6.95 (1-55037-626-8). High school senior Kip feels secure that he has saved enough money for college until he meets King, a magician and con artist who takes advantage of Kip's love of gambling. (Rev: BL 8/00; HBG 9/00; SLJ 9/00)

1442 Fox, Paula. *Monkey Island* (5–8). 1991, Watts LB $16.99 (0-531-08562-7). A homeless, abandoned 11-year-old boy in New York City contracts pneumonia and is cared for by a homeless African American teenager and retired teacher, who share

their place in the park with him. (Rev: BCCB 10/91*; BL 9/1/91*; HB 9–10/91*; SLJ 8/91)

1443 Fox, Paula. *A Place Apart* (7–9). 1993, Farrar paper $3.95 (0-374-45868-5). In a small town where she and her mother have moved after her father's death, Victoria meets the unusual Hugh Todd.

1444 Fox, Paula. *Western Wind* (5–9). 1993, Orchard LB $17.99 (0-531-08652-6). At first resentful of being sent to spend a summer with her grandmother on a Maine island, Elizabeth gradually adjusts and learns a great deal about herself. (Rev: BCCB 9/93; BL 10/15/93; SLJ 12/93*; VOYA 12/93)

1445 Franco, Betsy, ed. *Things I Have to Tell You: Poems and Writing by Teenage Girls* (7–12). Photos by Nina Nickles. 2001, Candlewick $15.99 (0-7636-0905-6); paper $8.99 (0-7636-1035-6). Teen girls reveal their aspirations, fears, and frustrations in this appealing collection of poems, stories, and essays. (Rev: BL 3/15/01; BR 11–12/01; HB 5–6/01; HBG 10/01; SLJ 5/01; VOYA 10/01)

1446 Frank, E. R. *Life Is Funny* (7–12). 2000, DK paper $19.99 (0-7894-2634-X). This novel of intersecting stories features the aspirations, problems, and everyday life of 11 teens growing up in Brooklyn. (Rev: BL 3/15/00; HB 5–6/00; HBG 9/00; SLJ 5/00; VOYA 6/00)

1447 Fredericks, Mariah. *The True Meaning of Cleavage* (7–10). 2003, Simon & Schuster $15.95 (0-689-85092-1). High school freshman Jess describes her friend Sari's obsession with an older student in this novel of sexuality, betrayal, and self-image. (Rev: BCCB 3/03; BL 3/15/03*; HB 7–8/03; HBG 10/03; SLJ 2/03; VOYA 4/03)

1448 Freeman, Martha. *The Year My Parents Ruined My Life* (6–9). 1997, Holiday $15.95 (0-8234-1324-1). Twelve-year-old Kate has many problems adjusting to her new home in a small Pennsylvania town and longs to return to the suburbs of Los Angeles, her friends, and dreamy boyfriend. (Rev: BL 12/1/97; HBG 3/98; SLJ 12/97)

1449 Freymann-Weyr, Garret. *My Heartbeat* (8–12). 2002, Houghton $15.00 (0-618-14181-2). Fourteen-year-old Ellen is in love with James, but James and her older brother Link are also involved. (Rev: BCCB 5/02; BL 6/1–15/02; HB 5–6/02*; HBG 10/02; SLJ 4/02; VOYA 4/02)

1450 Friel, Maeve. *Charlie's Story* (8–10). 1997, Peachtree $14.95 (0-56145-167-3). Charlie, who was abandoned by her mother as a child, now lives with her father in Ireland and, at age 14, is facing a group of bullies at school who accuse her of a theft and cause a terrible field hockey incident. (Rev: BL 1/1–15/98; VOYA 2/98)

1451 Friesen, Gayle. *Men of Stone* (5–8). 2000, Kids Can $16.95 (1-55074-781-9). While Ben Conrad traces his own family roots, he confronts a local bully in this story of a boy's journey to maturity. (Rev: HBG 3/01; SLJ 10/00; VOYA 2/01)

1452 Froese, Deborah. *Out of the Fire* (8–11). 2002, Sumach paper $7.95 (1-894549-09-0). Sixteen-year-old Dayle is badly burned at a riotous bonfire party and spends the painful months that follow reassessing her feelings about friends and family. (Rev: BL 7/02; SLJ 8/02)

1453 Fromm, Pete. *Monkey Tag* (4–7). 1994, Scholastic paper $14.95 (0-590-46525-2). When his twin is paralyzed from an accident, Eli feels partly responsible. (Rev: BCCB 12/94; BL 10/15/94; SLJ 10/94)

1454 Frost, Helen. *Keesha's House* (6–10). 2003, Farrar $16.00 (0-374-34064-1). Keesha reaches out to other teens in trouble as they describe their problems in brief, poetic vignettes. (Rev: BL 3/1/03; HBG 10/03; SLJ 3/03*; VOYA 4/03)

1455 Gabhart, Ann. *Bridge to Courage* (6–8). 1993, Avon paper $3.50 (0-380-76051-7). Luke is afraid of bridges and walks away from the initiation rites of the elite Truelanders, who then shun him. Luke finally learns self-confidence in this deftly plotted tale. (Rev: BL 5/15/93; VOYA 10/93)

1456 Gallo, Donald, ed. *On the Fringe* (7–10). 2001, Dial $17.99 (0-8037-2656-2). Stories about outsiders — geeks, nerds, loners, and other "misfits" — are the focus of this anthology of fiction by well-known YA authors. (Rev: BCCB 6/01; BL 3/15/01; HBG 10/01; SLJ 5/01; VOYA 4/01)

1457 Gallo, Donald R., ed. *Destination Unexpected* (7–12). 2003, Candlewick $16.99 (0-7636-1764-4). This is a collection of 10 excellent short stories about teens who are undergoing changes in their lives. (Rev: BL 4/1/03*; HBG 10/03; SLJ 5/03; VOYA 6/03)

1458 Gallo, Donald R., ed. *No Easy Answers: Short Stories About Teenagers Making Tough Choices* (6–12). 1997, Delacorte $16.95 (0-385-32290-9). A collection of short stories by some of today's best writers for young adults, including Ron Koertze and Gloria Miklowitz, about teenagers who face moral and ethical dilemmas. (Rev: BL 11/15/97; BR 5–6/98; SLJ 12/97; VOYA 10/97)

1459 Garden, Nancy. *Holly's Secret* (5–8). 2000, Farrar $16.00 (0-374-33273-8). When Holly and her family move to western Massachusetts, she decides to hide from her new classmates the fact that her parents are lesbians. (Rev: BCCB 9/00; BL 10/15/00; HB 9–10/00; HBG 3/01; SLJ 9/00; VOYA 4/01)

1460 Garden, Nancy. *The Year They Burned the Books* (7–12). 1999, Farrar $17.00 (0-374-38667-6). High school senior Jamie Crawford's problems as editor of the school newspaper under attack by a right-wing group are compounded when she realizes that she is a lesbian and falling in love with Tessa, a new girl in school. (Rev: BL 8/99; HBG 4/00; SLJ 9/99; VOYA 12/99)

1461 Garland, Sherry. *Letters from the Mountain* (6–10). 1996, Harcourt $12.00 (0-15-200661-3); paper $6.00 (0-15-200659-1). Tyler is unhappy spending the summer with elderly relatives and, through a series of letters to his mother and friends, he vents his anger and also tells of his gradual adjustment. (Rev: BL 10/1/96; BR 3–4/97; SLJ 11/96; VOYA 4/97)

1462 Gauthier, Gail. *The Hero of Ticonderoga* (6–8). 2001, Putnam $16.99 (0-399-23559-0). An assignment on Ethan Allen results in new self-confidence and an interest in history on the part of 6th-grader Tessy. (Rev: BCCB 3/01; BL 4/1/01; HBG 10/01; SLJ 2/01)

1463 Gelb, Alan. *Real Life: My Best Friend Died* (7–12). 1995, Pocket Books paper $3.50 (0-671-87273-7). A high school senior, living a happy, normal life, finds his world exploding when he feels responsible for his friend's death. (Rev: BL 4/1/95; SLJ 6/95; VOYA 5/95)

1464 Gifaldi, David. *Rearranging and Other Stories* (6–10). 1998, Simon & Schuster $16.00 (0-689-81750-9). In these nine short stories, young teens face problems related to adolescence and reaching maturity. (Rev: BL 4/15/98; BR 1–2/99; HBG 9/98; SLJ 6/98; VOYA 8/98)

1465 Gilbert, Barbara Snow. *Broken Chords* (8–12). 1998, Front Street $15.95 (1-886910-23-5). As she prepares for the piano competition that could lead to a place at Juilliard, Clara has doubts about a lifetime of sacrifice that a career in music would require. (Rev: BL 12/15/98; HB 11–12/98; HBG 3/99; SLJ 12/98; VOYA 2/99)

1466 Gilbert, Barbara Snow. *Stone Water* (5–9). 1996, Front Street $15.95 (1-886910-11-1). Fourteen-year-old Grant must decide if he will honor his ailing grandfather's wish to help him commit suicide. (Rev: BL 12/15/96; SLJ 12/96*; VOYA 4/97)

1467 Giles, Gail. *Shattering Glass* (8–10). 2002, Millbrook $15.95 (0-7613-1581-0). A suspenseful story of young people manipulating power and popularity that ends in stunning violence. (Rev: BCCB 5/02; BL 3/1/02; HBG 10/02; SLJ 4/02; VOYA 6/02)

1468 Glassman, Miriam. *Box Top Dreams* (4–7). 1998, Delacorte $14.95 (0-385-32532-0). Ari is devastated when her best friend moves away; but through this experience she learns independence. (Rev: BCCB 3/98; BL 2/1/98; HB 5–6/98; HBG 10/98; SLJ 3/98)

1469 Godden, Rumer. *An Episode of Sparrows* (7–10). 1993, Pan Books paper $16.95 (0-330-32779-8). In postwar London two waifs try to grow a secret garden. (Rev: SLJ 6/89)

1470 Golding, Theresa Martin. *Kat's Surrender* (5–8). 1999, Boyds Mills $16.95 (1-56397-755-9). Thirteen-year-old Kat misses her deceased mother terribly, but she tries to hide it in her friendships for an old man and a wacky girl. (Rev: BL 10/15/99; HBG 3/00; SLJ 11/99; VOYA 4/00)

1471 Goldman-Rubin, Susan. *Emily in Love* (6–9). 1997, Harcourt $14.00 (0-15-200961-2). Developmentally disabled Emily of *Emily Good as Gold* (o.p.), deludes herself and deceives those around her in her pursuit of a boyfriend. (Rev: BL 5/15/97; SLJ 5/97; VOYA 6/97)

1472 Gordon, Amy. *The Gorillas of Gill Park* (4–7). Illus. 2003, Holiday $16.95 (0-8234-1751-4). Shy, lonely Willie comes into his own when he spends the summer with his eccentric Aunt Bridget and meets her zany neighbors. (Rev: BL 6/1–15/03; HBG 10/03; SLJ 5/03)

1473 Gordon, Amy. *When JFK Was My Father* (5–9). 1999, Houghton $15.00 (0-395-91364-0). Georgia, who often imagines that President Kennedy is her caring father, has several problems including divorcing parents and adjustment to a Connecticut boarding school. (Rev: BL 6/1–15/99; HB 7–8/99; HBG 10/99; SLJ 4/99; VOYA 6/99)

1474 Grant, Cynthia D. *The Cannibals: Starring Tiffany Spratt* (7–10). 2002, Millbrook $15.95 (0-7613-1642-6). Tiffany's senior year is definitely not what she had hoped for in this satirical tale of a pretty student with grand aspirations. (Rev: BL 10/1/02; HBG 3/03; SLJ 9/02; VOYA 12/02)

1475 Gray, Dianne E. *Holding Up the Earth* (5–8). 2000, Houghton $15.00 (0-618-00703-2). Sarah, a foster child now living on a Nebraska farm, does some research and uncovers stories of the many generations of women who preceded her on the farm and their struggles and problems. (Rev: BL 1/1–15/01; HB 9–10/00; HBG 3/01; SLJ 10/00)

1476 Gray, Keith. *Creepers* (7–10). 1997, Putnam $15.95 (0-399-23186-2). Creeping is the sport of running the length of a neighborhood through backyards, and two teenagers engage in a particularly difficult creep in this suspenseful British novel. (Rev: BL 2/1/98; HBG 3/98)

1477 Greene, Constance C. *Monday I Love You* (7–10). 1988, HarperCollins $11.95 (0-06-022183-6). An overdeveloped bust is just one of the problems faced by 15-year-old Grace. (Rev: BL 7/88; VOYA 8/88)

1478 Greene, Constance C. *Your Old Pal, Al* (6–8). 1999, Viking paper $3.99 (0-14-036849-3). Al has problems with her father, a boy she recently met, and her best friend. Part of a series.

1479 Griffin, Adele. *Amandine* (6–9). 2001, Hyperion $15.99 (0-7868-0618-4). A chilling story of a dangerous friendship between shy, needy Delia and theatrical, manipulative Amandine. (Rev: BCCB 10/01; BL 9/15/01; HB 11–12/01; HBG 3/02; SLJ 11/01; VOYA 12/01)

1480 Grimes, Nikki. *Bronx Masquerade* (7–12). 2002, Dial $16.99 (0-8037-2569-8). Eighteen high school English students enjoy the weekly open-mike opportunity to express themselves in poetry and prose, revealing much about their lives and their maturing selves. (Rev: BCCB 3/02; BL 2/15/02; HB 3–4/02; HBG 10/02; SLJ 1/02; VOYA 2/02)

1481 Grove, Vicki. *Destiny* (5–9). 2000, Putnam $16.99 (0-399-23449-7). Destiny Louise, age 12, who is growing up in poverty with a mother who only watches TV, finds an outlet in her interest in art and two teachers who befriend her. (Rev: BCCB 9/00; BL 5/1/00; HBG 3/01; SLJ 4/00; VOYA 6/00)

1482 Grove, Vicki. *Reaching Dustin* (5–8). 1998, Putnam paper $5.99 (0-698-11839-1). As part of a 6th-grade assignment, Carly must get to know Dustin Groat, the class outcast, and as she learns more about him and his family, she realizes that her attitudes toward him in the past have helped create his problems. (Rev: BCCB 3/98; BL 5/1/98; BR 11–12/98; SLJ 5/98)

1483 Haas, Jessie. *Skipping School* (7–10). 1992, Greenwillow $14.00 (0-688-10179-8). A realistic, ultimately upbeat portrait of a boy's reluctant coming-of-age and of a family's eventual acceptance of death. (Rev: BL 11/15/92; SLJ 11/92)

1484 Haas, Jessie. *Unbroken: A Novel* (5–8). 1999, HarperCollins $14.95 (0-688-16260-6). A powerful story of a 13-year-old girl's adjustment to her mother's death and her efforts to train a stubborn colt so that she can ride him to school. (Rev: BL 3/15/99; HB 7–8/99; HBG 10/99; SLJ 4/99*; VOYA 8/99)

1485 Haas, Jessie. *Will You, Won't You?* (5–8). 2000, Greenwillow LB $15.89 (0-06-029197-4). Mad (short for Madison) is a shy middle-schooler who comes out of her shell during a summer she spends with her wise grandmother in the country. (Rev: BCCB 10/00; BL 2/1/01; HBG 3/01; SLJ 10/00)

1486 Haddix, Margaret P. *Just Ella* (7–12). 1999, Simon & Schuster $17.00 (0-689-82186-7). The story of Cinderella after the ball, when she finds out that castle life with Prince Charming isn't all it's cut out to be, meets a social activist tutor, and rethinks her priorities in life. (Rev: BCCB 11/99; BL 9/1/99; HBG 4/00; SLJ 9/99; VOYA 12/99)

1487 Hahn, Mary D. *Following My Own Footsteps* (5–8). 1996, Clarion $15.00 (0-395-76477-7). Living with a grandmother to escape a drunken, abusive father, Gordy has problems adjusting and becomes friends with the boy next door, who has polio and is wheelchair bound. (Rev: BCCB 10/96; BL 9/15/96*; HB 9–10/96; SLJ 11/96)

1488 Haines, J. D. *Vision Quest: Journey to Manhood* (6–9). 1999, Arrowsmith paper $11.95 (0-

9653119 0 2). A 13-year-old boy is mentored by his Native American grandfather when he and his mother move from gang-ridden Chicago to the wilderness of Oklahoma. (Rev: BL 9/1/99)

1489 Hall, Lynn. *Where Have All the Tigers Gone?* (7–12). 1989, Macmillan LB $13.95 (0-684-19003-6). A 50-year-old woman at her class reunion recalls her school years. (Rev: BL 4/15/89; BR 9–10/89; SLJ 5/89; VOYA 8/89)

1490 Halvorson, Marilyn. *Cowboys Don't Cry* (6–8). 1986, Dell paper $3.25 (0-440-91303-9). While drunk, Shane's father was involved in an accident in which his wife was killed and Shane cannot forgive him for the death of his mother. (Rev: SLJ 9/85; VOYA 6/85)

1491 Hamilton, Virginia. *Cousins* (5–8). 1990, Putnam $17.99 (0-399-22164-6). Cammy faces both guilt and grief when her cousin Patty Ann drowns. (Rev: BCCB 11/90*; HB 3–4/91; SLJ 12/90)

1492 Hartinger, Brent. *Geography Club* (7–12). 2003, HarperTempest $15.99 (0-06-001221-8). A group of gay teens form a secret support group in this frank novel full of humor and romance. (Rev: BCCB 2/03; BL 4/1/03; HB 3–4/03; HBG 10/03; SLJ 2/03; VOYA 4/03)

1493 Hautman, Pete. *Stone Cold* (7–12). 1998, Simon & Schuster paper $16.00 (0-689-81759-2). In this entertaining first-person narrative, Fenn becomes adept at gambling and soon finds that he is a gambling addict. (Rev: BL 9/15/98; BR 5–6/99; HB 11–12/98; HBG 3/99; SLJ 9/98; VOYA 2/99)

1494 Hawes, Louise. *Waiting for Christopher* (7–10). 2002, Candlewick $15.99 (0-7636-1371-1). Two very different teenage girls form an unlikely friendship and work together to care for a small boy who was being abused by his mother. (Rev: BCCB 9/02; BL 7/02; HB 9–10/02; HBG 10/02; SLJ 6/02; VOYA 4/02)

1495 Hawks, Robert. *The Twenty-Six Minutes* (6–10). 1988, Square One paper $4.95 (0-938961-03-9). Two teenage misfits join an anti-nuclear protest group. (Rev: SLJ 11/88; VOYA 4/89)

1496 Head, Ann. *Mr. and Mrs. Bo Jo Jones* (7–12). 1973, Signet paper $4.99 (0-451-16319-2). The perennial favorite of two teenagers madly in love but unprepared for the responsibilities of parenthood.

1497 Hearne, Betsy. *Listening for Leroy* (4–7). 1998, Simon & Schuster $16.00 (0-689-82218-9). When her family, dominated by her strict doctor father, moves from Alabama to Tennessee in the 1950s, Alice finds she doesn't fit in at school either physically (she is too tall and doesn't dress conventionally) or emotionally. (Rev: BL 11/15/98*; HBG 3/99; SLJ 11/98)

1498 Heide, Florence Parry. *Growing Anyway Up* (6–8). 1976, HarperCollins $12.95 (0-397-31657-7). Florence is shy when confronted with new situations but an aunt helps her conquer her fears.

1499 Henderson, Aileen K. *Treasure of Panther Peak* (4–7). Illus. 1998, Milkweed $15.95 (1-57131-618-3); paper $6.95 (1-57131-619-1). Twelve-year-old Ellie Williams gradually adjusts to her new home when her mother, fleeing an abusive husband, moves to Big Bend National Park to teach in a one-room school. (Rev: BL 12/1/98; HBG 3/99; VOYA 8/99)

1500 Heynen, Jim. *Being Youngest* (7–12). 1997, Holt $15.95 (0-8050-5486-3). Two Iowa farm kids, Henry and Gretchen, become friends when they realize that being the youngest in their respective families brings a certain number of problems. (Rev: BL 10/15/97; BR 5–6/98; HBG 3/98; SLJ 11/97; VOYA 4/98)

1501 High, Linda O. *The Summer of the Great Divide* (5–8). 1996, Holiday $15.95 (0-8234-1228-8). With the political events of 1969 as a backdrop, 13-year-old Wheezie sorts herself out at her relatives' farm. (Rev: BCCB 7–8/96; BL 6/1–15/96; BR 11–12/96; SLJ 4/96)

1502 Hill, David. *Time Out* (6–9). 2001, Cricket $15.95 (0-8126-2899-3). Kit is training for a race when a serious accident seems to send him into a parallel universe, where people and circumstances are eerily familiar. (Rev: BCCB 11/01; BR 1–2/02; HBG 3/02; SLJ 10/01; VOYA 2/02)

1503 Hite, Sid. *A Hole in the World* (7–9). 2001, Scholastic $16.95 (0-439-09830-0). When Paul spends the summer on a Virginia farm, he is introduced to hard work and to the memory of a man who committed suicide the year before. (Rev: BCCB 11/01; BL 11/15/01; HBG 3/02; SLJ 10/01; VOYA 10/01)

1504 Holeman, Linda. *Mercy's Birds* (6–10). 1998, Tundra paper $5.95 (0-88776-463-0). Fifteen-year-old Mercy lives a life of loneliness and hurt as she cares for a depressed mother and an alcoholic aunt while working after school in a flower shop. (Rev: BL 12/15/98; SLJ 3/99; VOYA 12/98)

1505 Holland, Isabelle. *The Man Without a Face* (7–10). 1972, HarperCollins paper $5.99 (0-06-447028-8). Charles's close relations with his reclusive tutor lead to a physical experience.

1506 Hopkins, Cathy. *Mates, Dates, and Cosmic Kisses* (6–10). 2003, Simon & Schuster paper $5.99 (0-689-85545-1). Teen anxieties about dating, friendship, and making decisions fill this funny novel about Izzy's attraction to a boy — and how her friends help her cope. (Rev: BL 2/1/03; SLJ 4/03)

1507 Hopkins, Cathy. *Mates, Dates, and Inflatable Bras* (6–10). 2003, Simon & Schuster paper $4.99

(0-689-85544-3). Lucy, 14, is concerned about her lack of development but, with the help of her friends, she is able to accept herself and even attract a cute boy. Other titles in this series include *Mates, Dates, and Designer Divas* (2003). (Rev: BL 2/1/03; SLJ 4/03)

1508 Hopper, Nancy J. *The Seven 1/2 Sins of Stacey Kendall* (7–9). 1982, Dell paper $2.25 (0-440-47736-0). Stacey finds out the true meaning of beauty when she goes into the ear-piercing business.

1509 Horvath, Penny. *Everything on a Waffle* (5–7). 2001, Farrar $16.00 (0-374-32236-8). Eleven-year-old Primrose Squarp does not believe her parents drowned during a storm. In the meantime she is moved from pillar to post, ending up as a foster child to an elderly couple. (Rev: BCCB 3/01*; BL 2/15/01; HB 5–6/01*; HBG 10/01; SLJ 4/01; VOYA 6/01)

1510 Howe, Norma. *Blue Avenger and the Theory of Everything* (8–10). Series: Blue Avenger. 2002, Cricket $17.95 (0-8126-2654-0). David Schumacher (aka Blue Avenger) faces a dilemma as he seeks to save his girlfriend from eviction. (Rev: BCCB 7–8/02; BL 5/15/02; HBG 3/03; SLJ 7/02; VOYA 12/02)

1511 Howe, Norma. *God, the Universe, and Hot Fudge Sundaes* (7–10). 1986, Avon paper $2.50 (0-380-70074-3). A 16-year-old girl would like to share her mother's born-again faith but can't.

1512 Howland, Ethan. *The Lobster War* (6–9). 2001, Front Street $15.95 (0-8126-2800-4). Sixteen-year-old Dain, who is struggling to keep his dead father's lobster business afloat, is upset to find that it is his own brother who is sabotaging his efforts. (Rev: BL 4/15/01; HBG 10/01; SLJ 5/01; VOYA 6/01)

1513 Hrdlitschka, Shelley. *Beans on Toast* (6–8). 1998, Orca paper $6.95 (1-55143-116-5). Thirteen-year-old Madison is having trouble accepting her parents' divorce and fitting in at summer Band Camp. (Rev: SLJ 2/99; VOYA 6/99)

1514 Hrdlitschka, Shelley. *Dancing Naked* (8–12). 2002, Orca paper $6.95 (1-55143-210-2). An absorbing story about a 16-year-old girl struggling to decide whether to end her pregnancy. (Rev: BL 3/15/02; SLJ 3/02*)

1515 Hrdlitschka, Shelley. *Disconnected* (7–12). 1999, Orca paper $6.95 (1-55143-105-X). The lives of Tanner, a hockey-playing teen who has recurring dreams of trying to escape an underwater attacker, and Alex, a boy escaping his father's abuse, connect in a most unusual way. (Rev: BL 4/1/99; SLJ 6/99; VOYA 6/99)

1516 Hughes, Dean. *Family Pose* (5–8). 1989, Macmillan LB $14.95 (0-689-31396-9). An 11-year-old runaway finds a home in a Seattle hotel where the employees shelter him. (Rev: BL 4/1/89; BR 9–10/89; SLJ 4/89; VOYA 8/89)

1517 Hurwitz, Johanna. *Even Stephen* (5–9). Illus. 1996, Morrow $15.00 (0-688-14197-8). Allison's older brother, Stephen, who excels in both sports and school work, is considered both confident and independent until his basketball coach dies and he sinks into a deep depression. (Rev: BL 4/1/96; BR 9–10/96; SLJ 3/96)

1518 Huser, Glen. *Stitches* (7–10). 2003, Groundwood $18.95 (0-88899-553-9); paper $9.95 (0-88899-578-4). Disfigured Chantelle and much-bullied Travis support each other through the difficult years of junior high school. (Rev: BCCB 2/04; HB 11–12/03*; SLJ 12/03)

1519 Huser, Glen. *Touch of the Clown* (7–10). 1999, Groundwood $15.95 (0-88899-343-9). Neglected sisters Barbara and Livvy get a new lease on life when they meet the eccentric Cosmo, who runs a teen clown workshop. (Rev: SLJ 11/99; VOYA 10/99)

1520 Ingold, Jeanette. *Pictures, 1918* (6–9). 1998, Harcourt $16.00 (0-15-201802-3). In this novel set in the final days of World War I, 16-year-old Asa faces many personal problems but finds release when she becomes an apprentice to the local portrait photographer. (Rev: BCCB 10/98; VOYA 2/99)

1521 Irwin, Hadley. *The Lilith Summer* (6–8). 1979, Feminist Pr. paper $8.95 (0-912670-52-5). Twelve-year-old Ellen learns about old age when she "lady sits" with 77-year-old Lilith Adams.

1522 Jenkins, A. M. *Breaking Boxes* (8–12). 1997, Delacorte $15.95 (0-385-32513-4). Charlie and Brandon form a friendship at high school, but when word gets out that Charlie's brother is gay, Brandon rejects both his friend and his family. (Rev: BL 9/1/97; BR 1–2/98; HBG 3/98; SLJ 10/97; VOYA 12/97)

1523 Jimenez, Francisco. *Breaking Through* (6–12). 2001, Houghton $15.00 (0-618-01173-0). In this sequel to *The Circuit: Stories from the Life of a Migrant Child* (2001), 14-year-old Francisco recounts his efforts to improve his lot in life and describes his school and romantic experiences. (Rev: BCCB 1/02; BL 9/1/01; HB 11–12/01; HBG 3/02; SLJ 9/01; VOYA 12/01)

1524 Johnson, Angela. *The First Part Last* (6–12). 2003, Simon & Schuster $15.95 (0-689-84922-2). Sixteen-year-old single-parent Bobby is overwhelmed and exhausted, but he loves his baby daughter. (Rev: BL 9/1/03*; HB 7–8/03; HBG 10/03; SLJ 6/03*; VOYA 6/03)

1525 Johnson, Lissa Halls. *Fast Forward to Normal* (6–10). Series: Brio Girls. 2001, Bethany paper $5.99 (1-56179-952-1). Becca, one of a quartet of high school juniors who call themselves the Brio Girls, isn't happy with her parents' idea of adopting the Guatemalan boy they have been fostering. Also in this series is *Stuck in the Sky* (2001). (Rev: BL 10/15/01)

1526 Johnston, Julie. *Adam and Eve and Pinch-Me* (7–9). 1994, Penguin paper $4.99 (0-14-037588-0). A neglected child learns the meaning of love in this coming-of-age story. (Rev: BL 5/15/94*; SLJ 7/94; VOYA 8/94)

1527 Johnston, Norma. *The Time of the Cranes* (7–10). 1990, Macmillan LB $14.95 (0-02-747713-4). A girl filled with self-doubt about her abilities receives an unexpected inheritance. (Rev: BL 4/1/90; SLJ 5/90; VOYA 6/88)

1528 Juby, Susan. *Alice, I Think* (8–12). 2003, HarperTempest $15.99 (0-06-051543-0). Alice, a quirky 15-year-old who has been homeschooled, enters public school and narrates in her diary all her new experiences. (Rev: BCCB 9/03; BL 8/03; HB 7–8/03; HBG 10/03; SLJ 7/03; VOYA 8/03)

1529 Jukes, Mavis. *Expecting the Unexpected: Human Interactions with Mrs. Gladys Furley, R.N.* (6–8). 1996, Delacorte $15.95 (0-385-32242-9). Twelve-year-old River is learning a lot about sex and family living in her human interactions class with Mrs. Flurey. Soon, she is beginning to apply this new knowledge to her own life, with mixed results. (Rev: BL 10/1/96; SLJ 9/96; VOYA 12/96)

1530 Kaplow, Robert. *Alessandra in Between* (8–12). 1992, HarperCollins LB $13.89 (0-06-023298-6). A young heroine has a lot on her mind, including her grandfather's deteriorating health, her friendships, and an unrequited love. (Rev: BL 9/15/92; SLJ 9/92)

1531 Kassem, Lou. *Secret Wishes* (6–8). 1989, Avon paper $2.95 (0-380-75544-0). A girl summons up her resources to try to lose weight to be a cheerleader. (Rev: BL 4/15/89; SLJ 4/89)

1532 Katz, Welwyn W. *Out of the Dark* (5–8). 1996, Simon & Schuster $16.00 (0-689-80947-6). A young boy escapes the painful present by imagining himself as a Viking shipbuilder. (Rev: BL 10/15/96; HB 11–12/96; SLJ 9/96; VOYA 12/96)

1533 Kaye, Marilyn. *The Atonement of Mindy Wise* (6–9). 1991, Harcourt $15.95 (0-15-200402-5). A Jewish girl reviews a year's worth of sins on Yom Kippur and realizes she isn't as bad as she thought. (Rev: BL 6/15/91)

1534 Kaye, Marilyn. *Cassie* (6–9). 1987, Harcourt paper $4.95 (0-15-200422-X). A shoplifting incident forces Cassie to examine her values. A companion volume is *Lydia*, about Cassie's older sister. (Rev: SLJ 12/87)

1535 Kaye, Marilyn. *Real Heroes* (5–7). 1993, Avon paper $3.50 (0-380-72283-6). Kevin finds he is in the middle of a situation involving quarrels between parents and between best friends, and a controversy about a teacher who is HIV positive. (Rev: BCCB 5/93; BL 4/1/93)

1536 Keene, Carolyn. *Love Times Three* (5–8). Series: River Heights. 1991, Pocket paper $3.50 (0-671-96703-7). Nikki has a crush on Tim, but Brittany wants him too. (Rev: BL 12/15/89)

1537 Kehret, Peg. *I'm Not Who You Think I Am* (6–9). 1999, Penguin $15.99 (0-525-46153-1). Thirteen-year-old Ginger has two problems, one concerning a deranged woman who thinks she is her daughter and the other involving her favorite teacher who is being harassed by a parent. (Rev: BCCB 3/99; BL 3/1/99; HBG 10/99; SLJ 4/99; VOYA 6/99)

1538 Keillor, Garrison, and Jenny L. Nilsson. *The Sandy Bottom Orchestra* (5–8). 1996, Hyperion LB $15.49 (0-7868-2145-0). Rachel, age 14, faces problems in growing up, including the ending of a treasured friendship. (Rev: BCCB 2/97; BL 1/1–15/97; BR 3–4/97; SLJ 1/97)

1539 Kerr, Dan. *Candy on the Edge* (5–8). 2002, Coteau paper $8.95 (1-55050-189-5). Candy, an 8th grader, finds herself drawn into a world of crime as she makes new friends and falls for Ramon. (Rev: SLJ 5/02)

1540 Kerr, M. E. *Dinky Hocker Shoots Smack!* (6–9). 1989, HarperCollins paper $5.99 (0-06-447006-7). Overweight and underloved Dinky finds a unique way to gain her parents' attention in this humorous novel.

1541 Kerr, M. E. *Gentlehands* (7–12). 1990, HarperCollins paper $5.99 (0-06-447067-9). Buddy Boyle wonders if the grandfather he has recently grown to love is really a Nazi war criminal in this novel set on the eastern tip of Long Island.

1542 Kerr, M. E. *I Stay Near You* (7–10). 1997, Harcourt paper $6.00 (0-15-201420-9). These three stories of love and self-acceptance span three generations in a small town. (Rev: BL 4/15/85; BR 1–2/86; SLJ 4/85; VOYA 6/85)

1543 Kerr, M. E. *Linger* (7–12). 1995, HarperCollins paper $4.95 (0-06-447102-0). In a story filled with wit and sadness, Kerr tells of kids entangled in love, war, and work. (Rev: BL 6/1–15/93; SLJ 7/93; VOYA 8/93)

1544 Kerr, M. E. *The Son of Someone Famous* (7–10). 1991, HarperCollins paper $3.95 (0-06-447069-5). In chapters alternately written by each, two teenagers in rural Vermont write about their friendship and their problems.

1545 Kerr, M. E. *What I Really Think of You* (7–10). 1982, HarperCollins $13.00 (0-06-023188-2); paper $3.50 (0-06-447062-8). The meeting of two teenagers who represent two kinds of religion — the evangelical mission and the TV pulpit. (Rev: BL 9/1/95)

1546 Ketchum, Liza. *Blue Coyote* (7–12). 1997, Simon & Schuster $16.00 (0-689-80790-2). High school junior Alex Beekman denies that he is gay, but, in time, he realizes the truth about himself. (Rev: BL 6/1–15/97; BR 9–10/97; SLJ 5/97; VOYA 8/97)

1547 Killien, Christi. *Artie's Brief: The Whole Truth, and Nothing But* (5–7). 1989, Avon paper $2.95 (0-380-71108-7). Sixth-grader Artie deals with the suicide of his older brother. (Rev: BL 5/15/89)

1548 Kindl, Patrice. *The Woman in the Wall* (7–10). 1997, Houghton $16.00 (0-395-83014-1). A dream-like story about a girl who emerges into the world after living alone for most of her 14 years in secret rooms in the family house. (Rev: BL 3/15/97; BR 9–10/97; SLJ 4/97; VOYA 8/97)

1549 Kinsey-Warnock, Natalie. *In the Language of Loons* (4–7). 1998, Cobblehill $15.99 (0-525-65237-X). During a summer on his grandfather's farm, Arlis gains self-confidence and learns how to tap his potential. (Rev: BCCB 4/98; HBG 10/98; SLJ 3/98)

1550 Klass, David. *Home of the Braves* (8–12). 2002, Farrar $18.00 (0-374-39963-8). Joe's plans for his senior year in high school are changed by the arrival of a Brazilian student who threatens Joe's position as soccer star and steals his would-be girl-friend too. (Rev: BCCB 12/02; BL 9/1/02; HB 1–2/03; HBG 3/03; SLJ 9/02)

1551 Klass, Sheila S. *Kool Ada* (5–7). 1991, Scholastic paper $13.95 (0-590-43902-2). Ada reacts only with her fists when she is sent to live in inner-city Chicago. (Rev: BL 10/15/91; SLJ 8/91*)

1552 Klass, Sheila S. *Next Stop: Nowhere* (6–10). 1995, Scholastic paper $14.95 (0-590-46686-0). Exiled to Vermont to live with her eccentric father, Beth must deal with separation from her close friend and from her new romantic interest, Josef, who's moved to Israel. (Rev: BL 1/15/95; SLJ 4/95; VOYA 2/95)

1553 Klass, Sheila S. *The Uncivil War* (6–9). 1997, Holiday $15.95 (0-8234-1329-2). An engaging novel about a 6th-grade girl who wants to get control of her life, which includes dealing with a life-long weight problem and the pending birth of a sibling. (Rev: BL 2/15/98; HBG 9/98; SLJ 4/98)

1554 Koertge, Ron. *The Arizona Kid* (8–12). 1989, Avon paper $3.99 (0-380-70776-4). Teenage Billy discovers that his uncle Wes is gay. (Rev: BL 5/1/88; BR 9–10/88; SLJ 6/88; VOYA 10/88)

1555 Koertge, Ron. *Confess-O-Rama* (7–9). 1996, Orchard LB $17.99 (0-531-08865-0). Beset with problems about his mother and his new school, Tony unburdens himself on Confess-O-Rama, a telephone hot line, only to discover he has told all to the school's weirdo, who then makes Tony her new

project. (Rev: BL 10/1/96; BR 3–4/97; SLJ 9/96*; VOYA 12/96)

1556 Koertge, Ron. *The Harmony Arms* (7–9). 1992, Avon paper $3.99 (0-380-72188-0). Gabriel and his father have gone to Los Angeles to break into the movies. By summer's end, Gabriel has embarked on his first romance and confronted death for the first time. (Rev: BL 10/15/92; SLJ 8/92*)

1557 Koja, Kathe. *Buddha Boy* (6–10). 2003, Farrar $16.00 (0-374-30998-1). Justin is intrigued by "Buddha Boy," a new student whose appearance and beliefs make him the target of bullies. (Rev: BL 2/15/03; HB 5–6/03; HBG 10/03; SLJ 2/03; VOYA 4/03)

1558 Koja, Kathe. *Straydog* (7–10). 2002, Farrar $16.00 (0-374-37278-0). Rachel, a lonely teenager who enjoys writing, is devastated when her favorite dog at the animal shelter is put to sleep and her anger affects the people closest to her. (Rev: BL 4/15/02; HB 5–6/02; HBG 10/02; SLJ 4/02; VOYA 6/02)

1559 Koller, Jackie F. *The Last Voyage of the Misty Day* (6–9). 1992, Atheneum $14.00 (0-689-31731-X). The story of a young girl and her friendship with an ailing neighbor. (Rev: BL 5/1/92; SLJ 6/92)

1560 Konigsburg, E. L. *Jennifer, Hecate, Macbeth, William McKinley, and Me, Elizabeth* (6–8). 1967, Macmillan $16.00 (0-689-30007-7); Dell paper $5.50 (0-440-44162-5). Elizabeth finds a new friend in Jennifer, an unusual girl who is interested in witchcraft.

1561 Konigsburg, E. L. *T-Backs, T-Shirts, Coat, and Suit* (5–8). 1993, Atheneum $16.95 (0-689-31855-3). When Chloe goes to visit her former flower-child aunt, she becomes part of a struggle for individual rights in the workplace. (Rev: BCCB 11/93; BL 11/1/93; SLJ 10/93*; VOYA 12/93)

1562 Konigsburg, E. L. *Throwing Shadows* (7–10). 1988, Macmillan paper $4.50 (0-02-044140-1). Five short stories about teenagers learning about themselves and their emotions.

1563 Kornblatt, Marc. *Izzy's Place* (4–7). 2003, Simon & Schuster $16.95 (0-689-84639-8). Summer with his grandmother proves more rewarding than 10-year-old Henry anticipated as he makes friends and gains a new outlook on life. (Rev: BL 6/1–15/03; HBG 10/03; SLJ 7/03)

1564 Koss, Amy Goldman. *The Girls* (5–9). 2000, Dial $16.99 (0-8037-2494-2). In chapters narrated by different protagonists, this book tells of Maya who has been dropped for no apparent reason from a clique of five popular girls in the middle school she attends. (Rev: BCCB 6/00; BL 8/00; HB 7–8/00; HBG 10/00; SLJ 6/00)

1565 Koss, Amy Goldman. *Smoke Screen* (5–8). 2000, Pleasant paper $5.95 (1-584-85201-1). A harmless fib gets out of control when Mitzi lies in order to impress a boy. (Rev: BL 9/15/00; HBG 10/01; SLJ 11/00)

1566 Krantz, Hazel. *Walks in Beauty* (6–9). 1997, Northland paper $6.95 (0-87358-671-9). The story of a 15-year-old Navajo girl and how she copes with such adolescent woes as popularity, boyfriends, prom dates, and family problems. (Rev: BL 8/97; BR 11–12/97; HBG 3/98; SLJ 10/97)

1567 Kropp, Paul. *Moonkid and Liberty* (6–9). 1990, Little, Brown $13.95 (0-316-50485-8). The teenage son and daughter of two hippies try to sort out their lives and plan for their future. (Rev: BL 6/15/90; SLJ 4/90; VOYA 6/90)

1568 Kropp, Paul. *Moonkid and Prometheus* (6–8). 1998, Stoddart paper $5.95 (0-7736-7465-9). In this sequel to *Moonkid and Liberty,* Moonkid takes on the job of tutoring a black student, Prometheus, in reading and Pro in turn teaches Moonkid techniques in basketball. (Rev: BL 6/1–15/98; SLJ 10/98)

1569 Krumgold, Joseph. *Onion John* (5–8). 1959, HarperCollins LB $16.89 (0-690-04698-7); paper $5.99 (0-06-440144-8). A Newbery Medal winner (1960) about a boy's friendship with an old man. Also use the Newbery winner . . . *And Now Miguel* (1954).

1570 Kurland, Morton L. *Our Sacred Honor* (7–12). 1987, Rosen LB $12.95 (0-8239-0692-2). A story from two points of view about a pregnant teenage girl, her boyfriend, and their decision for abortion. (Rev: SLJ 6/87)

1571 Laird, Elizabeth. *Secret Friends* (5–8). 1999, Putnam $14.99 (0-399-23334-2). Lucy tells the story of her ill-fated friendship with the class outsider who has been nicknamed Earwig because of her protruding ears. (Rev: BCCB 2/99; BL 1/1–15/99; BR 9–10/99; HBG 10/99; SLJ 3/99)

1572 Larimer, Tamela. *Buck* (7–10). 1986, Avon paper $2.50 (0-380-75172-0). The friendship between runaway Buck and Rich is threatened when Buck becomes friendly with Rich's girlfriend. (Rev: BL 4/87; SLJ 6/87; VOYA 4/87)

1573 Laser, Michael. *6–321* (4–7). 2001, Simon & Schuster $15.00 (0-689-83372-5). In this autobiographical novel set in 1963, 6th-grader Marc Chaikin falls in love, experiences his parents' divorce, and reacts to the assassination of John F. Kennedy. (Rev: BCCB 2/01; BL 1/1–15/01; HBG 10/01; SLJ 5/01; VOYA 4/01)

1574 Lawson, Julie. *Turns on a Dime* (5–8). 1999, Stoddart paper $7.95 (0-7737-5942-5). In this sequel to *Goldstone* (1998), set in British Columbia, 11-year-old Jo faces many new situations, including finding a boyfriend, discovering that she is adopted, and learning that her beloved babysitter is pregnant. (Rev: SLJ 6/99)

1575 Layton, George. *The Swap* (5–8). 1997, Putnam $16.95 (0-399-23148-X). A series of stories narrated by an 11-year-old working-class boy in the north of England, who is troubled by bullying and growing up without a father. (Rev: BL 10/1/97; BR 1–2/98; HBG 3/98; SLJ 9/97)

1576 Lemieux, Anne E. *All the Answers* (7–10). 2000, Avon $15.99 (0-380-97771-0). Unable to face the criticism of family and friends, 8th-grader Jason cheats on a math test to improve his grades but gets caught. (Rev: BL 1/1–15/00; HBG 9/00; SLJ 2/00; VOYA 4/00)

1577 Lemieux, Michele. *Stormy Night* (4–8). 1999, Kids Can $15.95 (1-55074-692-8). A long picture book in which a young girl who can't sleep ponders questions that are common to preteen girls. (Rev: BL 12/1/99; HBG 3/00; SLJ 12/99)

1578 L'Engle, Madeleine. *A House Like a Lotus* (7–12). 1984, Farrar $17.00 (0-374-33385-8); Dell paper $4.99 (0-440-93685-3). Polly O'Keefe, of previous L'Engle novels, is now 17 and encounters both lesbianism and a heterosexual romance in this probing novel.

1579 L'Engle, Madeleine. *A Ring of Endless Light* (7–10). 1980, Dell paper $5.99 (0-440-97232-9). The Austin family are again central characters in this novel in which Vicky must adjust to her grandfather's death while exploring her telepathic powers with dolphins. Newbery Honor Book, 1981.

1580 Lester, Alison. *The Quicksand Pony* (5–8). 1998, Houghton $15.00 (0-395-93749-3). In this novel set in Australia, 17-year-old Joycie fakes a drowning and seeks a new life in the bush with her infant son, but two young girls stumble on the truth nine years later. (Rev: BCCB 10/98; BL 12/15/98; HB 1–2/99; HBG 3/99; SLJ 10/98; VOYA 2/99)

1581 Lester, Jim. *Fallout* (7–10). 1996, Dell paper $3.99 (0-440-22683-X). A fast-paced novel told in a confessional format about the problems faced by Kenny Francis, self-styled "terminal goofball," when he transfers to a fancy prep school. (Rev: BL 1/1–15/96; BR 5–6/96; SLJ 2/96; VOYA 2/96)

1582 Leverich, Kathleen. *The New You* (5–8). 1998, Greenwillow $15.00 (0-688-16076-X). Abby, who recently moved to New York City and entered a new school, is unhappy and friendless until she begins to share her experiences with others. (Rev: BL 11/1/98; HBG 3/99; SLJ 11/98)

1583 Levy, Elizabeth. *Cheater, Cheater* (5–8). 1994, Scholastic paper $3.50 (0-590-45866-3). Lucy Lovello has been labeled a cheater and even her teachers don't trust her. When she finds her best friend cheating, she faces a moral dilemma. (Rev: BL 10/1/93; SLJ 10/93; VOYA 12/93)

1584 Levy, Marilyn. *Is That Really Me in the Mirror?* (7–10). 1991, Ballantine paper $4.99 (0-449-70343-6). Joanne is envious of her beautiful, popular older sister until an automobile accident and plastic surgery transform Joanne into a very pretty stranger. (Rev: BL 11/1/91)

1585 Lewis, Beverly. *Catch a Falling Star* (5–8). Series: Summerhill Secrets. 1995, Bethany paper $5.99 (1-55661-478-0). An Amish boy faces excommunication when he begins paying too much attention to a non-Amish girl. (Rev: BL 3/15/96)

1586 Lewis, Beverly. *Night of the Fireflies* (5–8). Series: Summerhill Secrets. 1995, Bethany House paper $5.99 (1-55661-479-9). In this sequel to *Catch a Falling Star* (1995), Levi, an Amish boy, tries to save his young sister, who has been struck by a car. (Rev: BL 3/15/96)

1587 Lewis, Linda. *Is There Life After Boys?* (6–9). 1990, Archway paper $2.95 (0-671-69559-2). When Linda transfers to an all-girl school she finds the social change unbearable. (Rev: SLJ 2/88)

1588 Littke, Lael. *Loydene in Love* (8–10). 1986, Harcourt $13.95 (0-15-249888-5). A high school junior from a small town gets a different view of life when she visits Los Angeles for the summer. (Rev: BL 2/15/87; SLJ 3/87)

1589 Littke, Lael. *Shanny on Her Own* (6–9). 1985, Harcourt $12.95 (0-15-273531-3). Shanny is sent to live with an aunt in rural Idaho to counteract her developing punkiness. (Rev: BL 1/1/86; SLJ 12/85; VOYA 4/86)

1590 Lowry, Lois. *A Summer to Die* (7–10). Illus. 1977, Houghton $16.00 (0-395-25338-1). Meg is confused and dismayed by her older sister's death. (Rev: BL 7/88)

1591 Lowry, Lois. *Taking Care of Terrific* (7–9). 1983, Houghton $16.00 (0-395-34070-5); Dell paper $4.99 (0-440-48494-4). A baby-sitting job leads to all sorts of hectic adventures for 14-year-old Enid.

1592 Lubar, David. *Dunk* (8–12). 2002, Clarion $15.00 (0-618-19455-X). Over the course of a summer, troubled young Chad learns a lot about himself and his anger. (Rev: BCCB 12/02; BL 9/1/02; HB 11–12/02; HBG 3/03; SLJ 8/02*)

1593 Lynch, Chris. *Blood Relations* (8–12). 1996, HarperCollins LB $13.89 (0-06-025399-1); paper $4.50 (0-06-447122-5). The beginning of a violent, disturbing trilogy about 15-year-old Mick, his working-class Irish family, his drug-ridden neighborhood, and the Latino classmates to whom he turns for help. Followed by *Dog Eat Dog* (1996) and *Mick* (1996). (Rev: BL 4/1/96; SLJ 3/96; VOYA 8/96)

1594 Lynch, Chris. *Extreme Elvin* (8–10). 1999, HarperCollins LB $15.89 (0-06-028210-X). Elvin of *Slot Machine* is back, and this time he has discovered girls and a whole new set of relationships.

(Rev: BL 2/1/99; HBG 9/99; SLJ 2/99; VOYA 10/99)

1595 Lynch, Chris. *Slot Machine* (8–10). 1995, HarperCollins LB $14.89 (0-06-023585-3). Elvin is a 13-year-old boy, overweight, and expected to perform with exuberance everything forced upon him. (Rev: BL 9/1/95*; SLJ 10/95; VOYA 12/95)

1596 Lynch, Chris. *Who the Man* (6–9). 2002, HarperCollins $15.99 (0-06-623938-9). Thirteen-year-old Earl Pryor's ideas about manhood are turned upside-down when he sees how his father reacts to problems in his marriage. (Rev: BCCB 1/03; BL 11/15/02; HBG 10/03; SLJ 12/02; VOYA 2/03)

1597 McCall, Edith. *Better Than a Brother* (6–9). 1988, Walker $14.85 (0-8027-6783-4). Hughie turns to her friend Jerry for help when she loses her new gold locket. (Rev: BR 9–10/88; SLJ 5/88)

1598 McDaniel, Lurlene. *The Girl Death Left Behind* (6–9). 1999, Bantam paper $4.99 (0-553-57091-9). A touching story of a girl's adjustment to the sudden death of her parents and starting a new life living with relatives. (Rev: SLJ 3/99; VOYA 4/99)

1599 McDaniel, Lurlene. *I'll Be Seeing You* (6–9). 1996, Bantam paper $4.99 (0-553-56718-7). Carley's face has been disfigured by the removal of a tumor and she tries to keep this secret from a blind boy with whom she has fallen in love. (Rev: BL 7/96; SLJ 12/96)

1600 McDaniel, Lurlene. *Starry, Starry Night* (6–10). 1998, Bantam $8.95 (0-553-57130-3). Three Christmas season stories about different heroines, each with a problem. One finally adjusts to her mother's pregnancy and then is devastated when the baby is born with severe brain damage; another discovers that a cancer patient has a crush on her; the third has difficulty with her boyfriend and must regain her perspective. (Rev: HBG 3/99; SLJ 10/98; VOYA 12/98)

1601 McDaniel, Lurlene. *Telling Christina Goodbye* (6–10). 2002, Bantam paper $4.99 (0-533-57087-0). Tucker, who had been driving recklessly, is the only person uninjured in the accident that kills Christina. (Rev: BL 3/15/02; SLJ 7/02)

1602 MacDonald, Caroline. *Speaking to Miranda* (7–10). 1992, HarperCollins LB $13.89 (0-06-021103-2). Set in Australia and New Zealand, Ruby, 18, leaves her boyfriend, travels with her father, and gradually decides to explore the mysteries of her life: Who was her mother? Who is her family? Who is she? (Rev: BL 12/15/92*; SLJ 10/92)

1603 McDonald, Joyce. *Swallowing Stones* (7–10). 1997, Bantam paper $4.99 (0-440-22672-4). When Michael accidentally kills a man with his rifle, he and his friend decide to hide the gun and feign ignorance. (Rev: BL 10/15/97; BR 11–12/97; SLJ 9/97; VOYA 12/97)

1604 McElfresh, Lynn E. *Can You Feel the Thunder?* (4–8). 1999, Simon & Schuster $16.00 (0-689-82324-X). Mic, a 7th grader, has trouble adjusting to his blind and deaf older sister and also finds that if he doesn't master mathematical fractions, he won't be allowed to play baseball at school. (Rev: BCCB 9/99; BL 6/1–15/99; HBG 10/99; SLJ 7/99; VOYA 8/99)

1605 McKenna, Colleen O'Shaughnessy. *The Brightest Light* (6–10). 1992, Scholastic paper $13.95 (0-590-45347-5). A young girl discovers the secret behind her hometown's strange behavior during one long, hot summer. (Rev: BL 9/15/92; SLJ 12/92)

1606 Mackler, Carolyn. *The Earth, My Butt, and Other Big Round Things* (7–10). 2003, Candlewick $15.99 (0-7636-1958-2). Virginia, a privileged New York 15-year-old, struggles with her weight, her lack of self confidence, her family, the absence of her best friend, and her aspiring boyfriend. (Rev: BL 9/1/03; HB 9–10/03; SLJ 9/03)

1607 MacLachlan, Patricia. *The Facts and Fictions of Minna Pratt* (5–7). 1988, HarperCollins LB $15.89 (0-06-024117-9); paper $5.99 (0-06-440265-7). A budding young cellist on the verge of adolescence experiences her first boyfriend. (Rev: BCCB 4/88; BL 6/15/88; SLJ 6–7/88)

1608 MacLachlan, Patricia. *Unclaimed Treasures* (5–8). 1984, HarperCollins paper $4.95 (0-06-440189-8). A romantic story of a young girl finding herself.

1609 McNaughton, Janet. *To Dance at the Palais Royale* (7–10). 1999, Stoddart paper $5.95 (0-7736-7473-X). The story of the loneliness and growing maturity of Aggie Maxwell who leaves her home in Scotland at age 17 to become a domestic servant with her sister in Toronto. (Rev: SLJ 5/99; VOYA 10/99)

1610 McNeal, Laura, and Tom McNeal. *Crooked* (7–12). 1999, Knopf $16.95 (0-679-89300-8). Ninth-graders Clara and Amos find they are falling in love and face the menace of the bullying Tripp brothers. (Rev: BL 10/15/99; HB 11–12/99; HBG 4/00; SLJ 11/99; VOYA 4/00)

1611 McVeity, Jen. *On Different Shores* (6–10). 1998, Orchard LB $17.99 (0-531-33115-6). The problems of a teenage Australian girl surface when the guerrilla environmental group to which she belongs is caught and a crisis develops over a beached whale. (Rev: BCCB 11/98; BL 11/15/98; BR 5–6/99; HBG 3/99; SLJ 3/99; VOYA 10/98)

1612 Maguire, Gregory. *Oasis* (7–10). 1996, Clarion $14.95 (0-395-67019-5). This story of grief and guilt involves 13-year-old Hand, his adjustment to his father's sudden death, and his mother's efforts to save the motel her husband had managed. (Rev: BL 9/15/96; BR 3–4/97; SLJ 11/96; VOYA 2/97)

1613 Mahon, K. L. *Just One Tear* (5–10). 1994, Lothrop $14.00 (0-688-13519-6). The diary of a 14-year-old girl tells the story of a 13-year-old boy whose father is shot in front of him and tells how the boy deals with his grief. (Rev: BL 5/15/94; SLJ 5/94; VOYA 10/94)

1614 Mahy, Margaret. *The Catalogue of the Universe* (8–12). 1987, Scholastic paper $2.75 (0-590-42318-5). Through their friendship, Angela, who longs to meet her absent father, and Tycho, who believes he is physically ugly, find tenderness and compassion. (Rev: BL 3/15/86; SLJ 4/86; VOYA 12/86)

1615 Mahy, Margaret. *The Other Side of Silence* (7–10). 1995, Viking $14.99 (0-670-86455-2). A gothic story with a menacing tone about a young woman's quest for individuality and personal power. (Rev: BL 10/1/95*; SLJ 10/95; VOYA 4/96)

1616 Makris, Kathryn. *A Different Way* (7–10). 1989, Avon paper $2.95 (0-380-75728-1). A newcomer in a Texas high school wonders if acceptance by the in crowd is worth the effort. (Rev: BL 10/15/89)

1617 Many, Paul. *Walk Away Home* (8–10). 2002, Walker $16.95 (0-8027-8828-9). Nick leaves home in search of more welcoming surroundings, and finds himself on an interesting journey of growth involving romance and alternative lifestyles. (Rev: HB 1–2/03; HBG 3/03; SLJ 9/02; VOYA 12/02)

1618 Marino, Jan. *Searching for Atticus* (7–10). 1997, Simon & Schuster $16.00 (0-689-80066-5). During a stay at an aunt's home with her exhausted father, a Vietnam War veteran, 15-year-old Tessa falls in love with handsome but dangerous Caleb. (Rev: BL 11/15/97; BR 3–4/98; HBG 3/98; SLJ 10/97; VOYA 12/97)

1619 Martin, Ann M. *The Slam Book* (6–9). 1987, Holiday $12.95 (0-8234-0666-0). Revealing the contents of a notebook in which students write freely about each other leads to broken friendships and a suicide. (Rev: SLJ 12/87; VOYA 2/88)

1620 Matthews, Phoebe. *Switchstance* (7–10). 1989, Avon paper $2.95 (0-380-75729-X). After her parents' divorce, Elvy moves in with her grandmother and forms friendships with two very different boys. (Rev: VOYA 2/90)

1621 Mayfield, Sue. *Drowning Anna* (8–12). 2002, Hyperion $15.99 (0-7868-0870-5). Anna is pretty and talented, but shy and an easy mark for master manipulator Hayley, whose bullying drives Anna to a suicide attempt. (Rev: BCCB 12/02; BL 10/15/02; HB 1–2/03; HBG 3/03; SLJ 12/02; VOYA 2/03)

1622 Maynard, Meredy. *Blue True Dream of Sky* (7–10). 1997, Polestar Bk. paper $7.95 (1-89609-

523-2). Nickie, a 14-year-old albino girl, faces new problems when her brother sinks into a coma after a car crash, and she begins a crusade to save a stand of trees near her Pacific Northwest home. (Rev: BR 1-2/98; VOYA 10/97)

1623 Mazer, Anne, ed. *Working Days: Stories About Teenagers and Work* (6–12). 1997, Persea paper $9.95 (0-89255-224-7). An anthology of 15 varied, multicultural short stories about teenagers at their jobs. (Rev: BL 7/97; HBG 3/98; SLJ 9/97; VOYA 12/97)

1624 Mazer, Harry. *Hey, Kid! Does She Love Me?* (7–12). 1986, Avon paper $2.95 (0-380-70025-5). Stage-struck Jeff falls in love with a woman who was once an aspiring actress in this romance that contains some sexually explicit language.

1625 Mazer, Norma Fox. *Out of Control* (7–12). 1993, Avon paper $5.99 (0-380-71347-0). This novel deals directly and realistically with the complexities of sexual harassment. (Rev: BL 6/1–15/93; VOYA 8/93)

1626 Mazer, Norma Fox. *Someone to Love* (7–12). 1985, Dell paper $3.25 (0-440-98062-3). A lonely college student moves in with her boyfriend, a dropout.

1627 Meyer, Carolyn. *Drummers of Jericho* (6–9). 1995, Harcourt $11.00 (0-15-200441-6); paper $6.00 (0-15-200190-5). Jewish Pazit Trujillo goes to live with her father in the small town of Jericho, but trouble breaks out when she objects to Christian symbols at school. (Rev: BL 6/1–15/95; SLJ 9/95; VOYA 5/95)

1628 Miles, Betty. *The Real Me* (6–8). 1975, Avon paper $2.75 (0-380-00347-3). Barbara rebels against all the restrictions placed on her life because she is a girl.

1629 Miles, Betty. *The Trouble with Thirteen* (6–9). 1979, Knopf $12.99 (0-394-93930-1). Divorce and death, among other changes, make two friends realize that they are growing up.

1630 Miller-Lachmann, Lyn. *Hiding Places* (8–12). 1987, Square One paper $4.95 (0-938961-00-4). Mark runs away from his suburban home and ends up in a shelter in New York City. (Rev: SLJ 5/87)

1631 Moiles, Steven. *The Summer of My First Pediddle* (7–9). 1995, Royal Fireworks paper $9.99 (0-88092-122-6). Set in a small Illinois town during 1953, this is 14-year-old Brad Thatcher's story of how he weathered two firsts in his life — first love and his first encounter with prejudice after his father is investigated during the McCarthy hearings. (Rev: BR 1-2/96; VOYA 2/96)

1632 Moore, Emily. *Whose Side Are You On?* (5–7). 1988, Farrar paper $5.95 (0-374-48373-6). Barbra is dismayed to find out that her math tutor is none other than T.J., the class pest. (Rev: BCCB 10/88; BL 1/15/89; SLJ 10/88)

1633 Morgenstern, Susie. *Three Days Off* (7–12). Trans. by Gill Rosner. 2001, Viking $14.99 (0-670-03511-4). William, suspended from school after making a suggestive remark to a teacher, spends three days aimlessly wandering through his small French town in this brief novel translated from the French. (Rev: BL 12/15/01; HB 11–12/01; HBG 3/02; SLJ 12/01; VOYA 10/01)

1634 Morris, Winifred. *Liar* (7–10). 1996, Walker $15.95 (0-8027-8461-5). Fourteen-year-old Alex starts life over on his grandparents' farm in Oregon, but there are many obstacles, including school bullies, a hostile principal, and an unloving grandfather. (Rev: BL 12/1/96; SLJ 1/97; VOYA 12/96)

1635 Mosier, Elizabeth. *My Life as a Girl* (8–12). 1999, Random $18.99 (0-679-99035-6). Jamie wants to become a new person when she enters Bryn Mawr as a freshman, but her precollege summer boyfriend reminds her that she must come to terms with persistent family problems, including a father who has driven the family into financial ruin. (Rev: BL 4/1/99; HBG 9/99; SLJ 6/99)

1636 Murphy, Claire Rudolf. *Free Radical* (7–10). 2002, Clarion $15.00 (0-618-11134-4). Luke, a baseball star in Fairbanks, Alaska, is stunned when his mother turns herself in for her role in a fatal bombing more than 30 years before. (Rev: BCCB 6/02; BL 3/15/02; HBG 10/02; SLJ 3/02; VOYA 6/02)

1637 Murray, Martine. *The Slightly True Story of Cedar B. Hartley (Who Planned to Live an Unusual Life)* (5–8). Illus. 2003, Scholastic $15.95 (0-439-48622-X). Cedar, 13, is indeed unusual in her questioning nature, her outlook on life, her advanced vocabulary, and her ability to connect with people of all sorts. (Rev: BCCB 9/03; BL 11/15/03*; HB 9–10/03; HBG 9–10/03; SLJ 8/03*; VOYA 10/03)

1638 Myers, Anna. *Ethan Between Us* (7–10). 1998, Walker $15.95 (0-8027-8670-7). The lives of two close friends growing up in a small Oklahoma town are changed and their friendship shattered when they become involved with a handsome, troubled young man to whom both are attracted. (Rev: BL 8/98; BR 1-2/99; HBG 9/99; SLJ 10/98)

1639 Myers, Walter Dean. *Handbook for Boys: A Novel* (8–12). 2002, HarperCollins $15.95 (0-06-029146-X). Jimmy, 16, is the recipient of a lot of unsought advice when he starts work in a Harlem barbershop as part of a mentoring program. (Rev: HBG 10/02; SLJ 5/02; VOYA 8/02)

1640 Myers, Walter Dean. *Won't Know Till I Get There* (7–10). 1982, Penguin paper $5.99 (0-14-032612-X). A young subway graffiti artist is sentenced to help out in a senior citizens' home.

1641 Myracle, Lauren. *Kissing Kate* (7–10). 2003, Dutton $16.99 (0-525-46917-6). Lissa, 16, and best friend Kate have very different reactions after they share a passionate kiss. (Rev: BCCB 5/03; BL 8/03; HBG 10/03; SLJ 4/03; VOYA 4/03)

1642 Namioka, Lensey. *Ties That Bind, Ties That Break* (7–10). 1999, Delacorte $15.95 (0-385-32666-1). In this novel set in early 20th-century China, a period of dramatic and political changes, Ailin rebels against traditions that repress women, and after a lonely and difficult journey to America, eventually achieves self-fulfillment. (Rev: BCCB 5/99; BL 5/15/99; HBG 9/99; SLJ 7/99)

1643 Naylor, Phyllis Reynolds. *Night Cry* (5–8). 1984, Macmillan $17.00 (0-689-31017-X); Dell paper $3.99 (0-440-40017-1). A 13-year-old Mississippi girl lives alone in the backwoods.

1644 Neenan, Colin. *Live a Little* (8–12). 1996, Harcourt $12.00 (0-15-201242-7); paper $6.00 (0-15-202143-5). Hale's last days in high school are plagued with disappointments and he experiences bouts of self-pity when he discovers that good friend Zoe is pregnant. (Rev: BL 9/1/96; BR 3–4/97; SLJ 3/97; VOYA 12/96)

1645 Nelson, Theresa. *The Beggar's Ride* (6–8). 1992, Orchard LB $17.99 (0-531-08496-5). A compelling chronicle of a runaway's time on the tawdry boardwalks of Atlantic City. (Rev: BL 11/1/92; SLJ 11/92*)

1646 Nelson, Vaunda M. *Possibles* (4–8). 1995, Putnam $15.95 (0-399-22823-3). Twelve-year-old Sheppy comes to accept the death of her father through caring for an unusual 36-year-old woman who has broken her leg. (Rev: BL 2/1/96; SLJ 10/95; VOYA 12/95)

1647 Neville, Emily C. *It's Like This, Cat* (7–9). Illus. 1963, HarperCollins LB $16.89 (0-06-024391-0); paper $5.99 (0-06-440073-5). A New York City 14-year-old boy has more in common with his cat than his father. Newbery Medal, 1964.

1648 Nixon, Joan Lowery. *Nobody's There* (7–12). 2000, Delacorte $15.95 (0-385-32567-3). Because of an act of vandalism, Abbie is sentenced to community service helping the cantankerous elderly Mrs. Merkel. (Rev: BCCB 7–8/00; BL 6/1–15/00; HBG 9/00; SLJ 7/00)

1649 Nolan, Han. *Send Me Down a Miracle* (6–9). 1996, Harcourt $13.00 (0-15-200979-5); paper $6.00 (0-15-200978-7). Fourteen-year-old Charity is caught in the middle when her preacher father objects violently when Charity's friend, artist Adrienne Dabney, claims to have had a vision of Jesus. (Rev: BL 3/15/96*; SLJ 4/96*; VOYA 6/96)

1650 Oates, Joyce Carol. *Big Mouth and Ugly Girl* (8–12). 2002, HarperCollins $16.95 (0-06-623756-4). Ursula ("Ugly Girl") stands up for Matt ("Big Mouth") when he is accused of plotting to blow up

the high school. (Rev: BL 5/15/02; HB 7–8/02; HBG 10/02; SLJ 5/02*)

1651 Oke, Janette. *A Quiet Strength* (7–9). Series: Prairie Legacy. 1999, Bethany House paper $12.99 (0-7642-2156-6). The problems and joys of the first days of marriage for Virginia Simpson and her beau from former days. (Rev: BL 9/15/99)

1652 Okimoto, Jean D. *The Eclipse of Moonbeam Dawson* (7–10). 1997, Tor $17.95 (0-312-86244-X). Fifteen-year-old Moonbeam Dawson rebels against his mother's unconventional ways and takes a job and an apartment at posh Stere Island Lodge, where he changes his name and tries to change his values. (Rev: HBG 9/98; SLJ 11/97; VOYA 4/98)

1653 Okimoto, Jean Davies. *To JayKae: Life Stinx* (8–12). 1999, Tor $18.95 (0-312-86732-8). In this sequel to *Jason's Women* (Tor, 1986), teenager Jason woos a girl over the Internet by pretending to be his handsome, very-popular stepbrother. (Rev: BL 12/15/99; HBG 4/00; SLJ 1/00; VOYA 2/00)

1654 O'Leary, Patsy Baker. *With Wings as Eagles* (7–10). 1997, Houghton $15.00 (0-395-70557-6). Set in rural North Carolina in 1938, this novel tells about young Bubba's becoming reacquainted with a father newly released from prison, his family's struggle with poverty, and Bubba's friendship with a black boy. (Rev: BL 10/15/97; BR 5–6/98; HBG 3/98; SLJ 12/97*)

1655 Park, Barbara. *Beanpole* (7–9). 1983, Avon paper $2.95 (0-380-69840-4). On her 13th birthday Lillian, who is extra tall for her age, makes three wishes and they seem to be coming true.

1656 Paulsen, Gary. *Alida's Song* (6–10). 1999, Delacorte $15.95 (0-385-32586-X). A 14-year-old boy discovers a new life away from his alcoholic parents when he accepts an invitation from his grandmother to spend time on her quiet northern Minnesota farm. (Rev: BL 6/1–15/99; BR 9–10/99; HBG 10/99; SLJ 7/99)

1657 Paulsen, Gary. *The Boy Who Owned the School* (6–9). 1990, Orchard paper $15.95 (0-531-05865-4). Jacob's main object in life is to be as invisible as possible and to avoid trouble. (Rev: BL 4/1/90; SLJ 4/90; VOYA 6/90)

1658 Paulsen, Gary. *Brian's Return* (5–8). 1999, Delacorte $15.95 (0-385-32500-2). Brian, the hero of *Brian's Winter,* becomes so disheartened with life at school away from the wilderness that he decides to leave society behind forever. (Rev: BL 2/1/99; HB 1–2/99; HBG 10/99; SLJ 2/99)

1659 Paulsen, Gary. *The Car* (6–9). 1994, Harcourt $17.00 (0-15-292878-2). The cross-country adventures of Terry, 14, and Waylon, a 45-year-old Vietnam vet who sometimes suffers flashback memories and becomes violent. (Rev: BL 4/1/94; SLJ 5/94; VOYA 6/94)

1660 Paulsen, Gary. *The Cookcamp* (5–7). 1991, Orchard paper $15.95 (0-531-05927-8). After a 5-year-old boy discovers his mother is having an affair, he is sent off to northern Minnesota in this World War II story. (Rev: BCCB 3/91; BL 3/1/91; HB 3–4/91; SLJ 2/91*)

1661 Paulsen, Gary. *The Crossing* (8–10). 1987, Dell paper $5.99 (0-440-20582-4). An alcoholic American soldier and a homeless street waif become friends in a Mexican border town. (Rev: BL 10/15/87; BR 1–2/88; SLJ 11/87; VOYA 10/87)

1662 Paulsen, Gary. *Dancing Carl* (7–9). 1987, Puffin paper $3.95 (0-685-19101-X). A young boy recalls his friendship with Carl, a troubled man who is an expert ice skater.

1663 Paulsen, Gary. *The Island* (7–10). 1988, Orchard paper $17.95 (0-531-05749-6). A 15-year-old boy finds peace and a meaning to life when he explores his own private island. (Rev: BL 3/15/88; BR 9–10/88; SLJ 5/88; VOYA 6/88)

1664 Paulsen, Gary. *Popcorn Days and Buttermilk Nights* (8–12). 1989, Penguin paper $4.99 (0-14-034204-4). Carley finds adventure after he is sent to his Uncle David's farm in Minnesota to sort himself out.

1665 Paulsen, Gary. *Sisters / Hermanas* (8–10). Trans. by Gloria de Aragón Andújar. 1993, Harcourt $10.95 (0-15-275323-0); paper $6.00 (0-15-275324-9). The bilingual story of two girls, age 14, in a Texas town, one an illegal Mexican immigrant prostitute, the other a superficial blond cheerleader. (Rev: BL 1/1/94; SLJ 1/94; VOYA 12/93)

1666 Paulsen, Gary. *Tracker* (7–9). 1984, Bradbury paper $3.95 (0-317-62280-3). John's encounters with nature help him accept the approaching death of his grandfather.

1667 Pearson, Gayle. *The Secret Box* (5–8). 1997, Simon & Schuster $16.00 (0-689-81379-1). Five short stories set in Oakland, California, about the pangs of growing up. (Rev: BCCB 7–8/97; BL 8/97; BR 3–4/98; HBG 3/98; SLJ 6/97)

1668 Peck, Richard. *Are You in the House Alone?* (7–10). 1977, Bantam paper $4.99 (0-440-90227-4). Gail is raped by a classmate while she is on a babysitting assignment. (Rev: BL 2/15/88)

1669 Pennebaker, Ruth. *Conditions of Love* (8–10). 1999, Holt $16.95 (0-8050-6104-5). In this first-person narrative, 14-year-old Sarah tells of her problems adjusting to her father's death and getting along with her mother, plus difficulties at her school where she is considered an outsider. (Rev: BL 5/15/99; HBG 9/99; SLJ 5/99; VOYA 6/99)

1670 Peters, Julie Anne. *Define "Normal"* (6–8). 2000, Little, Brown $16.95 (0-316-70631-0). Bright, over-achiever Antonia is paired, in a peer counseling situation, with a notorious punker Jas-mine Luther. (Rev: BL 5/15/00; HBG 9/00; SLJ 7/00; VOYA 6/00)

1671 Peterseil, Tehila. *The Safe Place* (5–8). 1996, Pitspopany $16.95 (0-943706-71-8); paper $12.95 (0-943706-72-6). A moving story of an Israeli girl and the problems she faces at school because of a learning disability. (Rev: SLJ 12/96)

1672 Pevsner, Stella. *Cute Is a Four-Letter Word* (7–9). 1980, Archway paper $2.75 (0-671-68845-6). The best-laid plans of Clara go awry.

1673 Pevsner, Stella. *Is Everyone Moonburned But Me?* (4–7). 2000, Clarion $15.00 (0-395-95770-2). In this lighthearted look at adolescent problems, 13-year-old Hannah shoulders many household responsibilities when her parents divorce. (Rev: BCCB 6/00; BL 5/1/00; HBG 10/00; SLJ 7/00)

1674 Pfeffer, Susan Beth. *Kid Power* (6–9). Illus. 1988, Scholastic paper $2.99 (0-590-42607-9). A group of youngsters join together to do jobs for money.

1675 Philbrick, Rodman. *The Fire Pony* (5–8). 1996, Scholastic paper $14.95 (0-590-55251-1). Rescued from a foster home by his half-brother Joe, Roy hopes that life will be better on the ranch where Joe finds work. (Rev: BCCB 7–8/96; BL 5/1/96; HB 7–8/96; SLJ 9/96; VOYA 10/96)

1676 Philbrick, Rodman. *Freak the Mighty* (7–10). 1993, Scholastic paper $15.95 (0-590-47412-X). When Maxwell Kane, the son of Killer Kane, becomes friends with Kevin, a new boy with a birth defect, he gains a new interest in school and learning. (Rev: BL 12/15/93; SLJ 12/93*; VOYA 4/94)

1677 Pinkney, Andrea D. *Raven in a Dove House* (6–10). 1998, Harcourt $16.00 (0-15-201461-6). Twelve-year-old Nell, who is spending the summer with an aunt in upstate New York, is terrified when her male cousin, Foley, takes up with a smooth-talking boy who hides a gun in her dollhouse. (Rev: BCCB 5/98; BL 2/15/98; HBG 10/98; SLJ 5/98; VOYA 10/98)

1678 Platt, Kin. *Crocker* (7–10). 1983, Harper-Collins $11.95 (0-397-32025-6). Dorothy is attracted to a new boy in school.

1679 Platt, Randall B. *The Cornerstone* (8–12). 1998, Catbird Pr. $21.95 (0-945774-40-0). Using flashbacks, this novel tells about the growth of a tough 15-year-old charity case at summer camp on a scholarship in 1944, where he meets a Navy man on medical leave who changes his life. (Rev: VOYA 2/99)

1680 Plum-Ucci, Carol. *What Happened to Lani Garver* (8–12). 2002, Harcourt $17.00 (0-15-216813-3). Claire, a popular 16-year-old who is battling private demons, finds support and a cause in a newly arrived, curiously androgynous student who disturbs her friends. (Rev: BCCB 11/02; BL 8/02; HBG 10/03; SLJ 10/02*; VOYA 12/02)

1681 Porter, Tracey. *A Dance of Sisters* (5–8). 2002, HarperCollins LB $17.89 (0-06-029239-3). When a young ballet dancer's dreams are dashed, she is comforted by her sister. (Rev: BCCB 1/03; BL 2/15/03; HBG 3/03; SLJ 1/03)

1682 Potok, Chaim. *Zebra and Other Stories* (7–12). Illus. 1998, Random $19.99 (0-679-95440-6); paper $4.99 (0-375-80686-5). An anthology of six stories about experiences that youngsters have that help them along the road to maturity. (Rev: BL 7/98; HBG 3/99; SLJ 9/98; VOYA 10/98)

1683 Reed, Don C. *The Kraken* (6–10). 1997, Boyds Mills paper $7.95 (1-56397-693-5). In Newfoundland in the late 1800s, a boy struggles to survive against the impersonal rich and the harsh environment. (Rev: BL 3/15/95; SLJ 2/95)

1684 Reynolds, Marilyn. *Detour for Emmy* (8–12). 1993, Morning Glory paper $8.95 (0-930934-76-8). Emmy is a good student and a hunk's girlfriend, but her home life includes a deserter father and an alcoholic mother. Emmy's pregnancy causes more hardship when she keeps the baby. (Rev: BL 10/1/93; SLJ 7/93; VOYA 12/93)

1685 Reynolds, Marilyn. *If You Loved Me: True-to-Life Series from Hamilton High* (8–12). 1999, Morning Glory paper $8.95 (1-885356-55-2). Seventeen-year-old Lauren, born to a drug-addicted mother now deceased, vows to abstain from drugs and sex, but the latter is particularly difficult because of an insistent boyfriend. (Rev: BL 9/1/99; HBG 4/00; VOYA 2/00)

1686 Reynolds, Marilyn. *Telling: True-to-Life Series from Hamilton High* (7–10). 1996, Morning Glory paper $8.95 (1-885356-03-X). Twelve-year-old Cassie is confused and embarrassed when her adult neighbor makes sexual advances towards her. (Rev: BL 4/1/96; SLJ 5/96; VOYA 6/96)

1687 Reynolds, Marilyn. *Too Soon for Jeff* (8–12). 1994, Morning Glory $15.95 (0-930934-90-3); paper $8.95 (0-930934-91-1). Jeff's hopes of going to college on a debate scholarship are put in jeopardy when his girlfriend happily announces she's pregnant. Jeff reluctantly prepares for fatherhood. (Rev: BL 9/15/94; SLJ 9/94; VOYA 12/94)

1688 Rhue, Morton. *The Wave* (7–10). 1981, Dell paper $5.50 (0-440-99371-7). A high school experiment to test social interaction backfires when an elitist group is formed.

1689 Roberts, Laura P. *Get a Life* (7–10). Series: Clearwater Crossing. 1998, Bantam Doubleday Dell paper $4.50 (0-553-57118-4). A group of teenagers, each with a problem or a family secret not to be shared, come together as volunteers planning a high school charity carnival. (Rev: BR 9–10/98; SLJ 11/98)

1690 Roberts, Willo Davis. *Secrets at Hidden Valley* (5–7). 1997, Simon & Schuster $16.00 (0-689-81166-7). Gradually, 11-year-old Steffi learns to fit in when she is sent to northern Michigan to live with a grandfather she has never met. (Rev: BL 3/15/97; SLJ 6/97)

1691 Rodowsky, Colby. *Remembering Mog* (7–12). 1996, Avon paper $3.99 (0-380-72922-9). With the death of her older sister and mentor, Annie must face the future alone and make her own decisions. (Rev: BL 2/1/96; BR 9–10/96; SLJ 3/96*; VOYA 6/96)

1692 Roos, Stephen. *Confessions of a Wayward Preppie* (7–10). 1986, Dell paper $2.75 (0-440-91586-4). Through an unusual bequest, Cary is able to attend a classy prep school but there his troubles begin. (Rev: BL 6/1/86; BR 9–10/86; SLJ 5/86; VOYA 8/86)

1693 Rosenberg, Liz. *Heart and Soul* (8–12). 1996, Harcourt $11.00 (0-15-200942-6); paper $5.00 (0-15-201270-2). It is only when Willie helps a troubled Jewish classmate that she is able to straighten out her own problems. (Rev: BL 6/1–15/96; VOYA 8/96)

1694 Rottman, S. L. *Head Above Water* (6–9). 1999, Peachtree $14.95 (1-56145-185-1). Skye's efforts to care for her mentally disabled brother, to work toward a swimming scholarship, and to deal with a violent boyfriend threaten to overwhelm her in this arresting novel. (Rev: BL 11/15/99; HBG 4/00)

1695 Rottman, S. L. *Hero* (5–8). 1997, Peachtree $14.95 (1-56145-159-2). When his home life becomes unbearable, Sean is sent to Carbondale Ranch, where his sense of self-worth gradually grows. (Rev: BL 12/1/97; HBG 3/98; SLJ 12/97; VOYA 12/97)

1696 Rottman, S. L. *Rough Waters* (7–12). 1998, Peachtree $14.95 (1-56145-172-X). After the deaths of their parents, teenage brothers Gregg and Scott move to Colorado to live with an uncle who runs a white-water rafting business. (Rev: BL 5/1/98; BR 11–12/98; HBG 9/98; SLJ 8/98; VOYA 8/98)

1697 Rottman, S. L. *Stetson* (6–12). 2002, Viking $16.99 (0-670-03542-4). Prankster Stetson tries to get his life on track and graduate from high school despite a troubled past. (Rev: BCCB 3/02; BL 4/1/02; HBG 10/02; SLJ 4/02; VOYA 2/02)

1698 Russo, Marisabina. *House of Sports* (5–8). 2002, Greenwillow LB $16.89 (0-06-623804-8). Twelve-year-old Jim faces many problems, from a fear of public speaking to dealing with a girl on the basketball team. (Rev: BCCB 3/02; BL 3/15/02; HBG 10/02; SLJ 4/02)

1699 Ryan, Mary C. *The Voice from the Mendelsohns' Maple* (5–7). 1990, Little, Brown $13.95 (0-316-76360-8). Penny tries to cope with many problems, including finding out the identity of the woman who is hiding in the neighbor's maple tree. (Rev: SLJ 12/89)

1700 Ryan, Mary E. *Me, My Sister, and I* (4–7). 1992, Simon & Schuster paper $15.00 (0-671-73851-8). Mattie is in a dilemma about whom to ask to the Sadie Hawkins dance in this story of the ups and downs of being twins. (Rev: BL 12/15/92)

1701 Ryden, Hope. *Wild Horse Summer* (5–8). Illus. 1997, Clarion $15.00 (0-395-77519-1). During a summer on her relatives' Wyoming ranch, Alison overcomes her anxieties and fears. (Rev: BL 8/97; HBG 3/98; SLJ 9/97)

1702 Rylant, Cynthia. *A Blue-Eyed Daisy* (5–8). 1985, Macmillan LB $15.00 (0-02-777960-2); Dell paper $3.25 (0-440-40927-6). Fourteen interrelated stories describe one year in the rather sad and troubled world of an 11-year-old girl growing up in West Virginia. (Rev: BCCB 9/85; BL 6/15/85; HB 7–8/85; SLJ 4/85)

1703 Rylant, Cynthia. *A Fine White Dust* (6–8). 1986, Bradbury LB $16.00 (0-02-777240-3). A 13-year-old boy falls under the spell of a traveling preacher with tragic results. (Rev: BL 9/1/86; BR 3–4/87; SLJ 9/86)

1704 Rylant, Cynthia. *Missing May* (5–8). 1992, Orchard LB $15.99 (0-531-08596-1); Dell paper $5.50 (0-440-40865-2). Caring about each other is the tender message in this story of 12-year-old Summer, who, along with her uncle, must cope with the death of her beloved aunt. Newbery Medal winner, 1993. (Rev: BCCB 3/92*; BL 2/15/92*; HB 3–4/92; SLJ 3/92*)

1705 Sachar, Louis. *Holes* (6–9). 1998, Farrar $17.00 (0-374-33265-7). This Newbery Medal–winning novel describes unfortunate Stanley Yelnats's stay at a juvenile detention home after he has been wrongfully found guilty of stealing a pair of sneakers. (Rev: BCCB 9/98; BL 6/1–15/98; BR 5–6/99; HB 9–10/98*; HBG 3/99; SLJ 9/98; VOYA 12/98)

1706 Sachar, Louis. *Stanley Yelnats' Survival Guide to Camp Green Lake* (5–7). 2003, Dell paper $4.99 (0-440-41947-6). In this companion book to *Holes* (1998), Stanley Yelnats provides additional information about the detention camp's idiosyncrasies and his fellow diggers, as well as survival tips such as how to identify rattlesnakes. (Rev: SLJ 9/03)

1707 Sachs, Marilyn. *Almost Fifteen* (6–8). 1988, Avon paper $2.95 (0-380-70357-2). A light story of a practical girl, her boyfriends, and her impractical parents. (Rev: BL 6/15/87; SLJ 5/87)

1708 Sachs, Marilyn. *Class Pictures* (7–9). 1980, Avon paper $2.95 (0-380-61408-1). The friendship from kindergarten through high school between two girls is recalled through old class pictures.

1709 Sachs, Marilyn. *Fourteen* (7–9). 1983, Avon paper $2.95 (0-380-69842-0). First love comes to Rebecca by way of a new neighbor.

1710 Sachs, Marilyn. *Peter and Veronica* (7–9). 1995, Puffin paper $5.99 (0-14-037082-X). Peter's friendship with non-Jewish Veronica faces a crisis over his bar mitzvah.

1711 Salinger, J. D. *The Catcher in the Rye* (7–12). 1951, Little, Brown $25.95 (0-316-76953-3); Bantam paper $3.95 (0-553-25025-6). For mature readers, the saga of Holden Caulfield and his three days in New York City. (Rev: BL 10/1/88)

1712 Salisbury, Graham. *Jungle Dogs* (5–9). 1998, Delacorte $15.95 (0-385-32187-2). In this novel set in a poor Hawaiian village, young Boy must face his fears and confront the dogs that terrorize him on his paper route. (Rev: BL 9/1/98; HB 9–10/98; HBG 3/99; VOYA 10/98)

1713 Savage, Deborah. *Under a Different Sky* (7–9). 1997, Houghton $16.00 (0-395-77395-4). Two troubled teenagers — Ben, a born horseman, and Lara, a newcomer in the area — find friendship in this novel set in a poor rural Pennsylvania community. (Rev: BL 3/15/97; BR 9–10/97; SLJ 5/97*; VOYA 6/97)

1714 Say, Allen. *The Sign Painter* (5–9). Illus. 2000, Houghton $17.00 (0-395-97974-9). An Asian American youth who wants to be a serious artist gets a job painting signboards scattered through the desert. (Rev: BL 10/1/00; HB 9–10/00; HBG 3/01; SLJ 9/00)

1715 Schenker, Dona. *The Secret Circle* (5–8). 1998, Knopf $16.00 (0-679-88989-2). When Jamie wants to join the exclusive Secret Circle at her new private school, she finds the tests she must pass are against her principles. (Rev: BCCB 10/98; BL 11/1/98; HBG 3/99; SLJ 10/98)

1716 Sebestyen, Ouida. *Out of Nowhere* (6–9). 1994, Orchard LB $17.99 (0-531-08689-5). The story of the bonding into a sort of family of a quirky group of characters, among them Harley, 13, who's left home; his dog Ishmael; Bill, a junk collector; and May, the "queen of clean." (Rev: BL 4/1/94; SLJ 3/94; VOYA 4/94)

1717 Sefton, Catherine. *Island of the Strangers* (7–9). 1985, Harcourt $12.95 (0-15-239100-2). City kids from Belfast clash with town toughs in this novel set on an island off Northern Ireland. (Rev: BL 1/1/86; SLJ 1/86)

1718 Seymour, Tres. *The Revelation of Saint Bruce* (7–12). 1998, Orchard paper $16.95 (0-531-30109-5). Because of his honesty, Bruce is responsible for the expulsion of several friends from school. (Rev: BL 10/15/98; BR 5–6/99; HBG 3/99; SLJ 9/98; VOYA 2/99)

1719 Sheldon, Dyan. *Planet Janet* (6–10). 2003, Candlewick $14.99 (0-7636-2048-3). Janet pours out to her diary the frustrations she and her friend Disha face in their dealings with family and friends in this entertaining novel set in London. (Rev: BCCB 3/03; BL 3/15/03; SLJ 5/03)

1720 Shoup, Barbara. *Stranded in Harmony* (7–10). 1997, Hyperion LB $18.49 (0-7868-2284-8). Lucas, an 18-year-old popular senior in high school, is discontented until he meets and becomes friendly with an older woman. (Rev: BL 7/97; BR 11–12/97; HBG 3/98; SLJ 6/97*)

1721 Shura, Mary Francis. *The Sunday Doll* (5–7). 1988, Avon paper $2.95 (0-380-70618-0). Thirteen-year-old Emmy is miffed when the family won't tell her what has happened to upset her older sister Jayne, until she learns that Jayne's boyfriend has committed suicide. (Rev: BCCB 7–8/88; BL 7/88; SLJ 8/88)

1722 Shyer, Marlene Fanta. *The Rainbow Kite* (6–8). 2002, Marshall Cavendish $15.95 (0-7614-5122-6). Matthew tells of his gay brother Bennett's "coming out," a process that began painfully but ended happily when Bennett was accepted by his family and friends. (Rev: BCCB 12/02; BL 12/15/02; HBG 3/03; SLJ 11/02; VOYA 6/03)

1723 Silverman. *Mirror Mirror: Twisted Tales* (5–8). 2002, Scholastic paper $15.95 (0-439-29593-9). Disturbing stories serve as metaphors for the problems of drug use, divorce, homelessness, and other ills. (Rev: BL 9/1/02; HBG 10/02; SLJ 8/02; VOYA 6/02)

1724 Singer, Marilyn, ed. *Stay True: Short Stories for Strong Girls* (7–12). 1998, Scholastic paper $16.95 (0-590-36031-0). There are 11 new short stories in this collection that explores the problems girls face growing up and how they discover inner strength. (Rev: BL 4/1/98; BR 11–12/98; HB 3–4/98; SLJ 5/98; VOYA 4/98)

1725 Skinner, David. *The Wrecker* (6–9). 1995, Simon & Schuster $14.00 (0-671-79771-9). A bully, a genius, and a newcomer (the narrator) are part of a story with elements as compelling as those of Robert Cormier or Stephen King. (Rev: BL 8/95*; SLJ 1/00; VOYA 5/95)

1726 Slade, Arthur. *Tribes* (7–10). 2002, Random $15.95 (0-385-73003-9). Percy Montmount views his senior classmates through the eyes of an anthropologist, giving some interesting and humorous insights. (Rev: BL 10/15/02; HB 1–2/03; HBG 3/03; SLJ 10/02; VOYA 2/03)

1727 Slepian, Jan. *The Broccoli Tapes* (5–8). 1989, Putnam $15.99 (0-399-21712-6); Scholastic paper $3.50 (0-590-43473-X). Sara uses tapes during her stay in Hawaii to keep up with her class oral history project. (Rev: BCCB 4/89; BL 4/15/89; SLJ 4/89; VOYA 6/89)

1728 Slepian, Jan. *The Mind Reader* (5–7). 1997, Putnam $15.95 (0-399-23150-1). A 12-year-old clairvoyant runs away from vaudeville and a drunken father to live with a cousin he has never met. (Rev: BL 9/15/97; HB 9–10/97; HBG 3/98; SLJ 9/97)

1729 Smith, Cynthia Leitich. *Rain Is Not My Indian Name* (5–9). 2001, HarperCollins LB $15.89 (0-06-029504-X). Native American girl Rain's love of photography helps her to overcome her terrible grief at the death of a friend. (Rev: BCCB 9/01; HBG 3/02; SLJ 6/01)

1730 Smith, Sherri L. *Lucy the Giant* (6–10). 2002, Delacorte $15.95 (0-385-72940-5). Lucy's height — 6 feet at the age of 15 — is a handicap until it helps her find a new life posing as an adult aboard a crabbing boat in Alaska. (Rev: BCCB 4/02; BL 2/15/02; HB 3–4/02*; HBG 10/02; SLJ 1/02)

1731 Snyder, Zilpha Keatley. *The Runaways* (4–8). 1999, Delacorte $15.95 (0-385-32599-1). Twelve-year-old Dani O'Donnell, angry at her mother for moving down to a desert town where she feels lost, makes plans to run away. (Rev: BL 1/1–15/99; BR 9–10/99; HBG 10/99; SLJ 3/99)

1732 Sonenklar, Carol. *My Own Worst Enemy* (5–8). 1999, Holiday $15.95 (0-8234-1456-6). In this first-person narrative, Eve Belkin finds there is a price to pay when she outdoes herself to be popular in her new school. (Rev: BL 5/15/99; HBG 9/99; SLJ 8/99; VOYA 10/99)

1733 Sones, Sonya. *What My Mother Doesn't Know* (6–10). 2001, Simon & Schuster $17.00 (0-689-84114-0). Sophie, 14, expresses her feelings about falling in and out of love in a poetic narrative that is humorous and romantic. (Rev: BCCB 12/01; BL 11/1/01; HBG 10/02; SLJ 10/01; VOYA 10/01)

1734 Soto, Gary. *Baseball in April and Other Stories* (5–9). 1990, Harcourt $16.00 (0-15-205720-X). A group of stories about young Hispanics growing up in Southern California. (Rev: BL 3/1/90; SLJ 6/90; VOYA 8/90)

1735 Soto, Gary. *Buried Onions* (8–12). 1997, Harcourt $17.00 (0-15-201333-4). A junior college dropout, 19-year-old Eddie is trying to support himself in this story set in the barrio of Fresno, California. (Rev: BL 11/15/97; HBG 3/98; SLJ 1/98; VOYA 10/97)

1736 Soto, Gary. *The Pool Party* (4–7). 1992, Delacorte $13.95 (0-385-30890-6). Rudy, part of a Mexican American family, has growing-up problems. (Rev: SLJ 6/93)

1737 Southgate, Martha. *Another Way to Dance* (6–8). 1996, Delacorte $15.95 (0-385-32191-0). A young African American girl is thrilled to spend a summer at the School of American Ballet in New York City but encounters unforeseen problems.

(Rev: BL 12/1/96; BR 11–12/96; SLJ 12/96; VOYA 10/96)

1738 Speregen, Devra. *Phone Call from a Flamingo* (5–7). Series: Full House. 1993, Pocket paper $3.99 (0-671-88004-7). Stephanie decides that the price of being popular with the in crowd is too high when it involves hurting others. Based on the TV series *Full House*. (Rev: SLJ 11/93)

1739 Spinelli, Jerry. *Jason and Marceline* (7–10). 2000, Little, Brown paper $6.99 (0-316-80662-5). Jason, now in the 9th grade, sorts out his feelings toward girls in general and Marceline in particular. Preceded by *Space Station Seventh Grade*. (Rev: BL 1/1/87; SLJ 2/87)

1740 Spinelli, Jerry. *Space Station Seventh Grade* (6–8). 2000, Little, Brown paper $6.99 (0-316-80605-6). Jason has many adventures, mostly hilarious, during his 7th-grade year.

1741 Spinelli, Jerry. *Stargirl* (6–9). 2000, Knopf $15.95 (0-679-88637-0). When the unusual Stargirl appears at Mica High School, things change and social relationships are questioned. (Rev: BL 6/1–15/00; HB 7–8/00; HBG 3/01; SLJ 8/00)

1742 Spinelli, Jerry. *Wringer* (4–7). 1997, HarperCollins LB $16.89 (0-06-024914-5). A sensitive boy must participate in the massacre of thousands of pigeons released at an annual fair. (Rev: BL 9/1/97*; HB 9–10/97; HBG 3/98; SLJ 9/97*)

1743 Springer, Nancy. *Secret Star* (7–10). 1997, Putnam $15.95 (0-399-23028-9). Fourteen-year-old Tess Mathis, strong but dirt-poor, can't remember anything before age 10, but when a scar-faced stranger comes to town, she must confront her past. (Rev: BL 4/1/97; BR 5–6/97; SLJ 5/97; VOYA 12/97)

1744 Stanley, Diane. *A Time Apart* (6–9). 1999, Morrow $15.95 (0-688-16997-X). A 13-year-old girl discovers she has inner strengths when she spends a summer with her father on an archaeological project to replicate an Iron Age village in England. (Rev: BCCB 10/99; BL 6/1–15/99; HBG 4/00; SLJ 9/99)

1745 Staples, Suzanne F. *Dangerous Skies* (7–10). 1996, Farrar $16.00 (0-374-31694-5). An interracial friendship, sexual abuse, and family secrets are themes in this novel about a white boy and a black girl growing up in the eastern shore of Virginia. (Rev: BL 9/1/96*; BR 1–2/97; SLJ 10/96; VOYA 12/96)

1746 Stevens, Diane. *Liza's Blue Moon* (6–8). 1995, Greenwillow $15.00 (0-688-13542-0). A coming-of-age story where a young girl feels she has been left behind by all that matters in life. (Rev: BL 4/1/95; SLJ 4/95)

1747 Stevens, Diane. *Liza's Star Wish* (6–10). 1997, Greenwillow $15.00 (0-688-15310-0). In this sequel to *Liza's Blue Moon*, Liza and her mother spend time in Rockport one summer, and Liza deals with vast changes in her life, including family relationships and friendships. (Rev: BL 9/15/97; HBG 3/98; SLJ 10/97)

1748 Stewart, Jennifer J. *The Bean King's Daughter* (5–7). 2002, Holiday $16.95 (0-8234-1644-5). Phoebe, a 12-year-old heiress, reluctantly learns about herself and her young stepmother while at an Arizona ranch. (Rev: BL 9/1/02; HBG 10/02; SLJ 7/02)

1749 Strasser, Todd. *CON-fidence* (5–8). 2002, Holiday $16.95 (0-8234-1394-2). Shy Lauren falls under the spell of the dazzling Celeste, failing to perceive Celeste's underlying motives. (Rev: BCCB 2/03; BL 4/15/03; HBG 10/03; SLJ 1/03; VOYA 4/03)

1750 Strasser, Todd. *How I Changed My Life* (7–12). 1995, Simon & Schuster paper $16.00 (0-671-88415-8). Introverted Bo, the theater department stage manager, works on her self-image and weight problem when handsome football captain Kyle joins a production. (Rev: BL 5/1/95; SLJ 5/95)

1751 Swallow, Pamela Curtis. *It Only Looks Easy* (4–7). 2003, Millbrook $15.95 (0-7613-1790-2). Kat's problems start when her dog is hit by a car and she "borrows" a bicycle to get to the vet only to have it stolen from her. (Rev: BL 4/15/03; HBG 10/03; SLJ 4/03)

1752 Swarthout, Glendon. *Bless the Beasts and Children* (7–12). 1995, Pocket Books paper $6.99 (0-671-52151-9). At summer camp a group of misfits prove they have the right stuff. (Rev: BL 9/1/97)

1753 Sweeney, Joyce. *Waiting for June* (8–11). 2003, Marshall Cavendish $15.95 (0-7614-5138-2). High school senior Sophie is pregnant, reluctant to disclose the identity of the father, and in danger, in this complex, suspenseful novel. (Rev: BL 9/1/03; SLJ 10/03)

1754 Tamar, Erika. *The Things I Did Last Summer* (7–9). 1994, Harcourt $10.95 (0-15-282490-1); paper $3.95 (0-15-200020-8). A teenager spending the summer on Long Island with his pregnant stepmother loses his virginity when he meets a deceptive older woman. (Rev: BL 3/15/94; SLJ 4/94; VOYA 6/94)

1755 Tanzman, Carol M. *The Shadow Place* (6–9). 2002, Millbrook $15.95 (0-7613-1588-8). When her friend Rodney's behavior spins out of control and she finds out he's obsessed with guns, Lissa must decide if she can trust him in this novel about friendship and peer pressure. (Rev: BCCB 10/02; BL 11/15/02; HBG 3/03; SLJ 10/02; VOYA 12/02)

1756 Tarbox, Katherine. *Katie.Com: My Story* (6–10). 2000, Dutton $19.95 (0-525-94543-1). Katie, a lonely 8th grader, forms an e-mail relationship with a man who turns out to be a 41-year-old pedophile. (Rev: BL 7/00; SLJ 9/00)

1757 Thesman, Jean. *Calling the Swan* (5–8). 2000, Viking $15.99 (0-670-88874-5). A troubled girl gets help when she forms a tentative friendship with kids in her summer school English class. (Rev: BL 6/1–15/00; HB 7–8/00; HBG 10/00; SLJ 5/00; VOYA 6/00)

1758 Thesman, Jean. *Cattail Moon* (6–9). 1994, Avon paper $4.50 (0-380-72504-5). Julia, 14, is at odds with her mother, who wants to transform her from a classical musician into a cheerleader. (Rev: BL 4/1/94; SLJ 5/94; VOYA 8/94)

1759 Thesman, Jean. *Couldn't I Start Over?* (7–10). 1989, Avon paper $2.95 (0-380-75717-6). Growing up in a caring family situation, teenager Shiloh still faces many problems in her coming of age. (Rev: BL 11/15/89; VOYA 2/90)

1760 Thesman, Jean. *The Rain Catchers* (7–12). 1991, Houghton $15.00 (0-395-55333-4). Grayling learns the importance of storytelling in keeping the past alive, understanding others and herself, and surviving difficult times. (Rev: BL 4/15/91*; SLJ 3/91)

1761 Thesman, Jean. *Summerspell* (7–10). 1995, Simon & Schuster $15.00 (0-671-50130-5). A web of lies and secrets are behind a girl's escape from sexual harassment to a cabin where life had been safe and happy in the past. (Rev: BL 5/1/95; SLJ 6/95)

1762 Thomas, Joyce C. *When the Nightingale Sings* (6–8). 1992, HarperCollins paper $3.95 (0-06-440524-9). Marigold's only joy in her stepfamily is singing, which leads her to audition for a Baptist church choir, where she discovers self-worth, her family, and happiness. (Rev: BL 1/1/93; SLJ 2/93)

1763 Thomas, Rob. *Rats Saw God* (8–12). 1996, Simon & Schuster paper $4.99 (0-689-80777-5). At the suggestion of his counselor, high school senior Steve York explores his life, his problems, and how things went wrong when he moved from Texas to California. (Rev: BL 6/1–15/96; BR 1–2/97; SLJ 6/96*; VOYA 6/96)

1764 Thompson, Julian. *Facing It* (7–9). 1989, Avon paper $2.95 (0-380-84491-5). An accident ruins the baseball chances of the star at Camp Raycroft. A reissue.

1765 Thompson, Julian. *Philo Fortune's Awesome Journey to His Comfort Zone* (8–12). 1995, Hyperion $16.95 (0-7868-0067-4). A story of a youth who discovers the possibilities of the man he might become. (Rev: BL 5/1/95; SLJ 5/95; VOYA 2/96)

1766 Tolan, Stephanie S. *Plague Year* (8–12). 1991, Fawcett paper $6.50 (0-449-70403-3). Nonconformist Bran, whose father is a mass murderer, faces

problems of acceptance at his new high school. (Rev: BL 4/1/90; SLJ 6/90)

1767 Tomey, Ingrid. *Nobody Else Has to Know* (8–10). 1999, Delacorte $15.95 (0-385-32624-6). Fifteen-year-old Webb, a high school track star, feels increasing guilt after he hits a young girl while driving without a license and his grandfather takes the blame. (Rev: BL 12/15/99; HBG 4/00; SLJ 9/99; VOYA 4/00)

1768 Tomey, Ingrid. *Savage Carrot* (7–9). 1993, Scribners $14.95 (0-684-19633-6). When the death of Carrot's father robs her of her hero, she withdraws from everyone except her developmentally disabled uncle. (Rev: BL 3/1/94; SLJ 2/94; VOYA 4/94)

1769 Torres, Laura. *November Ever After* (8–12). 1999, Holiday $16.95 (0-8234-1464-7). Still recovering from her mother's death, 16-yer-old Amy discovers that her best friend, Sara, is a lesbian and in love with a girl in her class. (Rev: BL 12/1/99; HBG 4/00; SLJ 1/00)

1770 Toten, Teresa. *The Onlyhouse* (5–8). 1996, Red Deer paper $7.95 (0-88995-137-3). Eleven-year-old Lucija, whose family was originally from Croatia, relocates to a new house in suburban Toronto after several years in a dense downtown neighborhood with a large immigrant population, and must adjust to a new school, peer pressures, and bullies. (Rev: SLJ 7/96)

1771 Trembath, Don. *The Tuesday Cafe* (6–9). 1996, Orca paper $6.95 (1-55143-074-6). Harper Winslow, a disaffected, wealthy teenager, learns about life and grows up when he is forced to join a local writing group called "The Tuesday Cafe." (Rev: BL 8/97; SLJ 9/96; VOYA 2/97)

1772 Tullson, Diane. *Edge* (7–10). 2003, Fitzhenry & Whiteside paper $6.95 (0-7737-6230-2). Tired of being bullied, Marlie Peters, 14, joins a group of other outcast students only to realize that they are involved in a dangerous plot. (Rev: BL 3/1/03; SLJ 10/03; VOYA 6/03)

1773 Ure, Jean. *Skinny Melon and Me* (5–7). Illus. 2001, Holt $16.00 (0-8050-6359-5). An interesting British novel about a young Cherry Waterton, who keeps a diary; her mother's boyfriend who sends Cherry rebus letters to win her over; and Cherry's teacher, who writes to a friend about the girl's problem behavior. (Rev: BCCB 3/01; BL 1/1–15/01; HBG 10/01; SLJ 1/01; VOYA 4/01)

1774 Vail, Rachel. *Do-Over* (5–9). 1992, Avon paper $3.99 (0-380-72180-5). The story of 13-year-old Whitman Levy's first crush, first kiss, first heartbreak, and first real boy-girl relationship, as well as assorted family problems. (Rev: BL 8/92*; SLJ 9/92)

1775 Vail, Rachel. *Ever After* (5–9). 1994, Orchard LB $16.99 (0-531-08688-7); Avon paper $3.99 (0-

380-72465-0). Fourteen-year-old Molly is trying to act maturely but always seems to mess things up. (Rev: BCCB 4/94; BL 3/1/94; HB 5–6/94, 7–8/94; SLJ 5/94*; VOYA 6/94)

1776 Vande Velde, Vivian. *Curses, Inc.: And Other Stories* (6–10). 1997, Harcourt $16.00 (0-15-201452-7). In the title story in this collection of tales with surprise endings, Bill Essler thinks he has found the perfect way to get even with his girlfriend, who humiliated him, by utilizing a web site, Curses, Inc. (Rev: SLJ 6/97*; VOYA 6/97)

1777 Van Oosting, James. *The Last Payback* (5–8). 1997, HarperCollins $14.95 (0-06-027491-3). The story of how Dimple gradually accepts the death of her twin brother, who has died of a gunshot wound. (Rev: BCCB 6/97; BL 6/1–15/97; HB 7–8/97; SLJ 7/97)

1778 Velasquez, Gloria. *Tommy Stands Alone* (7–10). 1995, Arte Publico $14.95 (1-55885-146-1); paper $9.95 (1-55885-147-X). An engaging story about a Latino gay teen who is humiliated and rejected but finds understanding from a Chicano therapist. (Rev: BL 10/15/95; SLJ 11/95; VOYA 12/95)

1779 Voigt, Cynthia. *Tell Me If the Lovers Are Losers* (7–10). 1982, Macmillan LB $17.00 (0-689-30911-2). Three college roommates clash until they find a common interest in volleyball. (Rev: BL 3/87)

1780 Walker, Alice. *To Hell with Dying* (4–7). Illus. 1988, Harcourt paper $8.00 (0-15-289074-2). The Walker family won't let old Mr. Sweet die. (Rev: BCCB 4/88; BL 4/15/88; HB 7–8/88)

1781 Walker, Paul R. *The Method* (8–12). 1990, Harcourt $14.95 (0-15-200528-5). A candid novel about a 15-year-old boy, his acting aspirations, and his sexual problems. (Rev: BL 8/90; SLJ 6/90)

1782 Wallace, Bill. *Aloha Summer* (7–9). 1997, Holiday $15.95 (0-8234-1306-3). Fourteen-year-old John Priddle moves with his family to Hawaii in 1925 and finds less than the island paradise he expected. However, his friendship with a Hawaiian classmate brings new meaning to his life. (Rev: BL 10/1/97; HBG 3/98; SLJ 10/97; VOYA 12/97)

1783 Wallace, Rich. *Losing Is Not an Option* (6–10). 2003, Knopf $15.95 (0-375-81351-9). Nine stories follow Ron, a high school athlete, through coming-of-age experiences including family problems, budding sexual attractions, and competition with his peers. (Rev: BL 8/03; HB 9–10/03; SLJ 9/03; VOYA 10/03)

1784 Walpole, Peter. *The Healer of Harrow Point* (4–7). 2000, Hampton Roads paper $11.95 (1-57174-167-4). A novel of love and compassion about a boy who is promised a hunting trip for his twelfth birthday but wonders if he can kill a deer, particularly after seeing one killed by poachers and

after meeting Emma, who can heal animals with her touch. (Rev: SLJ 10/00)

1785 Waltman, Kevin. *Nowhere Fast* (8–12). 2002, Scholastic paper $6.99 (0-439-09013-X). After stealing a car for joyriding, teenagers Gary and Wilson become entrapped in the activities of a former teacher with a dangerous agenda. (Rev: BL 2/1/03)

1786 Warner, Sally. *Totally Confidential* (4–7). 2000, HarperCollins LB $15.89 (0-06-028262-2). Twelve-year-old Quinney has a talent for giving good advice to others but this gift brings unforeseen responsibilities and problems. (Rev: BCCB 5/00; BL 6/1–15/00; HBG 10/00; SLJ 6/00)

1787 Wartski, Maureen C. *My Name Is Nobody* (7–10). 1988, Walker $15.95 (0-8027-6770-2). A victim of child abuse survives a suicide attempt and is given a second chance by a tough ex-cop. (Rev: BL 2/1/88; BR 9–10/88; SLJ 3/88; VOYA 4/88)

1788 Watts, Julia. *Finding H.F.* (7–12). 2001, Alyson paper $12.95 (1-55583-622-4). A humorous 16-year-old heroine named H.F. and her friend Bo, both gay, set off on a trip to that teaches them a lot about life outside their small Kentucky town. (Rev: BCCB 1/02; SLJ 2/02; VOYA 2/02)

1789 Weaver, Beth Nixon. *Rooster* (7–12). 2001, Winslow $15.95 (1-58837-001-1). In the 1960s, 15-year-old Kady is growing up in a confusing mix of poverty at home on a struggling orange grove, a devoted but disabled neighboring child, and a wealthy boyfriend who introduces her to marijuana. (Rev: BL 7/01; HB 7–8/01; HBG 10/01; SLJ 6/01; VOYA 2/02)

1790 Weiss, M. Jerry, and Helen S. Weiss, eds. *From One Experience to Another: Stories About Turning Points* (6–12). 1997, Tor $18.95 (0-312-86253-9). In 15 original stories, well-known young adult writers tell about incidents that were important turning points in their lives. (Rev: BL 2/1/98; BR 5–6/98; HBG 3/98; SLJ 11/97; VOYA 12/97)

1791 Wennick, Elizabeth. *Changing Jareth* (8–11). 2000, Polestar paper $6.95 (1-896095-97-6). Seventeen-year-old, street-smart Jareth is involved with two deaths, one of his younger brother and the other of a man who died of a heart attack while Jareth was robbing him. (Rev: BL 4/1/00; SLJ 5/00; VOYA 6/00)

1792 Wieler, Diana. *RanVan: A Worthy Opponent* (7–10). 1998, Douglas & McIntyre $16.95 (0-88899-271-8); paper $5.95 (0-88899-219-X). Nerdy 15-year-old RanVan finds his video game personality can spill over into real life. Preceded by *RanVan: The Defender* and followed by *RanVan: Magic Nation* (1998). (Rev: BL 11/15/98; SLJ 3/98)

1793 Wieler, Diana. *RanVan: The Defender* (7–12). 1997, Douglas & McIntyre $16.95 (0-88899-270-X). Orphaned Rhan Van, who lives with his grandmother in a city apartment, begins hanging out in bad company and soon finds he is vandalizing school and private property. (Rev: BL 2/1/98; SLJ 3/98)

1794 Williams, Carol L. *If I Forget, You Remember* (5–8). 1998, Delacorte $15.95 (0-385-32534-7). A first-person narrative about a self-centered 7th-grade girl who gains maturity after her grandmother, who is suffering from Alzheimer's disease, moves in. (Rev: BL 4/15/98; BR 9–10/98; HBG 10/98; SLJ 3/98; VOYA 10/98)

1795 Williams, Carol Lynch. *Carolina Autumn* (7–10). 2000, Delacorte $14.95 (0-385-32716-1). Slowly Caroline begins the healing process adjusting to the deaths of her father and sister and the distant behavior of her mother. (Rev: BL 9/1/00; HBG 10/01; SLJ 9/00)

1796 Williams, Lori Aurelia. *Shayla's Double Brown Baby Blues* (7–12). 2003, Pulse $17.00 (0-689-85670-9). In this sequel to *When Kambia Elaine Flew in from Neptune* (2000), 13-year-old Shayla must cope with problems including the arrival of a new half-sister, her friend Kambia's traumatic and abusive past, and her friend Lemm's alcoholism. (Rev: BL 7/01; BR 3–4/02; HB 9–10/01; SLJ 8/01)

1797 Williams, Lori Aurelia. *When Kambia Elaine Flew in from Neptune* (7–12). 2001, Pulse paper $17.00 (0-689-84593-6). In this first-person narrative, 12-year-old Shayla adjusts to the unhappy departure from the family of her older sister and finds escape in her friendship with an imaginative girl named Kambia. (Rev: BL 2/15/00)

1798 Williams-Garcia, Rita. *Like Sisters on the Homefront* (8–10). 1995, Lodestar $15.99 (0-525-67465-9). After 14-year-old Gayle Ann has an abortion to end her second pregnancy, her mother sends her down South to be rehabilitated by her God-fearing brother, a minister, whose family leads a very structured life and where Gayle Ann must follow rules and help care for her aged but strong-minded grandmother. (Rev: BL 9/1/95*; BR 1–2/96; SLJ 10/95; VOYA 4/96)

1799 Willis, Patricia. *Out of the Storm* (4–7). 1995, Clarion $15.00 (0-395-68708-X). In 1946, Mandy's family moves in with her difficult Aunt Bess, who makes her tend a flock of sheep. (Rev: BCCB 5/95; BL 4/15/95; SLJ 4/95)

1800 Wilson, Budge. *Sharla* (7–10). 1998, Stoddart paper $6.95 (0-7736-7467-5). A run-in with a polar bear, adjusting to a new school, trying to make friends, and getting used to severe weather are some of the problems 15-year-old Sharla faces when she moves with her family from Ottawa to Churchill, a small community in northern Manitoba. (Rev: SLJ 8/98)

1801 Wilson, Jacqueline. *Girls in Love* (7–10). Series: British Girls. 2002, Delacorte $9.95 (0-385-

72974-X). The romantic ups and downs of 13-year-od schoolmates Ellie, Magda, and Nadine are the focus of this first book in a trilogy set in Britain. (Rev: BCCB 2/02; BL 5/15/02; HBG 10/02; SLJ 1/02)

1802 Wilson, Jacqueline. *Girls Under Pressure* (7–10). Series: British Girls. 2002, Delacorte $9.95 (0-385-72975-8). The second volume in this trilogy finds the girls striving — sometimes excessively — to be thin, beautiful, and popular. The third book is titled *Girls Out Late* (2002). (Rev: BCCB 10/02; BL 5/15/02; HBG 10/02; SLJ 12/02; VOYA 12/02)

1803 Wilson, Johnniece M. *Poor Girl* (5–7). 1992, Scholastic $13.95 (0-590-44732-7). A first-person story about Miranda, who spends the summer trying to earn money for contact lenses before the fall. (Rev: BCCB 4/92; BL 8/92; SLJ 4/92)

1804 Winton, Tim. *Lockie Leonard, Human Torpedo* (6–8). 1992, Little, Brown $13.95 (0-316-94753-9). Set in Australia, the story of a 14-year-old surfer and his confusion as he begins a more intimate relationship with his girlfriend. (Rev: BL 12/15/91; SLJ 12/91)

1805 Wittlinger, Ellen. *Hard Love* (8–12). 1999, Simon & Schuster $16.95 (0-689-82134-4); paper $8.00 (0-689-84154-X). Two outsiders, John, a high school junior and fan of "zines," and Marisol, a self-proclaimed virgin lesbian, form an unusual relationship in this well-crafted novel that explores many teenage problems. (Rev: BL 10/1/99*; HB 7–8/99; HBG 9/99; SLJ 7/99; VOYA 8/99)

1806 Wittlinger, Ellen. *What's in a Name* (7–10). 2000, Simon & Schuster $16.00 (0-689-82551-X). Identity problems involving class, race, family, and sex are explored in these short stories about 10 different students at suburban Scrub Harbor High School. (Rev: BL 1/1–15/00; HB 3–4/00; HBG 9/00; SLJ 2/00; VOYA 4/00)

1807 Wittlinger, Ellen. *Zigzag* (8–12). 2003, Simon & Schuster $16.95 (0-689-84996-6). A summer cross-country car trip with her recently widowed aunt and two cousins poses many challenges for 17-year-old Robin. (Rev: BL 9/1/03; HB 7–8/03; SLJ 8/03; VOYA 10/03)

1808 Wojciechowska, Maia. *Shadow of a Bull* (5–8). 1964, Macmillan $16.95 (0-689-30042-5); paper $4.99 (0-689-71567-6). Manolo, surviving son of a great bullfighter, has his own "moment of truth" when he faces his first bull. Newbery Medal winner, 1965.

1809 Wood, June R. *The Man Who Loved Clowns* (5–8). 1992, Hyperion paper $4.95 (0-7868-1084-X). When Delrita's parents are killed in an auto accident, she grows close to her uncle, an adult with Down's syndrome. (Rev: BL 11/15/92; SLJ 9/92*)

1810 Wood, June R. *Turtle on a Fence Post* (5–8). 1997, Putnam paper $6.99 (0-698-11783-2). After the deaths of her parents and an uncle, Delrita, now living with an aunt and her husband, is so emotionally upset that it seems she will never love anyone again. A sequel to *The Man Who Loved Clowns* (1992). (Rev: BL 11/15/97; HBG 3/98; SLJ 9/97)

1811 Woods, Ron. *The Hero* (6–10). 2002, Knopf $15.95 (0-375-80612-1). When hapless young Dennis dies in a rafting incident in 1957, 14-year-old Jamie tells a lie intended to show the dead boy as a hero. (Rev: BCCB 3/02; BL 2/1/02; HB 3–4/02; HBG 10/02; SLJ 1/02; VOYA 8/02)

1812 Woodson, Jacqueline. *The House You Pass on the Way* (6–9). Illus. 1997, Puffin paper $5.99 (0-14-250191-3). A young girl from an interracial marriage feels left out and becomes a loner until she falls in love with a girl cousin who comes to visit. (Rev: BL 8/97; BR 3–4/98; SLJ 10/97; VOYA 10/97)

1813 Wright, Betty R. *The Summer of Mrs. MacGregor* (5–8). 1986, Holiday $15.95 (0-8234-0628-8). Meeting an exotic teenager who calls herself Mrs. Lillina MacGregor helps Linda solve her problem of jealousy toward her older sister. (Rev: BCCB 12/86; BL 11/1/86; SLJ 11/86; VOYA 4/87)

1814 Wright, Randall. *A Hundred Days from Home* (6–10). 2002, Holt $15.95 (0-8050-6885-6). Elam, 12, grief-stricken by the death of his best friend, slowly learns to trust a new friend when his family moves to the Arizona desert in the early 1960s. (Rev: BL 11/15/02; HBG 3/03; SLJ 9/02)

1815 Wyss, Thelma Hatch. *Ten Miles from Winnemucca* (6–8). 2002, HarperCollins $15.95 (0-06-029783-2). When his mother and new husband leave on their honeymoon, 16-year-old Martin decides to take a break from his new stepbrother and starts a new life for himself in Idaho. (Rev: BCCB 7–8/02; BL 2/1/02; HB 7–8/02; HBG 10/02; SLJ 6/02; VOYA 2/02)

1816 Yang, Margaret. *Locked Out* (6–9). 1996, Tudor $17.95 (0-936389-40-0). Gina is outraged and goaded into activism when she learns that the principal of her school, in an effort to curb smoking, has closed all the bathrooms except those close to his office. (Rev: SLJ 5/96)

1817 Young, Karen Romano. *Video* (6–12). 1999, Greenwillow $16.00 (0-688-16517-6). A multilayered story in which Janine confronts a flasher and gains the support of classmates who have been shunning her. (Rev: BL 10/1/99; HBG 4/00; SLJ 10/99)

1818 Young, Ronder T. *Moving Mama to Town* (5–8). 1997, Orchard LB $18.99 (0-531-33025-7). Although his father is a gambler and a failure, Fred never loses faith in him in this story of a boy who must help support his family although he's only 13. (Rev: BL 6/1–15/97; BR 9–10/97; HB 7–8/97; SLJ 6/97)

1819 Young, Ronder Thomas. *Objects in Mirror* (7–10). 2002, Millbrook $15.95 (0-7613-1580-2). Grace, 16, feels uncertain of her own image as she juggles the demands of a difficult family and high school friends. (Rev: BL 5/1/02; HBG 10/02; VOYA 6/02)

1820 Yumoto, Kazumi. *The Letters* (8–12). 2002, Farrar $16.00 (0-374-34383-7). Attending the funeral of her former landlady proves cathartic for Chaiki, a troubled young adult looking back at her childhood. (Rev: BCCB 7–8/02; BL 4/1/02; HB 9–10/02; HBG 10/02; SLJ 5/02)

1821 Zach, Cheryl. *Dear Diary: Runaway* (7–12). 1995, Berkley paper $4.50 (0-425-15047-X). In diary form, young, pregnant Cassie tells how she and her lover, Seth, become runaways seeking a place that will give them shelter and security. (Rev: BL 1/1–15/96)

1822 Zalben, Jane Breskin. *Unfinished Dreams* (6–9). 1996, Simon & Schuster $16.00 (0-689-80033-9). Jason, a 6th grader and aspiring violinist, discovers that his beloved school principal has AIDS. (Rev: BL 6/1–15/96; BR 1–2/97; SLJ 6/96; VOYA 8/96)

1823 Zalben, Jane Breskin. *Water from the Moon* (8–10). 1987, Random paper $4.99 (0-440-22855-7). Nicky Berstein, a high school sophomore, tries too hard to make friends and is hurt in the process. (Rev: BL 5/15/87; SLJ 5/87; VOYA 8/87)

1824 Zindel, Bonnie, and Paul Zindel. *A Star for the Latecomer* (7–10). 1980, HarperCollins $12.95 (0-06-026847-6). When her mother dies, Brooke is freed of the need to pursue a dancing career.

1825 Zindel, Paul. *A Begonia for Miss Applebaum* (7–12). 1990, Bantam paper $4.99 (0-553-28765-6). Two unconventional teens take under their wings a favorite teacher who is dying of cancer. (Rev: BL 3/15/89; BR 11–12/89; SLJ 4/89)

1826 Zindel, Paul. *Confessions of a Teenage Baboon* (7–9). 1984, Bantam paper $4.50 (0-553-27190-3). Chris has difficulty adjusting to his mother's employer, a somewhat bitter loner.

1827 Zindel, Paul. *David and Della* (7–12). 1995, Bantam paper $4.50 (0-553-56727-6). High school playwright David hires Della — who pretends to be blind and to have studied under Lee Strasberg — to be his coach until he overcomes writer's block. (Rev: BL 12/1/93; SLJ 12/93; VOYA 2/94)

1828 Zindel, Paul. *I Never Loved Your Mind* (8–12). 1970, Bantam paper $4.50 (0-553-27323-X). Two dropouts working in a hospital together suffer the pangs of love and loss.

1829 Zindel, Paul. *My Darling, My Hamburger* (8–12). 1969, Bantam paper $4.99 (0-553-27324-8). Two young couples in love face life's complications including one girl's abortion.

1830 Zinnen, Linda. *The Truth About Rats, Rules, and Seventh Grade* (5–7). 2001, HarperCollins LB $15.89 (0-06-028800-0). Larch, who faces multiple problems at home and at school, tries to live her life by a set of unemotional rules, but a friendly stray dog and the discovery of the truth about her father's death make these rules hard to keep. (Rev: BCCB 6/01; BL 4/1/01*; HBG 10/01; SLJ 2/01)

1831 Zolotow, Charlotte, ed. *Early Sorrow: Ten Stories of Youth* (8–12). 1986, HarperCollins $12.95 (0-06-026936-7). This excellent collection of 12 adult stories about growing up is a companion piece to *An Overpraised Season* (o.p.), another anthology about adolescence. (Rev: BL 10/1/86; BR 3–4/87; SLJ 1/87; VOYA 2/87)

World Affairs and Contemporary Problems

1832 Abelove, Joan. *Go and Come Back* (8–10). 1998, Puffin paper $5.99 (0-14-130694-7). The story of two female anthropologists studying a primitive Peruvian Indian village, written from the perspective of Alicia, one of the village teenagers. (Rev: BL 3/1/98; BR 1–2/99; SLJ 3/98*; VOYA 10/98)

1833 Anderson, Mary. *The Unsinkable Molly Malone* (7–10). 1991, Harcourt $16.95 (0-15-213801-3). Molly, 16, sells her collages outside New York's Metropolitan Museum, starts an art class for kids on welfare, and learns that her boyfriend is rich. (Rev: BL 11/15/91; SLJ 12/91)

1834 Beale, Fleur. *I Am Not Esther* (7–10). 2002, Hyperion $15.99 (0-7868-0845-4). The insidious nature of cults is clearly shown in this novel about a spirited New Zealand girl sent to live with her fanatical Uncle Caleb. (Rev: BCCB 12/02; BL 10/15/02; HB 1–2/03; HBG 3/03; SLJ 11/02; VOYA 2/03)

1835 Bledsoe, Lucy Jane. *Cougar Canyon* (5–8). 2001, Holiday $16.95 (0-8234-1599-6). A family story and environmental tale about a 13-year-old girl named Izzy who fights to save a cougar in the local park. (Rev: BCCB 2/02; BL 2/1/02; HBG 3/02; SLJ 2/02; VOYA 4/02)

1836 Carbone, Elisa. *The Pack* (8–11). 2003, Viking $15.99 (0-670-03619-6). Teen outcasts Becky and Omar take an interest in an unusual new student, Akhil, and the three of them struggle to deal with another student's plan for a violent attack at their school. (Rev: BCCB 3/03; BL 2/15/03; SLJ 3/03; VOYA 4/03)

1837 Carmi, Daniella. *Samir and Yonatan* (4–8). Trans. from Hebrew by Yael Lotan. 2000, Scholastic paper $15.95 (0-439-13504-4). Samir, a young Palestinian, is sent to a Jewish hospital for surgery and there he meets some Jewish contemporaries. (Rev: BCCB 4/00; BL 2/1/00; HBG 10/00; SLJ 3/00; VOYA 6/00)

1838 Carvell, Marlene. *Who Will Tell My Brother?* (7–10). 2002, Hyperion $15.99 (0-7868-0827-6). In free-verse poetry, part-Mohawk high school senior Evan relates his efforts to rid his school of its Indian mascot. (Rev: BCCB 10/02; BL 7/02; HBG 3/03; SLJ 7/02; VOYA 6/02)

1839 Castaneda, Omar S. *Among the Volcanoes* (7–10). 1996, Bantam paper $4.50 (0-440-91118-4). Set in a remote Guatemalan village, this story is about a Mayan woodcutter's daughter, Isabel, who is caught between her respect for the old ways and her yearning for something more. (Rev: BL 5/15/91; SLJ 3/91)

1840 Clinton, Cathryn. *A Stone in My Hand* (5–8). 2002, Candlewick $15.99 (0-7636-1388-6). Eleven-year-old Maalak's father is killed in the violence of 1988 Gaza, and she must worry about her brother's future. (Rev: BL 9/15/02; HBG 3/03; SLJ 11/02*; VOYA 2/03)

1841 Coleman, Evelyn. *Born in Sin* (7–12). 2001, Simon & Schuster $16.00 (0-689-83833-6). Keisha Wright, 14, has strong ambitions and is determined to escape the poverty, racism, and dangers of her life in the all-black projects. (Rev: BCCB 2/01; BL 2/15/01; HBG 10/01; SLJ 3/01; VOYA 4/01)

1842 Collins, Pat Lowery. *The Fattening Hut* (8–12). 2003, Houghton $16.00 (0-618-30955-1). Fourteen-year-old Helen sets off on a dangerous journey, running away from the tropical tribe that requires her to undergo female circumcision before her impending marriage. (Rev: BL 11/1/03; SLJ 11/03)

1843 Covington, Dennis. *Lasso the Moon* (7–10). 1996, Bantam $20.95 (0-385-30991-0). After April and her divorced doctor father move to Saint Simons Island, April takes a liking to Fernando, an illegal alien from El Salvador being treated by her father. (Rev: BL 1/15/95; SLJ 3/95; VOYA 4/95)

1844 D'Adamo, Francesco. *Iqbal: A Novel* (4–7). 2003, Simon & Schuster $15.95 (0-689-85445-5). The sad story of the death of Iqbal, the young child labor activist, is brought to life through the fictional narrative of a young Pakistani girl who worked with him in the carpet factories. (Rev: BL 11/1/03; HB 11–12/03; SLJ 11/03)

1845 Davis, Jenny. *Checking on the Moon* (6–9). 1991, Orchard LB $17.99 (0-531-08560-0). A 13-year-old, forced to spend the summer in a run-down Pittsburgh neighborhood with a grandmother she has never met, discovers community activism and her own abilities. (Rev: BL 9/15/91; SLJ 10/91*)

1846 DeFelice, Cynthia. *Under the Same Sky* (5–9). 2003, Farrar $16.00 (0-374-38032-5). Joe, the spoiled 14-year-old son of a New York state farmer, learns about a different kind of life when he starts working with the migrant laborers from Mexico. (Rev: BCCB 5/03; BL 6/03; HBG 10/03; LMC 8–9/03; SLJ 3/03; VOYA 4/03)

1847 Doyle, Brian. *Easy Avenue* (6–9). 1998, Douglas & McIntyre $14.95 (0-88899-338-2). The luck of Hulbert, who is used to a life of poverty and deprivation, mysteriously changes, and his homelife and relationships begin to erode and he finds that he is becoming a snob. (Rev: BL 12/1/98; SLJ 11/98; VOYA 6/99)

1848 Ellis, Deborah. *Mud City* (4–7). Series: Breadwinner Trilogy. 2003, Douglas & McIntyre $15.95 (0-88899-518-0). Feisty Afghan refugee Shauzia sets off on her own, dreaming of a life of freedom in France and prepared to dress as a boy and beg, but circumstances force her back to the camp on the Pakistan border in this final novel in the trilogy. (Rev: BL 11/15/03; SLJ 11/03)

1849 Esckilsen, Erik E. *The Last Mall Rat* (7–10). 2003, Houghton $15.00 (0-618-23417-9). Bored and penniless, 15-year-old Mitch agrees to harass rude shoppers. (Rev: BL 4/1/03; SLJ 6/03; VOYA 6/03)

1850 Flegg, Aubrey. *The Cinnamon Tree* (7–10). 2002, O'Brien paper $7.95 (0-86278-657-6). The horror of the injuries inflicted by landmines is brought to life in this story of a girl who loses a leg and goes on to teach others about the dangers of these weapons. (Rev: BL 8/02; SLJ 8/02)

1851 Fox, Paula. *Lily and the Lost Boy* (6–9). 1987, Watts LB $17.99 (0-531-08320-9). Using the tiny island of Thasos in Greece as a setting the author tells a story of the maturation of a 12-year-old American girl and her older brother. (Rev: BL 7/87; BR 1–2/88; VOYA 2/88)

1852 French, Jackie. *Hitler's Daughter* (4–7). 2003, HarperCollins $15.99 (0-06-008652-1). A story about a fictional daughter of Hitler inspires Mark, a young Australian, to wonder about evil and genocide. (Rev: BCCB 7–8/03; BL 9/15/03; HBG 10/03; SLJ 5/03; VOYA 8/03)

1853 Gauthier, Gail. *Saving the Planet and Stuff* (8–10). 2003, Putnam $17.99 (0-399-23761-5). Office politics turn out to be an unexpected pleasure for 16-year-old Michael when he spends the summer working for an environmental magazine. (Rev: BCCB 9/03; BL 5/15/03; HB 7–8/03; HBG 10/03; SLJ 6/03; VOYA 6/03)

1854 Golio, Janet, and Mike Golio. *A Present from the Past* (6–8). 1995, Portunus paper $8.95 (0-9641330-5-9). In this blend of fact and fiction, Sarah and her friend become concerned about their environment after they discover some petroglyphs. (Rev: BL 1/1–15/96)

1855 Hall, Lynn. *If Winter Comes* (7–10). 1986, Macmillan LB $17.00 (0-684-18575-X). Two teenagers spend what they believe to be their last weekend on earth because of the imminent threat of a nuclear war. (Rev: BL 6/1/86; SLJ 9/86; VOYA 8/86)

1856 Hentoff, Nat. *The Day They Came to Arrest the Book* (7–10). 1983, Dell paper $5.50 (0-440-91814-6). Some students at George Mason High think *Huckleberry Finn* is a racist book.

1857 Hesse, Karen. *Phoenix Rising* (6–8). 1994, Holt $16.95 (0-8050-3108-1). A 13-year-old and her grandmother on a Vermont farm hope to avoid radiation contamination from a nuclear plant. They are visited by Boston evacuees, one of them a boy with whom the girl falls in love. (Rev: BL 5/15/94; SLJ 6/94*; VOYA 8/94)

1858 Hiaasen, Carl. *Hoot* (5–8). 2002, Knopf $15.95 (0-375-82181-3). Roy Eberhart, the new kid in Coconut Cove, finds himself embroiled in a battle to save some owls. Newbery Honor Book, 2003. (Rev: BCCB 11/02; BL 10/15/02; HB 11–12/02; HBG 3/03; SLJ 8/02)

1859 Ho, Minfong. *Rice Without Rain* (7–12). 1990, Lothrop $16.99 (0-688-06355-1). Jinda, a 17-year-old girl, experiences personal tragedy and the awakening of love in this novel set during revolutionary times in Thailand during the 1970s. (Rev: BL 7/90; SLJ 9/90)

1860 Hobbs, Valerie. *Stefan's Story* (5–8). 2003, Farrar $16.00 (0-374-37240-3). Wheelchair-bound Stefan, 13, visits his friend Carolina in Oregon, where an environmental dispute is splitting the community in two. A sequel to *Carolina Crow Girl* (1999). (Rev: BL 9/15/03; SLJ 8/03)

1861 Jicai, Feng. *Let One Hundred Flowers Bloom* (7–10). Trans. by Christopher Smith. 1996, Viking $13.99 (0-670-85805-6). A bleak story about a talented artisan in contemporary China whose life is destroyed when he is accused of counterrevolutionary behavior. (Rev: BL 4/15/96; SLJ 6/96)

1862 Keizer, Garret. *God of Beer* (8–12). 2002, HarperCollins $15.95 (0-06-029456-6). A group of high schoolers form an association, Students Undermining a Drunk Society, in an effort to change their community's attitudes toward alcohol. (Rev: BCCB 5/02; HB 5–6/02; HBG 10/02; SLJ 2/02; VOYA 4/02)

1863 Laird, Elizabeth. *The Garbage King* (5–8). 2003, Barron's $14.95 (0-7641-5679-9); paper $5.95 (0-7641-2626-1). Two Ethiopian boys find themselves homeless and join a gang that begs and scavenges for a livelihood. (Rev: BL 12/1/03; SLJ 12/03)

1864 Levine, Anna. *Running on Eggs* (5–9). 1999, Front Street $15.95 (0-8126-2875-6). The story of two girls — one Jewish and the other Palestinian — and a friendship that withstands cultural and political differences. (Rev: BCCB 11/99; BL 1/1–15/00; HBG 3/00; SLJ 12/99; VOYA 2/00)

1865 Levitin, Sonia. *The Return* (6–10). 1987, Macmillan $16.00 (0-689-31309-8); Fawcett paper

$5.99 (0-449-70280-4). Seen from the viewpoint of a teenage girl, this is the story of a group of African Jews who journey from Ethiopia to the Sudan to escape persecution. (Rev: BL 4/15/87; BR 11–12/87; SLJ 5/87; VOYA 6/87)

1866 McDaniel, Lurlene. *Baby Alicia Is Dying* (8–10). 1993, Bantam paper $4.99 (0-553-29605-1). In an attempt to feel needed, Desi volunteers to care for HIV-positive babies and discovers a deep commitment in herself. (Rev: BL 10/1/93; SLJ 7/93; VOYA 8/93)

1867 McDonald, Janet. *Chill Wind* (7–12). 2002, Farrar $16.00 (0-374-39958-1). Nineteen-year-old Aisha is inventive and determined in her efforts to avoid workfare and still support herself and her two children. (Rev: BCCB 1/03; BL 9/1/02; HB 9–10/02; HBG 3/03; SLJ 11/02)

1868 Mankell, Henning. *Secrets in the Fire* (4–8). 2003, Annick $14.95 (1-55037-801-5); paper $7.95 (1-55037-800-7). This is the true story of Sofia, a courageous Mozambican girl who lost both legs — and her sister — when a landmine exploded. (Rev: BL 12/15/03*)

1869 Martin, Nora. *Perfect Snow* (8–12). 2002, Bloomsbury $16.95 (1-58234-788-3). Ben feels strong and confident when he participates in the violent intolerance of the local white supremacists until he meets Eden, a new — and Jewish — girl at school, in this novel set in a small Montana community. (Rev: BL 8/02; SLJ 9/02)

1870 Mazer, Norma Fox, and Harry Mazer. *Bright Days, Stupid Nights* (7–10). 1993, Bantam paper $3.50 (0-553-56253-3). Charts the course of four youths who are brought together for a summer newspaper internship. (Rev: BL 6/15/92; SLJ 7/92)

1871 Miklowitz, Gloria D. *The Enemy Has a Face* (5–8). 2003, Eerdmans $16.00 (0-8028-5243-2). Soon after Netta's family moves from Israel to Los Angeles, her brother goes missing and Netta automatically suspects Palestinian involvement. (Rev: BL 6/1–15/03; HBG 10/03; SLJ 7/03; VOYA 8/03)

1872 Mosher, Richard. *Zazoo* (6–9). 2001, Clarion $16.00 (0-618-13534-0). Zazoo, a French girl adopted from Vietnam, comes to understand the complexities of her adoptive Grand-Pierre's past in this absorbing, multilayered novel. (Rev: BL 12/15/01; HBG 3/02; SLJ 11/01*; VOYA 10/01)

1873 Myers, Anna. *Flying Blind* (4–8). 2003, Walker $16.95 (0-8027-8879-3). In the early 20th century, Ben, 13, and an unusually talented pet macaw deplore the killing of egrets for their feathers but understand the economic needs of the deprived hunters. (Rev: BL 9/15/03; SLJ 11/03; VOYA 10/03)

1874 Myers, Bill. *The Society* (7–9). Series: Forbidden Doors. 2001, Tyndale paper $2.99 (0-8423-

3987-6). Scott and Becka have left Brazil and begun the year at their new U.S. school when they discover that a local bookshop is the hub of a Ouija board cult. (Rev: BL 1/15/95)

1875 Naidoo, Beverly. *The Other Side of Truth* (5–9). 2001, HarperCollins $15.95 (0-06-029628-3). Two Nigerian children face a frightening sequence of events as they find themselves abandoned in London, afraid to trust anyone. Carnegie Medal winner, 2000. (Rev: BCCB 9/01; BL 9/1/01; HB 11–12/01*; HBG 3/02; SLJ 9/01*; VOYA 10/01)

1876 Neufeld, John. *A Small Civil War* (7–10). 1996, Simon & Schuster $16.00 (0-689-80770-8). A revised edition of the 1981 novel about 13-year-old Georgia and her fight against censorship when *The Grapes of Wrath* is challenged in her high school. (Rev: BL 10/15/96; BR 5–6/97; SLJ 11/96; VOYA 2/97)

1877 Neville, Emily C. *The China Year* (5–8). 1991, HarperCollins $15.95 (0-06-024383-X). Henri, 14, has left his New York City home, school, and friends to go to Peking University for a year with his father. (Rev: BL 5/1/91; SLJ 5/91)

1878 Paulsen, Gary. *The Rifle* (7–9). 1995, Harcourt $17.00 (0-15-292880-4). An exploration of the history of a flintlock rifle, from its use in the Revolutionary War into the 20th century, where it ends up killing a teen in a freak accident. (Rev: BL 9/15/95; SLJ 10/95; VOYA 2/96)

1879 Paulsen, Gary. *Sentries* (8–12). 1986, Bradbury LB $17.00 (0-02-770100-X); Penguin paper $3.95 (0-317-62279-X). The stories of four different young people are left unresolved when they are all wiped out by a superbomb. (Rev: BL 5/1/86; SLJ 8/86; VOYA 8/86)

1880 Peck, Richard. *The Last Safe Place on Earth* (7–10). 1996, Bantam paper $5.50 (0-440-22007-6). Todd has a crush on Laura, who baby-sits for his sister, but he discovers that she's a fundamentalist Christian who brainwashes and terrifies the child by telling her about witches and devils. (Rev: BL 1/15/95; SLJ 4/95; VOYA 2/95)

1881 Prose, Francine. *After* (8–10). 2003, HarperCollins $15.99 (0-06-008081-7). A school district hires an over-the-top crisis counselor to impose order in the name of safety after a massacre at a nearby high school. (Rev: HB 5–6/03; HBG 10/03; SLJ 5/03; VOYA 6/03)

1882 Rochman, Hazel, ed. *Somehow Tenderness Survives: Stories of Southern Africa* (8–12). 1988, HarperCollins $12.95 (0-06-025022-4); paper $5.99 (0-06-447063-6). Ten stories by such writers as Nadine Gordimer about growing up in South Africa. (Rev: BL 8/88; BR 5–6/89; SLJ 12/88; VOYA 12/88)

1883 Ruby, Lois. *Skin Deep* (8–12). 1994, Scholastic paper $14.95 (0-590-47699-8). Dan, the frustrated new kid in town, falls in love with popular senior Laurel, but he destroys their relationship when he joins a neo-Nazi skinhead group. (Rev: BL 11/15/94*; SLJ 3/95; VOYA 12/94)

1884 Silvey, Diane. *Raven's Flight* (7–12). 2001, Raincoast paper $6.95 (1-55192-344-0). When her sister's letters home suddenly stop, 15-year-old Raven sets off in pursuit, only to confront the horrors of drug addiction. (Rev: SLJ 12/01)

1885 Staples, Suzanne F. *Shabanu: Daughter of the Wind* (7–10). 1989, Knopf LB $18.99 (0-394-94815-7). The story of a young girl coming-of-age in a family living in a desert region of Pakistan. (Rev: BL 10/1/89; SLJ 11/89; VOYA 4/90)

1886 Strasser, Todd. *Give a Boy a Gun* (6–12). 2000, Simon & Schuster $16.00 (0-689-81112-8). The story of Gary and Brendan, who go on a shooting spree at their school, is revealed through the voices of those who knew them — parents, friends, teachers, and classmates. (Rev: BL 10/1/00; HBG 3/01; SLJ 9/00)

1887 Taylor, Theodore. *The Bomb* (7–10). 1995, Harcourt $15.00 (0-15-200867-5). In this tale — based on Taylor's memory of a visit to Bikini Atoll as it was being prepared for testing of the atomic bomb — a 14-year-old boy suspects that the Americans are less than honest about their plans. (Rev: BL 10/1/95*; SLJ 12/95; VOYA 4/96)

1888 Temple, Frances. *Grab Hands and Run* (6–12). 1993, Orchard LB $16.99 (0-531-08630-5). Jacinto opposes the oppressive government of El Salvador. When he disappears, his wife, Paloma, and their son, 12-year-old Felipe, try to escape to freedom in Canada. (Rev: BL 5/1/93*; SLJ 4/93*)

1889 Temple, Frances. *Tonight, by Sea* (6–10). 1995, Orchard LB $16.99 (0-531-08749-2). A docunovel about Haitian boat people who struggle for social justice and attempt harrowing escapes to freedom. (Rev: BL 3/15/95; SLJ 4/95)

1890 Williams-Garcia, Rita. *No Laughter Here* (4–8). 2003, HarperCollins $15.99 (0-688-16247-9). Akilah is shocked when her friend Victoria reveals she has undergone female circumcision while on vacation in Nigeria. (Rev: BL 12/1/03*)

1891 Yolen, Jane. *Children of the Wolf* (6–8). 1993, Puffin paper $4.99 (0-14-036477-3). Based on fact, this is the story of a Christian minister in India who finds two children who have been reared in the wild.

1892 Zephaniah, Benjamin. *Refugee Boy* (8–12). 2002, Bloomsbury $15.95 (1-58234-763-8). Abandoned in England by a father who believes he will be safer there, Alem — the son of an Eritrean mother and an Ethiopian father — struggles to cope with the judicial and social system as he seeks a new home. (Rev: BCCB 10/02; BL 9/1/02; SLJ 10/02)

Fantasy

1893 Adams, Richard. *Watership Down* (7–12). Illus. 1974, Macmillan $40.00 (0-02-700030-3); Avon paper $12.00 (0-380-00428-3). Rabbits, frightened by the coming destruction of their warren, journey across the English downs in search of a new home.

1894 Adler, C. S. *Good-bye Pink Pig* (5–7). 1986, Avon paper $2.75 (0-380-70175-8). Shy Amanda takes comfort in the make-believe world of her miniature pink pig — away from the elegant world of her mother and easygoing life of her brother — until trouble enters her real and imaginary worlds and she learns to assert herself. (Rev: BCCB 2/86; BL 12/15/85)

1895 Adler, C. S. *Help, Pink Pig!* (5–7). 1991, Avon paper $2.95 (0-380-71156-7). Unsure of herself with her mother, Amanda retreats into the world of her miniature pink pig. (Rev: BL 5/1/90; SLJ 5/90)

1896 Alcock, Vivien. *The Haunting of Cassie Palmer* (5–8). 1997, Houghton paper $6.95 (0-395-81653-X). Cassie finds she is blessed with second sight.

1897 Alcock, Vivien. *The Red-Eared Ghosts* (5–8). 1997, Houghton $15.95 (0-395-81660-2). Mary Frewin travels through time to solve a mystery involving her great-great-grandmother. (Rev: BL 3/1/97; BR 11–12/97; SLJ 4/97; VOYA 10/97)

1898 Alcock, Vivien. *The Stonewalkers* (5–8). 1998, Houghton paper $4.95 (0-395-81652-1). Statues come to life and begin stalking two girls.

1899 Alexander, Lloyd. *The Arkadians* (6–9). 1995, Dutton $17.99 (0-525-45415-2). A focus on the goddess culture and its role in history and myth. Lucian and Fronto are forced to flee a castle and hunt for the goddess who can help them. (Rev: BL 5/1/95; SLJ 5/95; VOYA 12/95)

1900 Alexander, Lloyd. *The Book of Three* (5–8). 1964, Dell paper $5.99 (0-440-40702-8). Welsh legend and universal mythology are blended in the tale of an assistant pig keeper who becomes a hero. Newbery Medal winner, 1969. Others in the Prydain cycle are *The Black Cauldron, The Castle of Llyr, Taran Wanderer*, and *The High King*.

1901 Alexander, Lloyd. *The Cat Who Wished to Be a Man* (5–6). 1973, Dell paper $3.99 (0-440-40580-7). A cat named Lionel, turned into a man by a magician, takes on the corrupt mayor of the town.

1902 Alexander, Lloyd. *The First Two Lives of Lukas-Kasha* (5–8). 1998, Puffin paper $6.99 (0-141-30057-4). Lukas awakens to find himself in a strange land.

1903 Alexander, Lloyd. *The Foundling and Other Tales of Prydain* (6–8). 1999, Holt $19.95 (0-8050-

6130-4). Six stories of Alexander's enchanted land of Prydain. (Rev: HBG 4/00)

1904 Alexander, Lloyd. *The Iron Ring* (6–9). 1997, Puffin paper $5.99 (0-14-130348-4). When he loses in a dice game, Tamar must fulfill a promise to journey to the kingdom of King Jaya in this fantasy based on Indian mythology. (Rev: BL 5/15/97; BR 11–12/97; SLJ 5/97*; VOYA 10/97)

1905 Alexander, Lloyd. *The Remarkable Journey of Prince Jen* (6–9). 1991, Dell paper $5.50 (0-440-40890-3). Prince Jen searches for the legendary court of T'ien-kuo, finds a flute girl, faces death at the hands of a bandit, and learns how to be a man and a ruler. (Rev: BL 12/1/91*; SLJ 12/91*)

1906 Alexander, Lloyd. *The Rope Trick* (4–7). 2002, Dutton $16.99 (0-525-47020-4). A young magician sets out on a challenging journey to master the difficult rope trick. (Rev: BCCB 1/03; BL 10/15/02; HB 11–12/02; HBG 3/03; SLJ 9/02; VOYA 12/02)

1907 Alexander, Lloyd. *The Wizard in the Tree* (5–8). Illus. 1988, Demco $11.04 (0-606-13070-5). Mallory finds a wizard in a tree and must help him when he is accused of murder.

1908 Allen, Will. *Swords for Hire: Two of the Most Unlikely Heroes You'll Ever Meet* (5–8). 2003, CenterPunch paper $6.95 (0-9724882-0-0). A spoof of a fantasy in which inexperienced warrior 16-year-old Sam Hatcher and his eccentric mentor Rigby Skeet set off to rescue King Olive, who has been unseated by his evil brother. (Rev: BCCB 6/03; SLJ 8/03)

1909 Almond, David. *Heaven Eyes* (5–8). 2001, Delacorte $15.95 (0-385-32770-6). A very ambitious novel about three young escapees from a detention center in England and the life they live in a forgotten warehouse where the watchman is a deranged man known as Heaven Eyes. (Rev: BCCB 4/01; BL 1/1–15/01*; HB 3–4/01; HBG 10/01; SLJ 3/01; VOYA 4/01)

1910 Almond, David. *Kit's Wilderness* (6–9). 2000, Delacorte $15.95 (0-385-32665-3). Set in an English coal-mining town, this fantasy involves 13-year-old Kit Watson who sees ghosts of his ancestors who died in mining accidents. (Rev: BCCB 1/00; BL 1/1–15/00; HB 3–4/00; HBG 9/00; SLJ 3/00; VOYA 4/00)

1911 Almond, David. *Secret Heart* (6–10). 2002, Delacorte $15.95 (0-385-72947-2). An unhappy stutterer's dreams about a tiger coincide with the arrival of a seedy circus that has strange appeal for him, especially the girl who sees in the boy a heart of courage, in this gripping blend of fantasy and realism. (Rev: BCCB 12/02; BL 10/1/02; HB 11–12/02; HBG 3/03; SLJ 10/02; VOYA 12/02)

1912 Almond, David. *Skellig* (5–8). 1999, Delacorte $16.95 (0-385-32653-X). Michael discovers a ragged man in his garage existing on dead flies in this novel that is part fantasy, part mystery, and part

family story. (Rev: BL 2/1/99*; HB 5–6/99; HBG 10/99; SLJ 2/99)

1913 Alton, Steve. *The Malifex* (5–8). 2002, Carolrhoda LB $17.95 (0-8225-0959-8). Sam's vacation in contemporary England is complicated by a Wiccan's daughter, the release of the ghost of Merlin's apprentice, and a battle between good and evil. (Rev: BL 9/1/02; HBG 10/03; SLJ 11/02)

1914 Amoss, Berthe. *Lost Magic* (5–7). 1993, Hyperion $14.95 (1-56282-573-9). Fantasy and history mingle in this story set in the Middle Ages about a young girl who knows how to use both healing herbs and magic. (Rev: BL 11/1/93)

1915 Arkin, Alan. *Cassie Loves Beethoven* (4–7). 2000, Hyperion LB $15.49 (0-7868-2489-1). A delightful story about the Kennedy family and an adopted cow that learns to play Beethoven on the piano. (Rev: BCCB 2/01; BL 12/15/00; HBG 10/01; SLJ 2/01)

1916 Arkin, Alan. *The Lemming Condition* (4–7). 1989, HarperCollins paper $9.00 (0-062-50048-1). Bubber opposes the mass suicide of his companions in this interesting fable.

1917 Atwater-Rhodes, Amelia. *Hawksong* (7–10). 2003, Delacorte $9.95 (0-385-73071-3). A gripping fantasy about two young leaders who seek to end the long war between their peoples — avian shapeshifters and serpent shapeshifters — and are prepared to consider marriage for the sake of peace. (Rev: SLJ 8/03*; VOYA 6/03)

1918 Atwater-Rhodes, Amelia. *Midnight Predator* (7–9). 2002, Delacorte $9.95 (0-385-32794-3). In a world where humans are slaves to vampires, teen vampire hunter Turquoise and her colleague pose as slaves in order to defeat an evil tyrant. (Rev: BL 8/02; HBG 10/02; SLJ 5/02; VOYA 6/02)

1919 Atwater-Rhodes, Amelia. *Shattered Mirror* (6–10). 2001, Delacorte $9.95 (0-385-32793-5). A story full of suspense about a young vampire hunter, Sarah Tigress Vida, who finds there are two vampires in her high school class, one of whom is very attractive. (Rev: BCCB 10/01; BL 9/1/01; HBG 3/02; SLJ 9/01; VOYA 12/01)

1920 Augarde, Steve. *The Various* (4–8). 2004, Random $15.95 (0-385-75029-3). Midge, a 12-year-old girl on vacation in the countryside, discovers a tribe of little people known as the Various, who are not as helpless as they seem. (Rev: BL 12/15/03)

1921 Avi. *Bright Shadow* (5–8). 1994, Simon & Schuster paper $4.99 (0-689-71783-0). At the death of the great wizard, Morenna finds she possesses the last five wishes in the world. (Rev: SLJ 12/85)

1922 Avi. *The Man Who Was Poe* (7–10). 1991, Avon paper $5.99 (0-380-71192-3). When Edmund goes out to search for his missing mother and sister, he encounters Edgar Allan Poe in disguise as detective Auguste Dupin. (Rev: BL 10/1/89; BR 5–6/90; SLJ 9/89; VOYA 2/90)

1923 Avi. *Perloo the Bold* (4–7). 1998, Scholastic paper $16.95 (0-590-11002-0). Perloo, a member of the jackrabbitlike Montmer tribe, is the unlikely hero of this fantasy about the rivalry between the Montmers and the Felbarts, a coyotelike tribe. (Rev: BCCB 11/98; BL 12/15/98; HB 1–2/99; HBG 3/99; SLJ 11/98)

1924 Babbitt, Natalie. *The Search for Delicious* (4–7). 1969, Farrar $17.00 (0-374-36534-2). The innocent task of polling the kingdom's subjects for personal food preferences provokes civil war in a zestful spoof of taste and society.

1925 Baker, E. D. *Dragon's Breath* (5–7). 2003, Bloomsbury $15.95 (1-58234-858-8). Esmeralda and Eadric help Aunt Grassina find ingredients needed to break the spell that turned Grassina's true love, Haywood, into an otter in this sequel to *The Frog Princess* (2002). (Rev: SLJ 12/03)

1926 Baker, E. D. *The Frog Princess* (5–8). 2002, Bloomsbury $15.95 (1-58234-799-9). When Princess Esmeralda kisses the frog, she turns into one herself in this humorous twist on the traditional saga. (Rev: BCCB 2/03; BL 11/15/02; SLJ 1/03; VOYA 12/02)

1927 Banks, Lynne Reid. *Angela and Diabola* (5–8). 1997, Avon $15.95 (0-380-97562-9). A wicked romp that chronicles the lives of twins, the angelic Angela and the truly horrible and destructive Diabola. (Rev: BR 9–10/97; SLJ 7/97)

1928 Banks, Lynne Reid. *The Key to the Indian* (4–8). Illus. Series: Indian in the Cupboard. 1998, Avon $16.00 (0-380-97717-6). In the fifth book of the Indian in the Cupboard series, Omri and Dad return to the time of Little Bear to help the Iroquois deal with European meddlers. (Rev: BL 11/15/98; HBG 3/99; SLJ 12/98)

1929 Banks, Lynne Reid. *Melusine* (8–12). 1997, Avon paper $4.99 (0-380-79135-8). While staying with his family in an old French chateau, Roger discovers Melusine, a supernatural creature that is half woman and half snake. (Rev: BL 10/1/89; SLJ 11/89; VOYA 2/90)

1930 Banks, Lynne Reid. *The Mystery of the Cupboard* (4–8). Illus. Series: Indian in the Cupboard. 1993, HarperCollins paper $5.99 (0-380-72013-2). In this, the fourth book in the series, the young hero Omri uncovers a diary that reveals secrets about his magical cupboard. (Rev: BCCB 6/93; BL 4/1/93; HB 7–8/93; SLJ 6/93; VOYA 10/93)

1931 Banks, Lynne Reid. *The Return of the Indian* (5–7). Series: Indian in the Cupboard. 1986, Doubleday $16.95 (0-385-23497-X); Avon paper $5.99 (0-380-70284-3). Omri brings his plastic Indian figures to life and discovers that his friend Little Bear has been wounded and needs his help. (Rev: BL 9/15/86; HB 11–12/86; SLJ 11/86)

1932 Barker, Clive. *Abarat* (7–12). Illus. 2002, HarperCollins $24.99 (0-06-028092-1). Bored teen Candy Quackenbush is carried away to a strange and magical world called Abarat and finds herself at the center of a struggle between good and evil in this novel enhanced by full-color art. (Rev: BCCB 3/03; BL 9/1/02; HBG 10/03; SLJ 10/02)

1933 Barron, T. A. *The Ancient One* (6–9). 1992, Putnam $19.99 (0-399-21899-8); Tor paper $5.99 (0-8125-3654-1). A fight to save a stand of Oregon redwoods occupies Kate, 13, in this time-travel fantasy. (Rev: BL 9/1/92; SLJ 11/92)

1934 Barron, T. A. *The Fires of Merlin* (7–10). Illus. Series: Lost Years of Merlin. 1998, Putnam $19.99 (0-399-23020-3). A complex sequel to *The Seven Songs of Merlin,* in which young Merlin once again faces the threat of the dragon Valdearg, who is preparing to conquer the land of Fincayra. (Rev: BL 9/1/98; BR 5–6/99; HBG 3/99; SLJ 3/99; VOYA 2/99)

1935 Barron, T. A. *The Lost Years of Merlin* (7–10). Series: Lost Years of Merlin. 1996, Putnam $19.99 (0-399-23018-1). The author has created a magical land populated by remarkable creatures in this first book of a trilogy about the early years of the magician Merlin. (Rev: BL 9/1/96; BR 3–4/97; SLJ 9/96; VOYA 10/96)

1936 Barron, T. A. *The Merlin Effect* (6–9). 1994, Putnam $19.99 (0-399-22689-3). Kate, 13, accompanies her father, a King Arthur expert, to a remote lagoon where they search a sunken ship for the magical horn of Merlin. A sequel to *Heartlight* (1990) and *The Ancient One* (1992). (Rev: BL 11/1/94; SLJ 11/94; VOYA 12/94)

1937 Barron, T. A. *The Mirror of Merlin* (7–10). Series: Lost Years of Merlin. 1999, Putnam $19.99 (0-399-23455-1). Young Merlin faces a deadly disease and confronts his future self as he continues his dangerous search for his sword. (Rev: BL 10/1/99; HBG 4/00; SLJ 10/99; VOYA 2/00)

1938 Barron, T. A. *The Seven Songs of Merlin* (7–10). Series: Lost Years of Merlin. 1997, Putnam $19.99 (0-399-23019-X). In this sequel to *The Lost Years of Merlin,* Emrys, who will become Merlin, must travel to the Otherworld to save his mother who has been poisoned. (Rev: BL 9/1/97; HBG 3/98; SLJ 9/97)

1939 Barron, T. A. *Tree Girl* (4–8). 2001, Putnam $14.99 (0-399-23457-8). Rowanna, 9, discovers she is descended from tree spirits after she is lured into the woods by a shape-shifting bear cub in this book for middle-graders. (Rev: BCCB 10/01; BL 11/1/01; HBG 3/02; SLJ 10/01; VOYA 10/01)

1940 Barron, T. A. *The Wings of Merlin* (7–10). Series: Lost Years of Merlin. 2000, Philomel $19.99 (0-399-23456-X). In this, the concluding volume of the saga, Merlin faces his most difficult decision.

(Rev: BL 10/1/00; HDG 3/01; SLJ 11/00; VOYA 12/00)

1941 Bauer, Marion Dane. *Touch the Moon* (5–7). 1987, Houghton $15.00 (0-89919-526-1). Angry when she doesn't get a real horse, Jennifer throws away her toy horse gift and learns a lesson in responsibility. (Rev: BCCB 9/87; BL 9/15/87; HB 9–10/87)

1942 Baum, L. Frank. *The Wizard of Oz* (4–8). 2000, Holt $34.95 (0-8050-6430-3). A gorgeous edition of the classic fantasy that is a reissue of the 1982 version with a few new illustrations. (Rev: BL 12/1/00; HBG 10/00)

1943 Baum, L. Frank. *The Wonderful Wizard of Oz* (4–8). 1987, Morrow $21.95 (0-688-06944-4). A reissue of the 1900 classic with original colorplates. (Rev: BL 11/1/87)

1944 Baum, L. Frank. *The Wonderful Wizard of Oz* (4–8). 2000, HarperCollins $24.99 (0-06-029323-3). A handsome facsimile of the 1900 publication on high-quality paper and featuring 24 original color plates and 130 two-color drawings. (Rev: BL 12/1/00)

1945 Baum, L. Frank. *The Wonderful Wizard of Oz: A Commemorative Pop-Up* (4–8). 2001, Simon & Schuster $24.95 (0-689-81751-7). An extraordinary pop-up version of the classic fantasy told in a condensed text. (Rev: BL 12/1/00; HB 9–10/00; HBG 3/01; SLJ 11/00)

1946 Beaverson, Aiden. *The Hidden Arrow of Maether* (7–9). 2000, Delacorte $14.95 (0-385-32750-1). Rather than marry a man of whom she disapproves, Linn runs away and finds herself among the lysefolk. (Rev: BCCB 2/01; BR 5–6/01; HBG 3/01; SLJ 12/00)

1947 Bedard, Michael. *A Darker Magic* (6–8). 1987, Avon paper $2.95 (0-380-70611-3). An intricate fantasy about the strange effects of a magic show run by Professor Mephisto. (Rev: BL 9/1/87; SLJ 9/87)

1948 Belden, Wilanne Schneider. *Mind-Hold* (6–9). 1987, Harcourt $14.95 (0-15-254280-9). After a violent earthquake, Carson and his sister, who has the gift of ESP, move into the desert hoping to find new friends. (Rev: BL 2/15/87; SLJ 3/87)

1949 Bell, Clare E. *Ratha's Challenge* (6–12). 1994, Macmillan paper $16.95 (0-689-50586-8). When a tribe of prehistoric cats faces challenges to survival, their leader, Ratha, hopes to domesticate the tusked face-tails to ensure a steady food supply. (Rev: BL 1/1/95; SLJ 1/95; VOYA 5/95)

1950 Bell, Hilari. *Flame* (6–10). Series: The Book of Sorahb. 2003, Simon & Schuster $16.95 (0-689-85413-7). Three young people — Jiaan, Soraya, and Kavi — play important roles in the country of Farsala's efforts to repel the Hrum in this first

installment of a series that draws on Persian legends. (Rev: BL 9/1/03*; HB 9–10/03; SLJ 11/03*)

1951 Bell, Hilari. *The Goblin Wood* (6–10). 2003, HarperCollins $16.99 (0-06-051371-3). A young hedgewitch befriends a band of goblins, and with them battles the evil Hierarchy in this novel that blends fantasy, intrigue, and romance. (Rev: BL 6/1–15/03; HB 5–6/03; HBG 10/03; SLJ 7/03; VOYA 8/03)

1952 Bellairs, John. *The Curse of the Blue Figurine* (5–8). 1984, Bantam paper $3.50 (0-553-15540-7). A boy steals an ancient book from a church and evil spells begin working in this blend of fantasy and mystery story. Two sequels are *The Mummy, the Will, and the Crypt* and *The Spell of the Sorcerer's Skull.*

1953 Bellairs, John. *The Ghost in the Mirror* (5–8). 1994, Puffin paper $5.99 (0-140-34934-0). Fourteen-year-old Rose and white witch Mrs. Zimmerman are transported in time to 1828 on a secret mission. (Rev: SLJ 3/93)

1954 Bellairs, John. *The Mansion in the Mist* (5–7). 1992, Puffin paper $5.99 (0-140-34933-2). Anthony Monday finds mystery and adventure on a remote island in northern Canada. (Rev: BL 8/92; SLJ 6/92)

1955 Bennett, Cherie. *Love Never Dies* (7–10). Series: Teen Angels. 1996, Avon paper $3.99 (0-380-78248-0). In this fantasy, a teen angel is sent back to earth to help a rock star bent on self-destruction. (Rev: VOYA 6/96)

1956 Berger, Barbara Helen. *Gwinna* (4–8). Illus. 1990, Putnam $24.99 (0-399-21738-X). A mystic coming-of-age fable when a couple's wish for a child is granted in the form of a daughter who grows wings. (Rev: BL 10/15/90; SLJ 12/90)

1957 Berry, Liz. *The China Garden* (8–12). 1996, HarperCollins paper $6.99 (0-380-73228-9). Mysterious occurrences involving villagers who appear to know Clare and a handsome young man on a motorcycle happen when she accompanies her mother to an estate named Ravensmere. (Rev: BL 3/15/96; BR 9–10/96; SLJ 5/96; VOYA 6/96)

1958 Billingsley, Franny. *The Folk Keeper* (5–8). 1999, Simon & Schuster $16.00 (0-689-82876-4); Aladdin paper $4.99 (0-689-84461-1). Orphaned Corinna disguises herself as a boy to become a Folk Keeper, one who guards the fierce Folk who live underground. (Rev: BCCB 10/99; BL 9/1/99; HB 11–12/99; HBG 3/00; SLJ 10/99; VOYA 12/99)

1959 Billingsley, Franny. *Well Wished* (5–8). 1997, Simon & Schuster $16.00 (0-689-81210-8). An intriguing fantasy that involves a lonely girl and a wishing well that grants each person a single wish. (Rev: BCCB 4/97; BL 6/1–15/97; HB 5–6/97; SLJ 5/97*)

1960 Black, Holly. *Tithe: A Modern Faerie Tale* (8–12). 2002, Simon & Schuster $16.95 (0-689-84924-9). Sixteen-year-old Kaye's adventures include rescuing a knight, Roiben, and being caught up in the battles between faerie kingdoms. (Rev: BL 2/15/03; HBG 3/03; SLJ 10/02)

1961 Blackwood, Gary. *The Year of the Hangman* (6–9). 2002, Dutton $16.99 (0-525-46921-4). After the British have defeated the colonists and captured General Washington, a 15-year-old English boy faces questions of loyalty in this exciting alternate history. (Rev: BCCB 12/02; BL 8/02; HBG 3/03; SLJ 9/02*)

1962 Blair, Margaret Whitman. *Brothers at War* (4–7). 1997, White Mane paper $7.95 (1-57249-049-7). Two brothers and their friend Sarah find themselves transported back in time to the Battle of Antietam in 1862. (Rev: BL 8/97)

1963 Block, Francesca L. *I Was a Teenage Fairy* (8–12). 1998, HarperCollins LB $14.89 (0-06-027748-3). Barbie Marks, at 16 a successful model, sorts herself out with the help of a fairy named Mab, after her father leaves and she is molested by a photographer. (Rev: BL 10/15/98; HB 11–12/98; HBG 3/99; SLJ 12/98*; VOYA 10/98)

1964 Block, Francesca L. *Missing Angel Juan* (8–12). Series: Weetzie Bat Saga. 1993, HarperCollins $14.89 (0-06-023007-X). Witch Baby, aided by her grandfather's ghost, roams New York City looking for Angel Juan, who's left her behind to play music on the city streets. (Rev: BL 10/15/93; SLJ 10/93*; VOYA 12/93)

1965 Bond, Nancy. *A String in the Harp* (6–8). 1978, Penguin paper $5.99 (0-14-032376-7). In Wales, the Morgan children find a magic harp-tuning key that takes them back in time. (Rev: BL 1/1/90)

1966 Botkin, Gleb. *Lost Tales: Stories for the Tsar's Children* (7–12). Trans. from Russian by Masha Tolstoya Sarandinaki. Illus. 1996, Random $12.99 (0-679-45142-0). This book contains three fantasies about a heroic bear who works to restore a monarch to his throne. They were written by the personal physician to Tsar Nicholas II and illustrated by his son to amuse the royal children held captive during the Russian Revolution. (Rev: SLJ 7/97)

1967 Bradbury, Ray. *The Halloween Tree* (7–12). 1972, Knopf $19.95 (0-394-82409-1). Nine boys discover the true meaning — and horror — of Halloween.

1968 Bradbury, Ray. *The Illustrated Man* (7–12). 1990, Bantam paper $7.50 (0-553-27449-X). A tattooed man tells a story for each of his tattoos.

1969 Bradshaw, Gillian. *The Land of Gold* (5–8). 1992, Greenwillow $14.00 (0-688-10576-9). In this sequel to *The Dragon and the Thief* (o.p.), a clever Egyptian thief and his sidekicks save a princess

from being sacrificed and help her reclaim her throne. (Rev: BCCB 10/92; BL 9/15/92; HB 3–4/93; SLJ 10/92)

1970 Bray, Libby. *A Great and Terrible Beauty* (8–12). 2003, Delacorte LB $17.99 (0-385-90161-5). Gemma, a troubled student in London, learns to control her visions and enter the Realms, a place of magic, in this multilayered novel that combines fantasy, mystery, and romance with a look at 19th-century manners. (Rev: BL 11/15/03)

1971 Breathed, Berkeley. *The Last Basselope: One Ferocious Story* (4–7). Illus. 2001, Little, Brown paper $5.95 (0-3161-2664-0). In this imaginative picture book for older readers, Opus and his reluctant adventurers are after the nearly extinct basselope. (Rev: BCCB 1/93; BL 12/15/92; SLJ 1/93)

1972 Brennan, Herbie. *Faerie Wars* (6–8). 2003, Bloomsbury $17.95 (1-58234-810-3). Henry Atherton becomes involved with an escaped fairy crown prince in this complex tale of parallel worlds. (Rev: BL 4/15/03; HBG 10/03; SLJ 7/03; VOYA 6/03)

1973 Brittain, Bill. *Wings* (5–7). 1995, HarperCollins paper $4.95 (0-064-40612-1). Troubles really begin for 12-year-old Ian when he sprouts wings. (Rev: BCCB 11/91; BL 1/1/91; SLJ 10/91)

1974 Britton, Susan McGee. *The Treekeepers* (4–7). 2003, Dutton $16.99 (0-525-46944-3). Bird, a plucky orphan, discovers she is the ordained opener of a locket containing a sacred seed and is plunged into a dangerous journey. (Rev: BL 4/15/03; HBG 10/03; SLJ 7/03)

1975 Brooks, Bruce. *Throwing Smoke* (4–7). 2000, HarperCollins LB $15.89 (0-06-028320-3). Whiz discovers that winning isn't everything when his dream team comes to life in this baseball fantasy. (Rev: BCCB 5/00; BL 5/15/00; HB 5–6/00; HBG 10/00; SLJ 6/00)

1976 Brown, Joseph F. *Dark Things* (6–9). 1995, Royal Fireworks paper $9.99 (0-88092-110-2). A fantasy that spans 130 years, from the Civil War to the present, about a boy who never grows old and who possesses magical powers. (Rev: VOYA 4/96)

1977 Browne, N. M. *Warriors of Alavna* (7–10). 2002, Bloomsbury $16.95 (1-58234-775-1). This historical fantasy pits 15-year-olds Dan and Ursula against invaders in Roman Britain. A sequel is *Warriors of Camlann* (2003). (Rev: BCCB 10/02; SLJ 1/03; VOYA 2/03)

1978 Buffie, Margaret. *Angels Turn Their Backs* (7–9). 1998, Kids Can $16.95 (1-55074-415-1). When 15-year-old Addy moves with her mother to Winnipeg, she suffers panic attacks at the thought of going to a new school and trying to make new friends, but she gets help from a ghost who speaks through a parrot. (Rev: BCCB 11/98; HBG 3/99; SLJ 11/98; VOYA 4/99)

1979 Buffie, Margaret. *The Haunting of Frances Rain* (7–10). 1989, Scholastic paper $12.95 (0-590-42834-9). Through a pair of magic spectacles, Lizzie is able to see events that occurred more than 50 years ago. (Rev: BL 10/1/89; SLJ 9/89)

1980 Buffie, Margaret. *The Seeker* (5–8). 2002, Kids Can $16.95 (1-55337-358-8). Emma is involved in a quest to reunite her family and becomes embroiled in interplanetary intrigue and gaming in this sequel to *The Watcher* (2000). (Rev: BL 10/1/02; HBG 10/03; SLJ 11/02; VOYA 4/03)

1981 Buffie, Margaret. *The Watcher* (5–8). 2000, Kids Can $16.95 (1-55074-829-7). Sixteen-year-old Emma discovers that she is really a changeling, a Watcher, whose mission is to protect her younger sister from warring factions. (Rev: BL 11/1/00; HBG 3/01; SLJ 10/00; VOYA 2/01)

1982 Calhoun, Dia. *Aria of the Sea* (6–9). 2003, Farrar paper $7.95 (0-374-40454-2). In the kingdom of Windward, 13-year-old Cerinthe joins the Royal Dancing School and finds herself having to choose between her talents: dancing and healing. (Rev: BR 11–12/00; SLJ 9/00)

1983 Calhoun, Dia. *Firegold* (7–12). 1999, Winslow $15.95 (1-890817-10-4). A fantasy in which a 13-year-old boy is persecuted in his village because of his different looks and behavior and is forced to travel to the Red Mountains, home of fierce barbarians. (Rev: BL 5/15/99; BR 9–10/99; SLJ 6/99; VOYA 8/99)

1984 Carroll, Lewis. *Alice's Adventures in Wonderland* (5–7). Illus. 2000, Chronicle $19.95 (0-8118-2274-5). This oversize edition of the complete text of Carroll's classic features illustrations from 29 artists. (Rev: BL 11/1/00; HBG 3/01; SLJ 11/00)

1985 Carroll, Lewis. *Alice's Adventures in Wonderland and Through the Looking Glass* (4–7). 1963, Putnam $16.99 (0-448-06004-3). One of many recommended editions of these enduring fantasies.

1986 Carroll, Lewis. *Through the Looking Glass, and What Alice Found There* (4–7). 1977, St. Martin's $14.95 (0-312-80374-5). The sequel to *Alice's Adventures in Wonderland*. One of many editions.

1987 Carroll, Thomas. *The Colony* (4–7). 2000, Sunstone $18.95 (0-86534-295-4). Fifth-grader Tony and his bullying arch-enemy Lawrence are shrunk to the size of ants by a Navajo charm and in their new environment join opposing forces. (Rev: HBG 3/01; SLJ 7/00)

1988 Chabon, Michael. *Summerland* (5–9). 2002, Hyperion $22.95 (0-7868-0877-2). Little Leaguer Ethan Feld is recruited to save the world from an old enemy in this fantasy adventure. (Rev: BCCB 1/03; HB 11–12/02; HBG 3/03; SLJ 11/02*; VOYA 2/03)

1989 Chan, Gillian. *The Carved Box* (5–8). 2001, Kids Can $16.95 (1-55074-895-5). The acquisition of a dog and a carved box ease the transition for orphaned Callum, 15, who has moved from Scotland to Canada to live with his uncle, in this novel which has an element of fantasy that comes to the fore in the dramatic ending. (Rev: BL 10/01; HBG 3/02; SLJ 10/01; VOYA 4/02)

1990 Charnas, Suzy McKee. *The Kingdom of Kevin Malone* (7–10). 1993, Harcourt $16.95 (0-15-200756-3). This novel melds the world of the teenage problem novel with that of fantasy in a story that pokes gentle fun at the conventions of fantasy fiction. (Rev: BL 6/1–15/93; SLJ 1/94; VOYA 8/93)

1991 Chetwin, Grace. *The Crystal Stair: From Tales of Gom in the Legends of Ulm* (6–8). 1988, Macmillan LB $14.95 (0-02-718311-4). Young Gom sets out to find a wizard who will teach him magic in this sequel to *The Riddle and the Rune*. (Rev: BL 4/1/88; SLJ 6/88)

1992 Clement-Davies, David. *Fire Bringer* (6–12). 2000, Dutton $19.95 (0-525-46492-1). A fawn with a destiny readies himself to challenge the ruling stag in this absorbing and suspenseful novel set in medieval Scotland. (Rev: BL 9/1/00; BR 5–6/01; HB 1–2/01; HBG 3/01; SLJ 12/00)

1993 Clement-Davies, David. *The Sight* (7–12). 2002, Dutton $21.99 (0-525-46723-8). A wolf pack in Transylvania is the focus of this story of good and evil that entwines fantasy, history, mythology, and the supernatural. (Rev: BCCB 4/02; BL 3/1/02; HB 7–8/02; HBG 10/02; SLJ 6/02; VOYA 6/02)

1994 Coleman, Alice Scovell. *Engraved in Stone* (4–7). 2003, Tiara Bks. $14.95 (0-9729846-0-7). A prince and princess who will do anything to avoid their planned marriage set off on a quest to get their fate changed in this humorous fantasy. (Rev: SLJ 12/03)

1995 Colfer, Eoin. *Artemis Fowl* (6–9). 2001, Hyperion $16.95 (0-7868-0801-2). Twelve-year-old genius and adventurous criminal entrepreneur Artemis Fowl captures a fairy investigator, with lively and hilarious results. (Rev: BL 4/15/01; HB 7–8/01; HBG 10/01; SLJ 5/01; VOYA 8/01)

1996 Colfer, Eoin. *Artemis Fowl: The Arctic Incident* (6–9). 2002, Hyperion $16.99 (0-7868-0855-1). Another madcap adventure in which Artemis and Captain Holly combine their talents to combat forces as diverse as the Russian mafia and a band of dangerous smugglers. (Rev: BCCB 7–8/01; BL 5/1/02; HBG 10/02; SLJ 7/02; VOYA 8/02)

1997 Colfer, Eoin. *Artemis Fowl: The Eternity Code* (6–9). 2003, Hyperion $16.95 (0-7868-1914-6). An action-packed adventure in which Artemis creates an unauthorized groundbreaking supercomputer with fairy technology, which becomes a threat when it is stolen. (Rev: BL 6/1–15/03; HBG 10/03; SLJ 7/03)

1998 Collins, Suzanne. *Gregor the Overlander* (4–7). 2003, Scholastic $16.95 (0-439-43536-6). When his baby sister disappears into an air vent, 11-year-old Gregor doesn't hesitate to follow and finds himself in a whole new world, an Underland where an unexpected role awaits him. (Rev: BCCB 1/04; BL 11/15/03*; HB 9–10/03; HBG 9–10/03; LMC 11–12/03; SLJ 11/03; VOYA 10/03)

1999 Conly, Jane L. *Racso and the Rats of NIMH* (5–7). 1986, HarperCollins LB $17.89 (0-06-021362-0). This sequel to the Newbery Medal winner involves once again the smart rodents who wish to live in peace in Thorn Valley. (Rev: BCCB 6/86; BL 6/1/86; SLJ 4/86)

2000 Conrad, Pam. *Zoe Rising* (4–7). 1996, HarperCollins LB $14.89 (0-06-027218-X). In a sequel to *Stonewords* (1990), Zoe's time traveling brings her an experience that almost causes her death. (Rev: BCCB 10/96; BL 8/96; BR 1–2/97; HB 11–12/96; SLJ 11/96; VOYA 12/96)

2001 Cooney, Caroline B. *For All Time* (6–10). Series: Time Travel. 2001, Delacorte $12.95 (0-385-32773-0). Annie and Strat's ill-timed romance continues in this stand-alone conclusion to the earlier trilogy as Annie tries to join Strat in 1899 and instead ends up in ancient Egypt. (Rev: BCCB 11/01; BL 9/15/01; HBG 3/02; SLJ 9/01; VOYA 12/01)

2002 Cooney, Caroline B. *Prisoner of Time* (6–10). Series: Time Travel. 1998, Laurel Leaf paper $5.50 (0-440-22019-X). In this conclusion to the trilogy, there is again a contrast between the lifestyles of today and those of 100 years ago as a girl is rescued from an unsuitable marriage. (Rev: BL 6/1–15/98; SLJ 5/98; VOYA 6/98)

2003 Cooper, Susan. *Green Boy* (4–8). 2002, Simon & Schuster $16.00 (0-689-84751-3). Two young boys discover a futuristic world in which natural resources are depleted and a war to save the environment is being waged. (Rev: BCCB 5/02; BL 3/1/02; HB 5–6/02; HBG 10/02; SLJ 2/02)

2004 Cooper, Susan. *King of Shadows* (5–8). 1999, Simon & Schuster $16.00 (0-689-82817-9). Nat Field time-travels to 1599 London and assumes the child-actor role of Puck in *A Midsummer Night's Dream*. (Rev: BL 10/15/99*; HB 11–12/99; HBG 3/00; SLJ 11/99)

2005 Cooper, Susan. *Over Sea, Under Stone* (6–9). Illus. Series: The Dark Is Rising. 1966, Harcourt $18.00 (0-15-259034-X); paper $3.95 (0-02-042785-9). Three contemporary children enter the world of King Arthur in this first volume of a series. Followed by *The Dark Is Rising* (1973), *Greenwitch* (1985), *The Grey King* (1975), and *Silver on the Tree* (1977).

2006 Cooper, Susan. *Silver on the Tree* (5–7). 1980, Macmillan $18.00 (0-689-50088-2); paper $4.99 (0-689-71152-2). In this fifth and last volume of a series, Will Stanton and his friends wage a final battle against the Dark, the powers of evil. The first four volumes are *Over Sea, Under Stone* (1966), *The Dark Is Rising* (1973), *The Grey King* (1975), and *Greenwitch* (1985). *The Grey King* won the 1976 Newbery Medal.

2007 Corbett, Sue. *12 Again* (5–8). 2002, Dutton $16.99 (0-525-46899-4). Patrick's mother becomes 12 again after drinking a magic potion, and it's up to Patrick to save her. (Rev: BCCB 10/02; BL 9/1/02; HBG 3/03; SLJ 7/02; VOYA 8/02)

2008 Corlett, William. *The Steps up the Chimney* (5–8). 2000, Pocket paper $4.99 (0-7434-1001-7). Children stuck in a remote mansion in Wales with an uncle and his pregnant, vegetarian girlfriend discover a secret room that houses a magician. (Rev: SLJ 5/01)

2009 Coville, Bruce, ed. *A Glory of Unicorns* (5–8). Illus. 1998, Scholastic paper $16.95 (0-590-95943-3). A collection of stories by fantasy authors, including the editor and his wife, that deal with unicorns. (Rev: BL 6/1–15/98; BR 5–6/98; HBG 10/98; SLJ 5/98; VOYA 8/98)

2010 Coville, Bruce. *Goblins in the Castle* (5–7). Illus. 1992, Pocket paper $4.99 (0-671-72711-7). William, now 11, has grown up in Toad-in-a-Cage Castle and knows many of its secret passages. (Rev: BL 2/1/93)

2011 Coville, Bruce, ed. *Half-Human* (7–10). 2001, Scholastic $15.95 (0-590-95944-1). Ten stories by well-known YA authors feature beings that are half-human, half-animal, accompanied by striking illustrations. (Rev: BL 12/15/01; HBG 10/02; SLJ 12/01; VOYA 12/01)

2012 Coville, Bruce. *Juliet Dove, Queen of Love: A Magic Shop Book* (4–8). 2003, Harcourt $17.00 (0-15-204561-9). Life changes for shy Juliet, 12, when she is given an amulet and the boys suddenly come flocking to her side. (Rev: BL 1/1–15/04; SLJ 12/03)

2013 Coville, Bruce. *The Skull of Truth* (5–7). Illus. Series: Magic Shop Books. 1997, Harcourt $17.00 (0-15-275457-1). A fantasy in which compulsive liar Charlie learns to tell the truth through the efforts of a wisecracking skull. (Rev: BL 10/1/97; HBG 3/98; SLJ 10/97*)

2014 Coville, Bruce. *Song of the Wanderer* (5–8). Series: Unicorn Chronicles. 1999, Scholastic paper $16.95 (0-590-45953-8). Cara and her friends undertake a dangerous mission — returning to Earth to bring her grandmother, the Wanderer, back to Luster. This is a sequel to *Into the Land of the Unicorn*. (Rev: BL 3/1/00; HBG 3/00; SLJ 12/99)

2015 Craddock, Sonia. *Sleeping Boy* (5–8). 1999, Simon & Schuster $16.95 (0-689-81763-0). This version of the Sleeping Beauty is set in Berlin around World War II. A wicked general curses a baby boy who is later saved from going to war by an aunt who puts him to sleep. (Rev: BL 2/1/00; HBG 3/00; SLJ 9/99)

2016 Crispin, A. C. *Voices of Chaos* (8–12). 1998, Ace paper $5.99 (0-441-00516-0). In this story of romance, political intrigue, and coming of age, the students and teachers at Starbridge Academy are introduced to a race of feline beings — expressive, intelligent, ambitious, and skillful at deception and manipulation — when Prince Khyriz and Shiksara, a girl from the merchant class, come to study. (Rev: BL 3/1/98; VOYA 6/98)

2017 Crocker, Carter. *The Tale of the Swamp Rat* (4–8). Illus. 2003, Putnam $16.99 (0-399-23964-2). Ossie the swamp rat, orphaned by a snake but rescued by an alligator, finds himself accused of causing the drought that is affecting his swamp. (Rev: BCCB 12/03; BL 11/15/03; SLJ 10/03)

2018 Cross, Gillian. *Pictures in the Dark* (5–8). 1996, Holiday $16.95 (0-8234-1267-9). A boy whose life is miserable uses supernatural means to escape the pressures. (Rev: BCCB 1/97; BL 1/1–15/97; BR 3–4/97)

2019 Crossley-Holland, Kevin. *At the Crossing Places* (5–8). 2002, Scholastic $17.95 (0-439-26598-3). The story started in *The Seeing Stone* (2001) continues, with Arthur now on a quest to find his mother and trying to make peace with his discoveries about his father and his own relationship with Arthur-in-the-stone. (Rev: BL 11/1/02; HB 11–12/02; HBG 3/03; SLJ 11/02; VOYA 2/03)

2020 Crossley-Holland, Kevin. *The Seeing Stone* (4–8). 2001, Scholastic $17.95 (0-439-26326-3). In the time of Richard the Lion-Hearted, a 13-year-old boy named Arthur finds that his life mirrors that of the legendary King Arthur. (Rev: BL 10/1/01; HB 11–12/01*; HBG 3/02; SLJ 10/01; VOYA 12/01)

2021 Curley, Marianne. *The Dark* (7–12). 2003, Bloomsbury $16.95 (1-58234-853-7). Isabel, Ethan, and Matt must rescue their mentor, Akarian, from a frightening underworld in this sequel to *The Named* (2002). (Rev: BL 10/1/03)

2022 Curley, Marianne. *The Named* (7–11). 2002, Bloomsbury $16.95 (1-58234-779-4). Ethan and Isabel time-travel through history on a difficult quest in this first volume of a multilayered trilogy recounting the battle against the Order of Chaos. (Rev: BL 11/15/02; SLJ 1/03)

2023 Curry, Jane L. *Dark Shade* (6–10). 1998, Simon & Schuster $16.00 (0-689-81812-2). Maggie Gilmour and her silent, withdrawn friend, Kip, travel in time to 1758 and the time of the French and Indian Wars. (Rev: BL 4/1/98; BR 1–2/99; HB 5–6/98; HBG 9/98; SLJ 5/98; VOYA 8/98)

2024 Curry, Jane L. *Moon Window* (5–8). 1996, Simon & Schuster $16.00 (0-689-80945-X). Joellen travels back in time and meets several of her ancestors. (Rev: BCCB 11/96; BL 10/15/96; SLJ 12/96)

2025 Curry, Jane Louise. *The Egyptian Box* (4–7). 2002, Simon & Schuster $16.00 (0-689-84273-2). A suspenseful mystery about a middle-schooler who discovers a magical servant, an Egyptian statue come to life, who will obey her wishes. (Rev: BCCB 5/02; BL 6/1–15/02; HBG 10/02; SLJ 3/02)

2026 Dadey, Debbie, and Marcia T. Jones. *Leprechauns Don't Play Basketball* (5–8). 1992, Scholastic paper $3.99 (0-590-44822-6). The Bailey Elementary 3rd grade thinks the gym teacher is a leprechaun. (Rev: BL 9/15/92)

2027 Dalkey, Kara. *Ascension* (7–10). Series: Water. 2002, Avon paper $4.99 (0-06-440808-6). Nia is an ambitious 16-year-old mermaid living in the city of Atlantis in this first installment in a richly detailed trilogy that blends fantasy, romance, and adventure. The sequels are *Reunion* and *Transformation*. (Rev: BCCB 4/02; BL 2/1/02; SLJ 3/02; VOYA 2/02)

2028 Dalkey, Kara. *The Heavenward Path* (7–12). 1998, Harcourt $17.00 (0-15-201652-X). In this sequel to *Little Sister,* 16-year-old Mitsuko escapes from an arranged marriage by flying away on the wings of her friend Goranu. (Rev: BL 6/1–15/98; HBG 9/98; SLJ 5/98; VOYA 6/98)

2029 Dalkey, Kara. *Little Sister* (7–10). 1996, Harcourt $17.00 (0-15-201392-X). In this historical fantasy, a Japanese girl from a noble family, who is a helper for her newly married oldest sister, travels into a hell-like land and back. (Rev: BL 10/1/96; BR 3–4/97; SLJ 12/96; VOYA 2/97)

2030 Danko, Dan, and Tom Mason. *The Minotaur* (4–8). Series: MythQuest. 2002, Bantam LB $12.99 (0-553-13009-9); paper $4.99 (0-553-48759-0). Alex is investigating his archaeologist father's disappearance when he is whisked away to ancient Crete and must do battle with the Minotaur. (Rev: HBG 10/02; SLJ 4/02)

2031 Davies, Valentine. *Miracle on 34th Street* (6–9). Illus. 1984, Harcourt $16.95 (0-15-254526-3). Kris Kringle, living in an old folks home, plays Santa at Macy's in this 1947 fantasy.

2032 Deem, James M. *The Very Real Ghost Book of Christina Rose* (7–9). 1996, Houghton $15.00 (0-395-76128-X). In this book that combines detection, the paranormal, and humor, 12-year-old Christina deals with her mother's death by immersing herself in the study of paranormal activities and wearing only dark, depressing colors. (Rev: BL 5/1/96; SLJ 5/96; VOYA 10/96)

2033 DeFelice, Cynthia. *The Strange Night Writing of Jessamine Colter* (6–9). 1988, Macmillan paper $13.95 (0-02-726451-3). A short tender novel about a woman who has the gift of seeing into the future. (Rev: BL 10/1/88; SLJ 11/88; VOYA 4/89)

2034 de Lint, Charles. *Waifs and Strays* (7–12). 2002, Viking $17.99 (0-670-03584-X). A collection of 16 de Lint fantasies — the majority previously published — featuring urban teen characters. (Rev: BCCB 12/02; BL 10/1/02; HBG 3/03; SLJ 11/02; VOYA 12/02)

2035 Dickinson, Peter. *The Lion-Tamer's Daughter and Other Stories* (6–9). 1997, Bantam Doubleday Dell $15.95 (0-385-32327-1). Four fantastic stories that deal with transformations, other worlds, and duplicate identities. (Rev: BL 4/1/97; SLJ 3/97*; VOYA 4/97)

2036 Dickinson, Peter. *The Ropemaker* (7–12). 2001, Delacorte $15.95 (0-385-72921-9). Two young people — Tilja and Tahl — and their grandparents set off on a perilous journey to find the magician who has protected their Valley from its enemies. (Rev: BCCB 1/02; BL 10/15/01; HB 11–12/01; HBG 3/02; SLJ 11/01*; VOYA 12/01)

2037 Dickinson, Peter. *The Tears of the Salamander* (6–9). 2003, Random $16.95 (0-385-73098-5). Alfredo, 13 and the possessor of a beautiful voice, goes to live on Mount Etna with his putative uncle after his family dies in a fire, only to find that his uncle is not what he seems and has evil plans for Alfredo. (Rev: BCCB 12/03; BL 5/15/03*; HB 7–8/03; SLJ 8/03)

2038 Divakaruni, Chitra Banerjee. *The Conch Bearer* (5–8). 2003, Millbrook $16.95 (0-7613-1935-2). A multilayered and richly descriptive story of a poor Indian boy, Anand, who sets off on a challenging quest to return a magic conch shell to its rightful home. (Rev: BL 9/15/03*; SLJ 12/03)

2039 Downer, Ann. *Hatching Magic* (4–7). 2003, Simon & Schuster $16.95 (0-689-83400-4). A procession of a pet dragon, a wizard, and his archenemy travel through time from the 13th century to the 21st century, where an 11-year-old Bostonian becomes involved in their disputes. (Rev: BL 4/15/03; HB 7–8/03; HBG 10/03; SLJ 8/03)

2040 Doyle, Debra, and James D. MacDonald. *The Knight's Wyrd* (6–9). 1992, Harcourt $16.95 (0-15-200764-4). On the eve of his knighting, young Will learns his wyrd (fate) from his father's wizard, which sets off a series of adventures. (Rev: BL 11/15/92; SLJ 11/92)

2041 Drake, Emily. *The Magickers* (5–6). 2001, DAW $19.95 (0-88677-935-9). Jason, who is 11, finds that Camp Ravenwyng is really a "magick" training ground and he is plunged into mystery and adventure. (Rev: BL 7/01; SLJ 12/01; VOYA 10/01)

2042 Drexler, Sam, and Fay Shelby. *Lost in Spillville* (5–9). Series: Erika and Oz Adventures in American History. 2000, Aunt Strawberry paper $6.99 (0-9669988-1-2). Two teenagers accidentally are transported to the 1930s and must locate an important clock maker to be returned to the 1990s. (Rev: SLJ 11/00; VOYA 12/00)

2043 Duane, Diane. *Deep Wizardry* (5–8). Series: Young Wizards. 2001, Magic Carpet Books LB $15.25 (0-613-36059-1); Harcourt paper $6.95 (0-15-216257-7). Nita and Kit, the two young wizards of *So You Want to Be a Wizard,* again use their powers to prevent a great catastrophe. (Rev: HB 5–6/85)

2044 Duane, Diane. *So You Want to Be a Wizard* (5–8). Series: Young Wizards. 2003, Harcourt $16.95 (0-15-204738-7); paper $6.95 (0-15-216250-X). Nita and friends embark on a journey to retrieve the Book of Night with Moon.

2045 Duane, Diane. *A Wizard Abroad* (6–9). Series: Young Wizards. 1997, Harcourt $15.00 (0-15-201209-5). The fourth book in the series concerns 14-year-old Nita and her struggle against the Fomori, monster people who are trying to destroy the ancient symbols of power in Ireland. (Rev: BL 10/1/97; HBG 3/98; SLJ 9/97)

2046 Duane, Diane. *A Wizard Alone* (6–10). Series: Young Wizards. 2002, Harcourt $17.00 (0-15-204562-7). The sixth book in the series of Nita and Kit's adventures in magic finds wizard Kit working on his own while Nita mourns the death of her mother. (Rev: BL 11/15/02; HBG 3/03; SLJ 2/03; VOYA 4/03)

2047 Duane, Diane. *The Wizard's Dilemma* (6–9). Series: Young Wizards. 2001, Harcourt $17.00 (0-15-202551-0). Young wizard Nita travels to other universes in search of a cure for her mother's cancer, and eventually must make a difficult decision. (Rev: BL 6/1–15/01; HBG 10/01; SLJ 8/01; VOYA 8/01)

2048 Duane, Diane. *Wizard's Holiday* (6–9). Series: Young Wizards. 2003, Harcourt $17.00 (0-15-204771-9). Plotlines alternate between teen wizards Nita and Kit's exploits on a distant planet and Nita's little sister and her father, who are hosting alien exchange students, as disaster approaches. (Rev: BL 1/1–15/04; SLJ 12/03)

2049 Duel, John. *Wide Awake in Dreamland* (5–8). Illus. 1992, Stargaze Publg. $15.95 (0-9630923-0-8). An evil warlock threatens to steal a 9-year-old's imagination unless the young boy can find a friendly wizard first. (Rev: BL 3/1/92; SLJ 5/92)

2050 Dunkle, Clare B. *The Hollow Kingdom* (5–8). 2003, Holt $16.95 (0-8050-7390-6). A beauty-and-the-beast story with a twist, in which Kate is persuaded to marry a goblin king and move to his underground world. (Rev: BL 11/15/03; SLJ 12/03)

2051 Dunlop, Eileen. *Websters' Leap* (4–7). 1995, Holiday $15.95 (0-8234-1193-1). In this time-slip fantasy, Jill gets involved with people who owned a

Scottish castle 400 years before. (Rev: BL 10/1/95; SLJ 10/95)

2052 Eberhardt, Thom. *Rat Boys: A Dating Experiment* (6–8). 2001, Hyperion $15.99 (0-7868-0696-6). Marci and Summer resort to magically turning rats into boys to compete with nasty, popular Jennifer. (Rev: BL 11/1/01; HBG 10/02; SLJ 11/01; VOYA 12/01)

2053 Ende, Michael. *The Neverending Story* (7–12). Trans. by Ralph Manheim. 1984, Penguin paper $11.95 (0-14-007431-7). An overweight boy with many problems enters the magic world of Fantastica in this charming fantasy.

2054 Etchemendy, Nancy. *The Power of Un* (4–7). 2000, Front Street $14.95 (0-8126-2850-0). Gib, a young boy, meets a strange old man who gives him an "unner," which can send him back in time in this thought-provoking fantasy. (Rev: BCCB 7–8/00; BL 5/1/00; HBG 10/00; SLJ 6/00; VOYA 6/00)

2055 Farber, Erica, and J. R. Sansevere. *The Secret in the Stones* (5–9). Series: Tales of the Nine Charms. 2001, Dell paper $4.50 (0-440-41820-8). In this second installment in a trilogy with an intricate plot, 13-year-old Zoe's blue trinket proves to be one of the famous Nine Charms, leading her into a fantastic adventure far from her home in California. (Rev: SLJ 9/01)

2056 Farjeon, Eleanor. *The Glass Slipper* (6–9). 1986, HarperCollins LB $11.89 (0-397-32181-3). A romantic retelling in prose of the Cinderella story. (Rev: BL 10/15/86)

2057 Favole, Robert J. *Through the Wormhole* (5–8). 2001, Flywheel $17.95 (1-930826-00-1). Detailed endnotes add historical weight to this story of Michael and Kate, who travel through time to 1778 to aid the Marquis de Lafayette and rescue one of Michael's ancestors. (Rev: BL 3/1/01; SLJ 4/01; VOYA 4/01)

2058 Fienberg, Anna. *The Witch in the Lake* (5–8). 2002, Annick LB $18.95 (1-55037-723-X); paper $7.95 (1-55037-722-1). This story of magic and suspense in 16th-century Italy interweaves fantasy with facts about the time. (Rev: HBG 3/03; SLJ 8/02; VOYA 8/02)

2059 Findon, Joanne. *When Night Eats the Moon* (4–7). 2000, Red Deer paper $7.95 (0-88995-212-4). Her flute music and some magic take Holly, a Canadian girl visiting England, back to prehistoric times at Stonehenge when the locals are being threatened with a Celtic invasion. (Rev: BL 8/00; VOYA 6/00)

2060 Fisk, Pauline. *Midnight Blue* (5–7). 2003, Bloomsbury $16.95 (1-58234-829-4). Bonnie happens upon a magical balloon that takes her to a parallel world that is very familiar yet very different, where she finds the happy family she has always dreamed of. (Rev: BL 10/1/03; SLJ 11/03)

2061 Fisk, Pauline. *The Secret of Sabrina Fludde* (6–10). 2002, Bloomsbury $15.95 (1-58234-754-9). A young girl with no memory floats into the Welsh town of Pengwern, where she takes the name Abren and eventually discovers the secret of her past. (Rev: BL 9/1/02; SLJ 7/02)

2062 Fletcher, Susan. *Dragon's Milk* (5–9). 1989, Macmillan LB $15.95 (0-689-31579-1). To save her brother, Kaeldra embarks on a quest to find dragon's milk. (Rev: BL 11/1/89; BR 3–4/90; SLJ 11/89; VOYA 12/89)

2063 Fletcher, Susan. *Flight of the Dragon Kyn* (5–7). 1993, Atheneum $17.00 (0-689-31880-4). A girl with a special talent to call down birds uses it to attract dragons for the king and his hunters. (Rev: BL 1/15/94; SLJ 11/93)

2064 Fletcher, Susan. *Sign of the Dove* (6–10). 1996, Atheneum $17.00 (0-689-80460-1). Lyf, her foster sister, Kaeldra, and Kaeldra's husband are dedicated to saving dragon hatchlings from the Krags in this allegory in which Lyf finds herself alone in a world of wild dragons. A sequel to *Dragon's Milk* (1989). (Rev: BL 5/1/96; BR 1–2/97; HB 9–10/96; SLJ 5/96; VOYA 8/96)

2065 Flieger, Verlyn. *Pig Tale* (7–10). 2002, Hyperion $16.99 (0-7868-0792-X). Mokie, an orphan pigtender, finds her life changed by a mysterious trio of gypsies after she is raped in this story that draws on Celtic mysticism. (Rev: BCCB 1/03; BL 11/15/02; HBG 3/03; SLJ 12/02; VOYA 2/03)

2066 Forrester, Sandra. *The Everyday Witch* (5–7). 2002, Barron's paper $4.95 (0-7641-2220-7). To establish her magic rating, 11-year-old witch Beatrice is assigned to rescue a famous sorcerer and his daughters from an evil villain. (Rev: SLJ 10/02)

2067 Fromental, Jean-Luc. *Broadway Chicken* (5–8). Trans. by Suzi Baker. Illus. 1995, Hyperion LB $15.49 (0-7868-2048-9). A tale of success and failure with, yes, a dancing chicken as the protagonist. (Rev: BL 12/15/95; SLJ 2/96)

2068 Funke, Cornelia. *Inkheart* (6–12). 2003, Scholastic $19.95 (0-439-53164-0). Twelve-year-old Meggie, the key character in this complex novel, is the daughter of a bookbinder who can release fictional characters from their books. (Rev: BL 9/1/03; SLJ 10/03)

2069 Furlong, Monica. *Juniper* (7–12). 1992, Demco $11.04 (0-606-01569-8). A rich coming-of-age novel about Ninnoc, the only child of King Mark of Cornwall, as Christianity is beginning to overcome the ancient Celtic religion of the Mother Goddess. (Rev: BL 2/15/91; SLJ 5/91)

2070 Gaiman, Neil. *Coraline* (5–8). 2002, HarperCollins LB $17.89 (0-06-623744-0). An Alice-in-Wonderland type of tale for older readers in which a girl finds an alternate world in the empty apartment next door. (Rev: BCCB 11/02; BL 8/02; HB 11–12/02; HBG 3/03; SLJ 8/02*)

2071 Garfield, Henry. *Tartabull's Throw* (7–10). 2001, Simon & Schuster $15.00 (0-689-83840-9). A 19-year-old baseball player and a mysterious young woman called Cassandra are the principal characters in this multifaceted story set in 1967 that entwines baseball, werewolves, romance, and suspense. (Rev: BL 5/15/01; HBG 10/01; SLJ 6/01; VOYA 8/01)

2072 Garland, Sherry. *Cabin 102* (5–8). 1995, Harcourt $11.00 (0-15-200663-X); paper $6.00 (0-15-200662-1). On a cruise ship with his family, Dusty encounters a mysterious girl from the extinct Taino tribe. (Rev: BL 11/15/95; SLJ 12/95)

2073 Gideon, Melanie. *The Map That Breathed* (5–8). 2003, Holt $16.95 (0-8050-7142-3). Dangerous and exciting adventures await Nora and Billy when they look into the alternate world of Sasarea. (Rev: BCCB 2/04; BL 11/15/03; SLJ 12/03)

2074 Gliori, Debi. *Pure Dead Brilliant* (4–8). 2003, Knopf $15.95 (0-375-81412-4). The fun continues at the Strega-Borgia castle as Titus anticipates a large windfall, Pandora finds a time-travel clock, and there are some strange house guests. (Rev: BL 11/1/03; SLJ 10/03)

2075 Gliori, Debi. *Pure Dead Magic* (4–8). 2001, Knopf LB $17.99 (0-375-91410-2). Life at the Strega-Borgia castle is an overwhelming riot of problems — a lost father, a mother at witch school, a new nanny, a dragon with an upset stomach, and a baby in Cyberspace — that only a little magic can solve. (Rev: BCCB 2/02; BL 8/01; HBG 10/02; SLJ 9/01)

2076 Gliori, Debi. *Pure Dead Wicked* (5–8). 2002, Knopf $15.95 (0-375-81411-6). Siblings Titus, Pandora, and Damp must leave their castle and move with their creepy extended family into the Auchenlochtermuchy Arms with disastrous but humorous consequences in this sequel to *Pure Dead Magic* (2001). (Rev: BL 9/15/02; HBG 10/03; SLJ 8/02)

2077 Gordon, Lawrence. *User Friendly* (7–10). Series: Ghost Chronicles. 1999, Karmichael paper $11.95 (0-9653966-0-6). Frank, a teenage ghost in limbo, contacts Eddie through the computer to get help to free himself and his friend, a runaway slave, from the purgatory in which they are living. (Rev: BL 1/1–15/99; SLJ 1/99)

2078 Gormley, Beatrice. *Best Friend Insurance* (5–7). 1988, Avon paper $2.50 (0-380-69854-4). Maureen finds that her mother has been transformed into a new friend named Kitty.

2079 Goto, Hiromi. *The Water of Possibility* (5–7). Series: In the Same Boat. 2002, Coteau paper $8.95 (1-55050-183-6). Sayuri, 12, and her younger brother discover a magical world full of danger in this fantasy that includes many elements of Japanese folklore. (Rev: SLJ 8/02)

2080 Grahame, Kenneth. *The Wind in the Willows* (4–7). 1983, Macmillan $19.95 (0-684-17957-1). The classic that introduced Mole, Ratty, and Mr. Toad. Two of many other editions are: illus. by Michael Hague (1980, Henry Holt); illus. by John Burningham (1983, Viking).

2081 Gray, Luli. *Falcon and the Charles Street Witch* (4–7). 2002, Houghton $15.00 (0-618-16410-3). In this fantasy follow-up to 1995's *Falcon's Egg*, a 12-year-old girl becomes reacquainted with a dragon she released over New York City and befriends a witch who lives in Greenwich Village. (Rev: BL 3/15/02*; HBG 10/02; SLJ 4/02; VOYA 4/02)

2082 Greenberg, Martin H., ed. *Elf Fantastic* (8–12). 1997, D A W Books paper $5.99 (0-88677-736-4). Each of the 19 short stories about elves in this collection offers a fresh insight into humankind. (Rev: VOYA 10/97)

2083 Greer, Gery, and Bob Ruddick. *Max and Me and the Time Machine* (5–8). 1983, HarperCollins paper $4.99 (0-06-440222-3). Steve and Max travel back in time to England during the Middle Ages.

2084 Griffin, Peni R. *A Dig in Time* (4–7). 1991, Macmillan $14.95 (0-689-50525-6). Twelve-year-old Nan and her brother spend the summer in San Antonio with their grandmother and find they can travel back in time to witness events in their family's history. (Rev: BCCB 10/91; BL 6/15/91; SLJ 6/91)

2085 Griffin, Peni R. *Switching Well* (5–9). 1993, Macmillan $17.00 (0-689-50581-7); Penguin paper $5.99 (0-14-036910-4). Two girls from different centuries trade places but soon regret their decisions. (Rev: BCCB 7–8/93; BL 6/1–15/93*; SLJ 6/93*; VOYA 8/93)

2086 Grove, Vicki. *Rimwalkers* (6–10). 1993, Putnam $14.95 (0-399-22430-0). On an Illinois farm for the summer, Tory develops self-esteem as she unravels a mystery involving the apparition of a small boy. (Rev: BL 10/15/93; SLJ 10/93; VOYA 12/93)

2087 Gutman, Dan. *Babe and Me* (4–7). Illus. 2000, Avon $15.99 (0-380-97739-7). Joe and his dad time-travel to the 1932 World Series to witness a historic moment with hitter Babe Ruth. (Rev: BL 2/1/00; HBG 10/00; SLJ 2/00; VOYA 4/00)

2088 Gutman, Dan. *Honus and Me: A Baseball Card Adventure* (4–7). 1997, Avon paper $5.99 (0-380-78878-0). Young Joe Stoshack finds a magical baseball card that allows him to travel through time and participate in the 1909 World Series. (Rev: BL 4/15/97; SLJ 6/97)

2089 Gutman, Dan. *Jackie and Me: A Baseball Card Adventure* (4–7). Illus. 1999, Avon $15.99 (0-380-97685-4). While time-traveling to research a paper on Jackie Robinson, Joe Stoshack becomes an

African American and experiences prejudice first hand. (Rev: BL 2/1/99; HBG 10/99; SLJ 3/99)

2090 Gutman, Dan. *Qwerty Stevens Back in Time with Benjamin Franklin* (4–7). 2002, Simon & Schuster $16.95 (0-689-84553-7). Benjamin Franklin is transported through time into Robert "Qwerty" Stevens's bedroom, and Qwerty and a friend accompany Franklin to 1776 to sign the Declaration of Independence. (Rev: BL 9/15/02; HBG 3/03; SLJ 8/02)

2091 Haddix, Margaret P. *Running Out of Time* (4–7). 1995, Simon & Schuster $16.95 (0-689-80084-3). Living in a historical site where the time is the 1840s, Jessie escapes into the present in this fantasy. (Rev: BCCB 11/95; BL 10/1/95; SLJ 10/95*)

2092 Haddix, Margaret Peterson. *Escape from Memory* (6–9). 2003, Simon & Schuster $16.95 (0-689-85421-8). Under hypnosis, Kira reveals memories of another place in another time, one that threatens both herself and her mother. (Rev: BL 9/1/03; VOYA 10/03)

2093 Hague, Michael, ed. *The Book of Dragons* (4–7). 1995, Morrow $21.99 (0-688-10879-2). Seventeen classic tales about dragons by such authors as Tolkien and Kenneth Grahame are included in this interesting anthology. (Rev: BL 10/1/95; SLJ 10/95)

2094 Hamilton, Virginia. *Justice and Her Brothers* (7–10). 1998, Scholastic paper $4.99 (0-590-36214-3). Four children with supernatural powers move in time in this complex novel. Sequels are *Dustland* and *The Gathering*.

2095 Hanley, Victoria. *The Healer's Keep* (7–12). 2002, Holiday $17.95 (0-8234-1760-3). A princess, a former slave girl, and their companions battle evil in a land full of magic. (Rev: BCCB 1/03; HBG 3/03; SLJ 12/02; VOYA 2/03)

2096 Hanley, Victoria. *The Seer and the Sword* (6–10). 2000, Holiday $17.95 (0-8234-1532-5). Romance, court politics, battles, and suspense all are essential parts of this fantasy featuring Princess Torina and Prince Landen. (Rev: BCCB 2/01; BL 12/15/00; HBG 10/01; SLJ 3/01; VOYA 4/01)

2097 Hansen, Brooks. *Caesar's Antlers* (5–8). Illus. 1997, Farrar $16.00 (0-374-31024-6). In this animal fantasy, Caesar the reindeer and his friend Bette the sparrow and her two offspring set out to contact some human friends to get help for the winter. (Rev: BL 10/1/97; BR 3–4/98; HBG 3/98; SLJ 11/97)

2098 Hantman, Clea. *Heaven Sent: Goddesses #1* (7–10). 2002, Avon paper $4.99 (0-06-440875-2). Zeus sends three teenage daughters to Earth — Athens, Georgia, to be precise — to learn some manners in this amusing and hip novel that combines mythology and teen culture. (Rev: BCCB 3/02; BL 2/15/02; SLJ 3/02; VOYA 2/02)

2099 Hautman, Pete. *Mr. Was* (8–12). 1996, Simon & Schuster $16.00 (0-689-81068-7). In this complex fantasy, Jack escapes his father's drunken rage by entering a door in his grandfather's house that takes him back to 1941. (Rev: BL 9/15/96; SLJ 10/96; VOYA 12/96)

2100 Hendry, Diana. *Harvey Angell* (4–7). 2001, Pocket paper $4.99 (0-7434-2828-5). A spirited story about an orphan, Henry, who lives in a dismal boarding house that brightens up when a new resident brings excitement and mystery. (Rev: BL 1/1–15/02; SLJ 12/01; VOYA 4/02)

2101 Heneghan, James. *Flood* (5–8). 2002, Farrar $16.00 (0-374-35057-4). The Little People save a boy from the flood that kills his parents, and save him from the neglectful father he never knew in this poignant story about loss and acceptance. (Rev: BCCB 4/02; BL 3/15/02; HB 7–8/02; HBG 10/02; SLJ 4/02)

2102 Heneghan, James. *The Grave* (7–10). 2000, Farrar $17.00 (0-374-32765-3). Fantasy and historical fiction blend as orphan Tom, 13, travels from 1974 Liverpool back to 19th-century Ireland and experiences both family life and the potato famine. (Rev: BCCB 3/01; BL 10/15/00; BR 3–4/01; HB 11–12/00; HBG 3/01; SLJ 11/00; VOYA 12/00)

2103 Highwater, Jamake. *Rama: A Legend* (5–9). 1997, Replica Books LB $24.95 (0-7351-0001-2). When he's wrongfully banished from his father's kingdom and his wife, Sita, is kidnapped, valiant Prince Rama charges back to avenge the evil that's befallen his world. (Rev: BL 11/15/94; SLJ 12/94; VOYA 2/95)

2104 Hill, Pamela Smith. *The Last Grail Keeper* (7–10). 2001, Holiday $17.95 (0-8234-1574-0). While visiting England with her mother, 16-year-old Felicity discovers she is an Arthurian "grail keeper" with magical powers. (Rev: BCCB 2/02; BL 11/15/01; HBG 3/02; SLJ 12/01; VOYA 6/02)

2105 Hite, Sid. *Answer My Prayer* (7–10). 1995, Holt $15.95 (0-8050-3406-4). A girl meets a fortune-teller who forecasts a strange future that includes a sleeping stranger. (Rev: BL 5/1/95*)

2106 Hite, Sid. *The Distance of Hope* (6–8). 1998, Holt $16.95 (0-8050-5054-X). Young prince Yeshe embarks on a perilous journey to find the White Bean Lama who will help him save his diminishing eyesight. (Rev: BL 3/15/98; HBG 9/98; SLJ 5/98; VOYA 6/98)

2107 Hite, Sid. *Dither Farm* (6–10). 1992, Holt $15.95 (0-8050-1871-9). An 11-year-old orphan is taken in by a farm family and discovers joys and miracles. (Rev: BL 5/15/92*; SLJ 5/92)

2108 Hoban, Russell. *The Mouse and His Child* (4–8). 2001, Scholastic paper $16.95 (0-439-09820-2). A toy mouse and his child embark on a quest to become "self-winding" and have sometimes scary, sometimes humorous adventures in this enchanting fantasy first published in 1967 and now updated with new illustrations. (Rev: BL 12/1/01; HBG 3/02)

2109 Hoban, Russell. *The Trokeville Way* (5–8). 1996, Knopf $1.99 (0-679-88148-4). A magical jigsaw puzzle leads Nick into a strange new universe. (Rev: BL 11/15/96; SLJ 12/96)

2110 Hobbs, Will. *Kokopelli's Flute* (6–9). 1995, Atheneum $16.00 (0-689-31974-6). A teen finds a bone flute at an ancient Anasazi cliff dwelling that grave robbers have plundered. Strange events occur each night when the boy plays this ancient flute. (Rev: BL 10/1/95; SLJ 10/95; VOYA 2/96)

2111 Hodges, Margaret. *Gulliver in Lilliput: From Gulliver's Travels by Jonathan Swift* (4–7). 1995, Holiday $16.95 (0-8234-1147-8). The story of Gulliver in the land of the little people is retold with bright, detailed illustrations. (Rev: BCCB 6/95; BL 4/15/95; HB 7–8/95; SLJ 6/95*)

2112 Hoeye, Michael. *The Sands of Time* (5–8). Series: A Hermux Tantamoq Adventure. 2002, Putnam $14.99 (0-399-23879-4). In this sequel to *Time Stops for No Mouse* (2002), the mouse watchmaker and a chipmunk friend believe that mice were once the slaves of cats. (Rev: HBG 3/03; SLJ 10/02; VOYA 12/02)

2113 Hoeye, Michael. *Time Stops for No Mouse* (5–9). Series: A Hermux Tantamoq Adventure. 2002, Putnam $14.99 (0-399-23878-6). Hermux Tantamoq, a mouse, leads a quiet life as a watchmaker until Linka Perflinger turns up and Hermux becomes entangled in mystery and suspense. (Rev: BL 3/15/02*; HB 7–8/02; HBG 10/02; SLJ 5/02; VOYA 6/02)

2114 Hoffman, Alice. *Aquamarine* (4–7). 2001, Scholastic paper $16.95 (0-439-09863-7). Twelve-year-old friends Hailey and Claire find a lonely mermaid named Aquamarine, and they try to give her love and adventure. (Rev: BCCB 2/01; BL 3/1/01; HBG 10/01; SLJ 3/01; VOYA 4/01)

2115 Hoffman, Alice. *Indigo* (4–7). Illus. 2002, Scholastic paper $16.95 (0-439-25635-6). Three outcasts save their town from a terrible flood in this aquatic fantasy. (Rev: BCCB 6/02; BL 8/02; HBG 10/02; SLJ 8/02; VOYA 8/02)

2116 Hoffman, Mary. *Stravaganza: City of Masks* (7–12). Series: Stravaganza. 2002, Bloomsbury $16.95 (1-58234-791-3). Cancer-stricken Lucien time-travels from the 21st century to a 16th-century city much like Venice, where he meets the lovely Arianna and has many adventures. (Rev: BL 10/15/02; SLJ 11/02; VOYA 12/02)

2117 Hoffman, Mary. *Stravaganza: City of Stars* (6–10). Series: Stravaganza. 2003, Bloomsbury $17.95 (1-58234-839-1). In this sequel to *Stravaganza: City of Masks* (2002), horse-loving Georgia

is transported to 16th-century Remora (Sienna), where she finds romance and intrigue. (Rev: BL 9/15/03*)

2118 Holch, Gregory. *The Things with Wings* (5–8). 1998, Scholastic paper $15.95 (0-590-93501-1). In this mystery fantasy, Newton and his classmate Vanessa learn about the Emerald Rainbow butterflies, become involved in the disappearance of a friend, and discover the magic of flying. (Rev: BL 8/98; HB 7–8/98; HBG 9/98; SLJ 5/98; VOYA 6/98)

2119 Holman, Felice. *Real* (8–12). 1997, Simon & Schuster $16.00 (0-689-80772-4). While still trying to accept the death of his mother, young Colly, who is spending time in the desert with his father, is befriended by some Native Americans and meets Sparrow, a Cahuilla Indian who, with his grandmother, is trapped in time. (Rev: BL 10/1/97; HBG 3/98; SLJ 11/97; VOYA 2/98)

2120 Hoobler, Dorothy, and Thomas Hoobler. *The Ghost in the Tokaido Inn* (6–12). 1999, Putnam $17.99 (0-399-23330-X). Set in 18th-century Japan, this is the story of 14-year-old Seikei, his dreams of becoming a samurai, and what happened after he saw a legendary ghost stealing a valuable jewel. (Rev: BL 6/1–15/99; HBG 4/00; SLJ 6/99; VOYA 10/99)

2121 Hood, David. *Wizard's Heir* (8–12). 1995, Ace paper $4.99 (0-441-00231-5). In this humorous fantasy, Liam insists he is not a wizard, but things keep happening that convince his neighbors otherwise. (Rev: VOYA 2/96)

2122 Hughes, Monica, sel. *What If? Amazing Stories* (5–10). 1998, Tundra paper $6.95 (0-88776-458-4). Fourteen fantasy and science fiction short stories by noted Canadian writers are included in this anthology, plus a few related poems. (Rev: BL 2/15/99; SLJ 6/99; VOYA 6/99)

2123 Hunter, Erin. *Fire and Ice* (6–9). Series: Warriors. 2003, HarperCollins $15.99 (0-06-000003-1). Ex-kittypet Firepaw (now known as Fireheart) is eager to prove himself on his first mission — to bring WindClan back to their territory — but faces many obstacles. (Rev: BL 9/1/03; HBG 10/03; SLJ 9/03)

2124 Hunter, Erin. *Forest of Secrets* (6–9). Series: Warriors. 2003, HarperCollins $15.99 (0-06-000004-X). Firepaw suspects Tigerclaw of treachery and works to expose him in this exciting installment featuring a flood, a tragic death, and clan rivalries. (Rev: BL 9/15/03; SLJ 10/03)

2125 Hunter, Erin. *Into the Wild* (6–9). Series: Warriors. 2003, HarperCollins $15.99 (0-06-000002-3). A young cat named Firepaw, formerly a pet, becomes an apprentice in the ThunderClan of wild warrior cats, which is in the midst of a struggle to retain its territory. (Rev: BL 2/15/03; HBG 10/03; SLJ 5/03)

2126 Hunter, Mollie. *The Mermaid Summer* (5–8). 1988, HarperCollins $15.89 (0-06-022628-5); paper $5.99 (0-06-440344-0). Eric Anderson refuses to recognize the power of the mermaid and leaves his Scottish fishing village after his boat is dashed to pieces on the rocks. (Rev: BCCB 5/88; BL 6/1/88; BR 1–2/89; SLJ 6–7/88)

2127 Hunter, Mollie. *A Stranger Came Ashore* (7–9). 1977, HarperCollins paper $5.99 (0-06-440082-4). In this fantasy set in the Shetland Islands, a bull seal takes human form and comes ashore.

2128 Hurmence, Belinda. *A Girl Called Boy* (5–8). 1982, Houghton paper $5.95 (0-395-55698-8). A contemporary African American girl travels back to the time of slavery.

2129 Ibbotson, Eva. *Island of the Aunts* (5–8). 2000, Dutton $15.99 (0-525-46484-0). Three elderly sisters kidnap three children to help them take care of their collection of exotic creatures, including mermaids. (Rev: BCCB 2/01; BL 12/1/00; HBG 3/01; SLJ 11/00)

2130 Ibbotson, Eva. *The Secret of Platform 13* (4–7). Illus. 1998, Dutton $15.99 (0-525-45929-4). In this fantasy, three unusual creatures — a wizard, an ogre, and a hag — set out to rescue from their enchanted kingdom a prince who has been kidnapped. (Rev: BL 2/15/98; HBG 10/98; SLJ 3/98*)

2131 Ibbotson, Eva. *Which Witch?* (5–8). 1999, Dutton $15.99 (0-525-46164-7). This British fantasy involves a wizard who holds a competition to find a wife, a sweet witch who wants to win the wizard's heart. (Rev: BCCB 9/99; BL 8/99; HBG 3/00; SLJ 8/99)

2132 Ingold, Jeanette. *The Window* (7–10). 1996, Harcourt $13.00 (0-15-201265-6); paper $6.00 (0-15-201264-8). While staying with relatives in Texas, a newly blinded girl time-travels to discover secrets about her family. (Rev: BL 11/1/96; BR 3–4/97; SLJ 12/96; VOYA 12/96)

2133 Irving, Washington. *Rip Van Winkle* (5–7). 1987, Morrow $22.95 (0-688-07459-6). Distinguished illustrations highlight this 1921 edition. (Rev: BL 9/1/87)

2134 Irving, Washington. *Rip Van Winkle and the Legend of Sleepy Hollow* (5–7). 1980, Sleepy Hollow $19.95 (0-912882-42-5). A handsome edition of these two classics.

2135 Jacques, Brian. *The Angel's Command: A Tale from the Castaways of the Flying Dutchman* (5–9). 2003, Putnam $23.99 (0-399-23999-5). This action-packed fantasy, set in the 17th century, is the sequel to *Castaways of the Flying Dutchman*. (Rev: BL

2/1/03; HB 3–4/03; HBG 10/03; SLJ 3/03; VOYA 4/03)

2136 Jacques, Brian. *The Bellmaker* (5–7). Illus. 1995, Putnam $23.99 (0-399-22805-5). This seventh tale in the Redwall series of animal fantasies features Mariel, a courageous, outspoken mouse. (Rev: BCCB 4/95; BL 4/1/95; HB 5–6/95; SLJ 8/95)

2137 Jacques, Brian. *Castaways of the Flying Dutchman* (5–9). 2001, Putnam $22.95 (0-399-23601-5). A mute boy stows away on the *Flying Dutchman*, a ship that is condemned to sail the seas forever, and there he meets the ghostly crew and the crazed captain in this story in which the boy has many adventures and eventually gains the power of speech and the gift of staying young forever. (Rev: BCCB 3/01; BL 3/1/01; HB 3–4/01; HBG 10/01; SLJ 3/01; VOYA 4/01)

2138 Jacques, Brian. *The Legend of Luke: A Tale from Redwall* (5–8). Illus. 2000, Putnam $22.95 (0-399-23490-X). This Redwall book focuses on the building of the abbey, Martin's search for his father Luke, and Luke's heroic career. (Rev: BL 12/15/99; HBG 10/00; SLJ 2/00; VOYA 4/00)

2139 Jacques, Brian. *Loamhedge* (5–8). Series: Redwall. 2003, Putnam $23.99 (0-399-23724-0). As Redwall stalwarts including Bragoon and Sarobando seek a cure for a haremaid's ills at Loamhedge Abbey, Redwall itself comes under attack. (Rev: BL 9/15/03; HB 11–12/03; SLJ 10/03)

2140 Jacques, Brian. *The Long Patrol* (5–8). Illus. 1998, Putnam $22.99 (0-399-23165-X). In this tenth Redwall adventure, the villainous Rapscallions decide to attack the peaceful Abbey of Redwall. (Rev: BCCB 4/98; BL 12/15/97; BR 3–4/98; HB 3–4/98; HBG 10/98; SLJ 1/98)

2141 Jacques, Brian. *Lord Brocktree* (5–8). 2000, Putnam $22.95 (0-399-23590-6). In this installment of the Redwall saga, the villainous Ungatt Trunn and his Blue Hordes invade and capture the mountain fortress Salamandastron. (Rev: BCCB 9/00; BL 9/1/00; HB 9–10/00; HBG 3/01; SLJ 9/00)

2142 Jacques, Brian. *Mariel of Redwall* (5–7). 1992, Putnam $23.99 (0-399-22144-1). Fourth in the saga of the animals of Redwall Abbey, this story tells how the great Joseph Bell is brought to the abbey. (Rev: BCCB 3/92; BL 1/15/92*; HB 9–10/92; SLJ 3/92)

2143 Jacques, Brian. *Marlfox* (5–8). Illus. 1999, Putnam $22.99 (0-399-23307-5). The famous tapestry depicting Martin and Warrior has been stolen from Redwall Abbey, and four young would-be heroes set out to recover it. (Rev: BL 12/15/98; BR 9–10/99; HB 1–2/99; HBG 10/99; SLJ 4/99; VOYA 2/99)

2144 Jacques, Brian. *Martin the Warrior* (5–7). 1994, Putnam $23.99 (0-399-22670-2). This Redwall book tells how the mouse Martin the Warrior became the bold, courageous fighter that he is. (Rev: BCCB 1/94; BL 3/1/94; HB 9–10/94; SLJ 1/94)

2145 Jacques, Brian. *Mattimeo* (5–8). 1990, Putnam $23.99 (0-399-21741-X). The evil fox kidnaps the animal children of Redwall Abbey in this continuation of *Mossflower* (1988) and *Redwall* (1987). (Rev: BL 4/15/90; SLJ 9/90; VOYA 8/90)

2146 Jacques, Brian. *Mossflower* (5–7). 1988, Putnam $23.99 (0-399-21549-2); Avon paper $5.99 (0-380-70828-0). How a brave and resourceful mouse took power from the evil wildcat. (Rev: BCCB 12/88; BL 11/1/88; SLJ 11/88)

2147 Jacques, Brian. *Outcast of Redwall* (5–8). Illus. Series: Redwall. 1996, Philomel $23.99 (0-399-22914-0). This episode in the Redwall saga involves the badger Sunflash, his buddy Skarlath the kestrel, and their enemy the ferret Swartt Sixclaw. (Rev: BCCB 3/96; BL 3/1/96; BR 3–4/96; SLJ 5/96; VOYA 10/96)

2148 Jacques, Brian. *The Pearls of Lutra* (5–8). 1997, Putnam $23.99 (0-399-22946-9). The evil marten Mad Eyes threatens the peaceful Redwall Abbey in this ninth book in the series. (Rev: BCCB 4/97; BL 2/15/97; SLJ 3/97*; VOYA 6/97)

2149 Jacques, Brian. *Salamandastron* (5–7). 1993, Putnam $23.99 (0-399-21992-7). These tales are centered on the badgers and hares of the castle of Salamandastron near the sea. (Rev: BCCB 7–8/93; BL 3/15/93; HB 5–6/93; SLJ 3/93)

2150 Jacques, Brian. *Taggerung* (5–8). Illus. 2001, Putnam $23.99 (0-399-23720-8). The 14th book in the Redwall series features an otter named Taggerung who was kidnapped from the abbey as a baby and raised by an outlaw ferret. (Rev: BL 8/01; HB 11–12/01; HBG 3/02; SLJ 10/01; VOYA 10/01)

2151 Jacques, Brian. *Triss* (5–8). 2002, Putnam $23.99 (0-399-23723-2). An action-packed installment in the Redwall series in which squirrel Triss, an escaped slave, meets up with the badger Sagax and his friend Scarum. (Rev: BL 9/1/02; HB 1–2/03; HBG 3/03; SLJ 10/02; VOYA 12/02)

2152 James, Mary. *Frankenlouse* (5–8). 1994, Scholastic paper $13.95 (0-590-46528-7). Nick, 14, is enrolled at Blister Military Academy, which is run by his father. He escapes into his own comic book creations featuring an insect named Frankenlouse. (Rev: BCCB 11/94; BL 10/15/94; SLJ 11/94; VOYA 12/94)

2153 James, Mary. *The Shuteyes* (4–7). 1994, Scholastic paper $3.25 (0-590-45070-0). Chester has some unusual experiences when he journeys to Alert, a land where no one sleeps. (Rev: SLJ 4/93)

2154 Jarvis, Robin. *The Crystal Prison: Book Two of the Deptford Mice Trilogy* (5–8). 2001, North-South $17.95 (1-58717-107-4). In this sequel to *The Dark Portal*, city mouse Audrey is adapting to country life when she is accused of committing murder. (Rev: BL 8/01; HBG 3/02; SLJ 11/01; VOYA 12/01)

2155 Jarvis, Robin. *The Dark Portal: Book One of The Deptford Mice* (5–8). 2000, North-South $17.95 (1-58717-021-3). In this tale of horror, valor, and adventure, Albert, one of the mice living in an old, empty house in Deptford, London, must leave his household and enter the slimy sewers inhabited by deadly rats. (Rev: BL 10/15/00; HBG 3/01; SLJ 12/00; VOYA 12/00)

2156 Jarvis, Robin. *The Final Reckoning: Book Three of the Deptford Mice Trilogy* (5–8). 2002, North-South $17.95 (1-58717-192-9). Jupiter returns to wreak havoc on the Deptford mice in this thrilling conclusion to the trilogy. (Rev: BL 8/02; HBG 3/03; SLJ 9/02)

2157 Jarvis, Robin. *Thorn Ogres of Hagwood* (5–8). 2002, Harcourt $16.00 (0-15-216752-8). Trouble is spreading through Hagwood, and a young, not-too-confident shape-shifting werling will play a role in a gripping battle between good and evil. (Rev: BCCB 12/02; BL 11/1/02; HBG 3/03; SLJ 11/02)

2158 Jennings, Richard W. *Orwell's Luck* (4–7). 2000, Houghton $15.00 (0-618-03628-8). After a 12-year-old girl saves a rabbit's life, she begins receiving coded messages from him that change her life. (Rev: BCCB 11/00; BL 10/15/00*; HB 9–10/00; HBG 3/01; SLJ 10/00)

2159 Jones, Diana Wynne. *The Crown of Dalemark* (6–9). Series: Dalemark Quartet. 1995, Greenwillow $17.00 (0-688-13363-0). Readers familiar with the first three books in this quartet will enjoy its conclusion about Noreth, a teen who believes she is destined to become queen, and Maewen, who is sent to impersonate her. New readers should start with book one. (Rev: BL 12/15/95; SLJ 8/96)

2160 Jones, Diana Wynne. *Dark Lord of Derkholm* (7–10). 1998, Greenwillow $16.95 (0-688-16004-2). A humorous, scary fantasy about the efforts of a band of inhabitants to stop the incursions of Mr. Chesney's Pilgrim Parties, who have been wreaking havoc on their lands for 40 years. (Rev: BL 9/1/98; BR 5–6/99; HB 11–12/98; HBG 3/99; SLJ 10/98; VOYA 2/99)

2161 Jones, Diana Wynne. *Dogsbody* (7–10). 1990, Random $3.50 (0-394-82031-2). The Dogstar, Sirius, is sent to Earth in the form of a dog to fulfill a dangerous mission. (Rev: BR 11–12/88; VOYA 2/89)

2162 Jones, Diana Wynne. *Fantasy Stories* (4–8). Illus. 1994, Kingfisher paper $7.95 (1-85697-982-2). A selection of fantasies from such authors as Kipling, C. S. Lewis, and Jane Yolen. (Rev: BL 3/1/95; SLJ 11/94)

2163 Jones, Diana Wynne. *Howl's Moving Castle* (7–12). 1986, Greenwillow $16.95 (0-688-06233-4). A fearful young girl is changed into an old woman and in that disguise moves into the castle of Wizard Howl. (Rev: BL 6/1/86; SLJ 8/86; VOYA 8/86)

2164 Jones, Diana Wynne. *The Lives of Christopher Chant* (5–9). 1998, Morrow paper $5.99 (0-688-16365-3). At night Christopher can leave his body and travel from London to other worlds. (Rev: BR 5–6/88; SLJ 5/88; VOYA 6/88)

2165 Jones, Diana Wynne. *The Merlin Conspiracy* (6–10). 2003, HarperCollins $16.99 (0-06-052318-2). Three teenagers blessed with magical powers collaborate to save the islands of Blest, an alternate England, from attack by wizards in this complex novel full of humor. (Rev: BL 4/15/03; HB 5–6/03; HBG 10/03; SLJ 5/03; VOYA 8/03)

2166 Jones, Diana Wynne. *Mixed Magics* (5–8). 2001, Greenwillow $15.89 (0-06-029706-9). This fantasy contains four short stories each involving an enchanter named Chrestomanci, who has nine lives and oversees the use of magic in his world. (Rev: BL 4/15/01; HB 5–6/01; HBG 10/01; SLJ 7/01)

2167 Jones, Diana Wynne. *The Time of the Ghost* (6–9). 1996, Greenwillow $15.00 (0-668-14598-1). Sally, the ghost of one of four sisters whose parents run a school for boys, tries to undo a bargain she made with an evil goddess when she was young. (Rev: BL 8/96; SLJ 11/96; VOYA 4/97)

2168 Jones, Diana Wynne. *Year of the Griffin* (7–10). 2000, Greenwillow $15.95 (0-688-17898-7). Pirates, assassins, and plain old magic are among the challenges faced by students at Wizard's University — including Elda, griffin daughter of the wizard Derk — in this sequel to the humorous *Dark Lord of Derkholm* (1998). (Rev: BL 11/1/00; HB 11–12/00; HBG 3/01; SLJ 10/00; VOYA 12/00)

2169 Jordan, Robert. *A Crown of Swords* (8–12). Series: Wheel of Time. 1996, Tor $29.95 (0-312-85767-5). In this seventh book of this series, Rand and his army of Aiel warriors prepare to do battle with the Dark One. (Rev: VOYA 2/97)

2170 Jordan, Sherryl. *The Hunting of the Last Dragon* (6–10). 2002, HarperCollins LB $15.89 (0-06-028903-1). In 14th-century England a monk records young peasant Jude's story of his quest, accompanied by a young Chinese woman, to kill a dragon. (Rev: BCCB 9/02; BL 4/15/02; HBG 10/02; SLJ 7/02)

2171 Jordan, Sherryl. *Secret Sacrament* (8–12). 2001, HarperCollins $15.95 (0-06-028904-X). In an ancient time, Gabriel trains at the Citadel to become a healer, hoping to intervene in the violence that surrounds him. (Rev: BCCB 3/01; BL 2/15/01; HBG 10/01; SLJ 2/01; VOYA 6/01)

2172 Kalman, Maira. *Swami on Rye: Max in India* (4–8). Illus. 1995, Viking $14.99 (0-670-84646-0).

A sophisticated comic novel about a dog who goes to India to find the meaning of life. (Rev: BL 10/15/95; SLJ 11/95)

2173 Kassem, Lou. *A Summer for Secrets* (5–7). 1989, Avon paper $2.95 (0-380-75759-1). Laura's ability to communicate with animals causes complications. (Rev: BL 10/1/89)

2174 Kay, Elizabeth. *The Divide* (5–9). 2003, Scholastic $15.95 (0-439-45696-7). Felix, a 13-year-old with a heart problem, passes out while on a trip to Costa Rica and wakes up in a world full of mythical creatures. (Rev: BL 6/1–15/03; SLJ 9/03; VOYA 8/03)

2175 Kelleher, Victor. *Brother Night* (7–9). 1991, Walker $16.95 (0-8027-8100-4). Rabon, 15, was raised by a foster father in a small town and ends up on a quest to the city with his dark, ugly twin, both learning about their heritage along the way. (Rev: BL 6/15/91; SLJ 5/91)

2176 Kempton, Kate. *The World Beyond the Waves: An Environmental Adventure* (5–7). Illus. 1995, Portunus $14.95 (0-9641330-6-7); paper $8.95 (0-9641330-1-6). After being washed overboard during a violent storm, Sam visits a land where she meets ocean animals that have been misused by humans. (Rev: BL 4/15/95; SLJ 3/95)

2177 Kendall, Carol. *The Gammage Cup* (4–7). 1990, Harcourt paper $6.00 (0-15-230575-0). A fantasy of the Minnipins, a small people of the "land between the mountains."

2178 Kennedy, Richard. *Amy's Eyes* (5–6). 1985, HarperCollins $15.00 (0-06-023219-6). Amy's doll, Captain, comes alive and runs away to sea. Before he returns, Amy herself changes into a doll, and Captain takes her with him for a journey of high adventure. (Rev: BCCB 4/85; BL 5/1/85; SLJ 5/85)

2179 Kimmel, Elizabeth C. *The Ghost of the Stone Circle* (5–8). 1998, Scholastic paper $15.95 (0-590-21308-3). Fourteen-year-old Cristyn, who is spending the summer in Wales with her historian father, discovers a ghost in the house her father has rented. (Rev: BCCB 3/98; BL 4/15/98; HBG 10/98; SLJ 4/98; VOYA 8/98)

2180 Kimmel, Eric A. *Website of the Cracked Cookies* (4–8). 2001, Dutton $15.99 (0-525-46799-8). A whirlwind, comic cyber-adventure that starts with a click on a Web site that houses an evil grandmother and a cast of familiar characters. (Rev: HBG 3/02; SLJ 9/01)

2181 Kindl, Patrice. *Goose Chase* (6–9). 2001, Houghton $15.00 (0-618-03377-7). A lively romp in true fairy-tale style that involves an enchanted Goose Girl who must escape a difficult choice between two unappealing suitors. (Rev: BCCB 4/01; BL 4/15/01; HB 7–8/01; HBG 10/01; SLJ 4/01; VOYA 6/01)

2182 Kindl, Patrice. *Owl in Love* (5–9). 1993, Houghton $16.00 (0-395-66162-5). Owl, a shapeshifter, is an ordinary high school girl by day, and she falls in love with her science teacher. (Rev: BL 9/1/93; VOYA 12/93)

2183 King-Smith, Dick. *The Roundhill* (5–7). Illus. 2000, Random paper $4.99 (0-440-41844-5). In the English countryside in 1936, 14-year-old Evan meets a mysterious girl who seems to be the Alice of *Alice in Wonderland*. (Rev: BL 1/1–15/01; HBG 3/01; SLJ 12/00)

2184 King-Smith, Richard. *Godhanger* (7–10). 1999, Crown $18.99 (0-517-80036-5). Skymaster, a Christlike bird, comes to Godhanger Wood to help save the animals from a merciless gamekeeper. (Rev: BL 3/1/99; HB 7–8/99; HBG 9/99; SLJ 2/99)

2185 Kirwan-Vogel, Anna. *The Jewel of Life* (6–8). Illus. 1991, Harcourt $15.95 (0-15-200750-4). Young orphan Duffy travels to other worlds, brings back a precious cockatrice feather, and creates the Philosopher's Stone. (Rev: BL 6/15/91; SLJ 6/91)

2186 Koller, Jackie F. *If I Had One Wish . . .* (5–8). 1991, Little, Brown $14.95 (0-316-50150-6). When 8th-grader Alec is granted his wish that his little brother had never been born, he learns a lesson about charity, kindness, and old-fashioned family values. (Rev: BCCB 12/91; BL 11/1/91; SLJ 11/91)

2187 Konigsburg, E. L. *Up from Jericho Tel* (6–9). 1986, Macmillan $17.00 (0-689-31194-X). The ghost of a dead actress named Tallulah makes Jeanmarie and friend Malcolm invisible in order to search for a necklace. (Rev: BL 5/1/86; SLJ 5/86; VOYA 12/86)

2188 Konwicki, Tadeusz. *The Anthropos-Specter-Beast* (7–9). Trans. by George and Audrey Korwin-Rodziszewski. 1977, S. G. Phillips $26.95 (0-87599-218-8). Peter is transported to a remote place by the talking dog Sebastian.

2189 Kortum, Jeanie. *Ghost Vision* (5–8). n.d., Scholastic paper $3.50 (0-614-19197-1). A Greenland Inuit realizes that his son has special mystical powers.

2190 La Fevers, R. L. *The Falconmaster* (6–8). 2003, Dutton $16.99 (0-525-46993-1). In medieval England, after rescuing a pair of baby falcons, a disabled boy named Wat meets Griswold, an old man attuned to nature who teaches him new powers. (Rev: BL 11/1/03)

2191 Lally, Soinbhe. *A Hive for the Honeybee* (8–12). Illus. 1999, Scholastic paper $16.95 (0-590-51038-X). An allegory about life and work that takes place in a beehive with such characters as Alfred, the bee poet, and Mo, a radical drone. (Rev: BL 2/1/99; HB 3–4/99; HBG 10/99; SLJ 5/99*; VOYA 4/99)

2192 Langton, Jane. *The Fledgling* (5–7). 1980, HarperCollins LB $16.89 (0-06-023679-5); paper $5.99 (0-06-440121-9). A young girl learns to fly with her Goose Prince. A sequel is *The Fragile Flag* (1984). Also use *The Diamond in the Window* (1962).

2193 Lasky, Kathryn. *The Capture* (5–8). 2003, Scholastic paper $4.99 (0-439-40557-2). Soren, a happy, well-adjusted young barn owl, falls from his nest and is stolen away by a group of owlet thieves bent on reeducation. (Rev: BL 9/15/03; SLJ 10/03)

2194 Lasky, Kathryn. *Double Trouble Squared* (5–7). 1991, Harcourt paper $8.00 (0-15-224127-2). The first in a series concerning the lively Starbuck family, with youngsters who can read one another's minds. (Rev: BCCB 2/92; BL 1/15/92; SLJ 2/92)

2195 Lawrence, Michael. *The Poppykettle Papers* (5–9). 2000, Pavilion $22.95 (1-86205-282-4). Two boys discover an ancient manuscript that tells of an adventure-filled voyage taken by five tiny people in a poppykettle, a vessel used to make tea for the gods. (Rev: SLJ 3/00)

2196 Lawson, Robert. *Rabbit Hill* (4–7). 1944, Puffin paper $5.99 (0-14-031010-X). A warm and humorous story about the small creatures of a Connecticut countryside — each with a distinct personality. Newbery Medal winner, 1945.

2197 Layefsky, Virginia. *Impossible Things* (5–8). 1998, Marshall Cavendish $14.95 (0-7614-5038-6). Twelve-year-old Brady has several personal and family problems to solve along with taking care of the dragonlike creature that he is hiding. (Rev: HBG 3/99; SLJ 11/98)

2198 Lee, Tanith. *Black Unicorn* (7–10). Illus. 1993, Tor paper $3.99 (0-8125-2459-4). The 16-year-old daughter of a sorceress reconstructs a unicorn from a cache of golden bones that impels her to run away from her desert home to a seaside city. (Rev: BL 10/15/91; SLJ 11/91)

2199 Lee, Tanith. *Gold Unicorn* (7–10). 1994, Atheneum $15.95 (0-689-31814-6). This sequel to *Black Unicorn* continues the adventures of Tanaquil, 16, runaway daughter of an odd sorceress, after she is captured by Empress Veriam, who turns out to be her half-sister. (Rev: BL 1/15/95; SLJ 2/95; VOYA 4/95)

2200 Lee, Tanith. *Islands in the Sky* (4–7). Series: Voyage of the Basset. 1999, Random paper $3.99 (0-679-89127-7). In this fantasy a boy and a girl are transported from Victorian England to a land where mythological beasts, gods, and people come to life. (Rev: SLJ 1/00)

2201 Lee, Tanith. *Red Unicorn* (7–10). 1997, St. Martin's paper $5.99 (0-7653-4568-4). This continuation of the fantasies *Black Unicorn* and *Gold Unicorn* tells of Tanaquil's encounters with her double,

Princess Tanakil, who lives in an alternate world. (Rev: BL 6/1–15/97; VOYA 12/97)

2202 Lee, Tanith. *Wolf Queen* (5–8). Series: Claidi Journals. 2002, Dutton $16.99 (0-525-46895-1). After *Wolf Tower* and *Wolf Star*, this concluding volume of the Claidi Journals trilogy tells how the fearless Claidi faces the power of the Raven Tower. (Rev: BCCB 6/02; BL 4/15/02; HBG 10/02; SLJ 6/02; VOYA 8/02)

2203 Lee, Tanith. *Wolf Star* (5–8). Series: Claidi Journals. 2001, Dutton $16.99 (0-525-46673-8). This sequel to *Wolf Tower* finds Claidi trapped in a castle with a strange prince who, in time, helps her find a way home. (Rev: BCCB 10/01; BL 4/15/01; HBG 10/01; SLJ 7/01; VOYA 10/01)

2204 Lee, Tanith. *Wolf Tower* (5–8). Series: Claidi Journals. 2000, Dutton $15.99 (0-525-46394-1). In this adventure-filled fantasy, a 16-year-old slave girl is chosen to rescue a young man captured when his hot-air balloon is shot down. (Rev: BL 4/15/00; HBG 10/00; SLJ 6/00)

2205 Lee, Tanith. *Wolf Wing* (5–8). Series: Claidi Journals. 2003, Dutton $16.99 (0-525-47162-6). Claidi and Argul, now married, set off on an exciting voyage to his mother's magical land in this novel that revisits many sites from previous volumes in the series. (Rev: BL 9/1/03; SLJ 10/03)

2206 Le Guin, Ursula K. *Tehanu: The Last Book of Earthsea* (7–10). Series: Earthsea. 1990, Macmillan $21.00 (0-689-31595-3). In the fourth and last of the Earthsea books, Tenar is summoned by a dying mage, or wise one, to teach a child the spells and magic that give the power to lead. (Rev: BL 3/1/90; SLJ 4/90; VOYA 6/90)

2207 Le Guin, Ursula K. *A Wizard of Earthsea* (8–12). Illus. Series: Earthsea. 1968, Bantam paper $7.50 (0-553-26250-5). An apprentice wizard accidentally unleashes an evil power onto the land of Earthsea. Followed by *The Tombs of Atuan* and *The Farthest Shore*.

2208 L'Engle, Madeleine. *An Acceptable Time* (8–12). 1989, Farrar $18.00 (0-374-30027-5). Polly O'Keefe time-travels (as her parents did years before in the Time trilogy) but this time to visit a civilization of Druids that lived 3,000 years ago. (Rev: BL 1/1/90; BR 5–6/90; SLJ 1/90; VOYA 4/90)

2209 Leroe, Ellen. *H.O.W.L. High* (4–7). 1991, Pocket paper $2.95 (0-671-68568-6). His classmates at H.O.W.L. Junior High do not realize that Drac is really a warlock. (Rev: SLJ 1/92)

2210 Levin, Betty. *The Banished* (5–8). 1999, Greenwillow $16.00 (0-688-16602-4). An engaging prequel to *The Ice Bear* in which Siri must make a dangerous sea journey to deliver an ice bear to her people's king. (Rev: BL 8/99; HB 11–12/99; HBG 3/00; SLJ 10/99)

2211 Levine, Gail C. *The Wish* (4–7). 2000, HarperCollins LB $15.89 (0-06-027901-X). When a kindly old lady grants Wilma's wish to become popular at school, the girl forgets that she is graduating in only three weeks. (Rev: BCCB 5/00; BL 4/1/00; HBG 10/00; SLJ 5/00)

2212 Levine, Gail Carson. *The Two Princesses of Bamarre* (4–7). 2001, HarperCollins LB $16.89 (0-06-029316-0). Princess Addie sets out on a quest to find a cure for the Grey Death, a sickness that is destroying her older sister. (Rev: BCCB 10/01; BL 4/15/01; HB 5–6/01; HBG 10/01; SLJ 5/01)

2213 Levitin, Sonia. *The Cure* (6–9). 1999, Harcourt $16.00 (0-15-201827-1). In the 25th century, Gemm, because he is unconventional, is sent to 14th-century Strasbourg, where, as a Jew, he experiences terrible anti-Semitism as part of his cure. (Rev: BL 6/1–15/99; BR 9–10/99; HB 5–6/99; HBG 9/99; SLJ 5/99; VOYA 6/99)

2214 Levy, Robert. *Escape from Exile* (4–8). 1993, Houghton $16.00 (0-395-64379-1). Daniel, 13, is struck by lightning and transported to Lithia, where his new telepathic powers help him cope with a bitter civil war. (Rev: BL 3/15/93; SLJ 5/93; VOYA 8/93)

2215 Lewis, C. S. *The Lion, the Witch and the Wardrobe* (5–8). Illus. Series: Narnia. 1988, Macmillan LB $22.95 (0-02-758200-0). Four children enter the kingdom of Narnia through the back of an old wardrobe. A special edition illustrated by Michael Hague. The other six volumes in this series are *Prince Caspian, The Voyage of the Dawn Treader, The Silver Chair, The Horse and His Boy, The Magician's Nephew*, and *The Last Battle*.

2216 Lewis, C. S. *The Lion, the Witch and the Wardrobe: A Story for Children* (4–7). 1988, Macmillan paper $7.95 (0-02-044490-7). A beautifully written adventure featuring four children who go into the magical land of Narnia.

2217 Lindbergh, Anne. *The Hunky-Dory Dairy* (5–7). 1986, Harcourt $14.95 (0-15-237449-3); Dell paper $2.75 (0-380-70320-3). Zannah visits a community magically removed from the 20th century and enjoys introducing the people to bubble gum, tacos, and other "modern" things. (Rev: BCCB 9/86; BL 4/1/86; SLJ 8/86)

2218 Lindbergh, Anne. *The Prisoner of Pineapple Place* (5–7). 1988, Harcourt $13.95 (0-15-263559-9); Avon paper $2.95 (0-380-70765-9). Pineapple Place is invisible to everyone except the inhabitants, and somehow finds itself landing in Connecticut. (Rev: BL 7/88; SLJ 8/88)

2219 Lindbergh, Anne. *Three Lives to Live* (5–8). 1995, Pocket paper $3.50 (0-671-86732-6). A teenager discovers that her laundry chute is a conduit through time and that she, her grandmother, and her little sister are all the same person. (Rev: SLJ 6/92)

2220 Lindgren, Astrid. *Ronia, the Robber's Daughter* (4–7). 1985, Puffin paper $5.99 (0-14-031720-1). Ronia becomes friendly with the son of her father's rival in this fantasy.

2221 Lisle, Janet T. *The Lampfish of Twill* (4–8). 1991, Orchard paper $16.95 (0-531-05963-4). Orphaned Eric faces forces of danger as he lives in the mysterious country of Twill. (Rev: BCCB 10/91; HB 1–2/92; SLJ 9/91*)

2222 Little, Kimberley Griffiths. *The Last Snake Runner* (6–9). 2002, Knopf $15.95 (0-375-81539-2). Kendall Drennan, introduced in *Enchanted Runner* (1999), travels back in time to 1598 New Mexico and witnesses bloody attacks on his ancestors by the Spanish. (Rev: BL 5/15/02; HBG 3/03; SLJ 8/02; VOYA 8/02)

2223 Littlefield, Bill. *The Circus in the Woods* (6–10). 2001, Houghton $15.00 (0-618-06642-X). Mystery and fantasy are combined in this quiet, reflective story about a 13-year-old girl who finds a strange circus in the Vermont woods where she spends her summers. (Rev: BCCB 12/01; HBG 10/02; SLJ 11/01; VOYA 12/01)

2224 Logue, Mary. *Dancing with an Alien* (8–10). 2000, HarperCollins $14.95 (0-06-028318-1). Tonia faces a tough decision when she falls in love with a boy from another planet who was sent to Earth to find a mate. (Rev: HBG 9/00; SLJ 7/00)

2225 Lowry, Lois. *Gathering Blue* (5–9). 2000, Houghton $16.00 (0-618-05581-9). In an inhospitable future world, young Kira must use her courage and her artistic talents. (Rev: BL 6/1–15/00*; HB 9–10/00; HBG 3/01; SLJ 8/00*)

2226 Lowry, Lois. *The Giver* (6–9). 1993, Houghton $16.00 (0-395-64566-2); Dell paper $6.50 (0-440-21907-8). A dystopian fantasy in which Jonas receives his life assignment as Receiver of Memory and learns that a land with no war, poverty, fear, or hardship is also one where "misfits" are killed. (Rev: BL 4/15/93*; SLJ 5/93*; VOYA 8/93)

2227 Lyon, George E. *Here and Then* (6–8). 1994, Orchard paper $15.95 (0-531-06866-8). Abby, 13, becomes connected across time to Eliza, a nurse she portrays in a Civil War reenactment, and goes back in time to help her. (Rev: BL 10/1/94; SLJ 10/94; VOYA 10/94)

2228 Lyon, George Ella. *Gina.Jamie.Father.Bear* (6–9). 2002, Simon & Schuster $15.95 (0-689-84370-4). A troubled girl enters a fantasy world when she consults a psychic in this beautifully written novel. (Rev: BCCB 12/02; BL 12/15/02; HB 9–10/02; HBG 3/03)

2229 Lyons, Mary. *Knockabeg: A Famine Tale* (4–7). 2001, Houghton $15.00 (0-618-09283-8). In order to protect the people of Knockabeg, faeries battle with the creatures who are causing the blight during the great Irish potato famine. (Rev: BL 11/15/01; HBG 3/02; SLJ 9/01; VOYA 10/01)

2230 Lytle, Robert A. *Three Rivers Crossing* (5–8). 2000, River Road $15.95 (0-938682-55-5). After he suffers an accident while fishing, 7th-grader Walker wakes to find he is in the 1820s village of his ancestors. (Rev: BL 5/15/00; SLJ 6/00)

2231 Macaulay, David. *Baaa* (6–10). Illus. 1985, Houghton LB $13.95 (0-395-38948-8); paper $5.95 (0-395-39588-7). An allegory about the world after humans have left and intelligent sheep take control. (Rev: BL 9/1/85; BR 3–4/86; SLJ 10/85)

2232 McCaffrey, Anne. *If Wishes Were Horses* (7–12). 1998, NAL $14.95 (0-451-45642-4). When Tirza turns 16 and earns her own magic crystal, she wishes for a horse for her twin brother — with unexpected results. (Rev: VOYA 2/99)

2233 McCaffrey, Anne. *No One Noticed the Cat* (5–8). 1996, Roc $13.95 (0-451-45578-9). Niffy, an extraordinary cat, protects her young master, Prince Jamas, when he is threatened by the wicked King Egdril. (Rev: VOYA 4/97)

2234 McCaffrey, Laura Williams. *Alia Waking* (5–7). 2003, Clarion $15.00 (0-618-19461-4). Alia, 12, and her best friend Kay long to be come "keen-ten," or warrior women. (Rev: BL 3/1/03; HBG 10/03; SLJ 6/03; VOYA 10/03)

2235 McCaughrean, Geraldine. *A Pack of Lies* (5–7). 1990, Macmillan $16.95 (0-7451-1154-8). Stories told by mysterious M.C.C. Berkshire, who wanders into an antique store run by adolescent Ailsa and her mother. (Rev: BCCB 5/89)

2236 McCaughrean, Geraldine. *The Stones Are Hatching* (5–8). 2000, HarperCollins LB $15.89 (0-06-028766-7). Eleven-year-old Phelim Green begins a quest with strange friends to kill the Stoor Worm and thus save the world. (Rev: HB 7–8/00; HBG 10/00; SLJ 6/00)

2237 McCusker, Paul. *Arin's Judgment* (5–8). 1999, Tommy Nelson paper $6.99 (1-56179-774-X). In 1945, while awaiting word about his father who is missing in action, Wade is transported to another world where his knowledge of World War II places him at risk. (Rev: SLJ 4/00)

2238 MacDonald, George. *At the Back of the North Wind* (4–7). 1989, Morrow $24.95 (0-688-07808-7). A facsimile edition of the 1919 printing of this classic fantasy.

2239 MacHale, D. J. *The Lost City of Faar* (5–8). Series: Pendragon. 2003, Simon & Schuster paper $5.99 (0-7434-3732-2). After saving Denduron from Saint Dane in *The Merchant of Death* (2002), 14-year-old Bobby must confront the shape-changer again in Cloral, a world covered by water. (Rev: SLJ 5/03)

2240 McKenzie, Ellen Kindt. *The Golden Band of Eddris* (6–9). 1998, Holt $16.95 (0-8050-4389-6). A brother and sister combat the forces of evil that are terrorizing the land of Adnor in this complex fantasy. (Rev: BL 2/15/98; HBG 9/98; SLJ 3/98; VOYA 4/98)

2241 McKillip, Patricia A. *The Changeling Sea* (7–9). 1989, Ballantine paper $4.99 (0-345-36040-0). An unhappy young girl causes a giant monster to rise from the sea. (Rev: BL 9/15/88; BR 1–2/89; SLJ 11/88; VOYA 12/88)

2242 McKinley, Robin. *The Blue Sword* (7–10). 1982, Greenwillow $16.99 (0-688-00938-7). The king of Damar kidnaps a girl to help in his war against the Northerners. A prequel to *The Hero and the Crown*. Newbery Medal 1985. (Rev: BL 12/15/89)

2243 McKinley, Robin. *The Door in the Hedge* (6–9). 2003, Firebird paper $6.99 (0-698-11960-6). Four tales, two of which originated in the folklore of the Grimm Brothers.

2244 McKinley, Robin. *Rose Daughter* (6–12). Illus. 1997, Greenwillow $16.95 (0-688-15439-5). As in her award-winning *Beauty*, (1955) the author returns to the Beauty and the Beast fairy tale in this outstanding reworking of the traditional story. (Rev: BL 8/97; BR 11–12/97; HBG 3/98; SLJ 9/97; VOYA 2/98) [398.2]

2245 McKinley, Robin. *Spindle's End* (7–12). 2000, Putnam $19.99 (0-399-23466-7). An engrossing expansion of the Sleeping Beauty story told with humor, wit, and spellbinding magic. (Rev: BL 4/15/00; HB 5–6/00; HBG 9/00; SLJ 6/00; VOYA 4/00)

2246 McKinley, Robin. *The Stone Fey* (6–10). Illus. 1998, Harcourt $17.00 (0-15-200017-8). A fantasy in which young Maddy temporarily falls in love with a stone fey while her fiance is away earning money for their future together. (Rev: BL 11/1/98; HBG 9/99; SLJ 1/99)

2247 Mahy, Margaret. *Alchemy* (7–10). 2003, Simon & Schuster $16.95 (0-689-85053-0). Sinister twists and horrifying thrills abound in this story of 17-year-old Roland, who has frightening dreams and finds the divide between dream and reality is beginning to blur. (Rev: BL 3/15/03; HB 5–6/03; HBG 10/03; SLJ 5/03; VOYA 6/03)

2248 Mahy, Margaret. *The Changeover: A Supernatural Romance* (8–12). 1984, Macmillan $16.00 (0-689-50303-2). To save her brother from an evil force, Laura must use the powers of witchcraft.

2249 Marsden, John. *Burning for Revenge* (8–12). Series: Tomorrow. 2000, Houghton $16.00 (0-395-96054-1). Ellie and her four Australian friends

attack an airfield held by the enemy in this continuing saga. (Rev: BL 10/1/00; HBG 3/01; SLJ 10/00)

2250 Marsden, John. *The Night Is for Hunting* (8–12). Series: Tomorrow. 2001, Houghton $15.00 (0-618-07026-5). This sixth book in the Tomorrow series continues the action-packed story of a group of teenagers fighting to defend Australia against a band of invaders. (Rev: BCCB 2/02; BL 11/1/01; HBG 10/02; SLJ 10/01; VOYA 12/01)

2251 Martin, Ann M., and Laura Godwin. *The Meanest Doll in the World* (5–8). 2003, Hyperion $15.99 (0-7868-0878-0). Through a series of mishaps, dolls Annabelle Doll and Tiffany Funcraft end up in the home of Mean Mimi, a doll with tyrannical tendencies, in this sequel to *The Doll People* (2000). (Rev: BL 10/15/03; HB 11–12/03; SLJ 10/03*)

2252 Massie, Elizabeth. *Maryland: The Night the Harbor Lights Went Out* (5–8). 1995, Z-Fave paper $3.50 (0-8217-5059-3). In this time travel story, two teenage girls, one an African American slave trying to escape from Baltimore in 1849, and the other a contemporary white 8th grader on a field trip to the Baltimore aquarium, exchange places. (Rev: VOYA 2/96)

2253 Masson, Sophie. *Serafin* (5–8). 2000, Saint Mary's paper $5.50 (0-88489-567-X). After he saves Calou from being lynched as a witch, Frederick is forced to flee his 17th-century French village with Calou and soon afterward realizes that the girl is a matagot, a half-angel half-human creature. (Rev: SLJ 8/00)

2254 Matas, Carol, and Perry Nodelman. *More Minds* (5–8). Series: Minds. 1996, Simon & Schuster paper $16.00 (0-689-80388-5). Rebellious Princess Lenora and her clairvoyant fiance, Coren, set out to find the giant that is terrorizing the land. (Rev: SLJ 10/96; VOYA 6/97)

2255 Matas, Carol, and Perry Nodelman. *Of Two Minds* (5–8). Series: Minds. 1995, Simon & Schuster paper $16.00 (0-689-80138-6). A princess and a shy prince, trapped in a strange land and stripped of their powers, must work together to triumph over evil. (Rev: SLJ 10/95*; VOYA 4/96)

2256 Matas, Carol, and Perry Nodelman. *Out of Their Minds* (5–8). Illus. Series: Minds. 1998, Simon & Schuster $16.00 (0-689-81946-3). In this fantasy (the third in the series), Princess Lenora and Prince Coren journey to Andilla to marry but find that some force is upsetting The Balance. (Rev: HBG 3/99; SLJ 9/98; VOYA 2/99)

2257 Melling, Orla. *The Druid's Tune* (6–10). 1993, O'Brien Pr. paper $9.95 (0-86278-285-6). Peter, a Druid lost in the 20th century, involves two teenagers in a time-travel spell that sends them back to Ireland's Iron Age. (Rev: BL 2/15/93)

2258 Molloy, Michael. *The Time Witches* (5–8). 2002, Scholastic paper $4.99 (0-439-42090-3). The characters from *The Witch Trade* (2002) return in this sequel in which Abby, a Light Witch, and her friends must travel into the past to foil a plot hatched by the nefarious Wolfbane. (Rev: BL 1/1–15/03; SLJ 8/03)

2259 Morpurgo, Michael. *Little Foxes* (6–9). 1987, David & Charles $15.95 (0-7182-3972-5). Two orphans — a boy and a fox — are helped by a swan in this magical story. (Rev: BR 1–2/88; SLJ 9/87)

2260 Morpurgo, Michael. *The War of Jenkins' Ear* (6–9). 1995, Putnam $16.99 (0-399-22735-0). In England at a prep school, Toby meets a boy who is different from the rest, taking the role of peacemaker. Could this unusual boy be Jesus disguised as a British schoolboy? (Rev: BL 9/1/95; SLJ 9/95; VOYA 12/95)

2261 Morris, Gerald. *Parsifal's Page* (5–8). 2001, Houghton $15.00 (0-618-05509-6). Piers becomes a page to Parsifal and accompanies the innocent young man on his quest to become a knight. (Rev: BCCB 4/01; BL 4/15/01; HB 5–6/01; HBG 10/01; SLJ 4/01; VOYA 6/01)

2262 Morris, Gerald. *The Savage Damsel and the Dwarf* (5–8). 2000, Houghton $16.00 (0-395-97126-8). Sixteen-year-old Lady Lynet travels to Camelot, in the company of a dwarf, to ask King Arthur's aid in defeating her sister's suitor. (Rev: BL 3/1/00; HB 5–6/00; HBG 10/00; SLJ 5/00; VOYA 6/00)

2263 Morris, Gilbert. *Journey to Freedom* (4–8). 2000, Crossway $12.99 (1-581-34191-1). Chip, an ordinary white-foot mouse, is chosen to lead his people against the invasions of warlike brown rats. (Rev: BL 12/15/00; HBG 10/01; VOYA 2/01)

2264 Mullin, Caryl Cude. *A Riddle of Roses* (4–7). 2000, Second Story Pr. paper $6.95 (1-896764-28-2). Meryl, who has been expelled from school for a year, goes on a quest to Avalon to find her own wisdom. (Rev: BL 2/15/01; VOYA 4/01)

2265 Murphy, Rita. *Harmony* (6–10). 2002, Delacorte $15.95 (0-385-72938-3). Harmony — who apparently fell from a star to land in a chicken coop in the mountains of Tennessee — has strange telekinetic powers that she tries to keep secret. (Rev: BL 9/15/02; HB 1/03; HBG 3/03; SLJ 10/02; VOYA 12/02)

2266 Murphy, Rita. *Night Flying* (8–12). 2000, Delacorte $14.95 (0-385-32748-X). Everyone in the Hansen family, including 15-year-old Georgia, can fly, and the rules are obeyed by all, but family relationships change when an outspoken aunt arrives from California. (Rev: BL 12/15/00; HB 9–10/00; HBG 3/01; SLJ 11/00)

2267 Myers, Walter Dean. *The Legend of Tarik* (6–9). 1991, Scholastic paper $3.50 (0-590-44426-

3). Tarik, a black teenager in Africa of years ago, acquires a magic sword.

2268 Napoli, Donna Jo. *Beast* (7–10). 2000, Simon & Schuster $17.00 (0-689-83589-2). Beast's life is the focus of this retelling of Beauty and the Beast, in which a Persian prince is turned into a lion and travels to live in a lonely castle in France. (Rev: BL 9/15/00; HB 9–10/00; HBG 3/01; SLJ 10/00)

2269 Napoli, Donna Jo. *Zel* (7–12). 1996, Dutton $15.99 (0-525-45612-0). Set in 15th-century Switzerland, this is a brilliant reworking of the Rapunzel fairy tale told from three different points of view. (Rev: BL 9/1/96; BR 9–10/97; SLJ 9/96; VOYA 4/97)

2270 Napoli, Donna Jo, and Richard Tchen. *Spinners* (8–12). 1999, Dutton $15.99 (0-525-46065-9). Fifteen-year-old Saskia is saved by the mysterious spinner Rumpelstiltskin, whose secret is that he is the girl's father. (Rev: BL 9/1/99; HBG 4/00; SLJ 9/99; VOYA 12/99)

2271 Naylor, Phyllis Reynolds. *The Grand Escape* (5–7). Illus. 1993, Macmillan $16.95 (0-689-31722-0). Two adventurous cats must solve three mysteries before they can join the Cats' Club of Mysteries. (Rev: BL 7/93; SLJ 8/93)

2272 Naylor, Phyllis Reynolds. *Sang Spell* (6–9). 1998, Simon & Schuster $16.00 (0-689-82007-0). Recently orphaned Josh wanders into a magical village inhabited by descendants of colonists who settled in North America before Jamestown. (Rev: BL 9/15/98; HB 11–12/98; HBG 3/99; SLJ 10/98; VOYA 2/99)

2273 Nicholson, William. *Firesong* (7–12). Series: The Wind on Fire. 2002, Hyperion $17.99 (0-7868-0571-4). Twins Bowman and Kestrel have succeeded in their goal of rescuing the Manth people from slavery and travel to what they believe is the promised land. (Rev: HBG 3/03; SLJ 1/03; VOYA 12/02)

2274 Nicholson, William. *Slaves of the Mastery* (7–12). Series: The Wind on Fire. 2001, Hyperion $17.99 (0-7868-0570-6). In this sequel to *The Wind Singer* (2000), 15-year-old twins Bowman and Kestrel must use magic and mettle to combat the Master who has enslaved their people. (Rev: BL 10/15/01; HBG 3/02; SLJ 12/01; VOYA 12/01)

2275 Nicholson, William. *The Wind Singer* (5–7). Illus. 2000, Hyperion $17.99 (0-7868-0569-2). In the structured community of Amaranth, ruled by a caste system, twin brother and sister Kestrel and Bowman rebel and try to get help from the Wind Singer. (Rev: BL 10/15/00; HBG 10/01; SLJ 12/00; VOYA 4/01)

2276 Nimmo, Jenny. *Charlie Bone and the Time Twister* (5–7). 2003, Scholastic $9.95 (0-439-49687-X). In 1916 Henry Yewbeam finds a strange marble and is transported to the present-day Bloor's

Academy, where Charlie Bone tests his magical abilities in an effort to send him home. A sequel to *Midnight for Charlie Bone* (2003). (Rev: BL 9/15/03; SLJ 10/03)

2277 Nimmo, Jenny. *Griffin's Castle* (5–8). 1997, Orchard LB $17.99 (0-531-33006-0). When Dinah and her young mother, Rosalie, move into the run-down mansion owned by Rosalie's boyfriend, Dinah brings to life several carved animals for protection. (Rev: SLJ 6/97; VOYA 8/97)

2278 Nimmo, Jenny. *Orchard of the Crescent Moon* (5–7). 1990, Troll paper $2.95 (0-8167-2265-X). Nia has begun to believe it when her family says "Nia-can't-do-nothing." (Rev: BL 8/89)

2279 Nix, Garth. *Abhorsen* (7–12). 2003, Harper-Collins $17.99 (0-06-027825-0). Two previous books, *Sabriel* (1996) and *Lirael* (2001), set the stage for the confrontation between Lirael and the evil Hedge, who now controls the dead and is seeking to release the Destroyer. (Rev: BCCB 3/03; BL 1/1–15/03; HB 3–4/03; HBG 10/03; SLJ 2/03; VOYA 2/03)

2280 Nix, Garth. *Above the Veil* (5–7). Series: The Seventh Tower. 2001, Scholastic paper $4.99 (0-439-17685-9). In episode four in this series, Tal and Milla continue their otherworldly adventures full of action, secrets, and surprising twists and turns. (Rev: SLJ 9/01)

2281 Nix, Garth. *Lirael: Daughter of the Clayr* (7–12). 2001, HarperCollins $16.95 (0-06-027823-4). In this sequel to *Sabriel* (1996), Lirael and Prince Sameth battle against a new evil that threatens the Old Kingdom. (Rev: BCCB 5/01; BL 4/15/01; HB 7–8/01; HBG 10/01; SLJ 5/01; VOYA 8/01)

2282 Nix, Garth. *Mister Monday* (5–8). Series: The Keys to the Kingdom. 2003, Scholastic paper $5.99 (0-439-55123-4). When 7th-grader Arthur Pen-haglion receives a healing key from a mysterious stranger, the gift turns out to be a mixed blessing that brings illness and strange creatures seeking to reclaim the key. (Rev: BCCB 1/04; SLJ 12/03)

2283 Nodelman, Perry. *A Completely Different Place* (5–8). 1997, Simon & Schuster paper $16.00 (0-689-80836-4). Johnny awakes from a nightmare and finds that he has shrunk in size and is in the land of the green-skinned Strangers. (Rev: BL 7/97; SLJ 6/97; VOYA 8/97)

2284 Nodelman, Perry. *The Same Place But Different* (5–9). 1995, Simon & Schuster paper $15.00 (0-671-89839-6). A teen visits the land of Strangers, evil fairies, to rescue his sister. In this reversal of expectations, good fairies and benevolent creatures become sinister and terrifying. (Rev: BL 10/1/95)

2285 Norton, Andre. *The Monster's Legacy* (1–10). 1996, Simon & Schuster $17.00 (0-689-80731-7). In this novel, part of the *Dragonflight* series, a

young apprentice embroiderer and her two friends flee invaders and escape to a land inhabited by Loden, a monster who preys on humans. (Rev: BL 4/1/96; SLJ 6/96; VOYA 8/96)

2286 O'Brien, Robert C. *Mrs. Frisby and the Rats of NIMH* (5–7). 1971, Macmillan $18.00 (0-689-20651-8); paper $5.50 (0-689-71068-2). Saga of a group of rats made literate and given human intelligence by a series of experiments, who escape from their laboratory to found their own community. Newbery Medal winner, 1972.

2287 Oppel, Kenneth. *Silverwing* (5–9). 1997, Simon & Schuster $17.00 (0-689-81529-8). The existence of the bat colony is threatened when a newborn Silverwing bat challenges a stronger bat to commit a forbidden act: looking at the sun. (Rev: HBG 3/98; SLJ 10/97; VOYA 4/98)

2288 Oppel, Kenneth. *Sunwing* (5–8). 2000, Simon & Schuster $17.00 (0-689-82674-5). In this sequel to *Silverwing*, Shade, the Silverwing bat, sets out to find his father and has a series of adventures including confronting the forces of evil. (Rev: BCCB 5/00; BL 1/1–15/00; HB 3–4/00; HBG 10/00; SLJ 2/00; VOYA 4/00)

2289 Orgel, Doris. *The Princess and the God* (7–10). 1996, Orchard LB $16.99 (0-531-08866-9); Bantam paper $4.50 (0-440-22691-0). A handsome retelling of the Cupid and Psyche myth in novel format, in which the power of pure love is shown conquering overwhelming obstacles. (Rev: BL 2/1/96; BR 9–10/96; SLJ 4/96)

2290 O'Shea, Pat. *The Hounds of the Morrigan* (5–8). 1986, HarperCollins paper $7.99 (0-06-447205-1). The forces of good and evil in Irish mythology battle over two children who are on a quest for a magic pebble. (Rev: BCCB 7–8/86; BL 4/1/86; HB 7–8/86; SLJ 3/86)

2291 Osterweil, Adam. *The Amulet of Komondor* (5–7). 2003, Front Street $15.95 (1-886910-81-2). Finding themselves in a parallel world of "Japani-mations," Joe and Katie face a mighty challenge, worry about how to get home, and continue their real-world romance in this lighthearted fantasy with *anime*-style illustrations. (Rev: BL 11/15/03; SLJ 12/03)

2292 Paolini, Christopher. *Eragon* (7–12). Series: Inheritance. 2003, Knopf $18.95 (0-375-82668-8). A 15-year-old boy called Eragon finds a stone that hatches a magnificent blue dragon, drawing him into a series of dangerous adventures as the two hunt killers and in turn are hunted. (Rev: BL 8/03*; SLJ 9/03; VOYA 8/03)

2293 Pattou, Edith. *East* (6–10). 2003, Harcourt $18.00 (0-15-204563-5). A great white bear carries Rose away from home to her destiny in this romantic novelization of the East o' the Sun and West o' the Moon fairy tale. (Rev: BL 9/1/03*; SLJ 12/03)

2294 Pattou, Edith. *Fire Arrow* (7–10). 1998, Harcourt $18.00 (0-15-201635-X); paper $6.00 (0-15-202264-3). In this sequel to *Hero's Song,* Brie sets out to avenge the death of her father by confronting his torturer. (Rev: BL 5/15/98; HBG 9/98; SLJ 7/98; VOYA 10/98)

2295 Pattou, Edith. *Hero's Song* (7–10). 1991, Harcourt $16.95 (0-15-233807-1). This fantasy-quest novel, infused with Irish myth and folklore, concerns a youth's search for his beloved sister, a wicked queen, and a clash between good and evil. (Rev: BL 10/15/91; SLJ 1/92)

2296 Pearce, Philippa. *Tom's Midnight Garden* (4–7). 1959, HarperCollins $15.89 (0-397-30477-3); Dell paper $5.95 (0-06-440445-5). When the clock strikes 13, Tom visits his garden and meets Hatty, a strange mid-Victorian girl.

2297 Pearson, Mary E. *David v. God* (6–9). 2000, Harcourt $16.00 (0-15-202058-6). David and his nerdy friend Marie are killed in a automobile accident and, on the way to heaven, they decide to debate God about being returned alive to earth. (Rev: BL 3/15/00; HBG 9/00; SLJ 4/00)

2298 Peck, Richard. *Voices After Midnight* (6–9). 1990, Dell paper $4.50 (0-440-40378-2). A 14-year-old boy and his family move to a brownstone in Manhattan and soon become involved with events and people of 100 years ago. (Rev: BL 10/1/89; BR 11–12/89; SLJ 9/89; VOYA 2/90)

2299 Perrin, Randy, et al. *Time Like a River* (5–7). 1997, RDR Books $14.95 (1-57143-061-X). Margie travels back in time to find a cure for her mother's mysterious illness. (Rev: HBG 3/98; SLJ 3/98)

2300 Philbrick, Rodman. *The Last Book in the Universe* (6–9). 2000, Scholastic paper $16.95 (0-439-08758-9). In this fast-paced but somber adventure-fantasy, Spaz, a young epileptic, travels with three companions through nightmarish territory to be with his foster sister, Bean. (Rev: BL 11/15/00; HBG 3/01; SLJ 11/00; VOYA 12/00)

2301 Pierce, Meredith Ann. *Treasure at the Heart of the Tanglewood* (6–10). 2001, Viking $16.99 (0-670-89247-5). Hannah, a young healer who lives in a forest with her animal companions, embarks on a fantastic journey of self-discovery after she falls in love with a handsome young knight. (Rev: BCCB 7–8/01; BL 4/15/01; HB 7–8/01; HBG 10/01; SLJ 6/01*; VOYA 6/01)

2302 Pierce, Tamora. *Briar's Book* (5–9). Series: Circle of Magic. 1999, Scholastic paper $15.95 (0-590-55359-3). In this fantasy, Briar, a former street urchin and petty thief, and his teacher, Rosethorn, search for the cause of a deadly plague that is sweeping through their land. (Rev: BL 2/15/99; HBG 10/99; SLJ 3/99; VOYA 6/99)

2303 Pierce, Tamora. *The Circle Opens: Magic Steps* (5–9). Series: Circle Opens. 2000, Scholastic

paper $16.95 (0-590-39588-2). Fourteen-year-old Sandry and her friend Pasco use their magic to stop the murders of local merchants. (Rev: BCCB 3/00; BL 3/1/00; HB 5–6/00; HBG 10/00; SLJ 4/00)

2304 Pierce, Tamora. *Cold Fire* (6–10). Series: The Circle Opens. 2002, Scholastic $16.95 (0-590-39655-2). Daja is studying in the chilly northern city of Kugisko, where her ability to handle fire comes in handy but also draws her into a relationship with an arsonist. (Rev: BL 9/1/02; HB 7–8/02; HBG 10/02; SLJ 8/02)

2305 Pierce, Tamora. *Daja's Book* (5–9). Series: Circle of Magic. 1998, Scholastic paper $15.95 (0-590-55358-5). Daja, a mage-in-training, uses her magical powers to create a living vine out of metal, and soon members of the nomadic Traders want to possess it. (Rev: BCCB 12/98; BL 12/1/98; HBG 3/99; SLJ 12/98; VOYA 2/99)

2306 Pierce, Tamora. *First Test* (4–7). 1999, Random LB $17.99 (0-679-98914-5). Keladry uses her wits and intelligence to conquer the many obstacles she encounters during her first year in knight training. (Rev: BCCB 7–8/99; BL 6/1–15/99; HBG 10/99; SLJ 7/99)

2307 Pierce, Tamora. *Lady Knight* (6–9). Series: Protector of the Small. 2002, Random $16.95 (0-375-81465-5). Now a knight, Kel is disappointed when her first assignment is to command a refugee camp. (Rev: BL 10/1/02; HBG 3/03; SLJ 12/02; VOYA 2/03)

2308 Pierce, Tamora. *Page: Protector of the Small* (5–8). 2000, Random $16.00 (0-679-88915-9). After successfully passing her first year of knight's training, Keladry moves on to the next three years as a page. (Rev: BCCB 9/00; BL 8/00; HBG 10/00; SLJ 8/00; VOYA 4/01)

2309 Pierce, Tamora. *The Realms of the Gods* (6–10). Series: The Immortals. 1996, Simon & Schuster $17.00 (0-689-31990-8). In this fourth volume of the series, Daine and the mage Numair triumph over evil Stormwing and Uusoae, the Queen of Chaos. (Rev: BL 10/15/96; SLJ 11/96; VOYA 4/97)

2310 Pierce, Tamora. *Sandry's Book* (6–9). Series: Circle of Magic. 1997, Scholastic paper $15.95 (0-590-55356-9). Four misfits are brought to Winding Circle Temple to learn new magical crafts in this first volume of a fantasy series. (Rev: BL 9/1/97; BR 11–12/97; HBG 3/98; SLJ 9/97; VOYA 12/97)

2311 Pierce, Tamora. *Shatterglass* (6–9). Series: The Circle Opens. 2003, Scholastic $16.95 (0-590-39683-8). Tris, 14, joins forces with another mage, Kethlun, whose glass-blowing skills help them solve a series of murders. (Rev: BL 3/1/03; HB 5–6/03; HBG 10/03; SLJ 7/03; VOYA 6/03)

2312 Pierce, Tamora. *Squire: Protector of the Small* (6–9). Series: Protector of the Small. 2001, Random

$15.95 (0-679-88916-7). In this third volume in the series, Keladry, now 14, wins a position as squire to Lord Raoul, a knight commander, and enjoys an exciting life of jousting and battles while preparing for the knighthood test in the Chamber of the Ordeal. (Rev: BL 9/1/01; HB 7–8/01; HBG 10/01; SLJ 8/01; VOYA 8/01)

2313 Pierce, Tamora. *Trickster's Choice* (7–12). Series: Daughter of the Lioness. 2003, Random $17.95 (0-375-81466-3). Aly, the 16-year-old daughter of Alanna the Lioness, uses her intelligence and magical powers to escape the trickster god Kyprioth's clutches. (Rev: BL 12/1/03; SLJ 12/03; VOYA 10/03)

2314 Pierce, Tamora. *Tris's Book* (5–9). Series: Circle of Magic. 1998, Scholastic paper $15.95 (0-590-55357-7). Tris and her three fellow mages combine forces to fight the pirates who are threatening to destroy their home in this sequel to *Sandry's Book*. (Rev: BCCB 4/98; BL 8/98; HBG 10/98; SLJ 4/98; VOYA 8/98)

2315 Pierce, Tamora. *Wild Magic* (6–10). Series: The Immortals. 1992, Atheneum $17.00 (0-689-31761-1). An exciting tale in which teenager Daine gradually accepts the fact that she possesses wild magic. (Rev: BL 10/15/92; SLJ 11/92)

2316 Pierce, Tamora. *Wolf-Speaker* (7–9). Series: The Immortals. 1994, Atheneum $16.00 (0-689-31833-2). A girl who speaks the language of animals works to help humans and animals move beyond species prejudice to prevent an ecological disaster. (Rev: BL 3/15/94; SLJ 5/94; VOYA 8/94)

2317 Porte, Barbara Ann. *Beauty and the Serpent: Thirteen Tales of Unnatural Animals* (6–10). 2001, Simon & Schuster $17.00 (0-689-84147-7). An eccentric school librarian introduces an exchange of offbeat stories about animals with strange, often dark, abilities and tendencies. (Rev: HBG 10/02; SLJ 11/01; VOYA 2/02)

2318 Porte, Barbara Ann. *Hearsay: Tales from the Middle Kingdom* (5–8). Illus. 1998, Greenwillow $15.00 (0-688-15381-X). Each of these 15 entertaining fantasies contains elements of Chinese folklore and culture. (Rev: BCCB 5/98; BR 11–12/98; HBG 10/98; SLJ 6/98)

2319 Pratchett, Terry. *The Amazing Maurice and His Educated Rodents* (6–9). Series: Discworld. 2001, HarperCollins $15.95 (0-06-001233-1). A cat, a boy with a whistle, and a group of intelligent rats try a Pied Piper-type scam, with suspenseful and comic results. (Rev: BCCB 2/02; BL 1/1–15/02; HB 3–4/02; HBG 10/02; SLJ 12/01*; VOYA 2/02)

2320 Pratchett, Terry. *The Wee Free Men* (6–10). Series: Discworld. 2003, HarperCollins $16.99 (0-06-001236-6). Nine-year-old Tiffany, an aspiring witch, teams up with some feisty characters to rescue her younger brother from Fairyland in a novel

that offers both humor and suspense. (Rev: BL 4/15/03; HB 5–6/03*; HBG 10/03; SLJ 5/03*; VOYA 8/03)

2321 Price, Reynolds. *A Perfect Friend* (5–8). 2000, Simon & Schuster $16.00 (0-689-83029-7). Set in the early part of the 20th century, this story tells how Ben, whose mother has died, communes with a young circus elephant who has also just lost a loved one. (Rev: BCCB 10/00; BL 11/15/00; HB 9–10/00; HBG 3/01; SLJ 2/01)

2322 Prince, Maggie. *The House on Hound Hill* (6–10). 1998, Houghton $16.00 (0-395-90702-0). When Emily and her family move to a historic house in London, she is gradually drawn into time-traveling to the 17th century and a London devastated by the bubonic plague. (Rev: BCCB 10/98; BL 11/15/98; HB 11–12/98; HBG 3/99; SLJ 9/98; VOYA 2/99)

2323 Prue, Sally. *Cold Tom* (4–8). 2003, Scholastic $15.95 (0-439-48268-2). Tom has disabilities that make him an outcast, and he flees from his elfin tribe to the city inhabited by demons (humans), where he is confronted with his human side. (Rev: BL 9/15/03; HB 7–8/03*; HBG 10/03; SLJ 9/03*; VOYA 10/03)

2324 Pullman, Philip. *The Amber Spyglass* (7–12). Series: His Dark Materials. 2000, Knopf $19.95 (0-679-87926-9). Lyra and Will are key figures in the battle between good and evil in this final volume in the prize-winning trilogy. (Rev: BL 10/1/00; BR 1–2/01; HB 11–12/00; HBG 3/01; SLJ 10/00)

2325 Pullman, Philip. *Clockwork* (4–7). Illus. 1998, Scholastic paper $14.95 (0-590-12999-6). Reality and fantasy interact when characters in a storyteller's tale come to life in this story set in a bygone German inn. (Rev: BCCB 12/98; BL 9/15/98*; BR 1–2/99; HB 11–12/98; HBG 3/99; SLJ 10/98; VOYA 12/98)

2326 Pullman, Philip. *The Golden Compass* (7–12). Series: His Dark Materials. 1996, Knopf $20.00 (0-679-87924-2); Ballantine paper $6.99 (0-345-41335-0). In this first book of a fantasy trilogy, young Lyra and her alter ego, a protective animal named Pantalaimon, escape from the child-stealing Gobblers and join a group heading north to rescue a band of missing children. (Rev: BL 3/1/96*; BR 9–10/96; SLJ 4/96)

2327 Pullman, Philip. *The Subtle Knife* (7–12). Series: His Dark Materials. 1997, Random $20.00 (0-679-87925-0); Ballantine paper $6.99 (0-345-41336-9). In this second volume of a trilogy, Will and Lyra travel from world to world searching for the mysterious Dust and Will's long-lost father. (Rev: BL 7/97; HBG 3/98; SLJ 10/97)

2328 Purtill, Richard. *Enchantment at Delphi* (6–9). 1986, Harcourt $14.95 (0-15-200447-5). On a trip to Delphi, Alice finds herself transported back in time to the days of Apollo and other Greek gods. (Rev: SLJ 11/86)

2329 Reiss, Kathryn. *Pale Phoenix* (7–10). 1994, Harcourt $10.95 (0-15-200030-5); paper $3.95 (0-15-200031-3). Miranda Browne's parents take in an orphan girl who can disappear at will and who was the victim of a tragedy in a past life in Puritan Massachusetts. (Rev: BL 3/15/94; SLJ 5/94; VOYA 6/94)

2330 Reiss, Kathryn. *Paperquake: A Puzzle* (5–8). 1998, Harcourt $17.00 (0-15-201183-8). In this novel set in contemporary San Francisco, Violet receives a message from a girl who lived during the 1906 earthquake warning her of a disaster soon to come. (Rev: BCCB 6/98; BL 5/15/98; HBG 9/98; SLJ 6/98; VOYA 6/98)

2331 Reiss, Kathryn. *Time Windows* (6–9). 1991, Harcourt $17.00 (0-15-288205-7). Miranda, age 13, finds a dollhouse in the attic that replicates the details of her new home. When she looks inside, she witnesses disturbing past events. (Rev: BL 11/1/91; SLJ 10/91)

2332 Richardson, Bill. *After Hamelin* (4–8). 2000, Annick $19.95 (1-55037-629-2). In this entertaining fantasy that is a follow-up to the Pied Piper of Hamelin story, Penelope gets the gift of Deep Dreaming and is able to enter the Piper's secret world in the hope of rescuing the children. (Rev: BL 2/15/01; SLJ 4/01; VOYA 4/01)

2333 Rinaldi, Ann. *Millicent's Gift* (5–8). 2002, HarperCollins LB $15.89 (0-06-029637-2). Millicent finds she has problems being in a family where spells and shape-shifting are learned skills. (Rev: BL 6/1–15/02; HBG 10/02; SLJ 6/02)

2334 Roberts, Katherine. *Crystal Mask* (5–8). Series: The Echorium Sequence. 2002, Scholastic paper $15.95 (0-439-33864-6). The Singers, a group of people who maintain peace in the world through their unusual powers, are confronted by evildoers known as the Frazhin. Also use *Dark Quetzal* (2003). (Rev: BL 4/15/02; HBG 10/02; SLJ 3/02)

2335 Roberts, Laura P. *Ghost of a Chance* (6–9). 1997, Delacorte $14.95 (0-385-32508-8). Melissa must deal with her feelings about her parents' divorce and jealousy of her best friend Chloe when they both fall in love with James, a ghost. (Rev: BR 3–4/98; HBG 3/98; SLJ 10/97)

2336 Rowling, J. K. *Fantastic Beasts: And Where to Find Them* (4–7). 2001, Scholastic paper $3.99 (0-439-29501-7). This guide to 75 magical beasts and their whereabouts is one of the texts that Harry Potter has studied, complete with his jottings in the margins. Similarly, *Quidditch Through the Ages* (2001) contains the game's history, rules, and league details. (Rev: BL 5/1/01; SLJ 6/01)

2337 Rowling, J. K. *Harry Potter and the Chamber of Secrets* (4–8). 1999, Scholastic $19.95 (0-439-06486-4). During his second year at Hogwarts School of Witchcraft and Wizardry, Harry is baffled when he hears noises no one else can. (Rev: BCCB 9/99; BL 5/15/99*; BR 9–10/99; HB 7–8/99; HBG 10/99; SLJ 7/99; VOYA 10/99)

2338 Rowling, J. K. *Harry Potter and the Goblet of Fire* (4–9). 2000, Scholastic $25.95 (0-439-13959-7). This, the fourth installment of Harry Potter's adventures, begins when Voldemort tries to regain the power he lost in his failed attempt to kill Harry. (Rev: BL 8/00*; HB 11–12/00; HBG 3/01; SLJ 8/00)

2339 Rowling, J. K. *Harry Potter and the Order of the Phoenix* (4–12). 2003, Scholastic $29.99 (0-439-35806-X). Adolescence, adult hypocrisy, and the deadly threat of Voldemort and his evil supporters combine to make Harry's fifth year at Hogwarts as eventful as ever. (Rev: BL 7/03; HB 9–10/03; HBG 10/03; SLJ 8/03; VOYA 8/03)

2340 Rowling, J. K. *Harry Potter and the Prisoner of Azkaban* (4–8). 1999, Scholastic $19.95 (0-439-13635-0). In this third thrilling adventure, a murderer has escaped from prison and is after our young hero. (Rev: BCCB 10/99; BL 9/1/99*; HB 11–12/99; HBG 3/00; SLJ 10/99)

2341 Rowling, J. K. *Harry Potter and the Sorcerer's Stone* (4–8). Illus. 1998, Scholastic $19.95 (0-590-35340-3). In this humorous and suspenseful story, 11-year-old Harry Potter attends the Hogwarts School for Witchcraft and Wizardry, where he discovers that he is a wizard just as his parents had been and that someone at the school is trying to steal a valuable stone with the power to make people immortal. (Rev: BCCB 11/98; BL 9/15/98; HB 1–2/99; HBG 3/99; SLJ 10/98; VOYA 12/98)

2342 Rubenstein, Gillian. *Foxspell* (7–9). Illus. 1996, Simon & Schuster $16.00 (0-689-80602-7). In this fantasy, a troubled boy is tempted by a fox spirit to receive peace and immortality if he will assume a fox shape forever. (Rev: BL 10/15/96; SLJ 9/96; VOYA 12/96)

2343 Rupp, Rebecca. *The Waterstone* (4–8). 2002, Candlewick $16.99 (0-7636-0726-6). Twelve-year-old Tad, who has special powers and memories, must find a crystal that will set the world to rights. (Rev: BCCB 10/02; HBG 10/03; SLJ 11/02; VOYA 2/03)

2344 Ruskin, John. *King of the Golden River or the Black Brother* (5–8). 1974, Dover paper $3.95 (0-486-20066-3). Two mean brothers incur the wrath of the South-West Wind.

2345 Russell, Barbara T. *The Taker's Stone* (7–12). 1999, DK $16.95 (1-7894-2568-8). When 14-year-old Fischer steals some glowing red gemstones from a man at a campsite, he unleashes the terrible evil of Belial, some catastrophic weather, and the beginning of the end of the world. (Rev: VOYA 10/99)

2346 Rylant, Cynthia. *The Heavenly Village* (4–7). 1999, Scholastic paper $15.95 (0-439-04096-5). A special book about the Heavenly Village — a place where some people stay who are not sure about going to heaven — and about some of the people who live in this in-between world. (Rev: BL 12/1/99*; HBG 3/00; SLJ 3/00; VOYA 2/00)

2347 Rylant, Cynthia. *The Islander* (5–8). 1998, DK paper $14.95 (0-7894-2490-8). Growing up on a lonely island off the coast of British Columbia with his grandfather, Daniel encounters a mermaid and, through her, learns about his family. (Rev: BCCB 5/98; BL 2/1/98; HB 5–6/98; HBG 10/98; SLJ 3/98; VOYA 8/98)

2348 Saint-Exupery, Antoine de. *The Little Prince* (5–9). Trans. by Katherine Woods. 1943, Harcourt paper $10.00 (0-15-646511-6). An airplane pilot crashes in a desert and encounters a little prince who seeks harmony for his planet.

2349 Sampson, Fay. *Pangur Ban: The White Cat* (5–8). Series: Pangur Ban. 2003, Lion Publg. paper $7.95 (0-7459-4763-8). A Welsh cat and an Irish monk encounter princesses and mermaids in this fantasy set in the Middle Ages. (Rev: BL 5/15/03; SLJ 11/03)

2350 Sampson, Fay. *Shape-Shifter: The Naming of Pangur Ban* (5–8). Series: Pangur Ban. 2003, Lion Publg. paper $7.95 (0-7459-4762-X). A Welsh cat pursued by witches befriends an Irish monk in this first book in the series. (Rev: BL 5/15/03)

2351 Schaeffer, Susan F. *The Dragons of North Chittendon* (5–7). 1986, Simon & Schuster paper $2.95 (0-685-14462-3). The story of Arthur, an unruly dragon, and his ESP relationship with the boy Patrick in a story of humans and dragons in and above North Chittendon, Vermont. (Rev: BL 8/86; SLJ 9/86)

2352 Schimel, Lawrence. *Camelot Fantastic* (8–12). 1998, D A W Books paper $5.99 (0-88677-790-9). A collection of original novelettes written by well-known authors of fantasy, science fiction, and mystery, that present different perspectives on characters and incidents associated with King Arthur's Camelot. (Rev: VOYA 12/98)

2353 Schmidt, Gary D. *Straw into Gold* (5–8). 2001, Clarion $15.00 (0-618-05601-7). Two boys set off to find the answer to the king's riddle and thereby save the lives of rebels, only to discover much more than they had expected. (Rev: BCCB 9/01; HBG 10/01; SLJ 8/01; VOYA 2/02)

2354 Scott, Deborah. *The Kid Who Got Zapped Through Time* (4–7). 1997, Avon $14.00 (0-380-97356-1). In this humorous time-travel fantasy, Flattop Kincaid is transported to England during the Middle Ages, where he becomes a serf. (Rev: BL 11/1/97; SLJ 9/97)

2355 Sedgwick, Marcus. *The Dark Horse* (5–8). 2003, Random $15.95 (0-385-73054-3). A fantasy in which young Sigurd, part of the ancient Storn tribe, helps his people fight the invading Dark Horse. (Rev: BL 2/1/03; HB 3–4/03; HBG 10/03; SLJ 3/03*; VOYA 4/03)

2356 Sedgwick, Marcus. *Floodland* (5–8). 2001, Delacorte $15.95 (0-385-32801-X). In this fantasy set in an England undergoing terrible floods, young Zoe is swept away to an island where she is held prisoner by people who have reverted to primitive ways. (Rev: BCCB 3/01; HB 3–4/01; HBG 10/01; SLJ 3/01)

2357 Selden, George. *The Genie of Sutton Place* (5–6). 1985, Farrar paper $7.95 (0-374-42530-2). The summer Tim lives with his Aunt Lucy on Sutton Place in New York City, he evokes his own magical genie who works not only miracles but mishaps.

2358 Service, Pamela F. *Vision Quest* (5–7). 1989, Fawcett paper $3.99 (0-449-70372-X). Mourning the death of her father, Kate is changed by an ancient Indian charm-stone. (Rev: BCCB 5/89; BL 4/15/89; SLJ 3/89)

2359 Sherman, Josepha. *Windleaf* (7–12). 1993, Walker $14.95 (0-8027-8259-0). Count Thierry falls in love with half-faerie Glinfinial, only to have her father, the Faerie Lord, steal her away. (Rev: BL 11/1/93*; SLJ 12/93; VOYA 2/94)

2360 Shetterly, Will. *Elsewhere* (8–12). 1991, Harcourt $16.95 (0-15-200731-8). Set in Bordertown, between the real world and Faerie world, home to runaway elves and humans, this is a fantasy of integration, survival, and coming of age. (Rev: BL 10/15/91; SLJ 11/91)

2361 Shetterly, Will. *Nevernever* (8–12). 1993, Harcourt $16.95 (0-15-257022-5); Tor paper $4.99 (0-8125-5151-6). This sequel to *Elsewhere* (1991) shows Wolfboy trying to protect Florida, the heir of Faerie, from gangs of Elves out to get her, while one of his friends is framed for murder. (Rev: BL 9/15/93; SLJ 10/93; VOYA 12/93)

2362 Shusterman, Neal. *Downsiders* (8–12). 1999, Simon & Schuster $16.95 (0-689-80375-3). A fantasy about the people who live in the Downside, the subterranean world beneath New York City, and a teenage boy who ventures Topside to get medicine for his sick sister, leading to a dangerous chain of events. (Rev: HBG 9/99; SLJ 7/99; VOYA 8/99)

2363 Singer, Marilyn. *Deal with a Ghost* (7–9). 1996, Holt $15.95 (0-8050-4797-2). Overly confident 15-year-old Deal meets her match when she is dumped on a grandmother she scarcely knows, encounters a ghost, and becomes involved with a boy who sees through her game. (Rev: BL 6/1–15/97; HBG 3/98; SLJ 6/97; VOYA 10/98)

2364 Sleator, William. *The Boxes* (5–8). 1998, Dutton $15.99 (0-525-46012-8). In spite of warnings from her Uncle Marco, Annie opens two mysterious boxes he has left her and, as a result, finds herself swept into a different set of relationships that will change her life. (Rev: BCCB 7–8/98; BL 6/1–15/98; HB 5–6/98; HBG 10/98; SLJ 6/98; VOYA 12/98)

2365 Sleator, William. *Marco's Millions* (5–9). 2001, Dutton $16.99 (0-525-46441-7). In this prequel to *The Boxes* (1998), 12-year-old Marco travels to an alien world. (Rev: BCCB 7–8/01; HB 5–6/01*; HBG 10/01; SLJ 6/01; VOYA 6/01)

2366 Sleator, William. *Rewind* (5–8). 1999, Dutton $15.99 (0-525-46130-2). Peter realizes how his behavior affects other people when, after he is killed in a car accident, he is given a chance to relive parts of his life and avoid his death. (Rev: BL 10/15/99; HB 7–8/99; HBG 4/00; SLJ 8/99; VOYA 10/99)

2367 Slepian, Jan. *Back to Before* (5–7). 1994, Scholastic paper $3.25 (0-590-48459-1). Cousins Linny and Hilary travel back to a time before Linny's mother's death and Hilary's parents' separation. (Rev: BCCB 9/93; BL 9/1/93*; SLJ 10/93)

2368 Smith, Sherwood. *Court Duel* (5–8). 1998, Harcourt $18.00 (0-15-201609-0). In this fantasy, Meliara has problems at court when she can't distinguish friends from enemies. A sequel to *Crown Duel* (1997). (Rev: BL 3/1/98; HBG 10/98; SLJ 4/98; VOYA 8/98)

2369 Smith, Sherwood. *Crown Duel* (5–8). 1997, Harcourt $17.00 (0-15-201608-2). Young Meliara and her brother Bran lead a small band of friends against the wicked King Galdran. (Rev: BCCB 7–8/97; BL 4/15/97; SLJ 8/97; VOYA 6/97)

2370 Smith, Sherwood. *Wren's Quest* (5–8). 1993, Harcourt $16.95 (0-15-200976-0). Wren takes time out from magician school to search for clues to her parentage. Sequel to *Wren to the Rescue* (1990). (Rev: BL 4/1/93*; SLJ 6/93)

2371 Smith, Sherwood. *Wren's War* (5–8). 1995, Harcourt $17.00 (0-15-200977-9). In this sequel to *Wren to the Rescue* and *Wren's Quest,* Princess Teressa struggles to control herself and her destiny when she finds her parents murdered. (Rev: BL 3/1/95*; SLJ 5/95)

2372 Sneve, Virginia Driving Hawk. *The Trickster and the Troll* (4–8). 1997, Univ. of Nebraska Pr. $25.00 (0-8032-4261-1). In this fantasy, two folktale characters, the Sioux trickster Iktomi and a troll who has followed a Norwegian family to this country, develop a friendship as they see the country grow and change. (Rev: BL 9/15/97; BR 1–2/98; HBG 3/98; SLJ 12/97)

2373 Snyder, Midori. *Hannah's Garden* (6–8). 2002, Viking $16.99 (0-670-03577-7). Seventeen-year-old Cassie's life with her mother seems fairly normal until the two travel to look after Cassie's

dying grandfather and find themselves in the middle of a battle between two clans of fairy people. (Rev: BCCB 2/03; BL 10/15/02; HBG 3/03; SLJ 10/02; VOYA 12/02)

2374 Somary, Wolfgang. *Night and the Candlemaker* (4–8). Illus. 2000, Barefoot $16.99 (1-84148-137-8). In this allegory, a candle maker continues with his trade in spite of threats he receives from Night. (Rev: BL 9/15/00; HBG 10/01; SLJ 1/01)

2375 Spalding, Andres. *The White Horse Talisman* (4–7). 2002, Orca $12.95 (1-55143-187-4). Two Canadian children vacationing in England help the magical White Horse fight the forces of the honey-tongued dragon. (Rev: BL 4/15/02; HBG 10/02; SLJ 11/02; VOYA 6/02)

2376 Spicer, Dorothy. *The Humming Top* (6–8). 1968, Phillips $26.95 (0-87599-147-5). An orphan finds she is able to predict future events.

2377 Springer, Nancy. *Red Wizard* (6–8). 1990, Macmillan $13.95 (0-689-31485-X). Ryan is called into another world by an inept wizard and must find the secret of the Deep Magic of colors before he can return. (Rev: SLJ 7/90; VOYA 4/90)

2378 Springer, Nancy, ed. *Ribbiting Tales* (5–7). Illus. 2002, Putnam Juvenile paper $5.99 (0-698-11952-5). This is an anthology of eight stories about frogs by such authors as Janet Taylor Lisle, Robert J. Harris, and Bruce Coville. (Rev: BL 11/1/00; SLJ 1/01)

2379 Stearns, Michael, ed. *A Wizard's Dozen: Stories of the Fantastic* (7–12). 1993, Harcourt $16.95 (0-15-200965-5). This collection of 13 strange and magical tales includes works by Vivian Vande Velde, Patricia Wrede, and Bruce Coville. (Rev: BL 12/15/93; SLJ 12/93; VOYA 4/94)

2380 Steele, Mary Q. *Journey Outside* (5–8). 1984, Peter Smith $20.25 (0-8446-6169-4); Puffin paper $4.99 (0-14-030588-2). Young Dilar, believing that his Raft People have been circling endlessly in their quest for a "Better Place," sets out to discover the origin and fate of his kind.

2381 Stevermer, Caroline. *River Rats* (7–10). 1992, Harcourt $17.00 (0-15-200895-0). This action-packed story begins in the years following a nuclear disaster when six orphans, living on an old paddle wheeler, are threatened by a fugitive with a menacing past. (Rev: BL 4/1/92; SLJ 8/92)

2382 Strasser, Todd. *Help! I'm Trapped in Obedience School* (5–8). 1995, Scholastic paper $4.50 (0-590-54209-5). Andy, trapped in a dog's body, must adjust to eating dog food and engaging in other typical canine activities. (Rev: BL 2/1/96; SLJ 2/96)

2383 Strasser, Todd. *Pastabilities* (5–8). 2000, Pocket paper $4.99 (0-671-03628-9). Heavenly Litebody, a modern-day nanny with mysterious powers, travels with her five charges to Italy for a vacation. (Rev: SLJ 8/00)

2384 Strauss, Victoria. *Guardian of the Hills* (7–10). 1995, Morrow $15.00 (0-688-06998-3). Pamela, who is part Quapaw Indian, experiences cultural conflict when her grandfather organizes an excavation of sacred burial grounds to learn more of their spiritual heritage. (Rev: BL 10/15/95*; SLJ 10/95)

2385 Strickland, Brad. *The Bell, the Book, and the Spellbinder* (5–8). 1997, Dial $14.99 (0-8037-1831-4). Fergie seems to fall under a strange spell when he opens a library book written by a sorcerer who has been kidnapping boys and taking possession of their bodies for the past 300 years. (Rev: BL 9/1/97; HBG 3/98; SLJ 8/97)

2386 Strickland, Brad. *The Hand of the Necromancer* (5–8). 1996, Dial $14.89 (0-8037-1830-6). Johnny Dixon and Professor Childermass combat a wicked magician, Mattheus Mergel, in a continuation of the series begun by John Bellairs. (Rev: BL 7/96; SLJ 9/96)

2387 Strickland, Brad. *The Wrath of the Grinning Ghost* (5–8). 1999, Dial $16.99 (0-8037-2222-2). The forces of good and evil clash as Johnny and his friend Professor Childermass journey to the realm of a magical falcon to destroy a force that is trying to destroy the world. (Rev: BL 9/15/99; HBG 3/00; SLJ 10/99)

2388 Stroud, Jonathan. *The Amulet of Samarkand* (6–12). 2003, Hyperion $17.95 (0-7868-1859-X). Nathaniel, an apprentice magician, plots to steal an amulet and sets powerful forces in motion in this fantasy set in London. (Rev: BL 9/1/03*; HB 11–12/03)

2389 Swados, Elizabeth. *Dreamtective: The Dreamy and Daring Adventures of Cobra Kite* (6–9). 1999, Genesis paper $5.95 (1-885478-54-3). A humorous and unusual adventure in which 12-year-old Cobra discovers she can visit other people's dreams. (Rev: BR 3–4/99; SLJ 10/99)

2390 *Swan Sister: Fairy Tales Retold* (5–10). Ed. by Ellen Datlow and Terri Windung. 2003, Simon & Schuster $16.95 (0-689-84613-4). Retellings by well-known authors of traditional stories are inventive and entertaining. (Rev: BCCB 11/03; BL 9/15/03; SLJ 12/03)

2391 Sweeney, Joyce. *Shadow* (7–10). 1995, Bantam $20.95 (0-385-30988-0). Sarah's cat, Shadow, has mysteriously returned from the dead. Sarah and Cissy, the psychic housemaid, try to figure out why. (Rev: BL 7/94; SLJ 9/94; VOYA 10/94)

2392 Tarr, Judith. *His Majesty's Elephant* (6–9). 1993, Harcourt $16.95 (0-15-200737-7). Set in the court of Charlemagne, this fantasy tells of a teenage princess who joins forces with a witch and an enchanted elephant to save her father. (Rev: BL 1/1/94; VOYA 2/94)

2393 Thesman, Jean. *The Other Ones* (7–9). 1999, Puffin paper $5.99 (0-14-131246-7). Bridget must decide if she should try to be a normal human or, because she possesses supernatural powers, remain part of the Other Ones. (Rev: BL 5/99; SLJ 6/99; VOYA 8/99)

2394 Thompson, Julian F. *Hard Time* (7–11). 2003, Simon & Schuster $16.95 (0-689-85424-2). A leprechaun that lives in Annie's Life Skills doll coaxes Annie to write an inventive essay that prompts punishments including a jail sentence for Annie and her best friend in this irreverent fantasy. (Rev: BCCB 1/04; BL 12/15/03)

2395 Thompson, Kate. *Midnight's Choice* (6–9). 1999, Hyperion LB $16.49 (0-7868-2329-1). In this sequel to *Switchers,* 15-year-old Tess must choose whether to remain human or assume a permanent animal form and, if the latter, whether to become immortal as a phoenix, the embodiment of good, or as a vampire, the embodiment of evil. (Rev: HBG 4/00; SLJ 7/99)

2396 Thompson, Kate. *Switchers* (5–8). 1998, Hyperion LB $15.49 (0-7868-2328-3); paper $5.99 (0-7868-1266-4). Two teens who are able to change shape and become any animal they wish, real or imaginary, set out to stop a group of mysterious ice creatures who are causing severe blizzards. (Rev: BCCB 9/98; BL 3/15/98; HBG 10/98; SLJ 5/98)

2397 Thompson, Kate. *Wild Blood* (5–8). 2000, Hyperion $16.49 (0-7868-2497-2). On her 15th birthday, Tess must choose the form she will retain for the rest of her life because, on that day, she will lose the power to "switch" and become other creatures. (Rev: BL 4/15/00; HBG 10/00; SLJ 7/00)

2398 Thornton, Duncan. *Kalifax* (5–9). 2000, Coteau paper $8.95 (1-55050-152-6). In this fantasy novel, young Tom, with the help of Grandfather Frost, saves the crew of his ship after it becomes trapped in ice. (Rev: SLJ 1/01)

2399 Tolan, Stephanie S. *Flight of the Raven* (5–8). 2001, HarperCollins LB $17.89 (0-06-029620-8). Amber, whose father is responsible for a terrorist attack, and Elijah, an African American boy who has mysterious powers, attempt to stop further violence in this novel that blends science fiction and suspense. (Rev: BCCB 12/01; BL 10/15/01; HBG 10/02; SLJ 10/01)

2400 Tolkien, J. R. R. *The Hobbit: Or, There and Back Again* (7–12). Illus. 1938, Houghton $16.00 (0-395-07122-4); Ballantine paper $7.99 (0-345-33968-1). In this prelude to *The Lord of the Rings,* the reader meets Bilbo Baggins, a hobbit, in a land filled with dwarfs, elves, goblins, and dragons.

2401 Tolkien, J. R. R. *Roverandom* (4–9). 1998, Houghton $17.00 (0-395-89871-4); paper $12.00 (0-395-95799-0). This fantasy deals with a dog named Roverandom who has the misfortune of insulting a wizard and having to pay the consequences. (Rev: BL 7/98; SLJ 6/98; VOYA 10/98)

2402 Townley, Roderick. *Into the Labyrinth* (5–7). 2002, Simon & Schuster $16.95 (0-689-84615-0). In this sequel to *The Great Good Thing* (2001), Princess Sylvie and the other characters in their novel become exhausted as their popularity grows and they must rush from chapter to chapter; when the book goes digital, things spiral out of control and Sylvie must defeat an evil "bot" that threatens to destroy them. (Rev: BL 11/1/02; HBG 10/03; SLJ 10/02)

2403 Townsend, John Rowe. *The Fortunate Isles* (7–12). 1989, HarperCollins LB $13.89 (0-397-32366-2). Eleni and her friend Andreas seek the living god in this novel set in a mythical land. (Rev: BL 10/15/89; SLJ 10/89)

2404 Townsend, Tom. *The Trouble with an Elf* (5–8). Series: Fairie Ring. 1999, Royal Fireworks paper $9.99 (0-88092-525-6). The adopted daughter of the king of the elves, Elazandra, journeys through a ring of mushrooms to the world of humans to stop the evil that will destroy both worlds. (Rev: SLJ 4/00)

2405 Turner, Ann. *Rosemary's Witch* (5–8). 1991, HarperCollins paper $3.95 (0-06-440494-3). Rosemary discovers that her new home is haunted by the spirit of a girl named Mathilda, who's become a witch because of her pain and anger. (Rev: BL 4/1/91; SLJ 5/91*)

2406 Turner, Megan W. *The Queen of Attolia* (5–8). 2000, Greenwillow $15.95 (0-688-17423-X). In this sequel to *The Thief*, Gen, a slippery rogue, once more gets involved in the rivalry between two city states. (Rev: BL 4/15/00; HB 7–8/00; HBG 10/00; SLJ 5/00)

2407 Turner, Megan W. *The Thief* (5–8). 1996, Greenwillow $16.99 (0-688-14627-9). To escape life imprisonment, Gen must steal a legendary stone in this first-person fantasy set in olden days. (Rev: BCCB 11/96; BL 1/1–15/97; BR 11–12/96; HB 11–12/96; SLJ 10/96; VOYA 6/97)

2408 Vande Velde, Vivian. *Dragon's Bait* (7–10). 1992, Harcourt $16.95 (0-15-200726-1). A young girl accused of being a witch and sentenced to be killed by a dragon becomes friends with a shapechanger who promises to help her take revenge. (Rev: BL 9/15/92; SLJ 9/92)

2409 Vande Velde, Vivian. *Magic Can Be Murder* (7–11). 2000, Harcourt $17.00 (0-15-202665-7). Teenage witch Nola finds romance while working to reveal the identity of a murderer. (Rev: BL 12/15/00; HBG 3/01; SLJ 11/00; VOYA 12/00)

2410 Vansickle, Lisa. *The Secret Little City* (5–8). 2000, Palmae $15.95 (1-930167-11-3). When 11-year-old Mackenzie moves with her family to a small town in Oregon, she discovers a whole civilization of inch-high people living beneath the floorboards of her new room. (Rev: SLJ 8/00)

2411 Venokur, Ross. *The Amazing Frecktacle* (4–7). 1998, Delacorte $14.95 (0-385-32621-1). Nicholas Bells, tired of being teased because of his abundant freckles, strikes a bargain with the villainous Mr. Piddlesticks to remove them, little knowing that his freckles are magical. (Rev: BCCB 9/98; BL 8/98; HBG 10/99; SLJ 9/98)

2412 Venokur, Ross. *The Autobiography of Meatball Finkelstein* (4–8). 2001, Delacorte $14.95 (0-385-32798-6). Meatball, a vegetarian, gains magic powers when he eats his first meatball in this funny and absorbing book with many twists and turns. (Rev: BCCB 9/01; HBG 3/02; SLJ 8/01)

2413 Vick, Helen H. *Tag Against Time* (6–9). 1996, Harbinger $15.95 (1-57140-006-0); paper $9.95 (1-57140-007-9). In this third volume about Tag, our hero thinks it is time to leave the 1200s and the Hopi culture he has grown to love and return to the present. (Rev: SLJ 10/96; VOYA 2/97)

2414 Vick, Helen H. *Walker's Journey Home* (7–10). 1995, Harbinger $14.95 (1-57140-000-1); paper $9.95 (1-57140-001-X). Walker leads the Sinagua Indians through treacherous challenges from both old enemies and new, and learns that greed and jealousy have been destructive forces throughout history. Sequel to *Walker of Time* (1993). (Rev: BL 8/95)

2415 Voigt, Cynthia. *Building Blocks* (7–10). 1985, Fawcett paper $3.99 (0-449-70130-1). A boy travels back in time to witness his father's childhood.

2416 Voigt, Cynthia. *Elske* (7–12). Series: The Kingdom. 1999, Simon & Schuster $18.00 (0-689-82472-6). In the fourth and final volume of this fantasy series, 12-year-old Elske accompanies Beriel, an exiled noblewoman, on her quest to recover her kingdom's throne. (Rev: BCCB 12/99; BL 9/1/99; HBG 4/00; SLJ 10/99; VOYA 10/99)

2417 Voigt, Cynthia. *The Wings of a Falcon* (7–12). 1993, Scholastic $15.95 (0-590-46712-3). Two boys escape from a remote island and face danger and adventure in this multilayered tale that includes themes of friendship, romance, and heroism. (Rev: SLJ 10/93*; VOYA 12/93)

2418 Walsh, Jill Paton. *A Chance Child* (7–9). 1978, Avon paper $1.95 (0-380-48561-3). In this English novel, a young boy who has been a prisoner all his life suddenly travels back in time. (Rev: BL 5/1/89)

2419 Wangerin, Walter, Jr. *The Book of the Dun Cow* (7–10). 1978, HarperCollins $12.95 (0-06-026346-6). A farmyard fable with talking animals that retells the story of Chanticleer the Rooster.

2420 Watson, Patrick. *Ahmek* (5–6). 1999, Stoddart $14.95 (0-7737-3145-8). Ahmek, a beaver, is forced to leave his beloved pond and travel north to find a new home and a mate for life. (Rev: SLJ 4/00)

2421 Waugh, Sylvia. *The Mennyms* (4–8). 1994, Greenwillow $16.00 (0-688-13070-4). When their owner dies, a family of rag dolls comes to life and takes over her house in this beginning volume of an extensive series. (Rev: BCCB 5/94; HB 7–8/94; SLJ 4/94)

2422 Weinberg, Karen. *Window of Time* (5–7). 1991, White Mane paper $9.95 (0-942597-18-4). Ben climbs through a window and finds himself 125 years back in time. (Rev: SLJ 7/91)

2423 Wesley, Mary. *Haphazard House* (5–7). 1993, Overlook $14.95 (0-87951-470-1). An artist's magic hat enables him to make money betting on the Derby race during a visit to England. (Rev: BCCB 10/93; BL 1/1/94)

2424 Westall, Robert. *The Promise* (6–10). 1991, Scholastic $13.95 (0-590-43760-7). Bob's friendship with beautiful, sickly Valerie becomes romantic; when she dies, only Bob knows that her spirit still lingers among the living. (Rev: BL 3/1/91; SLJ 3/91)

2425 White, T. H. *The Sword in the Stone* (7–12). 1993, Putnam $24.99 (0-399-22502-1); Dell paper $5.99 (0-440-98445-9). In this, the first part of *The Once and Future King,* the career of Wart is traced until he becomes King Arthur.

2426 Whitmore, Arvella. *Trapped Between the Lash and the Gun: A Boy's Journey* (5–8). 1999, Dial $16.99 (0-8037-2384-9). Jordan, an African American boy of 12, changes after he travels back in time and experiences the horror and terror of slavery and a trip to freedom on the Underground Railroad. (Rev: BCCB 2/99; BL 11/15/98; BR 9–10/99; HBG 10/99; SLJ 1/99; VOYA 4/99)

2427 Wilde, Oscar. *The Canterville Ghost* (7–12). Illus. 1996, North-South paper $6.95 (1-55858-611-3). An American family buys an English manor house and causes problems for the resident ghost in this classic fantasy. (Rev: BL 12/15/96; SLJ 1/97)

2428 Winthrop, Elizabeth. *The Battle for the Castle* (4–7). 1993, Holiday $15.95 (0-8234-1010-2). William and friend Jason time-travel to the Middle Ages, where they become involved in a struggle to prevent the return of evil as a ruling power. A sequel to *The Castle in the Attic* (1985). (Rev: BL 9/1/93; HB 7–8/93; SLJ 5/93)

2429 Winthrop, Elizabeth. *The Castle in the Attic* (5–7). 1985, Holiday $16.95 (0-8234-0579-6). In an effort to keep his sitter from returning to England, William miniaturizes her and then must find a way to undo the deed. (Rev: BCCB 10/85; BL 1/15/86; SLJ 2/86)

2430 Wood, Beverly, and Chris Wood. *Dog Star* (5–8). 1998, Orca paper $6.95 (0-896095-37-2). On a cruise to Alaska with his family, 13-year-old Jeff Beacon encounters a magical pet bull terrier who

transports him back in time to the Juneau of 1932. (Rev: BR 1–2/99; VOYA 8/98)

2431 Woodruff, Elvira. *Orphan of Ellis Island* (4–7). 1997, Scholastic paper $15.95 (0-590-48245-9). Left alone on Ellis Island, Dominic finds himself transported in time to the village in Italy his family came from. (Rev: BCCB 3/97; BL 6/1–15/97; SLJ 5/97)

2432 Wrede, Patricia C. *Book of Enchantments* (5–8). 1996, Harcourt $17.00 (0-15-201255-9). A collection of stories with various settings, each dealing with an enchantment. (Rev: BCCB 5/96; BL 5/15/96; SLJ 6/96; VOYA 8/96)

2433 Wrede, Patricia C. *Searching for Dragons* (6–10). Series: Enchanted Forest Chronicles. 1991, Harcourt $16.95 (0-15-200898-5). Cimorene goes on a quest with Mendanbar, king of the forest, to find the dragon king Kazul by borrowing a faulty magic carpet from a giant. (Rev: BL 10/1/91; SLJ 12/91)

2434 Wrede, Patricia C. *Talking to Dragons* (6–10). Series: Enchanted Forest Chronicles. 1993, Harcourt $16.95 (0-15-284247-0). The fourth book in the series opens 16 years after *Calling on Dragons* with King Menenbar still imprisoned in his castle by a wizard's spells. (Rev: BL 8/93; VOYA 12/93)

2435 Wynne-Jones, Tim. *Some of the Kinder Planets* (5–8). 1995, Orchard LB $16.99 (0-531-08751-4). Nine imaginative stories about ordinary boys and girls in offbeat situations. (Rev: BCCB 5/95; BL 3/1/95*; HB 1–2/95, 5–6/95, 9–10/95; SLJ 4/95*)

2436 Yarbro, Chelsea Q. *Beyond the Waterlilies* (6–10). Illus. 1997, Simon & Schuster $17.00 (0-689-80732-5). Geena Howe has a unique talent — blending into paintings — and has an amazing adventure when she enters a huge Monet painting of water lilies in a castle moat. (Rev: BL 6/1–15/97; SLJ 6/97; VOYA 8/97)

2437 Yep, Laurence. *Dragon Cauldron* (6–10). 1991, HarperCollins paper $7.99 (0-06-440398-X). Monkey narrates this sequel to *Dragon Steel,* continuing the quest of a band of humans and wizards and Shimmer, a dragon princess, to fulfill Shimmer's task of repairing the damaged cauldron. (Rev: BL 5/15/91; SLJ 6/91)

2438 Yep, Laurence. *Dragon of the Lost Sea* (5–8). 1982, HarperCollins paper $5.99 (0-06-440227-4). Shimmer, a dragon, in the company of a boy, Thorn, sets out to destroy the villain Civet.

2439 Yep, Laurence. *Dragon Steel* (6–10). 1985, HarperCollins $12.95 (0-06-026748-8). The dragon princess Shimmer tries to save her people who are forced to work in an undersea volcano in this sequel to *Dragon of the Lost Sea.* (Rev: BL 5/15/85; SLJ 9/85; VOYA 8/85)

2440 Yep, Laurence. *Dragon War* (6–10). 1992, HarperCollins paper $6.99 (0-06-440525-7). In this sequel to *Dragon Cauldron,* the heroes use shape-changing magic and the help of a Dragon King to save the day. (Rev: BL 4/15/92; SLJ 6/92)

2441 Yep, Laurence. *The Tiger's Apprentice* (5–7). 2003, HarperCollins $15.99 (0-06-001013-4). A scary, magical world envelops Tom Lee when his grandmother dies in this novel set in San Francisco that includes elements of Chinese legend and tradition. (Rev: BL 7/03; HBG 10/03; SLJ 4/03)

2442 Yolen, Jane. *Boots and the Seven Leaguers: A Rock-and-Troll Novel* (5–9). 2000, Harcourt $17.00 (0-15-202557-X). In this lighthearted fantasy with a contemporary twist, adolescent troll Gog and his sidekick set out on a quest to rescue Gog's kidnapped little brother, Magog. (Rev: BL 11/1/00; HBG 3/01; SLJ 10/00)

2443 Yolen, Jane. *Hobby: The Young Merlin Trilogy Book Two* (5–8). Illus. Series: Young Merlin Trilogy. 1996, Harcourt $16.00 (0-15-200815-2). The story of Merlin's youth, when he sets out alone into the medieval world, is held captive by a villain named Fowler, and eventually joins a traveling magic show, where he is known as Hobby and where the performers take advantage of his ability to look into the future. Book one is *The Passager* (1996). (Rev: BL 1/1–15/97; SLJ 9/96)

2444 Yolen, Jane. *Merlin* (5–8). Series: Young Merlin Trilogy. 1997, Harcourt $16.00 (0-15-200814-4); Scholastic paper $3.50 (0-590-37119-3). In this concluding volume of a trilogy, Hawk-Hobby (Merlin) escapes from his enemies with a young friend who will later become King Arthur. (Rev: BL 4/15/97; SLJ 5/97)

2445 Yolen, Jane. *The One-Armed Queen* (8–10). 1998, Tor $23.95 (0-312-85243-6). Scillia, the adopted daughter of Queen Jenna, is being groomed to rule when her younger brother decides that he should become king. (Rev: VOYA 4/99)

2446 Yolen, Jane. *Passager: The Young Merlin Trilogy, Book One* (4–7). 1996, Harcourt $16.00 (0-15-200391-6). In medieval England, an abandoned 8-year-old boy named Merlin is taken in by a friendly man who becomes his master. Book two of the trilogy is *Hobby* (1996). (Rev: BL 5/1/96; HB 7–8/96; SLJ 5/96*)

2447 Yolen, Jane. *A Sending of Dragons* (7–12). Series: Pit Dragon. 1987, Harcourt paper $6.00 (0-15-200864-0). In this concluding volume of the trilogy, hero and heroine Jakkin and Akki are captured by primitive people who live underground. Previous volumes are *Dragon's Blood* and *Heart's Blood.* (Rev: BL 11/1/87; BR 11–12/87; SLJ 1/88)

2448 Yolen, Jane. *The Transfigured Hart: Nan* (5–8). 1997, Harcourt paper $5.00 (0-15-201195-1). Richard, a lonely 12-year-old orphan who lives with his aunt and uncle, and outgoing, popular Heather, 13, become friends as they make plans to find and capture a mysterious animal they see in the Five Mile Wood. (Rev: VOYA 4/98)

2449 Yolen, Jane. *Twelve Impossible Things Before Breakfast: Stories by Jane Yolen* (6–9). 1997, Harcourt $17.00 (0-15-201524-8). Twelve fantastic short stories on a variety of topics, including a variation on Peter Pan, are included in this collection by this prolific author. (Rev: BL 11/1/97; HBG 3/98; SLJ 12/97; VOYA 12/97)

2450 Yolen, Jane. *The Wild Hunt* (6–12). 1995, Harcourt $17.00 (0-15-200211-1). The myth of the Wild Hunt is combined with other European legends when Jerold and Gerund become pawns in a game between the Horned King Winter and his wife. (Rev: BL 6/1–15/95; SLJ 6/95; VOYA 12/95)

2451 Yolen, Jane, et al., eds. *Dragons and Dreams* (6–10). 1986, HarperCollins $12.95 (0-06-026792-5). A collection of 10 fantasy and some science fiction stories that can be a fine introduction to these genres. (Rev: BR 11–12/86; SLJ 5/86; VOYA 6/86)

2452 Yolen, Jane, and Robert J. Harris. *Odysseus in the Serpent Maze* (4–7). 2001, HarperCollins LB $16.89 (0-06-028735-7). This adventure story involves Odysseus as a teenager, when he was captured by pirates and experienced perilous obstacles and narrow escapes. (Rev: BCCB 5/01; BL 4/15/01; HBG 10/01; SLJ 7/01)

2453 Yoshi. *The Butterfly Hunt* (5–8). Illus. 1991, Picture Book paper $14.95 (0-88708-137-1). In this fantasy, a young boy releases a butterfly and forevermore it becomes his own. (Rev: SLJ 6/91)

2454 Youmans, Marly. *The Curse of the Raven Mocker* (5–8). 2003, Farrar $18.00 (0-374-31667-8). In pursuit of her parents, Adanta heads into the mountains of the Blue Ridge and finds a land of magic and sorcery in this novel based on Cherokee legend and local lore. (Rev: BL 9/1/03; SLJ 12/03)

Graphic Novels

2455 Asamiya, Kia. *Dark Angel: The Path to Destiny* (8–12). Illus. Series: Dark Angel. 2000, CPM Comics paper $15.95 (1-56219-827-7). In this first volume of a series of graphic novels, a young swordsman named Dark travels through time and different worlds to complete his moral journey. (Rev: BL 12/1/00)

2456 Avi. *City of Light, City of Dark: A Comic-Book Novel* (6–9). Illus. 1995, Orchard paper $7.95 (0-531-07058-1). In black-and-white comic book format, Sarah and her friend Carlos must save her father from the evil Underton and pay tribute to the

Kurbs before Manhattan freezes. (Rev: BL 9/15/93; VOYA 2/94)

2457 Brennan, Michael. *Electric Girl*, Vol. 2 (5–8). Illus. 2002, Mighty Gremlin paper $13.95 (0-970355-51-3). In this graphic novel, Virginia, who can release bursts of electricity at will, locks horns with evil gremlin Oogleeoog. (Rev: BL 5/1/02; SLJ 5/02)

2458 Dini, Paul. *The Batman Adventures: Dangerous Dames and Demons* (6–12). Illus. 2003, DC Comics paper $14.95 (1-56389-973-6). A collection of Batman stories originally published as single magazines. (Rev: BL 9/1/03)

2459 Dixon, Chuck. *Way of the Rat: The Walls of Zhumar* (7–12). Illus. 2003, CrossGeneration paper $15.95 (1-931484-51-1). Boon has stolen a scholar's magic ring and the Book of Hell and is now being chased by villains in this fantasy set in Asia and enhanced by dynamic illustrations. (Rev: BL 2/1/03)

2460 *Fairy Tales of Oscar Wilde* (5–8). 1992, Nantier $15.95 (1-56163-056-X). Cartoon art enlivens the retelling of two of Wilde's short stories. (Rev: BL 1/15/93) [741.5973]

2461 Geary, Rick. *The Borden Tragedy: A Memoir of the Infamous Double Murder at Fall River, Mass., 1892* (8–12). 1997, NBM paper $8.95 (1-56163-189-2). The unsolved Lizzie Borden murder case has intrigued many readers over the years, and this visual presentation provides a creative new way to examine the theories. (Rev: BL 2/1/03) [741.5973]

2462 Irwin, Jane, and Jeff Berndt. *Vogelein: Clockwork Faerie* (5–12). Illus. 2003, Fiery Studios paper $12.95 (0-9743110-0-6). A beautiful 17th-century mechanical fairy who is immortal but depends on others to wind her up stars in this graphic novel. (Rev: BL 11/1/03)

2463 Kesel, Barbara. *Meridian: Flying Solo* (7–12). Illus. Series: Meridian. 2003, CrossGeneration paper $9.95 (1-931484-54-6). Sephie inherits her father's position as first minister of Meridian, a floating city, and must use her magical powers to battle an evil uncle. (Rev: BL 4/1/03)

2464 London, Jack. *Graphic Classics: Jack London* (5–8). Illus. 2003, Eureka paper $9.95 (0-9712464-5-9). Short stories by London are illustrated by diverse artists, some using a comic-book style, others with more traditional graphics. (Rev: BL 7/03; VOYA 10/03)

2465 McCaffrey, Anne. *Dragonflight* (6–12). Adapted by Brynne Stephens. Illus. Series: Dragonriders of Pern. 1991, Eclipse Books $4.95 (1-56060-074-8). Book one of a three-part graphic novel based on *Dragonflight* from the Dragonriders of Pern series. (Rev: BL 9/1/91)

2466 McCloud, Scott. *The New Adventures of Abraham Lincoln* (7–10). 1998, Homage Comics paper $19.00 (1-887-27987-3). Time travel, an encounter with Abraham Lincoln, and an alien attempt to rule America are some of the adventures faced by a middle-school student when he is sent to detention. (Rev: BL 2/1/03)

2467 Mizuno, Ryo. *Record of Lodoss War: The Grey Witch — Birth of a New Knight* (7–12). Series: Grey Witch Trilogy. 2000, CPM Comics $15.95 (1-56219-928-S). This graphic novel is the second volume of the Grey Witch Trilogy and tells how Pam struggles to learn the identity of his father in a universe where gods, goddesses, and goblins exist. (Rev: BL 12/1/00)

2468 Muth, Jon. *Swamp Thing: Roots* (8–12). 1998, DC Comics paper $7.95 (1-56389-377-0). Visual images enhance this story of the supernatural elements that influence life in a small community. (Rev: BL 2/1/03)

2469 Nishiyama, Yuriko. *Harlem Beat* (8–12). 1999, TokyoPop paper $9.95 (1-892-21304-4). Created and produced in Japan, this graphic novel follows the adventures of an urban, teenage boy who loves basketball. (Rev: BL 2/1/03)

2470 Russell, P. Craig. *Fairy Tales of Oscar Wilde, Vol. 3: The Birthday of the Infanta* (5–8). Illus. 1998, NBM $15.95 (1-56163-213-9). A graphic-novel version of Wilde's fairy tale about the misshapen dwarf who dies of a broken heart. (Rev: BL 4/1/99)

2471 Seto, Andy. *Crouching Tiger, Hidden Dragon* (7–12). Illus. 2002, ComicsOne paper $13.95 (1-58899-999-8). A comic book version of the first installment of the martial arts story that was made into a successful movie. (Rev: BL 4/1/03)

2472 Sfar, Joann. *Little Vampire Does Kung Fu!* (4–7). Illus. 2003, Simon & Schuster $12.95 (0-689-85769-1). An oversize comic book combining humor and fantasy in which Little Vampire rescues Michael from a bully and Michael learns martial arts. (Rev: BL 9/15/03; SLJ 12/03)

2473 Shanower, Eric. *Age of Bronze: A Thousand Ships* (8–12). 2001, Image Comics paper $19.95 (1-58240-200-0). Mythological images and events fill this fast-paced retelling of events connected to the Trojan War. (Rev: BL 2/1/03)

2474 Slott, Dan, et al. *Justice League Adventures* (5–8). Illus. 2003, DC Comics paper $9.95 (1-56389-954-X). Seven stories that each stand alone come from the comic book series of the same name and feature such familiar names as Superman, Batman, and Wonder Woman, battling the usual villains. (Rev: BL 8/03)

2475 Sturm, James. *The Golem's Mighty Swing* (7–12). 2001, Drawn & Quarterly paper $16.95 (1-89659-745-9). A Jewish baseball team's efforts to win in the 1920s lead to a dangerous stunt that features an African American player who is portrayed as a mythical Golem. (Rev: BL 2/1/03)

2476 Templeton, Ty. *Batman Gotham Adventures* (5–10). 2000, DC Comics paper $9.95 (1-56389-616-8). This graphic novel offers six short stories about Batman, Catwoman, Robin, and the usual villains, drawn by Rick Burkett and others. (Rev: BL 12/1/00)

2477 Tolkien, J. R. R. *The Hobbit; or, There and Back Again* (5–10). Adapted by Charles Dixon and Sean Deming. Illus. 1990, Eclipse Books paper $12.95 (0-345-36858-4). The classic story of Bilbo Baggins and his companions is introduced to reluctant readers in this full-color graphic novel. (Rev: BL 9/1/91)

2478 Waid, Mark. *Ruse: Inferno of Blue* (7–12). 2002, CrossGeneration paper $15.95 (1-931484-19-8). Mystery, action, and magical powers abound in this graphic novel set in an alternate universe and starring detective Simon Archard and sidekick Emma Bishop. (Rev: BL 8/02)

2479 Warner, Allen. *Ninja Boy: Faded Dreams* (8–12). 2003, DC Comics paper $14.95 (1-4012-0102-4). The first six issues of *Ninja Boy* are collected in this Japanese *anime* tale of Nakio, who is seeking to avenge his family, which has suffered at the hands of the evil Mikaboshi. (Rev: BL 11/1/03)

2480 Winick, Judd. *Pedro and Me: Friendship, Loss, and What I Learned* (8–12). Illus. 2000, Holt paper $16.00 (0-8050-6403-6). A graphic novel tribute to Pedro Zamora, an AIDS educator and actor who died of HIV complications at the age of 22. (Rev: BL 9/15/00; HB 11–12/00; HBG 3/01; SLJ 10/00)

Historical Fiction and Foreign Lands

Prehistory

2481 Brennan, J. H. *Shiva Accused: An Adventure of the Ice Age* (6–9). 1991, HarperCollins LB $16.89 (0-06-020742-6). In this sequel to *Shiva* (o.p.), a prehistoric orphan girl is accused of murder by a rival tribe. (Rev: BL 8/91; SLJ 11/91)

2482 Brennan, J. H. *Shiva's Challenge: An Adventure of the Ice Age* (6–9). 1992, HarperCollins LB $16.89 (0-06-020826-0). In the third entry in the series, Cro-Magnon Shiva is spirited away by the shamanistic Crones to test her powers and see if she can survive the ordeals that will make her a Crone, too. (Rev: BL 12/15/92)

2483 Cowley, Marjorie. *Anooka's Answer* (5–8). Illus. 1998, Clarion $16.00 (0-395-88530-2). Set in prehistoric times, this sequel to *Dar and the Spear-Thrower* introduces 13-year-old Anooka and her

quest to find her missing mother. (Rev: BL 11/15/98; BR 5–6/99; HBG 3/99; SLJ 12/98)

2484 Cowley, Marjorie. *Dar and the Spear-Thrower* (5–7). 1994, Clarion $15.00 (0-395-68132-4). This is the story of Dar, a boy growing up in the Cro-Magnon period, and the problems he faces when beginning to accept adult responsibilities. (Rev: BL 8/94; SLJ 9/94)

2485 Denzel, Justin. *Boy of the Painted Cave* (5–7). 1988, Putnam $17.99 (0-399-21559-X). The story of a boy who longs to be a cave artist, set in Cro Magnon times. (Rev: BL 11/1/88; SLJ 11/88)

2486 Dickinson, Peter. *A Bone from a Dry Sea* (7–10). 1993, Dell paper $4.99 (0-440-21928-0). The protagonists are Li, a girl in a tribe of "sea apes" living four million years ago, and Vinny, the teenage daughter of a modern-day paleontologist. (Rev: BL 2/1/93; SLJ 4/93*)

2487 Dickinson, Peter. *Noli's Story* (4–8). Series: The Kin. 1998, Grosset $14.99 (0-399-23328-8). Noli, his friend Suth, and three other orphaned children of a prehistoric clan experience many adventures before they are eventually reunited with the adults of their society. (Rev: HBG 3/99; SLJ 1/99)

2488 Dickinson, Peter. *Po's Story* (7–10). Series: The Kin. 1998, Grosset $14.99 (0-399-23349-0); paper $3.99 (0-448-41711-1). In prehistoric times, Po sets out to find water for his people and instead finds a different tribe of people. (Rev: VOYA 10/99)

2489 Dickinson, Peter. *Suth's Story* (4–7). Series: The Kin. 1998, Grosset $14.99 (0-399-23327-X). In this opening volume of the series, two orphans, Suth and Noli, along with some other children, find a lush new home in the crater of a volcano. (Rev: BL 8/98; HBG 3/99; SLJ 1/99)

2490 Turnbull, Ann. *Maroo of the Winter Caves* (4–7). 1984, Houghton paper $6.95 (0-395-54795-4). A story centered on semi-nomadic people who lived in southern Europe during the last Ice Age.

Ancient and Medieval History

GENERAL AND MISCELLANEOUS

2491 Branford, Henrietta. *The Fated Sky* (8–12). 1999, Candlewick $16.99 (0-7636-0775-4). Set in Viking times, this novel tells of 16-year-old Ran and how she is saved from becoming a human sacrifice by a blind musician, Toki, with whom she later falls in love. (Rev: BL 12/1/99; HB 11–12/99; HBG 4/00; SLJ 11/99)

2492 Cadnum, Michael. *Daughter of the Wind* (7–10). 2003, Scholastic $17.95 (0-439-35224-X). Norse culture and atmosphere are strong in this action-packed and violent story of three young people facing danger in the time of the Vikings. (Rev: BL 11/15/03; SLJ 12/03)

2493 Cadnum, Michael. *Raven of the Waves* (7–10). 2001, Scholastic $17.95 (0-531-30334-9). In this gory tale set in the 8th century, 17-year-old Viking Lidsmod takes part in a bloodthirsty raid on an English community but later helps a boy who is taken captive. (Rev: BL 4/1/01; HB 9–10/01; HBG 3/02; SLJ 7/01; VOYA 8/01)

2494 Carter, Dorothy Sharp. *His Majesty, Queen Hatshepsut* (6–9). 1987, HarperCollins LB $16.89 (0-397-32179-1). A fictionalized biography of Queen Hatshepsut, daughter of Thutmose I and the only female pharaoh of Egypt. (Rev: BR 3–4/88; SLJ 10/87; VOYA 12/87)

2495 Chen, Da. *Wandering Warrior* (8–12). 2003, Delacorte $15.95 (0-385-73020-9). Luka, 12, must survive on his own when he is separated from his teacher, Atami, in this adventure set in ancient China featuring monsters, kung fu, violent confrontations, and magic. (Rev: BL 2/15/03; SLJ 2/03; VOYA 6/03)

2496 Fletcher, Susan. *Shadow Spinner* (7–10). 1998, Simon & Schuster $17.00 (0-689-81852-1). The story of Shahrazad and how she collected the tales that kept her and her harem companions alive for 1,001 nights. (Rev: BCCB 7–8/98; BL 6/1–15/98; BR 1–2/99; HB 7–8/98; HBG 10/98; SLJ 6/98; VOYA 4/99)

2497 Gormley, Beatrice. *Miriam* (6–8). 1999, Eerdmans paper $6.00 (0-8028-5156-8). The story of how Moses' older sister, Miriam, was able to save her young brother's life and how she grew to enjoy living in the pharaoh's palace after she became a servant there. (Rev: BL 4/1/99; SLJ 5/99)

2498 Lester, Julius. *Pharaoh's Daughter: A Novel of Ancient Egypt* (6–9). 2000, Harcourt $17.00 (0-15-201826-3). The grandeur of ancient Egypt is re-created in this novel of young Moses and the sister who saved him. (Rev: BL 4/1/00; HB 7–8/00; HBG 9/00; SLJ 6/00; VOYA 6/00)

2499 Levitin, Sonia. *Escape from Egypt* (8–10). 1996, Puffin paper $5.99 (0-14-037537-6). Historical fiction related to the biblical tale of the Exodus told from the point of view of two teens. (Rev: BL 5/1/94*; SLJ 4/94; VOYA 4/94)

2500 McCaffrey, Anne. *Black Horses for the King* (5–8). 1996, Harcourt $17.00 (0-15-227322-0). In this historical novel set in 5th-century Roman Britain, young Galwyn is hired by Lord Artos (later King Arthur) to help find and transport giant Libyan horses from continental Europe to Britain, where Galwyn trains them for the wars against the Saxons. (Rev: BL 6/1–15/96; SLJ 6/96; VOYA 12/96)

2501 McCaughrean, Geraldine. *Casting the Gods Adrift: A Tale of Ancient Egypt* (5–8). 2003, Cricket $15.95 (0-8126-2684-2). History and fiction are intertwined in this well-illustrated, suspenseful novel about two boys who are content to be taken in by the Pharoah Akhenaten, and a father enraged by the Pharaoh's refusal to worship the traditional Egyptian gods. (Rev: BCCB 10/03; BL 10/15/03; SLJ 8/03)

2502 McCaughrean, Geraldine. *The Kite Rider* (6–9). 2002, HarperCollins $15.95 (0-06-623874-9). The shock of watching his father's death propels Haoyou, 12, into a series of adventures that include becoming a circus kite rider in this story set in ancient China. (Rev: BCCB 7–8/02; BL 5/15/02; HB 7–8/02; HBG 10/02; SLJ 6/02*; VOYA 6/02)

2503 Miklowitz, Gloria D. *Masada: The Last Fortress* (7–10). 1998, Eerdmans $16.00 (0-8028-5165-7). The siege of Masada comes alive through the eyes of a young Jewish man and a Roman commander. (Rev: BCCB 10/98; BL 10/1/98; HBG 3/99; SLJ 12/98; VOYA 2/99)

2504 Pfitsch, Patricia C. *The Deeper Song* (8–10). 1998, Simon & Schuster $16.00 (0-689-81183-7). In this story, set at the time of King Solomon, a high-spirited girl named Judith decides to write down the oral traditions of the Jewish people, thus creating a book that will become a cornerstone of Judaism. (Rev: BL 10/1/98; HBG 3/99; SLJ 11/98; VOYA 8/99)

2505 Speare, Elizabeth G. *The Bronze Bow* (7–10). 1961, Houghton paper $6.95 (0-395-13719-5). A Jewish boy seeks revenge against the Romans who killed his parents, but finally his hatred abates when he hears the messages and teachings of Jesus. Newbery Medal winner, 1962. (Rev: BL 9/1/95)

GREECE AND ROME

2506 Alcock, Vivien. *Singer to the Sea God* (5–8). 1995, Dell paper $3.99 (0-440-41003-7). Epic tales — from Scylla and Charybdis to Perseus and the Gorgon — are interwoven with the story of runaway slaves. (Rev: BCCB 2/93; BL 5/1/93; HB 7–8/93; SLJ 3/93)

2507 Blacklock, Dyan. *Pankration: The Ultimate Game* (5–8). 1999, Albert Whitman paper $5.95 (0-8075-6324-2). An exciting, far-fetched story set in ancient Greece about two friends, separated by a shipwreck, who are reunited at the Olympic Games during the Pankration, a combination wrestling and boxing sport. (Rev: BCCB 6/99; HBG 10/99; SLJ 4/99)

2508 Cooney, Caroline B. *Goddess of Yesterday* (7–12). 2002, Delacorte $15.95 (0-385-72945-6). Young Anaxandra adopts a false identity and is given a home by King Menelaus of Sparta despite the suspicions of the king's wife, Helen, in this exciting novel set in the build-up to the Trojan War. (Rev: BCCB 7–8/02; BL 6/1–15/02; HBG 10/02; SLJ 6/02; VOYA 8/02)

2509 McLaren, Clemence. *Aphrodite's Blessings: Love Stories from the Greek Myths* (7–12). 2002, Simon & Schuster $16.00 (0-689-84377-1). The lot of women in ancient Greece comes to life in three stories, based on mythology, about Atalanta, Andromeda, and Psyche. (Rev: BL 3/1/02; HBG 10/02; SLJ 1/02; VOYA 4/02)

2510 McLaren, Clemence. *Inside the Walls of Troy* (7–10). 1996, Simon & Schuster $17.00 (0-689-31820-0). The story of the Trojan War and the fall of Troy as told by Helen, the lover of Paris, and by Cassandra, who foresees the tragedy to come. (Rev: BL 10/15/96; BR 5–6/97; SLJ 10/96; VOYA 2/97)

2511 Napoli, Donna Jo. *The Great God Pan* (7–10). 2003, Random $15.95 (0-385-32777-2). A beautifully written novel about the life and aspirations of Pan, who was half man and half goat. (Rev: BL 4/15/03)

2512 Napoli, Donna Jo. *Sirena* (7–12). 1998, Scholastic $15.95 (0-590-38388-4); paper $4.99 (0-590-38389-2). This romantic expansion of the Greek myth of the Sirens describes the dilemma of an immortal mermaid who loves a mortal. (Rev: BL 1/1–15/03; BR 11–12/98; HBG 3/99; SLJ 10/98; VOYA 12/98)

2513 Rubalcaba, Jill. *The Wadjet Eye* (5–8). 2000, Clarion $15.00 (0-395-68942-2). After mummifying his dead mother, Damon sets off to find his father and is later hired by Cleopatra as a spy in this action-filled novel set in the Roman Empire of 45 B.C. (Rev: BL 5/15/00; HBG 10/00; SLJ 6/00; VOYA 6/00)

2514 Sutcliff, Rosemary. *The Eagle of the Ninth* (7–12). 1993, Farrar paper $5.95 (0-374-41930-2). A reissue of the historical novel about the Roman legion that went to battle and disappeared. (Rev: BR 1–2/87)

MIDDLE AGES

2515 Alder, Elizabeth. *The King's Shadow* (7–12). 1995, Bantam paper $5.50 (0-440-22011-4). In medieval Britain, mute Evyn is sold into slavery, but as Earl Harold of Wessex's squire and eventual foster son, he chronicles the king's life and becomes a storyteller. (Rev: BL 7/95; SLJ 7/95)

2516 Avi. *Crispin: The Cross of Lead* (5–9). 2002, Hyperion $16.49 (0-7868-2647-9). Thirteen-year-old orphan Crispin seeks protection from a juggler named Bear in this complex novel set in medieval England. Newbery Medal winner, 2003. (Rev: BL 5/15/02; HB 9–10/02; HBG 3/03; SLJ 6/02*)

2517 Barrett, Tracy. *Anna of Byzantium* (5–7). 1999, Delacorte $14.95 (0-385-32626-2). A novel about Anna Comnena, a medieval princess who was cheated out of her right to inherit the throne of Byzantium by her brother, John. (Rev: BL 4/1/99; HB 7–8/99; HBG 10/99; SLJ 7/99; VOYA 10/99)

2518 Cadnum, Michael. *The Book of the Lion* (7–12). 2000, Viking $15.99 (0-670-88386-7). Edmund, a young apprentice, is pressed into service as squire to a knight going to the Holy Land to fight in the Crusades. (Rev: BL 2/1/00; HB 3–4/00; HBG 9/00; SLJ 3/00; VOYA 4/00)

2519 Cadnum, Michael. *Forbidden Forest* (7–10). 2002, Scholastic $17.99 (0-439-31774-6). The story of Little John's entry into Robin Hood's band of merry men is told from John's point of view and combines realistic descriptions of medieval life with adventure and romance. (Rev: BL 4/15/02; HB 7–8/02; HBG 10/02; SLJ 6/02; VOYA 4/02)

2520 Cadnum, Michael. *In a Dark Wood* (7–10). 1998, Orchard LB $18.99 (0-531-33071-0). The story of Robin Hood as seen through the eyes of the sheriff of Nottingham and his young squire, Hugh. (Rev: BL 3/1/98; BR 11–12/98; HB 3–4/98; HBG 9/98; SLJ 4/98; VOYA 8/98)

2521 Cadnum, Michael. *The Leopard Sword* (7–10). 2002, Viking $15.99 (0-670-89908-9). Cadnum weaves realistic detail into this fictional story of crusaders returning to England after a long and dangerous journey only to meet new challenges. A sequel to *The Book of the Lion* (2000). (Rev: BCCB 1/03; BL 8/02; HBG 3/03; SLJ 10/02; VOYA 12/02)

2522 Crowley, Bridget. *Feast of Fools* (6–9). 2003, Simon & Schuster $15.95 (0-689-86512-0). In 13th-century England, a stonecarver's son, known as Peg-Leg for his injury in the accident that killed his father, struggles to defend Jews accused of murder. (Rev: BCCB 2/04; BL 11/15/03)

2523 Cushman, Karen. *Catherine, Called Birdy* (6–9). 1994, Clarion $16.00 (0-395-68186-3). Life in the last decade of the 12th century as seen through the eyes of a teenage girl. (Rev: BL 4/15/94; SLJ 6/94*; VOYA 6/94)

2524 Cushman, Karen. *Matilda Bone* (4–8). 2000, Clarion $15.00 (0-395-88156-0). Set in the 14th century, this novel describes the development of Matilda, 13, who serves as an assistant to the local bone setter in exchange for food and shelter. (Rev: BCCB 12/00; BL 8/00; HB 11–12/00; HBG 3/01; SLJ 9/00*; VOYA 12/00)

2525 Cushman, Karen. *The Midwife's Apprentice* (7–12). 1995, Clarion $12.00 (0-395-69229-6). A homeless young woman in medieval England becomes strong as she picks herself up and learns from a midwife to be brave. (Rev: BL 3/15/95*; SLJ 5/95)

2526 Dana, Barbara. *Young Joan* (6–10). 1991, HarperCollins $17.95 (0-06-021422-8); paper $6.99 (0-06-440661-X). A fictional account of Joan of Arc that questions how a simple French farm girl hears, assimilates, and acts upon a message from God. (Rev: BL 5/15/91*; SLJ 5/91)

2527 Goodman, Joan E. *The Winter Hare* (4–8). Illus. 1996, Houghton $17.00 (0-395-78569-3). In 12th-century England, Will becomes a page to the wicked Earl Aubrey. (Rev: BCCB 2/97; BL 11/15/96; BR 9–10/97; SLJ 11/96; VOYA 2/97)

2528 Goodman, Joan Elizabeth. *Peregrine* (7–10). 2000, Houghton $15.00 (0-395-97729-0). Fifteen-year-old Lady Edith, who has lost her husband and baby, escapes her problems by going on a pilgrimage from England to the Holy Land. (Rev: BL 4/1/00; HBG 9/00; SLJ 5/00; VOYA 6/00)

2529 Haahr, Berit. *The Minstrel's Tale* (6–9). 2000, Delacorte $15.95 (0-385-32713-7). In medieval England, musically talented young Judith runs away from her older husband to join a band of minstrels. (Rev: BL 7/00; HBG 3/01; SLJ 1/01; VOYA 2/01)

2530 Jordan, Sherryl. *The Raging Quiet* (8–12). 1999, Simon & Schuster $17.00 (0-689-82140-9). In this novel set in the Middle Ages, 16-year-old Marnie is shunned when she befriends the local madman, whom she discovers is only deaf, not mad. (Rev: BL 5/1/99; HBG 9/99; SLJ 5/99; VOYA 8/99)

2531 Malone, Patricia. *Legend of Lady Ilena* (6–9). 2002, Random $15.95 (0-385-72915-4). Fifteen-year-old warrior Ilena, living in 6th-century Britain, relates her adventures as she follows her dying father's instructions. (Rev: BL 1/1–15/02; HBG 10/02; SLJ 1/02; VOYA 2/03)

2532 Morressy, John. *The Juggler* (7–10). 1996, Holt $16.95 (0-8050-4217-2); paper $5.95 (0-06-447174-8). In this adventure story set in the Middle Ages, a young man regrets the bargain he has made with the devil to become the world's greatest juggler in exchange for his soul. (Rev: BR 11–12/96; SLJ 6/96; VOYA 8/96)

2533 Morris, Gerald. *The Ballad of Sir Dinadan* (5–9). 2003, Houghton $15.00 (0-618-19099-6). An amusing retelling from Arthurian legend that features the younger brother of Sir Tristram as a music lover and reluctant knight. (Rev: BL 5/1/03; HB 5–6/03; HBG 10/03; SLJ 4/03*; VOYA 6/03)

2534 Morris, Gerald. *The Squire, His Knight, and His Lady* (5–9). 1999, Houghton $15.00 (0-395-91211-3). This is a retelling, from the perspective of a knight's squire, of the classic story of Sir Gawain and the Green Knight. (Rev: BL 5/1/99; HBG 10/99; SLJ 5/99; VOYA 8/99)

2535 Morris, Gerald. *The Squire's Tale* (5–9). 1998, Houghton $15.00 (0-395-86959-5). The peaceful existence of 14-year-old Terence is shattered when he becomes the squire of Sir Gawain and becomes involved in a series of quests. (Rev: BL 4/15/98; BR 11–12/98; HB 7–8/98; SLJ 7/98; VOYA 8/98)

2536 O'Dell, Scott. *The Road to Damietta* (7–10). 1987, Fawcett paper $6.50 (0-449-70233-2). A novel set in 13th-century Italy and involving St. Francis of Assisi. (Rev: SLJ 12/85; VOYA 2/86)

2537 Pernoud, Regine. *A Day with a Miller* (4–7). Trans. by Dominique Clift. 1997, Runestone LB $22.60 (0-8225-1914-3). A description of the life of a miller and his family in the 12th century and how hydraulic energy was being introduced at that time. (Rev: HBG 3/98; SLJ 3/98)

2538 Pyle, Howard. *Men of Iron* (6–9). Adapted by Earle Hitchner. Illus. 1930, Troll paper $5.95 (0-8167-1872-5). The days of chivalry are re-created in this tale that takes place during the reign of King Henry IV. A reissue.

2539 Pyle, Howard. *Otto of the Silver Hand* (6–8). 1967, Dover paper $8.95 (0-486-21784-1). Life in feudal Germany, the turbulence and cruelty of robber barons, and the peaceful, scholarly pursuits of the monks are presented in the story of the kidnapped son of a robber baron.

2540 Rosen, Sidney, and Dorothy S. Rosen. *The Magician's Apprentice* (5–8). 1994, Carolrhoda LB $19.95 (0-87614-809-7). An orphan in a French abbey in the Middle Ages is accused of having a heretical document in his possession and is sent to spy on Roger Bacon, the English scientist. (Rev: BL 5/1/94; SLJ 6/94)

2541 Sauerwein, Leigh. *Song for Eloise* (8–10). 2003, Front Street $15.95 (1-886910-90-1). In the Middle Ages, an unhappy wife falls for a passing troubadour in a rich text full of historical detail. (Rev: BL 12/1/03; SLJ 12/03)

2542 Skurzynski, Gloria. *Spider's Voice* (8–12). 1999, Simon & Schuster $16.95 (0-689-82149-2). A retelling of the classic love story — set in 12th-century France — between the young teacher Abelard and his pupil, the beautiful Eloise. (Rev: BL 2/15/99; HBG 9/99; SLJ 3/99; VOYA 4/99)

2543 Springer, Nancy. *I Am Mordred: A Tale from Camelot* (7–12). 1998, Putnam $16.99 (0-399-23143-9). Told in the first person, this is the story of Mordred, bastard son of King Arthur, who is destined to kill his father. (Rev: BL 4/15/98; BR 1–2/99; HB 3–4/98; HBG 10/98; SLJ 5/98; VOYA 4/98)

2544 Springer, Nancy. *I Am Morgan le Fay: A Tale from Camelot* (6–10). 2001, Putnam $17.99 (0-399-23451-9). The legend of Morgan le Fay is expanded and enriched in this retelling, in which Morgan expresses her resentment of her older sister, Morgause, and her destructive love for Thomas. (Rev: BL 2/1/01; HB 1–2/01; HBG 10/01; SLJ 3/01; VOYA 2/01)

2545 Temple, Frances. *The Beduins' Gazelle* (7–10). 1996, Orchard LB $16.99 (0-531-08869-3). In this 14th-century adventure, a companion piece to *The*

Ramsey Scallop, young scholar Etienne becomes involved in the lives of two lovers when he goes to Fez to study at the university. (Rev: BL 2/15/96; BR 9–10/96; SLJ 4/96*; VOYA 12/96)

2546 Temple, Frances. *The Ramsay Scallop* (7–10). 1994, Orchard LB $19.99 (0-531-08686-0). In 1299, 14-year-old Elenor and her betrothed nobleman are sent on a chaste pilgrimage to Spain and hear the stories of their fellow travelers. (Rev: BL 3/15/94*; SLJ 5/94; VOYA 4/94)

2547 Thomson, Sarah L. *The Dragon's Son* (7–12). 2001, Scholastic $17.95 (0-531-30333-0). This historical novel, based on Welsh legends about King Arthur, tells the stories of family members and others who were involved in Arthur's life. (Rev: BCCB 7–8/01; BL 5/1/01; HBG 10/01; SLJ 7/01; VOYA 6/01)

2548 Tingle, Rebecca. *The Edge on the Sword* (7–10). 2001, Putnam $19.99 (0-399-23580-9). This fascinating novel set in Britain in the late 800s describes the exploits of 15-year-old Aethelflaed, daughter of King Alfred of West Saxony, who is engaged to an older man she doesn't know and is allowed the freedom to learn many skills. (Rev: BCCB 10/01; BL 4/15/01; HBG 10/01; SLJ 7/01*; VOYA 8/01)

2549 Tomlinson, Theresa. *The Forestwife* (8–12). 1995, Orchard LB $17.99 (0-531-08750-6). A Robin Hood legend with Marian as the benevolent Green Lady of the forest. (Rev: BL 3/1/95*; SLJ 3/95; VOYA 5/95)

2550 Voigt, Cynthia. *Jackaroo* (8–10). 1985, Macmillan $20.00 (0-689-31123-0). In this novel set in the Middle Ages, a 16-year-old girl assumes the identity of a Robin Hood-like character named Jackaroo. (Rev: BL 9/15/85; SLJ 12/85)

2551 Wein, Elizabeth E. *A Coalition of Lions* (7–12). Series: The Winter Prince. 2003, Viking $16.99 (0-370-03618-8). In the 6th century, a princess named Goewin travels from Britain to Africa on her way to an arranged marriage, in this absorbing sequel to *The Winter Prince* (1993). (Rev: BCCB 4/03; BL 2/15/03; SLJ 4/03)

2552 Williams, Laura. *The Executioner's Daughter* (5–8). 2000, Holt $16.95 (0-8050-6234-3). Set in England during the Middle Ages, this is the story of poor Lily who, after her mother dies, must assume the position of helping her father, an official executioner. (Rev: BCCB 5/00; BL 4/1/00; HBG 10/00; SLJ 6/00)

2553 Yolen, Jane, ed. *Sherwood: Original Stories from the World of Robin Hood* (4–9). 2000, Philomel $19.99 (0-399-23182-X). Nine short stories using Robin Hood and his men as the central characters. (Rev: BCCB 9/00; HBG 10/00; SLJ 8/00; VOYA 6/00)

2554 Yolen, Jane. *Sword of the Rightful King* (6–9). 2003, Harcourt $17.00 (0-15-202527-8). The story of Arthur and the sword in the stone gets a new ending in this novel peopled with the characters of legend. (Rev: BL 4/15/03*; HB 5–6/03; HBG 10/03; SLJ 7/03*; VOYA 6/03)

Africa

2555 Burns, Khephra. *Mansa Musa: The Lion of Mali* (4–7). 2001, Harcourt $18.00 (0-15-200375-4). Lavish illustrations complement this handsome, challenging book about Mansa Musa's journey from a rural village boyhood to becoming the king of Mali. (Rev: BL 12/1/01; HB 11–12/01; HBG 3/02; SLJ 10/01)

2556 Dickinson, Peter. *AK* (7–10). 1992, Dell paper $3.99 (0-440-21897-7). A young soldier survives a bloody civil war in an African country but must use his gun again after his father is kidnapped during a military coup. (Rev: BL 4/15/92; SLJ 7/92)

2557 Farmer, Nancy. *A Girl Named Disaster* (6–10). 1996, Orchard paper $19.95 (0-531-09539-8). Set in modern-day Africa, this is the story, with fantasy undertones, of Nhamo, who flees from her home in Mozambique to escape a planned marriage and settles with her father's family in Zimbabwe. (Rev: BL 9/1/96; SLJ 10/96*; VOYA 12/96)

2558 Ferreira, Anton. *Zulu Dog* (5–8). 2002, Farrar $16.00 (0-374-39223-4). Modern South Africa is the setting for this story, in which a racist white man has a change of heart when his daughter Shirley is rescued by a black boy's puppy. (Rev: BCCB 1/03; BL 9/15/02; HB 11–12/02; HBG 3/03; SLJ 9/02; VOYA 2/03)

2559 Gregory, Kristiana. *Cleopatra VII: Daughter of the Nile* (5–8). Series: Royal Diaries. 1999, Scholastic paper $10.95 (0-590-81975-5). This mock-diary recounts various events in the life of 12-year-old Cleopatra who, even at that age, was involved in palace intrigue. (Rev: BL 1/1–15/00; HBG 3/00; SLJ 10/99)

2560 Kehret, Peg. *The Secret Journey* (4–7). 1999, Pocket $16.00 (0-671-03416-2). In 1834, 12-year-old stowaway Emma is washed ashore on the coast of Liberia and must survive by learning from the chimps she observes. (Rev: BL 1/1–15/00; HBG 10/00; SLJ 3/00; VOYA 6/00)

2561 Kessler, Cristina. *No Condition Is Permanent* (8–12). 2000, Putnam $17.99 (0-399-23486-1). Fourteen-year-old Jodie, who has moved to Sierra Leone with her mother, tries to prevent the female circumcision of her new friend, Khadi. (Rev: BL 12/1/99; HBG 9/00; SLJ 2/00; VOYA 4/00)

2562 Kurtz, Jane. *Saba: Under the Hyena's Foot* (5–8). Series: Girls of Many Lands. 2003, Pleasant $15.95 (1-58485-829-X); paper $7.95 (1-58485-

747-1). Although she has been living a simple country life, 12-year-old Saba discovers she is in fact a member of the ruling family in this novel set in 19th-century Ethiopia and full of cultural and historical detail. (Rev: BL 10/1/03; SLJ 10/03)

2563 Kurtz, Jane. *The Storyteller's Beads* (5–8). Illus. 1998, Harcourt $15.00 (0-15-201074-2). Two Ethiopian refugees, one a girl from a traditional Ethiopian culture and the other a blind Jewish girl, overcome generations of prejudice against Jews when they face common danger as they flee war and famine during the 1980s. (Rev: BCCB 9/98; BL 5/1/98; HBG 10/98; SLJ 7/98; VOYA 10/98)

2564 Levitin, Sonia. *Dream Freedom* (5–9). 2000, Harcourt $17.00 (0-15-202404-2). A novel that graphically portrays the plight of Sudanese slaves, juxtaposed with the story of an American 5th-grade class that joins the fight to free them. (Rev: BL 11/1/00; HBG 3/01; SLJ 10/00; VOYA 12/00)

2565 McDaniel, Lurlene. *Angel of Hope* (7–10). 2000, Bantam paper $8.95 (0-553-57148-6). In this sequel to *Angel of Mercy,* Heather returns from missionary work in Uganda and, in her place, her younger, spoiled sister, Amber, continues the work in Africa. (Rev: BL 5/1/00; HBG 9/00)

2566 McDaniel, Lurlene. *Angel of Mercy* (7–10). 1999, Bantam $8.95 (0-553-57145-1). Heather is not prepared for the misery she finds in Uganda where she is a volunteer, but falling in love with handsome Ian, another volunteer, helps takes her mind off her problems. (Rev: BL 1/1–15/00; HBG 4/00; SLJ 1/00)

2567 McKissack, Patricia. *Nzingha: Warrior Queen of Matamba* (5–8). Illus. Series: Royal Diaries. 2000, Scholastic paper $10.95 (0-439-11210-9). Based on fact, this is the story of 17th-century African queen Nzingha who, in present-day Angola, resisted the Portuguese colonizers and slave traders. (Rev: BL 11/1/00; HBG 3/01; SLJ 12/00)

2568 Marston, Elsa. *The Ugly Goddess* (5–8). 2002, Cricket $16.95 (0-8126-2667-2). In 523 B.C. Egypt, a 14-year-old Egyptian princess, a young Greek soldier who is in love with her, and an Egyptian boy become embroiled in a mystery adventure that blends fact, fiction, and fantasy. (Rev: BL 1/1–15/03; HBG 3/03; SLJ 12/02)

2569 Naidoo, Beverley. *No Turning Back* (5–9). 1997, HarperCollins $15.89 (0-06-027506-5). Jaabu, a homeless African boy, looks for shelter in contemporary Johannesburg. (Rev: BCCB 2/97; BL 12/15/96*; BR 9–10/97; HB 3–4/97; SLJ 2/97; VOYA 10/97)

2570 Quintana, Anton. *The Baboon King* (8–12). Trans. by John Nieuwenhuizen. 1999, Walker $16.95 (0-8027-8711-8). After being exiled by his East African tribe after accidentally killing a tribesman, arrogant Morengru joins a troop of baboons, becomes their leader, and develops a sense of humanity. (Rev: HBG 9/99; SLJ 6/99; VOYA 10/99)

2571 Zemser, Amy B. *Beyond the Mango Tree* (6–12). 1998, Greenwillow $14.95 (0-688-16005-0). Trapped in her home by a domineering mother, Sarina, a 12-year-old white American girl living in Liberia, befriends a gentle African boy named Boima. (Rev: BL 11/1/98; HB 11–12/98; HBG 3/99; SLJ 10/98; VOYA 4/99)

Asia and the Pacific

2572 Bosse, Malcolm. *Deep Dream of the Rain Forest* (6–10). 1993, Farrar paper $5.95 (0-374-41702-4). Orphaned Harry Windsor goes to Borneo to be with his uncle, where he's forced to join a native warrior's dreamquest. (Rev: BL 10/1/93; SLJ 10/93*; VOYA 12/93)

2573 Bosse, Malcolm. *The Examination* (8–12). 1994, Farrar $18.00 (0-374-32234-1). During the Ming Dynasty, two very different Chinese brothers try to understand each other as they travel to Beijing, where one brother hopes to pass a government examination. (Rev: BL 11/1/94*; SLJ 12/94; VOYA 12/94)

2574 Bosse, Malcolm. *Tusk and Stone* (6–10). 1995, Front Street $15.95 (1-886910-01-4). Set in 7th-century India, this story tells about a young Brahman who is separated from his sister and sold to the military as a slave, goes on to gain recognition and fame for his skills and bravery as a warrior, and ultimately discovers his true talents and nature as a sculptor and stonecarver. (Rev: BL 12/1/95; VOYA 2/96)

2575 Choi, Sook N. *Year of Impossible Goodbyes* (6–10). 1991, Houghton $16.00 (0-395-57419-6). An autobiographical novel of two children in North Korea following World War II who become separated from their mother while attempting to cross the border into South Korea. (Rev: BL 9/15/91; SLJ 10/91*)

2576 Crew, Gary. *Mama's Babies* (6–9). 2002, Annick $18.95 (1-55037-725-6); paper $6.95 (1-55037-724-8). Set in Australia in 1897, this absorbing story of cruelty toward foster children — told from the point of view of 9-year-old Sarah — is based on true stories of "baby farmer" mothers who killed their young charges. (Rev: BCCB 9/02; BL 8/02; HBG 10/02; SLJ 6/02; VOYA 8/02)

2577 Disher, Garry. *The Bamboo Flute* (5–8). 1993, Ticknor $15.00 (0-395-66595-7). In this brief, quiet novel of self-discovery, an Australian boy, age 12, brings music back into the life of his impoverished family. (Rev: BL 9/1/93)

2578 Divakaruni, Chitra Banerjee. *Neela: Victory Song* (5–8). Series: Girls of Many Lands. 2002, Pleasant $12.95 (1-58485-597-5); paper $7.95 (1-

58485-521-5). Plucky Neela, 12, plunges into the frightening political fray of India in 1939, determined to help her father and a freedom fighter who are protesting British rule. (Rev: BL 11/15/02; HBG 3/03; SLJ 12/02)

2579 Ellis, Deborah. *The Breadwinner* (5–7). 2001, Groundwood $15.95 (0-88899-419-2). In Kabul under the strict rule of the Taliban, Parvana dresses as a boy so she can work to feed the remaining women in her family. (Rev: BL 3/1/01; HBG 10/01; SLJ 7/01; VOYA 6/01)

2580 Ellis, Deborah. *Parvana's Journey* (5–8). 2002, Douglas & McIntyre $15.95 (0-88899-514-8). This sequel to *The Breadwinner* (2001) shows 13-year-old Parvana, whose father has recently died, making a difficult journey across Taliban-ruled Afghanistan disguised as a boy. (Rev: BL 12/1/02; HBG 3/03; SLJ 12/02*; VOYA 2/03)

2581 Garland, Sherry. *Song of the Buffalo Boy* (7–10). 1992, Harcourt $16.00 (0-15-277107-7); paper $6.00 (0-15-200098-4). An Amerasian teenager wants to escape the prejudice of a Vietnam village and tries to find her father. (Rev: BL 4/1/92; SLJ 6/92)

2582 Gee, Maurice. *The Champion* (6–10). 1993, Simon & Schuster paper $16.00 (0-671-86561-7). Rex, 12, must overcome his own racism and recognize a true hero when an African American war veteran is sent to recuperate in Rex's New Zealand home. (Rev: BL 10/1/93*; SLJ 10/93; VOYA 2/94)

2583 Giles, Gail. *Breath of the Dragon* (4–7). Illus. 1997, Clarion $14.95 (0-395-76476-9). In this story set in Thailand, Malila faces rejection and loneliness because her father was a thief. (Rev: BCCB 4/97; BL 4/1/97; SLJ 6/97)

2584 Hartnett, Sonya. *Thursday's Child* (8–12). 2002, Candlewick $15.99 (0-7636-1620-6). An optimistic young girl tells the story of her Australian family's hapless struggles to weather the Great Depression, and of her brother's obsessive tunneling that results in the collapse of their shanty home. (Rev: BCCB 5/02; BL 7/02; HB 7–8/02; HBG 10/02; SLJ 5/02*; VOYA 6/02)

2585 Haugaard, Erik C. *The Boy and the Samurai* (6–9). 1991, Houghton $16.00 (0-395-56398-4). Despite his prejudice against samurai, Saru concocts a plot to rescue a samurai's imprisoned wife. (Rev: BL 5/1/91*; SLJ 4/91)

2586 Haugaard, Erik C. *The Revenge of the Forty-Seven Samurai* (7–12). 1995, Houghton $16.00 (0-395-70809-5). In a true story set in feudal Japan, a young servant is a witness to destiny when his master meets an unjust death. (Rev: BL 5/15/95; SLJ 4/95)

2587 Hausman, Gerald, and Loretta Hausman. *Escape from Botany Bay: The True Story of Mary Bryant* (6–10). 2003, Scholastic $16.95 (0-439-

40327-8). This is an absorbing fictionalized account of 18th-century Englishwoman Mary Bryant's early life of crime, her sentence to the prison colony of Botany Bay in Australia, and her daring escape. (Rev: BL 3/1/03; SLJ 4/03; VOYA 6/03)

2588 Ho, Minfong. *The Clay Marble* (5–9). 1991, Houghton $12.00 (0-395-77155-2). After fleeing from her Cambodian home in the early 1980s, 12-year-old Dara is separated from her family during an attack on a refugee camp on the Thailand border. (Rev: BL 11/15/91; SLJ 10/91)

2589 Ho, Minfong. *Gathering the Dew* (6–9). 2003, Scholastic $16.95 (0-439-38197-5). Twelve-year-old Nakri loses her beloved sister to the brutal Khmer Rouge regime in Cambodia and starts a new life in America, determined to uphold her sister's dedication to dance. (Rev: BL 3/1/03; HB 5–6/03; SLJ 3/03)

2590 Hoobler, Dorothy, and Thomas Hoobler. *The Demon in the Teahouse* (7–9). 2001, Putnam $17.99 (0-399-23499-3). Fourteen-year-old Seikei, who plans to become a samurai, investigates a series of fires and murders that appear to be connected to a popular geisha in this story set in 18th-century Japan, the sequel to *The Ghost in the Tokaido Inn* (1999). (Rev: BCCB 10/01; BL 5/1/01; HB 7–8/01; HBG 10/01; SLJ 6/01; VOYA 6/01)

2591 Huynh, Quang Nhuong. *The Land I Lost: Adventures of a Boy in Vietnam* (5–8). 1990, HarperCollins $15.89 (0-397-32448-0); paper $4.99 (0-06-440183-9). The story of a boy's growing up in rural Vietnam before the war.

2592 Ihimaera, Witi. *The Whale Rider* (7–12). 2003, Harcourt $17.00 (0-15-205017-5). Legend and contemporary Maori life are interwoven in this story of Kahu, a girl with a spiritual bent whose grandfather would have preferred a grandson to name as his successor. (Rev: BL 7/03; SLJ 9/03; VOYA 10/03)

2593 Kimmel, Eric A. *Sword of the Samurai: Adventure Stories from Japan* (4–8). 1999, Harcourt $15.00 (0-15-201985-5). A collection of 11 tales about the medieval Japanese warriors, their exploits, and their strict traditions. (Rev: BCCB 4/99; BL 3/15/99; HBG 9/99; SLJ 6/99)

2594 Lasky, Kathryn. *Jahanara: Princess of Princesses* (4–8). Series: Royal Diaries. 2002, Scholastic paper $10.95 (0-439-22350-4). Princess Jaharana, the daughter of Shah Jahan (who built the Taj Mahal) writes detailed diary accounts of her 17th-century life, with rich descriptions of her surroundings, palace intrigues, and dealing with her family. (Rev: BL 1/1–15/03; HBG 3/03; SLJ 1/03)

2595 Lewis, Elizabeth Foreman. *Young Fu of the Upper Yangtze* (5–8). 1973, Holt $18.95 (0-8050-0549-8); Dell paper $5.99 (0-440-49043-X). Young Fu must pay back a debt of $5 or face public shame. Newbery Medal winner, 1933.

2596 Marchetta, Melina. *Looking for Alibrandi* (8–10). 1999, Orchard LB $17.99 (0-531-33142-3). In this novel set in Sydney, Australia, teenage Josie Alibrandi is torn between her family's cultural ties to Italy and her Australian environment. (Rev: BL 2/15/99; BR 9–10/99; HB 5–6/99; HBG 9/99; SLJ 7/99; VOYA 6/99)

2597 Namioka, Lensey. *Den of the White Fox* (6–10). 1997, Harcourt $14.00 (0-15-201282-6); paper $6.00 (0-15-201283-4). Set in medieval Japan, this sequel to *The Coming of the Bear* (1992) continues the adventures of two ronin (unemployed samurai). In this tale, they try to solve the mystery of an elusive white fox. (Rev: BL 6/1–15/97; SLJ 6/97; VOYA 8/97)

2598 Namioka, Lensey. *An Ocean Apart, a World Away* (7–10). 2002, Delacorte $15.95 (0-385-73002-0). Yanyan, an independent teenager in the 1920s who rejects traditions such as the binding of feet, travels from her native China to study at Cornell, where she finds new challenges. (Rev: BCCB 10/02; BL 6/1–15/02; HBG 10/02; SLJ 7/02; VOYA 6/02)

2599 Park, Linda Sue. *Seesaw Girl* (4–7). Illus. 1999, Clarion $14.00 (0-395-91514-7). In 17th-century Korea, 12-year-old Jade Blossom wanders away from her aristocratic palace and discovers the reality and poverty of the world outside. (Rev: BCCB 12/99; BL 9/1/99; HBG 3/00; SLJ 9/99)

2600 Park, Linda Sue. *A Single Shard* (4–8). 2001, Clarion $15.00 (0-395-97827-0). This Newbery Medal winner describes a Korean boy's journey through unknown territory to deliver two valuable pots. (Rev: BCCB 3/01; BL 4/1/01*; HBG 10/01; SLJ 5/01*)

2601 Park, Linda Sue. *When My Name Was Keoko* (5–9). 2002, Clarion $16.00 (0-618-13335-6). A young brother and sister tell, in first-person accounts, what life was like during the Japanese occupation of Korea. (Rev: BCCB 5/02; BL 3/1/02; HB 5–6/02; HBG 10/02; SLJ 4/02)

2602 Paterson, Katherine. *The Master Puppeteer* (4–7). 1989, HarperCollins paper $5.99 (0-06-440281-9). Feudal Japan is the setting for this story about a young apprentice puppeteer and his search for a mysterious bandit.

2603 Paterson, Katherine. *Of Nightingales That Weep* (4–7). 1974, HarperCollins $14.00 (0-690-00485-0); paper $5.99 (0-06-440282-7). A story set in feudal Japan tells of Takiko, a samurai's daughter, who is sent to the royal court when her mother remarries.

2604 Paterson, Katherine. *Rebels of the Heavenly Kingdom* (7–9). 1983, Dutton $14.99 (0-525-66911-6); Avon paper $2.95 (0-380-68304-0). In 19th-century China a 15-year-old boy and a young girl engage in activities to overthrow the Manchu government.

2605 Paterson, Katherine. *The Sign of the Chrysanthemum* (5–7). 1973, HarperCollins LB $14.89 (0-690-04913-7); paper $5.99 (0-06-440232-0). At the death of his mother, a young boy sets out to find his samurai father in 12th-century Japan.

2606 Russell, Ching Yeung. *Child Bride* (4–7). Illus. 1999, Boyds Mills $15.95 (1-56397-748-6). Set in China in the early 1940s, this is the story of 11-year-old Ying, her arranged marriage, and an understanding bridegroom who allows her to go home to her ailing grandmother. (Rev: BL 3/1/99; HBG 10/99; SLJ 4/99)

2607 Russell, Ching Yeung. *Lichee Tree* (4–7). 1997, Boyds Mills $15.95 (1-56397-629-3). Growing up in China during the 1940s, Ying dreams of selling lichee nuts and visiting Canton. (Rev: BCCB 4/97; BL 3/15/97; SLJ 6/97)

2608 Soto, Gary. *Pacific Crossing* (6–9). 1992, Harcourt paper $8.00 (0-15-259188-5). As part of a summer exchange program, Lincoln Mendoza adapts to life on a Japanese farm, practices a martial art, embraces Japanese customs, and shares his own. (Rev: BL 11/1/92; SLJ 11/92)

2609 Sreenivasan, Jyotsna. *Aruna's Journeys* (4–7). Illus. 1997, Smooth Stone paper $6.95 (0-9619401-7-4). Aruna denies her Indian heritage until she spends a summer in Bangalore, India. (Rev: BL 7/97)

2610 Staples, Suzanne Fisher. *Shiva's Fire* (8–12). 2000, Farrar $18.00 (0-374-36824-4). The inspiring story of a mystical Indian girl who devotes her life to the dance. (Rev: BL 3/15/00; SLJ 4/00; VOYA 6/00)

2611 Watkins, Yoko K. *My Brother, My Sister, and I* (6–10). 1994, Bradbury paper $17.00 (0-02-792526-9). Tells of a once-secure middle-class child who is now homeless, hungry, and in danger in post-World War II Japan. A sequel to the fictionalized autobiography *So Far from the Bamboo Grove* (1986). (Rev: BL 5/1/94; SLJ 9/94; VOYA 8/94)

2612 Whelan, Gloria. *Homeless Bird* (5–8). 2000, HarperCollins LB $16.89 (0-06-028452-8). A novel set in contemporary India about a young girl and her arranged marriage to a young man who is dying of tuberculosis. (Rev: BL 3/1/00; HBG 10/00; SLJ 2/00)

2613 Whitesel, Cheryl Aylward. *Rebel: A Tibetan Odyssey* (5–8). 2000, HarperCollins $15.95 (0-688-16735-7). In Tibet about a century ago, a young boy named Thunder is sent to live with his uncle, an important lama in a Buddhist monastery. (Rev: BCCB 5/00; BL 4/15/00; HBG 3/01; SLJ 7/00)

2614 Wilson, Diane Lee. *I Rode a Horse of Milk White Jade* (6–10). 1998, Orchard paper $18.95 (0-

531-30024-2). This adventure story set in medieval China tells the story of Oyuna and her adventures delivering a package to the court of the great Kublai Khan. (Rev: BL 4/1/98; BR 1–2/99; HBG 9/98; SLJ 6/98; VOYA 8/98)

2615 Wu, Priscilla. *The Abacus Contest: Stories from Taiwan and China* (5–8). Illus. 1996, Fulcrum $15.95 (1-55591-243-5). Six simple short stories explore life in a Taiwanese city. (Rev: BL 7/96; SLJ 6/96)

2616 Yep, Laurence. *Lady of Ch'iao Kuo: Warrior of the South* (5–8). Illus. Series: Royal Diaries. 2001, Scholastic $10.95 (0-439-16483-6). In this volume of the Royal Diaries series, the teenage Princess Redbird of the Hsien tribe must use her diplomatic skills to save the lives of both her own people and Chinese colonists in the 6th century A.D. Historical notes add background information. (Rev: BL 11/1/01)

2617 Yep, Laurence. *Mountain Light* (8–12). 1997, HarperCollins paper $6.95 (0-06-440667-9). Yep continues to explore life in 19th-century China through the experience of a girl, Cassia, her father and friends, and their struggle against the Manchus in this sequel to *The Serpent's Children* (1984). (Rev: BL 9/15/85; SLJ 1/87; VOYA 12/85)

2618 Yep, Laurence. *Spring Pearl: The Last Flower* (4–7). Series: Girls of Many Lands. 2002, Pleasant $12.95 (1-58485-595-9); paper $7.95 (1-58485-519-3). An adventurous, intelligent orphan faces a difficult time when she goes to live with her artist father's patron in this novel set in the turmoil of 1857 China. (Rev: BL 12/15/02; HBG 3/03; SLJ 10/02)

2619 Yumoto, Kazumi. *The Friends* (5–8). 1996, Farrar $15.00 (0-374-32460-3). Three Japanese boys who are intrigued with death begin surveillance of an old man they think is about to die and find friendship instead. (Rev: BCCB 2/97; BL 10/15/96; HB 11–12/96; SLJ 12/96; VOYA 4/97)

Europe and the Middle East

2620 Almond, David. *Counting Stars* (5–9). 2002, Delacorte LB $18.99 (0-385-90034-1). In a series of vignettes based on personal experience, a man recalls growing up in a poor mining town in northern England. (Rev: BCCB 3/02; BL 1/1/02; HB 3–4/02; HBG 10/02; SLJ 3/02)

2621 Bagdasarian, Adam. *Forgotten Fire* (8–12). 2000, DK paper $19.99 (0-7894-2627-7). The heartbreaking story of a young boy, Vahan Kenderian, and his harrowing experiences during the Turkish genocide of the Armenians. (Rev: BL 7/00; BR 3–4/01; HB 11–12/00; HBG 3/01; SLJ 12/00; VOYA 12/00)

2622 Banks, Lynne Reid. *Broken Bridge* (7–12). 1995, Morrow $16.00 (0-688-13595-1). In this sequel to *One More River* (1992), a woman's daughter sees her cousin killed by an Arab terrorist while living on a kibbutz, posing some tough moral questions. (Rev: BL 3/15/95; SLJ 4/95; VOYA 5/95)

2623 Banks, Lynne Reid. *The Dungeon* (6–9). 2002, HarperCollins $15.99 (0-06-623782-3). Retribution is at the heart of this dark story about a bereaved 14th-century laird whose anger spurs him to abuse a Chinese child. (Rev: BL 10/1/02; HB 9/02; HBG 3/03; SLJ 12/02)

2624 Bawden, Nina. *The Real Plato Jones* (5–8). 1993, Clarion $15.00 (0-395-66972-3). British teen Plato Jones and his mother return to Greece for his grandfather's funeral, where Plato discovers that his grandfather may have been a coward and traitor while serving in the Greek Resistance. (Rev: BCCB 11/93; BL 10/15/93; SLJ 11/93*)

2625 Blackwood, Gary. *Shakespeare's Spy* (5–8). 2003, Dutton $16.99 (0-525-47145-6). Romance and intrigue are at hand as Widge continues his career at the Globe Theatre in this sequel to *The Shakespeare Stealer* (1998) and *Shakespeare's Scribe* (2000). (Rev: BL 9/1/03; HB 11–12/03; SLJ 10/03)

2626 Blackwood, Gary L. *Shakespeare Stealer* (5–8). 1998, NAL $15.99 (0-525-45863-8). A 14-year-old apprentice at the Globe Theater is sent by a rival theater company to steal Shakespeare's plays. (Rev: BL 6/1–15/98; HB 7–8/98; HBG 10/98; SLJ 6/98; VOYA 8/98)

2627 Blackwood, Gary L. *Shakespeare's Scribe* (5–8). 2000, Dutton $15.99 (0-525-46444-1). Set in Elizabethan England, this is the story of how young Widge discovers his true identity while traveling outside London with a theatrical troupe. (Rev: BL 9/1/00; HB 11–12/00; HBG 3/01; SLJ 9/00)

2628 Bowler, Tim. *River Boy* (6–10). 2000, Simon & Schuster $16.00 (0-689-82908-6). Jess helps her sick grandfather by returning with him to his remote boyhood home to complete the painting he has begun called *River Boy*. (Rev: BL 5/1/00; HBG 3/01; SLJ 8/00)

2629 Branford, Henrietta. *Fire, Bed, and Bone* (5–9). 1998, Candlewick $16.99 (0-7636-0338-4). This unusual novel, narrated from a dog's point of view, describes the oppression of the peasants in late 14th-century England and the revolt led by Wat Tyler and the preacher John Ball. (Rev: BCCB 5/98; BL 3/15/98; BR 9–10/98; HBG 10/98; SLJ 5/98; VOYA 10/98)

2630 Cadnum, Michael. *Ship of Fire* (6–8). 2003, Viking $16.99 (0-670-89907-0). Apprentice surgeon Thomas, 17, has to learn medicine and seafaring fast when he sails with Sir Francis Drake's fleet. (Rev: BL 9/15/03; SLJ 10/03)

2631 Casanova, Mary. *Cecile: Gates of Gold* (4–7). Illus. Series: Girls of Many Lands. 2002, Pleasant $12.95 (1-58485-594-0); paper $7.95 (1-58485-518-5). For 12-year-old Cecile, a peasant in 18th-century France, the chance to work at the Palace of Versailles seems like a dream come true until she faces some of the harsh realities of court life. (Rev: BL 10/15/02; HBG 3/03; SLJ 9/02)

2632 Casanova, Mary. *Curse of a Winter Moon* (5–8). 2000, Hyperion $15.99 (0-7868-0547-1). Set in 16th-century France, this novel tells of the conflict between the Huguenots and the Roman Catholics as seen from the point of view of young Marius. (Rev: BL 10/15/00; HBG 3/01; SLJ 10/00; VOYA 12/00)

2633 Cheaney, J. B. *The Playmaker* (7–10). 2000, Knopf $15.95 (0-375-80577-X). A well-written historical adventure story steeped in Elizabethan England and its theater and featuring a teenage boy caught up in dangerous political plots as he searches for his father. (Rev: BL 11/1/00; HB 1–2/01; HBG 3/01; SLJ 12/00; VOYA 4/01)

2634 Cheaney, J. B. *The True Prince* (7–10). 2002, Knopf $15.95 (0-375-81433-7). Richard Malory, a performer in Elizabethan England, becomes involved in mysterious and dangerous events. (Rev: BCCB 12/02; BL 1/1–15/03; HB 1–2/03; HBG 3/03; SLJ 11/02)

2635 Conlon-McKenna, Marita. *Fields of Home* (6–10). Illus. 1997, Holiday paper $15.95 (0-8234-1295-4). In this sequel to *Under the Hawthorn Tree* (1990) and *Wildflower Girl* (1992), the Irish O'Driscoll family saga continues as Michael and Eily try to make progress in spite of the hard times in Ireland. (Rev: BCCB 7–8/97; BL 4/15/97; BR 9–10/97; SLJ 6/97)

2636 Croutier, Alev Lytle. *Leyla: The Black Tulip* (6–8). 2003, Pleasant $15.95 (1-58485-831-1); paper $7.95 (1-58485-749-8). In the early 18th century, 12-year-old Leyla believes she is selling herself as a bride to support her family and finds that she instead becomes a slave at Topkapi Palace. (Rev: BL 12/1/03; SLJ 10/03)

2637 Curtis, Chara M. *No One Walks on My Father's Moon* (4–8). Illus. 1996, Voyage LB $16.95 (0-9649454-1-X). A Turkish boy is accused of blasphemy when he states that a man has walked on the moon. (Rev: BL 11/15/96)

2638 De Angeli, Marguerite. *The Door in the Wall* (5–7). 1990, Dell paper $5.50 (0-440-40283-2). Crippled Robin proves his courage in plague-ridden 19th century London. Newbery Medal winner, 1950.

2639 Degens, T. *Freya on the Wall* (6–9). 1997, Harcourt $19.00 (0-15-200210-3). After the Berlin Wall collapses, an American girl learns details about her distant cousin's childhood in East Germany under the Communists. (Rev: SLJ 6/97; VOYA 6/97)

2640 DeJong, Meindert. *Wheel on the School* (4–7). 1954, HarperCollins LB $16.89 (0-06-021586-0); paper $5.99 (0-06-440021-2). The storks are brought back to their island by the schoolchildren in a Dutch village. Newbery Medal winner, 1955.

2641 de Trevino, Elizabeth Borton. *I, Juan de Pareja* (6–9). 1987, Farrar paper $5.95 (0-374-43525-1). The story of the slave who became an inspiration for his master, the Spanish painter Velasquez. A Newbery Medal winner. A reissue.

2642 Dexter, Catherine. *Safe Return* (5–7). 1996, Candlewick $16.99 (0-7636-0005-9). On her island home in the Baltic Sea in 1824, an orphan anxiously awaits the return of her aunt, who has sailed to Stockholm, Sweden. (Rev: BCCB 11/96; BL 10/15/96; HB 11–12/96; SLJ 12/96)

2643 Dickinson, Peter. *Shadow of a Hero* (7–12). 1995, Doubleday $20.95 (0-385-30976-7). Letta's grandfather fights for the freedom of Varina, her family's Eastern European homeland. Living in England, she becomes interested in Varina's struggle. (Rev: BL 9/15/94*; SLJ 11/94; VOYA 10/94)

2644 Doherty, Berlie. *Street Child* (5–7). 1994, Orchard LB $18.99 (0-531-08714-X). The story of a street urchin in Victorian London who is forced to work on a river barge until he escapes. (Rev: BCCB 11/94; BL 9/1/94; SLJ 10/94)

2645 Dunlop, Eileen. *Tales of St. Patrick* (6–9). 1996, Holiday $15.95 (0-8234-1218-0). Using original sources when possible, the author has fashioned a fictionalized biography of Saint Patrick that focuses on his return to Ireland as a bishop and his efforts to convert the Irish. (Rev: BL 4/15/96; VOYA 8/96)

2646 Eisner, Will. *The Last Knight: An Introduction to Don Quixote by Miguel de Cervantes* (4–8). Illus. 2000, NBM $15.95 (1-56163-251-1). Using an engaging text and a comic book format, this is a fine retelling of Cervantes' classic. (Rev: BL 6/1–15/00; HBG 10/00; SLJ 7/00)

2647 Ellis, Deborah. *A Company of Fools* (5–8). 2002, Fitzhenry & Whiteside $15.95 (1-55041-719-3). Quiet Henri and free-spirited Micah try to cheer the people of a France devastated by the Black Death of 1348 by singing. (Rev: BCCB 1/03; BL 1/1–15/03; HB 1–2/03; HBG 3/03; VOYA 2/03)

2648 Elmer, Robert. *Chasing the Wind* (4–7). Series: Young Underground. 1996, Bethany paper $5.99 (1 55661 658 9). Three Danish children discover that after the Germans surrender some Nazis are still in their town diving for sunken treasure. (Rev: BL 5/1/96)

2649 Flegg, Aubrey. *Katie's War* (5–8). 2000, O'Brien paper $7.95 (0-86278-525-1). Set during Ireland's fight for independence from England, this story shows a girl torn between two sides when her father wants peace and her brother is preparing to use force. (Rev: BL 12/1/00)

2650 Gavin, Jamila. *Coram Boy* (6–9). Illus. 2001, Farrar $19.00 (0-374-31544-2). A complicated, suspenseful mystery set in 1741 and involving the fate of an abandoned infant. (Rev: BCCB 2/02; BL 12/15/01; HBG 3/02; SLJ 11/01; VOYA 12/01)

2651 Giff, Patricia Reilly. *Nory Ryan's Song* (4–7). 2000, Delacorte $15.95 (0-385-32141-4). Set in Ireland at the time of the great famine, 12-year-old Nory must fight starvation as well as care for her younger brother. (Rev: BL 9/15/00*; HB 1–2/01; HBG 3/01; SLJ 8/00; VOYA 2/01)

2652 Gilson, Jamie. *Stink Alley* (4–7). 2002, HarperCollins LB $15.89 (0-06-029217-2). Twelve-year-old orphan Lizzy Tinker, a Separatist who fled England with her family for Holland in 1608, is befriended by the boy who would one day be known as Rembrandt. (Rev: BCCB 9/02; BL 4/15/02; HB 9–10/02; HBG 3/03; SLJ 7/02)

2653 Gray, Elizabeth Janet. *Adam of the Road* (5–8). 1942, Puffin paper $5.99 (0-14-032464-X). Adventures of a 13th-century minstrel boy. Newbery Medal winner, 1943.

2654 Harrison, Cora. *The Famine Secret* (5–7). Series: Drumshee Timeline. 1998, Irish American paper $6.95 (0-86327-649-0). In 1847 the four McMahon children are orphaned and sent to an Irish workhouse, but their determination prevails and they are soon plotting to regain their home. (Rev: SLJ 12/98)

2655 Harrison, Cora. *The Secret of Drumshee Castle* (5–7). Series: Drumshee Timeline. 1998, Irish American paper $6.95 (0-86327-632-6). Grace Barry, the orphaned heiress to a castle in Ireland during Elizabethan times, flees to England to escape threats by her acquisitive guardians. (Rev: SLJ 12/98)

2656 Harrison, Cora. *The Secret of the Seven Crosses* (4–7). Illus. 1998, Wolfhound paper $6.95 (0-86327-616-4). In medieval Ireland, three youngsters hope to find hidden treasure by examining sources in their monastery library. Preceded by *Nauala and Her Secret Wolf* and followed by *The Secret of Drumshee Castle*. (Rev: BL 12/15/98)

2657 Holeman, Linda. *Search of the Moon King's Daughter* (8–11). 2002, Tundra $17.95 (0-88776-592-0). Fifteen-year-old Emmaline goes to London to search for her deaf brother, who has been sold into service by their laudanum-addicted mother in this story set in Victorian England. (Rev: BL 12/15/02; HBG 3/03; SLJ 3/03*; VOYA 2/03)

2658 Holub, Joseph. *The Robber and Me* (5–8). Trans. from German by Elizabeth D. Crawford. 1997, Holt $16.95 (0-8050-5591-1). On his way to live with his uncle, an orphan is helped by a mysterious stranger and he must later make a decision about whether to stand up to his uncle and the town authorities to clear the name of this man in this novel set in 19th-century Germany. (Rev: SLJ 12/97*)

2659 Hooper, Mary. *At the Sign of the Sugared Plum* (5–8). 2003, Bloomsbury $16.95 (1-58234-849-9). The horrors of the bubonic plague and the squalor of 17th-century London are brought to life in this story of Hannah and her sister Sarah, owner of a sweetmeats shop. (Rev: BL 9/15/03; SLJ 8/03; VOYA 10/03)

2660 Horowitz, Anthony. *The Devil and His Boy* (5–8). 2000, Putnam $16.99 (0-399-23432-2). In Elizabethan England, young Tom Falconer, a boy of the streets, ends up saving his queen. (Rev: BCCB 3/00; BL 1/1–15/00; HBG 10/00; SLJ 4/00; VOYA 4/00)

2661 Howard, Ellen. *The Gate in the Wall* (5–7). 1999, Simon & Schuster $16.00 (0-689-82295-2). In Victorian England, 10-year-old orphan Emma escapes the drudgery of factory work and gets a job on a canal boat where she helps load the cargo. (Rev: BCCB 5/99; BL 2/15/99; HB 3–4/99; HBG 10/99; SLJ 3/99)

2662 Hunter, Mollie. *The King's Swift Rider* (7–12). 1998, HarperCollins $16.95 (0-06-027186-8). A fast-paced historical novel about a young Scot, Martin Crawford, who became Robert the Bruce's page, confidante, and spy. (Rev: BL 9/15/98; HB 1–2/99; HBG 3/99; SLJ 12/98)

2663 Hunter, Mollie. *You Never Knew Her as I Did!* (7–10). Illus. 1981, HarperCollins $13.95 (0-06-022678-1). A historical novel about a plan to help the imprisoned Mary, Queen of Scots, to escape from prison.

2664 Jennings, Patrick. *The Wolving Time* (6–8). 2003, Scholastic $15.95 (0-439-39555-0). Fantasy and historical fiction are interwoven in this tale, set in 16th-century France, of two werewolves and their son. (Rev: BL 9/15/03)

2665 Jones, Terry. *The Lady and the Squire* (5–7). Illus. 2001, Pavilion $22.95 (1-86205-417-7). A beautiful aristocrat joins Tom and Ann as they make their way through a war-torn countryside to the papal court at Avignon. (Rev: BL 2/15/01; SLJ 3/01)

2666 Juster, Norton. *Alberic the Wise* (4–8). 1992, Picture Book $16.95 (0-88708-243-2). In this picture book set in the Renaissance, Alberic becomes an apprentice to a stained-glass maker. (Rev: BCCB 2/93; BL 1/15/93; SLJ 3/93)

144

2667 Kanefield, Teri. *Rivka's Way* (4–8). 2001, Front Street $15.95 (0-8126-2870-5). Daily life inside and outside the Prague ghetto in 1778 is explored in this novel about an unconventional Jewish girl, 15-year-old Rivka Liebermann. (Rev: BCCB 3/02; BL 4/1/01; HBG 10/01; SLJ 3/01; VOYA 10/01)

2668 Karr, Kathleen. *The 7th Knot* (6–9). 2003, Marshall Cavendish $15.95 (0-7614-5135-8). Brothers Wick, 15, and Miles, 12, romp through a series of adventures involving art and politics when they set off across Europe in pursuit of their uncle's kidnapped valet in the late 19th century. (Rev: BL 7/03; HBG 10/03; SLJ 8/03)

2669 Kelly, Eric P. *The Trumpeter of Krakow* (5–9). 1966, Macmillan $17.95 (0-02-750140-X); paper $4.99 (0-689-71571-4). Mystery surrounds a precious jewel and the youthful patriot who stands watch over it in a church tower in this novel of 15th-century Poland. Newbery Medal winner, 1929.

2670 Kirwan, Anna. *Victoria: May Blossom of Britannia* (5–8). Series: Royal Diaries. 2001, Scholastic paper $10.95 (0-439-21598-6). Young Victoria's fictional diary describes her over-regimented life at the ages of 10 and 11; background material adds some historical context to this account of the girl who grew up to rule England. (Rev: BL 12/1/01; HBG 10/02; SLJ 1/02; VOYA 2/02)

2671 Konigsburg, E. L. *A Proud Taste for Scarlet and Miniver* (7–9). Illus. 1973, Macmillan $18.95 (0-689-30111-1). Eleanor of Aquitaine tells her story in heaven while awaiting her second husband, Henry II.

2672 Konigsburg, E. L. *Second Mrs. Giaconda* (7–9). 1978, Macmillan paper $5.95 (0-689-70450-X). Leonardo da Vinci's valet narrates this story that tells the truth about Mona Lisa and her smile. (Rev: BL 3/1/90)

2673 Lasky, Kathryn. *Elizabeth I: Red Rose of the House of Tudor* (4–7). Series: Royal Diaries. 1999, Scholastic paper $10.95 (0-590-68484-1). Told in diary form, this is a fictionalized account of Elizabeth I's childhood after her mother was killed and she lived with her father, Henry VIII, and Catherine Parr. (Rev: BCCB 12/99; BL 9/15/99; HBG 3/00; SLJ 10/99)

2674 Lasky, Kathryn. *Marie Antoinette: Princess of Versailles* (5–8). Series: Royal Diaries. 2000, Scholastic paper $10.95 (0-439-07666-8). This fictional diary covers two years in the life of Marie Antoinette, beginning in 1769 when the 13-year-old was preparing for her fateful marriage. (Rev: BL 4/15/00; HBG 10/00; SLJ 5/00; VOYA 6/00)

2675 Lasky, Kathryn *Mary, Queen of Scots: Queen Without a Country* (5–8). Illus. Series: Royal Diaries. 2002, Scholastic paper $10.95 (0-439-19404-0). Part of the Royal Diary series, this is a fictional diary of the year 1553, when Mary was betrothed to the son of King Henry II of France. (Rev: BL 5/15/02; HBG 10/02; SLJ 6/02)

2676 Lasky, Kathryn. *The Night Journey* (6–9). Illus. 1986, Penguin paper $5.99 (0-14-032048-2). Nana tells her great-granddaughter about her escape from Czarist Russia. (Rev: BL 1/1/90)

2677 Lawrence, Iain. *The Buccaneers* (5–8). 2001, Delacorte $15.95 (0-385-32736-6). In this final volume in the trilogy that began with *The Wreckers* and *The Smugglers*, 16-year-old John Spencer and his captain rescue a castaway and appear headed for disaster. (Rev: BCCB 7–8/01; BL 5/15/01; HBG 3/02)

2678 Lawrence, Iain. *The Smugglers* (5–8). 1999, Delacorte $15.95 (0-385-32663-7). In this continuation of *The Wreckers*, 16-year-old John Spencer faces more adventures aboard the *Dragon*, where he faces powerful enemies and must bring the ship safely to port. (Rev: BCCB 7–8/99; BL 4/1/99*; HB 5–6/99; HBG 10/99; SLJ 6/99)

2679 Lawrence, Iain. *The Wreckers* (5–8). 1998, Delacorte $15.95 (0-385-32535-5); Bantam Doubleday Dell paper $5.50 (0-440-41545-4). In this historical novel, young John Spencer narrowly escapes with his life after the ship on which he is traveling is wrecked off the Cornish coast, lured to its destruction by a gang seeking to plunder its cargo. (Rev: BCCB 6/98; BL 6/1–15/98; BR 11–12/98; HB 7–8/98*; HBG 10/98; SLJ 6/98; VOYA 2/99)

2680 Lewin, Waldtraut. *Freedom Beyond the Sea* (5–9). 2001, Delacorte $15.95 (0-385-32705-6). Esther, a Jewish girl, disguises herself as a cabin boy on the *Santa Maria* to escape the Spanish Inquisition in this novel set in 1492. (Rev: BCCB 12/01; BL 9/15/01; HB 11–12/01; HBG 3/02; SLJ 1/02; VOYA 12/01)

2681 Lisson, Deborah. *Red Hugh* (6–12). 2001, O'Brien paper $7.95 (0-86278-604-5). A exciting tale of 16th-century Ireland's Hugh Roe O'Donnell, a teen whose life is endangered when he is caught up in clan violence. (Rev: BL 12/1/01; SLJ 12/01)

2682 McCaughrean, Geraldine. *The Pirate's Son* (7–10). 1998, Scholastic $16.95 (0-590-20344-4). In 1717 England, Nathan and his little sister, Maud, are taken aboard a pirate ship and sail to Madagascar in this terrific adventure story. (Rev: BL 8/98; BR 11–12/98; HB 11–12/98; HBG 3/99; SLJ 11/98; VOYA 2/99)

2683 Magorian, Michelle. *Back Home* (7–9). 1992, HarperCollins paper $6.95 (0-06-440411-0). A young English girl who returns to Britain after World War II wants to go back to her second home in the United States.

2684 Masefield, John. *Jim Davis: A High Sea Adventure* (5–8). 2002, Scholastic paper $15.95 (0-439-40436-3). This story about 12-year-old Jim and his adventures with smugglers is set in early-19th-century England and was originally published in 1911. (Rev: BL 11/15/02; HBG 3/03; VOYA 2/03)

2685 Matas, Carol. *The Garden* (8–12). 1997, Simon & Schuster paper $15.00 (0-689-80349-4). This novel, a continuation of *After the War*, follows Ruth Mendelson to a kibbutz in Palestine and describes the tensions she and other kibbutzniks face as the United Nations prepares to vote on a plan to partition Palestine into Jewish and Arab lands. (Rev: BL 4/1/97; BR 11–12/97; SLJ 5/97)

2686 Matas, Carol. *Sworn Enemies* (7–10). 1994, Dell paper $3.99 (0-440-21900-0). In czarist Russia, the enemies are Aaron, a young Jewish scholar, and Zev, hired to kidnap fellow Jews to fulfill military quotas. (Rev: BL 2/1/93; SLJ 2/93)

2687 Mead, Alice. *Girl of Kosovo* (5–10). 2001, Farrar $16.00 (0-374-32620-7). A moving novel about the ethnic wars in Kosovo as seen through the eyes of an 11-year-old Albanian girl who has witnessed the death of her father and two brothers and whose foot is smashed during the fighting. (Rev: BCCB 6/01; BL 3/15/01*; HBG 10/01; SLJ 3/01; VOYA 6/01)

2688 Menick, Stephen. *The Muffin Child* (5–7). 1998, Putnam $17.99 (0-399-23303-2). In a Balkan village, Tanya, an outcast at age 11, is wrongfully accused of kidnapping a child, but when she places blame on a band of Gypsies, she inadvertently causes a massacre in this tale of cruelty and kindness. (Rev: BCCB 10/98; BL 9/15/98; HB 1–2/99; HBG 3/99; SLJ 9/98)

2689 Meyer, Carolyn. *Anastasia: The Last Grand Duchess, Russia, 1914* (4–8). Series: Royal Diaries. 2000, Scholastic paper $10.95 (0-439-12908-7). Anastasia's fictional diary begins when she is 12 in 1914 and ends with her captivity in 1918. (Rev: HBG 10/01; SLJ 10/00; VOYA 4/01)

2690 Meyer, Carolyn. *Beware, Princess Elizabeth* (5–8). Series: Young Royals. 2001, Harcourt $17.00 (0-15-202659-2). A first-person account of the youth of Elizabeth I, whose mother was murdered by her father, Henry VIII, and whose life is surrounded with intrigue after Henry's death. (Rev: BL 3/1/01; HBG 10/01; SLJ 5/01; VOYA 6/01)

2691 Meyer, Carolyn. *Doomed Queen Anne* (6–9). Series: Young Royals. 2002, Harcourt $17.00 (0-15-216523-1). A first-person account of the short life of Anne Boleyn, who succeeds in stealing Henry VIII's affections only to lose her life. (Rev: BL 9/15/02; HBG 3/03; SLJ 10/02; VOYA 12/02)

2692 Meyer, Carolyn. *Mary, Bloody Mary* (6–9). 1999, Harcourt $17.00 (0-15-201906-5). A historical novel that traces the life of England's Queen Mary I from age 10 to 20. (Rev: BCCB 10/99; BL 9/15/99; HBG 4/00; SLJ 10/99; VOYA 2/00)

2693 Meyer, L. A. *Bloody Jack: Being an Account of the Curious Adventures of Mary "Jacky" Faber, Ship's Boy* (6–9). 2002, Harcourt $17.00 (0-15-216731-5). Orphaned by the plague, Mary Faber disguises herself as a boy and signs up to work on the *HMS Dolphin* to escape life on the streets of 18th-century London. (Rev: BL 3/1/03; HB 1–2/03; HBG 3/03; SLJ 9/02; VOYA 12/02)

2694 Miklowitz, Gloria D. *Secrets in the House of Delgado* (6–9). 2001, Eerdmans $16.00 (0-8028-5206-8). Miklowitz tells the story of the Spanish Inquisition of 1492 through the eyes of 14-year-old Maria, a Catholic orphan working in the home of converted Jews. (Rev: BCCB 11/01; BL 10/1/01; HBG 3/02; SLJ 10/01; VOYA 12/01)

2695 Mooney, Bel. *The Voices of Silence* (5–9). 1997, Bantam Doubleday Dell $14.95 (0-385-32326-3). In Communist Romania, 13-year-old Flora and her family are living under very harsh conditions when she overhears a conversation about plans by her father to run for freedom. (Rev: BL 4/1/97; BR 5–6/97; SLJ 3/97*)

2696 Morpurgo, Michael. *Joan of Arc* (6–8). Illus. 1999, Harcourt $23.00 (0-15-201736-4). Beginning in the present, this novel goes back in time and shows Joan of Arc as a real person who experiences both confidence in her divine mission and doubts as she faces a cruel death. (Rev: HBG 4/00; SLJ 5/99)

2697 Napoli, Donna Jo. *Breath* (8–12). 2003, Simon & Schuster $16.95 (0-689-86174-5). Salz, a sickly youth, seems to be immune to the sufferings of the people of Hameln in this reinterpretation of the Pied Piper story that conveys much of the atmosphere of 13th-century Europe. (Rev: BL 9/15/03; SLJ 11/03)

2698 Napoli, Donna Jo. *Daughter of Venice* (6–10). 2002, Random $16.95 (0-385-32780-3). In 1592 Venice, 14-year-old Donata rejects the limits placed on her life as daughter of a nobleman and, disguised as a boy, sets out to discover the world outside her palazzo. (Rev: BCCB 7–8/02; BL 3/1/02; HB 3–4/02; HBG 10/02; SLJ 3/02*; VOYA 8/02)

2699 Newth, Mette. *The Dark Light* (8–12). Trans. by Faith Ingwersen. 1998, Farrar $18.00 (0-374-31701-1). Set in early-19th-century Norway, this novel tells of Tora, afflicted with leprosy, and her harrowing stay at a hospital surrounded by the horror of the disease. (Rev: BCCB 5/98; BL 6/1–15/98; HB 7–8/98*; HBG 9/98; SLJ 6/98; VOYA 2/99)

2700 Newth, Mette. *The Transformation* (8–12). Trans. by Faith Ingwersen. 2000, Farrar $16.00 (0-374-37752-9). In 15th-century Greenland, the lives of Navarana, an Inuit girl, and Brendan, a monk from the mainland, intersect and together they form an unusual relationship. (Rev: BL 11/15/00; HB 1–2/01; HBG 3/01)

2701 Orlev, Uri. *The Lady with the Hat* (7–10). Trans. by Hillel Halkin. 1995, Houghton $16.00 (0-

395-69957-6). Yulek, a concentration camp survivor, encounters anti-Semitism on her return to Poland, while another Jewish girl, hidden from the Nazis, wants to be a nun. (Rev: BL 3/15/95; SLJ 5/95)

2702 Peyton, K. M. *Snowfall* (8–12). 1998, Houghton $16.00 (0-395-89598-7). Set in Victorian times, this novel tells of a young girl brought up in a vicarage and her escape into a world where she falls in love with three exciting men. (Rev: BL 9/15/98; HBG 3/99; SLJ 9/98; VOYA 4/99)

2703 Pressler, Mirjam. *Shylock's Daughter* (8–12). Trans. by Brian Murdoch. 2001, Penguin Putnam $17.99 (0-8037-2667-8). This novel based on *The Merchant of Venice* focuses on 16-year-old Jessica's love and aspirations, and gives readers insight into life in 16th-century Venice and into the motivations of Shakespeare's characters. (Rev: BCCB 7–8/01; BL 4/1/01; HBG 10/01; SLJ 6/01; VOYA 10/01)

2704 Pullman, Philip. *The Ruby in the Smoke* (8–10). 1987, Knopf paper $5.50 (0-394-89589-4). Sally Lockhart, alone in Dickensian London, encounters murder, opium dens, and romance in her search for her inheritance. Continued in *Shadow in the North* (1988) and *The Tiger in the Well*. (Rev: BL 3/1/87; BR 11–12/87; SLJ 4/87; VOYA 10/87)

2705 Richardson, V. A. *The House of Windjammer* (7–10). 2003, Bloomsbury $16.95 (1-58234-811-1). Seventeenth-century Amsterdam in the midst of the tulip craze is the setting of the multilayered, suspenseful story of the Windjammer family, whose business and social standing are in jeopardy. (Rev: BCCB 9/03; BL 5/15/03*; SLJ 9/03; VOYA 10/03)

2706 Schmidt, Gary D. *Anson's Way* (5–9). 1999, Houghton $15.00 (0-395-91529-5). During the reign of George II, Anson begins his proud career in the British army as part of the forces occupying Ireland, then becomes disillusioned as he develops a growing respect and concern for the Irish. (Rev: BL 4/1/99*; HBG 10/99; SLJ 4/99; VOYA 8/99)

2707 Schur, Maxine R. *The Circlemaker* (6–10). 1994, Dial $14.99 (0-8037-1354-1). A 12-year-old Jewish boy in a Ukrainian shtetl escapes 25 years of forced conscription in the czar's army in 1852. (Rev: BL 1/15/94; SLJ 2/94)

2708 Shafer, Anders C. *The Fantastic Journey of Pieter Bruegel* (5–7). Illus. 2002, Dutton $18.99 (0-525-46986-9). A fictional account of the 16th-century painter's trip from Antwerp to Rome, in the form of a diary. (Rev: BL 7/02; HBG 10/02; SLJ 7/02)

2709 Siegel, Deborah Spector. *The Cross by Day, the Mezuzzah by Night* (6–8). 1999, Jewish Publication Soc. $14.95 (0-8276-0597-8). In this gripping first-person narrative set in Spain in 1492 during the Inquisition, Ruth discovers that her family is secretly Jewish and that they must flee or face torture or

burning at the stake. (Rev: BL 8/99; HBG 4/00; VOYA 2/00)

2710 Sturtevant, Katherine. *At the Sign of the Star* (4–8). 2000, Farrar $16.00 (0-374-30449-1). Growing up with her bookseller father in London during 1677, high-spirited Meg finds it difficult to adjust when her father remarries. (Rev: BCCB 1/01; BL 10/15/00*; HB 9–10/00; HBG 3/01; SLJ 9/00; VOYA 12/00)

2711 Szablya, Helen M., and Peggy K. Anderson. *The Fall of the Red Star* (7–9). 1996, Boyds Mills paper $9.95 (1-563-97977-2). A novel, partially based on fact, about a 14-year-old Hungarian boy who becomes a freedom fighter during the rebellion against the Soviets in 1956. (Rev: BL 2/1/96; SLJ 2/96; VOYA 6/96)

2712 Town, Florida Ann. *With a Silent Companion* (7–12). 2000, Red Deer paper $7.95 (0-88995-211-6). Beginning in 1806, this novel based on fact tells how a young Irish girl hides her identity and becomes a "man" to pursue a medical career. (Rev: BL 4/15/00; VOYA 6/00)

2713 Vogiel, Eva. *Friend or Foe?* (5–8). 2001, Judaica $19.95 (1-880582-66-X). In this novel set in London during 1948, the girls of the Migdal Binoh School for Orthodox Jewish girls notice strange happenings when the Campbell family moves next door. (Rev: BL 4/1/01)

2714 Wallace, Barbara Brooks. *Sparrows in the Scullery* (5–7). 1997, Simon & Schuster $15.00 (0-689-81585-9). Without explanation, Colley finds himself in an orphan home in this novel set in the London of Dickens. (Rev: BL 9/15/97; HBG 3/98; SLJ 11/97)

2715 Westall, Robert. *Gulf* (6–9). 1996, Scholastic paper $14.95 (0-590-22218-X). A savage tale of a psychic child witnessing the terrors of the Gulf War through the eyes of Latif, a 13-year-old Iraqi soldier. (Rev: SLJ 1/96; VOYA 4/96)

2716 Wheeler, Thomas Gerald. *All Men Tall* (7–9). 1969, Phillips $26.95 (0-87599-157-2). An adventure tale set in early England about a 15-year-old boy's search for security.

2717 Wheeler, Thomas Gerald. *A Fanfare for the Stalwart* (7–9). 1967, Phillips $26.95 (0-87599-139-4). An injured Frenchman is left behind when Napoleon retreats from Russia.

2718 Whelan, Gerard. *The Guns of Easter* (6–10). 2000, O'Brien paper $7.95 (0-86278-449-2). Twelve-year-old Jimmy Conway grapples with the reasons for, and impact of, the violence erupting in Ireland in the early 20th century. (Rev: BL 3/1/01)

2719 Whelan, Gerard. *A Winter of Spies* (6–10). 2002, O'Brien paper $6.95 (0-86278-566-9). The story of the Conway family, begun in *The Guns of Easter* (2001), continues in this novel as 11-year-old

Sarah sees spies and counterspies all around her in 1920 Dublin. (Rev: BL 6/1–15/02)

2720 Whelan, Gloria. *Angel on the Square* (5–10). Illus. 2001, HarperCollins $15.95 (0-06-029030-7). The Russian Revolution, World War, and social upheaval totally change life for privileged young Katya, who learns to adapt in this story that starts in 1913. (Rev: BL 9/15/01; HBG 3/02; SLJ 10/01; VOYA 10/01)

2721 Whelan, Gloria. *The Impossible Journey* (5–8). 2003, HarperCollins LB $16.89 (0-06-623812-9). A 13-year-old girl named Marya and her younger brother journey to Siberia to find their exiled mother in this book set in Stalin's Russia that includes lots of historical detail. (Rev: BL 12/15/02; HB 3–4/03; HBG 10/03; SLJ 1/03)

2722 Williams, Laura E. *The Spider's Web* (5–7). Illus. 1999, Milkweed $15.95 (1-57131-621-3); paper $6.95 (1-57131-622-1). Lexi, a modern German girl, joins a racist skinhead organization and discovers the consequences of irrational hatred — from her own actions and from speaking with an older woman who was once a member of Hitler's Youth. (Rev: BL 6/1–15/99; HBG 10/99)

2723 Yolen, Jane, and Robert Harris. *Girl in a Cage* (6–10). 2002, Putnam $19.99 (0-399-23627-9). In 1306, the 11-year-old daughter of the Scottish king describes her plight when she is captured by the English. (Rev: BCCB 2/03; BL 9/15/02; HB 1–2/03; HBG 3/03; SLJ 10/02*)

2724 Yolen, Jane, and Robert J. Harris. *Queen's Own Fool* (7–12). 2000, Putnam $19.99 (0-399-23380-6). The story of Mary, Queen of Scots, as narrated by the royal jester, a woman named La Jardiniere. (Rev: BL 4/1/00; HB 5–6/00; HBG 9/00; SLJ 6/00; VOYA 6/00)

2725 Zucker, N. F. *Benno's Bear* (4–7). 2001, Dutton $16.99 (0-525-46521-9). Benno, a young pickpocket in Central Europe, is taken in by a kind family who help him discover the joys of reading. (Rev: BCCB 12/01; BL 11/15/01; HB 11–12/01; HBG 3/02; SLJ 10/01; VOYA 4/02)

Latin America and Canada

2726 Alvarez, Julia. *Before We Were Free* (7–10). 2002, Knopf $15.95 (0-375-81544-9). Twelve-year-old Anita describes growing up in the repressive Dominican Republic of 1960 and her increasing understanding and personal experience of the political crisis taking place. (Rev: BCCB 11/02; BL 8/02; HB 9–10/02*; HBG 3/03; SLJ 8/02; VOYA 8/02)

2727 Belpre, Pura. *Firefly Summer* (5–8). 1996, Pinata paper $9.95 (1-55885-180-1). This gentle novel depicts family and community life in rural Puerto Rico at the turn of the 20th century as experienced by young Teresa Rodrigo, who has just com-

pleted 7th grade. (Rev: BR 3–4/97; SLJ 2/97; VOYA 4/97)

2728 Brandis, Marianne. *The Quarter-Pie Window* (6–8). 2003, Tundra paper $9.95 (0-88776-624-2). Fourteen-year-old Emma and her younger brother, recently orphaned, go to live with their aunt and soon discover that the aunt is exploiting them in this novel set in 1830 Canada. (Rev: BL 7/03; VOYA 8/03)

2729 Caswell, Maryanne. *Pioneer Girl* (5–8). 2001, Tundra $16.95 (0-88776-550-5). In letters to her grandmother, a 14-year-old girl describes the hardships and interesting experiences of her journey from Ontario to the prairies in the late 1880s. (Rev: HBG 10/01; SLJ 10/01)

2730 Clark, Ann Nolan. *Secret of the Andes* (6–8). 1970, Penguin paper $4.99 (0-14-030926-8). In this Newbery Medal winner (1953), a young Inca boy searches for his birthright and his identity.

2731 Crook, Connie Brummel. *The Hungry Year* (5–8). 2001, Stoddart paper $7.95 (0-7737-6206-X). Twelve-year-old Kate must care for her brothers and handle the household chores during a severe Canadian winter in the late 1700s. (Rev: BL 1/1–15/02; SLJ 11/01)

2732 Dorris, Michael. *Morning Girl* (5–9). 1992, Hyperion $12.95 (1-56282-284-5). The lovely and surprising coming-of-age story of Morning Girl and Star Boy, Arawak Indians on the eve of Columbus's exploration of the West Indies. (Rev: BL 8/92*; SLJ 10/92)

2733 Downie, Mary Alice, and John Downie. *Danger in Disguise* (5–8). Series: On Time's Wing. 2001, Roussan paper $6.95 (1-896184-72-3). Young Jamie, a Scot raised in Normandy in secrecy, is scooped up to serve in the British navy and sent to Quebec to fight the French in this complex tale of adventure and intrigue set in the mid-18th century. (Rev: SLJ 5/01)

2734 Doyle, Brian. *Mary Ann Alice* (4–7). 2002, Groundwood $15.95 (0-88899-453-2). It's 1926 and a new dam brings many changes to the Canadian community that is home to Mary Ann Alice, a 7th grader with a love of rocks. (Rev: BCCB 6/02; HB 5–6/02*; HBG 10/02; SLJ 6/02; VOYA 6/02)

2735 Durbin, William. *The Broken Blade* (5–8). 1997, Delacorte $14.95 (0-385-32224-0). To help his family, 13-year-old Pierre becomes a *voyageur*, a fur trader working out of old Quebec. (Rev: BCCB 2/97; BL 3/1/97; BR 5–6/97; SLJ 2/97; VOYA 4/97)

2736 Durbin, William. *Wintering* (5–8). 1999, Bantam Doubleday Dell $14.95 (0-385-32598-3). In this companion to *The Broken Blade*, young Pierre LaPage again lives the exciting life of a *voyageur* and spends a winter in the Great Lakes area transporting furs. (Rev: BL 2/15/99*; BR 9–10/99; HBG 10/99; SLJ 2/99)

2737 Eboch, Chris. *The Well of Sacrifice* (5–8). Illus. 1999, Houghton $16.00 (0-395-90374-2). In this novel set during Mayan times, Eveningstar Macaw sets out to avenge the death of her older brother, Smoke Shell. (Rev: BL 4/1/99; HBG 10/99; SLJ 5/99; VOYA 2/00)

2738 Gantos, Jack. *Jack's New Power: Stories from a Caribbean Year* (5–8). 1995, Farrar $16.00 (0-374-33657-1); paper $5.95 (0-374-43715-7). Eight stories about the interesting people Jack meets when his family moves to the Caribbean. A sequel to *Heads or Tails* (1994). (Rev: BCCB 12/95; BL 12/1/95; SLJ 11/95*)

2739 Harrison, Troon. *A Bushel of Light* (5–8). 2001, Stoddart paper $7.95 (0-7737-6140-3). Fourteen-year-old orphan Maggie juggles her need to search for her twin sister and her responsibilities for 4-year-old Lizzy, in this novel set in Canada in the early 1900s. (Rev: SLJ 10/01)

2740 Haworth-Attard, Barbara. *Home Child* (5–8). 1996, Roussan paper $6.95 (1-896184-18-9). Set in Canada during the early 1900s, this is the story of 13-year-old Arthur Fellowes, a London orphan who is treated like an outcast when he joins the Wilson family as a home child (that is, a cheap farm laborer). (Rev: VOYA 8/97)

2741 Holeman, Linda. *Promise Song* (5–8). 1997, Tundra paper $6.95 (0-88776-387-1). In 1900, Rosetta, an English orphan who has been sent to Canada, becomes an indentured servant. (Rev: BL 6/1–15/97; SLJ 10/97)

2742 Ibbotson, Eva. *Journey to the River Sea* (5–8). 2002, Dutton $17.99 (0-525-46739-4). Orphaned Maia journeys from 1910 London to live with relatives in Brazil in this complex story that involves an unwelcoming family, a beloved governess, a child actor, a runaway, and the wonders of Brazil, all presented with a mix of drama and humor. (Rev: BCCB 4/02; BL 12/15/01; HB 1–2/02; HBG 10/02; SLJ 1/02*; VOYA 12/01)

2743 Jenkins, Lyll Becerra de. *So Loud a Silence* (7–10). 1996, Dutton $16.99 (0-525-67538-8). In contemporary Colombia, 17-year-old Juan leaves the city slums to find peace at his grandmother's mountain home, but instead becomes involved in the civil war conflict and the violence of the army and the guerrillas. (Rev: BL 9/15/96; BR 3–4/97; SLJ 12/96; VOYA 2/97)

2744 Lawson, Julie. *Goldstone* (5–8). 1998, Stoddart paper $7.95 (0-7737-5891-7). Karin, a 13-year-old Swedish Canadian girl, lives with her family in a mountainous town in British Columbia in 1910 when heavy winter snows bring avalanches that cause death and destruction. (Rev: BL 7/97; SLJ 5/98)

2745 Limon, Graciela. *Song of the Hummingbird* (6–10). 1996, Arte Publico paper $12.95 (1-55885-091-0). The conquest of the Aztec Empire by Cortes is told through the experiences of Huizitzilin (Hummingbird), a descendent of Mexican kings. (Rev: VOYA 8/97)

2746 O'Dell, Scott. *The Captive* (7–9). 1979, Houghton $17.00 (0-395-27811-2). During a voyage in the 1500s, a young Jesuit seminarian discovers that the crew of his ship plans to enslave a colony of Mayans. A sequel is *The Feathered Serpent* (1981).

2747 O'Dell, Scott. *The King's Fifth* (7–10). 1966, Houghton $17.00 (0-395-06963-7). In a story told in flashbacks, Esteban explains why he is in jail in the Mexico of the Conquistadors. Also use *The Hawk That Dare Not Hunt by Day* (1975).

2748 O'Dell, Scott. *My Name Is Not Angelica* (5–8). 1989, Houghton $18.00 (0-395-51061-9). A fictionalized account of the slave revolt in the Virgin Islands in 1733–1734. (Rev: BL 11/15/89*; BR 3–4/90; SLJ 10/89; VOYA 12/89)

2749 Reekie, Jocelyn. *Tess* (5–8). 2003, Raincoast paper $7.95 (1-55192-471-4). Thirteen-year-old Tess is a plucky, strong-willed girl who must leave her Scottish home and move to British Columbia in 1857. (Rev: BL 3/1/03; VOYA 6/03)

2750 Schwartz, Virginia Frances. *Messenger* (5–9). 2002, Holiday $17.95 (0-8234-1716-6). This story of the hardships and joys of a Croatian family living in Ontario's mining towns in the 1920s and 1930s is based on the lives of the author's mother and grandmother. (Rev: HBG 3/03; SLJ 11/02; VOYA 12/02)

2751 Slade, Arthur. *Dust* (8–12). 2003, Random $15.95 (0-375-73004-7). Eleven-year-old Robert wonders why people are so accepting of the recent disappearance of a number of children and so willing to listen to the mysterious Hamsich, who promises to bring rain to his drought-stricken Saskatchewan town in the 1930s. (Rev: BCCB 3/03; BL 2/15/03; HB 3–4/03; SLJ 3/03*; VOYA 2/03)

2752 Slaughter, Charles H. *The Dirty War* (6–9). 1994, Walker $15.95 (0-8027-8312-0). Arte, 14, lives in Buenos Aires, Argentina. When his father is taken prisoner by the government, his grandmother stages public protests. (Rev: BL 11/1/94; SLJ 12/94; VOYA 2/95)

2753 Stenhouse, Ted. *Across the Steel River* (6–8). 2001, Kids Can $16.95 (1-55074-891-2). In 1952, a Canadian boy and his Indian friend find the badly beaten body of an Indian man and, in the process of investigating his death, reassess their own relationship. (Rev: BCCB 1/02; BL 1/1–15/02; HBG 3/02; SLJ 10/01; VOYA 2/02)

2754 Stenhouse, Ted. *A Dirty Deed* (6–8). 2003, Kids Can $16.95 (1-55337-360-X). In this sequel to *Across the Steel River* (2001), friends Will Samson and Arthur, a Blackfoot Indian, have exciting adventures as they struggle to return a deed to its rightful owners. (Rev: BL 3/15/03; HBG 10/03; SLJ 5/03; VOYA 10/03)

2755 Strasser, Todd. *The Diving Bell* (4–7). Illus. 1992, Scholastic paper $13.95 (0-590-44620-7). When Spanish ships ladened with gold sink close to their island, some natives try to salvage them in this story set in the New World during the Spanish conquest. (Rev: SLJ 6/92)

2756 Talbert, Marc. *Heart of a Jaguar* (7–10). 1995, Simon & Schuster $16.00 (0-689-80282-X). A death-inducing drought takes its toll in the heart of a Mayan village. (Rev: BL 9/15/95; SLJ 11/95; VOYA 12/95)

2757 Temple, Frances. *Taste of Salt: A Story of Modern Haiti* (7–12). 1992, Orchard LB $17.99 (0-531-08609-7). A first novel simply told in the voices of two Haitian teenagers who find political commitment and love. (Rev: BL 8/92; SLJ 9/92*)

2758 Trottier, Maxine. *A Circle of Silver* (5–8). 2000, Stoddart paper $7.95 (0-7737-6055-5). Set in the 1760s, this is the story of 13-year-old John Mac-Neil who is sent to Canada by his father to toughen him up. (Rev: SLJ 9/00)

2759 Vande Griek, Susan. *A Gift for Ampato* (5–8). 1999, Groundwood $14.95 (0-88899-358-7). Set in the days of the ancient Incas, this story tells about a young girl, Tinta, who has been chosen to be a human sacrifice to the gods. (Rev: BCCB 1/00; SLJ 12/99)

2760 Weir, Joan. *The Brideship* (7–9). 1999, Stoddart paper $5.95 (0-7736-7474-8). Three plucky British teens journey to British Columbia as mail-order brides in the 1860s. (Rev: BR 11–12/99; SLJ 10/99)

2761 Weir, Joan. *The Witcher* (5–7). 1998, Polestar paper $6.95 (1-896095-44-5). In Canada's Gold Rush country, 12-year-old Lion and his older sister help their father solve the custody issues surrounding a young girl who possesses divining powers. (Rev: SLJ 3/99)

United States

NATIVE AMERICANS

2762 Ackerman, Ned. *Spirit Horse* (5–8). 1998, Scholastic paper $15.95 (0-590-39650-1). Set in Blackfoot territory in the 1700s, this novel traces the adventures of young Running Crane, his struggle for survival alone in the wilderness, and his taming of the magnificent wild horse named Spirit Horse. (Rev: BCCB 3/98; BL 6/1–15/98; BR 5–6/98; HBG 9/98; SLJ 4/98)

2763 Armstrong, Nancy M. *Navajo Long Walk* (4–7). Illus. 1994, Roberts Rinehart $8.95 (1-

879373-56-4). The story of the Long Walk of the Navajo in 1864 and their confinement in an internment camp are vividly told. (Rev: BL 10/1/94; SLJ 1/95)

2764 Benchley, Nathaniel. *Only Earth and Sky Last Forever* (6–9). 1972, HarperCollins paper $4.95 (0-06-440049-2). The Battle of Little Big Horn is a pivotal event in this novel of an Indian boy's journey to manhood.

2765 Bruchac, Joseph. *A Boy Called Slow: The True Story of Sitting Bull* (5–8). 1995, Putnam $16.99 (0-399-22692-3). The story of the boyhood of Sitting Bull, who, because of his sluggishness, had been called Slow. (Rev: BCCB 4/95; BL 3/15/95; HB 9–10/95; SLJ 10/95)

2766 Bruchac, Joseph. *The Journal of Jesse Smoke: The Trail of Tears, 1838* (5–8). Illus. Series: My Name Is America. 2001, Scholastic paper $10.95 (0-439-12197-3). Jesse, a 16-year-old Cherokee, chronicles in his diary the tribe's forced journey to Oklahoma and tries to understand the reasons behind this cruel action. (Rev: BL 7/01; HBG 10/01; SLJ 7/01; VOYA 8/01)

2767 Burks, Brian. *Runs with Horses* (5–9). 1995, Harcourt $12.00 (0-15-200264-2); paper $6.00 (0-15-200994-9). An adventure story set in 1886 in which 16-year-old Runs with Horses completes his Apache warrior training by performing feats of endurance, survival, and daring, and partly as a result of information he gathers during raids, his tribe realizes that they can no longer continue to resist the white man. (Rev: BL 11/1/95; BR 1–2/96; SLJ 11/95; VOYA 2/96)

2768 Burks, Brian. *Walks Alone* (5–9). 1998, Harcourt $16.00 (0-15-201612-0). An accurate, heartbreaking account of the decimation of the Apache Indians circa 1879 by the U.S. Army, as experienced by a 15-year-old Indian girl, Walks Alone. (Rev: BCCB 5/98; BL 5/1/98; HBG 10/98; SLJ 4/98; VOYA 4/99)

2769 Cornelissen, Cornelia. *Soft Rain: A Story of the Cherokee Trail of Tears* (4–7). 1998, Delacorte $14.95 (0-385-32253-4). Told from a Cherokee child's point of view, this novel tells how Soft Rain's family was separated, of the brutal roundups by white soldiers, and of the long, forced march west from North Carolina in 1838. (Rev: BL 8/98; HBG 10/99; SLJ 10/98)

2770 Dadey, Debbie. *Cherokee Sister* (4–7). 2000, Delacorte $14.95 (0-385-32703-X). In 1838, Cherokees are forced on a terrible march and, by mistake, include a 12-year-old white girl named Allie. (Rev: BL 4/1/00; HBG 3/01; SLJ 4/00)

2771 Dorris, Michael. *Sees Behind Trees* (4–8). 1996, Hyperion LB $15.49 (0-7868-2215-5). Set in the 15th century, this story about Native Americans features a young man with an unusual talent who journeys with a village elder to find the land of water. (Rev: BR 3–4/97; SLJ 10/96*)

2772 Doughty, Wayne Dyre. *Crimson Moccasins* (7–9). 1980, HarperCollins paper $2.95 (0-06-440015-8). During the Revolutionary War a white boy is raised as the son of an Indian chief.

2773 Duey, Kathleen. *Celou Sudden Shout, Idaho, 1826* (4–8). Series: American Diaries. 1998, Simon & Schuster paper $4.50 (0-689-81622-7). Crow Indians kidnap Celou's mother, who is a Shoshone, and Celou follows the raiding party, hoping to effect a rescue. (Rev: SLJ 6/98)

2774 Erdrich, Louise. *The Birchbark House* (4–8). Illus. 1999, Hyperion LB $15.49 (0-7868-2241-4). An Ojibwa Indian child living on an island in Lake Superior in 1847 describes the problems that began when white people arrived to take over their land. (Rev: BL 4/1/99; HB 5–6/99; HBG 10/99)

2775 Finley, Mary Peace. *Soaring Eagle* (5–9). 1993, Simon & Schuster paper $16.00 (0-671-75598-6). In this coming-of-age story, Julio searches for his heritage among mid-19th-century Cheyenne Indians. (Rev: BL 8/93; VOYA 2/94)

2776 Gall, Grant. *Apache: The Long Ride Home* (7–10). 1988, Sunstone paper $9.95 (0-86534-105-2). Pedro was only nine when Apache raiders kidnapped him and renamed him Cuchillo. (Rev: BL 9/15/87; BR 9–10/88)

2777 Gregory, Kristiana. *The Legend of Jimmy Spoon* (6–8). 1990, Harcourt $15.95 (0-15-200506-4). The story of a 12-year-old white boy who is adopted by the Shoshoni in 1855. (Rev: BL 7/90)

2778 Grutman, Jewel H., and Gay Matthaei. *The Ledgerbook of Thomas Blue Eagle* (4–8). 1994, Thomasson-Grant $17.95 (1-56566-063-3). A young Native American boy attends a white man's school but tries to retain his own identity and culture in this story that takes place in the West 100 years ago. (Rev: SLJ 12/94)

2779 Hausman, Gerald. *The Coyote Bead* (7–12). 1999, Hampton Roads paper $11.95 (1-57174-145-3). With the help of his grandfather and Indian magic, a young Navajo boy evades the American soldiers who killed his parents. (Rev: SLJ 1/00; VOYA 4/00)

2780 Highwater, Jamake. *Legend Days* (7–10). Series: Ghost Horse. 1984, HarperCollins $12.95 (0-06-022303-0). This story about a young Indian girl begins a moving trilogy about three generations of Native Americans and their fate in a white man's world. Followed by *The Ceremony of Innocence* and *I Wear the Morning Star.*

2781 Hudson, Jan. *Sweetgrass* (5–8). 1989, Scholastic paper $3.99 (0-590-43486-1). A description of the culture of the Dakota Indians in the 1830s. (Rev: BCCB 4/89; BL 4/1/89; SLJ 4/89)

2782 Matcheck, Diane. *The Sacrifice* (7–9). 1998, Putnam paper $5.99 (0-14-130640-8). Taken prisoner by the Pawnee, a young Indian girl makes her escape and returns to her tribe in this adventurous survival story. (Rev: BL 6/1–15/98; BR 11–12/98; SLJ 10/98; VOYA 2/99)

2783 Matthaei, Gay, and Jewel Grutman. *The Sketchbook of Thomas Blue Eagle* (4–7). Illus. 2001, Chronicle $16.95 (0-8818-2908-1). Through drawings and narration, the Lakota artist Thomas Blue Eagle tells how he joined Buffalo Bill's show, traveled to Europe, and made enough money to marry. (Rev: BCCB 5/01; BL 4/1/01)

2784 O'Dell, Scott. *Sing Down the Moon* (6–9). 1970, Houghton $18.00 (0-395-10919-1); Dell paper $5.99 (0-440-97975-7). A young Navaho girl sees her culture destroyed by Spanish slavers and white soldiers. (Rev: BL 11/1/87)

2785 O'Dell, Scott, and Elizabeth Hall. *Thunder Rolling in the Mountains* (5–9). 1992, Houghton $17.00 (0-395-59966-0); Dell paper $5.50 (0-440-40879-2). From the viewpoint of Chief Joseph's daughter, this historical novel concerns the forced removal of the Nez Perce from their homeland in 1877. (Rev: BL 6/15/92*; SLJ 8/92)

2786 Rees, Celia. *Sorceress* (7–11). 2002, Candlewick $15.99 (0-7636-1847-0). Agnes, a Native American who is beginning college, researches Mary Newbury, first seen in *Witch Child* (2001), and discovers a connection that results in a vision quest. (Rev: BL 1/1–15/03; HB 1–2/03; HBG 3/03; SLJ 12/02; VOYA 4/03)

2787 Sandoz, Mari. *The Horsecatcher* (7–9). 1957, Univ. of Nebraska Pr. paper $9.95 (0-8032-9160-4). A Cheyenne youth gains stature with his tribe and earns the name of Horsecatcher. (Rev: BL 11/1/87)

2788 Shefelman, Janice. *Comanche Song* (6–9). 2000, Eakin $17.95 (1-57168-397-6). Tsena, 16, is imprisoned with other Comanches after peace talks falter and 12 Indian chiefs are killed in this story based on a real event in 1840. (Rev: BL 2/15/01; HBG 10/01; SLJ 10/00)

2789 Smith, Patricia Clark. *Weetamoo: Heart of the Pocassets, Massachusetts — Rhode Island, 1653* (5–8). Illus. Series: Royal Diaries. 2003, Scholastic $10.95 (0-439-12910-9). Weetamoo prepares to succeed her father as leader of the tribe and describes relationships with the European settlers and how daily life changes with the seasons. (Rev: BL 12/15/03)

2790 Stewart, Elisabeth J. *On the Long Trail Home* (5–7). 1994, Clarion $15.00 (0-395-68361-0). A Cherokee girl escapes from the Trail of Tears and makes her way back to the Appalachian Mountains during the 1830s. (Rev: BCCB 12/94; BL 10/15/94; SLJ 12/94)

2791 Turner, Ann. *The Girl Who Chased Away Sorrow: The Diary of Sarah Nita, a Navajo Girl* (5–8). Illus. Series: Dear America. 1999, Scholastic $10.95 (0-590-97216-2). A Navajo woman describes to her granddaughter the Long Walk from Arizona to New Mexico that she survived as a child. (Rev: BL 11/15/99; HBG 3/00; SLJ 2/00; VOYA 2/00)

2792 Vick, Helen H. *Shadow* (5–7). Series: Courage of the Stone. 1998, Roberts Rinehart $15.95 (1-57098-218-X); paper $9.95 (1-57098-195-7). Shadow, an independent Pueblo Indian girl in pre-Columbian Arizona, leaves her home to rescue her father. (Rev: SLJ 10/98)

DISCOVERY AND EXPLORATION

2793 Garland, Sherry. *Indio* (7–10). 1995, Harcourt $11.00 (0-15-238631-9); paper $6.00 (0-15-200021-6). Ipa-ta-chi's life is destroyed when Spanish conquistadors enslave her. When her brother is injured and her sister raped in the silver mines, Ipa attempts to escape but is charged with murder. (Rev: BL 6/1–15/95; SLJ 6/95)

2794 Torrey, Michele. *To the Edge of the World* (5–8). 2003, Knopf LB $17.99 (0-375-92338-1). On board one of Magellan's ships as a cabin boy, Mateo encounters danger and excitement. (Rev: BL 2/1/03; SLJ 2/03)

COLONIAL PERIOD AND FRENCH AND INDIAN WARS

2795 Avi. *Night Journeys* (6–9). 1994, Morrow paper $4.95 (0-688-13628-1). In the Pennsylvania of 1767, a 12-year-old orphan boy joins a hunt for escaped bondsmen. Another novel set at the same time by this author is *Encounter at Easton* (1994).

2796 Bruchac, Joseph. *Pocahontas* (6–12). 2003, Harcourt $17.00 (0-15-216737-4). Pocahontas and John Smith take turns describing the relationship between the Jamestown colonists and the Powhatan Indians. (Rev: BL 9/15/03)

2797 Bruchac, Joseph. *The Winter People* (6–10). 2002, Dial $16.99 (0-8037-2694-5). A 14-year-old Abenaki boy searches for his mother and sisters after they are kidnapped by English soldiers in the French and Indian War. (Rev: BL 10/1/02*; HBG 3/03; SLJ 11/02*)

2798 Buckey, Sarah Masters. *Enemy in the Fort* (4–7). Series: History Mystery. 2001, Pleasant paper $5.95 (1-58485-306-9). Ten-year-old Rebecca, whose family has been separated by Abenaki Indians, solves a mystery at her New Hampshire fort. (Rev: BL 10/1/01; HBG 3/02; SLJ 12/01)

2799 Butler, Amy. *Virginia Bound* (4–7). 2003, Clarion $15.00 (0-618-24752-1). Thirteen-year-old Rob is kidnapped in London and shipped to Virginia as an indentured servant to work on a tobacco farm in 1627. (Rev: BL 3/1/03; HBG 10/03; SLJ 6/03)

2800 Clapp, Patricia. *Constance: A Story of Early Plymouth* (7–9). 1987, Morrow paper $6.99 (0-688-10976-4). An imaginary diary kept by a young Pilgrim girl who sailed on the *Mayflower*.

2801 Collier, James L., and Christopher Collier. *The Bloody Country* (7–10). 1985, Macmillan $12.95 (0-590-07411-3); Scholastic paper $4.50 (0-590-43126-9). A pioneer story about a family that settles in the 1750s in what is now Wilkes-Barre, Pennsylvania. Also use another fine historical novel by these authors *The Winter Hero* (1985).

2802 Collier, James Lincoln. *The Corn Raid: A Story of the Jamestown Settlement* (5–9). 2000, Jamestown paper $5.95 (0-8092-0619-6). History and fiction mix in this adventure tale set in the Jamestown settlement and featuring a 12-year-old indentured servant and his cruel master. (Rev: SLJ 4/00)

2803 Coombs, Karen M. *Sarah on Her Own* (6–10). 1996, Avon paper $3.99 (0-380-78275-8). Through the eyes of a sensitive English teenager who voyaged to America in 1620, the reader relives the harsh realities and joys of life in an early Virginia settlement. (Rev: SLJ 9/96)

2804 Cooney, Caroline. *The Ransom of Mercy Carter* (6–10). 2001, Delacorte $15.95 (0-385-32615-7). Eleven-year-old Mercy Carter is adopted by Mohawk Indians after her settlement in Massachusetts is raided in this historically accurate and detailed story based on a real event in 1704. (Rev: BL 4/1/01; HBG 10/01; SLJ 8/01; VOYA 4/01)

2805 Curry, Jane L. *A Stolen Life* (5–8). 1999, Simon & Schuster $16.00 (0-689-82932-9). A young Scottish teenager is kidnapped in 1758 and sent to America, where she has a number of adventures before returning home. (Rev: BCCB 11/99; BL 11/1/99; HBG 3/00; SLJ 11/99)

2806 Duey, Kathleen. *Sarah Anne Hartford* (4–7). Series: American Diaries. 1996, Simon & Schuster paper $4.99 (0-689-80384-2). A story set in Puritan New England about two girls who are placed in a pillory for playing on the Sabbath. (Rev: BCCB 5/96; BL 5/15/96; HB 9–10/96; SLJ 6/96)

2807 Durrant, Lynda. *The Beaded Moccasins: The Story of Mary Campbell* (5–9). 1998, Clarion $15.00 (0-395-85398-2). Told in the first person, this is a fictionalized account of the true story of 12-year-old Mary Campbell who was captured by the Delaware Indians in 1759. (Rev: BCCB 5/98; BL 3/15/98; HBG 10/98; SLJ 6/98; VOYA 12/98)

2808 Durrant, Lynda. *Echohawk* (5–9). 1996, Clarion $16.00 (0-395-74430-X). Raised by Mohican Indians after the death of his family in 1738, Jonathan Starr, renamed Echohawk, is eventually sent to a white teacher to learn English and becomes reacquainted with his true heritage. (Rev: BL 9/1/96; BR 3–4/97; SLJ 9/96)

2809 Durrant, Lynda. *Turtle Clan Journey* (5–9). 1999, Clarion $15.00 (0-395-90369-6). In this sequel to *Echohawk,* Jonathan is forced to leave the Indians who raised him and is sent to live in Albany with an aunt he doesn't know. (Rev: BL 5/1/99; HBG 10/99; SLJ 6/99)

2810 Edmonds, Walter. *The Matchlock Gun* (5–7). 1941, Putnam $16.99 (0-399-21911-0). Exciting, true story of a courageous boy who protected his mother and sister from the Indians of the Hudson Valley. Newbery Medal winner, 1942.

2811 Field, Rachel. *Calico Bush* (5–7). 1987, Macmillan $17.95 (0-02-734610-2); Bantam paper $4.99 (0-440-40368-5). This 1932 Newbery Honor Book is an adventure story of a French girl "loaned" to a family of American pioneers in Maine in the 1740s.

2812 Fleischman, Paul. *Saturnalia* (6–9). 1990, HarperCollins LB $14.89 (0-06-021913-0). The harshness of colonial life is seen through the eyes of a young Indian boy who is a printer's apprentice. (Rev: BL 5/1/90; SLJ 5/90; VOYA 6/90)

2813 Forrester, Sandra. *Wheel of the Moon* (5–8). 2000, HarperCollins LB $15.89 (0-06-029203-2). The story of Pen, a 14-year-old orphan, who is kidnapped from the streets of London and shipped to Virginia, where she is sold at auction as an indentured servant. (Rev: BL 11/15/00; HBG 3/01; SLJ 10/00)

2814 Greene, Jacqueline D. *Out of Many Waters* (6–8). 1988, Walker $16.95 (0-8027-6811-3). A historical novel that begins in Brazil and ends with a group of Jewish settlers who, after landing in New Amsterdam, began the first synagogue in America. (Rev: BL 1/15/89; BR 1–2/89; SLJ 10/88; VOYA 12/88)

2815 Grote, JoAnn A. *Queen Anne's War* (5–8). Series: The American Adventure. 1998, Chelsea LB $15.95 (0-7910-5045-9). During Queen Anne's War in 1710, Will Smith's family becomes involved in the attempt to drive the French out of New England, but 11-year-old Will is preoccupied with a jealous classmate. (Rev: HBG 3/99; SLJ 1/99)

2816 Harrah, Madge. *My Brother, My Enemy* (4–7). 1997, Simon & Schuster $16.00 (0-689-80968-9). Using Bacon's Rebellion in 1676 as a background, this novel involves a 14-year-old whose family is killed during an Indian raid on their cabin. (Rev: BCCB 7–8/97; BL 5/1/97; BR 11–12/97; SLJ 7/97; VOYA 10/97)

2817 Hurst, Carol Otis, and Rebecca Otis. *A Killing in Plymouth Colony* (5–7). 2003, Houghton $15.00 (0-618-27597-5). John Bradford, the son of the governor of Plymouth Colony, has always struggled to gain his father's approval and feels an affinity

toward an outcast who is accused of murder. (Rev: BL 12/1/03; SLJ 10/03)

2818 Jacobs, Paul S. *James Printer: A Novel of Rebellion* (5–8). 1997, Scholastic paper $15.95 (0-590-16381-7). Though he has been raised as an Englishman in colonial Cambridge, Massachusetts, an Indian boy feels he must choose sides when the English and Indians go to war. (Rev: BCCB 3/97; BL 4/15/97; SLJ 6/97; VOYA 6/98)

2819 Karwoski, Gail Langer. *Surviving Jamestown: The Adventures of Young Sam Collier* (5–7). 2001, Peachtree $14.95 (1-56145-239-4); paper $8.95 (1-56145-245-9). Full of facts, this novel tells the story of a 12-year-old English boy who sails in 1606 for the colony of Virginia, with details of the struggles the colonists faced. (Rev: HBG 10/01; SLJ 8/01; VOYA 8/01)

2820 Keehn, Sally M. *I Am Regina* (6–9). 1991, Putnam $17.99 (0-399-21797-5). In this novel based on a true story, a white girl who is kidnapped by Indians at the age of 10 becomes so assimilated into the tribe's culture that she can't remember anything about her early years when she is rescued nine years later. (Rev: BL 7/91; SLJ 6/91)

2821 Keehn, Sally M. *Moon of Two Dark Horses* (6–9). 1995, Puffin paper $5.99 (0-698-11949-5). A sensitively drawn friendship between a Native American boy and a white settler. (Rev: BL 11/15/95*; SLJ 11/95; VOYA 12/95)

2822 Kirkpatrick, Katherine. *Trouble's Daughter: The Story of Susanna Hutchinson, Indian Captive* (5–8). 1998, Doubleday $14.95 (0-385-32600-9). Based on fact, this outstanding historical novel recounts Susanna Hutchinson's life after she is kidnapped by Lenape Indians who massacre her family on Long Island in 1663. (Rev: BL 8/98*; HBG 3/99; SLJ 9/98; VOYA 4/99)

2823 Koller, Jackie F. *The Primrose Way* (7–10). 1992, Harcourt $15.95 (0-15-256745-3). A historical romance in which Rebekah, 16, falls in love with Mishannock, a Pawtucket holy man. (Rev: BL 10/15/92; SLJ 9/92)

2824 Laird, Marnie. *Water Rat* (7–9). Illus. 1998, Winslow $15.95 (1-890817-08-2). An action-filled adventure story set in colonial times about Matt, a 14-year-old orphan, and his struggle to survive and prove his worth. (Rev: SLJ 1/99; VOYA 2/99)

2825 Lasky, Kathryn. *Beyond the Burning Time* (7–12). 1994, Scholastic paper $14.95 (0-590-47331-X). In this docunovel that captures the ignorance, violence, and hysteria of the Salem witch trials, Mary, 12, tries to save her mother, accused of witchcraft. (Rev: BL 10/15/94; SLJ 1/95; VOYA 12/94)

2826 Lasky, Kathryn. *A Journey to the New World: The Diary of Remember Patience Whipple* (4–7). Series: Dear America. 1996, Scholastic paper

$10.95 (0-590-50214-X). Using diary entries as a format, this is the story of 12-year-old Mem Whipple, her journey on the *Mayflower*, and her first year in the New World. (Rev: BCCB 10/96; HB 9–10/96; SLJ 8/96; VOYA 10/96)

2827 Moore, Robin. *The Man with the Silver Oar* (6–12). 2002, HarperCollins $15.95 (0-380-97877-6). Daniel, a Quaker 15-year-old, stows away on a ship hunting pirates in this fine adventure story set in 1718. (Rev: BL 6/1–15/02; HBG 10/02; SLJ 7/02; VOYA 8/02)

2828 O'Dell, Scott. *The Serpent Never Sleeps: A Novel of Jamestown and Pocahontas* (6–9). Illus. 1987, Houghton $17.00 (0-395-44242-7); Fawcett paper $6.50 (0-449-70328-2). A young English girl becomes part of a settlement at Jamestown and there meets Pocahontas. (Rev: BL 11/1/87; BR 9–10/88; SLJ 9/87; VOYA 10/87)

2829 Ovecka, Janice. *Cave of Falling Water* (4–8). 1992, New England Pr. paper $10.95 (0-933050-98-4). A cave in the hills of Vermont plays a part in the lives of three girls, one an Indian and one white, both from colonial times, and the last, a contemporary adolescent. (Rev: BL 5/1/93)

2830 Petry, Ann. *Tituba of Salem Village* (6–8). 1988, HarperCollins paper $5.99 (0-06-440403-X). The story of the slave Tituba and her husband, John Indian, from the day they were sold in the Barbados until the tragic Salem witchcraft trials.

2831 Rees, Celia. *Witch Child* (8–12). 2001, Candlewick $15.99 (0-7636-1421-1). Young Mary Newbury, a witch, keeps a journal of her voyage to the New World and describes how the Puritan community views her with suspicion. (Rev: BCCB 7–8/01; BL 10/15/01; HB 9–10/01; HBG 3/02; SLJ 8/01; VOYA 10/01)

2832 Rinaldi, Ann. *A Break with Charity: A Story About the Salem Witch Trials* (7–10). 1992, Harcourt $17.00 (0-15-200353-3). This blend of history and fiction brings to life the dark period in American history of the Salem witch trials. (Rev: BL 10/1/92; SLJ 9/92)

2833 Rinaldi, Ann. *Hang a Thousand Trees with Ribbons* (7–12). 1996, Harcourt $14.00 (0-15-200876-4); paper $6.00 (0-15-200877-2). A well-researched novel about the life of Phillis Wheatley, who was bought by the Wheatleys in 1761 and who later became America's first black poet. (Rev: BL 9/1/96; BR 3–4/97; SLJ 11/96; VOYA 12/96)

2834 Rinaldi, Ann. *The Journal of Jasper Jonathan Pierce: A Pilgrim Boy, Plymouth, 1620* (4–8). 2000, Scholastic paper $10.95 (0-590-51078-9). This fictionalized account of the Pilgrims in journal format follows the adventures of a 14-year-old indentured servant aboard the *Mayflower* and during his first year in the New World. (Rev: BL 2/15/00; HBG 10/00; SLJ 7/00)

2835 Rinaldi, Ann. *Or Give Me Death: A Novel of Patrick Henry's Family* (7–9). 2003, Harcourt $17.00 (0-15-216687-4). The treatment of the mentally ill in the colonial era is shown in this novel narrated by the daughters of an insane mother. (Rev: BL 5/15/03; SLJ 7/03; VOYA 8/03)

2836 Rinaldi, Ann. *A Stitch in Time* (7–10). Series: Quilt Trilogy. 1994, Scholastic paper $13.95 (0-590-46055-2). This historical novel set in 18th-century Salem, Massachusetts, concerns the tribulations of a 16-year-old girl and her family. (Rev: BL 3/1/94; SLJ 5/94; VOYA 4/94)

2837 Speare, Elizabeth George. *Calico Captive* (6–9). 1957, Dell paper $4.99 (0-440-41156-4). In colonial America, the Johnson family are captured by Indians and forced on a long trek.

2838 Speare, Elizabeth George. *The Sign of the Beaver* (6–9). 1983, Houghton $16.00 (0-395-33890-5); Dell paper $5.99 (0-440-47900-2). In Maine in 1768, Matt, though only 12, is struggling to survive on his own until the Indians help him. (Rev: BL 3/1/88)

2839 Speare, Elizabeth George. *The Witch of Blackbird Pond* (6–9). 1958, Houghton $16.00 (0-395-07114-3); Dell paper $5.99 (0-440-99577-9). Historical romance set in Puritan Connecticut with the theme of witchcraft. Newbery Medal winner, 1959. (Rev: BL 7/88)

2840 Stainer, M. L. *The Lyon's Cub* (5–9). Illus. 1998, Chicken Soup Pr. LB $9.95 (0-9646904-5-4); paper $6.95 (0-9646904-6-2). This novel, a continuation of *The Lyon's Roar* (1997), tells what happened to the settlers of the lost colony of Roanoke and their life with peaceful Indian tribes. Continued in *The Lyon's Pride* (1998). (Rev: SLJ 8/98)

2841 Strickland, Brad. *The Guns of Tortuga* (5–8). 2003, Simon & Schuster paper $4.99 (0-689-85297-5). Young Davy helps the crew of the *Aurora* defeat a band of pirates in this sequel to *Mutiny!* (Rev: BL 2/1/03; SLJ 3/03)

2842 Strickland, Brad, and Thomas E. Fuller. *Heart of Steele* (5–8). 2003, Simon & Schuster paper $4.99 (0-689-85298-3). Davy, his uncle, and Captain Hunter continue their hunt for the evil Jack Steele, who has been falsely implicating Captain Hunter in his murderous piracy. (Rev: BL 9/1/03; SLJ 10/03)

2843 Strickland, Brad, and Thomas E. Fuller. *Mutiny!* (5–8). 2002, Simon & Schuster paper $4.99 (0-689-85296-7). Fourteen-year-old orphan Davy arrives in Jamaica to live with his Uncle Patch, only to find himself embroiled in a daring and complex effort to capture Caribbean pirates in a story embellished with interesting facts about the 1680s. (Rev: BL 12/1/02; SLJ 11/02)

2844 Wisler, G. Clifton. *This New Land* (5–9). 1987, Walker LB $14.85 (0-8027-6727-3). Twelve-year-old Richard and his family begin a new life in Plymouth, Massachusetts, in 1620. (Rev: BL 3/15/88; BR 5–6/88; SLJ 11/87)

2845 Wyeth, Sharon D. *Once on This River* (6–10). 1997, Knopf $16.00 (0-679-88350-9); paper $4.99 (0-679-89446-2). In this historical novel set in 1760, 11-year-old Monday de Groot travels from Madagascar to New York to save a man from slavery, only to find the shocking truth of her own birth. (Rev: BCCB 4/98; BL 12/15/97; BR 5–6/98; HBG 9/98; SLJ 4/98)

REVOLUTIONARY PERIOD AND THE YOUNG NATION (1775–1809)

2846 Alsheimer, Jeanette E., and Patricia J. Friedle. *The Trouble with Tea* (5–8). 2002, Pentland $15.95 (1-57197-299-4). When Patience visits her friend Anne in Boston in 1773, she witnesses many of the events that led to the American Revolution. (Rev: BL 6/1–15/02)

2847 Anderson, Joan. *1787* (7–10). 1987, Harcourt $14.95 (0-15-200582-X). The story of a teenager who became James Madison's aide during the 1787 Constitutional Convention in Philadelphia. (Rev: BL 5/87; VOYA 12/87)

2848 Anderson, Laurie Halse. *Fever 1793* (6–10). 2000, Simon & Schuster $16.00 (0-689-83858-1). Matilda must find the strength to go on when her family is killed by yellow fever in a 1793 outbreak in Philadelphia. (Rev: BCCB 10/00; BL 10/1/00; HB 9–10/00; HBG 3/01; SLJ 8/00*)

2849 Armstrong, Jennifer. *Thomas Jefferson: Letters from a Philadelphia Bookworm* (5–8). Illus. Series: Dear Mr. President. 2001, Winslow $8.95 (1-890817-30-9). Twelve-year-old Amelia and President Jefferson discuss the events of the times in a continuing exchange of letters. (Rev: BL 5/15/01; HBG 10/01; SLJ 6/01; VOYA 8/01)

2850 Avi. *The Fighting Ground* (5–9). 1984, HarperCollins LB $16.89 (0-397-32074-4); paper $5.99 (0-06-440185-5). Thirteen-year-old Jonathan marches off to fight the British. (Rev: BL 4/87)

2851 Ayres, Katherine. *Stealing South: A Story of the Underground Railroad* (5–8). 2001, Delacorte $14.95 (0-385-72912-X). In pre-Civil War days, 16-year-old Will pretends to be a peddler in Kentucky to help with the escape of two slaves via the Underground Railroad. (Rev: BL 4/1/01; HBG 10/01; SLJ 6/01)

2852 Bradley, Kimberly Brubaker. *Weaver's Daughter* (5–7). 2000, Delacorte $14.95 (0-385-32769-2). Set in the South in the 1790s, this is the story of 10-year-old Lizzy Baker who suffers from asthma that is so severe that she is sent to live with a family in Charleston, to be near the sea air. (Rev: BCCB 11/00; BL 8/00; HBG 3/01; SLJ 10/00)

2853 Bruchac, Joseph. *The Arrow over the Door* (4–7). Illus. 1998, Dial $15.99 (0-8037-2078-5). Two boys, one a Quaker and the other a Native American, share the narration of this story that takes place immediately before the Battle of Saratoga in 1777. (Rev: BCCB 4/98; BL 2/15/98; HBG 10/98; SLJ 4/98)

2854 Collier, James Lincoln, and Christopher Collier. *My Brother Sam Is Dead* (6–9). 1984, Simon & Schuster $17.95 (0-02-722980-7); Scholastic paper $5.99 (0-590-42792-X). The story, based partially on fact, of a Connecticut family divided in loyalties during the Revolutionary War.

2855 Demas, Corinne. *If Ever I Return Again* (5–8). 2000, HarperCollins LB $15.89 (0-06-028718-7). Twelve-year-old Celia describes life aboard a whaling ship in letters home to her cousin. (Rev: BCCB 6/00; BL 4/1/00; HBG 10/00; SLJ 8/00)

2856 Denenberg, Barry. *The Journal of William Thomas Emerson: A Revolutionary War Patriot* (4–8). Series: My Name Is America. 1998, Scholastic paper $10.95 (0-590-31350-9). This historical novel consists of journal entries kept in 1774 by 12-year-old orphan Will, who becomes involved in political intrigue while working in a tavern. (Rev: BCCB 11/98; BL 11/1/98; HBG 3/99; SLJ 5/99)

2857 Durrant, Lynda. *Betsy Zane, the Rose of Fort Henry* (5–8). 2000, Clarion $15.00 (0-395-97899-8). Toward the end of the Revolutionary War, Betsy sets out alone from Philadelphia to rejoin her five brothers in western Virginia. (Rev: BCCB 10/00; BL 9/15/00; HBG 3/01; SLJ 4/01)

2858 Fast, Howard. *The Immigrants* (7–12). 1998, Harcourt paper $12.00 (0-15-600512-3). During the early stages of the Revolutionary War, 15-year-old Adam Cooper becomes a man.

2859 Fleischman, Paul. *Path of the Pale Horse* (7–9). 1992, HarperCollins paper $3.95 (0-06-440442-0). Dr. Peale and his apprentice help fight a yellow fever epidemic in 1793 Philadelphia.

2860 Forbes, Esther. *Johnny Tremain: A Novel for Old and Young* (6–9). 1943, Houghton $16.00 (0-395-06766-9); Dell paper $6.50 (0-440-94250-0). The story of a young silversmith's apprentice who plays an important part in the American Revolution. Newbery Medal winner, 1944. (Rev: BL 1/1/90)

2861 Fritz, Jean. *Brady* (4–7). 1960, Puffin paper $5.99 (0-14-032258-2). When Brady discovers his father is an Underground Railroad agent, he learns to control his tongue and form his own opinion about slavery.

2862 Gaeddert, Louann. *Breaking Free* (5–8). 1994, Atheneum paper $16.00 (0-689-31883-9). In upstate New York in 1800, orphaned Richard is upset that there are slaves on his uncle's farm and is determined to help one escape. (Rev: BL 4/1/94; HB 9–10/94; SLJ 5/94; VOYA 8/94)

2863 Goodman, Joan E. *Hope's Crossing* (5–8). 1998, Houghton $16.00 (0-395-86195-0). Kidnapped by British loyalists during the Revolution, Hope must try to escape and find her way home. (Rev: BCCB 7–8/98; BL 6/1–15/98; HBG 10/98; SLJ 5/98; VOYA 8/98)

2864 Gregory, Kristiana. *The Winter of Red Snow: The Revolutionary War Diary of Abigail Jane Stewart* (5–8). Series: Dear America. 1996, Scholastic paper $10.95 (0-590-22653-3). The hardships faced by the Revolutionary Army at Valley Forge in 1777–1778 are seen through the eyes of a young girl whose family lives close to the encampment. (Rev: BCCB 10/96; HB 9–10/96; SLJ 9/96; VOYA 10/96)

2865 Guzman, Lila, and Rick Guzman. *Lorenzo's Revolutionary Quest* (6–9). 2003, Piñata paper $9.95 (1-55885-392-8). In this sequel to *Lorenzo's Secret Mission* (2001), Lorenzo has exciting adventures when he is charged with buying 500 head of cattle for the Revolutionary Army. (Rev: SLJ 5/03)

2866 Guzman, Lila, and Rick Guzman. *Lorenzo's Secret Mission* (6–9). 2001, Piñata paper $9.95 (1-55885-341-3). In 1776, 15-year-old Lorenzo Bannister leaves Texas in search of his Virginia grandfather he has never known, and finds himself working on behalf of the American rebels. (Rev: BR 5–6/02; SLJ 12/01)

2867 Hansen, Joyce. *The Captive* (5–8). 1994, Scholastic paper $13.95 (0-590-41625-1). The exciting story based on fact of a young African boy sold into slavery in Massachusetts and how he eventually escaped. (Rev: BCCB 3/94; HB 1–2/94, 5–6/94; SLJ 1/94)

2868 Johnston, Norma. *Over Jordan* (5–9). 1999, Avon $15.00 (0-380-97635-8). Fourteen-year-old Roxana takes her attendant, Joss, and Joss's beau, escaped slave Gideon, upriver to Cincinnati in the hope of finding refuge for them through the Underground Railroad. (Rev: BL 12/15/99; HBG 3/00; SLJ 12/99; VOYA 2/00)

2869 Lavender, William. *Just Jane: A Daughter of England Caught in the Struggle of the American Revolution* (6–9). 2002, Harcourt $17.00 (0-15-202587-1). A young English girl is sent to live in South Carolina in 1776 and is soon caught up in romance and intrigue. (Rev: BL 11/1/02; HBG 3/03; SLJ 12/02; VOYA 12/02)

2870 Lunn, Janet. *The Hollow Tree* (5–9). 2000, Viking $15.99 (0-670-88949-0). Torn between feelings for both the rebels and the Tories, Phoebe finally decides to join the refugees heading to Canada and safety. (Rev: BCCB 6/00; BL 4/15/00; HBG 10/00; SLJ 6/00)

2871 Moore, Ruth Nulton. *Distant Thunder* (5–8). 1991, Herald Pr. paper $6.99 (0-8361-3557-1). During the Revolution, when wounded Americans are sent to Pennsylvania to recover, young Kate experiences the horrors of war. (Rev: BCCB 1/92; SLJ 1/92)

2872 Myers, Anna. *The Keeping Room* (4–7). 1997, Walker $16.95 (0-8027-8641-3). In this tale set during the Revolutionary War, Joseph's home is taken over by the Redcoats after his father goes off to war. (Rev: BL 11/1/97; HBG 3/98; SLJ 12/97)

2873 Nordan, Robert. *The Secret Road* (5–9). 2001, Holiday $16.95 (0-8234-1543-0). Young Laura helps an escaped slave on a long and suspenseful journey to freedom by posing as her sister. (Rev: BL 9/15/01; HBG 3/02; SLJ 10/01; VOYA 12/01)

2874 O'Dell, Scott. *Sarah Bishop* (6–9). 1980, Houghton $16.00 (0-395-29185-2); Scholastic paper $4.99 (0-590-44651-7). A first-person narrative of a girl who lives through the American Revolution and its toll of suffering and misery. (Rev: BL 3/1/88)

2875 Reit, Seymour. *Guns for General Washington: A Story of the American Revolution* (6–8). 1992, Harcourt paper $6.00 (0-15-232695-2). The true account of Colonel Henry Knox's attempt to bring cannons and artillery to the Continental Army during the blockade of 1775-1776. (Rev: BL 1/1/91; SLJ 1/91)

2876 Rinaldi, Ann. *Cast Two Shadows* (5–9). Series: Great Episodes. 1998, Harcourt $16.00 (0-15-200881-0). When the Revolutionary War reaches her home in Camden, South Carolina, life changes for 14-year-old Caroline Whitaker, whose family is divided in its allegiances. (Rev: BCCB 9/98; BL 9/15/98; HBG 10/99; SLJ 9/98)

2877 Rinaldi, Ann. *The Fifth of March: A Story of the Boston Massacre* (7–12). 1993, Harcourt $13.00 (0-15-200343-6); paper $6.00 (0-15-227517-7). In 1770, 14-year-old Rachel, an indentured servant in the household of John Adams, becomes caught up in political turmoil when she befriends a young British soldier. (Rev: BL 1/15/94*; SLJ 1/94; VOYA 2/94)

2878 Rinaldi, Ann. *Finishing Becca: The Story of Peggy Shippen and Benedict Arnold* (7–10). 1994, Harcourt $12.00 (0-15-200880-2). Historical fiction based on the author's contention that it was Peggy Shippen Arnold, wife of Benedict, who was responsible for her husband's betrayal of the American Revolution. (Rev: BL 11/15/94; SLJ 12/94; VOYA 2/95)

2879 Rinaldi, Ann. *A Ride into Morning: The Story of Temple Wick* (7–10). 1991, Harcourt $15.95 (0-15-200573-0). The story of a woman who hid her horse in her house to keep it from rebellious soldiers during the Revolutionary War. (Rev: BL 8/91; SLJ 5/91)

2880 Rinaldi, Ann. *The Secret of Sarah Revere* (7–10). 1995, Harcourt $13.00 (0-15-200393-2); paper $6.00 (0-15-200392-4). The daughter of Paul Revere recalls the events of the past two years against a background of historically significant events. (Rev: BL 11/15/95; SLJ 11/95; VOYA 12/95)

2881 Rinaldi, Ann. *Wolf by the Ears* (8–12). 1991, Scholastic $13.95 (0-590-43413-6). Harriet Hemings — the alleged daughter of Thomas Jefferson and his slave mistress — faces moral dilemmas in regard to freedom, equal rights, and her future. (Rev: BL 2/1/91; SLJ 4/91)

2882 Robinet, Harriette G. *Washington City Is Burning* (5–7). 1996, Simon & Schuster $16.95 (0-689-80773-2). In this historical novel set in the Washington, D.C., of James and Dolley Madison, young Virginia helps slaves escape. (Rev: BCCB 12/96; BL 11/1/96; SLJ 11/96)

2883 Roop, Peter, and Connie Roop. *An Eye for an Eye: A Story of the Revolutionary War* (5–9). 2000, Jamestown paper $5.95 (0-8092-0628-5). During the Revolutionary War, Samantha, disguised as boy, sets out to save her brother who is being held prisoner on a British ship. (Rev: BCCB 7–8/00; SLJ 4/00)

2884 Rosenburg, John. *First in War: George Washington in the American Revolution* (7–10). Illus. 1998, Millbrook LB $25.90 (0-7613-0311-1). This second part of the fictionalized biography of George Washington covers his career from 1775, when he was elected commander-in-chief, to the end of 1783, when he resigned from his military duties. (Rev: HBG 9/98; SLJ 7/98; VOYA 4/99)

2885 Schwartz, Virginia Frances. *Send One Angel Down* (5–8). 2000, Holiday $15.95 (0-8234-1484-1). This is the story of a young slave girl, Eliza, the skills she learns on the plantation, and how this knowledge helps her when she gains freedom. (Rev: BL 6/1–15/00; HB 7–8/00; HBG 10/00; SLJ 8/00)

2886 Shaik, Fatima. *Melitte* (6–9). 1997, Dial $15.99 (0-8037-2106-4). A horrifying look at slavery as experienced by a young girl, Melitte, in late-18th-century Louisiana. (Rev: BL 10/15/97; BR 3–4/98; HBG 3/98; SLJ 10/97; VOYA 2/98)

2887 Sterman, Betsy. *Saratoga Secret* (5–8). 1998, Dial $16.99 (0-8037-2332-6). In the Upper Hudson River Valley in 1777, young Amity must warn the Continentals of an impending attack by General Burgoyne. (Rev: BL 11/1/98; HBG 3/99; SLJ 11/98)

2888 Thomas, Velma M. *Lest We Forget: The Passage from Africa to Slavery and Emancipation* (5–8). Illus. 1997, Crown $29.95 (0-609-60030-3). An interactive book about slavery based on material from the Black Holocaust Museum. (Rev: BL 12/15/97) [973.6]

2889 Turner, Ann. *Love Thy Neighbor: The Tory Diary of Prudence Emerson* (4–7). Series: Dear America. 2003, Scholastic $10.95 (0-439-15308-5). Prudence, a teenager in 1774 Massachusetts,

describes the conflicts between Tories and Patriots and the effects on families and friends. (Rev: BL 7/03; HBG 10/03; SLJ 8/03)

2890 Van Leeuwen, Jean. *Hannah's Winter of Hope* (4–8). Illus. Series: Pioneer Daughters. 2000, Penguin $14.99 (0-8037-2492-6). After the British burn down their home, the Perley family suffers even more privations in this story told from the viewpoint of 11-year-old Hannah Perley. (Rev: BL 8/00; HBG 10/00; SLJ 7/00)

2891 Wait, Lea. *Seaward Born* (4–7). 2003, Simon & Schuster $16.95 (0-689-84719-X). Michael, a young slave, makes a dangerous journey to Canada and freedom in this dramatic historical novel. (Rev: BL 2/15/03; HBG 10/03; SLJ 1/03)

2892 Wait, Lea. *Stopping to Home* (4–7). 2001, Simon & Schuster $16.00 (0-689-83832-8). When 11-year-old Abbie's mother dies of smallpox and her father disappears, Abbie takes a job as a housemaid to provide for herself and her young brother in this story set in early-19th-century Maine. (Rev: BCCB 12/01; BL 11/15/01; HB 1–2/02; HBG 3/02; SLJ 10/01)

2893 Walter, Mildred P. *Second Daughter: The Story of a Slave Girl* (6–10). 1996, Scholastic paper $15.95 (0-590-48282-3). A fictional account of the dramatic incident in Massachusetts during 1781 when a slave woman, Mum Bett, took her owner to court and won her freedom. (Rev: BL 2/15/96; BR 5–6/96; SLJ 2/96; VOYA 8/96)

2894 Wisler, G. Clifton. *Kings Mountain* (5–7). 2002, HarperCollins LB $15.89 (0-06-623793-9). Fourteen-year-old Francis gets caught up in the intrigue and danger of the Revolutionary War when he is sent to South Carolina to help his grandmother run her tavern. Maps and a chronology add context. (Rev: BL 3/15/02; HBG 10/02; SLJ 7/02)

NINETEENTH CENTURY TO THE CIVIL WAR (1809–1861)

2895 Alder, Elizabeth. *Crossing the Panther's Path* (6–8). 2002, Farrar $19.00 (0-374-31662-7). Fifteen-year-old Billy Calder, who is half Mohawk, assists Chief Tecumseh during the War of 1812 in this historical novel. (Rev: BCCB 9/02; BL 5/15/02; HBG 10/02; SLJ 7/02; VOYA 6/02)

2896 Armstrong, Jennifer. *Steal Away* (6–9). 1993, Scholastic paper $4.50 (0-590-46921-5). Two unhappy 13-year-old girls — one a slave, the other a white orphan — disguise themselves as boys and run away. (Rev: BL 2/1/92; SLJ 2/92)

2897 Auch, Mary Jane. *Frozen Summer* (4–8). 1998, Holt $16.95 (0-8050-4923-1). In this sequel to *Journey to Nowhere*, set in 1816 in upstate New York, 12-year-old Mem struggles to hold her family together in spite of her mother's bouts of severe depression. (Rev: BCCB 1/99; BL 1/1–15/99; BR 5–6/99; HB 1–2/99; HBG 3/99; SLJ 12/98; VOYA 8/99)

2898 Auch, Mary Jane. *Journey to Nowhere* (4–8). 1997, Holt $16.95 (0-8050-4922-3). In 1815, 11-year-old Mem and her family relocate from Connecticut to the wilderness of Genesee County in western New York. (Rev: BCCB 6/97; BL 4/15/97; HB 7–8/97; SLJ 5/97)

2899 Auch, Mary Jane. *The Road to Home* (5–8). 2000, Holt $16.95 (0-8050-4921-5). In this sequel to *Journey to Nowhere* and *Frozen Summer*, Mem, now 13, and two siblings live in a boarding house in Rome, New York, while their father goes to work on the building of the Erie Canal. (Rev: BCCB 6/00; BL 4/1/00; HB 7–8/00; HBG 3/01; SLJ 7/00)

2900 Avi. *Beyond the Western Sea: Book Two: Lord Kirkle's Money* (6–9). 1996, Orchard LB $19.99 (0-531-08870-7). In this sequel to *Beyond the Western Sea: The Escape from Home* (1996), Patrick and Maura O'Connell and their two friends arrive in America, end up in the mill town of Lowell, Massachusetts, and encounter the villains that pursued them in the first book. (Rev: SLJ 10/96; VOYA 12/96)

2901 Avi. *Beyond the Western Sea: The Escape from Home* (6–10). 1996, Orchard LB $19.99 (0-531-08863-4). Three immigrant youngsters — two poor Irish peasants and the third, an English stowaway — face dangers and hardships on their journey to America in this suspenseful adventure novel set in the 1850s. (Rev: BL 2/1/96*; BR 9–10/96; SLJ 6/96; VOYA 6/96)

2902 Avi. *The True Confessions of Charlotte Doyle* (6–9). 1990, Watts LB $17.99 (0-531-08493-0). An adventure story set in the 1850s about a 13-year-old girl and her voyage to America on a ship with a murderous crew. (Rev: BL 9/1/90; SLJ 9/90)

2903 Ayres, Katherine. *North by Night: A Story of the Underground Railroad* (6–10). 1998, Delacorte $15.95 (0-385-32564-9). Told in diary form, this is the story of 16-year-old Lucinda and her role in helping slaves escape via the Underground Railroad. (Rev: BL 10/1/98; HBG 3/99; SLJ 10/98; VOYA 2/99)

2904 Blos, Joan W. *A Gathering of Days: A New England Girl's Journal, 1830–32* (6–8). 1979, Macmillan $16.00 (0-684-16340-3); paper $4.99 (0-689-71419-X). A fictional diary kept by 13-year-old Catherine Cabot, who is growing up in the town of Meredith, New Hampshire. Newbery Medal winner, 1980.

2905 Bryant, Louella. *The Black Bonnet* (6–9). 1996, New England Pr. paper $12.95 (1-881535-22-3). An exciting story of two young escaped slaves, Charity and her older sister Bea, and their last stop on the Underground Railroad in Burlington, Ver-mont, which they find is crawling with slave hunters. (Rev: BL 2/1/97; SLJ 2/97)

2906 Bryant, Louella. *Father by Blood* (6–9). 1999, New England Pr. paper $12.95 (1-881535-33-9). The story of John Brown and his raid on Harper's Ferry as seen through the eyes of his daughter Annie. (Rev: SLJ 9/99)

2907 Carbone, Elisa. *Stealing Freedom* (7–10). 1998, Knopf $17.00 (0-679-89307-5). Based on fact, this historical novel tells of a young teenage slave in Maryland and her escape to Canada via the Underground Railway in the 1850s. (Rev: BL 1/1–15/99; HBG 3/99; SLJ 2/99)

2908 Charbonneau, Eileen. *Honor to the Hills* (8–10). 1996, Tor $18.95 (0-312-86094-3). Returning to her home in the Catskill Mountains in 1851, 15-year-old Lily Woods finds that her family is involved in the Underground Railroad. (Rev: VOYA 6/96)

2909 Charbonneau, Eileen. *In the Time of the Wolves* (6–9). 1994, Tor paper $3.99 (0-8125-3361-5). In this story set in New York State 170 years ago, twin Josh struggles for his identity within his family and copes with prejudice against his Dutch/English/French/Native American heritage. (Rev: BL 12/1/94; VOYA 4/95)

2910 Collier, James Lincoln, and Christopher Collier. *The Clock* (5–7). 1995, Dell paper $4.99 (0-440-40999-3). Fifteen-year-old Annie Steele contends with the harsh life of mill work in Connecticut in 1810. (Rev: BCCB 4/92; BL 2/1/92; HB 3–4/92)

2911 Dahlberg, Maurine F. *The Spirit and Gilly Bucket* (5–8). 2002, Farrar $18.00 (0-374-31677-5). Eleven-year-old Gilly longs to join her father in his search for gold, but must stay in Virginia on a plantation, where she befriends a young slave and helps her escape via the Underground Railroad in this novel full of suspense and surprises. (Rev: BL 1/1–15/03; HBG 3/03; SLJ 12/02; VOYA 2/03)

2912 DeFelice, Cynthia. *The Apprenticeship of Lucas Whitaker* (5–8). 1996, Farrar $16.00 (0-374-34669-0). In the mid-1800s, orphan Lucas becomes an apprentice to the local dentist/barber/undertaker. (Rev: BCCB 10/96; BL 10/1/96; BR 3–4/97; SLJ 8/96*)

2913 Denenberg, Barry. *So Far from Home: The Diary of Mary Driscoll, an Irish Mill Girl* (4–8). Series: Dear America. 1997, Scholastic paper $10.95 (0-590-92667-5). Using a diary format, this novel tells the story of Mary Driscoll's journey to the United States from Ireland and her ordeals as a worker in a Massachusetts textile mill in the 1800s. (Rev: BL 12/15/97; HBG 3/98; SLJ 10/97)

2914 Donaldson, Joan. *A Pebble and a Pen* (5–8). 2000, Holiday $15.95 (0-8234-1500-7). In 1853, to avoid an arranged marriage, 14-year-old Matty runs away to study penmanship at Mr. Spencer's famous Ohio school. (Rev: BCCB 12/00; BL 1/1–15/01; HBG 10/01; SLJ 12/00; VOYA 2/01)

2915 Duey, Kathleen, and Karen A. Bale. *Hurricane: Open Seas, 1844* (5–7). Series: Survival! 1999, Simon & Schuster paper $4.50 (0-689-82544-7). This exciting sea story, set in 1844, tells of two youngsters who are on a whaler when a killer hurricane strikes. (Rev: SLJ 8/99)

2916 Forrester, Sandra. *Dust from Old Bones* (5–7). 1999, Morrow $16.00 (0-688-16202-9). In this novel set in New Orleans before the Civil War, young Simone resents her mother's strict discipline and instead likes to hang out with an aunt from Paris, who persuades her to help two slaves escape. (Rev: BCCB 10/99; BL 8/99; HBG 3/00; SLJ 10/99)

2917 Fox, Paula. *The Slave Dancer* (6–9). Illus. 1973, Bradbury LB $16.95 (0-02-735560-8); Dell paper $5.50 (0-440-96132-7). A young fifer is kidnapped and forced to play his instrument to exercise slaves on a slave ship. Newbery Medal winner, 1974.

2918 Garland, Sherry. *In the Shadow of the Alamo* (5–8). Series: Great Episodes. 2001, Harcourt $17.00 (0-15-201744-5). Fifteen-year-old Lorenzo Bonifacio, a conscript in the Mexican army of Santa Ana, describes the harsh life of the soldiers and the family members who follow them on the trek to Texas and the battle of the Alamo. (Rev: BCCB 1/02; BL 10/15/01; HB 11–12/01; HBG 3/02; SLJ 12/01; VOYA 10/01)

2919 Garland, Sherry. *A Line in the Sand: The Alamo Diary of Lucinda Lawrence* (4–8). Illus. Series: Dear America. 1998, Scholastic paper $10.95 (0-590-39466-5). Lucinda relates events in Gonzales, Texas, in 1835 that lead to the Texas War of Independence and to the massacre at the Alamo. (Rev: BL 3/1/99; HBG 3/99; SLJ 1/99)

2920 Guccione, Leslie D. *Come Morning* (4–7). 1995, Carolrhoda LB $19.15 (0-87614-892-5). A young boy takes over his father's duties as a conductor on the Underground Railroad. (Rev: BCCB 1/96; HB 11–12/95; SLJ 11/95)

2921 Hill, Donna. *Shipwreck Season* (5–8). 1998, Clarion $15.00 (0-395-86614-6). In the 1800s, 16-year-old Daniel joins a crew of seamen who patrol America's eastern coastline, rescuing people and cargo from shipwrecks. (Rev: BCCB 7–8/98; BL 6/1–15/98; HBG 3/99; SLJ 6/98)

2922 Hilts, Len. *Timmy O'Dowd and the Big Ditch: A Story of the Glory Days on the Old Erie Canal* (5–7). 1988, Harcourt $13.95 (0-15-200606-0). Timmy and his cousin Dennis don't get along, but when the canals threaten to flood, they realize each other's strengths and stamina. (Rev: BCCB 12/88; BL 10/1/88; SLJ 12/88)

2923 Houston, Gloria. *Bright Freedom's Song: A Story of the Underground Railroad* (4–7). 1998, Harcourt $16.00 (0-15-201812-3). A tense, dramatic story about a girl who helps her parents operate a North Carolina station on the Underground Railroad. (Rev: BCCB 1/99; BL 11/1/98; BR 5–6/99; HBG 3/99; SLJ 12/98; VOYA 2/99)

2924 Hurst, Carol Otis. *Through the Lock* (5–8). 2001, Houghton $15.00 (0-618-03036-0). In this novel set in Connecticut in the first half of the 19th century, a young orphan named Etta shares many adventures with a boy who lives in an abandoned cabin by a canal. (Rev: BCCB 3/01; BL 4/1/01; HB 3–4/01; HBG 10/01; SLJ 3/01; VOYA 4/01)

2925 Joslyn, Mauriel Phillips. *Shenandoah Autumn: Courage Under Fire* (6–10). 1999, White Mane paper $8.95 (1-57249-137-X). During the Civil War, young Mattie and her mother, though afraid of the Union troops around their Virginia home, save a wounded Confederate soldier and return him to his companions. (Rev: BL 5/1/99)

2926 Karr, Kathleen. *The Great Turkey Walk* (4–8). 1998, Farrar $17.00 (0-374-32773-4). In 1860, 15-year-old Simon decides to make his fortune by walking 1,000 turkeys from Missouri to Denver, where meat is scarce. (Rev: BCCB 5/98; BL 6/1–15/98; BR 1–2/99; HBG 10/98; SLJ 3/98*)

2927 Karr, Kathleen. *Skullduggery* (5–7). 2000, Hyperion $16.49 (0-7868-2439-5). Set in New York in the 19th century, this is the story of a young orphan boy whose job with a phrenologist involves digging up skulls for the doctor's research. (Rev: BCCB 4/00; BL 4/1/00; HB 5–6/00; HBG 10/00; SLJ 3/00)

2928 Ketchum, Liza. *Orphan Journey Home* (5–7). Illus. 2000, Avon $15.99 (0-380-97811-3). When their parents die in southern Illinois in 1828, Jesse and her three siblings must find their way to their grandmother in eastern Kentucky. (Rev: BCCB 6/00; BL 6/1–15/00; HBG 10/00; SLJ 8/00)

2929 Krisher, Trudy. *Uncommon Faith* (7–10). 2003, Holiday $17.95 (0-8234-1791-3). The year 1837–1838 is a time of change in Millbrook, Massachusetts, and 10 of the residents narrate their experiences in a collage that connects the reader to the townspeople and to the history. (Rev: BL 10/15/03; SLJ 10/03*; VOYA 10/03)

2930 Lasky, Kathryn. *True North* (6–8). 1996, Scholastic paper $15.95 (0-590-20523-4). Lucy, a 14-year-old girl living in Boston in 1858, and an escaped slave named Afrika travel north to Canada via the Underground Railroad. (Rev: BL 11/15/96; BR 3–4/97; SLJ 12/96; VOYA 4/97)

2931 Lyons, Mary E. *Letters from a Slave Girl: The Story of Harriet Jacobs* (7–12). 1992, Scribners $16.00 (0-684-19446-5). Based on Jacobs's autobiography, these "letters," written to lost relatives and friends, provide a look at what slavery meant for a young female in the mid-1800s. (Rev: BL 10/1/92; SLJ 12/92*)

2932 Lyons, Mary E. *The Poison Place* (6–8). Illus. 1997, Simon & Schuster $16.00 (0-689-81146-2). While taking his daughter on a tour of Philadelphia's Peale Museum, freed slave Moses Williams tells how his family and the Peales were entwined in family intrigue. (Rev: BL 12/1/97; BR 3–4/98; HBG 3/98; SLJ 11/97; VOYA 12/97)

2933 McGill, Alice. *Miles' Song* (6–9). 2000, Houghton $15.00 (0-395-97938-2). The story of a slave, Miles, who secretly learns to read and write and later plans a daring escape. (Rev: BL 4/1/00; HBG 9/00; SLJ 4/00; VOYA 6/00)

2934 McKissack, Patricia, and Fredrick McKissack. *Let My People Go* (5–8). Illus. 1998, Simon & Schuster $20.00 (0-689-80856-9). This novel set in the early 19th century combines Bible stories and the hardships endured by slaves as told by Price Jefferson, a former slave who is now an abolitionist living in South Carolina. (Rev: BCCB 12/98; BL 10/1/98; HBG 3/99; SLJ 11/98)

2935 Pastore, Clare. *Fiona McGilray's Story: A Voyage from Ireland in 1849* (5–8). Series: Journey to America. 2001, Berkley $9.95 (0-425-17783-1). To escape the Irish potato famine, Fiona McGilray and her brother emigrate to America, where Fiona is befriended by a wealthy woman. (Rev: BL 3/15/01; VOYA 8/01)

2936 Paterson, Katherine. *Jip: His Story* (5–9). 1998, Puffin paper $5.99 (0-14-038674-2). Jip, a foundling boy in Vermont of the 1850s, wonders about his origins, particularly after he finds he is being watched by a mysterious stranger. (Rev: BCCB 12/96; BL 9/1/96*; BR 3–4/97; HB 11–12/96; SLJ 10/96*; VOYA 4/97)

2937 Patrick, Denise Lewis. *The Adventures of Midnight Son* (5–8). 1997, Holt $16.00 (0-8050-4714-X). Fleeing slavery on a horse given to him by his parents, Midnight rides to Mexico and freedom. (Rev: BL 12/15/97; BR 3–4/98; HBG 3/98; SLJ 12/97)

2938 Paulsen, Gary. *Nightjohn* (6–12). 1993, Delacorte $15.95 (0-385-30838-8). Told in the voice of Sarny, 12, Paulsen exposes the myths that African American slaves were content, well cared for, ignorant, and childlike, and that brave, resourceful slaves easily escaped. (Rev: BL 12/15/92)

2939 Rees, Douglas. *Lightning Time* (6–9). 1997, Puffin paper $4.99 (0-14-130317-4). In Concord in 1857, young Theodore is so impressed with the words and deeds of John Brown that he runs away from home to join him and later takes part in the events at Harper's Ferry. (Rev: BL 1/1–15/98; BR 3–4/98; SLJ 12/97; VOYA 4/98)

2940 Rinaldi, Ann. *The Blue Door* (5–8). Series: Quilt. 1996, Scholastic paper $15.95 (0-590-46051-X). In this final volume of the Quilt trilogy — following *A Stitch in Time* (1994) and *Broken Days* — Amanda is forced to take a mill job in Lowell, Massachusetts, after an adventurous trip north from her South Carolina home. (Rev: BL 11/1/96; BR 3–4/97; VOYA 2/97)

2941 Rinaldi, Ann. *Broken Days* (6–10). Series: Quilt. 1995, Scholastic $14.95 (0-590-46053-6). When her cousin steals the piece of quilt that will establish her identity, Walking Breeze, who has come to live with her white family in Massachusetts at the age of 14 after being raised by Shawnees, is demoted to servant status in this story that takes place during the War of 1812. The second part of the Quilt trilogy. (Rev: VOYA 4/96)

2942 Rinaldi, Ann. *Mine Eyes Have Seen* (8–12). 1998, Scholastic paper $16.95 (0-590-54318-0). The story of the raid at Harper's Ferry is retold through the eyes of John Brown's daughter Annie. (Rev: BL 2/15/98; BR 11–12/98; HBG 9/98; SLJ 2/98; VOYA 4/98)

2943 Robinet, Harriette Gillem. *Twelve Travelers, Twenty Horses* (4–7). 2003, Simon & Schuster $16.95 (0-689-84561-8). Ten slaves band together to foil their master's plan to prevent the delivery of a crucial message as they travel to California in 1860. (Rev: BL 2/15/03; HBG 10/03; SLJ 2/03; VOYA 2/03)

2944 Ruby, Lois. *Soon Be Free* (6–9). 2000, Simon & Schuster $17.00 (0-689-83266-4). Told in two parallel narratives (the past and present), this sequel to *Steal Away Home,* deals with a lost treaty that the U.S. government made with the Delaware Indians in 1857 and how a 13-year-old Quaker boy gets involved. (Rev: BCCB 7–8/00; BL 6/1–15/00; HB 9–10/00; HBG 3/01; SLJ 8/00)

2945 Ruby, Lois. *Steal Away Home* (6–9). 1994, Macmillan paper $16.00 (0-02-777883-5). Dana, 12, finds a skeleton in a secret room of her Kansas home that turns out to be the remains of Lizbet, a conductor on the Underground Railroad, in this story that moves from the present day to the 1850s. (Rev: BL 1/1/95; SLJ 2/95; VOYA 4/95)

2946 Schneider, Mical. *Annie Quinn in America* (5–9). 2001, Carolrhoda LB $19.15 (1-57505-510-4). In 1847, young Annie and her brother travel from Ireland, a land ravaged by the potato famine, to America, a land fraught with dangers of its own. (Rev: BL 11/15/01; HBG 3/02; SLJ 9/01)

2947 Schwartz, Virginia Frances. *If I Just Had Two Wings* (6–10). 2001, Stoddart $15.95 (0-7737-3302-7). Accompanied by a friend and her two children, a young slave named Phoebe makes a daring escape to Canada and freedom via the Underground Railroad. (Rev: BL 12/1/01; SLJ 12/01; VOYA 12/01)

2948 Smucker, Barbara. *Runaway to Freedom: A Story of the Underground Railway* (6–9). Illus. 1979, HarperCollins paper $5.99 (0-06-440106-5). Two young slave girls try for freedom via the Underground Railway.

2949 Stolz, Mary. *Cezanne Pinto: A Memoir* (6–10). 1994, Knopf $16.00 (0-679-84917-3). This fictionalized memoir of a runaway slave who became a soldier, cowboy, and teacher includes quotations and stories of the great figures of the time. (Rev: BL 1/15/94; SLJ 12/93; VOYA 6/94)

2950 Stowe, Cynthia M. *The Second Escape of Arthur Cooper* (5–7). 2000, Marshall Cavendish LB $14.95 (0-7614-5069-6). Based on a true story, this novel tells of Arthur Cooper, an escaped slave, and the Quakers on Nantucket Island who saved him from slave catchers in 1822. (Rev: BL 8/00; HBG 3/01; SLJ 10/00)

2951 Trottier, Maxine. *Under a Shooting Star* (5–8). Series: The Circle of Silver Chronicles. 2002, Stoddart paper $7.95 (0-7737-6228-0). During the War of 1812, a 15-year-old boy who is half English and half Oneida Indian struggles with conflicting loyalties as he tries to protect the two American girls he is escorting. (Rev: SLJ 5/02)

2952 Turner, Glennette Tilley. *Running for Our Lives* (5–7). Illus. 1994, Holiday $16.95 (0-8234-1121-4). A thoroughly researched novel about a boy and his family who escape slavery in the 1850s and traveled on the Underground Railroad to Canada. (Rev: BCCB 6/94; BL 6/1–15/94; SLJ 4/94)

2953 Wall, Bill. *The Cove of Cork* (5–9). 1999, Irish American paper $7.95 (0-85635-225-0). In this novel, the third in a trilogy revolving around the War of 1812, an Irish lad, the first mate of the American schooner *Shenandoah*, sees action in a battle against a British vessel and eventually wins the hand of the granddaughter of a shipbuilding magnate. (Rev: SLJ 7/99)

2954 Wanttaja, Ronald. *The Key to Honor* (5–9). 1996, Royal Fireworks paper $9.99 (0-88092-270-2). During the War of 1812, midshipman Nate Lawton has doubts about his courage in battle and worries about his father, who has been taken prisoner by the British. (Rev: VOYA 8/96)

2955 Watts, Leander. *Stonecutter* (7–10). 2002, Houghton $15.00 (0-618-16474-X). In rural New York State in 1835, a gifted 14-year-old stonecutter rescues a beautiful girl who is being kept a prisoner by her wealthy and powerful father. (Rev: BCCB 11/02; BL 9/15/02; HB 11–12/02; HBG 3/03; SLJ 12/02; VOYA 12/02)

2956 Whelan, Gloria. *Farewell to the Island* (5–8). 1998, HarperCollins $16.95 (0-06-027751-3). In this sequel to *Once on This Island,* Mary leaves her Michigan home after the War of 1812 and travels to

England where she falls in love with Lord Lindsay. (Rev: BL 12/1/98; HBG 3/99; SLJ 1/99)

2957 Whelan, Gloria. *Once on This Island* (4–7). 1995, HarperCollins LB $14.89 (0-06-026249-4). In 1812, Mary and her older brother and sister must tend the family farm on Mackinac Island when their father goes off to war. (Rev: BCCB 11/95; BL 10/1/95; BR 3–4/96; SLJ 11/95; VOYA 2/96)

2958 Wiley, Melissa. *On Tide Mill Lane* (4–8). Illus. 2001, HarperCollins $16.95 (0-06-027013-6). Charlotte experiences a number of household crises in Roxbury, Massachusetts, where she lives with her blacksmith father at the time of the War of 1812. (Rev: BL 2/15/01; HBG 10/01)

2959 Wood, Frances M. *Daughter of Madrugada* (7–10). 2002, Delacorte $15.95 (0-385-32719-6). Thirteen-year-old Cesa describes her privileged life in 1840s California, even as the social landscape is changing with the arrival of gold miners and as she herself faces pressures to abandon her tomboy freedom. (Rev: BCCB 6/02; BL 5/15/02; HBG 10/02; SLJ 5/02; VOYA 8/02)

THE CIVIL WAR (1861–1865)

2960 Armstrong, Jennifer. *The Dreams of Mairhe Mehan* (7–12). 1996, Knopf $18.00 (0-679-88152-2). A grim, challenging novel that takes place in Civil War Washington and involves a poor immigrant Irish serving maid and her family. (Rev: BL 1/1–15/97; BR 1–2/97; SLJ 10/96)

2961 Banks, Sara H. *Abraham's Battle: A Novel of Gettysburg* (4–7). 1999, Simon & Schuster $15.95 (0-689-81779-7). After the Battle of Gettysburg, Abraham Small, a former slave and ambulance driver, helps a wounded Confederate soldier whom he met prior to the battle. (Rev: BCCB 4/99; BL 3/1/99; HBG 10/99; SLJ 7/99)

2962 Bartoletti, Susan Campbell. *No Man's Land: A Young Soldier's Story* (5–9). 1999, Scholastic paper $15.95 (0-590-38371-X). The story of a young boy's life as a Confederate soldier after he lies about his age and joins the Okefenokee Rifles in 1861. (Rev: BCCB 6/99; BL 4/1/99; HBG 10/99; SLJ 6/99; VOYA 12/99)

2963 Beatty, Patricia. *Jayhawker* (6–9). 1995, Morrow paper $6.99 (0-688-14422-5). The story of 12-year-old Elijah, son of a Kansas abolitionist, who becomes a spy and infiltrates Charles Quantrill's infamous Bushwhacker network. (Rev: BL 9/1/91*; SLJ 9/91*)

2964 Beatty, Patricia. *Who Comes with Cannons?* (5–7). 1992, Morrow $15.99 (0-688-11028-2). The Civil War brings danger to Truth Hopkins and her Quaker family because they are pacifists. (Rev: BCCB 10/92; BL 1/1/93; HB 1–2/93; SLJ 10/92)

2965 Brenaman, Miriam. *Evvy's Civil War* (6–8). 2002, Putnam $18.99 (0-399-23713-5). Fourteen-year-old Evvy is a very unusual southern girl who defies social and racial conventions as the Civil War looms. (Rev: BL 4/15/02*; HBG 10/02; SLJ 2/02; VOYA 2/02)

2966 Brill, Marlene T. *Diary of a Drummer Boy* (4–7). 1998, Millbrook LB $23.90 (0-7613-0118-6). Using a diary format, this novel tells of a 12-year-old's experiences as a drummer in the Union Army during the Civil War. (Rev: BL 3/1/98; HBG 10/98; SLJ 5/98)

2967 Clapp, Patricia. *The Tamarack Tree: A Novel of the Siege of Vicksburg* (7–10). 1986, Lothrop $15.99 (0-688-02852-7). The siege of Vicksburg as seen through the eyes of a 17-year-old English girl who is trapped inside the city. (Rev: BL 11/15/86; BR 1–2/87; SLJ 10/86; VOYA 2/87)

2968 Collier, James L., and Christopher Collier. *With Every Drop of Blood: A Novel of the Civil War* (6–10). 1994, Dell paper $5.99 (0-440-21983-3). A Civil War docunovel about Johnny, a young Confederate soldier, and Cush, a black Union soldier who captures him. Together, the two experience the horrors of war and bigotry. (Rev: BL 7/94; SLJ 8/94; VOYA 12/94)

2969 Crisp, Marty. *Private Captain: A Story of Gettysburg* (6–8). 2001, Philomel $18.99 (0-399-23577-9). Ben, 12, and his dog, Captain, travel to find Ben's brother, who is fighting in the Civil War, and persuade him to come home. (Rev: BCCB 3/01; BL 4/1/01; HBG 10/01; SLJ 4/01; VOYA 4/01)

2970 Crist-Evans, Craig. *Moon over Tennessee: A Boy's Civil War Journal* (4–7). 1999, Houghton $15.00 (0-395-91208-3). In free-verse diary entries, 13-year-old Crist-Evans reports on the Civil War from his vantage point in a camp behind the front lines. (Rev: BCCB 6/99; BL 5/15/99; HBG 10/99; SLJ 8/99; VOYA 10/99)

2971 Donahue, John. *An Island Far from Home* (4–7). 1994, Carolrhoda LB $19.15 (0-87614-859-3). Joshua, a Union supporter, forms an unusual friendship through corresponding with a young Southern soldier who is a prisoner of war. (Rev: BCCB 2/95; BL 2/15/95; SLJ 2/95)

2972 Duey, Kathleen. *Amelina Carrett: Bayou Grand Coeur, Louisiana, 1863* (5–8). Series: American Diaries. 1999, Simon & Schuster paper $3.99 (0-689-82402-5). Growing up in Cajun country during the Civil War, Amelina has to make a difficult decision when she finds a wounded Yankee soldier hiding in the bayou. (Rev: SLJ 9/99)

2973 Ernst, Kathleen. *The Bravest Girl in Sharpsburg* (6–9). 1998, White Mane paper $8.95 (1-57249-083-7). Told from the viewpoint of three girls in Maryland during the Civil War, this is the story of friendships that are tested when the the girls

support different sides and what happens when the Confederate Army marches through their town, thrusting the community into the middle of the war. (Rev: SLJ 9/98)

2974 Ernst, Kathleen. *Ghosts of Vicksburg* (6–10). 2003, White Mane paper $8.95 (1-57249-322-4). Jamie and Elisha, 15-year-old Union Army soldiers from Wisconsin, experience the horrors of war as their forces march to Mississippi. (Rev: SLJ 12/03)

2975 Ernst, Kathleen. *The Night Riders of Harper's Ferry* (6–8). Illus. 1996, White Mane paper $7.95 (1-57249-013-6). Told from the standpoint of 17-year-old Solomon, this is a story of romance, divided families, and dangerous secrets, set on the border between North and South during the Civil War. (Rev: BL 1/1–15/97; SLJ 5/97)

2976 Ernst, Kathleen. *Retreat from Gettysburg* (5–8). Illus. 2000, White Mane LB $17.95 (1-57249-187-6). When a doctor orders 14-year-old Chig and his mother to care for a wounded Confederate soldier, the boy finds it hard to be kind to a man who belongs to the side that killed his father and brothers. (Rev: BL 9/15/00; HBG 10/01; SLJ 12/00)

2977 Fleischman, Paul. *Bull Run* (6–12). 1993, HarperCollins LB $16.89 (0-06-021447-3). Spotlights the diary entries of 16 fictional characters, 8 each from the South and the North, throughout the battle. (Rev: BCCB 3/93; BL 1/15/93*; SLJ 3/93*)

2978 Forman, James D. *Becca's Story* (5–8). 1992, Scribners LB $15.00 (0-684-19332-9). Forman uses his ancestors' Civil War-era letters and diaries to weave the story of Becca, who is courted by two young men who go off to fight in the Union Army. (Rev: BL 12/1/92; SLJ 11/92*)

2979 Garrity, Jennifer Johnson. *The Bushwhacker: A Civil War Adventure* (5–8). 1999, Peachtree paper $8.95 (1-56145-201-7). The clash of divided loyalties is the main conflict in this story of a boy torn between his Unionist feelings and the friendship he feels towards his protector, a Confederate sympathizer. (Rev: SLJ 4/00)

2980 Greenberg, Martin H., and Charles G. Waugh, eds. *Civil War Women II: Stories by Women About Women* (7–10). 1997, August House paper $9.95 (0-87483-487-2). A collection of short stories by such female writers as Louisa May Alcott and Edith Wharton that deal with women's lives during the Civil War. (Rev: SLJ 8/97)

2981 Hahn, Mary Downing. *Hear the Wind Blow: A Novel of the Civil War* (6–9). 2003, Clarion $15.00 (0-618-18190-3). A moving novel of the Civil War in which 13-year-old Haswell searches for his wounded older brother after his mother is killed and his farm destroyed. (Rev: BCCB 7–8/03; BL 5/15/03; HB 5–6/03; HBG 5–6/03; SLJ 5/03; VOYA 10/03)

2982 Hansen, Joyce. *Out from This Place* (6–9). 1992, Avon paper $5.99 (0-380-71409-4). In this volume, Easter, the companion of Obi, a slave who joined the Northern Army during the Civil War in *Which Way Freedom*, tells her story and how she spent much of the war with other former slaves in the Carolina Sea Islands. (Rev: BL 1/15/89; BR 1–2/89; SLJ 12/88; VOYA 2/89)

2983 Hart, Alison. *Fires of Jubilee* (5–7). 2003, Simon & Schuster paper $4.99 (0-689-85528-1). Abby, 13, is suddenly a free person when the Civil War ends and finally able to search for her mother, who left long before. (Rev: BL 11/1/03)

2984 Hesse, Karen. *A Light in the Storm: The Civil War Diary of Amelia Martin* (4–7). Series: Dear America. 1999, Scholastic paper $10.95 (0-590-56733-0). The story of Amelia Martin, the 15-year-old daughter of a lighthouse keeper in Delaware, and how her family became involved in the oncoming Civil War. (Rev: BL 10/15/99; HBG 3/00; SLJ 11/99; VOYA 2/00)

2985 Hill, Pamela S. *A Voice from the Border* (6–8). 1998, Holiday $16.95 (0-8234-1356-X). Set in Missouri, a border state during the Civil War, this novel introduces 15-year-old Reeves, whose family owns slaves and whose house is commandeered by Union forces after Reeves' father dies in battle. (Rev: BCCB 9/98; HBG 3/99; SLJ 9/98)

2986 Hite, Sid. *The Journal of Rufus Rowe: A Witness to the Battle of Fredericksburg* (5–7). Series: My Name Is America. 2003, Scholastic $10.95 (0-439-35364-5). The Battle of Fredericksburg takes place under the watchful eye of 16-year-old Rufus, who records moments of compassion as well as horror. (Rev: SLJ 11/03)

2987 Hoobler, Thomas, and Dorothy Hoobler. *Sally Bradford: The Story of a Rebel Girl* (4–7). Illus. 1997, Silver Burdett LB $14.95 (0-382-39258-2); paper $4.95 (0-382-39259-0). The Civil War changes the lives of Sally Bradford and her family, who operate a farm without slaves in Norfolk, Virginia. (Rev: BL 6/1–15/97; SLJ 8/97)

2988 Houston, Gloria. *Mountain Valor* (4–7). 1994, Putnam $15.95 (0-399-22519-6). In this Civil War novel, Valor lives up to her name by recovering the family's supplies after they have been stolen by Yankee soldiers. (Rev: BCCB 6/94; BL 4/1/94; SLJ 6/94)

2989 Hughes, Pat. *Guerrilla Season* (7–12). 2003, Farrar $18.00 (0-374-32811-0). This multilayered novel clearly conveys the confusion that Matt, 15, feels in the face of the approaching violence of the Civil War. (Rev: BL 8/03; SLJ 11/03)

2990 Hunt, Irene. *Across Five Aprils* (6–8). 1993, Silver Burdett paper $5.45 (0-8136-7202-3). A young boy's experiences during the Civil War in the backwoods of southern Illinois. One brother joins the Union forces, the other the Confederacy, and the family is divided.

2991 Johnson, Nancy. *My Brother's Keeper: A Civil War Story* (6–10). 1997, Down East $14.95 (0-89272-414-5). Two orphaned brothers from upstate New York, ages 15 and 13, join the Union Army, one as a soldier, the other a drummer boy, and soon find themselves surrounded by the blood and tragedy of battle in this story based on the experiences of the author's great-great-uncles. (Rev: BR 5–6/98; HBG 9/98; SLJ 1/98)

2992 Jones, Elizabeth McDavid. *Watcher in the Piney Woods* (5–7). Series: History Mystery. 2000, Pleasant $9.95 (1-58485-091-4); paper $5.95 (1-58485-090-6). In southern Virginia during the last year of the Civil War, 12-year-old Cassie sets out to solve the mystery of objects disappearing from her home and farm. (Rev: HBG 10/01; SLJ 1/01)

2993 Keehn, Sally M. *Anna Sunday* (4–8). 2002, Putnam $18.99 (0-399-23875-1). In 1863, 12-year-old Anna travels with her younger brother from Pennsylvania to Virginia to find her wounded father. (Rev: BCCB 9/02; BL 6/1–15/02; HBG 10/02; SLJ 6/02; VOYA 8/02)

2994 Keith, Harold. *Rifles for Watie* (6–9). 1957, HarperCollins paper $5.99 (0-06-447030-X). Jeff, a Union soldier, learns about the realities of war when he becomes a spy. Newbery Medal winner, 1958.

2995 Lasky, Kathryn. *Alice Rose and Sam* (4–7). 1998, Hyperion LB $16.49 (0-7868-2277-5). Growing up in Nevada during the Civil War, Alice Rose forms a friendship with young Samuel Clemens, and together they solve the mystery of a murdered drunk and uncover a Confederate plot. (Rev: BCCB 5/98; BL 4/15/98; HBG 10/98; SLJ 5/98)

2996 Love, D. Anne. *Three Against the Tide* (5–8). 1998, Holiday $15.95 (0-8234-1400-0). In this Civil War novel, 12-year-old Confederate Susanna Simons must care for her two younger brothers when Yankee troops invade South Carolina. (Rev: BL 12/1/98; HBG 10/99; SLJ 1/99)

2997 Lyons, Mary E., and Muriel M. Branch. *Dear Ellen Bee: A Civil War Scrapbook of Two Union Spies* (5–8). Illus. 2000, Atheneum $17.00 (0-689-82379-7). Set in Richmond, Virginia, before and during the Civil War, this novel, based on fact, tells how a strong-willed lady and her emancipated slave get involved in a spying adventure. (Rev: BCCB 10/00; BL 11/1/00; HBG 3/01; SLJ 10/00; VOYA 2/01)

2998 Matas, Carol. *The War Within* (5–8). 2001, Simon & Schuster $16.00 (0-689-82935-3). The story of a 13-year-old Jewish southern girl and her family during the Civil War is told through diary entries. (Rev: BL 4/1/01; HBG 10/01; SLJ 6/01; VOYA 6/01)

2999 Murphy, Jim. *The Journal of James Edmond Pease: A Civil War Union Soldier* (7–12). Series: My Name Is America. 1998, Scholastic paper $10.95 (0-590-43814-X). This novel takes the form of a journal kept by a misfit 16-year-old private in the New York Volunteers, describing his experiences, including the time he gets lost behind enemy lines. (Rev: BCCB 11/98; BL 11/15/98; HBG 3/99; SLJ 7/99)

3000 Nixon, Joan Lowery. *A Dangerous Promise* (6–8). Series: Orphan Train Adventures. 1996, Bantam paper $4.99 (0-440-21965-5). Mike Kelly, 12, and his friend Todd Blakely run away to help the Union forces in the Civil War and experience the terrors of war. (Rev: BL 9/1/94; SLJ 11/94; VOYA 10/94)

3001 Nixon, Joan Lowery. *Keeping Secrets* (5–8). Series: Orphan Train Adventures. 1996, Demco $11.04 (0-606-08789-3). In Missouri during the Civil War, Peg, 11, unwittingly becomes involved with a Union spy. (Rev: BL 3/1/95; SLJ 3/95; VOYA 4/95)

3002 Paulsen, Gary. *Sarny: A Life Remembered* (6–12). 1997, Delacorte $15.95 (0-385-32195-3). In this sequel to *Nightjohn*, the slave Sarny sets out during the Civil War to find her son and daughter, who were sold and are now impossible to locate. (Rev: BL 10/1/97; BR 11–12/97; HBG 3/98; SLJ 9/97; VOYA 2/98)

3003 Paulsen, Gary. *Soldier's Heart* (5–8). 1998, Delacorte $15.95 (0-385-32498-7). A powerful novel about the agony of the Civil War, based on the real-life experiences of a Union soldier who was only 15 when he went to war. (Rev: BCCB 9/98; BL 6/1–15/98*; HB 11–12/98; HBG 3/99; SLJ 9/98; VOYA 10/98)

3004 Peck, Richard. *The River Between Us* (7–12). 2003, Dial $16.99 (0-8037-2735-6). In 1861 Illinois, Tilly's family makes room for two young women of different complexions from the South. (Rev: BL 9/15/03*; HB 9–10/03; SLJ 9/03; VOYA 10/03)

3005 Pinkney, Andrea D. *Silent Thunder: A Civil War Story* (5–8). 1999, Hyperion LB $16.49 (0-7868-2388-7). The brutal oppression of slavery is revealed in this story told by two black children living on a Virginia plantation during the Civil War. (Rev: BL 9/1/99; HBG 3/00; SLJ 12/99)

3006 Pinkney, Andrea Davis. *Abraham Lincoln: Letters from a Slave Girl* (4–7). Illus. Series: Dear Mr. President. 2001, Winslow $8.95 (1-890817-60-0). Twelve-year-old Lettie Tucker, a slave, exchanges thought-provoking letters with President Abraham Lincoln in this story set in the 1860s packed with interesting illustrations. (Rev: BCCB 2/02; BL 9/1/01; HBG 3/02; SLJ 9/01)

3007 Reeder, Carolyn. *Across the Lines* (4–7). 1997, Simon & Schuster $17.00 (0-689-81133-0). Edward and his slave friend, Simon, are separated when Yankees capture their Virginia plantation in this Civil War novel. (Rev: BCCB 6/97; BL 4/1/97*; BR 11–12/97; SLJ 6/97; VOYA 8/97)

3008 Reeder, Carolyn. *Before the Creeks Ran Red* (6–9). 2003, HarperCollins $16.99 (0-06-623615-0). Three stories examine the impact of the Civil War on three young men, who all come to reassess their perspectives on war, valor, and duty. (Rev: BCCB 3/03; BL 2/15/03; HBG 10/03; SLJ 2/03)

3009 Reeder, Carolyn. *Captain Kate* (6–8). 1999, Avon $15.00 (0-380-97628-5). This is an unusual Civil War story about 12-year-old Kate, her stepbrother Seth, and their dangerous trip down the C&O Canal on the family's coal boat. (Rev: BL 1/1–15/99; HBG 10/99; SLJ 1/99)

3010 Reeder, Carolyn. *Shades of Gray* (4–7). 1989, Macmillan LB $16.00 (0-02-775810-9). The story of 12-year-old Will, the last surviving member of his family from the South during the Civil War, who must go to live with an uncle he considers a coward. (Rev: BCCB 1/90; BL 1/15/90; HB 3–4/90; SLJ 1/90; VOYA 2/90)

3011 Richardson, George C. *Drummer* (6–9). 2001, Writer's Showcase paper $9.95 (0-595-15359-3). A young slave survives a dangerous journey north and joins a Colored Infantry unit in Philadelphia, becoming a drummer boy. (Rev: SLJ 12/01)

3012 Rinaldi, Ann. *Amelia's War* (5–9). 1999, Scholastic paper $15.95 (0-590-11744-0). During the Civil War, young Amelia Grafton secretly finds a way to prevent the Confederate forces from destroying her Maryland town. (Rev: BL 11/15/99; HBG 3/00; SLJ 2/00)

3013 Rinaldi, Ann. *Girl in Blue* (5–8). 2001, Scholastic paper $15.95 (0-439-07336-7). A first-person novel about Sarah, who disguises herself as a boy and joins the Union Army. (Rev: BCCB 6/01; BL 4/1/01; HBG 10/01; SLJ 3/01; VOYA 4/01)

3014 Rinaldi, Ann. *In My Father's House* (7–10). 1993, Scholastic paper $14.95 (0-590-44730-0). A coming-of-age novel set during the Civil War about 7-year-old Oscie. (Rev: BL 2/15/93)

3015 Rinaldi, Ann. *Numbering All the Bones* (7–10). 2002, Hyperion $15.99 (0-7868-0533-1). During the Civil War, young slave Eulinda braves the horrors of Andersonville Prison to search for her brother. (Rev: BCCB 6/02; BL 5/15/02; HBG 10/02; SLJ 6/02; VOYA 8/02)

3016 Sappey, Maureen Stack. *Letters from Vinnie* (7–10). 1999, Front Street $16.95 (1-886910-31-6). A novel that mixes fact and fiction to tell the story of the tiny woman who sculpted the large statue of Abraham Lincoln found in the Capitol Building in Washington. (Rev: BL 9/15/99; HBG 4/00; SLJ 11/99; VOYA 2/00)

3017 Severance, John B. *Braving the Fire* (7–12). 2002, Clarion $15.00 (0-618-22999-X). Jem finds war is far from the "glory" described by others in this coming-of-age story set in the realistic horrors of the Civil War. (Rev: BL 10/1/02; HBG 10/03; SLJ 11/02)

3018 Thomas, Carroll. *Blue Creek Farm* (4–8). 2001, Smith & Kraus paper $9.95 (1-57525-243-0). In Kansas of the 1860s, Matty Trescott and her father manage a farm and feel the effects of the Civil War. (Rev: BL 4/1/01; VOYA 6/01)

3019 Williams, Jeanne. *The Confederate Fiddle* (6–9). 1997, Hendrick-Long $16.95 (1-885777-04-3). On his wagon train taking cotton to Mexico in 1862, 17-year-old Vin Clayburn is torn between fulfilling his duty to his family and joining his brother fighting for the South in the Civil War. (Rev: BL 3/15/98; HBG 9/98)

3020 Wisler, G. Clifton. *The Drummer Boy of Vicksburg* (5–8). 1997, Lodestar $15.99 (0-525-67537-X). The story of a drummer boy in the Union Army during the Civil War. (Rev: BL 12/1/96; BR 9–10/97; SLJ 3/97)

3021 Wisler, G. Clifton. *Mr. Lincoln's Drummer* (5–7). 1994, Dutton $15.99 (0-525-67463-2). Eleven-year-old Willie, a Vermonter, joins the Union Army as a drummer boy when his father enlists. (Rev: BCCB 1/95; BL 1/15/95)

3022 Wisler, G. Clifton. *Mustang Flats* (5–8). 1997, Dutton $14.99 (0-525-67544-2). Abby wants to help his family when his father returns from the Civil War a broken, bitter man. (Rev: BL 8/97; BR 1–2/98; HBG 3/98; SLJ 7/97)

3023 Wisler, G. Clifton. *Red Cap* (6–8). 1991, Penguin paper $5.99 (0-14-036936-8). An adolescent boy lies about his age to join the Union Army and ends up as a prisoner of war in the infamous Andersonville camp. (Rev: BL 8/91; SLJ 8/91)

3024 Wisler, G. Clifton. *Run the Blockade* (5–8). 2000, HarperCollins LB $15.89 (0-06-029208-3). An Irish lad signs aboard the steamship *Banshee*, whose mission is to try to break the Union shipping blockade during the Civil War. (Rev: BCCB 10/00; BL 9/15/00; HBG 3/01; SLJ 1/01)

3025 Wisler, G. Clifton. *Thunder on the Tennessee* (7–10). 1995, Puffin paper $5.99 (0-14-037612-7). A 16-year-old Southern boy learns the value of courage and honor during the Civil War.

WESTWARD EXPANSION AND PIONEER LIFE

3026 Altsheler, Joseph A. *Kentucky Frontiersman: The Adventures of Henry Ware, Hunter and Border Fighter* (6–10). Illus. 1988, Voyageur $16.95 (0-929146-01-8). A reissue of a fine frontier adventure story featuring young Henry Ware who is captured by an Indian hunting party. (Rev: BR 3–4/89; SLJ 3/89)

3027 Applegate, Stan. *The Devil's Highway* (5–8). 1998, Peachtree paper $8.95 (1-56145-184-3). In this adventure novel set in the early 1800s, 14-year-old Zeb and his horse, Christmas, set out on the bandit-infested Natchez Trail to search for the boy's grandfather. (Rev: SLJ 2/99)

3028 Arrington, Frances. *Prairie Whispers* (5–8). 2003, Philomel $17.99 (0-399-23975-8). Promising to look after a dying woman's baby, Colleen, 12, substitutes the child for her own stillborn sister, but there's trouble when the baby's father arrives in this story set in South Dakota in the 1860s. (Rev: BL 5/15/03*; HB 7–8/03; HBG 10/03; SLJ 5/03; VOYA 6/03)

3029 Avi. *The Barn* (5–8). 1994, Orchard paper $15.99 (0-531-08711-5). In this story set in 1850s Oregon, Ben and his siblings must run their farm alone after their father becomes paralyzed, and Ben decides they must fulfill their father's dream and build a barn. (Rev: BL 9/1/94*; SLJ 10/94)

3030 Ayres, Katherine. *Silver Dollar Girl* (4–8). 2000, Random paper $4.99 (0-440-41705-8). Set in the silver rush days of the 1880s, this story tells how Valentine Harper disguises herself as a boy and sets out from Pittsburgh to find her father in Colorado. (Rev: BL 11/15/00; SLJ 11/00)

3031 Bauer, Marion Dane. *Land of the Buffalo Bones: The Diary of Mary Elizabeth Rodgers, an English Girl in Minnesota* (4–8). Series: Dear America. 2003, Scholastic $12.95 (0-439-22027-0). Based on real-life events, Polly Rodgers's diary reveals the hardships endured by a group of English settlers who arrived in Minnesota in 1873. (Rev: BL 5/15/03; HBG 10/03)

3032 Benchley, Nathaniel. *Gone and Back* (7–9). 1971, HarperCollins paper $1.95 (0-06-440016-6). Obed's family moves west to take advantage of the Homestead Act, and he soon finds he must assume new family responsibilities.

3033 Benner, J. A. *Uncle Comanche* (5–8). 1996, Texas Christian Univ. Pr. paper $12.95 (0-87565-152-6). Based on fact, this is the story of the adventures of 12-year-old Sul Ross, who runs away from home in pre-Civil War Texas and is pursued by a family friend nicknamed Uncle Comanche. (Rev: VOYA 10/96)

3034 Blakeslee, Ann R. *A Different Kind of Hero* (5–7). 1997, Marshall Cavendish $14.95 (0-7614-5000-9). In 1881 Colorado, Renny is criticized for befriending and helping a Chinese boy new to town. (Rev: BL 9/1/97; HBG 3/98; SLJ 1/98)

3035 Bowers, Terrell L. *Ride Against the Wind* (7–10). 1996, Walker $21.95 (0-8027-4156-8). Set in Eden, Kansas, in the late 1800s, this sequel to *The Secret of Snake Canyon* (1993) involves Jerrod

Danmyer and his attachment to Marion Gates, daughter of his family's sworn enemies. (Rev: BL 12/15/96; VOYA 8/97)

3036 Bruchac, Joseph. *Sacajawea: The Story of Bird Woman and the Lewis and Clark Expedition* (7–10). 2000, Harcourt $17.00 (0-15-202234-1). Told in alternating chapters by Sacajawea and William Clark, this novel re-creates the famous cross-country journey of Lewis and Clark. (Rev: BL 4/1/00; HBG 9/00; SLJ 5/00)

3037 Burks, Brian. *Soldier Boy* (6–9). 1997, Harcourt $12.00 (0-15-201218-4); paper $6.00 (0-15-201219-2). To escape a crooked boxing ring in 1870s Chicago, Johnny joins the army to fight Indians and eventually finds himself at Little Big Horn with Custer. (Rev: BL 5/15/97; SLJ 5/97; VOYA 8/97)

3038 Burks, Brian. *Wrango* (5–8). 1999, Harcourt $16.00 (0-15-201815-8). In this historical novel, George, an African American boy, is forced out of town by the Klan and turns to the adventurous life of a cowboy. (Rev: BL 9/1/99; HBG 3/00; SLJ 12/99; VOYA 4/00)

3039 Calvert, Patricia. *Betrayed!* (5–8). 2002, Simon & Schuster $16.00 (0-689-83472-1). Tyler Bohannon of *Bigger* (1994) and *Sooner* (1998) is back, this time traveling west, where he is taken captive by Sioux Indians. (Rev: BL 7/02; HBG 10/02; SLJ 6/02; VOYA 4/02)

3040 Calvert, Patricia. *Bigger* (5–8). 1994, Scribners $16.00 (0-684-19685-9). Accompanied by an abused stray dog named Bigger, Tyler, 12, sets out on an 800-mile trip from Missouri to the Rio Grande to find his father after the Civil War. (Rev: BCCB 3/94; BL 4/1/94; HB 7–8/94; SLJ 4/94; VOYA 4/94)

3041 Calvert, Patricia. *Sooner* (5–9). 1998, Simon & Schuster $16.00 (0-689-81114-4). After the Civil War, Tyler's father leaves the family to seek his fortune in Mexico and 13-year-old Tyler must assume adult responsibilities in this prequel to *Bigger*. (Rev: BCCB 6/98; BL 6/1–15/98; BR 1–2/99; HBG 10/98; SLJ 6/98)

3042 Cannon, A. E. *Charlotte's Rose* (5–8). 2002, Random LB $17.99 (0-385-90057-0). Thirteen-year-old Charlotte and her father make a difficult journey from Wales to Utah with a group of Mormons in 1856 in a narrative that presents religion as an integral part of life. (Rev: BCCB 1/03; BL 10/1/02; HB 11–12/02; HBG 3/03; SLJ 9/02)

3043 Clements, Bruce. *I Tell a Lie Every So Often* (7–9). 1974, Farrar paper $5.95 (0-374-43539-1). Set on the Mississippi River during 1848, this is the story of two brothers, one of whom is known for stretching the truth.

3044 Collier, James Lincoln. *Wild Boy* (5–8). 2002, Marshall Cavendish $15.95 (0-7614-5126-9). After

knocking his father out during an argument, 12-year-old Jesse runs away from his frontier home to live in the mountains, where he has many adventures, learns many skills, and reflects on his own characteristics before finally deciding to return home in this story that appears to be set in the 19th century. (Rev: BL 11/1/02; HBG 10/03; SLJ 11/02)

3045 Conrad, Pam. *Prairie Songs* (5–9). Illus. 1985, HarperCollins LB $15.89 (0-06-021337-X); paper $5.99 (0-06-440206-1). On the wide Nebraska prairie, young Louisa forms a friendship with a doctor's wife whose hold on reality is slipping away. (Rev: BL 9/1/85; SLJ 10/85; VOYA 12/85)

3046 Cullen, Lynn. *Nelly in the Wilderness* (5–8). 2002, HarperCollins LB $15.89 (0-06-029134-6). Set in the Indiana frontier of 1821, 12-year-old Nelly and her brother, Cornelius, must adjust to a new stepmother after their beloved Ma dies. (Rev: BCCB 5/02; BL 4/1/02; HB 7–8/02; HBG 10/02; SLJ 2/02)

3047 Cushman, Karen. *The Ballad of Lucy Whipple* (5–8). 1996, Clarion $15.00 (0-395-72806-1). Lucy hates being stuck in the California wilderness with an overbearing mother who runs a boarding house. (Rev: BCCB 9/96; BL 8/96*; HB 9–10/96; SLJ 8/96*; VOYA 12/96)

3048 DeFelice, Cynthia. *Weasel* (7–9). 1990, Macmillan paper $15.00 (0-02-726457-2). Set in rural Ohio in 1839, this is the story of a boy's initiation into the cruel realities of life and death. (Rev: BL 5/15/90; SLJ 5/90; VOYA 6/90)

3049 Donahue, Marilyn Cram. *The Valley in Between* (6–9). 1987, Walker LB $15.85 (0-8027-6733-8). In a story that spans a four-year period, a young girl comes of age in California of the 1850s. (Rev: BL 11/1/87; BR 5–6/88; SLJ 11/87; VOYA 12/87)

3050 Duey, Kathleen. *Anisett Lundberg: California, 1851* (4–7). Series: American Diaries. 1996, Simon & Schuster paper $4.99 (0-689-80386-9). An adventure story featuring Anisett and her family, who live in the gold-mining region of California in 1851. (Rev: HB 9–10/96; SLJ 12/96)

3051 Durbin, William. *The Journal of Sean Sullivan: A Transcontinental Railroad Worker, Nebraska and Points West, 1867* (5–8). Series: My Name Is America. 1999, Scholastic paper $10.95 (0-439-04994-6). This novel describes the early days of railroad construction in America as seen through the eyes of young Sean, who works his way up from a "water carrier" to "spiker." (Rev: BL 10/15/99; HBG 3/00; SLJ 11/99)

3052 Durrant, Lynda. *The Sun, the Rain, and the Apple Seed: A Novel of Johnny Appleseed's Life* (5–8). 2003, Clarion $15.00 (0-618-23487-X). This fictionalized biography of John Chapman's life focuses on his eccentricities. (Rev: BL 5/15/03; HBG 10/03; SLJ 5/03)

3053 Ellsworth, Loretta. *The Shrouding Woman* (4–8). 2002, Holt $16.95 (0-8050-6651-9). in this novel set in 19th-century Minnesota, 11-year-old Evie resists the efforts of her Aunt Flo ("the shrouding woman") to take care of her after Evie's mother dies. (Rev: BCCB 9/02; BL 5/15/02; HBG 10/02; SLJ 4/02; VOYA 8/02)

3054 Ernst, Kathleen. *Trouble at Fort La Pointe* (4–8). 2000, Pleasant $9.95 (1-58485-087-6). In a fur trading post near Lake Superior in the early 18th century, 12-year-old Suzette sets out to investigate who is plotting against her father. (Rev: BL 10/1/00; HBG 10/01; SLJ 12/00)

3055 Finley, Mary Peace. *Meadow Lark* (5–8). Series: Santa Fe Trail trilogy. 2003, Filter $15.95 (0-86541-070-4). In this sequel to *Soaring Eagle* (1993) and *White Grizzly* (2000) set in 1845, Teresita Montoya, 13, has various adventures on the Santa Fe Trail as she searches for her older brother and for a new life for herself. (Rev: BL 12/1/03; SLJ 2/04)

3056 Finley, Mary Peace. *White Grizzly* (5–9). 2000, Filter $15.95 (0-86541-053-4); paper $8.95 (0-86541-058-5). Fifteen-year-old Julio sets out on an arduous journey along the Santa Fe Trail to discover his true identity. (Rev: BL 12/1/00; HBG 10/01; SLJ 1/01; VOYA 2/01)

3057 Fleischman, Paul. *The Borning Room* (5–8). 1991, HarperCollins paper $4.99 (0-06-447099-7). Georgina remembers important turning points in her life and the role played by the room set aside for giving birth and dying in her grandfather's house in 19th-century rural Ohio. (Rev: BCCB 9/91; BL 10/1/91*; HB 11–12/91*; SLJ 9/91*)

3058 Gaeddert, Louann. *Hope* (5–7). 1995, Simon & Schuster $14.00 (0-689-80128-9). While their father is panning for gold in California, Hope and brother John move to a Shaker community. (Rev: BL 12/15/95; SLJ 11/95)

3059 Garland, Sherry. *Valley of the Moon: The Diary of Rosalia de Milagros* (5–8). Illus. 2001, Scholastic paper $10.95 (0-439-08820-8). Rosalia, a 13-year-old orphan, keeps a diary about working on a California ranch in 1846. (Rev: BL 4/1/01; HBG 3/02; SLJ 4/01; VOYA 8/01)

3060 Gregory, Kristiana. *Across the Wide and Lonesome Prairie: The Oregon Trail Diary of Hattie Campbell* (4–7). Illus. Series: Dear America. 1997, Scholastic paper $10.95 (0-590-22651-7). In a diary format, this novel chronicles the hardships that pioneers endured during a trip west on the Oregon Trail. (Rev: SLJ 3/97)

3061 Gregory, Kristiana. *The Great Railroad Race: The Transcontinental Railroad Diary of Libby West* (1 8). Series: Dear America. 1999, Scholastic paper $10.95 (0-590-10991-X). The story of the building of the transcontinental railroad as seen through the eyes of a 14-year-old girl whose father is a reporter

following the progress of the massive undertaking. (Rev: BL 4/1/99; HBG 10/99; SLJ 8/99; VOYA 10/99)

3062 Gregory, Kristiana. *Jenny of the Tetons* (6–9). 1989, Harcourt $13.95 (0-15-200480-7). An orphaned girl is brought by a trapper into his house to help care for his children in this story based on fact. (Rev: BL 7/89; SLJ 6/89; VOYA 6/90)

3063 Gregory, Kristiana. *Jimmy Spoon and the Pony Express* (6–8). 1997, Scholastic paper $4.50 (0-590-46578-3). Jimmy answers an ad for Pony Express riders, but he's haunted by his previous life with the Shoshoni (see *The Legend of Jimmy Spoon*, Harcourt, 1991), especially the beautiful Nahanee. (Rev: BL 11/15/94; SLJ 11/94; VOYA 4/95)

3064 Gregory, Kristiana. *Seeds of Hope: The Gold Rush Diary of Susanna Fairchild* (4–8). 2001, Scholastic paper $10.95 (0-590-51157-2). After Susanna's mother dies in 1849, the 14-year-old takes over her journal and describes the hardships she and her sisters face when their father decides to move the family to California in search of gold. (Rev: BL 9/1/01; HBG 10/01; SLJ 7/01; VOYA 10/01)

3065 Hahn, Mary D. *The Gentleman Outlaw and Me — Eli: A Story of the Old West* (5–8). 1996, Clarion $15.00 (0-395-73083-X). In frontier days, Eliza, masquerading as a boy, travels west in search of her father. (Rev: BCCB 4/96; BL 4/1/96; BR 11–12/96; HB 9–10/96; SLJ 5/96; VOYA 6/96)

3066 Heisel, Sharon E. *Precious Gold, Precious Jade* (5–8). 2000, Holiday $16.95 (0-8234-1432-9). At the end of the Gold Rush in southern Oregon, two sisters create hostilities when they befriend a Chinese family that has moved to town. (Rev: BCCB 4/00; HBG 10/00; SLJ 4/00)

3067 Heitzmann, Kristen. *Honor's Pledge* (8–12). 1997, Bethany House paper $11.99 (0-7642-2031-4). Set in frontier America after the Civil War, this romance is about how, after a terrible storm, a kidnapping, encounters with local Comanches, and several deaths, Abbie finally gets the man she loves. (Rev: BL 5/1/98; VOYA 12/98)

3068 Hermes, Patricia. *Calling Me Home* (4–7). 1998, Avon $15.00 (0-380-97451-7). In the late 1850s, Abbie and her family are living in their sod house in Missouri when a cholera epidemic strikes and her brother dies. (Rev: BL 1/1–15/99; HBG 3/99; SLJ 12/98)

3069 Hickman, Janet. *Susannah* (5–8). 1998, Greenwillow $15.00 (0-688-14854-9). Set in the Ohio frontier, this novel explores the world of a sensitive girl who, after her mother's death, lives with her father in a Shaker community surrounded by hostile, unsympathetic settlers. (Rev: BCCB 11/98; BL 10/15/98; HB 1–2/99; HBG 3/99; SLJ 10/98)

3070 Hill, Pamela S. *Ghost Horses* (6–9). 1996, Holiday $15.95 (0-8234-1229-6). In this novel set in the late 19th century, Tabitha rebels at her preacher father's old-fashioned ideas and, disguised as a boy, joins an expedition digging for dinosaur bones in the American West. (Rev: BL 4/15/96; BR 11–12/96; SLJ 3/96)

3071 Hite, Sid. *Stick and Whittle* (5–8). 2000, Scholastic paper $16.95 (0-439-09828-9). At the end of the Civil War, two young men, who adopt the nicknames Stick and Whittle, travel together in Comanche Territory and encounter kidnapping, romance, Indians, and a tornado. (Rev: BCCB 10/00; BL 11/1/00; HB 1–2/01; HBG 3/01; SLJ 9/00; VOYA 12/00)

3072 Holland, Isabelle. *The Promised Land* (5–8). 1996, Scholastic paper $15.95 (0-590-47176-7). Orphaned Maggie and Annie, who have been happily living with the Russell family on the Kansas frontier for three years, are visited by an uncle who wants them to come home with him to Catholicism and their Irish heritage in New York City. A sequel to *The Journey Home*. (Rev: BL 4/15/96; SLJ 8/96; VOYA 6/96)

3073 Holling, Holling C. *Tree in the Trail* (4–7). 1942, Houghton $20.00 (0-395-18228-X); paper $11.95 (0-395-54534-X). The history of the Santa Fe Trail, described through the life of a cottonwood tree, a 200-year-old landmark to travelers and a symbol of peace to the Indians.

3074 Holm, Jennifer L. *Boston Jane: An Adventure* (5–8). 2001, HarperCollins LB $17.89 (0-06-028739-X). A well-bred young woman faces hardships as she searches the 19th-century Washington Territory for her lost fiancé. (Rev: BL 9/1/01; HB 9–10/01; HBG 3/02; SLJ 8/01)

3075 Holm, Jennifer L. *Boston Jane: Wilderness Days* (5–8). 2002, HarperCollins LB $18.89 (0-06-029044-7). Jane's continued adventures in 1854 Washington Territory include helping to stop a murderer and adjusting to the hardships of pioneer life. (Rev: BL 9/1/02; HB 9–10/02; HBG 3/03; SLJ 10/02)

3076 Holmas, Stig. *Apache Pass* (6–8). Trans. from Norwegian by Anne Born. Illus. Series: Chiricahua Apache. 1996, Harbinger $15.95 (1-57140-010-9); paper $9.95 (1-57140-011-7). The kidnapping of a white boy by Indians leads to confrontations and killings in this novel set in what is now New Mexico. (Rev: SLJ 1/97; VOYA 4/97)

3077 Irwin, Hadley. *Jim-Dandy* (5–7). 1994, Macmillan $15.00 (0-689-50594-9). When his father sells his horse to the army, Caleb joins Custer's Cavalry to be near his pet in this story set in the Kansas frontier. (Rev: BCCB 4/94; BL 4/15/94; HB 7–8/94; SLJ 5/94)

3078 Jones, J. Sydney. *Frankie* (5–8). 1997, Lodestar $16.99 (0-525-67574-4). At the time of a coal miners' strike in Ludlow, Colorado, a strange girl shows up in this novel that uses historical figures such as Mother Jones as characters. (Rev: BR 3–4/98; HBG 3/98; SLJ 11/97)

3079 Karr, Kathleen. *Gold-Rush Phoebe* (5–8). Series: The Petticoat Party. 1998, HarperTrophy paper $4.95 (0-06-440498-6). An adventure-filled historical novel in which Phoebe, disguised as a boy, leaves Oregon with her friend Robbie to find wealth in Gold-Rush California. (Rev: SLJ 1/99)

3080 Karr, Kathleen. *Oregon Sweet Oregon* (5–8). Series: Petticoat Party. 1997, HarperCollins LB $14.89 (0-06-027234-1). This novel, set in Oregon City, Oregon, from 1846 through 1848, recounts the adventures of 13-year-old Phoebe Brown and her family when they stake a land claim along the Willamette River. (Rev: BL 7/97; SLJ 7/98)

3081 Karwoski, Gail L. *Seaman: The Dog Who Explored the West with Lewis and Clark* (4–8). 1999, Peachtree paper $8.95 (1-56145-190-8). This historical novel dramatizes the story of Seaman, the Newfoundland dog that accompanied Lewis and Clark on their expedition. (Rev: BL 8/99; BR 9–10/99; HBG 10/03; SLJ 10/99)

3082 Kerr, Rita. *Texas Footprints* (4–7). Illus. 1988, Eakin $13.95 (0-89015-676-X). A tale of the author's great-great-grandparents who went to Texas in 1823. (Rev: BL 3/1/89)

3083 Kirkpatrick, Katherine. *The Voyage of the Continental* (6–9). 2002, Holiday $16.95 (0-8234-1580-5). A 17-year-old girl relates in her diary the events of her journey by ship from New England to Seattle in 1866, which involve her in adventure, mystery, and romance. (Rev: BL 12/15/02; HBG 3/03; SLJ 11/02; VOYA 12/02)

3084 Lasky, Kathryn. *Beyond the Divide* (7–9). 1983, Macmillan LB $17.00 (0-02-751670-9). A young girl and her father join the rush for gold in 1849. (Rev: BL 2/15/88)

3085 Lawson, Julie. *Destination Gold!* (6–12). 2001, Orca $16.95 (1-55143-155-6). Ned, Catherine, and Sarah are all on their way to the Klondike in 1897, spurred by different motivations, but their stories all come together in an exciting climax, made more realistic by the background information and maps provided. (Rev: BCCB 4/01; BL 2/15/01; HBG 10/01; SLJ 7/01; VOYA 4/01)

3086 Laxalt, Robert. *Dust Devils* (6–10). 1997, Univ. of Nevada Pr. paper $16.00 (0-87417-300-0). A Native American teenager named Ira sets out to retrieve his prize-winning horse that has been stolen by a rustler named Hawkeye. (Rev: BL 10/15/97; VOYA 12/98)

3087 Levine, Ellen. *The Journal of Jedediah Barstow: An Emigrant on the Oregon Trail* (4–7).

Series: My Name Is America. 2002, Scholastic $10.95 (0-439-06310-8). Jedediah continues his mother's journal about their experiences on the Oregon Trail after she and the rest of his family are drowned while crossing a river. (Rev: BL 2/15/03; HBG 10/03; SLJ 11/02)

3088 Levitin, Sonia. *Clem's Chances* (4–7). 2001, Scholastic paper $17.95 (0-439-29314-6). Fourteen-year-old Clem becomes acquainted with the hardships and rewards of frontier life when he travels to California to find his father in 1860. (Rev: BL 9/15/01; HB 11–12/01; HBG 3/02; SLJ 10/01)

3089 Loveday, John. *Goodbye, Buffalo Sky* (5–8). 1997, Simon & Schuster $16.00 (0-689-81370-8). Two girls are kidnapped by a vengeful Sioux warrior in this exciting adventure set in the Great Plains during the 1870s. (Rev: BL 1/1–15/98; BR 3–4/98; HBG 3/98; SLJ 11/97)

3090 Luger, Harriett M. *The Last Stronghold: A Story of the Modoc Indian War, 1872–1873* (5–8). 1995, Linnet paper $17.50 (0-208-02403-4). The Modoc Indian War of 1872–73 is re-created in this story involving three young people: Charka, a Modoc youth; Ned, a frontier boy; and Yankel, a Russian Jew who has been tricked into joining the army. (Rev: VOYA 6/96)

3091 MacBride, Roger L. *New Dawn on Rocky Ridge* (4–7). Illus. Series: Rocky Ridge. 1997, HarperCollins $15.95 (0-06-024971-4); paper $6.99 (0-06-440581-8). This part of the Wilder family story covers 1900–1903 and focuses on Rose's difficult early teen years. (Rev: BL 11/1/97; HBG 3/98; SLJ 2/98)

3092 McCaughrean, Geraldine. *Stop the Train!* (5–8). 2003, HarperCollins $15.99 (0-06-050749-7). The challenges facing early homesteaders are brought to life in this story of a family that boards a train to nowhere in 1893. (Rev: BL 8/03*; HB 7–8/03; HBG 10/03; SLJ 8/03*; VOYA 10/03)

3093 McClain, Margaret S. *Bellboy: A Mule Train Journey* (6–10). Illus. 1989, New Mexico $17.95 (0-9622468-1-6). Set in California in the 1870s, this is the story of a 12-year-old boy and his first job on a mule train. (Rev: BL 3/1/90; SLJ 3/90)

3094 McDonald, Brix. *Riding on the Wind* (5–10). 1998, Avenue paper $5.95 (0-9661306-0-X). In frontier Wyoming during the early 1860s, 15-year-old Carrie Sutton is determined to become a rider in the Pony Express after her family's ranch has been chosen as a relay station. (Rev: SLJ 1/99)

3095 McDonald, Megan. *All the Stars in the Sky: The Santa Fe Trail Diary of Florrie Mack Ryder* (4–7). Series: Dear America. 2003, Scholastic $10.95 (0-439-16963-1). Florrie and her family make a long and difficult journey from Missouri to Santa Fe in 1848. (Rev: SLJ 11/03)

3096 McKissack, Patricia. *Run Away Home* (4–7). 1997, Scholastic paper $14.95 (0-590-46751-4). In 1888 rural Alabama, a young African American girl helps shelter a fugitive Apache boy. (Rev: BL 10/1/97; HB 11–12/97; HBG 3/98; SLJ 11/97)

3097 Mazzio, Joann. *Leaving Eldorado* (6–9). 1993, Houghton $16.00 (0-395-64381-3). The adventures of Maude, 14, in 1896 New Mexico Territory. (Rev: BL 3/15/93; SLJ 5/93)

3098 Meyer, Carolyn. *Where the Broken Heart Still Beats: The Story of Cynthia Ann Parker* (7–12). 1992, Harcourt $16.95 (0-15-200639-7); paper $7.00 (0-15-295602-6). A fictional retelling of the abduction of Cynthia Parker, who was stolen by Comanches as a child and lived with them for 24 years, first as a slave, then as a chief's wife. (Rev: BL 12/1/92; SLJ 9/92)

3099 Milligan, Bryce. *With the Wind, Kevin Dolan: A Novel of Ireland and Texas* (5–7). Illus. 1987, Corona paper $7.95 (0-931722-45-4). The story of Kevin and Tom, brothers who leave the famine in Ireland in the 1830s and head for America. (Rev: BL 8/87; SLJ 9/87)

3100 Moeri, Louise. *Save Queen of Sheba* (5–7). 1990, Avon paper $3.50 (0-380-71154-0). Young David survives a wagon train massacre and must take care of his young sister.

3101 Moore, Robin. *The Bread Sister of Sinking Creek* (7–10). 1990, HarperCollins LB $14.89 (0-397-32419-7). An orphaned 14-year-old girl becomes a servant in Pennsylvania during pioneer days. (Rev: BL 7/90; SLJ 4/90; VOYA 8/90)

3102 Murphy, Jim. *My Face to the Wind: The Diary of Sarah Jane Price, a Prairie Teacher* (5–8). Series: Dear America. 2001, Scholastic paper $10.95 (0-590-43810-7). To avoid being sent to an orphanage, 12-year-old Jessica pretends to be 16 and takes over her father's job as teacher in a 19th-century Nebraska town. (Rev: BL 12/1/01; HBG 3/02; SLJ 12/01; VOYA 2/02)

3103 Murphy, Jim. *West to a Land of Plenty: The Diary of Teresa Angelino Viscardi, New York to Idaho Territory, 1883* (4–8). Series: Dear America. 1998, Scholastic paper $10.95 (0-590-73888-7). Written in diary format, this historical novel tells about Italian American Teresa Viscardi and her family as they travel west to relocate in the Idaho Territory. (Rev: BCCB 3/98; BL 4/1/98; BR 9–10/98; HBG 9/98; SLJ 4/98)

3104 Myers, Walter Dean. *The Journal of Joshua Loper: A Black Cowboy* (5–8). 1999, Scholastic paper $10.95 (0-590-02691-7). In this fictionalized biography, set in 1871, 16-year-old Joshua Loper learns that age, race, and background are unimportant when you are on a cattle drive on the Chisholm Trail. (Rev: BL 2/15/99; HBG 9/99; SLJ 4/99)

3105 Nixon, Joan Lowery. *Circle of Love* (5–8). Series: Orphan Train Adventures. 1997, Delacorte $15.95 (0-385-32280-1). Confused by the reluctance of her boyfriend, a wounded Civil War veteran, to commit to marriage, Frances agrees to chaperone 30 orphaned children on the train ride to New York, where they are to meet their relatives or adoptive families. (Rev: BL 4/1/97; BR 5–6/97; SLJ 5/97)

3106 Nixon, Joan Lowery. *In the Face of Danger* (5–8). 1996, Bantam paper $4.99 (0-440-22705-4). Megan fears she will bring bad luck to her adoptive family in this story set in the prairies of Kansas. This is the third part of the Orphan Train Quartet. (Rev: BR 11–12/88; SLJ 12/88; VOYA 12/88)

3107 O'Dell, Scott. *Carlota* (7–9). 1977, Dell paper $4.99 (0-440-90928-7). After the Mexican-American War some Californians continue to battle the U.S. Army.

3108 O'Dell, Scott. *Streams to the River, River to the Sea: A Novel of Sacagawea* (5–9). 1986, Houghton $16.00 (0-395-40430-4); Fawcett paper $5.99 (0-449-70244-8). A fictionalized portrait of the real-life Indian woman who traveled west with Lewis and Clark on their famous journey. (Rev: BL 3/15/86; BR 9–10/86; HB 9–10/86; SLJ 5/86; VOYA 6/86)

3109 Patrick, Denise Lewis. *The Longest Ride* (6–9). 1999, Holt $15.95 (0-8050-4715-8). This sequel to *The Adventures of Midnight Son* explores slavery and Indian-black relations when escaped Texas slave Midnight Sun becomes lost during a long cattle drive and is rescued by some Arapahos at the time of the Civil War. (Rev: BL 6/1–15/99; HBG 3/00; SLJ 12/99; VOYA 2/00)

3110 Paulsen, Gary. *Call Me Francis Tucket* (5–9). 1995, Delacorte $15.95 (0-385-32116-3). In this sequel to *Mr. Tucket*, 15-year-old Francis continues his journey westward, becomes separated from his wagon train headed for Oregon, and is hopelessly lost in the wilderness. (Rev: BL 7/95; SLJ 6/95; VOYA 5/95)

3111 Paulsen, Gary. *Mr. Tucket* (5–9). 1994, Delacorte $15.95 (0-385-31169-9). A 14-year-old boy strays from his family's wagon on the Oregon Trail and ends up with the Pawnees. A trapper helps him escape and teaches him much about life and survival. (Rev: BL 5/1/94; VOYA 4/94)

3112 Paulsen, Gary. *Tucket's Home* (4–8). 2000, Delacorte $15.95 (0-385-32648-3). In this, the fifth and last installment of the Tucket Adventures, Francis, Lottie, and Billy continue their journey on the Oregon Trail, where they meet an English adventurer and his servants. (Rev: BL 9/1/00; HBG 3/01; SLJ 9/00)

3113 Paulsen, Gary. *Tucket's Ride* (4–7). 1997, Delacorte $15.95 (0-385-32199-6). Fifteen-year-old Francis Tucket faces hair-raising dangers while traveling into the Old West with orphans Lottie and Billy. (Rev: BL 12/15/96; SLJ 3/97)

3114 Philbrick, Rodman. *The Journal of Douglas Allen Deeds: The Donner Party Expedition* (5–7). Series: My Name Is America. 2001, Scholastic paper $10.95 (0-439-21600-1). A fictional account of the Donner Party's hardships as written in a 15-year-old orphaned boy's journal. (Rev: BL 1/1–15/02; HBG 3/02; SLJ 12/01)

3115 Portis, Charles. *True Grit* (7–12). 1995, NAL paper $5.50 (0-451-18545-5). A 14-year-old girl in the old West sets out to avenge her father's death.

3116 Reiss, Kathryn. *Riddle of the Prairie Bride* (5–7). Series: History Mystery. 2001, Pleasant paper $5.95 (1-584-85308-5). Ida Kate discovers that her father's mail-order bride is actually an impostor. (Rev: BL 4/1/01; HBG 3/02; SLJ 5/01)

3117 Richter, Conrad. *The Light in the Forest* (6–9). 1953, Knopf $23.00 (0-394-43314-9). At age 15, a white boy returns to his family after living many years with Indians. (Rev: BL 11/1/87)

3118 Rinaldi, Ann. *The Second Bend in the River* (5–9). 1997, Scholastic paper $15.95 (0-590-74258-2). In Ohio in 1798, 7-year-old Rebecca begins a long-lasting friendship with the Shawnee chief Tecumseh that eventually leads to a marriage proposal. (Rev: BCCB 3/97; BL 2/15/97; BR 5–6/97; HBG 3/98; SLJ 6/97)

3119 Rinaldi, Ann. *The Staircase* (5–7). 2000, Harcourt $16.00 (0-15-202430-1). The exciting story of a 19th-century teenager named Lizzy, who rooms with conniving Elinora at their Catholic girls' school. (Rev: BL 11/1/00; HBG 3/01; VOYA 12/00)

3120 Roberts, Willo Davis. *Jo and the Bandit* (6–8). 1992, Atheneum $16.00 (0-689-31745-X). Orphans Jo and her brother are sent to live with their uncle in 1860s Texas. When the stagecoach is robbed, Jo hides the son of the gang leader and helps him escape. (Rev: BL 6/1/92; SLJ 7/92)

3121 Roop, Peter, and Connie Roop. *Girl of the Shining Mountains: Sacagawea's Story* (5–8). 1999, Hyperion LB $15.49 (0-7868-2422-0). In this fictionalized account, Sacagawea tells her son about her life and the remarkable expedition of Lewis and Clark. (Rev: HBG 3/00; SLJ 3/00)

3122 Ruckman, Ivy. *Cassie of Blue Hill* (5–8). 1998, Bantam Doubleday Dell $14.95 (0-385-32514-2). In turn-of-the-century Nebraska, the peace and quiet of the Tucker family and 11-year-old Cassie are shattered with the arrival of Evan, a cousin who has a mind of his own. (Rev: BL 8/98; SLJ 10/98)

3123 Schultz, Jan Neubert. *Horse Sense* (5–7). 2001, Carolrhoda LB $19.15 (1-57505-998-3); paper $6.95 (1-57505-999-1). Fourteen-year-old Will and his father do not get along, but they join a posse tracking dangerous outlaws in this adventure based on a true story. (Rev: BL 8/01; HBG 3/02; VOYA 12/01)

3124 Seeley, Debra. *Grasslands* (5–8). 2002, Holiday $16.95 (0-8234-1731-X). The hard life on the prairie disappoints a 13-year-old newcomer from Virginia until he has the chance to ride as a cowboy in this novel set in the late 19th century. (Rev: BL 11/1/02; HBG 3/03; SLJ 1/03*; VOYA 12/02)

3125 Smith, Roland. *The Captain's Dog: My Journey with the Lewis and Clark Tribe* (5–8). 1999, Harcourt $17.00 (0-15-201989-8). This is the story of the Lewis and Clark expedition as experienced by the Newfoundland dog that accompanied the two explorers. (Rev: BL 10/15/99; HBG 3/00; SLJ 11/99; VOYA 4/00)

3126 Spooner, Michael. *Daniel's Walk* (6–9). 2001, Holt $16.95 (0-8050-6750-7). Danger, hardship, and his father's death teach young Daniel about the plight of Native Americans as he travels the Oregon Trail. (Rev: BCCB 11/01; BL 12/15/01; HBG 3/02; SLJ 10/01; VOYA 12/01)

3127 Tamar, Erika. *The Midnight Train Home* (5–7). 2000, Knopf LB $18.99 (0-375-90159-0); Random paper $4.99 (0-440-41670-1). Diedre O'Roarke, age 11, is adopted from the Orphan Train but her new home situation with a minister and his wife is far from happy. (Rev: BCCB 5/00; BL 4/1/00; HB 7–8/00; HBG 10/00; SLJ 7/00)

3128 Travis, Lucille. *Redheaded Orphan* (4–7). 1995, Baker Book House paper $5.99 (0-8010-4023-X). In 1864, Ben Abee and his family move from New York City to Minnesota, where Ben befriends orphaned Jamie. (Rev: BL 2/15/96)

3129 Vick, Helen H. *Charlotte* (6–8). Series: Courage of the Stone. 1999, Roberts Rinehart $15.95 (1-57098-278-3); paper $9.95 (1-57098-282-1). After her parents are killed by Apache warriors in frontier Arizona Territory, 13-year-old Charlotte learns the ways of survival from an elderly Native American woman. (Rev: HBG 9/99; SLJ 7/99)

3130 Wallace, Bill. *Buffalo Gal* (6–8). 1992, Holiday $15.95 (0-8234-0943-0). Amanda's plans for an elegant 16th birthday party evaporate when her mother drags her to the wilds of Texas to search for buffalo with cowboys. (Rev: BL 6/15/92; SLJ 5/92)

3131 Whelan, Gloria. *Miranda's Last Stand* (4–7). 1999, HarperCollins LB $14.89 (0-06-028252-5). After her husband was killed at Little Big Horn, Miranda's mother can't bear to be around Indians, including Sitting Bull, who works with her at Buffalo Bill's Wild West Show. (Rev: BL 11/1/99; HBG 3/00; SLJ 11/99)

3132 Whelan, Gloria. *Return to the Island* (4–7). 2000, HarperCollins LB $15.89 (0-06-028254-1). In the early 19th century on Mackinac Island, Mary

must decide between two men who love her: White Hawk, an orphan raised by a white family, and James, an English painter. (Rev: BL 1/1–15/01; HBG 3/01; SLJ 12/00)

3133 Wilder, Laura Ingalls. *The Long Winter* (5–8). Illus. 1953, HarperCollins LB $17.89 (0-06-026461-6). Number six in the Little House books. In this one, the Ingalls face a terrible winter with only seed grain for food.

3134 Wills, Patricia. *Danger Along the Ohio* (4–7). 1997, Clarion $15.00 (0-395-77044-0). This action-packed historical novel set in Ohio in 1795 tells how Amos and his younger brother and sister are captured by Indians. (Rev: BCCB 5/97; BL 5/1/97; SLJ 5/97)

3135 Wisler, G. Clifton. *All for Texas: A Story of Texas Liberation* (4–8). 2000, Jamestown paper $5.95 (0-8092-0629-3). A thirteen-year-old boy tells about moving west with his family in 1838 to Texas, where his father has been promised land if he will fight against Mexico. (Rev: BCCB 7–8/00; SLJ 8/00)

3136 Yep, Laurence. *Dragon's Gate* (6–9). 1993, HarperCollins $16.99 (0-06-022971-3). The adventures of a privileged Chinese teenager who travels to California in 1865 to join his father and uncle working on the transcontinental railroad. (Rev: BL 1/1/94; SLJ 1/94; VOYA 12/93)

3137 Yep, Laurence. *The Journal of Wong Ming-Chung* (4–7). Illus. 2000, Scholastic paper $10.95 (0-590-38607-7). Told in diary format beginning in October 1851, this is the story of a Chinese boy nicknamed Runt who travels from his native country to join an uncle in the gold mining fields of America. (Rev: BL 4/1/00; HBG 10/00; SLJ 4/00; VOYA 6/00)

RECONSTRUCTION TO WORLD WAR I
(1865–1914)

3138 Alter, Judith. *Luke and the Van Zandt County War* (5–9). Illus. 1984, Texas Christian Univ. $14.95 (0-912646-88-8). Life in Reconstruction Texas as seen through the eyes of two 14-year-olds. (Rev: SLJ 3/85)

3139 Armstrong, Jennifer. *Mary Mehan Awake* (6–10). 1997, Knopf $18.00 (0-679-88276-6). After the Civil War, Mary escapes the trauma the war caused by moving from Washington, D.C., to upstate New York, where she meets a deaf war veteran, Henry Till. A sequel to *The Dreams of Mairhe Mehan*. (Rev: BL 12/1/97; BR 3–4/98; SLJ 1/98)

3140 Auch, Mary Jane. *Ashes of Roses* (7–12). 2002, Holt $16.95 (0-8050-6686-1). Rose, a young immigrant from Ireland, suffers hardships that culminate in the Triangle Shirtwaist Factory fire in this fact-filled historical novel. (Rev: BCCB 7–8/02; BL 4/1/02; HBG 10/02; SLJ 5/02; VOYA 8/02)

3141 Bartoletti, Susan Campbell. *A Coal Miner's Bride: The Diary of Anetka Kaminska* (5–9). Illus. 2000, Scholastic paper $10.95 (0-439-05386-2). Based on a series of true events, this gripping historical novel tells the story of a young Polish immigrant girl and her struggle to survive in a coal mining town in Pennsylvania in the late 1890s. (Rev: BL 4/1/00; HBG 10/00; SLJ 8/00; VOYA 4/01)

3142 Blos, Joan W. *Brooklyn Doesn't Rhyme* (5–7). Illus. 1994, Scribners $16.00 (0-684-19694-8). A young girl narrates this episodic story about a Polish-Jewish family new to New York City in the early 1900s. (Rev: BCCB 11/94; BL 9/15/94; HB 9–10/94; SLJ 9/94)

3143 Burleigh, Robert. *Into the Air: The Story of the Wright Brothers' First Flight* (5–8). Series: American Heroes. 2002, Harcourt paper $6.00 (0-15-216803-6). A high-interest, comic-book presentation of the first flight with fictionalized dialogue. (Rev: HBG 3/03; SLJ 9/02)

3144 Byars, Betsy. *Keeper of the Doves* (5–8). 2002, Viking $14.99 (0-670-03576-9). Young Amie McBee is a thoughtful child who loves to write and — unlike her older twin sisters — has the sensitivity to see the softer side of the mysterious Polish immigrant who lives on their estate and keeps doves in this story set at the turn of the 20th century and presented in 26 short, alphabetical chapters. (Rev: BCCB 1/03; BL 10/1/02*; HB 9–10/02*; HBG 3/03; SLJ 10/02)

3145 Carbone, Elisa. *Storm Warriors* (4–8). 2001, Knopf LB $18.99 (0-375-90664-9). An exciting adventure story set on the Outer Banks of North Carolina in 1895, about a boy who wants to become part of the nearby rescue station that is manned by an African American crew. (Rev: BL 1/1–15/01; HB 5–6/01; HBG 10/01; SLJ 2/01)

3146 Carter, Alden R. *Crescent Moon* (5–8). 1999, Holiday $16.95 (0-8234-1521-X). In the early part of the 20th century, Jeremy joins Great-Uncle Mac on a log drive where they become friends with a Native American and his daughter and, through them, experience the shame of racial prejudice. (Rev: BCCB 1/00; BL 2/15/00; HB 3–4/00; HBG 10/00; SLJ 3/00; VOYA 6/00)

3147 Cindrich, Lisa. *In the Shadow of the Pali: A Story of the Hawaiian Leper Colony* (6–9). 2002, Putnam $17.99 (0-399-23855-7). Liliha is only 12 when she is sent in the mid-19th century to the leper colony on the island of Molokai and must deal with the lawless thugs who live there. (Rev: BCCB 10/02; HBG 10/02; SLJ 6/02; VOYA 8/02)

3148 Clark, Clara Gillow. *Hill Hawk Hattie* (4–7). 2003, Candlewick $15.99 (0-7636-1963-9). After her mother's death in the late 1880s, 11-year-old Hattie dresses as a boy and joins her father on a dangerous logging trip down the Delaware. (Rev: BL 7/03*; HBG 10/03; SLJ 8/03)

3149 Collier, James L. *My Crooked Family* (6–8). 1991, Simon & Schuster paper $15.00 (0-671-74224-8). Roger, 14, living in the slums in the early 1900s, steals to feed himself and becomes involved with a gang that killed his father. (Rev: BL 12/1/91; SLJ 10/91)

3150 Cross, Gillian. *The Great American Elephant Chase* (5–8). 1993, Holiday $16.95 (0-8234-1016-1). In 1881, Tad, 15, and young friend Cissie attempt to get to Nebraska with her showman father's elephant, pursued by two unsavory characters who claim they have bought the animal. (Rev: BCCB 6/93; BL 3/15/93*; SLJ 5/93*; VOYA 10/93)

3151 Cushman, Karen. *Rodzina* (5–9). 2003, Clarion $16.00 (0-618-13351-8). On an orphan train going from Chicago to California in 1881, plucky Rodzina worries about her fate and aims to find a better life than some of the other children on the train. (Rev: BCCB 3/03; BL 3/1/03*; HB 5–6/03; HBG 10/03; SLJ 4/03*)

3152 Cutler, Jane. *The Song of the Molimo* (5–8). Illus. 1998, Farrar $16.00 (0-374-37141-5). During the St. Louis World's Fair of 1904, 12-year-old Harry gets to know a group of pygmies who are on exhibit and encounters questions of race, intelligence, and fair play. (Rev: BCCB 10/98; BL 10/15/98; HBG 3/99; SLJ 11/98; VOYA 6/99)

3153 Duey, Kathleen. *Alexia Ellery Finsdale: San Francisco, 1905* (6–8). 1997, Simon & Schuster paper $4.50 (0-689-81620-0). Set in San Francisco in 1905, this historical novel tells of motherless Alexia, her unscrupulous father, and the tough decisions she is forced to make because of his bad behavior. (Rev: SLJ 4/98)

3154 Duey, Kathleen. *Ellen Elizabeth Hawkins: Mobeetie, Texas, 1886* (4–7). Series: American Diaries. 1997, Simon & Schuster paper $4.99 (0-689-81409-7). In this novel set on a Texas cattle ranch in 1886, young Ellen wants to be a rancher in spite of her father's objections. (Rev: SLJ 8/97)

3155 Duey, Kathleen. *Nell Dunne: Ellis Island, 1904* (4–8). 2000, Simon & Schuster paper $4.99 (0-689-83555-8). This tells the story of an Irish immigrant family's trip across the Atlantic and their reception at Ellis Island. (Rev: SLJ 10/00)

3156 Duey, Kathleen, and Karen A. Bale. *Fire: Chicago, 1871* (4–7). Series: Survival! 1998, Simon & Schuster paper $4.50 (0-689-81310-4). The tragic fire of 1871 that swept through Chicago is experienced by Nate Cooper, an orphan, and Julie Flynn, daughter of an important merchant. (Rev: SLJ 9/98)

3157 Duey, Kathleen, and Karen A. Bale. *Shipwreck: The Titanic, 1912* (4–7). Series: Survival! 1998, Simon & Schuster paper $4.99 (0-689-81311-2). The voyage of the *Titanic,* as experienced by Gavin Reilly, who is working his way to America, and by Karolina Green, who is returning to the United States after the death of her parents in England. (Rev: SLJ 9/98)

3158 Duffy, James. *Radical Red* (5–8). 1993, Scribners $16.95 (0-684-19533-X). This shows the plight of women in 1894 through 12-year-old Connor O'Shea, who, along with her mother, is abused at home and is drawn into a suffrage demonstration. (Rev: BCCB 1/94; BL 12/1/93; SLJ 1/94; VOYA 2/94)

3159 Durbin, William. *Blackwater Ben* (5–8). 2003, Wendy Lamb Books $15.95 (0-385-72928-6). At the end of the 19th century, 13-year-old Ben learns about lumberjacks from a distance as he works as a cook's helper in a logging camp. (Rev: BL 10/15/03; SLJ 12/03)

3160 Durbin, William. *The Journal of Otto Peltonen: A Finnish Immigrant* (6–12). Illus. Series: My Name Is America. 2000, Scholastic paper $10.95 (0-439-09254-X). In a journal format, young Otto Peltonen describes his journey to America at the turn of the last century and his life in a Minnesota mining town. (Rev: BL 10/1/00; HBG 10/01; VOYA 12/00)

3161 Durbin, William. *Song of Sampo Lake* (6–9). 2002, Random $15.95 (0-385-32731-5). This portrayal of a young Finnish immigrant's life in Minnesota in 1900 interweaves typical adolescent problems and joys with information on customs, culture, and geography. (Rev: BL 10/15/02; HBG 3/03; SLJ 11/02)

3162 Easton, Richard. *A Real American* (4–7). 2002, Clarion $15.00 (0-618-03339-9). Against his father's wishes, 11-year-old Nathan befriends Arturo, the son of Italian immigrants newly arrived in a Pennsylvania coal-mining town. (Rev: BCCB 9/02; BL 5/15/02; SLJ 3/02)

3163 Fletcher, Susan. *Walk Across the Sea* (6–10). 2001, Simon & Schuster $16.00 (0-689-84133-7). In spite of her father's dislike of immigrants, 15-year-old Eliza Jane helps a Chinese boy who rescued her and her goat in this story set in California in the late 19th century. (Rev: BCCB 12/01; BL 11/1/01; HBG 3/02; SLJ 11/01; VOYA 6/02)

3164 Forrester, Sandra. *My Home Is Over Jordan* (7–10). 1997, Dutton $15.99 (0-525-67568-X). In this sequel to *Sound the Jubilee* (1995), the Civil War is over and Maddie and her family try to start life over in North Carolina, but some whites resent their intrusion. (Rev: BL 10/1/97; HBG 3/98; SLJ 12/97)

3165 Gray, Dianne E. *Together Apart* (5–9). 2002, Houghton $16.00 (0-618-18721-9). After surviving the blizzard of 1888, Isaac and Hannah discover their love for each other while working for feminist publisher Eliza Moore. (Rev: BCCB 11/02; BL 9/15/02; HB 11–12/02; HBG 3/03; SLJ 12/02; VOYA 2/03)

3166 Gregory, Kristiana. *Orphan Runaways* (5–7). 1998, Scholastic paper $15.95 (0-590-60366-3). Two brothers run away from a San Francisco orphanage in 1879 to look for an uncle in the gold fields. (Rev: BCCB 3/98; BL 2/15/98; HBG 10/98; SLJ 3/98)

3167 Gundisch, Karin. *How I Became an American* (4–8). Trans. by James Skofield. 2001, Cricket $15.95 (0-8126-4875-7). This is the story of Johann, a young German immigrant, who arrives in an Ohio steel town in the early 20th century. (Rev: BL 11/15/01; HBG 3/02; SLJ 12/01; VOYA 4/02)

3168 Haas, Jessie. *Westminster West* (6–9). 1997, Greenwillow $15.00 (0-688-14883-2). This novel, set in 1884 Vermont, features two very different sisters and their struggle for position and control within their farming family. (Rev: BL 4/15/97; BR 9–10/97; SLJ 5/97)

3169 Hansen, Joyce. *The Heart Calls Home* (6–9). 1999, Walker $16.95 (0-8027-8636-7). In this, the third story about Obi and Easter, the two black lovers have survived the Civil War and are trying to build a new life in Reconstruction America. (Rev: BL 12/1/99; HBG 4/00)

3170 Hansen, Joyce. *I Thought My Soul Would Rise and Fly: The Diary of Patsy, a Freed Girl* (4–8). Series: Dear America. 1997, Scholastic paper $10.95 (0-590-84913-1). In this novel in the form of a diary, a freed slave girl wonders what to do with her life after leaving the plantation. (Rev: BL 12/15/97; HBG 3/98; SLJ 11/97)

3171 Harris, Carol Flynn. *A Place for Joey* (4–8). 2001, Boyds Mills $16.95 (1-56397-108-9). Twelve-year-old Joey, an Italian immigrant living in Boston in the early 20th century, learns an important lesson through a heroic act. (Rev: BL 9/1/01; HBG 3/02; SLJ 9/01; VOYA 10/01)

3172 Hurwitz, Johanna. *Faraway Summer* (5–7). Illus. 1998, Morrow $14.95 (0-688-15334-8). In 1910, a Jewish orphan who lives in a tenement in New York City is thrilled at the thought of spending two weeks on a farm in Vermont, thanks to the Fresh Air Fund. (Rev: BL 3/1/98; HB 7–8/98; HBG 10/98; SLJ 5/98)

3173 Jackson, Dave, and Neta Jackson. *Danger on the Flying Trapeze* (6–8). 1995, Bethany House paper $5.99 (1-55661-469-1). A 14-year-old joins the circus with his family to escape a dreary life. The boy hears the great evangelist D. L. Moody and learns something about the meaning of courage and faith. (Rev: BL 9/1/95; SLJ 12/95)

3174 Jocelyn, Marthe. *Earthly Astonishments* (4–8). 212003, Tundra paper $7.95 (0-88776-628-5). The setting is New York City in the 1880s and the novel involves a girl who is only 22 inches tall and her career in a glorified freak show. (Rev: BCCB 2/00; HBG 10/00; SLJ 4/00)

3175 Joinson, Carla. *A Diamond in the Dust* (6–10). 2001, Dial $17.99 (0-8037-2511-6). Sixteen-year-old Katy yearns to leave the confines of her Illinois mining town and make a life for herself in the big city in this novel set in the early 1900s. (Rev: HBG 10/01; SLJ 6/01; VOYA 8/01)

3176 Karr, Kathleen. *The Boxer* (6–9). 2000, Farrar $16.00 (0-374-30921-3). In 1885, 15-year-old Johnny Woods wants to use his boxing skills to support his family. (Rev: BL 9/1/00; HB 9–10/00; HBG 3/01; SLJ 11/00)

3177 Kendall, Jane. *Miranda and the Movies* (6–9). Illus. 1989, Harcourt paper $6.00 (0-15-202057-8). Miranda and her world suddenly come alive when a movie company moves next door in the summer of 1914. (Rev: BL 10/1/89; BR 3–4/90; SLJ 10/89)

3178 Kimball, K. M. *The Secret of the Red Flame* (4–7). 2002, Simon & Schuster paper $4.99 (0-689-85174-X). In this complex novel, Jozef, a Polish American boy living in Chicago in 1871, joins a gang in an effort to thwart some local criminals. (Rev: BL 7/02; SLJ 8/02)

3179 Klass, Sheila S. *A Shooting Star: A Novel About Annie Oakley* (4–8). 1996, Holiday $15.95 (0-8234-1279-2). A fictionalized biography of the woman who rose from poverty to become a famous show-business sharpshooter. (Rev: BL 12/15/96; SLJ 5/97)

3180 Kline, Lisa Williams. *Eleanor Hill* (7–10). 1999, Front Street $15.95 (0-8126-2715-6). Set in the early 1900s, this is a story of 12-year-old Eleanor who is determined to escape from her small North Carolina town and see the world. (Rev: BCCB 1/00; BL 2/15/00; HBG 4/00; SLJ 2/00)

3181 Kroll, Steven. *When I Dream of Heaven: Angelina's Story* (5–8). Series: Jamestown's American Portraits. 2000, Jamestown paper $5.95 (0-8092-0623-4). Set at the beginning of the 20th century in New York City, this novel tells the story of a young Italian American girl who works in a sweatshop but longs for an education. (Rev: SLJ 9/00)

3182 Kurtz, Jane. *Bicycle Madness* (5–7). 2003, Holt $15.95 (0-8050-6981-X). Twelve-year-old Lillie is fascinated by the woman who is struggling to learn to ride a bicycle in this novel set in the late 1800s and based on the life of the feminist Frances Willard. (Rev: BCCB 11/03; BL 10/15/03; HB 9–10/03; SLJ 10/03)

3183 Lafaye, Alexandria. *Edith Shay* (6–10). 1998, Viking $15.99 (0-670-87598-8). The story of a girl who decides to leave her 1860s Wisconsin settlement and find a new life for herself in Chicago. (Rev: BCCB 12/98; BL 10/15/98; BR 5–6/99; HBG 3/99; SLJ 10/98; VOYA 4/99)

3184 Lasky, Kathryn. *Dreams in the Golden Country: The Diary of Zipporah Feldman, a Jewish Immigrant Girl* (4–8). 1998, Scholastic paper $10.95 (0-590-02973-8). Twelve-year-old Zipporah Feldman, a Jewish immigrant from Russia, keeps a diary about her life with her family on New York's Lower East Side around 1910. (Rev: BL 4/1/98; HBG 9/98; SLJ 5/98)

3185 Lowell, Susan. *I Am Lavina Cumming* (5–7). 1993, Milkweed $14.95 (0-915943-39-5); paper $6.95 (0-915943-77-8). Ten-year-old Lavina encounters a number of challenging adjustments when she is sent to live with an aunt in San Francisco at the time of the earthquake. (Rev: BCCB 2/94; SLJ 1/94)

3186 Lowry, Lois. *The Silent Boy* (6–10). 2003, Houghton $15.00 (0-618-28231-9). Young Katy, who has a comfortable existence as a doctor's daughter in early-20th-century New England, makes friends with a mentally backward boy and learns that there are tragedies in life. (Rev: BL 4/15/03; HB 5–6/03; HBG 10/03; SLJ 4/03)

3187 Marshall, Catherine. *Christy* (8–12). 1976, Avon paper $6.99 (0-380-00141-1). This story set in Appalachia in 1912 tells about a spunky young girl who goes there to teach. (Rev: BL 5/1/89)

3188 Martin, Nora. *Flight of the Fisherbird* (5–7). 2003, Bloomsbury $15.95 (1-58234-814-6). Life on an isolated island on the Washington coast in 1889 is dull until 13-year-old Clem becomes involved in the rescue of a Chinese immigrant. (Rev: BL 4/1/03; HBG 10/03; SLJ 5/03; VOYA 6/03)

3189 Marvin, Isabel R. *A Bride for Anna's Papa* (5–7). 1994, Milkweed paper $6.95 (0-915943-93-X). In this novel set in Minnesota in 1907, 13-year-old Anna takes over managing the household after her mother's death and tries to find a new bride for her father. (Rev: SLJ 7/94)

3190 Massie, Elizabeth. *1870: Not with Our Blood* (6–9). Series: Young Founders. 2000, Tor paper $4.99 (0-312-59092-9). After his father dies in the Civil War, Patrick and his family seek mill work, which is so discouraging that Patrick considers turning to burglary. (Rev: BL 4/1/00; SLJ 6/00)

3191 Mattern, Joanne. *Coming to America: The Story of Immigration* (4–8). 2000, Perfection Learning $14.95 (0-7807-9715-9); paper $8.95 (0-7891-2851-9). A fictional presentation centering on the Martini family and their journey from Italy at the turn of the 20th century to find a new home in America. (Rev: HBG 3/01; SLJ 2/01)

3192 Myers, Anna. *Graveyard Girl* (5–8). 1995, Walker $14.95 (0-8027-8260-4). During the yellow-fever epidemic in Memphis in 1878, young Eli, whose family has been decimated, forms a friendship with Grace, who rings the bell for the dead at the graveyard. (Rev: SLJ 10/95)

3193 Myers, Anna. *Stolen by the Sea* (5–8). 2001, Walker $16.95 (0-8027-8787-8). A 12-year-old girl forgets her resentment toward an orphaned 14-year-old boy as they struggle to rescue themselves and others from the devastating hurricane that hit Galveston in 1900. (Rev: HBG 3/02; SLJ 11/01)

3194 Nixon, Joan Lowery. *Land of Dreams* (6–9). Series: Ellis Island. 1994, Dell paper $3.99 (0-440-21935-3). A Swedish immigrant in rural Minnesota who longs to move to the city of Minneapolis learns the importance of community support when fire strikes her home. (Rev: BL 2/15/94; SLJ 2/94)

3195 Nixon, Joan Lowery. *Land of Hope* (6–9). Series: Ellis Island. 1993, Dell paper $4.99 (0-440-21597-8). Rebekah, 15, and her family escape persecution in Russia in the early 1900s and flee to New York City, where life is harsh but hopeful. (Rev: BL 12/15/92; SLJ 10/92)

3196 Nixon, Joan Lowery. *Land of Promise* (6–9). Series: Ellis Island. 1993, Dell paper $3.99 (0-440-21904-3). This novel focuses on Irish Rosie, one of three immigrant girls who arrive in the United States in the early 1900s, and her adjustment to life in Chicago. (Rev: BL 12/1/93; VOYA 10/93)

3197 Paterson, Katherine. *Preacher's Boy* (5–8). 1999, Clarion $15.00 (0-395-83897-5). In small-town Vermont in 1899, a time of new ideas and technological change, Robbie, the restless, imaginative, questioning son of a preacher, causes unforeseen trouble when he plans his own kidnapping for profit. (Rev: BCCB 10/99; BL 8/99; HB 9–10/99; HBG 3/00; SLJ 8/99)

3198 Perez, N. A. *Breaker* (6–9). 1988, Houghton $16.00 (0-395-45537-5). A teenage boy enters the mines in 1902 Pennsylvania when his father is killed in an accident. (Rev: BL 7/88; BR 11–12/88; SLJ 8/88; VOYA 10/88)

3199 Pfitsch, Patricia C. *Keeper of the Light* (5–8). 1997, Simon & Schuster $16.00 (0-689-81492-5). Set in 1872, this is the story of Faith, who after keeping a Lake Superior lighthouse light burning after her father's death, is replaced by an inexperienced keeper and moved from the island home where she grew up. (Rev: BL 11/1/97; BR 9–10/98; HBG 3/98; SLJ 5/98; VOYA 2/98)

3200 Pfitsch, Patricia Curtis. *Riding the Flume* (5–8). 2002, Simon & Schuster $16.95 (0-689-83823-9). This adventure story set in the late 19th century in California features a plucky and environmentally conscious 15-year-old called Francie who faces a dangerous ride on the log flume in her quest to solve a mystery. (Rev: BL 11/15/02; HBG 3/03; SLJ 11/02)

3201 Raphael, Marie. *Streets of Gold* (7 9). 1998, TreeHouse paper $7.95 (1-883088-05-4). After fleeing Poland and conscription in the Russian czar's army, Stefan and his sister Marisia begin a new life in America on the Lower East Side of New York City at the turn of the 20th century. (Rev: SLJ 12/98)

3202 Reiss, Kathryn. *The Strange Case of Baby H* (4–7). Series: History Mystery. 2002, Pleasant $10.95 (1-58485-534-7); paper $6.95 (1-58485-533-9). Twelve-year-old Clara and her family survive the San Francisco earthquake of 1906 only to find an abandoned baby whose identity must be discovered. (Rev: BL 12/1/02; HBG 3/03; SLJ 11/02; VOYA 2/03)

3203 Rinaldi, Ann. *Acquaintance with Darkness* (7–10). 1997, Harcourt $16.00 (0-15-201294-X). A coming-of-age historical novel about a 14-year-old girl living in Washington, D.C., who becomes involved in political intrigue after the assassination of Lincoln. (Rev: BL 9/15/97; HBG 3/98; SLJ 10/97; VOYA 2/98)

3204 Rinaldi, Ann. *The Coffin Quilt: The Feud Between the Hatfields and the McCoys* (6–10). 1999, Harcourt $16.00 (0-15-202015-2). The infamous Hatfield-McCoy feud is flamed into violence when a McCoy daughter elopes with a Hatfield in this novel set in the late 1800s in West Virginia/Kentucky. (Rev: BL 9/1/99; HBG 4/00; SLJ 5/00; VOYA 10/99)

3205 Robinet, Harriette G. *Children of the Fire* (4–7). 1991, Macmillan $16.00 (0-689-31655-0). Hallelujah, born into slavery, escapes to Chicago, where she spends one night following the path of the Great Fire. (Rev: BCCB 9/91; BL 10/15/91; SLJ 10/91)

3206 Robinet, Harriette G. *Forty Acres and Maybe a Mule* (4–7). 1998, Simon & Schuster $16.00 (0-689-82078-X). After the Civil War, Gideon and other freed slaves begin working the 40 acres of land each has been promised in spite of the opposition of white settlers. (Rev: BL 1/1–15/99; HBG 3/99; SLJ 11/98)

3207 Rogers, Lisa Waller. *Get Along, Little Dogies: The Chisholm Trail Diary of Hallie Lou Wells: South Texas, 1878* (4–7). 2001, Texas Tech $14.50 (0-89672-446-8); paper $8.95 (0-89672-448-4). Feisty 14-year-old Hallie Lou records in her diary the details and dangers of a cattle drive from Texas to Kansas. (Rev: HBG 10/01; SLJ 7/01)

3208 Schnur, Steven. *Beyond Providence* (6–9). 1996, Harcourt $12.00 (0-15-200982-5); paper $6.00 (0-15-200981-7). In this historical novel set in Rhode Island, 12-year-old Nathan tells about life on his family farm, the tense relations between his father and older brother, and two relatives, Kitty and

Zeke, who come to live with them. (Rev: BL 4/1/96; SLJ 4/96; VOYA 6/96)

3209 Sherman, Eileen B. *Independence Avenue* (5–9). 1990, Jewish Publication Soc. $14.95 (0-8276-0367-3). This story of Russian Jews who immigrate to Texas in 1907 has a resourceful, engaging hero, an unusual setting, and plenty of action. (Rev: BL 2/15/91; SLJ 1/91)

3210 Skurzynski, Gloria. *Rockbuster* (6–12). 2001, Simon & Schuster $16.00 (0-689-83991-X). Tommy, a young coal miner and guitarist, becomes entangled in the labor movement in the early 20th century. (Rev: BCCB 2/02; BL 12/1/01; HBG 3/02; SLJ 12/01; VOYA 12/01)

3211 Snyder, Zilpha Keatley. *Gib and the Gray Ghost* (4–7). 2000, Delacorte $15.95 (0-385-32609-2). In this companion volume to *Gib Rides Home* 11-year-old Gib returns to the Thornton ranch where he attends school, encounters bullies, and trains a horse that turns up at the ranch during a snowstorm. (Rev: BCCB 2/00; BL 1/1–15/00*; HB 5–6/00; HBG 10/00; SLJ 3/00)

3212 Steiner, Barbara. *Mystery at Chilkoot Pass* (5–8). Series: History Mystery. 2002, Pleasant $10.95 (1-58485-488-X); paper $6.95 (1-58485-487-1). Twelve-year-old Hetty and her father, uncle, and friends join the Klondike Gold Rush, encountering danger, physical hardships, and mysterious happenings along the way. (Rev: BL 9/1/02; HBG 10/02; SLJ 6/02; VOYA 8/02)

3213 Stone, Bruce. *Autumn of the Royal Tar* (5–8). 1995, HarperCollins $13.95 (0-06-021492-9). Young Nora's life changes suddenly when a ship carrying passengers and circus animals burns and capsizes close to her island home off the coast of Maine. (Rev: BL 1/1–15/96; BR 3–4/96; SLJ 2/96; VOYA 4/96)

3214 Tate, Eleanora E. *The Minstrel's Melody* (5–7). Series: History Mystery. 2001, Pleasant paper $5.95 (1-58485-310-7). In Missouri of 1904, Orphelia, an African American girl, runs away from home to begin a stage career during the St. Louis World's Fair. (Rev: BL 4/1/01; HBG 3/02; SLJ 8/01)

3215 Taylor, Mildred D. *The Land* (7–12). 2001, Penguin Putnam $17.99 (0-8037-1950-7). In this prequel to *Roll of Thunder, Hear My Cry* (1976), Taylor weaves her own family history into a moving story of a young man of mixed parentage facing prejudice, cruelty, and betrayal during the time of Reconstruction. (Rev: BCCB 10/01; BL 8/01; HB 9–10/01; HBG 3/02; SLJ 8/01; VOYA 10/01)

3216 Thesman, Jean. *Rising Tide* (6–9). 2003, Viking $16.99 (0-670-03656-0). Kate Keely of *A Sea So Far* (2001), returns from Ireland to San Francisco to start a small shop with her friend Ellen, and together the two struggle with business and pri-

vate problems. (Rev: BCCB 11/03; BL 1/1–15/04; SLJ 12/03)

3217 Thesman, Jean. *A Sea So Far* (5–8). 2001, Viking $15.99 (0-670-89278-5). Fourteen-year-old orphan Kate befriends dying Jolie in a story set during and after the 1906 San Francisco earthquake. (Rev: BCCB 11/01; BL 10/15/01; HBG 3/02; SLJ 10/01; VOYA 10/01)

3218 Tucker, Terry Ward. *Moonlight and Mill Whistles* (5–7). 1998, Summerhouse $15.00 (1-887714-32-4). Thirteen-year-old Tommy is unaware how his life will change after he meets a gypsy girl named Rhona in this novel set in an early 1900s South Carolina cotton mill town. (Rev: BL 3/1/99; SLJ 5/99)

3219 Twomey, Cathleen. *Charlotte's Choice* (6–8). 2001, Boyds Mills $15.95 (1-56397-938-1). In 1905 Missouri, 13-year-old Charlotte must decide whether to betray her friend Jesse's trust and reveal why Jesse has committed murder. (Rev: BL 1/1–15/02; HBG 3/02; SLJ 12/01; VOYA 2/02)

3220 Uchida, Yoshiko. *Samurai of Gold Hill* (5–8). 1984, Creative Arts paper $8.95 (0-916870-86-3). In this reissue of a 1972 title, a group of Japanese colonists try to farm an arid stretch of California in 1869.

3221 Wallace, Barbara Brooks. *Secret in St. Something* (5–7). 2001, Simon & Schuster $16.00 (0-689-83464-0). In late-19th-century New York, 11-year-old Robin takes his baby brother and runs away from their abusive stepfather, but later discovers his stepfather's secret. (Rev: BL 5/15/01; HB 9–10/01; HBG 3/02; SLJ 7/01)

3222 Warner, Sally. *Finding Hattie* (5–8). 2001, HarperCollins $15.95 (0-06-028464-1). Hattie Knowlton's 1882 journal describes Miss Bulkey's school in Tarrytown, New York, and the people she meets there, including her sophisticated, shallow but popular cousin Sophie. (Rev: BCCB 6/01; BL 2/1/01; HB 5–6/01; HBG 10/01; SLJ 2/01; VOYA 8/01)

3223 Whelan, Gloria. *The Wanigan: A Life on the River* (4–7). 2002, Knopf LB $16.99 (0-375-91429-3). Eleven-year-old Annabel and her family live and work on a logging boat on a Michigan river in 1878. (Rev: BL 5/15/02; HBG 10/02; SLJ 3/02)

3224 White, Ellen E. *Voyage on the Great Titanic: The Diary of Margaret Ann Brady* (4–8). Series: Dear America. 1998, Scholastic paper $10.95 (0-590-96273-6). A moving, powerful novel about a young girl who earns her passage to America to be with her brother by serving as a companion to a wealthy woman aboard the *Titanic*. (Rev: BL 10/15/98; HBG 3/99; SLJ 12/98)

3225 White, Ellen Emerson. *Kaiulani: The People's Princess* (5–8). Series: Royal Diaries. 2001, Scholastic paper $10.95 (0-439-12909-5). This story, told in diary form, begins in 1889, when 13-year-old Princess Kaiulani of Hawaii heads to England to finish her studies. (Rev: BL 4/1/01; HBG 10/01; SLJ 6/01; VOYA 10/01)

3226 Yep, Laurence. *The Traitor* (5–8). Series: Golden Mountain Chronicles. 2003, HarperCollins LB $17.89 (0-06-027523-5). Two boys who are outsiders (one because he is of Chinese heritage, the other because he is illegitimate), take turns voicing their versions of the increasingly violent struggle between American miners and Chinese immigrants in 1885 Wyoming Territory. (Rev: BL 1/1–15/03; HB 3–4/03; HBG 10/03; SLJ 3/03)

BETWEEN THE WARS AND THE GREAT DEPRESSION (1919–1941)

3227 Alexander, Lloyd. *The Gawgon and the Boy* (5–7). 2001, Dutton $17.99 (0-525-46677-0). Set in 1920s Philadelphia, this is the story of a young boy who is encouraged in his love of art by a fierce aunt, nicknamed "the Gawgon." (Rev: BCCB 6/01; BL 5/15/01; HB 7–8/01; HBG 10/01; SLJ 4/01*; VOYA 6/01)

3228 Ayres, Katherine. *Macaroni Boy* (5–8). 2003, Delacorte $15.95 (0-385-73016-0). Sixth-grader Mike is living in Pittsburgh during the Depression and has many worries: lack of money, a bully who calls him "Macaroni Boy," and the possible connection between dying rats and his grandfather's illness. (Rev: BCCB 3/03; BL 1/1–15/03; HBG 10/03; SLJ 2/03; VOYA 4/03)

3229 Beard, Darleen Bailey. *The Babbs Switch Story* (5–8). 2002, Farrar $16.00 (0-374-30475-0). A young girl saves her sister from a fire on Christmas Eve in 1924 in this fictional account of a real event. (Rev: BL 3/15/02; HBG 10/02; SLJ 3/02; VOYA 4/02)

3230 Blackwood, Gary L. *Moonshine* (5–8). 1999, Marshall Cavendish $14.95 (0-7614-5056-4). Thirteen-year-old Thad, growing up with his mother in rural Mississippi during the Depression, makes a little extra money by running an illegal still that produces moonshine for the locals. (Rev: BCCB 11/99; BL 9/1/99; HBG 3/00; SLJ 10/99)

3231 Blakeslee, Ann R. *Summer Battles* (5–8). 2000, Marshall Cavendish $14.95 (0-7614-5064-5). The story of Kath, age 11, growing up in a small town in Indiana in 1926 and of her father, a preacher, who is attacked for opposing the Ku Klux Klan. (Rev: BCCB 3/00; BL 4/1/00; HBG 10/00; SLJ 4/00)

3232 Bornstein, Ruth Lercher. *Butterflies and Lizards Beryl and Me* (5–7). 2002, Marshall Cavendish LB $14.95 (0-7614-5118-8). Eleven-year-old Charley befriends an odd woman named Beryl while her mother works hard to make it

through the Great Depression. (Rev: BL 5/15/02; HBG 10/02; SLJ 5/02)

3233 Brooke, Peggy. *Jake's Orphan* (7–10). 2000, DK paper $16.99 (0-7894-2628-5). In 1926, 12-year-old Tree leaves his younger brother behind in the orphanage for a trial adoption with the Gunderson family in North Dakota. (Rev: BCCB 4/00; BL 4/1/00; HB 7–8/00; HBG 9/00; SLJ 6/00; VOYA 6/00)

3234 Burandt, Harriet, and Shelley Dale. *Tales from the Homeplace: Adventures of a Texas Farm Girl* (4–8). 1997, Holt $15.95 (0-8050-5075-2). A family story that takes place on a Texas cotton farm during the Depression and features spunky 12-year-old heroine Irene and her six brothers and sisters. (Rev: BCCB 7–8/97; HB 5–6/97; SLJ 4/97*; VOYA 12/97)

3235 Collins, Pat Lowery. *Just Imagine* (6–8). 2001, Houghton $15.00 (0-618-05603-3). Twelve-year-old Mary Francis uses her ability to have out-of-body experiences as a means to cope with her unusual family situation and the financial difficulties of the Depression. (Rev: BCCB 4/01; BL 4/1/01; HBG 10/01; SLJ 5/01; VOYA 8/01)

3236 Crew, Linda. *Fire on the Wind* (6–9). 1995, Delacorte $14.95 (0-385-32185-6). A 13-year-old girl's maturation through her experiences as a "log camp kid" in Depression-era Oregon. (Rev: BL 8/95; SLJ 11/95)

3237 Cummings, Priscilla. *Saving Grace* (4–7). 2003, Dutton $16.99 (0-525-47123-5). Eleven-year-old Grace faces a tough dilemma when a wealthy family offers to adopt her while her own family is suffering grinding poverty and illness during the Depression. (Rev: BCCB 9/03; BL 5/15/03; HBG 10/03; SLJ 6/03; VOYA 10/03)

3238 DeFelice, Cynthia. *Nowhere to Call Home* (5–8). 1999, Farrar $16.00 (0-374-35552-5). During the Great Depression, and after her father has committed suicide, 12-year-old Frances decides to dress as a boy and ride the rails like the hobos she has heard about. (Rev: BL 4/1/99; BR 9–10/99; HB 3–4/99; HBG 10/99; SLJ 4/99; VOYA 10/99)

3239 Duey, Kathleen. *Agnes May Gleason: Walsenburg, Colorado, 1933* (4–7). Series: American Diaries. 1998, Simon & Schuster paper $4.50 (0-689-82329-0). Set during the Great Depression, this novel shows how 12-year-old Agnes and her family strive to keep their dairy farm operating. (Rev: SLJ 1/99)

3240 Durbin, William. *The Journal of C. J. Jackson: A Dust Bowl Migrant, Oklahoma to California, 1935* (4–7). Series: My Name Is America. 2002, Scholastic paper $10.95 (0-439-15306-9). Young C.J. Jackson chronicles his family's journey west from the Dust Bowl, portraying clearly the harsh conditions these travelers faced. (Rev: HBG 10/02; SLJ 9/02)

3241 Erickson, John R. *Moonshiner's Gold* (5–9). 2001, Viking $15.99 (0-670-03502-5). Fourteen-year-old Riley becomes embroiled in exciting intrigue involving moonshiners and corruption in this novel set in Texas in the 1920s. (Rev: HBG 3/02; SLJ 8/01; VOYA 10/01)

3242 Fisher, Leonard E. *The Jetty Chronicles* (5–9). Illus. 1997, Marshall Cavendish $15.95 (0-7614-5017-3). A series of vignettes based on fact about the unusual people the author met while growing up in Sea Gate, New York, at a time when the United States was drifting into World War II. (Rev: BL 10/15/97; BR 3–4/98; HBG 3/98; SLJ 12/97; VOYA 2/98)

3243 Franklin, Kristine L. *Grape Thief* (5–9). 2003, Candlewick $16.99 (0-7636-1325-8). In 1925 Washington State, a boy of Croatian heritage tries to find a way to stay in school even though his family is in financial difficulty. (Rev: BL 10/1/03; SLJ 9/03)

3244 Fuqua, Jonathon. *Darby* (4–7). 2002, Candlewick $15.99 (0-7636-1417-3). A 9-year-old white girl, Darby, and her family become the target of KKK violence after she protests the killing of a black sharecropper's son in 1926 South Carolina. (Rev: BCCB 7–8/02; BL 3/15/02; HB 3–4/02; HBG 10/02; SLJ 3/02; VOYA 4/02)

3245 Green, Connie Jordan. *Emmy* (5–8). 1992, Macmillan $13.95 (0-689-50556-6). A story of perseverance and survival in a 1924 Kentucky mining town revolving around Emmy, 11; her brother, Gene, 14; their depressed father; and their mother, who is forced to take in boarders to make ends meet. (Rev: BCCB 2/92; BL 12/1/92; HB 1–2/93; SLJ 12/92)

3246 Harlow, Joan Hiatt. *Joshua's Song* (5–8). 2001, Simon & Schuster $16.00 (0-689-84119-1). Thirteen-year-old Joshua has to adjust to many changes in this story that interweaves history and fiction: his father has died in the 1918 flu epidemic, his mother is taking in boarders, and Joshua has left school and is working as a newsboy and learning a different kind of life. (Rev: BL 12/15/01; HBG 3/02; SLJ 11/01)

3247 Harrar, George. *The Trouble with Jeremy Chance* (4–7). 2003, Milkweed $16.95 (1-57131-647-7); paper $6.95 (1-57131-646-9). Tired of friction with his father, 12-year-old Jeremy travels from New Hampshire to Boston to meet his brother's troop ship in this novel set in 1919 and full of historical detail. (Rev: BL 10/1/03)

3248 Haseley, Dennis. *The Amazing Thinking Machine* (5–7). 2002, Dial $16.99 (0-8037-2609-0). Brothers Patrick and Roy invent an "amazing thinking machine" to amuse themselves while they wait

for their father's return from his search for work in this novel set in the Great Depression. (Rev: BCCB 5/02; BL 5/15/02; HB 7–8/02; HBG 10/02; SLJ 5/02; VOYA 4/02)

3249 Hesse, Karen. *Letters from Rifka* (4–8). 1992, Holt $16.95 (0-8050-1964-2); Penguin paper $5.99 (0-14-036391-2). In letters back to Russia, Rifka, 12, recounts her long journey to the United States in 1919, starting with the dangerous escape over the border. (Rev: BCCB 10/92; BL 7/92; HB 9–10/92*; SLJ 8/92*)

3250 Hesse, Karen. *A Time of Angels* (5–8). 1995, Hyperion LB $16.49 (0-7868-2072-1). As influenza sweeps her city in 1918, killing thousands, Hannah tries to escape its ravages by moving to Vermont, where an old farmer helps her. (Rev: BCCB 1/96; BL 12/1/95; SLJ 12/95)

3251 Hesse, Karen. *Witness* (7–12). 2001, Scholastic paper $16.95 (0-439-27199-1). Hesse uses fictional first-person accounts in free verse to describe Ku Klux Klan activity in a 1924 Vermont town. (Rev: BCCB 11/01; BL 9/1/01; HB 11–12/01; HBG 3/02; SLJ 9/01*; VOYA 10/01)

3252 Houston, Gloria. *Littlejim's Dreams* (5–8). 1997, Harcourt $16.00 (0-15-201509-4). Littlejim wants to become a writer, but his father thinks he should be a farmer and logger like himself, in this novel set in Appalachia in 1920. A sequel to *Littlejim* (1990). (Rev: SLJ 7/97)

3253 Hunt, Irene. *No Promises in the Wind* (6–8). 1987, Berkley paper $4.99 (0-425-09969-5). During the Great Depression, Josh must assume responsibilities far beyond his years. A reissue.

3254 Janke, Katelan. *Survival in the Storm: The Dust Bowl Diary of Grace Edwards* (4–8). Series: Dear America. 2002, Scholastic paper $10.95 (0-439-21599-4). The fictional diary of a girl living in the Texas panhandle during the Dust Bowl years. (Rev: BL 2/15/03; HBG 10/03; SLJ 12/02)

3255 Kendall, Jane. *Miranda Goes to Hollywood: Adventures in the Land of Palm Trees, Cowboys, and Moving Pictures* (5–8). 1999, Harcourt $16.00 (0-15-202059-4). In 1915, young Miranda goes to Hollywood, hoping to become a star, and there she gets involved with personalities such as D.W. Griffith and Fatty Arbuckle. A sequel to *Miranda and the Movies*. (Rev: BL 4/1/99; HBG 10/99; SLJ 6/99)

3256 Koller, Jackie F. *Nothing to Fear* (5–7). 1991, Harcourt $14.95 (0-15-200544-7); paper $8.00 (0-15-257582-0). Danny Garvey is a first-generation Catholic Irish American growing up in New York City in the 1930s. (Rev: BCCB 3/91; BL 3/1/91; SLJ 5/91)

3257 Koller, Jackie French. *Someday* (5–8). 2002, Scholastic paper $16.95 (0-439-29317-0). Celie's allegiances are divided when her town is flooded to create a reservoir in Massachusetts during the

1930s. (Rev: BCCB 10/02; BL 6/1–15/02; HBG 10/02; SLJ 7/02; VOYA 6/02)

3258 Levine, Gail C. *Dave at Night* (5–9). 1999, HarperCollins LB $16.89 (0-06-028154-5). Set in New York City in 1926, this novel is about an orphan who escapes from the hellish Hebrew Home for Boys and, through a chance encounter, meets amazing characters of the Harlem Renaissance. (Rev: BCCB 9/99; BL 6/1–15/99; HBG 3/00; SLJ 9/99)

3259 Little, Jean. *His Banner over Me* (6–9). 1995, Viking $13.99 (0-670-85664-9). A child of missionaries moves from Taiwan to Canada, where her parents leave her for many years to grow up on her own, and a terminally ill woman changes her life dramatically. (Rev: BL 11/15/95; SLJ 12/95)

3260 McNichols, Ann. *Falling from Grace* (6–10). 2000, Walker $16.95 (0-8027-8750-9). In Prohibition-era Arkansas, 13-year-old Cassie is preoccupied by her sister's disappearance, her father's affair with the preacher's wife, and her growing feelings for an immigrant boy. (Rev: BL 10/15/00; BR 1–2/01; HBG 10/01; SLJ 11/00; VOYA 2/01)

3261 Mills, Claudia. *What About Annie?* (6–8). 1985, Walker $9.95 (0-8027-6573-4). A harrowing story of a family in Baltimore living through the Depression as seen through the eyes of a young teenage girl. (Rev: BL 9/1/85)

3262 Myers, Anna. *Tulsa Burning* (8–10). 2002, Walker $16.95 (0-8027-8829-7). In 1921 Oklahoma, a 15-year-old boy helps an African American man who is injured during race riots. (Rev: BCCB 12/02; BL 10/1/02*; HBG 3/03; SLJ 9/02; VOYA 12/02)

3263 O'Sullivan, Mark. *Wash-Basin Street Blues* (7–10). 1996, Wolfhound paper $6.95 (0-86327-467-6). In 1920s New York City, 16-year-old Nora is reunited with her two younger brothers but the reunion causes unforeseen problems. A sequel to *Melody for Nora* (1994). (Rev: BL 6/1–15/96)

3264 Peck, Robert Newton. *Arly* (5–8). 1989, Walker $16.95 (0-8027-6856-3). A teacher changes the life of a young boy in a migrant camp in Florida in 1927. (Rev: BL 7/89; BR 9–10/89; VOYA 8/89)

3265 Peck, Robert Newton. *Horse Thief* (7–12). 2002, HarperCollins $16.95 (0-06-623791-2). In 1938, Tullis Yoder is determined to save 13 doomed rodeo horses in this entertaining cowboy tale. (Rev: BL 5/15/02; HBG 10/02; SLJ 7/02*; VOYA 8/02)

3266 Porter, Tracey. *Treasures in the Dust* (5–7). 1997, HarperCollins LB $14.89 (0-06-027564-2). With alternating points of view, two girls from poor families in Oklahoma's Dust Bowl tell their stories. (Rev: BL 8/97; HB 9–10/97; HBG 3/98; SLJ 12/97*; VOYA 10/98)

3267 Poupeney, Mollie. *Her Father's Daughter* (7–12). 2000, Delacorte $15.95 (0-385-32760-9). This is the story of Maggie's childhood in poverty with an alcoholic father during the years immediately preceding World War II. (Rev: BL 6/1–15/00; HBG 9/00; SLJ 7/00)

3268 Rabe, Berniece. *Hiding Mr. McMulty* (5–8). 1997, Harcourt $18.00 (0-15-201330-X). This novel, set in southeast Missouri in 1937, tells a story of race and class conflicts as experienced by 11-year-old Rass. (Rev: BL 10/15/97; HBG 3/98; SLJ 12/97; VOYA 2/98)

3269 Ray, Delia. *Ghost Girl: A Blue Ridge Mountain Story* (5–8). 2003, Clarion $15.00 (0-618-33377-0). In rural Virginia during the Depression, young April longs to go to the new school built by President Hoover and learn to read, but her family circumstances do not make this easy. (Rev: BCCB 11/03; BL 11/15/03; HB 1–2/04*; SLJ 11/03*)

3270 Reeder, Carolyn. *Moonshiner's Son* (7–10). 1993, Macmillan LB $14.95 (0-02-775805-2). It's Prohibition, and Tom, 12, is learning the art of moonshining from his father — until he becomes friendly with the new preacher's daughter. (Rev: BL 6/1–15/93; SLJ 5/93; VOYA 8/93)

3271 Robinet, Harriette G. *Mississippi Chariot* (6–10). 1994, Atheneum $14.95 (0-689-31960-6). Life in the 1930s Mississippi Delta is vividly evoked in this story of Shortning Bread, 12, whose father has been wrongfully convicted of a crime and sentenced to a chain gang. (Rev: BL 11/15/94; SLJ 12/94; VOYA 5/95)

3272 Rossiter, Phyllis. *Moxie* (4–7). 1990, Macmillan $14.95 (0-02-777831-2). The story of a gallant family's fight against drought and foreclosure in the Dust Bowl of the 1930s. (Rev: SLJ 12/90)

3273 Rostkowski, Margaret I. *After the Dancing Days* (6–9). 1986, HarperCollins LB $15.89 (0-06-025078-X); paper $5.99 (0-06-440248-7). Annie encounters the realities of war when she helps care for wounded soldiers after World War I. (Rev: BL 10/15/86; SLJ 12/86; VOYA 4/87)

3274 Ryan, Pam M. *Esperanza Rising* (5–8). 2000, Scholastic paper $15.95 (0-439-12041-1). During the Great Depression, poverty forces Esperanza and her mother to leave Mexico and seek work in an agricultural labor camp in California. (Rev: BCCB 12/00; BL 12/1/00; HB 1–2/01; HBG 3/01; SLJ 10/00; VOYA 12/00)

3275 Snyder, Zilpha Keatley. *Gib Rides Home* (5–8). 1998, Delacorte $15.95 (0-385-32267-4). Set in post-World War I America, this is the story of an orphan boy and how he conquers hardships and deprivations. (Rev: BL 1/1–15/98; BR 9–10/98; HB 3–4/98; HBG 10/98; SLJ 1/98*)

3276 Stolz, Mary. *Ivy Larkin* (7–9). 1986, Harcourt $13.95 (0-15-239366-8). During the Depression in

New York City, 15-year-old Ivy's father loses his job and the family moves to the Lower East Side. (Rev: BL 11/1/86; SLJ 12/86)

3277 Sullivan, Paul. *Maata's Journal* (6–9). 2003, Simon & Schuster $16.95 (0-689-83463-2). Maata, a 17-year-old Inuit girl, relates a story of cultural conflict, discrimination, and hardship as white society encroaches on her community in the early 20th century. (Rev: BL 3/1/03; HBG 10/03; SLJ 4/03; VOYA 2/03)

3278 Taylor, Kim. *Cissy Funk* (6–9). 2001, Harper-Collins $15.95 (0-06-029041-2). Cissy is neglected and abused until her Aunt Vera arrives in this novel of complex family relationships that evokes the privations of the Depression years in Colorado. (Rev: BCCB 5/01; BL 8/01; HBG 10/01; SLJ 5/01; VOYA 8/01)

3279 Thesman, Jean. *The Ornament Tree* (7–10). 1996, Houghton $16.00 (0-395-74278-1). Fourteen-year-old Bonnie moves into a boardinghouse run by her female relatives in Seattle in 1914, and through the years she adjusts to these strong-willed ladies and meets several interesting guests. (Rev: BL 5/1/96; BR 1–2/97; SLJ 3/96; VOYA 8/96)

3280 Thesman, Jean. *The Storyteller's Daughter* (6–9). 1997, Houghton $16.00 (0-395-80978-9). During the Depression in Seattle, Quinn believes that her father is smuggling liquor from Canada to help supplement the dwindling family income. (Rev: BL 11/1/97; BR 5–6/98; HBG 3/98; SLJ 9/97; VOYA 2/98)

3281 Winthrop, Elizabeth. *Franklin Delano Roosevelt: Letters from a Mill Town Girl* (5–7). Illus. Series: Dear Mr. President. 2001, Winslow $9.95 (1-890817-61-9). Fictional letters between Franklin Delano Roosevelt and a 12-year-old girl illustrate living conditions and government policy during the Depression. (Rev: BL 2/1/02; HBG 3/02; SLJ 12/01)

3282 Wolfert, Adrienne. *Making Tracks* (5–7). Illus. Series: Adventures in America. 2000, Silver Moon LB $14.95 (1-893110-16-8). In this novel set in the Depression, young Henry leaves his foster home to ride the rails to Chicago to find his father. (Rev: BL 7/00; HBG 3/01; SLJ 11/00)

POST WORLD WAR II UNITED STATES (1945–)

3283 Armistead, John. *The Return of Gabriel* (6–9). 2002, Milkweed $17.95 (1-57131-637-X); paper $6.95 (1-57131-638-8). Friendships and family loyalties are tested when the civil rights movement comes to Mississippi and parents take sides in this story set in 1964. (Rev: BL 12/15/02; HBG 3/03; SLJ 12/02)

3284 Baker, Julie. *Up Molasses Mountain* (6–9). 2002, Random $15.95 (0-385-72908-1). Clarence and Elizabeth find themselves on opposite sides of a labor dispute involving their coal-mining fathers in this multilayered novel set in 1953 West Virginia. (Rev: BL 5/15/02; HBG 10/02; SLJ 7/02; VOYA 8/02)

3285 Clifton, Lucille. *The Times They Used to Be* (4–9). Illus. 2000, Bantam $12.95 (0-385-32126-0); Yearling paper $4.99 (0-440-41867-4). In this narrative poem set in 1948, Mama tells her African American children about the days when she was growing up in the segregated South through a series of stories that deal with happiness, sorrow, yearning, and humor. (Rev: BL 1/1–15/01; HBG 9/99)

3286 Collier, Kristi. *Jericho Walls* (6–10). 2002, Holt $16.95 (0-8050-6521-0). Preacher's kid Jo makes friends with an African American boy after her family moves to South Carolina in this story of racial tensions in the 1950s. (Rev: BL 4/1/02; HB 7–8/02; HBG 10/02; SLJ 4/02; VOYA 6/02)

3287 Crowe, Chris. *Mississippi Trial, 1955* (7–12). 2002, Penguin Putnam $17.99 (0-8037-2745-3). The story of the racist murder in 1955 of a 14-year-old black boy called Emmett Till is told through the eyes of Hiram, a white teenager. (Rev: BCCB 4/02; BL 2/15/02; HBG 10/02; SLJ 5/02; VOYA 4/02)

3288 Crum, Shutta. *Spitting Image* (5–8). 2003, Clarion $15.00 (0-618-23477-2). Jessie has a busy summer in 1967 in her Kentucky hometown, tackling family problems and dealing with well-meaning volunteers and reporters who view them as "rural poor." (Rev: BL 3/1/03; HBG 10/03; SLJ 4/03*)

3289 Matthews, Kezi. *Scorpio's Child* (7–10). 2001, Cricket $15.95 (0-8126-2890-X). In South Carolina in 1947, 14-year-old Afton has difficulty welcoming a taciturn, previously unknown uncle into her home despite her mother's pleas for compassion. (Rev: BCCB 10/01; BL 9/15/01; HB 1–2/02; HBG 3/02; SLJ 10/01; VOYA 4/02)

3290 Rogers, Kenny, and Donald Davenport. *Christmas in Canaan* (5–8). 2002, HarperCollins $15.99 (0-06-000746-X). In 1960s Texas, after a black boy and a white boy fight on the school bus, the adults decree that the two boys must spend time together, and a difficult start ends in the boys becoming fast friends when they help a wounded dog. (Rev: BL 11/1/02; HBG 3/03; SLJ 10/02; VOYA 4/03)

3291 Woods, Brenda. *The Red Rose Box* (5–8). 2002, Putnam $16.99 (0-399-23702-X). In 1953, Leah, a southern black girl, and her family travel to Los Angeles where they find a different culture and more progressive attitudes. (Rev: BCCB 7–8/02; BL 6/1–15/02; HBG 10/02; SLJ 6/02; VOYA 6/02)

3292 Young, Karen Romano. *Outside In* (6–10). 2002, HarperCollins $16.95 (0-688-17363-2). Cherie, 12, is almost overwhelmed by the headlines of the newspapers she delivers daily in 1968. (Rev: BL 4/1/02; HBG 10/02; SLJ 5/02)

Twentieth-Century Wars

WORLD WAR I

3293 Breslin, Theresa. *Remembrance* (7–12). 2002, Delacorte $16.95 (0-385-73015-2). Francis, Charlotte, Maggie, and their friends and family find their lives drastically changed by World War I in this story of class differences, romance, loss, and bravery. (Rev: BL 12/15/02; HBG 3/03; SLJ 10/02; VOYA 12/02)

3294 Jorgensen, Norman. *In Flanders Fields* (4–7). 2002, Fremantle Arts Centre $22.95 (1-86368-369-0). During a Christmas Day ceasefire in the World War I trenches, a soldier rescues a trapped robin. (Rev: SLJ 2/03)

3295 Lawrence, Iain. *Lord of the Nutcracker Men* (5–9). 2001, Delacorte $15.95 (0-385-72924-3). Ten-year-old Johnny experiences World War I through the letters and carved soldiers his father sends to him from the front lines. (Rev: BCCB 10/01; BL 11/1/01; HB 11–12/01; HBG 3/02; SLJ 11/01*; VOYA 12/01)

3296 McKay, Sharon E. *Charlie Wilcox* (5–8). 2000, Stoddart paper $7.95 (0-7737-6093-8). This is the story of a 14-year-old Canadian boy who becomes involved in the trench warfare in France during World War I. (Rev: SLJ 11/00)

3297 Magorian, Michelle. *Good Night, Mr. Tom* (7–9). 1981, HarperCollins LB $17.89 (0-06-024079-2); paper $6.99 (0-06-440174-X). A quiet recluse takes in an abused 8-year-old who has been evacuated from World War II London.

3298 Myers, Anna. *Fire in the Hills* (6–10). 1996, Walker $15.95 (0-8027-8421-6). In rural Oklahoma during World War I, 16-year-old Hallie takes care of her younger siblings after her mother's death and also tries to help a German family fight the prejudice of their neighbors. (Rev: BL 4/15/96*; BR 9–10/96; SLJ 4/96; VOYA 6/96)

3299 Wilson, John. *And in the Morning* (8–12). 2003, Kids Can $16.95 (1-55337-400-2). This absorbing story of fighting in the trenches of World War I, told in diary form by a teenage boy, is enhanced by newspaper headlines and clippings. (Rev: BL 3/15/03; HBG 10/03; SLJ 6/03)

WORLD WAR II AND THE HOLOCAUST

3300 Almagor, Gila. *Under the Domim Tree* (6–9). 1995, Simon & Schuster $15.00 (0-671-89020-4). An autobiographical novel about young Holocaust survivors in an agricultural youth village in Israel in 1953. (Rev: BL 5/1/95; SLJ 6/95)

3301 Atlema, Martha. *A Time to Choose* (8–12). 1995, Orca paper $7.95 (1-55143-045-2). While growing up in Holland under the Nazi occupation, 16-year-old Johannes tries to separate himself from his father, who is considered a collaborator. (Rev: VOYA 10/97)

3302 Avi. *Don't You Know There's a War On?* (4–7). 2001, HarperCollins LB $16.89 (0-06-029214-8). It's 1943 Brooklyn, and 11-year-old Howie Crispers sees war, intrigue, and potential romance on every corner. (Rev: BCCB 5/01; BL 6/1–15/01; HB 5–6/01; HBG 10/01; SLJ 6/01)

3303 Avi. *Who Was That Masked Man, Anyway?* (5–7). 1992, Orchard LB $17.99 (0-531-08607-0). In a story told through dialogue, 6th-grader Frankie lives through World War II by immersing himself in his beloved radio serials. (Rev: BCCB 10/92*; BL 8/92*; HB 3–4/93; SLJ 10/92*)

3304 Bawden, Nina. *Carrie's War* (6–9). Illus. 1973, HarperCollins LB $14.89 (0-397-31450-7). Carrie relives her days during World War II when she and her brothers were evacuated to Wales. (Rev: BL 3/1/88)

3305 Benchley, Nathaniel. *Bright Candles: A Novel of the Danish Resistance* (6–9). 1974, HarperCollins $13.95 (0-06-020461-3). The Danish underground during World War II. (Rev: BL 7/88)

3306 Bennett, Cherie, and Jeff Gottesfeld. *Anne Frank and Me* (6–8). 2001, Putnam $18.99 (0-399-23329-6). Nicole Burns is wounded on a class trip to an Anne Frank exhibit and awakens in World War II France where she experiences the horrors of war and eventually is taken to a concentration camp. (Rev: BCCB 3/01; BL 2/15/01; HBG 10/01; SLJ 3/01; VOYA 4/01)

3307 Bergman, Tamar. *Along the Tracks* (6–9). Trans. by Michael Swirsky. 1991, Houghton $16.00 (0-395-55328-8). The story of an 8-year-old Jewish boy who is separated from his parents during World War II and wanders through Russia for four years searching for them. (Rev: BL 9/15/91; SLJ 12/91)

3308 Booth, Martin. *War Dog* (6–8). 1997, Simon & Schuster $16.00 (0-689-81380-5). Such events as Dunkirk and the London blitz are incorporated into this tale of World War II England and Jet, a dog that is trained for combat duty. (Rev: BL 11/1/97; BR 3–4/98; HBG 3/98; SLJ 10/97; VOYA 2/98)

3309 Bradley, Kimberly Brubaker. *For Freedom: The Story of a French Spy* (6–12). 2003, Delacorte $15.95 (0-385-72961-8). This fascinating first-person novel about a young French girl who becomes a spy for the Resistance is based on a true story. (Rev: BL 4/1/03*; HB 7–8/03; HBG 10/03; SLJ 6/03; VOYA 6/03)

3310 Buckvar, Felice. *Dangerous Dream* (6–9). 1998, Royal Fireworks paper $9.99 (0-88092-277-X). In postwar Germany, 13-year-old Hella, a concentration camp survivor, mistakenly believes that a new arrival in the infirmary is her father. (Rev: SLJ 4/99; VOYA 8/99)

3311 Bunting, Eve. *Spying on Miss Miller* (6–8). 1995, Clarion $15.00 (0-395-69172-9). During World War II in Belfast, Jessie, 13, believes her half-German teacher is a spy. (Rev: BL 3/15/95*; SLJ 5/95)

3312 Carey, Janet. *Molly's Fire* (4–7). 2000, Simon & Schuster $16.00 (0-689-82612-5). During World War II, Molly learns that her father's plane has been shot down but she refuses to believe he is dead. (Rev: BCCB 4/00; BL 4/15/00; HBG 10/00; SLJ 5/00)

3313 Chan, Gillian. *A Foreign Field* (7–10). 2002, Kids Can $16.95 (1-55337-349-9). Friendship develops into love for 14-year-old Ellen and a young British pilot who is training at an air base near her home in Canada. (Rev: BCCB 12/02; BL 9/15/02; HBG 3/03; SLJ 11/02; VOYA 2/03)

3314 Chang, Margaret, and Raymond Chang. *In the Eye of War* (5–7). 1990, Macmillan $14.95 (0-689-50503-5). A novel based on true experiences of growing up in Shanghai during World War II. (Rev: BCCB 4/90; BL 3/15/90; SLJ 8/90)

3315 Cheng, Andrea. *Marika* (7–12). 2002, Front Street $16.95 (1-886910-78-2). Marika's earlier preoccupations disappear when the arrival of Nazis in 1944 Budapest changes her life. (Rev: BL 11/15/02; HB 11–12/02; HBG 3/03; SLJ 12/02; VOYA 2/03)

3316 Coerr, Eleanor. *Mieko and the Fifth Treasure* (4–7). 2003, Puffin paper $5.99 (0-698-11990-8). A Japanese girl believes that she will never draw again after she is injured during the atomic bomb attack on Nagasaki. (Rev: BCCB 4/93; BL 4/1/93*; SLJ 7/93)

3317 Cooper, Susan. *Dawn of Fear* (5–9). 1970, Harcourt $14.95 (0-15-266201-4); Aladdin paper $4.99 (0-689-71327-4). Three boys in a London suburb become friends amid the violence of World War II. (Rev: BL 4/87)

3318 Copeland, Cynthia. *Elin's Island* (5–7). 2003, Millbrook LB $22.90 (0-7613-2522-0). Raised since infancy by lighthouse keepers, 13-year-old Elin is left on her own to tend the house and light on an eventful night in 1941. (Rev: BL 3/15/03; HBG 10/03; SLJ 7/03)

3319 Dahlberg, Maurine F. *Play to the Angel* (5–9). 2000, Farrar $16.00 (0-374-35994-6). When Hitler invades Austria in 1938, Greta must help her Jewish music teacher escape. (Rev: BL 7/00; HBG 3/01; SLJ 9/00; VOYA 12/00)

3320 Davies, Jacqueline. *Where the Ground Meets the Sky* (6–9). 2002, Marshall Cavendish $15.95 (0-7614-5105-6). During World War II, 12-year-old Hazel lives a lonely life in a compound in the New Mexico desert while her father works on a top secret project, until she makes a friend and uncovers a secret. (Rev: BL 9/1/02; HBG 10/02; SLJ 4/02)

3321 DeJong, Meindert. *The House of Sixty Fathers* (6–9). 1956, HarperCollins LB $16.89 (0-06-021481-3); paper $5.99 (0-06-440200-2). In wartorn China, a young boy searches for his family as the Japanese invade his country.

3322 Denenberg, Barry. *The Journal of Ben Uchida: Citizen 13559 Mirror Lake Internment Camp* (5–8). Illus. Series: Dear America. 1999, Scholastic paper $10.95 (0-590-48531-8). In this fictional diary, Ben Uchida and his Japanese American family are shipped off to an internment camp after Pearl Harbor. (Rev: BL 12/15/99; HBG 3/00)

3323 Denenberg, Barry. *One Eye Laughing, The Other Weeping* (5–7). Series: Dear America. 2000, Scholastic paper $12.95 (0-439-09518-2). Thirteen-year-old Julie Weiss is able to flee Austria when the Nazis invade and travel to America to stay with her aunt, a famous stage star. (Rev: BL 7/00; HBG 3/01; SLJ 12/00; VOYA 2/01)

3324 Douglas, Kirk. *The Broken Mirror* (5–8). 1997, Simon & Schuster paper $13.00 (0-689-81493-3). This short novel by the famous actor depicts the despair and loss of faith experienced by a Jewish child whose loved ones have died in the Holocaust. (Rev: BL 10/1/97; HBG 3/98; SLJ 9/97; VOYA 2/98)

3325 Drucker, Malka, and Michael Halperin. *Jacob's Rescue: A Holocaust Story* (6–10). 1993, Dell paper $4.99 (0-440-40965-9). The fictionalized true story of two Jewish children saved from the Holocaust in Poland by "righteous Gentiles." (Rev: BL 2/15/93; SLJ 5/93)

3326 Duey, Kathleen. *Janey G. Blue: Pearl Harbor, 1941* (4–8). 2001, Simon & Schuster paper $4.99 (0-689-84404-2). Sixth-grader Janey lives through the terror of the attack on Pearl Harbor and her family helps a neighboring Japanese American girl who is separated from her parents. (Rev: SLJ 10/01)

3327 Duey, Kathleen. *Josie Poe: Palouse, Washington, 1943* (4–7). Series: American Diaries. 1999, Simon & Schuster paper $4.99 (0-689-82930-2). Josie's diary entries during World War II depict life on the home front and also include a mystery concerning her older brother's strange behavior. (Rev: SLJ 1/00)

3328 Elliott, L. M. *Under a War-Torn Sky* (6–9). 2001, Hyperion $15.99 (0-7868-0755-5). Henry Forester, a 19-year-old American, travels across Nazi-occupied France with the help of the French Resistance after his plane is shot down. (Rev: BCCB 1/02; BL 10/1/01; HBG 3/02; SLJ 10/01; VOYA 12/01)

3329 Elmer, Robert. *Into the Flames* (5–7). Series: Young Underground. 1995, Bethany paper $5.99 (1-

55661-376-8). Danish twins are captured by the Gestapo while trying to rescue their uncle during World War II. (Rev: BL 5/15/95; SLJ 8/95)

3330 Fox, Robert Barlow. *To Be a Warrior* (6–9). 1997, Sunstone paper $12.95 (0-86534-253-9). A Navajo boy joins the marines after the bombing of Pearl Harbor and becomes one of the celebrated "code talkers." (Rev: BL 9/1/97; BR 5–6/98)

3331 Frank, Anne. *Anne Frank's Tales from the Secret Annex* (8–12). 1994, Bantam paper $4.50 (0-553-56983-X). This is a collection of all of Anne Frank's writings (apart from the diary, that is): stories, sketches, and fairy tales. [839.3]

3332 Gaeddert, Lou Ann. *Friends and Enemies* (6–9). Illus. 2000, Simon & Schuster $16.00 (0-689-82822-5). As told by a 14-year-old Methodist preacher's son, this is the story of a Mennonite community in Kansas whose members, for religious reasons, were pacifists during World War II. (Rev: BCCB 2/00; BL 2/1/00; HBG 9/00; SLJ 3/00; VOYA 4/00)

3333 Giff, Patricia Reilly. *Lily's Crossing* (5–8). 1997, Delacorte $15.95 (0-385-32142-2). During World War II, motherless Lily loses her father when he is sent to fight in France but becomes friendly with Albert, an orphaned Hungarian refugee. (Rev: BCCB 4/97; BL 2/1/97; HB 3–4/97; SLJ 2/97)

3334 Griffis, Molly Levite. *The Feester Filibuster* (4–8). 2002, Eakin $16.95 (1-57168-541-3); paper $8.95 (1-57168-694-0). John Allen Feester is determined to show he's not a spy in this sequel to *The Rachel Resistance* (2001). (Rev: BL 11/1/02; HBG 10/01)

3335 Hahn, Mary D. *Stepping on the Cracks* (5–8). 1991, Houghton $16.00 (0-395-58507-4); Avon paper $5.99 (0-380-71900-2). The compelling story of a 6th-grade girl during World War II and her difficult decision whether to help a pacifist deserter. (Rev: BCCB 12/91*; BL 10/15/91*; HB 11–12/91; SLJ 12/91*)

3336 Hamisch, Siegfried. *The Bunker on Edelweiss Mountain* (5–8). 2001, Pentland $16.95 (1-57197-282-X). Thirteen-year-old Norman, the son of an Allied sergeant, is caught up in dangerous intrigue when he befriends a local boy in this novel based in post-World War II Germany. (Rev: BL 10/15/01)

3337 Harlow, Joan Hiatt. *Shadows on the Sea* (7–10). 2003, Simon & Schuster $16.95 (0-689-84926-5). Fourteen-year-old Jill, staying with her grandmother in Maine in 1942, finds a pigeon carrying a message in German and suspects U-boats may be close. (Rev: BL 9/15/03; SLJ 9/03)

3338 Harrison, Barbara. *Theo* (6–12). 1999, Clarion $15.00 (0-899-19959-3). In World War II Greece, Theo learns the meaning of heroism when he tries to save some of his fellow Jews from the Nazis. (Rev: BL 1/1–15/00; HB 11–12/99; HBG 4/00; SLJ 9/99)

3339 Hartling, Peter. *Crutches* (6–9). 1988, Lothrop $12.95 (0-688-07991-1). A young war refugee makes friends with a one-legged man in postwar Vienna. (Rev: BL 2/1/89; SLJ 11/88; VOYA 2/89)

3340 Heneghan, James. *Wish Me Luck* (5–8). 1997, Bantam Doubleday Dell paper $4.50 (0-440-22764-X). When Jamie is evacuated to Canada from England during World War II, the ship he is on is sunk by a German U-boat. (Rev: BL 6/1–15/97; BR 9–10/97; SLJ 6/97)

3341 Hertenstein, Jane. *Beyond Paradise* (6–10). 1999, Morrow $16.00 (0-688-16381-5). This historical novel recounts the horrors of life in Japanese internment camps in the Pacific during World War II as seen through the eyes of a missionary's daughter. (Rev: BCCB 9/99; BL 8/99; HBG 4/00; SLJ 9/99)

3342 Hesse, Karen. *Aleutian Sparrow* (7–12). 2003, Simon & Schuster $16.95 (0-689-86189-3). The unhappy story of the relocation of the Aleutian islanders during World War II is told in prose poetry from the perspective of young Vera. (Rev: BL 10/15/03; SLJ 10/03)

3343 Holm, Anne. *North to Freedom* (6–8). 1984, Harcourt paper $6.00 (0-15-257553-7). A boy who has never known anything except life in a concentration camp makes his way across Europe alone and escapes to freedom.

3344 Hopper, Nancy J. *Cassandra — Live at Carnegie Hall!* (5–7). Illus. 1998, Dial $15.99 (0-8037-2329-6). Set in New York City during World War II, this novel tells the story of 13-year-old Cassandra and her sisters, who must move from Connecticut to Carnegie Hall to live with their bandleader father and pretend to be his cousins to protect his dashing image. (Rev: BL 6/1–15/98; HBG 10/98; SLJ 8/98)

3345 Howard, Ellen. *A Different Kind of Courage* (7–12). 1996, Simon & Schuster $15.00 (0-689-80774-0). A complex novel about two youngsters from different parts of France and their perilous journey in 1940 to reach safety in the United States. (Rev: BL 9/15/96; SLJ 11/96)

3346 Hughes, Dean. *Soldier Boys* (7–9). 2001, Simon & Schuster $16.00 (0-689-81748-7). Parallel stories follow two teenage boys — one American, one German — through the horrors of World War II and the Battle of the Bulge. (Rev: BCCB 3/02; BR 5–6/02; HB 1–2/02; HBG 3/02; SLJ 11/01; VOYA 2/02)

3347 Isaacs, Anne. *Torn Thread* (6–12). 2000, Scholastic paper $15.95 (0-590-60363-9). Based on the author's mother-in-law's wartime experiences in World War II, this tells of Eva and her sister Rachel and their years in a Nazi labor camp for Jews in Czechoslovakia. (Rev: BL 3/1/00; HBG 9/00; SLJ 4/00; VOYA 4/00)

3348 Kerr, M. E. *Slap Your Sides* (7–10). 2001, HarperCollins $15.89 (0-06-029481-7). Pacifism during time of war is at the center of this novel about a Quaker family living in a small Pennsylvania town in the early 1940s. (Rev: BCCB 11/01; BL 10/1/01; HB 11–12/01; HBG 3/02; SLJ 10/01; VOYA 10/01)

3349 Laird, Christa. *But Can the Phoenix Sing?* (7–10). 1995, Greenwillow $16.00 (0-688-13612-5). A Holocaust survivor story in which a young boy learns that cruelty and tenderness can reside at the same time in one person. (Rev: BL 11/15/95; SLJ 10/95)

3350 Levitin, Sonia. *Annie's Promise* (6–10). 1993, Atheneum $15.00 (0-689-31752-2); paper $4.99 (0-689-80440-7). Set near the end of World War II, this sequel to *Silver Days* focuses on 13-year-old Annie's break from her overprotective Jewish immigrant parents. (Rev: BCCB 3/93; BL 2/1/93; SLJ 4/93*)

3351 Levitin, Sonia. *Journey to America* (5–8). 1970, Macmillan $16.00 (0-689-31829-4); paper $4.99 (0-689-71130-1). A Jewish mother and her three daughters flee Nazi Germany in 1938 and undertake a long and difficult journey to join their father in America. (Rev: BL 9/1/93)

3352 Levitin, Sonia. *Room in the Heart* (7–10). 2003, Dutton $16.99 (0-525-46871-4). Alternating characters in a multilayered novel show the Danes' assistance to Jews and resistance to the Nazis during World War II. (Rev: BL 11/1/03; SLJ 12/03)

3353 Levitin, Sonia. *Silver Days* (7–9). 1992, Simon & Schuster paper $4.99 (0-689-71570-6). The Platt family moves to California as World War II breaks out, and adjustments to the New World must be made. This is a sequel to *Journey to America*. (Rev: BL 4/1/89; BR 9–10/89; SLJ 5/89; VOYA 6/89)

3354 Lisle, Janet T. *The Art of Keeping Cool* (5–8). 2000, Simon & Schuster $17.00 (0-689-83787-9). Robert is staying with his grandparents in New England during World War II and forms a friendship with his cousin, Eliot, who is helping an outcast German painter whom Robert thinks might be a spy. (Rev: BL 9/15/00*; HB 11–12/00; HBG 3/01; SLJ 10/00; VOYA 12/00)

3355 Lowry, Lois. *Number the Stars* (5–7). 1989, Houghton $16.00 (0-395-51060-0); Dell paper $5.99 (0-440-40327-8). The story of war-torn Denmark and best friends Annemarie Johansen and Ellen Rosen. Newbery Medal winner, 1990. (Rev: BCCB 3/89; BL 3/1/89; SLJ 3/89)

3356 McSwigan, Marie. *Snow Treasure* (4–7). 1986, Scholastic paper $3.99 (0-590-42537-4). Children smuggle gold out of occupied Norway on their sleds.

3357 Manley, Joan B. *She Flew No Flags* (7–10). 1995, Houghton $16.00 (0-395-71130-4). A strong-ly autobiographical World War II novel about a 10-year-old's voyage from India to her new home in the United States and the people she meets on the ship. (Rev: BL 3/15/95; SLJ 4/95; VOYA 5/95)

3358 Matas, Carol. *After the War* (5–9). 1996, Simon & Schuster LB $16.00 (0-689-80350-8). A harrowing docunovel about 15-year-old Ruth, who after being liberated from Buchenwald in 1945, leads a group of children across Europe to eventual safety in Palestine. (Rev: BL 4/1/96*; BR 1–2/97; SLJ 5/96; VOYA 8/96)

3359 Matas, Carol. *Daniel's Story* (6–9). 1994, Scholastic paper $4.99 (0-590-46588-0). In this companion to an exhibit at the U.S. Holocaust Memorial Museum, Daniel symbolizes the millions of young people who suffered or died under Hitler's regime. (Rev: BL 5/15/93)

3360 Matas, Carol. *Greater Than Angels* (7–10). 1998, Simon & Schuster paper $16.00 (0-689-81353-8). Although told in a somewhat confused manner, this is a gripping account of one of the Jewish children hidden from the Nazis in the French village of Le Chambon. (Rev: BCCB 7–8/98; BL 4/15/98; BR 1–2/99; HB 5–6/98; HBG 9/98; SLJ 6/98; VOYA 10/98)

3361 Matas, Carol. *In My Enemy's House* (7–10). 1999, Simon & Schuster paper $16.00 (0-689-81354-6). Marisa, 15, Jewish but Aryan-looking, assumes a new identity during World War II after her family and friends are killed by the Nazis in Poland. (Rev: BL 2/1/99; HBG 9/99; SLJ 3/99; VOYA 4/99)

3362 Mazer, Harry. *A Boy at War: A Novel of Pearl Harbor* (7–9). 2001, Simon & Schuster $15.00 (0-689-84161-2). Young Adam Pelko, new to Honolulu, is pressed into action on the morning of the attack on Pearl Harbor while trying to find his father, in this absorbing novel that also looks at relations with Japanese Americans. (Rev: BL 4/1/01; HB 5–6/01; HBG 10/01; SLJ 5/01; VOYA 6/01)

3363 Mazer, Harry. *The Last Mission* (7–10). 1981, Dell paper $5.50 (0-440-94797-9). An underage Jewish American boy joins the Air Corps and is taken prisoner by the Germans. (Rev: BL 5/1/88)

3364 Mazer, Norma Fox. *Good Night, Maman* (5–9). 1999, Harcourt $16.00 (0-15-201468-3). A first-person account of a young Jewish girl's experiences in Europe during the Holocaust and later in a refugee camp in Oswego, New York. (Rev: BCCB 12/99; BL 8/99*; HB 11–12/99; HBG 3/00; SLJ 12/99; VOYA 2/00)

3365 Melnikoff, Pamela. *Prisoner in Time: A Child of the Holocaust* (6–10). 2001, Jewish Publication Soc. paper $9.95 (0-8276-0735-0). Melnikoff combines history, fantasy, and Jewish legend in this story of 12-year-old Jan, in hiding from the Nazis in

1942 Czechoslovakia. (Rev: BL 10/1/01; SLJ 12/01)

3366 Michener, James A. *South Pacific* (5–9). Illus. 1992, Harcourt $16.95 (0-15-200618-4). A retelling for young people of Michener's stories on which the musical *South Pacific* was based. (Rev: BCCB 11/92; BL 9/1/92; SLJ 11/92)

3367 Moranville, Sharelle Byars. *Over the River* (5–7). 2002, Holt $16.95 (0-8050-7049-4). Willa Mae's father finally returns from World War II, and although the 11-year-old is happy to have him home, family tensions and secrets persist. (Rev: BCCB 1/03; BL 11/15/02; HBG 3/03; SLJ 11/02; VOYA 2/03)

3368 Morpurgo, Michael. *Waiting for Anya* (5–8). 1991, Viking $14.99 (0-670-83735-0). In this story set in occupied France, 12-year-old Jo helps a group of Jewish children hide from the Germans and then escape over the mountains to Spain. (Rev: BL 5/15/91; SLJ 4/91*)

3369 Myers, Anna. *Captain's Command* (4–8). Illus. 1999, Walker $15.95 (0-8027-8706-1). In Oklahoma during 1943, 12-year-old Gail and her family cope with problems caused by World War II, including the news that their father has been declared missing in action in France. (Rev: BL 12/15/99; HBG 3/00; SLJ 10/99)

3370 Myers, Walter Dean. *The Journal of Scott Pendleton Collins: A World War II Soldier* (5–9). Illus. Series: My Name Is America. 1999, Scholastic paper $10.95 (0-439-05013-8). Through a series of letters, readers get to know 17-year-old Collins, an American soldier who participates in the D-Day invasion of Europe. (Rev: BL 6/1–15/99; HBG 10/99; SLJ 7/99)

3371 Napoli, Donna Jo. *Stones in Water* (5–8). 1997, Dutton $16.99 (0-525-45842-5). The exciting story of two Italian boys, one of whom is Jewish, who have been transported to work camps by the Nazis during World War II. (Rev: BL 10/1/97; BR 3–4/98; HBG 3/98; SLJ 11/97*; VOYA 2/98)

3372 Nolan, Han. *If I Should Die Before I Wake* (7–10). 1994, Harcourt $18.00 (0-15-238040-X). Teenager Hilary, who hangs out with neo-Nazis, is in a hospital after an accident. Next to her is a Holocaust survivor, Chana, and before Hilary regains consciousness, she slips into Chana's memory and travels back in time to Auschwitz. (Rev: BL 4/1/94; SLJ 4/94; VOYA 6/94)

3373 Orgel, Doris. *The Devil in Vienna* (7–10). 1978, Penguin paper $5.99 (0-14-032500-X). Two friends, one Jewish and the other the daughter of a Nazi, growing up in German-occupied Austria.

3374 Orlev, Uri. *The Island on Bird Street* (7–9). 1984, Houghton $16.00 (0-395-33887-5); paper $6.95 (0-395-61623-9). A young Jewish boy strug-

gles to survive inside the Warsaw ghetto during World War II. (Rev: BL 11/1/88)

3375 Orlev, Uri. *The Man from the Other Side* (6–10). Trans. by Hillel Halkin. 1991, Houghton $16.00 (0-395-53808-4). The story of a teenager in Nazi-occupied Warsaw who helps desperate Jews despite his dislike of them. (Rev: BL 6/15/91*; SLJ 9/91*)

3376 Orlev, Uri. *Run, Boy, Run* (7–12). 2003, Houghton $15.00 (0-618-16465-0). A Polish boy survives the Holocaust by pretending to be a Catholic in this harrowing book full of historical detail. (Rev: BCCB 12/03; BL 10/15/03*; HB 11–12/03; SLJ 11/03)

3377 Osborne, Mary Pope. *My Secret War: The World War II Diary of Madeline Beck* (5–9). Illus. Series: Dear America. 2000, Scholastic paper $10.95 (0-590-68715-8). Using a diary format, this novel set on Long Island during World War II tells of an 8th-grade girl who forms a club to help in the war effort. (Rev: BL 10/1/00; HBG 3/01; SLJ 10/00; VOYA 12/00)

3378 Pausewang, Gudrun. *The Final Journey* (8–12). Trans. by Patricia Crampton. 1996, Puffin paper $5.99 (0-14-130104-X). The story of an 11-year-old Jewish girl and her horrifying train ride in a crowded freight car to a Nazi death camp. (Rev: BL 10/1/96; BR 3–4/97; VOYA 4/97)

3379 Pressler, Mirjam. *Malka* (6–10). Trans. by Brian Murdoch. 2003, Putnam $18.99 (0-399-23984-7). Escaping from the Nazis in Poland, a mother is forced to leave one daughter behind in this story based on truth that alternates between the difficult experiences of the anguished mother and the abandoned child. (Rev: BL 4/1/03; HB 5–6/03*; HBG 10/03; SLJ 5/03; VOYA 10/03)

3380 Propp, Vera W. *When the Soldiers Were Gone* (4–9). 1999, Putnam $14.99 (0-399-23325-3). The heartrending story of a young Jewish boy who, after World War II, must return to his own people and leave behind the loving farm family in Holland who had protected him and saved his life. (Rev: BCCB 2/99; BL 1/1–15/99; HB 7–8/99; HBG 10/99; SLJ 2/99)

3381 Ray, Karen. *To Cross a Line* (7–10). 1994, Orchard LB $16.99 (0-531-08681-X). The story of a 17-year-old Jewish boy who is pursued by the Gestapo and encounters barriers in his desperate attempts to escape Nazi Germany. (Rev: BL 2/15/94; SLJ 6/94; VOYA 6/94)

3382 Reuter, Bjarne. *The Boys from St. Petri* (7–10). Trans. by Anthea Bell. 1994, Dutton $15.99 (0-525-45121-8). Danish teenager Lars and his friends fight the Nazi occupation of their hometown during World War II and plan to blow up a train. (Rev: BL 2/1/94; SLJ 2/94; VOYA 4/94)

3383 Richter, Hans Peter. *Friedrich* (7–9). Trans. by Edite Kroll. 1987, Penguin $4.99 (0-14-032205-1). The story of a Jewish boy and his family caught in the horror of the rise of the Nazi party and the Holocaust. (Rev: BL 4/1/90)

3384 Rinaldi, Ann. *Keep Smiling Through* (5–8). 1996, Harcourt $13.00 (0-15-200768-7); paper $6.00 (0-15-201072-6). Life on the home front in New Jersey as seen through the eyes of Kate, a lonely 10-year-old. (Rev: BL 7/96; SLJ 6/96; VOYA 8/96)

3385 Ross, Stewart. *The Star Houses: A Story from the Holocaust* (4–8). Illus. Series: Survivors. 2002, Barron's $12.95 (0-7641-5528-8); paper $4.95 (0-7641-2204-5). Bandi, a 14-year-old Jewish boy, describes his family's determination to survive the Nazis in this novel based on reality. (Rev: HBG 3/03; SLJ 4/03)

3386 Rylant, Cynthia. *I Had Seen Castles* (6–12). 1993, Harcourt $10.95 (0-15-238003-5). A strong message about the physical and emotional costs of war — in this story, the toll of World War II on John, a Canadian adolescent. (Rev: BL 9/1/93; VOYA 2/94)

3387 Salisbury, Graham. *Under the Blood-Red Sun* (5–9). 1994, Delacorte $15.95 (0-385-32099-X). Tomi, born in Hawaii of Japanese parents, struggles during World War II, facing suspicion and hatred from classmates. His father is sent to a U.S. prison camp. (Rev: BL 10/15/94*; SLJ 10/94; VOYA 10/94)

3388 Serraillier, Ian. *The Silver Sword* (6–8). 1959, Phillips $32.95 (0-87599-104-1). A World War II story of Polish children who are separated from their parents and finally reunited.

3389 Spinelli, Jerry. *Milkweed* (6–10). 2003, Knopf $15.95 (0-375-81374-8). A boy who is uncertain of his ethnic background and adopts the name of Misha struggles to survive in the Warsaw ghetto and is befriended by a generous family. (Rev: BCCB 11/03; BL 10/15/03*; HB 11–12/03; SLJ 11/03)

3390 Tamar, Erika. *Good-bye, Glamour Girl* (7–10). 1984, HarperCollins LB $12.89 (0-397-32088-4). Liesl and her family flee from Hitler's Europe and Liesl must now become Americanized. (Rev: BL 1/1/85)

3391 Taylor, Marilyn. *Faraway Home* (5–8). 2000, O'Brien paper $7.95 (0-86278-643-6). Taken from his Austrian homeland by the Kindertransport, 13-year-old Karl is sent to County Down in Ireland where he endures the hardship of country life and the hostility of the locals. (Rev: BL 3/1/01)

3392 Thesman, Jean. *Molly Donnelly* (6–9). 1993, Houghton $16.00 (0-395-64348-1); Avon paper $4.50 (0-380-72252-6). The saga of a young girl growing up in Seattle during World War II and coping not only with the changes wrought by war but

also with typical adolescent concerns. (Rev: BL 4/1/93; SLJ 5/93; VOYA 8/93)

3393 Tunnell, Michael O. *Brothers in Valor: A Story of Resistance* (6–10). 2001, Holiday $16.95 (0-8234-1541-4). Tunnell interweaves history and fiction in this account of three young Germans, members of the Mormon Church, who protest Hitler's actions and put their own lives at risk. (Rev: BL 5/1/01; HBG 3/02; SLJ 6/01; VOYA 8/01)

3394 Twomey, Cathleen. *Beachmont Letters* (8–12). 2003, Boyds Mills $16.95 (1-59078-050-7). During World War II, 17-year-old Eleanor reaches out to a soldier through the letters that she writes him although she holds back those that deal with her own pain and suffering. (Rev: BL 3/1/03; HBG 10/03; SLJ 3/03)

3395 Van Dijk, Lutz. *Damned Strong Love: The True Story of Willi G. and Stefan K.* (8–12). Trans. by Elizabeth D. Crawford. 1995, Holt $15.95 (0-8050-3770-5). Nazi persecution of homosexuals, based on the life of Stefan K., a Polish teenager. (Rev: BL 5/15/95; SLJ 8/95)

3396 Vander Els, Betty. *The Bombers' Moon* (5–7). 1992, Farrar paper $4.50 (0-374-30877-7). Missionary children Ruth and Simeon are evacuated to escape the Japanese invasion of China; they will not see their parents for four years. A sequel is *Leaving Point* (1987). (Rev: BCCB 9/85; BL 11/1/85; HB 9–10/85)

3397 Van Steenwyk, Elizabeth. *A Traitor Among Us* (6–9). 1998, Eerdmans $15.00 (0-8028-5150-9). Set in Nazi-occupied Holland in 1944, this thriller describes the resistance activities of 13-year-old Pieter including his hiding of a wounded American soldier. (Rev: BL 8/98; HBG 9/98; SLJ 8/98)

3398 Voigt, Cynthia. *David and Jonathan* (8–12). 1992, Scholastic paper $14.95 (0-590-45165-0). A Holocaust survivor darkens the life of his American cousin with gruesome stories of the prison camps. (Rev: BL 3/1/92; SLJ 3/92)

3399 Vos, Ida. *Anna Is Still Here* (5–7). Trans. by Terese Edelstein and Inez Smidt. 1993, Houghton $15.00 (0-395-65368-1). The story of a survivor of the Holocaust and her adjustment to freedom after years of solitude and terror. (Rev: BL 4/15/93*; HB 7–8/93; SLJ 5/93)

3400 Vos, Ida. *Dancing on the Bridge at Avignon* (5–8). Trans. by Terese Edelstein and Inez Smidt. 1995, Houghton $14.95 (0-395-72039-7). Rosa, a Jewish girl in the Netherlands during World War II, lives in constant fear that the Nazis will deport her and her family in this novel translated from Dutch. (Rev: BCCB 2/96; BL 10/15/95; SLJ 10/95; VOYA 2/96)

3401 Vos, Ida. *Hide and Seek* (4–8). Trans. by Terese Edelstein and Inez Smidt. 1991, Houghton $16.00 (0-395-56470-0). A first-person narrative of a Jewish girl in Holland during the Nazi occupation. (Rev: BCCB 3/91; BL 3/15/91*; HB 5–6/91; SLJ 5/91)

3402 Vos, Ida. *The Key Is Lost* (5–9). Trans. by Terese Eddelstein. 2000, HarperCollins $15.95 (0-688-16283-5). Based on the author's experiences as a child, this novel tells the story of a young Jewish girl and her sister who survive World War II in hiding in Holland. (Rev: BCCB 9/00; BL 4/1/00; HBG 10/00; SLJ 6/00)

3403 Walters, Eric. *Caged Eagles* (6–9). 2000, Orca $15.95 (1-55143-182-3). The story of how Tadashi Fukushima deals with being interned in Vancouver during World War II is a companion to *War of the Eagles* (1999). (Rev: BL 12/1/00; HBG 3/01; SLJ 11/00; VOYA 2/01)

3404 Watts, Irene. *Good-bye Marianne: A Story of Growing Up in Nazi Germany* (5–8). 1998, Tundra paper $7.95 (0-88776-445-2). In this autobiographical novel, 11-year-old Marianne Kohn is Jewish and experiencing Nazi persecution in 1938 Berlin when her parents decide to sent her to Britain as part of the Kindertransport rescue operation. (Rev: BCCB 7–8/98; BL 8/98; SLJ 8/98)

3405 Watts, Irene N. *Finding Sophie: A Search for Belonging in Postwar Britain* (5–8). 2002, Tundra paper $6.95 (0-88776-613-7). In this sequel to *Remember Me* (2000), World War II has ended and 13-year-old Sophie waits anxiously to hear news of her Jewish family in Germany, at the same time hoping she will not have to leave her happy life in London. (Rev: BL 1/1–15/03; SLJ 3/03; VOYA 8/03)

3406 Watts, Irene N. *Remember Me: A Search for Refuge in Wartime Britain* (5–8). 2000, Tundra paper $7.95 (0-88776-519-X). A heart-tugging story of an 11-year-old Jewish girl who, at the beginning of World War II, is transported from her home in Berlin to live in a Welsh mining town where she knows no one and speaks no English. (Rev: BL 12/1/00; SLJ 1/01; VOYA 2/01)

3407 Westall, Robert. *The Machine Gunners* (6–9). 1997, Morrow paper $5.95 (0-688-15498-0). A reissue of the prize-winning English novel about a boy during World War II who finds a downed German plane with a machine gun intact. (Rev: VOYA 8/90)

3408 Westall, Robert. *Time of Fire* (6–9). 1997, Scholastic $15.95 (0-590-47746-3). World War II becomes real for young Sonny in Manchester, England, when his mother is killed in a bombing raid and his father dies in the armed forces. (Rev: BL 8/97; BR 11–12/97; HBG 3/98; SLJ 7/97; VOYA 6/98)

3409 Williams, Laura E. *Behind the Bedroom Wall* (5–8). Illus. 1996, Milkweed $15.95 (1-57131-607-8); paper $6.95 (1-57131-606-X). Korinna, a young Nazi, discovers that her parents are hiding a Jewish

couple in wartime Germany. (Rev: BL 8/96; BR 1–2/97; SLJ 9/96)

3410 Winter, Kathryn. *Katarina* (7–12). 1998, Scholastic paper $4.99 (0-439-09904-8). A gripping autobiographical novel about a Jewish orphan in hiding in Slovakia during World War II. (Rev: BCCB 3/98; BL 3/1/98; BR 11–12/98; SLJ 7/98)

3411 Wiseman, Eva. *My Canary Yellow Star* (8–12). Illus. 2002, Tundra paper $7.95 (0-88776-533-5). Marta Weisz's privileged life as the daughter of a wealthy Jewish surgeon comes to an abrupt end when Hitler invades Hungary, but her life is spared through the efforts of Raoul Wallenberg. (Rev: BL 1/1–15/02; SLJ 6/02)

3412 Wulffson, Don. *Soldier X* (8–12). 2001, Viking $15.99 (0-670-88863-X). After a battle in World War II, a 16-year-old German boy switches uniforms with a dead Russian in a desperate effort to survive. (Rev: BCCB 3/01; BL 5/1/01; HB 7–8/01; HBG 10/01; SLJ 3/01; VOYA 4/01)

3413 Yep, Laurence. *Hiroshima* (4–7). 1995, Scholastic paper $9.95 (0-590-20832-2). A powerful work of fiction that explores the bombing of Hiroshima in 1945 and its aftermath. (Rev: BCCB 6/95; BL 3/15/95*; HB 9–10/95; SLJ 5/95)

3414 Yolen, Jane. *The Devil's Arithmetic* (7–12). 1988, Viking $15.99 (0-670-81027-4); Puffin paper $5.99 (0-14-034535-3). This time-warp story transports a young Jewish girl back to Poland in the 1940s, conveying the horrors of the Holocaust. (Rev: BL 9/1/88; BR 1–2/89; SLJ 11/88)

3415 Zeinert, Karen. *To Touch the Stars: A Story of World War II* (5–8). Series: Jamestown's American Portraits. 2000, Jamestown paper $5.95 (0-8092-0630-7). Eighteen-year-old Liz Erickson, who loves to fly airplanes, longs for independence while she investigates possible sabotage in the Women's Airforce Service pilots program. (Rev: SLJ 9/00)

3416 Zindel, Paul. *The Gadget* (6–12). 2001, HarperCollins $15.99 (0-06-027812-9). Stephen has left London to live with his father who is on a secret scientific assignment in New Mexico — the Manhattan Project. (Rev: BL 1/1–15/01; HBG 10/01; SLJ 2/01; VOYA 8/01)

KOREAN, VIETNAM, AND OTHER WARS

3417 Brown, Don. *Our Time on the River* (7–10). 2003, Houghton $15.00 (0-618-31116-5). Two brothers learn more about each other on a canoe trip that precedes the older brother's departure to fight in Vietnam. (Rev: BL 4/1/03; HBG 10/03; SLJ 4/03)

3418 Choi, Sook N. *Echoes of the White Giraffe* (6–10). 1993, Houghton $16.00 (0-395-64721-3). Sookan, 15, struggles for independence within the restrictions of life in a refugee camp during the

187

Korean War in this sequel to *Year of Impossible Goodbyes* (1991). (Rev: BL 4/1/93; SLJ 5/93; VOYA 8/93)

3419 Crist-Evans, Craig. *Amaryllis* (7–12). 2003, Candlewick $15.99 (0-7636-1863-2). Frank enlists to fight in Vietnam mainly to escape his alcoholic father's rages, and his younger brother is heartbroken when Frank becomes a heroin addict and then is listed as missing. (Rev: BL 11/1/03; SLJ 11/03)

3420 Easton, Kelly. *The Life History of a Star* (7–10). 2001, Simon & Schuster $16.00 (0-689-83134-X). In the early 1970s, 14-year-old Kristin uses her journal as an outlet for her worries about her maturing body, her friends, her parents, and — most of all — her older brother, who has been wounded in Vietnam. (Rev: BCCB 3/01; BL 4/15/01; HBG 10/01; SLJ 7/01; VOYA 4/01)

3421 Hobbs, Valerie. *Sonny's War* (6–10). 2002, Farrar $16.00 (0-374-37136-9). Cory's world is in turmoil when her father dies and her older brother goes off to fight in Vietnam. (Rev: BCCB 11/02; BL 11/1/02; HB 11–12/02; HBG 3/03; SLJ 11/02*; VOYA 12/02)

3422 Myers, Walter Dean. *Patrol: An American Soldier in Vietnam* (4–8). 2002, HarperCollins LB $17.89 (0-06-028364-5). A penetrating picture book for older readers told in narrative verse from the perspective of a teenage soldier in Vietnam. (Rev: BL 3/15/02; HB 7–8/02; HBG 10/02; SLJ 5/02)

3423 Rostkowski, Margaret I. *The Best of Friends* (7–12). 1989, HarperCollins $12.95 (0-06-025104-2). Three Utah teenagers have a growing interest in the Vietnam War and how it affects each of them. (Rev: BL 9/1/89; SLJ 9/89; VOYA 12/89)

3424 White, Ellen Emerson. *The Journal of Patrick Seamus Flaherty: United States Marine Corps* (6–9). Illus. Series: Dear America. 2002, Scholastic $10.95 (0-439-14890-1). White uses Patrick's journal to portray the life of a soldier in Vietnam, describing the horrors of war and the questions surrounding American involvement in the conflict. (Rev: BL 7/02; HBG 10/02; SLJ 10/02)

3425 White, Ellen Emerson. *The Road Home* (8–12). 1995, Scholastic paper $15.95 (0-590-46737-9). This story re-creates a Vietnam War medical base in claustrophobic and horrific detail, and features army nurse Rebecca Phillips, from the Echo Company book series. (Rev: BL 1/15/95; SLJ 4/95; VOYA 4/95)

3426 White, Ellen Emerson. *Where Have All the Flowers Gone? The Diary of Molly MacKenzie Flaherty, Boston, Massachusetts, 1968* (7–10). Series: Dear America. 2002, Scholastic paper $10.95 (0-439-14889-8). Fifteen-year-old Molly's brother is fighting in Vietnam, and she wrestles with pride, anxiety, and the antiwar sentiment around her. (Rev: BL 8/02; HBG 10/02; SLJ 7/02)

Horror Stories and the Supernatural

3427 Ahlberg, Allan. *My Brother's Ghost* (5–9). 2001, Viking $9.99 (0-670-89290-4). A small-format book that tells the story of a young boy who appears at his own funeral and shepherds his still-living siblings through a series of tough spots. (Rev: BCCB 4/01; SLJ 7/01)

3428 Aiken, Joan. *A Fit of Shivers: Tales for Late at Night* (7–10). 1995, Bantam paper $4.50 (0-440-41120-3). Vengeful ghosts, eerie dreams, and haunted houses abound in these 10 tales. (Rev: BL 9/1/92)

3429 *Alfred Hitchcock's Supernatural Tales of Terror and Suspense* (7–10). Illus. 1973, Random paper $4.99 (0-394-85622-8). Horrifying tales by such masters as Patricia Highsmith and Raymond Chandler.

3430 Alphin, Elaine Marie. *Ghost Soldier* (5–7). 2001, Holt $16.95 (0-8050-6158-4). Alex, who has special powers, meets a Civil War ghost and helps him discover what happened to his family. (Rev: BCCB 7–8/01; BL 8/01; HBG 10/02; SLJ 8/01; VOYA 8/01)

3431 Anderson, M. T. *Thirsty* (7–12). 1997, Candlewick paper $6.99 (0-7636-2014-9). In addition to all kinds of family problems, Chris discovers that he is turning into a vampire. (Rev: BR 9–10/97; SLJ 3/97)

3432 Asimov, Isaac, et al., eds. *Young Witches and Warlocks* (6–9). 1987, HarperCollins $12.95 (0-06-020183-5). A collection of 10 stories, most of them scary, about witches. (Rev: BL 7/87; SLJ 1/88)

3433 Atwater-Rhodes, Amelia. *Demon in My View* (6–10). 2000, Delacorte $9.95 (0-385-32720-X). Seventeen-year-old Jessica, who writes fiction about vampires and witches, finds her imagined world coming to life. (Rev: BR 11–12/00; HBG 9/00; SLJ 5/00)

3434 Atwater-Rhodes, Amelia. *In the Forests of the Night* (7–12). 1999, Delacorte $8.95 (0-385-32674-2). In this story written by a 13-year-old author, Risika, a 300-year-old vampire, takes revenge against Aubrey, another vampire and her age-old enemy, when Aubrey threatens to harm Risika's only friend, Tora, a Bengal tiger in a zoo. (Rev: BL 6/1–15/99; HBG 9/99; SLJ 7/99; VOYA 8/99)

3435 Avi. *Devil's Race* (7–9). 1984, Avon paper $3.50 (0-380-70406-4). John Proud is in constant battle with a demon who has the same name and was hanged in 1854.

3436 Avi. *Something Upstairs: A Tale of Ghosts* (5–7). 1988, Orchard LB $16.99 (0-531-08382-9); Avon paper $4.99 (0-380-70853-1). Kenny moves into a house in Rhode Island that is haunted by the ghost of a slave who was murdered in 1800. (Rev: BCCB 9/88; BL 11/1/88; SLJ 10/88)

3437 Barrett, Tracy. *Cold in Summer* (4–7). 2003, Holt $16.95 (0-8050-7052-4). An enjoyable story about a lonely girl who slowly comes to realize that her new friend is a ghost. (Rev: BL 4/1/03; HB 5–6/03; HBG 10/03; SLJ 7/03; VOYA 6/03)

3438 Bawden, Nina. *Devil by the Sea* (6–8). 1976, HarperCollins $12.95 (0-397-31683-6). Is the strange old man Hilary sees at the beach really the devil?

3439 Bedard, Michael. *Painted Devil* (7–10). 1994, Atheneum $15.95 (0-689-31827-8). A girl helping to renovate an old puppet theater discovers that the vicious-looking devil puppet has evil powers. (Rev: BL 3/1/94; SLJ 4/94; VOYA 6/94)

3440 Bial, Raymond. *The Fresh Grave: And Other Ghostly Stories* (5–7). 1997, Midwest Traditions paper $13.95 (1-883953-22-7). A series of ten short, humorous ghost stories featuring two teenage heroes and their escapades in a small midwestern town. (Rev: SLJ 12/97)

3441 Bial, Raymond. *The Ghost of Honeymoon Creek* (5–8). Illus. 1999, Midwest Traditions $18.95 (1-883953-28-6); paper $13.95 (1-883953-27-8). While investigating a strange light in a neighboring farm, 15-year-old Hank encounters a ghost. (Rev: BL 9/1/00; HBG 3/01; SLJ 1/01)

3442 Brown, Roberta Simpson. *The Queen of the Cold-Blooded Tales* (6–9). 1993, August House $19.95 (0-87483-332-9). A collection of 23 contemporary horror stories. (Rev: BL 9/1/93; VOYA 4/94)

3443 Buffie, Margaret. *The Dark Garden* (6–10). 1997, Kids Can $16.95 (1-55074-288-4). Thea, who suffers from amnesia after an accident, begins hearing voices, one of which belongs to a young woman who died tragically years before. (Rev: BL 10/15/97; BR 1–2/98; HBG 3/98; SLJ 10/97)

3444 Bunting, Eve. *The Presence: A Ghost Story* (6–10). 2003, Clarion $15.00 (0-618-26919-3). Catherine, 17, who is still grieving over the death of a friend, finds solace in a handsome young man but at the same time senses that something isn't quite right. (Rev: BL 10/15/03; SLJ 10/03)

3445 Burgess, Melvin. *The Ghost Behind the Wall* (5–7). 2003, Holt $16.95 (0-8050-7149-0). David finds more than he expects when he ventures into his building's ventilation system. (Rev: BCCB 2/03; BL 4/15/03; HBG 10/03; SLJ 7/03; VOYA 4/03)

3446 Butler, Charles. *The Darkling* (6–9). 1998, Simon & Schuster $16.00 (0-689-81796-7). Soon after Petra visits Mr. Century, a mysterious hermit, she finds that she is being taken over by the spirit of the old man's dead love, Euridice. (Rev: BL 4/1/98; BR 1–2/99; HB 7–8/98; HBG 9/98; SLJ 5/98)

3447 Cabot, Meg. *Haunted* (7–10). Series: The Mediator. 2003, HarperCollins $15.99 (0-06-029471-X). In this fifth installment in The Mediator series (earlier volumes were published under the pseudonym Jenny Carroll), Susannah falls for teen "mediator" Paul Slater, who has just joined her school. (Rev: BL 3/1/03; HBG 10/03; SLJ 1/03; VOYA 4/03)

3448 Cameron, Eleanor. *The Court of the Stone Children* (5–7). 1990, Puffin paper $5.99 (0-14-034289-3). Nina's move with her family to San Francisco is a disaster until she encounters a young ghost in a small museum.

3449 Cargill, Linda. *The Surfer* (6–9). 1995, Scholastic paper $3.99 (0-590-22215-5). After Nick meets Marina, a strange but beautiful surfer, he realizes that she is an immortal who has plotted against male members of his family for generations. (Rev: SLJ 1/96)

3450 Carroll, Jenny. *Darkest Hour* (7–10). Series: The Mediator. 2001, Simon & Schuster paper $4.99 (0-671-78847-7). Suze's ability to communicate with ghosts comes in handy as a skeleton turns up in her backyard and she falls for a phantom called Jesse. (Rev: SLJ 4/02)

3451 Carus, Marianne, ed. *That's Ghosts for You: 13 Scary Stories* (4–7). 2000, Front Street $15.95 (0-8126-2675-3). A fine collection of 13 chilling stories set in locations around the world, each with a supernatural twist. (Rev: BL 12/1/00; HBG 3/01; SLJ 12/00)

3452 Carusone, Albert R. *The Boy with Dinosaur Hands* (4–7). Illus. 1998, Clarion $14.00 (0-395-77515-9). An eerie collection of nine original horror stories — most with surprise endings. (Rev: BL 8/98; HBG 10/98; SLJ 7/98)

3453 Cassedy, Sylvia. *Behind the Attic Wall* (6–8). 1983, HarperCollins LB $15.89 (0-690-04337-6). Maggie Turner, a difficult girl, is contacted by ghosts in the large house where two great-aunts live.

3454 Clarke, Judith. *Starry Nights* (5–9). 2003, Front Street $15.95 (1-886910-82-0). When Jess's family moves to a new house, a ghost seems to be involved in the family's emotional upheavals. (Rev: BL 6/1–15/03; HB 9–10/03)

3455 Cohen, Daniel. *Dangerous Ghosts* (5–7). 1996, Putnam $14.99 (0-399-22913-2). Seventeen ghost stories, many with historical backgrounds. (Rev: BL 11/15/96; SLJ 4/97)

3456 Cohen, Daniel. *Ghostly Tales of Love and Revenge* (5–8). 1995, Pocket paper $3.50 (0-671-79523-6). An international collection of ghost stories that deal with vengeance and unhappy loves. (Rev: SLJ 7/92)

3457 Cohen, Daniel. *Phantom Animals* (6–9). 1993, Pocket Books paper $2.99 (0-671-75930-2). Short

189

selections featuring ghostly dogs, scary kangaroos, menacing birds, and phantom cats. (Rev: BL 8/91; SLJ 7/91)

3458 Colfer, Eoin. *The Wish List* (6–9). 2003, Hyperion $16.95 (0-7868-1863-8). Meg's mix of good and bad deeds leaves her poised between Heaven and Hell, and she is sent on a mission that will tip the balance one way or the other. (Rev: BL 10/1/03; SLJ 12/03*)

3459 Conrad, Pam. *Stonewords: A Ghost Story* (5–9). 1990, HarperCollins LB $16.89 (0-06-021316-7); paper $5.99 (0-06-440354-8). Zoe moves to her grandparents' home and finds a playmate, from another century, already living there. (Rev: BCCB 5/90; BL 3/1/90; HB 7–8/90; SLJ 5/90*; VOYA 6/90)

3460 Cooney, Caroline B. *Night School* (7–10). 1995, Scholastic paper $3.50 (0-590-47878-8). Four California teens enroll in a mysterious night school course and encounter an evil instructor and their own worst character defects. (Rev: BL 5/1/95)

3461 Coville, Bruce. *The Ghost Wore Gray* (5–8). 1988, Bantam paper $4.99 (0-553-15610-1). Nina and friend Chris investigate a haunted inn in the Catskill Mountains. (Rev: BL 9/15/88; SLJ 9/88)

3462 Coville, Bruce. *Oddly Enough* (6–9). 1994, Harcourt $15.95 (0-15-200093-3). Nine short horror stories involving blood drinking, elves, unicorns, ghosts, werewolves, and executioners. (Rev: BL 10/1/94; SLJ 12/94; VOYA 2/95)

3463 Cray, Jordan. *Gemini 7* (6–10). 1997, Simon & Schuster paper $4.50 (0-689-81432-1). In this horror story, Jonah Lanier begins to realize that his new friend, Nicole, might be responsible for the mysterious disasters that are befalling his family and other friends. (Rev: SLJ 1/98)

3464 Creedon, Catherine. *Blue Wolf* (4–8). 2003, HarperCollins $15.99 (0-06-050868-X). Fantasy lurks around each corner of this story of Jamie, a 14-year-old for whom running is a retreat from life and who sometimes feels that wolves are right at his heels. (Rev: BCCB 1/04; BL 11/15/03; SLJ 10/03)

3465 Crowley, Bridget. *Step into the Dark* (5–7). 2003, Hodder & Stoughton paper $8.95 (0-340-84416-7). This ghost story is set in a theater and conveys the attraction of the stage. (Rev: BL 12/1/03)

3466 Cusick, Richie Tankersley. *The House Next Door* (6–12). 2002, Simon & Schuster paper $4.99 (0-7434-1838-7). Emma dares to spend a night in a haunted house and becomes caught up in a struggle to free a spirit from the past in this tale of supernatural suspense. (Rev: BL 1/1–15/02; SLJ 2/02; VOYA 6/02)

3467 Dean, Jan. *Finders* (6–9). 1995, Macmillan paper $15.00 (0-689-50612-0). Helen Draper, 16,

inherits her grandfather's gift of "finding" people and things, but when kelpie Nicholas Morgan asks her to find a special stone, her life is in jeopardy. (Rev: BL 5/1/95)

3468 Duncan, Lois. *Gallows Hill* (6–9). 1997, Bantam Doubleday Dell $15.95 (0-385-32331-X); paper $4.99 (0-440-22725-9). Sarah is alarmed when her harmless "future telling" turns out to be true and she begins dreaming of the Salem witch trials. (Rev: BL 4/15/97; BR 5–6/97; HBG 3/98; SLJ 5/97; VOYA 4/97)

3469 Duncan, Lois. *Locked in Time* (7–10). 1985, Dell paper $4.99 (0-440-94942-4). Nore's father marries into a family that somehow never seems to age. (Rev: BL 7/85; BR 9–10/85; SLJ 11/85)

3470 Duncan, Lois, ed. *Night Terrors: Stories of Shadow and Substance* (6–12). 1996, Simon & Schuster paper $16.00 (0-689-80346-X). An anthology of 11 horror/supernatural stories by such popular writers as Joan Aiken, Chris Lynch, and Norma Fox Mazer. (Rev: BL 5/15/96; BR 1–2/97; SLJ 6/96; VOYA 8/96)

3471 Duncan, Lois. *Stranger with My Face* (7–10). 1984, Dell paper $5.50 (0-440-98356-8). A girl encounters her evil twin who wishes to take her place.

3472 Duncan, Lois. *Summer of Fear* (7–10). 1976, Dell paper $5.50 (0-440-98324-X). An orphaned cousin who comes to live with Rachel's family is really a witch.

3473 Durant, Alan, ed. *Vampire and Werewolf Stories* (5–10). Illus. Series: Kingfisher Story Library. 1998, Kingfisher paper $6.95 (0-7534-5152-2). Eighteen stories, many written originally for an adult audience, make up this classic Gothic horror anthology about vampires and werewolves. (Rev: BL 1/1–15/99)

3474 Ellis, Sarah. *Back of Beyond Stories* (6–10). 1997, Simon & Schuster $15.00 (0-689-81484-4). Each of the 12 stories in this collection begins with real-world problems but soon slips into the realm of the supernatural. (Rev: BL 1/1–15/98; HBG 3/98; SLJ 11/97*; VOYA 12/97)

3475 Etchemendy, Nancy. *Cat in Glass: And Other Tales of the Unnatural* (8–12). 2002, Cricket $15.95 (0-8126-2674-5). Eight spooky and suspenseful stories will captivate brave readers. (Rev: BL 11/15/02; HBG 3/03; SLJ 12/02; VOYA 4/03)

3476 Furlong, Monica. *Wise Child* (6–8). 1987, Demco $11.04 (0-606-04425-6). Set in ancient Scotland, this is a story of a young girl torn between the good and evil aspects of witchcraft. (Rev: BL 12/1/87; SLJ 9/87)

3477 Gabhart, Ann. *Wish Come True* (7–10). 1988, Avon paper $2.50 (0-380-75653-6). Lyssie receives as a gift a mirror that grants her wishes. (Rev: VOYA 6/89)

3478 Garretson, Jerri. *The Secret of Whispering Springs* (7–12). 2002, Ravenstone paper $6.99 (0-9659712-4-4). A ghost and a mysterious stranger alert Cassie to potential danger, and a potential fortune, in this suspenseful adventure. (Rev: BL 8/02; SLJ 8/02)

3479 Gifaldi, David. *Yours Till Forever* (7–10). 1989, HarperCollins LB $13.89 (0-397-32356-5). In this easily read novel, a high school senior sees disturbing similarities between his friends and his dead parents. (Rev: BL 10/1/89; SLJ 11/89; VOYA 2/90)

3480 Gorog, Judith. *Please Do Not Touch* (6–12). 1995, Scholastic paper $3.50 (0-590-46683-6). The reader enters a different fantasy for each of the 11 horror stories. (Rev: BL 9/1/93; VOYA 12/93)

3481 Gorog, Judith. *When Nobody's Home* (6–12). 1996, Scholastic paper $15.95 (0-590-46862-6). A collection of 15 terrifying (supposedly true) tales on the theme of baby-sitting. (Rev: BL 5/1/96; BR 9–10/96; SLJ 4/96; VOYA 12/96)

3482 Greenberg, Martin H., et al., eds. *Great Writers and Kids Write Spooky Stories* (5–8). Illus. 1995, Random $17.00 (0-679-87662-6). An anthology of 13 original horror stories by prominent authors who were commissioned to write the stories in collaboration with their children or grandchildren. (Rev: SLJ 2/96)

3483 Hahn, Mary D. *Look for Me by Moonlight* (7–10). 1995, Clarion $16.00 (0-395-69843-X). A 16-year-old girl seeking friendship meets a boy whose attention has dangerous strings attached. (Rev: BL 3/15/95; SLJ 5/95)

3484 Hahn, Mary D. *Wait Till Helen Comes: A Ghost Story* (5–7). 1986, Houghton $15.00 (0-89919-453-2); Avon paper $5.99 (0-380-70442-0). Things go from bad to worse for Molly and Michael and their stepsister Heather when Heather becomes involved in a frightening relationship with the ghost of a dead child. (Rev: BCCB 10/86; BL 9/1/86; SLJ 10/86)

3485 Hamilton, Virginia. *Sweet Whispers, Brother Rush* (7–10). 1982, Putnam $21.99 (0-399-20894-1). A 14-year-old girl who cares for her older retarded brother meets a charming ghost who reveals secrets of her past.

3486 Hawes, Louise. *Rosey in the Present Tense* (8–12). 1999, Walker $15.95 (0-8027-8685-5). After the death of his girlfriend, Rosey, 17-year-old Franklin can't stop living in the past until the ghost of Rosey and his family and friends help him accept his loss and begin to think of the present. (Rev: BL 4/1/99; BR 9–10/99; HBG 9/99; SLJ 5/99; VOYA 10/99)

3487 Hill, Mary, ed. *Creepy Classics: Hair-Raising Horror from the Masters of the Macabre* (6–10). 1994, Random paper $4.99 (0-679-86692-2). Gothic horror stories, poems, and novel excerpts by masters of the genre, including selections from Poe and an excerpt from Shelley's *Frankenstein*. (Rev: BL 10/15/94; SLJ 11/94)

3488 Hodges, Margaret, ed. *Hauntings: Ghosts and Ghouls from Around the World* (5–8). 1991, Little, Brown $16.95 (0-316-36796-6). A diverse collection of 16 familiar and lesser-known tales about the supernatural. (Rev: BL 11/15/91; HB 11–12/91; SLJ 11/91) [398.2]

3489 Hoffman, Nina Kiriki. *A Stir of Bones* (6–8). 2003, Viking $15.99 (0-670-03551-3). Human and ghostly friends help Susan to deal with her abusive father in this prequel to *A Red Heart of Memories* (2000) and *Past the Size of Dreaming* (2002). (Rev: BL 10/1/03; SLJ 12/03)

3490 Hughes, Dean. *Nutty's Ghost* (5–8). 1993, Atheneum $13.95 (0-689-31743-3). Nutty lands the lead in a terrible movie, and the ghost of a Shakespearean actor uses Nutty to get revenge on the movie's director. (Rev: BL 2/15/93; SLJ 5/93)

3491 Huntington, Geoffrey. *Sorcerers of the Nightwing* (7–10). Series: Ravenscliff. 2002, Regan $17.95 (0-06-001425-3). Magic and mystery abound in this horror story featuring a young teenager with superpowers who is a sorcerer in the Order of the Nightwing. (Rev: BL 8/02; SLJ 10/02; VOYA 2/03)

3492 Jackson, Shirley. *The Lottery* (8–12). 1949, Farrar paper $14.00 (0-374-51681-2). Macabre stories by this master that include the classic about a village and its horrifying annual tradition. (Rev: BL 9/1/97)

3493 Jacques, Brian. *Seven Strange and Ghostly Tales* (4–7). 1991, Avon paper $3.99 (0-380-71906-1). Seven genuinely scary stories with touches of humor. (Rev: BCCB 12/91; BL 1/1/91*; HB 5–6/92; SLJ 12/91)

3494 Jensen, Dorothea. *The Riddle of Penncroft Farm* (5–7). 1989, Harcourt $16.00 (0-15-200574-9). Lars finds a ghost from the American Revolution when his family moves to rural Pennsylvania near Valley Forge. (Rev: BCCB 11/89; BL 10/1/89; SLJ 10/89)

3495 Johnson, Charles. *Pieces of Eight* (5–7). 1989, Discovery $9.95 (0-944770-00-2). David and Mitchell rouse a sea captain's ghost and get to meet Blackbeard the pirate. (Rev: BL 3/15/89)

3496 Karr, Kathleen. *Playing with Fire* (5–7). 2001, Farrar $16.00 (0-374-23453-1). This story about the occult takes place in New York during the 1920s and involves Greer and her spiritualist mother. (Rev: BCCB 5/01; BL 4/1/01; HBG 10/01; SLJ 5/01; VOYA 6/01)

191

3497 Kelleher, Victor. *Del-Del* (7–12). Illus. 1992, Walker $17.95 (0-8027-8154-3). A family believes its son is possessed by an evil alien. (Rev: BL 3/1/92; SLJ 6/92)

3498 Klause, Annette Curtis. *The Silver Kiss* (8–12). 1992, Bantam paper $5.50 (0-440-21346-0). A teenage girl, beset with personal problems, meets a silver-haired boy who is a vampire in this suspenseful, sometimes gory, novel. (Rev: BL 10/15/90; SLJ 9/90)

3499 Klaveness, Jan O'Donnell. *The Griffin Legacy* (7–9). 1985, Dell paper $3.25 (0-440-43165-4). Two ghosts are laid to rest when the secret of the Griffin legacy is revealed.

3500 Klein, Robin. *Tearaways* (6–10). 1991, Viking $12.95 (0-670-83212-X). This short-story collection combines shivery horror with laughter. (Rev: BL 6/15/91; SLJ 6/91)

3501 Leroe, E. W. *Monster Vision* (4–7). Series: Friendly Corners. 1996, Hyperion paper $3.95 (0-7868-1095-5). Ghosts of people killed when a meteorite struck at Friendly Corners return to haunt the residents. Others in this series are *Nasty the Snowman, Pizza Zombies,* and *Hairy Horror* (all 1966). (Rev: SLJ 5/97)

3502 Littke, Lael. *Haunted Sister* (7–10). 1998, Holt $16.95 (0-8050-5729-3). After a near-death experience, Janine becomes involved with the ghost of her dead twin sister, who in time inhabits Janine's spirit and body. (Rev: BCCB 10/98; BL 10/1/98; HBG 9/99; SLJ 10/98; VOYA 2/99)

3503 McAllister, Margaret. *Ghost at the Window* (6–9). 2002, Dutton $15.99 (0-525-46852-8). Ewan's Scottish home not only has a habit of shifting back in time, it also contains a trapped young ghost who seeks release. (Rev: BCCB 6/02; BL 5/1/02; HBG 3/03; SLJ 8/02; VOYA 8/02)

3504 MacDonald, Caroline. *Hostilities: Nine Bizarre Stories* (7–10). 1994, Scholastic paper $13.95 (0-590-46063-3). A collection of nine tales with strange, unsettling themes and Australian locales. (Rev: BL 1/15/94; SLJ 3/94; VOYA 10/94)

3505 McDonald, Collin. *The Chilling Hour: Tales of the Real and Unreal* (6–8). 1992, Dutton $14.99 (0-525-65101-2). Eight scary stories with unexpected twists. (Rev: BL 12/1/92; SLJ 8/92)

3506 McDonald, Joyce. *Shades of Simon Gray* (6–8). 2001, Delacorte $15.95 (0-385-32659-9). After a crash that some see as a suicide attempt, Simon lies in a coma attended by a ghost, his bed watched over by contemporaries who are worried he will awake and reveal their cheating on tests. (Rev: BCCB 12/01; BL 1/1–15/02; HB 1–2/02; HBG 3/02; SLJ 11/01; VOYA 12/01)

3507 McKean, Thomas. *Into the Candlelit Room and Other Strange Tales* (6–9). 1999, Putnam $17.99 (0-399-23359-8). A collection of offbeat stories, some in the form of letters and diary entries, about five young people and their encounters with the "dark side." (Rev: BCCB 10/99; BL 7/99; HBG 4/00; SLJ 9/99; VOYA 10/99)

3508 McKissack, Patricia. *The Dark-Thirty: Southern Tales of the Supernatural* (5–8). Illus. 1992, Knopf $17.99 (0-679-91863-9). Ten original stories, rooted in African American history and the oral-storytelling tradition, deal with such subjects as slavery, belief in "the sight," and the Montgomery bus boycott. (Rev: BCCB 12/92; BL 12/15/92; HB 3–4/93; SLJ 12/92*)

3509 Mahy, Margaret, and Susan Cooper. *Don't Read This! And Other Tales of the Unnatural* (7–10). 1998, Front Street $15.95 (1-886910-22-7). Great stories of ghosts and the supernatural are included in this international collection that represents some of the top writers of scary fiction at work today. (Rev: BL 4/1/99; BR 9–10/99; HBG 9/99; SLJ 7/99; VOYA 6/99)

3510 Manns, Nick. *Operating Codes* (5–8). 2001, Little, Brown $15.95 (0-316-60465-8). A suspenseful tale of supernatural presences and espionage in which two young children and their father become embroiled. (Rev: BCCB 2/02; BL 12/15/01; HBG 3/02; SLJ 1/02; VOYA 2/02)

3511 Mayne, William, ed. *Supernatural Stories: A Hair-Raising Collection* (7–9). Illus. 1996, Kingfisher paper $6.95 (0-7534-5026-7). A collection of literate, supernatural stories by such authors as Kipling, Capote, Mark Twain, and Saki. (Rev: SLJ 4/97)

3512 Medearis, Angela Shelf. *Haunts: Five Hair-Raising Tales* (4–7). 1996, Holiday $15.95 (0-8234-1280-6). Five stories that contain elements of horror and the supernatural. (Rev: BL 2/1/97; SLJ 4/97)

3513 Montes, Marisa. *A Circle of Time* (6–8). 2002, Harcourt $17.00 (0-15-202626-6). In a coma after an accident, 14-year-old Allison Blair travels back in time to 1906 California to help two young people in trouble there. (Rev: BL 5/1/02; HBG 10/02; SLJ 8/02; VOYA 6/02)

3514 Montes, Marisa. *Something Wicked's in Those Woods* (4–7). 2000, Harcourt $17.00 (0-15-202391-7). Javier is lonely after leaving Puerto Rico and relocating in northern California until he meets the ghost of a boy killed decades ago in an unsolved crime. (Rev: BCCB 10/00; BL 10/15/00; HBG 10/01; SLJ 12/00)

3515 Morgan, Jill. *Blood Brothers* (5–8). 1996, HarperCollins paper $4.50 (0-06-440562-1). A fast-paced adventure in which identical twins are turned into vampires. (Rev: BL 12/1/96; SLJ 1/97)

3516 Morpurgo, Michael, ed. *Ghostly Haunts* (6–9). 1997, Trafalgar paper $16.95 (1-85793-833-6). Some of Britain's best writers for young people, including Dick King-Smith and Joan Aiken, have contributed to this collection of supernatural stories. (Rev: BL 3/15/97)

3517 Moser, Barry, ed. *Great Ghost Stories* (7–12). Illus. 1998, Morrow $24.99 (0-688-14587-6). A collection of 13 ghost stories, some by established authors, others less-well known, but all effective particularly because of the eerie illustrations by the editor. (Rev: BL 11/15/98; HBG 3/99; SLJ 10/98; VOYA 2/99)

3518 Mowry, Jess. *Ghost Train* (6–9). 1996, Holt $14.95 (0-8050-4440-X). Remi, a 13-year-old immigrant from Haiti who is interested in the supernatural, sees a ghost train and witnesses an unsolved murder that occurred 50 years ago. (Rev: BR 9–10/97; SLJ 12/96*; VOYA 2/97)

3519 Murphy, Jim. *Night Terrors* (6–9). 1993, Scholastic paper $13.95 (0-590-45341-6). Five gruesome horror stories dealing with vampires, mummies, cannibals, and other creatures. (Rev: BL 10/1/93; VOYA 12/93)

3520 Naylor, Phyllis Reynolds. *Jade Green: A Ghost Story* (5–8). 2000, Simon & Schuster $16.00 (0-689-82005-4). Set in South Carolina about 100 years ago, this ghost story involves Judith Sparrow, age 15, and the mystery surrounding the gruesome death of a girl named Jade Green. (Rev: BL 12/15/99; HBG 10/00; SLJ 2/00; VOYA 6/00)

3521 Nixon, Joan Lowery. *The Haunting* (6–10). 1998, Doubleday $15.95 (0-385-32247-X). Anne is determined to rid Graymoss, an old mansion, of ghosts so that her mother can convert it into a home for unwanted children. (Rev: BL 7/98; HB 11–12/98; HBG 3/99; SLJ 8/98; VOYA 12/98)

3522 Nixon, Joan Lowery. *Whispers from the Dead* (7–12). 1991, Bantam paper $4.99 (0-440-20809-2). After being saved from drowning, Sarah is able to communicate with dead spirits. (Rev: BL 9/15/89; BR 11–12/89; SLJ 9/89; VOYA 12/89)

3523 Norton, Andre, and Phyllis Miller. *House of Shadows* (7–9). 1984, Tor paper $2.95 (0-8125-4743-8). While staying with a great-aunt, three children learn about the family curse.

3524 Olson, Arielle North, and Howard Schwartz, eds. *Ask the Bones: Scary Stories from Around the World* (5–9). 1999, Viking $15.99 (0-670-87581-3). A collection of 22 scary stories about subjects ranging from ghosts to witches and voodoo spells, accompanied by spooky illustrations. (Rev: BCCB 4/99; BL 5/1/99; BR 9–10/99; HB 5–6/99; HBG 10/99; SLJ 4/99)

3525 Patneaude, David. *Dark Starry Morning: Stories of This World and Beyond* (5–8). 1995, Albert Whitman LB $13.95 (0-8075-1474-8). Six eerie tales about encounters with the unknown and the supernatural. (Rev: BL 9/1/95; SLJ 9/95)

3526 Pearce, Philippa. *Who's Afraid? And Other Strange Stories* (5–7). 1987, Greenwillow $11.95 (0-688-06895-2). Eleven stories that explore the disturbing dark side of life. (Rev: BCCB 4/87; BL 4/1/87; BR 5–6/87; HB 5–6/87; SLJ 5/87)

3527 Peck, Richard. *The Ghost Belonged to Me* (5–8). 1997, Viking paper $5.99 (0-14-038671-8). Richard unwillingly receives the aid of his nemesis, Blossom Culp, in trying to solve the mystery behind the ghost of a young girl. Two sequels are *Ghosts I Have Been* (1977); *The Dreadful Future of Blossom Culp* (1983).

3528 Pepper, Dennis, ed. *The New Young Oxford Book of Ghost Stories* (6–12). Illus. 1999, Oxford $22.95 (0-19-278154-5). Many of the 23 stories in this scary collection are new to print. (Rev: BL 10/15/99; HBG 4/00)

3529 Pike, Christopher. *Bury Me Deep* (6–10). 1991, Pocket Books paper $4.50 (0-671-69057-4). A scuba-diving vacation in Hawaii turns into an adventure involving murder, ghosts, and underwater thrills. (Rev: BL 9/1/91)

3530 Pines, T., ed. *Thirteen: 13 Tales of Horror by 13 Masters of Horror* (8–12). 1991, Scholastic paper $4.99 (0-590-45256-8). Popular horror writers' stories of revenge, lust, and betrayal. (Rev: BL 3/1/92)

3531 Pipe, Jim. *The Werewolf* (4–7). Illus. Series: In the Footsteps Of. 1996, Millbrook LB $24.90 (0-7613-0450-9). A horror story in which Bernard, a werewolf, commits terrible acts under the influence of a full moon. (Rev: SLJ 7/96)

3532 Poe, Edgar Allan. *The Pit and the Pendulum and Other Stories* (6–12). Illus. Series: Whole Story. 1999, Viking $25.99 (0-670-88706-4). This handsome collection of Poe's mystery stories is enhanced with striking illustrations, historical notes, sidebars, and material about the author's life and times. (Rev: BL 12/1/99; HBG 4/00)

3533 Preussler, Otfried. *The Satanic Mill* (7–10). 1987, Peter Smith $26.50 (0-8446-6196-1). A young apprentice outwits a strange magician in this fantasy first published in 1972. (Rev: BL 6/1–15/98)

3534 Price, Susan, ed. *Horror Stories* (6–12). 1995, Kingfisher paper $7.95 (1-85697-592-4). Two dozen Halloween read-alouds from such writers as Joan Aiken, Stephen King, Edgar Allan Poe, and John Steinbeck. (Rev: BL 10/15/95)

3535 Rees, Douglas. *Vampire High* (6–9). 2003, Delacorte $15.95 (0-385-73117-5). A flunking Cody is sent to Vlad Dracul Magnet School where he finds his classmates very strange, but he soon adapts to their vampire nature. (Rev: BCCB 11/03; BL 8/03; HB 9–10/03; SLJ 11/03)

3536 Roach, Marilynne K. *Encounters with the Invisible World* (5–9). 1977, Amereon $18.95 (0-

193

89190-874-9). Spooky stories about witches, demons, spells, and ghosts in New England.

3537 Roos, Stephen. *My Favorite Ghost* (5–8). 1988, Macmillan LB $13.95 (0-689-31301-2). Thirteen-year-old Derek's money-making scheme involves the legend of a local ghost. A Plymouth Island story. (Rev: BL 4/15/88; BR 9–10/88; HB 5–6/88; SLJ 4/88)

3538 Ruby, Laura. *Lily's Ghosts* (5–8). 2003, HarperCollins $16.99 (0-06-051829-4). Thirteen-year-old Lily and her mother move into a Victorian house in Cape May, New Jersey, only to find it harbors both secrets and ghosts. (Rev: BCCB 9/03; SLJ 12/03)

3539 Russell, Barbara T. *Blue Lightning* (4–8). 1997, Viking $14.99 (0-670-87023-4). Calvin dies but returns to life, only to find that the ghost of another boy, Rory, who "died" at the same time, has followed him and won't leave him alone. (Rev: BCCB 2/97; BL 2/15/97; HB 5–6/97; SLJ 2/97)

3540 San Souci, Robert D. *Dare to Be Scared: Thirteen Stories to Chill and Thrill* (4–8). 2003, Cricket $15.95 (0-8126-2688-5). A baker's dozen of spooky stories suitable for this age group that feature diverse characters. (Rev: BL 10/1/03; HBG 10/03; SLJ 9/03)

3541 Schnur, Steven. *The Shadow Children* (4–7). 1994, Morrow $16.99 (0-688-13281-2). The experiences of the Holocaust are relived by a boy when he visits an area in France where Jewish refugees lived before being sent to the death camps. (Rev: BCCB 12/94; BL 11/15/94; SLJ 10/94)

3542 Schwartz, Alvin. *Scary Stories 3: More Tales to Chill Your Bones* (4–7). 1991, HarperCollins LB $16.89 (0-06-021795-2); paper $5.99 (0-06-440418-8). A modernized version of spooky tales handed down through the years. (Rev: BL 8/91; HB 11–12/91; SLJ 11/91)

3543 Seabrooke, Brenda. *The Haunting at Stratton Falls* (5–8). 2000, Dutton $15.99 (0-525-46389-5). Eleven-year-old Abby, who has recently moved to Stratton Falls, New York, while her father is fighting in Germany during World War II, sees wet footprints in the hall and wonders if the stories about the house being haunted are true. (Rev: BCCB 9/00; BL 7/00; HBG 3/01; SLJ 8/00)

3544 Seabrooke, Brenda. *The Vampire in My Bathtub* (4–7). 1999, Holiday $15.95 (0-8234-1505-8). After 13-year-old Jeff moves to a new home with his mother, he finds a friendly vampire hidden inside an old trunk. (Rev: BL 1/1–15/00; HBG 3/00; SLJ 12/99)

3545 Shan, Darren. *Cirque Du Freak: A Living Nightmare* (5–8). Series: Cirque Du Freak. 2001, Little, Brown $15.95 (0-316-60340-6). A supernatural story about a young boy who visits the Cirque

Du Freak and is turned into a vampire. (Rev: BL 4/15/01; HBG 10/01; SLJ 5/01; VOYA 4/01)

3546 Shan, Darren. *Cirque Du Freak: The Vampire's Assistant* (5–8). Series: Cirque Du Freak. 2001, Little, Brown $15.95 (0-316-60610-3). The creepy, suspenseful second installment about a boy who is "half vampire" and his efforts to adjust to the world of a traveling freak show. (Rev: BL 10/15/01; HBG 3/02; SLJ 8/01; VOYA 10/01)

3547 Shan, Darren. *Cirque Du Freak: Vampire Mountain* (5–8). Series: Cirque Du Freak. 2002, Little, Brown $15.95 (0-316-60806-8). Darren Shan, teenage half-vampire, and his mentor travel to Vampire Mountain. The fifth and sixth installments in the series are *Trials of Death* and *The Vampire Prince* (both 2003). (Rev: BL 8/02; HBG 3/03; SLJ 9/02; VOYA 12/02)

3548 Shan, Darren. *Tunnels of Blood* (5–8). Series: Cirque Du Freak. 2002, Little, Brown $15.95 (0-316-60763-0). Darren Shan, teenage half-vampire, sets out to investigate a spate of recent killings for which he believes his vampire master might be responsible. (Rev: BL 8/02; HBG 10/02; SLJ 5/02; VOYA 6/02)

3549 Shreve, Susan. *Ghost Cats* (4–7). 1999, Scholastic paper $14.95 (0-590-37131-2). A boy, who is trying to adjust to a new family home and the loss of his five cats, is helped when the cats return as ghosts. (Rev: BCCB 12/99; BL 9/1/99; HBG 3/00; SLJ 11/99; VOYA 6/00)

3550 Shusterman, Neal. *Full Tilt* (6–10). 2003, Simon & Schuster $16.95 (0-689-80374-5). A suspenseful drama in which 16-year-old Blake must tackle frightening rides at a mysterious carnival and face his own worst fears in order to save his daredevil older brother Quinn. (Rev: BCCB 9/03; BL 5/15/03; HB 7–8/03; HBG 10/03; SLJ 6/03; VOYA 10/03)

3551 Shusterman, Neal. *Mindtwisters: Stories to Shred Your Head* (6–9). 1997, Tor paper $3.99 (0-812-55199-0). These eight short stories deal with such bizarre and supernatural occurrences as a boy who can make people disappear and a store that sells "what might have been." (Rev: SLJ 11/97; VOYA 10/97)

3552 Shusterman, Neal. *Scorpion Shards* (8–12). 1996, Tor paper $5.99 (0-8125-2465-9). A horror story in which six misfits and outsiders must face and exorcise the monsters that dwell within them. (Rev: BL 2/1/96; SLJ 3/96; VOYA 4/96)

3553 Slade, Arthur G. *The Haunting of Drang Island* (5–7). 1999, Orca paper $6.95 (1-55143-111-4). In this sequel to *Draugr* (1998), 14-year-old Michael and his writer father are on Drang Island, off the coast of British Columbia, when they become involved with an undead sorcerer and creatures from Icelandic mythology. (Rev: BL 4/1/99; SLJ 8/99)

3554 Sleator, William. *The Beasties* (6–9). 1997, Dutton $15.99 (0-525-45598-1). In this modern horror tale, Doug and his younger sister discover a race of weird underground people who remove the arms and legs of their victims. (Rev: BL 10/1/97; BR 5–6/98; HB 9–10/97; HBG 3/98; SLJ 12/97; VOYA 4/98)

3555 Sleator, William. *Dangerous Wishes* (5–9). 1995, Dutton $14.99 (0-525-45283-4). In this sequel to *The Spirit House* (1991), Dominic Kamen travels to Thailand, where he seeks to return a jade carving to escape a vengeful spirit. (Rev: BL 8/95; SLJ 11/95; VOYA 4/96)

3556 Snyder, Zilpha Keatley. *The Ghosts of Rathburn Park* (5–8). 2002, Delacorte LB $17.99 (0-385-90064-3). Eleven-year-old Matthew explores Rathburn Park and comes across a mysterious girl dressed in clothes from a bygone era in this suspenseful, well-crafted tale. (Rev: BCCB 2/03; HBG 3/03; SLJ 9/02)

3557 Snyder, Zilpha Keatley. *The Headless Cupid* (4–7). 1971, Macmillan $17.00 (0-689-20687-9); Dell paper $4.99 (0-440-43507-2). Amanda, a student of the occult, upsets her new family. A sequel is *The Famous Stanley Kidnapping Case* (1985).

3558 Snyder, Zilpha Keatley. *The Trespassers* (5–7). 1995, Delacorte $15.95 (0-385-31055-2). Grub, a 7-year-old, forms a friendship with a ghost after he and his older sister, Neely, explore a deserted mansion. (Rev: BCCB 10/95; BL 6/1–15/95; SLJ 8/95)

3559 Soto, Gary. *The Afterlife* (7–10). 2003, Harcourt $16.00 (0-15-204774-3). After he is stabbed to death, 17-year-old Chuy lingers long enough to watch the reactions of family and friends while getting to know some other ghosts. (Rev: BL 8/03*; HB 11–12/03; SLJ 11/03)

3560 Springer, Nancy. *Sky Rider* (5–8). 2000, HarperCollins paper $4.95 (0-380-79565-5). In this contemporary supernatural mystery, Dusty's beloved horse Tazz is cured by a visitor who turns out to be the angry ghost of a teenage boy recently killed on her father's property. (Rev: BCCB 10/99; HBG 3/00; SLJ 8/99)

3561 Starkey, Dinah, ed. *Ghosts and Bogles* (5–10). Illus. 1987, David & Charles $17.95 (0-434-96440-9). A collection of 16 British ghost stories, each nicely presented with illustrations. (Rev: SLJ 9/87)

3562 Stearns, Michael, ed. *A Nightmare's Dozen: Stories from the Dark* (6–9). Illus. 1996, Harcourt $17.00 (0-15-201247-8). A collection of original, bizarre, nightmarish stories by such YA authors as Bruce Coville and Jane Yolen. (Rev: BL 1/1–15/97; SLJ 12/96)

3563 Stine, R. L. *The Haunting Hour: Chill in the Dead of Night* (5–8). Illus. 2001, HarperCollins $14.89 (0-06-623605-3). Ten chilling short stories, each with an introduction by the author. (Rev: BCCB 11/01; BL 1/1–15/02; HBG 3/02)

3564 Stine, R. L. *Nightmare Hour* (4–7). Illus. 1999, HarperCollins $15.99 (0-06-028688-1). Ten scary stories by a master of mystery, with characters that include aliens, sorcerers, werewolves, witches, and ghosts. (Rev: BL 10/15/99; HBG 3/00; SLJ 12/99)

3565 Strasser, Todd. *Hey Dad, Get a Life!* (5–8). 1996, Holiday $15.95 (0-8234-1278-4). Twelve-year-old Kelly and her younger sister use the ghost of their dead father to accomplish their everyday chores and finally let their mother know about their secret helper. (Rev: BCCB 3/97; BL 2/15/97; SLJ 3/97)

3566 Strickland, Brad. *The Whistle, the Grave, and the Ghost* (5–8). 2003, Dial $16.99 (0-8037-2622-8). A silver whistle frees a woman vampire, drawing Lewis Barnevalt and his friends into suspenseful adventures battling an ancient threat. (Rev: BL 8/03; SLJ 8/03)

3567 Strickland, Brad, and John Bellairs. *The Specter from the Magician's Museum* (5–8). 1998, Dial $15.99 (0-8037-2202-8). When Rose Rita accidentally cuts her finger on an enchanted scroll, she and friend Lewis begin a series of supernatural adventures. This is part of a series of supernatural adventures by John Bellairs that has been continued by Brad Strickland. (Rev: BL 10/1/98; BR 5–6/99; HBG 3/99; SLJ 11/98; VOYA 6/99)

3568 Tiernan, Cate. *Sweep: Book of Shadows* (8–12). Series: Sweep. 2001, Penguin paper $4.99 (0-14-131046-4). Morgan isn't interested in witchcraft until she meets Cal, a high school senior who is a Wiccan and who draws Morgan into his world. (Rev: BL 2/15/01)

3569 Tolan, Stephanie S. *The Face in the Mirror* (6–9). 1998, Morrow $15.00 (0-688-15394-1). When Jared goes to live with his father, a theater director, he isn't prepared for the malicious pranks of his stepbrother or the encounters with George Marsden, a sympathetic ghost. (Rev: BCCB 9/98; BL 9/1/98; HBG 3/99; SLJ 11/98; VOYA 4/99)

3570 Tolan, Stephanie S. *Who's There?* (5–8). 1994, Morrow $15.00 (0-688-04611-8); paper $4.95 (0-688-15289-9). Fourteen-year-old Drew is convinced that there is a ghost in her crusty grandfather's house, where she and her brother Evan, who has been mute since their parents' deaths, are currently living. (Rev: BCCB 12/94; BL 9/1/94; SLJ 10/94)

3571 Tunnell, Michael O. *School Spirits* (5–8). 1997, Holiday $15.95 (0-8234-1310-1). Three students at creepy Craven Hill School, including the son of the new principal, discover a ghost and solve a decades-old murder mystery involving an 8-year-old boy.

(Rev: BCCB 3/98; BL 2/15/98; BR 11–12/98; HBG 3/98; SLJ 3/98; VOYA 8/98)

3572 Ury, Allen B. *Scary Stories for When You're Home Alone* (5–8). 1996, Lowell House paper $5.95 (1-56565-382-3). A collection of 10 truly scary stories that deal with paranormal and supernatural phenomena, including extraterrestrials, time warps, fetish dolls, and Ouija boards. (Rev: SLJ 7/96)

3573 Van Belkom, Edo, ed. *Be Afraid! Tales of Horror* (8–12). 2000, Tundra $6.95 (0-88776-496-7). Fifteen horror stories for and about teens feature sinister twists, hauntings, and violence. (Rev: BL 2/1/01; SLJ 3/01; VOYA 2/01)

3574 Vance, Susanna. *Sights* (7–9). 2001, Delacorte $15.95 (0-385-32761-7). Baby Girl has the ability to see the future, but this does not help her to cope with her abusive father or to escape the usual traumas of adolescence. (Rev: BCCB 4/01; BL 2/15/01; BR 9–10/01; HB 3–4/01; HBG 10/01; SLJ 7/01; VOYA 8/01)

3575 Vande Velde, Vivian. *Being Dead* (7–10). 2001, Harcourt $17.00 (0-15-216320-4). A collection of seven chilling stories about death and the supernatural. (Rev: BCCB 9/01; BL 9/1/01; HB 11–12/01; HBG 3/02; SLJ 9/01; VOYA 12/01)

3576 Vande Velde, Vivian. *A Coming Evil* (5–9). 1998, Houghton $17.00 (0-395-90012-3). Through encounters with the ghost of a 14th-century knight at her aunt's home in Nazi-occupied France, Lizette gains the courage to help her aunt hide several Jewish and Gypsy children. (Rev: BCCB 9/98; BL 10/1/98; HBG 3/99; SLJ 11/98; VOYA 10/98)

3577 Vande Velde, Vivian. *Companions of the Night* (7–10). 1995, Harcourt $17.00 (0-15-200221-9). A 16-year-old finds herself caught in a life-and-death chase after she helps an injured young man who may be a vampire. (Rev: BL 4/1/95; SLJ 5/95)

3578 Vande Velde, Vivian. *Never Trust a Dead Man* (7–12). 1999, Harcourt $17.00 (0-15-201899-9). A witch helps Selwyn escape the death penalty for a murder he didn't commit and, with the help of the ghost of the dead man, he solves the mystery. (Rev: BL 4/1/99; BR 9–10/99; HB 5–6/99; HBG 9/99; SLJ 5/99; VOYA 8/99)

3579 Vande Velde, Vivian. *There's a Dead Person Following My Sister Around* (6–9). 1999, Harcourt $16.00 (0-15-202100-0). When the ghosts of an African American mother and child appear to his 5-year-old sister in contemporary Rochester, New York, 12-year-old Ted starts an investigation that eventually uncovers his great-great-grandmother's role in the Underground Railroad. (Rev: BCCB 10/99; BL 9/1/99; HBG 3/00; SLJ 9/99; VOYA 12/99)

3580 Wallace, Rich. *Restless: A Ghost's Story* (8–12). 2003, Viking $15.99 (0-670-03605-6). Sports and the supernatural take center stage in 17-year-old Herbie's life after he becomes aware of a ghostly being on a run through a graveyard. (Rev: BL 9/15/03; SLJ 11/03; VOYA 10/03)

3581 Welch, R. C. *Scary Stories for Stormy Nights* (5–7). Illus. 1995, Lowell House paper $5.95 (1-56565-262-2). Ten contemporary horror stories that involve such characters as a werewolf and some pirates. (Rev: BL 5/1/95)

3582 Westall, Robert. *Ghost Abbey* (5–9). 1990, Scholastic paper $3.25 (0-590-41693-6). Maggi realizes that the abbey her father is restoring seems to have a life of its own. (Rev: BCCB 2/89; BL 2/1/89; SLJ 3/89; VOYA 6/89)

3583 Westall, Robert. *Shades of Darkness: More of the Ghostly Best Stories of Robert Westall* (7–12). 1994, Macmillan paper $11.95 (0-330-35318-7). Eleven eerie tales, not the guts-and-gore variety of supernatural fiction but haunting and insightful stories. (Rev: BL 4/15/94; SLJ 5/94; VOYA 8/94)

3584 Westwood, Chris. *Calling All Monsters* (7–12). 1993, HarperCollins LB $14.89 (0-06-022462-2). Joanne is a huge fan of a horror writer, so when she starts seeing nightmare creatures from his books, she recognizes them. (Rev: BL 6/1–15/93; SLJ 7/93; VOYA 12/93)

3585 Westwood, Chris. *He Came from the Shadows* (5–8). 1991, HarperCollins LB $14.89 (0-06-021659-X). In a cautionary tale about the dangers of wishing for too much, odd things start to happen after a stranger comes to town. (Rev: BL 4/1/91; SLJ 6/91)

3586 Whelan, Gerard. *Dream Invader* (5–7). 2002, O'Brien paper $7.95 (0-86278-516-2). Only Simon's grandmother can break the spell behind the bad dreams he's been having in this supernatural tale set in Ireland. (Rev: BL 9/1/02)

3587 Wiseman, David. *Jeremy Visick* (5–8). 1981, Houghton paper $7.95 (0-395-56153-1). Matthew helps the ghost of young Jeremy find rest.

3588 Wright, Betty R. *A Ghost in the House* (5–7). 1991, Scholastic paper $13.95 (0-590-43606-6). Bizarre happenings take place when Sarah's elderly aunt moves in. (Rev: BCCB 11/91; BL 1/1/91; SLJ 11/91)

3589 Wright, Betty Ren. *Crandalls' Castle* (4–7). 2003, Holiday $16.95 (0-8234-1726-3). This gripping suspense story combines supernatural elements with a look at teen girls' yearning to belong. (Rev: BL 4/1/03; HBG 10/03; SLJ 5/03)

3590 Yashinsky, Dan, ed. *Ghostwise: A Book of Midnight Stories* (7–12). 1997, August House $11.95 (0-87483-499-6). A collection of 35 short but chilling stories of the supernatural and ghosts. (Rev: BCCB 3/98; VOYA 2/98)

3591 Yolen, Jane. *Here There Be Ghosts* (5–9). Series: Here There Be. 1998, Harcourt $19.00 (0-

15-201566-3). A collection of not-very-scary short stories and a few poems about ghosts and lost souls. (Rev: BL 11/1/98; HBG 3/99; SLJ 11/98; VOYA 12/98)

3592 Yolen, Jane, and Martin H. Greenberg, eds. *Werewolves: A Collection of Original Stories* (6–9). 1988, HarperCollins $13.95 (0-06-026798-4). Fifteen mostly scary stories about all kinds of werewolves. (Rev: BL 7/88; BR 1–2/88; SLJ 9/88; VOYA 8/88)

3593 Young, Richard, and Judy Dockery Young. *Ozark Ghost Stories* (6–12). 1995, August House paper $12.95 (0-87483-410-4). Spooky Ozark stories are the focus of this horror anthology, including old favorites and less-well-known jokes and tales. (Rev: BL 6/1–15/95)

3594 Young, Richard, and Judy Dockery Young. *The Scary Story Reader* (6–9). 1993, August House $19.00 (0-87483-271-3). Forty-one scary urban legends are presented, including traditional tales of horror as well as less-well-known stories from Alaska and Hawaii. (Rev: BL 11/15/93; SLJ 5/94)

3595 Zindel, Paul. *The Doom Stone* (6–10). 1995, Hyperion paper $4.95 (0-7868-1157-9). A slimy, truly evil creature stalks the moors and inhabits the mind of the protagonist's aunt. (Rev: BL 12/15/95; SLJ 12/95; VOYA 4/96)

3596 Zindel, Paul. *Loch* (7–10). 1994, HarperCollins LB $15.89 (0-06-024543-3). Lovable, though human-eating, creatures trapped in a Vermont lake become prey for a ruthless man. (Rev: BL 11/15/94; SLJ 1/95; VOYA 4/95)

Humor

3597 Anderson, M. T. *Burger Wuss* (7–10). 1999, Candlewick paper $6.99 (0-7636-1567-6). In this funny novel, Anthony gets a job at a hamburger joint and battles his archrival and the fast-food franchise with the help of an activist co-worker. (Rev: BL 11/15/99)

3598 Ardagh, Philip. *Dreadful Acts* (4–7). Series: Eddie Dickens. 2003, Holt $14.95 (0-8050-7155-5). This zany sequel to *A House Called Awful End* (2002) throws more wild adventures at 12-year-old Eddie Dickens. (Rev: BL 4/15/03; HBG 10/03; SLJ 5/03)

3599 Ardagh, Philip. *A House Called Awful End* (4–7). 2002, Holt $14.95 (0-8050-6828-7). Lemony Snicket fans will enjoy this complex story of 11-year-old Eddie, who winds up in a series of bizarre adventures when he has to leave his sick parents and live with eccentric relatives. (Rev: BCCB 12/02; BL 11/15/02; HBG 3/03; SLJ 9/02)

3600 Avi. *Punch with Judy* (6–8). Illus. 1993, Bradbury LB $14.95 (0-02-707755-1). The orphan boy Punch encounters tragedy and comedy in his attempt to keep a medicine show alive with the help of the owner's daughter. (Rev: BL 3/15/93; SLJ 6/93; VOYA 8/93)

3601 Avi. *Romeo and Juliet: Together (and Alive) at Last!* (6–8). 1987, Watts LB $16.99 (0-531-08321-7); Avon paper $4.99 (0-380-70525-7). Ed Sitrow decides to help true love along by casting his friends as Romeo and Juliet in a school play. Sitrow is also the "genius" behind the soccer escapades in *S.O.R. Losers.* (Rev: BL 8/87; SLJ 10/87)

3602 Base, Graeme. *The Discovery of Dragons* (5–8). Illus. 1996, Abrams $16.95 (0-8109-3237-7). A humorous account of the three pioneers in dragon research. (Rev: BL 11/15/96; SLJ 11/96)

3603 Bechard, Margaret. *My Sister, My Science Report* (5–7). 1990, Puffin paper $4.99 (0-14-034408-X). In this humorous novel, Tess's sister becomes the object of a scientific study for a school project. (Rev: BL 5/15/90; HB 5/90 & 9–10/90; SLJ 5/90)

3604 Blume, Judy. *Starring Sally J. Freedman as Herself* (4–7). 1977, Macmillan $17.00 (0-02-711070-2); Dell paper $5.99 (0-440-48253-4). A story of a 5th-grader's adventures in New Jersey and Florida in the late 1940s.

3605 Brian, Kate. *The Princess and the Pauper* (6–8). 2003, Simon & Schuster $14.95 (0-689-86173-7). When the wealthy Crown Princess Carina of Vineland and poor scholarship student Julia, both 16, realize they look alike, they plan a substitution that inevitably goes awry. (Rev: BL 10/15/03; HBG 10/03; SLJ 8/03)

3606 Brooke, William J. *A Is for AARRGH!* (5–8). 1999, HarperCollins LB $14.89 (0-06-023394-X). A humorous story about a prehistoric boy, Mog, and his amazing discoveries about language and communication. (Rev: BCCB 11/99; BL 10/15/99; HB 9–10/99; HBG 3/00; SLJ 9/99)

3607 Browne, Anthony. *Willy's Pictures* (5–8). Illus. 2000, Candlewick $16.99 (0-7636-1323-1). In this imaginative picture book for older children, the author/artist changes famous paintings to tell new and wild stories. (Rev: BL 12/15/00; HBG 10/01; SLJ 12/00)

3608 Byars, Betsy. *Bingo Brown, Gypsy Lover* (6–8). 1990, Viking $12.95 (0-670-83322-3). In this installment of the Bingo Brown saga, our hero finds himself in love. (Rev: BL 5/1/90; SLJ 6/90)

3609 Byars, Betsy. *Bingo Brown's Guide to Romance* (5–8). 2000, Puffin paper $5.99 (0-14-036080-8). Romance, confusion, and comedy occur when Bingo Brown meets his true love in the produce section of the grocery store. (Rev: BL 4/1/92; SLJ 4/92)

3610 Byars, Betsy. *The Burning Questions of Bingo Brown* (6–8). 1990, Puffin paper $5.99 (0-14-032479-8). During Bingo's 6th-grade year, he falls in love three times for starters. (Rev: BCCB 4/88; BL 4/15/88; SLJ 5/88)

3611 Cabot, Meg. *The Princess Diaries* (7–10). Series: Princess Diaries. 2000, HarperCollins $15.99 (0-380-97848-2). Fourteen-year-old Mia's diary reveals a fairly interesting life even before she learns that she is actually a royal princess, heir to the throne of Genovia. (Rev: BCCB 12/00; BL 9/15/00; HBG 3/01; SLJ 10/00; VOYA 4/01)

3612 Cabot, Meg. *Princess in Love: The Princess Diaries*, Vol. 3 (6–9). Series: The Princess Diaries. 2002, HarperCollins $15.95 (0-06-029467-1). This action-packed installment follows Mia's life from Thanksgiving through her December departure for Genovia, with details of typical teen life and of her efforts to learn about her new country. (Rev: BCCB 5/02; BL 7/02; HBG 10/02; SLJ 10/02; VOYA 6/02)

3613 Cabot, Meg. *Princess in the Spotlight: The Princess Diaries, Volume II* (7–10). Series: Princess Diaries. 2001, HarperCollins $15.95 (0-06-029465-5). In this sequel to *The Princess Diaries* (2000), readers find out how Mia is coping with being a princess and with more typical teen concerns such as a pregnant mother and a romance. (Rev: BCCB 9/01; BL 9/1/01; HBG 3/02; SLJ 8/01; VOYA 10/01)

3614 Cabot, Meg. *Princess in Waiting* (5–7). Series: Princess Diaries. 2003, HarperCollins $15.99 (0-06-009607-1). Princess Mia gets in a royal mess when her duties interfere with her love life. (Rev: BL 5/15/03; HBG 10/03; SLJ 5/03; VOYA 6/03)

3615 Clark, Catherine. *Truth or Dairy* (7–12). 2000, HarperCollins paper $6.95 (0-380-81443-9). Told in diary form, this breezy narrative chronicles Courtney's senior year in her Colorado school. (Rev: BL 4/15/00; SLJ 7/00; VOYA 12/00)

3616 Clarke, J. *Al Capsella and the Watchdogs* (7–10). 1991, Holt $14.95 (0-8050-1598-1). Al Capsella, 15, and his Australian high school friends spend much of their time bemoaning the tactics their parents use to be involved in all phases of their lives. (Rev: BL 8/91; SLJ 8/91)

3617 Conford, Ellen. *The Alfred G. Graebner Memorial High School Handbook of Rules and Regulations* (6–9). 1976, Little, Brown $14.95 (0-316-15293-5). The trials and tribulations of student life in a typical high school. (Rev: BL 7/88)

3618 Conford, Ellen. *Dear Lovey Hart, I Am Desperate* (6–7). 1975, Little, Brown $14.95 (0-316-15306-0). Freshman reporter Carrie Wasserman gets into trouble with her advice column in the school newspaper. (Rev: BL 10/15/87)

3619 Conford, Ellen. *Seven Days to Be a Brand-New Me* (6–9). 1990, Scholastic paper $3.50 (0-590-43824-7). Maddy knows she will become a teenage vamp after following Dr. Dudley's program.

3620 Conford, Ellen. *Why Me?* (6–9). 1985, Little, Brown $14.95 (0-316-15326-5). G.G. Graffman has a crush on Hobie, who only has eyes for Darlene, who is ga-ga over Warren. (Rev: BL 10/15/85; BR 5–6/86; SLJ 11/85; VOYA 2/86)

3621 Corbet, Robert. *Fifteen Love* (7–10). 2003, Walker $16.95 (0-8027-8851-3). A humorous story about a 15-year-old boy and girl whose romantic feelings seem to be doomed. (Rev: BL 4/15/03; HB 7–8/03; HBG 10/03; SLJ 5/03; VOYA 8/03)

3622 Creech, Sharon. *Absolutely Normal Chaos* (5–8). 1995, HarperCollins LB $16.89 (0-06-026992-8). Mary Lou, 13, keeps a journal during summer vacation, chronicling the roller-coaster process of adolescence — evolving friendships, her first kiss, and the gradual appreciation of people different from her. (Rev: BCCB 11/95; BL 10/1/95; SLJ 11/95)

3623 Dahl, Roald. *The Umbrella Man and Other Stories* (8–12). 1998, Viking $16.99 (0-670-87854-5). A collection of 13 stories originally written for adults that display Dahl's wit and penchant for irony. (Rev: BL 5/15/98; BR 5–6/99; HBG 9/98; SLJ 8/98; VOYA 8/98)

3624 Danko, Dan, and Tom Mason. *Sidekicks* (6–8). 2003, Little, Brown $10.95 (0-316-16845-9); paper $4.99 (0-316-16844-0). Guy, 13 years old and the fastest runner in the world, is a member of the Side-kick Club, secret apprentice do-gooders who come into their own when a band of villains attacks. (Rev: SLJ 11/03)

3625 Danziger, Paula. *This Place Has No Atmosphere* (6–9). 1989, Bantam paper $3.99 (0-440-40205-0). In this humorous story set in 2057, Aurora and her family move to the moon. (Rev: BL 10/15/86; BR 3–4/87; SLJ 11/86; VOYA 2/87)

3626 Dent, Grace. *LBD: It's a Girl Thing* (7–9). 2003, Putnam $15.99 (0-399-24187-6). Ronnie narrates the activities of Les Bambinos Dangereuses, three teen girls who are determined to circumvent parental restrictions and have a longed-for music festival — with boy bands. (Rev: BCCB 11/03; BL 11/15/03; SLJ 12/03; VOYA 10/03)

3627 Feiffer, Jules. *The Man in the Ceiling* (5–7). Illus. 1993, HarperCollins $15.95 (0-06-205035-4); paper $7.99 (0-06-205907-6). Jimmy turns to cartooning in an effort to gain some recognition in a family that is intent on ignoring him. (Rev: BCCB 12/93; BL 11/15/93; SLJ 2/94*)

3628 Ferris, Jean. *Love Among the Walnuts* (7–10). 1998, Harcourt $16.00 (0-15-201590-6). A good-natured, hilarious spoof in which young Sandy and his rich family are forced to move to a loony bin to escape the schemes of relatives intent on stealing their money. (Rev: HB 1–2/99; HBG 3/99; SLJ 8/98; VOYA 2/99)

3629 Fine, Anne. *The True Story of Christmas* (5–7). 2003, Delacorte $15.95 (0-385-73130-2). Ralph's horrendous relatives all arrive on Christmas Day, with disastrous consequences, in this hilarious novel. (Rev: BCCB 10/03; BL 9/1/03; HB 11–12/03; SLJ 10/03*)

3630 Fitzgerald, John D. *The Great Brain* (4–7). 1985, Dell paper $4.99 (0-440-43071-2). A witty and tender novel in which narrator John recalls the escapades of older brother Tom whose perceptive and crafty schemes set him apart. Some sequels are *More Adventures of the Great Brain* (1969); *Me and My Little Brain* (1971); *The Great Brain at the Academy* (1972); *The Great Brain Reforms* (1973); *The Return of the Great Brain* (1974); *The Great Brain Does It Again* (1975).

3631 Fleischman, Paul. *A Fate Totally Worse Than Death* (7–12). Illus. 1995, Candlewick $15.99 (1-56402-627-2). An offbeat mix of horror story and satire about self-centered rich girls who want to teach a beautiful exchange student a lesson. (Rev: BL 10/15/95; SLJ 10/95; VOYA 4/96)

3632 Fleischman, Sid. *Chancy and the Grand Rascal* (5–7). 1966, Little, Brown $14.95 (0-316-28575-7); paper $4.95 (0-316-26012-6). The boy and his uncle, the grand rascal, combine hard work and quick wits to outsmart a scoundrel, hoodwink a miser, and capture a band of outlaws.

3633 Foley, June. *Susanna Siegelbaum Gives Up Guys* (5–8). 1992, Scholastic paper $3.25 (0-590-43700-3). Susanna, a flirt, makes a bet that she can give up guys for three months. (Rev: SLJ 8/91)

3634 Frank, Lucy. *The Annoyance Bureau* (5–8). 2002, Simon & Schuster $16.95 (0-689-84903-6). Lucas, 12, is already having a very annoying Christmas holiday in New York when he meets a Santa who says he works for the Annoyance Bureau, and the irritations begin to multiply. (Rev: BCCB 12/02; BL 11/1/02; HBG 3/03; SLJ 10/02)

3635 Friedman, Robin. *How I Survived My Summer Vacation: And Lived to Write the Story* (5–9). 2000, Front Street $15.95 (0-8126-2738-5). A humorous story about 13-year-old Jackie Monterey, his friends, family, and the vow he has made to write the great American novel. (Rev: BL 8/00; HBG 10/00; SLJ 6/00)

3636 Gleitzman, Morris. *Worry Warts* (6–8). 1993, Harcourt $12.95 (0-15-299666-4). In this sequel to *Misery Guts,* Keith tries — and fails — to save his parents' marriage by going off to Australian opal fields to make money. (Rev: BL 7/93; SLJ 5/93)

3637 Gorman, Carol. *Dork on the Run* (4–7). 2002, HarperCollins LB $16.89 (0-06-029410-8). Flack, a 6th grader, doesn't foresee the unusual and often

funny situations that will arise when he runs for class president. (Rev: BCCB 9/02; BL 6/1–15/02; HB 9–10/02; HBG 10/02; SLJ 6/02)

3638 Gorman, Carol. *Lizard Flanagan, Supermodel??* (4–7). 1998, HarperCollins $14.95 (0-06-024868-8). Sixth-grader Lizard Flanagan will do anything to make enough money to go by bus from her home in Iowa to a game in Wrigley Field, but is entering a local fashion show for teens going too far? (Rev: BL 11/15/98; HBG 3/99; SLJ 10/98)

3639 Griggs, Terry. *Cat's Eye Corner* (6–8). 2003, Raincoast paper $7.95 (1-55192-350-5). Wordplay stars in this entertaining novel full of eccentric characters whom Olivier finds on a scavenger hunt through his grandfather's old mansion. (Rev: BL 6/1–15/03; SLJ 8/03)

3640 Hayes, Daniel. *Eye of the Beholder* (5–8). 1992, Fawcett paper $6.99 (0-449-00235-7). Tyler and Lymie are in trouble again when they fake some works of a famous sculptor. (Rev: BL 2/1/93; SLJ 12/92)

3641 Hayes, Daniel. *Flyers* (8–12). Illus. 1996, Simon & Schuster $16.00 (0-689-80372-9). A funny and clever novel that involves 15-year-old Gabe, the movie he and his friends are making, and a series of odd events that change their lives. (Rev: BL 9/15/96; SLJ 11/96; VOYA 2/97)

3642 Henry, Chad. *DogBreath Victorious* (6–10). 1999, Holiday $16.95 (0-8234-1458-2). Tim's rock band, DogBreath, ends up competing against his mom's group, the Angry Housewives, in this entertaining story. (Rev: HBG 9/00; SLJ 2/00; VOYA 6/00)

3643 Hite, Sid. *Those Darn Dithers* (5–8). 1996, Holt $15.95 (0-8050-3838-8). A humorous novel about the dithering Dithers with adventures involving Porcellina the dancing pig and an eccentric who drifts out to sea on a rubber raft. (Rev: BL 12/15/96; BR 9–10/97; SLJ 12/96; VOYA 10/97)

3644 Honey, Elizabeth. *Don't Pat the Wombat* (4–7). Illus. 2000, Knopf LB $16.99 (0-375-90578-2). This Aussie import tells the breezy story of a group of kids at school and at summer camp. (Rev: BCCB 9/00; BL 5/15/00; HB 5–6/00; HBG 10/00; SLJ 7/00)

3645 Horvath, Polly. *The Happy Yellow Car* (5–7). 2004, Farrar paper $5.95 (0-374-42879-4). In a small Missouri town, where this humorous story takes place, 12-year-old Betty Grunt must find a dollar if she wants to be elected Pork-Fry Queen. (Rev: BCCB 11/94; BL 8/94; SLJ 9/94)

3646 Horvath, Polly. *When the Circus Came to Town* (5–8). 1996, FSG paper $5.95 (0-374-48367-1). Opinion is sharply divided in Ivy's town when a circus troupe decides to relocate there. (Rev: BCCB 12/96; BL 11/15/96; SLJ 12/96*)

3647 Howe, James. *The New Nick Kramer or My Life as a Baby-Sitter* (5–9). 1995, Hyperion LB $14.49 (0-7868-2053-5). Nick and rival Mitch make an unusual bet on who will win the affections of newcomer Jennifer. (Rev: BL 12/15/95; SLJ 1/96)

3648 Howe, Norma. *The Adventures of Blue Avenger* (8–10). 1999, Holt $16.95 (0-8050-6062-6). When David Schumacher, 16, changes his name to Blue Avenger, he finds he can tackle all sorts of problems. (Rev: BL 3/15/99; HBG 9/99; SLJ 4/99; VOYA 6/99)

3649 Howe, Norma. *Blue Avenger Cracks the Code* (7–12). 2000, Holt $17.00 (0-8050-6372-2). David (aka Blue Avenger) pursues several lines of interest, including romance and the question of the true authorship of Shakespeare's plays. (Rev: HBG 3/01; SLJ 9/00; VOYA 12/00)

3650 Ives, David. *Monsieur Eek* (4–7). 2001, HarperCollins LB $15.89 (0-06-029530-9). Thirteen-year-old Emmaline defends a monkey against criminal charges in the not-quite-right town of MacOongafoondsen, population 21. (Rev: BL 6/1–15/01; HBG 3/02; SLJ 6/01)

3651 Jennings, Richard W. *My Life of Crime* (4–8). 2002, Houghton $15.00 (0-618-21433-X). Nothing goes right when 6th-grader Fowler decides to "rescue" a caged parrot. (Rev: BL 1/1–15/03; HBG 3/03; VOYA 2/03)

3652 Kalman, Maira. *Max in Hollywood, Baby* (6–9). 1992, Viking $17.99 (0-670-84479-9). Max the dog has gone Hollywood; everybody's favorite pooch poet just couldn't resist the call of the big screen. The ongoing saga of Max the dog — in words, pictures, and typography. (Rev: BL 12/1/92*; SLJ 11/92)

3653 Keller, Beverly. *The Amazon Papers* (7–10). 1996, Harcourt $12.00 (0-15-201345-8); paper $6.00 (0-15-201346-6). Iris's life is transformed, not necessarily for the better, when she falls for a handsome, pizza-delivering, high school dropout named Foster Prizer. (Rev: BL 1/1–15/97; BR 3–4/97; SLJ 10/96; VOYA 12/96)

3654 Keller, Beverly. *Desdemona: Twelve Going on Desperate* (5–7). 1986, HarperCollins paper $5.99 (0-06-440226-6). Mishap after mishap befalls Desdemona, including running into the handsomest boy in school. A sequel is *Fowl Play, Desdemona* (1989). (Rev: BCCB 12/86; BL 10/1/86; SLJ 11/86)

3655 Kidd, Ronald. *Sammy Carducci's Guide to Women* (5–7). 1995, Dramatic Publg. $5.60 (0-87129-522-9). A somewhat sexist 6th grader discovers that, where women are concerned, perhaps he is not as irresistible as he thinks he is. (Rev: BCCB 1/92; BL 1/1/92; SLJ 1/92)

3656 Kiesel, Stanley. *The War Between the Pitiful Teachers and the Splendid Kids* (7–9). 1980, Avon paper $3.50 (0-380-57802-6). A humorous fantasy about schoolchildren who decide to wage war on their teachers.

3657 Kline, Suzy. *Orp Goes to the Hoop* (5–7). 1993, Avon paper $3.50 (0-380-71829-4). Seventh-grader Orp gets a chance to play a big part in the basketball team's big game. (Rev: BCCB 7–8/91; BL 7/91; SLJ 7/91)

3658 Kline, Suzy. *Who's Orp's Girlfriend?* (5–7). 1993, Putnam $13.95 (0-399-22431-9). Orp, who is attracted to two girls, makes a date with both of them for the same night. (Rev: BL 8/93; SLJ 7/93)

3659 Klise, Kate. *Letters from Camp* (5–8). Illus. 1999, Avon $15.99 (0-380-97539-4). A humorous mystery about three sets of quarreling siblings who are sent to Camp Happy Harmony to learn to get along. The story is told entirely through letters, memos, journal entries, telegrams, receipts, lists, and drawings. (Rev: BL 7/99; HBG 10/99; SLJ 6/99)

3660 Korman, Gordon. *Don't Care High* (7–10). 1986, Scholastic paper $2.50 (0-590-40251-X). A new student in a high school where apathy is so rife it's nicknamed Don't Care High decides to infuse some school spirit into the student body. (Rev: BL 10/15/85)

3661 Lawrence, Michael. *The Poltergoose* (4–7). 2002, Dutton $14.99 (0-525-46839-0). Jiggy McCue's new house is being haunted by the ghost of a cranky goose in this humorous story set in the English countryside. (Rev: BL 1/1–15/02; HBG 10/02; SLJ 3/02)

3662 Lawson, Robert. *Ben and Me* (5–8). 1939, Little, Brown $16.95 (0-316-51732-1); paper $5.99 (0-316-51730-5). The events of Benjamin Franklin's life, as told by his good mouse Amos, who lived in his old fur cap.

3663 Lawson, Robert. *Mr. Revere and I* (5–8). 1953, Little, Brown paper $6.99 (0-316-51729-1). A delightful account of certain episodes in Revere's life, as revealed by his horse Scheherazade.

3664 Lowry, Lois. *Anastasia at This Address* (5–9). 1991, Houghton $16.00 (0-395-56263-5); Dell paper $4.50 (0-440-40652-8). The irrepressible Anastasia answers a personal ad, using her mother's picture instead of her own, with typically hilarious results. (Rev: BCCB 3/91; BL 4/1/91; SLJ 8/91)

3665 Lowry, Lois. *Anastasia on Her Own* (5–7). Illus. 1985, Houghton $16.00 (0-395-38133-9); Dell paper $4.50 (0-440-40291-3). Seventh-grader Anastasia Krupnik must face both domestic crisis and romance. Another chapter in Anastasia's busy life is recounted in *Anastasia Has the Answers* (1986). (Rev: BL 5/15/85; HB 9–10/85; SLJ 8/85)

3666 Lowry, Lois. *Anastasia's Chosen Career* (5–7). 1987, Houghton $16.00 (0-395-42506-9); Bantam paper $4.50 (0-440-40100-3). Thirteen-year-old Anastasia gets some surprises when she begs to go to charm school to change her freaky looks. Anastasia's baby brother is featured in *All About Sam* (1988). (Rev: BCCB 9/87; BL 9/1/87; SLJ 9/87)

3667 Lowry, Lois. *The One Hundredth Thing About Caroline* (6–9). 1983, Houghton $16.00 (0-395-34829-3); Dell paper $4.50 (0-440-46625-3). Caroline tries everything and anything to break up her mother's new romance. (Rev: BL 5/15/89)

3668 Lowry, Lois. *Switcharound* (5–7). 1985, Houghton $16.00 (0-395-39536-4); Dell paper $4.50 (0-440-48415-4). Caroline and her nemesis brother J.P. must spend the summer with their divorced father's new family in Des Moines. A sequel to *The One Hundredth Thing About Caroline* (1983). (Rev: BCCB 1/86; BL 10/1/85; HB 1–2/86)

3669 Lowry, Lois. *Your Move, J.P.!* (6–8). 1990, Houghton $16.00 (0-395-53639-1). J. P. Tate, a 7th grader, is hopelessly in love with Angela. (Rev: BL 3/1/90; SLJ 5/90; VOYA 4/90)

3670 Lynch, Chris. *Political Timber* (7–10). 1996, HarperCollins LB $14.89 (0-06-027361-5). In this political satire, Mayor Foley, in prison on several counts of racketeering, coaches his 18-year-old grandson to win the mayoral election and become his successor. (Rev: BL 10/15/96; BR 3–4/97; SLJ 1/97; VOYA 2/97)

3671 MacDonald, Amy. *No More Nice* (4–7). Illus. 1996, Orchard LB $15.99 (0-531-08892-8). A humorous story about a spring vacation spent by a boy with his eccentric great-aunt and -uncle. (Rev: BCCB 10/96; BL 9/1/96; SLJ 9/96)

3672 McDonald, Megan. *The Sisters Club* (4–7). 2003, Pleasant $12.95 (1-58485-782-X). A funny novel about three sisters ages 8 to 12, who each contribute in different ways to their theater-absorbed family. (Rev: BL 12/1/03; SLJ 11/03)

3673 McFann, Jane. *Deathtrap and Dinosaur* (7–12). 1989, Avon paper $2.75 (0-380-75624-2). An unlikely pair works to force the departure of a disliked history teacher. (Rev: SLJ 10/89; VOYA 10/89)

3674 Mackay, Claire, sel. *Laughs* (5–8). 1997, Tundra paper $6.95 (0-88776-393-6). An anthology of humorous stories (and some poems) by several well-known Canadian writers. (Rev: SLJ 9/97)

3675 McKenna, Colleen O'Shaughnessy. *Mother Murphy* (5–7). 1993, Scholastic paper $2.95 (0-590-44856-0). With her mother confined to bed, 12-year-old Collette volunteers as mother-for-a-day with disastrous and funny results. (Rev: BCCB 2/92; BL 2/1/92; SLJ 2/92)

3676 Mackler, Carolyn. *Love and Other Four-Letter Words* (6–10). 2000, Delacorte $14.95 (0-385-32743-9). A humorous novel in which Sammie, an average 16-year-old, tries to make sense of family, friendships, and romance. (Rev: BL 8/00; HBG 3/01; SLJ 9/00)

3677 McManus, Patrick F. *Never Cry "Arp!" and Other Great Adventures* (6–9). 1996, Holt $16.95 (0-8050-4662-3). Based on fact, the 12 stories in this collection deal humorously with the problems of growing up in the mountains of Idaho. (Rev: BL 8/96; BR 11–12/96; SLJ 7/96)

3678 Manes, Stephen. *Comedy High* (7–10). 1992, Scholastic paper $13.95 (0-590-44436-0). A comic story of a new high school designed to graduate jocks, performers, gambling experts, and hotel workers. (Rev: BL 12/1/92; SLJ 11/92)

3679 Many, Paul. *These Are the Rules* (7–10). 1997, Walker $15.95 (0-8027-8619-7); Knopf paper $4.99 (0-679-88978-7). In this hilarious first-person narrative, Colm tries to figure out the rules of dating, driving, girls, and getting some direction in his life. (Rev: BL 5/1/97; HBG 3/98; SLJ 5/97)

3680 Merrill, Jean. *The Pushcart War* (6–9). 1987, Dell paper $5.50 (0-440-47147-8). Mack, driving a Mighty Mammoth, runs down a pushcart belonging to Morris the Florist and starts a most unusual war that is humorous and also reveals many human foibles. (Rev: BL 4/87)

3681 Mills, Claudia. *Alex Ryan, Stop That!* (4–7). Series: West Creek Middle School. 2003, Farrar $16.00 (0-374-34655-0). All Alex's efforts to attract classmate Marcia go awry in this humorous account of 7th-grade and son-father relations. (Rev: BL 4/1/03; HBG 10/03; SLJ 4/03)

3682 Mills, Claudia. *Dinah in Love* (4–7). 1993, Macmillan LB $14.00 (0-02-766998-X). Dinah can't believe that boorish Nick, who continually insults her, really likes her. (Rev: BL 11/15/93; SLJ 12/93)

3683 Mills, Claudia. *You're a Brave Man, Julius Zimmerman* (5–7). 1999, Farrar $16.00 (0-374-38708-7). Julius Zimmerman, of *Losers, Inc.* fame, has a busy summer ahead of him, taking French classes and babysitting Edison, who isn't toilet-trained. (Rev: BCCB 9/99; BL 10/15/99; HB 9–10/99; HBG 3/00; SLJ 9/99)

3684 Morgenstern, Susie. *Secret Letters from 0 to 10* (4–8). Trans. by Gill Rosner. Illus. 1998, Viking $16.99 (0-670-88007-8). Ten-year-old Ernest Morlaisse, whose mother is dead and father gone, is living a bleak existence with a grim grandfather until he meets Victoria and her 13 outgoing brothers. (Rev: BCCB 10/98; BL 10/1/98*; HB 11–12/98; HBG 3/99; SLJ 10/98; VOYA 8/99)

3685 Mulford, Philippa Greene. *Making Room for Katherine* (5–9). 1994, Macmillan $14.95 (0-02-767652-8). A 16-year-old is recovering from her father's death when a 13-year-old cousin arrives from Paris to visit for the summer. (Rev: BL 4/15/94; SLJ 5/94; VOYA 8/94)

3686 Naylor, Phyllis Reynolds. *The Agony of Alice* (5–7). 1985, Macmillan $17.00 (0-689-31143-5); Dell paper $4.99 (0-689-81672-3). Motherless 6th-grader Alice is longing for a female role model, and finally finds one in her teacher, Mrs. Plotkin. (Rev: BL 10/1/85; SLJ 1/86)

3687 Naylor, Phyllis Reynolds. *Alice Alone* (6–10). 2001, Simon & Schuster $15.00 (0-689-82634-6). Alice's story continues as she starts high school and deals with the misery of breaking up with her boyfriend. (Rev: BCCB 5/01; BL 5/15/01; HB 7–8/01; HBG 10/01; SLJ 6/01; VOYA 8/01)

3688 Naylor, Phyllis Reynolds. *Alice in April* (5–8). 1993, Atheneum $16.00 (0-689-31805-7); Dell paper $4.50 (0-440-91032-3). Alice is back, this time caught between her desire to be a perfect housekeeper and her fascination with her developing body. (Rev: BL 3/1/93; SLJ 6/93)

3689 Naylor, Phyllis Reynolds. *Alice In-Between* (5–7). 1994, Atheneum $16.95 (0-689-31890-1). Alice, now 13, along with her friends, is becoming very aware of her changing body and of boys in this humorous look at early adolescence. (Rev: BCCB 5/94; BL 5/1/94; HB 7–8/94; SLJ 6/94)

3690 Naylor, Phyllis Reynolds. *Alice in Lace* (6–8). 1996, Simon & Schuster $17.00 (0-689-80358-3). Alice, in her usual bumbling, endearing way, confronts society's greatest problems when her health class does a unit on "Critical Choices." (Rev: BL 3/1/96; BR 1–2/97; SLJ 4/96; VOYA 8/96)

3691 Naylor, Phyllis Reynolds. *Alice in Rapture, Sort Of* (5–8). 1989, Macmillan $16.00 (0-689-31466-3); Dell paper $3.99 (0-440-40462-2). Our young heroine, now in 7th grade, wonders how to behave with her boyfriend, Patrick. (Rev: BL 3/1/89; HB 5–6/89; SLJ 4/89)

3692 Naylor, Phyllis Reynolds. *Alice on the Outside* (6–9). 1999, Simon & Schuster $16.00 (0-689-80359-1). In this 11th book about Alice, our young heroine continues her adolescent exploration of the problems of growing up, particularly adjusting to the opposite sex. (Rev: BL 5/1/99; HB 7–8/99; HBG 9/99; SLJ 7/99; VOYA 12/99)

3693 Naylor, Phyllis Reynolds. *Alice the Brave* (5–7). 1995, Simon & Schuster $15.95 (0-689-80095-9); paper $4.99 (0-689-80598-5). Alice conquers her fear of deep water and also feels the pangs of growing up in this amusing continuation of a popular series. (Rev: BCCB 4/95; BL 5/1/95; HB 7–8/95; SLJ 5/95)

3694 Naylor, Phyllis Reynolds. *All But Alice* (5–8). 1992, Macmillan $15.95 (0-689-31773-5). Alice, now a 7th grader and still motherless, deals with the challenges of friendship and popularity. (Rev: BCCB 5/92; BL 3/1/92; HB 7–8/92; SLJ 5/92*)

3695 Naylor, Phyllis Reynolds. *The Grooming of Alice* (6–9). 2000, Simon & Schuster $16.00 (0-689-82633-8). In this, the twelfth Alice story, our heroine discovers what is meant by "normal" for girls and also helps a friend who is having trouble at home. (Rev: BL 6/1–15/00; HB 7–8/00; HBG 9/00; SLJ 5/00)

3696 Naylor, Phyllis Reynolds. *Outrageously Alice* (6–8). 1997, Simon & Schuster $15.95 (0-689-80354-0); paper $4.99 (0-689-80596-9). Thirteen-year-old Alice, now in the 8th grade, decides that she is too ordinary and wants to do something about it. (Rev: BCCB 7–8/97; BL 5/15/97; BR 11–12/97; HB 7–8/98; SLJ 6/97; VOYA 10/97)

3697 Naylor, Phyllis Reynolds. *Patiently Alice* (6–9). 2003, Simon & Schuster $15.95 (0-689-82636-2). Alice spends summer as a camp counselor and despite a lack of romance has lots of fun (including talk of sex) and learns about her disadvantaged charges. (Rev: BL 8/03; HB 7–8/03; HBG 10/03; SLJ 5/03; VOYA 8/03)

3698 Naylor, Phyllis Reynolds. *Reluctantly Alice* (5–8). 1991, Macmillan $16.00 (0-689-31681-X). Alice's life in the 7th grade seems full of embarrassment. (Rev: BCCB 4/91*; BL 2/1/91; HB 7–8/91; SLJ 3/91*)

3699 Naylor, Phyllis Reynolds. *Simply Alice* (6–9). 2002, Simon & Schuster $16.00 (0-689-82635-4). Now 14, Alice is in 9th grade and living a full life while learning to deal with family, friendships, and embarrassing situations. (Rev: BCCB 6/02; BL 6/1–15/02; HB 7–8/02; HBG 10/02; SLJ 5/02; VOYA 6/02)

3700 Nodelman, Perry. *Behaving Bradley* (8–10). 1998, Simon & Schuster $16.00 (0-689-81466-6). In this screwball comedy, junior Bradley Gold represents student interests when his high school prepares a code of conduct. (Rev: BL 6/1–15/98; HBG 3/99; SLJ 6/98; VOYA 8/98)

3701 Palatini, Margie. *The Web Files* (4–8). 2001, Hyperion LB $16.49 (0-7868-2366-6). A clever and humorous takeoff of "Dragnet" that involves Ducktective Web and his feathered partner Bill, who are working the barnyard shift. (Rev: BCCB 2/01; BL 5/1/01; HB 5–6/01; HBG 10/01; SLJ 11/01*)

3702 Park, Barbara. *Buddies* (5–8). 1986, Avon paper $2.95 (0-380-69992-3). Dinah's dreams of being popular at camp are dashed in this humorous novel because she is forever being accompanied by Fern, the camp nerd. (Rev: BCCB 5/85; BL 4/15/85; SLJ 5/85)

3703 Paulsen, Gary. *Harris and Me: A Summer Remembered* (6–10). 1993, Harcourt $16.00 (0-15-292877-4); paper $4.99 (0-440-40994-2). A humorous story in which the 11-year-old narrator often gets the blame for mischief caused by troublemaker Harris. (Rev: BL 12/1/93*; SLJ 2/00; VOYA 2/94)

3704 Paulsen, Gary. *The Schernoff Discoveries* (4–8). 1997, Delacorte $15.95 (0-385-32194-5). A humorous novel about the misadventures of two friends, both self-confessed geeks. (Rev: BCCB 7–8/97; BL 6/1–15/97; BR 9–10/97; SLJ 7/97; VOYA 10/97)

3705 Peck, Richard. *A Long Way from Chicago* (6–10). 1998, Dial $15.99 (0-8037-2290-7). Seven stories are included in this book, each representing a different summer from 1929 to 1935 that Joey spent visiting in Illinois with his lying, cheating, conniving, and thoroughly charming grandmother. (Rev: BCCB 10/98; BL 9/1/98; HB 11–12/98; HBG 3/99; SLJ 10/98*; VOYA 12/98)

3706 Peck, Richard. *A Year Down Yonder* (6–10). 2000, Dial $16.99 (0-8037-2518-3). In this 2001 Newbery Medal winner, 15-year-old Mary Alice visits her feisty, independent, but lovable Grandma Dowdel in rural Illinois during the Great Depression. A sequel to *A Long Way from Chicago* (1998). (Rev: BCCB 1/01; BL 10/15/00; HB 11–12/00; HBG 3/01; SLJ 9/00; VOYA 12/00)

3707 Peck, Robert Newton. *Higbee's Halloween* (5–7). 1990, Walker LB $14.85 (0-8027-6969-1). Higbee decides something must be done about the unruly Striker children. (Rev: SLJ 10/90)

3708 Peck, Robert Newton. *Soup* (5–8). 1974, Knopf $15.99 (0-394-92700-1); Dell paper $4.50 (0-440-48186-4). A humorous story about the friendship between two boys growing up in a small town some years ago. Also use *Soup for President* (1978) and *Soup in the Saddle* (1983). (Rev: BL 5/1/89)

3709 Ragz, M. M. *French Fries up Your Nose* (5–8). 1994, Pocket paper $3.99 (0-671-88410-7). When the class clown runs for student council president, he struggles to maintain his irresponsible image while developing serious, election-winning habits. (Rev: BL 3/15/94)

3710 Rennison, Louise. *Angus, Thongs and Full-Frontal Snogging: Confessions of Georgia Nicolson* (6–9). 2000, HarperCollins $15.99 (0-06-028814-0). In her diary, 14-year-old Georgia Nicolson writes with humor and charm of her latest crush, learning to kiss, hunting for her cat, and other teen concerns. (Rev: BL 7/00; HB 5–6/00; HBG 9/00; SLJ 7/00; VOYA 6/00)

3711 Rennison, Louise. *Knocked Out by My Nunga-Nungas* (7–10). 2002, HarperCollins $15.95 (0-06-623656-8). British teenager Georgia Nicolson is back with more saucy talk, recorded in the pages of her diary along with her latest troubles with her boyfriend, family, and schoolmates. (Rev: BL 4/15/02; HB 7–8/02; HBG 10/02; SLJ 5/02)

3712 Rennison, Louise. *On the Bright Side, I'm Now the Girlfriend of a Sex God: The Further Confessions of Georgia Nicholson* (7–10). 2001, Harper-

Collins $15.95 (0-06-028813-2). Georgia records in her diary the details of her daily life and of her crush on "Robbie the Sex God" and her hilarious machinations to snare him in this sequel to *Angus, Thongs, and Full-Frontal Snogging* (2000). (Rev: BL 5/15/01; HB 5–6/01; HBG 10/01; SLJ 5/01; VOYA 6/01)

3713 Riggs, Bob. *My Best Defense* (6–10). 1996, Ward Hill paper $5.95 (1-886747-01-6). Sarcasm is the best defense of the narrator in this humorous story of a family and the unusual characters they attract. (Rev: SLJ 8/96; VOYA 10/96)

3714 Robertson, Keith. *Henry Reed, Inc.* (5–7). 1989, Puffin paper $5.99 (0-14-034144-7). Told deadpan in diary form, this story of Henry's enterprising summer in New Jersey presents one of the most amusing boys since Tom and Huck. Others in the series *Henry Reed's Journey* (1963); *Henry Reed's Baby-Sitting Service* (1966); *Henry Reed's Big Show* (1970).

3715 Rodgers, Mary. *Freaky Friday* (4–7). 1972, HarperCollins LB $16.89 (0-06-025049-6); paper $5.99 (0-06-440046-8). Thirteen-year-old Annabel learns some valuable lessons during the day she becomes her mother. Two sequels are *A Billion for Boris* (1974) and *Summer Switch* (1982). (Rev: BL 4/15/89)

3716 Roos, Stephen. *Twelve-Year-Old Vows Revenge After Being Dumped by Extraterrestrial on First Date* (5–6). Illus. 1991, Dell paper $3.25 (0-440-40465-7). The rivalry between two girls reaches such a point that they take the matter to court. (Rev: BL 5/15/90; SLJ 7/90)

3717 Ryan, Mary C. *Who Says I Can't?* (7–10). 1988, Little, Brown $12.95 (0-316-76374-8). Tessa decides to get revenge on a boy who shows too much ardor in his romancing. (Rev: SLJ 11/88)

3718 Sachar, Louis. *Sideways Arithmetic from Wayside School* (4–8). Series: Wayside School. 1992, Scholastic paper $4.50 (0-590-45726-8). Sue learns a new kind of math and encounters some humorous brainteasers when she transfers to Wayside School. (Rev: BL 12/15/89)

3719 Scrimger, Richard. *Noses Are Red* (4–7). 2002, Tundra $14.95 (0-88776-610-2); paper $7.95 (0-88776-590-4). Norbert, the alien who likes to live in Alan's nose, works to Alan's benefit once again when Alan and a friend meet a variety of perils on a camping trip. (Rev: BL 1/1–15/03; HBG 3/03; SLJ 12/02; VOYA 2/03)

3720 Shaw, Tucker. *Flavor of the Week* (8–10). 2003, Hyperion $15.99 (0-7868-1890-5). Overweight, diffident, and in love, aspiring chef Cyril agrees to a culinary ruse that backfires, leaving a happy Cyril winning the girl. (Rev: BL 11/15/03; SLJ 12/03)

3721 Sheldon, Dyan. *Confessions of a Teenage Drama Queen* (6–9). 1999, Candlewick $16.99 (0-7636-0822-X). A very funny story that describes the adjustments a New York City teenager must make when her family moves to Dellwood, New Jersey. (Rev: BL 11/1/99; HBG 4/00; SLJ 10/99; VOYA 2/00)

3722 Sheldon, Dyan. *My Perfect Life* (7–10). 2002, Candlewick $16.99 (0-7636-1839-X). A hard-fought race for class president pits timid Ella against arrogant Carla in this humorous novel that reintroduces the characters from *Confessions of a Teenage Drama Queen* (1999). (Rev: BL 7/02; HBG 3/03; SLJ 8/02; VOYA 12/02)

3723 Smith, Edwin R. *Blue Star Highway, Vol. 1: A Tale of Redemption from North Florida* (7–12). 1997, Mile Marker Twelve Publg. paper $9.95 (0-9659054-0-3). In this humorous novel, 14-year-old Marty Crane tells of the events in his life leading up to being sentenced to a detention home in 1962. (Rev: BL 2/15/99)

3724 Smith, Greg Leitich. *Ninjas, Piranhas, and Galileo* (5–8). 2003, Little, Brown $15.95 (0-316-77854-0). Romance, a science fair, and dubious ethics are in the air as Elias, Shohei, and Honoria try to navigate the shoals of 7th grade. (Rev: BL 12/1/03)

3725 Snicket, Lemony. *The Bad Beginning* (4–7). Illus. Series: A Series of Unfortunate Events. 1999, HarperCollins $10.99 (0-06-440766-7). A humorous story about the ill-fated Beaudelaire orphans and the creepy, wicked villains they never seem to avoid. (Rev: BL 12/1/99; HBG 3/00; SLJ 11/99)

3726 Snicket, Lemony. *The Carnivorous Carnival* (4–8). Series: A Series of Unfortunate Events. 2002, HarperCollins LB $14.89 (0-06-029640-2). The Baudelaire orphans pose as carnival freaks in the ninth volume of this unhappily-ever-after series. (Rev: BL 12/15/02; HBG 3/03; SLJ 1/03)

3727 Snicket, Lemony. *Lemony Snicket: The Unauthorized Autobiography* (4–7). Illus. 2002, HarperCollins LB $14.89 (0-06-000720-6). Using fake documents, newspaper articles, and transcripts, the author of the funny Series of Unfortunate Events books reconstructs his life. (Rev: BL 6/1–15/02; HBG 10/02; SLJ 7/02)

3728 Snicket, Lemony. *The Wide Window* (4–7). Illus. Series: A Series of Unfortunate Events. 2000, HarperCollins $10.99 (0-06-440768-3). The three Baudelaire children have a new guardian, timid cousin Josephine, but they are pursued by former keeper Count Olaf. (Rev: BL 2/1/00; HBG 10/00; SLJ 1/00)

3729 Somtow, S. P. *The Vampire's Beautiful Daughter* (7–10). Illus. 1997, Simon & Schuster $17.00 (0-689-31968-1). Johnny meets Rebecca Teppish, a fascinating girl who is part vampire. (Rev: BL 9/1/97; HBG 3/98; SLJ 10/97)

3730 Soto, Gary. *Summer on Wheels* (5–8). 1995, Scholastic paper $13.95 (0-590-48365-X). In this sequel to *Crazy Weekend* (1994), Hector and Mando take a bike ride from their barrio home in Los Angeles to Santa Monica. (Rev: BL 1/15/95; SLJ 4/95; VOYA 4/95)

3731 Spinelli, Jerry. *The Library Card* (4–8). 1997, Scholastic paper $15.95 (0-590-46731-X). Four humorous, poignant stories about how books changed the lives of several youngsters. (Rev: BCCB 3/97; BL 2/1/97; BR 3–4/97; HB 3–4/97; SLJ 3/97; VOYA 10/97)

3732 Stanley, George E. *Hershell Cobwell and the Miraculous Tattoo* (4–8). 1991, Avon paper $2.95 (0-380-75897-0). A junior high boy decides to gain popularity by getting a tattoo. (Rev: BL 3/15/91)

3733 Strasser, Todd. *Girl Gives Birth to Own Prom Date* (7–10). 1996, Simon & Schuster LB $16.00 (0-689-80482-2). Telling their stories in alternating chapters, friends Nichole and Brad discuss the frantic high school social scene and the upcoming senior prom. (Rev: BL 10/1/96; SLJ 9/96; VOYA 4/97)

3734 Strasser, Todd. *Here Comes Heavenly* (5–8). Series: Here Comes Heavenly. 1999, Pocket paper $4.99 (0-671-03626-2). A slight story about a bizarre-looking nanny named Heavenly Litebody and how she manages to tame a family of five unruly children while their parents are away. (Rev: BL 1/1–15/00; SLJ 12/99)

3735 Strasser, Todd. *Kidnap Kids* (5–7). 1998, Putnam paper $5.99 (0-698-11801-4). Because two brothers rarely see their busy parents, they hatch a plan to kidnap them. (Rev: BCCB 3/98; BL 1/1–15/98; HBG 10/98; SLJ 3/98)

3736 Taha, Karen T. *Marshmallow Muscles, Banana Brainstorms* (6–8). 1988, Harcourt $13.95 (0-15-200525-0). A puny youngster tries a regime of body development through the help of his dream girl. (Rev: BL 1/1/89)

3737 Todd, Pamela. *Pig and the Shrink* (5–8). 1999, Delacorte $14.95 (0-385-32657-2). A humorous story in which Tucker, a 7th grader, uses his fat friend, Angelo Pighetti, as a subject for his science project on nutrition. (Rev: BCCB 11/99; BL 10/1/99; HBG 3/00; SLJ 9/99)

3738 Tolan, Stephanie S. *Surviving the Applewhites* (5–9). 2002, HarperCollins LB $17.89 (0-06-623603-7). The convention-flouting Applewhite family's Creative Academy helps a 13-year-old troublemaker to discover hidden talents. Newbery Honor Book, 2003. (Rev: BCCB 10/02; BL 11/1/02; HBG 3/03; SLJ 9/02*)

3739 Trahey, Jane. *The Clovis Caper* (5–8). 1990, Avon paper $2.95 (0-380-75914-4). Martin is so upset at leaving his dog, Clovis, when going to England that Aunt Hortense plots to smuggle the dog out of the country. (Rev: BL 7/90)

3740 Trembath, Don. *A Fly Named Alfred* (7–10). 1997, Orca paper $6.95 (1-55143-083-5). In this sequel to *The Tuesday Cafe,* Harper Winslow gets into more trouble when he write an anonymous column in the school newspaper that enrages the school bully. (Rev: BL 8/97; SLJ 9/96)

3741 Uderzo, Albert. *Asterix and Son* (4–8). Trans. by Anthea Bell and Derek Hockridge. Illus. 2002, Orion paper $9.95 (0-75284-775-9). In comic-book format, this is the entertaining story of French heroes Asterix and Obelix and how they became guardians of a kidnapped baby. Also use *Asterix and the Black Gold* (2002) and *Asterix and the Great Divide* (2002). (Rev: BL 4/15/02)

3742 Uderzo, Albert. *Asterix and the Actress* (4–7). Trans. by Anthea Bell and Derek Hockridge. Illus. 2001, Sterling $12.95 (0-75284-657-4). These pun-filled, graphic-novel exploits of Asterix the Gaul include a boisterous shared birthday with the rotund Obelix and a daring rescue of prisoners in a Roman jail. (Rev: BL 8/01)

3743 Voigt, Cynthia. *Bad, Badder, Baddest* (5–8). 1997, Scholastic paper $16.95 (0-590-60136-9). A hilarious mix of funny situations and outrageous dialogue feature two 6th-grade outsiders who deserve their reputation for being bad. A sequel to *Bad Girls.* (Rev: BL 11/1/97; HBG 3/98; SLJ 11/97)

3744 Ware, Cheryl. *Venola in Love* (4–7). 2000, Orchard LB $16.99 (0-531-33306-X). Told through diary entries, e-mail messages, and class notes, this humorous novel tells how 7th-grader Venola discovers the problems of falling in love. (Rev: BCCB 10/00; HBG 10/01; SLJ 10/00)

3745 Weeks, Sarah. *Guy Time* (5–7). 2000, HarperCollins LB $15.89 (0-06-028366-1). A humorous story about 13-year-old Guy, his separated parents, his mother who is constantly dating, and the girl who has a crush on him. (Rev: BCCB 5/00; BL 8/00; HB 5–6/00; HBG 10/00; SLJ 6/00)

3746 Wersba, Barbara. *You'll Never Guess the End* (7–12). 1992, HarperCollins $14.00 (0-06-020448-6). A send-up of the New York City literary scene, rich dilettantes, and Scientology. (Rev: BL 11/15/92; SLJ 9/92)

3747 Weston, Martha. *Act I, Act II, Act Normal* (4–7). 2003, Millbrook $15.95 (0-7613-1779-1). Topher wins the lead in the 8th-grade play but the glory is tempered by the realities of school life in this humorous novel. (Rev: BL 6/1–15/03; HBG 10/03; SLJ 6/03; VOYA 8/03)

3748 Weyn, Suzanne. *The Makeover Club* (7–9). 1986, Avon paper $2.50 (0-380-75007-4). Three girls decide they are going to be glamorous by forming the Makeover Club. (Rev: SLJ 1/87; VOYA 12/86)

3749 Whytock, Cherry. *My Cup Runneth Over: The Life of Angelica Cookson Potts* (6–9). Illus. 2003, Simon & Schuster $14.95 (0-689-86546-5). Clever wordplay and laugh-out-loud humor reign in this British story featuring Angelica, who wants to be a chef but most of all yearns for a bra that fits. (Rev: BCCB 11/03; BL 11/15/03; SLJ 9/03)

3750 Wibberley, Leonard. *The Mouse That Roared* (7–12). 1992, Buccaneer LB $27.95 (0-89966-887-9). To get foreign aid, the tiny Duchy of Grand Fenwick declares war on the United States.

3751 Williams, Carol Lynch. *A Mother to Embarrass Me* (6–8). 2002, Delacorte $15.95 (0-385-72922-7). Twelve-year-old Laura is mortified when her mother, who is embarrassing at the best of times, announces that she is pregnant. (Rev: HBG 10/02; SLJ 3/02)

3752 Winton, Tim. *Lockie Leonard, Scumbuster* (5–9). 1999, Simon & Schuster $16.00 (0-689-82247-2). A humorous Australian novel about the efforts of Lockie Leonard and his friend Egg Eggleston to clean up the waters of a polluted bay. (Rev: BCCB 6/99; BL 6/1–15/99; HB 11–12/99; HBG 10/99; SLJ 6/99)

Mysteries, Thrillers, and Spy Stories

3753 Aiken, Joan. *The Teeth of the Gale* (7–9). 1988, HarperCollins $14.95 (0-06-020044-8). Eighteen-year-old Felix tries to rescue three children who have been kidnapped. A sequel to *Go Saddle the Sea* and *Bridle the Wind.* (Rev: BL 9/15/88; BR 5–6/89; SLJ 11/88; VOYA 12/88)

3754 Alcock, Vivien. *The Mysterious Mr. Ross* (6–8). 1987, Delacorte $14.95 (0-385-29581-2). Felicity saves a man from drowning and finds herself in the middle of the mystery surrounding him. (Rev: BL 11/1/87; BR 11–12/87; SLJ 10/87; VOYA 12/87)

3755 Alcock, Vivien. *Stranger at the Window* (5–8). 1998, Houghton $16.00 (0-395-81661-0). After 11-year-old Lesley discovers that her neighbor's children are hiding an illegal immigrant child in the attic of their home in London, she eagerly enters the conspiracy. (Rev: BCCB 5/98; BL 5/15/98; HB 5–6/98; HBG 9/98; SLJ 6/98)

3756 Anastasio, Dina. *The Case of the Glacier Park Swallow* (4–7). Illus. 1994, Roberts Rinehart paper $6.95 (1-879373-85-8). Juliet, who wants to be a veterinarian, stumbles upon a drug-smuggling ring in this tightly knit mystery. (Rev: BL 12/1/94; SLJ 10/94)

3757 Anastasio, Dina. *The Case of the Grand Canyon Eagle* (5–8). Series: Juliet Stone Environmental Mystery. 1994, Roberts Rinehart paper $6.95 (1-879373-84-X). In this ecological mystery, 17-year-old Juliet Stone investigates the disappearance of eagle eggs. (Rev: SLJ 10/94)

3758 Anderson, Janet S. *The Last Treasure* (5–7). 2003, Dutton $17.99 (0-525-46919-2). A whole family becomes immersed in a saga of intrigue and suspense that reaches back into the 19th century. (Rev: BL 3/15/03; SLJ 6/03*; VOYA 4/03)

3759 Avi. *Wolf Rider: A Tale of Terror* (7–12). 1986, Macmillan paper $17.00 (0-02-707760-8). In this thrilling mystery, a 15-year-old boy tries to learn the identity of a telephone caller who claims he is a murderer. (Rev: BL 11/15/86; BR 5–6/87; SLJ 12/86)

3760 Babbitt, Natalie. *Goody Hall* (6–8). 1971, Sunburst paper $5.95 (0-374-42767-4). A student and his new tutor investigate the mysterious death of the boy's father.

3761 Babbitt, Natalie. *Kneeknock Rise* (4–7). 1970, Farrar paper $5.95 (0-374-44260-6). Young Egan sets out bravely to see the mysterious people-eating Megrimum.

3762 Beatty, Patricia. *The Coach That Never Came* (6–8). 1985, Morrow $15.95 (0-688-05477-3). While doing research on Colorado history, Paul unravels the mystery of a missing stagecoach. (Rev: BL 12/15/85; SLJ 11/85)

3763 Bennett, Jay. *Coverup* (8–10). 1992, Fawcett paper $5.99 (0-449-70409-2). Realizing his friend has killed a pedestrian on a deserted road after a party, Brad returns to the accident scene and meets a girl searching for her homeless father. (Rev: BL 11/1/91)

3764 Bennett, Jay. *The Dark Corridor* (7–12). 1990, Fawcett paper $4.50 (0-449-70337-1). Kerry believes that his girlfriend's death was not suicide but murder. (Rev: BR 3–4/89; SLJ 11/88; VOYA 2/89)

3765 Bennett, Jay. *The Haunted One* (7–12). 1987, Fawcett paper $3.99 (0-449-70314-2). Paul Barrett, an 18-year-old lifeguard, is haunted by the memory of the girl he loved, who drowned before his eyes. (Rev: BR 3–4/88; SLJ 11/87)

3766 Bennett, Jay. *Sing Me a Death Song* (7–12). 1991, Fawcett paper $6.50 (0-449-70369-X). Eighteen-year-old Jason wonders if his accused mother is really a murderer. (Rev: SLJ 4/90; VOYA 8/90)

3767 Bennett, Jay. *The Skeleton Man* (7–12). 1988, Fawcett paper $4.50 (0-449-70284-7). Ray receives money from his uncle just before his death — but the gambling syndicate claims it as theirs. (Rev: BL 11/1/86; BR 1–2/87; SLJ 10/86; VOYA 4/87)

3768 Bonners, Susan. *Above and Beyond* (5–7). 2001, Farrar $16.00 (0-374-30018-6). Jerry makes a new friend and discovers the truth about an incident that took place many years ago. (Rev: BCCB 12/01; HBG 10/02; SLJ 10/01; VOYA 12/01)

3769 Bowler, Tim. *Storm Catchers* (6–10). 2003, Simon & Schuster $16.95 (0-689-84573-1). A multilayered, suspenseful story of the kidnapping of a 13-year-old girl on the Cornwall coast, her brother's agonized guilt, and the discovery of a dark family secret. (Rev: BL 9/1/03; SLJ 5/03; VOYA 8/03)

3770 Brooks, Kevin. *Lucas* (8–10). 2003, Scholastic $16.95 (0-439-45698-3). The arrival of an attractive young stranger on Cait's remote British island signals the start of a series of calamitous events. (Rev: BL 5/1/03*; HB 3–4/03; HBG 10/03; SLJ 5/03; VOYA 4/03)

3771 Bruchac, Joseph. *Skeleton Man* (5–9). 2001, HarperCollins LB $16.89 (0-06-029076-5). After her parents' disappearance, 6th-grader Molly, a Native American, must escape from the spooky man claiming to be her great-uncle. (Rev: BCCB 9/01; BL 9/1/01; HBG 3/02; SLJ 8/01*)

3772 Bunting, Eve. *The Haunting of Safe Keep* (7–10). 1985, HarperCollins LB $12.89 (0-397-32113-9). In this romantic mystery, two college friends work out their family problems while investigating strange occurrences where they work. (Rev: BL 4/15/85; BR 11–12/85; SLJ 5/85; VOYA 8/85)

3773 Cappo, Nan Willard. *Cheating Lessons* (7–10). 2002, Simon & Schuster $16.00 (0-689-84378-X). Bernadette, star of the high school quiz team, faces a dilemma when she guesses that cheating may explain her team's success. (Rev: BCCB 4/02; BL 3/15/02; HB 3–4/02*; HBG 10/02; SLJ 3/02; VOYA 2/02)

3774 Cargill, Linda. *Pool Party* (7–10). 1996, Scholastic paper $3.99 (0-590-58111-2). Sharon's beach party at a resort with a reputation for being haunted ends in murder. (Rev: SLJ 1/97)

3775 Chandler, Elizabeth. *Dark Secrets: Legacy of Lies* (6–12). Series: Dark Secrets. 2000, Pocket paper $4.99 (0-7434-0028-3). Megan, 16, has finally met her grandmother, but she still feels like an outsider and her frightening dreams become more and more intense. (Rev: BCCB 2/01; BL 2/1/01; SLJ 1/01)

3776 Ciencin, Scott. *Faceless* (6–10). Series: The Lurker Files. 1996, Random paper $6.99 (0-679-88235-9). An online/offline complicated thriller involving university students, a chat room, cyber-identities, and e-mail threats from "Dethboy" who claims to be responsible for the disappearance and possible death of one of the students. (Rev: SLJ 4/97)

3777 Ciencin, Scott. *Know Fear* (7–9). Series: The Lurker Files. 1996, Random paper $6.99 (0-679-

88236-7). Access to a computer is necessary to understand the plot and characters of this second horror/suspense novel set at Wintervale University. (Rev: SLJ 5/97)

3778 Clark, Mary Higgins, ed. *The International Association of Crime Writers Presents Bad Behavior* (8–12). 1995, Harcourt $20.00 (0-15-200179-4). Features many stories with young characters and less overt violence than adult fare. Includes works by Sara Paretsky, P. D. James, Lawrence Block, and Liza Cody. (Rev: BL 7/95)

3779 Conrad, Hy. *Whodunit Crime Puzzles* (4–7). 2002, Sterling paper $6.95 (0-8069-9796-6). This collection of 25 mysteries involves Sherman Holmes, a descendant of Sherlock, and his sidekick Sergeant Wilson. (Rev: BL 11/1/02)

3780 Cooper, Ilene. *I'll See You in My Dreams* (6–9). 1997, Viking $15.99 (0-670-86322-X). Karen, whose dreams foretell the future, dreams about a tragedy that involves a new boy in school and his young brother. (Rev: BL 6/1–15/97; BR 1–2/98; HBG 3/98; SLJ 8/97)

3781 Cray, Jordan. *Dead Man's Hand* (5–9). Series: danger.com. 1998, Simon & Schuster paper $3.99 (0-689-82383-5). In this light read, Nick Annunciato and his stepsister, Annie Hanley, use their brains and a computer to solve a murder and escape a biological-weapons smuggling ring. (Rev: SLJ 2/99)

3782 Cray, Jordan. *Shiver* (5–8). Series: danger.com. 1998, Simon & Schuster paper $3.99 (0-689-82384-3). Six drama students are spending a weekend in the Green Mountains of Vermont, when one of the group is murdered. (Rev: SLJ 2/99)

3783 Cresswell, Helen, ed. *Mystery Stories: An Intriguing Collection* (8–12). Illus. 1996, Kingfisher paper $7.95 (0-7534-5025-9). A collection of 19 mystery stories from such writers as Sir Arthur Conan Doyle, Agatha Christie, Ray Bradbury, and Emily Brontë. (Rev: SLJ 2/97)

3784 Crew, Gary. *Angel's Gate* (8–12). 1995, Simon & Schuster paper $16.00 (0-689-80166-1). A murder mystery/coming-of-age story about a dead man's children who have escaped to live in the wild and a 13-year-old girl who draws them back to civilization. (Rev: BL 10/1/95; SLJ 10/95; VOYA 4/96)

3785 Crew, Gary. *No Such Country* (6–9). 1994, Simon & Schuster paper $15.00 (0-671-79760-3). A mystery with elements of fantasy about an Australian fishing village with a secret. The text is strong on adolescent self-questioning and aboriginal history. (Rev: BL 5/1/94; SLJ 7/94)

3786 Cross, Gillian. *Phoning a Dead Man* (6–10). 2002, Holiday $16.95 (0-8234-1685-2). This suspenseful novel set in Russia alternates between the story of John, an amnesiac who is fleeing danger, and that of his sister and wheelchair-bound fiancee who are searching for him. (Rev: BCCB 5/02; BL 5/1/02; HB 7–8/02; HBG 10/02; SLJ 5/02; VOYA 6/02)

3787 Crossman, David A. *The Mystery of the Black Moriah* (5–8). Series: A Bean and Ab Mystery. 2002, Down East $16.95 (0-89272-536-2). The ever-curious Bean and Ab become caught up in a mystery adventure involving pirates, kidnappers, and a legendary ghost. (Rev: HBG 3/03; SLJ 12/02)

3788 Crossman, David A. *The Secret of the Missing Grave* (5–8). Series: A Bean and Ab Mystery. 1999, Down East $16.95 (0-89272-456-0). Two girls investigate a haunted house and become involved in a mystery concerning a missing treasure and stolen paintings in this fast-paced novel set in Maine. (Rev: HBG 3/00; SLJ 1/00)

3789 Dahl, Michael. *The Coral Coffin* (5–8). Series: A Finnegan Zwake Mystery. 2002, Simon & Schuster paper $4.50 (0-7434-1698-8). Still in search of his archaeologist parents, 13-year-old Finn finds himself on a remote island on the Great Barrier Reef with a pirate mystery he must solve within 24 hours. (Rev: SLJ 7/02)

3790 Dahl, Michael. *The Horizontal Man* (5–9). Series: A Finnegan Zwake Mystery. 1999, Pocket paper $4.99 (0-671-03269-0). When a rodent-eaten body is discovered in the basement, 12-year-old Finnegan and his mystery-writer uncle set out to solve the crime. (Rev: BL 3/15/00; SLJ 12/99)

3791 Davidson, Nicole. *Dying to Dance* (8–12). 1996, Avon paper $3.99 (0-380-78152-2). Carrie, a competitor on the ballroom-dance circuit, is suspected of murdering her archrival. (Rev: SLJ 7/96)

3792 DeFelice, Cynthia. *Death at Devil's Bridge* (6–10). 2000, Farrar $16.00 (0-374-31723-2). On Martha's Vineyard, 13-year-old Ben Daggett and his friend Jeff become a little too involved with an older boy who is dealing in drugs. (Rev: BCCB 9/00; BL 8/00; HBG 3/01; SLJ 9/00; VOYA 12/00)

3793 Delaney, Mark. *Of Heroes and Villains* (7–10). 1999, Peachtree paper $5.95 (1-56145-178-9). Using the world of comic books as a backdrop, this mystery features four teen sleuths known as the Misfits and the puzzle of a stolen film starring comic book hero Hyperman. (Rev: BL 7/99)

3794 Delaney, Mark. *The Protester's Song* (5–9). Series: Misfits, Inc. 2001, Peachtree paper $5.95 (1-56145-244-0). Four teens keep themselves busy investigating an incident that occurred during riots in Ohio in 1970 and, in a subplot, try to stop the new principal from removing books from the library. (Rev: SLJ 8/01)

3795 Delaney, Mark. *The Vanishing Chip* (5–8). Series: Misfits, Inc. 1998, Peachtree paper $5.95 (1-56145-176-2). Four teens who don't fit in at school investigate the disappearance of the world's most powerful computer chip. (Rev: BL 12/15/98; SLJ 2/99)

3796 Doyle, Brian. *Spud Sweetgrass* (5–8). 1996, Douglas & McIntyre $14.95 (0-88899-164-9). Spud and two friends solve the mystery of who is dumping grease in the Ottawa River. A sequel is *Spud in Winter* (1996). (Rev: BCCB 7–8/96; BL 6/1–15/96; SLJ 9/96)

3797 Duncan, Lois. *Daughters of Eve* (7–10). 1979, Dell paper $4.99 (0-440-91864-2). A group of girls comes under the evil influence of the faculty sponsor of their club.

3798 Duncan, Lois. *Don't Look Behind You* (7–12). 1990, Bantam paper $5.50 (0-440-20729-0). April and her family are on the run trying to escape from a hired hit man. (Rev: BL 5/15/89; SLJ 7/89; VOYA 8/89)

3799 Duncan, Lois. *Down a Dark Hall* (7–10). 1974, Little, Brown paper $5.50 (0-440-91805-7). From the moment of arrival, Kit feels uneasy at her new boarding school.

3800 Duncan, Lois. *I Know What You Did Last Summer* (7–10). 1990, Pocket Books paper $3.99 (0-671-73589-6). Four teenagers try to hide a hit-and-run accident in which they were involved.

3801 Duncan, Lois. *Killing Mr. Griffin* (7–10). 1978, Dell paper $5.50 (0-440-94515-1). A kidnapping plot involving a disliked English teacher leads to murder. (Rev: BL 10/15/88)

3802 Duncan, Lois. *The Third Eye* (7–10). 1984, Little, Brown $15.95 (0-316-19553-7); Dell paper $5.50 (0-440-98720-2). Karen learns that she has mental powers that enable her to locate missing children. (Rev: BL 7/87)

3803 Duncan, Lois. *The Twisted Window* (7–10). 1987, Dell paper $5.50 (0-440-20184-5). Tracy grows to regret the fact that she has helped a young man kidnap his 2-year-old half-sister. (Rev: BL 9/1/87; BR 1–2/88; SLJ 9/87; VOYA 11/87)

3804 Elmer, Robert. *Far from the Storm* (4–7). Series: Young Underground. 1995, Bethany paper $5.99 (0-55661-377-6). At the end of World War II, Danish twins Peter and Elise set out to find the culprit who set their uncle's boat on fire. (Rev: BL 2/15/96)

3805 Emerson, Kathy L. *The Mystery of the Missing Bagpipes* (5–7). 1991, Avon paper $2.95 (0-380-76138-6). Kim tries to find the real culprit when a young boy is wrongfully accused of stealing a set of ancient bagpipes and some precious daggers. (Rev: BL 9/15/91)

3806 Emerson, Scott. *The Case of the Cat with the Missing Ear: From the Notebooks of Edward R. Smithfield, D.V.M.* (5–7). 2003, Simon & Schuster LB $15.95 (0-689-85861-2). This canine takeoff of the Sherlock Holmes format features Yorkshire terrier Samuel Blackthorne and his sidekick and chronicler Dr. Edward Smithfield, who investigate

mysteries with humor and deductive prowess. (Rev: BCCB 10/02; BL 12/1/03; SLJ 3/04)

3807 Evarts, Hal G. *Jay-Jay and the Peking Monster* (7–9). 1984, Peter Smith $15.75 (0-8446-6166-X). Two teenagers discover the bones of a prehistoric man, and then the criminals move in.

3808 Falcone, L. M. *The Mysterious Mummer* (5–7). 2003, Kids Can $16.95 (1-55337-376-6). When Joey, 13, arrives in Newfoundland to spend Christmas with his aunt, he finds some very mysterious goings-on. (Rev: SLJ 10/03)

3809 Farley, Carol. *The Case of the Vanishing Villain* (5–6). Illus. 1986, Avon paper $2.95 (0-380-89959-0). A 10-year-old solves the mystery of an escaped convict's disappearance. Also use *Mystery of the Melted Diamonds* (1986); *The Case of the Lost Lookalike* (1988). (Rev: BL 9/15/86; SLJ 11/86)

3810 Feder, Harriet K. *Death on Sacred Ground* (6–10). Series: Vivi Hartman. 2001, Lerner $14.95 (0-8225-0741-2). Teen sleuth Vivi Hartman encounters a mystery at the funeral of an Orthodox Jewish girl who died on sacred Indian ground. (Rev: BCCB 3/01; BL 11/15/01; HBG 10/01; SLJ 3/01)

3811 Feder, Harriet K. *Mystery of the Kaifeng Scroll* (6–9). 1995, Lerner LB $14.95 (0-8225-0739-0). In this sequel to *Mystery in Miami Beach*, Vivi Hartman, 15, must use her wits and knowledge of the Torah to save her mother from Palestinian terrorists. (Rev: BL 6/1–15/95)

3812 Ferguson, Alane. *Overkill* (7–10). 1992, Bradbury LB $14.95 (0-02-734523-8); Avon paper $3.99 (0-380-72167-8). Lacey is seeing a therapist about nightmares in which she stabs her friend Celeste; when Celeste is found dead, Lacey is falsely arrested for the crime. (Rev: BL 1/1/93; SLJ 1/93)

3813 Ferguson, Alane. *Show Me the Evidence* (7–12). 1989, Avon paper $3.99 (0-380-70962-7). In this mystery story, a 17-year-old girl is fearful that her best friend might be involved in the mysterious deaths of several children. (Rev: BL 4/1/89; BR 1–2/90; SLJ 3/89; VOYA 6/89)

3814 Gee, Maurice. *The Fat Man* (8–10). 1997, Simon & Schuster $16.00 (0-689-81182-9). At first, this small New Zealand town welcomes back Herbert, a mysterious fat man who supposedly made good in America, but soon everyone becomes suspicious of his motives. (Rev: BL 12/15/97; BR 5–6/98; HBG 3/98; SLJ 11/97*; VOYA 12/97)

3815 Gee, Maurice. *The Fire-Raiser* (6–12). 1992, Houghton $16.00 (0-395-62428-2). A thriller set in New Zealand during World War I dramatizes the secret fury of a pyromaniac and relates it to the mob violence let loose in the community by jingoism and war. (Rev: BL 10/15/92*; SLJ 9/92)

3816 Gerson, Corrine. *My Grandfather the Spy* (5–7). 1990, Walker $14.95 (0-8027-6955-1). When a man arrives on the family farm in Vermont with a briefcase full of money, Danny suspects his grandfather is a spy. (Rev: BL 6/15/90; SLJ 8/90)

3817 Giff, Patricia Reilly. *Have You Seen Hyacinth Macaw?* (6–9). 1982, Dell paper $4.50 (0-440-43450-5). Two junior detectives sort out some confusing clues in their search for Hyacinth Macaw.

3818 Giles, Gail. *Dead Girls Don't Write Letters* (6–9). 2003, Millbrook $15.95 (0-7613-1727-9). Sunny, a 9th grader, is dealing with the aftermath of her 18-year-old sister Jazz's death in an apartment fire — until one day, a mysterious new Jazz appears. (Rev: BCCB 3/03; BL 3/15/03; HBG 10/03; SLJ 5/03; VOYA 6/03)

3819 Gordon, Lawrence. *Haunted High* (6–9). Series: Ghost Chronicles. 2000, Karmichael Pr. paper $11.95 (0-9653966-1-4). Eddie discovers he is receiving messages on his computer from long-dead high school students. (Rev: SLJ 7/00; VOYA 4/00)

3820 Green, Timothy. *Twilight Boy* (7–10). 1998, Northland LB $12.95 (0-873586-70-0); paper $6.95 (0-873586-40-9). Navajo folkways form the background of this gripping mystery about a boy who is haunted by the memory of his dead brother and an evil that is preying on his Navajo community. (Rev: BL 4/15/98; HBG 9/98; VOYA 8/98)

3821 Gutman, Dan. *Shoeless Joe and Me* (4–7). Series: Baseball Card Adventure. 2002, HarperCollins LB $16.89 (0-06-029254-7). Thirteen-year-old Joe travels back in time to remedy the 1919 Black Sox scandal and save Shoeless Joe's reputation. (Rev: BL 1/1–15/02; HBG 10/02; SLJ 3/02)

3822 Guy, Rosa. *The Disappearance* (7–10). 1979, Delacorte paper $4.99 (0-440-92064-7). A 16-year-old African American boy is accused of a kidnapping. Follow by *New Guys Around the Block* and *And I Heard a Bird Sing*.

3823 Hahn, Mary D. *The Dead Man in Indian Creek* (6–8). 1990, Clarion $15.00 (0-395-52397-4). On a harmless camping trip, Matt and friend Parker find a body floating in Indian Creek. (Rev: BL 2/15/90; SLJ 4/90)

3824 Hahn, Mary D. *Following the Mystery Man* (5–7). 1988, Avon paper $4.99 (0-380-70677-6). Madigan is certain that her grandmother's new boarder is none other than her missing father. (Rev: BL 3/15/88; HB 7–8/88; SLJ 4/88)

3825 Hall, Lynn. *A Killing Freeze* (6–10). 1990, Avon paper $2.95 (0-380-75491-6). A loner endangers her own life to find a murderer. (Rev: BL 8/88; BR 1–2/89; SLJ 9/88; VOYA 12/88)

3826 Hall, Lynn. *Ride a Dark Horse* (7–10). 1987, Avon paper $2.95 (0-380-75370-7). A teenage girl is fired from her job on a horse-breeding farm because she is getting too close to solving a mystery. (Rev: BL 9/15/87; BR 11–12/87; SLJ 12/87; VOYA 10/87)

3827 Hamilton, Virginia. *The House of Dies Drear* (6–9). Illus. 1968, Macmillan $18.95 (0-02-742500-2); paper $5.99 (0-02-043520-7). First-rate suspense as history professor Small and his young son Thomas investigate their rented house, formerly a station on the Underground Railroad, unlocking the secrets and dangers from attitudes dating back to the Civil War. (Rev: BL 10/15/87)

3828 Hamilton, Virginia. *The Mystery of Drear House* (5–7). 1987, Greenwillow $16.95 (0-688-04026-8); Scholastic paper $4.50 (0-590-95627-2). The story of Thomas Small and the threat to the treasure of Drear House. The final installment in the saga of this station on the Underground Railroad. (Rev: BCCB 5/87; BL 6/15/87; SLJ 6–7/87)

3829 Hayes, Daniel. *The Trouble with Lemons* (5–8). 1991, Random paper $5.99 (0-449-70416-5). Tyler, 14, has all kinds of problems — allergies, asthma, and nightmares — and then he finds a dead body. (Rev: BL 5/1/91; SLJ 6/91)

3830 Haynes, Betsy. *Deadly Deception* (7–10). 1994, Dell paper $3.99 (0-440-21947-7). A 17-year-old gets involved in the murder of a favorite school counselor. (Rev: BL 5/15/94; SLJ 6/94)

3831 Henderson, Aileen K. *The Monkey Thief* (5–7). 1997, Milkweed $15.95 (1-57131-612-4). While working with his uncle in the Costa Rican rain forest, Ron uncovers a plot to plunder ancient burial sites. (Rev: BL 11/1/97; HBG 3/98; SLJ 12/97)

3832 Heyes, Eileen. *O'Dwyer and Grady Starring in Tough Act to Follow* (4–7). Series: O'Dwyer and Grady. 2003, Simon & Schuster paper $4.99 (0-689-84920-6). Young actors Billy and Virginia stumble into a mystery while searching for props for a show in this action-packed story set in the 1930s. (Rev: BL 5/15/03; SLJ 7/03)

3833 Hill, William. *The Vampire Hunters* (7–12). 1998, Otter Creek $19.95 (1-890611-05-0); paper $12.95 (1-890611-02-6). Members of a gang called the Graveyard Armadillos are convinced that Marcus Chandler is a vampire, and 15-year-old Scooter Keyshaw is determined to find the truth. (Rev: BL 10/15/98; SLJ 2/99)

3834 Holm, Jennifer L. *The Creek* (6–8). 2003, HarperCollins $15.99 (0-06-000133-X). When local bad boy Caleb Devlin returns to town, he quickly gains 12-year-old Penny's fascinated attention, but his return coincides with a series of increasingly alarming events. (Rev: BCCB 7–8/03; BL 8/03; HBG 10/03; SLJ 7/03; VOYA 10/03)

3835 Holmes, Barbara Ware. *Following Fake Man* (5–8). 2001, Knopf $15.95 (0-375-81266-0). Lonely 12-year-old Homer makes a friend while on holiday in Maine, and the two boys uncover secrets about Homer's dead father. (Rev: BCCB 7–8/01; BL 6/1–15/01; HB 7–8/01; HBG 10/01; SLJ 5/01*)

3836 Honey, Elizabeth. *Remote Man* (6–8). 2002, Knopf LB $17.99 (0-375-91413-7). Young Ned, 13, is a loner whose high-tech savvy and interest in reptiles lead him to a key role in creating an international network that uncovers a ring of wildlife poachers. (Rev: BCCB 10/02; BL 10/15/02; HBG 10/03; SLJ 8/02)

3837 Hopper, Nancy J. *Ape Ears and Beaky* (4–7). 1987, Avon paper $2.50 (0-380-70270-3). Scott and Beaky solve the mystery of the robberies in a condominium.

3838 Horowitz, Anthony. *Point Blank* (6–10). Series: Alex Rider Adventure. 2002, Putnam $16.99 (0-399-23621-X). Alex, the young British spy, infiltrates an exclusive Swiss boarding school in this action-filled adventure. (Rev: BL 4/1/02; HBG 10/02; SLJ 3/02; VOYA 2/02)

3839 Horowitz, Anthony. *Skeleton Key* (6–9). Series: Alex Rider Adventure. 2003, Philomel $17.99 (0-399-23777-1). Alex confronts and confounds a former Russian commander who intends to resurrect the Soviet Union in this action-packed novel a la James Bond. (Rev: BL 5/15/03; HBG 10/03; SLJ 5/03; VOYA 6/03)

3840 Horowitz, Anthony. *Stormbreaker* (5–9). Series: Alex Rider Adventure. 2001, Philomel $16.99 (0-399-23620-1). Fourteen-year-old Alex becomes embroiled in dangerous undercover exploits when his MI6 uncle is murdered. (Rev: BCCB 9/01; BL 9/1/01; HBG 10/01; SLJ 6/01; VOYA 8/01)

3841 Howe, James. *Dew Drop Dead: A Sebastian Barth Mystery* (4–7). 1990, Macmillan $16.00 (0-689-31425-6). A group of boys discover a corpse, but by the time the police arrive it has disappeared. (Rev: BL 3/1/90; SLJ 4/90)

3842 Howe, James. *Stage Fright* (6–8). 1995, Simon & Schuster paper $4.99 (0-689-80338-9). Thirteen-year-old Sebastian Barth, the detective of *What Eric Knew*, tackles the problem of who is trying to kill a famous movie actress. (Rev: BL 5/1/86; VOYA 2/87)

3843 Hrdlitschka, Shelley. *Tangled Web* (6–12). 2000, Orca paper $6.95 (1-55143-178-5). Telepathic twins Alex and Tanner again tangle with their former kidnapper in this fast-paced sequel to *Disconnected* (1999). (Rev: BL 10/15/00; SLJ 10/00; VOYA 12/00)

3844 Irwin, Hadley. *The Original Freddie Ackerman* (5–7). 1992, Macmillan $15.00 (0-689-50562-0). Twelve-year-old Trevor is dismayed to find himself on a Maine isle with two unknown great-aunts, no television, no theaters, and no malls. (Rev: BCCB 9/92; BL 1/1/92; SLJ 8/92*)

3845 Jennings, Richard W. *Mystery in Mt. Mole* (6–9). 2003, Houghton $15.00 (0-618-28478-8). The assistant principal has disappeared but nobody seems to care much except 13-year-old Andy. (Rev: BL 9/15/03*; SLJ 12/03)

3846 Johnson, Rodney. *The Secret of Dead Man's Mine* (5–7). Series: Rinnah Two Feathers Mystery. 2001, Uglytown paper $12.00 (0-9663473-3-1). Rinnah Two Feathers and two friends set out to solve the mystery of a suspicious stranger and find themselves in danger. (Rev: SLJ 9/01)

3847 Johnston, Norma. *The Dragon's Eye* (7–10). 1990, Four Winds LB $14.95 (0-02-747701-0). The life of high school junior Jenny begins to unravel when nasty, cryptic messages start appearing at school. (Rev: BL 1/15/91; SLJ 12/90)

3848 Jorgensen, Christine T. *Death of a Dustbunny: A Stella the Stargazer Mystery* (8–12). 1998, Walker $22.95 (0-8027-3315-8). An uncomplicated mystery in which sleuth Stella the Stargazer, who writes a combination astrology and advice-to-the-lovelorn column for a local newspaper, investigates the disappearance of her friend Elena Ruiz, an employee of the Dustbunnies housekeeping and nanny agency. (Rev: VOYA 8/98)

3849 Karas, Phyllis. *For Lucky's Sake* (5–8). 1997, Avon paper $3.99 (0-380-78647-8). In this mystery with an animal rights theme, Benjy investigates a fire in which two greyhounds rescued from a research lab are killed. (Rev: BL 10/1/97)

3850 Karas, Phyllis. *The Hate Crime* (7–10). 1995, Avon paper $3.99 (0-380-78214-6). A docunovel/whodunit about a teen who scrawls the names of seven concentration camps on a Jewish temple. (Rev: BL 12/1/95; VOYA 2/96)

3851 Kehret, Peg. *Danger at the Fair* (5–8). 1995, Dutton $15.99 (0-525-65182-9); Puffin paper $5.99 (0-14-230222-8). Ellen learns from the fortune-teller at the fair that her brother Corey is in danger in this exciting tale of suspense. (Rev: BCCB 2/95; BL 12/1/94; SLJ 2/95)

3852 Kehret, Peg. *Deadly Stranger* (6–8). 1997, Troll paper $3.95 (0-8167-1308-1). Two 12-year-old girls are being stalked by a mentally deranged man. (Rev: BL 6/1/87)

3853 Kerr, M. E. *Fell* (8–12). 1987, HarperCollins paper $4.95 (0-06-447031-8). In a bizarre identity switch, a teenager from a middle-class background enters a posh prep school. Followed by *Fell Back* and *Fell Down*. (Rev: BL 6/1/87; SLJ 8/87; VOYA 10/87)

3854 Kerr, M. E. *Fell Down* (7–12). 1991, HarperCollins $15.00 (0-06-021763-4). Fell has dropped out of prep school but is haunted by the death of his best friend there, so he returns, to find kidnapping, murder, and obsession. (Rev: BL 9/15/91*; SLJ 10/91)

3855 Kerr, M. E. *What Became of Her* (7–10). 2000, HarperCollins $15.95 (0-06-028435-8). Sixteen-year-old E.C. Tobbit's life is forever changed when he meets eccentric Rosalind Slaymaster, her niece Julie, and her doll, Peale. (Rev: BL 7/00; HB 5–6/00; HBG 9/00; SLJ 7/00)

3856 Klise, Kate. *Trial by Jury Journal* (5–8). 2001, HarperCollins LB $16.89 (0-06-029541-4). When she is given the opportunity to serve as her state's first juvenile juror, 12-year-old Lily's sleuthing skills solve a murder mystery and save the day. (Rev: BCCB 4/01; BL 9/1/01; HB 5–6/01; HBG 10/01; SLJ 6/01)

3857 Konigsburg, E. L. *Father's Arcane Daughter* (7–9). 1976, Macmillan LB $15.00 (0-689-30524-9). When Caroline reappears after an absence of 17 years, everyone wonders if she might be an imposter in this complex suspense tale.

3858 Konigsburg, E. L. *Silent to the Bone* (5–9). 2000, Simon & Schuster $16.00 (0-689-83601-5). A mystery story filled with suspense about a baby who's been dropped and a 13-year-old suspect who has lost his ability to speak. (Rev: BL 8/00*; HB 11–12/00; HBG 3/01; SLJ 9/00; VOYA 12/00)

3859 Kotzwinkle, William. *Trouble in Bugland: A Collection of Inspector Mantis Mysteries* (6–8). 1996, Godine paper $14.95 (1-56792-070-5). An all-insect cast in a takeoff on Sherlock Holmes mysteries.

3860 Kuraoka, Hannah. *Missing!* (6–8). 1995, Avon paper $3.99 (0-380-77374-0). A mystery set in Seattle involving Kelly Donovan, a high school student; a teen mother who attends Kelly's school; and a demented child kidnapper. (Rev: BCCB 11/00; SLJ 1/96)

3861 Lachtman, Ofelia Dumas. *The Summer of El Pintor* (7–10). 2001, Arte Publico paper $9.95 (1-55885-327-8). Sixteen-year-old Monica's father loses his job and the two move from their wealthy neighborhood to the barrio house in which her dead mother grew up, where Monica searches for a missing neighbor and discovers the truth of her past. (Rev: BL 8/01; SLJ 7/01; VOYA 12/01)

3862 Lamensdorf, Len. *The Raging Dragon* (6–9). Series: Will to Conquer. 2002, Seascape $22.95 (0-9669741-7-4). William and Louise become embroiled in exciting events in 1960s Paris, including an effort to counter Algerian terrorists, in this sequel to *The Crouching Dragon* (1999). (Rev: BL 10/1/02; SLJ 10/02)

3863 Lawrence, Caroline. *The Pirates of Pompeii* (4–7). Series: Roman Mysteries. 2003, Millbrook $15.95 (0-7613-1584-5). Flavia and her friends investigate the disappearance of children after the eruption of Vesuvius in the 1st century B.C.E. (Rev: BL 5/15/03; HBG 10/03; SLJ 7/03)

3864 Lawrence, Caroline. *The Thieves of Ostia: A Roman Mystery* (4–7). Series: Roman Mysteries. 2002, Millbrook LB $22.90 (0-7613-2602-2). This fast-paced mystery set in early Rome finds a young sleuth named Flavia Gemina and her friends searching for an animal killer. (Rev: BL 3/15/02*; HBG 10/02; SLJ 5/02*)

3865 Lehr, Norma. *The Shimmering Ghost of Riversend* (5–7). 1991, Lerner LB $19.95 (0-8225-0732-3). An engaging mystery concerning an old family mansion in Gold Rush country where Kathy has gone to spend the summer with her aunt. (Rev: BL 10/1/91)

3866 L'Engle, Madeleine. *Dragon in the Waters* (7–9). 1982, Dell paper $5.50 (0-440-91719-0). On board an ocean liner, 13-year-old Simon encounters murder and a mystery surrounding a stolen portrait.

3867 L'Engle, Madeleine. *Troubling a Star* (7–10). 1994, Farrar $19.00 (0-374-37783-9). Vicki Austin, 16, travels to Antarctica and meets a Baltic prince looking for romance, and the two try to solve a mystery involving nuclear waste. (Rev: BL 8/94; SLJ 10/94; VOYA 12/94)

3868 Leonhardt, Alice. *Return of the Gypsy Witch* (5–7). 2003, Simon & Schuster paper $4.99 (0-689-85527-3). An exciting mystery featuring two detecting sisters and five very valuable comic books. (Rev: BL 5/1/03; SLJ 4/03)

3869 Levin, Betty. *Island Bound* (5–7). Illus. 1997, Greenwillow $15.00 (0-688-15217-1). Two teenagers uncover the truth behind a 150-year-old tragedy while they spend time on a tiny Maine island. (Rev: BL 7/97; HBG 3/98; SLJ 10/97)

3870 Levin, Betty. *Shadow-Catcher* (4–7). 2000, Greenwillow $15.95 (0-688-17862-6). In Maine during the 1890s, young Jonathan Capewell has the opportunity to act the detective in a local mystery and behave like the heroes in the dime novels he reads. (Rev: BL 5/15/00*; HB 7–8/00; HBG 10/00; SLJ 6/00)

3871 Levin, Betty. *Shoddy Cove* (5–7). 2003, Greenwillow $15.99 (0-06-052271-2). Clare, 12, is working at a living-history museum when she meets two strange children and must solve two mysteries from different centuries. (Rev: BL 7/03; HBG 10/03; SLJ 6/03; VOYA 6/03)

3872 Levitin, Sonia. *Evil Encounter* (8–10). 1996, Simon & Schuster $17.00 (0-689-80216-1). Michelle must find the killer when her mother is wrongfully accused of murdering the charismatic leader of a therapy group to which they belong. (Rev: BL 5/1/96; BR 1–2/97; SLJ 5/96; VOYA 6/96)

3873 Levitin, Sonia. *Incident at Loring Groves* (7–12). 1988, Fawcett paper $5.50 (vol. 1); $2.95 (vol. 2) (0-449-70347-9). High school students find the body of a murdered classmate and decide to remain silent about it. (Rev: BL 9/1/88; BR 11–12/88; SLJ 6/88; VOYA 12/88)

3874 Littke, Lael. *Lake of Secrets* (7–10). 2002, Holt $16.95 (0-8050-6730-2). Carlene experiences strong and puzzling feelings of deja vu when she and her mother go to the town where Carlene's younger brother died 18 years earlier, before Carlene's birth. (Rev: BCCB 4/02; BL 3/1/02; HB 5–6/02; HBG 10/02; SLJ 3/02; VOYA 6/02)

3875 Lucashenko, Melissa. *Killing Darcy* (8–10). 1998, Univ. of Queensland Pr. paper $13.95 (0-7022-3041-3). In this complex supernatural murder mystery set in New South Wales, 16-year-old Filomena uncovers a family murder, discovers a camera that can take pictures of the past, and is helped by a gay Aboriginal boy to solve the mystery. (Rev: SLJ 2/99)

3876 McGraw, Eloise. *Tangled Webb* (5–7). 1993, Macmillan $13.95 (0-689-50573-6). Twelve-year-old Juniper has the feeling that her new stepmother is hiding something from her past, and she sets out to find out what it is. (Rev: BCCB 6/93; BL 6/1–15/93)

3877 MacGregor, Rob. *Hawk Moon* (7–10). 1996, Simon & Schuster paper $16.00 (0-689-80171-8). Sixteen-year-old Will Lansa, having returned to Aspen, Colorado, to learn more about his Hopi heritage, finds himself at the center of an investigation of the murder of his girlfriend. (Rev: SLJ 11/96*; VOYA 2/97)

3878 MacPhail, Catherine. *Dark Waters* (7–10). 2003, Bloomsbury $15.95 (1-58234-846-4). This exciting story set in Scotland features Col McCann, who saves a boy from drowning only to realize that his own brother may have played a dangerous role in the mishap. (Rev: BCCB 3/03; BL 3/15/03; HBG 10/03; SLJ 6/03; VOYA 6/03)

3879 Marsden, John. *Winter* (7–10). 2002, Scholastic $16.95 (0-439-36849-9). Winter, a 16-year-old Australian girl who believes that her parents died together in an accident, returns to her family home to find puzzling secrets. (Rev: BCCB 11/02; HBG 3/03; SLJ 8/02)

3880 Martin, Les. *Humbug* (5–8). Series: X-Files. 1996, HarperCollins paper $3.95 (0-06-440627-X). Even for veteran FBI agents Fox Mulder and Dana Scully, the murder of "The Alligator Man" is bizarre. (Rev: SLJ 6/96)

3881 Martin, Terri. *A Family Trait* (5–7). 1999, Holiday $15.95 (0-8234-1467-1). In this fast-paced story, Iris, 11 years old and incurably curious, has a number of mysteries to solve while trying to finish a book report. (Rev: BL 10/1/99; HBG 3/00; SLJ 10/99)

3882 Mazzio, Joann. *The One Who Came Back* (7–10). 1992, Houghton $17.00 (0-395-59506-1). A New Mexico teen must prove he didn't kill his best friend. (Rev: BL 4/1/92; SLJ 5/92)

3883 Mitchell, Marianne. *Finding Zola* (5–8). 2003, Boyds Mills $16.95 (1-59078-070-1). A 13-year-old girl in a wheelchair investigates the disappearance of an elderly woman who has been staying with her. (Rev: BL 5/15/03; HBG 10/03; SLJ 2/03; VOYA 10/03)

3884 Mundis, Hester. *My Chimp Friday* (4–7). 2002, Simon & Schuster $16.00 (0-689-83837-9). Rachel and her family grow to love their new pet, a chimp named Friday, but when kidnappers try to steal Friday, Rachel realizes he is not an ordinary chimp. (Rev: BL 6/1–15/02; HBG 10/02; SLJ 6/02)

3885 Murphy, T. M. *The Secrets of Code Z* (4–8). Series: A Belltown Mystery. 2001, J. N. Townsend paper $9.95 (1-880158-33-7). Orville Jacques becomes embroiled in a fast-paced mystery involving CIA cover-ups, a death powder, and an evil Russian. (Rev: BL 5/15/01; SLJ 7/01)

3886 Murphy, T. M. *The Secrets of Cranberry Beach* (5–8). Series: A Belltown Mystery. 1996, Silver Burdett paper $4.95 (0-382-39303-1). After an encounter with the murderer that almost costs him his life, amateur detective 16-year-old Orville Jacques solves a baffling crime. (Rev: SLJ 1/97)

3887 Murray, Susan, and Robert Davies. *Mayhem on Maui* (6–8). Series: K. C. Flanagan, Girl Detective. 1999, Robert Davies Multimedia paper $5.99 (1-55207-022-0). While vacationing in Maui, K. C. Flanagan and her older brother investigate a series of mysterious fires that appear to be the work of the Japanese mafia. (Rev: SLJ 7/99)

3888 Murray, Susan, and Robert Davies. *Panic in Puerto Vallarta* (7–9). Series: K. C. Flanagan, Girl Detective. 1998, Robert Davies Multimedia paper $8.99 (1-55207-015-8). After witnessing a murder in Puerto Vallarta, young K. C. Flanagan finds that the killers are out to get her. (Rev: SLJ 12/98)

3889 Napoli, Donna Jo. *Three Days* (6–8). 2001, Dutton $15.99 (0-525-46790-4). A harrowing story full of advice on keeping safe in which 11-year-old Jackie is kidnapped on a trip to Italy after her father dies at the wheel of their car. (Rev: BCCB 11/01; BL 10/1/01; HB 9–10/01; HBG 3/02; SLJ 8/01*; VOYA 8/01)

3890 Naylor, Phyllis Reynolds. *Bernie Magruder and the Bats in the Belfry* (4–7). 2003, Simon & Schuster $16.95 (0-689-85066-2). Bernie is investigating a bat with a fatal bite; could it be connected to the fact that the bells in the belfry are annoyingly stuck on the same tune? (Rev: BL 1/1–15/03; HBG 10/03; SLJ 4/03)

3891 Newman, Robert. *The Case of the Baker Street Irregular: A Sherlock Holmes Story* (6–8). 1984, Macmillan paper $4.95 (0-689-70766-5). Andrew becomes a Baker Street urchin who occasionally helps Sherlock Holmes or Scotland Yard inspector Peter Wyatt solve crimes. Others in this series are *The Case of the Threatened King* and *The Case of the Vanishing Corpse.*

3892 Nickerson, Sara. *How to Disappear Completely and Never Be Found* (4–8). 2002, HarperCollins LB $15.89 (0-06-029772-7). Two youngsters with problems, 12-year-old Margaret and her friend Boyd, explore a deserted mansion and solve the mystery of the supernatural terrors it supposedly contains. (Rev: BCCB 5/02; BL 4/1/02; HB 7–8/02; HBG 10/02; SLJ 4/02)

3893 Nixon, Joan Lowery. *A Candidate for Murder* (6–12). 1991, Dell paper $4.99 (0-440-21212-X). While Cary's father enters the political limelight, his daughter becomes embroiled in a series of strange events. (Rev: BL 3/1/91)

3894 Nixon, Joan Lowery. *The Dark and Deadly Pool* (7–12). 1989, Bantam paper $4.99 (0-440-20348-1). Mary Elizabeth becomes aware of strange happenings at the health club where she works. (Rev: BL 11/1/87; BR 11–12/87; SLJ 2/88; VOYA 12/87)

3895 Nixon, Joan Lowery. *Ghost Town* (4–7). 2000, Delacorte $14.95 (0-385-32681-5). This collection of stories combines the author's flair for writing mysteries with an interest in the Wild West. (Rev: BL 9/1/00; HBG 3/01; SLJ 10/00)

3896 Nixon, Joan Lowery. *The Ghosts of Now* (7–10). 1984, Dell paper $4.99 (0-440-93115-0). Angie investigates a hit-and-run accident that has left her brother in a coma.

3897 Nixon, Joan Lowery. *The Island of Dangerous Dreams* (7–12). 1989, Dell paper $4.99 (0-440-20258-2). Seventeen-year-old Andrea helps in the investigation of the murder of a judge in the Bahamas. (Rev: VOYA 8/89)

3898 Nixon, Joan Lowery. *The Kidnapping of Christina Lattimore* (7–9). 1979, Dell paper $4.99 (0-440-94520-8). Christina faces rumors that she engineered her own kidnapping.

3899 Nixon, Joan Lowery. *Murdered, My Sweet* (6–9). 1997, Delacorte $15.95 (0-385-32245-3). The son of a millionaire is murdered and young Jenny and her mystery-writer mother try to solve the case. (Rev: BL 9/1/97; BR 1–2/98; HBG 3/98; SLJ 9/97; VOYA 2/98)

3900 Nixon, Joan Lowery. *The Name of the Game Was Murder* (6–8). 1994, Dell paper $4.99 (0-440-21916-7). Teenager Samantha must work with her uncle's houseguests to find a damning manuscript and uncover the murderer of its author. (Rev: BL 3/1/93)

3901 Nixon, Joan Lowery. *Nightmare* (6–10). 2003, Delacorte $15.95 (0-385-73026-8). A suspenseful mystery featuring 10th-grader Emily, who has suf-

fered a recurring nightmare since childhood and now finds herself facing a killer at her summer camp. (Rev: BL 10/15/03; SLJ 10/03; VOYA 10/03)

3902 Nixon, Joan Lowery. *The Other Side of Dark* (7–10). 1986, Dell paper $4.99 (0-440-96638-8). After waking from a four-year coma, Stacy is now the target of the man who wounded her and killed her mother. (Rev: BL 9/15/86; BR 3–4/87; SLJ 9/86; VOYA 12/86)

3903 Nixon, Joan Lowery. *Playing for Keeps* (6–10). 2001, Delacorte $15.95 (0-385-32759-5). While on a cruise in the Caribbean, 16-year-old Rose falls for a Cuban refugee and becomes embroiled in suspenseful intrigue. (Rev: BCCB 7–8/01; BL 5/1/01; HBG 10/02; VOYA 8/01)

3904 Nixon, Joan Lowery. *The Seance* (7–10). 1981, Dell paper $4.99 (0-440-97937-4). An innocent seance leads to a double murder in this fast-paced mystery.

3905 Nixon, Joan Lowery. *Search for the Shadowman* (5–8). 1996, Delacorte $15.95 (0-385-32203-8). Using computer research, Andy tries to clear the name of a long-dead relative accused of treachery. (Rev: BL 10/1/96; BR 11–12/96; SLJ 11/96; VOYA 12/96)

3906 Nixon, Joan Lowery. *Shadowmaker* (7–9). 1995, Dell paper $4.99 (0-440-21942-6). When Katie's mother, an investigative journalist, probes evidence of toxic-waste dumping, Katie discovers that events at her school are related. (Rev: BL 3/1/94; SLJ 5/94; VOYA 8/94)

3907 Nixon, Joan Lowery. *The Specter* (7–10). 1993, Dell paper $4.99 (0-440-97740-1). Seventeen-year-old Dina protects a child who believes she is going to be murdered.

3908 Nixon, Joan Lowery. *Spirit Seeker* (6–9). 1995, Delacorte paper $15.95 (0-385-32062-0). Holly Campbell is pitted against her police detective father in a race to exonerate her boyfriend of a charge of double murder. (Rev: BL 9/15/95; SLJ 9/95; VOYA 2/96)

3909 Nixon, Joan Lowery. *The Trap* (5–8). 2002, Delacorte LB $17.99 (0-385-90063-5). A gripping mystery in which 16-year-old Julie investigates deaths and missing jewelry, and faces danger herself. (Rev: BL 9/15/02; HBG 3/03; SLJ 9/02; VOYA 2/03)

3910 Nixon, Joan Lowery. *The Weekend Was Murder!* (6–10). 1992, Dell paper $4.99 (0-440-21901-9). A teen sleuth and her boyfriend attend a murder mystery enactment weekend and discover a real murder. (Rev: BL 2/15/92; SLJ 3/92)

3911 Nixon, Joan Lowery. *Who Are You?* (6–10). 1999, Bantam Doubleday Dell $15.95 (0-385-32566-5); Bantam paper $5.95 (0-440-22757-7).

Teenager Kristi Evans sets out to solve the mystery of a murdered art collector and find out why he had been keeping a file on her. (Rev: BL 4/15/99; HBG 10/99; SLJ 6/99; VOYA 10/99)

3912 Pascal, Francine. *Twisted* (7–10). Series: Fearless. 2000, Pocket paper $5.99 (0-671-03944-X). Fearless Gaia, alone after her mother's death and her father's disappearance, finds she is being stalked in this fourth book in the series. (Rev: BL 4/1/00)

3913 Patneaude, David. *Someone Was Watching* (6–9). 1993, Albert Whitman LB $14.95 (0-8075-7531-3). Chris and his friend disobey parental orders and embark on a cross-country chase of possible kidnappers. (Rev: BL 7/93; SLJ 7/93)

3914 Peck, Richard. *Through a Brief Darkness* (7–9). 1997, Penguin paper $3.99 (0-14-038557-6). Karen must discover the truth about her father and hopes to find out when she visits relatives in England.

3915 Peretti, Frank. *Hangman's Curse* (6–8). Series: The Veritas Project. 2001, Tommy Nelson $14.99 (0-8499-7616-2). Twins Elisha and Elijah, who belong to a secret government investigative team with an evangelical foundation, attempt to solve the mystery madness that is taking over a high school in this suspenseful novel. (Rev: SLJ 7/01)

3916 Petersen, P. J. *Liars* (6–9). 1992, Simon & Schuster $15.00 (0-671-75035-6). When Sam, 14, discovers that he can tell when someone is lying, his ability makes him suspicious of almost everyone, even his father. (Rev: BL 6/1/92; SLJ 4/92*)

3917 Pike, Christopher. *Gimme a Kiss* (7–12). 1991, Pocket Books paper $4.50 (0-671-63682-5). A girl fakes her own death in a wild plot to get revenge. (Rev: BL 10/15/88; VOYA 4/89)

3918 Pike, Christopher. *Last Act* (7–10). 1991, Pocket Books paper $3.99 (0-671-73683-3). The blanks in Melanie's stage pistol turn out to be real. Is she really guilty of murder? (Rev: BL 6/15/88; SLJ 11/88; VOYA 8/88)

3919 Pike, Christopher. *Slumber Party* (7–10). 1985, Scholastic paper $3.50 (0-590-43014-9). Six teenage girls stranded in a winter vacation home experience mysterious occurrences that bring terror into their lives. (Rev: SLJ 12/86)

3920 Plum-Ucci, Carol. *The Body of Christopher Creed* (8–12). 2000, Harcourt $17.00 (0-15-202388-7). Torey and his friends are implicated in the disappearance of his classmate Chris, causing Torey to examine his life while trying to find Chris. (Rev: HBG 9/00; SLJ 7/00)

3921 Plum-Ucci, Carol. *The She* (8–12). 2003, Harcourt $17.00 (0-15-216819-2). Now a teenager, Evan, who lost his parents to an accident at sea when he was six, decides to investigate further. (Rev: BL 9/15/03*; SLJ 10/03)

3922 Priestley, Chris. *Death and the Arrow* (6–10). 2003, Knopf $15.95 (0-375-82466-9). In this historical mystery set in 1715 London, 15-year-old Tom Marlowe and Dr. Harker investigate a murder that has international implications. (Rev: BCCB 7–8/03; HBG 10/03; SLJ 7/03; VOYA 10/03)

3923 Pullman, Philip. *Count Karlstein* (6–9). 1998, Random $18.99 (0-679-99255-3). Fun and suspense mingle in this melodrama about efforts to prevent wicked Count Karlstein from sacrificing his young nieces to the Demon Huntsman. (Rev: BCCB 10/98; BL 8/98; HB 9–10/98; HBG 3/99; SLJ 9/98)

3924 Pullman, Philip, ed. *Detective Stories* (7–12). Illus. 1998, Larousse Kingfisher Chambers $14.95 (0-7534-5157-3); paper $6.95 (0-7534-5146-8). A collection of mystery and detective stories by such authors as Agatha Christie, Ellery Queen, Conan Doyle, Damon Runyan, and Dorothy Sayers. (Rev: BL 5/15/98; SLJ 9/98)

3925 Qualey, Marsha. *Thin Ice* (7–12). 1997, Delacorte $14.95 (0-385-32298-4). Arden Munro's brother appears to have been drowned after a snowmobile accident but no body has been found, and the girl believes he has simply escaped his dull life by running away. (Rev: BL 11/1/97; HBG 3/98; SLJ 11/97; VOYA 10/97)

3926 Raskin, Ellen. *The Westing Game* (6–9). 1978, Dutton $15.99 (0-525-42320-6); Avon paper $3.50 (0-380-67991-4). Sixteen possible heirs try to decipher an enigmatic will. Newbery Medal, 1979.

3927 Reaver, Chap. *A Little Bit Dead* (8–12). 1992, Delacorte $15.00 (0-385-30801-9); Dell paper $3.99 (0-440-21910-8). When Reece saves an Indian boy from lynching by U.S. marshals, lawmen claim that Reece murdered one of the marshals and he must clear himself. (Rev: BL 9/1/92; SLJ 9/92)

3928 Roberts, Willo Davis. *The Absolutely True Story: My Trip to Yellowstone Park with the Terrible Rupes (No Names Have Been Changed to Protect the Guilty) by Lewis Q. Dodge* (4–7). 1994, Atheneum $15.00 (0-689-31939-8). A humorous mystery about a trip to Yellowstone Park by Lewis and sister Alison with the strange Rupes family. (Rev: BCCB 2/95; BL 1/15/95; SLJ 3/95)

3929 Roberts, Willo Davis. *Baby-Sitting Is a Dangerous Job* (5–7). 1987, Fawcett paper $6.50 (0-449-70177-8). Darcy tries to cope with three bratty children, but a kidnapping puts her and her charges in the hands of three dangerous men. (Rev: BCCB 3/85; BL 5/1/85; SLJ 5/85)

3930 Roberts, Willo Davis. *Caught!* (4–7). 1994, Atheneum $16.00 (0-689-31903-7). Vickie and her younger sister run away to join their father in California, where they confront an intriguing mystery. (Rev: BL 4/1/94; SLJ 5/94)

3931 Roberts, Willo Davis. *Hostage* (4–7). Illus. 2000, Simon & Schuster $16.00 (0-689-81669-3).

When she returns home unexpectedly from school, Kaci is taken hostage, along with a snoopy neighbor, by a gang of thieves. (Rev: BCCB 2/00; BL 2/1/00; HBG 3/01; SLJ 2/00; VOYA 6/00)

3932 Roberts, Willo Davis. *The Kidnappers* (4–7). 1998, Simon & Schuster $15.00 (0-689-81394-5). Joel Bishop, a private-school student, can't get anyone to believe him when he witnesses a kidnapping. (Rev: BCCB 3/98; BL 2/1/98; HBG 10/98; SLJ 3/98)

3933 Roberts, Willo Davis. *Nightmare* (7–10). 1989, Macmillan $16.00 (0-689-31551-1). After a series of unusual occurrences, 17-year-old Nick finds he is being followed. (Rev: BL 9/15/89; BR 3–4/90; SLJ 9/89; VOYA 12/89)

3934 Roberts, Willo Davis. *Pawns* (5–8). 1998, Simon & Schuster $16.00 (0-689-81668-5). Pregnant Dori claims to be the wife of Mamie's dead son, but Teddi, whom Mamie has raised, thinks that Dori is lying and sets out to prove that she is right. (Rev: BL 11/15/98; BR 5–6/99; HBG 3/99; SLJ 11/98; VOYA 4/99)

3935 Roberts, Willo Davis. *Rebel* (6–8). 2003, Simon & Schuster $15.95 (0-689-85073-5). When they accidentally videotape a crime, 14-year-old Rebel (whose real name is Amanda Jane) and her friend Moses inadvisedly decide to investigate on their own. (Rev: SLJ 8/03)

3936 Roberts, Willo Davis. *Scared Stiff* (4–7). 1991, Macmillan $16.00 (0-689-31692-5). Two brothers have adventures in an abandoned amusement park. (Rev: BCCB 2/91; BL 2/15/91)

3937 Roberts, Willo Davis. *Twisted Summer* (6–8). 1996, Simon & Schuster $16.00 (0-689-80459-8). In this mystery set in rural Michigan, Cici helps 17-year-old Jake to clear his brother of a murder charge. (Rev: BL 3/15/96; BR 1–2/97; SLJ 4/96; VOYA 6/96)

3938 Roberts, Willo Davis. *Undercurrents* (7–10). 2002, Simon & Schuster $16.00 (0-689-81671-5). Fourteen-year-old Nikki is troubled when her father remarries only months after her mother's death and his new wife seems to be hiding facts about her unhappy past. (Rev: BCCB 4/02; BL 2/15/02; HBG 10/02; SLJ 2/02; VOYA 2/02)

3939 Roberts, Willo Davis. *The View from the Cherry Tree* (7–9). 1994, Simon & Schuster paper $4.99 (0-689-71784-9). A boy who witnesses a murder becomes targeted as the next victim.

3940 Ross, Ramon R. *Harper and Moon* (6–8). 1993, Atheneum $15.00 (0-689-31803-0). Set in 1942, the story of Harper and Moon deals with child abuse, animal abuse, suspected murder, and a suicide attempt. (Rev: BL 5/15/93; SLJ 9/93*)

3941 Rushford, Patricia H. *Abandoned* (6–9). Series: Jennie McGrady Mystery. 1999, Bethany House

paper $4.99 (0-7642-2120-5). In this twelfth Jennie McGrady mystery, teen detective Jennie is involved in murders of pro-life advocates while also trying to help a girl who has recently learned she was adopted after being abandoned in a dumpster. (Rev: BL 7/99)

3942 Rushford, Patricia H. *Betrayed* (6–10). Series: Jennie McGrady Mystery. 1996, Bethany House paper $4.99 (1-55661-560-4). Jennie encounters a long list of suspects when she tries to find the murderer of her uncle on a dude ranch in Montana. (Rev: BL 6/1–15/96; SLJ 6/96; VOYA 12/96)

3943 Rushford, Patricia H. *Dying to Win* (6–10). Series: Jennie McGrady Mystery. 1995, Bethany House paper $4.99 (1-55661-559-0). A suspenseful Jennie McGrady mystery about the disappearance of a rebellious schoolchum known as the "Rainbow Girl." (Rev: BL 1/1–15/96; SLJ 2/96; VOYA 6/96)

3944 Rushford, Patricia H. *Without a Trace: Nick Is Missing and Now They Are After Her . . .* (6–9). Series: Jennie McGrady Mystery. 1995, Bethany House paper $4.99 (1-55661-558-2). In the fifth book in the series, Jennie practices her sleuthing skills when her young brother and one of his friends disappear. (Rev: BL 9/1/95; SLJ 9/95; VOYA 2/96)

3945 Ryan, Mary E. *Alias* (6–10). 1997, Simon & Schuster $16.00 (0-689-80789-9); paper $4.99 (0-689-82264-2). Teenager Toby discovers that his mother's constant moves and change of identity are because she is wanted by the FBI for terrorist activities during the Vietnam War. (Rev: BL 4/15/97; BR 11–12/97; SLJ 7/97*; VOYA 8/97)

3946 Sedgwick, Marcus. *Witch Hill* (5–7). 2001, Delacorte $15.95 (0-385-32802-8). Jamie is haunted by dreams of a witch and by memories of a deadly fire in this suspense novel that includes a look at a British town's history. (Rev: BCCB 10/01; BL 10/1/01; HBG 3/02; SLJ 9/01)

3947 Seidler, Tor. *Brainboy and the Deathmaster* (4–7). 2003, HarperCollins $16.99 (0-06-029181-8). Recently orphaned in a fire, Darryl, a 12-year-old video game expert, finds himself in a shelter run by a man who plans to exploit the children's technological knowhow. (Rev: BL 9/15/03; SLJ 10/03; VOYA 10/03)

3948 Selznick, Brian. *The Boy of a Thousand Faces* (4–7). Illus. 2000, HarperCollins $14.95 (0-06-026265-6). Ten-year-old Alonzo King has a fixation on horror movies and makeup disguises, both of which help him when the The Beast comes to town. (Rev: BL 9/15/00; HBG 3/01; SLJ 9/00)

3949 Shaw, Diana. *Lessons in Fear* (6–9). 1987, Little, Brown $12.95 (0-316-78341-2). An unpopular teacher has a series of mysterious accidents and one of her students, Carter Colborn, decides she must investigate them. (Rev: BL 4/15/88; BR 9–10/87; SLJ 10/87)

3950 Singer, Nicky. *Feather Boy* (6–10). 2002, Delacorte $15.95 (0-385-72980-4). Robert, a timid and unpopular 12-year-old, spends a scary night in an abandoned house and makes some discoveries about himself. (Rev: BCCB 4/02; BL 5/1/02; HBG 3/03; SLJ 4/02)

3951 Skurzynski, Gloria, and Alane Ferguson. *Buried Alive* (4–7). Series: Mysteries in Our National Parks. 2003, National Geographic $15.95 (0-7922-6966-7); paper $5.95 (0-7922-6968-3). A hit man and an avalanche are only two of the challenges Jack and Ashley face while on vacation with their parents in Denali National Park. (Rev: HBG 10/03; SLJ 12/03)

3952 Skurzynski, Gloria, and Alane Ferguson. *Deadly Waters* (4–7). Illus. Series: Mysteries in Our National Parks. 1999, National Geographic $15.95 (0-7922-7037-1). The Landon kids — Jack, Ashley, and foster brother, Bridger — travel to the Florida Everglades where their parents are investigating the mysterious deaths of some manatees. (Rev: BL 10/15/99; HBG 3/00; SLJ 10/99)

3953 Skurzynski, Gloria, and Alane Ferguson. *The Hunted* (5–8). Illus. Series: Mysteries in Our National Parks. 2000, National Geographic $15.95 (0-7922-7053-3). The Landon family sets out to discover why young grizzly bears are disappearing from Glacier National Park. (Rev: BL 6/1–15/00; HBG 10/00; SLJ 8/00)

3954 Skurzynski, Gloria, and Alane Ferguson. *Wolf Stalker* (5–8). Series: Mysteries in Our National Parks. 1997, National Geographic $15.00 (0-7922-7034-7). Three youngsters solve the mystery of who is killing the wolves of Yellowstone Park. (Rev: BR 3–4/98; HBG 3/98; SLJ 1/98)

3955 Smith, Roland. *The Last Lobo* (5–9). 1999, Hyperion LB $16.49 (0-7868-2378-X). When Jake returns to his Hopi reservation in northern Arizona, he discovers that the tribe thinks that a Mexican wolf-lobo is killing their livestock. (Rev: BL 12/1/99; HBG 3/00; SLJ 11/99)

3956 Snyder, Zilpha Keatley. *Spyhole Secrets* (4–7). 2001, Delacorte $15.95 (0-385-32764-1). When Hallie and her mother move to a new town after her father's death, Hallie finds herself preoccupied with the life of a mysterious neighboring family. (Rev: BCCB 10/01; BL 5/1/01; HBG 10/01; SLJ 6/01)

3957 Spirn, Michele. *The Bridges in London: Going to London* (5–7). Series: Going To. 2000, Four Corners paper $7.95 (1-893577-00-7). When two sisters fly to London with their parents, they become involved in a mystery when they find a suitcase full of knives. (Rev: SLJ 3/00)

3958 Steiber, Ellen. *Squeeze* (7–9). Series: The X-Files. 1996, HarperCollins paper $4.50 (0-06-440621-0). In this novelization of a TV screenplay, FBI agents Dana Scully and Fox Mulder investigate three murders that took place in rooms locked from the inside and find a 10-inch-long fingerprint. Also use *Shapes* (1996). (Rev: VOYA 4/97)

3959 Steiner, Barbara. *Dreamstalker* (8–12). 1992, Avon paper $3.50 (0-380-76611-6). A girl wonders if she's psychic when her terrifying nightmares start coming true. (Rev: BL 3/15/92)

3960 Steiner, Barbara. *Spring Break* (7–10). 1996, Scholastic paper $3.99 (0-590-54419-5). Five high schoolers rent a haunted house where they contend with odd appearances and disappearances, arson, and a skeleton. (Rev: SLJ 12/96)

3961 Stengel, Joyce A. *Mystery of the Island Jewels* (5–8). 2002, Simon & Schuster paper $4.99 (0-689-85049-2). On a cruise to Martinique with her father and new stepfamily, 14-year-old Cassie and new friend Charles uncover a mystery. (Rev: SLJ 6/02)

3962 Sternberg, Libby. *Uncovering Sadie's Secrets: A Bianca Balducci Mystery* (6–9). Series: Bianca Balducci Mystery. 2003, Bancroft $16.95 (1-890862-23-1). Bianca Balducci is a sophomore in high school with all of the everyday teen anxieties as well as an interest in the mysterious circumstances surrounding her new friend, Sadie. (Rev: BL 1/1–15/03; SLJ 3/03; VOYA 4/03)

3963 Stevenson, James. *The Bones in the Cliff* (4–7). 1995, Greenwillow $15.99 (0-688-13745-8). Pete is sure that a hit man is stalking his father at their home on Cutlass Island. (Rev: BCCB 6/95; BL 5/1/95*; HB 7–8/95; SLJ 4/95)

3964 Stevenson, James. *The Unprotected Witness* (4–7). 1997, Greenwillow $15.00 (0-688-15133-7). In this sequel to *The Bones in the Cliff*, Pete and his friend Rootie try to unravel the mystery of where a treasure is buried by seeking cludes in a letter from Pete's dead father. (Rev: BL 10/1/97*; HB 11–12/97; HBG 3/98; SLJ 9/97)

3965 Stine, R. L. *The Overnight* (7–10). 1991, Pocket Books paper $3.99 (0-671-74650-2). While on an overnight camping trip, one of six campers accidentally kills a stranger she meets in the woods. Also use *The New Girl* (1991). (Rev: BL 12/15/89)

3966 Stine, R. L. *The Wrong Number* (5–9). 1990, Pocket Books paper $4.99 (0-671-69411-1). While making a crank telephone call, a teenager hears a murder being committed. (Rev: SLJ 6/90)

3967 Sukach, Jim. *Clever Quicksolve Whodunit Puzzles* (4–7). Series: Mini-Mysteries for You to Solve. 1999, Sterling $14.95 (0-8069-6569-X). Thirty-five mini-mysteries are presented with answers appended. (Rev: SLJ 1/00)

3968 Sumner, M. C. *Night Terrors* (7–10). 1997, Pocket Books paper $3.99 (0-671-00241-4). When her father disappears from his top-secret research facility and her friend begins having terrifying nightmares, Kathleen decides to investigate. (Rev: SLJ 8/97)

3969 Sykes, Shelley. *For Mike* (7–10). 1998, Delacorte $15.95 (0-385-32337-9). Mystery, suspense, and romance are combined in this novel in which Jeff and a girlfriend try to solve the mystery of the disappearance of Jeff's best friend, Mike. (Rev: BL 4/1/98; BR 9–10/98; HBG 9/98; SLJ 5/98; VOYA 4/98)

3970 Talbert, Marc. *Small Change* (5–9). 2000, DK paper $16.95 (0-7894-2531-9). A suspenseful novel set in Mexico and involving two kidnapped boys, one Mexican and the other American. (Rev: BCCB 6/00; BL 4/1/00; HBG 10/00; SLJ 6/00; VOYA 6/00)

3971 Taylor, Theodore. *Lord of the Kill* (6–10). 2002, Scholastic $16.95 (0-439-33725-9). Ben Jepson, 16, is involved in a murder mystery in which the suspects include big game hunters, an organized crime ring, and other groups who dislike the animal-rights activities of Ben's family. (Rev: BCCB 1/03; BL 1/1–15/03; HBG 3/03; SLJ 1/03; VOYA 4/03)

3972 Thesman, Jean. *Rachel Chance* (6–9). 1990, Houghton $16.00 (0-395-50934-3). Rachel's young brother has been kidnapped, but no one seems to be taking any action. (Rev: BL 5/1/90; SLJ 4/90)

3973 Twain, Mark. *The Stolen White Elephant* (4–8). Illus. 1882, Ayer $19.95 (0-8369-3486-5). The tale of the elephant's guardian who naively is impressed by a corrupt police detective. (Rev: BL 5/1/88; SLJ 2/88)

3974 Vance, Susanna. *Deep* (7–10). 2003, Delacorte $15.95 (0-385-73057-8). Two girls from very different backgrounds confront a psychopathic kidnapper in a taut story of suspense. (Rev: BL 4/15/03; HB 5–6/03; HBG 10/03; SLJ 6/03)

3975 Van Draanen, Wendelin. *Sammy Keyes and the Art of Deception* (5–8). Series: Sammy Keyes. 2003, Knopf $15.95 (0-375-81176-1). Sammy (with some help from Grams) solves a mystery involving an art thief. (Rev: BL 2/1/03; HBG 10/03; SLJ 3/03; VOYA 8/03)

3976 Van Draanen, Wendelin. *Sammy Keyes and the Curse of Moustache Mary* (6–9). Series: Sammy Keyes. 2000, Knopf $14.95 (0-375-80265-7). Sammy and her friends become involved in a feud between two families that dates back to pioneer days but has deadly modern-day repercussions. (Rev: BL 9/15/00; HBG 9/00; SLJ 8/00)

3977 Van Draanen, Wendelin. *Sammy Keyes and the Hollywood Mummy* (6–9). Series: Sammy Keyes. 2001, Knopf $14.95 (0-375-80266-5). Sammy and Marissa travel to Hollywood to reconnect with Sammy's mother and, while there, investigate a murder and confront unpleasant secrets. (Rev: BL 3/1/01; HB 5–6/01; HBG 10/01; SLJ 2/01)

3978 Van Draanen, Wendelin. *Sammy Keyes and the Runaway Elf* (5–8). Series: Sammy Keyes. 1999, Knopf LB $17.99 (0-679-98854-8). Young Sammy Keyes, a 7th-grade sleuth, is on the trail of the dog-nappers who snatched Marique, the famous calendar cover dog. (Rev: BL 9/1/99; HBG 3/00; SLJ 9/99)

3979 Van Draanen, Wendelin. *Sammy Keyes and the Search for Snake Eyes* (6–9). Series: Sammy Keyes. 2002, Knopf $15.95 (0-375-81175-3). A young mother abandons her baby in a shopping bag, and 7th-grader Sammy sets out to find her in this mystery story full of realistic humor. (Rev: BCCB 9/02; BL 5/1/02; HB 7–8/02; HBG 10/02; SLJ 4/02; VOYA 8/02)

3980 Van Draanen, Wendelin. *Sammy Keyes and the Sisters of Mercy* (5–8). Series: Sammy Keyes. 1999, Knopf LB $17.99 (0-679-98852-1). Wise-cracking 7th-grader Sammy Keyes tackles another mystery when a treasured papal cross is stolen and she notices a mysterious girl at the church's soup kitchen. (Rev: BL 4/1/99; HBG 9/99; SLJ 7/99; VOYA 4/00)

3981 Van Draanen, Wendelin. *Sammy Keyes and the Skeleton Man* (5–8). 1998, Random LB $16.99 (0-679-98850-5); Knopf paper $4.99 (0-375-80054-9). Sammy, the youthful sleuth, is challenged when she tries to solve the mystery of a man dressed in a skeleton costume. (Rev: BL 9/1/98; BR 11–12/98; HBG 3/99; SLJ 9/98)

3982 Voigt, Cynthia. *The Callender Papers* (5–8). 1983, Fawcett paper $4.50 (0-449-70184-0). Jean takes a summer job in the Berkshire hills of Massachusetts and finds adventure and mystery.

3983 Voigt, Cynthia. *The Vandemark Mummy* (6–9). 1991, Atheneum $18.95 (0-689-31476-0). This story involves a break-in at a museum of Egyptian antiquities and two teenage siblings who attempt to solve the mystery. (Rev: BL 9/1/91; SLJ 9/91)

3984 Wallace, Barbara Brooks. *Ghosts in the Gallery* (5–7). 2000, Simon & Schuster $16.00 (0-689-83175-7). Orphaned 11-year-old Jenny is sent to live with her wealthy grandfather in England and must work like a servant in a mansion where she is sure someone wants to kill her. (Rev: BCCB 7–8/00; BL 4/1/00; HB 7–8/00; HBG 10/00; SLJ 7/00)

3985 Wallens, Scott. *Shattered: Week 1* (6–12). Series: Sevens Series. 2002, Puffin paper $1.77 (0-14-230098-5). This first installment in a new series of suspense introduces seven teens who over the period of seven weeks will confront the terrible experiences of their pasts. (Rev: SLJ 11/02)

3986 Weir, Joan. *The Mysterious Visitor* (5–7). Series: Lion and Bobbi. 2002, Raincoast paper $6.99 (1-55192-404-4). Two Canadian youngsters, Lion and sister Bobbi, try to solve the mystery of strange events occurring on a friend's land. (Rev: BL 5/1/02)

3987 Werlin, Nancy. *Black Mirror* (7–12). 2001, Dial $16.99 (0-8037-2605-8). Lonely Frances, 16, struggles with her Jewish-Japanese heritage and with her guilt and puzzlement over her brother's suicide in this intriguing and suspenseful novel set in a private boarding school. (Rev: BCCB 10/01; BL 9/15/01; HB 9–10/01; HBG 3/02; SLJ 9/01*; VOYA 10/01)

3988 Werlin, Nancy. *The Killer's Cousin* (7–12). 1998, Bantam $15.95 (0-385-32560-6). A tautly plotted thriller about a boy who tries to escape the guilt related to the accidental death of his girlfriend by moving in with relatives, but instead uncovers some horrifying family secrets. (Rev: BL 9/1/98; BR 5–6/99; HB 1–2/99; HBG 3/99; SLJ 11/98; VOYA 10/98)

3989 Werlin, Nancy. *Locked Inside* (7–10). 2000, Delacorte $15.95 (0-385-32700-5). In this thriller, teenager Marnie is kidnapped and held prisoner by a demented teacher who thinks she is Marnie's half-sister. (Rev: BL 12/1/99; HBG 9/00; SLJ 3/00; VOYA 4/00)

3990 West, Tracy. *The Butterflies of Freedom* (6–9). 1988, Crosswinds paper $2.25 (0-373-98023-X). An easily read mystery involving a missing deed to valuable property. (Rev: VOYA 8/88)

3991 Wilson, Eric. *Code Red at the Supermall* (6–8). Series: A Tom and Liz Austen Mystery. 2000, Orca paper $4.99 (1-55143-172-6). The intrepid Tom and Liz Austen investigate criminal activities at the Edmonton supermall. Also recommended in this series is *Disneyland Hostage* (2000). (Rev: SLJ 6/00)

3992 Wilson, Eric. *Murder on the Canadian: A Tom Austen Mystery* (4–8). 2000, Orca paper $4.99 (1-55143-151-3). A fast-moving mystery starring an intrepid hero who is also featured in *Vancouver Nightmare: A Tom Austen Mystery* (2000). (Rev: SLJ 1/01)

3993 Woodson, Marion. *My Brother's Keeper* (5–7). 2002, Raincoast paper $6.95 (1-55192-488-9). On Vancouver Island, 13-year-old Sarah believes she is being haunted by a cult leader who founded a colony there in the 1930s. (Rev: BL 5/1/02; VOYA 8/02)

3994 Wright, Betty R. *The Dollhouse Murders* (4–7). 1983, Holiday $16.95 (0-8234-0497-8). Dolls in a dollhouse come to life in this mystery about long-ago murders.

3995 Wynne-Jones, Tim. *The Boy in the Burning House* (7–12). 2001, Farrar $16.00 (0-374-30930-2). Disturbed Ruth Rose and 14-year-old Jim investigate the mystery of his father's disappearance — was he killed by Ruth Rose's pastor stepfather?

(Rev: BCCB 11/01; BL 9/1/01; HB 11–12/01; HBG 3/02; SLJ 10/01; VOYA 10/01)

3996 Yep, Laurence. *The Case of the Firecrackers* (4–7). 1999, HarperCollins LB $15.89 (0-06-024452-6). In this Chinatown mystery, Tiger Lil and her great-niece Lily are on the trail of the murderer who killed the star of the television show in which they were extras. (Rev: BL 9/15/99; HBG 3/00; SLJ 9/99)

3997 Yep, Laurence. *The Case of the Goblin Pearls* (5–7). 1997, HarperCollins LB $15.89 (0-06-024446-1). Lily and her Aunt Tiger Lil, a former actress, solve the mystery of the stolen pearls. (Rev: BCCB 5/97; BL 1/1–15/97; BR 9–10/97; SLJ 3/97)

3998 Zambreno, Mary F. *Journeyman Wizard* (4–7). 1994, Harcourt $16.95 (0-15-200022-4). Student wizard Jeremy is studying the casting of spells with Lady Allons when an unfortunate death occurs and he is accused of murder. (Rev: BL 5/1/94; SLJ 6/94)

3999 Zindel, Paul. *The E-mail Murders* (5–8). Series: P.C. Hawke Mysteries. 2001, Hyperion paper $4.99 (0-7868-1579-5). P.C. and Mackenzie team up with an inspector's daughter to investigate a murder in Monaco. (Rev: SLJ 1/02)

4000 Zindel, Paul. *The Gourmet Zombie* (6–9). Series: P.C. Hawke Mysteries. 2002, Hyperion paper $4.99 (0-7868-1590-6). P.C. and Mackenzie come to the rescue when chefs start dying mysteriously in New York City. (Rev: SLJ 10/02)

4001 Zindel, Paul. *The Lethal Gorilla* (5–8). Series: P.C. Hawke Mysteries. 2001, Hyperion paper $4.99 (0-7868-1587-6). Amateur detective P.C. Hawke and his sidekick Mackenzie Riggs face hair-raising adventures as they solve the murder of a scientist at the Bronx Zoo. (Rev: BL 3/1/02)

4002 Zindel, Paul. *The Phantom of 86th Street* (6–9). Series: P.C. Hawke Mysteries. 2002, Hyperion/Volo paper $4.99 (0-7868-1591-4). P.C. and Mackenzie believe they are on the trail of a serial killer. (Rev: SLJ 3/03)

4003 Zindel, Paul. *Rats* (6–9). 1999, Hyperion $14.99 (0-7868-0339-8). A breathtaking thriller in which Sarah and Michael play a major role in the fight against a landfill that is spewing rats into New York City. (Rev: HBG 9/00; SLJ 10/99; VOYA 2/00)

4004 Zindel, Paul. *The Square Root of Murder* (5–7). 2002, Hyperion paper $4.99 (0-7868-1588-4). Amateur detective P.C. Hawke and her sidekick Mackenzie Riggs try to solve the mystery of the murder of a calculus teacher. (Rev: BL 5/1/02; SLJ 4/02)

4005 Zindel, Paul. *The Undertaker's Gone Bananas* (7–9). 1984, Bantam paper $4.50 (0-553-27189-X). Bobby and Lauri are convinced that their new neighbor is a murderer.

Romances

4006 Applegate, Katherine. *July's Promise* (7–10). 1995, Archway paper $3.99 (0-671-51031-2). Sixteen-year-old Summer finds romance and adventure when she visits her hostile cousin on Crab Claw Key in Florida. Preceded by *June Dreams* and followed by *August Magic*. (Rev: VOYA 2/96)

4007 Applegate, Katherine. *Sharing Sam* (7–10). 1995, Bantam paper $4.50 (0-553-56660-1). A sacrificial love story in which a girl's best friend is dying of a brain tumor and boyfriend Sam is shared. (Rev: BL 3/15/95; SLJ 2/95)

4008 Applegate, Katherine, et al. *See You in September* (7–9). 1995, Avon paper $3.99 (0-380-78088-7). Four chaste and charming short stories by four popular YA romance authors. (Rev: BL 1/1–15/96; SLJ 3/96)

4009 Bat-Ami, Miriam. *Two Suns in the Sky* (8–12). 1999, Front Street $15.95 (0-8126-2900-0). A docunovel set in upstate New York during 1944 about the love between a Catholic teenage girl and a Jewish Holocaust survivor from Yugoslavia who is living in a refugee camp. (Rev: BL 4/15/99; HB 7–8/99; HBG 9/99; SLJ 7/99; VOYA 10/99)

4010 Bauer, Joan. *Thwonk* (7–10). 1996, Bantam paper $4.50 (0-440-21980-9). "Thwonk" is the sound of Cupid's bow when A. J.'s wish that hunky Peter become hers alone comes true. Unfortunately, Peter's adoration is more than she bargained for. (Rev: BL 1/1/95; SLJ 1/95)

4011 Bennett, Cherie, and Jeff Gottesfeld. *Trash* (6–9). 1997, Berkley paper $3.99 (0-425-15851-9). Romance, intrigue, and action combine in this light novel about an 18-year-old girl who has been selected to be a summer intern at "Trash," a New York-based TV talk show. (Rev: SLJ 10/97)

4012 Bernardo, Anilu. *Loves Me, Loves Me Not* (7–10). 1998, Arte Publico $16.95 (1-55885-258-1). A teen romance that involves Cuban American Maggie, a basketball player named Zach, newcomer Justin, and Maggie's friend, Susie. (Rev: BL 1/1–15/99)

4013 Bertrand, Diane Gonzales. *Lessons of the Game* (7–10). 1998, Arte Publico paper $9.95 (1-55885-245-X). Student teacher Kaylene Morales is attracted to the freshman football coach but wonders if romance and her school assignments will mix. (Rev: BL 1/1–15/99; VOYA 10/99)

4014 Brooks, Martha. *Two Moons in August* (7–12). 1992, Little, Brown $15.95 (0-316-10979-7). A midsummer romance in the 1950s between a newcomer to a small Canadian community and a 16-year-old girl who is mourning her mother's death. (Rev: BL 11/15/91*; SLJ 3/92*)

4015 Cann, Kate. *Diving In* (7–9). 1997, Women's Pr. paper $9.95 (0-7043-4937-X). A British romantic novel about Collette's love for Art and her problem deciding if she should have sex with him. (Rev: SLJ 10/97)

4016 Cleary, Beverly. *Fifteen* (7–9). 1956, Morrow $16.89 (0-688-31285-3); Avon paper $5.99 (0-380-72804-4). A young adolescent discovers that having a boyfriend isn't the answer to all her social problems.

4017 Cleary, Beverly. *Jean and Johnny* (7–9). 1959, Morrow $15.95 (0-688-21740-0). Jean is shy and uncertain of herself around handsome Johnny.

4018 Cleary, Beverly. *The Luckiest Girl* (7–9). 1958, Morrow $17.89 (0-688-31741-3); Avon paper $5.99 (0-380-72806-0). New social opportunities arise when a young girl spends her senior year at a school in California.

4019 Daly, Maureen. *First a Dream* (7–10). 1990, Scholastic paper $12.95 (0-590-40846-1). The love that Retta and Dallas feel for each other is tested during a summer when they are separated in this sequel to *Acts of Love* (1986). (Rev: BL 4/1/90; SLJ 4/90; VOYA 4/90)

4020 Daly, Maureen. *Seventeenth Summer* (6–8). 1981, Harmony LB $19.95 (0-89967-029-6); Archway paper $5.99 (0-671-61931-4). Angie experiences an idyllic summer after she meets Jack in this classic 1942 novel.

4021 Danziger, Paula. *Thames Doesn't Rhyme with James* (7–10). 1994, Putnam $15.95 (0-399-22526-9). Kendra and her family take a joint vacation to London with the Lees and their son Frank, Kendra's boyfriend. (Rev: BL 12/1/94; SLJ 1/95; VOYA 4/95)

4022 Davis, Leila. *Lover Boy* (7–12). 1989, Avon paper $2.95 (0-380-75722-2). Ryan finds that his racy reputation is keeping him from the girl he really loves. (Rev: SLJ 10/89; VOYA 8/89)

4023 Dessen, Sarah. *This Lullaby* (8–12). 2002, Viking $16.99 (0-670-03530-0). Eighteen-year-old Remy's complex family life leads her to avoid deep romantic attachments until she meets Dexter. (Rev: BCCB 5/02; BL 4/1/02; HB 7–8/02; HBG 10/02; SLJ 4/02; VOYA 6/02)

4024 Dokey, Cameron. *Hindenburg, 1937* (7–10). 1999, Archway paper $4.99 (0-671-03601-7). On board the *Hindenburg* on its last voyage to America in 1937, Anna, a German girl fleeing from her Nazi brother who is pressuring her to accept an arranged marriage, is torn between two suitors who each suspect the other of being a spy. (Rev: VOYA 10/99)

4025 DuJardin, Rosamond. *Boy Trouble* (7–9). 1988, HarperCollins LB $12.89 (0-397-32263-1). A harmless romance first published in the 1960s and now back in print. (Rev: SLJ 2/88)

4026 Fiedler, Lisa. *Lucky Me* (6–10). 1998, Clarion $15.00 (0-395-89131-0). In this sequel to *Curtis Piperfield's Biggest Fan* (1995), Cecily Caruthers wants to be more adventurous sexually and this leads to a series of humorous situations. (Rev: BCCB 10/98; BL 11/15/98; BR 5–6/99; HB 11–12/98; HBG 3/99; SLJ 3/99; VOYA 6/99)

4027 Filichia, Peter. *Not Just Another Pretty Face* (7–10). 1988, Avon paper $2.50 (0-380-75244-1). A high school story in which the course of true love does not run smoothly for Bill Richards. (Rev: BL 3/1/88; SLJ 5/88)

4028 Frank, Lucy. *Will You Be My Brussels Sprout?* (7–10). 1996, Holiday $15.95 (0-8234-1220-2). In this continuation of *I Am an Artichoke,* Emily, now 16, studies the cello at a New York music conservatory and falls in love for the first time. (Rev: BL 4/15/96; SLJ 4/96; VOYA 10/96)

4029 Garwood, Julie. *A Girl Named Summer* (7–9). 1998, Pocket Books paper $4.50 (0-671-02342-X). To impress her new boyfriend, Summer tells lies that eventually catch up with her. (Rev: BL 1/1–15/99; SLJ 4/99)

4030 Geras, Adele. *Pictures of the Night* (7–12). 1993, Harcourt $16.95 (0-15-261588-1). A modern version of *Snow White,* with the heroine an 18-year-old singer in London and Paris. (Rev: BL 3/1/93; SLJ 6/93)

4031 Geras, Adele. *The Tower Room* (7–12). 1992, Harcourt $15.95 (0-15-289627-9). The fairy tale *Rapunzel* is updated and set in an English girls' boarding school in the 1960s. (Rev: BL 2/15/92; SLJ 5/92)

4032 Gerber, Merrill Joan. *Handsome as Anything* (8–12). 1990, Scholastic $13.95 (0-590-43019-X). Rachel is attracted to three different boys and in making her choice learns a lot about herself. (Rev: BL 9/15/90; SLJ 12/90)

4033 Gregory, Diana. *Two's a Crowd* (7–10). 1985, Bantam paper $3.50 (0-553-24992-4). Peggy finds that her business rival is a handsome young man. (Rev: BL 10/15/85; SLJ 9/85)

4034 Gunn, Robin Jones. *I Promise* (6–12). Series: Christy and Todd, The College Years. 2001, Bethany $10.99 (0-7642-2274-0). Christy and Todd are finally engaged, but the complicated wedding plans and accompanying turmoil threaten to derail their happiness. (Rev: BL 1/1–15/02; VOYA 12/01)

4035 Hahn, Mary D. *The Wind Blows Backward* (8–12). 1993, Clarion $16.00 (0-395-62975-6); Avon paper $4.95 (0-380-77530-1). Spencer's downward emotional spiral and Lauren's deep commitment evoke a fantasy love gone awry. (Rev: BL 5/1/93; SLJ 5/93)

4036 Hart, Bruce, and Carol Hart. *Waiting Games* (7–10). 1981, Avon paper $3.50 (0-380-79012-2).

Jessie and Michael are in love and must make difficult decisions about sex.

4037 Hart, Bruce, and Carole Hart. *Sooner or Later* (8–12). 1978, Avon paper $2.95 (0-380-42978-0). In order to fool her 17-year-old boyfriend into thinking she is older than 13, Jessie begins an intricate pattern of lies.

4038 Haynes, Betsy. *The Great Dad Disaster* (6–8). 1994, Bantam paper $3.50 (0-553-48169-X). When two girlfriends begin to date boys, one finds her father too strict and the other, too lenient. (Rev: BL 6/1–15/94)

4039 Hite, Sid. *Cecil in Space* (7–10). 1999, Holt $16.95 (0-8050-5055-8). At 17, Cecil begins to takes life seriously when he falls in love with the richest, sexiest girl in town. (Rev: BL 4/15/99; HBG 9/99; SLJ 5/99; VOYA 6/99)

4040 Hoh, Diane. *Titanic, the Long Night* (7–12). 1998, Scholastic paper $4.99 (0-590-33123-X). In this novel set on the ill-fated *Titanic* in 1912, wealthy first-class passenger Elizabeth Farr meets Max Whittaker, a wealthy but rebellious artist; in a parallel plot in third class, Irish rogue Paddy Kelleher and talented singer Katie Hanrahan fall in love. (Rev: BR 1–2/99; VOYA 2/99)

4041 Jenkins, Beverly. *Belle and the Beau* (6–12). Series: Avon True Romance. 2002, Avon paper $4.99 (0-06-447342-2). Jenkins incorporates historical detail and atmosphere in this story of romance between an escaped slave and the son of an African American abolitionist family. (Rev: BL 9/15/02; SLJ 5/02)

4042 Jukes, Mavis. *Cinderella 2000* (6–10). 1999, Delacorte paper $8.95 (0-385-32711-0). Fourteen-year-old Ashley is desperate to go to the New Year's Eve party with the love of her life, but her stepmother wants her to babysit for her stepsisters. (Rev: BCCB 1/00; BL 10/1/99; HBG 4/00; SLJ 11/99)

4043 Kaplow, Robert. *Alessandra in Love* (8–10). 1989, HarperCollins LB $12.89 (0-397-32282-8). Alessandra's boyfriend turns out to be a self-centered disappointment. (Rev: BL 4/15/89; SLJ 4/89; VOYA 8/89)

4044 Kirby, Susan. *Blue Moon* (7–9). 1997, Berkley paper $4.50 (0-425-15414-9). Dee hopes that her friendship with Michael will turn to romance, but the young man is preoccupied with caring for his grandfather, who has Alzheimer's disease. (Rev: SLJ 1/98)

4045 Klass, David. *Screen Test* (7–9). 1997, Scholastic paper $16.95 (0-590-48592-X). Sixteen-year-old Liz Weaton is whisked off to Hollywood, where she almost falls in love with her costar. (Rev: BL 12/1/97; BR 11–12/97; HBG 3/98; SLJ 10/97)

4046 Knudson, R. R. *Just Another Love Story* (7–10). 1983, Avon paper $2.50 (0-380-65532-2). Dusty takes up body building to help forget the girlfriend who has spurned him.

4047 Korman, Gordon. *Son of the Mob* (6–8). 2002, Hyperion $15.99 (0-7868-0769-5). The son of a Mafia boss falls for the daughter of an FBI agent and must make some difficult choices in this novel that combines humor, suspense, and romance. (Rev: BL 11/1/02; HB 1–2/03; HBG 3/03; SLJ 11/02; VOYA 2/03)

4048 Lachtman, Ofelia Dumas. *The Girl from Playa Bianca* (7–12). 1995, Arte Publico paper $9.95 (1-55885-149-6). A gothic romance in which a Mexican teenager and her young brother travel to Los Angeles in search of their father. (Rev: BL 11/15/95; SLJ 10/95; VOYA 12/95)

4049 McCants, William D. *Anything Can Happen in High School (and It Usually Does)* (6–8). 1993, Harcourt $10.95 (0-15-276604-9); paper $3.95 (0-15-276605-7). In his attempts to win back his summer love, Janet, by starting a school club, T. J. Burant realizes her shallowness isn't for him. (Rev: BL 10/1/93; SLJ 10/93; VOYA 12/93)

4050 McDaniel, Lurlene. *Angels Watching Over Me* (8–10). 1996, Bantam paper $4.99 (0-553-56724-1). Romance, mystery, and personal problems mingle in this novel about a girl who has bone cancer, the boy she is attracted to in the hospital, and a mysterious nurse. (Rev: BR 11–12/96; SLJ 3/97)

4051 McDaniel, Lurlene. *Don't Die, My Love* (7–12). 1995, Bantam paper $4.99 (0-553-56715-2). A young couple, Julie and Luke, "engaged" since 6th grade, discover that Luke has Hodgkin's lymphoma. (Rev: BL 9/15/95; SLJ 10/95; VOYA 12/95)

4052 McFann, Jane. *Maybe by Then I'll Understand* (7–9). 1987, Avon paper $2.50 (0-380-75221-2). Cath and Tony become a pair but Tony demands more attention and loyalty than she can give. (Rev: BL 11/15/87; SLJ 1/88; VOYA 12/87)

4053 Martin, Ann M. *Just a Summer Romance* (6–8). 1987, Holiday $13.95 (0-8234-0649-0). While spending a summer on Fire Island, 14-year-old Melanie becomes attracted to Justin. (Rev: BL 4/1/87; SLJ 6/87; VOYA 10/87)

4054 Matthews, Phoebe. *The Boy on the Cover* (6–8). 1988, Avon paper $2.75 (0-380-75407-X). Cyndi falls in love with a boy whose picture is on the cover of a book she owns. (Rev: VOYA 2/89)

4055 Mauser, Pat Rhoads. *Love Is for the Dogs* (7–10). 1989, Avon paper $2.50 (0-380-75723-0). Janna realizes that Brian, the boy next door, can be very desirable. (Rev: BL 4/15/89; SLJ 4/89)

4056 Mines, Jeanette. *Risking It* (7–9). 1988, Avon paper $2.75 (0-380-75401-0). Jeannie is attracted to Trent Justin, who has joined her senior class. (Rev: BL 9/1/88; SLJ 1/89; VOYA 6/88)

4057 Moore, Margaret. *Gwyneth and the Thief* (8–12). Series: Avon True Romance. 2002, Avon paper $4.99 (0-06-447337-6). In an effort to save her family estate from a predatory baron, Lady Gwyneth seeks the help of a young — and increasingly appealing — thief. (Rev: BL 9/15/02)

4058 Napoli, Donna Jo. *Love in Venice* (7–9). 1998, Delacorte $15.95 (0-385-32531-2). Two young adults, one an American and the other an Italian, fall in love but clash about their beliefs concerning the future of Venice, where they both live. (Rev: BL 5/1/98; HBG 9/98; SLJ 6/98; VOYA 10/98)

4059 O'Brien, Judith. *Timeless Love* (7–10). 2002, Simon & Schuster paper $4.99 (0-7434-1921-9). A 16th birthday present transports Sam to Tudor England where she finds romance and intrigue in this novel that blends fantasy and history. (Rev: SLJ 3/02)

4060 Pascal, Francine. *Can't Stay Away* (7–10). Series: Sweet Valley High Senior Year. 1999, Bantam paper $4.50 (0-553-49234-9). A better-than-average Sweet Valley High novel about new friendships and rivalries that result when the students of El Carro High have to finish the year at Sweet Valley because of an earthquake. (Rev: SLJ 2/99)

4061 Pascal, Francine, and Jamie Suzanne. *Get Real* (6–8). Series: Sweet Valley Jr. High. 1999, Bantam paper $4.50 (0-553-48603-9). A quick read about twins Jessica and Elizabeth Wakefield and the adjustments they must make when their middle school becomes a junior high, and they, as 8th-graders, are no longer top dogs. (Rev: BCCB 2/99; SLJ 2/99)

4062 Plummer, Louise. *The Unlikely Romance of Kate Bjorkman* (7–10). 1997, Bantam paper $4.50 (0-440-22704-6). A brainy teen foils a beautiful, evil temptress and gets the man of her dreams. (Rev: SLJ 10/95; VOYA 12/95)

4063 Powell, Randy. *Is Kissing a Girl Who Smokes Like Licking an Ashtray?* (7–12). 2003, Farrar paper $5.95 (0-374-43628-2). High school senior Biff has never had a girlfriend until he meets the wild, beautiful loner Heidi, who is as troubled and mouthy as he is shy and fumbling. (Rev: BL 6/1/92*; SLJ 6/92)

4064 Randle, Kristen D. *Breaking Rank* (7–12). 1999, Morrow $15.95 (0-688-16243-6). Told from alternating viewpoints, this is the story of 17-year-old Casey and her experiences after she has agreed to tutor the enigmatic rebel, Thomas, who belongs to a group of outsiders known as the Clan. (Rev: BL 5/1/99; HB 3–4/99; HBG 9/99; SLJ 5/99; VOYA 12/99)

4065 Rees, Elizabeth M. *Moving as One* (6–10). Series: Heart Beats. 1998, Aladdin paper $3.99 (0-689-81948-X). When teenage ballerina Sophy's dance school merges with a school of Latin dance run by attractive Carlos Vargas, everyone wonders if ballet and salsa will mix. (Rev: BL 8/98; SLJ 11/98)

4066 Rodowsky, Colby. *Lucy Peale* (8–12). 1992, Farrar paper $3.95 (0-374-44659-8). Lucy, a rape victim, is pregnant, alone, and terrified when she meets Jake, and their friendship slowly evolves into love. (Rev: BL 7/92; SLJ 7/92)

4067 Rostkowski, Margaret I. *Moon Dancer* (7–10). 1995, Harcourt $11.00 (0-15-276638-3); paper $6.00 (0-15-200194-8). A 15-year-old on a trek to view ancient canyon rock art feels connections to the images and to an accompanying boy. (Rev: BL 5/1/95; SLJ 9/95)

4068 Ryan, Mary C. *Frankie's Run* (6–8). 1987, Little, Brown $12.95 (0-316-76370-5). In this teen novel, Mary Frances falls for the new boy in town but also organizes a run to aid her local library. (Rev: BL 8/87; BR 9–10/87; SLJ 5/87)

4069 Sachs, Marilyn. *Thunderbird* (7–10). Illus. 1985, Dutton $10.95 (0-525-44163-8). Two high school seniors meet and fall in love in the public library. (Rev: BL 4/15/85; SLJ 10/85)

4070 Schreiber, Ellen. *Teenage Mermaid* (6–8). 2003, HarperCollins $15.99 (0-06-008204-6). Romance and entertainment abound in this story of a teen mermaid who rescues a young surfer. (Rev: BL 7/03; HBG 10/03; SLJ 8/03; VOYA 8/03)

4071 Sheldon, Dyan. *The Boy of My Dreams* (6–10). 1997, Candlewick $16.99 (0-7636-0004-0). Mike (short for Michelle) falls head over heels in love with sophisticated Bill and begins to neglect her true friends. (Rev: BL 11/1/97; BR 1–2/98; HBG 3/98; SLJ 10/97; VOYA 2/98)

4072 Sierra, Patricia. *One-Way Romance* (7–10). 1986, Avon paper $2.50 (0-380-75107-0). A talented girl who does well with carpentry and track seems to be losing out with her boyfriend. (Rev: BL 8/86; SLJ 11/86; VOYA 12/86)

4073 Stacey, Cherylyn. *Gone to Maui* (7–9). 1996, Roussan paper $8.95 (1-896184-14-6). In this novel, teenage Becky accompanies her mother on a trip to Maui, and there finds romance. (Rev: VOYA 4/97)

4074 Stanek, Lou W. *Katy Did* (8–12). 1992, Avon paper $2.99 (0-380-76170-X). A shy country girl and popular city boy fall in love, with tragic consequences. (Rev: BL 3/15/92)

4075 Strasser, Todd. *How I Spent My Last Night on Earth* (7–10). Series: Time Zone High. 1998, Simon & Schuster $16.00 (0-689-81113-6). Rumors spread that a giant asteroid is heading for Earth, and "Legs" Hanover finds romance with a handsome surfer classmate after being jilted by her boyfriend. (Rev: BL 11/1/98; BR 5–6/99; HBG 9/99; SLJ 11/98; VOYA 8/99)

4076 Sunshine, Tina. *An X-Rated Romance* (7–9). 1982, Avon paper $2.50 (0-380-79905-7). Two 13-year-old girls have a crush on their English teacher. A reissue.

4077 Thesman, Jean. *Jamie* (6–9). 1998, Avon paper $3.99 (0-380-78681-8). Jamie relies on help from her cousins, friends, and parents to end an unhealthy relationship with her boyfriend, Rick. First in a series about three cousins, Jamie, Meredith, and Teresa, who live in the Seattle area. (Rev: SLJ 9/98)

4078 Thesman, Jean. *Who Said Life Is Fair?* (7–9). 1987, Avon paper $3.50 (0-380-75088-0). Teddy is trying to cope with work on the school newspaper while keeping her love life in order. (Rev: BL 5/87; VOYA 8/87)

4079 Trembath, Don. *A Beautiful Place on Yonge Street* (8–10). 1999, Orca paper $6.95 (1-55143-121-1). Budding writer Harper Winslow falls in love with Sunny Taylor when he attends a summer writing camp, and experiences all the angst that goes with it. (Rev: BL 3/1/99; SLJ 7/99; VOYA 6/99)

4080 Watson, Jude. *Audacious: Ivy's Story* (7–9). Series: Brides of Wildcat County. 1995, Simon & Schuster paper $3.95 (0-689-80328-1). Leaving her Maine community because of family problems, Ivy begins teaching school in a California mining community but is tracked down by her former fiance, who reveals a secret she doesn't want anyone to know. (Rev: SLJ 3/96)

4081 Watson, Jude. *Dangerous: Savannah's Story* (7–10). Series: Brides of Wildcat County. 1995, Simon & Schuster paper $3.95 (0-689-80326-5). Savannah leaves the East and heads to a gold-mining town in California, where she finds romance in the arms of the son of a gold mine owner. (Rev: SLJ 2/96)

4082 Watson, Jude. *Scandalous: Eden's Story* (7–10). Series: Brides of Wildcat County. 1995, Simon & Schuster paper $3.95 (0-689-80327-3). Eden, who has a criminal background, arrives in Last Chance, a gold mining town in California, where her reputation as a cardshark threatens her love for rich Josiah Bullock. (Rev: SLJ 2/96; VOYA 4/96)

4083 Weyn, Suzanne. *The Makeover Summer* (6–8). 1988, Avon paper $2.95 (0-380-75521-1). An exchange student who needs help joins the three girls of the Makeover Club. (Rev: BL 2/15/89)

4084 Williams, Carol L. *My Angelica* (5–9). 1999, Bantam $15.95 (0-385-32622-X); Random paper $4.99 (0-440-22778-X). Sage is disappointed when her writing efforts are criticized but finds solace in her growing romantic feelings for her best friend,

George. (Rev: BL 12/15/98; BR 9–10/99; HB 1–2/99; HBG 10/99; SLJ 1/99; VOYA 8/99)

4085 Winfrey, Elizabeth. *My So-Called Boyfriend* (6–10). Series: Love Stories. 1996, Bantam paper $3.99 (0-553-56668-7). After a fall that causes snobbish Tashi Pendleton to lose her memory, a boy she once embarrassed concocts a scheme to get even in this light romance. (Rev: SLJ 8/96)

4086 Wittlinger, Ellen. *Lombardo's Law* (7–10). 1993, Houghton $16.00 (0-395-65969-8); Morrow paper $4.95 (0-688-05294-0). The conventions of romance are thrown aside when sophomore Justine and 8th-grader Mike find themselves attracted to each other, despite obstacles. (Rev: BL 9/15/93; VOYA 12/93)

4087 Woodson, Jacqueline. *If You Come Softly* (7–10). 1998, Putnam $15.99 (0-399-23112-9). The story of the love between a black boy and a white girl, their families, and the prejudice they encounter. (Rev: BL 10/1/98; HBG 9/99; SLJ 12/98; VOYA 12/98)

4088 Young, Karen R. *The Beetle and Me: A Love Story* (6–9). 1999, Morrow $15.95 (0-688-15922-2). While trying to sort out her love interests, 15-year-old Daisy Pandolfi tries to restore a 1957 purple Volkswagen Beetle to running order. (Rev: BL 4/15/99; HBG 9/99; SLJ 5/99; VOYA 10/99)

Science Fiction

4089 Anderson, Kevin J., ed. *War of the Worlds: Global Dispatches* (7–12). 1996, Bantam $22.95 (0-553-10352-9). This tribute to H. G. Wells's *War of the Worlds* features stories of Martian invasions that are either take-offs on the writing styles of such famous authors as Conrad, London, Verne, and Kipling, or the experiences of famous individuals, such as Teddy Roosevelt and Pablo Picasso, during a Martian invasion. (Rev: VOYA 10/96)

4090 Anthony, Piers. *Race Against Time* (7–12). 1986, Tor paper $5.99 (0-8125-3101-9). John Smith and an African girl named Ala are different from others because they are racially pure.

4091 Applegate, K. A. *Animorphs #1: The Invasion* (5–8). 1996, Scholastic paper $4.99 (0-590-62977-8). Jake, an average suburban kid, is confronted one night by a creature from space who teaches him how to morph into the forms of other creatures. (Rev: VOYA 12/96)

4092 Archer, Chris. *Alien Blood* (6–8). Series: Mindwarp. 1997, Pocket Books paper $3.99 (0-671-01483-8). Using her supersonic hearing and sight, Ashley Rose is able to foil an alien killer. (Rev: SLJ 3/98)

4093 Archer, Chris. *Alien Terror* (6–8). Series: Mindwarp. 1997, Pocket Books paper $3.99 (0-671-01482-X). On his 13th birthday, Ethan finds he possesses superhuman strength and unearthly fighting skills. (Rev: SLJ 3/98)

4094 Armstrong, Jennifer, and Nancy Butcher. *The Keepers of the Flame* (7–10). Series: Fire-Us. 2002, HarperCollins $15.99 (0-06-008049-3). The plucky children who survived the deadly virus that hit in *The Kindling* (2002) meet a group of strange grownups. (Rev: BL 8/02*; HBG 3/03; SLJ 12/02)

4095 Armstrong, Jennifer, and Nancy Butcher. *The Kindling* (7–10). Series: Fire-Us. 2002, Harper-Collins LB $15.89 (0-06-029411-6). In 2007, after a virus has killed the adults, a small band of children join together in a Florida town and try to carry on with life. (Rev: BCCB 6/02; BL 4/15/02; HBG 10/02; SLJ 10/02)

4096 Asimov, Isaac, et al., eds. *Young Extraterrestrials* (7–9). 1984, HarperCollins paper $7.95 (0-06-020167-3). Eleven stories by well-known authors about youngsters who are aliens from space.

4097 Asimov, Janet. *Norby and the Terrified Taxi* (4–8). 1997, Walker $15.95 (0-8027-8642-1). Norby, the bungling robot, is kidnapped, and while trying to find him, Jeff and his friends stumble on a plot by Garc the Great to take over the Federation. This is one of a large series of Norby books suitable for middle school readers. (Rev: BL 1/1–15/98; SLJ 12/97)

4098 Asimov, Janet. *The Package in Hyperspace* (5–7). Illus. 1988, Walker LB $14.85 (0-8027-6823-7). Two space-wrecked children must fend for themselves as they try to reach Merkina. (Rev: BL 1/1/89; SLJ 11/88)

4099 Asimov, Janet, and Isaac Asimov. *Norby and the Invaders* (5–8). 1985, Walker LB $10.85 (0-8027-6607-2). Jeff and his unusual robot Norby travel to a planet to help one of Norby's ancestors. Part of a series that includes *Norby's Other Secret*. (Rev: BL 3/1/86; SLJ 2/86)

4100 Asimov, Janet, and Isaac Asimov. *Norby and Yobo's Great Adventure* (5–8). 1989, Walker LB $13.85 (0-8027-6894-6). Norby the robot time-travels to help Admiral Yobo of Mars to trace his family roots. Part of a series that also includes *Norby Down to Earth*. (Rev: BL 10/15/89)

4101 Asimov, Janet, and Isaac Asimov. *Norby Finds a Villain* (4–8). 1987, Walker LB $13.85 (0-8027-6711-7). Norby the robot and his human friends set out to free Pera, who has been robot-napped by the traitor Ing, in this sixth book of the Norby series. Also use *Norby and the Queen's Necklace* (1986). (Rev: BL 1/1/88; SLJ 11/87)

4102 Ball, Margaret. *Lost in Translation* (8–12). 1995, Baen $5.99 (0-671-87638-0). American teenager Allie flies to France to attend a university

223

but lands in a fantasy world filled with spells of every kind, where people communicate through voice-bubbles and a group of terrifying monsters controls an important subterranean substance called landvirtue. (Rev: VOYA 4/96)

4103 Bawden, Nina. *Off the Road* (5–9). 1998, Clarion $16.00 (0-395-91321-7). In this science fiction novel set in a time when the elderly are exterminated, 11-year-old Tom follows his grandfather to the "savage jungle" Outside the Wall, where the old man hopes to escape his fate, and discovers a different kind of society. (Rev: BCCB 10/98; BL 9/15/98; BR 5–6/99; HBG 10/99; SLJ 11/98)

4104 Belden, Wilanne Schneider. *Mind-Find* (6–9). 1988, Harcourt $14.95 (0-15-254270-1). A 13-year-old girl adjusts with difficulty to her amazing powers of ESP. (Rev: BL 2/15/88; SLJ 8/88)

4105 Bell, Hilari. *A Matter of Profit* (6–10). 2001, HarperCollins $15.95 (0-06-029513-9). Eighteen-year-old Ahvren, who wants to give up his interplanetary military career, agrees to look into a threat against the leader of the T'Chin Empire in hopes of saving his sister from an unwanted marriage and winning his own independence. (Rev: BL 8/01; HB 1–2/02; HBG 3/02; SLJ 10/01; VOYA 10/01)

4106 Bell, Hilari. *Songs of Power* (5–8). 2000, Hyperion LB $16.49 (0-7868-2487-5). In this science fiction novel, young Annis, who is living with her parents in an undersea station, is convinced that a series of accidents are caused by spells not saboteurs. (Rev: HBG 10/00; SLJ 5/00)

4107 Blacker, Terence. *The Angel Factory* (6–8). 2002, Simon & Schuster $16.98 (0-689-85171-5). The fate of humankind rests in Thomas's hands when he discovers that his parents are really alien "angels," part of a project to save humans from themselves. (Rev: BCCB 1/03; BL 8/02; HBG 3/03; SLJ 8/02)

4108 Boulle, Pierre. *Planet of the Apes* (7–12). n.d., Random paper $6.99 (0-345-44798-0). Stranded on the planet Soror, Ulysse Merou discovers a civilization ruled by apes.

4109 Bradbury, Ray. *Farhenheit 451* (7–12). 1953, Ballantine paper $6.99 (0-345-34296-8). In this futuristic novel, book reading has become a crime.

4110 Bradbury, Ray. *The October Country* (7–12). 1999, Avon $16.00 (0-380-97387-1). Ordinary people are caught up in unreal situations in these 19 strange stories.

4111 Bradbury, Ray. *The Stories of Ray Bradbury* (8–12). 1980, Knopf $40.00 (0-394-51335-5). An imaginative group of stories that often bridge the gap between fantasy and science fiction.

4112 Brittain, Bill. *Shape-Changer* (5–8). 1995, HarperCollins paper $5.95 (0-06-440514-1). Three 7th-graders meet an extraterrestrial police officer from the planet Rodinam who is escorting a dangerous criminal to an asteroid. (Rev: BL 4/15/94; SLJ 6/94)

4113 Bunting, Eve. *The Cloverdale Switch* (7–9). 1979, HarperCollins LB $12.89 (0-397-31867-7). John and Cindy encounter unusual changes in their world and find a mysterious black box.

4114 Burroughs, Edgar Rice. *At the Earth's Core* (7–12). 1990, Ballantine paper $3.95 (0-345-36668-9). David Innes travels 500 miles into the earth and finds a subterranean world. Sequels *Pellucidar* and *Tamar of Pellucidar* are also included in this volume.

4115 Butler, Susan. *The Hermit Thrush Sings* (5–8). 1999, Bantam paper $5.50 (0-440-22896-4). Leora, who is living in a future civilization in North America, must leave the safety of her walled village, controlled by the Rulers, and find rebels who are working to overthrow the government. (Rev: BCCB 4/99; BL 2/15/99*; HBG 10/99; SLJ 4/99; VOYA 12/99)

4116 Butts, Nancy. *The Door in the Lake* (5–8). 1997, Front Street $15.95 (1-886910-27-8). Twenty-seven months after being abducted by aliens, Joey returns home to find that everything has changed while he has remained the same. (Rev: BCCB 7–8/98; BL 5/15/98; HBG 10/98; SLJ 6/98; VOYA 10/98)

4117 Cart, Michael, ed. *Tomorrowland: 10 Stories About the Future* (7–10). 1999, Scholastic paper $15.95 (0-590-37678-0). Ten writers, including Ron Koertge, Lois Lowry, and Katherine Paterson, have contributed original stories to this anthology that reflect their concepts of the future. (Rev: BCCB 12/99; BL 8/99; HBG 4/00; SLJ 9/99; VOYA 12/99)

4118 Castro, Adam-Troy. *Spider-Man: Secret of the Sinister Six* (7–12). 2002, BP $24.95 (0-7434-4464-7). Six supervillians attack New York City and Spider-Man comes to the rescue in this humorous and action-packed final installment in a trilogy. (Rev: SLJ 7/02)

4119 Christopher, John. *A Dusk of Demons* (6–9). 1994, Macmillan LB $14.95 (0-02-718425-0). In a primitive future society, Ben and Paddy set out to find their family, who disappeared after the Demons set fire to their home. (Rev: BL 6/1–15/94; SLJ 7/94; VOYA 12/94)

4120 Christopher, John. *When the Tripods Came* (6–9). 1990, Macmillan paper $4.99 (0-02-042575-9). In this prequel, the author explains how the Tripods first came to Earth. (Rev: BCCB 7–8/88; BL 7/88; BR 5–6/89; HB 9–10/88; SLJ 8/88; VOYA 8/88)

4121 Christopher, John. *The White Mountains* (7–10). Series: Tripods. 1967, Simon & Schuster $17.95 (0-02-718360-2); Macmillan paper $4.99 (0-

02-042711-5). The first of the Tripods trilogy, followed by *The City of Gold and Lead* and *The Pool of Fire*. (Rev: BL 9/15/98)

4122 Ciencin, Scott. *Dinoverse* (5–8). Illus. 1999, Random $18.00 (0-679-88842-X). Bertram's science project really works and he and his three schoolmates are caught in a time warp in which they become dinosaurs. (Rev: BL 4/1/99; HBG 10/99; SLJ 4/99)

4123 Clancy, Tom, and Steve Pieczenik. *Virtual Vandals* (7–12). Series: Net Force. 1999, Berkley paper $4.99 (0-425-16173-0). In 2025, after Matt Hunter and his computer friends attend an all-star virtual reality baseball game where terrorists shoot wildly at the stands, our hero and his pals set out to catch the culprits. Followed by *The Deadliest Game*. (Rev: BL 3/15/99)

4124 Clarke, Arthur C. *Childhood's End* (7–12). 1963, Harcourt $14.95 (0-15-117205-6); Ballantine paper $6.99 (0-345-34795-1). The overlords' arrival on Earth marks the beginning of the end for humankind.

4125 Clarke, Arthur C. *Expedition to Earth* (7–10). 1998, Ballantine paper $10.00 (0-345-43073-5). Eleven stories about space exploration.

4126 Clements, Andrew. *Things Not Seen* (7–10). 2002, Putnam $15.99 (0-399-23626-0). Bobby, 15, suddenly becomes invisible and must deal with all the problems his "disappearance" causes. (Rev: BCCB 6/02; BL 4/15/02; HB 3–4/02; HBG 10/02; SLJ 3/02; VOYA 2/02)

4127 Conly, Jane Leslie. *The Rudest Alien on Earth* (6–8). 2002, Holt $16.95 (0-8050-6069-3). Oluu, an alien on a mission to observe the creatures of Earth, finds it impossible to retain her objectivity and befriends two youngsters in rural Vermont. (Rev: BCCB 11/02; BL 9/1/02; HB 1/03; HBG 3/03; SLJ 10/02; VOYA 2/03)

4128 Cooper, Clare. *Ashar of Qarius* (5–8). 1990, Harcourt $14.95 (0-15-200409-2). A teenage girl, two children, and their pets are left alone in a space dome and must find a way to survive. (Rev: BL 5/15/90; SLJ 7/90)

4129 Coville, Bruce. *Aliens Stole My Body* (4–7). Illus. Series: Alien Adventures. 1998, Pocket $14.00 (0-671-02414-0). To safeguard Rod from BKR, the cruelest being in the universe, and protect the important weapons formula that Rod knows, the boy's brain is separated from his body and enters the body of a six-legged blue alien. (Rev: BL 11/1/98; SLJ 2/99)

4130 Coville, Bruce, ed. *Bruce Coville's Alien Visitors* (4–7). 1999, Avon paper $4.99 (0-380-80254-6). A collection of 14 short stories about aliens and alien encounters by such writers as Ray Bradbury. (Rev: BL 11/15/99)

4131 Coville, Bruce, comp. and ed. *Bruce Coville's UFOs* (4–8). 2000, HarperCollins paper $4.99 (0-380-80257-0). A collection of 13 new and previously published science fiction short stories by well-known authors. (Rev: SLJ 11/00)

4132 Cowley, Joy. *Starbright and the Dream Eater* (5–8). 2000, HarperCollins LB $14.89 (0-06-028420-X). A child born to a mentally disabled teenage mother and named Starbright is destined to save the earth from the Dream Eater. (Rev: BCCB 7–8/00; BL 4/15/00; HBG 10/00; SLJ 6/00)

4133 Crilley, Mark. *Akiko on the Planet Smoo* (4–7). Illus. 2000, Delacorte $9.95 (0-385-32724-2). A fast-paced science fiction novel about Akiko, a 4th grader, and her flight into space to find the kidnapped son of King Froptoppit. (Rev: BL 3/1/00; HBG 10/00; SLJ 2/00)

4134 David, Peter. *Babylon 5: In the Beginning* (7–10). 1998, Ballantine paper $6.99 (0-345-42452-2). This is a novelization of the first full-length movie in the TV science fiction series *Babylon 5*. (Rev: VOYA 8/98)

4135 De Haven, Tom. *The Orphan's Tent* (7–10). 1996, Simon & Schuster $18.00 (0-689-31967-3). After Del, a young singer-songwriter, mysteriously disappears, her two friends, while trying to trace her, find themselves transported to another world. (Rev: SLJ 10/96; VOYA 12/96)

4136 Del Rey, Lester. *The Best of Lester del Rey* (7–10). 1978, Ballantine paper $5.99 (0-345-32933-3). Sixteen stories by this master of science fiction writing. Some full-length novels by del Rey are *Attack from Atlantis; Moon from Atlantis; Mysterious Planet;* and *Rocket Jockey* (all 1982).

4137 DeVita, James. *Blue* (4–7). 2001, HarperCollins LB $15.89 (0-06-029546-5). Morgan follows a marlin that has entered his living room and soon finds he is turning into a fish. (Rev: BCCB 5/01; BL 4/15/01; HBG 10/01; SLJ 5/01)

4138 Dicks, Terrance. *Doctor Who and the Genesis of the Daleks* (7–9). 1979, Amereon $18.95 (0-8488-0151-2). Based on the TV series, this is the story of an unusual Time Lord and his adventures in space.

4139 Doyle, Debra, and James D. MacDonald. *Groogleman* (5–8). 1996, Harcourt $15.00 (0-15-200235-9). In this novel set in the future, 13-year-old Dan is immune to the plague that is devastating the countryside and sets out with friend Leesie to help tend the sick. (Rev: BCCB 12/96; BR 3–4/97; SLJ 12/96; VOYA 6/97)

4140 DuPrau, Jeanne. *The City of Ember* (5–7). 2003, Random $15.95 (0-375-82273-9). Lina and Doon work to find a way out of their isolated and decaying city, where the population is beginning to panic. (Rev: BL 4/15/03; HB 5–6/03; HBG 10/03; SLJ 5/03; VOYA 6/03)

4141 Farmer, Nancy. *The Ear, the Eye and the Arm* (7–10). 1994, Orchard LB $19.99 (0-531-08679-8). In Zimbabwe in 2194, the military ruler's son, 13, and his younger siblings leave their technologically overcontrolled home and embark on a series of perilous adventures. (Rev: BL 4/1/94; SLJ 6/94; VOYA 6/94)

4142 Farmer, Nancy. *House of the Scorpion* (7–10). 2002, Simon & Schuster $17.95 (0-689-85222-3). Young Matt, who has spent his childhood in cruel circumstances, discovers he is in fact a clone of the 142-year-old ruler of Opium, a land south of the U.S. border. (Rev: BL 9/15/02; HB 11–12/02; HBG 3/03; SLJ 9/02)

4143 Finch, Sheila. *Tiger in the Sky* (4–8). Series: Out of Time. 1999, Avon paper $4.99 (0-380-79971-5). Three youngsters from a much earlier time are sent to the edge of the solar system to deal with a plague of furry animals that are endangering a scientific station in the 2300s. (Rev: BL 9/1/99)

4144 Follett, Ken. *The Power Twins* (4–8). 1991, Scholastic paper $2.75 (0-590-42507-2). Three youngsters travel to a planet where large, gentle worms live. (Rev: SLJ 1/91)

4145 Foster, Alan Dean. *The Hand of Dinotopia* (6–10). Series: Dinotopia. 1999, HarperCollins $22.99 (0-06-028005-0). In this adventure involving dinosaurs, our heroes journey through the Great Desert and Outer Island to find the key to a sea route that will link Dinotopia to the rest of the world. (Rev: BL 5/1/99; HBG 10/99; SLJ 4/99)

4146 Foster, Alan Dean. *Splinter of the Mind's Eye* (8–12). 1978, Ballantine paper $6.99 (0-345-32023-9). A novel about Luke Skywalker and Princess Leia of *Star Wars* fame and their battle against the Empire.

4147 Fuller, Kimberly. *Home* (7–10). 1997, Tor $16.95 (0-312-86152-4). When an attractive alien lands on her planet, Maran Thopel is attracted to him and to his mission to regain the planet for the people from whom it was taken. (Rev: BR 9–10/97; SLJ 7/97; VOYA 8/97)

4148 Gauthier, Gail. *Club Earth* (4–7). 1999, Putnam $15.99 (0-399-23373-3). When the Denis home is chosen to be an interstellar resort, the family finds that each alien visitor has an unusual talent in this humorous science fiction novel. (Rev: HB 5–6/99; HBG 10/99; SLJ 8/99; VOYA 4/00)

4149 Gerrold, David. *Chess with a Dragon* (8–12). 1988, Avon paper $3.50 (0-380-70662-8). The entire human race becomes slaves of giant slugs and Yake must save them. (Rev: BL 6/15/87; BR 11–12/87; SLJ 9/87)

4150 Gilden, Mel. *Outer Space and All That Junk* (5–7). Illus. 1989, HarperCollins LB $12.89 (0-397-32307-7). Myron's uncle is collecting junk, which

he believes will help aliens return to their home in outer space. (Rev: BL 12/1/89; SLJ 12/89)

4151 Gilden, Mel. *The Pumpkins of Time* (4–7). 1994, Harcourt $10.95 (0-15-276603-0); paper $4.95 (0-15-200889-6). Myron, his friend Princess, and their cat do some stylish time-traveling. (Rev: BL 10/15/94; SLJ 10/94)

4152 Gilmore, Kate. *The Exchange Student* (6–9). 1999, Houghton $15.00 (0-395-57511-7). Set in the year 2094, this novel describes the problems faced by a group of exchange students from the planet Chela who are studying on Earth. (Rev: BL 9/15/99; HB 9–10/99; HBG 4/00; SLJ 10/99)

4153 Goodman, Alison. *Singing the Dogstar Blues* (7–12). 2003, Viking $16.99 (0-670-03610-2). Science fiction, adventure, mystery, and humor are all combined in this story of a spunky time-travel student who shares a room with an alien. (Rev: BL 4/15/03; HBG 10/03; SLJ 4/03*; VOYA 2/03)

4154 Griffith, Helen V. *Journal of a Teenage Genius* (5–8). 1987, Troll paper $2.50 (0-8167-1325-1). In diary form, a young hero tells of his encounter with a time machine. (Rev: BR 11–12/87; SLJ 10/87; VOYA 12/87)

4155 Gutman, Dan. *Cyberkid* (4–8). 1998, Hyperion LB $14.49 (0-7868-2344-5). Yip, a computer-savvy 12-year-old, and his sister, Paige, create a "virtual actor," or "vactor," who breaks out of cyberspace and reveals a serious flaw: his database does not include a conscience. (Rev: BL 6/1–15/98; SLJ 8/98)

4156 Gutman, Dan. *The Edison Mystery* (4–8). Series: Qwerty Stevens, Back in Time. 2001, Simon & Schuster $16.00 (0-689-84124-8). The time machine he finds in his backyard sends 13-year-old Robert "Qwerty" Stevens to 1879 to Thomas Edison's workshop. (Rev: HBG 3/02; SLJ 8/01)

4157 Haddix, Margaret P. *Among the Hidden* (5–8). 1998, Simon & Schuster $16.95 (0-689-81700-2). In a society where only two children are allowed per family, Luke, the third, endures a secret life hidden from authorities. (Rev: BR 5–6/99; HBG 3/99; SLJ 9/98; VOYA 10/98)

4158 Haddix, Margaret Peterson. *Among the Barons* (5–8). 2003, Simon & Schuster $16.95 (0-689-83906-5). Luke, a third child who has been living underground in this two-child society, comes close to exposure in this exciting installment in the series that began with *Among the Hidden* (1998). (Rev: BL 5/15/03; HBG 10/03; SLJ 6/03; VOYA 8/03)

4159 Haddix, Margaret Peterson. *Among the Betrayed* (5–9). 2002, Simon & Schuster $16.95 (0-689-83905-7). In this third novel in the series that started with *Among the Hidden* (1998), illegal third child Nina faces danger and difficult decisions. (Rev: BCCB 10/02; HBG 10/02; SLJ 6/02; VOYA 6/02)

4160 Haddix, Margaret Peterson. *Among the Imposters* (5–7). 2001, Simon & Schuster $16.00 (0-689-83904-9). As a third child in a society that allows only two per family, Luke has assumed a new identity and at age 12 enrolls in a nightmarish boarding school. (Rev: BCCB 9/01; BL 4/15/01; HBG 10/01; SLJ 7/01; VOYA 8/01)

4161 Haddix, Margaret Peterson. *Turnabout* (7–10). 2000, Simon & Schuster $17.00 (0-689-82187-5). Life is turned upside down as two centenarian nursing home residents opt at the start of the 21st century to grow younger rather than older, and by 2085, after complicated lives, realize they'll need care in their childhoods. (Rev: BL 10/15/00; HBG 3/01; SLJ 9/00)

4162 Halam, Ann. *Dr. Franklin's Island* (6–10). 2002, Random $12.95 (0-385-73008-X). Three British teens survive a plane crash on a remote island only to find they have fallen into the hands of a mad scientist. (Rev: BCCB 5/02; BL 7/02; HBG 10/02; SLJ 5/02)

4163 Heinlein, Robert A. *Between Planets* (7–10). 1984, Ballantine paper $6.99 (0-345-32099-9). A revolt on Venus against an interplanetary alliance causes painful decisions for Don.

4164 Heinlein, Robert A. *Citizen of the Galaxy* (6–8). 1987, Ballantine paper $6.99 (0-345-34244-5). First published in 1957, this science fiction classic tells about the adventures of a young boy rescued from slavery to fulfill an unusual mission. (Rev: BL 6/1/87)

4165 Heinlein, Robert A. *Farmer in the Sky* (7–10). 1985, Ballantine paper $6.99 (0-345-32438-2). A family decides to leave Earth to find better resources on another planet. A reissue.

4166 Heinlein, Robert A. *Have Space Suit, Will Travel* (7–9). 1977, Ballantine paper $6.50 (0-345-32441-2). Kip Russell realizes his dream of visiting the moon in his own spacesuit.

4167 Heinlein, Robert A. *Red Planet* (7–10). 1981, Ballantine paper $6.99 (0-345-34039-6). A novel about the first space exploration of the planet Mars.

4168 Heinlein, Robert A. *The Rolling Stones* (7–10). 1985, Ballantine paper $6.99 (0-345-32451-X). The Stone family takes on the universe in this unusual science fiction adventure. A reissue.

4169 Heinlein, Robert A. *Space Cadet* (7–10). 1984, Ballantine paper $5.99 (0-345-35311-0). In the year 2075, several members of the Solar Patrol have fantastic adventures.

4170 Heinlein, Robert A. *The Star Beast* (7–10). 1977, Macmillan $15.00 (0-684-15329-7) A pet smuggled to Earth never seems to stop growing.

4171 Heinlein, Robert A. *Starman Jones* (7–10). 1985, Ballantine paper $6.99 (0-345-32811-6). Eager for adventure, Max Jones stows away on an intergalactic spaceship. A reissue.

4172 Heintze, Ty. *Valley of the Eels* (5–8). 1993, Eakin $15.95 (0-89015-904-1). A dolphin leads two boys to an underwater station where friendly aliens are cultivating trees to replant on their own planet. (Rev: BL 3/1/94)

4173 Hill, William. *The Magic Bicycle* (5–8). 1998, Otter Creek paper $13.95 (1-890611-00-X). For helping an alien escape, Danny receives a magical bicycle that is capable of transporting him through time and space. (Rev: BL 1/1–15/98; SLJ 3/98)

4174 Howarth, Lesley. *MapHead: The Return* (5–9). 1997, Candlewick $16.99 (0-7636-0344-9). In this sequel to *MapHead* (1994), our 13-year-old hero from a parallel universe moves in with a family where his ability to control the minds of others causes trouble. (Rev: BCCB 3/98; BR 3–4/98; HBG 3/98; SLJ 1/98; VOYA 4/98)

4175 Hughes, Monica. *Invitation to the Game* (7–10). 1991, Simon & Schuster paper $4.99 (0-671-86692-3). In 2154, a high school graduate and her friends face life on welfare in a highly robotic society and are invited to participate in a sinister government "game." (Rev: BL 9/15/91)

4176 Jeapes, Ben. *The Xenocide Mission* (7–10). 2002, Viking $15.95 (0-385-75007-2). A complex and exciting adventure set in the distant future in which humans and their quadrupled companions must fight against ferocious aliens known as the Kin. (Rev: BCCB 6/02; BL 4/15/02; HBG 3/03; SLJ 6/02; VOYA 8/02)

4177 Jeter, K. W. *The Mandalorian Armor* (7–9). Series: The Bounty Hunter Wars. 1998, Bantam paper $6.99 (0-553-57885-5). This first installment in a trilogy involves Boba Fett, the bounty hunter who captured Han Solo in *The Empire Strikes Back*. (Rev: VOYA 2/99)

4178 Jones, Diana Wynne. *Hexwood* (8–12). 1994, Greenwillow $16.00 (0-688-12488-7). A complex science fiction story about virtual realism, time manipulation, and a young girl who investigates the disappearance of guests at Hexwood Farm. (Rev: BL 6/1–15/94; SLJ 3/94; VOYA 10/94)

4179 Kaye, Marilyn. *Amy, Number Seven: How Many Are Out There?* (6–10). Series: Replica. 1998, Bantam Doubleday Dell paper $4.50 (0-553-49238-1). When Amy finds that her personality is mysteriously changing, her mother is acting strangely, and she is developing extraordinary new abilities, she sets out to find the truth about her past. (Rev: BL 10/15/98; SLJ 10/98)

4180 Kaye, Marilyn. *Pursuing Amy* (6–8). Series: Replica. 1998, Bantam paper $4.50 (0-553-49239-X). Amy, Tasha's 12-year-old friend, is actually a clone from a genetic engineering project and now she not only has superhuman capabilities but also is

227

being pursued by the evil forces that funded the project. (Rev: BL 1/1–15/99; SLJ 7/99)

4181 Key, Alexander. *The Forgotten Door* (5–7). 1986, Scholastic paper $4.50 (0-590-43130-7). When little Jon falls to earth from another planet, he encounters suspicion and hostility as well as sympathy. A reissue.

4182 Kiesel, Stanley. *Skinny Malinky Leads the War for Kidness* (6–8). 1984, Avon paper $2.50 (0-380-69875-7). Skinny is about to be captured by a powerful mutant red ant.

4183 Kilworth, Garry. *The Electric Kid* (6–9). 1995, Orchard LB $15.99 (0-531-08786-7). Two homeless young people struggle for survival in a large city's oppressive underworld in this bleak novel set in the horrifying world of 2061. (Rev: BL 1/1–15/96; SLJ 10/95; VOYA 12/95)

4184 Klause, Annette Curtis. *Alien Secrets* (5–8). 1993, Delacorte $15.95 (0-385-30928-7). Modern variations on the best of 1950s–1960s science fiction by Heinlein, Norton, Bova, et al. (Rev: BL 6/1–15/93*; SLJ 9/93*; VOYA 8/93)

4185 Kress, Nancy. *Yanked!* (4–8). Series: Out of Time. 1999, Avon paper $4.99 (0-380-79968-5). Teenagers Jason and Sharon are "yanked" from the 1990s to the 2300s to help save youngsters lost on an alien planet. (Rev: BL 9/1/99)

4186 Kurts, Charles. *These Are the Voyages: A Three-Dimensional Star Trek Album* (4–7). Illus. 1996, Simon & Schuster $35.00 (0-671-55139-6). Pop-ups are used to re-create the Starfleet ships, including the U.S.S. *Enterprise*. (Rev: BL 12/15/97)

4187 Lassiter, Rhiannon. *Hex* (7–10). 2001, Simon & Schuster paper $4.99 (0-7434-2211-2). An exciting, futuristic action story about 24th-century teens who use their computer savvy to combat an evil government agency. (Rev: BL 1/1–15/02)

4188 Lassiter, Rhiannon. *Shadows* (7–10). 2002, Simon & Schuster paper $4.99 (0-7434-2212-0). Raven, the superhacker introduced in *Hex*, faces new dangers as the government seeks to destroy her and her fellow mutants. The last volume in the trilogy is *Ghosts* (2002). (Rev: BL 4/15/02; SLJ 4/02)

4189 Lawrence, Louise. *Andra* (6–10). 1991, HarperCollins $14.95 (0-06-023685-X). This novel is set 2,000 years in the future, when humanity, having destroyed Earth's environment, lives in rigidly governed, sealed underground cities. (Rev: BL 5/1/91; SLJ 5/91)

4190 Lawrence, Louise. *Dream-Weaver* (7–12). 1996, Clarion $15.00 (0-395-71812-0). The horror of psychic manipulation is explored in this science fiction thriller about a girl who, in her dream body, joins a spaceship full of colonists bound for her planet. (Rev: BL 10/1/96*; SLJ 10/96; VOYA 2/97)

4191 Lawrence, Louise. *The Patchwork People* (7–10). 1994, Clarion $14.95 (0-395-67892-7). This brooding story takes place in a bleak Wales of the future, where natural resources are nearly depleted and jobs are scarce. (Rev: BL 12/15/94*; SLJ 11/94)

4192 Layne, Steven L. *This Side of Paradise* (7–10). 2001, North Star $15.99 (0-9712336-9-1). Jack, a junior in high school, soon questions his father's motives for moving the family into a town called Paradise, where things are definitely not what they seem. (Rev: BL 2/1/02; SLJ 1/02; VOYA 2/02)

4193 Le Guin, Ursula K. *The Left Hand of Darkness* (7–12). 1969, Ace paper $7.99 (0-441-47812-3). An envoy is sent to the ice-covered planet Gethen where people can be either male or female at will.

4194 L'Engle, Madeleine. *Many Waters* (7–10). 1986, Farrar $18.00 (0-374-34796-4); Dell paper $6.50 (0-440-40548-3). The Murry twins, from the author's Wrinkle in Time trilogy, time-travel to the Holy Land prior to the Great Flood. (Rev: BL 8/86; SLJ 11/86; VOYA 12/86)

4195 L'Engle, Madeleine. *A Wrinkle in Time* (6–9). 1962, Farrar $17.00 (0-374-38613-7); Dell paper $6.50 (0-440-49805-8). Meg and Charles Wallace Murry, with the help of Calvin O'Keefe, set out in space to find their scientist father. Newbery Medal 1963. Followed by *A Wind in the Door* (1973), *A Swiftly Tilting Planet* (1978), and *A Ring of Endless Light* (1981).

4196 Lowenstein, Sallie. *Evan's Voice* (5–8). Illus. 1998, Lion Stone paper $15.00 (0-9658486-1-2). Teenager Jake cares for his catatonic younger brother while seeking civilization's last chance for survival in an area known as the Dead Zone. (Rev: BL 3/1/99; VOYA 6/99)

4197 Lowenstein, Sallie. *Focus* (5–9). Illus. 2001, Lion Stone paper $15.00 (0-9658486-3-9). The Haldrans leave their planet and relocate to Miners World, where humans live, in order to save their son from discrimination because of his creative intelligence. (Rev: BL 4/15/01; SLJ 8/01; VOYA 8/01)

4198 Lubar, David. *Flip* (5–8). 2003, Tor $17.95 (0-765-30149-0). A humorous science fiction novel in which 13-year-old underachiever Ryan, whose twin sister is overachiever Taylor, becomes entranced by a set of disks dropped by passing aliens that introduces him to the achievements of such earthly successes as Babe Ruth, Einstein, Elvis, and Queen Victoria. (Rev: BCCB 10/03; SLJ 8/03; VOYA 8/03)

4199 Luiken, Nicole. *Silver Eyes* (7–12). 2001, S & S Pulse paper $5.99 (0-7434-0078-X). Romance and suspenseful mystery combine with science fiction in this story set in the future about a girl endangered by her memory losses. (Rev: SLJ 5/02)

4200 Mackel, Kathy. *Can of Worms* (4–7). 2000, HarperCollins $15.99 (0-380-97681-1); paper $3.99 (0-380-80050-0). A humorous science fiction story about 7th-grader Mike Pillsbury, who receives several extraterrestrial responses to his intergalactic appeal to be rescued from this planet when things go wrong in his life. (Rev: HB 5–6/99; HBG 10/99; SLJ 6/99; VOYA 4/99)

4201 Mackel, Kathy. *Eggs in One Basket* (5–7). 2000, HarperCollins LB $17.89 (0-06-029213-X). Scott Schreiber has hallucinations that lead him to a birdlike alien who is being watched by a dangerous race of conquerors. (Rev: BL 9/15/00; HB 9–10/00; HBG 3/01; SLJ 11/00)

4202 Mackel, Kathy. *From the Horse's Mouth* (5–7). 2002, HarperCollins LB $15.89 (0-06-029415-9). Nick Thorpe is on another science fiction adventure involving a time warp and evil aliens that plan to destroy his town. (Rev: BL 5/1/02; HBG 10/02; SLJ 7/02)

4203 Matas, Carol, and Perry Nodelman. *A Meeting of the Minds* (5–9). 1999, Simon & Schuster $17.00 (0-689-81947-1). Princess Lenora and fiance Prince Coren, strangers from a different universe, find themselves trapped in a shopping mall. (Rev: BL 12/1/99; HBG 3/00; SLJ 11/99; VOYA 2/00)

4204 Metz, Melinda. *The Outsider* (6–9). Series: Roswell High. 1998, Pocket Books paper $1.99 (0-671-02374-8). The first book about Max and Isabel, two teenagers attending a high school in New Mexico who are actually aliens trying to hide their real identities. (Rev: SLJ 3/99)

4205 Nelson, O. T. *The Girl Who Owned a City* (7–9). 1977, Dell paper $4.99 (0-440-92893-1). A mysterious virus kills off Earth's population except for children under the age of 13.

4206 Nix, Garth. *Shade's Children* (7–12). 1997, HarperCollins LB $15.89 (0-06-027325-9). In this science fiction novel, when a person reaches age 16, he or she is sent to the Meat Factory, where body parts are turned into hideous creatures. (Rev: BL 10/1/97; BR 3–4/98; SLJ 8/97; VOYA 6/98)

4207 Norton, Andre. *Key Out of Time* (7–12). 1978, Ultramarine $25.00 (0-89366-186-4). Two Time Agents recreate the conflict that destroyed life on the planet Hawaika.

4208 O'Brien, Robert C. *Z for Zachariah* (7–10). 1975, Macmillan paper $4.99 (0-02-044650-0). After a nuclear holocaust, Ann believes she is the only surviving human — but is she? (Rev: BL 7/88)

4209 Oldham, June. *Found* (7–12). 1996, Orchard LB $17.99 (0-531-08893-6). In this novel set in the 21st century, Ren becomes lost in a bleak countryside, gets involved with three other misfits, and finds an abandoned baby. (Rev: BL 9/15/96; BR 3–4/97; SLJ 10/96; VOYA 2/97)

4210 Parker, Daniel. *April* (7–10). Series: Countdown. 1999, Simon & Schuster paper $3.99 (0-689-81822-X). In this fourth book in this complex series, teenagers find that they must take over the earth when a terrible plague kills everyone except those between 16 and 20 years of age. It is necessary to read all the books in sequence to follow the story. The others are *January, February,* and *March* (1999). (Rev: SLJ 6/99)

4211 Paulsen, Gary. *The Transall Saga* (7–12). 1998, Delacorte $15.95 (0-385-32196-1). While on a hiking trip, young Mark is transported to a primitive world in this science fiction novel with a strong survival theme. (Rev: BCCB 7–8/98; BL 5/15/98; BR 11–12/98; HBG 10/98; SLJ 5/98; VOYA 10/98)

4212 Peel, John. *The Zanti Misfits* (6–10). 1997, Tor paper $3.99 (0-8125-9063-5). This quick read, a product of *The Outer Limits* television show, tells how the planet Zanti sent to Earth a shipload of their worst criminals and how three teenagers wander into their landing area. Also use *The Choice* and *The Time Shifter* (both 1997). (Rev: VOYA 4/98)

4213 Pierce, Tamora. *Street Magic* (5–9). Series: Circle Opens. 2001, Scholastic paper $16.95 (0-590-39628-5). Briar, a 14-year-old former gang member, finds he is again caught between warring gangs when he helps a female street urchin in this futuristic novel. (Rev: BL 4/15/01; HB 3–4/01; HBG 10/01; SLJ 7/01; VOYA 4/01)

4214 Price, Susan. *The Sterkarm Handshake* (7–10). 2000, HarperCollins $17.95 (0-06-028959-7). Violent confrontations result when a 21st-century corporation makes inroads into the 16th-century Scottish Borders. (Rev: BL 10/1/00; BR 3–4/01; HBG 3/01; SLJ 12/00)

4215 Read Magazine, ed. *Read into the Millennium: Tales of the Future* (6–8). 1999, Millbrook LB $24.90 (0-7613-0962-4). This collection of 10 science fiction stories includes works by Robert Lipsyte, Kurt Vonnegut, and Lois Lowry, plus adaptations of Wells's *The Time Machine* and Shelley's *Frankenstein*. (Rev: BL 5/15/99; BR 9–10/99; HBG 9/99; SLJ 6/99)

4216 Rector, Rebecca Kraft. *Tria and the Great Star Rescue* (4–7). 2002, Delacorte $14.95 (0-385-72941-3). Tria, who has been unwilling to leave her home planet of Chiron, must use her technological savvy and face untold dangers in her quest to rescue her kidnapped mother and holographic best friend, Star. (Rev: BCCB 9/02; HB 5–6/02; HBG 10/02; SLJ 2/02)

4217 Reeve, Philip. *Mortal Engines* (7–10). 2003, HarperCollins $16.99 (0-06-008207-0). An imaginative story of cities on the rampage, in which London is seeking to devour smaller towns to fuel its ability to move about, and brave youngsters who resist. (Rev: BL 11/1/03; HB 11–12/03; SLJ 12/03*)

4218 Regan, Dian C. *Princess Nevermore* (5–7). 1995, Scholastic $14.95 (0-590-47582-6). A princess from another world gets her wish to visit Earth, where she is befriended by two teenagers, Sarah and Adam. (Rev: BCCB 11/95; SLJ 9/95)

4219 Rodda, Emily. *Finders Keepers* (4–7). 1991, Greenwillow $12.95 (0-688-10516-5). Patrick is transported onto the set of a quiz show in a parallel world beyond the "great barrier." (Rev: BCCB 12/91; BL 11/15/91; SLJ 8/91)

4220 Rubenstein, Gillian. *Galax-Arena* (7–10). 1995, Simon & Schuster paper $15.00 (0-689-80136-X). A 13-year-old girl and 20 other children from Earth are removed to another planet and trained to perform dangerous acrobatic tricks. (Rev: BL 10/15/95*; SLJ 10/95)

4221 Rubinstein, Gillian. *Under the Cat's Eye* (5–7). 1998, Simon & Schuster $16.00 (0-689-81800-9). A multilayered novel blending time travel, mystery, and fantasy in which Jai is sent to a boarding school where the fiendish headmaster uses technology to steal the futures of his pupils and deprive them of hope and a sense of purpose. (Rev: BCCB 11/98; BL 8/98; HB 11–12/98; HBG 3/99; SLJ 10/98; VOYA 10/98)

4222 Sargent, Pamela. *Alien Child* (8–12). 1988, HarperCollins $13.95 (0-06-025202-2). A teenage girl raised in an alien world discovers there is another human living in her complex. (Rev: BL 2/1/88; BR 9–10/88; SLJ 4/88; VOYA 8/88)

4223 Scrimger, Richard. *The Nose from Jupiter* (5–8). 1998, Tundra paper $5.95 (0-88776-428-2). Alan doesn't mind that Norbert, an alien from Jupiter, is living in his nose, but Norbert's outspoken remarks often get Alan into trouble. (Rev: BL 7/98; BR 11–12/98)

4224 Shelley, Mary. *Frankenstein* (8–12). Illus. Series: Whole Story. 1998, Viking $25.99 (0-670-87800-6). Illustrations plus period prints and maps enhance this complete version of the early science fiction thriller. (Rev: BL 9/1/98; HBG 9/99; SLJ 10/98)

4225 Simons, Jamie, and E. W. Scollon. *Goners: RU1:2* (4–7). Illus. 1998, Avon paper $3.99 (0-380-79729-1). In this science fiction comedy, four teenage aliens from the planet Roma time-travel to a modern-day high school. (Rev: BL 5/15/98)

4226 Simons, Jamie, and E. W. Scollon. *Goners: The Hunt Is On* (4–7). Illus. 1998, Avon paper $3.99 (0-380-79730-5). Four alien teens from the planet Roma time-travel to Monticello to fetch Thomas Jefferson. (Rev: BL 5/15/98)

4227 Skurzynski, Gloria. *The Clones: The Virtual War Chronologs* (6–9). 2002, Simon & Schuster $16.00 (0-689-84463-5). In this sequel to *Virtual War* (1997), in which Corgan successfully defended the Western Hemisphere Federation, Corgan's peaceful life is disturbed by the arrival of a pair of surprisingly different clones. (Rev: BL 4/15/02; VOYA 8/02)

4228 Skurzynski, Gloria. *Virtual War* (6–9). Illus. 1997, Simon & Schuster $16.00 (0-689-81374-0). Fourteen-year-old Corgan and two other youngsters are chosen by the Council to represent the Western Hemisphere Federation in a virtual war. (Rev: BL 8/97; SLJ 7/97; VOYA 8/97)

4229 Sleator, William. *Boltzmon!* (5–8). 1999, Dutton $15.99 (0-525-46131-0). A subatomic particle transports Chris to an alternate universe where he must complete dangerous quests to prevent his own death on earth. (Rev: HBG 3/00; SLJ 11/99; VOYA 2/00)

4230 Sleator, William. *The Boy Who Reversed Himself* (8–12). 1998, Puffin paper $5.99 (0-14-038965-2). Laura travels into the fourth dimension with her gifted neighbor and literally everything in her life becomes upside-down. (Rev: BL 10/15/86; BR 5–6/87; SLJ 11/86; VOYA 6/87)

4231 Sleator, William. *The Duplicate* (7–10). 1990, Bantam paper $3.99 (0-553-28634-X). A teenager discovers a machine that allows him the power to duplicate himself. (Rev: BL 5/15/88; SLJ 4/88; VOYA 12/88)

4232 Sleator, William. *House of Stairs* (7–10). 1991, Puffin paper $5.99 (0-14-034580-9). Five teenage orphans are kidnapped to become part of an experiment on aggression.

4233 Sleator, William. *Interstellar Pig* (7–10). 1996, Peter Smith $20.75 (0-8446-6898-2); Puffin paper $6.99 (0-14-037595-3). Barney plays an odd board game with strangers who are actually aliens from space.

4234 Sleator, William. *The Night the Heads Came* (6–9). 1996, Dutton $16.99 (0-525-45463-2). A thrilling science fiction adventure in which Leo has problems adjusting to normal life after being abducted by aliens. (Rev: BL 3/15/96; BR 9–10/96; SLJ 4/96)

4235 Sleator, William. *Parasite Pig* (7–10). 2002, Dutton $15.99 (0-525-46918-4). Barney and Katie continue playing the board game they began in *Interstellar Pig* and wind up on a planet called J'koot, threatened by crablike aliens with cannibal tendencies. (Rev: BCCB 2/03; BL 11/15/02; HB 11–12/02*; HBG 3/03; SLJ 10/02; VOYA 12/02)

4236 Sleator, William. *Singularity* (7–12). 1995, Puffin paper $5.99 (0-14-037598-8). Twin boys discover a playhouse on the property they have inherited that contains a mystery involving monsters from space and a new dimension in time. (Rev: BL 4/1/85; SLJ 8/85)

4237 Slote, Alfred. *My Robot Buddy* (5–8). Illus. 1986, HarperCollins $12.95 (0-397-31641-0); paper

$4.95 (0-06-440165-0). An easily read novel about Danny and the robot that is created for him. (Rev: BL 11/1/87)

4238 Stackpole, Michael A. *I, Jedi* (8–12). 1998, Random paper $6.99 (0-553-57873-1). In order to find his wife, Corran must take a quick course at the Jedi Academy founded by Luke Skywalker and learn to use his hidden powers. (Rev: VOYA 12/98)

4239 Stemp, Jane. *Waterbound* (6–10). 1996, Dial $15.99 (0-8037-1994-9). Gem, who lives in the tightly controlled culture of the future, discovers another world where the misfits are kept. (Rev: BL 8/96; BR 3–4/97; SLJ 9/96; VOYA 8/97)

4240 Stevenson, Robert Louis. *The Strange Case of Dr. Jekyll and Mr. Hyde* (5–8). Illus. Series: Whole Story. 2003, Barnes & Noble paper $3.95 (1-593-08054-9). Using lively ink-and-watercolor illustrations, this book offers the complete text of the classic in an attractive format. (Rev: BL 5/1/00; HBG 10/00)

4241 Tolan, Stephanie S. *Welcome to the Ark* (7–10). 1996, Morrow $15.00 (0-688-13724-5). Science fiction and adventure combine in the story of four young people who are able to act for good or evil through telecommunications. (Rev: BL 10/15/96; BR 11–12/96; SLJ 10/96; VOYA 4/97)

4242 Townsend, John Rowe. *The Creatures* (7–10). 1980, HarperCollins $12.95 (0-397-31864-2). Earth is dominated by creatures from another planet who believe in mind over emotion.

4243 Ure, Jean. *Plague* (7–12). 1991, Harcourt $16.95 (0-15-262429-5); Puffin paper $4.99 (0-14-036283-5). Three teenagers must band together to survive in a hostile, nearly deserted London after a catastrophe has killed almost everyone. (Rev: BL 11/15/91*; SLJ 10/91)

4244 Vande Velde, Vivian. *Heir Apparent* (6–9). 2002, Harcourt $17.00 (0-15-204560-0). When Giannine, 14, enters a virtual reality game set in medieval times, she doesn't expect the game to be damaged or her playing skill to become a matter of life and death. (Rev: BCCB 12/02; BL 2/1/03; HB 11–12/02; HBG 3/03; SLJ 10/02; VOYA 12/02)

4245 Verne, Jules. *Around the Moon* (8–12). 1968, Airmont paper $1.50 (0-8049-0182-1). An early science fiction relic about a trip to the moon. Also use *From the Earth to the Moon* (1984).

4246 Walsh, Jill Paton. *The Green Book* (4–7). 1982, Farrar paper $4.95 (0-374-42802-6). The exodus of a group of Britons from dying Earth to another planet.

4247 Wells, H. G. *First Men in the Moon* (7–12). 1993, Tuttle paper $7.95 (0-460-87304-0). The first men on the moon discover strange creatures living there.

4248 Wells, H. G. *The Invisible Man* (8–12). 1987, Buccaneer LB $21.95 (0-89966-377-X); Bantam paper $4.95 (0-553-21353-9). Two editions of many available of the story of a scientist who finds a way to make himself invisible.

4249 Wells, H. G. *Time Machine* (7–12). 1984, Bantam paper $4.95 (0-553-21351-2). This is one of the earliest novels to use traveling through time as its subject.

4250 Wells, H. G. *The War of the Worlds* (7–12). 1988, Bantam paper $4.95 (0-553-21338-5). In this early science fiction novel, first published in 1898, strange creatures from Mars invade England.

4251 Westwood, Chris. *Virtual World* (6–9). 1997, Viking $15.99 (0-670-87546-5). When 14-year-old Jack North plays a pirated copy of a computer game called Silicon Sphere, he suddenly finds he has been transported to the world of virtual reality. (Rev: BL 9/1/97; BR 3–4/98; HBG 3/98; SLJ 1/98; VOYA 6/98)

4252 Wismer, Donald. *Starluck* (6–8). 1982, Ultramarine $20.00 (0-89366-255-0). A boy with unusual powers tries to overthrow a wicked emperor.

4253 Yolen, Jane, et al., eds. *Spaceships and Spells* (5–9). 1987, HarperCollins $12.95 (0-06-026796-8). A collection of 13 original tales, mostly science fiction but also some fantasy. (Rev: BL 1/15/88; BR 3–4/88; SLJ 11/87)

Sports

4254 Adler, C. S. *Winning* (5–8). 1999, Clarion $14.00 (0-395-65017-8). Eighth-grader Vicky lacks the courage and self-confidence to challenge her tennis partner when she catches her cheating. (Rev: BCCB 10/99; BL 10/1/99; HBG 3/00; SLJ 9/99)

4255 Altman, Millys N. *Racing in Her Blood* (7–12). 1980, HarperCollins LB $12.89 (0-397-31895-2). A junior novel about a young girl who wants to succeed in the world of automobile racing.

4256 Avi. *S.O.R. Losers* (5–7). 1984, Macmillan $15.00 (0-02-793410-1). The most inept soccer team in the history of the South Orange River Middle School is formed.

4257 Barwin, Steven, and Gabriel David Tick. *Slam Dunk* (5–7). Series: Sports Stories. 1999, Orca paper $5.50 (1-55028-598-X). An easy read about a junior high basketball team in Canada that goes coed and the problems that result. (Rev: SLJ 1/00)

4258 Bauer, Joan. *Sticks* (5–8). 1996, Delacorte $15.95 (0-385-32165-1). Ten-year-old Mickey, who is recovering from his father's death, gets an old family friend to teach him pool tricks so that he will have a chance at the Pool Hall Youth Championship. (Rev: BL 5/1/96; SLJ 6/96)

4259 Bennett, James. *Blue Star Rapture* (7–12). 1998, Simon & Schuster $16.00 (0-689-81580-8). T. J., a basketball hopeful, goes to a basketball camp, where he meets a girl from a religious cult in this novel about sports, politicking, religion, and loyalty. (Rev: BL 4/15/98; BR 1–2/99; HBG 9/98; SLJ 6/98; VOYA 12/98)

4260 Bledsoe, Lucy Jane. *Hoop Girlz* (5–7). 2002, Holiday $16.95 (0-8234-1691-7). When 11-year-old River is denied a place on the girls' basketball team, she forms her own team, with her brother as the coach. (Rev: BL 9/1/02; HBG 10/03; SLJ 12/02)

4261 Bo, Ben. *The Edge* (5–8). 1999, Lerner LB $17.95 (0-8225-3307-3). Conflicted Declan is sent to a rehabilitation program in Canada's Glacier National Park, where he learns to snowboard and is drawn into a duel with the local champion. (Rev: BCCB 1/00; BL 10/15/99; HBG 3/00; SLJ 1/00; VOYA 4/00)

4262 Bo, Ben. *Skullcrack* (7–12). 2000, Lerner LB $14.95 (0-8225-3308-1). Jonah, an avid surfer, travels with his father to Florida to be united with his twin sister who was put up for adoption at birth. (Rev: BL 6/1–15/00; HBG 9/00; SLJ 6/00)

4263 Bowen, Fred. *The Final Cut* (4–7). Series: All-Star Sport Story. 1999, Peachtree paper $4.95 (1-56145-192-4). A fast-paced novel about four friends and their efforts to make the junior high school basketball team. (Rev: SLJ 7/99)

4264 Bowen, Fred. *On the Line* (4–7). 1999, Peachtree paper $4.95 (1-56145-199-1). A young boy learns about self-image and open-mindedness while trying to improve his foul shots in this novel about an 8th grader and his basketball skills. (Rev: SLJ 4/00)

4265 Brooks, Bruce. *Billy* (4–8). Series: Wolfbay Wings. 1998, HarperCollins LB $14.89 (0-06-027899-4); paper $4.50 (0-06-440707-1). Billy, part of the Wolfbay Wings hockey team, worries that his overbearing father will refuse him permission to join the gang at the beach during summer vacation. (Rev: HBG 3/99; SLJ 7/98)

4266 Brooks, Bruce. *Boot* (4–7). Series: Wolfbay Wings. 1998, HarperCollins paper $4.50 (0-06-440680-6). In this hockey story, a foster child named The Boot is reluctant to "hit" his opponents. (Rev: HBG 10/98; SLJ 3/98)

4267 Brooks, Bruce. *Dooby* (5–8). Series: Wolfbay Wings. 1998, HarperCollins LB $14.89 (0-06-027898-6); paper $4.50 (0-06-440708-X). Dooby sulks when he is not made captain of his Peewee hockey team, but is completely humiliated to learn

he has lost out to a girl. Also recommended in this series is *Reed* (1998). (Rev: HBG 3/99; SLJ 2/99)

4268 Brooks, Bruce. *The Moves Make the Man* (7–9). 1984, HarperCollins $15.00 (0-06-020679-9); paper $6.99 (0-06-447022-9). Jerome, the only African American student in his high school and a star basketball player, forms an unusual friendship with Bix. (Rev: BL 3/87)

4269 Brooks, Bruce. *Prince* (5–8). Series: Wolfbay Wings. 1998, HarperCollins LB $14.89 (0-06-027542-1); paper $4.50 (0-06-440600-8). Prince, the only African American boy on the Wolfbay Wings hockey team, is pressured by his middle school coach to switch to basketball. (Rev: HBG 10/98; SLJ 6/98)

4270 Brooks, Bruce. *Reed* (5–8). Series: Wolfbay Wings. 1998, HarperCollins LB $14.89 (0-06-028055-7); paper $4.50 (0-06-440726-8). Reed, a member of the Wolfbay Wings hockey team, is considered a "puck-hog" and must learn to be more of a team player. (Rev: HBG 3/99; SLJ 2/99)

4271 Brooks, Bruce. *Shark* (5–8). Series: Wolfbay Wings. 1998, HarperCollins LB $14.89 (0-06-027570-7); paper $4.50 (0-06-440681-4). In spite of being fat, slow, and confused, Shark becomes a valuable player on the Wolfbay Wings hockey team. (Rev: HBG 10/98; SLJ 6/98)

4272 Bruchac, Joseph. *The Warriors* (5–8). 2003, Darby Creek $15.95 (1-58196-002-6). Jake Forrest, a Native American teenager and lacrosse whiz, leaves the reservation to attend a private school and encounters many new situations, including a different attitude toward sports. (Rev: BL 12/1/03; SLJ 10/03)

4273 Butcher, Kristin. *Cairo Kelly and the Man* (4–8). 2002, Orca paper $6.95 (1-55143-211-0). When Midge discovers that his baseball team's umpire, Hal Mann, is illiterate, Midge and his friend Kelly set out to solve the problem. (Rev: BL 9/1/02; VOYA 4/03)

4274 Butler, Dori Hillestad. *Sliding into Home* (5–8). 2003, Peachtree $14.95 (1-56145-222-X). Joelle, 13, refuses to accept a ban on girls playing baseball when she moves to a small town in Iowa. (Rev: BL 5/1/03; HBG 10/03)

4275 Cadnum, Michael. *Redhanded* (8–10). 2000, Viking $15.99 (0-670-88775-7). In this gripping novel, teenager Steven tries to further his boxing career by getting involved with streetwise Chad and planning a robbery to raise money for tournament fees. (Rev: BL 9/1/00; HBG 3/01; SLJ 11/00)

4276 Carter, Alden R. *Bull Catcher* (7–10). 1997, Scholastic paper $15.95 (0-590-50958-6). High school friends Bull and Jeff seem to live for baseball and plan their futures around the sport, but one of them begins to move in a different direction. (Rev: BL 4/15/97; BR 5–6/97; SLJ 5/97; VOYA 10/97)

4277 Charbonnet, Gabrielle. *Competition Fever* (5–7). 1996, Bantam paper $3.50 (0-553-48295-5). In this novel, rivalry between two girls endangers a team's chances of victory in gymnastics competitions. (Rev: BL 9/1/96; SLJ 6/96)

4278 Christopher, Matt. *Mountain Bike Mania* (5–7). 1998, Little, Brown paper $4.50 (0-316-14292-1). Will is at loose ends with no after-school activities until he becomes involved in a mountain bike club. (Rev: BL 2/1/99; HBG 10/99; SLJ 3/99)

4279 Christopher, Matt. *Prime-Time Pitcher* (4–7). 1998, Little, Brown paper $4.50 (0-316-14213-1). Koby Caplin becomes arrogant about his winning streak on the baseball team and soon loses games because of his lack of teamwork. (Rev: HBG 3/99; SLJ 12/98)

4280 Christopher, Matt. *Return of the Home Run Kid* (4–7). 1994, Little, Brown paper $4.50 (0-316-14273-5). In this sequel to *The Kid Who Only Hit Homers* (1972), Sylvester learns to be more aggressive on the field but gets criticism from his friends. (Rev: BL 4/15/92; SLJ 5/92)

4281 Christopher, Matt. *Snowboard Maverick* (4–7). 1997, Little, Brown paper $4.50 (0-316-14203-4). Dennis overcomes his fears and begins snowboarding. (Rev: BL 4/1/98; HBG 3/98; SLJ 3/98)

4282 Christopher, Matt. *Spike It!* (5–8). 1999, Little, Brown $15.95 (0-316-13451-1). Eighth-grader Jamie must adjust to her new stepsister, Michaela, and to the fact that she is planning on joining Jamie's volleyball team. (Rev: HBG 10/99; SLJ 6/99)

4283 Cochran, Thomas. *Roughnecks* (8–12). 1997, Harcourt $15.00 (0-15-201433-0). Senior Travis Cody, the narrator, wonders if he will be able to redeem himself with his football teammates after being responsible for a crucial loss because of a missed block. (Rev: BL 9/15/97; HBG 3/98; SLJ 10/97; VOYA 12/97)

4284 Crutcher, Chris. *The Crazy Horse Electric Game* (7–12). 1987, Greenwillow $16.99 (0-688-06683-6); Dell paper $5.50 (0-440-20094-6). A motorboat accident ends the comfortable life and budding baseball career of a teenage boy. (Rev: BL 4/15/87; BR 9–10/87; SLJ 5/87; VOYA 6/87)

4285 Crutcher, Chris. *Ironman* (8–12). 1995, Greenwillow $16.99 (0-688-13503-X). A psychological sports novel in which a 17-year-old carries an attitude that fuels the plot. (Rev: BL 3/1/95*; SLJ 3/95; VOYA 5/95)

4286 Crutcher, Chris. *Running Loose* (7–10). 1983, Greenwillow $18.99 (0-688-02002-X); Bantam paper $5.50 (0-440-97570-0). A senior in high school faces problems when he opposes the decisions of a football coach. (Rev: BL 3/87)

4287 Deuker, Carl. *Heart of a Champion* (8–10). 1993, Avon paper $5.99 (0-380-72269-0). Explores the ups and downs of the five-year friendship between Seth and Jimmy, from their first meeting on a baseball field at age 12. (Rev: BL 6/1–15/93; SLJ 6/93)

4288 Deuker, Carl. *Night Hoops* (7–11). 2000, Houghton $15.00 (0-395-97936-6). When older brother Scott gives up basketball for music, Nick develops his own presence on the court. (Rev: BL 5/1/00; HB 5–6/00; HBG 9/00; SLJ 5/00)

4289 Deuker, Carl. *On the Devil's Court* (8–12). 1991, Avon paper $4.99 (0-380-70879-5). In this variation on the Faust legend, a senior high basketball star believes he has sold his soul to have a perfect season. (Rev: BL 12/15/88; BR 9–10/89; SLJ 1/89; VOYA 4/89)

4290 Deuker, Carl. *Painting the Black* (8–12). 1997, Houghton $14.95 (0-395-82848-1). Ryan's spot on the baseball team hinges on catching the pitches of Josh Daniels, a sharp new player who is adept in both baseball and football. (Rev: BL 6/1–15/97; BR 11–12/97; SLJ 5/97; VOYA 8/97)

4291 Drumtra, Stacy. *Face-Off* (4–8). 1992, Avon paper $3.50 (0-380-76863-1). T.J. and his twin Brad become rivals for friends and for status on the hockey team. (Rev: BL 4/1/93; VOYA 8/93)

4292 Durant, Alan, sel. *Sports Stories* (5–9). Series: Story Library. 2000, Kingfisher $14.95 (0-7534-5322-3). A collection of 21 previously published short stories by well-known authors dealing with a variety of sports. (Rev: HBG 10/01; SLJ 11/00)

4293 Dygard, Thomas J. *Backfield Package* (6–10). 1992, Morrow $15.99 (0-688-11471-7). Two high school football stars want to play together in college, but only one of them is offered a scholarship. (Rev: BL 9/15/92; SLJ 9/92)

4294 Dygard, Thomas J. *Game Plan* (6–9). 1993, Morrow $14.00 (0-688-12007-5). Beano, a high school football student manager, must coach the team when the team's coach is injured in a car accident. (Rev: BL 9/1/93; SLJ 10/93; VOYA 2/94)

4295 Dygard, Thomas J. *Infield Hit* (6–9). 1995, Morrow $16.00 (0-688-14037-8). A boy struggles to make new friends by playing baseball. (Rev: BL 4/15/95; SLJ 3/95)

4296 Dygard, Thomas J. *The Rebounder* (7–10). 1994, Morrow $16.00 (0-688-12821-1). Chris quits playing basketball after accidentally injuring an opponent. After transferring to a new school, he is guided back to the sport by a sensitive coach. (Rev: BL 9/1/94; SLJ 10/94)

233

4297 Dygard, Thomas J. *The Rookie Arrives* (7–12). 1989, Puffin paper $5.99 (0-14-034112-9). Ted Bell comes of age when he becomes a major-leaguer fresh from high school. (Rev: BL 3/1/88; BR 5–6/88; SLJ 3/88)

4298 Dygard, Thomas J. *Running Wild* (7–10). 1996, Morrow $15.00 (0-688-14853-0). When Pete is forced to attend football practices, he discovers that he really enjoys the game. (Rev: BL 8/96; SLJ 9/96)

4299 Dygard, Thomas J. *Second Stringer* (6–12). 1998, Morrow $15.99 (0-688-15981-8). A star quarterback's knee injury gives second-stringer Kevin Taylor the opportunity of a lifetime during his senior year in high school. (Rev: BL 9/1/98; HBG 3/99; SLJ 12/98; VOYA 2/99)

4300 Farrell, Mame. *Bradley and the Billboard* (5–8). 1998, Farrar $16.00 (0-374-30949-3). Brad Wilson, a precocious kid who plays amazing baseball, finds a new life when he enters the modeling world. (Rev: BCCB 4/98; BL 7/98; HB 7–8/98; HBG 10/98; SLJ 5/98)

4301 Flynn, Pat. *Alex Jackson: SWA* (6–10). 2002, Univ. of Queensland paper $13.50 (0-7022-3307-2). Alex flirts with physical danger and trouble with the police when he joins up with Skateboarders with Attitude. (Rev: SLJ 1/03)

4302 Godfrey, Martyn. *Ice Hawk* (7–12). Illus. 1986, EMC paper $13.50 (0-8219-0235-0). An easy-to-read story about a young minor league hockey player who balks at unnecessary use of violence. (Rev: BL 2/1/87)

4303 Hale, Daniel J., and Matthew LaBrot. *Red Card* (4–7). Series: Zeke Armstrong Mystery. 2002, Top paper $7.95 (1-929976-15-1). Someone is trying to kill the soccer coach, and young Zeke sets out to discover who and why. (Rev: SLJ 12/02; VOYA 12/02)

4304 Hirschfeld, Robert. *Goalkeeper in Charge* (5–7). Series: Christopher Sports. 2002, Little, Brown $15.95 (0-316-07552-3); paper $4.50 (0-316-07548-5). Seventh-grader Tina works to overcome her shyness on and off the soccer field. (Rev: BL 9/1/02; HBG 3/03)

4305 Hoffius, Stephen. *Winners and Losers* (7–10). 1993, Simon & Schuster paper $16.00 (0-671-79194-X). When star runner Daryl collapses during a meet, the coach, his father, starts to ignore him and push Daryl's friend Curt to train harder. (Rev: BL 7/93; VOYA 2/94)

4306 Holohan, Maureen. *Catch Shorty by Rosie* (4–8). Series: The Broadway Ballplayers. 1999, Broadway Ballplayers paper $6.95 (0-9659091-6-6). Sixth-grader Rosie Jones devotes her time to organizing an all-girls football league while coping with a series of minor personal problems at home and school. (Rev: SLJ 3/00)

4307 Hughes, Dean. *End of the Race* (5–7). 1993, Atheneum $13.95 (0-689-31779-4). Both Jared and his African American track team competitor, Davin, are pressured by their parents to win. (Rev: BL 11/1/93; SLJ 12/93)

4308 Johnson, Scott. *Safe at Second* (5–8). 1999, Putnam $17.99 (0-399-23365-2). The story of the friendship between Paulie and Todd, their love of baseball, and what happens after Todd is hit during a game and loses an eye. (Rev: BL 6/1–15/99; HBG 10/99; SLJ 7/99; VOYA 8/99)

4309 Klass, David. *Danger Zone* (7–12). 1996, Scholastic paper $16.95 (0-590-48590-3). Jimmy Doyle, a young basketball star, tries to prove to himself as well as to his mostly African American teammates that he deserves a place on the American High School Dream Team. (Rev: BL 4/1/96; BR 5–6/96; SLJ 3/96; VOYA 4/96)

4310 Knudson, R. R. *Fox Running* (7–9). Illus. 1977, Avon paper $2.50 (0-380-00930-7). Kathy and an Apache Indian girl find friendship and inspiration in their mutual love of running.

4311 Konigsburg, E. L. *About the B'nai Bagels* (6–8). 1973, Dell paper $4.50 (0-440-40034-1). In this easily read story, Mark is uncomfortable at the thought of his mother's being the manager of his Little League baseball team. (Rev: BL 5/1/89)

4312 Korman, Gordon. *The Zucchini Warriors* (6–8). 1991, Scholastic paper $4.50 (0-590-44174-4). Hank, a former football player, promises to build Bruno and Boots's school a recreation hall if their team has a winning season. (Rev: BR 1–2/89; VOYA 10/88)

4313 Levy, Marilyn. *Run for Your Life* (7–9). 1996, Houghton $15.00 (0-395-74520-9). Thirteen-year-old Kisha tries to escape the Oakland projects and her parents' crumbling marriage by joining a track team that has been started by a new community center director. (Rev: BL 4/1/96; BR 9–10/96; SLJ 3/96; VOYA 6/96)

4314 Lynch, Chris. *Gold Dust* (5–8). 2000, HarperCollins LB $16.89 (0-06-028175-8). Richard comes from a Boston working-class family and Napoleon is the son of a visiting professor from the Dominican Republic in this novel about friendship, baseball, and racial tensions. (Rev: BCCB 11/00; BL 9/1/00; HBG 3/01; SLJ 10/00)

4315 Lynch, Chris. *Iceman* (8–12). 1994, HarperCollins $15.00 (0-06-023340-0). An emotionally fragile teenager expresses his anger in violent hockey games and spends time at the local mortuary with a disturbed recluse who works there. (Rev: BL 2/1/94; SLJ 3/94; VOYA 4/94)

4316 McGinley, Jerry. *Joaquin Strikes Back* (6–9). 1998, Tudor $18.95 (0-936389-58-3). Joaquin forms a soccer team in his new school that eventually plays the team from his former school. (Rev: BL 3/15/98; SLJ 3/99)

4317 Mackel, Kathy. *A Season of Comebacks* (4–7). 1997, Putnam $15.99 (0-399-23026-2). Molly is jealous of her sister Allie, who plays a better game of baseball than she does. (Rev: BCCB 4/97; BL 8/97; SLJ 7/97)

4318 Manes, Stephen. *An Almost Perfect Game* (4–7). 1995, Scholastic paper $14.95 (0-590-44432-8). Jake and Randy enjoy visiting their grandparents each summer because all of them are avid baseball fans. (Rev: BL 6/1–15/95; SLJ 6/95)

4319 Myers, Walter Dean. *Hoops* (7–10). 1981, Dell paper $5.50 (0-440-93884-8). Lonnie plays basketball in spite of his coach, a has-been named Cal. Followed by *The Outside Shot* (1987).

4320 Myers, Walter Dean. *The Journal of Biddy Owens* (5–7). Series: My Name Is America. 2001, Scholastic paper $10.95 (0-439-09503-4). A fictional journal that tells of the last year of the Negro Leagues, and of 17-year-old Biddy Owens and his involvement with the Birmingham Black Barons. (Rev: BL 2/15/01; HBG 10/01; SLJ 4/01; VOYA 8/01)

4321 Myers, Walter Dean. *Me, Mop, and the Moondance Kid* (5–7). Illus. 1988, Dell paper $4.99 (0-440-40396-0). The efforts of T.J. and Moondance to get their friend Mop adopted. (Rev: BCCB 12/88; BL 2/1/89; SLJ 1/88)

4322 Norman, Rick. *Cross Body Block* (8–10). 1996, Colonial Pr. paper $9.95 (1-56883-060-2). An anguished story about a middle-aged football coach and his personal family tragedies, including the brutal death of a son. (Rev: BR 9–10/96; VOYA 8/96)

4323 Pascal, Francine. *Fearless* (6–9). 1999, Pocket paper $5.99 (0-671-03941-5). Gaia, a 17-year old who has a black belt in kung fu, discovers that she is her own worst enemy. (Rev: BL 2/1/00)

4324 Patneaude, David. *Haunting at Home Plate* (4–7). 2000, Albert Whitman LB $14.95 (0-8075-3181-2). Twelve-year-old Nelson is amazed when mysterious instructions are left on the playing field in this baseball novel about a losing team that suddenly seems to be getting help from a ghost. (Rev: BCCB 11/00; BL 9/1/00; HBG 3/01; SLJ 9/00)

4325 Peers, Judi. *Shark Attack* (5–7). Series: Sports Stories. 1999, Orca paper $6.50 (1-55028-620-X). An easily read story set in Canada, in which a young baseball player wants to impress his father but doesn't think he can ever reach his older brother's record. (Rev: SLJ 1/00)

4326 Platt, Kin. *Brogg's Brain* (6–9). 1981, Harper-Collins LB $11.89 (0-397-31946-0). Monty is a run-ner who is pushed by his father and his coach to win.

4327 Powell, Randy. *Dean Duffy* (8–12). 1995, Farrar paper $5.95 (0-374-41698-2). A Little League baseball great has problems with his pitching arm and sees his career collapse. (Rev: BL 4/15/95; SLJ 5/95)

4328 Powell, Randy. *The Whistling Toilets* (7–10). 1996, Farrar paper $5.95 (0-374-48369-8). When Stan tries to help his friend Ginny with her tennis game, he finds that something strange is troubling the rising young tennis star. (Rev: BL 9/15/96; BR 3–4/97; SLJ 10/96; VOYA 12/96)

4329 Quies, Werner. *Soccer Shots* (6–9). 1995, Frontier paper $10.95 (0-939116-37-5). A 16-year-old East German boy pursues his dream of becoming a professional soccer player in the West. (Rev: BL 12/1/95)

4330 Ritter, John H. *The Boy Who Saved Baseball* (5–7). 2003, Putnam $17.99 (0-399-23622-8). A small town depends on its baseball team to rescue it from big developers. (Rev: BL 5/1/03*; SLJ 6/03; VOYA 8/03)

4331 Ritter, John H. *Choosing Up Sides* (5–9). 1998, Putnam $17.99 (0-399-23185-4). Jake is a great southpaw in baseball, but his preacher father forbids the boy to use his left hand for pitching as it is the instrument of Satan. (Rev: BCCB 6/98; BL 5/1/98; HBG 10/98; SLJ 6/98; VOYA 12/98)

4332 Ritter, John H. *Over the Wall* (6–10). 2000, Putnam $17.99 (0-399-23489-6). Fleeing a family tragedy, 14-year-old Tyler goes to live with relatives in New York City and play on a baseball league in Central Park. (Rev: BCCB 5/00; BL 4/1/00; HBG 9/00; SLJ 6/00; VOYA 6/00)

4333 Romain, Joseph. *The Mystery of the Wagner Whacker* (7–12). 1997, Warwick Publg. paper $8.95 (1-895629-94-2). Matt, a baseball enthusiast, is upset at moving to a small Canadian town where the sport is all but unknown, but an accidental travel in time to 1928 changes the situation. (Rev: BL 7/98; SLJ 7/98)

4334 Scholz, Jackson. *The Football Rebels* (5–7). 1993, Morrow paper $4.95 (0-688-12643-X). Clint does his best on the intramural football team when he doesn't make the varsity. Also use *Rookie Quarterback* (1993). Both are reissues.

4335 Smith, Charles R. *Tall Tales: Six Amazing Basketball Dreams* (5–8). Illus. 2000, Dutton $17.99 (0-525-46172-8). This book consists of six fantasy short stories about basketball. In one, for example, people find out that the best player in the neighborhood is blind. (Rev: BCCB 5/00; BL 3/1/00; HBG 10/00; SLJ 9/00; VOYA 12/00)

4336 Smith, Charles R., Jr. *Rimshots: Basketball Pix, Rolls, and Rhythms* (5–9). 1999, Dutton $17.99

(0-525-46099-3). In a series of poems and prose pieces, the author-photographer explores different facets of basketball and conveys a deep love of the game. (Rev: BCCB 5/99; BL 3/15/99; HBG 10/99; SLJ 2/99; VOYA 2/00)

4337 Spinelli, Jerry. *There's a Girl in My Hammerlock* (5–8). 1991, Simon & Schuster paper $14.00 (0-671-74684-7). This story of a girl who goes out for junior high wrestling, to the consternation of almost everyone but her mother, raises questions about gender roles and personal identity. (Rev: BCCB 9/91; BL 10/15/91; HB 9–10/91; SLJ 9/91*)

4338 Sweeney, Joyce. *Players* (6–12). 2000, Winslow $16.95 (1-890817-54-6). Corey, leader of the basketball team, is determined to find out who is sabotaging their chances of success. (Rev: BL 10/1/00; HBG 10/01; SLJ 9/00; VOYA 12/00)

4339 Trembath, Don. *Frog Face and the Three Boys* (4–7). Series: Black Belt. 2001, Orca paper $6.95 (1-55143-165-3). Three very different 7th-graders are enrolled in a karate class to teach them discipline. (Rev: BL 3/1/01; SLJ 9/01; VOYA 8/02)

4340 Tunis, John R. *Keystone Kids* (6–9). 1990, Harcourt paper $6.00 (0-15-242388-5). A reissue of the classic 1943 baseball story about two exceptional brothers. Also use *Highpockets* (1948) and *World Series* (1941). (Rev: BL 4/1/90)

4341 Tunis, John R. *The Kid from Tomkinsville* (6–9). 1990, Harcourt $14.95 (0-15-242568-3); paper $6.00 (0-15-242567-5). This novel, first published in 1940, introduces Roy Tucker and his remarkable pitching arm. It is continued in *The Kid Comes Back* (1946). Also use *Rookie of the Year* (1944). (Rev: BL 8/87)

4342 Wallace, Bill. *Never Say Quit* (5–7). 1993, Holiday $16.95 (0-8234-1013-7). A group of misfits who don't make the soccer team decide to form one of their own. (Rev: BL 4/15/93)

4343 Wallace, Rich. *Playing Without the Ball: A Novel in Four Quarters* (7–11). 2000, Knopf $15.95 (0-679-88672-9). Senior Jay McLeod is obsessed with basketball in a life that also includes his job as a short-order cook, family problems, a lonely existence, and fleeting attachments to girls. (Rev: BCCB 3–4/01; BL 9/1/00; HB 11–12/00; HBG 3/01; SLJ 10/00)

4344 Wallace, Rich. *Shots on Goal* (7–10). 1997, Knopf $18.99 (0-679-98670-7). Set against the exciting world of high school soccer, this novel also deals with the friendship of two of the team's players and how trouble with girls is dividing them. (Rev: BL 9/15/97; BR 1–2/98; HBG 3/98; SLJ 11/97)

4345 Weaver, Will. *Farm Team* (7–12). 1995, HarperCollins LB $15.89 (0-06-023589-6). Shy Billy Baggs, with many responsibilities for his age, finds success playing baseball. A sequel to *Striking Out.* (Rev: BL 9/1/95)

4346 Weaver, Will. *Hard Ball* (7–12). 1998, HarperCollins LB $15.89 (0-06-027122-1). Young, poor Billy Baggs discovers that his rival for the star position on the freshman baseball team is also his rival for the attention of the girl he is attracted to. (Rev: BL 1/1–15/98; HBG 9/98; SLJ 4/98; VOYA 6/98)

4347 Weaver, Will. *Striking Out* (8–12). 1993, HarperCollins paper $6.99 (0-06-447113-6). When Minnesota farmboy Billy Baggs picks up a stray baseball and fires it back to the pitcher, his baseball career begins, but his family isn't enthusiastic. (Rev: BL 11/1/93; SLJ 10/93; VOYA 12/93)

4348 Webster-Doyle, Terrence. *Breaking the Chains of the Ancient Warrior: Tests of Wisdom for Young Martial Artists* (5–8). Illus. 1995, Martial Arts for Peace paper $14.95 (0-942941-32-2). A collection of inspirational stories, karate parables, and tests that promote ethical behavior, with accompanying follow-up questions and a message for adult readers. (Rev: SLJ 1/96)

4349 Wells, Rosemary. *When No One Was Looking* (8–12). 1987, Fawcett paper $2.95 (0-449-70251-0). This story about tennis is also a mystery involving the death of the heroine's archrival.

4350 Wolff, Virginia E. *Bat 6* (5–9). 1998, Scholastic paper $16.95 (0-590-89799-3). In this novel narrated by the members of the opposing teams, a Japanese American girl just out of an internment camp meets a bitter girl whose father was killed at Pearl Harbor, and the two become rivals in baseball. (Rev: BCCB 6/98; BL 5/1/98*; HBG 10/98; SLJ 5/98; VOYA 6/98)

4351 Wooldridge, Frosty. *Strike Three! Take Your Base* (5–9). 2001, Brookfield Reader $16.95 (1-930093-01-2); paper $6.95 (1-930093-07-1). Baseball provides the setting as two brothers deal individually with the sudden death of their umpire father. (Rev: SLJ 3/02)

4352 Wunderli, Stephen. *The Heartbeat of Halftime* (6–9). 1996, Holt $14.95 (0-8050-4713-1). Wing tries to forget his father's declining health by becoming totally absorbed in football. (Rev: BL 10/1/96; BR 3–4/97; SLJ 11/96; VOYA 10/96)

4353 Zirpoli, Jane. *Roots in the Outfield* (5–7). 1988, Houghton $16.00 (0-395-45184-1). Josh spends a summer with his newly married father in Wisconsin and discovers some baseball memorabilia that help him overcome his own fears and ineptness in right field. (Rev: BL 4/1/88; SLJ 5/88)

4354 Zusak, Markus. *Fighting Ruben Wolfe* (8–12). 2001, Scholastic $15.95 (0-439-24188-X). Two brothers, Ruben and Cameron, try to assist their struggling family by boxing under the direction of an unethical promoter. (Rev: BL 2/15/01; HB 3–4/01; HBG 10/01; SLJ 3/01; VOYA 4/01)

Short Stories and General Anthologies

4355 Armstrong, Jennifer, ed. *Shattered: Stories of Children and War* (6–9). 2002, Knopf $15.95 (0-375-81112-5). A collection of thought-provoking short stories by well-known writers about war and its impact. (Rev: BL 12/15/01; HB 5–6/02; HBG 10/02; SLJ 1/02)

4356 Asher, Sandy, ed. *But That's Another Story: Famous Authors Introduce Popular Genres* (6–8). 1996, Walker $16.95 (0-8027-8424-0). Thirteen stories are included in this anthology, each representing a different genre, such as science fiction, fantasy, and adventure, with each written by a well-known YA author. (Rev: BL 6/1–15/96; BR 11–12/96; SLJ 7/96; VOYA 8/96)

4357 Bauer, Marion Dane, ed. *Am I Blue?* (8–12). 1995, HarperCollins paper $6.99 (0-06-440587-7). Sixteen short stories from well-known YA writers who have something meaningful to share about gay awareness and want to present positive, credible gay role models. (Rev: BL 5/1/94*; SLJ 6/94; VOYA 8/94)

4358 Blume, Judy, ed. *Places I Never Meant to Be: Original Stories by Censored Writers* (7–12). 1999, Simon & Schuster $16.95 (0-689-82034-8). A collection of original stories by 12 authors who have been both honored and censored, among them Walter Dean Myers, Norma Fox Mazer, Julius Lester, Katherine Paterson, Harry Mazer, David Klass, Chris Lynch, and Paul Zindel. Royalties from this book go to the National Coalition Against Censorship. (Rev: BL 6/1–15/99; HBG 4/00; SLJ 8/99; VOYA 12/99)

4359 Brooks, Bruce. *All That Remains* (7–12). 2001, Simon & Schuster $16.00 (0-689-83351-2). Three darkly entertaining novellas tackle the topic of death and how young people cope with it. (Rev: BCCB 6/01; BL 5/1/01; HB 7–8/01; HBG 10/01; SLJ 5/01; VOYA 6/01)

4360 Canfield, Jack, et al., eds. *Chicken Soup for the Kid's Soul: 101 Stories of Courage, Hope and Laughter* (4–7). 1998, Health Communications paper $12.95 (1-55874-609-9). A collection of inspiring true stories, some by well-known people, but mostly by children who sent them to the editors. (Rev: BL 9/1/98; HBG 3/99) [158.1]

4361 Canfield, Jack, et al., eds. *Chicken Soup for the Preteen Soul: 101 Stories of Changes, Choices and Growing Up for Kids Ages 9–13* (5–7). Illus. 2000, Health Communications $24.00 (1-55874-801-6); paper $12.95 (1-55874-800-8). The usual mix of verse and prose written by and for preteens, with the aim of offering inspiration, comfort, and practical advice. (Rev: HBG 10/01; SLJ 4/01) [158.1]

4362 Carter, Anne Laurel. *No Missing Parts and Other Stories About Real Princesses* (7–12). 2003, Red Deer paper $9.95 (0-88995-253-1). Ten thoughtful stories from Canada portray young women who rely on their own resources in difficult situations. (Rev: BL 5/1/03; SLJ 5/03; VOYA 10/03)

4363 Carver, Peter, ed. *Close-Ups: Best Stories for Teens* (6–8). 2000, Red Deer paper $9.95 (0-88995-200-0). Self-image, sexuality, and a variety of other teen topics are presented in this collection of stories by Canadian authors. (Rev: BL 2/15/01; VOYA 4/01)

4364 Christensen, Bonnie, ed. *In My Grandmother's House: Award-Winning Authors Tell Stories About Their Grandmothers* (6–12). Illus. 2003, HarperCollins $18.99 (0-06-029109-5). A collection of stories by well-known authors including Beverly Cleary, Jean Craighead George, and Alma Flor Ada. (Rev: BL 6/1–15/03; HBG 10/03; SLJ 5/03; VOYA 10/03) [306.87]

4365 Clay, Julie. *The Stars That Shine* (4–7). Illus. 2000, Simon & Schuster $24.95 (0-689-82202-2). This is an attractive collection of 12 inspirational short stories suggested by celebrities including Dolly Parton, LeAnn Rimes, and Willy Nelson. (Rev: BL 1/1–15/01; HBG 3/01; SLJ 12/00)

4366 Coville, Bruce. *Odder Than Ever* (5–9). 1999, Harcourt $16.00 (0-15-201747-X). A satisfying anthology of nine stories from this master of science fiction and fantasy. (Rev: BL 5/15/99; BR 9–10/99; HBG 10/99; SLJ 6/99; VOYA 10/99)

4367 Dahl, Roald. *Skin and Other Stories* (7–12). 2000, Viking $15.99 (0-670-89184-3). Selected from the author's short stories for adults, these 13 bizarre tales will also delight younger readers. (Rev: BL 10/1/00; HBG 3/01; VOYA 12/00)

4368 Datlow, Ellen, and Terri Windling, eds. *The Green Man: Tales from the Mythic Forest* (7–12). 2002, Viking $18.99 (0-670-03526-2). Mythical beings with special relevance to the natural world are portrayed in a collection of stories and poems. (Rev: BL 4/15/02; HBG 10/02; SLJ 7/02; VOYA 6/02)

4369 Dietz, Heather, ed. *Newbery Girls: Selections from Fifteen Newbery Award–Winning Books Chosen Especially for Girls* (4–8). 2000, Simon & Schuster $18.00 (0-689-83931-6). Fifteen chapters from Newbery winners and honor books that stand almost as short stories are reprinted in this interesting anthology for girls. (Rev: BL 11/1/00; HBG 3/01; SLJ 10/00)

4370 *Eighth Grade: Stories of Friendship, Passage and Discovery by Eighth Grade Writers* (6–12). Ed. by Christine Lord. Series: American Teen Writer. 1996, Merlyn's Pen paper $9.95 (1-886427-08-9). This is a group of short stories collected by *Merlyn's Pen* magazine that were written by 8th-graders. Also in this series are *Freshman: Fiction, Fantasy, and Humor by Ninth Grade Writers* and *Sophomores: Tales of Reality, Conflict, and the Road,* plus eight other volumes (all 1996). Each is accompanied by an audiotape. (Rev: VOYA 6/98)

4371 Fleischman, Paul. *Graven Images: Three Stories* (7–9). Illus. 1982, HarperCollins paper $4.95 (0-06-440186-3). Three stories that explore various aspects of human nature.

4372 Fox, Carol, et al. *In Times of War: An Anthology of War and Peace in Children's Literature* (6–12). Illus. 2001, Pavilion $24.95 (1-86205-446-0). Educators in the United Kingdom, Belgium, and Portugal worked together on this anthology of fiction, memoirs, and poetry — most of which deals with World Wars I and II in Europe — that is presented in thematic groupings. (Rev: BL 4/15/01; SLJ 6/01)

4373 Fraustino, Lisa Rowe, ed. *Soul Searching: Thirteen Stories About Faith and Belief* (6–10). 2002, Simon & Schuster $17.95 (0-689-83484-5). Young people's beliefs and faith form the center of this collection of thought-provoking stories. (Rev: BL 10/1/02; HB 1–2/03; HBG 3/03; SLJ 12/02; VOYA 2/03)

4374 Gac-Artigas, Alejandro. *Off to Catch the Sun* (5–8). 2001, Ediciones Nuevo Espacio paper $11.95 (1-930879-28-8). Thirteen-year-old author Gac-Artigas explores serious issues through poetry, essays, and short stories. (Rev: BL 1/1–15/02)

4375 Giovanni, Nikki, ed. *Grand Fathers: Reminiscences, Poems, Recipes, and Photos of the Keepers of Our Traditions* (6–12). Illus. 1999, Holt $18.95 (0-8050-5484-7). A collection of family stories and memoirs, some by famous writers but most by ordinary people, with memories about fathers that range from the inspirational to the sad and angry. (Rev: BL 6/1–15/99; SLJ 7/99; VOYA 10/99)

4376 Haynes, David, and Julie Landsman, eds. *Welcome to Your Life: Writings for the Heart of Young America* (7–12). 1999, Milkweed paper $15.95 (1-57131-017-7). Nearly 50 award-winning contributors each tell of a pivotal childhood experience, most with a focus on race and ethnicity, that affected the rest of his or her life. Subjects include gangs, bigotry, enemies, parents, and friends. (Rev: BL 5/1/99)

4377 Howe, James, ed. *The Color of Absence: 12 Stories About Loss and Hope* (6–10). 2001, Simon & Schuster $16.00 (0-689-82862-4). Well-known YA authors including Walter Dean Myers, Norma Fox Mazer, and Naomi Shihab Nye have contributed widely varied stories to this volume dealing with loss and hope. (Rev: BL 7/01; HB 9–10/01; HBG 3/02; SLJ 9/01; VOYA 8/01)

4378 Howe, James, ed. *13: Thirteen Stories That Capture the Agony and Ecstasy of Being Thirteen* (6–9). 2003, Simon & Schuster $16.95 (0-689-82863-2). Thirteen stories by well-known YA authors — Ann Martin, Todd Strasser, and Ron Koertge to name just three — feature 13-year-olds and their concerns. (Rev: BCCB 1/04; BL 1/1–15/04; SLJ 10/03)

4379 Hudson, Wade, and Cheryl W. Hudson, eds. *In Praise of Our Fathers and Our Mothers* (6–12). Illus. 1997, Just Us $29.95 (0-940975-59-9); paper $17.95 (0-940975-60-2). Nearly 50 well-known African American writers, among them Walter Dean Myers, Virginia Hamilton, and Brian Pinkney, recall their family life in this anthology of poetry, essays, paintings, and interviews. (Rev: BL 4/1/97; HB 3–4/97; SLJ 6/97) [920]

4380 Jones, Diana Wynne. *Believing Is Seeing* (6–12). 1999, Greenwillow $16.00 (0-688-16843-4). Seven stories of fantasy, horror, and the supernatural vary dramatically in tone and content. (Rev: BL 11/15/99; HBG 4/00)

4381 Kulpa, Kathryn, ed. *Something Like a Hero* (6–10). 1995, Merlyn's Pen paper $9.95 (1-886427-03-8). A collection of 11 short stories from different genres reprinted from the national magazine of student writing, *Merlyn's Pen.* (Rev: VOYA 2/96)

4382 Lynch, Chris. *All the Old Haunts* (8–12). 2001, HarperCollins $15.95 (0-06-028178-2). This collection of 10 dark short stories frankly explores such "old haunts" as young love, unwanted pregnancy, and difficult family relationships. (Rev: BCCB 10/01; BR 3–4/02; HB 9–10/01; HBG 3/02; SLJ 11/01; VOYA 10/01)

4383 McKinley, Robin, and Peter Dickinson. *Water: Tales of Elemental Spirits* (7–12). 2002, Putnam $18.99 (0-399-23796-8). Six captivating and imaginative stories feature magical sea-beings and the humans who love or fight them. (Rev: BL 4/15/02; HB 7–8/02; HBG 10/02; SLJ 6/02*; VOYA 6/02)

4384 Macy, Sue, ed. *Girls Got Game: Sports Stories and Poems* (6–9). 2001, Holt $15.95 (0-8050-6568-7). A collection of original stories and poems about girls playing sports that range from team games to individual pursuits. (Rev: BL 6/1–15/01; HB 7–8/01; HBG 10/01; SLJ 7/01; VOYA 8/01)

4385 Mazer, Anne, ed. *America Street: A Multicultural Anthology of Stories* (5–8). 1993, Persea paper $7.95 (0-89255-191-7). Fourteen short stories about growing up in America's diverse society by Robert Cormier, Langston Hughes, Grace Paley, Gary Soto, and others. (Rev: BCCB 11/93; BL 9/1/93; SLJ 11/93; VOYA 12/93)

4386 Morpurgo, Michael, comp. *The Kingfisher Book of Great Boy Stories: A Treasury of Classics from Children's Literature* (4–8). Illus. 2000, Kingfisher $19.95 (0-7534-5320-7). An attractively illustrated collection of stories from authors including Carlo Collodi, Roald Dahl, Ted Hughes, C. S.

Lewis, A. A. Milne, Donald Sobol, and Mark Twain. (Rev: HBG 10/01; SLJ 4/01)

4387 Myers, Walter Dean. *A Time to Love: Stories from the Old Testament* (7–10). 2003, Scholastic $19.95 (0-439-22000-9). Six well-known Old Testament stories are told from unusual first-person perspectives and accompanied by colorful illustrations. (Rev: BCCB 9/03; BL 5/15/03; HBG 10/03; SLJ 5/03; VOYA 8/03)

4388 Naidoo, Beverley. *Out of Bounds: Seven Stories of Conflict and Hope* (6–10). 2003, HarperCollins $16.99 (0-06-050799-3). The seven stories in this book, with a foreword by Archbishop Tutu, look at the racism, apartheid, discrimination, and progress in South Africa from the 1950s to the present. (Rev: BL 2/15/03; HB 3–4/03*; HBG 10/03; SLJ 1/03; VOYA 6/03)

4389 November, Sharyn, ed. *Firebirds* (7–12). 2003, Putnam $19.99 (0-14-250142-5). An excellent collection of stories by authors who publish with the Firebird imprint, including Michael Cadnum, Garth Nix, and Meredith Ann Pierce. (Rev: BL 10/15/03)

4390 Paterson, Katherine, ed. *Angels and Other Strangers: Family Christmas Stories* (5–9). 1979, HarperCollins paper $5.95 (0-06-440283-5). A collection of nine short stories that explore the true meaning of Christmas.

4391 Paterson, Katherine. *A Midnight Clear: Stories for the Christmas Season* (5–10). 1995, Dutton $16.00 (0-525-67529-9). Stories that reveal the spirit of Christmas in contemporary life and provide hope and light in a dark, uncertain world. (Rev: BL 9/15/95)

4392 Paulsen, Gary. *How Angel Patterson Got His Name* (6–9). 2003, Random $12.95 (0-385-72949-9). The zany adventures of a daring group of 13-year-old boys are based on the author's childhood experiences. (Rev: BL 12/15/02; HB 1–2/03; HBG 10/03; SLJ 2/03*; VOYA 4/03)

4393 Paulsen, Gary, ed. *Shelf Life: Stories by the Book* (4–7). 2003, Simon & Schuster $16.95 (0-689-84180-9). Books are the stars of these 10 stories by well-known authors that show that reading can change lives. (Rev: BL 8/03; SLJ 8/03; VOYA 8/03)

4394 Pearce, Philippa. *Familiar and Haunting: Collected Stories* (5–8). 2002, HarperCollins LB $16.89 (0-06-623965-6). Thirty-seven short stories, many of them about ghosts and the supernatural, are included in this intriguing collection. (Rev: BL 5/1/02; HB 5–6/02*; HBG 10/02; SLJ 7/02)

4395 Randol, Susan, ed. *Dead Good Read: Classic Tales of Mystery and Horror* (5–9). Illus. 2001, Reader's Digest $24.95 (0-7621-0347-7). Stories by authors including Robert Louis Stevenson, Bram Stoker, and Elizabeth Gaskell are retold for readers who would find the originals too challenging, with

definitions of difficult vocabulary. (Rev: HBG 10/02; SLJ 1/02)

4396 Rice, David. *Crazy Loco* (7–12). 2001, Dial $16.99 (0-8037-2598-1). A collection of nine stories about Mexican American youngsters growing up in South Texas. (Rev: BCCB 9/01; BL 5/15/01; HB 9–10/01; HBG 3/02; SLJ 6/01; VOYA 6/01)

4397 Rosen, Roger, and Patra M. Sevastiades, eds. *On Heroes and the Heroic: In Search of Good Deeds* (7–12). Series: Icarus World Issues. 1993, Rosen LB $16.95 (0-8239-1384-8); paper $8.95 (0-8239-1385-6). Nine fiction and nonfiction pieces explore the concepts of heroes and antiheroes. (Rev: BL 9/15/93; SLJ 1/94; VOYA 12/93)

4398 Saldana, Rene. *Finding Our Way* (7–12). 2003, Random $15.95 (0-385-73051-9). Featuring several Hispanic characters, these short stories focus on critical decisions in the lives of young adults. (Rev: BL 2/15/03; HB 3–4/03; HBG 10/03; SLJ 3/03; VOYA 8/03)

4399 Salisbury, Graham. *Blue Skin of the Sea* (8–12). 1992, Delacorte $15.95 (0-385-30596-6). These 11 stories contain a strong sense of time and place, fully realized characters, stylish prose, and universal themes. (Rev: BL 6/15/92*; SLJ 6/92*)

4400 Salisbury, Graham. *Island Boyz: Short Stories* (7–12). 2002, Random $16.95 (0-385-72970-7). Hawaii is the setting for this collection of varied stories about teenage boys growing into maturity. (Rev: BL 4/15/02*; HB 3–4/02; HBG 10/02; SLJ 3/02*)

4401 *Second Sight: Stories for a New Millennium* (7–12). 1999, Putnam $14.99 (0-399-23458-6). A collection of eight stories that focus on the millennium by such writers as Avi, Natalie Babbitt, and Richard Peck. (Rev: BL 9/15/99; HBG 4/00; VOYA 2/00)

4402 Sherman, Josepha, ed. *Orphans of the Night* (6–10). 1995, Walker $16.95 (0-8027-8368-6). Brings together 11 short stories and two poems about creatures from folklore, most with teen protagonists. (Rev: BL 6/1–15/95; SLJ 6/95; VOYA 12/95)

4403 Singer, Isaac Bashevis. *Stories for Children* (7–9). 1984, Farrar paper $14.00 (0-374-46489-8). This collection includes 36 stories, most of which are fantasies about Jewish life in old Europe.

4404 Singer, Marilyn, comp. *I Believe in Water: Twelve Brushes with Religion* (7–10). 2000, HarperCollins $15.95 (0-06-028397-1). Short stories by writers including Virginia Euwer Wolff and M. E. Kerr look at religion from varied viewpoints. (Rev: BL 10/1/00; HBG 3/01; SLJ 11/00; VOYA 4/01)

4405 Snell, Gordon, ed. *Thicker than Water: Coming-of-Age Stories by Irish and Irish American Writers* (7–12). 2001, Delacorte $17.95 (0-385-32571-

1). Twelve stories dealing with such topics as abortion, eating disorders, and hazing will resonate with American teens. (Rev: BCCB 3/01; BL 1/1–15/01; HB 3–4/01*; HBG 10/01; SLJ 5/01)

4406 Spiegelman, Art, and Francoise Mouly, eds. *Little Lit: Strange Stories for Strange Kids* (4–9). Illus. 2001, HarperCollins paper $19.95 (0-06-028626-1). This collection of offbeat, imaginative, graphic stories includes something for everyone, from humor to fantasy to horror, from Maurice Sendak to David Sedaris. (Rev: BL 12/15/01; HB 1–2/02; HBG 3/02; SLJ 3/02) [741.5]

4407 Valgardson, W. D. *The Divorced Kids Club and Other Stories* (6–8). 1999, Douglas & McIntyre $15.95 (0-88899-369-2). Many subjects, including isolation, divorce, drug dealing, and the supernatural, are dealt with in this attractive anthology of stories by Valgardson. (Rev: BCCB 1/00; BL 12/15/99; SLJ 7/00; VOYA 4/00)

4408 Villasenor, Victor. *Walking Stars: Stories of Magic and Power* (7–12). 1994, Arte Publico $16.95 (1-55885-118-6). Short stories, based on fact, describing the everyday magic and family love found in the author's Mexican and Native American heritage. (Rev: BL 10/15/94; SLJ 11/94; VOYA 4/95)

4409 Weiss, M. Jerry, and Helen S. Weiss, eds. *Big City Cool: Short Stories About Urban Youth* (7–12). 2002, Persea paper $8.95 (0-89255-278-6). A variety of urban settings and cultural and racial experiences are portrayed in these 14 stories, half of which have previously appeared in print. (Rev: BL 10/15/02; SLJ 11/02; VOYA 12/02)

4410 Weiss, M. Jerry, and Helen S. Weiss, eds. *Lost and Found: Award-Winning Authors Sharing Real-Life Experiences Through Fiction* (8–12). 2000, Forge $19.95 (0-312-87048-5). Thirteen well-known YA authors' stories are prefaced by explanations of the real-life origins of each story. (Rev: BL 11/1/00; SLJ 11/00)

4411 Wynne-Jones, Tim. *Lord of the Fries* (6–10). 1999, DK paper $17.95 (0-7894-2623-4). A collection of short stories by the author about young people and the decisions they make. (Rev: BCCB 3/99; BL 2/15/99; HB 7–8/99; HBG 10/99; SLJ 4/99; VOYA 10/99)

4412 Yee, Paul. *Dead Man's Gold and Other Stories* (6–12). 2002, Groundwood $16.95 (0-88899-475-3). A collection of disturbing ghost stories featuring Chinese immigrants to America and Canada. (Rev: BL 11/1/02; HB 1–2/03*; HBG 3/03; SLJ 1/03)

4413 Young, Cathy, ed. *One Hot Second: Stories About Desire* (7–12). 2002, Knopf $10.95 (0-375-81203-2). A collection of stories, some witty and some moving, by YA writers about teen yearnings — for romance, for a first kiss, even for a dream car. (Rev: BL 6/1–15/02; HBG 10/02; SLJ 6/02; VOYA 6/02)

Plays

General and Miscellaneous Collections

4414 Bland, Joellen, adapt. *Stage Plays from the Classics* (6–9). 1987, Plays paper $15.95 (0-8238-0281-7). Fifteen plays adapted from such classics as *Oliver Twist, Dracula,* and *The Purloined Letter.* (Rev: BR 1–2/88; SLJ 3/88) [812]

4415 Carlson, Lori Marie, ed. *You're On! Seven Plays in English and Spanish* (3–7). Illus. 1999, Morrow $17.00 (0-688-16237-1). These plays by authors including Federico Garcia Lorca, Pura Belpre, and Gary Soto offer a range of styles suitable for young cast members. (Rev: BCCB 9/99; BL 10/1/99; HBG 4/00; SLJ 10/99) [812.008]

4416 Ellis, Roger, ed. *Audition Monologs for Student Actors II: Selections from Contemporary Plays* (8–12). 2001, Meriwether paper $15.95 (1-56608-073-8). Fifty monologues for both sexes from ages 10 to mid-20s are accompanied by scene-setting notes and acting tips. (Rev: SLJ 4/02)

4417 Ellis, Roger, ed. *International Plays for Young Audiences: Contemporary Works from Leading Playwrights* (7–12). 2000, Meriwether paper $16.95 (1-56608-065-7). The 12 short plays in this collection come from varied cultures and deal with situations of interest to young people. (Rev: SLJ 2/01)

4418 Fredericks, Anthony D. *Tadpole Tales and Other Totally Terrific Treats for Readers Theatre* (4–8). 1997, Libraries Unlimited paper $23.00 (1-56308-547-X). A delightful collection of scripts for young performers that are spin-offs from folktales, fables, and nursery rhymes. (Rev: BL 3/1/98) [372.67]

4419 Henderson, Heather H. *The Flip Side II: 60 More Point-of-View Monologs for Teens* (6–9). 2001, Meriwether paper $15.95 (1-56608-074-6). A second collection of paired monologues that present two sides of a variety of situations. (Rev: SLJ 7/02) [812]

4420 Jennings, Coleman A., and Aurand Harris, eds. *Plays Children Love, Volume II: A Treasury of Contemporary and Classic Plays for Children* (5–8). 1988, St. Martin's $19.95 (0-312-01490-2). A group of 20 plays requiring royalties based on such stories as Charlotte's Web, The Wizard of Oz, and The Wind in the Willows. [812.00809282]

4421 Kamerman, Sylvia, ed. *The Big Book of Large-Cast Plays: 27 One-Act Plays for Young Actors* (5–10). 1994, Plays $12.95 (0-8238-0302-3). Thirty short plays on varied subjects, arranged according to audience appeal. (Rev: BL 3/15/95) [812]

4422 Kamerman, Sylvia, ed. *Christmas Play Favorites for Young People* (6–10). 1983, Plays paper $13.95 (0-8238-0257-4). Eighteen one-act plays that can be used in both elementary, middle, and high schools. [812.08]

4423 Lamedman, Debbie. *The Ultimate Audition Book for Teens: 111 One-Minute Monologues*, vol. 4 (7–12). Series: Young Actors. 2003, Smith & Kraus paper $11.95 (1-57525-353-4). Monologues for both girls and boys give young actors ample opportunity to display their talent in a range of selections. (Rev: SLJ 4/03) [812]

4424 Latrobe, Kathy Howard, and Mildred Knight Laughlin. *Readers Theatre for Young Adults: Scripts and Script Development* (7–12). 1989, Libraries Unlimited paper $22.00 (0-87287-743-4). A collection of short scripts based on literary classics plus tips on how to do one's own adaptations. (Rev: BL 1/1/90) [808.5]

4425 Nolan, Paul T. *Folk Tale Plays Round the World: A Collection of Royalty-Free, One-Act Plays About Lands Far and Near* (4–7). 1982, Plays paper $15.00 (0-8238-0253-1). Johnny Appleseed and

Robin Hood are heroes featured in two of the 17 plays in this collection.

4426 Ratliff, Gerald L., ed. *Millennium Monologs: 95 Contemporary Characterizations for Young Actors* (8–12). 2002, Meriwether paper $15.95 (1-56608-082-7). High school thespians will appreciate this collection of monologues, which are arranged by theme, as well as the advice on auditions. (Rev: BL 3/15/03; SLJ 5/03) [792]

4427 Ratliff, Gerald L., and Theodore O. Zapel, eds. *Playing Contemporary Scenes: 31 Famous Scenes and How to Play Them* (8–12). 1996, Meriwether paper $16.95 (1-56608-025-8). A selection of scenes by contemporary playwrights, arranged according to age and gender. (Rev: VOYA 6/97) [812]

4428 Slaight, Craig, and Jack Sharrar, eds. *Great Scenes and Monologues for Children* (5–8). Series: Young Actors. 1993, Smith & Kraus paper $12.95 (1-880399-15-6). Includes selections from children's novels and fairy tales, as well as adult drama and short stories. (Rev: BL 10/1/93; SLJ 11/93) [808.82]

4429 Slaight, Craig, and Jack Sharrar, eds. *Short Plays for Young Actors* (8–12). 1996, Smith & Kraus paper $16.95 (1-880399-74-1). An impressive collection of short plays in a variety of genres plus material on how to approach acting as a serious pursuit. (Rev: BL 9/15/96; BR 1–2/97) [812]

4430 Smith, Marisa, ed. *The Seattle Children's Theatre: Six Plays for Young Audiences* (5–8). Series: Young Actors. 1997, Smith & Kraus $16.95 (1-57525-008-X). Six plays that contain young adolescents as characters, adapted from books like *Afternoon of the Elves* and *Anne of Green Gables*. (Rev: SLJ 6/97) [809]

4431 Stevens, Chambers. *Magnificent Monologues for Kids* (4–8). Ed. by Renee Rolle-Whatley. 1999, Sandcastle Publg. paper $13.95 (1-883995-08-6). A collection of 51 monologues — some best for girls, others for boys — representing different situations and emotions. (Rev: BL 4/1/99; SLJ 8/99) [808.82]

4432 Surface, Mary Hall. *Short Scenes and Monologues for Middle School Actors* (6–9). 2000, Smith & Kraus paper $11.95 (1-57525-179-5). This is an excellent collection of monologues and scenes for two actors on a variety of subjects and settings that are suitable for 12- to14-year-old actors. (Rev: BL 2/15/00; SLJ 7/00; VOYA 6/00) [812.5408.]

4433 Swortzell, Lowell, ed. *Theatre for Young Audiences: Around the World in Twenty-One Plays* (6–12). 1996, Applause Theatre $35.00 (1-55783-263-3). A collection of 21 plays, with background information, including 8 traditional and 13 contemporary works by such authors as Langston Hughes,

Ossie Davis, Gertrude Stein, and August Strindberg. (Rev: BL 6/1–15/97; SLJ 6/97) [808.82]

4434 Vigil, Angel. *¡Teatro! Hispanic Plays for Young People* (4–8). Illus. 1996, Teacher Ideas paper $25.00 (1-56308-371-X). This collection contains 14 English-language scripts that integrate elements of the Hispanic traditions of the Southwest. (Rev: BL 3/1/97; BR 3–4/97; VOYA 6/97) [812]

4435 Winther, Barbara. *Plays from Hispanic Tales: One-Act, Royalty-Free Dramatizations for Young People, from Hispanic Stories and Folktales* (6–10). 1998, Plays paper $14.95 (0-8238-0307-4). A nicely balanced collection of 11 short plays based on folktales and legends from Spain, South and Central America, and the Caribbean. (Rev: BL 11/15/98; SLJ 9/98) [812]

Geographical Regions

Europe

GREAT BRITAIN AND IRELAND

4436 Birch, Beverley. *Shakespeare's Stories: Histories* (5–8). Illus. 1988, Bedrick paper $6.95 (0-87226-226-X). Retelling the classic stories of Shakespeare. (Rev: BL 2/15/89; SLJ 2/89) [813.54]

4437 Birch, Beverley. *Shakespeare's Stories: Tragedies* (5–8). Illus. 1988, Bedrick paper $6.95 (0-87226-227-8). Retelling the great tragedies. (Rev: BL 2/15/89; SLJ 2/89) [813.54]

4438 Birch, Beverley. *Shakespeare's Tales* (5–8). 2002, Hodder $22.95 (0-340-79725-8). This appealing and accessible large-format book introduces modern teens to the plots and language of four Shakespeare plays — *Hamlet, Othello, Antony and Cleopatra*, and *The Tempest*. (Rev: BL 1/1–15/03; SLJ 4/03) [823.914]

4439 Coville, Bruce. *William Shakespeare's Macbeth* (4–8). Illus. 1997, Dial $18.99 (0-8037-1899-3); paper $16.89 (0-8037-1900-0). Using a picture-book format, the story of Macbeth is retold with emphasis on the supernatural aspects. (Rev: BL 11/1/97; HBG 3/98; SLJ 12/97) [822.3]

4440 Early, Margaret, and William Shakespeare. *Romeo and Juliet* (4–8). Illus. 1998, Harry N. Abrams $18.95 (0-8109-3799-9). A retelling in prose, illustrated with paintings in the style of Italian Renaissance art. (Rev: BL 5/1/98; BR 11–12/98; HBG 9/98; SLJ 6/98) [822]

4441 Ganeri, Anita. *The Young Person's Guide to Shakespeare: With Performances on CD by the Royal Shakespeare Company* (4–9). 1999, Harcourt $25.00 (0-15-202101-9). This heavily illustrated account covers both Shakespeare's life and plays with a CD of the most familiar speeches such as "To be or not to be." (Rev: SLJ 1/00) [822.3]

4442 Garfield, Leon. *Shakespeare Stories* (5–9). Illus. 1991, Houghton $26.00 (0-395-56397-6). Modern retellings of 12 of Shakespeare's most popular plays. (Rev: BL 1/1/86) [822.3]

4443 Kahle, Peter V. T. *Shakespeare's The Tempest: A Prose Narrative* (5–8). 1999, Seventy Fourth Street $22.95 (0-9655702-2-3). An illustrated retelling of Shakespeare's play that uses much of its dialogue. (Rev: SLJ 1/00) [822.3]

4444 Lamb, Charles, and Mary Lamb. *Tales from Shakespeare* (7–9). Illus. 1993, Buccaneer LB $24.95 (1-56849-117-4); NAL paper $5.95 (0-451-52391-1). The famous retelling of 20 of Shakespeare's plays in a version first published in 1807. [822.3]

4445 Miles, Bernard. *Favorite Tales from Shakespeare* (7–10). Illus. 1993, Checkerboard $14.95 (1-56288-257-0). Shakespeare's most famous plays in a modern retelling. [822.3]

4446 Rosen, Michael. *Shakespeare's Romeo and Juliet* (7–10). 2004, Candlewick $17.99 (0-7636-2258-3). Vivid, evocative illustrations and a conversational narrative accompany passages of Shakespeare in an appealing retelling of the popular story that includes references and glossaries. (Rev: BL 12/1/03) [823]

4447 Shakespeare, William. *William Shakespeare* (5–7). Ed. by David Scott Kastan and Marina Kastan. Illus. Series: Poetry for Young People. 2000, Sterling $14.95 (0-8069-4344-0). In a large format illustrated by paintings, this volume contains three sonnets and 23 short excerpts from the plays of William Shakespeare. (Rev: BL 1/1–15/01; HBG 3/01; SLJ 1/01) [821]

4448 Stevenson, Robert Louis. *Treasure Island* (5–9). Series: Scribner Storybook Classic. 2003, Simon & Schuster $18.95 (0-689-85468-4). This picture-book adaptation of the classic story features beautiful paintings by N. C. Wyeth. (Rev: BL 8/03)

4449 Williams, Marcia. *Bravo, Mr. William Shakespeare!* (5–8). Illus. 2000, Candlewick $16.99 (0-7636-1209-X). Using an oversize, comic book format, this book summarizes seven plays (in each frame, the characters' words are Shakespeare's with a plot summary below) including *King Lear*, *Twelfth Night*, *As You Like It*, and *Richard the Third*. (Rev: BL 3/1/01; HBG 3/01; SLJ 12/00) [822.3]

United States

4450 Fairbanks, Stephanie S. *Spotlight! Solo Scenes for Student Actors* (7–12). 1996, Meriwether paper $14.95 (1-56608-020-7). This book contains 55 excellent one- to three-page monologues, some specifically for girls, others for boys, and others nonspecific. (Rev: BL 12/1/96; SLJ 5/97) [812]

4451 Gallo, Donald R., ed. *Center Stage: One-Act Plays for Teenage Readers and Actors* (7–12). 1990, HarperCollins $17.00 (0-06-022170-4); paper $8.99 (0-06-447078-4). A collection of 10 one-act plays especially written for this collection by such authors as Walter Dean Myers and Ouida Sebestyen. (Rev: BL 12/1/90; SLJ 9/90) [812]

4452 Garner, Joan. *Stagings* (6–12). 1995, Teacher Ideas paper $27.00 (1-56308-343-4). A collection of royalty-free short plays suitable for teens, also including character and costume descriptions, set suggestions, staging options, and lesson plans. (Rev: BL 2/1/96; BR 3–4/96; VOYA 4/96) [812]

4453 Gibson, William. *The Miracle Worker: A Play for Television* (7–12). 1957, Knopf $20.00 (0-394-40630-3); Bantam paper $5.99 (0-553-24778-6). An expanded version of the TV play about Annie Sullivan and Helen Keller. [812]

4454 Goodrich, Frances. *The Diary of Anne Frank* (7–12). Illus. 1958, Dramatists Play Service paper $6.50 (0-8222-0307-3). A dramatic version of the famous diary. [812]

4455 *Great Scenes for Young Actors* (7–12). Series: Young Actors. 1997, Smith & Kraus paper $14.95 (1-57525-107-8). A variety of scenes representing different forms of drama are reprinted from such playwrights as Arthur Miller, George S. Kaufman, Horton Foote, and Paul Zindel. (Rev: BL 3/1/99; SLJ 6/99) [808.82]

4456 Hamlett, Christina. *Humorous Plays for Teen-Agers* (7–10). 1987, Plays paper $12.95 (0-8238-0276-0). Easily read one-act plays for beginners in acting. (Rev: BL 5/1/87; BR 5–6/87; SLJ 11/87) [812]

4457 Kamerman, Sylvia, ed. *The Big Book of Holiday Plays* (6–9). 1990, Plays $16.95 (0-8238-0291-4). An assortment of one-act plays and adaptations, both dramas and comedies, related to 14 holidays. (Rev: BL 2/1/91; SLJ 1/91) [812]

4458 Kamerman, Sylvia, ed. *Great American Events on Stage: 15 Plays to Celebrate America's Past* (5–8). 1996, Plays paper $15.95 (0-8238-0305-8). A collection of short plays, each of which revolves around a single incident or individual important in U.S. history. (Rev: BR 5–6/97; SLJ 5/97) [812]

4459 Kamerman, Sylvia, ed. *Plays of Black Americans: The Black Experience in America, Dramatized for Young People* (7–12). 1994, Plays paper $13.95 (0-8238-0301-5). Eleven dramas focus on the history of African Americans (Rev: BL 5/15/95; SLJ 2/95) [812]

4460 Laurents, Arthur. *West Side Story: A Musical* (7–12). Illus. 1958, Random $13.95 (0-394-40788-1). This contemporary variation on the Romeo and Juliet story contains the script and lyrics by Stephen Sondheim. (Rev: BL 10/1/88) [812]

4461 Lerner, Alan Jay. *Camelot* (7–12). 1961, Random $13.95 (0-394-40521-8). This musical tells of the tragic love of King Arthur and Guinevere. [812]

4462 McCullough, L. E. *Plays of America from American Folklore for Young Actors* (7–12). Series: Young Actors. 1996, Smith & Kraus paper $14.95 (1-57525-040-3). Ten original short plays based on folk traditions are included, along with suggestions for staging and costumes. (Rev: BL 8/96; SLJ 8/96) [812]

4463 Mason, Timothy. *The Children's Theatre Company of Minneapolis: 10 Plays for Young Audiences* (6–9). Series: Young Actors. 1997, Smith & Kraus paper $19.95 (1-57525-120-5). This is a collection of 10 plays, each about an hour long, adapted from such classics as *Pinocchio, Aladdin*, and *Huckleberry Finn*. (Rev: SLJ 8/98) [812]

4464 Simon, Neil. *Brighton Beach Memoirs* (7–12). 1984, Random $14.95 (0-394-53739-4). The first of three semiautobiographical plays about the growing pains of Brooklyn-born Eugene Jerome. The other two are *Biloxi Blues* (1986) and *Broadway Bound* (1988). (Rev: BL 6/87) [812]

4465 Smith, Ronn. *Nothing but the Truth* (7–10). 1997, Avon paper $4.99 (0-380-78715-6). This is a play version of Avi's novel about a 9th grader whose suspension from school becomes a national issue. (Rev: VOYA 8/97) [812]

4466 Soto, Gary. *Nerdlandia: A Play* (8–12). 1999, Penguin paper $55.99 (0-698-11784-0). Young love causes transformations in nerdy Martin and cool Ceci in this hip play full of Spanish dialogue. (Rev: BL 10/1/99) [812.4]

4467 Soto, Gary. *Novio Boy: A Play* (5–8). 1997, Harcourt paper $7.00 (0-15-201531-0). A lighthearted play about Rudy, a 9th-grade Hispanic American boy, and his date with an older girl. (Rev: BL 4/15/97; SLJ 6/97; VOYA 8/97) [812]

4468 Thoms, Annie, ed. *With Their Eyes: September 11th: The View from a High School at Ground Zero* (7–12). Photos by Ethan Moses. 2002, Harper-Collins paper $6.99 (0-06-051718-2). A collection of moving and dramatic monologues created after students at a high school near Ground Zero interviewed fellow students, faculty, and others about their experiences that day. (Rev: BL 9/1/02; SLJ 1/03) [812]

4469 Wasserman, Dale. *Man of La Mancha* (7–12). Illus. 1966, Random paper $9.95 (0-394-40619-2). Based loosely on Cervantes's novel, this is a musical play of the adventures of Don Quixote and his servant Sancho Panza. [812]

Poetry

General and Miscellaneous Collections

4470 Adoff, Arnold. *All the Colors of the Race* (4–7). 1982, Lothrop LB $15.93 (0-688-00880-1). Poems that deal with the many races of mankind.

4471 Anaya, Rudolfo A. *Elegy on the Death of Cesar Chavez* (4–7). Illus. 2000, Cinco Puntos $16.95 (0-938317-51-2). This is an elegiac poem that celebrates the life, work, and struggle of the respected labor leader. (Rev: BL 12/15/00; HBG 3/01; SLJ 1/01) [811]

4472 Appelt, Kathi. *Poems from Homeroom: A Writer's Place to Start* (7–12). 2002, Holt $16.95 (0-8050-6978-X). Poems that speak to the adolescent experience are accompanied by encouraging writing tips from the poet. (Rev: BL 11/15/02; SLJ 9/02) [811]

4473 Argueta, Jorge. *A Movie in My Pillow / Una Pelicula en Mi Almohada* (4–8). 2001, Children's $15.95 (0-89239-165-0). The author remembers in poetry his family's immigration to the United States from El Salvador, with each poem accompanied by the translation and rich illustrations. (Rev: BL 10/1/01; HBG 10/01; SLJ 5/01*) [861]

4474 Berry, James, ed. *Classic Poems to Read Aloud* (4–8). Illus. 1995, Kingfisher $18.95 (1-85697-987-3); paper $8.95 (0-7534-5069-0). Jamaican writer Berry has collected old favorites, mostly British, along with new voices usually excluded from the literary canon. (Rev: BL 5/1/95; SLJ 5/95) [811]

4475 Bloom, Harold, ed. *Poets of World War I: Wilfred Owen and Isaac Rosenberg* (7–12). Series: Bloom's Major Poets. 2002, Chelsea LB $21.95 (0-7910-5932-4). This introduction to the work of

these two poets includes four poems by each, with analysis. (Rev: BR 11–12/02; SLJ 7/02) [821]

4476 Brenner, Barbara, ed. *Voices: Poetry and Art from Around the World* (6–12). Illus. 2000, National Geographic $18.95 (0-7922-7071-1). A fine collection of world poetry and art, arranged geographically in a handsome oversized book. (Rev: BL 12/1/00; HBG 3/01; SLJ 3/01; VOYA 4/02) [808.81]

4477 Brewton, Sara, et al., eds. *My Tang's Tungled and Other Ridiculous Situations* (6–9). 1973, HarperCollins $12.95 (0-690-57223-9). A wonderful collection of humorous verse. [811]

4478 Brewton, Sara, et al., eds. *Of Quarks, Quasars and Other Quirks: Quizzical Poems for the Supersonic Age* (5–8). 1977, HarperCollins LB $13.89 (0-690-04885-8). Contemporary poems that poke fun at such modern innovations as transplants and water beds.

4479 Duffy, Carol Ann, ed. *Stopping for Death: Poems of Death and Loss* (7–10). Illus. 1996, Holt $14.95 (0-8050-4717-4). An anthology of poems from around the world, including many contemporary poets, that deal with dying, death, and loss. (Rev: BL 8/96; SLJ 8/96; VOYA 10/96) [808.81]

4480 Dunning, Stephen, et al., eds. *Reflections on a Gift of Watermelon Pickle and Other Modern Verse* (6–8). Illus. 1967, Lothrop $19.99 (0-688-41231-9). An attractive volume of 114 expressive poems by recognized modern poets, illustrated with striking photographs.

4481 Fleischman, Paul. *Big Talk: Poems for Four Voices* (4–7). Illus. 2000, Candlewick $17.99 (0-7636-0636-7). This collection of spirited, evocative poems for four voices to read aloud covers a variety of topics. (Rev: BCCB 4/00; BL 6/1–15/00; HB 5–6/00; HBG 10/00; SLJ 6/00) [811]

4482 Fletcher, Ralph. *Have You Been to the Beach Lately? Poems* (4–7). Photos by Andrea Sperling.

2001, Scholastic paper $15.95 (0-531-30330-6). More than 30 chatty poems, illustrated with black-and-white photographs, are written from the perspective of a smart and funny 11-year-old. (Rev: HBG 10/01; SLJ 8/01) [811]

4483 Fletcher, Ralph. *I Am Wings: Poems About Love* (5–7). 1994, Macmillan paper $15.00 (0-02-735395-8). Thirty-three simple, short poems depict a boy's falling in and out of love. (Rev: BCCB 6/94; BL 3/15/94; HB 7–8/94; SLJ 6/94*) [811]

4484 Fletcher, Ralph. *Relatively Speaking: Poems About Family* (5–7). Illus. 1999, Orchard LB $15.99 (0-531-33141-5). From an 11-year-old boy's point of view, these original poems explore relationships as family members go through periods of change. (Rev: BCCB 5/99; BL 7/99; HBG 10/99; SLJ 4/99) [811]

4485 Foster, John, ed. *Let's Celebrate: Festival Poems* (8–12). Illus. 1997, Oxford paper $11.95 (0-19-276085-8). With many illustrations, this handsome volume includes poems on many of the world's holidays by 41 English-speaking poets. (Rev: VOYA 8/90) [808.81]

4486 George, Kristine O'Connell. *Swimming Upstream: Middle School Poems* (5–8). 2002, Clarion $14.00 (0-618-15250-4). Brief poems describe how one girl navigates the rapids of middle school, discussing everything from school lunches and lockers to making friends and relationships with boys. (Rev: BL 1/1–15/03; HB 1–2/03; HBG 3/03; SLJ 9/02) [811]

4487 Gillooly, Eileen, ed. *Rudyard Kipling* (4–8). 2000, Sterling $14.95 (0-8069-4484-6). This book contains complete poems or excerpts from 28 poems by this well-liked writer including "If" and "The Ballad of East and West." (Rev: HBG 3/01; SLJ 5/00) [821]

4488 Gordon, Ruth, ed. *Peeling the Onion* (8–12). 1993, HarperCollins $15.89 (0-06-021728-6). A collection of 66 poems with multilayered meanings by world-famous contemporary poets. (Rev: BL 6/1–15/93*; SLJ 7/93; VOYA 8/93) [808.81]

4489 Gordon, Ruth, ed. *Pierced by a Ray of Sun* (7–12). 1995, HarperCollins LB $16.89 (0-06-023614-0). A compilation of poems from across cultures and eras on topics from the timely to the timeless and emotions from hope to despair. (Rev: BL 5/1/95*; SLJ 6/95) [808.81]

4490 Gordon, Ruth, sel. *Under All Silences: Shades of Love* (8–12). 1987, HarperCollins $13.00 (0-06-022154-2). Sixty-six love poems, dating from ancient Egypt to modern days. (Rev: BL 9/15/87; BR 3–4/88; SLJ 10/87; VOYA 4/88) [808.1]

4491 Greenberg, Jan, ed. *Heart to Heart: New Poems Inspired by Twentieth-Century American Art* (5–10). Illus. 2001, Abrams $19.95 (0-8109-4386-7). This book contains specially commissioned poems from well-known writers to accompany some of the finest artworks of the 20th century. (Rev: BL 3/15/01*; HBG 10/01; SLJ 4/01*; VOYA 8/01) [811]

4492 Hall, Donald. *The Man Who Lived Alone* (4–7). Illus. 1998, Godine paper $11.95 (1-56792-050-0). A narrative poem concerning a man who ran away from abuse to see the world and returns in later life.

4493 Harrison, Michael, and Christopher Stuart-Clark, eds. *One Hundred Years of Poetry for Children* (5–7). Illus. 1999, Oxford $25.00 (0-19-276190-0). Arranged by theme, this collection of 20th-century verse contains one poem from each of approximately 150 poets. (Rev: BL 9/1/99; HBG 3/00; SLJ 7/99) [821.9]

4494 Harrison, Michael, and Christopher Stuart-Clark, eds. *The Oxford Book of Christmas Poems* (7–12). Illus. 1999, Oxford paper $12.95 (0-19-276214-1). A total of 120 British and American poems are included. [808.81]

4495 Harrison, Michael, and Christopher Stuart-Clark, comps. *The Oxford Treasury of Time Poems* (4–9). 1999, Oxford LB $25.00 (1-19-276175-7). From John Milton and William Blake to W. H. Auden and Sylvia Plath, this anthology contains poetry and thoughts about time. (Rev: SLJ 7/99) [811]

4496 Harrison, Michael, and Christopher Stuart-Clark, eds. *The Young Oxford Book of Christmas Poems* (5–8). Illus. 2001, Oxford $19.95 (0-19-276247-8). A richly illustrated collection of poems with Christmas themes by poets including Ted Hughes, Sylvia Plath, and Seamus Heaney. (Rev: BCCB 2/02; BL 12/1/01; HBG 3/02) [821]

4497 Hirsch, Robin. *FEG: Stupid (Ridiculous) Poems for Intelligent Children* (5–8). 2002, Little, Brown $15.95 (0-316-36344-8). A collection of amusing, sometimes hilarious, original poems that rely on playing with words and their meanings. (Rev: BL 6/1–15/02; HBG 10/02; SLJ 4/02) [821.914]

4498 Hovey, Kate. *Arachne Speaks* (6–9). Illus. 2001, Simon & Schuster $17.95 (0-689-82901-9). This poetic retelling of the Greek myth of Arachne features a teenaged girl who defies the gods and goddesses and must face the consequences. (Rev: BCCB 3/01; BL 2/1/01; HB 1–2/01; HBG 10/01; SLJ 3/01; VOYA 10/01) [811]

4499 Janeczko, Paul B. *The Place My Words Are Looking For: What Poets Say About and Through Their Work* (4–9). Illus. 1990, Macmillan $17.95 (0-02-747671-5). A collection of works by some of the best contemporary poets. (Rev: BCCB 7–8/90; BL 5/1/90; HB 5–6/90*; SLJ 5/90; VOYA 6/90) [811]

4500 Janeczko, Paul B., ed. *Stone Bench in an Empty Park* (5–12). Illus. 2000, Orchard LB $16.99 (0-531-33259-4). An inspired collection of haiku from variety of poets illustrated with stunning black-and-white photographs. (Rev: BCCB 6/00; BL 3/15/00*; HB 3–4/00; HBG 10/00; SLJ 3/00) [811]

4501 Janeczko, Paul B., ed. *Wherever Home Begins: 100 Contemporary Poems* (8–12). 1995, Orchard LB $17.99 (0-531-08781-6). One hundred poems that express various approaches to a sense of place. (Rev: BL 10/1/95; SLJ 11/95; VOYA 12/95) [811]

4502 Johnson, Angela. *Running Back to Ludie* (5–8). 2001, Scholastic paper $15.95 (0-439-29316-2). A teenage girl's friends and family, including her wayward mother, are introduced through a series of free-verse poems. (Rev: BCCB 1/02; BL 1/1–15/02; HB 11–12/01; HBG 3/02; SLJ 12/01; VOYA 10/01)

4503 Koch, Kenneth, and Kate Farrell. *Talking to the Sun: An Illustrated Anthology of Poems for Young People* (5–9). Illus. 1985, Holt $35.00 (0-8050-0144-1). A collection of poems on many subjects, illustrated with reproductions from the Metropolitan Museum of Art. (Rev: BL 1/1/86; BR 9–10/86; SLJ 1/87) [808.81]

4504 Koertge, Ron. *Shakespeare Bats Cleanup* (7–10). 2003, Candlewick $15.99 (0-7636-2116-1). Recuperating from an illness, 14-year-old Kevin amuses himself writing poetry and recounts the triumphs and problems of his life in verse. (Rev: BL 4/1/03*; HB 7–8/03; HBG 10/03; SLJ 5/03*; VOYA 8/03) [811]

4505 Koontz, Dean. *The Paper Doorway: Funny Verse and Nothing Worse* (4–8). 2001, Harper-Collins LB $17.89 (0-06-029489-2). A humorous and imaginative collection of poems that feature clever word play. (Rev: HBG 3/02; SLJ 1/02) [811]

4506 Lach, William, ed. *Curious Cats: In Art and Poetry* (5–7). Illus. 1999, Simon & Schuster $16.00 (0-689-83055-6). A fine collection of poems about cats, including the works of such authors as Langston Hughes, William Blake, and Kate Greenaway. (Rev: BL 12/15/99; HBG 3/00; SLJ 2/00) [808.81]

4507 Larrick, Nancy, ed. *Piping Down the Valleys Wild: Poetry for the Young of All Ages* (6–9). Illus. 1999, Bantam paper $5.99 (0-440-41582-9). A collection of favorite poems that deal with subjects related to the experience of young people. [808.81]

4508 Livingston, Myra Cohn, ed. *Call Down the Moon: Poems of Music* (6–12). 1995, Macmillan $16.00 (0-689-80416-4). A collection of poems by Tennyson, Whitman, and others, who use words to express how we create and listen to music. (Rev: BL 10/1/95; SLJ 11/95; VOYA 2/96) [821.008]

4509 Livingston, Myra Cohn, ed. *I Like You If You Like Me: Poems of Friendship* (4–8). 1987, Macmillan $16.00 (0-689-50408-X). Ninety short poems on the theme of friendship, from many cultures and

time periods. (Rev: BL 4/1/87; HB 5–6/87; SLJ 4/87) [808.819353]

4510 Livingston, Myra Cohn, ed. *If the Owl Calls Again: A Collection of Owl Poems* (4–7). 1990, Macmillan $13.95 (0-689-50501-9). A wide range of owl poems from various sources. (Rev: BCCB 1/91; BL 10/1/90; SLJ 1/91) [808.81]

4511 Livingston, Myra Cohn, ed. *Lots of Limericks* (5–8). 1991, Simon & Schuster $16.95 (0-689-50531-0). Nonsense limericks and wordplay abound in this collection. (Rev: BL 10/1/91; SLJ 1/92) [821]

4512 Livingston, Myra Cohn, ed. *A Time to Talk: Poems of Friendship* (7–12). 1992, Macmillan paper $14.00 (0-689-50558-2). Poems from many times and places express how friends bring us joy and support; how they betray and leave us; how we miss them when they're gone; and other aspects of friendship. (Rev: BL 10/15/92; SLJ 11/92) [808.81]

4513 McCord, David. *All Day Long: Fifty Rhymes of the Never Was and Always Is* (4–7). 1975, Little, Brown paper $6.95 (0-316-55532-0). A collection of poems on a variety of subjects, chiefly times that are important in childhood.

4514 McCullough, Frances, ed. *Love Is Like a Lion's Tooth: An Anthology of Love Poems* (7–12). 1984, HarperCollins $12.95 (0-06-024138-1). A collection of love poems that span time from ancient days to the 20th century. [808.81]

4515 McGough, Roger, sel. *The Kingfisher Book of Funny Poems* (4–7). 2002, Kingfisher $19.00 (0-7534-5480-7). An anthology of poems arranged by theme that includes many by familiar names such as Ogden Nash, Lewis Carroll, and Shel Silverstein. (Rev: SLJ 6/02) [811]

4516 Morrison, Lillian, ed. *More Spice than Sugar: Poems About Feisty Females* (4–7). Illus. 2001, Houghton $15.00 (0-618-06892-9). This anthology of poems by many famous writers deals with women in three sections: women's identity, women in sports, and women's rights. (Rev: BL 3/15/01; HBG 10/01; SLJ 3/01) [811]

4517 Morrison, Lillian. *Way to Go! Sports Poems* (4–8). 2001, Boyds Mills $16.95 (1-56397-961-6). Sport lovers will appreciate this collection of poems full of rhythm and life, with vibrant illustrations. (Rev: HBG 3/02; SLJ 10/01) [811]

4518 Myers, Walter Dean. *Blues Journey* (5–8). 2003, Holiday $18.95 (0-8234-1613-5). Poems reflecting the soulfulness of blues music, accompanied by illustrations. (Rev: BL 2/15/03; HB 5–6/03; HBG 10/03; SLJ 4/03*; VOYA 4/03) [811]

4519 Nye, Naomi S. *19 Varieties of Gazelle: Poems of the Middle East* (5–10). 2002, Greenwillow $16.95 (0-06-009765-5). Poems by Palestinian American Nye confide details of her life and the impact of war and terrorism on the peoples of Middle Eastern heritage. (Rev: BL 4/1/02; HB 9–10/02*; HBG 10/02; SLJ 5/02*; VOYA 6/02) [811]

4520 Nye, Naomi S., ed. *This Same Sky: A Collection of Poems from Around the World* (7–12). 1992, Four Winds $20.00 (0-02-768440-7). An extraordinary collection of 129 poems by contemporary poets from 68 countries, with an index by country. (Rev: BL 10/15/92*; SLJ 12/92) [808.81]

4521 Nye, Naomi S. *What Have You Lost?* (6–12). Illus. 1999, Greenwillow $18.95 (0-688-16184-7). A collection of 140 poems about loss — some losses that are trivial, others that are serious. (Rev: BL 4/1/99; BR 9–10/99; HB 3–4/99; SLJ 4/99; VOYA 10/99) [811.008]

4522 Nye, Naomi S., and Paul B. Janeczko, eds. *I Feel a Little Jumpy Around You: A Book of Her Poems and His Poems Collected in Pairs* (8–12). 1996, Simon & Schuster paper $18.00 (0-689-80518-7). This anthology of some 200 poems explores how the genders sometimes view things differently and sometimes the same. (Rev: BL 4/1/96; BR 3–4/97; SLJ 5/96*; VOYA 8/96) [808.81]

4523 Okutoro, Lydia Omolola, ed. *Quiet Storm: Voices of Young Black Poets* (8–12). 1999, Hyperion $16.99 (0-7868-0461-0). This anthology features poems written by black youths ages 13 to 21 from the United States, Canada, England, the West Indies, and several African countries. (Rev: BL 6/1–15/99; SLJ 7/99; VOYA 12/99) [811.008]

4524 Opie, Iona, and Peter Opie, eds. *The Oxford Book of Children's Verses* (6–9). Illus. 1995, Oxford paper $16.95 (0-19-280188-0). Using a chronological arrangement, the editors have included 332 famous selections. [821.08]

4525 Philip, Neil, ed. *It's a Woman's World: A Century of Women's Voices in Poetry* (7–12). Illus. 2000, Dutton $17.99 (0-525-46328-3). An international collection of poetry that celebrates woman's many roles in society. (Rev: BL 3/15/00; HBG 9/00; SLJ 5/00) [808.81.]

4526 Philip, Neil, ed. *War and the Pity of War* (6–12). 1998, Clarion $20.00 (0-395-84982-9). An outstanding collection of poetry from different times and cultures that explores the cruelty, bravery, and tragedy of war. (Rev: BL 9/15/98; BR 5–6/99; HBG 10/99; SLJ 9/98; VOYA 2/99) [808.81]

4527 Prelutsky, Jack. *Nightmares: Poems to Trouble Your Sleep* (5–8). 1976, Greenwillow LB $16.89 (0-688-84053-1). Shuddery, macabre poems that will frighten but amuse a young audience. A sequel is *The Headless Horseman Rides Tonight: More Poems to Trouble Your Sleep* (1980).

4528 Prelutsky, Jack, ed. *The Random House Book of Poetry for Children* (6–9). Illus. 1983, Random LB $21.99 (0-394-95010-0). A selection of verse

suitable for children that concentrates on light verse written recently. [821.08]

4529 Rogasky, Barbara, ed. *Leaf by Leaf: Autumn Poems* (5–8). 2001, Scholastic paper $15.95 (0-590-25347-6). Verses by poets including Shelley, Yeats, and Whitman accompany stunning autumnal photographs. (Rev: BL 7/01; HBG 3/02; SLJ 9/01*) [811.008]

4530 Rosen, Michael, ed. *Classic Poetry: An Illustrated Collection* (6–8). 1998, Candlewick $21.99 (1-56402-890-9). A fine selection of poems by major writers, supplying a brief biography of each, plus one or two poems or excerpts from poems, and an illustration that evokes the poet's times or the mood of the poems. (Rev: BL 1/1–15/99; BR 5–6/99; HBG 3/99; SLJ 5/99) [821.008]

4531 Rosenberg, Liz, ed. *Earth-Shattering Poems* (7–12). 1997, Holt $17.00 (0-8050-4821-9). An anthology of poems from more than 40 poets that deal with life's serious moments and intense experiences. (Rev: BL 12/15/97; BR 9–10/98; SLJ 2/98; VOYA 2/98) [808.81]

4532 Rosenberg, Liz, ed. *Light-Gathering Poems* (6–12). 2000, Holt $15.95 (0-8050-6223-8). An excellent anthology of high-quality poems, mainly from classic writers such as Byron and Frost, but also from some newer voices. (Rev: BL 3/15/00; HB 5–6/00; HBG 9/00; SLJ 6/00; VOYA 6/00) [808.81.]

4533 Sidman, Joyce. *The World According to Dog: Poems and Teen Voices* (6–12). Illus. 2003, Houghton $15.00 (0-618-17497-4). Poems by the author and essays by teens celebrate dogs and the companionship they offer. (Rev: BL 4/1/03; HBG 10/03; SLJ 5/03; VOYA 4/03) [810.8]

4534 Simon, Seymour, ed. *Star Walk* (4–8). Illus. 1995, Morrow LB $14.93 (0-688-11887-7). Simple poems and outstanding photographs create an impressive introduction to stars and outer space. (Rev: BL 3/1/95; SLJ 4/95) [811]

4535 Smith, Charles R. *Short Takes: Fast-Break Basketball Poetry* (4–7). Illus. 2001, Dutton $17.99 (0-525-46454-9). Young fans of basketball will enjoy this collection of original poems that capture the sights, sounds, and excitement of the game. (Rev: BCCB 2/01; BL 2/15/01; HBG 10/01; SLJ 3/01; VOYA 2/02) [811]

4536 Sullivan, Charles, ed. *Imaginary Animals* (6–10). 1996, Abrams $22.95 (0-8109-3470-1). A collection of works by such writers as D. H. Lawrence, Ogden Nash, and William Butler Yeats, and by artists from Andy Warhol to Winslow Homer, featuring all kinds of delightful animals, imaginary and real, among them the Jabberwock, prancing centaurs, rearing dragons, the Loch Ness monster and Salvador Dali's lobster telephone. (Rev: SLJ 2/97) [811]

4537 Swenson, May. *The Complete Poems to Solve* (5–8). 1993, Macmillan $13.95 (0-02-788725-1). From simple riddles to more complex questions, each of these poems contains a puzzle. (Rev: HB 3–4/93; SLJ 5/93) [811]

4538 Testa, Maria. *Becoming Joe DiMaggio* (5–8). 2002, Candlewick $14.99 (0-7636-1537-4). The story of an Italian American boy and his family, told through a series of poems set against a backdrop of radio-broadcast baseball games. (Rev: BCCB 5/02; BL 2/15/02; HBG 3/03; SLJ 5/02) [811]

4539 Thayer, Ernest Lawrence. *Casey at the Bat: A Ballad of the Republic Sung in the Year 1888* (4–8). 2003, Simon & Schuster $16.95 (0-689-85494-3). An impossibly muscular Casey is the star of this version of the classic baseball poem. (Rev: BCCB 1/01*; BL 2/1/03; HBG 10/03; SLJ 3/03*) [811]

4540 Thomas, Joyce Carol. *A Mother's Heart, A Daughter's Love* (6–12). 2001, HarperCollins $14.95 (0-06-029649-6). Two poetic voices — a mother's and a daughter's — describe their life together from the birth of the daughter through the death of the mother. (Rev: BL 3/15/01; HBG 10/01; SLJ 9/01) [811]

4541 Tom, Karen, ed. *Angst! Teen Verses from the Edge* (8–12). 2001, Workman paper $8.95 (0-7611-2383-0). A compilation of poems of varied literary standard, and some containing strong language, culled from PlanetKiki.com. (Rev: SLJ 11/01; VOYA 2/02) [811]

4542 Vecchione, Patrice, ed. *Truth and Lies: An Anthology of Poems* (6–12). 2001, Holt $17.00 (0-8050-6479-6). A collection of poems from around the world, from a variety of eras, and from well-known and obscure authors, with biographical notes. (Rev: BL 12/15/00; BR 9–10/01; HBG 10/01; SLJ 2/01*; VOYA 2/01) [808]

4543 Viorst, Judith. *If I Were in Charge of the World and Other Worries: Poems for Children and Their Parents* (5–8). Illus. 1984, Macmillan paper $5.99 (0-689-70770-3). Easily read poems focus on topics familiar to young people. [811]

4544 Viorst, Judith. *Sad Underwear and Other Complications* (4–7). Illus. 1995, Atheneum $16.00 (0-689-31929-0). A series of imaginative poems, some humorous, some contemplative. (Rev: BCCB 4/95; BL 4/1/95; SLJ 5/95) [811]

4545 Wallace, Daisy, ed. *Ghost Poems* (4–7). 1979, Holiday paper $4.95 (0-8234-0849-3). New and old poems to delight and frighten young readers.

4546 Waters, Fiona, comp. *Dark as a Midnight Dream: Poetry Collection 2* (5–8). 1999, Evans Brothers $24.95 (0-237-51845-7). An extensive anthology of poetry arranged by subjects such as "Mythical Creatures" and "City Life" that features such writers as Robert Browning, William Shakespeare, William Butler Yeats, William Wordsworth,

Langston Hughes, and Carl Sandburg. (Rev: SLJ 11/99) [811]

4547 Watson, Esther Pearl, and Mark Todd, sels. *The Pain Tree: And Other Teenage Angst-Ridden Poetry* (7–12). 2000, Houghton $16.00 (0-618-01558-2); paper $6.95 (0-618-04758-1). Poem collected from teen Web sites and magazines and illustrated with paintings express a wide range of emotions. (Rev: BR 11–12/00; HBG 9/00; SLJ 9/00; VOYA 6/00) [811]

4548 Willard, Nancy, ed. *Step Lightly: Poems for the Journey* (7–12). 1998, Harcourt paper $12.00 (0-15-202052-7). These works from the pens of about 40 poets represent the poems that the editor particularly loves. (Rev: BL 10/1/98; BR 5–6/99; HBG 3/99; SLJ 11/98; VOYA 4/99) [811:008]

4549 Winter, Jeanette. *Emily Dickinson's Letters to the World* (4–7). Illus. 2002, Farrar $16.00 (0-374-32147-7). Brief biographical information is paired with 21 of Emily Dickinson's poems in this small-format picture book told from her sister's point of view. (Rev: BL 3/1/02; HBG 10/02; SLJ 3/02) [811]

4550 Wong, Janet S. *A Suitcase of Seaweed and Other Poems* (4–7). 1996, Simon & Schuster $15.95 (0-689-80788-0). A group of personal poems that deal with the author's cultural backgrounds — Korean, Chinese, and American. (Rev: BCCB 4/96; BL 4/1/96; HB 7–8/96; SLJ 9/96; VOYA 10/96) [811]

4551 Worthen, Tom, ed. *Broken Hearts . . . Healing: Young Poets Speak Out on Divorce* (5–9). Illus. Series: Young Poets Speak Out. 2001, Poet Tree $26.95 (1-58876-150-9); paper $14.95 (1-58876-151-7). This large selection of poems written by their peers about divorce, family breakups, and blended families will resonate with young readers. (Rev: SLJ 9/01; VOYA 10/01) [811]

4552 Yolen, Jane. *Sacred Places* (5–9). Illus. 1996, Harcourt $16.00 (0-15-269953-8). An international collection of informational poems about the places sacred to various faiths. (Rev: BCCB 12/00; BL 10/1/96; SLJ 3/96) [811]

Geographical Regions

Europe

GREAT BRITAIN AND IRELAND

4553 Chaucer, Geoffrey. *The Canterbury Tales* (5–9). Adapted by Geraldine McCaughrean. Illus. 1985, Checkerboard $14.95 (1-56288-259-7). An adaptation for young readers of 13 tales that still keep the flavor and spirit of the originals. (Rev: SLJ 2/86) [826]

4554 Coleridge, Samuel Taylor. *The Rime of the Ancient Mariner* (7–12). Illus. 1994, Random $8.99 (0-517-11849-1). A haunting interpretation of a 200-year-old poem that tells the story of a sailor locked in a living nightmare after he shoots an innocent albatross and watches all his shipmates die. (Rev: BL 3/15/92; SLJ 4/92) [821]

4555 Coleridge, Samuel Taylor. *Samuel Taylor Coleridge* (6–10). Ed. by James Engell. Series: Poetry for Young People. 2003, Sterling $14.95 (0-8069-6951-2). Biographical information introduces a sampling of Coleridge's most famous poems, which are accompanied by editorial notes and full-color illustrations. Also use *William Wordsworth* and *William Butler Yeats* (both 2003). (Rev: BL 4/1/03; SLJ 9/03) [821]

4556 Corrin, Sara, and Stephen Corrin. *The Pied Piper of Hamelin* (6–9). Illus. 1989, Harcourt $14.95 (0-15-261596-2). A fine edition of the Browning poem with stunning illustrations by Errol Le Cain. (Rev: BL 4/1/89) [398.2]

4557 Dahl, Roald. *Rhyme Stew* (7–10). Illus. 1999, Viking paper $3.99 (0-14-034365-2). Lots of silly poems and parodies charmingly illustrated by Quentin Blake. (Rev: BL 5/15/90; SLJ 9/90) [821]

4558 Gillooly, Eileen, ed. *Robert Browning* (7–12). Series: Poetry for Young People. 2001, Sterling $14.95 (0-8069-5543-0). A fine, well-illustrated introduction to the works of the English poet that gives historical context, references, and explanations of terms. (Rev: HBG 10/01; SLJ 10/01) [811]

4559 Kipling, Rudyard. *Gunga Din* (7–12). Illus. 1987, Harcourt $12.95 (0-15-200456-4). A splendid edition of this poem dealing with the Indian Mutiny of 1857 and the heroics of an abused water carrier. (Rev: BCCB 10/87; BL 11/1/87; SLJ 12/87) [821]

4560 Livingston, Myra Cohn, comp. *Poems of Lewis Carroll* (7–9). Illus. 1986, HarperCollins LB $11.89 (0-690-04540-9). A complete collection of rhymes, poems, and riddles from the creator of Alice. (Rev: SLJ 8/86) [821]

4561 Opie, Iona, and Peter Opie. *I Saw Esau: The Schoolchild's Pocket Book* (7–12). Illus. 1992, Candlewick $19.99 (1-56402-046-0). Traces schoolyard folk rhymes to their roots. (Rev: BL 4/15/92*; SLJ 6/92) [821]

4562 Thomas, Dylan. *A Child's Christmas in Wales* (5–8). 1985, Holiday $16.95 (0-8234-0565-6). A prose poem about the poet's childhood in a small Welsh village. [821.912]

United States

4563 Adoff, Arnold. *Slow Dance Heartbreak Blues* (7–10). 1995, Lothrop $15.95 (0-688-10569-6).

Gritty, hip-hop poetry for modern, urban teens. (Rev: BL 12/15/95; SLJ 9/95; VOYA 6/96) [811]

4564 Begay, Shonto. *Navajo: Visions and Voices Across the Mesa* (7–12). 1995, Scholastic paper $17.95 (0-590-46153-2). Poetry that speaks to the ongoing struggle of living in a "dual society" and paintings firmly rooted in Navajo culture. (Rev: BL 4/1/95; SLJ 3/95) [811]

4565 Berry, James. *Rough Sketch Beginning* (4–8). Illus. 1996, Harcourt $18.00 (0-15-200112-3). A poem about the work of a landscape artist is accompanied by expressive drawings and a concluding painting of the outdoors. (Rev: BL 5/1/96; SLJ 5/96*) [821]

4566 Bouchard, David. *If Sarah Will Take Me* (4–8). Illus. 1997, Orca $16.95 (1-55143-081-9). The author, who is paralyzed from the neck down, recalls his love of nature and his many inspiring experiences outdoors. (Rev: HBG 3/98; SLJ 8/97) [811]

4567 Burleigh, Robert. *Hoops* (4–8). Illus. 1997, Harcourt $16.00 (0-15-201450-0). A poem that expresses the joy, exhilaration, and excitement of basketball, as seen from the players' point of view. (Rev: BL 11/15/97*; HBG 3/98; SLJ 11/97*) [811]

4568 Carlson, Lori M., ed. *Cool Salsa: Bilingual Poems on Growing Up Latino in the United States* (7–12). 1994, Holt $16.95 (0-8050-3135-9). An anthology of poetry that describes the experience of growing up with a dual heritage. (Rev: BL 11/1/94; SLJ 8/94*; VOYA 2/95) [811]

4569 Clinton, Catherine, ed. *I, Too, Sing America: Three Centuries of African American Poetry* (6–10). Illus. 1998, Houghton $21.00 (0-395-89599-5). This heavily illustrated volume of 36 poems by 25 authors traces the history of African American poetry, from Phillis Wheatley to Rita Dove. (Rev: BL 11/15/98; BR 5–6/99; HBG 3/99; SLJ 11/98; VOYA 8/99) [712.2]

4570 Clinton, Catherine, ed. *A Poem of Her Own: Voices of American Women Yesterday and Today* (6–9). 2003, Abrams $17.95 (0-8109-4240-2). Biographical profiles enhance this collection of poems by 25 women in U.S. history. (Rev: BL 4/1/03*; HBG 10/03; SLJ 5/03; VOYA 8/03) [811.008]

4571 Dickinson, Emily. *I'm Nobody! Who Are You?* (6–9). Illus. 1978, Stemmer $21.95 (0-916144-21-6); paper $14.95 (0-916144-22-4). A well-illustrated edition of poems that young people can appreciate. [811]

4572 Dunbar, Paul Laurence. *The Complete Poems of Paul Laurence Dunbar* (7–12). 1980, Dodd paper $10.95 (0-396-07895-8). The definitive collection first published in 1913 of this African American poet's work. [811]

4573 Fleischman, Paul. *I Am Phoenix: Poems for Two Voices* (4–9). Illus. 1985, HarperCollins paper $5.99 (0-06-446092-4). A group of love poems about birds that are designed to be read by two voices or groups of voices. (Rev: BL 12/1/85; BR 3–4/86) [811]

4574 Fletcher, Ralph. *Buried Alive: The Elements of Love* (5–8). 1996, Simon & Schuster $14.00 (0-689-80593-4). A series of free-verse poems that explore various aspects of love — puppy and otherwise. (Rev: BCCB 6/96; BL 5/1/96; SLJ 5/96; VOYA 10/96) [811]

4575 Fletcher, Ralph. *Ordinary Things: Poems from a Walk in Early Spring* (5–9). Illus. 1997, Simon & Schuster $16.00 (0-689-81035-0). Thirty-three short poems that comment on objects in nature like birds' nests, leaves, birch trees, and snakeskins. (Rev: BL 4/15/97; BR 11–12/97; SLJ 5/97*; VOYA 12/97) [811]

4576 Fletcher, Ralph. *Room Enough for Love: The Complete Poems of I Am Wings and Buried Alive* (7–12). 1998, Simon & Schuster paper $4.99 (0-689-81976-5). A collection of simple, gentle poems about various aspects of romantic love, taken from Fletcher's earlier books. (Rev: VOYA 8/98) [811]

4577 Franco, Betsy, ed. *You Hear Me? Poems and Writings by Teenage Boys* (7–12). 2000, Candlewick $14.99 (0-7636-1158-1). A fine collection of poems about boys coming of age that covers such topics as sex, jealousy, drugs, rejection, bullying, and being gay. (Rev: BL 10/1/00; HBG 3/01; SLJ 10/00; VOYA 12/00) [810.8]

4578 Frost, Robert. *Birches* (4–8). Illus. 1988, Holt paper $5.95 (0-8050-1316-4). Frost's 1916 poem still entices new readers. (Rev: BL 10/1/88; SLJ 10/88) [811.52]

4579 Frost, Robert. *A Swinger of Birches* (6–9). Illus. 1982, Stemmer $21.95 (0-916144-92-5); paper $14.95 (0-916144-93-3). A collection of Frost's poems suitable for young readers in a well-illustrated edition. [811]

4580 Frost, Robert. *You Come Too: Favorite Poems for Young Readers* (6–9). Illus. 1959, Holt $18.00 (0-8050-0299-5); paper $8.95 (0-8050-0316-9). A fine introduction to this poet's works through 50 of his more accessible poems. [811]

4581 Gardner, Joann, ed. *Runaway with Words: Poems from Florida's Youth Shelters* (6–12). 1996, Anhinga Pr. paper $14.95 (0-938078-47-X). Joy, anger, confusion, and fear are some of the emotions expressed in this collection of poems culled from writing workshops for teens in Florida's shelters. (Rev: BL 6/1–15/97) [811]

4582 Giovanni, Nikki, ed. *Grand Mothers: Poems, Reminiscences, and Short Stories About the Keepers of Our Traditions* (7–12). 1994, Holt $17.95 (0-8050-2766-1). An anthology of 27 poems, memo-

ries, and stories about grandmothers, written in diverse styles and expressing a wide range of sentiments and experiences. (Rev: BL 9/15/94; SLJ 10/94; VOYA 12/94) [811]

4583 Glenn, Mel. *Jump Ball: A Basketball Season in Poems* (6–12). 1997, Dutton $15.99 (0-525-67554-X). In a series of poems, people involved in an inner city high school are introduced, including basketball players, parents, teachers, and friends. (Rev: BL 10/15/97; SLJ 11/97*; VOYA 12/97) [811]

4584 Glenn, Mel. *Who Killed Mr. Chippendale? A Mystery in Poems* (7–12). 1996, Dutton $14.99 (0-525-67530-2). Using free verse, the author explores the shooting death of a high school teacher from the point of view of several characters, including students in his class and investigating police officers. (Rev: BL 6/1–15/96; SLJ 7/96*; VOYA 12/96) [811]

4585 Grimes, Nikki. *A Dime a Dozen* (5–8). Illus. 1998, Dial $17.99 (0-8037-2227-3). Through a series of original poems, the writer explores her childhood: its happy moments, its painful memories — including divorce, foster homes, and parents with drinking and gambling problems — and her search for herself as a teenager. (Rev: BL 12/1/98; HBG 3/99; SLJ 11/98; VOYA 4/99) [811]

4586 Grimes, Nikki. *Hopscotch Love: A Family Treasury of Love Poems* (4–8). Illus. 1999, Lothrop $15.95 (0-688-15667-3). This collection of poems celebrates all kinds of love as experienced by African Americans, including sibling love, teenage crushes, parental love, and love of a husband and wife and a graying couple. (Rev: BL 2/15/99; HBG 9/99; SLJ 1/99) [811]

4587 Grimes, Nikki. *Stepping Out with Grandma Mac* (4–7). Illus. 2001, Orchard paper $16.95 (0-531-30320-9). A loving 10-year-old girl describes a very independent grandmother. (Rev: BL 5/15/01*; HBG 10/01; SLJ 7/01) [811.54]

4588 Hearne, Betsy. *Polaroid and Other Poems of View* (7–12). Illus. 1991, Macmillan $13.95 (0-689-50530-2). A collection of short poems using the camera as a metaphor, drawing connections between word pictures created by the poet and those taken by a photographer. (Rev: BL 8/91) [811]

4589 Herrera, Juan F. *Laughing Out Loud, I Fly (A Caracajadas Yo Vuelo): Poems in English and Spanish* (6–10). Illus. 1998, HarperCollins $15.99 (0-06-027604-5). In this series of poems in both English and Spanish, the poet celebrates incidents in his childhood. (Rev: SLJ 5/98; VOYA 6/99) [811]

4590 Holbrook, Sara. *Walking on the Boundaries of Change: Poems of Transition* (8–12). 1998, Boyds Mills paper $8.95 (1-56397-737-0). In this collection of 53 poems, the author explores the problems of being a teen with amazing insight into concerns and decisions. (Rev: VOYA 2/99) [811]

4591 Hopkins, Lee Bennett, ed. *Hand in Hand* (5–8). 1994, Simon & Schuster $21.95 (0-671-73315-X). An overview of the history of American poetry, with an interesting selection of poems arranged chronologically. (Rev: BCCB 1/95; BL 1/1/95; SLJ 12/94; VOYA 4/95) [811]

4592 Hopkins, Lee Bennett, sel. *Lives: Poems About Famous Americans* (4–8). Illus. 1999, Harper-Collins LB $16.89 (0-06-027768-8). Poetry brings to life 16 important Americans, among them Paul Revere, Eleanor Roosevelt, Babe Ruth, and Langston Hughes. (Rev: BCCB 5/99; HBG 9/99; SLJ 6/99) [811]

4593 Hopkins, Lee Bennett, ed. *Rainbows Are Made* (6–9). 1982, Harcourt $17.95 (0-15-265480-1). Poems by Carl Sandburg that are suitable for young readers are included in this anthology. [811]

4594 Hughes, Langston. *The Dream Keeper and Other Poems* (6–12). Illus. 1994, Knopf LB $14.99 (0-679-94421-4). A classic poetry collection by the renowned African American, originally published in 1932, is presented in an updated, illustrated edition. (Rev: BL 3/15/94; VOYA 6/94) [811]

4595 Janeczko, Paul B., ed. *Poetspeak: In Their Work, About Their Work* (7–12). Illus. 1991, Simon & Schuster paper $9.95 (0-02-043850-8). The works of 60 modern American poets are represented, plus comments by the poets themselves on their work. [811.08]

4596 Johnson, Angela. *The Other Side: Shorter Poems* (6–12). 1998, Orchard LB $16.99 (0-531-33114-8). This African American poet gives us glimpses of her childhood in Alabama, her family life, and her views on such issues as Vietnam, racism, and the Black Panthers. (Rev: BL 11/15/98; BR 5–6/99; HB 11–12/98; HBG 3/99; SLJ 9/98; VOYA 2/99) [811]

4597 Johnson, Dave, ed. *Movin': Teen Poets Take Voice* (5–10). 2000, Orchard $15.95 (0-531-30258-X); paper $6.95 (0-531-07171-5). An anthology of poems by teens who participated in New York Public Library workshops or submitted their work via the Web. (Rev: BL 3/15/00; HBG 10/00; SLJ 5/00; VOYA 6/00) [811]

4598 Katz, Bobbi. *We, the People: Poems* (5–8). 2000, Greenwillow LB $15.89 (0-688-16532-X). The author has written a collection of 65 first-person poems placing herself in the shoes of individuals covering the entire span of American history. (Rev: HBG 3/01; SLJ 12/00) [811]

4599 Knudson, R. R., and May Swenson, eds. *American Sports Poems* (7–12). 1988, Watts LB $19.99 (0-531-08353-5). An excellent collection that concentrates on such popular sports as baseball, football, and swimming. (Rev: BL 8/88; BR 3–4/89; SLJ 11/88; VOYA 10/88) [811]

4600 Koertge, Ron. *The Brimstone Journals* (7–12). 2001, Candlewick $15.99 (0-7636-1302-9). Fifteen students at Brimstone High describe in poetry the issues that trouble them, such as overambitious parents, sexual abuse, dating, bullies, racism, and violence. (Rev: BCCB 4/01; BL 4/15/01; HBG 10/01; SLJ 3/01; VOYA 8/01) [811]

4601 Lawrence, Jacob. *Harriet and the Promised Land* (6–12). 1993, Simon & Schuster $18.95 (0-671-86673-7). The efforts of Harriet Tubman's to lead slaves to freedom in the North is retold in rhythmic text and narrative paintings. (Rev: BL 10/1/93*) [811]

4602 Levin, Jonathan, ed. *Walt Whitman: Poetry for Young People* (5–9). Illus. 1997, Sterling $14.95 (0-8069-9530-0). After a brief biographical sketch, this volume contains 26 poems and excerpts from longer poems, each introduced with an analysis. (Rev: HBG 3/98; SLJ 11/97) [811]

4603 Lewis, J. Patrick. *Freedom Like Sunlight: Praisesongs for Black Americans* (5–12). Illus. 2000, Creative Co. $17.95 (1-56846-163-1). This collection of original poems pays tribute to such important African Americans as Sojourner Truth, Arthur Ashe, Rosa Parks, Marian Anderson, Malcolm X, and Langston Hughes. (Rev: BL 9/15/00*; HBG 3/01; SLJ 12/00) [811]

4604 Livingston, Myra Cohn. *Cricket Never Does: A Collection of Haiku and Tanka* (5–8). Illus. 1997, Simon & Schuster $16.95 (0-689-81123-3). Seasonal changes are explored in more than 60 short haiku and tanka. (Rev: BL 3/1/97; BR 11–12/97; SLJ 4/97) [811]

4605 Loewen, Nancy, ed. *Walt Whitman* (7–12). 1994, Creative Editions LB $23.95 (0-88682-608-X). A dozen selections from *Leaves of Grass* are juxtaposed with biographical vignettes and sepia photographs. (Rev: SLJ 7/94*) [811]

4606 Longfellow, Henry Wadsworth. *The Children's Own Longfellow* (5–8). Illus. 1908, Houghton $20.00 (0-395-06889-4). Eight selections from the best-known and best-loved of Longfellow's poems.

4607 Longfellow, Henry Wadsworth. *Hiawatha and Megissogwon* (4–7). 2001, National Geographic $16.95 (0-7922-6676-5). Artwork with an authentic Native American feel illustrates Hiawatha's exciting adventures in the "Pearl-Feather" section of Longfellow's epic poem. (Rev: BCCB 3/02; BL 11/15/01; HBG 3/02; SLJ 9/01) [811]

4608 Lyne, Sandford, comp. *Ten-Second Rainshowers: Poems by Young People* (4–9). Illus. 1996, Simon & Schuster $16.00 (0-689-80113-0). Through poetry written in free verse, 130 young people ages 8 to 18 give brief, evocative glimpses of life. (Rev: SLJ 12/96; VOYA 12/96) [811]

4609 Meltzer, Milton, ed. *Hour of Freedom: American History in Poetry* (6–12). 2003, Boyds Mills $16.95 (1-59078-021-3). Brief histories introduce many classic and some less-familiar poems — plus lyrics and speeches — that are grouped in chronological chapters, ranging from the colonial period to the 20th century. (Rev: BL 9/1/03; SLJ 7/03) [811.54]

4610 Millay, Edna St. Vincent. *Edna St. Vincent Millay's Poems Selected for Young People* (7–10). Illus. 1979, HarperCollins $14.00 (0-06-024218-3). A fine selection of the poet's work illustrated with woodcuts. [811]

4611 Moss, Jeff. *The Dad of the Dad of the Dad of Your Dad: Stories About Kids and Their Fathers* (4–8). Illus. 1997, Ballantine $18.00 (0-345-38591-8). Eight humorous poems trace the history of families, from a prehistoric father and his son to a futuristic dad and his brood. (Rev: SLJ 7/97) [811]

4612 Mullins, Tom, ed. *Running Lightly . . . : Poems for Young People* (4–9). 1998, Mercier paper $12.95 (1-85342-193-9). A charming collection of old songs and ballads, nonsense rhymes, and lyrics. (Rev: BL 5/15/98; SLJ 7/98) [811]

4613 Myers, Walter Dean. *Angel to Angel: A Mother's Gift of Love* (4–8). Illus. 1998, HarperCollins LB $15.89 (0-06-027722-X). A photo/poetry montage with 10 distinctly styled poems and photographs focusing on African American mothers and children, and reflecting the relationship between words and pictures. (Rev: BL 2/15/98; HBG 10/98; SLJ 6/98) [811]

4614 Nelson, Marilyn. *Carver: A Life in Poems* (8–12). 2001, Front Street $16.95 (1-886910-53-7). Historical photographs and lyrical free verse present the life of the man born into slavery who accomplished so much for himself and for others. (Rev: BL 5/1/01; BR 11–12/01; HB 9–10/01; HBG 3/02; SLJ 7/01; VOYA 8/01) [811]

4615 Poe, Edgar Allan. *Annabel Lee* (5–9). Illus. 1987, Tundra $19.95 (0-88776-200-X). A haunting rendition of the Poe poem with paintings by the French Canadian artist Gilles Tibo. (Rev: BL 10/15/87; SLJ 12/87) [811]

4616 Robb, Laura, sel. *Music and Drum: Voices of War and Peace, Hope and Dreams* (5–9). 1997, Philomel $16.95 (0-399-22024-0). An anthology of war poems that are strikingly illustrated with photographs reflecting their power and emotions. (Rev: BL 4/1/97; SLJ 5/97) [808]

4617 Rosenberg, Liz, ed. *The Invisible Ladder: An Anthology of Contemporary American Poems for Young Readers* (6–10). 1996, Holt $19.95 (0-8050-3836-1). As well as an excellent anthology of modern American poetry, this volume provides commentary by the poets, photographs of them, and suggestions for using each of the poems. (Rev: BL 9/15/96; BR 9–10/97; SLJ 2/97; VOYA 2/97) [811]

4618 Rylant, Cynthia. *Soda Jerk* (7–12). Illus. 1990, Watts LB $16.99 (0-531-08464-7). A group of poems about the inhabitants of a small town written from the viewpoint of a teenage soda jerk. (Rev: BL 2/15/90; SLJ 4/90; VOYA 6/90) [811]

4619 Rylant, Cynthia. *Something Permanent* (7–12). Illus. 1994, Harcourt $18.00 (0-15-277090-9). Combines Rylant's poetry with Walker Evans's photographs to evoke strong emotions of southern life during the Depression. (Rev: BL 7/94*; SLJ 8/94; VOYA 12/94) [811]

4620 Rylant, Cynthia. *Waiting to Waltz: A Childhood* (7–9). Illus. 1984, Bradbury $16.00 (0-02-778000-7). In 30 poems, the author conveys the experience of growing up in a small Appalachian town. [808.81]

4621 Sandburg, Carl. *Grassroots* (4–8). Illus. 1998, Harcourt $18.00 (0-15-200082-8). This collection of 16 poems describing the seasons in America's Midwest is illustrated with watercolor landscapes. (Rev: BCCB 6/98; BL 3/15/98; HBG 9/98; SLJ 6/98) [811]

4622 Sandburg, Carl. *The Sandburg Treasury: Prose and Poetry for Young People* (5–8). Illus. 1970, Harcourt $24.00 (0-15-202678-9). Sandburg's whimsical stories, poetry, and portions of his autobiography.

4623 Schmidt, Gary D., ed. *Robert Frost* (5–7). Series: Poetry for Young People. 1994, Sterling $14.95 (0-8069-0633-2). An anthology of 25 poems suitable for young people, with watercolor illustrations that picture the New England landscape that Frost loved. (Rev: BL 12/1/94; SLJ 2/95) [811]

4624 Schoonmaker, Frances, ed. *Henry Wadsworth Longfellow* (4–8). Illus. Series: Poetry for Young People. 1999, Sterling $14.95 (0-8069-9417-7). A generous, carefully selected presentation of Longfellow's poetry illustrated by full-color paintings and accompanied by biographical notes. (Rev: BL 3/15/99; HBG 9/99; SLJ 3/99) [811]

4625 Shields, Carol Diggory. *Brain Juice: American History Fresh Squeezed!* (4–8). 2002, Handprint $14.95 (1-929766-62-9). A timeline runs across the tops of these pages of poems about events in American history. (Rev: HBG 3/03; SLJ 1/03) [811]

4626 Silverstein, Shel. *A Light in the Attic* (6–9). Illus. 1981, HarperCollins LB $18.89 (0-06-025674-5). More than 100 humorous poems that deal with children's interests and need for fun. Also use the author's earlier *Where the Sidewalk Ends* (1974). [811]

4627 Smith, Charles R. *Perfect Harmony: A Musical Journey with the Boys Choir of Harlem* (4–7). Illus. 2002, Hyperion $15.99 (0-7868-0758-X). Photographs of the Boys Choir of Harlem provide a dynamic backdrop for these upbeat poems about songs and singing. (Rev: BL 8/02; HBG 3/03; SLJ 8/02) [811]

4628 Smith, Hope Anita. *The Way a Door Closes* (5–8). 2003, Holt $18.95 (0-8050-6477-X). A series of poems convey the feelings of a 13-year-old African American boy whose warm, loving home is destroyed when his father loses his job. (Rev: BL 5/1/03; HBG 10/03; SLJ 5/03*) [811]

4629 Soto, Gary. *A Fire in My Hands: A Book of Poems* (6–10). Illus. 1992, Scholastic paper $4.50 (0-590-44579-0). An illustrated collection of 23 poems, accompanied by advice to young poets. (Rev: BL 4/1/92; SLJ 3/92) [811]

4630 Stafford, William. *Learning to Live in the World: Earth Poems* (8–12). 1994, Harcourt $17.00 (0-15-200208-1). Fifty nature poems that will appeal to teens. (Rev: BL 1/1/95; SLJ 12/94) [811]

4631 Stavans, Ilan, ed. *Wachale! Poetry and Prose About Growing Up Latino in America* (5–8). 2001, Cricket $16.95 (0-8126-4750-5). A bilingual anthology about Latino experiences, both in the past and in the present. (Rev: BCCB 2/02; BL 2/1/02; HBG 10/02; SLJ 2/02; VOYA 6/02) [810.8]

4632 Steig, Jeanne. *Alpha Beta Chowder* (5–8). Illus. 1992, HarperCollins LB $14.89 (0-06-205007-9). A collection of nonsense verses celebrating the joy of words — their sound and meaning — with each verse playing with a letter of the alphabet. (Rev: BL 11/15/92; SLJ 12/92) [811]

4633 Strickland, Michael R., ed. *My Own Song: And Other Poems to Groove To* (6–12). Illus. 1997, Boyds Mills $14.95 (1-56397-686-2). A collection of poems about music and its relationship to such subjects as love, cities, and birds. (Rev: BL 10/15/97; HBG 3/98; SLJ 12/97) [811]

4634 Sullivan, Charles, ed. *Imaginary Gardens: American Poetry and Art for Young People* (6–10). Illus. 1989, Abrams $19.95 (0-8109-1130-2). A collection of well-known poems, from such poets as Ogden Nash and Walt Whitman, with accompanying illustrations that also represent a wide range of artists and styles. (Rev: BL 12/1/89; SLJ 2/89) [700]

4635 Turner, Ann. *Grass Songs: Poems* (7–12). Illus. 1993, Harcourt $16.95 (0-15-136788-4). Dramatic monologues in poetic form that express courage and despair, passion and loneliness, and the struggle to find a home in the wilderness. (Rev: BL 6/1–15/93; VOYA 8/93) [811]

4636 Turner, Ann. *Learning to Swim: A Memoir* (6–12). 2000, Scholastic paper $14.95 (0-439-15309-3). In this memoir told in free verse, the author looks back at the summer she learned to swim and was sexually abused by an older boy. (Rev: BL 10/1/00; BR 1–2/01; HBG 3/01; SLJ 11/00; VOYA 12/00) [811.54]

4637 Turner, Ann W. *A Lion's Hunger: Poems of First Love* (8–12). Illus. 1999, Marshall Cavendish $15.95 (0-7614-5035-1). Written from a young woman's point of view, this is a collection of poems by the author chronicling the joys and sorrows of first love. (Rev: BL 3/1/99; BR 5–6/99; HBG 3/99; SLJ 1/99; VOYA 2/99) [811]

4638 Wayland, April Halprin. *Girl Coming in for a Landing* (6–12). 2002, Knopf paper $14.95 (0-375-80158-8). A teenage girl expresses in appealing poetry the social and academic trials and tribulations of a year of high school. (Rev: BL 10/15/02; HB 9–10/02; HBG 3/03; SLJ 8/02) [811.54]

4639 Weatherford, Carole Boston. *Remember the Bridge: Poems of a People* (7–12). Illus. 2002, Putnam $17.99 (0-399-23726-7). This collection of poems celebrates African Americans from the era of slavery through today, with accompanying archival images. (Rev: BL 2/15/02; HBG 10/02; SLJ 1/02; VOYA 8/02) [811]

4640 *When the Rain Sings: Poems by Young Native Americans* (5–10). Illus. 1999, Simon & Schuster $16.00 (0-689-82283-9). A collection of 37 poems from Native Americans ranging in age from seven to 17. (Rev: BL 12/1/99; HBG 3/00; SLJ 11/99) [811]

4641 Whipple, Laura, ed. *Celebrating America: A Collection of Poems and Images of the American Spirit* (5–10). 1994, Putnam $19.95 (0-399-22036-4). An anthology of poetry and art that reflects the wide range of American cultures, styles, and periods. (Rev: BL 9/1/94*; SLJ 9/94) [811.008]

4642 Whitman, Walt. *Voyages: Poems by Walt Whitman* (7–12). Illus. 1988, Harcourt $15.95 (0-15-294495-8). An introductory biographical sketch is followed by 53 representative poems selected by Lee Bennett Hopkins. (Rev: BL 11/15/88; BR 3–4/89; SLJ 12/88; VOYA 1/89) [811.3]

4643 Wong, Janet S. *Behind the Wheel* (7–12). 1999, Simon & Schuster $15.00 (0-689-82531-5). In a series of free-verse poems, the author explores individuals and their relationships within families. (Rev: BL 1/1–15/00; HB 11–12/99; HBG 4/00; VOYA 2/00) [811.]

4644 Wong, Janet S. *The Rainbow Hand: Poems About Mothers and Children* (5–8). Illus. 1999, Simon & Schuster $15.00 (0-689-82148-4). This collection of 18 poems deals with maternal love, from the mother's point of view and from the child's. (Rev: BL 4/1/99; HBG 10/99; SLJ 4/99; VOYA 6/99) [811]

4645 Yolen, Jane, sel. *Once Upon Ice: And Other Frozen Poems* (4–8). 1997, Boyds Mills $17.95 (1-56397-408-8). A collection of 17 poems inspired by photographs of ice formations, which are also included. (Rev: BL 2/1/97; SLJ 3/97) [811]

Other Regions

4646 Berry, James R. *Everywhere Faces Everywhere* (6–10). Illus. 1997, Simon & Schuster $16.00 (0-689-80996-4). A collection of 46 of the author's poems that describe his childhood in Jamaica and his adult life in the United Kingdom. (Rev: BL 5/1/97; BR 11–12/97; SLJ 6/97; VOYA 10/97) [821]

4647 Field, Edward. *Magic Words* (5–9). Illus. 1998, Harcourt $17.00 (0-15-201498-5). This is a collection of free-verse narratives based on Inuit creation myths and songs. (Rev: BCCB 10/98; BL 10/15/98; HBG 3/99; SLJ 12/98) [811]

4648 Johnston, Tony. *The Ancestors Are Singing* (4–8). 2003, Farrar $16.00 (0-374-30347-9). Mexico's geography, history, and culture are portrayed in poems full of vivid images. (Rev: BL 4/1/03; HBG 10/03; SLJ 4/03; VOYA 10/03) [811]

4649 Liu, Siyu, and Orel Protopopescu. *A Thousand Peaks: Poems from China* (6–10). 2002, Pacific View $19.95 (1-881896-24-2). Thirty-five translations of Chinese poems are accompanied by information giving historical and cultural context, the original in Chinese characters and pinyin transliteration, a literal translation, and black-and-white drawings. (Rev: BL 3/15/02; SLJ 2/02*) [895.1]

4650 Mado, Michio. *The Animals: Selected Poems* (5–10). Trans. by the Empress Michiko of Japan. Illus. 1992, Simon & Schuster LB $16.95 (0-689-50574-4). Twenty Japanese poems about animals, with English versions on facing pages. (Rev: BL 12/1/92; SLJ 2/93) [895.6]

4651 Nye, Naomi S., ed. *The Space Between Our Footsteps: Poems and Paintings from the Middle East* (8–12). Illus. 1998, Simon & Schuster $21.95 (0-689-81233-7). More than 100 poets and artists from 19 countries in the Middle East are featured in this handsome volume of verse about families, friends, and everyday events. (Rev: BCCB 5/98; BL 3/1/98; HB 3–4/98; SLJ 5/98; VOYA 10/98) [808.81]

4652 O'Huigin, Sean. *Ghost Horse of the Mounties* (5–7). 1991, Godine $14.95 (0-87923-721-X). A long poem about a black midsummer night in 1874 on the empty plains of the Northwest Territories in Canada. (Rev: BCCB 7–8/91; BL 5/1/91) [811]

4653 Service, Robert W. *The Cremation of Sam McGee* (5–9). Illus. 1987, Greenwillow $17.95 (0-688-06903-7). The famous Gold Rush poem is amusingly illustrated by Ted Harrison. (Rev: BL 4/15/87; HB 5–6/87; SLJ 3/87) [811]

4654 Service, Robert W. *The Shooting of Dan McGrew* (6–9). Illus. 1995, Godine paper $10.95 (1-56792-065-9). A bunch of the boys are still whooping it up in this nicely illustrated edition. (Rev: BL 1/1/89; SLJ 12/88) [811]

Folklore and Fairy Tales

General and Miscellaneous

4655 Caduto, Michael J. *Earth Tales from Around the World* (5–8). Illus. 1997, Fulcrum paper $17.95 (1-55591-968-5). This collection of 48 folktales from around the world emphasizes respect for the natural world. (Rev: BL 4/1/98; SLJ 5/98; VOYA 4/98) [398.27]

4656 Climo, Shirley. *A Treasury of Mermaids: Mermaid Tales from Around the World* (4–8). Illus. 1997, HarperCollins $17.95 (0-06-023876-3). A fine retelling of eight folktales from around the world about mermaids and other enchanted sea creatures. (Rev: BL 11/15/97; HBG 3/98; SLJ 10/97) [398.2]

4657 Cole, Joanna, ed. *Best-Loved Folktales of the World* (7–12). Illus. 1982, Doubleday paper $17.00 (0-385-18949-4). A collection of 200 tales from around the globe, arranged geographically. [398.2]

4658 Datlow, Ellen, and Terri Windling, eds. *A Wolf at the Door and Other Retold Fairy Tales* (6–10). 2000, Simon & Schuster $16.00 (0-689-82138-7). This collection of variations on standard fairy tales by prominent authors includes such titles as "The Seven Stage Comeback" (Snow White) and "Cinder Elephant" about a lovely but very large girl. (Rev: BL 9/1/00; HBG 3/01; SLJ 8/00; VOYA 6/00)

4659 Ferris, Jean. *Once Upon a Marigold* (5–8). 2002, Harcourt $17.00 (0-15-216791-9). Christian falls in love with Princess Marigold and wins her heart through his bravery in this fairy tale full of fun. (Rev: BCCB 2/03; BL 9/15/02; HB 9–10/02; HBG 3/03; SLJ 11/02; VOYA 12/02)

4660 Forest, Heather. *Wisdom Tales from Around the World* (4–7). 1996, August House $27.95 (0-87483-478-3); paper $19.95 (0-87483-479-1). Fifty fables, folktales, and myths from around the world. (Rev: BCCB 2/97; BL 3/1/97) [398.2]

4661 Hale, Shannon. *The Goose Girl* (6–10). 2003, Bloomsbury $17.95 (1-58234-843-X). Crown Princess Ani, who can talk to the animals, is betrayed by her guards and disguises herself as a goose girl until she can reclaim her crown. (Rev: BL 8/03; SLJ 8/03*; VOYA 10/03)

4662 Hamilton, Martha, and Mitch Weiss. *How and Why Stories: World Tales Kids Can Read and Tell* (5–10). Illus. 1999, August House $21.95 (0-87483-562-3); paper $12.95 (0-87483-561-5). This excellent collection of 25 pourquoi (how and why) stories from around the world also contains a useful introduction on folklore plus tips on delivering each of the tales. (Rev: BL 5/15/00; HBG 3/00; SLJ 1/00) [398.2]

4663 Hirsch, Odo. *Bartlett and the Ice Voyage* (4–7). 2003, Bloomsbury $14.95 (1-58234-797-2). When a queen demands a far-off fruit, the intrepid explorer Bartlett is ready to oblige. (Rev: BL 2/1/03; HBG 10/03; SLJ 1/03*; VOYA 2/03)

4664 Jaffe, Nina, and Steve Zeitlin. *The Cow of No Color: Riddle Stories and Justice Tales from Around the World* (5–8). Illus. 1998, Holt $17.00 (0-8050-3736-5). A collection of folktales from around the world that deal with the theme of justice. (Rev: BCCB 12/98; BL 11/1/98; HBG 3/99; SLJ 12/98) [398.2]

4665 Lupton, Hugh, ed. *The Songs of Birds: Stories and Poems from Many Cultures* (4–7). Illus. 2000, Barefoot $19.95 (1-84148-045-2). A beautifully illustrated collection of stories (mostly creation myths) and poems about birds culled from a wide range of cultures. (Rev: BL 3/15/00; SLJ 9/00) [808.819]

4666 McCaughrean, Geraldine. *The Bronze Cauldron* (5–6). Illus. 1998, Simon & Schuster $19.95

(0-689-81758-4). Twenty-six myths and legends, such as the rise and fall of Faust, a Viking legend about the founding of London, and the story of Cupid and Psyche, are retold in this delightful collection. (Rev: BCCB 7–8/98; BL 5/15/98; HBG 10/98; SLJ 7/98) [398.2]

4667 McCaughrean, Geraldine. *The Silver Treasure: Myths and Legends of the World* (5–8). 1997, Simon & Schuster paper $21.00 (0-689-81322-8). A collection of 23 myths and legends that includes such familiar ones as *Rip Van Winkle* and *The Tower of Babel* as well as many lesser-known ones. (Rev: BCCB 6/97; BL 4/15/97; HBG 3/98; SLJ 4/97*; VOYA 8/97) [398.2]

4668 MacDonald, Margaret Read. *Peace Tales: World Folktales to Talk About* (5–7). Illus. 1992, Shoe String LB $25.00 (0-208-02328-3); paper $17.50 (0-208-02329-1). Stories and proverbs directed toward achieving world peace. (Rev: BL 6/15/92; SLJ 10/92) [398.2]

4669 Matthews, John. *The Barefoot Book of Knights* (4–7). 2002, Barefoot $19.99 (1-84148-064-9). This book contains retellings of seven tales of knights and chivalry from countries around the world. (Rev: BCCB 9/02; BL 4/15/02; HBG 10/02; SLJ 6/02) [398.2]

4670 Mayer, Marianna. *Women Warriors: Myths and Legends of Heroic Women* (4–8). 1999, Morrow $17.95 (0-688-15522-7). A collection of 12 myths and legends about folk heroines from India, Africa, Japan, North America, and the British Isles. (Rev: BCCB 10/99; BL 9/15/99; HBG 3/00; SLJ 9/99) [398.2]

4671 Mayo, Margaret. *When the World Was Young: Creation and Pourquoi Tales* (4–7). 1996, Simon & Schuster paper $19.95 (0-689-80867-4). Age-old questions are answered in this collection of folktales that give explanations for natural phenomena. (Rev: BCCB 2/97; BL 9/1/96; SLJ 12/96) [398.2]

4672 Opie, Iona, and Peter Opie, eds. *The Classic Fairy Tales* (4–8). Illus. 1992, Oxford paper $17.95 (0-19-520219-8). Contains the earliest published text of these tales.

4673 Pearson, Maggie. *The Headless Horseman and Other Ghoulish Tales* (4–7). Illus. 2001, Interlink $18.95 (1-56656-377-1). From Bluebeard to Baba Yaga and Ichabod Crane, this is a collection of 14 tales about eerie beings. (Rev: BL 3/1/01; HBG 10/01; SLJ 1/01) [398.2]

4674 Phelps, Ethel Johnston. *The Maid of the North: Feminist Folk Tales from Around the World* (7–9). 1982, Holt paper $13.00 (0-8050-0679-6). An international collection of folktales featuring many wily and clever heroines. [398]

4675 Philip, Neil. *The Little People: Stories of Fairies, Pixies, and Other Small Folk* (4–8). Illus. 2002, Abrams $24.95 (0-8109-0570-1). Beautiful illustrations accompany stories about fairies and other "magical beings" from Europe. (Rev: BL 2/15/03; HBG 3/03; SLJ 12/02) [398.21]

4676 Reneaux, J. J. *How Animals Saved the People* (4–8). Illus. 2001, HarperCollins $17.89 (0-688-16254-1). Eighty lively, evocative folk tales are included in this anthology about a variety of animals and and their ingenious schemes. (Rev: BCCB 3/01; BL 2/15/01; HB 3–4/01; HBG 10/01; SLJ 1/01) [398.2]

4677 Rosen, Michael J. *How the Animals Got Their Colors* (5–8). 1992, Harcourt $14.95 (0-15-236783-7). Tales from around the world that explain such things as a leopard's spots and the green on a frog's back. (Rev: BCCB 7–8/92; BL 6/15/92; SLJ 9/91) [398.2]

4678 Rossel, Seymour. *Sefer Ha-Aggadah: The Book of Legends for Young Readers* (4–7). 1996, UAHC paper $14.00 (0-8074-0603-1). A collection of legends based on stories about the Jewish people from the Old Testament. (Rev: SLJ 3/97) [398.2]

4679 San Souci, Robert D. *Even More Short and Shivery: Thirty Spine-Tingling Stories* (5–8). Illus. 1997, Delacorte $14.95 (0-385-32252-6). A collection of 30 scary stories, mostly folktales from around the world, that are great for reading aloud or giving presentations before a group. (Rev: BL 7/97; HBG 3/98; SLJ 10/97) [398.25]

4680 Schmidt, Gary. *Mara's Stories: Glimmers in the Darkness* (4–8). 2001, Holt $16.95 (0-8050-6794-9). Mara tells stories from Jewish folklore to comfort the women and children in her concentration camp. (Rev: BL 10/1/01; HB 1–2/02*; HBG 3/02; SLJ 12/01) [398.2]

4681 Schwartz, Howard. *The Day the Rabbi Disappeared: Jewish Holiday Tales of Magic* (4–7). Illus. 2000, Viking $15.99 (0-670-88733-1). A collection of short folktales that explore Jewish heritage and the role of mysticism in the religion. (Rev: BL 10/1/00*; HB 7–8/00; HBG 3/01; SLJ 8/00) [398.2]

4682 Sherman, Josepha. *Merlin's Kin: World Tales of the Heroic Magician* (5–8). 1998, August House paper $11.95 (0-87483-519-4). A splendid international collection of folktales that feature magicians, sorcerers, shamans, healers, and wizards. (Rev: BL 4/15/99; BR 1–2/99; SLJ 3/99; VOYA 12/98) [398.21]

4683 Singer, Isaac Bashevis. *The Fools of Chelm and Their History* (5–6). 1973, Farrar $14.00 (0-374-32444-1). Nonsense stories about the village that is the setting of other Singer tales. [398.2]

4684 Singer, Isaac Bashevis. *When Shlemiel Went to Warsaw and Other Stories* (4–7). 1986, Farrar paper $4.05 (0-374-48365-5). Illustrations and the eight stories retold here delightfully reveal the distinctive people of Chelm and their extraordinary, universally exportable wisdom. (Rev: BL 6/1–15/98) [398.2]

4685 Spencer, Ann. *And Round Me Rings: Bell Tales and Folklore* (4–7). 2003, Tundra paper $11.95 (0-88776-597-1). A collection of folklore, poetry, fact, and fiction about bells that includes entries from Europe, the Far East, and North Amreica. (Rev: BL 12/1/03) [398.27]

4686 Spiegelman, Art. *Little Lit: Folklore and Fairy Tale Funnies* (4–9). Illus. 2000, HarperCollins $19.95 (0-06-028624-5). In this presentation in graphic format, 15 different artists create brilliant variations on standard fairy and folk tales. (Rev: BL 1/1–15/01*; HB 9–10/00; HBG 3/01; SLJ 12/00)

4687 Thompson, Stith, ed. *One Hundred Favorite Folktales* (5–8). 1968, Indiana Univ. Pr. $39.95 (0-253-15940-7); paper $19.95 (0-253-20172-1). A selection from an international store of folktales. [398.2]

4688 Thurber, James. *The White Deer* (6–7). 1968, Harcourt paper $9.00 (0-15-696264-0). Three princes, a princess, and magic occurrences are highlights of this modern fairy tale.

4689 Williams, Rose. *The Book of Fairies: Nature Spirits from Around the World* (5–7). Illus. 1997, Beyond Words $18.95 (1-885223-56-0). Fairies play a major role in these eight stories from such countries as France, Ireland, and India. (Rev: BL 1/1–15/98; HBG 3/98; SLJ 1/98) [398.2]

4690 Yolen, Jane, ed. *Mightier than the Sword: World Folktales for Strong Boys* (4–8). 2003, Harcourt $19.00 (0-15-216391-3). Yolen has collected stories from countries including Afghanistan, Angola, and China that portray intelligence as an invaluable asset. (Rev: BL 4/1/03; HB 5–6/03; HBG 10/03; SLJ 5/03) [398.2]

4691 Yolen, Jane, and Shulamith Oppenheim. *The Fish Prince and Other Stories* (7–12). 2001, Interlink $29.95 (1-56656-389-5); paper $15.00 (1-56656-390-9). An absorbing and informative collection of stories of mermaids and mermen from around the world, accompanied by black-and-white illustrations. (Rev: BL 11/15/01) [398.21]

4692 Young, Richard A., and Judy Dockery Young, eds. *Stories from the Days of Christopher Columbus: A Multicultural Collection for Young Readers* (5–9). 1992, August House paper $8.95 (0-87483-198-9). An anthology of stories translated from a variety of languages, including Italian, Spanish, Portuguese, and Aztec. (Rev: BL 9/15/92; SLJ 7/92) [398.2]

4693 Zeitlin, Steve. *The Four Corners of the Sky: Creation Stories and Cosmologies from Around the World* (7–12). Illus. 2000, Holt $17.00 (0-8050-4816-2). This is a thoughtful collection of folktales about the beginning of the universe from 16 diverse cultures and religions. (Rev: BL 11/15/00; HB 1–2/01; HBG 3/01; SLJ 12/00) [291.2]

Geographical Regions

Africa

4694 Abrahams, Roger D., ed. *African Folktales: Traditional Stories of the Black World* (7–12). Illus. 1983, Pantheon paper $18.00 (0-394-72117-9). A collection of about 100 tales from south of the Sahara. [398.2]

4695 Arkhurst, Joyce Cooper. *The Adventures of Spider: West African Folktales* (4–7). 1992, Little, Brown paper $8.99 (0-316-05107-1). Six humorous stories featuring the crafty spider. [398.2]

4696 Ashabranner, Brent, and Russell Davis. *The Lion's Whiskers and Other Ethiopian Tales* (4–7). Illus. 1997, Linnet LB $19.95 (0-208-02429-8). A classic collection of 16 Ethiopian folktales originally published in 1995. (Rev: BL 10/1/97; SLJ 5/97*) [398.2]

4697 Badoe, Adwoa. *The Pot of Wisdom: Ananse Stories* (4–8). 2001, Groundwood $18.95 (0-88899-429-X). Ten well-written folktales from Ghana recounting the adventures of Ananse, the clever trickster spider. (Rev: BL 12/1/01; HB 1–2/02; HBG 3/02; SLJ 10/01) [398.266]

4698 Eisner, Will. *Sundiata: A Legend of Africa* (5–8). Illus. 2003, NBM $15.95 (1-56163-332-1). A retelling, in comic book style, of an African folktale about a lame prince who conquers an evil king. (Rev: BL 2/1/03; HBG 10/03; SLJ 2/03) [398.2]

4699 Giles, Bridget. *Myths of West Africa* (6–10). Series: Mythic World. 2002, Gale LB $17.98 (0-7398-4976-X). A general introduction to this area of Africa through text and pictures is followed by retellings of important myths and relevant background information. (Rev: BL 7/02; HBG 10/02; SLJ 5/02) [398.2]

4700 Greaves, Nick. *When Hippo Was Hairy: And Other Tales from Africa* (4–8). Illus. 1988, Barron's paper $11.95 (0-8120-4548-3). Thirty-one traditional African tales, a combination of folklore and fact. (Rev: BL 2/15/89; SLJ 2/89) [398.2]

4701 Green, Roger L. *Tales of Ancient Egypt* (5–9). 1972, Penguin paper $4.99 (0-14-036716-0). A collection of folktales from ancient Egypt including one about the source of the Nile. [398]

4702 Kituku, Vincent Muli Wa, retel. *East African Folktales: From the Voice of Mukamba* (6–9). Illus. 1997, August House $9.95 (0-87483-489-9). This bilingual book contains 18 folktales in English and Kikamba, the language of the Kamba community in Kenya. (Rev: SLJ 8/97) [398.2]

4703 Kurtz, Jane. *Trouble* (4–7). 1997, Harcourt $16.00 (0-15-200219-7). An Eritrean story about a young goatherd who has a knack for getting into trouble. (Rev: BL 3/15/97; SLJ 4/97) [398.2]

4704 McIntosh, Gavin. *Hausaland Tales from the Nigerian Marketplace* (4–9). Illus. 2002, Linnet $22.50 (0-208-02523-5). This collection of 12 Nigerian folktales skillfully interweaves details of contemporary Hausa society. (Rev: HBG 3/03; SLJ 11/02) [398.2]

4705 Mama, Raouf, retel. *Why Goats Smell Bad and Other Stories from Benin* (4–8). Illus. 1998, Linnet LB $21.50 (0-208-02469-7). A delightful collection of 20 folktales from the Fon culture of Benin, handsomely illustrated with woodcuts. (Rev: BCCB 5/98; BL 2/15/98; HBG 9/98; SLJ 4/98) [398.2]

4706 *Nelson Mandela's Favorite African Folktales* (6–12). Illus. 2002, Norton $24.95 (0-393-05212-5). Thirty-two folktales from the African continent are complemented by artwork as diverse as the stories. (Rev: BL 12/1/02; HBG 10/03; SLJ 2/03) [398.2]

4707 Tchana, Katrin. *The Serpent Slayer and Other Stories of Strong Women* (4–7). Illus. 2000, Little, Brown $21.95 (0-316-38701-0). A collection of 18 folktales from around the world featuring brave, creative, and strong women and girls. (Rev: BCCB 11/00*; BL 12/15/00; HB 11–12/00; HBG 3/01; SLJ 11/00) [398.2]

Asia and the Middle East

4708 Alderson, Brian. *The Arabian Nights; or, Tales Told by Sheherezade During a Thousand Nights and One Night* (4–8). 1995, Morrow $20.00 (0-688-14219-2). A fine collection of more than 30 tales written in a colloquial style and including parts of the stories of Sinbad, Ali Baba, and Aladdin. (Rev: BL 10/15/95; SLJ 9/95) [398.22]

4709 Carpenter, F. R. *Tales of a Chinese Grandmother* (5–7). 1973, Amereon LB $24.95 (0-89190-481-6); Tuttle paper $8.95 (0-8048-1042-7). A boy and a girl listen to 30 classic Chinese tales. [398.2]

4710 Chin, Yin-lien C., ed. *Traditional Chinese Folktales* (5–8). 1989, East Gate $44.95 (0-87332-507-9). This is a collection of 12 Chinese folktales that express a variety of themes and genres from faithful lovers to trickster tales. (Rev: SLJ 8/89) [398.2]

4711 Conover, Sarah, ed. *Kindness: A Treasury of Buddhist Wisdom for Children and Parents* (4–7). Illus. 2001, Eastern Washington Univ. paper $19.95 (0-910055-67-X). Thirty-one stories related to Buddhism, including Jataka tales about the Buddha's incarnations, have been effectively translated and adapted for this anthology. (Rev: BL 2/15/01; SLJ 3/01) [294.3]

4712 Dokey, Cameron. *The Storyteller's Daughter* (6–10). 2002, Simon & Schuster paper $5.99 (0-7434-2220-1). A retelling of the story of Shahrazad that interweaves fantasy, court intrigue, and romance. (Rev: SLJ 12/02)

4713 Fu, Shelley. *Ho Yi the Archer and Other Classic Chinese Tales* (6–9). Illus. 2001, Linnet LB $22.50 (0-208-02487-5). This collection of folktales and myths, some of which may be familiar, is introduced by a look at Chinese folklore and the influence of Taoism and Buddhism and includes a pronunciation guide, and list of characters. (Rev: BL 7/01; HB 9–10/01; HBG 3/02; SLJ 7/01) [398.2]

4714 Jaffrey, Madhur. *Seasons of Splendor: Tales, Myths, and Legends from India* (5–8). 1985, Puffin paper $7.95 (0-317-62172-6). Folktales and family stories as well as accounts of Rama and Krishna. (Rev: BCCB 1/86; BL 1/15/86) [398.2]

4715 Kendall, Carol, retel. *Haunting Tales from Japan* (6–9). Illus. 1985, Spencer Museum Publns. paper $6.00 (0-913689-22-X). A retelling of six Japanese folktales, some of which deal with murder and suicide. (Rev: SLJ 2/86) [398]

4716 Kendall, Carol, and Li Yao-wen. *Sweet and Sour: Tales from China* (5–7). Illus. 1990, Houghton paper $7.95 (0-395-54798-9). A choice collection of some enchanting Chinese folktales. [398.2]

4717 Krishnaswami, Uma, retel. *Shower of Gold: Girls and Women in the Stories of India* (6–10). 1999, Linnet LB $21.50 (0-208-02484-0). All of the enchanting tales in this fine collection of Indian folklore feature wise and powerful women. (Rev: BCCB 5/99; BL 3/15/99; HBG 3/00; SLJ 8/99) [891]

4718 Lang, Andrew. *The Arabian Nights Entertainments* (5–9). Illus. 1969, Dover paper $9.95 (0-486-22289-6). Aladdin and Sinbad are only two of the characters in these 26 tales of Arabia and the East. (Rev: BL 9/1/89) [398.2]

4719 Lee, Jeanne M. *The Song of Mu Lan* (5–8). Illus. 1995, Front Street $15.95 (1-886910-00-6). Mu Lan disguises herself as a boy and joins the emperor's army in this traditional Chinese tale. (Rev: BL 11/15/95; SLJ 12/95) [398.2]

4720 Lee, Jeanne M., reteller. *Toad Is the Uncle of Heaven: A Vietnamese Folk Tale* (4–7). 1985, Holt paper $6.95 (0-8050-1147-1). This book tells the story of Toad who collects companions on his way to see the King of Heaven, who makes rain. (Rev: BL 11/1/85; HB 3–4/86) [398.2]

4721 McCaughrean, Geraldine. *Gilgamesh the Hero* (6–9). 2003, Eerdmans $18.00 (0-8028-5262-9). McCaughrean retells the ancient epic story of Gilgamesh, a Sumerian king around 3000 B.C.E., in this volume illustrated with evocative paintings. (Rev: BL 9/1/03*; HB 9–10/03; SLJ 12/03*) [398.]

4722 Mayer, Marianna. *Turandot* (6–8). Illus. 1995, Morrow $16.00 (0-688-09073-7). The Chinese tale of the princess who will consent to marry only the one man who can answer her three riddles. Beautifully illustrated. (Rev: BL 10/15/95; SLJ 10/95) [398.2]

4723 Meeker, Clare Hodgson. *A Tale of Two Rice Birds: A Folktale from Thailand* (4–8). 1994, Sasquatch $14.95 (1-57061-008-8). Two rice birds are reincarnated as a princess and a farmer's son in this Thai folktale. (Rev: BL 1/15/95; SLJ 11/94) [398.2]

4724 Merrill, Jean. *The Girl Who Loved Caterpillars: A Twelfth-Century Tale from Japan* (5–8). 1992, Putnam $16.99 (0-399-21871-8). The story of a young Izumi who has no interest in lute playing or writing poetry but is fascinated with "creepy crawlies" instead. (Rev: BCCB 11/92; BL 9/1/92*; SLJ 9/92) [398.2]

4725 Riordan, James. *Tales from the Arabian Nights* (7–9). Illus. 1985, Checkerboard $14.95 (1-56288-258-9). Among the 10 stories retold are those of Sinbad, Ali Baba, and Aladdin. (Rev: SLJ 3/86) [398.2]

4726 Vuong, Lynette Dyer. *The Brocaded Slipper and Other Vietnamese Tales* (5–7). 1982, HarperCollins paper $4.95 (0-06-440440-4). Five Vietnamese fairy tales, some of which are similar to our own. [398.2]

4727 Yeoman, John. *The Seven Voyages of Sinbad the Sailor* (4–8). 1997, Simon & Schuster $19.95 (0-689-81368-6). In these adaptations of stories from *Arabian Nights*, Sinbad describes the seven amazing voyages that brought him horror, disaster, adventure, and eventually wealth. (Rev: BL 1/1–15/98; HB 3–4/98; HBG 3/98; SLJ 12/97) [398.2]

4728 Yep, Laurence. *The Rainbow People* (7–10). Illus. 1989, HarperCollins $16.00 (0-06-026760-7); paper $5.99 (0-06-440441-2). The retelling of 20 Chinese folktales with illustrations by David Wiesner. (Rev: BL 4/1/89; BR 11–12/90; SLJ 5/89) [398.2]

Australia and the Pacific Islands

4729 Flood, Bo, and Beret E. Strong. *Pacific Island Legends: Tales from Micronesia, Melanesia, Polynesia, and Australia* (6–12). 1999, Bess Pr. $22.95 (1-57306-084-4); paper $14.95 (1-57306-078-X). The ocean's impact on island life is a theme that runs through many of these tales, which are organized in geographical groupings with introductions on each one's culture and history. (Rev: HBG 4/00; SLJ 10/99) [398.2]

4730 Oodgeroo. *Dreamtime: Aboriginal Stories* (6–10). Illus. 1994, Lothrop $16.00 (0-688-13296-0). Traditional and autobiographical stories of Aboriginal culture and its roots. Also examines current Aboriginal life alongside white civilization. (Rev: BCCB 1/99; BL 10/1/94; SLJ 10/94) [398.2]

4731 Te Kanawa, Kiri. *Land of the Long White Cloud: Maori Myths, Tales and Legends* (7–12). Illus. 1997, Pavilion paper $17.95 (1-86205-075-9).

A group of magical Maori folktales about sea gods, fairies, monsters, and fantastic voyages, retold by the famous opera singer from New Zealand. (Rev: BL 9/1/97) [398.2]

Europe

4732 Afanasyev, Alexander, ed. *Russian Fairy Tales* (4–7). 1976, Pantheon paper $18.00 (0-394-73090-9). The definitive collection of folktales reissued in the 1945 edition. [398.2]

4733 Bell, Anthea. *Jack and the Beanstalk: An English Fairy Tale Retold* (8–12). Illus. 2000, North-South $15.95 (0-7358-1374-4). This picture book for older readers offers unusual illustrations and a modernized text. (Rev: BL 9/15/00; HBG 3/01; SLJ 12/00)

4734 Collodi, Carlo. *The Adventures of Pinocchio* (5–7). 2002, Simply Read $29.95 (0-9688768-0-3). The full text of the original is used here with effective black-and-white illustrations and several full-page watercolors. (Rev: BL 4/1/02)

4735 Creswick, Paul. *Robin Hood* (6–9). 1984, Macmillan $28.00 (0-684-18162-2). A classic edition, with superb illustrations by N. C. Wyeth, now reissued. [398.2]

4736 Crossley-Holland, Kevin. *The World of King Arthur and His Court: People, Places, Legend, and Lore* (5–7). Illus. 1999, Dutton $25.00 (0-525-46167-1). A beautifully illustrated book that presents material on King Arthur, his loves, his knights, and his feats of chivalry. (Rev: BL 11/15/99; HBG 10/00; SLJ 1/00) [942.01]

4737 Delamare, David. *Cinderella* (7–12). 1993, Simon & Schuster paper $15.00 (0-671-76944-8). The familiar story is set in a locale much like Venice and enhanced by Delamare's paintings, both realistic and surreal. (Rev: BCCB 11/00; BL 9/15/93; SLJ 12/93) [398.2]

4738 Eisner, Will. *The Princess and the Frog: By the Grimm Brothers* (4–7). Illus. 1999, NBM $15.95 (1-56163-244-9). A retelling of the familiar fairy tale in graphic-novel style. (Rev: BL 12/15/99; HBG 3/00) [398.2]

4739 Green, Roger L. *Adventures of Robin Hood* (5–9). 1994, Knopf $15.00 (0-679-43636-7); Puffin paper $4.99 (0-14-036700-4). The exploits of this folk hero are retold in this reissue of a classic version. [398]

4740 Grimm Brothers. *Household Stories of the Brothers Grimm* (4–7). n.d., Dover paper $8.95 (0-486-21080-4). First published in the United States in 1883. [398.2]

4741 Grimm Brothers. *The Three Feathers* (5–8). 1984, Creative Editions LB $13.95 (0-87191-941-

9). A version for older readers that is faithful to the original. [398.2]

4742 Hastings, Selina, reteller. *Sir Gawain and the Loathly Lady* (5–8). 1987, Lothrop paper $4.95 (0-688-07046-9). Noble Sir Gawain agrees to honor a pledge for a husband to a deformed old hag and discovers that he has broken an old spell and released a beautiful woman. (Rev: BCCB 11/85; BL 11/15/85) [398.2]

4743 Heaney, Marie, reteller. *The Names Upon the Harp: Irish Myth and Legend* (4–9). 2000, Scholastic $19.95 (0-590-68052-8). These stories from Ireland are filled with magic, conflict, and creatures and deal with such themes as overcoming obstacles, searching for identity, and finding true love. (Rev: BCCB 3/01; BL 1/1–15/01; HBG 3/01; SLJ 1/01) [398.2]

4744 Hodges, Margaret, and Margery Evernden, retellers. *Of Swords and Sorcerers: The Adventures of King Arthur and His Knights* (4–8). 1993, Macmillan $15.00 (0-684-19437-6). From Merlin as a young boy to the last battle, this is the story of King Arthur and the knights and ladies connected with his court. (Rev: SLJ 8/93) [398.2]

4745 Kilgannon, Eily. *Folktales of the Yeats Country* (5–8). Illus. 1990, Mercier paper $10.95 (0-85342-861-1). Seventeen folktales that originate in County Sligo in Ireland. (Rev: BL 8/90; SLJ 2/91) [398.2]

4746 Leavy, Una. *Irish Fairy Tales and Legends* (4–8). Illus. 1997, Roberts Rinehart $18.95 (1-57098-177-9). An attractive book that contains 10 Irish legends, some going back 2,000 years. (Rev: BL 2/1/98; HBG 10/98; SLJ 2/98) [398.2]

4747 Levine, Gail C. *Ella Enchanted* (5–8). 1997, HarperCollins LB $16.89 (0-06-027511-1). A spirited, cleverly plotted retelling of the Cinderella story in which Ella is finally paired with the Prince Charmant. (Rev: BCCB 5/97; BL 4/15/97*; BR 1–2/98; HB 5/6/97; SLJ 4/97*; VOYA 8/97)

4748 MacDonald, George. *The Princess and the Goblin* (4–7). 1986, Morrow $24.99 (0-688-06604-6). A full-color edition of the 1920 classic about the princess who is protected by the goblins beneath the castle. (Rev: BL 10/15/86)

4749 Miles, Bernard. *Robin Hood: His Life and Legend* (7–9). Illus. 1979, Checkerboard $12.95 (1-56288-412-3). A collection of tales about this English folk hero and his merry men. [398.2]

4750 Molnar, Irma. *One-Time Dog Market at Buda and Other Hungarian Folktales* (5–8). 2001, Linnet $25.00 (0-208-02505-7). A collection of 23 clever, thought-provoking Hungarian folktales for older readers. (Rev: BL 1/1–15/02; HBG 3/02; SLJ 2/02) [398.2]

4751 Morpurgo, Michael. *Arthur: High King of Britain* (4–7). 1995, Harcourt $22.00 (0-15-200080-1). King Arthur tells nine stories of his exploits to a 12-year-old boy. (Rev: BCCB 5/95; BL 8/95; SLJ 7/95)

4752 Napoli, Donna Jo. *Crazy Jack* (6–9). 1999, Delacorte $15.95 (0-385-32627-0). Jack climbs the beanstalk in search of clues to his father's mysterious death and finds himself confronting a wife-beating giant and his greedy spouse in this fairy tale with a twist set in medieval England. (Rev: BCCB 12/99; BL 10/1/99*; HBG 4/00; SLJ 11/99)

4753 Napoli, Donna Jo. *The Magic Circle* (6–12). 1993, Dutton $15.99 (0-525-45127-7). A "history" of the witch in *Hansel and Gretel*. (Rev: BL 7/93; VOYA 8/93) [398.2]

4754 Nye, Robert. *Beowulf: A New Telling* (7–9). 1982, Dell paper $4.99 (0-440-90560-5). A retelling in modern English of the monster Grendel and the hero Beowulf. [398.2]

4755 Philip, Neil. *Celtic Fairy Tales* (4–8). Illus. 1999, Viking $21.99 (0-670-88387-5). The 20 stories in this fine anthology originated in Ireland, Scotland, Brittany, Wales, Cornwall, and the Isle of Man. (Rev: BL 11/15/99; HBG 10/00) [398.2]

4756 Prokofiev, Sergei. *Peter and the Wolf* (4–8). Adapted by Miguelanxo Prado. 1998, NBM $15.95 (1-56163-200-7). A somber version of the Russian folktale filled with menacing situations and scary settings. (Rev: HBG 10/98; SLJ 6/98) [398.2]

4757 Pyle, Howard. *The Merry Adventures of Robin Hood of Great Renown in Nottinghamshire* (7–9). Illus. n.d., Peter Smith $25.00 (0-8446-2765-8); Dover paper $9.95 (0-486-22043-5). The classic (first published in 1883) retelling of 22 of the most famous stories. [398.2]

4758 Pyle, Howard. *The Story of King Arthur and His Knights* (6–9). Illus. n.d., Peter Smith $25.75 (0-8446-2766-6); Dover paper $9.95 (0-486-21445-1). A retelling that has been in print since its first publication in 1903. [398.2]

4759 Pyle, Howard. *The Story of Sir Launcelot and His Companions* (7–9). Illus. 1991, Dover paper $12.95 (0-486-26701-6). The story of one of Arthur's famous knights, with illustrations by Howard Pyle. [398.2]

4760 Pyle, Howard. *The Story of the Champions of the Round Table* (7–9). Illus. 1984, Macmillan LB $19.95 (0-684-18171-1). A reissue of the 1905 book about the feats of Launcelot, Tristram, and Percival. Also reissued is *The Story of the Grail and the Passing of Arthur* (1984). [398.2]

4761 Pyle, Howard. *The Story of the Grail and the Passing of Arthur* (5–8). 1985, Macmillan paper $10.95 (0-486-27361-X). The last title of a four-volume King Arthur series, first published in 1910. (Rev: BL 12/15/85) [398.2]

4762 Singer, Isaac Bashevis. *The Golem* (7–9). Illus. 1996, Farrar paper $8.95 (0-374-42746-1). A retelling of the 16th-century Jewish tale about the rabbi in old Prague who brought a statue to life to help his people. [398.2]

4763 Spariosu, Mihai I., and Dezso Benedek. *Ghosts, Vampires, and Werewolves: Eerie Tales from Transylvania* (6–10). 1994, Orchard LB $19.99 (0-531-08710-7). An anthology of horror tales by two authors who heard the stories as children living in the Transylvanian Alps. (Rev: BL 10/15/94; SLJ 10/94) [398.2]

4764 Sutcliff, Rosemary, reteller. *Beowulf* (5–8). 1984, Smith $20.75 (0-8446-6165-1). This is a reissue of the Anglo-Saxon tale published originally in 1962. Also use the King Arthur story, *The Sword and the Circle* (1981, Dutton). [398.2]

4765 Sutcliff, Rosemary. *Dragon Slayer* (5–9). 1976, Penguin paper $4.99 (0-14-030254-9). A simple retelling of the story of Beowulf and his battle against Grendel. [398]

4766 Sutcliff, Rosemary. *The Light Beyond the Forest: The Quest for the Holy Grail* (7–9). Illus. 1994, Puffin paper $4.99 (0-14-037150-8). The first volume of the trilogy about the search for the Holy Grail by King Arthur and his knights. Continued in *The Sword in the Circle* and *The Road to Camelann* (both 1981). [398.2]

4767 Talbott, Hudson. *Lancelot* (5–7). Illus. 1999, Morrow LB $15.89 (0-688-14833-6). A retelling of the life of Lancelot, from his rescue as a child by the Lady of the Lake to his love for Guinevere, marriage to Elaine, and fathering of Galahad. (Rev: BL 9/1/99; HBG 3/00; SLJ 10/99) [398.2]

4768 Thomas, Gwyn, and Kevin Crossley-Holland. *Tales from the Mabinogion* (5–8). 1985, Overlook $19.95 (0-87951-987-8). A translation of Welsh hero tales. (Rev: BCCB 6/85; BL 4/1/85) [398.2]

4769 Vande Velde, Vivian. *Tales from the Brothers Grimm and the Sisters Weird* (4–8). Illus. Series: Jane Yolen Books. 1995, Harcourt $17.00 (0-15-200220-0). Using a role-reversal technique, the author examines the nature of good and evil in some of the standard tales from the Brothers Grimm. (Rev: BCCB 10/95; SLJ 1/96) [398.2]

4770 Vivian, E. Charles. *The Adventures of Robin Hood* (6–9). n.d., Airmont paper $1.75 (0-8049-0067-1). The principal stories about Robin Hood and his men are retold in this inexpensive edition. [398]

4771 Vivian, E. Charles. *Robin Hood: A Classic Illustrated Edition* (4–7). Illus. 2002, Chronicle $19.95 (0-8118-3399-2). Illustrations ranging from medieval tapestries to comic book drawings by

artists including Howard Pyle and N. C. Wyeth give visual interest to this retelling of the beloved Robin Hood tale. (Rev: BL 12/1/02; HBG 3/03; SLJ 3/03) [398.2]

4772 Walker, Barbara K., ed. *A Treasury of Turkish Folktales for Children* (4–7). 1988, Shoe String LB $25.00 (0-208-02206-6). A witty collection interspersed with riddles. (Rev: BL 10/15/88; SLJ 10/88) [398.2]

4773 Whipple, Laura. *If the Shoe Fits* (5–8). 2002, Simon & Schuster $17.95 (0-689-84070-5). A handsome retelling of the Cinderella story using blank verse. (Rev: BCCB 3/02; BL 5/1/02; HBG 10/02; SLJ 8/02) [398.2]

4774 Wolfson, Evelyn. *King Arthur and His Knights in Mythology* (6–9). Series: Mythology. 2002, Enslow LB $20.95 (0-7660-1914-4). The myths and legends surrounding King Arthur are retold with valuable historical background material. (Rev: BL 12/15/02; HBG 3/03) [398]

4775 Wyly, Michael. *King Arthur* (7–10). Series: Mystery Library. 2001, Lucent LB $19.96 (1-56006-771-3). An engrossing account that explores the fact and fiction surrounding this legendary king of England and his knights. (Rev: BL 9/15/01) [942]

North America

GENERAL AND MISCELLANEOUS

4776 McManus, Kay. *Land of the Five Suns* (6–8). Series: Looking at Myths and Legends. 1997, NTC $12.95 (0-8442-4762-6). Classic Aztec myths, including creation stories and tales of Aztec gods, are retold in novelized format. (Rev: SLJ 4/98) [398.2]

4777 Madrigal, Antonio H. *The Eagle and the Rainbow: Timeless Tales from México* (4–7). 1997, Fulcrum $15.95 (1-55591-317-2). A collection of wise, wonderful, but little-known folktales from Mexico. (Rev: BL 7/97) [398.2]

4778 Philip, Neil, ed. *Horse Hooves and Chicken Feet: Mexican Folktales* (4–8). 2003, Clarion $19.00 (0-618-19463-0). Bright folk-art illustrations accompany 14 stories that feature humor and the importance of the Catholic church. (Rev: BL 10/15/03; SLJ 9/03) [398.2]

4779 Pohl, John M. D. *The Legend of Lord Eight Deer: An Epic of Ancient Mexico* (6–12). Illus. 2001, Oxford $17.95 (0-19-514020-6). A retelling of the complex story of Eight Deer, a Mixtec leader, with a final chapter that explains how Pohl interpreted the historical codices that contributed to this tale. (Rev: BL 1/1–15/02; HBG 3/02; SLJ 1/02) [398.2]

4780 Turenne Des Pres, Francois. *Children of Yayoute: Folktales of Haiti* (6–9). 1994, Universe

$19.95 (0-87663-791-8). Traditional folktales that depict Haitian history and customs. Includes paintings that illustrate island life. (Rev: BL 10/1/94; SLJ 1/95) [398.2]

NATIVE AMERICANS

4781 Bierhorst, John. *The Mythology of North America* (8–12). Illus. 1986, Morrow paper $13.00 (0-688-06666-6). A region-by-region examination of the folklore and mythology of the North American Indian. (Rev: BL 6/15/85; SLJ 8/85) [291.1]

4782 Bierhorst, John. *Native American Stories* (6–12). Illus. 1998, Morrow $16.00 (0-688-14837-9). A collection of 22 tales about "little people" from 14 Native American groups, including the Inuits, Aztecs, and Mayans. (Rev: BCCB 7–8/98; BL 5/15/98; HBG 9/98; SLJ 9/98) [398.208997]

4783 Bierhorst, John. *The Way of the Earth: Native America and the Environment* (7–12). 1994, Morrow $15.00 (0-688-11560-8). Explores the mythologic and folkloric patterns of Native American belief systems. (Rev: BL 5/15/94; SLJ 5/94; VOYA 10/94) [179]

4784 Bierhorst, John. *The White Deer and Other Stories Told by the Lenape* (8–12). 1995, Morrow $15.00 (0-688-12900-5). This collection of Lenape/Delaware tribal stories is organized by type and includes a history of the tribe. (Rev: BL 6/1–15/95; SLJ 9/95) [398.2]

4785 Bruchac, Joseph. *Flying with the Eagle, Racing the Great Bear: Stories from Native North America* (5–8). Illus. 1993, Troll paper $13.95 (0-8167-3026-1). Sixteen stories, arranged geographically, introduce coming-of-age rites for males in Native American cultures. (Rev: BL 12/15/93; SLJ 9/93) [398.2]

4786 Bruchac, Joseph. *Native American Animal Stories* (5–8). Illus. 1992, Fulcrum paper $12.95 (1-55591-127-7). Animal stories from various Native American tribes, for reading aloud and storytelling. (Rev: BL 9/1/92; SLJ 11/92) [398.2]

4787 Bruchac, Joseph. *Native Plant Stories* (4–8). Illus. 1995, Fulcrum paper $12.95 (1-55591-212-5). A collection of stories about plants that come from various Native American cultures in North and Central America. (Rev: BL 9/1/95) [398.24]

4788 Connolly, James E. *Why the Possum's Tail Is Bare: And Other North American Indian Nature Tales* (4–7). Illus. 1992, Stemmer $15.95 (0-88045-069-X); paper $7.95 (0-88045-107-6). Nature and folklore are combined in 13 Native American animal tales. (Rev: BL 9/1/85; SLJ 10/85) [398.2]

4789 Goble, Paul. *The Legend of the White Buffalo Woman* (4–8). Illus. 1998, National Geographic $16.95 (0-7922-7074-6). In this picture book for older readers recounting a Lakota Indian tale, an earth woman and an eagle mate after a great flood to produce a new people. (Rev: BL 3/15/98; HBG 10/98; SLJ 5/98) [398.2]

4790 Highwater, Jamake. *Anpao: An American Indian Odyssey* (5–8). 1993, HarperCollins paper $7.95 (0-06-440437-4). A young hero encounters great danger on his way to meet his father, the Sun, in this dramatic American Indian folktale. [398.2]

4791 Hillerman, Tony, ed. *The Boy Who Made Dragonfly: A Zuni Myth* (5–7). 1986, Univ. of New Mexico Pr. paper $8.95 (0-8263-0910-0). A Zuni boy and his little sister are left behind by their tribe and survive hunger and deprivation through the intervention of the Cornstalk Being. [398.2]

4792 Martin, Rafe. *The World Before This One* (5–8). 2002, Scholastic paper $16.95 (0-590-37976-3). Crow, a Seneca Indian, comes upon a storytelling stone that tells him about the origins of the earth in this series of stories. (Rev: BL 2/15/03; HBG 3/03; SLJ 12/02; VOYA 2/03) [398.2]

4793 Mayo, Gretchen Will. *Star Tales: North American Indian Stories About the Stars* (4–7). 1987, Walker LB $13.85 (0-8027-6673-0). Fourteen tales, each introduced by a one-page commentary on a constellation. (Rev: BL 6/15/87; SLJ 5/87) [398.2]

4794 Monroe, Jean Guard, and Ray A. Williamson. *They Dance in the Sky: Native American Star Myths* (4–8). Illus. 1987, Houghton $16.00 (0-395-39970-X). Numerous Native American legends about stars. (Rev: BL 9/1/87; SLJ 9/87) [398.2]

4795 Norman, Howard. *The Girl Who Dreamed Only Geese and Other Stories of the Far North* (4–8). Illus. 1997, Harcourt $22.00 (0-15-230979-9). A fine collection of Inuit tales, enhanced by illustrations resembling stone carvings. (Rev: BL 9/15/97*; SLJ 11/97*) [398.2]

4796 Norman, Howard. *Trickster and the Fainting Birds* (4–7). 1999, Harcourt $20.00 (0-15-200888-8). In these seven Algonquian tales from Manitoba, the trickster often takes the form of a man but it can also change its shape into various animal forms. (Rev: BCCB 1/00; BL 1/1–15/00; HB 11–12/99; HBG 3/00; SLJ 12/99) [398.2]

4797 Philip, Neil, ed. *The Great Mystery: Myths of Native America* (8–12). Illus. 2001, Clarion $25.00 (0-395-98405-X). A collection of creation and other stories from many Native American tribes, organized by region. (Rev: BL 11/15/01; HBG 10/02; SLJ 11/01) [398.2]

4798 Pijoan, Teresa. *White Wolf Woman: Native American Transformation Myths* (7–12). 1992, August House paper $11.95 (0-87483-200-4). Drawn from a wide range of Indian tribes, a collection of 37 stories about animal and human transformations and connections. (Rev: BL 10/1/92) [398.2]

4799 Shenandoah, Joanne, and Douglas M. George-Kanentiio. *Skywoman: Legends of the Iroquois* (4–8). Illus. 1998, Clear Light $14.95 (0-940666-99-5). Good writing and effective artwork are combined in this retelling of nine traditional Iroquois tales, including a series of creation stories. (Rev: HBG 10/99; SLJ 2/99) [398.2]

4800 Tingle, Tim. *Walking the Choctaw Road* (6–12). 2003, Cinco Puntos $16.95 (0-938317-74-1). A collection of stories that convey Choctaw traditions and culture, including experiences on the Trail of Tears. (Rev: BL 6/1–15/03) [398.2]

4801 Van Etten, Teresa. *Ways of Indian Magic* (7–12). Illus. 1985, Sunstone paper $8.95 (0-86534-061-7). A fine retelling of six legends of the Pueblo Indians. (Rev: BR 3–4/86) [398.2]

4802 Van Etten, Teresa. *Ways of Indian Wisdom* (7–10). 1987, Sunstone paper $10.95 (0-86534-090-0). A collection of 20 Pueblo tales that reflect the Southeastern Indians' culture and customs. (Rev: BR 1–2/88) [398.2]

4803 Webster, M. L., retel. *On the Trail Made of Dawn: Native American Creation Stories* (4–9). 2001, Linnet LB $19.50 (0-208-02497-2). The author retells 13 creation stories and places them in cultural context. (Rev: HBG 3/02; SLJ 12/01) [398.2]

4804 Wolfson, Evelyn. *Inuit Mythology* (5–9). Series: Mythology. 2001, Enslow LB $20.95 (0-7660-1559-9). Seven tales from Inuit folklore are accompanied by information on the history and culture of the Inuit peoples. (Rev: BL 4/15/02; HBG 3/02; SLJ 3/02) [398.2]

UNITED STATES

4805 Anaya, Rudolfo A. *My Land Sings: Stories from the Rio Grande* (5–9). 1999, Morrow $17.00 (0-688-15078-0). A magical collection of 10 stories, set mostly in New Mexico, that deal with Mexican and Native American folklore. (Rev: BL 8/99; HBG 10/00; SLJ 9/99) [398.2]

4806 Avila, Alfred. *Mexican Ghost Tales of the Southwest* (7–9). Ed. by Kat Avila. 1994, Arte Publico paper $9.95 (1-55885-107-0). A collection of Mexican tales of ghosts and the spirit world from the Southwest. (Rev: BL 10/1/94; SLJ 9/94; VOYA 4/95) [398.25]

4807 Brown, Marcia. *Backbone of the King: The Story of Paka'a and His Son Ku* (5–7). 1984, Univ. of Hawaii Pr. $9.95 (0-8248-0963-7). A reissue of the book based on a Hawaiian legend of a boy who wants to help his exiled father. [398.2]

4808 Cohen, Daniel. *Southern Fried Rat and Other Gruesome Tales* (6–10). Illus. 1989, Avon paper $3.50 (0-380-70655-5). A collection of stories — some funny, some grisly — about people living in urban areas today. [398.2]

4809 Hamilton, Virginia. *Her Stories: African American Folktales, Fairy Tales, and True Tales* (5–8). Illus. 1995, Scholastic paper $19.95 (0-590-47370-0). Nineteen tales about African American females are retold in the wonderful style of Virginia Hamilton. (Rev: BL 11/1/95*; SLJ 11/95*) [398.2]

4810 Hamilton, Virginia. *The People Could Fly: American Black Folk Tales* (4–9). 1985, Knopf LB $18.99 (0-394-96925-1); paper $13.00 (0-679-84336-1). A retelling of 24 folktales — some little known, others familiar, such as Tar Baby. (Rev: BCCB 7/85; BL 7/85; SLJ 11/85) [398.2]

4811 Jacobs, Jimmy. *Moonlight Through the Pines: Tales from Georgia Evenings* (5–7). Illus. 2000, Franklin-Sarrett paper $11.95 (0-9637477-3-8). A collection of humorous reminiscences, family stories, tall tales, and other examples of folklore, all from the South. (Rev: BL 8/00) [398.2]

4812 Lester, Julius. *The Last Tales of Uncle Remus* (5–9). Illus. Series: Uncle Remus. 1994, Dial $18.89 (0-8037-1304-5). This fourth volume in the series draws together 39 African American tall tales, ghost stories, and trickster tales, with many illustrations. (Rev: BL 12/15/93*; SLJ 1/94) [398.2]

4813 Lyons, Mary E., ed. *Raw Head, Bloody Bones: African-American Tales of the Supernatural* (5–7). 1991, Macmillan $15.00 (0-684-19333-7). A bone-chiller full of ghosts, devils, and ogres as well as less familiar demons such as Plat-Eye and the monstrous night doctor. (Rev: BCCB 2/92; BL 1/1/92; HB 1–2/92; SLJ 12/91*) [398.2]

4814 Osborne, Mary Pope. *American Tall Tales* (4–7). 1991, Knopf LB $23.99 (0-679-90089-6). Nine tall tales perfect for telling to all ages. (Rev: BCCB 1/92; BL 3/15/92; SLJ 12/91*) [398.2]

4815 Philip, Neil, ed. *American Fairy Tales: From Rip Van Winkle to the Rootabaga Stories* (6–8). Illus. 1996, Hyperion LB $23.49 (0-7868-2171-X). A collection of 12 stories by such famous authors as Hawthorne, Sandburg, Alcott, and Baum. (Rev: BL 12/15/96; SLJ 11/96) [398.2]

4816 Reneaux, J. J. *Cajun Folktales* (6–8). 1992, August House $19.95 (0-87483-283-7); paper $11.95 (0-87483-282-9). An assortment of Cajun folktales divided into broad groups: animal tales, fairy tales, funny folk tales, and ghost stories. (Rev: BL 9/15/92) [398.2]

4817 Reneaux, J. J. *Haunted Bayou: And Other Cajun Ghost Stories* (4–8). 1994, August House paper $9.95 (0-87483-385-X). Thirteen scary, entertaining folktales from Cajun country are retold effectively. (Rev: SLJ 12/94) [398.2]

4818 Rhyne, Nancy. *More Tales of the South Carolina Low Country* (7–9). 1984, Blair paper $6.95

(0-89587-042-8). A collection of eerie and unusual folktales. [398.2]

4819 Rounds, Glen. *Ol' Paul, the Mighty Logger* (6–8). Illus. 1976, Holiday paper $5.95 (0-8234-0713-6). The colorful saga of the great tall-tale hero of American folklore. [398.2]

4820 Schwartz, Alvin. *More Scary Stories to Tell in the Dark* (4–7). 1984, HarperCollins LB $16.89 (0-397-32082-5); paper $5.99 (0-06-440177-4). Brief tales from folk stories and hearsay with a scary bent. [398.2]

4821 Schwartz, Alvin. *Scary Stories to Tell in the Dark* (6–9). Illus. 1981, HarperCollins LB $16.89 (0-397-31927-4). Stories about ghosts and witches that are mostly scary but often also humorous. Continued in *More Scary Stories to Tell in the Dark* (1984). [398.2]

4822 Shepherd, Esther. *Paul Bunyan* (7–10). Illus. 1941, Harcourt $12.95 (0-15-259749-2); paper $6.95 (0-15-259755-7). This tall-tale lumberjack is brought to life by the text and the stunning illustrations by Rockwell Kent. [398.2]

South and Central America

4823 Aldana, Patricia, ed. *Jade and Iron: Latin American Tales from Two Cultures* (5–8). Trans. by Hugh Hazelton. Illus. 1996, Douglas & McIntyre $18.95 (0-88899-256-4). Fourteen folktales on a variety of subjects and from many regions in Latin America are retold in this large-format picture book. (Rev: BCCB 1/97; BL 12/1/96) [398.2]

4824 Delacre, Lulu, retel. *Golden Tales: Myths, Legends, and Folktales from Latin America* (4–8). Illus. 1996, Scholastic paper $18.95 (0-590-48186-X). Twelve important Latin American folktales from before and after the time of Columbus are featured. (Rev: BL 12/15/96; SLJ 9/96) [398.2]

4825 Dorson, Mercedes, and Jeanne Wilmot. *Tales from the Rain Forest: Myths and Legends from the Amazonian Indians of Brazil* (5–8). Illus. 1997,

Ecco $18.00 (0-88001-567-5). Ten entertaining folktales from the Amazonian Indians of Brazil. (Rev: BL 2/15/98; HB 3–4/98; HBG 10/98) [398.2]

4826 Ehlert, Lois. *Moon Rope: A Peruvian Folktale* (4–8). Illus. 1992, Harcourt $17.00 (0-15-255343-6). In both English and Spanish, this is the story of Fox, who wants to go to the moon and persuades his friend Mole to go along. (Rev: BCCB 12/92; BL 10/15/92*; HB 11–12/92; SLJ 10/92*) [398.2]

4827 Gerson, Mary-Joan. *Fiesta Feminina: Celebrating Women in Mexican Folktales* (4–8). Illus. 2001, Barefoot $19.99 (1-84148-365-6). This volume includes eight tales from Mexican folklore about strong and magical women, presented with bold illustrations, a pronunciation guide, and a glossary. (Rev: BL 9/15/01; HBG 3/02; SLJ 10/01) [398.2]

4828 Kimmel, Eric A. *The Witch's Face: A Mexican Tale* (7–12). Illus. 1993, Holiday $15.95 (0-8234-1038-2). Kimmel uses a picture book format for this Mexican tale of a man who rescues his love from becoming a witch, only to lose her to his own doubt. (Rev: BL 11/15/93; SLJ 2/94) [398.22]

4829 Montejo, Victor, reteller. *Popol Vuh: A Sacred Book of the Maya* (5–8). Trans. by David Under. 1999, Groundwood $19.95 (0-88899-334-X). A creation story from the Mayans in a beautifully designed book that features gods, giants, mortals, and animals. (Rev: HBG 3/00; SLJ 12/99) [398.2]

4830 Munduruku, Daniel. *Tales of the Amazon: How the Munduruku Indians Live* (5–8). Trans. by Jane Springer. 2000, Groundwood $18.95 (0-88899-392-7). This is an interesting view of the life of the human inhabitants of the Amazon rain forest with material on lifestyles, houses, languages, myths, and marriage. (Rev: HBG 3/01; SLJ 9/00) [981]

4831 Schuman, Michael A. *Mayan and Aztec Mythology* (6–9). Series: Mythology. 2002, Enslow LB $20.95 (0-7660-1409-6). As well as retelling famous myths from the Aztec and Mayan cultures, this account gives good historical background information. (Rev: BL 4/15/02; HBG 10/02) [398.2]

Mythology

General and Miscellaneous

4832 Bini, Renata. *A World Treasury of Myths, Legends, and Folktales: Stories from Six Continents* (6–9). Illus. 2000, Abrams $24.95 (0-8109-4554-1). Stories from around the world are organized geographically in this handsome, large-format volume full of rich illustrations. (Rev: BL 1/1–15/01; HBG 3/01; SLJ 12/00) [291.1]

4833 Dalal, Anita. *Myths of Oceania* (5–8). Series: Mythic World. 2002, Raintree Steck-Vaughn LB $27.12 (0-7398-4978-6). Information about Oceania and its people is included as well as 10 myths about the sea, fishing, and other unique aspects of island living. (Rev: BL 7/02; HBG 10/02) [398.3]

4834 Dalal, Anita. *Myths of Russia and the Slavs* (5–8). Series: Mythic World. 2002, Raintree Steck-Vaughn LB $27.12 (0-7398-4979-4). This lavishly illustrated, oversize volume contains 10 myths from Eastern Europe as well as material on the society that created them. (Rev: BL 7/02; HBG 10/02; SLJ 5/02) [398.2]

4835 Evslin, Bernard. *Pig's Ploughman* (7–12). Illus. 1990, Chelsea LB $19.95 (1-55546-256-1). In Celtic mythology, Pig's Ploughman is the huge hog who fights Finn McCool. (Rev: BL 8/90; SLJ 3/91) [398.2]

4836 Fisher, Leonard Everett. *Gods and Goddesses of the Ancient Maya* (4–7). Illus. 1999, Holiday $16.95 (0-8234-1427-2). This book provides a fascinating introduction to Mayan mythology by describing 10 gods and two goddesses. (Rev: BL 2/1/00; HBG 3/00; SLJ 12/99) [299]

4837 Gifford, Douglas. *Warriors, Gods and Spirits from Central and South American Mythology* (7–12). Illus. 1993, NTC paper $14.95 (0-87226-915-9). Latin American mythology from Aztec tales to those reflecting Western influences. [299]

4838 Green, Jen. *Myths of China and Japan* (5–8). Series: Mythic World. 2002, Raintree Steck-Vaughn LB $27.12 (0-7398-4977-8). This handsome, oversize book explores the ancient mythology of China and Japan and, in addition to the retelling of 10 myths, contains information on the societies that created them. (Rev: BL 7/02; HBG 10/02) [398.2]

4839 Hamilton, Dorothy. *Mythology* (8–12). Illus. 1942, Little, Brown $27.95 (0-316-34114-2). An introduction to the mythology of Greece and Scandinavia plus a retelling of the principal myths. [292]

4840 Hamilton, Virginia. *In the Beginning: Creation Stories from Around the World* (6–9). Illus. 1988, Harcourt $28.00 (0-15-238740-4). Twenty-five creation myths from around the world are retold with notes about the sources of each. (Rev: BL 9/15/88; SLJ 12/88; VOYA 6/89) [291.2]

4841 Harris, Geraldine. *Gods and Pharaohs from Egyptian Mythology* (5–8). 1992, Bedrick LB $24.95 (0-87226-907-8). A collection of myths and legends from ancient Egypt. [398.2]

4842 January, Brendan. *The New York Public Library Amazing Mythology: A Book of Answers for Kids* (5–8). Illus. 2000, Wiley paper $12.95 (0-471-33205-4). This compendium of information covers Middle Eastern, African, Mediterranean, Asian, Pacific, Northern European, and North and Central American mythology. (Rev: BL 11/1/00; SLJ 9/00) [291.1]

4843 Leeming, David A., ed. *The Children's Dictionary of Mythology* (4–7). 1999, Watts LB $33.00 (0-531-11708-1). A basic introduction to world mythology through alphabetically arranged characters, stories, and motifs from a wide variety of cultures. (Rev: BL 12/15/99; SLJ 11/99) [291.1]

4844 Muten, Burleigh, retel. *The Lady of Ten Thousand Names: Goddess Stories from Many Cultures* (4–7). 2001, Barefoot $19.99 (1-84148-048-7). Eight myths that feature goddesses from cultures around the world are retold in this appealing volume. (Rev: HBG 3/02; SLJ 11/01) [291.2]

4845 Nardo, Don. *Monsters* (7–12). Illus. Series: Discovering Mythology. 2001, Gale LB $27.45 (1-56006-853-1). Monsters of yore from mythologies around the world are presented with accounts of their exploits. (Rev: SLJ 1/02) [001.9]

4846 Philip, Neil. *The Illustrated Book of Myths: Tales and Legends of the World* (5–8). 1995, DK paper $19.99 (0-7894-0202-5). Ancient myths from both the Old World and the New World have been collected under such headings as creation, destruction, and fertility. (Rev: BL 12/1/95; SLJ 12/95; VOYA 4/96) [291.1]

4847 Philip, Neil. *Mythology* (4–9). Series: Eyewitness Books. 1999, Knopf $19.00 (0-375-80135-9). A lavishly illustrated volume that covers such topics in world mythology and folklore as creation, the sun, floods, fertility, birth, tricksters, death, and mythical beasts. (Rev: HBG 3/00; SLJ 9/99) [291.1]

4848 Ross, Anne. *Druids, Gods and Heroes of Celtic Mythology* (6–10). Illus. 1994, Bedrick LB $24.95 (0-87226-918-3); paper $14.95 (0-87226-919-1). An oversized book that gives detailed information on Irish and Welsh Celtic mythology as well as material on King Arthur. (Rev: SLJ 2/87) [291.1]

4849 Waldherr, Kris. *The Book of Goddesses* (4–7). Illus. 1996, Beyond Words $17.95 (1-885223-30-7). In an oversize volume, 26 goddesses from mythology are profiled. (Rev: BL 4/1/96; SLJ 5/96) [291.2]

Classical

4850 Aesop. *Aesop's Fables* (7–12). 1988, Scholastic paper $4.50 (0-590-43880-8). This is one of many editions of the short moral tales from ancient Greece. (Rev: BCCB 12/00) [398.2]

4851 Barber, Antonia, reteller. *Apollo and Daphne: Masterpieces of Greek Mythology* (5–9). 1998, Getty Museum $16.95 (0-89236-504-8). A stunning book that retells famous Greek myths, including stories of the Trojan War and the return of Odysseus, with full-page reproductions of 19 splendid paintings. (Rev: BL 10/15/98; HBG 3/99; SLJ 9/98) [398.2]

4852 Claybourne, Anna, and Kamini Khanduri, retellers. *Greek Myths: Ulysses and the Trojan War* (5–10). Illus. 1999, EDC $24.95 (0-7460-3361-3). A chatty retelling of the adventures of Ulysses on his way home from Troy, with illustrations that resemble comic-book drawings. (Rev: HBG 3/00; SLJ 6/99) [398.2]

4853 Colum, Padraic. *The Golden Fleece and the Heroes Who Lived Before Achilles* (5–7). 1983, Macmillan $18.00 (0-02-723620-X); paper $9.95 (0-02-042260-1). Jason's search for the Golden Fleece incorporates some of the best-known myths and legends of ancient Greece. [398.2]

4854 Coolidge, Olivia. *Greek Myths* (4–7). 2001, Houghton $16.00 (0-395-06721-9). Twenty-seven well-known myths dramatically retold with accompanying illustrations. [398.2]

4855 Evslin, Bernard. *The Adventures of Ulysses: The Odyssey of Homer* (8–12). 1989, Scholastic paper $4.50 (0-590-42599-4). A modern retelling of the adventures of Ulysses during the 10 years he wandered after the Trojan War. [292]

4856 Evslin, Bernard. *Anteus* (6–9). Illus. 1988, Chelsea LB $19.95 (1-55546-241-3). A retelling of the story of Hercules and his battle against the horrible giant Anteus. Also use by the same author *Hecate* (1988). (Rev: BL 9/1/88) [292]

4857 Evslin, Bernard. *Cerberus* (6–12). Illus. 1987, Chelsea LB $19.95 (1-55546-243-X). The story of the 3-headed dog in Greek mythology that guards the gates of Hell. Also in this series are *The Dragons of Boeotia* and *Geryon* (both 1987). (Rev: BL 11/15/87; SLJ 1/88) [398.2]

4858 Evslin, Bernard. *The Chimaera* (6–10). Illus. 1987, Chelsea LB $19.95 (1-55546-244-8). This ugly, dangerous creature is composed of equal parts lion, goat, and reptile. Another in the series is *The Sirens* (1987). (Rev: BL 3/1/88) [398.2]

4859 Evslin, Bernard. *The Cyclopes* (6–12). Illus. 1987, Chelsea LB $19.95 (1-55546-236-7). The story of the ferocious one-eyed monster and how he was blinded by Ulysses. Others in this series about mythical monsters are *Medusa; The Minotaur;* and *Procrustes* (all 1987). (Rev: BL 6/15/87; SLJ 8/87) [398.2]

4860 Evslin, Bernard. *The Furies* (7–12). Illus. 1989, Chelsea LB $19.95 (1-55546-249-9). In Greek mythology the Furies were three witches. This retelling also includes the story of Circe, the famous sorceress. (Rev: BL 12/15/89; SLJ 4/90) [398.21]

4861 Evslin, Bernard. *Heroes, Gods and Monsters of Greek Myths* (8–12). Illus. 1984, Bantam paper $5.99 (0-553-25920-2). The most popular Greek myths are retold in modern language. [292]

4862 Evslin, Bernard. *Ladon* (7–12). Illus. 1990, Chelsea LB $19.95 (1-55546-254-5). A splendid retelling of the Greek myth about the sea serpent called up by Hera to fight Hercules. (Rev: BL 8/90) [398.24]

4863 Evslin, Bernard. *The Trojan War: The Iliad of Homer* (8–12). 1988, Scholastic paper $2.95 (0-590-41626-X). The story of the 10-year war between the Greeks and the Trojans is retold for the modern reader. [292]

4864 Evslin, Bernard, et al. *Heroes and Monsters of Greek Myth* (7–12). 1984, Scholastic paper $3.99 (0-590-43440-3). A simple retelling of the most famous Greek myths. Also use *The Greek Gods* (1988). [292]

4865 Fleischman, Paul. *Dateline: Troy* (6–9). Illus. 1996, Candlewick $17.99 (1-56402-469-5). The story of the Trojan War is juxtaposed with recent newspaper articles on each page that cover similar current events, e.g., Paris chooses the most beautiful woman alongside coverage of a Miss Universe contest. (Rev: BL 3/15/96; BR 9–10/96; SLJ 5/96; VOYA 12/96) [398.2]

4866 Galloway, Priscilla, reteller. *Aleta and the Queen: A Tale of Ancient Greece* (5–8). Illus. 1995, Annick LB $29.95 (1-55037-400-1); paper $14.95 (1-55037-462-1). Told from the standpoint of a 12-year-old girl, this volume expands on and embellishes the story of Penelope and her wait for Odysseus. (Rev: BL 1/1–15/96; SLJ 1/96) [398.2]

4867 Galloway, Priscilla. *Daedalus and the Minotaur* (5–9). Illus. Series: Tales of Ancient Lands. 1997, Annick LB $27.95 (1-55037-459-1); paper $14.95 (1-55037-458-3). The dramatic story of Daedalus and his adventures in Crete are retold, ending as he and his son, Icarus, launch themselves in flight. (Rev: BL 1/1–15/98; SLJ 2/98) [398.2]

4868 Graves, Robert. *Greek Gods and Heroes* (6–8). 1973, Dell paper $5.50 (0-440-93221-1). Tales of 12 of the most important figures in Greek mythology in 27 short chapters. [292]

4869 Green, Jen. *Myths of Ancient Greece* (5–8). Illus. Series: Mythic World. 2001, Raintree Steck-Vaughn LB $27.12 (0-7398-3191-7). This volume for older readers separates myth from reality about ancient Greece. (Rev: BL 3/1/02; HBG 3/02; SLJ 12/01) [398.2]

4870 Hawthorne, Nathaniel. *Wonder Book and Tanglewood Tales* (5–7). 1972, Ohio State Univ. Pr. $72.95 (0-8142-0158-X). This is a highly original retelling of the Greek myths, originally published in 1853. [398.2]

4871 Kindl, Patrice. *Lost in the Labyrinth* (6–10). 2002, Houghton $16.00 (0-618-16684-X). Told by Xenodice, a 14-year-old princess and the younger sister of Ariadne, this is an expanded version of the legend of Theseus and the Minotaur. (Rev: BCCB 11/02; BL 1/1–15/03; HB 11–12/02; HBG 3/03; SLJ 11/02; VOYA 2/03)

4872 McCarty, Nick, reteller. *The Iliad* (4–8). 2000, Kingfisher $22.95 (0-7534-5330-4); paper $15.95 (0-7534-5321-5). This account of the Trojan War uses an exciting text and action-packed illustrations. (Rev: SLJ 1/01) [398.2]

4873 McCaughrean, Geraldine. *Greek Gods and Goddesses* (4–7). Illus. 1998, Simon & Schuster $20.00 (0-689-82084-4). This book, illustrated in ancient Greek style, contains a lively retelling of a number of Greek myths, including the story of Hermes. (Rev: BL 11/15/98; HBG 3/99; SLJ 10/98) [292.13]

4874 McCaughrean, Geraldine. *Roman Myths* (4–8). 2001, Simon & Schuster $21.00 (0-689-83822-0). Fifteen Roman myths are retold here in a lively manner, accompanied by appealing color illustrations. (Rev: BL 9/1/01; HB 7–8/01; HBG 10/01; SLJ 7/01) [398.2]

4875 Nardo, Don. *Egyptian Mythology* (6–12). Illus. Series: Mythology. 2001, Enslow $20.95 (0-7660-1407-X). Eight Egyptian myths are related here, with background historical and cultural information, question-and-answer sections, and commentary from scholars. (Rev: BL 5/15/01; SLJ 5/01) [299]

4876 Nardo, Don. *Greek and Roman Mythology* (5–8). Series: World History. 1997, Lucent LB $27.45 (1-56006-308-4). The author provides a background on classical mythology — where the myths came from and why they were an important part of each country's culture — and relates the most famous stories from ancient Greek and Roman times. (Rev: SLJ 5/98) [398.2]

4877 Osborne, Mary Pope. *The One-Eyed Giant* (4–8). Series: Tales from the Odyssey. 2002, Hyperion $9.99 (0-7868-0770-9). Osborne recounts the return from the Trojan War and Odysseus's encounter with the Cyclops, followed by guides to the Greek gods and to pronunciation and information on Homer. Also use *The Land of the Dead* (2002). (Rev: BL 11/15/02; HBG 3/03; SLJ 1/03) [883]

4878 Pickels, Dwayne E. *Roman Myths, Heroes, and Legends* (5–8). Series: Costume, Tradition, and Culture: Reflecting on the Past. 1998, Chelsea $19.75 (0-7910-5164-1). Using double-page spreads and old collectors' cards as illustrations, this work retells the major Roman myths and introduces their important characters. (Rev: BL 3/15/99; HBG 10/99) [398.2]

4879 Spies, Karen Bornemann. *Heroes in Greek Mythology* (6–9). Series: Mythology. 2002, Enslow LB $20.95 (0-7660-1560-2). Through an introduction to the heroes in Greek mythology, many of the most famous myths are retold. (Rev: BL 4/15/02; HBG 10/02) [292]

4880 Spies, Karen Bornemann. *The Iliad and the Odyssey in Greek Mythology* (6–9). Series: Mythology. 2002, Enslow LB $20.95 (0-7660-1561-0). The two great epics of Homer are retold with many original illustrations and with useful historical background material. (Rev: BL 12/15/02; HBG 3/03; VOYA 8/03) [292]

4881 Spinner, Stephanie. *Quiver* (7–12). 2002, Knopf $15.95 (0-375-81489-2). A deft retelling of the Greek myth of Atalanta, who will marry only a man who can outrun her. (Rev: BCCB 2/03; BL 1/1–15/03*; HB 1–2/03; HBG 3/03; SLJ 10/02; VOYA 12/02)

4882 Spires, Elizabeth. *I Am Arachne* (4–7). Illus. 2001, Farrar $15.00 (0-374-33525-7). Spires takes a fresh look at some ancient stories, breathing new life and humor into first-person tales of Midas, Pan, Narcissus, and Eurydice. (Rev: BL 6/1–15/01; HB 9–10/01; HBG 3/02; SLJ 5/01; VOYA 8/01) [813]

4883 Sutcliff, Rosemary. *Black Ships Before Troy: The Story of the Iliad* (6–12). Illus. 1993, Delacorte $24.95 (0-385-31069-2). A re-creation of the classic epic, with a compelling vision and sensitivity to language, history, and heroics. (Rev: BCCB 1/94; BL 10/15/93) [883]

4884 Sutcliff, Rosemary. *The Wanderings of Odysseus: The Story of the Odyssey* (5–8). Illus. 1996, Delacorte $24.95 (0-385-32205-4). An oversize volume that retells Homer's *Odyssey* and the adventures of Odysseus on his journey home from the Trojan War. (Rev: BCCB 9/96; BL 9/1/96; HB 5–6/96; SLJ 6/96*) [883]

4885 Switzer, Ellen. *Greek Myths: Gods, Heroes, and Monsters — Their Sources, Their Stories and Their Meanings* (7–12). Illus. 1988, Macmillan

$18.00 (0-689-31253-9). A collection of myths that includes 13 stories about such characters as Perseus, Odysseus, and Medusa. (Rev: BL 4/1/88; BR 1–2/89; SLJ 4/88) [292]

4886 Usher, Kerry. *Heroes, Gods and Emperors from Roman Mythology* (8–12). Illus. 1992, NTC LB $24.95 (0-87226-909-4). The origins of Roman mythology are given, plus retellings of famous myths. [292]

4887 Woff, Richard. *Bright-Eyed Athena: Stories from Ancient Greece* (5–8). Illus. 1999, Getty Museum paper $12.95 (0-89236-558-7). Using full-color illustrations from Greek sculpture and vase paintings, this book retells the important Greek myths involving Athena. (Rev: BL 11/15/99; HBG 3/00; SLJ 2/00) [398.2]

4888 Wolfson, Evelyn. *Roman Mythology* (6–9). Series: Mythology. 2002, Enslow LB $20.95 (0-7660-1558-0). This is a general introduction to Roman mythology with a retelling of the major stories and an introduction to important characters. (Rev: BL 12/15/02; HBG 3/03) [398]

4889 Yolen, Jane, and Robert J. Harris. *Hippolyta and the Curse of the Amazons* (4–8). Series: Young Heroes. 2002, HarperCollins LB $15.89 (0-06-028737-3). It falls to 13-year-old Hippolyta, an Amazon princess, to find a way to save her people when her mother refuses to sacrifice her second-born male child. (Rev: BCCB 4/02; HBG 10/02; SLJ 3/02) [398.2]

Speeches, Essays, and General Literary Works

4890 Halliburton, Warren J., ed. *Historic Speeches of African Americans* (7–12). Series: African American Experience. 1993, Watts LB $23.00 (0-531-11034-6). Chronologically organized speeches by such leaders as Sojourner Truth, Frederick Douglass, Marcus Garvey, James Baldwin, Angela Davis, and Jesse Jackson. (Rev: BL 4/15/93; SLJ 7/93) [815]

4891 Hurley, Jennifer A., ed. *Women's Rights* (7–12). Series: Great Speeches in History. 2001, Greenhaven LB $31.20 (0-7377-0773-9); paper $19.95 (0-7377-0772-0). This anthology of speeches by noted women including Elizabeth Cady Stanton, Susan B. Anthony, Gloria Steinem, and Phyllis Schlafly also offers historical context, analytical headnotes, and biographical details. (Rev: BL 10/15/01) [305.42]

4892 McIntire, Suzanne, ed. *American Heritage Book of Great American Speeches for Young People* (7–12). 2001, Wiley paper $14.95 (0-471-38942-0). More than 100 key speeches by individuals ranging from politicians to athletes are provided in this single volume. (Rev: SLJ 12/01) [815.008]

4893 Meyer, Stephanie H., and John Meyer, eds. *Teen Ink: Friends and Family* (6–12). 2001, Health Communications paper $12.95 (1-55874-931-4). This collection of fiction, poetry, and essays written by young people that appeared in *Teen Ink* magazine is organized by themes such as "Snapshots: Friends and Family" and "Out of Focus: Facing Challenges." (Rev: BL 1/1–15/02; SLJ 12/01) [810.8]

4894 Rosen, Roger, and Patra McSharry, eds. *East-West: The Landscape Within* (7–12). Series: World Issues. 1992, Rosen LB $16.95 (0-8239-1375-9); paper $8.95 (0-8239-1376-7). Short stories and nonfiction selections by diverse authors of varied nationalities on their cultures' beliefs and values, among them the Dalai Lama, Joseph Campbell, Lydia Minatoya, and Aung Aung Taik. (Rev: BL 12/15/92; SLJ 2/93) [909]

4895 Stone, Miriam. *At the End of Words: A Daughter's Memoir* (6–12). 2003, Candlewick $14.00 (0-7636-1854-3). Moving poetry and narrative describe the author's grief and emotional upheaval over her mother's death from cancer. (Rev: BL 4/15/03; HBG 10/03; SLJ 5/03) [362.1]

Literary History and Criticism

Fiction

General and Miscellaneous

4896 Barlowe, Wayne Douglas, and Neil Duskis. *Barlowe's Guide to Fantasy* (7–12). Illus. 1996, HarperCollins $ (0-06-105238-8); paper $19.95 (0-06-100817-6). Using double-page spreads, this handsome book covers the history of fantasy literature from ancient times to the present by highlighting 50 examples, among them *Beowulf, Wind in the Willows,* and *Mists of Avalon.* (Rev: VOYA 10/97)

4897 Miller, Ron. *The History of Science Fiction* (6–10). Illus. 2001, Watts LB $28.00 (0-531-11866-5). An enticing overview of the genre, its development, recurring themes, primary authors, TV and movie presentations, and most important awards. (Rev: BL 7/01; SLJ 7/01; VOYA 6/02) [809.3]

4898 O'Neill, Jane. *The World of the Brontës* (8–12). Illus. 1999, Carlton $24.95 (1-85868-341-6). This book describes the lives and works of Emily, Charlotte, and Anne Brontë and gives a good picture of 19th-century English society, quoting frequently from their diaries and letters as well as their novels. (Rev: BL 9/1/99; SLJ 2/00) [823.809]

4899 Rainey, Richard. *The Monster Factory* (6–12). 1993, Macmillan LB $19.00 (0-02-775663-7). A discussion of seven famous monster-story writers and their most-loved works. (Rev: BL 8/93; VOYA 10/93) [809.3]

4900 Reid, Suzanne Elizabeth. *Presenting Young Adult Science Fiction* (7–12). Series: Twayne's United States Authors. 1998, Twayne $29.00 (0-8057-1653-X). This comprehensive introduction to science fiction describes the history of the genre, profiles such classical masters as Asimov, Bradbury, Heinlein, and Le Guin, and presents members of the new generation, among them Orson Scott Card, Pamela Service, Piers Anthony, and Douglas Adams. (Rev: SLJ 6/99) [808.3]

4901 Rovin, Jeff. *Aliens, Robots, and Spaceships* (7–12). Illus. 1995, Facts on File $38.50 (0-8160-3107-X). Alphabetically arranged entries on characters, creatures, and places in the world of science fiction, with over 100 black-and-white illustrations. (Rev: BR 1–2/96; SLJ 12/95; VOYA 4/96) [813]

4902 Smith, Lucinda I. *Women Who Write*, Vol. 2 (8–12). 1994, Messner $15.00 (0-671-87253-2). Interviews and short biographies of contemporary women writers, including Margaret Atwood and Sue Grafton. Addresses the desire to write and provides tips for aspiring authors. (Rev: BL 10/15/94; SLJ 11/94; VOYA 12/94) [809.8]

4903 Stuprich, Michael, ed. *Horror* (8–12). Series: Literary Movements and Genres. 2001, Greenhaven $32.45 (0-7377-0667-8); paper $19.95 (0-7377-0666-X). A thorough introduction to the horror genre, with essays by writers including Stephen King and Joyce Carol Oates. (Rev: BL 8/1/01; SLJ 11/01) [823]

Europe

Great Britain and Ireland

4904 Bloom, Harold, ed. *Charlotte Brontë's Jane Eyre* (8–12). Series: Bloom's Notes. 1996, Chelsea LB $21.95 (0-7910-4063-1). In addition to a collection of critical essays on *Jane Eyre,* there is a biography of the author, a plot summary, and character sketches. (Rev: BL 1/1–15/97; SLJ 4/97) [823]

4905 Brontë, Charlotte. *Jane Eyre* (8–12). Series: Case Studies in Contemporary Criticism. 1964, Airmont paper $4.95 (0-8049-0017-5). Jane finds terror and romance when she becomes a governess for Mr. Rochester.

Other Countries

4906 Cunningham, Jesse G., ed. *Readings on The Plague* (8–12). Series: Literary Companion to World Literature. 2001, Greenhaven LB $28.70 (0-7377-0691-0); paper $18.70 (0-7377-0690-2). Discussions of the structure, meaning, and historical context of Camus's novel provide a variety of viewpoints and interpretations. (Rev: SLJ 11/01) [843]

United States

4907 Bloom, Harold, ed. *Maya Angelou's I Know Why the Caged Bird Sings* (8–12). Series: Bloom's Notes. 1996, Chelsea LB $21.95 (0-7910-3666-9). A collection of critical essays on this work by Maya Angelou, plus a detailed analysis of the book and its characters, accompanied by material on the author's life. (Rev: BL 1/1–15/97; SLJ 3/97) [818]

4908 Cart, Michael. *Presenting Robert Lipsyte* (8–12). 1995, Twayne $29.00 (0-8057-4151-8). A probing look at Lipsyte's life and work. (Rev: BL 6/1–15/95; BR 3–4/96; VOYA 6/96) [813]

4909 Cassedy, Patrice. *Understanding Flowers for Algernon* (7–12). Illus. Series: Understanding Great Literature. 2001, Lucent LB $19.96 (1-56006-784-5). Clear and thoughtful analysis of *Flowers for Algernon*, a science fiction YA novel by Daniel Keyes, is accompanied by biographical information, historical context, a timeline, and sources. (Rev: BL 3/1/01) [813]

4910 Crowe, Chris. *Presenting Mildred D. Taylor* (6–12). Illus. Series: United States Authors. 1999, Twayne $33.00 (0-8057-1687-4). As well as some biographical material, this book gives an analysis of Taylor's works, their historical context, and a history of racism and the civil rights movement in Mississippi. (Rev: BL 2/15/00; VOYA 6/00) [813.]

4911 Curry, Barbara K., and James Michael Brodie. *Sweet Words So Brave: The Story of African American Literature* (5–8). Illus. 1996, Zino $24.95 (1-55933-179-8). An outline of African American literature, from slave narratives to the great writers of today, such as Nikki Giovanni and Toni Morrison. (Rev: BL 2/15/97*; SLJ 4/97) [810.9]

4912 Engle, Steven. *Readings on the Catcher in the Rye* (7–12). Series: Literary Companions. 1998, Greenhaven LB $33.70 (1-56510-817-5); paper $22.45 (1-56510-816-7). A helpful collection about this coming-of-age classic that explores the novel's themes, imagery, issues, and the narrator, Holden Caulfield. (Rev: BL 8/98) [813.54]

4913 Felgar, Robert. *Understanding Richard Wright's Black Boy: A Student Casebook to Issues, Sources and Historical Documents* (8–12). Series: Literature in Context. 1998, Greenwood $45.00 (0-313-30221-9). This book analyzes *Black Boy* from various standpoints, including structure and themes, its position in relation to other important autobiographies, and its place in the cultural and social conditions of the time. (Rev: BR 1–2/99; SLJ 9/98) [818]

4914 Howard, Todd. *The Outsiders* (7–12). Series: Understanding Great Literature. 2001, Lucent $24.95 (1-56006-702-0). This classic in young adult literature is examined with material on its structure, characters, themes, concepts, importance, and the life of the author. (Rev: BL 8/1/01; SLJ 7/01) [813]

4915 Johnson-Feelings, Dianne. *Presenting Laurence Yep* (8–12). 1995, Twayne $29.00 (0-8057-8201-X). A biocritical study that uses material from the Chinese American artist Laurence Yep's autobiography *The Lost Garden*. (Rev: BL 12/15/95) [813]

4916 Keeley, Jennifer. *Understanding I Am the Cheese* (7–12). Series: Understanding Great Literature. 2000, Lucent LB $19.96 (1-56006-678-4). An introduction to Robert Cormier's book, discussing the plot and characters as well as the author's life and other works. (Rev: BL 3/1/01; SLJ 4/01) [813]

4917 Keeley, Jennifer. *The Yearling* (7–12). Series: Understanding Great Literature. 2001, Lucent $24.95 (1-56006-811-6). This book explores the famous tale published in 1938 about a boy and his pet fawn as well as material on the eccentric author who wrote it. (Rev: BL 8/1/01) [813]

4918 MacRae, Cathi Dunn. *Presenting Young Adult Fantasy Fiction* (7–12). 1998, Twayne $29.00 (0-8057-8220-6). An excellent survey of current writers of fantasy plus in-depth interviews with Terry Brooks, Barbara Hambly, Jane Yolen, and Meredith Ann Pierce. (Rev: BL 1/1–15/99; VOYA 8/98) [813]

4919 Pinsker, Sanford, and Ann Pinsker. *Understanding The Catcher in the Rye: A Student Casebook to Issues, Sources, and Historical Documents* (7–12). Series: Literature in Context. 1999, Greenwood $39.95 (0-313-30200-6). Excerpts from primary materials are used to convey a historical context to young readers of Holden Caulfield's story. (Rev: SLJ 6/00) [813]

4920 Vollstadt, Elizabeth Weiss. *Understanding Johnny Tremain* (6–12). Series: Understanding Great Literature. 2001, Lucent LB $24.95 (1-56006-849-3). As well as an analysis of the plot and characters of *Johnny Tremain*, Vollstadt provides insight into the life and viewpoint of the author. (Rev: SLJ 9/01) [813]

4921 Yunghans, Penelope. *Prize Winners: Ten Writers for Young Readers* (5–9). Series: World Writers. 1995, Morgan Reynolds LB $21.95 (1-883846-11-0). How some of the most popular writers of youth fiction came to pen their stories. (Rev: BL 12/15/95; SLJ 12/95; VOYA 2/96) [810.9]

Plays and Poetry

General and Miscellaneous

4922 Adoff, Jaime. *The Song Shoots out of My Mouth: A Celebration of Music* (6–9). 2002, Dutton $17.99 (0-525-46949-4). Colorful illustrations accompany free-verse poems celebrating music from classical and jazz to reggae and hip hop. (Rev: BL 1/1–15/03; HBG 3/03; SLJ 10/02; VOYA 4/03) [811.6]

4923 Deutsch, Babette. *Poetry Handbook: A Dictionary of Terms*. 4th ed. (7–12). 1981, Barnes & Noble paper $14.00 (0-06-463548-1). The standard introduction to the technical aspects of poetry through definitions of terms with examples. [808.1]

4924 Vecchione, Patrice, ed. *The Body Eclectic: An Anthology of Poems* (8–12). 2002, Holt $16.95 (0-8050-6935-6). A collection of poems, both contemporary and classic, that look at parts of the body from serious, comic, tragic, reflective, and romantic points of view. (Rev: BL 7/02; HB 7–8/02; HBG 10/02; SLJ 8/02; VOYA 8/02) [808.81]

Europe

Shakespeare

4925 Allison, Amy. *Shakespeare's Globe* (7–10). Series: Building History. 1999, Lucent LB $18.96 (1-56006-526-5). The story of the theater built on the south bank of the Thames in London by Shakespeare and his partners and how this building became a landmark in theatrical history. (Rev: BL 10/15/99; HBG 9/00; SLJ 2/00) [822.3]

4926 Birch, Beverley, retel. *Shakespeare's Stories: Comedies* (5–9). Illus. 1990, Bedrick paper $6.95 (0-87226-225-1). This is the first of three volumes that retell in attractive, straightforward prose the most popular of his plays. The others are *Shakespeare's Stories: Histories* and *Shakespeare's Stories: Tragedies* (both 1988). (Rev: BL 2/15/89; BR 1–2/89; SLJ 2/89) [813]

4927 Derrick, Thomas. *Understanding Shakespeare's Julius Caesar* (8–12). Illus. Series: Literature in Context. 1998, Greenwood $45.00 (0-313-29638-3). An entertaining approach to *Julius Caesar* that brings to life the diverse worlds of history, theater, language, metaphor, plot, and source material, and even includes a chapter on pop culture treatments of the play. (Rev: VOYA 10/99) [822.3]

4928 Garfield, Leon. *Shakespeare Stories II* (6–10). Illus. 1995, Houghton $26.00 (0-395-70893-1). Plot synopses of *Julius Caesar* and eight less familiar plays. (Rev: BL 4/1/95; SLJ 6/95) [823]

4929 Nardo, Don. *Hamlet* (7–12). Series: Understanding Great Literature. 2001, Lucent $24.95 (1-56006-830-2). As well as a discussion of this play's themes, characters, and plot, this work covers Shakespeare's life, work, and times. (Rev: BL 8/1/01; SLJ 4/01) [822.3]

4930 Olster, Fredi, and Rick Hamilton. *A Midsummer Night's Dream: A Workbook for Students* (8–12). Series: Discovering Shakespeare. 1996, Smith & Kraus paper $19.95 (1-57525-042-X). The text of the play is presented in a double-page, four-column format that provides stage directions, scene description, and the original text,plus a version in the vernacular. Supplemental background material is also appended. (Rev: BL 1/1–15/97; SLJ 12/96; VOYA 2/97) [822.3]

4931 Olster, Fredi, and Rick Hamilton. *Romeo and Juliet: A Workbook for Students* (8–12). Series: Discovering Shakespeare. 1996, Smith & Kraus paper $19.95 (1-57525-044-6). This Shakespearean tragedy is presented in a four-column format that gives the original text, stage directions, scene descriptions, and a reworking into modern English. (Rev: BL 1/1–15/97; VOYA 2/97) [822.3]

4932 Olster, Fredi, and Rick Hamilton. *The Taming of the Shrew* (7–12). Series: Discovering Shakespeare. 1997, Smith & Kraus paper $19.95 (1-57525-046-2). This guide to Shakespeare's comedy uses a paraphrased text opposite the original script with details on stage directions. (Rev: BL 2/15/97; BR 11–12/97; SLJ 6/97; VOYA 2/97) [822.3]

4933 Thrasher, Thomas. *Romeo and Juliet* (7–12). Series: Understanding Great Literature. 2001, Lucent $24.95 (1-56006-787-X). After introducing the life and times of Shakespeare, this work discusses, in depth, the background, plot, characters, and themes of this classic play. (Rev: BL 8/1/01; SLJ 6/01) [822.3]

4934 Williams, Marcia. *Tales from Shakespeare: Seven Plays* (5–8). Illus. 1998, Candlewick $16.99 (0-7636-0441-0). Using a comic-strip format, this oversize book describes what it would have been like to attend performances of such plays as *Hamlet*, *Macbeth*, and *A Midsummer Night's Dream* at the Globe Theatre. (Rev: BCCB 11/98; BL 11/1/98; HBG 3/99; SLJ 10/98) [741.5973]

United States

4935 Bush, Valerie Chow, ed. *Believe Me, I Know: Poetry and Photographs by WritersCorps Youth* (6–12). Illus. 2002, WritersCorps paper $14.95 (1-888048-08-5). These poems and photographs dealing with a wide range of subjects were created during a WritersCorps workshop attended by a multicultural group of students. (Rev: BL 8/02; SLJ 11/02*; VOYA 12/02) [811]

4936 Kappel, Lawrence, ed. *Readings on A Raisin in the Sun* (7–12). Series: Literary Companion to American Literature. 2000, Greenhaven LB $22.96 (0-7377-0368-7); paper $14.96 (0-7377-0367-9). The essays in this collection look at the play from the African American and female points of view as well as discussing its important themes and its relevance. (Rev: BL 11/15/00; SLJ 2/01) [823]

Language and Communication

Signs and Symbols

4937 Crampton, William. *Flag* (5–9). Illus. 1989, Knopf $20.99 (0-394-92255-7). Stunning photographs and text introduce the use and nature of flags with many accompanying examples. (Rev: BL 10/15/89) [929.9]

4938 Ferry, Joseph. *The American Flag* (5–7). Series: American Symbols and Their Meanings. 2002, Mason Crest LB $18.95 (1-59084-026-7). Designs that preceded the familiar flag accompany material on Betsy Ross and Francis Scott Key, illustrations of important flag raisings, and discussion of proper use and treatment of the flag, all in a package that will appeal to reluctant readers. (Rev: SLJ 4/02) [929.9]

4939 Radlauer, Ruth. *Honor the Flag: A Guide to Its Care and Display* (4–7). 1992, Forest LB $14.95 (1-878363-61-1). Lots of information about the American flag and its care. (Rev: BL 10/15/92) [929.92]

4940 Singh, Simon. *The Code Book: How to Make It, Break It, Hack It, Crack It* (7–12). Illus. 2002, Random $16.95 (0-385-72913-8). This abridged version of an adult book provides an absorbing introduction to codes and cryptography, giving historical examples and discussing contemporary Internet issues. (Rev: BL 1/1–15/02; HB 3–4/02; HBG 10/02; SLJ 5/02; VOYA 8/02) [652.8]

4941 Williams, Earl P. *What You Should Know About the American Flag* (4–8). Illus. 1989, Thomas Publns. paper $5.95 (0-939631-10-5). A comprehensive guide to facts and legends, history and traditions concerning the U.S. flag. (Rev: BL 11/15/87) [929.920973]

4942 Woods, Mary B., and Michael Woods. *Ancient Communication: From Grunts to Graffiti* (5–8). Series: Ancient Technologies. 2000, Runestone LB $25.26 (0-8225-2996-3). Beginning with cave paintings and hieroglyphics and ending with modern alphabets and universal languages, this account of the history of communication emphasizes ancient cultures. (Rev: BL 9/15/00; HBG 3/01; SLJ 1/01) [652]

Words and Languages

4943 Adams, Simon. *Code Breakers: From Hiero-glyphs to Hackers* (4–8). Series: Secret Worlds. 2002, DK $14.95 (0-7894-8529-X); paper $5.95 (0-7894-8530-3). A wealth of fascinating information is packed into this book that traces code breaking from the Rosetta Stone to the present world of computers. (Rev: BL 8/02; HBG 10/02) [652]

4944 Agee, Jon. *Elvis Lives! and Other Anagrams* (4–8). Illus. 2000, Farrar $15.00 (0-374-32127-2). An entertaining introduction to anagrams — words or phases that can be rearranged to form new words or phrases — for children and adults. (Rev: BCCB 3/00; BL 2/1/00; HB 3–4/00; HBG 10/00; SLJ 4/00) [793.734]

4945 Agee, Jon. *Sit on a Potato Pan, Otis! More Palindromes* (4–8). Illus. 1999, Farrar $14.41 (0-374-31808-5). A whimsical book illustrated with black-and-white cartoons that contains 60 humorous palindromes. (Rev: BCCB 2/99; BL 3/1/99; HB 3–4/99; HBG 9/99; SLJ 3/99) [418]

4946 Agee, Jon. *Who Ordered the Jumbo Shrimp? And Other Oxymorons* (5–10). Illus. 1998, Harper-Collins $15.95 (0-06-205159-8). An amusing collection of oxymorons such as "permanent temp" and "Great Depression," cleverly illustrated with black-and-white cartoons. (Rev: BCCB 12/98; HBG 3/99; SLJ 11/98) [412]

4947 Bailey, LaWanda. *Miss Myrtle Frag, the Grammar Nag* (5–9). 2000, Absey paper $13.95 (1-888842-19-9). A clever book that explains key grammar rules through a series of witty letters from Miss Myrtle Frag. (Rev: SLJ 2/01) [415]

4948 Cooper, Kay. *Why Do You Speak as You Do? A Guide to World Languages* (5–8). 1992, Children's LB $14.85 (0-8027-8165-9). A simple yet lively presentation of linguistics. (Rev: BCCB 2/93; BL 1/15/93) [400]

4949 Cox, Brenda S. *Who Talks Funny? A Book About Languages for Kids* (7–12). 1995, Linnet LB $25.00 (0-208-02378-X). Explores the importance of learning other languages, describes the development of languages and common elements, and provides interesting information, such as how to say the days of the week in 27 languages. (Rev: BL 7/95; SLJ 4/95) [400]

4950 Fakih, Kimberly O. *Off the Clock: A Lexicon of Time Words and Expressions* (6–10). 1995, Ticknor $16.00 (0-395-66374-1). A look at how we talk about time in folklore, anthropology, mythology, history, semantics, and physics. (Rev: BL 1/1/95; SLJ 3/95) [428.1]

4951 Fisher, Leonard E. *Alphabet Art: Thirteen ABC's from Around the World* (7–9). Illus. 1978, Macmillan LB $16.95 (0-02-735230-7). Thirteen alphabets — from Arabic to Tibetan — are pictured with their English equivalents. [745.6]

4952 Frazier, Walt. *Word Jam: An Electrifying, Mesmerizing, Gravity-Defying Guide to a Powerful and Awesome Vocabulary* (6–9). 2001, Troll paper $6.95 (0-8167-7156-1). The basketball star aims to inspire a love of words and etymology through this mix of humor, instruction, and autobiography. (Rev: SLJ 9/01) [428.1]

4953 Gay, Kathlyn. *Getting Your Message Across* (6–12). 1993, Macmillan LB $22.00 (0-02-735815-1). Factors in communication are examined, such as body language, facial expression, ability to listen, and clothing. Also covers advertising. (Rev: BL 10/1/93; SLJ 11/93; VOYA 2/94) [302.2]

4954 *In Few Words / En Pocas Palabras: A Compendium of Latino Folk Wit and Wisdom* (6–12). Trans. by Jose A. Burciaga. 1996, Mercury House paper $14.95 (1-56279-093-5). This bilingual collection features popular sayings, proverbs, maxims, and adages that permeate Hispanic culture. (Rev: VOYA 6/97) [468.1]

4955 Johnson, Stephen T. *Alphabet City* (4–7). Illus. 1995, Viking $16.99 (0-670-85631-2). A sophisticated alphabet book that consists of a series of paintings, each of which represents a letter. (Rev: BCCB 11/95; BL 1/1–15/96; HB 11–12/95; SLJ 1/96*) [421]

4956 Jones, Charlotte F. *Eat Your Words: A Fascinating Look at the Language of Food* (4–8). Illus. 1999, Delacorte $16.95 (0-385-32575-4). The relationship between food and language is explored in this delightful book that covers topics including food named for people (peach melba), places (buffalo wings), and animals (horseradish), plus trivia about sayings, word etymologies, and silly laws all dealing with food. (Rev: BCCB 9/99; BL 4/15/99; HBG 10/99; SLJ 7/99) [418]

4957 Lederer, Richard. *The Circus of Words: Acrobatic Anagrams, Parading Palindromes, Wonderful Words on a Wire, and More Lively Letter Play* (5–8). 2001, Chicago Review paper $12.95 (1-55652-380-7). Lovers of words will find lots of entertainment in this selection of challenging exercises. (Rev: SLJ 8/01) [428.1]

4958 Roberts, Michael. *Mumbo Jumbo: The Creepy ABC* (4–8). 2000, Callaway $24.95 (0-935112-49-9). A scary alphabet book that features such subjects as vampires, eyeball stew, quicksand, and bats. (Rev: HBG 3/01; SLJ 3/01) [428]

4959 Samoyault, Tiphaine. *Give Me a Sign! What Pictograms Tell Us Without Words* (4–8). Trans. by Esther Allen. Illus. 1997, Viking $13.99 (0-670-87466-3). This book explains road signs and travel signage, as well as other pictograms. (Rev: BL 10/15/97; HBG 3/98; SLJ 1/98) [302.23]

4960 Schwartz, Alvin. *Chin Music: Tall Talk and Other Talk* (7–9). Illus. 1979, HarperCollins LB $12.89 (0-397-31870-7). A collection of folk words and their meanings. [410]

4961 Terban, Marvin. *Building Your Vocabulary* (4–8). Illus. Series: Scholastic Guides. 2002, Scholastic paper $12.95 (0-439-28561-5). In addition to techniques for increasing vocabulary, Terban discusses etymology and how to use a dictionary and thesaurus, giving clear, often entertaining examples throughout. (Rev: SLJ 8/02) [428.1]

4962 Terban, Marvin. *The Dove Dove: Funny Homograph Riddles* (4–7). 1988, Houghton paper $7.95 (0-89919-810-4). Making homographs less puzzling. Also use *Mad As a Wet Hen! and Other Funny Idioms* (1987). (Rev: BL 1/1/89) [818.5402]

4963 Umstatter, Jack. *Where Words Come From* (4–8). 2002, Watts LB $34.00 (0-531-11902-5). Etymology is brought to life through this accessible and often entertaining introduction to a variety of words and their evolution. (Rev: SLJ 7/02) [422.03]

4964 Vinton, Ken. *Alphabetic Antics: Hundreds of Activities to Challenge and Enrich Letter Learners of All Ages* (5–8). Illus. 1996, Free Spirit paper $19.95 (1-57542-008-2). For each letter of the alphabet, there is a history, how it appears in different alphabets, important words that begin with the letter, a quotation from someone whose name starts with it, and a number of interesting related projects. (Rev: SLJ 1/97) [411]

4965 Wilbur, Richard. *Opposites* (5–7). 1991, Harcourt $11.95 (0-15-258720-9). Through verses and cartoonlike illustrations, antonyms are given for a series of words. [811.52]

4966 Young, Ed. *Voices of the Heart* (4–8). Illus. 1997, Scholastic paper $17.95 (0-590-50199-2). In this sumptuous picture book, the author lists and explains 26 Chinese characters, each of which expresses a different emotion. (Rev: BCCB 4/97; BL 4/15/97; HB 5–6/97; SLJ 6/97) [179]

Writing and the Media

General and Miscellaneous

4967 Bauer, Marion Dane. *Our Stories: A Fiction Workshop for Young Authors* (6–10). 1996, Clarion $16.00 (0-395-81598-3); paper $6.95 (0-395-81599-1). Using critiques of 30 selections by students, the author explores such writing techniques as character development, dialogue, and point of view. (Rev: BL 10/15/96; BR 3–4/97; SLJ 12/96; VOYA 12/96) [808.3]

4968 Colman, Penny. *Where the Action Was: Women War Correspondents in World War II* (6–9). Illus. 2002, Crown $17.95 (0-517-80075-6). A vivid presentation of the courage and contributions of reporters and photographers including Margaret Bourke-White and Martha Gellhorn. (Rev: BL 3/1/02; HB 3–4/02; HBG 10/02; SLJ 1/02) [070.4]

4969 Hackwell, W. John. *Signs, Letters, Words: Archaeology Discovers Writing* (6–9). Illus. 1987, Macmillan LB $14.95 (0-684-18807-4). The story of the development of writing and how this has affected civilization. (Rev: BL 8/87; SLJ 1/88; VOYA 10/87) [652]

4970 Jean, Georges. *Writing: The Story of Alphabets and Scripts* (7–12). Series: Discoveries. 1992, Abrams paper $12.95 (0-8109-2893-0). Traces the beginnings of writing from the development of alphabets to printing and bookmaking, emphasizing the technological rather than intellectual aspects of the process. (Rev: BL 7/92) [652.1]

4971 Nuwer, Hank. *To the Young Writer: Nine Writers Talk About Their Craft* (6–9). 2002, Watts LB $23.00 (0-531-11591-7). Aspiring writers will learn much about the mechanics of published writing and the different kinds of careers available through these interviews with writers including a screenwriter, a journalist, and an advertiser. (Rev: LMC 1/03; SLJ 1/03; VOYA 4/03) [808]

4972 Senn, Joyce. *The Young People's Book of Quotations* (5–10). 1999, Millbrook LB $39.90 (0-7613-0267-0). Beginning with "accomplishment" and ending with "zoos," this is a collection of 2,000 quotations of special interest to young people, arranged by topic. (Rev: BL 3/1/99*; SLJ 4/99) [082]

4973 Van Allsburg, Chris. *The Mysteries of Harris Burdick* (7–9). Illus. 1984, Houghton LB $18.95 (0-395-35393-9). Fourteen drawings and captions invite the reader to write stories that explain them. (Rev: BL 9/86) [808]

Books and Publishing

4974 Brookfield, Karen. *Book* (5–9). Series: Eyewitness Books. 1993, Knopf $20.99 (0-679-94012-X). The evolution of writing is traced and the formats in which it has been recorded are covered. (Rev: BL 10/1/93) [002]

4975 *Dear Author: Students Write About the Books That Changed Their Lives* (5–9). 1995, Conari Pr. paper $9.95 (1-57324-003-6). A collection of young adults' letters to authors, both dead and alive, expressing, with wit and honesty, how the authors' books have affected them. (Rev: BL 1/1–15/96; SLJ 11/95) [028.5]

4976 Garcia, John. *The Success of Hispanic Magazine* (7–10). Illus. Series: Success. 1996, Walker LB $16.85 (0-8027-8310-4). A behind-the-scenes look at the magazine business, from starting out to marketing research, staffing, sales, circulation, and distribution. Traces an article from initial conception to final version and publication. (Rev: BL 5/15/96; SLJ 4/96) [051]

4977 Glassman, Peter, ed. *Oz: The Hundredth Anniversary Celebration* (4–8). 2000, HarperCollins $24.95 (0-688-15915-X). In this tribute to the children's classic, authors and illustrators — fans of the Oz books — pay homage in words and pictures. (Rev: BL 12/1/00; HBG 3/01; SLJ 11/00) [807]

4978 Madama, John. *Desktop Publishing: The Art of Communication* (7–12). Series: Media Workshop. 1993, Lerner LB $21.27 (0-8225-2303-5). Introduces desktop publishing elements and terminology, with advice on writing, editing, layout, type, illustration, and printing. (Rev: BL 5/15/93; SLJ 6/93) [686.2]

4979 Marcus, Leonard S. *Side by Side: Five Favorite Picture-Book Teams Go to Work* (4–7). Illus. 2001, Walker LB $23.85 (0-8027-8779-7). A look at how members of five well-known collaborative teams work together to create picture books, from concept to finished product. (Rev: BL 11/15/01; HB 1–2/02; HBG 3/02; SLJ 11/01) [070.5]

4980 Swain, Gwenyth. *Bookworks: Making Books by Hand* (4–7). Illus. 1995, Carolrhoda LB $22.60 (0-87614-858-5). After a brief history of books and printing, this account gives directions for making paper and various kinds of books. (Rev: BL 7/95; SLJ 8/95*) [745.5]

4981 Toussaint, Pamela. *Great Books for African American Children* (6–12). 1999, NAL paper $12.95 (0-452-28044-3). This book lists 250 recommended books for African American children from preschool to young adults, each with a lengthy, informative annotation. (Rev: BL 2/15/99; SLJ 9/99) [810]

Print and Other Media

4982 Beatty, Scott. *Batman: The Ultimate Guide* (6–8). Illus. 2001, DK $19.95 (0-7894-7865-X). This large-format, comprehensive guide to Batman's life, gadgets, friends, and foes features bright spreads full of illustrations, captions, diagrams, and panels and covers from the original comic. (Rev: BL 1/1–15/02; HBG 3/02) [741.5]

4983 Beatty, Scott. *Superman: The Ultimate Guide to the Man of Steel* (6–12). Illus. 2002, DK $19.99 (0-7894-8853-1). This comprehensive guide to Superman's life, powers, and friends and foes juxtaposes illustrations from different eras. (Rev: BL 8/02; SLJ 9/02) [741.5]

4984 Cohen, Daniel. *Yellow Journalism: Scandal, Sensationalism, and Gossip in the Media* (6–12).

Illus. 2000, Twenty-First Century LB $22.90 (0-7613-1502-0). The history of tabloid journalism and sensation-driven media is the focus of this fascinating book that uses many modern cases as examples. (Rev: BL 5/15/00; SLJ 8/00) [302.23.]

4985 Cooper, Alison. *Media Power?* (6–8). Illus. Series: Viewpoints. 1997, Watts LB $23.00 (0-531-14452-6). Double-page spreads cover such topics as the use and misuse of the media by advertisers and governments, the effect of the media on recent trials, privacy issues, and the formation of public opinion. (Rev: BL 1/1–15/98; HBG 3/98) [302.23]

4986 Day, Nancy. *Sensational TV: Trash or Journalism?* (7–10). Illus. 1996, Enslow LB $20.95 (0-89490-733-6). A history of tabloid journalism both in print and on TV, plus a discussion of present-day controversies surrounding it. (Rev: BL 4/1/96; SLJ 4/96; VOYA 6/96) [791.45]

4987 DeFalco, Tom. *Hulk: The Incredible Guide* (6–12). Illus. 2003, DK $24.99 (0-7894-9771-9). Full-color illustrations spanning 40 years of comics portray the Hulk's life and escapades in this oversize volume. Also use *X-Men: The Ultimate Guide* (2003). (Rev: BL 5/1/03) [741.5]

4988 Fleming, Thomas. *Behind the Headlines: The Story of American Newspapers* (6–10). 1989, Walker LB $15.85 (0-8027-6891-1). A lively history of American newspapers from the Revolution on and an indication of their continued importance today. (Rev: BL 1/1/90; BR 5–6/90; SLJ 1/90; VOYA 12/90) [071.3]

4989 Gerdes, Louise I., ed. *Media Violence* (8–12). Series: Opposing Viewpoints. 2003, Gale LB $33.70 (0-7377-2011-5); paper $22.45 (0-7377-2012-3). Violence in television, motion pictures, music lyrics, and other media is explored in this collection of essays with material on how serious the problem is and what, if anything, should be done about it. (Rev: BL 1/1–15/04) [303.6]

4990 Ritchie, Donald A. *American Journalists: Getting the Story* (8–12). Illus. 1998, Oxford $50.00 (0-19-509907-9). Fifty-six biographical sketches of journalists, supplemented by photographs, illustrations, and brief items about other news media notables, provide a glimpse into the journalism profession from Benjamin Franklin's time to today. (Rev: BL 2/15/98; BR 5–6/98; SLJ 7/98; VOYA 10/98) [070]

4991 Senna, Carl. *The Black Press and the Struggle for Civil Rights* (7–12). Series: African American Experience. 1993, Watts LB $24.00 (0-531-11036-2). The history of African American publications and their role in the fight for freedom and civil rights is traced, from *Freedom's Journal* in 1827 to today. (Rev: BL 1/1/94; SLJ 1/94; VOYA 3/94) [071]

4992 Somervill, Barbara A. *Backstage at a Newscast* (5–8). Illus. Series: Backstage Pass. 2003, Children's LB $20.00 (0-516-24326-8); paper $6.95 (0-516-24388-8). Somerville provides information on how a newscast is created, along with guidance on careers in journalism. (Rev: BL 5/1/03) [070.1]

4993 Stay, Byron L., ed. *Mass Media* (8–12). 1999, Greenhaven LB $32.45 (0-7377-0055-6); paper $21.20 (0-7377-0054-8). How does television affect society? Is advertising harmful? How do the media influence politics? Should pornography on the Internet be regulated? Do TV content labels benefit children? These are some of the questions explored in this collection of writings about the mass media. (Rev: BL 4/15/99) [303.6]

4994 Wakin, Edward. *How TV Changed America's Mind* (7–12). 1996, Lothrop $15.00 (0-688-13482-3). This book chronicles the impact of television journalism on U.S. history over the past 50 years by analyzing how the major news stories of the time were reported. (Rev: SLJ 7/96) [070.1]

Biography, Memoirs, Etc.

Adventurers and Explorers

Collective

4995 Currie, Stephen. *Polar Explorers* (5–9). Series: History Makers. 2002, Gale LB $27.45 (1-56006-957-0). The polar explorers profiled here are Roald Amundsen, John Franklin, Matthew Henson, Robert Peary, and Robert Scott. (Rev: SLJ 7/02) [919.804]

4996 Doherty, Kieran. *Ranchers, Homesteaders, and Traders: Frontiersmen of the South-Central States* (6–10). Illus. 2001, Oliver LB $21.95 (1-881508-53-6). Seven important settlers — including Sam Houston, Daniel Boone, and Eli Thayer — are introduced with plenty of historical and geographical background material. (Rev: BL 5/1/02; HBG 10/02; SLJ 1/02) [976]

4997 Haskins, Jim. *Against All Opposition: Black Explorers in America* (5–9). 1992, Walker LB $14.85 (0-8027-8138-1). A collective biography of African and African American explorers. (Rev: BL 2/15/92; SLJ 6/92) [910]

4998 Holden, Henry M. *American Women of Flight: Pilots and Pioneers* (7–12). Series: Collective Biographies. 2003, Enslow LB $20.95 (0-7660-2005-3). This collection of profiles includes sketches on Harriet Quimby, Bessie Colman, Amelia Earhart, Anne Morrow Lindbergh, and Jacqueline Cochran. (Rev: BL 6/1–15/03; HBG 10/03) [920]

4999 Johnstone, Michael. *The History News: Explorers* (4–7). Illus. Series: History News. 1997, Candlewick $15.99 (0-7636-0314-7). Famous explorers and their discoveries are covered using a newspaper format that even includes advertisements and letters to the editor, such as one from Columbus telling about reaching an island close to Japan. (Rev: BL 2/1/98; HBG 3/98; SLJ 1/98) [910.92]

5000 Lomask, Milton. *Great Lives: Exploration* (6–9). Illus. 1989, Macmillan $25.00 (0-684-18511-

3). An account of 25 world explorers from the ancient Greeks to the Polar expeditions of the 20th century. (Rev: BL 3/15/89; SLJ 1/89) [910]

5001 McLean, Jacqueline. *Women of Adventure* (5–9). Series: Profiles. 2003, Oliver LB $19.95 (1-881508-73-0). Seven 19th- and 20th-century women with diverse interests who broke social barriers by exploring far from home are profiled here, with biographical information, photographs, and maps. (Rev: BCCB 5/03; HBG 10/03; SLJ 7/03; VOYA 8/03) [910]

5002 Murphy, Claire R., and Jane G. Haigh. *Gold Rush Women* (7–12). Illus. 1997, Alaska Northwest paper $16.95 (0-88240-484-9). This is a collective biography of several women in the late 19th century who went to the Yukon and Alaska, where they panned for gold, ran boarding houses, and worked as dance hall girls and prostitutes. (Rev: BL 8/97; BR 1–2/98; SLJ 11/97*) [920]

5003 Platt, Richard. *Explorers: Pioneers Who Broke New Boundaries* (4–8). Illus. Series: Secret Worlds. 2001, DK paper $5.95 (0-7894-7974-5). An engaging introduction to explorers — of land, sea, and space — with illustrations and interesting, often wacky, facts. (Rev: BL 10/15/01; HBG 3/02) [910.92]

5004 Richie, Jason. *Spectacular Space Travelers* (6–10). Series: Profiles. 2001, Oliver LB $19.95 (1-881508-71-4). Three Soviet cosmonauts and four American astronauts are profiled in this volume that provides a brief history of the space race. (Rev: HBG 10/02; SLJ 4/02) [629.45]

5005 Schraff, Anne. *American Heroes of Exploration and Flight* (5–9). Illus. Series: Collective Biographies. 1996, Enslow LB $20.95 (0-89490-619-4). From the Wright Brothers, Lindbergh, and Earhart to Neil Armstrong and Sally Ride, this is a history of 12 Americans who dared the unknown. (Rev: BL 4/15/96; BR 9–10/96; SLJ 5/96; VOYA 6/96) [920]

5006 Sharp, Anne Wallace. *Daring Pirate Women* (5–8). Series: Biography. 2002, Lerner LB $25.26 (0-8225-0031-0). Profiles are given of notorious and ruthless female pirates such as Anne Bonny, Mary Read, and Grace O'Malley. (Rev: BL 6/1–15/02; HBG 10/02; SLJ 8/02) [920]

5007 Stefoff, Rebecca. *Vasco da Gama and the Portuguese Explorers* (6–9). Series: World Explorers. 1993, Chelsea LB $21.95 (0-7910-1303-0). An account of how different Portuguese explorers beginning with Vasco da Gama were able to visit unknown territories, particularly in the New World. (Rev: BL 3/15/93) [920]

5008 Twist, Clint. *Magellan and da Gama: To the Far East and Beyond* (4–7). Illus. Series: Beyond the Horizons. 1994, Raintree Steck-Vaughn LB $24.26 (0-8114-7254-X). Describes the period in which these two explorers lived, as well as their voyages and accomplishments. (Rev: BL 8/94) [920]

5009 Weatherly, Myra. *Women Pirates: Eight Stories of Adventure* (4–7). Illus. 1998, Morgan Reynolds LB $21.95 (1-883846-24-2). These stories of eight women pirates from the 17th and 18th centuries — including Grace O'Malley, Maria Cobham, and Rachel Wall — are enlivened by period prints and portraits and good maps. (Rev: BCCB 4/98; BL 4/15/98; HBG 3/99; SLJ 7/98; VOYA 10/98) [920]

5010 Wren, Laura Lee. *Pirates and Privateers of the High Seas* (6–10). Series: Collective Biographies. 2003, Enslow LB $20.95 (0-7660-1542-4). The piratical exploits of seafarers including Sir Francis Drake, Jean Laffite, Anne Bonny, and Mary Read are related in a lively narrative. (Rev: BL 6/1–15/03; HBG 10/03; SLJ 9/03) [910.4]

5011 Wyborny, Sheila. *Astronauts* (6–9). Series: History Makers. 2000, Lucent LB $19.96 (1-56006-648-2). Brief profiles and portraits of some of the major astronauts are included in this collective biography. (Rev: BL 12/15/00) [920]

5012 Yount, Lisa. *Women Aviators* (6–9). 1995, Facts on File $25.00 (0-8160-3062-6). Profiles of 11 prominent female aviators. (Rev: BL 4/1/95) [920]

5013 Zohorsky, Janet R. *Medieval Knights and Warriors* (6–9). Series: History Makers. 2003, Gale LB $21.96 (1-56006-954-6). Richard the Lionheart and Saladin are among the knights and adventurers profiled here. (Rev: BL 6/1–15/03; SLJ 7/03) [940.1]

Individual

ANZA, JUAN BAUTISTA DE

5014 Bankston, John. *Juan Bautista de Anza* (5–7). Series: Latinos in American History. 2003, Mitchell Lane LB $19.95 (1-58415-196-X). The biography of the Spanish explorer of the American Southwest who was a governor of New Mexico in the late 18th century. (Rev: BL 1/1–15/04) [921]

ARMSTRONG, NEIL

5015 Goss, Tim. *Neil Armstrong* (6–9). Series: Trailblazers of the Modern World. 2002, World Almanac Library LB $26.60 (0-8368-5075-0); paper $10.95 (0-8368-5235-4). The story of the famous astronaut and his part in the moon landing of 1969 is retold in this fine biography. (Rev: BL 12/15/02) [921]

5016 Kramer, Barbara. *Neil Armstrong: The First Man on the Moon* (5–7). Illus. Series: People to Know. 1997, Enslow LB $20.95 (0-89490-828-6). This biography covers Armstrong's public and private life, with details on his specialized training and many space missions. (Rev: HBG 3/98; SLJ 12/97) [921]

BLUFORD, GUION

5017 Haskins, Jim, and Kathleen Benson. *Space Challenger: The Story of Guion Bluford* (4–7). Illus. 1984, Carolrhoda LB $30.35 (0-87614-259-5). The story of the first African American man in space. [629.4540924]

BOYD, LOUISE ARNER

5018 Anema, Durlynn. *Louise Arner Boyd: Arctic Explorer* (4–6). Series: Notable Americans. 2000, Morgan Reynolds $19.95 (1-883846-42-0). A wealthy woman, Boyd financed and led polar expeditions in the 1920s but received little recognition for her achievements and her photographs, maps, and specimens. (Rev: BCCB 11/00; HBG 9/00; SLJ 4/00) [910.92]

BYRD, ADMIRAL RICHARD EVELYN

5019 Burleigh, Robert. *Black Whiteness: Admiral Byrd Alone in the Antarctic* (4–8). 1998, Simon & Schuster $16.95 (0-689-81299-X). An outstanding picture biography, with generous quotations from Byrd's diary that describe his great endurance and his lonely vigil in a small underground structure in the Antarctic. (Rev: BL 1/1–15/98*; HB 3–4/98; HBG 10/98; SLJ 3/98) [921]

CABEZA DE VACA, ALVAR NUNEZ

5020 Menard, Valerie. *Alvar Nunez Cabeza de Vaca* (5–7). Series: Latinos in American History. 2002, Mitchell Lane LB $19.95 (1-58415-153-6). A biography of the 16th-century Spanish nobleman who lived with Native Americans for eight years and who claimed Florida, Louisiana, and Texas for Spain. (Rev: BL 2/15/03; HBG 10/03) [921]

CABOT, JOHN

5021 Shields, Charles J. *John Cabot and the Rediscovery of North America* (4–8). Series: Explorers of New Worlds. 2001, Chelsea $19.75 (0-7910-6438-7); paper $8.95 (0-7910-6439-5). An absorbing biography that focuses on Cabot's expeditions at the end of the 15th century in search of a passage to Asia. (Rev: SLJ 3/02) [921]

CHAMPLAIN, SAMUEL DE

5022 Sherman, Josepha. *Samuel de Champlain: Explorer of the Great Lakes Region and Founder of Quebec* (4–7). Series: The Library of Explorers and Exploration. 2003, Rosen LB $32.00 (0-8239-3629-5). In addition to covering Champlain's life, this volume places his explorations in historical context and gives interesting information on the fur trade and relations with Native Americans. (Rev: SLJ 9/03) [971.01]

CID, EL

5023 Koslow, Philip. *El Cid* (5–8). Illus. Series: Hispanics of Achievement. 1993, Chelsea LB $21.95 (0-7910-1239-5). The story of Spain's national hero, who gained fame fighting the Moors. (Rev: BL 9/15/93) [921]

CLEMENS, ARABELLA

5024 Greenberg, Judith E., and Helen C. McKeever, eds. *A Pioneer Woman's Memoir* (6–9). Series: In Their Own Words. 1995, Watts LB $23.00 (0-531-11211-X). Excerpts from Arabella Clemens's memoirs chronicle a trek by covered wagon to Oregon. Black-and-white illustrations. (Rev: BL 9/1/95; SLJ 10/95; VOYA 2/96) [921]

COCHRAN, JACQUELINE

5025 Smith, Elizabeth Simpson. *Coming Out Right: The Story of Jacqueline Cochran, the First Woman Aviator to Break the Sound Barrier* (5–8). Illus. 1991, Walker LB $15.85 (0-8027-6989-6). From her impoverished childhood to her triumphs in the air and later, this is the story of a female aviation pioneer. (Rev: BL 4/15/91; SLJ 5/91) [921]

COLEMAN, BESSIE

5026 Fisher, Lillian M. *Brave Bessie: Flying Free* (4–7). Illus. 1995, Hendrick-Long $16.95 (0-937460-94-X). This biography tells of the struggles of Bessie Coleman, who became the first African American aviatrix in the United States. (Rev: BL 2/15/96; SLJ 2/96) [921]

5027 Hart, Philip S. *Up In the Air: The Story of Bessie Coleman* (5–8). 1996, Carolrhoda LB $16.95 (0-87614-949-2). Forced by restrictions in the Unit-ed States to get her training in France in the 1920s, Coleman became the first African American female airplane pilot. (Rev: BL 8/96; SLJ 8/96) [921]

5028 Plantz, Connie. *Bessie Coleman: First Black Woman Pilot* (4–8). 2001, Enslow LB $20.95 (0-7660-1545-9). This is a readable biography that breathes life into Coleman's childhood, training as a pilot, and tragic death. (Rev: HBG 3/02; SLJ 1/02) [921]

COLUMBUS, CHRISTOPHER

5029 Clare, John D., ed. *The Voyages of Christopher Columbus* (5–8). Illus. Series: Living History. 1992, Harcourt $16.95 (0-15-200507-2). Using actors and backdrops of the period, this account reconstructs each of Columbus's New World voyages. (Rev: SLJ 11/92) [921]

5030 Meltzer, Milton. *Columbus and the World Around Him* (7–10). 1990, Watts LB $20.00 (0-531-10899-6). A handsome addition to the literature about Columbus that also deals with the culture and attitudes of the Spanish at the time. (Rev: BL 4/15/90; SLJ 7/90) [970.01]

5031 Pelta, Kathy. *Discovering Christopher Columbus: How History Is Invented* (5–7). Illus. 1991, Lerner LB $23.93 (0-8225-4899-2). After telling what we know about Columbus, the author examines how myths and legends about him have grown over the years. (Rev: BL 10/1/91) [921]

5032 Sundel, Al. *Christopher Columbus and the Age of Exploration in World History* (8–12). Illus. Series: In World History. 2001, Enslow LB $20.95 (0-7660-1820-2). A detailed biography of Columbus that looks at the political climate of the time and discusses the atrocities inflicted on native peoples. (Rev: BL 3/1/02; HBG 10/02) [970.01]

COOK, CAPTAIN JAMES

5033 Gaines, Ann Graham. *Captain Cook Explores the Pacific* (8–12). Series: In World History. 2002, Enslow LB $20.95 (0-7660-1823-7). A mature account of the life and exploits of the famous British explorer known principally for his voyages in the Pacific Ocean. (Rev: BL 4/1/02; HBG 10/02; SLJ 8/02) [921]

5034 Lawlor, Laurie. *Magnificent Voyage: An American Adventurer on Captain James Cook's Final Expedition* (7–12). Illus. 2002, Holiday $22.95 (0-8234-1575-9). This absorbing account of Captain Cook's ill-fated efforts to locate the Northwest Passage gives details of the various difficulties encountered and of Cook's violent death. (Rev: BL 1/1–15/03; HBG 10/03; SLJ 2/03; VOYA 4/03) [910]

5035 Meltzer, Milton. *Captain James Cook: Three Times Around the World* (5–8). Series: Great Explorations. 2001, Marshall Cavendish LB $28.50 (0-7614-1240-9). Using both text and illustrations, this is a fine biography of the English mariner and explorer who, among other feats, explored the west coast of North America. (Rev: BL 4/1/02; HBG 3/02) [921]

DA GAMA, VASCO

5036 Draper, Allison Stark. *Vasco da Gama: The Portuguese Quest for a Sea Route from Europe to India* (5–8). Illus. Series: Library of Explorers and Exploration. 2003, Rosen LB $31.95 (0-8239-3632-5). Da Gama's achievements and brutal behavior are given equal exposure in this well-illustrated volume. (Rev: BL 6/1–15/03) [910]

5037 Kratoville, Betty Lou. *Vasco da Gama* (4–7). Series: Trade Route Explorers. 2000, High Noon paper $17.00 (1-57128-168-1). The story of the famous explorer who rounded the Cape of Good Hope and visited India, told in a simple, interesting account. (Rev: SLJ 3/01) [921]

DAVIS, JAN

5038 Greenberg, Keith E. *Stunt Woman: Daredevil Specialist* (4–7). Illus. Series: Risky Business. 1996, Blackbirch LB $24.94 (1-56711-159-9). The story of Jan Davis, who, for fun and profit, engages in such activities as jumping from airplanes. (Rev: BL 2/1/97; SLJ 1/97) [921]

DE SOTO, HERNANDO

5039 Gaines, Ann Graham. *Hernando de Soto and the Search for Gold* (8–12). Series: In World History. 2002, Enslow LB $20.95 (0-7660-1821-0). The story of the famous Spanish conquistador who explored the southeastern United States in his search for gold. (Rev: BL 4/1/02; HBG 10/02; SLJ 8/02) [921]

5040 Whiting, Jim. *Hernando de Soto* (5–7). Series: Latinos in American History. 2002, Mitchell Lane LB $19.95 (1-58415-147-1). A simple biography of the Spanish explorer who discovered the Mississippi River in the 16th century while traveling through what is now the southern United States. (Rev: BL 2/15/03; HBG 10/03; SLJ 6/03) [921]

DRAKE, SIR FRANCIS

5041 Duncan, Alice Smith. *Sir Francis Drake and the Struggle for an Ocean Empire* (6–9). Series: World Explorers. 1993, Chelsea LB $21.95 (0-7910-1302-2). The story of the intrepid Elizabethan explorer and adventurer who helped establish England's claims in the New World. (Rev: BL 3/15/93) [921]

5042 Gallagher, Jim. *Sir Francis Drake and the Foundation of a World Empire* (4–8). Series: Explorers of New Worlds. 2000, Chelsea $19.75 (0-7910-5950-2); paper $8.95 (0-7910-6160-4). This appealing and readable biography of Sir Francis Drake presents his life from childhood and details his major accomplishments, with photographs, sidebar features, documents, and maps. (Rev: HBG 10/01; SLJ 4/01) [921]

5043 Marrin, Albert. *The Sea King: Sir Francis Drake and His Times* (6–10). 1995, Atheneum $20.00 (0-689-31887-1). This biography includes Drake's trip around the world, his life as a privateer, and his role in defeating the Spanish Armada. (Rev: BL 7/95; SLJ 9/95) [921]

5044 Rice, Earle, Jr. *Sir Francis Drake: Navigator and Pirate* (5–8). Series: Great Explorations. 2002, Benchmark LB $19.95 (0-7614-1483-5). A profile of the 16th-century British explorer who circumnavigated the globe and fought the Spanish Armada, with maps, timeline, and reproductions. (Rev: HBG 10/03; SLJ 6/03) [942.05]

EARHART, AMELIA

5045 Earhart, Amelia. *The Fun of It: Random Records of My Own Flying and of Women in Aviation* (7–12). 1990, Omnigraphics $42.00 (1-55888-980-9). Autobiographical in part, this account is also a tribute to other women aviation pioneers. First published in 1932. [921]

5046 Lauber, Patricia. *Lost Star: The Story of Amelia Earhart* (5–7). Illus. 1988, Scholastic paper $4.50 (0-590-41159-4). A candid biography of the famed lost aviator. (Rev: BL 10/1/88; SLJ 12/88) [921]

5047 Leder, Jane. *Amelia Earhart* (6–9). Illus. 1990, Greenhaven LB $16.95 (0-89908-070-7). A thorough biography and good coverage of theories about Earhart's disappearance. (Rev: BL 3/1/90; SLJ 5/90) [921]

5048 Parr, Jan. *Amelia Earhart: First Lady of Flight* (5–8). Illus. Series: Book Report Biographies. 1997, Watts LB $22.00 (0-531-11407-4). A short, useful biography that relates the public and private life of this adventurer who broke many records and helped open up the world of flight for women. (Rev: BL 11/15/97; HBG 3/98; SLJ 11/97) [921]

5049 Sloate, Susan. *Amelia Earhart: Challenging the Skies* (5–8). Illus. 1990, Fawcett paper $6.99 (0-449-90396-6). The aviator's life story is told along with an examination of all the theories concerning her disappearance. (Rev: SLJ 6/90) [921]

5050 Szabo, Corinne. *Sky Pioneer: A Photobiography of Amelia Earhart* (4–8). Illus. 1997, National Geographic $16.00 (0-7922-3737-4). A lavishly illustrated biography of Earhart that concentrates more on her accomplishments than her disappearance. (Rev: BL 2/15/97; SLJ 4/97) [921]

EXQUEMELIN

5051 Exquemelin, A. O. *Exquemelin and the Pirates of the Caribbean* (5–8). Ed. by Jane Shuter. Illus. Series: History Eyewitness. 1995, Raintree Steck-Vaughn LB $24.26 (0-8114-8282-0). An edited version of the exciting journal of the 17th-century Frenchman who joined a pirate gang as a barber-surgeon. (Rev: BL 4/15/95) [921]

FREMONT, JOHN CHARLES

5052 Faber, Harold. *John Charles Fremont: Pathfinder to the West* (5–8). Series: Great Explorations. 2002, Benchmark LB $19.95 (0-7614-1481-9). A profile of the 19th-century explorer who helped open the American West to settlers, with maps, timeline, and reproductions. (Rev: HBG 10/03; SLJ 6/03) [979]

GRAHAM, ROBIN LEE

5053 Graham, Robin Lee, and Derek Gill. *Dove* (7–12). Illus. 1991, HarperCollins paper $13.00 (0-06-092047-5). A five-year solo voyage around the world and a tender romance with a girl the author met in Fiji. [921]

HENRY THE NAVIGATOR

5054 Gallagher, Aileen. *Prince Henry the Navigator: Pioneer of Modern Exploration* (5–8). Illus. Series: Library of Explorers and Exploration. 2003, Rosen LB $31.95 (0-8239-3621-X). During the 15th century, Prince Henry of Portugal spurred others to seek a route to India, claim new territory, and spread Christianity. (Rev: BL 6/1–15/03) [946.9]

HENSON, MATTHEW

5055 Gilman, Michael. *Matthew Henson* (6–10). Illus. 1988, Chelsea LB $21.95 (1-55546-590-0). The life story of the African American explorer who accompanied Peary on expeditions in search of the North Pole. (Rev: BL 6/15/88; SLJ 4/88) [921]

HILLARY, SIR EDMUND

5056 Brennan, Kristine. *Sir Edmund Hillary: Modern-Day Explorer* (4–8). Series: Explorers of New Worlds. 2000, Chelsea $19.75 (0-7910-5953-7); paper $8.95 (0-7910-6163-9). An appealing overview of the life and accomplishments of the mountaineer and explorer, with photographs and maps. (Rev: SLJ 4/01) [796.52]

5057 Coburn, Broughton. *Triumph on Everest: A Photobiography of Sir Edmund Hillary* (5–8). 2000,

National Geographic $17.95 (0-7922-7114-9). Using many quotations and excellent photographs, this work records the lifetime accomplishments of one of the first men to reach the top of Mount Everest. (Rev: BCCB 9/00; HBG 3/01; SLJ 10/00) [921]

5058 Stewart, Whitney. *Sir Edmund Hillary: To Everest and Beyond* (5–8). Photos by Anne B. Keiser. Illus. Series: Newsmakers. 1996, Lerner LB $30.35 (0-8225-4927-1). The life of this famous mountain climber is presented with interesting details about his other interests, including bee keeping, conservation, and helping the Sherpa people. (Rev: SLJ 9/96) [921]

HUDSON, HENRY

5059 Saffer, Barbara. *Henry Hudson: Ill-Fated Explorer of North America's Coast* (4–8). Series: Explorers of New Worlds. 2001, Chelsea $19.95 (0-7910-6436-0); paper $8.95 (0-7910-6437-9). This absorbing biography focuses on Hudson's early 17th-century expeditions from England in search of a sea route to the Far East. (Rev: HBG 10/02; SLJ 3/02) [921]

JOHNSON, OSA

5060 Arruda, Suzanne Middendorf. *From Kansas to Cannibals: The Story of Osa Johnson* (6–8). Series: Avisson Young Adult. 2001, Avisson paper $19.95 (1-888105-50-X). This is the biography of an intrepid woman who, with her husband, traveled to remote areas of Africa and the South Pacific from the 1920s to the 1940s, coming across wild beasts and cannibal headhunters. (Rev: SLJ 11/01) [910]

LA SALLE, CAVELIER DE

5061 Faber, Harold. *La Salle: Down the Mississippi* (5–8). Series: Great Explorations. 2001, Marshall Cavendish LB $28.50 (0-7614-1239-5). The exciting story of the French explorer who traveled down the Mississippi River to the Gulf of Mexico and named the region Louisiana. (Rev: BL 4/1/02; HBG 3/02; SLJ 3/02) [921]

LEWIS AND CLARK

5062 Edwards, Judith. *Lewis and Clark's Journey of Discovery* (6–10). Series: In American History. 1998, Enslow LB $20.95 (0-7660-1127-5). This story of the overland expedition to find the Pacific Ocean begins with Lewis and Clark getting their commission from Jefferson and ends with their return home two years later. (Rev: BL 2/15/99; HBG 9/99) [921]

5063 Streissguth, Thomas. *Lewis and Clark: Explorers of the Northwest* (4–9). Series: Historical American Biographies. 1998, Enslow LB $20.95 (0-7660-1016-3). The story of the two intrepid explorers who made their way overland to the Pacific Ocean. (Rev: BL 8/98) [921]

LINDBERGH, CHARLES A.

5064 Denenberg, Barry. *An American Hero: The True Story of Charles A. Lindbergh* (8–12). Illus. 1996, Scholastic paper $16.95 (0-590-46923-1). Beginning with Lindbergh's transatlantic flight, this fascinating biography then recounts the story of his early years followed by details about his multifaceted life. (Rev: BL 3/15/96*; BR 9–10/96; SLJ 7/96; VOYA 6/96) [921]

5065 Giblin, James Cross. *Charles A. Lindbergh: A Human Hero* (6–12). Illus. 1997, Clarion $21.00 (0-395-63389-3). A book about the public and private life of one of America's heroes that deals with his pro-Nazi sympathies and anti-Semitism, the adoration he received for his transatlantic flight, and pity the public felt for the kidnapping and murder of his child. (Rev: BL 9/15/97; HBG 3/98; SLJ 11/97*; VOYA 6/98) [921]

5066 Kent, Zachary. *Charles Lindbergh and the Spirit of St. Louis* (6–10). Series: In American History. 2001, Enslow LB $20.95 (0-7660-1683-8). The life and accomplishment of Lindbergh are recreated, including the first solo trip by airplane across the Atlantic Ocean he made when only 25 years old. (Rev: BL 8/1/01; HBG 10/01) [921]

5067 Koopman, Andy. *Charles Lindbergh* (7–12). Series: The Importance Of. 2003, Gale LB $27.45 (1-59018-245-6). Using many original sources, this is a lively biography of the aviation hero who captured the hearts of Americans. (Rev: BL 6/1–15/03; SLJ 8/03) [921]

5068 Meachum, Virginia. *Charles Lindbergh: American Hero of Flight* (6–10). Series: People to Know. 2002, Enslow LB $20.95 (0-7660-1535-1). A well-illustrated, appealing biography of the American hero of aviation with insights into his personal life. (Rev: BL 9/15/02; HBG 10/02; SLJ 9/02) [921]

MACCREADY, PAUL B.

5069 Taylor, Richard L. *The First Human-Powered Flight: The Story of Paul B. MacCready and His Airplane, the Gossamer Condor* (4–8). Illus. Series: First Books. 1995, Watts LB $23.00 (0-531-20185-6). After an introduction to the history of human-powered flight, this account focuses on MacCready's amazing flight in 1977. (Rev: SLJ 11/95) [921]

MCNAIR, RONALD

5070 Naden, Corinne J. *Ronald McNair* (5–8). Illus. Series: Black Americans of Achievement. 1991,

Chelsea LB $21.95 (0-7910-1133-X). An inspirational biography of the second African American astronaut, a victim of the *Challenger* disaster. (Rev: BL 4/1/91; SLJ 3/91) [921]

MAGELLAN, FERDINAND

5071 Burnett, Betty. *Ferdinand Magellan: The First Voyage Around the World* (4–7). Series: The Library of Explorers and Exploration. 2003, Rosen LB $32.00 (0-8239-3617-1). In addition to covering Magellan's life, this volume places his 16th-century voyage in historical context and gives interesting information on the funding of such expeditions and life at sea. (Rev: SLJ 9/03) [910]

5072 Levinson, Nancy Smiler. *Magellan and the First Voyage Around the World* (5–8). Illus. 2001, Clarion $19.00 (0-395-98773-3). A straightforward biography of Magellan, with information on his times and insightful analysis of his character. (Rev: BCCB 2/02; BL 2/1/02; HB 1–2/02; HBG 3/02; SLJ 1/02) [910.92]

5073 Meltzer, Milton. *Ferdinand Magellan: First to Sail Around the World* (5–8). Illus. Series: Great Explorations. 2001, Benchmark LB $28.50 (0-7614-1238-7). An encompassing look at Magellan's achievements is complemented by excellent illustrations, a timeline, and Web site information. (Rev: BL 1/1–15/02; HBG 3/02; SLJ 3/02) [910]

5074 Stefoff, Rebecca. *Ferdinand Magellan and the Discovery of the World Ocean* (7–12). Illus. 1990, Chelsea LB $21.95 (0-7910-1291-3). Using many quotations from original sources, this is an engrossing account of the explorer and his voyage. (Rev: BL 6/15/90) [921]

MALLORY, GEORGE

5075 Salkeld, Audrey. *Mystery on Everest: A Photobiography of George Mallory* (5–8). Illus. Series: Photobiography. 2000, National Geographic $17.95 (0-7922-7222-6). The life of the famous English mountain climber George Mallory, who died in 1924 in a climbing accident on Mount Everest, written by a member of the team that discovered his body in 1999. (Rev: BCCB 9/00; BL 11/1/00; HBG 3/01; SLJ 11/00) [921]

MARKHAM, BERYL

5076 Gourley, Catherine. *Beryl Markham: Never Turn Back* (6–10). Series: Bernard Biography. 1997, Conari Pr. paper $6.95 (1-57324-073-7). An exciting biography of the unconventional Englishwoman who was the first person to fly the Atlantic from east to west. (Rev: BL 3/15/97; SLJ 5/97; VOYA 12/97) [921]

MARTIN, JESSE

5077 Martin, Jesse. *Lionheart: A Journey of the Human Spirit* (8–12). 2002, Allen & Unwin paper $14.95 (1-86508-347-X). Martin details the exciting events and extreme isolation of his inspiring round-the-world solo voyage at the age of 17. (Rev: SLJ 5/02; VOYA 6/02) [910.4]

MORGAN, SIR HENRY

5078 Marrin, Albert. *Terror of the Spanish Main: Sir Henry Morgan and His Buccaneers* (7–12). 1999, Dutton $21.99 (0-525-45942-1). The story of Henry Morgan, a murderous cutthroat who, in the name of the English flag, wreaked havoc on Spanish colonies, using Jamaica as his home base. (Rev: BL 1/1–15/99; HB 3–4/99; HBG 9/99; SLJ 1/99*; VOYA 8/99) [921]

O'GRADY, SCOTT

5079 O'Grady, Scott, and Michael French. *Basher Five-Two: The True Story of F-16 Fighter Pilot Captain Scott O'Grady* (5–9). Illus. 1997, Doubleday $16.95 (0-385-32300-X). The true story of Scott O'Grady's ordeal after his F-16 was shot down by the Serbs in Bosnia. (Rev: BCCB 7–8/97; BL 7/97; BR 11–12/97; HB 7–8/97; SLJ 7/97) [921]

PEARY, ROBERT E.

5080 Calvert, Patricia. *Robert E. Peary: To the Top of the World* (5–8). Series: Great Explorations. 2001, Marshall Cavendish LB $28.50 (0-7614-1242-5). The exciting story of the Arctic explorer who, after several attempts, reached the North Pole in 1909. (Rev: BL 4/1/02; HBG 3/02; SLJ 3/02) [921]

5081 Dwyer, Christopher. *Robert Peary and the Quest for the North Pole* (6–9). Series: World Explorers. 1992, Chelsea LB $21.95 (0-7910-1316-2). The exciting story of Peary's expeditions to reach the South Pole and of the courage and endurance displayed. (Rev: BL 2/1/93) [921]

PFETZER, MARK

5082 Pfetzer, Mark, and Jack Galvin. *Within Reach: My Everest Story* (7–12). 1998, Dutton $16.95 (0-525-46089-6). The autobiography of the youngest person to climb Mount Everest, with material on how he became interested in mountain climbing. (Rev: BL 11/15/98; SLJ 11/98; VOYA 2/99) [921]

POLO, MARCO

5083 Otfinoski, Steven. *Marco Polo: To China and Back* (4–8). Series: Great Explorations. 2002,

Benchmark LB $19.95 (0-7614-1480-0). Readable text accompanied by many illustrations and sidebar features traces Polo's life and adventures. (Rev: HBG 10/03; SLJ 5/03) [915.04]

PONCE DE LEÓN, JUAN

5084 Dolan, Sean. *Juan Ponce de León* (5–9). Series: Hispanics of Achievement. 1995, Chelsea LB $21.95 (0-7910-2023-1). The story of the Spanish explorer who after accompanying Columbus on his second voyage set out on his own and eventually became the discoverer of Florida. (Rev: BL 10/15/95) [921]

5085 Whiting, Jim. *Juan Ponce de Leon* (5–7). Series: Latinos in American History. 2002, Mitchell Lane LB $19.95 (1-58415-149-8). This is the story of the man who is credited with discovering Florida in 1513 while searching for the fountain of youth. (Rev: BL 2/15/03; HBG 10/03; SLJ 6/03) [921]

5086 Worth, Richard. *Ponce de Leon and the Age of Spanish Exploration in World History* (5–9). Series: In World History. 2003, Enslow LB $20.95 (0-7660-1940-3). As well as a biography of this great adventurer from Spain, this book describes the work of other Spanish explorers in the Americas. (Rev: BL 11/15/03) [921]

POWELL, JOHN WESLEY

5087 Bruns, Roger A. *John Wesley Powell: Explorer of the Grand Canyon* (5–8). Illus. Series: Historical American Biographies. 1997, Enslow LB $20.95 (0-89490-783-2). This biography tells about Powell's youth, education, and Civil War days, as well as his many expeditions and research activities. (Rev: SLJ 10/97) [921]

RALEIGH, SIR WALTER

5088 Aronson, Marc. *Sir Walter Ralegh and the Quest for El Dorado* (7–10). 2000, Clarion $20.00 (0-395-84827-X). The fascinating life and times of the colorful Elizabethan explorer, with illustrations, maps, and quotations from Sir Walter himself. (Rev: BL 8/00; HB 9–10/00; HBG 9/00; SLJ 7/00*) [942.05]

RIDE, SALLY

5089 Camp, Carole Ann. *Sally Ride: First American Woman in Space* (6–10). Illus. Series: People to Know. 1997, Enslow LB $20.95 (0-89490-829-4). A lively account of Sally Ride's work as an astronaut and astrophysicist, with material on her training, shuttle flight, and life in microgravity. (Rev: BL 1/1–15/98; HBG 3/98; SLJ 12/97) [921]

5090 Hurwitz, Jane, and Sue Hurwitz. *Sally Ride: Shooting for the Stars* (5–8). 1989, Ballantine paper $6.99 (0-449-90394-X). An interestingly written account in paperback format of the female space pioneer. (Rev: BL 12/15/89; BR 3–4/90; SLJ 2/90; VOYA 2/90) [921]

5091 Kramer, Barbara. *Sally Ride: A Space Biography* (4–8). Illus. Series: Countdown to Space. 1998, Enslow LB $18.95 (0-89490-975-4). A brief, well-written biography of Sally Ride that describes her training, experience, and space flights. (Rev: BL 4/1/98; BR 9–10/98; HBG 9/98; SLJ 5/98) [921]

SACAGAWEA

5092 White, Alana J. *Sacagawea: Westward with Lewis and Clark* (4–8). Series: Native American Biographies. 1997, Enslow LB $20.95 (0-89490-867-7). A well-written account of this gallant woman's life, accompanied by a reading list, chapter notes, and a chronology. (Rev: BL 4/15/97; SLJ 8/97; VOYA 8/97) [921]

SERRA, JUNÍPERO

5093 Dolan, Sean. *Junípero Serra* (5–9). Series: Hispanics of Achievement. 1991, Chelsea LB $21.95 (0-7910-1255-7). The story of the devoted Spanish Franciscan missionary who was responsible for founding the famous missions on the coast of California. (Rev: BL 11/1/91; SLJ 2/92) [921]

5094 Genet, Donna. *Father Junípero Serra* (6–9). Illus. Series: Hispanic Biographies. 1996, Enslow LB $20.95 (0-89490-762-X). This book divides its contents equally between a biography of Father Junípero Serra and the story of the founding, history, and significance of the California missions. (Rev: BL 10/15/96; SLJ 9/96) [979.4]

5095 Whiting, Jim. *Junípero José Serra* (5–7). Series: Latinos in American History. 2003, Mitchell Lane LB $19.95 (1-58415-187-0). The story of the monk who was responsible for founding nine California missions and converting thousands of Native Americans to Christianity. (Rev: BL 1/1–15/04) [921]

SHACKLETON, SIR ERNEST

5096 Calvert, Patricia. *Sir Ernest Shackleton: By Endurance We Conquer* (4–8). Series: Great Explorations. 2002, Benchmark LB $19.95 (0-7614-1485-1). Readable text accompanied by many illustrations and sidebar features traces Shackleton's life and adventures. (Rev: HBG 10/03; SLJ 5/03) [919.8904]

5097 Johnson, Rebecca. *Ernest Shackleton: Gripped by the Antarctic* (6–10). Illus. Series: Trailblazer Biographies. 2003, Carolrhoda LB $25.26 (0-87614-920-4). Photographs, anecdotes, and quotations are sprinkled throughout this exciting account of Shackleton's youth and famous expeditions. (Rev: BL 6/1–15/03; HBG 10/03; SLJ 8/03; VOYA 8/03) [919.8]

5098 Kostyal, K. M. *Trial by Ice: A Photobiography of Sir Ernest Shackleton* (4–8). Illus. 1999, National Geographic $17.95 (0-7922-7393-1). A biography that details the life of Sir Ernest Shackleton, his 1915 Antarctic expedition, and the survival of the explorers aboard the *Endurance*. (Rev: BCCB 12/99; BL 12/1/99; HBG 3/00; SLJ 3/00) [921]

SMITH, JOHN

5099 Doherty, Kieran. *To Conquer Is to Live: The Life of Captain John Smith of Jamestown* (6–8). 2001, Twenty-First Century LB $23.90 (0-7613-1820-8). A compelling biography that includes details of Smith's adventures before coming to the New World. (Rev: HBG 3/02; SLJ 12/01) [973.2]

Artists, Authors, Composers, and Entertainers

Collective

5100 Aronson, Virginia. *Literature* (6–9). Series: Female Firsts in Their Fields. 1999, Chelsea $18.65 (0-7910-5146-3). Biographies of pioneering women authors Phillis Wheatley, Edith Wharton, Pearl Buck, Toni Morrison, Alice Walker, and Judy Blume. (Rev: BL 5/15/99; HBG 9/99) [920]

5101 Barber, Nicola, and Patrick Lee-Browne. *Poets of the First World War* (7–9). Illus. Series: Writers in Britain. 2001, Evans Brothers $19.95 (0-237-52239-X). Poets including Wilfred Owen and Siegfried Sassoon are introduced with brief biographical information and excerpts from poems. (Rev: SLJ 2/02) [811]

5102 Barnes, Rachel. *Abstract Expressionists* (6–8). Series: Artists in Profile. 2003, Heinemann LB $25.64 (1-58810-644-6). An introduction to the art and artists of this period, with profiles of major artists and examples of their works. Also use *Harlem Renaissance Artists* (2003). (Rev: HBG 10/03; LMC 10/03; SLJ 7/03) [759.13]

5103 Benedict, Kitty, and Karen Covington. *The Literary Crowd: Writers, Critics, Scholars, Wits* (5–9). Series: Remarkable Women. 2000, Raintree Steck-Vaughn LB $32.82 (0-8172-5732-2). Profiles of 150 women writers and others associated with the literary world, including Virginia Woolf, Jane Austen, and Maya Angelou. (Rev: SLJ 8/00) [920]

5104 Bredeson, Carmen. *American Writers of the 20th Century* (5–8). Illus. 1996, Enslow LB $20.95 (0-89490-704-2). Ten writers for adults, including Toni Morrison and F. Scott Fitzgerald, are introduced in brief profiles. (Rev: BL 6/1 15/96; BR 9–10/96; SLJ 9/96) [920]

5105 Chiu, Christina. *Lives of Notable Asian Americans: Literature and Education* (6–10). Illus. Series: The Asian American Experience. 1995, Chelsea LB $19.95 (0-7910-2182-3). Brief biographies of important Asian American writers and educators. (Rev: BL 1/1–15/96; BR 9–10/96) [920]

5106 Covington, Karen. *Creators: Artists, Designers, Craftswomen* (5–9). Series: Remarkable Women. 2000, Raintree Steck-Vaughn LB $32.85 (0-8172-5725-X). Mary Cassatt, Georgia O'Keefe, Frido Kahlo, and Beatrix Potter are four of the 150 female artists celebrated in this collective biography. (Rev: BL 6/1–15/00; SLJ 8/00) [920]

5107 Datnow, Claire. *American Science Fiction and Fantasy Writers* (5–8). Illus. Series: Collective Biographies. 1999, Enslow LB $20.95 (0-7660-1090-2). Science fiction and fantasy writers profiled in this book include Asimov, Heinlein, Bradbury, Anderson, Norton, L'Engle, and Le Guin. (Rev: BL 4/15/99; VOYA 6/99) [920]

5108 Davidson, Sue. *Getting the Real Story: Nellie Bly and Ida B. Wells* (6–10). 1992, Seal Pr. paper $8.95 (1-878067-16-8). A dual biography of two women who broke down barriers in journalism and how their different races shaped their individual stories. (Rev: BL 3/1/92; SLJ 7/92) [920]

5109 Earls, Irene. *Young Musicians in World History* (7–12). 2002, Greenwood $44.95 (0-313-31442-X). Thirteen musicians whose skills were recognized before the age of 25 are profiled, ranging from Bach and Beethoven to Louis Armstrong, Bob Dylan, and John Lennon. (Rev: LMC 2/03; SLJ 1/03) [780]

5110 Ehrlich, Amy, ed. *When I Was Your Age* (5–8). 1996, Candlewick $15.99 (1-56402-306-0). Ten well known writers — including Avi, Susan Cooper, and Nicholasa Mohr — recall incidents from their childhoods. (Rev: BCCB 4/96; BL 4/15/96; BR 9–10/96; SLJ 8/96; VOYA 10/96) [810.9]

5111 Faber, Doris, and Harold Faber. *Great Lives: American Literature* (5–9). 1995, Simon & Schuster $24.00 (0-684-19448-1). Ten-page biographies of 30 noted U.S. writers, from Poe and Twain to Hemingway. (Rev: BL 9/1/95; SLJ 6/95; VOYA 12/95) [920]

5112 Ford, Carin T. *Legends of American Dance and Choreography* (5–7). Series: Collective Biographies. 2000, Enslow LB $20.95 (0-7660-1378-2). This collective work presents 10 short biographies of such dance luminaries as George Balanchine and Martha Graham. (Rev: BL 6/1–15/00; HBG 10/00; SLJ 7/00) [920]

5113 Gaines, Ann. *Entertainment and Performing Arts* (6–9). Series: Female Firsts in Their Fields. 1999, Chelsea $18.95 (0-7910-5145-5). Emphasizing their importance as role models, this book discusses the lives of six pioneering women in the fields of the performing arts and entertainment. (Rev: BL 5/15/99; HBG 9/99) [920]

5114 Gaines, Ann Graham. *American Photographers: Capturing the Image* (4–7). Series: Collective Biographies. 2002, Enslow LB $20.95 (0-7660-1833-4). The lives and contributions of 10 well-known photographers are presented with photographs and a brief history of photography. (Rev: HBG 10/02; SLJ 10/02) [921]

5115 Glenn, Patricia Brown. *Discover America's Favorite Architects* (6–9). Illus. 1996, Preservation paper $19.95 (0-471-14354-5). The lives and careers of 10 major American architects, including Thomas Jefferson, Frederick Law Olmsted, Louis Henri Sullivan, Frank Lloyd Wright, Julia Morgan, Philip Johnson, and I. M. Pei. (Rev: SLJ 1/97) [921]

5116 Gourse, Leslie. *Fancy Fretwork: The Great Jazz Guitarists* (8–12). Illus. Series: Art of Jazz. 1999, Watts LB $25.00 (0-531-11565-8). Gourse profiles some of the genre's best guitarists, providing quotations from the artists and a brief history of the art form. Also use *Timekeepers: The Great Jazz Drummers* (1999). (Rev: BL 11/15/99) [787.87]

5117 Gourse, Leslie. *Swingers and Crooners: The Art of Jazz Singing* (6–10). 1997, Watts LB $23.00 (0-531-11321-3). Through the biographies of such great singers as Ella Fitzgerald, Louis Armstrong, Bing Crosby, and Harry Connick, Jr., the history of jazz is covered, from its roots in gospel and blues, through the big band and bebop eras, to the singers of today. (Rev: SLJ 6/97) [920]

5118 Halliwell, Sarah, ed. *The 18th Century: Artists, Writers, and Composers* (6–9). Series: Who and When? 1997, Raintree Steck-Vaughn LB $29.97 (0-8172-4727-0). A discussion of the lives and works of artists including Watteau, Hogarth, and David; composers including Vivaldi, Bach, and Haydn; and writers including Defoe, Swift, and Voltaire. (Rev: BL 12/15/97; SLJ 2/98) [700]

5119 Halliwell, Sarah, ed. *The 17th Century: Artists, Writers, and Composers* (6–9). Series: Who and When? 1997, Raintree Steck-Vaughn LB $29.97 (0-8172-4726-2). This work profiles artists including Caravaggio, Rubens, Velazquez, and Rembrandt and discusses works by such writers as Shakespeare, Donne, and Milton and the composer Monteverdi. (Rev: BL 12/15/97; SLJ 2/98) [700]

5120 Hardy, P. Stephen, and Sheila Jackson Hardy. *Extraordinary People of the Harlem Renaissance* (5–9). Series: Extraordinary People. 2000, Children's LB $39.00 (0-516-21201-X); paper $16.95 (0-516-27170-9). Black-and-white photographs, reproductions of sheet music, and interesting artwork enhance the extensive information on the artists, photographers, musicians, writers, and poets of Harlem in the 1920s and 1930s. (Rev: BL 11/15/00; SLJ 6/01; VOYA 4/01) [700]

5121 Hasday, Judy L. *Extraordinary People in the Movies* (5–9). Series: Extraordinary People. 2003, Children's LB $39.00 (0-516-22348-8); paper $16.95 (0-516-27857-6). Brief biographies of individuals associated with the movie business are arranged chronologically by date of birth and interspersed with short essays on related topics. (Rev: SLJ 7/03) [791.43]

5122 Hill, Anne E. *Broadcasting and Journalism* (6–9). Series: Female Firsts in Their Fields. 1999, Chelsea $18.65 (0-7910-5139-0). The biographies of six pioneering women in the mass media and how their work became an inspiration for other women. (Rev: BL 5/15/99; HBG 9/99) [920]

5123 Hill, Anne E. *Ten American Movie Directors: The Men Behind the Camera* (7–12). Series: Collective Biographies. 2003, Enslow LB $20.95 (0-7660-1836-9). This collective biography features profiles of 10 famous movie directors, including Alfred Hitchcock, Frank Capra, Woody Allen, Martin Scorsese, George Lucas, Spike Lee, and Steven Spielberg. (Rev: BL 6/1–15/03; HBG 10/03) [920]

5124 Hill, Christine M. *Ten Hispanic American Authors* (6–12). Illus. Series: Collective Biographies. 2002, Enslow LB $20.95 (0-7660-1541-6). Ten Hispanic Americans — including Sandra Cisneros, Gary Soto, and Piri Thomas — are introduced here, with information on how they became successful writers. (Rev: BL 5/1/02; HBG 10/02; SLJ 6/02) [810.9]

5125 Hill, Christine M. *Ten Terrific Authors for Teens* (5–7). Series: Collective Biographies. 2000, Enslow LB $20.95 (0-7660-1380-4). Among the authors profiled are Judy Blume, Virginia Hamilton, Julius Lester, Lois Lowry, Katherine Paterson, Gary Soto, and Lawrence Yep. (Rev: BL 9/15/00; HBG 10/01; SLJ 12/00; VOYA 8/01) [920]

5126 Hipple, Ted. *Writers for Young Adults* (7–12). 1997, Macmillan $310.00 (0-684-80474-3). This resource presents biographical and critical essays on 129 classic and contemporary writers for young adults, from Joan Aiken to Paul Zindel. (Rev: BL 10/15/97; SLJ 8/98) [920]

5127 Hirschfelder, Arlene. *Artists and Craftspeople* (8–12). Illus. Series: American Indian Lives. 1994, Facts on File $25.00 (0-8160-2960-1). This book profiles 18 Native Americans including Nampeyo, Maria Martinez, and Oscar Howe, who are famous in history or contemporary times for their contributions to craftwork and art. (Rev: BL 11/15/94; SLJ 11/94; VOYA 4/95) [920]

5128 Holme, Merilyn, and Bridget McKenzie. *Expressionists* (5–9). Series: Artists in Profile. 2002, Heinemann LB $28.50 (1-58810-647-0). Introduces the movement and gives biographical information on the major artists and their key works, with reproductions and photographs. Also use *Impressionists* and *Pop Artists* (both 2002). (Rev: HBG 3/03; SLJ 3/03) [759.06]

5129 Horitz, Margot F. *A Female Focus: Great Women Photographers* (7–12). Illus. Series: Women Then — Women Now. 1996, Watts LB $25.00 (0-531-11302-7). This collective biography highlights the lives of several dozen female photographers, from early women who helped their photographer-husbands to photographers including Margaret Bourke-White, Dorothea Lange, and Annie Leibovitz. (Rev: BL 3/15/97; SLJ 2/97; VOYA 8/97) [920]

5130 Ishizuka, Kathy. *Asian American Authors* (5–9). Series: Collective Biographies. 2000, Enslow LB $20.95 (0-7660-1376-6). Writers for children (including Laurence Yep) and for adults (such as Amy Tan) are included in this collective biography of 10 Asian American writers. (Rev: HBG 10/01; SLJ 3/01) [920]

5131 Jackson, Nancy. *Photographers: History and Culture Through the Camera* (7–12). Illus. Series: American Profiles. 1997, Facts on File $25.00 (0-8160-3358-7). The life stories of eight famous photographers, including Mathew Brady, Alfred Stieglitz, Edward Steichen, Dorothea Lange, and Gordon Parks. (Rev: BL 5/1/97; SLJ 7/97) [920]

5132 Kallen, Stuart A. *Great Composers* (6–9). Series: History Makers. 2000, Lucent LB $18.96 (1-56006-669-5). Music is covered from the Renaissance through jazz and rock through brief profiles of such composers as Bach, Mozart, and Andrew Lloyd Webber. (Rev: BL 6/1–15/00; HBG 3/01) [920]

5133 Kallen, Stuart A. *Great Male Comedians* (6–9). Series: History Makers. 2001, Lucent $24.95 (1-56006-739-X). After a general background chapter, this book contains brief profiles of such comedians as Groucho Marx, Bill Cosby, Eddie Murphy,

John Belushi, and Jim Carrey. (Rev: BL 8/1/01) [920]

5134 Keeley, Jennifer. *Women Pop Stars* (6–9). Series: History Makers. 2001, Lucent $24.95 (1-56006-814-0). This short book profiles six women who gained importance in pop music, including Tina Turner, Madonna, and Lauren Hill. (Rev: BL 8/1/01) [920]

5135 Knapp, Ron. *American Legends of Rock* (6–9). Illus. 1996, Enslow LB $20.95 (0-89490-709-3). Brief biographies of such personalities as Chuck Berry, Elvis Presley, Buddy Holly, and Jimi Hendrix. (Rev: BL 11/15/96; SLJ 12/96; VOYA 2/97) [920]

5136 Krull, Kathleen. *Lives of the Musicians: Good Times, Bad Times (And What the Neighbors Thought)* (5–8). Illus. 1993, Harcourt $20.00 (0-15-248010-2). Biographies of 16 musical giants, from Vivaldi, Mozart, and Beethoven to Gershwin, Joplin, and Woody Guthrie. (Rev: BL 4/1/93*; SLJ 5/93*) [920]

5137 Lester, Julius. *The Blues Singers: Ten Who Rocked the World* (5–8). 2001, Hyperion $15.99 (0-7868-0463-7). Profiles of 10 African Americans who sang the blues or were influenced by the blues are accompanied by attention-grabbing illustrations and a good discography. (Rev: BL 6/1–15/01; HBG 10/01; SLJ 6/01*; VOYA 8/01) [781.643]

5138 Madison, Bob. *American Horror Writers* (7–12). Series: Collective Biographies. 2001, Enslow LB $20.95 (0-7660-1379-0). Edgar Allan Poe, H. P. Lovecraft, Dean Koontz, R. L. Stine, Anne Rice, and Stephen King are among the 10 writers profiled here. (Rev: HBG 10/01; SLJ 4/01) [813]

5139 Marquez, Heron. *Latin Sensations* (5–9). 2001, Lerner LB $25.26 (0-8225-4993-X); paper $12.75 (0-8225-9695-4). A collective biography that features profiles of Selena, Ricky Martin, Jennifer Lopez, Marc Anthony, and Enrique Iglesias. (Rev: HBG 10/01; SLJ 3/01) [920]

5140 Mass, Wendy. *Great Authors of Children's Literature* (6–10). Series: History Makers. 2000, Lucent LB $18.96 (1-56006-589-3). From early children's books to the present, this is a collection of brief biographies of trailblazers in the field of children's literature including Milne, Dahl, Dr. Seuss, Sendak, and Judy Blume. (Rev: BL 3/15/00; HBG 9/00; SLJ 6/00) [920]

5141 Mazer, Anne, ed. *Going Where I'm Coming From: Memoirs of American Youth* (8–12). 1995, Persea paper $7.95 (0-89255-206-9). Writers from different cultures talk about growing up and the incidents in their lives that helped to establish their identities. (Rev: BL 1/15/95; VOYA 5/95) [818]

5142 Meehan, Elizabeth. *Twentieth-Century American Writers* (6–9). Series: History Makers. 2000, Lucent LB $18.96 (1-56006-671-7). This brief volume contains profiles of a few of the major American writers of the past century. (Rev: BL 9/15/00; HBG 3/01; SLJ 11/00) [920]

5143 Mour, Stanley L. *American Jazz Musicians* (6–9). Series: Collective Biographies. 1998, Enslow LB $20.95 (0-7660-1027-9). Ten greats of jazz are profiled chronologically, including Scott Joplin, Louis Armstrong, Duke Ellington, Charlie Parker, Miles Davis, and John Coltrane. (Rev: HBG 3/99; SLJ 1/99) [920]

5144 Orgill, Roxane. *Shout, Sister, Shout! Ten Girl Singers Who Shaped a Century* (5–8). 2001, Simon & Schuster $19.95 (0-689-81991-9). Orgill has chosen one female singer to represent each decade of the 20th century, revealing much about social mores and technological innovations as well as musical styles. (Rev: BL 1/1–15/01*; HBG 10/01; SLJ 5/01; VOYA 4/01) [970]

5145 Otfinoski, Steven. *African Americans in the Performing Arts* (8–12). Illus. Series: A to Z of African Americans. 2003, Facts on File $44.00 (0-8160-4807-X). Profiles of African American actors, dancers, choreographers, composers, musicians, and singers, mostly from the 20th century, give personal and career information. (Rev: BL 8/03; SLJ 6/03) [791]

5146 Press, Skip. *Candice and Edgar Bergen* (4–8). Illus. Series: Star Families. 1995, Silver Burdett paper $7.95 (0-382-24940-2). The story of a father and daughter who had vastly different talents, yet each became a star. (Rev: SLJ 9/95) [920]

5147 Press, Skip. *Natalie and Nat King Cole* (4–8). Illus. Series: Star Families. 1995, Silver Burdett LB $15.95 (0-89686-879-6); paper $4.95 (0-382-24942-9). A short book that describes the upbringing and home life of Natalie Cole and her father's influence on her career. (Rev: SLJ 9/95) [920]

5148 Price-Groff, Claire. *Extraordinary Women Journalists* (7–10). Series: Extraordinary People. 1997, Children's Pr. LB $39.00 (0-516-20474-2). Over 50 well-known and lesser-known female reporters, publishers, humorists, columnists, photographers, and television journalists from colonial times to the present are profiled, including Nellie Bly, Hedda Hopper, Ann Landers, Abigail Van Buren, and Barbara Walters. (Rev: BR 5–6/98; SLJ 3/98; VOYA 4/98) [920]

5149 Rennert, Richard, ed. *Female Writers* (6–9). Series: Profiles of Great Black Americans. 1994, Chelsea paper $5.95 (0-7910-2064-9). Biographical overviews of such writers as Alice Walker, Maya Angelou, and Toni Morrison. (Rev: BL 2/15/94; SLJ 3/94) [920]

5150 Rennert, Richard, ed. *Jazz Stars* (6–9). Series: Profiles of Great Black Americans. 1993, Chelsea LB $18.65 (0-7910-2059-2). Profiles of eight jazz greats: Louis Armstrong, Count Basie, Charlie Park-

er, Ella Fitzgerald, Billie Holiday, Duke Ellington, Dizzy Gillespie, and John Coltrane. (Rev: BL 1/1/94; SLJ 12/93) [781.65]

5151 Rennert, Richard, ed. *Male Writers* (6–9). Series: Profiles of Great Black Americans. 1994, Chelsea LB $14.95 (0-7910-2061-4); paper $7.65 (0-7910-2062-2). Biographical overviews of such writers as James Baldwin, Alex Haley, and Richard Wright. (Rev: BL 2/15/94) [920]

5152 Rennert, Richard, ed. *Performing Artists* (6–9). Illus. Series: Profiles of Great Black Americans. 1994, Chelsea paper $7.65 (0-7910-2070-3). Alvin Ailey, Marian Anderson, Josephine Baker, Bill Cosby, Katerine Dunham, Lena Horne, Sidney Poitier, and Paul Robeson are the performing artists included in this collective biography. (Rev: BL 6/1–15/94) [920]

5153 Shirley, Lynn M. *Latin American Writers* (8–12). Illus. Series: Global Profiles. 1996, Facts on File $25.00 (0-8160-3202-5). This work profiles the life and works of eight prominent contemporary Latin American authors including Borges, Marquez, Amado, Fuentes, Vargas Llosa, and Isabel Allende. (Rev: BL 3/15/97) [920]

5154 Sills, Leslie. *In Real Life: Six Women Photographers* (6–12). Illus. 2000, Holiday $19.95 (0-8234-1498-1). This broad-ranging collective biography not only looks at the lives and works of artists including Dorothea Lange and Carrie Mae Weems but gives the reader guidance on appreciating the women's technique and artistry. (Rev: BL 12/1/00; BR 3–4/01; HB 1–2/01; HBG 3/01; SLJ 2/01; VOYA 2/01) [770]

5155 Sills, Leslie. *Visions: Stories About Women Artists* (5–8). Illus. 1993, Whitman LB $18.95 (0-8075-8491-6). The lives of four women artists — Cassatt, Saar, Carrington, and Frank — are covered in text and reproductions of their art. (Rev: BCCB 3/93; BL 4/1/93; HB 7–8/93; SLJ 5/93*) [920]

5156 Steffens, Bradley, and Robyn M. Weaver. *Cartoonists* (6–9). Series: History Makers. 2000, Lucent LB $18.96 (1-56006-668-7). Charles Schulz and Garry Trudeau are among the cartoonists featured in this volume that also traces the history of cartooning and the genre's importance in our society. (Rev: BL 6/1–15/00; HBG 9/00; SLJ 8/00) [920]

5157 Stewart, Gail B. *Great Women Comedians* (5–8). Series: History Makers. 2002, Gale LB $27.45 (1-56006-953-8). The comedians Gracie Allen, Lucille Ball, Whoopi Goldberg, Roseanne Barr, and Ellen DeGeneres are profiled in this account that focuses on their groundbreaking achievements. (Rev: SLJ 8/02) [921]

5158 Strickland, Michael R. *African-American Poets* (5–10). Illus. Series: Collective Biographies. 1996, Enslow LB $20.95 (0-89490-774-3). The lives and works of 10 prominent African American poets from Phillis Wheatley to Rita Dove are covered, with quotations from their works and a single full-length poem from each. (Rev: BL 2/15/97; SLJ 1/97) [920]

5159 Stux, Erica. *Eight Who Made a Difference: Pioneer Women in the Arts* (7–10). 1999, Avisson LB $19.95 (1-888105-37-2). This volume profiles eight famous women in the arts: Marian Anderson, Mary Cassatt, Nadia Boulanger, Margaret Bourke-White, Julia Morgan, Louise Nevelson, Beverly Sills, and Maria Tallchief. (Rev: BL 2/15/99; SLJ 5/99; VOYA 10/99) [920]

5160 Sullivan, George. *Black Artists in Photography, 1840–1940* (5–8). Illus. 1996, Dutton $16.99 (0-525-65208-6). This volume features seven important African American photographers who worked between 1840 and 1940. (Rev: BL 10/15/96; BR 3–4/97; SLJ 10/96) [920]

5161 Tate, Eleanora E. *African American Musicians* (4–7). Series: Black Stars. 2000, Wiley $24.95 (0-471-25356-1). This collective biography highlights both past and present contributions to different kinds of music by several African Americans. (Rev: BL 7/00; HBG 3/01; SLJ 7/00) [920]

5162 Terkel, Studs, and Milly Hawk Daniel. *Giants of Jazz.* 2nd ed. (7–10). 1992, HarperCollins LB $16.89 (0-690-04917-X). Thirteen subjects are highlighted including Benny Goodman, Louis Armstrong, Bessie Smith, and Dizzy Gillespie. [920]

5163 Ventura, Piero. *Great Composers* (5–9). Illus. 1989, Putnam $25.95 (0-399-21746-0). From ancient times to the Beatles, this large-format book gives thumbnail profiles of the world's greatest composers, with an emphasis on those from the West. (Rev: BL 1/15/90; SLJ 4/90) [780]

5164 Weitzman, David. *Great Lives: Theater* (8–12). Illus. 1996, Simon & Schuster $24.00 (0-689-80579-9). This collective biography gives thumbnail sketches of 26 people (mostly dead) who have contributed to the theater as actors, producers, or playwrights, including Edwin Booth, Sarah Bernhardt, and P. T. Barnum. (Rev: BL 2/1/97; BR 5–6/97; SLJ 11/96; VOYA 12/96) [920]

5165 Whitelaw, Nancy. *They Wrote Their Own Headlines: American Women Journalists* (6–10). 1994, Morgan Reynolds LB $21.95 (1-883846-06-4). Biographies of seven women journalists such as advice columnist Ann Landers and war correspondent Marguerite Higgins, examining the drive that brought success in a male-dominated field. (Rev: BL 7/94; SLJ 6/94; VOYA 8/94) [920]

5166 Wilds, Mary. *Raggin' the Blues: Legendary Country Blues and Ragtime Musicians* (6–9). Illus. 2001, Avisson paper $19.95 (1-888105-47-X). Although many readers will not be familiar with these musicians — including Lightnin' Hopkins, Skip James, Libba Cotton, and Blind Willie Johnson

— they will appreciate their contributions to the foundations of modern blues, jazz, and improvisational music. (Rev: BL 2/15/03) [781]

5167 Wilkinson, Brenda. *African American Women Writers* (4–7). Illus. Series: Black Stars. 1999, Wiley $22.95 (0-471-17580-3). Arranged chronologically, this collective biography contains short profiles of more than 20 important female African American writers. (Rev: BL 2/15/00; HBG 10/00; SLJ 2/00) [910]

5168 Woog, Adam. *Magicians and Illusionists* (6–10). Series: History Makers. 1999, Lucent LB $18.96 (1-56006-573-7). Eight illusionists — including Houdini and David Copperfield — are profiled, with discussion of their performances and many quotations from original sources. (Rev: BL 10/15/99; HBG 9/00; SLJ 3/00) [793.8]

5169 Woog, Adam. *Rock and Roll Legends* (6–9). Series: History Makers. 2001, Lucent $24.95 (1-56606-741-1). Included in this book of short profiles are Elvis Presley, John Lennon, Janis Joplin, Jimi Hendrix, Bruce Springsteen, and Kurt Cobain. (Rev: BL 8/1/01) [920]

Artists and Architects

ADAMS, ANSEL

5170 Gherman, Beverly. *Ansel Adams: America's Photographer* (6–10). Illus. 2002, Little, Brown $19.95 (0-316-82445-3). This splendid introduction to Adams's photography includes high-quality reproductions of his work and a lively account of his life and love of the natural world. (Rev: BL 6/1–15/03*; HBG 10/03) [770.92]

5171 Strangis, Joel. *Ansel Adams: American Artist with a Camera* (6–8). Series: People to Know. 2003, Enslow LB $20.95 (0-7660-1847-4). The life of the famous American photographer of landscapes who died in 1984. (Rev: BL 6/1–15/03; HBG 10/03) [921]

AUDUBON, JOHN JAMES

5172 Kastner, Joseph. *John James Audubon* (6–9). Series: First Impressions. 1992, Abrams $19.95 (0-8109-1918-4). Smooth, professional writing and fine art reproductions make for a fine account of Audubon's adventurous life, with many fine art reproductions. (Rev: BL 10/15/92; HB 3–4/93; SLJ 12/92) [921]

5173 Roop, Peter, and Connie Roop, eds. *Capturing Nature* (5–7). 1993, Walker LB $17.85 (0-8027-8205-1). Audubon's prints and original paintings and excerpts from his journals are combined to produce a stunning biography. (Rev: BCCB 12/93; BL 12/15/93; SLJ 1/94) [921]

BEARDEN, ROMARE

5174 Brown, Kevin. *Romare Bearden* (7–10). Series: Black Americans of Achievement. 1995, Chelsea LB $19.95 (0-7910-1119-4). The story of the Harlem-raised African American painter who tries to portray the everyday experiences of African Americans. (Rev: BL 3/15/95; SLJ 3/95) [921]

5175 Greenberg, Jan. *Romare Bearden: Collage of Memories* (3–9). Illus. 2003, Abrams $17.95 (0-8109-4589-4). Text and Bearden's own collages recount this African American artist's life — his youth in North Carolina, his years in Harlem, his love of jazz — in a handsome oversize volume. (Rev: BL 9/15/03*; HB 11–12/03; SLJ 9/03) [709.]

BERENSTAIN, JAN AND BERENSTAIN, STAN

5176 Berenstain, Stan, and Jan Berenstain. *Down a Sunny Dirt Road: An Autobiography* (5–8). Illus. 2002, Random $20.00 (0-375-81403-5). This engrossing joint biography of the co-creators of the Berenstain Bears is filled with photographs, early cartoons, and other fascinating artwork. (Rev: BL 12/15/02; HB 1–2/03; HBG 3/03; SLJ 12/02) [813]

BOURGEOIS, LOUISE

5177 Greenberg, Jan, and Sandra Jordan. *Runaway Girl: The Artist Louise Bourgeois* (8–12). Illus. 2003, Abrams $19.95 (0-8109-4237-2). The life of the famous sculptor, with details of her youth and her difficult relations with her parents, is accompanied by many black-and-white and color photographs. (Rev: BL 4/15/03*; HB 7–8/03; HBG 10/03; SLJ 5/03*; VOYA 8/03) [730]

BOURKE-WHITE, MARGARET

5178 Ayer, Eleanor. *Margaret Bourke-White: Photographing the World* (6–10). Series: People in Focus. 1992, Dillon LB $13.95 (0-87518-513-4). A lively account of the photographer's craft and technique, her long association with *Life* magazine, and the subjects she recorded, from the Depression and Buchenwald concentration camp to Gandhi. (Rev: BL 12/1/92; SLJ 11/92) [921]

5179 Daffron, Carolyn. *Margaret Bourke-White* (7–12). Illus. 1988, Chelsea LB $19.95 (1-55546-644-3). The life story of this famous photographer in an account well illustrated with the artist's work. (Rev: BL 5/1/88; BR 5–6/88; SLJ 8/88) [921]

5180 Rubin, Susan Goldman. *Margaret Bourke-White: Her Pictures Were Her Life* (6–12). Illus. 1999, Abrams $19.95 (0-8109-4381-6). An excellent biography of a courageous, highly disciplined photographer whose work remains a hallmark of quality in the field. (Rev: BL 11/1/99; HBG 4/00) [770]

5181 Welch, Catherine A. *Margaret Bourke-White: Racing with a Dream* (4–8). Illus. 1998, Carolrhoda LB $30.35 (1-57505-049-8). A fine biography of the important photographer whose subjects included skyscrapers, the Depression, Buchenwald, and South African miners. (Rev: BL 10/1/98; HBG 3/99; SLJ 7/98) [921]

5182 Wooten, Sara McIntosh. *Margaret Bourke-White: Daring Photographer* (6–10). Series: People to Know. 2002, Enslow LB $20.95 (0-7660-1534-3). An accessible biography of the adventurous photographer with many examples of her work. (Rev: BL 9/15/02; HBG 3/03; SLJ 11/02; VOYA 6/03) [921]

BRADY, MATHEW

5183 Pflueger, Lynda. *Mathew Brady* (5–8). Series: Historical American Biographies. 2001, Enslow LB $20.95 (0-7660-1444-4). A biography of the photographer known primarily for his coverage of the Civil War, illustrated with many of his works. (Rev: BL 1/1–15/02; HBG 10/01; SLJ 9/01; VOYA 2/02) [921]

5184 Sullivan, George. *Mathew Brady: His Life and Photographs* (6–10). 1994, Dutton $15.99 (0-525-65186-1). A biography of the photographer known for capturing the Civil War on film; includes reproductions of Brady's photographs. (Rev: BL 7/94; SLJ 12/94; VOYA 12/94) [921]

CALDER, ALEXANDER

5185 Lipman, Jean, and Margaret Aspinwall. *Alexander Calder and His Magical Mobiles* (6–9). Illus. 1981, Hudson Hills $19.95 (0-933920-17-2). A biography of the noted sculptor with many interesting incidents from his childhood. [921]

CARLE, ERIC

5186 Carle, Eric. *Flora and Tiger: 19 Very Short Stories from My Life* (4–8). Illus. 1997, Putnam $17.99 (0-399-23203-6). An autobiography of the famous picture book artist who was born in Germany but who has lived in the United States since 1952. (Rev: BL 12/15/97; HBG 3/98; SLJ 2/98) [921]

CARR, EMILY

5187 Bogart, Jo Ellen. *Emily Carr: At the Edge of the World* (4–8). 2003, Tundra $18.95 (0-88776-640-4). This picture book for older readers presents the life and work of the Canadian artist and writer who became famous for her depictions of the native peoples of the Pacific Coast. (Rev: BL 11/1/03; SLJ 12/03) [759.11]

5188 Debon, Nicolas. *Four Pictures by Emily Carr* (5–9). Illus. 2003, Douglas & McIntyre $15.95 (0-88899-532-6). This small comic-book biography uses four of Carr's paintings to introduce chapters that trace the Canadian artist's life and interest in Native Americans. (Rev: BL 12/1/03; HB 1–2/04; SLJ 11/03) [759.11]

CASSATT, MARY

5189 Brooks, Philip. *Mary Cassatt: An American in Paris* (4–7). Illus. Series: First Books. 1995, Watts LB $23.00 (0-531-20183-X). A biography of the American artist who found fulfillment painting in Paris. (Rev: BL 10/1/95; HB 1–2/95; SLJ 10/95) [921]

5190 Meyer, Susan E. *Mary Cassatt* (4–8). Illus. Series: First Impressions. 1991, Abrams $19.95 (0-8109-3154-0). The story of the American artist who spent her most productive painting years in France. (Rev: SLJ 5/91) [921]

5191 Plain, Nancy. *Mary Cassatt: An Artist's Life* (6–9). 1994, Silver Burdett LB $13.95 (0-87518-597-5). Includes clear explanations of artistic techniques and discusses Cassatt's relationships with other Impressionists. (Rev: BL 1/15/95; SLJ 2/95) [921]

5192 Streissguth, Thomas. *Mary Cassatt* (4–8). Series: Trailblazers. 1999, Lerner LB $30.35 (1-57505-291-1). Full-color illustrations enhance this biography of the American painter who was associated with the Impressionists and spent most of her adult life in France. (Rev: BL 5/1/99; HBG 10/99; SLJ 9/99) [921]

CÉZANNE, PAUL

5193 Sellier, Marie. *Cézanne from A to Z* (4–8). Trans. from French by Claudia Zoe Bedrick. Illus. Series: Artists from A to Z. 1996, Bedrick LB $14.95 (0-87226-476-9). An imaginative, well-executed account of the life and works of Cézanne, enhanced by reproductions of many of his paintings. (Rev: SLJ 5/96) [921]

CHAGALL, MARC

5194 Hopler, Brigitta. *Marc Chagall: Life Is a Dream* (4–7). Trans. by Catherine McCreadie. Illus. Series: Adventures in Art. 1999, Prestel $14.95 (3-7913-1986-8). This biography of the surrealist painter not only relates the artist's life story but also encourages the reader to discover the meanings behind the images. (Rev: BL 2/1/99; SLJ 2/99) [921]

5195 Lemke, Elisabeth, and Thomas David. *Marc Chagall: What Colour Is Paradise?* (4–8). Illus. Series: Adventures in Art. 2001, Prestel $14.95 (3-7913-2393-8). Using Chagall's biographical paintings as a focus, this innovative biography tells of his life, career, and work. (Rev: BL 1/1–15/01; SLJ 4/01) [921]

5196 Pozzi, Gianni. *Chagall* (6–12). Illus. Series: Masters of Art. 1998, Bedrick $22.50 (0-87226-527-7). The life and times of Chagall, along with his painting techniques, methods, and materials, are covered in text and full-color illustrations in this oversize book. (Rev: BL 3/1/98; SLJ 12/97) [709]

CHANG, WAH MING

5197 Riley, Gail B. *Wah Ming Chang: Artist and Master of Special Effects* (4–8). Illus. Series: Multicultural Junior Biographies. 1995, Enslow LB $20.95 (0-89490-639-9). A thorough, well-documented biography of this Chinese American who has gained prominence in the field of special effects. (Rev: BL 2/15/96; SLJ 2/96) [921]

CHONG, GORDON H.

5198 *The Success of Gordon H. Chong and Associates: An Architecture Success Story* (7–10). Illus. Series: Success. 1996, Walker $15.95 (0-8027-8307-4). The amazing rise of the contemporary American architect, with examples of his work. (Rev: BL 5/15/96; SLJ 9/96) [921]

CLOSE, CHUCK

5199 Greenberg, Jan, and Sandra Jordan. *Chuck Close, up Close* (7–12). 1998, DK paper $19.95 (0-7894-2486-X). This is the inspiring story of the artist Chuck Close, who, in spite of a spinal collapse that left him paralyzed and in a wheelchair, continued to paint with a brush strapped to his hand. (Rev: BCCB 5/98; BL 3/15/98; HB 5–6/98*; HBG 9/98; SLJ 3/98; VOYA 8/98) [921]

COROT, JEAN CAMILLE

5200 Larroche, Caroline. *Corot from A to Z* (5–8). Trans. from French by Claudia Zoe Bedrick. Series: Artists from A to Z. 1996, Bedrick LB $14.95 (0-87226-477-7). Although the text is somewhat confusing, the strength of this account of Corot's life and work is the full-color reproductions of his work. (Rev: SLJ 1/97) [921]

CURTIS, EDWARD S.

5201 Lawlor, Laurie. *Shadow Catcher: The Life and Work of Edward S. Curtis* (6–12). 1994, Walker LB $20.85 (0-8027-8289-2). The personal and professional highlights of the life of this little-known, largely unappreciated photojournalist who was determined to preserve the lore of Native Americans. (Rev: BL 12/1/94; SLJ 2/95; VOYA 12/94) [921]

DALI, SALVADOR

5202 Anderson, Robert. *Salvador Dali* (5–8). Illus. Series: Artists in Their Time. 2002, Watts LB $22.00 (0-531-12231-X); paper $6.95 (0-531-16624-4). This volume presents Dali's life and influence with many illustrations, news clippings, and useful information. (Rev: BL 10/15/02) [709]

DA VINCI, LEONARDO

5203 Herbert, Janis. *Leonardo da Vinci for Kids: His Life and Ideas* (4–8). Illus. 1998, Chicago Review paper $16.95 (1-55652-298-3). This biography of Leonardo da Vinci contains background information on history, art techniques, science, and philosophy. (Rev: BL 3/1/99; SLJ 4/99) [921]

5204 Kallen, Stuart A., and P. M. Boekkhoff. *Leonardo da Vinci* (7–12). Series: The Importance Of. 2000, Lucent LB $18.96 (1-56006-604-0). The life, accomplishments, and significance of this multi-talented genius are covered in this fine biography. (Rev: BL 8/00; HBG 9/00) [921]

5205 Kuhne, Heinz. *Leonardo da Vinci: Dreams, Schemes, and Flying Machines* (4–8). Illus. Series: Adventures in Art. 2000, Prestel $14.95 (3-7913-2166-8). This well-illustrated biography covers da Vinci's accomplishments as a scientist, engineer, inventor, and artist. (Rev: BL 7/00) [921]

5206 McLanathan, Richard. *Leonardo da Vinci* (7–12). 1990, Abrams $22.95 (0-8109-1256-2). A readable, inviting introduction to the master painter, inventor, and scientist. (Rev: BL 12/15/90; SLJ 2/91*) [921]

5207 Mason, Antony. *Leonardo da Vinci* (4–8). Illus. 1994, Barron's paper $7.95 (0-8120-1997-0). A brief biography that chronicles the achievements of this multifaceted genius and supplies pictures of some of his great triumphs. (Rev: BL 12/1/94) [921]

5208 O'Connor, Barbara. *Leonardo da Vinci: Renaissance Genius* (5–8). Series: Trailblazer Biographies. 2002, Carolrhoda LB $30.35 (0-87614-467-9). An excellent biography that details Leonardo's life from childhood, discusses some of his famous paintings, and looks at his inventions and experiments. (Rev: BL 3/15/03; HBG 3/03; SLJ 11/02; VOYA 8/03) [921]

5209 Romei, Francesca. *Leonardo da Vinci: Artist, Inventor and Scientist of the Renaissance* (6–12). Illus. Series: Masters of Art. 1995, Bedrick $22.50 (0-87226-313-4). Historical and artistic overview of Leonardo, his life, art, inventions, and other accomplishments. (Rev: BL 4/1/95; SLJ 2/95) [921]

DAY, TOM

5210 Lyons, Mary E. *Master of Mahogany: Tom Day, Free Black Cabinetmaker* (5–8). 1994, Scribners paper $15.95 (0-684-19675-1). Chronicles the life of an 18th-century African American cabinetmaker, using quotations from Day's diary and photographs of his work. (Rev: BL 10/1/94; HB 11–12/94; SLJ 10/94*) [921]

DEGAS, EDGAR

5211 Meyer, Susan E. *Edgar Degas* (7–12). 1994, Abrams $19.95 (0-8109-3220-2). The life and work of this French artist are examined in this well-illustrated volume that contains reproductions of both his paintings and sculpture. (Rev: BL 1/1/95; SLJ 10/94) [921]

DESJARLAIT, PATRICK

5212 Williams, Neva. *Patrick DesJarlait: Conversations with a Native American Artist* (5–7). Illus. 1994, Lerner LB $27.15 (0-8225-3151-8). A beautifully illustrated biography of the Native American artist who worked at the Red Lake Indian Reservation in Minnesota. (Rev: BL 1/1/95; SLJ 1/95) [921]

DISNEY, WALT

5213 Cole, Michael D. *Walt Disney: Creator of Mickey Mouse* (4–7). Illus. Series: People to Know. 1996, Enslow LB $20.95 (0-89490-694-1). A thoughtful biography of the great animator, perfectionist, and founder of an entertainment empire. (Rev: BL 6/1–15/96; SLJ 8/96) [921]

5214 Ford, Barbara. *Walt Disney* (4–8). Illus. 1989, Walker LB $17.00 (0-8027-6865-2). The story of Disney's youth and his struggle to fulfill his dreams. (Rev: BL 5/15/89) [791.430924]

5215 Greene, Katherine, and Richard Greene. *The Man Behind the Magic: The Story of Walt Disney* (6–9). 1991, Viking $18.99 (0-670-82259-0). This biography concentrates on the personal characteristics of Disney and life at the Disney studio, clearly differentiating the man from his creations. (Rev: BL 10/1/91; SLJ 10/91) [921]

5216 Nardo, Don. *Walt Disney* (4–8). Series: The Importance Of. 2000, Lucent LB $27.45 (1-56006-605-9). A well-researched biography of Walt Disney that quotes from many original and secondary sources, documents facts, and gives an honest appraisal of his work. (Rev: BL 1/1–15/00; HBG 10/00) [921]

EVANS, MINNIE

5217 Lyons, Mary E. *Painting Dreams: Minnie Evans, Visionary Artist* (4–8). 1996, Houghton $14.95 (0-395-72032-X). The life story of this deeply religious, visionary African American folk artist, whose family and friends considered her mentally unstable and who was discovered by a photographer in the 1960s. (Rev: BCCB 9/96; BL 7/96; SLJ 7/96) [921]

FABERGÉ, CARL

5218 von Habsburg-Lothringen, Geza. *Carl Fabergé* (6–10). 1994, Abrams $19.95 (0-8109-3324-1). The history of the creations of the Russian artisan known for the priceless Faberge eggs, with color photographs. (Rev: BL 7/94; SLJ 6/94) [921]

GAUGUIN, PAUL

5219 Anderson, Robert. *Paul Gauguin* (4–8). Series: Artists in Their Time. 2003, Watts LB $22.00 (0-531-12239-5); paper $6.95 (0-531-16647-3). An interesting life of Gauguin, with reproductions of his works and of those of fellow painters, with a timeline that adds historical context. (Rev: SLJ 6/03) [759.4]

5220 Greenfeld, Howard. *Paul Gauguin* (7–12). Series: First Impressions. 1993, Abrams $19.95 (0-8109-3376-4). An examination of the life and work of this sometime-friend of van Gogh who journeyed to the South Seas in search of artistic inspiration and freedom. (Rev: BL 12/1/93; SLJ 1/94) [921]

GEHRY, FRANK O.

5221 Greenberg, Jan, and Sandra Jordan. *Frank O. Gehry: Outside In* (4–7). 2000, DK paper $19.95 (0-7894-2677-3). A stunning profile of this innovative architect who was responsible for the Guggenheim Museum in Bilbao, Spain, and the Experience Music Project in Seattle. (Rev: BCCB 10/00; BL 10/1/00; HB 9–10/00; HBG 3/01; SLJ 9/00; VOYA 8/01) [921]

GIACOMETTI, ALBERTO

5222 Gaff, Jackie. *Alberto Giacometti* (5–8). Series: Artists in Their Time. 2002, Watts LB $22.00 (0-531-12224-7); paper $6.95 (0-531-16617-1). The life of this Italian artist noted for his elongated sculptures is re-created with comments on his social period and reproductions of his work. (Rev: BL 10/15/02) [921]

GORMAN, R. C.

5223 Hermann, Spring. *R. C. Gorman: Navajo Artist* (4–8). Illus. Series: Multicultural Junior Biographies. 1995, Enslow LB $20.95 (0-89490-638-0). The story of this contemporary Native American artist, who reflects his heritage in his work. (Rev: BL 2/15/96; SLJ 3/96) [921]

GOYA, FRANCISCO

5224 Schiaffino, Mariarosa. *Goya* (4–8). Series: Masters of Art. 2000, Bedrick $22.50 (0-87226-529-3). Each of the double-page spreads in this attractive book is devoted to an aspect of Goya's life or work; for example, his contemporaries and his drawings of the bullfight. (Rev: HBG 10/00; SLJ 3/00) [921]

5225 Waldron, Ann. *Francisco Goya* (5–8). Illus. Series: First Impressions. 1992, Abrams $19.95 (0-8109-3368-3). Covers the stormy life of Goya and the many intrigues at court, and includes many reproductions. (Rev: SLJ 12/92) [921]

HOMER, WINSLOW

5226 Beneduce, Ann Keay. *A Weekend with Winslow Homer* (4–9). Illus. Series: Weekend with the Artists. 1993, Rizzoli $19.95 (0-8478-1622-2). An introduction to the famous New England painter of landscapes and the sea, including samples of his work. (Rev: BL 12/15/93; SLJ 11/93) [921]

HOPPER, EDWARD

5227 Foa, Emma. *Edward Hopper* (4–8). Series: Artists in Their Time. 2003, Watts LB $22.00 (0-531-12240-9); paper $6.95 (0-531-16641-4). An interesting life of Hopper, with reproductions of his works and of those of fellow painters, and a timeline that adds historical context. (Rev: SLJ 6/03) [759.13]

5228 Lyons, Deborah. *Edward Hopper: Summer at the Seaside* (4–8). Series: Adventures in Art. 2003, Prestel $14.95 (3-7913-2737-2). The story of the American painter who died in 1967, with a good analysis of many of his important works. (Rev: BL 11/15/03; SLJ 9/03) [921]

HOUSTON, JAMES

5229 Houston, James. *Fire into Ice: Adventures in Glass Making* (5–9). Illus. 1998, Tundra $15.95 (0-88776-459-2). The author, who lived with and wrote about the Inuit, tells how he left the Arctic in the early 1960s and became a Steuben glass designer, incorporating his Inuit-influenced drawings into a new medium. (Rev: BL 4/15/99; HBG 3/99; SLJ 1/99) [921]

HUNTER, CLEMENTINE

5230 Lyons, Mary E. *Talking with Tebe: Clementine Hunter, Memory Artist* (7–12). 1998, Houghton $17.00 (0-395-72031-1). This richly illustrated book, which quotes extensively from taped interviews and is as much about social history as about painting, tells the story of the first illiterate, self-taught African American folk artist to receive national attention for her work. (Rev: BCCB 1/99; BL 8/98; BR 5–6/99; HB 9–10/98; HBG 3/99; SLJ 9/98) [921]

JACKSON, WILLIAM HENRY

5231 Lawlor, Laurie. *Window on the West: The Frontier Photography of William Henry Jackson* (5–8). 1999, Holiday $18.95 (0-8234-1380-2). In addition to tracing the life of this famous photographer who captured the life and spirit of frontier America, this account covers the history and development of the West and pioneer life. (Rev: BL 2/15/00; HB 3–4/00; HBG 10/00; SLJ 3/00; VOYA 12/00) [921]

KAHLO, FRIDA

5232 Cruz, Barbara C. *Frida Kahlo: Portrait of a Mexican Painter* (6–9). Illus. Series: Hispanic Biographies. 1996, Enslow LB $20.95 (0-89490-765-4). A biography of one of Mexico's greatest artists that includes material on her relationship with artist Diego Rivera. (Rev: BL 11/1/96; BR 1–2/97; SLJ 10/96) [921]

5233 Frazier, Nancy. *Frida Kahlo: Mysterious Painter* (5–7). Illus. Series: Library of Famous Women. 1993, Rosen $26.19 (1-56711-012-6). A biography of this enigmatic artist with examples of her work. (Rev: BL 2/15/93) [921]

5234 Garza, Hedda. *Frida Kahlo* (5–9). Series: Hispanics of Achievement. 1994, Chelsea LB $21.95 (0-7910-1698-6); paper $9.95 (0-7910-1699-4). Known once only as the wife of Diego Rivera, this painter, who lived most of her life in Mexico, is now considered a great artist. (Rev: BL 3/1/94) [921]

5235 Holzhey, Magdalena. *Frida Kahlo: The Artist in the Blue House* (4–8). Series: Adventures in Art. 2003, Prestel $14.95 (3-7913-2863-8). A colorful introduction to this Mexican painter with an interesting analysis of individual paintings. (Rev: BL 11/15/03; SLJ 9/03) [921]

5236 Laidlaw, Jill A. *Frida Kahlo* (5–8). Series: Artists in Their Time. 2003, Watts LB $22.00 (0-531-12236-0); paper $6.95 (0-531-16642-2). An interesting life of Kahlo, with reproductions of her works and a timeline and informative sidebars that add historical context. (Rev: SLJ 6/03) [759]

KLEE, PAUL

5237 Laidlaw, Jill A. *Paul Klee* (5–8). Series: Artists in Their Time. 2002, Watts LB $22.00 (0-531-12230-1); paper $6.95 (0-531-16623-6). Photographs, reproductions, maps, and a timeline that links world events with events in the artist's life make this suitable both for browsing and report writing. (Rev: BL 10/15/02; SLJ 1/03) [921]

KLIMT, GUSTAV

5238 Wenzel, Angela. *Gustav Klimt: Silver, Gold, and Precious Stones* (4–8). Illus. Series: Adventures in Art. 2000, Prestel $14.95 (3-7913-2328-8). The life of this Austrian artist is presented along with analysis of many of his paintings, including the famous *The Kiss.* (Rev: BL 7/00) [921]

LANGE, DOROTHEA

5239 Partridge, Elizabeth. *Restless Spirit: The Life and Work of Dorothea Lange* (6–12). 1998, Viking $22.99 (0-670-87888-X). Using over 60 photographs, this photoessay tells of the personal and professional life of photographer Lange, her many problems, and her artistic accomplishments, particularly during the Depression and World War II. (Rev: BCCB 12/98; BL 10/15/98; HB 3–4/99; HBG 3/99; SLJ 10/98; VOYA 8/99) [921]

LAWRENCE, JACOB

5240 Duggleby, John. *Story Painter: The Life of Jacob Lawrence* (5–8). Illus. 1998, Chronicle $16.95 (0-8118-2082-3). Using 50 color reproductions, this biography of the great African American illustrator and painter tells how he moved to Harlem in the 1930s and developed his own techniques and style. (Rev: BCCB 1/99; BL 10/15/98; HB 3–4/99; HBG 3/99; SLJ 12/98) [921]

5241 Leach, Deba Foxley. *I See You I See Myself: The Young Life of Jacob Lawrence* (5–9). 2002, Phillips Collection $20.00 (0-943044-26-X). A look at the early life and work of the African American artist, with information on his paintings as a teen. (Rev: SLJ 12/02) [759.13]

LEWIN, TED

5242 Lewin, Ted. *I Was a Teenage Professional Wrestler* (7–12). 1993, Hyperion paper $6.95 (0-7868-1009-2). Memoir of a children's book author/illustrator about his wrestling career in the 1950s, showing the human side of the sport. (Rev: BL 6/1–15/93*; SLJ 7/93*; VOYA 10/93) [921]

5243 Lewin, Ted. *Touch and Go: Travels of a Children's Book Illustrator* (6–9). Illus. 1999, Lothrop $15.00 (0-688-14109-9). The noted picture book illustrator tells about his unusual experiences around the world in search of subjects for his books. (Rev: BL 4/15/99; SLJ 7/99) [921]

LEWIS, EDMONIA

5244 Wolfe, Rinna. *Edmonia Lewis: Wildfire in Marble* (6–10). Illus. Series: People in Focus. 1998, Silver Burdett LB $18.95 (0-382-39713-4); paper $7.95 (0-382-39714-2). An excellent documentary about the life and work of a woman with African/

Chippewa Indian roots who overcame racism to get a college education, went to Europe to develop her talent, and became the first American woman of African/Chippewa heritage to achieve international acclaim as a sculptor. (Rev: SLJ 8/98; VOYA 8/98) [921]

LIN, MAYA

5245 Ling, Bettina. *Maya Lin* (5–7). Illus. Series: Contemporary Asian Americans. 1997, Raintree Steck-Vaughn LB $17.98 (0-8172-3992-8). A profile of the Asian American architect and an introduction to many of her projects, including the Vietnam War Memorial in Washington, D.C. (Rev: BL 5/1/97) [921]

MARTINEZ, MARIA

5246 Morris, Juddi. *Tending the Fire: The Story of Maria Martinez* (5–8). 1997, Northland paper $6.95 (0-87358-654-9). The life story of New Mexico's most famous potter, who was born in an Indian pueblo in 1887. (Rev: BL 12/1/97; BR 11–12/97; HBG 3/98; SLJ 12/97) [921]

MATISSE, HENRI

5247 Hollein, Max, and Nina Hollein. *Matisse: Cut-Out Fun with Matisse* (4–8). Series: Adventures in Art. 2003, Prestel $14.95 (3-7913-2858-1). This large-formatted book that originated in Germany, successfully introduces the life and work of the great French master. (Rev: BL 11/15/03) [921]

5248 Roddari, Florian. *A Weekend with Matisse* (4–9). Illus. Series: A Weekend. 1994, Rizzoli $19.95 (0-8478-1792-X). This is a fine introduction to the life and work of Matisse, with accompanying illustrations that show his major works and styles. (Rev: BL 9/15/94) [921]

5249 Welton, Jude. *Henri Matisse* (5–8). Series: Artists in Their Time. 2002, Watts LB $22.00 (0-531-12228-X); paper $6.95 (0-531-16621-X). The artistic and social periods during which Matisse worked are re-created along with a biography and several color examples of his work. (Rev: BL 10/15/02; SLJ 1/03) [2.2.2]

MICHELANGELO

5250 Di Cagno, Gabriella. *Michelangelo* (6–12). Illus. Series: Masters of Art. 1996, Bedrick $22.50 (0-87226-319-3). The life, times, and accomplishments of Michelangelo are covered through use of outstanding reproductions, brief text, and many illustrations. (Rev: BL 11/15/96; SLJ 12/96; VOYA 4/97) [921]

5251 McLanathan, Richard. *Michelangelo* (7–12). Series: First Impressions. 1993, Abrams $19.95 (0-

8109-3634-8). A handsomely illustrated volume that surveys the life, times, and art of this Italian master. (Rev: BL 6/1–15/93) [700921]

5252 Stanley, Diane. *Michelangelo* (5–8). Illus. 2000, HarperCollins LB $17.89 (0-688-15086-1). An intriguing biography of Michelangelo that also gives extensive coverage on the history of the Italian Renaissance. (Rev: BCCB 10/00; BL 8/00*; HBG 3/01; SLJ 8/00) [921]

MIRÓ, JOAN

5253 Higdon, Elizabeth. *Joan Miró* (7–12). Series: Rizzoli Art. 1993, Rizzoli paper $7.95 (0-8478-1667-2). A lavishly illustrated biography of this influential, innovative 20th-century Spanish painter. (Rev: BL 1/15/94) [921]

MONET, CLAUDE

5254 Hodge, Susie. *Claude Monet* (5–8). Illus. Series: Artists in Their Time. 2002, Watts LB $22.00 (0-531-12226-3); paper $6.95 (0-531-16619-8). Photographs, reproductions, maps, and a timeline that links world events with events in the artist's life make this suitable both for browsing and report writing. (Rev: SLJ 1/03) [921]

5255 Waldron, Ann. *Claude Monet* (7–12). Series: First Impressions. 1991, Abrams $19.95 (0-8109-3620-8). This illustrated biographical study of the pioneering Impressionist painter explores his fascination with nature and his experimentation with the effects of light. (Rev: BL 11/15/91; SLJ 1/92) [921]

MORGAN, JULIA

5256 James, Cary. *Julia Morgan: Architect* (7–10). Illus. 1990, Chelsea LB $19.95 (1-55546-669-9). The story of the outstanding female architect who now has over 700 projects to her credit. (Rev: SLJ 8/90) [921]

MOSES, GRANDMA

5257 Biracree, Tom. *Grandma Moses* (7–10). Illus. 1989, Chelsea LB $19.95 (1-55546-670-2). This primitive artist's life and works are discussed, and insets are provided of some of her paintings. (Rev: BL 12/1/89; BR 3–4/90; SLJ 1/90; VOYA 2/90) [921]

5258 Oneal, Zibby. *Grandma Moses: Painter of Rural America* (5–7). 1987, Puffin paper $4.99 (0-14-032220-5). The story of Anna Mary Robertson, who became famous as Grandma Moses. (Rev: BCCB 10/86; BL 11/1/86; SLJ 10/86) [921]

MOUNT, WILLIAM SIDNEY

5259 Howard, Nancy S. *William Sidney Mount: Painter of Rural America* (4–7). Illus. 1994, Sterling

$14.95 (1-87192-275-4). An interactive book that explores the work and paintings of the 19th-century American painter William Sidney Mount. (Rev: BL 1/15/95) [921]

NAST, THOMAS

5260 Pflueger, Lynda. *Thomas Nast: Political Cartoonist* (5–8). Series: Historical American Biographies. 2000, Enslow LB $20.95 (0-7660-1251-4). An informative, entertaining, and well-written biography of this influential political cartoonist and critic. (Rev: BL 9/15/00; HBG 10/01; SLJ 11/00) [921]

O'KEEFFE, GEORGIA

5261 Berry, Michael. *Georgia O'Keeffe: Painter* (7–12). Illus. 1988, Chelsea LB $19.95 (1-55546-673-7). Illustrated chiefly in black and white, this is the story of the artist who reached maturity painting subjects in the southwestern states. (Rev: BL 9/15/88; BR 5–6/89; SLJ 9/88; VOYA 2/89) [921]

5262 Brooks, Philip. *Georgia O'Keeffe: An Adventurous Spirit* (4–7). Illus. Series: First Books. 1995, Watts LB $23.00 (0-531-20182-1). An insightful portrait of the American artist and her internal struggle to paint what, how, and where she chose. (Rev: BL 10/1/95; SLJ 10/95) [921]

5263 Gherman, Beverly. *Georgia O'Keeffe: The Wideness and Wonder of Her World* (7–9). Illus. 1986, Macmillan LB $13.95 (0-689-31164-8). This biography emphasizes the total commitment this artist felt toward her work. (Rev: BL 4/1/86; SLJ 5/86) [921]

OROZCO, JOSE

5264 Cruz, Barbara C. *Jose Clemente Orozco: Mexican Artist* (7–12). Series: Hispanic Biographies. 1998, Enslow LB $20.95 (0-7660-1041-4). The story of the great artist Orozco, as well as an introduction to the mural painters of Mexico and how they used designs from Aztec and Mayan art. (Rev: BL 1/1–15/99; HBG 3/99; SLJ 3/99) [921]

PARKS, GORDON

5265 Parks, Gordon. *Half Past Autumn: A Retrospective* (7–12). 1997, Bulfinch $65.00 (0-8212-2298-8); paper $40.00 (0-8212-2503-0). Using nearly 300 photographs, this great photographer recounts and reflects on his life and struggles. (Rev: BL 8/97; VOYA 12/98) [921]

PEALE, CHARLES WILLSON

5266 Giblin, James Cross. *The Mystery of the Mammoth Bones* (4–8). 1999, HarperCollins $15.95 (0-06-027493-X). Artist, paleontologist, and museum curator Charles Willson Peale's study of mastodon (mammoth) fossil bones is told in the context of the cultural and intellectual history of the time. (Rev: BL 1/1–15/99*; HB 9–10/99; HBG 9/99; SLJ 4/99) [921]

5267 Wilson, Janet. *The Ingenious Mr. Peale: Painter, Patriot and Man of Science* (5–8). Illus. 1996, Simon & Schuster $16.00 (0-689-31884-7). A profile of the famous portrait painter of the colonial period, with details of his varied interests. (Rev: BCCB 6/96; BL 5/15/96; BR 1–2/97; SLJ 6/96*; VOYA 8/96) [921]

PICASSO, PABLO

5268 Beardsley, John. *Pablo Picasso* (7–12). Series: First Impressions. 1991, Abrams $19.95 (0-8109-3713-1). Succinctly describes Picasso's bohemian lifestyle and analyzes his ever-changing styles, methods, and subjects. (Rev: BL 11/15/91; SLJ 1/92) [921]

5269 Holland, Gini. *Pablo Picasso* (5–8). Series: Trailblazers of the Modern World. 2003, World Almanac LB $26.60 (0-8368-5084-X). A clear portrayal of Picasso's life and work that places him in historical and social context. (Rev: SLJ 7/03) [921]

5270 Loria, Stefano. *Picasso* (6–12). Illus. Series: Masters of Art. 1996, Bedrick $22.50 (0-87226-318-5). A stunning combination of text and excellent reproductions bring this Spanish artist's life and work into focus. (Rev: BL 5/15/96) [921]

5271 MacDonald, Patricia A. *Pablo Picasso: Greatest Artist of the 20th Century* (7–10). Illus. Series: Giants of Art and Culture. 2001, Blackbirch LB $21.95 (1-56711-504-7). Picasso's life and career are placed in historical context, with photographs, a timeline, a glossary, and lists of resources. (Rev: BL 8/01; HBG 3/02) [709]

5272 Meadows, Matthew. *Pablo Picasso* (5–7). Illus. Series: Art for Young People. 1996, Sterling $14.95 (0-8069-6160-0). In double-page spreads, presents the life and work of this multitalented Spanish artist. (Rev: BL 2/1/97; HB 5–6/96; SLJ 3/97) [921]

5273 Pfleger, Susanne. *A Day with Picasso* (4–7). Series: Adventures in Art. 2000, Prestel $14.95 (3-7913-2165-X). An introduction to the life and work of Picasso, including many full-color reproductions. (Rev: BL 2/15/00; SLJ 2/00) [921]

5274 Scarborough, Kate. *Pablo Picasso* (5–8). Series: Artists in Their Time. 2002, Watts LB $22.00 (0-531-12229-8); paper $6.95 (0-531-16622-8). This biography of the 20th century's most famous artist is accompanied by material on the social conditions of his time. (Rev: BL 10/15/02; SLJ 1/03) [921]

5275 Selfridge, John W. *Pablo Picasso* (5–9). Series: Hispanics of Achievement. 1993, Chelsea

LB $21.95 (0-7910-1777-X). A colorful biography of this great Spanish painter, who lived most of his life as a political exile in France, with some examples of his enormous output. (Rev: BL 3/1/94) [9212]

5276 Wallis, Jeremy. *Pablo Picasso* (5–8). Series: Creative Lives. 2001, Heinemann LB $27.07 (1-58810-206-8). Picasso's eccentricities are highlighted in this volume that covers his life, his family, and his work. (Rev: HBG 10/02; SLJ 3/02) [921]

PIPPIN, HORACE

5277 Lyons, Mary E. *Starting Home: The Story of Horace Pippin, Painter* (5–7). Illus. Series: African American Artists and Artisans. 1993, Scribners $15.95 (0-684-19534-8). The story of this self-taught African American painter who depicted the horrors of World War I in his work. (Rev: BL 11/15/93; SLJ 2/94) [921]

POLLOCK, JACKSON

5278 Oliver, Clare. *Jackson Pollock* (5–8). Series: Artists in Their Time. 2003, Watts LB $22.00 (0-531-12237-9); paper $6.95 (0-531-16644-9). An interesting life of Pollock, with reproductions of his works and of those of fellow painters, and a timeline that adds historical context. (Rev: SLJ 5/03) [759]

POWERS, HARRIET

5279 Lyons, Mary E. *Stitching Stars: The Story Quilts of Harriet Powers* (5–7). Illus. Series: African American Artists and Artisans. 1993, Scribners $17.00 (0-684-19576-3). After Emancipation, this former slave created two huge story quilts that hang today in the Smithsonian and Boston's Museum of Fine Arts. (Rev: BCCB 12/93; BL 11/15/93; SLJ 2/94) [921]

REMBERT, WINFRED

5280 Rembert, Winfred. *Don't Hold Me Back: My Life and Art* (4–7). Illus. 2003, Cricket $19.95 (0-8126-2703-2). Rembert reflects on his life in the South as a sharecropper's son — picking cotton, dealing with racism, the civil rights movement — and displays his evocative works of art with comments on their creation. (Rev: BL 11/1/03*; SLJ 12/03*) [759.1]

REMBRANDT VAN RIJN

5281 Bonafoux, Pascal. *A Weekend with Rembrandt* (5–9). Series: A Weekend With. 1992, Rizzoli $19.95 (0-8478-1441-6). This book introduces the artist on a personal level and also gives details on his life and work. (Rev: BL 8/92) [921]

5282 Pescio, Claudio. *Rembrandt and Seventeenth-Century Holland* (6–12). Illus. Series: Masters of Art. 1996, Bedrick $22.50 (0-87226-317-7). This excellent art book traces the flowering of Dutch art through text and reproductions by focusing on Rembrandt, his work, and his followers. (Rev: BL 5/15/96; SLJ 3/96*; VOYA 6/96) [921]

5283 Schwartz, Gary. *Rembrandt* (7–12). Series: First Impressions. 1992, Abrams $19.95 (0-8109-3760-3). This jargon-free, accessible biography presents Rembrandt with all his flaws and quirks. (Rev: BL 5/1/92; SLJ 6/92*) [921]

REMINGTON, FREDERIC

5284 Plain, Nancy. *Frederic Remington* (6–8). Illus. Series: Historical American Biographies. 2003, Enslow LB $20.95 (0-7660-1975-6). This look at Remington's life and accomplishments includes black-and-white reproductions of his works and period photographs that convey the flavor of the 1880s. (Rev: BL 6/1–15/03; SLJ 6/03) [709]

RENOIR, AUGUSTE

5285 Parsons, Tom. *Pierre Auguste Renoir* (5–7). Illus. Series: Art for Young People. 1996, Sterling $14.95 (0-8069-6162-7). The life and work of this prolific French artist are examined in a series of double-page spreads. (Rev: BL 2/1/97; SLJ 3/97) [921]

5286 Rayfield, Susan. *Pierre-Auguste Renoir* (7–12). Series: First Impressions. 1998, Abrams $19.95 (0-8109-3795-6). A stunning book that focuses on Renoir's development as an Impressionist painter, with detailed discussions about individual pictures, full-color, full-page reproductions, and two double-page foldouts. (Rev: BL 12/1/98; HBG 3/99) [921]

RIVERA, DIEGO

5287 Bankston, John. *Diego Rivera* (5–7). Series: Latinos in American History. 2003, Mitchell Lane LB $19.95 (1-58415-208-7). A biography of the famous 20th-century Mexican artist who is best known for his murals with political overtones. (Rev: BL 1/1–15/04) [921]

5288 Braun, Barbara. *A Weekend with Diego Rivera* (4–9). Illus. Series: Weekend with. 1994, Rizzoli $19.95 (0-8478-1749-0). A well-researched introduction to the life and work of this Mexican artist, best known as a muralist. (Rev: BL 9/15/94; SLJ 5/94) [921]

5289 Cockcroft, James D. *Diego Rivera* (5–9). Series: Hispanics of Achievement. 1991, Chelsea LB $21.95 (0-7910-1252-2). The life of this Mexican artist and activist, with several illustrations. (Rev: BL 11/1/91; SLJ 1/92) [921]

5290 Goldstein, Ernest. *The Journey of Diego Rivera* (7–10). Illus. 1996, Lerner LB $23.93 (0-8225-2066-4). Though short on biographical material, this profusely illustrated volume is a fine introduction to Rivera's art and its connections to the history of Mexico. (Rev: BL 4/15/96; SLJ 1/96; VOYA 10/96) [921]

5291 Gonzales, Doreen. *Diego Rivera: His Art, His Life* (6–9). Illus. Series: Hispanic Americans. 1996, Enslow LB $20.95 (0-89490-764-6). The story of the great Mexican painter and muralist and his relationship with Frida Kahlo. (Rev: BL 11/1/96; BR 1–2/97; SLJ 10/96) [921]

ROCKWELL, NORMAN

5292 Gherman, Beverly. *Norman Rockwell: Storyteller with a Brush* (4–7). Illus. 2000, Simon & Schuster $19.95 (0-689-82001-1). An appealing biography of this New England artist who reflected mid-20th-century American life and values in his many paintings. (Rev: BCCB 7–8/00; BL 2/15/00; HB 3–4/00; HBG 10/00; SLJ 2/00) [921]

ROUSSEAU, HENRI

5293 Pfleger, Susanne. *Henri Rousseau: A Jungle Expedition* (4–7). Trans. by Catherine McCreadie. Illus. Series: Adventures in Art. 1999, Prestel $14.95 (3-7913-1987-6). The story of Henri Rousseau and the art that evolved from his visits to a botanical garden. (Rev: BL 2/1/99; SLJ 2/99) [921]

SCHULKE, FLIP

5294 Schulke, Flip. *Witness to Our Times: My Life as a Photojournalist* (6–12). Illus. 2003, Cricket $19.95 (0-8126-2682-6). In this volume full of examples of his work, Schulke describes his early life and his career covering events of the 20th century including the space program and the civil rights movement. (Rev: BL 4/15/03; HBG 10/03; SLJ 6/03) [070.4]

SCHULTZ, CHARLES M.

5295 Schuman, Michael A. *Charles M. Schultz: Cartoonist and Creator of Peanuts* (6–10). Series: People to Know. 2002, Enslow LB $20.95 (0-7660-1846-6). A fine biography of the creator of Peanuts, complete with many illustrations and cartoons. (Rev: BL 9/15/02; HBG 10/02) [921]

SIMMONS, PHILIP

5296 Lyons, Mary E. *Catching the Fire: Philip Simmons, Blacksmith* (4–8). 1997, Houghton $17.00 (0-395-72033-8). A biography of the contemporary African American craftsman and artist from Charleston, South Carolina, with extensive quotations from personal interviews. (Rev: BL 9/1/97; HBG 3/98; SLJ 9/97) [921]

UNGERER, TOMI

5297 Ungerer, Tomi. *Tomi: A Childhood Under the Nazis* (6–10). 1998, Roberts Rinehart $29.95 (1-57098-163-9). Using many memorabilia of the time, this is the illustrator's story of his life during World War II after the Germans entered his Alsace town in 1940 when he was 8 years old. (Rev: BL 12/15/98; SLJ 3/99) [921]

VAN GOGH, VINCENT

5298 Bonafoux, Pascal. *Van Gogh: The Passionate Eye* (7–12). Series: Discoveries. 1992, Abrams paper $12.95 (0-8109-2828-0). An overview of the life and work of this disturbed Dutch painter. (Rev: BL 7/92) [021]

5299 Crispino, Enrica. *Van Gogh* (6–12). Illus. Series: Masters of Art. 1996, Bedrick $22.50 (0-87226-525-0). The story of van Gogh's life and art is covered in a concise text, excellent reproductions, and engrossing diagrams. (Rev: BL 11/15/96; SLJ 12/96; VOYA 4/97) [921]

5300 Green, Jen. *Vincent van Gogh* (5–8). Series: Artists in Their Time. 2002, Watts LB $22.00 (0-531-12238-7); paper $6.95 (0-531-16648-1). The life and times of this 20th-century artistic genius are covered, with a number of reproductions of his paintings. (Rev: BL 10/15/02) [921]

5301 Greenberg, Jan, and Sandra Jordan. *Vincent van Gogh: Portrait of an Artist* (7–12). Illus. 2001, Delacorte $14.95 (0-385-32806-0). This absorbing biography gives details of van Gogh's life and work, but also presents his complex personality, attributing his erratic behavior not to madness but to epilepsy. (Rev: BL 8/01*; HB 11–12/01; HBG 3/02; SLJ 9/01*) [759.9492]

5302 Tyson, Peter. *Vincent van Gogh: Artist* (8–12). Illus. Series: Great Achievers: Lives of the Physically Challenged. 1996, Chelsea LB $21.95 (0-7910-2422-9). This mature biography discusses van Gogh's life and work and his contributions to Impressionism, achieved despite the deterioration of his mental health. (Rev: BL 5/1/96; SLJ 8/96) [921]

WANG YANI

5303 Zhensun, Zheng, and Alice Low. *A Young Painter: The Life and Paintings of Wang Yani — China's Extraordinary Young Artist* (5–8). 1991, Scholastic paper $17.95 (0-590-44906-0). The story of a self-taught prodigy whose paintings are highly regarded in China. Includes many examples of her unique work, based on the traditional Chinese style. (Rev: BCCB 9/91; BL 10/1/91*; SLJ 8/91) [921]

WARHOL, ANDY

5304 Bolton, Linda. *Andy Warhol* (5–8). Series: Artists in Their Time. 2002, Watts LB $22.00 (0-531-12225-5); paper $6.95 (0-531-16618-X). This biography includes material on the social period in which Warhol worked. (Rev: BL 10/15/02) [921]

WHISTLER, JAMES MCNEILL

5305 Berman, Avis. *James McNeill Whistler* (7–12). Series: First Impressions. 1993, Abrams $19.95 (0-8109-3968-1). A failure at West Point and in the Coast Guard, Whistler later pursued a career in art in Paris, where he gained worldwide renown. This well-illustrated account traces his life and work. (Rev: BL 12/1/93) [921]

WILLIAMS, PAUL R.

5306 Hudson, Karen E. *The Will and the Way: Paul R. Williams, Architect* (5–7). Illus. 1994, Rizzoli $14.95 (0-8478-1780-6). The story of this African American architect who, in his career from the 1920s to the 1970s, designed more than 3,000 buildings. (Rev: BL 2/15/94; SLJ 3/94) [921]

WOOD, GRANT

5307 Duggleby, John. *Artist in Overalls: The Life of Grant Wood* (4–8). 1996, Chronicle $15.95 (0-8118-1242-1). The life of this American artist tells of his difficult struggle with poverty and his great attachment to the Midwest. (Rev: BCCB 6/96; BL 4/15/96; HB 7–8/96; SLJ 5/96) [921]

WOOD, MICHELE

5308 Igus, Toyomi. *Going Back Home: An Artist Returns to the South* (4–8). Illus. 1996, Children's $16.95 (0-89239-137-5). The author re-creates the family history and life of the African American illustrator Michele Wood. (Rev: BCCB 12/96; BL 9/15/96; SLJ 7/97) [921]

WRIGHT, FRANK LLOYD

5309 Boulton, Alexander O. *Frank Lloyd Wright, Architect: An Illustrated Biography* (8–12). 1993, Rizzoli $24.95 (0-8478-1683-4). Examines both Wright's architecture and his private life in detail. (Rev: BL 12/15/93; SLJ 11/93) [921]

5310 Davis, Frances A. *Frank Lloyd Wright: Maverick Architect* (5–9). Illus. 1996, Lerner LB $30.35 (0-8225-4953-0). A well-documented life of this influential 20th-century architect, with many black-and-white photographs of his most important buildings. (Rev: BL 1/1–15/97; SLJ 1/97) [921]

5311 Middleton, Haydn. *Frank Lloyd Wright* (5–8). Series: Creative Lives. 2001, Heinemann LB $27.07

(1-58810-203-3). An attractive look at the architect's life and career with illustrations and a useful timeline. (Rev: HBG 10/02; SLJ 3/02) [921]

WYETH, ANDREW

5312 Meryman, Richard. *Andrew Wyeth* (6–12). Series: First Impressions. 1991, Abrams $19.95 (0-8109-3956-8). Insights into the artist's childhood show how various events influenced his life in this introduction to the work of this contemporary American master. (Rev: BL 8/91) [921]

ZHANG, SONG NAN

5313 Zhang, Song Nan. *A Little Tiger in the Chinese Night: An Autobiography in Art* (5–8). Illus. 1993, Tundra $19.95 (0-88776-320-0). The biography of a Chinese artist who endured many hardships before he was able to relocate to Montreal. (Rev: BCCB 3/94; BL 1/1/94*; SLJ 5/94) [921]

Authors

ALCOTT, LOUISA MAY

5314 Ruth, Amy. *Louisa May Alcott* (4–7). Series: A&E Biography. 1999, Lerner LB $25.26 (0-8225-4938-7). A clear, readable life of the author who wrote from personal experience about family life at the time of the Civil War and later. (Rev: BL 3/15/00; HBG 3/99; SLJ 1/99) [921]

5315 Silverthorne, Elizabeth. *Louisa May Alcott* (4–7). Illus. Series: Who Wrote That? 2002, Chelsea $22.95 (0-7910-6721-1). A look at the life and works of author Louisa May Alcott, with particular emphasis on how her family influenced her work. (Rev: BL 10/15/02; HBG 3/03; SLJ 10/02) [813]

5316 Warrick, Karen Clemens. *Louisa May Alcott: Author of Little Women* (5–8). Series: Historical American Biographies. 2000, Enslow LB $20.95 (0-7660-1254-9). Using many direct quotations from Alcott, along with fact boxes, maps, a chronology, and chapter notes, this is an interesting biography of the prolific writer from Pennsylvania. (Rev: BL 3/15/00; HBG 10/00) [921]

ANGELOU, MAYA

5317 Cuffie, Terrasita A. *Maya Angelou* (4–8). Series: The Importance Of. 1999, Lucent LB $27.45 (1-56006-532-X). A biography that traces Maya Angelou's life from her childhood exposure to poverty and bigotry in the rural South to her eventual fame as a writer. (Rev: BL 9/15/99; SLJ 11/99) [921]

5318 Kirkpatrick, Patricia. *Maya Angelou* (5–9). Series: Voices in Poetry. 2003, Creative Co. LB $19.95 (1-58341-281-6). This picture-book biography introduces readers to Angelou's poetry and life from childhood. (Rev: BL 12/1/03; SLJ 12/03) [811]

5319 Kite, L. Patricia. *Maya Angelou* (6–9). Series: A&E Biography. 1999, Lerner LB $25.26 (0-8225-4944-1). Beginning in 1993, when Maya Angelou read her poetry at President Clinton's inauguration, this biography flashes back to her birth in 1928 and continues through 1996, covering personal aspects of her life and honors she has received, and including brief descriptions of her poetry and other writing. (Rev: BL 3/15/00; SLJ 7/99) [921]

5320 Lisandrelli, Elaine S. *Maya Angelou: More than a Poet* (7–12). Illus. Series: African-American Biographies. 1996, Enslow LB $20.95 (0-89490-684-4). A biography of the famous African American writer that includes her work as a dancer, singer, actress, and spokesperson for African American causes. (Rev: BL 9/1/96; BR 9–10/96; SLJ 6/96; VOYA 10/96) [921]

5321 Raatma, Lucia. *Maya Angelou: Author and Documentary Filmmaker* (4–8). Series: Ferguson's Career Biographies. 2001, Ferguson LB $16.95 (0-89434-336-X). As well as a life of Maya Angelou, this book includes information on how to become a writer, filmmaker, and director. (Rev: SLJ 2/01) [921]

5322 Shapiro, Miles. *Maya Angelou* (7–10). Illus. Series: Black Americans of Achievement. 1994, Chelsea LB $21.95 (0-7910-1862-8). A chronological narrative of the life of this amazing African American writer that tells of her hardships and triumphs. (Rev: BL 6/1–15/94; SLJ 6/94) [921]

ASIMOV, ISAAC

5323 Boerst, William J. *Isaac Asimov: Writer of the Future* (5–9). Illus. 1998, Morgan Reynolds LB $21.95 (1-883846-32-3). An engaging biography of the amazingly prolific author and scientist who was considered a misfit in his youth. (Rev: BL 12/1/98; BR 9–10/99; SLJ 1/99) [921]

5324 Judson, Karen. *Isaac Asimov: Master of Science Fiction* (5–9). Illus. 1998, Enslow LB $20.95 (0-7660-1031-7). A biography of Asimov that includes two chapters particularly helpful to researchers: on his importance as a writer of science fiction and on his work in other genres. (Rev: BL 12/1/98; HBG 3/99; SLJ 2/99) [921]

AUSTEN, JANE

5325 Ruth, Amy. *Jane Austen* (5–8). Series: A&E Biography. 2001, Lerner LB $25.26 (0-8225-4992-

1). This is the intriguing story of Jane Austen, who lived a quiet, obscure life yet produced some of the world's greatest novels. (Rev: BL 6/1–15/01; HBG 10/01; SLJ 11/01) [921]

AVI

5326 Markham, Lois. *Avi* (5–8). 1996, Learning Works paper $7.99 (0-88160-280-9). This profile of the gifted writer recounts his triumph over dysgraphia, a learning disability that makes writing difficult, and explores his creative process and the major themes of his work. (Rev: BL 4/1/96; SLJ 8/96) [921]

5327 Mercier, Cathryn M., and Susan P. Bloom. *Presenting Avi* (6–10). Series: Twayne's United States Authors. 1997, Macmillan $29.00 (0-8057-4569-6). This biography of the noted writer of books for children and young adults is divided into chapters based on a role he has assumed as a writer, including storyteller, stylist, magician, and historian, and explores his many beliefs about the significance of literature. (Rev: SLJ 6/98) [921]

BALDWIN, JAMES

5328 Gottfried, Ted. *James Baldwin: Voice from Harlem* (7–12). Series: Impact Biographies. 1997, Watts LB $20.00 (0-531-11318-3). This biography, enlivened with many photographs, discusses Baldwin's childhood, beliefs, gay identity, and principal works. (Rev: BL 5/15/97; SLJ 7/97; VOYA 10/97) [921]

BARRIE, J. M.

5329 Aller, Susan Bivin. *J. M. Barrie: The Magic Behind Peter Pan* (6–8). 1994, Lerner LB $25.26 (0-8225-4918-2). This biography of the author reveals Barrie's similarities to his character Peter Pan and also gives details of his failed marriages. (Rev: BL 11/1/94; SLJ 12/94) [921]

BAWDEN, NINA

5330 Bawden, Nina. *In My Own Time: Almost an Autobiography* (8–12). 1995, Clarion $25.95 (0-395-74429-6). Bawden, the British author of numerous well-loved children's stories, writes of her own life. (Rev: BL 12/1/95) [921]

BORGES, JORGE LUÍS

5331 Lennon, Adrian. *Jorge Luís Borges* (5–9). Series: Hispanics of Achievement. 1991, Chelsea LB $19.95 (0-7910-1236-0). A simple account that describes the life and work of one of South America's great contemporary writers. (Rev: BL 3/15/92; SLJ 7/92) [921]

BRONTË FAMILY

5332 Guzzetti, Paula. *A Family Called Brontë* (6–9). 1994, Dillon LB $13.95 (0-87518-592-4). An account of the Brontë family written specifically for teenagers. (Rev: BL 5/15/94; SLJ 8/94; VOYA 8/94) [921]

5333 Kenyon, Karen Smith. *The Brontë Family: Passionate Literary Geniuses* (5–9). Series: Lerner Biographies. 2002, Lerner LB $30.35 (0-8225-0071-X). An absorbing introduction to the individual members of this literary family, with many illustrations and quotations from letters. (Rev: HBG 3/03; SLJ 1/03; VOYA 2/03) [921]

BROOKS, GWENDOLYN

5334 Rhynes, Martha E. *Gwendolyn Brooks: Poet from Chicago* (6–10). Illus. Series: World Writers. 2003, Morgan Reynolds LB $21.95 (1-931798-05-2). The chronological presentation in this biography provides readers with an understanding of Brooks's changing views and themes. (Rev: BL 2/15/03; HBG 10/03; SLJ 4/03; VOYA 6/03) [811]

BUCK, PEARL S.

5335 La Farge, Ann. *Pearl Buck* (7–10). Illus. 1988, Chelsea LB $19.95 (1-55546-645-1). The life of the writer who introduced pre-Revolutionary China to millions of American readers. (Rev: BL 8/88) [921]

BURNETT, FRANCES HODGSON

5336 Carpenter, Angelica S., and Jean Shirley. *Frances Hodgson Burnett: Beyond the Secret Garden* (4–8). Illus. 1990, Lerner LB $30.35 (0-8225-4905-0). A glimpse into the private life of the woman who wrote *The Secret Garden*. (Rev: BCCB 12/90; BL 1/1/91; SLJ 3/91*) [921]

BURROUGHS, EDGAR RICE

5337 Boerst, William J. *Edgar Rice Burroughs: Creator of Tarzan* (5–8). Illus. Series: World Writers. 2000, Morgan Reynolds LB $21.95 (1-883846-56-0). A concise biography of the prolific author who created Tarzan and was a pioneer of the science fiction genre. (Rev: BL 7/00; HBG 3/01; SLJ 1/01) [921]

BYARS, BETSY

5338 Byars, Betsy. *The Moon and I* (4–7). Illus. 1996, Morrow paper $4.99 (0-688-13704-0). A memoir from this well-known children's author, which gives her the opportunity to tell how she likes both writing and snakes. (Rev: BCCB 3/92; BL 5/15/92; SLJ 4/92) [921]

5339 Cammarano, Rita. *Betsy Byars* (4–7). Series: Who Wrote That? 2002, Chelsea $22.95 (0-7910-6720-3). A profile in text and pictures of one of America's best-loved authors and winner of the Newbery and other prizes. (Rev: BL 10/15/02; HBG 3/03) [921]

CARROLL, LEWIS

5340 Carpenter, Angelica Shirley. *Lewis Carroll: Through the Looking Glass* (6–9). Series: Lerner Biographies. 2002, Lerner LB $25.26 (0-8225-0073-6). The mathematician and author who created Alice is introduced through a look at his youth, education, university career, and Oxford friendships. (Rev: BCCB 1/03; HBG 3/03; SLJ 3/03; VOYA 8/03) [828]

CATHER, WILLA

5341 Keene, Ann T. *Willa Cather* (7–12). 1994, Messner LB $15.00 (0-671-86760-1). A biography examining the writer's childhood, college years, jobs as editor and teacher, travels, and friends, as well as her reputed lesbianism. (Rev: BL 10/1/94; SLJ 11/94; VOYA 4/95) [813]

5342 O'Brien, Sharon. *Willa Cather* (7–12). Series: Lives of Notable Gay Men and Lesbians. 1994, Chelsea LB $19.95 (0-7910-2302-8); paper $9.95 (0-7910-2877-1). This biography of the author focuses on her reputed lesbianism and shows how Cather created a nurturing network of women friends and lovers. (Rev: BL 11/1/94; SLJ 11/94; VOYA 2/95) [921]

5343 Streissguth, Thomas. *Writer of the Plains: A Story About Willa Cather* (4–7). Illus. 1997, Carolrhoda LB $25.55 (1-57505-015-3). A simple introduction to the works of Willa Cather and the places where she lived and wrote. (Rev: BL 6/1–15/97; SLJ 10/97) [921]

CERVANTES, MIGUEL DE

5344 Goldberg, Jake. *Miguel de Cervantes* (5–9). Series: Hispanics of Achievement. 1993, Chelsea LB $21.95 (0-7910-1238-7). The absorbing story of the Spanish writer whose life rivaled that of his adventurous hero, Don Quixote. (Rev: BL 9/15/93) [921]

CHESNUTT, CHARLES

5345 Thompson, Cliff. *Charles Chesnutt* (7–10). Series: Black Americans of Achievement. 1992, Chelsea LB $19.95 (1-55546-578-1). The life of this pioneering African American writer who explored themes related to slavery and the Reconstruction period in his fiction. (Rev: BL 12/1/92) [921]

CHRISTIE, AGATHA

5346 Dommermuth-Costa, Carol. *Agatha Christie: Writer of Mystery* (5–9). Series: Biographies. 1997, Lerner LB $30.35 (0-8225-4954-9). A biography of the "First Lady of Crime," with material on her personal life, including her two marriages. (Rev: SLJ 8/97; VOYA 4/98)

CISNEROS, SANDRA

5347 Mirriam-Goldberg, Caryn. *Sandra Cisneros: Latina Writer and Activist* (5–8). Illus. Series: Hispanic Biographies. 1998, Enslow LB $19.95 (0-7760-1045-7). A biography, enlivened with many quotations, of the woman who received Cs and Ds in school and later became a first-rate author and leading Hispanic American activist. (Rev: BL 1/1–15/99; VOYA 10/99) [921]

CLEARY, BEVERLY

5348 Cleary, Beverly. *A Girl from Yamhill: A Memoir* (6–12). Illus. 1988, Morrow $21.99 (0-688-07800-1). Details the early life in the Northwest of one of the greats of children's literature. (Rev: BL 6/1/88; BR 5–6/88; SLJ 5/88; VOYA 6/88) [921]

5349 Cleary, Beverly. *My Own Two Feet* (7–12). 1995, Morrow $15.00 (0-688-14267-2). In the second part of Cleary's candid autobiography, she departs for college. Although most appreciated by adults who grew up with her books, it also has a place on youth shelves. (Rev: BL 8/95*; SLJ 9/95) [921]

CONRAD, JOSEPH

5350 Fletcher, Chris. *Joseph Conrad* (7–9). Illus. 1999, Oxford LB $22.95 (0-19-521441-2). Using many quotations from Conrad's letters and works plus excellent illustrations, this biography traces the life of the adventurous author whose second language was English. (Rev: BL 1/1–15/00; HBG 4/00; SLJ 1/00) [921]

COURLANDER, HAROLD

5351 Jaffe, Nina. *A Voice for the People: The Life and Work of Harold Courlander* (7–10). Illus. 1997, Holt $16.95 (0-8050-3444-7). A biography of the famous collector of folk tales from minority groups who was also a noted writer and storyteller. (Rev: BL 11/1/97; HBG 3/98; SLJ 12/97) [921]

CRUTCHER, CHRIS

5352 Crutcher, Chris. *King of the Mild Frontier: An Ill-Advised Autobiography* (8–12). 2003, Greenwillow $16.99 (0-06-050249-5). Crutcher describes his young years and tense relationship with his family with humor and honesty. (Rev: BL 4/15/03*; HB 5–6/03; HBG 10/03; SLJ 4/03; VOYA 6/03) [813]

5353 Davis, Terry. *Presenting Chris Crutcher* (6–10). 1997, Macmillan $29.00 (0-8057-8223-0). A warm biography of this important young adult author, who combines sports stories with important themes including tolerance and the meaning of friendship. (Rev: SLJ 6/98; VOYA 6/98) [921]

DAHL, ROALD

5354 Dahl, Roald. *Boy: Tales of Childhood* (7–12). Illus. 1984, Farrar $17.00 (0-374-37374-4). The famous author's autobiography — sometimes humorous, sometimes touching — of growing up in Wales with a Norwegian family. (Rev: BL 6/87) [921]

5355 Shields, Charles J. *Roald Dahl* (4–7). Series: Who Wrote That? 2002, Chelsea $22.95 (0-7910-6722-X). A brief biography of the master of whimsical stories that involve such strange elements as secretive chocolate factories and giant peaches. (Rev: BL 10/15/02; HBG 3/03) [921]

D'ANGELO, PASCAL

5356 Murphy, Jim. *Pick and Shovel Poet: The Journeys of Pascal D'Angelo* (6–12). Illus. 2000, Clarion $20.00 (0-395-77610-4). The story of the short, hard life of the Italian American poet who wrote an important autobiography about coming to the New World. (Rev: BCCB 12/00; BL 3/1/01; HB 1–2/01; HBG 3/01; SLJ 1/01; VOYA 2/02) [973.04]

DANZIGER, PAULA

5357 Krull, Kathleen. *Presenting Paula Danziger* (6–12). Series: United States Authors. 1995, Twayne $29.00 (0-8057-4153-4). Examines writer Danziger's personal problems, humorous teaching experiences, and group discussions of her books in six thematic chapters. (Rev: BL 9/1/95; VOYA 2/96) [921]

DICKENS, CHARLES

5358 Collins, David R. *Tales for Hard Times: A Story About Charles Dickens* (4–8). Series: Creative Minds. 1991, Carolrhoda LB $25.55 (0-87614-433-4). The life of Charles Dickens, including his poverty-ridden childhood. (Rev: SLJ 3/91) [921]

DICKINSON, EMILY

5359 Dommermuth-Costa, Carol. *Emily Dickinson: Singular Poet* (6–9). 1998, Lerner LB $25.26 (0-8225-4958-1). Extensive quotations from poems and letters add interesting details to this biography of Emily Dickinson. (Rev: BL 12/15/98; BR 1–2/99; HBG 3/99; SLJ 11/98) [921]

5360 Olsen, Victoria. *Emily Dickinson* (7–12). Illus. 1990, Chelsea LB $19.95 (1-55546-649-4). An illustrated biography that describes the life of Emily Dickinson as well as her work. (Rev: BL 7/90) [921]

DORRIS, MICHAEL

5361 Weil, Ann. *Michael Dorris* (4–7). Illus. Series: Contemporary Native Americans. 1997, Raintree Steck-Vaughn LB $17.98 (0-8172-3994-4). The life story of the late Native American writer and teacher and his crusade to fight alcohol abuse. (Rev: BL 6/1–15/97) [921]

DOYLE, SIR ARTHUR CONAN

5362 Adams, Cynthia. *The Mysterious Case of Sir Arthur Conan Doyle* (5–8). Illus. Series: World Writers. 1999, Morgan Reynolds LB $21.95 (1-883846-34-X). This book traces the life of Sir Arthur Conan Doyle from his Scottish boyhood and failed medical practice to success as a writer and creator of Sherlock Holmes. (Rev: BL 3/1/99; BR 9–10/99; SLJ 9/99; VOYA 10/99) [921]

5363 Pascal, Janet B. *Arthur Conan Doyle: Beyond Baker Street* (7–12). Illus. 2000, Oxford $28.00 (0-19-512262-3). This biography of the creator of Sherlock Holmes tells how he was also a defender of those unjustly accused of crimes, a spiritualist, and a prolific author in various genres. (Rev: BL 2/15/00; HBG 9/00; SLJ 6/00) [921]

DUNBAR, PAUL LAURENCE

5364 Gentry, Tony. *Paul Laurence Dunbar* (7–12). Illus. 1988, Chelsea LB $21.95 (1-55546-583-8). A richly illustrated biography of one of the chief poets of the Harlem Renaissance of the 1920s. (Rev: BL 2/15/89; BR 1–289; SLJ 3/89; VOYA 2/89) [921]

5365 Reef, Catherine. *Paul Laurence Dunbar: Portrait of a Poet* (6–9). Series: African-American Biographies. 2000, Enslow $20.95 (0-7660-1350-2). Dunbar's experiences with injustice are described in this biography of the poet who dedicated his work to portraying the lives of African Americans. (Rev: HBG 9/00; SLJ 9/00) [811]

FITZGERALD, F. SCOTT

5366 Lazo, Caroline Evensen. *F. Scott Fitzgerald: Voice of the Jazz Age* (6–9). Series: Lerner Biographies. 2002, Lerner LB $25.26 (0-8225-0074-4). Fitzgerald's life from childhood, marriage, and work are covered in this interesting account that includes many black and white photographs (Rev: HBG 3/03; SLJ 12/02; VOYA 2/03) [813]

5367 Stewart, Gail B. *F. Scott Fitzgerald* (4–8). Series: The Importance Of. 1999, Lucent LB $27.45 (1-56006-541-9). The story of the famous Jazz Age author whose enduring works reflect American life in his era. (Rev: BL 9/15/99) [921]

5368 Tessitore, John. *F. Scott Fitzgerald: The American Dreamer* (7–12). Illus. 2001, Watts LB $24.00 (0-531-13955-7). An absorbing biography that recounts the author's complicated and ultimately tragic life. (Rev: BL 11/1/01; SLJ 11/01) [813]

FLEISCHMAN, SID

5369 Fleischman, Sid. *The Abracadabra Kid: A Writer's Life* (6–12). Illus. 1996, Greenwillow $16.99 (0-688-14859-X). The exciting autobiography of the famous author who was also a magician, gold miner, and World War II sailor. (Rev: BL 9/1/96*; BR 9–10/96; SLJ 8/96*; VOYA 4/97) [921]

FRITZ, JEAN

5370 Fritz, Jean. *China Homecoming* (8–12). Illus. 1985, Putnam $19.99 (0-399-21182-9). This autobiographical account describes the return of this author to China, where she spent her childhood. (Rev: SLJ 8/85) [921]

5371 Fritz, Jean. *Homesick: My Own Story* (5–7). 1982, Putnam $16.99 (0-399-20933-6); Dell paper $4.99 (0-440-43683-4). Growing up in the troubled China of the 1920s. [921]

GANTOS, JACK

5372 Gantos, Jack. *Hole in My Life* (8–12). 2002, Farrar $16.00 (0-374-39988-3). The gritty story of the author's experiences in prison after being convicted for drug smuggling — and his successful efforts to live a better life. (Rev: BCCB 5/02; BL 4/1/02; HB 5–6/02*; HBG 10/02; SLJ 5/02*; VOYA 6/02) [813.54]

GEISEL, THEODOR

5373 Dean, Tanya. *Theodor Geisel (Dr. Seuss)* (4–7). Illus. Series: Who Wrote That? 2002, Chelsea $22.95 (0-7910-6724-6). A look at the life and works of the author and illustrator known as Dr. Seuss. (Rev: BL 10/15/02; HBG 3/03) [813]

GIOVANNI, NIKKI

5374 Josephson, Judith Pinkerton. *Nikki Giovanni: Poet of the People* (7–12). Series: African-American Biographies. 2000, Enslow LB $20.95 (0-7660-1238-7). The life and work of one of the most popular living poets, who has written both for adults and children, is covered in prose and pictures. (Rev: BL 9/15/00; HBG 3/01; SLJ 1/01) [921]

GRIMM BROTHERS

5375 Hettinga, Donald R. *The Brothers Grimm: Two Lives, One Legacy* (5–8). Illus. 2001, Clarion $22.00 (0-618-05599-1). An interesting biography that places the brothers' lives in the context of their time and discusses their skills as lexicographers and scholars. (Rev: BL 7/01; HB 1–2/02; HBG 3/02; SLJ 10/01) [430]

GRISHAM, JOHN

5376 Weaver, Robyn M. *John Grisham* (5–8). Illus. Series: People in the News. 1999, Lucent LB $27.45 (1-56006-530-3). An accessible, laudatory biography of the lawyer and politician turned best-selling author. (Rev: BL 10/1/99; HBG 3/00; SLJ 11/99) [921]

HALEY, ALEX

5377 Shirley, David. *Alex Haley* (7–10). Series: Black Americans of Achievement. 1993, Chelsea LB $21.95 (0-7910-1979-9); paper $8.95 (0-7910-1980-2). The story of the African American writer who gave us the family saga *Roots*. (Rev: BL 2/15/94) [921]

HANSBERRY, LORRAINE

5378 McKissack, Patricia, and Fredrick McKissack. *Young, Black, and Determined: A Biography of Lorraine Hansberry* (8–12). Illus. 1997, Holiday $18.95 (0-8234-1300-4). This is the story of the late African American playwright who skyrocketed to fame in 1959 when she was only 28 for the play *A Raisin in the Sun*, which opened on Broadway and won the Drama Critics Award. (Rev: BCCB 5/98; BL 2/15/98; SLJ 4/98; VOYA 8/98) [921]

5379 Scheader, Catherine. *Lorraine Hansberry: Playwright and Voice of Justice* (7–10). Illus. Series: African-American Biographies. 1998, Enslow LB $20.95 (0-89490-945-2). Raised on Chicago's South Side, Lorraine Hansberry, writer and civil rights activist, used this setting for her prize-winning play *Raisin in the Sun*. (Rev: BL 9/1/98; HBG 3/99; SLJ 11/98) [921]

5380 Sinnott, Susan. *Lorraine Hansberry: Award-Winning Playwright and Civil Rights Activist* (7–12). 1998, Conari Pr. paper $6.95 (1-57324-093-1). This story of the great African American playwright who grew up with a passion for theater and politics conveys a sense of the politics from the 1930s to the 1960s and the pressures of fame on an artist. (Rev: BL 2/15/99) [921]

HEMINGWAY, ERNEST

5381 McDaniel, Melissa. *Ernest Hemingway: The Writer Who Suffered from Depression* (8–12).

Series: Great Achievers: Lives of the Physically Challenged. 1996, Chelsea LB $19.95 (0-7910-2420-2). This personal and literary biography emphasizes the way Hemingway contributed to and changed American literature, using many excerpts from his works as well as quotations from reviewers and critics, while also discussing his problems with alcohol and battles with the emotional problems that eventually led to his suicide. (Rev: BR 5–6/97; SLJ 3/97) [921]

5382 Tessitore, John. *The Hunt and the Feast: A Life of Ernest Hemingway* (7–12). Illus. Series: Impact Biographies. 1996, Watts LB $24.00 (0-531-11289-6). An excellent introduction to the life and works of the writer considered to be one of America's great 20th-century masters. (Rev: BL 1/1–15/97; BR 3–4/97; SLJ 1/97) [921]

5383 Yannuzzi, Della A. *Ernest Hemingway: Writer and Adventurer* (6–10). Series: People to Know. 1998, Enslow LB $20.95 (0-89490-979-7). An engrossing biography of the tempestuous writer whose life and loves were as exciting as his novels. (Rev: BL 11/15/98; HBG 3/99; SLJ 4/99) [921]

HENRY, MARGUERITE

5384 Collins, David R. *Write a Book for Me: The Story of Marguerite Henry* (7–10). Illus. Series: World Writers. 1999, Morgan Reynolds LB $21.95 (1-883846-39-0). A short, simple biography of the writer of such memorable books for young people as *King of the Wind*. (Rev: BL 3/15/99; SLJ 9/99; VOYA 10/99) [921]

HUGHES, LANGSTON

5385 Hill, Christine M. *Langston Hughes: Poet of the Harlem Renaissance* (6–10). Series: African-American Biographies. 1997, Enslow LB $20.95 (0-89490-815-4). An easy-to-read, accurate look at the poet's life and times, with good-quality black-and-white photographs. (Rev: BR 3–4/98; SLJ 1/98) [921]

5386 Meltzer, Milton. *Langston Hughes: A Biography* (7–10). 1968, HarperCollins $14.95 (0-690-48525-5). A rounded biography of the great African American writer and poet who spoke with great pride of his race. [921]

5387 Meltzer, Milton. *Langston Hughes: An Illustrated Edition* (6–12). Illus. 1997, Millbrook paper $20.95 (0-7613-0327-8). This is a new, large, well-illustrated edition of the highly respected 1968 biography of Langston Hughes. (Rev: BL 8/97; BR 3–4/98; SLJ 11/97; VOYA 2/98) [920]

5388 Osofsky, Audrey. *Free to Dream: The Making of a Poet, Langston Hughes* (6–10). Illus. 1996, Lothrop $16.00 (0-688-10605-6). An attractive biography that covers the writer's life and works as well as general information on the Harlem Renaissance. (Rev: BL 4/1/96; BR 9–10/96; SLJ 7/96) [921]

5389 Rummel, Jack. *Langston Hughes* (8–10). Illus. Series: Black Americans of Achievement. 1988, Chelsea LB $21.95 (1-55546-595-1). A highly readable biography of the African American poet and fiction writer that is well illustrated and contains excerpts from his writings. (Rev: BL 12/1/87; BR 1–2/89; VOYA 10/88) [921]

HURSTON, ZORA NEALE

5390 Calvert, Roz. *Zora Neale Hurston* (5–8). Illus. Series: Black Americans of Achievement. 1993, Chelsea LB $15.95 (0-7910-1766-4). A lively account of the life of the famous writer and folklorist. (Rev: BL 5/1/93; SLJ 6/93) [921]

5391 Lyons, Mary E. *Sorrow's Kitchen: The Life and Folklore of Zora Neale Hurston* (7–12). 1990, Scribners $15.00 (0-684-19198-9). A brief biography of the African American novelist whose use of dialect sometimes brought criticism from other writers and who until recently was largely forgotten. (Rev: BL 12/15/90; SLJ 1/91*) [921]

5392 Porter, A. P. *Jump at de Sun: The Story of Zora Neale Hurston* (7–12). 1992, Carolrhoda paper $12.75 (0-87614-546-2). A brief, easy-to-read biography that places Hurston within the context of the racism of her era. (Rev: BL 12/15/92; SLJ 1/93*) [921]

5393 Yannuzzi, Della A. *Zora Neale Hurston: Southern Storyteller* (7–12). Illus. Series: African-American Biographies. 1996, Enslow LB $20.95 (0-89490-685-2). The story of the Harlem Renaissance author who died penniless but left a priceless legacy in her writings. (Rev: BL 9/1/96; BR 9–10/96; SLJ 6/96) [921]

IRVING, WASHINGTON

5394 Collins, David R. *Washington Irving: Storyteller for a New Nation* (4–8). Illus. Series: World Writers. 2000, Morgan Reynolds LB $21.95 (1-883846-50-1). This biography introduces the globetrotting American writer and gives details of his work and personality. (Rev: BL 4/1/00; HBG 3/00; SLJ 5/00; VOYA 6/01) [921]

KEHRET, PEG

5395 Kehret, Peg. *Five Pages a Day: A Writer's Journey* (4–7). 2002, Albert Whitman LB $14.95 (0-8075-8650-1). Aspiring young writers will particularly enjoy Kehret's account of her writing life, from starting a newspaper about the neighborhood dogs to entering writing contests to her career as an

author of children's books. (Rev: BL 12/15/02; HBG 3/03; SLJ 9/02) [813]

KERR, M. E.

5396 Nilsen, Alleen P. *Presenting M. E. Kerr*. Rev. ed. (8–12). Series: Twayne's United States Authors. 1997, Twayne $29.00 (0-8057-9248-1). A biography of this popular young adult writer that also discusses her works, with a detailed analysis of her five most popular books. (Rev: SLJ 4/98; VOYA 4/98) [810]

KING-SMITH, DICK

5397 King-Smith, Dick. *Chewing the Cud* (8–12). Illus. 2002, Knopf $16.95 (0-375-81459-0). King-Smith's humor and love of animals shine in this interesting and informative memoir of his career as a children's book writer and his various preceding jobs. (Rev: BCCB 1/03; BL 10/15/02; HB 1–2/03; HBG 3/03; SLJ 11/02) [823]

KING, STEPHEN

5398 Keyishian, Amy, and Marjorie Keyishian. *Stephen King* (7–12). Series: Pop Culture Legends. 1995, Chelsea LB $21.95 (0-7910-2340-0). Gives insight into the life of one of the world's most successful writers, covering King's childhood poverty and abandonment by his father, support by his mother, and influences on his work by such giants as C. S. Lewis, H. G. Wells, and Bram Stoker. (Rev: BL 12/15/95; BR 11–12/96; SLJ 1/96) [921]

5399 Wukovits, John F. *Stephen King* (6–10). Illus. Series: People in the News. 1999, Lucent LB $17.96 (1-56006-562-1). A biography of the rags-to-riches prize-winning author whose mysteries and supernatural stories have thrilled millions. (Rev: BL 12/15/99; HBG 4/00; SLJ 11/99) [921]

L'ENGLE, MADELEINE

5400 Gonzales, Doreen. *Madeleine L'Engle: Author of "A Wrinkle in Time"* (5–8). Series: People in Focus. 1991, Dillon LB $13.95 (0-87518-485-5). A short biography of the beloved writer of such juvenile favorites as *A Wrinkle in Time* and the many books about the Austin family. (Rev: BL 2/15/92; SLJ 3/92) [921]

LEWIS, C. S.

5401 Gormley, Beatrice. *C. S. Lewis: Christian and Storyteller* (6–9). Illus. 1997, Eerdmans paper $8.00 (0-8028-5069-3). This biography of the author of the Narnia saga tells about his problems as a child after his mother's death and his gradual journey from atheism to Christianity. (Rev: BL 3/15/98; SLJ 6/98; VOYA 6/98) [921]

LONDON, JACK

5402 Dyer, Daniel. *Jack London: A Biography* (7–10). Illus. 1997, Scholastic paper $17.95 (0-590-22216-3). The hard life and early death of author Jack London, an adventurous, passionate lover of life. (Rev: BL 9/15/97; BR 3–4/98; SLJ 9/97; VOYA 10/98) [921]

5403 Stefoff, Rebecca. *Jack London: An American Original* (7–10). Series: Oxford Portraits. 2002, Oxford LB $24.00 (0-19-512223-2). A profile of this American original, his life, his work, and his lasting importance. (Rev: BL 7/02; HBG 10/02; SLJ 8/02) [921]

5404 Streissguth, Tom. *Jack London* (4–7). Series: A&E Biography. 2000, Lucent LB $25.26 (0-8225-4987-5). The story of an adventurer and author who battled personal hardships and wrote eloquently about nature and survival. (Rev: BL 12/15/00; HBG 3/01; SLJ 3/01) [921]

LOVECRAFT, H. P.

5405 Schoell, William. *H. P. Lovecraft: Master of Weird Fiction* (5–8). Illus. 2003, Morgan Reynolds LB $21.95 (1-931798-15-X). Lovecraft, known for his stories of horror and the supernatural, was born into privilege that ended with his parents' early deaths; his works only received real acclaim after his death. (Rev: BL 9/15/03; SLJ 12/03) [813]

LOWRY, LOIS

5406 Lowry, Lois. *Looking Back: A Book of Memories* (4–8). Illus. 1998, Houghton $16.00 (0-395-89543-X). This autobiographical work centers around a series of photographs and the author's comments on each. (Rev: BL 11/1/98; BR 5–6/99; HB 1–2/99; HBG 3/99; SLJ 9/98; VOYA 4/99) [921]

5407 Markham, Lois. *Lois Lowry* (5–8). Series: Meet the Author. 1995, Learning Works paper $7.99 (0-88160-278-7). This biography of the Newbery Medal–winning author tells how she became a writer and looks at the personal experiences that are reflected in her books. (Rev: SLJ 1/96) [921]

MCCAFFREY, ANNE

5408 Trachtenberg, Martha P. *Anne McCaffrey: Science Fiction Storyteller* (6–10). Illus. Series: People to Know. 2001, Enslow LB $20.95 (0-7660-1151-8). Trachtenberg introduces readers to McCaffrey's life and writing career, detailing the setbacks the author faced before winning the Hugo Award in 1968. (Rev: BL 7/01; HBG 3/02; SLJ 9/01) [813]

MAGEE, JOHN

5409 Granfield, Linda. *High Flight: A Story of World War II* (5–7). Illus. 1999, Tundra $15.95 (0-88776-469-X). The moving story of John Magee, a young Canadian Air Force pilot who was killed in World War II and who is best known for writing the poem "High Flight." (Rev: BCCB 12/99; BL 1/1–15/00; HBG 3/00; SLJ 2/00) [921]

MARTÍ, JOSÉ J.

5410 West, Alan. *José Martí: Man of Poetry, Soldier of Freedom* (5–8). Illus. Series: Hispanic Heritage. 1994, Millbrook LB $23.90 (1-56294-408-8). The life story of the famous 19th-century Cuban poet, with excerpts from his work in both Spanish and English. (Rev: SLJ 1/95) [921]

MILLAY, EDNA ST. VINCENT

5411 Daffron, Carolyn. *Edna St. Vincent Millay* (7–12). Illus. 1989, Chelsea LB $19.95 (1-55546-668-0). The life and career of this noted poet with examples of her work. (Rev: BL 12/1/89; BR 3–4/90; SLJ 3/90) [921]

MONTGOMERY, L. M.

5412 Andronik, Catherine M. *Kindred Spirit: A Biography of L. M. Montgomery, Creator of Anne of Green Gables* (6–9). 1993, Atheneum $16.00 (0-689-31671-2). Montgomery's biography uses her journals to portray her childhood with her grandparents on Prince Edward Island, her literary career and friendships, and her midlife marriage to a minister. (Rev: BL 11/1/93; SLJ 11/93; VOYA 12/93) [921]

MORRISON, TONI

5413 Century, Douglas. *Toni Morrison* (8–12). Series: Black Americans of Achievement. 1994, Chelsea LB $21.95 (0-7910-1877-6). A biography of the Nobel Prize–winning African American author, examining her life and the major themes of her novels. (Rev: BL 9/1/94; SLJ 7/94; VOYA 8/94) [921]

5414 Haskins, Jim. *Toni Morrison: Telling a Tale Untold* (7–12). Illus. 2002, Millbrook LB $26.90 (0-7613-1852-6). Haskins adds discussion of each of Morrison's books to this account of her life and literary career. (Rev: BL 10/1/02; HBG 3/03; VOYA 12/02) [813]

5415 Kramer, Barbara. *Toni Morrison: Nobel Prize–Winning Author* (7–12). Series: African-American Biographies. 1996, Enslow LB $20.95 (0-89490-688-7). Using many quotations and first-person comments, this biography re-creates the life and important works of this African American Nobel

Prize winner. (Rev. BL 9/15/96, DR 1–2/97; SLJ 11/96; VOYA 6/97) [921]

MYERS, WALTER DEAN

5416 Jordan, Denise M. *Walter Dean Myers: Writer for Real Teens* (7–10). Series: African-American Biographies. 1999, Enslow LB $19.95 (0-7660-1206-9). Jordan tells the story of the prolific African American writers who continues a storytelling tradition. (Rev: BL 11/15/99; HBG 4/00; SLJ 1/00) [921]

5417 Myers, Walter Dean. *Bad Boy: A Memoir* (7–12). 2001, HarperCollins $15.95 (0-06-029523-6). Myers describes his turbulent youth in Harlem in the 1940s, his difficulties in school, and his lifelong love of books. (Rev: BL 5/1/01; HB 7–8/01; HBG 10/01; SLJ 5/01; VOYA 6/01) [813.54]

NAYLOR, PHYLLIS REYNOLDS

5418 Naylor, Phyllis Reynolds. *How I Came to Be a Writer*. Rev. ed. (4–9). 2001, Simon & Schuster paper $4.99 (0-689-83887-5). Naylor describes the joys and difficulties of life as a writer and includes excerpts of her work in this autobiographical account. (Rev: SLJ 5/01) [921]

NERUDA, PABLO

5419 Goodnough, David. *Pablo Neruda: Nobel Prize–Winning Poet* (6–12). Illus. 1998, Enslow LB $20.95 (0-7660-1042-2). A brief, interesting biography of the great Chilean poet that includes good background material on the rise and fall of the dictator Allende. (Rev: BL 8/98; HBG 3/99; SLJ 9/98; VOYA 10/98) [921]

NIXON, JOAN LOWERY

5420 Nixon, Joan Lowery. *The Making of a Writer* (6–8). 2002, Delacorte $14.95 (0-385-73000-4). Nixon weaves lots of tips about writing into a fascinating memoir of her childhood and early writing career. (Rev: BCCB 9/02; BL 6/1–15/02; HBG 10/02; SLJ 7/02; VOYA 8/02) [813]

ORWELL, GEORGE

5421 Agathocleous, Tanya. *George Orwell: Battling Big Brother* (8–12). Illus. Series: Oxford Portraits. 2000, Oxford $28.00 (0-19-512185-6). A concise, well-written life of this fascinating English writer and his contributions to world literature. (Rev: BL 10/1/00; HBG 10/01) [921]

5422 Boerst, William J. *Generous Anger: The Story of George Orwell* (6–9). 2001, Morgan Reynolds $20.95 (1-883846-74-9). Report writers will find this a useful source of information on Orwell's life

and career, with quotations from primary sources and full chapter notes. (Rev: BL 6/1–15/01; HBG 10/02; SLJ 10/01) [828]

PAREDES, AMERICO

5423 Murcia, Rebecca Thatcher. *Americo Paredes* (5–7). Series: Latinos in American History. 2003, Mitchell Lane LB $19.95 (1-58415-207-9). The story of the Mexican American author, folklorist, and professor at the University of Texas in Austin who is also famous for establishing a center for intercultural studies. (Rev: BL 1/1–15/04) [921]

PATERSON, KATHERINE

5424 Cary, Alice. *Katherine Paterson* (5–8). Illus. Series: Meet the Author. 1997, Learning Works paper $7.99 (0-88160-281-7). A biography of the two-time Newbery winner, with many quotations from interviews and autobiographical essays. (Rev: BL 5/1/97; SLJ 7/97) [921]

PAULSEN, GARY

5425 Fine, Edith Hope. *Gary Paulsen: Author and Wilderness Adventurer* (5–8). Series: People to Know. 2000, Enslow LB $20.95 (0-7660-1146-1). The story of an outdoorsman who turned many of his exciting adventures into stories for children and young adults. (Rev: BL 9/15/00; HBG 10/00; SLJ 9/00) [921]

5426 Paterra, Elizabeth. *Gary Paulsen* (4–7). Series: Who Wrote That? 2002, Chelsea $22.95 (0-7910-6723-8). A profile of the prolific author (of almost 200 books) who is best known for his young adult outdoor survival stories. (Rev: BL 10/15/02; HBG 3/03) [921]

5427 Paulsen, Gary. *Caught by the Sea* (5–8). 2001, Delacorte $15.95 (0-385-32645-9). The author describes his ongoing love of the sea and the adventures he's had, some funny, some scary. (Rev: BL 9/15/01; HBG 3/02; SLJ 10/01; VOYA 12/01) [818]

5428 Paulsen, Gary. *Guts: The True Stories Behind Hatchet and the Brian Books* (5–10). 2001, Delacorte $16.95 (0-385-32650-5). These six stories re-create childhood experiences of the author Gary Paulsen, who was born to alcoholic parents in 1939 and who spent much of his youth in the woods of Minnesota where he hunted and fished. (Rev: BL 2/15/01; HB 3–4/01; HBG 10/01; SLJ 2/01; VOYA 6/01) [813]

5429 Peters, Stephanie True. *Gary Paulsen* (4–8). Illus. 1999, Learning Works paper $7.99 (0-88160-324-4). A straightforward biography of the outdoorsman and author that tells about his books, his interests, his alcoholism, and his continuing health problems. (Rev: BL 6/1–15/99; SLJ 6/99) [921]

POE, EDGAR ALLAN

5430 Kent, Zachary. *Edgar Allan Poe* (5–8). Series: Historical American Biographies. 2001, Enslow LB $20.95 (0-7660-1600-5). An informative, well-presented biography of this writer whose unique stories changed the history of American literature. (Rev: BL 1/1–15/02; HBG 3/02; SLJ 9/01) [921]

5431 Meltzer, Milton. *Edgar Allan Poe* (6–12). Illus. 2003, Millbrook LB $31.90 (0-7613-2910-2). Poe's difficult life and literary accomplishments are described within the larger context of early 19th-century society in this well-illustrated and well-documented biography. (Rev: BL 11/15/03) [818]

5432 Streissguth, Tom. *Edgar Allan Poe* (5–8). Series: A&E Biography. 2001, Lerner LB $25.26 (0-8225-4991-3). The tortured life of this early master of the short story is brought to life in an interesting text and many black-and-white illustrations. (Rev: BL 6/1–15/01; HBG 10/01; SLJ 8/01) [921]

PYLE, ERNIE

5433 O'Connor, Barbara. *The Soldiers' Voice: The Story of Ernie Pyle* (4–7). Illus. 1996, Carolrhoda LB $30.35 (0-87614-942-5). The story of the renowned World War II correspondent who died in the South Pacific while covering the war. (Rev: BCCB 10/96; BL 9/1/96; SLJ 8/96) [921]

RODRIGUEZ, LUIS

5434 Schwartz, Michael. *Luis Rodriguez* (4–8). Illus. Series: Contemporary Hispanic Americans. 1997, Raintree Steck-Vaughn LB $17.98 (0-8172-3990-1). The life of this contemporary Hispanic American who went from gang leader and drug addict to writer, journalist, publisher, speaker, and youth activist. (Rev: BL 4/15/97; SLJ 6/97) [921]

ROWLING, J. K.

5435 Chippendale, Lisa A. *Triumph of the Imagination: The Story of Writer J. K. Rowling* (7–10). Illus. Series: Overcoming Adversity. 2001, Chelsea LB $21.95 (0-7910-6312-7). Rowling's period on public assistance and the legal challenges to the Harry Potter books are among the topics touched on in this biography. (Rev: BL 3/15/02; HBG 10/02; SLJ 5/02) [823]

5436 Shapiro, Marc. *J. K. Rowling: The Wizard Behind Harry Potter* (5–8). 2000, St. Martin's paper $4.99 (0-312-27224-3). The creator of Harry Potter is profiled, with material on university life, her year in Paris, and her struggle to keep writing. (Rev: BL 11/15/00; SLJ 12/00; VOYA 2/01) [921]

5437 Steffens, Bradley. *J. K. Rowling* (5–7). Series: People in the News. 2002, Gale LB $27.45 (1-56006-776-4). Rowling's early life and education

figure prominently in this account of her life that also looks at the plot and setting of her novels and wonders what she will do when the series is finished. (Rev: BCCB 2/02; SLJ 10/02) [921]

SANDBURG, CARL

5438 Meltzer, Milton. *Carl Sandburg: A Biography* (5–10). Illus. 1999, Millbrook LB $31.90 (0-7613-1364-8). The story of a literary giant who, in addition to his poetry, is noted for nonfiction works including a biography of Abraham Lincoln. (Rev: BL 12/15/99; HBG 10/00; VOYA 6/00) [921]

SEBESTYEN, OUIDA

5439 Monseau, Virginia R. *Presenting Ouida Sebestyen* (6–12). Series: United States Authors. 1995, Twayne $28.00 (0-8057-8224-9). Sebestyen's unorthodox writing habits enliven this text, with biographical information and detailed analysis of six novels. (Rev: BL 9/1/95) [921]

SHAKESPEARE, WILLIAM

5440 Aliki. *William Shakespeare and the Globe* (4–7). Illus. 1999, HarperCollins LB $15.89 (0-06-027821-8). Shakespeare and Elizabethan England come to life in this detailed picture book that uses many quotations from his plays and also tells of the recent rebuilding of the Globe theater. (Rev: BCCB 4/99; BL 6/1–15/99*; HB 5–6/99; HBG 10/99; SLJ 5/99) [921]

5441 Dommermuth-Costa, Carol. *William Shakespeare* (5–8). Series: Biography. 2001, Lerner LB $25.26 (0-8225-4996-4). A readable, well-illustrated biography of the Bard of Avon with material on many of his plays. (Rev: BL 4/1/02; HBG 10/02; SLJ 3/02) [921]

5442 Fandel, Jennifer. *William Shakespeare* (5–9). Photos by Marcel Imsand. Series: Voices in Poetry. 2003, Creative Editions LB $19.95 (1-58341-283-2). A brief and appealing introduction to Shakespeare's life and work, with examples of his poems, excerpts from his plays, and illustrations. (Rev: SLJ 12/03) [822.3]

5443 Rosen, Michael. *Shakespeare: His Work and His World* (5–9). Illus. 2001, Candlewick $19.99 (0-7636-1568-4). An insightful look at Elizabethan culture and the life of William Shakespeare, as well as several of his plays. (Rev: BL 11/1/01; HBG 3/02; SLJ 11/01*) [822.3]

5444 Thrasher, Thomas. *The Importance of William Shakespeare* (4–8). Series: The Importance Of. 1998, Lucent LB $27.45 (1-56006-374-2). This work discusses Shakespeare and his contribution to world culture. (Rev: BL 12/15/98; VOYA 6/99) [921]

SHELLEY, MARY WOLLSTONECRAFT

5445 Darrow, Sharon. *Through the Tempests Dark and Wild: A Story of Mary Shelley, Creator of Frankenstein* (4–7). 2003, Candlewick $16.99 (0-7636-0835-1). The dramatic story of Mary Shelley's troubled youth is told in this beautifully illustrated, fictionalized picture-book biography. (Rev: BL 6/1–15/03; HBG 10/03; SLJ 6/03) [823]

5446 Miller, Calvin C. *Spirit like a Storm: The Story of Mary Shelley* (7–10). Illus. 1996, Morgan Reynolds LB $21.95 (1-883846-13-7). The life story of the fascinating, talented creator of *Frankenstein,* who was also the wife of poet Percy Bysshe Shelley. (Rev: BL 2/15/96; BR 1–2/97; SLJ 3/96; VOYA 6/96) [921]

SINGER, ISAAC BASHEVIS

5447 Singer, Isaac Bashevis. *A Day of Pleasure: Stories of a Boy Growing Up in Warsaw* (6–8). 1969, Farrar paper $8.95 (0-374-41696-6). A Hasidic Jew's fond remembrances of the world in which he grew up. [921]

SPINELLI, JERRY

5448 Spinelli, Jerry. *Knots in My Yo-Yo String: The Autobiography of a Kid* (5–8). 1998, Knopf LB $16.99 (0-679-98791-6); paper $10.95 (0-679-88791-1). A frank, delightful memoir of growing up in Norristown, Pennsylvania, during the 1950s by the renowned Newbery Medal–winning writer of fiction for young people. (Rev: BCCB 7–8/98; BL 5/1/98; HBG 10/98; SLJ 6/98; VOYA 12/98) [921]

STEINBECK, JOHN

5449 Florence, Donne. *John Steinbeck: America's Author* (6–8). Illus. Series: People to Know. 2000, Enslow LB $19.95 (0-7660-1150-X). A biography of the American Nobel Prize winner for literature with material on each of his great works. (Rev: BL 4/15/00; HBG 9/00) [921]

5450 Reef, Catherine. *John Steinbeck* (7–12). Illus. 1996, Clarion $17.95 (0-395-71278-5). A handsome photobiography that not only covers salient aspects of Steinbeck's life but also explores the themes and locales of his work. (Rev: BL 5/1/96; BR 9–10/96; SLJ 3/96; VOYA 8/96) [921]

5451 Tessitore, John. *John Steinbeck: A Writer's Life* (8–10). 2001, Watts LB $25.00 (0-531-11707-3). This readable biography focuses on Steinbeck's career, giving excerpts from his work at the beginning of each chapter. (Rev: SLJ 7/01) [813]

STEVENSON, ROBERT LOUIS

5452 Carpenter, Angelica S., and Jean Shirley. *Robert Louis Stevenson: Finding Treasure Island* (5–8). Illus. 1997, Lerner LB $30.35 (0-8225-4955-7). A lively biography of this great writer, who was a disappointment to his family because he did not become a minister. (Rev: BL 11/15/97; HBG 3/98; SLJ 12/97) [921]

5453 Gherman, Beverly. *Robert Louis Stevenson: Teller of Tales* (5–8). Illus. 1996, Simon & Schuster $16.00 (0-689-31985-1). The story of the author of *Treasure Island* who, though always in poor health, lived a full, adventurous life. (Rev: BL 10/1/96; BR 5–6/97; SLJ 2/97) [921]

STINE, R. L.

5454 Cohen, Joel H. *R. L. Stine* (5–8). Series: People in the News. 2000, Lucent LB $27.45 (1-56006-608-3). This well-documented biography, illustrated with several black-and-white photographs, tells the story of an author who enjoys scaring his readers. (Rev: BL 6/1–15/00; HBG 10/00; SLJ 8/00) [921]

STOKER, BRAM

5455 Whitelaw, Nancy. *Bram Stoker: Author of Dracula* (6–10). Illus. 1998, Morgan Reynolds LB $21.95 (1-883846-30-7). A well-documented biography of the writer who was fascinated with horror even as a child and eventually wrote the classic vampire tale *Dracula.* (Rev: BL 10/1/98; SLJ 6/98; VOYA 10/99) [921]

STOWE, HARRIET BEECHER

5456 Coil, Suzanne M. *Harriet Beecher Stowe* (7–12). 1993, Watts LB $20.00 (0-531-13006-1). An admiring biography of the celebrated author that documents the writing of *Uncle Tom's Cabin* and includes excerpts from her letters and works. (Rev: BL 1/15/94; SLJ 1/94; VOYA 4/94) [921]

5457 Fritz, Jean. *Harriet Beecher Stowe and the Beecher Preachers* (5–9). 1994, Putnam $15.99 (0-399-22666-4). In addition to covering *Uncle Tom's Cabin,* this biography gives a full account of Harriet Beecher's private life, marriage, and extended family. (Rev: BCCB 10/94; BL 8/94; HB 9–10/94; SLJ 9/94*; VOYA 8/94) [921]

5458 Jakoubek, Robert E. *Harriet Beecher Stowe: Author and Abolitionist* (6–9). Illus. 1989, Chelsea LB $19.95 (1-55546-680-X). This account is valuable not only as a biography of this famous writer but also as an insight into the horrors of slavery. (Rev: SLJ 6/89) [921]

TAN, AMY

5459 Kramer, Barbara. *Amy Tan: Author of the Joy Luck Club* (6–12). Illus. 1996, Enslow LB $20.95 (0-89490-699-2). The story of the Chinese American writer who at first denied her immigrant background and later grew to accept and celebrate it in her fiction. (Rev: BL 6/1–15/96; SLJ 10/96; VOYA 10/96) [921]

5460 Shields, Charles J. *Amy Tan* (7–10). Illus. Series: Women of Achievement. 2001, Chelsea LB $21.95 (0-7910-5889-1); paper $9.95 (0-7910-5890-5). An appealing biography of Amy Tan that explores Tan's relationship with her mother and interest in her Chinese heritage. (Rev: BL 3/1/02; HBG 10/02; SLJ 6/02) [813]

TARBELL, IDA

5461 Somervill, Barbara A. *Ida Tarbell: Pioneer Investigative Reporter* (6–9). Illus. Series: World Writers. 2002, Morgan Reynolds LB $20.95 (1-883846-87-0). In addition to giving details of Tarbell's life and career as an influential journalist, Somervill's interesting text introduces the reader to labor conditions in the early 20th century. (Rev: BL 3/1/02; HBG 10/02; SLJ 6/02) [070.92]

TOLKIEN, J. R. R.

5462 Lynch, Doris. *J. R. R. Tolkien* (5–8). Illus. 2003, Watts LB $29.50 (0-531-12253-0). An attractive biography that reveals how much the author of *The Lord of the Rings* was influenced by his surroundings and experiences. (Rev: BL 12/15/03) [828]

TWAIN, MARK

5463 Aller, Susan Bivin. *Mark Twain* (5–8). Series: A&E Biography. 2001, Lerner LB $25.26 (0-8225-4994-8). The colorful life of one of America's favorite authors is re-created in accessible text, black-and-white photographs, and such additions as interesting sidebars and extensive reading lists. (Rev: BL 6/1–15/01; HBG 10/01) [921]

5464 Cox, Clinton. *Mark Twain: America's Humorist, Dreamer, Prophet* (5–9). 1995, Scholastic paper $14.95 (0-590-45642-3). A biography that includes a discussion of Twain's views on race and how they changed. (Rev: BL 9/15/95; SLJ 9/95; VOYA 12/95) [921]

5465 Howard, Todd, ed. *Mark Twain* (7–12). Series: People Who Made History. 2002, Gale LB $31.20 (0-7377-0896-4); paper $19.95 (0-7377-0897-2). Detailed essays that explore various aspects of Twain's life and writing are preceded by a general introductory that gives an overview of his life and times. (Rev: BL 4/1/02) [921]

5466 Lasky, Kathryn. *A Brilliant Streak: The Making of Mark Twain* (4–7). Illus. 1998, Harcourt $18.00 (0-15-252110-0). Using many quotations and anecdotes from the author's work, this nicely illustrated biography of Mark Twain concentrates on his first 30 years when he was a steamboat pilot,

prospector, reporter, and budding writer. (Rev: BCCB 7–8/98; BL 4/1/98; HB 5–6/98; HBG 10/98; SLJ 4/98) [921]

5467 Lyttle, Richard B. *Mark Twain: The Man and His Adventures* (7–12). 1994, Atheneum $15.95 (0-689-31712-3). A sturdy biography that concentrates on the adventurous life Twain led during his formative years. (Rev: BL 12/1/94; SLJ 1/95; VOYA 2/95) [921]

5468 Pflueger, Lynda. *Mark Twain* (5–8). Series: Historical American Biographies. 1999, Enslow LB $20.95 (0-7660-1093-7). A balanced, well-documented biography that includes chapter notes, a bibliography, glossary, and some period black-and-white illustrations. (Rev: BL 1/1–15/00; HBG 3/00; SLJ 1/00) [921]

5469 Ross, Stewart. *Mark Twain and Huckleberry Finn* (4–7). Illus. 1999, Viking $16.99 (0-670-88181-3). This picture book for older readers takes a candid look at the acclaimed author, mentions true incidents that he incorporated into his plots, and supplies interesting personal details, such as the fact that he could smoke 40 cigars a day. (Rev: BL 3/1/99; HBG 10/99; SLJ 5/99) [921]

VERNE, JULES

5470 Schoell, William. *Remarkable Journeys: The Story of Jules Verne* (4–8). Series: World Writers. 2002, Morgan Reynolds LB $21.95 (1-883846-92-7). Writing was not Verne's first love, as Schoell explains in this accessible biography. (Rev: BL 6/1–15/02; HBG 10/02; SLJ 9/02) [843.8]

5471 Teeters, Peggy. *Jules Verne: The Man Who Invented Tomorrow* (5–7). Illus. 1993, Walker LB $14.85 (0-8027-8191-8). The life of the famous writer of science fiction, including his childhood in France. (Rev: BL 3/15/93; SLJ 5/93) [921]

WALKER, ALICE

5472 Lazo, Caroline Evensen. *Alice Walker: Freedom Writer* (6–12). Illus. Series: Lerner Biographies. 2000, Lerner LB $25.26 (0-8225-4960-3). The personal life and literary career of the woman who won the Pulitzer Prize for *The Color Purple* is enhanced by the frequent use of quotations. (Rev: BL 8/00; HBG 9/00; SLJ 8/00; VOYA 2/01) [921]

WELLS, H. G.

5473 Boerst, William J. *Time Machine: The Story of H. G. Wells* (5–8). Illus. Series: World Writers. 1999, Morgan Reynolds LB $21.95 (1-883846-40-4). The story of the intriguing English author, including material on his childhood, romances, political views, and literary works. (Rev: BL 1/1–15/00; HBG 3/00) [921]

WERSBA, BARBARA

5474 Poe, Elizabeth Ann. *Presenting Barbara Wersba* (8–12). Series: United States Authors. 1998, Macmillan $29.00 (0-8057-4154-2). An excellent introduction to the life and works of this groundbreaking YA novelist. (Rev: BL 9/1/98; SLJ 9/98; VOYA 12/98) [921]

WHEATLEY, PHILLIS

5475 McLendon, Jacquelyn. *Phillis Wheatley: A Revolutionary Poet* (4–7). Series: Library of American Lives and Times. 2003, Rosen LB $31.95 (0-8239-5750-0). Kidnapped into slavery from Senegal, Phillis Wheatley became a major voice in the American literary scene. (Rev: BL 6/1–15/03; SLJ 5/03) [921]

5476 Richmond, Merle. *Phillis Wheatley* (7–10). Illus. 1988, Chelsea LB $19.95 (1-55546-683-4). A heavily illustrated account of this poet who triumphed over slavery. (Rev: BL 2/15/88; SLJ 4/88) [921]

5477 Salisbury, Cynthia. *Phillis Wheatley: Legendary African-American Poet* (5–8). Series: Historical American Biographies. 2001, Enslow LB $20.95 (0-7660-1394-4). The life story of the first important African American poet, who was brought to America as a slave and bought by a Quaker family who allowed her to develop her talents. (Rev: BL 3/1/01; HBG 10/01; SLJ 7/01) [921]

5478 Sherrow, Victoria. *Phillis Wheatley: Poet* (4–7). Illus. Series: Junior World Biography. 1992, Chelsea LB $15.95 (0-7910-1753-2). The biography of the poet who is considered to be the first important African American writer. (Rev: BL 8/92; SLJ 8/92) [921]

WHITE, E. B.

5479 Gherman, Beverly. *E. B. White: Some Writer!* (5–9). 1992, Atheneum $16.00 (0-689-31672-0). A look at the life of the author of *Charlotte's Web* reveals a man who loved words and craved solitude. (Rev: BL 4/15/92; SLJ 7/92) [921]

5480 Tingum, Janice. *E. B. White: The Elements of a Writer* (7–10). 1995, Lerner LB $30.35 (0-8225-4922-0). This quiet biography of the author of the much-beloved *Charlotte's Web* and other books discusses the underside of White's success: his shyness and depression. (Rev: BL 11/1/95) [921]

WHITMAN, WALT

5481 Meltzer, Milton. *Walt Whitman: A Biography* (6–12). Illus. 2002, Millbrook LB $31.40 (0-7613-2272-8). This life story of the American poet emphasizes his place in the country's history. (Rev:

BL 4/1/02; HB 9–10/02; HBG 3/03; SLJ 3/02; VOYA 6/03) [811]

5482 Reef, Catherine. *Walt Whitman* (7–12). 1995, Clarion $16.95 (0-395-68705-5). A biography of the 19th-century poet who sang of America and the self. (Rev: BL 5/1/95; SLJ 5/95) [921]

WIESEL, ELIE

5483 Lazo, Caroline. *Elie Wiesel* (4–7). Illus. 1994, Dillon paper $7.95 (0-382-24715-9). The story of the distinguished writer and spokesman on the Holocaust who won the Nobel Peace Prize in 1986. (Rev: BL 2/15/95; SLJ 7/95) [921]

WILDER, LAURA INGALLS

5484 Wadsworth, Ginger. *Laura Ingalls Wilder: Storyteller of the Prairie* (5–8). Series: Biography. 1997, Lerner LB $30.35 (0-8225-4950-6). A solid, readable biography of this author that clarifies the chronology in the Little House books. (Rev: BL 3/1/97; SLJ 4/97) [921]

WILLIAMS, WILLIAM CARLOS

5485 Berry, S. L. *William Carlos Williams* (5–9). Series: Voices in Poetry. 2003, Creative Co. LB $19.95 (1-58341-284-0). This picture-book biography introduces readers to Williams's poetry and life from childhood. (Rev: BL 12/1/03) [808]

WOODSON, CARTER G.

5486 Durden, Robert F. *Carter G. Woodson: Father of African-American History* (6–10). Series: African-American Biographies. 1998, Enslow LB $20.95 (0-89490-946-0). This balanced, documented account focuses on the successes and failures of this historian, pioneering writer, and publisher, who devoted his life to the study of African American history and culture. (Rev: BR 11–12/98; SLJ 1/99) [921]

WRIGHT, RICHARD

5487 Hart, Joyce. *Native Son: The Story of Richard Wright* (6–10). Illus. Series: World Writers. 2002, Morgan Reynolds LB $21.95 (1-931798-06-0). This biography describes best-selling African American author Richard Wright's controversial works and his development as a writer. (Rev: BL 2/15/03; HBG 3/03; SLJ 4/03) [813]

5488 Urban, Joan. *Richard Wright* (7–10). Illus. 1989, Chelsea LB $19.95 (1-55546-618-4). A well-illustrated biography that also tells a little about the author's work. (Rev: BL 6/15/89; BR 9–10/89; SLJ 8/89) [921]

5489 Westen, Robin. *Richard Wright: Author of Native Son and Black Boy* (7–10). Series: African-American Biographies. 2002, Enslow LB $20.95 (0-7660-1769-9). The life and achievements of the African American novelist known for opposition to racial discrimination. (Rev: HBG 3/03; SLJ 1/03) [813]

YEATS, WILLIAM BUTLER

5490 Allison, Jonathan, ed. *William Butler Yeats* (6–12). Series: Poetry for Young People. 2003, Sterling $14.95 (0-8069-6615-7). A handomely illustrated collection of Yeats's poems, each introduced with commentary and followed by explanations of any challenging vocabulary. (Rev: BL 4/1/03; HBG 10/03; SLJ 2/03) [811]

Composers

BEETHOVEN, LUDWIG VAN

5491 Balcavage, Dynise. *Ludwig Van Beethoven: Composer* (4–8). Series: Great Achievers: Lives of the Physically Challenged. 1997, Chelsea LB $21.95 (0-7910-2082-7). This is an information-rich account of the composer's public and private life, with good coverage of his compositions. (Rev: SLJ 7/97) [921]

BERNSTEIN, LEONARD

5492 Blashfield, Jean F. *Leonard Bernstein: Composer and Conductor* (4–7). Series: Ferguson's Career Biographies. 2001, Ferguson LB $16.95 (0-89434-337-8). Numerous black-and-white photographs accompany the easily read text in this interesting account of Bernstein's life and career. (Rev: SLJ 7/01) [780]

5493 Hurwitz, Johanna. *Leonard Bernstein: A Passion for Music* (4–8). 1993, Jewish Publication Soc. $14.95 (0-8276-0501-3). The career of this amazing conductor and composer who was also a gifted pianist and teacher. (Rev: BL 2/15/94; SLJ 12/93) [921]

5494 Lazo, Caroline Evensen. *Leonard Bernstein: In Love with Music* (7–12). Illus. 2002, Lerner LB $25.26 (0-8225-0072-8). This detailed portrait of Bernstein's life and musical accomplishments includes many black-and-white photographs. (Rev: BL 10/15/02; HBG 3/03; VOYA 12/02) [780]

DVORAK, ANTONIN

5495 Horowitz, Joseph. *Dvorak in America* (6–12). Illus. 2003, Cricket $17.95 (0-8126-2481-8). Dvo-

rak's life in the United States (he arrived from Prague in the 1890s) is the focus of this narrative, which also covers the composition of the New World symphony. (Rev: BL 6/1–15/03) [780]

GERSHWIN, GEORGE

5496 Reef, Catherine. *George Gershwin: American Composer* (5–8). Illus. Series: Masters of Music. 2000, Morgan Reynolds LB $21.95 (1-883846-58-7). This biography traces the life one of America's great composers, giving insight into his personality, family, and times. (Rev: BL 2/15/00; HBG 10/00; SLJ 3/00) [921]

5497 Vernon, Roland. *Introducing Gershwin* (5–7). Illus. 1996, Silver Burdett LB $14.95 (0-382-39161-6); paper $8.95 (0-382-39160-8). This oversize volume with copious illustrations re-creates the life and times of George Gershwin. (Rev: BL 5/1/96; SLJ 9/96) [921]

GUTHRIE, WOODY

5498 Neimark, Anne E. *There Ain't Nobody That Can Sing Like Me: The Life of Woody Guthrie* (6–12). Illus. 2002, Simon & Schuster $17.95 (0-689-83369-5). This biography of the famous folk singer draws on Guthrie's own words to tell the story of his life. (Rev: BL 12/15/02; HB 9–10/02; HBG 3/03; SLJ 10/02; VOYA 2/03) [782.42162]

5499 Partridge, Elizabeth. *This Land Was Made for You and Me: The Life and Songs of Woodie Guthrie* (6–12). Illus. 2002, Viking $21.99 (0-670-03535-1). The life, work, and times of the folk singer, from his childhood in the Dust Bowl to his death from Huntington's Disease. (Rev: BL 4/1/02; HB 3–4/02*; HBG 10/02; SLJ 4/02; VOYA 8/02) [782.42162]

5500 Yates, Janelle. *Woody Guthrie: American Balladeer* (6–10). 1995, Ward Hill LB $14.95 (0-9623380-0-1); paper $10.95 (0-9623380-5-2). Describes Guthrie's creative life and provides important historical information, including the many tragedies suffered by his family and his friendly relationship with labor, members of the Communist Party, and other musicians. (Rev: BL 2/1/95; SLJ 3/95) [921]

JONES, QUINCY

5501 Kavanaugh, Lee H. *Quincy Jones: Musician, Composer, Producer* (5–8). 1998, Enslow LB $20.95 (0-89490-814-6). This biography describes Quincy Jones's 50-year career in music and how he overcame poverty, racism, and health problems to become a musical director, composer, producer, arranger, and driving force behind many award-winning recordings. (Rev: VOYA 8/98) [921]

JOPLIN, SCOTT

5502 Preston, Katherine. *Scott Joplin: Composer* (7–10). Illus. 1988, Chelsea LB $21.95 (1-55546-598-6). The story of the talented musician, composer, and performer and the legacy of ragtime music he has left us. (Rev: BL 2/1/88; SLJ 5/88) [921]

MOZART, WOLFGANG AMADEUS

5503 Vernon, Roland. *Introducing Mozart* (5–7). Illus. 1996, Silver Burdett LB $14.95 (0-382-39159-4); paper $8.95 (0-382-39158-6). The life and times of Mozart are covered in the oversize, heavily illustrated volume. (Rev: BL 5/1/96; SLJ 1/97) [921]

STILL, WILLIAM GRANT

5504 Reef, Catherine. *William Grant Still: African American Composer* (6–9). Illus. 2003, Morgan Reynolds LB $21.95 (1-931798-11-7). Still, who was born in 1895, shunned his mother's advice and devoted himself to music, learning to play, compose, and arrange. (Rev: BL 7/03; HBG 10/03; SLJ 9/03) [780.9]

Performers (Actors, Musicians, etc.)

ABDUL, PAULA

5505 Zannos, Susan. *Paula Abdul* (4–8). Series: Real-Life Reader Biography. 1999, Mitchell Lane LB $15.95 (1-883845-74-2). A brief biography of this choreographer and recording artist that recounts her many problems, including a struggle with bulimia and a series of failed marriages. (Rev: BL 6/1–15/99) [921]

ALBA, JESSICA

5506 Rivera, Ursula. *Jessica Alba* (5–8). Series: Celebrity Bios. 2002, Children's LB $20.00 (0-516-23909-0); paper $6.95 (0-516-23482-X). A quickly read biography of the young actress who appeared in the Fox TV series "Dark Angel" and such movies as *Idle Hands* and *Paranoid*. (Rev: BL 6/1–15/02) [921]

ALLEN, TIM

5507 Wukovits, John. *Tim Allen* (6–9). Illus. Series: Overcoming Adversity. 1998, Chelsea paper $9.95 (0-7910-4697-4). A sympathetic portrait of the show business star who once went to jail for selling cocaine and rebounded to gain success on TV's *Home Improvement*. (Rev: HBG 3/99, SLJ 11/98) [921]

ALONSO, ALICIA

5508 Arnold, Sandra M. *Alicia Alonso: First Lady of the Ballet* (6–10). 1993, Walker LB $15.85 (0-8027-8243-4). Overcoming the lack of dance schools in her native Cuba and going blind in her 20s, Alicia Alonso became a prima ballerina and went on to teach, study, and perform in Cuba. (Rev: BL 12/15/93; SLJ 11/93; VOYA 2/94) [921]

ANDERSON, MARIAN

5509 Broadwater, Andrea. *Marian Anderson: Singer and Humanitarian* (7–12). Series: African-American Biographies. 2000, Enslow LB $19.95 (0-7660-1211-5). The story of the great African American singer who broke many color barriers in the world of music. (Rev: BL 4/15/00; HBG 9/00) [921]

5510 Tedards, Anne. *Marian Anderson* (6–10). Illus. 1987, Chelsea LB $19.95 (1-55546-638-9). The life story of the great singer-artist who helped destroy many color barriers. (Rev: BL 2/1/88; SLJ 4/88) [921]

ARMSTRONG, LOUIS

5511 Old, Wendie C. *Louis Armstrong: King of Jazz* (5–9). Series: African-American Biographies. 1998, Enslow LB $20.95 (0-89490-997-5). The life and accomplishments of the legendary jazz trumpeter know as Satchmo who lived from 1900 to 1971. (Rev: BL 11/15/98; SLJ 11/98) [921]

5512 Tanenhaus, Sam. *Louis Armstrong* (7–10). Illus. 1989, Chelsea LB $21.95 (1-55546-571-4). The story of the African American musician who rose from poverty in New Orleans to the heights of the jazz world. (Rev: BL 3/15/89) [921]

BALANCHINE, GEORGE

5513 Kristy, Davida. *George Balanchine: American Ballet Master* (5–9). Illus. Series: Biographies. 1996, Lerner LB $30.35 (0-8225-4951-4). The story of the Russian émigré choreographer and how he changed the world of American ballet. (Rev: BL 9/1/96; SLJ 8/96) [921]

BANKS, TYRA

5514 Levin, Pam. *Tyra Banks* (5–8). Illus. Series: Black Americans of Achievement. 1999, Chelsea $21.95 (0-7910-5195-1); paper $9.95 (0-7910-4964-7). This is the story of an "ugly duckling" who was awkward and uncoordinated as a child but who later became a supermodel. (Rev: BL 2/15/00; HBG 3/00) [921]

BARR, ROSEANNE

5515 Gaines, Ann. *Roseanne: Entertainer* (5–8). Series: Overcoming Adversity. 1999, Chelsea LB $21.95 (0-7910-4706-7); paper $8.95 (0-7910-4707-5). The story of how this overweight housewife made difficult decisions and many sacrifices to achieve her goal of becoming successful not just in show business, but also in the difficult field of comedy, and later as a TV personality. (Rev: VOYA 8/98) [921]

BASIE, COUNT

5516 Kliment, Bud. *Count Basie* (7–10). Series: Black Americans of Achievement. 1992, Chelsea LB $21.95 (0-7910-1118-6). The story of this trailblazing band leader and his contributions to jazz and popular music. (Rev: BL 9/15/92) [781.65]

BEATLES (MUSICAL GROUP)

5517 Martin, Marvin. *The Beatles: The Music Was Never the Same* (7–9). Illus. Series: Impact Biographies. 1996, Watts LB $18.95 (0-531-11307-8). In spite of a rather plodding style, this is an attractive biography of the Mersey four, with emphasis on how they changed the course of pop music. (Rev: BL 2/1/97; SLJ 3/97) [921]

5518 Roberts, Jeremy. *The Beatles* (5–8). Series: Biography. 2001, Lerner LB $25.26 (0-8225-4998-0). This is the story of the Beatles, from Liverpool to international stardom and eventual separation. (Rev: BL 4/1/02; HBG 10/02) [921]

5519 Woog, Adam. *The Beatles* (4–8). Series: Importance Of. 1997, Lucent LB $27.45 (1-56006-088-3). Outlines the lives and careers of these four Liverpool natives and their many achievements. (Rev: BL 10/15/97; SLJ 12/97) [921]

BEIDERBECKE, BIX

5520 Collins, David R. *Bix Beiderbecke: Jazz Age Genius* (7–12). Illus. Series: Notable Americans. 1998, Morgan Reynolds LB $21.95 (1-883846-36-6). This biography chronicles the risc and fall of the amazing jazz cornet player Bix Beiderbecke, who died of alcoholism at age 28. (Rev: BL 7/98; SLJ 1/99) [921]

BERLIN, IRVING

5521 Furstinger, Nancy. *Say It with Music: The Story of Irving Berlin* (5–9). Illus. Series: Masters of Music. 2003, Morgan Reynolds LB $21.95 (1-931798-12-5). Well-researched and very readable, this account traces Berlin's life from Russia to the United States and his popular and lasting success as a songwriter. (Rev: BL 6/1–15/03; SLJ 10/03) [780.92]

BLADES, RUBEN

5522 Cruz, Barbara C. *Ruben Blades: Salsa Singer and Social Activist* (4–9). Series: Hispanic Biographies. 1997, Enslow LB $20.95 (0-89490-893-6). The inspiring story of the Panama-born musician and his involvement in social activism and politics. (Rev: BR 5–6/98; HBG 3/98; SLJ 1/98; VOYA 2/98) [921]

5523 Marton, Betty A. *Rubén Blades* (5–9). Series: Hispanics of Achievement. 1992, Chelsea LB $21.95 (0-7910-1235-2). The story of the Panamanian salsa singer who is also a poet and activist. (Rev: BL 10/1/92; SLJ 11/92) [921]

BOONE, JOHN WILLIAM

5524 Harrah, Madge. *Blind Boone* (5–8). Illus. 2003, Carolrhoda LB $25.26 (1-57505-057-9). The son of a runaway slave, Boone became blind as an infant but soon revealed a musical talent and went on to become a composer and concert pianist. (Rev: BL 12/1/03) [781.64]

BRANDY (SINGER)

5525 Nerz, A. Ryan. *Brandy* (5–8). Illus. Series: Scene. 1999, Aladdin paper $6.99 (0-689-82545-5). A fanzine treatment of this star's life and career. (Rev: VOYA 6/99) [921]

5526 Newman, Michael. *Brandy* (5–8). Series: Galaxy of Superstars. 2000, Chelsea $19.75 (0-7910-5781-X). A biography of the famous singer and star of *Moesha*. (Rev: BL 12/15/00; HBG 10/01) [921]

BROOKS, GARTH

5527 Howey, Paul. *Garth Brooks: Chart-Bustin' Country* (4–7). Illus. Series: Achievers Biographies. 1998, Lerner LB $21.27 (0-8225-2898-3). Using interviews with Garth Brooks and his family plus many interesting photographs, this biography tells of the country-western musician's slow rise to fame, his persistence, and his courage to explore forbidden topics in his songs. (Rev: BL 8/98; HBG 10/98) [921]

5528 Powell, Phelan. *Garth Brooks: Award-Winning Country Music Star* (4–7). Series: Real-Life Reader Biographies. 1999, Mitchell Lane LB $15.95 (1-58415-004-1). A biography of the award-winning country music star and how he got there. (Rev: SLJ 1/00)

5529 Wren, Laura Lee. *Garth Brooks: Country Music Superstar* (6–10). Series: People to Know. 2002, Enslow LB $20.95 (0-7660-1672-2). The story of the country music star and his incredible rise to fame told in text and pictures. (Rev: BL 9/15/02; HBG 3/03; SLJ 1/03) [921]

BULLOCK, SANDRA

5530 Hill, Anne E. *Sandra Bullock* (5–8). Series: People in the News. 2000, Lucent LB $27.45 (1-56006-711-X). Quotations from Bullock and others expand this biography and explain how and why she has gained prominence as a Hollywood actress. (Rev: BL 9/15/00) [921]

BURKE, CHRIS

5531 Geraghty, Helen M. *Chris Burke* (5–9). Series: Great Achievers: Lives of the Physically Challenged. 1994, Chelsea LB $19.95 (0-7910-2081-9). This biography of the star of TV's *Life Goes On* looks at Burke's family life and career success despite Down's syndrome. (Rev: BL 10/15/94) [921]

CAREY, MARIAH

5532 Cole, Melanie. *Mariah Carey* (5–10). Series: A Real-Life Reader Biography. 1997, Mitchell Lane LB $15.95 (1-883845-51-3). For hi-lo collections, this biography of the popular singer tells of her difficulties in reaching the top and of her career since then. (Rev: BL 6/1–15/98; HBG 3/98; SLJ 2/98) [921]

5533 Nickson, Chris. *Mariah Carey: Her Story* (8–10). 1995, St. Martin's paper $9.95 (0-312-13121-6). Traces Carey's fairy-tale rise to stardom. (Rev: BL 6/1–15/95) [921]

5534 Parker, Judy. *Mariah Carey* (5–8). Illus. Series: Celebrity Bios. 2001, Children's LB $20.00 (0-516-23425-0); paper $6.95 (0-516-29600-0). An attractive simple introduction that looks at the popular singer's childhood and first breaks. (Rev: BL 12/15/01; VOYA 4/02) [782.42164]

CARREY, JIM

5535 Wukovits, John. *Jim Carrey* (5–9). Series: People in the News. 1999, Lucent LB $27.45 (1-56006-561-3). From his boyhood in Canada to stardom in such movies as *The Truman Show*, this biography reveals Carrey's efforts to become a multidimensional actor. (Rev: BL 8/99; HBG 3/00) [921]

CASALS, PABLO

5536 Garza, Hedda. *Pablo Casals* (5–9). Series: Hispanics of Achievement. 1993, Chelsea LB $21.95 (0-7910-1237-9). The story of the legendary Spanish cellist and his exile from his homeland during Franco's regime. (Rev: BL 4/1/93; SLJ 7/93; VOYA 8/93) [921]

CHAPLIN, CHARLIE

5537 Schroeder, Alan. *Charlie Chaplin: The Beauty of Silence* (7–12). Series: Impact Biographies. 1997, Watts LB $20.00 (0-531-11317-5). This biography re-creates a history of Hollywood in its golden days, while capturing the life and work of this comic artist who was able through his art and technique to explore the relationship between tragedy and humor in his films. (Rev: BL 6/1–15/97; SLJ 6/97) [921]

5538 Turk, Ruth. *Charlie Chaplin: Genius of the Silent Screen* (5–9). 2000, Lerner LB $30.35 (0-8225-4957-3). A competent overview of this great movie maker's life from his childhood in England to his exile in Switzerland. (Rev: BL 2/15/00; HBG 10/00; SLJ 4/00) [921]

CHARLES, RAY

5539 Ritz, David. *Ray Charles: Voice of Soul* (6–10). 1994, Chelsea LB $21.95 (0-7910-2080-0); paper $8.95 (0-7910-2093-2). The story of Ray Charles Robinson, who overcame the hardships of poverty, racism, drug addiction, and blindness to become one of America's most influential musicians. (Rev: BL 11/15/94) [921]

5540 Turk, Ruth. *Ray Charles: Soul Man* (5–8). Illus. Series: Newsmakers. 1996, Lerner LB $30.35 (0-8225-4928-X). A candid biography of the great blind entertainer that includes compelling details about his childhood. (Rev: SLJ 8/96) [921]

CHRISTENSEN, HAYDEN

5541 Friedman, Katherine. *Hayden Christensen* (5–8). Series: Celebrity Bios. 2002, Children's LB $20.00 (0-516-23907-4); paper $6.95 (0-516-23481-1). A high-interest, simple biography of the young Canadian actor who plays Anakin Skywalker in the *Star Wars* prequels. (Rev: BL 6/1–15/02) [921]

COLTRANE, JOHN

5542 Barron, Rachel Stiffler. *John Coltrane: Jazz Revolutionary* (6–10). 2001, Morgan Reynolds LB $20.95 (1-883846-57-9). Coltrane's love of music and jazz innovations are the main focus of this biography. (Rev: HBG 3/02; SLJ 1/02; VOYA 10/03) [788.7]

5543 Selfridge, John. *John Coltrane: A Sound Supreme* (7–12). 1999, Watts LB $24.00 (0-531-11542-9). An appealing biography that discusses jazz in general as well as profiling Coltrane and his contributions to the genre. (Rev: SLJ 11/99) [788.7]

COOK, RACHAEL LEIGH

5544 Rivera, Ursula. *Rachel Leigh Cook* (5–8). Series: Celebrity Bios. 2002, Children's LB $20.00 (0-516-23908-2); paper $6.95 (0-516-23484-6). Ms.

Cook, a Minnesota native, starred in such movies as *Get Carter* and *Josie and the Pussycats*. (Rev: BL 6/1–15/02) [921]

COSBY, BILL

5545 Haskins, Jim. *Bill Cosby: America's Most Famous Father* (5–7). Illus. 1988, Walker LB $17.00 (0-8027-6786-9). The childhood and career of this famous entertainer. (Rev: BL 6/1/88) [921]

5546 Schuman, Michael A. *Bill Cosby: Actor and Comedian* (6–12). Series: People to Know. 1995, Enslow LB $20.95 (0-89490-548-1). Describes the life and career of one of the most successful comedians in modern times. (Rev: BL 9/15/95; SLJ 2/96; VOYA 2/96) [921]

5547 Woods, Harold, and Geraldine Woods. *Bill Cosby: Making America Laugh and Learn* (4–7). Illus. 1988, Macmillan LB $13.95 (0-87518-240-2). A biography of the outstanding African American comedian, educator, and humanitarian. [921]

CRUISE, TOM

5548 Powell, Phelan. *Tom Cruise* (6–9). Series: Overcoming Adversity. 1999, Chelsea LB $21.95 (0-7910-4940-X); paper $9.95 (0-7910-4941-8). The story of this famous actor, his struggle with dyslexia and his parents' divorce, and his eventual fame in film. (Rev: BL 5/15/99; HBG 9/99) [921]

DAMON, MATT

5549 Busch, Kristen. *Golden Boy* (6–12). 1998, Ballantine paper $5.99 (0-345-42816-1). This is a well-researched, fun read about Matt Damon, the young star who was co-author and star of *Good Will Hunting* and star of *Saving Private Ryan*. (Rev: VOYA 12/98) [921]

5550 Diamond, Maxine, with Harriet Hemmings. *Matt Damon: A Biography* (6–12). 1998, Pocket Books paper $4.50 (0-671-02649-6). A fast read that gives a well-researched look at this likable, multitalented young movie star, with plenty of off-screen gossip. (Rev: VOYA 12/98) [921]

5551 Greene, Meg. *Matt Damon* (5–8). Series: Galaxy of Superstars. 2000, Chelsea $19.75 (0-7910-5779-8). An entertaining biography of the actor who gained star status as the cowriter and lead actor in *Good Will Hunting*. (Rev: BL 12/15/00; HBG 10/01) [921]

5552 Scott, Kieran. *Matt Damon* (5–8). Illus. Series: Scene. 1999, Aladdin paper $6.99 (0-689-82405-X). A fan magazine treatment of this popular young actor's life and career, with many color photographs. (Rev: VOYA 6/99) [921]

DAVIS, MILES

5553 Frankl, Ron. *Miles Davis* (7–10). Series: Black Americans of Achievement. 1995, Chelsea LB $21.95 (0-7910-2156-4). The story of the famous African American trumpeter and his contributions to jazz. (Rev: BL 11/15/95) [921]

DEAN, JAMES

5554 Oleksy, Walter. *The Importance of James Dean* (7–12). Series: The Importance Of. 2000, Lucent LB $19.96 (1-56006-698-9). Using a number of firsthand quotations, this book traces the life of James Dean, his tragic death, and his impact on motion pictures. (Rev: BL 3/1/01) [921]

DICAPRIO, LEONARDO

5555 Catalano, Grace. *Leonardo DiCaprio: Modern-Day Romeo* (5–9). 1997, Dell paper $4.99 (0-440-22701-1). A pre-*Titanic* look at the teen heartthrob, with details on his career. (Rev: VOYA 10/97) [921]

5556 Stauffer, Stacey. *Leonardo DiCaprio* (5–8). Illus. Series: Galaxy of Superstars. 1999, Chelsea $19.75 (0-7910-5151-X); paper $8.95 (0-7910-5326-1). The story of this young actor's life, with special attention to his role in *Titanic*. (Rev: BL 4/15/99; BR 9–10/99; HBG 10/99; SLJ 5/99) [921]

5557 Thompson, Douglas. *Leonardo DiCaprio* (6–12). 1998, Berkley paper $11.95 (0-425-16752-6). Sixty color photographs highlight this tribute to the young actor's life through *Titanic* and *Man in the Iron Mask*. (Rev: BR 11–12/98; VOYA 10/98) [921]

DION, CELINE

5558 Lutz, Norma Jean. *Celine Dion* (5–8). Series: Galaxy of Superstars. 2000, Chelsea $19.75 (0-7910-5777-1). The story of the amazing career of this French Canadian singer and how she gained worldwide popularity. (Rev: BL 10/15/00; HBG 10/01) [921]

DOMINGO, PLÁCIDO

5559 Stefoff, Rebecca. *Plácido Domingo* (5–9). Series: Hispanics of Achievement. 1992, Chelsea LB $21.95 (0-7910-1563-7). The story of the amazing Spanish-born tenor and his sensational international career, with some information on his private life. (Rev: BL 12/1/92; SLJ 1/93) [921]

DOWD, OLYMPIA

5560 Dowd, Olympia. *A Young Dancer's Apprenticeship: On Tour with the Moscow City Ballet* (6–9). 2003, Twenty-First Century LB $24.90 (0-

7613-2917-X). Dowd tells the story of how, at the age of only 14, she was offered the opportunity to dance with the Moscow City Ballet. (Rev: HBG 10/03; SLJ 5/03; VOYA 10/03) [792.8]

DUNCAN, ISADORA

5561 O'Connor, Barbara. *Barefoot Dancer: The Story of Isadora Duncan* (5–7). Illus. 1994, Carolrhoda LB $30.35 (0-87614-807-0). The story of this eccentric individualist who influenced and liberated a generation of dancers. (Rev: BCCB 10/94; BL 7/94) [921]

DUNHAM, KATHERINE

5562 O'Connor, Barbara. *Katherine Dunham: Pioneer of Black Dance* (5–8). Illus. 2000, Carolrhoda LB $30.35 (1-57505-353-5). A fine biography of the African American choreographer who used her study of anthropology to create works for her own dance company and for stage and screen productions. (Rev: BL 5/15/00; HBG 10/00; SLJ 7/00; VOYA 2/01) [921]

DYLAN, BOB

5563 Horn, Geoffrey M. *Bob Dylan* (6–9). Series: Trailblazers of the Modern World. 2002, World Almanac Library LB $26.60 (0-8368-5076-9); paper $10.95 (0-8368-5236-2). A biography of the great performer and composer who also inspired a generation of songwriters. (Rev: BL 12/15/02) [921]

5564 Richardson, Susan. *Bob Dylan* (7–12). Series: Pop Culture Legends. 1995, Chelsea paper $8.95 (0-7910-2360-5). The life of this creative icon who influenced both country and pop music. (Rev: BL 8/95) [921]

ELLINGTON, DUKE

5565 Brown, Gene. *Duke Ellington: Jazz Master* (7–10). Illus. Series: Giants of Art and Culture. 2001, Blackbirch LB $21.95 (1-56711-505-5). Ellington's life and career are placed in historical context, with photographs, a timeline, a glossary, and lists of resources. (Rev: BL 8/01; HBG 3/02) [781.65]

5566 Frankl, Ron. *Duke Ellington: Bandleader and Composer* (6–10). Illus. 1988, Chelsea LB $21.95 (1-55546-584-6). The story of the evolution of a great composer and of his life in music. (Rev: BR 1–2/89; SLJ 8/88) [921]

5567 Old, Wendie C. *Duke Ellington: Giant of Jazz* (7–12). Series: African-American Biographies. 1996, Enslow LB $20.95 (0-89490-691-7). An attractive biography of this giant of jazz who was a brilliant composer and arranger as well as an outstanding performer. (Rev: BL 9/15/96) [921]

ESTEFAN, GLORIA

5568 Gonzales, Doreen. *Gloria Estefan: Singer and Entertainer* (5–9). Series: Hispanic Biographies. 1998, Enslow LB $20.95 (0-89490-890-1). This story of the singer who started with the Miami Sound Machine and then branched out as a soloist also reveals her devotion to her family and many social causes. (Rev: BR 9–10/98; HBG 3/99; SLJ 10/98; VOYA 10/98) [921]

5569 Rodriguez, Janel. *Gloria Estefan* (4–8). Illus. Series: Contemporary Hispanic Americans. 1995, Raintree Steck-Vaughn LB $24.26 (0-8172-3982-0). A fine biography of this Cuban American entertainer who, at the height of her career, overcame severe medical problems and remained a star singer. (Rev: BL 3/15/96; SLJ 1/96) [921]

5570 Shirley, David. *Gloria Estefan* (4–7). Illus. Series: Hispanics of Achievement. 1994, Chelsea LB $15.95 (0-7910-2114-4); paper $7.65 (0-7910-2117-3). A nicely illustrated biography of the Cuban-born rock star. (Rev: BL 11/15/94; SLJ 10/94) [921]

5571 Stefoff, Rebecca. *Gloria Estefan* (5–9). Series: Hispanics of Achievement. 1991, Chelsea LB $21.95 (0-7910-1244-1). The story of the singer who broke her back in a 1990 accident but bounced back to success. (Rev: BL 8/91; SLJ 12/91) [782.42164]

FRANKLIN, ARETHA

5572 Gourse, Leslie. *Aretha Franklin, Lady Soul* (7–10). 1995, Watts LB $20.00 (0-531-13037-1). A biography of the now-legendary singer that recalls the problems in her life, including the disappearance of her mother when she was six, as well as her many concert triumphs. (Rev: SLJ 10/95; VOYA 2/96) [921]

5573 Sheafer, Silvia A. *Aretha Franklin: Motown Superstar* (6–10). Series: African-American Biographies. 1996, Enslow LB $20.95 (0-89490-686-0). The life story of one of America's most popular singers is told, accompanied by a discography, chronology, and index. (Rev: BL 12/15/96; SLJ 9/96) [921]

FREEMAN, MORGAN

5574 DeAngelis, Gina. *Morgan Freeman* (7–12). Series: Black Americans of Achievement. 1999, Chelsea LB $19.95 (0-7910-4963-9). The life and career of the African American actor who starred on Broadway, on television, and in movies. (Rev: HBG 4/00; SLJ 1/00) [791.43]

GILLESPIE, DIZZY

5575 Gourse, Leslie. *Dizzy Gillespie and the Birth of Bebop* (6–10). 1994, Atheneum $14.95 (0-689-

31869-3). Bebop became a national music trend due in part to the influence of this trumpet-playing jazz legend. (Rev: BL 1/1/95; SLJ 3/95) [921]

GOH, CHAN HON

5576 Goh, Chan Hon, and Cary Fagan. *Beyond the Dance: A Ballerina's Life* (6–12). 2002, Tundra LB $15.95 (0-88776-596-3). A readable account of Goh's childhood in Vancouver and rapid rise as a ballet dancer to become a prima ballerina with the National Ballet of Canada. (Rev: HBG 10/03; SLJ 4/03; VOYA 4/03) [792]

GOLDBERG, WHOOPI

5577 Blue, Rose, and Corinne J. Naden. *Whoopi Goldberg* (7–10). Series: Black Americans of Achievement. 1995, Chelsea LB $21.95 (0-7910-2152-1); paper $8.95 (0-7910-2153-X). A biography that tells how in spite of great odds, this unusual comedian and actress rose to the top. (Rev: BL 3/15/95) [921]

5578 Caper, William. *Whoopi Goldberg: Comedian and Movie Star* (6–9). Illus. 1999, Enslow LB $19.95 (0-7660-1205-0). Goldberg's journey from the New York housing projects to Hollywood is detailed here with black-and-white photographs and a chronology and filmography. (Rev: BL 10/1/99) [791.43]

5579 Gaines, Ann. *Whoopi Goldberg* (6–9). Series: Overcoming Adversity. 1999, Chelsea LB $21.95 (0-7910-4938-8); paper $9.95 (0-7910-4939-6). The story of Whoopi Goldberg, her struggle with dyslexia, and how she dropped out of school at the age of 13 and turned to a life of drugs and sex before finding acting and a new life. (Rev: BL 5/15/99; HBG 9/99) [921]

5580 Katz, Sandor. *Whoopi Goldberg: Performer with a Heart* (5–8). Series: Junior Black Americans of Achievement. 1996, Chelsea $18.65 (0-7910-2396-6). A look at Whoopi Goldberg's life and career, focusing on how she feels about her profession and the causes she believes in. (Rev: BL 10/15/96; SLJ 1/97) [921]

GRAHAM, MARTHA

5581 Freedman, Russell. *Martha Graham: A Dancer's Life* (4–8). 1998, Clarion $18.00 (0-395-74655-8). Martha Graham's amazing talents, driving force, and complex personality are well depicted in this handsomely illustrated biography. (Rev: BCCB 6/98; BL 4/1/98; SLJ 5/98; VOYA 8/98) [921]

5582 Pratt, Paula B. *Martha Graham* (4–8). Illus. Series: The Importance Of. 1995, Lucent LB $27.45 (1-56006-056-5). The life of this amazing dancer, choreographer, and dance company founder. (Rev: BL 1/15/95; SLJ 1/95) [921]

5583 Probosz, Kathilyn S. *Martha Graham* (6–10). Series: People in Focus. 1995, Silver Burdett paper $7.95 (0-382-24961-5). With high-quality photographs, the author describes the dancer's many accomplishments and gives details on her youth and the influences on her work. (Rev: BL 8/95; SLJ 10/95) [921]

GRATEFUL DEAD (MUSICAL GROUP)

5584 *The Grateful Dead* (7–9). Illus. Series: Pop Culture Legends. 1997, Chelsea $21.95 (0-7910-3250-7); paper $8.95 (0-7910-4454-8). A colorful portrait of this band that has become a rock and roll legend and of its many dedicated fans, who are known as Deadheads. (Rev: BL 7/97; BR 9–10/97; SLJ 7/97) [782.42]

HANKS, TOM

5585 Kramer, Barbara. *Tom Hanks: Superstar* (6–8). Series: People to Know. 2000, Enslow LB $20.95 (0-7660-1436-3). A portrait of this amazing multi-talented superstar is presented in a heavily-illustrated account. (Rev: BL 3/1/01; HBG 10/01) [921]

HANSON (MUSICAL GROUP)

5586 Matthews, Jill. *Hanson: Mmmbop to the Top* (5–9). 1997, Pocket Books paper $3.99 (0-671-01913-9). A look at the three brothers who make up this popular band, with color photographs. (Rev: VOYA 10/98) [921]

5587 Powell, Phelan. *Hanson* (5–8). Series: Galaxy of Superstars. 1999, Chelsea $19.75 (0-7910-5148-X); paper $8.95 (0-7910-5325-3). An attractive volume with information on the three-brother singing group that hails from Tulsa, Oklahoma. (Rev: BL 4/15/98; BR 9–10/99; HBG 10/99) [921]

HART, MELISSA JOAN

5588 Ciacobello, John. *Melissa Joan Hart* (5–8). Series: Celebrity Bios. 2002, Children's LB $20.00 (0-516-23906-6); paper $6.95 (0-516-23483-8). An easily read, heavily illustrated biography of the young actress who gained stardom as *Sabrina, the Teenage Witch*. (Rev: BL 6/1–15/02; SLJ 8/02) [921]

HENDRIX, JIMI

5589 Markel, Rita J. *Jimi Hendrix* (7–10). Illus. Series: A&E Biography. 2001, Lerner LB $25.26 (0-8225-4990-5); paper $7.95 (0-8225-9697-0). The unhappy life and drug-related death of rock guitarist Jimi Hendrix are related with evocative descriptions of his music, a bibliography, Web sites, and discography. (Rev: BL 2/15/01; HBG 10/01; SLJ 3/01) [787.87]

5590 Piccoli, Sean. *Jimi Hendrix* (6–9). 1996, Chelsea LB $21.95 (0-7910-2042-8). An objective account of Hendrix's phenomenal music career and the unfortunate circumstances surrounding his death. (Rev: SLJ 11/96) [921]

5591 Stockdale, Tom. *Jimi Hendrix* (7–9). Illus. Series: They Died Too Young. 1999, Chelsea LB $18.65 (0-7910-4632-X). Early musical influences, career-related events, and the effects of drugs and alcohol are covered in this biography of the entertainer and singer whose career highlights included a tour in 1968 and a performance at Woodstock. (Rev: SLJ 7/98) [921]

HILL, FAITH

5592 Hinman, Bonnie. *Faith Hill* (5–9). 2001, Chelsea $19.75 (0-7910-6471-9). A look at the life and career of the country music star, with information on Nashville's Grand Ole Opry. (Rev: HBG 10/02; SLJ 4/02) [921]

HILL, LAURYN

5593 Greene, Meg. *Lauryn Hill* (5–8). Series: Galaxy of Superstars. 1999, Chelsea $19.75 (0-7910-5495-0). A biography of the music superstar who won five Grammy Awards for her breakout solo album. (Rev: BL 3/15/00; HBG 10/00) [921]

HINES, GREGORY

5594 DeAngelis, Gina. *Gregory Hines* (4–7). Illus. Series: Black Americans of Achievement. 1999, Chelsea $21.95 (0-7910-5197-8); paper $9.95 (0-7910-5198-6). Though he is known primarily as a dancer, this biography of Gregory Hines points out his many other talents, including acting. (Rev: BL 2/15/00; HBG 3/00) [921]

HITCHCOCK, ALFRED

5595 Adair, Gene. *Alfred Hitchcock: Filming Our Fears* (7–10). Series: Oxford Portraits. 2002, Oxford LB $24.00 (0-19-511967-3). Hitchcock's youth in England is covered in addition to chronological details of his career from the silent movies through his classic creations. (Rev: HBG 3/03; SLJ 11/02) [791.43]

HOLIDAY, BILLIE

5596 Kliment, Bud. *Billie Holiday* (8–12). Illus. 1990, Chelsea LB $19.95 (1-55546-592-7). A stirring biography of one of the great ladies of song whose life ended tragically. (Rev: BL 2/15/90; SLJ 5/90; VOYA 5/90) [921]

HOUDINI, HARRY

5597 Cox, Clinton. *Houdini: Master of Illusion* (5–9). Illus. 2001, Scholastic paper $16.95 (0-590-94960-8). A fast-paced account of the life of the world-famous magician from childhood on, with eight pages of photographs and reproductions. (Rev: BL 11/15/01; HB 1–2/02; HBG 3/02; SLJ 12/01; VOYA 2/02) [793.8]

5598 Lalicki, Tom. *Spellbinder: The Life of Harry Houdini* (5–8). Illus. 2000, Holiday $18.95 (0-8234-1499-X). A biography of Elrich Weiss, aka Harry Houdini, and his career as a magician and escape artist. (Rev: BCCB 3/01; BL 9/1/00; HBG 3/01; SLJ 9/00; VOYA 12/00) [921]

HOUSTON, WHITNEY

5599 Cox, Ted. *Whitney Houston: Singer Actress* (5–8). Illus. Series: Black Americans of Achievement. 1997, Chelsea LB $21.95 (0-7910-4455-6); paper $8.95 (0-7910-4456-4). A readable biography that shows Whitney Houston growing up in New Jersey, the major influences in her life, her rise to fame, marriage, and philanthropic endeavors. (Rev: BL 8/98; HBG 10/98) [921]

HOWARD, RON

5600 Kramer, Barbara. *Ron Howard: Child Star and Hollywood Director* (7–10). Series: People to Know. 1998, Enslow LB $20.95 (0-89490-981-9). Using many photographs of Howard at work, this book traces his career from sitcoms such as *Happy Days* to becoming the director of fine films including *Apollo 13*. (Rev: BL 2/15/99; HBG 3/99; SLJ 3/99) [921]

JACKSON, JANET

5601 Dyson, Cindy. *Janet Jackson* (4–7). Series: Black Americans of Achievement. 2000, Chelsea $21.95 (0-7910-5283-4). The life story of the popular singer and the ups and downs of her career. (Rev: BL 6/1–15/00; HBG 10/00) [921]

JACKSON, MAHALIA

5602 Gourse, Leslie. *Mahalia Jackson: Queen of Gospel Song* (6–10). Illus. Series: Impact Biographies. 1996, Watts LB $24.00 (0-531-11228-4). Although she could have been a famous blues singer, Mahalia Jackson devoted her life to religious music and became the "Queen of Gospel Soul." (Rev: BL 8/96; BR 11–12/96; SLJ 8/96) [921]

5603 Orgill, Roxane. *Mahalia: A Life in Gospel Music* (5–9). Illus. 2002, Candlewick $19.99 (0-7636-1011-9). An impassioned biography about the life of gospel singer Mahalia Jackson set against the backdrop of social and political events of the times.

(Rev: BL 2/15/02; HBG 10/02; SLJ 1/02; VOYA 8/02) [782.25]

JACKSON, MICHAEL

5604 Graves, Karen Marie. *Michael Jackson* (5–8). Series: People in the News. 2001, Lucent LB $35.15 (1-56006-707-1). The unusual life of this show business legend is outlined in text and photographs. (Rev: BL 4/1/02) [921]

5605 Nicholson, Lois. *Michael Jackson* (4–8). Illus. Series: Black Americans of Achievement. 1994, Chelsea LB $21.95 (0-7910-1929-2); paper $8.95 (0-7910-1930-6). A biography of the pop star that examines his loneliness and his family ties, and touches on the allegations against him of sexual abuse. (Rev: BL 10/15/94; SLJ 10/94) [921]

JACKSON, SAMUEL L.

5606 Dils, Tracey E. *Samuel L. Jackson* (4–7). Series: Black Americans of Achievement. 2000, Chelsea $21.95 (0-7910-5281-8). The life story of the African American actor who has portrayed diverse characters in films including *Pulp Fiction* and *A Time to Kill*. (Rev: BL 6/1–15/00; HBG 10/00) [921]

JEWEL (SINGER)

5607 Kemp, Kristen. *Jewel: Pieces of a Dream* (6–10). 1998, Simon & Schuster paper $4.99 (0-671-02455-8). A somewhat sanitized version of the life of the phenomenal Jewel, musician and songwriter, that tells about her rugged childhood in Alaska; overcoming dyslexia; yodeling in bars with her folk-singing parents; a year in an exclusive boarding school; living out of a VW van while singing in coffee shops; and the release of her first successful CD. (Rev: SLJ 4/99) [921]

JONES, JAMES EARL

5608 Hasday, Judy. *James Earl Jones: Actor* (7–10). Illus. Series: Overcoming Adversity. 1999, Chelsea LB $21.95 (0-7910-4702-4). A story of the great African American actor, noted for his deep, resonant voice, who conquered stuttering and muteness as a child. (Rev: HBG 9/98; SLJ 8/98; VOYA 8/98) [921]

JULIA, RAUL

5609 Perez, Frank, and Ann Well. *Raul Julia* (4–8). Illus. Series: Contemporary Hispanic Americans. 1995, Raintree Steck-Vaughn LB $28.80 (0-8172-3984-7). The story of the brilliant stage and film actor who gained fame in *The Addams Family* and on *Sesame Street*. This biography was written

before his untimely death. (Rev: BL 3/15/96; SLJ 1/96) [921]

LATIFAH, QUEEN

5610 Bloom, Sara R. *Queen Latifah* (4–7). Series: Black Americans of Achievement. 2001, Chelsea $21.95 (0-7910-6287-2). Numerous photographs add interest to this biography of the amazing singer-actress and her rise to fame. (Rev: BL 4/1/02; HBG 10/02; SLJ 6/02) [921]

5611 Ruth, Amy. *Queen Latifah* (5–8). Series: A&E Biography. 2000, Lerner LB $25.26 (0-8225-4988-3). The story of the female rap singer who used her positive attitudes, hard work, and determination to get ahead. (Rev: BL 3/1/01; HBG 10/01) [921]

LEE, BRUCE

5612 Tagliaferro, Linda. *Bruce Lee* (5–10). Series: A&E Biography. 2000, Lerner LB $25.26 (0-8225-4948-4); paper $7.95 (0-8225-9688-1). This colorful biography of the famous action star is filled with information about him, his films, and his family. (Rev: HBG 10/00; SLJ 5/00) [921]

LEE, SPIKE

5613 Hardy, James Earl. *Spike Lee* (7–10). Series: Black Americans of Achievement. 1995, Chelsea LB $21.95 (0-7910-1875-X); paper $9.95 (0-7910-1904-7). The story of the African American film producer and director who has fought for the right to express his ideas in a tough motion picture world. (Rev: BL 11/15/95; SLJ 12/95) [921]

5614 Haskins, Jim. *Spike Lee: By Any Means Necessary* (6–10). Illus. 1997, Walker LB $16.85 (0-8027-8496-8). Compiling previously published biographical material, the author has produced an interesting profile of this important African American filmmaker, including a behind-the-cameras view of each of Lee's 10 films to see what it takes to make a movie. (Rev: BL 5/1/97; SLJ 6/97; VOYA 10/97) [921]

5615 McDaniel, Melissa. *Spike Lee: On His Own Terms* (5–8). Series: Book Report Biographies. 1998, Watts LB $22.00 (0-531-11460-0); paper $6.95 (0-531-15935-3). An objective portrait of this controversial director, writer, and promoter of motion pictures featuring black subjects. (Rev: BL 2/15/99; HBG 3/99; SLJ 12/98) [921]

5616 Shields, Charles J. *Spike Lee* (5–7). Illus. 2002, Chelsea $22.95 (0-7910-6715-7). This look at Spike Lee's career, working methods, and importance includes both strengths and weaknesses and includes many photographs and quotations. (Rev: BL 11/1/02; HBG 3/03) [791.43]

LENNON, JOHN

5617 Conord, Bruce W. *John Lennon* (7–12). Series: Pop Culture Legends. 1993, Chelsea LB $21.95 (0-7910-1739-7); paper $8.95 (0-7910-1740-0). Looks at Lennon's childhood in Liverpool, his career with the Beatles, and his life after their breakup. (Rev: BL 12/15/93; SLJ 11/93) [921]

5618 Wright, David K. *John Lennon: The Beatles and Beyond* (6–10). Series: People to Know. 1996, Enslow LB $20.95 (0-89490-702-6). This biography of the legendary founder of one of the most popular music groups of all time explores Lennon's background and his development as a songwriter and as a political activist, as well as recounting the history of the Beatles. (Rev: BL 10/15/96; SLJ 12/96; VOYA 2/97) [921]

LETTERMAN, DAVID

5619 Lefkowitz, Frances. *David Letterman* (7–9). Series: Pop Culture Legends. 1996, Chelsea LB $21.95 (0-7910-3252-3); paper $8.95 (0-7910-3253-1). This show-business biography traces Letterman's career and the evolution of his style, with an emphasis on entertainers who influenced him. (Rev: SLJ 12/96) [921]

LOPEZ, JENNIFER

5620 Hill, Anne E. *Jennifer Lopez* (5–8). Series: Galaxy of Superstars. 2000, Chelsea $19.75 (0-7910-5775-5). This book chronicles the career of the young Latina star who is a fine singer and actress. (Rev: BL 10/15/00; HBG 10/01) [921]

LUCAS, GEORGE

5621 Rau, Dana Meachen, and Christopher Rau. *George Lucas: Creator of Star Wars* (5–8). Series: Book Report Biographies. 1999, Watts LB $22.00 (0-531-11457-0). An entertaining look at the popular filmmaker's life and accomplishments, illustrated with black-and-white photographs. (Rev: HBG 10/99; SLJ 7/99) [921]

5622 Shields, Charles J. *George Lucas* (5–7). Illus. Series: Behind the Camera. 2002, Chelsea $22.95 (0-7910-6712-2). A profile of the famous filmmaker, with information on his strengths and weaknesses, his working methods, and his importance to the American film industry, backed up by many photographs and quotations. (Rev: BL 11/1/02; HBG 3/03) [791.43]

5623 White, Dana. *George Lucas* (5–8). Series: A&E Biography. 1999, Lerner LB $30.35 (0-8225-4975-1); paper $7.95 (0-8225-9684-9). This book covers the childhood and early career of this filmmaker but concentrates on his masterpiece, the creation of the *Star Wars* saga. (Rev: HBG 3/00; SLJ 3/00) [921]

MCGREGOR, EWAN

5624 Jones, Veda Boyd. *Ewan McGregor* (5–8). Series: Galaxy of Superstars. 1999, Chelsea $19.75 (0-7910-5501-9). A well-illustrated biography of the Scottish-born actor in the *Star Wars* prequels. (Rev: BL 3/15/00; HBG 10/00) [921]

MADONNA

5625 Claro, Nicole. *Madonna* (7–10). Series: Pop Culture Legends. 1994, Chelsea LB $21.95 (0-7910-2330-3); paper $8.95 (0-7910-2355-9). Examines the pop diva's childhood, the early death of her mother, her rise to stardom, her love affairs, and her controversial personality. (Rev: BL 10/15/94; SLJ 11/94; VOYA 12/94) [021]

MARLEY, BOB

5626 Dolan, Sean. *Bob Marley* (6–9). Series: Black Americans of Achievement. 1996, Chelsea LB $21.95 (0-7910-2041-X); paper $8.95 (0-7910-3255-8). The life story of the Jamaican entertainer, with historical background about his island home. (Rev: SLJ 11/96) [921]

MARX, GROUCHO

5627 Tyson, Peter. *Groucho Marx* (7–12). Illus. Series: Pop Culture Legends. 1995, Chelsea $18.95 (0-7910-2341-9). The story of Groucho Marx, from his childhood on the Lower East Side of Manhattan to stardom with his brothers and, lastly, to fame as a quiz show host. (Rev: BL 7/95) [921]

MONROE, MARILYN

5628 Krohn, Katherine E. *Marilyn Monroe: Norma Jeane's Dream* (6–9). Series: Newsmakers Biographies. 1997, Lerner LB $30.35 (0-8225-4930-1). A well-illustrated biography that gives a good overview of the actress's life without probing into the mystery surrounding her death. (Rev: SLJ 7/97) [921]

5629 Lefkowitz, Frances. *Marilyn Monroe* (7–12). Series: Pop Culture Legends. 1995, Chelsea LB $21.95 (0-7910-2342-7); paper $8.95 (0-7910-2367-2). The story of the Hollywood star who, despite immense popularity, lived a tragic life. (Rev: BL 8/95) [921]

5630 Woog, Adam. *Marilyn Monroe* (6–10). Series: Mysterious Deaths. 1996, Lucent LB $22.45 (1-56006-265-7). After a brief overview of the star's life and career, this account describes her last night alive, and the many theories surrounding her death. (Rev: SLJ 3/97; VOYA 8/97) [921]

MORENO, RITA

5631 Suntree, Susan. *Rita Moreno* (5–9). Series: Hispanics of Achievement. 1992, Chelsea LB $21.95 (0-7910-1247-6). A biography of the Peurto Rican entertainer and her successes on stage and screen. (Rev: BL 2/1/93) [921]

MORRISON, JIM

5632 Lewis, Jon E. *Jim Morrison* (7–9). Illus. Series: They Died Too Young. 1997, Chelsea LB $18.65 (0-7910-4631-1). The great talent of this rock legend is highlighted in this biography that does not minimize the effects of drugs and alcohol on his life. (Rev: SLJ 7/98) [921]

MUNIZ, FRANKIE

5633 Beyer, Mark. *Frankie Muniz* (5–8). Series: Celebrity Bios. 2002, Children's LB $20.00 (0-516-23910-4); paper $6.95 (0-516-23480-3). Using simple sentences and many color photographs, this is a brief biography of the young actor who scored a big hit in "Malcolm in the Middle." (Rev: BL 6/1–15/02; SLJ 8/02) [921]

MURPHY, EDDIE

5634 Wilburn, Deborah A. *Eddie Murphy* (7–10). Series: Black Americans of Achievement. 1993, Chelsea LB $21.95 (0-7910-1879-2); paper $9.95 (0-7910-1908-X). A nicely illustrated introduction to the life of this talented actor/comedian. (Rev: BL 1/1/94; SLJ 1/94) [921]

NEW KIDS ON THE BLOCK (MUSICAL GROUP)

5635 McGibbon, Robin. *New Kids on the Block: The Whole Story* (5–8). Illus. 1990, Avon paper $6.95 (0-380-76344-3). Stories about members of this band have been collected from a variety of sources, including the members themselves. (Rev: BL 10/1/90) [921]

NUREYEV, RUDOLF

5636 Maybarduk, Linda. *The Dancer Who Flew: A Memoir of Rudolf Nureyev* (5–9). Illus. 1999, Tundra $18.95 (0-88776-415-0). The author, a friend and colleague of Nureyev, not only gives a straightforward biography of the dancer but also tells many backstage stories and introduces his most important roles. (Rev: BL 1/1–15/00; HBG 3/00; SLJ 2/00; VOYA 4/00) [921]

OAKLEY, ANNIE

5637 Flynn, Jean. *Annie Oakley: Legendary Sharpshooter* (4–9). Series: Historical American Biogra-phies. 1998, Enslow LB $20.95 (0-7660-1012-0). Using a concise text, fact boxes, and a chronology, this is the story of the star attraction of Buffalo Bill's Wild West Show. (Rev: BL 8/98; SLJ 8/98) [921]

5638 Macy, Sue. *Bull's-Eye: A Photobiography of Annie Oakley* (5–8). Illus. 2001, National Geographic $17.95 (0-7922-7008-8). This book separates fact from fiction in the life of Phoebe Ann Moses Butler, who came to be known as Annie Oakley. (Rev: BL 11/15/01; HBG 3/02; SLJ 10/01; VOYA 4/02) [799.3]

5639 Wukovits, John. *Annie Oakley* (4–8). Series: Legends of the West. 1997, Chelsea LB $18.65 (0-7910-3906-4). A profile of the famous sharpshooter and her career with Buffalo Bill's Wide West Show. (Rev: SLJ 10/97) [921]

O'DONNELL, ROSIE

5640 Kallen, Stuart A. *Rosie O'Donnell* (4–8). Series: People in the News. 1999, Lucent LB $27.45 (1-56006-546-X). An interesting, well-researched biography of this popular actress, comedienne, and talk-show host, covering her personal and professional life. (Rev: BL 8/99; HBG 3/00) [921]

5641 Krohn, Katherine E. *Rosie O'Donnell* (4–8). Series: A&E Biography. 1998, Lerner LB $25.26 (0-8225-4939-5). A breezy look at O'Donnell's rise from stand-up comic to TV fame with glimpses into her personal life, her mother's death when she was a child, and her fulfilling adoption of two children. (Rev: HBG 3/99; SLJ 2/99) [921]

5642 Stone, Tanya L. *Rosie O'Donnell: America's Favorite Grown-Up Kid* (4–7). Illus. 2000, Millbrook LB $23.90 (0-7613-1724-4). A well-designed, chatty biography of the popular talk-show host and comedienne. (Rev: BL 12/15/00; HBG 3/01) [792.7]

OLMOS, EDWARD JAMES

5643 Carrillo, Louis. *Edward James Olmos* (4–8). Illus. Series: Contemporary Hispanic Americans. 1997, Raintree Steck-Vaughn LB $17.98 (0-8172-3989-8). Along with a timeline and glossary, this account traces the life of this contemporary human rights activist and actor. (Rev: BL 4/15/97) [921]

OZAWA, SEIJI

5644 Tan, Sheri. *Seiji Ozawa* (5–7). Illus. Series: Contemporary Asian Americans. 1997, Raintree Steck-Vaughn LB $17.98 (0-8172-3993-6). A profile of the Asian American musician who has been the chief conductor of the Boston Symphony for more than 20 years. (Rev: BL 5/1/97; SLJ 9/97) [921]

PARKER, CHARLIE

5645 Frankl, Ron. *Charlie Parker* (7–10). Series: Black Americans of Achievement. 1992, Chelsea LB $21.95 (0-7910-1134-8). The story of the "Bird," his alto sax, and his contributions to jazz, particularly bebop. (Rev: BL 2/1/93) [921]

PAVLOVA, ANNA

5646 Levine, Ellen. *Anna Pavlova: Genius of the Dance* (5–7). 1995, Scholastic paper $14.95 (0-590-44304-6). The life and career of this legendary ballerina, with coverage of the famous ballets in which she danced. (Rev: BCCB 5/95; BL 1/1/95; SLJ 4/95*) [921]

PITT, BRAD

5647 Dempsey, Amy. *Brad Pitt* (6–8). Illus. Series: Superstars of Film. 1999, Chelsea LB $18.65 (0-7910-4649-4). An easy-to-read biography about the teen idol and the hard work and seized opportunities that made him a star. (Rev: SLJ 10/98) [921]

PRESLEY, ELVIS

5648 Brown, Adele Q. *Elvis Presley* (6–9). Series: Trailblazers of the Modern World. 2003, World Almanac LB $26.60 (0-8368-5085-8); paper $14.60 (0-8368-5245-1). A biography of the international pop music star who reigned as king for many years. (Rev: BL 6/1–15/03) [921]

5649 Denenberg, Barry. *All Shook Up: The Life and Death of Elvis Presley* (6–9). 2001, Scholastic paper $16.95 (0-439-09504-2). This accessible biography of Elvis places him in historical and musical context and discusses both good and bad sides of his personal life and his mismanaged career. (Rev: BL 10/1/01; HB 1–2/02; HBG 3/02; SLJ 1/02; VOYA 4/02) [782.42166]

5650 Gentry, Tony. *Elvis Presley* (7–12). Series: Pop Culture Legends. 1994, Chelsea LB $21.95 (0-7910-2329-X); paper $8.95 (0-7910-2354-0). The life of the "King" is re-created in this nicely illustrated biography. (Rev: BL 9/15/94) [921]

5651 Krohn, Katherine E. *Elvis Presley: The King* (5–7). Illus. 1994, Lerner LB $18.60 (0-8225-2877-0). A somewhat sanitized biography of Elvis Presley that highlights important events in his career. (Rev: BL 7/94; SLJ 7/94) [921]

5652 Torr, James D., ed. *Elvis Presley* (7–12). Series: People Who Made History. 2001, Greenhaven LB $31.20 (0-7377-0644-9); paper $19.95 (0-7377-0643-0). This volume contains a selection of serious essays that assess the life, contributions and place in entertainment history of Elvis Presley. (Rev: BL 9/15/01; SLJ 9/01) [921]

QUINN, ANTHONY

5653 Amdur, Melissa. *Anthony Quinn* (5–9). Series: Hispanics of Achievement. 1993, Chelsea LB $19.95 (0-7910-1251-4). The life of this Mexican American actor is told with many interesting asides concerning his career and black-and-white stills from his movies. (Rev: BL 9/15/93) [921]

REESE, DELLA

5654 Dean, Tanya. *Della Reese* (4–7). Series: Black Americans of Achievement. 2001, Chelsea $21.95 (0-7910-6291-0). The life and career of this show business giant are outlined with special coverage on her recent successes in television. (Rev: BL 4/1/02) [921]

REEVE, CHRISTOPHER

5655 Finn, Margaret L. *Christopher Reeve: Actor and Activist* (6–10). 1997, Chelsea LB $21.95 (0-7910-4446-7); paper $8.95 (0-7910-4447-5). The story of the gallant film actor, his tragic accident, and the causes he champions. (Rev: BR 5–6/98; HBG 3/98; VOYA 2/98) [921]

5656 Howard, Megan. *Christopher Reeve* (6–9). 1999, Lerner LB $25.26 (0-8225-4945-X). This is an inspiring portrait of the film star, his career, and the emotional and physical hardships he faced following his crippling horse-riding accident. Despite limitations and initial depression, Reeve has learned to focus on what he can do, rather than on what he can't. (Rev: BL 8/99) [921]

RIMES, LEANN

5657 Catalano, Grace. *LeAnn Rimes: Teen Country Queen* (5–8). 1997, Dell paper $4.99 (0-440-22737-2). In fanzine-like prose, this is an introduction to country music's hot young star. (Rev: VOYA 10/97) [921]

5658 Sgammato, Jo. *Dream Come True: The LeAnn Rimes Story* (5–8). 1997, Ballantine paper $4.99 (0-345-41650-3). LeAnn Rimes is a country music phenomenon whose life is described here, with details on the country music circuit. (Rev: VOYA 10/97) [921]

5659 Zymet, Cathy Alter. *LeAnn Rimes* (5–8). Series: Galaxy of Superstars. 1999, Chelsea $19.75 (0-7910-5152-8); paper $8.95 (0-7910-5327-X). This book covers the rise to stardom and the career of this country-western singer who hails from Jackson, Mississippi. (Rev: BL 4/15/98; BR 9–10/99; HBG 10/99) [921]

ROBESON, PAUL

5660 Ehrlich, Scott. *Paul Robeson: Singer and Actor* (7–10). Illus. 1988, Chelsea LB $21.95 (1-

55546-608-7). A biography of this talented actor, singer, and athlete whose career suffered because of his civil rights activities and Communist affiliations. (Rev: BL 2/1/88; SLJ 5/88) [921]

5661 Wright, David K. *Paul Robeson: Actor, Singer, Political Activist* (5–9). Illus. Series: African-American Biographies. 1998, Enslow LB $20.95 (0-89490-944-4). This book details Robeson's personal and professional life and the hardships he faced because of his race and beliefs. (Rev: BL 11/15/98; SLJ 11/98) [921]

ROCK, CHRIS

5662 Blue, Rose, and Corinne J. Naden. *Chris Rock* (4–7). Series: Black Americans of Achievement. 2000, Chelsea $21.95 (0-7910-5277-X). The story of the comedian and actor who began his career on *Saturday Night Live* and is noted for his acerbic wit. (Rev: BL 6/1–15/00; HBG 10/00) [921]

RODRIGUEZ, ROBERT

5663 Marvis, Barbara. *Robert Rodriguez* (5–10). Series: A Real-Life Reader Biography. 1997, Mitchell Lane LB $15.95 (1-883845-48-3). This simple, attractive biography of the successful movie maker focuses on his problems growing up in a large family and clinging to his career dreams. (Rev: BL 6/1–15/98; HBG 3/98; SLJ 2/98) [921]

ROGERS, WILL

5664 Malone, Mary. *Will Rogers: Cowboy Philosopher* (4–7). Illus. Series: People to Know. 1996, Enslow LB $20.95 (0-89490-695-X). A lively look at the life and accomplishments of this cowboy and show business idol. (Rev: BL 5/15/96; SLJ 6/96) [921]

RONSTADT, LINDA

5665 Amdur, Melissa. *Linda Ronstadt* (5–9). Series: Hispanics of Achievement. 1993, Chelsea LB $21.95 (0-7910-1781-8). This biography of the popular Mexican American singer describes her roots and pride in her Hispanic heritage. (Rev: BL 9/15/93; SLJ 10/93) [921]

SANDLER, ADAM

5666 Seldman, David. *Adam Sandler* (5–8). Series: Galaxy of Superstars. 2000, Chelsea $19.75 (0-7910-5773-9). An entertaining biography of the actor and comedian who gained notoriety from his roles in *The Waterboy* and *Big Daddy*. (Rev: BL 12/15/00; HBG 10/01) [921]

SAVION

5667 Glover, Savion, and Bruce Weber. *Savion! My Life in Tap* (5–10). 2000, Morrow $19.95 (0-688-15629-0). A fascinating autobiography of the young dancer and choreographer whose tap dancing includes rap and hip-hop in a wonderful combination that has entranced audiences. (Rev: BCCB 2/00; BL 1/1–15/00; HBG 10/00; SLJ 3/00) [921]

SCHUMANN, CLARA

5668 Allman, Barbara. *Her Piano Sang: A Story About Clara Schumann* (4–7). Illus. 1996, Carolrhoda LB $25.55 (1-57505-012-9). The story of this groundbreaking composer and pianist who also championed her husband's music. (Rev: BL 1/1–15/97; SLJ 1/97) [921]

5669 Reich, Susanna. *Clara Schumann: Piano Virtuoso* (5–8). 1999, Houghton $18.00 (0-395-89119-1). A thorough, well-researched biography of this amazing pianist and composer that describes her life as a child prodigy, her marriage to Robert Schumann, and her life promoting his music after his death. (Rev: BL 8/99; HB 3–4/99; HBG 10/99; SLJ 4/99*; VOYA 4/00) [921]

SCHWARZENEGGER, ARNOLD

5670 Doherty, Craig A., and Katherine M. Doherty. *Arnold Schwarzenegger: Larger Than Life* (6–10). 1993, Walker LB $15.85 (0-8027-8238-8). This biography portrays Schwarzenegger as an "American hero," outlining his life and applauding his physical fitness and business sense. (Rev: BL 12/1/93; SLJ 2/94; VOYA 4/94) [921]

SELENA

5671 Jones, Veda Boyd. *Selena* (6–9). Series: Latinos in the Limelight. 2001, Chelsea LB $17.95 (0-7910-6112-4). The life and work of the award-winning Texas singer who was shot by the president of her fan club. (Rev: HBG 10/01; SLJ 8/01) [782.42164]

5672 Marvis, Barbara. *Selena* (5–10). Series: A Real-Life Reader Biography. 1997, Mitchell Lane LB $15.95 (1-883845-47-5). A simple, attractive biography of the singer, her supportive family, and her tragic death. (Rev: BL 6/1–15/98; HBG 3/98; SLJ 2/98) [921]

SMITH, WILL

5673 Anderson, Marilyn D. *Will Smith* (6–10). Series: People in the News. 2003, Gale LB $21.96 (1-59018-140-9). The story of Will Smith's youth, life as a rapper, and stardom in movies including *Men in Black* will appeal to his many fans. (Rev: SLJ 3/03) [791.43]

5674 Berrenson, Jan. *Will Power! A Biography of Will Smith, Star of Independence Day and Men in Black* (5–8). 1997, Pocket Books paper $3.99 (0-671-88784-X). An intimate look at the life of the rapper and TV and movie star Will Smith, who was known as the class clown because of his goofy antics. (Rev: VOYA 10/97) [921]

5675 Rodriguez, K. S. *Will Smith: From Fresh Prince to King of Cool* (6–10). 1998, HarperCollins paper $3.99 (0-06-107319-9). An appealing, easily read biography of this impressive TV/movie star and rap artist. (Rev: VOYA 4/99) [921]

5676 Stauffer, Stacey. *Will Smith* (6–10). Series: Black Americans of Achievement. 1998, Chelsea $21.95 (0-7910-4914-0); paper $9.95 (0-7910-4915-9). A serious biography of this popular star, beginning with *Independence Day* coverage, then moving back to Smith's childhood. (Rev: HBG 3/99; VOYA 8/99) [921]

5677 Stern, Dave. *Will Smith* (6–10). Illus. 1999, Aladdin paper $6.99 (0-689-82407-6). An oversize paperback with many color photographs that give a fan-magazine treatment to this star's life and career. (Rev: VOYA 8/99) [921]

SPEARS, BRITNEY

5678 Lutz, Norma Jean. *Britney Spears* (5–8). Series: Galaxy of Superstars. 1999, Chelsea $19.75 (0-7910-5499-3). A profile of the popular entertainer, telling how her childhood influenced her career path. (Rev: BL 3/15/00; HBG 10/00) [921]

SPICE GIRLS (MUSICAL GROUP)

5679 Shore, Nancy. *Spice Girls* (5–8). Series: Galaxy of Superstars. 1999, Chelsea $19.75 (0-7910-5149-8); paper $8.95 (0-7910-5328-8). Biographies of members of the popular singing group that took first Britain and then the world by storm. (Rev: BL 4/15/98; BR 9–10/99; HBG 10/99; SLJ 5/99) [921]

SPIELBERG, STEVEN

5680 Ferber, Elizabeth. *Steven Spielberg* (7–12). Illus. Series: Pop Culture Legends. 1996, Chelsea LB $21.95 (0-7910-3256-6); paper $9.95 (0-7910-3257-4). An account of America's popular filmmaker that includes material on *Jaws*, *E. T.*, and *Jurassic Park*, and ends with *Schindler's List*. (Rev: BL 11/15/96; SLJ 1/97) [921]

5681 Horn, Geoffrey M. *Steven Spielberg* (6–9). Series: Trailblazers of the Modern World. 2002, World Almanac Library LB $26.60 (0-8368-5080-7); paper $10.95 (0-8368-5240-0). The story of one of the most successful directors and movie makers in the history of the cinema. (Rev: BL 12/15/02) [921]

5682 Powers, Tom. *Steven Spielberg: Master Storyteller* (5–7). Illus. 1997, Lerner LB $25.26 (0-8225-4929-8). A candid biography of this successful filmmaker, illustrated with stills from many of his most famous pictures, e.g., *Jaws* and *Schindler's List*. (Rev: BL 6/1–15/97) [921]

5683 Rubin, Susan Goldman. *Steven Spielberg: Crazy for Movies* (5–8). Illus. 2001, Abrams $19.95 (0-8109-4492-8). Director Steven Spielberg's love of photography from his youth, his fascination with storytelling, and his successful movie career are presented in lively text and large photographs. (Rev: BL 12/1/01; HBG 3/02; SLJ 12/01) [791.43]

5684 Schoell, William. *Magic Man: The Life and Films of Steven Spielberg* (4–7). Illus. 1998, Tudor $18.95 (0-936389-57-5). This biography of Spielberg concentrates on how he produces the astonishing special effects for his movies. (Rev: BL 5/15/98; SLJ 2/99) [921]

SPRINGSTEEN, BRUCE

5685 Frankl, Ron. *Bruce Springsteen* (7–10). Illus. Series: Pop Culture Legends. 1994, Chelsea paper $9.95 (0-7910-2352-4). The compelling story of the famous rocker who has never forgotten his working-class roots. (Rev: BL 6/1–15/94) [921]

SUMMER, DONNA

5686 Haskins, Jim, and J. M. Stifle. *Donna Summer: An Unauthorized Biography* (7–12). Illus. 1983, Little, Brown $14.95 (0-316-35003-6). From a bit part in *Hair* to complete stardom, this account of Donna Summer's life ends in the early 1980s. [921]

SUPREMES (MUSICAL GROUP)

5687 Rivera, Ursula. *The Supremes* (4–8). Illus. Series: Rock and Roll Hall of Famers. 2002, Rosen LB $29.25 (0-8239-3527-2). The Supremes' rise to stardom — and eventual fall from fame without leader Diana Ross — is chronicled here with photographs, glossary, discography, and bibliography. (Rev: BL 10/1/02; SLJ 5/02) [782.421644]

TEMPTATIONS (MUSICAL GROUP)

5688 Cox, Ted. *The Temptations* (6–10). Series: African American Achievers. 1997, Chelsea LB $21.95 (0-7910-2587-X); paper $9.95 (0-7910-2588-8). A chronicle of the rise and fall of this musical group, with profiles of each of the members and insights into the influence of Motown records on the careers of many African American musicians in the 1960s. (Rev: HBG 3/98; SLJ 1/98) [921]

THREE STOOGES

5689 Scordato, Mark, and Ellen Scordato. *The Three Stooges* (7–12). Series: Pop Culture Legends. 1995, Chelsea LB $19.95 (0-7910-2344-3); paper $9.95 (0-7910-2369-9). A look at the six men who composed the Three Stooges at various times. Includes black-and-white photographs, a filmography, and a chronology. (Rev: BL 6/1–15/95) [921]

TWAIN, SHANIA

5690 Gallagher, Jim. *Shania Twain: Grammy Award-Winning Singer* (4–7). Series: Real-Life Reader Biographies. 1999, Mitchell Lane LB $15.95 (1-58415-000-9). The story of the entertainer who was adopted into the Ojibwa tribe, began singing in bars at age eight, and went on to marry producer Mutt Lange. (Rev: SLJ 1/00) [921]

VALENS, RITCHIE

5691 Mendheim, Beverly. *Ritchie Valens: The First Latino Rocker* (8–12). Illus. 1987, Bilingual Pr. paper $15.00 (0-916950-79-4). The story of the popular Latino rocker who died in a plane crash in 1959. (Rev: BL 12/15/87) [921]

VAN DER BEEK, JAMES

5692 McCracken, Kristin. *James Van Der Beek* (5–8). Illus. Series: Celebrity Bios. 2001, Children's LB $20.00 (0-516-23429-3); paper $6.95 (0-516-29604-3). The combination of easy text, photographs, gossip, and details of Van Der Beek's youth will appeal especially to reluctant readers. (Rev: BL 12/15/01) [791.45]

WALTERS, BARBARA

5693 Remstein, Henna. *Barbara Walters* (5–8). 1998, Chelsea $21.95 (0-7910-4716-4); paper $9.95 (0-7910-4717-2). The life story of Barbara Walters, who broke many barriers for women in the communications field and has become an icon in the field of journalism. (Rev: HBG 3/99; VOYA 4/99) [921]

WASHINGTON, DENZEL

5694 Hill, Anne E. *Denzel Washington* (7–10). Series: Black Americans of Achievement. 1998, Chelsea $21.95 (0-7910-4692-3); paper $9.95 (0-7910-4693-1). A complimentary biography of this versatile, attractive actor who quickly rose to the top of the acting profession. (Rev: HBG 3/99; SLJ 3/99) [921]

WILLIAMS, VANESSA

5695 Boulais, Sue. *Vanessa Williams* (4–8). Series: Real-Life Reader Biography. 1999, Mitchell Lane LB $15.95 (1-883845-75-0). The life story of the African American who lost her title of Miss America in 1983 but rebounded with a brilliant career in show business. (Rev: BL 6/1–15/99) [921]

WINFREY, OPRAH

5696 Krohn, Katherine. *Oprah Winfrey* (5–8). Series: Biography. 2001, Lerner LB $25.26 (0-8225-4999-9). The media genius and talk-show hostess is profiled in an interesting text with many photographs. (Rev: BL 4/1/02; HBG 10/02) [921]

5697 Nicholson, Lois. *Oprah Winfrey: Talking with America* (5–8). Series: Junior Black Americans of Achievement. 1997, Chelsea LB $18.65 (0-7910-2390-7); paper $4.95 (0-7910-4460-2). A biography that skims the life of this personality, with material on her difficult childhood, sexual abuse, college experiences, early career, weight problems, and success on television. (Rev: SLJ 8/97) [921]

5698 Stone, Tanya Lee. *Oprah Winfrey: Success with an Open Heart* (4–7). Illus. Series: Gateway Biography. 2001, Millbrook LB $23.90 (0-7613-1814-3). Oprah's story, with concise text and excellent photographs, will attract and inspire young readers. (Rev: BL 6/1–15/01; HBG 10/01) [791.45]

5699 Wooten, Sara McIntosh. *Oprah Winfrey: Talk Show Legend* (6–10). Illus. Series: African-American Biographies. 1999, Enslow LB $20.95 (0-7660-1207-7). The story of the amazing television personality who rose from a background of poverty, loneliness, and sexual abuse to become world-famous. (Rev: BL 9/15/99; HBG 4/00; VOYA 12/99) [921]

WONDER, STEVIE

5700 Williams, Tenley. *Stevie Wonder* (7–10). Illus. Series: Overcoming Adversity. 2001, Chelsea LB $21.95 (0-7910-5903-0). This look at the musician's life and career puts an emphasis on the difficulties he has had to overcome. (Rev: BL 3/15/02; HBG 10/02) [782.421644]

Miscellaneous Artists

BARNUM, P. T.

5701 Andronik, Catherine M. *Prince of Humbugs: A Life of P. T. Barnum* (6–9). 1994, Atheneum $15.95 (0-689-31796-4). The master of hockum and old-fashioned show business is revealed in this interesting biography. (Rev: BL 12/15/94; SLJ 2/95; VOYA 5/95) [921]

5702 Barnum, P. T. *Barnum's Own Story* (7–12). Illus. 1962, Peter Smith $33.00 (0-8446-4001-8).

The autobiography of the showman who could fool people like no one else. [921]

5703 Fleming, Alice. *P. T. Barnum: The World's Greatest Showman* (5–8). 1993, Walker LB $15.85 (0-8027-8235-3). A look at the circus owner's childhood and various successful entrepreneurial ventures. (Rev: BL 1/15/94; SLJ 12/93; VOYA 2/94) [921]

5704 Tompert, Ann. *The Greatest Showman on Earth: A Biography of P.T. Barnum* (5–8). Illus. 1987, Dillon LB $13.95 (0-87518-370-0). An entertaining profile of the flamboyant showman and a discussion of his many money-making schemes. (Rev: BL 2/15/88; SLJ 3/88) [921]

5705 Warrick, Karen Clemens. *P. T. Barnum: Genius of the Three-Ring Circus* (5–8). Series: Historical American Biographies. 2001, Enslow LB $20.95 (0-7660-1447-9). The story of the showman and creator of "The Greatest Show on Earth" who presented such attractions as General Tom Thumb and Jenny Lind. (Rev: BL 4/15/01; HBG 10/01; SLJ 7/01) [921]

GALAN, NELY

5706 Rodriguez, Janel. *Nely Galan* (4–8). Illus. Series: Contemporary Hispanic Americans. 1997, Raintree Steck-Vaughn LB $17.98 (0-8172-3991-X). The life of this contemporary Hispanic American who, as a Hollywood producer, is responsible for developing TV and video projects for other Hispanic Americans. (Rev: BL 4/15/97) [921]

Contemporary and Historical Americans

Collective

5707 Allen, Paula Gunn, and Patricia C. Smith. *As Long As the Rivers Flow: The Stories of Nine Native Americans* (5–8). Illus. 1996, Scholastic paper $15.95 (0-590-47869-9). Nine notable Native Americans are profiled, including Geronimo, Will Rogers, and Maria Tallchief. (Rev: BL 12/1/96; BR 1–2/97; SLJ 1/97; VOYA 4/97) [920]

5708 Alter, Judith. *Extraordinary Women of the American West* (6–10). 1999, Children's Pr. LB $39.00 (0-516-20974-4). Profiles of 50 women, from the 18th century to modern times, representing a variety of races, careers, and contributions. (Rev: BL 8/99; SLJ 9/99) [920]

5709 Altman, Susan. *Extraordinary African-Americans: From Colonial to Contemporary Times.* Rev. ed. (5–8). Series: Extraordinary People. 2001, Children's LB $39.00 (0-516-22549-9). This revision of a 1989 title adds 36 new profiles and offers a good starting point for research into important African Americans throughout history. (Rev: SLJ 3/02; VOYA 8/02) [921]

5710 Ashby, Ruth. *Extraordinary People* (5–8). Series: Civil War Chronicles. 2002, Smart Apple LB $28.50 (1-58340-182-2). Key military and civilian figures from both North and South are profiled. (Rev: HBG 3/03; SLJ 2/03; VOYA 4/03) [973.7]

5711 Barber, James, and Amy Pastan. *Presidents and First Ladies* (4–8). Illus. 2002, DK LB $19.99 (0-7894-8454-4); paper $12.99 (0-7894-8453-6). For each president and his First Lady, there are biographies, a list of key events, and a box highlighting an important event during that administration, plus plenty of color illustrations. (Rev: BL 4/1/02; HBG 10/02; SLJ 5/02) [920]

5712 Blassingame, Wyatt. *The Look-It-Up Book of Presidents* (6–9). Illus. 1990, Random $14.99 (0-679-90353-4); paper $9.95 (0-679-80358-0). The author devotes two to six pages to each president and covers all the salient facts about each. (Rev: HBG 10/01; SLJ 5/90) [920]

5713 Bolden, Tonya. *And Not Afraid to Dare: The Stories of Ten African American Women* (6–9). Illus. 1998, Scholastic paper $16.95 (0-590-48080-4). The compelling biographies of 10 African American women, including Ida B. Wells, Mary McLeod Bethune, and Toni Morrison. (Rev: BCCB 5/98; BL 2/15/98; BR 11–12/98; HBG 9/98; SLJ 3/98; VOYA 6/98) [920]

5714 Brooks, Philip. *Extraordinary Jewish Americans* (5–9). Series: Extraordinary People. 1998, Children's LB $39.00 (0-516-20609-5); paper $16.95 (0-516-26350-1). In chronological order, this book presents brief biographical sketches of 60 prominent Jews from a wide variety of fields including science, business, sports, the arts, entertainment, and politics. (Rev: HBG 3/99; SLJ 10/98; VOYA 6/99) [920]

5715 Bruning, John Robert. *Elusive Glory: African-American Heroes of World War II* (5–8). Illus. Series: Avisson Young Adult. 2001, Avisson paper $19.95 (1-888105-48-8). The true stories of African American servicemen, including six Tuskegee Airmen, who served the United States during World War II. (Rev: BL 1/1–15/02; SLJ 4/02) [940.54]

5716 Burleigh, Robert. *Who Said That? Famous Americans Speak* (5–8). Illus. 1997, Holt $16.95 (0-8050-4394-2). Brief, insightful profiles use quotations in presenting 33 famous personalities including Benjamin Franklin, Sojourner Truth, Marilyn Monroe, and Louis Armstrong. (Rev: BL 3/1/97*; SLJ 5/97) [920]

5717 Calvert, Patricia. *Great Lives: The American Frontier* (4–8). Illus. 1997, Simon & Schuster $25.00 (0-689-80640-X). A large book that contains profiles of 27 individuals who played significant roles in the opening up of the West. (Rev: BL 2/15/98; BR 5–6/98; SLJ 1/98) [920]

5718 Caravantes, Peggy. *Petticoat Spies: Six Women Spies of the Civil War* (5–8). Illus. 2002, Morgan Reynolds LB $21.95 (1-883846-88-9). An exciting volume about six women who spied for the Union and Confederacy during the Civil War, with photographs, source notes, a glossary, and a bibliography. (Rev: BL 3/15/02; HBG 10/02; SLJ 8/02) [973.7]

5719 Doherty, Kieran. *Explorers, Missionaries, and Trappers: Trailblazers of the West* (5–8). Series: Shaping America. 2000, Oliver LB $22.95 (1-881508-52-8). Nine important pioneers of the American West are profiled including a Spanish conquistador, two Spanish priests, John Sutter, Marcus and Narcissa Whitman, and Brigham Young. (Rev: HBG 10/00; SLJ 5/00) [920]

5720 Dumbeck, Kristina. *Leaders of Women's Suffrage* (6–9). Series: History Makers. 2000, Lucent LB $18.96 (1-56006-367-X). This account spans 72 years and contains profiles of the women who dedicated their lives to the fight in America to get the vote for women. (Rev: BL 9/15/00) [920]

5721 Emert, Phyllis R. *Top Lawyers and Their Famous Cases* (6–10). Series: Profiles. 1996, Oliver LB $19.95 (1-881508-31-5). Profiles of eight notable lawyers and their outstanding legal cases, from colonial days to the present, including Alexander Hamilton, Morris Dees, Abraham Lincoln, Robert H. Jackson, Joseph Welsh, and Bella Lockwood. (Rev: BR 1–2/97; SLJ 11/96; VOYA 6/97) [920]

5722 Faber, Doris, and Harold Faber. *Great Lives: American Government* (6–9). Illus. 1988, Macmillan $23.00 (0-684-18521-0). Arranged chronologically, there are many thumbnail sketches of famous American statesmen from Washington to Nixon. (Rev: BL 2/1/88; SLJ 1/89) [920]

5723 Franklin, John Hope, and August Meier, eds. *Black Leaders of the Twentieth Century* (7–12). Illus. 1982, Univ. of Illinois Pr. $34.95 (0-252-00870-7); paper $18.95 (0-252-00939-8). A total of 15 African Americans, including W. E. B. Du Bois, Marcus Garvey, and Whitney Young, Jr., are highlighted. A companion volume is *Black Leaders of the Nineteenth Century*. [920]

5724 Freedman, Russell. *Indian Chiefs* (6–9). Illus. 1987, Holiday $19.95 (0-8234-0625-3). Brief biographies of six Indian chiefs including Red Cloud, Sitting Bull, and Joseph of the Nez Perce. (Rev: BL 5/1/87; SLJ 5/87; VOYA 8/87) [920]

5725 Furbee, Mary R. *Women of the American Revolution* (7–9). Series: History Makers. 1999, Lucent LB $27.45 (1-56006-489-7). Profiles of six women — Abigail Smith Adams, Peggy Shippen Arnold, Esther DeBerdt Reed, Deborah Sampson, Mercy Otis Warren, and Phillis Wheatley — who played very different roles during the American Revolution, with material on the general role of women during the Revolution and an overview of events leading up to it. (Rev: HBG 4/00; SLJ 9/99) [920]

5726 Gourley, Catherine. *Society's Sisters: Stories of Women Who Fought for Social Justice in America* (6–9). Illus. 2003, Millbrook LB $26.90 (0-7613-2865-3). An oversize collective biography concentrating on 19th-century women reformers who may not be familiar to readers. (Rev: BL 11/15/03) [303.48]

5727 Green, Carl R., and William R. Sanford. *Confederate Generals of the Civil War* (5–8). Illus. Series: Collective Biographies. 1998, Enslow LB $20.95 (0-7660-1029-5). After a brief introduction to the Civil War, this book highlights the careers of 10 Southern generals and their contributions to the Confederate cause. (Rev: BL 8/98) [920]

5728 Green, Carl R., and William R. Sanford. *Union Generals of the Civil War* (5–8). Illus. 1998, Enslow LB $20.95 (0-7660-1028-7). Using period photographs and prints plus a concise text, this book outlines the careers of 10 Union generals and supplies background material on the Civil War, including charts and maps. (Rev: BL 8/98) [920]

5729 Hacker, Carlotta. *Great African Americans in History* (5–8). Series: Outstanding African Americans. 1997, Crabtree LB $22.60 (0-86505-805-9); paper $8.95 (0-86505-819-9). There are profiles of 13 great African Americans in American history, including Frederick Douglass, Harriet Tubman, W. E. B. Du Bois, Mary McLeod Bethune, and George Washington Carver. (Rev: BL 9/15/97; SLJ 1/98) [920]

5730 Hancock, Sibyl. *Famous Firsts of Black Americans* (7–12). Illus. 1983, Pelican $12.95 (0-88289-240-1). Biographies of 20 famous African Americans who have contributed in a unique way to our culture. [920]

5731 Hansen, Joyce. *Women of Hope: African Americans Who Made a Difference* (6–12). 1998, Scholastic paper $16.95 (0-590-93973-4). A large-size volume that celebrates the lives and accomplishments of 13 female African American leaders from various walks of life, including civil rights activists such as Fannie Lou Hamer and writers such as Maya Angelou. (Rev: BL 12/1/98; HBG 3/99; SLJ 10/98; VOYA 4/99) [920]

5732 Harmon, Rod. *American Civil Rights Leaders* (5–7). Series: Collective Biographies. 2000, Enslow LB $20.95 (0-7660-1381-2). This collective biography profiles 10 individuals who are currently or once were active in the civil rights movement in the

United States. (Rev: BL 12/15/00; HBG 10/01) [920]

5733 Harness, Cheryl. *Remember the Ladies* (4–7). Illus. 2001, HarperCollins $16.99 (0-688-17017-X). Brief profiles of 100 important American women are each accompanied by a portrait. (Rev: BL 4/15/01; HBG 10/01; SLJ 2/01) [920]

5734 Haskins, Jim. *African American Military Heroes* (7–12). Series: Black Stars. 1998, Wiley $24.95 (0-471-14577-7). Profiles of 33 African American servicemen and servicewomen and their contributions, from the 1760s to the 1990s, are given in this book that stresses the struggle for equality. (Rev: BL 9/1/98; HBG 3/99; SLJ 11/98) [355.008996073]

5735 Haskins, Jim. *One More River to Cross: The Stories of Twelve Black Americans* (4–8). Illus. 1992, Scholastic $13.95 (0-590-42896-9). Eight men and four women who defied the odds to achieve prominence in their fields are introduced, including Ralph Bunche, Shirley Chisholm, and Ron McNair. (Rev: BCCB 4/92; BL 2/1/92; SLJ 4/92) [920]

5736 Helmer, Diana Star. *Women Suffragists* (7–10). Series: American Profiles. 1998, Facts on File $25.00 (0-8160-3579-2). This is a fine introduction to 10 outspoken women in the struggle for women's rights including Sojourner Truth, Elizabeth Cady Stanton, Victoria Woodhull, Carrie Chapman Catt, and Alice Paul. (Rev: BL 8/98; BR 11–12/98; SLJ 12/98) [346]

5737 Hoose, Phillip. *We Were There, Too! Young People in U.S. History* (5–8). Illus. 2001, Farrar $28.00 (0-374-38252-2). Hoose tells the stories of dozens of young people who contributed to the making of America — some famous but many who will be new to readers. (Rev: BCCB 10/01; BL 8/01; HB 9–10/01*; HBG 3/02; SLJ 8/01*) [973]

5738 Hudson, Wade, and Valerie Wesley Wilson. *Afro-Bets Book of Black Heroes from A to Z: An Introduction to Important Black Achievers* (4–7). Illus. 1988, Just Us paper $7.95 (0-940975-02-5). Forty-nine African American men and women of outstanding accomplishment. (Rev: BL 1/1/89; SLJ 12/88) [920]

5739 Jacobs, William J. *Great Lives: Human Rights* (5–8). Illus. 1990, Macmillan $24.00 (0-684-19036-2). Profiles 30 historical figures "united in a commitment to individual rights." (Rev: BL 7/90; SLJ 9/90) [920]

5740 Jones, Veda Boyd. *Government and Politics* (6–9). Series: Female Firsts in Their Fields. 1999, Chelsea $18.65 (0-7910-5140-4). Using black-and-white illustrations and clear, concise prose, this book profiles six women who were pioneers in American politics and government. (Rev: BL 5/15/99; HBG 9/99; VOYA 8/99) [920]

5741 Kallen, Stuart A. *Native American Chiefs and Warriors* (6–10). Illus. Series: History Makers. 1999, Lucent LB $17.96 (1-56006-364-5). This collective biography gives basic information on some historically important Native American leaders. (Rev: BL 1/1–15/00; HBG 4/00; SLJ 1/00) [920]

5742 Katz, William L. *Black People Who Made the Old West* (6–9). Illus. 1992, Africa World $35.00 (0-86543-363-1); paper $14.95 (0-86543-364-X). Sketches of 35 black explorers, pioneers, etc., who helped open up the West. [920]

5743 Keenan, Sheila. *Scholastic Encyclopedia of Women in United States History* (4–9). 1996, Scholastic paper $17.95 (0-590-22792-0). More than 200 brief biographies of American women representing a variety of professions and accomplishments, organized into six chronologically arranged chapters. (Rev: BR 3–4/97; SLJ 2/97) [920]

5744 Kennedy, John F. *Profiles in Courage.* Memorial Ed. (7–12). 1964, Perennial Lib. paper $7.00 (0-06-080698-2). Sketches of several famous Americans who took unpopular stands during their lives. (Rev: BL 4/87) [920]

5745 Ketchum, Liza. *Into a New Country: Eight Remarkable Women of the West* (6–12). Illus. 2000, Little, Brown $18.95 (0-316-49597-2). The women featured in this book were pioneers, activists, and philanthropists who faced both the dangers of settling the West and prejudice toward women. (Rev: BCCB 10/00; BL 1/1–15/01; HBG 10/01; SLJ 12/00) [978]

5746 Knapp, Ron. *American Generals of World War II* (5–8). Series: Collective Biographies. 1998, Enslow LB $20.95 (0-7660-1024-4). The 10 U.S. generals profiled here are Henry Arnold, Omar Bradley, Dwight Eisenhower, Curtis LeMay, Douglas MacArthur, George Marshall, George Patton, Matthew Ridgway, Holland Smith, and Joseph Stilwell. (Rev: SLJ 9/98) [920]

5747 Kramer, Barbara. *Trailblazing American Women* (5–7). Series: Collective Biographies. 2000, Enslow LB $20.95 (0-7660-1377-4). This collection of biographies profiles women who dared to branch out into new fields and break new ground. (Rev: BL 9/15/00; HBG 10/01; SLJ 12/00) [920]

5748 Kramer, S. A. *The Look-It-Up Book of First Ladies* (4–8). 2000, Random LB $11.99 (0-679-99347-9); paper $9.95 (0-679-89347-4). A companion to *The Look-It-Up Book of Presidents* that provides concise biographies of first ladies and discusses their level of participation in the administration and influence on their husbands. (Rev: HBG 10/01; SLJ 6/01) [920]

5749 Kranz, Rachel, and Philip Koslow. *The Biographical Dictionary of African Americans* (6–12). 1999, Facts on File $44.00 (0-8160-3903-8); paper $18.95 (0-8160-3904-6). Arranged chronologically from colonial times on, this volume contains brief profiles of 230 African Americans ranging from our earliest times to entries for Queen Latifah and Tupac Shakur. (Rev: BL 4/15/99; SLJ 8/99) [973]

5750 Krull, Kathleen. *Lives of the Presidents: Fame, Shame (and What the Neighbors Thought)* (4–8). Illus. 1998, Harcourt $20.00 (0-15-200808-X). An entertaining collective biography that stresses the human side of U.S. presidents, with interesting, insightful tidbits and details that bring the presidents to life. (Rev: BL 8/98; HB 11–12/98; HBG 3/99; SLJ 9/98) [920]

5751 Lindop, Edmund. *Dwight D. Eisenhower, John F. Kennedy, Lyndon B. Johnson* (4–7). Illus. Series: Presidents Who Dared. 1996, Twenty-First Century LB $23.90 (0-8050-3404-8). The highlights of these three administrations are presented, preceded by an introduction to the American presidency. (Rev: BL 4/15/96; SLJ 6/96) [920]

5752 Lindop, Edmund. *George Washington, Thomas Jefferson, Andrew Jackson* (4–7). Illus. Series: Presidents Who Dared. 1995, Twenty-First Century LB $23.90 (0-8050-3401-3). After a general introduction on the duties of the president, brief biographies of three are given, with emphasis on their accomplishments in office. (Rev: BL 1/1–15/96; SLJ 11/95) [920]

5753 Lindop, Edmund. *James K. Polk, Abraham Lincoln, Theodore Roosevelt* (4–7). Illus. Series: Presidents Who Dared. 1995, Twenty-First Century LB $23.90 (0-8050-3402-1). Highlights and evaluations of the presidencies of Polk, Lincoln, and Theodore Roosevelt. (Rev: BL 1/1–15/96; SLJ 11/95) [920]

5754 Lindop, Edmund. *Richard M. Nixon, Jimmy Carter, Ronald Reagan* (4–8). Series: Presidents Who Dared. 1996, Twenty-First Century LB $23.90 (0-8050-3405-6). This account traces salient events in each of these presidents' terms, for example: Nixon and Watergate and relations with China; Carter and ending the war between Egypt and Israel; and Reagan and his arms agreement with the Soviet Union. (Rev: BL 4/15/96; SLJ 6/96) [920]

5755 Lindop, Edmund. *Woodrow Wilson, Franklin D. Roosevelt, Harry S. Truman* (5–8). Illus. Series: Presidents Who Dared. 1995, Twenty-First Century LB $23.90 (0-8050-3403-X). After an overview of the presidency and brief profiles of these men, this account looks at daring decisions they made as presidents. (Rev: BL 1/1–15/96; BR 3–4/96; SLJ 11/95; VOYA 6/96) [920]

5756 Lindop, Laurie. *Champions of Equality* (7–10). Illus. Series: Dynamic Modern Women. 1997, Twenty-First Century LB $24.00 (0-8050-4165-6). This collective biography includes 10 contemporary women who are feminist leaders, a head of the NAACP, and a children's rights activist. Some

names are Margarethe Cammermeyer, Marian Wright Edelman, Wilma Mankiller, and Eleanor Holmes Norton. (Rev: BL 9/1/97; BR 1–2/98; SLJ 9/97) [303.48]

5757 Lindop, Laurie. *Political Leaders* (6–12). Illus. Series: Dynamic Modern Women. 1996, Twenty-First Century LB $24.90 (0-8050-4164-8). Elizabeth Dole, Dianne Feinstein, Geraldine Ferraro, Ruth Bader Ginsburg, and Barbara Jordan are five of the 10 prominent women in politics profiled in this book, with details on the childhood, influences, education, and political career of each. (Rev: BL 1/1–15/97; SLJ 1/97; VOYA 2/97) [320]

5758 McLean, Jacqueline. *Women with Wings* (4–7). Illus. Series: Profiles. 2001, Oliver $19.95 (1-881508-70-6). An absorbing account of the achievements of women pilots, including Bessie Coleman, Amelia Earhart, and Anne Morrow Lindbergh. (Rev: BL 5/15/01; HBG 10/01; SLJ 10/01) [629.13]

5759 Marvis, Barbara. *Famous People of Asian Ancestry*, Vol. 4 (4–7). Illus. Series: Contemporary American Success Stories. 1994, Mitchell Lane paper $10.95 (1-883845-09-2). A collective biography of Asian Americans, including actor Dustin Nguyen, novelist Amy Tan, and businessman Rocky Aoki. Also use volumes 1 through 3 (2nd ed., 1997). (Rev: BL 10/1/94; SLJ 11/94) [920]

5760 Marvis, Barbara. *Famous People of Hispanic Heritage*, Vol. 1 (4–7). Illus. Series: Contemporary American Success Stories. 1995, Mitchell Lane LB $21.95 (1-883845-21-1); paper $12.95 (1-883845-20-3). This is the first of three volumes that give brief biographies of Hispanic Americans from all walks of life who have made significant contributions to our country. (Rev: BL 11/15/95; SLJ 1/96) [920]

5761 Marvis, Barbara. *Famous People of Hispanic Heritage*, Vol. 4 (5–9). Illus. 1996, Mitchell Lane paper $12.95 (1-883845-29-7). The lives of two Hispanic men and two women who have succeeded in their careers are presented in an easy-to-read style. Other volumes in this series by the same author are available. (Rev: BL 12/15/96; SLJ 1/97; VOYA 2/97) [920]

5762 Mayo, Edith P., ed. *The Smithsonian Book of the First Ladies: Their Lives, Times, and Issues* (6–10). Illus. 1996, Holt $29.95 (0-8050-1751-8). From Martha Washington to Hillary Rodham Clinton, this book examines the lives and accomplishments of each First Lady with a three- to four-page biography and pictures. (Rev: BL 6/1–15/96; BR 1–2/97; SLJ 6/96; VOYA 8/96) [920]

5763 Meisner, James, and Amy Ruth. *American Revolutionaries and Founders of the Nation* (5–7). Series: Collective Biographies. 1999, Enslow LB $20.95 (0-7660-1115-1). Ten brief biographies of prominent leaders of the American Revolution, each with a black-and-white portrait. (Rev: BL 9/15/99) [920]

5764 Morey, Janet Nomura, and Wendy Dunn. *Famous Hispanic Americans* (7–10). Illus. 1996, Dutton $16.99 (0-525-65190-X). Fourteen men and women of Hispanic heritage from science, sports, the arts, and other professions are featured in this collective biography. (Rev: BL 2/15/96; BR 9–10/96; SLJ 2/96; VOYA 8/96) [920]

5765 Morin, Isobel V. *Women Chosen for Public Office* (5–7). Illus. 1995, Oliver LB $19.95 (1-881508-20-X). Nine biographies of women who are involved in the federal government from the superintendent of army nurses to Supreme Court Justice Ruth Bader Ginsburg. (Rev: BL 5/1/95; SLJ 6/95) [920]

5766 Morin, Isobel V. *Women of the U.S. Congress* (6–10). 1994, Oliver LB $19.95 (1-881508-12-9). Lists all the women who have served in Congress as of 1994 and provides political biographies of seven of them, citing their accomplishments and their different backgrounds and views. (Rev: BL 7/94; SLJ 5/94; VOYA 6/94) [920]

5767 Morin, Isobel V. *Women Who Reformed Politics* (7–12). 1994, Oliver LB $19.95 (1-881508-16-1). Describes the political activism of eight American women, including Abby Foster's abolition fight, Carrie Catt's suffrage battle, and Gloria Steinem's feminist crusade. (Rev: BL 10/15/94; SLJ 11/94; VOYA 2/95) [920]

5768 Morris, Juddi. *At Home with the Presidents* (4–8). 1999, Wiley paper $12.95 (0-471-25300-6). In three to five pages each, this account profiles the presidents of the United States from Washington through Clinton. (Rev: SLJ 3/00) [920]

5769 Munson, Sammye. *Today's Tejano Heroes* (5–8). Illus. 2000, Eakin $13.95 (1-57168-328-3). In alphabetical order, this volume introduces 16 important 20th-century Mexican Americans who have contributed to the history and culture of Texas, including Vikki Carr, Attorney General Dan Morales, and federal judge Hilda Tagle. (Rev: BL 2/1/01) [920]

5770 Netzley, Patricia D. *Presidential Assassins* (6–9). Series: History Makers. 2000, Lucent LB $18.96 (1-56006-623-7). Profiles of people who have assassinated or attempted to assassinate American presidents are profiled with material on the consequences of their action on the nation. (Rev: BL 6/1–15/00; HBG 9/00; SLJ 8/00) [920]

5771 Pascoe, Elaine. *First Facts About the Presidents* (4–8). Illus. Series: First Facts About. 1996, Blackbirch $34.94 (1-56711-167-X). Divided into four historical periods, this book introduces each of the presidents, briefly describes his presidency, and looks at the major historical events of the time. (Rev: SLJ 5/96) [920]

5772 Pinkney, Andrea D. *Let It Shine: Stories of Black Women Freedom Fighters* (5–8). Illus. 2000, Harcourt $20.00 (0-15-201005-X). This work contains chatty profiles of 10 important African American women, including Sojourner Truth, Rosa Parks, and Shirley Chisholm. (Rev: BCCB 11/00; BL 11/15/00; HB 11–12/00; HBG 3/01; SLJ 10/00; VOYA 12/00) [921]

5773 Rennert, Richard, ed. *Book of Firsts: Leaders of America* (6–9). Illus. Series: Profiles of Great Black Americans. 1994, Chelsea paper $7.65 (0-7910-2066-5). This collective biography profiles the lives and works of nine African American leaders, including Ralph Bunche, Shirley Chisholm, William H. Hastie, Colin Powell, and L. Douglas Wilder. (Rev: BL 6/1–15/94) [920]

5774 Roberts, Russell. *Presidents and Scandals* (6–9). Series: History Makers. 2001, Lucent $24.95 (1-56006-642-3). This work discusses five American presidents whose term of office was tainted by scandal, including Grant, Harding, Nixon, Reagan, and Clinton. (Rev: BL 8/1/01; SLJ 6/01) [920]

5775 St. George, Judith. *Dear Dr. Bell . . . Your Friend, Helen Keller* (5–7). Illus. 1992, Morrow paper $4.95 (0-688-12814-9). A joint biography about the friendship between Alexander Graham Bell and Helen Keller. (Rev: BCCB 11–12/92 & 2/93; SLJ 12/92) [920]

5776 Satter, James. *Journalists Who Made History* (7–12). Illus. Series: Profiles. 1998, Oliver LB $19.95 (1-881508-39-0). Ten journalists famous for their fearless reporting are profiled, including Horace Greeley, Ida Tarbell, Carl Bernstein and Bob Woodward, William Randolph Hearst, and Edward R. Murrow. (Rev: BL 10/15/98; SLJ 11/98) [920]

5777 Straub, Deborah G., ed. *Hispanic American Voices* (6–12). 1997, Gale $52.00 (0-8103-9827-3). Profiles of 16 Hispanic Americans, most of whom are civil and human rights leaders, politicians, attorneys, or civil rights activists. (Rev: BR 9–10/97; SLJ 11/97) [920]

5778 Streissguth, Thomas. *Legendary Labor Leaders* (7–12). Illus. Series: Profiles. 1998, Oliver LB $19.95 (1-881508-44-7). The eight labor leaders profiled in this collective biography are Samuel Gompers, Cesar Chavez, A. Philip Randolph, Jimmy Hoffa, Eugene Debs, William Haywood, Mother Jones, and John L. Lewis. (Rev: BL 10/15/98; SLJ 1/99) [920]

5779 Taylor, Kimberly H. *Black Abolitionists and Freedom Fighters* (6–10). 1996, Oliver LB $19.95 (1-881508-30-7). Profiles are given for eight African Americans who fought to end slavery, some well-known (including Nat Turner and Harriet Tubman) and others less familiar, such as Richard Allen and Mary Terrell. (Rev: BR 1–2/97; SLJ 10/96) [920]

5780 Taylor, Kimberly H. *Black Civil Rights Champions* (6–12). Illus. 1995, Oliver LB $19.95 (1-881508-22-6). In separate chapters, seven civil rights leaders, including W. E. B. Du Bois, James Farmer, Ella Baker, and Malcolm X, are profiled, with an 8th final chapter that gives thumbnail sketches of many more. (Rev: BL 1/1–15/96; BR 1–2/97; SLJ 3/96; VOYA 6/96) [920]

5781 Taylor, Sherri Peel. *Influential First Ladies* (6–9). Series: History Makers. 2001, Lucent $24.95 (1-56006-740-3). This collective biography tells how such first ladies as Jacqueline Kennedy, Eleanor Roosevelt, Barbara Bush, and Hillary Clinton contributed to their husbands' administrations. (Rev: BL 8/1/01) [920]

5782 Thrasher, Thomas. *Gunfighters* (6–9). Series: History Makers. 2000, Lucent LB $27.45 (1-56006-570-2). A fascinating collective biography that introduces the West of olden days and gives profiles of Wild Bill Hickok, Ben Thompson, Wyatt Earp, John Wesley Hardin, Billy the Kid, and Tom Horn. (Rev: BL 3/15/00; HBG 10/00; SLJ 9/00) [920]

5783 Thro, Ellen. *Twentieth-Century Women Politicians* (7–12). Series: American Profiles. 1998, Facts on File $25.00 (0-8160-3758-2). Beginning in the mid-20th century, this work features 10 women who were elected to important public offices, including Margaret Chase Smith, Geraldine Ferraro, Dianne Feinstein, Christine Todd Whitman, and Ann Richards. (Rev: BL 12/15/98) [920]

5784 Ungar, Harlow G. *Teachers and Educators* (7–10). Illus. Series: American Profiles. 1994, Facts on File $25.00 (0-8160-2990-3). This book profiles eight great American educators of the past, including John Dewey, Horace Mann, Emma Willard, Booker T. Washington, and Henry Barnard. (Rev: BL 7/95; VOYA 5/95) [920]

5785 Uschan, Michael V. *America's Founders* (6–10). Series: History Makers. 1999, Lucent LB $18.96 (1-56006-571-0). These brief biographies of Washington, Franklin, Jefferson, John Adams, and Alexander Hamilton focus on their lasting contributions to this country. (Rev: BL 10/15/99; HBG 9/00) [920]

5786 Vernell, Marjorie. *Leaders of Black Civil Rights* (6–10). Illus. Series: History Makers. 1999, Lucent LB $18.96 (1-56006-670-9). After a review of the civil rights movements of the 1950s and 1960s, this collective biography features seven short sketches of such subjects as A. Philip Randolph, Malcolm X, Fannie Low Hamer, and Jesse Jackson. (Rev: BL 2/15/00; HBG 9/00) [921.]

5787 Weatherford, Carole Boston. *Great African-American Lawyers: Raising the Bar of Freedom* (7–12). Illus. Series: Collective Biography. 2003,

Enslow $20.95 (0-7660-1837-7). From Macon Allen, the first black lawyer in America, through more familiar names such as Thurgood Marshall and Marian Wright Edelman, this is an overview of the accomplishments of African American lawyers. (Rev: BL 2/15/03; HBG 10/03) [340.09]

5788 Wheeler, Jill C. *America's Leaders* (4–7). Series: War on Terrorism. 2002, ABDO LB $25.65 (1-57765-661-X). This book contains brief profiles of important American figures in the war against terrorism such as President Bush, Colin Powell, John Ashcroft, and Rudy Giuliani. (Rev: BL 5/15/02; HBG 10/02) [920]

5789 Woog, Adam. *Gangsters* (6–9). Series: History Makers. 2000, Lucent LB $18.96 (1-56006-638-5). A collective biography featuring gangsters including Al Capone. (Rev: BL 9/15/00; HBG 3/01) [920]

Civil and Human Rights Leaders

ABERNATHY, RALPH

5790 Reef, Catherine. *Ralph David Abernathy* (6–10). Series: People in Focus. 1995, Silver Burdett $13.95 (0-87518-653-X); paper $7.95 (0-382-24965-8). A straightforward biography that describes this civil rights leader's youth and many accomplishments. (Rev: BL 8/95; SLJ 10/95) [921]

ANTHONY, SUSAN B.

5791 Kendall, Martha E. *Susan B. Anthony: Voice for Women's Voting Rights* (6–8). Series: Historical American Biographies. 1997, Enslow LB $20.95 (0-89490-780-8). A biography of this amazing woman who campaigned for women's right to vote, hold political office, divorce, and own property, and for an end to slavery. (Rev: SLJ 8/97) [921]

5792 Stalcup, Brenda, ed. *Susan B. Anthony* (7–12). Series: People Who Made History. 2001, Gale LB $31.20 (0-7377-0890-5); paper $19.95 (0-7377-0891-3). The story of the American reformer and leader of the woman-suffrage movement is covered in this anthology of mature essays. (Rev: BL 4/1/02) [921]

5793 Weisberg, Barbara. *Susan B. Anthony* (6–10). Illus. 1988, Chelsea LB $19.95 (1-55546-639-7). The biography of the woman who led the early suffragette movement. (Rev: BL 12/1/88) [921]

BATES, DAISY

5794 Polakow, Amy. *Daisy Bates: Civil Rights Crusader* (6–12). Illus. 2003, Linnet $25.00 (0-208-02513-8). In 1957, Bates supported the Little Rock Nine students who were the first African Americans to take advantage of school integration. (Rev: BL 6/1–15/03; HBG 10/03; SLJ 8/03) [379.2]

BETHUNE, MARY MCLEOD

5795 Halasa, Malu. *Mary McLeod Bethune* (6–10). Illus. 1988, Chelsea LB $21.95 (1-55546-574-9). A stirring biography of the African American woman who fought for the right to a quality education for her people. (Rev: BL 3/15/89) [921]

5796 Meltzer, Milton. *Mary McLeod Bethune: Voice of Black Hope* (4–7). Illus. 1988, Puffin paper $4.99 (0-14-032219-1). An effective profile of the African American educator. (Rev: BCCB 5/87; BL 3/15/87; SLJ 3/87) [370.0924]

BOND, JULIAN

5797 Jordan, Denise M. *Julian Bond: Civil Rights Activist and Chairman of the NAACP* (6–8). 2001, Enslow LB $20.95 (0-7660-1549-1). A concise overview of the life and political career of the African American who protested against the Vietnam War and against racial discrimination. (Rev: HBG 3/02; SLJ 3/02) [323.1]

BROWN, JOHN

5798 Becker, Helaine. *John Brown* (4–7). Series: The Civil War. 2001, Gale LB $27.44 (1-56711-558-6). Brown's life is detailed from childhood through his adult achievements, and is carefully placed in the context of the time and his family background. (Rev: HBG 3/02; SLJ 4/02) [921]

5799 Cox, Clinton. *Fiery Vision: The Life and Death of John Brown* (7–10). Illus. 1997, Scholastic paper $15.95 (0-590-47574-6). A well-researched, detailed account of the life of the abolitionist who was hanged for the raid at Harper's Ferry. (Rev: BL 2/15/97; HBG 3/98; SLJ 6/97; VOYA 10/98) [921]

BURNS, ANTHONY

5800 Hamilton, Virginia. *Anthony Burns: The Defeat and Triumph of a Fugitive Slave* (7–12). 1988, Knopf $14.99 (0-394-98185-5). Burns, who lived only 28 years, rebelled against his slave status with repercussions felt around the country. (Rev: BL 6/1/88; BR 11–12/88; SLJ 6/88; VOYA 10/88) [921]

CATT, CARRIE CHAPMAN

5801 Somervill, Barbara A. *Votes for Women! The Story of Carrie Chapman Catt* (5–8). Illus. 2002, Morgan Reynolds LB $21.95 (1-883846-96-X). This is the story of Carrie Chapman Catt, who devoted her early life to the quest for women's right to vote and later turned her energies to helping Jew-

ish refugees. (Rev: BL 11/15/02; HBG 3/03; SLJ 1/03; VOYA 2/03) [324.6]

CHAVEZ, CESAR

5802 Gonzales, Doreen. *Cesar Chavez: Leader for Migrant Farm Workers* (6–10). Illus. Series: Hispanic Biographies. 1996, Enslow LB $20.95 (0-89490-760-3). This biography concentrates on Chavez's struggle to organize California farmworkers, his belief in nonviolence, and his inspirational leadership. (Rev: BL 10/1/96; SLJ 6/96) [921]

5803 Houle, Michelle E., ed. *Cesar Chavez* (7–12). Series: People Who Made History. 2003, Gale LB $33.70 (0-7377-1298-8); paper $22.45 (0-7377-1299-6). A compilation of essays about the champion of migrant workers that show his achievements from various points of view. (Rev: SLJ 10/03) [921]

5804 Tracy, Kathleen. *Cesar Chavez* (5–7). Series: Latinos in American History. 2003, Mitchell Lane LB $19.95 (1-58415-224-9). This biography covers the life and accomplishments of the Mexican American labor leader who founded the United Farm Workers. (Rev: BL 1/1–15/04) [921]

CHILD, LYDIA MARIA

5805 Kenschaft, Lori. *Lydia Maria Child: The Quest for Racial Justice* (6–10). Illus. Series: Oxford Portraits. 2002, Oxford LB $24.00 (0-19-513257-2). Lydia Maria Child, an activist for civil rights in the early and middle 1800s, is also known for her literary career. (Rev: BL 3/1/03; HBG 3/03; SLJ 1/03) [303.48]

DE LA CRUZ, JESSIE

5806 Soto, Gary. *Jessie de la Cruz: A Profile of a United Farm Worker* (7–12). 2000, Persea $17.95 (0-89255-253-0). De la Cruz grew up working in the fields of California with her migrant family and later became an organizer for the United Farm Workers. (Rev: BCCB 2/01; BL 11/15/00; BR 3–4/01; HBG 3/01; SLJ 1/01) [331.88]

DIX, DOROTHEA

5807 Herstek, Amy Paulson. *Dorothea Dix* (5–8). Series: Historical American Biographies. 2001, Enslow LB $20.95 (0-7660-1258-1). The life of this militant reformer who fought for more humane treatment of the insane. (Rev: BL 1/1–15/02; HBG 3/02; SLJ 1/02) [921]

DOUGLASS, FREDERICK

5808 Becker, Helaine. *Frederick Douglass* (4–7). Series: The Civil War. 2001, Gale LB $27.44 (1-56711-557-8). Readers of this biography that covers Douglass's life and work as an abolitionist will be particularly interested in the account of his youth as a slave in Maryland and his escape to freedom. (Rev: HBG 3/02; SLJ 4/02) [921]

5809 Burchard, Peter. *Frederick Douglass: For the Great Family of Man* (7–12). Illus. 2003, Simon & Schuster $18.95 (0-689-83240-0). This absorbing biography includes information about the impact of events in Douglass's early life on his development as an important human rights advocate. (Rev: BL 2/15/03; HB 3–4/03; HBG 10/03; SLJ 1/03; VOYA 2/03) [973.7]

5810 Douglass, Frederick. *Escape from Slavery: The Boyhood of Frederick Douglass in His Own Words* (5–10). Illus. 1994, Knopf $15.00 (0-679-84652-2); paper $6.99 (0-679-84651-4). This shortened version of the famous abolitionist's 1845 autobiography dramatizes the abomination of slavery and the struggle of a man to break free. (Rev: BL 2/15/94*; SLJ 2/94) [921]

5811 Meltzer, Milton, ed. *Frederick Douglass: In His Own Words* (8–12). Illus. 1995, Harcourt $22.00 (0-15-229492-9). An introduction to the articles and speeches of the great 19th-century abolitionist leader, arranged chronologically. (Rev: BL 12/15/94; SLJ 2/95) [305.8]

5812 Miller, Douglas T. *Frederick Douglass and the Fight for Freedom* (7–12). Illus. 1988, Facts on File $19.95 (0-8160-1617-8). An engrossing biography of the self-taught former slave who led the abolitionist movement. (Rev: BL 11/1/88; BR 1–2/89; SLJ 10/88; VOYA 2/89) [921]

DU BOIS, W. E. B.

5813 Moss, Nathaniel. *W. E. B. Du Bois: Civil Rights Leader* (5–8). Series: Junior World Biography. 1996, Chelsea LB $15.95 (0-7910-2382-6). A brief, somewhat superficial overview of this great pioneer in the civil rights movement and his accomplishments. (Rev: SLJ 7/96) [921]

5814 Rowh, Mark. *W.E.B. DuBois: Champion of Civil Rights* (7–12). Series: African-American Biographies. 1999, Enslow LB $19.95 (0-7660-1209-3). The inspiring biography of the African American educator and writer who helped found the NAACP. (Rev: BL 11/15/99; HBG 4/00) [921]

FARRAKHAN, LOUIS

5815 Haskins, Jim. *Louis Farrakhan and the Nation of Islam* (7–12). Illus. 1996, Walker LB $16.85 (0-8027-8423-2). Beginning with a history of African American nationalism and the Nation of Islam, this biography places the life of Farrakhan within the movement for black solidarity. (Rev: BL 10/1/96; BR 1–2/97; SLJ 1/97) [921]

FREEMAN, ELIZABETH

5816 Wilds, Mary. *MumBet: The Life and Times of Elizabeth Freeman: The True Story of a Slave Who Won Her Freedom* (7–12). Illus. 1999, Avisson LB $19.95 (1-888105-40-2). The story of MumBet (Elizabeth Freeman), a black slave who sued for her freedom in Massachusetts in 1781 after hearing a reading of the Declaration of Independence and won, helping to set the legal precedents that ended slavery in New England. (Rev: BL 6/1–15/99; SLJ 6/99; VOYA 2/00) [921]

GARVEY, MARCUS

5817 Lawler, Mary. *Marcus Garvey* (7–10). Illus. Series: Black Americans of Achievement. 1987, Chelsea LB $21.95 (1-55546-587-0). The story of the black leader who preached black separation and founded the Universal Negro Improvement Association. (Rev: BL 12/1/87; BR 1–2/89; VOYA 10/88) [921]

GRIMKE, SARAH AND ANGELINA

5818 McPherson, Stephanie S. *Sisters Against Slavery: A Story About Sarah and Angelina Grimke* (4–7). Series: Creative Minds Biographies. 1999, Carolrhoda LB $25.55 (1-57505-361-6). The story of the remarkable Grimke sisters from South Carolina who fought against slavery and later became suffragettes. (Rev: BCCB 1/00; HBG 3/00; SLJ 12/99) [921]

HARRIS, LA DONNA

5819 Schwartz, Michael. *La Donna Harris* (4–7). Illus. Series: Contemporary Native Americans. 1997, Raintree Steck-Vaughn LB $17.98 (0-8172-3995-2). The life story and accomplishments of this Native American, who has openly championed her people's rights before the Senate. (Rev: BL 6/1–15/97) [921]

HAYDEN, LEWIS

5820 Strangis, Joel. *Lewis Hayden and the War Against Slavery* (7–12). 1998, Shoe String LB $25.00 (0-208-02430-1). The dramatic story of the former slave who became an active abolitionist and a stationmaster on the Underground Railroad. (Rev: BL 2/15/99; BR 9–10/99; HBG 9/99; SLJ 5/99; VOYA 10/99) [921]

HESCHEL, ABRAHAM JOSHUA

5821 Rose, Or. *Abraham Joshua Heschel* (4–8). Illus. 2003, Jewish Publication Soc. paper $9.95 (0-8276-0758-X). A portrait of the rabbi and teacher who was born in Poland, emigrated to the United States, and became a leader in the civil rights movement. (Rev: BL 6/1–15/03) [290.092]

HUERTA, DOLORES

5822 Murcia, Rebecca Thatcher. *Dolores Huerta* (5–7). Series: Latinos in American History. 2002, Mitchell Lane LB $19.95 (1-58415-155-2). The story of the gallant woman who worked along with Cesar Chavez to protect the rights of farm workers. (Rev: BL 2/15/03; HBG 10/03) [921]

5823 Perez, Frank. *Dolores Huerta* (4–8). Illus. Series: Contemporary Hispanic Americans. 1995, Raintree Steck-Vaughn LB $28.80 (0-8172-3981-2). The accomplishments of Dolores Huerta, a Hispanic American who cofounded the United Farm Workers, are described in this informative biography. (Rev: BL 3/15/96) [921]

IDAR, JOVITA

5824 Gibson, Karen Bush. *Jovita Idar* (5–7). Series: Latinos in American History. 2002, Mitchell Lane LB $19.95 (1-58415-151-X). The inspiring story of the Latin American woman who started San Antonio's first free kindergarten and who founded the League of Mexican American women in 1911 to educate poor children. (Rev: BL 2/15/03; HBG 10/03) [921]

JACKSON, JESSE

5825 Haskins, James. *Jesse Jackson: Civil Rights Activist* (6–10). Series: African-American Biographies. 2000, Enslow LB $19.95 (0-7660-1390-1). A biography of the man who has been a defender of the poor, minorities, and underprivileged. (Rev: BL 9/15/00; HBG 3/01; SLJ 11/00) [921]

5826 Steffens, Bradley, and Dan Wood. *Jesse Jackson* (5–8). Series: People in the News. 2000, Lucent LB $27.45 (1-56006-631-8). This well-documented look at the life of the religious and civil rights leader gives interesting information on the events and people who influenced him. (Rev: BL 6/1–15/00; HBG 10/00) [921]

JACOBS, HARRIET A.

5827 Fleischner, Jennifer. *I Was Born a Slave: The Story of Harriet Jacobs* (4–8). Illus. 1997, Millbrook LB $26.90 (0-7613-0111-9). The turbulent life of Harriet Jacobs, who was born into slavery and lived for many years as a fugitive before winning her freedom and becoming an abolitionist. (Rev: BL 9/15/97; BR 1–2/98; HBG 3/98; SLJ 1/98) [921]

JONES, MOTHER

5828 Josephson, Judith P. *Mother Jones: Fierce Fighter for Workers' Rights* (6–10). Illus. 1997, Lerner LB $30.35 (0-8225-4924-7). The story of this early labor leader in coal country is also a histo-ry of the struggle against long work hours, unsafe working conditions, poor wages, and child labor. (Rev: BL 2/1/97; SLJ 4/97*) [921]

KENNEDY, ROBERT F.

5829 Mills, Judie. *Robert Kennedy* (8–12). Illus. 1998, Millbrook LB $36.90 (1-56294-250-6). A useful, informative biography that tells of Robert Kennedy's life and career and places them in the context of other historical events. (Rev: BL 8/98; SLJ 9/98) [921]

KING, CORETTA SCOTT

5830 Bankston, John. *Coretta Scott King and the Story Behind the Coretta Scott King Award* (4–8). Series: Great Achievement Awards. 2003, Mitchell Lane LB $19.95 (1-58415-202-8). The story of the widow of Martin Luther King, Jr., her continuing fight for civil rights, and the children's book prize named after her are covered in this biography. (Rev: BL 10/15/03; SLJ 10/03) [921]

5831 Rhodes, Lisa R. *Coretta Scott King* (5–8). Illus. Series: Black Americans of Achievement. 1999, Chelsea $21.95 (0-7910-4690-7); paper $9.95 (0-7910-4691-5). This biography of Coretta Scott King describes her childhood, education, marriage, participation in the civil rights movement, and her work since her husband's assassination. (Rev: BL 8/98; HBG 10/98; SLJ 8/98) [323.092]

5832 Schraff, Anne. *Coretta Scott King: Striving for Civil Rights* (7–12). Series: African-American Biographies. 1997, Enslow LB $20.95 (0-89490-811-1). The life story of the gallant woman who has, with her family, continued the struggle for civil rights begun by her husband. (Rev: BL 6/1–15/97) [921]

KING, MARTIN LUTHER, JR.

5833 Darby, Jean. *Martin Luther King, Jr.* (4–8). Illus. Series: Lerner Biographies. 1990, Lerner LB $30.35 (0-8225-4902-6). An in-depth look at King's life and the civil rights movement. (Rev: BL 7/90; SLJ 11/90) [921]

5834 Haskins, Jim. *I Have a Dream: The Life and Words of Martin Luther King, Jr.* (6–12). 1993, Millbrook LB $29.90 (1-56294-087-2). Describes King's early life, family, and education, and the impact of the civil rights movement and beliefs that he espoused. (Rev: BL 2/15/93; SLJ 6/93*) [921]

5835 Haskins, Jim. *The Life and Death of Martin Luther King, Jr.* (5–7). Illus. 1992, Morrow paper $6.95 (0-688-11690-6). Covering the life and career of the African American leader, with focus on the civil rights movement. [921]

5836 Jakoubek, Robert E. *Martin Luther King, Jr.* (6–9). Illus. 1989, Chelsea LB $21.95 (1-55546-597-8). A stirring biography that also gives a good history of the nonviolent civil rights movement. (Rev: BL 12/15/89; BR 1–2/90; SLJ 3/90; VOYA 2/90) [921]

5837 January, Brendan. *Martin Luther King Jr.: Minister and Civil Rights Activist* (4–8). Series: Ferguson's Career Biographies. 2001, Ferguson LB $16.95 (0-89434-342-4). This concise account focuses on King's career as a minister as well as his work as an advocate of civil rights and includes a section on training for the ministry. (Rev: SLJ 4/01) [921]

5838 Lambert, Kathy K. *Martin Luther King, Jr.* (4–7). Illus. Series: Junior World Biography. 1992, Chelsea LB $18.65 (0-7910-1759-1). A well-designed biography using many photographs to re-create the life of the great civil rights leader. (Rev: BL 11/1/92) [921]

5839 Milton, Joyce. *Marching to Freedom: The Story of Martin Luther King, Jr.* (5–7). Illus. 1987, Dell paper $3.99 (0-440-45433-6). A biography of his life, from childhood to civil rights leader. (Rev: BL 6/15/87; SLJ 10/87) [323.40924]

5840 Patrick, Diane. *Martin Luther King, Jr.* (4–8). Illus. 1990, Watts paper $21.00 (0-531-10892-9). A colorful format helps to make this look at King's life accessible to middle-grade readers. (Rev: BL 7/90; SLJ 9/90) [921]

5841 Patterson, Lillie. *Martin Luther King, Jr. and the Freedom Movement* (7–12). Illus. 1989, Facts on File $19.95 (0-8160-1605-4). A biography of the civil rights leader and the movement he led. (Rev: BL 7/89; BR 11–12/89; SLJ 9/89; VOYA 12/89) [921]

5842 Schuman, Michael A. *Martin Luther King, Jr.: Leader for Civil Rights* (5–8). Series: African-American Biographies. 1996, Enslow LB $20.95 (0-89490-687-9). A straightforward biography that covers the important events in King's life. (Rev: SLJ 12/96) [921]

5843 Siebold, Thomas, ed. *Martin Luther King, Jr.* (7–12). 2000, Greenhaven LB $21.96 (0-7377-0227-3); paper $13.96 (0-7377-0226-5). This collection of primary source documents concentrates on Dr. King's life, mission, and his effects on African Americans and the nation. (Rev: BL 4/15/00; SLJ 9/00) [921]

LADUKE, WINONA

5844 Silverstone, Michael. *Winona LaDuke: Restoring Land and Culture in Native America* (5–8). Series: Women Changing the World. 2001, Feminist Pr. $19.95 (1-55861-260-2). A candidate for the vice presidency under Ralph Nader in 2000, this author and environmental and Native American rights activist lives on a reservation in Minnesota, where she is dedicated to restoring the land and the culture. (Rev: BL 12/15/01; HBG 10/02) [921]

LYON, MARY

5845 Rosen, Dorothy S. *A Fire in Her Bones: The Story of Mary Lyon* (5–7). Illus. 1995, Carolrhoda LB $30.35 (0-87614-840-2). A biography of the woman who defied social barriers and founded Mount Holyoke Female Seminary, now known as Mount Holyoke College. (Rev: BL 6/1–15/95; SLJ 4/95) [921]

MALCOLM X

5846 Benson, Michael. *Malcolm X* (5–8). Series: Biography. 2001, Lerner LB $25.26 (0-8225-5025-3). An accessible text and many photographs are used to enliven this biography of the African American civil rights leader who was assassinated in 1965. (Rev: BL 4/1/02; HBG 3/02; SLJ 3/02) [921]

5847 Collins, David R. *Malcolm X: Black Rage* (5–9). 1992, Dillon LB $13.95 (0-87518-498-7). A short biography of the influential African American activist, tracing the early events that led to his belief that whites were the enemy. (Rev: BL 10/15/92; SLJ 1/93) [921]

5848 Diamond, Arthur. *Malcolm X: A Voice for Black America* (6–12). Illus. Series: People to Know. 1994, Enslow $18.95 (0-89490-453-3). A sympathetic but unbiased account of the man, once a convict, who became an important African American leader. (Rev: BL 6/1–15/94) [921]

5849 Malcolm X, and Alex Haley. *The Autobiography of Malcolm X* (7–12). 1999, Ballantine $20.00 (0-345-91536-4); paper $12.00 (0-345-91503-8). The story of the man who turned from Harlem drug pusher into a charismatic leader of his people. [921]

5850 Myers, Walter Dean. *Malcolm X: By Any Means Necessary* (6–12). 1993, Scholastic paper $13.95 (0-590-46484-1). An eloquent tribute to the brilliant, radical African American leader, quoting extensively from *The Autobiography of Malcolm X*. (Rev: BCCB 3/93; BL 11/15/92; SLJ 2/93) [921]

5851 Rummel, Jack. *Malcolm X* (6–9). Illus. 1989, Chelsea LB $21.95 (1-55546-600-1). A heavily illustrated portrait of the African American leader and the movement for civil rights for his people. (Rev: BL 5/15/89; BR 9–10/89; SLJ 6/89; VOYA 8/89) [921]

5852 Sagan, Miriam. *Malcolm X* (7–9). Illus. Series: Mysterious Deaths. 1997, Lucent LB $27.45 (1-56006-264-9). After a brief biography of Malcolm X, this book focuses on the circumstances of his death and his rivalry with Louis Farrakhan, who was thought by many to be responsible for Malcolm's death, and his family's subsequent relationship with Farrakhan. (Rev: BL 2/15/97; SLJ 3/97; VOYA 8/97) [921]

PARKS, ROSA

5853 Hull, Mary. *Rosa Parks* (7–10). Illus. Series: Black Americans of Achievement. 1994, Chelsea LB $21.95 (0-7910-1881-4). The story of the seemingly ordinary African American woman who had the courage to fight bus segregation in Montgomery, Alabama. (Rev: BL 6/1–15/94; SLJ 8/94; VOYA 8/94) [921]

5854 Nobleman, Mark Tyler. *Rosa Parks* (6–9). Illus. Series: Trailblazers of the Modern World. 2001, World Almanac Library LB $26.60 (0-8368-5071-8). The story of Parks's life and importance to our culture is told in narrative, illustrations, and excerpts from primary documents. (Rev: BL 5/1/02) [323]

5855 Parks, Rosa, and Jim Haskins. *Rosa Parks: My Story* (6–10). 1992, Dial $17.99 (0-8037-0673-1). This autobiography of the civil rights hero becomes an oral history of the movement, including her recollections of Martin Luther King, Jr., Roy Wilkins, and others. (Rev: BL 12/15/91; SLJ 2/92) [921]

5856 Siegel, Beatrice. *The Year They Walked: Rosa Parks and the Montgomery Bus Boycott* (6–8). 1992, Four Winds $16.00 (0-02-782631-7). The story behind the historic bus boycott and the committed work of African Americans and whites who made it a success. (Rev: BL 2/15/92; SLJ 8/92) [921]

RANDOLPH, A. PHILIP

5857 Hanley, Sally. *A. Philip Randolph* (5–9). 1988, Chelsea LB $19.95 (1-55546-607-9); paper $8.95 (0-7910-0222-5). The story of the African American labor leader who founded the Brotherhood of Sleeping Car Porters. (Rev: BL 10/1/88; BR 1–2/89; VOYA 2/89) [921]

RUSTIN, BAYARD

5858 Haskins, Jim. *Bayard Rustin: Behind the Scenes of the Civil Rights Movement* (5–8). Illus. 1997, Hyperion LB $15.49 (0-7868-2140-X). The life of the great civil rights leader and 50 years in the struggle for equality are presented in this exciting biography. (Rev: BL 2/15/97*; BR 9–10/97; SLJ 4/97; VOYA 2/98) [921]

SHABAZZ, BETTY

5859 Jeffrey, Laura S. *Betty Shabazz: Sharing the Vision of Malcolm X* (6–10). Series: African-American Biographies. 2000, Enslow LB $20.95 (0-7660-

1210-7). The wife of Malcolm X was only 31 years old when her husband was assassinated and she was left to raise six children and continue his fight for civil rights. (Rev: BL 9/15/00; HBG 3/01; SLJ 1/01) [320.54]

STANTON, ELIZABETH CADY

5860 Bohannon, Lisa Frederiksen. *Women's Rights and Nothing Less: The Story of Elizabeth Cady Stanton* (6–12). Illus. 2000, Morgan Reynolds LB $21.95 (1-883846-66-8). An engrossing biography of this great fighter for human rights and her relations with such people as Susan B. Anthony and Frederick Douglass. (Rev: BL 12/15/00; HBG 3/01; SLJ 12/00) [921]

5861 Cullen-DuPont, Kathryn. *Elizabeth Cady Stanton and Women's Liberty* (6–10). 1992, Facts on File $25.00 (0-8160-2413-8). Presents a humanistic picture of one of the founders of the women's rights movement and provides an intimate portrait of Stanton as wife, mother, and activist. (Rev: BL 10/1/92; SLJ 7/92) [921]

5862 Fritz, Jean. *You Want Women to Vote, Lizzie Stanton?* (4–7). Illus. 1995, Putnam $17.99 (0-399-22786-5). An exciting, witty re-creation of the life of Elizabeth Cady Stanton, fighter for women's rights, including suffrage. (Rev: BCCB 10/95; BL 8/95*; SLJ 9/95*) [921]

5863 Loos, Pamela. *Elizabeth Cady Stanton* (5–8). Illus. Series: Women of Achievement. 2000, Chelsea $19.95 (0-7910-5293-1). Drawing largely on Stanton's autobiography, this is the life story of the well-known suffragist of the 19th century. (Rev: BL 2/15/01; HBG 10/01) [921]

5864 Salisbury, Cynthia. *Elizabeth Cady Stanton: Leader of the Fight for Women's Rights* (5–8). Series: Historical American Biographies. 2002, Enslow LB $20.95 (0-7660-1616-1). The life of the fighter for women's suffrage and the organizer of the first women's rights convention. (Rev: BL 4/1/02; HBG 10/02; SLJ 5/02) [921]

5865 Sigerman, Harriet. *Elizabeth Cady Stanton: The Right Is Ours* (6–10). Illus. Series: Oxford Portraits. 2001, Oxford $24.00 (0-19-511969-X). The life of the pioneering suffragist, accompanied by photographs and historic documents such as newspaper articles and cartoons. (Rev: BL 12/15/01; HBG 3/02; SLJ 11/01; VOYA 2/02) [305.42]

STEINEM, GLORIA

5866 Daffron, Carolyn. *Gloria Steinem* (7–12). Illus. 1988, Chelsea LB $19.95 (1-55546-679-6). The story of the influential woman who founded *Ms.* magazine and who is also a leader in the feminist movement. (Rev: BL 11/1/87; BR 11–12/88; VOYA 2/89) [921]

5867 Hoff, Mark. *Gloria Steinem: The Women's Movement* (6–12). Series: New Directions. 1991, Millbrook LB $21.90 (1-878841-19-X). A biography of the famous feminist. (Rev: BL 2/1/91) [921]

5868 Lazo, Caroline. *Gloria Steinem: Feminist Extraordinaire* (5–7). Illus. Series: Lerner Biographies. 1998, Lerner LB $25.26 (0-8225-4934-4). The story of Steinem, who overcame a troubled childhood to become a great humanitarian, writer, and leader of the feminist movement. (Rev: BL 7/98; SLJ 7/98) [921]

5869 Wheaton, Elizabeth. *Ms: The Story of Gloria Steinem* (6–9). Illus. Series: Feminist Voices. 2002, Morgan Reynolds LB $20.95 (1-883846-82-X). A very readable account of Steinem's life that gives a clear portrait of her character as well as her many accomplishments. (Rev: BL 3/1/02; HBG 10/02; SLJ 6/02; VOYA 2/03) [305.42]

TERRELL, MARY CHURCH

5870 Fradin, Dennis Brindell, and Judith Bloom Fradin. *Fight On! Mary Church Terrell's Battle for Integration* (5–9). Illus. 2003, Clarion $17.00 (0-618-13349-6). Terrell's efforts to end discrimination are detailed in a readable, large-format biography that includes primary sources and lots of illustrations. (Rev: BL 6/1–15/03; HB 7–8/03; HBG 10/03; SLJ 5/03*; VOYA 6/03) [323]

5871 Lommel, Cookie. *Mary Church Terrell: Speaking Out for Civil Rights* (4–7). Series: African-American Biographies. 2003, Enslow LB $20.95 (0-7660-2116-5). This interesting account of Terrell's life and her passion for education and activism contains many black-and-white photographs. (Rev: SLJ 10/03) [323]

TRUTH, SOJOURNER

5872 Bernard, Catherine. *Sojourner Truth: Abolitionist and Women's Rights Activist* (5–8). Series: Historical American Biographies. 2001, Enslow LB $20.95 (0-7660-1257-3). The life story of the freed slave who traveled throughout the North preaching emancipation and women's rights before the Civil War. (Rev: BL 4/15/01; HBG 10/01) [921]

5873 Butler, Mary G. *Sojourner Truth: From Slave to Activist for Freedom* (4–8). Series: Library of American Lives and Times. 2003, Rosen LB $31.95 (0-8239-5736-5). A forerunner of the modern civil rights movement, Sojourner Truth rose from slavery to become a crusader for good race relations and women's rights. (Rev: BL 6/1–15/03; SLJ 5/03; VOYA 6/03) [921]

5874 Krass, Peter. *Sojourner Truth* (7–12). Illus. 1988, Chelsea LB $21.95 (1-55546-611-7). The life of a woman who began as a slave and ended as a respected abolitionist and feminist. (Rev: BL 10/1/88) [921]

5875 Macht, Norman L. *Sojourner Truth* (4–7). Illus. Series: Junior World Biography. 1992, Chelsea LB $18.65 (0-7910-1754-0). The story of the freed slave who traveled through the North preaching emancipation and women's rights. (Rev: BL 10/1/92; SLJ 12/92) [921]

5876 McKissack, Patricia, and Fredrick McKissack. *Sojourner Truth: Ain't I a Woman?* (5–8). 1992, Scholastic paper $13.95 (0-590-44690-8). Drawing on the 1850 autobiography *Narrative of Sojourner Truth: A Northern Slave,* the authors integrate her personal story with a history of slavery, resistance, and abolitionism. (Rev: BL 11/15/92; SLJ 2/93) [921]

5877 Rockwell, Anne. *Only Passing Through* (4–8). Illus. 2000, Knopf $16.95 (0-679-89186-2). A moving picture-book biography of Sojourner Truth, who was a pioneer in the struggle for racial equality and devoted her life to the abolitionist movement. (Rev: BCCB 1/01; BL 11/15/00; HB 11–12/00; HBG 3/01; SLJ 12/00) [921]

TUBMAN, HARRIET

5878 Bradford, Sarah. *Harriet Tubman, the Moses of Her People* (7–12). Illus. 1961, Peter Smith $18.75 (0-8446-1717-2). A biography first published in 1869 of this former slave who brought hundreds of slaves north to freedom. [921]

5879 Burns, Bree. *Harriet Tubman* (4–7). Illus. Series: Junior World Biography. 1992, Chelsea LB $18.65 (0-7910-1751-6). This is a straightforward account of the escaped slave who helped free more than 300 slaves via the Underground Railroad. (Rev: BL 10/1/92; SLJ 12/92) [921]

5880 Carlson, Judy. *Harriet Tubman: Call to Freedom* (5–8). 1989, Ballantine paper $5.99 (0-449-90376-1). A biography that is a lively account of the early fighter against slavery. (Rev: BL 12/15/89; BR 3–4/90; SLJ 2/90) [921]

5881 Schraff, Anne. *Harriet Tubman: Moses of the Underground Railroad* (4–8). Series: African-American Biographies. 2001, Enslow LB $20.95 (0-7660-1548-3). This is an absorbing account of the life of the Underground Railroad leader that covers her work as a nurse, a scout, and a spy. (Rev: HBG 3/02; SLJ 10/01) [921]

5882 Taylor, M. W. *Harriet Tubman* (5–8). Illus. Series: Black Americans of Achievement. 1990, Chelsea LB $21.95 (1-55546-612-5). The story of the famous conductor on the Underground Railroad. (Rev: SLJ 1/91) [921]

TURNER, NAT

5883 Bisson, Terry. *Nat Turner: Slave Revolt Leader* (7–10). Illus. 1988, Chelsea LB $21.95 (1-55546-613-3). A biography of the courageous black man who led one of the nation's most important slave revolts. (Rev: BL 8/88; BR 1–2/89; SLJ 2/89; VOYA 2/89) [921]

5884 Edwards, Judith. *Nat Turner's Slave Rebellion* (7–12). Illus. Series: In American History. 2000, Enslow LB $19.95 (0-7660-1302-2). After some general material on slavery and other slave rebellions, this account stresses the life of Nat Turner and the consequences of his belief that he was sent by God to free the slaves. (Rev: BL 2/15/00; HBG 9/00; SLJ 7/00) [921]

5885 Hendrickson, Ann-Marie. *Nat Turner: Rebel Slave* (4–7). Illus. Series: Junior World Biography. 1995, Chelsea LB $18.65 (0-7910-2386-9). An attractive biography of this slave who led a revolution and became a symbol of heroism for his people. (Rev: BL 10/15/95) [921]

VESEY, DENMARK

5886 Edwards, Lillie J. *Denmark Vesey: Slave Revolt Leader* (6–9). Illus. 1990, Chelsea LB $19.95 (1-55546-614-1). The story of the slave who bought his freedom and was later hanged for plotting a slave rebellion. (Rev: BL 7/90; SLJ 7/90) [921]

WASHINGTON, BOOKER T.

5887 Washington, Booker T. *Up from Slavery: An Autobiography by Booker T. Washington* (7–12). Illus. 1963, Airmont paper $3.95 (0-8049-0157-0). The story of the slave who later organized the Tuskegee Institute. [921]

WELLS, IDA B.

5888 Fradin, Dennis B., and Judith B. Fradin. *Ida B. Wells: Mother of the Civil Rights Movement* (5–10). 2000, Clarion $18.00 (0-395-89898-6). An inspiring biography of the African American who was born a slave and went on to become a school teacher, journalist, and an activist who fought for black women's right to vote and helped found the NAACP. (Rev: BL 2/15/00; HB 5–6/00; HBG 10/00; SLJ 4/00*) [921]

5889 Welch, Catherine A. *Ida B. Wells-Barnett: Powerhouse with a Pen* (5–8). Illus. Series: Trailblazer Biographies. 2000, Carolrhoda LB $30.35 (1-57505-352-7). This book introduces Wells-Barnett, who was born a slave and became a powerful journalist and activist as well as a spokesperson for all African Americans. (Rev: BL 6/1–15/00; HBG 10/00; SLJ 7/00; VOYA 2/01) [921]

WILLIAMS, ROGER

5890 Gaustad, Edwin S. *Roger Williams: Prophet of Liberty* (7–12). Illus. Series: Oxford Portraits. 2001, Oxford $22.00 (0-19-513000-6). Gaustad introduces the life and beliefs of the minister who was exiled from his New World community because he insisted on keeping his faith separate from politics. (Rev: BL 5/1/01; HBG 10/01; SLJ 7/01) [974.5]

ZITKALA-SA (RED BIRD)

5891 Rappaport, Doreen. *The Flight of Red Bird: The Life of Zitkala-Sa* (7–10). 1997, NewStar Media $15.99 (0-8037-1438-6). The remarkable story of Zitkala-Sa (Red Bird), who was born to a Sioux mother and a white father in 1876 and devoted her life to advocating the rights of Native Americans. (Rev: BL 7/97; SLJ 7/97; VOYA 10/98) [921]

Presidents and Their Families

ADAMS, ABIGAIL

5892 Bober, Natalie S. *Abigail Adams: Witness to a Revolution* (6–12). 1995, Atheneum $18.00 (0-689-31760-3). A portrait of a woman and the age she lived in. (Rev: BL 4/15/95*; SLJ 6/95) [921]

5893 Ching, Jacqueline. *Abigail Adams: A Revolutionary Woman* (4–7). Series: Library of American Lives and Times. 2001, Rosen $23.95 (0-8239-5723-3). This biography of Abigail Adams stresses the fact that her husband, John Adams, relied heavily on her advice and that her vision of equality and justice inspired the early consideration of women's rights. (Rev: BCCB 4/01; BL 10/15/01) [921]

5894 Davis, Kate. *Abigail Adams* (6–8). Series: Triangle Histories of the Revolutionary War: Leaders. 2003, Gale LB $21.95 (1-56711-610-8). The life and times of the influential wife of President John Adams and mother of President John Quincy Adams. (Rev: LMC 8–9/03; SLJ 5/03) [973.4]

5895 McCarthy, Pat. *Abigail Adams: First Lady and Patriot* (5–8). Series: Historical American Biographies. 2002, Enslow LB $20.95 (0-7660-1618-8). The life story of the prolific letter-writer who was wife of the second president of the United States, John Adams. (Rev: BCCB 4/01; BL 4/1/02; HBG 10/02; SLJ 7/02) [921]

5896 Osborne, Angela. *Abigail Adams* (6–10). Illus. 1988, Chelsea LB $19.95 (1-55546-635-4). The biography of the early feminist who was a strong influence on husband John and a fine recorder of American history. (Rev: BL 12/1/88; BR 5–6/89; SLJ 1/89) [921]

ADAMS, JOHN

5897 Feinstein, Stephen. *John Adams* (5–9). 2002, Enslow/MyReportLinks.com LB $19.95 (0-7660-5001-7). A well-written and accessible overview of Adams's life and contributions that is extended by a number of recommended Web sites. (Rev: SLJ 6/02) [921]

5898 Lukes, Bonnie L. *John Adams: Public Servant* (8–12). Illus. Series: Notable Americans. 2000, Morgan Reynolds LB $21.95 (1-883846-80-3). An excellent biography of the second president of the United States that reveals both his virtues and his flaws. (Rev: BL 12/1/00; HBG 3/01; SLJ 2/01) [921]

ADAMS, JOHN AND ABIGAIL

5899 St. George, Judith. *John and Abigail Adams: An American Love Story* (6–9). Illus. 2001, Holiday $22.95 (0-8234-1571-6). This story of the Adamses' partnership, drawing extensively on their letters to each other, will be useful for report writers. (Rev: BL 11/1/01; HB 1–2/02; HBG 3/02; SLJ 12/01; VOYA 2/02) [973.4]

ADAMS, JOHN QUINCY

5900 Feinstein, Stephen. *John Quincy Adams* (5–9). 2002, Enslow/MyReportLinks.com LB $19.95 (0-7660-5002-5). Adams's early and later life are covered in this concise biography that includes several pages of annotated Web site recommendations. (Rev: HBG 10/02; SLJ 10/02) [921]

ARTHUR, CHESTER A.

5901 Young, Jeff C. *Chester A. Arthur* (4–7). Series: Presidents. 2002, Enslow/MyReportLinks.com LB $19.95 (0-7660-5077-7). As well as an overview of the life and accomplishments of Chester A. Arthur, this book gives a pre-evaluated listing of Web sites where more material can be found. (Rev: BL 12/15/02) [921]

BUCHANAN, JAMES

5902 Young, Jeff C. *James Buchanan* (4–7). Series: Presidents. 2003, Enslow/MyReportLinks.com LB $19.95 (0-7660-5101-3). The story of the fifteenth president who had an extensive political career before becoming president. (Rev: BL 6/1–15/03; HBG 10/03) [921]

BUSH, GEORGE H. W.

5903 Anderson, Ken. *George Bush: A Lifetime of Service* (6–12). Illus. 2003, Eakin $17.95 (1-57168-663-0); paper $12.95 (1-57168-600-2). George Herbert Walker Bush, the forty-first president, is profiled in this biography that gives insights into his

relationship with his son, George W. Bush. (Rev: BL 1/1–15/03; HBG 10/03; SLJ 2/03) [973.928]

5904 Pemberton, William E. *George Bush* (6–12). Series: World Leaders. 1993, Rourke LB $25.27 (0-86625-478-1). A biography of the former vice-president and president of the United States and an assessment of his accomplishments in office. (Rev: BL 12/1/93) [921]

5905 Schuman, Michael A. *George H. W. Bush* (6–12). Illus. Series: United States Presidents. 2002, Enslow LB $20.95 (0-7660-1702-8). Bush's youth, family, education, career, and presidency are all covered here, as is his role raising children with strong political agendas. (Rev: BL 3/1/03; HBG 10/03) [973.928]

BUSH, GEORGE W.

5906 Gormley, Beatrice. *President George W. Bush* (4–7). Illus. 2001, Simon & Schuster paper $4.99 (0-689-84123-X). An appealing, chronological account of Bush's life that shows him against his family background and looks at his uneven record of achievement. (Rev: BL 5/15/01; SLJ 6/01) [973.931]

5907 Jones, Veda Boyd. *George W. Bush* (5–8). Series: Major World Leaders. 2002, Chelsea $23.95 (0-7910-6940-0). Using both color and sepia photographs, this account introduces George W. Bush and his family with coverage through the early part of his presidency. (Rev: BL 1/1–15/03; HBG 3/03) [921]

5908 McNeese, Tim. *George W. Bush: First President of the New Century* (6–10). Series: Notable Americans. 2001, Morgan Reynolds LB $20.95 (1-883846-85-4). This biography of the former Texas governor covers his life from childhood and gives details of the controversial 2000 presidential election. (Rev: HBG 3/02; SLJ 4/02) [973.931]

5909 Marquez, Heron. *George W. Bush* (5–8). Series: Biography. 2001, Lerner LB $25.26 (0-8225-4995-6). The life story of our president from birth through the turmoil of his presidential election. (Rev: BL 4/1/02; HBG 10/02) [921]

5910 Thompson, Bill, and Dorcas Thompson. *George W. Bush* (4–8). Illus. Series: Childhoods of the Presidents. 2003, Mason Crest $17.95 (1-59084-281-2). Bush's privileged childhood and education, his role as eldest son, and the death of his sister from leukemia are covered in an interesting narrative that highlights his character. (Rev: BL 6/1–15/03; SLJ 2/03) [973.931]

5911 Wheeler, Jill C. *George W. Bush* (4–7). Series: War on Terrorism. 2002, ABDO LB $25.65 (1-57765-662-8). A brief profile of President Bush with particular emphasis on his war on terrorism. (Rev: BL 5/15/02; HBG 10/02) [921]

5912 Wukovits, John F. *George W. Bush* (5–8). Series: People in the News. 2000, Lucent LB $27.45 (1-56006-693-8). Published before the 2000 election, this biography uses extensive quotations from Mr. Bush, his friends, and critics. (Rev: BL 9/15/00; HBG 3/01; SLJ 10/00) [921]

BUSH, LAURA WELCH

5913 Gormley, Beatrice. *Laura Bush: America's First Lady* (5–8). Illus. 2003, Simon & Schuster LB $11.89 (0-689-85628-8); paper $4.99 (0-689-85366-1). A chronological account of Laura Bush's life, with information on her childhood as well as her later public life. (Rev: BL 3/1/03; HBG 10/03; SLJ 5/03) [973.931]

CARTER, JIMMY

5914 Lazo, Caroline. *Jimmy Carter: On the Road to Peace* (4–7). Series: People in Focus. 1996, Silver Burdett LB $13.95 (0-382-39262-0); paper $7.95 (0-382-39263-9). Jimmy Carter's written words are used effectively in this biography that covers both his political career and his post-presidential humanitarian efforts. (Rev: BL 8/96; SLJ 8/96) [921]

5915 O'Shei, Tim. *Jimmy Carter* (5–9). 2002, Enslow/MyReportLinks.com LB $19.95 (0-7660-5051-3). This introduction to Carter's life, including his childhood, and his contributions contains a long list of recommended Web sites that extend the printed material. (Rev: HBG 10/02; SLJ 6/02) [921]

5916 Richman, Daniel A. *James E. Carter* (5–8). Series: Presidents of the United States. 1989, GEC LB $21.27 (0-944483-24-0). The story of this former U.S. president, his political career, family, and present charitable activities. (Rev: SLJ 9/89) [921]

5917 Santella, Andrew. *James Earl Carter Jr.* (4–7). Series: Profiles of the Presidents. 2002, Compass Point LB $23.93 (0-7565-0283-7). A straightforward profile that touches on Carter's southern roots, his successes and failures as president, and his subsequent work in the fields of human rights and democracy. (Rev: SLJ 1/03) [921]

5918 Slavin, Ed. *Jimmy Carter* (4–8). Illus. 1989, Chelsea LB $19.95 (1-55546-828-4). Introducing the 39th president of the United States. (Rev: BL 7/89) [973.9260924]

5919 Smith, Betsy. *Jimmy Carter, President* (5–7). Illus. 1986, Walker LB $13.85 (0-8027-6652-8). A profile of Jimmy Carter and his one-term presidency. (Rev: BL 2/15/87; SLJ 12/86) [973.9260924]

5920 Whitelaw, Nancy. *Jimmy Carter: President and Peacemaker* (7–10). Illus. 2003, Morgan Reynolds LB $21.95 (1-931798-18-4). From childhood in rural Georgia to his current work for charities and international peace, this is the story of the 39th president. (Rev: BL 12/15/03) [973.926]

CLEVELAND, GROVER

5921 Collins, David R. *Grover Cleveland: 22nd and 24th President of the United States* (7–9). Illus. 1988, Garrett LB $21.27 (0-944483-01-1). A fine introduction to this president and his career, with interesting sidebar features. (Rev: SLJ 9/88) [921]

CLINTON, BILL

5922 Cole, Michael D. *Bill Clinton: United States President* (6–9). 1994, Enslow LB $20.95 (0-89490-437-X). Surveys Clinton's life and accomplishments prior to his presidential election, emphasizing his tenure as governor of Arkansas. (Rev: BL 7/94; SLJ 7/94) [921]

5923 Cwiklik, Robert. *Bill Clinton: President of the 90's*. Rev. ed. (4–8). Series: Gateway Biography. 1997, Millbrook $22.90 (0-7613-0129-1); paper $8.95 (0-7613-0146-1). A readable biography that concentrates on Clinton's career as governor of Arkansas and his early years as president. (Rev: BL 9/15/97; SLJ 7/97) [921]

5924 Heinrichs, Ann. *William Jefferson Clinton* (4–8). Series: Profiles of the Presidents. 2002, Compass Point LB $28.75 (0-7565-0207-1). This absorbing account of Clinton's life and career covers both the good and bad sides of his presidency and includes a discussion of Hillary's role. (Rev: SLJ 6/02) [973.929092]

5925 Kelly, Michael. *Bill Clinton* (6–10). Series: Overcoming Adversity. 1998, Chelsea LB $21.95 (0-7910-4700-8). This book describes Bill Clinton's difficult childhood, including his abusive, alcoholic stepfather, but focuses on his political career, emphasizing the important role Hillary Rodham Clinton has played in his success, with a good balance between coverage of Clinton's achievements and problems, including the scandals. (Rev: HBG 3/99; SLJ 2/99) [921]

5926 Landau, Elaine. *Bill Clinton and His Presidency* (4–8). Series: First Books: Biographies. 1997, Watts LB $22.00 (0-531-20295-X). This biography traces the life and career of Bill Clinton through his first term as president. (Rev: BL 9/15/97; SLJ 9/97) [921]

5927 Marcovitz, Hal. *Bill Clinton* (4–8). Illus. Series: Childhoods of the Presidents. 2003, Mason Crest LB $17.95 (1-59084-273-1). This brief, well-illustrated overview of Clinton's childhood and adolescence looks in particular at his relationships with family members, his support for civil rights, and his popularity. (Rev: BL 6/1–15/03; SLJ 2/03) [973.929]

CLINTON, HILLARY RODHAM

5928 Guernsey, JoAnn B. *Hillary Rodham Clinton: A New Kind of First Lady* (4–7). Illus. 1993, Lerner LB $21.27 (0-8225-2875-4); paper $6.95 (0-8225-

9650-4). A behind-the-scenes biography of the First Lady that ends with her attempts to reform health care. (Rev: BL 11/1/93; SLJ 12/93) [921]

5929 Kozar, Richard. *Hillary Rodman Clinton* (6–9). Series: Women of Achievement. 1998, Chelsea $21.95 (0-7910-4712-1). Updated through July 1997, this biography emphasizes the many ways in which Hillary Rodham Clinton redefined the role of First Lady while she was in the White House. (Rev: BR 1–2/99; HBG 3/99; SLJ 10/98; VOYA 4/99) [921]

COOLIDGE, CALVIN

5930 Allen, Michael Geoffrey. *Calvin Coolidge* (6–12). Illus. Series: United States Presidents. 2002, Enslow LB $20.95 (0-7660-1703-6). Coolidge's youth, family, education, career, and presidency are all covered here, as are his character and his legacy. (Rev: BL 3/1/03; HBG 3/03; SLJ 2/03) [973.91]

EISENHOWER, DWIGHT D.

5931 Darby, Jean. *Dwight D. Eisenhower: A Man Called Ike* (6–9). Illus. Series: Lerner Biographies. 1989, Lerner LB $30.35 (0-8225-4900-X). An easily read account of the highlights in the life of this general and president. (Rev: BL 11/15/89; SLJ 9/89) [921]

5932 Deitch, Kenneth, and Joanne B. Weisman. *Dwight D. Eisenhower: Man of Many Hats* (5–7). 1990, Discovery LB $14.95 (1-878668-02-1). Each stage of Eisenhower's multifaceted career is represented. (Rev: SLJ 2/91) [921]

5933 Raatma, Lucia. *Dwight D. Eisenhower* (4–7). Series: Profiles of the Presidents. 2002, Compass Point LB $23.93 (0-7565-0279-9). A straightforward account that focuses on Eisenhower's military career and successes in World War II. (Rev: SLJ 1/03) [921]

5934 Sandberg, Peter Lars. *Dwight D. Eisenhower* (7–12). Illus. 1986, Chelsea LB $19.95 (0-87754-521-9). A brief biography of the president and war leader that emphasizes the human side of this historical figure. (Rev: SLJ 11/86) [921]

5935 Van Steenwyk, Elizabeth. *Dwight David Eisenhower, President* (5–8). Illus. 1987, Walker LB $13.85 (0-8027-6671-4). The focus is on the career of this war-hero president. (Rev: BL 5/15/87) [921]

5936 Young, Jeff C. *Dwight D. Eisenhower: Soldier and President* (6–12). Illus. 2001, Morgan Reynolds LB $20.95 (1-883846-76-5). This well-written and interesting biography of the 34th president covers his life from boyhood, his career, and his personality. (Rev: BL 11/15/01; HBG 3/02; SLJ 2/02) [973.921]

GARFIELD, JAMES A.

5937 Kingsbury, Robert. *The Assassination of James A. Garfield* (6–9). Series: The Library of Political Assassinations. 2002, Rosen LB $26.50 (0-8239-3540-X). The life and death of this lesser-known President are examined with material on the strange life of the assassin, Charles Guiteau. (Rev: BL 8/02) [921]

5938 Young, Jeff C. *James A. Garfield* (4–7). Series: Presidents. 2003, Enslow/MyReportLinks.com LB $19.95 (0-7660-5100-5). The story of the twentieth president of the U.S. who served as a major general during the Civil War and was assassinated while he was still in office. (Rev: BL 6/1–15/03) [921]

GORE, TIPPER

5939 Kramer, Barbara. *Tipper Gore* (4–7). Illus. Series: People to Know. 1999, Enslow LB $20.95 (0-7660-1142-9). The story of the life of the former vice president's wife and her activities as a mother, professional photographer, and social issues advocate. (Rev: BL 8/99) [921]

GRANT, ULYSSES S.

5940 Alter, Judy. *Ulysses S. Grant* (5–9). 2002, Enslow/MyReportLinks.com LB $19.95 (0-7660-5014-9). Grant's early and later life are covered in this concise and balanced biography that includes several pages of annotated Web site recommendations. (Rev: SLJ 10/02) [921]

5941 King, David C. *Ulysses S. Grant* (6–9). Series: The Civil War. 2001, Gale LB $19.95 (1-56711-555-1). Grant's achievements during the Civil War are the main focus of this well-illustrated volume that also touches on his early life and family. (Rev: HBG 3/02; SLJ 4/02) [973]

5942 Marrin, Albert. *Unconditional Surrender: U. S. Grant and the Civil War* (6–12). 1994, Atheneum LB $21.00 (0-689-31837-5). Part history, part biography, this is a fine study of Grant and his pivotal role in the Civil War. (Rev: BL 4/1/94*; SLJ 7/94*; VOYA 6/94) [921]

5943 Rickarby, Laura A. *Ulysses S. Grant and the Strategy of Victory* (4–7). Illus. Series: The Story of the Civil War. 1991, Silver Burdett paper $7.95 (0-382-24053-7). This book focuses mainly on Grant's role in the winning of the Civil War for the North. (Rev: BL 9/1/91) [921]

HOOVER, HERBERT

5944 Hilton, Suzanne. *The World of Young Herbert Hoover* (4–8). Illus. 1987, Walker LB $13.85 (0-8027-6709-5). This brief biography takes Hoover through his college years and gives some indication of events to follow. (Rev: SLJ 1/88) [921]

5945 Holford, David M. *Herbert Hoover* (5–8). Series: United States Presidents. 1999, Enslow LB $20.95 (0-7660-1035-X). An insightful look at the president who was orphaned as a child and gained a reputation for being rigid and insensitive. (Rev: SLJ 1/00) [921]

HOOVER, LOU

5946 Colbert, Nancy A. *Lou Hoover: The Duty to Serve* (5–8). Illus. 1997, Morgan Reynolds LB $21.95 (1-883846-22-6). President Hoover's wife was a most interesting person, who, among other accomplishments, was the first woman to get a degree in geology in this country, was the translator — with her husband — of a 16th-century Latin mining text, was an advocate of physical education for women, and was fluent in seven languages, including Chinese. (Rev: BL 2/15/98; HBG 3/98; SLJ 3/98) [973.91]

JACKSON, ANDREW

5947 Behrman, Carol H. *Andrew Jackson* (5–8). Series: Presidential Leaders. 2002, Lerner LB $31.95 (0-8225-0093-0). Jackson's life and character are brought to life in this narrative that points out his failings as well as his achievements. (Rev: HBG 3/03; SLJ 1/03) [921]

5948 Feinstein, Stephen. *Andrew Jackson* (5–9). 2002, Enslow/MyReportLinks.com LB $19.95 (0-7660-5003-3). A well-written and accessible overview of Jackson's life and contributions that is extended by a number of recommended Web sites. (Rev: SLJ 6/02; VOYA 8/02) [921]

5949 Meltzer, Milton. *Andrew Jackson and His America* (8–12). 1993, Watts LB $20.00 (0-531-11157-1). Presents a multifaceted picture of Jackson and his role in such historic operations as the Indian removal and in the abolitionist movement. (Rev: BL 1/15/94*; SLJ 1/94; VOYA 2/94) [921]

5950 Whitelaw, Nancy. *Andrew Jackson: Frontier President* (7–10). Illus. Series: Notable Americans. 2000, Morgan Reynolds LB $19.95 (1-883846-67-6). A fine biography of an interesting, multifaceted man who overcame many obstacles to achieve prominence. (Rev: BL 11/1/00; HBG 3/01; SLJ 2/01) [921]

JEFFERSON, THOMAS

5951 Aldridge, Rebecca. *Thomas Jefferson* (5–6). Series: Let Freedom Ring. 2001, Capstone LB $22.60 (0-7368-1035-8). An introduction to the life and work of Jefferson that touches on his attachment to Sally Hemmings. (Rev: HBG 3/02; SLJ 4/02) [921]

5952 Ferris, Jeri. *Thomas Jefferson: Father of Liberty* (5–8). 1998, Lerner LB $30.35 (1-57505-009-9).

This readable biography covers both the public and the private sides of Jefferson's life, with details on his personality and his family. (Rev: BL 3/1/99; HBG 3/99; SLJ 12/98) [921]

5953 Lanier, Shannon, and Jane Feldman. *Jefferson's Children: The Story of One American Family* (6–9). Illus. 2000, Random $19.95 (0-375-80597-4). In a photoessay, a descendant of Thomas Jefferson and his slave Sally Hemings relates the discoveries that he and others in the family made when DNA evidence confirmed their relationship. (Rev: BL 11/15/00; BR 5–6/01; HB 3–4/01; HBG 10/01; SLJ 11/00; VOYA 2/01) [921]

5954 Meltzer, Milton. *Thomas Jefferson: The Revolutionary Aristocrat* (6–10). 1991, Watts LB $18.95 (0-531-11069-9). A presentation of the major events of Jefferson's life and a discussion of some troubling inconsistencies, such as his ownership of slaves. (Rev: BL 12/15/91*; SLJ 12/91*) [921]

5955 Miller, Douglas T. *Thomas Jefferson and the Creation of America* (8–12). Series: Makers of America. 1997, Facts on File $25.00 (0-8160-3393-5). This biography presents Jefferson as a complex character who personified ideals of equality and liberty yet lived a life of many contradictions and conflicts. (Rev: BL 11/15/97; BR 3–4/98) [921]

5956 Old, Wendie C. *Thomas Jefferson* (5–8). Series: United States Presidents. 1997, Enslow LB $20.95 (0-89490-837-5). An account of the life and career of the multifaceted Jefferson. (Rev: BL 2/1/98; HBG 3/98; SLJ 3/98) [921]

5957 Reiter, Chris. *Thomas Jefferson* (4–7). Illus. Series: MyReportLinks.com. 2002, Enslow/MyReportLinks.com LB $19.95 (0-7660-5071-8). A concise biography suitable for students doing reports that provides extensive Web links for further research and uses Web site images among the many illustrations. (Rev: BL 9/1/02; HBG 3/03) [973.4]

5958 Severance, John B. *Thomas Jefferson; Architect of Democracy* (7–12). 1998, Clarion $18.00 (0-395-84513-0). A thoughtful, well-rounded biography that focuses on Jefferson's accomplishments and his beliefs, with many quotations from his writings. (Rev: BL 9/1/98; BR 5–6/99; HBG 3/99; SLJ 12/98; VOYA 4/99) [921]

5959 Whitelaw, Nancy. *Thomas Jefferson: Philosopher and President* (7–10). 2001, Morgan Reynolds LB $20.95 (1-883846-81-1). This concise and thorough biography, which covers Jefferson's strengths and weaknesses, will be useful for report writers. (Rev: HBG 3/02; SLJ 3/02) [973.4]

JOHNSON, ANDREW

5960 Alter, Judy. *Andrew Johnson* (5–8). 2002, Enslow/MyReportLinks.com LB $19.95 (0-7660-5007-6). This overview of Johnson's life and career contains a listing of about 30 Web sites that will extend the information contained in the book. (Rev: SLJ 6/02) [921]

5961 Stevens, Rita. *Andrew Johnson: 17th President of the United States* (5–7). Illus. 1989, Garrett LB $21.27 (0-944483-16-X). Story of the man who became president on Lincoln's assassination. (Rev: BL 5/1/89) [973.810924]

JOHNSON, LYNDON B.

5962 Colbert, Nancy A. *Great Society: The Story of Lyndon Baines Johnson* (4–8). Illus. 2002, Morgan Reynolds LB $21.95 (1-883846-84-6). A solid, readable life of the hardworking president that presents fairly both his virtues and defects. (Rev: BL 4/15/02; HBG 3/03; SLJ 8/02) [921]

5963 Eskow, Dennis. *Lyndon Baines Johnson* (8–12). Series: Impact Biographies. 1993, Watts paper $24.00 (0-531-13019-3). Well-chosen episodes and anecdotes illustrate the life of this Texas-born president. (Rev: BL 9/1/93; VOYA 10/93) [921]

5964 Falkof, Lucille. *Lyndon B. Johnson: 36th President of the United States* (5–8). Illus. 1989, Garrett LB $21.27 (0-944483-20-8). An informative biography that covers both the public and private life of this president. (Rev: BL 5/1/89; BR 9–10/89; SLJ 8/89) [921]

5965 Kaye, Tony. *Lyndon B. Johnson* (6–10). Illus. 1987, Chelsea LB $19.95 (0-87754-536-7). A biography of the president associated with Great Society legislation and the Vietnam War. (Rev: BL 1/15/88; SLJ 4/88) [921]

5966 Levy, Debbie. *Lyndon B. Johnson* (5–9). Series: Presidential Leaders. 2003, Lerner LB $31.95 (0-8225-0097-3). A look at the fascinating personal and political life of the president known for his support for civil rights and for increasing the U.S. involvement in Vietnam. (Rev: HBG 10/03; SLJ 2/03) [921]

5967 Schuman, Michael A. *Lyndon B. Johnson* (6–10). Series: United States Presidents. 1998, Enslow LB $20.95 (0-89490-938-X). This biography focuses on Johnson's public career, his presidential administration, and his legacy. (Rev: HBG 3/99; SLJ 3/99) [921]

KENNEDY FAMILY

5968 Uschan, Michael V. *The Kennedys* (7–12). 2001, Gale LB $27.45 (1-56006-875-2). The Kennedys presented here — with their achievements and their failings — are Joseph P.; his sons John, Robert, and Ted; and John's wife Jacqueline and son John Jr. (Rev: SLJ 1/02) [920]

KENNEDY, JOHN F.

5969 Cole, Michael D. *John F. Kennedy: President of the New Frontier* (4–7). Illus. Series: People to Know. 1996, Enslow LB $20.95 (0-89490-693-3). A profile of the life and accomplishments of this charismatic president. (Rev: BL 5/15/96; SLJ 6/96) [921]

5970 Cooper, Ilene. *Jack: The Early Years of John F. Kennedy* (7–12). 2003, Dutton $22.99 (0-525-46923-0). Jack's youth and school years — in particular his rivalry with his older brother — are described in a narrative peppered with anecdotes and quotations from family and friends. (Rev: BCCB 2/03; BL 1/1–15/03; HB 3–4/03; HBG 10/03; SLJ 2/03; VOYA 4/03) [973.922]

5971 Falkof, Lucille. *John F. Kennedy: 35th President of the United States* (6–9). Illus. 1988, Garrett LB $21.27 (0-944483-03-8). As well as the life and career of this president, the author gives good background material on the issues and general events of the times. (Rev: SLJ 10/88) [921]

5972 Netzley, Patricia. *The Assassination of President John F. Kennedy* (7–12). Series: American Events. 1994, Macmillan LB $18.95 (0-02-768127-0). An account of the events leading up to the assassination, the event itself, and the consequences. (Rev: BL 7/94) [921]

5973 Randall, Marta. *John F. Kennedy* (6–10). Illus. 1987, Chelsea LB $19.95 (0-87754-586-3). A biography of this beloved president that includes coverage of domestic and international crises. (Rev: BL 1/15/88; BR 9–10/88; VOYA 10/88) [921]

5974 Schultz, Randy. *John F. Kennedy* (4–7). Illus. Series: MyReportLinks.com. 2002, Enslow/MyReportLinks.com LB $19.95 (0-7660-5012-2). A basic, illustrated account of Kennedy's life and accomplishments that provides extensive Web links for students to do further research. (Rev: BL 9/1/02) [973.922]

5975 Selfridge, John W. *John F. Kennedy: Courage in Crisis* (5–8). 1989, Ballantine paper $4.99 (0-449-90399-0). A simple biography of the late president that tells about his youth as well as his presidency. (Rev: BL 12/15/89; BR 3–4/90; SLJ 2/90) [921]

5976 Spencer, Lauren. *The Assassination of John F. Kennedy* (6–10). Series: Library of Political Assassinations. 2001, Rosen LB $26.50 (0-8239-3541-8). This is a highly readable account of the assassination, its political buildup, and the social fallout. (Rev: BL 3/15/02; SLJ 6/02) [921]

5977 Swisher, Clarice, ed. *John F. Kennedy* (8–12). Illus. Series: People Who Made History. 1999, Greenhaven LB $21.96 (0-7377-0225-7); paper $13.96 (0-7377-0224-9). This collection of essays covers such topics as major influences on JFK, the presidential debates, the new frontier, foreign policy, and assessments of his presidency. (Rev: BL 2/1/00) [921]

5978 Uschan, Michael V. *John F. Kennedy* (6–10). Illus. 1998, Lucent LB $27.45 (1-56006-482-X). An objective account that uses quotations from many original sources, chronicling fairly and honestly Kennedy's rise to power, his triumphs, and his faults. (Rev: SLJ 4/99; VOYA 8/99) [921]

KENNEDY, JOHN F., JR.

5979 Landau, Elaine. *John F. Kennedy Jr.* (6–9). Illus. Series: Great Americans. 2000, Twenty-First Century LB $26.90 (0-7613-1857-7). Beginning with the tragic plane crash that ended his life, and moving back in time, this biography of JFK Jr. captures his personality and the aura that surrounded him. (Rev: BL 12/15/00; HBG 3/01; SLJ 3/01) [921]

LINCOLN, ABRAHAM

5980 Barter, James. *Abraham Lincoln* (7–12). Series: The Importance Of. 2003, Gale LB $21.96 (1-56006-965-1). This biography of Lincoln uses ample quotations from important sources and tries to evaluate Lincoln's importance by present-day standards. (Rev: BL 3/15/03) [921]

5981 Bracken, Thomas. *Abraham Lincoln: U.S. President* (7–9). Illus. Series: Overcoming Adversity. 1999, Chelsea paper $9.95 (0-7910-4705-9). A biography of Lincoln that stresses the many obstacles he overcame, including lack of formal education, financial difficulties, and bouts of depression. (Rev: HBG 3/99; SLJ 10/98) [921]

5982 Freedman, Russell. *Lincoln: A Photobiography* (4–8). Illus. 1987, Houghton $18.00 (0-89919-380-3); paper $7.95 (0-395-51848-2). A no-nonsense, unromanticized look at this beloved president. Newbery Medal winner, 1988. (Rev: BL 12/15/87; SLJ 12/87) [921]

5983 Holzer, Harold. *Abraham Lincoln: The Writer* (6–10). Illus. 2000, Boyds Mills $15.95 (1-56397-772-9). Following a brief biography, this resource contains letters, excerpts from speeches, notes, debates, and inaugural addresses, each with explanatory introductions that connect the snippet to his life. (Rev: BL 5/1/00; HBG 9/00; SLJ 6/00) [921]

5984 Ito, Tom. *Abraham Lincoln* (5–8). Illus. Series: Mysterious Deaths. 1996, Lucent LB $24.94 (1-56006-259-2). A look at the various conspiracy theories that surround Lincoln's death. (Rev: BL 2/15/97; SLJ 5/97) [921]

5985 Kops, Deborah. *Abraham Lincoln* (6–9). Series: The Civil War. 2001, Gale LB $19.95 (1-56711-535-7). Lincoln's achievements during the

Civil War are the main focus of this well-illustrated volume that also touches on his early life and family. (Rev: HBG 3/02; SLJ 4/02) [973]

5986 Marrin, Albert. *Commander in Chief Abraham Lincoln and the Civil War* (7–12). Illus. 1997, Dutton $25.00 (0-525-45822-0). This is not only a stirring biography of Lincoln but also a history of the Civil War, with profiles of people involved in the fight against slavery, such as John Brown. (Rev: BL 12/15/97; BR 5–6/98; SLJ 2/98*; VOYA 4/98) [921]

5987 Meltzer, Milton, ed. *Lincoln in His Own Words* (6–9). Illus. 1993, Harcourt $22.95 (0-15-245437-3). A collection of excerpts of Lincoln's statements, with facts about his life. (Rev: BL 9/1/93; VOYA 12/93) [921]

5988 O'Neal, Michael. *The Assassination of Abraham Lincoln* (6–10). Series: Great Mysteries. 1991, Greenhaven LB $18.96 (0-89908-092-8). Outlines known facts about Lincoln's assassination and poses questions about the mysteries that remain unsolved. (Rev: BL 3/1/92; SLJ 4/92) [921]

5989 Sandburg, Carl. *Abe Lincoln Grows Up* (6–9). 1975, Harcourt paper $8.00 (0-15-602615-5). From the pen of one of America's great poets, this is an account of the boyhood of his great hero. [921]

5990 Sloate, Susan. *Abraham Lincoln: The Freedom President* (5–8). 1989, Ballantine paper $15.00 (0-449-90375-3). An accessible account of the president who led his country through division back to unity. (Rev: BL 12/15/89; BR 3–4/90) [921]

5991 Sullivan, George. *Picturing Lincoln: Famous Photographs That Popularized the President* (5–8). Illus. 2000, Clarion $16.00 (0-395-91682-8). Using five images of Lincoln taken between 1846 and 1864, this book gives historical and biographical information on each and tells how they have been used for posters, button, ribbons, postage stamps, and currency. (Rev: BL 2/1/01; HB 3–4/01; HBG 10/01; SLJ 3/01) [921]

LINCOLN, MARY TODD

5992 Hull, Mary E. *Mary Todd Lincoln* (5–8). Series: Historical American Biographies. 2000, Enslow LB $20.95 (0-7660-1252-2). This biography faithfully records the tragic life of Lincoln's widow, whose emotional health declined after the deaths of her son and her husband. (Rev: BL 1/1–15/00; HBG 10/00; SLJ 5/00) [921]

MCKINLEY, WILLIAM

5993 Wilson, Antoine. *The Assassination of William McKinley* (6–9). Series: The Library of Political Assassinations. 2002, Rosen LB $26.50 (0-8239-3546-9). The life of this President is re-created with emphasis on details leading up to the crime and the characters involved. (Rev: BL 8/02) [921]

MADISON, DOLLEY

5994 Pflueger, Lynda. *Dolley Madison: Courageous First Lady* (5–8). Series: Historical American Biographies. 1999, Enslow LB $20.95 (0-7660-1092-9). The interesting biography of the woman who defined the role of First Lady and who was known for her political acumen and diplomatic and social skills as well as her patriotism and her ability to inspire others. (Rev: BR 5–6/99; SLJ 1/99) [921]

5995 Weatherly, Myra. *Dolley Madison: America's First Lady* (5–8). Illus. Series: Founders of the Republic. 2002, Morgan Reynolds LB $21.95 (1-883846-95-1). This portrait of Dolley Madison conveys her popularity and courage, with reproductions of period paintings, prints, and maps. (Rev: BL 11/1/02; HBG 3/03; SLJ 3/03) [973.5]

MADISON, JAMES

5996 Fritz, Jean. *The Great Little Madison* (5–8). Illus. 1989, Putnam $16.99 (0-399-21768-1). With wit and imagination the author captures the life of the fourth president. (Rev: BCCB 10/89; BL 10/1/89; BR 3–4/90; HB 3–4/90*; SLJ 11/89; VOYA 12/89) [921]

5997 Malone, Mary. *James Madison* (7–9). Series: United States Presidents. 1997, Enslow LB $20.95 (0-89490-834-0). This objective biography emphasizes Madison's intellectual and public-service contributions, with details on his role in drafting the Constitution and his two terms as president. (Rev: BL 9/15/97; HBG 3/98; SLJ 9/97) [921]

MONROE, JAMES

5998 Wetzel, Charles. *James Monroe* (6–10). Illus. 1989, Chelsea LB $19.95 (1-55546-817-9). The life of the Revolutionary War hero, his presidency, and the foreign policy named after him. (Rev: BL 7/89; BR 9–10/89) [921]

NIXON, RICHARD M.

5999 Barron, Rachel. *Richard Nixon: American Politician* (7–12). Illus. Series: Notable Americans. 1998, Morgan Reynolds LB $21.95 (1-883846-33-1). An objective biography of this contradictory figure who became the century's most controversial president. (Rev: BL 8/98; HBG 3/99; SLJ 12/98; VOYA 10/98) [921]

6000 Marquez, Heron. *Richard M. Nixon* (5–7). Series: Presidential Leaders. 2003, Lerner LB $31.95 (0-8225-0098-1). The Vietnam War, relations with China, and Watergate all feature promi-

nently in this look at Nixon's private and public life. (Rev: BL 4/15/03; HBG 10/03; SLJ 2/03) [921]

6001 Randolph, Sallie. *Richard M. Nixon, President* (6–9). Illus. 1989, Walker LB $14.85 (0-8027-6849-0). A straightforward account using many original sources that doesn't skirt the controversial issues. (Rev: BL 1/15/90; SLJ 12/90; VOYA 2/90) [921]

6002 Ripley, C. Peter. *Richard Nixon* (6–10). Illus. 1987, Chelsea LB $19.95 (0-87754-585-5). Beginning with his 1974 resignation, Nixon's life is retraced and an assessment of his career is given. (Rev: BL 12/1/87; BR 5–6/88; SLJ 12/87) [921]

ONASSIS, JACQUELINE KENNEDY

6003 Anderson, Catherine C. *Jackie Kennedy Onassis* (4–7). Illus. 1995, Lerner LB $21.27 (0-8225-2885-1). An adoring biography of the former First Lady, who was a model of courage and dignity. (Rev: BL 2/1/96) [921]

PIERCE, FRANKLIN

6004 Brown, Fern G. *Franklin Pierce* (5–8). Series: Presidents of the United States. 1989, GEC LB $21.27 (0-944483-25-9). The story of Pierce, his political life and presidency, plus material on his personal life. (Rev: SLJ 9/89) [921]

REAGAN, RONALD

6005 Hinkle, Donald Henry. *Ronald Reagan* (4–7). Series: Presidents. 2003, Enslow/MyReportLinks.com LB $19.95 (0-7660-5112-9). The life story of the fortieth president with material on the successes and failures of his two terms. (Rev: BL 6/1–15/03; HBG 10/03) [921]

6006 Sullivan, George. *Ronald Reagan* (5–8). Illus. 1991, Simon & Schuster $14.98 (0-671-74537-9). This revised edition adds new material on Reagan's second term. (Rev: BL 1/15/92) [921]

6007 Young, Jeff C. *Great Communicator: The Story of Ronald Reagan* (6–10). Illus. Series: Twentieth-Century Leaders. 2003, Morgan Reynolds LB $21.95 (1-931798-10-9). Reagan's career is the main focus of this biography that includes many quotations and black-and-white photographs and deals objectively with the former president's strengths and weaknesses. (Rev: BL 6/1–15/03; HBG 10/03; SLJ 10/03) [973.927]

ROOSEVELT, ELEANOR

6008 Brown, Jonatha A. *Eleanor Roosevelt* (6–9). Series: Trailblazers of the Modern World. 2002, World Almanac Library LB $26.60 (0-8368-5079-3); paper $10.95 (0-8368-5239-7). A fine biography of the amazing first lady who excelled in a number of pursuits. (Rev: BL 12/15/02) [921]

6009 Faber, Doris. *Eleanor Roosevelt: First Lady to the World* (5–7). 1986, Puffin paper $4.99 (0-14-032103-9). Eleanor Roosevelt's life before and after FDR is discussed. (Rev: BL 9/1/85; HB 9–10/85; SLJ 8/85) [973.9170924]

6010 Freedman, Russell. *Eleanor Roosevelt: A Life of Discovery* (5–9). 1993, Clarion $17.95 (0-89919-862-7). This admiring photobiography captures Roosevelt's public role and personal sadness. (Rev: BL 7/93*; SLJ 8/93*; VOYA 2/94) [921]

6011 Lazo, Caroline. *Eleanor Roosevelt* (4–7). Illus. Series: Peacemakers. 1993, Dillon $13.95 (0-87518-594-0). A biography of the famous First Lady that focuses on her many lasting contributions, particularly in promoting world peace. (Rev: BL 12/15/93; SLJ 1/94) [921]

6012 Spangenburg, Raymond, and Diane Moser. *Eleanor Roosevelt: A Passion to Improve* (8–12). Series: Makers of America. 1996, Facts on File $25.00 (0-8160-3371-4). A superior introduction to the life and significant achievements of Eleanor Roosevelt and her lifetime struggle for social equality for all people. (Rev: BL 1/1–15/97) [921]

6013 Toor, Rachel. *Eleanor Roosevelt* (6–10). Illus. 1989, Chelsea LB $19.95 (1-55546-674-5). An affectionate portrait of a first lady who was also a great humanitarian and internationalist. (Rev: BL 4/1/89; BR 5–6/89; SLJ 5/89; VOYA 8/89) [921]

6014 Westervelt, Virginia Veeder. *Here Comes Eleanor: A New Biography of Eleanor Roosevelt for Young People* (5–8). Series: Avisson Young Adult. 1999, Avisson paper $16.00 (1-888105-33-X). A clear account of the life of Eleanor Roosevelt that gives a fine assessment of her many contributions to humankind. (Rev: BL 2/15/99; SLJ 7/99; VOYA 10/99) [921]

6015 Winget, Mary. *Eleanor Roosevelt* (5–8). Series: A&E Biography. 2000, Lerner LB $25.26 (0-8225-4985-9). Growing up in a troubled but loving family, Eleanor Roosevelt showed that an ordinary woman can achieve greatness. (Rev: BL 3/1/01; HBG 10/01) [921]

ROOSEVELT, FRANKLIN D.

6016 Burgan, Michael. *Franklin D. Roosevelt* (4–8). Series: Profiles of the Presidents. 2002, Compass Point LB $28.75 (0-7565-0203-9). An absorbing introduction to Roosevelt's life and career, with details of his youth and education and the role that his illness played in shaping his character. (Rev: SLJ 6/02) [973.917092]

6017 Devaney, John. *Franklin Delano Roosevelt, President* (6–10). Illus. 1987, Walker $12.95 (0-8027-6713-3). An account that detailed Roosevelt's personality as well as his career. (Rev: SLJ 1/88; VOYA 12/87) [921]

6018 Freedman, Russell. *Franklin Delano Roosevelt* (5–8). Illus. 1990, Houghton $20.00 (0-89919-379-X). A carefully researched and well-illustrated account of the man and the times. (Rev: HB 3–4/90; SLJ 12/90*) [921]

6019 Greenblatt, Miriam. *Franklin D. Roosevelt: 32nd President of the United States* (5–8). Illus. 1989, Garrett LB $21.27 (0-944483-06-2). A clearly written, objective biography of the man who guided the country through World War II, with information on his family life. (Rev: BL 5/1/89; SLJ 8/89) [921]

6020 Knapp, Ron. *Franklin D. Roosevelt* (5–9). 2002, Enslow/MyReportLinks.com LB $19.95 (0-7660-5009-2). A listing of recommended Web sites extends the contents of this introduction to Roosevelt's life and presidency. (Rev: HBG 10/02; SLJ 6/02) [921]

6021 Morris, Jeffrey. *The FDR Way* (5–8). Illus. Series: Great Presidential Decisions. 1996, Lerner LB $23.93 (0-8225-2929-7). A straightforward, incisive analysis of far-reaching, often painful decisions that FDR made, and an assessment of their consequences. (Rev: BL 3/15/96) [921]

6022 Nardo, Don. *Franklin D. Roosevelt: U.S. President* (7–10). Series: Great Achievers: Lives of the Physically Challenged. 1995, Chelsea LB $21.95 (0-7910-2406-7). This biography of Roosevelt stresses the physical challenges he faced and his strong personality that allowed him to achieve great success. (Rev: BR 3–4/96; SLJ 1/96) [921]

6023 Schuman, Michael A. *Franklin D. Roosevelt: The Four-Term President* (4–7). Illus. Series: People to Know. 1996, Enslow LB $20.95 (0-89490-696-8). A thoughtful, serious look at this great president, his important decisions, and his significance in history. (Rev: BL 6/1–15/96; SLJ 8/96) [921]

ROOSEVELT, THEODORE

6024 Donnelly, Matt. *Theodore Roosevelt: Larger Than Life* (6–9). Illus. 2003, Linnet $27.50 (0-208-02510-3). Information about the presidency of Theodore Roosevelt is presented along with coverage of his childhood and early experiences in the West and as a public servant. (Rev: BL 1/1–15/03; HB 3–4/03; HBG 10/03; SLJ 3/03; VOYA 10/03) [973.91]

6025 Fritz, Jean. *Bully for You, Teddy Roosevelt!* (5–8). 1991, Putnam $16.99 (0-399-21769-X). An affectionate portrait of the president who considered himself a "true American." (Rev: BL 4/15/91; HB 7–8/91; SLJ 7/91*) [921]

6026 Kraft, Betsy Harvey. *Theodore Roosevelt: Champion of the American Spirit* (5–9). Illus. 2003, Clarion $19.00 (0-618-14264-9). The determination that carried Roosevelt through a difficult childhood and drove his successful career is emphasized in this engrossing biography of his life and survey of his diverse accomplishments. (Rev: BL 10/15/03; HB 11–12/03; SLJ 12/03*; VOYA 10/03) [973.9]

6027 Schuman, Michael A. *Theodore Roosevelt* (5–8). Series: United States Presidents. 1997, Enslow LB $20.95 (0-89490-836-7). An objective biography of the life of this active president whose life spanned both the Civil War and World War I, with good background information. (Rev: BL 2/1/98; HBG 3/98; SLJ 2/98) [921]

6028 Whitelaw, Nancy. *Theodore Roosevelt Takes Charge* (6–9). 1992, Albert Whitman LB $14.95 (0-8075-7849-5). A clear, credible biography of a larger-than-life American hero who was full of contradictions. (Rev: BL 6/1/92*; SLJ 7/92*) [921]

TAYLOR, ZACHARY

6029 Collins, David R. *Zachary Taylor: 12th President of the United States* (5–7). Illus. 1989, Garrett LB $21.27 (0-944483-17-8). Tells the life story of a military man elected president in 1848. (Rev: BL 5/1/89) [973.630924]

TRUMAN, HARRY S

6030 Feinberg, Barbara S. *Harry S Truman* (7–12). 1994, Watts paper $24.00 (0-531-13036-3). Examines Truman's life and presidential administration, analyzing the events of his two terms and his struggles and triumphs. (Rev: BL 9/1/94; SLJ 9/94) [921]

6031 Fleming, Thomas. *Harry S Truman, President* (6–12). 1993, Walker LB $15.85 (0-8027-8269-8). The author of this uncritical biography of the former president had access to family photographs and documents. (Rev: BL 1/1/94; SLJ 12/93; VOYA 2/94) [921]

6032 Greenberg, Morrie. *The Buck Stops Here: A Biography of Harry Truman* (5–9). Illus. 1989, Dillon LB $13.95 (0-87518-394-8). A competent retelling of the major events in Truman's life and of his importance as a U.S. president. (Rev: SLJ 4/89) [921]

6033 Lazo, Caroline Evensen. *Harry S Truman* (5–7). Illus. Series: Presidential Leaders. 2003, Lerner LB $26.60 (0-8225-0096-5). Truman's youth, education, family life, and career are all covered in this concise biography full of photographs. (Rev: BL 4/15/03; HBG 10/03) [973.918]

VAN BUREN, MARTIN

6034 Doak, Robin S. *Martin Van Buren* (4–7). 2003, Compass Point LB $17.95 (0-7565-0256-X). Van Buren's strengths and weakness receive equal weight in this balanced and readable biography that

covers his life from a young age. (Rev: SLJ 11/03) [973.5]

6035 Ellis, Rafaela. *Martin Van Buren: 8th President of the United States* (5–7). Illus. 1989, Garrett LB $21.27 (0-944483-12-7). The story of a New York governor who became president. (Rev: BL 5/1/89) [973.570924]

WASHINGTON, GEORGE

6036 Bruns, Roger. *George Washington* (6–10). Illus. 1986, Chelsea LB $19.95 (0-87754-584-7). A solid, readable biography of our first president. (Rev: BL 3/1/87; SLJ 5/87) [921]

6037 Falkof, Lucille. *George Washington: 1st President of the United States* (5–8). Illus. 1989, Garrett LB $21.27 (0-944483-19-4). An objective, readable portrait of the life and times of our first president. (Rev: BL 5/1/89; BR 9–10/89; SLJ 8/89) [921]

6038 Hilton, Suzanne. *The World of Young George Washington* (5–8). 1987, Walker $12.95 (0-8027-6657-9). Washington as a youth plus detailed information on life in pre-Revolutionary America. (Rev: BR 5–6/87; SLJ 4/87) [921]

6039 McClung, Robert M. *Young George Washington and the French and Indian War: 1753–1758* (6–9). Illus. 2002, Linnet $22.50 (0-208-02509-X). A portrait of Washington as a military leader who matures from youthful impetuosity to a more thoughtful outlook on life. (Rev: BL 8/02; HBG 3/03; SLJ 10/02) [973.2]

6040 Marrin, Albert. *George Washington and the Founding of a Nation* (7–12). Illus. 2001, Dutton $30.00 (0-525-46481-6). A detailed account of this complex leader that examines the facts and the myths. (Rev: BCCB 2/01; BL 1/1–15/01; HB 5–6/01; HBG 10/01; SLJ 1/01) [973.4]

6041 Old, Wendie C. *George Washington* (5–8). Illus. Series: United States Presidents. 1997, Enslow LB $20.95 (0-89490-832-4). Washington's personal life and political career are dealt with equally in this thoughtful biography. (Rev: BL 9/15/97; SLJ 12/97) [921]

6042 Rosenburg, John. *First in Peace: George Washington, the Constitution, and the Presidency* (7–10). 1998, Millbrook LB $25.90 (0-7613-0422-3). The last of the trilogy about Washington, this installment describes the emergence of the new nation and the role played by our first president. (Rev: HBG 3/99; SLJ 1/99) [921]

6043 Yoder, Carolyn P., ed. *George Washington: The Writer: A Treasury of Letters, Diaries, and Public Documents* (7–10). Illus. 2003, Boyds Mills $16.95 (1-56397-199-2). Washington's speeches, letters, will, and other documents — many excerpted — reveal much about his life and career. (Rev: BL 3/15/03; HBG 10/03; SLJ 2/03) [973.41]

WASHINGTON, MARTHA

6044 McPherson, Stephanie S. *Martha Washington: First Lady* (7–9). Series: Historical American Biographies. 1998, Enslow LB $20.95 (0-7660-1017-1). An affectionate portrait of the first First Lady, who was not well educated but put the skills she learned to good use running a household and living in polite society. (Rev: BL 1/1–15/99; SLJ 1/99) [921]

WILSON, WOODROW

6045 Collins, David R. *Woodrow Wilson: 28th President of the United States* (5–8). Illus. 1989, Garrett LB $21.27 (0-944483-18-6). A compact biography of a Nobel Peace Prize–winning president. (Rev: BL 5/1/89; SLJ 8/89) [921]

6046 Randolph, Sallie. *Woodrow Wilson, President* (5–9). Series: Presidential Biography. 1992, Walker LB $15.85 (0-8027-8144-6). Offers a concise overview of Wilson's tragic personal and political struggles, his achievements, and his place in history. (Rev: BL 12/15/91; SLJ 3/92) [921]

6047 Rogers, James T. *Woodrow Wilson: Visionary for Peace* (7–10). Illus. Series: Makers of America. 1997, Facts on File $25.00 (0-8160-3396-X). A thoughtful, in-depth biography the idealistic American president who overcame obstacles throughout his life and whose dream of an international League of Nations was shattered when the United States declined to join. (Rev: BL 5/15/97) [921]

6048 Schraff, Anne. *Woodrow Wilson* (5–8). Series: United States Presidents. 1998, Enslow LB $20.95 (0-89490-936-3). The story of the brilliant 28th president, his initial opposition to entering World War I, the defeat of his proposals concerning the League of Nations, and the stroke he suffered. (Rev: SLJ 9/98) [921]

Other Government and Public Figures

ADAMS, SAMUEL

6049 Davis, Kate. *Samuel Adams* (6–8). Series: Triangle Histories of the Revolutionary War: Leaders. 2003, Gale LB $21.95 (1-56711-612-4). The life and times of the political activist who advocated independence for America. (Rev: LMC 8–9/03; SLJ 5/03) [921]

6050 Fradin, Dennis B. *Samuel Adams: The Father of American Independence* (5–9). Illus. 1998, Houghton $18.00 (0-395-82510-5). An attractive biography of the amazing Sam Adams, whom Jefferson called "the Man of the Revolution." (Rev:

BCCB 7–8/98; BL 7/98; BR 11–12/98; SLJ 7/98; VOYA 2/99) [921]

ALBRIGHT, MADELEINE

6051 Burgan, Michael. *Madeleine Albright* (8–10). 1998, Millbrook LB $24.90 (0-7613-0367-7). The life of the first woman U.S. secretary of state and highest-ranking woman ever in the federal government that tells of her European childhood, her arrival as a refugee in this country, and her experiences as a student, journalist, activist, teacher, mother, ambassador, and, finally, secretary of state. (Rev: SLJ 6/99) [921]

6052 Byman, Jeremy. *Madam Secretary: The Story of Madeleine Albright* (5–9). Series: Notable Americans. 1997, Morgan Reynolds LB $21.95 (1-883846-23-4). The emphasis in this biography is on Albright's public life, first as adviser to various political figures, then as ambassador to the United Nations, and finally as secretary of state. (Rev: BL 12/15/97; SLJ 4/98; VOYA 6/98) [921]

6053 Hasday, Judy. *Madeleine Albright* (8–12). Series: Women of Achievement. 1998, Chelsea $21.95 (0-7910-4708-3); paper $8.95 (0-7910-4709-1). A well-rounded biography of Madeleine Albright, her career in American public service, and her childhood in Eastern Europe. (Rev: HBG 3/99; SLJ 3/99) [921]

6054 Kramer, Barbara. *Madeleine Albright: First Woman Secretary of State* (6–9). Illus. Series: People to Know. 2000, Enslow LB $19.95 (0-7660-1143-7). This account traces the life and career of Albright through early 1999 and the Kosovo bombings. (Rev: BL 1/1–15/00; HBG 9/00) [327.73.]

ARNOLD, BENEDICT

6055 Fritz, Jean. *Traitor: The Case of Benedict Arnold* (7–9). Illus. 1981, Putnam $16.99 (0-399-20834-8). A biography that tries to probe the many reasons for Arnold's actions. [921]

6056 Gaines, Ann Graham. *Benedict Arnold: Patriot or Traitor?* (5–8). Series: Historical American Biographies. 2001, Enslow LB $20.95 (0-7660-1393-6). Many facets of the character of this controversial American are examined in this well-illustrated volume. (Rev: BL 4/15/01; HBG 10/01; SLJ 6/01) [921]

6057 Gregson, Susan R. *Benedict Arnold* (5–6). Series: Let Freedom Ring. 2001, Capstone LB $22.60 (0-7368-1032-3). An introduction to Arnold's life and contributions, with discussion of the reasons why he became a traitor. (Rev: HBG 3/02; SLJ 4/02) [921]

6058 King, David C. *Benedict Arnold and the American Revolution* (5–9). Series: Notorious Americans and Their Times. 1998, Blackbirch LB $27.44 (1-56711-221-8). Benedict Arnold's life and military accomplishments are placed in the context of the period in which he lived and the conflicts he faced. (Rev: BL 12/15/98; HBG 3/99; SLJ 12/98) [921]

AUSTIN, STEPHEN F.

6059 Haley, James L. *Stephen F. Austin and the Founding of Texas* (5–8). Series: The Library of American Lives and Times. 2003, Rosen LB $31.95 (0-8239-5738-1). A concise biography of the pioneer who became one of the founders of Texas. (Rev: SLJ 5/03) [976.4]

BARTON, CLARA

6060 Hamilton, Leni. *Clara Barton* (5–10). Illus. 1987, Chelsea LB $19.95 (1-55546-641-9). The story of the Civil War nurse and how she prepared for the founding of the American Red Cross. (Rev: BL 11/1/87) [921]

6061 Whitelaw, Nancy. *Clara Barton: Civil War Nurse* (5–9). Series: Historical American Biographies. 1997, Enslow LB $20.95 (0-89490-778-6). Using material from her diaries and published books, this biography relates Barton's life story and amazing accomplishments. (Rev: BL 3/15/98; SLJ 2/98) [921]

BOONE, DANIEL

6062 Calvert, Patricia. *Daniel Boone: Beyond the Mountains* (5–8). Series: Great Explorations. 2001, Marshall Cavendish LB $28.50 (0-7614-1243-3). An attractive biography of the American pioneer who explored the Cumberland Gap region and helped settlers in the Kentucky region. (Rev: BCCB 3/02; BL 4/1/02; HBG 3/02; SLJ 3/02) [921]

6063 Faragher, John Mack. *Daniel Boone: The Life and Legend of an American Pioneer* (7–12). 1992, Holt paper $18.00 (0-8050-3007-7). A biography of the complex frontier pioneer/politician/maverick. (Rev: BL 11/1/92*; SLJ 5/93*) [921]

6064 Green, Carl R. *Blazing the Wilderness Road with Daniel Boone* (6–10). Series: In American History. 2000, Enslow LB $20.95 (0-7660-1346-4). The story of Daniel Boone, his role in opening up the west, and his role in the American Revolution. (Rev: BL 12/15/00; HBG 3/01) [921]

6065 McCarthy, Pat. *Daniel Boone* (5–8). Series: Historical American Biographies. 2000, Enslow LB $20.95 (0-7660-1256-5). A well-organized and thoroughly documented biography of the legendary pioneer and hero of the American Revolution who died in 1820. (Rev: BL 1/1–15/00; HBG 10/00; SLJ 5/00) [921]

BRADFORD, WILLIAM

6066 Doherty, Kieran. *William Bradford: Rock of Plymouth* (5–9). 1999, Twenty-First Century LB $24.90 (0-7613-1304-4). Using Bradford's own writings and other contemporary accounts as sources, this is an objective biography of the man who was the governor of the Plymouth Plantation. (Rev: BL 12/1/99; HBG 3/00; SLJ 1/00) [921]

6067 Schmidt, Gary. *William Bradford: Plymouth's Faithful Pilgrim* (5–8). 1999, Eerdmans $18.00 (0-8028-5151-7); paper $8.00 (0-8028-5148-8). The story of the famous Pilgrim who helped found the Plymouth colony and who led it for many years. (Rev: BL 7/99; SLJ 6/99; VOYA 12/99) [921]

BRADLEY, BILL

6068 Buckley, James, Jr. *Bill Bradley* (5–8). Illus. Series: Basketball Hall of Famers. 2002, Rosen LB $29.25 (0-8239-3479-9). An easy-to-read, detailed biography of the former athlete, with plenty of photographs. (Rev: BL 9/1/02) [796.323]

6069 Jaspersohn, William. *Senator: A Profile of Bill Bradley in the U.S. Senate* (6–10). 1992, Harcourt $19.95 (0-15-272880-5). An in-depth photoessay about Congress in general and Senator Bradley of New Jersey in particular, showing how his sports career led to the Senate. (Rev: BL 7/92; SLJ 10/92) [921]

BRANDEIS, LOUIS

6070 Freedman, Suzanne. *Louis Brandeis* (4–9). Illus. Series: Justices of the Supreme Court. 1996, Enslow LB $20.95 (0-89490-678-X). A biography of the great justice who advocated many public causes and was known as the "people's attorney." (Rev: BL 8/96; SLJ 11/96) [921]

BUNCHE, RALPH

6071 Schraff, Anne. *Ralph Bunche: Winner of the Nobel Peace Prize* (7–12). Series: African-American Biographies. 1999, Enslow LB $20.95 (0-7660-1203-4). The story of the great American diplomat who helped mediate several international disputes and won the Nobel peace prize in 1950. (Rev: BL 11/15/99; SLJ 8/99) [921]

BURR, AARON

6072 Ingram, W. Scott. *Aaron Burr and the Young Nation* (5–8). Series: Major World Leaders. 2002, Chelsea $27.44 (1-56711-250-1). The story of the controversial political leader who killed Alexander Hamilton in a duel and later was tried and found guilty of treason. (Rev: BL 1/1–15/03; SLJ 10/02) [921]

CAMPBELL, BEN NIGHTHORSE

6073 Henry, Christopher. *Ben Nighthorse Campbell: Cheyenne Chief and U.S. Senator* (5–8). Illus. Series: North American Indians of Achievement. 1994, Chelsea $19.95 (0-7919-2046-0). The story of the Cheyenne leader who gained prominence not only among his own people but also in the U.S. Congress. (Rev: BL 6/1–15/93) [921]

CHIEF JOSEPH

6074 Yates, Diana. *Chief Joseph: Thunder Rolling from the Mountains* (7–12). 1992, Ward Hill LB $14.95 (0-9623380-9-5); paper $10.95 (0-9623380-8-7). A sensitive distillation of the life and times of Chief Joseph of the Nez Perce. (Rev: BL 12/15/92; SLJ 12/92) [921]

CRAZY HORSE

6075 Brennan, Kristine. *Crazy Horse* (4–7). Series: Famous Figures of the American Frontier. 2001, Chelsea $19.75 (0-7910-6493-X); paper $8.95 (0-7910-6494-8). Report writers will find this a useful source of information on this Native American leader's adult life and achievements in battle. (Rev: HBG 10/02; SLJ 4/02) [921]

6076 Freedman, Russell. *The Life and Death of Crazy Horse* (6–12). Illus. 1996, Holiday $21.95 (0-8234-1219-9). This biography of Crazy Horse tells an uncompromising story of bloody wars, terrible grief, tragedy, and the Sioux's losing battle to preserve their independence and their land. (Rev: BL 6/1–15/96*; BR 11–12/96; SLJ 6/96*; VOYA 10/96) [921]

6077 Goldman, Martin S. *Crazy Horse: War Chief of the Oglala Sioux* (6–12). Series: American Indian Experience. 1996, Watts paper $24.00 (0-531-11258-6). This carefully researched biography recounts the life of this fascinating leader and of the decline of the Sioux. (Rev: SLJ 9/96) [921]

6078 St. George, Judith. *Crazy Horse* (7–10). 1994, Putnam $17.95 (0-399-22667-2). An account of the legendary Lakota leader who struggled to save his people's culture and way of life from destruction by white soldiers and settlers. (Rev: BL 10/1/94; SLJ 11/94; VOYA 2/95) [921]

CUSTER, GEORGE ARMSTRONG

6079 Kent, Zachary. *George Armstrong Custer* (5–8). Series: Historical American Biographies. 2000, Enslow LB $20.95 (0-7660-1255-7). Using extensive chapter notes, a glossary, bibliography, and index, this is a well-documented and objective assessment of Custer's life and deeds. (Rev: BL 1/1–15/00; HBG 10/00) [921]

DAVIS, BENJAMIN, JR.

6080 Reef, Catherine. *Benjamin Davis, Jr.* (5–8). Series: African American Soldiers. 1992, Twenty-First Century LB $14.95 (0-8050-2137-X). The story of the African American air force general and how he served his country in several wars beginning with World War II. (Rev: BL 12/15/92) [921]

DAVIS, JEFFERSON

6081 Burch, Joann J. *Jefferson Davis: President of the Confederacy* (5–8). Series: Historical American Biographies. 1998, Enslow LB $20.95 (0-7660-1064-3). Using personal documents and well-chosen illustrations, this lively biography describes Jefferson Davis's life as well as the causes and major events of the Civil War. (Rev: BL 10/15/98; SLJ 1/99) [921]

6082 Ingram, W. Scott. *Jefferson Davis* (5–8). Series: Triangle Histories of the Civil War. 2002, Gale LB $27.44 (1-56711-565-9). A useful account of Davis's life and career with a sidebar feature on the servant who perhaps was a spy. (Rev: SLJ 1/03) [921]

6083 King, Perry Scott. *Jefferson Davis* (7–10). Illus. 1990, Chelsea LB $21.95 (1-55546-806-3). With many illustrations, King re-creates the life and times of the president of the Confederacy. (Rev: BL 8/90; SLJ 8/90) [921]

DAY, DOROTHY

6084 Kent, Deborah. *Dorothy Day: Friend to the Forgotten* (7–12). Illus. 1996, Eerdmans $15.00 (0-8028-5117-7). The biography of the great friend of the poor and helpless whose own life's drama involved an abortion, a short-lived marriage, imprisonment, political involvement, and questioning of her deep religious beliefs. (Rev: BL 6/1–15/96; BR 1–2/97; SLJ 8/96) [921]

DE ZAVALA, LORENZO

6085 Tracy, Kathleen. *Lorenzo de Zavala* (5–7). Series: Latinos in American History. 2002, Mitchell Lane LB $19.95 (1-58415-154-4). The biography of the 19th-century Mexican who became vice president of the Republic of Texas and was one of the signers of its constitution. (Rev: BL 2/15/03; HBG 10/03) [921]

EARP, WYATT

6086 Green, Carl R., and William R. Sanford. *Wyatt Earp* (4–8). Illus. Series: Outlaws and Lawmen of the Wild West. 1992, Enslow LB $16.95 (0-89490-367-5). With maps and authentic illustrations, this biography tells the story of the deputy marshal who tried to clean up Tombstone, Arizona. (Rev: BL 10/1/92; SLJ 11/92) [921]

FARRAGUT, DAVID

6087 Shorto, Russell. *David Farragut and the Great Naval Blockade* (4–7). Illus. Series: The Story of the Civil War. 1991, Silver Burdett paper $7.95 (0-382-24050-2). The story of the outstanding naval commander who closed the Gulf ports to Confederate blockade-running during the Civil War. (Rev: BL 9/1/91) [921]

FRANKLIN, BENJAMIN

6088 Adler, David A. *B. Franklin, Printer* (4–8). Illus. 2001, Holiday $19.95 (0-8234-1675-5). Quotations, anecdotes, and wonderful illustrations round out this excellent volume about the life and accomplishments of Benjamin Franklin. (Rev: BCCB 2/02; BL 1/1–15/02; HBG 10/02; SLJ 2/02*; VOYA 4/02) [973.3]

6089 Cousins, Margaret. *Ben Franklin of Old Philadelphia* (6–8). 1963, Random paper $5.99 (0-394-84928-0). A well-rounded portrait of this major figure in American history. [921]

6090 Fleming, Candace. *Ben Franklin's Almanac: Being a True Account of the Gentleman's Life* (6–9). Illus. 2003, Simon & Schuster $19.95 (0-689-83549-3). Compiled in scrapbook style, this is an appealing biography full of anecdotes and graphic elements and covering Franklin's family life and scientific, literary, and political achievements. (Rev: BL 8/03; HB 9–10/03; SLJ 9/03*) [973.3]

6091 Foster, Leila M. *Benjamin Franklin: Founding Father and Inventor* (5–8). Series: Historical American Biographies. 1997, Enslow LB $20.95 (0-89490-784-0). An admiring biography that describes Franklin's many talents — as a printer, businessman, scientist, inventor, and statesman. (Rev: SLJ 11/97) [921]

6092 Lee, Tanja, ed. *Benjamin Franklin* (7–12). Series: People Who Made History. 2002, Gale LB $31.20 (0-7377-0898-0); paper $19.95 (0-7377-0899-9). After an introductory general essay that introduces Franklin, his life, and his times, there are other essays that explore his talents, contributions, accomplishments, and his place in world history. (Rev: BL 4/1/02) [921]

6093 Looby, Chris. *Benjamin Franklin* (6–10). Illus. 1990, Chelsea LB $21.95 (1-55546-808-X). A well-illustrated account of the life of this complex man that also introduces many of his contemporaries. (Rev: BL 8/90; SLJ 7/90; VOYA 8/90) [921]

6094 Streissguth, Tom. *Benjamin Franklin* (5–8). Series: Biography. 2001, Lerner LB $25.26 (0-8225-4997-2). A readable biography of the many-

faceted genius of the newly formed United States. (Rev: BL 4/1/02; HBG 10/02) [921]

GERONIMO

6095 Hermann, Spring. *Geronimo: Apache Freedom Fighter* (6–9). Series: Native American Biographies. 1997, Enslow LB $20.95 (0-89490-864-2). This is a fine, well-rounded portrait of the man who became an Apache leader, fought at Little Bighorn, and died a prosperous man at age 85. (Rev: BL 4/15/97; SLJ 6/97) [921]

6096 Thompson, Bill, and Dorcas Thompson. *Geronimo* (4–7). Series: Famous Figures of the American Frontier. 2001, Chelsea $19.75 (0-7910-6491-3); paper $8.95 (0-7910-6492-1). A balanced biography of the Apache leader that report writers will find a useful resource. (Rev: HBG 10/02; SLJ 4/02) [921]

GINSBURG, RUTH BADER

6097 Ayer, Eleanor. *Ruth Bader Ginsburg: Fire and Steel on the Supreme Court* (5–8). 1995, Dillon LB $22.00 (0-87518-651-3); paper $7.95 (0-382-24721-3). A biography of the second woman Supreme Court justice, with emphasis on the many obstacles she had to overcome. (Rev: BL 5/15/95; SLJ 4/95; VOYA 5/95) [921]

GIULIANI, RUDOLPH W.

6098 Freemont, Eleanor. *Rudolph W. Giuliani* (4–8). 2002, Simon & Schuster paper $4.99 (0-689-85423-4). The story of the man *Time* magazine called "the mayor of the world" including material on his personal life and his rise to prominence with the attacks on September 11, 2001. (Rev: BL 9/1/02; SLJ 9/02) [974.7]

GLENN, JOHN

6099 Cole, Michael D. *John Glenn: Astronaut and Senator* (5–8). Series: People to Know. 2000, Enslow LB $20.95 (0-7660-1532-7). A biography of the astronaut and politician with coverage of his two trips into space. (Rev: BL 9/15/00; HBG 3/01) [921]

6100 Streissguth, Thomas. *John Glenn* (5–8). Series: A&E Biography. 1999, Lerner LB $25.26 (0-8225-4947-6); paper $7.95 (0-8225-9685-7). This account of John Glenn's life includes childhood influences, his career with NASA, and his political life as a senator. (Rev: HBG 3/00; SLJ 3/00) [921]

6101 Vogt, Gregory L. *John Glenn's Return to Space* (4–7). Illus. 2000, Twenty-First Century LB $24.90 (0-7613-1614-0). As well as describing John Glenn's two space flights on the Mercury capsule and later the *Discovery*, this biography gives information on astronauts' training and equipment. (Rev: BL 9/15/00; HBG 10/01; SLJ 1/01) [921]

HALE, NATHAN

6102 Krizner, L. J., and Lisa Sita. *Nathan Hale: Patriot and Martyr of the American Revolution* (4–7). Series: Library of American Lives and Times. 2001, Rosen $23.95 (0-8239-5724-1). Nathan Hale, executed by the British in 1776, represented the life-and-death issues fought for in the Revolution and became a symbol of courage and patriotism. (Rev: BL 10/15/01) [921]

HAMILTON, ALEXANDER

6103 DeCarolis, Lisa. *Alexander Hamilton: Federalist and Founding Father* (4–7). Series: Library of American Lives and Times. 2003, Rosen LB $31.95 (0-8239-5736-7). The story of the military hero of the American Revolution who was the first secretary of the treasury and helped write the Federalist Papers. (Rev: BL 6/1–15/03) [921]

HENRY, PATRICK

6104 Kukla, Amy, and Jon Kukla. *Patrick Henry: Voice of the Revolution* (4–7). Illus. Series: Library of American Lives and Times. 2001, Rosen $23.95 (0-8239-5725-X). Detailed text, a variety of illustrations, and a timeline give readers a good understanding of Henry's importance. (Rev: BL 10/15/01) [973.3]

HOLLIDAY, DOC

6105 Green, Carl R., and William R. Sanford. *Doc Holliday* (5–8). Series: Outlaws and Lawmen of the Wild West. 1995, Enslow LB $16.95 (0-89490-589-9). The life and exploits of this colorful western hero are reproduced with the help of photographs and maps. (Rev: BL 6/1–15/95) [921]

HOOVER, J. EDGAR

6106 Streissguth, Tom. *J. Edgar Hoover: Powerful FBI Director* (5–8). Series: Historical American Biographies. 2002, Enslow LB $20.95 (0-7660-1623-4). Streissguth looks at Hoover's life from youth, his personality, and his work as head of the FBI, and explores the areas in which his influence was felt, including civil rights and politics. (Rev: HBG 10/02; SLJ 8/02) [363.25092]

HOUSTON, SAM

6107 Fritz, Jean. *Make Way for Sam Houston* (6–9). Illus. 1986, Putnam $7.95 (0-399-21304-X). An authentic portrait of this colorful figure who served the state of Texas faithfully. (Rev: BL 6/1/86; HB 5–6/86; SLJ 5/86; VOYA 6/86) [921]

6108 Woodward, Walter M. *Sam Houston: For Texas and the Union* (5–8). Series: The Library of American Lives and Times. 2003, Rosen LB $31.95 (0-8239-5739-X). A concise biography of the man credited with gaining Texas's independence. (Rev: SLJ 5/03) [976.4]

JACKSON, STONEWALL

6109 Bennett, Barbara J. *Stonewall Jackson: Lee's Greatest Lieutenant* (4–7). Illus. Series: The History of the Civil War. 1990, Silver Burdett paper $7.95 (0-382-24048-0). The story of the Confederate general who gained his nickname beause he stood "like a stone wall." (Rev: BL 9/1/91) [921]

6110 Fritz, Jean. *Stonewall* (7–10). Illus. 1979, Putnam $16.99 (0-399-20698-1). The great Confederate general portrayed realistically as the complex man he was. [921]

6111 Pflueger, Lynda. *Stonewall Jackson: Confederate General* (5–8). Illus. Series: Historical American Biographies. 1997, Enslow LB $20.95 (0-89490-781-6). This sympathetic biography of Jackson, who favored neither slavery nor secession but became a Confederate general in the Civil War, provides good material on his personal life and beliefs, quoting generously from firsthand sources. (Rev: BL 10/1/97) [921]

6112 Robertson, James I. *Standing like a Stone Wall: The Life of General Thomas J. Jackson* (5–8). Illus. 2001, Simon & Schuster $22.00 (0-689-82419-X). Readers will gain a good understanding of Jackson's early life and career before the Civil War as well as his leadership during the war years. (Rev: BL 5/1/01; HBG 10/01; SLJ 6/01; VOYA 12/01) [973.7]

JONES, JOHN PAUL

6113 Bradford, James C. *John Paul Jones and the American Navy* (4–7). Series: Library of American Lives and Times. 2001, Rosen $23.95 (0-8239-5726-8). This attractively designed volume combines the life story of the naval hero of the American Revolution with a history of the birth and growth of the American navy. (Rev: BL 10/15/01) [921]

6114 Tibbitts, Alison Davis. *John Paul Jones: Father of the American Navy* (5–8). Series: Historical American Biographies. 2002, Enslow LB $20.95 (0-7660-1448-7). The life of the American naval officer noted for his role in the Revolution and for the statement, "I have not yet begun to fight." (Rev: BL 4/1/02; HBG 10/02; SLJ 5/02) [921]

JORDAN, BARBARA

6115 Blue, Rose, and Corinne J. Naden. *Barbara Jordan* (7–10). Series: Black Americans of Achievement. 1992, Chelsea LB $21.95 (0-7910-1131-3).

The colorful life of this former congresswoman and educator is re-created in this illustrated biography. (Rev: BL 9/15/92; SLJ 11/92) [921]

6116 Jeffrey, Laura S. *Barbara Jordan: Congresswoman, Lawyer, Educator* (7–12). Illus. Series: African-American Biographies. 1997, Enslow LB $20.95 (0-89490-692-5). This biography covers both the personal and professional life of this amazing woman who overcame great obstacles to fulfill a multi-faceted career. (Rev: BL 5/15/97; SLJ 3/97) [921]

LEE, ROBERT E.

6117 Anderson, Paul Christopher. *Robert E. Lee: Legendary Commander of the Confederacy* (4–7). Series: Library of American Lives and Times. 2003, Rosen LB $31.95 (0-8239-5748-9). Extensive original sources are used to re-create the life of this Confederate general and the times in which he lived. (Rev: BL 6/1–15/03) [921]

6118 Brown, Warren. *Robert E. Lee* (6–10). Series: World Leaders — Past and Present. 1991, Chelsea LB $19.95 (1-55546-814-4). Using many illustrations and maps, this volume re-creates the life of the Confederate Civil War general. (Rev: BL 11/15/91) [921]

6119 Dubowski, Cathy E. *Robert E. Lee: The Rise of the South* (4–7). Illus. Series: The History of the Civil War. 1990, Silver Burdett paper $7.95 (0-382-24051-0). The life of the Confederate general who was a stirring commander and a man of great character. (Rev: BL 9/1/91) [921]

6120 Kerby, Mona. *Robert E. Lee: Southern Hero of the Civil War* (5–8). Illus. Series: Historical American Biographies. 1997, Enslow LB $20.95 (0-89490-782-4). This thorough, sympathetic biography of Lee points out that he did not approve of slavery or the South's secession from the Union. (Rev: BL 10/1/97; SLJ 9/97) [921]

6121 King, David C. *Robert E. Lee* (6–9). Series: The Civil War. 2001, Gale LB $19.95 (1-56711-554-3). Lee's achievements during the Civil War are the main focus of this well-illustrated volume that also touches on his early life and family. (Rev: HBG 3/02; SLJ 4/02) [973.7]

LONG, HUEY

6122 La Vert, Suzanne. *Huey Long: The Kingfish of Louisiana* (8–12). Series: Makers of America. 1995, Facts on File $25.00 (0-8160-2880-X). Looks at the motivations and political life of Huey Long, "Kingfish of Louisiana," including his assassination and the inner workings of the government. (Rev: BL 6/1–15/95) [921]

MACARTHUR, DOUGLAS

6123 Darby, Jean. *Douglas MacArthur* (6–9). Illus. Series: Lerner Biographies. 1989, Lerner LB $30.35 (0-8225-4901-8). The career of the controversial general who led the war in the Pacific is outlined in this volume. (Rev: BL 11/15/89; SLJ 9/89) [921]

6124 Finkelstein, Norman H. *The Emperor General: A Biography of Douglas MacArthur* (5–9). Illus. 1989, Dillon LB $13.95 (0-87518-396-4). The high points in the life of General MacArthur are covered in this attractive biography. (Rev: BL 3/1/89; SLJ 4/89) [921]

6125 Fox, Mary V. *Douglas MacArthur* (4–8). Series: The Importance Of. 1999, Lucent LB $27.45 (1-56006-545-1). The story of one of the nation's most prominent generals, whose unorthodox actions made him a controversial figure. (Rev: BL 9/15/99) [921]

6126 Gaines, Ann Graham. *Douglas MacArthur: Brilliant General, Controversial Leader* (5–8). Series: Historical American Biographies. 2001, Enslow LB $20.95 (0-7660-1445-2). Using many black-and-white photographs as illustrations, this account gives a well-rounded, unbiased picture of this controversial general. (Rev: BL 4/15/01; HBG 10/01; SLJ 6/01) [921]

6127 Scott, Robert A. *Douglas MacArthur and the Century of War* (7–12). Series: Makers of America. 1997, Facts on File $25.00 (0-8160-3098-7). From the battlefields of World War I to his opposition to the Vietnam War, this biography follows the life of one of the most famous generals in American history. (Rev: BL 11/15/97; BR 3–4/98) [9211]

MCCAIN, JOHN

6128 Feinberg, Barbara S. *John McCain: Serving His Country* (4–7). Illus. Series: Gateway. 2000, Millbrook LB $23.90 (0-7613-1974-3). A biography of the senator that tells about his youth and later political career but concentrates on his stint in the navy and his imprisonment during the Vietnam War. (Rev: BL 3/1/01; HBG 10/01) [921]

6129 Kozar, Richard. *John McCain* (8–12). Series: Overcoming Adversity. 2002, Chelsea LB $21.95 (0-7910-6299-6). The story of the prominent U.S. politician and how he survived the ordeal of a POW camp in Vietnam. (Rev: BL 4/15/02; HBG 10/02) [921]

MCCARTHY, JOSEPH

6130 Sherrow, Victoria. *Joseph McCarthy and the Cold War* (5–9). Illus. Series: Notorious Americans and Their Times. 1998, Blackbirch LB $27.44 (1-56711-219-6). The story of Washington's witch hunting under Joseph McCarthy includes good background information on the Cold War. (Rev: BL 12/15/98; HBG 3/99; SLJ 1/99) [973.921]

MARSHALL, THURGOOD

6131 Herda, D. J. *Thurgood Marshall: Civil Rights Champion* (6–10). Illus. Series: Justices of the Supreme Court. 1995, Enslow LB $20.95 (0-89490-557-0). The story of the first African American Supreme Court justice and his lifelong fight to champion the rights of the oppressed. (Rev: BL 3/15/96) [921]

6132 Prentzas, G. S. *Thurgood Marshall: Champion of Justice* (4–8). Illus. Series: Junior World Biography. 1993, Chelsea LB $15.95 (0-7910-1769-9); paper $4.95 (0-7910-1969-1). An interesting biography of Thurgood Marshall that touches on his civil rights work but focuses on his years as a Supreme Court justice. (Rev: SLJ 11/93) [921]

6133 Rowh, Mark. *Thurgood Marshall: Civil Rights Attorney and Supreme Court Justice* (6–8). Series: African-American Biographies. 2002, Enslow LB $20.95 (0-7660-1547-5). Marshall's youth, education, early career, family life, and experiences as a Supreme Court judge are all covered in this readable biography. (Rev: HBG 10/02; SLJ 10/02) [347.73]

MURROW, EDWARD R.

6134 Finkelstein, Norman H. *With Heroic Truth: The Life of Edward R. Murrow* (6–9). 1997, Houghton $17.95 (0-395-67891-9). A well-written biography of this pioneer in broadcasting, enhanced by interviews with his wife and son, that describes personal acts of courage, his unique, straightforward broadcasts from London during World War II, and his principled expose of Sen. Joe McCarthy. (Rev: BL 6/1–15/97; BR 9–10/97; SLJ 7/97) [921]

NADER, RALPH

6135 Bowen, Nancy. *Ralph Nader: Man with a Mission* (6–10). Illus. 2002, Millbrook LB $24.90 (0-7613-2365-1). An absorbing biography of the consumer advocate, environmentalist, and politician, with photographs. (Rev: BL 4/1/02; HBG 10/02; SLJ 4/02) [343.7307]

6136 Celsi, Teresa. *Ralph Nader: The Consumer Revolution* (6–12). Series: New Directions. 1991, Millbrook LB $21.90 (1-56294-044-9). The story of the consumer advocate who has taken on some of the largest corporations in America and won. (Rev: BL 10/1/91; SLJ 10/91) [921]

6137 Graham, Kevin. *Ralph Nader: Battling for Democracy* (6–12). 2000, Windom paper $9.95 (0-9700323-0-7). A readable biography of the man who has devoted his life to fighting for liberty and justice for all. (Rev: BL 12/1/00; SLJ 11/00) [371.34]

NAVA, JULIAN

6138 Nava, Julian. *Julian Nava: My Mexican-American Journey* (7–12). 2002, Arte Publico $16.95 (1-55885-364-2); paper $9.95 (1-55885-351-0). Nava tells the story of his life and his journey from the barrio to become the first Mexican American ambassador to Mexico. (Rev: BL 10/15/02) [370]

O'CONNOR, SANDRA DAY

6139 Herda, D. J. *Sandra Day O'Connor: Independent Thinker* (6–10). Illus. Series: Justices of the Supreme Court. 1995, Enslow LB $17.95 (0-89480-558-9). The story of the first female Supreme Court justice, including her personal life and her most import decisions since becoming a Supreme Court member in 1981. (Rev: BL 2/15/96) [921]

6140 Macht, Norman L. *Sandra Day O'Connor: Supreme Court Justice* (4–7). Illus. Series: Junior World Biography. 1992, Chelsea paper $8.95 (0-7910-0448-1). In clear text with many photographs, this is a simple account of the first female Supreme Court Justice. (Rev: BL 8/92; SLJ 8/92) [921]

OSCEOLA

6141 Bland, Celia. *Osceola, Seminole Rebel* (5–8). Illus. Series: North American Indians of Achievement. 1994, Chelsea LB $21.95 (0-7910-1716-8). The story of the Seminole leader who resisted the removal of his people from Florida in the 1830s and died under mysterious circumstances in 1838. (Rev: BL 6/1–15/94; VOYA 4/94) [921]

PAINE, THOMAS

6142 Kaye, Harvey J. *Thomas Paine: Firebrand of the Revolution* (6–10). Illus. 2000, Oxford LB $22.00 (0-19-511627-5). A readable, well-illustrated biography on the career, accomplishments, and lasting importance of this Revolutionary War personality with material on the social and political conditions of the period. (Rev: BL 3/1/00; HBG 9/00; SLJ 4/00) [921]

6143 McCarthy, Pat. *Thomas Paine: Revolutionary Poet and Writer* (5–8). Series: Historical American Biographies. 2001, Enslow LB $20.95 (0-7660-1446-0). A balanced, well-researched biography of the American political theorist and writer who created controversy throughout his lifetime. (Rev: BL 4/15/01; HBG 10/01) [921]

6144 McCartin, Brian. *Thomas Paine: Common Sense and Revolutionary Pamphleteering* (4–7). Series: Library of American Lives and Times. 2001, Rosen $23.95 (0-8239-5729-2). The story of the British-born colonialist who heard the cries for liberty around him and whose writings set the stage for the Declaration of Independence. (Rev: BL 10/15/01) [921]

6145 Vail, John. *Thomas Paine* (6–10). Illus. 1990, Chelsea LB $19.95 (1-55546-819-5). The story of the outspoken radical whose writings influenced the development of the American Revolution. (Rev: BL 8/90; SLJ 6/90; VOYA 8/90) [921]

PATTON, GEORGE

6146 Peifer, Charles. *Soldier of Destiny: A Biography of George Patton* (5–8). Illus. 1988, Macmillan LB $13.95 (0-87518-395-6). The life and times of the colorful general who commanded the Third Army in Europe during World War II. (Rev: BL 3/1/89; SLJ 4/89; VOYA 8/89) [921]

PERKINS, FRANCES

6147 Pasachoff, Naomi. *Frances Perkins: Champion of the New Deal* (6–12). Series: Oxford Portraits. 1999, Oxford LB $22.00 (0-19-512222-4). A biography of the first woman to become a cabinet member in the United States, including both her achievements and her flaws. (Rev: BR 11–12/99; HBG 4/00; SLJ 1/00) [973.917]

POWELL, COLIN

6148 Blue, Rose, and Corinne J. Naden. *Colin Powell: Straight to the Top*. Rev. ed. (4–8). Series: Gateway Biography. 1997, Millbrook LB $23.90 (0-7613-0256-5); paper $9.95 (0-7613-0242-5). A balanced biography of Colin Powell that focuses on his adult life and his stint as chairman of the Joint Chiefs of Staff. (Rev: BL 9/15/97; SLJ 1/98) [921]

6149 Brown, Warren. *Colin Powell* (7–10). Series: Black Americans of Achievement. 1992, Chelsea LB $21.95 (0-7910-1647-1). A nicely illustrated account of the African American general who distinguished himself during the Persian Gulf War. (Rev: BL 8/92) [921]

6150 Finlayson, Reggie. *Colin Powell* (5–8). Series: A&E Biography. 2003, Lerner LB $25.26 (0-8225-4966-2); paper $7.95 (0-8225-9698-9). This story of the rise of this leader from the military into the political and diplomatic world. (Rev: BL 1/1–15/04) [921]

6151 Finlayson, Reggie. *Colin Powell: People's Hero* (5–8). Series: Achievers Biographies. 1997, Lerner LB $25.55 (0-8225-2891-6). From his birth in Harlem to his distinguished military career, this is a fine biography of Colin Powell. (Rev: SLJ 4/97; VOYA 6/97) [921]

6152 Hughes, Libby. *Colin Powell: A Man of Quality* (7–9). Series: People in Focus. 1996, Silver Burdett LB $13.95 (0-382-39260-4); paper $7.95 (0-382-39261-2). Documentary materials and Powell's own words are used extensively in this account that gives good coverage of his youth and education as well as his military career. (Rev: SLJ 8/96) [921]

6153 Schraff, Anne. *Colin Powell: Soldier and Patriot* (7–12). Illus. Series: African-American Biographies. 1997, Enslow LB $20.95 (0-89490-810-3). The biography of the career soldier who lead our forces in war and peace, and became an inspiration to all America. (Rev: BL 5/15/97; SLJ 3/97; VOYA 6/97) [921]

6154 Senna, Carl. *Colin Powell: A Man of War and Peace* (4–8). Illus. 1992, Walker LB $16.85 (0-8027-8181-0). The life of the general who became the first African American chairman of the Joint Chiefs of Staff. (Rev: BL 3/15/93) [921]

6155 Wukovits, John F. *Colin Powell* (5–8). Series: People in the News. 2000, Lucent LB $27.45 (1-56006-632-6). This account of the African American military leader ends before he became part in the Bush administration, but it gives good coverage of his formative years and his early accomplishments. (Rev: BL 6/1–15/00; HBG 10/00) [921]

RICE, CONDOLEEZA

6156 Ditchfield, Christin. *Condoleeza Rice* (5–8). Illus. Series: Great Life Stories. 2003, Watts LB $29.50 (0-531-12307-3). This attractive biography details Rice's life from her childhood in Alabama to becoming the first woman to hold the post of national security adviser. (Rev: BL 12/15/03) [355]

6157 Wade, Mary Dodson. *Condoleezza Rice: Being the Best* (4–7). Illus. 2003, Millbrook LB $23.90 (0-7613-2619-7). An interesting profile with a focus on Rice's talented youth and southern upbringing. (Rev: BL 3/1/03; HBG 10/03; SLJ 4/03) [355]

RICHARDS, ANN

6158 Siegel, Dorothy S. *Ann Richards: Politician, Feminist, Survivor* (4–7). Illus. Series: People to Know. 1996, Enslow LB $20.95 (0-89490-497-3). In a conversational style, this biography covers the important events in the life of this Texas politician. (Rev: BL 5/15/96; SLJ 10/96) [921]

SCHWARZKOPF, NORMAN

6159 Hughes, Libby. *Norman Schwarzkopf: Hero with a Heart* (6–10). Series: People in Focus. 1992, Dillon LB $13.95 (0-87518-521-5). The story of the leader of the Persian Gulf War's Operation Desert Storm in 1991 and how he emerged a popular hero. (Rev: BL 1/15/93; SLJ 2/93) [921]

SEWARD, WILLIAM

6160 Kent, Zachary. *William Seward: The Master mind of the Alaska Purchase* (6–10). Series: Historical American Biographies. 2001, Enslow LB $20.95 (0-7660-1391-X). The story of the man who was appointed secretary of state by Lincoln and who engineered the purchase of Alaska is the focus of this biography full of period illustrations, maps, and cartoons. (Rev: BL 3/1/01; HBG 10/01; SLJ 5/01) [973.7]

SHERMAN, WILLIAM T.

6161 King, David C. *William T. Sherman* (5–8). Series: Triangle Histories of the Civil War. 2002, Gale LB $27.44 (1-56711-563-2). Sherman's march to the sea and relationship with Joseph Johnston, the confederate general, are among the topics covered in this solid introduction. (Rev: SLJ 1/03) [921]

6162 Whitelaw, Nancy. *William Tecumseh Sherman: Defender and Destroyer* (5–8). 1996, Morgan Reynolds LB $21.95 (1-883846-12-9). Both the personal and public life of this Civil War general, who brought destruction to the South, are detailed, using many quotations and photographs. (Rev: BL 3/15/96; BR 11–12/96; SLJ 6/96; VOYA 10/96) [921]

SITTING BULL

6163 Black, Sheila. *Sitting Bull and the Battle of the Little Bighorn* (4–7). Illus. Series: Biography Series of American Indians. 1989, Silver Burdett LB $12.95 (0-382-09572-3); paper $7.95 (0-382-09761-0). A biography of the Sioux leader who defeated Custer at the Little Bighorn. (Rev: BL 1/1/90; SLJ 4/90) [921]

6164 Marrin, Albert. *Sitting Bull and His World* (6–12). Illus. 2000, Dutton $27.50 (0-525-45944-8). A well-illustrated, carefully-researched biography of this misunderstood Sioux leader that is also the tragic history of the Plains Indians. (Rev: BL 5/1/00; HB 7–8/00; HBG 9/00; SLJ 7/00) [921]

6165 Schleichert, Elizabeth. *Sitting Bull: Sioux Leader* (6–9). Series: Native American Biographies. 1997, Enslow LB $20.95 (0-89490-868-5). A well-documented account of this important Sioux leader, including his reasons for participating in Buffalo Bill's Wild West Show. (Rev: BL 4/15/97; SLJ 6/97) [921]

STUART, JEB

6166 Pflueger, Lynda. *Jeb Stuart: Confederate Cavalry General* (5–8). Series: Historical American Biographies. 1998, Enslow LB $20.95 (0-7660-1013-9). The life of the brilliant general who had successes at the battles of Bull Run, Antietam, and Fredericksburg, but who committed a tactical error at Gettysburg. (Rev: BL 8/98; SLJ 8/98) [921]

TECUMSEH

6167 Stefoff, Rebecca. *Tecumseh and the Shawnee Confederacy* (6–10). Illus. Series: Library of American Indian History. 1998, Facts on File $25.00 (0-

8160-3648-9). Through an examination of the life of Tecumseh, the charismatic leader of the Shawnee Confederation, this volume presents the Shawnee culture and an illuminating history of the Indian wars in the Ohio River Valley. (Rev: SLJ 7/98) [921]

THOMAS, CLARENCE

6168 Macht, Norman L. *Clarence Thomas* (6–9). 1995, Chelsea LB $21.95 (0-7910-1883-0); paper $9.95 (0-7910-1912-8). Details Thomas's life, culminating in his controversial appointment to the Supreme Court, with frank coverage of the congressional hearings. (Rev: BL 8/95; SLJ 9/95) [347.73]

VALLEJO, MARIANO GUADALUPE

6169 Tracy, Kathleen. *Mariano Guadalupe Vallejo* (5–7). Series: Latinos in American History. 2002, Mitchell Lane LB $19.95 (1-58415-152-8). The story of the 19th-century military man who supported the U.S. annexation of California and later served in the state's first Senate. (Rev: BL 2/15/03; HBG 10/03) [921]

WARD, NANCY

6170 Furbee, Mary R. *Wild Rose: Nancy Ward and the Cherokee Nation* (6–9). Illus. Series: Women of the Frontier. 2001, Morgan Reynolds LB $20.95 (1-883846-71-4). This is the absorbing story of the Cherokee woman who became a much-respected leader and advocate for peaceful coexistence with the white settlers. (Rev: HBG 3/02; SLJ 9/01; VOYA 6/02) [975]

WARREN, EARL

6171 Compston, Christine L. *Earl Warren: Justice for All* (7–10). Illus. Series: Oxford Portraits. 2002, Oxford $24.00 (0-19-513001-4). In addition to Warren's family life and career, this portrait presents his belief in the rule of law and his dealings with successive presidents. (Rev: BL 4/15/02; HBG 10/02; SLJ 6/02) [347.73]

6172 Herda, D. J. *Earl Warren: Chief Justice for Social Change* (6–10). Illus. Series: Justices of the Supreme Court. 1995, Enslow LB $20.95 (0-89490-556-2). The story of the chief justice who led the Supreme Court during a period of great change, and who headed the commission that investigated President Kennedy's death. (Rev: BL 3/15/96; SLJ 3/96) [921]

WATTS, J. C.

6173 Lutz, Norma Jean. *J. C. Watts* (4–7). Series: Black Americans of Achievement. 2000, Chelsea $21.95 (0-7910-5338-5). The story of a former

Oklahoma University football player who entered politics and was first elected to the House of Representatives in 1994. (Rev: BL 6/1–15/00; HBG 10/00) [921]

WEBSTER, DANIEL

6174 Harvey, Bonnie Carman. *Daniel Webster* (5–8). Series: Historical American Biographies. 2001, Enslow LB $20.95 (0-7660-1392-8). An engrossing biography of the American statesman, lawyer, and orator who fought to save the Union. (Rev: BL 1/1–15/02; HBG 3/02; SLJ 12/01) [921]

WOODHULL, VICTORIA

6175 McLean, Jacqueline. *Victoria Woodhull: First Woman Presidential Candidate* (7–12). 1999, Morgan Reynolds LB $21.95 (1-883846-47-1). The fascinating story of Victoria Woodhull, an ardent suffragist and feminist who was nominated by the Equal Rights Party in 1872 as its presidential candidate. (Rev: BL 8/99; HBG 4/00; SLJ 10/99; VOYA 12/99) [921]

Miscellaneous Persons

ADDAMS, JANE

6176 Harvey, Bonnie Carman. *Jane Addams: Nobel Prize Winner and Founder of Hull House* (5–8). Illus. Series: Historic American Biographies. 1999, Enslow LB $20.95 (0-7660-1094-5). This biography of the Nobel Peace Prize winner and founder of Hull House traces her life and her outstanding achievements as a social worker. (Rev: BL 11/1/99; HBG 3/00; SLJ 11/99) [921]

6177 Hovde, Jane. *Jane Addams* (8–12). Illus. 1989, Facts on File $19.95 (0-8160-1547-3). The life and work of this early feminist and social worker. (Rev: BL 9/15/89; BR 11–12/89; VOYA 12/89) [921]

6178 Kittredge, Mary. *Jane Addams* (6–10). Illus. 1988, Chelsea LB $19.95 (1-55546-636-2). Jane Addams helped immigrants by founding the first settlement house, Hull House, in Chicago. (Rev: BL 6/15/88; BR 11–12/88; SLJ 1/89) [921]

6179 McPherson, Stephanie S. *Peace and Bread: The Story of Jane Addams* (5–8). 1993, Carolrhoda LB $30.35 (0-87614-792-9). An introduction to Jane Addams's work among the poor of Chicago and her leadership in international organizations on behalf of world peace. (Rev: BL 1/15/94; SLJ 2/94) [921]

6180 Wheeler, Leslie. *Jane Addams* (5–8). Illus. Series: Pioneers in Change. 1990, Silver Burdett LB $17.95 (0-382-09962-1); paper $6.95 (0-382-09968-0). The story of the outspoken social activist who

lived in turn-of-the-century Chicago. (Rev: BL 1/15/91; SLJ 4/91) [921]

ALEXANDER, SALLY HOBART

6181 Alexander, Sally H. *Taking Hold: My Journey into Blindness* (6–12). 1994, Macmillan paper $14.95 (0-02-700402-3). A true story of a 3rd-grade teacher who lost her sight but found independence. (Rev: BL 1/15/95; SLJ 4/95; VOYA 4/95) [921]

ALLEN, ETHAN

6182 Raabe, Emily. *Ethan Allen: The Green Mountain Boys and Vermont's Path to Statehood* (4–7). Series: Library of American Lives and Times. 2001, Rosen LB $23.95 (0-8239-5722-5). Extraordinary illustrations and fine text tell the story of the controversial founder of Vermont who led the Green Mountain Boys in the capture of Fort Ticonderoga and Crown Point. (Rev: BL 10/15/01) [921]

ALLEN, RICHARD

6183 Klots, Steve. *Richard Allen* (5–8). Illus. Series: Black Americans of Achievement. 1990, Chelsea LB $19.95 (1-55546-570-6). Born a slave in 1780, this convert to Christianity founded the first African American Methodist Church. (Rev: SLJ 2/91) [921]

BAILEY, ANNE

6184 Furbee, Mary R. *Anne Bailey: Frontier Scout* (6–12). Illus. 2001, Morgan Reynolds $20.95 (1-883846-70-6). This is the absorbing story of a courageous woman who became a scout in the Revolutionary War. (Rev: BL 12/1/01; HBG 3/02; SLJ 3/02) [975.4]

BALL, CHARLES

6185 Shuter, Jane, ed. *Charles Ball and American Slavery* (5–8). Illus. Series: History Eyewitness. 1995, Raintree Steck-Vaughn LB $24.26 (0-8114-8281-2). This autobiographical account in simple language brings the horrors of slavery to life, with period prints and maps. (Rev: BL 4/15/95; SLJ 5/95) [975]

BILLY THE KID

6186 Bruns, Roger A. *Billy the Kid* (5–8). Series: Historical American Biographies. 2000, Enslow LB $20.95 (0-7660-1091-0). A well-researched and thoroughly documented biography of America's famous outlaw. (Rev: BL 1/1–15/00; HBG 10/00; SLJ 5/00) [921]

6187 Green, Carl R., and William R. Sanford. *Billy the Kid* (4–8). Illus. Series: Outlaws and Lawmen of the Wild West. 1992, Enslow LB $16.95 (0-89490-

364-0). The life story of the outlaw William H. Bonney, who lived from 1859 to 1881. (Rev: BL 7/92; SLJ 8/92) [921]

BLY, NELLIE

6188 Fredeen, Charles. *Nellie Bly: Daredevil Reporter* (5–9). Series: Lerner Biographies. 2000, Lerner LB $25.26 (0-8225-4956-5). The story of the daring reporter who traveled around the world in 72 days and was a champion of the women's suffrage movement. (Rev: HBG 10/00; SLJ 3/00) [921]

6189 Peck, Ira, and Nellie Bly. *Nellie Bly's Book: Around the World in 72 Days* (6–8). 1998, Twenty-First Century LB $27.90 (0-7613-0971-3). An abridged version of the account written by the famous muckraking journalist about her trip around the world in which she beat Phileas Fogg's record by six days. (Rev: BL 2/15/99; HBG 10/99; SLJ 4/99) [921]

BONNEY, WILLIAM

6190 Cline, Don. *Alias Billy the Kid, the Man Behind the Legend* (8–12). Illus. 1986, Sunstone paper $12.95 (0-86534-080-3). The real story of Billy the Kid, clearing up many misconceptions. (Rev: BR 11–12/86) [921]

BOOTH, JOHN WILKES

6191 Otfinoski, Steven. *John Wilkes Booth and the Civil War* (5–9). Series: Notorious Americans and Their Times. 1998, Blackbirch LB $27.44 (1-56711-222-6). The colorful life and death of John Wilkes Booth, born into a theatrical family, who turned political over the slavery issue and plotted to kill President Lincoln. (Rev: BL 12/15/98; HBG 3/99; SLJ 12/98) [921]

BOWDITCH, NATHANIEL

6192 Latham, Jean Lee. *Carry On, Mr. Bowditch* (6–9). 1955, Houghton $16.00 (0-395-06881-9); paper $6.95 (0-395-13713-6). This fictionalized biography of the great American navigator is enlivened by fascinating material on sailing ships and the romance of old Salem. Newbery Medal winner, 1956. [921]

BOWIE, JIM

6193 Edmondson, J. R. *Jim Bowie: Frontier Legend, Alamo Hero* (4–7). Series: Library of American Lives and Times. 2003, Rosen LB $31.95 (0-8239-5734-9). As well as being a rogue, slave trader, and murderer, Jim Bowie was also a hero of the famous battle of the Alamo. (Rev: BL 6/1–15/03; SLJ 7/03) [921]

6194 Gaines, Ann Graham. *Jim Bowie* (5–8). Series: Historical American Biographies. 2000, Enslow LB $20.95 (0-7660-1253-0). A well-documented biography of Jim Bowie, a hero of the revolution in Texas who was best known for fighting in the battle of the Alamo. (Rev: BL 1/1–15/00; HBG 10/00; SLJ 5/00) [921]

BROADWICK, GEORGIA "TINY"

6195 Roberson, Elizabeth Whitley. *Tiny Broadwick: The First Lady of Parachuting* (4–8). Illus. 2001, Pelican paper $9.95 (1-56554-780-2). Less than 5 feet tall, "Tiny" Broadwick joined a hot-air balloon act as a teenager and became the first woman to jump with a parachute. (Rev: BL 7/01) [797.5]

BROWN, CLARA

6196 Lowery, Linda. *One More Valley, One More Hill: The Story of Aunt Clara Brown* (5–8). Illus. 2002, Random LB $17.99 (0-375-91092-1). A biography of the freed slave and pioneer who found success in Colorado. (Rev: BL 2/15/03; HBG 3/03; SLJ 2/03*) [978.8]

CALAMITY JANE

6197 Faber, Doris. *Calamity Jane: Her Life and Her Legend* (5–9). 1992, Houghton $16.00 (0-395-56396-8). The author carefully distinguishes what is certain, what is possible, and what is blatantly untrue in the legend of Calamity Jane and her later show business career. (Rev: BL 8/92; SLJ 10/92) [921]

CAPONE, AL

6198 King, David C. *Al Capone and the Roaring Twenties* (5–9). Illus. Series: Notorious Americans and Their Times. 1998, Blackbirch LB $27.44 (1-56711-218-8). In this biography of the gangster, the reader also gets information on the Jazz Age, the Ku Klux Klan, and other personalities of the time, such as Earhart and Lindbergh. (Rev: BL 12/15/98; HBG 3/99; SLJ 12/98) [921]

6199 Yancey, Diane. *Al Capone* (6–9). Series: Heroes and Villains. 2003, Gale LB $21.96 (1-56006-949-X). Capone's rise to power and descent to illness in prison are described with references to primary sources and black-and-white photographs. (Rev: SLJ 3/03) [364.1]

CASSIDY, BUTCH

6200 Green, Carl R., and William R. Sanford. *Butch Cassidy* (4–8). Series: Outlaws and Lawmen of the Wild West. 1995, Enslow LB $16.95 (0-89490-587-2). The Wild West is re-created in this brief account of the life of this colorful outlaw, whose death remains a mystery. (Rev: BL 6/1–15/95; SLJ 7/95) [921]

6201 Wukovits, John F. *Butch Cassidy* (4–7). Series: Legends of the West. 1997, Chelsea $18.65 (0-7910-3857-2). This biography of Robert Leroy Parker, who is better known as Butch Cassidy, emphasizes the fact that he was a ruthless criminal and not the idealized character of the movies. (Rev: HBG 3/98; SLJ 4/98) [921]

CHAPMAN, JOHN

6202 Warrick, Karen Clemens. *John Chapman: The Legendary Johnny Appleseed* (5–8). Series: Historical American Biographies. 2001, Enslow LB $20.95 (0-7660-1443-6). An engrossing, nicely illustrated portrait of the man who wandered the Midwest promoting apple cultivation. (Rev: BL 4/15/01; HBG 10/01; SLJ 4/01) [921]

CODY, BUFFALO BILL

6203 Spies, Karen B. *Buffalo Bill Cody: Western Legend* (5–8). Series: Historical American Biographies. 1998, Enslow LB $20.95 (0-7660-1015-5). An in-depth look at this legendary frontiersman and the Wild West show he founded. (Rev: BL 3/15/98; SLJ 5/98) [921]

EDMONDS, EMMA

6204 Reit, Seymour. *Behind Rebel Lines: The Incredible Story of Emma Edmonds, Civil War Spy* (5–8). 1988, Harcourt $12.95 (0-15-200416-5); paper $6.00 (0-15-200424-6). The remarkable Canadian-born spy who helped to defend the Union in the Civil War. (Rev: BL 3/1/88; SLJ 3/88) [973.785]

EDWARDS, JONATHAN

6205 Lutz, Norma Jean. *Jonathan Edwards: Colonial Religious Leader* (5–7). Series: Colonial Leaders. 2001, Chelsea $20.85 (0-7910-5961-8); paper $8.95 (0-7910-6118-3). The life of Edwards, a leader in the Great Awakening spiritual movement and preacher among Native American tribes, is presented here with discussion of his contributions and his failings. (Rev: SLJ 5/01) [921]

ESCALANTE, JAIME

6206 Byers, Ann. *Jaime Escalante: Sensational Teacher* (6–10). Illus. Series: Hispanic Biographies. 1996, Enslow LB $20.95 (0-89490-763-8). A profile of the unique, inspiring teacher whose career became the basis of the film *Stand and Deliver*. (Rev: BL 10/1/96; SLJ 9/96; VOYA 12/96) [910]

FORTUNE, AMOS

6207 Yates, Elizabeth. *Amos Fortune, Free Man* (6–9). 1950, Dutton $15.99 (0-525-25570-2); Puffin paper $5.99 (0-14-034158-7). The simplicity and dignity of the human spirit and its triumph over degradation are movingly portrayed in this portrait of a slave who bought his freedom. Newbery Medal winner, 1951. [974.4]

FRAUNCES, PHOEBE

6208 Griffin, Judith Berry. *Phoebe the Spy* (7–9). 1989, Scholastic paper $3.99 (0-590-42432-7). The story of the 13-year-old black girl who saved George Washington's life from an assassination attempt. [921]

GRAHAM, BILLY

6209 Wooten, Sara McIntosh. *Billy Graham: World-Famous Evangelist* (6–10). Illus. Series: People to Know. 2001, Enslow LB $20.95 (0-7660-1533-5). A well-rounded and interesting biography of Graham's life and career, with coverage of his boisterous youth and of his education. (Rev: BL 10/1/01; HBG 3/02) [269.2]

HEARST, WILLIAM RANDOLPH

6210 Whitelaw, Nancy. *William Randolph Hearst and the American Century* (6–12). Illus. 1999, Morgan Reynolds $19.95 (1-883846-46-3). Hearst's eccentricities and lively, thrusting approach to life are well portrayed in this vivid biography. (Rev: BL 10/1/99; HBG 4/00; VOYA 6/00) [070.5]

HICKOK, WILD BILL

6211 Green, Carl R., and William R. Sanford. *Wild Bill Hickok* (4–8). Illus. Series: Outlaws and Lawmen of the Wild West. 1992, Enslow LB $16.95 (0-89490-366-7). The life story of the famous frontier marshal in Kansas is retold in text and pictures. (Rev: BL 7/92; SLJ 8/92) [921]

HOOKER, FORRESTINE C.

6212 Hooker, Forrestine C. *Child of the Fighting Tenth: On the Frontier with the Buffalo Soldiers* (6–9). Ed. by Steve Wilson. 2003, Oxford $25.00 (0-19-516158-0). This fascinating memoir of growing up as the daughter of an officer with the Tenth U.S. Cavalry, a regiment of black troops led by white commanders, reveals much about life on the frontier and racial attitudes. (Rev: BL 12/15/03) [973.8]

371

HUTCHINSON, ANNE

6213 Ilgenfritz, Elizabeth. *Anne Hutchinson* (5–8). Illus. Series: American Women of Achievement. 1990, Chelsea LB $19.95 (1-55546-660-5). The story of the woman in pre-Revolutionary days who stood trial to defend religious liberty. (Rev: SLJ 4/91) [921]

INGLES, MARY DRAPER

6214 Furbee, Mary R. *Shawnee Captive: The Story of Mary Draper Ingles* (5–8). Illus. 2001, Morgan Reynolds LB $21.95 (1-883846-69-2). The tragic and exciting story of a pioneer woman captured by Shawnee Indians, her daring escape, and her long and difficult journey home. (Rev: BL 5/15/01; HBG 10/01; SLJ 6/01) [975.5]

ISHI

6215 Kroeber, Theodora. *Ishi, Last of the Tribe* (5–7). 1973, Bantam paper $5.99 (0-553-24898-7). A California Yahi, the last of his tribe, leaves his primitive life and enters the modern world. [979.4]

JAMES, JESSE

6216 Bruns, Roger. *Jesse James: Legendary Outlaw* (5–8). Series: Historical American Biographies. 1998, Enslow LB $20.95 (0-7660-1055-4). Using fact boxes, maps, a chronology, and chapter notes as well as an interesting text and black-and-white photographs, this book gives a fine biography of Jesse James and his exploits. (Rev: BL 10/15/98; SLJ 8/98) [921]

6217 Green, Carl R., and William R. Sanford. *Jesse James* (4–8). Illus. Series: Outlaws and Lawmen of the Wild West. 1992, Enslow LB $16.95 (0-89490-365-9). This easy-to-read text portrays the legendary gunman as both outlaw and hero. (Rev: BL 3/1/92; SLJ 5/92) [921]

6218 Wukovits, John F. *Jesse James* (5–8). Illus. Series: Legends of the West. 1996, Chelsea $18.65 (0-7910-3876-9). An action-packed biography that tries to probe the complex nature of the famous Western outlaw. (Rev: BR 5–6/97; SLJ 4/97) [921]

JOHNSON, ISAAC

6219 Marston, Hope I. *Isaac Johnson: From Slave to Stonecutter* (5–8). 1995, Dutton $14.99 (0-525-65165-9). Based on Johnson's 1901 autobiography, *Slavery Days in Old Kentucky,* Marston brings the story of Isaac Johnson to life. (Rev: BL 9/15/95; SLJ 9/95) [921]

KELLER, HELEN

6220 Dash, Joan. *The World at Her Fingertips: The Story of Helen Keller* (4–7). Illus. 2001, Scholastic paper $15.95 (0-590-90715-8). A straightforward account of the girl who was left blind and deaf at 19 months and of her determination to be independent. (Rev: BCCB 3/01; BL 2/15/01; HB 3–4/01; HBG 10/01; SLJ 4/01*; VOYA 6/01) [921]

6221 Ford, Carin T. *Helen Keller: Lighting the Way for the Blind and Deaf* (6–9). Series: People to Know. 2001, Enslow LB $20.95 (0-7660-1530-0). Ford traces Keller's life from birth through her college education, activism, and fund-raising work in a narrative that is both interesting and detailed enough for report writers. (Rev: HBG 10/01; SLJ 5/01) [362.4]

6222 Lawlor, Laurie. *Helen Keller: Rebellious Spirit* (4–8). Illus. 2001, Holiday $22.95 (0-8234-1588-0). This account puts Keller's life in the context of her time and looks at the opinions and beliefs that made her a "rebellious spirit," with photographs, quotations, a bibliography, and the manual alphabet. (Rev: BL 9/1/01; HB 9–10/01; HBG 3/02; SLJ 9/01*; VOYA 2/02) [362.4]

6223 Nicholson, Lois. *Helen Keller: Humanitarian* (7–10). Series: Great Achievers: Lives of the Physically Challenged. 1995, Chelsea LB $21.95 (0-7910-2086-X). The strong personality traits of Helen Keller that allowed her to rise above her physical handicaps are stressed in this biography of a remarkable woman. (Rev: BR 3–4/96; SLJ 1/96) [921]

6224 Wepman, Dennis. *Helen Keller* (6–10). Illus. 1987, Chelsea LB $19.95 (1-55546-662-1). The inspiring story of this handicapped woman and her struggle to help people like herself. (Rev: BL 8/87; SLJ 9/87) [921]

KING, HORACE

6225 Gibbons, Faye. *Horace King: Bridges to Freedom* (5–8). Illus. 2002, Crane Hill paper $9.95 (1-57587-199-8). The story of a slave who went on to become a builder and later a public servant in the post-Civil War South. (Rev: BL 2/15/03) [328.761]

KLECKLEY, ELIZABETH

6226 Rutberg, Becky. *Mary Lincoln's Dressmaker: Elizabeth Kleckley's Remarkable Rise from Slave to White House Confidante* (6–10). 1995, Walker $15.95 (0-8027-8224-8). The story of a slave, a fine seamstress, who was freed and became Mary Todd Lincoln's dressmaker. (Rev: BL 10/15/95; SLJ 12/95; VOYA 12/95) [921]

KOVIC, RON

6227 Moss, Nathaniel. *Ron Kovic: Antiwar Activist* (7–12). Series: Great Achievers: Lives of the Physically Challenged. 1994, Chelsea LB $19.95 (0-7910-2076-2). A biography of the disabled Vietnam veteran, antiwar activist, and author. (Rev: BL 1/15/94) [921]

LANDERS, ANN AND ABIGAIL VAN BUREN

6228 Aronson, Virginia. *Ann Landers and Abigail Van Buren* (6–9). Series: Women of Achievement. 2003, Chelsea $22.95 (0-7910-5297-4). A look at the lives from childhood of the twin sisters who have offered advice to millions, with excerpts from their columns and many photographs. (Rev: HBG 9/00; SLJ 7/00) [070]

MANKILLER, WILMA P.

6229 Glassman, Bruce. *Wilma Mankiller: Chief of the Cherokee Nation* (5–7). Illus. Series: Library of Famous Women. 1992, Blackbirch $17.95 (1-56711-032-0). This is an inspiring biography of the amazing woman who led her Cherokee Indians through difficult crises. (Rev: BL 6/1/92; SLJ 4/92) [921]

6230 Lazo, Caroline. *Wilma Mankiller* (4–7). Illus. Series: Peacemakers. 1995, Silver Burdett paper $7.95 (0-382-24716-7). The dramatic story of the woman who contributed to peace within the Native American community. (Rev: BL 7/95; SLJ 7/95) [921]

MANSON, CHARLES

6231 Steffens, Bradley, and Craig L. Staples. *The Trial of Charles Manson: California Cult Murders* (6–9). Series: Famous Trials. 2002, Gale LB $27.45 (1-56006-733-0). The story of the California cult leader and the murders that shocked the world. (Rev: BL 3/15/03; SLJ 9/02) [921]

MARION, FRANCIS

6232 Towles, Louis P. *Francis Marion: The Swamp Fox of the American Revolution* (4–7). Series: Library of American Lives and Times. 2001, Rosen LB $23.95 (0-8239-5728-4). The life of the Revolutionary War hero known as the Swamp Fox because of his stealthy retreats into the swamp lands. (Rev: BL 1/1–15/02) [921]

NATION, CARRY A.

6233 Harvey, Bonnie Carman. *Carry A. Nation: Saloon Smasher and Prohibitionist* (5–8). Series:

Historical American Biographies. 2002, Enslow LB $20.95 (0-7660-1907-1). A lively and balanced biography of the prohibitionist who fought alcohol with violence. (Rev: HBG 3/03; SLJ 1/03) [921]

NEWTON, JOHN

6234 Granfield, Linda. *Amazing Grace: The Story of the Hymn* (4–8). Illus. 1997, Tundra $15.95 (0-88776-389-8). The life story of John Newton, a sea captain in the slave trade who later rejected slavery, became a minister, and wrote several hymns, including "Amazing Grace." (Rev: SLJ 8/97) [921]

OATMAN, OLIVE

6235 Rau, Margaret. *The Ordeal of Olive Oatman: A True Story of the American West* (6–8). Illus. 1997, Morgan Reynolds LB $21.95 (1-883846-21-8). The biography of Olive Oatman, who was captured by Apaches while her family was crossing the Arizona desert and lived with them for six years. (Rev: BL 9/1/97; BR 11–12/98; HBG 3/98; SLJ 2/98; VOYA 12/97) [921]

OSBORN, SHANE

6236 Osborn, Shane, and Malcolm McConnell. *Born to Fly: The Heroic Story of Downed U.S. Navy Pilot Lt. Shane Osborn* (5–8). Adapted by Michael French. 2001, Delacorte LB $17.99 (0-385-90045-7). This adaptation of an adult book tells the story of Osborn's training as a pilot and the collision in 2001 that led to tensions between the United States and China, with lots of interesting career information. (Rev: HBG 3/02; SLJ 1/02) [921]

PAYNE, LUCILLE M. W.

6237 Rice, Dorothy M., and Lucille Payne. *The Seventeenth Child* (7–12). 1998, Linnet LB $18.50 (0-208-02414-X). A biography of an African American woman growing up in rural Virginia during the 1930s and 40s, as recorded and edited by her daughter. (Rev: HBG 3/99; SLJ 1/99; VOYA 6/99) [921]

PHILIP (SACHEM OF THE WAMPANOAGS)

6238 Averill, Esther. *King Philip: The Indian Chief* (5–8). 1993, Shoe String LB $20.00 (0-208-02357-7). The story of the Wampanoag chief who befriended the Pilgrims and later waged war against the settlers. (Rev: BL 7/93) [921]

6239 Cwiklik, Robert. *King Philip and the War with the Colonists* (4–7). Illus. Series: Biography Series of American Indians. 1989, Silver Burdett LB $12.95 (0-382-09573-1); paper $7.95 (0-382-09762-

9). A biography of the Wampanoag Indian chief who led his people in the most important Indian War in New England. (Rev: BL 1/1/90) [921]

PINKERTON, ALLAN

6240 Green, Carl R., and William R. Sanford. *Allan Pinkerton* (4–8). Illus. Series: Outlaws and Lawmen of the Wild West. 1995, Enslow LB $16.95 (0-89490-590-2). The story of the Scottish immigrant who organized Pinkerton's National Detective Agency, whose specialty was antiunion actions. (Rev: BL 11/15/95) [921]

6241 Josephson, Judith P. *Allan Pinkerton: The Original Private Eye* (5–8). Illus. 1996, Lerner LB $17.21 (0-8225-2923-9). The story of the famed criminal-catcher who founded the world-famous detective agency. (Rev: BL 10/15/96; SLJ 10/96) [921]

POCAHONTAS

6242 Holler, Anne. *Pocahontas: Powhatan Peacemaker* (5–8). Illus. Series: North American Indians of Achievement. 1993, Chelsea $21.95 (0-7910-1705-2); paper $9.95 (0-7910-1952-7). A brief biography of the woman who helped the English settlers survive at Jamestown. (Rev: SLJ 4/93) [921]

6243 Iannone, Catherine. *Pocahontas* (4–7). Illus. Series: Junior World Biography. 1995, Chelsea LB $18.65 (0-7910-2496-2); paper $18.65 (0-7910-2497-0). The fascinating story of the Native American who married a white man and was received by English royalty. (Rev: BL 10/15/95; SLJ 10/95) [921]

PRINTZ, MICHAEL

6244 Bankston, John. *Michael L. Printz and the Story of the Michael L. Printz Award* (4–8). Illus. Series: Great Achievement Awards. 2003, Mitchell Lane LB $19.95 (1-58415-182-X). Printz's career as a high school librarian is highlighted in this account of his establishment of the well-known award for YA literature, which includes a list of prize winners. (Rev: BL 10/15/03; SLJ 10/03) [020]

QUINTANILLA, GUADALUPE

6245 Wade, Mary D. *Guadalupe Quintanilla: Leader of the Hispanic Community* (4–8). Illus. Series: Multicultural Junior Biographies. 1995, Enslow LB $20.95 (0-89490-637-2). An inspiring story of a woman who once was considered mentally disabled and now is a leader in her Spanish American community. (Rev: BL 3/1/96; SLJ 2/96) [921]

REVERE, PAUL

6246 Randolph, Ryan P. *Paul Revere and the Minutemen of the American Revolution* (4–7). Series: Library of American Lives and Times. 2001, Rosen $23.95 (0-8239-5727-6). Fairly large type and many illustrations bring to life Paul Revere, a businessman and family man but also a soldier and spy, and the group of patriots known as the Minutemen. (Rev: BL 10/15/01) [921]

ROGERS, ROBERT

6247 Quasha, Jennifer. *Robert Rogers: Rogers' Rangers and the French and Indian War* (4–7). Series: Library of American Lives and Times. 2001, Rosen $23.95 (0-8239-5731-4). A beautifully illustrated biography of Major Robert Rogers, who recruited companies of soldiers known as Rogers' Rangers to fight for the British in the French and Indian War. (Rev: BL 10/15/01) [921]

ROSS, BETSY

6248 Randolph, Ryan P. *Betsy Ross: The American Flag and Life in a Young America* (4–7). Series: Library of American Lives and Times. 2001, Rosen $23.95 (0-8239-5730-6). This contemporary of George Washington was supposedly the seamstress of the American flag. (Rev: BL 1/1–15/02) [921]

SEIGEL, BUGSY

6249 Otfinoski, Steve. *Bugsy Siegel and the Postwar Boom* (7–10). Illus. Series: Notorious Americans and Their Times. 2000, Blackbirch LB $27.44 (1-56711-224-2). The story of the gangster and the times in which he and his fellow mobsters were active. (Rev: BL 12/1/00; HBG 3/01; SLJ 1/01) [921]

SEQUOYAH

6250 Cwiklik, Robert. *Sequoyah and the Cherokee Alphabet* (4–7). Illus. Series: Biography Series of American Indians. 1989, Silver Burdett LB $12.95 (0-382-09570-7). The story of the great Cherokee leader who was able to translate the language of his people to written form. (Rev: BL 1/1/90; SLJ 4/90) [921]

6251 Klausner, Janet. *Sequoyah's Gift: A Portrait of the Cherokee Leader* (4–7). Illus. 1993, HarperCollins LB $16.89 (0-06-021236-5). The life of this Cherokee leader is retold, with material on his invention of a written alphabet and his behavior during the Trail of Tears journey. (Rev: BL 9/1/93; HB 9–10/93; SLJ 11/93) [921]

SHREVE, HENRY MILLER

6252 McCall, Edith. *Mississippi Steamboatman: The Story of Henry Miller Shreve* (5–8). Illus. 1986, Walker $11.95 (0-8027-6597-1). The story of Henry Shreve, whose freight and passenger boats helped open up the Midwest. (Rev: BR 5–6/86; SLJ 3/86; VOYA 4/86) [921]

STARR, BELLE

6253 Naden, Corinne J., and Rose Blue. *Belle Starr and the Wild West* (5–9). Series: Notorious Americans and Their Times. 2000, Blackbirch LB $27.44 (1-56711-223-4). A fascinating biography of the legendary female outlaw who died a violent death at age 51. (Rev: HBG 3/01; SLJ 1/01) [921]

STEWART, BRIDGETT

6254 Stewart, Bridgett, and Franklin White. *No Matter What* (7–12). 2002, Blue/Black $14.99 (0-965-28271-6). Stewart relates in diary fashion the hardships of growing up poor in a shack in Georgia and the uphill battle she faced in her effort to get a full education. (Rev: BL 7/02) [920]

STILL, PETER

6255 Fradin, Dennis Brindell. *My Family Shall Be Free! The Life of Peter Still* (6–12). Illus. 2001, HarperCollins $16.95 (0-06-029595-3). Along with his brother, Peter Still was taken and sold into slavery; this compelling story of his struggle to win freedom and reunite with his family incorporates historical documents, interviews, and maps. (Rev: BCCB 5/01; BL 2/15/01; HBG 10/01; SLJ 4/01; VOYA 8/01) [305.5]

STINSON, KATHERINE

6256 Winegarten, Debra L. *Katherine Stinson: The Flying Schoolgirl* (4–7). 2001, Eakin $26.95 (1-57168-459-X). An absorbing introduction to Stinson's accomplishments, which include a whole series of "firsts," that interweaves fiction and fact. (Rev: HBG 10/01; SLJ 6/01) [629.13092]

STUYVESANT, PETER

6257 Krizner, L. J., and Lisa Sita. *Peter Stuyvesant: New Amsterdam, and the Origins of New York* (4–7). Series: Library of American Lives and Times. 2001, Rosen LB $38.35 (0-8239-5732-2). The story of New Amsterdam's best-known leader and how the Dutch presence in America influenced our culture for years to come. (Rev: BL 10/15/01; SLJ 7/01*) [921]

THOREAU, HENRY DAVID

6258 McCarthy, Pat. *Henry David Thoreau* (6–8). Illus. Series: Historical American Biographies. 2003, Enslow LB $20.95 (0-7660-1978-0). A detailed introduction to Thoreau's life, work, and legacy, with brief excerpts from his writings. (Rev: BL 6/1–15/03; HBG 10/03) [818]

TILLAGE, LEON

6259 Tillage, Leon W. *Leon's Story* (4–9). Illus. 1997, Farrar $15.00 (0-374-34379-9). An autobiographical account of growing up African American and poor in the segregated South and of participating in the civil rights movement. (Rev: BL 10/1/97*; BR 5–6/98; HB 11–12/97; HBG 3/98; SLJ 12/97) [975.6]

TWEED, WILLIAM "BOSS"

6260 Johnson, Suzan. *Boss Tweed and Tammany Hall* (5–8). Series: Major World Leaders. 2002, Chelsea LB $27.44 (1-56711-224-4). The amazing life of the corrupt New York politician who defrauded the city of more than $30 million and whose life ended in prison. (Rev: BL 1/1–15/03) [921]

WILSON, BILL

6261 White, Tom. *Bill W., a Different Kind of Hero* (4–7). Illus. 2003, Boyds Mills $16.95 (1-59078-067-1). The founder of Alcoholics Anonymous is the subject of this biography that describes his long battle with addiction. (Rev: BL 4/15/03; HBG 10/03; SLJ 2/03) [362.292]

WRIGHT, KATHARINE

6262 Maurer, Richard. *The Wright Sister* (5–9). Illus. 2003, Millbrook $18.95 (0-7613-1546-2). Katharine, the younger sister of Orville and Wilbur, devoted herself to supporting her brothers' aspirations despite the fact that she trained as a teacher. (Rev: BL 4/15/03*; HB 7–8/03; HBG 10/03; SLJ 6/03*) [629.13]

Science, Medicine, Industry, and Business Figures

Collective

6263 Aaseng, Nathan. *Black Inventors* (6–12). Illus. Series: American Profiles. 1997, Facts on File $25.00 (0-8160-3407-9). This work profiles 10 African American inventors, including Lewis Temple, Elijah McCoy, and Sarah Breedlove Walker, and tells how they were denied recognition for their achievements and overcame social and economic obstacles to achieve success. (Rev: BL 2/15/98; BR 1–2/98) [920]

6264 Aaseng, Nathan. *Business Builders in Computers* (5–8). Series: Business Builders. 2000, Oliver LB $22.95 (1-881508-57-9). Bill Gates, Steve Jobs of Apple, and Steve Case of AOL are among the individuals profiled in this interesting volume on the growth of the computer industry. (Rev: BL 2/1/01; HBG 10/01; SLJ 5/01) [338.4]

6265 Aaseng, Nathan. *Business Builders in Fast Food* (5–8). Series: Business Builders. 2001, Oliver $22.95 (1-881508-58-7). An interesting look at the creators of fast food empires such as McDonald's and Wendy's. (Rev: BL 9/15/01; HBG 10/01; SLJ 9/01) [381]

6266 Aaseng, Nathan. *Business Builders in Oil* (5–8). Series: Business Builders. 2000, Oliver LB $22.95 (1-881508-56-0). This lively introduction to the oil industry provides profiles of key individuals such as John D. Rockefeller, Andrew Mellon, and J. Paul Getty. (Rev: BL 2/1/01; HBG 10/01; SLJ 5/01) [338.2]

6267 Aaseng, Nathan. *Construction: Building the Impossible* (5–9). Illus. 2000, Oliver LB $21.95 (1-881508-59-5). This book profiles eight famous builders — from Imhotep, who built the first stone pyramids in Egypt, to Frank Crowe, the visionary behind the Hoover Dam. (Rev: BL 5/1/00; HBG 10/00; SLJ 10/00) [920]

6268 Altman, Linda J. *Women Inventors* (6–8). Illus. Series: American Profiles. 1997, Facts on File $25.00 (0-8160-3385-4). Relying heavily on primary sources, this book profiles nine women inventors, including Carrie Everson, Madam C. J. Walker, Bette Graham, and Ruth Handler. (Rev: BL 5/1/97; BR 9–10/97) [920]

6269 Anderson, Margaret J., and Karen F. Stephenson. *Scientists of the Ancient World* (6–9). Series: Collective Biographies. 1999, Enslow LB $20.95 (0-7660-1111-9). Ten early scientists are profiled, including Pythagoras, Hippocrates, Aristotle, Archimedes, Pliny, Galen, and Al-Khwarizmi. (Rev: BL 12/1/98) [920]

6270 Archer, Jules. *To Save the Earth: The American Environmental Movement* (5–9). 1998, Viking $17.99 (0-670-87121-4). A history of the environmentalist movement in this country is revealed through biographies of four key individuals: John Muir, Rachel Carson, David McTaggart, and Dave Foreman. (Rev: BL 9/15/98; HBG 3/99; SLJ 12/98; VOYA 2/99) [920]

6271 Bankston, John. *Francis Crick and James Watson: Pioneers in DNA Research* (5–7). Series: Unlocking the Secrets of Science. 2002, Mitchell Lane LB $17.95 (1-58415-122-6). An accessible account of the discovery of the structure of DNA and the lives of the two scientists involved. (Rev: HBG 10/03; SLJ 1/03) [576.5]

6272 Buchanan, Doug. *Air and Space* (6–9). Series: Female Firsts in Their Fields. 1999, Chelsea $18.65 (0-7910-5141-2). The biographies of six women who were pioneers in air and space technology. (Rev: BL 5/15/99; HBG 9/99) [920]

6273 Bussing-Burks, Marie. *Influential Economists* (7–12). Illus. 2003, Oliver $19.95 (1-881508-72-2).

The historical perspective of this book provides insights into economic theories and introduces some of the key people — including John Maynard Keynes and Milton Friedman — who have shaped the world's economy. (Rev: BL 3/1/03; HBG 10/03; SLJ 12/03) [330]

6274 Byrnes, Patricia. *Environmental Pioneers* (6–10). 1998, Oliver LB $19.95 (1-881508-45-5). This collective biography of early environmentalists includes profiles of John Muir, David Brower, Rachel Carson, Jay Darling, Rosalie Edge, Aldo Leopold, Olaus and Margaret Murie, and Gaylord Nelson. (Rev: BL 9/15/98; BR 1–2/99; SLJ 11/98) [920]

6275 Camp, Carole Ann. *American Astronomers: Searchers and Wonderers* (5–8). Series: Collective Biographies. 1996, Enslow LB $20.95 (0-89490-631-3). This volume presents brief profiles of important astronomers including Maria Mitchell, Edwin Hubble, and Carl Sagan. (Rev: BL 4/15/96; BR 9–10/96; SLJ 5/96) [920]

6276 Carruthers, Margaret W., and Susan Clinton. *Pioneers of Geology: Discovering Earth's Secrets* (5–9). Illus. Series: Lives in Science. 2001, Watts LB $20.00 (0-531-11364-7). Chronologically arranged biographies of important geologists give information on the individual's life and work and also on the state of scientific knowledge at the time. (Rev: SLJ 11/01) [550.922]

6277 Cooney, Miriam P. *Celebrating Women in Mathematics and Science* (6–10). 1996, National Council of Teachers of Math paper $26.95 (0-87353-425-5). Covering ancient times to the present, this collective biography celebrates the struggles and triumphs of women in the fields of mathematics and sciences. (Rev: SLJ 10/96) [920]

6278 Cox, Clinton. *African American Healers* (4–7). Illus. Series: Black Stars. 1999, Wiley $24.95 (0-471-24650-6). Using entries of two to three pages each, this work profiles more than 20 African Americans who have achieved prominence in medicine and related areas. (Rev: BL 2/15/00; HBG 10/00; SLJ 2/00) [910]

6279 Currie, Stephen. *Women Inventors* (6–9). Series: History Makers. 2001, Lucent $24.95 (1-56006-865-5). This collective biography highlights the lives and accomplishments of five American female inventors including Grace Hopper and Madam C. J. Walker. (Rev: BL 8/1/01; SLJ 12/01) [920]

6280 Curtis, Robert H. *Great Lives: Medicine* (5–8). Series: Great Lives. 1992, Scribners $24.00 (0-684-19321-3). Biographies of doctors and other medical professionals who made major contributions and discoveries throughout history. (Rev: BL 12/15/92; SLJ 6/93) [920]

6281 Dash, Joan. *The Triumph of Discovery: Four Nobel Women* (7–12). 1991, Messner paper $8.95 (0-671-69333-6). This collective biography highlights the work of four women who won the Nobel Prize in science, including Rita Levi-Montalcini, Maria Goepper Mayer, and Barbara McClintock. (Rev: BL 3/15/91) [920]

6282 DeAngelis, Gina. *Science and Medicine* (5–9). Series: Female Firsts in Their Fields. 1999, Chelsea $18.65 (0-7910-5143-9). The six women profiled here are Elizabeth Blackwell, Clara Barton, Marie Curie, Margaret Mead, Rachel Carson, and Antonia Novello. (Rev: BL 5/15/99; HBG 10/99; SLJ 9/99; VOYA 8/99) [920]

6283 Di Domenico, Kelly. *Super Women in Science* (6–8). Illus. 2002, Second Story paper $10.95 (1-896764-66-5). Ten women are featured for their contributions to the scientific community, among them environmentalist Rachel Carson, physicist Chien-Shiung Wu, researcher Rosalind Franklin, and astronaut Mae Jemison. (Rev: BL 3/1/03) [509]

6284 Evernden, Margery. *The Experimenters: Twelve Great Chemists* (6–8). Illus. 2001, Avisson paper $19.95 (1-888105-49-6). The lives and research of 12 chemists are introduced in this accessible volume that is suitable for report writers. (Rev: BL 1/1–15/01) [540]

6285 Faber, Doris, and Harold Faber. *Nature and the Environment* (5–8). Series: Great Lives. 1991, Macmillan $22.95 (0-684-19047-8). This book explores the lives of some of the great naturalists and conservationists. (Rev: BL 6/1/91; HB 7–8/91; SLJ 10/91) [920]

6286 Fox, Karen. *The Chain Reaction: Pioneers of Nuclear Science* (6–12). Series: Lives of Science. 1998, Watts LB $20.00 (0-531-11425-2). The world of nuclear science is introduced through profiles of seven men and women who have studied the atom, including Curie, Rutherford, Fermi, Lawrence, Oppenheimer, Goeppert-Mayer, and Sakharov. (Rev: BL 1/1–15/99; HBG 3/99; SLJ 2/99) [539.7]

6287 French, Laura. *Internet Pioneers: The Cyber Elite* (5–9). Series: Collective Biographies. 2001, Enslow LB $20.95 (0-7660-1540-8). French tells the stories of 10 Internet innovators — including Andrew Grove, Bill Gates, Larry Ellison, and Jeff Bezos — detailing their successes and revealing their very different backgrounds. (Rev: HBG 3/02; SLJ 9/01) [920]

6288 Fridell, Ron. *Solving Crimes: Pioneers of Forensic Science* (7–12). Illus. Series: Lives in Science. 2000, Watts LB $25.00 (0-531-11721-9). Six key figures in forensic science are profiled in an absorbing narrative that explains the science behind the evolving techniques. (Rev: BL 8/00; SLJ 6/00) [363.25]

6289 Green, Carl R., and William R. Sanford. *American Tycoons* (6–9). Series: Collective Biographies. 1999, Enslow LB $19.95 (0-7660-1112-7). The stories of 10 businessmen — including Henry Ford and Bill Gates — who built fortunes in America. (Rev: HBG 4/00; SLJ 3/00) [970]

6290 Greenberg, Lorna, and Margot F. Horwitz. *Digging into the Past: Pioneers of Archeology* (6–9). Series: Lives in Science. 2001, Watts LB $20.00 (0-531-11857-6). Chronologically arranged biographies of important archaeologists including Howard Carter and Kathleen Kenyon give information on the individual's life and work and also on the state of scientific knowledge at the time. (Rev: BL 11/15/01; SLJ 11/01) [930.1]

6291 Hansen, Ole Steen. *The Wright Brothers and Other Pioneers of Flight* (4–7). Series: The Story of Flight. 2003, Crabtree $23.93 (0-7787-1200-1). In text and pictures, this book introduces the pioneers of flight, with a concentration on the Wright brothers. (Rev: BL 10/15/03) [921]

6292 Harris, Laurie L., ed. *Biography Today: Profiles of People of Interest to Young Readers* (4–7). Illus. Series: Scientists and Inventors. 1996, Omnigraphics LB $39.00 (0-7808-0068-0). Profiles of 14 important contemporaries including Carl Sagan and Jane Goodall are accompanied by those of some lesser-known figures, such as geneticist and AIDS fighter Mathilde Krim. (Rev: SLJ 2/97) [920]

6293 Haskins, Jim. *African American Entrepreneurs* (6–12). Illus. Series: Black Stars. 1998, Wiley $24.95 (0-471-14576-9). This is a collective biography of more than 30 African Americans who have made their mark on the business community. (Rev: BL 2/15/98; BR 11–12/98; SLJ 7/98) [920]

6294 Haskins, Jim. *Outward Dreams: Black Inventors and Their Inventions* (7–12). 1991, Walker LB $14.85 (0-8027-6994-2). Examines the lives and inventions of African American men and women who, only after the Civil War, were given recognition for their contributions. (Rev: BL 5/15/91) [920]

6295 Hatt, Christine. *Scientists and Their Discoveries* (6–9). Illus. Series: Documenting History. 2001, Watts LB $22.00 (0-531-14614-6). An overview of the work of a number of famous scientists in various disciplines, drawing from sources including advertisements, interviews, and personal diaries. (Rev: BL 12/15/01) [509.2]

6296 Henderson, Harry. *Modern Mathematicians* (7–12). Illus. 1995, Facts on File LB $25.00 (0-8160-3235-1). Profiles of the lives and accomplishments of nine men and four women, among them George Boole, Alan Turing, and Sophia Kovalevsky, who have contributed to the development of modern mathematics. (Rev: BL 1/1–15/96; BR 5–6/96; SLJ 2/96; VOYA 2/96) [920]

6297 Hudson, Wade. *Book of Black Heroes: Scientists, Healers and Inventors* (5–8). Illus. 2002, Just Us $9.95 (0-940975-97-1). One historic or present-day African American figure is presented on each page of this collective biography of doctors, engineers, and inventors. (Rev: BL 2/15/03) [925]

6298 Jeffrey, Laura S. *American Inventors of the 20th Century* (6–9). Illus. Series: Collective Biographies. 1996, Enslow LB $20.95 (0-89490-632-1). Ten short biographies of famous modern inventors such as Philo Farnsworth (television) and William Lear (Learjet) are presented in this easily read book. (Rev: BL 7/96; BR 9–10/96; SLJ 5/96) [920]

6299 Jeffrey, Laura S. *Great American Businesswomen* (4–7). Illus. 1996, Enslow LB $20.95 (0-89490-706-9). Profiles of 10 successful American businesswomen, including Maggie L. Walker and Katharine Graham. (Rev: BL 9/1/96; SLJ 9/96) [920]

6300 Keene, Ann T. *Earthkeepers: Observers and Protectors of Nature* (4–8). Illus. 1993, Oxford $50.00 (0-19-507867-5). Profiles are given for more than 40 people throughout history who have worked to preserve the environment, beginning with the self-educated botanist John Bartram, who worked in the 1700s. (Rev: HB 11–12/93; SLJ 8/94*) [920]

6301 Kent, Jacqueline C. *Business Builders in Fashion* (6–9). Illus. Series: Business Builders. 2003, Oliver LB $22.95 (1-881508-80-3). Chanel, Dior, Worth, Mary Quant, and Ralph Lauren are among the designers introduced. (Rev: BL 5/1/03; HBG 10/03; SLJ 6/03) [746.9]

6302 Kirsh, Shannon, and Florence Kirsh. *Fabulous Female Physicians* (4–8). 2002, Second Story paper $7.95 (1-896764-43-6). Using short chapters and black-and-white photographs, this account profiles 10 mostly unknown female doctors and their accomplishments. (Rev: BL 6/1–15/02; VOYA 8/02) [921]

6303 Leuzzi, Linda. *Life Connections: Pioneers of Ecology* (6–9). Illus. 2000, Watts LB $25.00 (0-531-11566-6). This collective biography contains eight sketches of scientists who have developed the field of ecology including Alexander von Humboldt, Jacques-Yves Cousteau, Aldo Leopold, E. Lucy Braun, and Rachel Carson. (Rev: BL 5/1/00; SLJ 6/00) [920]

6304 Leuzzi, Linda. *To the Young Environmentalist: Lives Dedicated to Preserving the Natural World* (6–10). Illus. Series: To the Young . . . 1997, Watts LB $23.00 (0-531-11359-0). This work profiles eight individuals who have dedicated their lives to preserving the natural world. (Rev: BL 12/1/97; VOYA 6/98) [920]

6305 Lindop, Laurie. *Scientists and Doctors* (6–10). Series: Dynamic Women. 1997, Twenty-First Century LB $24.90 (0-8050-4166-4). This book contains biographies of women who have excelled in such areas as archaeology, physics, astronautics, and genetics, including Mildred Dresselhaus, Mae Jemison, Susan Love, Helen Taussig, and Rosalyn Yalow. (Rev: SLJ 9/97) [920]

6306 Lomask, Milton. *Great Lives: Invention and Technology* (5–8). Series: Invention and Technology. 1991, Scribners $23.00 (0-684-19106-7). Profiles of great names in invention and technology around the world. (Rev: BL 11/1/91; SLJ 1/92) [920]

6307 Lutz, Norma Jean. *Business and Industry* (6–9). Series: Female Firsts in Their Fields. 1999, Chelsea $18.65 (0-7910-5142-0). Six trail-blazing females in the business world are profiled: Madam C. J. Walker, Katharine Graham, Mary Kay Ash, Martha Stewart, Oprah Winfrey, and Sherry Lansing. (Rev: BL 5/15/99; HBG 10/99; SLJ 9/99; VOYA 8/99) [920]

6308 McClure, Judy. *Healers and Researchers: Physicians, Biologists, Social Scientists* (5–9). Series: Remarkable Women. 2000, Raintree Steck-Vaughn LB $32.85 (0-8172-5734-9). This book profiles 150 women from the scientific community including Barbara McClintock, Anna Freud, Jocelyn Elders, and Sushila Nyir. (Rev: SLJ 8/00) [920]

6309 Mayberry, Jodine. *Business Leaders Who Built Financial Empires* (5–8). Illus. Series: 20 Events. 1995, Raintree Steck-Vaughn LB $27.12 (0-8114-4934-3). The biographies of 19 financial wizards and entrepreneurs, beginning with Levi Strauss and Andrew Carnegie and ending with Steven Jobs and Anita Roddick. (Rev: SLJ 7/95) [920]

6310 Mulcahy, Robert. *Medical Technology: Inventing the Instruments* (5–8). Illus. Series: Innovators. 1997, Oliver LB $21.95 (1-881508-34-X). Seven short biographies of scientists who were responsible for such inventions as the X-ray, stethoscope, thermometer, and electrocardiograph. (Rev: BCCB 7–8/97; BR 11–12/97; SLJ 7/97) [920]

6311 Northrup, Mary. *American Computer Pioneers* (6–12). Illus. Series: Collective Biographies. 1998, Enslow LB $20.95 (0-7660-1053-8). This book profiles individuals who revolutionized modern technology, and gives a concise history of the evolution of computers and their capabilities. (Rev: BL 10/15/98; BR 11–12/98; HBG 3/99; SLJ 8/98) [004]

6312 Oleksy, Walter. *Hispanic-American Scientists* (7–10). Illus. Series: American Profiles. 1998, Facts on File $25.00 (0-8160-3704-3). Ten Hispanic American scientists are profiled, including Pedro Sanchez, Henry Diaz, Adriana Ocampo, and Francisco Dallmeier. (Rev: BL 3/1/99; BR 5–6/99; SLJ 2/99) [920]

6313 Pile, Robert B. *Top Entrepreneurs and Their Business* (6–12). 1993, Oliver LB $19.95 (1-881508-04-8). The rags-to-riches stories of nine

entrepreneurs, among them L. L. Bean, Walt Disney, and Sam Walton. With photographs. (Rev: BL 11/15/93; SLJ 1/94) [920]

6314 Pile, Robert B. *Women Business Leaders* (6–12). Illus. Series: Profiles. 1995, Oliver LB $19.95 (1-881508-24-2). Profiles of eight women, most of them not well known (except for Mary Kay Ash of the cosmetics firm), who have the "creativity, strength, and determination to run thriving businesses." (Rev: BL 1/1–15/96; SLJ 5/96; VOYA 4/96) [910]

6315 Polking, Kirk. *Oceanographers and Explorers of the Sea* (5–9). Series: Collective Biographies. 1999, Enslow LB $20.95 (0-7660-1113-5). Profiles 10 scientists and adventurers who have devoted their lives to the oceans, marine life, and ocean-related pursuits, including Maurice Ewing, who mapped the ocean floor, and Robert Ballard, discoverer of the *Titanic*. (Rev: BL 8/99; SLJ 9/99) [920]

6316 Rennert, Richard, ed. *Pioneers of Discovery* (6–9). Illus. Series: Profiles of Great Black Americans. 1994, Chelsea paper $7.65 (0-7910-2068-1). Eight African American leaders in science and technology profiled here, among them Benjamin Banneker, James Beckwourth, George Washington Carver, Charles Drew, and Matthew Henson. (Rev: BL 6/1–15/94) [920]

6317 Richie, Jason. *Space Flight: Crossing the Last Frontier* (5–9). Illus. Series: Innovators. 2002, Oliver LB $21.95 (1-881508-77-3). Biographies of seven men who were instrumental in the development of space flight — including Robert Goddard, Wernher von Braun, and Sergei Korolev — are arranged in chronological order. (Rev: HBG 3/03; LMC 4–5/03; SLJ 4/03) [629.4]

6318 Shell, Barry. *Great Canadian Scientists* (5–8). Illus. 1998, Polestar Book Publishers paper $14.95 (1-896095-36-4). In profiles that average five or six pages, 19 important contemporary Canadian scientists and their work are introduced; an additional section gives short profiles of over 100 more. (Rev: SLJ 9/98) [920]

6319 Sherman, Josepha. *Jerry Yang and David Filo: Chief Yahoos of Yahoo* (5–8). Series: Techies. 2001, Millbrook LB $23.90 (0-7613-1961-1). This is the story of the creators of Yahoo!, the world's most heavily trafficked Web site. (Rev: BL 4/1/02; HBG 3/02; SLJ 12/01) [921]

6320 Stanley, Phyllis M. *American Environmental Heroes* (4–7). Illus. 1996, Enslow LB $20.95 (0-89490-630-5). John Muir, Barry Commoner, Sylvia Earle, and seven other environmentalists are profiled. (Rev: BL 9/1/96; SLJ 7/96) [920]

6321 Sullivan, Otha R. *African American Inventors* (5–8). Ed. by Jim Haskins. Illus. Series: Black Stars. 1998, Wiley $24.95 (0-471-14804-0). Among the African American inventors profiled in two- and three-page spreads are Benjamin Banneker, Madam C. J. Walker, and Dr. Charles Drew, whose research laid the basis for blood donation. (Rev: BL 7/98; BR 11–12/98; SLJ 6/98) [920]

6322 Sullivan, Otha Richard. *African American Women Scientists and Inventors* (7–10). Series: Black Stars. 2001, Wiley $22.95 (0-471-38707-X). Twenty-six African American women born between 1849 and 1967 are profiled in this accessible book, with details of their lives and accomplishments. (Rev: SLJ 4/02) [608.9]

6323 Thimmesh, Catherine. *The Sky's the Limit: Stories of Discovery by Women and Girls* (5–7). 2002, Houghton $16.00 (0-618-07698-0). Details discoveries in the sciences, all made by women and girls. A sequel to *Girls Think of Everything* (2000). (Rev: BL 3/1/02; HB 5–6/02; HBG 10/02; SLJ 5/02; VOYA 6/02) [500]

6324 VanCleave, Janice. *Janice VanCleave's Scientists Through the Ages* (4–7). Illus. 2003, Wiley paper $12.95 (0-471-25222-0). A collective biography profiling 25 scientists, with explanations of each one's important work and a relevant experiment for the reader to perform. (Rev: BL 12/1/03) [509]

6325 Veglahn, Nancy. *Women Scientists* (7–10). Series: American Profiles. 1991, Facts on File LB $25.00 (0-8160-2482-0). This book profiles 11 women scientists of the 19th and 20th centuries, such as Alice Eastwood, Alice Hamilton, Margaret Mead, Barbara McClintock, and Rachel Carson. (Rev: BL 11/15/91; SLJ 3/92) [920]

6326 Yount, Lisa. *Asian-American Scientists* (6–10). Series: American Profiles. 1998, Facts on File $25.00 (0-8160-3756-6). This work features 12 Asian American scientists who have contributed to major scientific advances in the past century, among them Flossie Wong-Staal, Subrahmanyan Chandrasekhar, Tsutomo Shimomura, and David Da-i Ho. (Rev: BL 12/15/98; BR 5–6/99; SLJ 7/99) [920]

6327 Yount, Lisa. *Black Scientists* (7–12). Series: American Profiles. 1991, Facts on File LB $25.00 (0-8160-2549-5). Descriptions of the professional achievements of eight African American scientists and what led each to his/her particular field. (Rev: BL 11/15/91; SLJ 1/92) [920]

6328 Yount, Lisa. *Disease Detectives* (6–9). Series: History Makers. 2000, Lucent LB $19.96 (1-56006-738-1). This is a collection of profiles of medical pioneers who worked in the discovery, prevention, and treatment of diseases. (Rev: BL 1/1–15/01) [920]

6329 Yount, Lisa. *Twentieth-Century Women Scientists* (7–12). Illus. 1995, Facts on File $25.00 (0-8160-3173-8). For each of the 11 women highlighted, there are details on the obstacles they faced, as well as information on their contributions and

diverse backgrounds. (Rev: BL 4/15/96; SLJ 2/96; VOYA 4/96) [920]

6330 Zach, Kim K. *Hidden from History: The Lives of Eight American Women Scientists* (6–12). Illus. 2002, Avisson paper $19.95 (1-888105-54-2). The important achievements of eight women who made often unacknowledged contributions to the sciences are accompanied by some personal details. (Rev: BL 12/1/02; SLJ 4/03) [509.2]

Individual

ALVAREZ, LUIS

6331 Allison, Amy. *Luis Alvarez and the Development of the Bubble Chamber* (5–8). Series: Unlocking the Secrets of Science. 2002, Mitchell Lane LB $17.95 (1-58415-140-4). Alvarez was a scientist of wide-ranging interests who won a Nobel Prize for developing a bubble chamber to track atomic particles. (Rev: HBG 3/03; SLJ 2/03; VOYA 6/03) [921]

ANDREESSEN, MARC

6332 Ehrenhaft, Daniel. *Marc Andreessen: Web Warrior* (5–8). Illus. Series: The Techies. 2001, Twenty-First Century LB $23.90 (0-7613-1964-6). This biography introduces Marc Andreessen, who coauthored the Web-browsing software Mosaic, cofounded the firm Netscape, and was a multimillionaire at age 24. (Rev: BL 3/15/01; HBG 10/01; SLJ 7/01; VOYA 8/01) [921]

ANDREWS, ROY CHAPMAN

6333 Bausum, Ann. *Dragon Bones and Dinosaur Eggs: A Photobiography of Explorer Roy Chapman Andrews* (5–8). Illus. 2000, National Geographic $17.95 (0-7922-7123-8). A biography of the famous paleontologist who made several important dinosaur discoveries in central Asia and later became director of the American Museum of Natural History in New York City. (Rev: BCCB 5/00*; BL 3/15/00; HBG 10/00; SLJ 3/00) [921]

6334 Marrin, Albert. *Secrets from the Rocks: Dinosaur Hunting with Roy Chapman Andrews* (4–8). Illus. 2002, Dutton $18.99 (0-525-46743-2). This photo-biography of the famous paleontologist concentrates on his Mongolian expeditions in the 1920s and his great dinosaur discoveries. (Rev: BL 4/15/02; HB 7–8/02; HBG 10/02; SLJ 4/02; VOYA 12/02) [921]

ANNING, MARY

6335 Goodhue, Thomas. *Curious Bones: Mary Anning and the Birth of Paleontology* (5–8). Illus. 2002, Morgan Reynolds LB $21.95 (1-883846-93-

5). A readable biography of the groundbreaking female paleontologist (1799–1847) that places her achievements in historical context, with a glossary, bibliography, and timeline. (Rev: BL 7/02; HBG 3/03; SLJ 9/02) [560.92]

ARDEN, ELIZABETH

6336 Shuker, Nancy. *Elizabeth Arden: Beauty Empire Builder* (7–10). Illus. Series: Giants of American Industry. 2001, Blackbirch LB $21.95 (1-56711-510-1). A farmer's daughter, Elizabeth Arden was an assistant to a beauty specialist before opening her first salon. (Rev: BL 10/15/01; HBG 3/02) [338.7]

AVERY, OSWALD

6337 Severs, Vesta-Nadine, and Jim Whiting. *Oswald Avery and the Story of DNA* (4–7). Series: Unlocking the Secrets of Science. 2002, Mitchell Lane LB $17.95 (1-58415-110-2). The importance of Avery's early research is reinforced by a description of DNA evidence being used to free wrongly accused prisoners. (Rev: HBG 10/02; SLJ 6/02) [579.3092]

BANNEKER, BENJAMIN

6338 Conley, Kevin. *Benjamin Banneker* (5–9). Illus. 1989, Chelsea LB $9.95 (1-55546-573-0). Banneker was a remarkable 18th-century African American who excelled in mathematics and science. (Rev: BL 1/1/90; SLJ 5/90; VOYA 4/90) [921]

6339 Litwin, Laura Baskes. *Benjamin Banneker: Astronomer and Mathematician* (6–10). Illus. Series: African-American Biographies. 1999, Enslow LB $20.95 (0-7660-1208-5). The story of the self-taught African American scientist who lived during the days of slavery and was responsible for some brilliant scientific inventions. (Rev: BL 9/15/99; HBG 4/00) [921]

BELL, ALEXANDER GRAHAM

6340 Lewis, Cynthia C. *Hello, Alexander Graham Bell Speaking* (4–7). Illus. Series: Taking Part. 1991, Macmillan LB $13.95 (0-87518-461-8). This inventor studied human speech and created one of the greatest means of communication, the telephone. (Rev: BL 9/1/91; SLJ 12/91) [921]

6341 Pasachoff, Naomi. *Alexander Graham Bell: Making Connections* (6–9). Series: Oxford Portraits in Science. 1996, Oxford $28.00 (0-19-509908-7). A fine biography that focuses on Bell's work as a teacher of the deaf and his career as an inventor. (Rev: BR 11–12/96; SLJ 2/97*) [921]

6342 Pollard, Michael. *Alexander Graham Bell: Father of Modern Communication* (5–7). Series:

Giants of Science. 2000, Blackbirch LB $27.44 (1-56711-334-6). Known primarily for the invention of the telephone, Bell also invented the first hydrofoil, an air-conditioning system, and an early fax machine. (Rev: BL 1/1–15/01; HBG 3/01) [921]

6343 Weaver, Robyn M. *Alexander Graham Bell* (7–12). Series: The Importance Of. 2000, Lucent LB $18.96 (1-56006-603-2). The life and accomplishments of this scientific genius are covered with emphasis on Bell's lasting importance. (Rev: BL 8/00; HBG 9/00) [921]

BERNERS-LEE, TIM

6344 Gaines, Ann. *Tim Berners-Lee and the Development of the World Wide Web* (4–7). Series: Unlocking the Secrets of Science. 2001, Mitchell Lane LB $17.95 (1-58415-096-3). A profile of the man who created the user-friendly way of accessing much of the information on the Internet. (Rev: HBG 10/02; SLJ 2/02) [921]

6345 Stewart, Melissa. *Tim Berners-Lee: Inventor of the World Wide Web* (4–7). Series: Ferguson's Career Biographies. 2001, Ferguson LB $16.95 (0-89434-367-X). Young readers will be fascinated by the details of Berners-Lee's life and career and the accompanying information on the skills needed to become a computer programmer. (Rev: SLJ 10/01) [921]

BEZOS, JEFF

6346 Garty, Judy. *Jeff Bezos* (5–8). Illus. Series: Internet Biographies. 2003, Enslow LB $18.95 (0-7660-1972-1). A reader-friendly biography of the creator of Amazon.com, with plenty of information on his youth. (Rev: BL 3/15/03; HBG 10/03) [380.1]

6347 Sherman, Josepha. *Jeff Bezos: King of Amazon* (5–8). Illus. 2001, Twenty-First Century LB $23.90 (0-7613-1963-8). Jeff Bezos, the genius behind Amazon.com, is introduced along with information on his struggle to found a book company on the Web. (Rev: BL 3/15/01; HBG 10/01; SLJ 7/01; VOYA 8/01) [921]

BLACKWELL, ELIZABETH

6348 Brown, Jordan. *Elizabeth Blackwell* (7–10). Illus. 1989, Chelsea LB $19.95 (1-55546-642-7). The life story of the first woman doctor; she also organized a nursing service during the Civil War and helped provide educational opportunities for other young women. (Rev: BL 5/15/89) [921]

6349 Kline, Nancy. *Elizabeth Blackwell: A Doctor's Triumph* (5–9). Series: Barnard Biography. 1997, Conari Pr. paper $6.95 (1-57324-057-5). The story of the first woman doctor in America, with generous excerpts from her journal and letters. (Rev: BL

2/15/97; BR 9–10/97; SLJ 6/97; VOYA 12/97) [921]

BOHR, NIELS

6350 Pasachoff, Naomi. *Niels Bohr: Physicist and Humanitarian* (7–10). Illus. Series: Great Minds of Science. 2003, Enslow $20.95 (0-7660-1997-7). An appealing biography that explains Bohr's scientific achievements in clear, understandable terms and covers his protests against the Nazis and against the use of nuclear weapons. (Rev: BL 6/1–15/03; HBG 10/03) [530]

BRAHE, TYCHO

6351 Boerst, William J. *Tycho Brahe: Mapping the Heavens* (6–9). Illus. 2003, Morgan Reynolds LB $23.95 (1-883846-97-8). A concise biography with many illustrations of the man whose research on astronomy in the 1500s provided the foundation for future scientific inquiry. (Rev: BL 3/15/03; HBG 10/03; SLJ 8/03) [520]

BROWN, HELEN GURLEY

6352 Falkof, Lucille. *Helen Gurley Brown: The Queen of Cosmopolitan* (5–8). Series: Wizards of Business. 1992, Garrett LB $17.26 (1-56074-013-2). An interesting, accessible, and inspiring biography of the magazine magnate. (Rev: BL 6/15/92; SLJ 7/92) [921]

BURROUGHS, JOHN

6353 Wadsworth, Ginger. *John Burroughs: The Sage of Slabsides* (5–8). Illus. 1997, Clarion $16.95 (0-395-77830-1). A biography of the American naturalist and essayist who lived in a cabin in the Catskill Mountains and wrote about his observations. (Rev: BCCB 5/97; BL 3/15/97; BR 9–10/97; HB 7–8/97; SLJ 5/97) [508.73]

CARNEGIE, ANDREW

6354 Meltzer, Milton. *The Many Lives of Andrew Carnegie* (7–10). Illus. 1997, Watts LB $20.00 (0-531-11427-9). The amazing life of this complex, successful businessman and philanthropist who sought to project himself as a generous industrial leader but used unscrupulous business tactics and treated his workers ruthlessly. (Rev: BL 10/1/97; BR 5–6/98; HBG 3/98; SLJ 10/97; VOYA 10/98) [921]

CARSON, RACHEL

6355 Harlan, Judith. *Sounding the Alarm: A Biography of Rachel Carson* (5–7). Illus. Series: People in Focus. 1989, Macmillan LB $13.95 (0-87518-407-3). A good account of this founder of the modern

ecology movement. (Rev: BL 10/1/89; SLJ 11/89) [921]

6356 Jezer, Marty. *Rachel Carson* (6–9). 1988, Chelsea LB $19.95 (1-55546-646-X). The biography of the scientist who was one of the first to warn us of our environmental problems. (Rev: BL 9/1/88; BR 11–12/88; VOYA 2/89) [921]

6357 Presnall, Judith J. *Rachel Carson* (4–8). Illus. Series: The Importance Of. 1995, Lucent LB $27.45 (1-56006-052-2). The life of this innovative scientist whose writings, including *Silent Spring*, made the world aware of conservation and the erosion of our environment. (Rev: BL 1/15/95; SLJ 1/95) [921]

6358 Wadsworth, Ginger. *Rachel Carson: Voice for the Earth* (5–7). Illus. Series: Lerner Biographies. 1992, Lerner LB $30.35 (0-8225-4907-7). The life and work of the conservationist and author, best known for *Silent Spring*. (Rev: BL 6/1/92; HB 7–8/92; SLJ 7/92) [921]

6359 Wheeler, Leslie A. *Rachel Carson* (7–12). Series: Pioneers in Change. 1991, Silver Burdett LB $13.95 (0-382-24167-3); paper $6.95 (0-382-24174-6). A portrait of the pioneer conservationist whose expose on the lasting damage caused by widespread use of pesticides had a major impact. (Rev: BL 2/1/92) [921]

CASE, STEVE

6360 Ashby, Ruth. *Steve Case: America Online Pioneer* (5–8). Series: Techies. 2002, Millbrook LB $23.90 (0-7613-2655-3). The story of the Honolulu native who was a leader of AOL and the driving force behind its merger with Time-Warner. (Rev: BL 4/1/02; HBG 10/02) [921]

CLARK, EUGENIE

6361 Butts, Ellen R., and Joyce R. Schwartz. *Eugenie Clark: Adventures of a Shark Scientist* (5–8). Illus. 2000, Linnet $19.50 (0-208-02440-9). An interesting biography of a contemporary American scientist — an ichthyologist who has produced some startling research on sharks. (Rev: BCCB 2/00; BL 2/15/00; HBG 10/00; SLJ 7/00) [921]

COPERNICUS

6362 Andronik, Catherine M. *Copernicus: Founder of Modern Astronomy* (4–8). Illus. Series: Great Minds of Science. 2002, Enslow LB $20.95 (0-7660-1755-9). This absorbing biography that covers Copernicus's youth and succeeds in explaining necessary scientific concepts also includes activities that reinforce this understanding. (Rev: HBG 10/02; SLJ 6/02) [520.92]

6363 Goble, Todd. *Nicholas Copernicus and the Founding of Modern Astronomy* (6–8). 2003, Morgan Reynolds LB $23.95 (1-883846-99-4). The 16th-century Polish astronomer's life and work are placed in historical context, revealing the upsurge in scientific inquiry that took place during the Renaissance. (Rev: SLJ 10/03) [520]

CURIE, MARIE

6364 Birch, Beverley. *Marie Curie: Courageous Pioneer in the Study of Radioactivity* (5–7). Illus. Series: Giants of Science. 2000, Blackbirch LB $27.44 (1-56711-333-8). This biography of Marie Curie covers her youth, her struggles to get an education, her marriage, and her scientific career and accomplishments. (Rev: BL 1/1–15/01; HBG 3/01) [921]

6365 Pasachoff, Naomi. *Marie Curie and the Science of Radioactivity* (7–12). Illus. Series: Portraits in Science. 1996, Oxford $28.00 (0-19-509214-7). Combining details of her scientific research with information on her personal life, this is a fascinating biography of Madame Curie. (Rev: BL 9/1/96; SLJ 8/96) [921]

6366 Poynter, Margaret. *Marie Curie: Discoverer of Radium* (4–7). Illus. Series: Great Minds of Science. 1994, Enslow LB $20.95 (0-89490-477-9). The life and significance of this discoverer of radium are covered, with a chapter of suggested activities. (Rev: BL 1/1/95; SLJ 10/94) [921]

DAMADIAN, RAYMOND

6367 Kjelle, Marylou Morano. *Raymond Damadian and the Development of MRI* (5–7). Series: Unlocking the Secrets of Science. 2002, Mitchell Lane LB $17.95 (1-58415-141-2). This account focuses on Damadian's scientific accomplishments. (Rev: HBG 10/03; SLJ 1/03) [921]

DARWIN, CHARLES

6368 Anderson, Margaret J. *Charles Darwin: Naturalist* (4–7). Illus. Series: Great Minds of Science. 1994, Enslow LB $20.95 (0-89490-476-0). In addition to a biography of this controversial naturalist, there is a chapter on activities for the reader. (Rev: BL 1/1/95; SLJ 10/94) [921]

6369 Evans, J. Edward. *Charles Darwin: Revolutionary Biologist* (6–9). Series: Lerner Biographies. 1993, Lerner LB $23.93 (0-8225-4914-X). An account of Darwin's life that includes interesting anecdotes, such as the fact that he dropped out of medical school and that his father thought he would never amount to anything. (Rev: BL 12/1/93; SLJ 11/93) [921]

6370 Patent, Dorothy Hinshaw. *Charles Darwin: The Life of a Revolutionary Thinker* (7–12). Illus. 2001, Holiday $22.95 (0-8234-1494-9). An absorbing portrait of the man who came late to the career that made him famous, with information on his youth, education, family life, and interests in science and literature. (Rev: BL 8/01; HB 9–10/01; HBG 3/02; SLJ 8/01) [576.8]

6371 Senker, Cath. *Charles Darwin* (4–8). Illus. Series: Scientists Who Made History. 2002, Raintree Steck-Vaughn LB $27.12 (0-7398-4843-7). Darwin's life and contributions are presented in clear text and ample illustrations, with historical detail that places the information in context. (Rev: HBG 10/02; SLJ 9/02) [576.8092]

6372 Sis, Peter. *The Tree of Life: Charles Darwin* (4–7). Illus. 2003, Farrar $18.00 (0-374-45628-3). Highly illustrated, this imaginative and visual biography traces Darwin's life and development as a naturalist, with a focus on his voyages on the *Beagle*. (Rev: BL 10/15/03; HB 11–12/03*; SLJ 10/03*) [576.8]

6373 Sproule, Anna. *Charles Darwin: Visionary Behind the Theory of Evolution* (4–7). Illus. Series: Giants of Science. 2003, Gale $27.44 (1-56711-655-8). Darwin's life and accomplishments are presented in concise text. (Rev: SLJ 1/03) [921]

DE LA RENTA, OSCAR

6374 Carrillo, Louis. *Oscar de la Renta* (4–8). Illus. Series: Contemporary Hispanic Americans. 1995, Raintree Steck-Vaughn LB $28.80 (0-8172-3980-4). This account focuses on the professional life of the renowned Hispanic American fashion designer who was born in the Dominican Republic. (Rev: BL 3/15/96; SLJ 1/96) [921]

DE PASSE, SUZANNE

6375 Mussari, Mark. *Suzanne De Passe: Motown's Boss Lady* (5–8). Illus. Series: Wizards of Business. 1992, Garrett LB $17.26 (1-56074-026-4). The story of the woman who helped make Motown the great name in the music industry. (Rev: BL 6/15/92) [921]

DREW, CHARLES

6376 Mahone-Lonesome, Robyn. *Charles Drew* (6–10). Illus. 1990, Chelsea LB $21.95 (1-55546-581-1). The biography of the African American scientist who did pioneer work in blood preservation and the establishment of blood banks. (Rev: BL 2/15/90; BR 5–6/90) [921]

DYSON, ESTHER

6377 Jablonski, Carla. *Esther Dyson: Web Guru* (5–8). Series: Techies. 2002, Millbrook LB $23.90 (0-7613-2657-X). A leading light in the computer world, Dyson is the owner of EDventure Holdings, and is an active developer of emerging technologies and companies. (Rev: BL 4/1/02; HBG 10/02) [921]

6378 Morales, Leslie. *Esther Dyson: Internet Visionary* (5–8). Series: Internet Biographies. 2003, Enslow LB $18.95 (0-7660-1973-X). Dyson, a skillful businesswoman, has played an influential role in the development of the Internet as a tool suitable for everyday use. (Rev: HBG 10/03; SLJ 10/03) [338.4]

EARLE, SYLVIA

6379 Baker, Beth. *Sylvia Earle: Guardian of the Sea* (4–7). Illus. Series: Lerner Biographies. 2000, Lerner LB $30.35 (0-8225-4961-1). This is a thrilling biography of the famous underwater explorer and marine scientist who was one of the first humans to swim with whales. (Rev: BL 10/15/00; HBG 3/01; SLJ 11/00) [921]

EASTMAN, GEORGE

6380 Holmes, Burnham. *George Eastman* (7–12). Series: Pioneers in Change. 1992, Silver Burdett LB $13.95 (0-382-24170-3); paper $6.95 (0-382-24176-2). The story of the great inventor of photographic equipment, founder of Eastman Kodak Company, and renowned philanthropist. (Rev: BL 9/15/92) [921]

6381 Pflueger, Lynda. *George Eastman: Bringing Photography to the People* (7–10). Series: Historical American Biographies. 2002, Enslow LB $20.95 (0-7660-1617-X). Eastman's success in bringing photography to the masses is described, as are his philanthropy and personal life. (Rev: HBG 3/03; SLJ 11/02) [770]

EDISON, THOMAS ALVA

6382 Adair, Gene. *Thomas Alva Edison: Inventing the Electric Age* (7–10). Illus. 1996, Oxford $28.00 (0-19-508799-2). A biography of this astounding genius who not only invented the light bulb, but also was involved with improving the telegraph, inventing the phonograph, and developing early motion pictures. (Rev: BL 6/1–15/96; SLJ 6/96; VOYA 8/96) [921]

6383 Cramer, Carol, ed. *Thomas Edison* (7–12). Series: People Who Made History. 2001, Greenhaven LB $22.96 (0-7377-0428-4); paper $14.96 (0-7377-0427-6). An introductory overview of Edison's life and times is followed by a series of detailed chapters that explore various facets of his accomplishments and lasting contributions to society. (Rev: BL 4/15/01) [921]

6384 Dolan, Ellen M. *Thomas Alva Edison: Inventor* (5–8). Series: Historical American Biographies. 1998, Enslow LB $20.95 (0-7660-1014-7). Direct quotations, fact boxes, a chronology, and chapter notes make this an attractive life of the great inventor. (Rev: BL 8/98) [921]

6385 Sproule, Anna. *Thomas Edison: The World's Greatest Inventor* (5–7). Series: Giants of Science. 2000, Blackbirch paper $27.44 (1-56711-331-1). A prolific inventor, Edison not only worked on the electric light bulb but also the phonograph, the movie projector, and an early answering machine. (Rev: BL 1/1–15/01; HBG 3/01; SLJ 1/01) [921]

6386 Tagliaferro, Linda. *Thomas Edison: Inventor of the Age of Electricity* (6–9). 2003, Lerner LB $25.26 (0-8225-4689-2). Clear, lively language is used to give details of Edison's youth and trace his interest in science and invention throughout his life. (Rev: HBG 10/03; SLJ 7/03) [621.3]

EINSTEIN, ALBERT

6387 Bankston, John. *Albert Einstein and the Theory of Relativity* (5–8). Series: Unlocking the Secrets of Science. 2002, Mitchell Lane LB $17.95 (1-58415-137-4). Einstein's accomplishments and the many challenges he faced are explored in concise text with many black-and-white photographs. (Rev: SLJ 2/03) [921]

6388 Heinrichs, Ann. *Albert Einstein* (4–7). Series: Trailblazers of the Modern World. 2002, World Almanac LB $29.26 (0-8368-5069-6). The impact of Einstein's work on the scientists of the 20th century is highlighted in this biography describing his life and contributions. (Rev: SLJ 7/02) [530.092]

6389 MacDonald, Fiona. *Albert Einstein: The Genius Behind the Theory of Relativity* (5–7). Illus. Series: Giants of Science. 2000, Blackbirch LB $27.44 (1-56711-330-3). As well as his childhood, education, theories, personal life, and international awards, this biography of Albert Einstein assesses his lasting contributions to physics and mathematics. (Rev: BL 1/1–15/01; HBG 3/01; SLJ 1/01) [921]

6390 MacDonald, Fiona. *The World in the Time of Albert Einstein: 1879–1955* (6–9). Series: The World in the Time Of. 1998, Dillon LB $9.95 (0-382-39739-8). An overview of Einstein's life and accomplishments and an examination of the political, scientific, religious, and creative climate of the time. (Rev: SLJ 3/99) [921]

6391 MacLeod, Elizabeth. *Albert Einstein: A Life of Genius* (5–7). Illus. 2003, Kids Can $14.95 (1-55337-396-0); paper $6.95 (1-55337-397-9). Small photographs and illustrations accompany this attractive chronological introduction to the life of Einstein that focuses on the man rather than his theories. (Rev: BL 3/1/03; HBG 10/03; SLJ 5/03) [530]

6392 McPherson, Stephanie S. *Ordinary Genius: The Story of Albert Einstein* (4–7). Illus. 1995, Car-

olrhoda LB $30.35 (0-87614-788-0). Good histori-
cal background information is given on the life of
Einstein plus a clear explanation of his discoveries.
(Rev: BL 6/1–15/95; SLJ 9/95) [921]

6393 Pirotta, Saviour. *Albert Einstein* (6–8). Illus.
Series: Scientists Who Made History. 2002, Raintree Steck-Vaughn LB $18.98 (0-7398-4844-5). A
thorough account of Einstein's life and well-known
contributions, with clear scientific explanations and
discussion of his legacy. (Rev: HBG 10/02; SLJ
7/02) [530]

6394 Reef, Catherine. *Albert Einstein: Scientist of
the 20th Century* (4–7). Illus. Series: Taking Part.
1991, Macmillan LB $13.95 (0-87518-462-6). Ein-
stein gave the world a new way of looking at time,
space, gravity, and the nature of light. (Rev: BL
9/1/91; SLJ 12/91) [921]

6395 Severance, John B. *Einstein: Visionary Scientist* (7–12). Illus. 1999, Clarion $16.00 (0-395-
93100-2). This book covers Einstein's academic
theories as well as his private life and his life as a
celebrity. (Rev: BCCB 9/99; BL 9/1/99; HB 9–10/99;
HBG 4/00; SLJ 9/99) [921]

6396 Swisher, Clarice, ed. *Albert Einstein* (7–12).
Series: People Who Made History. 2002, Gale LB
$31.20 (0-7377-0892-1); paper $19.95 (0-7377-
0893-X). After an introductory overview chapter,
the remaining 19 essays explore different facets of
the life and accomplishments of this great scientist
and mathematician. (Rev: BL 4/1/02; SLJ 5/02)
[921]

ELLISON, LARRY

6397 Ehrenhaft, Daniel. *Larry Ellison: Sheer Nerve*
(5–8). Series: Techies. 2001, Millbrook LB $23.90
(0-7613-1962-X). The life story of one of the
world's richest men and co-founder of Oracle, the
world's leading supplier of software for information
management. (Rev: BL 4/1/02; HBG 3/02; SLJ
12/01) [921]

6398 Peters, Craig. *Larry Ellison: Database Genius
of Oracle* (5–8). Series: Internet Biographies. 2003,
Enslow LB $18.95 (0-7660-1974-8). A look at the
life and accomplishments of the cofounder of Oracle Corporation. (Rev: HBG 10/03; SLJ 10/03)
[338.7]

ERICSSON, JOHN

6399 Brophy, Ann. *John Ericsson: The Inventions of
War* (4–7). Illus. Series: The History of the Civil
War. 1990, Silver Burdett paper $7.95 (0-382-
24052-9). In clear text, this is the life story of the
Swedish engineer who designed and constructed the
Monitor. (Rev: BL 9/1/91) [921]

FANNING, SHAWN

6400 Mitten, Christopher. *Shawn Fanning: Napster
and the Music Revolution* (5–8). Series: Techies.
2002, Millbrook LB $23.90 (0-7613-2656-1). Using
many photographs and an interesting text, this is the
biography of the creator of Napster, a software
package for downloading music from computers.
(Rev: BL 4/1/02; HBG 10/02; SLJ 6/02) [921]

FARNSWORTH, PHILO

6401 McPherson, Stephanie S. *TV's Forgotten
Hero: The Story of Philo Farnsworth* (4–7). Illus.
1996, Carolrhoda LB $30.35 (1-57505-017-X). The
biography of the genius who invented electronic television when he was only 14. (Rev: BL 2/1/97; SLJ
2/97) [921]

FERMI, ENRICO

6402 Cooper, Dan. *Enrico Fermi: And the Revolutions of Modern Physics* (8–12). Series: Oxford Portraits in Science. 1999, Oxford $28.00 (0-19-
511762-X). A readable biography of the Italian
scientist, who immigrated to the United States in
1939 and worked on the first atomic bomb. Some of
the coverage of quantum and nuclear physics is
challenging. (Rev: SLJ 6/99) [921]

FLEMING, ALEXANDER

6403 Bankston, John. *Alexander Fleming and the
Story of Penicillin* (5–8). Series: Unlocking the
Secrets of Science. 2001, Mitchell Lane LB $17.95
(1-58415-106-4). This absorbing biography of the
Scottish Nobel Prize winner covers his personal life
as well as his scientific career. (Rev: HBG 3/02;
SLJ 1/02) [616.014092]

6404 Birch, Beverley. *Alexander Fleming: Pioneer
with Antibiotics* (4–7). Illus. Series: Giants of Science. 2003, Gale $27.44 (1-56711-656-6). Flem-
ing's life, education, research, and discovery of
penicillin are presented in concise text. (Rev: SLJ
1/03) [921]

6405 Gottfried, Ted. *Alexander Fleming: Discoverer
of Penicillin* (6–10). Illus. Series: Book Report
Biographies. 1997, Watts LB $22.00 (0-531-11370-
1). In 1928, bacteriologist Alexander Fleming discovered a blue mold growing on a culture dish in his
lab in London. This discovery lead to the development of the first antibiotic, penicillin, and a Nobel
Prize. (Rev: BL 12/1/97; HBG 3/98; SLJ 2/98)
[921]

6406 Hantula, Richard. *Alexander Fleming* (5–8).
Series: Trailblazers of the Modern World. 2003,
World Almanac LB $26.60 (0-8368-5083-1). An
absorbing introduction to the Nobel Prize winner's
life, achievements, and legacy, with quotations and

plenty of illustrations. (Rev: BL 6/1–15/03; SLJ 9/03) [921]

6407 Tocci, Salvatore. *Alexander Fleming: The Man Who Discovered Penicillin* (5–8). Series: Great Minds of Science. 2002, Enslow LB $20.95 (0-7660-1998-5). An absorbing account of Fleming's childhood and later life, with solid information on his contributions to medical science and his legacy. (Rev: HBG 10/02; SLJ 9/02) [921]

FORD, HENRY

6408 Burgan, Michael. *Henry Ford* (6–9). Illus. Series: Trailblazers of the Modern World. 2001, World Almanac Library LB $26.60 (0-8368-5070-X). The story of Ford's life and influence on our culture is told in narrative, illustrations, and excerpts from primary documents. (Rev: BL 5/1/02) [338.7]

6409 McCarthy, Pat. *Henry Ford: Building Cars for Everyone* (5–8). Series: Historical American Biographies. 2002, Enslow LB $20.95 (0-7660-1620-X). Ford is shown as an eccentric but successful father, engineer, and businessman, who made the automobile widely available but expected his workers to suffer difficult conditions. (Rev: HBG 3/03; SLJ 1/03) [338.76292092]

6410 Tilton, Rafael. *Henry Ford* (7–12). Series: The Importance Of. 2003, Gale LB $27.45 (1-56006-846-9). The designer of an efficient gasoline engine and developer of the assembly line is profiled in this biography that uses many quotations from original sources. (Rev: BL 6/1–15/03) [921]

FOSSEY, DIAN

6411 Gogerly, Liz. *Dian Fossey* (5–8). Illus. Series: Scientists Who Made History. 2003, Raintree Steck-Vaughn LB $27.12 (0-7368-5225-6). A riveting profile of the woman who became an expert on gorillas and the militant stance that may have led to her murder. (Rev: BL 3/1/03) [599.884]

6412 Nicholson, Lois P. *Dian Fossey: Primatologist* (7–12). Series: Women in Science. 2003, Chelsea LB $22.95 (0-7910-6907-9). An absorbing portrait of the woman who overcame obstacles to study and protect mountain gorillas in central Africa. (Rev: LMC 11–12/03; SLJ 7/03) [599.884]

FRANKLIN, ROSALIND

6413 Senker, Cath. *Rosalind Franklin* (5–8). Illus. Series: Scientists Who Made History. 2003, Raintree Steck-Vaughn $27.12 (0-7398-5226-4). An interesting biography of the woman who never gained credit for her contributions to the discovery of the structure of DNA. (Rev: BL 3/1/03; HBG 10/03; SLJ 4/03) [572.8]

FREUD, SIGMUND

6414 Reef, Catherine. *Sigmund Freud: Pioneer of the Mind* (7–12). Illus. 2001, Clarion $19.00 (0-618-01762-3). Reef looks at Freud's life and career, showing the ways in which his ideas evolved over time and the initial rejection of many of his revolutionary thoughts. (Rev: BL 7/01; HB 7–8/01*; HBG 10/01; SLJ 8/01; VOYA 10/01) [150.1]

FULTON, ROBERT

6415 Flammang, James M. *Robert Fulton: Inventor and Steamboat Builder* (5–8). Illus. Series: Historical American Biographies. 1999, Enslow LB $20.95 (0-7660-1141-0). Beginning with Fulton's 1807 demonstration of his steamboat, this biography moves back and forth in time to trace the complete career of this man who changed America's transportation history. (Rev: BL 11/1/99; HBG 3/00) [921]

6416 Pierce, Morris A. *Robert Fulton and the Development of the Steamboat* (4–8). Series: Library of American Lives and Times. 2003, Rosen LB $31.95 (0-8239-5737-3). The inventor of the steamboat was a man of determination and wide interests who also worked on naval weapons. (Rev: BL 6/1–15/03; SLJ 4/03) [921]

GALDIKAS, BIRUTE

6417 Gallardo, Evelyn. *Among the Orangutans: The Birute Galdikas Story* (4–7). Illus. Series: Great Naturalists. 1993, Chronicle paper $9.95 (0-8118-0408-9). The story of this important primate specialist who began studying orangutans in 1971. (Rev: BL 4/1/93; SLJ 6/93) [921]

GALILEO

6418 Boerst, William J. *Galileo Galilei and the Science of Motion* (6–10). Illus. Series: Great Scientists. 2003, Morgan Reynolds LB $23.95 (1-931798-00-1). Galileo's early insistence on adherence to scientific verification is emphasized in this detailed yet accessible biography that includes color period reproductions and a timeline. (Rev: BL 11/1/03; SLJ 12/03) [520.92]

6419 Hightower, Paul. *Galileo: Astronomer and Physicist* (4–7). Illus. Series: Great Minds of Science. 1997, Enslow LB $20.95 (0-89490-787-5). This biography not only includes material on the life and accomplishments of this courageous scientist but also contains several activities that give an understanding of his work. (Rev: BL 6/1–15/97) [921]

6420 MacLachlan, James. *Galileo Galilei: First Physicist* (6–10). Series: Oxford Portraits in Science. 1997, Oxford $28.00 (0-19-509342-9). A fine portrait of this mathematician/physicist and his accomplishments, and a good introduction to the Renaissance world. (Rev: SLJ 3/98) [921]

6421 Mason, Paul. *Galileo* (6–8). Illus. Series: Groundbreakers. 2001, Heinemann LB $25.54 (1-58810-052-9). Galileo's life, times, and achievements are covered here, with discussion of his failings as well as his attributes. (Rev: HBG 10/01; SLJ 7/01) [520]

6422 Swisher, Clarice, ed. *Galileo* (7–12). Series: People Who Made History. 2001, Greenhaven LB $31.20 (0-7377-0671-6); paper $19.95 (0-7377-0670-8). This series of essays explore the life of Galileo, his problems with the Inquisition, and his many contributions to mathematics, astronomy, and physics. (Rev: BL 9/15/01) [921]

6423 White, Michael. *Galileo Galilei: Inventor, Astronomer, and Rebel* (5–8). Series: Giants of Science. 1999, Blackbirch LB $27.44 (1-56711-325-7). The dramatic story of Galileo's life, his persecutions, accomplishments, and lasting contributions to science. (Rev: HBG 10/00; SLJ 2/00) [921]

GATES, BILL

6424 Boyd, Aaron. *Smart Money: The Story of Bill Gates* (6–10). 1995, Morgan Reynolds LB $21.95 (1-883846-09-9). A biography of Microsoft's billionaire mogul Bill Gates. (Rev: BL 4/1/95; SLJ 4/95; VOYA 2/96) [921]

6425 Dickinson, Joan D. *Bill Gates: Billionaire Computer Genius* (5–8). Series: People to Know. 1997, Enslow LB $20.95 (0-89490-824-3). This biography of the computer genius traces his life from his birth in 1955, showing how his personal drive made him into the richest man in America. (Rev: BL 10/15/97; BR 1–2/98; HBG 3/98; SLJ 12/97; VOYA 2/98) [921]

6426 Lee, Lauren. *Bill Gates* (6–9). Series: Trailblazers of the Modern World. 2002, World Almanac Library LB $26.60 (0-8368-5077-7); paper $10.95 (0-8368-5237-0). The story of the wealthy computer genius who founded Microsoft. (Rev: BL 12/15/02) [921]

6427 Peters, Craig. *Bill Gates* (5–8). Illus. Series: Internet Biographies. 2003, Enslow LB $18.95 (0-7660-1969-1). A reader-friendly biography of the creator of Microsoft, with information on his youth as well as his successful later life. (Rev: BL 3/15/03; HBG 10/03) [338.7]

6428 Woog, Adam. *Bill Gates* (4–7). Illus. Series: Famous People. 2003, Gale $23.70 (0-7377-1400-X). Woog covers Gates's childhood, education, interest in computers, and career, with photographs. (Rev: BL 6/1 15/03) [338.7]

6429 Woog, Adam. *Bill Gates* (7–9). Illus. 1998, Lucent LB $27.45 (1-56006-256-8). A biography of the controversial cofounder and CEO of Microsoft,

who has become not only the most important person in the computer industry, but also the richest man in America. (Rev: SLJ 4/99) [921]

GETTY, JOHN PAUL

6430 Glassman, Bruce S. *John Paul Getty: Billionaire Oilman* (7–10). Illus. Series: Giants of American Industry. 2001, Blackbirch LB $21.95 (1-56711-513-6). Glassman covers Getty's life from childhood, describing how he became a millionaire in his 20s and later was known for his philanthropy and art collection. (Rev: BL 10/15/01; HBG 3/02) [332]

GODDARD, ROBERT

6431 Bankston, John. *Robert Goddard and the Liquid Rocket Engine* (4–7). Series: Unlocking the Secrets of Science. 2001, Mitchell Lane LB $17.95 (1-58415-107-2). Bankston combines an introduction to Goddard's commitment to rocketry and his difficulty finding funding with an understandable explanation of the scientific challenges. (Rev: HBG 3/02; SLJ 2/02) [621.43]

6432 Streissguth, Thomas. *Rocket Man: The Story of Robert Goddard* (5–7). Illus. Series: Trailblazers. 1995, Carolrhoda LB $30.35 (0-87614-863-1). A history of rocketry, with emphasis on the life and accomplishments of Goddard. (Rev: BL 10/15/95; SLJ 9/95) [921]

GOODALL, JANE

6433 January, Brendan. *Jane Goodall: Animal Behaviorist and Writer* (4–7). Series: Ferguson's Career Biographies. 2001, Ferguson LB $16.95 (0-89434-370-X). This easily read biography will appeal in particular to reluctant readers and students seeking quick information for a report. (Rev: SLJ 9/01) [921]

6434 Kozleski, Lisa. *Jane Goodall: Primatologist/Naturalist* (7–12). Series: Women in Science. 2003, Chelsea LB $22.95 (0-7910-6905-2). An absorbing biography that discusses the primatologist's personal life as well as her dedicated work with chimpanzees in Tanzania. (Rev: LMC 11–12/03; SLJ 7/03) [590]

6435 Meachum, Virginia. *Jane Goodall: Protector of Chimpanzees* (6–10). Illus. Series: People to Know. 1997, Enslow LB $20.95 (0-89490-827-8). The story of the great naturalist who fulfilled her childhood dream and made groundbreaking observations of chimpanzee behavior. (Rev: BL 1/1–15/98; HBG 3/98) [921]

6436 Pratt, Paula B. *Jane Goodall* (4–8). Illus. Series: The Importance Of. 1997, Lucent LB $27.45 (1-56006-082-4). The story of the great naturalist who studied and protected the primates of Africa. (Rev: BL 1/1–15/97; BR 9–10/97; SLJ 2/97) [921]

GRAHAM, KATHARINE

6437 Asirvatham, Sandy. *Katharine Graham* (7–10). Illus. Series: Women of Achievement. 2001, Chelsea LB $21.95 (0-7910-6310-0); paper $9.95 (0-7910-6311-9). A concise and readable account of Graham's life and her success in taking over the *Washington Post* after her husband's suicide. (Rev: BL 3/1/02; HBG 10/02; SLJ 6/02) [070.5]

6438 Whitelaw, Nancy. *Let's Go! Let's Publish! Katharine Graham and the Washington Post* (7–10). 1998, Morgan Reynolds LB $21.95 (1-883846-37-4). The life story of the famous female editor of the *Washington Post,* who lead it through such turbulent times as the Pentagon Papers and Watergate. (Rev: BL 1/1–15/99; HBG 3/99; SLJ 5/99; VOYA 6/00) [921]

GROVE, ANDREW

6439 Byman, Jeremy. *Andrew Grove and the Intel Corporation* (6–12). 1999, Morgan Reynolds LB $21.95 (1-883846-38-2). A biography of the computer giant from his hiding with his mother from the Nazis in Budapest, to the story of Intel, the corporation that he cofounded and that changed computer history. (Rev: BL 3/15/99; SLJ 5/99) [338.7]

GUTENBERG, JOHANN

6440 Pollard, Michael. *Johann Gutenberg: Master of Modern Printing* (5–7). Series: Giants of Science. 2001, Blackbirch LB $27.44 (1-56711-335-4). Good use of illustrations and an interesting text are highlights of this life of the German printer who first used movable type. (Rev: BL 8/1/01; HBG 3/02) [921]

HARRIOT, THOMAS

6441 Staiger, Ralph C. *Thomas Harriot: Science Pioneer* (6–10). 1998, Clarion $19.00 (0-395-67296-1). The biography of the Elizabethan scientist who made contributions to navigation, optics, and astronomy and who accompanied Sir Walter Raleigh to Roanoke Island in 1585, where he studied the flora, fauna, and the native people. (Rev: BL 12/1/98; BR 5–6/99; HBG 3/99; SLJ 5/99; VOYA 2/99) [921]

HARVEY, WILLIAM

6442 Yount, Lisa. *William Harvey: Discoverer of How Blood Circulates* (4–8). Illus. Series: Great Minds of Science. 1994, Enslow LB $20.95 (0-89490-481-7). A biography of the 17th-century scientist that describes early theories about the blood

system and the importance of Harvey's discoveries. (Rev: SLJ 2/95) [921]

HERRIOT, JAMES

6443 Herriot, James. *All Creatures Great and Small* (8–12). 1972, Bantam paper $7.50 (0-553-26812-0). The first volume of Herriot's memories of being a veterinarian in Yorkshire, England, during the 1930s. Continued in *All Things Bright and Beautiful* (1974), *All Things Wise and Wonderful* (1977), and *The Lord God Made Them All* (1981). [921]

HEWLETT, WILLIAM

6444 Tracy, Kathleen. *William Hewlett: Pioneer of the Computer Age* (5–7). Series: Unlocking the Secrets of Science. 2002, Mitchell Lane LB $17.95 (1-58415-142-0). This accessible account focuses on Hewlett's scientific accomplishments and career in business. (Rev: SLJ 1/03) [921]

HUBBLE, EDWIN

6445 Datnow, Claire. *Edwin Hubble: Discoverer of Galaxies* (4–8). Illus. Series: Great Minds of Science. 1997, Enslow LB $20.95 (0-89490-934-7). A portrait of the great astronomer, noted for his amazing scientific abilities and quirky pretentions. (Rev: BL 12/1/97; HBG 3/98; SLJ 3/98; VOYA 12/97) [921]

6446 MacDonald, Fiona. *Edwin Hubble* (6–8). Illus. Series: Groundbreakers. 2001, Heinemann LB $25.54 (1-58810-054-5). MacDonald takes a frank look at Hubble's life, times, and achievements, discussing his difficult character as well as his important contributions. (Rev: SLJ 7/01) [520]

JEMISON, MAE

6447 Jemison, Mae. *Find Where the Wind Goes* (7–12). 2001, Scholastic $16.95 (0-439-13195-2). The fascinating autobiography of the first African American woman in space. (Rev: BL 11/1/01; HBG 10/01; SLJ 4/01; VOYA 8/01) [629.45]

JOBS, STEVE

6448 Brashares, Ann. *Steve Jobs: Thinks Different* (5–8). Series: Techies. 2001, Twenty-First Century LB $23.90 (0-7613-1959-X). The life story of the amazing creator of Apple computers and his phenomenal success as a businessman and entrepreneur. (Rev: BL 3/15/01; HBG 10/01) [921]

6449 Wilson, Suzan. *Steve Jobs: Wizard of Apple Computer* (5–8). Series: People to Know. 2001, Enslow LB $20.95 (0-7660-1536-X). An engrossing biography that will attract computer-lovers, in which Jobs's early passion for electronics is shown as paving the way for his success — and failures —

at Apple and other companies. (Rev: HBG 3/02; SLJ 3/02) [921]

JONES, CAROLINE

6450 Fleming, Robert. *The Success of Caroline Jones Advertising, Inc.* (7–10). Illus. Series: Success. 1996, Walker LB $16.85 (0-8027-8354-6). A biography of the amazing career of Caroline Jones and her rapid rise in the world of advertising. (Rev: BL 1/1–15/96; SLJ 4/96) [921]

KARAN, DONNA

6451 Tippins, Sherill. *Donna Karan: Designing an American Dream* (5–8). Illus. Series: Wizards of Business. 1992, Garrett LB $17.26 (1-56074-019-1). Along with the life story of one of America's top fashion designers is advice for those who wish to enter the field. (Rev: BL 6/15/92) [921]

KEPLER, JOHANNES

6452 Boerst, William J. *Johannes Kepler: Discovering the Laws of Celestial Motion* (6–9). Illus. Series: Renaissance Scientists. 2003, Morgan Reynolds LB $21.95 (1-883846-98-6). Astronomer and mathematician Kepler's life and achievements are placed in historical context, with details of the religious tensions of the time and the uncertainty of a scientific career. (Rev: BL 6/1–15/03; HBG 10/03; SLJ 8/03) [520]

6453 Voelkel, James R. *Johannes Kepler and the New Astronomy* (6–9). Illus. 1999, Oxford $28.00 (0-19-511680-1). The story of the tumultuous life of this astronomer and his many accomplishments, including discovering the three laws of planetary motion. (Rev: BL 11/1/99; HBG 9/00; SLJ 2/00) [921]

KOLFF, WILLEM

6454 Tracy, Kathleen. *Willem Kolff and the Invention of the Dialysis Machine* (5–8). Illus. Series: Unlocking the Secrets of Science. 2002, Mitchell Lane LB $17.95 (1-58415-135-8). Kolff invented the dialysis machine in 1942 in the Nazi-occupied Netherlands. (Rev: HBG 3/03; SLJ 12/02) [617.461059092]

LATIMER, LEWIS

6455 Norman, Winifred Latimer, and Lily Patterson. *Lewis Latimer* (7–10). Series: Black Americans of Achievement. 1993, Chelsea LB $21.95 (0-7910-1977-2). Follows Lattimer's career from Civil War veteran to executive at the Edison Company, where he helped Thomas Edison improve the light bulb and supervised the installation of electrical systems in several cities. (Rev: BL 11/15/93) [921]

LAVOISIER, ANTOINE

6456 Yount, Lisa. *Antoine Lavoisier: Founder of Modern Chemistry* (4–7). Illus. Series: Great Minds of Science. 1997, Enslow LB $20.95 (0-89490-785-9). In addition to providing an assessment of the life and works of Lavoisier, called the Father of Chemistry, this book includes several hands-on activities that depend on an understanding of his work. (Rev: BL 6/1–15/97) [921]

LEAKEY, LOUIS AND MARY

6457 Poynter, Margaret. *The Leakeys: Uncovering the Origins of Humankind* (5–8). Illus. Series: Great Minds of Science. 1997, Enslow LB $20.95 (0-89490-788-3). The story of the famous husband-and-wife team of scientists, Louis and Mary Leakey, and how they expanded our knowledge of evolution. (Rev: BL 12/1/97; HBG 3/98; SLJ 12/97) [921]

LEEUWENHOEK, ANTONI VAN

6458 Yount, Lisa. *Antoni van Leeuwenhoek: First to See Microscopic Life* (4–8). Series: Great Minds of Science. 1996, Enslow LB $20.95 (0-89490-680-1). A brief biography of the Dutch maker of microscopes, who was also the first to examine closely bacteria and blood cells. (Rev: BL 10/15/96; SLJ 12/96) [921]

LEOPOLD, ALDO

6459 Lorbiecki, Marybeth. *Of Things Natural, Wild, and Free: A Story About Aldo Leopold* (4–7). Illus. 1993, Carolrhoda LB $25.55 (0-87614-797-X). The story of a man who was a great hunter until he realized the importance of the balance in nature, and then turned a tract of farmland into a nature refuge. (Rev: BL 11/1/93; SLJ 11/93) [921]

LINNAEUS, CARL

6460 Anderson, Margaret J. *Carl Linnaeus: Father of Classification* (4–8). Series: Great Minds of Science. 1997, Enslow LB $20.95 (0-89490-786-7). This biography discusses the personal life of Linnaeus, including his explorations in Lapland, but the focus is on the development of his important biological classification system. (Rev: BL 12/1/97; HBG 3/98; SLJ 9/97) [921]

LOVELACE, ADA KING

6461 Wade, Mary D. *Ada Byron Lovelace: The Lady and the Computer* (5–8). Illus. 1995, Silver Burdett LB $13.95 (0-87518-598-3); paper $7.95 (0-382-24717-5). A biography of the poet Byron's amazing daughter, who was a distinguished mathematician and pioneer computer programmer. (Rev: BL 5/1/95) [921]

MCCLINTOCK, BARBARA

6462 Cullen, J. Heather. *Barbara McClintock: Geneticist* (6–12). Illus. Series: Women in Science. 2003, Chelsea LB $22.95 (0-7910-7248-7). Cullen explores the life and achievements of McClintock, who won a Nobel Prize in 1983 for research in genetics that she conducted decades earlier. (Rev: HBG 10/03; SLJ 10/03) [576.5]

6463 Fine, Edith Hope. *Barbara McClintock: Nobel Prize Geneticist* (6–8). Series: People to Know. 1998, Enslow LB $20.95 (0-89490-983-5). This biography of the famous female geneticist whose work on maize earned her a Nobel Prize gives interesting details on her youth and the many honors she received later in life. (Rev: BL 1/1–15/99; HBG 3/99; SLJ 3/99) [921]

6464 Tracy, Kathleen. *Barbara McClintock: Pioneering Geneticist* (4–7). Series: Unlocking the Secrets of Science. 2001, Mitchell Lane LB $17.95 (1-58415-111-0). An absorbing look at the life and research of this Nobel Prize winner. (Rev: HBG 3/02; SLJ 2/02) [921]

MALONE, ANNIE TURNBO

6465 Wilkerson, J. L. *Story of Pride, Power and Uplift: Annie T. Malone* (4–8). Illus. 2003, Acorn $9.95 (0-9664470-8-5). Malone, a child of slaves, created beauty products for African American women at the turn of the 20th century and became a wealthy woman and philanthropist. (Rev: BL 3/1/03; SLJ 7/03) [646.7]

MARCONI, GUGLIELMO

6466 Birch, Beverley. *Guglielmo Marconi: Radio Pioneer* (5–8). Series: Giants of Science. 2001, Gale LB $27.44 (1-56711-337-0). This account of Marconi and his accomplishments also looks at how his inventions have evolved. (Rev: HBG 3/02; SLJ 2/02) [921]

MAYER, MARIA GOEPPERT

6467 Ferry, Joseph P. *Maria Goeppert Mayer: Physicist* (6–12). Series: Women in Science. 2003, Chelsea LB $22.95 (0-7910-7247-9). Ferry explores the life and achievements of Mayer, who won a Nobel Prize in 1963 for research into the atomic nucleus. (Rev: HBG 10/03; SLJ 10/03) [530]

MEAD, MARGARET

6468 Mark, Joan. *Margaret Mead: Coming of Age in America* (6–10). Ed. by Owen Gingerich. Illus. Series: Oxford Portraits in Science. 1999, Oxford $28.00 (0-19-511679-8). An introduction to the life and work of the pioneering anthropologist and her research with people of the South Seas, particularly in Samoa. (Rev: BL 4/1/99; SLJ 3/99) [921]

6469 Pollard, Michael. *Margaret Mead: Bringing World Cultures Together* (5–8). Series: Giants of Science. 1999, Blackbirch LB $27.44 (1-56711-327-3). This biography stresses the contribution Margaret Mead made to anthropology through her work in the South Pacific. (Rev: HBG 10/00; SLJ 2/00) [921]

6470 Ziesk, Edra. *Margaret Mead* (5–8). Illus. Series: American Women of Achievement. 1990, Chelsea LB $19.95 (1-55546-667-2). A useful volume covering the career and personal life of this unconventional anthropologist. (Rev: BL 2/15/90; SLJ 9/90; VOYA 8/90) [921]

MEITNER, LISE

6471 Barron, Rachel Stiffler. *Lise Meitner: Discoverer of Nuclear Fission* (7–12). Series: Great Scientists. 2000, Morgan Reynolds LB $21.95 (1-883846-52-8). The story of the Jewish scientist who fled Nazi Germany to the U.S., where her findings concerning nuclear fission led to the first atomic bomb. (Rev: BL 3/15/00; HBG 4/00; SLJ 6/00) [921]

6472 Hamilton, Janet. *Lise Meitner: Pioneer of Nuclear Fission* (6–10). Illus. Series: Great Minds of Science. 2002, Enslow LB $20.95 (0-7660-1756-7). This readable biography of the nuclear physicist who fled Nazi Germany before the outbreak of World War II, and who subsequently refused to work on developing nuclear weapons, is notable for placing her life and work in historical context. (Rev: HBG 10/02; SLJ 10/02) [539]

MENDEL, GREGOR

6473 Edelson, Edward. *Gregor Mendel: And the Roots of Genetics* (7–10). Series: Oxford Portraits in Science. 1999, Oxford $28.00 (0-19-512226-7). This work describes Mendel's life and his work on plant heredity and the study of genetics in the context of the social, scientific,and political events of his time. (Rev: SLJ 7/99) [921]

6474 Klare, Roger. *Gregor Mendel: Father of Genetics* (5–7). Illus. Series: Great Minds of Science. 1997, Enslow LB $20.95 (0-89490-789-1). The science of genetics is introduced through the life of Mendel and his experimentation with peas. (Rev: BL 12/1/97; HBG 3/98; SLJ 12/97; VOYA 12/97) [921]

MITCHELL, MARIA

6475 Gormley, Beatrice. *Maria Mitchell: The Soul of an Astronomer* (6–9). 1995, Eerdmans paper

$8.00 (0-8028-5099-5). An authentic, interesting biography of the 19th-century female astronomer, with details on her accomplishments and an accompanying 16-page centerfold of photographs. (Rev: BL 9/1/95; BR 9–10/96; SLJ 1/96) [921]

MORGAN, J. P.

6476 Byman, Jeremy. *J. P. Morgan: Banker to a Growing Nation* (6–10). Series: American Business Leaders. 2001, Morgan Reynolds LB $20.95 (1-883846-60-9). An easily read introduction to Morgan's importance that places his contributions in political and social context. (Rev: BR 9–10/01; HBG 10/01; SLJ 7/01) [970]

MOSS, CYNTHIA

6477 Pringle, Laurence. *Elephant Woman: Cynthia Moss Explores the World of Elephants* (4–8). 1997, Simon & Schuster $16.00 (0-689-80142-4). A biography of the conservationist who studied elephants for 25 years at the Amboseli National Park in Kenya. The book contains information on how elephants live, why they are endangered, and how they can be saved, and conveys a sense of how researchers live and conduct their research. (Rev: BCCB 3/98; BL 11/15/97; HBG 3/98; SLJ 12/97*) [921]

MUIR, JOHN

6478 Ito, Tom. *The Importance of John Muir* (4–8). Illus. Series: The Importance Of. 1996, Lucent LB $27.45 (1-56006-054-9). A short biography of the great naturalist and traveler who pioneered the U.S. conservation movement. (Rev: BL 5/15/96) [921]

6479 Wadsworth, Ginger. *John Muir: Wilderness Protector* (6–12). 1992, Lerner LB $30.35 (0-8225-4912-3). Original photographs and Muir's letters, journals, and writings provide an overview of the conservationist's personal life, achievements, and contributions to the environmental movement. (Rev: BL 8/92) [921]

MURRAY, JOSEPH E.

6480 Mattern, Joanne. *Joseph E. Murray and the Story of the First Human Kidney Transplant* (5–8). Illus. Series: Unlocking the Secrets of Science. 2002, Mitchell Lane LB $17.95 (1-58415-136-6). A look at the work of the surgeon who performed the first successful kidney transplant. (Rev: SLJ 12/02; VOYA 6/03) [617.95092]

NEWTON, ISAAC

6481 Allan, Tony. *Isaac Newton* (6–8). Illus. Series: Groundbreakers. 2001, Heinemann LB $25.54 (1-58810-053-7). MacDonald takes a frank look at

Newton's life, times, and achievements, discussing his unpopularity as a teacher and his interest in alchemy. (Rev: SLJ 7/01) [530]

6482 Anderson, Margaret J. *Isaac Newton: The Greatest Scientist of All Time* (4–7). Illus. Series: Great Minds of Science. 1996, Enslow LB $20.95 (0-89490-681-X). The life of the great English mathematician and physicist who formulated the laws of motion and gravity. (Rev: BL 10/15/96; SLJ 12/96) [921]

6483 Christianson, Gale E. *Isaac Newton and the Scientific Revolution* (8–12). Illus. Series: Oxford Portraits in Science. 1996, Oxford $28.00 (0-19-509224-4). A challenging biography which gives the scientist's life history plus detailed explanations on theories of gravity, relativity, and calculus. (Rev: BL 12/1/96; SLJ 1/97; VOYA 2/97) [530]

6484 Mason, Paul. *Isaac Newton* (4–8). Illus. Series: Scientists Who Made History. 2002, Raintree Steck-Vaughn LB $27.12 (0-7398-4845-3). Newton's life and contributions are presented in clear text and ample illustrations, with historical detail that places the information in context. (Rev: HBG 10/02; SLJ 9/02) [530.092]

6485 White, Michael. *Isaac Newton: Discovering Laws That Govern the Universe* (5–8). Series: Giants of Science. 1999, Blackbirch LB $27.44 (1-56711-326-5). A visually appealing biography of the great English mathematician who was the first scientist to be knighted. (Rev: HBG 10/00; SLJ 2/00) [921]

OPPENHEIMER, ROBERT

6486 Rummel, Jack. *Robert Oppenheimer: Dark Prince* (7–12). 1992, Facts on File LB $19.95 (0-8160-2598-3). A straightforward biography of the physicist credited with developing the atomic bomb. (Rev: BL 9/15/92; SLJ 9/92) [921]

PASTEUR, LOUIS

6487 Birch, Beverley. *Louis Pasteur: Father of Modern Medicine* (5–7). Series: Giants of Science. 2001, Blackbirch LB $27.44 (1-56711-336-2). A readable, well-organized biography of the French chemist whose varied accomplishments include discovery of the process known now as pasteurization. (Rev: BL 8/1/01; HBG 3/02) [921]

6488 Gogerly, Liz. *Louis Pasteur* (6–8). Illus. Series: Scientists Who Made History. 2002, Raintree Steck-Vaughn LB $18.98 (0-7398-4846-1). Information on Pasteur's youth and his early fascination with science is included in this readable account of his life and accomplishments. (Rev: HBG 10/02; SLJ 7/02) [579]

6489 Robbins, Louise E. *Louis Pasteur and the Hidden World of Microbes* (8–12). Series: Oxford Portraits in Science. 2001, Oxford $24.00 (0-19-512227-5). A look at the life of the famous scientist, with glimpses of his personality as well as his research and discoveries. (Rev: BL 12/1/01; HBG 3/02; SLJ 12/01) [579]

6490 Smith, Linda W. *Louis Pasteur: Disease Fighter* (4–8). Illus. Series: Great Minds of Science. 1997, Enslow LB $20.95 (0-89490-790-5). The story of the "father of microbiology," who discovered pasteurization while working on a wine problem for Napoleon. (Rev: BL 12/1/97; HBG 3/98; SLJ 12/97) [921]

PLOTKIN, MARK

6491 Pascoe, Elaine, adapt. *Mysteries of the Rain Forest: 20th Century Medicine Man* (4–8). Series: The New Explorers. 1997, Blackbirch LB $18.95 (1-56711-229-3). An exploration of the life and discoveries of Mark Plotkin, an ethnobotanist fascinated by the plants and people of the Amazon. (Rev: HBG 3/98; SLJ 2/98) [921]

PULITZER, JOSEPH

6492 Whitelaw, Nancy. *Joseph Pulitzer and the New York World* (7–10). Illus. Series: Makers of the Media. 1999, Morgan Reynolds LB $21.95 (1-883846-44-7). The life story of the founder of "tabloid journalism," who revolutionized the newspaper industry by combining sensational news, visuals, and reports on political corruption to both attract readers and encourage social change, and after whom the Pulitzer Prize is named. (Rev: BL 6/1–15/99; SLJ 9/99) [921]

6493 Zannos, Susan. *Joseph Pulitzer and the Story Behind the Pulitzer Prize* (4–8). Illus. Series: Great Achievement Awards. 2003, Mitchell Lane LB $19.95 (1-58415-179-X). Pulitzer's difficulty personality and passion for journalism are highlighted in this account of his establishment of the well-known awards. (Rev: BL 10/15/03; SLJ 9/03) [070.9]

ROBERTS, EDWARD

6494 Zannos, Susan. *Edward Roberts and the Story of the Personal Computer* (5–7). Series: Unlocking the Secrets of Science. 2002, Mitchell Lane LB $17.95 (1-58415-118-8). This accessible account focuses on Roberts's accomplishments as an electronic engineer. (Rev: HBG 10/03; SLJ 1/03) [921]

ROCKEFELLER, JOHN D.

6495 Laughlin, Rosemary. *John D. Rockefeller: Oil Baron and Philanthropist* (5–8). Illus. Series: American Business Leaders. 2001, Morgan Reynolds LB $21.95 (1-883846-59-5). A biography of the determined and skilled businessman who made Standard Oil the dominant company in the oil industry and who was later noted for his philanthropy. (Rev: BL 3/1/01; HBG 10/01; SLJ 7/01) [921]

SAGAN, CARL

6496 Butts, Ellen R., and Joyce R. Schwarts. *Carl Sagan* (5–8). Series: A&E Biography. 2000, Lerner LB $25.26 (0-8225-4986-7). The story of the great astronomer who interested millions in the study of the stars and the question of whether there is life elsewhere in our universe. (Rev: BL 10/15/00; HBG 3/01; SLJ 10/00) [921]

6497 Byman, Jeremy. *Carl Sagan: In Contact with the Cosmos* (5–8). Illus. Series: Great Scientists. 2000, Morgan Reynolds LB $21.95 (1-883846-55-2). An informative biography of the scientist who popularized astronomy while maintaining a highly productive scholarly life. (Rev: BL 11/1/00; HBG 10/00; SLJ 8/00) [921]

SALK, JONAS

6498 McPherson, Stephanie Sammartino. *Jonas Salk: Conquering Polio* (5–8). Series: Lerner Biographies. 2001, Lerner LB $30.35 (0-8225-4964-6). An absorbing account of Salk's life and contributions to medicine that discusses his confrontation with Sabin and the early failures of Salk's vaccine. (Rev: HBG 3/02; SLJ 4/02) [921]

6499 Sherrow, Victoria. *Jonas Salk* (7–12). 1993, Facts on File $25.00 (0-8160-2805-2). Begins with a history of polio, moves on to Salk's education, research, and development of the polio vaccine, and ends with the Salk Institute's work on cancer and AIDS. (Rev: BL 9/15/93) [921]

6500 Tocci, Salvatore. *Jonas Salk: Creator of the Polio Vaccine* (4–7). Illus. Series: Great Minds of Science. 2003, Enslow LB $20.95 (0-7660-2097-5). This book covers the life of the scientist and the importance and impact of the vaccine he developed. (Rev: BL 5/15/03; HBG 10/03) [610]

STEWART, MARTHA

6501 Meachum, Virginia. *Martha Stewart: Successful Businesswoman* (6–10). Series: People to Know. 1998, Enslow LB $20.95 (0-89490-984-3). A well-documented biography of Martha Kostyra Stewart, the human dynamo who has achieved notoriety as a model, master chef, expert homemaker, entertainer, author, and TV celebrity. (Rev: HBG 3/99; SLJ 1/99) [921]

STRAUSS, LEVI

6502 Van Steenwyk, Elizabeth. *Levi Strauss: The Blue Jeans Man* (5–9). 1988, Walker LB $14.85 (0-8027-6796-6). A biography of the Bavarian immigrant, Levi Strauss, who became the blue jeans king of the western world. (Rev: BL 6/15/88; SLJ 10/88; VOYA 8/88) [921]

TELLER, EDWARD

6503 Bankston, John. *Edward Teller and the Development of the Hydrogen Bomb* (5–8). Series: Unlocking the Secrets of Science. 2001, Mitchell Lane LB $17.95 (1-58415-108-0). The life of the scientist born in Hungary who played a key role in the development of the H-bomb. (Rev: HBG 3/02; SLJ 1/02) [539.7092]

TESLA, NIKOLA

6504 Dommermuth-Costa, Carol. *Nikola Tesla: A Spark of Genius* (5–9). 1994, Lerner LB $30.35 (0-8225-4920-4). Traces the life and career of this pioneer in the field of electricity. (Rev: BL 12/15/94; SLJ 2/95) [921]

TORVALDS, LINUS

6505 Brashares, Ann. *Linus Torvalds: Software Rebel* (5–8). Series: Techies. 2001, Millbrook LB $23.90 (0-7613-1960-3). The story of the computer genius who created the Linux operating system. (Rev: BL 4/1/02; HBG 3/02; SLJ 12/01) [921]

TURNER, TED

6506 Byman, Jeremy. *Ted Turner: Cable Television Tycoon* (7–10). Illus. 1998, Morgan Reynolds LB $21.95 (1-883846-25-0). Known as the "mouth of the south," Ted Turner, a born rebel, introduced CNN in 1980 and hasn't stopped expanding his cable empire since. This is a biography of this media mogul. (Rev: BL 4/1/98; BR 1–2/99; HBG 9/98; SLJ 8/98) [921]

WAKSMAN, SELMAN

6507 Gordon, Karen. *Selman Waksman and the Discovery of Streptomycin* (5–7). Series: Unlocking the Secrets of Science. 2002, Mitchell Lane LB $17.95 (1-58415-138-2). An accessible account of Waksman's life and scientific research. (Rev: HBG 10/03; SLJ 1/03) [921]

WALKER, MADAM C. J.

6508 Bundles, A'Lelia Perry. *Madam C. J. Walker* (5–10). Series: Black Americans of Achievement. 1993, Chelsea LB $21.95 (1-55546-615-X); paper $9.95 (0-7910-0251-9). This biography, written by Walker's great great-granddaughter, tells of the developer of a line of hair care products whose entrepreneurial ability made her into the "foremost colored businesswoman in America." (Rev: BL 3/1/94) [921]

6509 Yannuzzi, Della A. *Madam C. J. Walker: Self-Made Businesswoman* (6–9). Illus. 2000, Enslow LB $19.95 (0-7660-1204-2). Born into poverty, the daughter of freed slaves, Walker made a fortune as an entrepreneur in hair-care products for African American women. (Rev: BL 2/15/00; HBG 9/00; SLJ 7/00) [921]

WALKER, MAGGIE

6510 Branch, Muriel M., and Dorothy M. Rice. *Pennies to Dollars: The Story of Maggie Lena Walker* (4–8). 1997, Linnet LB $19.50 (0-208-02453-0); paper $13.95 (0-208-02455-7). Maggie Walker, the daughter of a former slave, helped African Americans through her financial schemes, including the founding of the Penny Savings Bank. (Rev: BL 11/1/97; SLJ 10/97) [921]

WATT, JAMES

6511 Sproule, Anna. *James Watt: Master of the Steam Engine* (5–8). Series: Giants of Science. 2001, Gale LB $27.44 (1-56711-338-9). This exploration of Watt's life and accomplishments also looks at how his inventions have evolved. (Rev: HBG 3/02; SLJ 2/02) [921]

WEINBERG, ROBERT A.

6512 Gaines, Ann, and Jim Whiting. *Robert A. Weinberg and the Search for the Cause of Cancer* (4–7). Series: Unlocking the Secrets of Science. 2002, Mitchell Lane LB $17.95 (1-58415-095-5). The life and achievements of the scientist who specializes in the genetic causes of disease. (Rev: HBG 10/02; SLJ 6/02) [616.9940092]

WILLIAMS, DANIEL HALE

6513 Kaye, Judith. *The Life of Daniel Hale Williams* (5–8). Illus. Series: Pioneers in Health and Medicine. 1993, Twenty-First Century LB $16.90 (0-8050-2302-X). The life story of the famous doctor who pioneered heart surgery and also helped open up the medical profession to African Americans. (Rev: SLJ 1/94) [921]

WOZNIAK, STEPHEN

6514 Kendall, Martha E. *Steve Wozniak: Inventor of the Apple Computer* (6–9). 1995, Walker $15.85 (0-8027-8342-2). A biography of the eccentric genius who revolutionized personal computing. (Rev: BL 3/1/95; SLJ 3/95) [921]

6515 Riddle, John, and Jim Whiting. *Stephen Wozniak and the Story of Apple Computer* (4–7). Series: Unlocking the Secrets of Science. 2001, Mitchell Lane LB $17.95 (1-58415-109-9). A profile of the life and achievements of the co-founder of Apple, who is known for his philanthropy and teaching in elementary schools. (Rev: HBG 10/02; SLJ 2/02) [921]

WRIGHT, WILBUR AND ORVILLE

6516 Collins, Mary. *Airborne: A Photobiography of Wilbur and Orville Wright* (4–8). Illus. 2003, National Geographic $18.95 (0-7922-6957-8). Sixty photographs are only the beginning of this intriguing book packed with information about the brothers and their famous flight. (Rev: BL 2/1/03*; HB 3–4/03; HBG 10/03; SLJ 3/03) [629.13]

6517 Freedman, Russell. *The Wright Brothers: How They Invented the Airplane* (6–10). 1991, Holiday $22.95 (0-8234-0875-2). Chronicles the achievements of two brothers who built the first flying machine in an Ohio bicycle shop and ultimately saw their dream come true. (Rev: BL 6/15/91*; SLJ 6/91*) [921]

6518 Martin, Michael J. *The Wright Brothers* (7–12). Series: The Importance Of. 2003, Gale LB $27.45 (1-56006-847-7). With lengthy quotations from primary and secondary sources, this is a lively biography of Wilbur and Orville Wright and how they changed history at Kitty Hawk. (Rev: BL 6/1–15/03) [921]

6519 Old, Wendie C. *The Wright Brothers* (5–8). Series: Historical American Biographies. 2000, Enslow LB $20.95 (0-7660-1095-3). An accurate and objective biography of the heroes of Kitty Hawk, containing chapter notes, a bibliography, and a glossary. (Rev: BL 1/1–15/00; HBG 10/00; SLJ 7/00) [921]

6520 Reynolds, Quentin. *The Wright Brothers* (5–8). 1963, Random paper $5.99 (0-394-84700-8). An easily read account of the two young men and their dream of flight. [921]

6521 Sproule, Anna. *The Wright Brothers: The Birth of Modern Aviation* (5–8). Series: Giants of Science. 1999, Blackbirch LB $27.44 (1-56711-328-1). This slim biography with an inviting format stresses the lasting contributions of the Wright brothers to world transportation. (Rev: HBG 10/00; SLJ 2/00) [921]

6522 Taylor, Richard L. *The First Flight: The Story of the Wright Brothers* (5–8). Illus. 1990, Watts paper $22.00 (0-531-10891-0). The story of the famous brothers and the drive and determination that finally led them to Kitty Hawk. (Rev: BL 4/15/90; SLJ 9/90) [921]

Sports Figures

Collective

6523 Aaseng, Nathan. *African-American Athletes* (8–12). Series: A to Z of African Americans. 2003, Facts on File $44.00 (0-8160-4805-3). Profiles of more than 150 African American athletes, past and present and representing all kinds of sports, give personal and career information. (Rev: SLJ 6/03) [796]

6524 Aaseng, Nathan. *Athletes* (7–12). Series: American Indian Lives. 1995, Facts on File $25.00 (0-8160-3019-7). A collective biography that highlights the lives of 11 Native American athletes, including Jim Thorpe, Kitty O'Neil, Sonny Sixkiller, Billy Mills, and Henry Boucha. (Rev: BL 4/1/95) [920]

6525 Aaseng, Nathan. *Top 10 Basketball Scoring Small Forwards* (4–7). Series: Sports Top 10. 1999, Enslow LB $18.95 (0-7660-1152-6). Each of these 10 basketball forwards is covered by a two-page biography, a full-page picture, and a page of sports statistics. (Rev: BL 11/15/99; HBG 10/00) [920]

6526 Aaseng, Nathan. *True Champions* (5–9). 1993, Walker $14.95 (0-8027-8246-9). Tales of legendary athletes who have demonstrated heroism and self-sacrifice off the field. (Rev: BL 8/93; SLJ 6/93) [921]

6527 Aaseng, Nathan. *Women Olympic Champions* (5–9). Series: History Makers. 2000, Lucent LB $27.45 (1-56006-709-8). This collective biography contains profiles of women athletes who have excelled at the Olympic Games. (Rev: BL 12/15/00; SLJ 4/01) [796.0820922]

6528 Bayne, Bijan C. *Sky Kings: Black Pioneers of Professional Basketball* (6–9). Illus. Series: The African-American Experience. 1997, Watts LB $23.00 (0-531-11308-6). This book tells the stories of Chuck Cooper, Nat Clifton, and Earl Lloyd, the three African American players who integrated basketball in 1950. (Rev: BL 12/15/97; HBG 3/98; SLJ 12/97) [920]

6529 Breton, Marcos. *Home Is Everything: The Latino Baseball Story* (7–12). Trans. by Daniel Santacruz. Photos by Jos Luis Villegas. 2003, Cinco Puntos paper $25.95 (0-938317-70-9). The story of Miguel Tejada is spotlighted in this photoessay that also profiles Latino baseball players including Jose Santana, Orlando Cepeda, and Roberto Clemente. (Rev: SLJ 12/03) [796.357]

6530 Bryant, Jill. *Amazing Women Athletes* (4–8). Illus. Series: Women's Hall of Fame. 2002, Second Story paper $7.95 (1-896764-44-4). This book contains profiles of 10 distinguished women athletes including mountain climber Annie Smith Peck and tennis stars Venus and Serena Williams. (Rev: BL 6/1–15/02; SLJ 8/02) [920]

6531 Christopher, Andre. *Top 10 Men's Tennis Players* (4–7). Series: Sports Top 10. 1998, Enslow LB $17.95 (0-7600-1009-0). Brief biographies of past and present tennis greats, with fact boxes, career statistics, and chapter notes. (Rev: BL 3/15/98) [920]

6532 Crisfield, Deborah. *Louisville Slugger Book of Great Hitters* (4–8). Series: Mountain Lion. 1998, Wiley paper $12.95 (0-471-19772-6). One hundred brief profiles introduce baseball's outstanding hitters, past and present, with plenty of accompanying black-and-white portraits and action shots. (Rev: SLJ 4/98) [920]

6533 Deane, Bill. *Top 10 Baseball Home Run Hitters* (4–7). Illus. Series: Sports Top 10. 1997, Enslow LB $18.95 (0-89490-804-9). Ten brief biographies of baseball hitters, e.g., Hank Aaron, Mickey Mantle, Jimmie Foxx, and Frank Thomas. (Rev: BL 9/15/97; HBG 3/98) [920]

6534 Deane, Bill. *Top 10 Men's Baseball Hitters* (4–7). Series: Sports Top 10. 1998, Enslow LB $17.95 (0-7600-1007-4). Brief biographies of great past and present baseball hitters, with fact boxes, career statistics, and chapter notes. (Rev: BL 3/15/98) [920]

6535 Ditchfield, Christin. *Top 10 American Women's Olympic Gold Medalists* (4–7). Illus. Series: Sports Top 10. 2000, Enslow LB $18.95 (0-7660-1277-8). Along with the profiles of 10 female athletes, this book contains fact boxes, career statistics, and chapter notes. (Rev: BL 9/15/00; HBG 10/01) [920]

6536 Dolin, Nick, et al. *Basketball Stars* (4–8). Illus. 1997, Black Dog & Leventhal $24.98 (1-884822-61-4). This oversize book contains 50 double-page profiles with statistics of contemporary basketball stars. (Rev: BL 8/97) [920]

6537 Gaines, Ann. *Sports and Activities* (6–9). Series: Female Firsts in Their Fields. 1999, Chelsea $18.65 (0-7910-5144-7). A collection of six biographies of outstanding female trail blazers in athletics, focusing on how each achieved firsts for their sex. (Rev: BL 5/15/99; HBG 9/99) [920]

6538 Green, Septima. *Top 10 Women Gymnasts* (4–7). Series: Sports Top 10. 1999, Enslow LB $18.95 (0-89490-809-X). Each of these star gymnasts from the past and present gets a two-page biography, a page of important statistics, and a black-and-white photograph. (Rev: BL 11/15/99; HBG 10/00) [920]

6539 Gutman, Bill. *Teammates: Michael Jordan and Scottie Pippen* (7–10). 1998, Millbrook LB $23.90 (0-7613-0420-7). The life stories of these two NBA stars are told, with emphasis on how the personal and professional development of each and their dedication to basketball influenced their roles as teammates. (Rev: HBG 3/99; SLJ 1/99; VOYA 4/99) [920]

6540 Hasday, Judy L. *Extraordinary Women Athletes* (6–12). Illus. Series: Extraordinary People. 2000, Children's LB $37.00 (0-516-27039-7); paper $16.95 (0-516-21608-2). A collective biography of 45 women who have gained recognition in a wide variety of sports. (Rev: BL 10/1/00; VOYA 2/01) [920]

6541 Jacobs, William J. *They Shaped the Game* (6–9). 1994, Scribners $15.95 (0-684-19734-0). Profiles the lives of baseball greats Ty Cobb, Babe Ruth, and Jackie Robinson. (Rev: BL 1/15/95; SLJ 2/95) [920]

6542 Kaminsky, Marty. *Uncommon Champions: Fifteen Athletes Who Battled Back* (5–8). Illus. 2000, Boyds Mills $14.95 (1-56397-787-7). Profiles of 15 athletes in several different sports who have conquered such mental and physical problems as blindness and drug addiction to achieve their goals.

(Rev: BCCB 1/01; BL 11/1/00; HBG 3/01; SLJ 10/00; VOYA 12/00) [921]

6543 Knapp, Ron. *Top 10 American Men Sprinters* (4–7). Series: Sports Top 10. 1999, Enslow LB $18.95 (0-7660-1074-0). Profiles and photographs are given of 10 important American male sprinters past and present. (Rev: BL 3/15/99; HBG 10/99) [920]

6544 Knapp, Ron. *Top 10 American Men's Olympic Gold Medalists* (4–7). Illus. Series: Sports Top 10. 2000, Enslow LB $18.95 (0-7660-1274-3). This book of 10 American male Olympic stars covers a number of sports, including track and field and diving. (Rev: BL 9/15/00; HBG 10/00) [920]

6545 Knapp, Ron. *Top 10 NFL Super Bowl Most Valuable Players* (4–7). Series: Sports Top 10. 2000, Enslow LB $18.95 (0-7660-1273-5). This book profiles 10 of the past and present most valuable players in the National Football League's Super Bowl. (Rev: BL 12/15/00; HBG 10/01) [920]

6546 Krull, Kathleen. *Lives of the Athletes* (4–7). 1997, Harcourt $20.00 (0-15-200806-3). A collective biography that describes the public and private lives of 20 famous athletes, including Johnny Weissmuller, Red Grange, Babe Didrikson Zaharias, Sonja Henie, and Bruce Lee. (Rev: BCCB 6/97; BL 3/15/97; HB 5–6/97; SLJ 5/97) [920]

6547 Kuhn, Betsy. *Top 10 Jockeys* (4–7). Series: Sports Top 10. 1999, Enslow LB $18.95 (0-7660-1130-5). Important jockeys, both past and present, are featured with a short biography, a portrait, and a page of pertinent statistics. (Rev: BL 11/15/99; HBG 10/00) [920]

6548 Mattern, Joanne. *Basketball Greats* (6–10). Series: History Makers. 2003, Gale LB $27.45 (1-59018-228-6). Some of the Basketball heroes provided in this collection are Wilt Chamberlain, Kareem Abdul-Jabbar, Magic Johnson, John Stockton, and Michael Jordan. (Rev: BL 6/1–15/03) [920]

6549 Molzahn, Arlene Bourgeois. *Top 10 American Women Sprinters* (4–8). Series: Sports Top 10. 1998, Enslow LB $18.95 (0-7660-1011-2). An easily read survey of the lives and accomplishments of 10 important women runners in track and field. (Rev: BL 8/98; HBG 10/99; SLJ 1/99) [920]

6550 Pare, Michael A. *Sports Stars: Series 4* (6–10). 1998, Visible Ink Pr. LB $55.00 (0-7876-2784-4). Thirty minibiographies are included in this book that introduces some of today's important athletes such as Mark McGwire, Marion Jones, Dominik Hasek, and Martina Hingis. (Rev: BL 9/15/98; VOYA 2/99) [920]

6551 Pare, Michael A. *Sports Stars: Series 3* (6–10). 1997, Gale LB $55.00 (0-7876-1749-0). Like the others in this series, this volume introduces biographical material on athletes from a variety of sports. (Rev: BL 9/1/97; SLJ 2/98) [920]

6552 Pare, Michael A. *Sports Stars: Series 2* (6–10). 1996, Gale LB $158.40 (0-7876-0867-X). This second series of "Sports Stars" is in two volumes and contains biographical sketches of 60 leading professional and amateur figures from many different sports. (Rev: BL 9/1/97; BR 1–2/97; SLJ 2/97) [920]

6553 Pietrusza, David. *Top 10 Baseball Managers* (4–7). Series: Sports Top 10. 1999, Enslow LB $18.95 (0-7660-1076-7). This work gives brief profiles of 10 famous past and present managers of American baseball teams. (Rev: BL 1/1–15/99; HBG 10/99) [920]

6554 Porter, David L., ed. *African-American Sports Greats: A Biographical Dictionary* (8–12). 1995, Greenwood $67.95 (0-313-28987-5). This reference book contains realistic, readable profiles of all the African American sports greats, both well known and less well known, with information about their lives, who influenced them, and the challenges they faced on the road to success. (Rev: BR 9–10/96; VOYA 4/96) [796]

6555 Poynter, Margaret. *Top 10 American Women's Figure Skaters* (4–7). Series: Sports Top 10. 1998, Enslow LB $18.95 (0-7660-1075-9). This work offers brief profiles and photographs of 10 female figure skaters. (Rev: BL 11/15/98; HBG 10/99) [920]

6556 Rappoport, Ken. *Guts and Glory: Making It in the NBA* (4–8). 1997, Walker LB $16.85 (0-8027-8431-3). The 10 basketball players profiled in this book had to overcome obstacles to get to the top. (Rev: BL 8/97; BR 11–12/97; SLJ 7/97) [920]

6557 Rennert, Richard S., ed. *Book of Firsts: Sports Heroes* (5–8). Illus. Series: Profiles of Great Black Americans. 1993, Chelsea LB $15.95 (0-7910-2055-X); paper $7.65 (0-7910-2056-8). Contains profiles of these great African American athletes: Arthur Ashe, Chuck Cooper, Althea Gibson, Jesse Owens, Jackie Robinson, Jack Johnson, Frank Robinson, and Bill Russell. (Rev: SLJ 12/93) [920]

6558 Rutledge, Rachel. *The Best of the Best in Figure Skating* (4–7). Series: Women of Sports. 1998, Millbrook LB $24.90 (0-7613-1302-8). After a brief history of figure skating and mention of its women pioneers, this book devotes separate chapters to the sport's present-day female leaders. (Rev: BL 2/15/99; HBG 10/99) [920]

6559 Rutledge, Rachel. *The Best of the Best in Gymnastics* (5–8). Series: Women of Sports. 1999, Millbrook LB $24.90 (0-7613-1321-4); paper $7.95 (0-7613-0784-2). After an overview of the sport and its history, the author profiles eight important contemporary female gymnasts, five of whom are American. (Rev: HBG 10/99; SLJ 7/99; VOYA 2/00) [920]

6560 Rutledge, Rachel. *The Best of the Best in Soccer* (4–7). Series: Women of Sports. 1998, Millbrook LB $24.90 (0-7613-1315-X). A revised edition of the 1998 title, containing a brief history of women's soccer and profiles of the top women players of yesterday, today, and tomorrow. (Rev: BL 2/15/99; HBG 10/99) [920]

6561 Rutledge, Rachel. *The Best of the Best in Track and Field* (5–8). Series: Women of Sports. 1999, Millbrook LB $24.90 (0-7613-1300-1); paper $7.95 (0-7613-0446-0). A brief history of track and field is followed by profiles of eight female athletes from the United States and abroad, with material on their careers and off-the-field lives. (Rev: HBG 10/99; SLJ 7/99; VOYA 2/00) [920]

6562 Savage, Jeff. *Top 10 Basketball Point Guards* (4–7). Series: Sports Top 10. 1997, Enslow LB $18.95 (0-89490-807-3). Each of the athletes is presented in four pages containing a biography, statistics, and two photographs. Also use *Top 10 Basketball Power Forwards* (1997). (Rev: BL 9/15/97; VOYA 10/97) [920]

6563 Savage, Jeff. *Top 10 Football Sackers* (4–7). Series: Sports Top 10. 1997, Enslow LB $18.95 (0-89490-805-7). Each of the 10 football stars highlighted is covered in four pages that include a short biography, two photographs, and a statistics table. (Rev: BL 9/15/97) [920]

6564 Savage, Jeff. *Top 10 Heisman Trophy Winners* (4–7). Series: Sports Top 10. 1999, Enslow LB $18.95 (0-7660-1072-4). This work profiles 10 winners of the trophy given each year to the most outstanding college football player in America. (Rev: BL 1/1–15/99; HBG 10/99) [920]

6565 Savage, Jeff. *Top 10 Physically Challenged Athletes* (4–7). Series: Sports Top 10. 2000, Enslow LB $18.95 (0-7660-1272-7). Each of the 10 short biographies in this book on physically handicapped athletes has an accompanying photo (usually in color) and a page of statistics. (Rev: BL 2/15/00; HBG 10/00; SLJ 10/00) [920]

6566 Savage, Jeff. *Top 10 Professional Football Coaches* (6–9). Series: Sports Top 10. 1998, Enslow LB $18.95 (0-7660-1006-6). Profiles of 10 top football coaches are accompanied by statistics and photographs. (Rev: HBG 10/98; SLJ 9/98; VOYA 12/98) [920]

6567 Schnakenberg, Robert E. *Teammates: Karl Malone and John Stockton* (5–7). Illus. 1998, Millbrook LB $23.90 (0-7613-0300-6). Despite very different backgrounds, these two leading players on the Utah Jazz basketball team have become close personal friends. (Rev: BL 8/98; HBG 10/98; SLJ 5/98) [920]

6568 Sehnert, Chris W. *Top 10 Sluggers* (5–8). Illus. Series: Top 10 Champions. 1997, ABDO LB $25.65 (1-56239-797-4). An overview of the careers of such notable hitters as Babe Ruth, Hank Aaron, and Roberto Clemente. (Rev: BL 1/1–15/98; HBG 3/98) [920]

6569 Spiros, Dean. *Top 10 Hockey Goalies* (6–9). Series: Sports Top 10. 1998, Enslow LB $18.95 (0-7660-1010-4). This book profiles 10 top hockey goalies, with brief biographical sketches and career statistics. (Rev: BL 8/98; HBG 9/99; VOYA 12/98) [920]

6570 Sullivan, George. *Great Lives: Sports* (5–7). Illus. 1988, Macmillan $25.00 (0-684-18510-5). Introducing 27 sports stars from all fields. (Rev: BL 1/1/89; HB 3–4/89) [796.0922]

6571 Sullivan, George. *Power Football: The Greatest Running Backs* (4–9). 2001, Simon & Schuster $18.00 (0-689-82432-7). Profiles eighteen 20th-century running backs, including O. J. Simpson, Terrell Davis, and Emmitt Smith. (Rev: HBG 3/02; SLJ 11/01) [920]

6572 Sullivan, George. *Quarterbacks! 18 of Football's Greatest* (5–10). 1998, Simon & Schuster $18.00 (0-689-81334-1). In two- to four-page entries, the author profiles 18 quarterbacks (including Brett Favre, Troy Aikman, Sammy Baugh, and Sid Luckman), explains why he chose them, and highlights their contributions to the game. (Rev: HBG 3/99; SLJ 9/98) [796.48]

6573 Sullivan, George. *Sluggers!* (4–7). Illus. 1991, Macmillan $18.00 (0-689-31566-X). Profiles of the careers of 27 of baseball's best hitters. (Rev: SLJ 1/92) [920]

6574 Teitelbaum, Michael. *Grand Slam Stars: Martina Hingis and Venus Williams* (6–10). 1998, HarperCollins paper $4.50 (0-06-107100-5). An easy read that contains biographies of the two most prominent teen sensations in the tennis world, Martina Hingis and Venus Williams. (Rev: VOYA 4/99) [920]

6575 Torres, John A. *Top 10 Basketball Three-Point Shooters* (4–7). Series: Sports Top 10. 1999, Enslow LB $18.95 (0-7660-1071-6). A profile and a photograph of 10 star basketball players make up this slender volume. (Rev: BL 1/1–15/99; HBG 10/99) [920]

6576 Torres, John A. *Top 10 NBA Finals Most Valuable Players* (4–7). Illus. Series: Sports Top 10. 2000, Enslow LB $18.95 (0-7660-1276-X). Short profiles of these NBA players also include photographs and some sports statistics. (Rev: BL 9/15/00; HBG 10/00) [920]

6577 Uschan, Michael V. *Male Olympic Champions* (6–12). Illus. Series: History Makers. 1999, Lucent LB $18.96 (1-56006-614-8). This collective biography introduces the Olympic Games and seven champions including Jim Thorpe, Paavo Nurmi,

Jesse Owens, Mark Spitz, and Jean-Claude Killy. (Rev: BL 1/1–15/00; HBG 9/00; SLJ 5/00) [921]

6578 Young, Jeff C. *Top 10 Basketball Shot-Blockers* (4–7). Series: Sports Top 10. 2000, Enslow LB $18.95 (0-7660-1275-1). For each of the basketball stars profiled, there is a full-page picture, a two-page biography, and a page of statistics. (Rev: BL 2/15/00; HBG 10/00) [920]

Automobile Racing

ANDRETTI, MARIO

6579 Prentzas, G. S. *Mario Andretti* (6–9). Series: Car Racing Legends. 1996, Chelsea LB $18.65 (0-7910-3176-4). This biography of the racing hero reveals Andretti's drive and endurance in his rise to the top. (Rev: SLJ 8/96) [921]

EARNHARDT, DALE, JR.

6580 Stewart, Mark. *Dale Earnhardt Jr.: Driven by Destiny* (5–8). Series: Auto Racing's New Wave. 2003, Millbrook LB $22.90 (0-7613-2908-0). An exciting biography of the NASCAR driver who was voted the most popular driver of 2003. (Rev: BL 6/1–15/03; HBG 10/03; SLJ 10/03) [796.72]

PETTY FAMILY

6581 Stewart, Mark. *The Pettys: Triumphs and Tragedies of Auto Racing's First Family* (4–8). Illus. 2001, Millbrook LB $24.90 (0-7613-2273-6). Photographs, quotations, anecdotes, and informative text introduce readers to the famous Petty family and their sometimes tragic involvement in automobile racing. (Rev: BL 9/1/01; HBG 3/02) [796.72]

Baseball

AARON, HANK

6582 Rennert, Richard. *Henry Aaron* (7–10). Series: Black Americans of Achievement. 1993, Chelsea LB $19.95 (0-7910-1859-8). The story of the African American baseball great who broke Babe Ruth's batting record in 1974. (Rev: BL 5/1/93) [921]

6583 Spencer, Lauren. *Hank Aaron* (4–7). Series: Baseball Hall of Famers. 2003, Rosen LB $29.25 (0-8239-3600-7). In 1974, Hank Aaron, an African American, was crowned home run king, taking the title away from Babe Ruth. This is his story. (Rev: BL 6/1–15/03; SLJ 6/03) [921]

ABBOTT, JIM

6584 Johnson, Rick L. *Jim Abbott: Beating the Odds* (4–7). Illus. Series: Taking Part. 1991, Macmillan LB $13.95 (0-87518-459-6). This account re-creates the life of the baseball pitcher who overcame a severe disability. (Rev: BL 9/1/91) [921]

6585 Savage, Jeff. *Jim Abbott* (5–8). Series: Sports Greats. 1993, Enslow LB $17.95 (0-89490-395-0). The amazing career of the one-handed pitcher who came up with the California Angels and threw a no-hitter for the New York Yankees. (Rev: BL 3/1/93) [921]

ALOMAR, ROBERTO

6586 Macht, Norman L. *Roberto Alomar* (6–10). Series: Latinos in Baseball. 1999, Mitchell Lane LB $18.95 (1-883845-84-X). Using extensive interviews with Alomar, his family, friends, and colleagues, this profile of the famous Puerto Rican baseball player shows his strong self-discipline, work ethic, and close family ties. (Rev: BL 4/15/99; HBG 10/99; SLJ 5/99) [921]

ALOU, MOISES

6587 Muskat, Carrie. *Moises Alou* (6–10). Illus. Series: Latinos in Baseball. 1999, Mitchell Lane LB $18.95 (1-883845-86-6). This is the story of the baseball giant who came from a sports-minded family, and who faced a number of personal tragedies on his way to the the top. (Rev: BL 4/15/99; HBG 9/99) [921]

BELL, COOL PAPA

6588 McCormack, Shaun. *Cool Papa Bell* (4–7). Series: Baseball Hall of Famers of the Negro Leagues. 2002, Rosen LB $29.25 (0-8239-3474-8). A biography of James Thomas "Cool Papa" Bell of Negro League baseball, who is said to have stolen 175 bases in one season. (Rev: BL 7/02) [921]

BONDS, BARRY

6589 Savage, Jeff. *Barry Bonds: Mr. Excitement* (4–8). Series: Sports Achievers. 1996, Lerner paper $5.95 (0-8225-9748-9). The story of this fantastic baseball player who has won the Most Valuable Player Award three times and who grew up in the shadow of a famous father. (Rev: BL 4/15/97; SLJ 2/97) [921]

BONILLA, BOBBY

6590 Knapp, Ron. *Bobby Bonilla* (5–8). Illus. Series: Sports Greats. 1993, Enslow LB $17.95 (0-89490-417-5). Using easy-to-read prose and a number of action photographs, this is a lively introduc-

tion to baseball star Bobby Bonilla. (Rev: BL 9/15/93) [921]

6591 Rappoport, Ken. *Bobby Bonilla* (5–9). 1993, Walker LB $15.85 (0-8027-8256-6). A biography of the baseball player who rose from poverty in the South Bronx to superstardom and multimillionaire status. (Rev: BL 5/15/93; SLJ 5/93; VOYA 8/93) [921]

CANSECO, JOSÉ

6592 Aaseng, Nathan. *Jose Canseco: Baseball's Forty-Forty Man* (4–7). Illus. 1989, Lerner paper $4.95 (0-8225-9586-9). The ups and downs of this sometimes controversial baseball star of the Oakland A's. (Rev: BCCB 9/89; BL 7/89; SLJ 8/89) [921]

CLEMENTE, ROBERTO

6593 Gilbert, Tom. *Roberto Clemente* (5–8). Illus. 1991, Chelsea LB $21.95 (0-7910-1240-9). The life of the first Hispanic in the Baseball Hall of Fame. (Rev: BL 8/91) [921]

6594 Kingsbury, Robert. *Roberto Clemente* (4–7). Series: Baseball Hall of Famers. 2003, Rosen LB $29.25 (0-8239-3602-3). The story of the National League battling champion who faced racism and discrimination because of his Hispanic background. (Rev: BL 6/1–15/03; SLJ 6/03) [921]

6595 Walker, Paul R. *Pride of Puerto Rico: The Life of Roberto Clemente* (4–7). 1988, Harcourt $14.00 (0-15-200562-5); paper $6.00 (0-15-263420-7). The life of a baseball star and hero who died trying to help others. (Rev: BL 10/1/88; HB 9–10/88; SLJ 1/89) [921]

GIBSON, JOSH

6596 Holway, John B. *Josh Gibson* (7–10). Series: Black Americans of Achievement. 1995, Chelsea LB $19.95 (0-7910-1872-5). The inspiring story of this African American baseball hero. (Rev: BL 8/95) [921]

6597 Twemlow, Nick. *Josh Gibson* (4–7). Series: Baseball Hall of Famers of the Negro Leagues. 2002, Rosen LB $29.25 (0-8239-3475-6). In addition to racial prejudice in the world of baseball, Josh Gibson suffered many personal misfortunes as this life story recounts. (Rev: BL 7/02) [921]

HERSHISER, OREL

6598 Knapp, Ron. *Orel Hershiser* (5–8). Series: Sports Greats. 1993, Enslow LB $17.95 (0-89490-389-6). An easily read sports biography that re-creates the great moments in this baseball star's career up to 1993. (Rev: BL 4/1/93) [921]

IRVIN, MONTE

6599 Haegele, Katie. *Monte Irvin* (4–7). Series: Baseball Hall of Famers of the Negro Leagues. 2002, Rosen LB $29.25 (0-8239-3477-2). Though recruited into the Negro leagues when he was 17, Irvin, a very talented player, was past his prime when he finally became a major leaguer. (Rev: BL 7/02) [921]

JOHNSON, JUDY

6600 Billus, Kathleen. *Judy Johnson* (4–7). Illus. Series: Baseball Hall of Famers of the Negro Leagues. 2002, Rosen LB $29.25 (0-8239-3476-4). A biography of Johnson covering his years as player, coach, manager, and scout, with black-and-white photographs, glossary, timeline, and lists of additional resources. (Rev: BL 7/02) [796.357]

JOHNSON, MAMIE "PEANUT"

6601 Green, Michelle Y. *A Strong Right Arm: The Story of Mamie "Peanut" Johnson* (4–7). 2002, Dial $15.99 (0-8037-2661-9). The life story of the woman who was one of three to play professional baseball and of her career as pitcher with the Negro Leagues' Indianapolis Clowns. (Rev: BL 6/1–15/02*; HBG 3/03; SLJ 8/02; VOYA 8/02) [921]

JOHNSON, WALTER

6602 Kavanagh, Jack. *Walter Johnson* (4–8). Illus. Series: Baseball Legends. 1991, Chelsea LB $18.65 (0-7910-1179-8). A biography of a baseball giant, including coverage of important games and many black-and-white photographs. (Rev: BL 1/15/92) [921]

LEONARD, BUCK

6603 Payment, Simone. *Buck Leonard* (4–7). Series: Baseball Hall of Famers of the Negro Leagues. 2002, Rosen LB $29.25 (0-8239-3473-X). The story of one of the greatest baseball players of all time, who missed worldwide fame because of his color. (Rev: BL 7/02) [921]

MCGWIRE, MARK

6604 Hall, Jonathan. *Mark McGwire: A Biography* (6–10). 1998, Archway paper $4.99 (0-671-03273-9). This biography covers the batter's childhood, his progress through minor leagues, and earlier major league experiences, then focuses on the sensational 1998 season. (Rev: VOYA 4/99) [921]

6605 Thornley, Stew. *Mark McGwire: Star Home Run Hitter* (4–8). Series: Sports Reports. 1999, Enslow LB $20.95 (0-7660-1329-4). A look at the life and accomplishments of this exciting baseball player. (Rev: BL 3/15/99; HBG 9/99; SLJ 7/99; VOYA 8/99) [921]

MADDUX, GREG

6606 Christopher, Matt. *On the Mound with . . . Greg Maddux* (4–7). Illus. 1997, Little, Brown paper $4.95 (0-316-14191-7). The life of the famous player with the Chicago Cubs and Atlanta Braves, who has been called the best pitcher in baseball. (Rev: BL 7/97) [921]

6607 Thornley, Stew. *Greg Maddux* (5–8). Illus. Series: Sports Greats. 1997, Enslow LB $17.95 (0-89490-873-1). The life of this baseball great, supplemented by career statistics and many action photographs. (Rev: BL 2/15/97; VOYA 6/97) [921]

MARTINEZ, PEDRO

6608 Gallagher, Jim. *Pedro Martinez* (6–10). Series: Latinos in Baseball. 1999, Mitchell Lane LB $18.95 (1-883845-85-8). The life history and career highlights of Pedro Martinez, one of the many Hispanic Americans to become baseball stars. (Rev: BL 4/15/99; HBG 9/99) [921]

PAIGE, SATCHEL

6609 Schmidt, Julie. *Satchel Paige* (4–7). Illus. Series: Baseball Hall of Famers of the Negro Leagues. 2002, Rosen LB $29.25 (0-8239-3478-0). A biography of the famous pitcher who became the oldest rookie ever, with black-and-white photographs, glossary, timeline, and lists of additional resources. (Rev: BL 7/02; VOYA 6/02) [796.357]

6610 Shirley, David. *Satchel Paige* (7–10). Series: Black Americans of Achievement. 1993, Chelsea LB $19.95 (0-7910-1880-6). The story of the baseball Hall of Famer who was the first African American to pitch in the American League. (Rev: BL 5/1/93) [921]

RIPKEN, CAL, JR.

6611 Macnow, Glen. *Cal Ripken, Jr.* (5–8). Series: Sports Greats. 1993, Enslow LB $17.95 (0-89490-387-X). The story of the baseball giant who gained fame as the star shortstop for the Baltimore Orioles. (Rev: BL 4/1/93) [921]

ROBINSON, JACKIE

6612 Coombs, Karen Mueller. *Jackie Robinson: Baseball's Civil Rights Legend* (5–7). Illus. Series: African-American Biographies. 1997, Enslow LB $20.95 (0-89490-690-9). The story of the baseball great who stood up to racism in athletics. (Rev: BL 6/1–15/97) [921]

6613 DeAngelis, Gina. *Jackie Robinson: Overcoming Adversity* (5–8). Illus. Series: Overcoming Adversity. 2000, Chelsea $21.95 (0-7910-5897-2). Using a highly readable text and black-and-white photographs, this book gives a real picture of Robinson that touches on the reasons he felt extreme anger and his great determination to make a difference. (Rev: BL 2/15/01; HBG 10/01) [921]

6614 Scott, Richard. *Jackie Robinson* (5–10). Illus. 1987, Chelsea LB $21.95 (1-55546-609-5). A well-researched biography giving good material on Robinson's life outside of baseball. (Rev: BL 9/1/87; SLJ 9/87) [921]

6615 Weidhorn, Manfred. *Jackie Robinson* (6–12). 1993, Atheneum LB $15.95 (0-689-31644-5). This biography of the African American legend who integrated baseball in 1947 focuses on the personal qualities of the boy, the man, and the athlete. (Rev: BL 3/15/94; SLJ 2/94; VOYA 4/94) [921]

RODRIGUEZ, ALEX

6616 Macnow, Glen. *Alex Rodriguez* (5–8). Series: Sports Greats. 2002, Enslow LB $17.95 (0-7660-1845-8). An easy-to-read yet fairly detailed biography of the baseball player, with plenty of statistics and quotations. (Rev: BL 9/1/02; HBG 10/02) [796.357]

RUTH, BABE

6617 Nicholson, Lois. *Babe Ruth: Sultan of Swat* (5–8). Illus. 1995, Goodwood $17.95 (0-9625427-1-7). This well-written account of the famous slugger explains his lasting influence on baseball. (Rev: SLJ 7/95) [921]

RYAN, NOLAN

6618 Lace, William W. *Nolan Ryan* (5–8). Series: Sports Greats. 1993, Enslow LB $17.95 (0-89490-394-2). The amazing story of this baseball phenomenon who became the baseball strike-out king. (Rev: BL 6/1–15/93) [921]

SOSA, SAMMY

6619 Gutman, Bill. *Sammy Sosa: A Biography* (6–10). 1998, Archway paper $4.99 (0-671-03274-7). The life story of this sensational slugger, in both English and Spanish, with about half the book devoted to the exciting 1998 season. (Rev: VOYA 4/99) [921]

6620 Muskat, Carrie. *Sammy Sosa* (6–10). Illus. Series: Latinos in Baseball. 1999, Mitchell Lane LB $18.95 (1-883845-92-0). This account of Sosa's life tells of his beginning as a poor shoeshine boy in the Dominican Republic and his rise in baseball to his record-setting home run at age 29. (Rev: BL 4/15/99; HBG 10/99; SLJ 5/99) [921]

SUZUKI, ICHIRO

6621 Stewart, Mark. *Ichiro Suzuki: Best in the West* (4–7). Illus. Series: Sports New Wave. 2002, Millbrook LB $22.90 (0-7613-2616-2). A well-constructed biography of the famous Japanese Seattle Mariners player that offers information on the game itself as well as statistics, color photographs, and quotations that illustrate his achievements. (Rev: BL 9/1/02; HBG 3/03) [796.357]

THOMAS, FRANK

6622 Thornley, Stew. *Frank Thomas: Baseball's Big Hurt* (4–8). Series: Sports Achievers. 1997, Lerner LB $22.60 (0-8225-3651-X). As well as being a big-time hitter in baseball, this star — nicknamed "The Big Hurt" — devotes much of his spare time to the fight against leukemia. (Rev: BL 1/1–15/98; HBG 3/98) [921]

Basketball

ABDUL-JABBAR, KAREEM

6623 Kneib, Martha. *Kareem Abdul-Jabbar* (5–8). Series: Basketball Hall of Famers. 2002, Rosen LB $29.25 (0-8239-3483-7). An in-depth look at this basketball great's life, with highlights from his childhood through his NBA career. (Rev: BL 9/1/02) [921]

BARKLEY, CHARLES

6624 Dolan, Sean. *Charles Barkley* (5–7). Illus. Series: Basketball Legends. 1996, Chelsea LB $18.65 (0-7910-2433-4). The life of this basketball superstar, with details on his record on the court. (Rev: BL 7/96) [921]

6625 Macnow, Glen. *Charles Barkley* (5–8). Series: Sports Greats. 1992, Enslow LB $17.95 (0-89490-386-1). A short biography of this basketball star, with career statistics and action photographs. (Rev: BL 10/15/92) [921]

BIRD, LARRY

6626 Kavanagh, Jack. *Larry Bird* (4–8). Illus. Series: Sports Greats. 1992, Enslow LB $17.95 (0-89490-368-3). The extraordinary story of the basketball player who drove his team, the Boston Celtics, to five NBA finals. (Rev: BL 7/92; SLJ 10/92) [921]

BRYANT, KOBE

6627 Kennedy, Nick. *Kobe Bryant: Star Guard* (4–8). Series: Sports Reports. 2002, Enslow LB $20.95 (0-7660-1828-8). An accessible biography of the basketball player, with detailed descriptions of career highlights. (Rev: BL 9/1/02; HBG 3/03) [796.323]

6628 Savage, Jeff. *Kobe Bryant: Basketball Big Shot* (4–7). Illus. Series: Sports Biography. 2000, Lerner LB $27.15 (0-8225-3680-3). A very readable, attractive biography of the new NBA sensation that ends with the 1999–2000 season. (Rev: BL 1/1–15/01; HBG 10/01) [921]

6629 Stewart, Mark. *Kobe Bryant: Hard to the Hoop* (4–8). Series: Basketball's New Wave. 2000, Millbrook LB $20.90 (0-7613-1800-3). The life story of this basketball star who was the son of an NBA player and who became the youngest player in league history to star in the All-Star Game. (Rev: HBG 10/00; SLJ 8/00) [921]

CARTER, VINCE

6630 Savage, Jeff. *Vince Carter* (5–8). Series: Sports Greats. 2002, Enslow LB $17.95 (0-7660-1767-2). An accessible biography of the Toronto Raptors basketball player that will be useful for students writing reports. (Rev: BL 9/1/02; HBG 10/02) [796.323]

COOPER, CYNTHIA

6631 Schnakenberg, Robert E. *Cynthia Cooper* (5–9). Series: Women Who Win. 2000, Chelsea $19.75 (0-7910-5796-8). A biography of this basketball star that focuses on her career and game-related information. (Rev: HBG 3/01; SLJ 2/01; VOYA 4/01) [921]

DUNCAN, TIM

6632 Byman, Jeremy. *Tim Duncan* (4–8). Illus. Series: Great Athletes. 2000, Morgan Reynolds LB $18.95 (1-883846-43-9). This biography about a basketball hero who has been playing professionally for only a short time focuses on his college years, his outstanding talent, and his determination. (Rev: BL 6/1–15/00; HBG 3/01) [921]

6633 Rappoport, Ken. *Tim Duncan: Star Forward* (5–8). Series: Sports Reports. 2000, Enslow LB $20.95 (0-7660-1334-0). A look at one of basketball's star forwards, accompanied by statistics and action photographs. (Rev: BL 10/15/00; HBG 3/01) [921]

6634 Stewart, Mark. *Tim Duncan: Tower of Power* (4–8). Series: Basketball's New Wave. 1999, Millbrook LB $22.90 (0-7613-1513-6). Although this biography of basketball's rising star is brief, the information is ample and important topics are all covered. (Rev: HBG 10/00; SLJ 7/00) [921]

6635 Torres, John Albert. *Tim Duncan* (5–8). Series: Sports Greats. 2002, Enslow LB $17.95 (0-7660-1766-4). The life of this basketball star is re-created using an easy-reading text and many photographs. (Rev: BL 9/1/02; HBG 10/02) [921]

EWING, PATRICK

6636 Kavanagh, Jack. *Patrick Ewing* (5–8). Illus. Series: Sports Greats. 1992, Enslow LB $17.95 (0-89490-369-1). An easily read, candid look at the basketball great from Jamaica. (Rev: BL 9/1/92) [921]

GARNETT, KEVIN

6637 Bernstein, Ross. *Kevin Garnett: Star Forward* (4–8). Series: Sports Reports. 2002, Enslow LB $20.95 (0-7660-1829-6). An in-depth look at the life of this basketball star in a simple account suitable for reluctant readers. (Rev: BL 9/1/02; HBG 3/03) [921]

6638 Stewart, Mark. *Kevin Garnett: Shake Up the Game* (4–7). Series: Sports New Wave. 2002, Millbrook LB $22.90 (0-7613-2615-4). A short biography that chronicles the career of the new star of the Minnesota Timberwolves. (Rev: BL 9/1/02; HBG 10/02) [921]

HARDAWAY, ANFERNEE

6639 Rekela, George R. *Anfernee Hardaway* (5–8). Illus. Series: Sports Greats. 1996, Enslow LB $17.95 (0-89490-758-1). Career statistics and many black-and-white photographs enliven the biography of this famous basketball star. (Rev: BL 3/15/96) [921]

HILL, GRANT

6640 Gutman, Bill. *Grant Hill: A Biography* (6–10). 1997, Archway paper $3.99 (0-671-88738-6). This covers the life and career of the Detroit Pistons basketball star who is outstanding not only as an athlete but also as a modest, well-liked man. (Rev: VOYA 8/97) [921]

6641 Rappoport, Ken. *Grant Hill* (6–9). Illus. 1996, Walker LB $16.85 (0-8027-8456-9). The story of the basketball star, from the AAU National Basketball Championship at age 13 through high school, where he played on the varsity team as a freshman, and his college years playing at Duke, to the Detroit Pistons, where he was the NBA Rookie of the Year. (Rev: BL 1/1–15/97; BR 3–4/97; SLJ 1/97; VOYA 8/97) [796.323]

6642 Savage, Jeff. *Grant Hill: Humble Hotshot* (4–8). Series: Sports Achievers. 1996, Lerner LB $22.60 (0-8225-2893-2). A brief biography of this humble basketball star who was a mainstay both at Duke University and with the Detroit Pistons. (Rev: BL 4/15/97; SLJ 6/97; VOYA 8/97) [921]

HOLDSCLAW, CHAMIQUE

6643 Holdsclaw, Chamique, and Jennifer Frey. *Chamique Holdsclaw: My Story* (6–12). Illus. 2001, Simon & Schuster paper $4.99 (0-689-83592-2). Holdsclaw tells readers how her athletic ability at first hindered but later helped her, and attributes much of her success to the grandmother who raised her. (Rev: BL 9/1/01) [796.323]

HOWARD, JUWAN

6644 Savage, Jeff. *Juwan Howard* (5–8). Series: Sports Greats. 1998, Enslow LB $17.95 (0-7660-1065-1). The Washington Wizards basketball star is profiled in this lively account, supplemented by many black-and-white photographs. (Rev: BL 2/15/99; HBG 10/99; VOYA 6/99) [921]

6645 Sirak, Ron. *Juwan Howard* (5–8). 1998, Chelsea LB $18.65 (0-7910-4575-7). A biography of one of the great basketball players of the 1990s, with good material on his early years and the influence of his grandmother. (Rev: BR 11–12/98; HBG 3/99; VOYA 6/99) [921]

JOHNSON, MAGIC

6646 Dolan, Sean. *Magic Johnson* (7–10). 1993, Chelsea LB $21.95 (0-7910-1975-6). The story to 1992 of the Los Angeles Lakers star and his battle after testing HIV-positive. (Rev: BL 9/15/93) [921]

6647 Greenberg, Keith E. *Magic Johnson: Champion with a Cause* (4–7). Illus. Series: Achievers. 1992, Lerner LB $27.15 (0-8225-0546-0). The story of the gifted athlete for the L.A. Lakers, whose career was cut short when he discovered he was HIV-positive. (Rev: BL 8/92; SLJ 7/92) [921]

6648 Haskins, Jim. *Magic Johnson*. Rev. ed. (5–8). Series: Sports Greats. 1992, Enslow LB $17.95 (0-89490-348-9). This revised and updated edition includes a discussion of the basketball star's HIV status, his 1991 retirement from the Lakers, and his role in the fight against AIDS. (Rev: BL 10/15/92) [921]

JORDAN, MICHAEL

6649 Aaseng, Nathan. *Michael Jordan* (5–8). Illus. Series: Sports Greats. 1992, Enslow LB $17.95 (0-89490-370-5). Michael Jordan's life, his successes as guard of the Chicago Bulls, and his commercials

for TV are discussed in this easily read book. (Rev: BL 10/15/92) [921]

6650 Berger, Phil, and John Rolfe. *Michael Jordan* (4–7). Illus. 1990, Little, Brown paper $4.95 (0-316-09229-0). This account covers Jordan's childhood and his career development. (Rev: BL 12/15/90; SLJ 4/91) [921]

6651 Dolan, Sean. *Michael Jordan* (7–10). Series: Black Americans of Achievement. 1993, Chelsea paper $9.95 (0-7910-2151-3). The life of this basketball legend to 1992 and how his determination and family support helped him rise to the top. (Rev: BL 3/1/94; VOYA 6/94) [921]

6652 Gutman, Bill. *Michael Jordan: A Biography* (5–8). 1995, Pocket paper $4.99 (0-671-51972-7). This readable book contains good coverage of the formative years as well as the current accomplishments of this basketball hero. (Rev: SLJ 5/92) [921]

6653 Lovitt, Chip. *Michael Jordan* (6–10). 1998, Scholastic paper $4.50 (0-590-59644-6). This quick read, an update of the 1993 edition, traces Jordan's remarkable career from a young age to the end of the Chicago Bulls' 1998 season. (Rev: VOYA 4/99) [921]

KIDD, JASON

6654 Gray, Valerie A. *Jason Kidd: Star Guard* (5–8). Series: Sports Reports. 2000, Enslow LB $20.95 (0-7660-1333-2). The story of the basketball superstar with behind-the-scenes reporting on his life and career. (Rev: BL 10/15/00; HBG 10/00) [921]

6655 Torres, John A. *Jason Kidd* (5–8). Series: Sports Greats. 1998, Enslow LB $17.95 (0-7660-1001-5). An action-filled biography of this basketball star, complete with career statistics and black-and-white photographs of Kidd on the court. (Rev: BL 7/98; HBG 10/98) [921]

LESLIE, LISA

6656 Kelley, Brent. *Lisa Leslie* (5–9). Series: Women Who Win. 2000, Chelsea $19.75 (0-7910-5794-1). This profile of a pioneer in the Women's National Basketball Association contains much game-related information. (Rev: HBG 3/01; SLJ 2/01) [921]

LIEBERMAN-CLINE, NANCY

6657 Greenberg, Doreen, and Michael Greenberg. *A Drive to Win: The Story of Nancy Lieberman-Cline* (4–8). Series: Anything You Can Do — New Sports Heroes for Girls. 2000, Wish paper $9.95 (1-930546-40-8). Based on personal interviews, this is an informative biography of the basketball star Lieberman-Cline. (Rev: SLJ 3/01; VOYA 2/01) [921]

MILLER, REGGIE

6658 Thornley, Stew. *Reggie Miller* (5–8). Series: Sports Greats. 1996, Enslow LB $17.95 (0-89490-874-X). The life of this basketball star is traced, with special emphasis on key games. (Rev: BL 9/15/96) [921]

MOURNING, ALONZO

6659 Fortunato, Frank. *Alonzo Mourning* (5–8). Illus. Series: Sports Greats. 1997, Enslow LB $17.95 (0-89490-875-8). An easily read biography of this amazing basketball star. (Rev: BL 2/15/97; VOYA 6/97) [921]

MULLIN, CHRIS

6660 Morgan, Terri, and Shmuel Thaler. *Chris Mullin: Sure Shot* (4–8). Illus. Series: Sports Achievers. 1994, Lerner LB $10.13 (0-8225-2887-7). The story of this amazing basketball star who overcame many obstacles, including alcoholism. (Rev: BL 1/1/95; SLJ 1/95) [921]

NUNEZ, TOMMY

6661 Marvis, Barbara. *Tommy Nunez, NBA Referee: Taking My Best Shot* (6–10). Illus. 1996, Mitchell Lane paper $12.95 (1-883845-28-9). The story of the youngster who grew up in the poverty of Phoenix's barrio to become the first (and so far the only) Mexican American referee in the NBA. (Rev: BL 5/15/96; SLJ 3/96; VOYA 6/96) [921]

OLAJUWON, HAKEEM

6662 McMane, Fred. *Hakeem Olajuwon* (5–7). Series: Basketball Legends. 1997, Chelsea LB $18.65 (0-7910-4385-1). The story of this basketball star of the Houston Rockets, his boyhood in Nigeria, and his role as part of the U.S. Olympic "Dream Team." (Rev: BL 9/15/97) [921]

O'NEAL, SHAQUILLE

6663 Sullivan, Michael J. *Shaquille O'Neal* (5–8). Series: Sports Greats. 1998, Enslow LB $17.95 (0-7660-1003-1). The life and career of this well-known basketball star are covered in this easily read biography containing career statistics and many illustrations. (Rev: BL 2/15/99; HBG 10/99) [921]

6664 Ungs, Tim. *Shaquille O'Neal* (5–7). Illus. Series: Basketball Legends. 1996, Chelsea LB $18.65 (0-7910-2437-7). An interesting portrait of the unstoppable Lakers basketball superstar. (Rev: BL 7/96) [921]

PIPPEN, SCOTTIE

6665 Bjarkman, Peter C. *Scottie Pippen* (5–8). Series: Sports Greats. 1996, Enslow LB $17.95 (0-89490-755-7). Action photographs, career statistics, and an account of important games are highlights of this basketball biography. (Rev: BL 9/15/96) [921]

6666 McMane, Fred. *Scottie Pippen* (5–7). Illus. Series: Basketball Legends. 1996, Chelsea LB $18.65 (0-7910-2498-9). The life of this basketball star, highlighting his special abilities and his court record. (Rev: BL 7/96) [921]

6667 Pippen, Scottie, and Greg Brown. *Reach Higher* (4–7). 1997, Taylor $14.95 (0-87833-981-7). The story of the famous Chicago Bulls basketball star, who came from a family of 12 and whose original sports were baseball and football. (Rev: BL 10/1/97) [921]

RICHMOND, MITCH

6668 Grody, Carl W. *Mitch Richmond* (5–8). Series: Sports Greats. 1998, Enslow LB $17.95 (0-7660-1070-8). Using many black-and-white photographs and a lively text, this book re-creates the life of the basketball great. (Rev: BL 2/15/99; HBG 10/99) [921]

ROBINSON, DAVID

6669 Aaseng, Nathan. *David Robinson* (5–8). Illus. Series: Sports Greats. 1992, Enslow LB $17.95 (0-89490-373-X). This easily read biography highlights David Robinson of the San Antonio Spurs, the 1990 Rookie of the Year. (Rev: BL 10/15/92) [921]

6670 Bock, Hal. *David Robinson* (5–7). Series: Basketball Legends. 1997, Chelsea LB $18.65 (0-7910-4387-8). The story of this star of the San Antonio Spurs, who was a brilliant student and an officer in the U.S. Navy before turning to professional sports. (Rev: BL 9/15/97) [921]

6671 Green, Carl R., and Roxanne Ford. *David Robinson* (4–8). Illus. Series: Sports Headliners. 1994, Silver Burdett LB $13.95 (0-89686-839-7); paper $7.95 (0-382-24808-2). A slim biography of this basketball star, who gained fame during the 1987 Navy–Duke game. (Rev: BL 10/1/94) [921]

RODMAN, DENNIS

6672 Frank, Steven. *Dennis Rodman* (4–8). Series: Basketball Legends. 1997, Chelsea LB $18.65 (0-7910-4388-6). A candid look at the bad boy of basketball, his troubled youth, and rebellious attitudes. (Rev: HBG 3/98; SLJ 4/98) [921]

6673 Thornley, Stew. *Dennis Rodman* (5–8). Illus. Series: Sports Greats. 1996, Enslow LB $17.95 (0-89490-759-X). The life of this controversial basketball star is told in a brisk text with many black-and-white photographs. (Rev: BL 3/15/96) [921]

STILES, JACKIE

6674 Stewart, Mark. *Jackie Stiles: Gym Dandy* (4–7). Illus. Series: Sports New Wave. 2002, Millbrook LB $22.90 (0-7613-2614-6). A biography of the WNBA star, with information on her childhood and family, statistics, color photographs, and general material on the game itself. (Rev: BL 9/1/02; HBG 3/03) [796.323]

STOCKTON, JOHN

6675 Aaseng, Nathan. *John Stockton* (5–8). Illus. Series: Sports Greats. 1995, Enslow LB $17.95 (0-89490-598-8). A short biography of the basketball great John Stockton, with sports action and lively photographs. (Rev: BL 9/15/95) [921]

SWOOPES, SHERYL

6676 Rappoport, Ken. *Sheryl Swoopes* (4–8). Illus. Series: Sports Reports. 2002, Enslow LB $20.95 (0-7660-1827-X). An accessible biography of the basketball player, with detailed descriptions of career highlights. (Rev: BL 9/1/02; HBG 3/03) [976.323]

THOMAS, ISIAH

6677 Knapp, Ron. *Isiah Thomas* (5–8). Illus. Series: Sports Greats. 1992, Enslow LB $17.95 (0-89490-374-8). Using a standard chronological approach and many photographs, this is an accurate, appealing biography of this great African American basketball player. (Rev: BL 9/1/92) [921]

WEST, JERRY

6678 Ramen, Fred. *Jerry West* (5–8). Series: Basketball Hall of Famers. 2002, Rosen LB $29.25 (0-8239-3482-9). Facts, stories, and full-color photographs are used to bring alive the story of this basketball great, with material on his NBA career and beyond. (Rev: BL 9/1/02) [921]

WILKINS, DOMINIQUE

6679 Bjarkman, Peter C. *Dominique Wilkins* (5–8). Series: Sports Greats. 1996, Enslow LB $17.95 (0-89490-754-9). The story of this basketball star, with profiles of his most exciting games and career statistics. (Rev: BL 9/15/96) [921]

Boxing

ALI, MUHAMMAD

6680 Myers, Walter Dean. *The Greatest: Muhammad Ali* (6–10). Illus. 2001, Scholastic paper $16.95 (0-590-54342-3). This engaging biography explores Ali's life from childhood, his careers as boxer and political activist, and the impact he had on generations of African Americans. (Rev: BL 1/1–15/01; HB 1–2/01; HBG 10/01; SLJ 1/01; VOYA 2/01) [796.83]

6681 Random House, eds. *Muhammed Ali* (6–10). 1997, Random $20.00 (0-517-20080-5). Using plenty of sidebars, quotations from his poetry, and photographs, this excellent biography, based on A&E cable TV's *Biography* show, traces the boxer's life from his days as a scrawny kid named Cassius Clay, Jr. to his becoming "the greatest," ending with the 1996 lighting of the Olympic torch in Atlanta, Georgia. (Rev: VOYA 8/98) [921]

6682 Rummel, Jack. *Muhammad Ali* (6–10). Illus. 1988, Chelsea LB $21.95 (1-55546-569-2). A biography that emphasizes the boxer's professional career rather than his personal life. (Rev: BL 6/15/88) [921]

6683 Schulman, Arlene. *Muhammad Ali: Champion* (6–9). Series: Newsmakers. 1996, Lerner LB $25.26 (0-8225-4925-5). An accurate account of Ali's youth, his career, his Muslim beliefs, and his civil rights activities. (Rev: SLJ 6/96) [921]

6684 Tessitore, John. *Muhammad Ali: The World's Champion* (7–12). Series: Impact Biographies. 1998, Watts LB $20.00 (0-531-11437-6). Crowned heavyweight champion of the world three times, Muhammad Ali also stands out as a courageous humanitarian, a champion of peace and civil rights, and a role model for all people. (Rev: BL 11/15/98; HBG 3/99; SLJ 12/98) [921]

CHAVEZ, JULIO CESAR

6685 Dolan, Terrance. *Julio Cesar Chavez* (5–8). Illus. Series: Hispanics of Achievement. 1994, Chelsea LB $21.95 (0-7910-2021-5). A biography of the fighting boxer and his struggle to get to the top. (Rev: BL 9/15/94) [921]

DE LA HOYA, OSCAR

6686 Torres, John A. *Oscar De La Hoya* (5–8). Series: Sports Greats. 1998, Enslow LB $17.95 (0-7660-1066-X). A brief biography of the boxing sensation, with action photographs and career statistics. (Rev: BL 2/15/98; HBG 10/99) [921]

HAWKINS, DWIGHT

6687 Hawkins, Dwight, and Morrie Greenberg. *Survival in the Square* (7–10). Illus. 1989, Brooke-Richards paper $5.95 (0-9622652-0-9). A story of an African American who overcame a physical handicap and became a boxing champion. (Rev: BL 11/15/89; VOYA 12/89) [921]

LOUIS, JOE

6688 Jakoubek, Robert E. *Joe Louis* (6–9). Illus. 1990, Chelsea LB $19.95 (1-55546-599-4). Both the professional career of Joe Louis and his often unfortunate personal life are handled in this account. (Rev: BL 5/1/90) [921]

Football

AIKMAN, TROY

6689 Macnow, Glen. *Troy Aikman* (5–8). Illus. Series: Sports Greats. 1995, Enslow LB $17.95 (0-89490-593-7). The life story of the football great Troy Aikman, with good action photographs and sports statistics. (Rev: BL 9/15/95) [921]

BETTIS, JEROME

6690 Majewski, Stephen. *Jerome Bettis* (5–8). Illus. Series: Sports Greats. 1997, Enslow LB $17.95 (0-89490-872-3). The great football hero Jerome Bettis and his amazing career are highlighted in this easily read biography. (Rev: BL 2/15/97; VOYA 6/97) [921]

BRADY, TOM

6691 Stewart, Mark. *Tom Brady: Heart of the Huddle* (4–7). Series: Sports New Wave. 2003, Millbrook LB $22.90 (0-7613-2907-2). The story of the popular young football player who is quarterback for the New England Patriots. (Rev: BL 6/1–15/03; HBG 10/03) [921]

BRUNELL, MARK

6692 Steenkamer, Paul. *Mark Brunell: Star Quarterback* (4–8). Series: Sports Reports. 2002, Enslow LB $20.95 (0-7660-1830-X). The life story of the Jacksonville Jaguars quarterback, told with detailed summaries of his greatest moments. (Rev: BL 9/1/02; HBG 3/03) [921]

BRYANT, PAUL W.

6693 Smith, E. S. *Bear Bryant: Football's Winning Coach* (6–8). Illus. 1984, Walker $11.95 (0-8027-

6526-2). The story of one of the most famous coaches in football history. [921]

CULPEPPER, DAUNTE

6694 Stewart, Mark. *Daunte Culpepper: Command and Control* (4–7). Series: Sports New Wave. 2002, Millbrook LB $22.90 (0-7613-2613-8). This brief biography celebrates the career of the young African American footballer and his achievements as quarterback of the Minnesota Vikings. (Rev: BL 9/1/02; HBG 10/02) [921]

DAVIS, TERRELL

6695 Stewart, Mark. *Terrell Davis: Toughing It Out* (4–8). Series: Football's New Wave. 1999, Millbrook LB $22.90 (0-7613-1514-4). A brief biography of this football hero that uses color photographs and many fact boxes. (Rev: HBG 10/00; SLJ 7/00) [921]

FAVRE, BRETT

6696 Gutman, Bill. *Brett Favre* (4–8). 1998, Pocket Books paper $3.99 (0-671-02077-3). The story of the quarterback of the Green Bay Packers, with many insider details about his eventful life, play-by-play descriptions, and game strategies. (Rev: BL 12/1/98) [921]

6697 Mooney, Martin. *Brett Favre* (5–7). Illus. Series: Football Legends. 1997, Chelsea LB $18.65 (0-7910-4396-7). The story of the famous quarterback who took the Green Bay Packers to victory in the 1997 Super Bowl. (Rev: BL 1/1–15/98; HBG 3/98) [921]

6698 Rekela, George R. *Brett Favre: Star Quarterback* (5–8). Series: Sports Reports. 2000, Enslow LB $20.95 (0-7660-1332-4). A brief biography of one of football's star quarterbacks that provides good career statistics and behind-the-scenes reporting. (Rev: BL 10/15/00; HBG 10/00) [921]

6699 Savage, Jeff. *Brett Favre* (5–8). Series: Sports Greats. 1998, Enslow LB $17.95 (0-7660-1000-7). An exciting biography of the star quarterback of the Green Bay Packers. (Rev: BL 3/15/98; HBG 10/98) [921]

JACKSON, BO

6700 Devaney, John. *Bo Jackson: A Star for All Seasons* (5–7). Illus. 1992, Walker LB $15.85 (0-802-78179-9). Biography of the Kansas City Royals baseball star, who also played pro football for the Los Angeles Raiders. (Rev: BL 2/15/89; SLJ 1/89) [921]

6701 Gutman, Bill. *Bo Jackson: A Biography* (4–7). Illus. 1991, Pocket paper $2.99 (0-671-73363-X). This account covers such topics as Jackson's winning the Heisman trophy and injuries. (Rev: BL 6/15/91) [921]

6702 Knapp, Ron. *Bo Jackson* (5–8). Illus. Series: Sports Greats. 1990, Enslow LB $17.95 (0-89490-281-4). A standard biography that includes unexpected aspects of Jackson's personality. (Rev: BL 10/15/90; SLJ 3/91) [921]

KELLY, JIM

6703 Harrington, Denis J. *Jim Kelly* (5–8). Illus. Series: Sports Greats. 1996, Enslow LB $17.95 (0-89490-670-4). A short, action-filled biography of this former star quarterback, complete with career statistics. (Rev: BL 3/15/96) [921]

LOMBARDI, VINCE

6704 Roensch, Greg. *Vince Lombardi* (4–7). Series: Football Hall of Famers. 2003, Rosen LB $29.25 (0-8239-3610-4). A lively, detailed, and inspiring biography of the legendary coach for whom the Super Bowl trophy is named. (Rev: SLJ 4/03) [796.332]

MANNING, PEYTON

6705 Savage, Jeff. *Peyton Manning: Precision Passer* (4–7). Series: Sports Achievers Biographies. 2001, Lerner LB $27.15 (0-8225-3683-8); paper $5.95 (0-8225-9865-5). Sports statistics, action photographs, and an accessible text highlight this biography of the Indianapolis Colts quarterback. (Rev: BL 4/1/02; HBG 10/02) [921]

6706 Stewart, Mark. *Peyton Manning: Rising Son* (4–8). Series: Football's New Wave. 2000, Millbrook LB $22.90 (0-7613-1517-9). An easily read account of the professional football player's life and family, including a father who also played in the NFL. (Rev: HBG 10/00; SLJ 1/01) [921]

MONTANA, JOE

6707 Kavanagh, Jack. *Joe Montana* (4–8). Illus. Series: Sports Greats. 1992, Enslow LB $17.95 (0-89490-371-3). In simple text, this is the story of the quarterback who led his San Francisco 49ers to four Super Bowl championships. (Rev: BL 7/92; SLJ 10/92) [921]

MOSS, RANDY

6708 Bernstein, Ross. *Randy Moss: Star Wide Receiver* (4–8). Series: Sports Reports. 2002, Enslow LB $20.95 (0-7660-1503-3). A well-illustrated account of the life of this Minnesota Vikings star, told with plenty of sports action. (Rev: BL 9/1/02; HBG 10/02) [921]

6709 Stewart, Mark. *Randy Moss: First in Flight* (4–8). Illus. Series: Football's New Wave. 2000,

Millbrook LB $22.90 (0-7613-1518-7). The story of the footballer who came from a poor, segregated West Virginia town, was arrested as a young man, but went on to attend college and play professional football. (Rev: HBG 10/00; SLJ 1/01) [921]

PRIETO, JORGÉ

6710 Prieto, Jorge. *The Quarterback Who Almost Wasn't* (7–10). 1994, Arte Publico paper $9.95 (1-55885-109-7). The autobiography of a Mexican physician who struggled with poverty, racism, and political exile before he received a scholarship to play football at Notre Dame. (Rev: BL 8/94) [921]

RICE, JERRY

6711 Dickey, Glenn. *Jerry Rice* (5–8). Illus. Series: Sports Greats. 1993, Enslow LB $17.95 (0-89490-419-1). A brief biography of the star football player who gained fame with the San Francisco 49ers. (Rev: BL 9/15/93) [921]

SANDERS, BARRY

6712 Aaseng, Nathan. *Barry Sanders: Star Running Back* (4–7). Illus. Series: Sports Reports. 1994, Enslow LB $20.95 (0-89490-484-1). This biography of the football star of the Detroit Lions contains many quotations about him from his associates. (Rev: SLJ 8/94) [921]

6713 Knapp, Ron. *Barry Sanders* (5–8). Illus. Series: Sports Greats. 1993, Enslow LB $17.95 (0-89490-418-3). This brief biography of the star football player contains many action photographs and a separate section on his career statistics. (Rev: BL 9/15/93) [921]

SMITH, EMMITT

6714 Grabowski, John. *Emmitt Smith* (5–8). Series: Sports Greats. 1998, Enslow LB $17.95 (0-7660-1002-3). A high-interest biography of this football great that contains career statistics, action photographs, and exciting game action. (Rev: BL 7/98; HBG 10/98) [921]

6715 Thornley, Stew. *Emmitt Smith: Relentless Rusher* (4–8). Series: Sports Achievers. 1996, Lerner LB $27.15 (0-8225-2897-5). The professional life of one of the Dallas Cowboys is highlighted, supplemented by career statistics and action photographs. (Rev: BL 4/15/97; SLJ 8/97) [921]

TARKENTON, FRAN

6716 Hulm, David. *Fran Tarkenton* (4–7). Series: Football Hall of Famers. 2003, Rosen LB $29.25 (0-8239-3608-2). A lively, detailed, and inspiring biography of the star of the Minnesota Vikings and the New York Giants who went on to become a successful businessman. (Rev: SLJ 4/03; VOYA 4/03) [796.332]

THOMAS, THURMAN

6717 Savage, Jeff. *Thurman Thomas: Star Running Back* (4–7). Illus. Series: Sports Reports. 1994, Enslow LB $20.95 (0-89490-445-0). This life story of the football hero also contains action photographs, fact boxes, and statistics. (Rev: SLJ 8/94) [921]

WALKER, HERSCHEL

6718 Benagh, Jim. *Herschel Walker* (5–8). Illus. Series: Sports Greats. 1990, Enslow LB $17.95 (0-89490-207-5). This account tells how Walker grew up in Georgia and went on to a career in professional football. (Rev: BL 10/15/90; SLJ 3/91) [921]

YOUNG, STEVE

6719 Morgan, Terri, and Shmuel Thaler. *Steve Young: Complete Quarterback* (4–8). Illus. Series: Sports Achievers. 1995, Lerner paper $9.55 (0-8225-9716-0). A profile of the San Francisco 49ers quarterback, with material on his professional career, his character, and outside interests. (Rev: BL 11/15/95) [921]

Gymnastics

MOCEANU, DOMINIQUE

6720 Durrett, Deanne. *Dominique Moceanu* (5–8). Series: People in the News. 1999, Lucent LB $27.45 (1-56006-099-9). Drawing heavily on Moceanu's autobiography, this is the life story of the phenomenal gymnast, with behind-the scenes glimpses of competitions, training, scoring, and routines. (Rev: HBG 3/00; SLJ 8/99) [921]

6721 Quiner, Krista. *Dominique Moceanu: A Gymnastics Sensation* (4–7). Illus. 1997, Bradford paper $12.95 (0-9643460-3-6). The story of the United States' youngest gold medal winner in gymnastics, with a special 24-page insert of photographs. (Rev: SLJ 3/97) [921]

Ice Skating and Hockey

BOITANO, BRIAN

6722 Boitano, Brian, and Suzanne Harper. *Boitano's Edge: Inside the Real World of Figure Skating* (4–8). Illus. 1997, Simon & Schuster $25.00 (0-689-81915-3). In this autobiography, Boitano tells about his life, the 1988 Olympics, his training programs, touring, and preparing for competitions. (Rev: BCCB 3/98; BL 2/15/98; SLJ 4/98; VOYA 4/98) [921]

FORREST, ALBERT

6723 McFarlane, Brian. *The Youngest Goalie* (6–9). 1997, Warwick Publg. paper $8.95 (1-895629-95-0). This is an exciting, fictionalized biography of Albert Forrest, who was born in 1887 and became the youngest goalie to play in a Stanley Cup final. (Rev: VOYA 2/99) [921]

GORDEEVA, EKATERINA

6724 Hill, Anne E. *Ekaterina Gordeeva* (6–9). Series: Overcoming Adversity. 1999, Chelsea LB $21.95 (0-7910-4948-5); paper $9.95 (0-7910-4949-3). The story of the amazing Russian ice skater, her Olympic triumphs, and her adjustment to the sudden death of her husband and partner, who was also a gold-medal winner. (Rev: BL 5/15/99) [921]

6725 Shea, Pegi Deitz. *Ekatarina Gordeeva* (4–8). Series: Female Figure Skating Legends. 1999, Chelsea LB $18.65 (0-7910-5027-0). Sports lovers will enjoy this look at the life of the famous skater before and after the death of her partner and husband, Sergei Grinkov. (Rev: SLJ 4/99) [921]

GRETZKY, WAYNE

6726 Rappoport, Ken. *Wayne Gretzky* (5–8). Illus. Series: Sports Greats. 1996, Enslow LB $17.95 (0-89490-757-3). A brief biography of this hockey phenomenon, illustrated with black-and-white action photographs. (Rev: BL 3/15/96) [921]

HAMILTON, SCOTT

6727 Brennan, Kristine. *Scott Hamilton* (6–9). Series: Overcoming Adversity. 1999, Chelsea LB $21.95 (0-7910-4944-2); paper $9.95 (0-7910-4945-0). A biography of the 4-time winner of the men's world figure skating championship between 1981 and 1984, and his gallant battle against cancer. (Rev: BL 5/15/99) [921]

KWAN, MICHELLE

6728 Epstein, Edward Z. *Born to Skate* (6–12). 1997, Ballantine paper $5.99 (0-345-42136-1). This book describes the career of figure skater Michelle Kwan from her first steps on ice at age five to her world championship in 1996 and disappointments in 1997. (This book was written before her 1998 Olympic triumphs.) (Rev: VOYA 4/98) [921]

6729 James, Laura. *Michelle Kwan: Heart of a Champion* (4–8). Illus. 1997, Scholastic paper $14.95 (0-590-76340-7). A highly personal account of this figure-skating champion, who describes how she succeeded in placing second at the World Championships in 1997 only one month after two falls cost her the position of U.S. women's champion, and who reveals a maturity beyond her years. (Rev: BL 11/15/97; HBG 3/98; SLJ 11/97) [921]

LEMIEUX, MARIO

6730 O'Shei, Tim. *Mario Lemieux* (8–12). Series: Overcoming Adversity. 2002, Chelsea LB $21.95 (0-7910-6305-4). This biography of the renowned hockey legend, tells how he made an amazing comeback from Hodgkin's Disease. (Rev: BL 4/15/02) [921]

6731 Rossiter, Sean. *Mario Lemieux* (4–8). Illus. Series: Hockey Heroes. 2001, Sterling $12.95 (1-55054-870-0). A detailed look at the career of Pittsburgh Penguin Mario Lemieux. (Rev: BL 2/15/02) [796.962]

6732 Stewart, Mark. *Mario Lemieux: Own the Ice* (5–8). Illus. 2002, Millbrook LB $24.90 (0-7613-2555-7); paper $8.95 (0-7613-1687-6). A readable biography of the ice hockey star, with photographs, statistics, and information about the athlete's personal life and work ethic. (Rev: BL 9/15/02; HBG 3/03) [796.962]

LINDROS, ERIC

6733 Rappoport, Ken. *Eric Lindros* (5–8). Series: Sports Greats. 1997, Enslow LB $17.95 (0-89490-871-5). A biography of the famous hockey star that includes career statistics and action photographs. (Rev: BL 10/15/97) [921]

OHNO, APOLO ANTON

6734 Ohno, Apolo Anton, and Nancy Ann Richardson. *A Journey: The Autobiography of Apolo Anton Ohno* (7–12). Illus. 2002, Simon & Schuster $16.95 (0-689-85608-3). The story of the difficult childhood and rigorous preparation endured by Ohno, the winner of two medals for ice skating in the 2002 Olympics. (Rev: BL 12/1/02; HBG 3/03; SLJ 2/03; VOYA 2/03) [796.91]

WITT, KATARINA

6735 Coffey, Wayne. *Katarina Witt* (4–7). Illus. 1992, Blackbirch $16.45 (1-56711-001-0). This biography highlights the 1988 Olympic Games, where this figure skater became a star. (Rev: SLJ 11/92) [921]

6736 Kelly, Evelyn B. *Katerina Witt* (6–9). Series: Female Figure Skating Legends. 1999, Chelsea LB $18.65 (0-7910-5026-2). This is the story of figure skating champion Katerina Witt, from her childhood in East Germany under Communist rule to her many

Olympic competitions. (Rev: BL 3/1/99; VOYA 6/99) [921]

Tennis

AGASSI, ANDRE

6737 Knapp, Ron. *Andre Agassi: Star Tennis Player* (5–8). Series: Sports Reports. 1997, Enslow LB $20.95 (0-89490-798-0). An in-depth look at the life and career of this tennis star, with details of his childhood and his father's influence. (Rev: BL 8/97; SLJ 8/97) [921]

6738 Savage, Jeff. *Andre Agassi: Reaching the Top — Again* (4–8). Series: Sports Achievers. 1997, Lerner paper $9.55 (0-8225-9750-0). A short, easily read biography of this volatile tennis star. (Rev: BL 1/1–15/98; HBG 3/98) [921]

ASHE, ARTHUR

6739 Collins, David R. *Arthur Ashe: Against the Wind* (6–9). Series: People in Focus. 1994, Dillon LB $13.95 (0-87518-647-5). A portrait of the inspiring African American sports champion, humanitarian, and civil rights activist. (Rev: BL 2/1/95; SLJ 3/95; VOYA 5/95) [921]

6740 Lazo, Caroline. *Arthur Ashe* (4–7). Series: A&E Biography. 1999, Lerner $25.26 (0-8225-1932-8). The inspiring story of this great African American tennis star and humanitarian is told in a clear, well-organized text with several black-and-white photographs. (Rev: BL 3/15/00) [921]

6741 Martin, Marvin. *Arthur Ashe: Of Tennis and the Human Spirit* (6–12). 1999, Watts LB $18.95 (0-531-11432-5). In spite of incredible obstacles, Arthur Ashe achieved great heights in the tennis world, including becoming the first African American world champion, and became admired as much for his humanitarian efforts and his dignified struggle against racism as for his tennis achievements. (Rev: BL 7/99; SLJ 6/99) [921]

6742 Wright, David K. *Arthur Ashe: Breaking the Color Barrier in Tennis* (7–12). Illus. Series: African-American Biographies. 1996, Enslow LB $20.95 (0-89490-689-5). The life story of this revered tennis star, his professional career, and gallant struggle against AIDS. (Rev: BL 12/15/96; SLJ 10/96) [921]

CHANG, MICHAEL

6743 Ditchfield, Christin. *Michael Chang* (5–8). Series: Sports Greats. 1999, Enslow LB $17.95 (0-7660-1223-9). A biography of this tennis phenomenon, with career statistics and plenty of action photographs. (Rev: BL 3/15/99; HBG 10/99) [921]

GIBSON, ALTHEA

6744 Biracree, Tom. *Althea Gibson* (7–12). Illus. 1989, Chelsea LB $19.95 (1-55546-654-0). The rags-to-riches story of the African American athlete who was once the best woman tennis player in the world. (Rev: BL 2/15/90; BR 3–4/90; SLJ 2/90; VOYA 2/90) [921]

SAMPRAS, PETE

6745 Miller, Calvin C. *Pete Sampras* (6–10). Illus. 1998, Morgan Reynolds LB $18.95 (1-883846-26-9). A candid biography of this usually quiet and staid tennis professional, with details on his phenomenal career. (Rev: BL 4/1/98; BR 1–2/99; HBG 9/98) [921]

6746 Sherrow, Victoria. *Pete Sampras* (5–8). Illus. Series: Sports Greats. 1996, Enslow LB $17.95 (0-89490-756-5). The life story of this charismatic tennis star is told in brief text and many photographs, accompanied by career statistics. (Rev: BL 3/15/96) [921]

SELES, MONICA

6747 Blue, Rose, and Corinne J. Naden. *Monica Seles* (8–12). Series: Overcoming Adversity. 2002, Chelsea LB $21.95 (0-7910-5899-9). The biography of the courageous tennis star who returned to competition after being stabbed during a match. (Rev: BL 4/15/02; HBG 10/02) [921]

6748 Murdico, Suzanne J. *Monica Seles* (5–8). Illus. Series: Overcoming the Odds. 1998, Raintree Steck-Vaughn $28.80 (0-8172-4128-0). The story of the great tennis player and the courtside stabbing that resulted in a trauma difficult to overcome. (Rev: HBG 9/98; VOYA 8/98) [921]

WILLIAMS, VENUS AND SERENA

6749 Aronson, Virginia. *Venus Williams* (5–8). Illus. Series: Galaxy of Superstars. 1999, Chelsea $19.75 (0-7910-5153-6); paper $8.95 (0-7910-5329-6). The story of this superstar of tennis, how her father trained her, and how he made her education more important than her tennis. (Rev: BL 4/15/99; BR 9–10/99; HBG 10/99; SLJ 5/99; VOYA 4/00) [921]

6750 Buckley, James. *Venus and Serena Williams* (6–9). Series: Trailblazers of the Modern World. 2003, World Almanac LB $26.60 (0-8368-5086-6); paper $14.60 (0-8368-5246-X). The story of the amazing sister team who changed the history of tennis. (Rev: BL 6/1–15/03) [921]

6751 Fillon, Mike. *Young Superstars of Tennis: The Venus and Serena Williams Story* (4–8). Series: Avisson Young Adult. 1999, Avisson LB $19.95 (1-888105-43-7). This biography of the Williams sis-

ters tells about their childhood, the influence of their father, and their determination to get to the top in tennis. (Rev: BL 12/15/99; SLJ 3/00; VOYA 4/00) [921]

6752 Morgan, Terri. *Venus and Serena Williams: Grand Slam Sisters* (4–7). Series: Sports Achievers Biographies. 2001, Lerner LB $27.15 (0-8225-3684-6); paper $5.95 (0-8225-9866-3). An action-packed biography of the amazing tennis duo that covers their careers and their family. (Rev: BL 4/1/02; HBG 10/02) [921]

6753 Stewart, Mark. *Venus and Serena Williams: Sisters in Arms* (4–7). Series: Tennis's New Wave. 2000, Millbrook LB $22.90 (0-7613-1803-8). A simple biography of the amazing tennis-playing sisters with good coverage of their early lives. (Rev: HBG 3/01; SLJ 3/01) [921]

Track and Field

DEVERS, GAIL

6754 Worth, Richard. *Gail Devers* (8–12). Series: Overcoming Adversity. 2002, Chelsea LB $21.95 (0-7910-6307-0). While battling Bright's Disease, a serious thyroid disorder, Gail Devers won a gold medal in the 100-meter sprint during the 1992 Olympics. (Rev: BL 4/15/02) [921]

JONES, MARION

6755 Rutledge, Rachel. *Marion Jones: Fast and Fearless* (4–7). 2000, Millbrook LB $22.90 (0-7613-1870-4). A biography of the track-and-field star of the 2000 Sydney Olympics that stresses her drive and tenacity. (Rev: HBG 3/01; SLJ 3/01) [921]

JOYNER-KERSEE, JACKIE

6756 Green, Carl R. *Jackie Joyner-Kersee* (4–8). Illus. Series: Sports Headliners. 1994, Macmillan LB $13.95 (0-89686-838-9). A biography of the track star that uses quotations and photographs to highlight important events in her career. (Rev: BL 10/1/94) [921]

6757 Harrington, Geri. *Jackie Joyner-Kersee: Champion Athlete* (6–10). 1995, Chelsea LB $21.95 (0-7910-2085-1). Describes Joyner-Kersee's four Olympic championships, despite asthma attacks. (Rev: BL 10/1/95) [921]

LEWIS, CARL

6758 Aaseng, Nathan. *Carl Lewis: Legend Chaser* (4–8). Illus. 1985, Lerner LB $18.60 (0-8225-0496-0). Childhood, college, and Olympic performances are covered in this biography, including both praise and criticism about Lewis's attempt at the long-jump record. (Rev: BCCB 11/85; BL 7/85; SLJ 8/85) [796.420924]

6759 Klots, Steve. *Carl Lewis* (7–10). Series: Black Americans of Achievement. 1994, Chelsea LB $21.75 (0-7910-2164-5). Describes the childhood, college career, and Olympic performances of this athlete, including his attempts at the long-jump record. (Rev: BL 3/15/95) [921]

LEWIS, RAY

6760 Cooper, John. *Rapid Ray: The Story of Ray Lewis* (5–9). 2002, Tundra paper $8.95 (0-88776-612-9). An absorbing profile of the Canadian-born black athlete (and train porter) who won a bronze medal in the 1932 Olympics and the racial hurdles he had to overcome. (Rev: SLJ 6/03) [796.42]

LONGBOAT, TOM

6761 Batten, Jack. *The Man Who Ran Faster Than Everyone: The Story of Tom Longboat* (7–12). Illus. 2002, Tundra paper $12.95 (0-88776-507-6). A straightforward biography of the Onondaga Indian distance runner whose won fame in the early 20th century. (Rev: BL 4/1/02; SLJ 6/02) [796.42]

O'BRIEN, DAN

6762 Gutman, Bill. *Dan O'Brien* (5–8). Series: Overcoming the Odds. 1998, Raintree Steck-Vaughn $28.80 (0-8172-4129-9). A biography of this great decathlete that describes his struggles to overcome attention-deficit hyperactivity disorder as well as various injuries. (Rev: HBG 9/98; VOYA 8/98) [921]

OWENS, JESSE

6763 Gentry, Tony. *Jesse Owens: Champion Athlete* (6–9). Illus. 1990, Chelsea LB $21.95 (1-55546-603-6). The story of the African American track star who upset Hitler's master race theory at the Olympics. (Rev: SLJ 7/90; VOYA 8/90) [921]

6764 Josephson, Judith P. *Jesse Owens: Track and Field Legend* (6–10). Series: African-American Biographies. 1997, Enslow LB $20.95 (0-89490-812-X). The life of this track star is retold with details about the prejudice he faced throughout his personal and professional life and his performance at the 1936 Berlin Olympics, where he won four gold medals, defying Adolf Hitler's view of Aryans as the "Master Race." (Rev: SLJ 1/98) [921]

6765 Nuwer, Hank. *The Legend of Jesse Owens* (7–12). Series: Impact Biographies. 1998, Watts LB $20.00 (0-531-11356-6). The inspiring life of the track-and-field star who won a gold medal in the 1936 Olympics despite pervasive racism and a frail constitution. (Rev: BL 1/1–15/99; HBG 3/99; SLJ 1/99) [921]

6766 Rennert, Richard S. *Jesse Owens* (4–7). Illus. Series: Junior World Biography. 1991, Chelsea LB $16.95 (0-7910-1570-X). An attractive, well-illustrated account of this famous track-and-field star who embarrassed Hitler by winning four gold medals at the 1936 Olympic Games. (Rev: BL 9/1/91; SLJ 9/91) [921]

RUDOLPH, WILMA

6767 Biracree, Tom. *Wilma Rudolph* (7–12). Illus. 1987, Chelsea LB $19.95 (1-55546-675-3). The inspiring story of the African American athlete who conquered polio and won three Olympic gold medals in track in a single year. (Rev: BL 8/88) [921]

THORPE, JIM

6768 Long, Barbara. *Jim Thorpe: Legendary Athlete* (5–7). Illus. Series: Native American Biographies. 1997, Enslow LB $20.95 (0-89490-865-0). The story of the amazing Native American athlete whose career had tremendous highs and lows. (Rev: BL 6/1–15/97) [921]

Miscellaneous Sports

ARMSTRONG, LANCE

6769 Stewart, Mark. *Sweet Victory: Lance Armstrong's Incredible Journey* (6–10). Illus. Series: Inspiring People. 2000, Millbrook LB $24.90 (0-7613-1861-5). The inspiring story of Lance Armstrong who became an American hero when he fought and won a battle with cancer and triumphed at the Tour de France in 1999. (Rev: BL 8/00; HBG 10/00; SLJ 8/00) [921]

BASS, TOM

6770 Wilkerson, J. L. *From Slave to World-Class Horseman: Tom Bass* (4–8). 2000, Acorn paper $9.95 (0-9664470-3-4). A fast-paced narrative about the man who was born a slave and later became such a renowned horseman that he performed for Queen Victoria. (Rev: SLJ 4/00) [921]

BUTCHER, SUSAN

6771 Wadsworth, Ginger. *Susan Butcher: Sled Dog Racer* (4–7). Illus. Series: Sports Achievers. 1994, Lerner LB $18.60 (0-8225-2878-9). This exciting biography brings to life the four-time Iditarod winner and the rigors and courage each race involved. (Rev: SLJ 6/94) [921]

LEMOND, GREG

6772 Porter, A. P. *Greg LeMond: Premier Cyclist* (4–7). Illus. Series: Sports Achievers. 1990, Lerner LB $18.60 (0-8225-0476-6). Although he suffered severe injuries in a hunting accident, LeMond won the Tour de France bicycle race. (Rev: BL 6/15/90; SLJ 9/90) [921]

MACDONALD, ANDY

6773 MacDonald, Andy, and Theresa Foy Digeronimo. *Dropping in with Andy Mac: The Life of a Pro Skateboarder* (6–12). Illus. 2003, Simon & Schuster paper $9.99 (0-689-85784-5). Andy Mac describes his life from early childhood, telling readers about his family, his teen years, and his love of sports. (Rev: BL 6/1–15/03; VOYA 8/03) [796.22]

MONPLAISIR, SHARON

6774 Greenberg, Doreen, and Michael Greenberg. *Sword of a Champion: The Story of Sharon Monplaisir* (4–8). Series: Anything You Can Do — New Sports Heroes for Girls. 2000, Wish paper $9.95 (1-930546-39-4). The life story of the timid, shy high schooler who found her place in fencing via a coach who encouraged her to develop her natural talents. (Rev: SLJ 3/01; VOYA 2/01) [796.8]

NASH, KEVIN

6775 Mudge, Jacqueline. *Kevin Nash* (4–7). Series: Pro Wrestling Legends. 2000, Chelsea paper $8.95 (0-7910-5828-X). This is the biography of the wrestler known as "Diesel." (Rev: BL 10/15/00; HBG 3/01) [921]

PAK, SE RI

6776 Stewart, Mark. *Se Ri Pak: Driven to Win* (4–8). Series: Golf's New Wave. 2000, Millbrook LB $22.90 (0-7613-1519-5). The story of the South Korean who won the Ladies Professional Golf Association Championship in 1998. (Rev: HBG 10/00; SLJ 8/00) [921]

PELE

6777 Arnold, Caroline. *Pele: The King of Soccer* (4–8). Illus. Series: First Books. 1992, Watts paper $22.00 (0-531-20077-9). Traces Pele's soccer career from early promise to international superstardom. (Rev: BL 10/1/92) [921]

REECE, GABRIELLE

6778 Morgan, Terri. *Gabrielle Reece: Volleyball's Model Athlete* (4–7). Illus. Series: Sports Achievers. 1999, Lerner LB $22.60 (0-8225-3667-6). An accessible biography of the woman who is not only a volleyball champ but also a fashion model and TV personality. (Rev: BL 10/15/99; HBG 3/00) [921]

SIFFORD, CHARLIE

6779 Britt, Grant. *Charlie Sifford* (4–7). Illus. 1998, Morgan Reynolds LB $18.95 (1-883846-27-7). This biography of the African American golfer stresses the problems he faced breaking the color barrier when he entered the sport after World War II. (Rev: BL 2/15/98; HBG 10/98; SLJ 7/98) [921]

TREVINO, LEE

6780 Gilbert, Thomas. *Lee Trevino* (5–9). Series: Hispanics of Achievement. 1991, Chelsea LB $19.95 (0-7910-1256-5). The story of one of golf's all-time greats to 1990. (Rev: BL 3/15/92) [796.352]

VENTURA, JESSE

6781 Cohen, Daniel. *Jesse Ventura: The Body, the Mouth, the Mind* (6–10). Illus. 2001, Millbrook LB $25.90 (0-7613-1905-0). A comprehensive profile of Ventura's private life and his stints as Navy Seal, talk-show host, actor, wrestler, and politician. (Rev: BL 10/1/01; HBG 3/02; SLJ 12/01; VOYA 12/01) [977.6]

6782 Greenberg, Keith E. *Jesse Ventura* (5–8). Illus. Series: A&E Biography. 1999, Lerner LB $30.35 (0-8225-4977-8); paper $7.95 (0-8225-9680-6). A look at this larger-than-life pop culture hero who has been an actor, a professional wrestler, a Navy SEAL, and the governor of Minnesota. (Rev: BL 3/1/00; HBG 3/00; SLJ 2/00) [921]

6783 Uschan, Michael V. *Jesse Ventura* (5–8). Series: People in the News. 2001, Lucent LB $35.15 (1-56006-777-2). From a career in wrestling to a state governorship, this is the story of the amazing Jesse Ventura. (Rev: BL 4/1/02) [921]

WOODS, TIGER

6784 Boyd, Aaron. *Tiger Woods* (5–7). Illus. 1997, Morgan Reynolds LB $18.95 (1-883846-19-6). A brief, straightforward biography of this amazing golfer who was a young prodigy. (Rev: BL 5/1/97; HBG 3/98; SLJ 8/97; VOYA 10/97) [921]

6785 Collins, David R. *Tiger Woods, Golfing Champion* (5–8). 1999, Pelican $14.95 (1-56554-322-X). A chronologically arranged book ending in 1999 that reveals Tiger Woods's determination and love of the game. (Rev: SLJ 1/00) [921]

6786 Roberts, Jeremy. *Tiger Woods* (5–8). Series: Biography. 2002, Lerner LB $30.35 (0-8225-0030-2). The story of the likable wonder boy of golf is told in text and pictures. (Rev: BL 4/1/02; HBG 10/02) [921]

6787 Teague, Allison L. *Prince of the Fairway: The Tiger Woods Story* (8–12). 1997, Avisson LB $18.50 (1-888105-22-4). Written for young adults, this biography probes into Woods's childhood and the cultural values of his family as well as describing his golf training and career. (Rev: SLJ 10/97; VOYA 10/97) [921]

ZAHARIAS, BABE DIDRIKSON

6788 Cayleff, Susan E. *Babe Didrikson: The Greatest All-Sport Athlete of All Time* (7–12). Illus. 2000, Conari paper $8.95 (1-57324-194-6). A candid, honest look at the life of this difficult, brash, competitive golf legend. (Rev: BL 10/1/00; VOYA 8/01) [921]

6789 Freedman, Russell. *Babe Didrikson Zaharias: The Making of a Champion* (6–12). 1999, Clarion $18.00 (0-395-63367-2). Although this athlete was known to most for her golf career, this entertaining biography points out that Babe Didrikson Zaharias was also an Olympic athlete, a track star, leader of a women's amateur basketball team, and an entrepreneur. (Rev: BCCB 10/99; BL 7/99; HB 9–10/99; HBG 3/00; SLJ 7/99; VOYA 12/00) [921]

6790 Lynn, Elizabeth A. *Babe Didrikson Zaharias* (6–10). Illus. 1988, Chelsea LB $19.95 (1-55546-684-2). The story of the all-around athlete best known for her accomplishments in golf. (Rev: BL 12/1/88; BR 5–6/89) [921]

6791 Wakeman, Nancy. *Babe Didrikson Zaharias: Driven to Win* (4–7). Illus. Series: Biography. 2000, Lerner LB $25.26 (0-8225-4917-4). The account focuses on this sportswoman's professional career and her strong personality plus her accomplishments in track and field, basketball, and baseball. (Rev: BL 6/1–15/00; HBG 10/00; SLJ 7/00; VOYA 12/00) [921]

World Figures

Collective

6792 Aaseng, Nathan. *The Peace Seekers: The Nobel Peace Prize* (5–8). Illus. 1987, Lerner LB $18.60 (0-8225-0654-8); paper $7.95 (0-8225-9604-0). Martin Luther King, Jr., and Lech Walesa are among those whose lives and works are introduced. (Rev: BL 2/1/88) [327.1720922]

6793 Avakian, Monique. *Reformers: Activists, Educators, Religious Leaders* (5–9). Series: Remarkable Women. 2000, Raintree Steck-Vaughn LB $32.85 (0-8172-5733-0). This book contains 150 profiles of woman who, throughout history and from many cultures, have fought for human rights, including Harriet Tubman, Mother Teresa, and Dolores Huerta. (Rev: SLJ 8/00) [920]

6794 Axelrod-Contrada, Joan. *Women Who Led Nations* (7–10). Series: Profiles. 1999, Oliver LB $18.95 (1-881508-48-X). Corazon Aquino, Benazir Bhutto, and Golda Meir are among the seven women profiled in detail in this collective biography. (Rev: HBG 4/00; SLJ 10/99) [921]

6795 Baker, Rosalie, and Charles Baker. *Ancient Egyptians: People of the Pyramids* (6–12). Illus. Series: Oxford Profiles. 2001, Oxford $40.00 (0-19-512221-6). Detailed biographies of key figures such as Nefertiti, Hatshepsut, Tutankhamun, and Ramses give plenty of background social and cultural information and are accompanied by sidebar features and black-and-white photographs. (Rev: BL 9/15/01; HBG 10/02; SLJ 11/01) [920.032]

6796 Benson, Sonia G. *Korean War: Biographies* (6–10). 2001, Gale LB $52.00 (0-7876-5692-5). A collection of 25 biographies of individuals — Koreans, Americans, and other nationalities — who participated in or affected the course of the Korean War. (Rev: BL 3/15/02; SLJ 5/02) [951.904]

6797 Billinghurst, Jane. *Growing Up Royal: Life in the Shadow of the British Throne* (4–7). Illus. 2001, Annick $22.95 (1-55037-623-3); paper $12.95 (1-55037-622-5). A look at what it's like to be young and royal, with a focus on the lives of today's British royalty, with color photographs and interesting anecdotes. (Rev: BL 9/1/01; HBG 3/02; SLJ 11/01; VOYA 4/02) [971.082]

6798 Blue, Rose, and Corinne J. Naden. *People of Peace* (4–7). Illus. 1994, Millbrook LB $26.90 (1-56294-409-6). Brief biographies of 10 people in modern history who have made great sacrifices for world peace, including Mohandas Gandhi and Desmond Tutu. (Rev: BL 12/15/94; SLJ 2/95) [920]

6799 Brewster, Hugh, and Laurie Coulter. *To Be a Princess: The Fascinating Lives of Real Princesses* (4–8). Illus. 2001, HarperCollins $17.89 (0-06-000159-3). Twelve real-life princesses, historical and contemporary, are featured here in chapter-length profiles with timelines, reproductions of museum portraits, and historical details. (Rev: BCCB 12/01; BL 12/1/01; HBG 3/02; SLJ 10/01) [940]

6800 Glick, Susan. *Heroes of the Holocaust* (6–10). Series: History Makers. 2003, Gale LB $27.45 (1-59018-063-1). This work contains brief biographies of such heroes as Oskar Schindler, Raul Wallenberg, Vladka Reed, Hannah Senech, and Jan Karski. (Rev: BL 6/1–15/03; SLJ 7/03) [920]

6801 Goldman, Elizabeth. *Believers: Spiritual Leaders of the World* (7–9). Illus. 1996, Oxford $50.00 (0-19-508240-0). This oversize book contains profiles of 40 religious leaders, from the well known, such as Moses and Jesus, to the obscure, such as Hildegard of Bingen and Isaac Luria. (Rev: BL 4/15/96) [920]

6802 Green, Robert. *Dictators* (6–9). Series: History Makers. 2000, Lucent LB $18.96 (1-56006-594-X).

Several 20th-century dictators such as Stalin, Hitler, Mao Zedong, Franco, and Saddam Hussein are profiled. (Rev: BL 6/1–15/00; HBG 9/00) [920]

6803 Gulatta, Charles. *Extraordinary Women in Politics* (5–9). Series: Extraordinary People. 1998, Children's LB $37.50 (0-516-20610-9). From Cleopatra, Queen Victoria, and Catherine the Great to Margaret Thatcher, Bella Abzug, Sandra Day O'Connor, and Hillary Rodham Clinton, this book profiles 55 women who have had a powerful influence in the world's political arena. (Rev: BL 1/1–15/99; HBG 3/99; SLJ 1/99) [920]

6804 Hazell, Rebecca. *The Barefoot Book of Heroic Children* (4–7). Illus. 2000, Barefoot $19.95 (1-902283-23-6). This book presents the lives of 12 heroic children from different times and places, among them Anne Frank, Fanny Mendelssohn, Annie Sullivan, and Iqbal Masih. (Rev: BL 4/15/00) [920]

6805 Hazell, Rebecca. *Heroines: Great Women Through the Ages* (5–8). Illus. 1996, Abbeville $19.95 (0-7892-0210-7). This is a collective biography of 12 great women spanning the period from ancient Greece to modern times, including Sacagawea, Madame Sun Yat-Sen, Frido Kahlo, Joan of Arc, Harriet Tubman, and Marie Curie. (Rev: SLJ 12/96) [920]

6806 James, Lesley. *Women in Government: Politicians, Lawmakers, Law Enforcers* (6–10). Illus. Series: Remarkable Women. 2000, Raintree Steck-Vaughn LB $28.54 (0-8172-5730-6). A collection of illustrated, alphabetically-arranged biographies of famous queens, presidents, activists, and empresses. (Rev: BL 6/1–15/00) [920]

6807 Kjelle, Marylou Morano. *Hitler's Henchmen* (6–10). Series: History Makers. 2003, Gale LB $27.45 (1-59018-229-4). Hitler's assistants are profiled in this collective biography that includes Goebbels and Himmler. (Rev: BL 6/1–15/03; SLJ 7/03) [920]

6808 Krull, Kathleen. *Lives of Extraordinary Women: Rulers, Rebels (and What the Neighbors Thought)* (5–8). Illus. Series: Extraordinary Lives. 2000, Harcourt $20.00 (0-15-200807-1). Short biographies of women who affected the course of history, from Cleopatra to contemporary Burma's Aung San Suu Kyi. (Rev: BCCB 9/00; BL 9/1/00; HB 11–12/00; HBG 3/01; SLJ 9/00; VOYA 6/01) [920]

6809 Lace, William W. *Leaders and Generals* (5–10). Series: American War. 2000, Lucent LB $27.45 (1-56006-664-4). This book contains eight profiles of about 10 pages each of the following World War II leaders: Erwin Rommel, Georgi Zhukov, Erich von Manstein, Yamamoto Isoroku, Douglas MacArthur, Chester Nimitz, Dwight Eisenhower, and Bernard Law Montgomery. (Rev: BL 4/15/00; HBG 10/00; SLJ 6/00) [920]

6810 Leon, Vicki. *Outrageous Women of Ancient Times* (4–7). Illus. 1997, Wiley paper $12.95 (0-471-17006-2). Fifteen unusual women from ancient civilizations in Asia, Europe, and Africa are profiled, among them warriors, philosophers, empresses, artists, and professional poisoners, and including Cleopatra and Sappho. (Rev: BL 11/1/97; SLJ 12/97) [920]

6811 Leon, Vicki. *Outrageous Women of the Middle Ages* (4–7). Illus. 1998, Wiley paper $12.95 (0-471-17004-6). Using a witty writing style and modern comparisons, this fascinating book profiles a diverse group of amazing women who lived from the 6th through the 14th centuries in Europe, Asia, and Africa. (Rev: BL 4/15/98; SLJ 8/98) [920]

6812 Meltzer, Milton. *Ten Kings and the Worlds They Ruled* (5–8). 2002, Scholastic paper $21.95 (0-439-31293-0). Ten kings from around the world and across the ages are discussed in this attractive book that includes impressive portraits and other illustrations. Also use *Ten Queens* (1998). (Rev: BCCB 9/02; BL 7/02; HBG 10/02; SLJ 10/02*) [920.02]

6813 Meltzer, Milton. *Ten Queens: Portraits of Women of Power* (5–8). Illus. 1998, Dutton $24.99 (0-525-45643-0). In this handsome book enhanced by reproductions of many paintings, 10 queens are profiled, including Esther, Cleopatra, Eleanor of Aquitaine, Isabella of Spain, Elizabeth I, and Catherine the Great. (Rev: BCCB 7–8/98; BL 4/15/98; BR 1–2/99; HBG 3/99; SLJ 6/98; VOYA 4/99) [920]

6814 Nardo, Don. *Women Leaders of Nations* (6–10). Illus. Series: History Makers. 1999, Lucent LB $17.96 (1-56006-397-1). An overview of women in government, followed by chapters on several female leaders of nations, among them Cleopatra and Margaret Thatcher, and a chapter on other women leaders, including Amazon warriors and Queen Boudicca. (Rev: BL 6/1–15/99) [920]

6815 Price-Groff, Claire. *Great Conquerors* (6–10). Series: History Makers. 2000, Lucent LB $18.96 (1-56006-612-5). This work profiles seven world conquerors, including Alexander the Great and Napoleon, each representing a different time period and a different culture. (Rev: BL 3/15/00) [920]

6816 Price-Groff, Claire. *Twentieth-Century Women Political Leaders* (7–10). Series: Global Profiles. 1998, Facts on File LB $25.00 (0-8160-3672-1). This book contains profiles of 12 women political leaders in the second half of the 20th century: Golda Meir, Indira Gandhi, Eva Peron, Margaret Thatcher, Corazon Aquino, Winnie Mandela, Barbara Jordan, Violeta Chamorro, Wilma Mankiller, Gro Harlem Brundtland, Aung San Suu Kyi, and Benazir Bhutto. (Rev: BR 1–2/99; SLJ 1/99) [920]

6817 Rasmussen, R. Kent. *Modern African Political Leaders* (7–12). Illus. Series: Global Profiles. 1998,

Facts on File $25.00 (0-8160-3277-7). This book focuses on how personal incidents inspired the political actions of eight African leaders of the 20th century who played major roles in the political changes throughout the continent, including Haile Selassie, Gamal Abdel Nasser, Kwame Nkrumah, Robert Mugabe, and Nelson Mandela. (Rev: BL 8/98; BR 11–12/98; SLJ 9/98) [920]

6818 Shaw, Maura D. *Ten Amazing People: And How They Changed the World* (4–7). Illus. 2002, Skylight Paths $17.95 (1-893361-47-0). Shaw presents 10 well-illustrated biographies of 20th-century religious figures, each with timelines, a quotation, a glossary, and an emphasis on the individual's beliefs. (Rev: BL 10/1/02; HBG 3/03; SLJ 12/02) [200]

6819 Traub, Carol G. *Philanthropists and Their Legacies* (7–12). Illus. Series: Profiles. 1997, Oliver LB $19.95 (1-881508-42-0). Profiles — warts and all — of nine of the world's greatest benefactors, including Alfred Nobel, Andrew Carnegie, Cecil Rhodes, George Eastman, Will Kellogg, and John and Catherine MacArthur. (Rev: BL 2/15/98; BR 1–2/98; SLJ 2/98) [361.7]

6820 Wakin, Edward. *Contemporary Political Leaders of the Middle East* (6–12). Illus. Series: Global Profiles. 1996, Facts on File $25.00 (0-8160-3154-1). Profiles of eight Israeli and Arab leaders who have shaped events in the Middle East, including Saddam Hussein, Mubarek, Quadaffi, Rabin, and Peres. (Rev: BL 4/15/96; SLJ 3/96; VOYA 4/96) [956.05]

6821 Welden, Amelie. *Girls Who Rocked the World: Heroines from Sacagawea to Sheryl Swoopes* (4–8). Illus. 1998, Beyond Words paper $8.95 (1-885223-68-4). This collective biography contains short profiles of 33 women who achieved extraordinary things before age 20, arranged chronologically, starting with Cleopatra and ending with tennis star Martina Hingis. (Rev: BL 7/97; SLJ 7/98) [920]

Africa

ADAMSON, JOY

6822 Neimark, Anne E. *Wild Heart: The Story of Joy Adamson, Author of Born Free* (6–10). 1999, Harcourt $17.00 (0-15-201368-7). This biography of the author of *Born Free* tells about her childhood in Austria, her later work with wild animals in Kenya (including raising the lion cub Elsa), and her pioneer work in conservation. (Rev: BL 3/15/99; SLJ 6/99; VOYA 10/99) [921]

CLEOPATRA

6823 Brooks, Polly Schoyer. *Cleopatra: Goddess of Egypt, Enemy of Rome* (7–10). 1995, HarperCollins LB $16.89 (0-06-023608-6). As much an account of the Roman struggle for power as a biography of the Egyptian queen, an intelligent and capable leader. (Rev: BL 11/1/95; SLJ 12/95; VOYA 4/96) [921]

6824 Hoobler, Dorothy, and Thomas Hoobler. *Cleopatra* (6–10). Illus. 1986, Chelsea LB $21.95 (0-87754-589-8). Through recounting the story of this amazing queen, the author tells about life in ancient Egypt. (Rev: BL 2/1/87; SLJ 2/87) [921]

6825 Nardo, Don, ed. *Cleopatra* (7–12). Series: People Who Made History. 2000, Greenhaven LB $22.96 (0-7377-0322-9); paper $14.96 (0-7377-0321-0). This collection of essays focuses on the life of Cleopatra, her contributions, and her place in history. (Rev: BL 3/1/01; SLJ 3/01) [921]

6826 Streissguth, Thomas. *Queen Cleopatra* (4–7). Series: A&E Biography. 2000, Lerner LB $25.26 (0-8225-4946-8). The story of Cleopatra and her impact on world history. (Rev: BL 3/15/00; HBG 10/00; SLJ 5/00) [921]

HATSHEPSUT

6827 Greenblatt, Miriam. *Hatshepsut and Ancient Egypt* (6–8). Series: Rulers and Their Times. 1999, Benchmark LB $19.95 (0-7614-0911-4). To give the reader a feel for ancient Egypt, this biography of Hatshepsut also compares Hatshepsut's life with the life of a typical Egyptian. (Rev: HBG 9/00; SLJ 2/00) [932]

MANDELA, NELSON

6828 Connolly, Sean. *Nelson Mandela: An Unauthorized Biography* (5–7). 2000, Heinemann LB $24.22 (1-57572-225-9). An appealing biography that contains good background material on South Africa, past and present. (Rev: SLJ 1/01) [921]

6829 Finlayson, Reggie. *Nelson Mandela* (4–8). Illus. Series: A&E Biography. 1999, Lerner LB $25.26 (0-8225-4936-0). An overview that concentrates on Mandela's childhood, his training as a lawyer, and his rise through the ranks of the African National Congress, with only brief coverage of his imprisonment, release, and presidency. (Rev: BL 2/15/00; HBG 3/99; SLJ 2/99) [921]

6830 Holland, Gini. *Nelson Mandela* (6–9). Series: Trailblazers of the Modern World. 2002, World Almanac Library LB $26.60 (0-8368-5078-5); paper $10.95 (0-8368-5238-9). The story of the great South African leader who suffered a jail sentence to help free his people. (Rev: BL 12/15/02) [921]

6831 Hoobler, Dorothy, and Thomas Hoobler. *Mandela: The Man, the Struggle, the Triumph* (6–12).

1992, Watts paper $24.00 (0-531-11141-5). A review of the struggle against apartheid in South Africa from 1987 to 1992, which encompassed the repeal of the apartheid laws and the release of Nelson Mandela and other political prisoners from prison. (Rev: BL 5/15/92; SLJ 12/92) [921]

6832 Hughes, Libby. *Nelson Mandela: Voice of Freedom* (6–10). Series: People in Focus. 1992, Dillon LB $18.95 (0-87518-484-7). Integrates Mandela's political struggle against apartheid with his personal story. Extensive bibliography, photographs. (Rev: BL 12/1/92; SLJ 1/93) [921]

6833 Kramer, Ann. *Nelson Mandela* (6–10). Illus. Series: Twentieth Century History. 2003, Raintree Steck-Vaughn LB $32.85 (0-7398-5258-2). An attractive and absorbing account of Mandela's life and efforts to bring equality to his country. (Rev: BL 6/1–15/03; SLJ 7/03) [968.06]

MUGABE, ROBERT

6834 Worth, Richard. *Robert Mugabe of Zimbabwe* (5–8). Illus. Series: In Focus Biographies. 1990, Silver Burdett LB $13.95 (0-671-68987-8); paper $7.95 (0-671-70684-5). Tells the story of Zimbabwe's first prime minister, along with a history of this emerging country. (Rev: SLJ 2/91) [921]

RAMPHELE, MAMPHELA

6835 Harlan, Judith. *Mamphela Ramphele: Challenging Apartheid in South Africa* (5–8). Illus. Series: Women Changing the World. 2000, Feminist Pr. $19.95 (1-55861-227-0). This is the inspiring story of the black South African woman who fought racial segregation and injustice in her country and went on to be a doctor and educator. (Rev: BL 9/15/00; HBG 3/01; SLJ 12/00) [921]

Asia and the Middle East

ARAFAT, YASIR

6836 Ferber, Elizabeth. *Yasir Arafat: The Battle for Peace in Palestine* (7–12). 1995, Millbrook $23.90 (1-56294-585-8). A balanced presentation of Arafat's political career. (Rev: BL 10/1/95; SLJ 12/95) [921]

6837 Headlam, George. *Yasser Arafat* (5–8). Series: A&E Biography. 2003, Lerner LB $25.26 (0-8225-5004-0); paper $7.95 (0-8225-9902-3). The story of the Palestinian leader, his rise to power, and his current status. (Rev: BL 1/1–15/04)

6838 Williams, Colleen Madonna Flood. *Yasir Arafat* (5–8). Illus. 2002, Chelsea $23.95 (0-7910-6941-9); paper $9.95 (0-7910-7186-3). The contro-

versial PLO leader is shown as a man of conviction who struggles to balance the desires of his people and of the rest of the world. (Rev: BL 1/1–15/03; HBG 3/03) [956.9405]

BEGIN, MENACHEM

6839 Brackett, Virginia. *Menachem Begin* (5–8). Series: Major World Leaders. 2002, Chelsea $23.95 (0-7910-6946-X). The life of the important Israeli prime minister who was in office when peace was declared between Israel and Egypt. (Rev: BL 1/1–15/03; SLJ 2/03) [921]

BHATT, ELA

6840 Sreenivasan, Jyotsna. *Ela Bhatt: Uniting Women in India* (5–8). Illus. Series: Women Changing the World. 2000, Feminist Pr. $19.95 (1-55861-229-7). Inspired by Gandhi, this Indian lawyer founded an organization to help and protect the lives of her country's poorest women and organized a labor union for them. (Rev: BL 9/15/00; HBG 3/01; SLJ 12/00) [921]

BIN LADEN, OSAMA

6841 Landau, Elaine. *Osama bin Laden: A War Against the West* (6–10). Illus. 2002, Millbrook LB $23.90 (0-7613-1709-0). Landau combines what is known of Bin Laden's youth, fundamentalist beliefs, and terrorist organization with a look at his assumed involvement in the September 11, 2001, and other attacks. (Rev: BL 1/1–15/02; HBG 10/02; SLJ 3/02) [322.4]

6842 Louis, Nancy. *Osama bin Laden* (4–7). Series: War on Terrorism. 2002, ABDO LB $25.65 (1-57765-663-6). A brief biography of the terrorist leader told through a matter-of-fact text and many color photographs. (Rev: BL 5/15/02; HBG 10/02) [921]

6843 Woolf, Alex. *Osama Bin Laden* (5–8). Series: A&E Biography. 2003, Lerner LB $25.26 (0-8225-5003-2); paper $7.95 (0-8225-9900-7). The story of the leader of the Al Qaeda terrorist movement and his family background in Saudi Arabia. (Rev: BL 1/1–15/04) [921]

CHEN, DA

6844 Chen, Da. *China's Son: Growing Up in the Cultural Revolution* (6–9). 2001, Delacorte $15.95 (0-385-72929-4). Da Chen retells for younger readers the story of his difficult youth in a small village in southern China during the upheaval of the Cultural Revolution, previously presented in the memoir *Colors of the Mountain* (1996). (Rev: BL 7/01; HBG 3/02; SLJ 8/01; VOYA 10/01) [951.05]

CONFUCIUS

6845 Freedman, Russell. *Confucius: The Golden Rule* (4–8). 2002, Scholastic paper $15.95 (0-439-13957-0). This absorbing account of the life and philosophy of Confucius gives new insight into the character of the man who had so much influence on China. (Rev: BL 10/1/02*; HB 1–2/03; HBG 3/03; SLJ 9/02*) [181]

DALAI LAMA

6846 Perez, Louis G. *The Dalai Lama* (6–12). Series: World Leaders. 1993, Rourke LB $25.27 (0-86625-480-3). Tells of the Dalai Lama's lonely childhood, nonviolent struggle for his people, years in exile, his impact and life through 1992. (Rev: BL 12/1/93) [921]

6847 Stewart, Whitney. *The 14th Dalai Lama: Spiritual Leader of Tibet* (5–8). Series: Newsmakers. 1996, Lerner LB $30.35 (0-8225-4926-3). As well as describing the life and spiritual beliefs of the 14th Dalai Lama, this account describes the political situation in Tibet at the time. (Rev: SLJ 6/96; VOYA 10/96) [921]

DALOKAY, VEDAT

6848 Dalokay, Vedat. *Sister Shako and Kolo the Goat: Memories of My Childhood in Turkey* (5–7). Trans. by Guner Ener. 1994, Lothrop $14.00 (0-688-13271-5). A memoir by the former mayor of Ankara about growing up Muslim in rural Turkey in the 1930s and his friendship with an indomitable widow named Sister Shako. (Rev: BCCB 4/94; BL 5/1/94; SLJ 6/94) [921]

DAVID, KING OF ISRAEL

6849 Cohen, Barbara. *David: A Biography* (5–8). 1995, Clarion $15.95 (0-395-58702-6). Re-creates the events in the life of the biblical David, who began as a simple shepherd and ended as a warrior king. (Rev: BCCB 9/95; SLJ 7/95) [921]

GANDHI, INDIRA

6850 Dommermuth-Costa, Carol. *Indira Gandhi: Daughter of India* (7–12). Series: Lerner Biographies. 2001, Lerner LB $25.26 (0-8225-4963-8). A thorough profile that places Gandhi's life in historical context and provides a good history of modern India. (Rev: HBG 3/02; SLJ 3/02) [954.04]

GANDHI, MAHATMA

6851 Fisher, Leonard Everett. *Gandhi* (5–7). Illus. 1995, Simon & Schuster paper $16.00 (0-689-80337-0). In powerful black-and-white drawings and simple text, this is a handsome account of the life of the Indian leader. (Rev: BL 10/1/95; SLJ 10/95) [921]

6852 Furbee, Mary, and Mike Furbee. *Mohandas Gandhi* (7–12). Series: The Importance Of. 2000, Lucent LB $18.96 (1-56006-674-1). Using a number of quotations from original sources, this account traces the life and importance of the important Indian leader and his world significance. (Rev: BL 8/00; HBG 3/01) [921]

6853 Heinrichs, Ann. *Mahatma Gandhi* (4–7). Series: Trailblazers of the Modern World. 2001, World Almanac LB $29.26 (0-8368-5064-5). A clear and concise biography that focuses on Gandhi's personal life as well as his struggles to free India and belief in nonviolence. (Rev: SLJ 1/02) [921]

6854 Martin, Christopher. *Mohandas Gandhi* (4–7). Series: A&E Biography. 2000, Lucent LB $25.26 (0-8225-4984-0). The story of the man who sought to unite and free his people not through violence but by prayer, civil disobedience, and communication. (Rev: BL 12/15/00; HBG 3/01; SLJ 1/01) [921]

6855 Severance, John B. *Gandhi, Great Soul* (6–9). Illus. 1997, Clarion $17.00 (0-395-77179-X). The life and times of Gandhi are covered in this attractive, informative book, which explains Gandhi's philosophy of peaceful resistance and describes the evolution of his beliefs. (Rev: BL 2/15/97; BR 9–10/97; SLJ 4/97*) [921]

6856 Shields, Charles J. *Mohandas K. Gandhi* (8–12). Illus. Series: Overcoming Adversity. 2001, Chelsea LB $21.95 (0-7910-6301-1). This thorough account of Gandhi's beliefs and work also discusses his influence on other leaders and opposition to his ideas. (Rev: BL 2/15/02; HBG 10/02) [954.03]

GENGHIS KHAN

6857 Humphrey, Judy. *Genghis Khan* (6–10). Illus. 1987, Chelsea LB $21.95 (0-87754-527-8). The story of the fierce warrior who shaped the Mongolian empire in the 12th century. (Rev: BL 11/15/87; SLJ 12/87) [921]

HERZL, THEODOR

6858 Finkelstein, Norman H. *Theodor Herzl: Architect of a Nation* (7–12). 1991, Lerner LB $30.35 (0-8225-4913-1). The story of the respected playwright/journalist who dedicated himself to helping the Jewish people obtain their own country. (Rev: BL 4/15/92; SLJ 7/92) [921]

HUSSEIN, SADDAM

6859 Anderson, Dale. *Saddam Hussein* (5–8). Series: A&E Biography. 2003, Lerner LB $25.26 (0-8225-5005-9); paper $7.95 (0-8225-9901-5).

This biography of the Iraqi despot tells his story up to the decision that led to the American invasion. (Rev: BL 1/1–15/04) [921]

6860 Claypool, Jane. *Saddam Hussein* (6–12). Series: World Leaders. 1993, Rourke LB $25.27 (0-86625-477-3). Describes Hussein's violent childhood, his rise to power, his impact, and his life to 1992. (Rev: BL 12/1/93; SLJ 1/94) [921]

6861 Shields, Charles J. *Saddam Hussein* (5–8). Illus. Series: Major World Leaders. 2002, Chelsea $22.95 (0-7910-6943-5). An account of the Iraqi leader's regime, with information on the Iran-Iraq and Persian Gulf wars and on United Nations sanctions and weapons inspections. (Rev: BL 2/1/03; HBG 3/03; SLJ 4/03) [956.7044]

JIANG, JI-LI

6862 Jiang, Ji-li. *Red Scarf Girl: A Memoir of the Cultural Revolution* (6–10). 1997, HarperCollins $16.99 (0-06-027585-5). An engrossing memoir of a Chinese girl, her family, and how their lives became a nightmare during Chairman Mao's Cultural Revolution of the late 1960s. (Rev: BL 10/1/97; BR 3–4/98; SLJ 12/97; VOYA 6/98) [921]

KOLLEK, TEDDY

6863 Rabinovich, Abraham. *Teddy Kollek: Builder of Jerusalem* (5–8). Illus. 1996, Jewish Publication Soc. $14.95 (0-8276-0559-5); paper $9.95 (0-8276-0561-7). The story of the former mayor of Jerusalem, who supervised the city's unification after the Six Days War in 1967. (Rev: BL 5/15/96; BR 9–10/96) [921]

MASIH, IQBAL

6864 Kuklin, Susan. *Iqbal Masih and the Crusaders Against Child Slavery* (6–12). Illus. 1998, Holt $17.95 (0-8050-5459-6). The story of the Pakistani boy who after escaping slavery devoted his young life to a crusade against child labor abuse until he was murdered at age 12. (Rev: BCCB 11/98; BL 11/1/98; HB 1–2/99; HBG 3/99; SLJ 11/98; VOYA 4/99) [331.34092]

MUHAMMAD

6865 Demi. *Muhammad* (4–7). Illus. 2003, Simon & Schuster $19.95 (0-689-85264-9). This readable account of the life of the founding prophet of Islam is accompanied by quotations from the Koran and intricate illustrations. (Rev: BL 6/1–15/03*; HB 7–8/03; SLJ 8/03) [297.6]

6866 Oliver, Marilyn Tower. *Muhammad* (6–10). 2003, Gale LB $27.45 (1-59018-232-4). A thorough and balanced account of Muhammad's life and legacy as the founder of Islam. (Rev: SLJ 6/03) [297.6]

PAHLAVI, MOHAMMED REZA

6867 Barth, Linda. *Mohammed Reza Pahlavi* (5–8). Series: Major World Leaders. 2002, Chelsea $23.95 (0-7910-6948-6). An engrossing biography of the last Shah of Iran, who ruled during a tumultuous time in the region. (Rev: BL 1/1–15/03) [921]

SADAT, ANWAR

6868 Kras, Sara Louise. *Anwar Sadat* (5–8). Series: Major World Leaders. 2002, Chelsea $23.95 (0-7910-6949-4). An absorbing account of the life of the famous Egyptian leader who shared the 1978 Nobel Peace Prize with Israeli Prime Minister Menachem Begin. (Rev: BL 1/1–15/03; HBG 3/03) [921]

SALADIN

6869 Stanley, Diane. *Saladin: Noble Prince of Islam* (5–8). Illus. 2002, HarperCollins LB $18.89 (0-688-17136-2). A lavish picture-book biography of a noted Muslim commander during the Crusades that includes good background information on history, geography, and religion. (Rev: BL 9/1/02; HB 1–2/03; HBG 3/03; SLJ 9/02) [956]

SUU KYI, AUNG SAN

6870 Ling, Bettina. *Aung San Suu Kyi: Standing Up for Democracy in Burma* (6–9). Series: Women Changing the World. 1999, Feminist Pr. $19.95 (1-55861-196-7). A biography of the woman who has fought for democracy in Burma, spent many years under house arrest, and was awarded the Nobel Peace Prize in 1991. (Rev: BL 3/15/99; VOYA 4/00) [921]

6871 Stewart, Whitney. *Aung San Suu Kyi: Fearless Voice of Burma* (6–9). 1997, Lerner LB $30.35 (0-8225-4931-X). A thorough, well-documented biography of the Nobel Peace Prize winner and fearless Burmese leader in the struggle for democracy. (Rev: BL 4/1/97; SLJ 5/97; VOYA 12/97) [921]

TAMERLANE

6872 Wepman, Dennis. *Tamerlane* (6–10). Illus. 1987, Chelsea LB $19.95 (0-87754-442-5). The story of the barbaric Mongol chieftain who lived in the 14th century and was responsible for the death of millions. (Rev: BL 7/87; SLJ 8/87) [921]

TERESA, MOTHER

6873 Dils, Tracey E. *Mother Teresa* (4–8). Series: Women of Achievement. 2001, Chelsea $21.95 (0-7910-5887-5). An absorbing account of the humanitarian's life from her childhood in Albania through her early years in India and her international work with the Missionaries of Charity. (Rev: HBG 3/02; SLJ 11/01) [921]

6874 Johnson, Linda C. *Mother Teresa: Protector of the Sick* (5–8). Illus. Series: Library of Famous Women. 1991, Blackbirch $26.19 (1-56711-034-7). Tracing Mother Teresa's life from her childhood in Yugoslavia to her renowned efforts to aid the sick around the world. (Rev: BL 3/15/93) [921]

6875 Morgan, Nina. *Mother Teresa: Saint of the Poor* (4–7). Illus. 1998, Raintree Steck-Vaughn paper $7.95 (0-8172-7848-6). A biography of the nun whose work with the poor of India made her an international celebrity and earned her a Nobel Peace Prize. (Rev: BL 7/98; HBG 10/98; SLJ 7/98) [921]

6876 Pond, Mildred. *Mother Teresa: A Life of Charity* (4–7). Illus. Series: Junior World Biography. 1992, Chelsea LB $15.95 (0-7910-1755-9). The inspiring life story of the nun who gave her life to serve and help the poor, particularly in India. (Rev: BL 8/92; SLJ 7/92) [921]

6877 Rice, Tanya. *Mother Teresa* (5–8). Illus. Series: The Life and Times Of. 1999, Chelsea LB $18.65 (0-7910-4637-0). A straightforward account of the life of Mother Teresa, from her birth in Albania to devout Catholic parents and her religious calling as a child, to her work in India and her commitment to helping the poor, to the winning of the Nobel Peace Prize, and her death. (Rev: SLJ 8/98) [921]

6878 Tilton, Rafael. *Mother Teresa* (4–8). Series: The Importance Of. 2000, Lucent LB $18.96 (1-56006-565-6). This thoroughly researched account describes the life of Mother Teresa and gives an honest appraisal of her importance. (Rev: BL 1/1–15/00; HBG 9/00) [921]

XIAOPING, DENG

6879 Stewart, Whitney. *Deng Xiaoping: Leader in a Changing China* (4–7). Series: Lerner Biographies. 2001, Lerner LB $30.35 (0-8225-4962-X). An accessible biography of the most powerful man in China from the 1970s until his death, with details of how his reputation was tarnished by the Tiananmen Square massacre. (Rev: BL 9/15/01; HBG 10/01; SLJ 7/01) [921]

Australia and the Pacific Islands

KA'LIULANI, PRINCESS

6880 Linnea, Sharon. *Princess Ka'iulani: Hope of a Nation, Heart of a People* (5–8). 1999, Eerdmans $18.00 (0-8028-5145-2). The story of the Hawaiian princess who tried to prevent the annexation of her country by the United States and of her untimely death at age 22. (Rev: BL 7/99; SLJ 6/99; VOYA 10/99) [921]

Europe

ALEXANDER THE GREAT

6881 Greenblatt, Miriam. *Alexander the Great and Ancient Greece* (5–8). Illus. Series: Rulers and Their Times. 1999, Marshall Cavendish LB $28.50 (0-7614-0913-0). The first part of this biography introduces Alexander the Great and his accomplishments and the second tells about daily life in ancient Greece. (Rev: BL 1/1–15/00; HBG 10/00; SLJ 2/00) [921]

ANIELEWICZ, MORDECHAI

6882 Callahan, Kerry P. *Mordechai Anielewicz: Hero of the Warsaw Uprising* (5–8). Series: Holocaust Biographies. 2001, Rosen LB $26.50 (0-8239-3377-6). The story of Anielewicz and other members of the Jewish resistance in the Warsaw ghetto is told in gripping text accompanied by black-and-white photographs. (Rev: BL 10/15/01) [921]

ARTHUR, KING

6883 Nardo, Don. *King Arthur* (6–9). Illus. Series: Heroes and Villains. 2003, Gale LB $21.96 (1-56006-948-1). This biography recounts Arthur's story and examines the combination of legend and fact. (Rev: BL 1/1–15/03; SLJ 3/03) [942.01]

ATATURK, KEMAL

6884 Tachau, Frank. *Kemal Ataturk* (6–10). Illus. 1987, Chelsea LB $19.95 (0-87754-507-3). A biography of the man who transformed Turkey and brought it into the 20th century. (Rev: BL 1/1/88; SLJ 3/88) [921]

ATTILA

6885 Ingram, Scott. *Attila the Hun* (6–9). Series: History's Villains. 2003, Gale LB $23.95 (1-56711-628-0). A look at Attila's barbarous exploits and rampages through Europe. (Rev: SLJ 3/03)

BLAIR, TONY

6886 Hinman, Bonnie. *Tony Blair* (5–8). Series: Major World Leaders. 2002, Chelsea $23.95 (0-7910-6939-7). A profile of the leader of the British Labour Party who in 1997 became the youngest prime minister in nearly 200 years. (Rev: BL 1/1–15/03) [921]

BONAPARTE, NAPOLEON

6887 Carroll, Bob. *Napoleon Bonaparte* (4–8). Illus. Series: The Importance Of. 1994, Lucent LB $27.45 (1-56006-021-2). From humble beginnings on the island of Corsica to becoming emperor of the French and his final wartime defeat and exile, this is the story of Napoleon. (Rev: BL 5/15/94; SLJ 4/94) [921]

BRAILLE, LOUIS

6888 Bryant, Jennifer. *Louis Braille: Inventor* (5–7). Illus. 1994, Chelsea LB $21.95 (0-7910-2077-0). This well-researched biography of Braille tells about the horror of his own blindness as well as the development of the alphabet that allows blind people to read. (Rev: BL 7/94; SLJ 8/94) [921]

6889 Freedman, Russell. *Out of Darkness: The Story of Louis Braille* (4–8). Illus. 1997, Clarion $16.00 (0-395-77516-7). The story of the blind Frenchman who, more than 170 years ago, invented a system of reading using raised dots. (Rev: BCCB 5/97; BL 3/1/97; BR 9–10/97; HB 5–6/97; SLJ 3/97*) [686.2]

CAESAR, AUGUSTUS

6890 Forsyth, Fiona. *Augustus: The First Emperor* (6–9). Series: Leaders of Ancient Rome. 2003, Rosen LB $31.95 (0-8239-3588-4). A balanced biography of the emperor's achievements and failings. (Rev: LMC 8–9/03; SLJ 6/03) [937]

6891 Greenblatt, Miriam. *Augustus and Imperial Rome* (6–8). Series: Rulers and Their Times. 1999, Benchmark LB $19.95 (0-7614-0912-2). To give the reader a feel for ancient Rome, this biography of Caesar Augustus also compares his life with the life of a typical Roman. (Rev: HBG 9/00; SLJ 2/00) [937]

CAESAR, JULIUS

6892 Barter, James. *Julius Caesar and Ancient Rome in World History* (8–12). Illus. Series: In World History. 2001, Enslow LB $20.95 (0-7660-1461-4). A detailed look at Caesar's life and accomplishments, along with information about the empire he ruled and the political and social climate of the time; with quotations from primary sources. (Rev: BL 3/1/02; HBG 3/02; SLJ 1/02) [937]

6893 Bruns, Roger. *Julius Caesar* (6–10). Illus. 1987, Chelsea LB $21.95 (0-87754-514-6). Using many sources, the author creates an accurate picture of the rise and fall of this Roman leader. (Rev: BL 11/15/87; BR 9–10/88; SLJ 12/87; VOYA 10/88) [921]

6894 Green, Robert. *Julius Caesar* (5–8). Series: First Books: Ancient Biographies. 1996, Watts LB $23.00 (0-531-20241-0). The story of Caesar's

political and military careers, how he expanded the Roman Empire, and his lasting importance. (Rev: SLJ 2/97) [921]

CALVIN, JOHN

6895 Stepanek, Sally. *John Calvin* (6–10). Illus. 1986, Chelsea LB $21.95 (0-87754-515-4). A well-researched biography of the 16th-century leader of the Protestant Reformation. (Rev: BL 3/1/87; SLJ 3/87) [921]

CARY, ELIZABETH

6896 Brackett, Ginger Roberts. *Elizabeth Cary: Writer of Conscience* (7–10). Illus. 1996, Morgan Reynolds LB $21.95 (1-883846-15-3). The story of the 17th-century Englishwoman and brilliant writer who defied society by becoming a Roman Catholic in heavily Protestant England. (Rev: BL 10/1/96; SLJ 10/96; VOYA 6/97) [921]

CHARLEMAGNE, EMPEROR

6897 Greenblatt, Miriam. *Charlemagne and the Early Middle Ages* (8–12). Series: Rulers and Their Times. 2002, Marshall Cavendish LB $19.95 (0-7614-1487-8). The story of the King of the Franks and the founder of the Holy Roman Empire, who ruled at the beginning of the Middle Ages. (Rev: BL 1/1–15/03; HBG 3/03; SLJ 3/03) [921]

6898 Westwood, Jennifer. *Stories of Charlemagne* (7–9). 1976, Phillips $26.95 (0-87599-213-7). A biography of the famous emperor of the Holy Roman Empire, who was one of the most influential men of the Middle Ages. [921]

CHURCHILL, SIR WINSTON

6899 Ashworth, Leon. *Winston Churchill* (5–8). Illus. Series: British History Makers. 2002, Cherrytree $17.95 (1-84234-072-7). A balanced look at the life and career of the British statesman, with a useful timeline and excellent illustrations. (Rev: SLJ 8/02) [941.082092]

6900 Driemen, J. E. *Winston Churchill: An Unbreakable Spirit* (5–8). Illus. Series: People in Focus. 1990, Macmillan LB $13.95 (0-87518-434-0). A biography of this amazing statesman, leader, and writer. (Rev: SLJ 8/90) [921]

6901 MacDonald, Fiona. *Winston Churchill* (5–8). Series: Trailblazers of the Modern World. 2003, World Almanac LB $26.60 (0-8368-5082-3). An appealing biography of Churchill, with plenty of black-and-white photographs, that reveals his youthful deficiencies as well as his adult accomplishments. (Rev: SLJ 8/03) [921]

6902 Severance, John B. *Winston Churchill: Soldier, Statesman, Artist* (5–8). Illus. 1996, Clarion

$17.95 (0-395-69853-7). A well-organized, clearly written account of the life and works of Britain's great statesman. (Rev: BL 4/15/96; HB 7–8/96; SLJ 4/96*; VOYA 6/96) [941.084]

CLEMENCEAU, GEORGES

6903 Gottfried, Ted. *Georges Clemenceau* (6–10). Illus. 1987, Chelsea LB $21.95 (0-87754-518-9). A biography of the French political leader who served his country with distinction during World War I. (Rev: BL 11/15/87; SLJ 3/88) [921]

CONSTANTINE I, EMPEROR

6904 Morgan, Julian. *Constantine: Ruler of Christian Rome* (6–9). Series: Leaders of Ancient Rome. 2003, Rosen LB $31.95 (0-8239-3592-2). The story of the 4th-century emperor who was the first Roman ruler to convert to Christianity. (Rev: SLJ 6/03) [937]

DE GAULLE, CHARLES

6905 Whitelaw, Nancy. *Charles de Gaulle: "I Am France"* (5–8). 1991, Dillon LB $13.95 (0-87518-486-3). Details the life and accomplishments of France's controversial leader. (Rev: BL 2/15/92) [921]

DIANA, PRINCESS OF WALES

6906 Brennan, Kristine. *Diana, Princess of Wales* (5–8). Series: Women of Achievement. 1998, Chelsea $21.95 (0-7910-4714-8); paper $9.95 (0-7910-4715-6). This book covers the facts about Diana's life, disappointing marriage, struggle for happiness, and untimely death. (Rev: HBG 3/99; VOYA 4/99) [921]

6907 Cerasini, Marc. *Diana: Queen of Hearts* (5–7). Illus. 1997, Random paper $4.99 (0-679-89214-1). A breezy, easily read account of the life of this princess. (Rev: BL 12/1/97) [921]

6908 Oleksy, Walter. *Princess Diana* (5–8). Series: People in the News. 2001, Lucent LB $27.45 (1-56006-579-6). A well-documented life of this tragic, troubled princess, with many quotations and black-and-white photographs. (Rev: BCCB 10/98; BL 4/1/02; HBG 3/01) [921]

6909 Whitelaw, Nancy. *Lady Diana Spencer: Princess of Wales* (4–7). Illus. 1998, Morgan Reynolds LB $21.95 (1-883846-35-8). A quick read that gives details about Diana's privileged but troubled background and the many problems she faced as a member of the royal family. (Rev: BCCB 7–8/98; BL 8/98; BR 1–2/99; HBG 10/98; SLJ 6/98; VOYA 10/98) [921]

6910 Wood, Richard. *Diana: The People's Princess* (4–7). Illus. 1998, Raintree Steck-Vaughn paper $7.95 (0-8172-7849-4). A biography that reveals some personal information about this multifaceted woman and details the many causes she supported. (Rev: BL 7/98; HBG 10/98; SLJ 8/98) [921]

ELIZABETH I, QUEEN OF ENGLAND

6911 Green, Robert. *Queen Elizabeth I* (4–7). Illus. Series: First Books. 1997, Watts LB $23.00 (0-531-20302-6). This account of the life of Elizabeth I also includes material on the religious conflicts of the day, her suitors, and the war with Spain. (Rev: BL 2/1/98; HBG 3/98; SLJ 1/98) [921]

6912 Havelin, Kate. *Elizabeth I* (5–8). Series: Biography. 2002, Lerner LB $25.26 (0-8225-0029-9). The story of one of the most powerful queens in history and how she learned, at an early age, the politics of survival. (Rev: BCCB 12/99; BL 6/1–15/02; HBG 10/02; SLJ 7/02) [921]

6913 Price-Groff, Claire. *The Importance of Queen Elizabeth I* (7–12). Series: The Importance Of. 2000, Lucent LB $19.96 (1-56006-700-4). As well as tracing the life of this famous monarch, this account comments on her lasting importance in world history. (Rev: BL 3/1/01; SLJ 2/01) [921]

6914 Thomas, Jane Resh. *Behind the Mask: The Life of Queen Elizabeth I* (5–8). Illus. 1998, Clarion $20.00 (0-395-69120-6). A behind-the-scenes look at the long-lived queen, discussing her childhood, how she overcame opposition to become queen, and her subsequent manipulation of people, the court, and foreigners to attain greatness. (Rev: BL 12/15/98; BR 5–6/99; HB 1–2/99; HBG 3/99; SLJ 12/98*; VOYA 4/99) [921]

ELIZABETH II, QUEEN OF GREAT BRITAIN

6915 Auerbach, Susan. *Queen Elizabeth II* (6–12). Series: World Leaders. 1993, Rourke LB $25.27 (0-86625-481-1). Queen Elizabeth's childhood during World War II, how she came to the throne, and the major events in her reign up to 1993. (Rev: BL 12/1/93) [921]

FRANCIS OF ASSISI, SAINT

6916 dePaola, Tomie. *Francis: The Poor Man of Assisi* (4–7). 1982, Holiday $18.95 (0-8234-0435-8); paper $9.95 (0-8234-0812-4). A simple retelling of the life of St. Francis with fine pictures by dePaola. [921]

FRANK, ANNE

6917 Alagna, Magdalena. *Anne Frank: Young Voice of the Holocaust* (5–8). Series: Holocaust Biographies. 2001, Rosen LB $26.50 (0-8239-3373-3). This book describes Anne's childhood, her time spent in hiding, her diary, and her life in the concentration camps. (Rev: BL 10/15/01) [921]

6918 Anne Frank House, comp. *Anne Frank in the World: 1929–1945* (7–12). 2001, Knopf $18.95 (0-375-81177-X). This photoessay, based on the Frank family's experiences, clearly shows the Nazis' impact on the lives of Jewish families and includes many photographs that will be new to readers. (Rev: BCCB 3/02; BL 9/1/01; HBG 3/02; SLJ 10/01; VOYA 12/01) [921]

6919 Frank, Anne. *Anne Frank: The Diary of a Young Girl* (5–8). 1967, Pocket paper $3.95 (0-685-05466-7). The moving diary of a young Jewish girl hiding from the Nazis in World War II Amsterdam. [921]

6920 Frank, Anne. *The Diary of a Young Girl* (7–12). Trans. by B. M. Mooyaart. Illus. 1967, Doubleday $25.95 (0-385-04019-9). The world-famous diary of the young Jewish girl kept while she was being hidden with her family from the Nazis. (Rev: BL 2/15/88) [921]

6921 Frank, Anne. *The Diary of a Young Girl: The Definitive Edition* (7–12). Trans. by Susan Massotty. 1995, Doubleday $27.50 (0-385-47378-8). This edition contains all of the writings of Anne Frank, including some short passages in the diary that had been formerly suppressed. (Rev: BL 4/15/95) [921]

6922 Frank, Anne. *The Diary of Anne Frank: The Critical Edition* (7–12). Illus. 1989, Doubleday $60.00 (0-385-24023-6). The most complete version of the diary to appear in English plus a history of the volume. (Rev: BL 5/15/89) [921]

6923 Gold, Alison L. *Memories of Anne Frank: Reflections of a Childhood Friend* (4–8). Illus. 1997, Scholastic paper $16.95 (0-590-90722-0). Anne Frank's story as told through recollections of her best friend in Amsterdam, Hannah Goslar, a survivor of the Holocaust. (Rev: BL 9/1/97; BR 11–12/97; HBG 3/98; SLJ 11/97) [921]

6924 Hurwitz, Johanna. *Anne Frank: Life in Hiding* (4–7). 1989, Jewish Publication Soc. $13.95 (0-8276-0311-8). This biography describes Anne's life in hiding. (Rev: BL 4/15/89) [921]

6925 Lindwer, Willy. *The Last Seven Months of Anne Frank* (8–12). 1992, Doubleday paper $12.95 (0-385-42360-8). Moving testimony from six women interned in a concentration camp with Anne Frank tells of the tragic conclusion of the young diarist's life. (Rev: BL 3/15/91) [921]

6926 Wukovits, John. *Anne Frank* (6–10). Series: The Importance Of. 1998, Lucent LB $27.45 (1-56006-353-X). This biographical account also supplies good background material on Nazism, the death camps, the writing of the diary, and the controversy surrounding it. (Rev: BL 1/1–15/99; VOYA 8/99) [940.53]

GARIBALDI, GIUSEPPI

6927 Viola, Herman J., and Susan P. Viola. *Giuseppi Garibaldi* (6–10). Illus. 1987, Chelsea LB $21.95 (0-87754-526-X). Garibaldi was a hero, patriot, and the man who led the movement to unify his country, Italy. (Rev: BL 11/15/87; SLJ 3/88) [921]

HAMMARSKJOLD, DAG

6928 Sheldon, Richard N. *Dag Hammarskjold* (6–10). Illus. 1987, Chelsea LB $19.95 (0-87754-529-4). The life story of the Swedish man who served as the secretary general of the United Nations for eight years. (Rev: BL 9/1/87; SLJ 10/87) [921]

HANNIBAL

6929 Green, Robert. *Hannibal* (5–8). Series: First Books: Ancient Biographies. 1996, Watts LB $22.00 (0-531-20240-2). An engrossing account of the military genius who trekked across the Alps with elephants and threatened to topple the might of the Roman Empire. (Rev: SLJ 2/97) [921]

HENRY VIII, KING OF ENGLAND

6930 Dwyer, Frank. *Henry VIII* (7–12). Illus. 1988, Chelsea LB $21.95 (0-87754-530-8). This is a fact-crammed biography with a great deal of English history given for background. (Rev: BL 1/15/88; SLJ 3/88) [921]

HINDENBURG, PAUL VON

6931 Berman, Russell A. *Paul von Hindenburg* (6–10). Illus. 1987, Chelsea LB $19.95 (0-87754-532-4). The story of the German military and political leader who became famous during World War I. (Rev: BL 8/87; SLJ 11/87) [921]

HITLER, ADOLF

6932 Ayer, Eleanor. *Adolf Hitler* (4–8). Illus. Series: The Importance Of. 1996, Lucent LB $27.45 (1-56006-072-7). This study of Hitler's rise and impact on Germany and the world includes analyses of the dictator's mental state, leadership qualities, and personality traits. (Rev: BL 3/15/96; SLJ 1/96) [921]

6933 Giblin, James Cross. *The Life and Death of Adolf Hitler* (7–9). 2002, Clarion $21.00 (0-395-90371-8). This absorbing biography examines the forces that shaped Hitler's personality and philosophy and rise to power, covers Hitler's behavior during the war, and looks at today's neo-Nazis. (Rev: BL 4/1/02; HB 5–6/02; HBG 10/02; SLJ 5/02*; VOYA 6/02) [943.086]

6934 Harris, Nathaniel. *Hitler* (8–12). Illus. 1989, David & Charles $19.95 (0-7134-5961-1). This biography surveys the life and times of Hitler and his impact on history. (Rev: SLJ 12/89) [921]

6935 Nardo, Don. *Adolf Hitler* (6–9). Illus. Series: Heroes and Villains. 2003, Gale LB $21.96 (1-56006-951-1). Quotations and sidebars add primary source material to Nardo's description of Hitler's abuse of power. (Rev: BL 1/1–15/03) [943.086]

6936 Stalcup, Brenda, ed. *Adolf Hitler* (7–12). Series: People Who Made History. 2000, Greenhaven LB $21.96 (0-7377-0223-0); paper $13.96 (0-7377-0222-2). This life of Adolf Hitler is shown through a collection of documents that give special emphais to his role in World War II and the Holocaust and the impact on the German people. (Rev: BL 4/15/00; SLJ 11/00) [921]

JACOBSEN, RUTH

6937 Jacobsen, Ruth. *Rescued Images: Memories of a Childhood in Hiding* (6–12). 2001, Mikaya $19.95 (1-931414-00-9). The author, who was eight years old when her family fled the Nazis and went into hiding in the Netherlands, relates memories evoked by family photographs, which are also included. (Rev: BCCB 2/02; BL 1/1–15/02; HBG 3/02; SLJ 1/02; VOYA 2/02) [940.53]

JAMES I, KING OF ENGLAND

6938 Dwyer, Frank. *James I* (6–10). Illus. 1988, Chelsea LB $19.95 (1-55546-811-X). The story of the first Stuart king of both England and Scotland. (Rev: BL 6/15/88) [921]

JOAN OF ARC

6939 Lee, William W. *Joan of Arc and the Hundred Years' War in World History* (5–9). Series: In World History. 2003, Enslow LB $20.95 (0-7660-1938-1). This combination of biography and history tells the story of Joan of Arc and gives details on the long conflict between France and England. (Rev: BL 6/1–15/03; HBG 10/03; SLJ 9/03) [921]

6940 Stanley, Diane. *Joan of Arc* (4–8). Illus. 1998, Morrow $16.89 (0-688-14330-X). Using glorious illustrations, this picture book for older readers gives a detailed history of the life and times of Joan of Arc. (Rev: BCCB 9/98; BL 8/98; HB 9–10/98*; HBG 3/99; SLJ 9/98) [921]

JOHN PAUL II, POPE

6941 Sullivan, George. *Pope John Paul II: The People's Pope* (7–9). Illus. 1984, Walker $11.95 (0-8027-6523-8). A very readable biography of this beloved pope and his activities for world peace. [921]

KOLBE, SAINT MAXIMILIAN

6942 Mohan, Claire J. *Saint Maximilian Kolbe: The Story of the Two Crowns* (4–8). Illus. 1999, Young Sparrow paper $8.95 (0-962-15003-7). The story of a Polish Catholic monk who took the place of a fellow prisoner who was condemned to die at Auschwitz. (Rev: BL 2/1/00) [921]

KOSSMAN, NINA

6943 Kossman, Nina. *Behind the Border* (5–7). 1994, Lothrop $14.00 (0-688-13494-7). This book contains 12 episodes about the author's childhood in Communist Russia before emigrating to the United States. (Rev: BCCB 10/94; BL 8/94; SLJ 10/94) [921]

LENIN, VLADIMIR ILICH

6944 Haney, John. *Vladimir Ilich Lenin* (6–10). Illus. 1988, Chelsea LB $19.95 (0-87754-570-7). A biography of the man who led the Russia Revolution and established the U.S.S.R. (Rev: BL 4/1/88) [921]

6945 Rawcliffe, Michael. *Lenin* (7–10). Illus. 1989, David & Charles $19.95 (0-7134-5611-6). Besides supplying a biography of this Russian leader, this book evaluates Lenin's significance in history. (Rev: SLJ 5/89) [921]

LLOYD GEORGE, DAVID

6946 Shearman, Deidre. *David Lloyd George* (7–12). Illus. 1987, Chelsea LB $21.95 (0-87754-581-2). The biography of the Welsh statesman who was British prime minister during World War I. (Rev: BL 1/15/88) [921]

MARSHAL, WILLIAM

6947 Weatherly, Myra. *William Marshal: Medieval England's Greatest Knight* (5–8). Illus. 2001, Morgan Reynolds LB $21.95 (1-883846-48-X). The story of the brave medieval English knight whose accomplishments numbered fighting in tournaments, traveling to the Holy Land, helping to draw up the Magna Carta, and serving as regent when Henry III was a child. (Rev: BCCB 3/01; BL 1/1–15/01; HBG 10/01; SLJ 3/01) [921]

MARY, QUEEN OF SCOTS

6948 Stepanek, Sally. *Mary, Queen of Scots* (6–10). Illus. 1987, Chelsea LB $21.95 (0-87754-540-5). The tragic story of this ill-fated queen, in prose and many pictures. (Rev: BL 6/1/87; SLJ 12/87) [921]

MEDICI, LORENZO DE

6949 Greenblatt, Miriam. *Lorenzo de' Medici* (8–12). Series: Rulers and Their Times. 2002, Marshall Cavendish LB $19.95 (0-7614-1490-8). This towering figure of the Renaissance was known as the Magnificent because he was a great politician, patron, poet, and scholar. (Rev: BL 1/1–15/03; HBG 3/03) [921]

MENGELE, JOSEF

6950 Cefrey, Holly. *Dr. Josef Mengele: The Angel of Death* (6–9). Series: Holocaust Biographies. 2001, Rosen LB $19.95 (0-8239-3374-1). Mengele's interest in genetics and natural selection and his activities at Auschwitz are the focus of this frank biography. (Rev: SLJ 1/02) [921]

MUSSOLINI, BENITO

6951 Hartenian, Larry. *Benito Mussolini* (6–10). Illus. 1988, Chelsea LB $19.95 (0-87754-572-3). A fascinating biography of the Italian Fascist leader who brought his country to defeat in World War II. (Rev: BL 6/1/88) [921]

NAPOLEON I, EMPEROR OF THE FRENCH

6952 Obstfeld, Raymond, and Loretta Obstfeld, eds. *Napoleon Bonaparte* (7–12). Series: People Who Made History. 2001, Greenhaven LB $22.96 (0-7377-0423-3); paper $14.96 (0-7377-0422-5). After an introductory overview chapter covering Napoleon's career, there are a number of specialized essays that focus on his contributions and place in history. (Rev: BL 4/15/01) [921]

NOBEL, ALFRED

6953 Bankston, John. *Alfred Nobel and the Story of the Nobel Prize* (4–8). Series: Great Achievement Awards. 2003, Mitchell Lane LB $19.95 (1-58415-168-4). An intriguing biography of the inventor of dynamite and the founder of the famous prizes. (Rev: BL 10/15/03; SLJ 9/03) [921]

PADEREWSKI, IGNACY

6954 Lisandrelli, Elaine S. *Ignacy Jan Paderewski: Polish Pianist and Patriot* (6–9). 1998, Morgan Reynolds LB $21.95 (1-883846-29-3). An engaging biography of the great pianist, world diplomat, and lover of his native land Poland, which he helped regain a world position between the two World Wars. (Rev. BL 1/1–15/99; IIBG 3/99; SLJ 5/99) [921]

PETER THE GREAT

6955 Greenblatt, Miriam. *Peter the Great and Tsarist Russia* (5–8). Illus. Series: Rulers and Their Times. 1999, Marshall Cavendish LB $28.50 (0-7614-0914-9). A biography of the czar who westernized Russia is followed by a section on daily life during his reign. (Rev: BL 1/1–15/00; HBG 10/00; SLJ 2/00) [921]

PULASKI, CASIMIR

6956 Collins, David R. *Casimir Pulaski: Soldier on Horseback* (4–8). Illus. 1995, Pelican $14.95 (1-56554-082-4). A smoothly written biography of the Polish patriot who, though he could scarcely speak English, became an important figure helping the colonists during the Revolutionary War. (Rev: BL 2/15/96) [921]

PUTIN, VLADIMIR

6957 Shields, Charles J. *Vladimir Putin* (5–8). Illus. Series: Major World Leaders. 2002, Chelsea $22.95 (0-7910-6945-1). Putin's family life, ambitions to be a spy, and accession to power are all covered in this fine biography. (Rev: BL 2/1/03; HBG 3/03; SLJ 3/03) [947.086]

RINGELBLUM, EMMANUEL

6958 Beyer, Mark. *Emmanuel Ringelblum: Historian of the Warsaw Ghetto* (5–8). Illus. Series: Holocaust Biographies. 2001, Rosen LB $26.50 (0-8239-3375-X). This true story of a man who recorded events in the Warsaw Ghetto during the Holocaust includes black-and-white photographs. (Rev: BL 10/15/01) [940.53]

ROMANOV, ANASTASIA

6959 Brewster, Hugh. *Anastasia's Album* (5–8). Illus. 1996, Hyperion $17.95 (0-7868-0292-8). The story of the youngest daughter of the last of the Romanov czars and of her family. (Rev: BCCB 1/97; BL 10/1/96*; SLJ 12/96*) [921]

SCHINDLER, OSKAR

6960 Thompson, Bruce, ed. *Oskar Schindler* (7–12). Series: People Who Made History. 2002, Gale LB $31.20 (0-7377-0894-8); paper $19.95 (0-7377-0895-6). The life and times of a hero of the Jewish Holocaust are explored in a series of essays that deal with different aspects of his career and contributions. (Rev: BL 4/1/02; SLJ 7/02) [921]

6961 Wukovits, John F. *Oskar Schindler* (6–9). Series: Heroes and Villains. 2003, Gale LB $21.96

(1-56006-952-X). A biography of the businessman who risked his life to save Jews during the Holocaust. (Rev: SLJ 3/03) [362.87]

SCHOLL, HANS AND SOPHIE

6962 Axelrod, Toby. *Hans and Sophie Scholl: German Resisters of the White Rose* (7–12). Series: Holocaust Biographies. 2001, Rosen LB $19.95 (0-8239-3316-4). The Scholls, brother and sister, were arrested and executed for their role in organizing the group known as the White Rose, which worked to expose the Nazis' atrocities. (Rev: SLJ 6/01) [943.086]

SULEIMAN THE MAGNIFICENT

6963 Greenblatt, Miriam. *Süleyman the Magnificent and the Ottoman Empire* (8–12). Series: Rulers and Their Times. 2002, Marshall Cavendish LB $19.95 (0-7614-1489-4). The story of the great sultan who ruled during the 16th century and brought the Ottoman Empire to its height of power. (Rev: BL 1/1–15/03; HBG 3/03) [921]

THATCHER, MARGARET

6964 Hughes, Libby. *Madam Prime Minister: A Biography of Margaret Thatcher* (5–7). Illus. 1989, Macmillan LB $13.95 (0-87518-410-3). This solid biography shows both the public and private sides of the former British prime minister. (Rev: BL 11/1/89*; SLJ 1/90) [921]

TITO, JOSIP BROZ

6965 Schiffman, Ruth. *Josip Broz Tito* (6–10). Illus. 1987, Chelsea LB $19.95 (0-87754-443-3). The story of this unusual Yugoslavian leader and of the unique Communist regime he founded. (Rev: BL 6/15/87; SLJ 8/87) [921]

VAN BEEK, CATO BONTJES

6966 Friedman, Ina R. *Flying Against the Wind: The Story of a Young Woman Who Defied the Nazis* (6–10). 1995, Lodgepole Pr. paper $11.95 (1-886721-00-9). The story of Cato Bontjes van Beek, who grew up in a progressive German household and was executed by the Nazis with her boyfriend for joining an underground movement. (Rev: BL 7/95; VOYA 4/96) [921]

VICTORIA, QUEEN

6967 Chiflet, Jean-Loup, and Alain Beaulet. *Victoria and Her Times* (6–10). Trans. from French by George Wen. Series: W5. 1996, Holt $19.95 (0-8050-5084-1). This oversized volume contains double-page spreads that describe various aspects of the

life and times of Queen Victoria. (Rev: SLJ 3/97) [921]

6968 Price-Groff, Claire. *Queen Victoria and Nineteenth-Century England* (8–12). Series: Rulers and Their Times. 2002, Marshall Cavendish LB $19.95 (0-7614-1488-6). The story of the great British monarch who gave her name to the age she dominated. (Rev: BL 1/1–15/03; HBG 3/03) [921]

WALESA, LECH

6969 Lazo, Caroline. *Lech Walesa* (4–7). Illus. Series: Peacemakers. 1993, Dillon LB $13.95 (0-87518-525-8). The story of the Polish Solidarity labor movement leader is told with generous quotes from Walesa's autobiography and speeches. (Rev: BL 12/15/93; SLJ 1/94) [921]

WALLENBERG, RAOUL

6970 Linnea, Sharon. *Raoul Wallenberg: The Man Who Stopped Death* (5–7). Illus. 1993, Jewish Publication Soc. paper $9.95 (0-8276-0448-3). This Swedish architect saved thousands of Jews in Hungary from the Nazi Holocaust. (Rev: BL 6/1–15/93) [940]

6971 Streissguth, Thomas. *Raoul Wallenberg: Swedish Diplomat and Humanitarian* (7–12). Series: Holocaust Biographies. 2001, Rosen LB $19.95 (0-8239-3318-0). Wallenberg's efforts to save Hungarian Jews during World War II and his subsequent disappearance are described here. (Rev: SLJ 6/01) [943]

WIESENTHAL, SIMON

6972 Altman, Linda Jacobs. *Simon Wiesenthal* (7–12). Series: The Importance Of. 2000, Lucent LB $18.96 (1-56006-490-0). A frank and compelling biography of the Holocaust survivor and his efforts to bring Nazis to justice. (Rev: BL 7/00; HBG 9/00; SLJ 8/00) [940.53]

6973 Jeffrey, Laura S. *Simon Wiesenthal: Tracking Down Nazi Criminals* (6–9). Series: People to Know. 1997, Enslow LB $20.95 (0-89490-830-8). The story of the great investigator of Holocaust crimes who was responsible for bringing to justice such infamous war criminals as Adolph Eichmann. (Rev: BR 5–6/98; HBG 3/98; SLJ 3/98) [921]

WILLIAM, PRINCE

6974 Dougherty, Terry. *Prince William* (5–8). Series: People in the News. 2001, Lucent LB $27.45 (1-56006-982-1). Using many quotes, good photographs, and an interesting text, this is a biography of the royal Prince Charming. (Rev: BL 4/1/02) [921]

6975 Wyborny, Sheila. *Prince William* (4–7). Illus. Series: Famous People. 2003, Gale $23.70 (0-7377-

1401-8). An interesting biography of the young prince that covers his mother's death and the difficulties of living in the limelight, with lots of color photographs. (Rev: BL 6/1–15/03) [941.085]

WOLLSTONECRAFT, MARY

6976 Miller, Calvin C. *Mary Wollstonecraft and the Rights of Women* (7–12). Illus. 1999, Morgan Reynolds LB $21.95 (1-883846-41-2). This is a biography of the passionate English fighter for women's rights who was motivated by the grinding poverty, discrimination, and lack of opportunity suffered by women in the late 18th and early 19th centuries. (Rev: BL 5/1/99; BR 9–10/99; SLJ 5/99; VOYA 12/99) [921]

YELTSIN, BORIS

6977 Miller, Calvin C. *Boris Yeltsin: First President of Russia* (6–9). 1994, Morgan Reynolds LB $20.95 (1-883846-08-0). The biography of the controversial Russian leader up to 1993. (Rev: BL 12/1/94; SLJ 4/95; VOYA 2/95) [921]

South and Central America, Canada, and Mexico

BOLIVAR, SIMON

6978 Goodnough, David. *Simon Bolivar: South American Liberator* (7–12). Series: Hispanic Biographies. 1998, Enslow LB $20.95 (0-7660-1044-9). The inspiring story of the young military leader who led the fight to free several South American countries from the oppression of the Spaniards. (Rev: BL 1/1–15/99; HBG 3/99; VOYA 10/99) [921]

CASTRO, FIDEL

6979 Bentley, Judith. *Fidel Castro of Cuba* (7–12). Series: In Focus Biographies. 1991, Messner LB $13.95 (0-671-70198-3); paper $7.95 (0-671-70199-1). Relates the Cuban leader's personal story to a detailed history of his country, its problems and achievements, and the changing international scene up to 1991. (Rev: BL 11/1/91) [921]

6980 Platt, Richard. *Fidel Castro: From Guerrilla to World Statesman* (5–7). Series: Twentieth-Century History Makers. 2003, Raintree Steck-Vaughn LB $32.85 (0-7398-6141-7). Platt traces Castro's life from childhood through today, presenting opposing opinions of his achievements in a chapter called "Hero or Monster?" (Rev: SLJ 9/03) [973.9106]

6981 Press, Petra. *Fidel Castro: An Unauthorized Biography* (5–7). Series: Heinemann Profiles. 2000, Heinemann LB $24.22 (1-57572-497-9). An interesting introduction to the life of Cuba's dictator, with photographs that show urban and rural Cuba. (Rev: SLJ 6/01) [972.91064092]

6982 Woog, Adam. *Fidel Castro* (6–8). Series: The Importance Of. 2003, Gale LB $27.45 (1-59018-231-6). A thorough and readable biography that looks objectively at Castro and his country and wonders what the future will bring. (Rev: BL 6/1–15/03; SLJ 9/03) [973.9106]

DE PORTOLA, GASPAR

6983 Whiting, Jim. *Gaspar de Portola* (5–7). Series: Latinos in American History. 2002, Mitchell Lane LB $19.95 (1-58415-148-X). The story of the Latino governor of "Las Californias" from 1768 to 1770 who was responsible for expelling Jesuits from the area. (Rev: BL 2/15/03; HBG 10/03) [921]

DUVALIER, FRANÇOIS AND JEAN-CLAUDE

6984 Condit, Erin. *The Duvaliers* (6–9). Illus. 1989, Chelsea $21.95 (1-55546-832-2). A history of modern Haiti is given as well as the life stories of these two dictators. (Rev: BL 8/89; VOYA 12/89) [921]

FOX, VICENTE

6985 Paprocki, Sherry Beck. *Vicente Fox* (5–8). Series: Major World Leaders. 2002, Chelsea $23.95 (0-7910-6944-3). The story of the man who became president of Mexico in July 2000, the first opposition candidate to gain presidential office in more than 70 years. (Rev: BL 1/1–15/03) [921]

GUEVARA, CHE

6986 Neimark, Anne E. *Ch'e! Latin America's Legendary Guerrilla Leader* (7–10). Illus. 1989, HarperCollins LB $13.89 (0-397-32309-3). A portrait of the Latin American revolutionary who tried to help the oppressed and poor of the nations in Spanish America. (Rev: BL 5/15/89; SLJ 5/89) [921]

L'OUVERTURE, TOUSSAINT

6987 Myers, Walter Dean. *Toussaint L'Ouverture: The Fight for Haiti's Freedom* (4–8). 1996, Simon & Schuster $16.00 (0-689-80126-2). Powerful paintings by Jacob Lawrence highlight this story of the black leader who fought to free Haiti. (Rev: BCCB 1/97; BL 9/1/96; SLJ 11/96*) [921]

MARTI, JOSE

6988 Goodnough, David. *Jose Marti: Cuban Patriot and Poet* (6–10). Illus. Series: Hispanic Biographies. 1996, Enslow LB $20.95 (0-89490-761-1).

This biography of the Cuban revolutionary who fought against Spanish rule also contains samples of his poetry in both Spanish and English. (Rev: BL 9/1/96; BR 9–10/96; SLJ 6/96) [921]

MUÑOZ MARÍN, LUIS

6989 Bernier-Grand, Carmen T. *Poet and Politician of Puerto Rico: Don Luis Muñoz Marín* (5–8). 1995, Orchard LB $16.99 (0-531-08737-9). This story of the life of the man who helped make Puerto Rico a commonwealth also includes a history of the island. (Rev: BL 5/15/95; SLJ 4/95) [921]

SANTA ANNA, ANTONIO LOPEZ DE

6990 Bankston, John. *Antonio López de Santa Anna* (5–7). Series: Latinos in American History. 2003, Mitchell Lane LB $19.95 (1-58415-209-5). A biography of the Mexican general, president, and statesman who is best known for his part in the Battle of the Alamo. (Rev: BL 1/1–15/04) [921]

SILVA, MARINA

6991 Hildebrant, Ziporah. *Marina Silva: Defending Rainforest Communities in Brazil* (5–8). Series: Women Changing the World. 2001, Feminist Pr. $19.95 (1-55861-292-9). Though battling a serious illness, this gallant women, once a leader of the native Amazonians, has become a leading figure in protecting the forests of Brazil. (Rev: BL 12/15/01) [921]

TUM, RIGOBERTA MENCHU

6992 Schulze, Julie. *Rigoberta Menchú Túm: Champion of Human Rights* (8–12). Illus. Series: Contemporary Profile and Policy. 1998, John Gordon Burke $20.00 (0-934272-42-5); paper $12.95 (0-934272-43-3). This biography combines the life story of Nobel Peace Prize-winner Rigoberta Menchu Tum with the story of the struggle of the Mayan people for equality in Guatemala and throughout Central America. (Rev: BL 4/1/98) [921]

VILLA, PANCHO

6993 O'Brien, Steven. *Pancho Villa* (5–9). Series: Hispanics of Achievement. 1994, Chelsea LB $21.95 (0-7910-1257-3). The life and accomplishments of this Mexican freedom fighter. (Rev: BL 9/15/94; VOYA 8/94) [921]

Miscellaneous Interesting Lives

Collective

6994 Berson, Robin Kadison. *Young Heroes in World History* (7–12). 1999, Greenwood $45.00 (0-313-30257-X). Real people — of both sexes and many nationalities — who achieved amazing things before the age of 25 are profiled, with quotations and black-and-white illustrations. (Rev: SLJ 1/00; VOYA 4/00) [920.02]

6995 Cox, Clinton. *African American Teachers* (4–7). Series: Black Stars. 2000, Wiley $22.95 (0-471-24649-2). A collection of short profiles of important African American teachers who have inspired their students and championed the cause of education. (Rev: BL 7/00; HBG 3/01; SLJ 7/00) [920]

6996 Drimmer, Frederick. *Incredible People: Five Stories of Extraordinary Lives* (4–7). Illus. 1997, Simon & Schuster $16.00 (0-689-31921-5). The stories of five people who were considered outsiders, including seven-and-a-half-foot-tall Jack Earle and conjoined twins Daisy and Violet Hilton. (Rev: BCCB 7–8/97; BL 6/1–15/97; SLJ 5/97; VOYA 8/97) [920]

6997 Gifford, Clive, et al. *1000 Years of Famous People* (6–10). Illus. 2002, Kingfisher $24.95 (0-7534-5540-4). Brief descriptions of famous men and women in sports, medicine, politics, the arts, and other fields are included in this large-format book that is organized by subject and provides historical overviews of each discipline. (Rev: BL 12/1/02; HBG 3/03; SLJ 2/03; VOYA 6/03) [920.02]

6998 Gonzales, Doreen. *AIDS: Ten Stories of Courage* (6–10). Illus. Series: Collective Diographies. 1996, Enslow LB $20.95 (0-89490-766-2). This is a collection of 10 biographies of people including Ryan White and Magic Johnson who have helped people understand AIDS and its effects. (Rev: BL 4/15/96; SLJ 5/96; VOYA 6/96) [920]

6999 Hazell, Rebecca. *Heroes: Great Men Through the Ages* (5–8). Illus. 1997, Abbeville $19.95 (0-7892-0289-1). A collection of 12 biographies, from Socrates to Martin Luther King, Jr., and including Shakespeare, Mohandas Gandhi, Leonardo da Vinci, and Jorge Louis Borges. (Rev: SLJ 6/97) [920]

7000 Kamen, Gloria, ed. *Heading Out: The Start of Some Splendid Careers* (6–12). 2003, Bloomsbury $15.95 (1-58234-787-5). Twenty-four famous figures — including artists, athletes, politicians — tell in their own words how they became what they are today. (Rev: BL 12/1/02; HBG 10/03; SLJ 2/03; VOYA 4/03) [331.7]

7001 Masters, Anthony. *Heroic Stories* (4–8). Illus. Series: Story Library. 1994, Kingfisher paper $6.95 (1-85697-983-0). Various kinds of courage are explored through the lives of 23 individuals, including Charles Lindbergh and Anne Frank. (Rev: BL 3/1/95) [920]

7002 Sinnott, Susan. *Extraordinary Asian Americans and Pacific Islanders*. Rev. ed. (5–9). Series: Extraordinary People. 2003, Children's LB $39.00 (0-516-22655-X); paper $16.95 (0-516-29355-9). Brief biographies of Asian Americans and Pacific Islanders representing many walks of life are arranged chronologically by date of birth and interspersed with short essays on related topics. (Rev: SLJ 7/03) [920]

7003 Warren, Andrea. *We Rode the Orphan Trains* (4–8). Illus. 2001, Houghton $18.00 (0-618-11712-1). Eight moving biographical accounts of men and women, now in their 80s and 90s, who traveled to the Midwest to find new homes and families. (Rev: BCCB 11/01; BL 11/1/01; HBG 3/02; SLJ 11/01; VOYA 12/01) [362.73]

Individual

BITTON-JACKSON, LIVIA

7004 Bitton-Jackson, Livia. *My Bridges of Hope: Searching for Life and Love After Auschwitz* (8–12). 1999, Simon & Schuster $17.00 (0-689-82026-7). The true story of the author's life after her Holocaust experiences until she and her mother manage to migrate to the U.S. in 1951. (Rev: BL 5/1/99; SLJ 5/99; VOYA 6/99) [921]

BONETTA, SARAH FORBES

7005 Myers, Walter Dean. *At Her Majesty's Request: An African Princess in Victorian England* (5–8). Illus. 1999, Scholastic paper $15.95 (0-590-48669-1). The intriguing story of the African princess who at age 7 was saved from becoming a sacrifice and sent her to England, where she became the ward of Queen Victoria. (Rev: BCCB 2/99; BL 4/1/99; HBG 10/99; SLJ 1/99; VOYA 4/99) [921]

EQUIANO, OLAUDAH

7006 Cameron, Ann. *The Kidnapped Prince: The Life of Olaudah Equiano* (5–8). 1995, Knopf $16.00 (0-679-85619-6). Adapted from his autobiography, this is the story of Olaudah Equiano, an African prince sold into slavery as a young boy in the 18th century. (Rev: BCCB 4/95; BL 1/1/95; SLJ 2/95) [921]

GAC-ARTIGAS, ALEJANDRO

7007 Gac-Artigas, Alejandro. *Yo, Alejandro* (5–7). 2000, Ediciones Nuevo Espacio paper $11.95 (1-930879-21-0). This is a collection of personal essays written by the author before his 12th birthday about his life in Puerto Rico, the state of Georgia, and later New York City. (Rev: BL 3/1/01) [921]

GARNER, ELEANOR

7008 Garner, Eleanor Ramrath. *Eleanor's Story: An American Girl in Hitler's Germany* (7–12). 1999, Peachtree $14.95 (1-56145-193-2). The author recounts her family's struggle to survive in Germany during World War II. (Rev: BL 10/1/99*; BR 1/00; HBG 4/00; SLJ 3/00) [940.54]

HAUTZIG, ESTHER

7009 Hautzig, Esther. *The Endless Steppe: Growing Up in Siberia* (7–12). 1968, HarperCollins paper $5.99 (0-06-447027-X). The autobiography of the Polish girl who, with her family, was exiled to Siberia during World War II. [921]

KHERDIAN, JERON

7010 Kherdian, Jeron. *The Road from Home: The Story of an Armenian Girl* (6–8). 1979, Greenwillow LB $16.89 (0-688-84205-4); Morrow paper $5.99 (0-688-14425-X). A portrait of the youth of the author's mother, an Armenian girl who suffered many hardships and finally arrived in America as a mail-order bride. [921]

LAFAYETTE, MARQUIS DE

7011 Fritz, Jean. *Why Not, Lafayette?* (5–8). Illus. 1999, Putnam $16.99 (0-399-23411-X). Using plenty of quotations, interesting anecdotes, and dry humor, this is a fine biography of General Lafayette, the French-born hero of the American Revolution. (Rev: BCCB 12/99; BL 9/15/99; HB 11–12/99; HBG 3/00; SLJ 12/99) [921]

7012 Payan, Gregory. *Marquis de Lafayette: French Hero of the American Revolution* (4–7). Illus. Series: Library of American Lives and Times. 2001, Rosen $23.95 (0-8239-5733-0). Payan introduces the French general who assisted the American cause, with illustrations, maps, and other aids to understanding his times. (Rev: BL 10/15/01) [944.04]

LEKUTON, JOSEPH LEMASOLAI

7013 Lekuton, Joseph Lemasolai. *Facing the Lion: Growing Up Maasai on the African Savanna* (5–12). 2003, National Geographic $15.95 (0-7922-5125-3). Lekuton, a member of a nomadic Masai tribe and now a teacher in Virginia, remembers his youth in Kenya. (Rev: BL 9/15/03; SLJ 10/03*) [967.62]

LEONOWENS, ANNA

7014 Landon, Margaret. *Anna and the King of Siam* (7–12). Illus. 1944, HarperCollins $16.95 (0-381-98136-3). The career of the indomitable schoolteacher whose life became the basis of a play, a musical, and two movies. [921]

MACE, NANCY

7015 Mace, Nancy, and Mary Jane Ross. *In the Company of Men: A Woman at the Citadel* (7–12). 2001, Simon & Schuster $18.00 (0-689-84002-0). Nancy Mace, the first woman graduate of the Citadel, describes the humiliations and harassment she endured in this previously all-male military college. (Rev: BL 10/1/01; HB 1–2/02; HBG 3/02; SLJ 12/01; VOYA 12/01) [355]

MAH, ADELINE YEN

7016 Mah, Adeline Yen. *Chinese Cinderella: The True Story of an Unwanted Daughter* (6–12). 1999,

Delacorte $16.95 (0-385-32707-2). The author recounts her sad childhood in China in the 1940s and 1950s and her struggle to succeed in spite of her father's disdain and her stepmother's neglect. (Rev: BCCB 11/99; BL 10/1/99; HBG 4/00; SLJ 10/99) [979.4]

MANJIRO

7017 Blumberg, Rhoda. *Shipwrecked! The True Adventures of a Japanese Boy* (5–9). Illus. 2001, HarperCollins $16.95 (0-688-17484-1). The story of a shipwrecked Japanese boy who was adopted by an American sea captain, brought to Massachusetts for an education, and became the first Japanese person to live in the United States. (Rev: BCCB 3/01; BL 2/1/01*; HB 3–4/01; HBG 10/01; SLJ 2/01) [921]

MONTESSORI, MARIA

7018 Shephard, Marie T. *Maria Montessori: Teacher of Teachers* (5–7). Illus. 1996, Lerner LB $30.35 (0-8225-4952-2). A biography of the Italian educator and her unusual teaching methods for the young. (Rev: BL 8/96; SLJ 9/96) [921]

NIGHTINGALE, FLORENCE

7019 Gorrell, Gena K. *Heart and Soul: The Story of Florence Nightingale* (5–8). Illus. 2000, Tundra $18.95 (0-88776-494-0). A readable biography of Florence Nightingale that details her drive and determination and how she became known as "the lady with the lamp." (Rev: BL 1/1–15/01; HB 1–2/01; HBG 3/01; SLJ 12/00; VOYA 2/01) [921]

NIR, YEHUDA

7020 Nir, Yehuda. *The Lost Childhood* (8–12). 2002, Scholastic $16.95 (0-439-16389-7). The author presents disturbing memories of his years disguised as a Catholic in World War II Poland. (Rev: BL 4/1/02; HB 3–4/02; HBG 10/02; SLJ 7/02; VOYA 4/02) [940.53]

REISS, JOHANNA

7021 Reiss, Johanna. *The Upstairs Room* (7–10). 1972, HarperCollins $16.99 (0-690-85127-8); paper $5.99 (0-06-447043-1). The author's story of her years spent hiding from the Nazis in occupied Holland. Followed by *The Journey Back* (1976). (Rev: BL 3/1/88) [921]

RICHTER, HANS PETER

7022 Richter, Hans Peter. *I Was There* (7–9). Trans. by Edite Kroll. 1987, Penguin paper $4.99 (0-14-032206-X). The author tells of his youth in Nazi Germany as a member of Hitler Youth and later in the army. [921]

SHERBURNE, ANDREW

7023 Sherburne, Andrew. *The Memoirs of Andrew Sherburne: Patriot and Privateer of the American Revolution* (5–8). Ed. by Karen Zeinert. Illus. 1993, Linnet LB $17.50 (0-208-02354-2). This excerpt from Sherburne's autobiography of the war years describes his early life at sea and his capture and imprisonment by the British. (Rev: BL 5/15/93; SLJ 7/93) [921]

SIEGAL, ARANKA

7024 Siegal, Aranka. *Upon the Head of the Goat: A Childhood in Hungary* (7–10). 1981, Farrar $16.00 (0-374-38059-7). A childhood in Hungary during Hitler's rise to power. (Rev: BL 12/15/89) [921]

SUGIHARA, CHIUNE

7025 Gold, Alison L. *A Special Fate: Chiune Sugihara: Hero of the Holocaust* (5–10). 2000, Scholastic paper $15.95 (0-590-39525-4). The life story of the Japanese diplomat who saved thousands of Jewish lives during the Holocaust while he was stationed in Lithuania. (Rev: BCCB 5/00; BL 4/1/00; HB 5–6/00; HBG 10/00; SLJ 5/00; VOYA 6/00) [921]

SUZUKI, SHINICHI

7026 Collins, David R. *Dr. Shinichi Suzuki: Teaching Music from the Heart* (4–8). 2001, Morgan Reynolds LB $21.95 (1-883846-49-8). This account covers Suzuki's childhood, his interest in music, and his development of a successful method of teaching music, especially the violin, to young children. (Rev: BL 12/15/01; HBG 3/02; SLJ 4/02; VOYA 10/03) [780]

The Arts and Entertainment

General and Miscellaneous

7027 Alter, Judith. *Beauty Pageants: Tiaras, Roses, and Runways* (4–8). Illus. 1997, Watts LB $23.00 (0-531-20253-4). After introducing various kinds of pageants, this book describes in detail the Miss America pageant, its history, and organization. (Rev: BL 12/1/97; SLJ 9/97) [791.6]

7028 Bigham, Julia. *The 60s: The Plastic Age* (5–7). Series: 20th Century Design. 2000, Gareth Stevens LB $25.26 (0-8368-2708-2). A heavily illustrated title that looks at design and technology in the 1960s with coverage of fashion, art, household appliances, furniture, and architecture. (Rev: HBG 10/01; SLJ 3/01) [700]

7029 Gaff, Jackie. *1900–20: The Birth of Modernism* (5–7). Series: 20th Century Design. 2000, Gareth Stevens LB $25.26 (0-8368-2705-8). This account traces developments in the worlds of art, design, and technology for the first 20 years of the past century. (Rev: HBG 10/01; SLJ 3/01) [708]

7030 Jones, Helen. *40s and 50s: War and Postwar Years* (5–7). Series: 20th Century Design. 2000, Gareth Stevens LB $25.26 (0-8368-2707-4). Developments in art, design, and technology during and after World War II are chronicled in this heavily illustrated book. (Rev: HBG 10/01; SLJ 3/01) [708]

Architecture and Building

General and Miscellaneous

7031 Corbishley, Mike. *The World of Architectural Wonders* (5–8). Illus. Series: The World Of. 1997, Bedrick $19.95 (0-87226-279-0). The story of 14 architectural wonders worldwide, including Stonehenge, the pyramids of Egypt, Chartes Cathedral, the Taj Mahal, and Hoover Dam. (Rev: BL 6/1–15/97; SLJ 7/97) [720]

7032 Glenn, Patricia Brown. *Under Every Roof: A Kid's Style and Field Guide to the Architecture of American Houses* (5–8). 1993, Preservation $16.95 (0-89133-214-6). An introduction to the history and styles of architecture of American homes, with a look at more than 70 houses. (Rev: BL 7/94; SLJ 6/94) [728]

7033 Rubin, Susan Goldman. *There Goes the Neighborhood: Ten Buildings People Loved to Hate* (4–7). 2001, Holiday $18.95 (0-8234-1435-3). Many buildings create an uproar from their earliest design but later become nostalgic favorites, among them the Eiffel Tower and Guggenheim Museum, which are profiled here in an absorbing, colorful account that discusses materials and methods of construction. (Rev: BCCB 9/01; BL 8/01; HBG 3/02; SLJ 9/01; VOYA 10/01) [720]

7034 Weaver, Janice. *Building America* (5–8). 2002, Tundra $17.95 (0-88776-606-4). This brief history of architecture in America, from the 17th century to today, features detailed renderings, an illustrated timeline, and a useful glossary. (Rev: HBG 3/03; SLJ 5/03) [721]

History of Architecture

7035 Bergin, Mark. *A Medieval Castle* (5–8). Illus. 2003, McGraw-Hill $20.95 (1-57768-980-1). Cutaway illustrations and insets provide magnified views of castles and explain their design, construction, defense, and the nature of the people who inhabited them. (Rev: BL 9/15/03) [728.8]

7036 DuTemple, Lesley A. *The Pantheon* (6–9). Illus. Series: Great Building Feats. 2003, Lerner LB $27.93 (0-8225-0376-X). An interesting look at the Pantheon, with background information on Rome at the time of its construction and Thomas Jefferson's admiration of the design. (Rev: HBG 10/03; LMC 4–5/03; SLJ 4/03*) [726]

7037 Gravett, Christopher. *Castle* (5–9). Series: Eyewitness Books. 1994, Knopf $20.99 (0-679-96000-7). A look at the evolution of the castle, its functions, parts, and construction. (Rev: BL 10/15/94) [623]

7038 Lace, William W. *The Medieval Cathedral* (7–10). Series: Building History. 2000, Lucent LB $19.96 (1-56006-720-9). The whys and hows of cathedral building in the Middle Ages are explained with many color illustrations, diagrams, and examples of existing structures. (Rev: BL 4/15/01) [726]

7039 Macaulay, David. *Building the Book Cathedral* (5–9). 1999, Houghton $29.95 (0-395-92147-3). The author retells the fascinating story behind the creation of the original *Cathedral* book 25 years ago and adds numerous changes as he leads a tour of the cathedral, such as alterations in scale and page placement. (Rev: BCCB 12/99; BL 11/15/99; HB 9–10/99; SLJ 9/99) [726]

7040 Macaulay, David. *Castle* (5–8). 1977, Houghton $18.00 (0-395-25784-0); paper $8.95 (0-395-32920-5). Another of the author's brilliant, detailed works, this one on the planning and building of a Welsh castle. [940.1]

7041 Macaulay, David. *Cathedral: The Story of Its Construction* (6–8). 1973, Houghton $18.00 (0-395-17513-5). Gothic architecture as seen through a detailed examination of the construction of an imaginary cathedral. [726]

7042 Macaulay, David. *Mill* (5–8). 1983, Houghton $18.00 (0-395-34830-7); paper $9.95 (0-395-52019-3). Rhode Island textile mills of the 19th century are described in text and excellent drawings. [690]

7043 Macaulay, David. *Mosque* (6–12). Illus. 2003, Houghton $18.00 (0-618-24034-9). Macaulay follows a 16th-century mosque through initial design and planning, construction, and the uses of the finished structure and all its associated support buildings. (Rev: BL 10/1/03*; HB 11–12/03; SLJ 11/03*) [726]

7044 Macaulay, David. *Pyramid* (7–12). Illus. 1975, Houghton $18.00 (0-395-21407-6); paper $9.95 (0-395-32121-2). In beautiful line drawings, the author describes how an ancient Egyptian pyramid was constructed. [726]

7045 Milo, Francesco. *The Story of Architecture* (4–8). Illus. 2000, Bedrick $22.50 (0-87226-528-5). The wealth of information on building materials, cultures, and trends in this book lend a historical perspective to the discussion of world architecture. It is colorfully illustrated with drawings, photographs, and diagrams. (Rev: BL 6/1–15/00; HBG 10/00; SLJ 8/00) [720.9]

7046 Moorcroft, Christine. *The Taj Mahal* (5–8). Series: Great Buildings. 1998, Raintree Steck-Vaughn LB $27.12 (0-8172-4920-6). A beautifully illustrated book that describes the history of the Taj Mahal, its design, its construction, and its importance in architecture. (Rev: BL 2/1/98; HBG 3/98; SLJ 7/98) [954]

7047 Nardo, Don. *The Medieval Castle* (6–10). Illus. Series: Building History. 1997, Lucent LB $27.45 (1-56006-430-7). This study presents a history of the medieval European castle, including its structure, design, usage, and construction. (Rev: SLJ 5/98) [940.1]

7048 Williams, Brian. *Forts and Castles* (5–8). Series: See Through History. 1995, Viking $16.99 (0-670-85898-6). This lavishly illustrated book is a general introduction to the construction, parts, and uses of forts and castles. (Rev: BL 10/15/95) [728.81]

Painting, Sculpture, and Photography

General and Miscellaneous

7049 Ancona, George. *Murals: Walls That Sing* (5–8). Illus. 2003, Marshall Cavendish $17.95 (0-7614-5131-5). A photoessay showing murals stretching back from today's urban frescos to the cave paintings of Lascaux. (Rev: BL 4/15/03; SLJ 5/03) [751.7]

7050 Billout, Guy. *Something's Not Quite Right* (6–12). Illus. 2002, Godine $18.95 (1-56792-230-9). The detailed illustrations in this book, reminiscent of Dali and Escher, offer intriguing perspectives on the world and will encourage creative writing. (Rev: BL 2/15/03; HB 1–2/03; HBG 3/03; SLJ 1/03) [741.6]

7051 Capek, Michael. *Artistic Trickery: The Tradition of Trompe l'Oeil Art* (5–8). Illus. 1995, Lerner LB $22.60 (0-8225-2064-8). The art of creating images so perfect that the viewer thinks they are real is introduced, with many historical and contemporary examples. (Rev: BCCB 7–8/95; BL 6/1–15/95; SLJ 7/95) [758]

7052 Davidson, Rosemary. *Take a Look: An Introduction to the Experience of Art* (5–9). 1994, Viking $18.99 (0-670-84478-0). This overview, with examples from many cultures, describes how art fits into everyday experience and how we use it to express ourselves. (Rev: BL 3/1/94; SLJ 2/94; VOYA 6/94) [701]

7053 Delafosse, Claude. *Landscapes* (4–7). Illus. Series: First Discovery Art. 1996, Scholastic $11.95 (0-590-50216-6). The art and techniques of landscape painting are introduced, with many examples from the masters in various historical periods. (Rev: BL 6/1–15/96; SLJ 7/96) [750]

7054 Delafosse, Claude. *Paintings* (4–7). Illus. Series: First Discovery Art. 1996, Scholastic $11.95

(0-590-55201-5). A general introduction to painting, with many reproductions and lessons in art appreciation. (Rev: BL 6/1–15/96; SLJ 7/96) [750]

7055 Fritz, Jean. *Leonardo's Horse* (4–7). 2001, Putnam $16.99 (0-399-23576-0). The story of a Leonardo da Vinci sculpture that was begun in 1493 and finally completed — thanks to the efforts of Charles Dent — in 1999, along with biographical information about da Vinci and examples of his work. (Rev: BCCB 10/01; BL 10/15/01; HB 9–10/01; HBG 3/02; SLJ 9/01) [730]

7056 Greenway, Shirley. *Art: An A–Z Guide* (6–12). 2000, Watts LB $32.50 (0-531-11729-4). An alphabetical introduction to art history and techniques, with full-color photographs. (Rev: SLJ 4/01)

7057 Pekarik, Andrew. *Painting: Behind the Scenes* (4–7). Illus. 1992, Hyperion LB $19.49 (1-56282-297-7). Exploring the art of painting, including basic elements involved in each process. (Rev: BL 2/1/93; SLJ 2/93) [750]

7058 Richardson, Joy. *Looking at Pictures: An Introduction to Art for Young People* (5–8). Illus. 1997, Harry N. Abrams $19.95 (0-8109-4252-6). A large-size volume that introduces art appreciation to middle-graders and describes different types of pictures and techniques. (Rev: BCCB 7–8/97; BL 4/15/97; SLJ 6/97*) [750]

7059 Roalf, Peggy. *Dogs* (5–8). Illus. Series: Looking at Paintings. 1993, Hyperion paper $6.95 (1-56282-530-5). Various ways that dogs have been represented in paintings are reproduced, with explanations, in this attractive book on art appreciation. (Rev: BL 2/15/94; SLJ 2/94) [758.3]

7060 White, Matt. *Cameras on the Battlefield: Photos of War* (5–7). Series: High Five Reading. 2002, Capstone LB $22.60 (0-7368-4004-4). For reluctant readers, this is an appealing look at photographs of war, both those that celebrate war and those that document its horrors. (Rev: SLJ 8/02) [779.9355]

7061 Wilkinson, Philip. *The Art Gallery: Faces: The Fascinating History of Faces in Art* (5–8). Series: Art Gallery. 2000, Bedrick $14.95 (0-87226-633-8). From ancient to modern art, this book focuses on the depiction of the face in art with a special focus on ten self-portraits by such artists as da Vinci, Holbein, Velasquez, Vermeer, van Gogh, and Kahlo. (Rev: HBG 10/01; SLJ 12/00; VOYA 2/01) [701]

History of Art

7062 Barter, James. *A Renaissance Painter's Studio* (5–9). Series: The Working Life. 2003, Gale LB $21.96 (1-59018-178-6). An exploration of daily life for a painter at a time when art was growing in social importance. (Rev: SLJ 5/03) [759.5]

7063 Beckett, Wendy. *The Duke and the Peasant: Life in the Middle Ages* (4–8). Series: Adventures in Art. 1997, Prestel $14.95 (3-7913-1813-6). The 12 calendar paintings from the Duc de Berry's *Books of Hours* are reproduced, with explanations of each and an introduction to the art of the Middle Ages. (Rev: BL 8/97; SLJ 10/97) [940.1]

7064 Belloli, Andrea. *Exploring World Art* (7–12). Illus. 1999, J. Paul Getty Museum $24.95 (0-89236-510-2). Using examples from world art and artifacts, this work introduces a variety of media and images under such chapter headings as "Daily Life" and "History and Myth." (Rev: BL 1/1–15/00; HBG 4/00; SLJ 4/00) [709.]

7065 Capek, Michael. *Murals: Cave, Cathedral, to Street* (5–8). Illus. 1996, Lerner LB $28.80 (0-8225-2065-6). A history of mural painting, from cave painting to such modern masters as Diego Rivera. (Rev: BL 6/1–15/96; SLJ 10/96; VOYA 10/96) [751.7]

7066 Corrain, Lucia. *The Art of the Renaissance* (6–12). Illus. Series: Masters of Art. 1998, Bedrick $22.50 (0-87226-526-9). An oversize volume packed with lots of small, full-color pictures and information-packed text introducing Renaissance artists and their times. (Rev: BL 3/1/98; SLJ 2/98) [709]

7067 Corrain, Lucia. *Giotto and Medieval Art* (6–12). Series: Masters of Art. 1995, Bedrick $22.50 (0-87226-315-0). A beautifully illustrated book that explores the art of Giotto and other masters of the Middle Ages. (Rev: BL 11/15/95) [759.5]

7068 Gaff, Jackie. *1920–40: Realism and Surrealism* (4–8). Series: 20th Century Art. 2001, Gareth Stevens LB $25.26 (0-8368-2850-X). This appealing overview of art movements — mainly in Europe — offers accessible text, high-quality color repro-

ductions, and black-and-white photographs of important individuals. Also use *1900–10: New Ways of Seeing* and *1910–20: The Birth of Abstract Art* (both 2001). (Rev: HBG 10/01; SLJ 7/01) [708]

7069 Govignon, Brigitte, ed. *The Beginner's Guide to Art* (8–12). Trans. from French by John Goodman. 1998, Abrams $24.95 (0-8109-4002-7). Using a broad subject approach (architecture, sculpture, painting), this is a comprehensive guide to world art and artists, with generous use of color illustrations. (Rev: SLJ 3/99) [709]

7070 Halliwell, Sarah, ed. *Impressionism and Postimpressionism: Artists, Writers, and Composers* (6–9). Illus. Series: Who and When? 1998, Raintree Steck-Vaughn LB $19.98 (0-8172-4730-0). Clear reproductions and a concise text introduce such artists as Pissarro, Monet, Renoir, Gauguin, and van Gogh as well as writers including Zola and the composer Debussy. (Rev: BL 12/15/97) [700]

7071 Harris, Nathaniel. *Renaissance Art* (6–10). Series: Art and Artists. 1994, Thomson Learning LB $24.26 (1-56847-217-X). A general overview of this rich period in art history, with illustrations of paintings, sculpture, and architecture. (Rev: BL 11/15/94; SLJ 10/94) [709]

7072 Heslewood, Juliet. *The History of Western Painting: A Young Person's Guide* (5–9). Illus. 1995, Raintree Steck-Vaughn LB $25.68 (0-8172-4000-4). Beginning with cave paintings, this large-format book gives a cursory overview of Western painting, with several pages devoted to contemporary artists and movements. (Rev: BL 1/1–15/96; SLJ 12/95) [759]

7073 Heslewood, Juliet. *The History of Western Sculpture* (5–9). Illus. 1995, Raintree Steck-Vaughn LB $25.68 (0-8172-4001-2). This oversize, heavily illustrated book traces the history of Western sculpture from the ancient Greeks to contemporary masters. (Rev: BL 1/1–15/96; SLJ 12/95) [730]

7074 Isaacson, Philip M. *A Short Walk Around the Pyramids and Through the World of Art* (5–8). 1993, Knopf $20.99 (0-679-91523-0). Art is shown in its broadest sense as a part of the everyday world, using examples of sculpture, architecture, photography, and painting. (Rev: BL 9/15/93; SLJ 8/93*) [700]

7075 Janson, H. W. *History of Art.* 3rd ed. (8–12). Illus. 1986, Abrams $49.50 (0-8109-1094-2). This standard history of art contains a timeline integrating important events in art history with those in other fields. (Rev: BL 5/1/86) [709]

7076 Janson, H. W., and Anthony F. Janson. *History of Art for Young People.* 5th ed. (7–12). Illus. 1997, Abrams $49.50 (0-8109-4150-3). A much-expanded, thoroughly revised edition of the standard history of art for young people that now includes the 1990s. (Rev: BL 2/1/97; BR 9–10/97) [709]

7077 Knapp, Ruthie, and Janice Lehmberg. *Greek and Roman Art* (5–9). Series: Off the Wall Museum Guides for Kids. 2001, Davis paper $9.95 (0-87192-549-4). Using many photographs, this account highlights a number of art objects, explains relevant terms associated with them, describes their uses, and gives details on Greek and Roman culture. (Rev: BL 8/1/01) [936]

7078 Knapp, Ruthie, and Janice Lehmberg. *Impressionist Art* (5–9). Illus. Series: Off the Wall Museum Guides for Kids. 1999, Davis paper $9.95 (0-87192-385-8). This pocket-size guide supplies an overview of Impressionism and brief introductions to major artists, including Sisley and Monet. (Rev: BL 1/1–15/99) [709.03]

7079 Knapp, Ruthie, and Janice Lehmberg. *Modern Art* (5–9). Series: Off the Wall Museum Guides for Kids. 2001, Davis paper $9.95 (0-87192-458-6). A lively and colorful survey of 20th-century art including examples from expressionists, cubists, surrealists, and pop artists. (Rev: BL 8/1/01) [709]

7080 Lauber, Patricia. *Painters of the Caves* (4–8). 1998, National Geographic $17.95 (0-7922-7095-9). This lavishly illustrated book describes the paintings in the Chauvet cave in southeastern France and the life of the Neanderthal people who produced them. (Rev: BL 5/1/98; HBG 10/98; SLJ 3/98*) [759.0112094482]

7081 Mason, Antony. *In the Time of Michelangelo: The Renaissance Period* (7–10). Series: Art Around the World. 2001, Millbrook LB $23.90 (0-7613-2455-0). Full of full-color reproductions, this volume not only looks at the work of major artists of the Renaissance but also profiles artists in other parts of the world during the 15th and 16th centuries. Also use *In the Time of Renoir: The Impressionist Era* (2001). (Rev: HBG 10/02; SLJ 3/02) [709]

7082 Merlo, Claudio. *The History of Art: From Ancient to Modern Times* (4–7). Trans. from Italian by Nathaniel Harris. Series: Masters of Art. 2000, Bedrick $29.95 (0-87226-531-5). This ambitious volume, which tries to cover world art in all media in a single volume, is particularly valuable for its color illustrations. (Rev: HBG 10/00; SLJ 4/00) [750]

7083 Opie, Mary-Jane. *Sculpture* (7–12). Series: Eyewitness Art. 1994, DK $16.95 (1-56458-613-8). A handsome book filled with color illustrations introducing the world of sculpture, its history, and its various forms and materials. (Rev: BL 12/1/94; SLJ 6/95; VOYA 5/95) [730]

7084 Powell, Jillian. *Ancient Art* (6–10). Series: Art and Artists. 1994, Thomson Learning LB $24.26 (1-56847-216-1). This book covers the ancient civilizations and their contributions to the history of art. (Rev: BL 11/15/94; SLJ 10/94) [709]

7085 Rebman, Renee C. *The Sistine Chapel* (7–10). Series: Building History. 2000, Lucent LB $19.96 (1-56006-640-7). This account includes material on Michelangelo's original creation, his conflicts with the Pope, and the recent restorations of the ceiling. (Rev: BL 9/15/00; HBG 3/01) [945]

7086 Romei, Francesca. *The Story of Sculpture* (6–12). Series: Masters of Art. 1995, Bedrick $22.50 (0-87226-316-9). Using outstanding illustrations, this book covers a world history of sculpture with many examples of various styles and materials. (Rev: BL 11/15/95) [730]

7087 Sabbeth, Carol. *Monet and the Impressionists for Kids* (6–9). Illus. 2002, Chicago Review paper $17.95 (1-55652-397-1). Sabbeth introduces the life and work of seven impressionist artists — Monet, Renoir, Degas, Cassatt, Cezanne, Gauguin, and Seurat — and provides 21 related activities. (Rev: BL 7/02; SLJ 6/02) [759.05]

7088 Sandler, Martin W. *Photography: An Illustrated History* (6–12). Illus. 2002, Oxford $29.95 (0-19-512608-4). An overview of photography's major figures and developments, from its invention to new technologies, featuring many photographs. (Rev: BL 4/15/02; HBG 3/03; SLJ 6/02; VOYA 4/02) [770.9]

7089 Steffens, Bradley. *Photography: Preserving the Past* (6–10). Series: Encyclopedia of Discovery and Invention. 1991, Lucent LB $52.44 (1-56006-212-6). A history of photography that describes its impact on the modern world and profiles men and women involved in it. (Rev: BL 4/15/92) [770]

7090 Wakin, Edward, and Daniel Wakin. *Photos That Made U.S. History, Vol. 1: From the Civil War Era to the Atomic Age* (6–9). 1993, Walker LB $13.85 (0-8027-8231-0). Photographs that altered the perceptions of people and governments during times of military and social crisis. Also use *Photos That Made U.S. History, Vol. 2: From the Cold War to the Space Age* (1993). (Rev: BL 5/1/94; SLJ 2/94) [973.9]

Regions

Africa

7091 Finley, Carol. *The Art of African Masks: Exploring Cultural Traditions* (5–9). Series: Art Around the World. 1999, Lerner LB $23.93 (0-8225-2078-8). This account on African mask making past and present focuses on the western Sudan, the Guinea Coast, and Central Africa. (Rev: HBG 10/99; SLJ 11/99) [745.5]

7092 Knapp, Ruthie, and Janice Lehmberg. *Egyptian Art* (5–9). Illus. Series: Off the Wall Museum Guides for Kids. 1999, Davis paper $9.95 (0-87192-

384-X). This pocket-size art appreciation book discusses mummies, sculpture, hieroglyphs, and other artifacts from Egyptian art. (Rev: BL 1/1–15/99) [709.32]

Asia and the Pacific

7093 Finley, Carol. *Aboriginal Art of Australia: Exploring Cultural Traditions* (5–9). Series: Art Around the World. 1999, Lerner LB $23.93 (0-8225-2076-1). The author covers aboriginal art, aboriginal beliefs, and the contemporary works that reflect the Australian natives' struggle for equality. (Rev: HBG 3/00; SLJ 11/99) [701]

7094 Finley, Carol. *Art of Japan: Wood Block Color Prints* (6–9). Series: Art Around the World. 1998, Lerner LB $28.75 (0-8225-2077-X). This richly illustrated book describes the 18th- and 19th-century wood block prints made in Japan, with background material on Japanese history and culture. (Rev: BL 4/1/99; HBG 3/99) [769.952]

Europe

7095 Blanquet, Claire-Helene. *Miró: Earth and Sky* (5–7). Trans. from French by John Goodman. Illus. Series: Art for Children. 1994, Chelsea LB $15.95 (0-7910-2813-5). Using a conversational style and some fictitious characters, the life and works of the famous 20th-century French painter Miró are introduced. (Rev: SLJ 12/94) [709]

7096 Jockel, Nils. *Bruegel's Tower of Babel: The Builder with the Red Hat* (4–7). Illus. Series: Adventures in Art. 1998, Prestel $14.95 (3-7913-1941-8). A detailed analysis of Pieter Bruegel's surreal masterpiece, using one of the characters in the painting to supply a point of view and an examination of the meaning of its contents. (Rev: BL 8/98; SLJ 8/98) [759.9493]

7097 Loumaye, Jacqueline. *Chagall: My Sad and Joyous Village* (4–8). Trans. from French by John Goodman. Illus. Series: Art for Children. 1994, Chelsea LB $15.95 (0-7910-2807-0). A youngster learns about Chagall and his paintings from a violinist who grew up in the artist's home town in Russia. (Rev: SLJ 8/94) [709]

7098 Loumaye, Jacqueline. *Degas: The Painted Gesture* (4–8). Trans. from French by John Goodman. Illus. Series: Art for Children. 1994, Chelsea LB $15.95 (0-7910-2809-7). Using a series of workshops for children at the Orsay Museum (Paris) as a focus, the life and works of Degas are introduced. (Rev: SLJ 8/94) [709]

7099 Loumaye, Jacqueline. *Van Gogh: The Touch of Yellow* (4–8). Trans. from French by John Goodman. Illus. Series: Art for Children. 1994, Chelsea LB $15.95 (0-7910-2817-8). Two youngsters visit

the museums in Amsterdam to learn about van Gogh, his tragic life, and his paintings. (Rev: SLJ 8/94) [709]

7100 Muhlberger, Richard. *What Makes a Raphael a Raphael?* (5–10). Series: What Makes a . . . 1993, Viking $9.95 (0-670-85204-X). An in-depth look at the paintings of Raphael and distinguishing features. (Rev: BL 1/15/94; SLJ 12/93) [759.5]

7101 Muhlberger, Richard. *What Makes a Rembrandt a Rembrandt?* (5–10). Series: What Makes a . . . 1993, Viking $9.95 (0-670-85199-X). The basic characteristics of this great Dutch master's work are pinpointed through a series of reproductions. (Rev: BL 1/15/94) [759.9492]

7102 Salvi, Francesco. *The Impressionists: The Origins of Modern Painting* (6–12). Series: Masters of Art. 1995, Bedrick $22.50 (0-87226-314-2). An overview of Paris during the Impressionist period that includes many large, handsome reproductions. (Rev: BL 4/1/95; VOYA 5/95) [759.05]

7103 Wenzel, Angela. *Rene Magritte: Now You See It — Now You Don't* (4–7). Illus. Series: Adventures in Art. 1998, Prestel $14.95 (3-7913-1873-X). An examination of some of the works of Belgian surrealist Rene Magritte. (Rev: BL 8/98; SLJ 8/98) [759.949]

North America

UNITED STATES

7104 Butler, Jerry. *A Drawing in the Sand: A Story of African American Art* (4–7). Illus. 1999, Zino $24.95 (1-55933-216-6). This oversize book contains two narratives; the first is a history of African American art and artists, the second, an autobiography of Jerry Butler, the African American artist. (Rev: BL 2/15/99*) [704.03]

7105 Cockcroft, James D., and Jane Canning. *Latino Visions: Contemporary Chicano, Puerto Rican, and Cuban American Artists* (7–12). 2000, Watts LB $26.00 (0-531-11312-4). The central themes of modern Latino art and the interests of individual artists are explored in this comprehensive survey that includes sections of full-color plates and many black-and-white illustrations and photographs. (Rev: SLJ 2/01; VOYA 6/01) [704.03]

7106 Cummings, Pat. *Talking with Artists*, Vol. 3 (4–8). Series: Talking with Artists. 1999, Clarion $20.00 (0-395-89132-9). This is the third volume of interviews with children's artists and includes Peter Sis, Betsy Lewin, and Paul O. Zelinsky, with examples of their works. (Rev: BCCB 4/99; BL 3/15/99; HB 5 6/99; HBG 10/99; SLJ 4/99) [741.6]

7107 Finch, Christopher. *The Art of Walt Disney. From Mickey Mouse to the Magic Kingdoms* (7–12). Illus. 1973, Crown $4.99 (0-517-66474-7). The life and career of Walt Disney are covered, but the main attraction in this book is a collection of almost 800 illustrations from his work. [791.43]

7108 Goldstein, Bobbye S., ed. *Mother Goose on the Loose: Cartoons from the New Yorker* (6–12). Illus. 2003, Abrams $18.95 (0-8109-4239-9). Eighty cartoons that appeared in the *New Yorker* are accompanied by original nursery rhymes written by the editor. (Rev: BL 4/15/03; SLJ 5/03) [398.8]

7109 Greenberg, Jan, and Sandra Jordon. *The American Eye: Eleven Artists of the Twentieth Century* (6–12). 1995, Delacorte $22.50 (0-385-32173-2). The art of these 11 artists is analyzed without jargon or pretension. A list of museums displaying their artwork is included. (Rev: BL 9/1/95*; SLJ 11/95) [709]

7110 Hainey, Michael. *Blue* (5–10). Illus. 1997, Addison-Wesley paper $12.99 (0-201-87396-6). Collages, cartoons, and funky art are used with a clever text to illustrate uses of the color blue in American culture. (Rev: BL 2/1/98) [535.6]

7111 Horwitz, Elinor Lander. *Contemporary American Folk Artists* (7–9). Illus. 1975, HarperCollins paper $3.95 (0-397-31627-5). An explanation of what folk art is plus samples of the products of many artists. [709]

7112 Howard, Nancy S. *Jacob Lawrence: American Scenes, American Struggles* (4–7). Illus. 1996, Davis $14.95 (0-87192-302-5). The narrative paintings of this contemporary African American artist

are featured, with several suggested follow-up activities. (Rev: BL 11/1/96) [759.13]

7113 Joyce, William. *The World of William Joyce Scrapbook* (4–7). Illus. 1997, HarperCollins $18.95 (0-06-027432-8). A scrapbook collected by the author-artist that contains handwritten memoirs, sketches, finished artwork, and personal photographs. (Rev: BL 1/1–15/98; HBG 10/98; SLJ 2/98) [813]

7114 Knapp, Ruthie, and Janice Lehmberg. *American Art* (5–9). Series: Off the Wall Museum Guides for Kids. 1999, Davis paper $9.95 (0-87192-386-6). An informal pocket-size art appreciation book that features portraits from several centuries of American art, plus various artifacts and furniture. (Rev: BL 1/1–15/99) [709.73]

South and Central America

7115 Chaplik, Dorothy. *Latin American Arts and Cultures* (5–8). Illus. 2001, Davis $26.95 (0-87192-547-8). An encompassing look at Latin American art, architecture, and culture, from pre-Columbian to present-day, complete with pronunciation guide and captioned reproductions or photographs on each page. (Rev: BL 11/1/01) [700.9]

7116 Presilla, Maricel E. *Mola: Cuna Life Stories and Art* (5–7). Illus. 1996, Holt $17.95 (0-8050-3801-9). An examination of the life and art of the Cuna Indians, who live on islands off the coast of Panama. (Rev: BCCB 1/97; BL 10/1/96; SLJ 10/96) [305.48]

Music

General and Miscellaneous

7117 Barber, Nicola. *Music: An A–Z Guide* (4–8). Illus. 2001, Watts LB $33.00 (0-531-11898-3). Basic information on everything from performers and instruments to various forms of music is presented with illustrations and sidebar features. (Rev: SLJ 9/01) [780]

7118 Cefrey, Holly. *Backstage at a Music Video* (5–8). Illus. Series: Backstage Pass. 2003, Children's LB $20.00 (0-516-24324-1); paper $6.95 (0-516-24386-1). The history of music videos is coupled with information on how they are financed and produced, along with guidance on careers in the music business. (Rev: BL 5/1/03) [791.45]

7119 Ench, Rick, and Jay Cravath. *North American Indian Music* (5–7). Illus. Series: Watts Library: Indians of the Americas. 2002, Watts LB $24.00 (0-531-11772-3); paper $8.95 (0-531-16230-3). This title looks at the importance of music in the rituals of North American Indian tribes and describes the forms of beat, rhythm, and melody, with illustrations, a glossary, bibliography, and timeline. (Rev: BL 7/02) [782.62]

7120 Garty, Judy. *Marching Band Competition* (6–9). Series: Let's Go Team. 2003, Mason Crest LB $19.95 (1-59084-539-0). Students considering joining a marching band will learn about the kinds of competitions that take place and the planning and rehearsing necessary. Also use *Techniques of Marching Bands* (2003). (Rev: SLJ 11/03) [784.8]

7121 Garty, Judy. *Techniques of Marching Bands* (5–8). Series: Let's Go Team. 2003, Mason Crest LB $19.95 (1-59084-538-2). The slim volume supplies a look at the functions of a marching band, how they operate, and the joys of playing in one. (Rev: BL 10/15/03; SLJ 11/03) [785.06]

7122 Igus, Toyomi. *I See the Rhythm* (5–8). Illus. 1998, Children's $15.95 (0-89239-151-0). Using a timeline to set the social context, this title traces African American contributions to such musical forms as the blues, big band, jazz, bebop, gospel, and rock. (Rev: BCCB 7–8/98; BL 2/15/98; SLJ 6/98) [780]

7123 Morris, Neil. *Music and Dance* (5–8). Illus. Series: Discovering World Cultures. 2001, Crabtree paper $8.95 (0-7787-0249-9). A heavily illustrated overview of musical instruments and forms of dance around the world. (Rev: SLJ 5/02) [780]

7124 Price, Leontyne, reteller. *Aida* (4–8). 1990, Harcourt $20.00 (0-15-200405-X). The story of one of the grandest of operas retold by one of opera's grandest divas. (Rev: BCCB 10/90; HB 3–4/91; SLJ 11/90*) [782.1]

7125 Rowe, Julian. *Music* (4–7). Illus. Series: Science Encounters. 1997, Rigby paper $25.55 (1-57572-091-4). This book shows how scientific principles are used in music, musical instruments, hearing, and recording devices. (Rev: SLJ 10/97) [780]

7126 Schaefer, A. R. *Forming a Band* (5–8). Illus. Series: Rock Music Library. 2003, Capstone LB $22.60 (0-7368-2146-5). A hip and practical guide suitable for reluctant readers. Also use *Booking a First Gig* (2003). (Rev: BL 12/1/03) [784.100]

History of Music

7127 Kallen, Stuart A. *The History of Classical Music* (6–10). Illus. Series: Music Library. 2002, Gale LB $21.96 (1-59018-123-9). This overview covers classical music and composers starting with the Middle Ages, providing interesting excerpts from primary documents. Also use *The History of Jazz* (2002). (Rev: BL 11/1/02) [781.6]

Jazz and Popular Music (Country, Rap, Rock, etc.)

7128 Aquila, Richard. *That Old Time Rock and Roll: A Chronicle of an Era, 1954–1963* (8–12). 1989, Schirmer $25.00 (0-02-870082-1). A history complete with important biographies from the first decade of rock. (Rev: BL 9/15/89) [784.5]

7129 Asirvatham, Sandy. *The History of Jazz* (7–12). Series: American Mosaic. 2003, Chelsea LB $22.95 (0-7910-7265-7). Jazz, a unique American musical form shaped largely by African Americans, is covered from its beginnings in New Orleans to the present. (Rev: BL 10/15/03; HBG 10/03; SLJ 8/03) [781.61]

7130 Asirvatham, Sandy. *The History of the Blues* (6–10). Series: American Mosaic. 2003, Chelsea LB $22.95 (0-7910-7266-5). The origin, style, and technique of blues, along with its evolution and key figures, are presented with drawings and photographs. Also use *The History of Jazz* (2003). (Rev: BL 10/15/03; HBG 10/03; SLJ 8/03) [781.643]

7131 Ayazi-Hashjin, Sherry. *Rap and Hip Hop: The Voice of a Generation* (4–7). Illus. Series: Library of African American Arts and Culture. 1999, Rosen LB $19.95 (0-8239-1855-6). This account traces the history of rap and hip hop music from their origins in spirituals, jazz, blues, and storytelling traditions; it also gives some information on musicians. (Rev: BL 2/15/00; SLJ 1/00) [782.4]

7132 Brunning, Bob. *Heavy Metal* (5–8). Series: Sound Trackers. 2000, Bedrick $15.95 (0-87226-580-3). This work contains profiles of such bands as Black Sabbath, Cream, Guns 'n' Roses, Iron Maiden, Kiss, and Metallica. For biographies of stars such as Madonna and Prince, use the companion volume *Pop* (1999). (Rev: BL 4/15/00; HBG 10/00; SLJ 3/00) [781]

7133 Brunning, Bob. *1960s Pop* (5–9). Series: Sound Trackers. 1999, Bedrick $15.95 (0-87226-576-5). After a brief history of pop music in the 1960s, this account profiles dozens of individuals and groups that were prominent during that time. Also use *1970s Pop* (1999). (Rev: HBG 3/00; SLJ 11/99) [780]

7134 Brunning, Bob. *1970s Pop* (6–8). Illus. Series: Sound Trackers. 1999, Bedrick $15.95 (0-87226-578-1). This volume on 1970s pop music covers such bands as ABBA, Jethro Tull, the Bee Gees, Fleetwood Mac, and the Sex Pistols, as well as individuals such as Rod Stewart. (Rev: BL 10/15/99; HBG 4/00; SLJ 11/99) [781.66]

7135 Brunning, Bob. *1980s Pop* (6–8). Series: Sound Trackers. 2000, Bedrick $15.95 (0-87226-579-X). A revue of the stars and the music involved in rock during the 1980s. (Rev: BL 4/15/00; HBG 9/00; SLJ 3/00) [781.66]

7136 Brunning, Bob. *Rock 'n' Roll* (5–9). Series: Sound Trackers. 1999, Bedrick $15.95 (0-87226-575-7). This book gives a two-page history of rock music and biographies of a few paragraphs each for about a dozen prominent artists including Elvis Presley and Chuck Berry. A similar format is used in *Reggae* (1999). (Rev: HBG 3/00; SLJ 11/99) [780]

7137 Collier, James L. *Jazz: An American Saga* (7–10). 1997, Holt $18.00 (0-8050-4121-4). A concise history of this uniquely American art form, from its African and European roots to the present day, and including the influences of various musicians on its development. (Rev: SLJ 1/98; VOYA 4/98) [781.65]

7138 Elmer, Howard. *Blues: Its Birth and Growth* (6–9). Illus. Series: Library of African American Arts and Culture. 1999, Rosen LB $31.95 (0-8239-1853-X). This book traces the blues back to the song traditions of Africa, shows how it was influenced by the African American experience, and highlights the careers of such pioneers as Robert Johnson, Bessie Smith, and Muddy Waters. (Rev: BR 9–10/99; SLJ 8/99; VOYA 8/99) [781.66]

7139 George-Warren, Holly. *Shake, Rattle and Roll: The Founders of Rock and Roll* (4–7). 2001, Houghton $15.00 (0-618-05540-1). After an informative introduction on the history of rock and roll, there is a series of one-page biographies of famous personalities. (Rev: BL 3/1/01; HBG 10/01; SLJ 5/01*) [781.66]

7140 Gourse, Leslie. *Blowing on the Changes: The Art of the Jazz Horn Players* (8–12). Series: The Art of Jazz. 1997, Watts LB $23.00 (0-531-11357-4). This book explores the influence on jazz of great artists of the trumpet, saxophone, trombone, clarinet, and other wind instruments. (Rev: BR 5–6/98; HBG 3/98; SLJ 11/97) [784]

7141 Gourse, Leslie. *Deep Down in Music: The Art of the Great Jazz Bassists* (7–10). Series: The Art of Jazz. 1998, Watts LB $23.00 (0-531-11410-4). By tracing the work of the great innovators on the bass fiddle, this book explores the development of jazz bass techniques and how these low sounds supply the foundation of the music. (Rev: BR 11–12/98; SLJ 7/98; VOYA 10/99) [781.65]

7142 Gourse, Leslie. *Striders to Beboppers and Beyond: The Art of Jazz Piano* (7–10). 1997, Watts LB $23.00 (0-531-11320-5). In this history of jazz pianists, the author profiles 23 great performers, including Jelly Roll Morton, Mary Lou Williams,

Thelonius Monk, and Bud Powell. (Rev: SLJ 7/97) [786.4]

7143 Haskins, James. *One Love, One Heart: A History of Reggae* (7–12). Illus. 2002, Hyperion $15.99 (0-7868-0479-3). The story of the birth and growth of this musical genre, including its roots in Jamaica and the Rastafarian religion. (Rev: BL 4/15/02; HBG 10/02; SLJ 5/02; VOYA 12/02) [781.646]

7144 Haskins, James. *One Nation Under a Groove: Rap Music and Its Roots* (4–9). 2000, Hyperion $15.99 (0-7868-0478-5). Students seeking information on rap's musical roots will find well-researched details in this volume that includes lyrics and photographs. (Rev: BL 2/15/01; HBG 10/01; SLJ 4/01; VOYA 6/01) [782.421649]

7145 Kallen, Stuart A. *The History of Rock and Roll* (6–10). Series: The Music Library. 2002, Gale LB $21.96 (1-59018-126-3). Beginning in the early 1950s, this account traces the history of rock and roll, profiles many musicians involved, and describes the unique characteristics of this form of music. (Rev: BL 3/15/03) [781.66]

7146 Keely, Jennifer. *Rap Music* (6–12). Series: Overview. 2001, Lucent LB $27.45 (1-56006-504-4). This richly llustrated book gives an in-depth overview of rap music and profiles of many celebrities connected with it. (Rev: BL 9/15/01; SLJ 10/01) [782.42]

7147 Lee, Jeanne. *Jam! The Story of Jazz Music* (4–7). Illus. Series: Library of African American Arts and Culture. 1999, Rosen LB $31.95 (0-8239-1852-1). This book tells about the African American musicians who were responsible for the early development of jazz and blues. (Rev: BL 2/15/00; SLJ 1/00) [781.65]

7148 Reisfeld, Randi. *This Is the Sound: The Best of Alternative Rock* (7–9). Illus. 1996, Simon & Schuster paper $7.99 (0-689-80670-1). Although it is now somewhat dated, this is a rundown on the hottest alternative rock bands as of 1996. (Rev: BL 6/1–15/96; SLJ 7/96; VOYA 12/96) [791.66]

7149 Shirley, David. *The History of Rock and Roll* (6–9). 1997, Watts LB $23.00 (0-531-11332-9). A history of rock and roll that includes trends, stories, scandals, and personalities as well as coverage of such genres as rockabilly, folk rock, and glam rock. (Rev: BL 4/15/97; SLJ 6/97; VOYA 10/97) [781.66]

7150 Talevski, Nick. *The Unofficial Encyclopedia of the Rock and Roll Hall of Fame* (8–12). 1998, Greenwood $65.95 (0-313-30032-1). This book provides background on the Rock and Roll Hall of Fame in Cleveland and covers, in alphabetical order, the first 150 inductees, with interesting personal as well as professional information, anecdotes, comments, and insights. (Rev: VOYA 2/99) [781.66]

7151 Weatherford, Carole Boston. *The Sound That Jazz Makes* (5–9). 2000, Walker LB $17.85 (0-802-

78721-5). The history of jazz, tied in with the history of African Americans and told in rhythmic text. (Rev: BCCB 5/00; BL 2/15/03; HBG 9/00; SLJ 7/00) [781.6509]

7152 Woog, Adam. *The History of Rock and Roll* (6–9). Series: World History. 1999, Lucent LB $27.45 (1-56006-498-6). The history of rock from its origins in blues, country, and gospel music to its present forms in rap, hip hop, and grunge. (Rev: BL 9/15/99; SLJ 11/99) [781.66]

Opera and Musicals

7153 Englander, Roger. *Opera: What's All the Screaming About?* (7–12). Illus. 1983, Walker $12.95 (0-8027-6491-6). After a general introduction to the history and conventions of opera, 50 popular operas are introduced. (Rev: BL 9/1/87) [782.1]

7154 Ganeri, Anita, and Nicola Barber. *The Young Person's Guide to the Opera: With Music from the Great Operas on CD* (4–8). 2001, Harcourt $25.00 (0-15-216498-7). A bright and friendly introduction to opera that provides historical information and profiles some of the important singers and opera houses, with a companion CD of vocal and instrumental tracks. (Rev: HBG 3/02; SLJ 12/01) [792.1]

7155 Gatti, Anne, reteller. *The Magic Flute* (4–8). 1997, Chronicle $17.95 (0-8118-1003-8). An elegant retelling of the Mozart opera, with each scene given a full-color painting and a page of text. The accompanying CD has 16 selections coded to each page. (Rev: SLJ 1/98*) [782.1]

7156 Sullivan, Arthur. *I Have a Song to Sing, O! An Introduction to the Songs of Gilbert and Sullivan* (5–8). Ed. by John Langstaff. Illus. 1994, Macmillan $17.95 (0-689-50591-4). An introduction to the lives and accomplishments of Gilbert and Sullivan as well as a songbook of some of their greatest gems. (Rev: BL 12/1/94; SLJ 10/94) [781]

Orchestra and Musical Instruments

7157 Ardley, Neil. *Music* (5–9). Illus. 1989, Knopf $20.99 (0-394-92259-X). A profusely illustrated account that concentrates on musical instruments and their history. (Rev: BL 7/89; BR 11–12/89; SLJ 8/89) [781.91]

7158 Dearling, Robert, ed. *The Illustrated Encyclopedia of Musical Instruments* (8–12). 1996, Schirmer $90.00 (0-02-864667-3). In addition to material on the history, development, and characteristics of each musical instrument, this oversize, well-illustrated book gives a history of music-making, plus coverage of composers and performers. (Rev: BL 1/1–15/97; SLJ 5/97) [784.19]

7159 Evans, Roger. *How to Play Guitar: A New Book for Everyone Interested in Guitar* (8–12). Illus. 1980, St. Martin's paper $9.95 (0-312-36609-0). An easily followed basic guidebook on how to play the guitar with information on such topics as buying equipment and reading music. [787.6]

7160 Hayes, Ann. *Meet the Orchestra* (4–7). 1991, Harcourt $16.00 (0-15-200526-9). Animals in evening dress introduce young readers to the orchestra. (Rev: BCCB 3/91; BL 4/15/91; SLJ 5/91) [784.19]

7161 Levine, Robert. *The Story of the Orchestra* (5–7). 2001, Black Dog & Leventhal $19.98 (1-57912-148-9). Orchestra Bob introduces young readers to orchestra history, famous conductors and their eras, and instruments, in a guided tour that includes amusing cartoons, illustrations, and links to selections on the accompanying CD. (Rev: BL 12/15/01; SLJ 9/01) [784.2]

7162 Miles, J. C. *First Book of the Keyboard* (5–8). Series: First Music. 1993, EDC paper $10.95 (0-7460-0962-3). A beginner's guide to the electronic keyboard. (Rev: SLJ 7/93) [786]

7163 Sabbeth, Alex. *Rubber-Band Banjos and a Java Jive Bass: Projects and Activities on the Science of Music and Sound* (4–7). Illus. 1997, Wiley paper $12.95 (0-471-15675-2). Describes the basic elements of music while giving directions for making a variety of homemade instruments. (Rev: BL 3/15/97; SLJ 6/97) [781]

7164 Thyacott, Louise. *Musical Instruments* (5–7). Illus. Series: Traditions Around the World. 1995, Thomson Learning LB $24.26 (1-56847-228-5). A continent-by-continent survey of the many kinds of musical instruments found in various cultures. (Rev: BCCB 11/94; BL 9/15/95) [784.3]

Songs and Folk Songs

7165 Axelrod, Alan. *Songs of the Wild West* (5–9). 1991, Simon & Schuster paper $19.95 (0-671-74775-4). A collection of 45 songs from the Old West, with an overview of the Western expansionist movement and brief essays linking the music with art and history. (Rev: BL 12/15/91; SLJ 1/92) [784.7]

7166 Berger, Melvin. *The Story of Folk Music* (6–9). Illus. 1976, Phillips LB $29.95 (0-87599-215-3). The story of the origins and characteristics of American folk music, with biographical information on singers from Woody Guthrie to John Denver. [781.7]

7167 Blood-Patterson, Peter, ed. *Rise Up Singing* (8–12). Illus. 1988, Sing Out LB $39.95 (0-9626704-8-0); paper $17.95 (0-9626704-9-9). Words, chords, and some background material on 1,200 songs, some folk, others pop. (Rev: BL 12/15/88; BR 3–4/89) [784.5]

7168 Cooper, Michael L. *Slave Spirituals and the Jubilee Singers* (6–9). Illus. 2001, Clarion $16.00 (0-395-97829-7). All about the songs of American slavery and the Fisk University Jubilee Singers, who kept the songs alive after slavery ended. With photographs and sheet music. (Rev: BL 12/1/01; HB 1–2/02; HBG 3/02; SLJ 12/01; VOYA 2/02) [782.42162]

7169 Downes, Belinda. *Silent Night: A Christmas Carol Sampler* (7–12). 1995, Knopf $18.00 (0-679-86959-X). This 32-page collection of Christmas carols is illustrated with a full-page embroidered tapestry facing each carol. Words and piano music are provided. (Rev: BL 9/15/95*) [782.281]

7170 McGill, Alice. *In the Hollow of Your Hand: Slave Lullabies* (5–7). Illus. 2000, Houghton $18.00 (0-395-85755-4). Family life in the days of slavery is revealed in this moving collection of 13 folk lullabies; a CD of the songs is also included. (Rev: BCCB 1/01; BL 11/15/00; HBG 3/01; SLJ 12/00) [811.008]

7171 McNeil, Keith, and Rusty McNeil, eds. *California Songbook with Historical Commentary* (6–10). Illus. 2001, WEM Records $15.95 (1-878360-27-2). Music, chords, lyrics, and background information are given for a large selection of songs that originated in California. (Rev: BL 8/01) [782.42]

7172 McNeil, Keith, and Rusty McNeil. *Colonial and Revolution Songbook: With Historical Commentary* (4–7). 1996, WEM Records paper $11.95 (1-878360-08-6). This songbook contains 39 traditional songs from the 17th century through the War of 1812, with brief historical comments for each. (Rev: SLJ 12/96) [973]

7173 McNeil, Keith, and Rusty McNeil. *Moving West Songbook: With Historical Commentary* (7–10). Illus. 2003, WEM Records $15.95 (1-878360-30-2). Historical information, anecdotes, illustrations, and guitar chords accompany this large-format selection of about 50 songs of the early to mid-19th century. (Rev: BL 7/03; SLJ 11/03) [782.42]

7174 Sandburg, Carl. *The American Songbag* (7–12). Illus. 1970, Harcourt paper $24.00 (0-15-605650-X). A fine collection of all kinds of American folk songs with music and background notes from Mr. Sandburg. [784.7]

7175 Sieling, Peter. *Folk Music* (6–9). Illus. Series: North American Folklore. 2003, Mason Crest LB $22.95 (1-59084-342-8). Sieling defines the essence of folk music, looks at the instruments used, and explores its roots in the Old World, and the ways in which it has evolved in the New World. Also use *Folk Songs* (2003), which has a chapter on children's songs. (Rev: SLJ 6/03) [781.62]

7176 Silverman, Jerry. *Songs and Stories of the Civil War* (6–9). Illus. 2002, Twenty-First Century LB $29.90 (0-7613-2305-8). Lyrics, music, and recommended recordings are given for a dozen Civil War songs, each introduced by information on its history and on its relevance to the soldiers and civilians of the time. (Rev: BL 2/1/02; HBG 10/02; SLJ 7/02) [782.42]

Theater, Dance, and Other Performing Arts

General and Miscellaneous

7177 Alter, Judith. *Wild West Shows: Rough Riders and Sure Shots* (4–7). Illus. 1997, Watts LB $23.00 (0-531-20274-7). A brief photoessay that covers the history of the Wild West show, with a special focus on the contributions of Buffalo Bill to this form of entertainment. (Rev: BL 10/1/97; SLJ 8/97) [791.8]

7178 Presnall, Judith J. *Circuses: Under the Big Top* (4–7). Illus. Series: First Books. 1996, Watts LB $23.00 (0-531-20235-6). A history of circuses from ancient times to today with material on star performers. (Rev: SLJ 3/97) [791.3]

7179 Presnall, Judith Janda. *Circus Animals* (4–7). Series: Animals with Jobs. 2002, Gale LB $23.70 (0-7377-1360-7). This colorful book describes the training and performance of such circus animals as elephants, lions, tigers, and horses. (Rev: BL 2/15/03) [791.3]

Dance (Ballet, Modern, etc.)

7180 Augustyn, Frank, and Shelley Tanaka. *Footnotes: Dancing the World's Best-Loved Ballets* (5–8). Illus. 2001, Millbrook LB $24.90 (0-7613-2323-6). A readable account that introduces ballet from a backstage perspective, with material on how it feels to be a dancer in a large ballet company. (Rev: BL 4/15/01; HBG 10/01; SLJ 6/01*; VOYA 8/01) [792.8]

7181 Balanchine, George, and Francis Mason. *101 Stories of the Great Ballets* (7–12). 1975, Doubleday paper $16.00 (0-385-03398-2). Both the classics and newer ballets are introduced plus general background material such as a brief history of ballet. [792.8]

7182 Berger, Melvin. *The World of Dance* (6–8). Illus. 1978, Phillips $29.95 (0-87599-221-8). An overview of the subject that begins in prehistoric times and ends with today's social dancing and ballet. [792]

7183 Ephron, Amy, reteller. *Swan Lake* (4–9). Photos by Nancy Ellison. 2000, Abrams $19.95 (0-8109-4192-9). A straightforward retelling of the ballet story using stunning full-page, color photographs. (Rev: HBG 10/00; SLJ 7/00) [792]

7184 Feldman, Jane. *I Am a Dancer* (4–7). Photos by author. Series: Young Dreamers. 1999, Random $14.99 (0-679-88665-6). An attractive photoessay about 12-year-old Eva Lipman, a student at the School of American Ballet in New York City. (Rev: HBG 10/99; SLJ 8/99) [792.8]

7185 Ganeri, Anita. *The Young Person's Guide to the Ballet: With Music from the Nutcracker, Swan Lake, and the Sleeping Beauty* (5–8). 1998, Harcourt $25.00 (0-15-201184-6). Complete with a CD of familiar ballet music, this is a basic introduction to ballet, including its history, choreography, behind-the-scenes activities such as sewing costumes and making sets, and great ballet dancers, famous choreographers, composers, and ballet companies. (Rev: BL 11/1/98; SLJ 9/98; VOYA 2/99) [792.84]

7186 Grau, Andrea. *Dance* (4–9). Series: Eyewitness Books. 1998, Knopf $20.99 (0-679-99316-9). A stunning introduction to the world of dance, including ballet. (Rev: BL 8/98; HBG 3/99; SLJ 1/99) [792]

7187 Haskins, Jim. *Black Dance in America: A History Through Its People* (7–12). 1990, HarperCollins LB $14.89 (0-690-04659-6). Beginning with the dances brought from Africa by the slaves, this history moves to the present with the contributions of such people as Gregory Hines and Alvin Ailey. (Rev: BL 8/90; SLJ 6/90; VOYA 6/90) [792.8]

7188 Johnson, Anne E. *Jazz Tap: From African Drums to American Feet* (4–7). Series: The Library of African American Arts and Culture. 1999, Rosen LB $19.95 (0-8239-1856-4). This book traces the history of jazz tap from a variety of African dances to its emergence in the 1920s and its later development in night clubs, on Broadway, and in movies. (Rev: SLJ 1/00) [793.3]

7189 Pilobolus. *Twisted Yoga* (8–12). Photos by John Kane. 2002, North-South $9.95 (1-58717-136-8). Members of the Pilobolus Dance Theatre pose in eye-catching, contortionist positions. (Rev: SLJ 8/02) [792.8]

7190 Tythacott, Louise. *Dance* (5–7). Illus. Series: Traditions Around the World. 1995, Thomson Learning LB $24.26 (1-56847-275-7). The ways people dance around the world and the reasons they do are presented with many color photographs. (Rev: BL 6/1–15/95; SLJ 9/95) [793.3]

Motion Pictures

7191 Brackett, Leigh, and Lawrence Kasdan. *The Empire Strikes Back: The Illustrated Screenplay* (8–12). 1998, Ballantine paper $12.00 (0-345-42070-5). The shooting script for the second of the original *Star Wars* trilogy, with action direction and drawings of action scenes, preceded by an introduction that includes background and thoughts about the movie trilogy from the perspectives of people who were involved with the first release of the films. (Rev: SLJ 12/98) [791.43]

7192 Fingeroth, Danny. *Backstage at an Animated Series* (4–8). Series: Backstage Pass. 2003, Children's LB $20.00 (0-516-24323-3); paper $6.95 (0-516-24385-3). Fingeroth explores the world of animated films, discussing their history, recent technological advances, and the mechanics of production, and suggesting ways to become involved. Also use *Backstage at a Movie Set* (2003). (Rev: SLJ 10/03) [791.43]

7193 *James Cameron's Titanic* (6–12). Illus. 1997, HarperCollins $50.00 (0-06-757516-1); paper $20.00 (0-00-649060-3). A behind-the-scenes look at the creation of this blockbuster movie, with material and pictures on subjects including set design, costuming, and digital imaging. (Rev: VOYA 8/98) [791.43]

7194 Johnson, Shane. *Technical Star Wars Journal* (7–12). Illus. 1995, Del Rey $35.00 (0-345-40182-4). An intriguing look at the ships, droids, armor, and appliances that were developed for and featured

in the original *Star Wars* trilogy. (Rev: VOYA 4/96) [791.43]

7195 Jones, Sarah. *Film* (7–10). Illus. Series: Media-Wise. 2003, Smart Apple LB $28.50 (1-58340-256-X). The world of film making is clearly explained, with information on everything from initial concept to financing to the mechanics of production. (Rev: BL 10/15/03; SLJ 11/03) [791.43]

7196 Kasdan, Lawrence, and George Lucas. *Return of the Jedi: The Illustrated Screenplay* (8–12). 1998, Ballantine paper $12.00 (0-345-42079-9). The third of the original *Star Wars* trilogy is featured, with screenplay, background information, and drawings of action scenes from the film. (Rev: SLJ 12/98) [791.43]

7197 Mast, Gerald. *A Short History of the Movies*. 6th ed. (8–12). Illus. 1992, Macmillan $35.00 (0-02-580510-X). A lavishly illustrated history that deals with both the creative and technical aspects of movie history. (Rev: BL 1/15/87) [791.43]

7198 Platt, Richard. *Film* (5–9). Series: Eyewitness Books. 1992, Knopf $20.99 (0-679-91679-2). A discussion of the development of motion pictures and the use of film in other media. (Rev: BL 6/1/92; SLJ 2/93) [791.43]

7199 Reynolds, David West. *Star Wars: Incredible Cross-Sections* (4–8). 1998, DK $19.95 (1-7894-3480-6). This large-format book includes cross-sections of the TIE fighter, the X-wing fighter, the AT-AT, the Millennium Falcon, Jabba's sail barge, and the Death Star. (Rev: BL 12/15/98) [791.43]

7200 Reynolds, David West. *Star Wars: The Visual Dictionary* (4–8). 1998, DK $19.95 (0-7894-3481-4). Using a large-format dictionary approach, the people, creatures, and droids of the *Star Wars* saga are presented, with large photographs of the characters and many stills from the movies. (Rev: BL 12/15/98; HBG 3/99; SLJ 2/99) [791.43]

7201 Reynolds, David West. *Star Wars Episode I: Incredible Cross-Sections: The Definitive Guide to the Craft of Star Wars Episode I* (4–8). 1999, DK $19.95 (0-7894-3962-X). An excellent guidebook that features cross-sections of vehicles and spacecraft featured in *Star Wars: Episode I*. (Rev: HBG 3/00; SLJ 12/99) [791]

7202 Reynolds, David West. *Star Wars Episode I: The Visual Dictionary* (4–8). Illus. 1999, DK $19.95 (0-7894-4701-0). In this large-format book, a follow-up to *Star Wars: The Visual Dictionary,* the author, an archaeologist, reports on creatures and events in *Episode 1,* using movie stills and posed photographs to explain the galaxy's history, technology, anthropology, and politics. (Rev: BL 8/99) [791.43]

7203 Richards, Andrea. *Girl Director: A How-to Guide for the First-Time Flat-Broke Film Maker (and Video Maker)* (7–12). 2001, Alloy $17.95 (1-

9314-9700-1). Technical tips, inspiration, and instruction for would-be directors, with plenty of illustrations and other graphic elements. (Rev: BL 11/1/01; VOYA 6/01) [791.43]

7204 Schroeder, Russell. *Mickey Mouse: My Life in Pictures* (4–8). 1997, Disney LB $15.49 (0-7868-5059-0). After his meeting with Walt Disney, Mickey tells of his career decade by decade, using very brief text and numerous captioned illustrations of cartoon shorts, comic strips, TV programs, and feature films in which he appeared. (Rev: HBG 3/98; SLJ 2/98) [791.43]

7205 Shipman, David. *A Pictorial History of Science Fiction Films* (8–12). Illus. 1986, Salem House $17.95 (0-600-38520-5). From the French 19th-century efforts to today's works by Lucas and Spielberg, this is a heavily illustrated account of science fiction and fantasy movies. (Rev: BL 2/15/86) [791.435]

7206 Wallace, Daniel. *Star Wars: The Essential Guide to Planets and Moons* (6–12). Illus. 1998, Del Rey paper $19.95 (0-345-42068-3). This volume provides fascinating information on 110 different planets and moons in the *Star Wars* universe, arranged alphabetically from Abregado-rae, a popular stop for smugglers, to Zhar, a gas-filled giant, covering each world's inhabitants, climate, language, points of interest, and history. (Rev: VOYA 6/99) [791.45]

Radio, Television, and Video

7207 Catalano, Grace. *Meet the Stars of Dawson's Creek* (6–10). 1998, Bantam Doubleday Dell paper $4.99 (0-440-22821-2). This book describes how the *Dawson's Creek* television show was developed, profiles its stars and creator/producer, and summarizes the first six episodes. (Rev: VOYA 12/98) [791.45]

7208 Cavelos, Jeanne. *The Science of The X-Files* (8–12). 1998, Berkley paper $12.95 (0-425-16711-9). Combining pop culture and hard science, this book analyzes specific episodes of the *X-Files* from a scientific perspective. (Rev: VOYA 4/99) [791.45]

7209 Killick, Jane. *Babylon 5: The Coming of Shadows* (7–12). 1998, Ballantine paper $11.00 (0-345-42448-4). This is the second of a five-volume guide to this popular television series. (Rev: VOYA 12/98) [791.45]

7210 Kraus, Lawrence M. *The Physics of Star Trek* (7–12). Illus. 1996, HarperPerennial paper $13.00 (0-06-097710-8). Warp, transporter beams, antimatter, and other scientific concepts popularized in the TV series are examined, with speculations on their possible application in the future. (Rev: VOYA 8/97) [791.45]

7211 Krull, Kathleen. *The Night the Martians Landed: Just the Facts (Plus the Rumors) About Invaders from Mars* (4–7). 2003, HarperCollins LB $15.89 (0-688-17247-4); paper $4.25 (0-688-17246-6). The fascinating story of the 1938 radio broadcast of H. G. Wells's "The War of the Worlds" is amplified by a discussion of hoaxes in general and our tendency to believe them. (Rev: BCCB 10/03; SLJ 10/03)

7212 Lommel, Cookie. *African Americans in Film and Television* (7–12). Series: American Mosaic. 2003, Chelsea LB $22.95 (0-7910-7268-1). The history of the struggle of African Americans to be accepted in films and television and their position in these media today. (Rev: BL 10/15/03; HBG 10/03) [791.45]

7213 Wallner, Rosemary. *Fresh Prince of Bel-Air: The History of the Future* (7–10). 1992, ABDO LB $18.48 (1-56239-140-2). The story behind the TV series, now in reruns, that made a star of Will Smith. (Rev: BL 3/1/93; SLJ 11/93) [791.45]

Theater and Other Dramatic Forms

7214 Bany-Winters, Lisa. *On Stage: Theater Games and Activities for Kids* (4–7). Illus. 1997, Chicago Review paper $14.95 (1-55652-324-6). This book provides a number of theater games involving improvisation, creating characters, using and becoming objects, and ideas for pantomime and puppetry. (Rev: BL 2/1/98; SLJ 3/98) [327.12]

7215 Caruso, Sandra, and Susan Kosoff. *The Young Actor's Book of Improvisation: Dramatic Situations from Shakespeare to Spielberg: Ages 12–16* (6–12). 1998, Heinemann paper $22.95 (0-325-00049-2). This work supplies hundreds of situations suitable for improvisation culled from all forms of literature, plays, and movie scripts, arranged by themes such as confrontation and relationships. (Rev: BL 9/15/98; SLJ 1/99) [793]

7216 Currie, Stephen. *An Actor on the Elizabethan Stage* (7–10). Illus. 2003, Gale LB $27.45 (1-59018-174-3). An entertaining look at the Elizabethan theater and the skills that the all-male actors required. (Rev: SLJ 11/03) [792]

7217 Currie, Stephen. *Life in a Wild West Show* (6–10). Series: The Way People Live. 1998, Lucent LB $27.45 (1-56006-352-1). Personal struggles, individual jobs, and daily routines are stressed in this account of traveling shows that depicted life on the wild American frontier. (Rev: BL 11/15/98) [791.8]

7218 Cushman, Kathleen, and Montana Miller. *Circus Dreams* (6–12). Illus. 1990, Little, Brown $15.95 (0-316-16561-1). A look at the professional college for circus artists in France, following the experiences of one of its students. (Rev: BL 1/15/91; SLJ 1/91) [791.3]

7219 Friedman, Lise. *Break a Leg! The Kid's Guide to Acting and Stagecraft* (4–7). 2002, Workman $24.95 (0-7611-2590-6); paper $14.95 (0-7611-2208-7). Some of the topics covered for young would-be actors include analyzing a script, memorizing lines, stage fright, body language, and monologues. (Rev: BL 5/1/02; HBG 10/02) [292]

7220 Haskins, Jim, and Kathleen Benson. *Conjure Times: Black Magicians in America* (6–12). Illus. 2001, Walker $16.95 (0-8027-8762-2). The authors explore the substantial contributions of black performers to the early theater in America. (Rev: BL 7/01; HBG 3/02; SLJ 11/01; VOYA 4/02) [793.8]

7221 Helfer, Ralph D. *Mosey: The Remarkable Friendship of a Boy and His Elephant* (5–8). 2002, Scholastic paper $16.95 (0-439-29313-8). The adventure-filled story of an enduring friendship between a boy and his elephant, based on actual events in the early 20th century. (Rev: BL 7/02; HBG 3/03; SLJ 7/02; VOYA 8/02) [791.3]

7222 Kipnis, Claude. *The Mime Book* (7–12). Illus. 1988, Meriwether paper $16.95 (0-916260-55-0). One of the world's greatest mimes explains what it is and how it is done. [792.3]

7223 Lee, Robert L. *Everything About Theatre! The Guidebook of Theatre Fundamentals* (7–12). Illus. 1996, Meriwether paper $19.95 (1-56608-019-3). This excellent introduction to the backstage world includes material ranging from theater history to stagecraft, acting, and play production. (Rev: BL 12/1/96; SLJ 2/97) [792]

7224 Miller, Kimberly M. *Backstage at a Play* (4–8). Series: Backstage Pass. 2003, Children's LB $20.00 (0-516-24327-6); paper $6.95 (0-516-24389-6). Miller explores the world of theater, discussing how they are produced and the degree of commitment necessary, and suggesting ways to become involved. (Rev: SLJ 10/03) [792]

7225 Morley, Jacqueline. *A Shakespearean Theater* (5–8). Series: Magnifications. 2003, McGraw-Hill $20.95 (1-57768-979-8). Cutaway illustrations and insets provide magnified views of theaters in Shakespeare's days, with details on the history of drama, the actors, and the grimy state of 16th-century London. (Rev: BL 9/15/03) [792]

7226 Schindler, George. *Ventriloquism: Magic with Your Voice* (8–12). Illus. 1986, McKay paper $6.95 (0-679-14127-8). This book not only explains how to throw one's voice but also gives material on stage techniques, kinds of puppet figures, and writing routines. [793.8]

7227 Stevens, Chambers. *Sensational Scenes for Teens: The Scene Studyguide for Teen Actors!* (7–10). Illus. Series: Hollywood 101. 2001, Sandcastle paper $14.95 (1-883995-10-8). Acting coach Stevens includes more than 30 scenes — both comedy and drama — suitable for two teen actors, with choices for boy-girl, boy-boy, and girl-girl combinations. (Rev: BL 5/15/01; SLJ 4/01) [812.6]

7228 Stolzenberg, Mark. *Be a Clown!* (7–12). Illus. 1989, Sterling paper $10.95 (0-8069-5804-9). A how-to manual that describes how to create a clown character and supplies a number of routines. (Rev: BL 1/1/90) [791.3]

7229 Straub, Cindie, and Matthew Straub. *Mime: Basics for Beginners* (7–12). Illus. 1984, Plays paper $13.95 (0-8238-0263-9). The fundamentals of traditional mime are explained in text, line drawings, and photographs. (Rev: BL 2/1/85) [792.3]

History and Geography

General History and Geography

Miscellaneous Works

7230 Aaseng, Nathan. *You Are the Explorer* (4–8). Illus. Series: Great Decisions. 2000, Oliver LB $19.95 (1-881508-55-2). In this interactive book about famous explorers, the reader is asked to make decisions similar to those made by real explorers such as Columbus, Cortes, Champlain, and Robert Scott. (Rev: BL 5/1/00; HBG 10/00; SLJ 9/00) [910]

7231 Arnold, Caroline. *The Geography Book: Activities for Exploring, Mapping, and Enjoying Your World* (4–7). 2001, Wiley paper $12.95 (0-471-41236-8). An organized introduction to several geography concepts along with step-by-step instructions for projects and experiments. (Rev: BL 2/15/02; SLJ 3/02) [910]

7232 Burger, Leslie, and Debra L. Rahm. *Sister Cities in a World of Difference* (4–8). Illus. 1996, Lerner LB $22.60 (0-8225-2697-2). The pairing of cities internationally is covered with material on the results, mostly positive. (Rev: BL 9/1/96; SLJ 9/96; VOYA 4/97) [303.48]

7233 Cunha, Stephen F. *National Geographic Bee Official Study Guide* (4–8). 2002, National Geographic paper $9.95 (0-7922-7850-X). Tips on preparing for the geography bee, questions from former bees, and the competition rules and format are all presented in accessible text with plenty of helpful illustrations. (Rev: SLJ 9/02) [910.7973]

7234 Demarco, Neil. *The Children's Atlas of World History* (4–7). 2000, Bedrick $19.95 (0-87226-603-6). Double-page spreads introduce a series of maps and explanatory text that cover the history of the world. (Rev: HBG 10/00; SLJ 8/00) [910]

7235 Gardner, Robert. *Where on Earth Am I?* (8–12). Illus. 1996, Watts LB $20.00 (0-531-11297-

7). Topics relating to geography and geology, such as the earth's shape and motion, maps, and distance and direction, are explored in 45 projects and activities. (Rev: BL 2/15/97; SLJ 2/97) [526]

7236 Matthews, Rupert. *Explorer* (5–9). Series: Eyewitness Books. 1991, Knopf $20.99 (0-679-91460-9). The world of exploration is introduced with highlights from the careers of the most famous. (Rev: BL 12/1/91) [910]

7237 Pascoe, Elaine, and Deborah Kops. *Scholastic Kid's Almanac for the 21st Century* (4–7). 1999, Scholastic paper $12.95 (0-590-30724-X). An almanac that covers subjects including aerospace, animals, chemistry, computers, energy, geography, plants, religion, and sports. (Rev: SLJ 2/00) [900]

7238 Siegel, Alice, and Margo McLoone. *The Blackbirch Kid's Almanac of Geography* (4–7). 2000, Blackbirch $49.94 (1-56711-300-1). A good browsing book that contains information on such topics as natural and manmade wonders, countries, currencies, events, weather, languages, foods, and culture. (Rev: HBG 3/01; SLJ 2/01) [910]

7239 Wyse, Elizabeth, and Caroline Lucas, eds. *Dorling Kindersley Children's Atlas* (4–8). Illus. 2000, DK paper $24.99 (0-7894-5845-4). An excellent all-purpose atlas that includes material on history, climate, vegetation, population, and more. (Rev: BL 10/15/00; HBG 10/01; SLJ 5/01) [912]

Atlases, Maps, and Mapmaking

7240 Bramwell, Martyn. *How Maps Are Made* (3–8). Illus. Series: Maps and Mapmakers. 1998, Lerner LB $22.60 (0-8225-2920-3). The difficulties in representing the globe on a flat surface are explored, plus details on how maps are made —

both by hand and by computer — and on the use of aerial photography in mapmaking. (Rev: BL 3/15/99; HBG 3/99; SLJ 2/99) [526]

7241 Bramwell, Martyn. *Mapping Our World* (4–8). Illus. Series: Maps and Mapmakers. 1998, Lerner LB $22.60 (0-8225-2924-6). This work shows how different kinds of maps can be used to illustrate topography, geology, climate, vegetation, population, geography, minerals, trade, pollution, and habitat. (Rev: BL 3/15/99; SLJ 2/99) [912]

7242 Bramwell, Martyn. *Mapping the Seas and Airways* (5–8). Series: Maps and Mapmakers. 1998, Lerner LB $22.60 (0-8225-2921-1). This volume deals with special kinds of maps prepared and used by oceanographers and by airline cartographers. (Rev: BL 3/15/99; HBG 3/99) [912]

7243 Bramwell, Martyn. *Maps in Everyday Life* (5–8). Illus. Series: Maps and Mapmakers. 1998, Lerner LB $22.60 (0-8225-2923-8). This book explains how different maps are used for different purposes, e.g., tourist maps and climate maps. (Rev: BL 3/15/99; HBG 3/99) [912]

7244 Johnson, Sylvia A. *Mapping the World* (4–7). Illus. 1999, Simon & Schuster $16.95 (0-689-81813-0). A history of maps and mapmaking from Ptolemy in ancient Greece to the satellite and computer images of today. (Rev: BCCB 11/99; BL 12/1/99; HBG 3/00; SLJ 12/99*) [912]

7245 Jouris, David. *All Over the Map: An Extraordinary Atlas of the United States* (8–10). 1994, Ten Speed paper $11.95 (0-89815-649-1). A U.S. atlas that explores the history of the names of towns and cities, including such places as Peculiar, Ding Dong, Vendor, and Joy. (Rev: BL 7/94) [910]

7246 Oleksy, Walter. *Mapping the World* (5–7). Series: Watts Library: Geography. 2002, Watts LB $24.00 (0-531-12029-5); paper $8.95 (0-531-16636-8). A history of how maps have been made, from the explorers, merchants, and mapmakers of old to the accurate modern products that use new technology. Also use *Mapping the Seas* and *Maps in History* (both 2002). (Rev: BL 10/15/02) [912]

7247 Pratt, Paula B. *Maps: Plotting Places on the Globe* (6–10). Series: Encyclopedia of Discovery and Invention. 1995, Lucent LB $52.44 (1-56006-255-X). Traces the evolution of mapmaking/cartography from ancient times to the present. (Rev: BL 4/15/95; SLJ 3/95) [912]

7248 Ross, Val. *The Road to There: Mapmakers and Their Stories* (7–10). Illus. 2003, Tundra $19.95 (0-88776-621-8). Mapmakers of different eras and nationalities, well-known figures such as Henry the Navigator and less familiar individuals, and the charts they created are featured in this interesting volume with period illustrations and many maps. (Rev: BCCB 1/04; BL 12/15/03; SLJ 12/03*) [912]

7249 Smith, A. G. *Where Am I? The Story of Maps and Navigation* (4–8). Illus. 1997, Stoddart paper $13.95 (0-7737-5836-4). Important discoveries and innovations in the history of mapmaking are explained. (Rev: BL 9/1/97) [910]

7250 Young, Karen Romano. *Small Worlds: Maps and Mapmaking* (7–12). 2002, Scholastic $17.95 (0-439-09545-X). Maps of all kinds — from airport diagrams and neighborhood plans to a full globe and a chart of the universe — are introduced with many illustrations and historical and scientific explanations. (Rev: SLJ 6/03) [912]

Paleontology

7251 Aaseng, Nathan. *American Dinosaur Hunters* (6–9). Illus. 1996, Enslow LB $20.95 (0-89490-710-7). A history of paleontology, the story of major discoveries, and brief biographies of such scientists as Edward Hitchcock and Roy Chapman Andrews. (Rev: BL 11/15/96; BR 1–2/97; SLJ 12/96) [560]

7252 Agenbroad, Larry D., and Lisa Nelson. *Mammoths: Ice-Age Giants* (5–8). Illus. Series: Discovery! 2002, Lerner LB $31.95 (0-8225-2862-2). A detailed look at mammoths, theories on mammoth extinction, and mammoth discoveries, with sidebar features on topics such as human hunters in the Ice Age, and geologic timelines. (Rev: BL 6/1–15/02; HBG 10/02; SLJ 7/02) [569]

7253 Arnold, Caroline. *Dinosaur Mountain: Graveyard of the Past* (4–7). Illus. 1990, Ticknor $16.00 (0-89919-693-4). A visit to the Dinosaur National Monument quarry in Utah. (Rev: BL 5/15/89) [567.910979221]

7254 Barrett, Paul. *National Geographic Dinosaurs* (6–10). Illus. 2001, National Geographic $29.95 (0-7922-8224-8). This comprehensive and attractive guide provides a wealth of information about dinosaurs, their timeframe and evolution, individual species, and eventual extinction, with maps, fact boxes, and graphics. (Rev: BL 7/01; SLJ 10/01) [567.9]

7255 Berger, Melvin. *Mighty Dinosaurs* (4–8). Illus. 1990, Avon paper $2.95 (0-380-76052-5). Covers various kinds of dinosaurs and includes the latest research on their extinction. (Rev: BL 12/15/90) [567.9]

7256 Brett-Surman, Michael, and Thomas R. Holtz, Jr. *James Gurney: The World of Dinosaurs* (5–8). 1998, GWP paper $19.95 (0-86713-046-6). This story of the 15 dinosaur stamps designed for the U.S. Postal Service includes a description of each of the beasts. (Rev: SLJ 9/98) [567.9]

7257 Christian, Spencer, and Antonia Felix. *Is There a Dinosaur in Your Backyard? The World's Most Fascinating Fossils, Rocks, and Minerals* (5–8). Series: Spencer Christian's World of Wonders. 1998, Wiley paper $12.95 (0-471-19616-9). In addition to discussing dinosaurs, this fascinating book introduces earth science, with interesting details about rocks, minerals, and fossils. (Rev: BL 9/1/98; SLJ 10/98) [552]

7258 Clark, Neil, and William Lindsay. *1001 Facts About Dinosaurs* (7–12). Series: Backpack Books. 2002, DK paper $8.95 (0-7894-8448-X). Lively prose and more than 500 colorful illustrations present basic facts about various kinds of dinosaurs. (Rev: BL 3/15/02) [567.9]

7259 Clinton, Susan. *Reading Between the Bones: The Pioneers of Dinosaur Paleontology* (6–10). Series: Lives in Science. 1997, Watts LB $25.00 (0-531-11324-8). The lives and work of eight major scientists involved in dinosaur paleontology are profiled in this carefully documented book. (Rev: BL 5/1/97; SLJ 6/97; VOYA 12/97) [560]

7260 Cooley, Brian, and Mary Ann Wilson. *Make-a-Saurus: My Life with Raptors and Other Dinosaurs* (4–8). Photos by Gary Campbell. 2000, Annick LB $24.95 (1-55037-645-4); paper $14.95 (1-55037-644-6). A two-part book giving a step-by-step description of how museum-quality models of dinosaurs are made using the latest discoveries in paleontology, followed by an exploration of how these techniques can be adapted so the reader can make models at home. (Rev: HBG 3/01; SLJ 9/00) [567.9]

7261 Currie, Philip, and Kevin Padian, eds. *Encyclopedia of Dinosaurs* (8–12). Illus. 1997, Academic Pr. $116.95 (0-12-226810-5). An adult reference book, written by scientists, with interesting, alphabetically arranged articles on dinosaurs, digs, and sites. (Rev: BL 11/1/97; SLJ 5/98) [567.9]

7262 Currie, Philip J., and Colleayn O. Mastin. *The Newest and Coolest Dinosaurs* (4–8). Illus. 1998, Grasshopper $18.95 (1-895910-41-2). Using double-page spreads, this useful volume introduces 15 of the most recent finds in the world of dinosaurs. (Rev: SLJ 1/99) [560]

7263 Cutchins, Judy, and Ginny Johnston. *Giant Predators of the Ancient Seas* (4–7). Illus. Series: Southern Fossil Discoveries. 2001, Pineapple $14.95 (1-56164-237-1). A look at the reptiles, fish, whales, sharks, and sea snakes that were found in the seas that once covered much of North America, as well as a discussion of the methods scientists used to reconstruct them. (Rev: HBG 3/02; SLJ 12/01) [566]

7264 Dal Sasso, Cristiano. *Animals: Origins and Evolution* (4–8). Illus. Series: Beginnings — Origins and Evolution. 1995, Raintree Steck-Vaughn LB $24.26 (0-8114-3333-1). This well-illustrated account traces the development of animals from bacteria to the invertebrates and then fish, amphibians, reptiles, birds, and mammals. (Rev: BL 5/1/95; SLJ 6/95) [591]

7265 Dingus, Lowell, and Luis Chiappe. *The Tiniest Giants: Discovering Dinosaur Eggs* (5–8). Illus. 1999, Doubleday $17.95 (0-385-32642-4). An account of the discovery of a huge dinosaur nest area in Patagonia and the eggs that contained fossilized remains of sauropod embryos. (Rev: BCCB 7–8/99; BL 6/1–15/99; HBG 9/99; SLJ 6/99) [567.9]

7266 Dixon, Dougal. *Dinosaurs: The Good, the Bad, and the Ugly* (4–8). Series: Secret Worlds. 2001, DK $5.99 (0-7894-7972-9). Dramatic color illustrations and a lively text are used to create interest in this introduction to dinosaurs and their world. (Rev: BL 10/15/01; HBG 3/02) [567.9]

7267 Dixon, Dougal. *Dougal Dixon's Dinosaurs* (4–8). Illus. 1998, Boyds Mills $19.95 (1-56397-722-2). This updated revision of the 1993 volume remains a good basic resource on dinosaurs. (Rev: HBG 10/98; SLJ 6/98) [567.9]

7268 Dixon, Dougal. *The Search for Dinosaurs* (4–7). Illus. Series: Digging Up the Past. 1995, Thomson Learning LB $24.26 (1-56847-396-6). A history of the various discoveries that paleontologists have made about dinosaurs and other prehistoric beasts. (Rev: SLJ 2/96) [567.9]

7269 Farlow, James O. *Bringing Dinosaur Bones to Life: How Do We Know What Dinosaurs Were Like?* (4–7). Illus. 2001, Watts LB $25.00 (0-531-11403-1). An interesting look at the life of dinosaurs and at the methods paleontologists use to learn about the beasts, pointing out that although scientists can reconstruct animals from skeletons and fossil evidence, they must always differentiate between fact and educated guesses. (Rev: BL 12/15/01; SLJ 12/01) [567.9]

7270 Gallant, Jonathan R. *The Tales Fossils Tell* (5–9). Series: The Story of Science. 2000, Benchmark LB $28.50 (0-7614-1153-4). A fascinating introduction to paleontology that explains how the importance of fossils was only clearly understood after the ideas of evolution and extinction were accepted. (Rev: BL 12/15/00; HBG 10/01; SLJ 2/01) [560]

7271 Gee, Henry. *A Field Guide to Dinosaurs: The Essential Handbook for Travelers in the Mesozoic* (6–12). Illus. 2003, Barron's $24.95 (0-7641-5511-3). Fact and speculation are interwoven in this guide to dinosaur species that follows the format of a field guide to birds. (Rev: BL 8/03; HBG 10/03; SLJ 9/03) [567.9]

7272 Holmes, Thom, and Laurie Holmes. *Armored, Plated, and Bone-Headed Dinosaurs: The Ankylosaurs, Stegosaurs, and Pachycephalosaurs* (6–10). Series: Dinosaur Library. 2002, Enslow LB $20.95 (0-7660-1453-3). A well-organized introduction to these dinosaurs and their adaptation of anatomical defenses, with illustrations, graphic elements, a timeline of scientific discoveries, and a glossary. (Rev: BL 8/02; HBG 10/02; SLJ 10/02) [567.915]

7273 Holmes, Thom, and Laurie Holmes. *Feathered Dinosaurs: The Origin of Birds* (6–10). Series: Dinosaur Library. 2002, Enslow LB $20.95 (0-7660-1454-1). A well-organized introduction to these dinosaurs and their relationship to today's birds, with illustrations, graphic elements, a timeline of scientific discoveries, and a glossary. (Rev: BL 8/02; HBG 10/02; SLJ 10/02) [567.9]

7274 Holmes, Thom, and Laurie Holmes. *Horned Dinosaurs: The Ceratopsians* (6–10). Series: The Dinosaur Library. 2001, Enslow LB $20.95 (0-7660-1451-7). A detailed survey of psittacosaurs, protoceratopsids, and ceratopsids. Another recommended title in the series is *Peaceful Plant-Eating Dinosaurs: The Iguanodonts, Duckbills, and Other Ornithopods* (2001). (Rev: HBG 3/02; SLJ 11/01) [567.915]

7275 Krueger, Richard. *The Dinosaurs* (5–8). Illus. Series: Prehistoric North America. 1996, Millbrook LB $22.90 (1-56294-548-3). With plenty of color illustrations, this chatty overview tells about North American dinosaurs. (Rev: BL 5/15/96; SLJ 4/96) [567.9]

7276 Lambert, David. *A Field Guide to Dinosaurs* (7–12). Illus. 1983, Avon paper $9.95 (0-380-83519-3). A well-illustrated guide to more than 340 different dinosaurs arranged by family groups. [567.9]

7277 Lessem, Don. *Dinosaur Worlds: New Dinosaurs, New Discoveries* (5–8). Illus. 1996, Boyds

Mills $19.95 (1-56397-597-1). The reader visits various dinosaur digs worldwide in a review of what we know about these amazing creatures. (Rev: BL 11/15/96; BR 5–6/97; SLJ 12/96*) [567.9]

7278 Llamas, Andreu. *The Era of the Dinosaurs* (4–8). Illus. Series: Development of the Earth. 1996, Chelsea LB $17.55 (0-7910-3452-6). Various kinds of dinosaurs are introduced, with an emphasis on their evolution and on how geology and climate affected their development. (Rev: SLJ 7/96) [567.9]

7279 Llamas, Andreu. *The First Amphibians* (4–8). Illus. Series: Development of the Earth. 1996, Chelsea LB $17.55 (0-7910-3453-4). Using many color illustrations, this book begins with the earliest land vertebrates and gives clear explanations of their adaptations over time. (Rev: SLJ 7/96) [567.9]

7280 McGowan, Christopher. *T-Rex to Go* (7–12). Illus. 1999, HarperPerennial paper $14.00 (0-06-095281-4). Along with a great deal of information about dinosaurs, particularly Tyrannosaurus Rex, this fascinating book explains in great detail how to make a model of the dinosaur using chicken bones and simple tools. (Rev: VOYA 10/99) [567.9]

7281 Mannetti, William. *Dinosaurs in Your Backyard* (5–8). 1982, Macmillan $15.00 (0-689-30906-6). The latest discoveries and theories concerning dinosaurs and their history are incorporated into this account. [567.9]

7282 Nardo, Don. *Dinosaurs: Unearthing the Secrets of Ancient Beasts* (6–10). Series: Encyclopedia of Discovery and Invention. 1995, Lucent LB $52.44 (1-56006-253-3). Describes dinosaurs and their habitats and highlights the dedicated men and women who have made significant discoveries about them. (Rev: BL 4/15/95) [567.9]

7283 Norman, David, and Angela Milner. *Dinosaur* (4–8). Illus. Series: Eyewitness Books. 1989, Knopf $20.99 (0-394-92253-0). Rich illustrations highlight various dinosaurs, with details on structure and habits. (Rev: BCCB 6/00; BL 10/15/89; SLJ 1/90) [567.9]

7284 Nye, Bill, and Ian G. Saunders. *Bill Nye the Science Guy's Great Big Dinosaur Dig* (5–6). 2002, Hyperion $17.49 (0-7868-2472-7). The Science Guy fills us in on dinosaurs, what we learn from their fossils, and the animals' eventual evolution into birds. (Rev: HBG 3/03; SLJ 1/03) [567.9]

7285 Parker, Steve, and Jane Parker. *Collecting Fossils: Hold Prehistory in the Palm of Your Hand* (5–8). Illus. 1998, Sterling $14.95 (0-8069-9762-1). After a discussion of how fossils are formed, this work introduces different types of fossils, explains important terms, and tells how to collect and organize them. (Rev: BL 6/1–15/98; SLJ 6/98) [560]

7286 Patent, Dorothy Hinshaw. *In Search of Maiasaurs* (4–7). Series: Frozen in Time. 1998, Benchmark LB $27.07 (0-7614-0787-1). This book on dinosaurs describes the recent find of a huge bed of bones and Jack Horner's work to retrieve the fossils and learn from them. (Rev: HBG 10/99; SLJ 3/99) [567.9]

7287 Sloan, Christopher. *Supercroc and the Origin of Crocodiles* (5–8). Illus. 2002, National Geographic $18.95 (0-7922-6691-9). A fascinating account of the discovery in Africa of the fossil *Sarcosuchus*, or Supercroc, with additional information on paleontology and crocodile evolution. (Rev: BCCB 5/02; BL 9/15/02; HBG 10/02; SLJ 7/02*) [567.9]

7288 Stein, Wendy. *Dinosaurs* (6–10). Series: Great Mysteries. 1994, Greenhaven $18.96 (1-56510-096-4). An introduction to dinosaurs and an examination of the various theories about their extinction. (Rev: BL 4/15/94) [567.9]

7289 Tanaka, Shelley. *Graveyards of the Dinosaurs: What It's Like to Discover Prehistoric Creatures* (4–7). Illus. 1998, Hyperion $16.95 (0-7868-0375-4). This introduction to paleontology introduces readers to key paleontologists and the major dinosaur bone sites around the world. (Rev: BL 9/1/98; HBG 10/98; SLJ 7/98) [567.9]

7290 Thompson, Ida. *The Audubon Society Field Guide to North American Fossils* (7–12). Illus. 1982, Knopf $19.95 (0-394-52412-8). An illustrated guide to the identification of North American fossils plus some background information on their formation. [560]

7291 Thompson, Sharon E. *Death Trap: The Story of the La Brea Tar Pits* (4–8). Illus. 1995, Lerner LB $28.75 (0-8225-2851-7). A history of the 40,000-year-old tar pits in Los Angeles and of the many species of prehistoric animals that were trapped in them, with color photographs. (Rev: BL 6/1–15/95; SLJ 5/95) [560]

7292 VanCleave, Janice. *Dinosaurs for Every Kid: Easy Activities That Make Learning Science Fun* (4–7). Illus. Series: Science for Every Kid. 1994, Wiley paper $12.95 (0-471-30812-9). With accompanying activities, this book explores the world of dinosaurs and how paleontology has discovered, through fossils, how they lived. (Rev: BL 4/1/94; SLJ 7/94) [567.9]

Anthropology and Evolution

7293 Ackroyd, Peter. *The Beginning* (4–8). Illus. Series: Voyages Through Time. 2003, DK $19.99 (0-7894-9836-7). An attractive and readable tour of the early years of our planet, through the emergence of Cro-Magnon man, with eye-catching and amazingly realistic images of dinosaurs as they are currently envisaged. (Rev: BL 12/15/03*) [576.8]

7294 Batten, Mary. *Anthropologist: Scientist of the People* (4–7). Illus. Series: Scientists in the Field. 2001, Houghton $16.00 (0-618-08368-5). Striking photographs of a Paraguayan tribe of hunter-gatherers serve as a powerful backdrop to this explanation of the work of anthropologists. (Rev: BL 8/01; HB 1–2/02*; HBG 3/02; SLJ 9/01) [627]

7295 Corbishley, Mike. *What Do We Know About Prehistoric People?* (4–7). Illus. Series: What Do We Know About. 1996, Bedrick LB $18.95 (0-87226-383-5). Using double-page spreads, this book explores the known facts about human prehistoric life around the world. (Rev: BL 6/1–15/96) [930.1]

7296 Crump, Donald J., ed. *Giants from the Past: The Age of Mammals* (7–10). Illus. 1983, National Geographic LB $12.50 (0-87044-429-8). A description of early animals, such as the mastodon, and how they evolved during the Ice Age. [569]

7297 Facchini, Fiorenzo. *Humans: Origins and Evolution* (4–8). Illus. Series: Beginnings — Origins and Evolution. 1995, Raintree Steck-Vaughn LB $24.26 (0-8114-3336-6). Theories and facts explaining human evolution are presented in a straightforward way, with extensive artwork and diagrams. (Rev: BL 4/15/95; SLJ 6/95) [573.2]

7298 Gallant, Roy A. *Early Humans* (5–8). Series: The Story of Science. 1999, Benchmark LB $28.50 (0-7614-0960-2). Neanderthals, Homo erectus, and early hominids are covered in this work on human evolution and important anthropological finds. (Rev: BL 2/15/00; HBG 3/00; SLJ 3/00) [573.2]

7299 Gallant, Roy A. *The Origins of Life* (6–10). Series: The Story of Science. 2000, Marshall Cavendish LB $19.95 (0-7614-1151-8). This prize-winning author presents a clear, attractive introduction to the beginning of life on this earth. (Rev: BL 12/15/00; HBG 10/01) [575]

7300 Garassino, Alessandro. *Life, Origins and Evolution* (5–8). Series: Beginnings — Origins and Evolution. 1995, Raintree Steck-Vaughn LB $24.26 (0-8114-3335-8). Using informative visuals, the author presents theories concerning the beginnings of life in the world. (Rev: BL 5/1/95) [575]

7301 Lauber, Patricia. *Who Came First? New Clues to Prehistoric Americans* (5–10). Illus. 2003, National Geographic $18.95 (0-7922-8228-0). An attractive, oversized volume that encompasses anthropology, archaeology, genetics, and linguistics in its discussion of the provenance of the peoples of the Americas. (Rev: BL 7/03*; HB 7–8/03; HBG 10/03; SLJ 8/03*) [970.01]

7302 Lindsay, William. *Prehistoric Life* (4–8). Illus. Series: Eyewitness Books. 1994, Knopf $20.99 (0-679-96001-5). Prehistoric life is described, as well as the process of evolution and the methods used by anthropologists. (Rev: BL 10/15/94; SLJ 8/94) [560]

7303 McCutcheon, Marc. *The Beast in You! Activities and Questions to Explore Evolution* (4–8). Series: A Kaleidoscope Kids Book. 1999, Williamson paper $10.95 (1-885593-36-8). In a humorous, creative presentation, the author shows the similarities between humans and other animals and introduces the topic of evolution, our early ancestors, and their development. (Rev: SLJ 3/00) [575]

7304 McGowen, Tom. *Giant Stones and Earth Mounds* (4–8). Illus. 2000, Millbrook LB $25.90 (0-7613-1372-9). A history of the New Stone Age of about 9,000 years ago and the constructions that still exist in the United States today from that period. (Rev: BL 10/1/00; HBG 10/01; SLJ 10/00) [930.1]

7305 Merriman, Nick. *Early Humans* (5–9). Illus. 1989, Knopf $20.99 (0-394-92257-3). An account of prehistoric life in text and lavish pictures. (Rev: BL 7/89; BR 11–12/89) [930.1]

7306 Netzley, Patricia. *The Stone Age* (6–10). Illus. 1997, Lucent LB $27.45 (1-56006-316-5). This book describes the major epochs in the evolution of humans and the development of stone-tool technology. (Rev: BL 5/15/98; SLJ 6/98) [930.12]

7307 Patent, Dorothy Hinshaw. *Mystery of the Lascaux Cave* (4–7). Series: Frozen in Time. 1998, Benchmark LB $27.07 (0-7614-0784-7). As well as displaying these remarkable cave paintings, this book covers what is known or surmised about the prehistoric people who produced these artistic wonders. (Rev: HBG 10/99; SLJ 3/99) [930.12]

7308 Patent, Dorothy Hinshaw. *Secrets of the Ice Man* (4–7). Series: Frozen in Time. 1998, Benchmark LB $27.07 (0-7614-0782-0). The author discusses life during the Ice Age with material from recent discoveries. (Rev: HBG 10/99; SLJ 3/99) [937]

7309 Pickering, Robert. *The People* (5–8). Illus. Series: Prehistoric North America. 1996, Millbrook LB $22.90 (1-56294-550-5). An account of the development of the prehistoric North American tribes that may have crossed the land bridge from Asia to the Americas. (Rev: SLJ 4/96) [973.01]

7310 Pye, Claire. *The Wild World of the Future* (4–8). Illus. 2003, Firefly $24.95 (1-55297-727-7); paper $14.95 (1-55297-725-0). This lively, attractive volume speculates on the animals of the future, basing the projections on previous evolutionary development. (Rev: BL 7/03; SLJ 6/03) [576.8]

7311 Sloan, Christopher. *Bury the Dead: Tombs, Corpses, Mummies, Skeletons, and Rituals* (5–9). Illus. 2002, National Geographic $18.95 (0-7922-7192-0). Young readers will be fascinated by this serious account of burial practices throughout the ages, with timelines, color photographs, diagrams, and clear descriptions of rites around the world. (Rev: BL 12/1/02; HBG 3/03; SLJ 10/02*) [393]

7312 Sonder, Ben. *Evolutionism and Creationism* (8–12). Illus. 1999, Watts LB $24.00 (0-531-11416-3). A well-researched, unbiased look at the history and present status of the conflict between evolutionists and creationists. (Rev: BL 12/1/99; SLJ 1/00; VOYA 2/00) [231.7]

7313 Stein, Sara Bonnett. *The Evolution Book* (6–8). Illus. 1986, Workman paper $12.95 (0-89480-927-X). A history of evolution that covers time from 4,000 million years ago to the present. (Rev: BL 2/15/87; BR 5–6/87; SLJ 3/87; VOYA 4/87) [508]

7314 Thorndike, Jonathan L. *Epperson v. Arkansas: The Evolution–Creationism Debate* (6–10). Series: Landmark Supreme Court Cases. 1999, Enslow LB $20.95 (0-7660-1084-8). This book examines the issues involved in this case of evolution versus creationism, traces the case from lower courts to the Supreme Court, and discusses the present-day impact of the court's decision. (Rev: BL 3/15/99) [116]

7315 Webster, Stephen. *The Kingfisher Book of Evolution* (6–8). Illus. 2000, Kingfisher $21.95 (0-7534-5271-5). Double-page spreads cover such subjects as the theory of evolution, the history of life on earth, the evolution of behavior, and the future of evolution. (Rev: BL 12/1/00; HBG 10/01; SLJ 2/01) [576.8]

7316 Westrup, Hugh. *The Mammals* (5–8). Illus. Series: Prehistoric North America. 1996, Millbrook LB $22.90 (1-56294-546-7). The woolly mammoth and saber-toothed tiger are two of the prehistoric mammals described in words and pictures. (Rev: BL 5/15/96; SLJ 4/96) [569]

7317 Wilkinson, Philip, and Jacqueline Dineen. *The Early Inventions* (5–8). Illus. 1995, Chelsea LB $21.95 (0-7910-2766-X). A look at the invention of early tools and processes, mostly for human survival purposes — eating and staying warm. (Rev: BR 5–6/96; SLJ 11/95; VOYA 2/96) [930]

Archaeology

7318 Arnold, Caroline. *Stone Age Farmers Beside the Sea: Scotland's Prehistoric Village of Skara Brae* (5–8). 1997, Clarion $15.95 (0-395-77601-5). A stunning volume that tells the story of the Stone Age village of Skara Brae, dating to about 3000 B.C., that was unearthed in the Orkney Islands in 1850. (Rev: BCCB 4/97; BL 4/15/97; SLJ 7/97) [930]

7319 Avi-Yonah, Michael. *Dig This! How Archaeologists Uncover Our Past* (5–8). Series: Buried Worlds. 1993, Lerner LB $28.75 (0-8225-3200-X). A history of the discipline of archaeology, an examination of excavating methods, and a look at several ancient civilizations. (Rev: BL 1/15/94; SLJ 2/94) [930.1]

7320 Buell, Janet. *Ancient Horsemen of Siberia* (6–9). Series: Time Travelers. 1998, Millbrook LB $25.90 (0-7613-3005-4). This account describes the excavation of a 2,500-year-old burial site in the Altai Mountains in southern Siberia and recounts how the Russian archeologists were able to re-create the life of these primitive peoples through an examination of their artifacts. (Rev: SLJ 10/98) [930]

7321 Buell, Janet. *Greenland Mummies* (5–8). Series: Time Travelers. 1998, Twenty-First Century LB $25.90 (0-7613-3004-6). By examining mummified human corpses found in Greenland, archaeologists have been able to reconstruct the life and culture of Inuits who lived 500 years ago. (Rev: SLJ 10/98) [930]

7322 Buell, Janet. *Ice Maiden of the Andes* (5–8). Illus. Series: Time Travelers. 1997, Twenty-First Century paper $25.90 (0-8050-5185-6). The story of the discovery of the frozen body of a young Inca girl who died 500 years ago and of how forensic methods such as DNA testing have revealed insights into Inca society, its religion, and gender roles. (Rev: BL 2/1/98; SLJ 3/98) [985]

7323 Caselli, Giovanni. *In Search of Troy* (4–7). Illus. Series: In Search Of. 1999, Bedrick $18.95 (0-87226-542-0). Each of the two-page spreads in this book focuses on different aspects of Heinrich Schliemann's quest to find the city of Troy and on the archaeological discoveries he made. (Rev: BL 10/15/99; HBG 3/00; SLJ 8/99) [939]

7324 *Dazzling! Jewelry of the Ancient World* (5–8). Illus. Series: Buried Worlds. 1995, Lerner LB $28.75 (0-8225-3203-4). An exploration of the jewels that archaeologists have retrieved from various ancient sites. (Rev: BL 7/95; SLJ 4/95) [739.27]

7325 Deem, James M. *Bodies from the Bog* (5–8). Illus. 1998, Houghton $16.00 (0-395-85784-8). With striking color and black-and-white photographs, this is a riveting book about the various humans from past European cultures who were mummified in bogs and discovered centuries later. (Rev: BCCB 6/98; BL 5/15/98; HBG 10/98; SLJ 4/98) [569.9]

7326 Echo-Hawk, Roger C., and Walter R. Echo-Hawk. *Battlefields and Burial Grounds: The Indian Struggle to Protect Ancestral Graves in the United States* (7–10). 1994, Lerner LB $22.60 (0-8225-2663-8); paper $8.95 (0-8225-9722-5). A solid discussion of the conflict over Indian graves that have been plundered in the name of scientific research. (Rev: BL 5/15/94; SLJ 7/94*) [393]

7327 Funston, Sylvia. *Mummies* (5–7). Series: Strange Science. 2000, Owl $19.95 (1-894379-03-9); paper $9.95 (1-894379-04-7). All kinds of mummified human remains are discussed, from those in ancient Egypt to the 1999 discovery of George Mallory's body on Mount Everest. (Rev: HBG 3/01; SLJ 11/00) [909]

7328 Greene, Meg. *Buttons, Bones, and the Organ-Grinder's Monkey: Tales of Historical Archaeology* (5–8). Illus. 2001, Linnet LB $25.00 (0-208-02498-

0). This introduction to historical archaeology looks at finds at five different sites in the United States. (Rev: BL 10/1/01; HBG 10/02; SLJ 1/02; VOYA 4/02) [973]

7329 Guiberson, Brenda Z. *Mummy Mysteries: Tales from North America* (4–7). Series: A Red-feather Chapter Book. 1998, Holt $15.95 (0-8050-5369-7). Reading like a mystery story, this book focuses on mummies found in North America, how and where they were found, and the information they reveal. (Rev: BCCB 2/99; HBG 3/99; SLJ 12/98) [937]

7330 Hoobler, Dorothy. *Lost Civilizations* (5–7). 1992, Walker LB $15.85 (0-8027-8153-5). Interesting discussion of Stonehenge, the Mound Builders, and other lost ancient civilizations. (Rev: BL 5/1/92; SLJ 9/92) [930]

7331 Jameson, W. C. *Buried Treasures of the Atlantic Coast: Legends of Sunken Pirate Treasures, Mysterious Caches, and Jinxed Ships — From Maine to Florida* (4–8). Series: Buried Treasure. 1997, August House $11.95 (0-87483-484-8). An account of how buried treasures were acquired and lost and the modern efforts to locate and retrieve them. Also use *Buried Treasures of New England* (1997). (Rev: BR 5–6/99; SLJ 10/97) [910.4]

7332 Kallen, Stuart A. *Mummies* (4–7). Illus. Series: Wonders of the World. 2003, Gale LB $18.96 (0-7377-1031-7). Coverage of various types of mummies, the mummification process, and mummies of note will be especially useful for report writers. (Rev: BL 5/1/03) [393]

7333 Lauber, Patricia. *Tales Mummies Tell* (5–8). Illus. 1985, HarperCollins LB $17.89 (0-690-04389-9). A fascinating account of how people and animals were mummified and what mummies can tell scientists. (Rev: BCCB 7/85; BL 6/15/85; HB 5–6/85; SLJ 8/85) [930]

7334 Lourie, Peter. *The Mystery of the Maya: Uncovering the Lost City of Palenque* (5–8). Illus. 2001, Boyds Mills $19.95 (1-56397-839-3). The author relates his interesting and often exciting experiences at a dig in Mexico and describes the work of the archaeologists and the history of the site. (Rev: BL 9/15/01; HBG 3/02; SLJ 11/01) [972.75]

7335 MacDonald, Fiona, and Alison Roberts. *The Stone Age News* (4–8). 1998, Candlewick $16.99 (0-7636-0451-8). Using a newspaper format, this clever, oversize volume introduces life during the Stone Age through society pages, religious news, real estate ads, and humor columns, such as "A Cave of One's Own," which suggests ways to make a cave a comfortable living space. (Rev: BL 5/15/98; HBG 3/99; SLJ 6/98) [560]

7336 McIntosh, Jane. *The Practical Archaeologist* (8–12). 1986, Facts on File $26.95 (0-8160-1400-0); paper $15.95 (0-8160-1814-6). A discussion of how an archaeologist operates with particular emphasis on how sites are found and excavated. (Rev: BR 1–2/89; VOYA 10/88) [930.1]

7337 Malam, John. *Mummies* (5–8). Illus. Series: Kingfisher Knowledge. 2003, Kingfisher $11.95 (0-7534-5623-0). A highly illustrated, readable exploration of preserved bodies of all eras and areas of the world. (Rev: SLJ 12/03) [393]

7338 Malone, Caroline, and Nancy Stone Bernard. *Stonehenge* (7–10). Illus. Series: Digging for the Past. 2002, Oxford $19.95 (0-19-514314-0). This fascinating look at Stonehenge's history and at the work of archaeologists there over the years will attract report writers and browsers. (Rev: BL 10/15/02; HBG 10/03; SLJ 12/02) [936.2]

7339 O'Neal, Michael. *Pyramids* (6–9). Series: Great Mysteries: Opposing Viewpoints. 1995, Greenhaven LB $22.45 (1-56510-216-9). Different perspectives on the purpose and meaning of pyramids and the mysteries surrounding them. (Rev: BL 4/15/95; SLJ 3/95) [726]

7340 Panchyk, Richard. *Archaeology for Kids: Uncovering the Mysteries of Our Past with 25 Activities* (5–8). Illus. 2001, Chicago Review paper $14.95 (1-55652-395-5). An introduction for older readers to the history and scientific method of archaeology, full of illustrations and with interesting activities. (Rev: BL 1/1–15/02; SLJ 12/01) [930.1]

7341 Place, Robin. *Bodies from the Past* (4–7). Illus. Series: Digging Up the Past. 1995, Thomson Learning LB $24.26 (1-56847-397-4). Explores the preserved remains of people around the world from burial sites in China and mummies in peat bogs to the Ice Man recently discovered in the Alps. (Rev: SLJ 2/96) [567.9]

7342 Reid, Struan. *The Children's Atlas of Lost Treasures* (4–7). Illus. Series: Children's Atlases. 1997, Millbrook paper $14.95 (0-7613-0240-9). Using a double-page spread for each site, this book supplies a survey of the world-famous discoveries of treasures that began as religious offerings, pirate booty, and items lost in war or by natural disasters. (Rev: HBG 3/98; SLJ 3/98) [930.1]

7343 Reinhard, Johan. *Discovering the Inca Ice Maiden: My Adventures on Ampato* (5–8). Illus. 1998, National Geographic $19.95 (0-7922-7142-4). In this oversize book featuring many photographs, the anthropologist who discovered the Inca girl buried in the Andes for more than 500 years reconstructs her life and death. (Rev: BCCB 5/98; BL 5/15/98; HBG 10/98; SLJ 5/98) [985]

7344 Scarre, Chris, and Rebecca Stefoff. *Palace of Minos at Knossos* (7–10). Series: Digging for the Past. 2002, Oxford $19.95 (0-19-514272-1). After a map and timeline, this account describes various archaeological digs at Knossos and tells how the palace was built and gives material on the original structure. (Rev: BL 10/15/02) [930]

7345 Scheller, William. *Amazing Archaeologists and Their Finds* (6–10). 1994, Oliver LB $19.95 (1-881508-17-X). This work presents the discoveries of eight archaeologists, including the walls of Troy, the tomb of King Tut, Jericho, and Incan ruins. (Rev: BL 11/1/94; SLJ 2/95; VOYA 2/95) [930.1]

7346 Smith, K. C. *Exploring for Shipwrecks* (5–7). Series: Shipwrecks. 2000, Watts LB $24.00 (0-531-20377-8). This book explains and explores the world of underwater archaeology, the techniques and training involved, and gives many examples from specific shipwreck studies. (Rev: BL 10/15/00) [930.1]

7347 Smith, K. C. *Shipwrecks of the Explorers* (5–7). Illus. Series: Watts Library: Shipwrecks. 2000, Watts LB $24.00 (0-531-20378-6); paper $8.95 (0-531-16485-3). A look at underwater archaeology tells how scientists locate shipwrecks and what the ships reveal about the explorers who sailed in them. There are also descriptions of famous voyages including those of Columbus and Amundsen. (Rev: BL 10/15/00) [910.4]

7348 Tanaka, Shelley. *Discovering the Iceman: What Was It Like to Find a 5,300-Year-Old Mummy?* (4–7). Illus. 1997, Hyperion $16.95 (0-7868-0284-7). The story of discovering the 5,300-year-old Iceman in the Swiss Alps in 1991 and his importance to science. (Rev: BCCB 5/97; BL 4/15/97; SLJ 6/97) [937]

7349 Vivian, R. Gwinn, and Margaret Anderson. *Chaco Canyon* (7–10). Illus. Series: Digging for the Past. 2002, Oxford $19.95 (0-19-514280-2). An interesting overview of Chaco Canyon's history and the work of archaeologists there over the years. (Rev: BL 10/15/02; HBG 10/02; SLJ 10/02) [973]

7350 Wilcox, Charlotte. *Mummies and Their Mysteries* (5–7). Illus. 1993, Carolrhoda LB $28.75 (0-87614-767-8). An account of how throughout history many civilizations and religions have attempted to preserve bodies. (Rev: BCCB 7–8/93*; BL 6/1–15/93*) [393.3]

7351 Wilcox, Charlotte. *Mummies, Bones, and Body Parts* (4–7). Illus. 2000, Lerner paper $12.75 (1-57505-486-8). The study of human remains is covered, including material on how death is treated in various cultures, embalming practices, and the work of archaeologists and anthropologists. (Rev: BCCB 9/00; BL 9/1/00; HBG 10/01; SLJ 10/00) [393]

World History and Geography

General

7352 Aaseng, Nathan. *You Are the General II: 1800–1899* (6–9). Series: Great Decisions. 1995, Oliver LB $19.95 (1-881508-25-0). In this account of famous battles such as Waterloo, Gettysburg, and Little Bighorn, the reader is asked to become a field marshal and interact with history. (Rev: SLJ 2/96) [900]

7353 Barnard, Bryn. *Dangerous Planet: Natural Disasters That Changed History* (5–8). Illus. 2003, Crown $17.95 (0-375-82249-6). A fascinating look at nine natural disasters that hit our planet, with maps, full-page illustrations, and speculation about the impact of global warming. (Rev: BCCB 11/03; BL 12/1/03*; SLJ 11/03) [363.34]

7354 Blackwood, Gary L. *Highwaymen* (5–8). Illus. Series: Bad Guys. 2001, Marshall Cavendish LB $28.50 (0-7614-1017-1). Period artwork, photographs, and intriguing tales bring real highway robbers, and the times they lived in, to life. (Rev: BL 1/1–15/02; HBG 3/02; SLJ 1/02) [364.15]

7355 Blackwood, Gary L. *Swindlers* (5–8). Illus. Series: Bad Guys. 2001, Marshall Cavendish LB $28.50 (0-7614-1031-7). The author presents famous swindlers and cheats throughout history, providing illustrations, source notes, and recommended Web sites and further reading. (Rev: BL 1/1–15/02; HBG 3/02) [364.16]

7356 Burleigh, Robert. *Earth from Above for Young Readers* (4–9). Photos by Yann Arthus-Bertrand. 2002, Abrams $14.95 (0-8109-3486-8). Large aerial views show landscapes around the world, from remote areas of natural beauty to New York's Yankee Stadium. (Rev: HBG 3/03; SLJ 1/03) [779]

7357 Chambers, Catherine. *Africa* (4–7). Illus. Series: Origins. 1997, Watts LB $21.00 (0-531-

14416-X). The story of emigration from Africa, the slave trade, and the conditions that African Americans have faced through history on their arrival in the United States. (Rev: BL 4/15/97; SLJ 7/97) [960]

7358 *Children's History of the 20th Century* (5–9). Illus. Series: DK Millennium. 2001, DK paper $29.95 (0-7894-4722-3). An attractive, colorful presentation of the major world events of the past century. (Rev: BL 11/15/99; SLJ 2/00) [909.82]

7359 Chisholm, Jane. *The Usborne Book of World History Dates: The Key Events in History* (4–8). 1998, EDC paper $22.95 (0-7460-2318-9). Timelines and double-page spreads with brief topical essays present a panorama of world history. (Rev: SLJ 5/99) [910]

7360 Claybourne, Anna, and Caroline Young. *The Usborne Book of Treasure Hunting* (4–7). Illus. 1999, Usborne paper $14.95 (0-7460-3445-8). In a series of short chapters, this book covers famous treasures that were buried underground, lost at sea, or existed in ancient times — with coverage of such subjects as the clay soldiers in Huang Di's tomb and the restoration of the Tudor ship *Mary Rose*. (Rev: BL 4/1/99) [622.19]

7361 Currie, Stephen. *Pirates* (6–10). Series: World History. 2001, Lucent LB $19.96 (1-56006-807-8). Although pirates of all eras are mentioned, the "Golden Age of Piracy" in the 17th and 18th centuries is the focus of this detailed overview. (Rev: SLJ 7/01) [910.4]

7362 Gelber, Carol. *Masks Tell Stories* (5–7). Illus. Series: Beyond Museum Walls. 1993, Millbrook LB $24.90 (1-56294-224-7). Explores the nature, meaning, and uses of masks in different cultures at various times. (Rev: BL 8/93) [391]

7363 Gold, Susan D. *Governments of the Western Hemisphere* (5–8). Illus. Series: Comparing Continents. 1997, Twenty-First Century LB $24.90 (0-8050-5602-5). This book examines the struggles for independence in the United States, Canada, Mexico, Central America, and South America and the different directions taken by each once independence was achieved, highlighting the diversity across the nations. (Rev: BL 2/1/98; SLJ 3/98) [320.3]

7364 Harris, Nicholas. *The Incredible Journey to the Beginning of Time* (4–7). 1998, Bedrick $18.95 (0-87226-293-6). Beginning with the present and working backward, this book recounts world history in various locations and times as far back as 10 billion years ago. (Rev: HBG 3/99; SLJ 3/99) [900]

7365 Hart, Avery, and Paul Mantell. *Who Really Discovered America? Unraveling the Mystery and Solving the Puzzle* (5–7). Series: A Kaleidoscope Kids Book. 2001, Williamson paper $10.95 (1-885593-46-5). Several theories are presented about the discovery of America, and students are urged to examine them with open minds, using activities that help them to question and explore. (Rev: SLJ 10/01) [970.01]

7366 Hinds, Kathryn. *The Celts of Northern Europe* (7–10). Series: Cultures of the Past. 1996, Benchmark LB $28.50 (0-7614-0092-3). This book gives a history of the Celts, their religion, social structure, art, folklore, and how they helped keep Christianity alive in Ireland. (Rev: SLJ 3/97) [940.1]

7367 Horrell, Sarah. *The History of Emigration from Eastern Europe* (4–8). Series: Origins. 1998, Watts LB $21.00 (0-531-14449-6). Seven short chapters cover emigration from Eastern Europe from the 17th century to the present and its impact on such areas as North America, Western Europe, and Israel. (Rev: HBG 10/98; SLJ 9/98) [940]

7368 Kallen, Stuart A. *Life Among the Pirates* (6–10). Series: The Way People Live. 1998, Lucent LB $27.45 (1-56006-393-9). A fascinating history of world piracy with an emphasis on the "Golden Age" from 1519 until the 1720s. (Rev: BL 11/15/98; SLJ 3/99) [910.45]

7369 Lassieur, Allison. *The Celts* (6–9). Series: Lost Civilizations. 2001, Lucent LB $24.95 (1-56006-746-X). This well-researched account covers the history, culture and artistic contributions of the ancient Celts during the period from 600 B.C. through 600 A.D. (Rev: BL 8/1/01) [940.1]

7370 Levy, Elizabeth. *Awesome Ancient Ancestors! Mound Builders, Maya, and More* (5–8). Series: America's Horrible Histories. 2001, Scholastic $12.95 (0-439-30349-4); paper $4.99 (0-590-10795-X). A humorous and chatty cockroach introduces the early inhabitants of North America and Mesoamerica. (Rev: HBG 10/02; SLJ 5/02) [970.01]

7371 Mason, Antony. *People Around the World* (5–7). Illus. 2002, Kingfisher $24.95 (0-7534-5497-1). An oversize guide to people of different cultures around the world, organized by continent, featuring hundreds of full-color photographs and illustrations, and detailing such topics as diet, language, employment, and leisure of urban and rural dwellers. (Rev: BL 5/1/03; HBG 10/03; SLJ 4/03; VOYA 6/03) [305.8]

7372 Maynard, Christopher. *The History News: Revolution* (4–7). Illus. 1999, Candlewick $16.99 (0-7636-0491-7). Using a tabloid-newspaper format, this book covers four revolutions: the American, French, Russian, and Chinese. (Rev: BL 12/15/99; HBG 3/00; SLJ 10/99) [909]

7373 Meltzer, Milton. *Piracy and Plunder: A Murderous Business* (6–9). 2001, Dutton $24.99 (0-525-45857-3). The violent realities of piracy are the centerpiece of this attractive book, which includes a history of pirates, tales of famous pirates, and analysis of pirates' ties to government and industry. (Rev: BL 12/15/01; HBG 3/02; SLJ 12/01*; VOYA 12/01) [910.4]

7374 Meltzer, Milton. *Witches and Witch-Hunts: A History of Persecution* (5–9). 1999, Scholastic paper $16.95 (0-590-48517-2). This is a record of scapegoating through history on the basis of gender, religion, or politics, beginning with witches in the Middle Ages and continuing through the 20th century to Hitler's Germany and Senator McCarthy's hearings. (Rev: BCCB 10/99; BL 11/1/99; HB 11–12/99; HBG 3/00; SLJ 11/99) [303]

7375 Millard, Anne. *A Street Through Time* (4–8). Illus. 1998, DK $17.99 (0-7894-3426-1). Western European history is traced in this oversize book that contains 14 views of the same riverside location at various times in history, including the Stone Age, Viking times, the Roman period, the Middle Ages, and modern times. (Rev: BL 1/1–15/99; HB 1–2/99; HBG 3/99; SLJ 12/98) [936]

7376 Platt, Richard. *Pirate* (5–9). Series: Eyewitness Books. 1995, Knopf $19.00 (0-679-87255-8). A history of piracy, with profiles of some of the major buccaneers of the past, in an account that separates truth from myth. (Rev: BL 8/95; SLJ 8/95) [364.1]

7377 Prior, Natalie Jane. *The Encyclopedia of Preserved People: Pickled, Frozen, and Mummified Corpses from Around the World* (5–8). Illus. 2003, Crown $14.95 (0-375-82287-9). Egyptian mummies and bog bodies feature here, but so do Lenin and Einstein's brain as part of the discussion of what we can learn from preserved corpses as opposed to skeletons. (Rev: SLJ 4/03)

7378 Reid, Struan. *Cultures and Civilizations* (5–9). Illus. Series: The Silk and Spice Routes. 1994, Silver Burdett LB $15.95 (0-02-726315-0). An attractive, oversize introduction to the many historic cultures that thrived along the ancient trade route to the East, with stunning illustrations. (Rev: BL 12/15/94; SLJ 12/94) [909]

7379 Reid, Struan. *Inventions and Trade* (5–8). Illus. Series: Silk and Spice Routes. 1994, Silver Burdett LB $15.95 (0-02-726316-9). A history of the trade between China and Europe along the Spice Route and of the technological advances that occurred because of this cultural exchange. (Rev: BL 12/15/94; SLJ 12/94) [382.09]

7380 Ross, Stewart. *Conquerors and Explorers* (5–7). Illus. Series: Fact or Fiction? 1996, Millbrook LB $26.90 (0-7613-0532-7). The subtitle of this work is "The Greed, Cunning, and Bravery of the Travelers and Plunderers Who Opened Up the World." (Rev: BL 10/15/96; SLJ 4/97) [910]

7381 Ross, Stewart. *The Industrial Revolution* (6–9). Illus. Series: Documenting History. 2001, Watts LB $22.00 (0-531-14609-X). This well-illustrated volume traces the history of industrialization and looks at the economic and social impact through the 20th century. (Rev: SLJ 3/02) [330.9]

7382 Ruggiero, Adriane. *The Ottoman Empire* (5–8). Series: Cultures of the Past. 2002, Marshall Cavendish $19.95 (0-7614-1494-0). A handsome account that traces the rise and fall of the great Ottoman Empire from its beginning in the 15th century to its collapse and the formation of modern Turkey after World War I. (Rev: BL 1/1–15/03; HBG 3/03; SLJ 2/03) [956]

7383 Rutsala, David. *The Sea Route to Asia* (4–7). Series: Exploration and Discovery. 2002, Mason Crest LB $19.95 (1-59084-046-1). Rutsala presents Portuguese explorers' efforts to find a route around Africa to Asia, with information on Prince Henry the Navigator, Bartholomeu Dias, and Vasco da Gama. (Rev: SLJ 12/02) [910]

7384 St. Antoine, Sara, ed. *Stories from Where We Live: The Great North American Prairie* (4–8). 2001, Milkweed $19.95 (1-57131-630-2). A collection of historical and contemporary stories, poems, essays, and journal entries about life on the prairie, with informative appendixes. (Rev: BL 5/15/01) [978]

7385 Smith, Bonnie G. *Imperialism: A History in Documents* (6–12). Series: Pages from History. 2000, Oxford $36.95 (0-19-510801-9). This detailed account of how powerful nations spread their influence around the globe draws on many primary sources and includes eye-catching photographs and a useful timeline. (Rev: BL 11/15/00; HBG 10/01; SLJ 4/01) [325]

7386 Swanson, Diane. *Tunnels!* (5–8). Series: True Stories from the Edge. 2003, Annick $18.95 (1-55037-781-7); paper $6.95 (1-55037-780-9). Ten thrilling stories of tunnel escapes and escapades are accompanied by maps. (Rev: BL 4/15/03, SLJ 5/03) [624.1]

7387 Weitzman, David. *My Backyard History Book* (4–7). 1975, Little, Brown paper $13.95 (0-316-92902-6). A guide to re-creating history that occurred close to home by interviewing, for example, family and friends.

7388 Williams, Brian. *The Modern World: From the French Revolution to the Computer Age* (5–8). Illus. Series: Timelink. 1994, Bedrick LB $18.95 (0-87226-312-6). An overview of the 200 years of world history that outlines major events, with useful timelines and maps. (Rev: SLJ 1/95) [909]

7389 Williams, Brian, and Brenda Williams. *The Age of Discovery: From the Renaissance to American Independence* (5–8). Illus. Series: Timelink. 1994, Bedrick LB $18.95 (0-87226-311-8). An overview of world history from the Renaissance through the American Revolution presented in 50-year segments. (Rev: SLJ 1/95) [909]

Ancient History

General and Miscellaneous

7390 Ash, Russell. *Great Wonders of the World* (4–7). Series: Eyewitness Books. 2000, DK paper $19.99 (0-7894-6505-1). The seven wonders of the ancient world are presented with material comparing them to other ancient and modern technological marvels. (Rev: HBG 10/01; SLJ 9/00) [930]

7391 Avi-Yonah, Michael. *Piece by Piece! Mosaics of the Ancient World* (5–8). Illus. Series: Buried Worlds. 1993, Lerner LB $28.75 (0-8225-3204-2). This book shows how and where mosaics were made in the ancient world and how, through the wonders of archaeology, they are still being uncovered today. (Rev: BL 1/15/94; SLJ 3/94) [738.5]

7392 Brewer, Paul. *Warfare in the Ancient World* (7–10). Series: History of Warfare. 1999, Raintree Steck-Vaughn LB $29.97 (0-8172-5442-0). This account describes important wars and battles in the ancient world, from Egypt through the Roman Empire. (Rev: HBG 3/99; SLJ 3/99) [930]

7393 Burrell, Roy. *Oxford First Ancient History* (4–7). Illus. 1994, Oxford $37.95 (0-19-521058-1). A survey of ancient civilizations, particularly those of the Mediterranean but also including the Chinese and Assyrians. (Rev: BL 7/94) [930]

7394 Caselli, Giovanni. *The First Civilizations* (6–8). Illus. 1985, Bedrick $18.95 (0-911745-59-9). This account traces the early history of man, from the first toolmakers to the civilizations of Egypt and Greece, through the objects that were made and used. (Rev: BL 11/15/85; BR 3–4/86; SLJ 1/87) [930]

7395 Corbishley, Mike. *How Do We Know Where People Came From?* (5–8). Series: How Do We Know. 1995, Raintree Steck-Vaughn LB $24.26 (0-8114-3880-5). Using double-page spreads, this book covers early cultures and touches on such subjects as early writing, Stonehenge, the Great Wall of China, the Easter Island statues, and the pyramids. (Rev: SLJ 1/96) [930]

7396 DeAngelis, Therese. *Wonders of the Ancient World* (5–8). Illus. Series: Costume, Tradition, and Culture: Reflecting on the Past. 1998, Chelsea $19.75 (0-7910-5170-6). This work features, in double-page spreads, such wonders as the Great Pyramids, Easter Island, and Stonehenge. (Rev: BL 3/15/99; HBG 10/99) [930]

7397 Gaines, Ann. *Herodotus and the Explorers of the Classical Age* (6–9). Illus. Series: World Explorers. 1993, Chelsea LB $21.95 (0-7910-1293-X). A description of the exploration of the Mediterranean Sea region by adventurers of the ancient world, including the "father of history," Herodotus. (Rev: BL 12/15/93; SLJ 11/93) [909]

7398 Gonen, Rivka. *Fired Up! Making Pottery in Ancient Times* (5–8). Illus. Series: Buried Worlds. 1993, Lerner LB $28.75 (0-8225-3202-6). This book explains how pottery was made in ancient times, showing examples from different cultures, and tells how archaeologists are uncovering more and more examples. (Rev: BL 1/15/94; SLJ 4/94) [738.3]

7399 Greene, Jacqueline D. *Slavery in Ancient Greece and Rome* (4–7). Series: Watts Library: History of Slavery. 2000, Watts LB $24.00 (0-531-11693-X). Topics covered include the treatment of slaves in Greece and Rome, how they thrived in Greece's democracy, the slave fire brigades, battles of slave gladiators, and the attitudes toward slavery in the early Christian church. (Rev: BL 3/1/01; SLJ 3/01) [930]

7400 Gregory, Tony. *The Dark Ages* (4–7). Illus. 1993, Facts on File $25.00 (0-8160-2787-0). Beginning with human evolution, this account traces the history of early settlements to about 200 B.C. (Rev: SLJ 7/93) [938]

7401 Hall, Eleanor J. *Ancient Chinese Dynasties* (7–10). Series: World History. 2000, Lucent LB $18.96 (1-56006-624-5). This well-illustrated account describes the dynasties that laid the foundations of Chinese culture and highlights their unsurpassed works of art, architecture, and philosophy. (Rev: BL 6/1–15/00; HBG 9/00; SLJ 6/00) [951]

7402 Haywood, John. *The Encyclopedia of Ancient Civilizations of the Near East and the Mediterranean* (8–12). Illus. 1997, M.E. Sharpe $95.00 (1-56324-799-2). Divided into three parts — ancient Near East and Egypt, the Greek world, and the Roman world — this adult narrative presents basic history and, through the use of sidebars, provides material on important places, cultural advances, scientific progress, religious practices, and military advances. (Rev: SLJ 8/98) [909]

7403 Martell, Hazel M. *The Kingfisher Book of the Ancient World: From the Ice Age to the Fall of Rome* (4–8). Illus. 1995, Kingfisher $24.95 (1-85697-565-7). An attractive book that describes the ancient civilizations in 11 geographical regions, including the Mediterranean, Fertile Crescent, Middle and Far East, America, Africa, and Oceania. (Rev: BL 2/1/96; BR 5–6/96; SLJ 1/96) [930]

7404 Nardo, Don. *Greek and Roman Sport* (5–10). Series: World History. 1999, Lucent LB $27.45 (1-56006-436-6). A very detailed account, using many quotations from classical sources, that gives a realistic picture of the place of sports in both ancient Greece and Rome, the different events, and the rewards and hardships of participants. (Rev: BL 7/99; SLJ 8/99) [930]

7405 Odijk, Pamela. *The Phoenicians* (4–7). Illus. Series: Ancient World. 1989, Silver Burdett LB $14.95 (0-382-09891-9). The ancient traders of the Mediterranean Sea are introduced. (Rev: BL 1/15/90; SLJ 5/90) [939.44]

7406 Service, Pamela F. *300 B.C.* (5–8). Series: Around the World In. 2002, Benchmark $19.95 (0-7614-1080-5). The author explores what was going on in Europe, Africa, Asia, and the Americas in the year 300 B.C. Also use *1200* (2002). (Rev: HBG 3/03; SLJ 2/03) [930]

7407 Smith, K. C. *Ancient Shipwrecks* (5–7). Series: Shipwrecks. 2000, Watts LB $24.00 (0-531-20381-6). From the Bronze Age through the Roman Empire, this volume explores the fascinating stories behind ancient wrecks found in the Mediterranean and explored by archaeologists. (Rev: BL 10/15/00) [930]

7408 Wilkinson, Philip, and Jacqueline Dineen. *The Mediterranean* (4–7). Series: Mysterious Places. 1994, Chelsea LB $21.95 (0-7910-2751-1). Ten sites around the Mediterranean are investigated, including Knossos, Rhodes, Delphi, Mistra, the Topkapi Palace, and Hagia Sophia. (Rev: BL 1/15/94; SLJ 5/94) [930.3]

7409 Woods, Michael, and Mary Woods. *Ancient Agriculture: From Foraging to Farming* (5–8). Series: Ancient Technologies. 2000, Runestone LB $25.26 (0-8225-2995-5). Beginning with prehistoric food-gathering peoples, this book traces the history of plant cultivation and agriculture through each of the great ancient civilizations. (Rev: BL 8/00; HBG 10/00; SLJ 6/00) [630]

7410 Woods, Michael, and Mary Woods. *Ancient Machines from Wedges to Waterwheels* (5–8). Series: Ancient Technologies. 1999, Lerner LB $25.26 (0-8225-2994-7). This heavily illustrated account describes the important machines that came into being from ancient history to the fall of the Western Roman Empire. (Rev: BL 1/1–15/00; HBG 10/00; SLJ 6/00; VOYA 6/00) [936]

7411 Woods, Michael, and Mary B. Woods. *Ancient Medicine: From Sorcery to Surgery* (5–8). Illus. Series: Ancient Technologies. 2000, Lerner LB $25.26 (0-8225-2992-0). Medical practices in ancient times and cultures — the Stone Age, ancient Egypt, and early Hindu cultures, for example — are discussed in this volume. (Rev: BL 1/1–15/00; HBG 10/00; SLJ 5/00; VOYA 6/00) [610]

7412 Woods, Michael, and Mary B. Woods. *Ancient Transportation: From Camels to Canals* (5–8). Illus. Series: Ancient Technologies. 2000, Lerner LB $25.26 (0-8225-2993-9). This book covers such topics related to early transportation as the first bridges and roads, early skis and sleds, primitive wagons, and the beginnings of maps. (Rev: BL 1/1–15/00; HBG 10/00; SLJ 6/00; VOYA 6/00) [629.04]

Egypt and Mesopotamia

7413 Alcraft, Rob. *Valley of the Kings* (5–7). Series: Visiting the Past. 1999, Heinemann LB $24.22 (1-57572-860-5). This account uses double-page spreads to cover topics including the history, landscape, beliefs, and daily life of the ancient Egyptians. (Rev: SLJ 3/00) [932]

7414 Berger, Melvin, and Gilda Berger. *Mummies of the Pharaohs: Exploring the Valley of the Kings* (4–7). Illus. 2001, National Geographic $17.95 (0-7922-7223-4). Beginning with King Tut's tomb and continuing through other sites, this book uses stunning photographs and a clear text to describe workings of archaeological digs that are studying Egypt's past. (Rev: BL 2/1/01) [932]

7415 Broida, Marian. *Ancient Egyptians and Their Neighbors: An Activity Guide* (4–8). Illus. 1999, Chicago Review paper $16.95 (1-55652-360-2). The lives and times of the ancient Egyptians, Nubians, Hittites, and Mesopotamians are examined using text and a series of 40 fascinating projects. (Rev: BL 3/15/00; SLJ 2/00) [939]

7416 Caselli, Giovanni. *In Search of Tutankhamun: The Discovery of a King's Tomb* (4–7). Series: In Search Of. 1999, Bedrick $18.95 (0-87226-543-9). As well as supplying information on King Tut's tomb, this heavily illustrated book supplies good general material on the culture and history of the ancient Egyptian civilization. (Rev: BL 10/15/99; HBG 3/00; SLJ 8/99) [932]

7417 Chapman, Gillian. *The Egyptians* (4–8). Series: Crafts from the Past. 1997, Heinemann LB $25.64 (1-57572-556-8). A variety of craft projects related to the ancient Egyptians are introduced and placed within their cultural context. (Rev: SLJ 4/98) [932]

7418 Charley, Catherine. *Tombs and Treasures* (4–8). Illus. Series: See Through History. 1995,

Viking $19.99 (0-670-85899-4). An overview of ancient burial practices and the wealth often interred with the body, as in the cases of King Tut and other Egyptian pharaohs. (Rev: BL 1/1–15/96; SLJ 1/96) [393.1]

7419 Chrisp, Peter. *Ancient Egypt Revealed* (4–8). Illus. 2002, DK paper $12.99 (0-7894-8883-3). This absorbing introduction to ancient Egypt uses a crisp text, a variety of beautiful photographs, computer graphics, and transparent cutaways to reveal the secrets of tombs and temples, and to inform readers about culture, writing methods, myths, and so forth. (Rev: BL 1/1–15/03; HBG 3/03; SLJ 3/03) [932]

7420 Crosher, Judith. *Technology in the Time of Ancient Egypt* (4–8). Series: Technology in the Time Of. 1998, Raintree Steck-Vaughn LB $27.12 (0-8172-4875-7). Each double-page spread presents an aspect of technology in ancient Egypt in such areas as food production, transportation, and building. (Rev: HBG 10/98; SLJ 3/99) [932]

7421 Day, Nancy. *Your Travel Guide to Ancient Egypt* (4–8). Series: Passport to History. 2000, Runestone LB $26.60 (0-8225-3075-9). Written in the style of a modern-day travel guide, this book on ancient Egypt covers such subjects as sites to see, food, clothing, religious beliefs, politics, and daily life. (Rev: BL 11/15/00; HBG 3/01; SLJ 5/01; VOYA 8/01) [932]

7422 Giblin, James Cross. *The Riddle of the Rosetta Stone: Key to Ancient Egypt* (5–7). Illus. 1990, HarperCollins LB $15.89 (0-690-04799-1). Beginning with the British museum, where the Rosetta Stone is now, this is an explanation of its importance. (Rev: BCCB 11/90; BL 9/15/90*; HB 11–12/90; SLJ 9/90) [493]

7423 Greene, Jacqueline D. *Slavery in Ancient Egypt and Mesopotamia* (4–7). Series: Watts Library: History of Slavery. 2000, Watts LB $24.00 (0-531-11692-1). This unusual book covers the earliest forms of slavery, how the pharaohs used slaves to construct the pyramids, and the place of slavery in Hebrew society. (Rev: BL 3/1/01; SLJ 3/01) [930]

7424 Harris, Geraldine. *Ancient Egypt* (5–8). Illus. 1990, Facts on File $19.95 (0-8160-1971-1). This account of Egyptian history is enlivened by excellent maps, photographs, and drawings. (Rev: SLJ 8/90) [932]

7425 Haynes, Joyce. *Egyptian Dynasties* (6–9). Series: First Books: African Civilizations. 1999, Watts LB $23.00 (0-531-20280-1). A history of the great ancient kingdoms of Egypt and their rulers. (Rev: BL 9/15/99; HBG 9/99; SLJ 8/99) [962]

7426 Jovinelly, Joann, and Jason Netelkos. *The Crafts and Culture of the Ancient Egyptians* (5–8). Series: Crafts of the Ancient World. 2002, Rosen LB $29.25 (0-8239-3509-4). As well as learning about the mysteries of ancient Egypt, readers can engage in such craft projects as designing a pharaoh's headdress and necklace and re-creating an ancient marbles game. (Rev: BL 5/15/02; SLJ 6/02) [932]

7427 Kallen, Stuart A. *Pyramids* (7–10). Series: Mystery Library. 2002, Gale LB $27.45 (1-56006-773-X). This work explores the mysterious and intriguing aspects of the purposes behind and the construction of the Egyptian pyramids. (Rev: BL 7/02; SLJ 7/02) [932]

7428 Katan, Norma Jean, and Barbara Mintz. *Hieroglyphs: The Writings of Ancient Egypt* (7–9). Illus. 1981, Macmillan $16.00 (0-689-50176-5). An explanation of hieroglyphics is given — how they originated and how the Rosetta Stone helped solve their mystery. [493]

7429 Lassieur, Allison. *The Ancient Egyptians* (6–9). Series: Lost Civilizations. 2001, Lucent LB $24.95 (1-56006-755-1). This book covers the rise, fall, and lasting contributions of the civilization that ruled the Nile River valley for 4,000 years. (Rev: BL 8/1/01; SLJ 6/01) [932]

7430 McCall, Henrietta. *Gods and Goddesses: In the Daily Life of the Ancient Egyptians* (4–7). Illus. 2002, McGraw-Hill $18.95 (0-87226-635-4). A colorful overview of religion in ancient Egypt in a series of double-page spreads that cover particular gods, religious practices, and various pharaohs. (Rev: BL 5/1/02; HBG 10/02) [200]

7431 McNeese, Tim. *The Pyramids of Giza* (6–8). Series: Building History. 1997, Lucent LB $27.45 (1-56006-426-9). Although crammed with too much detail, this volume gives interesting information on what is known, and theorized, about how these massive monuments to the dead were built. (Rev: BR 1–2/98; HBG 3/98; SLJ 8/97) [932]

7432 McNeill, Sarah. *Ancient Egyptian People* (4–8). Illus. Series: People and Places. 1997, Millbrook LB $21.90 (0-7613-0056-2). This basic introduction to the people of ancient Egypt and how they lived consists of several attractive double-page spreads and a brief text. (Rev: BL 2/15/97; SLJ 3/97) [932]

7433 McNeill, Sarah. *Ancient Egyptian Places* (4–8). Illus. Series: People and Places. 1997, Millbrook LB $21.90 (0-7613-0057-0). Some of the great constructions of ancient Egypt are pictured in a series of elegant double-page spreads with a simple text. (Rev: BL 2/15/97; SLJ 3/97) [932]

7434 Malam, John. *Ancient Egypt* (5–8). Series: Remains to Be Seen. 1998, Evans Brothers $19.95 (0-237-51839-2). This introduction to ancient Egypt's culture and history is organized in double-page spreads and is noteworthy for its many sidebars, charts, and illustrations. (Rev: SLJ 9/98) [932]

7435 Malam, John. *Ancient Egyptian Jobs* (5–7). Illus. 2002, Heinemann LB $25.64. (1-4034-0311-

2). The daily activities of workers such as scribes, bakers, dancers, jewelers, pyramid builders, and embalmers are described in this slim volume that also offers a general introduction to ancient Egypt. (Rev: HBG 10/03; SLJ 4/03) [331.7]

7436 Malam, John. *Mesopotamia and the Fertile Crescent: 10,000 to 539 B.C.* (5–8). Series: Looking Back. 1999, Raintree Steck-Vaughn $19.98 (0-8172-5434-X). The story of the ancient civilizations that grew up in the rich area around the Tigris and Euphrates rivers. (Rev: BL 5/15/99; SLJ 7/99) [930]

7437 Malam, John. *Mummies and the Secrets of Ancient Egypt* (4–8). Series: Secret Worlds. 2001, DK paper $5.99 (0-7894-7976-1). As well as fascinating information on ancient Egypt, its religion, and mummification practices, this book contains a fine Web site listing and an eight-page reference section. (Rev: BL 10/15/01; HBG 3/02) [932]

7438 Mann, Elizabeth. *The Great Pyramid* (4–7). Illus. Series: Wonders of the World. 1996, Mikaya $19.95 (0-9650493-1-0). The building of this architectural marvel is told graphically, with details on the society of ancient Egypt. (Rev: BL 2/1/97; SLJ 6/97*) [932]

7439 Manning, Ruth. *Ancient Egyptian Women* (5–8). Illus. Series: People in the Past. 2002, Heinemann LB $27.07 (1-40340-313-9). A look at the life of, and options open to, women in ancient Egypt. (Rev: BL 3/1/03; SLJ 4/03) [305.42]

7440 Marston, Elsa. *The Ancient Egyptians* (5–8). Series: Cultures of the Past. 1995, Benchmark LB $28.50 (0-7614-0073-7). With photographs of artifacts, monuments, and historical scenes, this book tells of ancient Egyptian history and culture, the rise and fall of the dynasties, and the people's religious beliefs and practices. (Rev: BR 9–10/96; SLJ 6/96) [932]

7441 Meltzer, Milton. *In the Days of the Pharaohs: A Look at Ancient Egypt* (6–12). Illus. 2001, Watts LB $33.50 (0-531-11791-X). A series of color plates add to the visual appeal of this look at ancient Egypt and how archaeological discoveries have contributed to our knowledge of this intriguing society. (Rev: BL 12/1/01; SLJ 12/01) [932]

7442 Millard, Anne. *Going to War in Ancient Egypt* (5–7). Illus. 2001, Watts LB $24.00 (0-531-14589-1). Soldiers, weapons, and military strategies of ancient Egypt are presented with many illustrations and a timeline. (Rev: SLJ 10/01) [355.00932]

7443 Morgan, Julian. *Cleopatra: Ruling in the Shadow of Rome* (6–8). Series: Leaders of Ancient Egypt. 2003, Rosen LB $31.95 (0-8239-3591-4). Cleopatra's relations with Julius Caesar and Mark Anthony are central to this account that homes in on their individual characteristics and provides ample historical context. (Rev: SLJ 9/03) [921]

7444 Morley, Jacqueline. *How Would You Survive as an Ancient Egyptian?* (4–7). Illus. Series: How Would You Survive? 1995, Watts LB $26.00 (0-531-14345-7). Everyday life in Egypt of 1500 B.C. is covered, with material on the preparation of mummies, crops harvested, and the types of food eaten. (Rev: BL 6/1–15/95; SLJ 8/95) [932]

7445 Morris, Neil. *The Atlas of Ancient Egypt* (4–8). Series: Atlas. 2000, Bedrick $19.95 (0-87226-610-9). Using many illustrations as well as maps, this is an attractive, colorful account of ancient Egypt that covers history, people, culture, lifestyles, and geography. (Rev: HBG 3/01; SLJ 3/01) [932]

7446 Nardo, Don. *Ancient Alexandria* (6–10). Illus. Series: A Travel Guide To. 2003, Gale LB $21.96 (1-59018-142-5). Readers are treated to a guidebook-style survey of ancient Alexandria's attractions, with a focus on weather, transport, hotels, shopping, festivals and sporting events, institutions, and people. (Rev: SLJ 6/03) [962]

7447 Nardo, Don. *Ancient Egypt* (7–12). Illus. Series: The History of Weapons and Warfare. 2003, Gale LB $21.96 (1-59018-066-6). The Battle of Kadesh is a central part of this account that discusses the ancient Egyptians' military weapons and techniques. (Rev: SLJ 2/03) [355]

7448 Nardo, Don. *Ancient Egypt* (5–8). Illus. Series: History of the World. 2001, Gale LB $23.70 (0-7377-0774-7). Topics covered in this basic introduction to ancient Egypt include customs of worship and burial, the role of the pharaoh, Egyptian history, and important artifacts. (Rev: BL 4/1/02) [932]

7449 Nardo, Don. *Empires of Mesopotamia* (6–9). Series: Lost Civilizations. 2001, Lucent LB $24.95 (1-56006-820-5). A well-researched account that traces the history and accomplishments of the various peoples who controlled the fertile crescent in ancient times. (Rev: BL 8/1/01; SLJ 6/01) [930]

7450 Odijk, Pamela. *The Egyptians* (4–7). Illus. Series: Ancient World. 1989, Silver Burdett LB $14.95 (0-382-09886-2). An introduction to the history of ancient Egypt. (Rev: BL 1/15/90; SLJ 5/90) [932]

7451 Odijk, Pamela. *The Sumerians* (4–7). Illus. Series: Ancient World. 1990, Silver Burdett LB $14.95 (0-382-09892-7). History and contributions of the Sumerians in the Fertile Crescent. (Rev: BL 11/1/90; SLJ 1/91) [935.01]

7452 Payne, Elizabeth. *The Pharaohs of Ancient Egypt* (6–8). Illus. 1981, Random paper $5.99 (0-394-84699-0). A fascinating study of this important period in Egyptian history. [932]

7453 Perl, Lila. *Mummies, Tombs, and Treasure: Secrets of Ancient Egypt* (5–7). Illus. 1987, Houghton $16.00 (0-89919-407-9). An inviting look at the fascinating preservation techniques of the early Egyptians. (Rev: BCCB 6/87; BL 6/15/87; SLJ 8/87) [932]

7454 Putnam, James. *Mummy* (5–9). Photos by Peter Hayman. Series: Eyewitness Books. 1993, Knopf $20.99 (0-679-93881-8). The process of mummification is discussed, with emphasis on the mummies of ancient Egypt. (Rev: BL 8/93) [393]

7455 Quie, Sarah. *The Myths and Civilization of the Ancient Egyptians* (4–8). Illus. Series: Myths and Civilization. 1999, Bedrick $16.95 (0-87226-282-0). Using the popular myths of the ancient Egyptians as a beginning, this book introduces the culture, history, and artifacts of this era. (Rev: HBG 10/99; SLJ 3/99) [932]

7456 Roberts, Russell. *Rulers of Ancient Egypt* (7–10). Series: History Makers. 1999, Lucent LB $27.45 (1-56006-438-2). The author uses both primary and secondary sources to describe the contributions and personalities of Hatshepsut, Akhenaten, Tutankhamon, Ramses II, and Cleopatra and to provide further insight into this period's culture and power structure. (Rev: SLJ 8/99) [932]

7457 Service, Pamela F. *Ancient Mesopotamia* (6–9). Series: Cultures of the Past. 1998, Marshall Cavendish LB $28.50 (0-7614-0301-9). This book explores the cultures of ancient Mesopotamia, their sacred tales and legends, their histories, and their legacy. (Rev: BL 12/15/98; BR 5–6/99; HBG 9/99; SLJ 4/99) [935]

7458 Shuter, Jane. *Egypt* (5–10). Series: Ancient World. 1998, Raintree Steck-Vaughn LB $27.12 (0-8172-5058-1). Ancient Egypt's mysterious hieroglyphics, treasure-filled tombs, puzzling pyramid construction, and embalming techniques, as well as its history, politics, ideas, religion, art, architecture, science, and everyday life are covered in this introductory volume. (Rev: BL 1/1–15/99; HBG 3/99; SLJ 3/99) [932]

7459 Smith, Brenda. *Egypt of the Pharaohs* (6–9). Series: World History. 1996, Lucent LB $27.45 (1-56006-241-X). This book explores ancient Egypt through periods of ascent and decline, its culture and contributions, and how the pharaohs helped shape the nation. (Rev: BL 2/15/96; SLJ 4/96) [932]

7460 Smith, Carter. *The Pyramid Builders* (5–8). Series: Turning Points in World History. 1991, Silver Burdett LB $14.95 (0-382-24131-2); paper $7.95 (0-382-24137-1). A testimonial to a brilliant culture at its peak. (Rev: BL 3/15/92) [932]

7461 Smith, Stuart Tyson, and Nancy Stone Bernard. *Valley of the Kings* (7–10). Series: Digging for the Past. 2002, Oxford $19.95 (0-19-514770-7). After a map, timeline, and some historical background material, this account describes the tombs in the Valley of the Kings, how they were built, and what they contained. (Rev: BL 10/15/02; HBG 10/03; SLJ 2/03) [932]

7462 Stalcup, Brenda, ed. *Ancient Egyptian Civilization* (7–12). Series: Turning Points in World History. 2001, Greenhaven LB $22.96 (0-7377-0480-2); paper $14.96 (0-7377-0479-9). Following an introductory overview, this anthology of essays presents various aspects of the history of ancient Egypt, its culture and its contributions of world civilization. (Rev: BL 6/1–15/01; SLJ 7/01) [932]

7463 Steedman, Scott. *The Egyptian News: The Greatest Newspaper in Civilization* (4–8). 1997, Candlewick $15.99 (1-56402-873-9). Using a modern newspaper format, this book gives a sense of daily life in ancient Egypt as well as the pyramids, mummies, and pharaohs. (Rev: SLJ 9/97) [932]

7464 Streissguth, Thomas. *Life in Ancient Egypt* (6–10). Series: The Way People Live. 2000, Lucent LB $19.96 (1-56006-643-1). Everyday life within the different social classes that existed in ancient Egypt is covered in this account that contains many black-and-white illustrations. (Rev: BL 3/1/01) [932]

7465 Tagholm, Sally. *Ancient Egypt: A Guide to Egypt in the Time of the Pharaohs* (4–7). Series: Sightseers. 1999, Kingfisher $8.95 (0-7534-5182-4). In the form of a tourist guide to ancient Egypt, this book tells the traveler what to wear, see, eat, and buy. (Rev: HBG 10/99; SLJ 8/99) [932]

7466 Tiano, Oliver. *Ramses II and Egypt* (6–10). Series: W5. 1996, Holt $19.95 (0-8050-4659-3). Using all sorts of gimmicky illustrations and diagrams, this work presents basic facts about ancient Egypt, its culture, and its people. (Rev: SLJ 12/96) [932]

7467 *What Life Was Like on the Banks of the Nile, Egypt 3050–30 BC* (8–12). Illus. 1996, Time-Life Books $34.95 (0-8094-9378-0). An illustrated account that concentrates on everyday life in ancient Egypt, with information on several important kings. (Rev: BL 11/1/96; BR 1–2/97; SLJ 12/96) [932]

7468 Woods, Geraldine. *Science in Ancient Egypt* (4–8). Series: Science of the Past. 1998, Watts LB $26.00 (0-531-20341-7); paper $8.95 (0-531-15915-9). The many contributions to science by the ancient Egyptians, including architecture, astronomy, and mathematics, are outlined in this richly illustrated volume. (Rev: BL 6/1–15/98; BR 11–12/98; HBG 10/98; SLJ 6/98) [932]

Greece

7469 *At the Dawn of Democracy: Classical Athens, 525–332 BC* (7–12). Illus. 1997, Time-Life Books $34.95 (0-7835-5453-2). Using lavish color illustrations, this book re-creates the world of ancient Athens with coverage of daily life, sports, laws, politics, art, and religion. (Rev: BL 2/1/98; SLJ 5/98) [938]

7470 Blacklock, Dyan. *Olympia: Warrior Athletes of Ancient Greece* (5–8). 2001, Walker $17.95 (0-8027-8790-8). A lavishly illustrated introduction to the ancient Olympic Games. (Rev: BL 9/15/01; HBG 3/02; SLJ 10/01) [796.48]

7471 Chapman, Gillian. *The Greeks* (4–7). Series: Crafts from the Past. 1998, Heinemann LB $25.64 (1-57572-733-1). Double-page spreads each outline a project inspired by an art object, i.e. a Greek vase yields pâpier-maché pottery. (Rev: SLJ 2/99) [938]

7472 Day, Nancy. *Your Travel Guide to Ancient Greece* (4–8). Illus. Series: Passport to History. 2000, Runestone LB $26.60 (0-8225-3076-7). An outstanding introduction to ancient Greece arranged in the format of a guided tour and covering topics · including geography, history, customs, and places to visit in an exciting, interesting way. (Rev: BL 10/15/00*; HBG 3/01; SLJ 2/01) [938]

7473 Hart, Avery, and Paul Mantell. *Ancient Greece! 40 Hands-On Activities to Experience This Wondrous Age* (4–7). Illus. 1999, Williamson paper $10.95 (1-885593-25-2). A concise text and several craft projects introduce us to the world of ancient Greece, its geography, history, people, culture, and lasting contributions. (Rev: BL 9/15/99; SLJ 8/99) [938]

7474 Hodge, Susie. *Ancient Greek Art* (4–8). Series: Art in History. 1998, Heinemann LB $24.22 (1-57572-551-7). A solid introduction to ancient Greek art, covering painting, mosaics, pottery, architecture, and sculpture. (Rev: HBG 3/98; SLJ 5/98) [938]

7475 Hull, Robert. *Greece* (5–10). Series: The Ancient World. 1998, Raintree Steck-Vaughn LB $27.12 (0-8172-5055-7). This brief introduction to ancient Greece touches on its religion and mythology, its great philosophers, important historical events, and its contributions to world culture. (Rev: BL 1/1–15/99; HBG 3/99) [938]

7476 Jovinelly, Joann, and Jason Netelkos. *The Crafts and Culture of the Ancient Greeks* (5–8). Series: Crafts of the Ancient World. 2002, Rosen LB $29.25 (0-8239-3510-8). As well as basic information on ancient Greece, this book outlines many craft projects. (Rev: BL 5/15/02) [938]

7477 MacDonald, Fiona. *Women in Ancient Greece* (4–7). Series: The Other Half of History. 1999, Bedrick $17.95 (0-87226-568-4). The status of women in ancient Greece and their occupations and contributions are discussed in this colorful account. (Rev: HBG 3/00; SLJ 2/00) [938]

7478 Malam, John. *Exploring Ancient Greece* (5–8). Series: Remains to Be Seen. 1999, Evans Brothers $19.95 (0-237-51994-1). Particularly noteworthy in this basic account of the history of ancient Greece are the stunning photographs of temples, theaters, artifacts, and landscapes. (Rev: SLJ 1/00) [938]

7479 Malam, John. *Gods and Goddesses* (4–7). Series: Ancient Greece. 2000, Bedrick $18.95 (0-87226-598-6). This book identifies and describes each of the major gods and goddesses of ancient Greece and retells the myths in which they are characters. (Rev: BL 1/1–15/01; HBG 10/00; SLJ 8/00) [938]

7480 Martell, Hazel M. *The Myths and Civilization of the Ancient Greeks* (4–8). Illus. Series: Myths and Civilization. 1999, Bedrick $16.95 (0-87226-283-9). A handsome volume that combines Greek myths and legends with information about ancient Greek artifacts, culture, and history. (Rev: HBG 10/99; SLJ 3/99) [938]

7481 Nardo, Don. *Ancient Athens* (5–8). Illus. Series: A Travel Guide To. 2002, Gale $27.45 (1-59018-016-X). This fact-filled "guidebook" introduces aspiring travelers to everyday life in ancient Athens, in addition to information on climate, geography, important sights, and so forth. (Rev: BL 1/1–15/03; SLJ 2/03) [914.75]

7482 Nardo, Don. *Ancient Greece* (7–10). Series: The History of Weapons and Warfare. 2003, Gale LB $21.96 (1-59018-004-6). A look at weapons, techniques, and strategies of the anicent Greeks — both on land and at sea — with quotations from a variety of sources and maps, diagrams, and other illustrations. (Rev: SLJ 1/03) [355]

7483 Nardo, Don, ed. *Ancient Greece* (6–12). Illus. Series: Complete History Of. 2001, Greenhaven LB $99.00 (0-7377-0425-X). This anthology provides a well-organized and balanced look at Ancient Greece with more than 90 selections on a wide variety of topics. (Rev: BL 11/1/01; SLJ 7/01) [938]

7484 Nardo, Don. *The Ancient Greeks* (6–9). Illus. Series: Lost Civilizations. 2000, Lucent LB $19.96 (1-56006-705-5). The history, organization, culture, and daily life of ancient Greece are presented, including the importance of the city-states. (Rev: BL 2/15/01) [938]

7485 Nardo, Don. *The Battle of Marathon* (6–10). Illus. 1996, Lucent LB $26.20 (1-56006-412-9). A colorful, well-illustrated account that describes the causes, events, and aftermath of the battle in which the ancient Greeks repelled the Persian invasion. (Rev: BL 4/15/96; BR 9–10/96; SLJ 1/96) [938]

7486 Nardo, Don, ed. *The Decline and Fall of Ancient Greece* (8–12). Series: Turning Points in World History. 2000, Greenhaven LB $21.96 (0-7377-0241-9); paper $13.96 (0-7377-0240-0). This anthology discusses the leaders and military campaigns of the various Greek states and the events that led to their complete overthrow by the Romans. (Rev: BL 5/15/00; SLJ 11/00) [938]

7487 Nardo, Don. *Greek Temples* (5–7). Illus. Series: Famous Structures. 2002, Watts LB $24.00 (0-531-12035-X); paper $8.95 (0-531-16225-7).

Nardo looks at the construction, elements, use, and importance of ancient Greek temples, with illustrations. (Rev: BL 9/1/02; SLJ 8/02) [726]

7488 Nardo, Don. *Life in Ancient Athens* (6–10). Series: Way People Live. 1999, Lucent LB $18.96 (1-56006-494-3). This account describes how people lived in ancient Athens with material on how they dressed, worked, ate, socialized, played, and went to school. (Rev: BL 10/15/99; HBG 9/00) [938]

7489 Nardo, Don. *The Parthenon of Ancient Greece* (6–10). 1998, Lucent LB $27.45 (1-56006-431-5). The how and why of the construction of the Parthenon, its legacy as a symbol of classical Greek society and artistry, and its influence on Roman, American, and European architecture. (Rev: BL 12/15/98; BR 5–6/99; SLJ 3/99) [726]

7490 Nardo, Don. *Philip II and Alexander the Great Unify Greece in World History* (6–10). Illus. Series: In World History. 2000, Enslow LB $19.95 (0-7660-1399-5). Primary and secondary sources are used in this survey of relations between the city-states of Greece in the 4th century B.C.E. (Rev: HBG 9/00; SLJ 6/00) [938]

7491 Nardo, Don. *Women of Ancient Greece* (7–10). Series: World History. 2000, Lucent LB $18.96 (1-56006-646-6). The story of the place of women in ancient Greek society, how they lacked political rights and lived sheltered lives yet performed many important duties. (Rev: BL 6/1–15/00; HBG 3/01) [938]

7492 Odijk, Pamela. *The Greeks* (4–7). Illus. Series: Ancient World. 1989, Silver Burdett LB $14.95 (0-382-09884-6). An oversize book that covers history, art, architecture, clothing, and other aspects of ancient Greece. (Rev: BL 1/15/90; SLJ 5/90) [938]

7493 Pearson, Anne. *Ancient Greece* (5–9). Series: Eyewitness Books. 1992, Knopf $20.99 (0-679-91682-2). This attractively laid out book covers the history, religion, people and customs, occupations, recreation, and warfare of ancient Greece. (Rev: BL 11/1/92; SLJ 12/92) [938]

7494 Robinson, C. E. *Everyday Life in Ancient Greece* (7–12). Illus. n.d., AMS $45.00 (0-404-14592-2). The classic account, first published in 1933, of how people lived during various periods in ancient Greek history. [938]

7495 Ross, Stewart. *Daily Life* (4–7). Illus. Series: Ancient Greece. 2000, Bedrick $18.95 (0-87226-599-4). An attractive volume that explores daily life in ancient Greece with coverage of topics including food, dress, eating habits, war, and religion. (Rev: BL 1/1–15/01; HBG 10/00) [938]

7496 Ross, Stewart. *Greek Theatre* (4–7). Series: Ancient Greece. 2000, Bedrick $18.95 (0-87226-597-8). This book describes ancient Greek theaters and their parts and introduces the major playwrights and their works. (Rev: BL 1/1–15/01; HBG 10/00; SLJ 9/00) [938]

7497 Schomp, Virginia. *The Ancient Greeks* (5–8). Series: Cultures of the Past. 1995, Benchmark LB $28.50 (0-7614-0070-2). Using quotations from period literature and many photographs and drawings, this volume examines the history of ancient Greece, its culture, and the importance of the numerous Greek gods and goddesses. (Rev: BR 9–10/96; SLJ 6/96) [938]

7498 Shuter, Jane. *The Acropolis* (5–7). Series: Visiting the Past. 1999, Heinemann LB $24.22 (1-57572-855-9). As well as describing the main buildings found in ancient Greece, this account uses double-page spreads to introduce the daily life and culture of the Athenians. (Rev: SLJ 3/00) [938]

7499 Tyler, Deborah. *The Greeks and Troy* (4–7). Illus. Series: Hidden Worlds. 1993, Dillon $13.95 (0-87518-537-1). The story of the Trojan War is retold, along with a tour of the ruins of Troy and a re-creation of what it once was. (Rev: BL 12/1/93) [938]

7500 Woodford, Susan. *The Parthenon* (6–10). Illus. 1983, Cambridge Univ. Pr. paper $16.00 (0-521-22629-5). A history of the famous temple in Athens and of the religion of ancient Greece. [938]

Middle East

7501 Broida, Marian. *Ancient Israelites and Their Neighbors: An Activity Guide* (4–7). Illus. 2003, Chicago Review paper $16.95 (1-55652-457-9). Readers will find out what life was like for the ancient Israelis, Phoenicians, and Philistines through the information and activities in this attractive book. (Rev: BL 5/15/03; SLJ 8/03) [933]

7502 Jenkins, Earnestine. *A Glorious Past: Ancient Egypt, Ethiopia and Nubia* (7–10). Series: Milestones in Black History. 1995, Chelsea LB $21.95 (0-7910-2258-7); paper $8.95 (0-7910-2684-1). A social and political survey of ancient Egypt, Nubia, the civilization to the south, and Ethiopia. (Rev: BL 4/15/95; SLJ 4/95) [932]

7503 Jovinelly, Joann, and Jason Netelkos. *The Crafts and Culture of the Ancient Hebrews* (5–8). Illus. Series: Crafts of the Ancient World. 2002, Rosen LB $29.25 (0-8239-3511-6). The crafts of the ancient Hebrews and projects related to them are used to give basic information on their history and how they lived. (Rev: BL 4/1/02) [932]

7504 Mann, Kenny. *The Ancient Hebrews* (6–9). Series: Cultures of the Past. 1998, Marshall Cavendish LB $28.50 (0-7614-0302-7). A fine introduction to the history of the ancient Jews, their culture, religion, and legacy. (Rev: BL 12/15/98; BR 5–6/99; HBG 9/99; SLJ 4/99) [909]

7505 Odijk, Pamela. *The Israelites* (4–7). Illus. Series: Ancient World. 1990, Silver Burdett LB $14.95 (0-382-09888-9). Covers the early history of the Jewish people, from their origins in Canaan through the Diaspora. (Rev: BL 7/90; SLJ 8/90) [956.94]

7506 Trumble, Kelly. *The Library of Alexandria* (5–7). 2003, Clarion $17.00 (0-395-75832-7). An introduction to the famous library, its collection, its scholars, and its destruction by fire. (Rev: BCCB 1/04; BL 11/15/03) [027.032]

7507 Zeinert, Karen. *The Persian Empire* (7–10). Series: Cultures of the Past. 1996, Benchmark LB $28.50 (0-7614-0089-3). A brief history of the Persian Empire, with material on the kings Cyrus, Darius, and Xerxes, is followed by chapters on daily life, culture, religion, and lasting contributions the empire made to human achievement. (Rev: SLJ 3/97) [935]

Rome

7508 Butterfield, Moira. *Going to War in Roman Times* (5–7). Illus. Series: Armies of the Past. 2001, Watts LB $24.00 (0-531-14591-3); paper $6.95 (0-531-16352-0). Soldiers, weapons, and military strategies of Roman times are presented with many illustrations and a timeline. (Rev: SLJ 10/01) [355.00937]

7509 Chapman, Gillian. *The Romans* (4–7). Series: Crafts from the Past. 1998, Heinemann LB $25.64 (1-57572-734-X). Using double-page spreads, this work describes Roman culture while outlining several craft projects inspired by art objects, places, or people. (Rev: HBG 10/99; SLJ 2/99) [937]

7510 DuTemple, Lesley A. *The Colosseum* (4–7). Series: Great Building Feats. 2003, Lerner LB $27.93 (0-8225-4693-0). Using many colorful diagrams and illustrations, this is the story of the construction of the famous colosseum in Rome. (Rev: BL 11/15/03) [937]

7511 Ganeri, Anita. *How Would You Survive as an Ancient Roman?* (4–7). Illus. Series: How Would You Survive? 1995, Watts LB $26.00 (0-531-14349-X). Typical entertainment, education, and religious beliefs in ancient Rome are covered, with sidebars on the proper way to appear before a court of law or how to become a Vestal Virgin. (Rev: BL 6/1–15/95; SLJ 8/95) [937]

7512 Hinds, Kathryn. *The Ancient Romans* (7–10). Series: Cultures of the Past. 1996, Benchmark LB $28.50 (0-7614-0090-7). A well-illustrated volume that tells about the Roman Empire, the architectural feats of the Romans, their religion and entertainment, and their lasting contributions to world civilization. (Rev: SLJ 3/97) [937]

7513 Hodge, Susie. *Ancient Roman Art* (4–8). Series: Art in History. 1997, Heinemann LB $24.22 (1-57572-552-5). This slim, well-illustrated volume outlines Roman contributions to architecture, sculpture, pottery, and mosaics. (Rev: SLJ 5/98) [937.6]

7514 Jovinelly, Joann, and Jason Netelkos. *The Crafts and Culture of the Romans* (5–8). Series: Crafts of the Ancient World. 2002, Rosen LB $29.25 (0-8239-3513-2). The daily life and contributions of the ancient Romans are covered, as well as such craft projects as designing a toga. (Rev: BL 5/15/02; SLJ 6/02) [937]

7515 Langley, Andrew, and Philip de Souza. *The Roman News: The Greatest Newspaper in Civilization* (5–8). 1996, Candlewick $15.99 (0-7636-0055-5). Using the format of a tabloid newspaper, this book highlights the history of ancient Rome. (Rev: BL 10/1/96; SLJ 1/97) [937]

7516 Macaulay, David. *City: A Story of Roman Planning and Construction* (6–10). Illus. 1974, Houghton $18.00 (0-395-19492-X); paper $8.95 (0-395-34922-2). In text and detailed drawing, the artist explores an imaginary Roman city over approximately 125 years. [711]

7517 MacDonald, Fiona. *Women in Ancient Rome* (4–8). Series: The Other Half of History. 2000, NTC $17.95 (0-87226-570-6). Topics about women in ancient Rome include their roles at home and at work, their health and beauty, and famous individuals. (Rev: HBG 3/01; SLJ 9/00) [937]

7518 Malam, John. *Gladiator: Life and Death in Ancient Rome* (4–8). Series: Secret Worlds. 2002, DK $14.95 (0-7894-8531-1); paper $5.95 (0-7894-8532-X). The world of the Roman gladiator is presented with fascinating, gory details, and everyday life in ancient Rome is described in a lively text with full-color illustrations. (Rev: BL 8/02; HBG 10/02; SLJ 6/02) [937]

7519 Mann, Elizabeth. *The Roman Colosseum* (4–7). Illus. Series: Wonders of the World. 1998, Mikaya $19.95 (0-9650493-3-7). An oversize book that is crammed with factual material on the Colosseum in Rome. (Rev: BL 12/15/98; SLJ 2/99) [937]

7520 Nardo, Don. *The Ancient Romans* (6–9). Illus. Series: Lost Civilizations. 2000, Lucent LB $19.96 (1-56006-706-3). The history, organization, culture, and daily life of ancient Rome are presented, with information on its legacy, particularly through its legal system. (Rev: BL 2/15/01; SLJ 3/01) [937]

7521 Nardo, Don. *The Battle of Zama* (6–10). Illus. 1996, Lucent LB $26.20 (1-56006-420-X). An exciting account of the 202 B.C. battle in North Africa in which Hannibal's forces were defeated by the Romans during the second Punic War. (Rev: BL 4/15/96; BR 9–10/96; SLJ 4/96) [937]

7522 Nardo, Don. *Caesar's Conquest of Gaul* (7–10). Series: World History. 1996, Lucent LB $27.45 (1-56006-301-7). This is the story of how Caesar's conquest of Gaul destroyed one culture and created a new one that was to influence the development of modern Europe. (Rev: BL 2/15/96; SLJ 2/96) [937]

7523 Nardo, Don. *The Decline and Fall of the Roman Empire* (6–9). Illus. Series: World History. 1998, Lucent LB $27.45 (1-56006-314-9). This book describes the gradual decline of the Roman Empire, which culminated in A.D. 476 when the last emperor was deposed by the superior forces of the Goths. (Rev: BL 6/1–15/98; SLJ 8/98) [937.06]

7524 Nardo, Don, ed. *The End of Ancient Rome* (7–12). Series: Turning Points in World History. 2000, Greenhaven LB $22.96 (0-7377-0372-5); paper $14.96 (0-7377-0371-7). This collection of essays from recognized historians traces the decline and fall of the Roman Empire and the reason for that fall. (Rev: BL 12/15/00; SLJ 1/01) [937]

7525 Nardo, Don. *The Fall of the Roman Empire* (7–12). Illus. Series: Opposing Viewpoints Digests. 1997, Greenhaven LB $27.45 (1-56510-739-X); paper $17.45 (1-56510-738-1). Theories about why Rome fell are presented in a pro and con format. (Rev: BL 3/1/98) [937]

7526 Nardo, Don. *Games of Ancient Rome* (6–10). Series: The Way People Live. 2000, Lucent LB $18.96 (1-56006-655-5). Nardo gives an interesting overview of popular sports in ancient Rome (gladiators, wild animal shows, and chariot races, for example), their importance in daily life, and the reasons for their decline. (Rev: BL 1/1–15/00; HBG 9/00; SLJ 5/00) [937]

7527 Nardo, Don. *The Punic Wars* (8–12). Illus. Series: World History. 1996, Lucent LB $27.45 (1-56006-417-X). A description of the three wars between Rome and Carthage, Hannibal and other leaders, and the significance of Rome's victory. (Rev: BL 2/15/96; SLJ 2/96) [937]

7528 Nardo, Don, ed. *The Rise of the Roman Empire* (7–12). Series: Turning Points in World History. 2001, Greenhaven LB $31.20 (0-7377-0756-9); paper $19.95 (0-7377-0757-7). After an introductory overview, this anthology of essays explores various facets of the rise and growth of the Roman Empire and its social and cultural effects on life in the ancient world. (Rev: BL 3/15/02; SLJ 4/02) [937]

7529 Nardo, Don. *Roman Amphitheaters* (5–7). Illus. Series: Famous Structures. 2002, Watts LB $24.00 (0-531-12036-8); paper $8.95 (0-531-16224-9). A clear overview of the construction, elements, use, and importance of ancient Roman amphitheaters, with illustrations. (Rev: BL 9/1/02; SLJ 8/02) [725]

7530 Nardo, Don. *Women of Ancient Rome* (6–10). Illus. Series: Women in History. 2002, Gale LB

$21.96 (1-59018-169-7). The daily lives of Roman women, from slaves to aristocrats, are portrayed here, with details of social status, work, attire, religion, and even sexuality. (Rev: BL 10/15/02; SLJ 1/03) [305.4]

7531 Ochoa, George. *The Assassination of Julius Caesar* (5–8). Series: Turning Points in World History. 1991, Silver Burdett LB $14.95 (0-382-24130-4); paper $7.95 (0-382-24136-3). A study of the circumstances surrounding the murder of the Roman leader and its historical impact. (Rev: BL 3/15/92) [937]

7532 Odijk, Pamela. *The Romans* (4–7). Illus. Series: Ancient World. 1989, Silver Burdett LB $14.95 (0-382-09885-4). An oversize book about the ancient Romans and their way of life. (Rev: BL 1/15/90; SLJ 5/90) [937]

7533 Patent, Dorothy Hinshaw. *Lost City of Pompeii* (4–7). Series: Frozen in Time. 1999, Benchmark LB $27.07 (0-7614-0785-5). The story of the ancient city of Pompeii, its destruction, and how its excavation has given us a wealth of information about ancient Rome. (Rev: BL 2/1/00; HBG 10/00; SLJ 3/00) [937]

7534 Ridd, Stephen, ed. *Julius Caesar in Gaul and Britain* (5–8). Illus. Series: History Eyewitness. 1995, Raintree Steck-Vaughn LB $24.26 (0-8114-8283-9). An edited version of Caesar's fascinating accounts of the Gallic Wars, with pictures and maps. (Rev: BL 4/15/95; SLJ 5/95) [937.05]

7535 Sheehan, Sean, and Pat Levy. *Rome* (5–10). Series: The Ancient World. 1998, Raintree Steck-Vaughn LB $27.12 (0-8172-5057-3). A brief history of Rome and the Roman Empire, including its culture, buildings, amusements, and emperors. (Rev: BL 1/1–15/99; HBG 3/99; SLJ 3/99) [937]

7536 Snedden, Robert. *Technology in the Time of Ancient Rome* (4–8). Series: Technology in the Time Of. 1998, Raintree Steck-Vaughn LB $27.12 (0-8172-4876-5). Weaving, food production, construction, transportation, and metalwork are covered in this discussion of Roman technology. (Rev: HBG 10/98; SLJ 3/99) [937]

7537 Solway, Andrew. *Rome: In Spectacular Cross-Section* (4–7). 2003, Scholastic paper $18.95 (0-439-45546-4). An inside look at life in ancient Rome, with views of a private home, the Colosseum, the docks, and a bustling festival. (Rev: BL 2/15/03; HBG 10/03; SLJ 7/03) [937]

7538 Steele, Philip. *Food and Feasts in Ancient Rome* (4–8). Illus. Series: Food and Feasts. 1994, New Discovery LB $14.95 (0-02-726321-5). A description of food and food preparation in ancient Rome and how it differed among the classes, as well as a selection of tasty recipes. (Rev: BCCB 10/94; SLJ 12/94) [937]

7539 Stroud, Jonathan. *Ancient Rome: A Guide to the Glory of Imperial Rome* (4–7). Series: Sightseers. 2000, Kingfisher $8.95 (0-7534-5235-9). This book on ancient Rome is presented like a handbook for tourists, with material on such topics as accommodations, shopping, key sites, etc. (Rev: HBG 3/01; SLJ 9/00) [937]

7540 Tanaka, Shelley. *The Buried City of Pompeii* (4–7). Illus. Series: I Was There. 1997, Hyperion $16.95 (0-7868-0285-5). The facts concerning the destruction of the city of Pompeii are told through the fictionalized account of one of its victims. (Rev: BL 12/1/97; HBG 3/98; SLJ 3/98)

7541 Time-Life Books, eds. *When Rome Ruled the World: The Roman Empire, 100 B.C.–A.D. 200* (8–12). Series: What Life Was Like. 1997, Time-Life Books $34.95 (0-7835-5452-4). A wordy introduction to everyday life during the Roman Empire that is noteworthy for its excellent illustrations of art and artifacts. (Rev: SLJ 3/98) [937]

7542 Watkins, Richard. *Gladiator* (5–8). Illus. 1997, Houghton $18.00 (0-395-82656-X). In 12 brief chapters, 700 years of Roman gladiator sports are described, including equipment, animals used, contests, and the architecture and construction of the great amphitheaters. (Rev: BL 11/1/97; BR 9–10/98; HBG 3/98; SLJ 10/97*) [937]

7543 Williams, Brian. *Ancient Roman Women* (5–8). Illus. Series: People in the Past. 2002, Heinemann LB $27.07 (1-58810-632-2). A look at the life of, and options open to, women in ancient Rome. (Rev: BL 3/1/03; HBG 10/03; SLJ 4/03) [305.8]

Middle Ages Through the Renaissance (500–1700)

7544 Barter, James. *Artists of the Renaissance* (6–10). Illus. Series: History Makers. 1999, Lucent LB $27.45 (1-56006-439-0). Following an overview of the Renaissance, including explanations of humanism and classicism, this book focuses on several great artists, among them Giotto, Leonardo da Vinci, and Michelangelo. (Rev: BL 6/1–15/99; SLJ 7/99) [709]

7545 Barter, James. *Renaissance Florence* (5–8). Illus. Series: A Travel Guide To. 2002, Gale $27.45 (1-59018-145-X). Travel back in time to Renaissance Florence with this guidebook that gives period-appropriate historical and sight-seeing information as well as a flavor of everyday life in the city. (Rev: BL 1/1–15/03; SLJ 4/03) [914.4]

7546 Blackwood, Gary L. *Life in a Medieval Castle* (6–10). Series: The Way People Live. 1999, Lucent LB $18.96 (1-56006-582-6). The daily life and personal problems involved in living in a castle during the Middle Ages are two of the topics discussed in this book that uses quotations from original sources. (Rev: BL 11/15/99) [940.1]

7547 Brewer, Paul. *Warfare in the Renaissance World* (7–10). Series: History of Warfare. 1999, Raintree Steck-Vaughn LB $29.97 (0-8172-5444-7). Using diagrams and other illustrations, this is an account of the wars and battles fought during the Renaissance period. (Rev: HBG 3/99; SLJ 3/99) [940.2]

7548 Corbishley, Mike. *The Medieval World* (5–7). Illus. Series: Timelink. 1993, Bedrick LB $18.95 (0-87226-362-2). Using a chronological approach, this book covers the years 450 through 1500 in Europe, Asia, Africa, and the Americas. (Rev: SLJ 8/93) [940.1]

7549 Corbishley, Mike. *The Middle Ages* (6–9). Illus. 1990, Facts on File $19.95 (0-8160-1973-8). An overview of medieval Europe is given, covering history and culture with some material on stained glassmaking. (Rev: SLJ 9/90) [909]

7550 Corrick, James A. *The Early Middle Ages* (8–12). Illus. Series: World History. 1995, Lucent LB $27.45 (1-56006-246-0). This account tells how Europe recovered and regrouped its power structure into a feudal economy after the barbarian invasions destroyed the Roman Empire. (Rev: BL 2/15/95) [940.1]

7551 Corrick, James A. *Life of a Medieval Knight* (6–10). Series: The Way People Live. 2001, Lucent LB $19.96 (1-56006-817-5). With a generous use of quotations from primary and secondary sources, the daily life and routines of knights are chronicled plus coverage of their more sensational exploits and struggles. (Rev: BL 6/1–15/01) [941]

7552 Dawson, Imogen. *Food and Feasts in the Middle Ages* (4–8). Series: Food and Feasts. 1994, New Discovery LB $14.95 (0-02-726324-X). This account re-creates the culinary aspects of the Middle Ages, with material on farming, dishes, and town and city fare plus several recipes and many attractive illustrations. (Rev: BCCB 10/94; SLJ 12/94) [940.1]

7553 Day, Nancy. *Your Travel Guide to Renaissance Europe* (4–8). Series: Passport to History. 2000, Lerner LB $26.60 (0-8225-3080-5). This book uses a travel guide format to introduce the reader to the life and people of Europe from 1350 to 1550 with coverage of culture, style, inventions, religious beliefs, and scientific discoveries. (Rev: BL 3/1/01; HBG 10/01) [940.2]

7554 De Hahn, Tracee. *The Black Death* (6–8). Series: Great Disasters. 2001, Chelsea LB $21.95 (0-7910-6326-7). The story of the terrible plague that swept through Europe and parts of Asia in the 14th century and of the changes it produced in society. (Rev: BL 6/1–15/02; HBG 10/02) [614.5]

7555 Doherty, Katherine M., and Craig A. Doherty. *King Richard the Lionhearted and the Crusades* (8–12). Series: In World History. 2002, Enslow LB $20.95 (0-7660-1459-2). Combining both biography and history, this account re-creates the life of Richard the Lionhearted and his contributions to freeing the Holy Land during the Crusades. (Rev: BL 4/1/02; HBG 10/02; SLJ 6/02) [921]

7556 Dunn, John M. *Life During the Black Death* (5–9). Series: The Way People Live. 2000, Lucent LB $27.45 (1-56006-542-7). This account traces the spread of the Black Death from Mongolia in 1320 to Western Europe and its lasting effects on history, society, and culture. (Rev: HBG 10/00; SLJ 6/00) [940]

7557 George, Linda S. *800* (5–8). Illus. Series: Around the World. 2003, Marshall Cavendish LB $28.50 (0-7614-1085-6). This absorbing look at civilizations around the world in the year 800 includes color reproductions, photographs, a timeline, a glossary, and lists of resources. (Rev: BL 6/1–15/03; HBG 3/03) [909.07]

7558 Gravett, Christopher. *The World of the Medieval Knight* (5–10). Illus. 1997, Bedrick $19.95 (0-87226-277-4). Various aspects of knighthood — from armor and jousting to castle life and the Crusades — are presented in this richly illustrated book. (Rev: BL 1/1–15/97; SLJ 3/97) [940.1]

7559 Halliwell, Sarah, ed. *The Renaissance: Artists and Writers* (6–9). Illus. Series: Who and When? 1998, Raintree Steck-Vaughn LB $19.98 (0-8172-4725-4). This account covers the artistic life of the Renaissance and includes profiles of 13 artists and writers, including Giotto, Botticelli, Bosch, Dante, Chaucer, and Cervantes. (Rev: BL 12/15/97; SLJ 1/98) [700]

7560 Hanawalt, Barbara. *The Middle Ages: An Illustrated History* (8–12). Illus. 1999, Oxford $29.95 (0-19-510359-9). A carefully researched account of the Roman Empire and its gradual fall, the rise of the church, its use of power, and feudal society, including such topics as castles, the Crusades, the Black Death, the rise of guilds and universities, and the growth of the middle class. (Rev: BL 3/1/99; HBG 3/99; SLJ 4/99) [909.07]

7561 Hay, Jeff, ed. *The Early Middle Ages* (7–12). Series: Turning Points in World History. 2001, Greenhaven LB $22.96 (0-7377-0482-9); paper $14.96 (0-7377-0481-0). After a general introduction to this period in western history, several detailed essays present various aspects of the history, culture, and social conditions during the early middle ages. (Rev: BL 6/1–15/01) [940.1]

7562 Hinds, Kathryn. *The Castle* (5–8). Series: Life in the Middle Ages. 2000, Marshall Cavendish LB $28.50 (0-7614-1007-4). A book that explores the construction and parts of the medieval castle as well as the lifestyles of those who lived in them, from kings and knights to humble servants. (Rev: BL 3/1/01; HBG 3/01; SLJ 3/01) [940]

7563 Hinds, Kathryn. *The Church* (5–8). Series: Life in the Middle Ages. 2000, Marshall Cavendish LB $28.50 (0-7614-1008-2). Explains the role of the church and the clergy in medieval life as well as giving examples of church construction. (Rev: BL 3/1/01; HBG 3/01; SLJ 3/01) [940]

7564 Hinds, Kathryn. *The City* (5–8). Illus. Series: Life in the Middle Ages. 2000, Marshall Cavendish LB $28.50 (0-7614-1005-8). A beautifully designed book that tells about daily life in medieval cities and their functions as centers of learning, commerce, worship, construction, and recreation as well as disease and disaster. (Rev: BL 2/15/01; HBG 3/01; SLJ 3/01) [940.1]

7565 Hinds, Kathryn. *The Countryside* (5–8). Illus. Series: Life in the Middle Ages. 2000, Marshall Cavendish LB $28.50 (0-7614-1006-6). The author explains manorialism — a primary social structure in rural areas during the Middle Ages — and describes a medieval village, its residents, and their work and pastimes. (Rev: BL 2/15/01; HBG 3/01; SLJ 3/01) [940.1]

7566 Howarth, Sarah. *What Do We Know About the Middle Ages?* (4–7). Illus. Series: What Do We Know About. 1996, Bedrick $18.95 (0-87226-384-3). The way people lived in the Middle Ages in Western Europe is described in a series of double-page spreads. (Rev: BL 6/1–15/96) [940.1]

7567 Hunt, Jonathan. *Bestiary: An Illuminated Alphabet of Medieval Beasts* (4–8). Illus. 1998, Simon & Schuster $17.00 (0-689-81246-9). A total of 26 wondrous, mostly scary, beasts from medieval times, among them the griffin, phoenix, sphinx, and ziphius, are pictured and described in this eye-catching volume. (Rev: BL 9/1/98; HBG 3/99; SLJ 9/98) [940]

7568 January, Brendan. *Science in the Renaissance* (4–7). Illus. Series: Science of the Past. 1999, Watts LB $26.00 (0-531-11526-7). Covers the reawakening of science during the Renaissance in such areas as astronomy, medicine, physics, anatomy, and geometry and perspective in art. (Rev: BL 3/15/99; HBG 10/99) [509.4]

7569 Jones, Madeline. *Knights and Castles* (6–9). Series: How It Was. 1991, Batsford $19.95 (0-7134-6352-X). A re-creation of castles and knights and the time in which they existed. (Rev: BL 1/15/92; SLJ 3/92) [941]

7570 Jordan, William Chester, ed. *The Middle Ages: A Watts Guide for Children* (4–7). 2000, Watts LB $36.50 (0-531-11715-4); paper $19.95 (0-531-16488-8). A basic guide to life in the Middle Ages

with alphabetically arranged entries on major events, important places, and significant people. (Rev: SLJ 7/00) [940]

7571 Knight, Judson. *Middle Ages: Almanac* (6–10). Series: UXL Middle Ages Reference Library. 2000, Gale LB $45.00 (0-7876-4856-6). A comprehensive review of events around the world during the Middle Ages, with material on Africa and Asia as well as on Europe and the Middle East. Also use *Middle Ages: Biographies* and *Middle Ages: Primary Sources* (both 2000). (Rev: BL 4/1/01; SLJ 5/01) [940.1]

7572 Lace, William W. *Defeat of the Spanish Armada* (6–10). Series: Battles. 1996, Lucent LB $26.20 (1-56006-458-7). The story of the war between England and Spain during the time of Elizabeth I, and how the defeat of Spain established England as a major sea power. (Rev: BL 4/15/97; BR 11–12/97; SLJ 6/97) [947]

7573 Langley, Andrew. *Medieval Life* (4–9). Illus. Series: Eyewitness Books. 1996, Knopf $20.99 (0-679-98077-6). This book goes behind the scenes of life in a castle during the Middle Ages, explaining and illustrating its parts and how people lived within its walls. (Rev: BL 6/1–15/96; SLJ 7/96) [940.1]

7574 Langley, Andrew. *Renaissance* (4–9). Photos by Andy Crawford. Series: Eyewitness Books. 1999, Knopf $20.99 (0-375-90136-1). A concise account, illustrated with photographs, that describes such aspects of the Renaissance as city-states, trade, daily dress, art, architecture, and religion. (Rev: HBG 3/00; SLJ 9/99) [909.07]

7575 MacDonald, Fiona. *Women in Medieval Times* (4–8). Series: The Other Half of History. 2000, NTC $17.95 (0-87226-569-2). Using a topical arrangement this book discusses the role of women in medieval times in the castle, in the workplace, and at court. (Rev: HBG 3/01; SLJ 9/00) [940]

7576 MacDonald, Fiona. *The World in the Time of Charlemagne: AD 700–900* (6–9). Series: The World in the Time Of. 1998, Dillon $9.95 (0-382-39737-1). After background material on Charlemagne's life and achievements, this book describes important developments in the arts, science, and religion during the 200-year period influenced by his reign. (Rev: SLJ 3/99) [921]

7577 Marshall, Chris. *Warfare in the Medieval World* (7–10). Series: History of Warfare. 1999, Raintree Steck-Vaughn LB $29.97 (0-8172-5443-9). The Hundred Years' War is one of the wars highlighted in this book that focuses on individual battles and is illustrated with many full-color maps and reproductions. (Rev: HBG 3/99; SLJ 3/99; VOYA 2/00) [940.1]

7578 Marston, Elsa. *The Byzantine Empire* (5–8). Series: Cultures of the Past. 2002, Marshall Cavendish $19.95 (0-7614-1495-9). Well-written text and colorful graphics present the history and culture of the surviving eastern part of the Roman Empire. (Rev: BL 1/1–15/03; HBG 3/03; SLJ 2/03) [949.5]

7579 Morgan, Gwyneth. *Life in a Medieval Village* (5–7). 1991, HarperCollins paper $14.00 (0-06-092046-7). A story of activities in a medieval village and of the church's importance in life in the Middle Ages. [306.094265]

7580 Nicolle, David. *Medieval Knights* (4–8). Series: See Through History. 1997, Viking $19.99 (0-670-87463-9). An introduction to knights, their functions, weapons, quests, training, and accomplishments. (Rev: BL 10/15/97; HBG 3/98; SLJ 1/98) [940]

7581 Pernoud, Regine. *A Day with a Noblewoman* (5–8). Trans. by Dominique Clift. Illus. Series: A Day With. 1997, Runestone LB $27.15 (0-8225-1916-X). After a brief introduction to the Middle Ages, this book describes a busy day in the life of Blanche, the countess of Champagne, a French widow in the 13th century. (Rev: BL 1/1–15/98; HBG 3/98; SLJ 2/98) [940.1]

7582 Prum, Deborah Mazzotta. *Rats, Bulls, and Flying Machines: A History of Renaissance and Reformation* (4–8). Illus. Series: Core Chronicles. 1999, Core Knowledge $21.95 (1-890517-19-4); paper $11.95 (1-890517-18-6). A handsome volume that gives a basic history of the Renaissance and Reformation and highlights the accomplishments of people such as the Medici family, Machiavelli, Michelangelo, Cervantes, Shakespeare, and Gutenberg. (Rev: BL 12/15/99) [909.08]

7583 Rice, Earle, Jr. *Life During the Crusades* (8–10). Illus. Series: The Way People Live. 1998, Lucent LB $27.45 (1-56006-379-3). The period of the Crusades (1096–1272) is introduced, with material on feudal life, knighthood, reasons for the Crusades, Muslim culture, and key events of each of the Crusades. (Rev: BL 3/15/98; SLJ 5/98) [909.07]

7584 Rice, Earle, Jr. *Life During the Middle Ages* (6–10). Series: Way People Live. 1998, Lucent LB $27.45 (1-56006-386-6). An account of how serfs, lords, and clergy lived under feudalism in the Middle Ages, enduring warfare, famine, and disease. (Rev: BL 7/98; SLJ 8/98) [941]

7585 Schomp, Virginia. *1500* (5–8). Illus. Series: Around the World. 2003, Marshall Cavendish LB $28.50 (0-7614-1082-1). This absorbing look at civilizations around the world in the year 1500 includes color reproductions, photographs, a timeline, a glossary, and lists of resources. (Rev: BL 6/1–15/03; HBG 3/03) [909]

7586 Schomp, Virginia. *The Italian Renaissance* (5–8). Series: Cultures of the Past. 2002, Marshall Cavendish $19.95 (0-7614-1492-4). A handsome volume that gives a balanced, well-organized account of the Italian Renaissance, its history, personalities, art, and artifacts. (Rev: BL 1/1–15/03; HBG 3/03) [940.2]

7587 Sherrow, Victoria. *Life in a Medieval Monastery* (5–9). Series: The Way People Live. 2001, Lucent LB $27.45 (1-56006-791-8). An absorbing account of religious life in the Middle Ages, with details of clothing, diet, and hairstyles as well as maps and black-and-white reproductions. (Rev: BL 6/1–15/01; SLJ 8/01) [271]

7588 Stalcup, Brenda, ed. *The Inquisition* (7–12). Series: Turning Points in World History. 2001, Greenhaven LB $22.96 (0-7377-0486-1); paper $14.96 (0-7377-0485-3). The history of this form of religious intolerance and persecution in Western Europe is traced in a series of essays that cover its beginnings in the 13th century and its eventual abolition. (Rev: BL 6/1–15/01; SLJ 7/01) [940]

7589 Steele, Philip. *Castles* (5–7). Illus. 1995, Kingfisher $16.95 (1-85697-547-9). In this oversized, well-designed book, castles, jousting, armor, and feast days are described. (Rev: BL 8/95; SLJ 4/95) [940.1]

7590 Sypeck, Jeff. *The Holy Roman Empire and Charlemagne in World History* (8–12). Series: In World History. 2002, Enslow LB $20.95 (0-7660-1901-2). This combination of biography and history tells the story of the life and reign of Charlemagne and the foundation of the Holy Roman Empire, which lasted for more than 700 years. (Rev: BL 3/15/03; HBG 3/03) [940.1]

7591 Tanaka, Shelley. *In the Time of Knights: The Real-Life Story of History's Greatest Knight* (4–7). Series: I Was There. 2000, Hyperion $16.99 (0-7868-0651-6). This fictionalized account of the life of William Marshal, who became a famous knight during the 12th century, also gives a great deal of information on life during the Middle Ages. (Rev: BCCB 2/01; HBG 10/01; SLJ 3/01) [921]

7592 Taylor, Robert. *Life in Genghis Khan's Mongolia* (6–10). Series: The Way People Live. 2001, Lucent LB $19.96 (1-56006-348-3). As well as a life of this 13th-century Mongol conqueror and his empire, this account, which uses many original sources, describes the daily life of his subjects. (Rev: BL 6/1–15/01; SLJ 6/01) [951]

7593 Wood, Tim. *The Renaissance* (5–8). Series: See Through History. 1993, Viking $19.99 (0-670-85149-3). A series of double-page spreads explore the day-to-day lives of people during the Renaissance, including Far East trade, Italian city-states, women at court, art, and technology. (Rev: BL 12/15/93; SLJ 2/94) [940.2]

Eighteenth Through Nineteenth Centuries (1700–1900)

7594 Bachrach, Deborah. *The Charge of the Light Brigade* (6–10). Illus. Series: Battles. 1996, Lucent LB $26.20 (1-56006-455-2). An account of the "death charge of the 600" at Balaclava on Sept. 20, 1854, during the Crimean War. (Rev: BL 4/15/97; BR 11–12/97; SLJ 6/97) [947]

7595 Bachrach, Deborah. *The Crimean War* (8–12). Illus. Series: World History. 1997, Lucent LB $27.45 (1-56006-315-7). An easy-to-read account of the causes, main events, and consequences of the Crimean War, the first war to be extensively covered by the press, fought from 1853 to 1856 and involving Great Britain, France, Russia, Sardinia, and Turkey. (Rev: SLJ 6/98) [947]

7596 Cooper, Paul. *Going to War in the 18th Century* (4–7). Illus. Series: Armies of the Past. 2001, Watts LB $24.00 (0-531-14593-X). All about the armies and navies involved in the American Revolution and major conflicts in Europe — forms of recruitment, artillery, cavalry, uniforms, strategies, camp life, and so forth. Also use *Going to War in the 19th Century* (2001). (Rev: SLJ 2/02) [355.009033]

7597 Corrick, James A. *The Industrial Revolution* (7–10). Illus. Series: World History. 1998, Lucent LB $27.45 (1-56006-318-1). Using more than 20 original documents, this work examines the changes in technology and working conditions brought about by the Industrial Revolution in England, Europe, and America, and explores its far-reaching social impact spanning the 18th, 19th, and 20th centuries. (Rev: BL 9/1/98) [909.81]

7598 Dunn, John M. *The Enlightenment* (6–9). Series: World History. 1998, Lucent LB $27.45 (1-56006-242-8). A look at Western Europe's emergence from the Dark Ages and the rediscovery of ancient scholarship. (Rev: BL 12/15/98; BR 5–6/99) [940.2]

7599 Haskins, Jim, and Kathleen Benson. *Bound for America: The Forced Migration of Africans to the New World* (4–9). Illus. Series: From African Beginnings. 1999, Lothrop LB $17.89 (0-688-10259-X). This stirring account traces the fate of African slaves from capture, imprisonment, and branding to the brutal conditions on slave ships and finally to the survivors' arrival in the New World. (Rev: BCCB 3/99; BL 12/15/98; BR 5–6/99; HBG 10/99; SLJ 1/99*) [382]

7600 Killingray, David. *The Transatlantic Slave Trade* (7–12). Illus. 1987, Batsford $19.95 (0-7134-

5469-5). This book gives detailed coverage of the causes, history, and end of the international slave trade and how it has affected demographics today. (Rev: SLJ 1/88) [380.1]

7601 MacDonald, Fiona. *Women in 19th-Century Europe* (4–8). Series: The Other Half of History. 1999, Bedrick $17.95 (0-87226-565-X). Describes women's progress and contributions in 19th-century Europe and gives biographies of famous women of the time. (Rev: HBG 3/00; SLJ 11/99) [940.2]

7602 Monaghan, Tom. *The Slave Trade* (6–10). Series: Events and Outcomes. 2002, Raintree Steck-Vaughn LB $28.54 (0-7398-5802-5). An interesting overview of the supply of slaves to the New World from its early days through its abolition, with information on key abolitionists and discussion of the economic reasons for this trade. (Rev: HBG 3/03; SLJ 4/03) [306.3]

7603 Pietrusza, David. *The Battle of Waterloo* (6–10). Illus. Series: Great Battles in History. 1996, Lucent LB $26.20 (1-56006-423-4). The story of the last battle of the Napoleonic Wars is told with a generous use of graphics, including a timeline and maps. (Rev: BL 4/15/96; BR 9–10/96; SLJ 4/96) [940.2]

7604 Sommerville, Donald. *Revolutionary and Napoleonic Wars* (8–10). Series: History of Warfare. 1998, Raintree Steck-Vaughn LB $29.97 (0-8172-5446-3). This well-illustrated book looks at the wars fought from the late-18th through mid-19th centuries, focusing primarily on the Americans and the French and their wars of independence and subsequent battles with other enemies. (Rev: HBG 3/99; SLJ 1/99) [909]

7605 Westwell, Ian. *Warfare in the 18th Century* (8–10). Series: History of Warfare. 1998, Raintree Steck-Vaughn LB $29.97 (0-8172-5445-5). A look at wars fought from the Great Northern War in 1700 to the death of Catherine the Great in 1796, including wars fought with Native Americans and over the fate of India. (Rev: HBG 3/99; SLJ 1/99) [909]

7606 Wilkinson, Philip, and Jacqueline Dineen. *The Industrial Revolution* (6–9). Illus. 1995, Chelsea LB $21.95 (0-7910-2767-8). This simple account shows how harnessing energy and the development of industry during the 19th century and afterward changed the way people lived and created a new social structure. (Rev: BR 5–6/96; VOYA 2/96) [909.8]

7607 Woog, Adam. *A Sweatshop During the Industrial Revolution* (5–9). Series: The Working Life. 2003, Gale LB $21.96 (1-59018-179-4). An exploration of daily life for a sweatshop worker during a time of social change, with material on the roles of women, minorities, and organized labor. (Rev: SLJ 5/03) [331.25]

Twentieth Century

General and Miscellaneous

7608 Clare, John D. *Growing Up in the People's Century* (6–12). 1998, BBC Books $20.00 (0-563-40410-8). Wonderful for browsers, this book uses double-page spreads with pictures and quotations to present a quick view of events of historical or cultural significance in the 20th century. (Rev: BL 1/1–15/99) [909.82]

7609 *Events That Shaped the Century* (7–12). 1998, Time-Life Books $29.95 (0-7835-5502-4). Using outstanding photographs, this volume describes 125 events since 1900 that transformed America and affected all aspects of American life. (Rev: BR 11–12/98; SLJ 9/98) [909.82]

7610 Jennings, Peter, and Todd Brewster. *The Century for Young People* (7–10). Illus. 1999, Doubleday $29.95 (0-385-32708-0). An attractive presentation of the major events of 1900–1998, with photographs and first-person accounts. (Rev: BL 11/15/99; HBG 4/00; SLJ 11/99*; VOYA 2/00) [909.82]

7611 McGowen, Tom. *Assault from the Sea: Amphibious Invasions in the Twentieth Century* (5–8). Series: Military Might. 2002, Twenty-First Century LB $26.90 (0-7613-1811-9). Invasions launched from the sea during World Wars I and II and the Korean War are the subject of this introduction that includes black-and-white photographs and maps. Also use *Assault from the Sky: Airborne Infantry of World War II* (2002). (Rev: HBG 10/02; SLJ 6/02) [355.460904]

7612 Ross, Stewart. *Oxford Children's Book of the 20th Century: A Concise Guide to a Century of Contrast and Change* (4–9). 1999, Oxford $18.95 (0-19-521488-9). Using double-page spreads, this book focuses on the people, places, and events of the 20th century, with interesting text, photographs, maps, and timelines. (Rev: HBG 9/99; SLJ 7/99) [909.82]

7613 Stolley, Richard B., ed. *Life: Our Century in Pictures for Young People* (5–12). Illus. 2000, Little, Brown $25.45 (0-316-81577-2). Adapted from an adult coffee-table book, this survey of the last century is divided into nine chronological, heavily illustrated chapters with contributions from many children's writers including Lois Lowry and Robert Cormier. (Rev: BL 12/15/00) [909.82]

7614 Wilson, Janet. *Imagine That!* (4–8). 2000, Stoddart $14.95 (0-7737-3221-7). In the form of a reminiscence by 100-year-old Auntie Violet, this is a brief history of the past century, with major events highlighted. (Rev: SLJ 11/00) [909]

World War I

7615 Adams, Simon. *World War I* (6–12). Illus. 2001, DK $15.95 (0-7894-7939-7). This attractive large-format book is full of information and graphics relating to the war. (Rev: BL 12/15/01) [940.3]

7616 Bosco, Peter. *World War I* (7–12). Series: America at War. 1991, Facts on File $25.00 (0-8160-2460-X). Highlights the major battles and personalities of World War I and discusses events leading to a declaration of war and the changes following the peace. (Rev: BL 10/15/91; SLJ 8/91) [940.3]

7617 Clare, John D., ed. *First World War* (5–8). Illus. Series: Living History. 1995, Gulliver $16.95 (0-15-200087-9). Excellent visuals and a vivid text are used in this history of World War I. (Rev: SLJ 6/95) [940.53]

7618 Coetzee, Frans, and Marilyn Shevin-Coetzee. *World War I: A History in Documents* (7–12). Series: Pages from History. 2002, Oxford LB $32.95 (0-19-513746-9). Letters, poems, posters, quotations, and other documents are accompanied by advice on evaluating their content. (Rev: SLJ 8/02) [940.3]

7619 Currie, Stephen. *Life in the Trenches* (6–12). Series: American War Library: World War I. 2002, Gale LB $27.45 (1-56006-838-8). This volume describes daily life for American servicemen in European battlefields and behind the scenes during World War I. (Rev: BL 6/1–15/02) [940.3]

7620 Dudley, William, ed. *World War I* (6–12). Illus. Series: Opposing Viewpoints: American History. 1997, Greenhaven LB $32.45 (1-56510-703-9); paper $21.20 (1-56510-702-0). The disagreements, debates, and international problems related to the First World War, including U.S. war preparedness, neutrality, and the League of Nations, are covered in this collection of viewpoints. (Rev: BL 5/15/98) [940.3]

7621 Gay, Kathlyn, and Martin Gay. *World War I* (5–8). Illus. Series: Voices from the Past. 1995, Twenty-First Century LB $25.90 (0-8050-2848-X). The causes, major battles, and effects of World War I are covered, with many excerpts from personal accounts. (Rev: BL 12/15/95; SLJ 2/96) [940.3]

7622 George, Linda S. *World War I* (5–8). Series: Letters from the Homefront. 2001, Benchmark LB $28.50 (0-7614-1096-1). Life at the front and at home during the First World War is depicted through letters and other firsthand accounts. (Rev: BL 10/15/01; HBG 3/02) [973.9]

7623 Granfield, Linda. *Where Poppies Grow: A World War I Companion* (4–7). 2002, Stoddart $16.95 (0-7737-3319-1). The horrors of war in the trenches are portrayed in this scrapbook full of photographs, propaganda, and ephemera that includes accounts of two Canadian soldiers. (Rev: BL 6/1–15/02; HBG 10/02; SLJ 7/02) [940.3]

7624 Grant, Reg. *World War I: Armistice 1918* (5–8). Series: The World Wars. 2001, Raintree Steck-Vaughn LB $27.12 (0-7398-2753-7). The negotiations that ended World War I are detailed here, with discussion of the failure of the League of Nations and the lead-up to World War II. (Rev: SLJ 6/01) [940.3]

7625 Hansen, Ole Steen. *Military Aircraft of WWI* (4–7). Series: The Story of Flight. 2003, Crabtree $23.93 (0-7787-1201-X). This book introduces in text and pictures the aircraft used by the allies and enemies during World War I. (Rev: BL 10/15/03) [940.3]

7626 Hansen, Ole Steen. *World War I: War in the Trenches* (5–8). Series: The World Wars. 2001, Raintree Steck-Vaughn LB $27.12 (0-7398-2752-9). The causes of World War I are introduced, followed by information on the major battles and descriptions of the misery of life in the trenches, with plenty of photographs, reproductions, maps, sidebars, and excerpts from primary sources. (Rev: SLJ 6/01) [940.3]

7627 Hatt, Christine. *World War I: 1914–18* (6–9). Illus. Series: Documenting History. 2001, Watts LB $22.00 (0-531-14611-1). This overview of the war draws on sources including advertisements, interviews, and personal diaries, and offers maps, charts, and photographs. (Rev: BL 12/15/01; SLJ 12/01) [940.3]

7628 Murphy, Donald J., ed. *World War I* (7–12). Series: Turning Points in World History. 2002, Gale LB $31.20 (0-7377-0932-4); paper $19.95 (0-7377-0933-2). The causes, campaigns, battles, effects, and personal aspects of World War I are explored in this anthology of important essays for the serious student. (Rev: BL 6/1–15/02) [940.3]

7629 Preston, Diana. *Remember the Lusitania!* (5–8). Illus. 2003, Walker $22.95 (0-8027-8846-7). This gripping account of the sinking of the *Lusitania* includes many personal stories that will hold young readers' attention. (Rev: BL 4/15/03; HB 7–8/03; HBG 10/03; SLJ 7/03) [940.4]

7630 Rice, Earle, Jr. *The Battle of Belleau Wood* (6–10). Illus. Series: Great Battles in History. 1996, Lucent LB $19.95 (1-56006-424-2). The story of the victory over the Germans in June 1918 by chiefly American troops is told with a generous use of illustrations, maps, and a timeline. (Rev: BL 4/15/96; BR 9–10/96) [940.4]

7631 Ross, Stewart. *Assassination in Sarajevo: The Trigger for World War I* (4–9). Series: Point of Impact. 2001, Heinemann LB $24.22 (1-58810-074-X). The assassination of the Archduke of Austria, a precipitating factor in World War I, is put into con-

text and the alliances among the world's nations at the time are clearly explained. (Rev: HBG 10/01; SLJ 7/01) [940.3]

7632 Ross, Stewart. *Causes and Consequences of World War I* (7–10). Series: Causes and Consequences. 1998, Raintree Steck-Vaughn LB $29.97 (0-8172-4057-8). This volume analyzes the factors that led to World War I and the conflict's short-term and long-term effects, accompanied by contemporary illustrations. (Rev: BL 8/98; SLJ 6/98) [940.311]

7633 Ross, Stewart. *Leaders of World War I* (4–8). Illus. Series: World Wars. 2003, Raintree Steck-Vaughn LB $28.56 (0-7398-5481-X). Stewart presents concise details on the large cast of world and military leaders involved in this conflict. (Rev: BL 12/1/03; HBG 10/03) [023]

7634 Ross, Stewart. *The Technology of World War I* (4–8). Illus. Series: World Wars. 2003, Raintree Steck-Vaughn LB $28.56 (0-7398-5482-8). New technologies used during World War I included torpedoes, mines, submarines, tanks, planes with machine guns, and mustard gas; all are shown here with maps, diagrams, period reproductions, and posters. (Rev: BL 12/1/03; HBG 10/03; SLJ 7/03) [023]

World War II and the Holocaust

7635 Aaseng, Nathan. *Navajo Code Talkers* (6–9). 1992, Walker LB $16.85 (0-8027-8183-7). Describes how Navajos were recruited during World War II to create an unbreakable code that allowed the marines to transmit information quickly, accurately, and safely. (Rev: BL 12/1/92; SLJ 12/92) [940.54]

7636 Aaseng, Nathan. *Paris* (6–12). Series: Cities at War. 1992, Macmillan LB $18.00 (0-02-700010-9). Remembrances from people who experienced World War II in Paris. (Rev: BL 10/15/92) [944]

7637 Adams, Simon. *World War II* (4–8). Illus. 2000, DK $15.95 (0-7894-3298-2). Each double-page spread presents a different aspect of World War II, such as the Battle of Britain, military equipment, women at work, and conditions inside the Soviet Union. (Rev: BL 11/1/00) [940.53]

7638 Adler, David A. *We Remember the Holocaust* (4–7). 1995, Holt paper $14.95 (0-8050-3715-2). Through interview excerpts, the terrible days of the Holocaust are remembered. (Rev: SLJ 12/89) [940.54]

7639 Allen, Thomas B. *Remember Pearl Harbor: American and Japanese Survivors Tell Their Stories* (5–9). Illus. 2001, National Geographic $17.95 (0-7922-6690-0). First-person accounts by Japanese and American men and women give readers a close-up view of the 1941 Japanese attack on Pearl Harbor, with maps and photographs. (Rev: BL 9/1/01; HBG 3/02; SLJ 9/01*; VOYA 10/01) [940.54]

7640 Altman, Linda Jacobs. *Forever Outsiders: Jews and History from Ancient Times to August 1935* (6–12). Illus. Series: Holocaust. 1997, Blackbirch LB $27.44 (1-56711-200-5). An authoritative look at anti-Semitism throughout history, ending with Hitler's rise to power and the beginnings of his Final Solution. (Rev: BL 10/15/97; BR 1–2/98; HBG 3/98; SLJ 2/98) [940.53]

7641 Altman, Linda Jacobs. *The Forgotten Victims of the Holocaust* (5–10). Illus. Series: Holocaust in History. 2003, Enslow LB $20.95 (0-7660-1993-4). Altman looks at the populations victimized by the Nazis who are often overlooked: Poles, Russians, gypsies, homosexuals, and the disabled. Also use *The Jewish Victims of the Holocaust* (2003), which describes Hitler's genocide of the Jews. (Rev: BL 7/03; SLJ 10/03) [940.53]

7642 Altman, Linda Jacobs. *The Holocaust Ghettos* (8–12). Series: The Holocaust Series. 1998, Enslow LB $20.95 (0-89490-994-0). This volume explains the role that ghettos played in the Nazis' scheme to isolate and control the Jews in preparation for relocation to death camps. (Rev: BR 9–10/98; SLJ 7/98; VOYA 8/98) [940.54]

7643 Altman, Linda Jacobs. *The Holocaust, Hitler, and Nazi Germany* (6–12). Illus. Series: Holocaust Remembered. 1999, Enslow LB $19.95 (0-7660-1230-1). This book explores the many causes and forces, including Hitler and the Nazis, that produced the Holocaust. (Rev: BL 4/1/00; HBG 4/00; SLJ 5/00) [943.08.]

7644 Altshuler, David A. *Hitler's War Against the Jews: A Young Reader's Version of The War Against the Jews, 1933–1945, by Lucy S. Dawidowicz* (7–10). Illus. 1995, Behrman paper $14.95 (0-87441-298-6). The tragic story of Hitler's Final Solution and its aftermath. [940.54]

7645 Ambrose, Stephen E. *The Good Fight: How World War II Was Won* (7–12). Illus. 2001, Simon & Schuster $19.95 (0-689-84361-5). Historian Ambrose presents an appealing and well-written overview of World War II, from its origins through the Marshall Plan, with many photographs, fact boxes, and maps. (Rev: BL 7/01; HBG 10/01; SLJ 5/01; VOYA 6/01) [940.53]

7646 Anflick, Charles. *Resistance: Teen Partisan and Resisters Who Fought Nazi Tyranny* (5–9). Series: Teen Witnesses to the Holocaust. 1999, Rosen LB $26.50 (0-8239-2847-0). This volume celebrates the teenagers who fought against the Nazis in ghettos, concentration camps, inside Germany, and in the lands that the Nazis conquered. (Rev: BL 4/15/98; BR 9–10/99; VOYA 8/99) [940.54]

7647 Anthony, Nathan, and Robert Gardner. *The Bombing of Pearl Harbor in American History* (6–10). Series: In American History. 2001, Enslow LB $20.95 (0-7660-1126-7). This is a well-researched account that covers the bombing of Pearl Harbor by the Japanese in 1941 and its earth-shaking results. (Rev: BL 3/1/01; HBG 10/01) [940.54]

7648 Auerbacher, Inge. *I Am a Star: Child of the Holocaust* (5–7). Illus. 1993, Puffin paper $5.99 (0-14-036401-3). The memoirs of a former child survivor of the Terezin concentration camp in Czechoslovakia. (Rev: BCCB 7–8/87; BL 6/1/87; SLJ 4/87) [940.5]

7649 Axelrod, Toby. *In the Camps: Teens Who Survived the Nazi Concentration Camps* (5–9). Series: Teen Witnesses to the Holocaust. 1999, Rosen LB $18.50 (0-8239-2844-6). These are the stories of teenagers who survived the death camps, their despair and sadness, and the hope they maintained despite the horror around them. (Rev: BL 7/99) [940.54]

7650 Axelrod, Toby. *Rescuers Defying the Nazis: Non-Jewish Teens Who Rescued Jews* (5–8). Series: Teen Witnesses to the Holocaust. 1999, Rosen LB $26.50 (0-8239-2848-9). Inspiring stories of teenage gentiles in Poland, Denmark, and Germany who risked their lives to rescue Jews from the Holocaust. (Rev: BL 7/99; SLJ 8/99) [940.54]

7651 Ayer, Eleanor. *Berlin* (6–12). Series: Cities at War. 1992, Macmillan LB $18.00 (0-02-707800-0). A photoessay on the lives of ordinary people in Berlin during World War II, with eyewitness quotations. (Rev: BL 6/15/92; SLJ 9/92) [940.53]

7652 Ayer, Eleanor. *A Firestorm Unleashed: January 1942 to June 1943* (6–12). Illus. Series: Holocaust. 1997, Blackbirch LB $27.44 (1-56711-204-8). Historical narratives and personal accounts are blended in this story of the Holocaust that covers the first year and a half of American participation in the war. (Rev: BL 10/15/97; BR 1–2/98; HBG 3/98; SLJ 2/98) [940.53]

7653 Ayer, Eleanor. *In the Ghettos: Teens Who Survived the Ghettos of the Holocaust* (5–8). Series: Teens Witnesses to the Holocaust. 1999, Rosen LB $26.50 (0-8239-2845-4). The harrowing stories of courageous teenagers who survived life in the ghettos of Lodz, Theresienstadt, and Warsaw. (Rev: BL 7/99; SLJ 8/99) [940.54]

7654 Ayer, Eleanor. *Inferno: June 1943 to May 1945* (6–12). Illus. Series: Holocaust. 1997, Blackbirch LB $27.44 (1-56711-205-6). During the two-year period covered in this part of the series, Hitler and the Nazis fully implement their plans to destroy European Jews and the death camps reach their peak of activity. (Rev: BL 10/15/97; BR 1–2/98; HBG 3/98; SLJ 2/98) [940.53]

7655 Ayer, Eleanor, et al. *Parallel Journeys* (7–12). 1995, Atheneum $16.00 (0-689-31830-8). Personal narratives in alternative chapters of a Jewish woman and a former ardent member of the Hitler Youth, who grew up a few miles from each other. (Rev: BL 5/15/95*; SLJ 6/95) [943.086]

7656 Bachrach, Susan D. *Tell Them We Remember: The Story of the Holocaust* (5–9). 1994, Little, Brown $21.95 (0-316-69264-6). A photohistory focusing on the young who struggled through the brutality of the Holocaust following the destruction of their world of family and friends. (Rev: BL 7/94*; SLJ 11/94; VOYA 12/94) [940.54]

7657 Ballard, Robert D. *Exploring the Bismarck* (5–8). Illus. 1991, Scholastic $15.95 (0-590-44268-6). This is an account of the history and rediscovery of the German battleship *Bismarck*, which was sunk more than 50 years ago. (Rev: BL 1/1/91; SLJ 8/91) [943]

7658 Bard, Mitchell, ed. *The Nuremberg Trial* (8–12). Series: History Firsthand. 2002, Gale LB $31.20 (0-7377-1075-6); paper $19.95 (0-7377-1076-4). Well-introduced primary documents give background and insight to the war crimes trial following World War II. (Rev: BL 8/02; SLJ 7/02) [341.6]

7659 Bard, Mitchell G., ed. *The Holocaust* (6–12). Illus. Series: Complete History Of. 2001, Greenhaven LB $99.00 (0-7377-0373-3). This anthology of more than 90 entries presents a well-organized and balanced look at the Holocaust. (Rev: BL 11/1/01; SLJ 8/01) [940.53]

7660 Bard, Mitchell G., ed. *The Holocaust* (7–12). Series: Turning Points in World History. 2001, Greenhaven LB $22.96 (0-7377-0576-0); paper $14.96 (0-7377-0575-2). The Jewish genocide in Nazi Germany is explored in an anthology of essays, each of which examines a different aspect of this terrible period in history. (Rev: BL 6/1–15/01) [940.54]

7661 Bitton-Jackson, Livia. *I Have Lived a Thousand Years: Growing Up in the Holocaust* (7–12). 1997, Simon & Schuster $17.00 (0-689-81022-9). Abridged from the author's adult book, this is the story of a 13-year-old Hungarian Jewish girl and how she survived Auschwitz. (Rev: BL 3/15/97; BR 9–10/97; SLJ 5/97; VOYA 6/97) [940.54]

7662 Black, Wallace B., and Jean F. Blashfield. *Bataan and Corregidor* (5–7). Illus. Series: World War II 50th Anniversary. 1991, Macmillan LB $12.95 (0-89686-557-6). Using documentary photographs, this book examines the major events in the struggle over the Philippines in World War II. (Rev: BL 12/1/91; SLJ 2/92) [940.54]

7663 Black, Wallace B., and Jean F. Blashfield. *Battle of Britain* (5–7). Illus. Series: World War II 50th Anniversary. 1991, Macmillan LB $12.95 (0-89686-553-3). The story of Britain's valiant stand against the German power. Also use *Blitzkrieg* (1991). (Rev: BL 6/15/91; SLJ 9/91) [940.53]

7664 Black, Wallace B., and Jean F. Blashfield. *Battle of the Atlantic* (5–7). Illus. Series: World War II 50th Anniversary. 1991, Macmillan LB $12.95 (0-89686-558-4). The war in the Atlantic Ocean during World War II, when the Allies tried to keep the seas open for the movement of troops and supplies, is retold in text and pictures. (Rev: BL 12/1/91; SLJ 2/92) [940.54]

7665 Black, Wallace B., and Jean F. Blashfield. *Battle of the Bulge* (5–7). Illus. Series: World War II 50th Anniversary. 1993, Macmillan LB $12.95 (0-89686-568-1). This account describes Hitler's desperate offensive and his gamble to split the Allied army in two. (Rev: BL 4/15/93) [940.54]

7666 Black, Wallace B., and Jean F. Blashfield. *Bombing Fortress Europe* (5–7). Illus. Series: World War II 50th Anniversary. 1992, Macmillan LB $12.95 (0-89686-562-2). The thrilling, heroic exploits of British and American airmen and their war over the skies of Europe are retold in this illustrated account. (Rev: BL 8/92; SLJ 1/93) [940.54]

7667 Black, Wallace B., and Jean F. Blashfield. *D-Day* (5–7). Illus. Series: World War II 50th Anniversary. 1992, Macmillan LB $12.95 (0-89686-566-5). The fateful day when the Allied forces invaded France during World War II. (Rev: BL 2/1/93; SLJ 4/93) [940.54]

7668 Black, Wallace B., and Jean F. Blashfield. *Desert Warfare* (5–7). Illus. Series: World War II 50th Anniversary. 1992, Macmillan LB $12.95 (0-89686-561-4). This account chronicles the Allied campaigns in North Africa against the desert forces of the Germans and Italians. (Rev: BL 8/92; SLJ 1/93) [940.54]

7669 Black, Wallace B., and Jean F. Blashfield. *Flattops at War* (5–7). Illus. Series: World War II 50th Anniversary. 1991, Macmillan LB $12.95 (0-89686-559-2). The use of aircraft carriers in the Pacific area of combat is described in this account. (Rev: BL 12/1/91) [940.54]

7670 Black, Wallace B., and Jean F. Blashfield. *Guadalcanal* (5–7). Illus. Series: World War II 50th Anniversary. 1992, Macmillan LB $12.95 (0-89686-560-6). The war in the South Pacific, as revealed in the battle of Guadalcanal during 1942–1943, is retold in text and pictures. (Rev: BL 8/92; SLJ 1/93) [940.54]

7671 Black, Wallace B., and Jean F. Blashfield. *Hiroshima and the Atomic Bomb* (5–7). Illus. Series: World War II 50th Anniversary. 1993, Macmillan LB $12.95 (0-89686-571-1). This is a chronicle of President Truman's decision to drop the atomic bomb on Hiroshima and Nagasaki and the results of that decision. (Rev: BL 4/15/93; SLJ 10/93) [940.54]

7672 Black, Wallace B., and Jean F. Blashfield. *Invasion of Italy* (5–7). Illus. Series: World War II

50th Anniversary. 1992, Macmillan LB $12.95 (0-89686-565-7). This book describes the campaign by the Allied forces to liberate Italy from the Axis. (Rev: BL 2/1/93; SLJ 4/93) [940.54]

7673 Black, Wallace B., and Jean F. Blashfield. *Island Hopping in the Pacific* (5–7). Illus. Series: World War II 50th Anniversary. 1992, Macmillan LB $12.95 (0-89686-567-3). The campaign to retake Pacific islands from the Japanese is described in brief text and many photographs. (Rev: BL 2/1/93; SLJ 4/93) [940.54]

7674 Black, Wallace B., and Jean F. Blashfield. *Iwo Jima and Okinawa* (5–7). Illus. Series: World War II 50th Anniversary. 1993, Macmillan LB $12.95 (0-89686-569-X). The story of the savage battles that the Allies faced while taking these two islands from the Japanese during World War II. (Rev: BL 4/15/93; SLJ 10/93) [940.54]

7675 Black, Wallace B., and Jean F. Blashfield. *Jungle Warfare* (5–7). Illus. Series: World War II 50th Anniversary. 1992, Macmillan LB $12.95 (0-89686-563-0). This generously illustrated account re-creates the World War II campaigns waged in the jungle of southeastern Asia. (Rev: BL 8/92; SLJ 1/93) [940.54]

7676 Black, Wallace B., and Jean F. Blashfield. *Pearl Harbor!* (5–7). Illus. Series: World War II 50th Anniversary. 1991, Macmillan LB $4.95 (0-89686-555-X). The Japanese surprise attack that shocked the United States into World War II. (Rev: BL 6/15/91; SLJ 9/91) [940.53]

7677 Black, Wallace B., and Jean F. Blashfield. *Russia at War* (5–7). Illus. Series: World War II 50th Anniversary. 1991, Macmillan LB $12.95 (0-89686-556-8). Describes the role played by Russia in World War II and how they stopped the Germans in spite of terrible losses, with many documentary photographs. (Rev: BL 12/1/91; SLJ 2/92) [940.54]

7678 Black, Wallace B., and Jean F. Blashfield. *Victory in Europe* (5–7). Illus. Series: World War II 50th Anniversary. 1993, Macmillan LB $12.95 (0-89686-570-3). This account outlines the events that led to the Allied victory in Europe including the Russian advance and the fall of Berlin. (Rev: BL 4/15/93) [940.54]

7679 Black, Wallace B., and Jean F. Blashfield. *War Behind the Lines* (5–7). Illus. Series: World War II 50th Anniversary. 1992, Macmillan LB $12.95 (0-89686-564-9). This book tells about the many gallant underground movements that tried to undermine the Fascist powers from within. (Rev: BL 2/1/93; SLJ 4/93) [940.54]

7680 Bliven, Bruce, Jr. *Story of D-Day, June 6, 1944* (6–8). 1963, Random $8.99 (0-394-90362-5). An accurate but simple hour-by-hour account of the Allied invasion of Normandy. [940.53]

7681 Boas, Jacob. *We Are Witnesses: The Diaries of Five Teenagers Who Died in the Holocaust* (7–12). 1995, Holt $17.95 (0-8050-3702-0). Boas, born in 1943 in a Nazi camp, tells about being a Holocaust survivor and of the deaths of five other young inmates. (Rev: BL 5/15/95*) [940.53]

7682 Boraks-Nemetz, Lillian, and Irene N. Watts, eds. *Tapestry of Hope: Holocaust Writing for Young People* (6–12). 2003, Tundra $24.99 (0-88776-638-2). Two Holocaust survivors have collected fiction, poetry, drama, and nonfiction excerpts that detail the experiences of those who went into hiding, were sent to the camps, joined the resistance movement, and made their way to other countries. (Rev: BL 6/1–15/03; HBG 10/03; SLJ 8/03; VOYA 10/03) [810.8]

7683 Brager, Bruce L. *The Trial of Adolf Eichmann: The Holocaust on Trial* (8–12). Series: Famous Trials. 1999, Lucent LB $27.45 (1-56006-469-2). The story of the search for the infamous war criminal and of his trial in Israel in 1961, during which the horror of the Holocaust was relived. (Rev: BL 5/1/99; SLJ 8/99) [364.15]

7684 Brash, Sarah, ed. *World War II* (7–12). Illus. Series: The American Story. 1997, Time-Life Books $19.95 (0-7835-6253-5). The causes, events, and outcomes of World War II are covered in this well-illustrated account that emphasizes American participation. (Rev: BL 5/15/97) [940.53]

7685 Butterfield, Moira. *Going to War in World War II* (5–7). Illus. 2001, Watts LB $24.00 (0-531-14596-4). Soldiers, weapons, and military strategies of World War II are briefly presented with many illustrations and a timeline. (Rev: SLJ 10/01) [940.54]

7686 Byers, Ann. *The Holocaust Camps* (8–12). Series: The Holocaust Remembered. 1998, Enslow LB $18.95 (0-89490-955-9). This work traces the evolution of political prison camps to labor camps and eventually to death camps during the Nazi regime. (Rev: BR 9–10/98; VOYA 8/98) [940.54]

7687 Cretzmeyer, Stacy. *Your Name Is Renée: Ruth Kapp Hartz's Story as a Hidden Child in Nazi-Occupied France* (5–8). 2003, Bt. Bound $22.50 (0-613-56879-6). The story of a German Jewish family living in France during the Holocaust, how they survived, and how young Ruth hid in an orphanage run by Catholic nuns. (Rev: BCCB 7–8/99; SLJ 8/99) [940.54]

7688 Cross, Robin. *Children and War* (4–7). Illus. Series: World War II. 1994, Thomson Learning LB $24.26 (1-56847-180-7). True case histories of children in various circumstances during World War II, including in a gulag, the resistance movement, and a death camp. (Rev: BL 12/15/94; SLJ 2/95) [940.53]

7689 Daily, Robert. *The Code Talkers: American Indians in World War II* (4–8). Illus. Series: First

Books. 1995, Watts LB $23.00 (0-531-20190-2). Describes the roles that Native Americans played in World War II, both as soldiers and as translators. (Rev: SLJ 10/95) [940.54]

7690 DeAngelis, Therese. *Pearl Harbor: Deadly Surprise Attack* (6–9). Illus. Series: American Disasters. 2002, Enslow LB $18.95 (0-7660-1783-4). A concise account of the attack that brought the United States into World War II. (Rev: BL 1/1–15/03; HBG 3/03; SLJ 10/02) [940.54]

7691 Devaney, John. *America Fights the Tide: 1942* (6–10). 1991, Walker $17.95 (0-8027-6997-7). Using a diary format and anecdotal accounts, this volume focuses on the United States' entry into World War II in both the European and the Pacific theaters. (Rev: BL 10/15/91; SLJ 10/91) [940.54]

7692 Devaney, John. *America Goes to War: 1941* (5–8). 1991, Walker LB $17.85 (0-8027-6980-2). An illustrated, datelined, day-by-day account that covers personal and public events of America's first year of World War II. (Rev: BL 10/1/91; SLJ 8/91) [940.53]

7693 Devaney, John. *America on the Attack: 1943* (6–10). Series: Walker's World War II. 1992, Walker LB $18.85 (0-8027-8195-0). This well-illustrated account describes America's active participation in World War II once the war effort got underway. (Rev: BL 12/1/92) [940.53]

7694 Devaney, John. *America Storms the Beaches: 1944* (6–10). Series: World War II. 1993, Walker LB $18.85 (0-8027-8245-0). The story of D-day and the other invasions of Europe by the Allies in 1944 that spelled the beginning of the end of Nazi Germany. (Rev: BL 12/15/93; SLJ 12/93; VOYA 2/94) [940.54]

7695 Drucker, Olga L. *Kindertransport* (5–8). 1995, Holt paper $8.95 (0-8050-4251-2). A true account of a Jewish girl sent from Germany to live in England until she could join her parents in New York City in 1945. (Rev: BCCB 1/93; SLJ 11/92) [940.54]

7696 Dudley, William, ed. *World War II* (7–12). Series: Opposing Viewpoints in American History. 1996, Greenhaven LB $32.45 (1-56510-528-1); paper $16.20 (1-56510-527-3). A thought-provoking anthology of different viewpoints on various aspects of World War II, representative of that time, including whether the United States should enter the war, the use of the atomic bomb, women's roles, and the internment of Japanese Americans but not German Americans or Italian Americans. (Rev: SLJ 3/97) [940.54]

7697 Durrett, Deanne. *Unsung Heroes of World War II: The Story of the Navajo Code Talkers* (7–12). Illus. Series: Library of American Indian History. 1998, Facts on File $25.00 (0-8160-3603-9). The story of the gallant Native American servicemen who developed a unique, unbreakable code based on

the Navajo's complex, inflection-sensitive language, and transmitted and translated more than 800 messages in 48 hours without error during the battle of Iwo Jima. (Rev: BL 11/1/98; SLJ 1/99) [940.548673]

7698 Dvorson, Alexa. *The Hitler Youth: Marching Toward Madness* (5–9). Illus. Series: Teen Witnesses to the Holocaust. 1999, Rosen LB $26.50 (0-8239-2783-0). This volume describes how thousands of German boys and girls joined the Hitler Youth, why they were seduced into obeying the Nazis, and how their dreams were eventually shattered. (Rev: BL 4/15/99; BR 9–10/99) [943.086]

7699 Fisch, Robert O. *Light from the Yellow Star: A Lesson of Love from the Holocaust* (7–12). Illus. 1996, Univ. of Minnesota Pr. $14.95 (1-885116-00-4); paper $9.95 (0-9644896-0-0). A biographical account that uses the author's abstract paintings to tell about his childhood in Budapest and his Holocaust death camp experiences. (Rev: BL 4/15/96) [940.53]

7700 Fox, Anne L., and Eva Abraham-Podietz. *Ten Thousand Children: True Stories Told by Children Who Escaped the Holocaust on the Kindertransport* (5–8). Illus. 1998, Behrman paper $12.95 (0-87441-648-5). The moving stories of 21 survivors who were part of the rescue operation known as the Kindertransport that took 10,000 Jewish children from Nazi-occupied Europe to freedom during late 1938 and 1939. (Rev: BL 1/1–15/99) [940.53]

7701 Freeman, Charles. *The Rise of the Nazis* (7–12). Series: New Perspectives. 1998, Raintree Steck-Vaughn $28.54 (0-8172-5015-8). Presents differing views on Hitler and the Nazi Party as expressed by German politicians, leaders, and ordinary citizens. (Rev: BL 3/15/98; BR 1–2/99; HBG 9/98; SLJ 7/98) [940.54]

7702 Fremon, David K. *The Holocaust Heroes* (6–10). Series: Holocaust Remembered. 1998, Enslow LB $20.95 (0-7660-1046-5). This account of the Holocaust focuses on Resistance fighters, such as the people of the Warsaw Ghetto, and people including Raoul Wallenberg and the Danish nation who took risks to help Jews escape. (Rev: BL 9/15/98; BR 1–2/99; HBG 3/99; SLJ 12/98) [940.5318]

7703 Galloway, Priscilla, ed. *Too Young to Fight: Memories from Our Youth During World War II* (6–12). 2000, Stoddart $22.95 (0-7737-3190-3). Eleven Canadian authors of books for young people describe what it was like growing up on the home front during World War II. (Rev: BL 5/1/00; SLJ 7/00) [940.53.]

7704 Giddens, Sandra. *Escape: Teens Who Escaped the Holocaust to Freedom* (5–9). Series: Teen Witnesses to the Holocaust. 1999, Rosen LB $26.50 (0-8239-2843-8). This volume focuses on the ordeals of four Jewish teens who were able to elude the

Nazis during the Holocaust. (Rev: BL 4/15/98; BR 9–10/99; VOYA 8/99) [940.54]

7705 Gies, Miep, and Alison L. Gold. *Anne Frank Remembered: The Story of Miep Gies, Who Helped to Hide the Frank Family* (8–12). Illus. 1987, Simon & Schuster paper $14.00 (0-671-66234-1). The story of the woman who helped the Frank family during World War II and of the Resistance movement in the Netherlands. (Rev: BL 4/1/87; SLJ 11/87; VOYA 12/87) [940.53]

7706 Gonzales, Doreen. *The Manhattan Project and the Atomic Bomb in American History* (6–12). Illus. Series: American History. 2000, Enslow LB $19.95 (0-89490-879-0). This work traces the events that produced the atomic bomb, introduces the people involved, and gives details on the impact of its use during World War II. (Rev: BL 1/1–15/00; HBG 9/00; SLJ 9/00) [355.8]

7707 Gottfried, Ted. *Children of the Slaughter: Young People of the Holocaust* (7–12). Illus. Series: Holocaust. 2001, Twenty-First Century LB $28.90 (0-7613-1716-3). Gottfried provides a clear and thought-provoking account of the suffering of children at the hands of the Nazis, looking not only at the genocide of Jewish children but also at the experiences of German youngsters forced into Hitler Youth, spying on their families, and dying in battle. Also use *Heroes of the Holocaust* (2001), which tells the stories of heroic rescuers. (Rev: BL 5/15/01; HBG 10/01; SLJ 6/01) [940.53]

7708 Gottfried, Ted. *Displaced Persons: The Liberation and Abuse of Holocaust Survivors* (6–12). Illus. 2001, Twenty-First Century LB $28.90 (0-7613-1924-7). Survivors of the Holocaust went on to suffer many indignities and rejections, as Gottfried shows in this account of continued racism, displaced persons camps, and denial of shelter by countries including the United States. (Rev: BL 9/1/01; HBG 3/02) [940]

7709 Gottfried, Ted. *Martyrs to Madness: The Victims of the Holocaust* (8–12). Illus. Series: The Holocaust. 2000, Twenty-First Century LB $21.68 (0-7613-1715-5). After a brief overview of the Holocaust, the author devotes separate chapters to each group of victims including Jews, the Slavs, gypsies, homosexuals, and POWs. (Rev: BL 7/00; HBG 10/01; SLJ 12/00; VOYA 6/01) [940.53]

7710 Gottfried, Ted. *Nazi Germany: The Face of Tyranny* (8–12). Illus. Series: The Holocaust. 2000, Twenty-First Century LB $21.68 (0-7613-1714-7). Gottfried describes the Nazis' rise to power, their expansion through Europe, and the systematic attacks against Jews and other groups. (Rev: BL 7/00; HBG 10/01; SLJ 12/00; VOYA 6/01) [940.53]

7711 Grant, R. G. *Hiroshima and Nagasaki* (7–12). Illus. Series: New Perspectives. 1998, Raintree Steck-Vaughn $28.54 (0-8172-5013-1). This account of the dropping of atomic bombs on Japan examines the different viewpoints of the scientists, politicians, and air crews involved, and the people who survived it. (Rev: BL 3/15/98; BR 1–2/99; HBG 9/98) [940.54]

7712 Grant, R. G. *The Holocaust* (7–12). Series: New Perspectives. 1998, Raintree Steck-Vaughn $19.98 (0-8172-5016-6). The story of the Holocaust, one of history's darkest moments, as shaped by the German perpetrators, witnessed by onlookers, and recalled by survivors. (Rev: BL 3/15/98; BR 1–2/99; HBG 9/98; SLJ 7/98) [940.54]

7713 Green, Robert. *"Vive La France": The French Resistance During World War II* (5–8). Illus. Series: First Books. 1995, Watts LB $23.00 (0-531-20192-9). The story of the role played by the French underground during World War II. (Rev: SLJ 10/95) [940.54]

7714 Greenfeld, Howard. *After the Holocaust* (6–12). Illus. 2001, Greenwillow $15.95 (0-688-17752-2). Greenfeld tells the stories of eight Jewish survivors of the Holocaust, describing the conditions in the camps for displaced persons, the search for a new home, and the very different ways in which people react to adversity. (Rev: BCCB 1/02; BL 10/1/01*; HB 11–12/01; HBG 3/02; SLJ 11/01*; VOYA 12/01) [804.48]

7715 Greenfeld, Howard. *The Hidden Children* (5–10). 1993, Ticknor $18.00 (0-395-66074-2). This account of what it was like to be a Jewish child hiding from the Nazis in World War II includes painful personal narratives of survivors. (Rev: BL 1/1/94*; SLJ 5/94*; VOYA 6/94) [940.53]

7716 Grossman, Mendel. *My Secret Camera: Life in the Lodz Ghetto* (4–8). Illus. 2000, Harcourt $16.00 (0-15-202306-2). Using a hidden camera, a young Jewish man recorded life in the Lodz ghetto in Poland; he later died during a forced march in 1945. Sixteen of his photographs are reproduced here with a brief text. (Rev: BCCB 5/00; BL 4/1/00; HB 5–6/00; HBG 10/00; SLJ 5/00; VOYA 2/01) [940.53]

7717 Handler, Andrew, and Susan V. Meschel, eds. *Young People Speak: Surviving the Holocaust in Hungary* (7–12). 1993, Watts paper $24.00 (0-531-11044-3). Memoirs of 11 Holocaust survivors who were children in Hungary during the Nazi occupation at the end of World War II. (Rev: BL 6/1–15/93; SLJ 7/93; VOYA 10/93) [940.53]

7718 Hanmer, Trudy J. *Leningrad* (6–12). Series: Cities at War. 1992, Macmillan $18.00 (0-02-742615-7). The story of the city of Leningrad during World War II and the terrible siege that destroyed a large percentage of the city and its inhabitants. (Rev: BL 10/15/92) [947]

7719 Hargrove, Hondon. *Buffalo Soldiers in Italy: Black Americans in World War II* (8–12). 1985, McFarland LB $39.95 (0-89950-116-8). A history of the last all-black U.S. army division and its record during World War II. (Rev: BR 9–10/85) [940.53]

7720 Harris, Jacqueline L. *The Tuskegee Airmen: Black Heroes of World War II* (6–9). Illus. 1996, Dillon $13.95 (0-382-39215-9); paper $7.95 (0-382-39217-5). The story of how African American fliers in the service fought prejudice and eventually formed the extraordinary all-black Fighter Squadron during World War II. (Rev: BL 9/1/96; SLJ 9/96) [940.54]

7721 Hatt, Christine. *World War II: 1939–45* (6–9). Series: Documenting History. 2001, Watts LB $22.00 (0-531-14612-X). A visual and balanced look at the causes and key battles of the war, with material on the homefront, propaganda, and the role of women and with excerpts from primary documents. (Rev: BR 3/02; SLJ 12/01) [940.53]

7722 Hills, C. A. R. *The Second World War* (7–12). Illus. 1986, David & Charles $19.95 (0-7134-4531-9). A brief but comprehensive history of World War II as seen through the eyes of its leaders. (Rev: SLJ 11/86) [940.53]

7723 Hipperson, Carol Edgemon. *The Belly Gunner* (6–9). Illus. 2001, Twenty-First Century LB $27.90 (0-7613-1873-9). This is the absorbing story, told in the first person and enhanced by informative side notes, of one man's experiences in World War II as a B-17 gunner and in a German prison camp. (Rev: HBG 3/02; SLJ 8/01) [940.54]

7724 Hook, Jason. *Hiroshima: August 6, 1945* (6–8). Series: Days That Shook the World. 2003, Raintree Steck-Vaughn LB $27.12 (0-7398-5234-5). With many color and black-and-white photographs, this slim volume looks at the development of the atom bomb, the circumstances that led to its use, the destruction it caused in Hiroshima, and the aftermath. (Rev: HBG 10/03; SLJ 10/03) [940.54]

7725 Immell, Myra H., ed. *World War II* (7–12). Series: Turning Points in World History. 2001, Greenhaven LB $31.20 (0-7377-0699-6); paper $19.95 (0-7377-0698-8). This collection of scholarly documents and essays explores various aspects of the Second World War. (Rev: BL 3/15/02) [940.54]

7726 Ippisch, Hanneke. *Sky: A True Story of Resistance During World War II* (6–10). Illus. 1996, Simon & Schuster $18.00 (0-689-80508-X). An autobiographical account by the author who, as a teenage girl in 1943, joined the Dutch underground resistance movement and, after participating in many dangerous missions against the Nazis, was caught by the Germans and sent to prison. (Rev: BL 4/15/96; BR 1–2/97; SLJ 6/96; VOYA 8/96) [940.53]

7727 Isserman, Maurice. *World War II* (7–12). Series: America at War. 1991, Facts on File $25.00 (0-8160-2374-3). The major battles and personalities of World War II, events leading to war, and discussion of changes following the conflict. (Rev: BL 10/15/91; SLJ 8/92) [940.53]

7728 Jones, Catherine. *Navajo Code Talkers: Native American Heroes* (6–10). 1998, Tudor $12.95 (0-936389-51-6); paper $7.95 (0-936389-52-4). This is the story of the Navajo Code Talkers of the Marine Corps who, during World War II in the Pacific, used their secret language to communicate in a code that neither the Japanese or Americans could decipher. (Rev: SLJ 4/98) [940.54]

7729 Jones, Steven L. *The Red Tails: World War II's Tuskegee Airmen* (4–8). Illus. Series: Cover-to-Cover. 2002, Perfection Learning $15.95 (0-7569-0251-7); paper $8.95 (0-7891-5487-0). The story of the heroic African American squadron of World War II fighter pilots, their successful missions, and the prejudices they faced. (Rev: BL 5/1/02) [940.5404]

7730 Keeley, Jennifer. *Life in the Hitler Youth* (7–12). Illus. Series: Way People Live. 1999, Lucent LB $18.96 (1-56006-613-X). A compelling narrative using many eyewitness accounts of the training and indoctrination of Hitler's Youth and of the part they played in World War II. (Rev: BL 1/1–15/00; HBG 9/00; SLJ 3/00) [943.086.]

7731 Kodama, Tatsuharu. *Shin's Tricycle* (5–8). Trans. by Kazuko Hokumen-Jones. 1995, Walker LB $16.85 (0-8027-8376-7). A father recalls the life of his young son, who was killed in the bombing of Hiroshima. (Rev: BCCB 12/95; BL 9/1/95*; SLJ 12/95) [940.54]

7732 Kopf, Hedda Rosner. *Understanding Anne Frank's The Diary of a Young Girl: A Student Casebook to Issues, Sources, and Historical Documents* (7–12). 1997, Greenwood $45.00 (0-313-29607-3). In addition to examining Anne Frank's diary as literature, this collection of materials supplies great amounts of background information on the Holocaust, anti-Semitism, the Frank family, and World War II. (Rev: SLJ 3/98) [940.54]

7733 Kronenwetter, Michael. *London* (6–12). Series: Cities at War. 1992, Macmillan $18.00 (0-02-751050-6). A photoessay on the lives of ordinary people in London during World War II, with eyewitness quotations. (Rev: BL 6/15/92; SLJ 9/92) [942.1084]

7734 Kuhn, Betsy. *Angels of Mercy* (5–8). Illus. 1999, Simon & Schuster $18.00 (0-689-82044-5). A series of narratives on courage and bravery gives us a fascinating look at the contributions of nurses in World War II. (Rev: BCCB 12/99; BL 10/15/99; HBG 3/00; SLJ 11/99; VOYA 4/00) [940.54]

7735 Kustanowitz, Esther. *The Hidden Children of the Holocaust: Teens Who Hid from the Nazis* (5–9). Series: Teen Witnesses to the Holocaust. 1999, Rosen LB $26.50 (0-8239-2562-5). Many first-person narratives are used in this account of teenage Jews who hid in homes, barns, and forests or disguised themselves as non-Jews to escape the Nazis. (Rev: BL 7/99; SLJ 8/99) [940.54]

7736 Lace, William W. *Hitler and the Nazis* (6–12). Series: American War Library. 2000, Lucent LB $18.96 (1-56006-372-6). The story of the rise of Adolf Hitler and the emergence of the Nazi Party. (Rev: BL 4/15/00; HBG 9/00) [940.54]

7737 Landau, Elaine, ed. *Holocaust Memories: Speaking the Truth* (6–9). Illus. Series: In Their Own Voices. 2001, Watts LB $23.50 (0-531-11742-1). Landau combines survivors' stories of Kristallnacht, the Warsaw Ghetto rebellion, and concentration camps with background information and black-and-white photographs to present a moving whole that includes a story of her own grandfather. (Rev: BL 9/1/01; SLJ 9/01; VOYA 4/02) [940.53]

7738 Landau, Elaine. *The Warsaw Ghetto Uprising* (7–10). 1992, Macmillan LB $19.00 (0-02-751392-0). Recounts the horrors of the month-long battles between Nazis and Jews in 1943 Poland. (Rev: BL 2/15/93) [940.53]

7739 Landau, Elaine. *We Survived the Holocaust* (7–10). 1991, Watts paper $24.00 (0-531-11115-6). A series of personal accounts of survivors who were children during World War II that presents a picture of ethnic and religious persecution and courageous endurance. (Rev: BL 9/15/91; SLJ 10/91) [940.53]

7740 Langley, Wanda. *Flying Higher: The Women Airforce Service Pilots of World War II* (5–8). Illus. 2002, Linnet $25.00 (0-208-02506-5). The women who flew in World War II gained little glory for performing many vital tasks; this arresting volume focuses on the director of the service, Jacqueline Cochran, and one of the pilots. (Rev: BL 11/1/02; HBG 3/03; SLJ 8/02; VOYA 12/02) [940.54]

7741 Lawson, Don. *The French Resistance* (5–9). 1984, Messner LB $8.79 (0-671-50832-6). The story of the many gallant French men and women who defied death to oppose the German forces that occupied their country. [940.53]

7742 Lawton, Clive. *The Story of the Holocaust* (5–8). Illus. 2000, Watts LB $26.00 (0-531-14524-7). A graphically illustrated account of the rise of anti-Semitism in Germany, a trend that culminated in the horror of the concentration camps. (Rev: BL 7/00) [940.53]

7743 Leapman, Michael. *Witnesses to War: Eight True-Life Stories of Nazi Persecution* (8–12). Illus. 1998, Viking $16.99 (0-670-87386-1). Eight case histories of children who suffered at the hands of the Nazis, some by being selected for "Germanization" and others who survived death camps and Nazi massacres. (Rev: BL 10/1/98; HBG 3/99; SLJ 11/98; VOYA 12/98) [940.53]

7744 Levine, Ellen. *Darkness over Denmark: The Danish Resistance and the Rescue of the Jews* (6–12). Illus. 2000, Holiday $19.95 (0-8234-1447-7).

This is a straightforward history that uses many first-person accounts to relate the remarkable efforts of the Danish people to save their Jewish citizens during World War II. (Rev: BL 7/00; HB 9–10/00; HBG 10/00; SLJ 8/00; VOYA 2/01) [940.531809489]

7745 Levine, Karen. *Hana's Suitcase* (5–8). Illus. 2003, Albert Whitman $15.95 (0-8075-3148-0). A Japanese curator of a Holocaust exhibit traces the owner of a suitcase and learns the story of young Hana, who died in Auschwitz. (Rev: BL 3/15/03; HB 5–6/03; HBG 10/03) [940.53]

7746 Levy, Pat. *Causes* (5–9). Series: The Holocaust. 2001, Raintree Steck-Vaughn LB $28.54 (0-7398-3257-3). Levy discusses the causes of the Holocaust, looking at historical, religious, political, social, and economic factors. Also use *The Death Camps* (2002). (Rev: HBG 10/02; SLJ 2/02; VOYA 4/02) [940.5318]

7747 Lobel, Anita. *No Pretty Pictures: A Child of War* (6–12). 1998, Greenwillow $17.99 (0-688-15935-4). The author, today a successful illustrator, tells the gripping story of her childhood during World War II in Poland — five years in hiding beginning at the age of five, then her capture and transport, with her younger brother disguised as a girl, to a concentration camp. (Rev: BCCB 10/98; BL 8/98; HB 11–12/98; HBG 3/99; SLJ 9/98; VOYA 2/99) [940.5318092]

7748 Lord, Walter. *Day of Infamy* (8–12). Illus. 1998, NTC paper $12.99 (1-85326-670-1). An hour-by-hour re-creation of the attack on Pearl Harbor with extensive background information. [940.54]

7749 McGowen, Tom. *Carrier War: Aircraft Carriers in World War II* (5–7). Series: Military Might. 2001, Twenty-First Century LB $26.90 (0-7613-1808-9). An introduction to the importance of aircraft carriers in World War II, with coverage of Pearl Harbor and major battles in the Pacific. (Rev: HBG 10/01; SLJ 6/01) [940.54]

7750 McGowen, Tom. *Germany's Lightning War: Panzer Divisions of World War II* (5–8). Series: Military Might. 1999, Twenty-First Century LB $26.90 (0-7613-1511-X). After a general history of tank warfare, this account focuses on the Germans' Panzer tank divisions and the part they played in World War II. (Rev: HBG 3/00; SLJ 9/99) [940.54]

7751 McGowen, Tom. *Sink the Bismarck: Germany's Super-Battleship of World War II* (5–8). Series: Military Might. 1999, Twenty-First Century LB $26.90 (0-7613-1510-1). A history of German sea power during World War II and the many (eventually successful) British efforts to sink the *Bismarck*. (Rev: HBG 3/00; SLJ 9/99) [940.54]

7752 McKain, Mark, ed. *Making and Using the Atomic Bomb* (8–12). Series: History Firsthand. 2003, Gale LB $25.96 (0-7377-1412-3); paper $16.96 (0-7377-1413-1). A collection of documents relating to the discovery of fission, the Manhattan Project, the decision to use the bomb and the choice of targets, and stories of survivors of Hiroshima and Nagasaki. (Rev: SLJ 7/03) [355.8]

7753 McKissack, Patricia, and Fredrick McKissack. *Red-Tail Angels: The Story of the Tuskegee Airmen of World War II* (6–8). Illus. 1995, Walker LB $20.85 (0-8027-8293-0). A carefully researched account of the formation and training of the 332nd Fighter Group of African American aviators and their exploits during World War II in the North African and European theaters of war. (Rev: BL 2/15/96*; SLJ 2/96; VOYA 4/96) [940.54]

7754 McNeese, Tim. *The Attack on Pearl Harbor* (5–8). Illus. Series: First Battles. 2001, Morgan Reynolds LB $21.95 (1-883846-78-1). This book details the 1941 attack on Pearl Harbor and explains the conditions in Japan that led to the assault. (Rev: BL 10/1/01; HBG 3/02; SLJ 1/02; VOYA 12/01) [940.54]

7755 Maruki, Toshi. *Hiroshima No Pika* (7–10). Illus. 1982, Lothrop $17.99 (0-688-01297-3). One family's experiences during the day the bomb dropped on Hiroshima told in text and moving illustrations by the author. (Rev: BL 3/87) [940.54]

7756 Marx, Trish. *Echoes of World War II* (5–8). Illus. 1994, Lerner LB $19.93 (0-8225-4898-4). The true stories of six children around the world whose lives were changed dramatically by World War II. (Rev: BCCB 5/94; BL 9/15/94; SLJ 5/94) [940.53]

7757 Meltzer, Milton. *Never to Forget: The Jews of the Holocaust* (8–12). 1976, HarperCollins LB $15.89 (0-06-024175-6). A history of the murder of 6 million Jews and of anti-Semitism. [940.54]

7758 Meltzer, Milton. *Rescue: The Story of How Gentiles Saved Jews in the Holocaust* (6–9). 1988, HarperCollins paper $7.99 (0-06-446117-3). The uplifting story of those courageous few who helped save Jews from Nazi death camps. (Rev: BL 10/1/88; BR 1–2/89; SLJ 8/88; VOYA 8/88) [940.53]

7759 Milman, Barbara. *Light in the Shadows* (5–9). Illus. 1997, Jonathan David paper $14.95 (0-8246-0401-6). Illustrated with powerful woodcut prints, this book tells the story of five Holocaust survivors. (Rev: BL 11/15/97) [940.53]

7760 Nardo, Don. *World War II in the Pacific* (7–10). Series: World History. 2002, Gale LB $27.45 (1-59018-015-1). From Pearl Harbor to Japan's surrender, this is a history of the battles, decisions, and important people involved in the war in the Pacific. (Rev: BL 8/02) [940.54]

7761 Nathan, Amy. *Yankee Doodle Gals: Women Pilots of World War II* (6–9). Illus. 2001, National Geographic $21.00 (0-7922-8216-7). The fascinating story of the Women's Airforce Service Pilots (WASPs) of World War II, with photographs and

biographical information on individuals. (Rev: BL 12/15/01; VOYA 8/02) [940.54]

7762 Nelson, Pete. *Left for Dead: A Young Man's Search for Justice for the U.S.S. Indianapolis* (6–12). Illus. 2002, Delacorte $15.95 (0-385-72959-6). The gripping story of young Hunter Scott's efforts to clear the name of the captain of the U.S.S. Indianapolis, which was sunk by the Japanese during World War II. (Rev: BL 5/1/02; HB 7–8/02; HBG 10/02; SLJ 4/02; VOYA 8/02) [940.54]

7763 Newman, Amy. *The Nuremburg Laws* (7–12). Illus. Series: Words That Changed History. 1998, Lucent LB $27.45 (1-56006-354-8). An overview of the Holocaust, including the roots and growth of Nazism and the war against the Jews, and a discussion of contemporary ethnic violence, laws that promote bigotry, and the power of words. (Rev: BL 4/15/99; SLJ 9/99) [342.43]

7764 Newton, David E. *Tokyo* (6–12). Series: Cities at War. 1992, Macmillan LB $18.00 (0-02-768235-8). Remembrances from people who experienced World War II in Tokyo. (Rev: BL 10/15/92; SLJ 1/93) [952]

7765 Oleksy, Walter. *Military Leaders of World War II* (7–10). Series: American Profiles. 1994, Facts on File $25.00 (0-8160-3008-1). Profiles of 10 American World War II leaders, including Claire Lee Chennault, Douglas MacArthur, Chester Nimitz, Jacqueline Cochran, Curtis LeMay, and George Patton. (Rev: BL 1/1/95; SLJ 3/95; VOYA 5/95) [940.54]

7766 Panchyk, Richard. *World War II for Kids: A History with 21 Activities* (5–7). Illus. 2002, Chicago Review paper $14.95 (1-55652-455-2). Features on such topics as living on rations for a day, growing a victory garden, and tracking a ship's movements depict conditions in America and Europe during the war. (Rev: SLJ 12/02) [940.53]

7767 Perl, Lila, and Marion B. Lazan. *Four Perfect Pebbles: A Holocaust Story* (5–9). Illus. 1996, Greenwillow $15.99 (0-688-14294-X). A memoir of the horror and incredible tribulations suffered by the author's family in the detention camps and later death camps during the Holocaust. (Rev: BL 4/1/96; BR 9–10/96; SLJ 5/96) [940.53]

7768 Pettit, Jayne. *A Time to Fight Back: True Stories of Wartime Resistance* (5–8). 1996, Houghton $14.95 (0-395-76504-8). Eight true stories about courageous acts involving young people during World War II. (Rev: BCCB 3/96; BL 4/1/96; BR 11–12/96; SLJ 4/96; VOYA 6/96) [940.53]

7769 Pfeifer, Kathryn B. *The 761st Tank Battalion* (5–8). Series: African American Soldiers. 1994, Twenty-First Century LB $24.90 (0-8050-3057-3). The history of an outfit of African American soldiers who served with distinction during World War

II but were marginalized by racism. (Rev: BL 9/1/94; SLJ 11/94) [940.54]

7770 Rice, Earle. *Strategic Battles in the Pacific* (6–12). Series: American War Library. 2000, Lucent LB $18.96 (1-56006-537-0). Beginning with the rise of Japanese power in the Pacific, this account traces the war in this area from Pearl Harbor through such crucial battles as Midway. (Rev: BL 4/15/00; HBG 9/00) [940.54]

7771 Rice, Earle, Jr. *The Battle of Britain* (6–10). Illus. Series: Great Battles in History. 1996, Lucent LB $19.95 (1-56006-414-3). This account of the air battle in the skies over Britain during 1940 quotes many primary sources and uses extensive illustrations. (Rev: BL 4/15/96; BR 9–10/96) [940.54]

7772 Rice, Earle, Jr. *The Bombing of Pearl Harbor* (7–10). Series: World History. 2000, Lucent LB $19.96 (1-56006-652-0). This account covers the causes, effects, and significance in world history of the attack on Pearl Harbor by the Japanese. (Rev: BL 12/15/00; SLJ 2/01) [940.54]

7773 Rice, Earle, Jr. *The Nuremberg Trials* (6–10). Illus. Series: Famous Trials. 1996, Lucent LB $27.45 (1-56006-269-X). Beginning with an account of the Nazi atrocities during World War II, this book describes the trials of the war criminals during 1945–1946, the background of the accused, and their fate. (Rev: BL 3/15/97; BR 11–12/97; SLJ 3/97) [341.6]

7774 Rice, Earle, Jr. *Strategic Battles in Europe: World War II* (6–12). Series: American War Library. 2000, Lucent LB $18.96 (1-56006-536-2). This gripping account that includes many firsthand narratives chronicles the major battles of World War II as fought in Europe. (Rev: BL 9/15/00; HBG 9/00) [940.54]

7775 Rice, Earle, Jr. *The Third Reich: Demise of the Nazi Dream* (8–12). Series: History's Great Defeats. 2000, Lucent $27.45 (1-56006-630-X). Rice explores the factors that led to the Nazis' defeat, pointing at Hitler's overconfidence and strategic errors and detailing key battles. (Rev: BL 10/15/00; BR 3–4/01; HBG 3/01; SLJ 9/00) [943.086]

7776 Rochman, Hazel, and Darlene Z. McCampbell, eds. *Bearing Witness: Stories of the Holocaust* (7–12). 1995, Orchard LB $16.99 (0-531-08788-3). This anthology of 24 works revolving around the Holocaust includes memoirs, poetry, short stories, a film script, a letter, and a comic strip. (Rev: BL 6/1–15/95; SLJ 9/95; VOYA 12/95) [808]

7777 Rogasky, Barbara. *Smoke and Ashes: The Story of the Holocaust.* Rev. ed. (6–12). 2002, Holiday $27.50 (0-8234-1612-7); paper $14.95 (0-8234-1677-1). In this new edition, Rogasky updates information where new facts have come to light and expands the details of resistance efforts. (Rev: BL 10/15/02; HBG 3/03; SLJ 10/02) [940.53]

7778 Rogers, James T. *The Secret War* (8–12). Series: World Espionage. 1991, Facts on File LB $16.95 (0-8160-2395-6). A well-supported thesis stating that the British and Americans were more successful at espionage, counterespionage, and detection than either the Germans or the Japanese. (Rev: BL 3/1/92; SLJ 5/92) [940.54]

7779 Rogow, Sally M. *Faces of Courage: Young Heroes of World War II* (5–9). 2003, Granville Island $12.95 (1-894694-20-1). Based on true stories, this volume presents 12 fictionalized accounts of heroic actions by teenagers under Nazi rule in Europe. (Rev: BL 10/15/03) [940.53]

7780 Roleff, Tamara L., ed. *The Atom Bomb* (8–12). Series: Turning Points in World History. 2000, Greenhaven LB $21.96 (0-7377-0215-X); paper $13.96 (0-7377-0214-1). This anthology of thoughtful essays covers the development of the bomb, the scientists who worked on it, and its impact and legacy. (Rev: BL 5/15/00) [940.54]

7781 Ross, Stewart. *World War II* (7–12). Series: Causes and Consequences. 1995, Raintree Steck-Vaughn LB $29.97 (0-8172-4050-0). This book identifies the factors that led to the outbreak of World War II and discusses its outcome, using eyewitness documents. (Rev: BL 12/15/95) [940.53]

7782 Roubickova, Eva M. *We're Alive and Life Goes On: A Theresienstadt Diary* (8–12). Trans. by Zaia Alexander. 1997, Holt $16.95 (0-8050-5352-2). A translation of a diary kept by a young Jewish woman during her four years in a Nazi concentration camp. (Rev: BL 11/1/97; BR 5–6/98; SLJ 2/98) [940.53]

7783 Rubin, Susan G. *Fireflies in the Dark: The Story of Friedl Dicker-Brandeis and the Children of Terezin* (5–10). Illus. 2000, Holiday $18.95 (0-8234-1461-2). A heartbreaking picture book that reproduces some of the artwork and writings of the children imprisoned at the Terezin concentration camp, where only 100 of 15,000 children survived. (Rev: BCCB 11/00; BL 7/00*; HB 9–10/00; HBG 10/00; SLJ 8/00) [940.53]

7784 Rubin, Susan Goldman. *Searching for Anne Frank: Letters from Amsterdam to Iowa* (5–12). 2003, Abrams $19.95 (0-8109-4514-2). A brief pen-pal exchange between two sisters in Iowa and Anne Frank and her sister serves as the basis for a comparison between life in America and life for Jews in Europe. (Rev: BL 11/1/03; HB 11–12/03; SLJ 11/03; VOYA 10/03) [940.5]

7785 Saldinger, Anne Green. *Life in a Nazi Concentration Camp* (6–10). Series: The Way People Live. 2000, Lucent LB $19.96 (1-56006-185-1). Daily life and death in Nazi death camps is covered in this shocking chronicle of inhumanity during World War II. (Rev: BL 3/1/01) [940.54]

7786 Shapiro, Stephen, and Tina Forrester. *Ultra Hush-Hush: Espionage and Special Missions* (5–8). Series: Outwitting the Enemy. 2003, Annick LB $29.95 (1-55037-779-5); paper $14.95 (1-55037-778-7). Undercover activities during World War II are the focus of this volume that covers such groups and missions as the Navajo Code Talkers and Britain's double agents. (Rev: BL 8/03) [940.54]

7787 Sheehan, Sean. *D-Day: June 6, 1944* (6–8). Series: Days That Shook the World. 2003, Raintree Steck-Vaughn LB $27.12 (0-7398-5232-9). With many color and black-and-white photographs and quotations from combatants on both sides, this slim volume looks at the Allied landings in Normandy. (Rev: HBG 10/03; SLJ 10/03) [940.54]

7788 Sheehan, Sean. *The Technology of World War II* (5–8). 2003, Raintree Steck-Vaughn LB $28.56 (0-7398-6064-X). New technologies introduced during World War II include radar, microwave transmissions, V-1 and V-2 rockets, the jet, codes, chemical and biological weapons, and the atom bomb. (Rev: HBG 10/03; SLJ 7/03) [940.54]

7789 Sherrow, Victoria. *Amsterdam* (6–12). Series: Cities at War. 1992, Macmillan LB $18.00 (0-02-782465-9). A photoessay on the lives of ordinary people in Amsterdam during World War II, with quotations by eyewitnesses. (Rev: BL 6/15/92; SLJ 9/92) [940.53]

7790 Sherrow, Victoria. *The Blaze Engulfs: January 1939 to December 1941* (6–12). Illus. Series: Holocaust. 1997, Blackbirch LB $27.44 (1-56711-202-1). This account, book three of the Holocaust series, describes the first two years of World War II, when Hitler's racial programs were being put into place. (Rev: BL 10/15/97; BR 1–2/98; HBG 3/98; SLJ 2/98) [940.53]

7791 Sherrow, Victoria. *Hiroshima* (6–12). 1994, Silver Burdett LB $14.95 (0-02-782467-5). Chronicles the birth of the atomic age, concluding with graphic descriptions of the World War II bombing of Hiroshima. (Rev: BL 10/1/94; SLJ 11/94) [940.54]

7792 Sherrow, Victoria. *Smoke to Flame: September 1935 to December 1938* (6–12). Illus. Series: Holocaust. 1997, Blackbirch LB $27.44 (1-56711-201-3). This volume covers the growing anti-Semitism of Hitler's first years in power until the beginning of World War II, by which time his war against "undesirables" was gaining momentum. (Rev: BL 10/15/97; HBG 3/98; SLJ 2/98) [940.53]

7793 Shulman, William L., ed. *Resource Guide: A Comprehensive Listing of Media for Further Study* (6–12). Illus. Series: Holocaust. 1997, Blackbirch LB $27.44 (1-56711-208-0). This eighth and last volume of the Holocaust series is a guide to other sources on the subject including CD-ROMS, books,

videos, museums, and other resource centers. (Rev: BL 10/15/97; BR 1–2/98; SLJ 2/98) [940.53]

7794 Shulman, William L., ed. *Voices and Visions: A Collection of Primary Sources* (6–12). Illus. Series: Holocaust. 1997, Blackbirch LB $27.44 (1-56711-207-2). A collection of primary sources, including eyewitness accounts, of the Holocaust and its many targets. (Rev: BL 10/15/97; BR 1–2/98; HBG 3/98; SLJ 2/98) [940.53]

7795 Shuter, Jane. *The Camp System* (7–12). Illus. Series: Holocaust. 2003, Heinemann LB $28.50 (1-4034-0809-2). This book explores the horrific procedures and life in the concentration camps of the Holocaust. (Rev: BL 3/1/03; SLJ 4/03) [940.53]

7796 Shuter, Jane, ed. *Christabel Bielenberg and Nazi Germany* (5–8). Illus. Series: History Eyewitness. 1996, Raintree Steck-Vaughn LB $24.26 (0-8114-8285-5). Using a first-person narrative as a framework, this account traces the growth, flowering, and defeat of Nazism in Germany. (Rev: BL 5/15/96; SLJ 6/96) [943.086]

7797 Shuter, Jane. *Resistance to the Nazis* (7–12). Illus. Series: Holocaust. 2003, Heinemann LB $28.50 (1-4034-0814-9). An account of the acts of heroism by the many people who risked and lost their lives resisting the Nazis and their Holocaust agenda. (Rev: BL 3/1/03; SLJ 4/03) [943.086]

7798 Stalcup, Ann. *On the Home Front: Growing up in Wartime England* (6–10). Illus. 1998, Shoe String LB $19.50 (0-208-02482-4). A vivid first-person account about growing up in a small English town in Shropshire during World War II. (Rev: BCCB 9/98; BL 10/15/98; BR 11–12/98; HBG 9/98; SLJ 7/98) [940.54]

7799 Stein, R. Conrad. *World War II in Europe: "America Goes to War"* (5–7). Illus. Series: American War. 1994, Enslow LB $20.95 (0-89490-525-2). An unbiased account of the European theater of war during World War II, with emphasis on American participation. (Rev: BL 10/15/94; SLJ 1/95) [940.54]

7800 Stein, R. Conrad. *World War II in the Pacific: Remember Pearl Harbor* (5–7). Illus. Series: American War. 1994, Enslow LB $20.95 (0-89490-524-4). A well-organized, concise account of the Pacific war from the attack on Pearl Harbor to V-J Day that describes key battles and important personnel. (Rev: BL 7/94; SLJ 7/94) [940.54]

7801 Steins, Richard. *The Allies Against the Axis: World War II (1940–1950)* (5–8). Series: First Person America. 1994, Twenty-First Century LB $20.90 (0-8050-2586-3). An introduction to World War II and early postwar conditions, with generous use of primary sources. (Rev: BL 5/15/94; SLJ 12/94) [940.53]

7802 Strahinich, Helen. *The Holocaust: Understanding and Remembering* (6–10). Illus. Series: Issues in Focus. 1996, Enslow LB $20.95 (0-89490-

725-5). A fully documented account that covers such topics as the roots of anti-Semitism, the rise of Nazism, ghetto life, the roundups, death camps, liberation, and the Nuremberg trials. (Rev: BL 9/15/96; SLJ 10/96; VOYA 10/96) [940.53]

7803 Sullivan, George. *Strange but True Stories of World War II* (7–12). Illus. 1983, Walker $14.95 (0-8027-6489-4). Eleven true stories of bizarre incidents during World War II. [940.53]

7804 Talbott, Hudson. *Forging Freedom* (4–7). Illus. 2000, Putnam $15.99 (0-399-23434-9). This is the story of Jaap Penraat, a young architectural student in Amsterdam during the Nazi occupation who saved hundreds of Jews from deportation by forging papers and smuggling them out of the city. (Rev: BCCB 11/00; BL 7/00; HB 1–2/01; HBG 3/01; SLJ 11/00) [940.53]

7805 Tames, Richard. *Fascism* (6–8). Series: Ideas of the Modern World. 2001, Raintree Steck-Vaughn LB $17.98 (0-7398-3159-3). The story of the regimes in Germany, Italy, and Japan that promoted one-person rule and aggressive military policies. (Rev: BL 4/15/02; VOYA 4/02) [940.54]

7806 Tanaka, Shelley. *Attack on Pearl Harbor: The True Story of the Day America Entered World War II* (5–8). Illus. Series: I Was There. 2001, Hyperion $19.99 (0-7868-0736-9). An absorbing account of Pearl Harbor that presents the real-life, and very different, experiences of four young men who were there. (Rev: BL 8/01; HBG 10/01; SLJ 11/01; VOYA 12/01) [940.54]

7807 Taylor, Theodore. *Air Raid — Pearl Harbor: The Story of December 7, 1941* (5–8). 1991, Harcourt paper $6.00 (0-15-201655-4). A fine account of why the attack occurred and the effects that were felt around the world. A revised edition. (Rev: SLJ 12/91) [940.54]

7808 Taylor, Theodore. *Battle in the English Channel* (7–10). Illus. 1983, Avon paper $3.50 (0-380-85225-X). The retelling of the exciting World War II incident when Hitler tried to free three of his battleships from French waters. [940.54]

7809 Taylor, Theodore. *The Battle of Midway Island* (7–10). Illus. 1981, Avon paper $3.95 (0-380-78790-3). The story of the brilliant victory of U.S. forces at Midway is excitingly retold. [940.54]

7810 Taylor, Theodore. *H.M.S. Hood vs. Bismarck: The Battleship Battle* (7–10). Illus. 1982, Avon paper $3.95 (0-380-81174-X). The subject of this book is the sinking of the battleship *Bismarck* by the Royal Navy. [940.54]

7811 Tito, E. Tina. *Liberation: Teens in the Concentration Camps and the Teen Soldiers Who Liberated Them* (5–9). Illus. Series: Teen Witnesses to the Holocaust. 1999, Rosen LB $26.50 (0-8239-2846-2). A harrowing account in which two teenage Nazi camp survivors and two American soldiers who

were also teenagers during World War II tell their respective stories. (Rev: BL 4/15/99; BR 9–10/99; VOYA 8/99) [940.53]

7812 Tregaskis, Richard. *Guadalcanal Diary* (6–9). Illus. 1993, Buccaneer LB $25.95 (1-56849-231-6). This is a simplified version of the adult book that tells of the Marine landing at Guadalcanal in 1942. [940.54]

7813 Verhoeven, Rian, and Ruud van der Rol. *Anne Frank: Beyond the Diary: A Photographic Remembrance* (6–12). Trans. by Tony Langham and Plym Peters. 1993, Viking $18.99 (0-670-84932-4). Includes photographs of people who knew Anne and of the places she lived and hid in, with excerpts from her diary. (Rev: BL 10/1/93*; SLJ 12/93*) [940.53]

7814 Warren, Andrea. *Surviving Hitler: A Boy in the Nazi Death Camps* (5–10). Illus. 2001, HarperCollins LB $17.89 (0-06-029218-0). The true story of Jack Mandelbaum who as a teenager survived three years in Nazi death camps through a combination of luck, courage, and friendship. (Rev: BCCB 3/01; BL 1/1–15/01; HB 3–4/01; HBG 10/01; SLJ 3/01) [940.53]

7815 Wassiljewa, Tatjana. *Hostage to War: A True Story* (6–10). 1997, Scholastic paper $15.95 (0-590-13446-9). The World War II diary of a young Russian girl who endured hunger, cold, disease, brutality during the German occupation of Leningrad, and then spent years in forced labor camps and factories in Germany. (Rev: BL 4/15/97; SLJ 6/97; VOYA 12/98) [940.54]

7816 *Weapons of War: World War II* (6–10). Series: American War Library. 2000, Lucent LB $27.45 (1-56006-584-2). The weapons used by the American Army, Navy, and Air Force during World War II are covered in both text and pictures. (Rev: BL 9/15/00; HBG 10/00; SLJ 7/00) [940.54]

7817 Whitman, Sylvia. *Uncle Sam Wants You!* (5–7). Illus. 1993, Lerner LB $30.35 (0-8225-1728-0). This work describes the experiences of the many men and women who served in the various armed forces during World War II. (Rev: BL 5/1/93) [940.54]

7818 Wills, Charles A. *Pearl Harbor* (5–7). Illus. Series: Turning Points. 1991, Silver Burdett LB $14.95 (0-382-24125-8); paper $7.95 (0-382-24119-3). The "Day of Infamy" that brought America into World War II is re-created through text and pictures. (Rev: BL 1/15/92) [940.54]

7819 Winston, Keith. *Letters from a World War II G.I.* (8–12). Ed. by Judith E. Greenberg and Helen Carey McKeever. 1995, Watts LB $23.00 (0-531-11212-8). A collection of letters home speaking of the hardships of life as a soldier. (Rev: BL 9/15/95; SLJ 9/95; VOYA 12/95) [940.54]

7820 Wukovits, John F. *Life as a POW: World War II* (6–12). Series: American War Library. 2000, Lucent LB $27.45 (1-56006-665-2). Using archival photographs and many firsthand accounts, this work explores the treatment of World War II prisoners of war by the Germans and Japanese, the emotional upheavals the prisoners suffered, and the transition to freedom after release. (Rev: BL 9/15/00; HBG 10/00; SLJ 7/00) [940.54]

7821 Wukovits, John F. *Life of an American Soldier in Europe* (6–10). Series: American War Library. 2000, Lucent LB $27.45 (1-56006-666-0). As well as giving a history of World War II and the major battles involving Americans in Europe, this account describes the soldiers' training, daily life, and living conditions. (Rev: BL 4/15/00; HBG 10/00; SLJ 6/00) [940.54]

7822 Yancey, Diane. *The Internment of the Japanese* (7–10). Series: World History. 2002, Gale LB $27.45 (1-59018-013-5). An accessible account of the causes of the internment of many Japanese Americans during World War II, the conditions they endured, and the aftermath. (Rev: BL 8/02; SLJ 8/02) [940.54]

Modern World History (1945–)

7823 Aaseng, Nathan. *The Space Race* (6–9). Series: World History. 2001, Gale LB $27.45 (1-56006-809-4). Narrative about the Cold War, technological advances, and the space race is interspersed with informative illustrations and sidebar features. (Rev: SLJ 1/02) [629.4]

7824 Ayer, Eleanor, and Stephen D. Chicoine. *From the Ashes: May 1945 and After* (6–12). Illus. Series: Holocaust. 1997, Blackbirch LB $27.44 (1-56711-206-4). This account of the Holocaust covers the end of the war, its aftermath, the war crimes trials, and the stories of death camp survivors. (Rev: BL 10/15/97; BR 1–2/98; HBG 3/98; SLJ 2/98) [940.53]

7825 Benson, Sonia G. *Korean War: Almanac and Primary Sources* (6–10). 2001, Gale LB $52.00 (0-7876-5691-7). After an almanac section that traces the progress of the war, a selection of primary materials — speeches, memoirs, government documents, and so forth — are presented with introductions that place them in historical context. (Rev: SLJ 5/02) [951.904]

7826 Bjornlund, Britta. *The Cold War* (7–10). Series: World History. 2002, Gale LB $27.45 (1-59018-003-8). With ample quotations from original sources and a timeline, Bjornlund looks at the origins and development of the Cold War, and details the crises and periods of reduced tension that marked the length of the conflict. (Rev: BL 8/02; SLJ 10/02) [909.83]

7827 Brubaker, Paul. *The Cuban Missile Crisis in American History* (6–10). Series: In American History. 2001, Enslow LB $20.95 (0-7660-1414-2). This is a gripping account of how diplomacy and quick-thinking averted a war when the Soviets brought missiles to Cuba in 1962. (Rev: BL 8/1/01; HBG 10/01; SLJ 7/01) [973.992]

7828 Chrisp, Peter. *The Cuban Missile Crisis* (5–8). Illus. Series: Cold War. 2002, World Almanac LB $31.93 (0-8368-5273-7). This look at the Cold War crisis focuses on the events leading up to the stand-off and the reasons for the deteriorating relationship between Moscow and Washington. Also use *The Causes of the Cold War, The Vietnam War*, and *The End of the Cold War* (all 2002). (Rev: BL 11/15/02; SLJ 7/02) [973.922]

7829 Denenberg, Barry. *Voices from Vietnam* (7–12). 1995, Scholastic paper $16.95 (0-590-44267-8). Personal narratives of the Vietnam War from the late 1940s to 1975. (Rev: BL 2/15/95*; SLJ 3/95) [959.704]

7830 Dolan, Edward. *America in the Korean War* (7–12). 1998, Millbrook LB $30.90 (0-7613-0361-8). This study of the Korean War focuses on the battles, strategies, technological limitations, and personalities involved. (Rev: BL 1/1–15/99; HBG 3/99; SLJ 3/99) [951.904]

7831 Dowswell, Paul. *The Vietnam War* (6–8). Series: The Cold War. 2002, World Almanac LB $29.27 (0-8368-5274-5). The history, conduct, and end of the Vietnam War are presented in clear context, with information on the key figures, a timeline, and helpful maps. (Rev: BL 11/15/02; SLJ 7/02) [959.7]

7832 Fisher, Trevor. *The 1960s* (8–12). Illus. 1989, David & Charles $19.95 (0-7134-5603-5). Under a broad subject arrangement, the major news stories and trends of the 1960s are chronicled. (Rev: SLJ 5/89) [973.92]

7833 Gay, Kathlyn, and Martin Gay. *Korean War* (6–8). Illus. Series: Voices from the Past. 1996, Twenty-First Century LB $25.90 (0-8050-4100-1). A discussion of the often forgotten Korean War — its causes, its battles, and the people involved. (Rev: BL 11/15/96; SLJ 12/96; VOYA 4/97) [951.904]

7834 Gay, Kathlyn, and Martin Gay. *Persian Gulf War* (6–8). Illus. Series: Voices from the Past. 1996, Twenty-First Century LB $25.90 (0-8050-4102-8). A clearly written, objective overview of the Gulf War that gives material on the recent history of Iraq and Saddam Hussein's rise to power and contains many quotations from reporters, soldiers, military leaders, and ordinary people on every aspect of the war. (Rev: BL 11/15/96; SLJ 2/97; VOYA 6/97) [956.7044]

7835 Gay, Kathlyn, and Martin Gay. *Vietnam War* (6–8). Illus. Series: Voices from the Past. 1996, Twenty-First Century LB $25.90 (0-8050-4101-X). An objective overview of the Vietnam War, illustrated with black-and-white photographs. (Rev: BL 11/15/96; SLJ 12/96; VOYA 2/97) [959.704]

7836 Gerdes, Louise I., ed. *The Cold War* (6–12). Series: Great Speeches in History. 2003, Gale LB $32.45 (0-7377-0869-7); paper $21.20 (0-7377-0868-9). Winston Churchill and Che Guevara are among the world leaders whose words are given in this collection that examines the confrontation between East and West. (Rev: BL 5/1/03; SLJ 9/03) [909.82]

7837 Hillstrom, Kevin, and Laurie Collier Hillstrom. *Vietnam War: Almanac* (7–12). Series: UXL Vietnam War Reference Library. 2000, Gale LB $45.00 (0-7876-4883-3). An absorbing and comprehensive overview of the causes, conduct, and aftermath of the war that includes interesting sidebars and black-and-white photographs. Also use *Vietnam War: Biographies* and *Vietnam War: Primary Sources* (both 2000). (Rev: BL 3/15/01; SLJ 5/01) [959.704]

7838 Holden, Henry M. *The Persian Gulf War* (4–8). Series: U.S. Wars. 2003, Enslow/MyReportLinks.com LB $19.95 (0-7660-5109-9). This concise, interesting account of the conflict in the early 1990s is enhanced by Internet access to a set of monitored Web links. (Rev: HBG 10/03; SLJ 8/03) [956.7]

7839 Isserman, Maurice. *The Korean War* (7–12). Series: America at War. 1992, Facts on File $25.00 (0-8160-2688-2). A thorough re-creation of the Korean War, the first armed conflict of the Cold War. (Rev: BL 11/1/92) [951.904]

7840 Isserman, Maurice. *The Vietnam War: America at War* (7–12). Series: America at War. 1992, Facts on File $25.00 (0-8160-2375-1). A riveting account of the Vietnam War from its roots after World War II to U.S. withdrawal in 1975, and a review of the lessons learned. (Rev: BL 3/1/92) [959.7]

7841 Kent, Zachary. *The Persian Gulf War: "The Mother of All Battles"* (5–7). Illus. 1994, Enslow LB $20.95 (0-89490-528-7). The story of the 1991 Gulf War, its causes and effects, told with striking action photographs. (Rev: BL 4/15/95; SLJ 2/95) [956.7]

7842 King, John. *The Gulf War* (7–10). 1991, Dillon $13.95 (0-87518-514-2). A factual account of the Iraqi invasion of Kuwait, wartime operations, and the aftermath. (Rev: BL 3/1/92; SLJ 4/92) [956.704]

7843 Nardo, Don. *The War Against Iraq* (6–12). Series: American War Library: The Persian Gulf War. 2000, Lucent LB $35.15 (1-56006-715-2).

This vividly written and nonjudgmental account of the Gulf War of 1991 includes a good final chapter on the results of the war. (Rev: BL 3/1/01; SLJ 3/01) [956.7]

7844 Rice, Earle. *Point of No Return: Tonkin Gulf and the Vietnam War* (7–12). Illus. 2003, Morgan Reynolds LB $21.95 (1-931798-16-8). Rice presents the events that led up to the passage in 1964 of the Tonkin Gulf Resolution, which gave Lyndon Johnson authority to take action against North Vietnam. (Rev: BL 9/1/03; SLJ 11/03) [959.704]

7845 Rice, Earle, Jr. *The Inchon Invasion* (6–10). Illus. Series: Great Battles in History. 1996, Lucent LB $26.20 (1-56006-418-8). The invasion of this Korean city on Sept. 15, 1950, during the Korean War is highlighted in this well-illustrated account that contains many quotations from primary and secondary sources. (Rev: BL 4/15/96) [951.904]

7846 Rice, Earle, Jr. *The Tet Offensive* (6–10). Illus. Series: Battles. 1996, Lucent LB $26.20 (1-56006-422-6). The story of the bloody Vietnam War battle and its consequences, with some general background coverage of the war. (Rev: BL 1/1–15/97; BR 11–12/97; SLJ 8/97) [959.704]

7847 Roberts, Russell. *Leaders and Generals* (6–12). Series: American War Library: The Vietnam War. 2001, Lucent LB $19.96 (1-56006-717-9). Ho Chi Minh, Lyndon Johnson, Richard Nixon, and Henry Kissinger are among the leaders whose roles in the Vietnam War are examined here. (Rev: BL 3/15/01; SLJ 6/01) [957.704]

7848 Saenger, Diana, and Bradley Steffens. *Life as a POW* (6–12). Series: American War Library: The Vietnam War. 2001, Lucent LB $19.96 (1-56006-716-0). The treatment and morale of prisoners of war during the Vietnam War is covered with many references to actual case histories. (Rev: BL 3/15/01) [959.704]

7849 Schaffer, David. *The Iran-Iraq War* (5–8). Illus. Series: World History. 2002, Gale LB $27.45 (1-59018-184-0). Schaffer traces the causes and progress of this long war, incorporating useful primary and secondary source material plus interesting sidebar features. (Rev: BL 5/1/03) [955.05]

7850 Smith, Carter. *The Korean War* (4–7). Illus. Series: Turning Points. 1990, Silver Burdett LB $14.95 (0-382-09953-2); paper $7.95 (0-382-09949-4). Covers the causes and events of the Korean War, as well as its significance in American history. (Rev: BL 3/1/91; SLJ 5/91) [951]

7851 Stein, R. Conrad. *The Korean War: "The Forgotten War"* (5–7). Illus. 1994, Enslow LB $20.95 (0-89490-526-0). This well organized account of the Korean War presents a balanced picture of the war and includes personal observations. (Rev: BL 4/15/95; SLJ 2/95) [951]

7852 Taylor, David. *The Cold War* (5–9). Illus. Series: 20th Century Perspectives. 2001, Heinemann LB $25.64 (1-57572-434-0). An easily understood account of the causes of tension between the Soviet Union and the West and the major crises of the "war." (Rev: HBG 3/02; SLJ 11/01) [909.825]

7853 Uschan, Michael V. *The Korean War* (6–10). Series: World History. 2001, Lucent LB $19.96 (1-56006-704-7). This book traces the causes and course of the war, starting in 1946 with the beginning of the Cold War, and includes maps, archival photographs, sidebar features, and quotations. (Rev: SLJ 9/01) [951.904]

7854 Willoughby, Douglas. *The Vietnam War* (5–9). Series: 20th Century Perspectives. 2001, Heinemann LB $27.07 (1-57572-439-1). An easily understood and attractive account of Vietnam's relations with China, and of French and U.S. involvement in the country's affairs. (Rev: SLJ 11/01) [959]

7855 Wills, Charles A. *The Tet Offensive* (6–9). Illus. 1989, Silver Burdett LB $14.95 (0-382-09849-8); paper $7.95 (0-382-09855-2). The story of the 1968 campaign in Vietnam plus general material about the war and the Memorial in Washington, D.C. (Rev: BL 11/1/89; BR 1–2/90) [959.704]

7856 Wright, David K. *War in Vietnam* (5–10). 1998, Children's Pr. paper $20.60 (0-516-02287-3). This is the first volume of an excellent four-volume set. The other volumes are *War in Vietnam, Book II: A Wider War; War in Vietnam, Book III: Vietnamization;* and *War in Vietnam, Book IV: Fall of Vietnam* (all 1989, available only as a set). (Rev: BL 6/1/89; SLJ 6/89) [959.704]

7857 Wukovits, John F. *Leaders and Generals* (6–12). Series: American War Library: The Persian Gulf War. 2001, Lucent LB $19.96 (1-56006-714-4). Key personnel who led the army during the Persian Gulf War of 1991 are profiled in this work that comments on the contributions of each. (Rev: BL 3/15/01) [956.7044]

7858 Yancey, Diane, ed. *The Vietnam War* (7–12). Series: Turning Points in World History. 2001, Greenhaven LB $22.96 (0-7377-0614-7); paper $14.96 (0-7377-0613-9). In a series of separate essays, some from scholarly works, various aspects of the Vietnam War are covered and different points of view expressed. (Rev: BL 6/1–15/01) [959.704]

7859 Yeatts, Tabatha. *The Holocaust Survivors* (6–10). Series: Holocaust Remembered. 1998, Enslow LB $20.95 (0-89490-993-2). This work concentrates on the liberation of the Nazi death camps, the capture of war criminals, the Nuremberg trials, the founding of Israel, and the lives of individual survivors. (Rev: BL 9/15/98; BR 1–2/99; HBG 3/99; SLJ 12/98) [940.5318]

7860 Young, Marilyn B., and John J. Fitzgerald. *The Vietnam War: A History in Documents* (6–12). Series: Pages from History. 2002, Oxford $32.95 (0-19-512278-X). Primary sources cover the conflict in Vietnam from French involvement through the U.S. withdrawal and include everything from official documents, speeches, and transcripts of White House tapes to North Vietnamese political cartoons and U.S. anti-war posters. (Rev: BCCB 9/02; BL 6/1–15/02; HBG 10/02; SLJ 9/02) [959.704]

Geographical Regions

Africa

General and Miscellaneous

7861 Ayo, Yvonne. *Africa* (5–8). Series: Eyewitness Books. 1995, Knopf $20.99 (0-679-97334-6). An introduction to the continent of Africa, with its amazing diversity of people, places, wildlife, and cultures. (Rev: BL 12/15/95; SLJ 1/96) [960]

7862 Baroin, Catherine. *Tubu: The Teda and the Daza* (7–12). Illus. Series: Heritage Library of African Peoples. 1997, Rosen LB $28.75 (0-8239-2000-3). The history and contemporary life of these peoples of Chad, Libya, Niger, and the Sudan are presented in easy-reading text. (Rev: BL 4/15/97) [967.43]

7863 Harrison, Peter, ed. *African Nations and Leaders* (7–12). Illus. Series: History of Africa. 2003, Facts on File $30.00 (0-8160-5066-X). Double-page spreads provide a wealth of information on the nations of Africa, their leaders, and important historical events. (Rev: BL 9/15/03) [900]

7864 Jones, Constance. *A Short History of Africa: 1500–1900* (8–12). 1993, Facts on File $19.95 (0-8160-2774-9). Jones describes the Islamic cultures of North Africa, the city-states and kingdoms of East Africa, the rich traditions of West Africa, and the roots of apartheid in South Africa. (Rev: BL 3/1/93; SLJ 10/93) [960]

7865 Martell, Hazel M. *Exploring Africa* (4–8). Illus. Series: Voyages of Discovery. 1998, Bedrick $18.95 (0-87226-490-4). Double-page spreads, maps, and illustrations are used in this introduction to the history and geography of Africa, including an overview of early trade, European exploration and colonization, and African independence movements. (Rev: HBG 10/98; SLJ 4/98) [960]

7866 Rich, Susan, et al. *Africa South of the Sahara: Understanding Geography and History Through Art* (5–9). Series: Artisans Around the World. 1999, Raintree Steck-Vaughn LB $27.12 (0-7398-0118-X). After a brief overview of the history and geography of southern Africa, this book presents a colorful introduction to such crafts as beadwork from Kenya, a carved wooden mask from Congo, and a wire toy from South Africa. Most will require adult help or supervision. (Rev: HBG 3/00; SLJ 1/00) [960]

7867 Russman, Edna R. *Nubian Kingdoms* (6–9). Series: First Books: African Civilizations. 1999, Watts LB $23.00 (0-531-20283-6). The story of the growth and decline of the ancient civilization that grew up south of Egypt. (Rev: BL 9/15/99; HBG 10/99; SLJ 8/99) [967]

7868 Sheehan, Sean. *Great African Kingdoms* (5–10). Series: The Ancient World. 1998, Raintree Steck-Vaughn LB $27.12 (0-8172-5124-3). Coverage of the great African kingdoms includes the spectacular palace of Great Zimbabwe, the majestic sculptures of Benin, and the Zulu empire' struggle for survival. (Rev: BL 1/1–15/99; HBG 3/99) [960]

7869 Shillington, Kevin. *Causes and Consequences of Independence in Africa* (6–9). Series: Causes and Consequences. 1998, Raintree Steck-Vaughn LB $29.97 (0-8172-4060-8). A concise overview of African history before, during, and after colonialism. (Rev: BL 7/98; SLJ 6/98) [960.32]

7870 Wekesser, Carol, and Christina Pierce. *Africa* (7–12). Series: Opposing Viewpoints. 1992, Greenhaven paper $16.20 (0-89908-161-4). The history and present conditions of Africa, from politics to social issues, are discussed in essays offering varying perspectives. (Rev: BL 5/15/92; SLJ 7/92) [960]

7871 Wepman, Dennis. *Africa: The Struggle for Independence* (7–10). 1993, Facts on File $25.00 (0-8160-2820-6). Focuses on the arbitrary division of the African continent by European countries and the struggles in different regions against colonial rule. (Rev: BL 2/15/94; VOYA 6/94) [960]

7872 Worth, Richard. *Stanley and Livingstone and the Exploration of Africa in World History* (6–9). Series: In World History. 2000, Enslow LB $19.95 (0-7660-1400-2). Worth chronicles the explorers' expeditions into Africa and their historical context and consequences. (Rev: HBG 9/00; SLJ 7/00) [916.704]

Central and Eastern Africa

7873 Allen, Christina. *Hippos in the Night: Autobiographical Adventures in Africa* (4–8). 2003, HarperCollins $16.99 (0-688-17826-X). An appealing account of a camping trip through Kenya and Tanzania, with details of the exciting animals and fascinating people encountered on the way. (Rev: BL 4/15/03; HBG 10/03; SLJ 4/03) [591.96]

7874 Ayodo, Awuor. *Luo* (4–7). Illus. Series: Heritage Library of African Peoples. 1995, Rosen LB $17.95 (0-8239-1758-4). A portrait of the culture, history, and society of the Luo people, who lived on the shores of Lake Victoria in Kenya. (Rev: BL 3/1/96) [967.8]

7875 Bangura, Abdul Karim. *Kipsigis* (5–8). Illus. Series: Heritage Library of African Peoples. 1994, Rosen LB $17.95 (0-8239-1765-7). An attractive title that deals with the history and present status of the Kipsigis people of Kenya. (Rev: SLJ 5/95) [967.62]

7876 Bessire, Aimee, and Mark Bessire. *Sukuma* (5–8). Series: Heritage Library of African Peoples. 1997, Rosen LB $17.95 (0-8239-1992-7). Describes the history, culture, leaders, customs, and present situation of the Sukuma people of Tanzania. (Rev: BL 9/15/97; VOYA 12/97) [967.6]

7877 Blauer, Ettagale, and Jason Lauré. *Uganda* (5–8). Illus. Series: Enchantment of the World. 1997, Children's paper $32.00 (0-516-20306-1). This introduction to Uganda covers such topics as geography, climate, plants and animals, history, religion, culture, and daily life. (Rev: BL 7/97; HBG 3/98) [967.61]

7878 Bodnarchuk, Kari. *Rwanda: Country Torn Apart* (7–10). Illus. Series: World in Conflict. 1999, Lerner LB $25.26 (0-8225-3557-2). This history of Rwanda concentrates on the Tutsi/Hutu civil war in 1994 that left over a million people dead. (Rev: BL 1/1–15/00; HBG 4/00) [967.571.]

7879 Broberg, Catherine. *Kenya in Pictures* (6–10). Series: Visual Geography. 2002, Lerner LB $27.93 (0-8225-1957-7). Information on all aspects of life in this African country, including extensive coverage of its history, is accompanied by plenty of pho-

tographs and a Web site that offers up-to-date links. (Rev: BL 10/15/02; HBG 3/03; SLJ 12/02) [967]

7880 Burnham, Philip. *Gbaya* (7–12). Illus. Series: Heritage Library of African Peoples. 1997, Rosen LB $17.95 (0-8239-1995-1). These African people who live in Cameroon, Central African Republic, Congo, and Zaire, are introduced through illustrations and simple text. (Rev: BL 4/15/97) [967]

7881 Corona, Laurel. *Ethiopia* (5–8). Series: Modern Nations of the World. 2000, Lucent LB $27.45 (1-56006-823-X). An attractive, well-organized introduction to Ethiopia that gives its history, geography, and culture plus national statistics, a chronology, and bibliographies. (Rev: BL 3/1/01) [963]

7882 Corona, Laurel. *Kenya* (5–8). Illus. Series: Modern Nations of the World. 1999, Lucent LB $27.45 (1-56006-590-7). A profile of this poor African country that is a study in contrasts and cultures, with material on such subjects as geography, economics, people, and current problems. (Rev: BL 2/15/00; HBG 10/00) [967.62]

7883 Creed, Alexander. *Uganda* (6–12). Series: Major World Nations. 1998, Chelsea LB $21.95 (0-7910-4770-9). This book presents background material on the history and geography of Uganda and good current information on the country's economic, cultural, and social conditions. (Rev: BL 9/15/98; BR 1–2/99) [967.61]

7884 Diouf, Sylviane. *Kings and Queens of Central Africa* (4–7). Series: Watts Library: Africa — Kings and Queens. 2000, Watts LB $24.00 (0-531-20372-7). This look at the political and social evolution of central Africa describes some of its important royalty including the 15th-century Afonso and Bolongongo, the legendary Bakuba king, with a final chapter on the region today. (Rev: BL 3/1/01) [960]

7885 Diouf, Sylviane. *Kings and Queens of East Africa* (4–7). Illus. Series: Watts Library: Africa — Kings and Queens. 2000, Watts LB $24.00 (0-531-20373-5). This book gives biographical information about royalty in East Africa and through these sketches re-creates the history of this part of Africa. (Rev: BL 2/15/01) [967.6]

7886 *Ethiopia in Pictures* (5–8). Illus. Series: Visual Geography. 1994, Lerner LB $21.27 (0-8225-1836-8). Land, history and government, culture, education, religion, and health are covered. (Rev: BL 2/1/89) [963]

7887 Fox, Mary V. *Somalia* (5–8). Illus. Series: Enchantment of the World. 1996, Children's Pr. paper $32.00 (0-516-20019-4). An introduction to the land and people of this Muslim republic, which occupies the eastern horn of Africa. (Rev: BL 1/1–15/97) [967.73]

7888 Freeman, Charles. *Crisis in Rwanda* (7–12). Series: New Perspectives. 1998, Raintree Steck-Vaughn LB $28.54 (0-8172-5020-4). This book tells of the genocide of the Tutsi, the movements of Hutu refugees, and the actions of the international community from the viewpoints of survivors, aid workers, politicians, historians, and journalists. (Rev: BL 12/15/98; HBG 3/99; SLJ 2/99) [967.57]

7889 Gaertner, Ursula. *Elmolo* (7–10). Series: Heritage Library of African Peoples. 1995, Rosen LB $17.95 (0-8239-1764-9). Looks at the customs, daily life, and values of the Elmolo tribe in Kenya. (Rev: BL 7/95; SLJ 5/95) [967.62]

7890 Giles, Bridget. *Kenya* (4–8). Series: Nations of the World. 2001, Raintree Steck-Vaughn LB $34.26 (0-7398-1290-4). From snow-capped mountains to scorching deserts, this geographically and culturally diverse African nation is attractively introduced in this volume. (Rev: BL 12/15/01; HBG 3/02; SLJ 12/01) [967.62]

7891 Gish, Steven. *Ethiopia* (4–7). Illus. Series: Cultures of the World. 1996, Marshall Cavendish LB $35.64 (0-7614-0276-4). After general background information on Ethiopia, such topics as lifestyles, religion, and language are discussed. (Rev: BL 8/96; SLJ 8/96) [963]

7892 Holtzman, Jon. *Samburu* (7–10). Series: Heritage Library of African Peoples. 1995, Rosen LB $17.95 (0-8239-1759-2). Discusses in detailed but simple text the culture and lifestyle of the Samburu people of Kenya. (Rev: BL 7/95; SLJ 5/95) [967]

7893 Hussein, Ikram. *Teenage Refugees from Somalia Speak Out* (7–12). Series: Teenage Refugees Speak Out. 1997, Rosen LB $16.95 (0-8239-2444-0). Teenage refugees from Somalia recount the violent anarchy and acute famine in their country and their journey from Africa to the United States. (Rev: BL 12/15/97; SLJ 12/97) [967]

7894 Ifemesia, Chieka. *Turkana* (7–10). Illus. Series: Heritage Library of African Peoples. 1996, Rosen LB $17.95 (0-8239-1761-4). Using a simple text and color photographs, this account describes the past and present of the Turkana people, who now live in Ethiopia, Kenya, Sudan, and Uganda. (Rev: BL 2/15/95) [960]

7895 Jones, Schuyler. *Pygmies of Central Africa* (5–8). Illus. 1989, Rourke LB $16.67 (0-86625-268-1). A vivid look into the lives of these fascinating people. (Rev: BL 5/15/89) [967.00496]

7896 Kabira, Wanjiku M. *Agikuyu* (7–10). Series: Heritage Library of African Peoples. 1995, Rosen LB $17.95 (0-8239-1762-2). Presents social and cultural aspects of the Agikuyu community of Kenya in ways that make them accessible to Western readers. (Rev: BL 7/95; SLJ 6/95) [967]

7897 Kurtz, Jane. *Ethiopia: The Roof of Africa* (5–8). Illus. Series: Discovering Our Heritage. 1991, Macmillan LB $14.95 (0-87518-483-9). Beginning with a map and two pages of basic facts, this is an interesting introduction to the land, people, and

modern problems of Ethiopia. (Rev: BL 2/1/92; SLJ 5/92) [963]

7898 McNair, Sylvia, and Lynne Mansure. *Kenya* (4–7). Series: Enchantment of the World. 2001, Children's LB $34.50 (0-516-21078-5). A superior introduction to the land and people of Kenya with material on such topics as history, culture, problems, climate, resources, and religion. (Rev: BL 1/1–15/02) [967.62]

7899 McQuail, Lisa. *The Masai of Africa* (4–7). Illus. Series: First Peoples. 2001, Lerner LB $23.93 (0-8225-4855-0). McQuail provides information about the Masai people, covering their history, customs, and contemporary daily life, with photographs. (Rev: BL 10/15/01; HBG 3/02; SLJ 3/02) [967.6]

7900 *Malawi in Pictures* (5–8). Illus. Series: Visual Geography. 1989, Lerner LB $25.55 (0-8225-1842-2). An overview of climate, history, geography, culture, education, and other aspects of life. (Rev: BL 2/1/89) [968.97]

7901 Ng'weno, Fleur. *Kenya* (4–7). Illus. Series: Focus On. 1992, Trafalgar $22.95 (0-237-60194-X). Discusses Kenya's history, peoples, and lifestyles. (Rev: SLJ 8/92) [967.6]

7902 Nnoromele, Salome. *Somalia* (5–8). Series: Modern Nations of the World. 2000, Lucent LB $27.45 (1-56006-396-3). An introduction to this East African country with material on its history and geography and a large section on daily life. (Rev: BL 5/15/00; HBG 10/00) [967.73]

7903 Nwaezeigwe, Nwankwo T. *Ngoni* (7–12). Illus. Series: Heritage Library of African Peoples. 1997, Rosen LB $17.95 (0-8239-2006-2). The history, traditions, and struggle for freedom of this African group in Malawi are laid out in accessible text. (Rev: BL 4/15/97) [968.97]

7904 Ojo, Onukaba A. *Mbuti* (7–10). Illus. Series: Heritage Library of African Peoples. 1996, Rosen LB $17.95 (0-8239-1998-6). The Mbuti people of Zaire are introduced with details on their environment, history, customs, and present situation. (Rev: BL 2/15/96; SLJ 7/96) [305.896]

7905 Okeke, Chika. *Kongo* (7–12). Illus. Series: Heritage Library of African Peoples. 1997, Rosen LB $17.95 (0-8239-2001-1). The Kongo people of Angola, Congo, and Zaire in Central Africa are featured in easy-reading text with material on their land, kingdoms, political life, and culture. (Rev: BL 4/15/97) [967]

7906 Parris, Ronald. *Rendille* (5–8). Illus. Series: Heritage Library of African Peoples. 1994, Rosen LB $17.95 (0-8239-1763-0). With extensive use of black-and-white and color photographs, introduces the history and customs of the Rendille people of Kenya. (Rev: SLJ 5/95) [967.62]

7907 Pateman, Robert. *Kenya* (4–7). Illus. Series: Cultures of the World. 1993, Marshall Cavendish LB $35.64 (1-85435-572-4). The background story of Kenya is revealed through color photographs and a text that also covers present concerns. (Rev: BL 8/93) [967.62]

7908 Peffer, John. *States of Ethiopia* (6–9). Series: First Books: African Civilizations. 1998, Watts LB $23.00 (0-531-20278-X). A history of this kingdom that converted to Christianity in the 4th century and then became Muslim in the 7th century, and of the turmoil this produced over the centuries. (Rev: BL 1/1–15/99; HBG 9/99) [963]

7909 *Peoples of Central Africa* (8–12). Series: Peoples of Africa. 1997, Facts on File $28.00 (0-8160-3486-9). A description of the history, culture, and present status of 17 African peoples who live in and around the present-day countries of Angola, Congo, and Zaire. (Rev: BR 11–12/97; SLJ 2/98) [967]

7910 *Peoples of East Africa* (6–12). Series: Peoples of Africa. 1997, Facts on File $28.00 (0-8160-3484-2). This book gives a concise overview of 15 ethnic groups of eastern Africa, with details on history, language, way of life, society, religion, and culture. Included are Falasha, Ganda, Hutus and Tutsis, Masai, Nyoro, Somalis, and Swahili. (Rev: BR 11–12/97; SLJ 10/97) [967]

7911 Roberts, Mary N., and Allen F. Roberts. *Luba* (6–10). Series: Heritage Library of African Peoples. 1997, Rosen LB $17.95 (0-8239-2002-X). The Luba people of Zaire are introduced with material on their history, present conditions, and cultural resources. (Rev: BL 9/15/97) [967]

7912 Schnapper, LaDena. *Teenage Refugees from Ethiopia Speak Out* (5–10). Series: Teenage Refugees Speak Out. 1997, Rosen LB $16.95 (0-8239-2438-6). Ethiopian teens now living in America tell of the violence, famine, and civil war that drove them from their country and of their reception in America. (Rev: SLJ 2/98) [963]

7913 *Sudan in Pictures* (5–8). Illus. Series: Visual Geography. 1990, Lerner LB $25.55 (0-8225-1839-2). An overview of history, culture, geography, economy, education, and health. (Rev: BL 2/1/89) [962.4]

7914 Swinimer, Ciarunji C. *Pokot* (5–8). Illus. Series: Heritage Library of African Peoples. 1994, Rosen LB $17.95 (0-8239-1756-8). Using a good balance of text and visuals, this account describes the history, culture, and present status of the Pokot people of Kenya. (Rev: SLJ 5/95) [967.62]

7915 *Tanzania in Pictures* (5–8). Illus. Series: Visual Geography. 1989, Lerner LB $25.55 (0-8225-1838-4). Part of the Visual Geography series, contains information on history, geography, economy, religion, and culture. (Rev: BL 2/1/89) [967.8104]

7916 Twagilimana, Aimable. *Hutu and Tutsi* (5–9). Series: The Heritage Library of African Peoples. 1997, Rosen LB $28.75 (0-8239-1999-4). A large section of this book is devoted to the current struggle between the Hutu and Tutsi people of central Africa, along with chapters on art and religion. (Rev: BR 9–10/98; SLJ 3/98) [967]

7917 Twagilimana, Aimable. *Teenage Refugees from Rwanda Speak Out* (5–10). Series: Teenage Refugees Speak Out. 1997, Rosen LB $16.95 (0-8239-2443-2). Teenage refugees from Rwanda describe the warfare between Tutsi and Hutu peoples and the terrible living conditions that forced them to leave their country and discuss the challenges and difficulties they have experienced in the United States. (Rev: SLJ 2/98) [967]

7918 Wangari, Estgher. *Ameru* (7–10). Illus. Series: The Heritage Library of African Peoples. 1995, Rosen LB $17.95 (0-8239-1766-5). An introduction to the history, traditions, and culture of the Ameru people of Kenya in easy-reading text. (Rev: BL 9/15/95; SLJ 11/95) [967.6]

7919 Wilson, Thomas H. *City-States of the Swahili Coast* (6–9). Series: First Books: African Civilizations. 1998, Watts LB $23.00 (0-531-20281-X). The history of the separate kingdoms that grew up along the eastern coast of Africa from present-day Somalia to Mozambique. (Rev: BL 1/1–15/99; HBG 9/99) [963]

7920 Zeleza, Tiyambe. *Akamba* (7–10). Illus. Series: The Heritage Library of African Peoples. 1995, Rosen LB $17.95 (0-8239-1768-1). The history, traditions, and fight for freedom of the Akamba people of Kenya are covered in this book with many color illustrations. (Rev: BL 7/95; SLJ 6/95) [960]

7921 Zeleza, Tiyambe. *Maasai* (5–8). Illus. Series: Heritage Library of African Peoples. 1994, Rosen LB $17.95 (0-8239-1757-6). An introduction to these people of Kenya and Tanzania, their culture, customs, and history. (Rev: SLJ 5/95) [967.62]

7922 Zeleza, Tiyambe. *Mijikenda* (7–10). Series: Heritage Library of African Peoples. 1995, Rosen LB $17.95 (0-8239-1767-3). Combines history and anthropology to provide an easy-to-read portrait of the Mijikenda people. (Rev: BL 9/15/95; SLJ 11/95) [967]

North Africa

7923 Azuonye, Chukwuma. *Dogon* (7–10). Illus. Series: Heritage Library of African Peoples. 1995, Rosen LB $28.75 (0-8239-1976-5). Provides information on the history, culture, and lifestyles of the Dogon people of Mali. (Rev: BL 2/15/96) [966.23]

7924 Barter, James. *The Nile* (5–8). Series: Rivers of the World. 2003, Gale $27.45 (1-56006-935-X). An appealing and informative description of the Nile's source, tributaries, and path; history from ancient times; and the long-term environmental problems affecting the river and actions that are being taken to preserve the river. (Rev: SLJ 1/03) [962]

7925 Blauer, Ettagale, and Jason Lauré. *Morocco* (4–7). Series: Enchantment of the World. 1999, Children's LB $34.50 (0-516-20961-2). In this fine introduction to Morocco topics include history, government, economics, people, religion, culture, and the arts. (Rev: BL 9/15/99) [964]

7926 Cumming, David. *The Nile* (4–7). Series: Great Rivers of the World. 2003, World Almanac LB $26.60 (0-8368-5445-4). An exploration of the Nile's flow, history, and animals and plants, with discussion of the settlements along its banks, the industries it supports, recreation on its waters, and environmental threats to the river. (Rev: SLJ 9/03)

7927 Fox, Mary V. *Tunisia* (5–8). Illus. Series: Enchantment of the World. 1990, Children's paper $32.00 (0-516-02724-7). Introduces this North African country. (Rev: BL 1/1/91) [961.1]

7928 Kagda, Falaq. *Algeria* (4–7). Illus. Series: Cultures of the World. 1997, Marshall Cavendish LB $35.64 (0-7614-0680-8). This book on Algeria emphasizes the people and how they live. (Rev: BL 8/97) [965]

7929 Malcolm, Peter. *Libya* (4–7). Illus. 1993, Marshall Cavendish LB $35.64 (1-85435-573-2). Well-chosen photographs and readable text give good background information as well as material on present problems. (Rev: BL 8/93) [961.2]

7930 *Peoples of North Africa* (8–12). Series: Peoples of Africa. 1997, Facts on File $28.00 (0-8160-3483-4). This book describes the history and cultures of North African peoples, including Arabs, Baggara, Beja, Berbers, Copts, Dinka, Muba, Nuer, Shilluk, and Tuareg. (Rev: BR 11–12/97; SLJ 2/98) [961]

7931 Raskin, Lawrie, and Debora Pearson. *52 Days by Camel: My Sahara Adventure* (4–8). Illus. 1998, Annick $24.95 (1-55037-519-9); paper $14.95 (1-55037-518-0). An engaging account of a trip from Fez to Timbuktu by bus, jeep, train, truck, and camel, with details on desert life and culture. (Rev: BL 6/1–15/98; SLJ 7/98) [964]

Southern Africa

7932 Bessire, Mark. *Great Zimbabwe* (6–9). Series: First Books: African Civilizations. 1999, Watts LB $23.00 (0-531-20285-2). The story of the rise and fall of the civilization that flourished in the southern part of Africa. (Rev: BL 9/15/99; HBG 9/99) [968]

7933 Biesele, Megan, and Kxao Royal. *San* (7–10). Series: Heritage Library of African Peoples. 1997, Rosen LB $17.95 (0-8239-1997-8). The San people

of Botswana, Namibia, and South Africa are featured in this accessible account that describes their rich tradition and struggle for freedom. (Rev: BL 9/15/97) [960]

7934 Blauer, Ettagale, and Jason Lauré. *Madagascar* (4–7). Series: Enchantment of the World. 2000, Children's LB $34.50 (0-516-21634-1). Madagascar, the island nation off the coast of Africa, is introduced. Topics addressed include its land and people, wildlife, history, traditions, daily life, and economy. (Rev: BL 12/15/00) [969]

7935 Blauer, Ettagale, and Jason Lauré. *South Africa* (5–10). Series: Enchantment of the World. 1998, Children's LB $34.50 (0-516-20606-0). An introduction to South Africa that gives good coverage of the struggle of black Africans for freedom and the problems facing the population today. (Rev: HBG 3/99; SLJ 11/98) [968]

7936 Blauer, Ettagale, and Jason Lauré. *Swaziland* (5–8). Illus. Series: Enchantment of the World. 1996, Children's Pr. paper $32.00 (0-516-20020-8). This landlocked kingdom north of South Africa is introduced with material on its physical features, history, and economy. (Rev: BL 1/1–15/97) [968.87]

7937 Bolaane, Maitseo, and Part T. Mgadla. *Batswana* (6–10). Series: Heritage Library of African Peoples. 1997, Rosen LB $17.95 (0-8239-2008-9). This work discusses the history, culture, and present status of the Batswana people of southern Africa. (Rev: BL 1/1–15/98) [968]

7938 Brandenburg, Jim. *Sand and Fog: Adventures in Southern Africa* (5–8). Illus. 1994, Walker LB $17.85 (0-8027-8233-7). A stunning photoessay about the wildlife found in Namibia. (Rev: BCCB 5/94; BL 3/1/94*; HB 5–6/94; SLJ 5/94) [968.1]

7939 Canesso, Claudia. *South Africa* (6–10). Series: Major World Nations. 1998, Chelsea LB $21.95 (0-7910-4766-0). An accurate, informative, and unbiased account of the social, political, and economic conditions in South Africa today, supplemented by illustrations and maps. (Rev: BL 9/15/98; BR 1–2/99; HBG 3/99; SLJ 6/99) [968.06]

7940 Diouf, Sylviane. *Kings and Queens of Southern Africa* (4–7). Illus. Series: Watts Library: Africa — Kings and Queens. 2000, Watts LB $24.00 (0-531-20374-3). Through the lives of Shaka the Zulu king, Moshoeshoe of the Sotho kingdom, and others, the reader gets a good history of this region before and during the colonial period. (Rev: BL 2/15/01) [968]

7941 Fish, Bruce, and Becky Durost Fish. *South Africa: 1880 to the Present: Imperialism, Nationalism, and Apartheid* (6–12). 2000, Chelsea LB $24.95 (0-7910-5676-7). This survey of South African history is careful to highlight changes and achievements that did not involve European influence; it includes many Royal Geographic Society black-and-white photographs. (Rev: BR 9–10/01; HBG 3/01; SLJ 2/01) [968]

7942 Flint, David. *South Africa* (5–8). Illus. Series: Modern Industrial World. 1996, Raintree Steck-Vaughn $24.26 (0-8172-4554-5). The present economic status of South Africa is studied through personal narratives and case studies. (Rev: BL 2/15/97; SLJ 8/97) [968]

7943 Green, Jen. *South Africa* (4–8). Series: Nations of the World. 2001, Raintree Steck-Vaughn LB $34.26 (0-7398-1282-3). A profile of the strongest industrial nation in Africa, with material on its geography, resources, environment, government, economy, and future. (Rev: BL 6/1–15/01; HBG 10/01) [968]

7944 Green, Rebecca L. *Merina* (7–12). Illus. Series: Heritage Library of African Peoples. 1997, Rosen LB $17.95 (0-8239-1991-9). The history and culture of the Merina people of Madagascar are covered in simple text and many illustrations. (Rev: BL 4/15/97; VOYA 6/97) [969.1]

7945 Harrison, Peter, ed. *History of Southern Africa* (7–12). Illus. Series: History of Africa. 2003, Facts on File $30.00 (0-8160-5065-1). From prehistory to today, this volume covers in detail the history of southern Africa, detailing in particular European settlement, independence, and apartheid. (Rev: BL 9/15/03) [968]

7946 Inserra, Rose, and Susan Powell. *The Kalahari* (5–8). Series: Ends of the Earth. 1997, Heinemann LB $25.45 (0-431-06932-8). An introduction to the history, animal and vegetable life, and future of this desert region of southern Botswana, eastern Namibia, and western South Africa. (Rev: SLJ 11/97) [968]

7947 Kaschula, Russel. *Xhosa* (7–12). Series: Heritage Library of African Peoples. 1997, Rosen LB $17.95 (0-8239-2013-5). The Xhosa people of South Africa are introduced with stunning photographs and simple text describing their past as well as present culture and lifestyles. (Rev: BL 1/1–15/98) [968]

7948 Klopper, Sandra. *The Zulu Kingdom* (6–9). Series: First Books: African Civilizations. 1999, Watts LB $23.00 (0-531-20286-0). This book traces the growth of the Zulu empire in the south of Africa and how it was destroyed chiefly by Europeans. (Rev: BL 9/15/99; HBG 9/99) [968]

7949 Lauré, Jason. *Angola* (5–8). Illus. Series: Enchantment of the World. 1990, Children's paper $32.00 (0-516-02721-2). The troubled history of Angola is given, and geography and key people are introduced. (Rev: BL 1/1/91) [967.3]

7950 Lauré, Jason. *Botswana* (5–8). Illus. Series: Enchantment of the World. 1993, Children's paper $32.00 (0-516-02616-X). An introduction to this republic that gained independence in 1964 and is famous for its gold and wildlife preserves. (Rev: BL 11/1/93; SLJ 4/94) [968.83]

7951 Lauré, Jason. *Namibia* (5–8). Series: Enchantment of the World. 1993, Children's Pr. paper $32.00 (0-516-02615-1). A description of the land and people of Namibia, which was once administered by South Africa and gained full independence in 1990. (Rev: BL 8/93) [968.81]

7952 Lauré, Jason. *Zimbabwe* (4–7). Illus. 1989, Children's paper $32.00 (0-516-02704-2). The history, culture, people, and customs of this African land. (Rev: BL 8/88) [968.91]

7953 *Madagascar in Pictures* (5–8). Illus. Series: Visual Geography. 1988, Lerner LB $25.55 (0-8225-1841-4). Covers geography, history, culture, economics, religion, and health. (Rev: BL 2/1/89) [969.1]

7954 Mann, Kenny. *Monomotapa, Zulu, Basuto: Southern Africa* (8–12). Series: African Kingdoms of the Past. 1996, Silver Burdett LB $15.95 (0-87518-659-9); paper $7.95 (0-382-39300-7). The history of three southern African kingdoms using striking layouts, plenty of color, and clear writing. (Rev: SLJ 2/97; VOYA 2/97) [968]

7955 Nagle, Garrett. *South Africa* (6–12). Series: Country Studies. 1999, Heinemann LB $27.07 (1-57572-896-6). An excellent overview of South Africa, with particularly good coverage of current conditions and problems. (Rev: BL 8/99) [968]

7956 Ngwane, Zolani. *Zulu* (7–12). Series: Heritage Library of African Peoples. 1997, Rosen LB $17.95 (0-8239-2014-3). This readable work introduces the history and culture of the Zulus of South Africa. (Rev: BL 9/15/97; VOYA 12/97) [968]

7957 Njoku, Onwuka N. *Mbundu* (7–12). Illus. Series: Heritage Library of African Peoples. 1997, Rosen LB $28.75 (0-8239-2004-6). An easy-to-read introduction to the history and contemporary culture of this people of Angola. (Rev: BL 4/15/97) [967.3]

7958 Oluikpe, Benson O. *Swazi* (7–12). Illus. Series: Heritage Library of African Peoples. 1997, Rosen LB $28.75 (0-8239-2012-7). This accessible book describes the history, traditions, and struggles for freedom of the Swazi people of Swaziland and South Africa. (Rev: BL 4/15/97; SLJ 12/97) [968]

7959 *Peoples of Southern Africa* (6–12). Series: Peoples of Africa. 1997, Facts on File $28.00 (0-8160-3487-7). The history, geography, culture, religion, and social life of 17 different South African peoples are highlighted, including Afrikaners, Cape Coloreds, Cape Malays, Indian South Africans, Ndebele, Swazi, Tswana, Venda, and Zulu. (Rev: BR 11–12/97; SLJ 10/97) [968]

7960 Rogers, Barbara Radcliffe, and Stillman D. Rogers. *Zimbabwe* (4–7). Series: Enchantment of the World. 2002, Children's LB $34.50 (0-516-

21113-7). This troubled African land is introduced with material on topics including history, geography, people, government, and resources. (Rev: BL 5/15/02; SLJ 7/02) [968.9]

7961 Rosemarin, Ike. *South Africa* (4–7). Illus. Series: Cultures of the World. 1993, Marshall Cavendish LB $35.64 (1-85435-575-9). Historical and modern concerns are covered in this look at South Africa. (Rev: BL 8/93) [968]

7962 Schneider, Elizabeth Ann. *Ndebele* (7–12). Illus. Series: Heritage Library of African Peoples. 1997, Rosen LB $17.95 (0-8239-2009-7). Topics covered about the Ndebele people of South Africa include environment, history, religion, social organization, politics, and customs. (Rev: BL 4/15/97) [968]

7963 Smith, Chris. *Conflict in Southern Africa* (6–12). Series: Conflicts. 1993, Macmillan LB $22.00 (0-02-785956-8). An overview of the politics of southern Africa: Angola, Mozambique, Zambia, Namibia, and South Africa. (Rev: BL 7/93; SLJ 12/93) [968]

7964 *South Africa in Pictures* (5–8). Illus. Series: Visual Geography. 1996, Lerner LB $25.55 (0-8225-1835-X). Focusing on climate, geography, wildlife, and the history of this troubled country. (Rev: BL 8/88) [968.06]

7965 Stark, Al. *Zimbabwe: A Treasure of Africa* (4–7). Illus. 1986, Macmillan $14.95 (0-87518-308-5). The colorful history, culture, wildlife, geography, and diversity of the people of Zimbabwe are detailed. (Rev: BL 6/15/86; SLJ 5/86) [968]

7966 Stein, R. Conrad. *Cape Town* (5–8). Series: Cities of the World. 1998, Children's Pr. LB $27.00 (0-516-20781-4). A photoessay that shows this modern, multicultural, multiracial South African capital with its rich diversity of people at work, at school, and at play. (Rev: BL 12/15/98; HBG 3/99) [968.7]

7967 Udechukwu, Ada. *Herero* (7–10). Series: Heritage Library of African Peoples. 1996, Rosen LB $17.95 (0-8239-2003-8). In simple text, this book introduces the three Herero subgroups that share a similar language and culture in today's Botswana, Angola, and Namibia, with an emphasis on their political history. (Rev: BL 3/15/96; SLJ 6/96) [968]

7968 Van Wyk, Gary N. *Basotho* (5–7). Illus. Series: Heritage Library of African Peoples. 1996, Rosen LB $17.95 (0-8239-2005-4). Describes the Basotho people, who live in Lesotho and South Africa, with simple text on their history, religion, social organization, and customs. (Rev: BL 11/15/96; SLJ 3/97) [968]

7969 Van Wyk, Gary N., and Robert Johnson. *Shona* (5–7). Series: Heritage Library of African Peoples. 1997, Rosen LB $17.95 (0-8239-2011-9). The Shona people of Zimbabwe are presented in

outstanding photographs, with a text that covers their past, their culture, and their present living conditions and problems. (Rev: BL 1/1–15/98) [968]

7970 *Zimbabwe* (5–9). Illus. Series: Major World Nations. 1999, Chelsea LB $19.95 (0-7910-4753-9). A good introduction to Zimbabwe's history, geography, government, people, pastimes, economy, and culture. (Rev: SLJ 8/98) [968]

7971 *Zimbabwe in Pictures* (5–8). Illus. Series: Visual Geography. 1997, Lerner LB $25.55 (0-8225-1825-2). Many photographs highlight this overview of Zimbabwe's history, climate, wildlife, and culture. (Rev: BL 4/15/88) [968]

West Africa

7972 Adeeb, Hassan, and Bonnetta Adeeb. *Nigeria: One Nation, Many Cultures* (4–8). Illus. Series: Exploring Cultures of the World. 1995, Benchmark LB $27.07 (0-7614-0190-3). Opening with an account of a legendary figure, this book continues with an introduction to Nigeria that emphasizes its culture and how the people live. (Rev: SLJ 6/96) [966.9]

7973 Adeleke, Tunde. *Songhay* (5–7). Illus. Series: Heritage Library of African Peoples. 1996, Rosen LB $28.75 (0-8239-1986-2). Both historical information and material on contemporary life are given in this account of the African people who live chiefly in Mali, Niger, and Benin. (Rev: BL 11/15/96) [960]

7974 Anda, Michael O. *Yoruba* (7–10). Series: Heritage Library of African Peoples. 1996, Rosen LB $17.95 (0-8239-1988-9). This work describes one of the largest sub-Sahara ethnic groups, whose influence, because of the slave trade, spread to the New World, especially Brazil. (Rev: BL 3/15/96; SLJ 6/96) [966.9]

7975 Azuonye, Chukwuma. *Edo: The Bini People of the Benin Kingdom* (7–10). Illus. Series: Heritage Library of African Peoples. 1996, Rosen LB $28.75 (0-8239-1985-4). A review of the history, culture, society, and the struggle for freedom of the Bini people, whose empire was part of present-day Nigeria. (Rev: BL 3/15/96) [966.9]

7976 Beaton, Margaret. *Senegal* (5–8). Series: Enchantment of the World. 1997, Children's Pr. paper $32.00 (0-516-20304-5). An introduction to this West African nation, its people, and its cities, including the capital of Dakar. (Rev: BL 7/97; HBG 3/98) [916.63]

7977 Blauer, Ettagale, and Jason Lauré. *Ghana* (4–7). Series: Enchantment of the World. 1999, Children's LB $34.50 (0-516-20962-0). A geographical and cultural exploration of the African nation of Ghana, once a center of the slave trade. (Rev: BL 12/15/99) [966.7]

7978 Blauer, Ettagale, and Jason Lauré. *Nigeria* (4–7). Series: Enchantment of the World. 2001, Children's LB $34.50 (0-516-22281-3). An interesting and well-illustrated introduction to the nation that is dominated by the delta of the Niger River. (Rev: BL 1/1–15/02) [966.9]

7979 Boateng, Faustine Ama. *Asante* (5–7). Illus. Series: Heritage Library of African Peoples. 1996, Rosen LB $17.95 (0-8239-1975-7). This African people living in present-day Ghana is described, with information on history, traditions, and lifestyle. (Rev: BL 11/15/96; SLJ 3/97) [966.7]

7980 Brace, Steve. *Ghana* (4–8). Illus. Series: Economically Developing Countries. 1995, Thomson Learning LB $24.26 (1-56847-242-0). Rich and poor rural and urban families are introduced in this attractive book on Ghana, its past, and its present. (Rev: SLJ 7/95) [966.7]

7981 Brook, Larry. *Daily Life in Ancient and Modern Timbuktu* (5–7). Illus. 1999, Lerner LB $25.26 (0-8225-3215-8). A fascinating look at this ancient West African city that was once a center of commerce and learning. (Rev: BL 9/1/99; HBG 10/99; SLJ 7/99) [966.23]

7982 Chambers, Catherine. *West African States: 15th Century to the Colonial Era* (5–8). Series: Looking Back. 1999, Raintree Steck-Vaughn $19.98 (0-8172-5427-7). A brief overview of the history and culture of the great empires of West Africa and how they disappeared with the arrival of the Europeans. (Rev: BL 5/15/99; VOYA 2/00) [966.2]

7983 Conrad, David. *The Songhay Empire* (6–9). Series: First Books: African Civilizations. 1998, Watts LB $23.00 (0-531-20284-4). This African empire founded in Mali in western Africa around 700 A.D. by Berbers reached the height of its power about 1500. (Rev: BL 1/1–15/99; HBG 9/99) [966.7]

7984 *Cote d'Ivoire (Ivory Coast) in Pictures* (5–8). Illus. Series: Visual Geography. 1988, Lerner LB $25.55 (0-8225-1828-7). Covering all aspects of life in this overview, with pictorial emphasis and coverage of possible future developments. (Rev: BL 4/15/88; SLJ 11/88) [966.68]

7985 Diouf, Sylviane. *Kings and Queens of West Africa* (4–7). Series: Watts Library: Africa — Kings and Queens. 2000, Watts LB $24.00 (0-531-20375-1). Some of the royal figures covered in this historical survey of West Africa are Emperor Mansa Musa of Mali and Nsate Yalla Mbodj, queen of the Walo of Senegal. (Rev: BL 3/1/01) [960]

7986 *Ghana* (5–9). Illus. Series: Major World Nations. 1999, Chelsea LB $21.95 (0-7910-4739-3). Basic facts about Ghana's history, geography, politics, government, economy, natural resources, education, and people. (Rev: HBG 9/98; SLJ 8/98) [966.7]

7987 Greene, Rebecca L. *The Empire of Ghana* (6–9). Series: First Books: African Civilizations. 1998, Watts LB $23.00 (0-531-20276-3). This book describes the medieval African kingdom that grew up in what is now eastern Senegal, southwest Mali, and southern Mauritania, and how it flourished because it was on the trans-Sahara caravan routes. (Rev: BL 1/1–15/99; HBG 9/99) [966.7]

7988 Harmon, Daniel E. *Nigeria: 1880 to the Present: The Struggle, the Tragedy, the Promise* (6–12). 2000, Chelsea LB $29.95 (0-7910-5452-7). This survey of Nigerian history is careful to highlight changes and achievements that did not involve European influence; it includes many Royal Geographic Society black-and-white photographs. (Rev: BR 9–10/01; HBG 3/01; SLJ 2/01) [966.9]

7989 Hathaway, Jim. *Cameroon in Pictures* (5–8). Illus. Series: Visual Geography. 1992, Lerner LB $25.55 (0-8225-1857-0). With numerous charts, maps, and photographs, the country of Cameroon is introduced. (Rev: BL 9/15/89) [967]

7990 Heale, Jay. *Democratic Republic of the Congo* (5–9). Series: Cultures of the World. 1998, Marshall Cavendish LB $35.64 (0-7614-0874-6). A history of this nation that has been stricken with civil wars and political instability, with descriptions of its history, economy, government, people, and culture. (Rev: HBG 9/99; SLJ 6/99) [967]

7991 Heinrichs, Ann. *Niger* (4–7). Series: Enchantment of the World. 2001, Children's LB $34.50 (0-516-21633-3). Niger, a predominately Muslim country that is one of the hottest places in the world, is described in this attractive volume with material on topics such as resources, history, and culture. (Rev: BL 1/1–15/02) [967]

7992 Jordan, Manuel. *The Kongo Kingdom* (6–9). Series: First Books: African Civilizations. 1999, Watts LB $23.00 (0-531-20282-8). The story of the ancient African civilization that grew up around the banks of the Congo River. (Rev: BL 9/15/99; HBG 9/99) [966]

7993 Koslow, Philip. *Asante: The Gold Coast* (6–9). Illus. Series: Kingdoms of Africa. 1996, Chelsea LB $17.95 (0-7910-3139-X). The history of the mighty West African people who acquired great wealth from their gold mines and who were known worldwide for their artwork. (Rev: BL 6/1–15/96; BR 11–12/96) [966.7018]

7994 Koslow, Philip. *Benin: Lords of the River* (6–9). Illus. Series: Kingdoms of Africa. 1995, Chelsea paper $8.95 (0-7910-3134-9). A history of the people who lived around the Benin River, their conflicts with Europeans, and their lasting imperial grandeur. (Rev: BL 6/1–15/96) [966.9]

7995 Koslow, Philip. *Dahomey: The Warrior Kings* (5–8). Illus. Series: The Kingdoms of Africa. 1996, Chelsea LB $20.85 (0-7910-3137-3); paper $8.95

(0-7910-3138-1). A history of the West African kingdom that flourished in the 17th and 18th centuries, describing how the slave trade affected it. (Rev: BR 11–12/96; SLJ 12/96) [960]

7996 Koslow, Philip. *Lords of the Savanna: The Bambara, Fulani, Igbo, Mossi, and Nupe* (7–10). Series: The Kingdoms of Africa. 1997, Chelsea paper $8.95 (0-7910-3142-X). A strong narrative style and attractive illustrations are used to present the history and culture of these West African peoples of present-day Nigeria, Cameroon, and Burkina Faso. (Rev: SLJ 1/98) [966]

7997 Koslow, Philip. *Songhay: The Empire Builders* (6–9). Illus. Series: The Kingdoms of Africa. 1995, Chelsea LB $17.95 (0-7910-3128-4); paper $8.95 (0-7910-2943-3). This account concentrates on the 10th through 15th centuries, and tells about the great Songhay empire in West Africa that flourished under King Sunni Ali and later King Askia Muhammad, and produced such thriving cities as Timbuktu. (Rev: BL 2/15/96) [966.2]

7998 Koslow, Philip. *Yorubaland: The Flowering of Genius* (6–9). Illus. Series: The Kingdoms of Africa. 1995, Chelsea LB $17.95 (0-7910-3131-4); paper $9.95 (0-7910-3132-2). This account traces the 1,500-year history of the Yorubaland civilization in West Africa that dates back to the 4th century B.C. and produced an early sophisticated system of government. (Rev: BL 2/15/96; BR 11–12/96; SLJ 2/96) [960]

7999 Kummer, Patricia K. *Cote d'Ivoire* (5–8). Illus. Series: Enchantment of the World. 1996, Children's paper $32.00 (0-516-02641-0). An introduction to the small French-speaking African republic of Ivory Coast, which gained its freedom in 1960 and is now known as Cote d'Ivoire. (Rev: BL 7/96) [966.68]

8000 Levy, Patricia. *Nigeria* (4–7). Illus. Series: Cultures of the World. 1993, Marshall Cavendish LB $35.64 (1-85435-574-0). Information on history, geography, lifestyles, people, and culture. (Rev: BL 8/93) [966.9]

8001 *Liberia in Pictures* (5–8). Illus. Series: Visual Geography. 1996, Lerner LB $25.55 (0-8225-1837-6). Covers climate, geography, wildlife, vegetation, and natural resources. (Rev: BL 8/88) [966.62]

8002 MacDonald, Fiona. *Ancient African Town* (4–7). Series: Metropolis. 1998, Watts LB $25.00 (0-531-14480-1). Using a well-written text and colorful drawings, this work describes life in a 17th-century African community based on Benin City of the Edo empire in present-day Nigeria. (Rev: HBG 3/99; SLJ 1/99) [966.9]

8003 Mack William, Kibibi V. Morri (7–10). Illus. Series: Heritage Library of African Peoples. 1996, Rosen LB $28.75 (0-8239-1984-6). The history, social organization, and culture of the Mossi people

of West Africa are described. (Rev: BL 3/15/96) [966.25]

8004 Malaquais, Dominique. *The Kingdom of Benin* (6–9). Series: First Books: African Civilizations. 1998, Watts LB $23.00 (0-531-20279-8). Benin, formerly Dahomey, was the center of a thriving kingdom known particularly for its arts before European intervention. (Rev: BL 1/1–15/99; HBG 9/99) [966.9]

8005 Mann, Kenny. *Ghana, Mali, Songhay: The Western Sudan* (4–8). Series: African Kingdoms of the Past. 1996, Silver Burdett $15.95 (0-87518-656-4); paper $7.95 (0-382-39176 4). An eloquently written book about the once powerful empires of Ghana, Mali, and Songhay, with information on the beginnings of Islam Africa and how the slave trade gradually took over. (Rev: SLJ 9/96) [960]

8006 Mann, Kenny. *Kongo Ndongo: West Central Africa* (8–12). Series: African Kingdoms of the Past. 1996, Silver Burdett $15.95 (0-87518-658-0); paper $7.95 (0-382-39298-1). A visually attractive book that outlines the history of this West African kingdom and utilizes many excellent sources. (Rev: SLJ 2/97; VOYA 2/97) [966]

8007 Mann, Kenny. *Oyo, Benin, Ashanti: The Guinea Coast* (6–10). Series: African Kingdoms of the Past. 1996, Silver Burdett $15.95 (0-87518-657-2); paper $7.95 (0-382-39177-2). Through legends and history, the author re-creates the story of these three West Africa kingdoms and their culture. (Rev: SLJ 6/96) [960]

8008 Ndukwe, Pat I. *Fulani* (7–10). Illus. Series: Heritage Library of African Peoples. 1995.64p, Rosen LB $28.75 (0-8239-1982-X). A description of the history, surroundings, politics, customs, and current conditions of the Fulani people, who live in Cameroon, Mali, and Nigeria. (Rev: BL 2/15/96; SLJ 7/96) [966]

8009 *Nigeria in Pictures* (5–8). Illus. Series: Visual Geography. 1995, Lerner LB $25.55 (0-8225-1826-0). A visual focus on this African land. (Rev: BL 8/88) [966.9]

8010 Nnoromele, Salome. *Life Among the Ibo Women of Nigeria* (4–7). Illus. 1998, Lucent LB $27.45 (1-56006-344-0). A beautifully written account of women's role in Nigeria's Ibo society, tracing the country's history, social structure, and changes brought about by contacts with Western culture. (Rev: BL 9/1/98) [305.48]

8011 Nwanunobi, C. O. *Malinke* (5–7). Illus. Series: Heritage Library of African Peoples. 1996, Rosen LB $28.75 (0-8239-1979-X). Features the culture, history, and contemporary lifeways of the Malinke people, now living along the western coast of Africa. (Rev: BL 11/15/96) [966.23]

8012 Nwanunobi, C. O. *Soninke* (5–7). Illus. Series: Heritage Library of African Peoples. 1996, Rosen

LB $28.75 (0-8239-1978-1). A discussion of the African people found in such countries as Ghana, Mali, Nigeria, and Senegal, with material on history, customs, and present living conditions. (Rev: BL 11/15/96) [966]

8013 Ogbaa, Kalu. *Igbo* (7–10). Series: Heritage Library of African Peoples. 1995, Rosen LB $17.95 (0-8239-1977-3). An introduction to the Igbo people, one of the three most important ethnic groups in Nigeria. (Rev: BL 9/15/95; SLJ 11/95) [966.9]

8014 Parris, Ronald. *Hausa* (5–7). Illus. Series: Heritage Library of African Peoples. 1996, Rosen LB $28.75 (0-8239-1983-8). A look at the Hausa people of Niger and Nigeria, with material on history and contemporary life. (Rev: BL 11/15/96) [966]

8015 *Peoples of West Africa* (6–12). Series: Peoples of West Africa. 1997, Facts on File $28.00 (0-8160-3485-0). Extensive background material is provided on the history, geography, languages, art, music, religion, and society of 13 West African peoples, including Asante, Bambara, Dogon, Fon, Hausa, Moors, Mossi, and Yoruba. (Rev: BL 8/97; BR 11–12/97; SLJ 10/97) [966]

8016 Reef, Catherine. *This Our Dark Country: The American Settlers of Liberia* (7–12). 2002, Clarion $17.00 (0-618-14785-3). This chronological account of Liberia's history makes good use of excerpts from letters and diaries. (Rev: BL 11/15/02; HBG 3/03; SLJ 12/02; VOYA 6/03) [966.62]

8017 Sallah, Tijan M. *Wolof* (7–12). Series: Heritage Library of African Peoples. 1996, Rosen LB $17.95 (0-8239-1987-0). Using maps, many color illustrations, and simple text, this book introduces the Wolof people of Senegal and their history, social and political life, customs, religious beliefs, and relations with other peoples in their region. (Rev: BL 3/15/96; SLJ 7/96) [966.3]

8018 *Senegal in Pictures* (5–8). Illus. Series: Visual Geography. 1989, Lerner LB $25.55 (0-8225-1827-9). A look at the geography, history, culture, and economics of Senegal. (Rev: BL 4/15/89; SLJ 11/88) [966.3]

8019 Sheehan, Patricia. *Côte d'Ivoire* (5–8). 1999, Marshall Cavendish LB $35.64 (0-7614-0980-7). The Ivory Coast is presented with coverage of its geography, history, government, economy, and social and cultural life. (Rev: HBG 10/00; SLJ 4/00) [966.68]

8020 Tenquist, Alasdair. *Nigeria* (5–8). Illus. Series: Economically Developing Countries. 1996, Raintree Steck-Vaughn LB $24.26 (0-8172-4527-8). This introduction to Nigeria emphasizes present-day government and economic conditions. (Rev: BL 3/1/97; SLJ 9/97) [330.9669]

8021 Thompson, Carol. *The Asante Kingdom* (6–9). Series: First Books: African Civilizations. 1999, Watts LB $22.00 (0-531-20287-9). This is the histo-

ry of the kingdom that emerged in the 1690s to become the largest and most powerful of the chiefdoms of Ghana. (Rev: BL 9/15/99; HBG 9/99) [966]

8022 Thompson, Carol. *The Empire of Mali* (6–9). 1998, Watts LB $23.00 (0-531-20277-1). This book chronicles the rise of the great Mali Empire that flourished in western Africa from the 13th to the 16th century and describes its universities, legal system, and remarkable architecture, art, and crafts. (Rev: BL 1/1–15/99; HBG 9/99) [966.2]

8023 Zimmermann, Robert. *The Gambia* (5–8). Illus. Series: Enchantment of the World. 1994, Children's paper $32.00 (0-516-02625-9). This tiny West African country is introduced in text and color photographs that cover all major topics related to this nation. (Rev: BL 12/15/94; SLJ 4/95) [966.51]

Asia

General and Miscellaneous

8024 Bramwell, Martyn. *Southern and Eastern Asia* (4–8). Illus. Series: The World in Maps. 2001, Lerner LB $23.93 (0-8225-2916-5). For each country in these geographical areas, readers will find a color map, the flag, a box containing important facts, and brief discussions of geography, industry, and economy. Also use *Northern and Western Asia* (2001). (Rev: HBG 10/01; SLJ 7/01) [915]

8025 Dramer, Kim. *The Mekong River* (4–8). Series: Watts Library. 2001, Watts LB $24.00 (0-531-11854-1). A fact-filled introduction to the history of the Mekong and to the landscape and industry found along it. (Rev: SLJ 5/01) [959.7]

8026 Franck, Irene M., and David M. Brownstone. *Across Asia by Land* (6–10). Series: Travel and Trade Routes. 1991, Facts on File $17.95 (0-8160-1874-X). Specific trade and travel routes tell historical tales from ancient times to the present. (Rev: BL 1/15/91; SLJ 6/91) [380.1]

8027 Greenblatt, Miriam. *Genghis Khan and the Mongol Empire* (5–8). Series: Rulers and Their Times. 2001, Marshall Cavendish LB $28.50 (0-7614-1027-9). This handsomely illustrated book presents, in three parts, a life of Genghis Khan, a section on conditions in Russia during his reign, and a selection of documents of the time. (Rev: BL 1/1–15/02; HBG 3/02; SLJ 2/02) [947]

8028 Major, John S., and Betty J. Belanus. *Caravan to America: Living Arts of the Silk Road* (5–8). Illus. 2002, Cricket $24.95 (0-8126-2666-4); paper $15.95 (0-8126-2677-X). The traditions and skills emanating from the ancient trade routes are shown as surviving today in the work of a rug restorer in New York, an artist-monk in Los Angeles, a cook from Iran, and other examples in this fascinating approach to an interesting subject. (Rev: BL 11/1/02; HB 1–2/03; HBG 3/03; SLJ 2/03; VOYA 6/03) [745]

8029 Pascoe, Elaine. *The Pacific Rim: East Asia at the Dawn of a New Century* (7–12). 1999, Twenty-First Century LB $25.90 (0-7613-3015-1). Brief historical information and current economic figures are given for Japan, China, Taiwan, the Koreas, Indonesia, Singapore, Malaysia, and the Philippines. (Rev: BL 7/99; SLJ 9/99) [950.4]

8030 Sayre, April Pulley. *Asia* (5–8). Illus. Series: Seven Continents. 1999, Twenty-First Century LB $25.90 (0-7613-1368-0). Using maps, photographs, and sidebars, this concise work discusses Asia's people, geography and geology, climate and oceans, flora and fauna. (Rev: BL 8/99; HBG 3/00) [915]

8031 Wilkinson, Philip, and Michael Pollard. *The Magical East* (4–7). Series: Mysterious Places. 1994, Chelsea LB $21.95 (0-7910-2754-6). An oversize volume that highlights several places and cities of importance in the history of the Orient. (Rev: BL 1/15/94; SLJ 4/94) [930.1]

China

8032 Allison, Amy. *Life in Ancient China* (6–10). Series: The Way People Live. 2000, Lucent LB $19..96 (1-56006-694-6). After a general history of ancient China, this account focuses on the daily life of the people, their struggles, and their accomplishments. (Rev: BL 3/1/01) [951]

8033 Baldwin, Robert F. *Daily Life in Ancient and Modern Beijing* (4–7). Series: Cities Through Time. 1999, Runestone LB $25.26 (0-8225-3214-X). Topics introduced in this contrast between Beijing past and present include the arts, religion, school, history, and daily life. (Rev: HBG 10/99; SLJ 7/99) [951]

8034 Behnke, Alison. *China in Pictures*. Rev. ed. (6–10). Illus. Series: Visual Geography. 2002, Lerner LB $27.93 (0-8225-0370-0). An excellent introduction to China that includes material on geography, history, people, economy, and culture with maps, photographs, and illustrations. (Rev: BL 10/15/02; HBG 3/03; SLJ 3/03) [951]

8035 Beshore, George. *Science in Ancient China* (4–7). Series: Science of the Past. 1998, Watts LB $26.00 (0-531-11334-5). Photographs of period artifacts, documents, and artworks illustrate this exploration of ancient China's important scientific contributions. (Rev: BL 6/1–15/98; HBG 10/98; SLJ 8/98) [509]

8036 Cozic, Charles P., ed. *U.S. Policy Toward China* (8–12). Series: At Issue. 1996, Greenhaven LB $35.15 (1-56510-389-0); paper $17.45 (1-56510-388-2). Differences between China and the

U.S. on such issues as human rights and copyright policies are explored from various points of view in this collection of articles. (Rev: BL 1/1–15/96; SLJ 5/96) [327.73]

8037 Dramer, Kim. *People's Republic of China* (4–7). Series: Enchantment of the World. 1999, Children's LB $34.50 (0-516-21077-7). A revision of a standard source on China, including its history, government, people, languages, culture, and current conditions. (Rev: BL 9/15/99) [951]

8038 DuTemple, Lesley A. *The Great Wall of China* (4–7). Illus. Series: Great Building Feats. 2003, Lerner LB $27.93 (0-8225-0377-8). This absorbing account tells the story of the building and importance of the Great Wall of China, with a good selection of illustrations, sidebar features, and maps. (Rev: BL 1/1–15/03; HBG 10/03; SLJ 4/03*) [931]

8039 Ferroa, Peggy. *China* (4–7). Illus. Series: Cultures of the World. 1991, Marshall Cavendish LB $35.64 (1-85435-399-3). Unusual facts highlight this look at China, with emphasis on culture. (Rev: BL 2/15/92; SLJ 3/92) [951]

8040 Field, Catherine. *China* (4–8). Illus. Series: Nations of the World. 2000, Raintree Steck-Vaughn LB $34.26 (0-8172-5781-0). This is a fine introduction to China's past and present that supplies even more interesting information through the use of sidebars. (Rev: BL 10/15/00; HBG 10/00) [951.21]

8041 Fritz, Jean. *China's Long March: 6,000 Miles of Danger* (6–9). Illus. 1988, Putnam $16.99 (0-399-21512-3). A description of the legend-making 6,000-mile march of the Chinese Communists during the 1930s. (Rev: BL 3/1/88; SLJ 5/88) [951.04]

8042 Goh, Sui Noi. *China* (4–8). Series: Countries of the World. 1998, Gareth Stevens LB $29.26 (0-8368-2124-6). An overview of the country's history, government, economy, geography, people, and the arts, followed by a "Closer Look" section that examines contemporary issues such as the role of women, secret societies, Tibet, Tiananman Square, and a final section on relations with North America. (Rev: BL 12/15/98; HBG 10/99; SLJ 6/99) [951]

8043 Green, Robert. *China* (6–10). Series: Modern Nations of the World. 1999, Lucent LB $27.45 (1-56006-440-4). A well-organized overview of China and its emergence as a major political and economic power. (Rev: SLJ 8/99) [051]

8044 Immell, Myra. *The Han Dynasty* (6–10). Illus. Series: Lost Civilizations. 2003, Gale LB $21.96 (1-59018-096-8). An informative and readable overview of the long Han dynasty and the social and agricultural systems of the time. (Rev: SLJ 5/03) [931]

8045 Israel, Fred L., and Arthur M. Schlesinger, Jr., eds. *Peking* (6–10). Illus. Series: The World 100 Years Ago. 1999, Chelsea LB $29.95 (0-7910-4666-4). This is an edited version of travel essays by Burton Holmes, a popular traveler-lecturer during the first half of the 20th century, about the sights he saw in Peking. (Rev: SLJ 7/98) [951]

8046 Kagda, Falaq. *Hong Kong* (5–8). Series: Cultures of the World. 1998, Marshall Cavendish LB $35.64 (0-7614-0692-1). An attractive book that introduces us to Hong Kong's history and geography, its people, and their culture and lifestyles. (Rev: HBG 3/98; SLJ 6/98) [951]

8047 Lazo, Caroline. *The Terra Cotta Army of Emperor Qin* (5–8). Illus. 1993, Macmillan LB $14.95 (0-02-754631-4). The story of the 7,500 terracotta figures that guard the tomb of China's first emperor. (Rev: BL 7/93; SLJ 8/93) [931]

8048 McLenighan, Valjean. *China: A History to 1949* (5–8). Illus. 1983, Children's paper $32.00 (0-516-02754-9). China from its earliest days to the founding of the People's Republic in 1949. [951]

8049 Mann, Elizabeth. *The Great Wall: The Story of Thousands of Miles of Earth and Stone* (4–8). Illus. Series: Wonders of the World. 1997, Mikaya $19.95 (0-9650493-2-9). The story behind the building of this massive structure, which began as far back as 200 B.C. and involves historical battles for land and power between the Chinese and the nomadic Mongols. (Rev: BL 1/1–15/98; SLJ 12/97) [951]

8050 Odijk, Pamela. *The Chinese* (4–7). Illus. Series: Ancient World. 1991, Silver Burdett LB $14.95 (0-382-09894-3). Brief, informative, and eye-catching treatment of the Chinese, including their influences on medicine and architecture. (Rev: BL 1/15/92) [951]

8051 Patent, Dorothy Hinshaw. *The Incredible Story of China's Buried Warriors* (4–7). Series: Frozen in Time. 1999, Benchmark LB $27.07 (0-7614-0783-9). This book explores the mystery of the creation of China's buried warriors, the thousands of terracotta statues that belonged to the first emperor of China and were uncovered in 1974. (Rev: BL 2/1/00; HBG 10/00; SLJ 3/00) [951]

8052 Pollard, Michael. *The Yangtze* (5–7). Series: Great Rivers. 1997, Benchmark LB $22.79 (0-7614-0505-4). Covers historical and geographical aspects of the Yangtze River and discusses current dam-building projects. (Rev: HBG 3/98; SLJ 4/98) [951]

8053 Prior, Katherine. *The History of Emigration from China and Southeast Asia* (4–7). Series: Origins. 1997, Watts LB $21.00 (0-531-14442-9). Outlines the political, social, and economic conditions in China that led to people leaving during different periods in its history, as well as material on where they went and their reception. (Rev: BL 12/15/97; HBG 3/98; SLJ 2/98) [951]

8054 Shemie, Bonnie. *Houses of China* (4–7). Illus. Series: Native Dwellings. 1996, Tundra $13.95 (0-88776-369-3). The various cultures of China, past

and present, are introduced through an examination of 10 traditional houses. (Rev: SLJ 2/97) [951]

8055 Tao, Wang. *Exploration into China* (4–7). Illus. Series: Exploration. 1996, Dillon LB $15.95 (0-02-718087-5); paper $7.95 (0-382-39185-3). The story of Chinese history until the opening up of the country by Europeans is given, with a brief overview of its recent history and contemporary life. (Rev: BL 8/96) [951]

8056 Waterlow, Julia. *China* (4–7). Illus. Series: Country Insights. 1997, Raintree Steck-Vaughn LB $27.12 (0-8172-4787-4). Compares the social conditions — home life, employment, schooling, and recreation — in a large city and a rural village in China. (Rev: BL 7/97; SLJ 8/97) [951]

8057 Waterlow, Julia. *The Yangtze* (4–7). Series: Great Rivers of the World. 2003, World Almanac LB $26.60 (0-8368-5447-0). An exploration of the Yangtze's flow, history, and animals and plants, with discussion of the settlements along its banks, the industries it supports, recreation on its waters, and environmental threats to the river. (Rev: SLJ 9/03) [951]

8058 Williams, Brian. *Ancient China* (6–9). Series: See Through History. 1996, Viking $19.99 (0-670-87157-5). Detailed illustrations and some overlays provide a glimpse at ancient China's farming, religion, clothing, architecture, and daily life. (Rev: SLJ 3/97) [951]

8059 Zhang, Song Nan. *Cowboy on the Steppes* (4–7). Illus. 1997, Tundra $15.95 (0-88776-410-X). The true story of an 18-year-old Chinese boy and the first eight months he spent living in the steppes of Mongolia, where he has been sent during the Cultural Revolution to herd sheep. (Rev: BL 2/15/98; HBG 3/98; SLJ 2/98) [951.7]

8060 Zurlo, Tony. *Life in Hong Kong* (6–10). Series: The Way People Live. 2002, Gale LB $27.45 (1-56006-384-X). Contemporary life in Hong Kong at many levels of wealth and position is the topic explored in this fascinating narrative with many illustrations and some historical coverage. (Rev: BL 7/02; SLJ 6/02) [951]

India, Pakistan, and Bangladesh

8061 Brace, Steve. *Bangladesh* (4–8). Illus. Series: Economically Developing Countries. 1995, Thomson Learning LB $24.26 (1-56847-243-9). An overview of life in Bangladesh told in a simple, large-print text and many color photographs. (Rev: SLJ 7/95) [954.9]

8062 Brace, Steve. *India* (7–10). Series: Country Studies. 1999, Heinemann LB $27.07 (1-57572-893-1). An excellent introduction to India that gives current information on such subjects as population, environment, problems, and economy. (Rev: BL 8/99) [954]

8063 Chatterjee, Manini, and Anita Roy. *India* (4–8). Illus. Series: Eyewitness Books. 2002, DK paper $19.99 (0-7894-9029-3). An informative and attractive overview of all aspects of India's history and culture. (Rev: HBG 3/03; SLJ 12/02) [954.002]

8064 Crompton, Samuel Willard. *Pakistan* (7–12). Series: Modern World Nations. 2002, Chelsea LB $24.95 (0-7910-7098-0). An overview of the history, geography, people, politics, and religion of Pakistan, with discussion of current difficulties such as ethnic strife, population problems, and disputes with India. (Rev: SLJ 2/03) [954.91]

8065 Cumming, David. *The Ganges Delta and Its People* (5–8). Illus. Series: People and Places. 1994, Thomson Learning LB $24.26 (1-56847-168-8). An introduction to the Ganges delta, the people who live there, the economy it supports, and the tragedy of its frequent flooding. (Rev: BL 10/15/94) [954]

8066 Cumming, David. *India* (4–7). Illus. Series: Our Country. 1998, Raintree Steck-Vaughn LB $27.12 (0-8172-4797-1). Several young inhabitants introduce India and describe life, customs, food, and their homes. (Rev: BL 12/1/89; HBG 10/98; SLJ 3/92) [954]

8067 Dalal, Anita. *India* (4–8). Series: Nations of the World. 2001, Raintree Steck-Vaughn LB $34.26 (0-7398-1289-0). A fine introduction to this vast, populous country with chapters on the land and cities, past and present, the economy, arts and living, and the future. (Rev: BL 12/15/01; HBG 3/02) [954]

8068 DuTemple, Lesley A. *The Taj Mahal* (4–7). Series: Great Building Feats. 2003, Lerner LB $27.93 (0-8225-4692-0). Using many illustrations, this account traces the building of the magnificent tomb that was inspired by one man's love for his wife. (Rev: BL 11/15/03) [954]

8069 Goodwin, William. *India* (5–8). Series: Modern Nations of the World. 2000, Lucent LB $27.45 (1-56006-598-2). An admirable introduction to India that gives material on the land and its past but concentrates on today's population, living conditions, and problems. (Rev: BL 3/15/00; HBG 10/00) [954]

8070 Goodwin, William. *Pakistan* (6–12). Illus. Series: Modern Nations of the World. 2002, Gale LB $21.96 (1-59018-218-9). An overview of Pakistan's geography, history, culture, and society, with biographical information on key individuals. (Rev: BL 11/15/02; SLJ 1/03) [954.91]

8071 Haque, Jameel. *Pakistan* (4–8). Series: Countries of the World. 2002, Gareth Stevens LB $29.27 (0-8368-2352-4). A useful source of the standard information on Pakistan plus a discussion of relations with the United States and some interesting

sidebar features on such topics as pollution and cricket. (Rev: HBG 3/03; SLJ 1/03) [954.91]

8072 Lauré, Jason. *Bangladesh* (5–8). Series: Enchantment of the World. 1992, Children's Pr. paper $32.00 (0-516-02609-7). The history, culture, and economic problems of this crowded Asian land are covered. (Rev: BL 12/15/92; SLJ 1/93) [954.9]

8073 McNair, Sylvia. *India* (5–8). Illus. Series: Enchantment of the World. 1991, Children's paper $32.00 (0-516-02719-0). Such topics as civilization, ethnic groups, and history are treated in this lively introduction to India. (Rev: SLJ 5/91) [954]

8074 *Pakistan in Pictures* (5–8). Illus. Series: Visual Geography. 1996, Lerner LB $25.55 (0-8225-1850-3). Photographs, charts, and maps help to introduce the country of Pakistan. (Rev: BL 9/15/89) [954.9]

8075 Pollard, Michael. *The Ganges* (5–7). Series: Great Rivers. 1997, Benchmark LB $22.79 (0-7614-0504-6). This work describes the course of the Ganges from the Himalayas to its muddy delta, covers its history, and touches on the poverty and pollution that is found around it today. (Rev: HBG 3/98; SLJ 4/98) [954]

8076 Prior, Katherine. *Indian Subcontinent* (4–7). Illus. Series: Origins. 1997, Watts LB $21.00 (0-531-14418-6). Describes the conditions in India, Pakistan, and Bangladesh that led to emigration, where their people went, and their reception in such countries as the United States and Great Britain. (Rev: BL 4/15/97; SLJ 7/97) [304.8]

8077 Sheehan, Sean. *Pakistan* (5–8). Illus. Series: Cultures of the World. 1993, Marshall Cavendish LB $35.64 (1-85435-583-X). This informative account describes the history and culture of Pakistan, with coverage of its economy and how its people live. (Rev: SLJ 2/94) [954.9]

8078 Srinivasan, Radhika, and Leslie Jermyn. *India*. 2nd ed. (4–8). Illus. Series: Cultures of the World. 2001, Benchmark LB $35.64 (0-7614-1354-5). An updated edition of the 1990 title, covering the history, geography, politics, people, arts, culture, and environmental concerns of India. (Rev: HBG 3/02; SLJ 3/02) [954]

8079 Stewart, Melissa. *Science in Ancient India* (4–8). Series: Science of the Past. 1999, Watts LB $26.00 (0-531-11626-3). Using a chronological approach beginning with the ancient cities of Mohenjo-daro and Harappa (both now in Pakistan), this account traces the growth of science in India with material on medicine, mathematics, astronomy, and physics. (Rev: HBG 10/99; SLJ 6/99) [954]

8080 Swan, Erin Pembrey. *India* (4–7). Series: Enchantment of the World. 2002, Children's LB $31.50 (0-516-21121-8). This visually attractive introduction to the past and present of India includes coverage of languages, culture, the people, economy, and government. (Rev: BL 5/15/02) [954]

8081 Viswanath, R. *Teenage Refugees and Immigrants from India Speak Out* (7–12). Series: Teenage Refugees Speak Out. 1997, Rosen LB $16.95 (0-8239-2440-8). A description of the ethnic and religious conflicts and economic conditions that have caused the displacement of tens of thousands of Indians, plus the stories of those who came to the United States, told in first-person teenage accounts. (Rev: BL 12/15/97; SLJ 4/98) [954]

8082 Wagner, Heather Lehr. *India and Pakistan* (6–12). Illus. Series: People at Odds. 2002, Chelsea LB $21.95 (0-7910-6709-2). An easy-to-understand, chronological summary of the ongoing conflict between the two nations, with photographs and maps. (Rev: BL 11/1/02; HBG 3/03; SLJ 12/02) [954.03]

8083 Weston, Mark. *The Land and People of Pakistan* (6–9). Series: Land and People Of. 1992, HarperCollins LB $17.89 (0-06-022790-7). Pakistan's geography, ethnicity, and history as well as an exploration of political, social, economic, and cultural life. (Rev: BL 8/92; SLJ 12/92*) [954.91]

8084 Whyte, Mariam. *Bangladesh* (5–9). Series: Cultures of the World. 1998, Marshall Cavendish LB $35.64 (0-7614-0869-X). A sympathetic look at the history and geography of Bangladesh, with details of the country's rich background and current problems. (Rev: HBG 10/99; SLJ 6/99) [954.9]

8085 Yusufali, Jabeen. *Pakistan: An Islamic Treasure* (4–8). Illus. Series: Discovering Our Heritage. 1990, Macmillan LB $14.95 (0-87518-433-2). This book covers the country of Pakistan from its foundation in 1947 to the present, with coverage of economy, geography, and more. (Rev: BL 7/90; SLJ 8/90) [954.91]

Japan

8086 Behnke, Alison. *Japan in Pictures* (6–10). Series: Visual Geography. 2002, Lerner LB $27.93 (0-8225-1956-9). This revised edition of an old title contains all new material on Japan's history, government, people, customs, economy, and culture. (Rev: BL 10/15/02; HBG 3/03) [952]

8087 Blumberg, Rhoda. *Commodore Perry in the Land of the Shogun* (5–8). Illus. 1985, Lothrop $18.95 (0-688-03723-2). Japan was a mysterious country when Perry arrived in 1853 to open its harbors to American ships. (Rev: BL 11/1/85; SLJ 10/85) [952.025]

8088 Bornoff, Nick. *Japan* (4–7). Illus. Series: Country Insights. 1997, Raintree Steck-Vaughn LB $27.12 (0-8172-4786-6). This description of modern life in the city of Okazaki and in the village of Narai compares home life, employment, schooling, and recreation. (Rev: BL 7/97; SLJ 8/97) [952]

8089 Case, Robert. *Japan* (6–10). Series: Countries of the World. 2003, Facts on File $30.00 (0-8160-5381-2). An attractive introduction to Japan that includes material on history, geography, economy, people, and culture. (Rev: BL 1/1–15/04) [952]

8090 Green, Jen. *Japan* (4–8). Series: Nations of the World. 2001, Raintree Steck-Vaughn LB $34.26 (0-8172-5783-7). An attractive, fact-filled introduction to this island nation, its rich culture, advanced technology, and wealthy economy. (Rev: BL 6/1–15/01; HBG 10/01) [952]

8091 Hall, Eleanor J. *Life Among the Samurai* (6–10). Series: The Way People Live. 1998, Lucent LB $27.45 (1-56006-390-4). A history of the feudal period in Japanese history that focuses on the warrior class and their exploits. (Rev: BL 11/15/98) [952]

8092 Hamanaka, Sheila, and Ayano Ohmi. *In Search of the Spirit: The Living National Treasures of Japan* (4–8). Illus. 1999, Morrow LB $16.89 (0-688-14608-2). In the 1950s, the Japanese government, concerned that ancient traditions were dying out, created a National Living Treasures program to honor elders practicing age-old crafts and performing arts and to give them grants to continue their work and to train apprentices. This book features six such elders: a sword maker, a puppet master, a yuzen dyer who decorates silk kimonos, a bamboo weaver, a Noh actor, and a potter. (Rev: BCCB 4/99; BL 3/1/99; HBG 9/99; SLJ 5/99) [952]

8093 Kallen, Stuart A. *Life in Tokyo* (6–10). Series: The Way People Live. 2001, Lucent LB $19.96 (1-56006-797-7). After a brief historical introduction, life in present-day Tokyo is featured with material on such topics as daily life, education, entertainment, jobs, food, and culture. (Rev: BL 6/1–15/01; SLJ 6/01) [952]

8094 Netzley, Patricia D. *Japan* (5–8). Series: Modern Nations of the World. 1999, Lucent LB $27.45 (1-56006-599-0). Background historic and geographic information is given in this introduction to Japan, but the emphasis is on modern history, the people today, and current living conditions and problems. (Rev: BL 2/15/00; HBG 10/00) [952]

8095 Odijk, Pamela. *The Japanese* (4–7). Illus. Series: Ancient World. 1991, Silver Burdett LB $14.95 (0-382-09898-6). This brief, informative volume includes sections on famous figures and places. (Rev: BL 1/15/92) [952]

8096 Pilbeam, Mavis. *Japan Under the Shoguns, 1185–1868* (5–8). Series: Looking Back. 1999, Raintree Steck-Vaughn $19.98 (0-8172-5431-5). A handsome, detailed overview of the shogun society of Japan from 1185 to 1868, featuring color photographs and reproductions of original art. (Rev: BL 5/15/99) [452]

8097 Roberson, John R. *Japan Meets the World: The Birth of a Super Power* (7–12). 1998, Millbrook LB $24.90 (0-7613-0407-X). Beginning with the shoguns of the 16th century, this book traces Japanese history through various stages of progress, its development into an economic superpower, and its current economic crisis and social stresses. (Rev: BL 1/1–15/99; HBG 3/99; SLJ 2/99) [952]

8098 Ross, Stewart. *The Rise of Japan and the Pacific Rim* (7–12). Series: Causes and Consequences. 1995, Raintree Steck-Vaughn LB $29.97 (0-8172-4054-3). A thorough, unbiased account of the remarkable history of Japan since World War II, with well-documented details on the political, social, and economic conditions that made it possible, and also including material on the economic rise of other Pacific Rim nations. (Rev: BL 12/15/95; BR 3–4/96; SLJ 2/96) [952]

8099 Say, Allen. *Tea with Milk* (4–8). Illus. 1999, Houghton LB $17.00 (0-395-90495-1). A picture book about the author's mother, who was forced by her father to leave her California residence and return to the family's original home in Japan. (Rev: BCCB 6/99; BL 3/15/99*; HB 7–8/99; HBG 10/99; SLJ 5/99) [952]

8100 Schomp, Virginia. *Japan in the Days of the Samurai* (5–8). Illus. Series: Cultures of the Past. 2001, Marshall Cavendish LB $28.50 (0-7614-0304-3). A well-illustrated look at the history of Japan, including information on such cultural topics as the tea ceremony and samurai women. (Rev: BL 2/15/02; HBG 3/02; SLJ 3/02) [952]

8101 Shelley, Rex, and Teo Chuu Yong. *Japan*. 2nd ed. (5–8). Illus. Series: Cultures of the World. 2001, Benchmark LB $35.64 (0-7614-1356-1). An updated edition of the 1996 title, covering the history, geography, politics, people, arts, culture, and environmental concerns of Japan. (Rev: HBG 3/02; SLJ 3/02) [952]

8102 Stefoff, Rebecca. *Japan* (6–10). Series: Major World Nations. 1998, Chelsea LB $21.95 (0-7910-4761-X). With emphasis on the present social, economic, and cultural conditions, this is a readable, informative introduction to Japan. (Rev: BL 9/15/98; BR 1–2/99) [952.04]

8103 Tames, Richard. *Exploration into Japan* (5–7). Illus. Series: Exploration. 1996, Dillon LB $15.95 (0-02-751390-4); paper $7.95 (0-382-39186-1). A brief history of Japan is given, including the effects of early Western influences. (Rev: BL 8/96) [952]

8104 Whyte, Harlinah. *Japan* (4–8). Series: Countries of the World. 1998, Gareth Stevens LB $29.26 (0 8368 2126 2). After a section that presents standard introductory information about Japan, this account describes interesting aspects of Japanese culture including sumo wrestling, sushi, and eti-

quette. (Rev: BL 12/15/98; HBG 9/99; SLJ 6/99) [952]

8105 Zurlo, Tony. *Japan: Superpower of the Pacific* (5–8). Illus. Series: Discovering Our Heritage. 1991, Macmillan LB $14.95 (0-87518-480-4). A book that highlights aspects of Japan's history and culture as well as its economic growth and living conditions to 1990. (Rev: BL 2/1/92; SLJ 4/92) [952]

Other Asian Countries

8106 *Afghanistan in Pictures* (5–8). Illus. Series: Visual Geography. 1997, Lerner LB $25.55 (0-8225-1849-X). Includes sections on vegetation and wildlife, minerals, cities, history, and government. (Rev: BL 5/1/89) [958.1]

8107 Ali, Sharifah Enayat. *Afghanistan* (4–7). Illus. Series: Cultures of the World. 1995, Marshall Cavendish LB $35.64 (0-7614-0177-6). After general background information, this account focuses on the arts, leisure activities, and festivals of the people of Afghanistan. (Rev: BL 1/1–15/96; SLJ 4/96) [958.1]

8108 Burbank, Jon. *Nepal* (4–7). Illus. Series: Cultures of the World. 1991, Marshall Cavendish LB $35.64 (1-85435-401-9). The emphasis is on culture as well as the basics of geography, history, government, and people. (Rev: BL 2/15/92) [954.96]

8109 Clifford, Mary Louise. *The Land and People of Afghanistan* (5–7). Illus. 1989, HarperCollins LB $14.89 (0-397-32339-5). An introduction to past life in this central Asian country. A reissue. [958.1]

8110 Cole, Wendy M. *Vietnam* (6–10). Illus. Series: Major World Nations. 1999, Chelsea LB $21.95 (0-7910-4751-2). A revised edition of the author's 1989 introduction to Vietnam, with chapters on history, geography, people, culture, cities and villages, government and social services, resources and economy, and transportation and communications. (Rev: SLJ 5/98) [959.7]

8111 Corona, Laurel. *Afghanistan* (6–12). Illus. Series: Modern Nations of the World. 2002, Gale LB $21.96 (1-59018-217-0). This book covers the cultural, geographical, religious, and other aspects of Afghanistan, with discussion of the Taliban and the role of women. (Rev: BL 11/15/02; SLJ 12/02) [958.1]

8112 Cromie, Alice. *Taiwan* (5–8). Illus. Series: Enchantment of the World. 1994, Children's Pr. paper $32.00 (0-516-02627-5). An attractive introduction, with many color photographs, to Taiwan's history, government, people, and economy. (Rev: BL 12/15/94) [951.24]

8113 Gogol, Sara. *A Mien Family* (4–7). Illus. Series: Journey Between Two Worlds. 1996, Lerner LB $22.60 (0-8225-3407-X); paper $8.95 (0-8225-

9745-4). The story of a refugee family from the mountainous area of Laos and their journey to the United States. (Rev: BL 11/15/96; SLJ 1/97) [306.85]

8114 Goodman, Jim. *Thailand* (5–9). Series: Cultures of the World. 1991, Marshall Cavendish LB $35.64 (1-85435-402-7). Thailand's history, land, and culture. (Rev: BL 3/15/92) [959.3]

8115 Green, Robert. *Cambodia* (5–9). Series: Modern Nations of the World. 2003, Gale LB $27.45 (1-59018-109-3). As well as general material on Cambodia including geography, history and culture, this account gives a detailed chronology, national statistics, and extensive sidebars. (Rev: BL 11/15/03; SLJ 8/03) [959.5]

8116 Green, Robert. *Taiwan* (5–8). Series: Modern Nations of the World. 2001, Lucent LB $27.45 (1-56006-819-1). Once known as Formosa, this island nation is introduced with material on its history, geography, climate, people, and economy. (Rev: BL 6/1–15/01) [951.24]

8117 Gritzner, Jeffrey A. *Afghanistan* (7–12). Series: Modern World Nations. 2002, Chelsea LB $24.95 (0-7910-6774-2). An overview of the history, geography, people, politics, and religion of Afghanistan, with discussion of the current antiterrorist and rebuilding efforts. (Rev: SLJ 2/03) [958.1]

8118 Guruswamy, Krishnan. *Sri Lanka* (4–8). Series: Countries of the World. 2002, Gareth Stevens LB $29.27 (0-8368-2354-0). History, geography, government, and people are all covered here, with special sections on such topics as the status of women and relations with the United States. Also use *South Korea* (2002). (Rev: HBG 3/03; SLJ 2/03) [954.93]

8119 Hansen, Ole Steen. *Vietnam* (5–8). Illus. Series: Economically Developing Countries. 1996, Raintree Steck-Vaughn LB $24.26 (0-8172-4526-X). This introduction to Vietnam includes background information and material on its emerging economy. (Rev: BL 3/1/97) [959.7]

8120 Heinrichs, Ann. *Nepal* (5–8). Illus. Series: Enchantment of the World. 1996, Children's Pr. paper $32.00 (0-516-02642-9). Using color photographs on each page, this attractive book introduces the history, geography, and people of Nepal. (Rev: BL 7/96) [954.96]

8121 Heinrichs, Ann. *Tibet* (5–8). Illus. Series: Enchantment of the World. 1996, Children's Pr. LB $32.00 (0-516-20155-7). An introduction to the history, people, and geography of this country, now occupied by China. (Rev: BL 1/1–15/97) [951]

8122 Jacobs, Judy. *Indonesia: A Nation of Islands* (4–8). Illus. Series: Discovering Our Heritage. 1990, Macmillan LB $14.95 (0-87518-423-5). History and geography of the major Indonesian islands. (Rev: SLJ 9/90) [959.8]

8123 Jung, Sung-Hoon. *South Korea* (5–8). Series: Economically Developing Countries. 1997, Raintree Steck-Vaughn LB $24.26 (0-8172-4530-8). This overview of economic conditions in South Korea describes the country's success with electronic exports and provides case studies of family-run companies. (Rev: BL 5/15/97) [951.95]

8124 Kazem, Halima. *Afghanistan* (4–8). Illus. 2003, Gareth Stevens LB $29.26 (0-8368-2357-5). Afghanistan's geography, history, government, people, and culture are introduced, with material on women, sports, and clothing, a map, and a glossary. (Rev: HBG 10/03; SLJ 7/03) [58.1]

8125 Kendra, Judith. *Tibetans* (5–8). Series: Threatened Cultures. 1994, Thomson Learning LB $24.25 (1-56847-152-1). Discusses Tibetan culture and religion, with emphasis on the denial by China of Tibetans' rights. Follows the daily lives of two Tibetan children, one living in the country, one in the city. (Rev: BL 7/94) [951]

8126 Kizilos, Peter. *Tibet: Disputed Land* (7–10). Series: World in Conflict. 2000, Lerner LB $25.26 (0-8225-3563-7). The history of Tibet and its present political divisions are covered in this well-illustrated account. (Rev: BL 10/15/2000; HBG 3/01) [951.1]

8127 Layton, Lesley. *Singapore* (5–8). Illus. Series: Cultures of the World. 1990, Marshall Cavendish LB $35.64 (1-85435-295-4). As well as history and economy, this introduction to Singapore includes coverage of lifestyles and current problems. (Rev: BL 3/1/91; SLJ 6/91) [959.57]

8128 Levy, Patricia. *Tibet* (4–7). Illus. Series: Cultures of the World. 1996, Marshall Cavendish LB $35.64 (0-7614-0277-2). Tibet is introduced with general background information, followed by material on its people and their culture, festivals, and food. (Rev: BL 8/96; SLJ 9/96) [951.1]

8129 Lorbiecki, Marybeth. *Children of Vietnam* (4–7). Photos by Paul P. Rome. Series: The World's Children. 1997, Carolrhoda LB $28.75 (1-57505-034-X). Beginning in the north and working south, this photoessay describes the people of Vietnam and the lives of their children. (Rev: HBG 3/98; SLJ 2/98) [959.7]

8130 McNair, Sylvia. *Malaysia* (4–7). Series: Enchantment of the World. 2002, Children's LB $34.50 (0-516-21009-2). This Southeast Asian nation is presented in text and many color photographs that introduce its history, geography, people, culture, and present status. (Rev: BL 9/15/02) [959.505]

8131 *Malaysia in Pictures* (5–8). Illus. Series: Visual Geography. 1997, Lerner LB $25.55 (0-8225-

1854-6). A basic, visual overview of this nation and its people. (Rev: BL 5/1/89) [959.5]

8132 Mirpuri, Gouri, and Robert Cooper. *Indonesia.* 2nd ed. (5–8). Illus. Series: Cultures of the World. 2001, Marshall Cavendish LB $35.64 (0-7614-1355-3). An encompassing look at the history, culture, society, and geography of Indonesia. (Rev: BL 3/1/02; HBG 3/02; SLJ 4/02) [959.8]

8133 Moiz, Azra. *Taiwan* (4–7). Illus. Series: Cultures of the World. 1995, Marshall Cavendish LB $35.64 (0-7614-0180-6). The accomplishments, lifestyle, and religious festivals of the people of Taiwan are covered, along with its history and geography. (Rev: BL 1/1–15/96; SLJ 9/96) [957.24]

8134 Munan, Heidi. *Malaysia* (5–8). Illus. Series: Cultures of the World. 1990, Marshall Cavendish LB $35.64 (1-85435-296-2). Cultural diversity and lifestyles of the people are two topics covered in this introduction to Malaysia. (Rev: BL 3/1/91) [959.5]

8135 Pang, Guek-Cheng. *Mongolia* (5–8). Series: Cultures of the World. 1999, Marshall Cavendish LB $35.64 (0-7614-0954-8). A clear, well-illustrated introduction to this remote land that includes good background information as well as coverage of modern life. (Rev: HBG 10/99; SLJ 10/99) [957]

8136 Rowell, Jonathan. *Malaysia* (5–8). Illus. Series: Economically Developing Countries. 1997, Raintree Steck-Vaughn LB $24.26 (0-8172-4531-6). The growth and development of Malaysia are traced, with material on its high-tech sector. (Rev: BL 5/15/97) [959.505]

8137 Salter, Christopher. *North Korea* (6–12). Illus. 2003, Chelsea LB $24.95 (0-7910-7233-9). A thorough and concise overview of North Korea's geography, history, government, politics, economics, language, peoples, and religion, with maps, photographs, and a look at the future. (Rev: BL 9/15/03; HBG 10/03) [951.93]

8138 Schwabach, Karen. *Thailand: Land of Smiles* (5–8). Illus. Series: Discovering Our Heritage. 1991, Macmillan LB $14.95 (0-87518-454-5). Explores the land and people of Thailand, with a chapter on the immigrants who have come to the United States. (Rev: BL 4/1/91; SLJ 7/91) [959.3]

8139 Sheehan, Sean. *Cambodia* (4–7). Illus. Series: Cultures of the World. 1996, Marshall Cavendish LB $35.64 (0-7614-0281-0). The troubled land of Cambodia is introduced, with emphasis on its people, their lifestyles, and culture. (Rev: BL 8/96; SLJ 9/96) [959]

8140 Sis, Peter. *Tibet: Through the Red Box* (7–12). Illus. 1998, Farrar $25.00 (0-374-37552-6). Using a journal kept by the author's filmmaker father when he journeyed to Tibet long ago, old tales, and pictures of landscapes and intriguing illustrations inspired by the Tibetan wheel of life, the author

writes about the past and present of this land, its culture, and its religion. (Rev: BCCB 12/98; BL 9/15/98; BR 5–6/99; HB 11–12/98; HBG 3/99; SLJ 10/98) [954.96]

8141 Smith, Roland, and Michael J. Schmidt. *In the Forest with the Elephants* (4–7). 1998, Harcourt paper $9.00 (0-15-201290-7). A photoessay that takes a look at the timber elephants of Myanmar, their *oozies* or trainers, and the logging industry that keeps them busy. (Rev: HBG 10/98; SLJ 4/98) [954]

8142 *South Korea in Pictures* (5–7). Series: Visual Geography. 1997, Lerner LB $25.55 (0-8225-1868-6). An introduction to South Korea that focuses on its politics and economy. (Rev: SLJ 5/90) [951.9]

8143 Tull, Mary, et al. *Northern Asia* (4–7). Illus. Series: Artisans Around the World. 1990, Raintree Steck-Vaughn LB $27.12 (0-7398-0119-8). This book introduces Mongolia and its neighbors, with descriptions of arts and crafts and many projects. (Rev: BL 10/15/99; HBG 3/00; SLJ 1/00) [745.5]

8144 *Vietnam in Pictures* (5–8). Illus. Series: Visual Geography. 1994, Lerner LB $25.55 (0-8225-1909-7). This well-illustrated account of Vietnam covers its history, geography, people, government, and economy. (Rev: BL 11/1/94) [915.97]

8145 Wanasundera, Nanda P. *Sri Lanka* (4–7). Illus. Series: Cultures of the World. 1991, Marshall Cavendish LB $213.86 (1-85435-397-7). The history, geography, and culture of Sri Lanka are introduced with an emphasis on contemporary problems. (Rev: BL 2/15/92) [954.93]

8146 Willis, Karen. *Vietnam* (5–8). Illus. Series: Modern Nations of the World. 2000, Lucent LB $27.45 (1-56006-635-0). A thorough history of Vietnam, this work also focuses on progress after the war and daily life in modern Vietnam. (Rev: BL 9/15/00; HBG 3/01) [959.7]

8147 Willis, Terri. *Vietnam* (4–7). Series: Enchantment of the World. 2002, Children's LB $34.50 (0-516-22150-7). This attractive volume presents basic material on Vietnam's history, geography, and culture, with an emphasis on progress after the war. (Rev: BL 9/15/02; SLJ 12/02) [959.7]

8148 Withington, William A. *Southeast Asia* (5–8). Illus. 1988, Gateway $16.95 (0-934291-32-2). Sections on lifestyle, land and climate, history and government, festivals, sports, arts, and crafts. (Rev: BL 12/1/88)

8149 Wright, David K. *Burma* (5–8). Illus. Series: Enchantment of the World. 1991, Children's paper $32.00 (0-516-02725-5). The land and people of Myanmar (Burma), together with its culture and history, are covered in this colorful introduction. (Rev: BL 8/91; SLJ 9/91) [788.9]

8150 Wright, David K. *Vietnam* (4–7). Illus. 1989, Children's paper $32.00 (0-516-02712-3). Standard information is highlighted by color illustrations and war coverage. (Rev: BL 8/89; SLJ 1/90) [959.7]

8151 Yin, Saw Myat. *Myanmar*. Rev. ed. (4–8). Illus. Series: Cultures of the World. 2001, Benchmark LB $35.64 (0-7614-1353-7). An introduction to every aspect of Myanmar with useful information on daily life and phonetic pronunciations of many foreign words. Also use *Indonesia* (2001). (Rev: HBG 3/02; SLJ 4/02) [959.1]

8152 Yu, Ling. *Taiwan in Pictures* (5–8). Illus. Series: Visual Geography. 1997, Lerner LB $25.55 (0-8225-1865-1). The history and geography of Taiwan are introduced, with coverage of cities, culture, religion, and economy. (Rev: BL 9/15/89) [915.1]

8153 Zwier, Lawrence J. *Sri Lanka: War Torn Island* (8–12). Illus. Series: World in Conflict. 1998, Lerner LB $25.26 (0-8225-3550-5). The author describes the war and political struggle in Sri Lanka, with good historical information and material on the present standoff. (Rev: BL 4/15/98) [305.8]

Australia and the Pacific Islands

8154 Arnold, Caroline. *Easter Island: Giant Stone Statues Tell of a Rich and Tragic Past* (4–7). Illus. 2000, Clarion LB $15.00 (0-395-87609-5). This chronological history of Easter Island tells how the stone statues got there and what they mean. (Rev: BCCB 4/00; BL 3/15/00; HB 5–6/00; HBG 10/00; SLJ 4/00) [996.1]

8155 Arnold, Caroline. *Uluru: Australia's Aboriginal Heart* (4–8). 2003, Clarion $16.00 (0-618-18181-4). Uluru, formerly known as Ayers Rock, is a giant sandstone monolith that changes color in the setting sun and is a spiritual landmark for the native people of the central Australian desert. (Rev: BCCB 12/03; BL 12/15/03; HB 11–12/03; HBG 11–12/03) [994.01]

8156 Arnold, Caroline. *A Walk on the Great Barrier Reef* (4–7). Illus. 1988, Lerner LB $23.93 (0-87614-285-4). Exploring one of the great natural wonders of the world. (Rev: BL 7/88; SLJ 8/88) [574.91943]

8157 Bartlett, Anne. *The Aboriginal Peoples of Australia* (4–7). Illus. Series: First Peoples. 2001, Lerner LB $23.93 (0-8225-4854-2). An introduction to the indigenous people of Australia, including their history, customs, and daily life, with photographs. (Rev: BL 10/15/01; HBG 3/02; SLJ 3/02) [994]

8158 Darian-Smith, Kate. *Exploration into Australia* (5–7). Illus. Series: Exploration. 1996, Dillon LB $15.95 (0-02-718088-3); paper $7.95 (0-382-39227-2). Descriptions are given of the prehistory of Aus-

tralia and the changes made after European exploration. (Rev: BL 8/96; SLJ 9/96) [994]

8159 Darian-Smith, Kate, and David Lowe. *The Australian Outback and Its People* (4–7). Illus. Series: People and Places. 1995, Thomson Learning LB $24.26 (1-56847-337-0). A well-organized guide to the Australian outback, its exploration and history, flora and fauna, mining, environmental issues, and people. (Rev: SLJ 7/95) [994]

8160 Darlington, Robert. *Australia* (4–8). Series: Nations of the World. 2001, Raintree Steck-Vaughn LB $34.26 (0-7398-1280-7). Australia, the world's largest island, is introduced in this attractive volume that gives material on geography, climate, terrain, history, economy, and lifestyles. (Rev: BL 6/1–15/01; HBG 10/01) [994]

8161 Fox, Mary V. *New Zealand* (5–8). Illus. Series: Enchantment of the World. 1991, Children's paper $32.00 (0-516-02728-X). This island country is introduced in text and pictures that cover geography, history, the people, and key attractions. (Rev: BL 10/1/91) [992]

8162 Franklin, Sharon, et al. *Southwest Pacific* (4–7). Series: Artisans Around the World. 1999, Raintree Steck-Vaughn LB $27.12 (0-7398-0120-1). The influence of traditions and geography is shown in this survey of folk art from Australia, New Guinea, New Zealand, and Indonesia, with directions for projects such as a Maori woven band and a batik wall hanging. (Rev: BL 10/15/99; HBG 3/00; SLJ 1/00) [994]

8163 Grabowski, John F. *Australia* (5–8). Series: Modern Nations of the World. 2002, Gale LB $27.45 (1-56006-566-4). The continent Down Under is introduced with coverage of history, natural resources, landmarks, economy, and people. (Rev: BL 12/15/02) [994]

8164 Keyworth, Valerie. *New Zealand: Land of the Long White Cloud* (4–7). Illus. Series: Discovering Our Heritage. 1990, Macmillan LB $14.95 (0-87518-414-6). New Zealand is introduced with information on people, history, culture, and geography. (Rev: SLJ 1/91) [993.1]

8165 Lepthien, Emilie U. *The Philippines* (4–7). 1986, Children's paper $32.00 (0-516-02782-4). These islands are introduced through a discussion of their history, geography, and culture.

8166 Lowe, David, and Andrea Shimmen. *Australia* (4–8). Illus. Series: Modern Industrial World. 1996, Raintree Steck-Vaughn LB $24.26 (0-8172-4553-7). Australia's economic status, living standards, educational system, and industry are covered. (Rev: BL 2/15/97) [919.4]

8167 Macdonald, Robert. *Islands of the Pacific Rim and Their People* (5–8). Illus. Series: People and Places. 1994, Thomson Learning LB $24.26 (1-56847-167-X). An overview of the islands of the

Pacific Ocean and their people, different environments, and economies. (Rev: BL 10/15/94; SLJ 10/94) [990]

8168 McGuinn, Taro. *East Timor: Island in Turmoil* (7–10). Series: World in Conflict. 1998, Lerner LB $25.26 (0-8225-3555-6). The country of East Timor, an island east of Indonesia, is introduced, with material on its internal ethnic and political conflicts. (Rev: BL 10/15/98; BR 1–2/99; HBG 3/99; SLJ 10/98) [959.86]

8169 NgCheong-Lum, Roseline. *Tahiti* (4–7). Illus. Series: Cultures of the World. 1997, Marshall Cavendish LB $35.64 (0-7614-0682-4). Background material on history and geography is given, with information on how Tahitians live today. (Rev: BL 8/97; HBG 3/98) [919.62]

8170 Nile, Richard. *Australian Aborigines* (4–7). Illus. Series: Threatened Cultures. 1993, Raintree Steck-Vaughn LB $24.26 (0-8114-2303-4). The aboriginal culture of Australia is presented. (Rev: BL 8/93; SLJ 8/93) [305]

8171 Oleksy, Walter. *The Philippines* (4–7). Series: Enchantment of the World. 2000, Children's LB $34.50 (0-516-21010-6). These South Pacific islands are presented with coverage of history, geography, economy, the people, current problems, culture, and recreation. (Rev: BL 7/00) [959.9]

8172 Pelta, Kathy. *Rediscovering Easter Island* (5–9). Series: How History Is Invented. 2001, Lerner LB $28.75 (0-8225-4890-9). An assortment of illustrations, maps, and inserts add to this exploration of the mysteries of Easter Island. (Rev: BCCB 7–8/01; HBG 10/01; SLJ 2/02) [996.18]

8173 Rajendra, Vijeya, and Sundran Rajendra. *Australia* (4–7). Illus. Series: Cultures of the World. 1991, Marshall Cavendish LB $35.64 (1-85435-400-0). Beyond the basics, this volume highlights contemporary problems and concerns in the Land Down Under. (Rev: BL 2/15/92; SLJ 3/92) [994]

8174 Sharp, Anne Wallace. *Australia* (5–9). Series: Indigenous Peoples of the World. 2003, Gale $27.45 (1-59018-091-7). In addition to discussing the customs and traditions of the aboriginal people of Australia, the author looks at their harsh treatment by the European settlers. (Rev: SLJ 1/03) [305.89915]

8175 Shepherd, Donna Walsh. *New Zealand* (4–7). Series: Enchantment of the World. 2002, Children's LB $34.50 (0-516-21099-8). Some of the subjects covered in this fine introduction to New Zealand are history, people and languages, economy, government, culture, natural resources, and climate. (Rev: BL 5/15/02; SLJ 10/02) [992]

8176 Sullivan, Margaret. *The Philippines: Pacific Crossroads* (4–8). Illus. Series: Discovering Our Heritage. 1993, Macmillan LB $14.95 (0-87518-548-7). A history with a focus on relations with the

United States and current developments. (Rev: SLJ 8/93) [959.9]

8177 Tope, Lily R. *Philippines* (4–7). Illus. Series: Cultures of the World. 1991, Marshall Cavendish LB $35.64 (1-85435-403-5). With emphasis on contemporary problems and concerns, the land and culture of the Philippines are introduced in text and well-chosen color photographs. (Rev: BL 2/15/92) [959.9]

Europe

General and Miscellaneous

8178 Allan, Tony. *The Rhine* (4–7). Series: Great Rivers of the World. 2003, World Almanac LB $26.60 (0-8368-5446-2). An exploration of the Rhine's flow, history, and animals and plants, with discussion of the settlements along its banks, the industries it supports, recreation on its waters, and environmental threats to the river. (Rev: SLJ 9/03) [943]

8179 Baralt, Luis A. *Turkey* (5–8). Illus. Series: Enchantment of the World. 1997, Children's paper $32.00 (0-516-20305-3). A visually attractive book that covers such topics as Turkey's population, natural resources, historic landmarks, and people. (Rev: BL 8/97; HBG 3/98) [915.61]

8180 *Cyprus in Pictures* (5–8). Illus. Series: Visual Geography. 1992, Lerner LB $25.55 (0-8225-1910-0). The divided island of Cyprus is introduced, with good background information and material on the standoff between Greece and Turkey up to 1992. (Rev: BL 2/1/93) [956.45]

8181 Feinstein, Steve. *Turkey in Pictures* (5–8). Illus. 1989, Lerner LB $25.55 (0-8225-1831-7). An overview of Turkey and its people that includes lots of images. (Rev: BL 8/88) [956.1]

8182 Fox, Mary V. *Cyprus* (5–8). Illus. Series: Enchantment of the World. 1993, Children's paper $32.00 (0-516-02617-8). An introduction to this Mediterranean island, its troubled history, and its present division between Turkey and Greece. (Rev: BL 11/1/93; SLJ 3/94) [956.93]

8183 Kallen, Stuart A. *The Rhine* (5–8). Series: Rivers of the World. 2003, Gale LB $27.45 (1-59018-062-3). A comprehensive look at this important river's history, geology, agricultural and industrial significance, environmental problems, and the floods that threaten surrounding communities. (Rev: SLJ 9/03) [943]

8184 Pollard, Michael. *The Rhine* (5–8). Series: Great Rivers. 1997, Benchmark LB $22.79 (0-7614-0500-3). After explaining how the Rhine was formed, this attractive book describes its history, importance, tributaries, tourism, and present-day role. (Rev: HBG 3/98; SLJ 3/98) [943]

8185 Sheehan, Sean. *Malta* (5–9). Series: Cultures of the World. 2000, Marshall Cavendish LB $35.64 (0-7614-0993-9). This work covers the culture, geography, and history of Malta with material on such subjects as government, economy, people, lifestyles, and leisure. (Rev: HBG 10/00; SLJ 11/00) [945]

8186 Sheehan, Sean. *Turkey* (4–7). Illus. Series: Cultures of the World. 1993, Marshall Cavendish LB $35.64 (1-85435-576-7). This introduction to Turkey covers history, culture, economics, and present-day concerns. (Rev: BL 8/93) [956.1]

Eastern Europe and the Balkans

8187 Andryszewski, Tricia. *Kosovo: The Splintering of Yugoslavia* (5–8). Illus. Series: Headliners. 2000, Millbrook LB $25.90 (0-7613-1750-3). Introduced by refugees' accounts of the horror in Kosovo, this book traces the origins of ethnic conflicts in Yugoslavia, with a concentration on events of the past 10 years. (Rev: BL 6/1–15/00; HBG 10/00; SLJ 6/00) [949.7]

8188 Burke, Patrick. *Eastern Europe: Bulgaria, Czech Republic, Hungary, Poland, Romania, Slovakia* (5–8). Series: Country Fact Files. 1997, Raintree Steck-Vaughn LB $27.12 (0-8172-4628-2). In chapters two to four pages long, the impact of geography on the landscape, daily life, natural resources, transportation, and other aspects of life is examined for these six countries. (Rev: SLJ 8/97) [947]

8189 Carran, Betty B. *Romania* (4–7). Illus. 1988, Children's paper $32.00 (0-516-02703-4). Coverage includes geography, culture, history, and politics. (Rev: BL 8/88) [949.8]

8190 Corona, Laurel. *Poland* (5–8). Illus. Series: Modern Nations of the World. 2000, Lucent LB $27.45 (1-56006-600-8). A good history of Poland that also covers Polish achievements and daily life. (Rev: BL 9/15/00; HBG 3/01) [943.8]

8191 Fireside, Harvey, and Bryna J. Fireside. *Young People From Bosnia Talk About War* (6–9). Illus. Series: Issues in Focus. 1996, Enslow LB $20.95 (0-89490-730-1). Several students from Bosnia who have been brought to this country to study by the Bosnian Student Project tell about the effects of the war on them, their families, and their country. (Rev: BL 10/15/96; BR 1–2/97; SLJ 10/96; VOYA 2/97) [949.702]

8192 Harbor, Bernard. *Conflict in Eastern Europe* (6–12). Series: Conflicts. 1993, Macmillan LB $13.95 (0-02-742626-2). An overview of events that led to the demise of the Soviet empire in Eastern Europe and what transpired subsequently, up to 1993. (Rev: BL 10/1/93; SLJ 12/93) [947]

8193 Harris, Nathaniel. *The War in Former Yugoslavia* (7–12). Illus. Series: New Perspectives. 1998, Raintree Steck-Vaughn LB $28.54 (0-8172-5014-X). Different perspectives on this war are expressed through the viewpoints of political leaders, ordinary citizens, soldiers, militiamen, foreign diplomats, rescue workers, and news reporters. (Rev: BL 3/15/98; BR 1–2/99; HBG 9/98) [940.54]

8194 Humphreys, Rob. *Czech Republic* (4–7). Illus. Series: Country Insights. 1998, Raintree Steck-Vaughn LB $27.12 (0-8172-4795-5). Discusses developments in the Czech Republic since the fall of Communism and contrasts city/village life. (Rev: BL 5/1/98; HBG 10/98) [943.71]

8195 *Hungary in Pictures* (5–8). Illus. Series: Visual Geography. 1993, Lerner LB $25.55 (0-8225-1883-X). Concise text and extensive photographs introduce the land, history, and people of Hungary. (Rev: BL 12/1/93; SLJ 12/93) [943.9]

8196 Otfinoski, Steven. *Bulgaria* (6–10). Series: Nations in Transition. 1998, Facts on File $25.00 (0-8160-3705-1). This book reviews the history, politics, people, and culture of Bulgaria, now undergoing transition as a result of the fall of communism in Eastern Europe, plus material on relationships with Gypsies and other minorities. (Rev: BL 3/1/99; BR 5–6/99; SLJ 6/99) [949.903]

8197 Otfinoski, Steven. *Poland* (6–10). Series: Nations in Transition. 1995, Facts on File $25.00 (0-8160-3063-4). This work explains Poland's past and covers its present situation, with chapters on religion, economy, culture, and daily life. (Rev: BR 9–10/96; VOYA 8/96) [943]

8198 Pfeiffer, Christine. *Poland: Land of Freedom Fighters* (5–8). Illus. 1991, Macmillan LB $14.95 (0-87518-464-2). An introduction to the land and people of Poland and of their migration to the United States. [943.8]

8199 Reger, James P. *The Rebuilding of Bosnia* (6–8). Illus. Series: Overview. 1997, Lucent LB $27.45 (1-56006-190-1). After a discussion of the ethnic and religious strife in the Balkans for 1,500 years, this book focuses on the recent war in Bosnia and the uneasy peace following 1995's Dayton Accords. (Rev: BL 9/1/97; SLJ 8/97) [949.703]

8200 Ricchiardi, Sherry. *Bosnia: The Struggle for Peace* (5–8). Illus. 1996, Millbrook LB $25.90 (0-7613-0031-7). An account that gives background information but concentrates on the recent (through 1995) history of Bosnia. (Rev: BL 7/96; SLJ 7/96) [949.702]

8201 Rollyson, Carl S. *Teenage Refugees from Eastern Europe Speak Out* (7–12). Series: Teenage Refugees Speak Out. 1997, Rosen LB $16.95 (0-8239-2437-8). Young refugees from Slovakia, Bulgaria, Hungary, Romania, Poland, Yugoslavia, and the former East Germany tell about conditions in their homelands and their receptions in the United States. (Rev: BL 12/15/97) [947]

8202 *Romania in Pictures* (5–8). Illus. Series: Visual Geography. 1993, Lerner LB $25.55 (0-8225-1894-5). In addition to background material on history and geography, this account gives a good picture of contemporary life in Romania. (Rev: BL 9/1/93) [949.8]

8203 Sioras, Efstathia. *Czech Republic* (7–10). Series: Cultures of the World. 1998, Marshall Cavendish LB $35.64 (0-7614-0870-3). An attractive volume that covers the standard topics: geography, history, government, economy, leisure, festivals, and food, and includes full-color photographs, colorful sidebars, maps, charts, and recipes. (Rev: HBG 9/99; SLJ 6/99) [943.7]

8204 Willis, Terri. *Romania* (4–7). Series: Enchantment of the World. 2001, Children's LB $34.50 (0-516-21635-X). Packed with photographs, original maps, and browser-friendly sidebars, this is a fine introduction to Romania that explores a number of aspects of the past and present of this country. (Rev: BL 1/1–15/02) [949.8]

8205 Yancey, Diane. *Life in War-Torn Bosnia* (6–9). Illus. Series: The Way People Live. 1996, Lucent LB $27.45 (1-56006-326-2). Though now a few years old, this account gives valuable background material on the Balkans, tracing their history and problems from the Middle Ages. (Rev: BL 3/15/96; BR 9–10/96; SLJ 4/96) [949.7]

France

8206 Barter, James. *The Palace of Versailles* (6–10). Series: Building History. 1998, Lucent LB $27.45 (1-56006-433-1). An informative account of the building of the palace for King Louis XIV of France, which took 40 years and represents a pinnacle of opulence and grandeur. (Rev: BL 12/15/98; BR 5–6/99; SLJ 2/99) [944]

8207 Benedict, Kitty C. *The Fall of the Bastille* (5–8). Series: Turning Points in World History. 1991, Silver Burdett LB $14.95 (0-382-24129-0); paper $7.95 (0-382-24135-5). A study of the event that symbolized a tremendous change in French society. (Rev: BL 3/15/92) [944.04]

8208 Cooper, Margaret. *Exploring the Ice Age* (5–8). Illus. 2001, Simon & Schuster $19.95 (0-689-82556-0). Details the everyday lives, from tools and shelter to clothing and art, of humans living in the last Ice Age in southwestern France. (Rev: BL 11/1/01; HB 1–2/02; HBG 3/02; SLJ 10/01) [936]

8209 Corona, Laurel. *France* (5–8). Series: Modern Nations of the World. 2002, Gale LB $27.45 (1-56006-760-8). A comprehensive introduction to the land and people of France with material on history,

geography, culture, and lifestyles. (Rev: BL 12/15/02) [944]

8210 Dunford, Mick. *France* (5–8). Illus. Series: Modern Industrial World. 1994, Thomson Learning LB $24.26 (1-56847-263-3). An introduction to modern France that gives information about government, people, economic conditions, and recent history. (Rev: BL 1/15/95) [944]

8211 Fisher, Teresa. *France: City and Village Life* (4–7). Illus. Series: Country Insights. 1997, Raintree Steck-Vaughn LB $27.12 (0-8172-4788-2). A specific city and village are used to compare and contrast two lifestyles in contemporary France. (Rev: SLJ 8/97) [944]

8212 Gofen, Ethel C. *France* (4–7). Illus. Series: Cultures of the World. 1992, Marshall Cavendish LB $35.64 (1-85435-449-3). This account provides information on the history, culture, and people of France and discusses the current problems and concerns. (Rev: BL 10/15/92) [944]

8213 Greene, Meg. *The Eiffel Tower* (7–10). Series: Building History. 2000, Lucent LB $19.96 (1-56006-826-4). This account describes the building of this Paris landmark with coverage of both the social and technical obstacles that confronted its builders. (Rev: BL 4/15/01; SLJ 6/01) [944]

8214 Hoban, Sarah. *Daily Life in Ancient and Modern Paris* (4–7). Illus. 2000, Runestone LB $25.26 (0-8225-3222-0). This well-illustrated history of Paris is divided chronologically into seven sections, beginning with early Paris and working through the Middle Ages to World War II and the Paris of today. (Rev: BL 2/1/01; HBG 3/01; SLJ 2/01) [944]

8215 Ingham, Richard. *France* (4–8). Illus. 2000, Raintree Steck-Vaughn LB $34.26 (0-8172-5782-9). A fine introduction to France — its past, its present, and its people — that is particularly noteworthy for its use of graphics. (Rev: BL 10/15/00; HBG 10/00; SLJ 7/00) [944]

8216 Libby, Megan M. *Postcards from France* (8–12). 1998, HarperCollins paper $5.99 (0-06-101170-3). A compilation of 12 columns written for a local newspaper, this book tells of the experiences of Megan Libby, a high school student from Connecticut during her junior year in France. (Rev: BL 4/15/97) [944]

8217 Nardo, Don. *France* (4–7). Series: Enchantment of the World. 2000, Children's LB $34.50 (0-516-21052-1). This attractively formatted and illustrated new edition gives solid information about France, its land, and its people. (Rev: BL 7/00) [944]

8218 Nardo, Don. *The Trial of Joan of Arc* (7–10). Series: Famous Trials. 1997, Lucent LB $27.45 (1-56006-466-8). A scholarly discussion and analysis of Joan of Arc's trial and execution, with a brief introductory biography. (Rev: SLJ 10/97) [944]

8219 NgCheong-Lum, Roseline. *France* (5–7). Series: Countries of the World. 1999, Gareth Stevens LB $29.26 (0-8368-2260-9). A wide range of topics including history, government, people, customs, and geography are covered in this colorful introduction to France. (Rev: BL 9/15/99; SLJ 8/99) [944]

8220 Plain, Nancy. *Louis XVI, Marie-Antoinette and the French Revolution* (5–8). Series: Rulers and Their Times. 2001, Marshall Cavendish LB $28.50 (0-7614-1029-5). In three well-illustrated parts, this book offers a biography of Marie Antoinette, a history of France and its people during the French Revolution, and a generous selection of original documents of the period. (Rev: BL 1/1–15/02; HBG 3/02; SLJ 3/02) [944]

8221 Powell, Jillian. *A History of France Through Art* (5–8). Illus. Series: History Through Art. 1996, Thomson Learning LB $5.00 (1-56847-441-5). The basic history of France is covered in 21 double-page spreads, each dealing with an important event or subject and each containing works of art and informative background text. (Rev: BL 3/1/96; SLJ 2/96) [944]

8222 Prosser, Robert. *France* (6–10). Series: Countries of the World. 2003, Facts on File $30.00 (0-8160-5380-4). This basic introduction to the land and people of France includes material on economy, culture, and present-day problems. (Rev: BL 1/1–15/04) [944]

8223 Shuter, Jane, ed. *Helen Williams and the French Revolution* (5–8). Illus. Series: History Eyewitness. 1996, Raintree Steck-Vaughn LB $24.26 (0-8114-8287-1). An abridged, well-illustrated firsthand account describes the causes and the course of the French Revolution. (Rev: BL 5/15/96; SLJ 6/96) [944.04]

8224 Wright, Rachel. *Paris 1789: A Guide to Paris on the Eve of the Revolution* (4–7). Series: Sightseers. 1999, Kingfisher $8.95 (0-7534-5183-2). Using the format of a tourist guide, this book tells you what to see, eat, wear, and buy in the Paris of the late 18th century. (Rev: HBG 10/99; SLJ 8/99) [944]

Germany, Austria, and Switzerland

8225 Ayer, Eleanor. *Germany* (6–9). Series: Modern Nations of the World. 1998, Lucent LB $27.45 (1-56006-355-6). A fine introduction to Germany's history, geography, and culture that does not gloss over the atrocities of the Nazi regime and the problems of reunification. (Rev: BL 12/1/98) [943]

8226 Cartlidge, Cherese, and Charles Clark. *Life of a Nazi Soldier* (6–10). Series: The Way People Live. 2000, Lucent LB $19.96 (1-56006-484-6). The living conditions and military requirements of German soldiers during World War II are the primary focus of this volume, which condemns the atrocities that took place while attempting to explain why they were allowed to happen. (Rev: BL 3/1/01; SLJ 7/01) [940.54]

8227 Fuller, Barbara. *Germany* (4–7). Illus. Series: Cultures of the World. 1992, Marshall Cavendish LB $35.64 (1-85435-530-9). In addition to the usual information on the history and geography of Germany, this account stresses how the people live and their traditions. (Rev: BL 1/1/93) [943]

8228 *Germany in Pictures* (5–8). Illus. Series: Visual Geography. 1994, Lerner LB $21.27 (0-8225-1873-2). The new united Germany is introduced with a basic text and copious illustrations, including maps, charts, and attractive photographs. (Rev: BL 1/15/95) [943]

8229 Grant, R. G. *The Berlin Wall* (7–12). Series: New Perspectives. 1998, Raintree Steck-Vaughn LB $28.54 (0-8172-5017-4). This presentation of various perspectives on the Berlin Wall, its uses, and its destruction in 1989, is also an overview of the history of the Cold War in Europe and the collapse of communism there. (Rev: BL 1/1–15/99; HBG 3/99) [943.1]

8230 Hargrove, Jim. *Germany* (5–8). Illus. Series: Enchantment of the World. 1991, Children's paper $32.00 (0-516-02601-1). German geography, people, culture, and history through reunification are covered in text and pictures. (Rev: BL 2/1/92) [943]

8231 McGowen, Tom. *Frederick the Great, Bismarck, and the Building of the German Empire in World History* (8–12). Series: In World History. 2002, Enslow LB $20.95 (0-7660-1822-9). From Frederick, ruler of Prussia through the careers of Otto von Bismarck and William I, this is the story of the unification of Germany. (Rev: BL 3/15/03; HBG 3/03; SLJ 12/02) [943]

8232 Mirable, Lisa. *The Berlin Wall* (5–8). Series: Turning Points. 1991, Silver Burdett LB $14.95 (0-382-24133-9); paper $7.95 (0-382-24140-1). How the fall of the Berlin Wall dramatically changed German history. (Rev: BL 3/15/92) [943.1]

8233 Nardo, Don, ed. *The Rise of Nazi Germany* (7–12). Series: Turning Points in World History. 1999, Greenhaven LB $32.45 (1-56510-965-1); paper $21.20 (1-56510-964-3). This anthology of writings examines the emergence of fascism and National Socialism in Germany, the personality of Hitler, his use of propaganda, and his political maneuvering to seize control in 1933. (Rev: BL 6/1–15/99; SLJ 5/99) [943.086]

8234 Netzley, Patricia D. *Switzerland* (5–8). Series: Modern Nations of the World. 2001, Lucent LB $27.45 (1-56006-821-3). Interesting sidebars, a chronology, and excellent photographs supplement informative text introducing this small country. (Rev: BL 6/1–15/01) [949.3]

8235 Nickles, Greg, and Niki Walker. *Germany* (4–8). Series: Nations of the World. 2001, Raintree Steck-Vaughn LB $34.26 (0-7398-1285-8). A profile of this recently united, highly industrialized, and urbanized country, with material on its past, present, and future. (Rev: BL 6/1–15/01; HBG 10/01) [943]

8236 Rogers, Lura. *Switzerland* (4–7). Series: Enchantment of the World. 2001, Children's LB $34.50 (0-516-21080-7). A highly visual introduction to Switzerland that covers such topics as people and languages, history, natural resources, and climate. (Rev: BL 1/1–15/02) [949.4]

8237 Schrepfer, Margaret. *Switzerland: The Summit of Europe* (4–7). Illus. Series: Discovering Our Heritage. 1989, Macmillan LB $14.95 (0-87518-405-7). Four ethnic groups plus Switzerland's ancient and modern history are covered in this introduction. (Rev: BL 7/89; SLJ 10/89) [949.4]

8238 Sheehan, Sean. *Austria* (4–7). Illus. Series: Cultures of the World. 1992, Marshall Cavendish LB $35.64 (1-85435-454-X). This introduction to Austria covers its history, lifestyles of the people, and contemporary problems. (Rev: BL 10/15/92) [943.6]

8239 Stein, R. Conrad. *Austria* (4–7). Series: Enchantment of the World. 2000, Children's LB $34.50 (0-516-21049-1). A thorough introduction to Austria with material on such subjects as history, the land, government, people, culture, cities, and daily life. (Rev: BL 1/1–15/01) [943.6]

8240 *Switzerland in Pictures* (5–8). Series: Visual Geography. 1996, Lerner LB $25.55 (0-8225-1895-3). With a generous number of color pictures, this account traces the history and geography of Switzerland, with emphasis on the modern nation and its people. (Rev: BL 9/15/96; SLJ 8/98) [949.4]

8241 Symynkywicz, Jeffrey B. *Germany: United Again* (6–9). Series: The Fall of Communism. 1995, Silver Burdett LB $14.95 (0-87518-634-3); paper $7.95 (0-382-39190-X). This account of German history from Kaiser Wilhelm to the present focuses on the fall of the Berlin Wall and the reunification of Germany. (Rev: SLJ 7/96) [943]

Great Britain and Ireland

8242 Allan, Tony. *The Irish Famine: The Birth of Irish America* (4–9). Series: Point of Impact. 2001, Heinemann LB $24.22 (1-58810-077-4). Allan traces the causes of the crisis that started in Ireland in 1845, the subsequent wave of emigration to the United States, and the ill feelings created between Britain and Ireland. (Rev: HBG 10/01; SLJ 7/01) [941.5081]

8243 Ashby, Ruth. *Elizabethan England* (5–9). Series: Cultures of the Past. 1998, Benchmark LB $28.50 (0-7614-0269-1). Ashby looks at the cultural aspects of Elizabethan England, providing material on the art and literature of the period plus coverage of daily life, religion, and major personalities. (Rev: BL 12/15/98; BR 5–6/99; HBG 10/99; SLJ 2/99) [942]

8244 Ashby, Ruth. *Victorian England* (5–8). Series: Cultures of the Past. 2002, Marshall Cavendish $19.95 (0-7614-1493-2). The political, historical, and cultural aspects of life in England during the reign of Victoria are covered in this handsome volume. (Rev: BL 1/1–15/03; HBG 3/03) [942]

8245 Atkins, Sinclair. *From Stone Age to Conquest* (7–10). Illus. 1986, Hulton paper $14.95 (0-7175-1305-X). A well-illustrated account of British history from prehistoric times to the Norman Conquest. (Rev: SLJ 4/86) [941.01]

8246 Bartoletti, Susan Campbell. *Black Potatoes: The Story of the Great Irish Famine, 1845–1850* (6–12). Illus. 2001, Houghton $18.00 (0-618-00271-5). First-person narratives and a chronological account of events interspersed with illustrations, letters, and news reports clearly portray the sufferings of the Irish people during the famine of the late 1840s. (Rev: BL 10/15/01; HB 1–2/02; HBG 3/02; SLJ 11/01*; VOYA 12/01) [941.5081]

8247 Bernard, Catherine. *The British Empire and Queen Victoria in World History* (8–12). Series: In World History. 2002, Enslow LB $20.95 (0-7660-1824-5). Combining both biography and history, this account describes Victoria's 63-year reign and how, during it, the British Empire flourished. (Rev: BL 3/15/03; HBG 10/03; SLJ 7/03) [941]

8248 Black, Eric. *Northern Ireland: Troubled Land* (8–12). Illus. Series: World in Conflict. 1998, Lerner LB $25.26 (0-8225-3552-1). An information-packed, illustrated account of the historical background of the conflict in Northern Ireland and current developments. (Rev: BL 4/15/98; HBG 9/98) [941.6]

8249 Blashfield, Jean F. *England* (4–7). Illus. Series: Enchantment of the World. 1997, Children's LB $34.50 (0-516-20471-8). This fine introduction to England gives material on its history, politics, the royal family, religion, and daily life. (Rev: BL 2/1/98; HBG 10/98) [942]

8250 Blashfield, Jean F. *Ireland* (4–7). Series: Enchantment of the World. 2002, Children's LB $34.50 (0-516-21127-7). Using many visual aids and a lively text, this is an introduction to Ireland — the land, the people, and the culture. (Rev: BL 5/15/02; SLJ 12/02) [941.5]

8251 Bowden, Rob. *United Kingdom* (6–10). Series: Countries of the World. 2003, Facts on File $30.00 (0-8160-5383-9). An attractive volume that presents basic material about Great Britain including history, geography, and present social conditions. (Rev: BL 1/1–15/04) [941]

8252 Buscher, Sarah, and Bettina Ling. *Mairead Corrigan and Betty Williams: Making Peace in Northern Ireland* (5–8). Illus. 1999, Feminist Pr. $19.95 (1-55861-200-9); paper $9.95 (1-55861-201-7). The story of the two women in Northern Ireland who won the Nobel Peace Prize for their efforts to help end the civil strife in their country. (Rev: BL 3/15/00; SLJ 2/00; VOYA 4/00) [941]

8253 Childress, Diana. *Chaucer's England* (7–12). Illus. 2000, Linnet LB $25.00 (0-208-02489-1). A fascinating glimpse into the social life, community structure, landscape, and economy of 14th-century England. (Rev: BL 9/15/00; BR 5–6/01; HBG 10/01; SLJ 10/00; VOYA 4/01) [942.03]

8254 Corona, Laurel. *Scotland* (5–8). Series: Modern Nations of the World. 2000, Lucent LB $27.45 (1-56006-703-9). The history, geography, and culture of Scotland are discussed along with material on daily life in modern Scotland. (Rev: BL 3/1/01) [941]

8255 Dahl, Roald. *The Mildenhall Treasure* (7–12). 2000, Knopf $22.95 (0-375-81035-8). A British farmer's discovery of ancient Roman artifacts in 1942 leads to intrigue and greed in this fascinating nonfiction action. (Rev: BL 2/1/01; HBG 3/01; SLJ 12/00) [642]

8256 Davis, Kenneth C. *Don't Know Much About the Kings and Queens of England* (4–7). Series: Don't Know Much About. 2002, HarperCollins LB $15.89 (0-06-028612-1). Humorous questions and answers supply information that browsers will enjoy. (Rev: HBG 10/02; SLJ 7/02) [941.0099]

8257 Dolan, Edward F. *The Irish Potato Famine: The Story of Irish-American Immigration* (6–9). Series: Great Journeys. 2002, Marshall Cavendish LB $21.95 (0-7614-1323-5). The story of the terrible Irish famine that lasted from 1845 through 1851 and caused a mass exodus, particularly to America. (Rev: BL 3/15/03; HBG 3/03) [941.7]

8258 Flint, David. *Great Britain* (5–8). Illus. Series: Modern Industrial World. 1996, Raintree Steck-Vaughn LB $24.26 (0-8172-4555-3). Modern Great Britain is the focus of this volume, which concentrates on the economy and industrial development. (Rev: BL 2/15/96; SLJ 8/97) [330.941]

8259 Fradin, Dennis B. *The Republic of Ireland* (4–7). Illus. 1984, Children's paper $32.00 (0-516-02767-0). An introduction to this country that touches briefly on many subjects. [941]

8260 Gallagher, Carole. *The Irish Potato Famine* (6–8). Series: Great Disasters. 2001, Chelsea LB $21.95 (0-7910-5788-7). The horrors of the terrible blight that destroyed the potato crops of Ireland from 1845 to 1849 are re-created, with discussion of the monumental changes that followed. (Rev: BL 6/1–15/02; HBG 10/02) [941.7]

8261 Gottfried, Ted. *Northern Ireland: Peace in Our Time?* (5–8). Series: Headliners. 2002, Millbrook LB $25.90 (0-7613-2252-3). This attractive book gives current and background information on the struggles within Northern Ireland and the causes and possible solutions. (Rev: BL 4/15/02; HBG 10/02; SLJ 3/02) [941]

8262 Greenblatt, Miriam. *Elizabeth I and Tudor England* (5–8). Series: Rulers and Their Times. 2001, Marshall Cavendish LB $28.50 (0-7614-1028-7). After a biography of Elizabeth I, this colorful account traces everyday life in Elizabethan times and supplies a selection of primary documents. (Rev: BL 1/1–15/02; HBG 3/02; SLJ 3/02) [942.1]

8263 Hestler, Anna. *Wales* (5–9). Illus. Series: Cultures of the World. 2001, Marshall Cavendish LB $35.64 (0-7614-1195-X). Geography, history, government, arts and culture, and lifestyle are all covered in this interesting and attractive volume. (Rev: HBG 10/01; SLJ 11/01) [942.9]

8264 Hirst, Mike. *The History of Emigration from Scotland* (4–7). Series: Origins. 1997, Watts LB $21.00 (0-531-14441-0). Details on the political, social, and economic conditions in Scotland through various periods in its history that led to emigration to the United States and other lands. (Rev: BL 12/15/97; HBG 3/98; SLJ 2/98) [941.106]

8265 Innes, Brian. *United Kingdom* (4–8). Series: Nations of the World. 2001, Raintree Steck-Vaughn LB $34.26 (0-7398-1288-1). An in-depth look at the nation's geography, climate. terrain, history, government, and lifestyles. (Rev: BL 12/15/01) [941]

8266 *Ireland in Pictures* (5–8). Illus. Series: Visual Geography. 1997, Lerner LB $25.55 (0-8225-1878-3). Contemporary Ireland is highlighted in this illustrated account. (Rev: BL 12/1/90) [941.5]

8267 Lace, William W. *The British Empire* (6–12). Illus. Series: History's Great Defeats. 2000, Lucent LB $23.70 (1-56006-683-0). Subtitled "The End of Colonialism," this account traces the rise and growth of the British Empire, its accomplishments and failures, and its decline and fall. (Rev: BL 11/1/00; HBG 3/01; SLJ 10/00) [909]

8268 Lace, William W. *Elizabeth I and Her Court* (6–10). Series: The Lucent Library of Historical Eras: Elizabethan England. 2002, Gale LB $27.45 (1-59018-098-4). A well-written account of life at court during Elizabeth I's reign, with black-and-white reproductions and photographs. Also recommended in this series are *Life in Elizabethan London* and *Primary Sources* (both 2002). (Rev: LMC 11–12/03; SLJ 9/03)

8269 Lace, William W. *England* (7–10). Series: Modern Nations of the World. 1997, Lucent LB $27.45 (1-56006-194-4). A compact introduction to the past and present of England, arranged in six theme-based chapters, with good illustrations and interesting sidebars. (Rev: SLJ 9/97) [941]

8270 Lace, William W. *The Little Princes in the Tower* (7–9). Illus. Series: Mysterious Deaths. 1997, Lucent LB $27.45 (1-56006-262-2). The unsolved murders of Edward V and his brother in the Tower of London and the possible involvement of Richard III are explored in this book. (Rev: BL 2/15/96; BR 9–10/97; SLJ 3/97) [942.04]

8271 Lace, William W. *Oliver Cromwell and the English Civil War in World History* (8–12). Series: In World History. 2002, Enslow LB $20.95 (0-7660-1937-3). The story of the English Civil War leader who defeated both Charles I and Charles II and became, for a time, Lord Protector of England. (Rev: BL 3/15/03; HBG 10/03; VOYA 8/03) [941]

8272 Levy, Patricia. *Ireland* (4–7). Illus. Series: Cultures of the World. 1993, Marshall Cavendish LB $35.64 (1-85435-580-5). An account that traces the role of women in Irish history to the present day. (Rev: SLJ 2/94) [941]

8273 Lister, Maree, and Marti Sevier. *England* (5–8). Series: Countries of the World. 1998, Gareth Stevens LB $29.26 (0-8368-2125-4). In addition to basic information on the geography, history, economy, culture, and people of England, this book has a special section that describes characteristics that make this country unique, including particular places, people, and traditions. (Rev: BL 12/15/98; HBG 9/99; SLJ 2/99) [941]

8274 Lyons, Mary E., ed. *Feed the Children First: Irish Memories of the Great Hunger* (4–8). Illus. 2002, Simon & Schuster $17.00 (0-689-84226-0). Text, full-color reproductions, and occasional photographs clearly document the suffering of ordinary people during the Irish potato famine. (Rev: BL 12/15/01; HB 3–4/02; HBG 10/02; SLJ 3/02*) [941.5081]

8275 Marvel, Laura, ed. *Elizabethan England* (7–12). Series: Turning Points in World History. 2001, Greenhaven LB $31.20 (0-7377-0483-7); paper $19.95 (0-7377-0484-5). Well-written essays by well-known historians, and a collection of original documents, are featured in this account that explores various aspects of the Elizabethan age including cultural and social topics. (Rev: BL 3/15/02; SLJ 4/02)

8276 Mitchell, Graham. *The Napoleonic Wars* (5–9). Illus. 1990, Batsford $19.95 (0-7134-5729-5). This British import tells about the war chiefly from the British point of view and uses many quotations from original sources. (Rev: BR 3–4/90; SLJ 3/90) [944.05]

8277 *Northern Ireland in Pictures* (5–8). Series: Visual Geography. 1991, Lerner LB $25.55 (0-8225-1898-8). This beautiful but troubled land is introduced in text and pictures. (Rev: BL 2/15/92) [941.6]

8278 Prior, Katherine. *Ireland* (4–7). Illus. Series: Origins. 1997, Watts LB $21.00 (0-531-14415-1). Tells of the conditions in Ireland that led to emigration, where the Irish went, and their reception in Great Britain, the United States, and elsewhere. (Rev: BL 4/15/97) [941.5]

8279 Ross, Stewart. *Elizabethan Life* (6–9). Series: How It Was. 1991, Batsford $19.95 (0-7134-6356-2). Laws, journals, and other historical sources from the period help re-create a vivid picture of Elizabethan life. (Rev: BL 1/15/92) [941]

8280 Sancha, Sheila. *The Luttrell Village: Country Life in the Middle Ages* (7–10). Illus. 1983, Harper-Collins LB $13.89 (0-690-04324-4). Life and activities in an English village of 1328 are revealed in words and excellent drawings by the author. [942.03]

8281 Shields, Charles J. *The Great Plague and Fire of London* (6–8). Series: Great Disasters. 2001, Chelsea LB $21.95 (0-7910-6324-0). This is the story of the plague that ravished England in 1665 and of the fire the following year that nearly destroyed the entire city of London. (Rev: BL 6/1–15/02; SLJ 6/02) [941]

8282 Smith, Nigel. *The Houses of Parliament* (4–7). Illus. Series: Great Buildings. 1997, Raintree Steck-Vaughn LB $27.12 (0-8172-4921-4). As well as giving a history of the British Houses of Parliament, this book tells about the British form of government. (Rev: BL 2/1/98; HBG 3/98) [725]

8283 Stein, R. Conrad. *Scotland* (4–7). Series: Enchantment of the World. 2001, Children's LB $34.50 (0-516-21112-9). Numerous pictures, charts, maps, and drawings contribute to a fascinating portrait of Scotland's past and present. (Rev: BL 1/1–15/02) [931]

8284 Swisher, Clarice. *Victorian England* (7–10). Series: World History. 2000, Lucent LB $19.96 (1-56006-323-8). Quotations and period reproductions enhance this interesting survey of the long and eventful reign of Queen Victoria, a time of technological and social innovation and of growing power for Great Britain. (Rev: BL 12/15/00; SLJ 3/01) [942]

8285 Toht, Betony, and David Toht. *Daily Life in Ancient and Modern London* (6–9). Series: Cities Through Time. 2001, Lerner LB $25.26 (0-8225-3223-9). London's evolution from earliest times to today is presented in double-page spreads, with information on political, social, and religious life. (Rev: BL 4/15/01; HBG 10/01; SLJ 7/01) [942]

8286 *Wales in Pictures* (5–8). Illus. 1994, Lerner LB $25.55 (0-8225-1877-5). Wales is introduced and material is given on history and current conditions. (Rev: BL 12/1/90) [942.9]

8287 Yancey, Diane. *Life in Charles Dickens's England* (6–10). Series: The Way People Live. 1998, Lucent LB $27.45 (1-56006-098-0). From terrible squalor and grinding poverty to great wealth and comfort, the spectrum of British society, rural and urban, is explored during the days of Charles Dickens. (Rev: BL 10/15/98; SLJ 1/99; VOYA 12/99) [942]

Greece

8288 Dubois, Jill, and Xenia Skoura. *Greece*. 2nd ed. (5–8). Illus. Series: Cultures of the World. 2003, Benchmark LB $24.95 (0-7614-1499-1). In addition to coverage of the geography, history, and economics of Greece, this volume looks at the people and the culture of this Mediterranean nation and provides recipes. (Rev: HBG 10/03; SLJ 8/03) [949.5]

8289 *Greece in Pictures* (5–8). Illus. Series: Visual Geography. 1996, Lerner LB $25.55 (0-8225-1882-1). Photographs, maps, charts, and concise text introduce the land and people of Greece. (Rev: BL 10/1/92) [949.5]

8290 Heinrichs, Ann. *Greece* (4–7). Series: Enchantment of the World. 2002, Children's LB $34.50 (0-516-22271-6). With many color illustrations, this book gives a fascinating portrait of Greece's past and present with coverage of topics including natural resources, culture, climate, and religion. (Rev: BL 9/15/02; SLJ 12/02) [949.5]

8291 Kotapish, Dawn. *Daily Life in Ancient and Modern Athens* (5–8). Illus. Series: Cities Through Time. 2000, Runestone LB $25.26 (0-8225-3216-6). Kotapish explores everyday life, government, and culture in Athens through the ages. (Rev: HBG 3/01; SLJ 5/01) [949.5]

8292 Nardo, Don. *Greece* (5–8). Series: Modern Nations of the World. 2000, Lucent LB $27.45 (1-56006-587-7). Although there is coverage of ancient Greece, this account stresses modern history, the people today, and current living conditions and problems. (Rev: BL 2/15/00; HBG 10/00; SLJ 6/00) [949.5]

8293 Stein, R. Conrad. *Greece* (4–7). Illus. 1988, Children's paper $32.00 (0-516-02759-X). Photographs and maps highlight this overview of an ancient land. (Rev: BL 5/15/88) [938]

8294 Zinovieff, Sofka. *Greece* (4–7). Illus. Series: Origins. 1997, Watts LB $21.00 (0-531-14417-8). A look at the conditions in Greece at various times in history that led to emigration to the United States and Canada, and the experiences of these immigrants. (Rev: BL 4/15/97) [949.5]

Italy

8295 Barter, James. *The Tower of Pisa* (7–10). Series: Building History. 2001, Lucent $24.95 (1-56006-874-4). The story of the construction and history of the famous Pisan landmark that was begun in 1173 unfortunately on sandy subsoil. (Rev: BL 8/1/01) [945]

8296 Behnke, Alison. *Italy in Pictures*. Rev. ed. (4–8). Illus. Series: Visual Geography. 2002, Lerner LB $27.93 (0-8225-0368-9). An excellent introduction to Italy that includes material on geography, history, people, economy, and culture with maps, photographs, and illustrations. (Rev: HBG 3/03; SLJ 3/03) [914.5]

8297 Blashfield, Jean F. *Italy* (4–7). Series: Enchantment of the World. 1999, Children's LB $34.50 (0-516-20960-4). The topics covered in this book about Italy range from history, geography, and government to mythology, culture, daily life, and sports. (Rev: BL 1/1–15/00) [945]

8298 Cassidy, Picot. *Italy* (4–8). Series: Nations of the World. 2001, Raintree Steck-Vaughn LB $34.26 (0-7398-1287-4). A fine overall picture of Italy, its past, its land, its people, its culture, and present-day problems. (Rev: BL 12/15/01; HBG 3/02) [945]

8299 Foster, Leila M. *Italy* (5–9). Series: Modern Nations of the World. 1998, Lucent LB $27.45 (1-56006-481-1). A fine introduction to Italy's past and present with an overview of its amazing history, modern popular culture, achievements, daily life, and geography. (Rev: SLJ 5/99) [945]

8300 Hinds, Kathryn. *Venice and Its Merchant Empire* (5–8). Illus. Series: Cultures of the Past. 2001, Marshall Cavendish LB $28.50 (0-7614-0305-1). A well-illustrated overview of the history of Venice with a focus on the city's glory during the Renaissance. (Rev: BL 2/15/02; HBG 3/02) [945]

8301 Macaulay, David. *Rome Antics* (5–8). Illus. 1997, Houghton $18.00 (0-395-82279-3). The reader gets a pigeon-eye view of vistas and buildings as the bird flies over Rome. (Rev: BL 9/15/97; SLJ 11/97*) [945]

8302 Martin, Fred. *Italy* (5–8). Series: Country Studies. 1999, Heinemann LB $27.07 (1-57572-894-X). Using double-page spreads filled with charts, graphs, drawings, maps, and photographs, this book provides basic material about Italy with a focus on contemporary issues. (Rev: BL 8/99; SLJ 8/99) [945]

8303 Nardo, Don. *Roman Roads and Aqueducts* (7–10). Series: Building History. 2000, Lucent LB $19.96 (1-56006-721-7). This look at the highways, roads, and aqueducts of the ancient Roman Empire combines history and scientific and technological principles. (Rev: BL 4/15/01; SLJ 3/01) [930]

8304 Winter, Jane K. *Italy* (5–8). Illus. Series: Cultures of the World. 1992, Marshall Cavendish LB $35.64 (1-85435-453-1). Gives geographic and historical information about Italy and tells about its people and their concerns. (Rev: BL 10/15/92) [945]

The Netherlands and Belgium

8305 Burgan, Michael. *Belgium* (4–7). Series: Enchantment of the World. 2000, Children's LB $34.50 (0-516-21006-8). This new edition of a standard title contains up-to-date material on such topics as geography and climate, plants and animals, people and culture, the arts, and sports. (Rev: BL 7/00) [949.3]

8306 Hintz, Martin. *The Netherlands* (4–7). Series: Enchantment of the World. 1999, Children's LB $34.50 (0-516-21053-X). An up-to-date, well-illustrated, and comprehensive introduction to the Netherlands. (Rev: BL 12/15/99) [949.2]

8307 Pateman, Robert. *Belgium* (4–7). Illus. Series: Cultures of the World. 1995, Marshall Cavendish LB $35.64 (0-7614-0176-8). After a brief introduction to the history and geography of Belgium, this book focuses on the populace, how they live, and their major contributions to the world. (Rev: BL 1/1–15/96; SLJ 9/96) [949.3]

8308 Sheehan, Patricia. *Luxembourg* (4–7). Illus. Series: Cultures of the World. 1997, Marshall Cavendish LB $35.64 (0-7614-0685-9). Includes information on this tiny European country's history, culture, and lifestyles. (Rev: BL 8/97) [914.935]

Russia and Other Former Soviet Republics

8309 *Armenia* (5–8). Series: Then and Now. 1992, Lerner LB $23.93 (0-8225-2806-1). The story up to 1991 of the former Soviet republic that faced many internal problems after it gained independence. (Rev: BL 2/1/93; SLJ 3/93) [956.6]

8310 *Azerbaijan* (5–8). Series: Then and Now. 1993, Lerner LB $23.93 (0-8225-2810-X). This book introduces the small republic of Azerbaijan, once the Soviet Union's most important oil producing area. (Rev: BL 2/15/93) [947]

8311 Bassis, Volodymyr. *Ukraine* (4–7). Illus. Series: Cultures of the World. 1997, Marshall Cavendish LB $35.64 (0-7614-0684-0). An introduction to this former Soviet state, with emphasis on current history and culture. (Rev: BL 8/97; SLJ 10/97) [947.7]

8312 Batalden, Stephen K., and Sandra L. Batalden. *The Newly Independent States of Eurasia: Handbook of Former Soviet Republics.* 2nd ed. (7–12). 1997, Oryx paper $45.00 (0-89774-940-5). Arranged by geographical region, this volume examines each of the newly formed republics created from the former USSR, with details on their past, their culture, and key problems facing each today. (Rev: SLJ 11/97) [947]

8313 *Belarus* (5–8). Series: Then and Now. 1993, Lerner LB $23.93 (0-8225-2811-8). An introduction to the history and status as of 1993 of the former Soviet republic of Belarus, which borders on Ukraine. (Rev: BL 5/15/93) [947]

8314 Carrion, Esther. *The Empire of the Czars* (4–7). Illus. Series: World Heritage. 1994, Children's LB $15.00 (0-516-08319-0). An overview of Russian history from early times to the breakup of the Soviet Union, with special material on Russia's famous sights, such as Red Square, the Kremlin, and St. Petersburg. (Rev: SLJ 5/95) [947.07]

8315 Cartlidge, Cherese. *The Central Asian States* (6–12). Illus. Series: Modern Nations of the World: Former Soviet Republics. 2001, Lucent LB $19.96 (1-56006-735-7). This well-illustrated introduction to the former Soviet republics of Kazakhstan, Turkmenistan, Uzbekistan, Kyrgyzstan, and Tajikistan presents material on physical features, people, culture, economy, history, and efforts to enter the global market. (Rev: BL 8/01; SLJ 9/01) [958]

8316 Corona, Laurel. *Life in Moscow* (6–10). Series: The Way People Live. 2000, Lucent LB $19.96 (1-56006-795-0). After background historical information, this account introduces modern Moscow and the daily lives of its citizens. (Rev: BL 3/1/01; SLJ 3/01) [947]

8317 Corona, Laurel. *The Russian Federation* (6–12). Illus. Series: Former Soviet Republics. 2001, Lucent LB $19.96 (1-56006-675-X). Corona introduces readers to the dramatic changes that took place in Russia during the 20th century and looks at the economic and political challenges facing the country today. (Rev: BL 7/01; SLJ 9/01) [958]

8318 Corona, Laurel. *Ukraine* (5–8). Series: Modern Nations of the World. 2001, Lucent LB $27.45 (1-56006-737-3). This well-illustrated introduction to the former Soviet republic presents material on the people, culture, economy, history, and physical features. (Rev: BL 6/1–15/01) [947]

8319 Cumming, David. *Russia* (5–8). Illus. Series: Modern Industrial World. 1994, Thomson Learning LB $24.26 (1-56847-240-4). An introduction to Russia that stresses the economic upheaval caused by the breakup of the USSR. (Rev: BL 1/15/95; SLJ 3/95) [947]

8320 Dhilawala, Sakina. *Armenia* (4–7). Illus. Series: Cultures of the World. 1997, Marshall Cavendish LB $35.64 (0-7614-0683-2). An introduction to this troubled land that describes how its people live, their lifestyles, and culture. (Rev: BL 8/97; HBG 3/98) [945.56]

8321 *Estonia* (5–8). 1992, Lerner LB $23.93 (0-8225-2803-7). Following an introduction about the fall of communism, the book provides an overview of the land and its peoples. (Rev: BL 2/1/93; SLJ 12/92) [914.7]

8322 *Georgia* (5–8). Illus. Series: Then and Now. 1994, Lerner LB $23.93 (0-8225-2807-X). This former Soviet republic is introduced, with information on its geography, ethnic makeup, history, economy, and future challenges. (Rev: BL 2/1/94; SLJ 3/94) [947]

8323 Gottfried, Ted. *The Road to Communism* (8–12). 2002, Millbrook LB $28.90 (0-7613-2557-3). This first volume on the rise and fall of the Soviet Union traces in depth the developments that led to the establishment of a communist state. The second volume is titled *Stalinist Empire*. (Rev: BL 10/15/02; HBG 3/03; SLJ 11/02) [957]

8324 Harbor, Bernard. *The Breakup of the Soviet Union* (6–12). Series: Conflicts. 1993, Macmillan LB $22.00 (0-02-742625-4). An overview of the conflicts and changes in the region. (Rev: BL 7/93; SLJ 12/93) [947.08]

8325 Israel, Fred L., and Arthur M. Schlesinger, Jr., eds. *Moscow* (6–10). Illus. Series: The World 100 Years Ago. 1999, Chelsea $29.95 (0-7910-4658-3). This book describes what Burton Holmes, a traveler-lecturer during the first half of the 20th century, saw when he visited Moscow around the beginning of the century, including a trip to the Kremlin, a visit to the public baths, and a breakfast with Leo Tolstoy. (Rev: SLJ 7/98) [947]

8326 Kagda, Sakina. *Lithuania* (4–7). Illus. Series: Cultures of the World. 1997, Marshall Cavendish LB $35.64 (0-7614-0681-6). An introduction to Lithuania, with material on geography, history, government, culture, daily life, and festivals. (Rev: BL 8/97; SLJ 10/97) [947.93]

8327 *Kazakhstan* (5–8). Series: Then and Now. 1993, Lerner LB $23.93 (0-8225-2815-0). An introduction to the second-largest republic in the former USSR, with information on its status as of 1993. (Rev: BL 9/1/93; SLJ 9/93) [958]

8328 Kort, Michael G. *The Handbook of the Former Soviet Union* (7–12). Illus. 1997, Millbrook LB $39.90 (0-7613-0016-3). An expert in Russian history gives an overview of the former Soviet Union, the problems each state faces today and the important personalities involved. (Rev: BL 2/1/98; BR 5–6/98; SLJ 1/98; VOYA 6/98) [947]

8329 Kort, Michael G. *Russia*. Rev. ed. (7–12). Series: Nations in Transition. 1998, Facts on File $25.00 (0-8160-3776-0). This book explains the rapid changes in Russia's economy, politics, social conditions, and daily life in recent years and reviews the country's complex history and its impact on today. (Rev: BL 3/15/99; SLJ 4/99) [947.085]

8330 Kummer, Patricia. *Ukraine* (4–7). Series: Enchantment of the World. 2001, Children's LB $34.50 (0-516-21101-3). A fine introduction to the past and present of the Ukraine with well-chosen illustrations and material on such topics as re-

sources, daily life, landmarks, languages, and economy. (Rev: BL 1/1–15/02; SLJ 12/01) [947.7]

8331 *Latvia* (5–8). 1992, Lerner LB $23.93 (0-8225-2802-9). Following an introduction about the fall of communism, this book provides an overview of the land and its peoples. (Rev: BL 2/1/93; SLJ 12/92) [947]

8332 *Lithuania* (5–8). Series: Then and Now. 1992, Lerner LB $23.93 (0-8225-2804-5). This Baltic Sea republic is described, including its history, people, and conditions in the period immediately following its independence in 1990. (Rev: BL 2/1/93) [947]

8333 Lustig, Michael M. *Ukraine* (7–12). Series: Nations in Transition. 1999, Facts on File $25.00 (0-8160-3757-4). A slim volume that traces the history of Ukraine and its people, with emphasis on today — its faltering economy, corruption in government, Crimean independence, and other current problems. (Rev: BL 4/15/99; SLJ 6/99) [947.7]

8334 Matthews, John R. *The Rise and Fall of the Soviet Union* (7–9). Illus. Series: World History. 1999, Lucent LB $18.96 (1-56006-567-2). A brief but effective overview of the history of Soviet Communism beginning with the fall of the tzars and ending with the breakup of the Soviet Union in 1991. (Rev: BL 2/15/00; HBG 9/00; SLJ 4/00) [947.]

8335 *Moldova* (5–8). Series: Then and Now. 1992, Lerner LB $23.93 (0-8225-2809-6). The history of this small, landlocked republic, parts of which at one time or another have belonged to the Ottoman Turks, Romania, Russia, and the USSR, and which is now independent. (Rev: BL 2/1/93; SLJ 3/93) [947]

8336 Murrell, Kathleen B. *Russia* (4–8). Illus. Series: Eyewitness. 1998, Random $20.99 (0-679-99118-2). Double-page spreads with many color illustrations explore Russia from the earliest times to the present. (Rev: BL 7/98; HBG 10/98; SLJ 8/98) [947]

8337 Pavlenkov, Victor, and Peter Pappas, eds. *Russia: Yesterday, Today, Tomorrow: Voice of the Young Generation* (8–12). Illus. 1997, FC-Izdat paper $12.95 (0-9637035-5-2). This is a collection of essays written by Russian high school students who reflect on the past, present, and future of their country. (Rev: BL 2/15/97) [947.08]

8338 Resnick, Abraham. *The Commonwealth of Independent States: Russia and the Other Republics* (5–8). Illus. Series: Enchantment of the World. 1993, Children's paper $32.00 (0-516-02613-5). Following a description of the fall of Communism, this title introduces the geography, history, society, and economies of each of the independent republics. (Rev: SLJ 9/93) [947]

8339 Rice, Earle. *The Cold War: Collapse of Communism* (8–12). Illus. Series: History's Great Defeats. 2000, Lucent LB $23.70 (1-56006-634-2).

A detailed account that traces the events and trends that caused the collapse of communism in the USSR from World War II through Gorbachev's reforms. (Rev: BL 11/1/00; HBG 3/01; SLJ 12/00) [372.47]

8340 Rogers, Stillman D. *Russia* (4–7). Series: Enchantment of the World. 2002, Children's LB $34.50 (0-516-22494-8). This portrait of Russia in text and illustrations covers such basic subjects as history, resources, geography, people, problems, economy, and culture. (Rev: BL 9/15/02; SLJ 10/02) [947]

8341 *Russia* (5–8). Series: Then and Now. 1992, Lerner LB $23.93 (0-8225-2805-3). A brief history of Russia with emphasis on its status in the period immediately following the fall of the USSR in 1991. (Rev: BL 2/1/93; SLJ 12/92) [947]

8342 Sallnow, John, and Tatyana Saiko. *Russia* (5–8). Series: Country Fact Files. 1997, Raintree Steck-Vaughn LB $27.12 (0-8172-4625-8). The impact of geography on different aspects of life in Russia, including natural resources, daily life, the landscape, and transportation, is explored. (Rev: SLJ 8/97) [947]

8343 Sheehan, Patricia. *Moldova* (5–9). Series: Cultures of the World. 2000, Marshall Cavendish LB $35.64 (0-7614-0997-1). This book on the former Soviet republic that borders on the Ukraine covers such topics as culture, land, people, history, resources, and government. (Rev: HBG 10/00; SLJ 11/00) [947]

8344 Spilling, Michael. *Estonia* (7–10). Series: Cultures of the World. 1999, Marshall Cavendish LB $35.64 (0-7614-0951-3). An overview of this Baltic land that covers basic information and contemporary life and culture. (Rev: HBG 9/99; SLJ 7/99) [947]

8345 Spilling, Michael. *Georgia* (6–10). Series: Cultures of the World. 1997, Marshall Cavendish LB $35.64 (0-7614-0691-3). A detailed introduction to the former Soviet republic of Georgia, its geography, history, government, and culture. (Rev: HBG 3/98; SLJ 2/98) [947]

8346 Streissguth, Thomas. *Life in Communist Russia* (6–10). Series: The Way People Live. 2001, Lucent LB $19.96 (1-56006-378-5). From the revolution of 1917 through its collapse in the 1980s, the history of Communist Russia is told with emphasis on social and economic conditions and everyday life. (Rev: BL 6/1–15/01; SLJ 7/01) [947]

8347 Streissguth, Thomas, ed. *The Rise of the Soviet Union* (7–12). Series: Turning Points in World History. 2002, Gale LB $31.20 (0-7377-0928-6); paper $19.95 (0-7377-0929-4). Following an overview of Russian and Soviet history, each of the essays in this anthology explores a different aspect of the rise of Communism and the creation of the Soviet Union. (Rev: BL 6/1–15/02; SLJ 6/02) [947]

8348 Strickler, Jim. *Russia of the Tsars* (6–12). Series: World History. 1997, Lucent LB $22.45 (1-56006-295-9). This history of Russia's ruling dynasty gives special material on Peter the Great, and Catherine as well as the events and tsars immediately preceding the Russian Revolution. (Rev: BL 12/15/97; SLJ 11/97) [947]

8349 *Tajikistan* (5–8). Illus. Series: Then and Now. 1993, Lerner LB $23.93 (0-8225-2816-9). An introduction to the land and people of this remote former Soviet republic located north of Afghanistan. (Rev: BL 10/15/93; SLJ 11/93) [958.6]

8350 *Ukraine* (5 8). Series: Then and Now. 1992, Lerner LB $23.93 (0-8225-2808-8). The history of this Black Sea republic and its status in the period immediately following its independence in 1991. (Rev: BCCB 3/93; BL 2/1/93; SLJ 3/93) [947]

8351 *Uzbekistan* (5–8). Series: Then and Now. 1993, Lerner LB $23.93 (0-8225-2812-6). A history of this Muslim republic, its economic situation, and prospects for the future as of 1993. (Rev: BL 5/15/93) [958.7]

8352 Vail, John. *"Peace, Land, Bread?": A History of the Russian Revolution* (7–12). Illus. Series: World History Library. 1996, Facts on File $25.00 (0-8160-2818-4). This volume, illustrated with photographs and maps, covers the period in Russian history from the revolt against the czar to the rise of Joseph Stalin. (Rev: BL 2/15/96; BR 9–10/96; SLJ 2/96; VOYA 4/96) [947.084]

8353 Wilson, Neil. *Russia* (4–8). Series: Nations of the World. 2001, Raintree Steck-Vaughn LB $34.26 (0-7398-1281-5). Colorful photographs, charts, and maps enrich chapters on Russia's past and present, land and cities, economy, art and culture, and possible future developments. (Rev: BL 6/1–15/01; HBG 10/01) [947]

Scandinavia, Iceland, and Greenland

8354 Berger, Melvin, and Gilda Berger. *The Real Vikings: Craftsmen, Traders, and Fearsome Raiders* (4–8). Illus. 2003, National Geographic $18.95 (0-7922-5132-6). A highly illustrated introduction to the Vikings and their world, with information on their political and social ideals — including democracy — as well as their more fearsome and acquisitive traits. (Rev: BL 12/1/03) [948]

8355 Blashfield, Jean F. *Norway* (4–7). Series: Enchantment of the World. 2000, Children's LB $34.50 (0-516-20651-6). An introduction to Norway that covers such subjects as geography and climate, history and government, mythology and culture, and people and economy. (Rev: BL 7/00) [948.1]

8356 Butler, Robbie. *Sweden* (4–8). Series: Nations of the World. 2001, Raintree Steck-Vaughn LB $34.26 (0-8172-5784-5). Colorful maps, charts and

525

graphs, and photographs supplement the text in this fine profile of Sweden. (Rev: BL 6/1–15/01; HBG 10/01) [948.5]

8357 Carlsson, Bo Kage. *Sweden* (5–8). Series: Modern Industrial World. 1995, Thomson Learning LB $24.26 (1-56847-436-9). A survey of modern Sweden and its industries, economy, resources, and people. (Rev: BL 12/15/95) [949.4]

8358 Corona, Laurel. *Norway* (5–8). Series: Modern Nations of the World. 2000, Lucent LB $27.45 (1-56006-647-4). Norway is introduced with coverage of history, geography, and culture plus material on everyday modern life. (Rev: BL 3/1/01) [948.1]

8359 *Denmark in Pictures* (5–8). Illus. Series: Visual Geography. 1997, Lerner LB $25.55 (0-8225-1880-5). In photographs, maps, charts, and concise text, the land of Denmark and its people are introduced. (Rev: BL 4/1/91; SLJ 7/91) [948]

8360 DuTemple, Lesley A. *Sweden* (5–8). Series: Modern Nations of the World. 2000, Lucent LB $27.45 (1-56006-588-5). A general introduction to Sweden that includes its history and geography but stresses today's living conditions and the people's lifestyles. (Rev: BL 3/15/00; HBG 10/00) [948.5]

8361 Franklin, Sharon, et al. *Scandinavia* (4–7). Series: Artisans Around the World. 1999, Raintree Steck-Vaughn LB $27.12 (0-7398-0122-8). This book, which contains many hands-on activities, surveys Scandinavian crafts and shows how geography has influenced this area's artisans. (Rev: BL 10/15/99; HBG 3/00; SLJ 1/00) [948]

8362 Gan, Delice. *Sweden* (4–7). Illus. Series: Cultures of the World. 1992, Marshall Cavendish LB $35.64 (1-85435-452-3). This introduction to Sweden gives special coverage of the people and their lifestyles. (Rev: BL 10/15/92) [948.5]

8363 Hansen, Ole Steen. *Denmark* (4–7). Series: Country Insights. 1998, Raintree Steck-Vaughn LB $27.12 (0-8172-4794-7). This book provides a broad description of the country — its lifestyle, culture, and traditions — and contrasts Denmark's rural and urban environments. (Rev: BL 6/1–15/98; HBG 10/98) [948]

8364 *Iceland in Pictures* (5–8). Illus. Series: Visual Geography. 1996, Lerner LB $25.55 (0-8225-1892-9). The history, government, people, and economy of the northern republic of Iceland are covered in words and pictures. (Rev: BL 8/91) [949.12]

8365 Janeway, Elizabeth. *The Vikings* (6–8). 1981, Random paper $5.99 (0-394-84885-3). The exploits, explorations, and contributions of the Vikings are given. [936]

8366 Jovinelly, Joann, and Jason Netelkos. *The Crafts and Culture of the Vikings* (5–8). Series: Crafts of the Ancient World. 2002, Rosen LB $29.25 (0-8239-3514-0). In addition to giving a tour

of ancient Scandinavia, this book outlines such craft projects as designing a battle shield and helmet, minting coins, and playing an ancient board game. (Rev: BL 5/15/02) [948]

8367 Kagda, Sakina. *Norway* (4–7). Illus. Series: Cultures of the World. 1995, Marshall Cavendish LB $35.64 (0-7614-0181-4). After general information on Norway's geography and history, this account concentrates on the Norwegian people, how they live, and their artistic accomplishments. (Rev: BL 1/1–15/96; SLJ 9/96) [948.1]

8368 Lasky, Kathryn. *Surtsey: The Newest Place on Earth* (5–9). Photos. 1992, Hyperion LB $16.49 (1-56282-301-9). Conveys the dramatic beginnings of the island of Surtsey, which sprang up off the coast of Iceland in 1963. Many full-page photographs. (Rev: BL 1/1/93*; SLJ 2/93*) [508.4912]

8369 Lassieur, Allison. *The Vikings* (6–9). Series: Lost Civilizations. 2001, Lucent LB $24.95 (1-56006-816-7). Using archaeological evidence, this account re-creates the history and culture of the Vikings from their glory days to their ultimate demise. (Rev: BL 8/1/01) [948]

8370 Lee, Tan Chung. *Finland* (4–7). Illus. Series: Cultures of the World. 1996, Marshall Cavendish LB $35.64 (0-7614-0280-2). The small country of Finland with its thousands of lakes is introduced, with emphasis on the people and how they live. (Rev: BL 8/96; SLJ 7/96) [984.97]

8371 Martell, Hazel M. *The Vikings and Jorvik* (4–7). Illus. Series: Hidden Worlds. 1993, Dillon LB $13.95 (0-87518-541-X). A detailed account of how the Vikings lived, based on sound archaeological research. (Rev: BL 10/15/93; SLJ 8/93) [942.8]

8372 Mason, Antony. *Viking Times* (4–7). Series: If You Were There. 1997, Simon & Schuster paper $16.95 (0-689-81198-5). Using many illustrations, a timeline, and a pictorial map, this account describes the homeland of the Vikings and their wars, explorations, trade, and Christianization. (Rev: HBG 3/98; SLJ 12/97) [948]

8373 Morley, Jacqueline. *How Would You Survive as a Viking?* (4–7). Illus. Series: How Would You Survive? 1995, Watts LB $25.00 (0-531-14344-9). The way Vikings lived in A.D. 1000 is discussed, with information on such topics as their food, forms of worship, and how they settled disputes. (Rev: BL 6/1–15/95; SLJ 8/95) [948]

8374 Odijk, Pamela. *The Vikings* (4–7). Illus. Series: Ancient World. 1990, Silver Burdett LB $14.95 (0-382-09893-5). The exploits, explorations, and contributions of the Vikings. (Rev: BL 7/90; SLJ 8/90) [936]

8375 Schaffer, David. *Viking Conquests* (7–10). Series: World History. 2002, Gale LB $27.45 (1-56006-322-X). Though the Vikings were known mainly for their raids and pillaging, this account also gives details on their lasting contributions to the world. (Rev: BL 8/02) [948]

8376 Streissguth, Thomas. *Life Among the Vikings* (7–10). Series: The Way People Live. 1998, Lucent LB $27.45 (1-56006-392-0). Using a topical approach, this book covers the Vikings' everyday life, warfare, ships, farming, language, art, and poetry. (Rev: SLJ 6/99) [948]

8377 *Sweden in Pictures* (5–8). Illus. Series: Visual Geography. 1993, Lerner LB $21.27 (0-8225-1872-4). Gives the background geography and history of Sweden, along with contemporary material. (Rev: BL 12/1/90) [948.5]

8378 Wilcox, Jonathan. *Iceland* (4–7). Series: Cultures of the World. 1996, Marshall Cavendish LB $35.64 (0-7614-0279-9). The history, geography, people, and culture of this remote island republic are introduced, with many color photographs. (Rev: SLJ 7/96) [949.12]

Spain and Portugal

8379 Anderson, Wayne. *The ETA: Spain's Basque Terrorists* (4–8). Series: Inside the World's Most Infamous Terrorist Organizations. 2003, Rosen LB $26.50 (0-8239-3818-2). This is the history and present status of the violent organization committed to creating an ethnic homeland separate from Spain. (Rev: BL 10/15/03; SLJ 9/03) [946]

8380 Blauer, Ettagale, and Jason Lauré. *Portugal* (4–7). Series: Enchantment of the World. 2002, Children's LB $34.50 (0-516-21109-9). This highly visual introduction to Portugal includes accessible information on topics including history, people and language, customs, and economy. (Rev: BL 9/15/02) [946.9]

8381 Champion, Neil. *Portugal* (5–8). Illus. Series: Modern Industrial World. 1995, Thomson Learning LB $24.26 (1-56847-435-0). Modern Portugal is highlighted in text and pictures, with coverage of its economy, industries, and resources. (Rev: BL 12/15/95) [946.904]

8382 Goodman, Joan Elizabeth. *A Long and Uncertain Journey: The 27,000-Mile Voyage of Vasco da Gama* (4–8). 2001, Mikaya $19.95 (0-9650493-7-X). Details of Vasco da Gama's explorations and their historical context are accompanied by biographical information, illustrations, journal entries, a map, and a timeline. (Rev: BL 9/1/01; HBG 10/01; SLJ 6/01*; VOYA 8/01) [910]

8383 Grabowski, John F. *Spain* (5–8). Series: Modern Nations of the World. 1999, Lucent LB $27.45 (1 56006 602 4). This fact filled introduction to Spain emphasizes both history and current life and contains black-and-white photographs and interesting sidebars. (Rev: BL 2/15/00; HBG 10/00) [946]

8384 Heale, Jay. *Portugal* (5–8). Illus. Series: Cultures of the World. 1995, Marshall Cavendish LB $35.64 (0-7614-0169-5). Present-day conditions in Portugal are emphasized in this account, which also covers history, geography, and culture. (Rev: SLJ 11/95) [914.9]

8385 Kohen, Elizabeth. *Spain* (4–7). Illus. Series: Cultures of the World. 1992, Marshall Cavendish LB $35.64 (1-85435-451-5). With text, photographs, maps, and fact sheets, the land and people of Spain are introduced. (Rev: BL 10/15/92) [946]

8386 McDowall, David. *The Spanish Armada* (8–12). Illus. 1988, David & Charles $19.95 (0-7134-5671-X). A British import that tells about the events surrounding this Spanish fleet and also supplies many short biographies of the people involved. (Rev: BR 11–12/88; SLJ 3/89) [946]

8387 Mann, Kenny. *Isabel, Ferdinand and Fifteenth-Century Spain* (5–8). Series: Rulers and Their Times. 2001, Marshall Cavendish LB $28.50 (0-7614-1030-9). Following biographies of these great Spanish rulers, there is a section on the life and culture of their times plus a generous selection of original documents of the period. (Rev: BL 1/1–15/02; HBG 3/02; SLJ 3/02) [946]

8388 Melchiore, Susan McCarthy. *The Spanish Inquisition* (6–8). Series: Great Disasters. 2001, Chelsea LB $21.95 (0-7910-6327-5). The story of this institution established by Spanish monarchs in 1478, and its ruthless treatment of Jews and Muslims as well as Christians suspected of heresy. (Rev: BL 6/1–15/02; HBG 10/02; SLJ 6/02) [946]

8389 Millar, Heather. *Spain in the Age of Exploration* (5–8). Series: Cultures of the Past. 1998, Benchmark LB $28.50 (0-7614-0303-5). This book covers Spanish history from the time of Columbus to about 1700, with an emphasis on art and literature plus material on daily life and major personalities. (Rev: BL 12/15/98; BR 5–6/99; HBG 10/99; SLJ 2/99) [946]

8390 *Portugal in Pictures* (5–8). Illus. Series: Visual Geography. 1996, Lerner LB $25.55 (0-8225-1886-4). Current conditions and problems in Portugal are introduced along with the standard material on history, geography, and social conditions. (Rev: BL 12/15/91) [946.9]

8391 Rogers, Lura. *Spain* (4–7). Series: Enchantment of the World. 2001, Children's LB $34.50 (0-516-21123-4). A well-designed book that uses clear text, numerous charts, maps, drawings, and photographs to introduce a number of topics related to Spain and its people. (Rev: BL 1/1–15/02) [946]

8392 Selby, Anna. *Spain* (4–7). Illus. Series: Country Fact Files. 1994, Raintree Steck Vaughn LB $27.12 (0-8114-1848-0). A well-illustrated introduction to Spain, with coverage of such subjects as current social conditions, the economy, food and farming, and the environment. (Rev: SLJ 7/94) [946]

8393 Shubert, Adrian. *The Land and People of Spain* (6–9). Series: Land and People Of. 1992, HarperCollins LB $17.89 (0-06-020218-1). A comprehensive, detailed history of Spain. (Rev: BL 8/92) [946]

8394 *Spain in Pictures* (5–8). Illus. Series: Visual Geography. 1995, Lerner LB $25.55 (0-8225-1887-2). Modern Spain is the focus of this introduction, which includes many photographs, charts, and maps. (Rev: BL 11/15/95) [914.6]

8395 Worth, Richard. *The Spanish Inquisition in World History* (8–12). Series: In World History. 2002, Enslow LB $20.95 (0-7660-1825-3). This account describes the formation of the Spanish Inquisition, the work of Torquemada, and how the Catholic Church tried to punish those who went against the teachings of Christianity. (Rev: BL 3/15/03; HBG 10/03; SLJ 4/03) [946]

Middle East

General and Miscellaneous

8396 Beshore, George. *Science in Early Islamic Culture* (4–7). Illus. Series: Science of the Past. 1998, Watts LB $26.00 (0-531-20355-7). This book traces the many contributions to science made by the early Muslims, including mathematics, alchemy, astronomy, and medicine. (Rev: BL 6/1–15/98; HBG 10/98; SLJ 8/98) [509]

8397 Dudley, William, ed. *The Middle East* (7–10). Series: Opposing Viewpoints. 1992, Greenhaven paper $16.20 (0-89908-160-6). Articles and essays examine the background causes of the Middle East conflicts. (Rev: BL 6/15/92; SLJ 7/92) [320.956]

8398 Due, Andrea. *The Atlas of the Bible Lands: History, Daily Life and Traditions* (4–9). Illus. 1999, Bedrick $19.95 (0-87226-559-5). This atlas presents an encyclopedic amount of information on the history and culture of the Middle East from prehistory to modern times, with maps supplemented by clearly written text and extensive artwork. (Rev: BR 9–10/99; HBG 10/99; SLJ 3/99) [956]

8399 Harik, Ramsay M., and Elsa Marston. *Women in the Middle East*. Rev. ed. (7–12). Illus. 2003, Watts LB $29.50 (0-531-12222-0). A chapter on the women of Afghanistan has been added to this revised and updated edition that looks at topics including health, education, and family and public life. (Rev: BL 4/15/03; SLJ 5/03; VOYA 8/03) [305.42]

8400 King, John. *Conflict in the Middle East* (6–12). Series: Conflicts. 1993, Macmillan LB $13.95 (0-02-785955-X). This book gives good background information and history on the origins of the current problems in the Middle East. (Rev: BL 10/1/93; SLJ 12/93) [956.04]

8401 Kort, Michael G. *The Handbook of the Middle East* (7–12). Illus. 2002, Twenty-First Century LB $39.90 (0-7613-1611-6). History, geography, culture, politics (current and future), and religion are all covered in this overview of the region that includes maps, flags, a timeline, and material on key figures. (Rev: HBG 10/02; SLJ 3/02; VOYA 6/02) [956]

8402 Long, Cathryn J. *The Middle East in Search of Peace*. Rev. ed. (4–7). Illus. Series: Headliners. 1996, Millbrook LB $25.90 (0-7613-0105-4). An objective account of the conflict between Arabs and Jews in the Middle East, with good historical information and a description of various peace plans. (Rev: SLJ 1/97) [956]

8403 Tubb, Jonathan N. *Bible Lands* (5–9). Series: Eyewitness Books. 1991, Knopf $20.99 (0-679-91457-9). A history of the Middle Eastern lands that figured in the Bible and a description of their status at the beginning of the 1990s. (Rev: BL 12/1/91) [220.9]

8404 Wagner, Heather Lehr. *Israel and the Arab World* (6–12). Illus. Series: People at Odds. 2002, Chelsea LB $21.95 (0-7910-6705-X). An easy-to-understand summary of the conflict between the two groups, with illustrative photographs. (Rev: BL 11/1/02; HBG 3/03) [956.9405]

8405 Whitcraft, Melissa. *The Tigris and Euphrates Rivers* (4–8). Series: Watts Library. 1999, Watts LB $24.00 (0-531-11741-3). Describes the historical importance of these rivers and their ancient civilizations and traces their course today through Turkey, Iraq, and Syria. (Rev: BL 1/1–15/00; SLJ 2/00) [956]

Egypt

8406 Barghusen, Joan. *Daily Life in Ancient and Modern Cairo* (6–9). Series: Cities Through Time. 2001, Lerner LB $25.26 (0-8225-3221-2). Cairo's evolution from earliest times to today is presented in richly illustrated double-page spreads with information on political, social, and religious life as well as women's issues, with a timeline and quotations. (Rev: BL 4/15/01; HBG 10/01; SLJ 7/01) [962.16]

8407 Diamond, Arthur. *Egypt: Gift of the Nile* (5–9). Series: Discovering Our Heritage. 1992, Dillon $14.95 (0-87518-511-8). An introduction to Egypt that includes history, culture, folktales, maps, recipes, and a discussion of Egyptian immigrants in the United States. (Rev: BL 8/92; SLJ 11/92) [962]

8408 Heinrichs, Ann. *Egypt* (4–7). Illus. Series: Enchantment of the World. 1997, Children's LB $34.50 (0-516-20470-X). This fine introduction to

Egypt gives substantial information on ancient and modern history, with coverage of religion, daily life, politics, and relations with Israel. (Rev: BL 2/1/98; HBG 10/98; SLJ 5/98) [962]

8409 Kallen, Stuart A. *Egypt* (4–8). Series: Modern Nations of the World. 1999, Lucent LB $27.45 (1-56006-535-4). Sidebars are used for specialized topics in this overview that is particularly strong on the history of Egypt. (Rev: HBG 3/00; SLJ 10/99) [962]

8410 Loveridge, Emma. *Egypt* (5–8). Series: Country Fact Files. 1997, Raintree Steck-Vaughn LB $27.12 (0-8172-4626-6). This book gives standard basic information about Egypt, including its climate, landscape, trade, industry, and daily life. (Rev: SLJ 9/97) [962]

8411 Orr, Tamra. *Egyptian Islamic Jihad* (4–8). Series: Inside the World's Most Infamous Terrorist Organizations. 2003, Rosen LB $26.50 (0-8239-3819-0). Dedicated to the overthrow of the secular Egyptian government, this terrorist organization has links to the Al Qaeda terrorist network. (Rev: BL 10/15/03) [962]

8412 Pateman, Robert. *Egypt* (4–7). Illus. Series: Cultures of the World. 1992, Marshall Cavendish LB $35.64 (1-85435-535-X). Egypt past and present is introduced in this account that stresses how the people live. (Rev: BL 1/1/93) [962]

8413 Stewart, Gail. *The Suez Canal* (7–10). Series: Building History. 2001, Lucent $24.95 (1-56006-842-6). This is the dramatic story of the construction and utilization of the Suez Canal, one of the great engineering marvels of the 19th century. (Rev: BL 8/1/01) [962]

8414 Tenquist, Alasdair. *Egypt* (5–7). Illus. Series: Economically Developing Countries. 1995, Thomson Learning LB $24.26 (1-56847-385-0). A look at present-day conditions in Egypt and its concerns and problems. (Rev: SLJ 2/96) [962]

8415 Wilson, Neil. *Egypt* (4–8). Series: Nations of the World. 2001, Raintree Steck-Vaughn LB $34.26 (0-7398-1283-1). An excellent introduction to the country that housed one of the world's oldest civilizations and is currently a center of Islamic culture and religion. (Rev: BL 6/1–15/01; HBG 10/01) [962]

8416 Zuehlke, Jeffrey. *Egypt in Pictures*. Rev. ed. (4–8). Illus. Series: Visual Geography. 2002, Lerner LB $27.93 (0-8225-0367-0). Covers Egypt's geography, history, people, economy, and culture with maps, photographs, and illustrations. (Rev: SLJ 3/03) [962]

Israel and Palestine

8417 Altman, Linda J. *The Creation of Israel* (6–9). Series: World History. 1998, Lucent LB $27.45 (1-56006-288-6). Founded as a home for the Jews fleeing war and persecution, this is the story of the nation that is now more than 50 years old. (Rev: BL 6/1–15/98) [956.94]

8418 Bernards, Neal. *The Palestinian Conflict: Identifying Propaganda Techniques* (4–7). Illus. 1990, Greenhaven LB $22.45 (0-89908-602-0). Such skills as distinguishing between fact and fiction and detecting bias are stressed in this book. (Rev: BL 6/15/91) [956.04]

8419 Corona, Laurel. *Israel* (6–9). Illus. Series: Modern Nations of the World. 2003, Gale $27.45 (1-59018-115-8). A thorough overview of the geography, history, and people of the land of Israel, with informative and interesting sidebars on historical and contemporary topics. (Rev: BL 4/15/03; SLJ 8/03) [956.94]

8420 Corzine, Phyllis. *The Palestinian-Israeli Accord* (6–10). Series: Overview. 1996, Lucent LB $27.45 (1-56006-181-2). This work explores the historical roots of the Israeli-Palestinian conflict, discusses the foundation of Israel and its need for land, and traces the rise of Yasir Arafat. (Rev: BR 11–12/97; SLJ 5/97) [956.94]

8421 Dubois, Jill. *Israel* (4–7). Illus. Series: Cultures of the World. 1992, Marshall Cavendish LB $35.64 (1-85435-531-7). This introduction to Israel emphasizes its culture and the lifestyles of the people. (Rev: BL 1/1/93) [956.94]

8422 Feinstein, Steve. *Israel in Pictures* (5–8). Illus. 1992, Lerner LB $25.55 (0-8225-1833-3). An overview of geography, climate, wildlife, and vegetation with photographs, maps, and charts. (Rev: BL 8/88) [956.9405]

8423 Finkelstein, Norman H. *Friends Indeed: The Special Relationship of Israel and the United States* (7–12). 1998, Millbrook LB $24.90 (0-7613-0114-3). This book explores the close, often rocky, relationship between Israel and the U.S. through 10 administrations and several wars. (Rev: BL 8/98; BR 9–10/98; SLJ 6/98) [327.73]

8424 Green, Jen. *Israel* (4–8). Series: Nations of the World. 2001, Raintree Steck-Vaughn LB $34.26 (0-7398-1286-6). A fine, attractive introduction to the land and people of Israel, the nation that was created as a homeland for the Jewish people after World War II. (Rev: BL 6/1–15/01; HBG 10/01) [956.94]

8425 Hintz, Martin, and Stephen Hintz. *Israel* (4–7). Series: Enchantment of the World. 1999, Children's LB $34.50 (0-516-21108-0). This attractive account provides current information on many topics related to Israel, including history, geography, people, religion, and problems. (Rev: BL 9/15/99) [956.94]

8426 Marchood, Nabil. *Palestinian Teenage Refugees and Immigrants Speak Out* (7–12). Series: Teenage Refugees Speak Out. 1997, Rosen LB $17.95 (0-8239-2442-4). The exodus of Palestinians, many to the United States, and their reasons for leaving their homes are recounted through the stories of several teenage immigrants. (Rev: BL 12/15/97) [956.04]

8427 Mozeson, I. E., and Lois Stavsky. *Jerusalem Mosaic: Young Voices from the Holy City* (6–12). 1994, Four Winds paper $15.95 (0-02-767651-X). Thirty-six lively monologues based on interviews with teenagers living in Jerusalem in the early 1990s — Jew and Arab, Muslim and Christian. (Rev: BL 12/1/94; SLJ 1/95) [305.23]

8428 Ross, Stewart. *The Arab-Israeli Conflict* (7–12). Series: Causes and Consequences. 1995, Raintree Steck-Vaughn LB $29.97 (0-8172-4051-9). This conflict is presented in a historical context, using a magazine format, maps, and photographs, and lays the basis for understanding the current continuing hostility. (Rev: BL 12/15/95; BR 3–4/96; SLJ 2/96) [956.94]

8429 Scharfstein, Sol. *Understanding Israel* (5–7). Illus. 1994, KTAV paper $14.95 (0-88125-428-2). A heavily illustrated introduction to Israel that covers history, religion, government, culture, and current concerns. (Rev: SLJ 10/94) [956.94]

8430 Sha'Ban, Mervet A., and Galit Fink. *If You Could Be My Friend: Letters of Mervet Akram Sha'Ban and Galit Fink* (6–9). Trans. by Beatrice Khadige. Illus. 1998, Orchard LB $16.99 (0-531-33113-X). Two teenage girls — one an Israeli and the other a Palestinian — share their feelings and fears in a series of letters they exchanged from 1988 to 1991. (Rev: BCCB 11/98; BL 10/15/98; HB 9–10/98; HBG 3/99; SLJ 11/98; VOYA 12/98) [956.94054]

8431 Silverman, Maida. *Israel: The Founding of a Modern Nation* (4–7). Illus. 1998, Dial LB $15.00 (0-8034-2136-6). This account covers 3,000 years of Jewish history, with emphasis on recent centuries, and includes a timeline showing Israel's history from 1948 to 1998. (Rev: BL 5/1/98) [956.94]

8432 Slavik, Diane. *Daily Life in Ancient and Modern Jerusalem* (6–9). Illus. Series: Cities Through Time. 2000, Lerner $17.95 (0-8225-3218-2). Slavik traces the history of Jerusalem from the earliest times, exploring what life was like for the inhabitants of each period. (Rev: BL 3/1/01; HBG 10/01; SLJ 9/01) [956.94]

8433 Stefoff, Rebecca. *West Bank / Gaza Strip* (7–12). Series: Major World Nations. 1999, Chelsea LB $21.95 (0-7910-4771-7). This work describes the long, confrontational history of this area, with information on its people, economics, geography, and the outlook for the future. (Rev: HBG 3/99; SLJ 6/99) [956.94]

8434 Taitz, Emily, and Sondra Henry. *Israel: A Sacred Land* (5–7). Illus. 1988, Macmillan LB $14.95 (0-87518-364-6). The focus is on everyday

life in this Middle East land. (Rev: BL 2/15/88) [956.94054]

Other Middle East Countries

8435 Augustin, Byron. *United Arab Emirates* (4–7). Series: Enchantment of the World. 2002, Children's LB $34.50 (0-516-20473-4). This important nation is introduced with material on topics including history, natural resources, climate, and people. (Rev: BL 5/15/02; SLJ 9/02) [953]

8436 Augustin, Byron, and Rebecca A. Augustin. *Qatar* (5–8). Illus. Series: Enchantment of the World. 1997, Children's LB $32.00 (0-516-20303-7). An introduction to the small oil-producing country on the Persian Gulf that describes its history under British rule and how the people now live. (Rev: BL 7/97; HBG 3/98) [953.63]

8437 Balcavage, Dynise. *Iraq* (5–8). Illus. Series: Countries of the World. 2003, Gareth Stevens LB $29.27 (0-8368-2359-1). Report writers will find solid information on Iraq's history, geography, government, and society in this volume that includes discussion of Iraq's relations with the United States. (Rev: BL 5/1/03; HBG 10/03) [956.7]

8438 Bodnarchuk, Karl J. *Kurdistan: Region Under Siege* (7–10). Series: World in Conflict. 2000, Lerner LB $25.26 (0-8225-3556-4). This work gives an unbiased historical picture of this mountainous region of the Middle East and tells of the frequent upheavals that mark its past and present. (Rev: BL 6/1–15/00; HBG 3/01; SLJ 12/00) [955]

8439 Broberg, Catherine. *Saudi Arabia in Pictures* (6–10). Illus. Series: Visual Geography. 2002, Lerner LB $27.93 (0-8225-1958-5). Full-color photographs complement information on the country's geography, history, government, economy, people, and culture. (Rev: BL 10/15/02; HBG 3/03) [953.8]

8440 Byers, Ann. *Lebanon's Hezbollah* (4–8). Series: Inside the World's Most Infamous Terrorist Organizations. 2003, Rosen LB $26.50 (0-8239-3821-2). This is the story of the Lebanese terrorist organization dedicated to installing a conservative Islamic government in Lebanon and to the destruction of Israel. (Rev: BL 10/15/03; SLJ 9/03) [956.92]

8441 Cartlidge, Cherese. *Iran* (5–8). Series: Modern Nations of the World. 2002, Gale LB $27.45 (1-56006-971-6). This colorful account gives a comprehensive overview of Iran, including history, geography, and culture. (Rev: BL 12/15/02; SLJ 1/03) [955]

8442 Clark, Charles. *Iran* (7–12). Series: Nations in Transition. 2002, Gale LB $21.96 (0-7377-1096-9). Iran's internal political upheavals and difficult relationship with the rest of the world are the focus of this thorough and concise volume that includes biographical and cultural features. (Rev: SLJ 1/03) [955]

8443 Eboch, Chris. *Turkey* (5–9). Series: Modern Nations of the World. 2003, Gale LB $27.45 (1-59018-122-0). This account presents a broad spectrum of material about Turkey including history, geography, and culture. (Rev: BL 11/15/03; SLJ 6/03) [961]

8444 Foster, Leila M. *Iraq* (4–9). Series: Enchantment of the World. 1997, Children's Pr. LB $34.50 (0-516-20584-6). This book describes the land of Iraq, its history starting with Mesopotamia, the role of Islam, and daily life of normal Iraqi citizens, and comments on Saddam Hussein. (Rev: HBG 3/99; SLJ 4/99) [956]

8445 Foster, Leila M. *Jordan* (5–8). Illus. Series: Enchantment of the World. 1991, Children's paper $32.00 (0-516-02603-8). An introduction in text and pictures to the geography, history, culture, and important people of Jordan. (Rev: BL 2/1/92) [956.95]

8446 Foster, Leila M. *Kuwait* (5–10). Series: Enchantment of the World. 1998, Children's LB $34.50 (0-516-20604-4). An introduction to Kuwait for older readers, with extensive coverage of the Gulf War. (Rev: SLJ 11/98) [956]

8447 Foster, Leila M. *Oman* (4–7). Series: Enchantment of the World. 1999, Children's LB $34.50 (0-516-20964-7). A fine introduction to this oil-producing country, covering topics such as history, geography, government, religion, and the economy. (Rev: BL 9/15/99) [956]

8448 Foster, Leila M. *Saudi Arabia* (5–8). Series: Enchantment of the World. 1993, Children's Pr. paper $32.00 (0-516-02611-9). The huge, oil-rich Middle Eastern kingdom of Saudi Arabia is presented, with material on its economic conditions, relationship with the West, and social and religious beliefs. (Rev: BL 8/93; SLJ 8/93) [953.8]

8449 Fox, Mary V. *Bahrain* (5–8). Series: Enchantment of the World. 1992, Children's Pr. paper $32.00 (0-516-02608-9). An in-depth introduction to Bahrain, including geological, meteorological, historical, and engineering aspects. (Rev: BL 12/15/92; SLJ 1/93) [953.65]

8450 Fox, Mary V. *Iran* (5–8). Illus. Series: Enchantment of the World. 1991, Children's paper $32.00 (0-516-02727-1). The history of the country once known as Persia is presented along with discussion of conditions at the end of the 1980s and brief biographies of famous people. (Rev: BL 10/1/91) [955]

8451 Goodwin, William. *Saudi Arabia* (5–8). Series: Modern Nations of the World. 2001, Lucent LB $27.45 (1-56006-762-2). The land ruled by the Saud dynasty is presented with details on history, government, geography, resources, and world importance. (Rev: BL 6/1–15/01) [953.8]

8452 Greenblatt, Miriam. *Iran* (5–9). Illus. 2003, Children's LB $34.00 (0-516-22375-5). Iran's geography, history, economy, religion, culture, lifestyle, and people are among the topics covered in this comprehensive volume that will be useful for reports. (Rev: SLJ 11/03) [955]

8453 Hassig, Susan M. *Iraq* (4–7). Illus. Series: Cultures of the World. 1992, Marshall Cavendish LB $35.64 (1-85435-533-3). This introduction stresses the lifestyles of the people, their religion, and culture. (Rev: BL 1/1/93) [956.7]

8454 Heinrichs, Ann. *Saudi Arabia* (4–7). Series: Enchantment of the World. 2002, Children's LB $34.50 (0-516-22287-2). Topics covered in the highly visual introduction to Saudi Arabia include history, religion, language, economy, and government. (Rev: BL 9/15/02) [953.8]

8455 Hestler, Anna. *Yemen* (5–8). Series: Cultures of the World. 1999, Marshall Cavendish LB $35.64 (0-7614-0956-4). A fine introduction to this country on the Gulf of Aden with good background information and an overview of modern life. (Rev: HBG 10/99; SLJ 10/99) [956]

8456 Hutchison, Linda. *Lebanon* (6–9). Illus. Series: Modern Nations of the World. 2003, Gale $27.45 (1-59018-116-6). Report writers will appreciate this thorough overview of the geography, history, and people of Lebanon, with information on contemporary society and strife since the 1970s. (Rev: BL 4/15/03) [956.92]

8457 *Iran in Pictures* (5–8). Illus. Series: Visual Geography. 1992, Lerner LB $21.27 (0-8225-1848-1). Basic coverage on this Middle Eastern land and its people. (Rev: BL 5/1/89) [955]

8458 Isiorho, Solomon A. *Kuwait* (7–12). Series: Modern World Nations. 2002, Chelsea LB $24.95 (0-7910-6781-5). An overview of the history, geography, people, politics, and religion of Kuwait, with discussion of the importance of Islam. Also use *Bahrain* (2002). (Rev: SLJ 2/03) [953.67]

8459 Janin, Hunt. *Saudi Arabia* (4–7). Illus. Series: Cultures of the World. 1992, Marshall Cavendish LB $35.64 (1-85435-532-5). The history, geography, economy, language, and people are discussed in this book about Saudi Arabia. (Rev: BL 1/1/93) [953.8]

8460 *Jordan in Pictures* (5–8). Illus. 1992, Lerner LB $25.55 (0-8225-1834-1). Young readers learn what life is like in this Middle East land. (Rev: BL 2/1/89; SLJ 2/89) [956.9504]

8461 Kheirabadi, Masoud. *Iran* (6–12). Illus. Series: Modern World Nations. 2003, Chelsea LB $24.95 (0-7910-7234-7). A thorough and concise overview of Iran's geography, history, government, politics, economics, language, peoples, and religion, with maps, photographs, and a look at the future. (Rev: BL 9/15/03; HBG 10/03) [955]

8462 *Lebanon in Pictures* (5–8). Illus. Series: Visual Geography. 1992, Lerner LB $25.55 (0-8225-1832-5). A country torn apart by strife is the focus of this edition. (Rev: BL 2/1/89) [956.9204]

8463 Marcovitz, Hal. *Jordan* (7–12). Series: Creation of the Modern Middle East. 2002, Chelsea LB $30.95 (0-7910-6507-3). This volume on the history of Jordan, its importance in the Middle East, and its relations with the United States will be useful for report writers. Also use *Syria*, *Oman*, and *The Kurds* (all 2002). (Rev: LMC 4–5/03; SLJ 2/03) [956.9504]

8464 Marcovitz, Hal. *Kuwait* (5–8). Illus. Series: Modern Middle East Nations. 2003, Mason Crest LB $24.95 (1-59084-510-2). A thorough introduction to the geography, history, and people of Kuwait, whose wealth makes it an unusual country. (Rev: BL 6/1–15/03; SLJ 10/03) [953.67]

8465 Marston, Elsa. *Lebanon: New Light in an Ancient Land* (5–8). Illus. Series: Discovering Our Heritage. 1994, Dillon LB $14.95 (0-87518-584-3). A well-organized, readable introduction to the history, geography, and people of Lebanon, together with material on the impact of Lebanese immigration on the United States. (Rev: SLJ 7/94) [956]

8466 Orr, Tamra. *Turkey* (5–8). Illus. Series: Enchantment of the World, Second Series. 2003, Children's LB $34.00 (0-516-22679-7). A visually attractive book that covers such topics as the geography, history, government, culture, and people, with a timeline, fast facts, and a recipe. (Rev: SLJ 5/03) [915]

8467 Rajendra, Vijeya, and Gisela Kaplan. *Iran* (4–7). Illus. Series: Cultures of the World. 1992, Marshall Cavendish LB $35.64 (1-85435-534-1). As well as standard introductory information about Iran, this book tells about how the people live and what the country's present problems are. (Rev: BL 1/1/93) [955]

8468 Reed, Jennifer Bond. *The Saudi Royal Family* (5–8). Illus. Series: Major World Leaders. 2002, Chelsea $23.95 (0-7910-7063-8); paper $9.95 (0-7910-7187-1). Saudi Arabia's ruling royal family is profiled, detailing its rise to power, its Islamic policies, and the various individual rulers, with a look at the contrast between the family's extravagant lifestyle and its religious beliefs. (Rev: BL 1/1–15/03; SLJ 4/03) [953.8]

8469 Sheehan, Sean. *Lebanon* (5–10). Series: Cultures of the World. 1996, Marshall Cavendish LB $35.64 (0-7614-0283-7). A lively, well-written introduction to this war-ravaged country with details on history, economy, culture, religion and foods, including a recipe for a typical dish. (Rev: SLJ 6/97) [569.2]

8470 South, Coleman. *Jordan* (5–10). Series: Cultures of the World. 1996, Marshall Cavendish LB $35.64 (0-7614-0287-X). Everyday life in Jordan is the focus of this book that also covers history, religion, culture, geography, festivals, and foods; a single recipe is included. (Rev: SLJ 6/97) [569.5]

8471 Spencer, William. *Iraq: Old Land, New Nation in Conflict* (7–12). Illus. 2000, Twenty-First Century LB $23.90 (0-7613-1356-7). This account traces the history of Iraq from its Mesopotamian origins to Saddam Hussein's rule prior to the American invasion. (Rev: BL 11/15/00; HBG 3/01; SLJ 12/00) [956.7]

8472 Spencer, William. *The United States and Iran* (7–12). Illus. 2000, Twenty-First Century LB $23.90 (0-7613-1554-3). After covering Iranian culture and history, this account explores Iran's rocky relations with the U.S. to the beginning of 2000, with material on the hostage crisis of 1979. (Rev: BL 4/15/00; HBG 9/00; SLJ 7/00; VOYA 6/01) [327.73055.]

8473 Wills, Karen. *Jordan* (5–8). Series: Modern Nations of the World. 2001, Lucent LB $27.45 (1-56006-822-1). A good profile of Jordan is presented, with basic background material and information on present conditions and the people today. (Rev: BL 6/1–15/01) [956.95]

8474 *Yemen in Pictures* (5–8). Illus. Series: Visual Geography. 1993, Lerner LB $25.55 (0-8225-1911-9). In introduction to this Muslim republic on the Gulf of Aden, with material on its economic and social conditions. (Rev: BL 12/1/93; SLJ 12/93) [953.3]

North and South America (excluding the United States)

General and Miscellaneous

8475 Barden, Renardo. *The Discovery of America* (6–9). Illus. 1990, Greenhaven LB $22.45 (0-89908-071-5). The exploits of the Vikings as well as exploits in Irish, Welsh, and African legends are retold in this search for the first discoverers of the New World. (Rev: BL 3/1/90; SLJ 5/90) [970.1]

8476 Dalal, Anita. *Myths of Pre-Columbian America* (5–8). Illus. Series: Mythic World. 2002, Raintree Steck-Vaughn LB $27.12 (0-7398-3193-3). This volume for older readers separates myth from reality about cultures present in America in pre-Columbian times. (Rev: BL 3/1/02; HBG 3/02; SLJ 12/01) [398.2]

8477 Jones, Charlotte F. *Yukon Gold: The Story of the Klondike Gold Rush* (4–8). 1999, Holiday $18.95 (0-8234-1403-5). A solid account of the Alaska/Yukon Gold Rush that is enlivened by black-and-white photographs and intriguing asides and anecdotes. (Rev: BCCB 6/99; HB 7–8/99; HBG 10/99; SLJ 5/99; VOYA 12/99) [979.8]

8478 Long, Catheryn J. *Ancient America* (7–10). Series: World History. 2002, Gale LB $27.45 (1-56006-889-2). The story of the hunter-gatherers, agriculturalists, and city dwellers of North and South America from the arrival of the first humans in America to Columbus. (Rev: BL 8/02) [970]

8479 Murphy, Jim. *Gone a-Whaling: The Lure of the Sea and the Hunt for the Great Whale* (7–12). Illus. 1998, Clarion $18.00 (0-395-69847-2). Diary entries are used to describe American whale hunting and life aboard whaling vessels from the 19th century to the present. (Rev: BCCB 4/98; BL 3/15/98; BR 11–12/98; HB 5–6/98; SLJ 5/98; VOYA 12/98) [306.3]

8480 O'Neill, Thomas. *Lakes, Peaks, and Prairies: Discovering the United States-Canadian Border* (7–12). Illus. 1984, National Geographic LB $12.95 (0-87044-483-2). A trip across the continent that reveals much about the diversity of these regions. [973]

8481 Patent, Dorothy Hinshaw. *Treasures of the Spanish Main* (6–10). Series: Frozen in Time. 1999, Marshall Cavendish LB $27.07 (0-7614-0786-3). This lavishly illustrated book describes the sinking of Spanish galleons near the Florida Keys in the 1600s and how their excavation has brought us amazing information about life and culture in the New World at that time. (Rev: BL 2/15/00; HBG 10/00; SLJ 3/00) [930]

8482 Wood, Geraldine. *Science of the Early Americas* (4–8). Series: Science of the Past. 1999, Watts LB $26.00 (0-531-11524-0). A survey of the scientific knowledge accrued by the early inhabitants of North and South America in such fields as medicine, mathematics, engineering, astronomy, and agriculture. (Rev: BL 3/15/99; HBG 10/99; SLJ 6/99) [970]

North America

CANADA

8483 Barlas, Robert, and Norman Tompsett. *Canada* (5–8). Series: Countries of the World. 1998, Gareth Stevens LB $29.26 (0-8368-2123-8). Using maps, illustrations, concise text, and a quick facts section, this book gives basic information about Canada, with particular attention to education and politics. (Rev: BL 12/15/98; HBG 9/99; SLJ 2/99) [971]

8484 Beattie, Owen, and John Geiger. *Buried in Ice: The Mystery of a Lost Arctic Expedition* (4–7). Series: Time Quest. 1993, Scholastic paper $6.95 (0-590-43849-2). The story of Sir John Franklin's unsuccessful 1845 expedition from England to find the Northwest Passage. (Rev: BCCB 3/92; BL 4/1/92; SLJ 4/92*) [919.804]

8485 Bowers, Vivien. *Only in Canada! From the Colossal to the Kooky* (4–8). Series: Wow Canada! 2002, Maple Tree $24.95 (1-894379-37-3); paper $14.95 (1-894379-38-1). Facts of all kinds about Canada and the Canadians are presented in lively text with a wide range of illustrations plus maps and timelines. (Rev: SLJ 2/03) [971]

8486 Braun, Eric. *Canada in Pictures*. Rev. ed. (5–9). Illus. Series: Visual Geography. 2003, Lerner LB $27.93 (0-8225-4679-5). An informative and interesting overview of Canada's history, geography, government, economy, and people suitable for both research and browsing. (Rev: HBG 10/03; SLJ 7/03) [971.064]

8487 Campbell, Marjorie Wilkins. *The Nor'westers: The Fight for the Fur Trade* (6–12). Illus. 2003, Fitzhenry & Whiteside paper $12.95 (1-894004-97-3). An absorbing account of the Canadian fur trade in the 19th century, with details of company politics and relations between traders and the Native Americans. (Rev: BL 4/1/03) [380.1]

8488 Cooper, Michael. *Klondike Fever: The Famous Gold Rush of 1898* (5–8). Illus. 1990, Houghton paper $6.95 (0-395-54784-9). The events that turned a remote part of the Yukon into a three-ring circus of gold-hungry prospectors. (Rev: BCCB 1/90; BL 11/15/89; HB 1–2/90) [971.9]

8489 Coulter, Tony. *Jacques Cartier, Samuel de Champlain, and the Explorers of Canada* (5–8). Illus. Series: World Explorers. 1993, Chelsea LB $21.95 (0-7910-1298-0). This book about the early exploration of Canada includes material on Cartier, Champlain, Cabot, and Hudson, among others. (Rev: BL 1/1/93) [971]

8490 *Destination Vancouver* (6–9). Illus. Series: Port Cities of North America. 1998, Lerner LB $23.93 (0-8225-2787-1). A small volume that is full of information about Vancouver, its history, economy, and details about materials and goods that are shipped in and out of this port city. (Rev: HBG 9/98; SLJ 8/98) [971]

8491 Ferry, Steven. *Ontario* (6–9). Illus. Series: Exploring Canada. 2003, Gale LB $21.96 (1-59018-050-X). Ontario's geography, history, people, politics, and potential are presented in a well-organized volume that will be useful for report writers. (Rev: BL 7/03; SLJ 6/03) [971.3]

8492 Grabowski, John. *Canada* (5–8). Illus. Series: Overview: Modern Nations of the World. 1997, Lucent LB $27.45 (1-56006-520-6). A fine introduction to Canada and its people with coverage of major cities, industry, art and culture, government, and the separatist movement in Quebec. (Rev: BL 6/1–15/98; SLJ 8/98) [971]

8493 Greenwood, Barbara. *Gold Rush Fever: A Story of the Klondike, 1898* (4–7). 2001, Kids Can $18.95 (1-55074-852-1); paper $12.95 (1-55074-

850-5). Thirteen-year-old Tim and his older brother trek to the Yukon to try to win their fortune in this account that interweaves fact and fiction, with many details about the hardships the miners faced. (Rev: BL 12/15/01; HBG 10/02; SLJ 10/01) [971.91]

8494 Kizilos, Peter. *Quebec: Province Divided* (7–10). Series: World in Conflict. 2000, Lerner LB $25.26 (0-8225-3562-9). The history of the French Canadian province and the separatist movement that wishes to create a separate state. (Rev: BL 10/15/2000; HBG 4/00; VOYA 8/01) [971]

8495 Murphy, Claire R., and Jane G. Haigh. *Children of the Gold Rush* (6–9). 1999, Roberts Rinehart paper $14.95 (1-57098-257-0). The story of the Yukon Gold Rush of 1878–1898 from the perspectives of the children involved, using diary excerpts, advertisements of the day, archival photographs, maps, and illustrations. (Rev: HB 7–8/99; HBG 9/99; SLJ 9/99) [971]

8496 Palana, Brett J. *British Columbia* (6–9). Illus. Series: Exploring Canada. 2003, Gale LB $21.96 (1-59018-046-1). A concise look at British Columbia's geography, history, people, and politics, with information on the large population of Asian immigrants and on environmental concerns. (Rev: BL 7/03) [971.1]

8497 Rogers, Barbara Radcliffe, and Stillman D. Rogers. *Canada* (4–7). Series: Enchantment of the World. 2000, Children's LB $34.50 (0-516-21076-9). This fine introduction to Canada, its land and its people, also contains coverage of its history, economy, plants and animals, languages, sports, and the arts. (Rev: BL 1/1–15/01) [971]

8498 Shepherd, Jennifer. *Canada* (4–7). Illus. 1988, Children's paper $32.00 (0-516-02757-3). Geography, history, climate, and people are discussed in this look at the northern U.S. neighbor. (Rev: BL 5/15/88; SLJ 8/88) [971]

8499 Thompson, Alexa. *Nova Scotia* (4–8). Series: Hello Canada. 1995, Lerner LB $19.93 (0-8225-2759-6). Nova Scotia's history, geography, and the economy are covered, with material on the various peoples and cultures. (Rev: SLJ 3/96) [971.6]

8500 Whitcraft, Melissa. *The Niagara River* (4–8). Series: Watts Libraray. 2001, Watts LB $24.00 (0-531-11903-3). This absorbing and readable account with maps and historical and contemporary photographs looks at the river's history, industry, and impact on the surrounding region. (Rev: SLJ 5/01) [971.3]

8501 Yates, Sarah. *Alberta* (4–8). Series: Hello Canada. 1995, Lerner LB $19.93 (0-8225-2763-4). A colorful, slim volume that crams many facts about this western Canadian province's culture, history, geography, and resources into a few attractive pages. (Rev: BL 12/15/95; SLJ 3/96) [971.23]

CENTRAL AMERICA

8502 Adams, Faith. *Nicaragua: Struggling with Change* (5–8). Illus. 1987, Macmillan LB $14.95 (0-87518-340-9). A balanced telling of a troubled Central American country's story. (Rev: BL 5/15/87; SLJ 8/87) [972.85]

8503 Brill, Marlene T., and Harry R. Targ. *Guatemala* (5–8). Illus. Series: Enchantment of the World. 1993, Children's paper $32.00 (0-516-02614-3). This introduction to Guatemala covers history, geography, people, and culture. (Rev: BL 8/93) [972.8]

8504 Day, Nancy. *Your Travel Guide to Ancient Mayan Civilization* (4–8). Series: Passport to History. 2000, Lerner LB $26.60 (0-8225-3077-5). Using the format of a modern-day travel guide, this book explores the ancient Mayan cities of Uzmal, Tikal, Copan, and others to discover the lifestyles of the Maya, their food, clothes, religion, discoveries, and behavior. (Rev: BL 3/1/01; HBG 10/01; SLJ 4/01) [972]

8505 Franklin, Kristine L., and Nancy McGirr, eds. *Out of the Dump: Writings and Photographs by Children from Guatemala* (4–8). Illus. 1996, Lothrop LB $18.93 (0-688-13924-8). A photographic essay that focuses on the poor children who exist by scavenging in the garbage dump of Guatemala City. (Rev: BCCB 3/96; BL 3/15/96*; SLJ 4/96*) [861]

8506 Freedman, Russell. *In the Days of the Vaqueros: America's First True Cowboys* (5–9). Illus. 2001, Clarion $18.00 (0-395-96788-0). Vivid artwork complements this history of the earliest cowboys, the Central American vaqueros who first rode the range in the late 15th century. (Rev: BL 11/15/01*; HB 1–2/02; HBG 3/02; SLJ 9/01) [636.2]

8507 Gaines, Ann. *The Panama Canal in American History* (4–8). Series: In American History. 1999, Enslow LB $20.95 (0-7660-1216-6). This is a carefully researched history of the building of the Panama Canal, including a review of events before U.S. involvement, how the United States established the country of Panama and gained control of the Canal Zone, details of the many difficulties encountered, and a description of how the canal locks operate. (Rev: BL 3/1/99; HBG 10/99; SLJ 8/99) [972.87]

8508 Gold, Susan D. *The Panama Canal Transfer: Controversy at the Crossroads* (7–10). 1999, Raintree Steck-Vaughn $19.98 (0-8172-5762-4). The first half of this book describes the building of the canal and the second half traces the process of returning the Canal Zone to Panama, including the 1978 treaty providing for the return, the positions of both countries, and the ill will and controversy that developed. (Rev: SLJ 8/99) [972.8]

8509 Hadden, Gerry. *Teenage Refugees from Guatemala Speak Out* (7–12). Series: Teenage Refugees

Speak Out. 1997, Rosen LB $16.95 (0-8239-2439-4). Teens from Guatemala who now live in the U.S. describe the violent military campaigns that destroyed villages and lives in their homeland. (Rev: BL 10/15/97; SLJ 1/98) [972.8]

8510 Hassig, Susan M. *Panama* (4–7). Illus. Series: Cultures of the World. 1996, Marshall Cavendish LB $35.64 (0-7614-0278-0). The troubled history of Panama is covered, with material on geography and the lifestyle and culture of its people. (Rev: BL 8/96) [972.87]

8511 Haverstock, Nathan A. *Nicaragua in Pictures* (5–8). Illus. 1993, Lerner LB $25.55 (0-8225-1817-1). A visit to this controversial country is highlighted by color photographs and clear text. (Rev: BL 10/15/87) [972.85]

8512 *Honduras in Pictures* (4–7). Illus. Series: Visual Geography. 1994, Lerner LB $25.55 (0-8225-1804-X). Chapters focus on history, culture, education, people, geography, and lifestyles. (Rev: BL 8/87)

8513 Jermyn, Leslie. *Belize* (5–9). Series: Cultures of the World. 2001, Marshall Cavendish LB $35.64 (0-7614-1190-9). Geography, history, government, arts and culture, and lifestyle are all covered in this interesting and attractive volume. (Rev: HBG 10/01; SLJ 11/01) [972.82]

8514 Kallen, Stuart A. *The Mayans* (7–12). Illus. Series: Lost Civilizations. 2001, Lucent LB $19.96 (1-56006-757-8). Kallen covers all aspects of Mayan civilization and emphasizes the ongoing archaeological discoveries that add to our knowledge. (Rev: SLJ 5/01) [972.81]

8515 Lindop, Edmund. *Panama and the United States: Divided by the Canal* (5–8). Illus. 1997, Twenty-First Century LB $23.40 (0-8050-4768-9). A history of United States-Panama relations, from the building of the canal to the present. (Rev: BL 8/97; BR 11–12/97; SLJ 7/97) [327.7307287]

8516 McGaffey, Leta. *Honduras* (5–9). Series: Cultures of the World. 1999, Marshall Cavendish LB $35.64 (0-7614-0955-6). After background material on the history and geography of Honduras, this book focuses on modern times and such topics as the economy, population, religion, holidays, and recreation. (Rev: HBG 10/99; SLJ 11/99) [972.8]

8517 McNeese, Tim. *The Panama Canal* (5–8). Illus. Series: Building History. 1997, Lucent LB $27.45 (1-56006-425-0). A description of the building of the Panama Canal that also supplies valuable insights into the economic and social conditions of the times. (Rev: BL 8/97; BR 1–2/98; HBG 3/98; SLJ 7/97) [386]

8518 Malone, Michael. *A Guatemalan Family* (4–7). Illus. Series: Journey Between Two Worlds. 1996, Lerner paper $8.95 (0-8225-9742-X). The story of a refugee family from Guatemala and of its resettle-

ment in the United States. (Rev: BL 11/15/96; SLJ 1/97) [975.9]

8519 Mann, Elizabeth. *Tikal: The Center of the Maya World* (4–8). Series: Wonders of the World. 2002, Mikaya $19.95 (1-931414-05-X). Mann provides an overview for older readers of the Mayan city of Tikal, covering the location, the people, the architecture, the culture, and their sometimes bloodthirsty customs. (Rev: BL 12/15/02; HBG 3/03; SLJ 1/03) [972.81]

8520 Markun, Patricia M. *It's Panama's Canal!* (5–9). Illus. 1999, Linnet LB $22.50 (0-208-02499-9). This account gives a good background history of the canal plus current information on Panama's control of the zone and its plans for successful management. (Rev: BL 1/1–15/00; HBG 3/00) [972.87]

8521 Morrison, Marion. *Belize* (5–8). Illus. Series: Enchantment of the World. 1996, Children's paper $32.00 (0-516-02639-9). An introduction to the small Central American nation, formerly called British Honduras. (Rev: BL 7/96) [972.82]

8522 Morrison, Marion. *Nicaragua* (4–7). Series: Enchantment of the World. 2002, Children's LB $34.50 (0-516-20963-9). Such topics as geography, history, people, language, economy, and government are covered in this introduction to Nicaragua. (Rev: BL 5/15/02) [972.8]

8523 Netzley, Patricia D. *Maya Civilization* (6–9). 2002, Gale LB $21.96 (1-56006-806-X). Primary and secondary sources are incorporated into the text of this introduction to the Mayans and their culture that emphasizes the role of historians. (Rev: SLJ 12/02) [972]

8524 Odijk, Pamela. *The Mayas* (4–7). Illus. Series: Ancient World. 1990, Silver Burdett LB $14.95 (0-382-09890-0). The history and accomplishments of the Mayas are covered in this illustrated account. (Rev: BL 11/1/90; SLJ 1/91) [972.81]

8525 *Panama in Pictures* (4–7). Illus. Series: Visual Geography. 1996, Lerner LB $25.55 (0-8225-1818-X). The life and culture, history, and geography of the people of Panama. (Rev: BL 8/87) [972.87]

8526 Sharer, Robert J. *Daily Life in Maya Civilization* (8–12). Series: Daily Life Through History. 1996, Greenwood $49.95 (0-313-29342-2). The latest research is included in this thorough study of Maya civilization from its beginnings to the Spanish conquest. (Rev: BR 5–6/97; SLJ 2/97) [972.81]

8527 Sheehan, Sean. *Guatemala* (6–10). Series: Cultures of the World. 1998, Marshall Cavendish LB $35.64 (0-7614-0812-6). A solid introduction to Guatemala's geography, politics, and culture. (Rev: HBG 9/98; SLJ 2/99) [972.8]

8528 Shields, Charles J. *Belize* (5–7). Illus. Series: Discovering Central America. 2002, Mason Crest LB $19.95 (1-59084-092-5). Students needing facts

535

about Belize will find everything here: geography, history, people, and culture, all backed up by maps, photographs, a timeline, and even recipes. (Rev: BL 1/1–15/03) [972.82]

8529 Shields, Charles J. *Central America: Facts and Figures* (5–7). Illus. Series: Discovering Central America. 2002, Mason Crest LB $19.95 (1-59084-099-2). This look at Central America as a whole covers history, geography, inhabitants, and cultures. (Rev: BL 1/1–15/03) [972.8]

8530 Silverstone, Michael. *Rigoberta Menchu: Defending Human Rights in Guatemala* (5–8). Illus. 1999, Feminist Pr. $19.95 (1-55861-198-3); paper $9.95 (1-55861-199-1). In addition to a biography of Nobel Peace Prize winner Rigoberta Menchu, this account presents Guatemala, its civil war, and the efforts to end it. (Rev: BL 3/15/00) [972.81]

8531 Vazquez, Ana Maria B. *Panama* (5–8). Illus. Series: Enchantment of the World. 1991, Children's paper $32.00 (0-516-02604-6). In addition to historical and geographic information, this book discusses the importance of the canal. (Rev: BL 2/1/92) [972.87]

MEXICO

8532 Ancona, George. *Charro* (4–8). 1999, Harcourt $18.00 (0-15-201047-5); paper $9.00 (0-15-201046-7). A handsome photoessay that focuses on Mexican cowboys called *charros* and *la charreada*, a rodeolike competition where they display their skills. (Rev: BCCB 5/99; BL 5/15/99; HBG 10/99; SLJ 6/99) [972]

8533 Baquedano, Elizabeth. *Aztec, Inca and Maya* (4–8). Illus. Series: Eyewitness Books. 1993, Knopf $20.99 (0-679-93883-4). An overview of the history of these Indian civilizations of the Americas, their cultures, and their fate at the hands of the invading Spaniards. (Rev: BL 10/1/93; SLJ 12/93) [972]

8534 Barghusen, Joan D. *The Aztecs: End of a Civilization* (6–10). Series: History's Great Defeats. 2000, Lucent LB $19.96 (1-56006-620-2). The defeat of the large Aztec population by a small number of Spanish invaders is detailed using primary and secondary sources. (Rev: BR 3–4/01; HBG 3/01; SLJ 12/00) [972]

8535 Burr, Claudia, et al. *Broken Shields* (4–8). Illus. 1997, Douglas & McIntyre $15.95 (0-88899-303-X); paper $6.95 (0-88899-304-8). From firsthand eyewitness accounts, this is the story of the betrayal of Montezuma at the hands of the Spanish conqueror Cortez. (Rev: BL 12/1/97; HB 11–12/97; HBG 3/98; SLJ 1/98) [972]

8536 Castillo, Ana. *My Daughter, My Son, the Eagle, the Dove* (7–12). Illus. 2000, Dutton $12.99 (0-525-45856-5). In this series of short poems that originated with the Aztecs, each of which is illus-

trated by traditional figures, the cultural life of the Aztecs comes alive. (Rev: BL 6/1–15/00; HBG 9/00; SLJ 6/00; VOYA 6/00) [398.2.]

8537 Chapman, Gillian. *The Aztecs* (4–8). Series: Crafts from the Past. 1997, Heinemann LB $25.64 (1-57572-555-X). A craft book with instructions for a variety of Aztec ornaments and artifacts, including textiles and statues. (Rev: SLJ 4/98) [745]

8538 Flowers, Charles. *Cortés and the Conquest of the Aztec Empire in World History* (6–10). Illus. Series: In World History. 2001, Enslow LB $20.95 (0-7660-1395-2). This accessible and interesting account describes Cortes's incursion into the Aztec empire and explains how the Aztecs' beliefs contributed to the ease of this conquest. (Rev: HBG 10/01; SLJ 8/01) [972]

8539 Franklin, Sharon, et al. *Mexico and Central America* (4–7). Illus. Series: Artisans Around the World. 1999, Raintree Steck-Vaughn LB $27.12 (0-7398-0121-X). This craft book, with related projects, describes the folk art of each of the countries in Central America and Mexico. (Rev: BL 10/15/99; HBG 3/00; SLJ 1/00) [745.5]

8540 Hadden, Gerry. *Teenage Refugees from Mexico Speak Out* (7–12). Series: Teenage Refugees Speak Out. 1997, Rosen LB $16.95 (0-8239-2441-6). Teens who have left Mexico and come to the United States to escape economic conditions and political instability tell about their experiences. (Rev: BL 10/15/97; SLJ 1/98) [972]

8541 Hamilton, Janice. *Mexico in Pictures*. Rev. ed. (4–8). Illus. Series: Visual Geography. 2002, Lerner LB $27.93 (0-8225-1960-7). An excellent introduction to Mexico that includes material on geography, history, people, economy, and culture with maps, photographs, and illustrations. (Rev: HBG 3/03; SLJ 3/03) [972]

8542 Helly, Mathilde, and Rémi Courgeon. *Montezuma and the Aztecs* (7–10). 1996, Holt $19.95 (0-8050-5060-4). Although the presentation is somewhat disorganized, this account describes the Aztecs, their culture, political structure, everyday life, and human sacrifices, as well as European invaders, and the ruler Montezuma. (Rev: BR 1–2/98; SLJ 3/97) [972]

8543 Hull, Robert. *The Aztecs* (5–10). Series: The Ancient World. 1998, Raintree Steck-Vaughn LB $27.12 (0-8172-5056-5). This history of the Aztecs and their culture tells about their great pyramids, feathered headdresses, gods, human sacrifices, and the coming of the Spanish. (Rev: BL 1/1–15/99; HBG 3/99) [972]

8544 Jermyn, Leslie. *Mexico* (5–8). Series: Countries of the World. 1998, Gareth Stevens LB $29.26 (0-8368-2127-0). Good basic information about Mexico, particularly in the areas of education and politics, is presented through clear text, full-page illustrations, maps, and a quick facts section. (Rev: BL 12/15/98; HBG 9/99; SLJ 2/99) [972]

8545 Jovinelly, Joann, and Jason Netelkos. *The Crafts and Culture of the Aztecs* (5–8). Illus. Series: Crafts of the Ancient World. 2002, Rosen LB $29.25 (0-8239-3512-4). The culture of the Aztecs is covered through a discussion of their crafts and a variety of easily accomplished projects related to them. (Rev: BL 4/1/02; VOYA 6/02) [972]

8546 Kent, Deborah. *Mexico: Rich in Spirit and Tradition* (4–8). Series: Exploring Cultures of the World. 1995, Benchmark LB $27.07 (0-7614-0187-3). This book begins with a Mexican folktale, then gives an overview of the country's people, culture, history, and problems. (Rev: SLJ 6/96) [972]

8547 Lewington, Anna. *Mexico* (5–8). Illus. Series: Economically Developing Countries. 1996, Raintree Steck-Vaughn LB $24.26 (0-8172-4528-6). A fine general profile of Mexico that includes jobs, industries, and other economic indicators. (Rev: BL 3/15/97; SLJ 2/97) [330.972]

8548 Libura, Krystyna, et al. *What the Aztecs Told Me* (4–8). Illus. 1997, Douglas & McIntyre $15.95 (0-88899-305-6); paper $6.95 (0-88899-306-4). Based on an original 12-volume work written in the 16th century, this book describes the Aztec people from observation and eyewitness accounts. (Rev: BL 12/1/97; HB 11–12/97; HBG 3/98; SLJ 12/97) [972]

8549 MacDonald, Fiona. *How Would You Survive as an Aztec?* (4–7). Illus. Series: How Would You Survive? 1995, Watts LB $26.00 (0-531-14348-1). Food, clothing, and everyday life in an Aztec community are covered in a series of double-page spreads. (Rev: BL 6/1–15/95) [972]

8550 Marquez, Heron. *Destination Veracruz* (5–8). Series: Port Cities of North America. 1998, Lerner LB $23.93 (0-8225-2791-X). A description of this port city on the Gulf of Mexico that reviews its history, everyday life, the effects of development on the environment, and the city's economy, including the impact of NAFTA and a discussion of international trade, economic systems, and free trade. (Rev: HBG 3/99; SLJ 3/99) [972]

8551 Marrin, Albert. *Aztecs and Spaniards: Cortes and the Conquest of Mexico* (7–10). Illus. 1986, Macmillan $15.95 (0-689-31176-1). The story of the decline and fall of the Aztec civilization and the Spanish conquistadors who caused it. (Rev: BL 4/15/86; SLJ 8/86; VOYA 2/87) [972.01]

8552 Mason, Antony. *Aztec Times* (4–7). Series: If You Were There. 1997, Simon & Schuster $16.95 (0-689-81199-3). Using many illustrations, a timeline, and a pictorial map, this account describes the origins of this civilization, its daily life, customs, and the arrival the Spaniards. (Rev: HBG 3/98; SLJ 12/97) [972]

8553 Ochoa, George. *The Fall of Mexico City* (6–9). Illus. 1989, Silver Burdett LB $14.95 (0-382-09836-6); paper $7.95 (0-382-09853-6). An account of the U.S. occupation of Mexico City during 1847 and 1848. (Rev: BL 11/1/89; BR 1–2/90; SLJ 12/89) [973]

8554 Odijk, Pamela. *The Aztecs* (4–7). Illus. Series: Ancient World. 1990, Silver Burdett LB $14.95 (0-382-09887-0). A well-illustrated account of the rise and fall of the ancient Mexican civilization. (Rev: BL 7/90; SLJ 8/90) [972]

8555 Pascoe, Elaine. *Mexico and the United States: Cooperation and Conflict* (7–12). Illus. 1996, Twenty-First Century LB $24.90 (0-8050-4180-X). After a history of the stormy relations between Mexico and the U.S., the author discusses current problems, such as drug trafficking, oil, the peso, and immigration. (Rev: BL 12/1/96; BR 3–4/97; SLJ 1/97) [303.48]

8556 Reilly, Mary J. *Mexico* (5–8). Illus. Series: Cultures of the World. 1991, Marshall Cavendish LB $35.64 (1-85435-385-3). This account emphasizes the geography, history, economy, and lifestyles of the Mexican people. (Rev: BL 4/1/91) [972]

8557 Rosenblum, Morris. *Heroes of Mexico* (5–8). 1972, Fleet $9.50 (0-8303-0082-1). A collected group of profiles of people important in the history of Mexico. (Rev: BL 6/87) [972]

8558 Rummel, Jack. *Mexico* (6–10). Series: Major World Nations. 1998, Chelsea LB $19.95 (0-7910-4763-6). A well-illustrated account that emphasizes current economic, political, and cultural conditions, supplemented by good background information. (Rev: BL 9/15/98; BR 1–2/99; HBG 3/99; SLJ 12/98) [917.2]

8559 Sanna, Ellyn. *Mexico: Facts and Figures* (5–8). Series: Mexico: Our Southern Neighbor. 2002, Mason Crest LB $19.95 (1-59084-088-7). An introduction to Mexico and its states, with material on history, people and culture today, and issues of importance such as poverty. Also use *The Geography of Mexico*, *The Economy of Mexico*, and *The Government of Mexico*. (Rev: SLJ 12/02) [972]

8560 Stefoff, Rebecca. *Independence and Revolution in Mexico, 1810–1940* (7–12). 1993, Facts on File $19.95 (0-8160-2841-9). The history of Mexico's 130-year struggle for independence is explored, highlighting notable events and people. (Rev: BL 12/1/93) [972]

8561 Stein, R. Conrad. *The Aztec Empire* (5–8). Series: Cultures of the Past. 1995, Benchmark LB $28.50 (0-7614-0072-9). The Aztecs' history, beliefs, and lifestyles are examined in this book, with quotations from original sources and many color photographs of artifacts, monuments, and historical sites. (Rev: BR 9–10/96; SLJ 6/96) [972]

8562 Stein, R. Conrad. *The Mexican Revolution, 1910–1920* (7–9). 1994, Macmillan LB $14.95 (0-02-786950-4). An examination of significant political, emotional, economic, and ideological issues of the period, with profiles of the main leaders. (Rev: BL 3/1/94; SLJ 8/94; VOYA 8/94) [972.08]

8563 Stein, R. Conrad. *Mexico* (4–7). Series: Enchantment of the World. 1998, Children's LB $34.50 (0-516-20650-8). As well as the history, geography, and economy of Mexico, this account covers modern culture, holidays, the arts, and religion. (Rev: HBG 3/99; SLJ 1/99) [972]

8564 Tanaka, Shelley. *Lost Temple of the Aztecs: What It Was Like When the Spaniards Invaded Mexico* (4–7). Series: An I Was There Book. 1998, Hyperion $16.95 (0-7868-0441-6). A readable text that centers on the Great Temple of Tenochtitlan and details the life of the Aztecs from the arrival of the Spaniards until the capital city's destruction in 1521. (Rev: BCCB 1/99; HBG 3/99; SLJ 2/99) [972]

PUERTO RICO, CUBA, AND OTHER CARIBBEAN ISLANDS

8565 Anthony, Suzanne. *West Indies* (6–12). Series: Major World Nations. 1998, Chelsea LB $19.95 (0-7910-4772-5). An introduction to the people, geography, history, and economy of the West Indies, with a focus on current conditions. (Rev: BL 9/15/98; BR 1–2/99) [975.9]

8566 Davis, Lucile. *Puerto Rico* (5–8). Series: America the Beautiful. 2000, Children's LB $34.00 (0-516-21042-4). This introduction to Puerto Rico contains information on the island's history, geography, economy, people, culture, and current concerns. (Rev: BL 5/15/00) [972.95]

8567 Fernandez, Ronald M., et al. *Puerto Rico Past and Present: An Encyclopedia* (8–12). 1998, Greenwood $67.95 (0-313-29822-X). A browsable book that contains biographies of famous Puerto Ricans as well as political terms and groups, buildings, important court decisions, and other information on the island's cultural and historical developments. (Rev: BL 7/97; VOYA 10/98) [972.95]

8568 Greenberg, Keith E. *A Haitian Family* (4–7). Illus. Series: Journey Between Two Worlds. 1998, Lerner LB $22.60 (0-8225-3410-X). The story of the Beaubrun family, the political oppression they suffered in Haiti, and their eventual journey to freedom in the United States. (Rev: BL 3/1/98; HBG 10/98) [305.9]

8569 Harlan, Judith. *Puerto Rico: Deciding Its Future* (7–10). Illus. 1996, Twenty-First Century LB $23.40 (0-8050-4372-1). The statehood-commonwealth-independence question is presented with clarity, simplicity, and objectivity. (Rev: BL 1/1–15/97; SLJ 7/97) [972.95]

8570 Haverstock, Nathan A. *Cuba in Pictures* (5–8). Illus. Series: Visual Geography. 1997, Lerner LB $25.55 (0-8225-1811-2). A look at America's island neighbor, with color photographs. Also use *Dominican Republic in Pictures* (1997). (Rev: BL 10/15/87) [972.91064]

8571 *Jamaica in Pictures* (5–8). Illus. Series: Visual Geography. 1997, Lerner LB $25.55 (0-8225-1814-7). Color photographs highlight this visit to a popular and beautiful island. (Rev: BL 10/15/87) [972.92]

8572 Marquez, Heron. *Destination San Juan* (5–8). Series: Port Cities of North America. 1998, Lerner LB $23.93 (0-8225-2792-8). A matter-of-fact introduction to San Juan that describes the city, people, economy, and port activities. (Rev: HBG 3/99; SLJ 3/99) [972.95]

8573 Morrison, Marion. *Cuba* (4–7). Illus. Series: Country Insights. 1998, Raintree Steck-Vaughn LB $27.12 (0-8172-4796-3). An introduction to contemporary life in Cuba, showing the contrast between life in a big city (Havana) and in a country village. (Rev: BL 5/1/98; HBG 10/98) [972.91]

8574 Morrison, Marion. *Cuba* (5–9). Illus. Series: Enchantment of the World. 1999, Children's LB $34.50 (0-516-21051-3). A fine, colorful introduction to Cuba past and present, with material on climate, industry, government, daily life, social customs, and religions. (Rev: BL 12/15/99) [972.91]

8575 *Puerto Rico in Pictures* (4–7). Illus. Series: Visual Geography. 1995, Lerner LB $25.55 (0-8225-1821-X). Everyday life, history, culture, and geography are introduced. (Rev: BL 8/87) [972.95]

8576 Rogers, Barbara Radcliffe, and Lure Rogers. *The Dominican Republic* (4–7). Series: Enchantment of the World. 1999, Children's LB $34.50 (0-516-21125-0). An introduction to the Dominican Republic with coverage of such topics as history, climate, geography, people, religion, culture, daily life, and landmarks. (Rev: BL 12/15/99) [972.93]

8577 Sheehan, Sean. *Jamaica* (5–8). Illus. Series: Cultures of the World. 1993, Marshall Cavendish LB $35.64 (1-85435-581-3). This informative account describes many facets of Jamaican life, including history, religion, and reggae music. (Rev: SLJ 2/94) [972.92]

8578 Sherrow, Victoria. *Cuba* (7–12). Illus. 2001, Twenty-First Century LB $24.40 (0-7613-1404-0). Fidel Castro is a key figure in this overview of Cuba's internal affairs and relations with the outside world that will be useful for report writers. (Rev: BL 9/15/01; HBG 3/02; SLJ 12/01; VOYA 12/01) [973.91]

8579 Tuck, Jay, and Norma C. Vergara. *Heroes of Puerto Rico* (5–8). 1969, Fleet $9.50 (0-8303-0070-8). A series of profiles of famous Puerto Ricans. (Rev: BL 6/87) [972.9]

8580 Turck, Mary C. *Haiti: Land of Inequality* (8–12). Series: World in Conflict. 1999, Lerner $25.26 (0-8225-3554-8). Though now out-of-date, this well-illustrated book gives good background information on this troubled land and its history. (Rev: BL 10/15/99; HBG 4/00; SLJ 2/00) [975.9]

8581 Wagner, Michele. *Haiti* (4–8). 2002, Gareth Stevens LB $29.27 (0-8368-2351-6). History, geography, government, and people are all covered here, with special sections on such topics as the status of women and relations with the United States. (Rev: HBG 3/03; SLJ 2/03) [972.94]

8582 Will, Emily Wade. *Haiti* (5–8). Series: Modern Nations of the World. 2001, Lucent LB $27.45 (1-56006-761-6). The history, geography, and culture of this island country are presented with colorful prose and pictures plus unusual facts contained in sidebars. (Rev: BL 6/1–15/01) [972.94]

South America

8583 *Argentina in Pictures* (5–8). Illus. Series: Visual Geography. 1994, Lerner LB $25.55 (0-8225-1807-4). An overview of climate, wildlife, cities, vegetation, and mineral resources. (Rev: BL 4/15/88; SLJ 5/88) [982]

8584 Augustin, Byron. *Bolivia* (4–7). Series: Enchantment of the World. 2001, Children's LB $34.50 (0-516-21050-5). With each page containing a color illustration, this attractive book introduces the land and people, economy, culture, and natural resources of Bolivia. (Rev: BL 1/1–15/02) [984]

8585 Barter, James. *The Amazon* (5–9). Illus. 2003, Gale $27.45 (1-56006-934-1). In addition to covering the river's location and importance, Barter reviews the history of the peoples living along the Amazon, early exploration by outsiders, and the environmental problems of the area. (Rev: BL 3/15/03; SLJ 1/03) [981]

8586 Barter, James. *The Galapagos Islands* (7–10). Series: Endangered Animals and Habitats. 2002, Gale LB $27.45 (1-56006-920-1). In text and many color illustrations, this endangered habitat and its history are described with material on the methods employed to save these unique islands from destruction. (Rev: BL 5/15/02) [508.866]

8587 Bender, Evelyn. *Brazil* (6–12). Series: Major World Nations. 1998, Chelsea LB $21.95 (0-7910-4758-X). Current economic and social conditions in Brazil are emphasized, supplemented by background material on history and geography. (Rev: BL 9/15/98; BR 1–2/99; HBG 3/99) [981]

8588 Bernhard, Brendan. *Pizarro, Orellana, and the Exploration of the Amazon* (6–9). Series: World Explorers. 1991, Chelsea LB $21.95 (0-7910-1305-7). An account of the hardships, dangers, and rewards faced by the early explorers of the Amazon. (Rev: BL 9/15/91; SLJ 12/91) [981]

8589 Cameron, Sara. *Out of War: True Stories from the Front Lines of the Children's Movement for Peace in Colombia* (7–12). 2001, Scholastic $15.95 (0-439-29721-4). Nine teen members of the Colombian peace movement describe their lives in this war-torn country and express their desire for peace rather than retribution. (Rev: BL 9/1/01; HBG 3/02; SLJ 8/01; VOYA 10/01) [305.23]

8590 Carpenter, Mark L. *Brazil: An Awakening Giant* (5–7). Illus. 1988, Macmillan LB $14.95 (0-87518-366-2). A wide range of information is included, with the focus on everyday life. (Rev: BL 2/15/88) [981]

8591 Castner, James L. *Native Peoples* (6–12). Illus. Series: Deep in the Amazon. 2001, Marshall Cavendish LB $18.95 (0-7614-1128-3). This volume looks at the people of the Amazon, their way of life, and the encroachment of outsiders. Also use *Rainforest Researchers* (2001). (Rev: BL 12/15/01; HBG 3/02) [981]

8592 *Colombia in Pictures* (5–8). Illus. Series: Visual Geography. 1996, Lerner LB $25.55 (0-8225-1810-4). Many photographs highlight this visit to a South American nation. (Rev: BL 10/15/87) [986.1]

8593 Corona, Laurel. *Brazil* (5–8). Series: Modern Nations of the World. 1999, Lucent LB $27.45 (1-56006-621-0). A lively account of Brazil's history, geography, famous people, and conditions today. (Rev: BL 2/15/00; HBG 10/00) [981]

8594 Corona, Laurel. *Peru* (5–8). Series: Modern Nations of the World. 2001, Lucent LB $27.45 (1-56006-862-0). Detailed sidebars, a chronology, and national statistics supplement the general information presented in this colorful introduction to Peru. (Rev: BL 6/1–15/01) [985]

8595 Dalal, Anita. *Argentina* (4–8). Series: Nations of the World. 2001, Raintree Steck-Vaughn LB $34.26 (0-7398-1279-3). A colorful, interesting introduction to Argentina that covers its land and cities, history, culture, present economic conditions, and possible future developments. (Rev: BL 6/1–15/01; HBG 10/01) [982]

8596 Dalal, Anita. *Brazil* (4–8). Series: Nations of the World. 2001, Raintree Steck-Vaughn LB $34.26 (0-7398-1284-X). A profile of the home of Carnival, the Amazon, and Pele with material attractively presented on its past and present, its people, and its culture. (Rev: BL 6/1–15/01; HBG 10/01) [981]

8597 Dubois, Jill. *Colombia* (5–8). Illus. Series: Cultures of the World. 1991, Marshall Cavendish LB $35.64 (1-85435-384-5). Background information on Colombia is given as well as coverage of contemporary concerns. (Rev: BL 4/1/91) [986.1]

8598 Falconer, Kieran. *Peru* (4–7). Illus. Series: Cultures of the World. 1995, Marshall Cavendish LB $35.64 (0-7614-0179-2). The focus of this book is on the people of Peru, their lifestyles, artistic endeavors, religion, and leisure activities. (Rev: BL 1/1–15/96; SLJ 4/96) [985]

8599 Foley, Erin. *Ecuador* (5–8). Illus. Series: Cultures of the World. 1995, Marshall Cavendish LB $35.64 (0-7614-0173-3). This book supplies good background material on Ecuador but is strongest in describing contemporary conditions. (Rev: SLJ 11/95) [980]

8600 Gofen, Ethel C. *Cultures of the World: Argentina* (5–8). Illus. Series: Cultures of the World. 1991, Marshall Cavendish LB $213.86 (1-85435-380-2). This book provides standard information on history and geography and tells about the contemporary lifestyles of the people. (Rev: BL 4/1/91) [962]

8601 *Guyana in Pictures* (5–8). Illus. Series: Visual Geography. 1997, Lerner LB $25.55 (0-8225-1815-5). History, climate, wildlife, and major cities are covered in this overview. (Rev: BL 4/15/88) [988.1]

8602 Haverstock, Nathan A. *Brazil in Pictures* (4–7). Illus. Series: Visual Geography. 1997, Lerner LB $25.55 (0-8225-1802-3). Current data on the political scene, plus chapters on history, people, and culture in this revised text. Also use *Chile in Pictures* (1988). (Rev: BL 8/87)

8603 Haverstock, Nathan A. *Paraguay in Pictures* (5–8). Illus. Series: Visual Geography. 1995, Lerner LB $25.55 (0-8225-1819-8). This overview of Paraguay includes its history to 1987 and possible future developments. (Rev: BL 4/15/88) [989.2]

8604 Heisey, Janet. *Peru* (5–8). Illus. Series: Countries of the World. 2001, Gareth Stevens LB $29.26 (0-8368-2333-8). An informative overview of Peru's history, geography, government, culture, and relationship with other countries in the Western Hemisphere. (Rev: HBG 10/01; SLJ 4/01) [985]

8605 Jermyn, Leslie. *Paraguay* (5–8). 1999, Marshall Cavendish LB $35.64 (0-7614-0979-3). This book about Paraguay covers history, geography, government, and economy as well as such social and cultural topics as religion, the arts, food, and recreation. (Rev: HBG 10/00; SLJ 4/00) [989]

8606 Jermyn, Leslie. *Uruguay* (7–10). Series: Cultures of the World. 1998, Marshall Cavendish LB $35.64 (0-7614-0873-8). An attractive book that covers all the basic topics related to Uruguay, plus material on leisure activities, festivals, and food. (Rev: HBG 9/99; SLJ 6/99) [980]

8607 Kendall, Sarita. *The Incas* (5–6). Illus. Series: World of the Past. 1992, Macmillan LB $21.00 (0-02-750160-4). A history of the Incas before, during, and after the Spanish conquest. (Rev: SLJ 11/92) [940.54]

8608 Lepthien, Emilie U. *Peru* (5–8). Series: Enchantment of the World. 1992, Children's Pr. paper $32.00 (0-516-02610-0). An illustrated discussion of Peru's history, economy, and politics through 1990. (Rev: BL 2/1/93; SLJ 2/93) [985]

8609 Litteral, Linda L. *Boobies, Iguanas, and Other Critters: Nature's Story in the Galapagos* (6–10). 1994, American Kestrel $23.00 (1-883966-01-9). After a historical overview of the Galapagos Islands, this richly illustrated book covers the islands' animals, plants, and geology. (Rev: BL 6/1–15/94; SLJ 9/94) [508.866]

8610 Lourie, Peter. *Lost Treasure of the Inca* (4–7). Illus. 1999, Boyds Mills $18.95 (1-56397-743-5). A thrilling narrative of a modern search for the gold supposedly hidden by the Incas in the Ecuadorian mountains. (Rev: BCCB 11/99; BL 10/15/99; HBG 3/00; SLJ 11/99) [986.6]

8611 MacDonald, Fiona. *Inca Town* (4–7). Series: Metropolis. 1998, Watts LB $25.00 (0-531-14481-X). Double-page spreads, a well-organized text, and colorful drawings present life in an Inca town in the 15th century. (Rev: SLJ 1/99) [985]

8612 McNair, Sylvia. *Chile* (4–7). Series: Enchantment of the World. 2000, Children's LB $34.50 (0-516-21007-6). This attractive new edition of an old title includes material on Chile's land and people, history and government, economics and landmarks, daily life, and sports. (Rev: BL 7/00) [983]

8613 Martell, Hazel M. *Civilizations of Peru, Before 1535* (5–8). Illus. Series: Looking Back. 1999, Raintree Steck-Vaughn $19.98 (0-8172-5428-5). This book covers the history and culture of the Inca empire that stretched far beyond the boundaries of Peru. (Rev: BL 5/15/99; SLJ 7/99) [985]

8614 Morrison, Marion. *Brazil* (4–7). Illus. Series: Country Insights. 1997, Raintree Steck-Vaughn LB $27.12 (0-8172-4785-8). Compares the home life, employment, schooling, and recreation in a large city and in a small village in Brazil. (Rev: BL 7/97; SLJ 8/97) [918.1]

8615 Morrison, Marion. *Colombia* (4–7). Series: Enchantment of the World. 1999, Children's LB $34.50 (0-516-21106-4). A revision of a standard introduction to this South American country that covers such topics as history, government, people, economy, and current issues. (Rev: BL 9/15/99; HBG 3/00) [986.1]

8616 Morrison, Marion. *Ecuador* (4–7). Series: Enchantment of the World. 2000, Children's LB $34.50 (0-516-21544-2). This book examines the geography and climate of Ecuador, its history, government, language, economy, and people. (Rev: BL 1/1–15/01) [986]

8617 Morrison, Marion. *Guyana* (5–8). Illus. Series: Enchantment of the World, Second Series. 2003, Children's LB $34.00 (0-516-22377-1). A visually attractive book that covers such topics as the geography, history, government, culture, and people with a timeline, fast facts, and a recipe. (Rev: SLJ 5/03) [966.7]

8618 Morrison, Marion. *Paraguay* (5–8). Series: Enchantment of the World. 1993, Children's Pr. paper $32.00 (0-516-02619-4). An introduction to Paraguay's history, geography, economy, and culture. (Rev: BL 11/1/93; SLJ 3/94) [989.2]

8619 Morrison, Marion. *Peru* (4–7). Series: Enchantment of the World. 2000, Children's LB $34.50 (0-516-21545-0). History, geography and climate, daily life and ancient civilizations, cities, culture, and traditions are some of the topics covered in this attractive introduction to Peru. (Rev: BL 7/00) [985]

8620 Morrison, Marion. *Uruguay* (5–8). Series: Enchantment of the World. 1992, Children's Pr. paper $36.00 (0-516-02607-0). An introduction to Uruguay's people, history, climate, geography, and government. (Rev: BL 6/1/92) [989.5]

8621 Morrison, Marion. *Venezuela* (5–8). Illus. Series: Enchantment of the World. 1989, Children's paper $32.00 (0-516-02711-5). Economy, geography, history, and people are some of the topics covered. (Rev: BL 8/89; SLJ 2/90) [987]

8622 Myers, Lynne B., and Christopher A. Myers. *Galapagos: Islands of Change* (4–7). Illus. 1995, Hyperion LB $17.49 (0-7868-2061-6). The formation of these islands and the evolution of life on them are covered in text and amazing photographs. (Rev: BL 12/15/95; SLJ 11/95) [508]

8623 Nishi, Dennis. *The Inca Empire* (7–10). Series: World History. 2000, Lucent LB $18.96 (1-56006-538-9). This book discusses the mightiest of the Andean civilizations and how it spread over a great part of South America and created an intricate social structure. (Rev: BL 6/1–15/00; HBG 9/00; SLJ 7/00) [985]

8624 Odijk, Pamela. *The Incas* (4–7). Illus. Series: Ancient World. 1990, Silver Burdett LB $14.95 (0-382-09889-7). In addition to a history of the civilization that prospered in Peru, there is a timeline, glossary, and list of famous names. (Rev: BL 7/90; SLJ 8/90) [985]

8625 Parker, Edward. *The Amazon* (5–9). Illus. Series: Great Rivers of the World. 2003, World Almanac LB $29.26 (0-8368-5442-X). A comprehensive look at the river, its flora and fauna, its importance to mankind throughout history, and efforts to control outside factors threatening its survival. (Rev: BL 3/15/03) [981]

8626 Parker, Edward. *Peru* (5–8). Illus. 1996, Raintree Steck-Vaughn LB $24.26 (0-8172-4525-1). After a general introduction to Peru, this account discusses such current economic indicators as the job market, industry, and agriculture. (Rev: BL 3/15/97; SLJ 2/97) [985]

8627 Pateman, Robert. *Bolivia* (4–7). Illus. Series: Cultures of the World. 1995, Marshall Cavendish LB $35.64 (0-7614-0178-4). The people of Bolivia, how they live, and their traditions are some of the topics covered in this general introduction. (Rev: BL 1/1–15/96; SLJ 4/96) [984]

8628 Peck, Robert McCracken. *Headhunters and Hummingbirds: An Expedition into Ecuador* (7–10). Illus. 1987, Walker LB $14.85 (0-8027-6646-3). An account of an ill-fated scientific expedition into the land of the Jívaro Indians in Ecuador. (Rev: SLJ 6/87; VOYA 8/87) [986]

8629 *Peru in Pictures* (5–8). Illus. Series: Visual Geography. 1997, Lerner LB $25.55 (0-8225-1820-1). An introduction to this South American land, highlighted by color photographs. (Rev: BL 10/15/87) [985]

8630 Rawlins, Carol B. *The Orinoco River* (4–7). Illus. Series: World of Water. 1999, Watts LB $24.00 (0-531-11740-5). An introduction to this important Venezuelan river, with material on its history and current status and the areas through which it passes. (Rev: BL 1/1–15/00) [987.06]

8631 Richard, Christopher. *Brazil* (5–8). Illus. Series: Cultures of the World. 1991, Marshall Cavendish LB $35.64 (1-85435-382-9). Brazil is introduced with information on such topics as history, economics, people, and modern problems. (Rev: BL 4/1/91) [981]

8632 Robinson, Roger. *Brazil* (5–8). Series: Country Studies. 1999, Heinemann LB $27.07 (1-57572-892-3). Using colorful charts, graphs, drawings, maps, and photographs in double-page spreads, this book provides basic information about Brazil, with emphasis on regional contrasts and contemporary issues, such as population changes and the growth of agribusiness. (Rev: BL 8/99; SLJ 8/99) [981]

8633 Sayer, Chloe. *The Incas* (5–10). Series: Ancient World. 1998, Raintree Steck-Vaughn LB $27.12 (0-8172-5125-1). An in-depth look at Inca life, from their beautiful gold ornaments to their unique form of record keeping and impressive citadels and forts. (Rev: BL 1/1–15/99; HBG 3/99) [985]

8634 Siy, Alexandra. *The Waorani: People of the Ecuadoran Rain Forest* (4–7). Illus. Series: Global Villages. 1993, Macmillan LB $14.95 (0-87518-550-9). Presents the history, culture, and prospects for the future of these people. (Rev: SLJ 8/93) [980]

8635 Steele, Philip. *The Incas and Machu Picchu* (4–7). Illus. Series: Hidden Worlds. 1993, Dillon LB $13.95 (0-87518-536-3). A history of the Inca people and a tour of their ruined fortress city in Peru are included in this fascinating account. (Rev: BL 12/1/93) [985.37]

8636 Tagliaferro, Linda. *Galapagos Islands: Nature's Delicate Balance at Risk* (4–8). Illus. 2001, Lerner LB $25.26 (0-8225-0648-3). This is a detailed but accessible introduction to the history, geology, wildlife, and ecology of the Galapagos Islands, with maps and photographs. (Rev: BL 9/15/01; HBG 3/02; SLJ 11/01; VOYA 12/01) [561.9866]

8637 *Venezuela in Pictures* (4–7). Illus. Series: Visual Geography. 1993, Lerner LB $21.27 (0-8225-1824-4). The land, people, and government of this oil-rich country are explored in maps, text, and photographs. (Rev: BL 1/1/88) [987]

8638 Winter, Jane K. *Chile* (5–8). Illus. Series: Cultures of the World. 1991, Marshall Cavendish LB $35.64 (1-85435-383-7). The geography, history, government, and economy of Chile are some of the topics covered in this fine introduction. (Rev: BL 4/1/91) [983]

8639 Winter, Jane K. *Venezuela* (5–8). Illus. Series: Cultures of the World. 1991, Marshall Cavendish LB $35.64 (1-85435-386-1). In detailed text and color photographs, the land, people, and contemporary problems and concerns of Venezuela are introduced. (Rev: BL 4/1/91) [987]

8640 Wood, Tim. *The Incas* (6–9). Series: See Through History. 1996, Viking $16.99 (0-670-87037-4). A beautifully illustrated history of the Incas, their empire, and the eventual conquest by the Spaniards. (Rev: SLJ 3/97) [985.37]

8641 Worth, Richard. *Pizarro and the Conquest of the Incan Empire in World History* (6–9). Series: In World History. 2000, Enslow LB $19.95 (0-7660-1396-0). The explorer's conquest and its historical context and consequences are described. (Rev: HBG 9/00; SLJ 7/00) [985.019]

Polar Regions

8642 Aldis, Rodney. *Polar Lands* (5–8). Series: Ecology Watch. 1992, Dillon LB $13.95 (0-87518-494-4). The lands around both the North and South Poles are introduced, with discussion of their similarities and differences. (Rev: BL 11/1/92) [574.5]

8643 Armstrong, Jennifer. *Shipwreck at the Bottom of the World: The True Story of the Endurance Expedition* (7–12). 1999, Crown LB $19.99 (0-517-80014-4). A gripping account of Sir Ernest Shackleton's trans-Antarctic expedition, during which he and his team were trapped for 19 months in the frozen Antarctic wasteland, enduring extreme cold, dangerous ice, and a perilous 800-mile open-boat journey — all without losing a single man. (Rev: BL 12/1/98; HBG 9/99; SLJ 4/99) [919.8]

8644 Armstrong, Jennifer. *Spirit of Endurance* (4–8). Illus. 2000, Crown $17.95 (0-517-80091-8). An oversize book that tells the incredible survival story of Shackleton in the Antarctic. (Rev: BCCB 10/00; BL 9/15/00; HBG 3/01; SLJ 10/00) [919.8]

8645 Bial, Raymond. *The Inuit* (5–8). Series: Lifeways. 2001, Marshall Cavendish LB $32.79 (0-7614-1212-3). Using clear language and many intriguing illustrations, this is a fine introduction to the Inuit that begins with a folk story on the origins of the people and continues with material on a variety of basic topics. (Rev: BL 1/1–15/02; HBG 3/02; SLJ 4/02) [979.8]

8646 Billings, Henry. *Antarctica* (5–8). Illus. Series: Enchantment of the World. 1994, Children's paper $32.00 (0-516-02624-0). With color photographs on each page, this book explores the history and geography of the Antarctic region, with material on plant and animal life. (Rev: BL 12/15/94) [998.2]

8647 Bocknek, Jonathan. *Antarctica: The Last Wilderness* (5–8). Series: Understanding Global Issues. 2003, Smart Apple $19.95 (1-58340-356-6). This nicely-illustrated book introduces Antarctica with material on climate, animals, exploration, and possible future developments. (Rev: BL 11/15/03; SLJ 12/03) [998.9]

8648 Bredeson, Carmen. *After the Last Dog Died: The True-Life, Hair-Raising Adventures of Douglas Mawson and his 1911–1914 Antarctic Expedition* (5–8). Illus. 2003, National Geographic $18.95 (0-7922-6140-2). This enthralling story of courage in the face of starvation and harsh conditions draws on primary materials including the writings of expedition leader Mawson himself. (Rev: BL 11/1/03; SLJ 1/04*) [919.8]

8649 Fine, Jil. *The Shackleton Expedition* (5–8). Series: Survivor. 2002, Children's LB $20.00 (0-516-23904-X); paper $6.95 (0-516-23489-7). For reluctant readers, this is an accessible and exciting account of how Shackleton's men survived the perils of shipwreck in the ice. (Rev: SLJ 9/02) [919.8904]

8650 Green, Jen. *Exploring the Polar Regions* (4–8). Series: Voyages of Discovery. 1998, Bedrick $18.95 (0-87226-489-0). After an introduction to the polar regions, this book covers the exploration of these areas from the days of Eric the Red in A.D. 998 through 1993. (Rev: HBG 10/98; SLJ 4/98) [998]

8651 Hooper, Meredith. *Antarctic Journal: The Hidden Worlds of Antarctica's Animals* (5–7). 2001, National Geographic $16.95 (0-7922-7188-2). An exciting account of a summer the author spent at Palmer Station in the Antarctic and the wildlife there. (Rev: BL 6/1–15/01; HBG 10/01; SLJ 3/01) [988]

8652 Kimmel, Elizabeth C. *Ice Story: Shackleton's Lost Expedition* (4–7). Illus. 1999, Clarion $18.00 (0-395-91524-4). A fine, accurate, and engrossing description of Shackleton's Imperial Transatlantic Expedition to the Antarctic — one of the great survival stories of all time. (Rev: BL 4/1/99; HBG 10/99; SLJ 4/99) [910.9]

8653 Lambert, David. *Polar Regions* (5–8). Illus. 1988, Silver Burdett LB $12.95 (0-382-09502-2). Striking color photographs, maps, and diagrams highlight this description of the world's polar regions. (Rev: BL 4/1/88) [919.8]

8654 Loewen, Nancy, and Ann Bancroft. *Four to the Pole!* (6–9). Illus. 2001, Linnet $25.00 (0-208-02518-9). Diary entries, interviews, and expedition newsletters bring to life the physical and mental strength required of the first all-woman team to reach the South Pole. (Rev: BL 9/1/01; HBG 3/02; SLJ 8/01*; VOYA 10/01) [919.8904]

8655 Oberman, Sheldon. *The Shaman's Nephew: A Life in the Far North* (4–8). Illus. 2000, Stoddart $18.95 (0-7737-3200-4). This first-person narrative explores Inuit art and culture as experienced by Tookoome, an Inuit artist, who reflects on the daily life, beliefs, and myths of his people as presented in his work. (Rev: BL 6/1–15/00; SLJ 7/00) [971.9]

8656 Sayre, April P. *Antarctica* (5–8). Series: Seven Continents. 1998, Twenty-First Century LB $25.90 (0-7613-3227-8). A well-written and well-illustrated introduction to the Antarctic environment, including its geology, plants, animals, and research facilities. (Rev: BL 2/1/99; HBG 9/99; SLJ 4/99) [919.89]

8657 Senungetuk, Vivian, and Paul Tiulana. *A Place for Winter: Paul Tiulana's Story* (7–12). Illus. 1988, CIRI Foundation $17.95 (0-938227-02-5). The story of a King Island Eskimo boy, his childhood, and his people. (Rev: BL 5/15/88) [917.98]

8658 Shepherd, Donna Walsh. *Tundra* (4–8). Series: First Book: Science. 1996, Watts LB $23.00 (0-531-20249-6). The climate, life forms, and people of the Arctic tundra are introduced. (Rev: BL 2/1/97; SLJ 4/97) [551.4]

8659 Steger, Will, and Jon Bowermaster. *Over the Top of the World: Explorer Will Steger's Trek Across the Arctic* (4–7). Illus. 1997, Scholastic paper $17.95 (0-590-84860-7). Describes the grueling, dangerous adventures involved in a journey across the Arctic Ocean. (Rev: BCCB 2/97; BL 4/15/97; SLJ 4/97*) [919.804]

8660 Taylor, Barbara. *Arctic and Antarctic* (5–9). Series: Eyewitness Books. 1995, Knopf $19.00 (0-679-87257-4). Spectacular photographs and diagrams explain ice formations, tundra, and plant, sea, and wildlife of each region. (Rev: BL 8/95; SLJ 9/95) [508.311]

8661 Tessendorf, K. C. *Over the Edge: Flying with the Arctic Heroes* (4–8). Illus. 1998, Simon & Schuster $17.00 (0-689-31804-9). Beginning with Salomon Andree's ill-fated helium-balloon expedition to the North Pole, this chronicle includes other aerialists such as Roald Amundsen and Richard Byrd who also accepted the challenge. (Rev: BL 12/15/98; HB 11–12/98; SLJ 12/98) [910]

8662 Wallace, Mary. *The Inuksuk Book* (4–8). Illus. 1999, Owl $19.95 (1-895688-90-6); paper $12.95 (1-895688-91-4). Arctic life is introduced through an explanation of inuksuks (stone constructions, sometimes in the shape of human beings, that can act in place of people) and their role in Inuit culture. (Rev: BL 9/1/99; HBG 9/99; SLJ 6/99) [979.8]

8663 Warrick, Karen Clemens. *The Race for the North Pole in World History* (8–12). Series: In World History. 2002, Enslow LB $20.95 (0-7660-1933-0). Various explorers of the Arctic are introduced with emphasis of Robert Peary and Frederick Cook, both of whom claimed to be the first to reach the North Pole. (Rev: BL 3/15/03; HBG 10/03; VOYA 8/03) [979.8]

8664 Winckler, Suzanne. *Our Endangered Planet: Antarctica* (4–7). Illus. Series: Our Endangered Planet. 1992, Lerner LB $27.15 (0-8225-2506-2). Introduces the continent of Antarctica, including current environmental concerns. (Rev: BL 5/15/92) [918.8]

8665 Winner, Cherie. *Life in the Tundra* (5–8). Series: Ecosystems in Action. 2003, Lerner LB $26.60 (0-8225-4686-8). In text and pictures, the Arctic tundra is presented with material on the organisms that live there and how human life has changed this ecosystem. (Rev: BL 9/15/03; HBG 10/03) [551.4]

8666 Yue, Charlotte, and David Yue. *The Igloo* (6–8). Illus. 1988, Houghton $16.00 (0-395-44613-9). This account describes the geography of the Arctic and the life led by the native Inuit. (Rev: BL 9/1/88; BR 9–10/89; SLJ 12/88) [970.004]

United States

General History and Geography

8667 Andryszewski, Tricia. *Step by Step Along the Appalachian Trail* (4–8). 1998, Twenty-First Century LB $24.90 (0-7613-0273-5). A state-by-state tour of the Appalachian Trail, with material on the terrain, elevations, landmarks, and sites along the way. (Rev: BL 3/1/99; HBG 9/99; SLJ 4/99) [973]

8668 Baines, John. *The United States* (4–8). Illus. Series: Country Fact Files. 1994, Raintree Steck-Vaughn LB $27.12 (0-8114-1857-X). In a series of double-page spreads, basic information about the United States is given, including geography, economy, population, industry, education, government, and environment. (Rev: SLJ 7/94) [973]

8669 Baker, Patricia. *Fashions of a Decade: The 1940s* (7–12). Illus. Series: Fashions of a Decade. 1992, Facts on File $25.00 (0-8160-2467-7). Each book in the Fashions of a Decade series connects political and social history with particular modes of dress. Part of an 8-volume set that covers fashion from the 1920s through the 1990s. (Rev: BL 4/1/92) [391]

8670 Bolden, Tonya, ed. *33 Things Every Girl Should Know About Women's History: From Suffragettes to Skirt Lengths to the E. R. A.* (6–9). Illus. 2002, Random paper $12.95 (0-375-81122-2). This well-designed follow-up to *33 Things Every Girl Should Know* (1998) is an appealing compilation of articles, fiction, poetry, diary entries, charts, and a timeline that reveal much about women's roles in America — from the struggle for equal rights to fashion and 1960s singing groups. (Rev: BL 3/1/02; HB 7–8/02; HBG 10/02; SLJ 4/02; VOYA 12/02) [305.4]

8671 Boorstin, Daniel J., ed. *An American Primer* (7–12). 1968, NAL paper $19.95 (0-452-00922-7). Eighty-three documents vital to our history are reproduced plus accompanying background articles. [973]

8672 Brown, Gene. *Conflict in Europe and the Great Depression: World War I (1914–1940)* (5–8). Series: First Person America. 1994, Twenty-First Century LB $20.90 (0-8050-2585-5). The period from 1914 to 1940 is re-created through excerpts from original source material and texts describing events and social conditions. (Rev: BL 5/15/94; SLJ 11/94) [973.9]

8673 Burgan, Michael. *Colonial and Revolutionary Times: A Watts Guide* (5–8). 2003, Watts LB $40.00 (0-531-15453-X). An appealing, alphabetical guide to the people, places, ideas, and events of colonial and revolutionary times. (Rev: LMC 11–12/03; SLJ 7/03) [973.2]

8674 Collier, Christopher, and James Lincoln Collier. *The Rise of the Cities: 1820–1920* (5–8). Illus. Series: The Drama of American History. 2001, Marshall Cavendish LB $29.93 (0-7614-1051-1). In this highly illustrated volume, the Colliers paint a broad picture of the process of urbanization in the United States, tracing the problems involved and the growing prominence of cities in American life. (Rev: BL 3/15/01; HBG 10/01; SLJ 7/01) [973]

8675 Collier, Christopher, and James Lincoln Collier. *The United States Enters the World Stage: From the Alaska Purchase Through World War I* (5–8). Series: The Drama of American History. 2001, Marshall Cavendish LB $29.93 (0-7614-1053-8). Covering the years 1867 through 1918, this well-illustrated account traces America's emergence as a world power. (Rev: BL 3/15/01; HBG 10/01) [973.9]

8676 Colman, Penny. *Girls: A History of Growing Up Female in America* (5–8). Illus. 2000, Scholastic paper $18.95 (0-590-37129-0). Using diaries, mem-

oirs, letters, magazine articles, and other sources, the author presents a history of girls in America from the first females to cross the Bering Strait to the present day. (Rev: BCCB 2/00; BL 2/1/00; HBG 10/00; SLJ 3/00) [305.23]

8677 Cooper, Jason. *Árboles / Trees* (4–8). Trans. by Blanca Rey. Illus. Series: La Guía de Rourke Para los Símbolos de los Estados/Rourke's Guide to State Symbols. 2002, Rourke LB $29.93 (1-58952-399-7). The 50 state trees are introduced in bilingual text and illustrations. Also use *Aves / Birds*, *Banderas / Flags*, and *Flores / Flowers*. (Rev: SLJ 3/03) [582]

8678 Currie, Stephen. *The Mississippi* (5–8). Series: Rivers of the World. 2003, Gale LB $27.45 (1-59018-061-5). A comprehensive look at this important river's history, geology, agricultural and industrial significance, environmental problems, and the floods that threaten surrounding communities. (Rev: SLJ 9/03) [977]

8679 Dolan, Edward F. *The American Indian Wars* (5–8). Illus. 2003, Millbrook LB $29.90 (0-7613-1968-9). Four hundred years of conflict are covered in this volume that looks at the causes, details the key battles and events, and provides portraits of the key participants. (Rev: BL 12/1/03) [973.04]

8680 Druckman, Nancy. *American Flags: Designs for a Young Nation* (8–12). Illus. 2003, Abrams $16.95 (0-8109-4506-1). Photographs of more than 60 flags form the basis of this guide to the evolution of the national symbol. (Rev: BL 11/1/03; SLJ 10/03) [929.9]

8681 Dudley, William, ed. *The 1960s* (6–12). Series: America's Decades. 2000, Greenhaven LB $29.96 (0-7377-0306-7); paper $17.96 (0-7377-0305-9). The Vietnam War, the moon landing, assassinations, Woodstock, and the civil rights movement are some of the topics covered in this collection of articles on the 1960s. (Rev: BL 7/00) [073.9]

8682 Dudley, William, ed. *Opposing Viewpoints in American History, Vol. 1: From Colonial Times to Reconstruction* (8–12). Illus. Series: Opposing Viewpoints. 1996, Greenhaven LB $37.44 (1-56510-348-3); paper $27.45 (1-56510-347-5). Alternative primary source opinions are given for such issues in early American history as Native American rights, acceptance of the Bill of Rights, and slavery. (Rev: BL 3/15/96) [973]

8683 Dudley, William, ed. *Opposing Viewpoints in American History, Vol. 2: From Reconstruction to the Present* (8–12). Illus. Series: Opposing Viewpoints. 1996, Greenhaven LB $37.44 (1-56510-350-5); paper $36.75 (1-56510-349-1). Conflicting opinions from primary sources are presented on such topics as women's rights, U.S. participation in World War I, the dropping of the atomic bomb, the

New Deal, and the Cold War. (Rev: BL 3/15/96) [973]

8684 Ehlert, Willis J. *America's Heritage: Capitols of the United States* (6–12). 1993, State House Publg. paper $10.95 (0-9634908-3-4). Provides data on state capitals and capitol buildings, descriptions of architectural details, brief state histories, state symbols, and an extensive bibliography. (Rev: BL 4/15/93) [725]

8685 English, June A., and Thomas D. Jones. *Scholastic Encyclopedia of the United States at War* (5–8). 1998, Scholastic paper $18.95 (0-590-59959-3). A heavily illustrated volume that traces America's wars from the Revolution to the Gulf War, with each chapter including a timeline, a map, and a discussion of causes, battles, new technologies, and the aftermath. (Rev: BL 10/15/98; SLJ 2/99) [973]

8686 Feinstein, Stephen. *The 1910s: From World War I to Ragtime Music* (5–8). Series: Decades of the 20th Century. 2001, Enslow LB $17.95 (0-7660-1611-0). The events of the 1910s are covered in chapters on lifestyle and fashion, arts and entertainment, sports, politics, and science, technology, and medicine. Also use *The 1920s: From Prohibition to Charles Lindbergh* (2001). (Rev: HBG 10/02; SLJ 2/02) [973.9]

8687 Feinstein, Stephen. *The 1940s: From World War II to Jackie Robinson* (5–8). Illus. Series: Decades of the 20th Century. 2000, Enslow LB $17.95 (0-7660-1428-2). A lively look at events of the 1940s, covering everything from fashion and fads to politics, science, technology, medicine, and sports. Also use *The 1930s: From the Great Depression to the Wizard of Oz* (2001) and *The 1950s: From the Korean War to Elvis* (2000). (Rev: HBG 3/01; SLJ 5/01) [973.9]

8688 Feinstein, Stephen. *The 1960s: From the Vietnam War to Flower Power* (4–7). Illus. Series: Decades of the 20th Century. 2000, Enslow LB $17.95 (0-7660-1426-6). An account of America's turbulent 1960s that includes lifestyles, politics, fashion, fads, and entertainment. (Rev: BL 10/15/00; HBG 3/01; SLJ 12/00) [973.92]

8689 Feinstein, Stephen. *The 1970s: From Watergate to Disco* (4–7). Series: Decades of the 20th Century. 2000, Enslow LB $17.95 (0-7660-1425-8). This book covers the people and events of the 1970s along with developments in such areas as politics, science, and sports. (Rev: BL 10/15/00; HBG 3/01; SLJ 12/00) [973.9]

8690 Feinstein, Stephen. *The 1990s: From the Persian Gulf War to Y2K* (5–8). Series: Decades of the 20th Century. 2001, Enslow LB $17.95 (0-7660-1613-7). The events of the 1990s are covered in chapters on lifestyle and fashion; arts and entertainment; sports; politics; and science, technology, and medicine. (Rev: HBG 10/02; SLJ 2/02) [973.9]

8691 Findling, John E., and Frank W. Thackeray, eds. *Events That Changed America in the Eighteenth Century* (7–12). 1998, Greenwood $45.00 (0-313-29082-2). Using an essay format, this overview of the 18th century covers the French and Indian War, the Stamp Act, the Boston Tea Party, the American Revolution, and the Constitutional Convention. (Rev: BR 1–2/99; SLJ 5/99) [973.3]

8692 Fischer, Maureen M. *Nineteenth Century Lumber Camp Cooking* (4–7). Series: Exploring History Through Simple Recipes. 2000, Capstone LB $22.60 (0-7368-0604-0). After describing life in a lumber camp more than a hundred years ago, this book supplies some authentic recipes. (Rev: BL 3/1/01; HBG 10/01; SLJ 4/01) [973.8]

8693 Foster, Genevieve, and Joanna Foster. *George Washington's World*. Rev. ed. (5–8). Illus. 1997, Beautiful Feet paper $15.95 (0-9643803-4-X). A new edition of this 50-year-old book that re-creates what was happening in the world during Washington's life, now with expanded coverage on minorities. (Rev: SLJ 3/98) [909]

8694 Fyson, Nance Lui. *The 1940s* (6–9). Illus. 1990, Batsford $19.95 (0-7134-5628-0). The story of World War II and its aftermath are covered plus developments in such areas as sports, the arts, science, and invention. (Rev: SLJ 7/90) [973.9]

8695 Garrington, Sally. *The United States* (6–10). Series: Countries of the World. 2003, Facts on File $30.00 (0-8160-5385-5). This basic work supplies on overview of information on the United States with emphasis on present conditions. (Rev: BL 1/1–15/04) [973]

8696 Gay, Kathlyn, and Martin Gay. *After the Shooting Stops: The Aftermath of War* (7–12). 1998, Millbrook LB $24.90 (0-7613-3006-2). A look at the political, economic, and social changes that have followed U.S. involvement in various wars. (Rev: BL 8/98; HBG 3/99; SLJ 9/98) [355.00973]

8697 Gerdes, Louise I., ed. *The 1940s* (6–12). Series: America's Decades. 2000, Greenhaven LB $29.96 (0-7377-0302-4); paper $17.96 (0-7377-0301-6). This anthology of articles and essays deal with the beginning of the atomic age, the growth of motion pictures, and World War II: its causes, effects, home front activities, and the battles. (Rev: BL 7/00) [973.9]

8698 Giblin, James Cross, ed. *The Century That Was: Reflections on the Last One Hundred Years* (6–12). Illus. 2000, Simon & Schuster $20.00 (0-689-82281-2). Eleven well-known writers for young people, including Katherine Paterson, Walter Dean Myers, and Laurence Pringle, write about the last century in America and cover such topics as civil rights, religion, conservation, and sports. (Rev: BL 3/1/00; HB 3–4/00; HBG 9/00; SLJ 7/00) [973.91.]

8699 Grant, R. G. *The Seventies* (4–7). Series: A Look at Life In. 2000, Raintree Steck-Vaughn LB $27.12 (0-7398-1340-4). After the major news events of the 1970s, this book describes important developments in science, the arts, and popular culture. Also use *The Sixties* (2000). (Rev: HBG 10/00; SLJ 9/00) [973.9]

8700 Gross, Ernie. *The American Years: A Chronology of United States History* (6–12). 1998, Scribners $130.00 (0-684-80590-1). A chronology of events, developments, and trends from 1776 to 1997, in the following categories: international, national, transportation, religion, entertainment, education, arts/music, sports, business/industry/inventions, science/medicine, and literature/journalism. (Rev: BL 7/99; BR 9–10/99; SLJ 8/99) [973]

8701 Haban, Rita D. *How Proudly They Wave: Flags of the Fifty States* (4–9). Illus. 1989, Lerner LB $23.93 (0-8225-1799-X). Pictures of the state flags are accompanied by background information. (Rev: BL 12/15/89; SLJ 3/90) [929.9]

8702 Hakim, Joy. *An Age of Extremes.* 2nd ed. (5–8). Series: A History of Us. 1999, Oxford LB $19.95 (0-19-512765-X); paper $13.95 (0-19-512766-8). A thorough and accurate history of the United States' coming of age after Reconstruction — from 1870 through World War I. (Rev: BL 12/15/99) [973.8]

8703 Hakim, Joy. *Sourcebook: Documents that Shaped the American Nation* (5–8). Series: A History of Us. 1999, Oxford $219.45 (0-19-512773-0). This, the final volume of the outstanding A History of Us series, consists of the complete texts of 94 essential documents in American history, with a commentary on each. (Rev: BL 12/15/99; SLJ 5/00) [973]

8704 Hakim, Joy. *War, Peace, and All That Jazz.* 2nd ed (5–8). Series: A History of Us. 1999, Oxford LB $19.95 (0-19-512767-6). Political, social, and cultural events and developments are traced in this fascinating account of life in the United States between the world wars and through World War II, with coverage of the Jazz Age, the Great Depression, and the war itself. (Rev: BL 12/15/99) [973.9]

8705 Head, Judith. *America's Daughters: 400 Years of American Women* (6–12). Illus. 1999, Perspectives paper $16.95 (0-9622036-8-8). This overview of the part played by women in American history highlights the work of many who have been unjustly ignored. (Rev: BL 1/1–15/00; SLJ 3/00) [305.4.]

8706 Heinemann, Sue. *The New York Public Library Amazing Women in History* (6–10). Illus. 1998, Wiley paper $12.95 (0-471-19216-3). Using a question-and-answer format, this work supplies hundreds of facts about women in American history, arranged by topics that include activism, sports,

recreation, and racial and ethnic groups. (Rev: BL 4/15/98; BR 11–12/98; SLJ 8/98) [973]

8707 Hoobler, Dorothy, and Thomas Hoobler. *Real American Girls Tell Their Own Stories* (4–7). Illus. 1999, Simon & Schuster $12.95 (0-689-82083-6). Excerpts from personal diaries and autobiographies are used to introduce a number of young American girls from colonial times to the 1950s. (Rev: BCCB 12/99; BL 10/15/99; HBG 3/00; SLJ 12/99; VOYA 4/00) [305.23]

8708 Isaacs, Sally Senzell. *America in the Time of Franklin Delano Roosevelt: The Story of Our Nation from Coast to Coast, from 1929 to 1948* (4–8). Series: America in the Time Of. 1999, Heinemann LB $30.35 (1-57572-761-7). Using the life of Roosevelt as a framework, this account describes life in America during the Great Depression and World War II. (Rev: SLJ 5/00) [973.9]

8709 Isaacs, Sally Senzell. *America in the Time of Susan B. Anthony: The Story of Our Nation from Coast to Coast, from 1845 to 1928* (4–8). 1999, Heinemann LB $30.35 (1-57572-763-3). Using the life of Susan B. Anthony as a framework, this work covers topics including woman's suffrage, poverty, and World War I. (Rev: SLJ 5/00) [973.9]

8710 Jaffe, Steven H. *Who Were the Founding Fathers? Two Hundred Years of Reinventing American History* (7–12). Illus. 1996, Holt $18.95 (0-8050-3102-2). An exploration of our nation's founding fathers and how their ideas have been interpreted and reinterpreted by groups as diverse as suffragettes, the Ku Klux Klan, McCarthyites, and the yippies to promote their programs and theories. An excellent source for material on the Revolution, the Constitution, and issues associated with civil rights, immigration, citizenship, and slavery. (Rev: BL 12/1/96*; BR 3–4/97; SLJ 1/97*; VOYA 4/97) [973.3]

8711 Johnston, Robert D. *The Making of America* (5–8). Illus. 2002, National Geographic $29.95 (0-7922-6944-6). An informative and balanced overview of American history, this appealing volume divides American history into eight periods; in addition to the narrative, each period includes profiles of two major figures and examines important issues of the time. (Rev: BL 1/1–15/03; HBG 3/03; SLJ 12/02*) [973]

8712 Jones, Rebecca C. *The President Has Been Shot! True Stories of the Attacks on Ten U.S. Presidents* (4–8). Illus. 1996, Dutton $15.99 (0-525-45333-4). In chronological order, ten attacks on U.S. presidents are presented in a very readable text. (Rev: BCCB 9/96; BL 7/96; SLJ 9/96) [364.1]

8713 Kalman, Bobbie, and Greg Nickles. *Spanish Missions* (4–7). Illus. Series: Historic Communities. 1996, Crabtree LB $21.28 (0-86505-436-3); paper $7.95 (0-86505-466-5). In double-page spreads, this book covers the building of the mission in the southern United States and of its functions: teaching Christianity, educating children, and supplying housing and food. (Rev: SLJ 4/97) [973]

8714 Katz, William L. *Exploration to the War of 1812, 1492–1814* (7–10). Series: History of Multicultural America. 1993, Raintree Steck-Vaughn LB $27.11 (0-8114-6275-7). Discusses America from before European colonization through the formation of the new nation, exploration of new territory, and the War of 1812. Includes the role and treatment of Native Americans, women, slaves, and free blacks. (Rev: BL 6/1–15/93) [973]

8715 King, David C. *First Facts About U.S. History* (4–8). Illus. Series: First Facts. 1996, Blackbirch $34.94 (1-56711-168-8). A brief chronological survey of major events in U.S. history. (Rev: BL 7/96; SLJ 7/96) [973]

8716 Langdon, William Chauncey. *Everyday Things in American Life, 1776–1876* (7–12). Illus. 1941, Macmillan $45.00 (0-684-17416-2). This illustrated account covers such topics as clothing, machinery, canals, bridges, and turnpikes. [973]

8717 McCormick, Anita Louise. *The Industrial Revolution in American History* (5–8). Illus. Series: In American History. 1998, Enslow LB $20.95 (0-89490-985-1). A description of the causes of the Industrial Revolution and the changes that it brought to the United States up to 1946. (Rev: BL 9/1/98; BR 11–12/98) [338.0973]

8718 MacDonald, Fiona. *Women in 19th-Century America* (4–8). Series: The Other Half of History. 1999, Bedrick $17.95 (0-87226-566-8). A very brief account of the history of women and their progress during the 19th century with information on some important individuals. (Rev: HBG 3/00; SLJ 11/99) [973.6]

8719 Mee, Sue. *1900–20: Linen and Lace* (5–10). Series: 20th Century Fashion. 2000, Gareth Stevens LB $25.26 (0-8368-2598-5). The fashion and design of the first two decades of the last century are pictured and described in this book that also contains a great deal of social history. (Rev: HBG 10/00; SLJ 6/00) [973.9]

8720 Miller, Marilyn. *Words That Built a Nation: A Young Person's Collection of Historic American Documents* (4–8). Illus. 1999, Scholastic paper $18.95 (0-590-29881-X). A collection of 37 documents important in American history — from the Mayflower Compact and the Declaration of Independence to Hillary Rodham Clinton's address to the United Nations Conference on Women and Malcolm X's "The Ballot or the Bullet" speech. (Rev: BL 10/15/99; HBG 3/00; SLJ 2/00) [973]

8721 Moser, Diane, and Raymond Spangenburg. *Political and Social Movements* (7–12). Illus. Series: American Historic Places. 1998, Facts on

File $25.00 (0-8160-3404-4). Important political, philosophical, and social movements that changed America are traced using as a backdrop the places where they originated or took place, such as Valley Forge, Ellis Island, Ford's Theater, Clara Barton's house, and Wounded Knee, from the Revolution through the civil rights era. (Rev: BL 5/15/98; SLJ 8/98) [973]

8722 Nash, Gary B. *Landmarks of the American Revolution* (5–8). Series: American Landmarks. 2003, Oxford LB $30.00 (0-19-512849-4). Landmark sites such as Independence Hall, Valley Forge National Historic Park, Faneuil Hall, and Yorktown Battlefield are introduced with excerpts from primary documents such as letters and broadsides. (Rev: SLJ 8/03) [973.3]

8723 Pollard, Michael. *The Mississippi* (5–8). Illus. Series: Great Rivers. 1997, Benchmark LB $22.79 (0-7614-0502-X). A history of this great river and its influence on American history, with photographs, maps, and diagrams. (Rev: HBG 3/98; SLJ 3/98) [917.7]

8724 Rawlins, Carol B. *The Colorado River* (4–8). Series: Watts Library. 1999, Watts LB $24.00 (0-531-11738-3). With full-color photographs and maps that complement the text, this book traces the famous Rocky Mountain waterway from north-central Colorado through the Southwest into the Gulf of California and covers its history and uses. (Rev: BL 1/1–15/00; SLJ 2/00) [973]

8725 Ruth, Maria Mudd. *The Mississippi River* (7–12). Illus. Series: Ecosystems of North America. 2000, Benchmark LB $18.95 (0-7614-0934-3). A detailed look at the largest river in North America, its flora and fauna, and the effects of human development on the ecosystem. (Rev: HBG 3/01; SLJ 4/01) [577.6]

8726 St. George, Judith. *In the Line of Fire* (6–9). Illus. 1999, Holiday $18.95 (0-8234-1428-0). This book describes each of the attempts to assassinate U.S. presidents, some successful and some not, and gives information on both the targets and the criminals. (Rev: BCCB 1/00; BL 12/1/99; HBG 4/00) [364.15]

8727 Sandak, Cass R. *The United States* (4–8). Illus. Series: Modern Industrial World. 1996, Raintree Steck-Vaughn LB $24.26 (0-8172-4556-1). An examination of the economic and industrial situation in the United States, with additional information on education, living standards, and related subjects. (Rev: BL 2/15/97; SLJ 8/97) [973]

8728 Sheafer, Silvia A. *Women in America's Wars* (6–12). Illus. 1996, Enslow LB $20.95 (0-89490-553-8). From the American Revolution to the Persian Gulf War, this account profiles 10 women and the amazingly diversified roles they played in U.S.

wars. (Rev: BL 4/15/96; BR 9–10/96; SLJ 5/96; VOYA 6/96) [355]

8729 Smith-Baranzini, Marlene, and Howard Egger-Bovet. *Brown Paper School USKids History: Book of the New American Nation* (5–7). Illus. 1995, Little, Brown paper $14.95 (0-316-22206-2). From George Washington to the building of the Erie Canal, key issues and people in American history are introduced. (Rev: BL 8/95; SLJ 8/95) [973.5]

8730 Sonneborn, Liz. *The American West: An Illustrated History* (6–12). Illus. 2002, Scholastic $19.95 (0-439-21970-1). An inviting introduction to the settlement of the American West, beginning with the first Native Americans and ending in the present day. (Rev: BL 12/15/02; HBG 3/03; SLJ 2/03) [978]

8731 Stewart, Gail B. *1900s* (5–8). Illus. Series: Timelines. 1990, Macmillan LB $11.95 (0-89686-471-5). Events and trivia of the decade, with many illustrations. Also use *1910s; 1920s; 1930s* (all 1989). (Rev: SLJ 6/90) [973.9]

8732 Stienecker, David L. *First Facts About the States* (4–8). Series: First Facts. 1996, Blackbirch $34.94 (1-56711-166-1). Using a double-page spread for each state, this account gives basic information on such topics as state symbols, mottos, history, geography, and landmarks. (Rev: SLJ 7/96) [973]

8733 Stone, Tanya Lee. *The Great Depression and World War II* (5–8). Series: Making of America. 2001, Raintree Steck-Vaughn LB $28.54 (0-8172-5710-1). Concise text and attractive illustrations recreate the history of America from 1929 through World War II. (Rev: BL 9/15/01; HBG 10/01) [973.9]

8734 Stone, Tanya Lee. *The Progressive Era and World War I* (5–8). Series: Making of America. 2001, Raintree Steck-Vaughn LB $28.54 (0-8172-5709-8). Roughly the first 20 years of the 20th century in American history are retold in this history that also looks at home life, culture, and entertainment. (Rev: BL 9/15/01; HBG 10/01; SLJ 6/01) [973.9]

8735 Streissguth, Thomas. *Utopian Visionaries* (7–12). Illus. 1999, Oliver LB $19.95 (1-881508-47-1). This account presents material on attempts to build utopian communities in the U.S. during the 18th and 19th centuries by such visionaries as Ann Lee, a Shaker, and John Humphrey Noyes, who created the Oneida community. (Rev: BL 12/15/99; HBG 4/00; SLJ 11/99) [321]

8736 Thro, Ellen, and Andrew K. Frank. *Growing and Dividing* (5–8). Series: The Making of America. 2001, Raintree Steck-Vaughn LB $28.54 (0-8172-5704-7). The story of the development of the eastern United States from the early days of the Republic through the clashes that led to the Civil War. (Rev: BL 4/15/01; HBG 10/01) [973.5]

8737 *United States in Pictures* (5–8). Illus. Series: Visual Geography. 1995, Lerner LB $25.55 (0-8225-1896-1). An attractive basic introduction to the geography, history, and people of the United States. (Rev: BL 8/95) [973]

8738 Uschan, Michael V. *The 1910s* (7–10). Illus. 1998, Lucent LB $27.45 (1-56006-551-6). This volume presents an overview of the 1910s, highlighting social and technical developments as well as the U.S. role in world affairs and World War I. (Rev: SLJ 4/99) [973.9]

8739 Uschan, Michael V. *The 1940s* (5–10). Series: Cultural History of the United States. 1998, Lucent LB $18.96 (1-56510-554-0). Life at home and abroad during World War II dominate this book, which also discusses the Great Depression, the New Deal, events leading up to U.S. participation in the war, the beginnings of the Cold War, the growth of suburban living, and the rise of television, with sidebars on such topics as the Holocaust, the influences of radio, movies, and comics, 1940s slang, and the first computers. (Rev: SLJ 1/99) [973.9]

8740 Van Zandt, Eleanor. *A History of the United States Through Art* (5–8). Illus. Series: History Through Art. 1996, Thomson Learning LB $5.00 (1-56847-443-1). American history is covered in 21 double-page spreads that feature text and famous artworks. (Rev: BL 3/1/96; SLJ 2/96) [973]

8741 Wacker, Grant. *Religion in Nineteenth Century America* (5–8). Series: Religion in American Life. 2000, Oxford $28.00 (0-19-511021-8). This is the story of how religion in America affected such 19th-century events as the westward movement, the Civil War, and immigration, with additional coverage of the careers of such people as Sojourner Truth and Mary Baker Eddy. (Rev: BL 6/1–15/00; HBG 10/00; SLJ 8/00) [973]

8742 Walsh, Kieran J. *The Mississippi* (4–7). Series: Great Rivers of the World. 2003, World Almanac LB $26.60 (0-8368-5444-6). An exploration of the Mississippi's flow, history, and animals and plants, with discussion of the settlements along its banks, the industries it supports, recreation on its waters, and environmental threats to the river. (Rev: SLJ 9/03) [977]

8743 Webb, Marcus. *The United States* (5–8). Series: Modern Nations of the World. 2000, Lucent LB $27.45 (1-56006-663-6). A mature look at the past and present United States with an extended section on modern culture. (Rev: BL 5/15/00; HBG 10/00) [973]

8744 Wilbur, Keith C. *Revolutionary Medicine, 1700–1800* (4–8). Illus. Series: Illustrated Living History. 1996, Chelsea $21.95 (0-7910-4532-3). In a large-book format, this account gives a great deal of information — some gruesome, some funny —

about medicine in 18th-century America. (Rev: BL 6/1–15/97; SLJ 7/97) [973.3]

8745 Wormser, Richard. *American Childhoods: Three Centuries of Youth at Risk* (7–12). Illus. 1996, Walker LB $17.85 (0-8027-8427-5). A graphic, realistic picture of childhood and growing up in America from the repressive Puritans to the present day with chapters on work, crime, disease, education, sex, and related topics. (Rev: BL 9/15/96; BR 11–12/96; SLJ 9/96; VOYA 12/96) [305.23]

8746 Wormser, Richard. *Hoboes: Wandering in America, 1870–1940* (6–12). Illus. 1994, Walker $17.95 (0-8027-8279-5). This account covers the history, rules, literature, songs, and customs of those who rode the rails from the end of the Civil War to the outbreak of World War II. (Rev: BL 6/1–15/94; SLJ 7/94) [305.5]

8747 Wukovits, John F., ed. *The 1910s* (6–12). Series: America's Decades. 2000, Greenhaven LB $29.96 (0-7377-0296-6); paper $17.96 (0-7377-0295-8). Articles in this anthology cover important events of the decade, including World War I, and introduce such personalities as Charlie Chaplin, Alvin York, Woodrow Wilson, and Henry Ford. (Rev: BL 7/00) [973.9]

8748 Wukovits, John F., ed. *The 1920s* (6–12). Series: America's Decades. 2000, Greenhaven LB $29.96 (0-7377-0298-2); paper $17.96 (0-7377-0297-4). This anthology of articles about the 20s covers such topics as prohibition, the stock market crash of 1929, and the rising importance of radio. (Rev: BL 7/00; SLJ 9/00) [973.9]

Historical Periods

NATIVE AMERICANS

8749 Aaseng, Nathan. *Cherokee Nation v. Georgia: The Forced Removal of a People* (6–9). Illus. Series: Famous Trials. 2000, Lucent paper $16.20 (1-56510-628-8). This account chronicles the struggle between settlers and Native Americans that led to the court case and the decision, under President Andrew Jackson, that set the course of Native American relations for the next half century. (Rev: BL 9/15/00; SLJ 7/97) [973]

8750 Ake, Anne. *The Apache* (7–10). Series: Indigenous Peoples of North America. 2000, Lucent LB $19.96 (1-56006-616-4). The savage warriors of the American Southwest are featured with material on their history, religion, culture, and present affairs. (Rev: BL 9/15/00) [973]

8751 Anderson, Dale. *The Anasazi Culture at Mesa Verde* (5–8). Series: Landmark Events in American History. 2003, World Almanac LB $26.60 (0-8368-5371-7). The story of the native people from the region around the Four Corners and of their many cultural accomplishment including basketry, pot-

tery, and urban architecture. (Rev: BL 10/15/03) [973]

8752 Arnold, Caroline. *The Ancient Cliff Dwellers of Mesa Verde* (4–7). 1992, Houghton $16.00 (0-395-56241-4). This is the fascinating story of the Anasazi of southwestern Colorado, who made their homes in the cliffs of steep canyons and later abandoned them. (Rev: BL 5/1/92; SLJ 7/92*) [978.8]

8753 Ashabranner, Brent. *A Strange and Distant Shore: Indians of the Great Plains in Exile* (6–9). 1996, Cobblehill $16.99 (0-525-65201-9). This is the story of 72 Plains Indians from different tribes who were imprisoned in St. Augustine, Florida, between 1875 and 1878 and of the art they produced. (Rev: BL 7/96; BR 3–4/97; SLJ 9/96) [973.8]

8754 Ayer, Eleanor. *The Anasazi* (6–9). 1993, Walker LB $15.85 (0-8027-8185-3). An in-depth look at the Anasazi Indians of the Southwest, who came to this country about 2,000 years ago. (Rev: BL 3/1/93; SLJ 11/93) [979]

8755 Barth, Kelly. *Native Americans of the Northwest Plateau* (7–10). Series: Indigenous Peoples of North America. 2002, Gale LB $27.45 (1-56006-877-9). This work explores the social, cultural, and political history and contemporary life of these groups of Native Americans found in the central Northwest. (Rev: BL 4/15/02) [970.004]

8756 Bial, Raymond. *The Apache* (5–8). Series: Lifeways. 2000, Benchmark LB $32.79 (0-7614-0939-4). Presents the dramatic, often tragic history of the Apache Indians, with biographies of leaders such as Geronimo and a description of the social and cultural life of these nomadic people. (Rev: BL 11/15/00; HBG 3/01; SLJ 3/01) [973]

8757 Bial, Raymond. *The Cheyenne* (5–8). Series: Lifeways. 2000, Benchmark LB $32.79 (0-7614-0938-6). Part of the Great Plains Indian group, the Cheyenne's daily life, religious beliefs, social system, and history are introduced in this book. (Rev: BL 11/15/00; HBG 3/01; SLJ 3/01) [973]

8758 Bial, Raymond. *The Comanche* (4–8). Series: Lifeways. 1999, Benchmark LB $32.79 (0-7614-0864-9). This impressive volume gives an accurate picture of the social and political life of the Comanche from their early history to the present day. (Rev: BL 3/15/00; HBG 10/00; SLJ 3/00) [973]

8759 Bial, Raymond. *The Haida* (5–8). Series: Lifeways. 2000, Benchmark LB $32.79 (0-7614-0937-8). This book describes these Native Americans of the Northwest and introduces their artistic and carving skills, their social system, beliefs, history, and daily life. (Rev: BL 11/15/00; HBG 3/01; SLJ 3/01) [973]

8760 Bial, Raymond. *The Huron* (5–8). Series: Lifeways. 2000, Benchmark LB $32.79 (0-7614-0940-8). Color pictures and clear text describe this Indian group's past and present and give details of their daily life, religion, and rituals. (Rev: BL 11/15/00; HBG 3/01; SLJ 3/01) [973]

8761 Bial, Raymond. *The Long Walk: The Story of Navajo Captivity* (6–9). Series: Great Journeys. 2002, Marshall Cavendish LB $21.95 (0-7614-1322-7). The story of the Navajo nation and the imprisonment that lasted until 1868 when they were given their own reservation. (Rev: BL 3/15/03; HBG 3/03; SLJ 3/03) [973]

8762 Bial, Raymond. *The Nez Perce* (5–8). Series: Lifeways. 2001, Marshall Cavendish LB $32.79 (0-7614-1210-7). This attractively illustrated account gives basic material on the historical and social aspects of this Native American tribe, including their food, clothing, and culture. (Rev: BL 1/1–15/02; HBG 3/02; SLJ 4/02) [973]

8763 Bial, Raymond. *The Ojibwe* (5–8). Illus. Series: Lifeways. 1999, Marshall Cavendish LB $32.79 (0-7614-0863-0). Topics covered in this introduction to the Ojibwe nation include history, traditions, beliefs, and the nation today. (Rev: BL 3/1/00; HBG 10/00; SLJ 3/00) [977]

8764 Bial, Raymond. *The Powhatan* (5–8). Series: Lifeways. 2001, Marshall Cavendish LB $32.79 (0-7614-1209-3). The story of the Powhatan tribe of Virginia, whose members included Pocahontas, with material on their history and various aspects of their culture. (Rev: BL 1/1–15/02; HBG 3/02) [973]

8765 Bial, Raymond. *The Pueblo* (5–8). Illus. Series: Lifeways. 1999, Marshall Cavendish LB $32.79 (0-7614-0861-4). Good photographs and a lucid text combine to produce a fine introduction to the Pueblo Indians, their history, culture, traditions, present status, and notable members of the nation. (Rev: BL 3/1/00; HBG 10/00; SLJ 3/00) [978.9]

8766 Bial, Raymond. *The Seminole* (4–8). Series: Lifeways. 1999, Benchmark LB $32.79 (0-7614-0862-2). Topics covered in this account of the Seminole Indians include history, daily life, religious beliefs, sacred rituals, and attitudes toward themselves. (Rev: BL 3/15/00; HBG 10/00; SLJ 3/00) [973]

8767 Bial, Raymond. *The Shoshone* (5–8). Series: Lifeways. 2001, Marshall Cavendish LB $32.79 (0-7614-1211-5). The story of the Native American tribe of buffalo hunters who lived in the Northwest, with material on their history, culture, language, food, and clothing. (Rev: BL 1/1–15/02; HBG 3/02) [973]

8768 Bjornlund, Lydia. *The Iroquois* (7–10). Series: Indigenous Peoples of North America. 2000, Lucent LB $19.96 (1-56006-618-0). This volume gives material on the history, culture, and present condition of the Indian nation that was the most powerful Native American group in the 17th century. (Rev: BL 9/15/00) [973]

8769 Bond, Fred G. *Flatboating on the Yellowstone, 1877* (7–12). 1998, Ward Hill $19.95 (1-886747-03-2). A first-person account of the relocation in 1877 of Chief Joseph and other Nez Perce Indians from Oregon to Oklahoma by raft down the Yellowstone and Missouri Rivers, written by their pilot, who documented the trip for the New York Public Library in 1925. (Rev: BL 12/15/98) [973]

8770 Bonvillain, Nancy. *The Inuit* (6–9). Series: Indians of North America. 1995, Chelsea paper $9.95 (0-7910-0380-9). A history of the present residents of the tundra and arctic regions of North America, with material on their daily life, beliefs, culture, and origins. (Rev: BL 10/15/95) [971]

8771 Bonvillain, Nancy. *Native American Medicine* (6–9). Series: Indians of North America. 1997, Chelsea LB $21.95 (0-7910-4041-0). This volume follows the course of Native American medical practices, healing rituals, and treatments through history and offers an interesting account of America's first doctors. (Rev: BL 11/15/97; BR 1–2/98) [973]

8772 Bonvillain, Nancy. *Native American Religion* (6–10). Series: Indians of North America. 1995, Chelsea LB $21.95 (0-7910-2652-3); paper $9.95 (0-7910-3479-8). Explanations of native spiritual life, emphasizing the natural world and the earth. Also discusses holistic approaches toward illness and well-being. (Rev: BL 3/1/96; SLJ 2/96) [973]

8773 Bonvillain, Nancy. *The Sac and Fox* (6–9). Series: Indians of North America. 1995, Chelsea $19.95 (0-7910-1684-6). The tragic story of these Native American peoples whose fight to maintain their lands eventually led to the Black Hawk War and their resettlement in the Midwest. (Rev: BL 7/95) [977.1]

8774 Bonvillain, Nancy. *The Santee Sioux* (6–9). Series: Indians of North America. 1996, Chelsea LB $21.95 (0-7910-1685-4); paper $9.95 (0-7910-3482-8). This account of the Native American tribe that lived on the Great Plains covers their way of life, history, and culture, as well as current issues and conflicts. (Rev: BL 12/15/96) [973]

8775 Bonvillain, Nancy. *The Teton Sioux* (6–9). Series: Indians of North America. 1994, Chelsea LB $21.95 (0-7910-1688-9). A look at the largest group of the Sioux confederacy, the Teton Dakotas, including the battle at Wounded Knee. (Rev: BL 10/15/94; VOYA 2/95) [977]

8776 Bonvillain, Nancy. *The Zuni* (6–9). Series: Indians of North America. 1995, Chelsea LB $19.95 (0-7910-1689-7). The history of the Zuni Indians of western New Mexico, including their crafts such as basket weaving and turquoise jewelry. (Rev: BL 10/15/95) [973]

8777 Bruchac, Joseph. *Lasting Echoes: An Oral History of Native American People* (7–12). Illus.

1997, Harcourt $16.00 (0-15-201327-X). Beginning with the welcoming speeches that Indian leaders delivered to the first Europeans, this work traces the history of Native Americans through their own words. (Rev: BCCB 3/98; BL 12/15/97; HBG 3/98; SLJ 3/98; VOYA 10/98) [973]

8778 Bruchac, Joseph. *Navajo Long Walk: The Tragic Story of a Proud People's Forced March from Their Homeland* (4–8). 2002, National Geographic $18.95 (0-7922-7058-4). Using revealing words and pictures, this large picture book for older readers re-creates the shameful story of the deadly marches of the Navajo in the 1860s. (Rev: BL 5/1/02; HBG 10/02; SLJ 7/02) [979.1]

8779 Calloway, Colin G. *Indians of the Northeast* (6–10). Series: First Americans. 1991, Facts on File LB $26.35 (0-8160-2389-1). Focuses on the major tribes of the region. Coverage includes the French and Indian Wars and the government's policy toward Native Americans today. (Rev: BL 1/15/92) [974]

8780 Calvert, Patricia. *Standoff at Standing Rock: The Story of Sitting Bull and James McLaughlin* (6–12). Illus. 2001, Twenty-First Century LB $24.90 (0-7613-1360-5). The confrontation between these two determined men serves as the central focus of an examination of the treatment of Native Americans, the Indian Wars, boarding schools, and the efforts to impose new beliefs. (Rev: BL 2/15/01; HBG 10/01; VOYA 12/01) [978.004]

8781 Carew-Miller, Anna. *Native American Cooking* (4–7). Illus. Series: Native American Life. 2002, Mason Crest LB $19.95 (1-59084-131-X). The role of the environment in Native American food choices is emphasized in this overview that is organized by region. Also use *Native American Tools and Weapons* and *What the Native Americans Wore* (both 2002). (Rev: SLJ 2/03) [641.5979]

8782 Collins, David R., and Kris Bergren. *Ishi: The Last of His People* (5–8). Illus. 2000, Morgan Reynolds LB $21.95 (1-883846-54-4). This is the story of Ishi, the ill-clad and half-starved man who emerged from the wilderness in California in 1911 and who was believed to be a survivor of the lost Yahi tribe. (Rev: BL 12/1/00; HBG 10/00) [979.4004]

8783 Cooper, Michael L. *Indian School: Teaching the White Man's Way* (5–10). Illus. 1999, Clarion $16.00 (0-395-92084-1). A moving photoessay about Native American children and how they have been removed from their homes and uprooted from their culture to attend Indian boarding schools in an effort to "civilize" them. (Rev: BL 12/1/99; HBG 3/00; SLJ 2/00; VOYA 4/00) [370]

8784 Cory, Steven. *Pueblo Indian* (5–8). Illus. Series: American Pastfinder. 1996, Lerner LB $25.55 (0-8225-2976-9). Color illustrations and maps accompany this account of the Pueblo Indians

and the incredible cities they built. (Rev: BL 7/96) [973]

8785 Crum, Robert. *Eagle Drum: On the Powwow Trail with a Young Grass Dancer* (4–7). Illus. 1994, Four Winds paper $16.95 (0-02-725515-8). The preparation and execution of a powwow dance is told through the eyes of a nine-year-old Kalispel Indian in Montana. (Rev: BL 10/1/94; SLJ 12/94) [394.3]

8786 Delgado, James P. *Native American Shipwrecks* (5–7). Illus. Series: Watts Library: Shipwrecks. 2000, Watts LB $24.00 (0-531-20379-4); paper $8.95 (0-531-16473-X). This book covers the boats that Native Americans made, their uses and voyages, the culture of these peoples, and how underwater archaeologists have explored their wrecks. (Rev: BL 10/15/00) [623.8]

8787 Denny, Sidney G., and Ernest L. Schusky. *The Ancient Splendor of Prehistoric Cahokia* (4–8). 1997, Ozark paper $3.95 (1-56763-272-6). Using the findings at the Cahokia Mounds in southern Illinois as a beginning, the author re-creates the life and culture of these prehistoric American Indians. (Rev: BL 5/1/97) [977.3]

8788 Dramer, Kim. *Native Americans and Black Americans* (7–10). Illus. Series: Indians of North America. 1997, Chelsea LB $19.95 (0-7910-2653-1). This work gives a historic overview of the relationship between these two groups through slavery, the Civil War, land battles, segregation, and various political movements, as well as a basic history of each group's struggle for civil rights. (Rev: BL 8/97; SLJ 9/97) [303.48]

8789 Durrett, Deanne. *Healers* (8–12). Series: American Indian Lives. 1997, Facts on File $17.95 (0-8160-3460-0). This work profiles 12 Native American healers, ranging from the traditional medicine man to modern physicians and nurses. (Rev: VOYA 8/97) [973]

8790 Elish, Dan. *The Trail of Tears: The Story of the Cherokee Removal* (6–9). Illus. Series: Great Journeys. 2001, Marshall Cavendish LB $31.36 (0-7614-1228-X). The economic and social reasons for the Cherokees' forced exile to lands in the West are presented in text, quotations from primary sources, and many illustrations and maps. (Rev: BL 1/1–15/02; HBG 10/02; SLJ 3/02) [973]

8791 Ferrell, Nancy W. *The Battle of the Little Bighorn* (5–9). Series: In American History. 1996, Enslow LB $20.95 (0-89490-768-9). A detailed account of the Battle of Little Bighorn from various points of view on both sides, along with a review of the conflicts between the U.S. government and Native Americans, the different cultures of various tribes, key figures such as Crazy Horse and Sitting Bull, and the aftermath of the battle. (Rev: BR 1–2/97; SLJ 12/96) [973.8]

8792 Fowler, Verna. *The Menominee* (4–7). Series: Indian Nations. 2000, Raintree Steck-Vaughn LB $25.69 (0-8172-5458-7). Opening with a folk tale, this book describes the Menominee Indians, their life and culture, and how they were overrun in the 19th century and pushed onto a reservation in northern Wisconsin. (Rev: BL 3/15/01; HBG 10/01) [973]

8793 Freedman, Russell. *An Indian Winter* (6–9). 1992, Holiday $21.95 (0-8234-0930-9); paper $12.95 (0-8234-1158-3). A German naturalist/explorer and a Swiss artist recorded in words and pictures their 1832 observations of Mandan and Hidatsa Indian tribes in North Dakota. (Rev: BL 6/1/92*; HB 7–8/92; SLJ 6/92*) [917.804]

8794 Girod, Christina M. *Native Americans of the Southeast* (7–10). Series: Indigenous Peoples of North America. 2000, Lucent LB $19.96 (1-56006-610-5). The native peoples of the Southeast are featured with material on systems of government, lifestyles, struggle for survival, and attempts to preserve their unique heritage and culture. (Rev: BL 9/15/00) [973]

8795 Gleason, Katherine. *Native American Literature* (6–9). Series: Junior Library of American Indians. 1996, Chelsea LB $19.75 (0-7910-2477-6). This is an excellent introduction to the long history of Native American oral and written literature that begins with chants, myths, and prayers and ends with such famous contemporary writers as Louis Erdrich and Michael Dorris. (Rev: SLJ 3/97) [973]

8796 Gold, Susan D. *Indian Treaties* (5–8). Illus. Series: Pacts and Treaties. 1997, Twenty-First Century LB $24.90 (0-8050-4813-8). A history of the successive treaties under which the Native Americans gradually lost their homes and livelihood. (Rev: BL 5/15/97; BR 9–10/97; SLJ 6/97) [323.1]

8797 Gorsline, Marie, and Douglas Gorsline. *North American Indians* (5–8). 1978, Random paper $3.25 (0-394-83702-9). Major tribes are identified and briefly described. [973]

8798 Griffin, Lana T. *The Navajo* (4–7). Illus. Series: Indian Nations. 1999, Raintree Steck-Vaughn LB $25.69 (0-8172-5463-3). This book describes the history of the Navajo, their everyday life, customs, and tribal government, and includes two Navajo creation stories. (Rev: BL 2/15/00; HBG 10/00; SLJ 4/00) [979.1]

8799 Gunderson, Mary. *American Indian Cooking Before 1500* (4–7). Series: Exploring History Through Simple Recipes. 2000, Capstone LB $22.60 (0-7368-0605-9). This book describes the everyday life of Native Americans before Europeans arrived and gives a few simple recipes. (Rev: BL 3/1/01; HBG 10/01; SLJ 7/01) [973]

8800 Hakim, Joy. *The First Americans*. 2nd ed. (5–8). Series: A History of Us. 1999, Oxford LB $19.95 (0-19-512751-X). The first volume in this outstanding series traces the history of America from prehistory through the coming of the Europeans, with emphasis on the development of Native American culture. (Rev: BL 12/15/99; VOYA 4/00) [973.1]

8801 Hoig, Stan. *Night of the Cruel Moon: Cherokee Removal and the Trail of Tears* (7–10). Illus. Series: Library of American Indian History. 1996, Facts on File $25.00 (0-8160-3307-2). Using original sources and first-person narratives, this well-documented account describes the tragic Cherokee Trail of Tears and the complexities of the situation. (Rev: BL 7/96) [976.6]

8802 Hoyt-Goldsmith, Diane. *Potlatch: A Tsimshian Celebration* (4–8). 1997, Holiday $16.95 (0-8234-1290-3). A 13-year-old boy explains the meaning of potlatch for the Tsimshian tribe in Alaska and describes the many rituals and activities it involves. (Rev: BL 5/1/97; SLJ 6/97) [394.2]

8803 Hubbard-Brown, Janet. *The Shawnee* (6–9). Series: Indians of North America. 1995, Chelsea paper $9.95 (0-7910-3475-5). The history of the Native American tribe that resisted white expansion, sided with the British in the American Revolution and again in the War of 1812, and who were led by Tecumseh, the warrior who sought to unite all northwestern Indians to fight for their land. (Rev: BL 7/95) [973]

8804 Jones, Constance. *The European Conquest of North America* (7–12). 1995, Facts on File $25.00 (0-8160-3041-3). A detailed account of Native American cultures and the methods used by European conquerors to subdue them. (Rev: BL 5/1/95) [970.01]

8805 Jones, Veda Boyd. *Native Americans of the Northwest Coast*. (7–10). Series: Indigenous Peoples of North America. 2000, Lucent LB $19.96 (1-56006-691-1). This account features the native peoples of the Pacific coast from Alaska south to Washington and how they created a unique culture and art including totem poles. (Rev: BL 9/15/00) [973]

8806 Kallen, Stuart A. *Native Americans of the Great Lakes* (7–10). Illus. Series: Indigenous Peoples of North America. 1999, Lucent LB $18.96 (1-56006-568-0). This book covers the history, culture, and famous people connected with the Six Nations of the Iroquois in the east around the Great Lakes and the Algonquins in the west. (Rev: BL 3/1/00; HBG 9/00) [977.004.]

8807 Kallen, Stuart A. *Native Americans of the Northeast* (7–10). Series: Indigenous Peoples of North America. 2000, Lucent LB $18.96 (1-56006-629-6). Kallen looks at the history, culture, religion, and conflicts of these Indians, with material on their daily lives in the past and today. (Rev: BL 3/15/00; BR 11–12/00; HBG 9/00; SLJ 5/00) [973]

8808 Kallen, Stuart A. *Native Americans of the Southwest* (7–10). Series: Indigenous Peoples of North America. 2000, Lucent LB $18.96 (1-56006-681-4). This account covers the daily lives, past and present, and culture of tribes including the Hopi, Navajo, and Zuni. (Rev: BL 8/00; HBG 3/01; SLJ 9/00) [973]

8809 Kallen, Stuart A. *The Pawnee* (7–10). Series: Indigenous Peoples of North America. 2002, Gale LB $27.45 (1-56006-825-6). The history and contributions of this Native American group who lived in the Midwest and were the enemies of their neighbors, the Cheyenne. (Rev: BL 4/15/02) [970.004]

8810 Katz, Jane B., ed. *We Rode the Wind: Recollections of Native American Life*. Rev. ed. (6–10). 1995, Lerner LB $22.60 (0-8225-3154-2). A collection of the autobiographical writings of eight notable Native Americans, among them Charles Eastman and Black Elk, who grew up on the Great Plains. (Rev: BL 2/1/96; SLJ 12/95) [978]

8811 Kavasch, E. Barrie. *The Seminoles* (4–7). Illus. Series: Indian Nations. 1999, Raintree Steck-Vaughn LB $25.69 (0-8172-5464-1). This account gives a history of the Seminole Indians, with material on their society, customs, festivals, government, present-day conditions, and one of their creation myths. (Rev: BL 2/15/00; HBG 10/00; SLJ 4/00) [975.9]

8812 King, Sandra. *Shannon: An Ojibway Dancer* (4–7). 1993, Lerner $19.95 (0-8225-2752-2); paper $11.15 (0-8225-9643-1). Thirteen-year-old Shannon Anderson, an Ojibway girl, prepares for the summer powwow and her part in the shawl dance. (Rev: BCCB 1/94; BL 1/15/94; SLJ 2/94) [394]

8813 Kirk, Connie Ann. *The Mohawks of North America* (4–7). Series: First Peoples. 2001, Lerner LB $23.93 (0-8225-4853-4). This book focuses on the history and cultural practices of the Mohawk people and their present status in America. (Rev: BL 10/15/01; HBG 3/02) [973]

8814 Klots, Steve. *Native Americans and Christianity* (7–10). Illus. Series: Indians of North America. 1997, Chelsea paper $9.95 (0-7910-4463-7). The story of how early explorers and settlers tried to convert Native Americans to Christianity, the forms that this religion took, and the many ways Native Americans practice their religion today. (Rev: BL 8/97; SLJ 9/97) [277]

8815 Krehbiel, Randy. *Little Bighorn* (4–8). Series: Battlefields Across America. 1997, Twenty-First Century LB $26.90 (0-8050-5236-4). A review of the historical background and events leading up to the Battle of Little Bighorn, followed by a description of the battle itself and the site as it is today. (Rev: SLJ 1/98) [973.8]

8816 Lacey, Theresa Jensen. *The Blackfeet* (6–9). Series: Indians of North America. 1995, Chelsea LB $21.95 (0-7910-1681-1). The story of the nomadic Native Americans of the northern Great Plains and their history of struggles with the European settlers. (Rev: BL 7/95) [970.004]

8817 La Pierre, Yvette. *Native American Rock Art: Messages from the Past* (4–8). Illus. 1994, Thomasson-Grant $16.95 (1-56566-064-1). Different types and techniques of Native American rock art are discussed, with additional information on the cultures that produced this phenomenon. (Rev: BL 12/1/94; SLJ 11/94) [709]

8818 Lassieur, Allison. *Before the Storm: American Indians Before the Europeans* (7–12). Series: Library of American Indian History. 1998, Facts on File $25.00 (0-8160-3651-9). This unique study reports on the flourishing civilizations of seven "precontact Native American" peoples before contact with the European invaders. (Rev: BL 11/15/98; BR 1–2/99; SLJ 9/98) [970]

8819 Lavender, David. *Mother Earth, Father Sky: Pueblo Indians of the American Southwest* (5–8). Illus. 1998, Holiday $16.95 (0-8234-1365-9). After introducing the geographical area of the Southwest known as Four Corners — where Arizona, New Mexico, Colorado, and Utah meet — this book traces the history and culture of the Pueblo Indians who live there. (Rev: BL 9/1/98; BR 5–6/99; HBG 10/99; SLJ 11/98) [978]

8820 Limberland, Dennis, and Mary Em Parrilli. *The Cheyenne* (4–7). Series: Indian Nations. 2000, Raintree Steck-Vaughn LB $25.69 (0-8172-5469-2). This history of the Cheyenne Indians begins with a folk tale and goes on to describe their lifestyles before and after being sent to reservations in Oklahoma and Montana. (Rev: BL 3/15/01; HBG 10/01) [973]

8821 Liptak, Karen. *Indians of the Southwest* (6–10). Series: First Americans. 1991, Facts on File $26.35 (0-8160-2385-9). Describes the first Indian inhabitants of the area and highlights their social, political, and religious life before and after contact with Europeans. (Rev: BL 1/15/92) [979]

8822 Littlechild, George. *This Land Is My Land* (6–9). 1993, Children's $16.95 (0-89239-119-7). Littlechild draws on his Plains Cree background in this presentation of 17 of his full-color paintings that focus on Native American history. (Rev: BL 11/1/93; SLJ 1/94) [971]

8823 Long, Cathryn J. *The Cherokee* (7–10). Series: Indigenous Peoples of North America. 2000, Lucent LB $18.96 (1-56006-617-2). The story of the Cherokee from their origins in the southern Appalachian mountains, through the Trail of Tears to Oklahoma, to their present status. (Rev: BL 3/15/00; HBG 9/00; VOYA 6/01) [973]

8824 McCarthy, Cathy. *The Ojibwa* (4–7). Series: Indian Nations. 2000, Raintree Steck-Vaughn LB $25.69 (0-8172-5460-9). A history of the Ojibwa Indians that includes material on the daily life and traditions of this group that now lives in Minnesota, Wisconsin, and central Canada. (Rev: BL 3/15/01; HBG 10/01) [973]

8825 McCormick, Anita Louise. *Native Americans and the Reservation in American History* (7–10). Illus. Series: American History. 1996, Enslow LB $20.95 (0-89490-769-7). An overview of the relationship between whites and Native Americans that covers hundreds of years of history and discusses the cruelty of forced marches and life on the reservations. (Rev: BL 1/1–15/97; BR 3–4/97; SLJ 2/97) [973]

8826 McLester, L. Gordon, and Elisabeth Towers. *The Oneida* (4–7). Series: Indian Nations. 2000, Raintree Steck-Vaughn LB $25.69 (0-8172-5457-9). The Oneida left their New York lands for Wisconsin and Canada. Beginning with a folk tale, this account describes their past and present with some indication of what the future holds. (Rev: BL 3/15/01; HBG 10/01) [973]

8827 Margolin, Malcolm, and Yolanda Montijo, eds. *Native Ways: California Indian Stories and Memories* (5–8). Illus. 1996, Heyday paper $8.95 (0-930588-73-8). Reminiscences and stories reflect California Indian culture, both past and present. (Rev: BL 7/96) [979.4]

8828 Marrin, Albert. *Plains Warrior: Chief Quanah Parker and the Comanches* (6–10). Illus. 1996, Simon & Schuster $18.00 (0-689-80081-9). The story of the great Comanche leader and his clashes with U.S. policy toward Native Americans makes for fine historical writing enlivened with many photographs. (Rev: BL 6/1–15/96*; BR 3–4/97; SLJ 6/96; VOYA 8/96) [973]

8829 Martell, Hazel M. *Native Americans and Mesa Verde* (4–7). Illus. Series: Hidden Worlds. 1993, Dillon LB $13.95 (0-87518-540-1). The history of the Pueblo Indians, their amazing cliff dwellings, and the Mesa Verde National Park. (Rev: BL 10/15/93; SLJ 8/93) [948.8]

8830 Mayfield, Thomas Jefferson. *Adopted by Indians: A True Story* (5–8). Ed. by Malcolm Margolin. Illus. 1997, Heyday paper $10.95 (0-930588-93-2). This is an adaption of the memoirs of a white man who lived with the Choinumne Indians in California for 10 years, beginning in 1850 when he was 8 years old. (Rev: BL 3/1/98) [979.4]

8831 Meyers, Madeleine, ed. *Cherokee Nation: Life Before the Tears* (4–8). Series: Perspectives on History. 1994, Discovery paper $6.95 (1-878668-26-9). A history of the Cherokees that emphasizes the leadership of Sequoyah and the life of the tribe

before their forced displacement. (Rev: BL 8/94) [970.3]

8832 Monroe, Jean Guard, and Ray A. Williamson. *First Houses: Native American Homes and Sacred Structures* (6–9). 1993, Houghton $17.00 (0-395-51081-3). A description in words and pictures of the dwellings of early Native Americans. (Rev: BL 10/15/93; VOYA 2/94) [299]

8833 Mooney, Martin. *The Comanche Indians* (4–7). Illus. Series: Junior Library of American Indians. 1993, Chelsea LB $19.75 (0-7910-1653-6). A historical account of the Comanches from about 1700 to the present. (Rev: SLJ 4/93) [970]

8834 Murdoch, David. *North American Indian* (4–9). Illus. Series: Eyewitness Books. 1995, Knopf $19.00 (0-679-86169-6). Full-color illustrations and a brisk text are used to introduce the history, culture, and present status of the North American Indians. (Rev: BL 8/95; SLJ 9/95) [970.004]

8835 Nies, Judith. *Native American History: A Chronology of a Culture's Vast Achievements and Their Links to World Events* (6–12). 1997, Ballantine paper $15.00 (0-345-39350-3). This chronology of Native North American history and culture from 28,000 B.C. through 1996, using a split-page format to juxtapose simultaneous political, social, religious, and military developments occurring in North America and in other parts of the world. (Rev: SLJ 5/97) [970.003]

8836 Philip, Neil, ed. *A Braid of Lives: Native American Childhood* (4–8). Illus. 2000, Clarion $20.00 (0-395-64528-X). Twenty vignettes of one or two pages in length give a many-faceted picture of growing up Native American in different parts of the county. (Rev: BL 10/1/00; HBG 10/01; SLJ 6/01; VOYA 4/01) [973]

8837 Philip, Neil, ed. *In a Sacred Manner I Live: Native American Wisdom* (4–8). Illus. 1997, Clarion $20.00 (0-395-84981-0). More than 30 Native American leaders — including Geronimo and Cochise — are quoted on topics relating to the conduct of life and their beliefs. (Rev: BL 7/97; BR 5–6/98; HBG 3/98; SLJ 12/97) [973]

8838 Powell, Suzanne. *The Pueblos* (4–7). Illus. Series: First Books. 1993, Watts paper $6.95 (0-531-15703-2). Covers the history and present status of the Pueblos and their ability to survive the harsh weather and terrain of the American Southwest. (Rev: BL 2/15/94) [978.9]

8839 Remington, Gwen. *The Cheyenne* (7–10). Series: Indigenous Peoples of North America. 2000, Lucent LB $19.96 (1-56006-750-0). The story of the past and present of the nomadic rulers of the High Plains who were considered to be the most civilized of the Great Plains Indians. (Rev: BL 9/15/00) [973]

8840 Remington, Gwen. *The Sioux* (5–9). Series: Indigenous Peoples of North America. 1999, Lucent LB $27.45 (1-56006-615-6). A thorough discussion of the history of the Sioux tribe, their origins, and their traditions and culture, with good coverage of conflicts such as Wounded Knee, their forced assimilation, and their style of life since 1920. (Rev: SLJ 3/00) [973.1]

8841 Roessel, Monty. *Kinaalda: A Navajo Girl Grows Up* (4–7). Illus. 1993, Lerner LB $25.55 (0-8225-2655-7); paper $11.15 (0-8225-9641-5). Celinda McKelvey, a Navajo girl, returns to the reservation to participate in her Kinaalda, the coming-of-age ceremony. (Rev: BCCB 1/94; BL 1/15/94; SLJ 2/94) [392.1]

8842 Sattler, Helen R. *The Earliest Americans* (5–7). 1993, Houghton $19.00 (0-395-54996-5). This account of early human life in North America also discusses the controversy about the origin of the first hunters to arrive here. (Rev: BCCB 6/93; BL 5/1/93; SLJ 6/93*) [970.1]

8843 Seymour, Tryntje Van Ness. *The Gift of Changing Woman* (5–8). 1993, Holt $16.95 (0-8050-2577-4). A description of the Apache initiation rite for young women in picture-book format, illustrated by Apache artists. (Rev: BL 11/15/93; SLJ 3/94) [299]

8844 Sherrow, Victoria. *Cherokee Nation v. Georgia: Native American Rights* (6–10). Series: Landmark Supreme Court Cases. 1997, Enslow LB $20.95 (0-89490-856-1). This book re-creates vividly the important case of 1831 when the Supreme Court ruled that the Cherokee tribe was a "domestic, dependent nation" and not liable to regulation by the state of Georgia. (Rev: BL 10/15/97; HBG 3/98) [973]

8845 Shuter, Jane, ed. *Francis Parkman and the Plains Indians* (5–8). Illus. Series: History Eyewitness. 1995, Raintree Steck-Vaughn LB $24.26 (0-8114-8280-4). An edited and abridged version of Parkman's autobiographical writing about the social customs, family life, and hunting practices of the Plains Indians. (Rev: BL 4/15/95) [978]

8846 Siegel, Beatrice. *Indians of the Northeast Woodlands* (4–8). 1991, Walker LB $14.85 (0-8027-8157-8). In question-and-answer format — following the original 1972 edition — this volume contains much information on Native Americans in New England. (Rev: BL 11/15/92) [973]

8847 Siy, Alexandra. *The Eeyou: People of Eastern James Bay* (4–7). Illus. Series: Global Villages. 1993, Macmillan $14.95 (0-87518-549-5). Introduces the Indian culture of the Eeyou, a people with their own writing system. (Rev: BCCB 7 8; SLJ 8/93) [970]

8848 Sonneborn, Liz. *The New York Public Library Amazing Native American History: A Book of*

Answers for Kids (5–8). 1999, Wiley paper $12.95 (0-471-33204-6). Organized by regions and using a question-and-answer approach, this is a fine overview of the history of Native Americans, ending with a chapter on contemporary conditions. (Rev: BL 5/1/00; SLJ 7/00) [970.004]

8849 Steedman, Scott. *How Would You Survive as an American Indian?* (4–7). Illus. Series: How Would You Survive? 1996, Watts LB $26.00 (0-531-14383-X). The life of the Plains Indians is described, with material on hunting, meals, shelter, and festivals. (Rev: BL 5/15/96) [978]

8850 Steele, Philip. *Little Bighorn* (5 8). Series: Great Battles and Sieges. 1992, Macmillan $21.00 (0-02-786885-0). How General George Custer was defeated by Cheyenne and Sioux Indians in 1876. (Rev: BL 10/1/92; SLJ 2/93) [973.8]

8851 *The Story of the Blackfoot People: Nitsitapi-isinni* (7–12). Illus. 2001, Firefly paper $15.95 (1-55297-583-5). Blackfoot leaders reveal details of their people's history, beliefs, social structure, traditions, and culture, with numerous photographs and a glossary of Blackfoot terms. (Rev: BL 2/15/02; SLJ 3/02) [970.004]

8852 Streissguth, Thomas. *The Comanche* (7–10). Series: Indigenous Peoples of North America. 2000, Lucent LB $18.96 (1-56006-633-4). The history of these fierce raiders and expert horsemen who became the "Masters of the South," and one of the most feared of all Native American tribes. (Rev: BL 8/00; HBG 3/01) [973]

8853 Streissguth, Thomas. *Wounded Knee, 1890: The End of the Plains Indian Wars* (7–12). Illus. Series: Library of American Indian History. 1998, Facts on File $25.00 (0-8160-3600-4). Using primary sources from soldiers, pioneers, missionaries, reporters, and Lakota Indians, this is the story of the events of 1890 that led to the devastation of an entire race. (Rev: BL 10/1/98; BR 1–2/99) [973.8]

8854 Tehanetorens. *Roots of the Iroquois* (7–10). Illus. 2000, Native Voices paper $9.95 (1-57067-097-8). A lively, detailed look at the history of the Iroquois Confederation before and after the arrival of European settlers. (Rev: BL 11/15/00) [974.004]

8855 Torr, James D., ed. *Primary Sources* (5–9). Series: Indigenous Peoples of North America. 2002, Gale LB $27.45 (1-59018-010-0). An anthology of excerpts from primary documents, with a timeline, that covers Native American history and culture since the arrival of Europeans. (Rev: SLJ 8/02) [970.00497]

8856 Uschan, Michael V. *The Battle of Little Bighorn* (5–8). Illus. Series: Landmark Events in American History. 2003, World Almanac LB $29.26 (0-8368-5338-5). The significance and key events of the famous battle are described from both white and Indian points of view, with extracts from primary sources, maps, and many illustrations. (Rev: BL 10/15/03; SLJ 2/03) [973.]

8857 Viola, Herman J. *It Is a Good Day to Die: Indian Eyewitnesses Tell the Story of the Battle of the Little Bighorn* (5–8). Illus. 1998, Crown $19.99 (0-517-70913-9). Taken from first-person accounts of Native Americans, this is the authentic story of the 1876 Battle of Little Bighorn, which ended in General Custer's defeat. (Rev: BCCB 9/98; BL 9/1/98; HB 9–10/98; HBG 10/98; SLJ 7/98) [973.8]

8858 Waldman, Neil. *Wounded Knee* (5–9). Illus. 2001, Simon & Schuster $18.00 (0-689-82559-5). This balanced account traces the clash of values, misunderstandings, and lack of cultural knowledge that led to the bloody conflict at Wounded Knee where, in 1890, the U.S. Army killed many Sioux Indians. (Rev: BL 3/15/01; HB 7–8/01; HBG 10/01; SLJ 5/01) [973.8]

8859 White Deer of Autumn. *The Native American Book of Knowledge* (5–8). 1992, Beyond Words paper $5.95 (0-941831-42-6). A description of Native American hero figures before Columbus is part of the information in this native view of history and life-styles. (Rev: BL 10/15/92) [970]

8860 White Deer of Autumn. *The Native American Book of Life* (5–8). 1992, Beyond Words paper $5.95 (0-941831-43-4). In this look at lifestyles from the Native American point of view, the focus is on child rearing. (Rev: BL 10/15/92) [970]

8861 Wolfson, Evelyn. *Growing Up Indian* (5–7). Illus. 1986, Walker LB $11.85 (0-8027-6644-7). What it was like to grow up Indian in traditional American culture before the influence of the white race. (Rev: BL 1/15/87; SLJ 3/87) [306.08997073]

8862 Wood, Nancy. *Sacred Fire* (7–12). Illus. 1998, Bantam Doubleday Dell $25.00 (0-385-32515-0). This meditation on the world of the Pueblo Indians, their beliefs about nature, and the drastic change in their lives after the Spanish invasion in 1540, is illustrated with breathtakingly beautiful paintings by Frank Howell. (Rev: BL 7/98; HBG 3/99; SLJ 10/98) [973]

8863 Woods, Geraldine. *The Navajo* (5–7). Illus. Series: Watts Library: Indians of the Americas. 2002, Watts LB $24.00 (0-531-13950-6); paper $8.95 (0-531-16227-3). This account includes information on history and contemporary issues and covers the Navajo code talkers, land disputes, traditions, housing, and clothing. (Rev: BL 7/02) [979.1]

8864 Young, Robert. *A Personal Tour of Mesa Verde* (4–7). Illus. Series: How It Was. 1999, Lerner LB $30.35 (0-8225-3577-7). This book gives a special glimpse into the lives of the Native Americans known as the Puebloans, how they lived, and the culture they developed. (Rev: BL 6/1–15/99; HBG 10/99; SLJ 7/99) [978.8]

8865 Yue, Charlotte, and David Yue. *The Wigwam and the Longhouse* (4–9). 2000, Houghton $15.00 (0-395-84169-0). A well-balanced account that describes the life and history of several tribes of Native Americans from the eastern woodlands. (Rev: HB 7–8/00; HBG 10/00; SLJ 10/00; VOYA 12/00) [973]

DISCOVERY AND EXPLORATION

8866 Arenstam, Peter, et al. *Mayflower 1620: A New Look at a Pilgrim Voyage* (5–9). 2003, National Geographic $17.95 (0-7922-6142-9). A large-format photoessay of a voyage of the *Mayflower II* — recreating the original journey — is the backdrop for detail about the 1620 passengers, supplies, navigation techniques, and the new country they arrived in. (Rev: BL 11/1/03; SLJ 11/03) [974.4]

8867 Asikinack, Bill, and Kate Scarborough. *Exploration into North America* (5–7). Illus. Series: Exploration. 1996, Dillon LB $15.95 (0-02-718086-7); paper $7.95 (0-382-39228-0). This account tells the history of North America from prehistory to European exploration and settlement. (Rev: BL 8/96; SLJ 9/96) [970]

8868 Aykroyd, Clarissa. *Exploration of the California Coast* (4–7). Series: Exploration and Discovery. 2002, Mason Crest LB $19.95 (1-59084-043-7). Explorers such as Cortes and Drake are covered in this look at 16th-century California. (Rev: SLJ 12/02) [917.94041]

8869 Blumberg, Rhoda. *York's Adventures with Lewis and Clark: An African-American's Part in the Great Expedition* (4–8). Illus. 2003, HarperCollins $17.99 (0-06-009111-8). York, a slave, was the only African American included on Lewis and Clark's trip but is credited with great strength and agility, attributes that impressed the Native Americans. (Rev: BL 12/1/03) [971.804]

8870 Faber, Harold. *The Discoverers of America* (6–12). 1992, Scribners $17.95 (0-684-19217-9). Discusses the exploration of North and South America, focusing on the period from Columbus to Lewis and Clark. (Rev: BL 5/15/92; SLJ 6/92) [970.01]

8871 Faber, Harold. *Lewis and Clark: From Ocean to Ocean* (5–8). Illus. Series: Great Explorations. 2001, Benchmark LB $28.50 (0-7614-1241-7). This concise, artfully illustrated volume about the journey of Lewis and Clark includes journal entries, a timeline, and Web site information. (Rev: BL 1/1–15/02; HBG 3/02; SLJ 3/02) [917.804]

8872 Lepore, Jill. *Encounters in the New World: A History in Documents* (7–12). Series: Pages from History. 1999, Oxford LB $32.95 (0-19-510513-3). Documents including letters, journals, and advertisements make relations between Native Americans and European arrivals more real to readers. (Rev: BR 3–4/00; HBG 9/00; SLJ 3/00) [970]

8873 McGrath, Patrick. *The Lewis and Clark Expedition* (5–8). Illus. 1986, Silver Burdett LB $14.95 (0-382-06828-9); paper $7.95 (0-382-09899-4). A straightforward account illustrated with maps, photographs, paintings, and diary entries. (Rev: BCCB 6/86) [921]

8874 Patent, Dorothy Hinshaw. *Animals on the Trail with Lewis and Clark* (4–8). 2002, Clarion $18.00 (0-395-91415-9). A handsome account of the Lewis and Clark expedition with emphasis on the animals that were discovered during the journey. (Rev: BCCB 5/02; BL 4/15/02*; HB 5–6/02; HBG 10/02; SLJ 4/02) [917.804]

8875 Patent, Dorothy Hinshaw. *The Lewis and Clark Trail: Then and Now* (4–8). 2002, Dutton $19.99 (0-525-46912-5). The hardships faced by the members of the famous expedition are given a new focus, comparing the conditions and landscapes of today to those Lewis and Clark discovered. (Rev: BL 1/1–15/03; HB 1–2/03; HBG 3/03; SLJ 1/03) [917.804]

8876 Roberts, Russell. *Pedro Menendez de Aviles* (5–7). Illus. Series: Latinos in American History. 2002, Mitchell Lane LB $19.95 (1-58415-150-1). This account of explorer Pedro Menendez de Aviles's efforts to procure Florida for Spain uses some fictionalized narrative to illustrate the times. (Rev: BL 10/15/02; HBG 3/03; SLJ 10/02) [975.9]

8877 Schouweiler, Thomas. *The Lost Colony of Roanoke* (6–10). Series: Great Mysteries. 1991, Greenhaven LB $22.45 (0-89908-093-6). Outlines what is known about the colony that disappeared and poses questions about its unsolved mysteries. (Rev: BL 3/1/92) [975.6]

8878 Stefoff, Rebecca. *Exploring the New World* (4–7). Illus. Series: North American Historical Atlases. 2000, Benchmark LB $24.21 (0-7614-1056-2). Using historical maps and reproductions, the important explorers and their accomplishments are covered in this slim, attractive volume. (Rev: HBG 3/01; SLJ 1/01) [970.01]

8879 Stefoff, Rebecca. *Lewis and Clark* (4–7). Illus. 1992, Chelsea LB $18.65 (0-7910-1750-8). A simple text and pictures of the Lewis and Clark expedition, which helped open up the West. (Rev: BL 7/92) [978.02]

8880 Steins, Richard. *Exploration and Settlement* (5–8). Illus. Series: Making of America. 2000, Raintree Steck-Vaughn LB $28.54 (0-8172-5700-4). This account begins with prehistoric migrations to North America and continues with European explorers, including the Spanish, English, French, and Dutch. (Rev: BL 5/1/00; HBG 10/00; SLJ 9/00) [970.01]

8881 Whiting, Jim. *Francisco Vasquez de Coronado* (5–7). Illus. Series: Latinos in American History. 2002, Mitchell Lane LB $19.95 (1-58415-146-3). This account of Francisco Vasquez de Coronado's search for the lost cities of gold, and his subsequent trial for cruelty to Native Americans, uses some fictionalized narrative. (Rev: BL 10/15/02; HBG 3/03; SLJ 10/02; VOYA 6/03) [979]

8882 Wittmann, Kelly. *The European Rediscovery of America* (4–7). Series: Exploration and Discovery. 2002, Mason Crest LB $19.95 (1-59084-052-6). Wittmann looks at the explorers of the 15th and 16th centuries, including Columbus and Cabot. (Rev: SLJ 12/02) [970]

COLONIAL PERIOD AND FRENCH AND INDIAN WARS

8883 Allman, Melinda, ed. *Primary Sources* (5–8). Series: Thirteen Colonies. 2002, Gale LB $27.45 (1-59018-011-9). A fascinating collection of primary source material for the young researcher. (Rev: BL 9/15/02; SLJ 10/02) [873.2]

8884 Asirvatham, Sandy. *The Salem Witch Trials* (6–8). Series: Great Disasters. 2001, Chelsea LB $21.95 (0-7910-6328-3). A historically accurate account of the hysteria that swept New England and resulted in the execution of 20 suspected witches in 1692. (Rev: BL 6/1–15/02; HBG 10/02) [973.2]

8885 Bjornlund, Lydia J. *Massachusetts* (5–8). Series: The Thirteen Colonies. 2001, Lucent LB $27.45 (1-56006-879-5). The story of the colony of Massachusetts with particular emphasis on its role in the Revolution and creation of a new nation. (Rev: BL 3/15/02) [973.2]

8886 Blohm, Craig E. *New Hampshire* (5–8). Series: Thirteen Colonies. 2002, Gale LB $27.45 (1-56006-991-0). Clear writing and reproductions of period illustrations are the highlights of this history of the New Hampshire colony. (Rev: BL 9/15/02; SLJ 4/02) [973.2]

8887 Brown, Gene. *Discovery and Settlement: Europe Meets the New World (1490–1700)* (5–7). Series: First Person America. 1993, Twenty-First Century LB $20.90 (0-8050-2574-X). Using excerpts from original documents, this book covers the exploration of the United States, the Puritans, and the role of Native Americans, African Americans, and women in early colonial days. (Rev: SLJ 3/94) [973.2]

8888 Butler, Jon. *Religion in Colonial America* (5–8). Series: Religion in American Life. 2000, Oxford $28.00 (0-19-511998-3). This book describes the mix of Catholics, Jews, Africans, Native Americans, Puritans, and various Protestant faiths that coexisted during colonial times. (Rev: BL 6/1–15/00; HBG 10/00) [973.2]

8889 Collier, Christopher, and James L. Collier. *Clash of Cultures: Prehistory–1638* (5–8). Illus. Series: Drama of American History. 1998, Marshall

Cavendish LB $29.93 (0-7614-0436-8). This well-illustrated examination of the cultures on both sides of the Atlantic — Native American and European — in the years before and during the formation of the colonies. (Rev: BL 4/15/98*; BR 11–12/98; HBG 10/98) [970.00497]

8890 Collier, Christopher, and James L. Collier. *The Paradox of Jamestown: 1585–1700* (5–8). Illus. Series: Drama of American History. 1998, Marshall Cavendish LB $29.93 (0-7614-0437-6). The paradox of Jamestown's history is that it gave democratic freedom through its elected legislature while introducing the first African slaves into the colonies. (Rev: BL 4/15/98*; BR 11–12/98; HBG 10/98) [975.5]

8891 Collier, Christopher, and James Lincoln Collier. *The French and Indian War* (5–8). Illus. Series: Drama of American History. 1998, Marshall Cavendish LB $28.50 (0-7614-0439-2). A nicely illustrated book providing a broad perspective on the French and Indian War, and noting the conflict's importance on both sides of the Atlantic. (Rev: BL 4/15/98*; BR 11–12/98; HBG 10/98) [973.2]

8892 Collier, Christopher, and James Lincoln Collier. *Pilgrims and Puritans: 1620–1676* (5–8). Illus. Series: Drama of American History. 1997, Marshall Cavendish LB $29.93 (0-7614-0438-4). This volume describes the routes the Pilgrims and Puritans took to America, their beliefs and practices, and how present-day American life continues to be influenced by them. (Rev: BL 4/15/98*; BR 11–12/98; HBG 10/98) [974.4]

8893 Daugherty, James. *The Landing of the Pilgrims* (5–7). 1981, Random paper $5.99 (0-394-84697-4). Based on his own writings, this is the story of the Pilgrims from the standpoint of William Bradford. [974.4]

8894 Day, Nancy. *Your Travel Guide to Colonial America* (4–8). Series: Passport to History. 2000, Lerner LB $26.60 (0-8225-3079-1). Using a modern-day guidebook format, this account takes the reader back to colonial times with glimpses of the *Mayflower* and visits to such colonies as Jamestown, Virginia, and Plymouth, Massachusetts. (Rev: BL 3/1/01; HBG 10/01; SLJ 4/01) [973.2]

8895 Dean, Ruth, and Melissa Thomson. *Life in the American Colonies* (4–8). Illus. Series: The Way People Live. 1999, Lucent LB $27.45 (1-56006-376-9). A description of life in the American colonies that covers immigrants, slaves, cities, farms, the frontier, home, crafts, professions, science, technology, and encounters with Native Americans. (Rev: BL 5/1/99; SLJ 7/99) [973.2]

8896 Doherty, Kieran. *Puritans, Pilgrims, and Merchants: Founders of the Northeastern Colonies* (4–8). Illus. 1999, Oliver LB $22.95 (1-881508-50-1). A history of each of the northeastern colonies is

supplemented with brief biographies of such people as William Bradford, John Winthrop, Peter Stuyvesant, Anne Hutchinson, and William Penn. (Rev: BL 8/99; HBG 3/00; SLJ 1/00) [974]

8897 Doherty, Kieran. *Soldiers, Cavaliers, and Planters: Settlers of the Southeastern Colonies* (4–8). 1999, Oliver LB $22.95 (1-881508-51-X). This book focuses on the early southern colonies and their founders and leaders, among them Captain John Smith, Sir Walter Raleigh, and Pedro Menendez de Aviles. (Rev: BL 8/99; HBG 3/00; SLJ 10/99) [975]

8898 Dosier, Susan. *Colonial Cooking* (4–7). Illus. Series: Exploring History Through Simple Recipes. 2000, Capstone LB $22.60 (0-7368-0352-1). This work covers the home life of the colonialists in the North, with material on kitchens, celebrations, food, and some recipes. (Rev: BL 8/00; HBG 10/00) [394.1]

8899 Dunnahoo, Terry. *Boston's Freedom Trail* (4–7). Illus. Series: Places in American History. 1994, Dillon LB $22.00 (0-87518-623-8); paper $7.95 (0-382-24762-0). An explanation of the historical events of the colonial period that are commemorated in the famous Boston walking tour. (Rev: BL 1/1/95; SLJ 3/95) [917.4]

8900 Edwards, Judith. *Jamestown: John Smith and Pocahontas in American History* (6–10). Series: In American History. 2002, Enslow LB $20.95 (0-7660-1842-3). This is a well-documented account that describes this crucial period in American colonial history and the key people involved. (Rev: BL 5/15/02; HBG 10/02) [973.2]

8901 Egger-Bovet, Howard, and Marlene Smith-Baranzini. *US Kids History: Book of the American Colonies* (5–7). Illus. Series: Brown Paper School. 1996, Little, Brown paper $14.99 (0-316-22201-1). In an informal writing style with plenty of drawings and activities, the American colonial period is introduced. (Rev: BL 8/96; SLJ 8/96) [973.2]

8902 Fradin, Dennis B. *The Georgia Colony* (4–7). Illus. Series: The Thirteen Colonies. 1989, Children's LB $33.50 (0-516-00392-5). This account traces the history of Georgia from prehistory to ratification of the Constitution. (Rev: BL 1/15/90) [975]

8903 Fradin, Dennis B. *The Maryland Colony* (5–8). Illus. Series: The Thirteen Colonies. 1990, Children's LB $33.50 (0-516-00394-1). The history of the Maryland colony from its first settlers to statehood. (Rev: BL 1/1/91) [975.2]

8904 Fradin, Dennis B. *The New Hampshire Colony* (4–7). Illus. 1988, Children's LB $33.50 (0-516-00388-7). The history of the first of the original 13 colonies to form its own government. (Rev: BL 5/15/88) [974.202]

8905 Fradin, Dennis B. *The New Jersey Colony* (5–8). Illus. Series: The Thirteen Colonies. 1991, Children's LB $33.50 (0-516-00395-X). Life in colonial New Jersey is discussed in this account that ends with the gaining of statehood. (Rev: BL 8/91; SLJ 10/91) [974]

8906 Fradin, Dennis B. *The New York Colony* (4–7). Illus. 1988, Children's LB $33.50 (0-516-00389-5). Traces the development of New York, beginning in the 1300s with the Algonquian and Iroquois Indian tribes. (Rev: BL 10/1/88) [974.702]

8907 Fradin, Dennis B. *The Pennsylvania Colony* (4–7). Illus. 1988, Children's LB $33.50 (0-516-00390-9). A history of the Keystone state from the early 1600s. (Rev: BL 3/15/89; SLJ 4/89)

8908 Fradin, Dennis B. *The Rhode Island Colony* (4–7). Illus. Series: The Thirteen Colonies. 1989, Children's LB $33.50 (0-516-00391-7). This is an introduction to the smallest U.S. state — Rhode Island. (Rev: BL 8/89; SLJ 11/89) [974.5]

8909 Fradin, Dennis B. *The South Carolina Colony* (5–8). Illus. Series: The Thirteen Colonies. 1992, Children's LB $33.50 (0-516-00397-6). This illustrated account tells the story of South Carolina from the first settlements to statehood. (Rev: BL 9/1/92) [975.7]

8910 Girod, Christina M. *Connecticut* (5–8). Illus. Series: Thirteen Colonies. 2001, Lucent LB $27.45 (1-56006-892-2). This frank history of the Connecticut area covers the period from 1613 to statehood in 1788, with period illustrations, photographs, a map, source notes, and recommended resources. (Rev: BL 12/1/01) [974.6]

8911 Girod, Christina M. *Georgia* (5–8). Series: The Thirteen Colonies. 2001, Lucent LB $27.45 (1-56006-990-2). The story of the last of the 13 colonies to be founded is told in a clear, forthright text with many black-and-white period illustrations. (Rev: BL 3/15/02; SLJ 8/02) [973.2]

8912 Girod, Christina M. *South Carolina* (5–8). Series: Thirteen Colonies. 2002, Gale LB $27.45 (1-56006-994-5). A history of the colony of South Carolina and its people from the early settlements to admission into the United States, told in concise prose with numerous black-and-white illustrations. (Rev: BL 9/15/02) [973.2]

8913 Hakim, Joy. *From Colonies to Country*. 2nd ed. (5–8). Series: A History of Us. 1999, Oxford LB $19.95 (0-19-512755-2). The colonial period and Revolutionary War are covered in this outstanding account that uses many quotations, profiles of personalities, and vivid details. (Rev: BL 12/15/99) [973.2]

8914 Hakim, Joy. *Making Thirteen Colonies*. 2nd ed. (5–8). Illus. Series: A History of Us. 1999, Oxford $19.95 (0-19-512753-6). This excellent history of the colonial period is a reissue of the 1993 volume with some revisions and new illustrations. (Rev: BL 12/15/99) [973.2]

8915 Hale, Anna W. *The Mayflower People: Triumphs and Tragedies* (5–8). Illus. 1995, Harbinger $15.95 (1-57140-002-8); paper $9.95 (1-57140-003-6). A human account of the Pilgrims that begins with their departure from Southampton, England, in 1620 and ends two years later in the New World with the death of Squanto. (Rev: BL 1/1–15/96) [974.4]

8916 Hossell, Karen Price. *Virginia* (5–8). Series: Thirteen Colonies. 2002, Gale LB $27.45 (1-56006-995-3). A cogently written history of the early years of Virginia, its people, and their lifestyle, plus sketches of their most famous colonial personalities. (Rev: BL 9/15/02) [973.2]

8917 Howarth, Sarah. *Colonial Places* (4–8). Illus. Series: People and Places. 1994, Millbrook LB $22.90 (1-56294-513-0). Highlights various places of importance in everyday colonial life, such as the meetinghouse and the church. (Rev: BL 5/15/95; SLJ 3/95) [973]

8918 Hubbard-Brown, Janet. *The Secret of Roanoke Island* (4–7). Illus. 1991, Avon paper $3.50 (0-380-76223-4). An intriguing look at this bit of history in colonial times. (Rev: BL 12/15/91) [975.63]

8919 Jackson, Shirley. *The Witchcraft of Salem Village* (4–7). Illus. 1963, Random paper $5.99 (0-394-89176-7). An account of the witch-hunting hysteria that hit Salem Village. [133.43097445]

8920 January, Brendan. *Science in Colonial America* (4–8). Series: Science of the Past. 1999, Watts LB $26.00 (0-531-11525-9). An attractive title that surveys the progress of science in colonial times with material on such key figures as Cotton Mather, Thomas Jefferson, David Rittenhouse, and Ben Franklin. (Rev: HBG 10/99; SLJ 6/99) [973.2]

8921 Kallen, Stuart A. *Delaware* (5–8). Series: Thirteen Colonies. 2002, Gale LB $27.45 (1-56006-989-9). This history of colonial Delaware offers a clearly written account plus black-and-white portraits, engravings, paintings, some photographs, and a map of the colonies. (Rev: BL 9/15/02; SLJ 4/02) [973.2]

8922 Kallen, Stuart A. *The Salem Witch Trials* (5–8). Series: World History. 1999, Lucent LB $27.45 (1-56006-544-3). After a general history of witch-hunting, this book describes the Salem trials and quotes extensively from firsthand accounts and trial notes. (Rev: BL 9/15/99; SLJ 9/99) [973.2]

8923 Kent, Deborah. *In Colonial New England* (4–8). Series: How We Lived. 1999, Benchmark LB $27.07 (0-7614-0905-X). Topics such as home life, childhood, religion, problems, and amusements are covered for the colonial period in New England. Companion volumes are *In the Middle Colonies* and *In the Southern Colonies* (1999). (Rev: HBG 10/00; SLJ 2/00) [973.2]

8924 Kling, Andrew A. *Rhode Island* (5–8). Series: The Thirteen Colonies. 2001, Lucent LB $27.45 (1-56006-873-6). In text and period prints, the story of colonial Rhode Island is told from its beginning to its stormy path to Constitution ratification. (Rev: BL 3/15/02; SLJ 8/02) [973.2]

8925 Loeper, John J. *Going to School in 1776* (7–9). Illus. 1973, Macmillan $16.00 (0-689-30089-1). A description of what schools were like during the late colonial period. [370.9]

8926 Lukes, Bonnie L. *Colonial America* (7–10). Illus. 1999, Lucent LB $18.96 (1-56006-321-1). Using extensive quotations from many sources, this book traces the basic history of colonial America, and gives good material on the obstacles settlers faced and their relations with Native Americans. (Rev: BL 2/15/00; HBG 9/00; SLJ 3/00) [940.2.]

8927 Marrin, Albert. *Struggle for a Continent: The French and Indian Wars, 1690–1760* (6–9). Illus. 1987, Macmillan LB $15.95 (0-689-31313-6). A vivid re-creation of the events and personalities of these wars and how they helped lead to the Revolution. (Rev: BL 1/15/88; SLJ 12/87; VOYA 10/87) [973.2]

8928 Masoff, Joy. *Colonial Times, 1600–1700* (4–7). Series: Chronicle of America. 2000, Scholastic paper $16.95 (0-439-05107-X). As well as describing why the colonists came to America, this work covers life aboard ships crossing the Atlantic and the challenges these people faced on arrival in the New World. (Rev: BCCB 9/00; HBG 3/01; SLJ 10/00) [973.2]

8929 Miller, Brandon Marie. *Good Women of a Well-Blessed Land: Women's Lives in Colonial America* (5–8). Series: People's History. 2003, Lerner LB $25.26 (0-8225-0032-9). The lives and roles of women from all layers of early American society are presented in this well-written account that includes many quotations, maps, and period reproductions. (Rev: BL 5/15/03; HBG 10/03; SLJ 7/03) [305.4]

8930 Miller, Brandon Marie. *Growing Up in a New World* (5–8). Series: Our America. 2002, Lerner LB $31.95 (0-8225-0658-0). The thrill of landing in the New World for the first time is re-created through true-life adventures of young people. (Rev: BL 2/15/03; HBG 3/03; SLJ 7/03) [973.2]

8931 Nardo, Don. *Braving the New World, 1619–1784: From the Arrival of the Enslaved Africans to the End of the American Revolution* (7–10). Series: Milestones in Black History. 1995, Chelsea LB $21.95 (0-7910-2259-5); paper $9.95 (0-7910-2685-X). How and why the slave trade became established in North America and the legacy of the slave culture. (Rev: BL 4/15/95) [973.2]

8932 Ochoa, George. *The Fall of Quebec and the French and Indian War* (5–7). Illus. Series: Turning

Points. 1990, Silver Burdett LB $14.95 (0-382-09954-0); paper $7.95 (0-382-09950-8). Illustrated account of the French and Indian Wars and the importance of the defeat of Montcalm and the taking of Quebec under Wolfe. (Rev: BL 3/1/91) [973.2]

8933 O'Neill, Laurie A. *The Boston Tea Party* (4–8). Series: Spotlight on American History. 1996, Millbrook LB $24.90 (0-7613-0006-6). The causes and effects of the Boston Tea Party are discussed, along with material on the Battles of Lexington and Concord. (Rev: BL 1/1–15/97; SLJ 3/97) [973.3]

8934 Perl, Lila. *Slumps, Grunts, and Snickerdoodles: What Colonial America Ate and Why* (7–9). Illus. 1975, Clarion $16.00 (0-395-28923-8). A description of what was eaten in the various colonies plus 13 recipes from the period. [641.5]

8935 Rice, Earle, Jr. *The Salem Witch Trials* (7–10). Series: Famous Trials. 1996, Lucent LB $27.45 (1-56006-272-X). This account of the Salem trials discusses dozens of the people involved in the proceedings and provides a social, political, and legal context. (Rev: BR 11–12/97; SLJ 6/97; VOYA 8/97) [973.2]

8936 Riehecky, Janet. *The Settling of Jamestown* (5–8). Series: Landmark Events in American History. 2003, World Almanac LB $26.60 (0-8368-5341-5). The story of the first permanent English settlement in North America and how its was established near the mouth of Chesapeake Bay. (Rev: BL 10/15/03) [975.5]

8937 Roach, Marilynne K. *In the Days of the Salem Witchcraft Trials* (4–8). Illus. 1996, Houghton $16.00 (0-395-69704-2). The Salem witch trials are discussed in the context of how people lived in this period and what they believed. (Rev: BL 5/15/96; SLJ 7/96) [973.3]

8938 Roop, Connie, and Peter Roop, eds. *Pilgrim Voices: Our First Year in the New World* (4–7). Illus. 1995, Walker LB $17.85 (0-8027-8315-5). Using first-person sources, the experiences of the Pilgrims from their sea journey to the first Thanksgiving are re-created. (Rev: BL 2/1/96; SLJ 1/96) [974.4]

8939 Sherrow, Victoria. *Huskings, Quiltings, and Barn Raisings: Work-Play Parties in Early America* (4–7). 1992, Walker LB $14.85 (0-8027-8188-8). How people in early America helped each other with difficult tasks, such as clearing land and raising barns. (Rev: BL 1/15/93) [973.2]

8940 Sherrow, Victoria. *Pennsylvania* (5–8). Series: Thirteen Colonies. 2002, Gale LB $27.45 (1-56006-993-7). The history of the colony of Pennsylvania from early settlements to achieving statehood. (Rev: BL 9/15/02) [973.2]

8941 Slavicek, Louise Chipley. *Life Among the Puritans* (4–8). Series: The Way People Live. 2001,

Lucent LB $27.45 (1-56006-869-8). Slavicek discusses the religious beliefs of the Puritans and how these affected the everyday life and policies of the Plymouth Colony and Massachusetts Bay Colony. (Rev: SLJ 9/01) [974.02]

8942 Smith, Carter, ed. *The Arts and Sciences: A Sourcebook on Colonial America* (5–8). Illus. Series: American Albums. 1991, Millbrook $25.90 (1-56294-037-6). Through many well-captioned illustrations and brief text, this sourcebook traces cultural and scientific life during the U.S. colonial period. (Rev: BL 1/1/92) [973.2]

8943 Smith, Carter. *The Jamestown Colony* (5–7). Illus. Series: Turning Points. 1991, Silver Burdett LB $14.95 (0-382-24121-5); paper $7.95 (0-382-24116-9). An introduction in text and excellent illustrations to the ill-fated early colony in Virginia. (Rev: BL 1/15/92) [975.5]

8944 Steen, Sandra, and Susan Steen. *Colonial Williamsburg* (4–7). Illus. 1993, Macmillan LB $14.95 (0-87518-546-0). The historic town of Williamsburg, the birthplace of the Bill of Rights, has been restored to its colonial state through John D. Rockefeller's generosity. (Rev: BL 5/15/93; SLJ 6/93) [975.5]

8945 Stefoff, Rebecca. *The Colonies* (4–7). Series: North American Historical Atlases. 2000, Benchmark LB $24.21 (0-7614-1057-0). A slim, clearly written account that gives a history of the American colonies, important places, and outstanding people. (Rev: HBG 3/01; SLJ 1/01) [973.2]

8946 Steins, Richard. *Colonial America* (5–8). Series: Making of America. 2000, Raintree Steck-Vaughn LB $28.54 (0-8172-5701-2). A brief history of the colonies from 1607 to 1763 with details of their founding, composition, and history. (Rev: HBG 10/00; SLJ 8/00) [973.2]

8947 Stevens, Bernardine S. *Colonial American Craftspeople* (5–8). Series: Colonial America. 1993, Watts LB $24.00 (0-531-12536-X). A description of colonial trades and the apprenticeship system, illustrated with period engravings and paintings. (Rev: BL 1/1/94; SLJ 2/94) [680]

8948 Streissguth, Thomas. *New Jersey* (5–8). Series: Thirteen Colonies. 2002, Gale LB $27.45 (1-56006-872-8). Using many well-chosen quotations and interesting black-and-white illustrations, this is a solid account of colonial New Jersey and its people. (Rev: BL 9/15/02) [973.2]

8949 Terkel, Susan N. *Colonial American Medicine* (5–8). Illus. Series: Colonial America. 1993, Watts LB $24.00 (0-531-12539-4). An exploration of the practice of medicine in colonial America, with material on physicians, barbers, midwives, and astrologers. (Rev: BL 1/1/94; SLJ 11/93) [362.1]

8950 Uschan, Michael V. *North Carolina* (5–8). Series: The Thirteen Colonies. 2001, Lucent LB $27.45 (1-56006-885-X). A straightforward text is combined with many period illustrations and lists of related media to tell North Carolina's early history. (Rev: BL 3/15/02) [973.2]

8951 Warner, John F. *Colonial American Home Life* (5–8). Illus. Series: Colonial America. 1993, Watts LB $24.00 (0-531-12541-6). Topics covered in this book about colonial life include housing, clothing, food, work, and schools. (Rev: BL 1/1/94; SLJ 2/94; VOYA 4/94) [973.2]

8952 Washington, George. *George-isms* (5–10). 2000, Atheneum $7.95 (0-689-84082-9). This is a collection of the rules of behavior copied out by George Washington as a teenager and includes dos and don'ts in such areas as dress, table manners, and polite conversation. (Rev: BL 10/15/00; HBG 3/01; SLJ 8/00) [973.4]

8953 Wilson, Lori L. *The Salem Witch Trials: How History Is Invented* (6–12). Illus. Series: How History Is Invented. 1997, Lerner LB $23.93 (0-8225-4889-5). The story of the famous trial of 100 people in Massachusetts during 1692, and the hysteria and falsehoods that led to 20 people being put to death. (Rev: BL 9/1/97; HBG 3/98; SLJ 8/97*) [133.4]

8954 Wood, Peter H. *Strange New Land: African Americans 1617–1776* (7–12). Illus. Series: Young Oxford History of African Americans. 1996, Oxford $24.00 (0-19-508700-3). A well-organized description of slavery during the colonial period and early Revolution. A chronology and illustrations add to the book's usefulness. (Rev: BL 2/15/96; SLJ 3/96) [973]

8955 Woog, Adam. *New York* (5–8). Series: The Thirteen Colonies. 2001, Lucent LB $27.45 (1-56006-992-9). Well-chosen quotations as well as black-and-white illustrations and maps help bring to life the story of colonial New York State. (Rev: BL 3/15/02) [973.2]

REVOLUTIONARY PERIOD AND THE YOUNG NATION (1775–1809)

8956 Allison, Robert J., ed. *American Eras: The Revolutionary Era (1754–1783)* (7–12). 1998, Gale $115.00 (0-7876-1480-7). A good reference source that opens with an overview of world events during the Revolutionary period, followed by chapters on specific topics such as the arts; business and the economy; law and justice; lifestyles, social trends, and fashions; religion; and sports and recreation. (Rev: SLJ 2/99) [973.3]

8957 Beller, Susan Provost. *The Revolutionary War* (5–8). Series: Letters from the Homefront. 2001, Benchmark LB $28.50 (0-7614-1094-5). An attractive volume that brings events and living conditions during the Revolution alive through a collection of letters and other personal documents. (Rev: BL 10/15/01; HBG 3/02) [973.3]

8958 Beller, Susan Provost. *Yankee Doodle and the Redcoats: Soldiering in the Revolutionary War* (5–8). 2003, Millbrook LB $26.90 (0-7613-2612-X). This attractive book covers the plight of the Revolutionary War soldier, with artwork as well as soldiers' letters and other documents adding to the presentation. (Rev: BL 5/15/03; HBG 10/03) [973.]

8959 Bennett, William J., ed. *The Country's Founders: A Book of Advice for Young People* (7–12). 1998, Simon & Schuster $17.00 (0-689-82106-9). The guiding principles of the founders of the U.S. are revealed in this collection of writings by Washington, Jefferson, Adams, and others. (Rev: BL 8/98; HBG 3/99; SLJ 10/98) [973.099]

8960 Bliven, Bruce, Jr. *The American Revolution, 1760–1783* (6–9). Illus. 1958, Random $9.99 (0-394-90383-8); paper $5.99 (0-394-84696-6). A concise account of the causes, battles, and results of the Revolution. [973.3]

8961 Blumberg, Rhoda. *What's the Deal? Jefferson, Napoleon, and the Louisiana Purchase* (5–9). Illus. 1998, National Geographic $18.95 (0-7922-7013-4). A dramatic retelling of the events surrounding the Louisiana Purchase, the people involved, the greed and double-dealing it induced, and what might have happened had Napoleon refused to sell it. (Rev: BL 11/1/98*; HB 11–12/98; HBG 3/99; SLJ 10/98) [973.4]

8962 Bober, Natalie S. *Countdown to Independence: A Revolution of Ideas in England and Her American Colonies, 1760–1776* (7–12). Illus. 2001, Simon & Schuster $26.95 (0-689-81329-5). Bober offers a concise, scholarly, and readable overview of the events, influences, and personalities that spurred the American Revolution. (Rev: BCCB 3/01; BL 5/15/01; HB 3–4/01; HBG 10/01; SLJ 6/01*; VOYA 4/01) [973.3]

8963 Brenner, Barbara. *If You Were There in 1776* (4–8). Illus. 1994, Bradbury $17.95 (0-02-712322-7). The year 1776 is explored, with particular emphasis on the everyday life of young people in the colonies. (Rev: BCCB 6/94; BL 5/15/94; SLJ 6/94) [973.3]

8964 Burgan, Michael. *The Louisiana Purchase* (5–8). Series: We the People. 2002, Compass Point LB $27.15 (0-7565-0210-1). An accessible, well-illustrated account of the purchase that doubled the size of the United States. (Rev: SLJ 7/02) [973.46]

8965 Chase, John Churchill. *Louisiana Purchase: An American Story.* Rev. ed. (5–8). Illus. 2002, Pelican paper $12.95 (1-58980-084-2). The story of the Louisiana Purchase, engagingly told in comic-strip format. (Rev: BL 2/1/03) [973.4]

8966 Collier, Christopher, and James L. Collier. *The American Revolution: 1763–1783* (5–8). Series: Drama of American History. 1998, Marshall Cavendish LB $29.93 (0-7614-0440-6). Using period illustrations, this is a basic history of the Revolution, with material on how the colonialists felt, major battles, and major figures. (Rev: BL 4/15/98*; BR 11–12/98; HBG 10/98) [973.3]

8967 Collier, Christopher, and James Lincoln Collier. *Building a New Nation, 1789–1801* (5–8). Illus. Series: Drama of American History. 1998, Marshall Cavendish LB $29.93 (0-7614-0777-4). An account of how the Federalists began to use the Constitution as a blueprint for guiding the young nation. (Rev: BL 2/15/99) [973.4]

8968 Collier, Christopher, and James Lincoln Collier. *Slavery and the Coming of the Civil War, 1831–1861* (5–8). Illus. 1999, Marshall Cavendish LB $29.93 (0-7614-0817-7). A reliable, interesting account the traces the history of slavery in the United States, with an emphasis on the events leading up to the Civil War. (Rev: BL 2/15/00; HBG 10/00; SLJ 3/00) [973.7]

8969 Corrick, James A. *The Louisiana Purchase* (7–10). Series: World History. 2000, Lucent LB $19.96 (1-56006-637-7). The story of the transaction of 1803 that doubled the size of the United States, assured expansion westward, and changed the destinies of France, Spain, and the United States. (Rev: BL 10/15/2000; SLJ 1/01) [973.6]

8970 Cox, Clinton. *Come All You Brave Soldiers: Blacks in the Revolutionary War* (5–7). Illus. 1999, Scholastic paper $15.95 (0-590-47576-2). Beginning with the Boston Massacre and ending with the Battle of Yorktown, this is an exciting account of the participation and contributions of more than 5,000 blacks in the American Revolution. (Rev: BL 2/15/99; HBG 10/99; SLJ 2/99; VOYA 6/99) [973.3]

8971 Davis, Burke. *Black Heroes of the American Revolution* (7–9). Illus. 1976, Harcourt $14.95 (0-15-208560-2). A book that highlights the contributions of a group of black patriots who fought for freedom. [973.3]

8972 De Pauw, Linda Grant. *Founding Mothers: Women in America in the Revolutionary Era* (7–10). Illus. 1975, Houghton $18.00 (0-395-21896-9). The role of women during the Revolutionary War period. [305.4]

8973 Diouf, Sylviane A. *Growing Up in Slavery* (6–12). 2001, Millbrook LB $25.90 (0-7613-1763-5). A compelling account that dispels any myths about happy slave children and describes the hard life on the plantation as well as the atrocious conditions on slave ships. (Rev: BL 3/1/01; HBG 10/01; SLJ 6/01) [380.1]

8974 Doherty, Craig A., and Katherine M. Doherty. *The Erie Canal* (4–7). Illus. Series: Building America. 1996, Blackbirch LB $26.19 (1-56711-112-2). Photographs and maps are used effectively in this introduction to the Erie Canal, an engineering marvel. (Rev: BL 2/15/97; SLJ 2/97) [386]

8975 Dolan, Edward F. *The American Revolution: How We Fought the War of Independence* (6–9). 1995, Millbrook LB $30.40 (1-56294-521-1). This heavily illustrated, clearly written, battle-by-battle history of the Revolution looks at the causes, places, campaigns, and people, as well as the bloodiest battles. (Rev: BL 12/15/95; BR 5–6/96; SLJ 1/96) [973.3]

8976 Erickson, Paul. *Daily Life on a Southern Plantation 1853* (4–7). 1998, Bt. Bound $16.45 (0-613-28459-3). Gives an hour-by-hour tour of a Southern plantation in Louisiana in 1853, revealing how both the landowners and the slaves lived. (Rev: HBG 10/98; SLJ 12/98) [973.5]

8977 Ferrie, Richard. *The World Turned Upside Down: George Washington and the Battle of Yorktown* (5–9). Illus. 1999, Holiday $18.95 (0-8234-1402-7). A lavishly illustrated account of the battle that was the turning point in the Revolution, with details on strategies, personalities, and period warfare. (Rev: BL 9/1/99; HBG 3/00; SLJ 10/99) [973.3]

8978 Fink, Sam. *The Declaration of Independence: The Words That Made America* (4–8). Illus. 2002, Scholastic paper $19.95 (0-439-40700-1). The Declaration of Independence is broken down and examined phrase by phrase, with illustrations that will attract attention and useful appendixes. (Rev: BCCB 10/02; BL 9/15/02; HBG 3/03; SLJ 10/02) [973.313]

8979 Freedman, Russell. *Give Me Liberty! The Story of the Declaration of Independence* (4–7). Illus. 2000, Holiday $24.95 (0-8234-1448-5). Beginning with the Boston Tea Party, this stirring account introduces characters including Patrick Henry and Paul Revere, events such as the battles at Lexington and Concord, and ends with the Continental Congress and the drawing up of the Declaration of Independence. (Rev: BCCB 10/00; BL 10/1/00*; HB 1–2/01; HBG 3/01; SLJ 10/00) [973.3]

8980 Gaines, Ann Graham. *The Louisiana Purchase in American History* (7–10). Series: In American History. 2000, Enslow LB $19.95 (0-7660-1301-4). A well-documented and illustrated account of the 1803 purchase of southern land from the French government. (Rev: BL 1/1–15/00; HBG 9/00) [973.5]

8981 Greenberg, Judith E., and Helen C. McKeever. *Journal of a Revolutionary War Woman* (6–10). Illus. Series: In Their Own Words. 1996, Watts LB $23.00 (0-531-11259-4). An intimate view of the American Revolution through the eyes of the wife of an officer in the Continental Army. (Rev: BL 9/1/96; BR 11–12/96; SLJ 8/96; VOYA 2/97) [973.3]

8982 Gunderson, Mary. *Southern Plantation Cooking* (4–7). Illus. 2000, Capstone LB $22.60 (0-7368-0357-2). This book explores life on Southern plantations during the days of slavery with emphasis on the importance of food and food preparation. A few representative recipes are provided. (Rev: BL 8/00; HBG 10/00) [394.1]

8983 Hakim, Joy. *Liberty for All?* 2nd ed. (5–8). Series: A History of Us. 1999, Oxford LB $19.95 (0-19-512759-5); paper $13.95 (0-19-512760-9). An excellent account of American history from 1800 to the outbreak of the Civil War, with emphasis on the slave economy and events leading up to the war. (Rev: BL 12/15/99) [973.5]

8984 Herbert, Janis. *The American Revolution for Kids* (5–8). Illus. 2002, Chicago Review paper $14.95 (1-55652-456-0). A comprehensive look at the American Revolution from its causes through the early 18th century, with biographical information and interesting features. (Rev: BL 10/1/02; SLJ 11/02) [973.3]

8985 Hull, Mary. *The Boston Tea Party in American History* (6–10). Series: In American History. 1999, Enslow LB $20.95 (0-7660-1139-9). A look at the events leading up to this act of defiance that sparked the American Revolution. (Rev: BL 2/15/99; HBG 9/99) [973.3115]

8986 Hull, Mary. *Shays' Rebellion and the Constitution in American History* (6–10). Series: In American History. 2000, Enslow LB $20.95 (0-7660-1418-5). The story of the economic depression of the 1780s and the resulting violent protests and government reforms. (Rev: BL 2/15/00; HBG 10/00; SLJ 6/00) [973.4]

8987 Kallen, Stuart A. *Life During the American Revolution* (6–10). Series: The Way People Live. 2002, Gale LB $27.45 (1-59018-007-0). Everyday life on the home front during the American Revolution is recreated in this account that uses primary and secondary source quotations extensively. (Rev: BL 7/02) [973.3]

8988 Karapalides, Harry J. *Dates of the American Revolution: Who, What, and Where in the War for Independence* (7–12). 1998, Burd Street paper $19.95 (1-57249-106-X). A chronological record tracing the American Revolution from 1760, when King George II inherited the British throne, to 1799, with George Washington's death, with an emphasis on military action and commanders. (Rev: SLJ 2/99) [973.3]

8989 Kent, Deborah. *The American Revolution: "Give Me Liberty, or Give Me Death!"* (5–7). Illus. Series: American War. 1994, Enslow LB $20.95 (0-89490-521-X). A succinct history of the Revolution that uses many firsthand quotations and period illustrations and maps. (Rev: BL 7/94; SLJ 7/94) [973.3]

8990 King, David C. *Saratoga* (5–8). Illus. Series: Battlefields Across America. 1998, Twenty-First Century LB $26.90 (0-7613-3011-9). The significance of the battle at Saratoga in 1777, in which General Burgoyne's British army was defeated, and where and how the history of this battle is preserved today. (Rev: HBG 9/98; SLJ 8/98) [973.3]

8991 Lukes, Bonnie L. *The Boston Massacre* (6–9). Illus. Series: Famous Trials. 1998, Lucent LB $27.45 (1-56006-467-6). This book explores the dramatic trial of the British soldiers who fired on rioting protesters in Boston, killing six outright and fatally wounding two others. (Rev: BL 4/15/98; SLJ 7/98) [973.3]

8992 Maltz, Leora, ed. *The Founding of America* (7–12). Series: Great Speeches in History. 2002, Gale LB $31.20 (0-7377-0871-9); paper $19.95 (0-7377-0870-0). After introductory essays, this anthology of about 20 important speeches (each with its own introduction) recreates the important events and issues involved in the creation of the United States. (Rev: BL 4/15/02) [973.2]

8993 Masoff, Joy. *American Revolution: 1700–1800* (4–7). Series: Chronicle of America. 2000, Scholastic paper $16.95 (0-439-05109-6). A successful basic introduction to the American Revolution. (Rev: BCCB 9/00; HBG 3/01; SLJ 10/00) [973.3]

8994 Miller, Brandon Marie. *Growing Up in the Revolution and the New Nation* (4–7). Illus. Series: Our America. 2002, Lerner LB $31.95 (0-8225-0078-7). An in-depth examination of the lives of children during and immediately after the American Revolution, including biographical information about real youngsters. (Rev: BL 10/15/02; HBG 3/03; SLJ 12/02) [973.3]

8995 Minks, Louise, and Benton Minks. *The Revolutionary War* (7–12). Series: America at War. 1992, Facts on File $25.00 (0-8160-2508-8). A colorful account of the causes, main battles, and outcomes of the Revolutionary War. (Rev: BL 2/1/93) [973.3]

8996 Murphy, Jim. *An American Plague: The True and Terrifying Story of the Yellow Fever Epidemic of 1793* (6–12). Illus. 2003, Clarion $17.00 (0-395-77608-2). Narrative, newspaper articles, and archival prints and photographs combine to tell the dramatic story of the epidemic that hit Philadelphia in the late 18th century. (Rev: BL 6/1–15/03; HB 7–8/03; HBG 10/03; SLJ 6/03*) [614.5]

8997 Murphy, Jim. *A Young Patriot: The American Revolution as Experienced by One Boy* (5–8). Illus. 1996, Clarion $16.00 (0-395-60523-7). The American Revolution as seen through the eyes of a 15-year-old volunteer. (Rev: BCCB 6/96; BL 6/1–15/96*; HB 9–10/96; SLJ 6/96*) [973.3]

8998 Nardo, Don. *The American Revolution* (7–12). Series: Opposing Viewpoints Digests. 1998, Greenhaven LB $27.45 (1-56510-755-1); paper $17.45 (1-56510-754-3). Quoting from dozens of primary and secondary sources, this book explores issues related to the Revolution, such as prewar disputes, patriotic vs. loyalist views, wartime concerns, and modern attitudes. (Rev: BL 5/15/98; SLJ 6/98) [973.3]

8999 Nardo, Don. *Weapons of War* (6–9). Illus. Series: American War Library: The American Revolution. 2003, Gale LB $21.96 (1-59018-226-X). A look at the equipment of war — from muskets and bayonets to naval ships — and the tactics of war and intelligence gathering during the Revolutionary War. Also use *Life of a Soldier in Washington's Army* (2003), which discusses training, equipment, supplies, medicine, and so forth. (Rev: SLJ 4/03) [973.3]

9000 *The Revolutionaries* (7–12). Illus. Series: American Story. 1996, Time-Life Books $19.95 (0-7835-6250-0). Illustrations and personal narratives enhance this detailed chronological account of the drive for independence and the military high points of the American Revolution. (Rev: BL 12/15/96; BR 3–4/97; SLJ 1/97) [973.3]

9001 Simonds, Christopher. *Samuel Slater's Mill and the Industrial Revolution* (5–7). Illus. Series: Turning Points. 1990, Silver Burdett LB $14.95 (0-382-09951-6); paper $7.95 (0-382-09947-8). Describes how the pioneer in the cotton textile industry reproduced English machinery and how the Industrial Revolution began in this country. (Rev: BL 3/1/91) [338]

9002 Slavicek, Louise Chipley. *The Women of the American Revolution* (6–10). Illus. Series: Women in History. 2002, Gale LB $21.96 (1-59018-172-7). An absorbing, well-illustrated account of the roles women played during the Revolutionary War — on the battlefield and on the home front. (Rev: BL 10/15/02) [973.3]

9003 Smith, Carter, ed. *The Revolutionary War: A Sourcebook on Colonial America* (5–8). Series: American Albums. 1991, Millbrook $25.90 (1-56294-039-2). This volume illustrates the major events leading up to the Revolution and the battles and personalities involved. (Rev: BL 1/1/92) [973.38]

9004 Stefoff, Rebecca. *Revolutionary War* (4–7). Illus. Series: North American Historical Atlases. 2000, Benchmark LB $24.21 (0-7614-1058-9). Using historical maps and reproductions plus a clear text, this is a basic account of the American Revolution. (Rev: HBG 3/01; SLJ 1/01) [973.3]

9005 Stewart, Gail B. *Weapons of War* (6–12). Series: American War Library. 2000, Lucent LB $18.96 (1-56006-616-1). This book discusses weapons used during the American Revolution including muskets, swords, rifles, warships and even intelligence and espionage. (Rev: BL 2/15/00) [973.3]

9006 Weber, Michael. *The American Revolution* (5–8). Series: Making of America. 2000, Raintree Steck-Vaughn LB $28.54 (0-8172-5702-0). A fine overview of the American Revolution from the French and Indian War to the creation of the United States. (Rev: BL 7/00; HBG 10/00; SLJ 8/00) [973.3]

9007 Weber, Michael. *Yorktown* (4–7). Illus. Series: Battlefields Across America. 1997, Twenty-First Century LB $26.90 (0-8050-5226-7). Background material on the Revolutionary War is given, along with details of the battle and the present-day condition of its site. (Rev: SLJ 1/98) [973.3]

9008 Weber, Michael. *The Young Republic* (5–8). Illus. Series: Making of America. 2000, Raintree Steck-Vaughn LB $28.54 (0-8172-5703-9). This well-illustrated account begins in the 1780s with the creation of the federal system, the ratification of the Constitution, and the inauguration of Washington as president in 1789. (Rev: BL 5/1/00; HBG 10/00; SLJ 9/00) [973]

9009 Whitelaw, Nancy. *The Shot Heard Round the World: The Battles of Lexington and Concord* (5–8). Illus. 2001, Morgan Reynolds LB $21.95 (1-883846-75-7). Whitelaw details events from the Boston Massacre in 1770 to the first battles of the Revolution in 1775, with profiles of some of the key players. (Rev: BL 5/15/01; HBG 10/01; SLJ 7/01; VOYA 6/01) [973.3]

9010 Wilbur, Keith C. *The Revolutionary Soldier, 1775–1783* (4–8). Series: Illustrated Living History. 1996, Chelsea LB $21.95 (0-7910-4533-1). Topics covered in this book about the Continental Army include clothing, weapons, camp life, food, hospitals, and leisure activities. (Rev: BL 6/1–15/97; SLJ 7/97) [973.3]

9011 Zall, P. M. *Becoming American: Young People in the American Revolution* (8–12). 1993, Linnet LB $25.00 (0-208-02355-0). Letters, journal entries, and testimonies by young people describing their lives, events, and social conditions in the years immediately before, during, and immediately after the Revolution. (Rev: BL 5/1/93; VOYA 8/93) [973.3]

9012 Zeinert, Karen. *Those Remarkable Women of the American Revolution* (5–8). Illus. 1996, Millbrook LB $29.90 (1-56294-657-9). A fascinating account of the conditions and status of women in colonial America and their important contributions to the Revolution, from fighting and spying to fund raising. (Rev: BL 12/1/96; SLJ 3/97; VOYA 4/97) [973.3]

NINETEENTH CENTURY TO THE CIVIL WAR (1809–1861)

9013 Baldwin, Robert F. *New England Whaler* (5–8). Illus. Series: American Pastfinder. 1996, Lerner LB $25.55 (0-8225-2978-5). Life on a 19th-century whaling ship is detailed, with many maps and color photographs. (Rev: BL 7/96; SLJ 6/96) [638.2]

9014 Bentley, Judith. *"Dear Friend": Thomas Garrett and William Still, Collaborators on the Underground Railroad* (5–9). Illus. 1997, Dutton $15.99 (0-525-65156-X). This account of the "eastern line" of the network that helped bring slaves from the South to the North and freedom focuses on the courageous collaboration of Thomas Garrett, a white Quaker, and William Still, a free black. (Rev: BCCB 2/97; BL 2/15/97; SLJ 6/97; VOYA 12/97) [973.7]

9015 Bial, Raymond. *The Strength of These Arms: Life in the Slave Quarters* (5–8). 1997, Houghton $16.00 (0-395-77394-6). This photoessay re-creates daily life in the slave quarters on large plantations, contrasts it with the luxurious lifestyles of the slave holders, and documents how slaves tried to preserve their heritage, dignity, and hope. (Rev: BL 9/15/97; HBG 3/98; SLJ 11/97) [975]

9016 Bial, Raymond. *The Underground Railroad* (4–7). Illus. 1995, Houghton $17.00 (0-395-69937-1). This photoessay re-creates the places involved in the Underground Railroad and the heroism of the people involved. (Rev: BCCB 3/95; BL 4/1/95; HB 7–8/95; SLJ 4/95) [973.7]

9017 Bredeson, Carmen. *The Battle of the Alamo: The Fight for Texas Territory* (5–8). Series: Spotlight on American History. 1996, Millbrook LB $24.90 (0-7613-0019-8). A well-organized account of the causes, events, and campaigns of the war in which much of California, Texas, and the Southwest became part of the United States. (Rev: SLJ 4/97) [973.6]

9018 Carey, Charles W. *The Mexican War: "Mr. Polk's War"* (6–9). Series: American War. 2002, Enslow LB $20.95 (0-7660-1853-9). A thorough and very readable account of the Mexican-American War and the key figures of the time. Also in this series is *The War of 1812: "We Have Met the Enemy and They Are Ours"* (2002). (Rev: HBG 3/03; SLJ 1/03) [973.6]

9019 Collier, C., and J. L. Collier. *Andrew Jackson's America, 1824–1850* (5–8). Illus. Series: Drama of American History. 1998, Marshall Cavendish LB $29.93 (0-7614-0779-0). The Colliers trace American history over an eventful 26 years that encompass great change, from the Industrial Revolution to the Trail of Tears. (Rev: BL 2/15/99; HBG 10/99) [973.56]

9020 Collier, C., and J. L. Collier. *The Jeffersonian Republicans, 1800–1823* (5–8). Illus. Series: Drama of American History. 1998, Marshall Cavendish LB $29.93 (0-7614-0778-2). This lively account describes 23 eventful years in our history that include the Louisiana Purchase, the Lewis and Clark Expedition, and the War of 1812. (Rev: BL 2/15/99; HBG 10/99; SLJ 4/99) [973.46]

9021 Collier, Christopher, and James Lincoln Collier. *Hispanic America, Texas and the Mexican War, 1835–1850* (5–8). Illus. Series: Drama of American History. 1998, Marshall Cavendish LB $29.93 (0-7614-0780-4). This account covers the history of Europeans in the Southwest, the Hispanic culture in the region, the doctrine of Manifest Destiny, the Mexican War, and the settling of California. (Rev: BL 2/15/99; HBG 10/99; SLJ 4/99) [979]

9022 Currie, Stephanie. *Life of a Slave on a Southern Plantation* (6–10). Series: Way People Live. 1999, Lucent LB $18.96 (1-56006-539-7). Using many quotations from original sources, this book on everyday life on a southern slave plantation covers family life, food and housing, work, play, and methods of escape. (Rev: BL 10/15/99; HBG 9/00; SLJ 1/00) [975]

9023 Currie, Stephen. *Thar She Blows: American Whaling in the Nineteenth Century* (6–9). Illus. Series: People's History. 2001, Lerner LB $25.26 (0-8225-0646-7). A concise text with many quotations from primary sources such as diaries, letters, and newspaper articles brings to life the grim conditions aboard whaling ships. (Rev: BL 1/1–15/02; HBG 10/02; SLJ 4/02; VOYA 4/02) [639.2]

9024 Draper, Charla L. *Cooking on Nineteenth Century Whaling Ships* (4–7). Series: Exploring History Through Simple Recipes. 2000, Capstone LB $22.60 (0-7368-0602-4). As well as learning about life on a whaling ship, this book provides a series of simple recipes. (Rev: BL 3/1/01; HBG 10/01; SLJ 4/01) [974.8]

9025 Dudley, William, ed. *American Slavery* (8–12). Series: Turning Points in World History. 2000, Greenhaven LB $21.96 (0-7377-0223-3); paper $13.96 (0-7377-0212-5). This anthology of essays covers the rise of slavery in America and how this issue became the cause of the Civil War at a time when there were more than 4 million African American slaves in the South. (Rev: BL 5/15/00; SLJ 10/00) [973.7]

9026 Fleischner, Jennifer. *The Dred Scott Case: Testing the Right to Live Free* (5–8). Series: Spotlight on American History. 1997, Millbrook $24.90 (0-7613-0005-8). An account of the life of the slave Dred Scott and the historic court case of 1857 against his owner, John Sanford. (Rev: BL 5/1/97; SLJ 4/97) [342.73]

9027 Forten, Charlotte. *A Free Black Girl Before the Civil War: The Diary of Charlotte Forten, 1854* (4–8). Ed. by Kerry Graves. Illus. Series: Diaries, Letters, and Memoirs. 2000, Capstone LB $22.60 (0-7368-0345-9). This first-person account based on actual sources describes, in diary format, the life of a 16-year-old African American girl living in Massachusetts before the Civil War and her participation in the antislavery movement. (Rev: BL 10/15/00; HBG 10/00; SLJ 9/00) [974.4]

9028 Fradin, Dennis Brindell. *Bound for the North Star: True Stories of Fugitive Slaves* (8–12). Illus. 2000, Clarion $20.00 (0-395-97017-2). Personal experiences form the basis of these moving profiles that spare no details of the horrors suffered by escaping slaves and the courage of their helpers. (Rev: BL 1/1–15/01; HB 1–2/01; HBG 3/01; SLJ 11/00; VOYA 10/01) [973.7]

9029 Freedman, Florence B. *Two Tickets to Freedom: The True Story of Ellen and William Craft, Fugitive Slaves* (4–8). 1971, Bedrick $12.95 (0-87226-330-4); paper $5.95 (0-87226-221-9). An exciting story of slavery, escape, and pursuit that is based on fact. A reissue. (Rev: BR 3–4/90) [973.5]

9030 Gay, Kathlyn, and Martin Gay. *War of 1812* (5–8). Series: Voices of the Past. 1995, Twenty-First Century LB $25.90 (0-8050-2846-3). Excerpts from letters, memoirs, and official reports highlight this well-illustrated history of the War of 1812 and its consequences. (Rev: BL 12/15/95; SLJ 3/96) [973.5]

9031 Gorrell, Gena K. *North Star to Freedom: The Story of the Underground Railroad* (5–10). Illus. 1997, Delacorte $17.95 (0-385-32319-0). A handsome, readable account that captures the danger and excitement connected to the Underground Railroad and the heroism and dedication of abolitionists in Canada as well as in the United States who helped slaves escape from the South. (Rev: BL 2/15/97; BR 9–10/97; SLJ 1/97*) [973.7]

9032 Greenblatt, Miriam. *The War of 1812* (7–12). Illus. Series: America at War. 1994, Facts on File $25.00 (0-8160-2879-6). A lively account of how our young nation tried to rid itself of foreign influences, tracing the causes of the war and describing the battles fought on land and sea. (Rev: BL 11/15/94; SLJ 12/94) [973.5]

9033 Hansen, Joyce, and Gary McGowan. *Freedom Roads: Searching for the Underground Railroad* (5–8). 2003, Cricket $18.95 (0-8126-2673-7). This look at the history of the Underground Railroad emphasizes how much of our knowledge consists of speculation and anecdotal material rather than hard evidence. (Rev: BL 5/1/03; HB 7–8/03; HBG 10/03; SLJ 9/03*) [973.7]

9034 Heidler, David S., and Jeanne T. Heidler. *The War of 1812* (8–12). Series: Greenwood Guides to

Historic Events, 1500–1900. 2002, Greenwood $44.95 (0-313-31687-2). This thorough and detailed description of the causes, events, and key figures of the War of 1812 will be useful for report writers. (Rev: BL 10/15/02; SLJ 10/02) [973.5]

9035 Herda, D. J. *The Dred Scott Case: Slavery and Citizenship* (6–10). Illus. Series: Landmark Supreme Court Cases. 1994, Enslow LB $20.95 (0-89490-460-4). An examination of the pre-Civil War case in which a slave was denied his freedom, and its consequences. (Rev: BL 6/1–15/94) [342.73]

9036 January, Brendan. *The Dred Scott Decision* (5–8). Illus. Series: Cornerstones of Freedom. 1998, Children's Pr. LB $21.00 (0-516-20833-0); paper $5.95 (0-516-26457-5). Using many photographs and reproductions, this book explores the landmark 1857 Supreme Court decision on slavery that helped lead the United States into civil war. (Rev: BR 11–12/98; HBG 9/98; SLJ 8/98) [973.7]

9037 Jurmain, Suzanne. *Freedom's Sons: The True Story of the Amistad Mutiny* (5–8). Illus. 1998, Lothrop $15.95 (0-688-11072-X). Told with true storytelling skill, this fascinating chapter in American history is re-created brilliantly, with a special focus on the nobility of Cinque and his men. (Rev: BCCB 5/98; BL 2/15/98; HBG 10/98; SLJ 4/98) [326]

9038 Kallen, Stuart A. *Life on the Underground Railroad* (6–10). Series: The Way People Live. 2000, Lucent LB $27.45 (1-56006-667-9). After a brief history of slavery in America, this account covers the organization of and people involved in the Underground Railroad, the journeys made on it, and its impact on the future. (Rev: BL 2/15/00; HBG 10/00; SLJ 5/00) [973.6]

9039 King, David C. *New Orleans* (5–8). Illus. Series: Battlefields Across America. 1998, Twenty-First Century LB $26.90 (0-7613-3010-0). The story of the famous 1815 battle in New Orleans in which the British were decisively defeated, including the background of the War of 1812, the role of Andrew Jackson, and the significance of this defeat to the British. (Rev: HBG 9/98; SLJ 8/98) [973.6]

9040. Landau, Elaine, ed. *Slave Narratives: The Journey to Freedom* (6–9). Illus. Series: In Their Own Voices. 2001, Watts LB $22.50 (0-531-11743-X). Four first-person accounts, presented with historical background and period photographs and prints, paint a vivid picture of life as a slave and of the dangers of escaping to freedom. (Rev: BL 8/01; SLJ 8/01; VOYA 10/01) [973]

9041 Levy, Janey. *The Alamo: A Primary Source History of the Legendary Texas Mission* (5–8). Illus. Series: Primary Sources in American History. 2003, Rosen LB $29.25 (0-8239-3681-3). Primary sources — including maps and paintings — tell the story of the Battle of the Alamo. (Rev: BL 5/15/03; SLJ 5/03) [976.4]

9042 McKissack, Patricia, and Fredrick McKissack. *Rebels Against Slavery: American Slave Revolts* (5–8). Illus. 1996, Scholastic paper $15.95 (0-590-45735-7). A fascinating account of the men and women who led revolts against slavery, including Toussaint L'Ouverture, Cinque, Harriet Tubman, and Nat Turner. (Rev: BCCB 6/96; BL 2/15/96; BR 3–4/96; SLJ 3/96; VOYA 4/96) [970]

9043 McNeese, Tim. *The Alamo* (6–9). Illus. Series: Sieges That Changed the World. 2003, Chelsea LB $22.95 (0-7910-7101-4). The attack on the Alamo that resulted in the death of many Texans at the hands of Santa Ana's troops is placed in historical context. (Rev: HBG 10/03; SLJ 10/03) [976.4]

9044 Mancall, Peter C., ed. *American Eras: Westward Expansion (1800–1860)* (8–12). 1999, Gale $115.00 (0-7876-1483-1). The period of growth and change in America from the early 19th century up to the Civil War is examined. (Rev: SLJ 8/99) [973.6]

9045 Marquette, Scott. *War of 1812* (4–7). Illus. Series: America at War. 2002, Rourke LB $27.93 (1-58952-389-X). This book for middle-graders studies the war itself and the events that led up to it. (Rev: BL 10/15/02) [973.5]

9046 Murphy, Jim. *Inside the Alamo* (4–8). Illus. 2003, Delacorte LB $18.99 (0-385-90092-9). A gripping narrative combines with solid facts to give readers a good understanding of the events at the Alamo, their causes, and their aftermath. (Rev: BL 3/15/03*; HB 7–8/03; HBG 10/03; SLJ 5/03*) [976.4]

9047 Myers, Walter Dean. *Amistad: A Long Road to Freedom* (5–9). Illus. 1998, Dutton $16.99 (0-525-45970-7). The fascinating story of the 1839 mutiny and its consequences, told in a skillful narrative that emphasizes the courage, strength, and dignity of the mutineers. (Rev: BCCB 5/98; BL 2/15/98; HBG 10/98; SLJ 5/98; VOYA 6/98) [326]

9048 Nardo, Don. *The Mexican-American War* (6–9). Series: World History. 1999, Lucent LB $27.45 (1-56006-495-1). The author reviews the events leading up to this war involving Texas, Colorado, and California, the major battles, the large antiwar movement in the United States, and the bitterness that still exists among some Mexicans. (Rev: BL 9/15/99; HBG 4/00; SLJ 9/99) [973.6]

9049 Nardo, Don. *The War of 1812* (8–12). Series: World History. 1999, Lucent LB $18.96 (1-56006-581-8). A well-organized account of "Mr. Madison's War" that includes primary-source material, a timeline, maps, and other interesting elements. (Rev: BL 11/15/99; HBG 9/00; SLJ 2/00) [973.5]

9050 Nofi, Albert A. *The Underground Railroad and the Civil War* (4–8). Series: Untold History of the Civil War. 2000, Chelsea $19.75 (0-7910-5434-

9). A history of the dangers, devotion, excitement, and daring involved in this collaborative system that was developed to help fugitive Southern slaves reach freedom in the North or in Canada. (Rev: BL 5/15/00; HBG 10/00; SLJ 6/00) [973.7]

9051 Paulson, Timothy J. *Days of Sorrow, Years of Glory, 1831–1850: From the Nat Turner Revolt to the Fugitive Slave Law* (5–9). Series: Milestones in Black American History. 1994, Chelsea paper $14.93 (0-7910-2552-7). An examination of the Underground Railroad, slave resistance, the Seminole Wars, and the abolition movement. (Rev: BL 11/1/94; SLJ 4/95; VOYA 12/94) [973]

9052 Richards, Caroline Cowles. *A 19th Century Schoolgirl: The Diary of Caroline Cowles Richards, 1852–1855* (4–8). Ed. by Kerry Graves. Illus. Series: Diaries, Letters, and Memoirs. 2000, Capstone LB $22.60 (0-7368-0342-4). This diary of a young girl living in western New York State in the early 1850s describes her daily life, schooling, and her reaction to the women's rights movement. (Rev: BL 10/15/00; HBG 10/00; SLJ 9/00) [974.7]

9053 Sawyer, Kem K. *The Underground Railroad in American History* (7–10). Illus. Series: In American History. 1997, Enslow LB $20.95 (0-89490-885-5). A description of the formation of the Underground Railroad, its functions, key people connected with it, and its importance in American history. (Rev: BL 7/97; BR 9–10/97) [973.7]

9054 Sigerman, Harriet. *An Unfinished Battle: American Women 1848–1865* (8–12). Illus. Series: The Young Oxford History of Women in the United States. 1994, Oxford $24.00 (0-19-508110-2). This volume explores the social and political conditions of women during the years prior to the Civil War and their contributions to and participation in the war. (Rev: BL 12/15/94; SLJ 1/95) [305.4]

9055 Sisson, Mary Barr. *The Gathering Storm: From the Framing of the Constitution to Walker's Appeal, 1787–1829* (7–10). Illus. Series: Milestones in Black American History. 1996, Chelsea LB $21.95 (0-7910-2252-8); paper $9.95 (0-7910-2678-7). The story of slavery in the early days of the Republic with emphasis on civil disobedience, militant action, and important figures of the period. (Rev: BL 10/15/96; BR 1–2/97; SLJ 2/97) [973]

9056 Sorrels, Roy. *The Alamo in American History* (6–8). Illus. Series: In American History. 1996, Enslow LB $20.95 (0-89490-770-0). This book gives an account of the events leading up to the battle plus detailed coverage of the siege of the Alamo and its significance in American history. (Rev: BL 3/1/97; BR 3–4/97) [976.4]

9057 Stefoff, Rebecca. *The War of 1812* (4–7). Illus. Series: North American Historical Atlases. 2000, Benchmark LB $24.21 (0-7614-1060-0). A clearly written text plus historical maps and reproductions are used to give an easy-to-read account of the War of 1812. (Rev: HBG 3/01; SLJ 1/01) [973.8]

9058 Stein, R. Conrad. *John Brown's Raid on Harpers Ferry* (7–10). Series: In American History. 1999, Enslow LB $20.95 (0-7660-1123-2). This account gives an in-depth look at this important moment in American history and its effects on the events to come. (Rev: BL 9/15/99; HBG 4/00) [973.6]

9059 Turner, Glennette Tilley. *The Underground Railroad in Illinois* (5–8). Illus. 2001, Newman Educational Publg. paper $16.95 (0-938990-05-5). Using a question-and-answer format, this book focuses on the Underground Railroad in Illinois, the historical period, the problems, people who worked on the effort, and the many heroic deeds. (Rev: BL 2/15/01) [973.7]

9060 White, Deborah Gray. *Let My People Go: African Americans, 1804–1860* (7–12). Illus. Series: Young Oxford History of African Americans. 1996, Oxford $24.00 (0-19-508769-0). The story of slavery in the United States during the 19th century, attempts to end it, efforts to rescue slaves, and events leading up to the Civil War. (Rev: BL 5/15/96; SLJ 6/96; VOYA 8/96) [973]

9061 Young, Mary, and Gerald Horne. *Testaments of Courage: Selections from Men's Slave Narratives* (7–12). Series: African-American Slave Narratives. 1995, Watts LB $25.00 (0-531-11205-5). Chilling and illuminating excerpts from the writings of slaves, beginning with one from 1831. (Rev: BR 1–2/96; SLJ 2/96) [973.6]

9062 Zeinert, Karen. *The Amistad Slave Revolt and American Abolition* (7–10). Illus. 1997, Shoe String LB $21.50 (0-208-02438-7); paper $12.95 (0-208-02439-5). The dramatic story of Cinque and 52 other slaves onboard the Spanish ship *Amistad* in 1839 and of their historic mutiny and subsequent trial. (Rev: BL 7/97; SLJ 6/97) [326]

9063 Zeinert, Karen. *Tragic Prelude: Bleeding Kansas* (6–10). Illus. 2001, Linnet $25.00 (0-208-02446-8). An accessible account of the conflict that erupted in Kansas over the question of slavery, with information on individuals including John Brown and Hannah Ropes, a timeline, extracts from primary documents, photographs, and references. (Rev: BL 6/1–15/01; HBG 10/01; SLJ 6/01; VOYA 2/02) [978.1]

CIVIL WAR (1861–1865)

9064 Arnold, James R., and Roberta Wiener. *Divided in Two: The Road to Civil War* (4–7). Series: The Civil War. 2002, Lerner LB $25.26 (0-8225-2312-4). A well-designed oversize book that describes the events of 1861 that led to the outbreak of the Civil War. (Rev: BL 10/15/02; HBG 10/02; SLJ 7/02) [973.7]

9065 Arnold, James R., and Roberta Wiener. *Life Goes On: The Civil War at Home* (4–7). Series: The Civil War. 2002, Lerner LB $25.26 (0-8225-2315-9). Many easy-to-follow maps and illustrations are used with a simple text to describe life on the home front in both South and North during the Civil War. (Rev: BL 10/15/02; HBG 10/02; SLJ 7/02) [973.7]

9066 Arnold, James R., and Roberta Wiener. *Lost Cause: The End of the Civil War* (4–7). Series: The Civil War. 2002, Lerner LB $25.26 (0-8225-2317-5). Beginning with the campaign of 1864, this well-illustrated account traces the Civil War to Appomattox and beyond. (Rev: BL 10/15/02; HBG 10/02; SLJ 6/02) [973.7]

9067 Arnold, James R., and Roberta Wiener. *On to Richmond: The Civil War in the East, 1861–1862* (4–7). Illus. Series: Civil War. 2002, Lerner LB $25.26 (0-8225-2313-2). Early battles in the Civil War are the subject of this volume for older readers that includes timelines, notes, and lists of Web sites and battlefields to visit. (Rev: BL 10/15/02; HBG 10/02; SLJ 6/02; VOYA 6/03) [973.7]

9068 Arnold, James R., and Roberta Wiener. *River to Victory: The Civil War in the West* (4–7). Series: The Civil War. 2002, Lerner LB $25.26 (0-8225-2314-0). The Civil War in the West from 1861 through 1863 is re-created in text and illustrations with many maps and sidebars on personalities and events. (Rev: BL 10/15/02; HBG 10/02; SLJ 6/02; VOYA 6/03) [973.7]

9069 Arnold, James R., and Roberta Wiener. *This Unhappy Country: The Turn of the Civil War* (4–7). Illus. Series: Civil War. 2002, Lerner LB $25.26 (0-8225-2316-7). Maps and other period illustrations flesh out the events of 1863, a pivotal year in the Civil War, in this volume for older readers. (Rev: BL 10/15/02; HBG 10/02; SLJ 7/02) [973.7]

9070 Ashby, Ruth. *Gettysburg* (5–8). Series: Civil War Chronicles. 2002, Smart Apple LB $28.50 (1-58340-186-5). The three days of battle are covered in some detail, and the text and photographs convey the horrible conditions. (Rev: HBG 3/03; SLJ 2/03; VOYA 4/03) [973]

9071 Bailey, Ronald H. *The Bloodiest Day: The Battle of Antietam* (7–12). Illus. 1984, Silver Burdett LB $25.93 (0-8094-4741-X). The story of Lee's defeat in the battle that caused terrible losses on both sides. [973.7]

9072 Barney, William L. *The Civil War and Reconstruction: A Student Companion* (7–12). Series: Oxford Student Companions to American History. 2001, Oxford LB $45.00 (0-19-511559-7). An alphabetically arranged series of articles covering all aspects of the Civil War and Reconstruction, illustrated with photographs, maps, and reproductions. (Rev: BL 9/15/01; SLJ 6/01) [973.7]

9073 Beller, Susan P. *Billy Yank and Johnny Reb: Soldiering in the Civil War* (5–8). Illus. 2000, Twenty-First Century LB $26.90 (0-7613-1869-0). Solid, interesting information is provided in this illustrated account that describes the everyday life of soldiers on both sides of the Civil War. (Rev: BL 10/15/00; HBG 3/01; SLJ 12/00; VOYA 2/01) [973.7]

9074 Beller, Susan P. *The Confederate Ladies of Richmond* (5–8). Illus. 1999, Twenty-First Century LB $26.90 (0-7613-1470-9). The Civil War seen through the eyes and activities of the upper-class women of Richmond, the capital of the Confederacy. (Rev: BCCB 1/00; BL 12/15/99; HBG 3/00; SLJ 1/00) [973.7]

9075 Beller, Susan P. *To Hold This Ground: A Desperate Battle at Gettysburg* (8–12). 1995, Simon & Schuster $15.00 (0-689-50621-X). After a brief history of the Civil War to July 2, 1863, the author combines narrative and primary sources to recount the Battle of Gettysburg, with alternate chapters focusing on each regiment involved, telling their histories, giving brief biographies of their commanders, and describing the battle as opportunities were taken and lost. (Rev: BR 3–4/96; SLJ 12/95; VOYA 4/96) [973.7]

9076 Beller, Susan Provost. *The Civil War* (5–8). Series: American Voices From. 2002, Benchmark LB $22.95 (0-7614-1204-2). A collection of primary sources that includes speeches by Lincoln and Lee and represents people from all walks of life commenting on different aspects of the Civil War. (Rev: HBG 10/03; SLJ 4/03) [973.7]

9077 Biel, Timothy L. *Life in the North During the Civil War* (6–10). Illus. Series: Way People Live. 1997, Lucent LB $27.45 (1-56006-334-3). This book tells how civilians in the North lived during the Civil War, far from the battles but nevertheless deeply affected by the war's terrible toll. (Rev: BL 3/15/97; SLJ 5/97) [973.7]

9078 Bolotin, Norman. *Civil War A to Z: A Young Reader's Guide to Over 100 People, Places, and Points of Importance* (4–8). Illus. 2002, Dutton $19.99 (0-525-46268-6). An encyclopedia-style text on the Civil War, with brief entries on important battles; politicians, generals, and other key figures; and crucial issues of the time, with photographs, a glossary, a timeline, and information on further resources. (Rev: BL 7/02; SLJ 7/02) [973.7]

9079 Brooks, Victor. *African Americans in the Civil War* (4–8). Illus. Series: Untold History of the Civil War. 2000, Chelsea $19.75 (0-7910-5435-7). This book describes African American soldiers' roles in the Civil War, on both the Confederate and Union sides. (Rev: BL 5/15/00; HBG 10/00; SLJ 6/00) [355.7]

9080 Brooks, Victor. *Civil War Forts* (4–8). Illus. Series: Untold History of the Civil War. 2000, Chelsea $19.75 (0-7910-5438-1). Describes the important roles played by such forts as Fort Sumter and Fort Wagner in South Carolina, Fort Fischer in North Carolina, Fort Henry and Fort Donelson in Tennessee, and the city of Vicksburg, Mississippi. (Rev: BL 5/15/00; HBG 10/00; SLJ 7/00) [973.7]

9081 Brooks, Victor. *Secret Weapons in the Civil War* (4–8). Series: Untold History of the Civil War. 2000, Chelsea $19.75 (0-7910-5433-0). Covers such secret weapons and maneuvers as underwater transportation, advanced artillery, communications devices, and explosive materials. (Rev: BL 5/15/00; HBG 10/00; SLJ 7/00) [973.7]

9082 Burchard, Peter. *Lincoln and Slavery* (6–10). 1999, Simon & Schuster $17.00 (0-689-81570-0). This book discusses the predominance of slavery as a political and moral issue in 19th-century America and traces the evolution of Lincoln's ideas on slavery and how he put his beliefs into practice. (Rev: HB 7–8/99; SLJ 7/99; VOYA 8/99) [973.7]

9083 Catton, Bruce. *The Civil War* (7–12). Illus. 1985, Houghton paper $16.00 (0-8281-0305-4). A well-illustrated book that deals with the major events and personalities of the war. [973.7]

9084 *Chancellorsville* (7–12). Illus. Series: Voices of the Civil War. 1996, Time-Life Books $24.95 (0-7853-4708-0). A handsome description of this key Civil War battle, featuring regimental histories, letters, diaries, and memoirs. (Rev: BL 1/1–15/97) [973.7]

9085 *Charleston* (7–12). Series: Voices of the Civil War. 1997, Time-Life Books $29.95 (0-7835-4709-9). The story of the siege of Charleston and its fall to Union forces in February 1865, with quotations from original sources. (Rev: BL 5/15/97) [973.7]

9086 *Chickamauga* (7–12). Series: Voices of the Civil War. 1997, Time-Life Books $29.95 (0-7835-4710-2). Using many original sources, this is the story of the 1863 battle in northern Georgia after which the Union Army fell back to Chattanooga. (Rev: BL 7/97) [973.7]

9087 Clinton, Catherine. *Scholastic Encyclopedia of the Civil War* (4–7). Illus. 1999, Scholastic paper $18.95 (0-590-37227-0). Using many black-and-white illustrations, this narrative gives a good chronological introduction to the Civil War, with interesting supplementary information. (Rev: BL 1/1–15/00; HBG 3/00; SLJ 5/00) [973.7]

9088 Colbert, Nancy. *The Firing on Fort Sumter: A Splintered Nation Goes to War* (6–12). Illus. 2000, Morgan Reynolds LB $19.95 (1-883846-51-X). An intriguing, detailed account, told in lively prose and many photographs, of the incident that began the Civil War. (Rev: BL 10/1/00; HBG 3/01; VOYA 6/01) [973.7.]

9089 Collier, Christopher, and James Lincoln Collier. *The Civil War, 1860–1865* (5–8). Series: Drama of American History. 1999, Marshall Cavendish LB $29.93 (0-7614-0818-5). A dramatic, accurate account that covers causes, leaders, battles, effects, and the immediate aftermath of the Civil War. (Rev: BL 2/15/00; HBG 10/00; SLJ 3/00) [973.7]

9090 Corrick, James A. *The Battle of Gettysburg* (6–10). Illus. Series: Great Battles in History. 1996, Lucent LB $26.20 (1-56006-451-X). This account of the decisive battle of the Civil War contains useful maps and timelines plus many excerpts from primary sources. (Rev: BL 4/15/96; SLJ 7/96) [973.7]

9091 Corrick, James A. *Life Among the Soldiers and Cavalry* (6–12). Illus. Series: American War Library. 1999, Lucent LB $18.96 (1-56006-491-9). This concise account examines soldiers' everyday life during the Civil War with material on topics like enlistment, clothing, weapons, training, and recreation. (Rev: BL 1/1–15/00; HBG 9/00; SLJ 3/00) [973]

9092 Damon, Duane. *Growing Up In the Civil War: 1861 to 1865* (5–8). Series: Our America. 2002, Lerner LB $31.95 (0-8225-0656-4). The lives of children in this period are described with many quotations and excerpts from diaries, letters, and memoirs. (Rev: BL 2/15/03; HBG 3/03; SLJ 2/03) [973.7]

9093 Damon, Duane. *When This Cruel War Is Over* (5–8). Illus. 1996, Lerner LB $30.35 (0-8225-1731-0). The human side of the Civil War is stressed as the reader goes behind the scenes at the battlefields and learns about conditions on the home front. (Rev: BL 8/96; SLJ 8/96*) [973.7]

9094 Day, Nancy. *Your Travel Guide to Civil War America* (4–8). Series: Passport to History. 2000, Lerner LB $26.60 (0-8225-3078-3). Using the format of a guide book, this account takes the reader back to the Civil War with coverage of topics including food, civil and military clothing, Lincoln's office, Gettysburg, and various battlefields. (Rev: BL 3/1/01; HBG 10/01; SLJ 4/01; VOYA 8/01) [073.7]

9095 Dolan, Edward F. *The American Civil War: A House Divided* (5–8). Illus. 1997, Millbrook LB $29.90 (0-7613-0255-7). A chronologically arranged, well-organized account of the Civil War, beginning with the shots fired at Fort Sumter. (Rev: BL 3/1/98; HBG 3/98; SLJ 3/98) [973.7]

9096 Dosier, Susan. *Civil War Cooking: The Confederacy* (4–7). Series: Exploring History Through Simple Recipes. 2000, Capstone LB $22.60 (0-7368-0350-5). As well as simple, authentic recipes of Civil War times, this book tells of customs, family roles, and everyday life during this period. Also use *Civil War Cooking: The Union* (2000). (Rev: BL 8/00; HBG 10/00; SLJ 9/00) [973.7]

9097 Egger-Bovet, Howard, and Marlene Smith-Baranzini. *Book of the American Civil War* (5–7). Series: Brown Paper School. 1998, Little, Brown paper $12.95 (0-316-22243-7). Facts, photographs, illustrations, stories and appealing activities are combined in this overview of the Civil War. (Rev: SLJ 12/98) [973.7]

9098 Feinberg, Barbara S. *Abraham Lincoln's Gettysburg Address: Four Score and More . . .* (4–8). Illus. 2000, Twenty-First Century LB $24.40 (0-7613-1410-8). Illustrated with period photographs, this well-researched volume reveals surprising facts about the Gettysburg Address and its delivery. (Rev: BL 11/15/00) [973.7]

9099 *First Manassas* (7–12). Series: Voices of the Civil War. 1997, Time-Life Books $29.95 (0-7835-4712-9). The story of the first Battle of Bull Run fought close to the town of Manassas in north Virginia, told with extensive use of personal narratives. (Rev: BL 10/15/97) [973.7]

9100 Fleming, Thomas. *Band of Brothers: West Point in the Civil War* (6–9). Illus. 1988, Walker LB $14.85 (0-8027-6741-9). The influence in the Civil War of such men as Grant and Lee, all of whom were graduates of West Point. (Rev: BL 2/1/88) [973.7]

9101 Fraser, Mary Ann. *Vicksburg: The Battle That Won the Civil War* (4–8). Illus. 1999, Holt $17.95 (0-8050-6106-1). The focus of this book is the Battle of Vicksburg, the events surrounding it, the participants, and its importance. (Rev: BCCB 1/00; BL 3/1/00; HBG 3/00; SLJ 3/00; VOYA 4/00) [973.7]

9102 Friend, Sandra. *Florida in the Civil War: A State in Turmoil* (5–8). Illus. 2001, Millbrook LB $25.90 (0-7613-1973-5). An account of Florida's involvement in the Civil War, with maps and photographs. (Rev: BL 10/15/01; HBG 3/02; SLJ 2/02; VOYA 12/01) [973.7]

9103 Gaines, Ann Graham. *The Battle of Gettysburg in American History* (6–10). Series: In American History. 2001, Enslow LB $20.95 (0-7660-1455-X). The causes and events related to this, the most momentous battle of the Civil War, are retold with a fine interweaving of personal stories. (Rev: BL 8/1/01; HBG 10/01) [973.7]

9104 *Gettysburg* (8–12). Series: Voices of the Civil War. 1995, Time-Life Books $29.95 (0-7835-4700-5). The Battle of Gettysburg, with illustrations showing the human dimension of the battle. (Rev: BL 5/15/95) [973.7]

9105 Golay, Michael. *The Civil War* (7–12). Series: America at War. 1992, Facts on File $25.00 (0-8160-2514-2). A comprehensive chronicle of the war, from the issues that gave rise to it to Lee's surrender at Appomattox. (Rev: BL 10/15/92) [973.7]

9106 Hakim, Joy. *War, Terrible War.* 2nd ed. (5–8). Illus. Series: A History of Us. 1999, Oxford $19.95 (0-19-512761-7). This excellent history of the Civil War is basically a reissue of the 1994 edition with a few minor revisions and changes in illustrations. (Rev: BL 12/15/99) [973.7]

9107 Haskins, Jim. *Black, Blue, and Gray: African Americans in the Civil War* (5–8). Illus. 1998, Simon & Schuster $18.95 (0-689-80655-8). A concise and rewarding picture of the role of African Americans before, during, and after the Civil War. (Rev: BL 2/15/98; HBG 10/98; SLJ 3/98*; VOYA 10/98) [973.7]

9108 Haskins, Jim. *The Day Fort Sumter Was Fired On: A Photo History of the Civil War* (5–8). Illus. 1995, Scholastic paper $6.95 (0-590-46397-7). A short, well-illustrated history of the Civil War, with coverage of the roles of women and African Americans. (Rev: BL 7/95) [973.7]

9109 Heinrichs, Ann. *The Emancipation Proclamation* (5–8). Series: We the People. 2002, Compass Point LB $27.15 (0-7565-0209-8). An accessible examination of the proclamation's creation that reveals Lincoln's careful attention to detail. (Rev: SLJ 7/02) [973.7]

9110 Herbert, Janis. *The Civil War for Kids: A History with 21 Activities* (4–8). Illus. 1999, Chicago Review paper $14.95 (1-55652-355-6). As well as supplying information about leaders, battles, daily life, and the contributions of women and African Americans, this book on the Civil War includes activities such as reenactments of battles, most of which are geared toward groups. (Rev: SLJ 12/99) [973.7]

9111 Holford, David M. *Lincoln and the Emancipation Proclamation in American History* (5–8). Series: In American History. 2002, Enslow LB $20.95 (0-7660-1456-8). A well-researched account that gives background material and traces the significance of this document. (Rev: BL 1/1–15/03; HBG 3/03) [973.7]

9112 Hughes, Christopher. *Antietam* (5–8). Series: Battlefields Across America. 1998, Millbrook LB $26.90 (0-7613-3009-7). This book describes the battle at Antietam in detail, discusses its impact on the outcome of the war and on the future of the United States, profiles the major people involved, and provides information on where the history of this battle is preserved. (Rev: HBG 9/98; SLJ 8/98) [973.7]

9113 Hull, Mary E. *The Union and the Civil War in American History* (6–10). Series: In American History. 2000, Enslow LB $19.95 (0-7660-1416-9). This account explains how the North tried to keep the nation together through Civil War and highlights how different groups — from nurses and soldiers to people on the home front — helped the war effort. (Rev: BL 7/00; HBG 3/01) [973.7]

9114 Kantor, MacKinlay. *Gettysburg* (6–9). Illus. 1952, Random paper $5.99 (0-394-89181-3). The story of the crucial battle of the Civil War that could have meant a total victory for the Confederacy. [973.7]

9115 Kent, Zachary. *The Civil War: "A House Divided"* (5–7). Illus. Series: American War. 1994, Enslow LB $20.95 (0-89490-522-8). Using many original quotations, period illustrations, and maps, this account gives a concise history of the Civil War. (Rev: BL 7/94; SLJ 9/94) [973.7]

9116 *Lee Takes Command: From Seven Days to Second Bull Run* (7–12). Illus. 1984, Silver Burdett LB $25.93 (0-8094-4805-X). A graphic account complemented with many illustrations of Lee's campaign during 1862. [973.7]

9117 McPherson, James M. *Fields of Fury: The American Civil War* (6–8). Illus. 2002, Simon & Schuster $22.95 (0-689-84833-1). Packed with interesting illustrations and sidebars, this large-format book gives an overview of the Civil War that will attract both report writers and casual browsers. (Rev: BL 11/15/02; HBG 3/03; SLJ 10/02*) [973.7]

9118 Marinelli, Deborah A. *The Assassination of Abraham Lincoln* (6–9). Series: The Library of Political Assassinations. 2002, Rosen LB $26.50 (0-8239-3539-6). In addition to describing the assassination itself, Marinelli covers the Civil War and Lincoln's legacy. (Rev: BL 8/02; SLJ 8/02) [976]

9119 Morrison, Taylor. *Civil War Artist* (5–7). Illus. 1999, Houghton $16.00 (0-395-91426-4). Explains the long and complex process involved in transmitting drawings of Civil War scenes from the field to the public via a newspaper. (Rev: BL 4/15/99; HBG 3/00; SLJ 5/99) [070.4]

9120 Murphy, Jim. *The Boys' War: Confederate and Union Soldiers Talk About the Civil War* (6–12). Series: Icarus World Issues. 1990, Clarion $18.00 (0-89919-893-7). Diaries, journals, and letters of young soldiers on both sides of the Civil War are used to describe their military role, early impressions of the war, life in the camps and field, and return home. (Rev: BL 12/1/90; SLJ 1/91*) [973.7]

9121 Murphy, Jim. *The Long Road to Gettysburg* (6–9). 1992, Clarion $17.00 (0-395-55965-0). An account of the Civil War from both the Union and Confederate perspectives. (Rev: BL 5/15/92*; SLJ 6/92*) [973.7]

9122 Nofi, Albert A. *Spies in the Civil War* (5–8). Series: Untold History of the Civil War. 2000, Chelsea $19.75 (0-7910-5427-6). In this account readers meet famous spies (including Allan Pinkerton and Belle Boyd) and lesser-known spies of the Civil War. (Rev: HBG 10/00; SLJ 7/00) [973.7]

9123 Ray, Delia. *Behind the Blue and Gray: The Soldier's Life in the Civil War* (5–10). Series: Young Readers' History of the Civil War. 1991, Dutton $17.99 (0-525-67333-4). This sequel to *A Nation Torn* uses personal accounts to describe the life of the common soldier on both sides of the Civil War. (Rev: BL 9/1/91; SLJ 8/91*) [973.7]

9124 Reger, James P. *The Battle of Antietam* (6–10). Illus. Series: Battles. 1996, Lucent LB $26.20 (1-56006-454-4). The story of the bloody 1862 Civil War battle that cost both sides dearly but stopped the northern invasion of General Lee. (Rev: BL 1/1–15/97; SLJ 7/97) [973.7]

9125 Reger, James P. *Life in the South During the Civil War* (6–10). Illus. Series: Way People Live. 1997, Lucent LB $27.45 (1-56006-333-5). A behind-the-battlefront look at life in the cities and on the plantations of the South during the Civil War and how the war affected people's everyday lives. (Rev: BL 3/15/97; SLJ 3/97) [975]

9126 Roberts, Russell. *Lincoln and the Abolition of Slavery* (5–12). Series: American War. 1999, Lucent LB $27.45 (1-56006-580-X). This gripping, fully documented account describes the events leading to the Civil War and Lincoln's role in these events. (Rev: BL 1/1–15/00; HBG 10/00) [973.7]

9127 Robertson, James I., Jr. *Civil War! America Becomes One Nation* (6–10). 1992, Knopf $16.99 (0-394-92996-9). A basic history of the Civil War, with each chapter devoted to one calendar year of the conflict. (Rev: BL 4/1/92; SLJ 5/92) [973.7]

9128 Savage, Douglas J. *Ironclads and Blockades in the Civil War* (4–8). Series: Untold History of the Civil War. 2000, Chelsea $19.95 (0-7910-5429-2). A clear text and period illustrations introduce the huge ships used in the Union and Confederate navies and their efforts to block different ports during the Civil War. (Rev: BL 7/00; HBG 10/00; SLJ 9/00) [973.7]

9129 Savage, Douglas J. *Prison Camps in the Civil War* (4–8). Series: Untold History of the Civil War. 2000, Chelsea $19.75 (0-7910-5428-4). This account describes the prisoner-of-war camps on both sides during the Civil War, the appalling conditions in them, and the acts of heroism that sometimes occurred. (Rev: BL 7/00; HBG 10/00; SLJ 9/00) [973.7]

9130 Savage, Douglas J. *Women in the Civil War* (4–8). Series: Untold History of the Civil War. 2000, Chelsea $19.75 (0-7910-5436-5). This book describes the roles played by women in the Civil War as nurses, suppliers of support services, and crusaders for issues including suffrage and abolition. (Rev: BL 7/00; HBG 10/00; SLJ 9/00) [973.7]

9131 Schomp, Virginia. *The Civil War* (5–8). Illus. Series: Letters from the Homefront. 2001, Marshall Cavendish LB $28.50 (0-7614-1095-3). After placing the conflict in historical context, Schomp uses excerpts from letters and other accounts that bring the period to life. (Rev: BL 10/15/01; HBG 3/02; SLJ 3/02) [973.7]

9132 *Second Manassas* (8–12). Illus. Series: Voices of the Civil War. 1995, Time-Life Books $29.95 (0-7835-4701-3). The gripping story of the important Civil War battle, the Second Battle of Bull Run, in 1862, re-created with extensive use of original documents. (Rev: BL 7/95) [973.7]

9133 *Shiloh* (7–12). Illus. Series: Voices of the Civil War. 1996, Time-Life Books $29.95 (0-7835-4707-2). The horror and gallantry associated with the Battle of Shiloh come alive through this account rich in excerpts from military histories, letters, diary entries, and memoirs. (Rev: BL 1/1–15/97; BR 3–4/97) [973.7]

9134 Smith, Carter, ed. *One Nation Again: A Sourcebook on the Civil War* (5–8). Series: American Albums. 1993, Millbrook LB $25.90 (1-56294-266-2). This heavily illustrated sourcebook chronicles the peace at Appomattox and the period immediately following. (Rev: BL 3/1/93) [973.8]

9135 Smith, Carter, ed. *The Road to Appomattox: A Sourcebook on the Civil War* (5–8). Series: American Albums. 1993, Millbrook $25.90 (1-56294-264-6). The last battles of the Civil War are covered in this album that uses period illustrations and excerpts from first-person accounts. (Rev: BL 3/1/93) [973.7]

9136 Somerlott, Robert. *The Lincoln Assassination* (5–8). Series: In American History. 1998, Enslow LB $20.95 (0-89490-886-3). Using primary sources, the author has created a gripping story of the causes of the assassination, the shooting itself, and its aftermath. (Rev: BL 7/98; BR 9–10/98; SLJ 6/98) [973.7]

9137 Stanchak, John. *Civil War* (5–8). Illus. Series: Eyewitness Books. 2000, DK paper $15.99 (0-7894-6302-4). This highly visual treatment presents topics related to the Civil War such as causes, battles, slavery, states' rights, weapons, and uniforms in a series of double-page spreads. (Rev: BL 1/1–15/01; HBG 3/01; SLJ 12/00) [973.7]

9138 Sullivan, George. *The Civil War at Sea* (5–8). Illus. 2001, Twenty-First Century LB $27.90 (0-7613-1553-5). This book tells of the struggle between the Union and Confederate forces in American bays, harbors, and rivers with material on famous ships and their commanders, important battles, and the daily life of the sailors. (Rev: BL 2/1/01; HBG 10/01; SLJ 3/01) [973.7]

9139 Tackach, James, ed. *The Battle of Gettysburg* (8–12). Illus. Series: At Issue in History. 2002, Greenhaven paper $18.70 (0-7377-0826-6). Excerpts from historical documents and contemporary writings portray events at Gettysburg from both Union

and Confederate points of view, with maps, photographs, and other illustrations. (Rev: BL 5/1/02) [973.7]

9140 Tackach, James. *The Emancipation Proclamation: Abolishing Slavery in the South* (8–12). Illus. Series: Words That Changed History. 1999, Lucent LB $27.45 (1-56006-370-X). This is the story of the short proclamation that changed U.S. history, with material on slavery, Abraham Lincoln, the Civil War, and the document's historical legacy. (Rev: BL 6/1–15/99; HBG 4/00; SLJ 8/99) [973.7]

9141 *Vicksburg* (7–12). Illus. Series: Voices of the Civil War. 1997, Time-Life Books $29.95 (0-7835-4713-7). The story of the siege of Vicksburg in 1863 and the Union victory that cut the Confederacy in two. (Rev: BL 1/1–15/97) [973.7]

9142 *War Between Brothers* (7–12). Illus. 1996, Time-Life Books $19.95 (0-7835-6251-9). A discussion of the Civil War, including secession of the Confederate states, key Civil War battles, and the assassination of Abraham Lincoln, using vivid text, first-person narratives, and numerous illustrations. (Rev: BL 12/15/96; BR 3–4/97) [973.7]

9143 Weber, Michael. *Civil War and Reconstruction* (5–8). Series: The Making of America. 2001, Raintree Steck-Vaughn LB $19.98 (0-8172-5707-2). Using many illustrations, interesting sidebars, and an accessible text, this is a concise history of the Civil War and its immediate aftermath. (Rev: BL 4/15/01) [973.7]

9144 Wisler, G. Clifton. *When Johnny Went Marching: Young Americans Fight the Civil War* (5–8). Illus. 2001, HarperCollins LB $18.89 (0-06-029242-3). Stories of young men and women under the age of 18 who enlisted illegally in the Civil War, with period photographs and diary excerpts. (Rev: BL 11/15/01; HB 9–10/01; HBG 3/02; SLJ 11/01) [973.7]

9145 Yancey, Diane. *Strategic Battles* (5–12). Series: American War. 1999, Lucent LB $27.45 (1-56006-496-X). The key battles of the Civil War are covered in chronological order with maps and other illustrations. (Rev: BL 1/1–15/00; HBG 10/00) [973.7]

9146 Zeinert, Karen. *The Lincoln Murder Plot* (6–12). 1999, Shoe String LB $22.50 (0-208-02451-4). A detailed, well-documented retelling of the first assassination of a U.S. president and its world-shaking results. (Rev: BL 3/1/99; BR 9–10/99; HB 7–8/99; SLJ 5/99; VOYA 4/99) [973.7]

9147 Zeinert, Karen. *Those Courageous Women of the Civil War* (5–8). Illus. 1998, Millbrook LB $29.90 (0-7613-0212-3). This account relates the contributions of women during the Civil War, with details on how they served as nurses, spies, writers, and workers on the home front. (Rev: BL 6/1–15/98; HBG 3/99) [973.7]

WESTWARD EXPANSION AND PIONEER LIFE

9148 Altman, Linda Jacobs. *The California Gold Rush in American History* (4–8). Illus. Series: In American History. 1997, Enslow LB $20.95 (0-89490-878-2). After a brief history of the California Gold Rush, this book covers topics including frontier injustice, racial discrimination, and the place of women. (Rev: BR 1–2/98; HBG 3/98; SLJ 3/98) [979.4]

9149 Anderson, Dale. *Westward Expansion* (5–8). Series: The Making of America. 2001, Raintree Steck-Vaughn LB $28.54 (0-8172-5705-5). An attractive, balanced history of the expansion of the United States to the Pacific with many biographies of pioneers given in sidebars. (Rev: BL 4/15/01; HBG 10/01) [978]

9150 Bentley, Judith. *Brides, Midwives, and Widows* (6–9). Series: Settling the West. 1995, Twenty-First Century LB $24.90 (0-8050-2994-X). The story of the women who helped settle the West, using diaries and other primary sources. (Rev: BL 8/95; SLJ 9/95) [978]

9151 Bentley, Judith. *Explorers, Trappers, and Guides* (6–9). Series: Settling the West. 1995, Twenty-First Century LB $24.90 (0-8050-2995-8). Unusually well-told stories about lesser-known explorers taken from first-person accounts. (Rev: BL 8/95; SLJ 11/95) [979.5]

9152 Blackwood, Gary L. *Life on the Oregon Trail* (5–8). Series: The Way People Live. 1999, Lucent LB $27.45 (1-56006-540-0). Using many excerpts from diaries, this is a thorough, appealing account of life on the Oregon Trail, which took pioneers from Missouri to the Pacific Ocean. (Rev: HBG 3/00; SLJ 8/99) [978]

9153 Calabro, Marian. *The Perilous Journey of the Donner Party* (5–8). Illus. 1999, Houghton $20.00 (0-395-86610-3). The story of the ill-fated Donner Party, as seen through the eyes of 12-year-old Virginia Reed. (Rev: BL 4/1/99*; HB 5–6/99; SLJ 5/99; VOYA 2/00) [979.4]

9154 Collier, Christopher, and James Lincoln Collier. *Indians, Cowboys, and Farmers: And the Battle for the Great Plains* (5–8). Series: The Drama of American History. 2001, Marshall Cavendish LB $29.93 (0-7614-1052-X). This excellently written and illustrated account covers the history of the Great Plains from the end of the Civil War to 1910, by which time the Native Americans had been scattered and the ranchers and farmers had reached a truce. (Rev: BL 3/15/01; HBG 10/01; SLJ 7/01) [973.8]

9155 DeAngelis, Gina. *The Black Cowboys* (4–8). Illus. Series: Legends of the West. 1997, Chelsea LB $21.95 (0-7910-2589-6); paper $9.95 (0-7910-2590-X). A look at the contributions of African

Americans such as Jim Beckwourth and Edward Rose to the exploration and settlement of the American West. (Rev: BL 2/15/98; HBG 3/98) [978]

9156 DeAngelis, Gina. *The Wild West* (5–8). Series: Costume, Tradition, and Culture: Reflecting on the Past. 1998, Chelsea $19.75 (0-7910-5169-2). Illustrated with historical collectors' cards, this account relates the legends and stories of the Wild West — its explorers, lawmen, outlaws, and Native Americans. (Rev: BL 3/15/99; HBG 10/99) [978]

9157 Delgado, James P. *Shipwrecks from the Westward Movement* (5–7). Series: Shipwrecks. 2000, Watts LB $24.00 (0-531-20380-8). A discussion and exploration of the shipwrecks — from small canoes to steam-powered riverboats — that occurred as European settlers moved across America. (Rev: BL 10/15/00) [978]

9158 Dolan, Edward F. *Beyond the Frontier: The Story of the Trails West* (6–10). Series: Great Journeys. 1999, Benchmark LB $31.36 (0-7614-0969-6). As well as describing life on the Santa Fe, Oregon, and California trails, and the sea routes taken west, this account covers such specific topics as the Donner Party and life in western settlements. (Rev: BL 1/1–15/00; HBG 3/00; SLJ 2/00) [978]

9159 Duncan, Dayton. *People of the West* (5–10). Illus. 1996, Little, Brown $19.95 (0-316-19627-4). Individual people — both famous and less well known — tell in their own words about the opening up of the West. Based on the PBS series. (Rev: BL 8/96; SLJ 10/96) [978]

9160 Freedman, Russell. *Buffalo Hunt* (7–10). 1988, Holiday $21.95 (0-8234-0702-0). A history of how the buffalo were hunted from the times of the Indians to the slaughter by whites that brought on the near extinction of this animal. (Rev: BL 10/1/88; SLJ 10/88) [973]

9161 Freedman, Russell. *Children of the Wild West* (5–9). Illus. 1983, Clarion $18.00 (0-89919-143-6). A look at the life of the children of pioneers. (Rev: BL 1/1/90) [978]

9162 Freedman, Russell. *Cowboys of the Wild West* (5–8). Illus. 1990, Houghton paper $9.95 (0-395-54800-4). Text and excellent historical photographs describe these romantic figures. (Rev: BCCB 12/85; HB 3–4/86) [978.02]

9163 Goldsmith, Connie. *Lost in Death Valley: The True Story of Four Families in California's Gold Rush* (5–8). Illus. 2001, Twenty-First Century LB $24.90 (0-7613-1915-8). Using original sources, the author has re-created the story of an ill-fated pioneer trek and the shortcut that led them into Death Valley. (Rev: BL 4/1/01; HBG 10/01; SLJ 4/01; VOYA 10/01) [979.4]

9164 Green, Carl R. *The California Trail to Gold in American History* (6–10). Series: In American History. 2000, Enslow LB $20.95 (0-7660-1347-2).

Searchers for gold in California first used the Oregon Trail to go west, then they made their own separate, more direct trail. This is the history of that trail. (Rev: BL 10/15/2000; HBG 3/01) [978]

9165 Green, Carl R., and William R. Sanford. *The Dalton Gang* (4–8). Illus. Series: Outlaws and Lawmen of the Wild West. 1995, Enslow LB $16.95 (0-89490-588-0). The story of the gang of outlaws who roamed the West during pioneer days. (Rev: BL 11/15/95) [978]

9166 Gunderson, Mary. *Oregon Trail Cooking* (4–7). Series: Exploring History Through Simple Recipes. 2000, Capstone LB $22.60 (0-7368-0355-6). This book tells about journeys on the Oregon Trail, the lifestyles of the pioneers, the foods they ate, and some of the recipes that they used. Also use *Cowboy Cooking* (2000). (Rev: BL 8/00; HBG 10/00; SLJ 12/00) [973.5]

9167 Hakim, Joy. *The New Nation*. 2nd ed. (5–8). Series: A History of Us. 1999, Oxford LB $19.95 (0-19-512757-9). Political and social developments, including territorial expansion and pioneer life, are covered in this excellent history of America from 1789 through 1850. (Rev: BL 12/15/99) [973.5]

9168 Harris, Edward D. *John Charles Fremont and the Great Western Reconnaissance* (6–9). Illus. 1990, Chelsea LB $21.95 (0-7910-1312-X). An account of the exploration of the West that concentrates on the five major journeys taken by Fremont. (Rev: BL 9/15/90) [973.6]

9169 Harvey, Brett. *Farmers and Ranchers* (6–9). Illus. Series: Settling the West. 1995, Twenty-First Century LB $24.90 (0-8050-2999-0). Westward migration and homesteading are covered in this history that uses first-person accounts and the experiences of people of various backgrounds. (Rev: BL 8/95; SLJ 11/95) [978.02]

9170 Hatt, Christine. *The American West: Native Americans, Pioneers and Settlers* (4–7). Series: History in Writing. 1999, Bedrick $19.95 (0-87226-290-1). A broad overview of frontier life in America with material on such topics as the Louisiana Purchase, Indian relocations, the Gold Rush, and a settler's daily life. (Rev: HBG 3/00; SLJ 5/99) [978]

9171 Herb, Angela. *Beyond the Mississippi: Early Westward Expansion of the United States* (7–12). Illus. Series: Young Readers' History of the West. 1996, Dutton $16.99 (0-525-67503-5). This large-size, heavily illustrated history of westward expansion covers such subjects as traders and trappers, missionaries, the treatment of Native Americans, homesteaders, the Mexican War, the gold rush, and the Oregon Trail. (Rev: BL 10/15/96; SLJ 11/96; VOYA 2/97) [978]

9172 Hevly, Nancy. *Preachers and Teachers* (6–9). Illus. Series: Settling the West. 1995, Twenty-First Century LB $24.90 (0-8050-2996-6). The bringing of religion and education to the western pioneers is the subject of this book that relies heavily of first-person accounts. (Rev: BL 8/95; SLJ 11/95) [278]

9173 Hilton, Suzanne. *Miners, Merchants, and Maids* (6–9). Illus. Series: Settling the West. 1995, Twenty-First Century LB $24.90 (0-8050-2998-2). Three kinds of employment that helped open up the West are discussed, with quotations from many primary sources representing people of different backgrounds. (Rev: BL 8/95; SLJ 11/95) [978]

9174 Hirschfelder, Arlene B. *Photo Odyssey: Solomon Cavalho's Remarkable Western Adventure, 1853–54* (6–10). Illus. 2000, Clarion $18.00 (0-395-89123-X). The story of the last westward journey of John C. Fremont as seen through the eyes of a painter/photographer who was a member of the expedition. (Rev: BCCB 9/00; BL 7/00; HBG 9/00; SLJ 8/00*; VOYA 12/00) [917.8]

9175 Kallen, Stuart A. *Life on the American Frontier* (6–10). Series: The Way People Live. 1998, Lucent LB $27.45 (1-56006-366-1). Thematically arranged chapters offer material on everyday life on the American frontier and on such groups as the trailblazers, the mountain men, the miners, the railroad men, the sodbusters, and the cattlemen. (Rev: BL 10/15/98; SLJ 1/99; VOYA 12/99) [978]

9176 Katz, William L. *Black Pioneers: An Untold Story* (7–12). 1999, Simon & Schuster $17.00 (0-689-81410-0). The account describes the stories of the many determined black Americans who defied prejudice, slavery, and severe legal restrictions such as the Northwest Territory's "Black Laws" to make a new life for themselves in the frontier of pre-Civil War days. (Rev: BL 7/99; HB 7–8/99; HBG 9/99; SLJ 9/99; VOYA 8/99) [977]

9177 Katz, William L. *Black Women of the Old West* (6–9). 1995, Atheneum $19.95 (0-689-31944-4). The role black women played in the settlement of the West — a topic virtually ignored in history books. (Rev: BL 12/15/95; SLJ 12/95; VOYA 4/96) [978]

9178 Katz, William L. *The Civil War to the Last Frontier: 1850–1880s* (7–9). Series: History of Multicultural America. 1993, Raintree Steck-Vaughn LB $27.11 (0-8114-6277-3). A history of the United States during this period, from a multicultural perspective. (Rev: BL 9/1/93; VOYA 8/93) [973.5]

9179 Kimball, Violet T. *Stories of Young Pioneers: In Their Own Words* (6–9). Illus. 2000, Mountain Press paper $14.00 (0-87842-423-7). Using diaries and memoirs as sources, the editor brings to life the experiences of youngsters who traveled westward in the mid 19th century. (Rev: BL 12/15/00; VOYA 4/01) [978]

9180 Klausmeier, Robert. *Cowboy* (4–7). Illus. Series: American Pastfinder. 1996, Lerner LB

$25.55 (0-8225-2975-0). This account focuses on the huge cattle drives and the men who led them in the years following the Civil War. (Rev: BL 3/1/96; SLJ 3/96) [636.2]

9181 Lavender, David. *Snowbound: The Tragic Story of the Donner Party* (6–10). Illus. 1996, Holiday $18.95 (0-8234-1231-8). With extensive use of primary documents and excellent illustrations, this account vividly reconstructs the hardships and horror of the Donner Party's attempt to cross the Rockies. (Rev: BL 6/1–15/96; SLJ 7/96; VOYA 8/96) [978]

9182 McCormick, Anita Louise. *The Pony Express in American History* (6–10). Series: In American History. 2001, Enslow LB $20.95 (0-7660-1296-4). This account traces the development and the short life of this phenomenon that linked the East to the West and created an American legend. (Rev: BL 8/1/01; HBG 10/01) [383]

9183 Marrin, Albert. *Cowboys, Indians, and Gunfighters: The Story of the Cattle Kingdom* (6–10). 1993, Atheneum $22.95 (0-689-31774-3). An exciting account of the Old West, including Comanche vengeance, buffalo hunts, and frontier lawlessness. (Rev: BL 8/93; VOYA 10/93) [978]

9184 Matthews, Leonard J. *Indians* (6–9). Illus. Series: Wild West in American History. 1988, Rourke LB $23.93 (0-86625-364-5). An overview of how Indians lived during the days of the Wild West. (Rev: SLJ 6/89) [970.004]

9185 Matthews, Leonard J. *Pioneers* (6–9). Illus. Series: Wild West in American History. 1988, Rourke LB $18.00 (0-86625-362-9). A tribute to the homesteaders who risked their lives to find a new home in the West. Also use in the same series *Railroaders and Soldiers* (both 1989). (Rev: SLJ 6/89) [973.5]

9186 Miller, Brandon M. *Buffalo Gals: Women of the Old West* (4–7). Illus. 1995, Lerner LB $30.35 (0-8225-1730-2). A realistic portrait of the hardships faced by women pioneers during the 19th century on the western frontier. (Rev: BCCB 7–8/95; BL 5/1/95; SLJ 6/95*) [978]

9187 Morley, Jacqueline. *How Would You Survive in the American West?* (4–7). Illus. Series: How Would You Survive? 1996, Watts LB $26.00 (0-531-14382-1). Information about supplies and shelter are given in this imaginary journey through the American West, with encounters with Native Americans, buffalo, and various obstacles. (Rev: BL 5/15/96) [978]

9188 Morris, Juddi. *The Harvey Girls: The Women Who Civilized the West* (6–9). Illus. 1994, Walker $15.95 (0-8027-8302-3). The story of the waitresses at Fred Harvey's restaurants along the Santa Fe railroad, and how they left their homes in the East in search of adventure and independence. (Rev: BL 6/1–15/94; SLJ 7/94) [979]

9189 Murdoch, David. *Cowboy* (5–9). Series: Eyewitness Books. 1993, Knopf $20.99 (0-679-94014-6). An illustrated history of cowboys in the American West and around the world. (Rev: BL 10/1/93) [978]

9190 Murphy, Virginia R. *Across the Plains in the Donner Party* (6–10). Ed. by Karen Zeinert. 1996, Linnet LB $21.50 (0-208-02404-2). As well as being a condensation of the memoirs of a teenage survivor of the Donner Party, this account gives good background information and excerpts from other original sources. (Rev: BL 6/1–15/96; BR 1–2/97; SLJ 8/96; VOYA 8/96) [979.4]

9191 O'Donnell, Kerri. *The Gold Rush: A Primary Source History of the Search for Gold in California* (4–8). Series: Primary Sources in American History. 2003, Rosen LB $29.25 (0-8239-3682-1). Timelines and reproductions of period photographs and relevant items add to the narrative in this introduction to the Gold Rush, the life of the miners, and the lawless character of the West. (Rev: SLJ 5/03) [979.4]

9192 Pelta, Kathy. *Cattle Trails: "Get Along Little Dogies"* (5–8). Series: American Trails. 1997, Raintree Steck-Vaughn LB $19.98 (0-8172-4073-X). A discussion of the cattle drives that were part of the history of the American West from 1850 to 1890. (Rev: SLJ 12/97) [978]

9193 Pelta, Kathy. *The Royal Roads: Spanish Trails in North America* (5–8). Series: American Trails. 1997, Raintree Steck-Vaughn LB $19.98 (0-8172-4074-8). The story of the Spanish trails in Florida, California, New Mexico, and Texas, and the people who traveled them looking for spiritual or material gain. (Rev: SLJ 12/97) [970.01]

9194 Rau, Margaret. *The Wells Fargo Book of the Gold Rush* (6–10). 2001, Simon & Schuster $18.00 (0-689-83019-X). This comprehensive account of the California Gold Rush, which includes many period photographs and illustrations from the Wells Fargo archives, looks at the miners themselves, their techniques, daily life, the impact on the environment, and the relations among various ethnic groups. (Rev: BCCB 6/01; BL 7/01; HBG 10/01; SLJ 6/01; VOYA 10/01) [979.4]

9195 Reinfeld, Fred. *Pony Express* (7–12). Illus. 1973, Univ. of Nebraska Pr. paper $10.95 (0-8032-5786-4). A history of the communication system that linked the East and West and the courageous riders who manned it. [383]

9196 Richards, Colin. *Sheriff Pat Garrett's Last Days* (8–12). Illus. 1986, Sunstone paper $8.95 (0-86534-079-X). A history of the Wild West drawn into focus by the death of the man who shot Billy the Kid. (Rev: BR 11–12/86) [978]

9197 Ritchie, David. *Frontier Life* (5–7). Illus. Series: Life in America 100 Years Ago. 1995, Chelsea $21.95 (0-7910-2842-9). A concise overview of life on the American frontier that does not gloss over the harsh and often violent aspects. (Rev: SLJ 1/96) [973.5]

9198 Ross, Stewart. *Cowboys* (5–7). Illus. Series: Fact or Fiction? 1995, Millbrook LB $26.90 (1-56294-618-8). The life of cowboys during the late 1800s is covered, with information that tries to separate fact from fable. (Rev: BL 7/95; SLJ 5/95) [978.02]

9199 Saffer, Barbara. *The California Gold Rush* (5–7). Series: The American West. 2002, Mason Crest LB $19.95 (1-59084-060-7). Reluctant readers will be drawn to this attractive account of the hardships of traveling to California and the life in the mining camps. (Rev: SLJ 4/02) [979.4]

9200 Sandler, Martin W. *Vaqueros: America's First Cowmen* (6–9). Illus. 2001, Holt $17.95 (0-8050-6019-7). Before the cowboys came the skillful vaqueros, whose circumstances, myths, and traditions are presented here. (Rev: BL 1/1–15/01; HB 1–2/01; HBG 10/01; SLJ 1/01) [973]

9201 Sanford, William R. *The Chisholm Trail* (6–10). Series: In American History. 2000, Enslow LB $20.95 (0-7660-1345-6). A look at this important trail that stretched from Texas to Kansas, and became the main route for driving longhorn cattle to the North. (Rev: BL 7/00; HBG 3/01; SLJ 12/00) [978]

9202 Sanford, William R. *The Natchez Trace Historic Trail* (6–9). Series: In American History. 2001, Enslow LB $20.95 (0-7660-1344-8). Sanford looks at the history of this ancient Native American trail that became important from the 1780s to 1830s, the people who used it, and confrontations between newcomers and the indigenous people. (Rev: BL 12/15/01; HBG 3/02; SLJ 3/02) [976]

9203 Sanford, William R. *The Santa Fe Trail in American History* (6–10). Series: In American History. 2000, Enslow LB $20.95 (0-7660-1348-0). The story of the trail from Missouri to New Mexico that opened in 1821 and became an important continental trade route. (Rev: BL 10/15/2000; HBG 3/01) [978]

9204 Savage, Candace. *Born to Be a Cowgirl: A Spirited Ride Through the Old West* (6–9). 2001, Tricycle Pr. $15.95 (1-58246-019-1); paper $9.95 (1-58246-020-5). An appealing package of fascinating text, excerpts from letters and journals, and period illustrations that introduces female cowhands and their lifestyle. (Rev: BL 5/15/01; HB 7–8/01; HBG 10/01; SLJ 6/01; VOYA 12/01) [978]

9205 Savage, Jeff. *Cowboys and Cow Towns of the Wild West* (4–7). Illus. Series: Trailblazers of the Wild West. 1995, Enslow LB $16.95 (0-89490-603-

8). Through the experiences of a single cowboy, the reader learns about his equipment, dangers, leisure time, cattle drives, and roundups. (Rev: SLJ 2/96) [978]

9206 Schilissel, Lillian. *Black Frontiers: A History of African American Heroes of the Old West* (5–8). 1995, Simon & Schuster $18.00 (0-689-80285-4). Almost a dozen men and women, including cowboy Nat Love, rodeo rider Bill Pickett, and real estate tycoon Biddy Mason, are introduced in this informative account of the Old West. (Rev: BL 1/1–15/96; SLJ 12/95; VOYA 4/96) [978]

9207 Schroeder, Lisa Golden. *California Gold Rush Cooking* (4–7). Series: Exploring History Through Simple Recipes. 2000, Capstone LB $22.60 (0-7368-0603-2). This book discusses the California Gold Rush and everyday life of the period with details of the kinds of food eaten and some simple recipes. (Rev: BL 3/1/01; HBG 10/01; SLJ 4/01) [979.4]

9208 Sherrow, Victoria. *Life During the Gold Rush* (5–9). Series: The Way People Live. 1998, Lucent LB $27.45 (1-56006-382-3). This story of the California Gold Rush, from Sutter's Mill to the advent of huge companies, gives good information on the daily life of the forty-niners. (Rev: BL 8/98; SLJ 12/98) [979.5]

9209 Shuter, Jane, ed. *Sarah Royce and the American West* (5–8). Illus. Series: History Eyewitness. 1996, Raintree Steck-Vaughn LB $24.26 (0-8114-8286-3). The ordeals and achievements of American pioneers are chronicled in this first-person account, accompanied by many splendid illustrations. (Rev: BL 5/15/96; SLJ 6/96) [978]

9210 Sigerman, Harriet. *Land of Many Hands: Women in the American West* (7–12). 1998, Oxford $24.95 (0-19-509942-7). A well-researched account that uses many original documents to tell the story of women's role in the opening up of the West, their struggles and triumphs, and how different ethnic groups were treated. (Rev: BL 2/15/98; BR 5–6/98; HBG 3/99; SLJ 4/98; VOYA 4/98) [978]

9211 Stanley, Jerry. *Cowboys and Longhorns: A Portrait of the Long Drive* (5–12). Illus. 2003, Crown $18.95 (0-375-81565-1). Stanley debunks the popular view of cowboys, using the long cattle drives from Texas to Kansas to illustrate the dangers and discomforts of an unglamorous life on horseback. (Rev: BL 7/03*; SLJ 8/03) [636.2]

9212 Stanley, Jerry. *Frontier Merchants: Lionel and Barron Jacobs and the Jewish Pioneers Who Settled the West* (5–10). 1998, Crown $20.99 (0-517-80020-9). This fascinating biography of the Jacobs brothers, who set up a successful business venture in Tucson in 1867, illustrates business development in pioneer communities and the role of Jewish immigrants in building the economic foundation of the West. (Rev: BR 5–6/99; HBG 3/99; SLJ 3/99) [973.8]

9213 Stanley, Jerry. *Hurry Freedom: African Americans in Gold Rush California* (6–8). 2000, Crown $18.95 (0-517-80094-2). Prejudice followed African Americans west to the gold fields, but some blacks managed to succeed despite the odds; this volume profiles two blacks who prospered. (Rev: BCCB 1/01; HB 1–2/01; HBG 3/01; SLJ 1/01*) [979.4]

9214 Stefoff, Rebecca. *First Frontier* (4–7). Series: North American Historical Atlases. 2000, Benchmark LB $24.21 (0-7614-1059-7). This book presents an illustrated view of the western expansion and its effects on Native Americans, frontiersmen, speculators, and soldiers. (Rev: HBG 3/01; SLJ 1/01) [978]

9215 Stefoff, Rebecca. *The Opening of the West* (5–8). 2002, Benchmark LB $22.95 (0-7614-1201-8). A collection of primary sources that includes excerpts from letters, newspaper articles, and journal entries commenting on different aspects of frontier life, exploration, and the plight of Native Americans. (Rev: HBG 10/03; SLJ 4/03) [978]

9216 Stefoff, Rebecca. *The Oregon Trail in American History* (6–10). Illus. Series: In American History. 1997, Enslow LB $20.95 (0-89490-771-9). The story of the Oregon Trail and the everyday life of the settlers who traveled it are re-created, with a guide to the trail as it exists today. (Rev: BL 2/1/98; HBG 3/98; SLJ 2/98) [978]

9217 Stefoff, Rebecca. *Women Pioneers* (6–12). Series: American Profiles. 1995, Facts on File $25.00 (0-8160-3134-7). Nine profiles of pioneer women noted for their courage, ingenuity, and triumphs are presented in this readable account that gives details of life on the American frontier. (Rev: BL 1/1–15/96; SLJ 2/96; VOYA 4/96) [973.8]

9218 Stein, R. Conrad. *In the Spanish West* (4–8). Series: How We Lived. 1999, Benchmark LB $27.07 (0-7614-0906-8). This well-balanced account describes the American West under Spanish control and influence with material on history, social life, agriculture, and home life. (Rev: HBG 10/00; SLJ 3/00) [978]

9219 Stein, R. Conrad. *On the Old Western Frontier* (4–8). Series: How We Lived. 1999, Benchmark LB $27.07 (0-7614-0909-2). An interesting book that gives an overview of the history and living conditions on the American frontier with material on everyday life, farming and ranching, social life, religion, Native Americans, and slaves. (Rev: HBG 10/00; SLJ 3/00) [978]

9220 Stewart, Gail B. *Cowboys in the Old West* (6–9). Series: The Way People Live. 1995, Lucent LB $27.45 (1-56006-077-8). A description of the life of the cowboy from 1865 to 1890. (Rev: BL 5/1/95; SLJ 5/95) [978]

9221 Stovall, TaRessa. *The Buffalo Soldiers* (6–10). Illus. Series: African American Achievers. 1997, Chelsea LB $21.95 (0-7910-2595-0); paper $9.95 (0-7910-2596-9). The story of the stirring achievements of the black U.S. Army regiments that distinguished themselves during numerous campaigns and played a vital role in the settlement of the American West. (Rev: BL 12/1/97; HBG 3/98) [978]

9222 Torr, James D., ed. *The American Frontier* (7–12). Series: Turning Points in World History. 2001, Greenhaven LB $31.20 (0-7377-0785-2); paper $19.95 (0-7377-0786-0). A collection of essays that explores the opening up of the West, the nature of the pioneer spirit, and the changes this development brought to our history. (Rev: BL 3/15/02) [973.7]

9223 Torr, James D., ed. *Westward Expansion* (7–12). Series: Interpreting Primary Documents. 2003, Gale LB $16.96 (0-7377-1134-5); paper $21.20 (0-7377-1133-7). A broad selection of primary sources present different perspectives on issues related to the United States' westward expansion (the Indian Wars, building the transcontinental railroad, the gold rush, and so forth). (Rev: BL 1/1–15/03; SLJ 2/03) [978]

9224 Uschan, Michael V. *Westward Expansion* (7–10). Series: World History. 2000, Lucent LB $19.96 (1-56006-690-3). The story of how the quest for economic opportunities, land, and personal freedom stretched the boundaries of the United States to the Pacific Ocean. (Rev: BL 10/15/2000; SLJ 1/01) [978]

9225 Wadsworth, Ginger. *Words West: Voices of Young Pioneers* (5–8). 2003, Clarion $18.00 (0-618-23475-6). Excerpts from journals and other documents give a clear picture of the experiences of young people traveling west between 1840 and 1870. (Rev: SLJ 12/03) [917.804]

9226 Walker, Paul R. *Great Figures of the Wild West* (7–10). Series: American Profiles. 1992, Facts on File LB $25.00 (0-8160-2576-2). A vivid picture of the history of the American West, with profiles of such people as Jesse James, Sitting Bull, Wyatt Earp, Geronimo, Judge Roy Bean, and Belle Starr. (Rev: BL 9/1/92; SLJ 8/92) [978]

9227 Werther, Scott P. *The Donner Party* (5–7). Illus. 2002, Children's LB $20.00 (0-516-23901-5). The fate of the Donner Party is described against the backdrop of life in America in the 1840s and the dangers of travel to the West and the Pacific. (Rev: SLJ 10/02) [979.4]

9228 Winslow, Mimi. *Loggers and Railroad Workers* (6–9). Illus. Series: Settling the West. 1995, Twenty-First Century LB $24.90 (0-8050-2997-4). First-person accounts from workers in logging and on the railroad are woven together to give a portrait of these fledgling industries in the Old West. (Rev: BL 7/95; SLJ 9/95) [338.7]

9229 Worth, Richard. *Westward Expansion and Manifest Destiny* (6–10). Series: In American History. 2001, Enslow LB $20.95 (0-7660-1457-6). This account chronicles events after the Revolution when Americans believed that westward expansion was their destiny and acted on this impulse. (Rev: BL 8/1/01; HBG 10/01; SLJ 7/01) [978]

9230 Yancey, Diane. *Life in the Pony Express* (6–10). Series: The Way People Live. 2001, Lucent LB $19.96 (1-56006-793-4). Though only in existence for 18 months, this transcontinental mail service, presented well in both text and pictures, made a great impact on American history. (Rev: BL 6/1–15/01; SLJ 8/01) [383]

RECONSTRUCTION TO WORLD WAR I
(1865–1914)

9231 Arnold, Caroline. *Children of the Settlement Houses* (4–7). Illus. Series: Picture the American Past. 1998, Carolrhoda LB $27.15 (1-57505-242-3). Using historical photographs and a simple text, this book introduces the turn-of-the-20th-century settlement house, where the poor and new immigrants found shelter and a place to learn, explore the arts, and develop a sense of belonging. (Rev: BL 9/15/98; HBG 3/99; SLJ 1/99) [362.5]

9232 Axelrod-Contrada, Joan. *The Lizzie Borden "Axe Murder" Trial: A Headline Court Case* (5–9). Series: Headline Court Cases. 2000, Enslow LB $20.95 (0-7660-1422-3). A well-documented account of the famous 1892 trial, the events that led up to it, and its aftermath. (Rev: HBG 3/01; SLJ 1/01) [973.8]

9233 Bartoletti, Susan C. *Growing Up in Coal Country* (5–8). Illus. 1996, Houghton $17.00 (0-395-77847-6). The life of child laborers in the coal mines of Pennsylvania 100 years ago is covered in this brilliant photoessay. (Rev: BCCB 2/97; BL 12/1/96*; BR 11–12/97; SLJ 2/97*) [331.3]

9234 Bartoletti, Susan Campbell. *Kids on Strike!* (5–8). Illus. 1999, Houghton $20.00 (0-395-88892-1). This book chronicles the history of child labor in America during the 19th and early 20th centuries and features such personalities as William Randolph Hearst, Pauline Newman, and Mother Jones. (Rev: BCCB 12/99; BL 12/1/99; HBG 3/00; SLJ 12/99*; VOYA 2/00) [973.8]

9235 Cohen, Daniel. *The Alaska Purchase* (4–8). Series: Spotlight on American History. 1996, Millbrook $24.90 (1-56294-528-9). The story of the purchase of Alaska from Russia in 1867 and how it changed the course of American history. (Rev: BL 3/15/96; SLJ 5/96) [979.8]

9236 Collier, Christopher, and James Lincoln Collier. *Reconstruction and the Rise of Jim Crow, 1864–1896* (5–8). Series: Drama of American History. 1999, Marshall Cavendish LB $29.93 (0-7614-0819-3). A clear, objective account of the problems facing the country after the Civil War and how they were resolved. (Rev: BL 2/15/00; HBG 10/00; SLJ 3/00) [973.8]

9237 Collier, Christopher, and James Lincoln Collier. *The Rise of Industry, 1860–1900* (5–8). Illus. Series: Drama of American History. 1999, Marshall Cavendish LB $29.93 (0-7614-0820-7). A readable account of 40 years of industrialism and its effect on the United States. (Rev: BL 2/15/00; HBG 10/00; SLJ 3/00) [338.0973]

9238 Currie, Stephen. *We Have Marched Together: The Working Children's Crusade* (7–12). Series: People's History. Set), Lerner LB $30.35 (0-8225-1733-7). The focus of this book is on child labor in the United States and the protest march from Philadelphia to New York led by Mother Jones in 1903. (Rev: BL 5/1/97; SLJ 7/97) [331.3]

9239 DeAngelis, Gina. *The Triangle Shirtwaist Company Fire of 1911* (7–12). Illus. Series: Great Disasters: Reforms and Ramifications. 2000, Chelsea $19.95 (0-7910-5267-2). This is a dramatic and detailed account of the fire, the conditions that made such a disaster possible, and the union protests that followed. (Rev: BL 10/15/00; HBG 3/01; SLJ 2/01; VOYA 2/01) [974.7]

9240 Dolan, Edward F. *The Spanish-American War* (5–8). Illus. 2001, Millbrook LB $28.90 (0-7613-1453-9). This chronological account of the Spanish-American War includes profiles of military personnel, maps, and historical photographs. (Rev: BL 11/1/01; HBG 3/02; SLJ 11/01) [973.8]

9241 Fireside, Bryna J. *The Haymarket Square Riot Trial* (6–10). Series: Headline Court Cases. 2002, Enslow LB $20.95 (0-7660-1761-3). This is an account of the trial that resulted from the arrest of several people after a bomb-throwing incident during a labor protest rally in Chicago on May 4, 1886. (Rev: BL 3/15/03; HBG 3/03) [973.8]

9242 Fremon, David K. *The Alaska Purchase in American History* (7–10). Series: In American History. 1999, Enslow LB $20.95 (0-7660-1138-0). This account covers both the purchase of Alaska in 1867 and an early history of the Native Americans who lived there. (Rev: BL 11/15/99; HBG 3/00; SLJ 3/00) [979.8]

9243 Fry, Annette R. *The Orphan Trains* (7–12). Series: American Events. 1994, Macmillan LB $14.95 (0-02-735721-X). Interviews, letters, and photographs chronicle how slum children were sent on "orphan trains" to live in the West and how the move affected them. (Rev: BL 7/94; SLJ 1/95) [362.7]

9244 Gan, Geraldine. *Communication* (6–9). Series: Life in America 100 Years Ago. 1997, Chelsea LB $21.95 (0-7910-2845-3). An exploration of the growing importance of mail, books, newspapers, magazines, telegraphs, and telephones at the turn of the 20th century. (Rev: BL 10/15/97; SLJ 9/97) [973.8]

9245 Gourley, Catherine. *Good Girl Work: Factories, Sweatshops, and How Women Changed Their Role in the American Workforce* (7–10). 1999, Millbrook LB $26.90 (0-7613-0951-9). This history of the exploitation of female children around the turn of the 20th century includes dramatic, in-depth personal testimonies and first-person accounts from letters, diaries, memoirs, and newspaper interviews. (Rev: BL 5/1/99; BR 9–10/99; SLJ 8/99) [331.3]

9246 Greenwood, Janette Thomas. *The Gilded Age: A History in Documents* (6–12). Illus. 2000, Oxford LB $36.95 (0-19-510523-0). Documents of all kinds are used to show readers the many changes that took place in American society in the last years of the 19th century. (Rev: BL 10/1/00; HBG 3/01; SLJ 10/00) [973.8]

9247 Hakim, Joy. *Reconstruction and Reform.* 2nd ed. (5–8). Series: A History of Us. 1999, Oxford LB $19.95 (0-19-512763-3); paper $13.95 (0-19-512764-1). The years immediately following the Civil War (1865–1896) are covered in this outstanding history that uses many quotes, anecdotes, and excellent illustrations. (Rev: BL 12/15/99) [973.8]

9248 Hansen, Joyce. *"Bury Me Not in a Land of Slaves": African-Americans in the Time of Reconstruction* (6–10). Illus. 2000, Watts LB $25.00 (0-531-11539-9). An excellent overview of the complex era that followed the Civil War and how compromises were reached on giving civil rights to African Americans. (Rev: BL 6/1–15/00; SLJ 6/00) [973.]

9249 Haskins, Jim. *Geography of Hope: Black Exodus from the South After Reconstruction* (7–12). Illus. 1999, Twenty-First Century LB $31.90 (0-7613-0323-5). After information on slavery and the Reconstruction, the author describes the migrations of African Americans to the North, their leaders, and the politics that made life in the South intolerable. (Rev: BL 10/15/99; HBG 4/00; SLJ 11/99; VOYA 6/00) [973]

9250 Havens, John C. *Government and Politics* (6–9). Illus. Series: Life in America 100 Years Ago. 1997, Chelsea LB $21.95 (0-7910-2847-X). This book focuses on the influences on politics at the turn of the 20th century, such as the end of the Civil War, the rise of big business and the growing power of industry, and government scandals. (Rev: BL 6/1–15/97) [973]

9251 Immell, Myra H., ed. *The 1900s* (6–12). Series: America's Decades. 2000, Greenhaven LB

$29.96 (0-7377-0294-X); paper $17.96 (0-7377-0293-1). After an overview chapter, the articles in this anthology cover the important events of this decade and highlight cultural and technological trends. (Rev: BL 7/00; SLJ 9/00) [973.9]

9252 *Industry and Business* (6–9). Illus. Series: Life in America 100 Years Ago. 1996, Chelsea LB $21.95 (0-7910-2846-1). A look at the Industrial Revolution that transformed the United States from a rural to an urban nation and set it on a course toward becoming a world power. (Rev: BL 6/1–15/97) [338.0973]

9253 Isserman, Maurice. *Journey to Freedom* (7–12). Illus. Series: Library of African American History. 1997, Facts on File $25.00 (0-8160-3413-3). An account of the African American men and women who traveled north at the beginning of the 20th century filled with hope and looking for freedom, dignity, and economic opportunity, and of the impact on the nation's politics and culture. (Rev: BL 2/15/98; BR 3–4/98) [975]

9254 Josephson, Judith Pinkerton. *Growing Up in a New Century* (5–8). Illus. Series: Our America. 2002, Lerner LB $31.95 (0-8225-0657-2). A look at the lives of American children of different backgrounds and situations at the dawn of the 20th century. (Rev: BL 2/1/03; HBG 3/03; SLJ 7/03) [973.91]

9255 Leuzzi, Linda. *Education* (6–9). Series: Life in America 100 Years Ago. 1998, Chelsea LB $21.95 (0-7910-2849-6). With fascinating examples and detailed descriptions, this book discusses practices in turn-of-the-century schools and classrooms. (Rev: BL 3/15/98; BR 11–12/98; HBG 9/98) [973.8]

9256 McNeese, Tim. *Remember the Maine: The Spanish-American War Begins* (6–12). Illus. Series: First Battles. 2001, Morgan Reynolds LB $20.95 (1-883846-79-X). The story of the sinking of the battleship *Maine*, an event that led to the Spanish-American War in 1898. (Rev: BL 11/1/01; HBG 3/02; SLJ 4/02) [973.8]

9257 Maurer, Richard. *The Wild Colorado: The True Adventures of Fred Dellenbaugh, Age 17, on the Second Powell Expedition into the Grand Canyon* (5–9). 1999, Crown $19.99 (0-517-70946-5). A firsthand account, with authentic photographs, of Major John Wesley Powell's 16-month journey down the Colorado River in the 1870s, as recorded by a teenage crew member. (Rev: HBG 3/00; SLJ 8/99) [973.8]

9258 Mettger, Zak. *Reconstruction: America After the Civil War* (5–8). Series: Young Readers' History of the Civil War. 1994, Dutton $17.99 (0-525-67490-X). Describes the political, economic, and social upheaval during Reconstruction and the fight for the civil rights of the former slaves. (Rev: BL 10/1/94; SLJ 2/95) [973.8]

9259 Miller, Marilyn. *The Transcontinental Railroad* (5–8). Illus. 1987, Silver Burdett paper $12.36 (0-382-09912-5). The great event that linked East and West by rail is portrayed with numerous illustrations. (Rev: BL 7/87; SLJ 9/87) [385.0979]

9260 Murphy, Jim. *Blizzard! The Storm that Changed America* (5–9). Illus. 2000, Scholastic paper $18.95 (0-590-67309-2). A brilliant narrative about the great storm that hit the Northeast on March 10, 1888, and brought 31 inches of snow and 800 deaths in New York City alone. (Rev: BL 2/15/01*; HB 1–2/01; HBG 3/01; SLJ 12/00; VOYA 6/01) [974.7]

9261 Sherrow, Victoria. *The Triangle Factory Fire* (5–8). Series: Spotlight on American History. 1995, Millbrook LB $24.90 (1-56294-572-6). The story of the deadly factory fire that exposed the shameful labor exploitation in this country and led to needed reforms. (Rev: BR 1–2/96; SLJ 3/96) [363.37]

9262 Smith, Karen M. *New Paths to Power: American Women 1890–1920* (8–12). Series: Young Oxford History of Women in the United States. 1994, Oxford $24.00 (0-19-508111-0). A history of women from the end of the 19th century to 1920, the year U.S. women finally won the right to vote. (Rev: BL 12/15/94; SLJ 1/95) [305.4]

9263 Somerlott, Robert. *The Spanish-American War: "Remember the Maine!"* (6–12). Illus. Series: American War. 2002, Enslow LB $20.95 (0-7660-1855-5). This overview of the Spanish-American War's key events and individuals includes information on President William McKinley, Teddy Roosevelt and his Rough Riders, and Clara Barton. (Rev: BL 3/1/03; HBG 3/03; SLJ 6/03) [973.8]

9264 Stalcup, Brenda, ed. *Reconstruction* (8–12). Illus. Series: Opposing Viewpoints: American History. 1995, Greenhaven LB $32.45 (1-56510-227-4). An anthology of writings that present various points of view on the period of social transformation and controversy from 1865 through 1877 that is known as Reconstruction. (Rev: BL 3/15/95; SLJ 5/95) [973.8]

9265 Stein, R. Conrad. *The Transcontinental Railroad in American History* (6–10). Illus. Series: In American History. 1997, Enslow LB $20.95 (0-89490-882-0). This is a lively account of the building of the transcontinental railroad and the people involved, including the essential role of Chinese Americans. (Rev: BL 2/1/98; HBG 3/98; SLJ 1/98) [385]

9266 Wells, Donna. *America Comes of Age* (5–8). Series: The Making of America. 2001, Raintree Steck-Vaughn LB $28.54 (0-8172-5708-X). A handsomely illustrated account that traces U.S. history from Reconstruction to the beginning of the 20th century. (Rev: BL 4/15/01; HBG 10/01) [973.8]

9267 Wilder, Laura Ingalls. *West from Home: Letters of Laura Ingalls Wilder, San Francisco 1915* (7–9).

1974, HarperCollins $16.99 (0-06-024110-1); paper $5.99 (0-06-440081-6). The author describes her trip from Missouri to San Francisco in 1915. [973.9]

9268 Woog, Adam. *The 1900's* (7–10). Illus. 1998, Lucent LB $27.45 (1-56006-550-8). This overview of the 1900s includes material on the economy, working and living conditions, politics, important events and personalities, and the growing influences of advertising, movies, and mass transportation. (Rev: SLJ 4/99) [973.9]

9269 Wukovits, John F. *The Spanish-American War* (7–10). Series: World History. 2002, Gale LB $27.45 (1-56006-682-2). The story of the 1898 war that freed Cuba and ceded Puerto Rico and Guam to the U.S. (Rev: BL 4/15/02; SLJ 1/02) [973.8]

9270 Ziff, Marsha. *Reconstruction Following the Civil War in American History* (7–10). Series: In American History. 1999, Enslow LB $19.95 (0-7660-1140-2). A look at the events, personalities, and movements associated with the period from 1865 to 1877. (Rev: BL 11/15/99; HBG 4/00; SLJ 3/00) [973.8]

WORLD WAR I

9271 Ruggiero, Adriane. *World War I* (6–9). Series: American Voices From. 2002, Benchmark LB $22.95 (0-7614-1203-4). Excerpts from primary documents including letters, newspaper articles, speeches, and journals present a variety of different experiences of those who lived through World War I. (Rev: HBG 10/03; SLJ 3/03) [940.3]

9272 Torr, James D., ed. *Primary Sources* (6–12). Series: American War Library: World War I. 2002, Gale LB $27.45 (1-59018-008-9). This is a collection of documents, letters, and memorabilia that describe key events and America's participation in World War I. (Rev: BL 6/1–15/02) [940.1]

9273 Wukovits, John F. *Flying Aces* (6–12). Series: American War Library: World War I. 2002, Gale LB $27.45 (1-56006-810-8). With an emphasis on American airmen, this account describes the war in the air and the people involved during World War I. (Rev: BL 6/1–15/02) [940.3]

9274 Wukovits, John F. *Strategic Battles* (6–12). Series: American War Library: World War I. 2002, Gale LB $27.45 (1-56006-836-1). The important battles of World War I are described with an emphasis on those involving Americans in an account that includes firsthand accounts, maps, and archival photographs. (Rev: BL 6/1–15/02) [940.3]

BETWEEN THE WARS AND THE GREAT DEPRESSION (1918–1941)

9275 Aaseng, Nathan. *The Crash of 1929* (6–9). Series: World History. 2001, Gale LB $19.96 (1-56006-804-3). This engrossing account of the stock market crash and its aftermath introduces many of the key characters and tells many personal stories. (Rev: SLJ 12/01) [338.5]

9276 Appelt, Kathi, and Jeanne Cannella Schmitzer. *Down Cut Shin Creek* (6–9). Illus. 2001, Harper-Collins $16.95 (0-06-029135-4). An absorbing account of the dedicated pack-horse librarians who braved difficult conditions to deliver books and other materials to needy families in the hills of Kentucky during the Depression. (Rev: BL 7/01; HB 5–6/01; HBG 10/01; SLJ 5/01*) [716.15]

9277 Blackman, Cally. *The 20s and 30s: Flappers and Vamps* (5–10). Series: 20th Century Fashion. 2000, Gareth Stevens LB $25.26 (0-8368-2599-3). Social history is combined with fashion and design in this account of the 1920s and 1930s that is illustrated with period photographs and magazine covers. (Rev: HBG 10/00; SLJ 6/00) [973.9]

9278 Blumenthal, Karen. *Six Days in October: The Stock Market Crash of 1929* (7–12). Illus. 2002, Simon & Schuster $17.95 (0-689-84276-7). An absorbing look at the factors that led to the infamous crash and the fortunes that were lost, with clear definitions of economic concepts and interesting illustrations. (Rev: BL 11/1/02; HB 1–2/03; HBG 3/03; SLJ 10/02; VOYA 12/02) [332.64]

9279 Candaele, Kerry. *Bound for Glory: From the Great Migration to the Harlem Renaissance, 1910–1930* (7–10). Illus. Series: Milestones in Black American History. 1996, Chelsea LB $21.95 (0-7910-2261-7); paper $9.95 (0-7910-2687-6). This account covers the mass movement of African Americans from the rural South to the northern cities in the early 20th century and their achievements in the arts, politics, business, and sports, with emphasis on the origins of the Harlem Renaissance. (Rev: BL 10/15/96; BR 1–2/97; SLJ 2/97) [973]

9280 Carter, Ron. *The Youngest Drover* (5–9). 1995, Harbour $19.95 (0-9643672-1-1); paper $14.95 (0-9643672-0-3). In 1923, when he was 15, the author's father participated in an exciting cattle drive from Alberta to Montana. (Rev: BL 1/1–15/96) [978]

9281 Chambers, Veronica. *The Harlem Renaissance* (7–12). Illus. Series: African American Achievers. 1997, Chelsea LB $21.95 (0-7910-2597-7); paper $9.95 (0-7910-2598-5). This history discusses the emergence of Harlem as a cultural center in the 1920s in the context of the social and political forces of the time, weaving in accounts of such greats as Langston Hughes, Countee Cullen, Zora Neale Hurston, and others who were part of this artistic and intellectual movement. (Rev: BL 2/15/98; BR 3–4/98; HBG 3/98; SLJ 4/98) [700]

9282 Collier, Christopher, and James Lincoln Collier. *Progressivism, the Great Depression, and the New Deal* (5–8). Illus. Series: The Drama of Ameri-

can History. 2001, Marshall Cavendish LB $29.93 (0-7614-1054-6). A highly readable account that covers such topics as the stock market crash, the reformation of business practices, the Great Depression, and the social policies of the New Deal. (Rev: BL 3/15/01; HBG 10/01) [973.91]

9283 Cryan-Hicks, Kathryn, ed. *Pride and Promise: The Harlem Renaissance* (4–8). Illus. Series: Perspectives on History. 1994, Discovery Enterprises paper $6.95 (1-878668-30-7). The story of the great artistic awakening in New York's Harlem and of its many leaders, including Langston Hughes. (Rev: BL 8/94) [305.896]

9284 Damon, Duane. *Headin' for Better Times: The Arts of the Great Depression* (6–8). Illus. Series: People's History. 2002, Lerner LB $25.26 (0-8225-1741-8). Damon introduces readers to the wide range of literature, music, art, drama, and entertainment that was produced during this time of hardship in the United States. (Rev: BL 3/15/02; HBG 10/02; SLJ 5/02) [700]

9285 Davies, Nancy M. *The Stock Market Crash of 1929* (7–12). Series: American Events. 1994, Macmillan LB $14.95 (0-02-726221-9). The causes and effects of the devastating stock market crash of 1929 are traced, with a discussion of safeguards that were put in place. (Rev: BL 7/94) [338.5]

9286 DeAngelis, Therese, and Gina DeAngelis. *The Dust Bowl* (6–8). Illus. Series: Great Disasters. 2002, Chelsea LB $21.95 (0-7910-6323-2). Photographs and excerpts from letters add realism to this portrait of the hardships of life in the Midwest during the Depression. (Rev: BL 4/15/02; HBG 10/02) [978]

9287 Dudley, William, ed. *The Great Depression: Opposing Viewpoints* (7–12). Illus. Series: Opposing Viewpoints Digests. 1994, Greenhaven LB $17.95 (1-56510-084-0). This account uses dozens of quotations from primary and secondary sources to explore various facets of the Great Depression, including its causes, its effects, and the New Deal. (Rev: BL 2/1/94) [973.9]

9288 Edwards, Judith. *The Lindbergh Baby Kidnapping* (7–10). Series: In American History. 2000, Enslow LB $19.95 (0-7660-1299-9). The 1932 kidnapping and subsequent trial are covered in detail, followed by a discussion of capital punishment and the pressures involved in this celebrity case. (Rev: BL 1/1–15/00; HBG 9/00; SLJ 4/00) [973.9]

9289 Feinberg, Barbara S. *Black Tuesday: The Stock Market Crash of 1929* (4–7). Illus. Series: Spotlight on American History. 1995, Millbrook LB $24.90 (1-56294-574-2). The causes and consequences of the great stock market crash of 1929 are interestingly retold with many photographs and illustrations. (Rev: BL 10/15/95) [338.5]

9290 Fremon, David K. *The Great Depression* (7–10). Series: In American History. 1997, Enslow LB $20.95 (0-89490-881-2). The Great Depression, its causes, its effects, and how it was ended, told with a lively text and many black-and-white photographs. (Rev: BL 5/15/97; BR 9–10/97) [338.5]

9291 Gerdes, Louise I., ed. *The Great Depression* (7–12). Series: Great Speeches in History. 2002, Gale LB $31.20 (0-7377-0873-5); paper $19.95 (0-7377-0872-7). Various viewpoints on internal U.S. history from 1928 through 1939, are expressed in this collection of 21 speeches by such notables as Franklin Roosevelt, Huey Long, and Will Rogers. (Rev: BL 4/15/02; SLJ 4/02) [973.91]

9292 Gerdes, Louise I., ed. *The 1930s* (6–12). Series: America's Decades. 2000, Greenhaven LB $29.96 (0-7377-0030-8); paper $17.96 (0-7377-0299-0). After an overview chapter, this collection of essays covers such topics the Great Depression, the New Deal, the Lindbergh kidnapping, labor disputes, and the importance of radio. (Rev: BL 7/00; SLJ 9/00) [973.9]

9293 Grant, R. G. *The Great Depression* (6–12). Illus. Series: Lives in Crisis. 2003, Barron's $14.95 (0-7641-5601-2). Period photographs and excerpts from letters, articles, and speeches add to the narrative about the economic collapse in the 1920s and 1930s, both in the United States and abroad. (Rev: BL 10/15/03*; SLJ 9/03) [303.9]

9294 Harris, Nathaniel. *The Great Depression* (7–12). Illus. 1988, David & Charles $19.95 (0-7134-5658-2). This account describes the 1930s not only in the United States but also in Britain and Europe. (Rev: SLJ 1/89) [973.91]

9295 Herald, Jacqueline. *Fashions of a Decade: The 1920s* (7–12). Series: Fashions of a Decade. 1991, Facts on File $25.00 (0-8160-2465-0). An illustrated overview of fashions and trends of the 1920s as they reflected the development of modern life after World War I. (Rev: BL 12/15/91; SLJ 2/92) [391]

9296 Hintz, Martin. *Farewell, John Barleycorn: Prohibition in the United States* (6–10). Illus. Series: People's History. 1996, Lerner LB $25.26 (0-8225-1734-5). A well-organized, readable account that traces the history of alcohol use in the United States, covers the 18th Amendment and its effects, and ends with repeal of Prohibition. (Rev: BL 8/96; SLJ 10/96) [363.4]

9297 Hoffman, Nancy. *Eleanor Roosevelt and the Arthurdale Experiment* (5–8). Illus. 2001, Linnet LB $22.50 (0-208-02504-9). Hoffman includes quotations and black-and-white photographs in her account of the story of Arthurdale, a government-planned community of the 1930s. (Rev: BL 10/15/01; HBG 3/02; SLJ 12/01) [975.4]

9298 Jacques, Geoffrey. *Free Within Ourselves: The Harlem Renaissance* (7–10). Illus. Series: The African-American Experience. 1996, Watts LB $22.00 (0-531-11272-1). The important African American artists of the late 1920s, including writers, painters, musicians, actors, and sculptors, are profiled in this history of the Harlem Renaissance. (Rev: BL 2/15/97; SLJ 1/97) [700]

9299 Katz, William L. *The New Freedom to the New Deal: 1913–1939* (7–9). Series: History of Multicultural America. 1993, Raintree Steck-Vaughn LB $27.11 (0-8114-6279-X). An examination from a multicultural perspective of events inside the U.S. from World War I through the beginning of World War II. (Rev: BL 9/1/93) [973.91]

9300 Lawson, Don. *FDR's New Deal* (7–9). 1979, HarperCollins $12.95 (0-690-03953-0). The story of how President Roosevelt's policies helped this country out of the Great Depression. [973.91]

9301 McArthur, Debra. *The Dust Bowl and the Depression* (6–10). Series: In American History. 2002, Enslow LB $20.95 (0-7660-1838-5). A well-researched and well-documented account of the Great Depression in the Midwest, the plight of the farmers, and the lasting effects. (Rev: BL 5/15/02; HBG 10/02; SLJ 7/02) [973.91]

9302 Meltzer, Milton. *Brother, Can You Spare a Dime? The Great Depression, 1929–1933* (7–12). Series: Library of American History. 1991, Facts on File $19.95 (0-8160-2372-7). Through firsthand accounts of workers, farmers, sharecroppers, veterans, and professionals, the author re-creates how this economic catastrophe affected millions of ordinary people. (Rev: BL 5/15/91; SLJ 10/91) [330.973]

9303 Meltzer, Milton. *Driven from the Land: The Story of the Dust Bowl* (4–8). Series: Great Journeys. 1999, Benchmark LB $31.36 (0-7614-0968-8). Traces the development of the Dust Bowl, its effects on the land and the people, and how many were forced to leave their farms and seek a new life elsewhere. (Rev: BL 1/1–15/00; HBG 3/00; SLJ 2/00) [973.9]

9304 Nardo, Don, ed. *The Great Depression* (7–12). Series: Turning Points in World History. 2000, Greenhaven LB $21.96 (0-7377-0231-1); paper $13.96 (0-7377-0230-3). After a general overview of the Great Depression, this collection of informative essays and eyewitness accounts explores various aspects of this bleak period. (Rev: BL 5/15/00; SLJ 3/00) [338.]

9305 Nardo, Don. *The Great Depression* (7–12). Illus. Series: Opposing Viewpoints Digests. 1997, Greenhaven paper $17.45 (1-56510-742-X). This volume presents various viewpoints on why the Depression occurred, the role of the government, and the pros and cons surrounding the New Deal as they were argued at the time, followed by modern historians' assessments. (Rev: BL 3/1/98; SLJ 4/98; VOYA 2/99) [973.917]

9306 Nardo, Don. *The Scopes Trial* (6–10). Illus. Series: Famous Trials. 1996, Lucent LB $27.45 (1-56006-268-1). The story of the "Great Monkey Trial" of 1925 that revolved around a schoolteacher named Scopes and the teaching of evolution in schools, and involved a confrontation between two great orators, attorneys Clarence Darrow and William Jennings Bryan. (Rev: BL 5/1/97; BR 11–12/97; SLJ 4/97) [345.73]

9307 Nishi, Dennis, ed. *The Great Depression* (6–12). Illus. Series: History Firsthand. 2001, Greenhaven LB $22.96 (0-7377-0411-X); paper $14.96 (0-7377-0410-1). More than 20 first-person accounts introduce readers to life during the Depression — on Wall Street, among the unemployed and the homeless, and the New Deal efforts of President Roosevelt. (Rev: BL 5/15/01) [338.5]

9308 Pietrusza, David. *The Roaring '20s* (7–10). Illus. Series: World History. 1997, Lucent LB $27.45 (1-56006-309-2). Prohibition, the Teapot Dome scandal, jazz, the economy and the stock market, the automobile, the speak-easy, and the Scopes Trial are among the topics covered in this history of the prosperous 1920s, when America became an urban society and headed for the Great Depression. (Rev: SLJ 7/98) [973.9]

9309 Ross, Stewart. *Causes and Consequences of the Great Depression* (7–10). Series: Causes and Consequences. 1998, Raintree Steck-Vaughn LB $29.97 (0-8172-4059-4). A thorough analysis that uses illustrations including cartoons, posters, photographs, and statistical charts as well as quotations from historians, documents, and world leaders. (Rev: BL 8/98; SLJ 6/98; VOYA 2/99) [338.542]

9310 Ruth, Amy. *Growing Up in the Great Depression* (5–8). Series: Our America. 2002, Lerner LB $31.95 (0-8225-0655-6). With many sidebars and quotations from original sources, this narrative re-creates the despair and courage of children growing up during the Great Depression. (Rev: BL 2/15/03; HBG 3/03) [973.9]

9311 Sonnenfeld, Kelly. *Memories of Clason Point* (6–12). 1998, Dutton $16.99 (0-525-45961-8). This candid memoir by a daughter in a Jewish immigrant family living in the Bronx during the Great Depression recalls the material and emotional hardships it brought to her family and neighbors. (Rev: BL 2/1/98; SLJ 3/98; VOYA 4/98) [974.7]

9312 Stanley, Jerry. *Children of the Dust Bowl: The True Story of the School at Weedpatch Camp* (5–8). 1992, Crown LB $15.99 (0-517-58782-3). Records, with photographs, the enormity of the Dust Bowl, the migrants' desperate flight, and the story of the Weedpatch School and the "Okie" children who built it. (Rev: BCCB 10/92; BL 9/1/92*; HB 1–2/93*; SLJ 11/92*) [371.96]

9313 Stewart, Gail B. *The New Deal* (6–9). 1993, Macmillan LB $14.95 (0-02-788369-8). Explains the causes of the Great Depression and how President Roosevelt tried to turn the economy and national morale around through the New Deal. (Rev: BL 11/15/93; VOYA 2/94) [973.917]

9314 Stewart, Gail B. *1920s* (5–9). Illus. 1990, Crestwood LB $11.95 (0-89686-473-1). A chronological description of the Great War and its aftermath plus material on the trivia associated with this period. Also use *1930s* (1990). (Rev: SLJ 6/90) [973.9]

9315 Warren, Andrea. *Orphan Train Rider: One Boy's True Story* (4–8). 1996, Houghton $17.00 (0-395-69822-7). Between 1854 and 1930, more than 200,000 orphaned and abandoned children from cities on the East Coast were "placed out" to new homes and families in midwestern and western states. This is an account of one of them. (Rev: BL 7/96; SLJ 8/96*) [362.7]

9316 Woog, Adam. *Roosevelt and the New Deal* (7–10). Illus. Series: World History. 1997, Lucent LB $27.45 (1-56006-324-6). Through double-page spreads, sidebars, and political cartoons, photographs, reproductions, and first-person accounts, this book discusses Roosevelt's efforts to end the Great Depression through the New Deal, its impact on the nation, and what it did and did not accomplish. (Rev: SLJ 8/98) [973.9]

9317 Wormser, Richard. *Growing Up in the Great Depression* (6–12). 1994, Atheneum $15.95 (0-689-31711-5). Letters, photographs, and interviews examine children's lives during the Great Depression. Includes accounts of job loss, child labor, and the struggles of African Americans. (Rev: BL 10/15/94; SLJ 12/94; VOYA 2/95) [973.91]

9318 Wroble, Lisa A. *The New Deal and the Great Depression in American History* (5–8). Series: In American History. 2002, Enslow LB $20.95 (0-7660-1421-5). A timeline, maps, chapter notes, and research topics are found in this well-researched account that concentrates on Roosevelt's economic policies during the 1930s. (Rev: BL 1/1–15/03; HBG 3/03) [973.9]

WORLD WAR II

9319 Alonso, Karen. *Korematsu v. United States: Japanese-American Internment Camps* (7–12). Illus. Series: Landmark Supreme Court Cases. 1998, Enslow LB $20.95 (0-89490-966-5). The book tells of the Japanese American internments during World War II and focuses on Fred Korematsu's case challenging the government's right to remove him from his home and imprison him simply because he was a Japanese American. (Rev: BL 5/1/98; BR 9–10/98; SLJ 8/98; VOYA 2/99) [323.1]

9320 Black, Wallace B., and Jean F. Blashfield. *America Prepares for War* (5–7). Illus. Series: World War II 50th Anniversary. 1991, Macmillan LB $12.95 (0-89686-554-1). The U.S. entry into World War II, with numerous photographs. (Rev: BL 6/15/91; SLJ 9/91) [940.53]

9321 Bradley, James, and Ron Powers. *Flags of Our Fathers: Heroes of Iwo Jima* (7–10). Adapted by Michael French. 2001, Delacorte $15.95 (0-385-72932-4). The son of one of the Marines who raised the flag at Iwo Jima tells the story behind the event in this adaptation of an adult bestseller. (Rev: BL 4/1/01; BR 11/01; HBG 10/01; SLJ 5/01*; VOYA 10/01) [940.54]

9322 Brimner, Larry Dane. *Voices from the Camps: Internment of Japanese Americans During World War II* (7–12). Illus. 1994, Watts LB $17.70 (0-531-11179-2). The shameful treatment of Japanese Americans in California during the Second World War is re-created through interviews with survivors and their children. (Rev: BL 6/1–15/94) [940.53]

9323 Colman, Penny. *Rosie the Riveter* (6–12). 1995, Crown $20.99 (0-517-59791-8). An overview of the new role women played in the wartime workplace. (Rev: BL 4/15/95; SLJ 5/95) [331.4]

9324 Cooper, Michael L. *Fighting for Honor: Japanese Americans and World War II* (6–12). Illus. 2000, Clarion $16.00 (0-395-91375-6). The experiences of Japanese Americans who were sent to internment camps or faced anti-Asian attacks in their communities are well-documented here. (Rev: BCCB 2/01; BL 1/1–15/01; HB 3–4/01; HBG 10/01; SLJ 3/01) [940.53]

9325 Cooper, Michael L. *Remembering Manzanar: Life in a Japanese Relocation Camp* (4–8). Illus. 2002, Clarion $15.00 (0-618-06778-7). This evocative account of life in a Japanese American World War II internment center tells its tale through personal accounts of survivors, quotations from the camp newspaper, and revealing photographs. (Rev: BL 1/1–15/03; HBG 10/03; SLJ 2/03) [940.54]

9326 Dudley, William, ed. *Japanese American Internment Camps* (7–12). Series: At Issue in History. 2002, Gale LB $27.45 (0-7377-0821-2); paper $18.70 (0-7377-0820-4). Primary texts revealing different attitudes toward the internment of Japanese Americans are introduced by statements explaining the historical context. (Rev: SLJ 3/02) [940.53]

9327 Fremon, David K. *Japanese-American Internment in American History* (7–10). Illus. Series: In American History. 1996, Enslow LB $20.95 (0-89490-767-0). Drawing on a wide range of personal narratives, the author re-creates the shameful period during World War II when Japanese Americans were forcibly evacuated to internment camps. (Rev: BL 1/1–15/97; BR 3–4/97; SLJ 6/97; VOYA 12/96) [940.53]

9328 Grapes, Bryan J., ed. *Japanese American Internment Camps* (6–12). Series: History Firsthand. 2000, Greenhaven LB $22.96 (0-7377-0413-6); paper $14.96 (0-7377-0412-8). Essays, speeches, and firsthand accounts tell the story of the relocation of Japanese Americans during World War II. (Rev: BL 3/1/01; SLJ 4/01) [940.53]

9329 Hasday, Judy L. *The Tuskegee Airmen* (7–12). Series: American Mosaic. 2003, Chelsea LB $22.95 (0-7910-7267-3). During World War II, few could match the obstacles and rewards of the Tuskegee Airmen, a group of African American pilots. (Rev: BL 10/15/03; HBG 10/03) [940.54]

9330 Josephson, Judith Pinkerton. *Growing Up in World War II* (5–8). Illus. Series: Our America. 2002, Lerner LB $26.60 (0-8225-0660-2). A look at the lives of American children of different backgrounds and situations during World War II. (Rev: BL 2/1/03; HBG 3/03) [940.533]

9331 Kallen, Stuart A. *The War at Home* (6–12). Illus. 1999, Lucent LB $18.96 (1-56006-531-1). This book describes conditions within the United states during World War II and covers topics such as daily life, the changing workplace and workforce, civil defense, and racial discrimination. (Rev: BL 1/1–15/00; HBG 9/00; SLJ 2/00) [940.53]

9332 Komatsu, Kimberly, and Kaleigh Komatsu. *In America's Shadow* (5–8). Illus. 2003, Thomas George $35.00 (0-9709829-0-9). This account of the internment of Japanese Americans during World War II draws on the memories and archives of the authors' family. (Rev: BL 4/1/03) [940.531]

9333 Levine, Ellen. *A Fence Away from Freedom: Japanese Americans and World War II* (7–12). 1995, Putnam $18.99 (0-399-22638-9). Many voices tell of their bitter experiences as Japanese Americans were forced into internment camps during World War II. (Rev: BL 10/1/95; SLJ 12/95; VOYA 2/96) [940.53]

9334 McGowen, Tom. *"Go for Broke": Japanese-Americans in World War II* (5–8). Illus. Series: First Books. 1995, Watts LB $23.00 (0-531-20195-3). An attractive, accessible presentation that describes the fate of Japanese Americans during World War II. (Rev: SLJ 10/95) [940.54]

9335 Nicholson, Dorinda M. *Pearl Harbor Child: A Child's View of Pearl Harbor — from Attack to Peace* (5–8). 1998, Woodson House paper $9.95 (1-892858-00-2). This photoessay describes a child's experience during the bombing of Pearl Harbor, the temporary evacuation, and everyday life growing up in Hawaii during World War II. (Rev: BL 1/1–15/99) [996.9]

9336 Perl, Lila. *Behind Barbed Wire: The Story of Japanese-American Internment During World War II* (6–9). Series: Great Journeys. 2002, Marshall Cavendish LB $21.95 (0-7614-1321-9). The story of the causes, events, and effects related to the internment of many Japanese Americans during World War II. (Rev: BL 3/15/03; HBG 3/03) [940.5472]

9337 Ruggiero, Adriane. *World War II* (6–9). Series: American Voices From. 2002, Benchmark LB $22.95 (0-7614-1206-9). Excerpts from primary documents including letters, newspaper articles, speeches, and journals present a variety of different experiences of those who lived through World War II. (Rev: HBG 10/03; SLJ 3/03) [940.53]

9338 Schomp, Virginia. *World War II* (5–8). Illus. Series: Letters from the Homefront. 2001, Marshall Cavendish LB $28.50 (0-7614-1098-8). Schomp uses letters written during World War II, accompanied by relevant illustrations, to give readers a real understanding of the difficulties of life on the homefront. (Rev: BL 10/15/01; HBG 3/02) [940.54]

9339 Simon, Charnan. *Hollywood at War: The Motion Picture Industry and World War II* (4–8). Illus. Series: First Books. 1995, Watts LB $23.00 (0-531-20193-7). Chronicles the role of the movie industry during World War II in supplying propaganda and entertainment. (Rev: SLJ 10/95) [940.54]

9340 Sinnott, Susan. *Doing Our Part: American Women on the Home Front During World War II* (4–8). Illus. Series: First Books. 1995, Watts LB $23.00 (0-531-20198-8). The role of women at home and in defense industries during World War II is covered in this interesting account. (Rev: SLJ 10/95) [940.54]

9341 Sinnott, Susan. *Our Burden of Shame: Japanese-American Internment During World War II* (5–8). Illus. Series: First Books. 1995, Watts LB $23.00 (0-531-20194-5). The story of the heartbreaking internment of Japanese Americans during World War II is told in this easily understood, well-illustrated volume. (Rev: SLJ 10/95) [940.54]

9342 Streissguth, Thomas, ed. *The Attack on Pearl Harbor* (7–10). Series: At Issue in History. 2002, Gale LB $27.45 (0-7377-0752-6); paper $18.70 (0-7377-0751-8). Primary sources present many opposing views on the attack and who was responsible for the lack of preparation for such a possibility. (Rev: SLJ 7/02) [940.54]

9343 Tunnell, Michael O., and George W. Chilcoat. *The Children of Topaz: The Story of a Japanese-American Internment Camp Based on a Classroom Diary* (6–10). Illus. 1996, Holiday $18.95 (0-8234-1239-3). This book consists of 20 excerpts from a classroom diary kept by a 3rd-grade Japanese American schoolteacher during her confinement in a desert relocation camp during 1943. (Rev: BL 7/96; SLJ 8/96*; VOYA 12/96) [769.8]

9344 Whitman, Sylvia. *V Is for Victory: The American Home Front During World War II* (4–7). Illus. 1993, Lerner LB $30.35 (0-8225-1727-2). Rosie the Riveter, ration stamps, and the relocation of Japan-

ese Americans are among the topics covered in this look at the United States in another time. (Rev: BL 2/15/93) [973.9]

9345 Yancey, Diane. *Life in a Japanese American Internment Camp* (6–12). Illus. Series: Way People Live. 1997, Lucent LB $27.45 (1-56006-345-9). Black-and-white photographs and excerpts from personal narratives are used to describe the upheaval in the lives of Japanese Americans during World War II. (Rev: BL 1/1–15/98) [940.53]

POST WORLD WAR II UNITED STATES
(1945–)

9346 Alonso, Karen. *The Chicago Seven Political Protest Trial* (6–10). Series: Headline Court Cases. 2002, Enslow LB $20.95 (0-7660-1764-8). This is an account of the trial of the Chicago Seven, a group that was arrested during a demonstration at the Democratic National Convention in Chicago. (Rev: BL 3/15/03; HBG 10/03) [973.92]

9347 Anderson, Dale. *America into a New Millennium* (5–8). Series: Making of America. 2001, Raintree Steck-Vaughn LB $28.54 (0-8172-5712-8). This last part of a 12-volume series presents American history from the end of the Cold War to the beginning of the 21st century. (Rev: BL 9/15/01; HBG 10/01; SLJ 6/01) [973.9]

9348 Anderson, Dale. *The Cold War Years* (5–8). Series: Making of America. 2001, Raintree Steck-Vaughn LB $28.54 (0-8172-5711-X). A concise, easy-to-understand text tells America's story from the end of World War II to the 1990s. (Rev: BL 9/15/01; HBG 10/01; SLJ 6/01) [973.9]

9349 Archer, Jules. *The Incredible Sixties: The Stormy Years That Changed America* (7–12). 1986, Harcourt $17.95 (0-15-238298-4). A topically arranged overview of the events, trends, and significance of the 1960s and how they have shaped our future. (Rev: BL 5/15/86; SLJ 9/86; VOYA 4/87) [973.922]

9350 Baker, Patricia. *Fashions of a Decade: The 1950s* (7–12). Series: Fashions of a Decade. 1991, Facts on File $25.00 (0-8160-2468-5). An illustrated overview of fashions of the 1950s and the political, economic, and social developments of the time. (Rev: BL 12/15/91; SLJ 2/92) [391]

9351 Brown, Gene. *The Nation in Turmoil: Civil Rights and the Vietnam War (1960–1973)* (5–8). Series: First Person America. 1994, Twenty-First Century LB $20.90 (0-8050-2588-X). An overview of the civil rights movement and the Vietnam War, highlighting excerpts from letters, diaries, and speeches. (Rev: BL 5/15/94) [973.92]

9352 Brown, Gene. *The 1992 Election* (5–8). Illus. Series: Headliners. 1993, Millbrook LB $25.90 (1-56294-080-5). This book presents the issues and highlights of the campaigns and presidential election. (Rev: BL 4/1/93; SLJ 7/93) [973.9]

9353 Ching, Jacqueline. *The Assassination of Martin Luther King Jr.* (6–10). Series: The Library of Political Assassinations. 2002, Rosen LB $26.50 (0-8239-3543-4). A look at the life and death of Martin Luther King, Jr., and his legacy. (Rev: SLJ 8/02) [976]

9354 Ching, Juliet. *The Assassination of Robert F. Kennedy* (6–10). Series: The Library of Political Assassinations. 2002, Rosen LB $26.50 (0-8239-3545-0). In addition to discussing the assassination and the events preceding it, the author looks at the rumors of a conspiracy and allegations of incompetence on the part of the Los Angeles police force. (Rev: BL 8/02; SLJ 8/02) [976]

9355 Cunningham, Jesse G., ed. *The McCarthy Hearings* (8–12). Series: At Issue in History. 2003, Gale LB $21.96 (0-7377-1346-1); paper $14.96 (0-7377-1347-X). An objective look at the activities of the senator from Wisconsin that gives clear historical context. (Rev: SLJ 4/03) [973.921]

9356 Dolan, Sean. *Pursuing the Dream: From the Selma-Montgomery March to the Formation of PUSH (1965–1971)* (7–10). Illus. Series: Milestones in Black American History. 1995, Chelsea LB $19.95 (0-7910-2254-4); paper $8.95 (0-7910-2680-9). This chronicle of the civil rights movement of the 1960s describes the demonstrations and confrontations and gives background information on participation of blacks in sports and the arts. (Rev: BL 7/95) [323.1]

9357 Draper, Allison Stark. *The Assassination of Malcolm X* (6–10). Series: The Library of Political Assassinations. 2002, Rosen LB $31.95 (0-8239-3542-6). A description of the assassination and its aftermath is followed by information on Malcolm X's life and beliefs. (Rev: BL 2/15/02; SLJ 7/02) [976.2]

9358 Epstein, Dan. *The 80s: The Decade of Plenty* (7–10). Series: 20th Century Pop Culture. 2000, Chelsea LB $17.95 (0-7910-6088-8). A mix of popular entertainment and fashion with key news events, all arranged chronologically and accompanied by lots of color photographs. Other books in the series include *The 50s: America Tunes In* and *The 60s: A Decade of Change: The Flintstones to Woodstock*. (Rev: SLJ 6/01) [973.9]

9359 Feinstein, Stephen. *The 1980s: From Ronald Reagan to MTV* (4–7). Series: Decades of the 20th Century. 2000, Enslow LB $17.95 (0-7660-1424-X). Presents the decade's major events, important people, and developments in such areas as politics, science, the arts, and sports. (Rev: BL 10/15/00; HBG 10/00; SLJ 12/00) [973.9]

9360 Finkelstein, Norman H. *Thirteen Days / Ninety Miles: The Cuban Missile Crisis* (8–12). 1994,

Messner LB $18.95 (0-671-86622-2). Declassified materials, letters, and memoirs describe the tension-filled Cuban missile crisis, documenting the actions and ideologies of Kennedy and Khrushchev and revealing how narrowly nuclear war was averted. (Rev: BL 7/94*; SLJ 6/94) [973.992]

9361 Finkelstein, Norman H. *The Way Things Never Were: The Truth About the "Good Old Days"* (5–8). 1999, Simon & Schuster $16.00 (0-689-81412-7). The 1950s and 1960s are revisited in this social history that describes a time of Cold War jitters, less reliable automobiles, poorer diet, and inferior health and long-term care. (Rev: BCCB 9/99; BL 9/1/99; HBG 3/00; SLJ 7/99; VOYA 4/00) [973.92]

9362 Fremon, David K. *The Watergate Scandal in American History* (7–10). Series: In American History. 1997, Enslow LB $20.95 (0-89490-883-9). A clear, logically arranged, and objective account of the famous political scandal that ended the Nixon presidency. (Rev: BL 4/15/98; SLJ 5/98) [973.9]

9363 Hakim, Joy. *All the People*. 2nd ed. (5–8). Series: A History of Us. 1999, Oxford LB $19.95 (0-19-512769-2); paper $13.95 (0-19-512770-6). An outstanding history of the political and social events, trends, and developments in the United States from the end of World War II through 1998. (Rev: BL 12/15/99; VOYA 4/00) [973.9]

9364 Hampton, Wilborn. *Kennedy Assassinated! The World Mourns* (5–8). Illus. 1997, Candlewick $17.99 (1-56402-811-9). A gripping first-person account of John Kennedy's assassination by a veteran newspaper reporter who was in Dallas that day. (Rev: BL 9/15/97; BR 3–4/98; HBG 3/98; SLJ 10/97) [364.1]

9365 Harding, Vincent, et al. *We Changed the World: African Americans, 1945–1970* (7–12). Illus. Series: Young Oxford History of African Americans. 1997, Oxford $24.00 (0-19-508796-8). This volume covers African American history immediately after World War II and traces the beginnings of the modern civil rights movement. (Rev: BL 9/1/97; BR 11–12/97) [973]

9366 Haskins, Jim. *Power to the People: The Rise and Fall of the Black Panther Party* (7–12). Illus. 1997, Simon & Schuster paper $16.00 (0-689-80085-1). A somewhat plodding account of this radical 1960s political organization whose leaders included Huey Newton and Bobby Seale. (Rev: BL 3/15/97; SLJ 3/97; VOYA 8/97) [322.4]

9367 Hendler, Herb. *Year by Year in the Rock Era* (7–12). 1983, Greenwood $62.95 (0-313-23456-6). A year-by-year chronicle of social events matched with information about artists, hits, and so on, of the rock era from 1954 through 1981. [973.92]

9368 Herda, D. J. *United States v. Nixon: Watergate and the President* (6–10). Illus. Series: Landmark

Supreme Court Cases. 1996, Enslow LB $20.95 (0-89490-753-0). The Watergate scandal is reviewed with special emphasis on the legal aspects of this case that brought down the presidency of Richard Nixon. (Rev: BL 8/96; SLJ 7/96) [342.73]

9369 Hull, Mary. *Struggle and Love, 1972–1997* (7–10). Illus. Series: Milestones in Black American History. 1996, Chelsea LB $21.95 (0-7910-2262-5); paper $9.95 (0-7910-2688-4). This book covers the past quarter of a century in African American history, highlighting the lives and careers of prominent individuals including Jesse Jackson, Colin Powell, and Michael Jordan. (Rev: BL 3/15/97; SLJ 6/97) [973]

9370 Hurley, Jennifer A. *The 1960s* (7–12). Series: Opposing Viewpoints Digests. 1999, Greenhaven LB $21.96 (0-7377-0211-7); paper $13.96 (0-7377-0210-9). The Vietnam War and the many social changes of the 1960s are discussed from different perspectives; an appendix of original documents includes excerpts from news articles, speeches, government papers, and other primary materials of interest. (Rev: SLJ 4/00) [306]

9371 Isaacs, Sally Senzell. *America in the Time of Martin Luther King Jr.: The Story of Our Nation from Coast to Coast, from 1948 to 1976* (4–8). Series: America in the Time Of. 1999, Heinemann LB $30.35 (1-57572-780-3). As well as describing the accomplishment of Martin Luther King, Jr., this account traces important developments during his time including the 1960s peace movement, the Vietnam War, space travel, and the Watergate scandal. (Rev: SLJ 5/00) [973.9]

9372 Johnson, Darv. *The Reagan Years* (7–10). Series: World History. 2000, Lucent LB $18.96 (1-56006-592-3). This account of the two-term president focuses on conservatism, his economic agenda, and relations with the Soviet Union, the Middle East, and Central America. (Rev: BL 6/1–15/00; HBG 9/00; SLJ 9/00) [973.9]

9373 Kallen, Stuart A., ed. *The Baby Boom* (7–12). Series: Turning Points in World History. 2001, Greenhaven LB $31.20 (0-7377-0924-3); paper $19.95 (0-7377-0925-1). This collection of essays and documents arranged in chronological order, explores the social, economic, and cultural effects of the large generation of babies that were born in the United States after World War II. (Rev: BL 3/15/02; SLJ 7/02) [973.9]

9374 Kallen, Stuart A. *Life in America During the 1960s* (6–10). Series: The Way People Live. 2001, Lucent LB $19.96 (1-56006-790-X). Using as a backdrop the presidencies of Kennedy and Johnson, the civil rights movement and the Vietnam War, this work focuses in pictures and text on the daily life of Americans during this difficult period. (Rev: BL 6/1–15/01) [973.9]

9375 Kallen, Stuart A. *The 1950s* (5–8). Series: Cultural History of the United States. 1998, Lucent LB $27.45 (1-56006-555-9). Readable text and many photographs are used to survey the contrasting political and cultural trends, events, and movements of the 1950s in the United States and examine what life was like for teenagers at that time. (Rev: BL 1/1–15/99; SLJ 3/99) [973.921]

9376 Kallen, Stuart A., ed. *The 1950s* (6–12). Series: America's Decades. 2000, Greenhaven LB $29.96 (0-7377-0304-0); paper $17.96 (0-7377-0303-2). This history of the 1950s in America covers such topics as fear about a nuclear war, the growth of suburbia, racial tensions, and the importance of television and rock and roll. (Rev: BL 7/00; SLJ 9/00) [973.9]

9377 Kallen, Stuart A., ed. *The 1990s* (6–12). Illus. Series: American Decades. 2000, Greenhaven LB $29.96 (0-7377-0312-1); paper $17.96 (0-7377-0311-3). Major events of the 1990s are discussed and arranged under six subjects: politics, war, violence, race and gender, pop culture, and technology. (Rev: BL 6/1–15/00) [973.929.]

9378 Katz, William L. *The Great Society to the Reagan Era: 1964–1990* (7–9). Series: History of Multicultural America. 1993, Raintree Steck-Vaughn LB $27.11 (0-8114-6282-X). A history of race relations in the United States that covers the struggles, gains, and setbacks from the mid-1960s to 1990, spanning the Johnson, Nixon, Carter, and Reagan administrations. (Rev: BL 9/1/93) [973.92]

9379 Kronenwetter, Michael. *America in the 1960s* (6–9). Illus. Series: World History. 1997, Lucent LB $27.45 (1-56006-294-0). A re-creation of this tumultuous decade rocked by the antiwar and civil rights movements and a vast reassessment of social values by individuals and the nation as a whole. (Rev: BL 6/1–15/98; SLJ 8/98) [973.923]

9380 Landsman, Susan. *Who Shot JFK?* (6–8). Series: History Mystery. 1992, Avon paper $3.50 (0-380-77063-6). A look at the controversial subject of JFK's assassination, examining the maze of theories, charges, and countercharges. (Rev: BL 4/1/93) [364.1]

9381 Lindop, Edmund. *America in the 1950s* (6–10). Illus. 2002, Millbrook LB $25.90 (0-7613-2551-4). Lindop looks at the lighter sides of life in the 1950s — including the influence of TV on popular culture, the move to the suburbs, and sports — as well as the political and social upheavals of the Korean War, the Cold War, McCarthyism, and desegregation. (Rev: BL 9/1/02; HBG 3/03; SLJ 10/02) [973.921]

9382 Lomas, Clare. *The 80s and 90s: Power Dressing to Sportswear* (5–10). Series: 20th Century Fashion. 2000, Gareth Stevens LB $25.26 (0-8368-2603-5). Power dressing, androgyny, sportswear, and grunge characterize the world of fashion during the 1980s and 1990s in this book that covers both design and social history. (Rev: HBG 10/00; SLJ 6/00) [973.9]

9383 Meltzer, Milton, ed. *The American Promise: Voices of a Changing Nation* (8–12). Illus. 1990, Bantam $15.95 (0-553-07020-7). In a series of excerpts from books, speeches, and interviews, the major movements affecting American life since World War II are outlined. (Rev: BL 12/15/90; SLJ 2/91) [973.92]

9384 Morris, Jeffrey. *The Reagan Way* (6–9). Series: Great Presidential Decisions. 1996, Lerner LB $23.93 (0-8225-2931-9). By examining Reagan's major presidential decisions, the author presents an even-handed look at Reagan's strengths and weaknesses. (Rev: SLJ 2/96) [973.9]

9385 Powe-Temperley, Kitty. *The 60s: Mods and Hippies* (5–10). Series: 20th Century Fashion. 2000, Gareth Stevens LB $25.26 (0-8368-2601-9). Mods, hippies, miniskirts, Eastern influences, and art as fashion are covered in this overview of clothing fads of the 1960s, along with background information. (Rev: HBG 10/00; SLJ 6/00) [973.9]

9386 Reynolds, Helen. *The 40s and 50s: Utility to New Look* (5–10). Series: 20th Century Fashion. 2000, Gareth Stevens LB $25.26 (0-8368-2600-0). Using a lively style and many period illustrations, this book highlights the world of fashion and design during and after World War II and gives some background social history. (Rev: HBG 10/00; SLJ 6/00) [973.9]

9387 Ribeiro, Myra. *The Assassination of Medgar Evers* (6–10). Series: The Library of Political Assassinations. 2002, Rosen LB $26.50 (0-8239-3544-2). A description of the assassination and its aftermath is followed by information on Evers's life and beliefs. (Rev: BL 2/15/02; SLJ 7/02) [976]

9388 *The Rock and Roll Generation: Teen Life in the '50s* (7–12). Illus. Series: Our American Century. 1998, Time-Life Books $29.95 (0-7835-5501-6). Outstanding photographs and short, simple text document important developments in the 1950s, including the birth of rock music, the beat generation, television, the Cold War and Korean War, McCarthyism, and the beginnings of the civil rights movement, and provides insights into teen life. (Rev: BR 9–10/98; SLJ 9/98) [973.9]

9389 Schmidt, Mark Ray, ed. *The 1970s* (6–12). Series: America's Decades. 2000, Greenhaven LB $29.96 (0-7377-0308-3); paper $17.96 (0-7377-0307-5). This anthology contains articles on topics including environmental and energy issues, racial integration, the Watergate scandal, and interracial conflicts (Rev: BL 7/00; SLJ 7/00) [973.9]

9390 Steins, Richard. *The Postwar Years: The Cold War and the Atomic Age (1950–1959)* (5–8). Series: First Person America. 1994, Twenty-First Century

LB $20.90 (0-8050-2587-1). Coverage of the 1950s includes first-person material on the Cold War and the Korean conflict. (Rev: BL 5/15/94; SLJ 12/94) [973.92]

9391 Torr, James D., ed. *The 1980s* (6–12). Series: America's Decades. 2000, Greenhaven LB $29.96 (0-7377-0310-5); paper $17.96 (0-7377-0309-2). The election of Reagan, the appearance of AIDS, the rise of personal computers, and the fall of the Berlin Wall in 1989, are some of the topics covered in this anthology of articles. (Rev: BL 7/00; SLJ 7/00) [973.9]

9392 Walsh, Frank. *The Montgomery Bus Boycott* (5–8). Series: Landmark Events in American History. 2003, World Almanac LB $26.60 (0-8368-5375-X). The story of what happened when Rosa Parks refused to give up her seat on a Montgomery, Alabama, bus in 1955. (Rev: BL 10/15/03; SLJ 9/03) [305.8]

9393 Warren, James A. *Cold War: The American Crusade Against World Communism, 1945–1991* (7–12). Illus. 1996, Lothrop $16.00 (0-688-10596-3). A meticulously researched account that covers the events, strategies, and personalities involved in the nation's 50-year effort to contain and subvert communism around the world. (Rev: BL 1/1–15/97; BR 11–12/96; SLJ 10/96*; VOYA 4/97) [327.73047]

9394 Westerfeld, Scott. *Watergate* (5–7). Illus. Series: Turning Points. 1991, Silver Burdett paper $7.95 (0-382-24120-7). An objective account in text and pictures of the Watergate break-in during Nixon's presidency and its consequences. (Rev: BL 1/15/92) [364.1]

9395 Zeinert, Karen. *McCarthy and the Fear of Communism* (7–10). Series: In American History. 1998, Enslow LB $20.95 (0-89490-987-8). The story of the reign of terror inflicted on America during the 1950s by the senator from Wisconsin. (Rev: BL 8/98; HBG 9/99; SLJ 12/98) [973.9]

KOREAN, VIETNAM, AND GULF WARS

9396 Campbell, Geoffrey A. *Life of an American Soldier* (5–9). Series: American War Library: The Persian Gulf War. 2001, Lucent LB $27.45 (1-56006-713-6). Interviews with Gulf War veterans bring a personal touch to this volume, which includes many photographs of soldiers and equipment along with a history of the war and discussion of the reasons for the conflict. (Rev: SLJ 8/01) [956.7044]

9397 Freedman, Suzanne. *Clay v. United States: Muhammad Ali Objects to War* (6–10). Series: Landmark Supreme Court Cases. 1997, Enslow LB $20.95 (0-89490-855-3). A thorough examination of Muhammad Ali's court case involving the Vietnam War. (Rev: BL 10/15/97; HBG 3/98; SLJ 12/97) [959.704]

589

9398 Galt, Margot Fortunato. *Stop This War! American Protest of the Conflict in Vietnam* (8–12). Series: People's History. 2000, Lerner LB $30.35 (0-8225-1740-X). The author cites her husband, a conscientious objector, among those who protested the war from the early 1960s until its end, and details key events and student and other groups. (Rev: BL 7/00; HBG 9/00; SLJ 8/00) [959.704]

9399 Granfield, Linda. *I Remember Korea: Veterans Tell Their Stories of the Korean War, 1950–53* (6–12). Illus. 2003, Clarion $16.00 (0-618-17740-X). First-person accounts by American combatants that reveal a wide variety of experiences are accompanied by brief introductory notes, photographs, and a short account of the war itself. (Rev: BCCB 2/04; BL 12/15/03) [951.904]

9400 Kallen, Stuart A. *The Home Front: Americans Protest the War* (6–12). Series: American War Library: The Vietnam War. 2000, Lucent LB $19.96 (1-56006-718-7). Campus protests against the war, peace marches, the burning of draft cards, and Woodstock are among the topics covered in this informative volume. (Rev: BL 3/1/01; SLJ 4/01) [959.704]

9401 Kent, Deborah. *The Vietnam War: "What Are We Fighting For?"* (5–7). Illus. Series: American War. 1994, Enslow LB $20.95 (0-89490-527-9). An objective overview of this war, its causes, progression, and results. (Rev: BL 10/15/94; SLJ 11/94) [959.704]

9402 McCloud, Bill. *What Should We Tell Our Children About Vietnam?* (7–12). 1989, Univ. of Oklahoma Pr. paper $14.95 (0-8061-3240-X). More than 120 individuals, including the first President Bush and Gary Trudeau, tell what they think young people should know about the war. (Rev: BL 9/15/89) [959.704]

9403 McCormick, Anita Louise. *The Vietnam Antiwar Movement* (6–12). Illus. Series: In American History. 2000, Enslow LB $19.95 (0-7660-1295-6). Historical photographs and clear prose are used in this account of the many anti-Vietnam War protests in the United States and their effect on the course of history. (Rev: BL 1/1–15/00; HBG 9/00; SLJ 4/00) [959.704.]

9404 Schomp, Virginia. *The Vietnam War* (5–8). Series: Letters from the Homefront. 2001, Benchmark LB $28.50 (0-7614-1099-6). Conditions on the home front during the Vietnam War are re-created through primary documents such as letters and period photographs. (Rev: BL 10/15/01; HBG 3/02; SLJ 3/02) [973.9]

9405 Yancey, Diane. *Life of an American Soldier* (6–12). Series: American War Library: The Vietnam War. 2001, Lucent LB $19.96 (1-56006-676-8). A candid, well-illustrated look at the problems faced by American soldiers during their service in Vietnam and after their return to the United States, with many firsthand accounts. (Rev: BL 3/15/01; SLJ 6/01) [957.704]

9406 Zeinert, Karen. *The Valiant Women of the Vietnam War* (5–8). Illus. 2000, Millbrook LB $29.90 (0-7613-1268-4). Provides a good overview of the Vietnam War and highlights the contributions of women at home and abroad during this conflict. (Rev: BL 4/1/00; HBG 10/00; SLJ 5/00) [959.704]

Regions

MIDWEST

9407 Aylesworth, Thomas G., and Virginia L. Aylesworth. *Eastern Great Lakes: Indiana, Michigan, Ohio* (4–7). Illus. Series: State Reports. 1995, Chelsea $19.95 (0-7910-3409-7). Information is given for each of the three states covered, including major cities, history, geography, and climate. (Rev: BL 3/15/92) [977]

9408 Balcavage, Dynise. *Iowa* (5–8). Illus. Series: From Sea to Shining Sea, Second Series. 2002, Children's LB $29.50 (0-516-22481-6). An attractive overview of Iowa's land, history, culture, economy, and people. (Rev: SLJ 3/03) [977.7]

9409 Baldwin, Guy. *Oklahoma* (4–8). Series: Celebrate the States. 2000, Marshall Cavendish LB $142.57 (0-7614-1061-9). The beauties and hidden treasures of Oklahoma are covered in this colorful introduction to the state, its past, its present, and its people. (Rev: BL 12/15/00) [976.6]

9410 Bennett, Michelle. *Missouri* (4–8). Series: Celebrate the States. 2001, Benchmark LB $35.64 (0-7614-1063-5). A logically organized, thorough introduction to Missouri with material on such topics as history, people, landmarks, and famous natives. (Rev: BL 9/15/01; HBG 10/01) [977.8]

9411 Bjorklund, Ruth. *Kansas* (4–8). Series: Celebrate the States. 2000, Marshall Cavendish LB $35.64 (0-7614-0646-8). A broad introduction to Kansas — its geography and history, its government and people, its songs and folktales, and a few of its recipes. (Rev: BL 6/1–15/00; HBG 10/00) [978.1]

9412 Blashfield, Jean F. *Wisconsin* (5–8). Series: America the Beautiful. 1998, Children's LB $34.00 (0-516-20640-0). Important facts about Wisconsin include its history, famous people, dates, places, and economy. (Rev: BL 1/1–15/99; SLJ 4/99) [977.5]

9413 Boekhoff, P. M., and Stuart A. Kallen. *Illinois* (4–7). Illus. Series: Seeds of a Nation. 2002, Gale LB $30.35 (0-7377-0279-6). This is a compact history of the territory that would become Illinois, with fine coverage of Native American culture and history. (Rev: BL 4/1/02; SLJ 3/02) [977.3]

9414 Brill, Marlene T. *Illinois* (4–8). Illus. Series: Celebrate the States. 1996, Marshall Cavendish LB

$35.64 (0-7614-0113-X). Maps, diagrams, and photographs enliven this introduction to Illinois that gives good coverage of history, geography, and social conditions. (Rev: BL 2/1/97; SLJ 2/97) [913.73]

9415 Brill, Marlene T. *Indiana* (4–8). Illus. Series: Celebrate the States. 1997, Marshall Cavendish LB $35.64 (0-7614-0147-4). An introduction to this Midwest state's agriculture, industries, famous natives, history, and geography. (Rev: BL 7/97; SLJ 8/97) [977.2]

9416 Carlson, Jeffrey D. *A Historical Album of Minnesota* (5–8). Illus. Series: Historical Albums. 1993, Millbrook LB $24.40 (1-56294-006-6). A heavily illustrated volume that traces the history of Minnesota from Native American communities through exploration and settlement to present-day concerns. (Rev: SLJ 10/93) [977.6]

9417 Dornfeld, Margaret. *Wisconsin* (4–7). Series: It's My State! 2003, Marshall Cavendish LB $18.95 (0-7614-1524-6). Using many quotations from various sources, this account supplies a basic introduction to Wisconsin, its people, and its past and present. (Rev: BL 9/15/03; SLJ 11/03) [977.5]

9418 Edge, Laura B. *A Personal Tour of Hull-House* (4–7). Series: How It Was. 2001, Lerner LB $25.26 (0-8225-3583-3). A firsthand account of the settlement house founded in Chicago by Jane Addams. (Rev: BL 8/1/01) [977.3]

9419 Hahn, Laura. *Mount Rushmore* (4–8). Illus. Series: American Symbols and Their Meanings. 2002, Mason Crest LB $18.95 (1-59084-027-5). Hahn describes Gutzon Borglum's struggle to build his monument, with a helpful timeline and many illustrations. (Rev: SLJ 9/02) [730]

9420 Heinrichs, Ann. *Indiana* (5–8). Series: America the Beautiful. 2000, Children's LB $34.00 (0-516-21038-6). Topics covered in this excellent introduction to Indiana include geography, history, government, economy, people, and places. (Rev: BL 5/15/00) [977]

9421 Heinrichs, Ann. *Ohio* (5–8). Series: America the Beautiful. 1999, Children's LB $34.00 (0-516-20995-7). Clear writing plus many color illustrations and maps are used to cover a wide range of topics about Ohio, including history, geography, famous residents, cities, economy, and government. (Rev: BL 11/15/99) [977.1]

9422 Hintz, Martin. *Iowa* (5–8). Series: America the Beautiful. 2000, Children's LB $34.00 (0-516-21070-X). This introduction to Iowa includes such topics as its history, government, celebrities, and sports teams. (Rev: BL 5/15/00) [977.8]

9423 Hintz, Martin. *Minnesota* (5–8). Series: America the Beautiful. 2000, Children's LB $34.00 (0-516-21040-8). This revision of the standard work on Minnesota gives expanded coverage and includes a

timeline, fact sheets, and extensive lists of outside resources. (Rev: BL 5/15/00) [977.6]

9424 Hintz, Martin. *Missouri* (5–8). Series: America the Beautiful. 1999, Children's LB $34.00 (0-516-20836-5). This colorful introduction to Missouri covers such topics as geography, history, government, economy, famous personalities, people, and culture. (Rev: BL 11/15/99) [977.8]

9425 Hintz, Martin. *North Dakota* (5–8). Series: America the Beautiful. 2000, Children's LB $34.00 (0-516-21072-6). An introduction to North Dakota that includes the economy, land, people, history, state symbols, and sports teams. (Rev: BL 11/15/00) [978.4]

9426 Jameson, W. C. *Buried Treasures of the Great Plains* (5–8). Series: Buried Treasure. 1997, August House $11.95 (0-87483-486-4). Stories of buried treasure are organized by the individual states of the Great Plains region. (Rev: BR 5–6/99; SLJ 7/97) [977]

9427 Martin, Michael A. *Ohio: The Buckeye State* (4–7). Series: World Almanac Library of the States. 2002, World Almanac LB $29.26 (0-8368-5124-2). Facts, statistics, a pleasing layout, and color photographs make this a useful choice for report writers. Also use *Iowa: The Hawkeye State* (2002). (Rev: SLJ 9/02) [977.1]

9428 Masters, Nancy Robinson. *Kansas* (5–8). Series: America the Beautiful. 1999, Children's LB $34.00 (0-516-20993-0). An introduction to Kansas that covers its history and government, geography and people, tourism and state symbols, culture, and celebrities. (Rev: BL 12/15/9) [978.1]

9429 Murphy, Jim. *The Great Fire* (5–9). 1995, Scholastic paper $17.95 (0-590-47267-4). A dramatic re-creation of the great Chicago fire that combines documents, personal accounts, illustrations, photographs, and street maps to give an in-depth view of the disaster. (Rev: BCCB 5/95; BL 6/1–15/95; HB 5–6/95, 9–10/95; SLJ 7/95) [977.3]

9430 Presnall, Judith Janda. *Mount Rushmore* (7–10). Series: Building History. 1999, Lucent LB $18.96 (1-56006-529-X). Conceived by Doune Robinson and sculpted by Gutzon Borglum, this mountainside monument has become a national landmark. (Rev: BL 10/15/99; HBG 9/00) [978.3]

9431 Reedy, Jerry. *Oklahoma* (5–8). Series: America the Beautiful. 1998, Children's Pr. LB $34.00 (0-516-20639-7). Basic material on Oklahoma, plus a special reference section that includes key statistics, important dates, famous people, and maps. (Rev: BL 1/1–15/99; SLJ 2/99) [976.6]

9432 St. Antoine, Sara, ed. *Stories from Where We Live: The Great Lakes* (4–8). 2003, Milkweed $19.95 (1-57131-639-6). Fiction, poetry, journal entries, and essays celebrate the flora, fauna, topology, and traditions of the Great Lakes region. (Rev: BL 12/1/03) [810.8]

9433 Santella, Andrew. *Illinois* (5–8). Illus. Series: America the Beautiful. 1998, Children's LB $34.00 (0-516-20633-8). This comprehensive account of Illinois includes its history and geography, principal cities and important landmarks, and culture and people. (Rev: BL 1/1–15/99) [977.3]

9434 Schonberg, Lisa. *People of Ohio* (4–7). Illus. Series: Heinemann State Studies. 2003, Heinemann LB $27.07 (1-4034-0668-5). Schonberg looks at groups of Ohioans from the original native peoples to later arrivals and at individuals who have contributed to all fields of endeavor, with many color photographs. (Rev: BL 10/15/03; SLJ 10/03) [305.]

9435 Schwabacher, Martin. *Minnesota* (4–7). Series: Celebrate the States. 1999, Benchmark LB $35.64 (0-7614-0658-1). Minnesota is introduced in six chapters that cover history, geography, government and economy, people, achievements, and landmarks. (Rev: HBG 10/99; SLJ 10/99) [977.6]

9436 Wills, Charles A. *A Historical Album of Illinois* (4–8). Illus. Series: Historical Albums. 1994, Millbrook LB $24.40 (1-56294-482-7). A brief history of Illinois that touches on the most important events from before the white man to the 1990s. (Rev: SLJ 3/95) [977.3]

9437 Wills, Charles A. *A Historical Album of Michigan* (4–7). Illus. Series: Historical Albums. 1996, Millbrook LB $24.40 (0-7613-0036-8). Using many archival prints, drawings, photographs, and ample text, the history of Michigan is told. (Rev: BL 10/15/96) [977]

MOUNTAIN AND PLAINS STATES

9438 Ayer, Eleanor. *Colorado* (4–8). Illus. Series: Celebrate the States. 1997, Marshall Cavendish LB $35.64 (0-7614-0148-2). An introduction to the Centennial State, with information on its history, geography, and people. (Rev: BL 7/97; SLJ 8/97) [978.8]

9439 Blashfield, Jean F. *Arizona* (5–8). Series: America the Beautiful. 2000, Children's LB $34.00 (0-516-21068-8). This excellent guide to Arizona covers all the basic topics about the southwestern state. (Rev: BL 9/15/00) [979.1]

9440 Blashfield, Jean F. *Colorado* (5–8). Series: America the Beautiful. 1999, Children's LB $34.00 (0-516-20684-2). A solid introduction to Colorado that contains the standard historical and geographical information plus state symbols, a government chart, about a dozen maps, and a historical timeline. (Rev: BL 11/15/99; HBG 10/99; SLJ 10/99) [978.8]

9441 George, Charles, and Linda George. *Idaho* (5–8). Series: America the Beautiful. 2000, Children's LB $34.00 (0-516-21037-8). A fine introduc-

tion to Idaho that includes such topics as geography, history, government, landmarks, people, recreation, and culture. (Rev: BL 9/15/00) [978]

9442 George, Charles, and Linda George. *Montana* (5–8). Series: America the Beautiful. 2000, Children's LB $34.00 (0-516-21092-0). A broad introduction to the state of Montana, including its history and geography, cities and landmarks, people, and economy. (Rev: BL 11/15/00) [978.6]

9443 Kent, Deborah. *Utah* (5–8). Series: America the Beautiful. 2000, Children's LB $34.00 (0-516-21045-9). A guide to this mountain state, covering all the basics plus information on sports, religion, celebrities, and the Indian tribes that lived there. (Rev: BL 5/15/00) [979.2]

9444 Kent, Deborah. *Wyoming* (5–8). Series: America the Beautiful. 2000, Children's LB $34.00 (0-516-21075-0). An introduction to Wyoming, including its geography, history, government, economy, people, sports, and celebrities. (Rev: BL 9/15/00) [978.7]

9445 Lourie, Peter. *In the Path of Lewis and Clark: Traveling the Missouri* (6–9). Illus. 1996, Silver Burdett LB $19.95 (0-382-39307-4); paper $14.95 (0-382-39308-2). A day-by-day account of the 1,700-mile trip on the Missouri River that the author took in 1995 with William Least Heat-Moon, mostly by motorboat, during Moon's cross-country trip, with relevant bits of history and river lore and numerous color photographs. (Rev: BL 2/15/97; SLJ 4/97) [917.804]

9446 McCarthy, Betty. *Utah* (5–7). Illus. Series: America the Beautiful. 1989, Children's LB $28.00 (0-516-00490-5). The story of Utah is told in pictures and text covering such topics as economy, history, geography, and recreation. (Rev: BL 1/1/90) [979.2]

9447 McDaniel, Melissa. *Arizona* (4–8). Series: Celebrate the States. 2000, Marshall Cavendish LB $35.64 (0-7614-0647-6). This introduction to Arizona discusses its land, history, economy, festivals, cultural diversity, and landmarks. (Rev: BL 6/1–15/00; HBG 10/00; SLJ 9/00) [979.1]

9448 Minor, Wendell. *Grand Canyon: Exploring a Natural Wonder* (4–8). Illus. 1998, Scholastic paper $16.95 (0-590-47968-7). In watercolors and lyrical text, the author presents a grand portrait of the Grand Canyon. (Rev: BL 9/15/98; BR 1–2/99; HBG 3/99; SLJ 8/98) [978.8]

9449 Stefoff, Rebecca. *Idaho* (4–8). Series: Celebrate the States. 2000, Benchmark LB $35.64 (0-7614-0663-8). Interesting charts, graphs, and maps are used to illustrate such topics as the people, land, history, and culture of Idaho. (Rev: BL 1/1–15/00; HBG 10/00) [978.8]

9450 Stefoff, Rebecca. *Nevada* (4–8). Series: Celebrate the States. 2001, Benchmark LB $35.64 (0-

7614-1073-2). This well-organized introduction to Nevada gives general information followed by a timeline and special material on tourist attractions, famous natives of Nevada, and local festivals. (Rev: BL 9/15/01; HBG 10/01) [979.3]

9451 Stefoff, Rebecca. *Utah* (4–8). Series: Celebrate the States. 2000, Marshall Cavendish LB $35.64 (0-7614-1064-3). Utah's unique characteristics and places are highlighted in this account that also covers the state's history, geography, and government. (Rev: BL 12/15/00; HBG 3/01; SLJ 2/01) [979.2]

9452 Stein, R. Conrad. *Nevada* (5–8). Series: America the Beautiful. 2000, Children's LB $34.00 (0-516-21041-6). A good introduction to Nevada's history and geography, economy, culture, people, sights, and entertainment. (Rev: BL 5/15/00) [979.3]

9453 Wills, Charles A. *A Historical Album of Colorado* (4–7). Illus. Series: Historical Albums. 1996, Millbrook $24.40 (1-56294-592-0); paper $6.95 (1-56294-858-X). Using many old engravings and photographs, the history of Colorado is traced, beginning with its Native American population. (Rev: BL 7/96; SLJ 7/96) [978.8]

NORTHEASTERN AND MID-ATLANTIC STATES

9454 Aaseng, Nathan. *The White House* (7–10). Series: Building History. 2000, Lucent LB $19.96 (1-56006-708-X). The history of this Washington landmark is given plus material on the presidents and architects who shaped this building through the years. (Rev: BL 9/15/00) [975.3]

9455 Arnosky, Jim. *Nearer Nature* (6–12). Illus. 1996, Lothrop $18.00 (0-688-12213-2). In 26 short chapters and using his own pencil sketches, the author introduces the animals and the beauty of life found on a wooded sheep farm in rural Vermont. (Rev: BL 8/96; SLJ 11/96; VOYA 4/97) [508.743]

9456 Ashabranner, Brent. *Badge of Valor: The National Law Enforcement Officers Memorial* (5–8). Illus. 2000, Twenty-First Century LB $25.90 (0-7613-1522-5). This history of the memorial, from the original proposal in the 1970s to its opening in 1991, also discusses what it stands for and reveals the heroic deeds of some important law enforcement officers. (Rev: BL 10/1/00; HBG 3/01; SLJ 1/01) [363.2]

9457 Ashabranner, Brent. *A Date with Destiny: The Women in Military Service for America Memorial* (5–8). Illus. 2000, Twenty-First Century LB $25.90 (0-7613-1472-5). This book tells the story of the memorial outside Arlington National Cemetery that honors American women in the military and retells some of the stories of these servicewomen. (Rev: BL 2/1/00; HBG 10/00; SLJ 4/00) [355.1]

9458 Ashabranner, Brent. *No Better Hope: What the Lincoln Memorial Means to America* (4–8). Illus. Series: Great American Memorials. 2001, Twenty-First Century LB $25.90 (0-7613-1523-3). As well as telling about Lincoln and his importance to the country, this volume describes the building of the memorial and the important events that have occurred on the site. (Rev: BL 3/1/01; HBG 10/01; SLJ 7/01; VOYA 10/01) [975.3]

9459 Ashabranner, Brent. *On the Mall in Washington, D.C.: A Visit to America's Front Yard* (5–7). 2002, Twenty-First Century LB $23.90 (0-7613-2351-1). An entertaining and informative tour of the National Mall in Washington, D.C. (Rev: BL 3/15/02; HBG 10/02; SLJ 4/02) [917.5304]

9460 Ashabranner, Brent. *Remembering Korea: The Korean War Veterans Memorial* (4–8). Series: Great American Memorials. 2001, Twenty-First Century LB $25.90 (0-7613-2156-X). Ashabranner explains who the memorial honors, how much it cost, and what it represents. (Rev: BL 9/15/01; HBG 3/02; SLJ 12/01) [951.904]

9461 Ashabranner, Brent. *The Washington Monument: A Beacon for America* (4–8). Series: Great American Memorials. 2002, Millbrook LB $25.90 (0-7613-1524-1). Ashabranner presents the story behind the monument, including its planning, design, and construction, with full-color photographs and black-and-white period reproductions. (Rev: BL 9/1/02; HBG 3/03; SLJ 11/02) [975.3]

9462 Avakian, Monique. *A Historical Album of Massachusetts* (4–8). Illus. Series: Historical Albums. 1994, Millbrook LB $24.40 (1-56294-481-9). A history of Massachusetts that begins with the Native American culture and ends with the 1900s, including basic material on major events and personalities. (Rev: SLJ 2/95) [974.4]

9463 Avakian, Monique, and Carter Smith, III. *A Historical Album of New York* (5–8). Illus. Series: Historical Albums. 1993, Millbrook $24.40 (1-56294-005-8). An overview of New York State history from Native American settlements to the present day, using extensive archival illustrations. (Rev: SLJ 10/93) [974.7]

9464 Barenblat, Rachel. *Massachusetts: The Bay State* (4–7). Series: World Almanac Library of the States. 2002, World Almanac LB $29.26 (0-8368-5123-4). History, politics, government, culture, and state symbols are all covered, with charts, maps, photographs, biographical sketches, and a list of important events and attractions. (Rev: SLJ 6/02) [974.4]

9465 Bial, Raymond. *Tenement: Immigrant Life on the Lower East Side* (5–8). Illus. 2002, Houghton $16.00 (0-618-13849-8). Historic photographs complement the simple, descriptive text about life in New York City tenement housing in the late 1800s and early 1900s. (Rev: BL 10/15/02; HB 11–12/02; HBG 3/03; SLJ 9/02) [307.76]

9466 Blashfield, Jean F. *Delaware* (5–8). Series: America the Beautiful. 2000, Children's LB $34.00 (0-516-21090-4). Delaware's geography and history are explored in this attractive volume, which also discusses its culture, people, and lifestyle. (Rev: BL 11/15/00) [975.1]

9467 Burchard, Sue. *The Statue of Liberty: Birth to Rebirth* (7–9). Illus. 1985, Harcourt $13.95 (0-15-279969-9). After a tour of present-day Liberty Island the author describes the history behind the statue. (Rev: BL 12/1/85; SLJ 12/85) [941.7]

9468 Burgan, Michael. *Connecticut* (4–7). Series: It's My State! 2003, Marshall Cavendish LB $18.95 (0-7614-1523-8). This New England state is introduced with material on its people, geography, history, cities, products, and resources. (Rev: BL 9/15/03) [974.6]

9469 Cowan, Mary Morton. *Timberrr: A History of Logging in New England* (5–8). Illus. 2003, Millbrook LB $25.90 (0-7613-1866-6). Cowan highlights timber's historical importance in many walks of life — trade, politics, and construction, for example — and looks at changes brought by new technologies and the impact on ecology and the environment. (Rev: BL 11/15/03) [634.9]

9470 Cytron, Barry. *Fire! The Library Is Burning* (4–7). Illus. 1988, Lerner LB $15.93 (0-8225-0525-8). How workers and volunteers helped to restore the Jewish Theological Seminary in New York City when it was nearly destroyed by fire. (Rev: BL 7/88; SLJ 9/88) [027.63089924097471]

9471 Dornfeld, Margaret. *Maine* (4–8). Series: Celebrate the States. 2001, Benchmark LB $35.64 (0-7614-1071-6). An attractive, fact-filled introduction to the state of Maine with material on history, famous places and people, and current concerns. (Rev: BL 9/15/01; HBG 10/01) [974.1]

9472 Elish, Dan. *New York* (4–7). Illus. Series: My State. 2003, Marshall Cavendish $18.95 (0-7614-1419-3). Color photographs accompany information on the state's topography, wildlife, climate, population, government, industries, and resources. (Rev: BL 3/1/03; HBG 10/03) [974.7]

9473 Elish, Dan. *Vermont* (4–8). Illus. Series: Celebrate the States. 1997, Marshall Cavendish LB $35.64 (0-7614-0146-6). An introduction to this New England state, including famous sights, history, and how the people live. (Rev: BL 7/97; SLJ 8/97) [974.3]

9474 Elish, Dan. *Washington, D.C.* (5–8). Series: Celebrate the States. 1998, Benchmark LB $35.64 (0-7614-0423-6). An attractive introduction to the people and government of the U.S. capital with material on parks, landmarks, history, economics,

and racial problems. (Rev: HBG 10/98; SLJ 1/99) [975.3]

9475 Fisher, Leonard E. *Niagara Falls: Nature's Wonder* (7–9). Illus. 1996, Holiday $16.95 (0-8234-1240-7). Beginning with the European discovery of the Falls in 1678, the author focuses on this natural wonder as a cultural and historical institution. (Rev: BL 9/1/96; SLJ 10/96) [971.3]

9476 Fradin, Dennis B. *The Connecticut Colony* (5–8). Illus. Series: The Thirteen Colonies. 1990, Children's LB $33.50 (0-516-00393-3). A history of Connecticut from the first settlements to statehood. (Rev: BL 8/90) [974.6]

9477 Goldstein, Ernest. *The Statue Abraham Lincoln: A Masterpiece by Daniel Chester French* (5–8). Series: Art Beyond Borders. 1998, Lerner LB $28.80 (0-8225-2067-2). This book provides a detailed description of the Lincoln Memorial and an introduction to the life and accomplishments of its sculptor, Daniel Chester French. (Rev: SLJ 5/98) [975.3]

9478 Grace, Catherine O'Neill. *The White House: An Illustrated History* (4–8). Illus. 2003, Scholastic $19.95 (0-439-42971-4). Plenty of photographs are featured in this attractive and detailed volume devoted to the building's history and its residents over the years, with profiles of the people who work there. (Rev: BL 12/1/03; SLJ 12/03) [975.3]

9479 Graham, Amy. *Maine* (4–7). Illus. Series: States. 2002, Enslow/MyReportLinks.com LB $19.95 (0-7660-5017-3). This well-illustrated volume offers report writers basic information on the state's land, climate, economy, government, and history, plus recommendations of Web sites that will extend their knowledge. Also use *New York* (2002). (Rev: SLJ 9/02) [974.1]

9480 Heinrichs, Ann. *Pennsylvania* (5–8). Series: America the Beautiful. 2000, Children's LB $34.00 (0-516-20692-3). A basic introduction to Pennsylvania that also covers such topics as state symbols, sports teams, and regional food. (Rev: BL 5/15/00) [975]

9481 Herda, D. J. *Environmental America: The Northeastern States* (4–7). Illus. Series: American Scene. 1991, Millbrook LB $22.40 (1-878841-06-8). This volume discusses the condition of the environment and presents information on such topics as water and land pollution in the northeastern states. (Rev: BL 8/91; SLJ 7/91) [639.9]

9482 Herda, D. J. *Ethnic America: The Northeastern States* (5–7). Illus. Series: American Scene. 1991, Millbrook LB $22.40 (1-56294-014-7). In this heavily illustrated account, the ethnic groups of the area, including Native Americans, are described and their accomplishments detailed. (Rev: BL 2/1/92; SLJ 2/92) [572.973]

9483 Ingram, Scott. *Pennsylvania: The Keystone State* (4–7). Series: World Almanac Library of the States. 2002, World Almanac LB $29.26 (0-8368-5120-X). Facts, statistics, a pleasing layout, and color photographs make this a useful choice for report writers. (Rev: SLJ 9/02) [974.8]

9484 Jameson, W. C. *Buried Treasures of New England: Legends of Hidden Riches, Forgotten War Loots, and Lost Ship Treasures* (4–8). Series: Buried Treasure. 1997, August House $11.95 (0-87483-485-6). This account describes how these treasures were amassed and lost, and furnishes maps to indicate their general location. (Rev: BR 5–6/99; SLJ 10/97) [910.4]

9485 Katz, William L. *Black Legacy: A History of New York's African Americans* (6–10). Illus. 1997, Simon & Schuster $19.00 (0-689-31913-4). A history of New York City's African American community is chronicled, beginning with New Amsterdam and continuing through the Revolution and Civil War to the Harlem Renaissance, and ending with the mayoralty of David Dinkins in the early 1990s. (Rev: BL 2/15/97; BR 1–2/98; SLJ 10/97*; VOYA 6/97) [974.7]

9486 Kent, Deborah. *Maine* (5–8). Series: America the Beautiful. 1999, Children's LB $34.00 (0-516-20994-9). A standard account of the history, geography, and people of Maine, with additional information on state symbols, famous personalities, annual events, and weather. (Rev: BL 11/15/99) [974.1]

9487 LeVert, Suzanne. *Massachusetts* (4–8). Series: Celebrate the States. 2000, Benchmark LB $35.64 (0-7614-0666-2). A fine introduction to the people and places of the Bay State that also includes recipes, folktales, and songs. (Rev: BL 1/1–15/00; HBG 10/00; SLJ 5/00) [974.4]

9488 Levy, Janey. *The Erie Canal: A Primary Source History of the Canal That Changed America* (5–8). 2003, Rosen LB $29.25 (0-8239-3680-5). The story of the construction of the Erie Canal and its impact on commerce is revealed through primary documents and many period illustrations. (Rev: SLJ 5/03) [974.7]

9489 Locker, Thomas. *In Blue Mountains: An Artist's Return to America's First Wilderness* (6–12). Illus. 2000, Bell Pond $18.00 (0-88010-471-6). This picture book is a tribute to nature chronicling the author-artist's return to Kaaterskill Cove in New York State to find inspiration. (Rev: BL 7/00; SLJ 11/00) [974.7]

9490 Louis, Nancy. *Ground Zero* (4–7). Series: War on Terrorism. 2002, ABDO LB $16.95 (1-57765-675-1). This heavily illustrated, factually accurate account describes the search, recovery, and cleanup that took place after September 11, 2001, in New York City. (Rev: BL 5/15/02) [974.7]

9491 Lourie, Peter. *Erie Canal: Canoeing America's Great Waterway* (5–8). Illus. 1997, Boyds Mills $17.95 (1-56397-669-2). This colorful book about a journey along the Erie Canal also supplies historical facts about its construction and uses. (Rev: BL 7/97; HBG 3/98; SLJ 9/97) [974.7]

9492 McNair, Sylvia. *Connecticut* (5–8). Series: America the Beautiful. 1999, Children's LB $34.00 (0-516-20832-2). Color photographs and about a dozen maps are included in this survey of Connecticut that covers history, geography, economy, famous sights, recreation, and state symbols. (Rev: BL 11/15/99) [974.6]

9493 McNair, Sylvia. *Massachusetts* (5–8). Series: America the Beautiful. 1998, Children's Pr. LB $34.00 (0-516-20635-4). With a special reference section and a fine use of graphics, this book introduces the Bay State's history, geography, and important people. (Rev: BL 1/1–15/99; HBG 3/99) [974.4]

9494 McNair, Sylvia. *Rhode Island* (5–8). Series: America the Beautiful. 2000, Children's LB $34.00 (0-516-21043-2). An accessible fund of knowledge is contained in this book on Rhode Island that gives well-organized, basic information on this tiny state, its past, its present, and its people. (Rev: BL 5/15/00) [974.5]

9495 McNeese, Tim. *The New York Subway System* (6–10). Illus. Series: Building History. 1997, Lucent LB $27.45 (1-56006-427-7). The story of the building of the 722 miles of tunnels that compose the subway system of New York City, the longest underground system in the world. (Rev: BL 12/1/97; BR 1–2/98; HBG 3/98; SLJ 11/97) [388.4]

9496 Marcovitz, Hal. *The Liberty Bell* (4–8). Illus. Series: American Symbols and Their Meanings. 2002, Mason Crest LB $18.95 (1-59084-025-9). The history and condition of the bell are presented through text, illustrations, and a useful timeline. Also use *The White House* (2002). (Rev: SLJ 9/02) [974.8]

9497 Marcus, Leonard S. *Storied City: A Children's Book Walking-Tour Guide to New York City* (4–9). 2003, Dutton paper $12.99 (0-525-46924-9). This historical and geographic guide to tours of New York City that are based on children's literature features an eclectic mix of fiction, nonfiction, maps, illustrations, and trivia that will enhance the enjoyment of any visit. (Rev: BCCB 6/03; LMC 11–12/03; SLJ 7/03) [016.9747]

9498 Morgane, Wendy. *New Jersey* (4–8). Series: Celebrate the States. 2000, Benchmark LB $35.64 (0-7614-0673-5). This excellent introduction to New Jersey covers its history, land, government, economy, unique characteristics, and famous residents. (Rev: BL 1/1–15/00; HBG 10/00) [974.9]

9499 Myers, Walter Dean. *Harlem* (6–12). Illus. 1997, Scholastic paper $16.95 (0-590-54340-7). This book is an impressionistic appreciation of Harlem and its culture as seen through the eyes of author Walter Dean Myers and his artist son, Christopher. (Rev: BL 2/15/97; SLJ 2/97; VOYA 10/97) [811]

9500 Peters, Stephen. *Pennsylvania* (4–7). Series: Celebrate the States. 2000, Marshall Cavendish LB $35.64 (0-7614-0644-1). An overview of the history, geography, and culture of Pennsylvania with additional material on state symbols, industry, the people, and the economy. (Rev: BL 6/1–15/00; SLJ 9/00) [974.8]

9501 Quiri, Patricia R. *The White House* (4–8). Series: First Books. 1996, Watts LB $22.00 (0-531-20221-6). A well-illustrated history of the White House, with a description of the exterior design and the rooms inside, interesting items such as the introduction of running water, and information about the families that have lived there. (Rev: BL 6/1–15/96; SLJ 8/96) [975.3]

9502 Rebman, Renee C. *Life on Ellis Island* (5–8). Series: The Way People Live. 1999, Lucent LB $27.45 (1-56006-533-8). With extensive use of first-hand accounts, this book relates the purpose of Ellis Island, the processing of immigrants, and the joys and hardships involved. (Rev: BL 10/15/99; HBG 10/00; SLJ 1/00) [325.1]

9503 St. Antoine, Sara, ed. *The North Atlantic Coast* (5–8). Illus. Series: Stories from Where We Live. 2000, Milkweed $19.95 (1-57131-627-2). This anthology presents stories, essays, folktales, journal entries, songs, and poems related to the north coast of the Atlantic Ocean from Newfoundland to Delaware. (Rev: BL 1/1–15/01; VOYA 4/01) [974]

9504 Schnurnberger, Lynn. *Kids Love New York! The A-to-Z Resource Book* (4–8). Illus. 1990, Congdon & Weed paper $133.65 (0-312-92415-1). A group of suggestions for various activities in New York City.

9505 Schomp, Virginia. *New York* (4–8). Illus. Series: Celebrate the States. 1996, Marshall Cavendish LB $37.07 (0-7614-0108-3). The Empire State is introduced, with information on history, geography, people, landmarks, and distinguished New Yorkers. (Rev: BL 2/15/97; SLJ 2/97) [917.47]

9506 Schuman, Michael. *Delaware* (4–8). Series: Celebrate the States. 2000, Marshall Cavendish LB $35.64 (0-7614-0645-X). Beginning with quotations about Delaware and its people, this account covers the basic topics plus information on folklore, food, and festivals. (Rev: BL 6/1–15/00; HBG 10/00) [975.1]

9507 Stein, R. Conrad. *New Hampshire* (5–8). Series: America the Beautiful. 2000, Children's LB $34.00 (0-516-21071-8). A basic introduction to New Hampshire, including its people, history, geography, economy, government, and state symbols. (Rev: BL 11/15/00) [974.2]

9508 Stein, R. Conrad. *New Jersey* (5–8). Series: America the Beautiful. 1998, Children's LB $34.00 (0-516-20637-0). Full-color graphics and a clear text highlight this introduction to New Jersey's history, geography, economy, people, and culture. (Rev: BL 1/1–15/99) [974.9]

9509 Stein, R. Conrad. *Washington, D.C.* (5–8). Series: America the Beautiful. 1999, Children's LB $34.00 (0-516-21046-7). The District of Columbia is covered in text, color photographs, sidebars, maps, and a timeline, with material on its history, government, people, economy, sights, and related subjects. (Rev: BL 12/15/99) [975.3]

9510 Sullivan, George. *How the White House Really Works* (5–8). Illus. 1990, Scholastic paper $3.95 (0-590-43403-9). Home, office, museum, and tourist attraction — how the White House operates. (Rev: BCCB 5/89; BL 5/15/89; HB 7–8/89) [975.3]

9511 Tagliaferro, Linda. *Destination New York* (4–8). Series: Port Cities of North America. 1998, Lerner LB $23.93 (0-8225-2793-6). Written with a focus on New York's economic life and its handling of goods moving in and out of the port, this book also gives information on the city's history, geography, and daily life. (Rev: HBG 3/99; SLJ 1/99) [974.7]

9512 Whitcraft, Melissa. *The Hudson River* (4–7). Illus. Series: World of Water. 1999, Watts LB $24.00 (0-531-11739-1). A handsome volume that traces the history of New York State's most important river and how it currently affects people's lives. (Rev: BL 1/1–15/00) [974.7]

9513 Wills, Charles A. *A Historical Album of Pennsylvania* (4–8). Series: Historical Albums. 1996, Millbrook LB $24.40 (1-56294-595-5). Beginning with its Native American origins and settlement by Europeans and the Quakers, this book traces the history of Pennsylvania from the First Continental Congress and the ratification of the United States Constitution, through the Battle of Gettysburg and President Lincoln's famous Gettysburg Address, and up to today. (Rev: BL 7/96; SLJ 7/96) [974.8]

PACIFIC STATES

9514 Abbink, Emily. *Missions of the Monterey Bay Area* (4–7). Series: California Missions. 1996, Lerner LB $28.75 (0-8225-1928-3). Covers the history of the missions at San Carlos Borromeo de Carmelo, San Juan Bautista, and Santa Cruz. (Rev: BL 2/15/97) [979.4]

9515 Altman, Linda J. *California* (4–8). Illus. Series: Celebrate the States. 1996, Marshall Cavendish LB $35.64 (0-7614-0111-3). A richly illustrated book that contains material on California's geography, history, economic life, contemporary challenges, society, contributions, and landmarks. (Rev: BL 2/1/97; SLJ 2/97) [979.4]

9516 Anderson, Dale. *The California Missions* (5–8). Series: Landmark Events in American History. 2003, World Almanac LB $26.60 (0-8368-5339-3). The story of the California missions, how they were founded, their purposes, and their contributions to opening up this state. (Rev: BL 10/15/03; SLJ 1/03) [979.4]

9517 Ansary, Mir Tamim. *People of California* (4–7). Illus. Series: Heinemann State Studies. 2003, Heinemann LB $27.07 (1-4034-0342-2). Ansary looks at groups of people who have settled in California and offers brief biographies of individuals who have contributed to all fields of endeavor, with many color photographs. (Rev: BL 10/15/03; SLJ 11/03) [305.]

9518 Barter, James. *Alcatraz* (7–10). Series: Building History. 2000, Lucent LB $18.96 (1-56006-596-6). The story of how and why buildings were placed on Alcatraz Island and how it functions today as a popular park. (Rev: BL 1/1–15/00; HBG 9/00) [979.4]

9519 Barter, James. *The Golden Gate Bridge* (7–10). Series: Building History. 2001, Lucent $24.95 (1-56006-856-6). Using many quotations from firsthand sources, this account presents both the human and technological aspects of the construction and use of San Francisco's landmark bridge. (Rev: BL 8/1/01) [979.4]

9520 Behler, Deborah A. *The Rain Forests of the Pacific Northwest* (7–12). Illus. Series: Ecosystems of North America. 2000, Benchmark LB $18.95 (0-7614-0926-2). A detailed look at the flora and fauna of this ecosystem that covers each layer of the forest from top to bottom as well as the impact of human activities. (Rev: HBG 3/01; SLJ 4/01) [577.34]

9521 Behrens, June. *Missions of the Central Coast* (4–7). Series: California Missions. 1996, Lerner LB $28.75 (0-8225-1930-5). The missions at Santa Barbara, Santa Ines, and La Purisima Concepción are discussed, with material on their history and importance. (Rev: BL 2/15/97) [979.4]

9522 Boekhoff, P. M., and Stuart A. Kallen. *California* (4–7). Illus. Series: Seeds of a Nation. 2002, Gale LB $30.35 (0-7377-0946-4). The history of California before statehood is presented with material on Native Americans, missionaries, settlers, and prospectors. (Rev: BL 4/1/02) [979.4]

9523 Bredeson, Carmen. *Fire in Oakland, California: Billion-Dollar Blaze* (4–8). Series: American Disasters. 1999, Enslow LB $18.95 (0-7660-1220-4). A high-interest book that tells of the terrible fire in Oakland and the massive destruction it caused. (Rev: BL 10/15/99; HBG 3/00) [976.8]

9524 Brower, Pauline. *Missions of the Inland Valleys* (4–7). Series: California Missions. 1996, Lerner LB $28.75 (0-8225-1929-1). Examines four missions, including San Luis Obispo and San Miguel Arcangel, with material on their early history and their impact on the existing cultures. (Rev: BL 2/15/97) [979.4]

9525 Brown, Tricia. *Children of the Midnight Sun: Young Native Voices of Alaska* (4–7). Illus. 1998, Graphic Arts Center $16.95 (0-88240-500-4). This illustrated book gives a fine introduction to various aspects of the Alaskan environment, describing the lives of eight preteens from different regions and ethnic backgrounds. (Rev: BL 7/98; HBG 10/98; SLJ 9/98) [979.8]

9526 Chippendale, Lisa A. *The San Francisco Earthquake of 1906* (7–12). Series: Great Disasters: Reforms and Ramifications. 2001, Chelsea $21.95 (0-7910-5270-2). An interesting account full of photographs, eyewitness accounts, and good background information on earthquakes and California history that focuses on the appropriateness of the responses to the disaster by the various authorities and the lessons learned. (Rev: BL 4/15/01; HBG 10/01; SLJ 6/01) [979.4]

9527 Corral, Kimberly. *A Child's Glacier Bay* (4–8). Illus. 1998, Graphic Arts Center $15.95 (0-88240-503-9). A photoessay chronicling a three-week kayak trip in Alaska's Glacier Bay, told from the perspective of a 13-year-old girl. (Rev: BL 7/98; HBG 10/98; SLJ 8/98) [978.652]

9528 Ferrell, Nancy W. *Destination Valdez* (6–9). Illus. Series: Port Cities of North America. 1997, Lerner LB $23.93 (0-8225-2790-1). A fact-filled book that describes the history, economy, and people of the port city of Valdez in Alaska, including an examination of the effect of the billion-dollar oil shipping industry on a tiny, remote town in Alaska. (Rev: HBG 9/98; SLJ 8/98) [979]

9529 Fraser, Mary Ann. *A Mission for the People: The Story of La Purisima* (4–8). Illus. 1998, Holt $15.95 (0-8050-5050-7). Using the mission of La Purisima as an example of early California history, this account describes life among the natives before and after the arrival of Spanish missionaries. (Rev: BL 5/1/98; HBG 10/98; SLJ 4/98) [979.4]

9530 Goldberg, Jake. *Hawaii* (5–8). Series: Celebrate the States. 1998, Benchmark LB $35.64 (0-7614-0203-9). Using fine illustrations, fact boxes, graphs, and maps, this attractive book gives an excellent introduction to Hawaii, with the added bonus of a recipe and two songs. (Rev: HBG 10/98; SLJ 1/99) [996.9]

9531 Green, Carl R. *The Mission Trails* (6–10). Series: In American History. 2001, Enslow LB $20.95 (0-7660-1349-9). A well-researched and documented history of the southwestern Spanish missions and the trails that were built to connect them. (Rev: BL 12/15/01; HBG 3/02; SLJ 3/02) [979.4]

9532 Heinrichs, Ann. *California* (5–8). Series: America the Beautiful. 1998, Children's LB $34.00 (0-516-20631-1). A fine introduction to California's history, geography, economy, arts, and recreation. (Rev: BL 1/1–15/99; HBG 3/99; SLJ 2/99) [979.4]

9533 Heinrichs, Ann. *The California Missions* (5–8). Series: We the People. 2002, Compass Point LB $27.15 (0-7565-0208-X). An accessible, well-illustrated account of the creation of Spanish missions in California and the impact on the native peoples of the region. (Rev: SLJ 7/02) [979.402]

9534 Herda, D. J. *Environmental America: The Northwestern States* (4–7). Illus. Series: American Scene. 1991, Millbrook LB $22.40 (1-878841-10-6). This account presents information on such topics as pollution, waste, logging, and the general condition of the environment in Idaho, Montana, Oregon, Washington, and Wyoming. (Rev: BL 8/91; SLJ 7/91) [639.9]

9535 Hintz, Martin. *Hawaii* (5–8). Series: America the Beautiful. 1999, Children's LB $34.00 (0-516-20686-9). An introduction to Hawaii — its land and people, its government and economy, its state symbols and famous sights. (Rev: BL 11/15/99; HBG 10/99) [996.9]

9536 Ingram, W. Scott. *Oregon* (5–8). Series: America the Beautiful. 2000, Children's LB $34.00 (0-516-20996-5). An attractive guide to Oregon that is packed with facts about its history, geography, population, economy, culture, cities, and recreation. (Rev: BL 5/15/00) [979.5]

9537 Knapp, Ron. *Oregon* (4–7). Illus. Series: MyReportLinks.com. 2002, Enslow LB $19.95 (0-7660-5021-1). An introduction to the government, geography, and history of the state, with helpful Web sites. (Rev: BL 2/1/03; HBG 3/03; VOYA 4/03) [979.5]

9538 Lemke, Nancy. *Missions of the Southern Coast* (4–7). Illus. Series: California Missions. 1996, Lerner LB $28.75 (0-8225-1925-9). The three missions described here are San Diego de Alcala, San Luis Rey de Francia, and San Juan Capistrano. (Rev: BL 9/15/96; SLJ 8/96) [979.4]

9539 Levi, Steven C. *Cowboys of the Sky: The Story of Alaska's Bush Pilots* (5–9). Illus. 1996, Walker LB $18.85 (0-8027-8332-5). The exciting life of the people who deliver medical supplies, mail, and passengers to remote areas in Alaska is vividly re-created. (Rev: BL 6/1–15/96; BR 9–10/96; SLJ 7/96; VOYA 8/96) [629.13]

9540 MacMillan, Dianne. *Missions of the Los Angeles Area* (4–7). Illus. Series: California Missions. 1996, Lerner LB $28.75 (0-8225-1927-5). This volume gives a description and history of three mis-

sions: San Gabriel Arcangel, San Fernando Rey de España, and San Buenaventura. (Rev: BL 9/15/96; SLJ 8/96) [979.4]

9541 Meyer, Carolyn. *In a Different Light: Growing Up in a Yup'ik Eskimo Village in Alaska* (6–9). Illus. 1996, Simon & Schuster $17.00 (0-689-80146-7). The author revisits a Yupik Eskimo village in Alaska after an 18-year absence and details how life has changed as the residents adopt modern ways of life and gradually forget their traditional arts and customs. (Rev: BL 5/1/96; BR 1–2/97; SLJ 6/96; VOYA 8/96) [979.8]

9542 Oliver, Marilyn Tower. *Alcatraz Prison* (4–8). Series: In American History. 1998, Enslow LB $20.95 (0-89490-990-8). After years as first a settlement and then a fort and a lighthouse, the "Rock" became a military and federal prison. This is its history, including famous prisoners, escape attempts, and its evolution into a top tourist attraction. (Rev: HBG 3/99; SLJ 1/99) [979.4]

9543 Otfinoski, Steve. *Washington* (4–7). Series: It's My State! 2003, Marshall Cavendish LB $18.95 (0-7614-1522-X). The state of Washington, its geography, history, people, and economic development are some of the topics covered in this introduction to this Pacific state. (Rev: BL 9/15/03) [979.9]

9544 Pratt, Helen Jay. *The Hawaiians: An Island People* (6–8). Illus. 1991, Tuttle paper $9.95 (0-8048-1709-X). An account of early Hawaii and its inhabitants, with emphasis on folk customs.

9545 Rice, Oliver D. *Lone Woman of Ghalas-Hat* (5–7). 1993, California Weekly LB $13.00 (0-936778-52-0); paper $6.00 (0-936778-51-2). The true story of the Indian woman who lived alone on a California island for 18 years. This was the basis of *Island of the Blue Dolphins*. A reissue. [979.7]

9546 Ruth, Maria Mudd. *The Pacific Coast* (7–12). Illus. Series: Ecosystems of North America. 2000, Benchmark LB $18.95 (0-7614-0935-1). A detailed look at the tides, plants, animals, and ecosystems found along the Pacific Coast from Alaska south to Mexico. (Rev: HBG 3/01; SLJ 4/01) [577.5]

9547 St. Antoine, Sara, ed. *Stories from Where We Live: The California Coast* (4–7). 2001, Milkweed $19.95 (1-57131-631-0). A compilation of poetry and prose focusing on the California coastal region and its plant and animal life. (Rev: BL 1/1–15/02; HBG 10/02) [979.4]

9548 Seibold, J. Otto, and Vivian Walsh. *Going to the Getty: A Book About the Getty Center in Los Angeles* (4–7). Illus. 1997, Getty Museum $16.95 (0-89236-493-9). This introduction to the Getty Museum in Los Angeles is a patchwork of impressions, photographs, drawings, and reproductions of artworks. (Rev: BL 2/15/98; HBG 10/98) [708]

9549 Senungetuk, Vivian. *Wise Words of Paul Tiulana: An Inupiat Alaskan's Life* (5–8). 1998, Watts LB $23.50 (0-531-11448-1). The story of Paul Tiulana's life and the culture of the natives who have lived for centuries on a tiny island in the Bering Sea between Siberia and Alaska. (Rev: BL 1/1–15/99; HBG 10/99; SLJ 2/99) [979.8]

9550 Sherrow, Victoria. *The Exxon Valdez: Tragic Oil Spill* (4–8). Series: American Disasters. 1998, Enslow LB $18.95 (0-7660-1058-9). The dramatic story of the *Exxon Valdez* oil spill and the damage it caused to the Alaskan coast and its wildlife. (Rev: BL 1/1–15/99; BR 5–6/99; HBG 3/99; SLJ 3/99; VOYA 4/99) [979.8]

9551 Sherrow, Victoria. *San Francisco Earthquake, 1989: Death and Destruction* (4–8). Illus. Series: American Disasters. 1998, Enslow LB $18.95 (0-7660-1060-0). This account of the San Francisco earthquake incorporates many eyewitness reports. (Rev: BL 1/1–15/99; HBG 3/99; SLJ 6/99) [363.34]

9552 Stefoff, Rebecca. *Oregon* (4–8). Illus. Series: Celebrate the States. 1997, Marshall Cavendish LB $35.64 (0-7614-0145-8). A look at life in this Pacific state, along with its history, famous sights, cities, and industries. (Rev: BL 7/97; SLJ 7/97) [917.95]

9553 Stepanchuk, Carol. *Exploring Chinatown* (4–8). 2002, Pacific View LB $22.95 (1-881896-25-0). This "walk" through San Francisco's Chinatown explores the Chinese culture and customs, and offers historical facts as well as a few hands-on projects. (Rev: BL 8/02; SLJ 9/02) [305.8951073]

9554 Takaki, Ronald. *Raising Cane: The World of Plantation Hawaii* (6–10). Adapted by Rebecca Stefoff. Illus. Series: Asian American Experience. 1994, Chelsea LB $19.95 (0-7910-2178-5). A fascinating look at the part that Asian immigrants played in the development of the economy of Hawaii. (Rev: BL 6/1–15/94; SLJ 7/94) [996.9]

9555 Turnbull, Andy, and Debora Pearson. *By Truck to the North: My Arctic Adventure* (4–8). 1998, Annick LB $24.95 (1-55037-551-2); paper $14.95 (1-55037-550-4). An exciting account of an overland trip by truck from Vancouver, British Columbia, to the Arctic villages of Inuvik and Tuktoyaktuk. (Rev: BL 1/1–15/99; SLJ 1/99) [979.8]

9556 Uschan, Michael V. *The California Gold Rush* (5–8). Series: Landmark Events in American History. 2003, World Almanac LB $26.60 (0-8368-5374-1). An attractive account of the California gold rush, famous people involved, and its consequences. (Rev: BL 10/15/03) [979.4]

9557 White, Tekla N. *Missions of the San Francisco Bay Area* (4–7). Illus. Series: California Missions. 1996, Lerner LB $28.75 (0-8225-1926-7). The history of five Spanish missions in the San Francisco Bay Area, including Santa Clara de Asis and San Rafael Arcangel. (Rev: BL 9/15/96; SLJ 8/96) [979.4]

9558 Wills, Charles A. *A Historical Album of California* (4–8). Illus. Series: Historical Albums. 1994, Millbrook LB $24.40 (1-56294-479-7). A slim volume that covers the basic history of California, with material on major events and important personalities. (Rev: SLJ 3/95) [979.4]

9559 Wills, Charles A. *A Historical Album of Oregon* (4–8). Series: Historical Albums. 1995, Millbrook $24.40 (1-56294-594-7). A good, broad overview of Oregon's history and current political and economic situation, places to see, and other information, with many illustrations. (Rev: BL 12/15/95; SLJ 1/96) [979.5]

9560 Young, Robert. *A Personal Tour of La Purisima* (4–7). Series: How It Was. 1999, Lerner LB $30.35 (0-8225-3576-9). A you-are-there visit to La Purisima — one of the 21 missions built by the Spanish in California — in which the reader experiences life in the mission as it was in 1820. (Rev: BL 6/1–15/99; HBG 10/99) [979.4]

SOUTH

9561 Altman, Linda Jacobs. *Arkansas* (4–8). Series: Celebrate the States. 2000, Benchmark LB $35.64 (0-7614-0672-7). An broad introduction to the culture, land, government, history, and unique characteristics of Arkansas, with emphasis on its inhabitants. (Rev: BL 1/1–15/00; HBG 10/00) [976.7]

9562 Barrett, Tracy. *Kentucky* (4–7). Series: Celebrate the States. 1999, Benchmark LB $35.64 (0-7614-0657-3). An attractive, concise introduction to Kentucky that covers geography, history, government and economy, people, achievements, and landmarks. (Rev: HBG 10/99; SLJ 10/99) [976.9]

9563 Barrett, Tracy. *Virginia* (4–8). Illus. Series: Celebrate the States. 1996, Marshall Cavendish LB $35.64 (0-7614-0110-5). An introduction to Virginia, including its history, culture, famous sites, and important Virginians. (Rev: BL 2/15/97; SLJ 6/97) [975.5]

9564 Bial, Raymond. *Cajun Home* (4–7). Illus. 1998, Houghton $16.00 (0-395-86095-4). This is the story of the people who left France to find freedom in Canada, only to be transported to Louisiana where they settled in the backwood swamp areas. (Rev: BL 3/15/98; HB 5–6/98; HBG 10/98; SLJ 5/98) [976.3]

9565 Bial, Raymond. *Mist Over the Mountains: Appalachia and Its People* (4–8). 1997, Houghton $14.95 (0-395-73569-6). The people and culture of Appalachia are introduced, with material on history, agriculture, and folk arts. (Rev: BCCB 6/97; BL 3/1/97; SLJ 5/97) [976.1]

599

9566 Blashfield, Jean F. *Virginia* (5–8). Series: America the Beautiful. 1999, Children's LB $34.00 (0-516-20831-4). A solid account of the land and people of Virginia, with full-color maps, sidebars, a timeline, and a discussion of its state symbols. (Rev: BL 11/15/99) [975.5]

9567 Branch, Muriel M. *The Water Brought Us: The Story of the Gullah-Speaking People* (5–9). 1995, Dutton $16.99 (0-525-65185-3). About the Gullah people who live on the sea islands off the coast of South Carolina and Georgia and who are descendants of slaves. (Rev: BL 9/15/95; SLJ 10/95) [975.8]

9568 Burgan, Michael. *Maryland* (5–8). Series: America the Beautiful. 1999, Children's LB $34.00 (0-516-21039-4). History and government, economy and population, famous sights, and annual events are only a few of the topics covered in this fine introduction to Maryland. (Rev: BL 11/15/99) [975]

9569 Chang, Perry. *Florida* (5–8). Series: Celebrate the States. 1998, Benchmark LB $35.64 (0-7614-0420-1). A fine introduction to the history, geography, people, landmarks, and government of Florida, with material on the cultural diversity of its people. (Rev: HBG 9/98; SLJ 1/99) [975.9]

9570 Cocke, William. *A Historical Album of Virginia* (4–8). Series: Historical Albums. 1995, Millbrook paper $6.95 (1-56294-856-3). A broad overview of Virginia's history, using many period prints and paintings, with equal space given to past and current events, and including general information on the state. (Rev: SLJ 1/96) [975.5]

9571 Fazio, Wende. *West Virginia* (5–8). Series: America the Beautiful. 2000, Children's LB $34.00 (0-516-21074-2). As well as the standard information on history, geography, and the people, this colorful introduction covers topics such as state symbols and famous West Virginians. (Rev: BL 5/15/00) [975.5]

9572 Fisher, Leonard Everett. *Monticello* (4–7). 1988, Holiday $18.95 (0-8234-0688-1). Touring the famous home of the third president. (Rev: BCCB 6/88; BL 6/1/88; SLJ 6–7/88) [973.460924]

9573 Gaines, Ann Graham. *Kentucky* (4–7). Series: It's My State! 2003, Marshall Cavendish LB $18.95 (0-7614-1525-4). Full-color photographs, trivia, and recipes and crafts are included along with the standard information required for reports. (Rev: BL 9/15/03; SLJ 9/03) [976.9]

9574 Heinrichs, Ann. *Florida* (4–8). Series: America the Beautiful. 1998, Children's Pr. LB $34.00 (0-516-20632-X). This book provides background on the history, geography, and economy of Florida and describes the recent influx of people there, its major cities, and endangered wildlife. (Rev: BL 10/15/98; SLJ 1/99) [975.9]

9575 Herda, D. J. *Environmental America: The South Central States* (4–7). Illus. Series: American Scene. 1991, Millbrook LB $22.40 (1-878841-09-2). This account discusses the general state of the environment and presents information on animal species, pollution, waste, and urban sprawl for 10 states, including Georgia, Kansas, Missouri, and Texas. (Rev: BL 8/91; SLJ 7/91) [639.9]

9576 Hess, Debra. *Florida* (4–7). Series: It's My State! 2003, Marshall Cavendish LB $18.95 (0-7614-1527-0). Products, resources, plants and animals, and important background material are some of the topics covered in this general introduction to Florida. (Rev: BL 9/15/03; SLJ 9/03) [975.9]

9577 Hintz, Martin. *Louisiana* (5–8). Series: America the Beautiful. 1998, Children's LB $34.00 (0-516-20634-6). With a good use of graphics and clear writing, this book provides a wealth of information about Louisiana, past and present. (Rev: BL 1/1–15/99; SLJ 2/99) [975.6]

9578 Hintz, Martin, and Stephen Hintz. *North Carolina* (5–8). Illus. Series: America the Beautiful. 1998, Children's LB $34.00 (0-516-20638-9). A revised edition of a comprehensive introduction to North Carolina's history and geography, natural resources and industry, people and landmarks. (Rev: BL 1/1–15/99; SLJ 4/99) [975.6]

9579 Hoffman, Nancy. *South Carolina* (4–8). Series: Celebrate the States. 2000, Marshall Cavendish LB $35.64 (0-7614-1065-1). An interesting introduction to South Carolina, with material on its land and waterways, history, government, economy, landmarks, and success stories. (Rev: BL 12/15/00; HBG 3/01) [975.7]

9580 LeVert, Suzanne. *Louisiana* (4–8). Illus. Series: Celebrate the States. 1997, Marshall Cavendish LB $35.64 (0-7614-0112-1). An interesting introduction that covers the standard material needed for reports. (Rev: BL 7/97; SLJ 7/97) [976.3]

9581 Martin, Michael A. *Alabama: The Heart of Dixie* (4–7). Series: World Almanac Library of the States. 2002, World Almanac LB $29.26 (0-8368-5127-7). Full-color photographs and graphic elements this informative introduction to the state. Also use *Virginia* (2002). (Rev: SLJ 2/03) [976.1]

9582 Odinoski, Steve. *Georgia* (4–8). Series: Celebrate the States. 2000, Marshall Cavendish LB $35.64 (0-7614-1062-7). An informative, attractive introduction to Georgia with material on its land, history, people, social issues, and hidden treasures. (Rev: BL 12/15/00; HBG 3/01; SLJ 2/01) [975.8]

9583 Rauth, Leslie. *Maryland* (5–9). Series: Celebrate the States. 1999, Benchmark LB $35.64 (0-7614-0671-9). This book explores Maryland with material on topics including land and waterways, government, economy, festivals, and people. (Rev: BL 1/1–15/00; HBG 10/00; SLJ 5/00) [975.2]

9584 St. Antoine, Sara, ed. *Stories from Where We Live: The Gulf Coast* (7–12). Illus. 2002, Milkweed $19.95 (1-57131-636-1). A variety of literary forms including poetry, essays, and stories describe experiences in the Gulf Coast. (Rev: BL 1/1–15/03; HBG 10/03) [976]

9585 Shirley, David. *Alabama* (4–8). Series: Celebrate the States. 2000, Marshall Cavendish LB $35.64 (0-7614-0648-4). An introduction to Alabama that covers its land and waterways; its history, government, and economy; and its culture and success stories. (Rev: BL 6/1–15/00; HBG 10/00) [976.1]

9586 Shirley, David. *North Carolina* (4–8). Series: Celebrate the States. 2001, Benchmark LB $35.64 (0-7614-1072-4). A fine introduction to the land, history, economy, and people of North Carolina. (Rev: BL 9/15/01; HBG 10/01) [975.6]

9587 Stein, R. Conrad. *South Carolina* (5–8). Series: America the Beautiful. 1999, Children's LB $34.00 (0-516-20997-3). A comprehensive and well-illustrated introduction to South Carolina — its history and geography, its government and economy, its people and important places. (Rev: BL 11/15/99) [975.2]

9588 Streissguth, Thomas. *Maryland* (5–8). Series: The Thirteen Colonies. 2001, Lucent LB $27.45 (1-56006-871-X). Source notes, annotated bibliographies, and lists of Internet resources complement this history of Maryland from its beginnings to statehood. (Rev: BL 3/15/02) [973.2]

9589 Weatherford, Carole Boston. *Sink or Swim: African-American Lifesavers of the Outer Banks* (4–8). Illus. 1999, Coastal Carolina $15.95 (1-928556-01-9); paper $12.95 (1-928556-03-5). A history of the African Americans who participated in lifesaving efforts on the Outer Banks of North Carolina, known as "the graveyard of the Atlantic." (Rev: BL 12/15/99) [363.28]

9590 Wills, Charles A. *A Historical Album of Alabama* (4–8). Series: Historical Albums. 1995, Millbrook LB $23.40 (1-56294-591-2); paper $6.95 (1-56294-854-7). Using many period prints and engravings, the author traces the history of Alabama from prehistoric days to today, including the impact of the shift away from cotton as a main crop, the civil rights movement, and the importance of football in the state. (Rev: BL 12/15/95; SLJ 1/96) [976.1]

9591 Wills, Charles A. *A Historical Album of Florida* (4–8). Illus. Series: Historical Albums. 1994, Millbrook LB $24.40 (1-56294-480-0). This compressed history of Florida deals with major events from prehistory through the 1990s. (Rev: SLJ 2/95) [975.9]

9592 Wills, Charles A. *A Historical Album of Georgia* (4–7). Illus. Series: Historical Albums. 1996,

Millbrook LB $24.40 (0-7613-0035-X). With many period illustrations, some in color, and a simple text, the history and geography of Georgia are presented. (Rev: BL 12/15/96) [975.8]

9593 Young, Robert. *A Personal Tour of Monticello* (4–7). Illus. Series: How It Was. 1999, Lerner LB $30.35 (0-8225-3575-0). Through the eyes of Jefferson, his daughter, and one of his slaves, the reader is introduced to the home of the third president of the United States. (Rev: BL 6/1–15/99; HBG 10/99; SLJ 7/99) [975.5]

SOUTHWEST

9594 Alter, Judy. *New Mexico* (4–7). Illus. Series: MyReportLinks.com. 2002, Enslow LB $19.95 (0-7660-5098-X). An introduction to the government, geography, and history of the state, with helpful Web sites. (Rev: BL 2/1/03; SLJ 4/03; VOYA 4/03) [978.9]

9595 Bjorklund, Ruth. *New Mexico* (4–7). Series: It's My State! 2003, Marshall Cavendish LB $18.95 (0-7614-1526-2). Actual quotations from both famous and unknown residents of New Mexico are used to introduce this state, its people, history, wildlife, and resources. (Rev: BL 9/15/03) [978.9]

9596 Bredeson, Carmen. *The Spindletop Gusher: The Story of the Texas Oil Boom* (4–7). Illus. Series: Spotlight on American History. 1996, Millbrook LB $24.90 (1-56294-916-0). A discussion of the Texas oil boom, its effects on the state and its economy, and the present status of the oil industry. (Rev: BL 3/15/96) [338.4]

9597 Bredeson, Carmen. *Texas* (4–8). Illus. Series: Celebrate the States. 1996, Marshall Cavendish LB $35.64 (0-7614-0109-1). Basic information about Texas is presented in an attractive format with many color photographs, maps, and diagrams. (Rev: BL 2/15/97; SLJ 6/97) [976.4]

9598 Heinrichs, Ann. *Texas* (5–8). Series: America the Beautiful. 1999, Children's LB $34.00 (0-516-20998-1). Photographs and maps illustrate this account of Texas — its history and geography, economy and government, people and resources. (Rev: BL 11/15/99) [976.4]

9599 Herda, D. J. *Environmental America: The Southwestern States* (4–7). Illus. Series: American Scene. 1991, Millbrook LB $22.40 (1-878841-11-4). This account, which discusses the state of the environment and how it can be changed for the better, covers Arizona, California, Colorado, Nevada, New Mexico, and Utah. (Rev: BL 8/91; SLJ 7/91) [639.9]

9600 Lee, Sally. *San Antonio* (4–7). Illus. Series: Downtown America. 1992, Macmillan LB $13.95 (0-87518-510-X). This introduction to San Antonio covers history, people, festivals, and interesting landmarks such as the Alamo, the river walk, and Spanish missions. (Rev: BL 4/15/92; SLJ 5/92) [976]

9601 Lourie, Peter. *The Lost World of the Anasazi: Exploring the Mysteries of Chaco Canyon* (5–8). Illus. 2003, Boyds Mills $19.95 (1-56397-972-1). With many full-color photographs, the author describes his trip to the ruins of Chaco Canyon and discusses the mysterious disappearance of its Anasazi residents. (Rev: BL 9/1/03) [978.9]

9602 McCarry, Charles. *The Great Southwest* (7–12). Illus. 1980, National Geographic LB $12.95 (0-87044-288-0). In pictures and text, descriptions are given of such states as New Mexico, Colorado, and Arizona. [979.1]

9603 Marcovitz, Hal. *The Alamo* (4–8). Illus. Series: American Symbols and Their Meanings. 2002, Mason Crest LB $18.95 (1-59084-037-2). A basic and readable introduction to the history of the Alamo and its importance to Americans, with illuminating illustrations and inset features. (Rev: SLJ 9/02) [976]

9604 Marrin, Albert. *Empires Lost and Won* (6–10). Illus. 1997, Simon & Schuster $19.00 (0-689-80414-8). Beginning with the destruction of Pueblo Indian cities and ending with the war between the U.S. and Mexico, this book provides a fascinating history of the 300-year struggle for control of the Southwest. (Rev: BL 7/97; BR 9–10/97; SLJ 6/97*; VOYA 6/97) [979]

9605 Tweit, Susan J. *Meet the Wild Southwest: Land of Hoodoos and Gila Monsters* (4–8). Illus. 1996, Alaska Northwest paper $14.95 (0-88240-468-7). An impressive collection of facts and curiosities about the natural history of the Southwest, with many appendixes that supply more-traditional information. (Rev: BL 3/1/96) [508.79]

9606 Wills, Charles A. *A Historical Album of Texas* (4–7). Illus. Series: Historical Albums. 1995, Millbrook LB $24.40 (1-56294-504-1). This account of the history of Texas from earliest times to today is also particularly noteworthy for its many illustrations. (Rev: SLJ 6/95) [976.4]

Philosophy and Religion

Philosophy

9607 Law, Stephen. *Philosophy Rocks!* (7–12). 2002, Hyperion paper $12.99 (0-7868-1699-6). A lighthearted approach is used in tackling eight basic philosophical questions, including "What is real?" and "Does God exist?" (Rev: LMC 2/03; SLJ 10/02; VOYA 12/02)

9608 Weate, Jeremy. *A Young Person's Guide to Philosophy* (6–12). 1998, DK paper $16.99 (0-7894-3074-6). After a discussion of what constitutes philosophy, this well-illustrated volume tells about the life, times, and thoughts of 25 of the world's great thinkers. (Rev: BL 12/15/98; BR 5–6/99; HBG 3/99; SLJ 1/99) [100]

World Religions and Holidays

General and Miscellaneous

9609 Andryszewski, Tricia. *Communities of the Faithful: American Religious Movements Outside the Mainstream* (6–10). 1997, Millbrook LB $24.90 (0-7613-0067-8). Seven religious orders — Old Order Amish, Shakers, Mormons, Catholic Workers, Nation of Islam, Lubavitcher Hasidim, and Quakers — are introduced, with material on their beliefs and contributions to American culture. (Rev: BR 5–6/98; SLJ 2/98) [200]

9610 Asimov, Isaac. *Asimov's Guide to the Bible* (7–12). 1981, Crown $19.99 (0-517-34582-X). This is a book-by-book guide to both the Old and New Testaments. [220.7]

9611 Bahree, Patricia. *Hinduism* (6–9). Illus. 1985, Batsford $19.95 (0-7134-3654-9). The basic beliefs and gods of Hinduism are discussed under 100 subjects arranged alphabetically. (Rev: BL 5/1/85) [294.5]

9612 Balmer, Randall. *Religion in Twentieth-Century America* (6–12). Illus. Series: Religion in American Life. 2001, Oxford LB $22.00 (0-19-511295-4). Balmer looks at the evolution of religious movements across America, including the emergence of the Religious Right and televangelism, and at important events such as the Scopes Trial and the FBI attack on the Branch Davidians. (Rev: BL 8/01; HBG 10/01; SLJ 6/01) [200]

9613 Barnes, Trevor. *The Kingfisher Book of Religions: Festivals, Ceremonies, and Beliefs from Around the World* (4–9). 1999, Kingfisher $22.95 (0-7534-5199-9). Short chapters and many attractive photographs and reproductions are used to introduce an array of religions and their customs with emphasis on Judaism, Christianity, and Islam. (Rev: HBG 10/00; SLJ 1/00) [200]

9614 Batchelor, Mary, ed. *Children's Prayers: From Around the World* (4–7). Illus. 1995, Augsburg $13.99 (0-8066-2830-8). Two hundred prayers for children from many sources worldwide, with some for special holidays and holy days. (Rev: BL 9/1/95) [242]

9615 Bernos de Gasztold, Carmen. *Prayers from the Ark* (4–7). Trans. by Rumer Godden. 1995, Puffin paper $5.99 (0-140-54585-9). A poem written during World War II by a woman who is now a nun. (Rev: BCCB 12/92; BL 9/1/92; HB 11–12/92) [841]

9616 Birdseye, Debbie H., and Tom Birdseye. *What I Believe: Kids Talk About Faith* (4–7). 1996, Holiday $15.95 (0-8234-1268-7). Children from six faiths explain what their religion means to them. (Rev: BL 12/15/96; SLJ 2/97) [200]

9617 Braude, Ann. *Women and American Religion* (8–12). Illus. Series: Religion in America. 2000, Oxford LB $22.00 (0-19-510676-8). Beginning with Native American and Puritan women and continuing to the present, this account traces the many contributions women have made to religion in America. (Rev: BL 3/15/00; HBG 3/01; SLJ 5/00) [200.]

9618 Breuilly, Elizabeth, et al. *Religions of the World: The Illustrated Guide to Origins, Beliefs, Traditions and Festivals* (7–12). Illus. 1997, Facts on File $29.95 (0-8160-3723-X). This well-illustrated work defines religion generally, discusses each of the world's major religions, points out similarities, and links each religion to current events and international politics. (Rev: BL 10/1/97; HBG 3/98; SLJ 2/98) [291]

9619 Brown, Alan, and Andrew Langley. *What I Believe: A Young Person's Guide to the Religions of the World* (4–7). Illus. 1999, Millbrook LB $24.90 (0-7613-1501-2). Young people of eight major faiths explain their religion's principal tenets, rituals, holy days, and celebrations. (Rev: BL 10/1/99; HBG 3/00; SLJ 2/00) [291]

9620 Brunelli, Roberto. *A Family Treasury of Bible Stories: One for Each Week of the Year* (4–8). Illus. 1997, Abrams $24.95 (0-8109-1248-7). A collection of 52 short stories from the Old and New Testaments. (Rev: BL 10/1/97; SLJ 2/98) [220.9]

9621 Carlson, Melody. *Piercing Proverbs: Wise Words for Today's Teens* (7–12). 2002, Multnomah paper $7.99 (1-57673-895-7). The author presents a selection of proverbs and asks readers to consider their relevance to circumstances today. (Rev: BL 7/02) [223]

9622 Chaikin, Miriam. *Angels Sweep the Desert Floor: Bible Legends About Moses in the Wilderness* (4–7). 2002, Clarion $19.00 (0-395-97825-4). This collection of stories mixes religious history and rabbinic literature to tell the story of the Israelites' 40 years in the wilderness. (Rev: BL 10/1/02; HB 11–12/02; HBG 3/03; SLJ 9/02) [296.1]

9623 Chaikin, Miriam. *Clouds of Glory: Legends and Stories About Bible Times* (4–8). Illus. 1998, Clarion $19.00 (0-395-74654-X). Illustrated with charming woodcuts, this collection of stories mixes Bible accounts with Jewish parallel legends (midrashim) to create an unusual retelling of Genesis tales. (Rev: BL 4/1/98; HBG 10/98; SLJ 4/98) [296.1]

9624 Chaikin, Miriam. *Joshua in the Promised Land* (4–8). 1990, Houghton paper $7.95 (0-395-54797-0). The story of Moses' success and the Israelites' journey to the Holy Land.

9625 Cooper, Ilene. *The Dead Sea Scrolls* (5–8). Illus. 1997, Morrow $15.00 (0-688-14300-8). An account of the discovery of the Dead Sea Scrolls, their contents, and their archaeological importance. (Rev: BCCB 5/97; BL 3/1/97; HB 9–10/97; SLJ 6/97) [296.1]

9626 Cotner, June, ed. *Teen Sunshine Reflections: Words for the Heart and Soul* (6–12). 2002, HarperCollins $15.95 (0-06-000525-4); paper $9.95 (0-06-000527-0). This anthology of poems and quotations that celebrate spiritual beliefs and appreciation of the world about us includes the works of the well-known (such as Saint Francis, Gandhi, and Anne Frank) and the unknown. (Rev: BL 7/02; HBG 10/02; SLJ 8/02) [082]

9627 Dhanjal, Beryl. *Sikhism* (7–10). Illus. 1987, David & Charles $19.95 (0-7134-5202-1). The major tenets, doctrines, and personages of this religion are discussed in alphabetical order. (Rev: SLJ 9/87) [294.6]

9628 Dillon, Leo, and Diane Dillon. *To Every Thing There Is a Season: Verses from Ecclesiastes* (4–7). Illus. 1998, Scholastic paper $16.95 (0-590-47887-7). Using verses from Ecclesiastes such as "A time to be born and a time to die," the artists have created

a stunning picture book on the cycle of life. (Rev: BCCB 11/98; BL 10/1/98*; HB 9–10/98; HBG 3/99; SLJ 9/98) [223]

9629 Dudley, William, ed. *Religion in America* (7–12). Illus. Series: Opposing Viewpoints. 2001, Greenhaven LB $31.20 (1-56510-003-4); paper $19.95 (1-56510-002-6). Essays assess the importance of religion in America today, with debate of such questions as the proper role for religion in education, how to accommodate religious freedom, and whether religion can solve social problems. (Rev: BL 10/1/01) [200]

9630 Ellwood, Robert S., and Gregory D. Alles, eds. *The Encyclopedia of World Religions* (7–12). Illus. 1998, Facts on File $45.00 (0-8160-3504-0). Though basically intended as a reference book, this is an absorbing work that offers information on religions past and present and on general topics of interest, such as the sun, moon, music, and science. (Rev: BL 9/1/98; SLJ 11/98) [200]

9631 Ford, Michael Thomas. *Paths of Faith: Conversations About Religion and Spirituality* (8–12). 2000, Simon & Schuster $17.00 (0-689-82263-4). In a series of interviews, 12 young people discuss religion, what it means to them, and the nature of their spiritual journeys. (Rev: BL 10/1/00; HB 1–2/01; HBG 3/01; SLJ 1/01) [291]

9632 Ganeri, Anita. *Out of the Ark: Stories from the World's Religions* (4–7). 1996, Harcourt $18.00 (0-15-200943-4). Traditional tales from seven of the world's major religions are retold in this thematically arranged book. (Rev: BCCB 4/96; SLJ 4/96) [200]

9633 Ganeri, Anita. *What Do We Know About Buddhism?* (4–7). Illus. Series: What Do We Know About. 1997, Bedrick $18.95 (0-87226-389-4). Using double-page spreads, basic facts about Buddha's life and teachings are covered, with information on Buddhist beliefs, sacred texts, festivals, and the art and folk literature connected with this religion. (Rev: HBG 3/98; SLJ 10/97) [294]

9634 Gellman, Marc. *God's Mailbox: More Stories About Stories in the Bible* (4–7). 1996, Morrow $15.00 (0-688-13169-7). Some stories retold from the Bible, including the Creation, Garden of Eden, Jacob's ladder, the Exodus, and Moses receiving the Ten Commandments. (Rev: BCCB 5/96; SLJ 3/96) [222]

9635 Gellman, Marc, and Thomas Hartman. *How Do You Spell God? Answers to the Big Questions from Around the World* (5–8). 1995, Morrow $17.99 (0-688-13041-0). A priest and a rabbi have written this introduction to the world's most important religions: Judaism, Christianity, Islam, Buddhism, and Hinduism. (Rev: BCCB 7–8/95; BL 6/1–15/95; SLJ 5/95) [200]

9636 Gold, Susan D. *Religions of the Western Hemisphere* (5–8). Illus. Series: Comparing Continents. 1997, Twenty-First Century $23.40 (0-8050-5603-3). This work explores the history and influence of religions, beliefs, and customs on life in the United States, Canada, and Latin America, with discussion of the roles of religious leaders in government, economy, and everyday life. (Rev: BL 2/1/98; SLJ 3/98) [200]

9637 Goldin, Barbara D. *Journeys with Elijah: Eight Tales of the Prophet* (4–7). 1999, Harcourt $20.00 (0-15-200445-9). Eight tales depict the prophet Elijah in his many roles as teacher, miracle worker, and mysterious stranger. (Rev: BCCB 4/99; BL 4/15/99; HB 3–4/99; HBG 10/99; SLJ 6/99) [222]

9638 Hartz, Paula. *Baha'i Faith* (6–10). Series: World Religions. 2002, Facts on File $30.00 (0-8160-4729-4). A look at the history and beliefs of the Baha'i Faith and its spread from Persia to the rest of the world. (Rev: HBG 3/03; SLJ 12/02) [297.9]

9639 Hartz, Paula R. *Taoism* (6–9). Illus. Series: World Religions. 1993, Facts on File $30.00 (0-8160-2448-0). A clear, objective explanation of the Chinese religion Taoism, with details on its metamorphosis from mysticism to a more secular form. (Rev: BL 7/93) [299]

9640 Hartz, Paula R. *Zoroastrianism* (8–12). Illus. Series: World Religions. 1999, Facts on File $26.95 (0-8160-3877-5). A thorough description of the beliefs and customs of followers of Zarathushtra. (Rev: BR 1–2/00; HBG 4/00; SLJ 1/00) [295]

9641 Hastings, Selina. *The Children's Illustrated Bible* (4–7). Illus. 1994, DK paper $22.99 (1-56458-472-0). Several stories from both testaments of the Bible are retold, with some background material on history and geographical settings. (Rev: BL 6/1–15/94) [220.9]

9642 Hoobler, Thomas, and Dorothy Hoobler. *Confucianism* (6–9). Series: World Religions. 1993, Facts on File $30.00 (0-8160-2445-6). Describes how the teachings of Confucius evolved from a social order to a religion, permeating all phases of Chinese life for 2,000 years. (Rev: BL 3/1/93) [299]

9643 Ikeda, Daisaku. *The Way of Youth* (6–12). 2000, Middleway paper $14.95 (0-9674697-0-8). The great questions of human behavior — such as the nature of love, friendship, and compassion — are discussed from a Buddhist perspective. (Rev: BL 12/1/00) [294.3]

9644 Joselit, Jenna Weissman. *Immigration and American Religion* (6–12). Illus. Series: Religion in American Life. 2001, Oxford $22.00 (0-19-511083-8). Joselit looks at Protestant, Catholic, Jewish, and Asian immigrants to the United States and how their religious beliefs and practices have evolved to suit their new circumstances. (Rev: BL 5/15/01; HBG 10/01; SLJ 8/01) [200.86]

9645 Kallen, Stuart A. *Shinto* (6–9). Series: Religions of the World. 2001, Gale LB $27.45 (1-56006-988-0). This book explores the beliefs, customs, and historical roots of Shinto, the indigenous religion of Japan. (Rev: BL 8/02; SLJ 6/02) [299]

9646 Kimmel, Eric A. *Be Not Far from Me: The Oldest Love Story: Legends from the Bible* (4–8). Illus. 1998, Simon & Schuster $25.00 (0-689-81088-1). A collection of stories about heroes and heroines from the Old Testament with incidents and details from ancient midrashic tradition. Illustrated by Caldecott winner David Diaz. (Rev: BCCB 5/98; BL 4/1/98; SLJ 6/98) [220]

9647 Kingsbury, Karen. *A Treasury of Miracles for Teens : True Stories of God's Presence Today* (7–12). 2003, Warner $12.95 (0-446-52962-1). Kingsbury recounts stories in which teens seek God's help and are rewarded. (Rev: BL 7/03) [231.7]

9648 Krishnaswami, Uma. *The Broken Tusk: Stories of the Hindu God Ganesha* (4–8). Illus. 1996, Linnet $19.95 (0-208-02242-5). A collection of tales about the elephant-headed Hindu god Ganesha, the god of good beginnings. (Rev: SLJ 7/97) [294.5]

9649 Lach, William, ed. *I Imagine Angels: Poems and Prayers for Parents and Children* (4–8). Illus. 2000, Simon & Schuster $16.00 (0-689-84080-2). Handsomely reproduced pictures illustrate this collection of prayers and thoughtful poems from many sources, including the Bible. (Rev: BL 10/1/00; HBG 10/01; SLJ 1/01) [808.81]

9650 Langley, Myrtle. *Religion* (4–7). Illus. Series: Eyewitness Books. 1996, Knopf $20.99 (0-679-98123-3). Each double-page spread introduces a different religion, including those of ancient Egypt and Greece as well as Hinduism, Buddhism, Confucianism, Taoism, Sikhism, Judaism, Christianity, and Islam. (Rev: SLJ 12/96) [291]

9651 Lester, Julius. *When the Beginning Began: Stories About God, the Creatures, and Us* (4–8). Illus. 1999, Harcourt $17.00 (0-15-201138-9). Using parts of Genesis and creation stories from Jewish legends, this wondrous retelling adds thought-provoking human interest to the stories that end with Adam and Eve. (Rev: BL 4/15/99*; SLJ 5/99) [296.1]

9652 Lincoln, Frances. *A Family Treasury of Prayers* (4–8). 1996, Simon & Schuster $16.00 (0-689-80956-5). Classic art works illustrate this lovely collection of prayers from famous sources. (Rev: BL 10/1/96; SLJ 10/96; VOYA 6/97) [242]

9653 Lincoln, Frances. *Stories from The Old Testament: With Masterwork Paintings Inspired by the Stories* (5–8). 1996, Simon & Schuster $18.00 (0-689-80955-7). Scenes from the Old Testament (the

Hebrew Bible) are told in the King James version and are illustrated with masterpieces of world art. (Rev: BL 10/1/96; SLJ 10/96; VOYA 6/97) [222]

9654 Lugira, Aloysius. *African Religion* (7–10). Illus. Series: World Religions. 1999, Facts on File $30.00 (0-8160-3876-7). The author gives a fine over view of the major religious beliefs of the different ethnic groups in Africa plus material on organized religion, witchcraft, and the influence of Western religions on the area. (Rev: BL 1/1–15/00; HBG 4/00; SLJ 1/00) [299.]

9655 McCaughrean, Geraldine. *God's People: Stories from the Old Testament* (4–7). Illus. 1997, Simon & Schuster $19.95 (0-689-81366-X). A brilliant retelling of the major stories found in the Old Testament. (Rev: BL 3/1/98*; HBG 3/98; SLJ 3/98) [221.9]

9656 McFarlane, Marilyn, retel. *Sacred Myths: Stories of World Religions* (6–10). 1996, Sibyl $26.95 (0-9638327-7-8). A collection of myths from a number of religions, including Judaism, Christianity, Islam, and Hinduism. (Rev: BL 10/1/96; SLJ 1/97) [200]

9657 MacMillan, Dianne M. *Diwali: Hindu Festival of Lights* (4–8). Series: Best Holiday Books. 1997, Enslow LB $18.95 (0-89490-817-0). This book on the Hindu Diwali festival discusses its significance and relationship to the history, culture, and people of India, and includes material on the food, crafts, instruments, and costumes of the festival. (Rev: SLJ 8/97) [294.5]

9658 Maestro, Betsy. *The Story of Religion* (4–7). 1996, Clarion LB $16.00 (0-395-62364-2). Traces the history of religion from the beliefs of primitive peoples to the development of such modern religions as Islam and Christianity. (Rev: BL 10/1/96; SLJ 9/96*) [291]

9659 Mann, Gruinder Singh, et al. *Buddhists, Hindus, and Sikhs in America* (6–12). Illus. Series: Religion in American Life. 2002, Oxford $24.00 (0-19-512442-1). Photographs, anecdotes, and excerpts from primary sources add appeal to this survey of how three major religions have affected, and been affected by, life in America. (Rev: BL 1/1–15/02; HBG 10/02; SLJ 1/02; VOYA 4/02) [294]

9660 Manushkin, Fran. *Daughters of Fire* (4–7). 2001, Harcourt $20.00 (0-15-201869-7). Rich, striking illustrations accompany a selection of stories about biblical women. (Rev: BL 12/15/01; HBG 3/02; SLJ 10/01) [221.9]

9661 Martin, Joel W. *Native American Religion* (7–12). 1999, Oxford LB $22.00 (0-19-511035-8). An overview of historical and contemporary Native American religious beliefs and practices, their importance in daily life, and the conflicts introduced by the Europeans. (Rev: HBG 4/00; SLJ 9/99; VOYA 10/99) [299]

9662 Mayer, Marianna. *Remembering the Prophets of Sacred Scripture* (6–10). Illus. 2003, Penguin Putnam $16.99 (0-8034-2727-5). Old Testament prophets — from Daniel and Moses to Amos and Obadiah — are introduced in this handsome picture book for older readers. (Rev: BL 7/03; SLJ 8/03) [224]

9663 Metcalf, Franz. *Buddha in Your Backpack: Everyday Buddhism for Teens* (7–12). 2002, Ulysses paper $12.95 (1-56975-321-0). This humorous and informative guide will satisfy young adults' interest in the spiritual world of Buddhism. (Rev: BL 1/1–15/03; SLJ 2/03) [294.3]

9664 Morgan, Peggy. *Buddhism* (7–10). Illus. 1987, David & Charles $19.95 (0-7134-5203-X). In a dictionary format, the major points concerning this religion and its founder are described. (Rev: SLJ 9/87) [294.3]

9665 Morris, Neil. *The Life of Moses* (6–9). Illus. Series: Art Revelations. 2003, Enchanted Lion $18.95 (1-59271-001-2). The works of artists including Botticelli and Michelangelo, hieroglyphs, and artifacts form a handsome backdrop to the story of Moses in this large-format book that looks at important events in double-page spreads. Also use *The Life of Jesus* (2003). (Rev: BL 8/03) [704.9]

9666 Murphy, Claire Rudolf, et al. *Daughters of the Desert: Stories of Remarkable Women from Christian, Jewish, and Muslim Traditions* (7–10). 2003, Skylight Paths $19.95 (1-893361-72-1). Five authors contributed to these 18 stories, based on the Bible and Koran, of the lives of women including Eve, Esther, Mary Magdalene, Sarah, and Khadiji, the wife of Mohammed. (Rev: BL 10/15/03) [220.9]

9667 Netzley, Patricia D. *Angels* (7–10). Series: Mystery Library. 2001, Lucent LB $19.96 (1-56006-768-3). A serious examination of sources and occurrences that have been used to prove or disprove the existence of angels. (Rev: BL 9/15/01) [291.2]

9668 Osborne, Mary Pope. *One World, Many Religions: The Ways We Worship* (4–7). Illus. 1996, Knopf LB $21.99 (0-679-93930-X). Six of the world's major religions are introduced in an account that emphasizes their similarities. (Rev: BCCB 1/97; BL 10/1/96; SLJ 11/96) [291]

9669 Pandell, Karen, and Barry Bryant. *Learning from the Dalai Lama: Secrets of the Wheel of Time* (5–8). 1995, Dutton $16.99 (0-525-45063-7). An excellent introduction to the essentials of Buddhism and the Kalachakra teaching, including instructions for creating a sand mandala and supplemented by photographs. (Rev: BL 1/1–15/96; SLJ 3/96) [294.3]

9670 Paterson, John, and Katherine Paterson. *Images of God: Views of the Invisible* (5–8). Illus. 1998, Houghton $20.00 (0-395-70734-X). After explaining the differences between the Hebrew and the Christian Bibles, the authors describe the images of God in these texts, as well as the portrayal of such elements as light, water, wind, fire, rocks, and clouds. (Rev: BL 5/1/98; BR 11–12/98; HBG 10/98; SLJ 4/98) [231]

9671 Philip, Neil. *In the House of Happiness: A Book of Prayer and Praise* (6–9). 2003, Clarion $17.00 (0-618-23481-0). Reflective verses are accompanied by images of nature in this book of inspirational messages. (Rev: BL 2/1/03; HBG 10/03; SLJ 7/03) [291.4]

9672 Ries, Julien. *The Many Faces of Buddhism* (7–10). Illus. Series: Religions of Humanity. 2002, Chelsea LB $17.55 (0-7910-6626-6). This brief overview covers the history, beliefs, and various forms of Buddhism, with information on the spread of this religion from India into neighboring countries and on how Buddhism has evolved. (Rev: SLJ 10/02) [294.3]

9673 Seeger, Elizabeth. *Eastern Religions* (7–12). Illus. 1973, HarperCollins $14.95 (0-690-25342-7). A fine overview of such religions as Hinduism, Buddhism, Confucianism, and Taoism. [291]

9674 Simpson, Nancy. *Face-to-Face with Women of the Bible* (6–8). Illus. 1996, Chariot-Victor $16.99 (0-7814-0251-4). Both well-known and obscure women from the Bible are introduced in two or three pages per subject. (Rev: BL 10/15/96) [220.92]

9675 Singh, Nikky-Guninder Kaur. *Sikhism* (6–9). Series: World Religions. 1993, Facts on File $30.00 (0-8160-2446-4). Describes the development of Sikhism an outgrowth of Hinduism and discusses its traditions, customs, and beliefs. (Rev: BL 7/93) [294.6]

9676 Sita, Lisa. *Worlds of Belief: Religion and Spirituality* (5–8). Series: Our Human Family. 1995, Blackbirch LB $31.19 (1-56711-125-4). Using many illustrations, this book gives a tour of the world's religions, with an emphasis on the similarities rather than the differences. (Rev: SLJ 1/96) [200]

9677 Slavicek, Louise Chipley. *Confucianism* (6–9). Series: Religions of the World. 2001, Gale LB $27.45 (1-56006-984-8). After a biography of Confucius, this account discusses the principles of this faith and how it is being practiced throughout the world today. (Rev: BL 8/02; SLJ 6/02) [299]

9678 Stein, Stephen J. *Alternative American Religions* (8–12). Series: Religion in American Life. 2000, Oxford LB $22.00 (0-19-511196-6). From Puritan dissenters to cults like Heaven's Gate, this is a look at the alternative religions that have attracted followers in the America. (Rev: HBG 9/00; SLJ 4/00; VOYA 12/00) [291.9]

9679 Sweeney, Jon M., ed. *God Within: Our Spiritual Future — As Told by Today's New Adults*

(8–12). 2001, Skylight Paths paper $14.95 (1-893361-15-2). Writers in their teens and 20s, who reflect a wide variety of beliefs, present very personal essays on their faiths and their paths to spirituality. (Rev: BL 1/1–15/02) [200]

9680 Wagner, Katherine. *Life in an Amish Community* (6–10). Series: Way People Live. 2001, Lucent $27.45 (1-56006-654-7). Wagner explains the traditions of the Amish, traces their history, and discusses some of the contemporary disagreements within the community and problems with outsiders. (Rev: BL 10/1/01; SLJ 1/02) [973]

9681 Waldman, Neil. *The Promised Land: The Birth of the Jewish People* (4–7). Illus. 2002, Boyds Mills $21.95 (1-56397-332-4). Waldman interweaves information on religious tradition and the experiences of the Jewish people over time in this handsome volume. (Rev: BL 10/1/02; HBG 3/03; SLJ 9/02) [909]

9682 Wangu, Madhu Bazaz. *Buddhism* (6–9). Series: World Religions. 1993, Facts on File $19.95 (0-8160-2442-1). Describes Buddha's life, the spread of Buddhism, and its existence today. (Rev: BL 3/1/93; SLJ 6/93) [294.3]

9683 Wangu, Madhu Bazaz. *Hinduism* (6–9). Series: World Religions. 1991, Facts on File $30.00 (0-8160-2447-2). A detailed, in-depth look at this major religion, with particular emphasis on how it is practiced in India. (Rev: BL 4/15/92; SLJ 3/92) [294.5]

9684 Winston, Diana. *Wide Awake: A Buddhist Guide for Teens* (6–10). 2003, Putnam paper $13.95 (0-399-52897-0). In a conversational style, the author introduces the tenets of Buddhism, explains her own beliefs and how she arrived at them, and looks at ways teens can apply Buddhist teachings to their own experiences. (Rev: BL 10/1/03) [294.]

Christianity

9685 Aaseng, Rolfe E. *Augsburg Story Bible* (4–8). 1992, Augsburg LB $19.99 (0-8066-2607-0). This copiously illustrated version of the Bible is only slightly abridged. (Rev: SLJ 7/92) [222]

9686 Bolick, Nancy O., and Sallie Randolph. *Shaker Inventions* (6–8). Illus. 1990, Walker LB $13.85 (0-8027-6934-9). This book describes the Shaker religion and explores the many contributions of the Shakers to American life, such as the clothespin and washing machine. (Rev: BL 8/90) [289]

9687 Bolick, Nancy O., and Sallie Randolph. *Shaker Villages* (6–8). Illus. 1993, Walker LB $13.85 (0-8027-8210-8). This history offers insights into one of the world's longest-lived communal societies, its founder, its faith, its daily life, and its village organization. (Rev: BL 3/15/93; SLJ 6/93) [289]

9688 Capek, Michael. *A Personal Tour of a Shaker Village* (4–7). Series: How It Was. 2001, Lerner LB $30.35 (0-8225-3584-X). An account of life in a Shaker village, seen through the eyes of people who lived there. (Rev: BL 8/1/01; HBG 10/01; SLJ 8/01) [289.8]

9689 *Christmas in Colonial and Early America* (4–7). Illus. 1996, World Book $19.00 (0-7166-0875-8). The evolution of Christmas celebrations is traced through more than 100 years of American history to the end of the 19th century. (Rev: BL 11/1/96) [394.26]

9690 *Christmas in Greece* (5–10). Illus. Series: Christmas Around the World. 2000, World Book $19.00 (0-7166-0859-6). This account focuses on the religious practices of the Greek Orthodox Church at Christmastime, which begins with a long fasting period. (Rev: BL 9/1/00) [398.2]

9691 Corzine, Phyllis. *The King James Bible: Christianity's Definitive Text* (7–12). 2000, Lucent LB $18.96 (1-56006-673-3). The author traces the history of translations of the Bible into English and looks at the cultural and religious climate at the time of the King James version (1611), giving examples of differing translations of specific passages. (Rev: HBG 9/00; SLJ 8/00)

9692 *The Easter Story: According to the Gospels of Matthew, Luke, and John from the King James Bible* (4–8). Illus. 1999, Holt $19.95 (0-8050-5052-3). Using passages from various books of the New Testament and stunning paintings, this is the story of Holy Week from the cleansing of the temple to Christ's appearance to the disciples after the Resurrection. (Rev: BL 3/15/99; HBG 9/99; SLJ 3/99) [232.9]

9693 Erickson, John H. *Orthodox Christians in America* (7–12). Illus. Series: Religion in American Life. 1999, Oxford LB $22.00 (0-19-510852-3). A detailed account of the growth of Eastern Orthodox churches —and of the various ethnic groups they serve — in the United States. (Rev: HBG 4/00; SLJ 1/00) [281.9]

9694 Fisher, James T. *Catholics in America* (5–9). Illus. Series: Religion in American Life. 2000, Oxford $28.00 (0-19-511179-6). This account traces the history of Roman Catholicism in America, its adherents, their role in public affairs, and debates over topics such as abortion. (Rev: BL 6/1–15/00; HBG 3/01; SLJ 12/00) [282]

9695 Harik, Ramsay M. *Jesus of Nazareth: Teacher and Prophet* (5–8). Illus. Series: Book Report Biographies. 2001, Watts paper $6.95 (0-531-15552-8). Harik presents the life and ministry of Jesus. (Rev: BL 8/01) [232.9]

9696 Israel, Fred L. *The Amish* (5–8). Illus. Series: Immigrant Experience. 1996, Chelsea LB $21.95 (0-7910-3368-6). The story of this conservative division of the Mennonites, why they settled in the United States, and their contributions to the nation. (Rev: BL 7/96; SLJ 10/96) [305.6]

9697 Jeffers, H. Paul. *Legends of Santa Claus* (4–7). Series: A&E Biography. 2000, Lucent LB $25.26 (0-8225-4983-2). This book recounts the tales, legends, and myths about Santa Claus and sorts the truth from the fiction. (Rev: BL 12/15/00; HBG 3/01) [394.2]

9698 *Jesus of Nazareth: A Life of Christ Through Pictures* (5–7). Illus. 1994, Simon & Schuster $16.00 (0-671-88651-7). The life of Jesus Christ, with words from the King James Bible and illustrations from Washington's National Gallery. (Rev: BL 1/1/95; SLJ 3/95) [232]

9699 John Paul II. *Every Child a Light: The Pope's Message to Young People* (4–7). Ed. by Jerome M. Vereb. Illus. 2002, Boyds Mills $16.95 (1-56397-090-2). Using photographs and snippets from Pope John Paul II's writings for children and teens, this is an inspirational book of comments and advice for youngsters. (Rev: BL 6/1–15/02; HBG 10/02; SLJ 5/02) [248.8]

9700 Kenna, Kathleen. *A People Apart* (5–8). Illus. 1995, Houghton $18.00 (0-395-67344-5). A thoughtful photoessay on the lives of the Mennonites by a woman who attended the church as a child. Interviews and the history of the group flesh out the text. (Rev: BL 11/1/95*; SLJ 12/95*) [289.7]

9701 Lutz, Norma Jean. *The History of the Black Church* (5–8). Illus. Series: African American Achievers. 2001, Chelsea $21.95 (0-7910-5822-0); paper $9.95 (0-7910-5823-9). Historical and contemporary photographs illustrate this history of African American religious life and institutions. (Rev: BL 10/1/01; HBG 3/02; SLJ 12/01) [277.3]

9702 McCaughrean, Geraldine. *God's Kingdom* (4–7). Illus. 2000, Simon & Schuster $20.00 (0-689-82488-2). This is a fine retelling of the major stories in the New Testament, including some of the parables of Jesus. (Rev: BL 1/1–15/00; HBG 10/00; SLJ 4/00) [226]

9703 Mayer, Marianna. *Seeing Jesus in His Own Words* (4–8). Illus. 2002, Penguin $16.99 (0-8037-2742-9). A range of styles of paintings illustrate this collection of sayings of Jesus that are restated in words young people will understand. (Rev: BL 10/1/02; HBG 3/03; SLJ 1/03) [232.9]

9704 Mitchell, Stephen. *Jesus: What He Really Said and Did* (8–12). 2002, HarperCollins $15.95 (0-06-623836-6). This abridged version of *The Gospel According to Jesus* (1991) gives Mitchell's controversial interpretation of the Gospels, looking at topics such as resurrection and spiritual healing. (Rev:

BL 3/15/02; HB 9–10/02; HBG 3/03; SLJ 8/02; VOYA 2/03) [232.9]

9705 Mulvihill, Margaret. *The Treasury of Saints and Martyrs* (5–7). Illus. 1999, Viking $19.99 (0-670-88789-7). A handsome, oversize book about the lives of 40 saints from the beginning of Christianity to the present day. (Rev: BL 10/1/99; HBG 10/00; SLJ 3/00) [270.029]

9706 Noll, Mark. *Protestants in America* (7–12). Illus. Series: Religion in America. 2000, Oxford $28.00 (0-19-511034-X). From the arrival of the Puritans to today, this is a well-organized overview of Protestantism and how it has evolved, changed, and splintered in America. (Rev: BL 10/1/00; HBG 3/01; SLJ 2/01) [280]

9707 Paul, John. *For the Children: Words of Love and Inspiration from His Holiness John Paul II* (4–7). Illus. 2000, Scholastic paper $16.95 (0-439-14902-9). Letters and speeches by Pope John Paul II and photographs of children from around the world are used to illustrate inspirational messages about such subjects as hope, faith, and school. (Rev: BL 3/1/00; HBG 10/00; SLJ 3/00) [248.8]

9708 Penney, Sue. *Christianity* (6–8). Series: World Beliefs and Cultures. 2000, Heinemann LB $25.64 (1-57572-355-7). A balanced introduction to the history and practice of this major religion, with material on its sacred texts, worship, pilgrimage sites, key figures, festivals, and subgroups. (Rev: HBG 10/01; SLJ 4/01) [230]

9709 Rollins, Charlemae Hill, ed. *Christmas Gif': An Anthology of Christmas Poems, Songs, and Stories* (5–10). Illus. 1993, Morrow $14.00 (0-688-11667-1). A reissue of this Christmas anthology of African American songs, stories, poems, spirituals, and recipes, newly illustrated by Ashley Bryan. (Rev: BL 7/93) [810.8]

9710 Ross, Lillian H. *Daughters of Eve: Strong Women of the Bible* (5–7). Illus. 2000, Barefoot $19.99 (1-902283-82-1). Fictionalized accounts that expand on the material given in the Bible and Apocrypha about 12 strong women and their deeds. (Rev: BL 10/1/00; HBG 10/01; SLJ 11/00) [220.9]

9711 Schmidt, Gary D., retel. *The Blessing of the Lord: Stories from the Old and New Testaments* (5–8). Illus. 1997, Eerdmans $20.00 (0-8028-3789-1). Using 25 Old and New Testament stories as a focus, these insightful accounts describe how biblical personalities react to such events as Daniel's struggle with the lions and Jesus causing nets to be filled with fish. (Rev: BL 11/1/97; HBG 3/98; SLJ 10/97) [222]

9712 *Stories from the Bible* (5–7). 2002, North-South $19.95 (0-7358-1413-9). Sophisticated paintings illustrate verbatim excerpts from the King James version of both the Old and New Testaments.

(Rev: BCCB 9/02; BL 4/1/02; HB 7–8/02; HBG 10/02; SLJ 5/02) [220.5]

9713 Teresa, Mother. *Words to Love By* (7–12). 1983, Ave Maria Pr. paper $9.95 (0-87793-261-1). A collection of the writing and meditations of the Nobel Prize–winning nun. [242]

9714 Williams, Jean K. *The Amish* (6–9). Illus. 1996, Watts LB $25.00 (0-531-11275-6). This book tells about the Amish, their history, beliefs, social structure, and how their lifestyle differs from that of most other Americans. (Rev: BL 10/1/96; SLJ 1/97) [289.7]

9715 Williams, Jean K. *The Christian Scientists* (7–12). Series: The American Religious Experience. 1997, Watts LB $25.00 (0-531-11309-4). This serves as both a history and exploration of the Christian Science faith and a biography of founder Mary Baker Eddy, who believed that mind is spirit and that sin and disease should be conquered solely by prayer. (Rev: SLJ 8/97) [289.5]

9716 Williams, Jean K. *The Mormons* (6–9). Illus. 1996, Watts LB $25.00 (0-531-11276-4). How the Church of Jesus Christ of Latter-day Saints began is told, plus information on the beliefs and practices of its members. (Rev: BL 10/1/96; SLJ 1/97) [289.3]

9717 Williams, Jean K. *The Quakers* (6–12). Illus. Series: American Religious Experience. 1998, Watts LB $25.00 (0-531-11377-9). From the time they left England and came to this country in the 17th century, this is the story of the Quakers, their beliefs and doctrines, and the role they have played in American history. (Rev: BL 10/1/98; HBG 3/99; SLJ 1/99) [289.6]

9718 Williams, Jean K. *The Shakers* (6–10). Illus. Series: American Religious Experience. 1997, Watts LB $25.00 (0-531-11342-6). The story of this religious sect, its origins in England, how members came to America in the late 1700s, its history here, and the group's emphasis on hard work, celibacy, orderliness, and simplicity. (Rev: BL 12/1/97; SLJ 2/98) [289]

9719 Winthrop, Elizabeth, adapt. *He Is Risen: The Easter Story* (4–7). 1985, Holiday $16.95 (0-8234-0547-8). The Easter story taken from parts of the King James version of the Bible and dramatically illustrated. (Rev: BCCB 4/85; HB 7–8/85; SLJ 4/85)

Islam

9720 Child, John. *The Rise of Islam* (6–8). 1995, Bedrick $17.95 (0-87226-116-6). A historical approach to Islam's impact on world history. Discusses its beginnings and middle development but only briefly discusses Islam today. (Rev: BL 9/1/95; SLJ 8/95) [297]

9721 Clark, Charles. *Islam* (6–9). Illus. Series: Religions of the World. 2002, Gale LB $27.45 (1-56006-986-4). Clark explains the history and practice of Islam and discusses the challenges facing this religion today, with interesting sidebars on topics including dietary laws and dress for women. (Rev: BL 8/02; SLJ 7/02) [297]

9722 Gordon, Matthew S. *Islam* (6–9). Series: World Religions. 1991, Facts on File $19.95 (0-8160-2443-X). An overview of the history of Islam, its branches, the Koran, and Islam's place in the modern world. (Rev: BL 4/15/92; SLJ 1/92) [297]

9723 Hurley, Jennifer A., ed. *Islam* (8–12). Illus. Series: Opposing Viewpoints. 2000, Greenhaven LB $22.96 (0-7377-0514-0); paper $14.96 (0-7377-0513-2). Essays offer widely contrasting viewpoints on Islam, looking in particular at the religion's basic values, women's role in Muslim society, terrorism, and relations with the West. (Rev: SLJ 2/01) [297]

9724 Husain, Shahrukh. *What Do We Know About Islam?* (4–7). Illus. Series: What Do We Know About. 1997, Bedrick $18.95 (0-87226-388-6). Covers the major aspects of Islam, including its history, the lifestyles of its believers, holidays, dietary obligations, and the Haj pilgrimage to Mecca. (Rev: SLJ 5/97) [297]

9725 Ojeda, Auriana, ed. *Islamic Fundamentalism* (6–12). Series: At Issue. 2002, Gale LB $20.96 (0-7377-1332-5); paper $13.96 (0-7377-1331-3). The essays in this collection describe the beliefs associated with Islam and those embraced by more extreme Islamic fundamentalists. (Rev: BL 3/15/03; SLJ 7/03) [297]

9726 Spencer, William. *Islam Fundamentalism in the Modern World* (7–10). 1995, Millbrook LB $24.90 (1-56294-435-5). Explains the tenets of Islam and the general nature of religious fundamentalism. (Rev: BL 4/15/95; SLJ 5/95) [320.5]

9727 Tames, Richard. *Islam* (8–10). Illus. 1985, David & Charles $18.95 (0-7134-3655-7). A topically arranged overview of Islam that covers such topics as marriage, mosques, festivals, and beliefs. (Rev: BL 8/85; SLJ 1/86) [297]

9728 Wilkinson, Philip. *Islam* (4–8). Illus. Series: Eyewitness Books. 2002, DK paper $19.99 (0-7894-8871-X). This overview of Islam gives readers a good understanding of the history and tenets of Islam as well as the ways in which it is practiced today. (Rev: BL 10/1/02; HBG 3/03; SLJ 1/03) [297]

9729 Wormser, Richard. *American Islam: Growing Up Muslim in America* (7–12). 1994, Walker $16.85 (0-8027-8344-9). A portrait of Muslim American youth and their faith. (Rev: BL 12/15/94; SLJ 3/95; VOYA 2/95) [297]

Judaism

9730 Adler, David A. *The Kids' Catalog of Jewish Holidays* (4–7). Illus. 1996, Jewish Publication Soc. paper $15.95 (0-8276-0581-1). Thirteen major and several minor Jewish holidays are introduced, along with activities, songs, and recipes. (Rev: BL 12/15/96; SLJ 3/97) [296.4]

9731 Burns, Marilyn. *The Hanukkah Book* (4–7). 1991, Avon paper $3.99 (0-380-71520-1). Not only the history and traditions of this holiday but also attitudes Jewish children have about Christmas are discussed. [296.4]

9732 Burstein, Chaya M. *The Jewish Kids Catalog* (7–9). 1983, Jewish Publication Soc. paper $15.95 (0-8276-0215-4). All sorts of information is given on Jewish culture and history including holidays, folktales, and even some recipes. [296]

9733 Chaikin, Miriam. *Menorahs, Mezuzas, and Other Jewish Symbols* (5–9). 1990, Clarion $17.00 (0-89919-856-2). A Jewish historian explains some of the symbols of the faith. (Rev: BL 1/15/91; HB 5–6/91; SLJ 1/91) [296.4]

9734 Corona, Laurel. *Judaism* (6–9). Series: Religions of the World. 2003, Gale LB $27.45 (1-56006-987-2). The history, teachings, and contemporary customs of Judaism are clearly presented, with information on some famous Jews. (Rev: BL 11/15/03; SLJ 11/03) [296]

9735 David, Jo, and Daniel B. Syme. *The Book of the Jewish Life* (5–8). Illus. 1997, UAHC paper $12.95 (0-8074-0628-7). This book explores common Jewish traditions in such areas as birth and naming, religious schools, bar/bat mitzvahs, confirmation, marriage, and mourning. (Rev: SLJ 9/98) [296]

9736 Feinstein, Edward. *Tough Questions Jews Ask: A Young Adult's Guide to Building a Jewish Life* (5–7). 2003, Jewish Lights $14.95 (1-58023-139-X). Rabbi Feinstein effectively answers hypothetical questions posed by an imagined class of thoughtful young students. (Rev: BL 4/1/03) [296.7]

9737 Fisher, Leonard E. *To Bigotry No Sanction: The Story of the Oldest Synagogue in America* (5–8). Illus. 1998, Holiday $16.95 (0-8234-1401-9). Beginning with the expulsion of the Jews from Spain in 1492, the author traces the history of Jews in America, including the 1763 building — with George Washington's blessing — of the Touro Synagogue. (Rev: BCCB 4/99; BL 2/1/99; HBG 10/99; SLJ 3/99) [296.097457]

9738 Fishman, Cathy G. *On Rosh Hashanah and Yom Kippur* (4–7). 1997, Simon & Schuster $16.00 (0-689-80526-8). Explores and explains the traditions associated with Jewish High Holidays, with particular emphasis of Rosh Hashanah. (Rev: BL 10/1/97; HBG 3/98; SLJ 10/97) [296.4]

9739 Isaacs, Ron. *Ask the Rabbi: The Who, What, Where, Why, and How of Being Jewish* (7–12). 2003, Jossey-Bass paper $22.95 (0-7879-6784-X). Questions and answers are divided into thematic chapters and provide information on practices in different denominations. (Rev: BL 10/15/03) [296]

9740 Kimmel, Eric A., ed. *A Hanukkah Treasury* (5–8). 1998, Holt $19.95 (0-8050-5293-3). A diverse collection of Hanukkah stories, songs, poems, and activities, such as making a menorah, playing dreidel games, and cooking special foods associated with the holiday. (Rev: BL 12/1/98; HBG 3/99; SLJ 10/98) [296.4]

9741 Morrison, Martha, and Stephen F. Brown. *Judaism* (6–9). Illus. Series: World Religions. 1991, Facts on File $30.00 (0-8160-2444-8). An illustrated study of the impact Judaism has had on civilization and a look at its evolution, branches, holidays, and traditions. (Rev: BL 4/15/92; SLJ 3/92) [296]

9742 Penney, Sue. *Judaism* (6–8). Series: World Beliefs and Cultures. 2000, Heinemann LB $25.64 (1-57572-358-1). A balanced introduction to the history and practice of this major religion, with material on its sacred texts, worship, pilgrimage sites, key figures, festivals, and subgroups. (Rev: HBG 10/01; SLJ 4/01) [296]

9743 Salkin, Jeffrey K. *For Kids — Putting God on Your Guest List: How to Claim the Spiritual Meaning of Your Bar or Bat Mitzvah* (6–8). Illus. 1998, Jewish Lights Publg. paper $14.95 (1-58023-015-6). Rabbi Salkin explains the religious and cultural significance of this rite of passage in the Jewish religion. (Rev: BL 3/1/99) [296.4]

9744 Scharfstein, Sol. *Understanding Jewish History I* (6–9). Illus. 1996, KTAV paper $15.95 (0-88125-545-9). Using many colorful illustrations, this work traces Jewish history from biblical times to the expulsion of the Jews from Spain in the 15th century. (Rev: BL 10/1/96; SLJ 1/97) [909]

9745 Scharfstein, Sol. *Understanding Jewish Holidays and Customs: Historical and Contemporary* (4–7). Illus. 1999, KTAV $27.50 (0-88125-634-X); paper $18.95 (0-88125-626-9). From ancient Jewish traditions to the present day, this highly visual volume describes the history, customs, and teaching of Judaism. (Rev: BL 10/1/99; HBG 3/00; SLJ 2/00) [296.4]

9746 Wood, Angela. *Being a Jew* (6–10). Illus. 1988, David & Charles $19.95 (0-7134-4668-4). This book deals with the history, religion, customs, and traditions of Jewish people around the world. (Rev: SLJ 8/88) [296]

9747 Wood, Angela. *Judaism* (5–8). Illus. Series: World Religions. 1995, Thomson Learning LB $24.26 (1-56847-376-1). An informative, clearly written text on Judaism, with a glossary, bibliography, and map of regions in which the religion flourishes. (Rev: BL 9/1/95; SLJ 11/95) [296]

Religious Cults

9748 Barghusen, Joan D. *Cults* (7–12). Illus. Series: Overview. 1997, Lucent LB $27.45 (1-56006-199-5). The author recounts the history of cults in America, attempts to demystify them through an examination of their beliefs, recruitment methods, funding, and various practices, and reviews the anticult movement, including the practice of deprogramming. (Rev: BL 5/1/98; SLJ 8/98) [291.0460973]

9749 Cohen, Daniel. *Cults* (7–10). 1994, Millbrook LB $23.40 (1-56294-324-3). This work describes cults throughout American history, including Pilgrims, Quakers, Moonies, and Satanists, and examines their recruiting methods. (Rev: BL 11/1/94; SLJ 2/95; VOYA 2/95) [291.9]

9750 Cole, Michael D. *The Siege at Waco: Deadly Inferno* (5–9). Series: American Disasters. 1999, Enslow LB $18.95 (0-7660-1218-2). The story of the disaster that ended the 51-day siege at Waco and resulted in the deaths of cult leader David Koresh and 73 of his followers. (Rev: BL 2/15/99; HBG 10/99) [976.4284063]

9751 DeAngelis, Gina. *Jonestown Massacre: Tragic End of a Cult* (6–9). Illus. Series: American Disasters. 2002, Enslow LB $18.95 (0-7660-1784-2). The circumstances behind the mass suicide at Jonestown, Guyana, are examined here. (Rev: BL 1/1–15/03; HBG 3/03; SLJ 4/03) [988.1]

9752 Gay, Kathlyn. *Communes and Cults* (7–12). 1997, Twenty-First Century LB $24.40 (0-8050-3803-5). After tracing the history of cults that rely on communal living, the author discusses contemporary cults, their similarities and differences, their appeal, and their problems. (Rev: BL 9/1/97; BR 11–12/97; SLJ 7/97; VOYA 10/97) [280]

9753 Goodnough, David. *Cult Awareness: A Hot Issue* (5–8). Series: Hot Issues. 2000, Enslow LB $21.95 (0-7660-1196-8). This book explains the nature of cults and how they differ as well as giving information on many groups including Jehovah's Witnesses, Unification Church, Hare Krishna, Shakers, Mormons, and Church of Scientology. (Rev: BL 6/1–15/00; HBG 10/00; SLJ 6/00) [291.9]

9754 Kellaher, Karen Burns. *Cult Leaders* (6–9). Illus. Series: History Makers. 1999, Lucent LB $18.96 (1-56006-593-1). This work profiles six cult leaders including Shaker founder Mother Ann Lee, David Koresh of Branch Davidian fame, and Jim

Jones who followed his cult members in death. (Rev: BL 3/15/00; HBG 9/00; SLJ 4/00) [200.]

9755 Roleff, Tamara L., ed. *Satanism* (6–12). Series: At Issue. 2002, Gale $24.95 (0-7377-0807-7); paper $16.20 (0-7377-0806-9). A series of essays examine Satanism and the beliefs and rituals of the Church of Satan. (Rev: BL 5/15/02; SLJ 7/02) [113.4]

9756 Streissguth, Thomas. *Charismatic Cult Leaders* (7–12). 1995, Oliver LB $19.95 (1-881508-18-8). A balanced presentation of a potentially sensa-tional topic. Includes biblical references where appropriate in the discussion of various cults and their leaders. (Rev: BL 8/95; SLJ 5/95) [291]

9757 Zeinert, Karen. *Cults* (7–12). Illus. Series: Issues in Focus. 1997, Enslow LB $20.95 (0-89490-900-2). Following a history of cults in America from the days of the Salem witches on, this book discusses all forms of present-day cults, from the more establishment (Jehovah's Witnesses and Mormonism) to the extremist (Branch Davidians and the Freemen of Montana). (Rev: BL 6/1–15/97; BR 11–12/97; VOYA 10/97) [291.9]

Society and the Individual

Government and Political Science

General and Miscellaneous

9758 Downing, David. *Democracy* (5–8). Illus. Series: Political and Economic Systems. 2002, Heinemann LB $28.50 (1-40340-317-1). Downing explains the history of democracy and looks at its weaknesses and benefits. Also use *Dictatorship* (2002). (Rev: BL 1/1–15/03; HBG 3/03) [321.8]

9759 Harris, Nathaniel. *Democracy* (6–8). Series: Ideas of the Modern World. 2001, Raintree Steck-Vaughn LB $17.98 (0-7398-3160-7). This account traces the history of democracy from ancient Greece through its flowering after the American and French revolutions and ends with the defeat of communism in the Cold War. (Rev: BL 4/15/02) [320.5]

9760 Nardo, Don. *Democracy* (6–8). Illus. Series: Overview. 1994, Lucent LB $27.45 (1-56006-147-2). This book explains the basic principles of government by and for the people, its evolution through history, and its status in the world today. (Rev: BL 7/94) [321.8]

9761 Tames, Richard. *Monarchy* (5–8). Series: Political and Economic Systems. 2002, Heinemann LB $28.50 (1-40340-320-1). A description of the concept of monarchy, followed by a history of its application, its current status, and its various forms. (Rev: BL 1/1–15/03; HBG 3/03) [321.8]

United Nations and Other International Organizations

9762 Burger, Leslie, and Debra L. Rahm. *Red Cross / Red Crescent: When Help Can't Wait* (5–7). Illus. 1996, Lerner $22.60 (0-8225-2698-0). The story of the Red Cross and the role it plays in helping people today. (Rev: BL 1/1–15/97; SLJ 1/97; VOYA 4/97) [361.7]

9763 Jacobs, William J. *Search for Peace: The Story of the United Nations* (7–10). 1994, Scribners paper $14.95 (0-684-19652-2). Describes the formation of the United Nations and discusses the difficulties the organization has faced in its efforts to maintain peace. (Rev: BL 7/94; SLJ 8/94) [341.23]

9764 Ostopowich, Melanie. *Greenpeace* (4–8). Series: International Organizations. 2002, Weigl LB $24.25 (1-59036-020-6). An introduction to the goals, structure, members, and volunteers who work with this international organization. Also use *Peace Corps* (2003). (Rev: HBG 3/03; SLJ 4/03) [333.72]

9765 Ross, Stewart. *The United Nations* (7–12). Illus. Series: 20th Century Perspectives. 2003, Heinemann LB $25.64 (1-4034-0152-7). An overview of the history, importance, abilities, and current activities of the United Nations, including efforts of UN agencies such as the World Health Organization. (Rev: BL 3/1/03; HBG 10/03; SLJ 5/03) [341.23]

9766 *The United Nations* (8–12). Series: At Issue. 1996, Greenhaven paper $17.45 (1-56510-547-8). This book traces the history, composition, and functions of the United Nations in such areas as population control, pollution, hunger, and economic development. (Rev: BL 5/15/97; SLJ 7/97) [341.23]

9767 *A World in Our Hands: In Honor of the 50th Anniversary of the United Nations* (6–8). 1995, Ten Speed paper $15.95 (1-883672-31-7). The history and accomplishments of the United Nations are the focus of this collection of prose, poetry, and art by young people from around the world. (Rev: BL 2/1/96) [341.23]

International Relations, Peace, and War

9768 Altman, Linda J. *Genocide: The Systematic Killing of a People* (7–12). Series: Issues in Focus. 1995, Enslow LB $20.95 (0-89490-664-X). Discusses the history of genocide and explores the Us-Them mentality and racist stereotypes that are still used today to execute genocidal policies. (Rev: BL 10/15/95; SLJ 11/95; VOYA 12/95) [364.15]

9769 Carter, Jimmy. *Talking Peace: A Vision for the Next Generation* (8–12). 1995, Puffin paper $6.99 (0-14-037440-X). Carter encourages youth to work for world peace by improving human rights, civil liberties, environmental protection, and aid for the poor. The 1995 revised edition updates events in some of the wartorn areas Carter discussed previously and includes a chapter about his peace missions to Korea, Haiti, Bosnia, and Sudan. (Rev: BL 8/93; SLJ 10/93*) [327.1]

9770 Cheney, Glenn. *Nuclear Proliferation: The Problems and Possibilities* (8–12). 1999, Watts LB $22.00 (0-531-11431-7). This account traces the history of nuclear weapons and radioactive materials, describes the treaties to control them, and discusses the current problems in controlling their use, the role of rogue nations, and illegal trade in radioactive materials. (Rev: BL 7/99; SLJ 6/99) [327.1]

9771 Chippendale, Neil. *Crimes Against Humanity* (7–10). Series: Crime, Justice, and Punishment. 2001, Chelsea LB $19.95 (0-7910-4254-5). A clearly written, informative account that explores such international crimes as genocide. (Rev: BL 6/1–15/01; HBG 3/01; SLJ 2/01) [341]

9772 Dudley, William, ed. *Genocide* (8–12). Series: Opposing Viewpoints. 2001, Greenhaven LB $22.96 (0-7377-0681-3); paper $14.96 (0-7377-0680-5). This is an unflinching examination of genocides and "ethnic cleansings" in history. (Rev: BL 12/1/01) [304.6]

9773 Gold, Susan D. *Arms Control* (6–9). Illus. Series: Pacts and Treaties. 1997, Twenty-First Century LB $24.90 (0-8050-4812-X). Beginning with the 1868 Declaration of St. Petersburg calling for a ban on the use of explosive projectiles, the author tells of the many subsequent attempts by world leaders to limit the sale and use of arms. (Rev: BL 9/1/97; SLJ 12/97) [327.1]

9774 Grant, R. G. *Genocide* (5–10). Illus. Series: Talking Points. 1999, Raintree Steck-Vaughn LB $27.12 (0-8172-5314-9). This book covers the Holocaust in World War II as well as more recent massacres in Cambodia, Rwanda, and Bosnia, and probes such controversies as who is guilty of genocide — the person who pulls the trigger or those who plan and organize it, and what about the bystander? (Rev: BL 9/1/99; BR 9–10/99) [304.6]

9775 Landau, Elaine. *Big Brother Is Watching: Secret Police and Intelligence Services* (7–12). 1992, Walker LB $15.85 (0-8027-8161-6). Describes the activities and methods of intelligence and police services in several Western and former Eastern-bloc nations, including the KGB, the Mossad, the CIA, and Honduran death squads. (Rev: BL 6/1/92; SLJ 8/92) [363.2]

9776 Loescher, Gil, and Ann D. Loescher. *The Global Refugee Crisis* (7–12). Series: Contemporary World Issues. 1995, ABC-CLIO LB $45.00 (0-87436-753-0). This volume introduces the problem of refugees and discusses how the United States and the international community have dealt with it. (Rev: BR 9–10/96; SLJ 1/96) [341.4]

9777 Ousseimi, Maria. *Caught in the Crossfire: Growing Up in a War Zone* (6–10). 1995, Walker LB $20.85 (0-8027-8364-3). Examines the effects of violence on children and how violence changes children's perception of the world. (Rev: BL 9/1/95; SLJ 9/95; VOYA 12/95) [305.23]

9778 Roleff, Tamara L., ed. *War* (8–12). Series: Opposing Viewpoints. 1999, Greenhaven paper $21.20 (0-7377-0060-2). An anthology of varying viewpoints on topics related to the causes and prevention of war, international intervention, and the role of the U.S. as a peace broker. (Rev: BL 3/15/99) [341.6]

9779 Spangenburg, Ray, and Kit Moser. *The Crime of Genocide: Terror Against Humanity* (8–12). Series: Issues in Focus. 2000, Enslow LB $20.95 (0-7660-1249-2). Separate chapters address the mass killings of the 20th century — during the Holocaust and in Armenia, Bosnia and Kosovo, Cambodia, and Rwanda. (Rev: HBG 3/01; SLJ 3/01) [364.15]

9780 Winters, Paul A., ed. *Interventionism* (7–12). Series: Current Controversies. 1995, Greenhaven LB $32.45 (1-56510-233-9). Various kinds of international intervention — military, trade, economic sanctions, and humanitarian aid — are explored in this collection of documents. (Rev: BL 6/1–15/95) [341.5]

United States Government and Institutions

General and Miscellaneous

9781 Kronenwetter, Michael. *How Democratic Is the United States?* (7–12). Series: Democracy in Action. 1994, Watts paper $24.00 (0-531-11155-5). Presents the problems of politics and government in the United States and discusses proposals for change. (Rev: BL 11/15/94; SLJ 1/95) [324.6]

9782 Ventura, Jesse, and Heron Marquez. *Jesse Ventura Tells It Like It Is: America's Most Outspoken Governor Speaks Out About Government* (5–8). Illus. 2002, Lerner LB $19.15 (0-8225-0385-9). A look at the U.S. government and politicians from the viewpoint of wrestler-turned-Minnesota-governor Jesse Ventura. (Rev: BL 8/02; HBG 3/03; SLJ 9/02) [977.6]

9783 Weizmann, Daniel. *Take a Stand!* (5–8). Illus. 1996, Price Stern Sloan $6.95 (0-8431-7997-X). This book introduces and describes American government and tells how young people can get involved through grassroots activities, letter writing, or volunteering, with an emphasis on environmental and human-care issues. (Rev: SLJ 12/96) [324]

The Constitution

9784 Banfield, Susan. *The Fifteenth Amendment: African-American Men's Right to Vote* (7–12). Illus. Series: Constitution. 1998, Enslow LB $20.95 (0-7660-1033-3). This is the stormy history of the constitutional amendment passed during Reconstruction that barred states from denying voting rights to black males. (Rev: BL 9/1/98) [324.6208996073]

9785 Bjornlund, Lydia. *The Constitution and the Founding of America* (6–9). Series: World History. 2000, Lucent LB $18.96 (1-56006-586-9). A clearly written account with many quotations from original sources that traces the development of the U.S. Constitution after the Revolution. (Rev: BL 2/15/00; HBG 9/00) [342.73]

9786 Bjornlund, Lydia. *The U.S. Constitution* (8–12). Illus. Series: Words That Changed History. 1999, Lucent LB $27.45 (1-56006-486-2). Topics covered in this volume include the need for the Constitution, factors considered in deciding on the structure of the government, important figures in its history, controversies and compromises, amendments, and an evaluation of its success. (Rev: BL 6/1–15/99; SLJ 8/99) [342.73]

9787 Collier, Christopher, and James L. Collier. *Creating the Constitution, 1787* (5–8). Illus. Series: Drama of American History. 1998, Marshall Cavendish LB $29.93 (0-7614-0776-6). This history of the U.S. Constitution describes the background and importance of the document and the compromises made to win ratification. (Rev: BL 2/15/99) [342.73029]

9788 Farish, Leah. *The First Amendment: Freedom of Speech, Religion, and the Press* (6–9). Illus. 1998, Enslow LB $20.95 (0-89490-897-9). Using many actual cases as examples, the author explores the complexities of the First Amendment to the Constitution, which guarantees basic freedoms. (Rev: BL 3/15/98; BR 9–10/98; SLJ 6/98) [342.73]

9789 Feinberg, Barbara S. *Constitutional Amendments* (5–8). Series: Inside Government. 1996, Twenty-First Century LB $22.40 (0-8050-4619-4). After presenting a brief history of the Constitution, this work examines the Bill of Rights and then covers the remaining amendments in chapters arranged by topic. (Rev: SLJ 12/96) [342.73]

9790 Feinberg, Barbara Silberdick. *The Articles of Confederation: The First Constitution of the United States* (7–10). Illus. 2002, Twenty-First Century LB $24.90 (0-7613-2114-4). Feinberg presents the history and text of the constitution that was in force from 1776 to 1787, along with a list of the signers, a timeline, and source notes. (Rev: BL 2/1/02; HBG 10/02; SLJ 3/02) [342.73]

9791 Freedman, Russell. *In Defense of Liberty: The Story of America's Bill of Rights* (5–10). 2003, Holiday $24.95 (0-8234-1585-6). A succinct explanation of the history of the Bill of Rights, discussing each amendment in turn and its particular relevance to today's controversies, with many references to cases involving young people. (Rev: BCCB 10/03*; BL 10/1/03*; HB 9–10/03*; SLJ 10/03*) [342.73]

9792 Gerberg, Mort. *The U.S. Constitution for Everyone* (8–12). Illus. 1987, Putnam paper $6.95 (0-399-51305-1). The text of the Constitution and amendments is analyzed with many interesting asides and background information. (Rev: BL 5/1/87) [342.73]

9793 Haesly, Richard, ed. *The Constitutional Convention* (6–9). Series: History Firsthand. 2001, Gale LB $31.20 (0-7377-1072-1); paper $19.95 (0-7377-1071-3). Excerpts from personal accounts bring to life the events and key characters surrounding the writing of the U.S. Constitution. (Rev: SLJ 2/02) [342.73]

9794 Hanson, Freya Ottem. *The Second Amendment: The Right to Own Guns* (6–8). Series: The Constitution. 1998, Enslow LB $20.95 (0-89490-925-8). Using historical background material, case studies, legal decisions, and statistics, the author presents a balanced account of the controversy surrounding the owning of arms and the demand for gun control. (Rev: BR 11–12/98; SLJ 12/98) [347]

9795 Hudson, David L. *The Bill of Rights* (5–8). Illus. Series: The Constitution. 2002, Enslow LB $20.95 (0-7660-1903-9). A look at the first 10 amendments to the Constitution and how they have affected the citizens of the United States. (Rev: BL 2/15/03; HBG 3/03) [342.73]

9796 Hudson, David L. *The Fourteenth Amendment: Equal Protection Under the Law* (5–8). Illus. Series: The Constitution. 2002, Enslow LB $20.95 (0-7660-1904-7). What the 14th amendment to the Constitution entails and how it has affected the citizens of the United States. (Rev: BL 2/15/03; HBG 10/03) [342.73]

9797 Judson, Karen. *The Constitution of the United States* (7–10). Series: American Government in Action. 1996, Enslow LB $20.95 (0-89490-586-4). This book focuses on the historical background of the constitutional convention and the issues that were debated. (Rev: SLJ 5/96) [342.73]

9798 Krull, Kathleen. *A Kids' Guide to America's Bill of Rights: Curfews, Censorship, and the 100-Pound Giant* (5–8). Illus. 1999, Avon $15.99 (0-380-97497-5). After a description of the first 10 amendments, this book details famous court cases and what each amendment means to young people. (Rev: BL 12/1/99; HBG 3/00; VOYA 4/00) [342.73]

9799 Lucas, Eileen. *The Eighteenth and Twenty-First Amendments: Alcohol, Prohibition, and Repeal* (7–12). Illus. Series: Constitution. 1998, Enslow LB $20.95 (0-89490-926-6). An account of the circumstances that led to the passage of Prohibition, its effects, and later repeal. (Rev: BL 9/1/98) [344.730541]

9800 Nardo, Don. *The U.S. Constitution* (5–8). Illus. Series: History of the World. 2001, Gale LB $23.70 (0-7377-0776-3). A history of the Constitution and the Bill of Rights is given plus a discussion of their importance today. (Rev: BL 4/1/02) [342.73]

9801 Schleichert, Elizabeth. *The Thirteenth Amendment: Ending Slavery* (8–10). 1998, Enslow LB $20.95 (0-89490-923-1). The stormy history of this constitutional amendment that ended slavery and fundamentally changed American society. (Rev: BL 8/98; BR 11–12/98; HBG 3/99; SLJ 1/99) [342.73]

9802 Weidner, Daniel. *The Constitution: The Preamble and the Articles* (5–8). Series: The Constitution. 2002, Enslow LB $20.95 (0-7660-1906-3). The history of the U.S. Constitution and its meanings are explored through personal stories and examples. (Rev: BL 2/15/03; HBG 3/03; SLJ 1/03) [342.73]

9803 Weidner, Daniel. *Creating the Constitution: The People and Events That Formed the Nation* (5–8). Series: The Constitution. 2002, Enslow LB $20.95 (0-7660-1905-5). This informative volume describes how the U.S. Constitution was written and the debates that preceded its adoption. (Rev: BL 2/15/03; HBG 3/03; SLJ 1/03) [342.73]

9804 Wetterer, Charles M. *The Fourth Amendment: Search and Seizure* (8–10). 1998, Enslow LB $20.95 (0-89490-924-X). Though enacted early in this country's history, this amendment on privacy has continued to have an important impact throughout the years. (Rev: BL 8/98) [342.73]

The Presidency

9805 Aaseng, Nathan. *The Impeachment of President Clinton* (6–9). Illus. Series: Famous Trials. 2000, Lucent LB $18.96 (1-56006-651-2). This book covers the Clinton impeachment with a discus-sion of his behavior and the question of whether it was a constitutional violation or merely a moral issue. (Rev: BL 9/15/00; HBG 9/00; SLJ 8/00; VOYA 2/01) [973.9]

9806 Aaseng, Nathan. *You Are the President* (7–10). 1994, Oliver LB $19.95 (1-881508-10-2). Devotes one chapter each to a crisis faced by eight presidents in the 20th century, among them Theodore Roosevelt, Eisenhower, and Nixon. (Rev: BL 4/1/94; SLJ 7/94; VOYA 8/94) [973.9]

9807 Aaseng, Nathan. *You Are the President II: 1800–1899* (7–10). Illus. Series: Great Decisions. 1994, Oliver LB $19.95 (1-881508-15-3). This work discusses the powers of the presidency during the 19th century and the major decisions made by presidents during that time. (Rev: BL 11/15/94; SLJ 12/94) [973.5]

9808 Bernstein, Richard B., and Jerome Agel. *The Presidency* (8–12). Illus. 1989, Walker LB $13.85 (0-8027-6831-8). A basic history of this institution with some biographical information and a final section that explores the advisability of concentrating such power in one office. (Rev: BL 5/1/89; BR 3–4/89; SLJ 1/89; VOYA 4/89) [353.03]

9809 Black, Christine M. *The Pursuit of the Presidency: '92 and Beyond* (7–12). 1993, Oryx paper $24.50 (0-89774-845-X). Using the presidential campaign of 1992, the author examines the inner workings of a political campaign and how campaigns relate to actual governing. (Rev: BL 4/15/94) [324.973]

9810 Cohen, Daniel. *The Impeachment of William Jefferson Clinton* (6–12). 2000, Twenty-First Century LB $23.90 (0-7613-1711-2). Extensive background information sets the stage for this account of the impeachment proceedings. (Rev: HBG 9/00; SLJ 6/00; VOYA 2/01) [973.929]

9811 Fernandez, Justin. *High Crimes and Misdemeanors: The Impeachment Process* (7–10). Illus. Series: Crime, Justice, and Punishment. 2000, Chelsea LB $19.95 (0-7910-5450-0). Attorney Fernandez explains this process, looking at the early history and at the impeachment of Bill Clinton. (Rev: BL 1/1–15/01; HBG 3/01; SLJ 12/00; VOYA 2/01) [342.73]

9812 Hardesty, Von. *Air Force One: The Aircraft That Shaped the Modern Presidency* (6–12). 2003, NorthWord $29.95 (1-55971-894-3). From FDR's first presidential flights through today's dependence on air travel, this highly visual book describes the interior redesigns and other evolutions in this symbol of prestige. (Rev: SLJ 11/03*) [387.7]

9813 Judson, Karen. *The Presidency of the United States* (7–10). Series: American Government in Action. 1996, Enslow LB $20.95 (0-89490-585-6). This introduction to the American presidency includes material on the roles of the president, the constitutional basis of the office, the operations of the White House, and the organization of the executive branch. (Rev: SLJ 5/96) [353.03]

9814 Morin, Isobel V. *Impeaching the President* (8–12). 1996, Millbrook LB $24.90 (1-56294-668-4). This book, written before the Clinton impeachment, explains what impeachment is, its processes, and its role in American history. (Rev: BR 9–10/96; SLJ 6/96; VOYA 10/96) [336.73]

9815 Nardo, Don. *The U.S. Presidency* (6–8). Series: Overview. 1995, Lucent LB $27.45 (1-56006-157-X). This book explores the events that shaped the presidency and the changing views of the president's role in legislative affairs, foreign policy, war, and the appointment process. (Rev: BL 7/95) [353.03]

9816 Phillips, Louis. *Ask Me Anything About the Presidents* (5–8). 1992, Avon paper $5.99 (0-380-76426-1). A collection of unusual facts about various aspects of the U.S. presidency, presented in a question-and-answer format. (Rev: BL 4/15/92) [920]

9817 Rubel, David. *Scholastic Encyclopedia of the Presidents and Their Times*. Rev. ed. (4–8). Illus. 1997, Scholastic paper $18.95 (0-590-49366-3). This fine reference book introduces each of the presidents and his administration and supplies material on related historical events, movements, and personalities. (Rev: BR 9–10/97; HBG 10/01; SLJ 5/97) [920]

9818 Schlesinger, Arthur M., Jr., ed. *The Election of 2000 and the Administration of George W. Bush* (8–12). Series: Major Presidential Elections and the Administrations That Followed. 2003, Mason Crest LB $24.95 (1-59084-365-7). The circumstances of Bush's election and the major events of his administration through 2002 are presented with reference to many primary sources; brief biographical facts about the president and his cabinet are also included. (Rev: SLJ 10/03) [324.973]

9819 Smith, Carter, ed. *Presidents in a Time of Change: A Sourcebook on the U.S. Presidency* (5–8). Illus. Series: American Albums. 1993, Millbrook $25.90 (1-56294-362-6). A heavily illustrated, attractive review of the presidency from Truman to Clinton. (Rev: BL 12/1/93; SLJ 4/94; VOYA 4/94) [973.92]

9820 Smith, Carter, ed. *Presidents of a Divided Nation: A Sourcebook on the U.S. Presidency* (5–8). Series: American Albums. 1993, Millbrook $25.90 (1-56294-360-X). A visual sourcebook about the presidents during the Civil War and immediately after, from the Library of Congress collection on U.S. presidents. Also use *Presidents of a Growing Country* (Rev: BL 12/1/93) [973.0]

9821 Smith, Carter, ed. *Presidents of a Growing Country: A Sourcebook on the U.S. Presidency*

(5–8). Illus. Series: American Albums. 1993, Millbrook $25.90 (1-56294-358-8). Through extensive use of pictorials, a thorough timeline, and concise text, this attractive book traces the presidency from Hayes through McKinley. (Rev: BL 12/1/93; SLJ 4/94) [973.8]

9822 Smith, Carter, ed. *Presidents of a Young Republic: A Sourcebook on the U.S. Presidency* (5–8). Illus. Series: American Albums. 1993, Millbrook $25.90 (1-56294-359-6). A well-illustrated account that traces U.S. history from the presidency of John Quincy Adams through James Buchanan. (Rev: BL 12/1/93; SLJ 4/94) [973.5]

9823 Waldman, Michael, comp. *My Fellow Americans: The Most Important Speeches of American Presidents from George Washington to George W. Bush* (7–12). 2003, Sourcebooks paper $45.00 (1-4022-0027-7). A collection of more than 40 speeches by 17 presidents, some of which are shown with early drafts; two accompanying CDs contain all the speeches, with the actual voices of presidents starting with Teddy Roosevelt. (Rev: SLJ 10/03*) [352.23]

9824 Woronoff, Kristen. *American Inaugurals: The Speeches, the Presidents, and Their Times* (7–10). Illus. 2002, Gale $64.94 (1-56711-854-5). An attractive, well-illustrated, large-format presentation of all the inaugural speeches, with background information, fast-fact sidebars, and commentary. (Rev: BL 8/02; SLJ 11/02) [352.23]

Federal Government, Its Agencies, and Public Administration

9825 Aaseng, Nathan. *You Are the Senator* (7–10). Illus. Series: Great Decisions. 1997, Oliver LB $19.95 (1-881508-36-6). This book describes the duties and responsibilities of a U.S. senator and the nature of the decisions that senators make. (Rev: BL 4/15/97; BR 11–12/97; SLJ 8/97; VOYA 8/97) [328.73]

9826 Balcavage, Dynise. *The Federal Bureau of Investigation* (7–9). Series: Your Government: How It Works. 2000, Chelsea LB $17.95 (0-7910-5530-2). Famous cases introduce this examination of the FBI, its history, and crime detection equipment and strategies. (Rev: HBG 9/00; SLJ 8/00) [363.25]

9827 Bernstein, Richard B., and Jerome Agel. *The Congress* (7–12). Illus. 1989, Walker LB $13.85 (0-8027-6833-4). An introduction to this branch of the government with material arranged chronologically and including some coverage of scandals and decline in prestige. (Rev: BL 5/1/89; SLJ 1/89; VOYA 4/89) [328.73]

9828 Cothran, Helen, ed. *The Central Intelligence Agency* (6–12). Series: At Issue. 2003, Gale LB $26.60 (0-7377-1725-4); paper $17.45 (0-7377-

1726-2). This collection of essays examines the purpose and scope of operations of the CIA, especially in light of September 11, 2001. (Rev: BL 5/15/03) [327.127]

9829 Dolan, Edward F., and Margaret M. Scariano. *Shaping U.S. Foreign Policy: Profiles of Twelve Secretaries of State* (7–12). Illus. Series: Democracy in Action. 1996, Watts LB $22.00 (0-531-11264-0). A look at five secretaries of state who made major acquisitions of land, and seven who dealt with the search for peace or with the Cold War. (Rev: BL 6/1–15/96; SLJ 7/96) [327.73]

9830 Feinberg, Barbara S. *The National Government* (4–8). Illus. Series: First Books. 1993, Watts LB $22.00 (0-531-20155-4). After an introduction to the federal government, this book explains the functions of each department and how they work together. (Rev: SLJ 1/94) [336.73]

9831 Harmon, Daniel E. *The Environmental Protection Agency* (6–9). Series: Your Government: How It Works. 2002, Chelsea LB $20.75 (0-7910-6792-0). A readable examination of the purpose of the agency and its internal workings, with an emphasis on the kinds of challenges our environment faces. (Rev: HBG 3/03; SLJ 1/03) [354.3]

9832 Harmon, Daniel E. *The FBI* (7–10). Series: Crime, Justice, and Punishment. 2001, Chelsea LB $19.95 (0-7910-4289-8). The highest branch of criminal investigation in the United States is discussed with material on powers, methods, and personnel. (Rev: BL 6/1–15/01; HBG 10/01) [363.2]

9833 Kassinger, Ruth. *U.S. Census: A Mirror of America* (5–8). Illus. 1999, Raintree Steck-Vaughn $28.54 (0-7398-1217-3). Written before the 2000 census began, this book describes the history of the census and the methods used to count Americans. (Rev: BL 12/15/99; HBG 3/00) [304]

9834 Mintzer, Rich. *The National Institutes of Health* (6–9). 2002, Chelsea LB $20.75 (0-7910-6793-9). An absorbing overview of the role of this institution and the importance of public health. (Rev: HBG 3/03; SLJ 1/03) [362.1]

9835 Nardo, Don. *The U.S. Congress* (6–8). Illus. Series: Overview. 1994, Lucent LB $27.45 (1-56006-155-3). A clearly written introduction to the composition, responsibilities, and problems of Congress. (Rev: BL 6/1–15/94) [328.73]

9836 Richie, Jason. *Secretaries of State: Making Foreign Policy* (7–10). Illus. Series: Cabinet. 2002, Oliver LB $22.95 (1-881508-65-X). Succinct profiles of eight secretaries of state, ranging chronologically from John Quincy Adams to James Baker, look at their beliefs and how they influenced the nation's foreign policy. Also recommended in this series is *Secretaries of War, Navy, and Defense: Ensuring National Security* (2002). (Rev: BL 10/15/02; HBG 3/03; SLJ 4/03) [327.73]

9837 Ritchie, Donald A. *The Congress of the United States: A Student Companion.* 2nd ed. (8–12). Series: Oxford Student Companions to American Government. 2002, Oxford LB $45.00 (0-19-515007-4). An alphabetically arranged series of articles covering all aspects of Congress, illustrated with photographs, maps, and reproductions. (Rev: SLJ 5/02) [328.73]

9838 Sandak, Cass R. *Congressional Committees* (7–9). Series: Inside Government. 1995, Twenty-First Century LB $24.90 (0-8050-3425-0). An overview of how congressional committees came into existence and their role, including how they control legislation. (Rev: BL 12/15/95; SLJ 1/96) [336.73]

9839 Sandak, Cass R. *Lobbying* (7–9). Series: Inside Government. 1995, Twenty-First Century LB $24.90 (0-8050-3424-2). A look at how legislation is influenced, including a brief history of lobbies and descriptions of domestic and foreign public interest groups. (Rev: BL 12/15/95; SLJ 1/96) [328.73]

9840 Sandak, Cass R. *The National Debt* (5–8). Series: Inside Government. 1996, Twenty-First Century LB $22.40 (0-8050-3423-4). The origins and causes of the national debt are covered, with options for the future. (Rev: BL 5/15/96; BR 9–10/96; SLJ 8/96) [336.3]

State and Municipal Governments and Agencies

9841 Feinberg, Barbara S. *State Governments* (4–8). Illus. Series: First Books. 1993, Watts LB $22.00 (0-531-20154-6). Introduces the various parts of a state government, explains how each works, and stresses the need for cooperation among the components. (Rev: SLJ 1/94) [320]

9842 Gorrell, Gena K. *Catching Fire: The Story of Firefighting* (7–10). 1999, Tundra paper $16.95 (0-88776-430-4). This is a history of firefighting, from the bucket brigades of the past to the sophisticated equipment of today, with related information on how fires burn, important fires in history, equipment, firefighting tactics, forms of arson, wildfires, and more. (Rev: BCCB 5/99; BL 6/1–15/99; SLJ 6/99) [363.3]

9843 Levinson, Isabel Simone. *Gibbons v. Ogden: Controlling Trade Between States* (8–10). Series: Landmark Supreme Court Cases. 1999, Enslow LB $20.95 (0-7660-1086-4). States' rights and autonomy were the subject of this important Supreme Court case that focused on trade between the states. (Rev: BL 8/99) [353]

9844 Ryan, Bernard. *Serving with Police, Fire, and EMS* (7–12). Series: Community Service for Teens. 1998, Ferguson LB $15.95 (0-89434-232-0). This work explains how teens can play an active and productive role in police, fire, and allied community agencies. (Rev: BL 9/15/98; BR 11–12/98; SLJ 2/99) [361.8]

Libraries and Other Educational Institutions

9845 Lerner, Fred. *Libraries Through the Ages* (7–10). Illus. 1999, Continuum $15.95 (0-8264-1201-7). A history of libraries, the books they hold, and their readers, adapted from the adult title *The Story of Libraries*. (Rev: BL 11/15/99) [027]

9846 Thomson, Peggy, and Barbara Moore. *The Nine-Ton Cat: Behind the Scenes at an Art Museum* (5–10). 1997, Houghton paper $14.95 (0-395-82683-7). An inside look at the workings of the National Gallery in Washington, with descriptions in photographs and text of the contributions of workers including curators, conservators, and gardeners. (Rev: BCCB 4/97; BL 3/15/97*; HB 5–6/97; SLJ 4/97) [069]

The Law and the Courts

9847 Aaseng, Nathan. *The O. J. Simpson Trial: What It Shows Us About Our Legal System* (6–9). 1996, Walker LB $16.85 (0-8027-8405-4). The author uses the Simpson trial to explain such aspects of the American judicial system as investigative techniques, the grand jury, defense, prosecution, the media's role, and emerging technologies. (Rev: BL 5/1/96; SLJ 4/96) [345.73]

9848 Aaseng, Nathan. *You Are the Juror* (6–10). 1997, Oliver LB $19.95 (1-881508-40-4). The author re-creates eight famous criminal trials of the 20th century, including the Lindbergh kidnapping case, the Patty Hearst and O. J. Simpson trials, and the Ford Pinto case, and asks the reader to become a jury member and make a decision. (Rev: SLJ 1/98) [347.73]

9849 Aaseng, Nathan. *You Are the Supreme Court Justice* (7–10). Illus. Series: Great Decisions. 1994, Oliver LB $19.95 (1-881508-14-5). A description of how the Supreme Court works and the decisions and responsibilities involved in being a Justice. (Rev: BL 11/15/94; SLJ 12/94) [347.73]

9850 Alonso, Karen. *The Alger Hiss Communist Spy Trial* (6–10). Series: Headline Court Cases. 2001, Enslow LB $20.95 (0-7660-1481-9). Alonso provides a clear explanation of the political climate of the time and of the intricacies of this important trial, with a glossary, discussion questions, and excerpts from recently declassified documents. (Rev: BL 12/15/01; HBG 3/02; SLJ 11/01) [345]

9851 Alonso, Karen. *Loving v. Virginia: Interracial Marriage* (7–12). Series: Landmark Supreme Court Cases. 2000, Enslow LB $19.95 (0-7660-1338-3). A thorough examination of the case that overturned Virginia's law forbidding interracial marriage. (Rev: HBG 3/01; SLJ 10/00) [346.7301]

9852 Anderson, Kelly C. *Police Brutality* (6–10). Series: Overview. 1995, Lucent LB $27.45 (1-56006-164-2). A discussion of the reasons for police behavior, the stress and danger of the job and the possible misuse of power. (Rev: BL 4/15/95; SLJ 3/95) [363.2]

9853 Andryszewski, Tricia. *School Prayer: A History of the Debate* (8–12). Illus. Series: Issues in Focus. 1997, Enslow LB $20.95 (0-89490-904-5). A thorough, balanced account that explores all sides of the controversy concerning school prayer, with material on the separation of church and state. (Rev: BL 10/1/97; SLJ 3/98; VOYA 2/98) [344.73]

9854 Arnest, Lauren Krohn. *Children, Young Adults, and the Law: A Dictionary* (8–12). 1998, ABC-CLIO LB $55.00 (0-87436-879-0). Using a dictionary arrangement, this volume contains about 200 articles on legal issues involving children and young adults, with entries on important court cases and decisions. (Rev: BL 10/15/98; SLJ 2/99; VOYA 6/99) [346.73]

9855 Berger, Leslie. *The Grand Jury* (7–12). Illus. Series: Crime, Justice, and Punishment. 2000, Chelsea $21.95 (0-7910-4290-1). This work traces the history of the grand jury system, outlines procedures at the local and national level, and cites famous grand jury hearings including the Monica Lewinsky case. (Rev: BL 8/00) [345.73]

9856 Bernstein, Richard B., and Jerome Agel. *The Supreme Court* (8–12). Illus. 1989, Walker LB $13.85 (0-8027-6835-0). An account that gives a history of the Supreme Court, details on landmark cases, and an outline of how it operates today. (Rev: BL 5/1/89; BR 3–4/89; SLJ 1/89; VOYA 4/89) [347]

9857 Billitteri, Thomas J. *The Gault Case: Legal Rights for Young People* (7–12). Series: Landmark Supreme Court Cases. 2000, Enslow LB $20.95 (0-7660-1340-5). Children's rights and due process were the focus of this 1960s case — involving a 15-year-old — that was eventually decided by the Supreme Court. (Rev: HBG 3/01; SLJ 2/01) [345.73]

9858 Calabro, Marian. *Great Courtroom Lawyers: Fighting the Cases That Made History* (6–9). 1996, Facts on File $25.00 (0-8160-3323-4). This book provides profiles of nine important lawyers, including Clarence Darrow, Thurgood Marshall, and William Kunstler, and presents highlights of such important cases as Roe v. Wade and the O. J. Simpson trial. (Rev: BL 10/15/96; VOYA 6/97) [349.73]

9859 Campbell, Andrew. *Rights of the Accused* (7–10). Series: Crime, Justice, and Punishment. 2001, Chelsea LB $19.95 (0-7910-4303-7). A cleverly written, informative exploration of how and why the judicial system tries to safeguard the rights of accused criminals. (Rev: BL 6/1–15/01; HBG 3/01; SLJ 2/01; VOYA 12/01) [345]

9860 Campbell, Geoffrey A. *The Pentagon Papers: National Security Versus the Public's Right to Know* (6–9). Illus. Series: Famous Trials. 2000, Lucent LB $18.96 (1-56006-692-X). Campbell relates the Nixon administration's efforts to stop the *New York Times* from publishing secret government documents relating to the war in Vietnam. (Rev: BL 9/15/00; HBG 3/01; SLJ 10/00) [347.3]

9861 Carrel, Annette. *It's the Law! A Young Person's Guide to Our Legal System* (8–12). 1994, Volcano Pr. paper $12.95 (1-884244-01-7). The book's goal is voter responsibility through understanding of the laws, how they developed, and how they can be changed. (Rev: BL 2/15/95; VOYA 12/95) [349.73]

9862 Chadwick, Bruce. *Infamous Trials* (6–9). Illus. Series: Crime, Justice, and Punishment. 1997, Chelsea LB $21.95 (0-7910-4293-6). This book highlights eight cases in the history of American justice, from the Salem witchcraft trials to the Chicago Seven, including Benedict Arnold's court-martial, the Scopes "monkey trial," and the Scottsboro boys. (Rev: BL 9/1/97; BR 11–12/97; SLJ 10/97) [345.73]

9863 Ciment, James. *Law and Order* (6–9). Series: Life in America 100 Years Ago. 1995, Chelsea LB $21.95 (0-7910-2843-7). An examination of how the rule of law was established in the U.S. and how basic institutions involving the courts, law enforcement officials, and the legal profession evolved. (Rev: BL 2/1/96) [349.73]

9864 Cothran, Helen, ed. *Police Brutality* (7–12). Illus. Series: Opposing Viewpoints. 2001, Greenhaven LB $22.96 (0-7377-0516-7); paper $14.96 (0-7377-0515-9). Contributors address various aspects of police conduct and overview, with a special interest in the treatment of teen suspects and a focus on New York City and Los Angeles. (Rev: BL 5/15/01) [363.2]

9865 Day, Nancy. *The Death Penalty for Teens: A Pro/Con Issue* (6–10). Illus. Series: Hot Pro/Con Issues. 2000, Enslow LB $19.95 (0-7660-1370-7). Strong, opposing opinions on juvenile justice and the death penalty are accompanied by a historical overview and comparisons between the United States and other countries. (Rev: BL 2/15/01; HBG 3/01; SLJ 4/01; VOYA 6/01) [364.66]

9866 DeVillers, David. *The John Brown Slavery Revolt Trial: A Headline Court Case* (8–12). 2000, Enslow $20.95 (0-7660-1385-5). An account of the trial of the abolitionist who was hanged for treason and murder. (Rev: HBG 3/01; SLJ 9/00) [306.3]

9867 DeVillers, David. *Marbury v. Madison: Powers of the Supreme Court* (6–10). Series: Landmark Supreme Court Cases. 1998, Enslow LB $20.95 (0-89490-967-3). The steps, arguments, and personalities in this early court case that helped define the powers of the Supreme Court. (Rev: BL 2/15/98; SLJ 6/98) [3437]

9868 Dudley, Mark E. *Engel v. Vitale (1962): Religion and the Schools* (5–9). Series: Supreme Court Decisions. 1995, Twenty-First Century LB $25.90 (0-8050-3916-3). The story of the Supreme Court case on school prayer that originated with two Jewish youngsters who objected to being forced to pray every morning in a New York City school. (Rev: BL 11/15/95; SLJ 1/96; VOYA 4/96) [347]

9869 Dudley, Mark E. *Gideon v. Wainwright (1963): Right to Counsel* (6–10). Series: Supreme Court Decisions. 1995, Twenty-First Century LB $25.90 (0-8050-3914-7). Reviews how the case was built, argued, and decided, and discusses its impact. (Rev: BL 6/1–15/95; SLJ 8/95) [347.3]

9870 Dudley, Mark E. *United States v. Nixon (1974)* (6–10). Illus. Series: Supreme Court Decisions. 1994, Twenty-First Century LB $25.90 (0-8050-3658-X). This landmark Supreme Court case concerning the definition of presidential powers is reported on in a step-by-step analysis of the arguments in the Watergate case. (Rev: BL 12/15/94; SLJ 2/95) [342.73]

9871 Egendorf, Laura K., ed. *The Death Penalty* (7–12). Illus. Series: Examining Issues Through Political Cartoons. 2002, Gale $24.95 (0-7377-1102-7); paper $16.20 (0-7377-1101-9). Egendorf uses cartoons focusing on the death penalty as the basis for a discussion of the controversies surrounding this practice. Also recommended in this series is *Euthanasia* (2002). (Rev: BL 8/02) [364.44]

9872 Freedman, Suzanne. *United States v. Amistad: Rebellion on a Slave Ship* (6–9). Series: Landmark Supreme Court Cases. 2000, Enslow LB $20.95 (0-7660-1337-5). A look at the slave rebellion from the perspective of the trial that followed, laying out the presentations of the prosecution and defense. (Rev: HBG 3/01; SLJ 2/01)

9873 Gold, Susan D. *Miranda v. Arizona (1966)* (6–10). Series: Supreme Court Decisions. 1995, Twenty-First Century LB $25.90 (0-8050-3915-5). This book describes the court case that defined the rights of suspects, with good historical background and a discussion of its impact through 1994. (Rev: BL 6/1–15/95; SLJ 8/95) [345.73]

9874 Gottfried, Ted. *Capital Punishment: The Death Penalty Debate* (6–12). Illus. Series: Issues in Focus. 1997, Enslow LB $20.95 (0-89490-899-5). The author presents strong arguments on all sides of the death penalty controversy, including material on its history, moral justification, purpose, legal procedures, and questions of race and geography. (Rev: BL 2/1/97; SLJ 7/97) [345.73]

9875 Gottfried, Ted. *The Death Penalty: Justice or Legalized Murder?* (7–12). Illus. 2002, Twenty-First Century LB $24.90 (0-7613-2155-1). Gottfried presents an absorbing and balanced examination of the arguments for and against the death penalty, with historical information and details of specific cases. (Rev: BL 3/15/02; HBG 10/02; SLJ 3/02) [364.66]

9876 Gottfried, Ted. *Police Under Fire* (7–12). Illus. 1999, Twenty-First Century LB $22.90 (0-7613-1313-3). A well-balanced account that gives a history of policing, police culture, pressures on police personnel, corruption, and cases of police brutality. (Rev: BL 12/15/99; HBG 4/00; SLJ 1/00) [363.2]

9877 Grabowski, John F. *The Death Penalty* (5–8). Series: Overview. 1999, Lucent LB $27.45 (1-56006-371-8). A fair, unbiased review of the history, pro and con arguments, and present status of the death penalty in America. (Rev: BL 8/99) [364.6]

9878 Haas, Carol. *Engel v. Vitale: Separation of Church and State* (6–10). 1994, Enslow LB $20.95 (0-89490-461-2). A discussion of the arguments presented by both sides in this landmark Supreme Court case concerning the separation of church and state as it applies to religion in public schools. (Rev: BL 11/15/94; VOYA 12/94) [344.73]

9879 Hanson, Freya Ottem. *The Scopes Monkey Trial: A Headline Court Case* (6–10). Illus. Series: Headline Court Cases. 2000, Enslow LB $20.95 (0-7660-1388-X). The story of the famous trial of a Tennessee high school teacher for teaching evolution. (Rev: BL 10/1/00; HBG 3/01; SLJ 9/00) [345.73]

9880 Harmon, Daniel E. *Defense Lawyers* (7–10). Series: Crime, Justice, and Punishment. 2001, Chelsea LB $21.95 (0-7910-4284-7). This introduction to the roles of defense attorney and public defender provides brief profiles of figures including Clarence Darrow and Alan Dershowitz. (Rev: HBG 10/02; SLJ 4/02) [345.73]

9881 Henson, Burt, and Ross R. Olney. *Furman v. Georgia: The Constitution and the Death Penalty* (7–10). Series: Historic Supreme Court Cases. 1996, Watts LB $25.00 (0-531-11285-3). In this 1972 case, the Supreme Court ruled that the imposition of the death penalty as then applied was unconstitutional. This account gives the legal background, a history of capital punishment, and pros and cons of the death penalty. (Rev: SLJ 4/97) [345]

9882 Herda, D. J. *Furman v. Georgia: The Death Penalty Case* (6–10). Series: Landmark Supreme Court Cases. 1994, Enslow LB $20.95 (0-89490-489-2). Summarizes the historical background of this case, the case itself, and the impact it has had. (Rev: BL 11/15/94; SLJ 11/94) [345.73]

9883 Herda, D. J. *New York Times v. United States: National Security and Censorship* (6–10). Illus. Series: Landmark Supreme Court Cases. 1994, Enslow LB $20.95 (0-89490-490-6). This exciting, controversial Supreme Court case involved the Pentagon Papers and helped define freedom of the press when it conflicts with what may be considered national security. (Rev: BL 11/15/94; SLJ 1/95) [342.73]

9884 Herda, D. J. *Roe v. Wade: The Abortion Question* (6–10). Illus. Series: Landmark Supreme Court Cases. 1994, Enslow LB $20.95 (0-89490-459-0). This book describes the arguments on both sides of the abortion debate, how the justices of the Supreme Court reacted, their decision, and its consequences. (Rev: BL 6/1–15/94; SLJ 7/94; VOYA 8/94) [344.73]

9885 Jacobs, Thomas A. *Teens on Trial: Young People Who Challenged the Law — and Changed Your Life* (8–12). 2000, Free Spirit paper $14.95 (1-57542-081-3). Student rights and responsibilities are explored through this examination of 21 cases in which teens participated in the legal process. (Rev: BL 1/1–15/01; SLJ 1/01; VOYA 4/01) [346.7301]

9886 Jones-Brown, Delores D. *Race, Crime, and Punishment* (7–12). Illus. Series: Crime, Justice, and Punishment. 2000, Chelsea $19.95 (0-7910-4273-1). This book explores the double standard often applied to black and white offenders and also discusses police brutality as related to race. (Rev: BL 8/00; HBG 9/00) [364]

9887 Kraft, Betsy H. *Sensational Trials of the 20th Century* (6–10). Illus. 1998, Scholastic paper $16.95 (0-590-37205-X). This book profiles eight important American trials including Sacco and Vanzetti, the Rosenbergs, Scopes, Watergate, O. J. Simpson, and John Hinckley. (Rev: BL 3/1/99; HBG 3/99; SLJ 11/98; VOYA 6/99) [347.73]

9888 Kronenwetter, Michael. *The Supreme Court of the United States* (7–10). Series: American Government in Action. 1996, Enslow LB $20.95 (0-89490-536-8). After presenting an example of the power of the Supreme Court, the author describes the judicial system and a brief history of the court, discusses how it operates and the increasingly political nature of appointments and decisions, and details some of its most significant decisions. (Rev: SLJ 5/96) [347]

9889 Kuklin, Susan. *Trial: The Inside Story* (8–12). Illus. 2001, Holt $17.95 (0-8050-6457-5). The story of a kidnapping of illegal Chinese immigrants and the subsequent trial is used to illustrate legal concepts, the trial process, and the roles of attorneys, police, and witnesses. (Rev: BL 12/15/00; HBG 10/01; SLJ 1/01; VOYA 2/01) [345.73]

9890 Loren, Julia C. *Engel v. Vitale: Prayer in the Public Schools* (6–9). Series: Famous Trials. 2001, Lucent LB $27.45 (1-56006-732-2). This engrossing narrative covers the people and issues of the 1962 Supreme Court case concerning the constitutionality of prayer in American public schools. (Rev: BL 12/15/01; SLJ 7/01) [322]

9891 Manaugh, Sara. *Judges and Sentencing* (7–10). Series: Crime, Justice, and Punishment. 2001, Chelsea LB $21.95 (0-7910-4296-0). An introduction to the role of judges and to the sentencing process, with material on sentencing reform. (Rev: HBG 10/02; SLJ 4/02) [345.73]

9892 Mitchell, Hayley R., ed. *The Death Penalty* (6–12). Illus. Series: Complete History Of. 2001, Greenhaven LB $99.00 (0-7377-0426-8). This anthology provides a well-organized and balanced look at the death penalty, with selections that offer differing viewpoints. (Rev: BL 11/1/01; SLJ 8/01) [364.6]

9893 Mitchell, Hayley R., ed. *The Death Penalty* (7–12). Series: Contemporary Issues Companion. 2001, Greenhaven LB $17.96 (0-7377-0458-6); paper $11.96 (0-7377-0457-8). Diverse viewpoints on the death penalty are presented in this well-organized text, which includes historical, legal, and personal insights. (Rev: BL 3/1/01; SLJ 4/01) [364.66]

9894 Monroe, Judy. *The Sacco and Vanzetti Controversial Murder Trial: A Headline Court Case* (6–10). Illus. Series: Headline Court Cases. 2000, Enslow $19.95 (0-7660-1387-1). The story of the murder trials of two Italian immigrants in 1921, the long-questioned conviction, and the abuse and protection of suspects' rights then and today. (Rev: BL 10/1/00; BR 1–2/01; HBG 9/00; SLJ 1/01) [345.73]

9895 Moss, Francis. *The Rosenberg Espionage Case* (6–9). Illus. Series: Famous Trials. 1999, Lucent LB $18.96 (1-56006-578-8). A well-rounded account of this controversial trial that had overtones of cold war hysteria and anti-Semitism. (Rev: BL 3/1/00; HBG 9/00; SLJ 4/00) [345.73.]

9896 Netzley, Patricia D. *Issues in Crime* (7–10). Illus. Series: Contemporary Issues. 2000, Lucent LB $18.96 (1-56006-480-3). A general presentation of issues that pit the rights of individuals against the rights of society, such as gun control, mandatory sentencing, and juvenile justice rules. (Rev: HBG 9/00; SLJ 8/00) [364.973]

9897 Owens, L. L. *American Justice: Seven Famous Trials of the 20th Century* (6–8). Illus. Series: Cover-to-Cover. 2000, Perfection Learning $13.95 (0-7807-7831-6); paper $8.95 (0-7891-2869-1). Kidnappings, murder, and a classic civil rights case are among the trials presented here. (Rev: BL 1/1–15/01) [345.73]

9898 Paddock, Lisa. *Facts About the Supreme Court of the United States* (8–12). 1996, H.W. Wilson $105.00 (0-8242-0896-X). A one-stop reference source for information about the Supreme Court,

from individual justices to the court's history and important cases. (Rev: VOYA 12/96) [347]

9899 Peacock, Nancy. *Great Prosecutions* (8–12). Illus. Series: Crime, Justice, and Punishment. 2001, Chelsea LB $21.95 (0-7910-4292-8). Accounts of five famous trials — including those of the Manson "family" and Al Capone — show readers how prosecutors work to prove guilt. (Rev: BL 1/1–15/02) [345]

9900 Pellowski, Michael J. *The O. J. Simpson Murder Trial: A Headline Court Case* (7–12). Series: Headline Court Cases. 2001, Enslow LB $20.95 (0-7660-1480-0). An objective summary of the murder investigation, the murder trial and the civil trial, the personalities involved. (Rev: HBG 3/02; SLJ 12/01) [345.73]

9901 Persico, Deborah A. *Mapp vs. Ohio: Evidence and Search Warrants* (6–10). Illus. Series: Landmark Supreme Court Cases. 1997, Enslow LB $20.95 (0-89490-857-X). A step-by-step account of the Supreme Court decision that established a citizen's rights concerning search warrants and the collection of evidence. (Rev: BL 4/15/97; SLJ 6/97) [345.73]

9902 Persico, Deborah A. *New Jersey v. T.L.O.: Drug Searches in Schools* (7–12). Illus. Series: Landmark Supreme Court Cases. 1998, Enslow LB $20.95 (0-89490-969-X). This Supreme Court case lasted five years and explored the rights of a student, identified as T.L.O., whose handbag was searched by a school administrator who found marijuana and articles that indicated the student was selling drugs. (Rev: BL 8/98; HBG 9/98; SLJ 8/98; VOYA 2/99) [345.73]

9903 Persico, Deborah A. *Vernonia School District v. Acton: Drug Testing in Schools* (7–12). Series: Landmark Supreme Court Cases. 1999, Enslow LB $19.95 (0-7660-1087-2). An examination of an Oregon court case involving random drug testing introduces the reader to important legal concepts. (Rev: HBG 4/00; SLJ 1/00) [344.73]

9904 Reef, Catherine. *The Supreme Court* (4–7). Illus. Series: Places in American History. 1994, Dillon paper $7.95 (0-382-24722-1). An introduction to the Supreme Court, its powers, composition, and landmark decisions. (Rev: BL 1/1/95) [347.73]

9905 Riley, Gail B. *Miranda v. Arizona: Rights of the Accused* (6–10). Illus. 1994, Enslow LB $18.95 (0-89490-404-X). This account analyzes the Supreme Court case that defined the rights of an accused person based on what became known as Miranda rights. (Rev: BL 11/15/94) [345.73]

9906 Roleff, Tamara L., ed. *The Legal System* (8–12). Series: Opposing Viewpoints. 1996, Greenhaven LB $26.20 (1-56510-405-6); paper $16.20 (1-56510-404-8). This collection of original sources tackles such questions as: Does the legal system work? Does it need reforms? Is there too much litigation in this country? Is the criminal justice system fair? and How do the media affect the legal system? (Rev: BL 7/96) [347.73]

9907 Schonebaum, Steve, ed. *Does Capital Punishment Deter Crime?* (8–12). Series: At Issue. 1998, Greenhaven LB $26.20 (1-56510-791-8); paper $17.45 (1-56510-091-3). This anthology presents arguments by those who maintain the death penalty deters crime and by others with statistics, studies, and other evidence that point to the opposite conclusion. (Rev: BL 6/1–15/98) [364.6]

9908 Steffens, Bradley. *Furman v. Georgia: Fairness and the Death Penalty* (6–9). Series: Famous Trials. 2001, Lucent LB $27.45 (1-56006-470-6). The Supreme Court case of 1972 that stuck down the death penalty as cruel and unusual punishment is investigated with good background material and information about this case's significance. (Rev: BL 12/15/01) [345]

9909 Steins, Richard. *The Death Penalty: Is It Justice?* (6–9). Series: Issues of Our Time. 1993, Twenty-First Century LB $22.90 (0-8050-2571-5). Jumping off from Gary Gilmore's execution, this book looks at the death penalty through history and presents the current debate. (Rev: BL 11/1/93) [364.6]

9910 Stevens, Leonard A. *The Case of Roe v. Wade* (8–12). 1996, Putnam $16.99 (0-399-22812-8). Complete with fascinating details and numerous quotations, this account gives an objective account of this landmark court case and its ramifications. (Rev: BL 10/1/96*; BR 11–12/96; SLJ 1/97; VOYA 12/96) [344.73]

9911 Tompkins, Nancy. *Roe v. Wade: The Fight over Life and Liberty* (7–12). Illus. Series: Supreme Court Cases. 1996, Watts LB $25.00 (0-531-11286-1). This account of the landmark Supreme Court case focuses on the case itself and the controversy that the decision has caused. (Rev: BL 2/1/97; SLJ 2/97) [344.73]

9912 Trespacz, Karen L. *Ferrell v. Dallas I. S. D.* (6–10). Series: Landmark Supreme Court Cases. 1998, Enslow LB $20.95 (0-7660-1054-6). The dramatic story of the school district case that was adjudicated by the Supreme Court. (Rev: BL 8/98; BR 11–12/98; HBG 3/99; SLJ 1/99; VOYA 2/99) [347]

9913 Truly, Traci. *Teen Rights: A Legal Guide for Teens and the Adults in Their Lives* (7–12). 2002, Sphinx paper $22.95 (1-57248-221-4). This book examines issues and outcomes of legal actions of specific interest to young adults. (Rev: BL 1/1–15/03; SLJ 11/02) [346.7301]

9914 Wice, Paul B. *Miranda v. Arizona* (7–12). Series: Historic Supreme Court Cases. 1996, Watts LB $25.00 (0-531-11250-0). A reconstruction of the important Supreme Court case in which a confession was judged invalid because the suspect had not been informed of his rights. (Rev: SLJ 9/96) [347]

9915 Wolf, Robert V. *Capital Punishment* (6–9). Series: Crime, Justice, and Punishment. 1997, Chelsea $21.95 (0-7910-4311-8). This book reviews the history of capital punishment, explores the moral, philosophical, and legal issues involved, and presents case studies of several death-row inmates. (Rev: BR 1–2/98; SLJ 2/98) [364.6]

9916 Worth, Richard. *The Insanity Defense* (7–10). Series: Crime, Justice, and Punishment. 2001, Chelsea LB $19.95 (0-7910-4294-4). After some historical background material, this account uses specific examples to explore facets of the question, how far does mental illness go in excusing criminal behavior. (Rev: BL 6/1–15/01; HBG 10/01; SLJ 7/01; VOYA 6/02) [345]

Politics

GENERAL AND MISCELLANEOUS

9917 Archer, Jules. *Special Interests: How Lobbyists Influence Legislation* (7–12). Illus. 1997, Millbrook LB $24.90 (0-7613-0060-0). This timely account looks at special interest groups, why lobbyists have so much power, how lobbies were created, and the role they play in influencing policy. (Rev: BL 12/15/97; BR 3–4/98; SLJ 1/98; VOYA 2/98) [324]

9918 Audryszewski, Tricia. *The Reform Party* (5–8). Series: Headliners. 2000, Millbrook LB $25.90 (0-7613-1906-9). This book describes the formation of the Reform Party and highlights the work of Ross Perot, Pat Buchanan, and Jesse Ventura. (Rev: BL 8/00; HBG 10/01; SLJ 1/01) [324.273]

9919 Boyers, Sara Jane. *Teen Power Politics: Make Yourself Heard* (7–12). 2000, Twenty-First Century LB $25.90 (0-7613-1307-9); paper $9.95 (0-7613-1391-5). An in-depth and inspiring look at the ways in which teens too young to vote can nonetheless exert their influence. (Rev: BR 3–4/01; HBG 3/01; SLJ 1/01; VOYA 4/01) [323]

9920 Cozic, Charles P., ed. *Politicians and Ethics* (7–12). Series: Current Controversies. 1996, Greenhaven LB $32.45 (1-56510-407-2). This collection of original sources covers various points of view concerning the behavior and ethics of politicians, the problems of scrutiny, and the degree that legal measures should be used. (Rev: BL 6/1–15/96) [172]

9921 Gay, Kathlyn. *Who's Running the Nation? How Corporate Power Threatens Democracy* (7–12). Series: Impact. 1998, Watts LB $23.00 (0-531-11489-9). In this analysis of business influence on government, the author explains in a fairly objective tone exactly how corporations use campaign contributions and lobbying to influence policies, and demonstrates how this disenfranchises ordinary citizens. (Rev: HBG 3/99; SLJ 3/99) [324.2]

9922 Kronenwetter, Michael. *Political Parties of the United States* (6–9). Illus. 1996, Enslow LB $20.95 (0-89490-537-6). A history of political parties and how they function plus how they influence every aspect of the country's political life. (Rev: BL 6/1–15/96; BR 9–10/96; SLJ 6/96) [324.273]

9923 Lindop, Edmund. *Political Parties* (5–8). Series: Inside Government. 1996, Twenty-First Century LB $24.90 (0-8050-4618-6). This work traces the origins of political parties and the role they play in presidential elections. (Rev: BL 9/15/96; SLJ 12/96) [324.273]

9924 Lutz, Norma Jean. *The History of the Republican Party* (7–9). Series: Your Government: How It Works. 2000, Chelsea LB $17.95 (0-7910-5540-X). A look at the history and structure of the Republican Party, with anecdotes and information on key figures. (Rev: HBG 9/00; SLJ 8/00) [324.2734]

9925 Morin, Isobel V. *Politics, American Style: Political Parties in American History* (6–12). Illus. 1999, Twenty-First Century $24.90 (0-7613-1267-6). An engaging account of the history of American political parties, accompanied by political cartoons. (Rev: BL 11/15/99; HBG 4/00; SLJ 1/00) [324.273]

9926 Winters, Paul A., ed. *The Media and Politics* (8–12). 1996, Greenhaven LB $11.95 (1-56510-383-6); paper $17.45 (1-56510-382-3). A collection of articles about the relationship between the media and politics and how messages can be influenced by the agendas of journalists, politicians, and special interest groups. (Rev: BL 3/15/96; SLJ 4/96; VOYA 8/96) [302.23]

9927 Zeinert, Karen. *Women in Politics: In the Running* (6–9). 2002, Twenty-First Century LB $29.90 (0-7613-2253-1). From 1774 to the present, the author looks at women who have been elected to office or who have been influential in the political field, and discusses the possibility of a woman president. (Rev: BL 12/1/02; HBG 3/03; SLJ 11/02) [320]

ELECTIONS

9928 Gottfried, Ted. *The 2000 Election* (5–8). Illus. 2002, Millbrook LB $25.90 (0-7613-2406-2). A well-designed and detailed look at the controversial presidential election of 2000, with background information, sidebars on important people, and an electoral map and other graphics. (Rev: BL 7/02; HBG 10/02; SLJ 4/02) [324.973]

9929 Hewson, Martha S. *The Electoral College* (5–9). 2002, Chelsea $19.75 (0-7910-6790-4). Covers the history of the electoral college and details of elections of particular interest, including the 2000 Bush–Gore decision. (Rev: HBG 3/03; SLJ 2/03) [324.6]

9930 Israel, Fred L. *Student's Atlas of American Presidential Elections 1789 to 1996* (7–12). 1997, Congressional Quarterly $45.00 (1-56802-377-4). Each of the 53 presidential elections in U.S. history are described on a page or two, accompanied by maps to illustrate election results. (Rev: BL 11/15/97; SLJ 11/97) [973]

9931 Reische, Diana. *Electing a U.S. President* (7–12). 1992, Watts paper $24.00 (0-531-11043-5). A straightforward look at the presidential campaign process and the people involved in it. (Rev: BL 4/15/92; SLJ 8/92) [324.0973]

9932 Winters, Paul A., ed. *Voting Behavior* (8–12). Series: At Issue. 1996, Greenhaven LB $26.20 (1-56510-413-7); paper $23.95 (1-56510-412-9). Various opinions are represented on such topics as citizen participation in a democracy, the role of public opinion polls and the media, and the significance of campaign politics. (Rev: BL 8/96; SLJ 8/96; VOYA 12/96) [324.973]

The Armed Forces

9933 Aaseng, Nathan. *You Are the General* (7–12). Illus. Series: Great Decisions. 1994, Oliver $14.95 (1-881-50811-0). This book deals with decisions that have to be made by members of the military, with many examples. (Rev: BL 6/1–15/94) [355]

9934 Doherty, Kieran. *Congressional Medal of Honor Recipients* (6–9). Illus. 1998, Enslow LB $20.95 (0-7660-1026-0). This work profiles 11 winners of this prestigious medal, beginning with Jacob Parrott, who earned the first medal in 1863. (Rev: BL 3/15/98) [355.1]

9935 Fine, Jil. *Life Inside the Naval Academy* (7–12). Series: Insider's Look. 2002, Children's LB $20.00 (0-516-23922-8); paper $6.95 (0-516-24005-6). The story of the Naval Academy at Annapolis, Maryland, and of its history, traditions, and programs. (Rev: BL 10/15/02) [359]

9936 Goldberg, Jan. *Green Berets: The U.S. Army Special Forces* (5–7). Series: Inside Special Operations. 2003, Rosen LB $19.95 (0-8239-3808-5). An overview of the history, mission, training, and equipment of the Special Forces. (Rev: BL 7/03) [356]

9937 McNab, Chris. *Protecting the Nation with the U.S. Army* (6–10). Series: Rescue and Prevention: Defending Our Nation. 2003, Mason Crest LB $22.95 (1-59084-414-9). This series about the specific roles the various services play in defending

U.S. interests at home and abroad also discusses each service's history, structure, equipment, and recent operations. Also use *Protecting the Nation with the U.S. Air Force* and *Protecting the Nation with the U.S. Navy* (2003). (Rev: SLJ 7/03) [355]

9938 Stremlow, Mary V. *Coping with Sexism in the Military* (7–12). 1990, Rosen LB $17.95 (0-8239-1025-3). An analysis of the military from the per-spective of the female recruit that reflects conditions in the late 1980s. (Rev: BL 2/15/91) [355]

9939 Worth, Richard. *Women in Combat: The Battle for Equality* (7–12). Series: Issues in Focus. 1999, Enslow LB $20.95 (0-7660-1103-8). A study of the changing role of women in the armed forces from the First World War to the Gulf War. (Rev: BL 5/1/99) [355]

Citizenship and Civil Rights

General and Miscellaneous

9940 Luthringer, Chelsea. *So What Is Citizenship Anyway?* (5–8). Series: A Student's Guide to American Civics. 1999, Rosen LB $23.95 (0-8239-3097-1). Describes and defines the roles and responsibilities of citizens in a democracy and encourages young people to become active in political and social affairs and issues. (Rev: HBG 10/00; SLJ 3/00; VOYA 4/00) [323.6]

9941 Meltzer, Milton. *Ain't Gonna Study War No More: The Story of America's Peace Seekers* (6–9). Illus. 2002, Random LB $10.99 (0-375-92260-1); paper $5.99 (0-375-82260-7). This revision of a title first published in 1985 updates the story of the peace movement in America and adds a discussion guide and conversation with the author. (Rev: BL 10/15/02; HBG 10/03) [303.6]

Civil and Human Rights

9942 Adams, Colleen. *Women's Suffrage: A Primary Source History of the Women's Rights Movement in America* (5–8). Illus. Series: Primary Sources in American History. 2003, Rosen LB $29.25 (0-8239-3685-6). Primary sources — including pamphlets and newspaper articles — tell the story of the women's rights movement in America. (Rev: BL 5/15/03) [305.42]

9943 Allen, Zita. *Black Women Leaders of the Civil Rights Movement* (6–9). Illus. 1996, Watts LB $23.00 (0-531-11271-3). An overview of the civil rights movement from 1900 to 1964 that focuses on the many and varied contributions that African American women made to the cause. (Rev: BL 2/15/97; SLJ 1/97) [323.3]

9944 Alonso, Karen. *Schenck v. United States: Restrictions on Free Speech* (7–10). Series: Landmark Supreme Court Cases. 1999, Enslow LB $20.95 (0-7660-1089-9). A re-creation of this landmark Supreme Court case that explored the limitations of free speech, including a follow-up on its consequences. (Rev: BL 8/99) [323.44]

9945 Altman, Linda Jacobs. *Human Rights: Issues for a New Millennium* (7–10). 2002, Enslow LB $20.95 (0-7660-1689-7). A general introduction to the topic of human rights, with historical information and a survey of international organizations working in this area today. (Rev: HBG 10/03; SLJ 5/03; VOYA 8/03) [323]

9946 Altman, Linda Jacobs. *Slavery and Abolition in American History* (7–10). Series: In American History. 1999, Enslow LB $19.95 (0-7660-1124-0). A well-researched and well-documented account of slavery and the abolitionist movement in the United States. (Rev: BL 11/15/99; HBG 4/00; SLJ 3/00) [973.7]

9947 Andryszewski, Tricia. *Gay Rights* (6–12). Illus. 2000, Twenty-First Century LB $23.90 (0-7613-1568-3). The author present many viewpoints in this book that discusses gay rights in relation to the law, the military, the church, marriage, the family, government, and politics. (Rev: BL 10/15/00; HBG 10/01; SLJ 10/00; VOYA 12/00) [305.9]

9948 Bender, David, and Bruno Leone, eds. *Feminism* (7–12). Series: Opposing Viewpoints. 1995, Greenhaven paper $16.20 (1-56510-179-0). Essays supporting different viewpoints are presented. Topics include feminism's effects on women and society and its future and goals. (Rev: BL 7/95; SLJ 2/95) [305.42]

9949 Berg, Barbara J. *The Women's Movement and Young Women Today: A Hot Issue* (6–9). Series: Hot Issues. 2000, Enslow LB $19.95 (0-7660-1200-X). A look at the history of the women's movement and at the many inequalities still facing women today. (Rev: HBG 9/00; SLJ 8/00) [305.42]

9950 Booker, Christopher C. *African-Americans and the Presidency: A History of Broken Promises* (6–12). Illus. 2000, Watts $25.00 (0-531-11882-7). A chronological survey of U.S. presidents' promises and actions regarding equal rights for African Americans. (Rev: BL 2/15/01; SLJ 3/01; VOYA 6/01) [973]

9951 Bradley, Catherine. *Freedom of Movement* (5–8). Illus. Series: What Do We Mean by Human Rights? 1998, Watts LB $23.00 (0-531-14447-X). This lavishly illustrated book uses double-page spreads to explore immigration, nationalism, and refugees. (Rev: BL 4/1/98; BR 11–12/98; HBG 10/98) [323]

9952 Bradley, David, and Shelley Fisher Fishkin, eds. *The Encyclopedia of Civil Rights in America* (5–10). 1997, Sharpe Reference $299.00 (0-7656-8000-9). This three-volume set contains 683 alphabetically arranged articles that explore the history, meaning, and application of civil rights issues in the United States. (Rev: SLJ 5/98) [323]

9953 Bridges, Ruby. *Through My Eyes* (3–9). Illus. 1999, Scholastic $16.95 (0-590-18923-9). Ruby Bridges tells what it was like to be the first African American child at an integrated school in 1960; photographs add to the attractive presentation. (Rev: BCCB 1/00*; BL 11/15/99*; HBG 4/00; SLJ 12/99*) [379.2]

9954 Brill, Marlene T. *Women for Peace* (6–10). Series: Women Then — Women Now. 1997, Watts LB $23.00 (0-531-11328-0). A chronicle of the involvement of women in peace movements from ancient Greece to the Vietnam War. (Rev: BL 5/15/97; SLJ 4/97; VOYA 12/97) [327.1]

9955 Bullard, Sara. *Free at Last: A History of the Civil Rights Movement and Those Who Died in the Struggle* (6–10). 1993, Oxford $28.00 (0-19-508381-4). Following an overview of the history of African Americans, an in-depth look at the civil rights movement is presented, with 40 biographies of civil rights martyrs. (Rev: BL 11/1/93; VOYA 8/93) [323.1]

9956 Cary, Eve. *The Rights of Students* (6–12). Series: ACLU Handbooks for Young Americans. 1997, Penguin paper $8.99 (0-14-037784-0). Published with the cooperation of the American Civil Liberties Union, this book outlines the rights of young people at home, at school, and in the workplace. (Rev: BL 1/1–15/98) [344.73]

9957 Ching, Jacqueline, and Juliet Ching. *Women's Rights* (7–9). Illus. Series: Individual Rights and Civic Responsibility. 2001, Rosen LB $19.95 (0-8239-3233-8). A concise account of the struggle for women's rights in America. (Rev: BL 12/1/01) [305.42]

9958 Colbert, Jan, and Ann M. Harms, eds. *Dear Dr. King: Letters from Today's Children to Dr. Martin Luther King, Jr.* (4–7). Illus. 1998, Hyperion $14.95 (0-7868-0417-3). This is a selection of letters written by white and black Memphis schoolchildren to Dr. King, telling him about themselves and how conditions have changed since his death. (Rev: BCCB 5/98; BL 2/15/98; HBG 10/98; SLJ 5/98) [323]

9959 Crowe, Chris. *Getting Away with Murder: The True Story of the Emmett Till Case* (7–12). Illus. 2003, Penguin Putnam $18.99 (0-8037-2804-2). A gripping and detailed account of the brutal murder of 14-year-old Emmett Till, an African American boy from Chicago who was visiting relatives in Mississippi in 1954, with discussion of the impact of his death and the ensuing trial on the civil rights movement. (Rev: BL 2/15/03; HB 7–8/03; HBG 10/03; SLJ 5/03*) [364.15]

9960 Currie, Stephen. *Slavery* (7–12). Series: Opposing Viewpoints Digests. 1998, Greenhaven LB $27.45 (1-56510-881-7); paper $17.45 (1-56510-880-9). Diverse opinions are presented in this anthology on issues related to slavery and human rights, morality, justice, abolition, and resistance. (Rev: BL 4/15/99) [177]

9961 Davidson, Tish. *Prejudice* (4–8). Series: Life Balance. 2003, Watts LB $19.50 (0-531-12252-2); paper $6.95 (0-531-15572-2). This book explore the causes, types, and effects of prejudice, how it can change a person's mental health, and how it has influenced human history. (Rev: BL 10/15/03) [305.8]

9962 De Capua, Sarah E. *Abolitionists: A Force for Change* (4–7). Series: Journey to Freedom. 2002, Child's World LB $28.50 (1-56766-644-2). An overview of the efforts of abolitionists in America from the 17th through 19th centuries. (Rev: SLJ 12/02) [326.80973]

9963 Dolan, Edward F. *Your Privacy: Protecting It in a Nosy World* (7–12). 1995, Dutton $14.99 (0-525-65187-X). A historical and practical look at one of our most important rights. (Rev: BL 1/1/95; SLJ 2/95) [323.44]

9964 Dunn, John M. *The Civil Rights Movement* (7–9). Illus. Series: World History. 1998, Lucent LB $27.45 (1-56006-310-6). After summarizing the civil rights struggle of African Americans, the author focuses on the civil rights movement of the 20th century, with boxed excerpts from writings and speeches. (Rev: BL 2/15/98; SLJ 3/98) [323.1]

9965 Durrett, Deanne. *Teen Privacy Rights: A Hot Issue* (7–9). 2001, Enslow LB $19.95 (0-7660-

1374-X). Durrett traces the history of efforts to preserve privacy and explores how this issue affects teens today. (Rev: HBG 10/01; SLJ 6/01) [346.7301]

9966 Edelman, Marian Wright. *Stand for Children* (5–8). Illus. 1998, Hyperion LB $16.49 (0-7868-2310-0). A picture book for older readers in which collages, photographs, and excerpts from the author's speech at a rally are used to illuminate the rights of children and how they can be protected. (Rev: BL 7/98; HBG 10/98; SLJ 8/98) [305.2]

9967 Egendorf, Laura K., ed. *Human Rights* (8–12). Series: Opposing Viewpoints. 2003, Gale LB $33.70 (0-7377-1689-4); paper $22.45 (0-7377-1690-8). This collection of essays covers a definition of human rights, the state of these rights today, and ways in which the United States and the world can respond to human rights abuse. (Rev: BL 1/1–15/04) [323.4]

9968 Faherty, Sara. *Victims and Victims' Rights* (7–12). Series: Justice and Punishment. 1998, Chelsea LB $21.95 (0-7910-4308-8). A multifaceted overview of the victims' rights movement in the United States and its development over the past 25 years. (Rev: BL 3/15/99) [362.88]

9969 Farish, Leah. *Tinker vs. Des Moines: Student Protest* (6–10). Illus. Series: Landmark Supreme Court Cases. 1997, Enslow LB $20.95 (0-89490-859-6). This book traces step-by-step this case that was argued in the Supreme Court and that determined the rights of students in schools and campuses. (Rev: BL 4/15/97; SLJ 5/97) [341.4]

9970 Finkelstein, Norman H. *Heeding the Call: Jewish Voices in the Civil Rights Struggle* (6–9). 1997, Jewish Publication Soc. paper $14.95 (0-8276-0590-9). Beginning with the 1600s when both Africans and Jews first came to first country, this book traces the bond between these groups as they fought for civil rights. (Rev: BL 2/15/98) [323.1]

9971 Finlayson, Reggie. *We Shall Overcome: The History of the American Civil Rights Movement* (6–10). Illus. Series: People's History. 2003, Lerner $25.26 (0-8225-0647-5). In chronological order, this book explores important civil rights events of the 1950s and 1960s — including demonstrations, marches, lynchings, assassinations, and violent protests — and provides historical context and key quotations. (Rev: BL 2/15/03; HBG 3/03; SLJ 1/03) [323.1]

9972 Fireside, Harvey. *The "Mississippi Burning" Civil Rights Murder Conspiracy Trial* (6–10). Series: Headline Court Cases. 2002, Enslow LB $20.95 (0-7660-1762-1). This account describes the vicious murder of three young civil rights workers in Mississippi in 1964 and how their killers were brought to justice. (Rev: BL 3/15/03; HBG 3/03; SLJ 3/03) [973.9]

9973 Fireside, Harvey. *New York Times v. Sullivan: Affirming Freedom of the Press* (6–10). Series: Landmark Supreme Court Cases. 1999, Enslow LB $20.95 (0-7660-1085-6). The limits to freedom of the press was the subject of this Supreme Court case that had far-reaching results in the world of journalism. (Rev: BL 8/99) [347.3]

9974 Fireside, Harvey. *Plessy vs. Ferguson: Separate but Equal?* (6–10). Illus. Series: Landmark Supreme Court Cases. 1997, Enslow LB $20.95 (0-89490-860-X). This book gives a step-by-step account of the hearings in the Supreme Court of this case that challenged the basic underpinnings of segregation laws. (Rev: BL 7/97; HBG 3/98; SLJ 10/97) [342.73]

9975 Fireside, Harvey, and Sarah B. Fuller. *Brown v. Board of Education: Equal Schooling for All* (6–10). Series: Landmark Supreme Court Cases. 1994, Enslow LB $20.95 (0-89490-469-8). Presents background information, the case itself, and the far-reaching impact it has had. (Rev: BL 11/15/94) [344.73]

9976 Fleming, Maria, ed. *A Place at the Table: Struggles for Equality in America* (7–12). Illus. 2002, Oxford LB $28.00 (0-19-515036-8). Profiles of individuals who have fought for equality since colonial times are interspersed with excerpts from primary sources and photographs. (Rev: BL 2/1/02; HBG 10/02; SLJ 5/02; VOYA 2/02) [323]

9977 Freedman, Estelle B. *No Turning Back: The History of Feminism and the Future of Women* (8–12). 2002, Ballantine $15.95 (0-345-45054-X). Cultural, economic, educational, and historical information are provided in this overview of the feminist movement around the world. (Rev: BL 3/1/03)

9978 Fremon, David K. *The Jim Crow Laws and Racism* (6–10). Series: In American History. 2000, Enslow LB $20.95 (0-7660-1297-2). This is a history of racism in America from the end of the Civil War to the death of Martin Luther King, Jr., in 1968. (Rev: BL 10/15/2000; HBG 3/01; SLJ 12/00) [973]

9979 Frost-Knappman, Elizabeth, and Kathryn Cullen-DuPont. *Women's Rights on Trial: 101 Historic Trials from Anne Hutchinson to the Virginia Military Institute Cadets* (6–12). 1997, Gale $95.00 (0-7876-0384-8). The description of each of these landmark trials defining women's rights includes background information, partial transcripts, courtroom action, and the decision and its significance. (Rev: SLJ 5/97) [346]

9980 Galas, Judith C. *Gay Rights* (6–9). Illus. Series: Overview. 1996, Lucent LB $27.45 (1-56006-176-6). After a brief discussion of the nature of homosexuality, the author gives a history of the gay rights movement and the fight for equality in

634

the family, workplace, and the military. (Rev: BL 3/1/96; SLJ 2/96; VOYA 8/96) [305.9]

9981 George, Charles. *Life Under the Jim Crow Laws* (6–9). Series: The Way People Live. 1999, Lucent LB $18.96 (1-56006-499-4). A look at racial segregation laws and what life was like for African Americans before the civil rights movement. (Rev: BL 10/15/99; HBG 9/00; SLJ 1/00) [305.896075]

9982 Gold, Susan D. *Human Rights* (6–9). Illus. Series: Pacts and Treaties. 1997, Twenty-First Century LB $23.40 (0-8050-4811-1). This is a history of the fight for worldwide human rights that begins with the Geneva Convention of 1863 and ends with the present-day efforts by both political and private organizations. (Rev: BL 9/1/97; SLJ 7/97) [341.4]

9983 Gold, Susan D. *In Re Gault (1967): Juvenile Justice* (5–9). Series: Supreme Court Decisions. 1995, Twenty-First Century LB $25.90 (0-8050-3917-1). Inequalities in juvenile sentencing were the subject of this Supreme Court case, an appeal of a six-year reform school sentence given to a juvenile for making an obscene phone call. (Rev: BL 11/15/95; SLJ 1/96; VOYA 4/96) [347]

9984 Gottfried, Ted. *Homeland Security Versus Constitutional Rights* (8–12). Illus. 2003, Millbrook LB $24.90 (0-7613-2862-9). Gottfried addresses important questions, both historical and contemporary, in the balancing of safety versus civil liberties. (Rev: BL 11/15/03; SLJ 12/03) [303.3]

9985 Gottfried, Ted. *Privacy: Individual Rights v. Social Needs* (8–12). 1994, Millbrook LB $25.90 (1-56294-403-7). Discusses debates on privacy in relation to law enforcement, surveillance, abortion, AIDS, and the media. (Rev: BL 9/15/94; SLJ 10/94; VOYA 2/95) [342.73]

9986 Grant, R. G. *The African-American Slave Trade* (6–12). Illus. Series: Lives in Crisis. 2003, Barron's $14.95 (0-7641-5604-7). While focusing on the slave trade to the United States, this book also looks at the international context and at the history of slavery, providing eyewitness accounts. (Rev: BL 10/15/03*; SLJ 8/03) [306.]

9987 Grapes, Bryan J., ed. *Affirmative Action* (8–12). Series: At Issue. 1999, Greenhaven LB $21.96 (0-7377-0290-7); paper $13.96 (0-7377-0289-3). A wide range of opinions are included about this principle that favors preferential treatment for women and minority groups in employment and education. (Rev: BL 11/15/99) [331.13]

9988 Greenberg, Keith E. *Adolescent Rights: Are Young People Equal Under the Law?* (5–8). Illus. Series: Issues of Our Time. 1995, Twenty-First Century LB $22.00 (0-8050-3877-9). This unbiased account of the controversial subject encourages readers to form their own conclusions. (Rev: SLJ 9/95) [323]

9989 Guernsey, JoAnn B. *Voices of Feminism: Past, Present, and Future* (7–10). Illus. Series: Frontline. 1996, Lerner LB $19.95 (0-8225-2626-3). After a 150-year history of feminism, this account covers the complicated issues and concerns surrounding this subject and discusses past and present leaders in the movement. (Rev: BL 9/15/96; SLJ 7/97; VOYA 4/97) [305.42]

9990 Haskins, Jim. *The Day Martin Luther King, Jr., Was Shot: A Photo History of the Civil Rights Movement* (4–9). 1992, Scholastic paper $5.99 (0-590-43661-9). A photographic history of the African American struggle from the time of slavery to the early 1990s. (Rev: BL 2/1/92; SLJ 5/92) [323.4]

9991 Haskins, Jim. *Freedom Rides: Journey for Justice* (5–7). Illus. 1995, Hyperion LB $15.49 (0-7868-2037-3). This account focuses on a single dramatic aspect of the civil rights movement: the integration of buses and trains. (Rev: BL 1/1/95; SLJ 4/95) [323.1]

9992 Haskins, Jim. *Separate But Not Equal: The Dream and the Struggle* (7–10). Illus. 1998, Scholastic paper $15.95 (0-590-45910-4). A history of African Americans' struggle for equality in education beginning from the time of slavery, with coverage of key court cases and incidents and the beliefs of such leaders as W. E. B. Du Bois and Booker T. Washington. (Rev: BL 2/15/98; HBG 9/98; SLJ 2/98; VOYA 10/98) [379.2]

9993 Haughton, Emma. *Equality of the Sexes?* (6–8). Illus. Series: Viewpoints. 1997, Watts LB $23.00 (0-531-14443-7). Brief two-page spreads introduce women's place in the workplace, at home, in marriage, and under the law, with sections on women in government, religion, sports, and the arts. (Rev: BL 1/1–15/98; HBG 3/98; SLJ 12/97) [305.3]

9994 Heinrichs, Ann. *The Ku Klux Klan: A Hooded Brotherhood* (4–7). Series: Journey to Freedom. 2002, Child's World LB $28.50 (1-56766-646-9). This brief introduction to the Klan covers the group's origins and history, and touches on the Internet's role in spreading hate messages. (Rev: SLJ 12/02) [322.420973]

9995 Hirst, Mike. *Freedom of Belief* (4–8). Illus. Series: What Do We Mean by Human Rights? 1997, Watts LB $23.00 (0-531-14435-6). An information-packed overview of religious and political freedom and the people who fought and sometimes died for it. (Rev: BL 1/1–15/98; HBG 3/98) [323.44]

9996 Hu, Evaleen. *A Level Playing Field: Sports and Race* (5–8). Illus. Series: Sports Issues. 1995, Lerner LB $28.75 (0-8225-3302-2). A frank, thorough examination of the problems involving race in sports and how different athletes have dealt with them. (Rev: BL 1/1–15/96; SLJ 9/95) [796]

635

9997 Jacobs, Thomas A. *What Are My Rights? 95 Questions and Answers About Teens and the Law* (7–12). 1997, Free Spirit paper $14.95 (1-57542-028-7). Using a question-and-answer format, this topically arranged manual describes in simple terms concerns relating to teens' rights within the family, at school, and on the job. (Rev: BL 4/1/98; SLJ 4/98; VOYA 6/98) [346.7301]

9998 Katz, William L. *World War II to the New Frontier: 1940–1963* (7–9). Series: History of Multicultural America. 1993, Raintree Steck-Vaughn LB $27.11 (0-8114-6280-3). From the beginning of World War II through the Kennedy Era, this is a history of race relations and the struggle for civil rights in this country. (Rev: BL 9/1/93) [305.8]

9999 Kendall, Martha E. *Failure Is Impossible: The History of American Women's Rights* (5–8). Illus. Series: People's History. 2001, Lerner LB $30.35 (0-8225-1744-2). The status of women in the United States is discussed from the time of the Puritans to the present, including information on life for slaves, Native American women, and mill girls, and on equal pay and equal opportunity. (Rev: BL 5/1/01; HBG 10/01; SLJ 6/01; VOYA 8/01) [305.42]

10000 King, Casey. *Oh, Freedom! Kids Talk About the Civil Rights Movement with the People Who Made It Happen* (5–9). 1997, Knopf $19.99 (0-679-95856-8); Random paper $12.95 (0-679-89005-X). In 31 interviews, children ask family members, neighbors, and friends about the part they played in the civil rights movement. (Rev: BL 4/1/97; BR 11–12/97; SLJ 6/97*) [973]

10001 King, David C. *Freedom of Assembly* (4–8). Series: Land of the Free. 1997, Millbrook LB $22.90 (0-7613-0064-3). This book covers this basic civil right with examples throughout U.S. history and landmark court cases that helped define its limits. (Rev: BL 5/15/97; SLJ 10/97) [342.73]

10002 King, David C. *The Right to Speak Out* (4–8). Series: Land of the Free. 1997, Millbrook LB $22.90 (0-7613-0063-5). Background material on the freedom of speech is given, its use and abuse, and landmark courts cases that have defined it. (Rev: BL 5/15/97; SLJ 10/97) [351.81]

10003 King, Martin Luther, Jr. *I Have a Dream* (4–8). Illus. 1997, Scholastic paper $16.95 (0-590-20516-1). The full text of Dr. King's speech is reprinted, with illustrations by 15 award-winning African American artists. (Rev: BL 2/15/98; HBG 3/98; SLJ 11/97) [305.896]

10004 King, Martin Luther, Jr. *The Words of Martin Luther King, Jr.* (7–12). Illus. 1983, Newmarket $15.95 (0-937858-28-5). A selection from the writings and speeches of Dr. King that covers a great number of topics. [323.4]

10005 Kleinman, Joseph, and Eileen Kurtis-Kleinman. *Life on an African Slave Ship* (6–10). Series: The Way People Live. 2000, Lucent LB $27.45 (1-56006-653-9). The author uses quotations from primary sources and many illustrations in this portrayal of the terrible conditions endured by slaves bound for America. (Rev: BL 3/1/01; SLJ 5/01) [973.6]

10006 Kowalski, Kathiann M. *Teen Rights: At Home, at School, Online* (6–12). Illus. Series: Issues in Focus. 2000, Enslow LB $19.95 (0-7660-1242-5). The author lays out teens' rights in areas ranging from school drug testing and Internet use to healthcare and freedom of expression. (Rev: BL 8/00; HBG 9/00; SLJ 8/00; VOYA 2/01) [305.235]

10007 Kuklin, Susan. *Irrepressible Spirit* (7–12). 1996, Putnam $18.95 (0-399-22762-8); paper $9.95 (0-399-23045-9). This moving document profiles, through interviews, 11 activists from around the world and describes each one's struggle for civil rights and social justice. (Rev: BL 5/1/96*; BR 3–4/97; SLJ 4/96; VOYA 2/97) [323]

10008 Landau, Elaine. *Your Legal Rights: From Custody Battles to School Searches, the Headline-Making Cases That Affect Your Life* (6–10). 1995, Walker LB $14.85 (0-8027-8360-0). A review of advances in protection of the legal rights of children and teenagers. (Rev: BL 5/15/95; SLJ 8/95) [346.7301]

10009 Levine, Ellen. *Freedom's Children: Young Civil Rights Activists Tell Their Own Stories* (6–12). 1993, Avon paper $4.99 (0-380-72114-7). In this collection of oral histories, 30 African Americans who, as children or teenagers, were part of the civil rights struggles in the 1950s–1960s South recall their experiences. (Rev: BL 12/15/92*; SLJ 3/93*) [973]

10010 Levy, Debbie. *Bigotry* (6–12). 2002, Gale LB $27.45 (1-56006-500-1). Specific examples of racism, anti-Semitism, and homophobia are accompanied by discussion of the incidence of bigotry in America, its history, and the influence of the media. (Rev: BL 2/1/02) [179]

10011 Levy, Debbie. *Civil Liberties* (7–12). Illus. Series: Overview. 1999, Lucent LB $18.96 (1-56006-611-3). This introduction to civil liberties presents the Bill of Rights and covers freedom of speech and assembly, media freedom, religious liberties, and the right to privacy. (Rev: BL 2/1/00; HBG 9/00) [342.73.]

10012 Long, Barbara. *United States v. Virginia: Virginia Military Institute Accepts Women* (7–10). Series: Landmark Supreme Court Cases. 2000, Enslow LB $19.95 (0-7660-1342-1). Virginia Military Institute's battle to continue excluding women cadets is documented here with quotations and excerpts from primary documents. (Rev: HBG 3/01; SLJ 11/00) [344.73]

10013 Lucas, Eileen. *Civil Rights: The Long Struggle* (6–10). Illus. Series: Issues in Focus. 1996, Enslow LB $20.95 (0-89490-729-8). After a discussion of the first ten amendments to the U.S. Constitution, this account focuses on the civil rights struggles of African Americans. (Rev: BL 9/15/96; BR 5–6/97; SLJ 12/96) [323]

10014 Lusane, Clarence. *No Easy Victories: Black Americans and the Vote* (8–12). Illus. Series: The African-American Experience. 1996, Watts LB $25.00 (0-531-11270-5). This history of African Americans' struggle for the right to vote begins with the Revolutionary War and continues through the Civil War, Reconstruction, the New Deal, and the Voting Rights Acts of 1965, and on to Jesse Jackson's bid for the Democratic nomination for president and the struggles of the early 1990s. (Rev: BL 2/15/97; SLJ 4/97) [323.1]

10015 McDonald, Laughlin, and John A. Powell. *The Rights of Racial Minorities* (6–10). Series: ACLU Handbooks for Young Americans. 1998, Penguin paper $9.99 (0-14-037785-9). This handbook traces how the rights of racial minorities have gained legal protection and provides information on current laws. (Rev: BL 5/15/98; SLJ 6/98) [323.4]

10016 McKissack, Patricia, and Fredrick McKissack. *Days of Jubilee: The End of Slavery in the United States* (5–8). 2003, Scholastic $18.95 (0-590-10764-X). A combination of clear, interesting narrative, relevant quotations from primary sources, thorough historical approach, and well-chosen illustrations make this a worthwhile volume on the gradual end of slavery. (Rev: BCCB 4/03; BL 5/15/03; HBG 10/03; LMC 8–9/03; SLJ 5/03; VOYA 4/03) [973.7]

10017 Meltzer, Milton. *There Comes a Time: The Struggle for Civil Rights* (7–12). Illus. Series: Landmark Books. 2001, Random $16.95 (0-375-80407-2). Slavery, Reconstruction, school desegregation, marches, strikes, and speeches are among the topics that are explored in this book, which follows the civil rights movement through the work and assassination of Dr. King. (Rev: BL 2/1/01; HBG 10/01; SLJ 1/01) [973]

10018 Meltzer, Milton. *They Came in Chains: The Story of the Slave Ships* (6–10). Illus. Series: Great Journeys. 1999, Benchmark LB $21.95 (0-7614-0967-X). Slavery is treated in a global context with material on the horrors of the Middle Passage, and the life of slaves before and after the voyage. (Rev: BL 1/1–15/00; HBG 4/00; SLJ 2/00) [382.]

10019 Meyers, Madeleine, ed. *Forward into Light: The Struggle for Woman's Suffrage* (4–8). Illus. Series: Perspectives on History. 1994, Discovery paper $6.95 (1-878668-25-0). The story of the long struggle for women's right to vote, including the contributions of Elizabeth Cady Stanton, Susan B. Anthony, Sojourner Truth, and other leaders. (Rev: BL 8/94) [324.6]

10020 Milios, Rita. *Working Together Against Racism* (7–12). Series: Library of Social Activism. 1995, Rosen LB $16.95 (0-8239-1840-8). A history of civil rights in America and ways to protect citizens from racism. (Rev: BL 4/15/95; SLJ 4/95) [305.8]

10021 Miller, James, ed. *American Slavery* (6–12). Illus. Series: Complete History Of. 2001, Greenhaven LB $99.00 (0-7377-0424-1). This anthology provides a well-organized and balanced look at slavery in America and includes contributions on a variety of topics by writers including Frederick Douglass and Nat Turner. (Rev: BL 11/1/01; SLJ 8/01) [973.04]

10022 Monroe, Judy. *The Nineteenth Amendment: Women's Right to Vote* (6–8). Illus. 1998, Enslow LB $20.95 (0-89490-922-3). Beginning with the historic Seneca Falls meeting in 1848, this book highlights the events, movements, and people involved in the passage of the 19th Amendment giving women the right to vote. (Rev: BL 4/15/98; BR 9–10/98; SLJ 6/98; VOYA 4/98) [324-6]

10023 Monroe, Judy. *The Susan B. Anthony Women's Voting Rights Trial* (6–10). Series: Headline Court Cases. 2002, Enslow LB $20.95 (0-7660-1759-1). Monroe explores the fight for women's suffrage and the trial of Susan B. Anthony for voting illegally in the 1872 election. (Rev: BL 3/15/03; HBG 3/03; SLJ 12/02) [324.6]

10024 Nash, Carol R. *The Fight for Women's Right to Vote* (7–10). Series: In American History. 1998, Enslow LB $20.95 (0-89490-986-X). The struggle for women's right to vote is told concisely and clearly, with thumbnail sketches of the leading personalities involved. (Rev: BL 8/98; BR 1–2/99; HBG 9/99; SLJ 1/99) [324.6]

10025 Newman, Shirlee P. *The African Slave Trade* (4–7). Illus. Series: Watts Library: History of Slavery. 2000, Watts LB $24.00 (0-531-11694-8). From the brutality of capture through the unimaginable horrors of the Middle Passage and the humiliation of slave life, to the Emancipation Proclamation and slavery's lasting effects, this is a riveting narrative. (Rev: BL 2/15/01; SLJ 3/01) [380.1]

10026 O'Connor, Maureen. *Equal Rights* (5–8). Illus. Series: What Do We Mean by Human Rights? 1998, Watts LB $23.00 (0-531-14448-8). Uses an illustrated, double-page format to explore subjects including racism, freedom, and various types of prejudice. (Rev: BL 4/1/98; BR 11–12/98) [323]

10027 Oliver, Marilyn Tower. *Gay and Lesbian Rights: A Struggle* (7–12). 1998, Enslow LB $20.95 (0-89490-958-4). After recounting two incidents of gay bashing, the author reviews the history of gay rights from the ancient Greeks to today, with material on discrimination, law, health, and family

SOCIETY AND THE INDIVIDUAL

issues. (Rev: BL 12/1/98; SLJ 2/99; VOYA 10/99) [305.9]

10028 Parks, Rosa, and Gregory J. Reed. *Dear Mrs. Parks: A Dialogue with Today's Youth* (5–8). 1996, Lee & Low $16.95 (1-880000-45-8). This book contains a sampling of the thousands of letters sent to civil rights leader Rosa Parks and her replies. (Rev: BL 12/1/96; SLJ 12/96) [323]

10029 Patterson, Charles. *The Civil Rights Movement* (6–12). Series: Social Reform Movement. 1995, Facts on File $25.00 (0-8160-2968-7). Chronicles the civil rights movement in the United States, including a time line, chapter notes, and a reading list. (Rev: BL 11/15/95; SLJ 11/95; VOYA 12/95) [323.1196]

10030 Peck, Rodney. *Working Together Against Human Rights Violations* (7–12). Series: Library of Social Activism. 1995, Rosen LB $16.95 (0-8239-1778-9). Presents the struggles over a wide range of human rights issues. (Rev: BL 4/15/95; SLJ 4/95) [323]

10031 Powledge, Fred. *We Shall Overcome: Heroes of the Civil Rights Movement* (7–10). 1993, Scribners $17.00 (0-684-19362-0). A history of the civil rights movement: why it began, the system of segregation that existed with the government's tacit approval, and the movement's milestones and heroes. (Rev: BL 6/1–15/93; VOYA 8/93) [323.1]

10032 Rasmussen, R. Kent. *Farewell to Jim Crow: The Rise and Fall of Segregation in America* (8–12). Series: Library of African American History. 1997, Facts on File $25.00 (0-8160-3248-3). This is a history of segregation in the United States in such areas as housing, education, employment, transportation, and public accommodations, and efforts to end it. (Rev: BR 1–2/98; VOYA 2/98) [973]

10033 Rhym, Darren. *The NAACP* (6–9). Illus. Series: African American Achievers. 2001, Chelsea LB $21.95 (0-7910-5812-3). This history of the NAACP and the civil rights movement in America includes black-and-white photographs and a timeline. (Rev: BL 2/15/02; HBG 10/02; SLJ 5/02) [305.896]

10034 Ritchie, Nigel. *The Civil Rights Movement* (6–12). Series: Lives in Crisis. 2003, Barron's $14.95 (0-7641-5602-0). Using a number of well-documented quotations, this account traces the civil rights movement in this country, particularly in the late 20th century. (Rev: BL 10/15/03; SLJ 8/03) [331.1196]

10035 Rogers, James T. *The Antislavery Movement* (7–12). Series: Social Reform Movements. 1994, Facts on File $25.00 (0-8160-2907-5). This work traces slavery and its repercussions from 1619 to the present and provides insights into the conflicting interests and positions. (Rev: BL 1/1/95; SLJ 12/94; VOYA 5/95) [973]

10036 Roleff, Tamara L., ed. *Civil Liberties* (8–12). Series: Opposing Viewpoints. 1998, Greenhaven LB $32.45 (1-56510-937-6). This collection of essays explores potential restrictions on freedom of expression, the right to privacy, the separation of church and state, and freedom to use the Internet. (Rev: BL 8/98; SLJ 1/99; VOYA 6/99) [342]

10037 Seidman, David. *Civil Rights* (7–9). Series: Individual Rights and Civic Responsibility. 2001, Rosen LB $26.50 (0-8239-3231-1). Civil rights are defined, with material on key issues and a discussion of landmark cases including the Civil Rights Act of 1964. (Rev: BL 3/15/02; SLJ 2/02; VOYA 2/02) [323.1]

10038 Somerlott, Robert. *The Little Rock School Desegregation Crisis* (6–10). Series: In American History. 2001, Enslow LB $20.95 (0-7660-1298-0). Beginning on September 5, 1957, when nine African American schoolchildren were refused entrance to a Little Rock school, this account looks at the Arkansas school desegregation crisis. (Rev: BL 12/15/01; HBG 3/02; SLJ 9/01) [344.73]

10039 Springer, Jane. *Listen to Us: The World's Working Children* (7–12). Illus. 1997, Douglas & McIntyre $24.95 (0-88899-291-2). This impressive photoessay looks at the exploitation of children around the world in industry, agriculture, the home, the military, and on the street. (Rev: BL 1/1–15/98; SLJ 3/98) [331.3]

10040 Stalcup, Brenda, ed. *Women's Suffrage* (8–12). Series: Turning Points in World History. 2000, Greenhaven LB $21.96 (0-7377-0326-1); paper $13.96 (0-7377-0325-3). This collection of essays traces the history of the women's suffrage movement from the declaration of women's rights signed in New York State in 1848 through the impact of the passage of the nineteenth amendment on American history. (Rev: BL 5/15/00; SLJ 8/00) [346]

10041 *Stand Up, Speak Out: A Book About Children's Rights* (6–8). Illus. 2002, Two-Can $14.95 (1-58728-540-1); paper $9.95 (1-58728-541-X). Children's artwork and writings address children's rights issues around the world, with information on the U.N.'s Convention on the Rights of the Child, UNICEF, and other aid organizations. (Rev: BL 4/15/02; HBG 10/02; SLJ 6/02) [323]

10042 Stearman, Kaye. *Slavery Today* (6–10). Series: Talking Points. 1999, Raintree Steck-Vaughn LB $18.98 (0-8172-5320-3). Examples of modern slavery include child labor, trafficking in people, prostitution, migrant workers who are exploited, and other forms of forced labor. (Rev: BL 12/15/99; HBG 9/00; SLJ 5/00) [326]

10043 Stearman, Kaye. *Women's Rights: Changing Attitudes, 1900–2000* (6–9). Series: 20th Century Issues. 2000, Raintree Steck-Vaughn LB $28.55 (0-8172-5892-2). Stearman traces the history of the women's rights movement and looks at its achievements, the status of women around the world today, and possible future efforts. (Rev: BL 11/15/00; BR 3–4/00; HBG 9/00; SLJ 4/00) [323.1]

10044 Sullivan, George. *The Day the Women Got the Vote: A Photo History of the Women's Rights Movement* (5–8). Illus. 1994, Scholastic paper $6.95 (0-590-47560-6). The history of the struggle for women's rights is covered in a series of 24 short photoessays. (Rev: BL 6/1–15/94; SLJ 7/94) [323.34]

10045 Tackach, James. *The Abolition of American Slavery* (7–10). Series: World History. 2002, Gale LB $27.45 (1-59018-002-X). This comprehensive survey of slavery and the abolition movement includes information on key figures and events, with closing information on segregation and the civil rights movement of the 20th century. (Rev: BL 8/02; SLJ 9/02) [973.7]

10046 Thomas, Joyce Carol, ed. *Linda Brown, You Are Not Alone: The Brown v. Board of Education Decision* (6–12). 2003, Hyperion $15.99 (0-7868-0821-7). Well-known children's and YA writers contributed to this collection of fiction, poetry, and memoirs about the important court ruling and its impact on education in the United States. (Rev: BL 12/1/03) [344.73]

10047 Treanor, Nick, ed. *Desegregation* (8–12). Series: Interpreting Primary Documents. 2003, Gale LB $25.96 (0-7377-1302-X); paper $16.96 (0-7377-1308-8). An introduction discussing segregation precedes excerpts from speeches, documents, and other materials by individuals including John F. Kennedy, Martin Luther King, and George Wallace. (Rev: SLJ 5/03) [305.8]

10048 Turck, Mary C. *The Civil Rights Movement for Kids: A History with 21 Activities* (4–8). 2000, Chicago Review paper $14.95 (1-55652-370-X). The story of the civil rights movement with coverage of key events and personalities plus a number of related activities. (Rev: SLJ 10/00) [973.9]

10049 Turner, Chérie. *Everything You Need to Know About the Riot Grrrl Movement: The Feminism of a New Generation* (6–10). Illus. Series: Need to Know Library. 2001, Rosen LB $17.95 (0-8239-3400-4). A look at the movement that evolved from a 1970s aggressive punk attitude to a 1990s emphasis on equality and self-esteem. (Rev: SLJ 12/01) [781.66]

10050 Walter, Mildred P. *Mississippi Challenge* (7–12). 1992, Bradbury $18.95 (0-02-792301-0). An in-depth history of the civil rights struggle in Mississippi that tells how ordinary people worked to change the political system. (Rev: BL 11/1/92; SLJ 1/93) [305.896]

10051 Watkins, Richard Ross. *Slavery: Bondage Throughout History* (7–12). 2001, Houghton $18.00 (0-395-92289-5). Watkins traces the history of slav-

ery from ancient Babylon through current practices including child prostitution in Southeast Asia. (Rev: BL 2/15/01; HBG 10/01; SLJ 4/01) [306.3]

10052 Wawrose, Susan C. *Griswold v. Connecticut: Contraception and the Right of Privacy* (6–10). Illus. Series: Historic Supreme Court Cases. 1996, Watts LB $25.00 (0-531-11249-7). Many issues involving women's rights, sex, and personal privacy are raised in this discussion of the case against Estelle Griswold, of the Planned Parenthood League in Connecticut, who broke a state law prohibiting distribution of contraceptives. (Rev: BL 7/96; SLJ 9/96; VOYA 10/96) [342.746]

10053 Weatherford, Carole Boston. *The African-American Struggle for Legal Equality* (6–10). Series: In American History. 2000, Enslow LB $20.95 (0-7660-1415-0). From slavery to the present, the account traces the amazing changes that brought African Americans equality before the law. (Rev: BL 10/15/2000; HBG 3/01) [973]

10054 Webb, Sheyann, and Rachel W. Nelson. *Selma, Lord, Selma: Girlhood Memories of the Civil-Rights Days* (7–12). Illus. 1980, Univ. of Alabama Pr. $17.95 (0-8173-0031-7). Recollections of two girls who, when only ages 8 and 9, participated in the Selma civil rights struggle. (Rev: BL 9/1/87) [323.4]

10055 Weber, Michael. *Causes and Consequences of the African-American Civil Rights Movements* (6–10). Series: Causes and Consequences. 1998, Raintree Steck-Vaughn LB $29.97 (0-8172-4058-6). The author traces the legal and social history of African Americans that led up to the historic 1963 March on Washington, recounts events of the 1950s and 1960s such as the integration of schools, the growing urban tensions, and the rise of the black power movement, and discusses the movement's lasting achievements and current problems. (Rev: SLJ 6/98) [973]

10056 Wepman, Dennis. *The Struggle for Freedom* (7–12). Illus. Series: Library of African American History. 1996, Facts on File $19.95 (0-8160-3270-X). This well-researched work, using many maps and primary sources, traces slavery from ancient Sumerian times and continues through the centuries, exploring the slave trade triangle involving Africa, American, and England, the role of public opinion, slave revolts, working conditions and treatment, the Underground Railroad, the Civil War, and the revolt of Caribbean slaves led by Toussaint L'Ouverture. (Rev: VOYA 10/96) [973]

10057 Williams, Mary E., ed. *Civil Rights* (7–12). Series: Examining Issues Through Political Cartoons. 2002, Gale LB $24.95 (0-7377-1100-0); paper $16.20 (0-7377-1099-3). This limited but unusual approach to exploration of the civil rights movement looks at political cartoons in four thematic chapters. (Rev: BR 11–12/02; SLJ 10/02) [323.1]

10058 Williams, Mary E., ed. *Discrimination* (8–12). Series: Opposing Viewpoints. 2002, Gale LB $25.96 (0-7377-1226-0); paper $16.96 (0-7377-1225-2). Williams presents articles and speeches that condemn, defend, and even deny the existence of forms of discrimination including prejudice against women and gays, affirmative action, racial profiling, and reverse discrimination. (Rev: BL 10/1/02) [305]

10059 Wilson, Reginald. *Our Rights: Civil Liberties and the U.S.* (7–12). Illus. 1988, Walker $14.85 (0-8027-6751-6). A book that explains what civil rights are, how we have these freedoms, and how to protect them. (Rev: SLJ 8/88; VOYA 8/88) [323.4]

10060 Wilson, Reginald. *Think About Our Rights: Civil Liberties and the United States* (5–8). Illus. 1991, Walker LB $15.85 (0-8027-8127-6); paper $9.95 (0-8027-7371-0). The focus is on such civil rights questions as integration, affirmative action, and women's rights. (Rev: SLJ 1/92) [323.4]

10061 Winters, Paul A., ed. *The Civil Rights Movement* (8–12). Series: Turning Points in World History. 2000, Greenhaven LB $21.96 (0-7377-0217-6); paper $13.96 (0-7377-0216-8). The collection of essays covers the civil rights struggles of the 1950s and 1960s with material on the leaders, important debates, events, and the continuing struggle. (Rev: BL 2/15/00; SLJ 4/00) [323.1.]

10062 Wormser, Richard. *The Rise and Fall of Jim Crow: The African-American Struggle Against Discrimination, 1865–1954* (7–12). Illus. 1999, Watts LB $24.00 (0-531-11443-0). This is a history of the legalized segregation that existed in the United States from the end of the Civil War to the civil rights movements of the 1950s. (Rev: BL 2/15/00; SLJ 4/00) [305.896073.]

10063 Worth, Richard. *Cinqué of the Amistad and the Slave Trade* (6–10). Series: In World History. 2001, Enslow LB $20.95 (0-7660-1460-6). An accessible overview of slave trading from Roman times through the U.S. Civil War, with black-and-white photographs and reproductions and excerpts from source documents. (Rev: HBG 10/01; SLJ 8/01) [326]

10064 Zeinert, Karen. *Free Speech: From Newspapers to Music Lyrics* (7–10). 1995, Enslow LB $20.95 (0-89490-634-8). The censorship battle in the context of various mediums, from a historical perspective. (Rev: BL 4/1/95; SLJ 6/95) [323.44]

Immigration

10065 Anderson, Dale. *Arriving at Ellis Island* (5–8). Illus. Series: Landmark Events in American History. 2003, World Almanac LB $29.26 (0-8368-5337-7).

In addition to describing the experience of arriving at Ellis Island, this volume looks at the people who worked there, from cooks and nurses to interpreters and immigration officials. (Rev: BL 10/15/03; SLJ 1/03) [304.]

10066 Andryszewski, Tricia. *Immigration: Newcomers and Their Impact on the U.S.* (7–9). 1995, Millbrook $24.90 (1-56294-499-1). A detailed study of immigration as it pertains to the United States. (Rev: BL 1/15/95; SLJ 5/95) [304.8]

10067 Archibald, Erika F. *A Sudanese Family* (4–7). Illus. Series: Journey Between Two Worlds. 1997, Lerner paper $8.95 (0-8225-9753-5). Introduces Dei Jock Dei and his family, who left Sudan to escape religious persecution and, through the help of a church, settled in Atlanta, Georgia. (Rev: BL 6/1–15/97; SLJ 7/97) [975.8]

10068 Ashabranner, Brent. *Our Beckoning Borders: Illegal Immigration to America* (6–10). Illus. 1996, Dutton $15.99 (0-525-65223-X). Individual case studies and good photographs are used to explain the problems of illegal immigration, border patrols, and the involvement of human rights groups. (Rev: BL 4/15/96; BR 11–12/96; SLJ 5/96) [304.8]

10069 Ashabranner, Brent. *Still a Nation of Immigrants* (7–12). 1993, Dutton $15.99 (0-525-65130-6). Looks at the present influx of immigrants and discusses why they come and what they bring with them. (Rev: BL 9/1/93; VOYA 2/94) [325.73]

10070 Berg, Lois Anne. *An Eritrean Family* (4–7). Illus. Series: Journey Between Two Worlds. 1997, Lerner LB $22.60 (0-8225-3405-3); paper $8.95 (0-8225-9755-1). The story of the Kiklu family, which fled Eritrea in eastern Africa in 1978, spent 10 years in a refugee camp, and resettled in Minnesota. (Rev: BL 6/1–15/97; SLJ 8/97) [304.895]

10071 Bode, Janet. *The Colors of Freedom: Immigrant Stories* (7–12). 1999, Watts LB $24.00 (0-531-11530-5); paper $9.95 (0-531-15961-2). Using students' writing, artwork, interviews, and poems, the author has collected material on the feelings of young adult immigrants to this country from such areas as Latin America, Europe, and Asia. (Rev: BL 1/1–15/00; SLJ 3/00) [305.8.]

10072 Budhos, Marina. *Remix: Conversations with Immigrant Teenagers* (7–12). 1999, Holt $16.95 (0-8050-5113-9). This book contains interviews with 20 older teens from around the world who comment on their experiences as immigrants in the United States and the cultural differences they have encountered. (Rev: BL 9/15/99; HBG 4/00; SLJ 11/99; VOYA 12/99) [341.4]

10073 Caroli, Betty Boyd. *Immigrants Who Returned Home* (6–10). Illus. 1990, Chelsea LB $19.95 (0-87754-864-1). An account of immigrants who found life in the United States less than expected and returned home to their countries. (Rev: BL 4/15/90; SLJ 8/90) [304.8]

10074 Collier, Christopher, and James Lincoln Collier. *A Century of Immigration, 1820–1924* (5–8). Series: Drama of American History. 1999, Marshall Cavendish LB $29.93 (0-7614-0821-5). A compelling account that focuses on 100 years of migration to this country, with material on where the immigrants came from, why they emigrated, where they settled, and the problems of assimilation. (Rev: BL 2/15/00; HBG 10/00; SLJ 3/00) [973]

10075 Cothran, Helen, ed. *Illegal Immigration* (8–12). Series: Current Controversies. 2001, Greenhaven LB $22.96 (0-7377-0685-6); paper $14.96 (0-7377-0684-8). Cothran presents arguments on both sides of the questions of the treatment and impact of illegal immigrants into the United States. (Rev: SLJ 8/01) [304.873]

10076 Cox, Vic. *The Challenge of Immigration* (7–12). Series: Multicultural Issues. 1995, Enslow LB $20.95 (0-89490-628-3). An introduction to the controversial issues concerning immigration. (Rev: BL 5/1/95; SLJ 5/95) [325.73]

10077 Currie, Stephen. *Issues in Immigration* (7–12). Illus. Series: Contemporary Issues. 2000, Lucent LB $19.96 (1-56006-377-7). Questions involving immigration, including bilingual education, are examined from various points of view using quotations from primary sources. (Rev: BL 10/15/00; HBG 3/01; SLJ 12/00) [325.73]

10078 Daniels, Roger. *American Immigration: A Student Companion* (6–12). Series: Oxford Student Companions to American History. 2001, Oxford LB $40.00 (0-19-511316-0). An alphabetically arranged series of articles covering all aspects of immigration to the United States and the various ethnic groups that have made the journey, illustrated with photographs, maps, and reproductions. (Rev: SLJ 6/01) [304.8]

10079 Dudley, William, ed. *Illegal Immigration* (7–12). Series: Opposing Viewpoints. 2002, Gale LB $31.20 (0-7377-0911-1); paper $19.95 (0-7377-0910-3). A balanced collection of essays on the topic of illegal arrivals in the United States and the treatment of these immigrants, updated from the 1994 edition. (Rev: BL 4/15/02; SLJ 8/02) [325.73]

10080 Emsden, Katharine, ed. *Coming to America: A New Life in a New Land* (4–8). Series: Perspectives on History. 1993, Discovery paper $6.95 (1-878668-23-4). Diaries, journals, and letters of immigrants from many countries are used to provide insights into their lives. (Rev: BL 11/15/93) [325.73]

10081 Goldish, Meish. *Immigration: How Should It Be Controlled?* (6–9). Illus. Series: Issues of Our Time. 1994, Twenty-First Century LB $22.90 (0-8050-3182-0). An unbiased, clear look at current

positions and solutions to the immigration problem, particularly as they apply to the United States. (Rev: BL 6/1–15/94; SLJ 7/94) [325.73]

10082 Greenberg, Judith E. *Newcomers to America: Stories of Today's Young Immigrants* (7–10). Illus. 1996, Watts LB $23.00 (0-531-11256-X). An overview of the new wave of immigration to this country, followed by excerpts from 14 interviews of recent immigrants who came here as teens. (Rev: BL 6/1–15/96; BR 11–12/96; SLJ 8/96; VOYA 2/97) [304.8]

10083 Hauser, Pierre. *Illegal Aliens* (5–8). Series: Immigrant Experience. 1996, Chelsea LB $21.95 (0-7910-3363-5). A history of attitudes toward immigration is followed by a discussion of illegal immigrants, where they come from, why they came, and the government's policy toward them. (Rev: SLJ 2/97) [932]

10084 Hay, Jeff, ed. *Immigration* (7–12). Series: Turning Points in World History. 2001, Greenhaven LB $31.20 (0-7377-0639-2); paper $19.95 (0-7377-0638-4). In a series of engaging essays, the phenomenon of immigration is explored and how shifting populations have changing world history. (Rev: BL 3/15/02) [325]

10085 Hoobler, Dorothy, and Thomas Hoobler. *We Are Americans: Voices of the Immigrant Experience* (5–9). 2003, Scholastic $21.95 (0-439-16297-1). This chronological exploration of immigration, voluntary and forced, to North America since prehistoric times includes many personal accounts and archival photographs. (Rev: BCCB 1/04; BL 1/1–15/04*; SLJ 12/03) [304.8]

10086 Hopkinson, Deborah. *Shutting Out the Sky* (5–12). Illus. 2003, Scholastic $17.95 (0-439-37590-8). Five personal stories of young immigrants, striking photographs, and excerpts from primary documents form the backbone of this history of immigration to New York City in the late 19th century. (Rev: BL 11/1/03*; SLJ 12/03*) [307.76]

10087 Knight, Margy B. *Who Belongs Here? An American Story* (4–7). 1993, Tilbury $16.95 (0-88448-110-7). The story of ten-year-old Nari, who survived the killing fields of Cambodia and found a new life in the United States. (Rev: BL 3/1/94; SLJ 10/93) [305.895]

10088 Kosof, Anna. *Living in Two Worlds: The Immigrant Children's Experience* (7–12). Illus. 1996, Twenty-First Century LB $23.40 (0-8050-4083-8). After a brief introduction on the history of immigration, this book describes the problems and the reception of present-day teenage immigrants, using many first-person accounts. (Rev: BL 10/1/96; BR 11–12/96; SLJ 10/96; VOYA 2/97) [305.23]

10089 Leinwand, Gerald. *American Immigration: Should the Open Door Be Closed?* (7–12). 1995, Watts paper $24.00 (0-531-13038-X). A historical perspective on the current immigration debate reveals the racism that still underlies the melting-pot argument. (Rev: BL 8/95; VOYA 12/95) [325.73]

10090 Levine, Herbert M. *Immigration* (7–12). Illus. Series: American Issues Debated. 1997, Raintree Steck-Vaughn LB $31.40 (0-8172-4353-4). Questions involving immigration and the economy, the rights of illegal immigrants, and English-only laws are covered from various points of view. (Rev: BL 11/15/97; BR 1–2/98) [304.873]

10091 Meltzer, Milton. *Bound for America: The Story of the European Immigrants* (6–10). Series: Great Journeys. 2001, Benchmark LB $21.95 (0-7614-1227-1). An absorbing examination of the reasons for migration within and from Europe in the 19th and early 20th centuries, and of the hardships these travelers suffered. (Rev: BCCB 3/99; HBG 10/02; SLJ 3/02) [325.73]

10092 Morrow, Robert. *Immigration: Blessing or Burden?* (7–10). Illus. Series: Pro/Con Issues. 1998, Lerner LB $30.35 (0-8225-2613-1). This book examines our changing attitudes toward immigration, how we regard immigration laws, and the controversy over multiculturalism vs. assimilation. (Rev: BL 3/15/98; SLJ 4/98) [304.8]

10093 Murphy, Nora. *A Hmong Family* (4–7). Illus. Series: Journey Between Two Worlds. 1997, Lerner LB $27.15 (0-8225-3406-1); paper $8.95 (0-8225-9756-X). After fleeing Laos in 1975 to escape the Communists, this family spent time in a refugee camp in Thailand before settling in Minneapolis, Minnesota. (Rev: BL 6/1–15/97; SLJ 8/97) [305.895]

10094 O'Connor, Karen. *Dan Thuy's New Life in America* (4–8). Illus. 1992, Lerner LB $19.93 (0-8225-2555-0). A photoessay of a 13-year-old Vietnamese girl and her family, newly arrived in San Diego. (Rev: BL 9/15/92; SLJ 9/92) [325]

10095 O'Connor, Karen. *A Kurdish Family* (5–8). Series: Journey Between Two Worlds. 1996, Lerner LB $22.60 (0-8225-3402-9); paper $8.95 (0-8225-9743-8). This work describes the living conditions endured by a Kurdish family in their homeland and their new life in the United States. (Rev: BCCB 12/96; BL 11/1/96; SLJ 11/96) [305.891]

10096 Reimers, David M. *A Land of Immigrants* (5–8). Series: Immigrant Experience. 1995, Chelsea LB $21.95 (0-7910-3361-9). An overview of immigration to the United States and Canada and how the influx influenced the culture. (Rev: BL 10/15/95; SLJ 12/95) [304.8]

10097 Roleff, Tamara L., ed. *Immigration* (8–12). Series: Opposing Viewpoints. 1998, Greenhaven LB $16.20 (1-56510-798-5). Questions concerning restrictions on immigration, the extent of the immigration problem, how to cope with illegal immigrants, and possible reforms in our policies are

discussed in this anthology of differing opinions. (Rev: BL 6/1–15/98) [341.4]

10098 Santos, Edward J. *Everything You Need to Know If You and Your Parents Are New Americans* (7–12). Illus. Series: Need to Know Library. 2002, Rosen LB $23.95 (0-8239-3547-7). A useful and attractive guide for immigrant teens that gives practical advice on dealing with various facets of American life and emphasizes the possibility of retaining one's heritage while fitting in to a new culture. (Rev: BL 6/1–15/02; SLJ 4/02; VOYA 2/03) [304.8]

10099 Sawyer, Kem K. *Refugees: Seeking a Safe Haven* (7–12). Series: Multicultural Issues. 1995, Enslow LB $20.95 (0-89490-663-1). This book describes the lives and problems of refugees admitted into this country, with material on why they left their homelands and their reception here. (Rev: BL 6/1–15/95; SLJ 8/95) [362.87]

10100 Strom, Yale. *Quilted Landscape: Conversations with Young Immigrants* (5–8). Illus. 1996, Simon & Schuster paper $18.00 (0-689-80074-6). Young immigrants from 15 countries talk about their homelands and the lives they now lead in the United States. (Rev: BCCB 2/97; BL 10/15/96; SLJ 12/96) [305.8]

10101 Torr, James D., ed. *Primary Sources* (6–10). Illus. Series: Immigrants in America. 2002, Gale LB $27.45 (1-59018-009-7). Excerpts from primary documents are organized in chapters that address the conditions that prompted migrants to leave their homes, the attractions they perceived in America, and the treatment they received on arrival. (Rev: BR 9–10/02; SLJ 9/02) [304.8]

Ethnic Groups and Prejudice

General and Miscellaneous

10102 Altman, Linda Jacobs. *Racism and Ethnic Bias: Everybody's Problem* (6–9). Illus. Series: Teen Issues. 2001, Enslow LB $17.95 (0-7660-1578-5). Racism, racial profiling, and ethnic stereotyping are all discussed here, with examples of these behaviors and tips on how people can work against racism. (Rev: BL 1/1–15/02; HBG 3/02) [305.8]

10103 Birdseye, Debbie H., and Tom Birdseye. *Under Our Skin: Kids Talk About Race* (4–8). 1997, Holiday $15.95 (0-8234-1325-X). In separate chapters, six 8th-grade students in Oregon from different racial and ethnic backgrounds talk about race and what racism means to them. (Rev: HBG 3/98; SLJ 4/98) [572.973]

10104 *CityKids Speak on Prejudice* (7–12). 1995, Random paper $5.99 (0-679-86552-7). Identifies areas in which intolerance is common and cites unexpected examples of discrimination as seen through the eyes of young people. (Rev: BL 5/1/95) [303.3]

10105 Cole, Carolyn Kozo, and Kathy Kobayashi. *Shades of L.A.: Pictures from Ethnic Family Albums* (7–12). 1996, New Pr. paper $20.00 (1-56584-313-4). A collection of photographs of African American, Mexican American, Asian American, and Native American family life in Los Angeles' ethnic and racial neighborhoods prior to 1965. (Rev: BL 8/96; VOYA 2/97) [979.4]

10106 Cruz, Barbara C. *Multiethnic Teens and Cultural Identity: A Hot Issue* (6–10). Series: Hot Issues. 2001, Enslow LB $19.95 (0-7660-1201-8). A concise examination of the challenges facing teens of mixed racial heritage that looks at ethnic diversity during American history and profiles individuals such as Tiger Woods and Halle Berry. (Rev: HBG 10/01; SLJ 7/01) [305.23]

10107 Garg, Samidha, and Jan Hardy. *Racism* (6–10). Illus. Series: Global Issues. 1996, Raintree Steck-Vaughn LB $19.98 (0-8172-4548-0). This study of racism, supplementing statistics and facts with personal experiences, discusses prejudice, immigration, and citizenship, with separate chapters on Europe, South Africa, the United States, and Australia. (Rev: BL 2/1/97) [305.8]

10108 Garza, Hedda. *African Americans and Jewish Americans: A History of Struggle* (8–12). Illus. Series: African American Experience. 1995, Watts paper $24.00 (0-531-11217-9). An overview of the relationship between Jews and African Americans past and present, with material on how relations between these two groups have become strained because of current social developments. (Rev: BL 4/1/96) [973]

10109 Gaskins, Pearl Fuyo, ed. *What Are You? Voices of Mixed-Race Young People* (7–12). 1999, Holt $18.95 (0-8050-5968-7). In essays, interviews, and poetry, 45 mixed-race young people ages 14 to 26 talk about themselves and growing up. (Rev: BL 5/15/99; HB 7–8/99; SLJ 7/99; VOYA 10/99) [973]

10110 Gay, Kathlyn. *I Am Who I Am: Speaking Out About Multiracial Identity* (7–12). 1995, Watts LB $25.00 (0-531-11214-4). A look at what it's like to grow up in a mixed-race environment, including cultural, historical, and political perspectives and opinions from experts. (Rev: BL 6/1–15/95; SLJ 8/95) [305.8]

10111 Gillam, Scott. *Discrimination: Prejudice in Action* (7–12). Series: Multicultural Issues. 1995, Enslow LB $20.95 (0-89490-643-7). This book shows how racial discrimination is still practiced in this country and discusses how it can be combated. (Rev: BL 6/1–15/95; SLJ 9/95) [303.3]

10112 Grant, R. G. *Racism: Changing Attitudes, 1900–2000* (6–9). Illus. Series: Twentieth Century

Issues. 1999, Raintree Steck-Vaughn LB $27.11 (0-8172-5567-2). A brief discussion of racism and its various aspects is the focus of this account that includes material on colonialism, civil rights, and black power. (Rev: BL 3/15/00; HBG 9/00; SLJ 4/00) [305.8.]

10113 Hull, Mary. *Ethnic Violence* (5–8). Illus. Series: Overview. 1997, Lucent LB $27.45 (1-56006-184-7). Gives a history of racial prejudice that has led to violence and discusses decisions and policies that currently guide our behavior and attitudes toward this problem. (Rev: BL 8/97; BR 1–2/98; SLJ 9/97) [305.8]

10114 Hurley, Jennifer A., ed. *Racism* (7–12). 1998, Greenhaven LB $32.45 (1-56510-809-4). How prevalent is racism in U.S. society? How does racism affect minorities? Is affirmative action effective? How can racism by combated? These are some of the questions explored in this collection of essays. (Rev: BL 8/98) [305.8]

10115 Kassam, Nadya, ed. *Telling It Like It Is: Young Asian Women Talk* (7–12). 1998, Livewire paper $11.95 (0-7043-4941-8). These 22 short, informal essays reveal various attitudes toward sexism and racism as experienced by Hindu and Moslem girls whose families are from the Indian subcontinent but are now living in Britain. (Rev: BL 9/15/98; SLJ 8/98) [305.8914]

10116 Katz, William L. *The Great Migrations: History of Multicultural America* (7–12). Series: History of Multicultural America. 1993, Raintree Steck-Vaughn LB $22.83 (0-8114-6278-1). Shows the impact that women and minorities have had in the formation and development of this country. (Rev: BL 6/1–15/93; VOYA 10/93) [973]

10117 Newman, Gerald, and Eleanor N. Layfield. *Racism: Divided by Color* (7–12). Series: Multicultural Issues. 1995, Enslow LB $20.95 (0-89490-641-0). A well-documented history of color barriers in America and efforts to eradicate them. (Rev: BL 9/15/95; SLJ 12/95; VOYA 2/96) [305.8]

10118 O'Hearn, Claudine Chiawei, ed. *Half and Half: Writers on Growing Up Biracial and Bicultural* (7–12). 1998, Pantheon paper $13.00 (0-375-70011-0). This work contains 18 personal essays by people who live and work in the U.S., but because they are biracial and bicultural are not sure of where they belong. (Rev: BL 9/1/98) [306.84]

10119 Pascoe, Elaine. *Racial Prejudice: Why Can't We Overcome?* (7–12). Series: Impact. 1997, Watts paper $24.00 (0-531-11402-3). This title explores the causes and effects of racial prejudice through separate chapters on African Americans, Hispanic Americans, Asian Americans, and Native Americans. (Rev: BL 5/15/97) [305.8]

10120 Sharp, Anne Wallace. *The Gypsies* (8–12). Illus. Series: Indigenous Peoples of the World.

2003, Gale $21.96 (1-59018-239-1). The history and culture of the Roma are detailed here, with information on the fate of these groups during World War II and on continuing prejudices. (Rev: BL 4/15/03; SLJ 7/03) [909]

10121 Williams, Mary, ed. *Interracial America* (6–12). Illus. Series: Opposing Viewpoints. 2001, Greenhaven LB $22.96 (0-7377-0658-9); paper $14.96 (0-7377-0657-0). This collection of essays presents various viewpoints on such topics as the advisability of emphasizing ethnic differences, affirmative action, interracial marriage, and transracial adoption. (Rev: BL 7/01) [305.8]

10122 Williams, Mary E. *Issues in Racism* (7–12). Series: Contemporary Issues. 2000, Lucent LB $27.45 (1-56006-478-1). This volume discusses contemporary conditions regarding racism in America and explores such topics as affirmative action, racial profiling, hate crimes, and other issues. (Rev: BL 9/1/00; HBG 3/01) [305.8]

African Americans

10123 Altman, Susan. *The Encyclopedia of African-American Heritage* (6–12). 1997, Facts on File $40.00 (0-8160-3289-0). An alphabetically arranged series of entries that covers African American history from the standpoint of famous people, places, culture, events, and politics. (Rev: BL 3/15/97; BR 1–2/99; SLJ 2/98; VOYA 6/97) [973]

10124 Ashabranner, Brent. *The New African Americans* (5–9). Illus. 1999, Linnet LB $22.50 (0-208-02420-4). After a brief history of early African immigration and slavery, this account focuses on present-day immigrants — where they come from and their reception in the United States. (Rev: BCCB 12/99; BL 10/15/99; HB 11–12/99; HBG 3/00; VOYA 12/00) [304.87]

10125 Banks, William H., Jr. *The Black Muslims* (5–10). Series: African American Achievers. 1996, Chelsea LB $21.95 (0-7910-2593-4); paper $9.95 (0-7910-2594-2). The story of the founding of the Nation of Islam, its leaders, the Million Man March, and the reign of Louis Farrakhan. (Rev: SLJ 5/97) [323]

10126 Bolden, Tonya. *Tell All the Children Our Story: Memories and Mementos of Being Young and Black in America* (4–8). Illus. 2002, Abrams $24.95 (0-8109-4496-0). From the first recorded birth of a black child in the United States to the Million Man March, this book describes the African American experience through both personal and historical accounts, using a scrapbook format. (Rev: BL 2/15/02; HB 3–4/02; HBG 10/02; SLJ 3/02*; VOYA 4/02) [973]

10127 Boyle, David. *African Americans* (7–10). Series: Coming to America. 2003, Barron's $14.95

(0-7641-5628-4). This account gives an overview of African American history and the many contributions African Americans have made to the economy and culture. (Rev: BL 10/15/03; SLJ 12/03) [973]

10128 Buckley, Gail. *American Patriots: The Story of Blacks in the Military from the Revolution to Desert Storm* (6–9). 2003, Crown $15.95 (0-375-82243-7). This book describes the segregation, hardships, and triumphs experienced by African Americans in the U.S. military. (Rev: BL 2/15/03; SLJ 2/03) [355]

10129 Clinton, Catherine. *The Black Soldier: 1492 to the Present* (5–8). Illus. 2000, Houghton $17.00 (0-395-67722-X). This history of African Americans in the army begins with colonial slaves who were given muskets to fight the Indians and continues through each of America's wars to the present with emphasis on the slow progress toward equality in the ranks. (Rev: BCCB 10/00; BL 9/15/00; HBG 3/01; SLJ 10/00; VOYA 2/01) [355]

10130 Cole, Harriette, and John Pinderhuges. *Coming Together: Celebrations for African American Families* (4–12). Illus. 2003, Hyperion $22.99 (0-7868-0753-9). Traditions surrounding celebrations including Christmas, Kwanzaa, and naming ceremonies are covered here, with accompanying crafts, menu suggestions, and activities. (Rev: BL 12/15/03) [306.8]

10131 Cole, Michael D. *The Los Angeles Riots: Rage in the City of Angels* (5–9). Series: American Disasters. 1999, Enslow LB $18.95 (0-7660-1219-0). An account of the police beating of Rodney King in Los Angeles and the subsequent riots, the worst in U.S. history. (Rev: BL 2/1/99; HBG 10/99; SLJ 6/99) [979.494053]

10132 Cooper, Michael L. *Bound for the Promised Land* (5–9). 1995, Dutton $15.99 (0-525-67476-4). A short history of the African Americans who left the South for a better life in the North, and in the process changed the face of the nation. (Rev: BL 11/1/95; SLJ 12/95*; VOYA 4/96) [973]

10133 DeAngelis, Therese. *Louis Farrakhan* (6–10). Series: Black Americans of Achievement. 1998, Chelsea $21.95 (0-7910-4688-5); paper $9.95 (0-7910-4689-3). This book provides information about Farrakhan and explains the evolution of his leadership, but it is more a history of the Nation of Islam movement, with information on African American leaders including Malcolm X, Elijah Muhammad, and Roy Wilkins. (Rev: HBG 3/99; SLJ 2/99) [305.8]

10134 Dornfeld, Margaret. *The Turning Tide: From the Desegregation of the Armed Forces to the Montgomery Bus Boycott* (7–10). Series: Milestones in Black American History. 1995, Chelsea LB $21.95 (0-7910-2255-2); paper $9.95 (0-7910-2681-7). This work surveys the period in African American history from 1948 through 1956 and includes Rosa Parks, Ralph Ellison, Charlie Parker, and Adam Clayton Powell, Jr. (Rev: BL 8/95) [973]

10135 Ebony, eds. *Ebony Pictorial History of Black America* (7–12). Illus. 1971, Johnson Pub. $54.95 (set) (0-87485-049-5). These three volumes trace African American history from slavery to today's fight for integration and equality. [305.8]

10136 Feelings, Tom. *Tommy Traveler in the World of Black History* (5–8). 1991, Black Butterfly $13.95 (0-86316-202-9). A history of African Americans seen through the eyes of a boy who imagines himself participating in the important events. (Rev: BL 9/15/91; SLJ 2/92) [973]

10137 Ferry, Joe. *The History of African-American Civic Organizations* (7–12). Illus. Series: American Mosaic: African-American Contributions. 2003, Chelsea LB $22.95 (0-7910-7270-3). Social, business, and other clubs and groups for African American men, women, and children are explored, with information on membership and rituals. (Rev: BL 10/15/03) [36]

10138 Frank, Andrew. *The Birth of Black America: The Age of Discovery and the Slave Trade* (6–8). Series: Milestones in Black American History. 1996, Chelsea LB $21.95 (0-7910-2257-9). This work covers slavery during the colonization of the Americas, the birth of African American culture, and the end of the slave trade. (Rev: SLJ 10/96) [973.2]

10139 Freund, David M. P., and Marya Annette McQuirter. *Biographical Supplement and Index* (7–12). Series: Young Oxford History of African Americans. 1997, Oxford $24.00 (0-19-510258-4). In this, the last volume of the fine series, there is an index to the 10-volume set plus brief biographies of key people mentioned in the set. (Rev: BL 9/1/97; BR 11–12/97; VOYA 12/97) [973]

10140 Garrison, Mary. *Slaves Who Dared: The Stories of Ten African-American Heroes* (7–12). Illus. 2002, White Mane LB $19.95 (1-57249-272-4). Historical prints and quotations from original texts lend authenticity to these moving accounts of famous and less-well-known men and women who escaped from slavery. (Rev: BL 9/1/02; HBG 3/03; SLJ 7/02) [973]

10141 Greene, Meg. *Slave Young, Slave Long: The American Slave Experience* (5–8). Illus. Series: People's History. 1999, Lerner LB $30.35 (0-8225-1739-6). Using quotations from both victims and perpetrators, and illustrated by historical prints and photographs, this book presents the story of slavery in the United States. (Rev: BL 4/1/99; HBG 10/99; SLJ 10/99) [973.0496]

10142 Greenfield, Eloise, and Lessie Jones Little. *Childtimes: A Three-Generation Memoir* (5–8). 1979, HarperCollins LB $16.89 (0-690-03875-5);

paper $9.99 (0-06-446134-3). The childhoods of three generations of African American women.

10143 Hamilton, Virginia. *Many Thousand Gone: African Americans from Slavery to Freedom* (5–9). Illus. 1993, Random LB $18.99 (0-394-92873-3). Combining history with personal slave narratives and biography, Hamilton tells of the famous — Douglass, Truth, Tubman — and the unknown — slaves, rebels, and conductors. (Rev: BL 12/1/92*; SLJ 5/93*) [973.7]

10144 Hansen, Joyce, and Gary McGowan. *Breaking Ground, Breaking Silence: The Story of New York's African Burial Ground* (8–12). 1998, Holt $19.95 (0-8050-5012-4). The graphic story of the finding, in 1991, of the mid-18th-century African Burial Ground in Manhattan and what it reveals about the lives of slaves in New York. (Rev: BL 5/15/98; HBG 10/98; SLJ 5/98; VOYA 8/98) [974.7]

10145 Haskins, James, and Kathleen Benson. *Out of the Darkness: The Story of Blacks Moving North, 1890–1940* (6–8). Series: Great Journeys. 1999, Benchmark LB $21.95 (0-7614-0970-X). The stories of two individuals personalize this discussion of the "Great Migration." (Rev: BL 1/1–15/00; HBG 4/00; SLJ 2/00) [304.8]

10146 Hatt, Christine. *Slavery: From Africa to the Americas* (5–8). 1998, Bedrick $19.95 (0-87226-552-8). A broad overview of slavery in America that covers slave ships, plantation life, abolitionism, the Civil War, and Reconstruction, with maps, illustrations, and reproductions of documents. (Rev: HBG 10/98; SLJ 5/98) [973]

10147 Hauser, Pierre. *Great Ambitions: From the "Separate but Equal" Doctrine to the Birth of the NAACP (1896–1909)* (7–10). Series: Milestones in Black American History. 1995, Chelsea $21.95 (0-7910-2264-1); paper $9.95 (0-7910-2690-6). The history of African Americans at the end of the 19th and beginning of the 20th century, with coverage of such political and cultural pioneers as W. E. B. Du Bois, Charles Chesnutt, Paul Laurence Dunbar, and Scott Joplin. (Rev: BL 2/15/95) [323.1]

10148 Henry, Christopher. *Forever Free: From the Emancipation Proclamation to the Civil Rights Bill of 1875 (1863–1875)* (7–10). Series: Milestones in Black American History. 1995, Chelsea LB $21.95 (0-7910-2253-6); paper $8.95 (0-7910-2679-5). The history of African Americans during Reconstruction, covering the tearing down of racial barriers and the journey from political impotence to civil power. (Rev: BL 7/95; SLJ 10/95) [323.1]

10149 Hine, Darlene Clark. *The Path to Equality: From the Scottsboro Case to the Breaking of Baseball's Color Barrier (7–10).* Series: Milestones in Black American History. 1995, Chelsea LB $19.95 (0-7910-2251-X); paper $9.95 (0-7910-2677-9). This section of African American history covers the

Great Depression and World War II, and features the accomplishments of such people as Marion Anderson, Thurgood Marshall, A. Philip Randolph, and Jackie Robinson. (Rev: BL 8/95) [973]

10150 Holliday, Laurel, ed. *Dreaming in Color, Living in Black and White: Our Own Stories of Growing Up Black in America* (8–12). 2000, Pocket paper $4.99 (0-671-04127-4). This is a moving collection of first-person accounts by African Americans who tell of the racism they faced while growing up. (Rev: BL 2/15/00; SLJ 4/00; VOYA 4/00) [305.896.]

10151 Hurmence, Belinda, ed. *Slavery Time When I Was Chillun* (8–12). Illus. 1997, Putnam $9.99 (0-399-23194-3). A disturbing collection of 12 slave narratives that give firsthand accounts of brutality, family separation, and hard labor, as well as some of kindly masters and happy times. (Rev: BL 3/15/98) [975]

10152 Jacob, Iris. *My Sisters' Voices: Teenage Girls of Color Speak Out* (7–12). 2002, Holt paper $13.00 (0-8050-6821-X). Teen girls of color describe their feelings, aspirations, and disappointments in prose and poetry. (Rev: BL 3/1/02; SLJ 10/02; VOYA 12/02) [305.235]

10153 King, Wilma. *Toward the Promised Land: From Uncle Tom's Cabin to the Onset of the Civil War (1851–1861)* (7–10). Series: Milestones in Black American History. 1995, Chelsea paper $9.95 (0-7910-2691-4). This work examines the major trends and personalities in the struggle to end slavery before the Civil War, with material on Frederick Douglass, Sojourner Truth, Harriet Beecher Stowe, and John Brown. (Rev: BL 7/95; SLJ 10/95; VOYA 12/95) [973]

10154 Lester, Julius. *From Slave Ship to Freedom Road* (5–10). Illus. 1998, Dial $17.99 (0-8037-1893-4). This book combines art, history, and commentary to produce a graphically gripping history of slavery. (Rev: BL 2/15/98; HBG 9/98; SLJ 2/98*) [759.13]

10155 Lester, Julius. *To Be a Slave* (6–9). 1968, Dial $16.99 (0-8037-8955-6); Scholastic paper $4.50 (0-590-42460-2). A powerful account of what it means to be a slave drawn largely from primary documents. [326]

10156 Macht, Norman L., and Mary Hull. *The History of Slavery* (6–9). Illus. Series: World History. 1997, Lucent LB $27.45 (1-56006-302-5). This overview of slavery in the United States contains extensive quotations from original sources and a chronology. (Rev: BL 8/97; BR 11–12/97; SLJ 11/97) [306.3]

10157 McKissack, Patricia, and Fredrick McKissack. *Black Hands, White Sails: The Story of African-American Whalers* (6–10). Illus. 1999, Scholastic paper $15.95 (0-590-48313-7). This account of African American involvement in the whaling

industry from colonial times through the 19th century also touches on the abolitionist movement, the Underground Railroad, and the Civil War. (Rev: BCCB 11/99; BL 9/1/99; BR 9–10/99; HB 11–12/99; HBG 4/00; VOYA 2/00) [639.2]

10158 Newman, Shirlee P. *Slavery in the United States* (4–7). Series: Watts Library: History of Slavery. 2000, Watts LB $24.00 (0-531-11695-6). This account covers the shameful American record concerning slavery with coverage from the African slave trade through plantation life, the Underground Railroad, and abolitionists to the Civil War and emancipation. (Rev: BL 3/1/01) [973]

10159 Patrick, Diane. *The New York Public Library Amazing African American History: A Book of Answers for Kids* (5–9). Illus. 1998, Wiley paper $12.95 (0-471-19217-1). Using a question-and-answer format, this book traces the history of African Americans from slavery to the present day. (Rev: BL 2/15/98; SLJ 4/98) [973]

10160 Peltak, Jennifer. *The History of African-American Colleges and Universities* (7–12). Illus. Series: American Mosaic: African-American Contributions. 2003, Chelsea LB $22.95 (0-7910-7269-X). This volume looks at the history of black colleges and universities, enrollment trends, and the struggle for equality in education. (Rev: BL 10/15/03) [378.7]

10161 Rappaport, Doreen. *No More! Stories and Songs of Slave Resistance* (4–7). 2002, Candlewick $17.99 (0-7636-0984-6). A collection of narratives, prose, poetry, and songs that describe the African slave experience and the various forms of rebellion that took place. (Rev: BCCB 4/02; BL 2/15/02; HB 3–4/02; HBG 10/02; SLJ 2/02*) [306.3]

10162 Reef, Catherine. *Africans in America: The Spread of People and Culture* (6–9). Series: Library of African American History. 1999, Facts on File $25.00 (0-8160-3772-8). The author traces the dispersion of African peoples and cultures in the New World as a result of the slave trade and their influence on the Americas. (Rev: BL 2/15/99; SLJ 6/99) [970.00496]

10163 Straub, Deborah G., ed. *African American Voices* (5–8). Illus. 1996, Gale $105.00 (0-8103-9497-9). This is a collection of excerpts from important speeches delivered by a vast array of African Americans, past and present. (Rev: SLJ 2/97) [973]

10164 Sullivan, Charles, ed. *Children of Promise: African-American Literature and Art for Young People* (4–8). Illus. 1991, Abrams $24.95 (0-8109-3170-2). Through poems, songs, literary excerpts, and illustrations, the history of African Americans is traced. (Rev: BL 11/16/91; SLJ 1/92) [973]

10165 Van Peebles, Mario, et al. *Panther: A Pictorial History of the Black Panthers and the Story Behind the Film* (8–12). 1995, Newmarket paper

$16.95 (1-55704-227-6). The first part of this heavily illustrated book recounts the beginnings of the Black Panther Party and its eventual collapse; the second half describes the making of the movie about the party. (Rev: VOYA 2/96) [973]

10166 Weisbrot, Robert. *Marching Toward Freedom* (7–12). Series: Milestones in Black American History. 1994, Chelsea paper $8.95 (0-7910-2682-5). This history covers African American affairs from the founding of the Southern Christian Leadership Conference to the assassination of Malcolm X (1957–1965), with material on Martin Luther King, Jr., James Farmer, Elijah Muhammad, and Malcolm X, among others. (Rev: BL 11/15/94; SLJ 9/94; VOYA 10/94) [973]

10167 Woodson, Jacqueline, ed. *A Way out of No Way: Writings About Growing Up Black in America* (8–12). Illus. 1996, Holt $15.95 (0-8050-4570-8). A fine collection of prose and poetry, fiction and nonfiction about growing up in America, from some of the best African American writers, among them James Baldwin, Paul Beatty, Jamaica Kincaid, and Langston Hughes. (Rev: BL 2/15/97; BR 11–12/97; SLJ 7/97; VOYA 6/97) [808.898]

Asian Americans

10168 Bandon, Alexandra. *Chinese Americans* (6–12). Series: Footsteps to America. 1994, Silver Burdett LB $13.95 (0-02-768149-1). A look at Chinese people in the United States, beginning with their first large immigration in the mid-19th century to the 1990s. (Rev: BL 10/15/94; SLJ 11/94; VOYA 2/95) [973]

10169 Bandon, Alexandra. *Filipino Americans* (6–10). Series: Footsteps to America. 1993, Macmillan LB $13.95 (0-02-768143-2). Examines why Filipino Americans left their homeland and describes their culture, politics, education, religion, and holidays in the United States. (Rev: BL 12/15/93; SLJ 12/93) [973]

10170 Daley, William. *The Chinese Americans* (5–8). Illus. 1995, Chelsea LB $21.95 (0-7910-3357-0); paper $9.95 (0-7910-3379-1). The background and culture of this group are explained, as well as its adjustment to life in America. (Rev: BL 1/1/88) [973.04951]

10171 Dudley, William, ed. *Asian Americans* (7–12). Series: Opposing Viewpoints in American History. 1997, Greenhaven LB $32.45 (1-56510-524-9). A collection of documents tracing attitudes and policies toward Asian immigrants and Asian American citizens from the 1850s to the present. (Rev: BL 12/15/96) [973]

10172 Hamanaka, Sheila. *The Journey: Japanese Americans, Racism and Renewal* (5–9). 1990, Orchard LB $20.99 (0-531-08449-3). With brief

text, this book is a series of paintings from a large mural that describes the injustices suffered by Japanese Americans at the beginning of World War II. (Rev: BL 3/15/90; HB 5–6/90; SLJ 5/90; VOYA 6/90) [940.54]

10173 Kitano, Harry. *The Japanese Americans*. 2nd ed. (5–8). Photos by Richard Hewett. Series: Land of Immigrants. 1995, Chelsea LB $19.95 (0-7910-3358-9); paper $9.95 (0-7910-3380-5). The story of Japanese Americans and their traditions and contributions to American life and culture. (Rev: BL 10/15/95; VOYA 2/96) [305]

10174 Nam, Vickie, ed. *Yell-Oh Girls! Emerging Voices Explore Culture, Identity, and Growing up Asian American* (8–12). Illus. 2001, HarperCollins paper $13.00 (0-06-095944-4). An anthology of fiction and poetry written by Asian American high school and college students, revealing their feelings about topics including heritage, stereotypes, adoption, and interracial dating. (Rev: SLJ 10/01; VOYA 2/02) [305.235]

10175 Omoto, Susan. *Hmong Milestones in America: Citizens in a New World* (5–8). Illus. 2003, John Gordon Burke $27.00 (0-934272-57-3); paper $15.00 (0-934272-56-5). The author introduces the Hmong people's history and traditions and traces the steps of Hmong refugees who migrated to the United States, profiling five individuals who have found success in their new country. (Rev: BL 4/15/03) [973]

10176 Perl, Lila. *To the Golden Mountain: The Story of the Chinese Who Built the First Transcontinental Railroad* (6–9). Series: Great Journeys. 2002, Marshall Cavendish LB $21.95 (0-7614-1324-3). The immigration of Chinese to build the transcontinental railroad and their treatment form the basis of this account that includes many firsthand sources. (Rev: BL 3/15/03; HBG 3/03; SLJ 2/03) [973]

10177 Ragaza, Angelo. *Lives of Notable Asian Americans: Business, Politics, Science* (6–10). Series: Asian American Experience. 1995, Chelsea LB $18.95 (0-7910-2189-0). Asian Americans who have contributed in the business, political, and scientific arenas. (Rev: BL 8/95; VOYA 12/95) [973]

10178 St. Pierre, Stephanie. *Teenage Refugees from Cambodia Speak Out* (7–12). 1995, Rosen LB $16.95 (0-8239-1848-3). Grim stories of the escape from the "killing fields" and powerful testimony to the reality of refugee life. (Rev: BL 5/15/95; SLJ 5/95) [973]

10179 She, Colleen. *Teenage Refugees from China Speak Out* (7–12). Series: In Their Own Voices. 1995, Rosen LB $16.95 (0-8239-1847-5). Interviews with native Chinese teenagers who are now living in the United States. (Rev: BL 6/1–15/95; SLJ 5/95) [305.23]

10180 Springstubb, Tricia. *The Vietnamese Americans* (6–12). Illus. Series: Immigrants in America. 2002, Gale $27.45 (1-56006-964-3). A look at how this ethnic group is faring in America, with stories of individual immigrants adding interest. (Rev: BL 4/1/02; SLJ 6/02) [305.895]

10181 Stanley, Jerry. *I Am an American: A True Story of Japanese Internment* (5–10). 1994, Crown LB $17.99 (0-517-59787-X). A photoessay detailing the experiences of Japanese Americans during World War II. Focuses on war hysteria and the unjust use of internment camps. (Rev: BL 10/15/94*; SLJ 11/94*) [940.53]

10182 Takaki, Ronald. *Ethnic Islands: The Emergence of Urban Chinese America* (6–10). Series: Asian American Experience. 1994, Chelsea LB $19.95 (0-7910-2180-7). First-person accounts of the Chinese American experience in the 20th century. (Rev: BL 9/15/94; SLJ 9/94) [973]

10183 Takaki, Ronald. *From Exiles to Immigrants: The Refugees from Southeast Asia* (6–10). Series: Asian American Experience. 1995, Chelsea LB $19.95 (0-7910-2185-8). Personal histories of Southeast Asian refugees in the United States. (Rev: BL 8/95; VOYA 12/95) [978]

10184 Takaki, Ronald. *From the Land of Morning Calm: The Koreans in America* (6–10). Series: Asian American Experience. 1994, Chelsea LB $19.95 (0-7910-2181-5). Oral histories and local documents challenge stereotypes that plague Korean Americans. (Rev: BL 9/1/94; SLJ 9/94; VOYA 12/94) [973]

10185 Takaki, Ronald. *In the Heart of Filipino America: Immigrants from the Pacific Isles* (6–10). Series: Asian American Experience. 1994, Chelsea LB $19.95 (0-7910-2187-4). A historic overview of Filipinos in the United States. (Rev: BL 12/15/94; VOYA 4/95) [973]

10186 Takaki, Ronald. *India in the West: South Asians in America* (6–10). Series: Asian American Experience. 1994, Chelsea LB $19.95 (0-7910-2186-6). This overview of the Asian Indian experience in the United States describes how, when, and why South Asians came to this country and the problems they have confronted. (Rev: BL 12/15/94; SLJ 3/95) [970]

10187 Wapner, Kenneth. *Teenage Refugees from Vietnam Speak Out* (7–12). Series: In Their Own Voices. 1995, Rosen LB $16.95 (0-8239-1842-4). Interviews with Vietnamese teenagers who are now living in the United States. (Rev: BL 6/1–15/95; SLJ 5/95) [305.23]

10188 Wu, Dana Ying-Hui, and Jeffrey Dao-Sheng Tung. *The Chinese-American Experience* (5–7). Illus. Series: Coming to America. 1993, Millbrook LB $22.40 (1-56294-271-9). The story of Chinese immigration to the United States, from exploitation, prejudice, and discrimination to gradual acceptance. (Rev: BL 6/1–15/93) [973]

10189 Yamaguchi, Yoji. *A Student's Guide to Japanese American Genealogy* (8–12). 1996, Oryx $29.95 (0-89774-979-0). This book describes Japanese immigration to the United States and where they settled, followed by information on general genealogical research and on researching Japanese Americans' genealogies. (Rev: VOYA 8/96) [973]

10190 Zurlo, Tony. *The Japanese Americans* (6–12). Series: Immigrants in America. 2003, Gale LB $27.45 (1-59018-001-1). From Hawaii's sugar plantations to California's truck farms, this is the story of Japanese Americans and how they fought for full acceptance in America. (Rev: BL 11/15/03) [973]

Hispanic Americans

10191 Aliotta, Jerome J. *The Puerto Ricans* (5–8). Series: Land of Immigrants. 1995, Chelsea LB $21.95 (0-7910-3360-0). This account provides an extensive history of Puerto Ricans living in the United States, their struggles, traditions, and way of life. (Rev: BL 10/15/95) [305.868]

10192 Bandon, Alexandra. *Dominican Americans* (5–8). Illus. Series: Footsteps to America. 1995, New Discovery $22.00 (0-02-768152-1). A readable account of why many residents of the Dominican Republic left their country to come to the United States and the conditions they found. (Rev: SLJ 8/95) [973]

10193 Bandon, Alexandra. *Mexican Americans* (6–10). Series: Footsteps to America. 1993, Macmillan LB $14.95 (0-02-768142-4). A look at Mexico and the culture of Mexican American immigrants in the United States, with first-person narratives of immigrant experiences. (Rev: BL 12/15/93; SLJ 12/93; VOYA 2/94) [305.868]

10194 Catalano, Julie. *The Mexican Americans* (5–8). Illus. Series: Immigrant Experience. 1995, Chelsea LB $21.95 (0-7910-3359-7); paper $9.95 (0-7910-3381-3). This book traces the reasons for leaving Mexico, the immigrants' reception in the United States, and their contributions and achievements. (Rev: BL 11/15/95; SLJ 1/96) [973]

10195 Cerar, K. Melissa. *Teenage Refugees from Nicaragua Speak Out* (7–12). Series: In Their Own Voices. 1995, Rosen LB $16.95 (0-8239-1849-1). The horror of the contra war, after the corrupt rule of the Somoza family was ended by the Sandinistas, is recalled by Nicaraguan teens who fled their country, leaving their families, to seek refuge in the United States. (Rev: BL 6/1–15/95) [973]

10196 Cockcroft, James D. *The Hispanic Struggle for Social Justice: The Hispanic Experience in the Americas* (8–12). Series: Hispanic Experience in the Americas. 1994, Watts paper $24.00 (0-531-11185-

7). After a discussion of the diverse experiences of Mexican Americans, Puerto Ricans, and other Latinos in this country, the author examines their ethnic history and struggles around labor, immigration, civil rights, and women's rights issues. (Rev: BL 2/1/95) [305.868]

10197 Cofer, Judith Ortiz, ed. *Riding Low on the Streets of Gold* (6–12). 2003, Arte Publico $14.95 (1-55885-380-4). Latino writers consider issues close to teen hearts in this collection of fiction, poetry, and memoirs. (Rev: BL 12/1/03) [810]

10198 Cole, Melanie, et al. *Famous People of Hispanic Heritage* (4–7). Series: Contemporary American Success Stories. 1997, Mitchell Lane LB $21.95 (1-883845-44-0); paper $12.95 (1-883845-43-2). This useful series, now in nine volumes, profiles famous Hispanics, past and present, from around the world. (Rev: BL 3/15/98; HBG 3/98) [920]

10199 Gay, Kathlyn. *Leaving Cuba: From Operation Pedro Pan to Elian* (6–12). Illus. 2000, Twenty-First Century LB $22.90 (0-7613-1466-0). The plight of young Elian Gonzalez brought attention to Cubans' efforts to escape their oppressive regime and the uncertain welcome they face in the United States. (Rev: BL 3/1/01; HBG 3/01; SLJ 1/01; VOYA 6/01) [362.87]

10200 Gernand, Renee. *The Cuban Americans* (5–8). Illus. 1995, Chelsea LB $21.95 (0-791-03354-6); paper $9.95 (0-791-03376-7). The contributions of Cuban Americans and reasons why they came to America. (Rev: BL 2/1/89) [973.0468729]

10201 Mendez, Adriana. *Cubans in America* (5–7). Illus. Series: In America. 1994, Lerner LB $19.93 (0-8225-1953-4). An account that describes why Cubans left their homeland, where they live in the United States, their lifestyles, and their contributions to society. (Rev: BL 8/94; SLJ 8/94) [973]

10202 Ochoa, George. *The New York Public Library Amazing Hispanic American History: A Book of Answers for Kids* (4–9). 1998, Wiley paper $12.95 (0-471-19204-X). Using a question-and-answer format, this work explores such topics as Hispanic American identity and history, cultural groups, accomplishments, and immigrant experiences. (Rev: BL 12/1/98; SLJ 11/98) [973]

10203 Perl, Lila. *North Across the Border: The Story of the Mexican Americans* (5–9). Series: Great Journeys. 2001, Benchmark LB $31.36 (0-7614-1226-3). The economic and social reasons for Mexican migration to the north through history are presented in text, quotations from primary sources, and many illustrations and maps. (Rev: BL 1/1–15/02; HBG 10/02; SLJ 3/02) [973.0468]

10204 Ryskamp, George R., and Peggy Ryskamp. *A Student's Guide to Mexican American Genealogy* (6–10). Series: Oryx Family Tree. 1996, Oryx $24.95 (0-89774-981-2). This book provides an

interesting review of Mexican American history as well as an introduction to genealogy and a discussion of nontraditional families. (Rev: SLJ 2/97) [973]

10205 Sonneborn, Liz. *The Cuban Americans* (6–12). Illus. Series: Immigrants in America. 2002, Gale $27.45 (1-56006-902-3). A look at how this ethnic group is faring in America, with stories of individual immigrants adding interest. (Rev: BL 4/1/02) [973]

10206 Sullivan, Charles, ed. *Here Is My Kingdom: Hispanic-American Literature and Art for Young People* (7–12). 1994, Abrams $24.95 (0-8109-3422-1). A collection of Latino prose, poetry, painting, and photography, with profiles of leading figures from Cervantes to singer Gloria Estefan. (Rev: BL 7/94*)

Jewish Americans

10207 Finkelstein, Norman H. *Forged in Freedom: Shaping the Jewish-American Experience* (6–12). Illus. 2002, Jewish Publication Soc. $24.95 (0-8276-0748-2). Text and photographs present an overview of Jews' contributions to the United States, their influence on the culture, and the problems they have faced. (Rev: BL 8/02; HBG 3/03) [973.04]

10208 Horton, Casey. *The Jews* (4–8). Series: We Came to North America. 2000, Crabtree LB $21.28 (0-7787-0187-5); paper $8.95 (0-7787-0201-4). As well as discussing the reasons why Jews left Europe, this account describes the trip across the Atlantic, reception in America, and the many contributions to the United States. (Rev: SLJ 10/00) [973]

10209 Leder, Jane. *A Russian Jewish Family* (5–8). Series: Journey Between Two Worlds. 1996, Lerner LB $22.60 (0-8225-3401-0); paper $8.95 (0-8225-9744-6). This account compares the living conditions of a Jewish family in Russia and in their new American home. (Rev: BL 11/1/96; SLJ 11/96) [977.3]

10210 Lingen, Marissa. *The Jewish Americans* (4–7). Illus. Series: We Came to America. 2002, Mason Crest LB $19.95 (1-59084-109-3). Lingen traces the history of Jewish migration to the United States and provides a list of Jewish Americans of note. (Rev: SLJ 9/02) [973.049]

10211 Muggamin, Howard. *The Jewish Americans* (5–8). Series: Immigrant Experience. 1995, Chelsea LB $19.95 (0-7910-3365-1); paper $9.95 (0-7910-3387-2). An examination of Jewish Americans, their history of immigration and their reception in this country, and their achievements and contributions. (Rev: BL 11/15/95) [973]

10212 Schleifer, Jay. *A Student's Guide to Jewish American Genealogy* (7–12). Series: American Family Tree. 1996, Oryx $29.95 (0-89774-977-4).

An in-depth survey of Jewish history serves as a framework for realistic genealogical information, with plenty of valuable sources cited. (Rev: SLJ 1/97) [973]

10213 Shamir, Ilana, and Shlomo Shavit, eds. *The Young Reader's Encyclopedia of Jewish History* (5–10). Illus. 1987, Viking $17.95 (0-670-81738-4). From a home for nomadic tribes to the present, this is a history of Israel and the Jewish people in many brief chapters. (Rev: BL 3/15/88; SLJ 2/88) [909]

10214 Stein, Robert. *Jewish Americans* (7–10). Illus. Series: Coming to America. 2003, Barron's $14.95 (0-7641-5626-8). In an absorbing text with compelling illustrations and first-person anecdotes, Stein looks at the reasons for Jewish emigration, the conditions the emigres found when they arrived in the United States, and their contributions to their new country. (Rev: BL 10/15/03*; SLJ 12/03) [973]

Native Americans

10215 Adare, Sierra. *Mohawk* (4–8). Illus. 2003, Gareth Stevens LB $22.60 (0-8368-3665-0). An introduction to the history, culture, and current status of the Mohawk people, with photographs, maps, and interesting sidebar features that will be useful for reports. Also use *Apache* and *Nez Perce* (both 2003). (Rev: HBG 10/03; SLJ 9/03) [974.7004]

10216 Bial, Raymond. *The Mandan* (5–9). Series: Lifeways. 2002, Benchmark LB $22.95 (0-7614-1415-0). Two traditional stories, a recipe, and a language guide accompany information on the history, culture, beliefs, and key figures of the Mandan people. (Rev: HBG 3/03; LMC 8–9/03; SLJ 6/03) [978.004]

10217 Hirschfelder, Arlene, and Beverly R. Singer, eds. *Rising Voices: Writings of Young Native Americans* (5–8). 1992, Macmillan $14.00 (0-684-19207-1). Young Native Americans write in prose, poetry, essays, and song about identity, family, homelands, rituals, education, and other subjects. (Rev: BCCB 9/92; BL 7/92; SLJ 12/92*) [810.8]

10218 Hoig, Stan. *People of the Sacred Arrows: The Southern Cheyenne Today* (6–8). 1992, Dutton $15.00 (0-525-65088-1). A portrayal of the modern life of the southern Cheyenne. (Rev: BL 9/1/92; SLJ 11/92) [976.6]

10219 Secakuku, Susan. *Meet Mindy: A Native Girl from the Southwest* (5–8). Photos by John Harrington. Photos. Series: My World: Young Native Americans Today. 2003, Beyond Words paper $15.95 (1-58270-091-5). A Hopi teen named Mindy talks about her life and heritage in this full-color photoessay. (Rev: BL 4/1/03; SLJ 3/03) [979.1004]

10220 Straub, Deborah G., ed. *Native North American Voices* (6–12). 1997, Gale $55.00 (0-8103-9819-2). This is a collection of important speeches

delivered by 20 Native Americans, beginning with one by Joseph Brant in 1794 and ending with the 1944 speech of Ada Deer of the Bureau of Indian Affairs. (Rev: BR 9–10/97; SLJ 11/97) [973]

Other Ethnic Groups

10221 Ashabranner, Brent. *Children of the Maya: A Guatemalan Indian Odyssey* (6–9). Illus. 1986, Dodd $14.95 (0-396-08786-8). The story of the Mayan Indians from Guatemala who are refugees in Florida. (Rev: BL 3/87; SLJ 8/86) [341.4]

10222 Bandon, Alexandra. *Asian Indian Americans* (5–8). Illus. Series: Footsteps to America. 1995, New Discovery LB $13.95 (0-02-768144-0). An account of the conditions that have caused emigration from India and a description of life in the United States for the immigrants. (Rev: SLJ 8/95) [973]

10223 Bandon, Alexandra. *West Indian Americans* (5–10). Series: Footsteps to America. 1994, Silver Burdett LB $13.95 (0-02-768148-3). Describes why some West Indians left their islands to come to the United States, their reception, and their present lifestyles and contributions to their new nation. (Rev: BL 10/15/94; SLJ 12/94) [973]

10224 Brockman, Terra Castiglia. *A Student's Guide to Italian American Genealogy* (7–12). Series: American Family Tree. 1996, Oryx $29.95 (0-89774-973-1). This book, a guide to searching for Italian American ancestors, contains web sites, computer programs, addresses, and other sources of information. (Rev: SLJ 10/96) [929]

10225 Cavan, Seamus. *The Irish-American Experience* (5–7). Illus. Series: Coming to America. 1993, Millbrook LB $23.40 (1-56294-218-2). Beginning with the potato famine that forced millions of Irish to come to America, this is the story of the rise of Irish Americans to positions of prominence. (Rev: BCCB 4/93; BL 6/1–15/93) [973]

10226 Deignan, Tom. *Irish Americans* (7–10). Illus. Series: Coming to America. 2003, Barron's $14.95 (0-7641-5627-6). An absorbing look at the reasons for Irish emigration, the conditions the emigres found when they arrived in the United States, and their contributions to their new country. (Rev: BL 10/15/03*) [873]

10227 Di Franco, J. Philip. *The Italian Americans* (5–8). Illus. 1995, Chelsea LB $21.95 (0-791-03353-8); paper $9.95 (0-7910-3375-9). A heavily illustrated discussion of the culture that Italian immigrants left behind and their contributions to American life. (Rev: BL 1/1/88) [973.0451]

10228 Franck, Irene M. *The German-American Heritage* (7–12). Illus. 1988, Facts on File $25.00 (0-8160-1629-1). This book contains not only an account of the progress of Germans in this country but also a brief history of Germany. (Rev: BL 3/15/89; BR 5–6/89) [973]

10229 Galicich, Anne. *The German Americans* (5–8). Illus. Series: Immigrant Experience. 1995, Chelsea LB $19.95 (0-7910-3362-7); paper $9.95 (0-7910-3384-8). This account traces the history of German Americans, from their reasons for leaving Germany and their initial reception in the United States to their present status. (Rev: BL 4/1/89) [973]

10230 Halliburton, Warren J. *The West Indian-American Experience* (7–10). 1994, Millbrook LB $23.90 (1-56294-340-5). Tells the story of a Jamaican family's emigration to the United States in the 1980s, the history of the Caribbean, and immigration to the United States. (Rev: BL 4/1/94; SLJ 7/94) [973]

10231 Hossell, Karen Price. *The Irish Americans* (6–12). Series: Immigrants in America. 2003, Gale LB $27.45 (1-56006-752-7). The story of the thousands of Irish people who migrated to America, where they faced discrimination before being assimilated into society and being accepted as true Americans. (Rev: BL 11/15/03) [973]

10232 Johnson, Anne E. *A Student's Guide to British American Genealogy* (7–12). Series: American Family Tree. 1995, Oryx $29.95 (0-89774-982-0). This book gives instructions on how to start a genealogical search, explains English, Scottish, and Welsh history and traditions, and describes names, nobility, clans, and the history of British immigration to America. (Rev: SLJ 4/96) [973]

10233 Katz, William L. *Black Indians: A Hidden Heritage* (7–10). 1986, Macmillan $17.95 (0-689-31196-6). A history of the group that represented a mixture of the Indian and black races and its role in opening up the West. (Rev: BL 6/15/86; SLJ 8/86) [970]

10234 Kuropas, Myron B. *Ukrainians in America* (5–7). Illus. Series: In America. 1996, Lerner LB $19.93 (0-8225-1043-X). The story of Ukrainian immigrants to the United States, their cultural traditions, and their contributions to American life. (Rev: BL 3/15/96; SLJ 3/96) [973]

10235 Lock, Donna. *The Polish Americans* (5–8). Illus. Series: We Came to America. 2002, Mason Crest LB $19.95 (1-59084-112-3). A look at the customs and contributions of this ethnic group, including information on famous Polish Americans, with a bibliography, glossary, timeline, and resources for tracing ancestors. (Rev: BL 7/02) [305.891]

10236 McGill, Allyson. *The Swedish Americans* (5–8). Series: Immigrant Experience. 1997, Chelsea $19.95 (0-7910-4551-X); paper $9.95 (0-7910-4552-8). Explains why Swedes have emigrated from their homeland, their reception in the United States, and their contributions to the nation. (Rev: BL 10/15/97) [322.4]

10237 McKenna, Erin. *A Student's Guide to Irish American Genealogy* (7–12). Illus. 1996, Oryx $29.95 (0-89774-976-6). Along with giving practical tips on how to trace Irish ancestors, this book traces Irish history, immigration, Irish culture, and contributions. (Rev: BL 3/1/97; VOYA 4/97) [973]

10238 Magocsi, Paul R. *The Russian Americans* (5–8). Illus. Series: Immigrant Experience. 1995, Chelsea LB $21.95 (0-7910-3367-8). Coverage includes reasons for leaving Russia, customs and traditions, contributions to their new nation, and famous Russian Americans. (Rev: BL 11/15/95; SLJ 1/96) [973]

10239 Moreno, Barry. *Italian Americans* (7–10). Series: Coming to America. 2003, Barron's $14.95 (0-7641-5624-1). This is the story of how and why Italians migrated to this country, their reception, assimilation, and contributions. (Rev: BL 10/15/03) [973]

10240 Naff, Alixa. *The Arab Americans* (6–10). Series: The Immigrant Experience. 1998, Chelsea $21.95 (0-7910-5051-3); paper $9.95 (0-7910-5053-X). After a brief description of Arab culture and homelands, this book describes the different cycles in Arab immigration to this country, the reception Arabs received, their new identities and contributions, and famous Arab Americans such as Ralph Nader and Donna Shalala. (Rev: HBG 3/99; SLJ 1/99) [305.8]

10241 Paddock, Lisa, and Carl S. Rollyson. *A Student's Guide to Scandinavian American Genealogy* (7–12). Series: American Family Tree. 1996, Oryx $29.95 (0-89774-978-2). An introduction to the Scandinavian countries, people, and emigration to America, and information on how to research specific nationalities. (Rev: SLJ 10/96) [929]

10242 Sawyers, June S. *Famous Firsts of Scottish-Americans* (4–8). Illus. 1996, Pelican $13.95 (1-56554-122-7). Brief biographies of 30 Americans of Scottish descent, including Neil Armstrong, Alexander Calder, Herman Melville, and Patrick Henry. (Rev: BL 6/1–15/97) [920]

10243 Schouweiler, Thomas. *Germans in America* (5–7). Illus. Series: In America. 1994, Lerner LB $19.93 (0-8225-0245-3). The causes and results of German immigration to the United States are outlined, with good coverage of their contributions and important figures. (Rev: BL 1/15/95; SLJ 12/94) [973]

10244 Silverman, Robin L. *A Bosnian Family* (4–7). Illus. Series: Journey Between Two Worlds. 1997, Lerner LB $27.15 (0-8225-3404-5); paper $8.95 (0-8225-9754-3). The story of Velma Dusper, her homeland of Bosnia, and her journey with her family to freedom and a new home in North Dakota. (Rev: BL 6/1–15/97; SLJ 7/97) [304.8]

10245 Strazzabosco-Hayn, Gina. *Teenage Refugees from Iran Speak Out* (7–12). 1995, Rosen LB $16.95 (0-8239-1845-9). Iranian teens tell their grim stories as powerful testimony to the reality of refugee life. (Rev: BL 5/15/95; SLJ 5/95) [973]

10246 Tekavec, Valerie. *Teenage Refugees from Haiti Speak Out* (7–12). Series: In Their Own Voices. 1995, Rosen LB $16.95 (0-8239-1844-0). Interviews with native Haitian teenagers who are now living in the United States. (Rev: BL 6/1–15/95; SLJ 6/95) [305.23]

10247 Temple, Bob. *The Arab Americans* (5–8). Illus. Series: We Came to America. 2002, Mason Crest LB $19.95 (1-59084-102-6). Temple reviews the history of Arab immigration to North America, the group's customs and contributions, and famous Arab Americans, with the aid of photographs, a timeline, and glossary. (Rev: BL 7/02; SLJ 9/02) [305.892]

10248 Ueda, Reed, and Sandra Stotsky, eds. *Irish-American Answer Book* (6–10). 1999, Chelsea LB $19.75 (0-7910-4795-4); paper $9.95 (0-7910-4796-2). Using a question-and-answer format, this book examines the history, culture, politics, and religion of Irish Americans from the 1800s to the present. (Rev: VOYA 2/99) [973]

10249 Watts, J. F. *The Irish Americans* (5–8). Series: Immigrant Experience. 1995, Chelsea paper $9.95 (0-7910-3388-0). A lively, informative account of why the Irish came to America, the conditions they found here, and how they have fared. (Rev: BL 10/15/95) [973]

10250 Zamenova, Tatyana. *Teenage Refugees from Russia Speak Out* (7–12). Series: In Their Own Voices. 1995, Rosen LB $16.95 (0-8239-1846-7). Teenage Russian refugees describe their lives under socialism, leaving Russia, and adjusting to life in North America. (Rev: BL 6/1–15/95) [973]

Social Concerns and Problems

General and Miscellaneous

10251 Able, Deborah. *Hate Groups*. Rev. ed. (7–9). Series: Issues in Focus. 2000, Enslow LB $19.95 (0-7660-1245-X). An in-depth look at hate groups in America, what motivates them, their targets, and ways to combat them, with details of recent incidents and court cases, and of the growing use of the Internet in this area. (Rev: HBG 3/01; SLJ 1/01) [305.8]

10252 Ancona, George. *Harvest* (4–7). Illus. 2001, Marshall Cavendish $15.95 (0-7614-5086-6). This volume examines the difficult lives and work of Mexican migrant workers and the crops they harvest, ending with a look at the contributions of labor leader Cesar Chavez. (Rev: BL 1/1–15/02; HBG 3/02; SLJ 4/02) [331.5]

10253 Andryszewski, Tricia. *The Militia Movement in America: Before and After Oklahoma City* (7–12). Illus. 1997, Millbrook LB $24.90 (0-7613-0119-4). This work traces the roots of the anti-government militia movement in the United States from the late 1800s to the present, with coverage of events in Ruby Ridge, Waco, Oklahoma City, and elsewhere. (Rev: BL 2/15/97; BR 9–10/97; SLJ 3/97; VOYA 2/98) [320.4]

10254 Bekoff, Marc, and Carron A. Meaney, eds. *Encyclopedia of Animal Rights and Animal Welfare* (7–12). 1998, Greenwood $67.95 (0-313-29977-3). Signed entries explore different aspects of the animal rights issue, including such topics as hunting, genetic engineering, and laboratory use. (Rev: BL 9/15/98; SLJ 2/99; VOYA 2/99) [179]

10255 Brimner, Larry. *A Migrant Family* (4–8). Illus. 1992, Lerner LB $23.95 (0-8225-2554-2). The daily life of 12-year-old Juan and his Mexican American family is captured in this photoessay. (Rev: BCCB 10/92; BL 9/15/92) [305.5]

10256 Cann, Kate. *Living in the World* (5–9). Illus. Series: Life Education. 1997, Watts paper $19.00 (0-531-14430-5). Cartoon drawings, photographs, anecdotes, and pointed questions combine to explore group and interpersonal interactions, including such issues as peer pressure, racism, prejudice, and social activism. (Rev: HBG 3/98; SLJ 1/98) [305.8]

10257 Cohen, Daniel. *Animal Rights: A Handbook for Young Adults* (6–9). 1993, Millbrook LB $24.90 (1-56294-219-0). Discusses the use of animals for medical experimentation, zoos, marine theme parks, rodeos, factory farming and hunting, puppy mills, and classroom dissection. (Rev: BL 7/93; VOYA 2/94) [179]

10258 Cozic, Charles P., ed. *The Militia Movement* (8–12). Series: At Issue. 1996, Greenhaven LB $26.20 (1-56510-542-7); paper $17.45 (1-56510-541-9). A presentation of a broad spectrum of opinions on the militia movement, from those who say it is racist, extremist, and potentially violent to advocates who stress the constitutional right to bear arms. (Rev: BL 3/1/97; SLJ 4/97) [322.4]

10259 Cozic, Charles P., and Paul A. Winters, eds. *Gambling* (7–12). Series: Current Controversies. 1995, Greenhaven LB $26.20 (1-56510-235-5); paper $16.20 (1-56510-234-7). A collection of viewpoints on gambling, on why people become addicted, and on its social and economic effects. (Rev: BL 8/95; SLJ 10/95) [363.4]

10260 D'Angelo, Laura. *Hate Crimes* (6–9). Illus. Series: Crime, Justice, and Punishment. 1997, Chelsea LB $21.95 (0-7910-4266-9). This book examines the nature and causes of hate crimes based on differences in race, ethnicity, religion, or sexual preference, and the individuals or groups responsible for them, with interesting case studies and psychological profiles. (Rev: BL 5/15/98; VOYA 4/00) [364.1]

10261 Desetta, Al, and Sybil Wolin, eds. *The Struggle to Be Strong: True Stories by Teens About Overcoming Tough Times* (6–12). Illus. 2000, Free Spirit paper $14.95 (1-57542-079-1). Teens talk about problems such as addicted and abusive parents, AIDS, drugs and alcohol, school, health, and so forth. (Rev: BR 11–12/00; SLJ 8/00)

10262 Dolan, Edward F., and Margaret M. Scariano. *Guns in the United States* (7–12). 1994, Watts LB $24.00 (0-531-11189-X). Discusses rising gun violence in America, without taking sides in the gun-control debate, to encourage readers to investigate and take a knowledgeable stand on gun control. (Rev: BL 1/15/95; VOYA 5/95) [363.3]

10263 Egendorf, Laura K., ed. *Violence* (6–12). Series: Opposing Viewpoints. 2001, Greenhaven LB $22.96 (0-7377-0660-0); paper $14.96 (0-7377-0659-7). Differing views are offered on a variety of topics ranging from youth violence and contributing factors to gun control; drug abuse, and American culture in general. (Rev: BL 7/01) [303.6]

10264 Ennew, Judith. *Exploitation of Children* (6–10). Illus. Series: Global Issues. 1996, Raintree Steck-Vaughn LB $19.98 (0-8172-4546-4). This book presents historical material, statistical data, case studies, and differing viewpoints on how children are exploited in many countries of the world. (Rev: BL 2/1/97; VOYA 6/97) [305.23]

10265 Freedman, Russell. *Kids at Work: Lewis Hine and the Crusade Against Child Labor* (5–9). Photos. 1994, Clarion $20.00 (0-395-58703-4). This photoessay describes child labor in the United States at the beginning of the century and how Lewis Hine fought for reforms. (Rev: BCCB 10/94; BL 8/94; HB 11–12/94; SLJ 9/94*) [331.3]

10266 Gay, Kathlyn. *Militias: Armed and Dangerous* (7–12). Illus. Series: Issues in Focus. 1997, Enslow LB $20.95 (0-89490-902-9). A disturbing look at the militia movement in the U.S. and the attraction it holds for such malcontents as survivalists, neo-Nazis, white supremacists, Christian fanatics, and government haters. (Rev: BL 11/15/97; VOYA 2/98) [322.4]

10267 Gay, Kathlyn. *Neo-Nazis: A Growing Threat* (8–12). Illus. Series: In Focus. 1997, Enslow LB $20.95 (0-89490-901-0). After a discussion of eight recent neo-Nazi-related crimes, the author describes the philosophy and goals of this movement, current groups, and how to fight hate crimes. (Rev: BL 9/1/97; BR 11–12/97; SLJ 10/97) [320.53]

10268 Gottfried, Ted. *Deniers of the Holocaust: Who They Are, What They Do, Why They Do It* (6–12). Illus. 2001, Twenty-First Century LB $28.90 (0-7613-1950-6). Gottfried provides ample evidence to dismiss the arguments of those who deny that the Holocaust took place and discusses the racism of white supremacists, the existence of Internet hate sites, and issues of free speech. (Rev: BL 9/1/01; HBG 3/02) [940.53]

10269 Gourley, Catherine. *Media Wizards: A Behind-the-Scenes Look at Media Manipulations* (5–9). 1999, Twenty-First Century LB $26.90 (0-7613-0967-5). An informative account of how the media can manipulate the truth. (Rev: HBG 3/00; SLJ 2/00; VOYA 4/00) [380.3]

10270 Haddock, Patricia. *Teens and Gambling: Who Wins?* (7–12). Illus. Series: Issues in Focus. 1996, Enslow LB $20.95 (0-89490-719-0). The controversial subject of gambling is introduced — its lure, addiction, and problems, particularly as related to teenagers. (Rev: BL 8/96; SLJ 8/96; VOYA 10/96) [363.4]

10271 Harnack, Andrew, ed. *Animal Rights* (8–12). Series: Opposing Viewpoints. 1996, Greenhaven LB $17.96 (1-56510-399-8). Topics discussed in this well-balanced anthology cover such questions as: Do animals have rights? Should they be used in experiments? Should animals be used for food and other commodities? Is wildlife protection necessary? and What are the issues that need to be resolved in the animal rights movement? (Rev: SLJ 9/96; VOYA 10/96) [179]

10272 Haughen, David M., ed. *Animal Experimentation* (8–12). Series: At Issue. 1999, Greenhaven LB $21.96 (0-7377-0149-8); paper $13.96 (0-7377-0148-X). A collection of essays by experts that explore various viewpoints concerning animal rights and experimentation on animals. (Rev: BL 11/15/99; SLJ 1/00) [179]

10273 Hjelmeland, Andy. *Legalized Gambling: Solution or Illusion?* (8–12). Series: Pro/Con Issues. 1998, Lerner LB $30.35 (0-8225-2615-8). After a brief history of gambling since ancient times, this book discusses current legal forms of gambling, including lotteries and casinos, and the attendant topics of controversy. (Rev: HBG 3/99; SLJ 12/98) [795]

10274 Hoyt-Goldsmith, Diane. *Migrant Worker: A Boy from the Rio Grande Valley* (4–7). Illus. 1996, Holiday $15.95 (0-8234-1225-3). A photoessay about the grim living conditions endured by an 11-year-old Mexican American migrant worker. (Rev: BCCB 3/96; BL 3/1/96; SLJ 5/96) [331.5]

10275 Hurley, Jennifer A. *Animal Rights* (7–12). Series: Opposing Viewpoints Digests. 1998, Greenhaven paper $17.45 (1-56510-868-X). The rights of animals are defined and their place in experimentation and hunting and slaughter for human consumption explored in this book that presents different attitudes and opinions. (Rev: BL 4/15/99) [179]

10276 Hyde, Margaret O. *Gambling: Winners and Losers* (6–10). 1995, Millbrook LB $23.40 (1-56294-532-7). A timely subject gets rather dry treatment in this book that tells of the history, types, and psychology of gambling, with quotations from many case studies. (Rev: BL 12/15/95; BR 5–6/96; SLJ 3/96) [363.4]

10277 James, Barbara. *Animal Rights* (5–10). Series: Talking Points. 1999, Raintree Steck-Vaughn LB $27.12 (0-8172-5317-3). Various aspects of the animal rights controversy are explored in an objective, straightforward manner. (Rev: BL 8/99; BR 9–10/99) [179.3]

10278 Kronenwetter, Michael. *Encyclopedia of Modern American Social Issues* (7–12). 1997, ABC-CLIO LB $65.00 (0-87436-779-4). In alphabetically arranged articles, this book presents well-balanced information on such controversial issues as abortion, child abuse, drug testing, gun control, Head Start, same-sex marriage, Ebonics, and secondhand smoke. (Rev: BR 9–10/98; SLJ 5/98) [306]

10279 Landau, Elaine. *Land Mines: 100 Million Hidden Killers* (6–12). Series: Issues in Focus. 2000, Enslow LB $20.95 (0-7660-1240-9). This is an overview of where land mines are found, how they got there, and ways in which the danger they present can be overcome. (Rev: BL 9/15/00; HBG 3/01; VOYA 2/01) [363.3]

10280 Lang, Paul. *The English Language Debate: One Nation, One Language?* (7–12). Illus. 1995, Enslow LB $20.95 (0-89490-642-9). A well-documented account that explores such multicultural topics as the English-only movement, bilingual education, and other current political aspects of the teaching, status, and use of English in this country. (Rev: BL 6/1–15/95) [306.4]

10281 Levine, Herbert M. *Animal Rights* (7–12). Illus. Series: American Issues Debated. 1997, Raintree Steck-Vaughn LB $31.40 (0-8172-4350-X). Should animals be banned from use in science? Should hunting be illegal? Should people be ashamed of wearing fur? These and other questions related to animals are explored from different points of view. (Rev: BL 11/15/97; BR 1–2/98; VOYA 2/98) [179]

10282 Levine, Herbert M. *Gun Control* (7–12). Illus. Series: American Issues Debated. 1997, Raintree Steck-Vaughn LB $31.40 (0-8172-4351-8). The debate on the effectiveness of gun control in reducing crime is presented, along with questions concerning handgun bans, waiting periods, and penalties for illegal gun use. (Rev: BL 11/15/97; BR 1–2/98) [363.3]

10283 MccGwire, Scarlett. *Surveillance: The Impact on our Lives* (7–9). Illus. Series: 21st Century Debates. 2001, Raintree Steck-Vaughn LB $18.98 (0-7398-3172-0). An overview of the various ways in which our lives are monitored — by government, law enforcement authorities, companies, and so forth — and the benefits and dangers of such technologies as wire tapping and Web tracking. (Rev: BL 7/01; SLJ 7/01) [323.44]

10284 Newman, Shirlee P. *Child Slavery in Modern Times* (4–7). Illus. Series: Watts Library: History of Slavery. 2000, Watts LB $24.00 (0-531-11696-4). From Europe to Asia and Africa, this book explores the deplorable lives of servitude forced on child laborers and slaves, and how some have escaped. (Rev: BL 2/15/01; SLJ 3/01) [306.3]

10285 Ojeda, Auriana, ed. *Technology and Society* (6–12). Series: Opposing Viewpoints. 2002, Gale LB $31.20 (0-7377-0913-8); paper $19.95 (0-7377-0912-X). Technology's contributions to — and negative impact on — society are discussed here, with mention of Internet access, e-mail privacy, biotechnology, government regulation, the divide between rich and poor, and increasing social isolation. (Rev: BL 6/1–15/02; SLJ 6/02) [306.4]

10286 O'Neill, Terry. *Gun Control* (6–12). Illus. Series: Opposing Viewpoints Digests. 2000, Greenhaven LB $21.96 (1-56510-879-5); paper $13.96 (1-56510-878-7). This book explores different questions about gun control and supplies a number of essays that express conflicting viewpoints on each question. (Rev: BL 7/00; SLJ 6/00) [363.3]

10287 Owen, Marna. *Animal Rights: Yes or No?* (6–10). 1993, Lerner LB $30.35 (0-8225-2603-4). A discussion of the various positions on animal rights. (Rev: BL 1/15/94; SLJ 3/94) [179]

10288 Parker, David L., et al. *Stolen Dreams: Portraits of Working Children* (6–12). Illus. 1997, Lerner LB $23.95 (0-8225-2960-2). This compelling photoessay deals with child labor around the world, particularly in the Far East. (Rev: BL 11/1/97; HB 3–4/98; VOYA 2/98) [331.3]

10289 Patterson, Charles. *Animal Rights* (6–10). 1993, Enslow LB $20.95 (0-89490-468-X). A thorough examination of the topic, including a history of animal rights movements. (Rev: BL 10/15/93; SLJ 11/93; VOYA 2/94) [179]

10290 Pringle, Laurence. *The Animal Rights Controversy* (7–12). Illus. 1989, Harcourt $16.95 (0-15-203559-1). A book about the way animals are abused and misused that covers topics such as factory farming, experimentation, and zoos. (Rev: BL 1/15/90; SLJ 5/90; VOYA 4/90) [197]

10291 Rochford, Dierdre. *Rights for Animals?* (4–8). Series: Viewpoints. 1997, Watts LB $23.00 (0-531-14414 3). A presentation of different viewpoints on the use of animals in cosmetic and drug testing, blood sports, and hunting, with additional material on endangered animals and zoos. (Rev: SLJ 5/97) [179.3]

10292 Roleff, Tamara L., ed. *Extremist Groups* (6–12). Series: Opposing Viewpoints. 2001, Greenhaven LB $22.96 (0-7377-0656-2); paper $14.96 (0-7377-0655-4). Contributors give spirited pro and con arguments on topics including religious fundamentalism, white supremacy, animal rights, and socialism. (Rev: BL 9/15/01) [303.48]

10293 Roleff, Tamara L., ed. *Hate Crimes* (6–12). Series: Current Controversies. 2000, Greenhaven LB $22.96 (0-7377-0454-3); paper $14.96 (0-7377-0453-5). After describing what constitutes a hate crime, these essays focus on specific examples, laws, and the threat posed by groups that promote extreme, violent behaviors. (Rev: BL 2/15/01; SLJ 3/01) [364.1]

10294 Roleff, Tamara L. *Hate Groups* (7–12). Series: Opposing Viewpoints Digests. 2001, Greenhaven $19.96 (0-7377-0677-5); paper $12.96 (0-7377-0676-7). A concise and thought-provoking exploration of the problems of group hate and restrictions of free speech. (Rev: BL 1/1–15/02) [364.1]

10295 Roleff, Tamara L., ed. *The Rights of Animals* (6–12). Series: Current Controversies. 1999, Greenhaven LB $20.96 (0-7377-0069-6); paper $12.96 (0-7377-0068-8). This collection of provocative essays discusses such topics as: do animals have rights, cloning, animal organ transplants, hunting, trapping, and using animals in entertainment and experimentation. (Rev: BL 10/15/99) [179]

10296 Saunders, Carol Silverman. *Straight Talk About Teenage Gambling* (7–12). Series: Straight Talk. 1999, Facts on File $27.45 (0-8160-3718-3). This book details the physical and emotional stakes involved with games of chance and what happens when teens become completely preoccupied with gambling. (Rev: BL 1/1–15/99; BR 9–10/99; SLJ 8/99) [362.2]

10297 Schwartz, Ted. *Kids and Guns: The History, the Present, the Dangers, and the Remedies* (7–12). 1999, Watts LB $23.00 (0-531-11723-5). This book describes the issue of kids and guns, the scope of the problem, issues involved in gun ownership, teenage violence and the media, and how to create safe schools. (Rev: BL 7/99; SLJ 9/99) [303.6]

10298 Sherman, Aliza. *Working Together Against Violence Against Women* (6–10). Series: Library of Social Activism. 1996, Rosen LB $16.95 (0-8239-2258-8). This work introduces violence against women, including date rape, stranger rape, assault, and domestic violence, explores actions being taken by both government and private agencies, and offers advice on how teenagers can help themselves, a friend, and their communities. (Rev: SLJ 2/97; VOYA 6/97) [303.6]

10299 Sherry, Clifford J. *Animal Rights* (7–12). Series: Contemporary World Issues. 1995, ABC-CLIO LB $45.00 (0-87436-733-6). A well-organized volume that introduces the philosophical basis for the animal rights movement, present day problems, and the pros and cons of using animals in research. (Rev: SLJ 1/96) [346]

10300 Sonder, Ben. *The Militia Movement: Fighters of the Far Right* (7–9). Illus. 2000, Watts LB $25.00 (0-531-11405-8). This is an impressive portrait of contemporary right-wing hate groups with coverage of their ideologies and activities plus material on such tragedies as Ruby Ridge, Waco, and Oklahoma City. (Rev: BL 5/1/00; SLJ 8/00) [322.4.]

10301 Stewart, Gail B. *Militias* (7–12). Illus. Series: Overview. 1997, Lucent LB $27.45 (1-56006-501-X). This book traces the historical development of the militia movement and discusses prominent contemporary militia groups, their purposes, the beliefs and attitudes of their members and leaders, their activities, and why they are flourishing. (Rev: BL 1/1–15/98; HBG 9/98) [322.4]

10302 Streissguth, Thomas. *Hatemongers and Demagogues* (6–9). 1995, Oliver LB $19.95 (1-881508-23-4). A survey of American leaders who have used hate and inflammatory language to incite violence, along with an examination of the conditions that led people to support these demagogues, from the individuals who provoked the Salem witch hunts to Louis Farrakhan. (Rev: BL 12/15/95; BR 9–10/96; SLJ 2/96; VOYA 6/96) [305.8]

10303 Streissguth, Tom. *Gun Control: The Pros and Cons* (6–9). Illus. Series: Hot Issues. 2001, Enslow LB $20.95 (0-7660-1673-0). A dispassionate look at both sides of the gun control debate, with a rundown of the status quo in each state and a glossary of gun-related terms. (Rev: BL 1/1–15/02; HBG 3/02) [344.73]

10304 Tipp, Stacey L. *Child Abuse: Detecting Bias* (5–7). Series: Opposing Viewpoints Juniors. 1991, Greenhaven LB $22.45 (0-89908-611-X). Four different issues involving child abuse (e.g., whether abusers should be sent to prison) are presented from various points of view. (Rev: BL 5/15/92; SLJ 3/92) [362.7]

10305 Torr, James D., ed. *Gambling* (7–12). Series: Opposing Viewpoints. 2002, Gale $31.20 (0-7377-0907-3); paper $19.95 (0-7377-0906-5). Essays examine the addictive nature of gambling, the benefits to the Native American tribes that run casinos, sports betting, state lotteries, Internet gambling, and so forth. (Rev: BL 4/15/02) [306.4]

10306 Torr, James D., ed. *Gun Violence* (6–12). Illus. Series: Opposing Viewpoints. 2001, Greenhaven LB $31.20 (0-7377-0713-5); paper $19.95 (0-7377-0712-7). Twenty-four essays present varied opinions on guns, gun ownership, and gun violence. (Rev: BL 12/1/01) [363.3]

10307 Wand, Kelly, ed. *The Animal Rights Movement* (8–12). Series: American Social Movements. 2002, Gale LB $25.96 (0-7377-1046-2); paper $16.96 (0-7377-1045-4). This collection of essays traces this movement from the advocates of animal welfare of the 18th century through the development of the concept of animal rights of the late-20th century. (Rev: BL 1/1–15/03; SLJ 2/03) [179]

10308 Williams, Mary E., ed. *Culture Wars* (8–12). Series: Opposing Viewpoints. 2003, Gale LB $33.70 (0-7377-1679-7); paper $22.45 (0-7377-1680-0). These essays explore American cultural values, multiculturalism, popular culture, and the question of a decline in culture from various viewpoints. (Rev: BL 1/1–15/04) [306]

10309 Williams, Mary E., ed. *The White Separatist Movement* (8–12). Series: American Social Movements. 2002, Gale LB $31.20 (0-7377-1054-3); paper $19.95 (0-7377-1053-5). This collection of essays, speeches, book excerpts, and personal observations looks at groups ranging from the Ku Klux Klan to neo-Nazi skinheads and discusses the reasons why people are attracted to such organizations. (Rev: BL 9/15/02) [305.8]

10310 Williams, Mary E., ed. *Working Women* (8–12). Series: Opposing Viewpoints. 1997, Greenhaven LB $26.20 (1-56510-677-6). Differing viewpoints on the impact of women entering the work force, sexual harassment, discrimination, and women in the military are presented in this anthology of articles. (Rev: BL 11/15/97; VOYA 6/98) [5.4.1]

10311 Wiloch, Tom. *Everything You Need to Know About Protecting Yourself and Others from Abduction* (6–9). Illus. Series: Need to Know Library. 1998, Rosen LB $25.25 (0-8239-2553-6). This book describes the dangers of abduction and its frequency in America and provides safety tips for home, at school, while babysitting, jogging, and bicycling, and using the Internet. (Rev: BR 9–10/98; SLJ 9/98) [364]

Environmental Issues

General and Miscellaneous

10312 Aldis, Rodney. *Towns and Cities* (5–8). Series: Ecology Watch. 1992, Dillon LB $13.95 (0-87518-496-0). A discussion of urban life and environmental problems that it creates. (Rev: BL 12/15/92) [574.5]

10313 Andryszewski, Tricia. *The Environment and the Economy: Planting the Seeds for Tomorrow's Growth* (7–12). 1995, Millbrook LB $24.90 (1-56294-524-6). Traces the emergence of environ-

ment-versus-economy issues. (Rev: BL 12/1/95; SLJ 11/95) [363.7]

10314 Barbour, Scott. *The Environment* (6–12). Series: Opposing Viewpoints Digests. 2001, Greenhaven LB $28.70 (1-56510-873-6); paper $14.95 (1-56510-872-8). Teens interested in environmental issues including pollution, ozone, global warming will find this a useful resource, with a list of organizations and a bibliography. (Rev: BL 2/15/01) [363.7]

10315 Bowden, Rob. *Water Supply: Our Impact on the Planet* (5–8). Illus. Series: 21st Century Debates. 2003, Raintree Steck-Vaughn LB $28.56 (0-7398-5506-9). A thought-provoking examination of the status of the world's water supply, predictions of a looming water crisis, and measures that could be taken to avert this. (Rev: BL 8/03; HBG 10/03) [363.6]

10316 Chandler, Gary, and Kevin Graham. *Environmental Causes* (5–10). Series: Celebrity Activists. 1997, Twenty-First Century LB $25.90 (0-8050-5232-1). This book discusses how entertainers including Robert Redford, Sting, and Chevy Chase and other celebrities such as Al Gore, Ted Turner, and Jerry Greenfield support environmental causes. (Rev: BR 3–4/98; SLJ 1/98) [363.7]

10317 Collard, Sneed B. *Alien Invaders: The Continuing Threat of Exotic Species* (6–12). Illus. 1996, Watts LB $25.00 (0-531-11298-5). An account that explores the dangers of introducing nonindigenous or "exotics" into a new environment. (Rev: BL 11/1/96; BR 3–4/97; SLJ 1/97) [574.5824]

10318 Cothran, Helen, ed. *Energy Alternatives* (6–12). Series: Opposing Viewpoints. 2002, Gale LB $31.20 (0-7377-0905-7); paper $19.95 (0-7377-0904-9). Discussion of the pros and cons of fossil fuels and nuclear power is followed by a look at various alternatives, including solar power, geothermal energy, fuel cells, wind farms, and "biomass" or garbage conversion. (Rev: BL 7/02) [333.79]

10319 Fleisher, Paul. *Ecology A to Z* (6–10). 1994, Dillon LB $14.95 (0-87518-561-4). Defines words and phrases related to ecology and to our interaction with the environment. (Rev: BL 4/1/94; SLJ 5/94; VOYA 6/94) [363.7]

10320 Fridell, Ron. *Global Warming* (6–12). Illus. 2002, Watts LB $24.00 (0-531-11900-9). A detailed look at weather patterns of the past and how they may be used to predict future problems, with discussion of actions we can take to avoid disastrous global warming. (Rev: BL 10/15/02) [363.738]

10321 Gartner, Bob. *Working Together Against the Destruction of the Environment* (7–12). Series: Library of Social Activism. 1995, Rosen LB $16.95 (0-8239-1774-6). Describes efforts to protect the environment, such as recycling, emission laws, and sewage dump restrictions, and provides suggestions for how everyone can help. (Rev: BL 4/15/95) [363.7]

10322 Gay, Kathlyn. *Saving the Environment: Debating the Costs* (8–12). Illus. Series: Impact. 1996, Watts $22.50 (0-531-11263-2). This book explores environmental issues in which there is a conflict between the health of the environment and cost to the economy, such as saving endangered species, and property rights vs. pollution. (Rev: BL 9/1/96; BR 11–12/96; SLJ 10/96; VOYA 10/96) [363.7]

10323 Haddock, Patricia. *Environmental Time Bomb: Our Threatened Planet* (6–12). Series: Issues in Focus. 2000, Enslow LB $20.96 (0-7660-1229-8). Up-to-date information is given on current dangers to our environment. (Rev: BL 9/15/00; HBG 3/01; SLJ 12/00) [363.7]

10324 Johnson, Rebecca L. *Investigating the Ozone Hole* (5–8). 1994, Lerner LB $28.75 (0-8225-1574-1). Using interviews, documents, and firsthand research, the author charts the development and possible consequences of an ozone hole above the Antarctic. (Rev: BL 3/1/94) [551.5]

10325 Krensky, Stephen. *Four Against the Odds: The Struggle to Save Our Environment* (5–8). 1992, Scholastic paper $2.99 (0-590-44743-2). Introduces the work of four individuals who fought to raise public awareness about important environmental issues: John Muir, Chico Mendes, Rachel Carson, and Lois Gibb. (Rev: BL 6/1/92; SLJ 10/92) [363.7]

10326 Malaspina, Ann. *Saving the American Wilderness* (8–12). Illus. Series: Overview. 1999, Lucent LB $17.96 (1-56006-505-2). A look at American conservationism and environmentalism and how they have affected the country's land and wildlife. (Rev: BL 11/15/99; HBG 4/00) [333.78]

10327 Netzley, Patricia. *Environmental Groups* (6–10). Illus. Series: Our Endangered Planet. 1997, Lucent LB $27.45 (1-56006-195-2). This objective source introduces conflicting attitudes toward protection of species, lobbying tactics, economic issues, and scientific findings related to environmental issues. (Rev: SLJ 9/98) [363.7]

10328 Netzley, Patricia. *Issues in the Environment* (7–10). Series: Contemporary Issues. 1997, Lucent LB $27.45 (1-56006-475-7). Proponents and detractors state their cases in this volume that explores methods used to protect the environment, their cost, their effectiveness, and the possible use of other, less drastic alternatives. (Rev: SLJ 4/98) [363.7]

10329 Oxlade, Chris. *Global Warming* (5–7). Illus. Series: Our Planet in Peril. 2002, Capstone LB $22.60 (0-7368-1361-6). Attractive double-page spreads explore the concern about global warning, its causes, and options for the future. Also use *Nuclear Waste* (2003). (Rev: HBG 3/03; SLJ 4/03) [363.738]

10330 Parker, Janice, ed. *The Disappearing Forests* (5–8). Illus. Series: Understanding Global Issues. 2002, Smart Apple LB $19.95 (1-58340-168-7). A great deal of information about forest use, abuse, and conservation is packed into double-paged spreads with color illustrations. (Rev: BL 10/15/02; HBG 3/03; SLJ 12/02) [634.9]

10331 Peters, Celeste, ed. *The Energy Dilemma* (5–8). Illus. Series: Understanding Global Issues. 2002, Smart Apple LB $19.95 (1-58340-169-5). The information about energy sources, use, and conservation packed into these double-paged spreads with color illustrations will spark debate. (Rev: BL 10/15/02) [333.79]

10332 Petrikin, Jonathan S., ed. *Environmental Justice* (8–12). Series: At Issue. 1995, Greenhaven LB $19.95 (0-56510-264-9). A collection of essays exploring whether the wealthy and powerful are risking the health and living conditions of others while protecting their own resources. (Rev: BL 3/15/95) [363.7]

10333 Pringle, Laurence. *The Environmental Movement: From Its Roots to the Challenges of a New Century* (5–8). Illus. 2000, HarperCollins $16.95 (0-688-15626-6). This is a fine history of environmentalism in America, beginning with the conflicts between Native Americans and early settlers concerning natural resources and ending with current issues. (Rev: BL 4/1/00; HBG 10/00; SLJ 6/00) [363.7]

10334 Pringle, Laurence. *Global Warming: The Threat of Earth's Changing Climate* (4–8). Illus. 2001, North-South $16.95 (1-58717-009-4). A straightforward account that covers topics including the causes of global warming, the signs that it is occurring, and possible solutions. (Rev: BL 4/1/01; HBG 10/01; SLJ 6/01) [363.738]

10335 Pringle, Laurence. *Vanishing Ozone: Protecting Earth from Ultraviolet Radiation* (4–8). Illus. Series: Save-the-Earth Books. 1995, Morrow LB $15.89 (0-688-04158-2). The exciting but disturbing story of the thinning ozone layer and the conflicts it is producing among governments, environmentalists, and industry. (Rev: SLJ 9/95*) [363.73]

10336 Robbins, Ocean, and Sol Solomon. *Choices for Our Future* (7–12). 1994, Book Publg. paper $9.95 (1-57067-002-1). The founders of Youth for Environmental Sanity believe that young people can convince other young people to adopt more ecologically responsible life-styles. This book explains how we can all help. (Rev: BL 3/15/95) [363.7]

10337 Roleff, Tamara L., ed. *Global Warming* (8–12). Series: Opposing Viewpoints. 1997, Greenhaven LB $32.45 (1-56510-512-5). An anthology of writings that explores the gravity of global warming, its possible effects, and measures that can be taken to combat it. (Rev: BL 12/15/96; BR 5–6/97) [363.73]

10338 Ryan, Bernard. *Protecting the Environment* (7–12). Series: Community Service for Teens. 1998, Ferguson LB $15.95 (0-89434-228-2). After a general introduction on volunteerism, the author describes how teens can become involved in existing conservation projects and begin their own. (Rev: BL 9/15/98; BR 11–12/98; SLJ 2/99; VOYA 8/99) [363.7]

10339 Shaw, Jane. *Global Warming* (7–12). Illus. Series: Critical Thinking About Environmental Issues. 2002, Gale $21.96 (0-7377-1270-8). Readers will find a variety of opinions about the causes and severity of global warming. (Rev: BL 12/15/02) [363.738]

10340 Stefoff, Rebecca. *The American Environmental Movement* (7–10). 1995, Facts on File $25.00 (0-8160-3046-4). A study of efforts to preserve the environment from the 15th century to the present, with discussion of prominent figures and events in the movement. (Rev: BL 9/1/95; SLJ 9/95) [363.7]

10341 Stouffer, Marty. *Marty Stouffer's Wild America* (8–12). 1988, Times Books $30.00 (0-8129-1610-7). A wildlife documentary maker discusses his career and the importance of conservation. (Rev: BR 3–4/89; VOYA 4/89) [320.5]

10342 Suzuki, David, and Kathy Vanderlinden. *Eco-Fun* (5–8). Illus. 2001, Douglas & McIntyre paper $10.95 (1-55054-823-9). The activities in this collection reinforce some basic scientific concepts about air, water, earth, and fire, and encourage young readers to think about environmental issues and avoid pollution. (Rev: BL 6/1–15/01; SLJ 8/01) [577]

10343 Tesar, Jenny. *The Waste Crisis* (5–9). Series: Our Fragile Planet. 1991, Facts on File $19.95 (0-8160-2491-X). This well-illustrated account describes all types of waste, emphasizes the urgency of the problem, and suggests possible solutions. (Rev: BL 11/15/91; SLJ 11/91) [363.72]

10344 VanCleave, Janice. *Janice VanCleave's Ecology for Every Kid* (4–7). Illus. 1996, Wiley paper $10.95 (0-471-10086-2). Clear instructions and many diagrams introduce a series of experiments that highlight environmental issues. (Rev: BL 3/1/96; SLJ 4/96) [574.5]

10345 Whitman, Sylvia. *This Land Is Your Land: The American Conservation Movement* (5–7). Illus. 1994, Lerner LB $30.35 (0-8225-1729-9). A history of the conservation movement from its beginnings in 1870 when there were efforts to save Yellowstone and ending with today's major problems such as oil spills and trash disposal. (Rev: BL 12/15/94; HB 3–4/94; SLJ 12/94) [363.7]

Pollution

10346 Bang, Molly. *Nobody Particular: One Woman's Fight to Save the Bays* (6–12). Illus. 2001, Holt $18.00 (0-8050-5396-4). Teens will connect to this appealingly presented account about Diane Wilson, who became an environmental activist working to restore the ecology of the bays around her Texas home. (Rev: BCCB 2/01; BL 2/1/01; HB 1–2/01; HBG 10/01; SLJ 1/01; VOYA 4/02) [363.738]

10347 Brown, Paul. *Global Pollution* (5–8). Illus. Series: Face the Facts. 2003, Raintree Steck-Vaughn LB $28.56 (0-7398-6433-5). The effects of pollution on the environment are described in understandable terms, and practical responses from young people are suggested. (Rev: BL 11/15/03; HBG 10/03; SLJ 9/03) [303.73]

10348 Chapman, Matthew, and Rob Bowden. *Air Pollution* (5–8). Series: 21st Century Debates. 2002, Raintree Steck-Vaughn LB $27.12 (0-7398-4874-7). The causes of air pollution, the present situation, and possible future solutions are presented in this well-illustrated book that presents various points of view and offers topics for debate. (Rev: BL 6/1–15/02) [363.73]

10349 Collinson, Alan. *Pollution* (5–8). Series: Repairing the Damage. 1992, Macmillan LB $21.00 (0-02-722995-5). A historical overview of nuclear waste, river pollution, overpopulation, and other aspects of pollution. (Rev: BL 9/15/92) [363.73]

10350 Dolan, Edward F. *Our Poisoned Waters* (7–12). Illus. 1997, Dutton $14.99 (0-525-65220-5). With extensive use of first-person accounts, this book tells of the impact that humans have had on the water supply and about attempts to conserve and clean our water. The last chapter tells how readers can help the cause. (Rev: BL 3/1/97; BR 11–12/97; SLJ 3/97; VOYA 10/97) [363.739]

10351 Gay, Kathlyn. *Air Pollution* (7–12). Series: Impact. 1991, Watts paper $24.00 (0-531-13002-9). An examination of the alarming ecological effects and health risks of atmospheric pollution and an outline of combative strategies. (Rev: BL 12/1/91) [363.73]

10352 Hayley, James, ed. *Pollution* (8–12). Series: Current Controversies. 2002, Gale LB $25.96 (0-7377-1188-4); paper $16.96 (0-7377-1187-6). This book features in-depth essays by individuals — environmentalists, politicians, EPA representatives, and others — who present opposing views on the problem of pollution. (Rev: BL 12/15/02) [363.73]

10353 Hoff, Mary, and Mary M. Rodgers. *Our Endangered Planet: Groundwater* (4–7). Illus. Series: Our Endangered Planet. 1991, Lerner LB $22.60 (0-8225-2500-3). A discussion of the supply, access, uses, and pollution of groundwater around the world. (Rev: BL 6/15/91; SLJ 5/91) [333.91]

10354 Kidd, J. S., and Renee A. Kidd. *Into Thin Air: The Problem of Atmospheric Pollution* (7–12). Series: Into Thin Air. 1998, Facts on File $25.00 (0-8160-3585-7). This book evaluates how scientists have studied atmospheric chemistry and explores controversial theories on the effects of pollution, acid rain, the greenhouse effect, global warming, and El Niño. (Rev: BL 12/1/98) [363.739]

10355 Miller, Christina G., and Louise A. Berry. *Acid Rain: A Sourcebook for Young People* (6–8). Illus. 1986, Messner LB $12.95 (0-671-60177-6). An account that describes the origins of acid rain, its effects, and what can be done about it. (Rev: BL 2/15/87; SLJ 1/87) [363.7]

10356 Miller, Christina G., and Louise A. Berry. *Air Alert: Rescuing the Earth's Atmosphere* (5–9). Illus. 1996, Simon & Schuster $16.00 (0-689-31792-1). A clear overview of such atmospheric problems as acid rain, smog, the greenhouse effect, and depletion of the ozone layer. (Rev: BL 3/1/96; BR 1–2/97; SLJ 5/96; VOYA 12/96) [363.73]

10357 O'Neill, Mary. *Air Scare* (4–7). Series: SOS Planet Earth. 1991, Troll paper $5.95 (0-8167-2083-5). An oversize book that deals with the important environmental issue of air pollution. (Rev: BL 6/15/91) [363]

10358 Pringle, Laurence. *Oil Spills: Damage, Recovery, and Prevention* (5–8). 1993, Morrow LB $14.89 (0-688-09861-4). A discussion of damage caused by oil spills, cleanup, and prevention efforts, with a description of how petroleum forms, how it is removed from the ground, and its uses as background. (Rev: BL 9/15/93) [363.73]

10359 Reed, Jennifer Bond. *Love Canal* (6–12). Series: Great Disasters: Reforms and Ramifications. 2002, Chelsea LB $22.95 (0-7910-6742-4). The story of the town that had to be evacuated in the 1970s when hazardous wastes leaked from a disposal site. (Rev: HBG 3/03; SLJ 12/02) [363.738]

10360 Riddle, John. *Bhopal* (6–10). Series: Great Disasters: Reforms and Ramifications. 2002, Chelsea LB $22.95 (0-7910-6741-6). The story of the leak of pesticide gas from a Union Carbide plant that killed more than 3,000 people in India in 1984. (Rev: HBG 3/03; SLJ 12/02; VOYA 12/02) [363.17]

10361 Roleff, Tamara L., ed. *Pollution: Disputed Land* (8–12). Series: Opposing Viewpoints. 1999, Greenhaven LB $21.96 (0-7377-0135-8); paper $13.96 (0-7377-0134-X). Some of the questions explored in this anthology of articles include, is pollution a serious problem? do chemical pollutants present a health risk? and is recycling an effective response? (Rev: BL 11/15/99) [363.73]

10362 Zipko, Stephen J. *Toxic Threat: How Hazardous Substances Poison Our Lives* (5–7). 1990, Simon & Schuster paper $5.95 (0-671-69331-X).

Many environmental pollutants, including radon and PCBs, are introduced. (Rev: SLJ 8/90) [363.7]

Recycling

10363 Cozic, Charles P., ed. *Garbage and Waste* (7–12). Series: Current Controversies. 1997, Greenhaven LB $32.45 (1-56510-566-4). An anthology of articles about the seriousness of the waste problem, the dangers of toxic waste, the usefulness of recycling, and the extent that government should interfere in this problem. (Rev: BL 7/97; SLJ 10/97) [363.72]

10364 *50 Simple Things Kids Can Do to Recycle* (4–7). Illus. 1994, EarthWorks paper $6.95 (1-879682-00-1). A collection of projects and activities that can help recycling efforts at home, at school, and in the community. (Rev: BL 7/94; SLJ 8/94) [363.7]

10365 Hall, Eleanor J. *Garbage* (5–8). Illus. Series: Overview. 1997, Lucent LB $27.45 (1-56006-188-X). A history of how waste disposal has been handled, and current ecological and environmental approaches, including recycling. (Rev: BL 8/97; BR 1–2/98; HBG 3/98) [363.72]

Population Issues

General and Miscellaneous

10366 Allison, Anthony. *Hear These Voices: Youth at the Edge of the Millennium* (7–12). 1999, Dutton $22.99 (0-525-45353-9). Testimonies from troubled teenagers around the world, such as a 14-year-old Thai girl whose stepfather sold her into prostitution, comprise this harrowing anthology of case studies, accompanied by short, follow-up interviews with adults who have tried to help. (Rev: BL 1/1–15/99*; HBG 3/99; SLJ 2/99; VOYA 4/99) [305.235]

10367 Bowden, Rob. *An Overcrowded World?* (5–8). Series: 21st Century Debates. 2002, Raintree Steck-Vaughn LB $27.12 (0-7398-4872-0). Using a well-organized text, plus sidebars for additional facts and statements of opinion, this colorfully illustrated volume explores the current problems of overpopulation and the dire strain it causes on the earth's supplies. (Rev: BL 6/1–15/02) [304.6]

10368 Cox, Vic. *Guns, Violence, and Teens* (7–12). Illus. Series: Issues in Focus. 1997, Enslow LB $20.95 (0-89490-721-2). Topics covered in this book include the evolution of gun use in America, gun control, teenage violence, and the impact that guns have on teenagers. (Rev: BL 10/15/97; BR 11–12/97; SLJ 1/98; VOYA 2/98) [363.4]

10369 Gallant, Roy A. *The Peopling of Planet Earth: Human Population Growth Through the Ages*

(7–12). Illus. 1990, Macmillan LB $15.95 (0-02-735772-4). A history of patterns of world population, the present conditions in relation to resources, and the different future we face. (Rev: BL 3/1/90; VOYA 4/90) [304.6]

10370 Gedatus, Gus. *Violence in Public Places* (5–8). Series: Perspectives on Violence. 2000, Capstone LB $23.93 (0-7368-0428-5). This examines violence in public places from hate crimes to road rage. Also use in the same series *Violence in the Media* (2000). (Rev: HBG 10/00; SLJ 8/00) [362]

10371 Gellman, Marc, and Thomas Hartman. *Bad Stuff in the News: A Family Guide to Handling the Headlines* (4–7). 2002, North-South $14.95 (1-58717-132-5). A reassuring book about difficult current issues, including terrorism, accidents, school violence, and more. (Rev: BL 5/15/02; HBG 10/02; SLJ 3/02) [302.23]

10372 Grapes, Bryan J., ed. *School Violence* (6–12). Series: Contemporary Issues Companion. 2000, Greenhaven LB $21.96 (0-7377-0331-8); paper $13.96 (0-7377-0332-6). Personal stories add to the urgency of the thought-provoking solutions suggested for school violence. (Rev: BL 10/15/00; SLJ 9/00) [371.7]

10373 Grapes, Bryan J., ed. *Violent Children* (8–12). Series: At Issue. 1999, Greenhaven LB $21.96 (0-7377-0159-5); paper $13.96 (0-7377-0158-7). In a series of articles that express many viewpoints, the problem of violent children at home and school is explored. (Rev: BL 11/15/99) [363.4]

10374 Hohm, Charles F., ed. *Population* (6–12). Series: Opposing Viewpoints. 2000, Greenhaven LB $21.96 (0-7377-0292-3); paper $13.96 (0-7377-0291-5). A collection of essays that explore problems with world population, its growth, and its possible control. (Rev: BL 9/15/00) [306]

10375 Holliday, Laurel, ed. *Why Do They Hate Me? Young Lives Caught in War and Conflict* (7–12). 1999, Pocket paper $4.99 (0-671-03454-5). Using diaries, letters, and other first-person accounts the editor has captured the turmoil of growing up during the Holocaust, World War II, and present-day Northern Ireland. (Rev: BL 11/1/99; SLJ 11/99) [920]

10376 Proulx, Brenda, ed. *The Courage to Change: A Teen Survival Guide* (7–12). Illus. 2002, Second Story paper $16.95 (1-896764-41-X). A thought-provoking compilation of personal stories, poems, and photographs created by teens who participate in Canada's L.O.V.E. (Leave Out ViolencE) program. (Rev: BL 9/1/02; SLJ 7/02; VOYA 8/02) [364.4]

10377 Roberts, Anita. *Safe Teen: Powerful Alternatives to Violence* (7–12). 2001, Polestar paper $15.95 (1-896095-99-2). The author offers practical advice for teens looking for peaceful ways to solve

potentially dangerous problems. (Rev: BL 12/15/01; SLJ 4/02; VOYA 2/02) [155.5]

10378 Warner, Rachel. *Refugees* (6–10). Illus. Series: Global Issues. 1996, Raintree Steck-Vaughn LB $19.98 (0-8172-4547-2). After a brief history of the refugee problem, current case studies are used to explore this issue and how it is being confronted in today's world. (Rev: BL 3/15/97) [362.87]

10379 Winckler, Suzanne, and Mary M. Rodgers. *Our Endangered Planet: Population Growth* (4–7). Illus. Series: Our Endangered Planet. 1991, Lerner LB $27.15 (0-8225-2502-X). A discussion of the effects that rapid population growth has had on the environment. (Rev: BL 6/15/91; SLJ 5/91) [304.6]

10380 Zeaman, John. *Overpopulation* (8–12). 2002, Watts LB $24.00 (0-531-11893-2). Zeaman reviews the causes of the tremendous rise in population in the last century and discusses measures we might take to curtail the negative impact. (Rev: BL 8/02; SLJ 8/02) [363.9]

Aging and Death

10381 Cozic, Charles P., ed. *An Aging Population* (8–12). Series: Opposing Viewpoints. 1996, Greenhaven LB $26.20 (1-56510-395-5). A collection of documents expressing various points of view on how the aged will affect America in the future, their entitlement programs, quality of life, health care, and society's acceptance of the elderly. (Rev: BL 7/96; BR 1–2/97; SLJ 8/96; VOYA 10/96) [305.26]

10382 Gignoux, Jane Hughes. *Some Folk Say: Stories of Life, Death, and Beyond* (6–12). Illus. 1998, Foulketale $29.95 (0-9667168-0-9). A collection of 38 literary selections on various aspects of death and how people adjust to it, taken from world folklore and such writers as Shakespeare and Walt Whitman. (Rev: BL 2/15/99) [398.27]

Crime, Gangs, and Prisons

10383 Aaseng, Nathan. *Teens and Drunk Driving* (6–12). Illus. Series: Teen Issues. 1999, Lucent LB $18.96 (1-56006-518-4). A straightforward look at the problem of teens who drink and how this impairs their ability to drive, with relevant statistics and information on the law and strategies used to contain this problem. (Rev: BL 3/15/00; HBG 9/00; SLJ 3/00) [363.12]

10384 Aaseng, Nathan. *Treacherous Traitors* (5–9). Series: Profiles. 1997, Oliver LB $19.95 (1-881508-38-2). This book profiles 12 Americans who were tried for treason, including Benedict Arnold, John Brown, Alger Hiss, Julius and Ethel Rosenberg, and Aldrich Ames. (Rev: BR 1–2/98; SLJ 2/98) [355.3]

10385 Ballinger, Erich. *Detective Dictionary: A Handbook for Aspiring Sleuths* (4–8). Illus. 1994,

Lerner LB $19.93 (0-8225-0721-8). An unusual A-to-Z book that looks at various techniques used in crime detection and includes deductive puzzles and instructions for creating a crime lab. (Rev: BL 9/15/94) [363.2]

10386 Bayer, Linda. *Drugs, Crime, and Criminal Justice* (7–10). Series: Crime, Justice, and Punishment. 2001, Chelsea LB $19.95 (0-7910-4262-6). This book, written by an analyst from the Office of National Drug Control Policy, looks at the relationship between drugs and crime and its impact on our judicial system. (Rev: BL 9/15/01; HBG 3/02) [364]

10387 Black, Andy. *Organized Crime* (7–12). Series: Crime and Detection. 2003, Mason Crest LB $22.95 (1-59084-367-3). Organized crime in the United States and other countries including Russia and Britain is the main focus of this well-illustrated, large-format volume that will appeal to reluctant readers. Also use *Cyber Crime* and *Major Unsolved Crimes* (2003). (Rev: SLJ 10/03) [364.1]

10388 Blackwood, Gary L. *Gangsters* (4–7). Series: Bad Guys. 2001, Benchmark LB $28.50 (0-7614-1016-3). Al Capone is just one of the evildoers profiled in this volume that gives historical context for each "bad guy." Also use *Outlaws* and *Highwaymen* (both 2001). (Rev: HBG 3/02; SLJ 1/02) [364.106]

10389 Bode, Janet, and Stanley Mack. *Hard Time* (7–12). Illus. 1996, Delacorte $16.95 (0-385-32186-4). A series of horrifying and heartbreaking case histories about teens, including many who are in prison, who have been either the perpetrators or the victims of excessive violence. (Rev: BL 4/1/96; BR 9–10/96; SLJ 4/96*; VOYA 4/96) [364.3]

10390 Bosch, Carl. *Schools Under Siege: Guns, Gangs, and Hidden Dangers* (7–12). Illus. Series: Issues in Focus. 1997, Enslow LB $20.95 (0-89490-908-8). This work surveys teenage crime, its history and causes, the juvenile justice system, pertinent Supreme Court decisions, and types of school violence. (Rev: BL 8/97; SLJ 9/97) [363.119371]

10391 Brownlie, Alison. *Crime and Punishment: Changing Attitudes, 1900–2000* (6–9). Illus. Series: Twentieth Century Issues. 1999, Raintree Steck-Vaughn LB $27.11 (0-8172-5573-7). A compact, well-illustrated book that explores the concepts of crime and punishment with emphasis on today's organized crime and its international connections. (Rev: BL 3/15/00; HBG 9/00) [364]

10392 Coppin, Cheryl Branch. *Everything You Need to Know About Healing from Rape Trauma* (7–12). Series: Need to Know Library. 2000, Rosen $25.25 (0-8239-3122-6). Emphasizing that rape is about power not sex and that the victim is blameless, the author looks in particular at prevention and recovery. (Rev: SLJ 9/00) [362.883]

10393 Cothran, Helen, ed. *Sexual Violence* (8–12). Series: Opposing Viewpoints. 2003, Gale LB $32.45 (0-7377-1240-6); paper $21.20 (0-7377-1239-2). Twenty-five essays explore the reasons why people abuse others, the impact on the victims, the different forms of violence, and differing opinions on the extent of this phenomenon. (Rev: BL 6/1–15/03) [364.15]

10394 Cozic, Charles P., ed. *America's Prisons* (8–12). Illus. Series: Opposing Viewpoints. 1997, Greenhaven LB $16.20 (1-56510-549-4). A series of articles expressing differing opinions about the effectiveness of America's prisons, their purposes, and alternatives. (Rev: BL 4/15/97; BR 1–2/98) [365]

10395 Cozic, Charles P., ed. *Gangs* (8–12). Series: Opposing Viewpoints. 1995, Greenhaven LB $26.20 (1-56510-363-7); paper $22.45 (1-56510-362-9). A thought-provoking, alarming, and moving discussion of gangs and violence in the United States. (Rev: BL 12/15/95; VOYA 6/96) [364.1]

10396 Day, Nancy. *Violence in Schools: Learning in Fear* (7–12). Illus. Series: Issues in Focus. 1996, Enslow LB $20.95 (0-89490-734-4). Such forms of violence in schools as guns, sexual harassment, gay bashing, and gang fighting are discussed with material on their causes, effects, and the recent formation of student advocacy groups. (Rev: BL 6/1–15/96; SLJ 7/96) [371.5]

10397 DeAngelis, Gina. *White-Collar Crime* (6–9). Illus. Series: Crime, Justice, and Punishment. 1999, Chelsea $21.95 (0-7910-4279-0). Such crimes as frauds, hoaxes, and computer hacking are described in this volume that shows that betraying the public trust is as much a crime as murder. (Rev: BL 12/15/99; HBG 4/00) [364.16]

10398 De Hahn, Tracee. *Crimes Against Children: Child Abuse and Neglect* (7–12). Series: Crime, Justice, and Punishment. 1999, Chelsea LB $19.95 (0-7910-4253-7). Laws concerning child abuse, the definition of child abuse, and protecting children against abuse are some of the topics covered in this volume. (Rev: HBG 4/00; SLJ 3/00) [362.76]

10399 Egendorf, Laura K., ed. *Gangs* (6–12). Illus. Series: Opposing Viewpoints. 2000, Greenhaven LB $22.96 (0-7377-0510-8); paper $14.96 (0-7377-0509-4). Diverse viewpoints are offered on wide-ranging topics including gang behavior, racist tendencies, girl gangs, and the various laws and efforts to quell gang activities. (Rev: BL 3/1/01; SLJ 4/01) [364.1]

10400 Espejo, Roman, ed. *America's Prisons* (6–12). Series: Opposing Viewpoints. 2001, Gale LB $31.20 (0-7377-0788-7); paper $19.95 (0-7377-0787-9). Balanced essays examine the effectiveness of prisons and the treatment of prison inmates. (Rev: BL 4/1/02) [365]

10401 Farman, John. *The Short and Bloody History of Spies* (5–8). Illus. 2002, Lerner LB $23.95 (0-

8225-0845-1); paper $9.55 (0-8225-0846-X). A witty and fascinating account of the intriguing lives of spies, with descriptions of spying techniques and gadgets. (Rev: BL 1/1–15/03; HBG 3/03) [327.12]

10402 Fodor, Margie Druss. *Megan's Law: Protection or Privacy?* (6–8). Illus. Series: Issues in Focus. 2001, Enslow LB $20.95 (0-7660-1586-6). A look at both sides of the difficult question of children's safety versus privacy for convicted sex offenders who have served their time. (Rev: BL 1/1–15/02; HBG 10/02; SLJ 3/02) [362.7]

10403 Fridell, Ron. *Spying: The Modern World of Espionage* (7–12). Illus. 2002, Millbrook LB $21.40 (0-7613-1662-0). What spies do, the technology they use, and the politics of espionage are all covered in this concise volume. (Rev: BL 5/1/02; HBG 10/02; SLJ 4/02; VOYA 12/02) [327.1273]

10404 Friedlander, Mark P., Jr., and Terry M. Phillips. *When Objects Talk: Solving a Crime with Science* (5–8). Illus. Series: Discovery! 2001, Lerner LB $26.60 (0-8225-0649-1). A fictional mystery serves to introduce criminal investigation techniques such as fingerprints and DNA. (Rev: HBG 3/02; SLJ 2/02; VOYA 2/02) [363.25]

10405 Gaines, Ann. *Prisons* (8–12). Series: Crime, Justice, and Punishment. 1998, Chelsea LB $21.95 (0-7910-4315-0). A thought-provoking look inside America's prisons, with background material on the history and philosophy of incarceration and an examination of issues in penology. (Rev: VOYA 4/99) [365]

10406 Gardner, Robert. *Crime Lab 101: Experimenting with Crime Detection* (6–9). 1992, Walker LB $14.85 (0-8027-8159-4). Details how law enforcement agencies use science and technology to solve crimes, with 25 crime lab activities and eight exercises. (Rev: BL 8/92; SLJ 10/92) [363.2]

10407 Gedatus, Gus. *Gangs and Violence* (6–9). 2000, LifeMatters $0.00 (0-7368-0423-4); paper $0.0 (0-7368-0427-7). A look at the structure and activities of gangs, and the best ways to deal with them. (Rev: HBG 9/00; SLJ 9/00) [366.1]

10408 Goldentyer, Debra. *Street Violence* (4–8). Series: Preteen Pressures. 1998, Raintree Steck-Vaughn LB $25.69 (0-8172-5028-X). This book discusses types of street violence and how young people can protect themselves, as well as gang issues and alternatives to participation. (Rev: BL 5/15/98; HBG 10/98; SLJ 6/98) [364]

10409 Goodnough, David. *Stalking: A Hot Issue* (7–10). Series: Hot Issues. 2000, Enslow LB $19.95 (0-7660-1364-2). The motivations of stalkers, their strategies, how to deal with stalkers, and the legal actions that can be taken are all examined in this slim volume. (Rev: HBG 3/01; SLJ 12/00) [364.15]

10410 Goodwin, William. *Teen Violence* (7–10). Illus. Series: Overview: Teen Issues. 1997, Lucent

LB $27.45 (1-56006-511-7). A clear, in-depth discussion of the scope, causes, and prevention of teen violence; the relationships between the media, gangs, and violence; and the treatment of juvenile offenders in the justice system. (Rev: BL 5/15/98) [364.36]

10411 Graham, Ian. *Crime-Fighting* (5–8). Illus. Series: Science Spotlight. 1995, Raintree Steck-Vaughn LB $24.26 (0-8114-3840-6). A discussion of scientific methods used in analyzing evidence at crime scenes, such as DNA testing. (Rev: SLJ 7/95) [364]

10412 Graham, Ian. *Fakes and Forgeries* (5–8). Illus. Series: Science Spotlight. 1995, Raintree Steck-Vaughn LB $24.26 (0-8114-3843-0). Examines famous scandals in history involving such fakes as the Loch Ness monster, counterfeit money, and the forged Hitler diaries. (Rev: SLJ 7/95) [364]

10413 Grapes, Bryan J., ed. *Prisons* (8–12). Series: Current Controversies. 2000, Greenhaven LB $21.96 (0-7377-0147-1); paper $13.96 (0-7377-0146-3). This collection of sources explores facets of the penal system with material on the effectiveness of incarceration, the treatment of prisoners, privatization questions, and inmate labor. (Rev: BL 3/1/00) [365.]

10414 Greenberg, Keith E. *Out of the Gang* (5–8). Illus. 1992, Lerner LB $19.93 (0-8225-2553-4). A realistic portrait of gang life, revealed by a man who escaped it and a boy who managed to stay out of it. (Rev: BCCB 6/92; BL 6/15/92; SLJ 9/92) [364.1]

10415 Guernsey, JoAnn B. *Youth Violence: An American Epidemic?* (7–10). Series: Frontline. 1996, Lerner LB $19.95 (0-8225-2627-1). Chapters in this book include discussions on violence at home and school, gangs and gang violence, and the influence of such factors as guns, drugs, alcohol. poverty, race, and discrimination. (Rev: SLJ 1/97; VOYA 2/97) [364.3]

10416 Hjelmeland, Andy. *Prisons: Inside the Big House* (4–8). Illus. Series: Pro/Con Issues. 1996, Lerner LB $30.35 (0-8225-2607-7). Opposing viewpoints are presented on the purposes of prisons, prison conditions, and alternate forms of rehabilitation. (Rev: BL 8/96; SLJ 9/96) [365]

10417 Hyde, Margaret O. *Kids in and out of Trouble* (6–9). 1995, Dutton $13.99 (0-525-65149-7). A dark picture of the juvenile justice system and juvenile violence. (Rev: BL 5/15/95; SLJ 5/95; VOYA 12/95) [364.3]

10418 Innes, Brian. *Forensic Science* (8–12). 2003, Mason Crest LB $22.95 (1-59084-373-8). A well-illustrated exploration of historic and international crime investigations, with a look at evolving techniques and the importance of evidence in court cases. (Rev: SLJ 6/03) [363.25]

10419 Jackson, Donna M. *The Bone Detectives: How Forensic Anthropologists Solve Crimes and Uncover Mysteries of the Dead* (5–9). 1996, Little, Brown $17.95 (0-316-82935-8). A look at the role of forensic anthropologists in solving crimes including murder. (Rev: BCCB 4/96; BL 4/1/96; HB 5–6/96; SLJ 5/96*; VOYA 8/96) [363.2]

10420 Johnson, Julie. *Why Do People Join Gangs?* (5–8). Series: Exploring Tough Issues. 2001, Raintree Steck-Vaughn LB $25.69 (0-7398-3236-0). Johnson looks at gangs — who joins them and why, and how to get out of one — in the United States and abroad, and includes a chapter on dealing with bullies. Also use *Why Do People Fight Wars?* and *Why Are People Prejudiced?* (both 2002). (Rev: SLJ 11/01) [364.1]

10421 Johnson, Toni E. *Handcuff Blues: Helping Teens Stay Out of Trouble with the Law* (6–9). Illus. 1999, Goofy Foot paper $10.95 (1-885535-43-0). Twelve case histories about teens in trouble for drunk driving, vandalism, shoplifting, and drive-by shootings are given with background information, details of the crime, and finally the legal action taken and the outcome. (Rev: SLJ 8/99; VOYA 12/99) [364.3]

10422 Jones, Charlotte F. *Fingerprints and Talking Bones: How Real Life Crimes Are Solved* (5–8). Illus. 1997, Delacorte $16.95 (0-385-32299-2). A clear, concise account of what forensic science means and how it has been applied in real cases. (Rev: BCCB 6/97; BL 6/1–15/97; SLJ 8/97) [363.2]

10423 Kerrigan, Michael. *The History of Punishment* (7–12). Series: Crime and Detection. 2003, Mason Crest LB $22.95 (1-59084-386-X). A detailed and interesting overview of the kinds of punishments that have been imposed over the centuries on those who fail to adhere to a wide variety of laws and codes of conduct. (Rev: SLJ 12/03) [364.6]

10424 Kim, Henny H., ed. *Youth Violence* (7–12). 1998, Greenhaven LB $32.45 (1-56510-811-6). This book presents different opinions on the seriousness of youth violence, its causes, how it can be reduced, and punishments for young offenders. (Rev: BL 8/98) [302.3]

10425 Klee, Sheila. *Working Together Against School Violence* (6–10). Series: The Library of Social Activism. 1996, Rosen LB $16.95 (0-8239-2262-6). This guide introduces the increase in school violence and its causes in the context of violence in society, and shows students what they can do to reduce it in their schools. (Rev: SLJ 2/97) [371.5]

10426 Kopka, Deborah L. *School Violence* (7–12). Series: Contemporary World Issues. 1997, ABC-CLIO LB $45.00 (0-87436-861-8). An overview of juvenile violence over the last 30 years, potential risk factors in youth violence, and efforts to curb

school violence. (Rev: BR 3–4/98; SLJ 2/98) [371.5]

10427 Landau, Elaine. *Stalking* (7–12). Illus. 1996, Watts LB $25.00 (0-531-11295-0). All kinds of stalking and stalkers, e.g., former husbands, ex-boyfriends, fans, and total strangers, are discussed, with examples from actual case studies. (Rev: BL 2/15/97; SLJ 2/97) [364.1]

10428 Larsen, Anita. *Psychic Sleuths* (5–7). 1994, Macmillan LB $14.95 (0-02-751645-8). Pros and cons concerning the use of psychics in solving crimes are discussed, with many case studies. (Rev: BL 10/1/94; SLJ 11/94) [363.2]

10429 Lewis, Brenda Ralph. *Hostage Rescue with the FBI* (6–10). Illus. Series: Rescue and Prevention: Defending Our Nation. 2003, Mason Crest LB $22.95 (1-59084-403-3). Famous hostage situations such as the Achille Lauro incident are mentioned in this well-illustrated survey of the process of rescuing hostages, negotiating with their takers, and the use of snipers. Also use *Police Crime Prevention* (2003). (Rev: SLJ 7/03) [364.15]

10430 Lock, Joan. *Famous Prisons* (7–12). Series: Crime and Detection. 2003, Mason Crest LB $22.95 (1-59084-380-0). Alcatraz, Sing Sing, San Quentin, and Dartmoor are among the prisons described, with historical and anecdotal information and accounts of famous inmates. (Rev: SLJ 12/03) [365]

10431 Margolis, Jeffrey A. *Teen Crime Wave: A Growing Problem* (7–12). Illus. Series: Issues in Focus. 1997, Enslow LB $20.95 (0-89490-910-X). The teenage crime phenomenon is examined, with material on frequency, causes, the juvenile justice system, Supreme Court decisions, and historical background. (Rev: BL 8/97; SLJ 9/97) [364.36]

10432 Marzilli, Alan. *Famous Crimes of the 20th Century* (8–12). Series: Crime, Justice, and Punishment. 2002, Chelsea LB $22.95 (0-7910-6788-2). The author looks at six well-known events — including the assassination of Martin Luther King Jr., the Watergate burglary, and the O. J. Simpson trial — and discusses the social importance of each. (Rev: SLJ 2/03)

10433 Meltzer, Milton. *Crime in America* (6–10). 1990, Morrow $12.95 (0-688-08513-X). Survey of crime, law enforcement, and the justice system, including the strengths and weaknesses of the current judicial structure. (Rev: BL 1/1/91; SLJ 12/90) [364.973]

10434 Newton, David E. *Teen Violence: Out of Control* (7–10). Illus. Series: Issues in Focus. 1995, Enslow LB $20.95 (0-89490-506-6). A well-researched account that covers all types of teen violence, the nature-nuture controversy, ways of preventing teen violence, and types of punishment currently being used. (Rev: BL 3/1/96; SLJ 6/96; VOYA 2/96) [364.3]

10435 Oliver, Marilyn Tower. *Gangs: Trouble in the Streets* (5–8). 1995, Enslow LB $20.95 (0-89490-492-2). Discusses the roots of gangs in the 19th century, aspects of modern gang life, and how members manage to quit gangs. (Rev: BL 8/95) [364.1]

10436 Oliver, Marilyn Tower. *Prisons: Today's Debate* (7–12). Series: Issues in Focus. 1997, Enslow LB $20.95 (0-89490-906-1). The debate concerning the effectiveness of America's prisons and their purposes is presented clearly, with all sides represented fairly. (Rev: BL 11/15/97; SLJ 12/97) [365]

10437 Orr, Tamra. *Violence in Our Schools: Halls of Hope, Halls of Fear* (6–12). 2003, Watts LB $29.50 (0-531-12268-9). Strategies for avoiding and defusing violence before it erupts are a focus of this volume that traces violent incidents back to the 1920s and looks at topics including bullying, gun control, homeschooling, and current school efforts in these areas. (Rev: BL 1/1–15/04; SLJ 12/03) [371.7]

10438 Owen, David. *Police Lab: How Forensic Science Tracks Down and Convicts Criminals* (6–12). Illus. 2002, Firefly $19.95 (1-55297-620-3); paper $9.95 (1-55297-619-X). The nitty-gritty of forensic science is covered here, with information about the investigations of some well-known crimes and criminals and attention-grabbing photographs, some of them grisly. (Rev: BL 12/15/02; HBG 3/03; SLJ 5/03) [363.25]

10439 Owens, Lois Smith, and Vivian Verdell Gordon. *Think About Prisons and the Criminal Justice System* (6–10). Series: Think. 1991, Walker LB $15.85 (0-8027-8121-7); paper $9.95 (0-8027-7370-2). Basic information on incarceration, crime and its consequences, the criminal justice system, and the basis for laws. (Rev: BL 6/1/92; SLJ 2/92) [364.973]

10440 Platt, Richard. *Spy* (4–9). Illus. 1996, Knopf $20.99 (0-679-98122-5). All aspects of spying, including equipment and techniques, are described, along with profiles of famous spies. (Rev: BL 12/1/96; SLJ 6/97) [327.12]

10441 Powell, Phelan. *Major Unsolved Crimes* (6–9). Illus. Series: Crime, Justice, and Punishment. 1999, Chelsea $19.95 (0-7910-4277-4). Such crimes as the riddle of Jack the Ripper, the Zodiac killer, the Tylenol murders, and the Kennedy assassination are discussed in this fascinating volume. (Rev: BL 12/15/99; HBG 4/00) [364.15]

10442 Rabiger, Joanna. *Daily Prison Life* (7–12). Series: Crime and Detection. 2003, Mason Crest LB $22.9 (1-59084-384-3). Readers learn about the daily routine for prisoners in jails across America. (Rev: SLJ 12/03) [365]

10443 Rainis, Kenneth G. *Crime-Solving Science Projects: Forensic Science Experiments* (5–9). 2000, Enslow LB $20.95 (0-7660-1289-1). After defining forensic science, this book contains experi-

ments and projects involving such areas as fingerprints, inks, writing samples, fibers, forgeries, and blood evidence. (Rev: HBG 10/01; SLJ 2/01) [363.2]

10444 Roleff, Tamara L., ed. *Guns and Crime* (8–12). Series: At Issue. 1999, Greenhaven LB $21.96 (0-7377-0153-6); paper $13.96 (0-7377-0152-8). Both primary and secondary sources are included in this anthology that explores the relationship between guns and crime and the topic of gun control. (Rev: BL 12/15/99) [363.3]

10445 Roleff, Tamara L., ed. *Police Corruption* (6–12). Series: At Issue. 2003, Gale $20.96 (0-7377-1172-8); paper $13.96 (0-7377-1171-X). This is a thought-provoking exploration of the reasons why corruption can flourish within the law enforcement community. (Rev: BL 4/15/03) [353.4]

10446 Ross, Stewart. *Spies and Traitors* (5–8). Series: Fact or Fiction? 1995, Millbrook LB $26.90 (1-56294-648-X). A history of the people who have placed themselves above their country in the dangerous game of espionage and betrayal. (Rev: BL 11/15/95; SLJ 3/96) [355.3]

10447 Sadler, A. E., and Scott Barbour, eds. *Juvenile Crime* (6–12). Series: Opposing Viewpoints. 1997, Greenhaven LB $26.20 (1-56510-516-8). Excerpts from books and articles probe different viewpoints on juvenile violence and crime — its causes, frequency, and punishments. (Rev: BL 2/1/97; BR 5–6/97; SLJ 4/97) [364.3]

10448 Salak, John. *Violent Crime: Is It out of Control?* (6–8). Series: Issues of Our Time. 1995, Twenty-First Century LB $22.90 (0-8050-4239-3). An honest presentation of why violent crimes are being committed more frequently and how young people are becoming increasingly involved in them. (Rev: BL 2/1/96; SLJ 2/96) [364.1]

10449 Silverstein, Herma. *Kids Who Kill* (7–10). Illus. 1997, Twenty-First Century LB $25.90 (0-8050-4369-1). This volume examines the reasons for the escalation in the number of juvenile killers, who they are, why they kill, the environmental factors involved, and how the court system deals with underage criminals. (Rev: BL 12/15/97; SLJ 1/98; VOYA 2/98) [364.14]

10450 Silverstein, Herma. *Threads of Evidence: Using Forensic Science to Solve Crimes* (7–12). 1996, Twenty-First Century LB $26.90 (0-8050-4370-5). A discussion of the new forensic technology now available to criminologists, such as the use of DNA, blood splatters, fibers, and shell casings, and the role this science has played in solving famous cases. (Rev: BL 12/1/96; SLJ 2/97; VOYA 6/97) [363.2]

10451 Solomon, Louis. *The Ma and Pa Murders and Other Perfect Crimes* (7–9). 1976, HarperCollins $12.95 (0-397-31577-5). This is an account of six unsolved crimes including the murders involving Lizzie Borden. [364]

10452 Steele, Philip. *Smuggling* (5–9). Series: Past and Present. 1993, Macmillan LB $20.00 (0-02-786884-2). A colorful history of smuggling through the ages. (Rev: BL 8/93) [364.1]

10453 Stewart, Gail B. *Drug Trafficking* (6–8). 1990, Lucent LB $27.45 (1-56006-116-2). The author follows marijuana, cocaine, and heroin from the fields through the refinement process to their sale on the streets. (Rev: BL 4/15/91; SLJ 3/91) [363.4]

10454 Stewart, Gail B. *Gangs* (8–10). Illus. Series: The Other America. 1997, Lucent LB $27.45 (1-56006-340-8). Four gang members reveal in interviews why they joined, what gang life is like, and problems trying to leave gangs. (Rev: BL 5/15/97; BR 11–12/97; SLJ 3/97; VOYA 4/98) [364.3]

10455 Stewart, Gail B. *Gangs* (7–12). 1998, Greenhaven LB $27.45 (1-56510-751-9); paper $17.45 (1-56510-750-0). Issues discussed in this volume include why gangs attract members, how to control them, and the seriousness of the problem. (Rev: BL 5/15/98; BR 9–10/98; SLJ 6/98) [364.1]

10456 Streissguth, Thomas. *Hoaxers and Hustlers* (7–10). 1994, Oliver LB $19.95 (1-881508-13-7). Chronicles con artists and con games from the 1800s to the present, including pyramid schemes, the "Martian invasion" radio hoax, and Jim and Tammy Faye Bakker's real-estate scam. (Rev: BL 9/1/94; SLJ 7/94) [364.1]

10457 Szumski, Bonnie, and Neal Bernards. *Prisons: Detecting Bias* (4–7). Illus. Series: Opposing Viewpoints Juniors. 1991, Greenhaven LB $22.45 (0-89908-604-7). Can prisons rehabilitate and how do they affect criminals are two of several issues explored. (Rev: BL 6/15/91) [365]

10458 Thomas, Peggy. *Talking Bones: The Science of Forensic Anthropology* (6–9). Series: Science Sourcebooks. 1995, Facts on File $25.00 (0-8160-3114-2). This work provides an accessible introduction to the history and technology of forensic anthropology, with material on how forensic anthropologists are able to solve crimes through the analysis of human bones. (Rev: BL 10/15/95; BR 3–4/96; SLJ 1/96; VOYA 4/96) [613]

10459 Trapani, Margi. *Working Together Against Gang Violence* (4–8). Series: The Library of Social Activism. 1996, Rosen LB $16.95 (0-8239-2260-X). After a general discussion on gang behavior, the author gives pointers to help young people cope with the threat of gangs and suggestions for working with others against gang violence. (Rev: SLJ 2/97) [302.3]

10460 Wiese, Jim. *Detective Science: 40 Crime-Solving, Case-Breaking, Crook-Catching Activities for Kids* (4–7). 1996, Wiley paper $12.95 (0-471-11980-6). Presents 40 experiments and activities

that illustrate techniques in forensic science related to observing, collecting, and analyzing evidence. (Rev: BL 4/15/96; SLJ 6/96) [363.2]

10461 Wilker, Josh. *Classic Cons and Swindles* (6–9). Illus. Series: Crime, Justice, and Punishment. 1997, Chelsea LB $21.95 (0-7910-4251-0). This book explains such common con games and swindles as the pigeon drop and the bunco scam. (Rev: BL 9/1/97; BR 11–12/97; VOYA 12/97) [364.163]

10462 Williams, Stanley, and Barbara C. Becnel. *Gangs and the Abuse of Power* (4–8). Series: Tookie Speaks Out Against Gang Violence. 1996, Rosen LB $17.25 (0-8239-2346-0). A former active gang member in Los Angeles tells what his life was like as a member and how to avoid his mistakes. Also use in this series *Gangs and Wanting to Belong* (1996). (Rev: SLJ 1/97) [302.3]

10463 Williams, Stanley, and Barbara C. Becnel. *Gangs and Weapons* (4–8). Series: Tookie Speaks Out Against Gang Violence. 1996, Rosen LB $17.25 (0-8239-2342-8). The use of weapons in gangs to gain and maintain power and how they are obtained are two of the topics covered in this cautionary account written by a former gang member who was seriously wounded in a shootout. Also use *Gangs and Your Friends* (1996). (Rev: SLJ 1/97) [302.3]

10464 Williams, Stanley, and Barbara C. Becnel. *Gangs and Your Neighborhood* (4–8). Series: Tookie Speaks Out Against Gang Violence. 1996, Rosen LB $17.25 (0-8239-2347-9). How gangs grow in neighborhoods and how they change them are two of the topics covered in this book about the dangers of gangs and how to avoid joining one. (Rev: SLJ 1/97) [302.3]

10465 Winters, Paul A., ed. *Crime* (8–12). Series: Current Controversies. 1997, Greenhaven LB $32.45 (1-56510-687-3); paper $21.20 (1-56510-686-5). A collection of articles debating the causes of crime, methods of prevention, whether or not it is increasing, and juvenile crime. (Rev: BL 2/1/98) [364]

10466 Wolff, Lisa. *Gangs* (7–9). Illus. Series: Overview. 2000, Lucent LB $18.96 (1-56006-660-1). This book explores why gangs are formed, their criminal activities, and how the legal system and social agencies deal with them. (Rev: BL 4/15/00; HBG 9/00; SLJ 6/00) [364.1.]

10467 Woodford, Chris. *Criminal Investigation* (4–8). Illus. Series: Science Fact Files. 2001, Raintree Steck-Vaughn LB $27.12 (0-7398-1016-2). A concise introduction to the forensic science with information on the newest equipment and techniques. (Rev: HBG 10/01; SLJ 1/02) [363.2]

10468 Wormser, Richard. *Juveniles in Trouble* (8–12). 1994, Messner $15.00 (0-671-86775-X). Extensive use of first-person narratives of troubled youths, with hard-hitting facts on important choices kids in trouble need to make. (Rev: BL 5/15/94; SLJ 6/94; VOYA 12/94) [364.3]

10469 Worth, Richard. *Children, Violence, and Murder* (7–10). Series: Crime, Justice, and Punishment. 2001, Chelsea LB $19.95 (0-7910-5154-4). Specific cases of young people who murder are presented, including Columbine High School, in this fascinating account that presents opposing views on the subject. (Rev: BL 6/1–15/01; HBG 10/01; SLJ 7/01) [364]

10470 Wright, Cynthia. *Everything You Need to Know About Dealing with Stalking* (7–12). Series: Need to Know Library. 2000, Rosen LB $17.95 (0-8239-2841-1). What to do if you're being stalked, as well as where to get help. (Rev: HBG 9/00; SLJ 3/00) [362.88]

10471 Yeatts, Tabatha. *Forensics: Solving the Crime* (6–9). Illus. Series: Innovators. 2001, Oliver LB $21.95 (1-881508-75-7). An absorbing exploration of the development of forensics and the contributions of individual scientists, with clear explanations of some new technologies. (Rev: BCCB 2/02; HBG 10/02; SLJ 4/02) [363.25]

10472 Zeinert, Karen. *Victims of Teen Violence* (7–12). Illus. Series: Issues in Focus. 1996, Enslow LB $20.95 (0-89490-737-9). An exploration of teen violence that focuses of guns, gangs, sexual harassment, and gay bashing, and includes causes, consequences, victims, and solutions. (Rev: BL 6/1–15/96; SLJ 7/96; VOYA 8/96) [362.88]

10473 Ziff, John. *Espionage and Treason* (7–10). Series: Crime, Justice, and Punishment. 1999, Chelsea LB $19.95 (0-7910-4263-4). The Rosenbergs, Aldrich Ames, and Kim Philby are among the 20th-century spies covered in this survey of espionage and the motivations that drive traitors. (Rev: HBG 9/00; SLJ 4/00) [327.12]

Poverty, Homelessness, and Hunger

10474 Ayer, Eleanor. *Homeless Children* (5–8). Illus. Series: Overview. 1997, Lucent LB $27.45 (1-56006-177-4). The causes and consequences of homelessness are explored, with a focus on children and the ways the problem is being handled. (Rev: BL 3/15/97; BR 11–12/97) [362.7]

10475 Balkin, Karen, ed. *Poverty* (8–12). Series: Opposing Viewpoints. 2003, Gale LB $33.70 (0-7377-1697-5); paper $22.45 (0-7377-1698-3). This anthology describes the 36 million Americans living in poverty, debates the seriousness of the problem, explores how people get out of poverty, and how the poor can be helped. (Rev: BL 1/1–15/04) [362.5]

10476 Barbour, Scott, ed. *Hunger* (7–12). Series: Current Controversies. 1995, Greenhaven LB $32.45 (1-56510-239-8). This compilation of arti-

cles, essays, and book excerpts written by journalists, scholars, and activists will challenge young people to evaluate the information and develop their own conclusions about world hunger, the extent of the problem, and how it can be reduced. (Rev: BL 8/95; SLJ 10/95) [363.8]

10477 Berck, Judith. *No Place to Be: Voices of Homeless Children* (7–12). 1992, Houghton $17.00 (0-395-53350-3). Honest testimony of homeless young people, with excerpts from their writing, including poetry. (Rev: BL 4/1/92*; SLJ 6/92) [362.7]

10478 Bowden, Rob. *Food Supply* (5–8). Series: 21st Century Debates. 2002, Raintree Steck-Vaughn LB $27.12 (0-7398-4871-2). Trends and issues regarding the food supply, and possible solutions for shortages, are presented in this look at pros and cons. (Rev: BL 6/1–15/02) [338.19]

10479 Cozic, Charles P., ed. *Welfare Reform* (8–12). Series: At Issue. 1997, Greenhaven LB $26.20 (1-56510-546-X); paper $17.45 (1-56510-545-1). This anthology of different opinions on welfare reform explores such alternatives as workfare, establishment of orphanages, and reliance on private charities. (Rev: BL 1/1–15/97; SLJ 6/97) [361.973]

10480 Cozic, Charles P., and Paul A. Winters, eds. *Welfare* (8–12). Series: Opposing Viewpoints. 1997, Greenhaven LB $32.45 (1-56510-520-6). In this anthology of 35 essays, prominent politicians and writers debate questions about welfare, including its necessity, abuse, and reform. (Rev: BL 12/15/96; BR 5–6/97; SLJ 2/97) [362.5]

10481 De Koster, Katie, ed. *Poverty* (7–12). Series: Opposing Viewpoints. 1994, Greenhaven paper $16.20 (1-56510-065-4). Differing viewpoints are presented on such questions as what causes poverty and why women and minorities suffer from higher rates of poverty than white males. (Rev: BL 1/1/94) [362.5]

10482 Egendorf, Laura K., ed. *Poverty* (8–12). Series: Opposing Viewpoints. 1998, Greenhaven LB $32.45 (1-56510-947-3); paper $21.20 (1-56510-946-5). The seriousness of poverty today, its causes, and how it can be alleviated are covered in this collection of differing opinions on the subject. (Rev: BL 8/98) [362.5]

10483 Erlbach, Arlene. *Everything You Need to Know If Your Family Is on Welfare* (6–10). Series: Need to Know Library. 1997, Rosen LB $25.25 (0-8239-2433-5). This book explains the welfare system and details recipients' rights as well as offering tips on how to cope with being on welfare and the social stigma often associated with it. (Rev: SLJ 4/98) [362.5]

10484 Flood, Nancy Bohac. *Working Together Against World Hunger* (7–12). Series: Library of Social Activism. 1995, Rosen LB $16.95 (0-8239-

1773-8). A rundown on world hunger, the conditions that cause it, and ways of becoming active in fighting it. (Rev: BL 4/15/95) [363.8]

10485 Fyson, Nance Lui. *Feeding the World* (6–8). Illus. 1985, Batsford $19.95 (0-7134-4264-6). An introduction to the world's increasing food problems, with material on staple crops and a discussion of food production and distribution. (Rev: BL 5/15/85) [338.19]

10486 Garlake, Teresa. *Poverty: Changing Attitudes, 1900–2000* (6–9). Series: 20th Century Issues. 1999, Raintree Steck-Vaughn LB $28.55 (0-8172-5894-9). Garlake looks at the causes of poverty, events around the world that have contributed to poverty, attitudes toward this problem, and government efforts to contain it. (Rev: BL 11/15/00; BR 3–4/00; HBG 9/00; SLJ 5/00) [362.5]

10487 Gottfried, Ted. *Homelessness: Whose Problem Is It?* (6–12). Series: Issue and Debate. 1999, Millbrook LB $25.90 (0-7613-0953-5). After reviewing the history of homelessness in the United States, opposing views are presented on the causes of homelessness today, the responsibility of government and the individual, and methods of countering it. (Rev: BL 4/1/99; BR 9–10/99; SLJ 9/99) [305.569]

10488 Hubbard, Jim. *Lives Turned Upside Down: Homeless Children in Their Own Words and Photographs* (4–8). 1996, Simon & Schuster LB $17.00 (0-689-80649-3). Case studies of four youngsters give insights into homeless families. (Rev: BCCB 1/97; BL 11/15/96; SLJ 12/96) [362.7]

10489 Johnson, Joan J. *Children of Welfare* (6–10). Illus. 1995, Twenty-First Century LB $23.40 (0-8050-2985-0). A look at the emergence of the welfare system, what it is today, and its impact on young people. (Rev: BL 6/1–15/97; BR 11–12/97; SLJ 6/97) [362.71]

10490 Kowalski, Kathiann M. *Poverty in America: Causes and Issues* (6–12). Series: Issues in Focus. 2003, Enslow LB $20.95 (0-7660-1945-4). An exploration of unequal standards of living in America that looks at differences in levels of poverty and at homelessness, welfare, government efforts to alleviate the problem, and private-sector aid. (Rev: SLJ 11/03) [362.5]

10491 LeVert, Marianne. *The Welfare System* (7–12). 1995, Millbrook LB $25.90 (1-56294-455-X). A look at various issues that form part of the great welfare debate. (Rev: BL 4/15/95; SLJ 4/95) [361.6]

10492 McCauslin, Mark. *Homelessness* (6–9). 1994, Macmillan paper $4.95 (0-382-24757-4). A survey of the decline of affordable housing over the past few decades, along with other economic and employment factors that have led to homelessness. (Rev: BL 2/1/95; SLJ 3/95) [362.5]

10493 Nichelason, Margery G. *Homeless or Hopeless?* (5–8). Illus. Series: Pro/Con Issues. 1994,

Lerner LB $30.35 (0-8225-2606-9). After an explanation of the roots and causes of homelessness, clearly written statements debate who is responsible for homelessness and how it should be handled. (Rev: BL 6/1–15/94; SLJ 7/94) [362.5]

10494 O'Neill, Terry. *The Homeless: Distinguishing Between Fact and Opinion* (4–7). Illus. Series: Opposing Viewpoints Juniors. 1991, Greenwillow LB $16.20 (0-89908-605-5). Homelessness is explored, with different points of view on how serious the problem is and who is to blame. (Rev: BL 6/15/91) [362.5]

10495 Parker, Julie. *Everything You Need to Know About Living in a Shelter* (8–12). 1995, Rosen LB $25.25 (0-8239-1874-2). A straightforward account that describes life for teens living in shelters, with material on what they can do to control at least some aspects of their lives. (Rev: SLJ 12/95; VOYA 2/96) [362.5]

10496 Roleff, Tamara L., ed. *The Homeless* (8–12). Illus. Series: Opposing Viewpoints. 1996, Greenhaven LB $26.20 (1-56510-361-0); paper $16.20 (1-56510-360-2). Is homelessness a serious problem? Who are the homeless? What causes homelessness? How can society and government help the homeless? These are some of the questions discussed in this collection of articles representing different opinions on this subject. (Rev: BL 3/15/96; BR 9–10/96; SLJ 2/96; VOYA 6/96) [362.5]

10497 Roleff, Tamara L., ed. *Inner-City Poverty* (8–12). Series: Contemporary Issues Companion. 2003, Gale LB $25.96 (0-7377-0841-7); paper $16.96 (0-7377-0840-9). This examination of theories about the causes of urban poverty, the resulting crime and drug use, the impact of the welfare system, and the potential for effective reform provides lots of material for students doing research. (Rev: LMC 4–5/03; SLJ 2/03) [362.5]

10498 Rozakis, Laurie. *Homelessness: Can We Solve the Problem?* (6–9). Series: Issues of Our Time. 1995, Twenty-First Century LB $22.90 (0-8050-3878-7). A well-rounded discussion that will encourage readers to form their own conclusions. (Rev: BL 7/95; SLJ 9/95) [362.5]

10499 Seymour-Jones, Carole. *Homelessness* (5–9). Series: Past and Present. 1993, Macmillan $20.00 (0-02-786882-6). A discussion of the causes of homelessness, the extent of the problem and who is affected, and ways to end it. (Rev: BL 8/93) [362.5]

10500 Stavsky, Lois, and I. E. Mozeson. *The Place I Call Home: Faces and Voices of Homeless Teens* (8–12). Illus. 1990, Shapolsky $14.95 (0-944007-81-3). A series of interviews with homeless teens reveals lives of violence, poverty, and drugs. (Rev: BL 11/15/90; SLJ 2/91) [362.7]

10501 Stearman, Kaye. *Homelessness* (5–10). Illus. Series: Talking Points. 1999, Raintree Steck-

Vaughn LB $27.12 (0-8172-5312-2). A worldwide view of homelessness, its causes — including eviction, natural disasters, and war — and international efforts to combat it. (Rev: BL 9/1/99; BR 9–10/99; SLJ 8/99) [363.5]

10502 Stearman, Kaye. *Why Do People Live on the Streets?* (5–7). Series: Exploring Tough Issues. 2001, Raintree Steck-Vaughn LB $25.69 (0-7398-3232-8). Among reasons given for homelessness are poverty and discrimination. (Rev: HBG 10/01; SLJ 7/01) [305.569]

10503 Stewart, Gail B. *Homeless Teens* (8–10). Series: The Other America. 1999, Lucent LB $17.96 (1-56006-398-X). The plight of teens without homes is explored through an overview chapter and a series of interviews with five teens. (Rev: BL 9/15/99; SLJ 8/99) [362.5]

10504 Worth, Richard. *Poverty* (5–8). Illus. Series: Overview. 1997, Lucent LB $27.45 (1-56006-192-8). A carefully researched title that gives a history of poverty in America, changing attitudes toward it, and current policies and practices. (Rev: BL 8/97; SLJ 9/97) [362.5]

Unemployment

10505 Alpern, Michele. *The Effects of Job Loss on the Family* (6–12). Illus. Series: Focus on Family Matters. 2002, Chelsea LB $19.75 (0-7910-6690-8). Personal teen experiences draws reader into this straightforward account of the financial and emotional upheavals caused by unemployment. (Rev: BL 10/15/02; HBG 3/03) [306.4]

Public Morals

10506 Carnes, Jim. *Us and Them: A History of Intolerance in America* (7–12). Illus. 1996, Oxford $28.00 (0-19-510378-5). Each chapter focuses on an episode of intolerance and prejudice in our history, such as the Cherokee Trail of Tears, the internment of Japanese Americans during World War II, recent race riots in New York City, and the murder of a gay man in Maine. (Rev: BL 6/1–15/96; BR 11–12/96) [305.8]

10507 Cothran, Helen, ed. *Pornography* (8–12). Illus. Series: Opposing Viewpoints. 2001, Gale LB $31.20 (0-7377-0761-5); paper $19.95 (0-7377-0760-7). Debating teams will plenty of arguments to defend both sides of questions about the evils of pornography and whether it should be regulated and/or censored. (Rev: SLJ 12/01) [363.4]

10508 Day, Nancy. *Censorship or Freedom of Expression?* (7–12). Series: Pro/Con Issues. 2000, Lerner LB $25.26 (0-8225-2628-X). An exploration

of censorship in areas including schools and the arts and entertainment, with discussion of age appropriateness and use of the Internet. (Rev: HBG 3/01; SLJ 1/01) [363.3]

10509 Dudley, William, ed. *Media Violence* (8–12). Series: Opposing Viewpoints. 1998, Greenhaven LB $32.45 (1-56510-945-7); paper $21.20 (1-56510-944-9). This exploration of violence in television, motion pictures, song lyrics, and other media questions its extent, effects, and proposals to restrict it. (Rev: BL 8/89) [384]

10510 Gold, John C. *Board of Education v. Pico (1982)* (6–10). Illus. Series: Supreme Court Decisions. 1994, Twenty-First Century LB $25.90 (0-8050-3660-1). A thorough analysis of the Supreme Court case that began in a Long Island school and involved censoring library materials. (Rev: BL 11/15/94; SLJ 1/95) [344.73]

10511 McGwire, Scarlett. *Censorship: Changing Attitudes 1900–2000* (6–9). Series: 20th Century Issues. 1999, Raintree Steck-Vaughn LB $27.11 (0-8172-5574-5). McGwire looks at censorship at the beginning of the 20th century, global events around the world that contributed to censorship, the advent of movie rating systems, and the Internet. (Rev: BR 3/00; HBG 9/00; SLJ 5/00) [363.3]

10512 Miller, J. Anthony. *Texas vs. Johnson: The Flag-Burning Case* (6–10). Illus. Series: Landmark Supreme Court Cases. 1997, Enslow LB $20.95 (0-89490-858-8). The limits of civil disobedience was the subject of this important Supreme Court case. (Rev: BL 7/97; BR 11–12/97) [342.73]

10513 Roleff, Tamara L., ed. *Censorship* (6–12). Series: Opposing Viewpoints. 2001, Gale $31.20 (1-56510-957-0); paper $19.95 (1-56510-956-2). Thoughtful essays address censorship and free speech as they relate to art, pornography, schools, and libraries. (Rev: BL 4/1/02; SLJ 12/01) [363.3]

10514 Sherrow, Victoria. *Censorship in Schools* (6–9). Illus. Series: Issues in Focus. 1996, Enslow LB $20.95 (0-89490-728-X). After defining censorship, the author discusses when, how, and why it occurs in schools, with several citations of famous cases. (Rev: BL 1/1–15/97; BR 3–4/97; SLJ 12/96; VOYA 4/97) [025.213]

10515 Stay, Byron L., ed. *Censorship* (8–12). Series: Opposing Viewpoints. 1997, Greenhaven LB $32.45 (1-56510-508-7). This new edition of the 1990 title presents arguments on such controversial areas of the censorship battle as antipornography laws, campus speech codes, and use of the V-chip. (Rev: BL 12/15/96; BR 5–6/97; VOYA 6/97) [363.3]

10516 Stefens, Bradley. *Censorship* (7–10). Illus. 1996, Lucent LB $27.45 (1-56006-166-9). A historical survey that presents the conflict between freedom and censorship, beginning with the Ten

Commandments and the Bill of Rights and ending with today's controversy over rock lyrics. (Rev: BL 2/15/96; SLJ 3/96) [363.3]

10517 Steins, Richard. *Censorship: How Does It Conflict with Freedom?* (5–9). Series: Issues of Our Time. 1995, Twenty-First Century LB $22.90 (0-8050-3879-5). A clearly written introduction to censorship, its history, and the various positions possible toward it. (Rev: BL 7/95; SLJ 9/95) [363.3]

10518 Torr, James D., ed. *Is Media Violence a Problem?* (6–12). Series: At Issue. 2001, Greenhaven paper $16.20 (0-7377-0802-6). Brief essays look at the kinds of violence found on television and in movies, video games, and rap music, and assess whether this violence engenders further violence. (Rev: BL 1/1–15/02; SLJ 3/02) [302.23]

10519 Wekesser, Carol, ed. *Pornography* (8–12). Series: Opposing Viewpoints. 1997, Greenhaven paper $21.20 (1-56510-517-6). What is pornography? Is it harmful? Should it be censored? Can it be controlled on the Internet? These are some of the questions explored in this collection of writings representing different points of view. (Rev: BL 12/15/96; BR 5–6/97; SLJ 2/97) [363.7]

10520 Whitehead, Fred. *Culture Wars* (8–12). Series: Opposing Viewpoints. 1994, Greenhaven LB $26.20 (1-56510-101-4); paper $16.20 (1-56510-100-6). Includes essays by a variety of writers on such cultural topics as intellectual freedom, artistic quality, values, and public morality. (Rev: BL 5/1/94; SLJ 3/94; VOYA 4/94) [306]

Sex Roles

10521 Chipman, Dawn, et al. *Cool Women: The Reference* (6–9). 1998, Girl Pr. paper $19.95 (0-9659754-0-1). This work spotlights an eclectic variety of heroines, past and present, real and fictional, from around the world, ranging from athletes and spies to Amazons and comic book queens, chosen for their uniqueness, strength, tenacity, contributions, and ability to blaze new trails for women. (Rev: VOYA 2/99) [305.4]

10522 Hanmer, Trudy J. *The Gender Gap in Schools: Girls Losing Out* (7–12). Illus. Series: Issues in Focus. 1996, Enslow LB $20.95 (0-89490-718-2). Sex discrimination at the school level is introduced with an objective presentation of the many facets of this complex question. (Rev: BL 8/96; SLJ 6/96) [376]

10523 Ross, Mandy. *The Changing Role of Women* (6–9). Series: 20th Century Perspectives. 2002, Heinemann LB $25.64 (1-58810-660-8). An exploration of the ways in which women's roles changed

around the world during the 20th century. (Rev: SLJ 10/02) [305.42]

10524 Stearman, Kaye, and Nikki van der Gaag. *Gender Issues* (6–10). Illus. Series: Global Issues. 1996, Raintree Steck-Vaughn LB $19.98 (0-8172-4545-6). Using historical background material, statistics, and case studies, the various issues involving gender roles and sex discrimination around the world are explored. (Rev: BL 3/15/97; VOYA 6/97) [305.3]

Social Action, Social Change, and Futurism

10525 Brownlie, Alison. *Charities — Do They Work?* (6–10). Series: Talking Points. 1999, Raintree Steck-Vaughn LB $18.98 (0-8172-5319-X). In this brief account, the role of charities in American society is explored along with a discussion on their problems and accomplishments. (Rev: BL 12/15/99; HBG 9/00) [361]

10526 Coon, Nora E., ed. *It's Your Rite: Girls' Coming-of-Age Stories* (6–12). 2003, Beyond Words paper $9.95 (1-58270-074-5). Young authors from around the world describe practical and ceremonial milestones that mark their coming of age, and the associated worries and joys. (Rev: SLJ 10/03) [305.235]

10527 Fleming, Robert. *Rescuing a Neighborhood: The Bedford-Stuyvesant Volunteer Ambulance Corps* (4–8). Illus. 1995, Walker LB $16.85 (0-8027-8330-9). The story of how two determined, dedicated men organized emergency response services in their inner-city neighborhood. (Rev: BL 5/1/95; SLJ 9/95) [362]

10528 Hovanec, Erin M. *Get Involved! A Girl's Guide to Volunteering* (5–8). Series: Girls' Guides. 1999, Rosen LB $23.95 (0-8239-2985-X). Two case studies of successful volunteers are given in this account that explains where to volunteer, how to approach organizations, and how to determine one's interests. (Rev: HBG 10/00; SLJ 1/00; VOYA 2/00) [361]

10529 Isler, Claudia. *Volunteering to Help in Your Neighborhood* (6–10). Series: Service Learning. 2000, Children's LB $19.00 (0-516-23374-2); paper $6.95 (0-516-23574-5). For reluctant readers, this volume suggests ways in which teens can help others in their communities. Also use *Volunteering to Help with Animals* (2001). (Rev: SLJ 2/01)

10530 Karnes, Frances A., and Suzanne M. Bean. *Girls and Young Women Leading the Way: 20 True Stories About Leadership* (5–8). Illus. 1993, Free Spirit paper $12.95 (0-915793-52-0). Contains case histories of 20 girls who changed their communities by starting projects such as collecting food for the homeless or starting a recycling program. (Rev: SLJ 12/93) [307.1]

10531 Kronenwetter, Michael. *Protest!* (7–12). Illus. 1996, Twenty-First Century LB $23.40 (0-8050-4103-6). This book describes various forms of protest, from simple actions in everyday life to those related to political and social issues aimed at changing social conditions in the U.S. and around the world, providing a historical, sociological, and psychological context. (Rev: BL 1/1–15/97; SLJ 1/97; VOYA 6/97) [303.48]

10532 Kurian, George Thomas, and Graham T. T. Molitor, eds. *The 21st Century* (8–12). 1999, Macmillan $130.00 (0-02-864977-X). This book makes predictions for future developments in such areas as abortion, artificial intelligence, crime, extinction, household appliances, sexual behavior, and utopias. (Rev: BL 4/1/99; SLJ 8/99) [133.3]

10533 Lesko, Wendy Schaetzel. *Youth: The 26% Solution* (7–12). 1998, Information U. S. A. paper $14.95 (1-878346-47-4). A community action handbook for teens prepared by Project 2000 that provides basic, workable advice, based on the premise that the 26 percent of the population of the United States under the age of 18 can make a difference. (Rev: BL 11/1/98; VOYA 12/98) [361.8]

10534 Lewis, Barbara A. *The Kid's Guide to Service Projects: Over 500 Service Ideas for Young People Who Want to Make a Difference* (4–7). 1995, Free Spirit paper $12.95 (0-915793-82-2). After an introduction on how to organize and conduct service projects, this book gives details on 500 ideas from running errands for seniors to working for voter registration. (Rev: SLJ 7/95) [307]

10535 Lewis, Barbara A. *The Kid's Guide to Social Action: How to Solve the Social Problems You Choose — and Turn Creative Thinking into Positive Action.* Rev. ed. (4–8). 1998, Free Spirit paper $18.95 (1-57542-038-4). An inspirational guide that shows how young people can make a difference by becoming involved in social action, such as instigating a cleanup of toxic waste, lobbying, or youth rights campaigns. (Rev: SLJ 1/99) [361.6]

10536 Markley, Oliver W., and Walter R. McCuan, eds. *21st Century Earth* (7–12). Series: Opposing Viewpoints. 1996, Greenhaven LB $26.20 (1-56510-415-3); paper $21.20 (1-56510-414-5). An assortment of forecasts for the near future, including the effects of overpopulation and new technologies. (Rev: BL 4/1/96; SLJ 3/96) [303.49]

10537 Meltzer, Milton. *Who Cares? Millions Do . . . A Book About Altruism* (7–10). 1994, Walker LB $16.85 (0-8027-8325-2). Stories of people who help their fellow beings, both individually and through organizations. (Rev: BL 11/15/94; VOYA 2/95) [171]

10538 Mintzer, Rich. *Helping Hands: How Families Can Reach Out to Their Community* (6–12). Series:

Focus on Family Matters. 2002, Chelsea LB $20.75 (0-7910-6952-4). This is a basic introduction to volunteerism with tips on how teens can get involved in activities and projects that complement their interests and abilities. (Rev: BL 1/1–15/03) [361.8]

10539 Ryan, Bernard. *Caring for Animals* (7–12). 1998, Ferguson LB $15.95 (0-89434-227-4). After a general introduction to volunteerism, this book outlines ways that teens can help care for unwanted and abandoned animals in their neighborhood. (Rev: BL 9/15/98; BR 11–12/98; SLJ 11/98; VOYA 8/99) [361.8]

10540 Ryan, Bernard. *Expanding Education and Literacy* (7–12). Series: Community Service for Teens. 1998, Ferguson LB $15.95 (0-89434-231-2). This book describes literacy and reading programs in the United States and how teens can participate in them. (Rev: BL 9/15/98; BR 11–12/98; SLJ 11/98) [361.3]

10541 Ryan, Bernard. *Helping the Ill, Poor and the Elderly* (7–12). Series: Community Service for Teens. 1998, Ferguson LB $15.95 (0-89434-229-0). Outlines the many ways that teens can help the less fortunate in their communities both informally and working through service agencies. (Rev: BL 9/15/98; BR 11–12/98; SLJ 11/98) [361.8]

10542 Ryan, Bernard. *Promoting the Arts and Sciences* (7–12). Series: Community Service for Teens. 1998, Ferguson LB $15.95 (0-89434-234-7). This work tells how teens can become involved in local agencies that promote the arts and sciences and how their services can make a difference both to the community and themselves. (Rev: BL 9/15/98; BR 11–12/98; SLJ 2/99) [361.8]

10543 Ryan, Bernard, Jr. *Participating in Government: Opportunities to Volunteer* (7–12). Series: Community Service for Teens. 1998, Ferguson LB $15.95 (0-89434-230-4). An upbeat guide that advises teens about how they can volunteer in the areas of government and politics and become involved in their community. Also use *Promoting the Arts and Sciences: Opportunities to Volunteer* (1998). (Rev: BR 11–12/98; SLJ 2/99) [302.14]

10544 Seo, Danny. *Generation React: Activism for Beginners* (7–12). 1997, Ballantine paper $10.95 (0-345-41242-7). This book gives step-by-step directions for starting an activist group, with material on fund raising, protesting and boycotting, lobbying, publicity, and related topics. (Rev: BL 10/1/97; VOYA 2/98) [303.4]

Social Customs and Holidays

10545 Breuilly, Elizabeth, and Joanne O'Brien. *Festivals of the World: The Illustrated Guide to Celebrations, Customs, Events and Holidays* (6–12).

Illus. 2002, Checkmark $29.95 (0-8160-4481-3). Festivals around the world are organized by religion, with maps, photographs, and interesting sidebar features. (Rev: SLJ 4/03) [394.2]

10546 Bruchac, Joseph. *Squanto's Journey: The Story of the First Thanksgiving* (4–8). 2000, Harcourt $16.00 (0-15-201817-4). A picture book for older readers about the Pilgrims, the first Thanksgiving, and the important role played by the Paluxet Indian Squanto in helping the colony survive. (Rev: BL 9/1/00; HBG 3/01; SLJ 11/00) [394.2]

10547 Gelber, Carol. *Love and Marriage Around the World* (5–7). 1998, Millbrook LB $23.90 (0-7613-0102-X). From courtship to the wedding, this book introduces marriage customs from around the world and among different ethnic groups. (Rev: BCCB 7–8/98; HBG 10/98; SLJ 6/98) [392]

10548 Graham-Barber, Lynda. *Doodle Dandy! The Complete Book of Independence Day Words* (4–7). 1992, Macmillan LB $13.95 (0-02-736675-8). Thirty-four words and phrases that reflect our history and government and explain how they came to be. (Rev: BCCB 7–8/92; BL 7/92; SLJ 3/92) [394]

10549 Graham-Barber, Lynda. *Mushy! The Complete Book of Valentine Words* (4–8). 1993, Avon paper $3.50 (0-380-71650-X). An explanation of the words, symbols, and customs concerning Valentine's Day. (Rev: BCCB 3/91; BL 2/15/91; SLJ 5/91) [394.2]

10550 Harris, Zoe, and Suzanne Williams. *Pinatas and Smiling Skeletons* (4–8). Illus. 1998, Pacific View LB $19.95 (1-881896-19-6). This book introduces six festivals celebrated in Mexico: the Feast of the Virgin of Guadalupe, Christmas, Carnaval, Corpus Christi, Independence Day, and the Day of the Dead. (Rev: BL 3/15/99; BR 5–6/99; HBG 3/99; SLJ 3/99) [394.26972]

10551 Johnson, Dolores. *The Children's Book of Kwanzaa: A Guide to Celebrating the Holiday* (4–7). Illus. 1996, Simon & Schuster $16.00 (0-689-80864-X). This account discusses African American history and the origins of Kwanzaa, its meaning, and its rituals. (Rev: BCCB 11/96; BL 9/1/96) [394.2]

10552 Karenga, Maulana. *Kwanzaa: A Celebration of Family, Community and Culture, Special Commemorative Edition* (6–12). Illus. 1997, Univ. of Sankore Pr. $24.95 (0-943412-21-8). This complete book on Kwanzaa explains its African and African American origins, devotes a chapter to each of its seven principles, suggests activities, and gives answers to the most frequently asked questions about this holiday. (Rev: SLJ 10/98) [394.2]

10553 King, Elizabeth. *Quinceanera: Celebrating Fifteen* (5–8). Illus. 1998, Dutton $16.99 (0-525-45638-4). This photoessay traces the everyday life of two beautiful young Latin American women as

they prepare for quinceanera, a coming-of-age ritual. (Rev: BCCB 10/98; BL 8/98; HBG 3/99; SLJ 12/98; VOYA 2/99) [395.2]

10554 Limburg, Peter R. *Weird! The Complete Book of Halloween Words* (4–7). 1989, Macmillan LB $13.95 (0-02-759050-X). This book defines 41 words and expressions, such as trick or treat, associated with Halloween. (Rev: BL 9/1/89; SLJ 9/89) [394]

10555 MacMillan, Dianne M. *Thanksgiving Day* (4–8). Series: Best Holiday Books. 1997, Enslow LB $18.95 (0-89490-822-7). In spite of a dull format, this book gives solid information about Thanksgiving, its history, common traditions, and modern observances. (Rev: SLJ 8/97) [394.2]

10556 Perl, Lila. *Piñatas and Paper Flowers: Holidays of the Americas in English and Spanish* (6–9). Illus. 1983, HarperCollins paper $7.95 (0-89919-155-X). The origins and customs of eight holidays celebrated in the Americas are outlined in a bilingual text. [394.2]

10557 Taylor, Charles A. *Juneteenth: A Celebration of Freedom* (5–8). 2002, Open Hand $19.95 (0-940880-68-7). A well-organized account of this holiday, which celebrates emancipation, with a discussion of the history of slavery. (Rev: SLJ 11/02) [394.2]

10558 Wilkinson, Philip. *A Celebration of Customs and Rituals of the World* (5–8). Illus. 1996, Facts on File $44.00 (0-8160-3479-6). A discussion of customs and rituals connected with birth, death, marriage, and coming-of-age. (Rev: BL 4/1/96; VOYA 6/96) [394.2]

10559 Wilson, Sule Greg C. *Kwanzaa! Africa Lives in a New World Festival* (4–7). Series: The Library of African American Arts and Culture. 1999, Rosen LB $31.95 (0-8239-1857-2). This book begins with a history of slavery and the civil rights movement, then explains the origins and meaning of Kwanzaa. (Rev: SLJ 10/99) [641.59]

Terrorism

10560 Andryszewski, Tricia. *Terrorism in America* (6–10). Illus. Series: Headliners. 2002, Millbrook LB $25.90 (0-7613-2803-3). An overview of attacks against Americans both at home and abroad, with an interesting discussion of the difficulties of protecting civil rights while fighting terrorism. (Rev: BCCB 9/02; BL 8/02; HBG 3/03; SLJ 12/02) [363.3]

10561 Cart, Michael, et al., eds. *911: The Book of Help* (8–12). Illus. 2002, Cricket $17.95 (0-8126-2659-1); paper $9.95 (0-8126-2676-1). A collection of essays, stories, and poems by well-known writers

SOCIAL CONCERNS AND PROBLEMS: *Terrorism*

presented in sections titled "Healing," "Searching for History," "Asking Why? Why? Why?," and "Reacting and Recovering." (Rev: BL 7/02; HB 9–10/02; HBG 3/03; SLJ 9/02*) [818]

10562 Currie, Stephen. *Terrorists and Terrorist Groups* (6–12). Series: Lucent Terrorism Library. 2002, Gale LB $21.96 (1-59018-207-3). A thorough, well-researched survey of terrorist organizations that looks at their structures, beliefs, tactics, and key figures. (Rev: SLJ 11/02) [973.931]

10563 Fridell, Ron. *Terrorism: Political Violence at Home and Abroad* (6–9). Illus. Series: Issues in Focus. 2001, Enslow LB $20.95 (0-7660-1671-4). A balanced look at pre-September 2001 terrorism both at home and abroad, at the operations of terrorist networks, and at worldwide efforts to track and contain terrorists. (Rev: HBG 3/02; SLJ 3/02; VOYA 12/01) [303.6]

10564 Gaines, Ann. *Terrorism* (7–12). Series: Crime, Justice, and Punishment. 1998, Chelsea LB $21.95 (0-7910-4596-X). Beginning with the bombing of Pan Am flight 103 over Lockerbie, Scotland, in 1988, this thorough account discusses terrorism around the world and the groups that are responsible. (Rev: BL 12/15/98; SLJ 3/99) [364.1]

10565 Goodman, Robin, and Andrea Henderson Fahnestock. *The Day Our World Changed: Children's Art of 9/11* (7–12). 2002, Abrams $19.95 (0-8109-3544-9). Children's words and art are the main focus of this handsome volume. (Rev: BL 9/15/02) [700]

10566 Gow, Mary. *Attack on America: The Day the Twin Towers Collapsed* (8–12). Illus. Series: American Disasters. 2002, Enslow LB $18.95 (0-7660-2118-1). This dramatic account of the events of September 11, 2001, includes many survivor and eyewitness accounts. (Rev: BL 9/1/02; HBG 3/03; SLJ 1/03) [973.931]

10567 Hamilton, John. *Behind the Terror* (4–7). Series: War on Terrorism. 2002, ABDO LB $16.95 (1-57765-679-8). Using an accessible text and color photographs, this book reports on various international terrorist organizations, their leaders, and their tactics. (Rev: BL 5/15/02) [909.9]

10568 Hamilton, John. *Operation Enduring Freedom* (4–7). Series: War on Terrorism. 2002, ABDO LB $25.65 (1-57765-665-2). Using many color photographs and a matter-of-fact text, this book covers various aspects of the U.S. war against terrorism. (Rev: BL 5/15/02; HBG 10/02) [973.9]

10569 Hamilton, John. *Operation Noble Eagle* (4–7). Series: War on Terrorism. 2002, ABDO LB $25.65 (1-57765-664-4). A look at U.S. efforts to police and defend its borders as part of the war on terrorism. (Rev: BL 5/15/02; HBG 10/02) [973.9]

10570 Hampton, Wilborn. *September 11, 2001: Attack on New York City* (6–9). Illus. 2003, Can-

dlewick $17.99 (0-7636-1949-3). Personal stories give depth to a description of the tragedy in New York City and speculation about the motivation of the perpetrators. (Rev: BL 7/03; HB 9–10/03; SLJ 7/03) [974.7]

10571 Kreger, Clare, ed. *White Supremacy Groups* (8–12). Series: At Issue. 2003, Gale LB $20.96 (0-7377-1364-X); paper $13.96 (0-7377-1365-8). The White Supremacy movement and the bombing of Oklahoma City are among the topics examined in this book on threats and terrorism. (Rev: BL 2/1/03) [305.8]

10572 Lalley, Patrick. *9.11.01: Terrorists Attack the U.S.* (4–7). Illus. 2002, Raintree Steck-Vaughn LB $31.40 (0-7398-6021-6). A compact look at the terrorist attacks of September 11, 2001, their causes, the world of Islam, the history of the World Trade Center, and personal stories related to the attacks. (Rev: BL 4/1/02; HBG 10/02; SLJ 5/02; VOYA 8/02) [303.6250]

10573 Levitas, Mitchel, ed. *A Nation Challenged: A Visual History of 9/11 and Its Aftermath: Young Reader's Edition* (6–12). 2002, Scholastic paper $18.95 (0-439-48803-6). This is a selection of material first published in the *New York Times* that has been chosen as suitable for young readers. (Rev: BL 9/1/02; HBG 10/03; SLJ 9/02*) [973.931]

10574 Louis, Nancy. *Heroes of the Day* (4–7). Series: War on Terrorism. 2002, ABDO LB $25.65 (1-57765-658-X). This account of September 11, 2001, describes through pictures and case studies the gallant feats of firefighters, police, and those who fought back on Flight 93. (Rev: BL 5/15/02; HBG 10/02; SLJ 6/02) [973.9]

10575 Louis, Nancy. *United We Stand* (4–7). Series: War on Terrorism. 2002, ABDO LB $25.65 (1-57765-660-1). In text and pictures, this account describes the support offered to the victims of the terrorist attacks of September 11, 2001, and their families. (Rev: BL 5/15/02; HBG 10/02) [909.9]

10576 Margulies, Phillip. *Al-Qaeda: Osama Bin Laden's Army of Terrorists* (5–7). Illus. Series: Inside the World's Most Infamous Terrorist Organizations. 2003, Rosen LB $26.50 (0-8239-3817-4). Al-Qaeda's history, missions, methods, and structure are described, with a detailed profile of Osama Bin Laden. (Rev: BL 10/15/03) [973.93]

10577 Marquette, Scott. *America Under Attack* (4–7). Illus. Series: America at War. 2002, Rourke LB $27.93 (1-58952-386-5). This book for middle graders explains in simple terms the September 11, 2001, attacks and other acts of terrorism against the United States, as well as discussing resulting legislation and changing opinions in America. (Rev: BL 10/15/02) [973.931]

10578 Meltzer, Milton. *The Day the Sky Fell: A History of Terrorism* (6–9). Illus. 2002, Random LB

$10.99 (0-375-92250-4); paper $5.99 (0-375-82250-X). This absorbing account of domestic and international terrorism adds a new foreword and five new chapters to the book originally published in 1983 as *The Terrorists*. (Rev: BL 10/15/02; HBG 3/03) [363.3]

10579 Mitch, Frank. *Understanding September 11th: Answering Questions About the Attacks on America* (7–12). Illus. 2002, Viking $16.99 (0-670-03582-3). A thoughtful and thought-provoking, question-and-answer look at terrorism and the forces that can provoke such attacks, with information on Islam and the history of American involvement in the Middle East. (Rev: BL 9/1/02; HBG 3/03; SLJ 9/02; VOYA 12/02) [973.931]

10580 Pellowski, Michael J. *The Terrorist Trial of the 1993 Bombing of the World Trade Center: A Headline Court Case* (6–8). Series: Headline Court Cases. 2003, Enslow LB $20.95 (0-7660-2045-2). After a description of the bombing itself, Pellowski describes the search for the perpetrators, the trials of the accused, and the links between Islamic fundamentalism and continuing terrorist activities. (Rev: SLJ 11/03) [974.7]

10581 Roleff, Tamara L., ed. *America Under Attack: Primary Sources* (6–12). Illus. Series: Lucent Terrorism Library. 2002, Gale LB $21.96 (1-59018-216-2). Interviews, speeches, articles, and other items relating to the terrorist attacks of September 11, 2001, are collected in a volume that researchers will find useful. (Rev: BL 11/1/02; SLJ 9/02) [973.931]

10582 Rosaler, Maxine. *Hamas: Palestinian Terrorists* (5–7). Illus. Series: Inside the World's Most Infamous Terrorist Organizations. 2003, Rosen LB $26.50 (0-8239-3820-4). Hamas's history, missions, methods, and structure are described, with profiles of key figures. (Rev: BL 10/15/03) [950.940]

10583 Sherrow, Victoria. *The Oklahoma City Bombing: Terror in the Heartland* (4–8). Illus. Series: American Disasters. 1998, Enslow LB $18.95 (0-7660-1061-9). Using many first-person descriptions, this account of the Oklahoma City bombing ends with the sentencing of Timothy McVeigh and Terry Nichols. (Rev: BL 1/1–15/99; BR 5–6/99; HBG 3/99; SLJ 3/99) [364.16]

10584 Sherrow, Victoria. *The World Trade Center Bombing: Terror in the Towers* (4–8). Illus. Series: American Disasters. 1998, Enslow LB $18.95 (0-7660-1056-2). An illustrated discussion of the

events and individuals leading up to the 1993 World Trade Center bombing. (Rev: BL 1/1–15/99; BR 5–6/99; HBG 3/99; SLJ 3/99; VOYA 4/99) [363.2]

10585 Shields, Charles J. *The 1993 World Trade Center Bombing* (6–8). Illus. 2001, Chelsea LB $21.95 (0-7910-5789-5). The author delves into the whys and hows of the first World Trade Center bombing and connects it to the attack of September 11, 2001. (Rev: BL 4/15/02; HBG 10/02; SLJ 8/02) [374.1]

10586 Stewart, Gail. *America Under Attack: September 11, 2001* (6–12). Series: Lucent Terrorism Library. 2002, Gale LB $21.96 (1-59018-208-1). Accounts of the terrorist attacks of September 11, 2001, include disturbing eyewitness testimonies. (Rev: BL 11/1/02; SLJ 9/02) [973.931]

10587 Streissguth, Thomas. *International Terrorists* (6–10). Illus. Series: Profiles. 1993, Oliver LB $19.95 (1-881508-07-2). This book describes the causes of international terrorism, the responsible organizations, and famous incidents. (Rev: BL 10/15/93; SLJ 1/94; VOYA 2/94) [909.82]

10588 Taylor, Robert. *The History of Terrorism* (6–12). Illus. Series: Lucent Terrorism Library. 2002, Gale LB $21.96 (1-59018-206-5). A chronological look at the history of terrorism around the globe, with discussion of the reasons it has been so widespread and of terrorists' motivation. (Rev: BL 11/1/02; SLJ 11/02) [303.6]

Urban and Rural Life

10589 Barr, Roger. *Cities* (6–8). Series: Overview. 1995, Lucent LB $35.15 (1-56006-158-8). A historical as well as a contemporary look at cities. (Rev: BL 7/95; SLJ 4/95) [307.76]

10590 DeAngelis, Therese. *Blackout! Cities in Darkness* (4–8). Series: American Disasters. 2003, Enslow LB $18.95 (0-7660-2110-6). This book chronicles the events and people involved in some of the important blackouts that have crippled America's cities. (Rev: BL 11/15/03) [307.7]

10591 Leuzzi, Linda. *Urban Life* (6–9). 1995, Chelsea LB $21.95 (0-7910-2841-0). A look at urban life in U.S. cities a century ago, from both a contemporary perspective and the viewpoint of someone living then. (Rev: BL 7/95; SLJ 9/95) [973]

Economics and Business

General and Miscellaneous

10592 Green, Meg. *The Young Zillionaire's Guide to Investments and Savings* (5–8). Series: Be a Zillionaire. 2000, Rosen LB $23.95 (0-8239-3261-3). A guide to the investment markets and methods of saving with good use of examples and case studies. (Rev: HBG 10/01; SLJ 3/01) [338.5]

10593 Karnes, Frances A., and Suzanne M. Bean. *Girls and Young Women Entrepreneurs: True Stories About Starting and Running a Business Plus How You Can Do It Yourself* (6–10). Illus. 1997, Free Spirit paper $12.95 (1-57542-022-8). This inspirational book introduces dozens of young women ages 9 to 25 who have started business ventures, and provides advice and information for young females who would also like to become entrepreneurs. (Rev: BR 9–10/98; SLJ 6/98) [338]

10594 Oleksy, Walter. *Business and Industry* (6–12). Illus. Series: Information Revolution. 1996, Facts on File $25.00 (0-8160-3075-8). This book describes how companies use Powerbook computers, supercomputers, modems, and videophones to distribute information, increase productivity, and make better business decisions. (Rev: BL 2/15/96; BR 9–10/96; VOYA 6/96) [650]

10595 Seidman, David. *The Young Zillionaire's Guide to Supply and Demand* (5–7). Series: Be a Zillionaire. 2000, Rosen LB $23.95 (0-8239-3264-8). The basic principles of supply and demand are explained, with information on how they are influenced by producers and consumers and how they help create economic conditions. (Rev: SLJ 2/01) [330]

10596 Wilson, Antoine. *The Young Zillionaire's Guide to Distributing Goods and Services* (5–7). Series: Be a Zillionaire. 2000, Rosen LB $23.95 (0-8239-3259-1). This book explains how goods and services are distributed, the importance of retailing and wholesaling, how transportation affects prices and availability, and how the Internet might change these conditions. (Rev: SLJ 2/01) [330]

Economic Systems and Institutions

General and Miscellaneous

10597 Aaseng, Nathan. *You Are the Corporate Executive* (7–10). Illus. Series: Great Decisions. 1997, Oliver LB $19.95 (1-881508-35-8). This book describes the work of a company's CEO and the nature and consequences of the decisions that CEOs have to make. (Rev: BL 6/1–15/97; BR 11–12/97; SLJ 6/97) [658.4]

10598 Downing, David. *Capitalism* (5–8). Series: Political and Economic Systems. 2002, Heinemann LB $28.50 (1-40340-315-5). In an attractive format, this book explains the capitalistic economic system, its history, key thinkers, and present status. (Rev: BL 1/1–15/03; HBG 3/03; SLJ 2/03) [330.12]

10599 Downing, David. *Communism* (5–8). Series: Political and Economic Systems. 2002, Heinemann LB $28.50 (1-40340-316-3). The theoretical basis of communism is explained with material on its application, history, important thinkers and leaders, and different movements. (Rev: BL 1/1–15/03; HBG 3/03; SLJ 2/03) [335.43]

10600 O'Neill, Terry, and Karin L. Swisher, eds. *Economics in America* (7–10). Series: Opposing Viewpoints. 1992, Greenhaven paper $16.20 (0-89908-162-2). A look at the state of the U.S. economy, the budget deficit, taxation, the banking system, and the future of labor as of 1990. (Rev: BL 6/15/92) [338.973]

10601 Trahant, LeNora B. *The Success of the Navajo Arts and Crafts Enterprise* (7–10). Illus. Series: Success. 1996, Walker LB $16.85 (0-8027-8337-6). After a brief history of the Navajo Nation, the author describes how the arts and crafts of the Navajos have prospered under a manufacturing and marketing cooperative. (Rev: BL 5/15/96; SLJ 7/96) [381]

Stock Exchanges

10602 Bamford, Janet. *Street Wise: A Guide for Teen Investors* (8–12). 2000, Bloomberg paper $16.95 (1-57660-039-4). In clear prose, the author provides excellent material for the beginning stock trader or novice with bonds and mutual funds, with fine background material and sage conservative advice. (Rev: BL 10/1/00; SLJ 3/01) [332.6]

10603 Brennan, Kristine. *The Stock Market Crash of 1929* (8–12). Series: Great Disasters: Reforms and Ramifications. 2000, Chelsea LB $19.95 (0-7910-5268-0). This account of the crash and its causes and aftermath looks carefully at the economy of the time and discusses the changes of a similar crash happening today. (Rev: BR 1–2/01; HBG 3/01; SLJ 12/00) [338.5]

10604 Caes, Charles J. *The Young Zillionaire's Guide to the Stock Market* (5–8). Series: Be a Zillionaire. 2000, Rosen LB $23.95 (0-8239-3265-6). Basic information on the inner workings of the stock market is presented with many examples from the corporate world. (Rev: HBG 10/01; SLJ 3/01) [332.6]

10605 Liebowitz, Jay. *Wall Street Wizard: Advice from a Savvy Teen Investor* (6–12). Illus. 2000, Simon $16.00 (0-689-83401-2). This book about Wall Street, the stock market, and investing was written by a 19-year-old money whiz. (Rev: BL 9/1/00; BR 3–4/01; HBG 10/01; SLJ 10/00) [332.65]

10606 McGowan, Eileen Nixon, and Nancy Lagow Dumas. *Stock Market Smart* (5–8). Illus. 2002, Millbrook LB $23.90 (0-7613-2113-6). An accessible question-and-answer presentation on the stock market and different types of investors, with illustrations, tips on saving, activities, a glossary, and list of resources. (Rev: BL 9/1/02; HBG 3/03; SLJ 10/02) [332.63]

Consumerism

10607 Schmitt, Lois. *Smart Spending: A Consumer's Guide* (5–9). 1989, Macmillan $13.95 (0-684-19035-4). A thorough account incorporating teen-oriented case studies that covers such topics as advertising promotions, consumer fraud, mail-order problems, budgets, warranties, and consumerism. (Rev: BL 5/1/89; BR 11–12/89; SLJ 7/89; VOYA 12/89) [640.73]

Employment and Jobs

10608 Atkin, S. Beth, ed. *Voices from the Fields: Children of Migrant Farmworkers Tell Their Stories* (7–12). 1993, Little, Brown $18.95 (0-316-05633-2). Oral histories from nine children. Each interview demonstrates a strong sense of family devotion and provides a reminder that education is the key to escaping the fields. (Rev: BL 5/1/93*; VOYA 2/94) [305.23]

Labor Unions and Labor Problems

10609 Bendor, David, and Bruno Leone, eds. *Work* (7–12). Illus. Series: Opposing Viewpoints. 1995, Greenhaven LB $32.45 (1-56510-219-3); paper $16.20 (1-56510-218-5). A collection of essays explores problems related to workers and society such as the education of the workforce, government intervention, and inequality in the workplace. (Rev: BL 7/95; SLJ 8/95) [331]

10610 de Ruiz, Dana C., and Richard Larios. *La Causa: The Migrant Farmworkers' Story* (4–7). 1992, Raintree Steck-Vaughn LB $30.40 (0-8114-7231-0). The story of the founding of the United Farm Workers highlights the work of Cesar Chavez and Dolores Huerta. (Rev: BL 6/1–15/93) [331]

10611 Laughlin, Rosemary. *The Pullman Strike of 1894: American Labor Comes of Age* (7–12). 1999, Morgan Reynolds LB $21.95 (1-883846-28-5). An engrossing account of this bitter railroad strike, with good background material on the railroad industry, the planned city of Pullman, the depression of 1893, and the personalities involved, including Eugene Debs. (Rev: BL 7/99; SLJ 8/99; VOYA 4/00) [331.892]

10612 McKissack, Patricia, and Fredrick McKissack. *A Long Hard Journey* (5–9). Illus. 1989, Walker LB $18.85 (0-8027-6885-7). A 150-year saga of the organization of porters into the first black American union, the Brotherhood of Sleeping Car Porters. (Rev: BL 9/15/89; SLJ 1/90; VOYA 12/89) [331]

10613 Simonds, Patricia. *The Founding of the AFL and the Rise of Organized Labor* (5–7). Illus. Series: Turning Points. 1991, Silver Burdett LB $14.95 (0-382-24123-1); paper $7.95 (0-382-24118-5). The inspiring story of the beginning of the labor movement in the United States and its impact on American history and society. (Rev: BL 1/15/92) [331.88]

10614 Stein, R. Conrad. *The Pullman Strike and the Labor Movement in American History* (6–10). Series: In American History. 2001, Enslow LB $20.95 (0-7660-1300-6). This account traces the history of the 1894 strike (one of America's longest) and the parts played by President Grover Cleveland, George Pullman, Eugene Debs, and social worker Jane Addams. (Rev: BL 8/1/01; HBG 10/01; SLJ 5/01) [331.892]

Money and Trade

10615 Godfrey, Neale S. *Neale S. Godfrey's Ultimate Kids' Money Book* (5–8). Illus. 1998, Simon & Schuster $19.00 (0-689-81717-7). An outstanding book that combines history, fables, games, and vocabulary to give young readers a history of money and economics. (Rev: BL 11/1/98*; HBG 3/99; SLJ 2/99) [332.024]

10616 Menhard, Francha Roffe. *Teen Consumer Smarts: Shop, Save, and Steer Clear of Scams* (7–12). Series: Teen Issues. 2002, Enslow LB $17.95 (0-7660-1667-6). A useful guide to money management that recommends regular saving and alerts readers to the dangers of credit cards and fraudulent scams. (Rev: HBG 3/03; SLJ 1/03) [332.024]

10617 Resnick, Abraham. *Money* (6–8). Series: Overview. 1995, Lucent LB $27.45 (1-56006-165-0). A history of money from ancient times when barter was used to today, when the movement is toward a cashless society and the elimination of money. (Rev: BL 7/95) [332.4]

10618 *Sold! The Origins of Money and Trade* (5–8). Series: Buried Worlds. 1994, Runestone LB $28.75 (0-8225-3206-9). Explains the world origins of commerce and money, with coverage of how the earliest coins were made in the West and how other cultures developed unique forms of currency. (Rev: BL 9/15/94; SLJ 9/94) [737.4]

Marketing and Advertising

10619 Day, Nancy. *Advertising: Information or Manipulation?* (6–12). Series: Issues in Focus. 1999, Enslow LB $20.95 (0-7660-1106-2). In addition to presenting an introduction to advertising, its history, and its impact on U.S. society, this book questions many advertising practices, provides information on advertising methods and targeting, and offers tips on how to evaluate advertising critically. (Rev: BL 7/99) [659.1]

10620 Graydon, Shari. *Made You Look: How Advertising Works and Why You Should Know* (5–9). 2003, Annick $24.95 (1-55037-815-5); paper $14.95 (1-55037-814-7). The 8- to 14-year-old age group is an advertising target, and this title teaches readers to recognize the various techniques used and to assess products' value. (Rev: BL 12/1/03*; SLJ 12/03) [659.1]

10621 Mierau, Christina. *Accept No Substitutes! The History of American Advertising* (6–9). 2000, Lerner $25.26 (0-8225-1742-6). A social history of advertising in America starting with early handbills and progressing through catalogues and television to the Internet. (Rev: BCCB 6/00; BL 7/00; HBG 9/00; SLJ 9/00) [659.1]

10622 Petley, Julian. *Advertising* (7–10). Illus. Series: MediaWise. 2003, Smart Apple LB $28.50 (1-58340-255-1). A good introduction to the world of advertising, with discussion of creative and financial concerns. (Rev: BL 10/15/03; SLJ 11/03) [659.1]

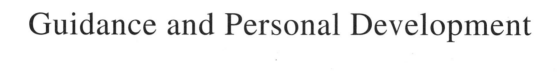

Guidance and Personal Development

Education and Schools

General and Miscellaneous

10623 Armstrong, Thomas. *You're Smarter Than You Think: A Kid's Guide to Multiple Intelligences* (5–8). 2003, Free Spirit paper $15.95 (1-57542-113-5). Eight different intelligences are defined in understandable terms, with quizzes that help readers investigate their own strengths. (Rev: BL 4/15/03; SLJ 6/03; VOYA 6/03) [153.9]

10624 Banfield, Susan. *The Bakke Case: Quotas in College Admissions* (6–10). Series: Landmark Supreme Court Cases. 1998, Enslow LB $20.95 (0-89490-968-1). The court case that challenged quotas in higher education to correct racial inequality is chronicled in this dramatic account that gives good background information. (Rev: BL 2/15/98; BR 9–10/98; SLJ 6/98) [378]

10625 Cruz, Barbara C. *School Dress Codes: A Pro/Con Issue* (6–10). Series: Hot Pro/Con Issues. 2001, Enslow LB $19.95 (0-7660-1465-7). Cruz presents the case for and against dress codes from the students' and the adults' points of view. (Rev: HBG 3/02; SLJ 7/01) [371.8]

10626 Cruz, Barbara C. *Separate Sexes, Separate Schools* (7–10). Illus. Series: Hot Pro/Con Issues. 2000, Enslow LB $19.95 (0-7660-1366-9). This examination of the issues connected with same-sex schools is well-organized and presents differing points of view on this complex topic. (Rev: BCCB 10/00; BL 2/1/01; HBG 3/01; SLJ 12/00; VOYA 6/01) [371.82]

10627 Davidson, Tish. *School Conflict* (4–8). Series: Life Balance. 2003, Watts LB $19.50 (0-531-12251-4); paper $6.95 (0-531-15571-4). This book examines the various conflicts, including violence, that exist in public education today and how these affect the lives and mental health of students. (Rev: BL 10/15/03) [370]

10628 Farrell, Juliana, and Beth Mayall. *Middle School: The Real Deal* (5–7). Illus. 2001, HarperCollins paper $7.99 (0-380-81313-0). Advice on coping with school work, teachers, and social life is presented in an appealing format. (Rev: BL 6/1–15/01; VOYA 8/01) [373.18]

10629 Feldman, Ruth Tenzer. *Don't Whistle in School: The History of America's Public Schools* (6–10). Illus. 2001, Lerner LB $25.26 (0-8225-1745-0). A broad overview of American public education that includes everything from regional differences to education trends and landmark court rulings, with illustrations and photographs. (Rev: BL 11/1/01; HBG 3/02; SLJ 11/01; VOYA 4/02) [370]

10630 Greene, Rebecca. *The Teenagers' Guide to School Outside the Box* (8–12). Illus. 2000, Free Spirit paper $15.95 (1-57542-087-2). Many learning opportunities are available to teens including travel, volunteer work, serving as an intern or apprentice, mentoring, and job shadowing. (Rev: BL 2/15/01; SLJ 3/01; VOYA 4/01) [373.2]

10631 Hurwitz, Sue. *High Performance Through Effective Scheduling* (8–12). Illus. Series: Learning-a-Living Library. 1996, Rosen LB $17.95 (0-8239-2204-9). This book discusses the basic skill of scheduling time and how it helps students at school, in extracurricular activities, and on the job. (Rev: BL 8/96; BR 1–2/97; SLJ 12/96; VOYA 2/97) [640]

10632 Pendleton, Scott. *The Ultimate Guide to Student Contests, Grades 7–12* (6–12). Illus. 1997, Walker paper $15.95 (0-8027-7512-8). This is a guide to various academically oriented contests open to young adults, arranged by subjects such as mathematics and foreign languages. (Rev: BL 8/97) [373.18]

10633 Pickering, Marianne. *Lessons for Life: Education and Learning* (5–8). Series: Our Human Family. 1995, Blackbirch LB $31.19 (1-56711-127-0). A look at educational practices around the world that shows great similarities regardless of the culture. (Rev: SLJ 1/96) [370]

10634 Schneider, Meg. *Help! My Teacher Hates Me* (5–8). 1994, Workman paper $7.95 (1-56305-492-2). Helpful hints for developing a positive attitude in school. (Rev: BL 3/15/95) [371.8]

10635 Sherrow, Victoria. *Challenges in Education* (7–12). Series: Issues for the 90s. 1991, Messner paper $13.95 (0-671-70556-3). An overview of the major questions and concerns facing today's educators. (Rev: BL 11/1/91; SLJ 11/91) [370]

10636 Terkel, Marni, and Susan Neiburg Terkel. *What's an "A" Anyway? How Important Are Grades?* (8–12). Illus. 2001, Watts $24.00 (0-531-11417-1). An examination of the academic grading system, addressing such issues as cheating, grade inflation, unusual grading systems, and whether success in school leads to success in life. (Rev: BL 11/1/01; SLJ 11/01) [371.27]

10637 Williams, Mary E., ed. *Education: Region Under Siege* (8–12). Series: Opposing Viewpoints. 1999, Greenhaven LB $21.95 (0-7377-0125-0); paper $13.96 (0-7377-0124-2). School choice, multicultural education, and educational reforms are three of the topics covered in this collection of different points of view on the subject of education. (Rev: BL 11/15/99) [370]

Development of Academic Skills

Study Skills

10638 Heiligman, Deborah. *The New York Public Library Kid's Guide to Research* (5–8). 1998, Scholastic paper $14.95 (0-590-30715-0). A fine introduction to research techniques including material on taking notes, using print and nonprint resources, conducting interviews and surveys, searching the Internet, and locating toll-free numbers. (Rev: HBG 3/99; SLJ 2/99) [808.023]

10639 Marks, Lillian S. *Touch Typing Made Simple.* Rev. ed. (8–12). Illus. 1985, Doubleday paper $12.95 (0-385-19426-9). A clear manual that gives information on specialized topics including types of letters, tabulations, and addressing envelopes. Part of a lengthy series. (Rev: BL 2/15/86) [652.3]

10640 Nathan, Amy. *Surviving Homework: Tips from Teens* (5–8). Illus. 1997, Millbrook LB $24.90 (1-56294-185-2). Using answers on questionnaires given to high school juniors and seniors, this book supplies many useful study tips and suggestions on

how to organize one's time. (Rev: BL 6/1–15/97; BR 11–12/96; SLJ 7/97) [372.12]

10641 Schumm, Jeanne Shay. *School Power: Strategies for Succeeding in School* (5–8). Illus. 1992, Free Spirit paper $15.95 (0-915793-42-3). Sensible suggestions for improving study skills: organization, note taking, improving reading, and writing reports. (Rev: BL 3/1/93) [371.3]

10642 Simpson, Carolyn. *High Performance Through Organizing Information* (8–12). Illus. Series: Learning-a-Living Library. 1996, Rosen LB $17.95 (0-8239-2207-3). This book discusses the importance of an organized work environment, whether in school, at home, or on the job, and how to create one using filing systems, to-do lists, data sources, and other strategies. (Rev: BL 8/96; BR 1–2/97; SLJ 8/96; VOYA 2/97) [640]

Tests and Test Taking

10643 Kern, Roy, and Richard Smith. *The Grade Booster Guide for Kids* (7–9). 1987, Hilton Thomas paper $7.95 (0-944162-00-2). This book covers the proper strategies and techniques to use for successful test-taking. (Rev: BR 5–6/88) [371.3]

Writing and Speaking Skills

10644 Asher, Sandy. *Where Do You Get Your Ideas? Helping Young Writers Begin* (5–7). Illus. 1987, Walker LB $13.85 (0-8027-6691-9). Keeping a journal and other interesting ideas for would-be journalists. (Rev: BCCB 12/87; BL 9/15/87; SLJ 9/87) [808.02]

10645 Bauer, Marion Dane. *What's Your Story? A Young Person's Guide to Writing Fiction* (5–10). 1992, Clarion paper $7.95 (0-395-57780-2). An award-winning writer gives advice to young authors, including suggestions for planning, writing, and revising. (Rev: BL 4/15/92; SLJ 6/92*) [808.3]

10646 Bauer, Marion Dane. *A Writer's Story from Life to Fiction* (5–8). 1995, Clarion $14.95 (0-395-72094-X); paper $6.95 (0-395-75053-9). Readers and aspiring writers will enjoy this famous author's explanations of how she draws on her own experiences to develop her works. (Rev: BL 9/15/95; SLJ 10/95; VOYA 2/96) [813]

10647 Bentley, Nancy, and Donna Guthrie. *Writing Mysteries, Movies, Monster Stories, and More* (5–8). Illus. 2001, Millbrook LB $24.90 (0-7613-1452-0). This book gives solid information on all kinds of fictional writing, including novels, short stories, fantasy, science fiction, humor, and even movie scripts. (Rev: BL 3/15/01; HBG 10/01; SLJ 4/01; VOYA 8/01) [808]

10648 Betz, Adrienne, comp. *Scholastic Treasury of Quotations for Children* (4–8). 1998, Scholastic paper $16.95 (0-590-27146-6). From Socrates to Bill Clinton, this is a useful compendium of quotations arranged under 75 subjects. (Rev: SLJ 2/99) [080]

10649 Block, Francesca L., and Hillary Carlip. *Zine Scene: The Do-It-Yourself Guide to Zines* (8–12). Illus. 1998, Girl Pr. paper $14.95 (0-9659754-3-6). This is a step-by-step guide to producing one's own magazine, from getting started and writing to layout, production, and marketing. (Rev: VOYA 8/99) [808]

10650 Bodart, Joni Richards. *The World's Best Thin Books: What to Read When Your Book Report Is Due Tomorrow* (6–12). 2000, Scarecrow paper $16.95 (1-57886-007-5). For each of the books listed, the author provides background material, themes, characters, and possible book talk or book report ideas. (Rev: BL 1/1–15/00) [028.1.]

10651 Brantley, C. L. *The Princeton Review Write Smart Junior* (6–8). Illus. 1995, Random paper $12.00 (0-679-76131-4). From writing haiku to keeping a journal, this entertaining manual explains how to write well. (Rev: VOYA 4/96) [808]

10652 Bruchac, Joseph. *Tell Me a Tale* (4–8). 1997, Harcourt $16.00 (0-15-201221-4). A master storyteller reveals tricks of the trade, tells where to find stories, and explores their origins and effects, with many examples from various cultures. (Rev: BL 3/15/97; SLJ 8/97) [808.5]

10653 Cibula, Matt. *How to Be the Greatest Writer in the World* (4–8). 1999, Zino $11.95 (1-55933-276-X). A spiral-bound book that presents 88 interesting and engaging exercises to help youngsters who feel they have nothing to write about. (Rev: SLJ 2/00) [808]

10654 Craig, Steve. *Sports Writing: A Beginner's Guide* (6–12). Illus. 2002, Discover Writing paper $15.00 (0-9656574-9-3). A fine introduction to writing news and features about sports, to conducting good interviews, and to the training of journalists. (Rev: BL 9/1/02; VOYA 4/03) [070.449]

10655 Detz, Joan. *You Mean I Have to Stand Up and Say Something?* (7–12). 1986, Macmillan LB $13.95 (0-689-31221-0). An entertaining guide to effective speaking and overcoming the fear of facing an audience. (Rev: BCCB 2/87; BL 2/87; SLJ 3/87) [808.5]

10656 Dragisic, Patricia. *How to Write a Letter* (7–12). Series: Speak Out, Write On! 1998, Watts LB $23.00 (0-531-11391-4). A readable, practical guide to writing personal notes, business letters, resumes, applications, memos, e-mail, and other forms of written communication. (Rev: BL 11/15/98; HBG 3/99; SLJ 1/99) [808.6]

10657 Dubrovin, Vivian. *Storytelling Adventures: Stories Kids Can Tell* (4–7). 1997, Storycraft paper $14.95 (0-9638339-2-8). This book not only

includes a selection of stories to tell but also suggests appropriate props to use, with directions on how to make them. (Rev: SLJ 5/97) [808.5]

10658 Dubrovin, Vivian. *Storytelling for the Fun of It* (4–8). 1994, Storycraft paper $16.95 (0-9638339-0-1). This useful guide is divided into three parts that give general information, where and what kinds of stories to tell, and how to learn and perform them. (Rev: SLJ 4/94) [808.5]

10659 Ehrlich, Amy, ed. *When I Was Your Age: Original Stories About Growing Up*, Vol. 2 (5–9). Illus. 1999, Candlewick $16.99 (0-7636-0407-0). Ten well-known writers for young people, including Norma Fox Mazer and Paul Fleischman, relate childhood experiences and describe how key incidents affected their writing. (Rev: BCCB 6/99; BL 4/15/99*; SLJ 7/99; VOYA 10/99) [810.9]

10660 Estepa, Andrea, and Philip Kay, eds. *Starting with "I": Personal Essays by Teenagers* (7–12). 1997, Persea paper $13.95 (0-89255-228-X). This is a collection of 35 brief essays written by teenagers about their families, neighborhoods, race, and culture. (Rev: BL 9/15/97; BR 1–2/98; SLJ 10/97; VOYA 10/97) [305.235]

10661 Everhart, Nancy. *How to Write a Term Paper* (7–12). 1995, Watts LB $23.00 (0-531-11200-4). This revised edition of *So You Have to Write a Term Paper* (1987) includes new information on electronic sources and data management by computer. (Rev: BL 6/1–15/95; SLJ 5/95) [808]

10662 Fletcher, Ralph. *How Writers Work: Finding a Process That Works for You* (4–8). 2000, HarperTrophy paper $4.99 (0-380-79702-X). Using a conversational style, the author explains the process of writing with material on brainstorming, rough drafts, revising, proofreading, and publishing. (Rev: SLJ 12/00) [808]

10663 Fletcher, Ralph. *Poetry Matters: Writing a Poem from the Inside Out* (4–7). 2002, HarperTrophy paper $4.99 (0-380-79703-8). A how-to book for young poets, with ideas on how to make images and "music" with words. (Rev: BL 5/15/02; HBG 10/02; SLJ 2/02*) [808.1]

10664 Graham, Paula W. *Speaking of Journals: Children's Book Writers Talk About Their Diaries, Notebooks and Sketchbooks* (5–8). Illus. 1999, Boyds Mills paper $14.95 (1-56397-741-9). A book that discusses the how-tos and the rewards of keeping a personal journal, and features interviews with 27 writers including Jim Arnosky, Pam Conrad, and Jean George. (Rev: BL 3/1/99; BR 9–10/99; SLJ 5/99; VOYA 2/00) [818]

10665 Grant, Janet. *The Young Person's Guide to Becoming a Writer*. Rev. Ed. (5–8). 1995, Free Spirit paper $13.95 (0-915793-90-3). This comprehensive beginner's guide provides information young people interested in writing as a career should know, such as ways to explore writing, different writing genres in the publishing industry and how an individual might be drawn toward one or another, practical information about the writing industry, how to find a publisher, manuscript preparation, and marketing. (Rev: SLJ 12/95; VOYA 2/96) [808]

10666 Guthrie, Donna, and Nancy Bentley. *The Young Journalist's Book: How to Write and Produce Your Own Newspaper* (4–7). Illus. 1998, Millbrook $24.40 (0-7613-0360-X). The authors explain what a journalist does and, in addition to explaining the parts of a newspaper, tells how to start one. (Rev: BL 3/1/99; HBG 3/99; SLJ 12/98) [070.1]

10667 Hambleton, Vicki, and Cathleen Greenwood. *So, You Wanna Be a Writer? How to Write, Get Published, and Maybe Even Make It Big!* (5–9). Series: So, You Wanna Be. 2001, Beyond Words paper $8.95 (1-58270-043-5). Practical advice is offered in straightforward text with lots of examples, sample letters, interviews with published writers, details of writing contests, and lists of magazines that accept submissions from young writers. (Rev: SLJ 10/01; VOYA 2/02) [808]

10668 Hamilton, Fran Santoro. *Hands-On English* (4–8). Illus. 1998, Portico paper $9.95 (0-9664867-0-6). A user-friendly volume that takes a visual approach to illustrate sentence patterns, such as using icons to represent the eight parts of speech, with clear, interesting explanations. Also included are irregular verbs, using modifiers, spelling rules, punctuation and capitalization, homonyms, and how to make outlines. (Rev: SLJ 2/99; VOYA 4/99) [415]

10669 Hamilton, Martha, and Mitch Weiss. *Stories in My Pocket: Tales Kids Can Tell* (4–7). Illus. 1997, Fulcrum paper $15.95 (1-55591-957-X). This handbook of storytelling for young storytellers includes 30 tales to begin with. (Rev: BL 1/1–15/97) [372.6]

10670 Harmon, Charles, ed. *Using the Internet, Online Services, and CD-ROMs for Writing Research and Term Papers* (7–12). Illus. Series: NetGuide. 1996, Neal-Schuman paper $32.95 (1-55570-238-4). This book shows all of the steps in writing a report, from selecting and narrowing a topic to collecting information electronically to preparing the final copy. (Rev: BL 4/15/96; SLJ 6/97) [371.2]

10671 Henderson, Kathy. *The Young Writer's Guide to Getting Published: Over 150 Listings of Opportunities for Young Writers*. Rev. ed. (5–12). Illus. 2001, Writer's Digest paper $18.99 (1-58297-057-2). This guide provides useful tips on identifying the best opportunities for budding writers, and relates some young writers' success stories. (Rev: BL 6/1–15/01; SLJ 11/01) [808]

10672 James, Elizabeth, and Carol Barkin. *How to Write a Term Paper* (7–12). 1980, Lothrop paper $3.95 (0-688-45025-3). A practical step-by-step approach to good report writing that uses many examples. [808]

10673 James, Elizabeth, and Carol Barkin. *How to Write Super School Reports*. Rev. ed. (4–9). Series: A School Survival Guide Book. 1998, Lothrop $15.00 (0-688-16132-4). This research guide takes readers through the steps involved in writing a research paper with material on choosing a topic, finding facts, using a library, organizing notes, and putting the report together. (Rev: HBG 3/99; SLJ 2/99) [808.023]

10674 Janeczko, Paul B. *How to Write Poetry* (4–8). Series: Scholastic Guides. 1999, Scholastic paper $12.95 (0-590-10077-7). An enthusiastic, clearly written how-to manual that uses many examples from well-known poems. (Rev: BL 3/15/99; HBG 10/99; SLJ 7/99; VOYA 8/99) [808.1]

10675 Janeczko, Paul B., comp. *Poetry from A to Z: A Guide for Young Writers* (4–8). Illus. Series: NetGuide. 1994, Simon & Schuster $16.95 (0-02-747672-3). This book of 72 poems, alphabetized by topic, gives examples to get young writers started, and the 23 poets represented give advice on how to become a better poet. (Rev: BCCB 3/95; BL 12/15/94; VOYA 5/95) [808.1]

10676 Janeczko, Paul B., ed. *Seeing the Blue Between: Advice and Inspiration for Young Poets* (7–10). 2002, Candlewick $17.99 (0-7636-0881-5). More than 30 poets who write for young people give advice on writing, reading, and simply enjoying poetry, with selected poems and biographical information. (Rev: BL 3/15/02; HB 7–8/02; HBG 10/02; SLJ 5/02; VOYA 6/02) [811]

10677 Kerr, M. E. *Blood on the Forehead: What I Know About Writing* (6–10). 1998, HarperCollins paper $14.95 (0-06-446207-2). This writer shares where she gets ideas for her stories and books and describes the writing process, which is far from easy, as the title would suggest. (Rev: BL 4/1/98; SLJ 5/98; VOYA 6/99) [808.3]

10678 Otfinoski, Steven. *Speaking Up, Speaking Out: A Kid's Guide to Making Speeches, Oral Reports, and Conversation* (5–8). Illus. 1996, Millbrook LB $24.90 (1-56294-345-6). All kinds of public-speaking situations are introduced, with suggestions on how to be a success at each. (Rev: BL 1/1–15/97; SLJ 1/97) [808.5]

10679 Rosen, Lucy. *High Performance Through Communicating Information* (8–12). Illus. Series: Learning-a-Living Library. 1996, Rosen LB $16.95 (0-8239-2201-4). Such communication skills as writing and speaking are discussed with tips on how to improve them and apply them effectively. (Rev: BL 8/96; BR 1–2/97; SLJ 3/97; VOYA 2/97) [153.6]

10680 Ryan, Elizabeth A. *How to Build a Better Vocabulary* (5–9). 1991, Troll paper $3.95 (0-8167-2461-X). A traditional study of prefixes, suffixes, and roots, with sections on foreign words. (Rev: BL 4/1/92; SLJ 4/92) [372.6]

10681 Ryan, Margaret. *How to Give a Speech* (7–12). 1995, Watts LB $22.00 (0-531-11199-7). This revision of *So You Have to Give a Speech* (1987) includes new information on electronic sources and data management by computer. (Rev: BL 6/1–15/95; SLJ 6/95) [808.5]

10682 Ryan, Margaret. *How to Write a Poem* (7–12). Illus. 1996, Watts LB $23.00 (0-531-11252-7); paper $7.95 (0-531-15788-1). From the idea to the final product, this helpful guide covers the techniques of writing, along with imagery, form, meter, and other aspects of poetry, and provides tips on entering poetry contests and getting published. (Rev: BL 2/1/97; SLJ 1/97) [808.1]

10683 Sullivan, Helen, and Linda Sernoff. *Research Reports: A Guide for Middle and High School Students* (6–10). 1996, Millbrook LB $24.90 (1-56294-694-3). A well-organized, concise book on writing reports that covers each step from selecting a topic to compiling the final bibliography. (Rev: BR 3–4/97; SLJ 9/96) [372.6]

10684 Terban, Marvin. *Checking Your Grammar* (5–8). Series: Scholastic Guides. 1993, Scholastic paper $10.95 (0-590-49454-6). An attractive, witty guide to effective writing of all sorts of letters, book reports, essays, and reviews. (Rev: BL 10/1/93; SLJ 2/94) [428.2]

10685 Terban, Marvin. *Punctuation Power: Punctuation and How to Use It* (4–9). 2000, Scholastic paper $12.95 (0-590-38673-5). After a description of each punctuation mark and its uses, this account covers topics including bibliographies, quotations, play scripts, and sentences, and the kinds of punctuation they require. (Rev: SLJ 7/00) [410]

10686 Veljkovic, Peggy, and Arthur Schwartz, eds. *Writing from the Heart: Young People Share Their Wisdom* (5–9). 2001, Templeton Foundation paper $12.95 (1-890151-48-3). A collection of the best essays by young people that have been submitted to the Laws of Life program since it began in 1987. (Rev: SLJ 6/01) [170]

10687 Vinton, Ken. *Alphabet Antics: Hundreds of Activities to Challenge and Enrich Letter Learners of All Ages* (5–8). 1996, Free Spirit paper $19.95 (0-915793-98-9). For each letter of the alphabet, there is a history, how it appears in different alphabets, important words that begin with that letter, a quotation from someone whose name starts with it, and a number of interesting related projects. (Rev: SLJ 1/97) [411]

10688 Wilber, Jessica. *Totally Private and Personal: Journaling Ideas for Girls and Young Women* (7–12). 1996, Free Spirit paper $9.95 (1-57542-005-8). The author, 14 years old when she wrote this book, offers advice for keeping a journal, including how, why, and what to put in it, with examples from her own journal. (Rev: VOYA 2/97) [808]

10689 Wooldridge, Susan Goldsmith. *Poemcrazy: Freeing Your Life with Words* (6–12). 1996, Clarkson N. Potter $22.00 (0-517-70370-X); paper $13.00 (0-609-80098-1). The author tries to show young people how to free their minds and spirits to write poetry and shares her own poetic experiences and inspirations as well as those of other poets. (Rev: VOYA 12/97) [811]

10690 Young, Sue. *Writing with Style* (5–8). Series: Scholastic Guides. 1997, Scholastic $12.95 (0-590-50977-2). A guide for the novice writer, with chapters on planning, presenting, and publishing one's work. (Rev: BL 3/1/97; SLJ 5/97) [372.6]

Academic Guidance

General and Miscellaneous

10691 Lieberman, Susan A. *The Real High School Handbook: How to Survive, Thrive, and Prepare for What's Next* (8–12). 1997, Houghton paper $12.00 (0-395-79760-8). A book of tips about prospering in high school and making it enjoyable, with material on topics including grade points, testing, course selection, and getting into a college. (Rev: BL 10/15/97) [373.18]

10692 Vollstadt, Elizabeth Weiss. *Teen Dropouts* (6–12). Series: Overview: Teen Issues. 2000, Lucent LB $18.96 (1-56006-625-3). The causes, effects, and possible solutions of teenagers dropping out of schools are discussed in this realistic account. (Rev: BL 6/1–15/00; HBG 9/00) [371.2]

Colleges and Universities

10693 Funk, Gary. *A Balancing Act: Sports and Education* (5–8). Illus. Series: Sports Issues. 1995, Lerner LB $28.75 (0-8225-3301-4). A frank, thorough discussion of the many issues involved in sports and their place in educational institutions. (Rev: BL 1/1–15/96; SLJ 9/95) [796.04]

Scholarships and Financial Aid

10694 Minnis, Whitney. *How to Get an Athletic Scholarship: A Student-Athlete's Guide to Collegiate Athletics* (6–12). 1995, ASI paper $12.95 (0-9645153-0-X). Basic information on athletic scholarships and the recruitment process, plus tips on training and academic considerations. (Rev: BL 2/1/96) [796]

Careers and Occupational Guidance

General and Miscellaneous

10695 Alagna, Magdalena. *Life Inside the Air Force Academy* (7–12). Illus. Series: Insider's Look. 2002, Children's $20.00 (0-516-23924-4); paper $6.95 (0-516-24001-3). This look inside the Air Force Academy — which explores the rituals, traditions, and rhythm of daily life at this institution — is intended for reluctant readers and explains the requirements for admittance. Also in this series is *Life Inside the Military Academy* (2002). (Rev: BL 10/15/02) [358.4]

10696 McGlothlin, Bruce. *High Performance Through Understanding Systems* (7–10). Series: Learning-a-Living Library. 1996, Rosen LB $17.95 (0-8239-2210-3). Aimed primarily at youths preparing to directly enter the world of work after graduation, this book explains systems ("any combination of elements that operate together and form a whole") in the family, at school, and at work, and tells how individuals can diagnose problems, predict outcomes, and improve the systems. (Rev: SLJ 3/97) [001.6]

10697 Strazzabosco, Jeanne M. *High Performance Through Dealing with Diversity* (8–12). Illus. Series: Learning-a-Living Library. 1996, Rosen LB $17.95 (0-8239-2202-2). Through applying attitudes of tolerance and positive feelings, this book prepares students to work with diverse populations in a multicultural workplace. (Rev: BL 8/96; BR 1–2/97) [650.1]

10698 *Young Person's Occupational Handbook.* 4th ed. (6–8). Illus. 2002, JIST Works $19.95 (1-56370-905-8). From the Department of Labor, a handbook of occupations in a wide variety of fields, with information about working conditions and the necessary training. (Rev: BL 12/15/02; VOYA 4/03) [331.7]

Careers

General and Miscellaneous

10699 Alagna, Magdalena. *War Correspondents: Life Under Fire* (5–10). Series: Extreme Careers. 2003, Rosen LB $26.50 (0-8239-3798-4). The dangers of wartime assignments are emphasized in this volume that also stresses job requirements that include a good education and broad knowledge of world events. (Rev: BL 9/15/03; SLJ 11/03) [808]

10700 Bowman-Kruhm, Mary. *Careers in Child Care* (7–12). Series: Careers Library. 2000, Rosen LB $18.95 (0-8239-2891-8). A comprehensive, accessible overview of the types of jobs that are available for people who enjoy working with children, with practical guidance on finding employment. (Rev: HBG 10/01; SLJ 3/01)

10701 *Broadcasting.* 2nd ed. (7–12). Series: Careers in Focus. 2002, Ferguson LB $14.50 (0-89434-440-4). Careers in animation, lighting, reporting, editing, and weather forecasting are just a few of those covered in this concise introduction to the world of broadcasting and its educational requirements, employment outlook, and potential salaries. Also use *Fashion* (2002). (Rev: SLJ 7/01) [384.54]

10702 Curless, Maura. *Kids* (6–9). Series: Careers Without College. 1993, Peterson's Guides $7.95 (1-56079-251-5). Describes professions that deal with children, such as teacher aides, caregivers, and museum staff. (Rev: BL 10/1/93) [649]

10703 Duncan, Jane Caryl. *Careers in Veterinary Medicine* (8–12). Illus. 1994, Rosen LB $16.95 (0-8239-1678-2); paper $9.95 (0-8239-1719-3). A veterinarian gives an honest description of her profession and many practical tips. (Rev: BL 9/1/88; SLJ 10/88; VOYA 10/88) [636.089]

10704 Ferguson, J. G. *What Can I Do Now? Preparing for a Career in Journalism* (7–12). 1998, Ferguson $16.95 (0-89434-251-7). This book introduces careers in journalism and related fields, describes the preparation and aptitudes necessary, and suggests how teens can get involved in journalism while still in school. (Rev: SLJ 4/99) [070]

10705 Frydenborg, Kay. *They Dreamed of Horses: Careers for Horse Lovers* (6–9). 1994, Walker LB $16.85 (0-8027-8284-1). Suggests career possibilities that involve working with horses, telling the stories of 13 women who love and work with them. (Rev: BL 7/94; SLJ 7/94; VOYA 8/94) [636.1]

10706 Giacobello, John. *Careers in the Fashion Industry* (7–12). Series: Exploring Careers. 1999, Rosen LB $17.95 (0-8239-2890-X). This book explains what it takes to get started in a variety of fashion-related careers, and includes tips on writing resumes, interviewing, and so forth. (Rev: SLJ 2/00) [746.9]

10707 Girod, Christina. *Aeronautics* (6–12). Series: Careers for the Twenty-First Century. 2002, Gale LB $27.45 (1-56006-894-9). A few of the careers introduced and discussed are pilots, flight attendant, air traffic controllers, aircraft mechanics, and astronauts. (Rev: BL 10/15/02) [629.13]

10708 Greene, Meg. *Careers in the National Guard's Search and Rescue Unit* (5–9). Series: Careers in Search and Rescue Operations. 2003, Rosen LB $26.50 (0-8239-3836-6). This account describes the vital role that citizen-soldiers play in the line of defense and tells of the their search and rescue activities during the terrorist attacks of September 11, 2001. (Rev: BL 10/15/03) [335]

10709 Haegele, Katie. *Nature Lovers* (7–12). Series: Cool Careers Without College. 2002, Rosen $30.60 (0-8239-3504-3). Jobs profiled here include Christmas tree farmer, ranch hand, fisherman, park ranger, and river guide with accompanying information of training, pay, opportunities, and related occupations. (Rev: BL 5/15/02; SLJ 7/02) [331.7]

10710 Hayhurst, Chris. *Astronauts: Life Exploring Outer Space* (4–7). Series: Extreme Careers. 2001, Rosen LB $26.50 (0-8239-3364-4). A high-interest look at the extensive skills required to become an astronaut, with brief coverage of space exploration and profiles of astronauts. (Rev: SLJ 1/02) [629]

10711 Hayhurst, Chris. *Cool Careers Without College for Animal Lovers* (7–12). Illus. Series: Cool Careers Without College. 2002, Rosen LB $30.60 (0-8239-3500-0). Veterinary technician, groomer, and pet photographer are some of the options explored in this book that gives information on training and on-the-job activities. (Rev: BL 5/15/02; SLJ 7/02) [636]

10712 *History* (4–8). Illus. Series: Discovering Careers for Your Future. 2001, Ferguson LB $15.95 (0-89434-391-2). A useful introduction to the career opportunities in this field, with information on the skills required, potential earnings, and job outlook. (Rev: SLJ 11/01) [331.702]

10713 Hurwitz, Jane. *Choosing a Career in Animal Care* (4–8). Illus. Series: World of Work. 1996, Rosen LB $17.95 (0-8239-2268-5). Various careers in working with animals are described, along with the education required, desirable character traits, and ways to break into the field. (Rev: SLJ 8/97) [371.7]

10714 Jacobs, Shannon K. *Healers of the Wild: People Who Care for Injured and Orphaned Wildlife* (4–7). Illus. 1998, Coyote Moon paper $19.95 (0-9661070-0-4). The process of helping orphaned, injured, or displaced wildlife is covered thoroughly under three operational headings: rescue, rehabilitation, and release. (Rev: BL 10/1/98) [339.946]

10715 Jaspersohn, William. *A Week in the Life of an Airline Pilot* (4–8). Illus. 1991, Little, Brown $14.95 (0-316-45822-8). A close-up look at the duties and lives of members of an airline crew. (Rev: BL 3/15/91; HB 5–6/91; SLJ 5/91) [629.132]

10716 Lee, Barbara. *Working with Animals* (4–8). Illus. Series: Exploring Careers. 1996, Lerner LB $28.75 (0-8225-1759-0). Profiles of 12 careers involving animals, such as veterinarian, animal shelter worker, or pet sitter. (Rev: BL 2/15/97) [591]

10717 Lytle, Elizabeth Stewart. *Careers in Cosmetology* (7–12). 1999, Rosen LB $17.95 (0-8239-2889-6). A survey of career options in the field of cosmetology, with descriptions of training and qualifications, profiles of cosmetologists, and general advice on job seeking. (Rev: SLJ 4/00) [646.7]

10718 Manley, Claudia B. *Secret Agents: Life as a Professional Spy* (4–7). Series: Extreme Careers. 2001, Rosen LB $26.50 (0-8239-3369-5). A high-interest look at the extensive skills required to become an intelligence agent and the kinds of intelligence that are gathered (strategic, tactical, counter-intelligence), with material on the history of espionage and on real-life and fictional spies. (Rev: SLJ 1/02) [327.12]

10719 Mason, Helen. *Great Careers for People Interested in Food* (6–10). Series: Career Connections. 1996, Gale $40.00 (0-7876-0860-2). All kinds of food-related careers are described in this book, along with career-path recommendations, training and experience requirements, and outlooks for the future. (Rev: BR 9–10/96; SLJ 9/96) [355.6]

10720 Maynard, Thane. *Working with Wildlife: A Guide to Careers in the Animal World* (6–10). Illus. 1999, Watts LB $26.00 (0-531-11538-0). Many different jobs working with animals are discussed, including training wild animals, working with insects, and being part of a conservation team. (Rev: BCCB 1/00; BL 1/1–15/00; SLJ 3/00) [636.]

10721 Nelson, Corinna. *Working in the Environment* (6–8). Series: Exploring Careers. 1999, Lerner LB $28.75 (0-8225-1763-9). A recycling manager, a fisheries technician, and a nonprofit organization director are among the 12 people profiled in this title that describes the wide range of jobs related to the environment. (Rev: BL 7/99; SLJ 10/99) [363.7]

10722 Parks, Peggy J. *The News Media* (6–12). Illus. Series: Careers for the Twenty-First Century. 2002, Gale LB $27.45 (1-59018-205-7). A comprehensive look at careers in journalism, with historical information as well as descriptions of the day-to-day requirements and challenges and discussion of the benefits and drawbacks of the profession. (Rev: BL 10/15/02) [070.4]

10723 Pasternak, Ceel. *Cool Careers for Girls with Animals* (5–8). Series: Cool Careers for Girls. 1998, Impact $19.95 (1-57023-108-7); paper $12.95 (1-57023-105-2). Veterinarian, pet sitter, bird handler, animal trainer, and horse-farm owner are among the careers covered, supplemented by interviews with women who work in each field. (Rev: SLJ 4/99; VOYA 8/99) [371.7]

10724 Pasternak, Ceel, and Linda Thornburg. *Cool Careers for Girls in Air and Space* (6–12). Series: Cool Careers for Girls. 2001, Impact LB $19.95 (1-57023-147-8); paper $12.95 (1-57023-146-X). This account discusses various careers open to women in the aircraft and space industries with information on qualifications, working conditions, and compensation. (Rev: BL 4/15/01; SLJ 4/01) [629]

10725 Pasternak, Ceel, and Linda Thornburg. *Cool Careers for Girls in Food* (5–10). Series: Cool Careers for Girls. 2000, Impact $19.95 (1-57023-127-3); paper $12.95 (1-57023-120-6). The 11 women featured in this book are involved in various aspects of the food industry such as cheese making, baking, wine making, selling health food, and cooking for the military. (Rev: SLJ 2/00) [641]

10726 Reeves, Diane L. *Career Ideas for Kids Who Like Art* (5–9). Illus. Series: Career Ideas for Kids Who Like. 1998, Facts on File $23.00 (0-8160-3681-0); paper $12.95 (0-8160-3687-X). An upbeat book that explores a variety of art-related careers, including many peripheral ones such as chef, animator, and photojournalist, with suggestions on how to test one's suitability for each area and reports from people working in the field. (Rev: SLJ 10/98; VOYA 8/98) [791]

10727 Reeves, Diane L. *Career Ideas for Kids Who Like Writing* (5–9). Illus. Series: Career Ideas for Kids Who Like. 1998, Facts on File $23.00 (0-8160-3685-3); paper $12.95 (0-8160-3691-8). A look at 15 careers related to writing, among them advertising copywriter, author, bookseller, editor, grant writer, journalist, librarian, literary agent, and publicist, with a self-test for each one and a profile

of a person working in the field. (Rev: BR 5–6/99; SLJ 3/99) [808]

10728 Reeves, Diane Lindsey. *Career Ideas for Kids Who Like Math* (4–8). 2000, Facts on File $23.00 (0-8160-4095-8). Presents an amazing array of careers available for the mathematically inclined, arranged alphabetically with good solid information on each. (Rev: HBG 10/00; SLJ 9/00) [510]

10729 Reeves, Diane Lindsey. *Career Ideas for Kids Who Like Talking* (5–9). Series: Career Ideas for Kids. 1998, Facts on File $23.00 (0-8160-3683-7); paper $12.95 (0-8160-3689-6). This is a guide to careers in communications, from hotel manager to publicist to broadcaster, with reports from people in the field, tests to check one's aptitude, and lists of resources. (Rev: SLJ 10/98) [331.7]

10730 Reeves, Diane Lindsey, and Gayle Bryan. *Career Ideas for Kids Who Like Money* (6–10). Illus. Series: Career Ideas. 2001, Facts on File $23.00 (0-8160-4319-1). An attractive introduction to careers such as business manager, e-merchant, entrepreneur, and investment banker, with personal profiles of individuals in the various fields and attractive cartoons. (Rev: BL 7/01; HBG 3/02; SLJ 8/01) [332]

10731 Reeves, Diane Lindsey, and Gayle Bryan. *Career Ideas for Kids Who Like Travel* (6–10). Series: Career Ideas for Kids. 2001, Checkmark $23.00 (0-8160-4325-6); paper $12.95 (0-8160-4326-4). A number of careers in the travel industry are presented with coverage of qualifications, training, rewards, and working conditions. (Rev: BL 3/15/02; HBG 10/02) [331.7]

10732 Reeves, Diane Lindsey, and Nancy Heubeck. *Career Ideas for Kids Who Like Adventure* (6–10). Series: Career Ideas for Kids. 2001, Facts on File LB $23.00 (0-8160-4321-3). An attractive introduction to careers such as fire fighting, scuba diving, oil rig work, and piloting, with personal profiles of individuals in the various fields and attractive cartoons. (Rev: BL 7/01; HBG 3/02; SLJ 8/01) [331.7]

10733 Reeves, Diane Lindsey, and Nancy Heubeck. *Career Ideas for Kids Who Like Animals and Nature* (6–10). 2000, Facts on File $18.95 (0-8160-4097-4). Careers explored in this volume that includes practical advice plus profiles of workers in these jobs range from veterinarian and animal trainer to arborist and botanist. (Rev: BR 11–12/00; HBG 9/00; SLJ 12/00) [570]

10734 Roza, Greg. *Careers in the Coast Guard's Search and Rescue Unit* (5–9). Series: Careers in Search and Rescue Operations. 2003, Rosen LB $26.50 (0-8239-3835-2). This book covers the search and rescue operations involving the Coast Guard with particular emphasis on their vital role during the September 11, 2001 attacks. (Rev: BL 10/15/03) [355]

10735 Schwager, Tina, and Michele Schueger. *Cool Women, Hot Jobs — And How You Can Go for it, Too!* (7–12). Illus. 2002, Free Spirit paper $15.95 (1-57542-109-7). Profiles of women who work in a wide variety of jobs — from dolphin training and Egyptology to flying fighter planes and planning weddings — are accompanied by details of the job itself and suggestions for setting and achieving goals. (Rev: BL 6/1–15/02; SLJ 7/02; VOYA 8/02) [650.14]

10736 Seidman, David. *Careers in Journalism* (6–12). Illus. Series: Exploring Careers. 2000, Rosen LB $18.95 (0-8239-3298-2). Print journalism, broadcast journalism, writing, editing, and design are all covered in this introduction to a widely varied field. (Rev: BL 3/15/01; HBG 10/01; SLJ 2/01) [070.4]

10737 Talbert, Marc. *Holding the Reins: A Ride Through Cowgirl Life* (5–7). Photos by Barbara Van Cleve. 2003, HarperCollins $16.99 (0-06-029255-5). The demanding but exhilarating lives of modern-day cowgirls are shown here as the author follows four teens through the seasons. (Rev: BCCB 4/03; BL 1/1–15/03; HBG 10/03; SLJ 4/03) [978]

10738 Turner, Chérie. *Adventure Tour Guides: Life on Extreme Outdoor Adventures* (5–10). Series: Extreme Careers. 2003, Rosen LB $26.50 (0-8239-3793-3). A look at the profession of tour guiding on excursions such as white-water rafting and mountain climbing, with material on qualifications and future possibilities. (Rev: BL 9/15/03) [908]

10739 Vogt, Peter. *Career Opportunities in the Fashion Industry* (7–12). 2002, Facts on File $49.50 (0-8160-4616-6). More than 60 jobs in the fashion industry are described with details of daily activities, salary potential, necessary training, and future outlook. (Rev: SLJ 2/03) [746.9]

10740 Weiss, Ann E. *The Glass Ceiling: A Look at Women in the Workforce* (8–12). 1999, Twenty-First Century LB $23.90 (0-7613-1365-6). After a brief history of women's place in the world of work, this book focuses on recent changes and new opportunities (and dangers) for women in the work force. (Rev: BL 6/1–15/99; SLJ 9/99) [331.4]

10741 Weiss, Ellen. *Odd Jobs: The Wackiest Jobs You've Never Heard Of!* (4–8). Photos by Damon Ross. 2000, Simon & Schuster paper $8.99 (0-689-82934-5). Describes such unusual occupations as roller-coaster designer, comedy writer, movie sound-effects producer, food stylist, and storm chaser. (Rev: SLJ 7/00) [331.7]

10742 Willett, Edward. *Careers in Outer Space: New Business Opportunities* (4–9). Series: The Career Resource Library. 2002, Rosen LB $25.25 (0-8239-3358-X). An interesting look at opportunities in the fields of science, math, engineering, technology, communication, and, of course, aeronautics,

with information on required skills and training and on the pros and cons of working in the public and private sectors. (Rev: SLJ 6/02) [629.4]

10743 Wilson, Wayne. *Careers in Publishing and Communications* (8–12). Series: Latinos at Work. 2001, Mitchell Lane LB $22.95 (1-58415-088-2). This career guide for Latinos explores job opportunities for authors, copy editors, disc jockeys, artists, and agents, and includes personal interviews with successful Hispanic Americans in these fields. (Rev: BL 10/15/01; HBG 3/02) [808]

10744 Zannos, Susan. *Careers in Science and Medicine* (8–12). Series: Latinos at Work. 2001, Mitchell Lane LB $22.95 (1-58415-084-X). Descriptions of careers in these fields are accompanied by information on salary and qualifications as well as profiles of Latino men and women who have found success in a variety of career positions. (Rev: BL 10/15/01; HBG 3/02; SLJ 11/01) [502]

10745 Zannos, Susan. *Latino Entrepreneurs* (8–12). Series: Latinos at Work. 2001, Mitchell Lane LB $22.95 (1-58415-089-0). This book looks at the many possibilities for self-employment for Hispanics with personal interviews of successful Latinos in a variety of fields. (Rev: BL 3/15/02; HBG 10/02; SLJ 3/02) [650.1]

Arts, Entertainment, and Sports

10746 Aaseng, Nathan. *Wildshots: The World of the Wildlife Photographer* (5–8). Illus. 2001, Millbrook LB $29.90 (0-7613-1551-9). This account describes the work of a wildlife photographer and tells exciting stories about unusual encounters. (Rev: BL 3/1/01*; HBG 10/01; SLJ 3/01; VOYA 10/01) [778.9]

10747 Amara, Philip. *So, You Wanna Be a Comic Book Artist?* (5–8). 2001, Beyond Words paper $9.95 (1-58270-058-3). A comprehensive, engaging look at the world of comic-book illustration, with tips on everything from buying supplies to submitting work to publishers. (Rev: BL 1/1–15/02; SLJ 4/02) [808]

10748 Apel, Melanie Ann. *Cool Careers Without College for Film and Television Buffs* (6–9). Series: Cool Careers Without College. 2002, Rosen LB $30.60 (0-8239-3501-9). A variety of options are presented for students interested in jobs in this sector, from actor and agent to grip, gaffer, makeup artist, animator, and puppeteer. (Rev: SLJ 7/02; VOYA 2/03) [331.7]

10749 *Art* (4–8). Illus. Series: Discovering Careers for Your Future. 2001, Ferguson LB $15.95 (0-89434-388-2). A useful introduction to career opportunities in art, with information on the skills required, potential earnings, and job outlook. (Rev: SLJ 11/01) [702.373]

10750 Bartlett, Gillian. *Great Careers for People Interested in Art and Design* (6–10). Series: Career Connections. 1996, Gale $40.00 (0-7876-0863-7). Using case studies of six people who have succeeded in careers related to art and design, this book discusses opportunities, career-path recommendations, qualifications, and the outlook for the future. (Rev: BR 9–10/96; SLJ 9/96) [746.9]

10751 *Careers in Focus — Sports* (8–12). Series: Careers in Focus. 1998, Ferguson $14.50 (0-89434-247-9). Over 20 careers related to sports, from golf-course superintendent to professional athlete to stadium vendor, are included in this volume, with information on qualifications, working conditions, salaries, opportunities, rewards, and methods of exploring and entering the field. (Rev: BR 9–10/98; SLJ 8/98) [796]

10752 Flender, Nicole. *People Who Love Movement* (7–12). Series: Cool Careers Without College. 2002, Rosen $30.60 (0-8239-3505-1). Some of the non-college degree careers discussed are dancers, dance and yoga teachers, and fitness instructors in this book which also covers salaries, and job opportunities. (Rev: BL 5/15/02) [613.7]

10753 Hinton, Kerry. *Cool Careers Without College for Music Lovers* (7–12). Illus. Series: Cool Careers Without College. 2002, Rosen LB $30.60 (0-8239-3503-5). Music store clerk, promoter, and instrument repairman are some of the options explored in this book that gives information on training and on-the-job activities. (Rev: BL 5/15/02; SLJ 7/02) [780]

10754 Jay, Annie, and Luanne Feik. *Stars in Your Eyes . . . Feet on the Ground: A Practical Guide for Teenage Actors (and Their Parents!)* (7–12). Illus. 1999, Theatre Directories paper $16.95 (0-933919-42-5). A young actress gives practical advice on how to break into show business, including information on publicity photographs, auditions, managers, agents, publicity packages, resumes, and casting calls. (Rev: BL 6/1–15/99) [792.02]

10755 Johnson, Marlys H. *Careers in the Movies* (5–9). Series: Career Resource Library. 2001, Rosen LB $18.95 (0-8239-3186-2). Job descriptions and qualifications are clearly laid out in this guide for aspiring filmmakers that also discusses the history of the industry and the basic steps in film production. (Rev: SLJ 8/01) [791.43]

10756 Lantz, Francess. *Rock, Rap, and Rad: How to Be a Rock or Rap Star* (6–12). 1992, Avon paper $3.99 (0-380-76793-7). The author takes aspiring rock stars through the basic steps of choosing an instrument, finding other musicians and a place to play, lining up gigs, and on up to the top. (Rev: BL 7/93) [781.66]

10757 Lee, Barbara. *Working in Music* (4–8). Illus. Series: Exploring Careers. 1996, Lerner LB $23.93 (0-8225-1761-2). Such careers as composing, performing, music retailing, and violin making are covered in this book profiling 12 people who work in the music field. (Rev: BL 2/15/97; SLJ 2/97) [780]

10758 Lee, Barbara. *Working in Sports and Recreation* (5–9). Illus. Series: Exploring Careers. 1996, Lerner LB $28.75 (0-8225-1762-0). Twelve people involved in careers related to sports and recreation talk candidly about their professions. (Rev: BL 2/15/97) [796]

10759 Libal, Joyce, and Rae Simons. *Professional Athlete and Sports Official* (5–9). Series: Careers with Character. 2003, Mason Crest LB $22.95 (1-59084-321-5). The importance of character traits such as integrity, respect, fairness, and self-discipline when seeking careers in sports is emphasized here. (Rev: HBG 10/03; SLJ 4/03) [796]

10760 McDaniels, Pellom. *So, You Want to Be a Pro?* (6–12). Illus. 1999, Addax $14.95 (1-886110-77-8). Atlanta Falcons player McDaniels offers encouragement to would-be professional athletes without encouraging unrealistic expectations. (Rev: BL 11/15/99; SLJ 3/00) [613.7]

10761 Mayfield, Katherine. *Acting A to Z: The Young Person's Guide to a Stage or Screen Career* (6–12). Illus. 1998, Back Stage Books paper $16.95 (0-8230-8801-4). This slim, eye-catching paperback explores all facets of an acting career, from the general to the practical and the specific, including networking, casting, education, self-esteem, budgeting, resumes, and promotional photographs. (Rev: VOYA 6/99) [792]

10762 Menard, Valerie. *Careers in Sports* (8–12). Series: Latinos at Work. 2001, Mitchell Lane LB $22.95 (1-58415-086-6). This book explores the career possibilities for Hispanic Americans in a variety of sports with several interesting case studies of Latinos who did well in them. (Rev: BL 3/15/02; HBG 10/02) [796]

10763 Moss, Miriam. *Fashion Model* (6–9). 1991, Macmillan LB $13.95 (0-89686-609-2). The prestige and perks as well as the downside of fashion modeling. (Rev: BL 5/15/91; SLJ 7/91) [659.1]

10764 Moss, Miriam. *Fashion Photographer* (6–9). 1991, Macmillan LB $13.95 (0-89686-608-4). Points out the prestige and perks, as well as the downside, of fashion photography. (Rev: BL 5/15/91; SLJ 7/91) [778.9]

10765 Nagle, Jeanne. *Careers in Coaching* (7–12). Series: Careers Library. 2000, Rosen LB $16.95 (0-8239-2966-3). This guide to how to become a successful coach covers all aspects of the job. (Rev: SLJ 7/00) [796]

10766 Nathan, Amy. *The Young Musician's Survival Guide: Tips from Teens and Pros* (5–8). 2000, Oxford $18.95 (0-19-512611-4); paper $9.95 (0-19-512612-2). A thorough study of how to break into the music world, with information on working with music teachers, conductors, and peers, and tips on practicing, choosing an instrument, and handling fears and frustrations. (Rev: BL 4/1/00; HBG 10/00; SLJ 6/00) [780]

10767 Parks, Peggy. *Music* (6–12). Series: Careers for the Twenty-First Century. 2002, Gale LB $27.45 (1-59018-223-5). This book provides a close look at six music-related careers — musician, composer, recording engineer, music therapist, music publicist, and music educator. (Rev: BL 10/15/02) [780]

10768 Pasternak, Ceel, and Linda Thornburg. *Cool Careers for Girls in Sports* (5–10). Series: Cool Careers for Girls. 1999, Impact $19.95 (1-57023-107-9); paper $12.95 (1-57023-104-4). A golf pro, basketball player, ski instructor, sports broadcaster, trainer, sports psychologist, and athletic director are among the 10 women profiled in this overview of careers for women in sports. (Rev: SLJ 7/99; VOYA 8/99) [796]

10769 Reeves, Diane L., and Peter Kent. *Career Ideas for Kids Who Like Sports* (5–9). Illus. Series: Career Ideas for Kids Who Like. 1998, Facts on File $23.00 (0-8160-3684-5); paper $12.95 (0-8160-3690-X). The 15 sports-related careers highlighted in this volume include coach, athlete, agent, sportscaster, and sports equipment manufacturer, with accompanying material on necessary skills, opportunities, duties, and a report from someone in the field. (Rev: BR 5–6/99; SLJ 6/99) [796]

10770 Reeves, Diane Lindsey, and Gayle Bryan. *Career Ideas for Kids Who Like Music and Dance* (6–10). Series: Career Ideas for Kids. 2001, Checkmark $23.00 (0-8160-4323-X); paper $12.95 (0-8160-4324-8). This work present a number of career opportunities in music and dance with material on training, qualifications, and working conditions. (Rev: BL 3/15/02; HBG 10/02) [790]

10771 Ritzenthaler, Carol L. *Teen Guide to Getting Started in the Arts* (8–12). 2001, Greenwood $39.95 (0-313-31392-X). This is a practical handbook that describes a variety of careers (actor, artist, dancer, writer, and so forth) and the skills required, with useful contact information and advice for parents. (Rev: SLJ 7/02; VOYA 12/02) [700]

10772 Sharon, Donna, and Jo Anne Sommers. *Great Careers for People Interested in Travel and Tourism* (6–10). Series: Career Connections. 1996, Gale $40.00 (0-7876-0862-9). Tour director and travel agent are among the jobs discussed in this overview of careers related to travel and tourism, with information on qualifications, training, and opportunities. (Rev: BR 9–10/96; SLJ 9/96) [658]

10773 Sommers, Michael A. *Wildlife Photographers: Life Through a Lens* (5–10). Series: Extreme Careers. 2003, Rosen LB $26.50 (0-8239-3638-4). A concise explanation of the work of wildlife pho-

tographers, the attributes needed, and the training and tenacity required to enter this field. (Rev: BL 9/15/03; SLJ 5/03) [771]

10774 Torres, John, and Susan Zannos. *Careers in the Music Industry* (8–12). Series: Latinos at Work. 2001, Mitchell Lane LB $22.95 (1-58415-085-8). Along with personal interviews with Hispanics who did well in the music world, there are descriptions of such related careers as singers, songwriters, managers, and agents. (Rev: BL 3/15/02; HBG 10/02) [780]

10775 Vitkus-Weeks, Jessica. *Television* (4–8). Illus. Series: Now Hiring. 1994, Crestwood LB $14.95 (0-89686-783-8). Using real people as case histories, this book describes such TV careers as grip, camera operator, production assistant, costume designer, and actor. (Rev: SLJ 8/94) [621.388]

10776 Weigant, Chris. *Careers as a Disc Jockey* (8–12). Series: Careers. 1997, Rosen LB $16.95 (0-8239-2528-5). This informative book gives many practical tips on how to get started and be successful in radio, with material on making demo tapes, applying for jobs and internships, and working oneself up. There are interviews with eight DJs. Careers in management, sales, technical areas, talk shows, and others are included. (Rev: BR 3–4/98; SLJ 12/97; VOYA 2/98) [384.54]

10777 Williamson, Walter. *Early Stages: The Professional Theater and the Young Actor* (6–9). 1986, Walker LB $12.85 (0-8027-6630-7). Through examining the careers of several young actors, tips are given on how to enter show business. (Rev: BL 7/86; BR 11–12/86; SLJ 5/86) [792]

10778 Wilson, Wayne. *Careers in Entertainment* (8–12). Series: Latinos at Work. 2001, Mitchell Lane LB $22.95 (1-58415-083-1). With an emphasis on Hispanic American success stories, this book features careers in film, television, and theater. (Rev: BL 10/15/01; HBG 3/02) [791]

10779 Wormser, Richard. *To the Young Filmmaker: Conversations with Working Filmmakers* (7–12). Series: To the Young . . . 2002, Watts LB $23.00 (0-531-11727-8). Profiles of eight movie industry workers — including a writer, producer, director, and actress — are intended to encourage young people that they too can make films. (Rev: LMC 1/03; SLJ 9/02; VOYA 4/03) [791.43]

Construction and Mechanical Trades

10780 Paige, Joy. *Cool Careers Without College for People Who Love to Build Things* (7–12). Series: Cool Careers Without College. 2002, Rosen LB $30.60 (0-8239-3506-X). Twenty careers in construction are outlined with useful information about salary, future prospects, and training. (Rev: BL 1/1–15/03; SLJ 7/02) [690]

10781 Pasternak, Ceel, and Linda Thornburg. *Cool Careers for Girls in Construction* (6–12). Illus. Series: Cool Careers for Girls. 2000, Impact $19.95 (1-57023-135-4); paper $12.95 (1-57023-131-1). From architect to ironworker, this book profiles a number of careers in construction for women with material on salaries, working conditions, and qualifications needed. (Rev: BL 3/15/00; SLJ 7/00) [624.]

Education and Librarianship

10782 Cassedy, Patrice. *Education* (6–12). Series: Careers for the Twenty-First Century. 2002, Gale LB $27.45 (1-56006-898-1). This work explores the duties, training, pay, working conditions and the job outlook for teachers, principals, counselors, and media specialists. (Rev: BL 10/15/02; SLJ 7/03) [371.7]

10783 Zannos, Susan. *Careers in Education* (8–12). Series: Latinos at Work. 2001, Mitchell Lane LB $22.95 (1-58415-081-5). Descriptions of careers in this field are accompanied by information on salary and qualifications as well as profiles of Latino men and women who have found success in a variety of career positions. (Rev: BL 10/15/01; HBG 3/02; SLJ 11/01; VOYA 6/02) [370]

Law, Police, and Other Society-Oriented Careers

10784 Bankston, John. *Careers in Community Service* (8–12). Series: Latinos at Work. 2001, Mitchell Lane LB $22.95 (1-58415-082-3). Aimed at Latino youths, this career guide features a multitude of jobs in non-profit agencies, including legal and medical fields, with accompanying stories of success. (Rev: BL 10/15/01; HBG 3/02; SLJ 1/02) [353.001]

10785 Beil, Karen M. *Fire in Their Eyes: Wildfires and the People Who Fight Them* (5–7). Illus. 1999, Harcourt $18.00 (0-15-201043-2). Excellent photographs and text tell the story of smoke jumpers and the tools, methods, and training they receive for their exciting but dangerous job. (Rev: BCCB 4/99; BL 5/1/99; HB 3–4/99; HBG 10/99; SLJ 7/99) [363.37]

10786 Binney, Greg A. *Careers in the Federal Emergency Management Agency's Search and Rescue Unit* (5–9). Illus. Series: Careers in Search and Rescue Operations. 2003, Rosen LB $26.50 (0-8239-3832-8). Starting with September 11, 2001, this volume explores the work of the teams that specialize in search and rescue after disasters such as tornadoes, hazardous materials spills, and building collapses, with material on the training required. (Rev: BL 10/15/03) [363.3]

10787 Cassedy, Patrice. *Law Enforcement* (6–12). Illus. Series: Careers for the Twenty-First Century. 2002, Gale LB $27.45 (1-56006-899-X). An attractive volume that covers the history of law enforcement and introduces the rewards and challenges of such professions as the police, federal agents, crime scene workers, and probation and correctional officers. (Rev: BL 10/15/02) [363.2]

10788 Croce, Nicholas. *Detectives: Life Investigating Crimes* (5–10). Series: Extreme Careers. 2003, Rosen LB $26.50 (0-8239-3796-8). As well as exploring the exciting side of detective work, this account explains the qualifications and training needed and the techniques that help do this job well. (Rev: BL 9/15/03) [340]

10789 Davis, Mary L. *Working in Law and Justice* (6–8). Series: Exploring Careers. 1999, Lerner LB $28.75 (0-8225-1766-3). Twelve people are profiled representing various jobs and careers in law and related fields, among them a female deputy sheriff, a male law librarian, a bail bond agent, and a security firm owner. (Rev: BL 7/99; SLJ 10/99) [340]

10790 Fall, Mitchell. *Careers in Fire Departments' Search and Rescue Unit* (5–9). Series: Careers in Search and Rescue Operations. 2003, Rosen LB $26.50 (0-8239-3833-6). This account pays tribute to the heroism of fire departments' search and rescue operations particularly during the September 11, 2001 attacks and also gives a career guide to this occupation. (Rev: BL 10/15/03) [363]

10791 Freedman, Jeri. *Careers in Emergency Medical Response Team's Search and Rescue Unit* (5–9). Illus. Series: Careers in Search and Rescue Operations. 2003, Rosen LB $26.50 (0-8239-3831-X). Starting with September 11, 2001, this volume explores the various roles played by emergency response teams, the use of equipment including helicopters and ambulances, and the training required. (Rev: BL 10/15/03) [616.0]

10792 Giacobello, John. *Bodyguards: Life Protecting Others* (5–10). Series: Extreme Careers. 2003, Rosen LB $26.50 (0-8239-3795-X). This book explores the duties and responsibilities of a bodyguard and includes information how to stay safe on the job and get ahead in this profession. (Rev: BL 9/15/03; SLJ 11/03) [340]

10793 Males, Anne Marie, and Julie Czerneda. *Great Careers for People Fascinated by Government and the Law* (6–9). Series: Career Connections. 1996, Gale $40.00 (0-7876-0858-0). Six people whose jobs involve various aspects of the law and government are profiled, with information on related careers, opportunities, and education and training requirements. (Rev: BR 9–10/96; SLJ 11/96) [345]

10794 Meltzer, Milton. *Case Closed: The Real Scoop on Detective Work* (5–9). Illus. 2001, Scholastic paper $18.95 (0-439-29315-4). Meltzer introduces the methods that detectives (both police and private) use to investigate crimes and provides case studies and a look at the history of detective agencies. (Rev: BL 9/15/01; HBG 10/02; SLJ 9/01; VOYA 4/02) [363.25]

10795 Oleksy, Walter. *Choosing a Career as a Firefighter* (6–9). Series: The World of Work. 2000, Rosen LB $17.95 (0-8239-3245-1). The details of a firefighter's life and of the training, duties, and educational and physical requirements of this and related careers will interest both browsers and report writers. (Rev: HBG 3/01; SLJ 3/01)

10796 Pasternak, Ceel, and Linda Thornburg. *Cool Careers for Girls in Law* (6–12). Series: Cool Careers for Girls. 2001, Impact LB $19.95 (1-57023-160-5); paper $12.95 (1-57023-157-5). Ten women who have succeeded in various areas of the legal profession are highlighted with material on qualifications, salaries, and working conditions. (Rev: BL 4/15/01; SLJ 7/01) [340]

10797 Plum, Jennifer. *Careers in Police Departments' Search and Rescue Unit* (5–9). Series: Careers in Search and Rescue Operations. 2003, Rosen LB $26.50 (0-8239-3834-4). This account highlights the role of police officers in search and rescue operations particularly their acts of heroism during the attacks of September 11, 2001. (Rev: BL 10/15/03) [363]

10798 Schulman, Arlene. *Cop on the Beat: Officer Steven Mayfield in New York City* (7–12). Illus. 2002, Dutton $18.99 (0-525-47064-6); paper $12.99 (0-525-46527-8). The day-to-day professional life of a New York City police officer is accompanied by a brief history of the department and a look at issues including police corruption and violence. (Rev: BL 11/15/02; HBG 3/03; SLJ 12/02; VOYA 12/02) [363.2]

10799 Wade, Linda R. *Careers in Law and Politics* (8–12). Series: Latinos at Work. 2001, Mitchell Lane LB $22.95 (1-58415-080-7). Along with interviews of successful Hispanic Americans in the fields of law and politics, this book describes such careers as lawyer, law professor, judge, police officer, and state representative. (Rev: BL 3/15/02; HBG 10/02; SLJ 3/02) [340]

10800 Wirths, Claudine G. *Choosing a Career in Law Enforcement* (6–10). Series: World of Work. 1996, Rosen LB $17.95 (0-8239-2274-X). Careers in law enforcement, such as police officer, security guard, and private investigator, are explored. (Rev: SLJ 3/97) [363]

Medicine and Health

10801 Asher, Dana. *Epidemiologists: Life Tracking Deadly Diseases* (5–10). Series: Extreme Careers. 2003, Rosen LB $26.50 (0-8239-3633-3). A concise explanation of the work of epidemiologists, the history of this discipline, and the training required to enter this field, with a case study. (Rev: BL 5/15/03; SLJ 5/03) [614.4]

10802 *Careers in Focus — Medical Tech* (8–12). Series: Careers in Focus. 1998, Ferguson $14.50 (0-89434-246-0). Over 20 careers in medical technology are described, covering the nature of the job, educational requirements, rewards, salaries, working conditions, and how to get into the field. (Rev: BR 9–10/98; SLJ 8/98) [610]

10803 Field, Shelly. *Career Opportunities in Health Care.* 2nd ed. (7–12). 2002, Facts on File $49.50 (0-8160-4816-9). Information on 80 or so careers is organized in 16 categories, and includes a job profile, salary outlook, and details of necessary education and skills. (Rev: SLJ 1/03) [610.69]

10804 Lee, Barbara. *Working in Health Care and Wellness* (4–8). Illus. Series: Exploring Careers. 1996, Lerner LB $28.75 (0-8225-1760-4). This book profiles 12 people who are in health care professions, and includes the pros and cons of each career. (Rev: BL 2/15/97) [610.69]

10805 Parks, Peggy. *Medicine* (6–12). Series: Careers for the Twenty-First Century. 2002, Gale LB $27.45 (1-56006-888-4). Such positions as physician, nurse, pharmacist, physical therapist, medical technologist, and emergency medical technician are described with material on working conditions and future possibilities. (Rev: BL 10/15/02; SLJ 9/02) [610.69]

10806 Pasternak, Ceel, and Linda Thornburg. *Cool Careers for Girls in Health* (5–9). Series: Cool Careers for Girls. 1999, Impact $19.95 (1-57023-125-7); paper $12.95 (1-57023-118-4). This book describes health-related careers for girls — as doctors, nurses, dentists, personal trainers, medical technologists, physical therapists, and dietitians. (Rev: SLJ 10/99) [610]

Science and Engineering

10807 Bortz, Alfred B. *To the Young Scientist: Reflections on Doing and Living Science* (6–12). Series: Venture. 1997, Watts LB $23.00 (0-531-11325-6). The author, five other men, and six women discuss their varied careers in science, why they chose them, and the rewards their professions have given them. (Rev: BL 6/1–15/97; SLJ 6/97; VOYA 4/98) [509]

10808 Burnett, Betty. *Math and Science Wizards* (7–12). Series: Cool Careers Without College. 2002, Rosen $30.60 (0-8239-3502-7). Jobs in medicine and science that do not require college degrees, such as chemical lab workers, miners, and doctors' helpers, are described with information on salaries, duties, training, and future outlooks. (Rev: BL 5/15/02; SLJ 7/02) [520]

10809 Cassedy, Patrice. *Engineering* (6–12). Series: Careers for the Twenty-First Century. 2002, Gale LB $27.45 (1-56006-897-3). Various branches of engineering are introduced with material on education necessary, working conditions, salaries, and the outlook for the future. (Rev: BL 10/15/02) [620]

10810 Hayhurst, Chris. *Arctic Scientists: Life Studying the Arctic* (5–10). Series: Extreme Careers. 2003, Rosen LB $26.50 (0-8239-3794-1). This guide to the life and work of Arctic scientists indicates the exciting study possibilities such as the plant and animal life and the effects of global warming. (Rev: BL 9/15/03; SLJ 11/03) [500]

10811 Hayhurst, Chris. *Volcanologists: Life Exploring Volcanoes* (5–10). Series: Extreme Careers. 2003, Rosen LB $26.50 (0-8239-3637-6). This career guide explains what is necessary to become a serious student of volcanoes and what to expect when one becomes a volcanologist. (Rev: BL 9/15/03) [551.2]

10812 Pasternak, Ceel, and Linda Thornburg. *Cool Careers for Girls in Engineering* (5–8). Series: Cool Careers for Girls. 1999, Impact $19.95 (1-57023-126-5); paper $12.95 (1-57023-119-2). Examines engineering specializations — such as computer, biomedical, civil, and agricultural — and the opportunities for women in these fields. (Rev: SLJ 1/00) [620]

10813 Reeves, Diane Lindsey. *Career Ideas for Kids Who Like Science* (5–9). Series: Career Ideas for Kids. 1998, Facts on File $23.00 (0-8160-3680-2); paper $12.95 (0-8060-3686-1). An upbeat, breezy introduction to 15 careers, providing aptitude tests and information on educational requirements, working conditions, activities, etc. (Rev: SLJ 9/98) [500]

10814 Swinburne, Stephen R. *The Woods Scientist* (4–8). Photos by Susan C. Morse. Illus. Series: Scientists in the Field. 2003, Houghton $16.00 (0-618-04602-X). Swinburne describes his fascinating expeditions in the company of a conservationist and ecologist in the woods of Vermont, and provides lots of information on risks to wildlife. (Rev: BCCB 3/03; BL 3/15/03; HBG 10/03; SLJ 4/03) [591.73]

10815 Vincent, Victoria. *Great Careers for People Interested in the Past* (6–10). Series: Career Connections. 1996, Gale $40.00 (0-7876-0861-0). Careers in history, paleontology, and anthropology are among the many careers described in this occupational guide book that provides information on common and lesser-known jobs related to this field and how to get them. (Rev: SLJ 9/96) [930]

10816 *What Can I Do Now? Preparing for a Career in Engineering* (7–12). Series: What Can I Do Now? 1998, Ferguson $16.95 (0-89434-248-7). Following a general introduction to engineering, the book describes jobs in the field, education and skill requirements, and salary ranges, and tells students what they can do now, emphasizing volunteer opportunities and internships. (Rev: SLJ 4/99) [620]

Technical and Industrial Careers

10817 Apel, Melanie Ann. *Careers in Information Technology* (6–12). Illus. Series: Exploring Careers. 2000, Rosen LB $18.95 (0-8239-2892-6). Testimonials from working professionals add to this survey of opportunities in information technology that gives details on skills required and employment outlook. (Rev: BL 3/15/01; HBG 10/01; SLJ 2/01) [004]

10818 Bonnice, Sherry. *Computer Programmer* (8–12). Series: Careers with Character. 2003, Mason Crest LB $22.95 (1-59084-312-6). An explanation of the job requirements and opportunities of computer programmers is accompanied by discussion of the importance of integrity and ethical behavior. (Rev: LMC 4–5/03; SLJ 2/03) [005.1]

10819 Brown, Marty. *Webmaster* (4–8). Series: Coolcareers.com. 2000, Rosen LB $23.95 (0-8239-3111-0). This volume describes a Web page, types of networks, servers, browsers, and protocols and introduces some careers in Web-related areas. (Rev: SLJ 6/00) [004]

10820 Buell, Tonya. *Web Surfers* (7–12). Series: Cool Careers Without College. 2002, Rosen $30.60 (0-8239-3507-8). This book presents 12 careers for computer buffs with information about salaries, future prospects, and further research possibilities. (Rev: BL 5/15/02; SLJ 7/02; VOYA 2/03) [004.6]

10821 *Computers* (4–8). Illus. Series: Discovering Careers for Your Future. 2001, Ferguson LB $15.95 (0-89434-389-0). A useful introduction to the career opportunities in this field, with information on the skills required, potential earnings, and job outlook. (Rev: SLJ 11/01) [004.02373]

10822 Czerneda, Julie, and Victoria Vincent. *Great Careers for People Interested in Communications Technology* (6–9). Series: Career Connections. 1996, Gale $40.00 (0-7876-0859-9). Using case studies of six people, this career book explores the many fields related to communications technology and the requisite job qualifications. (Rev: BR 9–10/96; SLJ 11/96) [621.38]

10823 Fulton, Michael T. *Exploring Careers in Cyberspace* (7–12). Series: Careers. 1997, Rosen LB $18.95 (0-8239-2633-8). A worthwhile source of information on how to prepare oneself to work in cyberspace, the types of jobs available, and the way to make a solid impression. (Rev: BL 6/1–15/98; BR 9–10/98; SLJ 7/98) [004.07802373]

10824 Garcia, Kimberly. *Careers in Technology* (8–12). Series: Latinos at Work. 2001, Mitchell

Lane LB $22.95 (1-58415-087-4). An easy-to-read guide to careers in computer technology such as Web designers, programmers, and Internet marketing, with particular emphasis on Hispanic success stories in these fields. (Rev: BL 10/15/01; HBG 3/02; SLJ 1/02) [004.6]

10825 Henderson, Harry. *Career Opportunities in Computers and Cyberspace* (7–12). 1999, Facts on File $29.95 (0-8160-3773-6); paper $26.95 (0-8160-3774-4). A well-organized resource that covers nearly 200 professions and jobs in computer-related fields. (Rev: BL 6/1–15/99) [004]

10826 Hovanec, Erin M. *Careers as a Content Provider for the Web* (5–8). Series: The Library of E-Commerce and Internet Careers. 2001, Rosen LB $19.95 (0-8239-3418-7). A basic guide to career opportunities in the high-tech sector, with personal stories, information on skills needed and how to get started, and lists of recommended resources, many of which are on the Web. Also use *E-Tailing: Careers Selling Over the Web* (2001). (Rev: SLJ 4/02) [004]

10827 McGinty, Alice B. *Software Designer* (4–8). Series: Coolcareers.com. 2000, Rosen LB $23.95 (0-8239-3149-8). This book explains what a software engineer does, the skills required, education needed, and future prospects. (Rev: SLJ 6/00) [004]

10828 Mazor, Barry. *Multimedia and New Media Developer* (4–8). Series: Coolcareers.com. 2000, Rosen LB $23.95 (0-8239-3102-1). This work explains the nature of multimedia careers, the training and skills necessary, and the job opportunities. (Rev: SLJ 6/00) [004]

10829 O'Donnell, Annie. *Computer Animator* (4–8). Series: Coolcareers.com. 2000, Rosen LB $23.95 (0-8239-3101-3). This book gives a brief history of animation and explains how it is used today, the specialized roles of animators, educational require-ments, and the future of the industry. (Rev: SLJ 6/00) [004]

10830 Oleksy, Walter. *Video Game Designer* (4–8). Series: Coolcareers.com. 2000, Rosen LB $23.95 (0-8239-3117-X). This account explains how video games work and how they are designed, with material on the careers involved and the qualifications necessary. (Rev: SLJ 6/00) [794.8]

10831 Oleksy, Walter. *Web Page Designer* (4–8). Series: Coolcareers.com. 2000, Rosen LB $23.95 (0-8239-3112-9). This well-illustrated account, which features case studies of several teenagers, gives information on Web page construction, what a designer does, the training required, and the job outlook. (Rev: SLJ 6/00) [004]

10832 Pasternak, Ceel, and Linda Thornburg. *Cool Careers for Girls in Computers* (7–12). Illus. 1999, Impact paper $12.95 (1-57023-103-6). This career book for girls features interviews with 10 women in computer-related fields, including a software engineer, sales executive, online specialist, technology trainer, and network administrator. (Rev: SLJ 4/00; VOYA 8/99) [004.6]

10833 Reeves, Diane Lindsey, and Peter Kent. *Career Ideas for Kids Who Like Computers* (5–9). Series: Career Ideas for Kids. 1998, Facts on File $23.00 (0-8160-3682-9); paper $12.95 (0-8160-3688-8). An upbeat, breezy introduction to careers related to computers, providing aptitude tests and information on educational requirements, working conditions, activities, etc. (Rev: BR 5–6/99; SLJ 6/99) [004]

10834 White, Katherine. *Oil Rig Workers: Life Drilling for Oil* (5–10). Series: Extreme Careers. 2003, Rosen LB $26.50 (0-8239-3797-6). This career book examines the lives of oil rig workers and provides a look at day-to-day activities on an oil rig. (Rev: BL 9/15/03) [665.5]

Personal Finances

Money-Making Ideas

General and Miscellaneous

10835 Bernstein, Daryl. *Better Than a Lemonade Stand! Small Business Ideas for Kids* (5–8). Illus. 1992, Beyond Words paper $9.95 (0-941831-75-2). The author, a 15-year-old entrepreneur, provides ideas for starting 51 different small businesses and offers advice on start-up costs, billing, and customer relations. (Rev: BL 10/1/92; SLJ 1/93) [650.1]

10836 Byers, Patricia, et al. *The Kids Money Book: Great Money Making Ideas* (7–10). 1983, Liberty paper $4.95 (0-89709-041-1). A wide variety of jobs are introduced that can be part-time and money-producing. [658.1]

10837 Drew, Bonnie, and Noel Drew. *Fast Cash for Kids* (4–7). Illus. 1995, Career Pr. paper $13.99 (1-564-14154-3). The authors present a variety of possible ways to make money. (Rev: BL 6/15/87) [658.041]

10838 Kravetz, Stacy. *Girl Boss: Running the Show Like the Big Chicks* (7–10). Illus. 1999, Girl Pr. paper $19.95 (0-9659754-2-8). This book gives practical advice and tips for teenage girls who want to start a business of their own. (Rev: VOYA 8/99) [658.1]

10839 Mariotti, Steve, and Tony Towle. *The Young Entrepreneur's Guide to Starting and Running a Business* (7–12). Illus. 1996, Times Books $15.00 (0-8129-2627-7). A thorough, practical guide to starting a business, from the fundamentals of setting up procedures to details on marketing, record keeping, and legal structure. (Rev: BL 2/15/96) [658.1]

10840 Otfinoski, Steven. *The Kid's Guide to Money: Earning It, Saving It, Spending It, Growing It, Shar-ing It* (4–8). Illus. 1996, Scholastic paper $4.95 (0-590-53853-5). This practical guide for kids on how to earn money and manage it responsibly includes budgeting, standard consumer advice, basic information about the stock market, credit cards, and sharing. (Rev: BL 4/1/96; SLJ 6/96; VOYA 6/96) [332.4]

Baby-sitting

10841 Barkin, Carol, and Elizabeth James. *The New Complete Babysitter's Handbook* (5–7). Illus. 1995, Clarion paper $7.95 (0-395-66558-2). A fine manual that covers such topics as first aid, ways to amuse children, and how to get jobs baby sitting. (Rev: BL 5/1/95; SLJ 6/95) [649.1]

10842 Kuch, K. D. *The Babysitter's Handbook* (5–10). Illus. Series: KidBacks. 1997, Random paper $0.99 (0-679-88369-X). This is a fact-filled manual on all aspects of baby-sitting including feeding and playing with babies, emergency measures, games and songs, and basic first aid. (Rev: SLJ 7/97) [649]

10843 Weintraub, Aileen. *Everything You Need to Know About Being a Baby-Sitter: A Teen's Guide to Responsible Child Care* (5–8). 2000, Rosen LB $25.25 (0-8239-3085-8). This book covers all facets of baby-sitting from preparation, responsibilities, and safety precautions to employment opportunities. (Rev: SLJ 7/00) [649]

10844 Zakarin, Debra M. *The Ultimate Baby-Sitter's Handbook: So You Wanna Make Tons of Money?* (4–8). Illus. 1997, Price Stern Sloan paper $4.99 (0-8431-7936-8). A practical, easily read guide to baby-sitting and setting up a business. (Rev: BL 9/15/97; SLJ 12/97) [649]

Managing Money

10845 Bateman, Katherine R. *The Young Investor: Projects and Activities for Making Your Money Grow* (8–12). Illus. 2001, Chicago Review paper $13.95 (1-55652-396-3). The basics of investing are introduced in a straightforward, reassuring manner, with anecdotes about young investor "Billy Ray Fawns" to hold the reader's interest. (Rev: BL 12/15/01; SLJ 2/02) [332.6]

10846 Guthrie, Donna, and Jan Stiles. *Real World Math: Money, Credit, and Other Numbers in Your Life* (6–9). Illus. 1998, Millbrook $26.90 (0-7613-0251-4). A practical and entertaining guide that shows how math is used in everyday situations including shopping, managing money, buying a car, and using credit wisely. (Rev: BL 6/1–15/98; BR 11–12/98; HBG 9/98; SLJ 6/98; VOYA 8/98) [332.024]

10847 Hurwitz, Jane. *High Performance Through Effective Budgeting* (8–12). Illus. Series: Learning-a-Living Library. 1996, Rosen LB $17.95 (0-8239-2203-0). Basic budgeting skills are presented for both personal and on-the-job application. (Rev: BL 8/96; BR 1–2/97; SLJ 10/96; VOYA 2/97) [332.024]

10848 Karlitz, Gail, and Debbie Honig. *Growing Money: A Complete Investing Guide for Kids* (4–8). 1999, Price Stern Sloan paper $6.99 (0-8431-7481-1). This work explains such terms as investing and compound interest, decodes the financial page of the newspaper, and gives advice to budding entrepreneurs. (Rev: SLJ 9/99) [658.1]

10849 Nathan, Amy. *The Kids' Allowance Book* (4–7). Illus. 1998, Walker $15.95 (0-8027-8651-0). Children ages 9 to 14 present the pros and cons of allowances and money management. (Rev: BCCB 6/98; BL 7/98; HBG 10/98; SLJ 10/98) [332.02]

10850 Rendon, Marion, and Rachel Kranz. *Straight Talk About Money* (7–12). Series: Straight Talk. 1992, Facts on File LB $27.45 (0-8160-2612-2). Provides a brief history and description of money and the U.S. economy, followed by suggestions young adults can use when earning and managing money. (Rev: BL 6/15/92) [332.4]

Health and the Human Body

General and Miscellaneous

10851 Apel, Melanie Ann. *Coping with Stuttering* (6–10). Series: Coping. 2000, Rosen LB $17.95 (0-8239-2970-1). Practical advice for stutterers and for listeners is accompanied by information on celebrities who have conquered this problem. (Rev: SLJ 4/00) [616.85]

10852 Costello, Patricia. *Female Fitness Stars of TV and the Movies* (7–12). Series: Legends of Health and Fitness. 2000, Mitchell Lane LB $24.95 (1-58415-050-5). Cher, Goldie Hawn, and Demi Moore are among the actors profiled here as examples of professionals who put fitness high on their list of priorities. (Rev: SLJ 2/01)

10853 Debenedette, Valerie. *Caffeine* (7–10). Series: Drug Library. 1996, Enslow LB $20.95 (0-89490-741-7). A well-documented, well-organized look at caffeine, where it is found, its effects, and its abuse. (Rev: BL 9/15/96; SLJ 9/96) [615]

10854 Foley, Ronan. *World Health: The Impact on Our Lives* (5–8). Illus. Series: 21st Century Debates. 2003, Raintree Steck-Vaughn LB $28.56 (0-7398-5507-7). A thorough and thought-provoking exploration of the health status of countries around the world and the reasons for the wide disparity between wealthy and poor nations. (Rev: BL 8/03; HBG 10/03; SLJ 7/03) [362.1]

10855 Gilbert, Richard J. *Caffeine: The Most Popular Stimulant* (8–12). Illus. 1986, Chelsea LB $19.95 (0-87754-756-4). Tea, coffee, and chocolate are covered in this account of what the author calls "the most popular drug in the world." (Rev: BL 7/86) [615]

10856 Gutman, Bill. *Harmful to Your Health* (5–8). Illus. Series: Focus on Safety. 1996, Twenty-First Century LB $24.90 (0-8050-4144-3). This volume outlines the problems inherent in drugs, alcohol, AIDS, steroids, and sexual abuse, with material on how to be alert to their dangers. (Rev: BL 2/1/97; SLJ 2/97) [616.86]

10857 Hurley, Jennifer A., ed. *Addiction* (6–12). Illus. Series: Opposing Viewpoints. 1999, Greenhaven LB $21.96 (0-7377-0117-X); paper $13.96 (0-7377-0116-1). A collection of essays and opinions that explores various viewpoints on addiction including causes, treatments, and government intervention. (Rev: BL 3/15/00) [362.29.]

10858 Isler, Charlotte, and Alwyn T. Cohall. *The Watts Teen Health Dictionary* (7–12). Illus. 1996, Watts LB $24.95 (0-513-11236-5); paper $16.00 (0-531-15792-X). This book in dictionary format contains articles on such subjects as STDs, contraceptives, medications, diseases, eating disorders, breast exams, and immunization. (Rev: BR 11–12/96; VOYA 10/96) [613]

10859 Jukes, Mavis. *The Guy Book: An Owner's Manual* (6–12). Illus. 2002, Crown LB $18.99 (0-679-99028-3); paper $12.95 (0-679-89028-9). Jukes takes an appealing, frank-talking approach to sex, health, and hygiene for young men, covering everything from dating and birth control to choosing clothes and slow dancing. (Rev: BL 1/1–15/02; HBG 10/02; SLJ 3/02; VOYA 6/02) [305.235]

10860 Jukes, Mavis, and Lilian Cheung. *Be Healthy! It's a Girl Thing: Food, Fitness, and Feeling Great* (5–8). 2003, Crown LB $18.99 (0-679-99029-1); paper $12.95 (0-679-89029-7). The authors take a matter-of-fact, motivational approach to changes that arrive with puberty and the steps girls can take to be healthy and avoid weight gain and eating disorders. (Rev: BL 1/1–15/04; SLJ 12/03) [613]

10861 McCarthy-Tucker, Sherri. *Coping with Special-Needs Classmates* (5–8). 1993, Rosen LB $25.25 (0-8239-1598-0). First-person accounts describe physical, mental, and emotional problems faced by some young people. (Rev: SLJ 8/93) [616]

10862 McHugh, Mary. *Special Siblings: Growing Up with Someone with a Disability* (7–12). 1999, Hyperion $23.95 (0-7868-6285-8). This book discusses a variety of physical and mental disabilities and how to cope with these handicaps when they affect a member of your family. (Rev: BL 2/15/99; SLJ 1/00; VOYA 8/99) [616]

10863 O'Neill, Terry. *Biomedical Ethics* (7–12). Series: Opposing Viewpoints Digests. 1998, Greenhaven LB $27.45 (1-56510-875-2); paper $17.45 (1-56510-874-4). This concise overview of biomedical ethics covers topics such as cloning, organ transplants, experiments, and research. (Rev: BL 4/15/99; SLJ 6/99) [575.1]

10864 Powell, Phelan. *Trailblazers of Physical Fitness* (7–12). Series: Legends of Health and Fitness. 2000, Mitchell Lane LB $24.95 (1-58415-024-6). Jack LaLanne and Richard Simmons are among the individuals profiled here as leading proponents of physical fitness. (Rev: SLJ 2/01)

10865 Roleff, Tamara L., ed. *Biomedical Ethics* (8–12). Series: Opposing Viewpoints. 1998, Greenhaven LB $32.45 (1-56510-793-4); paper $21.20 (1-56510-792-6). An anthology of opinions on the ethical considerations related to cloning, human transplants, modern reproductive techniques, and genetic research. (Rev: BL 6/1–15/98) [573.2]

10866 Sommers, Annie Leah. *Everything You Need to Know About Looking and Feeling Your Best: A Guide for Girls* (6–12). Series: Need to Know Library. 2000, Rosen LB $17.95 (0-8239-3079-3). This book aims to boost girls' self-images as well as their knowledge of health and hygiene. (Rev: HBG 9/00; SLJ 3/00) [613]

10867 Torr, James D., ed. *Health Care: Province Divided* (8–12). Series: Opposing Viewpoints. 1999, Greenhaven LB $21.96 (0-7377-0129-3); paper $13.96 (0-7377-0128-5). The problems of the healthcare system in the United States are presented from a variety of points of view including doctors and health policy experts. (Rev: BL 11/15/99; SLJ 2/00) [362.1]

Aging and Death

10868 Altman, Linda Jacobs. *Death: An Introduction to Medical-Ethical Dilemmas* (6–12). 2000, Enslow LB $19.95 (0-7660-1246-8). Physical, cultural, moral, and psychological issues related to death are explored in this insightful, informative book. (Rev: BL 6/1–15/00; HBG 9/00; SLJ 8/00) [179.4.]

10869 Cavan, Seamus. *Euthanasia: The Debate Over the Right to Die* (6–8). Series: Focus on Science and Society. 2000, Rosen LB $19.95 (0-8239-3215-X). This volume discusses ethical and legal considerations on both sides of the debate concerning euthanasia. (Rev: SLJ 1/01) [179.7]

10870 Colman, Penny. *Corpses, Coffins, and Crypts: A History of Burial* (7–12). Illus. 1997, Holt $19.95 (0-8050-5066-3). Customs associated with death and burial traditions in various cultures and times are covered in a text enlivened with many photographs. (Rev: BL 11/1/97; HBG 3/98; SLJ 12/97*) [393]

10871 Digiulio, Robert, and Rachel Kranz. *Straight Talk About Death and Dying* (7–12). Series: Straight Talk. 1995, Facts on File $27.45 (0-8160-3078-2). Among the topics covered in this book about death and dying are Kubler-Ross's five psychological stages experienced by the dying and various aspects of mourning. (Rev: BL 9/15/95; SLJ 12/95) [155.9]

10872 Egendorf, Laura K., ed. *Assisted Suicide* (7–12). Series: Current Controversies. 1998, Greenhaven LB $32.45 (1-56510-807-8). An anthology of opinions on topics related to assisted suicide, including its morality, legal status, and individual rights. (Rev: BL 8/98; SLJ 1/99) [179]

10873 Fry, Virginia. *Part of Me Died, Too: Stories of Creative Survival Among Bereaved Children and Teenagers* (5–8). 1995, Dutton $19.99 (0-525-45068-8). Each of the 11 true-life stories is followed by a selection of self-help activities to aid the bereaved. (Rev: BL 1/1/95; SLJ 2/95) [155.9]

10874 Gay, Kathlyn. *The Right to Die: Public Controversy, Private Matter* (7–12). Series: Issue and Debate. 1993, Millbrook LB $24.90 (1-56294-325-1). Discusses euthanasia and assisted suicide in depth — from Greek times to the present — and includes actual recent cases. (Rev: BL 10/1/93) [179]

10875 Giddens, Sandra, and Owen Giddens. *Coping with Grieving and Loss* (6–10). 2000, Rosen LB $17.95 (0-8239-2894-2). Practical advice about the process of grieving and funerals is accompanied by personal teen stories. (Rev: SLJ 4/00) [155.9]

10876 Grollman, Earl A. *Straight Talk About Death for Teenagers: How to Cope with Losing Someone You Love* (7–12). 1993, Beacon paper $13.00 (0-8070-2501-1). Grollman validates the painful feelings teens experience following the death of a loved one, conveying a sense of the grief as well as getting on with life. (Rev: BL 4/1/93; SLJ 6/93; VOYA 8/93) [155.9]

10877 Hawkins, Gail N., ed. *Physician-Assisted Suicide* (6–12). Series: At Issue. 2002, Gale LB $24.95 (0-7377-1056-X); paper $16.20 (0-7377-1044-1). There's plenty of material to spark debate in these essays about the morality, ethics, and possible legalization of physician-assisted suicide. (Rev: BL 6/1–15/02) [174]

10878 Hyde, Margaret O., and Lawrence E. Hyde. *Meeting Death* (5–8). 1989, Walker LB $15.85 (0-8027-6874-1). After a history of how various cultures regard death, the authors discuss this phenomenon, the concept of grieving, and how to face death. (Rev: BL 1/1/90; SLJ 11/89) [306.9]

10879 Knox, Jean. *Death and Dying* (8–12). Illus. Series: 21st Century Health and Wellness. 2000, Chelsea LB $24.95 (0-7910-5986-3). This comprehensive and detailed volume looks at the variety of rituals that accompany death, at the role of doctors and others in supporting the dying and their families, and at the possibility of an afterlife. (Rev: BL 11/15/00; HBG 10/01; SLJ 2/01)

10880 Krementz, Jill. *How It Feels When a Parent Dies* (4–7). Illus. 1988, Knopf paper $15.00 (0-394-75854-4). Eighteen experiences of parental death are recounted.

10881 Landau, Elaine. *The Right to Die* (7–12). 1993, Watts LB $24.00 (0-531-13015-0). A balanced, in-depth examination of the controversial issue, including a chapter on the rights of adolescents to refuse medical treatment. (Rev: BL 1/15/94; SLJ 2/94; VOYA 2/94) [174]

10882 Leone, Daniel, ed. *Physician-Assisted Suicide* (8–12). Series: At Issue. 1997, Greenhaven $26.20 (1-56510-019-0); paper $17.45 (1-56510-018-2). Authors represented in this anthology debate whether doctors should be allowed to help terminally ill patients end their lives rather than suffer prolonged pain. (Rev: BL 5/15/98; SLJ 5/98) [179.7]

10883 LeShan, Eda. *Learning to Say Good-bye: When a Parent Dies* (5–7). 1976, Avon paper $8.00 (0-380-40105-3). A sympathetic explanation of the many reactions children have to death.

10884 Rebman, Renee C. *Euthanasia and the "Right to Die": A Pro/Con Issue* (5–8). Illus. Series: Pro/Con Issues. 2002, Enslow LB $21.95 (0-7660-1816-4). An objective examination of both sides of the issue of euthanasia. (Rev: BL 9/1/02; HBG 3/03) [179.7]

10885 Schleifer, Jay. *Everything You Need to Know When Someone You Know Has Been Killed* (6–12). Illus. Series: Need to Know Library. 1998, Rosen LB $25.25 (0-8239-2779-2). This book helps young people deal with sudden death, describes the grieving process, and gives advice concerning the painful issues associated with death. (Rev: BL 10/1/98) [155.9]

10886 Wagner, Heather Lehr. *Dealing with Terminal Illness in the Family* (6–12). Series: Focus on Family Matters. 2002, Chelsea $20.75 (0-7910-6692-4). This account explores the different emotions produced by the terminal illness of a loved one and

how to cope with them. (Rev: BL 10/15/02; SLJ 10/02) [618]

10887 Walker, Richard. *A Right to Die?* (4–8). Series: Viewpoints. 1997, Watts LB $23.00 (0-531-14413-5). This objective book discusses traditional views of death, describes the impact of modern medicine on life spans, and presents different points of view on suicide, euthanasia, life-support systems, doctors' duties and responsibilities in terminal situations, hospice programs, living wills, and funeral choices. (Rev: SLJ 5/97) [306.88]

10888 Wekesser, Carol, ed. *Euthanasia* (7–12). Series: Opposing Viewpoints. 1995, Greenhaven LB $35.15 (1-56510-244-4). The ethical aspects of euthanasia, whether or not it should be legalized, physician-assisted suicide, and who should make decisions in these matters are addressed from a variety of viewpoints. (Rev: BL 7/95; SLJ 9/95; VOYA 12/95) [179]

10889 Wilson, Antoine. *You and a Death in Your Family* (5–8). Series: Family Matters. 2001, Rosen LB $23.95 (0-8239-3355-5). Wilson provides concise, readable advice on coping with the death of a relative or pet and stresses that youngsters should seek help when necessary. (Rev: SLJ 8/01) [155.9]

10890 Winters, Paul A., ed. *Death and Dying* (8–12). Series: Opposing Viewpoints. 1997, Greenhaven LB $32.45 (1-56510-671-7); paper $21.20 (1-56510-670-9). Topics dealt with in this anthology of articles include the treatment of terminally ill patients, the right to die, how to cope with death, and whether death is the end of life. (Rev: BL 10/15/97; SLJ 2/98) [179]

10891 Yount, Lisa, ed. *Euthanasia* (6–12). Series: Contemporary Issues. 2002, Gale LB $31.20 (0-7377-0829-8); paper $19.95 (0-7377-0828-X). This volume explores the often controversial positions of those who are for and against euthanasia, presenting statistics and information on the laws both in the United States and abroad. (Rev: BL 5/1/02) [179.7]

10892 Yount, Lisa. *Euthanasia* (6–12). Illus. 2000, Lucent LB $19.96 (1-56006-697-0). Diverse opinions are presented in this book, allowing readers to formulate their own ideas about this issue. (Rev: BL 1/1–15/01) [179.7]

Alcohol, Drugs, and Smoking

10893 Alagna, Magdalena. *Everything You Need to Know About the Dangers of Binge Drinking* (6–10). Illus. Series: Need to Know Library. 2001, Rosen LB $23.95 (0-8239-3289-3). Warnings about the physical and psychological dangers of alcohol are interwoven with fictional examples. (Rev: BL 5/1/02) [362.292]

10894 Algeo, Philippa. *Acid and Hallucinogens* (5–8). Illus. 1990, Watts paper $20.80 (0-531-10932-1). This book discusses the composition and effects of such drugs as LSD, mescaline, marijuana, and angel dust. (Rev: BL 8/90; SLJ 10/90) [615]

10895 Alvergue, Anne. *Ecstasy: The Danger of False Euphoria* (6–10). Illus. Series: Drug Prevention Library. 1997, Rosen LB $17.95 (0-8239-2506-4). A discussion of how the drug MDMA, known as ecstasy, affects the mind and body, outlining the dangers. (Rev: SLJ 5/98) [6.5.3]

10896 Avraham, Regina. *The Downside of Drugs* (8–12). Illus. 1988, Chelsea LB $19.95 (1-55546-232-4). This account covers the effects of such drugs as nicotine, alcohol, narcotics, stimulants, and hallucinogens. (Rev: SLJ 6/88) [613.8]

10897 Avraham, Regina. *Substance Abuse* (8–12). 1988, Chelsea LB $19.95 (1-55546-219-7). This account describes how drugs affect behavior and how addiction is treated. (Rev: BR 1–2/89; VOYA 4/89) [616.86]

10898 Ayer, Eleanor. *Teen Smoking* (6–12). 1998, Lucent LB $27.45 (1-56006-442-0). In spite of warnings, nearly two million teens smoke. This book traces the influences that make them start and gives advice on how to quit. (Rev: BL 1/1–15/99) [362.29]

10899 Banfield, Susan. *Inside Recovery: How the Twelve-Step Program Can Work for You* (7–10). Series: Drug Abuse Prevention Library. 1998, Rosen LB $17.95 (0-8239-2634-6). Using first-hand knowledge, the author describes the 12-step program and the many problems one can face going through this program, which has been a successful route for many on the road to recovery from addiction. (Rev: VOYA 2/99) [613.8]

10900 Barbour, Scott, ed. *Alcohol* (8–12). Series: Opposing Viewpoints. 1997, Greenhaven LB $26.20 (1-56510-675-X). Excerpts from books and articles explore questions involving the degree of harm that alcohol causes, treatments for alcoholism, the responsibility of the alcohol industry, and how to reduce alcohol-related problems. (Rev: BL 10/15/97; SLJ 1/98; VOYA 6/98) [613.8]

10901 Barbour, Scott, ed. *Drug Legalization* (6–12). Series: Current Controversies. 2000, Greenhaven LB $21.96 (0-7377-0335-0); paper $13.96 (0-7377-0336-9). In this collection of essays, the drug legalization controversy is examined from various points of view. (Rev: BL 10/15/00) [364.1]

10902 Barter, James. *Hallucinogens* (8–12). Illus. Series: Drug Education Library. 2002, Gale LB $27.45 (1-56006-915-5). This absorbing and comprehensive book explains the effects of hallucinogens on the body, traces their use — in ancient rituals, in medical treatments, and as a recreational drug — and looks at the debates over their legaliza-

tion. Also in this series is *Marijuana*. (Rev: BL 6/1–15/02; SLJ 6/02) [362.29]

10903 Bayer, Linda. *Strange Visions: Hallucinogen-Related Disorders* (6–10). Illus. Series: Encyclopedia of Psychological Disorders. 2000, Chelsea $27.45 (0-7910-5315-6). This volume explains how the abuse of certain drugs can produce hallucinations and possible permanent brain damage. (Rev: BL 11/1/00; HBG 9/00) [616.86]

10904 Beal, Eileen. *Ritalin: Its Use and Abuse* (7–10). Series: Drug Abuse Prevention. 1999, Rosen LB $17.95 (0-8239-2775-X). This book explores the drug Ritalin, widely used for attention deficit disorder, and presents the controversies surrounding it. (Rev: BL 5/15/99; VOYA 4/00) [616.85]

10905 Berger, Gilda. *Alcoholism and the Family* (8–12). Series: Changing Family. 1993, Watts LB $25.00 (0-531-12548-3). This discussion of alcoholism, presented in question-and-answer format, focuses on its effects on the family and covers causes, prevention, treatment, and recovery. (Rev: BL 1/15/94; SLJ 12/93; VOYA 2/94) [362.29]

10906 Berger, Gilda, and Nancy Levitin. *Crack* (6–12). 1995, Watts LB $24.00 (0-531-11188-1). Emphasizes the dangers of crack to users, the cost to society, and crack's ability to claim innocent victims: crack babies. (Rev: BL 5/1/95) [362.29]

10907 Biggers, Jeff. *Transgenerational Addiction* (6–9). Series: Drug Abuse Prevention Library. 1998, Rosen LB $17.95 (0-8239-2757-1); Hazelden Information & Educational Services paper $6.95 (1-56838-247-2). This book deals with entire families that battle addiction to drugs and alcohol, and how each member must deal with the challenge individually. (Rev: BL 5/15/98) [362.2913]

10908 Boyd, George A. *Drugs and Sex* (5–10). Illus. Series: Drug Abuse Prevention Library. 1994, Rosen LB $17.95 (0-8239-1538-7). A careful examination of the hazards of combining drugs and sex, including unsafe sex, pregnancy, AIDS, and other sexually transmitted diseases. (Rev: BL 6/1–15/94; SLJ 5/94) [613.9]

10909 Claypool, Jane. *Alcohol and You*. 3rd ed. (6–10). Series: Impact Books: Drugs and Alcohol. 1997, Watts LB $23.00 (0-531-11351-5). A readable new edition of a standard, well-respected work on alcohol and teenage drinking problems. (Rev: BR 5–6/98; SLJ 2/98) [613.8]

10910 Clayton, Lawrence. *Alcohol Drug Dangers* (4–7). Illus. Series: Drug Dangers. 1999, Enslow LB $21.95 (0-7660-1159-3). Using real-life case histories, this book describes the effects of alcohol on the body and mind. (Rev: BL 8/99; HBG 10/99) [362.292]

10911 Clayton, Lawrence. *Diet Pill Drug Dangers* (5–9). Series: Drug Dangers. 1999, Enslow LB $19.95 (0-7660-1158-5). With liberal use of case histories, this book explores the dangers of diet pill use, their effects on the human body, and prevention techniques. (Rev: HBG 10/99; SLJ 9/99) [362.29]

10912 Clayton, Lawrence. *Tranquilizers* (7–10). Illus. Series: Drug Library. 1997, Enslow LB $20.95 (0-89490-849-9). Information is presented about tranquilizers, their beneficial effects, and the potential consequences of abuse and addiction. (Rev: BL 3/15/97; SLJ 6/97) [615]

10913 Clayton, Lawrence. *Working Together Against Drug Addiction* (6–10). 1996, Rosen LB $16.95 (0-8239-2263-4). In addition to discussing drugs and addiction, this work takes an activist approach by providing ways for teens to locate drug and alcohol counselors and programs and ways they can become involved and make a difference. (Rev: SLJ 5/97) [362]

10914 Connelly, Elizabeth Russell. *Through a Glass Darkly: The Psychological Effects of Marijuana and Hashish* (8–12). Series: Encyclopedia of Psychological Disorders. 1999, Chelsea $27.45 (0-7910-4897-7). After an overview of the history of marijuana and hashish, this volume surveys their medicinal and recreational use, effects of interaction with other drugs, potential disorders from their use, the dangers of addiction, and treatments available. (Rev: VOYA 8/99) [362.29]

10915 Connolly, Sean. *Amphetamines* (7–9). Series: Just the Facts. 2000, Heinemann LB $22.79 (1-57572-254-2). An attractive look at the use and mis-use of these drugs, with many illustrations. (Rev: BL 3/1/01; SLJ 2/01) [362.29]

10916 Connolly, Sean. *Cocaine* (7–9). Series: Just the Facts. 2000, Heinemann LB $22.79 (1-57572-255-0). This book introduces cocaine, its history, the culture surrounding it, its effects on the brain and body, and recovery issues. (Rev: BL 3/1/01; HBG 10/01; SLJ 2/01) [362.29]

10917 Connolly, Sean. *LSD* (7–9). Series: Just the Facts. 2000, Heinemann LB $22.79 (1-57572-258-5). This attractive book describes the history of LSD, and gives material on the emotional, mental, and physical problems with its use. (Rev: BL 3/1/01) [362.29]

10918 Connolly, Sean. *Steroids* (7–9). Series: Just the Facts. 2000, Heinemann LB $22.79 (1-57572-259-3). This attractively illustrated book introduces steroids, their use and abuse, and their effects on both the body and the brain. (Rev: BL 3/1/01; HBG 10/01; SLJ 2/01) [362.29]

10919 Connolly, Sean. *Tobacco* (7–9). Illus. Series: Just the Facts. 2000, Heinemann LB $22.79 (1-57572-260-7). The history of tobacco use is presented along with related health concerns, details of lawsuits against tobacco companies, and the sale of cigarettes to Third World countries. (Rev: BL 2/15/01; HBG 10/01) [362.29]

10920 Croft, Jennifer. *Drugs and the Legalization Debate* (6–10). Illus. Series: Drug Abuse Prevention Library. 1997, Rosen LB $17.95 (0-8239-2509-9). A well-balanced presentation of the pros and cons of legalizing drugs, along with a discussion of drug abuse and penalties and a brief look at how other countries deal with the issue. (Rev: SLJ 5/98) [362.29]

10921 Croft, Jennifer. *PCP: High Risk on the Streets* (7–10). Series: Drug Abuse Prevention Library. 1998, Rosen LB $17.95 (0-8239-2774-1). This book provides readers with important information about phencyclidine, or angel dust, the behavior it produces, and its dangers. (Rev: BL 11/15/98; BR 1–2/99; SLJ 12/98) [362.29]

10922 Dudley, William, ed. *Drugs and Sports* (6–12). Series: At Issue. 2000, Greenhaven LB $17.96 (1-56510-697-0); paper $11.96 (1-56510-696-2). An interesting and thought-provoking exploration of the extensive use of performance-enhancing drugs by amateur and professional athletes. (Rev: BL 4/1/01) [362.29]

10923 Egendorf, Laura K., ed. *Teen Alcoholism* (6–12). Series: Contemporary Issues Companion. 2001, Greenhaven LB $22.96 (0-7377-0683-X); paper $14.96 (0-7377-0682-1). Essays explore teen abuse of alcohol, looking at its causes and the effects on the young people themselves and on society as a whole, with contributions from individuals who have close experience with this problem. (Rev: BL 9/1/01) [362.292]

10924 Galas, Judith C. *Drugs and Sports* (5–8). Illus. Series: Overview. 1997, Lucent LB $27.45 (1-56006-185-5). A look at the kinds of illegal drugs taken by athletes, the reasons for their use, and the ways in which their use can be detected. (Rev: BL 3/15/97; BR 11–12/97) [362.29]

10925 Glass, George. *Drugs and Fitting In* (6–9). Illus. Series: Drug Abuse Prevention Library. 1998, Rosen LB $17.95 (0-8239-2554-4). After a description of teen culture and its pressures to conform and be popular, this book presents alternatives and advice on how to remain drug-free. (Rev: BL 3/15/98; BR 9–10/98; VOYA 6/98) [362.29]

10926 Glass, George. *Narcotics: Dangerous Painkillers* (6–9). Illus. Series: Drug Abuse Prevention Library. 1998, Rosen LB $17.95 (0-8239-2719-9). This book explains the dangers of abusing prescribed painkilling drugs and their street derivatives and discusses issues relating to addiction and treatment. (Rev: BL 5/15/98; SLJ 10/98) [616.8632]

10927 Goldish, Meish. *Dangers of Herbal Stimulants* (6–10). Illus. Series: Drug Abuse Prevention Library. 1997, Rosen LB $17.95 (0-8239-2555-2). Teens are enticed to use herbal substances to get high, lose weight, or solve other emotional and physical problems. This book describes the products available, their potential dangers, and the laws that regulate their use. (Rev: SLJ 5/98; VOYA 2/99) [362.29]

10928 Gottfried, Ted. *Should Drugs Be Legalized?* (6–12). Illus. 2000, Twenty-First Century LB $23.90 (0-7613-1314-1). This work features a description of various kinds of drugs, their effects, their harmful aspects, and a discussion of the problems and benefits of legalizing their use. (Rev: BL 4/1/00; HBG 9/00; SLJ 7/00) [362.29.]

10929 Grabish, Beatrice R. *Drugs and Your Brain* (6–10). Illus. Series: Drug Abuse Prevention Library. 1998, Rosen paper $6.95 (1-56838-214-6). This book describes how drugs affect the brain and the risks of permanent as well as short-term damage. (Rev: BL 4/15/98; BR 9–10/98; SLJ 6/98) [616.86]

10930 Grosshandler-Smith, Janet. *Working Together Against Drinking and Driving* (4–8). Series: The Library of Social Activism. 1996, Rosen LB $16.95 (0-8239-2259-6). With an emphasis on prevention, the author presents a general discussion on drinking and driving and its consequences, followed by pointers on how to avoid embarrassing situations, how to handle peer pressure about drinking. (Rev: SLJ 2/97) [613.8]

10931 Gwynne, Peter. *Who Uses Drugs?* (7–10). Illus. 1987, Chelsea LB $19.95 (1-55546-223-5). An overview of different kinds of drugs and who uses them. (Rev: BL 5/1/88) [362.2]

10932 Hanan, Jessica. *When Someone You Love Is Addicted* (5–9). Series: Drug Abuse Prevention Library. 1999, Rosen LB $17.95 (0-8239-2831-4). A short book that begins with teenage case histories and then discusses treatments and resources for young people with drug problems. (Rev: SLJ 7/99) [362.29]

10933 Harris, Jonathan. *This Drinking Nation* (7–12). 1994, Four Winds $15.95 (0-02-742744-7). Discusses America's alcohol consumption from 1607 to the present, including information on the Prohibition period of 1920–1933. Also examines teenage drinking and alcoholism. (Rev: BL 7/94; SLJ 9/94; VOYA 10/94) [394.1]

10934 Haughton, Emma. *Alcohol* (7–10). Series: Talking Points. 1999, Raintree Steck-Vaughn LB $27.12 (0-8172-5318-1). A candid look at the use and abuse of alcohol and its physical and emotional effects. (Rev: BL 8/99; BR 9–10/99) [613.8]

10935 Haughton, Emma. *A Right to Smoke?* (4–8). Series: Viewpoints. 1997, Watts LB $23.00 (0-531-14412-7). Using double-page spreads, this book offers different viewpoints on who smokes, why they start, the physical dangers, second-hand smoke, the tobacco industry giants, taxes on cigarettes, advertising, and programs to discourage people

from smoking. (Rev: BL 6/1–15/97; SLJ 5/97) [362.2]

10936 Heyes, Eileen. *Tobacco, USA: The Industry Behind the Smoke* (8–12). Illus. 1999, Twenty-First Century LB $23.90. (0-7613-0974-8). A concise study of the U.S. tobacco industry with material on its history, current farming techniques, government support and regulations, marketing ploys, and the industry's defensive battle against medical facts. (Rev: BL 12/15/99; HBG 4/00; SLJ 1/00) [338.2]

10937 Hirschfelder, Arlene. *Kick Butts! A Kid's Action Guide to a Tobacco-Free America* (5–8). Illus. 1998, Silver Burdett $19.95 (0-382-39632-4); paper $9.95 (0-382-39633-2). A look at the history of smoking in the United States and its connection with various diseases, followed by examples of steps taken by young activists to create a smoke-free environment. (Rev: BL 6/1–15/98; HBG 10/98; SLJ 7/98; VOYA 2/99) [613.8]

10938 Hoobler, Thomas, and Dorothy Hoobler. *Drugs and Crime* (7–12). Illus. 1987, Chelsea LB $19.95 (1-55546-228-6). An account of how drug traffic is fostered by layers of crime and corruption both international and local. (Rev: BL 3/15/88; SLJ 5/88) [364.2]

10939 Hyde, Margaret O. *Drug Wars* (7–12). 1990, Walker LB $12.85 (0-8027-6901-2). This account discusses the violence and despair that crack cocaine has brought to America and ways in which its production and distribution can be halted. (Rev: SLJ 6/90; VOYA 6/90) [616.86]

10940 Hyde, Margaret O. *Know About Drugs*. 4th ed. (5–8). 1995, Walker LB $15.85 (0-8027-8395-3). An introduction to drugs including marijuana, alcohol, PCP, inhalants, crack/cocaine, heroin, and nicotine. (Rev: BL 7/90; SLJ 3/96) [362.2]

10941 Hyde, Margaret O. *Know About Smoking*. Rev. ed. (5–8). Illus. 1995, Walker LB $14.85 (0-8027-8400-3). After a history of tobacco and nicotine, this book describes their effects on the body, addiction prevention, and the role of advertising in smoking. (Rev: BL 7/90; SLJ 9/95) [362.2]

10942 Hyde, Margaret O., and John F. Setaro. *Alcohol 101: An Overview for Teens* (5–10). 1999, Twenty-First Century LB $24.90 (0-7613-1274-9). Kinds of alcohol and their effects are described, with material on alcoholism and binge drinking. (Rev: HBG 3/00; SLJ 3/00; VOYA 12/00) [613.8]

10943 Hyde, Margaret O., and John F. Setaro. *Drugs 101: An Overview for Teens* (7–12). 2003, Twenty-First Century LB $25.90 (0-7613-2608-1). This well-researched and accessible introduction to the nature of addiction, illicit drugs, and the harmful results of their use features useful photographs, diagrams, and charts. (Rev: BL 5/15/03; HBG 10/03; SLJ 5/03; VOYA 10/03) [362.29]

10944 Jamiolkowski, Raymond M. *Drugs and Domestic Violence* (7–12). Series: Drug Abuse Prevention Library. 1996, Rosen LB $17.95 (0-8239-2062-3). This volume points out that domestic violence increases when drugs are used in the home and gives pointers to teens in these situations on how to stay safe. (Rev: SLJ 3/96) [362.2]

10945 Jones, Ralph. *Straight Talk: Answers to Questions Young People Ask About Alcohol* (7–9). 1989, TAB paper $4.95 (0-8306-9005-0). Fifty questions concerning alcohol and physical and psychological effects are answered in this short, straightforward book. (Rev: VOYA 12/89) [661]

10946 Keyishian, Elizabeth. *Everything You Need to Know About Smoking* (6–10). Illus. 1989, Rosen $24.50 (0-8239-1017-2). This book covers such topics as why people smoke, its effects, and how to quit. (Rev: SLJ 2/90) [613.8]

10947 Klein, Wendy. *Drugs and Denial* (7–10). Series: Drug Abuse Prevention Library. 1998, Rosen LB $17.95 (0-8239-2773-3). This book describes the signs of addiction and the stages of adolescent drug use, helps teens to admit it if they have a drug problem, and provides tips for teens to help people they know who may be in denial. (Rev: BL 11/15/98) [362.29]

10948 Knox, Jean McBee. *Drinking, Driving and Drugs* (7–10). Illus. 1988, Chelsea LB $19.95 (1-55546-231-6). An overview of this national problem with a focus on teenage offenders and victims. (Rev: BL 7/88; BR 1–2/89; SLJ 9/88) [363.1]

10949 Kranz, Rachel. *Straight Talk About Smoking* (6–12). Series: Straight Talk. 1999, Facts on File LB $27.45 (0-8160-3976-3). This no-nonsense account explains why people start smoking, what smoking does to the body, the nature of addiction, and how to give up smoking. (Rev: BL 2/15/00; HBG 4/00; SLJ 3/00) [362.29.]

10950 Landau, Elaine. *Hooked: Talking About Addiction* (5–10). Illus. 1995, Millbrook LB $22.90 (1-56294-469-X). This account defines addiction broadly — from use of alcohol and drugs to various forms of compulsive behavior — and gives suggestions for recovery. (Rev: BL 1/1–15/96; SLJ 1/96) [362.29]

10951 Landau, Elaine. *Teenage Drinking* (7–12). Series: Issues in Focus. 1994, Enslow LB $20.95 (0-89490-575-9). This book focuses on the causes and effects of teenage drinking and prevention measures that have worked. (Rev: BL 11/15/94; SLJ 11/94; VOYA 12/94) [362.29]

10952 Lawler, Jennifer. *Drug Testing in Schools: A Pro/Con Issue* (5–8). Series: Hot Issues. 2000, Enslow LB $21.95 (0-7660-1367-7). The pros and cons of drug testing in schools are presented in an unbiased manner with sections on methods of drug testing, policies of various organizations, and the opinions of students, teachers, and parents. (Rev: HBG 3/01; SLJ 12/00) [362.29]

10953 Lee, Mary Price, and Richard S. Lee. *Drugs and Codependency* (6–10). Series: Drug Abuse Prevention Library. 1995, Rosen LB $17.95 (0-8239-2065-8). This book explores the vulnerability of teens who live in a household where drugs are abused. (Rev: BL 9/15/95; SLJ 10/95) [616.869]

10954 Lee, Mary Price, and Richard S. Lee. *Drugs and the Media* (5–10). Illus. Series: Drug Abuse Prevention Library. 1994, Rosen LB $17.95 (0-8239-1537-9). This book shows that the media often unintentionally glamorize drug use and describes how teens can evaluate the media's mixed messages. (Rev: BL 6/1–15/94; SLJ 5/94) [070.4]

10955 Levine, Herbert M. *The Drug Problem* (7–12). Illus. Series: American Issues Debated. 1997, Raintree Steck-Vaughn $31.40 (0-8172-4354-2). The pros and cons of issues related to drugs are presented fairly, with discussion on the effectiveness of the war on drugs, decriminalizing drugs, and the possible discrimination against minorities in our drug policies. (Rev: BL 11/15/97; BR 1–2/98; VOYA 4/98) [362.2]

10956 Littell, Mary Ann. *Heroin Drug Dangers* (5–8). Series: Drug Dangers. 1999, Enslow LB $21.95 (0-7660-1156-9). A short, well-illustrated book that describes the physiological effects of heroin, the dangers of its use, and how to resist its temptations. (Rev: BL 9/15/99; HBG 3/00) [362.29]

10957 Littell, Mary Ann. *LSD* (6–9). Illus. Series: The Drug Library. 1996, Enslow LB $20.95 (0-89490-739-5). A history of the drug, details on how it is made, its different forms, and the physical and psychological effects of its use. (Rev: BL 12/1/96; BR 3–4/97; SLJ 4/97) [362.29]

10958 Lukas, Scott E. *Steroids* (7–10). Series: Drug Library. 1994, Enslow LB $20.95 (0-89490-471-X). An exploration of the physical, psychological, and legal consequences of using steroids. (Rev: BL 1/1/95; HBG 10/01; SLJ 1/95; VOYA 4/95) [362.29]

10959 McGuire, Paula. *Alcohol* (4–8). Illus. Series: Preteen Pressures. 1998, Raintree Steck-Vaughn LB $25.69 (0-8172-5026-3). Topics discussed in this practical account include peer pressure to drink, the physical effects of alcohol, underage drinking, alcoholic parents, and ways to seek help. (Rev: BL 4/15/98; HBG 10/98) [362.29]

10960 McLaughlin, Miriam S., and Sandra P. Hazouri. *Addiction: The "High" That Brings You Down* (7–12). Series: Teen Issues. 1997, Enslow LB $20.95 (0-89490-915-0). This honest, accurate book lists causes of addiction, characteristics, and the results of compulsive, uncontrolled behavior, with an emphasis on where teen addicts can find help and support at school and in the community. (Rev: SLJ 8/97; VOYA 10/97) [362.29]

10961 McMillan, Daniel. *Teen Smoking: Understanding the Risk* (6–12). Series: Issues in Focus. 1998, Enslow LB $20.95 (0-89490-722-0). An interesting, informative account that discusses nicotine addiction, secondhand smoke, health hazards, smoking prevention, and treatments for people who want to stop. (Rev: VOYA 8/98) [362.2]

10962 Madsen, Christine. *Drinking and Driving* (6–10). Illus. 1989, Watts paper $20.80 (0-531-10799-X). The effects of alcohol are outlined in relation to driving. Material on how society is penalizing drunk drivers is also presented. (Rev: SLJ 4/90) [613.8]

10963 Masline, Shelagh Ryan. *Drug Abuse and Teens* (6–12). Illus. Series: Hot Issues. 2000, Enslow LB $19.95 (0-7660-1372-3). A clear, straightforward account that describes different drugs, ways they are abused, and how one can get help for drug problems. (Rev: BL 11/15/00; HBG 3/01) [362.29]

10964 Meer, Jeff. *Drugs and Sports* (7–12). Illus. 1987, Chelsea LB $19.95 (1-55546-226-X). An account that explains how various drugs affect an athlete's performance and how this abuse is being viewed by segments of the athletic world. (Rev: BL 11/1/87) [613]

10965 Miller, Maryann. *Drugs and Date Rape* (6–10). Series: Drug Abuse Prevention Library. 1995, Rosen LB $17.95 (0-8239-2064-X). This book shows how drugs can break down important inhibitors, possibly leading to date rape, and how to avoid becoming a victim. (Rev: BL 9/15/95; SLJ 10/95) [362.88]

10966 Miller, Maryann. *Drugs and Gun Violence* (6–10). Series: Drug Abuse Prevention Library. 1995, Rosen LB $17.95 (0-8239-2060-7). This book explores the connection between violent crimes and drug use, with lessons that teens can use for survival. (Rev: BL 9/15/95; SLJ 10/95) [364.2]

10967 Miller, Maryann. *Drugs and Violent Crime* (6–10). Series: Drug Abuse Prevention Library. 1996, Rosen LB $17.95 (0-8239-2282-0). This book gives general information about drugs and their effects and explores the relationship between drug use and violent crime. (Rev: SLJ 3/97) [362.29]

10968 Mitchell, Hayley R. *Teen Alcoholism* (7–12). Illus. Series: Teen Issues. 1997, Lucent LB $27.45 (1-56006-514-1). This book defines alcoholism and explains its causes, prevention, symptoms, and recovery programs. (Rev: BL 2/1/98) [362.29]

10969 Monroe, Judy. *Antidepressants* (7–10). Series: The Drug Library. 1997, Enslow LB $20.95 (0-89490-848-0). Current information is given about these frequently abused drugs, actual case studies are cited, and discussion questions provided. (Rev: BL 5/15/97) [616.85]

10970 Monroe, Judy. *Inhalant Drug Dangers* (5–9). 1999, Enslow LB $21.95 (0-7660-1153-4). Using case histories — such as the story of Ian, who is addicted to inhaling fabric protector — this slim volume tells of the effects and dangers of inhalants. (Rev: BL 8/99; HBG 10/99; SLJ 9/99) [362.29]

10971 Monroe, Judy. *Nicotine* (7–10). Series: Drug Library. 1995, Enslow LB $20.95 (0-89490-505-8). This provides a concise, easy-to-use look at nicotine, where it is found, its effects, and how to avoid its use. (Rev: BL 7/95; SLJ 9/95) [613.85]

10972 Monroe, Judy. *Steroid Drug Dangers* (5–8). Illus. Series: Drug Dangers. 1999, Enslow LB $21.95 (0-7660-1154-2). Case histories, facts, and statistics introduce the reader to steroid drugs and their legal and illegal uses, their effects and dangers, and the organizations that promote safe usage. (Rev: BL 9/15/99; HBG 3/00) [362.29]

10973 Murdico, Suzanne J. *Drug Abuse* (4–8). Series: Preteen Pressures. 1998, Raintree Steck-Vaughn LB $25.69 (0-8172-5027-1). This work discusses drug abuse, with emphasis on healthy alternatives and solutions to typical drug-related problems faced by many young people. (Rev: BL 5/15/98; HBG 10/98) [362.2]

10974 Myers, Arthur. *Drugs and Emotions* (6–10). Series: Drug Abuse Prevention Library. 1996, Rosen LB $17.95 (0-8239-2283-9). This book explains how teens may be attracted to drugs as a way of dealing with feelings of sadness, pain, confusion, and frustration, and how they can become hooked to both legal and illegal drugs. Much of the discussion deals with how to recognize that a problem exists and where to get help. (Rev: SLJ 3/97) [362.29]

10975 Myers, Arthur. *Drugs and Peer Pressure* (6–10). Series: Drug Abuse Prevention Library. 1995, Rosen LB $17.95 (0-8239-2066-6). An exploration of peer pressure as a major reason that teens begin to use drugs, with suggestions for resisting it. (Rev: BL 9/15/95; SLJ 10/95) [362.29]

10976 Newman, Gerald, and Eleanor N. Layfield. *PCP* (7–10). Series: Drug Library. 1997, Enslow LB $20.95 (0-89490-852-9). Case studies, discussion questions, and chapter notes are highlights of this informative book on PCP, a frequently abused drug. (Rev: BL 12/15/97; BR 3–4/98; HBG 3/98; SLJ 12/97) [362.2]

10977 Newton, David E. *Drug Testing: An Issue for School, Sports and Work* (6–12). Illus. Series: In Focus. 1999, Enslow LB $20.95 (0-89490-954-1). The question of civil rights vs. drug testing is explored in this volume that presents extreme positions and viewpoints in between. (Rev: BL 4/1/99; BR 5–6/99; SLJ 4/99) [658.3]

10978 Ojeda, Auriana, ed. *Smoking* (8–12). Series: Current Controversies. 2002, Gale LB $31.20 (0-

7377-0857-3); paper $19.95 (0-7377-0856-5). A collection of writings that presents both sides of the debates on the controversial aspects of smoking — the provable health risks, the influence of advertising on young smokers, and so forth. (Rev: BL 7/02) [363.4]

10979 Packard, Helen C. *Prozac: The Controversial Cure* (6–9). Illus. Series: Drug Abuse Prevention Library. 1998, Rosen LB $17.95 (0-8239-2551-X). This book explores the controversy around this antidepressant, called the miracle drug of the 1990s, and gives teens sound advice concerning its use and misuse. (Rev: BL 5/15/98; SLJ 10/98) [616.8527061]

10980 Packer, Alex J. *Highs! Over 150 Ways to Feel Really, REALLY Good . . . Without Alcohol or Other Drugs* (6–12). Illus. 2000, Free Spirit paper $14.95 (1-57542-074-0). Grouped into three areas (serenity, physical improvement, and creativity), the author describes 150 ways by which teenagers can feel good about themselves. (Rev: BL 11/1/00; BR 11–12/00; SLJ 9/00) [158]

10981 Pringle, Laurence. *Drinking: A Risky Business* (6–9). Illus. 1997, Morrow $16.00 (0-688-15044-6). A well-documented book about the toll that alcohol has taken on society over the years, its pervasiveness, and how alcohol peddling is a big business. (Rev: BL 12/15/97; BR 3–4/98; SLJ 1/98) [362.292]

10982 Pringle, Laurence. *Smoking: A Risky Business* (5–10). 1996, Morrow $16.00 (0-688-13039-9). After a history of tobacco, this book describes the dangers of smoking and the advertising strategies used to get people to smoke. (Rev: BL 12/1/96; SLJ 1/97; VOYA 4/97) [362.2]

10983 Richard, Pamela G. *Alcohol* (7–9). Series: Just the Facts. 2000, Heinemann LB $22.79 (1-57572-253-4). This account gives a history of alcohol use, how it affects the body and the brain, and treatments available for people who become addicted. (Rev: BL 3/1/01) [613.8]

10984 Robbins, Paul R. *Crack and Cocaine Drug Dangers* (5–9). Series: Drug Dangers. 1999, Enslow LB $21.95 (0-7660-1155-0). Charts, photographs, fact boxes, and a succinct text are used to discuss crack cocaine, its effects, and how to avoid its use. (Rev: BL 9/15/99; HBG 3/00) [362.29]

10985 Robbins, Paul R. *Designer Drugs* (7–12). Series: Drug Library. 1995, Enslow LB $20.95 (0-89490-488-4). An exploration of the growing problem of drugs made by "kitchen chemists." (Rev: BL 5/1/95; SLJ 5/95) [362.29]

10986 Robbins, Paul R. *Hallucinogens* (7–10). Illus. Series: Drug Library. 1996, Enslow LB $20.95 (0-89490-743-3). Drugs that cause auditory and visual hallucinations are described, along with their availability, dangerous effects, and current use. (Rev: BL 6/1–15/96; SLJ 7/96; VOYA 8/96) [362.29]

10987 Rogak, Lisa A. *Steroids: Dangerous Game* (6–9). 1992, Lerner LB $19.95 (0-8225-0048-5). Discusses what steroids are and why they are so dangerous physically and psychologically. Covers drug testing, use of steroids in sports, and tips for training without them. (Rev: BL 2/15/93; SLJ 12/92) [362.29]

10988 Roleff, Tamara L., and Mary Williams, eds. *Tobacco and Smoking* (8–12). Series: Opposing Viewpoints. 1998, Greenhaven LB $32.45 (1-56510-803-5); paper $21.20 (1-56510-802-7). This anthology presents different opinions on such topics as the health effects of smoking, the influence of tobacco advertising, government intervention, and possible controls on the tobacco industry. (Rev: BL 6/1–15/98) [613.8]

10989 Salak, John. *Drugs in Society: Are They Our Suicide Pill?* (6–9). Series: Issues of Our Time. 1993, Twenty-First Century LB $22.90 (0-8050-2572-3). Current opinions and treatments for drug addiction are discussed in this easily read book that examines how common drugs of all types are used and abused in our society. (Rev: BL 1/15/94; SLJ 2/94) [362.29]

10990 Sanders, Pete. *Smoking* (4–7). Illus. Series: What Do You Know About. 1996, Millbrook LB $23.90 (0-7613-0536-X). Covers the effects of smoking and ways in which youngsters can avoid getting hooked. (Rev: SLJ 3/97) [362.2]

10991 Sanders, Pete, and Steve Myers. *Drinking Alcohol* (4–8). Illus. Series: What Do You Know About. 1997, Millbrook LB $23.90 (0-7613-0573-4). An introduction to alcohol use and abuse, with material on how alcohol affects the body and behavior. (Rev: SLJ 10/97) [613.8]

10992 Santamaria, Peggy. *Drugs and Politics* (6–10). Series: Drug Abuse Prevention Library. 1994, Rosen LB $17.95 (0-8239-1703-7). A discussion of the influence of drugs on politics, such as in Colombia, where the government is involved with and intimidated by powerful drug interests. (Rev: BL 3/15/95; SLJ 3/95) [363.4]

10993 Schleichert, Elizabeth. *Marijuana* (7–10). Illus. Series: Drug Library. 1996, Enslow LB $20.95 (0-89490-740-9). This easy-to-read account discusses the history of marijuana use, its effects, availability, and controversies surrounding it, such as whether to legalize it. (Rev: BL 6/1–15/96; SLJ 7/96; VOYA 8/96) [362.29]

10994 Schleifer, Jay. *Methamphetamine: Speed Kills* (5–9). Series: Drug Abuse Prevention Library. 1999, Rosen LB $17.95 (0-8239-2512-9). An introduction to this drug, its effects, the crime and violence associated with it, and agencies and organizations where help is available. (Rev: SLJ 7/99; VOYA 4/00) [362.29]

10995 Schnoll, Sidney. *Getting Help: Treatments for Drug Abuse* (7–12). Illus. 1986, Chelsea LB $19.95 (0-87754-775-0). This book concentrates on the many kinds of treatments available and the agencies involved in supplying this help. (Rev: BL 2/15/87) [362.2]

10996 Serry, Clifford. *Drugs and Eating Disorders* (5–10). Illus. Series: Drug Abuse Prevention Library. 1994, Rosen LB $17.95 (0-8239-1540-9). The book shows how diet pills and other weight-loss products can lead to drug abuse and, in some cases, addiction. (Rev: BL 6/1–15/94; SLJ 6/94) [616.85]

10997 Sherry, Clifford J. *Inhalants* (5–10). 1994, Rosen LB $17.95 (0-8239-1704-5). Definitions of inhalants are given, where they are found, and how they affect the body. (Rev: BL 2/15/95; SLJ 3/95) [362.29]

10998 Shuker, Nancy. *Everything You Need to Know About an Alcoholic Parent*. Rev. ed. (7–12). Illus. 1998, Rosen LB $30.35 (0-8239-2869-1). After a general discussion of alcoholism, Shuker explains how it changes human relationships and how young people can cope with it. (Rev: BL 1/15/90; BR 3–4/90; VOYA 4/90) [362.29]

10999 Silverstein, Alvin, and Virginia Silverstein. *Alcoholism* (7–10). 1975, HarperCollins LB $12.89 (0-397-31648-8). Alcohol use and abuse are introduced, plus alcoholism and the problems it causes. [613.8]

11000 Simpson, Carolyn. *Methadone* (5–9). Series: Drug Abuse Prevention Library. 1997, Rosen LB $17.95 (0-8239-2286-3). The dangers of heroin are discussed, followed by an objective discussion of the pros and cons of methadone, the legal drug used to combat heroin addiction. (Rev: SLJ 11/97) [362.29]

11001 Somdahl, Gary L. *Marijuana Drug Dangers* (5–8). Series: Drug Dangers. 1999, Enslow LB $21.95 (0-7660-1214-X). After introducing marijuana and its effects, this account covers its misuse and abuse and ways to resist it. (Rev: BL 11/15/99; HBG 3/00) [362.29]

11002 Steffens, Bradley. *Addiction: Distinguishing Between Fact and Opinion* (5–7). Illus. Series: Opposing Viewpoints Juniors. 1994, Greenhaven LB $22.45 (1-56510-094-8). Critical thinking is encouraged by having the reader study a variety of attitudes and opinions about addiction. (Rev: BL 1/1/94) [362.29]

11003 Stewart, Gail B., ed. *Drugs and Sports* (7–10). Series: Opposing Viewpoints Digests. 1998, Greenhaven LB $27.45 (1-56510-749-7); paper $17.45 (1-56510-748-9). Covering topics including the prevention and prevalence of drug use and abuse, and the legitimacy of drug testing, this volume explores drugs in both amateur and professional sports. (Rev: BL 8/98) [362.29]

11004 Stewart, Gail B. *Teen Addicts* (7–12). Illus. Series: Other America. 1999, Lucent LB $18.96 (1-56006-574-5). Four teenage drug addicts of different backgrounds share their stories. (Rev: BL 11/15/99; HBG 9/00) [362.29]

11005 Stewart, Gail B. *Teen Alcoholics* (6–12). Illus. Series: Other America. 1999, Lucent LB $18.96 (1-56006-606-7). This book focuses on case studies of four teenage alcoholics, how and why they began drinking, and how they are handing their addiction. (Rev: BL 3/15/00; HBG 9/00; SLJ 1/00) [362.292.]

11006 Strazzabosco-Hayn, Gina. *Drugs and Sleeping Disorders* (7–12). Series: Drug Abuse Prevention Library. 1996, Rosen LB $17.95 (0-8239-2144-1). This book describes sleep disorders and potential problems and dangers of using drugs for sleep. (Rev: SLJ 3/96) [362.2]

11007 Thompson, Stephen P., ed. *War on Drugs* (7–12). Series: Opposing Viewpoints. 1998, Greenhaven LB $32.45 (1-56510-805-1). In this anthology of various opinions, questions are raised about the techniques used in the war against drugs, the nature of new strategies, and whether some drugs, particularly marijuana, should be legalized under certain conditions. (Rev: BL 7/98) [363.4]

11008 Torr, James D., ed. *Alcoholism* (6–12). Series: Current Controversies. 2000, Greenhaven LB $21.96 (0-7377-0139-0); paper $13.96 (0-7377-0138-2). Various viewpoints on the causes and treatments and on the alcohol industry are voiced in this valuable collection of primary sources about alcoholism. (Rev: BL 4/1/00) [362.292.]

11009 Torr, James D., ed. *Drug Abuse* (8–12). Series: Opposing Viewpoints. 1999, Greenhaven LB $32.45 (0-7377-0051-3); paper $21.20 (0-7377-0050-5). This collection of articles and essays debates such topics as how serious the nation's drug problem is, what programs are effective, the value of government policies, and the legalization of selected drugs. (Rev: BL 4/15/99) [362.29]

11010 Torr, James D., ed. *Teens and Alcohol* (6–12). Series: Current Controversies. 2001, Gale LB $31.20 (0-7377-0859-X); paper $19.95 (0-7377-0858-1). A thought-provoking collection of essays on alcohol, drunk driving, health, the media, and the law that will be equally useful for report writers and the interested reader. (Rev: BL 5/1/02) [362.292]

11011 Trapani, Margi. *Inside a Support Group: Help for Teenage Children of Alcoholics* (6–9). Illus. Series: Drug Abuse Prevention Library. 1997, Rosen LB $17.95 (0-8239-2508-0). Teens with alcoholic parents get helpful information from this inside look at Alateen, an organization designed to help teens cope with a loved one's addiction to alcohol. (Rev: BL 12/15/97; SLJ 1/98) [362.292]

11012 Washburne, Carolyn K. *Drug Abuse* (5–8). Illus. Series: Overview. 1996, Lucent LB $27.45 (1-56006-169-3). A carefully researched account that gives important background information on drug abuse and present-day practices and problems. (Rev: BL 1/1–15/96; VOYA 8/96) [362.29]

11013 Wax, Wendy. *Say No and Know Why: Kids Learn About Drugs* (4–7). 1992, Walker LB $13.85 (0-8027-8141-1). A serious look at drug problems as a 6th-grade class in the Bronx, New York, gets a visit from a local nurse and an assistant district attorney. (Rev: BL 1/15/93; SLJ 10/92) [362.29]

11014 Webb, Margot. *Drugs and Gangs* (7–12). Series: Drug Abuse Prevention Library. 1996, Rosen LB $17.95 (0-8239-2059-3). This book describes the connections between gangs and drugs, in both selling and using, and provides teens with tips on how to avoid these dangers. (Rev: SLJ 3/96; VOYA 6/96) [362.29]

11015 Weitzman, Elizabeth. *Let's Talk About Smoking* (4–8). Illus. Series: Let's Talk. 1996, Rosen LB $17.25 (0-8239-2307-X). This book explains why people smoke, its effects, and ways to avoid starting, with tips on how to give up. (Rev: BL 3/15/97; SLJ 1/97) [362.29]

11016 Wekesser, Carol, ed. *Chemical Dependency* (8–12). Illus. Series: Opposing Viewpoints. 1997, Greenhaven paper $21.20 (1-56510-551-6). Such topics as the magnitude of chemical dependency, the causes, treatments, and the possible reforming of drug laws are discussed in this collection of articles. (Rev: BL 7/97; BR 1–2/98) [362.29]

11017 Wekesser, Carol, ed. *Smoking* (8–12). Series: At Issue. 1999, Greenhaven LB $21.96 (0-7377-0157-9); paper $13.96 (0-7377-0156-0). From many perspectives including government reports, eyewitness accounts, and scientific journal articles, a wide range of opinions on smoking is explored. (Rev: BL 11/15/99) [362.2]

11018 Wekesser, Carol, ed. *Smoking* (7–12). Series: Current Controversies. 1996, Greenhaven LB $32.45 (1-56510-534-6); paper $21.20 (1-56510-533-8). This collection of various opinions about smoking covers health risks, the amount of blame that tobacco companies should assume, measures to combat smoking, and the degree that the government can interfere. (Rev: BL 12/15/96; BR 11–12/97; SLJ 3/97) [362.29]

11019 Westcott, Patsy. *Why Do People Take Drugs?* (5–7). Series: Exploring Tough Issues. 2001, Raintree Steck-Vaughn LB $25.69 (0-7398-3231-X). Drugs from caffeine to cocaine are explored, with discussion of society's attitudes toward drugs, legal issues, and the reasons some people are more tempted to abuse substances. (Rev: HBG 10/01; SLJ 7/01) [362.29]

11020 Wilkinson, Beth. *Drugs and Depression* (6–12). Illus. Series: Drug Abuse Prevention Library. 1994, Rosen LB $30.35 (0-8239-3004-1). Some young people turn to drugs to deal with their depression. This book shows the dangers in this approach and offers positive ways of handling depression and places to get assistance. (Rev: BL 6/1–15/94) [616.86]

11021 Winters, Paul A., ed. *Teen Addiction* (7–12). Series: Current Controversies. 1997, Greenhaven LB $32.45 (1-56510-536-2). The causes, effects, prevention, and regulation of teenage drug, tobacco, and alcohol consumption are explored in a series of documents expressing different opinions. (Rev: BL 2/15/97; SLJ 3/97) [362.29]

11022 Woods, Geraldine. *Heroin* (7–10). Series: Drug Library. 1994, Enslow LB $20.95 (0-89490-473-6). A well-researched, clearly written, and carefully sourced book about heroin use and addiction. (Rev: BL 1/1/95; SLJ 1/95; VOYA 4/95) [362.29]

11023 Ziemer, Maryann. *Quaaludes* (7–10). Illus. Series: Drug Library. 1997, Enslow LB $20.95 (0-89490-847-2). The uses and effects of these frequently prescribed drugs are discussed, along with problems of misuse and addiction. (Rev: BL 3/15/97; SLJ 6/97) [613.8]

Bionics and Transplants

11024 Beecroft, Simon. *Super Humans: A Beginner's Guide to Bionics* (5–7). Series: Future Files. 1998, Millbrook LB $23.40 (0-7613-0621-8). This work explores such futuristic topics as cloning humans, gene manipulation, electronic body parts, and life extension. (Rev: HBG 10/98; SLJ 10/98) [617.9]

11025 Fullick, Ann. *Rebuilding the Body* (5–8). Illus. Series: Science at the Edge. 2002, Heinemann LB $27.86 (1-58810-700-0). An insightful volume about transplant procedures, including a section on how the organs of the body function and a discussion about ethics. (Rev: BL 10/15/02; HBG 3/03; SLJ 4/03) [617.9]

11026 McClellan, Marilyn. *Organ and Tissue Transplants: Medical Miracles and Challenges* (7–12). Series: Issues in Focus. 2003, Enslow LB $20.95 (0-7660-1943-8). The story of a critically injured teen draws readers into this discussion of transplants of organs and tissues and the ethical issues involved. (Rev: HBG 10/03; SLJ 5/03) [617.9]

11027 Murphy, Wendy. *Spare Parts: From Peg Legs to Gene Splices* (6–12). Illus. 2001, Twenty-First Century LB $23.90 (0-7613-1355-9). A history of medical advances that acknowledges the role of war in the development of increasingly advanced designs, with the moving story of one boy's anguish. (Rev: BCCB 3/01; BL 3/15/01; HBG 10/01) [617.9]

11028 Rosaler, Maxine. *Bionics* (5–9). Series: Science on the Edge. 2003, Gale LB $20.95 (1-56711-784-8). This account explores the science of fusing artificial parts with human parts to aid body functions and comments on the controversy surround this new science. (Rev: BL 10/15/03) [174]

11029 Torr, James D., ed. *Organ Transplants* (6–12). Series: At Issue. 2002, Gale $20.96 (0-7377-1162-0); paper $13.96 (0-7377-1161-2). Contributors examine the positive and negative issues related to transplanting organs. (Rev: BL 1/1–15/03) [174]

Diseases and Illnesses

11030 Aaseng, Nathan. *Multiple Sclerosis* (7–10). Illus. 2000, Watts LB $25.00 (0-531-11531-3). Annette Funicello's experiences with MS draw teens into this study of this neurological disease and its symptoms, diagnosis, and treatment. (Rev: BL 7/00; SLJ 6/00) [616.8]

11031 Abramovitz, Melissa. *Leukemia* (5–8). Illus. Series: Diseases and Disorders. 2002, Gale LB $27.45 (1-56006-863-9). A look at the different types of leukemia, the possible causes, diagnosis, treatment, and the serious nature of the disease. (Rev: SLJ 3/03) [616.99419]

11032 Abrams, Liesa. *Chronic Fatigue Syndrome* (5–7). Illus. Series: Diseases and Disorders. 2003, Gale LB $27.45 (1-59018-039-9). The symptoms of and treatments for this mysterious condition and related medical problems are covered here, along with the research being undertaken. (Rev: SLJ 7/03) [616]

11033 Akers, Charlene. *Obesity* (7–12). Illus. 2000, Lucent $27.45 (1-56006-662-8). A look at obesity and its physiological, psychological, and sociological impact, with assessments of various treatment options. (Rev: HBG 3/01; SLJ 9/00) [616.3]

11034 Altman, Linda J. *Plague and Pestilence: A History of Infectious Disease* (6–12). Illus. Series: Issues in Focus. 1998, Enslow LB $20.95 (0-89490-957-6). A history of plagues and epidemics in world history, from the Black Death and leprosy to AIDS and spinal meningitis. (Rev: BL 3/1/99; HBG 3/99; SLJ 1/99) [614.4]

11035 Altman, Linda Jacobs. *Alzheimer's Disease* (7–9). Series: Diseases and Disorders. 2001, Lucent LB $19.96 (1-56006-695-4). In clear, concise prose, this account explains what Alzheimer's disease is, traces its causes, and gives current information on treatments. (Rev: BL 1/1–15/02) [616.8]

11036 Aronson, Virginia. *The Influenza Pandemic of 1918* (7–12). Illus. Series: Great Disasters: Reforms and Ramifications. 2000, Chelsea $21.95 (0-7910-5263-X). This detailed look at the deadly flu of 1918 serves as a reminder that modern travel makes such an event even more likely. (Rev: BL 10/15/00; HBG 3/01; SLJ 11/00; VOYA 2/01) [614.5]

11037 Benowitz, Steven I. *Cancer* (7–12). Series: Diseases and People. 1999, Enslow LB $20.95 (0-7660-1181-X). A discussion of the nature and treatment of various forms of cancer and of possible cures in the future. (Rev: BL 9/15/99; HBG 4/00) [616.994]

11038 Beshore, George. *Sickle Cell Anemia* (7–12). 1994, Watts LB $18.95 (0-531-12510-6). An informative overview that includes a history of the disease, how it is transmitted from parent to child, and the importance of genetic testing. (Rev: BL 1/1/95; SLJ 1/95; VOYA 4/95) [616.1]

11039 Biskup, Michael D., and Karin L. Swisher, eds. *AIDS* (7–12). Series: Opposing Viewpoints. 1992, Greenhaven paper $16.20 (0-89908-165-7). The ethical questions surrounding AIDS are discussed, along with the effectiveness of testing and treatment, and the prevention of the disease's spread. (Rev: BL 11/15/92) [362.1]

11040 Bode, Janet. *Food Fight: A Guide to Eating Disorders for Pre-teens and Their Parents* (5–10). 1997, Simon & Schuster $16.00 (0-689-80272-2). A clearly written account of the physical, psychological, and social aspects of anorexia and bulimia, plus practical suggestions for help. (Rev: BL 6/1–15/97; BR 11–12/97; HB 1–2/97; SLJ 8/97*; VOYA 8/97) [618.92]

11041 Bowman-Kruhm, Mary. *Everything You Need to Know About Down Syndrome* (4–7). Series: Need to Know Library. 2000, Rosen LB $25.25 (0-8239-2949-3). Describes the causes, symptoms, and treatment of Down syndrome, and looks at the education and family life of individuals with this condition. (Rev: HBG 10/00; SLJ 3/00) [362.1]

11042 Brill, Marlene Targ. *Tourette Syndrome* (6–12). Illus. Series: Twenty-First Century Medical Library. 2002, Millbrook LB $24.90 (0-7613-2101-2). This volume provides historical and medical information on the disorder named for neurologist Georges Gilles de la Tourette, presenting the stories of three teenagers who suffer from it. (Rev: BL 3/1/02; HBG 10/02; SLJ 4/02) [375]

11043 Brodman, Michael, et al. *Straight Talk About Sexually Transmitted Diseases* (7–12). Series: Straight Talk. 1993, Facts on File $19.95 (0-8160-2864-8). Discusses the ways sexually transmitted diseases are contracted, symptoms, possible consequences, and treatment. (Rev: BL 3/15/94; SLJ 6/94) [616.95]

11044 Bryan, Jenny. *Eating Disorders* (6–10). Series: Talking Points. 1999, Raintree Steck-Vaughn LB $18.98 (0-8172-5321-1). Statistics and quotations from experts are used in this book that introduces various eating disorders, their causes, and treatments. (Rev: BL 12/15/99; HBG 9/00) [616.85]

11045 Burby, Liza N. *Bulimia Nervosa: The Secret Cycle of Bingeing and Purging* (6–10). Series: Teen Health Library of Eating Disorder Prevention. 1998, Rosen LB $26.50 (0-8239-2762-8). Bulimia is an eating disorder characterized by bingeing and purging. This book describes various eating disorders, then focuses on bulimia, its causes, physical and psychological effects, the roles of peer pressure, media images, family relationships, and genetics, and treatment and recovery. (Rev: BR 5–6/99; SLJ 1/99) [616.85]

11046 Byers, Ann. *Sexually Transmitted Diseases* (6–9). Illus. Series: Hot Issues. 1999, Enslow LB $19.95 (0-7660-1192-5). As well as a description of various sexually transmitted diseases, this work discusses transmission, symptoms, treatment, and risks. (Rev: BL 4/1/00; HBG 4/00) [616.95.]

11047 Carson, Mary Kay. *Epilepsy* (7–12). Series: Diseases and People. 1998, Enslow LB $20.95 (0-7660-1049-X). This book describes the causes of epilepsy, gives a history of society's attitude toward epileptics, and describes current treatments and drugs used to control it. (Rev: BL 7/98; BR 1–2/99; SLJ 9/98; VOYA 2/99) [616.8]

11048 Cefrey, Holly. *Coping with Cancer* (6–12). Illus. Series: Coping. 2000, Rosen LB $25.25 (0-8239-2849-7). As well as discussing how cancer develops in various parts of the body, this book gives self-help advice for anyone who is diagnosed with the disease. (Rev: BL 1/1–15/01; SLJ 12/00) [616.99]

11049 Cefrey, Holly. *Syphilis and Other Sexually Transmitted Diseases* (5–8). Illus. Series: Epidemics. 2001, Rosen LB $19.95 (0-8239-3488-8). Cefrey describes historic outbreaks and treatments, as well as the symptoms and cure, of syphilis and other sexually transmitted diseases. (Rev: BL 3/15/02) [616.95]

11050 Cefrey, Holly. *Yellow Fever* (5–8). Series: Epidemics. 2002, Rosen LB $19.95 (0-8239-3489-6). Yellow fever, spread by mosquitoes, was the cause of several epidemics in American cities during the 19th century before a cure was found by dedicated doctors who risked their lives. (Rev: BL 8/02) [616]

11051 Check, William A. *AIDS* (8–12). Illus. Series: Encyclopedia of Health. 1999, Chelsea LB $24.95 (0-7910-4885-3). This updated and revised edition gives a history of the AIDS epidemic, the latest information on breakthrough HIV treatment meth-ods, and advice on how to avoid contracting the disease. (Rev: BL 8/98; SLJ 9/98) [616.9]

11052 Chiu, Christina. *Eating Disorder Survivors Tell Their Stories* (7–12). Series: Teen Health Library of Eating Disorder Prevention. 1998, Rosen LB $26.50 (0-8239-2767-9); Hazelden Information & Educational Services paper $6.95 (1-56838-259-6). In candid interviews, survivors of eating disorders share their experiences, treatments, and roads to recovery, and offer advice to other teens who might need help. (Rev: BL 3/1/99; BR 5–6/99; SLJ 1/99; VOYA 4/99) [616.85]

11053 Cotter, Alison. *Anorexia and Bulimia* (7–9). Series: Diseases and Disorders. 2001, Lucent LB $19.96 (1-56006-725-X). Various eating disorders are defined with material on causes, treatments, and how to live with them. (Rev: BL 1/1–15/02) [618.92]

11054 Crisfield, Deborah. *Eating Disorders* (6–9). 1994, Macmillan paper $4.95 (0-382-24756-6). A look at psychological/behavioral disorders including anorexia nervosa, bulimia, and overeating. (Rev: BL 3/1/95; SLJ 3/95) [616.85]

11055 Curran, Christine Perdan. *Sexually Transmitted Diseases* (7–12). 1998, Enslow LB $20.95 (0-7660-1050-3). This work discusses various kinds of sexually transmitted diseases, including those that are bacterial, like syphilis, those that are viral, like HIV, and those that are neither, like scabies and pubic lice. (Rev: BL 12/15/98; VOYA 2/99) [616.95]

11056 Daugirdas, John T. *S.T.D. Sexually Transmitted Diseases, Including HIV/AIDS.* 3rd ed. (8–12). 1992, MedText $14.95 (0-9629279-1-0). This overview simplifies the language and prunes unnecessary medical terminology. (Rev: BL 10/1/92; SLJ 11/92) [616.951]

11057 Day, Nancy. *Killer Superbugs: The Story of Drug-Resistant Diseases* (6–9). Illus. Series: Issues in Focus. 2001, Enslow LB $20.95 (0-7660-1588-2). Day examines the factors that have led to the development of "superbugs," the role of antibiotics in the fight against disease, and the potential use of bacteria as weapons. (Rev: HBG 10/02; SLJ 1/02) [616]

11058 Donnellan, William L. *The Miracle of Immunity* (5–8). Illus. Series: The Story of Science. 2002, Benchmark LB $19.95 (0-7614-1425-8). A history of mankind's discoveries about diseases and about the body's vulnerabilities and abilities to fend off infections, from the earliest times through AIDS. (Rev: HBG 3/03; LMC 4–5/03; SLJ 5/03) [616.07]

11059 Donnelly, Karen. *Coping with Lyme Disease* (6–12). Series: Coping. 2001, Rosen LB $18.95 (0-8239-3199-4). This introduction to the symptoms, diagnosis, treatment, and prevention of Lyme disease includes personal stories. (Rev: SLJ 7/01) [616.9]

11060 Donnelly, Karen. *Everything You Need to Know About Lyme Disease* (5–8). Illus. Series: Need to Know Library. 2000, Rosen LB $25.25 (0-8239-3216-8). This book explains how Lyme disease was discovered, how it is transmitted, its symptoms, and its treatments. (Rev: BL 12/1/00) [616.9]

11061 Donnelly, Karen. *Leprosy (Hansen's Disease)* (5–8). Series: Epidemics. 2002, Rosen LB $19.95 (0-8239-3498-5). This is the story of leprosy, the disease that created social outcasts of its victims, and of a man named Hansen who discovered an effective treatment. (Rev: BL 8/02) [616.9]

11062 Draper, Allison Stark. *Ebola* (5–8). Illus. Series: Epidemics. 2002, Rosen LB $19.95 (0-8239-3496-9). Discusses the Ebola virus in both scientific and human terms. Also use *Mad Cow Disease* (2002). (Rev: BL 8/02; SLJ 6/02) [616.9]

11063 Dudley, William, ed. *Epidemics* (8–12). Series: Opposing Viewpoints. 1998, Greenhaven LB $32.45 (1-56510-941-4). Topics covered in this anthology of different points of view include the threat of infectious diseases, the AIDS epidemic, vaccination programs, and the prevention of food-borne illnesses. (Rev: BL 11/15/98) [616.9]

11064 Edelson, Edward. *Allergies* (7–12). Illus. 1989, Chelsea LB $19.95 (0-7910-0055-9). Various types of allergies are described, including their effects and treatments that have been found to help sufferers. (Rev: BL 9/1/89; BR 11–12/89; SLJ 12/89) [616.97]

11065 Edelson, Edward. *The Immune System* (6–12). Illus. Series: 21st Century Health and Wellness. 2000, Chelsea LB $24.95 (0-7910-5525-6). A revised edition of Edelson's presentation on the immune system and what happens when it fails to function. (Rev: BL 4/15/00; BR 5–6/00; HBG 9/00; SLJ 6/00) [616.07]

11066 Eisenpreis, Bettijane. *Coping with Scoliosis* (7–10). Series: Coping. 1999, Rosen LB $25.25 (0-8239-2557-9). The author explores the physical and emotional issues involved in the diagnosis and treatment of scoliosis, curvature of the spine, using scientific explanations and firsthand accounts. (Rev: SLJ 5/99) [616]

11067 Epstein, Rachel. *Eating Habits and Disorders* (7–12). Illus. 1990, Chelsea LB $19.95 (0-7910-0048-6). A little history on eating disorders is given, but the major focus of this book is on the kinds of eating disorders and their treatments. (Rev: BL 6/1/90; SLJ 8/90) [616.85]

11068 Erlanger, Ellen. *Eating Disorders: A Question and Answer Book About Anorexia Nervosa and Bulimia Nervosa* (6–8). Illus. 1988, Lerner LB $19.93 (0-8225-0038-8). Case studies are used to introduce the causes, symptoms, and treatment of these disorders. (Rev: BL 3/15/88; SLJ 4/88) [616.85]

11069 Farrell, Jeanette. *Invisible Enemies: Stories of Infectious Disease* (7–12). 1997, Farrar $17.00 (0-374-33637-7). This is a dramatic retelling of human reactions to such diseases as malaria, leprosy, tuberculosis, and AIDS, and of the medical breakthroughs associated with each. (Rev: BL 6/1–15/98; SLJ 7/98; VOYA 10/98) [616.909]

11070 Feldman, Douglas A., and Julia Wang Miller. *The AIDS Crisis: A Documentary History* (8–12). Series: Primary Documents in American History and Contemporary Issues. 1998, Greenwood LB $49.95 (0-313-28715-5). Beginning with the first medical report on AIDS in 1981, this is a fine collection of documents related to the disease and people involved with it. (Rev: BR 1–2/99; VOYA 2/99) [616]

11071 Fine, Judylaine. *Afraid to Ask: A Book About Cancer* (7–12). 1986, Lothrop paper $6.95 (0-688-06196-6). In this straightforward account about the nature, causes, and treatment of cancer, the author tries to minimize the fear and emotion surrounding the topic. (Rev: BL 3/1/86; BR 5–6/86; VOYA 8/86) [616.99]

11072 Flynn, Tom, and Karen Lound. *AIDS: Examining the Crisis* (7–12). 1995, Lerner LB $19.93 (0-8225-2625-5). An informative explanation in clear language about HIV and AIDS. (Rev: BL 5/1/95; SLJ 6/95) [362.1]

11073 Ford, Michael T. *100 Questions and Answers About AIDS: A Guide for Young People* (8–12). 1992, Macmillan LB $14.95 (0-02-735424-5). Answers to common queries that clarify background, distinguish misinformation, and guide readers toward safer behaviors. (Rev: BL 8/92; SLJ 1/93*) [616.97]

11074 Ford, Michael T. *The Voices of AIDS* (8–12). 1995, Morrow $15.00 (0-688-05322-X). Dedicated to getting the word out about AIDS, told by 12 men and women. (Rev: BL 8/95*; SLJ 11/95) [362.1]

11075 Frankenberger, Elizabeth. *Food and Love: Dealing with Family Attitudes About Weight* (7–12). Series: Teen Health Library of Eating Disorder Prevention. 1998, Rosen LB $26.50 (0-8239-2760-1). This book explores the role the family plays in developing a healthy self-image and affecting a teenager's attitudes toward food. (Rev: BR 5–6/99; VOYA 4/99) [616.85]

11076 Friedlander, Mark P. *Outbreak: Disease Detectives at Work*. Rev. ed. (6–9). Illus. Series: Discovery! 2002, Lerner LB $25.26 (0-8225-0948-2). Friedlander presents an overview of past and present epidemics and of the efforts on the part of public health workers to control them and find cures, and adds a discussion of bioterrorism. (Rev: HBG 10/03; SLJ 3/03; VOYA 6/03) [614.4]

11077 Friedlander, Mark P., and Terry M. Phillips. *The Immune System: Your Body's Disease-Fighting Army* (6–10). 1997, Lerner LB $23.93 (0-8225-2858-4). Topics included in this introduction to the immune system include the makeup of the immune system, how it reacts to invaders, vaccination, nutrition, allergies, disorders of the system, and medicines that help it. (Rev: BL 6/1–15/98) [616.079]

11078 Frissell, Susan, and Paula Harney. *Eating Disorders and Weight Control* (7–10). Illus. 1998, Enslow LB $17.95 (0-89490-919-3). This book covers anorexia, bulimia, binge eating disorders, and weight control issues with material on how to cope with them in a healthy, realistic manner. (Rev: BL 4/15/98; BR 5–6/98; HBG 9/98; SLJ 3/98) [616.85]

11079 Gay, Kathlyn, and Sean McGarrahan. *Epilepsy: The Ultimate Teen Guide* (7–12). Illus. Series: Ultimate Teen Guide. 2003, Scarecrow LB $32.50 (0-8108-4339-0). This informative look at this seizure disease and its impact on typical teen activities (sports, jobs, driving, and so forth) includes the personal experiences of coauthor McGarrahan, who was diagnosed with epilepsy at the age of 16. (Rev: BL 10/15/03; SLJ 10/03) [616.]

11080 Gedatus, Gustav Mark. *Mononucleosis* (7–12). Series: Perspectives on Disease and Illness. 1999, Capstone LB $16.95 (0-7368-0283-5). An introduction to this disease, its transmission, and possible treatments. (Rev: SLJ 4/00) [616.9]

11081 Gilman, Laura Anne. *Coping with Cerebral Palsy* (5–9). Series: Coping. 2001, Rosen LB $25.25 (0-8239-3150-1). This is a self-help book that looks at ways to deal with school, work, and travel as well as coping with other people and their attitudes. (Rev: SLJ 2/02) [616.836]

11082 Gold, Susan D. *Alzheimer's Disease* (4–7). Illus. Series: Health Watch. 1995, Silver Burdett LB $15.95 (0-89686-857-5). Using a case study as the focus, this account introduces Alzheimer's disease, its treatment, and current research. (Rev: BL 5/15/96; SLJ 1/96) [362.19]

11083 Gold, Susan Dudley. *Sickle Cell Disease* (4–7). Illus. Series: Health Watch. 2001, Enslow LB $18.95 (0-7660-1662-5). Readers are introduced to the symptoms and treatment of this disease through the true story of a young African American boy called Keone who received a successful stem-cell transplant. (Rev: HBG 3/02; SLJ 12/01) [616.1]

11084 Goldsmith, Connie. *Neurological Disorders* (6–10). Illus. Series: Amazing Brain. 2001, Blackbirch LB $21.95 (1-56711-422-9). Conditions such as Alzheimer's, autism, cerebral palsy, and schizophrenia are presented, with information on how the disease affects the brain and on the treatments available now. Also use *Addiction* (2001), which looks at the ways in which chemicals affect the brain and

induce dependency. (Rev: BL 10/15/01; HBG 3/02; SLJ 9/01; VOYA 10/01) [616.8]

11085 Goldstein, Margaret J. *Everything You Need to Know About Multiple Sclerosis* (5–8). Series: Need to Know Library. 2001, Rosen LB $25.25 (0-8239-3292-3). An introduction to multiple sclerosis, its symptoms and treatment, and how it affects the nervous system, along with information on the importance of treating the emotional impact of this disease. (Rev: SLJ 5/01) [616]

11086 Goodnough, David. *Eating Disorders: A Hot Issue* (5–8). Series: Hot Issues. 1999, Enslow LB $21.95 (0-7660-1336-7). This is a clear introduction to anorexia nervosa, bulimia, and binge eating with material and case studies on symptoms, causes, and consequences but little coverage of prevention and treatment. (Rev: HBG 3/00; SLJ 1/00) [618.92]

11087 Gravelle, Karen, and Bertram A. John. *Teenagers Face to Face with Cancer* (7–12). 1986, Messner paper $5.95 (0-671-65975-8). From the accounts of 16 young people ages 13 to 21, one discovers what it is like to live with cancer. (Rev: BL 1/15/87; SLJ 2/87) [618.92]

11088 Greenberg, Alissa. *Asthma* (6–12). Illus. 2000, Watts $25.00 (0-531-11331-0). In this thorough presentation on asthma, readers will learn about the history, treatment, and management of this illness that often attacks people in their youth. (Rev: BL 2/15/01; SLJ 3/01) [616.2]

11089 Harmon, Dan. *Anorexia Nervosa: Starving for Attention* (8–12). Series: Encyclopedia of Psychological Disorders. 1999, Chelsea $27.45 (0-7910-4901-9). Citing many case studies, some of prominent people, this work defines anorexia nervosa, discusses its causes and the physical consequences, and covers the treatments available. (Rev: VOYA 8/99) [616.85]

11090 Harmon, Dan. *Life out of Focus: Alzheimer's Disease and Related Disorders* (7–12). 1999, Chelsea $27.45 (0-7910-4896-9). This title demonstrates the devastating effect of Alzheimer's disease on sufferers and their caregivers, and provides biological and psychological explanations of the symptoms as well as solid data and analysis on research and various treatments. (Rev: BL 8/99) [616.8]

11091 Harris, Jacqueline. *Sickle Cell Disease* (6–10). 2001, Twenty-First Century LB $24.90 (0-7613-1459-8). After introducing three young victims of this disease, the author describes its symptoms and treatment and traces its history. (Rev: BL 9/15/01; HBG 3/02; SLJ 12/01) [616.1]

11092 Hawkins, Trisha. *Everything You Need to Know About Measles and Rubella* (4–8). Series: Need to Know Library. 2001, Rosen LB $25.25 (0-8239-3322-9). Simple text and photographs describe the diseases and methods of prevention and treatment, and discuss public-health issues. Also use

Everything You Need to Know About Chicken Pox and Shingles (2001). (Rev: SLJ 8/01) [616.9]

11093 Hayhurst, Chris. *Cholera* (5–9). Series: Epidemics. 2001, Rosen LB $26.50 (0-8239-3345-8). In a readable style, Hayhurst discusses the history of cholera, formerly a deadly disease, and explains how its treatment was developed. Also use *Polio* and *Smallpox* (both 2001). (Rev: SLJ 7/01) [616.9]

11094 Huegel, Kelly. *Young People and Chronic Illness: True Stories, Help, and Hope* (6–12). 1998, Free Spirit paper $14.95 (1-57542-041-4). After a series of case histories of young people suffering from such chronic illnesses as diabetes and asthma, this book discusses topics including getting support, coping with hospital stays, and planning for the future. (Rev: BL 11/15/98; SLJ 10/98; VOYA 2/99) [618.92]

11095 Hyde, Margaret O., and Elizabeth Forsyth. *AIDS: What Does It Mean to You?* Rev. ed. (6–10). 1995, Walker LB $15.85 (0-8027-8398-8). This book traces the process of infection and the progress of the disease in the body, along with material on its history, treatment, prevention, and worldwide statistics. (Rev: SLJ 3/96; VOYA 4/96) [616.97]

11096 Hyde, Margaret O., and Elizabeth Forsyth. *The Disease Book: A Kid's Guide* (5–8). Illus. 1997, Walker LB $17.85 (0-8027-8498-4). A simple, straightforward overview of the causes, symptoms, and treatments of more than 100 physical and mental diseases. (Rev: BL 9/15/97; BR 3–4/98; HBG 3/98; SLJ 11/97) [616]

11097 Isle, Mick. *Everything You Need to Know About Food Poisoning* (4–8). Illus. Series: Need to Know Library. 2001, Rosen LB $25.25 (0-8239-3396-2). Safe ways to prepare food are the main focus of this book, which also describes the symptoms and treatment of food poisoning. (Rev: SLJ 10/01) [615.954]

11098 Johannsson, Phillip. *Heart Disease* (7–12). Series: Diseases and People. 1998, Enslow LB $20.95 (0-7660-1051-1). The causes and types of heart disease are described, along with an overview of current treatments and potential future advances. (Rev: BL 7/98) [616.1]

11099 Kittredge, Mary. *The Common Cold* (7–12). Illus. Series: 21st Century Health and Wellness. 2000, Chelsea House LB $24.95 (0-7910-5985-5). An interesting history of cold cures introduces this overview of the causes, prevention, and treatment of this perennial nuisance. (Rev: BL 11/15/00; HBG 10/01; SLJ 3/01)

11100 Kittredge, Mary. *Teens with AIDS Speak Out* (8–12). 1992, Messner paper $8.95 (0-671-74543-3). Combines facts and interviews on AIDS, its history, transmission, treatment, and prevention, as well as safer-sex practices and discrimination against people with AIDS. (Rev: BL 6/1/92; SLJ 7/92) [362.1]

11101 Lamb, Kirsten. *Cancer* (5–8). Series: Health Issues. 2002, Raintree Steck-Vaughn LB $28.54 (0-7398-5219-1). An informative account that covers various kinds of cancer, giving real-life stories, and also deals with issues and choices facing teens today. (Rev: BL 12/15/02; HBG 3/03; SLJ 3/03) [616.99]

11102 Landau, Elaine. *Allergies* (4–7). Illus. Series: Understanding Illness. 1994, Twenty-First Century LB $24.90 (0-8050-2989-3). After a case history that explores allergies in personal terms, an objective presentation is given of their causes, effects, and treatment. (Rev: BL 12/15/94; SLJ 2/95) [616.97]

11103 Landau, Elaine. *Alzheimer's Disease* (7–12). Illus. Series: Venture: Health and the Human Body. 1996, Watts LB $25.00 (0-531-11268-3). Designed to help young people cope with having an Alzheimer's patient in the family, this book presents several case studies and discusses the cause, nature, and progression of the disease, various treatments, and what family members can do. (Rev: BL 10/15/96; SLJ 8/96) [362.1]

11104 Landau, Elaine. *Cancer* (4–7). Illus. Series: Understanding Illness. 1994, Twenty-First Century LB $24.90 (0-8050-2990-7). This book explains the many types of cancer, their causes, present-day treatments, and possible developments in the future. (Rev: BL 12/15/95; SLJ 2/95) [616.99]

11105 Landau, Elaine. *Epilepsy* (4–7). Illus. Series: Understanding Illness. 1994, Twenty-First Century LB $24.90 (0-8050-2991-5). Following the story of a youngster who has epilepsy, this account describes the disorder, its emotional and medical aspects, and treatments. (Rev: BL 12/15/94; SLJ 2/95) [616.8]

11106 Landau, Elaine. *Parkinson's Disease* (7–12). 1999, Watts LB $20.00 (0-531-11423-6). A well-organized overview that explains the various motor, emotional, and speech symptoms of Parkinson's, with material on the different treatments available and why some are controversial. (Rev: BL 7/99; SLJ 6/99) [616.8]

11107 Landau, Elaine. *Tourette's Syndrome* (6–12). Series: Venture: Health and the Human Body. 1998, Watts LB $20.00 (0-531-11399-X). Tourette's syndrome is a neurological condition involving uncontrollable verbalization and involuntary tics. This book explains its causes and treatments and gives profiles of many people, some of them famous, who are afflicted. (Rev: BL 7/98; BR 11–12/98; SLJ 7/98; VOYA 12/98) [616.8]

11108 Landau, Elaine. *Tuberculosis* (6–10). 1995, Watts LB $20.00 (0-531-12555-6). The author reviews the history and nature of tuberculosis and its treatments, and warns of the danger presented by the rise of new drug-resistant strains today. (Rev: BL 6/1–15/95; SLJ 8/95; VOYA 2/96) [616]

11109 Landau, Elaine. *Why Are They Starving Themselves? Understanding Anorexia Nervosa and Bulimia* (7–10). 1983, Messner paper $5.95 (0-671-49492-9). Case studies are used as a focal point for explaining these eating disorders. [616.8]

11110 Latta, Sara L. *Allergies* (6–10). Series: Diseases and People. 1998, Enslow LB $20.95 (0-7660-1048-1). Using a number of case studies, this book describes the nature of allergies, their symptoms, methods of detection, and treatments. (Rev: BL 7/98) [616.9]

11111 Latta, Sara L. *Food Poisoning and Foodborne Diseases* (7–12). Series: Diseases and People. 1999, Enslow LB $20.95 (0-7660-1183-6). Using case studies and questions and answers, this book describes the causes, effects, and treatments for food poisoning and related illnesses. (Rev: BL 9/15/99; HBG 4/00; SLJ 11/99) [615.9]

11112 Lennard-Brown, Sarah. *Asthma* (5–8). Illus. Series: Health Issues. 2002, Raintree Steck-Vaughn LB $28.54 (0-7398-5218-3). Color photographs and straightforward text explain the symptoms, diagnosis, and treatment of asthma. (Rev: BL 12/15/02; HBG 3/03) [616.2]

11113 Leone, Daniel, ed. *Anorexia* (6–12). Series: At Issue. 2001, Greenhaven LB $22.45 (0-7377-0468-3); paper $14.95 (0-7377-0467-5). Revealing personal accounts provide different perspectives on coping with this condition. (Rev: BL 3/15/01) [616.85]

11114 Leone, Daniel, ed. *The Spread of AIDS* (8–12). Series: At Issue. 1997, Greenhaven paper $17.45 (1-56510-537-0). This anthology of different opinions explores the successes and failures of various educational strategies, health care programs, and political policies designed to prevent the spread of AIDS. (Rev: BL 1/1–15/97; SLJ 4/97) [362.1]

11115 LeVert, Marianne. *AIDS: A Handbook for the Future* (7–12). Illus. 1996, Millbrook LB $24.90 (1-56294-660-9). This book covers the basic facts about AIDS, its causes, prevention, present treatments, and current research. (Rev: BL 12/15/96; BR 3–4/97; SLJ 11/96; VOYA 6/97) [616.97]

11116 Little, Marjorie. *Diabetes* (7–12). Series: Encyclopedia of Health. 1990, Chelsea LB $19.95 (0-7910-0061-3). A clear, organized account that covers the history of diabetes, its causes, and present-day treatments. (Rev: BL 3/15/91) [616.4]

11117 McGuire, Paula. *AIDS* (4–8). Series: Preteen Pressures. 1998, Raintree Steck-Vaughn LB $25.69 (0-8172-5025-5). Straight facts and statistics are given on AIDS, including methods of prevention and stories of people with HIV/AIDS, such as Magic Johnson and the late Ryan White. (Rev: BL 5/15/98; HBG 10/98) [616,97]

11118 Majure, Janet. *AIDS* (7–10). 1998, Enslow LB $20.95 (0-7660-1182-8). This informative book describes AIDS, who gets it and how, symptoms, treatment, prevention, and prospects for the future, and touches on related social, economic, and legal issues. (Rev: VOYA 2/99) [616]

11119 Majure, Janet. *Breast Cancer* (7–12). Illus. 2000, Enslow LB $19.95 (0-7660-1312-X). A straightforward look at this disease's diagnosis and treatment, and at its social implications and its incidence around the world. (Rev: HBG 9/00; SLJ 10/00*) [616.99]

11120 Manning, Karen. *AIDS: Can This Epidemic Be Stopped?* (6–8). Series: Issues of Our Time. 1995, Twenty-First Century LB $22.90 (0-8050-4240-7). A frank, unbiased look at AIDS, its causes, effects on society, and perspectives for the future. (Rev: BL 2/1/96; SLJ 2/96; VOYA 4/96) [616.97]

11121 Marrin, Albert. *Dr. Jenner and the Speckled Monster: The Search for the Smallpox Vaccine* (4–8). Illus. 2002, Dutton $17.99 (0-525-46922-2). This highly readable and detailed account describes the impact of smallpox from the time of the Aztecs, major outbreaks over the years, the way the virus works, the work of Jenner in developing a vaccine, and the virus's potential as a weapon of mass destruction. (Rev: BL 11/15/02; HB 11–12/02; HBG 3/03; SLJ 1/03; VOYA 12/02) [614.5]

11122 Massari, Francesca. *Everything You Need to Know About Cancer* (5–9). Series: Need to Know Library. 2000, Rosen LB $25.25 (0-8239-3164-1). This book defines what cancer is and looks at its causes, prevention, symptoms, diagnosis, and treatment. (Rev: HBG 10/00; SLJ 8/00) [616.99]

11123 Medina, Loreta M., ed. *Bulimia* (6–12). Series: At Risk. 2003, Gale LB $20.96 (0-7377-1164-7); paper $13.96 (0-7377-1163-9). The essays in this book examine issues related to bulimia including symptoms, effects, and suggestions for intervention. (Rev: BL 1/1–15/03) [616.85]

11124 Miller, Martha J. *Kidney Disorders* (7–12). Series: Encyclopedia of Health. 1992, Chelsea LB $19.95 (0-7910-0066-4). This book explains the function of the kidneys, how they can malfunction, and treatments that are available, including transplants. (Rev: BL 12/1/92) [616.6]

11125 Moe, Barbara. *Coping with Eating Disorders* (7–10). 1999, Rosen $26.50 (0-8239-2974-4). Actual case histories are used to explain the characteristics of bulimia, anorexia, and compulsive-eating patterns. Practical coping suggestions are also offered. (Rev: BL 7/91; SLJ 11/91) [616.85]

11126 Moe, Barbara. *Coping with PMS* (7–12). Series: Coping. 1998, Rosen LB $25.25 (0-8239-2716-4). Supplemented by personal accounts, this book explains how PMS can be a manageable problem, with material on physiology, diet, life-style, attitude, and the relationship between nutrition and PMS control (recipes are included). (Rev: BL 5/15/98; SLJ 5/98) [618.172]

11127 Moe, Barbara. *Coping with Tourette Syndrome and Tic Disorders* (6–10). 2000, Rosen LB $18.95 (0-8239-2976-0). Solid information and many case studies are used in this examination of Tourette's syndrome, tic disorders, and related problems with material on how they affect moods, learning, activities, and sleep. (Rev: BL 7/00) [616.8]

11128 Moe, Barbara. *Everything You Need to Know About Migraines and Other Headaches* (7–12). Series: Need to Know Library. 2000, Rosen LB $17.95 (0-8239-3291-5). An accessible and thorough exploration of the symptoms, treatment, and prevention of migraines and other headaches. (Rev: HBG 10/01; SLJ 4/01) [616.8]

11129 Moe, Barbara. *Inside Eating Disorder Support Groups* (6–10). Series: Teen Health Library of Eating Disorder Prevention. 1998, Rosen LB $26.50 (0-8239-2769-5). After a general discussion of eating disorders and available treatments, this book explains the dynamics of support groups and how they can help teens recover from eating disorders and come to terms with their problems. (Rev: BR 5–6/99; SLJ 1/99) [616.85]

11130 Moehn, Heather. *Everything You Need to Know When Someone You Know Has Leukemia* (5–10). Series: Need to Know Library. 2000, Rosen LB $25.25 (0-8239-3121-8). The basic facts about leukemia are covered with material on its various types and treatments, possible causes, and the emotional aspects of the illness. (Rev: SLJ 9/00) [616.99]

11131 Moehn, Heather. *Understanding Eating Disorder Support Groups* (7–12). Series: Teen Eating Disorder Prevention Library. 2000, Rosen LB $18.95 (0-8239-2992-2). Extensive information on the diagnosis, symptoms, and treatment of eating disorders precedes discussion of the types of support available; case studies appear throughout. (Rev: HBG 10/01; SLJ 2/01)

11132 Monroe, Judy. *Cystic Fibrosis* (5–9). Illus. Series: Perspectives on Disease and Illness. 2001, Capstone LB $23.93 (0-7368-1026-9). A straightforward account of the symptoms, diagnosis, and treatment of this disease, with discussion of the impact on the life of the patient and other family members. Also use *Breast Cancer* (2001). (Rev: HBG 3/02; SLJ 3/02) [616.3]

11133 Moragne, Wendy. *Allergies* (5–8). Series: Twenty-First Century Medical Library. 1999, Twenty-First Century LB $26.90 (0-7613-1359-1). After general material on allergies, their causes and treatment, this account describes specific allergies involving food, skin, rhinitis, drugs, and insects. (Rev: HBG 3/00; SLJ 3/00) [616.97]

11134 Morgan, Sally. *Germ Killers: Fighting Disease* (5–8). Series: Science at the Edge. 2002, Heinemann LB $27.86 (1-58810-699-3). Current advances in fighting disease are outlined with their current applications and future possibilities. (Rev: BL 10/15/02; HBG 3/03) [616]

11135 Mulcahy, Robert. *Diseases: Finding the Cure* (7–9). 1996, Oliver LB $21.95 (1-881508-28-5). After a general introduction on disease fighting, single chapters explore the breakthroughs of such scientists as Edward Jenner, Louis Pasteur, Alexander Fleming, and Jonas Salk, with a special afterword on AIDS. (Rev: SLJ 10/96) [616]

11136 Murphy, Wendy. *Asthma* (7–12). Series: Millbrook Medical Library. 1998, Millbrook LB $26.90 (0-7613-0364-2). Beginning with the causes of asthma, this book describes what happens during an attack, how the disease is controlled, and various avenues of medical treatment. (Rev: BL 1/1–15/99; HBG 3/99; SLJ 1/99) [616.2]

11137 Murphy, Wendy. *Orphan Diseases: New Hope for Rare Medical Conditions* (7–12). Illus. 2002, Millbrook LB $26.90 (0-7613-1919-0). Autism, cystic fibrosis, and dwarfism are among the conditions discussed, with information on origin, causes, treatment, and how patients cope with the condition. (Rev: BL 10/15/02; HBG 3/03) [362.1]

11138 Nash, Carol R. *AIDS: Choices for Life* (7–12). Illus. Series: Issues in Focus. 1997, Enslow LB $20.95 (0-89490-903-7). This book offers information about AIDS and protease inhibitors, drug cocktails, the AIDS virus, current and future medical concerns, and prevention tactics, plus a history of the disease. (Rev: BL 12/1/97; SLJ 12/97; VOYA 6/98) [616.97]

11139 Nourse, Alan E. *The Virus Invaders* (8–10). 1992, Watts paper $24.00 (0-531-12511-4). Virology is explained in lay terms, including a history of viruses and the prognosis for treatment of killers like malaria and AIDS. (Rev: BL 9/15/92; SLJ 7/92) [616]

11140 O'Brien, Eileen. *Starving to Win: Athletes and Eating Disorders* (6–12). Series: Teen Health Library of Eating Disorder Prevention. 1998, Rosen LB $26.50 (0-8239-2764-4). This book describes the pressures on athletes to gain or lose weight and the temptation, particularly in track, gymnastics, ballet, and wrestling, to resort to dangerous crash diets, fasts, or drugs. The author stresses that health is more important than weight. (Rev: BR 5–6/99; SLJ 2/99) [616.85]

11141 Ouriou, Katie. *Love Ya Like a Sister: A Story of Friendship* (8–12). Ed. by Julie Johnston. 1999, Tundra paper $7.95 (0-88776-454-1). After her death from leukemia when only 16 years old, Katie Ouriou's life and thoughts during her last months were reconstructed from journal entries and e-mail correspondence with her many friends. (Rev: SLJ 5/99; VOYA 6/99) [616.95]

11142 Peacock, Judith. *Diabetes* (7–12). Series: Perspectives on Disease and Illness. 1999, Capstone LB $16.95 (0-7368-0277-0). An introduction to this disease, its transmission, and possible treatments, with material on how to manage it at home and at school. Also use *Juvenile Arthritis* (1999). (Rev: SLJ 4/00) [616.4]

11143 Pincus, Dion. *Everything You Need to Know About Cerebral Palsy* (4–7). Series: Need to Know Library. 2000, Rosen LB $25.25 (0-8239-2960-4). The causes and characteristics of cerebral palsy are discussed with material on the treatments and the daily life of those affected. (Rev: HBG 10/00; SLJ 3/00) [618.92]

11144 Pipher, Mary. *Hunger Pains: The Modern Woman's Tragic Quest for Thinness* (7–12). 1997, Ballantine paper $12.00 (0-345-41393-8). This book explains eating disorders, probes into their basic causes, and offers suggestions for help, with separate chapters on bulimia, anorexia, obesity, and diets. (Rev: VOYA 8/97) [616.95]

11145 Powers, Mary C. *Arthritis* (7–12). Series: Encyclopedia of Health. 1992, Chelsea LB $19.95 (0-7910-0057-5). Illustrated with black-and-white pictures, this book describes the causes of arthritis, therapies, and treatments. (Rev: BL 10/1/92) [616.7]

11146 Ramen, Fred. *Sleeping Sickness and Other Parasitic Tropical Diseases* (5–8). Series: Epidemics. 2002, Rosen LB $26.50 (0-8239-3499-3). After a history of parasitic diseases around the globe and the role played by bloodsucking killers like the tsetse fly, this account describes the treatments now available. (Rev: BL 8/02; SLJ 7/02) [616]

11147 Ray, Kurt. *Typhoid Fever* (5–8). Illus. Series: Epidemics. 2002, Rosen LB $19.95 (0-8239-3572-8). An introduction to the history and treatment of typhoid fever, including coverage of Typhoid Mary. (Rev: BL 3/15/02) [614.5]

11148 Ridgway, Tom. *Mad Cow Disease: Bovine Spongiform Encephalopathy* (6–8). Series: Epidemics. 2002, Rosen LB $26.50 (0-8239-3487-X). A fascinating account of how this disease affects its victims, how it spreads, and how scientists raced to discover more about it. (Rev: BL 8/02; SLJ 6/02) [616.8]

11149 Robbins, Paul R. *Anorexia and Bulimia* (7–12). Series: Diseases and People. 1998, Enslow LB $20.95 (0-7660-1047-3). The history of anorexia, bulimia, and binge eating is given, with material on symptoms, possible causes, prevention, and treatment. (Rev: BL 1/1–15/99; SLJ 1/99) [616.85]

11150 Rocha, Toni L. *Understanding Recovery from Eating Disorders* (6–10). Series: Teen Eating Disorder Prevention Library. 1999, Rosen $17.95 (0-8239-2884-5). This book offers first-person accounts

of survivors of various types of eating disorders and also offers advice for teens with are in recovery programs. (Rev: BL 10/15/99; HBG 9/00; SLJ 7/00) [616.85]

11151 Roleff, Tamara L., ed. *AIDS* (7–12). Illus. Series: Opposing Viewpoints. 2003, Gale LB $33.70 (0-7377-1136-1); paper $22.45 (0-7377-1135-3). Articles address the spread of HIV and the current status of the epidemic, treatment — including recommendations for pregnant women and infants, needle-exchange programs, and partner notification. (Rev: SLJ 11/03) [616.977]

11152 Sanders, Pete, and Steve Myers. *Anorexia and Bulimia* (4–8). Series: What Do You Know About. 1999, Millbrook LB $23.90 (0-7613-0914-4). Using an actual case study as a beginning, this book explores the causes, effects, and treatment of these eating disorders and covers the behavioral patterns of those afflicted. (Rev: HBG 10/99; SLJ 10/99) [618.92]

11153 Schwartz, Robert H., and Peter M. G. Deane. *Coping with Allergies* (4–7). Series: Coping. 1999, Rosen LB $25.25 (0-8239-2511-0). After a rundown of the types and causes of allergies, this account describes their physical and emotional impact and current treatments. (Rev: BL 2/15/00) [616.97]

11154 Shader, Laurel, and Jon Zonderman. *Mononucleosis and Other Infectious Diseases* (7–12). Illus. 1989, Chelsea LB $19.95 (0-7910-0069-9). Although many diseases including syphilis and smallpox are discussed, the emphasis is on mononucleosis, a disease that often attacks teens. (Rev: BL 1/15/90; BR 11–12/89; SLJ 11/89) [616.9]

11155 Sheen, Barbara. *Diabetes* (5–7). Illus. Series: Diseases and Disorders. 2003, Gale LB $27.45 (1-59018-244-8). The symptoms of and treatments for diabetes are covered here, with discussion of alternative treatments, how diabetics manage their disease, and the research being undertaken. (Rev: SLJ 7/03) [616.4]

11156 Shein, Lori. *AIDS* (5–8). Series: Overview. 1998, Lucent LB $27.45 (1-56006-193-6). A concise overview of the AIDS epidemic in the late 20th century, the attempts to treat and restrict the spread of the disease, and the controversies surrounding it. (Rev: BL 8/98) [616.99]

11157 Sherrow, Victoria. *Polio Epidemic: Crippling Virus Outbreak* (4–7). Series: American Disasters. 2001, Enslow LB $18.95 (0-7660-1555-6). In this readable account, Sherrow looks at the history of polio, its treatment, the epidemic in the United States that started in 1952, and the creation of the polio vaccine. (Rev: HBG 3/02; SLJ 3/02) [362.1]

11158 Siegel, Dorothy, and David E. Newton. *Leukemia* (7–12). 1994, Watts LB $20.00 (0-531-12509-2). An introduction to leukemia, emphasizing the advances in research and the cure rate. (Rev: BL 2/15/95; SLJ 1/95; VOYA 4/95) [616.99]

11159 Silverstein, Alvin, et al. *AIDS: An Allabout Guide for Young Adults* (6–12). Illus. Series: Issues in Focus. 1999, Enslow LB $19.95 (0-89490-716-6). In addition to discussing the history, diagnosis, treatment, and prevention of AIDS, the authors present interesting sidebar features and profiles of celebrities who have contracted the disease. (Rev: BL 11/15/99; HBG 4/00; SLJ 11/99) [616.97]

11160 Silverstein, Alvin, et al. *Asthma* (7–12). Illus. Series: Diseases and People. 1997, Enslow LB $20.95 (0-89490-712-3). This book discusses the nature, causes, and treatment of asthma and possible cures. (Rev: BL 2/15/97; SLJ 4/97; VOYA 6/97) [616.2]

11161 Silverstein, Alvin, et al. *Chickenpox and Shingles* (6–10). Series: Diseases and People. 1998, Enslow LB $20.95 (0-89490-715-8). The nature and treatment of these two diseases are discussed, supplemented by case studies. (Rev: BL 7/98) [616]

11162 Silverstein, Alvin, et al. *Diabetes* (7–12). Illus. Series: Diseases and People. 1994, Enslow LB $20.95 (0-89490-464-7). An examination of the causes and treatment of diabetes, with material on how to detect it and sources of possible cures. (Rev: BL 10/15/94; SLJ 12/94; VOYA 12/94) [616.4]

11163 Silverstein, Alvin, et al. *Leukemia* (6–10). Illus. Series: Diseases and People. 2000, Enslow $20.95 (0-7660-1310-3). A look at the history, symptoms, diagnosis, treatment, social impact, and future of this disease. (Rev: HBG 10/01; SLJ 9/00) [616.99]

11164 Silverstein, Alvin, et al. *Lyme Disease* (4–7). Illus. 2000, Watts LB $24.00 (0-531-11751-0); paper $8.95 (0-531-16531-0). This book introduces Lyme disease, its symptoms, history, the tick that carries it, prevention, and treatments. (Rev: BL 10/15/00) [616.9]

11165 Silverstein, Alvin, et al. *Mononucleosis* (7–10). Series: Diseases and People. 1994, Enslow LB $20.95 (0-89490-466-3). Examines this disease's history, causes, treatment, prevention, and societal response. (Rev: BL 1/15/95; HBG 10/01; SLJ 3/95) [616.9]

11166 Silverstein, Alvin, et al. *Sickle Cell Anemia* (6–12). Illus. Series: Diseases and People. 1997, Enslow LB $20.95 (0-89490-711-5). A clear, concise description of the causes, effects, and treatment of this condition, with information on why it attacks African Americans in particular. (Rev: BL 2/15/97; SLJ 2/97; VOYA 6/97) [616.1]

11167 Silverstein, Alvin, and Virginia Silverstein. *Allergies* (7–10). Illus. 1977, HarperCollins $13.00 (0-397-31758-1). The types of allergies — such as hay fever and asthma — as well as their causes, effects, and treatments are discussed. [616.97]

11168 Silverstein, Alvin, and Virginia Silverstein. *Measles and Rubella* (6–12). Illus. Series: Diseases and People. 1997, Enslow LB $20.95 (0-89490-714-X). The authors examine the nature of measles and rubella, their treatment, and the possibility of a cure. (Rev: BL 3/1/98; SLJ 5/98) [616.9]

11169 Silverstein, Alvin, and Virginia Silverstein. *Runaway Sugar: All About Diabetes* (7–10). Illus. 1981, HarperCollins LB $12.89 (0-397-31929-0). Among other topics, this book discusses what causes diabetes and how it can be controlled. [616.4]

11170 Simpson, Carolyn. *Coping with Asthma* (4–7). 1995, Rosen LB $17.95 (0-8239-2069-0). After discussing the respiratory system and the causes of asthma, this book deals with how to treat this illness. (Rev: BL 9/15/95) [616.2]

11171 Simpson, Carolyn. *Coping with Sleep Disorders* (7–12). Series: Coping. 1995, Rosen LB $25.25 (0-8239-2068-2). This book discusses sleeping disorders from snoring to insomnia and offers a wide range of possible solutions. (Rev: SLJ 6/96; VOYA 8/96) [613.7]

11172 Simpson, Carolyn. *Everything You Need to Know About Asthma* (5–10). Illus. Series: Need to Know Library. 1998, Rosen LB $25.25 (0-8239-2567-6). Vital background information is given about the causes and effects, symptoms, and treatments of asthma. (Rev: SLJ 10/98) [616.2]

11173 Smart, Paul. *Everything You Need to Know About Mononucleosis* (5–9). Series: Need to Know Library. 1998, Rosen LB $25.25 (0-8239-2550-1). A straightforward presentation about the "kissing disease," which is often undiagnosed or mistaken for the flu and which requires long periods of rest for recovery. (Rev: SLJ 10/98) [616]

11174 Smith, Erica. *Anorexia Nervosa: When Food Is the Enemy* (6–10). Series: Teen Health Library of Eating Disorder Prevention. 1998, Rosen LB $26.50 (0-8239-2766-0). The author describes anorexia nervosa and its symptoms and treatment, and discusses what to do if you suspect someone is suffering from the eating disorder. Society's attitudes toward weight and body image and the role of peer pressure, media images, family relationships, and genetics are examined, along with how to deal with these influences. (Rev: BR 5–6/99; SLJ 1/99) [616.85]

11175 Snedden, Robert. *Fighting Infectious Diseases* (6–10). Illus. Series: Microlife. 2000, Heinemann LB $22.79 (1-57572-243-7). The body's immune system and other forms of defense against diseases are discussed in this well-illustrated account. (Rev: BL 9/15/00) [616.8]

11176 Sparks, Beatrice, ed. *It Happened to Nancy* (7–12). 1994, Avon paper $5.99 (0-380-77315-5). In diary format, this is the story of 14-year-old Nancy who was raped by her boyfriend and infected

718

with the HIV virus. (Rev: BL 6/1–15/94; SLJ 6/94; VOYA 10/94) [362.196]

11177 Spray, Michelle. *Growing Up with Scoliosis: A Young Girl's Story* (5–9). 2002, Book Shelf paper $12.95 (0-9714160-3-6). An autobiographical account of the treatment of scoliosis and the emotional impact on the patient, with clear illustrations. (Rev: SLJ 12/02) [362.19673]

11178 Stanley, Debbie. *Understanding Anorexia Nervosa* (6–12). Series: Teen Eating Disorder Prevention Library. 1999, Rosen LB $17.95 (0-8239-2877-2). Why people get anorexia, how to get help for it, the dangers of this condition, and some of the myths surrounding it are all covered in this volume. (Rev: HBG 9/00; SLJ 2/00) [616.85]

11179 Stanley, Debbie. *Understanding Bulimia Nervosa* (6–10). Series: Teen Eating Disorder Prevention Library. 1999, Rosen $17.95 (0-8239-2878-0). A look at this eating disorder, in which a person binges and purges, with material on contributing factors and guidance to help recovery. (Rev: BL 10/15/99; HBG 9/00; SLJ 7/00) [616.85]

11180 Stewart, Gail B. *Sleep Disorders* (5–8). Illus. Series: Diseases and Disorders. 2002, Gale LB $27.45 (1-56006-909-0). Insomnia, narcolepsy, apnea, and night terrors are among the problems discussed here, with material on treatments, new research, and attitudes toward people who are always tired. (Rev: SLJ 3/03) [616.8498]

11181 Stewart, Gail B. *Teens with Cancer* (7–10). Photos by Carl Franzn. Series: The Other America. 2001, Gale LB $27.45 (1-56006-884-1). The first-person stories of four young people with life-threatening cancers reveal the hard realities such teens face. (Rev: SLJ 12/01)

11182 Stewart, Gail B. *Teens with Eating Disorders* (7–12). Illus. Series: Other America. 2000, Lucent LB $19.96 (1-56006-764-0). Four young adults describe their battles with eating disorders, which become particularly problematic in high school and at college. (Rev: BL 2/1/01) [616.85]

11183 Stone, Tanya L. *Medical Causes* (5–10). Series: Celebrity Activists. 1997, Twenty-First Century LB $25.90 (0-8050-5233-X). The contributions of such celebrity activists as Elizabeth Taylor, Elton John, Paul Newman, Jerry Lewis, and Linda Ellerbee to various medical causes are highlighted, with material on each of their causes. (Rev: BR 3–4/98; SLJ 1/98) [616]

11184 Storad, Conrad J. *Inside AIDS: HIV Attacks the Immune System* (8–12). 1998, Lerner LB $23.93 (0-8225-2857-6). An unusual book about the HIV virus that tells about the cellular structure of the body, its immune system, and how the virus tricks the host cells into replicating it. (Rev: BL 12/15/98; HBG 3/99; SLJ 1/99) [616.97]

11185 Strada, Jennifer L. *Eating Disorders* (6–12). Illus. 2000, Lucent LB $19.96 (1-56006-659-8). Anorexia, bulimia, and binge eating are all described in this easy-to-read text, with discussion of causes, risk factors, treatment, and prevention. (Rev: BL 3/1/01; SLJ 4/01) [616.85]

11186 Strauss, Peggy Guthart. *Relieve the Squeeze* (5–7). Illus. 2000, Viking $14.99 (0-670-89330-7). This book about asthma explains what it is, what triggers it, kinds of medication, and how to cope with it. (Rev: BL 1/1–15/01; HBG 3/01; SLJ 1/01) [616.2]

11187 Susman, Edward. *Multiple Sclerosis* (4–7). Series: Diseases and People. 1999, Enslow LB $20.95 (0-7660-1185-2). A description of this debilitating disease that attacks the nervous system. (Rev: HBG 3/00; SLJ 2/00) [616]

11188 Veggeberg, Scott. *Lyme Disease* (7–12). 1998, Enslow LB $20.95 (0-7660-1052-X). An overview of the symptoms, diagnosis, treatment, and prevention of Lyme disease. (Rev: BL 7/98; HBG 10/98; SLJ 9/98) [616.7]

11189 Vogel, Carole Garbuny. *Breast Cancer: Questions and Answers for Young Women* (6–12). Illus. 2001, Twenty-First Century LB $25.90 (0-7613-1855-0). Teen readers will find clear answers to both emotional and physiological questions about breasts, breast development, and breast cancer. (Rev: HBG 10/01; SLJ 5/01; VOYA 8/01) [616.99]

11190 Vollstadt, Elizabeth Weiss. *Teen Eating Disorders* (7–12). Series: Teen Issues. 1999, Lucent LB $27.45 (1-56006-516-8). This book defines the various kinds of teenage eating disorders and, using many anecdotes, describes their causes, effects, treatment, and prevention. (Rev: BL 7/99; HBG 4/00; SLJ 8/99) [616.85]

11191 Wade, Mary Dodson. *ALS: Lou Gehrig's Disease* (6–12). Illus. Series: Diseases and People. 2001, Enslow LB $20.95 (0-7660-1594-7). The story of Lou Gehrig's illness introduces this incurable disease and its symptoms, treatment, and the research being conducted in search of a cure. (Rev: BL 1/1–15/02; HBG 10/02; SLJ 2/02) [616.8]

11192 Wainwright, Tabitha. *You and an Illness in Your Family* (5–8). Series: Family Matters. 2001, Rosen LB $23.95 (0-8239-3352-0). Concise, readable advice is accompanied by full-page photographs of young teens and the recommendation to seek help when necessary. (Rev: SLJ 8/01) [610]

11193 Walker, Pamela. *Everything You Need to Know About Body Dysmorphic Disorder: Dealing with a Distorted Body Image* (6–9). Series: Need to Know Library. 1999, Rosen LB $17.95 (0-8239-2954-X). Body dysmorphic disorder usually hits boys and girls in adolescence; symptoms, warning signs, ways of detection, and treatment are all covered here. (Rev: HBG 9/00; SLJ 8/00) [616.89]

11194 Walker, Pamela. *Understanding the Risk of Diet Drugs* (6–10). Series: Teen Eating Disorder Prevention Library. 2000, Rosen LB $18.95 (0-8239-2991-4). This book examines teen concerns about body image and overall appearance and provides information about eating disorders and weight-loss products. (Rev: BL 2/15/01; SLJ 1/01) [616.85]

11195 Ward, Brian. *Epidemic* (4–7). Illus. Series: Eyewitness Books. 2000, DK $15.95 (0-7894-6296-6). This book covers the nature of epidemics, their causes, how they are spread and contained, and gives examples from history. (Rev: BL 12/1/00; HBG 10/01) [614.4]

11196 Weeldreyer, Laura. *Body Blues: Weight and Depression* (6–12). Series: Teen Health Library of Eating Disorder Prevention. 1998, Rosen LB $26.50 (0-8239-2761-X). This book uses case studies of three teenagers who are trying to come to terms with food and their bodies to explore the relationship between weight and depression, and encourages teenagers to learn to accept their bodies rather than aspiring to some media ideal. (Rev: BR 5–6/99; SLJ 2/99) [155.5]

11197 Weiss, Jonathan H. *Breathe Easy: Young People's Guide to Asthma* (4–7). Illus. 1994, Magination paper $9.95 (0-945354-62-2). An account that describes the causes of asthma, what happens during an attack, and how to manage this condition. (Rev: BL 2/15/95) [618.92]

11198 Whelan, Jo. *Diabetes* (5–8). Series: Health Issues. 2002, Raintree Steck-Vaughn LB $28.54 (0-7398-5220-5). Case histories of youngsters with diabetes are used to explain the nature of this disease, the problems it produces, and the treatments available. (Rev: BL 12/15/02; HBG 3/03) [616.4]

11199 Willett, Edward. *Alzheimer's Disease* (6–12). Series: Diseases and People. 2002, Enslow LB $20.95 (0-7660-1596-3). As well as discussing the nature, treatment, and possible cures of Alzheimer's disease, this account uses many case studies, including that of President Reagan. (Rev: BL 8/02; HBG 10/02; SLJ 8/02) [616.8]

11200 Williams, Mary E., ed. *Terminal Illness* (7–12). Series: Opposing Viewpoints. 2001, Greenhaven LB $22.96 (0-7377-0526-4); paper $18.70 (0-7377-0525-6). Euthanasia, the right to die, pain management, and the legalization of marijuana for the terminally ill are all discussed here, as are the choices of care available. (Rev: BL 5/1/01; SLJ 4/01) [362.1]

11201 Woods, Samuel G. *Everything You Need to Know About Sexually Transmitted Disease* (7–12). Illus. Series: Need to Know Library. 1990, Rosen $12.95 (0-8239-1010-5). Various kinds of venereal diseases are introduced, with their symptoms and treatments. (Rev: SLJ 9/90; VOYA 8/90) [305.4]

11202 Yancey, Diane. *STDs: What You Don't Know Can Hurt You* (6–12). 2002, Millbrook LB $24.90 (0-7613-1957-3). The facts on common sexually transmitted diseases are combined with stories of teenagers with STDs, a section on prevention, and tests to help the reader determine his or her risk of becoming infected. (Rev: BL 4/1/02; HBG 10/02; SLJ 5/02) [616.95]

11203 Yancey, Diane. *Tuberculosis* (7–12). Series: Twenty-First Century Medical Library. 2001, Twenty-First Century LB $24.90 (0-7613-1624-8). Interesting illustrations and case studies draw the reader into this account of the historical and contemporary incidence of this disease. (Rev: HBG 10/01; SLJ 5/01) [616]

11204 Yount, Lisa. *Cancer* (5–8). Series: Overview. 1999, Lucent LB $27.45 (1-56006-363-7). This objective overview explains how cancer cells develop, types of cancer, causes, and past and present treatments, both traditional and alternative. (Rev: BL 9/15/99; HBG 3/00; SLJ 7/99) [616.994]

11205 Yount, Lisa. *Epidemics* (7–10). Illus. 1999, Lucent LB $18.96 (1-56006-441-2). An interesting overview of epidemics of the past, their causes, and the potential for future epidemics, including ones caused by biological weapons. (Rev: HBG 9/00; SLJ 4/00) [614.4]

Doctors, Hospitals, and Medicine

11206 Billitteri, Thomas J. *Alternative Medicine* (7–10). Series: Twenty-First Century Medical Library. 2001, Twenty-First Century LB $24.90 (0-7613-0965-9). This overview of alternative therapies such as hypnosis, acupuncture, and homeopathy balances success stories with solid information on the lack of rigorous scientific investigation and of FDA oversight. (Rev: HBG 3/02; SLJ 12/01; VOYA 4/02) [615.5]

11207 Cosner, Shaaron. *War Nurses* (6–9). Illus. 1988, Walker $17.85 (0-8027-6828-8). A history of the important role nurses have played tending the wounded from the Civil War through the Vietnam conflict. (Rev: BL 12/1/88; BR 3–4/89; SLJ 12/88) [355.3]

11208 Dowswell, Paul. *Medicine* (5–8). Illus. Series: Great Inventions. 2001, Heinemann LB $25.64 (1-58810-213-0). A chronological look at new medical instruments and procedures over the ages, with diagrams and information on the inventors. (Rev: HBG 3/02; SLJ 2/02) [610]

11209 Fleischman, John. *Phineas Gage: A Gruesome But True Story About Brain Science* (7–10). Illus. 2002, Houghton $16.00 (0-618-05252-6). This riveting story of the amiable man whose personality changed when an iron rod shot through his brain presents lots of information on brain science and medical knowledge in the 19th century. (Rev: BL 3/1/02; HB 5–6/02; HBG 10/02; SLJ 3/02; VOYA 6/02) [362.1]

11210 Gates, Phil. *The History News: Medicine* (4–7). Illus. Series: History News. 1997, Candlewick $15.99 (0-7636-0316-3). The history of doctors and medicine is covered using a newspaper format that even includes "advertisements" (one announces leeches for sale) and letters. (Rev: BL 2/1/98; HBG 3/98; SLJ 1/98) [610.9]

11211 Giddens, Sandra, and Owen Giddens. *Future Techniques in Surgery* (6–9). Illus. Series: Library of Future Medicine. 2003, Rosen LB $26.50 (0-8239-3667-8). A look at the new techniques and equipment that make less invasive procedures possible and reduce recovery time. (Rev: BL 10/15/03; LMC 10/03; SLJ 5/03) [617]

11212 Hyde, Margaret O., and Elizabeth H. Forsyth. *Vaccinations: From Smallpox to Cancer* (6–12). Illus. 2000, Watts LB $20.00 (0-531-11746-4). This fine account traces the history of epidemics from ancient times, explains how diseases attack humans, and how vaccines help the immune system. (Rev: BL 11/15/00) [615]

11213 Ichord, Loretta Frances. *Toothworms and Spider Juice: An Illustrated History of Dentistry* (5–8). Illus. 2000, Millbrook LB $24.90 (0-7613-1465-2). A history of dentistry that reveals many of the barbaric treatments of the past and how superstition and ignorance gradually gave way to modern practices. (Rev: BCCB 2/00; BL 2/15/00; HBG 10/00; SLJ 2/00) [617.6]

11214 Jefferis, David. *Bio Tech: Frontiers of Medicine* (4–8). Illus. Series: Megatech. 2001, Crabtree LB $22.60 (0-7787-0051-8); paper $8.95 (0-7787-0061-5). An eye-catching look at future medical possibilities such as artificial body parts, enhanced use of robots, special foods, and so forth. (Rev: SLJ 6/02) [660.6]

11215 Judson, Karen. *Medical Ethics: Life and Death Issues* (7–10). 2001, Enslow LB $20.95 (0-7660-1585-8). After defining ethics, Judson presents a balanced overview of the potential positive and negative impacts of medical decisions, and discusses such topics as organ donation and the financial aspects of health care. (Rev: HBG 3/02; SLJ 9/01) [174]

11216 Kidd, J. S., and Renee A. Kidd. *Mother Nature's Pharmacy: Potent Medicines from Plants* (7–12). Illus. Series: Science and Society. 1998, Facts on File $25.00 (0-8160-3584-9). An interesting account of the long history of natural plant remedies, the individuals whose discoveries brought plant remedies to public attention, and the expanding role of the government in researching and sanc-

tioning their use, along with information on recent advances. (Rev: BL 10/15/98; SLJ 1/99; VOYA 2/99) [615.32]

11217 Kowalski, Kathiann M. *Alternative Medicine: Is It for You?* (7–9). Illus. Series: Issues in Focus. 1998, Enslow LB $20.95 (0-89490-955-X). After explaining the differences between traditional and alternative medicine, this book describes homeopathy, chiropractic medicine, medical practices from India and China, nutritional therapies, biofeedback, and healing based on prayer and meditation. (Rev: BL 10/1/98; BR 1–2/99; SLJ 12/98) [615.5]

11218 Levy, Debbie. *Medical Ethics* (6–12). Series: Overview. 2001, Lucent LB $27.45 (1-56006-547-8). Such topics as genetic engineering, experimental treatments, assisted suicide, and organ transplants are introduced and their relationship to medical ethics explored. (Rev: BL 9/15/01; SLJ 4/01) [174]

11219 Masoff, Joy. *Emergency!* (4–8). 1999, Scholastic paper $16.95 (0-590-97898-5). In a series of double-page spreads, this book explores various aspects of a medical emergency, from getting help to victims with an explanation of what goes on in an emergency room to giving advice on precautions youngsters can take to be prepared for an emergency. (Rev: BCCB 2/99; BL 1/1–15/99; HB 3–4/99; HBG 9/99; SLJ 8/99) [362.1]

11220 Miller, Brandon M. *Just What the Doctor Ordered: The History of American Medicine* (5–8). Series: People's History. 1997, Lerner LB $30.35 (0-8225-1737-X). A history of American medicine from early Indian ceremonies and remedies to today's use of laser surgery, placing medical developments in a historical context, such as the role disease played in the Revolutionary and Civil Wars. (Rev: SLJ 5/97*) [610.9]

11221 Moe, Barbara. *The Revolution in Medical Imaging* (6–9). Illus. Series: Library of Future Medicine. 2003, Rosen LB $26.50 (0-8239-3672-4). A look at breakthroughs such as CAT, PET, and MRI scans and the benefits they offer to both diagnostician and patient. (Rev: BL 10/15/03; SLJ 5/03) [61]

11222 Murphy, Patricia J. *Everything You Need to Know About Staying in the Hospital* (5–8). Series: Need to Know Library. 2001, Rosen LB $25.25 (0-8239-3325-3). This volume explains the basic hospital process from admission to discharge and follows a patient through a typical day. (Rev: SLJ 5/01) [362.1]

11223 Murphy, Wendy, and Jack Murphy. *Nuclear Medicine* (7–12). Series: Encyclopedia of Health. 1993, Chelsea LB $19.95 (0-7910-0070-2). This work presents current information on the role played by nuclear research in health care, including radiation treatments. (Rev: BL 12/1/93) [616.07]

11224 Nardo, Don, ed. *Vaccines* (7–10). Illus. Series: Great Medical Discoveries. 2001, Gale LB $27.45

(1-56006-932-5). The history of inoculations (back to ancient China), the discoveries of scientists including Sabine and Salk, and current efforts to find new vaccines are all discussed here. (Rev: BL 3/1/02; SLJ 5/02) [615]

11225 Oleksy, Walter. *Science and Medicine* (6–12). Series: Information Revolution. 1995, Facts on File $25.00 (0-8160-3076-6). A summary of computer technology used in medicine and in science classrooms. (Rev: BL 11/15/95; SLJ 11/95) [502]

11226 Powledge, Fred. *Pharmacy in the Forest* (5–8). 1998, Simon & Schuster $17.00 (0-689-80863-1). Writing from an environmental point of view, the author discusses medicinal plants, with examples of plants that have been useful in treating disease, and shows the reader how to identify potentially useful plants. (Rev: BL 8/98; BR 1–2/99; HBG 9/98; SLJ 6/98; VOYA 2/99) [610]

11227 Rattenbury, Jeanne. *Understanding Alternative Medicine* (7–10). Illus. 1999, Watts LB $20.00 (0-531-11413-9). An attractive book that supplies information on topics including osteopathy, chiropractic treatments, homeopathy, acupuncture, herbal medicine, and mind–body therapy. (Rev: BL 6/1–15/99; SLJ 7/99) [615]

11228 Snedden, Robert. *Medical Ethics: Changing Attitudes 1900–2000* (4–7). 1999, Raintree Steck-Vaughn LB $28.54 (0-8172-5893-0). Beginning with Hippocrates, this book gives a history of bioethics and follows with coverage of topics including reproductive rights, euthanasia, organ donation, psychiatry, eugenics, and cloning. (Rev: HBG 10/00; SLJ 5/00) [616]

11229 Stille, Darlene R. *Extraordinary Women of Medicine* (6–8). Illus. Series: Extraordinary People. 1997, Children's Pr. LB $39.00 (0-516-20307-X). A profile of 50 women who have reached prominence in medicine from the well-known, including the legendary Florence Nightingale, to many lesser-known, present-day achievers, spanning two centuries and organized according to groups or themes. (Rev: BL 10/1/97; HBG 3/98) [610]

11230 Tesar, Jeremy. *Stem Cells* (5–9). Illus. Series: Science on the Edge. 2003, Gale $20.95 (1-56711-787-2). Clear, accessible text and photographs describe stems cells and present the pros and cons of their use. (Rev: BL 10/15/03) [616]

11231 Van Steenwyk, Elizabeth. *Frontier Fever: The Silly, Superstitious — and Sometimes Sensible — Medicine of the Pioneers* (5–8). Illus. 1995, Walker LB $16.85 (0-8027-8403-8). A history of medicine in the United States from colonial times through the 19th century, including information on the training of caregivers. (Rev: BL 7/95; SLJ 12/95; VOYA 12/95) [610]

11232 Viegas, Jennifer. *Stem Cell Research* (6–10). Illus. Series: The Library of Future Medicine. 2003,

Rosen LB $26.50 (0-8239-3669-4). A look at the the composition of cells, the unique qualities of stem cells, and recent scientific discoveries about the use of embryonic stem cells and the growth of new human tissue, with discussion of possible future developments and the accompanying controversies. (Rev: SLJ 6/03) [616.02774]

11233 Winkler, Kathy. *Radiology* (4–8). Series: Inventors and Inventions. 1996, Benchmark LB $25.64 (0-7614-0075-3). This work outlines the history of radiology, provides short profiles of leaders in the field, and describes the effects of too many x-rays on tissue, how x-rays are made, their use in diagnosis and treatment, and other medical imaging such as ultrasound and MRIs. (Rev: BL 7/96; SLJ 9/96) [616.07]

11234 Yount, Lisa. *The History of Medicine* (6–9). Illus. Series: World History. 2001, Gale LB $27.45 (1-56006-805-1). Four thousand years of developments in medicine are covered here, with informative illustrations and sidebar features. (Rev: SLJ 1/02) [610]

11235 Yount, Lisa. *Medical Technology* (6–12). Series: Milestones in Discovery and Invention. 1998, Facts on File $25.00 (0-8160-3568-7). An overview of medical inventors, including interesting accounts about the lives and work of such technologists as William Morton, Joseph Lister, Christian Barnard, and Norman Shumway. (Rev: BL 5/15/98; SLJ 6/98) [610.9]

Genetics

11236 Allan, Tony. *Understanding DNA: A Breakthrough in Medicine* (5–8). Illus. Series: Point of Impact. 2002, Heinemann LB $25.64 (1-58810-557-1). A history of genetics with profiles of the important scientists and discussion of future uses of this knowledge in cloning, medicine, and production of food. (Rev: SLJ 9/02) [572.8609]

11237 Beatty, Richard. *Genetics* (4–8). Illus. Series: Science Fact Files. 2001, Raintree Steck-Vaughn LB $27.12 (0-7398-1015-4). Cells, chromosomes, genes, and genetic engineering are covered here, with profiles of key scientists. (Rev: HBG 10/01; SLJ 1/02) [660]

11238 Boon, Kevin Alexander. *The Human Genome Project: What Does Decoding DNA Mean for Us?* (8–12). Illus. Series: Issues in Focus. 2002, Enslow LB $20.95 (0-7660-1685-4). A discussion of the benefits of and legal and ethical concerns about the Human Genome Project is preceded by information on genes and genetics. (Rev: HBG 3/03; SLJ 11/02) [599.93]

11239 Bornstein, Sandy. *What Makes You What You Are: A First Look at Genetics* (5–8). 1989, Silver Burdett paper $6.95 (0-671-68650-X). This book affords a fine introduction to cell structure, dominant and recessive traits, and heredity. (Rev: SLJ 1/90) [573.2]

11240 Bryan, Jenny. *Genetic Engineering* (7–9). 1995, Thomson Learning LB $24.26 (1-56847-268-4). Recounts the advances of gene research, including a discussion of the ethical questions involved. (Rev: BL 8/95; SLJ 8/95) [575.1]

11241 Butterfield, Moira. *Genetics* (5–8). Illus. Series: 21st Century Science. 2003, Smart Apple LB $18.95 (1-58340-350-7). An accessible, large-format volume on genetics, cloning, and the use of genes in medicine and food engineering, with attractive full-color photographs. (Rev: BL 12/1/03) [576.5.]

11242 DuPrau, Jeanne. *Cloning* (7–12). Illus. 1999, Lucent LB $23.70 (1-56006-583-4). This examination delves into the ethical issues involved in human cloning as well as cloning's use in plants and animals. (Rev: BL 11/15/99; HBG 9/00) [6606]

11243 Gallant, Roy A. *The Treasure of Inheritance* (5–8). Illus. Series: The Story of Science. 2002, Benchmark LB $19.95 (0-7614-1426-6). A history of mankind's discoveries about genetics and heredity, starting with the earliest efforts to improve crops and animals, with material on today's and future genetic engineering and the mapping of the human genome. (Rev: HBG 3/03; LMC 4–5/03; SLJ 5/03) [576.5]

11244 Gardner, Robert. *Health Science Projects About Heredity* (7–12). Illus. Series: Science Projects. 2001, Enslow LB $20.95 (0-7660-1438-X). Projects that include tracing an inherited trait and creating a family tree are accompanied by explanatory information and useful charts and diagrams. (Rev: HBG 3/02; SLJ 9/01) [576.5]

11245 George, Linda. *Gene Therapy* (5–9). Series: Science on the Edge. 2003, Gale LB $20.95 (1-56711-786-4). This book explain how genetic engineering can not only have applications in health and industry but also can arouse a great deal of controversy. (Rev: BL 10/15/03) [660]

11246 Hyde, Margaret O., and John F. Setaro. *Medicine's Brave New World: Bioengineering and the New Genetics* (7–12). Illus. 2001, Millbrook LB $27.90 (0-7613-1706-6). Cloning, stem cell research, and other breakthroughs in genetics are explored in this accessible book that also discusses the ethical issues faced by scientists in this field. (Rev: BL 12/15/01; HBG 10/02; SLJ 12/01; VOYA 2/02) [610]

11247 Jefferis, David. *Cloning: Frontiers of Genetic Engineering* (5–7). Series: Megatech. 1999, Crabtree LB $22.60 (0-7787-0048-8); paper $8.95 (0-

7787-0058-5). This account discusses the history of genetic discoveries and theories, cell reproduction, and the present and possible future of genetic engineering with plants, animals, and humans. (Rev: SLJ 9/99) [174.957]

11248 Judson, Karen. *Genetic Engineering: Debating the Benefits and Concerns* (6–9). Illus. Series: Issues in Focus. 2001, Enslow LB $20.95 (0-7660-1587-4). An exploration of the pros and cons of genetic engineering, cloning, gene therapy, genetic testing, and the implications of genetic discrimination. (Rev: HBG 10/02; SLJ 12/01) [660.6]

11249 Kidd, J. S., and Renee A. Kidd. *Life Lines: The Story of the New Genetics* (7–12). Series: Science and Society. 1999, Facts on File $25.00 (0-8160-3586-5). This work explores the history of genetic research, from Mendel's early experiments to recent debates about cloning and genetic engineering. (Rev: BL 12/1/98; BR 9–10/99; SLJ 7/99; VOYA 10/99) [576.5]

11250 Marshall, Elizabeth L. *The Human Genome Project: Cracking the Code Within Us* (8–12). Illus. 1996, Watts LB $18.95 (0-531-11299-3). Concepts in genetic research are discussed along with a history of the international Human Genome Project, which is to be completed in 2005. (Rev: BL 12/1/96; SLJ 8/97) [547.87]

11251 Morgan, Sally. *Body Doubles: Cloning Plants and Animals* (5–8). Illus. Series: Science at the Edge. 2002, Heinemann LB $27.86 (1-58810-698-5). A discussion of the scientific and ethical issues of cloning, with excellent diagrams. (Rev: BL 10/15/02; HBG 3/03) [660.6]

11252 Nardo, Don. *Cloning* (5–9). Illus. Series: Science on the Edge. 2003, Gale $20.95 (1-56711-782-1). A concise overview of the techniques involved in cloning and the ways this science can be applied, with a balanced presentation of the pro and con arguments. (Rev: BL 10/15/03) [660.6]

11253 Nardo, Don, ed. *Cloning* (7–10). Illus. Series: Great Medical Discoveries. 2001, Gale LB $27.45 (1-56006-927-9). The science underlying plant and animal cloning and the controversy over potential human cloning are covered in this balanced and accessible volume. (Rev: BL 3/1/02; SLJ 5/02) [660.6]

11254 Richardson, Hazel. *How to Clone a Sheep* (4–8). 2001, Watts LB $14.50 (0-531-14645-6); paper $4.95 (0-531-16200-1). Historical developments in the area of biotechnology are accompanied by scientific explanations and information about the scientists who do this kind of research. (Rev: SLJ 6/02) [174.957]

11255 Silverstein, Alvin, et al. *DNA* (4–8). Series: Science Concepts. 2002, Millbrook LB $26.90 (0-7613-2257-4). This book examines the structure of DNA and clearly explains its components and functions and includes current topics such as the genome project, genetic engineering, gene therapy, and cloning. (Rev: BL 9/15/02; HBG 3/03; SLJ 11/02) [574.87]

11256 Snedden, Robert. *Cell Division and Genetics* (6–9). Illus. Series: Cells and Life. 2002, Heinemann LB $27.86 (1-58810-672-1). Cell structure and development, DNA, and patterns of inheritance are covered in this overview that uses diagrams and photographs to good effect in explaining complex topics. Also use *DNA and Genetic Engineering* (2002). (Rev: HBG 3/03; SLJ 1/03) [571.8]

11257 Tagliaferro, Linda. *Genetic Engineering: Progress or Peril?* (7–10). Illus. Series: Pro/Con Issues. 1997, Lerner LB $21.27 (0-8225-2620-7). This book presents the complex issues in the controversy over the manipulation of genes, such as the possibility of finding cures for hereditary diseases on the one hand, and on the other, the possibility of abusing it to create a made-to-order human race. (Rev: BL 9/1/97; SLJ 8/97) [575.1]

11258 Wilcox, Frank H. *DNA: The Thread of Life* (7–10). Illus. 1988, Lerner LB $23.93 (0-8225-1584-9). The basic DNA structure and functions are explained. (Rev: SLJ 6/88) [574.87]

11259 Winters, Paul A. *Cloning* (8–12). Series: At Issue. 1997, Greenhaven LB $26.20 (1-56510-753-5); paper $17.45 (1-56510-752-7). The successful cloning of a sheep has ignited many ethical questions concerning its application to humans. This controversy is explored in this anthology of various points of view. (Rev: BL 5/15/98; SLJ 1/99; VOYA 8/98) [174.957]

11260 Yount, Lisa. *Biotechnology and Genetic Engineering* (6–12). 2000, Facts on File LB $45.00 (0-8160-4000-1). An excellent resources that gives an overview of genetic engineering plus chapters on scientific achievements, ethnical concerns, court battles, health issues, and scientific problems. (Rev: BL 7/00) [303.48]

11261 Yount, Lisa, ed. *Cloning* (8–12). Series: Contemporary Issues Companion. 2000, Greenhaven LB $21.96 (0-7377-0330-X); paper $13.96 (0-7377-0329-6). The science and ethics of cloning are covered in this collection of more than 20 articles that cover developments through 1999. (Rev: BL 12/15/00) [571.8]

11262 Yount, Lisa, ed. *Genetic Engineering* (6–12). Series: Current Controversies. 2002, Gale LB $32.45 (0-7377-1124-8); paper $21.20 (0-7377-1123-X). This anthology explores various aspects and attitudes toward this controversial subject, with a good representation of differing viewpoints from known authorities. (Rev: BL 8/02) [575.1]

11263 Yount, Lisa. *Genetics and Genetic Engineering: Milestones in Discovery and Invention* (6–12). Illus. Series: Milestones in Discovery and Invention.

1997, Facts on File $25.00 (0-8160-3566-0). A clear explanation of genetics and its key concepts, with materials on heredity, gene mapping, the structure of DNA, disease-causing genes, and gene therapy. (Rev: BL 12/1/97) [576.5]

Grooming, Personal Appearance, and Dress

11264 Altman, Douglas. *For Guys* (6–9). Illus. 1989, Rourke LB $19.93 (0-86625-284-3). This is a good grooming manual for boys that covers such topics as diet, exercise, clothes, and hygiene. (Rev: SLJ 6/89) [646.7]

11265 Bressler, Karen W., and Susan Redstone. *D.I.Y. Beauty* (7–12). Illus. 2000, Penguin paper $5.99 (0-14-130918-0). Beauty experts respond to teen comments on areas including skin care, hair care, and makeup, with an emphasis on safety and interviews with beauty celebrities. (Rev: SLJ 12/00)

11266 Dawson, Mildred L. *Beauty Lab: How Science Is Changing the Way We Look* (5–10). 1997, Silver Moon $14.95 (1-881889-84-X). This work on health and hygiene contains chapters on skin, eyes, teeth, fitness, and hair. (Rev: BR 5–6/97; SLJ 3/97) [613.7]

11267 Douglas, Ann, and Julie Douglas. *Body Talk: The Straight Facts on Fitness, Nutrition and Feeling Great About Yourself!* (6–8). Series: Girl Zone. 2002, Firefly $19.95 (1-894379-27-6); paper $12.95 (1-894379-28-4). Tips on health, nutrition, skin care, and cosmetic surgery are accompanied by a timeline showing the evolution of standards of beauty and discussion of the roles of advertising and celebrities. (Rev: SLJ 3/03) [613]

11268 Gay, Kathlyn, and Christine Whittington. *Body Marks: Tattooing, Piercing, and Scarification* (6–12). Illus. 2002, Millbrook LB $29.90 (0-7613-2352-X); paper $14.95 (0-7613-1742-2). A look at the history of body modification around the world, with color photographs and discussion of current trends. (Rev: BL 12/1/02; HBG 3/03; SLJ 10/02) [391.6]

11269 Glicksman, Jane. *The Art of Mehndi* (6–12). Illus. 2000, NTC paper $4.95 (0-7373-0458-8). The practice of drawing on the body with henna is discussed with material on its history and easy do-it-yourself projects. (Rev: BL 10/15/00) [391.6]

11270 Hinds, Maurene J. *Focus on Body Image: How You Feel About How You Look* (6–9). Illus. Series: Teen Issues. 2002, Enslow LB $17.95 (0-7660-1915-2). A look at body image and self-esteem that discusses social pressures, eating disorders, the use of steroids, and a disorder known as muscle dysmorphia. (Rev: HBG 3/03; SLJ 1/03; VOYA 6/03) [306.4]

11271 Odes, Rebecca, et al. *The Looks Book: A Whole New Approach to Beauty, Body Image, and Style* (7–10). Illus. 2002, Penguin paper $18.00 (0-14-200211-9). Teens looking to learn more about style trends and beauty tips will find ideas in this attractive, colorful book. (Rev: BL 1/1–15/03) [646.7]

11272 Silverstein, Alvin, et al. *Overcoming Acne: The How and Why of Healthy Skin Care* (7–12). 1990, Morrow $16.00 (0-688-08344-7). This should be a popular book considering that 90 percent of adolescents suffer from some form of acne and that this account is thorough and well balanced. (Rev: BL 4/15/90; SLJ 6/90) [616.5]

11273 Sommers, Michael A. *Everything You Need to Know About Looking and Feeling Your Best: A Guide for Guys* (6–9). Series: Need to Know Library. 1999, Rosen LB $17.95 (0-8239-3080-7). Good hygiene and grooming are not difficult or time-consuming, according to this book that also looks at the benefits of exercise and diet. (Rev: SLJ 8/00) [613]

11274 Tym, Kate. *Totally You! Every Girl's Guide to Looking Good* (6–8). 1999, Element Books paper $4.95 (1-902618-44-0). Sleep, exercise, diet, make-up, aromatherapy, and other methods of pampering oneself are presented with practical, down-to-earth advice. (Rev: SLJ 4/00) [646.7]

11275 Weiss, Stefanie Iris. *Coping with the Beauty Myth: A Guide for Real Girls* (7–12). Series: Coping. 2002, Rosen LB $26.50 (0-8239-3757-7). Readers are urged to ignore unrealistic images presented in the media and to accept their own attributes and deficiencies as well as those of others. (Rev: SLJ 8/00) [155.5]

11276 Weiss, Stephanie Iris. *Everything You Need to Know About Mehndi, Temporary Tattoos, and Other Temporary Body Art* (8–12). Illus. Series: Need to Know Library. 2000, Rosen LB $17.95 (0-8239-3086-6). This account explores the cultural backgrounds associated with drawing on the body with henna, suggests methods of applying henna, and gives suggestions for patterns. (Rev: BL 7/00) [391.6]

The Human Body

General and Miscellaneous

11277 Allison, Linda. *Blood and Guts: A Working Guide to Your Own Little Insides* (5–8). 1976, Little, Brown paper $14.99 (0-316-03443-6). An off-putting title but a fine explanation of the functions of the human body.

11278 Brewer, Sarah, and Naomi Craft. *1001 Facts About the Human Body* (7–12). Illus. Series: Backpack Books. 2002, DK paper $8.95 (0-7894-8451-

X). A handy-sized book full of illustrations that gives basic, encyclopedia-style information on the human body. (Rev: BL 3/15/02) [612]

11279 Bruun, Ruth Dowling, and Bertel Bruun. *The Human Body* (5–8). 1982, Random LB $15.99 (0-394-94424-0); paper $12.99 (0-394-84424-6). A simple account that concentrates on parts of the body and its systems. [612]

11280 Brynie, Faith Hickman. *101 Questions About Your Immune System You Felt Defenseless to Answer . . . Until Now* (7–12). Illus. 2000, Twenty-First Century $27.90 (0-7613-1569-1). A question-and-answer format is used to explain the functioning and vulnerabilities of the immune system. (Rev: BL 6/1–15/00; HBG 9/00; SLJ 9/00; VOYA 4/01) [616.07]

11281 Brynie, Faith Hickman. *101 Questions About Your Skin* (7–12). Series: 101 Questions. 1999, Twenty-First Century LB $25.90 (0-7613-1259-5). This comprehensive, well-illustrated look at the composition, care, and diseases of the skin also includes information on tattooing, the effects of the sun, and aging and will attract both report writers and browsers. (Rev: HBG 4/00; SLJ 11/99) [612.7]

11282 Crelinstein, Jeffrey. *To the Limit* (5–8). Illus. Series: Wide World. 1992, Harcourt $17.95 (0-15-200616-8). The effects of exercise on the human body are explored in this book containing amazing photographs. (Rev: SLJ 10/92) [932]

11283 Davidson, Sue, and Ben Morgan. *Human Body Revealed* (5–8). Illus. 2002, DK paper $12.99 (0-7894-8882-5). Overlays, cutaway photographs, diagrams, and captions are all used effectively to give a picture of what's contained in various parts of the body. (Rev: BL 12/1/02; HBG 3/03) [611]

11284 Day, Trevor. *The Random House Book of 1001 Questions and Answers About the Human Body* (5–8). Illus. Series: 1001 Questions and Answers. 1994, Random $15.00 (0-679-85432-0). A profusely illustrated question-and-answer book that provides information on the parts of the body, its systems, and how they work. (Rev: BL 12/1/94; SLJ 7/94) [612]

11285 Gardner, Robert. *Science Projects About the Human Body* (5–7). 1992, Enslow LB $20.95 (0-89490-443-4). Simple experiments and activities are used to illustrate various areas of the human body, such as the senses, bones, teeth, and hair. (Rev: SLJ 11/93) [612]

11286 *The Human Body: Understanding and Taking Care of Your Body* (5–9). Illus. 1998, Barron's $21.95 (0-7641-5078-2). A well-illustrated book that gives a general introduction to the human body, with separate chapters on each system. (Rev: VOYA 4/99) [612]

11287 Kim, Melissa L. *The Endocrine and Reproductive Systems* (5–10). Illus. Series: Human Body Library. 2003, Enslow LB $18.95 (0-7660-2020-7).

Kim uses a conversational style to introduce detailed facts about these two body systems, with useful graphics and some practical advice. (Rev: BL 4/15/03; HBG 10/03) [612.4]

11288 Landau, Elaine. *Joined at Birth: The Lives of Conjoined Twins* (4–7). Illus. Series: A First Book. 1997, Watts LB $23.00 (0-531-20331-X). This book explains the phenomenon of conjoining and gives several famous examples of these twins. (Rev: BL 9/15/97; SLJ 8/97) [616.043]

11289 Landau, Elaine. *Short Stature: From Folklore to Fact* (4–7). Illus. Series: A First Book. 1997, Watts LB $23.00 (0-531-20265-8). After giving good historical information, this account explains dwarfism and gives several case histories. (Rev: BL 9/15/97; SLJ 8/97) [573.8]

11290 Landau, Elaine. *Standing Tall: Unusually Tall People* (4–7). Series: A First Book. 1997, Watts LB $23.00 (0-531-20257-7). This introduction to tall people gives a history of society's attitudes toward them and coverage of the challenges that they must face even today. (Rev: BL 9/15/97; SLJ 7/97) [612]

11291 Llamas, Andreu. *Digestion and Reproduction* (8–12). Illus. Series: Human Body. 1998, Gareth Stevens LB $23.93 (0-8368-2111-4). Using double-page spreads and lavish illustrations, the digestive and reproductive systems are explained. (Rev: BL 12/15/98; HBG 9/99; SLJ 3/99) [612]

11292 Llamas, Andreu. *Respiration and Circulation* (8–12). Illus. Series: Human Body. 1998, Gareth Stevens LB $23.93 (0-8368-2110-6). Double-page spreads and lavish illustrations are used to introduce the human respiration and circulation systems. (Rev: BL 12/15/98; HBG 9/99; SLJ 3/99) [612.1]

11293 Nilsson, Lennart. *Behold Man: A Photographic Journey of Discovery Inside the Body* (7–12). Illus. 1974, Little, Brown $29.95 (0-316-60751-7). An unusually illustrated book (many photographs represent magnifications of 45,000 times) on the body and its systems. [612]

11294 Rowan, Pete. *Big Head! A Book About Your Brain and Head* (5–9). Illus. 1998, Random $20.00 (0-679-89018-1). Using double-page spreads, this is a useful introduction to the anatomy, functions, and physiology of the head and neck, including such topics as hearing, speaking, emotions, and balance. (Rev: BCCB 1/99; BL 10/1/98; BR 1–2/99; HBG 3/99; SLJ 9/98) [612.8]

11295 Sneddon, Pamela Shires. *Body Image: A Reality Check* (6–10). Series: Issues in Focus. 1999, Enslow LB $20.95 (0-89490-960-6). This book discusses body image and actions, often destructive, that people take to control it, including anorexia, bulimia, steroid use, cosmetic surgery, and body piercing. (Rev: BL 5/1/99; SLJ 7/99) [155.9]

11296 Stein, Sara Bonnett. *The Body Book* (6–9). 1992, Workman paper $11.95 (0-89480-805-2). Fol-

lows human development from conception to birth and discusses what shapes us and how our bodies work. (Rev: BL 11/1/92; SLJ 12/92) [612]

11297 Tocci, Salvatore. *High-Tech IDs* (8–12). Illus. 2000, Watts LB $25.00 (0-531-11752-9). This work explores the science of biometrics (using physical or behavioral features to identify a person) with coverage of DNA use, fingerprinting, etc. and problems with the right to privacy. (Rev: BL 4/15/00; SLJ 8/00) [599.9.]

11298 VanCleave, Janice. *The Human Body for Every Kid: Easy Activities That Make Learning Science Fun* (5–7). Illus. Series: Science for Every Kid. 1995, Wiley $32.50 (0-471-02413-9); paper $12.95 (0-471-02408-2). The various systems in the human body are introduced and decribed, with many projects and experiments. (Rev: BL 4/15/95; SLJ 5/95) [612]

11299 Walker, Pam, and Elaine Wood. *The Immune System* (8–12). Illus. Series: Understanding the Human Body. 2002, Gale LB $21.96 (1-59018-151-4). This is a report-worthy text with useful information about this system in the human body, including some of the diseases relating to it. (Rev: BL 11/1/02; SLJ 2/03) [616.07]

11300 Walker, Richard. *Body: Bones, Muscle, Blood and Other Body Bits* (4–8). Series: Secret Worlds. 2001, DK $14.99 (0-7894-7967-2); paper $5.95 (0-7894-7968-0). A lively, unusual introduction to human anatomy that uses attractive layouts and lively text as well as providing a listing of tested Web sites and a special reference section. (Rev: BL 10/15/01; HBG 3/02) [612]

11301 Wiese, Jim. *Head to Toe Science: Over 40 Eye-Popping, Spine-Tingling, Heart-Pounding Activities That Teach Kids* (4–8). Illus. 2000, Wiley paper $12.95 (0-471-33203-8). A collection of experiments and projects that is arranged by body systems (e.g., nervous, digestive), accompanied by good instructions and scientific explanations. (Rev: BL 7/00; SLJ 7/00) [612]

Brain and Nervous System

11302 Andrews, Linda Wasmer. *Intelligence* (4–8). Series: Life Balance. 2003, Watts LB $19.50 (0-531-12220-4); paper $6.95 (0-531-16608-2). This book explores the concept of intelligence, how it is measured, and how it affects daily life. (Rev: BL 10/15/03) [612]

11303 Barrett, Susan L. *It's All in Your Head: A Guide to Understanding Your Brain and Boosting Your Brain Power* (6–10). Illus. 1992, Free Spirit paper $10.95 (0-915793-45-8). Covers subjects as diverse as brain anatomy, intelligence, biofeedback, creativity, ESP, and brain scans. (Rev: BL 2/15/93) [153]

11304 Bayer, Linda. *Sleep Disorders* (6–12). Series: Encyclopedia of Psychological Disorders. 2000, Chelsea LB $24.95 (0-7910-5314-8). Insomnia, sleepwalking, and other sleep-related disorders are discussed. (Rev: BL 1/1–15/01; HBG 10/01; SLJ 2/01) [612.8]

11305 Berger, Melvin. *Exploring the Mind and Brain* (7–10). Illus. 1983, HarperCollins LB $12.89 (0-690-04252-3). A book about the functions — both normal and abnormal — of the brain. [612]

11306 Brynie, Faith. *Perception* (6–10). Series: The Amazing Brain. 2001, Blackbirch LB $21.95 (1-56711-423-7). An introduction to the brain's role in perception and to disorders that can occur. (Rev: BL 10/15/01; HBG 3/02) [612]

11307 Brynie, Faith. *The Physical Brain* (6–10). Series: The Amazing Brain. 2001, Blackbirch $29.94 (1-56711-424-5). Photographs and absorbing text introduce the physical characteristics of the brain. Also use *Neurological Disorders* (2001). (Rev: BL 10/15/01; HBG 3/02; SLJ 9/01; VOYA 10/01) [612.8]

11308 Edelson, Edward. *Sleep* (7–10). Series: Encyclopedia of Health. 1991, Chelsea LB $19.95 (0-7910-0092-3). This book discusses the uses of sleep, people's sleeping habits, and sleeping disorders. (Rev: BL 11/15/91) [612.8]

11309 Garfield, Patricia. *The Dream Book: A Young Person's Guide to Understanding Dreams* (5–8). 2002, Tundra paper $9.95 (0-88776-594-7). The author, a psychologist, explains the meanings of common (and uncommon) dreams and suggests how to use dreams to good effect. (Rev: BL 9/15/02; SLJ 9/02; VOYA 8/02) [154.6]

11310 Hayhurst, Chris. *The Brain and Spinal Cord: Learning How We Think, Feel, and Move* (5–9). Series: 3-D Library of the Human Body. 2002, Rosen LB $26.50 (0-8239-3528-0). Exceptional illustrations and a clear text are used to explain the composition of the brain with explanations of how it works and how emotions influence our thoughts. (Rev: BL 7/02; SLJ 7/02) [612.8]

11311 Hyde, Margaret O., and John F. Setaro. *When the Brain Dies First* (8–12). Illus. 2000, Watts LB $25.00 (0-531-11543-7). This book explores different kinds of brain damage, including skull fractures and Alzheimer's, as well as discussing brain death and giving advice on preventative measures. (Rev: BL 4/15/00; SLJ 7/00) [616.8.]

11312 Innes, Brian. *Powers of the Mind* (4–7). Series: Unsolved Mysteries. 1999, Raintree Steck-Vaughn LB $25.69 (0-8172-5488-9). A balanced account that explores the powers of the brain in such controversial areas as moving objects, planting thoughts, and predicting events. (Rev: BL 5/15/99; HBG 10/99) [612.8]

11313 Lambert, Mark. *The Brain and Nervous System* (5–7). Illus. 1988, Silver Burdett LB $12.95 (0-382-09703-3). Diagrams and photographs highlight this description. (Rev: BL 4/1/89) [612.8]

11314 Llamas, Andreu. *The Nervous System* (8–12). Illus. Series: Human Body. 1998, Gareth Stevens LB $23.93 (0-8368-2113-0). The human nervous system is described with double-page spreads and lavish illustrations. (Rev: BL 12/15/98; HBG 9/99; SLJ 3/99) [612.8]

11315 McPhee, Andrew T. *Sleep and Dreams* (7–12). Illus. 2001, Watts LB $25.00 (0-531-11735-9). Normal sleep patterns, sleep deprivation, and sleep disorders (sleep walking and sleep apnea) are discussed along with the nature and symbolism of dreams. (Rev: BL 6/1–15/01; SLJ 8/01) [616.8]

11316 Parker, Steve. *The Brain and the Nervous System* (5–8). Series: The Human Body. 1997, Raintree Steck-Vaughn LB $18.98 (0-8172-4802-1). Double-page spreads introduce parts of the brain and their functions, brain waves, the nature of sleep and dreams, and other aspects of the brain and the nervous system. (Rev: BL 6/1–15/97; SLJ 8/97) [612.8]

11317 Policoff, Stephen P. *The Dreamer's Companion: A Beginner's Guide to Understanding Dreams and Using Them Creatively* (8–12). Illus. 1997, Chicago Review paper $12.95 (1-55652-280-0). This book covers mastering the art of lucid dreaming, the causes of dreams, how to analyze them, and how to keep a dream journal. (Rev: BL 5/15/98; SLJ 6/98) [154.63]

11318 Silverstein, Alvin, et al. *The Nervous System* (5–8). Illus. Series: Human Body Systems. 1994, Twenty-First Century LB $28.90 (0-8050-2835-8). The human nervous system and how it functions and can malfunction are described, with information on the systems of other animals. (Rev: BL 3/15/95; SLJ 5/95) [612.8]

11319 Silverstein, Alvin, and Virginia Silverstein. *Sleep and Dreams* (7–9). 1974, HarperCollins LB $12.89 (0-397-31325-X). Research into sleep is reviewed along with a description of our sleep patterns, dreams, and what dreams mean. [154.6]

11320 Walker, Pam, and Elaine Wood. *The Brain and Nervous System* (8–12). Series: Understanding the Human Body. 2003, Gale LB $21.96 (1-59018-148-4). The roles of the nervous system and the brain in collecting information, processing it, and sending responses to the various parts of the body, are explained in this attractive introduction to this body system. (Rev: BL 3/15/03) [612]

11321 Walker, Richard. *Brain: Inner Workings of the Gray Matter* (4–8). Series: Secret Worlds. 2002, DK $14.95 (0-7894-8527-3); paper $5.95 (0-7894-8528-1). This book contains a wealth of information (some quite detailed) on the structure and functions of the brain, all presented in a pleasing layout with excellent illustrations. (Rev: BL 8/02; HBG 10/02) [612.82]

Circulatory System

11322 Ballard, Carol. *The Heart and Circulatory System* (5–8). Illus. Series: The Human Body. 1997, Raintree Steck-Vaughn LB $18.98 (0-8172-4800-5). Topics discussed in this nicely illustrated volume include how blood is made, how it is pumped through the body, and how the heart and circulation system work together. (Rev: BL 6/1–15/97; SLJ 8/97) [612.1]

11323 Brynie, Faith Hickman. *101 Questions About Blood and Circulation: With Answers Straight from the Heart* (6–10). Series: 101 Questions. 2001, Twenty-First Century LB $25.90 (0-7613-1455-5). A clear and comprehensive overview of the circulatory system, how it works, and the importance of proper diet and exercise. (Rev: HBG 10/01; SLJ 4/01) [612.1]

11324 Parramon, Merce. *How Our Blood Circulates* (5–7). Series: Invisible World. 1994, Chelsea LB $17.55 (0-7910-2127-0). Double-page spreads introduce the circulatory system and discuss such topics as blood cells, clotting, the heart and its functions, and the lymphatic system. (Rev: SLJ 8/94) [612]

11325 Silverstein, Alvin, and Virginia Silverstein. *Heart Disease: America's #1 Killer*. Rev. ed. (7–10). Illus. 1985, HarperCollins LB $12.89 (0-397-32084-1). After a description of heart diseases, the authors present material on treatments and preventative measures. (Rev: BR 5–6/86; SLJ 1/86) [611]

11326 Silverstein, Alvin, and Virginia Silverstein. *Heartbeats: Your Body, Your Heart* (7–10). Illus. 1983, HarperCollins LB $13.89 (0-397-32038-8). Following a description of the heart and how it works, there are sections on heart disease and research. [612]

11327 Viegas, Jennifer. *The Heart: Learning How Our Blood Circulates* (5–9). Illus. Series: 3-D Library of the Human Body. 2002, Rosen LB $26.50 (0-8239-3532-9). An introduction to the anatomy and function of the human heart and the circulatory system that includes illustrations, diagrams, a glossary, and other aids. (Rev: BL 7/02) [612.1]

Digestive and Excretory Systems

11328 Ballard, Carol. *The Stomach and Digestive System* (5–8). Illus. Series: The Human Body. 1997, Raintree Steck-Vaughn LB $25.68 (0-8172-4801-3). Topics discussed in this nicely illustrated volume include the digestive organs, how they work together, how food is tasted, and where nutrients are stored. (Rev: BL 6/1–15/97; SLJ 8/97) [612.3]

11329 Brynie, Faith Hickman. *101 Questions About Food and Digestion That Have Been Eating at You . . . Until Now* (5–8). Illus. 2002, Millbrook LB $27.90 (0-7613-2309-0). A question-and-answer format succeeds in conveying lots of food for thought, with details on digestive functions, digestive disorders, food safety, fat cells, Mad Cow disease, vitamins, and so forth. (Rev: BL 1/1–15/03; HBG 3/03; SLJ 3/03) [612.3]

11330 Burgess, Jan. *Food and Digestion* (5–8). Illus. Series: How Our Bodies Work. 1988, Silver Burdett LB $12.95 (0-382-09704-1). Advice for staying healthy is provided in this addition to the How Our Bodies Work series. (Rev: BL 4/15/89) [612.3]

11331 Haduch, Bill. *Food Rules! The Stuff You Munch, Its Crunch, Its Punch, and Why You Sometimes Lose Your Lunch* (4–7). Illus. 2001, Dutton $19.99 (0-525-46419-0). An amusing book about food and the digestive process that also gives nutritional information, historical material, and humorous facts. (Rev: BL 3/15/01; HBG 10/01; SLJ 6/01) [613.]

11332 Monroe, Judy. *Coping with Ulcers, Heartburn, and Stress-Related Stomach Disorders* (7–12). Series: Coping. 2000, Rosen LB $17.95 (0-8239-2971-X). Fictional case histories convey lots of information about a variety of uncomfortable stomach conditions, stressing the importance of prevention and early treatment. (Rev: SLJ 6/00) [616.3]

11333 Silverstein, Alvin, et al. *The Excretory System* (5–8). Illus. Series: Human Body Systems. 1994, Twenty-First Century LB $29.90 (0-8050-2834-X). A discussion on the human system of waste elimination. (Rev: BL 3/15/95; SLJ 3/95) [612.4]

11334 Toriello, James. *The Stomach: Learning How We Digest* (5–9). Series: 3-D Library of the Human Body. 2002, Rosen LB $26.50 (0-8239-3536-1). Using outstanding diagrams and clear explanations, the digestive system is highlighted with material on each of its parts and their functions. (Rev: BL 7/02; SLJ 7/02) [612.3]

11335 Walker, Pam, and Elaine Wood. *The Digestive System* (8–12). Illus. Series: Understanding the Human Body. 2002, Gale LB $21.96 (1-59018-150-6). This is a report-worthy text with useful information about the digestive system, some of the diseases relating to it, and the ways in which problems are diagnosed. (Rev: BL 11/1/02; SLJ 2/03) [612.3]

Musculoskeletal System

11336 Ballard, Carol. *The Skeleton and Muscular System* (5–8). Illus. Series: Human Body. 1997, Raintree Steck-Vaughn $18.98 (0-8172-4805-6). This well-organized book introduces in text and pictures such topics as muscles and how they work, joint diseases, bones, and skeletal diseases. (Rev: SLJ 2/98) [612]

11337 Dineen, Jacqueline. *The Skeleton and Movement* (5–7). Illus. 1988, Silver Burdett $12.95 (0-382-09702-5). An explanation of human body movement. (Rev: BL 4/15/89) [612.75]

11338 Feinberg, Brian. *The Musculoskeletal System* (7–12). Series: Encyclopedia of Health. 1993, Chelsea LB $19.95 (0-7910-0028-1). An introduction to the muscles and bones in the human body and how they work together to form a single system. (Rev: BL 12/1/93) [612.7]

11339 Gold, Susan Dudley. *The Musculoskeletal System and the Skin* (5–10). Illus. Series: Human Body Library. 2003, Enslow LB $18.95 (0-7660-2023-1). Gold uses a conversational style to introduce detailed facts about the skeletal system, with useful graphics and some practical advice. (Rev: BL 4/15/03; HBG 10/03; SLJ 10/03) [612.7]

11340 Landau, Elaine. *Spinal Cord Injuries* (6–12). Illus. 2001, Enslow LB $20.95 (0-7660-1474-6). Stories of people who have suffered spinal cord injuries, including Gloria Estefan and Christopher Reeve, are interwoven with information on how spinal injuries affect the body and how patients cope. (Rev: BL 2/1/02; HBG 10/02) [617.4]

11341 Llamas, Andreu. *Muscles and Bones* (8–12). Series: Human Body. 1998, Gareth Stevens LB $23.93 (0-8368-2112-2). The musculoskeletal system is introduced in a series of double-page spreads with lavish illustrations. (Rev: BL 12/15/98; HBG 9/99; SLJ 3/99) [612]

11342 Oleksy, Walter. *The Head and Neck: Learning How We Use Our Muscles* (5–9). Series: 3-D Library of the Human Body. 2002, Rosen LB $26.50 (0-8239-3531-0). The muscles of the head and neck and their roles in controlling the sense organs, chewing and swallowing, facial expressions, and conveying emotions are explained in this well-illustrated account. (Rev: BL 7/02) [612.7]

11343 Sherman, Josepha. *The Upper Limbs: Learning How We Use Our Arms, Elbows, Forearms, and Hands* (5–9). Series: 3-D Library of the Human Body. 2002, Rosen LB $26.50 (0-8239-3537-X). The parts of the arm and hand are examined with illustrated material on how the muscles in these areas function and receive support from the skeletal structure. (Rev: BL 7/02) [612.7]

11344 Silverstein, Alvin, et al. *The Muscular System* (5–8). Illus. Series: Human Body Systems. 1994, Twenty-First Century $29.90 (0-8050-2836-6). Full-color diagrams, drawings, and photographs highlight this survey of the human muscular system. (Rev: BL 3/15/95; SLJ 5/95) [612.7]

11345 Viegas, Jennifer. *The Lower Limbs: Learning How We Use Our Thighs, Knees, Legs, and Feet* (5–9). Series: 3-D Library of the Human Body. 2002, Rosen LB $26.50 (0-8239-3533-7). The bones and muscles of the legs and feet and their functions are described in a clear text and exceptional illustrations. (Rev: BL 7/02; SLJ 7/02) [612.7]

TEETH

11346 Lee, Jordan. *Coping with Braces and Other Orthodontic Work* (4–9). Series: Coping. 1998, Rosen LB $25.25 (0-8239-2721-0). A book about braces, their purposes, and the problems they can cause. (Rev: SLJ 11/98) [612.3]

11347 Siegel, Dorothy. *Dental Health* (7–12). Series: Encyclopedia of Health. 1994, Chelsea LB $19.95 (0-7910-0014-1). An explanation of what teeth are made of, their uses, diseases, and how to take care of them. (Rev: BL 1/1/94) [617.6]

11348 Silverstein, Alvin, and Virginia Silverstein. *So You're Getting Braces: A Guide to Orthodontics* (6–9). 1978, HarperCollins LB $12.89 (0-397-31786-7). The dental specialization of orthodontics is explained as well as why braces are often needed. [617.6]

Respiratory System

11349 Hayhurst, Chris. *The Lungs: Learning How We Breathe* (5–9). Series: 3-D Library of the Human Body. 2002, Rosen LB $26.50 (0-8239-3534-5). Amazing computer graphics are used to explain the composition of the lungs, how they work, and what keeps them healthy. (Rev: BL 7/02) [612.6]

11350 Lambert, Mark. *The Lungs and Breathing* (5–7). Illus. 1988, Silver Burdett LB $12.95 (0-382-09701-7). Profusely illustrated addition to the How Our Bodies Work series. (Rev: BL 4/15/89)

11351 Parker, Steve. *The Lungs and Respiratory System* (5–8). Illus. Series: The Human Body. 1997, Raintree Steck-Vaughn LB $18.98 (0-8172-4803-X). This nicely illustrated volume examines the organs used in breathing, tells how the respiratory system works, and explains what happens when it fails. (Rev: BL 6/1–15/97; SLJ 8/97) [612.2]

11352 Silverstein, Alvin, et al. *The Respiratory System* (5–8). Illus. Series: Human Body Systems. 1994, Twenty-First Century LB $29.90 (0-8050-2831-5). The purpose and process of breathing are discussed, with the text and illustrations focusing on the human respiratory system. (Rev: BL 3/15/95; SLJ 4/95) [612.2]

Senses

11353 Cobb, Vicki. *How to Really Fool Yourself: Illusions for All Your Senses* (7–9). Illus. 1999, Wiley paper $12.95 (0-471-31592-3). A book about perception, how illusions are created, and how they are present in everyday life. [152.1]

11354 Martin, Paul D. *Messengers to the Brain: Our Fantastic Five Senses* (6–9). Illus. 1984, National Geographic LB $12.50 (0-87044-504-9). A well-illustrated introduction to the five senses and how they work. [612]

11355 Sherman, Josepha. *The Ear: Learning How We Hear* (5–9). Series: 3-D Library of the Human Body. 2002, Rosen LB $26.50 (0-8239-3529-9). Using amazing illustrations and clear explanations, Sherman introduces the ear, its anatomy, uses, operation, and problems that can develop. (Rev: BL 7/02) [612.8]

11356 Silverstein, Alvin, et al. *Smelling and Tasting* (6–8). Illus. 2002, Millbrook LB $25.90 (0-7613-1667-1). Human and animal senses of smell and taste are covered in this well-organized and readable volume. Also use *Touching and Feeling* (2002). (Rev: BL 3/15/02; HBG 10/02; SLJ 8/02) [612.8]

11357 Silverstein, Alvin, and Virginia Silverstein. *Glasses and Contact Lenses: Your Guide to Eyes, Eyewear, and Eye Care* (6–9). Illus. 1989, HarperCollins LB $14.89 (0-397-32185-6). A description of how the eye functions, disorders connected with it, and how glasses can help. (Rev: BL 6/15/89; BR 1–2/90; SLJ 6/89; VOYA 8/89) [617.7]

11358 Simon, Seymour. *Eyes and Ears* (5–8). Illus. 2003, HarperCollins LB $16.89 (0-688-15304-6). Simon explains in clear, straightforward terms our ability to see and hear. (Rev: BL 3/15/03*; HBG 10/03; SLJ 6/03) [612.8]

11359 Simon, Seymour. *The Optical Illusion Book* (7–9). Illus. 1984, Morrow paper $6.95 (0-688-03254-0). How optical illusions are created and the part that the brain as well as the eye plays in their perception. [152.1]

11360 Viegas, Jennifer. *The Eye: Learning How We See* (5–9). Illus. Series: 3-D Library of the Human Body. 2002, Rosen LB $26.50 (0-8239-3530-2). This volume on the anatomy and function of the human eye includes illustrations, diagrams, a glossary, and other aids. (Rev: BL 7/02) [612.8]

11361 Viegas, Jennifer. *The Mouth and Nose: Learning How We Taste and Smell* (5–9). Series: 3-D Library of the Human Body. 2002, Rosen LB $26.50 (0-8239-3535-3). The mouth and nose are featured in this heavily illustrated account that covers their composition, functions, and how they work together. (Rev: BL 7/02) [612]

Hygiene and Physical Fitness

11362 Ball, Jacqueline A. *Hygiene* (6–9). Illus. 1989, Rourke LB $19.93 (0-86625-285-1). This book is aimed at preteen and teenage girls and gives tips on care of nails, skin, hair, and so on. (Rev: SLJ 6/89) [613]

11363 Barbour, Scott, and Karin L. Swisher, eds. *Health and Fitness* (7–12). Series: Opposing Viewpoints. 1996, Greenhaven $26.20 (1-56510-403-X). Using carefully selected articles, this book explores different attitudes and controversies concerning diet, physical fitness, and exercise. (Rev: BL 9/15/96; BR 1–2/97; SLJ 8/96; VOYA 10/96) [613]

11364 Crump, Marguerite. *Don't Sweat It! Every Body's Answers to Questions You Don't Want to Ask: A Guide for Young People* (5–9). 2002, Free Spirit paper $13.95 (1-57542-114-3). Crump tackles potentially embarrassing questions about personal hygiene. (Rev: SLJ 1/03; VOYA 2/03) [613.0433]

11365 Frost, Simon. *Fitness for Young People* (4–8). Series: Flowmotion. 2003, Sterling paper $9.95 (0-8069-9373-1). Using a number of excellent stop-action photographs, the routines, techniques, and exercises involved with young people keeping fit are presented. (Rev: BL 10/15/03) [613]

11366 Gedatus, Gus. *Exercise for Weight Management* (4–7). Series: Nutrition and Fitness. 2001, Capstone LB $23.93 (0-7368-0706-3). As well as outlining a simple, practical exercise program, this volume stresses good nutrition and contains some healthy recipes. (Rev: BL 9/15/01; HBG 10/01) [613.7]

11367 Jenner, Bruce, and Bill Dobbins. *The Athletic Body: A Complete Fitness Guide for Teenagers — Sports, Strength, Health, Agility* (7–12). Illus. 1984, Simon & Schuster $17.95 (0-671-46549-X). A guide to physical fitness through sports, weight training, and good nutrition. [613.7]

11368 Johnson, Marlys. *Understanding Exercise Addiction* (7–12). Series: Teen Eating Disorder Prevention Library. 2000, Rosen LB $17.95 (0-8239-2990-6). This book offers teens the opportunity to assess whether attitudes toward exercise, eating, and the human body are normal. (Rev: SLJ 7/00) [616.86]

11369 Kaminker, Laura. *Exercise Addiction: When Fitness Becomes an Obsession* (6–10). Series: Teen Health Library of Eating Disorder Prevention. 1998, Rosen LB $26.50 (0-8239-2759-8). Some teens become addicted to exercise and exercise too much for the wrong reasons. This book defines the problem, risks, and causes, describes the symptoms, and tells where to get help and support if needed. (Rev: BL 3/1/89; BR 5–6/99; SLJ 1/99) [613.7]

11370 Miller, Shannon, and Nancy Ann Richardson. *Winning Every Day: Gold Medal Advice for a Happy, Healthy Life!* (5–9). Illus. 1998, Bantam paper $12.95 (0-553-09776-8). The 1996 Olympic gold medal gymnast describes her life and training and offers tips on stress management, good sportsmanship, and a healthy lifestyle. (Rev: BL 6/1–15/98; SLJ 7/98) [921]

11371 Savage, Jeff. *Fundamental Strength Training* (5–9). Photos by Jimmy Clarke. Series: Fundamental Sports. 1998, Lerner LB $26.40 (0-8225-3461-4). This beginner's manual discusses weight machines, training without weights, and various exercises for developing specific parts of the body. (Rev: HBG 10/99; SLJ 2/99) [613.7]

11372 Simon, Nissa. *Good Sports: Plain Talk About Health and Fitness for Teens* (7–10). Illus. 1990, HarperCollins LB $14.89 (0-690-04904-8). This book covers a variety of topics including nutrition, different kinds of exercise, and sports injuries. (Rev: BCCB 12/99; BL 9/15/90) [613]

11373 Stiefer, Sandy. *A Risky Prescription* (7–12). Illus. Series: Sports Issues. 1997, Lerner LB $28.75 (0-8225-3304-9). This book explores the relationship between sports and health, how some sports activities can lead to disabilities, and how performance-enhancing drugs can compromise or even ruin one's health. (Rev: BL 12/1/97; HBG 3/98; SLJ 3/98) [631.7]

11374 Turck, Mary. *Food and Emotions* (4–7). Series: Nutrition and Fitness. 2001, Capstone LB $23.93 (0-7368-0711-X). This book explains the relationship between nutrition and a healthy emotional life and gives many tips and recipes for healthy living. (Rev: BL 9/15/01; HBG 10/01; SLJ 7/01) [613.2]

11375 Vedral, Joyce L. *Toning for Teens: The 20-Minute Workout That Makes You Look Good and Feel Great!* (7–12). 2002, Warner paper $15.95 (0-446-67815-5). Three sets of dumbbells and a bench or step are the only items required for this daily workout; nutritional and fitness tips are included. (Rev: SLJ 8/02)

Mental Disorders and Emotional Problems

11376 Abeel, Samantha. *What Once Was White* (5–8). 1993, Village Pr. $19.95 (0-941653-13-7). The author is a 13-year-old learning-disabled student who can't tell time but writes sensitive interpretations of a group of watercolor paintings. (Rev: SLJ 9/93*) [618.62]

11377 Adler, Joe Anne. *Stress: Just Chill Out!* (7–10). 1997, Enslow LB $17.95 (0-89490-918-5). This book identifies three types of stress frequently experienced by teenagers — life transition stress, enduring life stress, and chronic daily stress — with chapters on their causes and treatment. (Rev: SLJ 10/97) [152.4]

11378 Axelrod, Toby. *Working Together Against Teen Suicide* (6–10). Series: The Library of Social Activism. 1996, Rosen LB $16.95 (0-8239-2261-8). The author examines the reasons for teenage suicide, suggests ways teens can cope with problems, and explains how telephone hotlines, community agencies, and institutions work to combat teen suicide and how teenagers can help. (Rev: SLJ 5/97) [394]

11379 Bayer, Linda. *Out of Control: Gambling and Other Impulse-Control Disorders* (6–12). Series: Encyclopedia of Psychological Disorders. 2000, Chelsea LB $24.95 (0-7910-5313-X). This account explores the nature, causes, and treatment of such types of compulsive behavior as gambling, kleptomania, pyromania, and hair pulling. (Rev: BL 1/1–15/01; HBG 3/01) [363.4]

11380 Bayer, Linda. *Personality Disorders* (6–12). Illus. Series: Encyclopedia of Psychological Disorders. 2000, Chelsea LB $27.45 (0-7910-5317-2). Ten types of personality disorders including paranoid, schizoid, and antisocial are defined and discussed in this informative account. (Rev: BL 6/1–15/00; HBG 9/00; SLJ 9/00) [616.89.]

11381 Beal, Eileen. *Everything You Need to Know About ADD ADHD* (6–8). Illus. Series: Need to Know Library. 1998, Rosen LB $25.25 (0-8239-2748-2). In six short chapters, the author describes attention deficit disorder and attention deficit hyperactivity disorder, their symptoms, the pros and cons of behavior modification and medications, and how teens can manage these disorders and use them to tap into special talents. (Rev: SLJ 9/98; VOYA 8/99) [371.9]

11382 Beckelman, Laurie. *Body Blues* (6–9). Illus. Series: Hot Line. 1994, Silver Burdett LB $17.95 (0-8968-0842-7). This book is designed to help adolescents understand the changes that are occurring to their body and give reassurance through interviews with other teenagers experiencing the same changes. (Rev: BL 2/15/95) [155.5]

11383 Beckelman, Laurie. *Stress* (6–9). Illus. Series: Hot Line. 1994, Silver Burdett $13.95 (0-89686-848-6). Through interviews with teenagers and quotations from professionals, the world of adolescent stress is explored, with tips on how to deal with it. (Rev: BL 2/15/94) [155.9]

11384 Bellenir, Karen, ed. *Mental Health Information for Teens: Health Tips About Mental Health and Mental Illness* (7–12). Series: Teen Health. 2001, Omnigraphics $48.00 (0-7808-0442-2). A comprehensive and easy-to-use overview of topics ranging from self esteem and physical appearance to abuse, addiction, and specific disorders and phobias, with tips on getting treatment. (Rev: BL 1/1–15/02; SLJ 1/02) [616.89]

11385 Borenstein, Gerri. *Therapy* (4–8). Illus. Series: Life Balance. 2003, Watts LB $19.50 (0-531-12269-7); paper $6.95 (0-531-15585-4). This friendly, reassuring introduction explains what therapy consists of, the different kinds of professionals involved, and the ways in which privacy is maintained. (Rev: BL 10/15/03; SLJ 12/03) [616.89]

11386 Bowman-Kruhm, Mary, and Claudine G. Wirths. *Everything You Need to Know About Learning Disabilities* (6–12). Series: Need to Know Library. 1999, Rosen LB $17.95 (0-8239-2956-6). An introduction to learning disabilities and how people cope with them at school and in everyday life, with fictionalized case studies and information on getting help. (Rev: SLJ 1/00; VOYA 4/00) [616.85]

11387 Clarke, Alicia. *Coping with Self-Mutilation: A Helping Book for Teens Who Hurt Themselves* (7–10). Series: Coping. 1999, Rosen LB $25.25 (0-8239-2559-5). This volume defines various forms of self-mutilation, such as cutting and burning, examines the causes and the physiological and psychological effects, and discusses available treatments and self-help measures. (Rev: SLJ 5/99) [362.2]

11388 Cobain, Bev. *When Nothing Matters Anymore: A Survival Guide for Depressed Teens* (7–12). 1998, Free Spirit paper $13.95 (1-57542-036-8). The author, a psychiatric nurse who works with teens, discusses the types, causes, and warning signs of depression, the dangers of addictions and eating disorders, and the relationship between depression and suicide, and provides information on treatment options and suggestions for developing good mental and physical health. (Rev: SLJ 3/99; VOYA 2/99) [155]

11389 Crook, Marion. *Teenagers Talk About Suicide* (7–12). 1988, NC Pr. paper $12.95 (1-55021-013-0). Interviews with 30 Canadian teenagers who have tried suicide are reprinted. (Rev: BR 9–10/88) [362.2]

11390 Davis, Brangien. *What's Real, What's Ideal: Overcoming a Negative Body Image* (7–12). Series: Teen Health Library of Eating Disorder Prevention. 1998, Rosen LB $26.50 (0-8239-2771-7). Because teenager's bodies are changing so quickly, many become confused about an ideal figure. This book describes why teens develop negative body images and offers suggestions for overcoming self-defeating perceptions. (Rev: BR 5–6/99; VOYA 4/99) [305.23]

11391 Demetriades, Helen A. *Bipolar Disorder, Depression, and Other Mood Disorders* (6–12). Series: Diseases and People. 2002, Enslow LB $20.95 (0-7660-1898-9). The causes and nature of unnatural mood swings and states of depression are examined and treatments that are currently available are discussed. (Rev: BL 12/15/02; HBG 3/03) [616.85]

11392 Dinner, Sherry H. *Nothing to Be Ashamed Of: Growing Up with Mental Illness in Your Family* (5–10). 1989, Lothrop LB $12.93 (0-688-08482-6). A psychologist gives good advice to those who must live with a mentally ill person. (Rev: BL 6/1/89; BR 11–12/89; SLJ 4/89; VOYA 8/89) [616.89]

11393 Donnelly, Karen. *Coping with Dyslexia* (6–9). Series: Coping. 2000, Rosen LB $18.95 (0-8239-2850-0). This volume offers short profiles of celebrities who have dyslexia as well as guidance on coping with this problem and choosing careers. (Rev: HBG 3/01; SLJ 12/00) [616.85]

11394 Fisher, Gary L., and Rhoda Woods Cummings. *The Survival Guide for Kids with LD (Learning Differences)* (5–8). Illus. 1990, Free Spirit paper $9.95 (0-915793-18-0). A book that explains various kinds of learning disabilities and how to cope with them. (Rev: BL 7/90; SLJ 6/90) [371.9]

11395 Giacobello, John. *Everything You Need to Know About Anxiety and Panic Attacks* (5–9). Series: Need to Know Library. 2000, Rosen LB $25.25 (0-8239-3219-2). This book explains anxiety attacks' causes, symptoms, and treatments in a reassuring tone. (Rev: SLJ 1/01) [616]

11396 Giacobello, John. *Everything You Need to Know About the Dangers of Overachieving: A Guide for Relieving Pressure and Anxiety* (6–9). Series: Need to Know Library. 2000, Rosen $25.25 (0-8239-3107-2). Stress-reduction techniques are among the strategies here for limiting the disadvantages of a compelling desire to achieve. (Rev: SLJ 9/00) [155.9]

11397 Girod, Christina M. *Down Syndrome* (7–9). Series: Diseases and Disorders. 2001, Lucent LB $19.96 (1-56006-824-8). The causes of this condition that usually produces mental retardation are discussed with material on how people live with it and how it affects children and their families. (Rev: BL 1/1–15/02; SLJ 4/01) [362.1]

11398 Girod, Christina M. *Learning Disabilities* (7–9). Illus. Series: Diseases and Disorders. 2001, Lucent LB $19.96 (1-56006-844-2). This introduction to learning disabilities and their diagnosis and treatment is enhanced by the stories of adults, such as Cher, who have overcome this problem. Also use *Autism* (2001). (Rev: BL 10/15/01; SLJ 9/01) [371.9]

11399 Gold, Susan D. *Attention Deficit Disorder* (4–8). Series: Health Watch. 2000, Enslow LB $18.95 (0-7660-1657-9). This account focuses on one boy from childhood to college and how he coped with attention deficit disorder. Several young people are profiled in the companion volume *Bipolar Disorder and Depression* (2000). (Rev: HBG 10/01; SLJ 2/01) [618.92]

11400 Goodfellow, Gregory. *Epilepsy* (7–9). Series: Diseases and Disorders. 2001, Lucent LB $19.96 (1-

56006-701-2). The author describes the causes of epilepsy, how it is currently being treated, and how people live with this condition. (Rev: BL 1/1–15/02; SLJ 4/01) [616.8]

11401 Gordon, James S. *Stress Management* (8–12). Illus. Series: 21st Century Health and Wellness. 2000, Chelsea LB $24.95 (0-7910-5987-1). This is a comprehensive and detailed examination of the causes of stress, the negative impact of stress, and ways to reduce stress. (Rev: BL 11/15/00; BR 3–4/01; HBG 10/01; SLJ 2/01)

11402 Gregson, Susan R. *Stress Management: Managing and Reducing Stress* (5–8). Series: Perspectives on Mental Health. 2000, Capstone LB $23.93 (0-7368-0432-3). This book discusses the causes of stress, explains its positive and negative effects on the body and mind, and outlines strategies for reducing and managing it. (Rev: HBG 10/00; SLJ 8/00) [152.4]

11403 Grollman, Earl A., and Max Malikow. *Living When a Young Friend Commits Suicide: Or Even Starts Talking About It* (6–12). 1999, Beacon $24.00 (0-8070-2502-X); paper $12.00 (0-8070-2503-8). Using simple prose and a compassionate attitude, this book examines suicide from many standpoints and gives good advice on the grieving process. (Rev: BL 11/1/99; SLJ 1/00; VOYA 2/00) [368.28]

11404 Hall, David E. *Living with Learning Disabilities: A Guide for Students* (5–8). 1993, Lerner LB $19.93 (0-8225-0036-1). This book explains what learning disabilities are, what causes them, how they can be detected, and today's techniques for treatment. (Rev: BL 1/1/94; SLJ 4/94) [371.9]

11405 Hermes, Patricia. *A Time to Listen: Preventing Youth Suicide* (8–12). 1987, Harcourt $13.95 (0-15-288196-4). Through questions and answers plus many case studies, the author explores many aspects of suicidal behavior and its causes. (Rev: BL 4/1/88; SLJ 3/88; VOYA 6/88) [362.2]

11406 Hurley, Jennifer A., ed. *Mental Health* (7–12). Series: Current Controversies. 1999, Greenhaven LB $32.45 (1-56510-953-8); paper $21.20 (1-56510-952-X). This anthology explores such questions as what constitutes good mental health, what treatments should be used for mentally ill patients, and how should society and the legal system respond to mentally ill people. (Rev: BL 7/99) [616.89]

11407 Hyde, Margaret O., and Elizabeth H. Forsyth. *Depression: What You Need to Know* (6–12). Illus. 2002, Watts $24.00 (0-531-11892-4). Information on celebrities and important figures who have experienced depression add to the details on the history, symptoms, and treatment of the condition. (Rev: BL 10/15/02; SLJ 12/02) [616.85]

11408 Hyman, Bruce M., and Cherry Pedroch. *Obsessive-Compulsive Disorder* (7–10). 2003, Mill-

brook LB $26.90 (0-7613-2758-4). Profiles of teens with OCD introduce a discussion of the condition that will aid understanding and will be useful for teens experiencing anxieties. (Rev: BL 12/15/03) [616.85]

11409 Kahn, Ada P., and Ronald M. Doctor. *Phobias* (4–8). Series: Life Balance. 2003, Watts LB $19.50 (0-531-12256-5); paper $6.95 (0-531-15575-7). This book discusses the causes of phobias, the different types, how they affect people, and their treatment. (Rev: BL 10/15/03) [616.85]

11410 Kent, Deborah. *Snake Pits, Talking Cures, and Magic Bullets: A History of Mental Illness* (6–12). Illus. 2003, Millbrook LB $26.90 (0-7613-2704-5). The madhouses of old, shock treatments, psychotherapy, psychoanalysis, and today's effective drug therapies are among the topics discussed in this volume. (Rev: BL 5/1/03; SLJ 7/03) [616.89]

11411 Klebanoff, Susan. *Ups and Downs: How to Beat the Blues and Teen Depression* (5–9). Illus. Series: Plugged In. 1998, Price Stern Sloan $13.89 (0-8431-7460-9). Written in an informal style, this is an informative, useful discussion of teen depression, its causes, and treatments. (Rev: BL 4/15/99; BR 9–10/99; SLJ 10/99; VOYA 8/99) [616.85]

11412 Kuklin, Susan. *After a Suicide: Young People Speak Up* (7–12). 1994, Putnam $16.95 (0-399-22605-2). Focuses on failed suicide attempts. Also looks at friends and family members who suffer shock, guilt, and loss when suicide succeeds. (Rev: BL 10/15/94; SLJ 12/94; VOYA 2/95) [362.2]

11413 Landau, Elaine. *Autism* (7–12). Illus. 2001, Watts $24.00 (0-531-11780-4). This straightforward look at the history, symptoms, and treatment of autism includes personal stories. (Rev: BL 4/1/02; SLJ 12/01) [616.89]

11414 Lauren, Jill. *Succeeding with LD: 20 True Stories About Real People with LD* (5–8). Illus. 1997, Free Spirit paper $14.95 (1-57542-012-0). Case studies of 20 people ages 10 to 61 who have overcome various learning difficulties. (Rev: BL 6/1–15/97; SLJ 7/97; VOYA 8/97) [371.92]

11415 Leder, Jane. *Dead Serious: A Book for Teenagers About Teenage Suicide* (7–12). 1987, Avon paper $3.50 (0-380-70661-X). This book deals specifically with the symptoms of a suicidal situation and how to cope with the aftereffects of the suicide of a relative or friend. (Rev: SLJ 8/87; VOYA 6/87) [179]

11416 Lee, Mary Price, and Richard S. Lee. *Everything You Need to Know About Natural Disasters and Post-Traumatic Stress Disorder* (5–9). Series: Need to Know Library. 1996, Rosen LB $17.95 (0-8239-2053-4). This book explains how such disasters as hurricanes, floods, and earthquakes can cause post-traumatic stress disorder and how to get help and counseling. (Rev: SLJ 6/96; VOYA 8/96) [155.5]

11417 Leigh, Vanora. *Mental Illness* (5–10). Series: Talking Points. 1999, Raintree Steck-Vaughn LB $27.12 (0-8172-5311-4). This book defines mental illness, gives examples, and discusses causes, treatments, and how to stay mentally healthy. (Rev: BL 8/99; BR 9–10/99; SLJ 8/99) [362.2]

11418 Levine, Mel. *Keeping a Head in School: A Student's Book About Learning Abilities and Learning Disorders* (8–12). Illus. 1990, Educators Publg. paper $24.75 (0-8388-2069-7). This account deals with all sorts of learning disorders, how they affect the learning process, and how they can be treated. (Rev: BL 6/15/90) [371.9]

11419 Moe, Barbara. *Coping with Mental Illness* (7–10). Series: Coping. 2001, Rosen LB $18.95 (0-8239-3205-2). The diagnosis, symptoms, and treatment of major forms of mental illness are discussed, along with the types of professionals who can help. Also use *Schizophrenia* (2001). (Rev: SLJ 8/01) [616.89]

11420 Moehn, Heather. *Social Anxiety* (7–12). 2001, Rosen LB $25.25 (0-8239-3363-6). A strong fear of social situations often manifests itself during adolescence, and Moehn combines case studies and coping strategies with an overview of the condition itself and a look at treatment alternatives. (Rev: BL 3/1/02; SLJ 5/02) [616.85]

11421 Monroe, Judy. *Phobias: Everything You Wanted to Know, But Were Afraid to Ask* (6–10). Series: Issues in Focus. 1996, Enslow LB $20.95 (0-89490-723-9). This book on phobias contains an "A to Z" list detailing each phobia as well as information on causes, treatments, and where to get help. (Rev: SLJ 6/96; VOYA 8/96) [616.85]

11422 Moragne, Wendy. *Depression* (7–12). Illus. Series: Medical Library. 2001, Twenty-First Century LB $24.90 (0-7613-1774-0). Signs, symptoms, diagnosis, and treatment of depression are introduced clearly and concisely with case histories of seven teenagers. (Rev: BL 5/15/01; HBG 10/01; SLJ 4/01; VOYA 10/01) [616.85]

11423 Paquette, Penny Hutchins, and Cheryl Gerson Tuttle. *Learning Disabilities: The Ultimate Teen Guide* (7–12). Series: It Happened to Me. 2003, Scarecrow LB $32.50 (0-8108-4261-0). Teens suffering from conditions including ADHD and dyslexia will find practical information on these disabilities, success stories, and advice on career and employment choices and strategies. (Rev: SLJ 10/03) [371.9]

11424 Partner, Daniel. *Disorders First Diagnosed in Childhood* (6–12). Series: Encyclopedia of Psychological Disorders. 2000, Chelsea LB $24.95 (0-7910-5312-1). This work discusses the symptoms, causes, and treatments for such disorders as autism

and Tourette's syndrome. (Rev: BL 1/1–15/01; HBG 10/01; SLJ 2/01) [616.8]

11425 Peacock, Judith. *Bipolar Disorder: A Roller Coaster of Emotions* (5–8). Series: Perspectives on Mental Health. 2000, Capstone LB $23.93 (0-7368-0434-X). Manic depression is defined with material on its various types and how it is diagnosed and treated in both youngsters and adults. (Rev: HBG 10/00; SLJ 8/00) [616.85]

11426 Peacock, Judith. *Depression* (5–8). Illus. Series: Perspectives on Mental Health. 2000, Capstone LB $23.93 (0-7368-0435-8). The causes and effects of mental depression are introduced, with material on how to handle it and its effects on the human body. (Rev: BL 8/00; HBG 10/00; SLJ 8/00) [616.85]

11427 Porterfield, Kay Marie. *Straight Talk About Learning Disabilities* (6–12). 1999, Facts on File $27.45 (0-8160-3865-1). By using three fictional case studies, the author is able to discuss various kinds of learning disabilities, their symptoms, methods of diagnosis, and available treatments. (Rev: BL 2/15/00; HBG 4/00; SLJ 2/00; VOYA 4/00) [371.92.]

11428 Powell, Mark. *Stress Relief: The Ultimate Teen Guide* (7–12). Series: Ultimate Teen Guide. 2003, Scarecrow LB $32.50 (0-8108-4433-8). Typical causes of teen stress — relationships, homework, money, and so forth — are examined and practical suggestions for dealing with them are spelled out. (Rev: BL 10/15/03; SLJ 7/03; VOYA 4/03) [155.5]

11429 Quinn, Patricia O. *Adolescents and ADD: Gaining the Advantage* (6–12). Illus. 1996, Magination paper $12.95 (0-945354-70-3). As well as citing many case studies, this book on teens and attention deficit disorder provides useful background information plus tips on how to adjust to this condition and how to create a lifestyle that accommodates it. (Rev: BL 1/1–15/96; SLJ 3/96; VOYA 8/96) [371.94]

11430 Roleff, Tamara L., ed. *Suicide* (8–12). Series: Opposing Viewpoints. 1997, Greenhaven LB $32.45 (1-56510-665-2); paper $21.20 (1-56510-664-4). Twenty-four articles express various points of view concerning the ethical and legal aspects of suicide, with special attention to the causes of teen suicide and how it can be prevented. (Rev: BL 11/1/97; BR 11–12/97; SLJ 1/98; VOYA 10/98) [362.28]

11431 Roleff, Tamara L., and Laura Egendorf, eds. *Mental Illness* (6–12). Illus. Series: Opposing Viewpoints. 2000, Greenhaven LB $21.96 (0-7377-0347-4); paper $13.96 (0-7377-0348-2). Differing opinions are offered on a variety of issues relating to mental illness, including diagnosis, treatment, and therapy. (Rev: BL 1/1–15/01) [616.89]

11432 Rosen, Marvin. *The Effects of Stress and Anxiety on the Family* (6–12). Series: Focus on Family Matters. 2002, Chelsea LB $20.75 (0-7910-6950-8). After describing situations that produce stress and anxiety in families, this account outlines effective coping strategies for healthy management of these emotions. (Rev: BL 1/1–15/03; HBG 3/03) [152.4]

11433 Rosen, Marvin. *Understanding Post-Traumatic Stress Disorder* (6–12). Series: Focus on Family Matters. 2003, Chelsea $20.75 (0-7910-6951-6). After a discussion of trauma and situations that cause it in teenagers, this book examines PTSD, its symptoms, and ways in which one can get help. (Rev: BL 10/15/02; SLJ 6/03) [616.89]

11434 Rosenberg, Marsha Sarah. *Coping When a Brother or Sister Is Autistic* (7–12). Series: Coping. 2001, Rosen LB $18.95 (0-8239-3194-3). Siblings of autistic children will find facts about the diagnosis and treatment of the disorder, as well as sympathetic, no-nonsense advice on dealing with the pressures of the situation. (Rev: SLJ 9/01) [618.92]

11435 Rosenberg, Marsha Sarah. *Everything You Need to Know When a Brother or Sister Is Autistic* (5–9). Series: Need to Know Library. 2000, Rosen LB $25.25 (0-8239-3123-4). Autism is defined and described, with material on its diagnosis and treatment plus coverage of how this condition can affect other members of the family. (Rev: SLJ 8/00) [616.8]

11436 Sanders, Pete, and Steve Myers. *Dyslexia* (4–8). Series: What Do You Know About. 1999, Millbrook LB $23.90 (0-7613-0915-2). Using a case study, this book explores one boy's problems with dyslexia, its causes, symptoms, and treatment. (Rev: HBG 10/99; SLJ 10/99) [617.7]

11437 Sebastian, Richard. *Compulsive Behavior* (7–12). Series: Encyclopedia of Health. 1993, Chelsea LB $19.95 (0-7910-0044-3). This book explores the origins of compulsive behavior, its consequences, and its treatment. (Rev: BL 1/1/93) [616.85]

11438 Sheen, Barbara. *Attention Deficit Disorder* (6–10). Series: Diseases and Disorders. 2001, Lucent LB $19.96 (1-56006-828-0). A comprehensive look at the history, causes, diagnosis, symptoms, and treatment of ADD, with quotations from individuals who suffer from the disorder. (Rev: SLJ 9/01) [616.85]

11439 Sherrow, Victoria. *Mental Illness* (6–9). Illus. Series: Overview. 1996, Lucent LB $27.45 (1-56006-168-5). After a general review of what constitutes mental illness, the author focuses on the history of society's treatment of the mentally ill, followed by a discussion of current controversies and approaches to therapy. (Rev: BL 3/1/96; SLJ 2/96; VOYA 8/96) [362.2]

11440 Shields, Charles. *Mental Illness and Its Effects on School and Work Environments* (6–10). Illus. Series: Encyclopedia of Psychological Disorders. 2000, Chelsea $24.95 (0-7910-5318-0). As well as giving a general introduction to the nature of mental illness, this work discusses how the mentally ill affect American society. (Rev: BL 11/1/00) [616.8]

11441 Silverstein, Alvin. *Depression* (6–10). Illus. Series: Diseases and People. 1997, Enslow LB $20.95 (0-89490-713-1). Topics covered in this appealing examination of depression include types, symptoms, and treatments. An extensive bibliography includes Internet sites. (Rev: BL 2/1/98; SLJ 4/98) [616.85]

11442 Silverstein, Alvin, and Virginia Silverstein. *Epilepsy* (7–10). Illus. 1975, HarperCollins $12.95 (0-397-31615-1). Sweeping aside all the untruths associated with this problem, the authors describe the cause and effect of seizures and their treatment. [616.8]

11443 Simpson, Carolyn, and Dwain Simpson. *Coping with Post-Traumatic Stress Disorder* (7–10). Series: Coping. 1997, Rosen LB $25.25 (0-8239-2080-1). Post-traumatic stress disorder (PTSD) affects people who have experienced natural disasters, rape, war, or other traumatic events. This book explains the causes and primary signs of PTSD and how it affects family and friends, as well as the victim, and provides useful information on treatment. (Rev: SLJ 10/97) [362]

11444 Sprung, Barbara. *Stress* (4–8). Illus. Series: Preteen Pressures. 1998, Raintree Steck-Vaughn LB $25.69 (0-8172-5033-6). A concise, practical account of the types and causes of stress in young people and how to manage it. (Rev: BL 4/15/98; HBG 10/98; SLJ 6/98) [155.4]

11445 Stewart, Gail B. *People with Mental Illness* (7–12). Series: The Other America. 2003, Gale LB $21.96 (1-59018-237-5). Personal stories of individuals with different conditions show how they cope with daily life and the impact on the families as well as the patients. (Rev: SLJ 6/03) [616.89]

11446 Stewart, Gail B. *Phobias* (7–9). Series: Diseases and Disorders. 2001, Lucent LB $19.96 (1-56006-726-8). The meaning of "phobia" is explained, with material on common phobias, what causes them, and how they can be treated. (Rev: BL 1/1–15/02; SLJ 10/01) [616.85]

11447 Stewart, Gail B. *Teen Dropouts* (7–12). Series: The Other America. 1998, Lucent LB $27.45 (1-56006-399-8). Four troubled teenagers — two girls and two boys — tell their sad stories about how and why they have become alienated from the mainstream and have withdrawn from life. (Rev: BL 4/15/99; SLJ 4/99) [373.12]

11448 Stewart, Gail B. *Teens and Depression* (6–12). Illus. Series: Other America. 1997, Lucent LB

$27.45 (1-56006-577-X). A discussion of possible causes of teenage clinical depression and how to recognize and treat it as early as possible, supplemented by case studies of four teens and their battles to overcome the condition. (Rev: BL 5/15/98; SLJ 6/98; VOYA 10/98) [616.852700835]

11449 Tocci, Salvatore. *Down Syndrome* (7–12). Illus. 2000, Watts LB $25.00 (0-531-11589-5). This introduces the causes, symptoms, and treatments for the form of mental retardation that bears the name of Dr. John Langdon Down, who identified it in the 1860s. (Rev: BL 5/1/00; SLJ 7/00) [616.85.]

11450 Williams, Julie. *Attention-Deficit / Hyperactivity Disorder* (6–12). Illus. Series: Diseases and People. 2001, Enslow LB $20.95 (0-7660-1598-X). Williams presents the symptoms, diagnosis, and treatment of ADHD, as well as its history, profiles of people who suffer from the condition, research that is being conducted, and the controversies that surround the condition. (Rev: BL 1/1–15/02; HBG 10/02; SLJ 2/02) [618.92]

11451 Williams, Julie. *Pyromania, Kleptomania, and Other Impulse-Control Disorders* (6–12). Series: Diseases and People. 2002, Enslow LB $20.95 (0-7660-1899-7). Various forms of abnormal mental obsessions are discussed with material on causes and treatments. (Rev: BL 12/15/02; HBG 3/03) [616.8]

11452 Wiltshire, Paula. *Dyslexia* (5–8). Illus. Series: Health Issues. 2002, Raintree Steck-Vaughn LB $28.54 (0-7398-5221-3). Color photographs and straightforward text introduce dyslexia's symptoms and treatment and explain how it affects learning, with tips on how to cope with the disability. (Rev: BL 12/15/02; HBG 3/03; SLJ 3/03) [616.85]

11453 Winkler, Kathleen. *Teens, Depression, and the Blues* (6–9). Series: Hot Issues. 2000, Enslow LB $19.95 (0-7660-1369-3). The stories of two teen girls suffering from depression introduce a discussion of causes, symptoms, treatment, and dangers of this condition. (Rev: BL 9/15/00; HBG 9/00; SLJ 8/00) [616.85]

11454 Wolff, Lisa. *Teen Depression* (6–12). Series: Overview: Teen Issues. 1998, Lucent LB $27.45 (1-56006-519-2). The complexities of teen depression and its causes, symptoms, and treatment are discussed. (Rev: BL 1/1–15/99) [616.85]

11455 Woog, Adam. *Suicide* (5–8). Illus. Series: Overview. 1997, Lucent LB $27.45 (1-56006-187-1). An in-depth view of suicide, including causes, frequency, consequences, and detectable warning signs. (Rev: BL 3/15/97; SLJ 4/97) [362.2]

11456 Zeinert, Karen. *Suicide: Tragic Choice* (6–12). Illus. Series: Issues in Focus. 1999, Enslow LB $19.95 (0-7660-1105-4). All aspects of suicide are covered including history, demographic patterns, causes, the grief of survivors, cluster suicide, and

assisted suicide. (Rev: BL 12/15/99; HBG 4/00; VOYA 4/00) [362.28]

11457 Zucker, Faye. *Depression* (4–8). Series: Life Balance. 2003, Watts LB $19.50 (0-531-12259-X); paper $6.95 (0-531-15578-1). This friendly, reassuring introduction explains the causes, diagnosis, and treatment of depression. (Rev: BL 10/15/03; SLJ 12/03) [616.85]

Nutrition and Diet

11458 Bellenir, Karen, ed. *Diet Information for Teens: Health Tips About Diet and Nutrition, Including Facts About Nutrients, Dietary Guidelines, Breakfasts, School Lunches, Snacks, Party Food, Weight Control, Eating Disorders, and More* (7–12). 2001, Omnigraphics $48.00 (0-7808-0441-4). General nutrition information is amplified by topics of particular interest to teens, such as snacking, school lunches, and eating disorders. (Rev: SLJ 6/01; VOYA 8/01) [613.2]

11459 Bijlefeld, Marjolijn, and Sharon K. Zoumbaris. *Food and You: A Guide to Healthy Habits for Teens* (7–12). 2001, Greenwood $45.00 (0-313-31108-0). A comprehensive guide to healthy eating, weight, and exercise that provides lots of information for report writers. (Rev: SLJ 11/01; VOYA 2/02) [613.7]

11460 Drohan, Michele I. *Weight-Loss Programs: Weighing the Risks and Realities* (6–10). Illus. Series: Teen Health Library of Eating Disorder Prevention. 1998, Rosen LB $26.50 (0-8239-2770-9). This book explores weight-loss programs, sheds light on potential dangers, and discusses safe and sensible approaches to weight loss. (Rev: BL 3/1/99; SLJ 1/99) [616.85]

11461 Krizmanic, Judy. *A Teen's Guide to Going Vegetarian* (7–12). 1994, Viking $14.99 (0-670-85114-0); paper $10.99 (0-14-036589-3). Explains the health, ethical, and environmental benefits of switching to a vegetarian diet. Discusses nutrition and provides recipes. (Rev: BL 10/1/94; SLJ 2/95; VOYA 2/95) [613.2]

11462 Landau, Elaine. *A Healthy Diet* (4–7). Series: Watts Library. 2003, Watts LB $24.00 (0-531-12027-9); paper $8.95 (0-531-16668-6). Landau explains the basics of good nutrition; the benefits of vitamins, minerals, and exercise; and the dangers of fad diets. (Rev: SLJ 9/03) [613.2]

11463 Lukes, Bonnie L. *How to Be a Reasonably Thin Teenage Girl: Without Starving, Losing Your Friends or Running Away from Home* (5–8). Illus. 1986, Macmillan $15.00 (0-689-31269-5). A commonsense guide that addresses the particular weight problems of young teenagers. (Rev: BCCB 10/86; BL 1/1/87; SLJ 11/86; VOYA 4/87) [613.2]

11464 Moe, Barbara. *Understanding Negative Body Image* (6–10). Series: Teen Eating Disorder Prevention Library. 1999, Rosen $17.95 (0-8239-2865-9). Our culture stresses body weight and shape, and this book explores the many causes and harmful consequences of a negative body image. (Rev: BL 10/15/99; HBG 9/00; SLJ 1/00; VOYA 2/00) [613.4]

11465 Monroe, Judy. *Understanding Weight-Loss Programs* (6–10). Series: Teen Eating Disorder Prevention Library. 1999, Rosen LB $25.25 (0-8239-2866-7). This book discusses good and bad weight loss programs, how to evaluate them, and how to be on guard for bogus products. (Rev: BL 10/15/99; HBG 9/00; SLJ 1/00) [613.7]

11466 Nardo, Don. *Vitamins and Minerals* (7–12). Series: Encyclopedia of Health. 1994, Chelsea LB $19.95 (0-7910-0032-X). A description of the vitamins and minerals needed by the human body and the importance of each. (Rev: BL 8/94; VOYA 6/94) [613.2]

11467 Parr, Jan. *The Young Vegetarian's Companion* (6–12). Illus. 1996, Watts LB $22.00 (0-531-11277-2). A guide to vegetarianism (with some horrifying descriptions of the meat industry) that stresses health and nutrition and provides a fine directory of further information sources such as films, online sites, and organizations. (Rev: BL 10/15/96; BR 3–4/97; SLJ 12/96; VOYA 6/97) [641.5]

11468 Peavy, Linda, and Ursula Smith. *Food, Nutrition, and You* (7–10). Illus. 1982, Macmillan LB $16.00 (0-684-17461-8). A discussion of digestion, food values, weight, and weight problems. [613.2]

11469 Pierson, Stephanie. *Vegetables Rock! A Complete Guide for Teenage Vegetarians* (7–12). 1999, Bantam paper $13.95 (0-553-37924-0). Animal rights and health issues are touched on in this book that describes philosophical and practical aspects of vegetarianism and provides a guide to good foods and balancing nutritional needs. (Rev: BL 3/1/99) [613.2]

11470 Schwartz, Ellen. *I'm a Vegetarian: Amazing Facts and Ideas for Healthy Vegetarians* (5–8). 2002, Tundra paper $9.95 (0-88776-588-2). The social aspects of being a vegetarian are handled here with humor and sensitivity. (Rev: BL 7/02; SLJ 9/02) [613.2]

11471 Serafin, Kim. *Everything You Need to Know About Being a Vegetarian* (5–8). Series: Need to Know Library. 1999, Rosen LB $25.25 (0-8239-2951-5). This book explains vegetarianism and its various varieties, the reasons why people become vegetarians, the nature of their diets, social problems involved, and names celebrities who are vegetarians. (Rev: SLJ 1/00; VOYA 4/00) [613.2]

11472 Spence, Annette. *Nutrition* (7–9). Illus. 1989, Facts on File $18.95 (0-8160-1670-4). After general information on nutrition, this account gives details on the use of food to improve and maintain health. (Rev: VOYA 8/89) [641.1]

11473 Tattersall, Clare. *Understanding Food and Your Family* (6–10). Series: Teen Eating Disorder Prevention Library. 1999, Rosen $17.95 (0-8239-2860-8). Using many facts and references to case studies, this book describes family dynamics and how eating patterns are developed within the family structure. (Rev: BL 10/15/99; HBG 9/00; SLJ 11/99; VOYA 2/00) [616.85]

11474 Turck, Mary. *Healthy Eating for Weight Management* (4–7). Series: Nutrition and Fitness. 2001, Capstone LB $23.95 (0-7368-0709-8). Good nutrition is emphasized as an effective method of controlling one's weight, and readers will find a fitness plan and several tempting recipes. (Rev: BL 9/15/01; HBG 10/01; SLJ 7/01) [613.2]

11475 Turck, Mary. *Healthy Snack and Fast-Food Choices* (4–7). Series: Nutrition and Fitness. 2001, Capstone LB $23.93 (0-7368-0710-1). Making healthy eating decisions is the focus of this guide to good nutrition that contains some delicious recipes. (Rev: BL 9/15/01; HBG 10/01) [613.2]

11476 VanCleave, Janice. *Janice VanCleave's Food and Nutrition for Every Kid: Easy Activities That Make Learning Science Fun* (4–8). Illus. Series: Science for Every Kid. 1999, Wiley $32.50 (0-471-17666-4); paper $12.95 (0-471-17665-6). Each of the 25 chapters in this book contains information about food, including food groups, the relationship between energy and food, how to read nutrition labels, and vitamins and minerals, plus dozens of easily performed projects that demonstrate these facts and concepts. (Rev: SLJ 8/99) [641.3]

11477 Weiss, Stefanie Iris. *Everything You Need to Know About Being a Vegan* (5–8). Series: Need to Know Library. 1999, Rosen LB $25.25 (0-8239-2958-2). This book discusses vegans, people who do not eat or use animal products (usually for religious reasons), their lifestyles, diets, and possible social problems. (Rev: SLJ 1/00; VOYA 4/00) [613.2]

Physical Disabilities and Problems

11478 Alexander, Sally H. *Do You Remember the Color Blue? And Other Questions Kids Ask About Blindness* (5–8). Illus. 2000, Viking $16.99 (0-670-88043-4). The writer, a blind person, tells about her daily life — how she tells time and works with her guide dog and how she and others have reacted to her disability. (Rev: BCCB 3/00; BL 3/15/00; HBG 10/00; SLJ 4/00) [305.9]

11479 Brown, Fern G. *Special Olympics* (4–7). Illus. 1992, Watts paper $22.00 (0-531-20062-0). The history of the Special Olympics, which began in 1963. (Rev: BCCB 5/92; BL 6/1/92; SLJ 7/92) [796]

11480 Cheney, Glenn. *Teens with Physical Disabilities: Real-Life Stories of Meeting the Challenges* (6–9). 1995, Enslow LB $20.95 (0-89490-625-9). Accounts of teens' daily lives as they struggle and triumph over the challenges imposed by disabilities. Includes short biographies and photographs. (Rev: BL 8/95; SLJ 8/95) [362.4]

11481 Costello, Elaine. *Signing: How to Speak with Your Hands* (7–9). Illus. 1995, Bantam paper $19.95 (0-553-37539-3). A simple explanation of and a guide to the use of sign language for the deaf. [001.56]

11482 Kent, Deborah. *American Sign Language* (5–7). Series: Watts Library: Disabilities. 2003, Watts LB $24.00 (0-531-12018-X); paper $8.95 (0-531-16662-7). This work covers the history of sign language, explains how it works, and tells how it has help countless deaf people. (Rev: BL 10/15/03; SLJ 6/03) [001.56]

11483 Landau, Elaine. *Blindness* (4–7). Illus. Series: Understanding Illness. 1994, Twenty-First Century LB $24.90 (0-8050-2992-3). Both the emotional and scientific aspects of blindness are covered, with an excellent chapter on prevention. (Rev: BL 12/15/94; SLJ 2/95) [617.7]

11484 Landau, Elaine. *Deafness* (4–7). Illus. Series: Understanding Illness. 1994, Twenty-First Century LB $24.90 (0-8050-2993-1). Beginning with the story of a deaf child, this book explores the causes of deafness, the scientific and emotional factors involved, treatments, and problems in adjusting. (Rev: BL 12/15/94; SLJ 2/95) [617.8]

11485 Landau, Elaine. *Living with Albinism* (5–8). Illus. Series: Living With. 1997, Watts LB $23.00 (0-531-20296-8). This book defines albinism, discusses its genetic causes and the accompanying problems related to vision and skin care, and tells how to live with this condition. (Rev: BL 11/15/98; HBG 9/98; SLJ 8/98) [616]

11486 Lutkenhoff, Marlene, and Sonya G. Oppenheimer, eds. *SPINAbilities: A Young Person's Guide to Spina Bifida* (8–12). Illus. 1997, Woodbine paper $16.95 (0-933149-86-7). A collection of essays on spina bifida — the nature of the disability, daily care concerns, and social adjustments. (Rev: BL 2/15/97; SLJ 4/97) [616.8]

11487 Stalcup, Brenda, ed. *The Disabled* (7–12). Series: Current Controversies. 1997, Greenhaven LB $32.45 (1-56510-530-3). This collection of documents explores such questions as the effectiveness of the Americans with Disabilities Act, the degree that the disabled should be helped, and the advisa-

bility of mainstreaming of children. (Rev: BL 2/15/97) [362.4]

11488 Stewart, Gail B. *Teens with Disabilities* (8–12). Photos by Carl Franzén. Series: The Other America. 2000, Lucent LB $19.96 (1-56006-815-9). The personal — and positive — stories of four teens with physical disabilities show how people with these problems can be accommodated in family and social settings. (Rev: SLJ 3/01)

Reproduction and Child Care

11489 Alpern, Michele. *Teen Pregnancy* (6–12). Series: Focus on Family Matters. 2002, Chelsea $20.75 (0-7910-6695-9). This account explores various aspects of teen pregnancy particularly as it effects the entire family. (Rev: BL 10/15/02; HBG 3/03; SLJ 9/02) [618.2]

11490 Bode, Janet. *Kids Still Having Kids: Talking About Teen Pregnancy*. Rev. ed. (7–12). 1999, Watts LB $22.50 (0-531-11588-7). Birth control, miscarriage, abortion, adoption, foster care, and parenting are among the topics discussed in this guide that highlights the experiences of individual teens. (Rev: SLJ 10/99) [306.7]

11491 Byers, Ann. *Teens and Pregnancy: A Hot Issue* (6–12). Series: Hot Issues. 2000, Enslow LB $19.95 (0-7660-1365-0). Various aspects of teen pregnancy are discussed — from social factors that put teens at risk to the financial ramifications of single parenthood to ways in which teens can avoid pregnancy. (Rev: HBG 3/01; SLJ 1/01) [306.874]

11492 Coles, Robert. *The Youngest Parents* (8–12). Illus. 1997, Norton $27.50 (0-393-04082-8). The first two-thirds of this adult book consists of interviews by the author, a child psychiatrist, with teenagers who are or about to be parents, and the last part is a moving photoessay that includes many rural, underprivileged teen parents and their children as subjects. (Rev: BL 2/1/97; VOYA 6/98) [306.85]

11493 Cozic, Charles P., and Johnathan Petrikin, eds. *The Abortion Controversy* (7–12). Series: Current Controversies. 1995, Greenhaven LB $26.20 (1-56510-229-0); paper $16.20 (1-56510-228-2). The morality of abortion and access to it is argued from many points of view. (Rev: BL 3/15/95; SLJ 5/95) [363.4]

11494 Currie, Stephen. *Abortion* (8–12). Illus. Series: Opposing Viewpoints Digests. 2000, Greenhaven $0.00 (0-7377-0229-X); paper $0.00 (0-7377-0228-1). Using primary sources as a foundation, the author presents varied viewpoints on the morality of abortion, laws limiting abortion, and research using aborted fetal tissue. (Rev: SLJ 9/00) [363.46]

11495 Day, Nancy. *Abortion: Debating the Issue* (8–12). Series: Issues in Focus. 1995, Enslow LB $20.95 (0-89490-645-3). A balanced presentation of the subject, with black-and-white photographs, glossary, and extensive notes. (Rev: BL 8/95; SLJ 12/95) [363.4]

11496 *Daycare and Diplomas: Teen Mothers Who Stayed in School* (7–12). Illus. 2001, Fairview paper $9.95 (1-57749-098-3). A group of young women who attend an unusual school that offers childcare relate the difficulties they have experienced in combining parenthood and education. (Rev: BL 5/15/01; VOYA 4/01) [306.874]

11497 Edelson, Paula. *Straight Talk About Teenage Pregnancy* (7–12). Series: Straight Talk. 1998, Facts on File $27.45 (0-8160-3717-5). A frank, nonjudgmental discussion on such topics as abstinence, safe sex, abortion, adoption, and teen parenting, to help young people make wise decisions and take responsibility for their actions. (Rev: BL 3/1/99; BR 9–10/99; SLJ 2/99) [306.874]

11498 Fullick, Ann. *Test Tube Babies: In Vitro Fertilization* (5–8). Series: Science at the Edge. 2002, Heinemann LB $27.86 (1-58810-703-5). This attractive book balances hard science with thought-provoking discussion on this controversial topic. (Rev: BL 10/15/02; HBG 3/03; SLJ 4/03) [613.9]

11499 Gay, Kathlyn. *Pregnancy: Private Decisions, Public Debates* (7–12). 1994, Watts LB $22.00 (0-531-11167-9). Discusses topics involving reproductive freedom, including the pro-choice/pro-life debate, reproductive technologies, population growth, and childbirth methods. (Rev: BL 8/94; SLJ 7/94; VOYA 10/94) [363.9]

11500 Gottfried, Ted. *Teen Fathers Today* (8–12). 2001, Twenty-First Century LB $23.90 (0-7613-1901-8). Real-life stories add immediacy to this practical guide to the challenges of becoming a father during the teen years. (Rev: HBG 3/02; SLJ 12/01; VOYA 2/02) [306.874]

11501 Gravelle, Karen, and Leslie Peterson. *Teenage Fathers* (7–12). 1992, Messner paper $5.95 (0-671-72851-2). Thirteen teenage boys describe their situations and feelings when they became fathers, with comments by the authors. (Rev: BL 10/15/92) [306.85]

11502 Hughes, Tracy. *Everything You Need to Know About Teen Pregnancy* (7–12). Illus. Series: Need to Know Library. 1988, Rosen $24.50 (0-8239-0810-0). A simple unbiased introduction to teen pregnancy and the options available. (Rev: SLJ 4/89) [612]

11503 Hurley, Jennifer A. *Teen Pregnancy* (7–10). Illus. Series. Opposing Viewpoints Digests. 2000, Greenhaven LB $22.96 (0-7377-0366-0); paper $14.96 (0-7377-0365-2). The author has effectively summarized the different points of view and stances about teenage pregnancy. (Rev: BL 11/1/00) [306.874]

11504 Iannucci, Lisa. *Birth Defects* (7–12). Illus. 2000, Enslow LB $19.95 (0-7660-1186-0). The stories of two babies with problems introduce this survey of birth defects and their causes, prevention, diagnosis, and treatment, along with discussion of the impact on the mothers. (Rev: HBG 9/00; SLJ 8/00) [616]

11505 Jackson, Donna M. *Twin Tales: The Magic and Mystery of Multiple Birth* (5–8). Illus. 2001, Little, Brown $16.95 (0-316-45431-1). A clear account of current scientific knowledge about multiple births, with anecdotes from children of multiple births and their families. (Rev: BCCB 2/01; BL 5/15/01; HB 3–4/01; HBG 10/01; SLJ 5/01*) [618.2]

11506 Jakobson, Cathryn. *Think About Teenage Pregnancy* (7–12). Illus. 1993, Walker LB $15.85 (0-8027-8128-4); paper $9.95 (0-8027-7372-9). Problems of teenagers who are pregnant. All possible options are presented plus the social issues involved. (Rev: SLJ 8/88; VOYA 10/88) [612]

11507 Keller, Kristin Thoennes. *Parenting an Infant* (8–12). Series: Skills for Teens Who Parent. 2000, Capstone LB $22.60 (0-7368-0702-0). Keller offers straightforward, accessible guidance to teens who are caring for very young children, with quotations from teen parents. Also use *Parenting a Toddler* (2000). (Rev: BR 5–6/01; HBG 10/01; SLJ 7/01) [649]

11508 Lang, Paul, and Susan S. Lang. *Teen Fathers* (7–12). 1995, Watts LB $25.00 (0-531-11216-0). A fact book not often seen concerning the dilemmas teen fathers face. (Rev: BL 9/1/95; SLJ 12/95) [306.85]

11509 Lindsay, Jeanne W. *Challenge of Toddlers: For Teen Parents — Parenting Your Child from One to Three* (8–12). Illus. Series: Teens Parenting. 1998, Morning Glory $18.95 (1-885356-38-2); paper $12.95 (1-885356-39-0). A practical, updated manual on how teens can raise children from ages one to three, including information on developmental problems. (Rev: BL 10/15/98; HBG 3/99) [649]

11510 Lindsay, Jeanne W. *Pregnant? Adoption Is an Option: Making an Adoption Plan for a Child* (7–12). Illus. 1996, Morning Glory paper $11.95 (1-885356-08-0). Using quotations from many case studies, this book describes the steps in the adoption process and how to develop an adoption plan. (Rev: BL 12/1/96; SLJ 2/97; VOYA 4/97) [362.7]

11511 Lindsay, Jeanne W. *Teen Dads: Rights, Responsibilities and Joys* (7–12). Illus. 1993, Morning Glory $15.95 (0-930934-77-6); paper $9.95 (0-930934-78-4). Teenage fatherhood is explored with good quotations from case histories. (Rev: BL 10/15/93; SLJ 10/93; VOYA 2/94) [649.1]

11512 Lindsay, Jeanne W. *Your Baby's First Year: A Guide for Teenage Parents* (8–12). Illus. Series: Teens Parenting. 1998, Morning Glory $18.95 (1-885356-32-3); paper $12.95 (1-885356-33-1). This book discusses growth changes that occur in babies from birth to age one and how teenage parents can handle these changes and adjust to them. (Rev: BL 10/15/98; HBG 3/99; SLJ 2/99; VOYA 8/99) [649]

11513 Lindsay, Jeanne W., and Jean Brunelli. *Your Pregnancy and Newborn Journey: A Guide for Pregnant Teens* (8–12). Illus. 1998, Morning Glory $18.95 (1-885356-29-3); paper $12.95 (1-885356-30-7). This guide for teens explains the stages of pregnancy, what health care measures should be taken, the process of giving birth, and the special needs of some babies. (Rev: BL 10/15/98; HBG 3/99; SLJ 12/98; VOYA 8/99) [618.2]

11514 Lindsay, Jeanne W., and Sally McCullough. *Discipline from Birth to Three: How Teen Parents Can Prevent and Deal with Discipline Problems with Babies and Toddlers* (8–12). Illus. Series: Teens Parenting. 1998, Morning Glory $18.95 (1-885356-35-8); paper $12.95 (1-885356-36-6). This volume gives practical advice for teen parents on how to handle behavioral problems with their children ages one to three. (Rev: BL 10/15/98; HBG 3/99) [649.64]

11515 Lowenstein, Felicia. *The Abortion Battle: Looking at Both Sides* (7–12). Illus. Series: Issues in Focus. 1996, Enslow LB $20.95 (0-89490-724-7). After a presentation of the facts, the author analyzes arguments on both sides of the abortion controversy. Appended are a glossary, hotline numbers, and a reading list. (Rev: BL 7/96; BR 9–10/96; SLJ 9/96; VOYA 8/96) [363.4]

11516 Moe, Barbara. *A Question of Timing: Successful Men Talk About Having Children* (6–12). Illus. Series: The Teen Pregnancy Prevention Library. 1997, Rosen LB $23.95 (0-8239-2253-7). Men from a variety of backgrounds talk abut why they waited to have children and how they feel about that choice. (Rev: BL 6/1–15/97; BR 9–10/97; VOYA 10/97) [306.874]

11517 Orr, Tamra B. *Test Tube Babies* (5–9). Series: Science on the Edge. 2003, Gale LB $20.95 (1-56711-788-0). This book discusses in vitro fertilization, and how it has helped many but also caused a great deal of controversy. (Rev: BL 10/15/03) [612]

11518 Parker, Steve. *The Reproductive System* (5–8). Illus. Series: Human Body. 1997, Raintree Steck-Vaughn LB $18.98 (0-8172-4806-4). A well-organized, straightforward account that covers male and female anatomy, genes, fertility problems, contraception, STDs, and human development from conception to adolescence. (Rev: SLJ 2/98) [613.9]

11519 Silverstein, Alvin, et al. *The Reproductive System* (5–8). Illus. Series: Human Body Systems. 1994, Twenty-First Century LB $16.95 (0-8050-2838-2). Reproduction in the plant and animal worlds is introduced, focusing on the human system and body parts. (Rev: BL 3/15/95) [612.6]

11520 Silverstein, Herma. *Teenage and Pregnant: What You Can Do* (7–12). 1989, Messner paper $5.95 (0-671-65222-2). Options available to pregnant teens are discussed plus related material on such subjects as contraception and care for the expectant mother. (Rev: BL 3/15/89; BR 9–10/89; SLJ 1/89; VOYA 8/89) [306.7]

11521 Stewart, Gail B. *Teen Fathers* (7–12). Illus. Series: Other America. 1998, Lucent LB $27.45 (1-56006-575-3). Using case studies and many photographs, this account reveals the various levels of responsibility assumed by teens when they become fathers. (Rev: BL 4/15/98; SLJ 6/98) [306.874]

11522 Stewart, Gail B. *Teen Parenting* (6–12). Series: Overview: Teen Issues. 2000, Lucent LB $18.96 (1-56006-517-6). This overview discusses the demographics of teen parents, what their lives are like, the implications for their children, and social responses to teen parenting. (Rev: BL 6/1–15/00; HBG 9/00) [649]

11523 Trapani, Margi. *Listen Up: Teenage Mothers Speak Out* (6–12). Illus. Series: The Teen Pregnancy Prevention Library. 1997, Rosen LB $23.95 (0-8239-2254-5). Young women speak candidly about why they had children at an early age and the impact this has had on their lives. (Rev: BL 6/1–15/97; BR 9–10/97; SLJ 6/97; VOYA 10/97) [306.874]

11524 Trapani, Margi. *Reality Check: Teenage Fathers Speak Out* (7–10). 1997, Rosen LB $23.95 (0-8239-2255-3). Case studies of teenage fathers who did not plan on becoming parents are discussed in this book that does not shun the hardships of being a teenage parent. (Rev: BL 6/1–15/97; SLJ 6/97; VOYA 10/97) [306.85]

11525 Wekesser, Carol, ed. *Reproductive Technologies* (7–12). Series: Current Controversies. 1996, Greenhaven LB $32.45 (1-56510-377-7). The fact that science has enabled infertile couples to have children has raised a number of ethical and legal concerns. These are explored in this collection of original sources. (Rev: BL 6/1–15/96; SLJ 3/96) [176]

11526 Wilks, Corinne Morgan, ed. *Dear Diary, I'm Pregnant: Teenagers Talk About Their Pregnancy* (7–12). Illus. 1997, Annick paper $9.95 (1-55037-440-0). Ten teenage girls talk about how they got pregnant, what they decided to do about it, and how the pregnancy has changed their lives. (Rev: BL 2/1/98; BR 11–12/97; SLJ 8/97; VOYA 12/97) [306.874]

11527 Williams, Kara. *Fertility Technology: The Baby Debate* (6–8). Illus. Series: Focus on Science and Society. 2000, Rosen LB $19.95 (0-8239-3210-

9). An interesting exploration of the types of fertility treatment available, the science behind them, and the controversies surrounding their use. (Rev: SLJ 1/01) [618.1]

Safety and First Aid

11528 Arnold, Caroline. *Coping with Natural Disasters* (7–10). Illus. 1988, Walker LB $14.85 (0-8027-6717-6). Natural disasters such as earthquakes, hurricanes, and blizzards are discussed, with information on how to react in these emergencies. (Rev: BCCB 6/88; BL 6/15/88; SLJ 6/88; VOYA 10/88) [904]

11529 Chaiet, Donna, and Francine Russell. *The Safe Zone: A Kid's Guide to Personal Safety* (4–7). Illus. 1998, Morrow paper $6.95 (0-688-16091-3). This book alerts youngsters to danger signs, gives advice on body language and self-esteem, and offers tips on how to avoid threatening situations. (Rev: BL 4/1/98; HBG 10/98) [613.6]

11530 Goedecke, Christopher J., and Rosmarie Hausherr. *Smart Moves: A Kid's Guide to Self-Defense* (6–8). 1995, Simon & Schuster $16.00 (0-689-80294-3). A martial arts instructor offers this sourcebook of safety and survival strategies. (Rev: BL 9/15/95; SLJ 12/95; VOYA 2/96) [613.6]

11531 Gutman, Bill. *Be Aware of Danger* (5–8). Illus. Series: Focus on Safety. 1996, Twenty-First Century LB $24.90 (0-8050-4142-7). Situations that could be dangerous to young people are highlighted and preventive measures outlined. (Rev: BL 2/1/97; SLJ 2/97) [613.6]

11532 Gutman, Bill. *Hazards at Home* (4–8). Series: Focus on Safety. 1996, Twenty-First Century LB $24.90 (0-8050-4141-9). A look at sources of potential accidents in the home with information on prevention and first-aid procedures. (Rev: BR 11–12/96; SLJ 9/96) [363.1]

11533 Gutman, Bill. *Recreation Can Be Risky* (4–8). Series: Focus on Safety. 1996, Holt LB $24.90 (0-8050-4143-5). The author gives practical suggestions for enjoying such activities as baseball, biking, or hiking while also keeping safe through warm-up exercises, proper equipment, correct clothing, etc. (Rev: BL 7/96; BR 11–12/96; SLJ 9/96; VOYA 10/96) [790]

11534 Roberts, Robin. *Sports Injuries: How to Stay Safe and Keep on Playing* (5–8). Series: Get in the Game! With Robin Roberts. 2001, Millbrook LB $23.90 (0-7613-2116-0). This general sports book that targets girls as a primary audience discusses safety in a variety of sports and how to cope with injuries. (Rev: BL 9/15/01; HBG 3/02; SLJ 1/02) [790]

11535 Wells, Donna K., and Bruce C. Morris. *Live Aware, Not in Fear: The 411 After 9-11 — A Book For Teens* (6–12). 2002, Health Communications paper $9.95 (0-7573-0013-8). The authors offer practical advice for teenagers who want to feel safe again, such as preparing escape routes and keeping a survival kit handy. (Rev: BL 5/15/02; VOYA 6/02) [363.3]

Sex Education and Sexual Identity

11536 Akagi, Cynthia G. *Dear Michael: Sexuality Education for Boys Ages 11–17* (6–10). Illus. 1996, Gylantic $12.95 (1-880197-16-2). Written by a mother to her adolescent son, these letters effectively explore male puberty, the male's role in conception, concerns about dating, and the problems involved in sexual relationships. (Rev: BL 1/1–15/97; VOYA 6/97) [613.9]

11537 Ball, Jacqueline A. *Puberty* (6–9). Illus. 1989, Rourke LB $19.93 (0-86625-283-5). This account aimed at young girls covers such topics as maturation, social problems, and menstruation. (Rev: SLJ 6/89) [305.2]

11538 Blackstone, Margaret, and Elissa Haden Guest. *Girl Stuff: A Survival Guide to Growing Up* (5–7). Illus. 2000, Harcourt $14.95 (0-15-201830-1); paper $8.95 (0-15-202644-4). Coverage of such topics as puberty, physical changes, sex, birth control, and sexually transmitted diseases helps girls learn about becoming young women. (Rev: BL 5/15/00; HBG 10/00; SLJ 6/00) [613]

11539 Bourgeois, Paulette, and Martin Wolfish. *Changes in You and Me: A Book About Puberty, Mostly for Boys* (4–7). Illus. 1994, Andrews & McMeel paper $14.95 (0-8362-2814-6). A straightforward account about the changes, problems, and challenges associated with puberty. A companion volume is *Changes . . . for Girls* (1994). (Rev: BL 2/1/95; SLJ 3/95) [612]

11540 Brody, Janis. *Your Body: The Girls' Guide* (5–10). 2000, St. Martin's paper $4.99 (0-312-97563-5). This book on puberty and body changes covers such subjects as self-image, menstruation, sexuality, sports participation, nutrition, eating disorders, substance abuse, and counseling. (Rev: SLJ 10/00) [612]

11541 Brynie, Faith Hickman. *101 Questions About Sex and Sexuality: With Answers for the Curious, Cautious, and Confused* (6–12). Illus. Series: 101 Questions. 2003, Twenty-First Century LB $27.90 (0-7613-2310-4). Information on abstinence, contraception, sexually transmitted diseases, and other issues of importance to teens is provided in a question-and-answer format with detailed black-and-white illustrations. (Rev: HBG 10/03; SLJ 6/03) [306.7]

11542 Bull, David. *Cool and Celibate? Sex or No Sex* (8–12). 1998, Element Books paper $4.95 (1-901881-17-2). In this discussion of sex, the author argues against teens having sex until they are in stable married relationships. (Rev: SLJ 3/99) [362.29]

11543 Diamond, Shifra N. *Everything You Need to Know About Going to the Gynecologist* (7–12). Series: Need to Know Library. 1999, Rosen LB $25.25 (0-8239-2839-X). This book explains what a gynecologist does, when teenage girls should see one, and how to find one. There is helpful information on menstruation, breast self-examinations, treatments for common reproductive problems, contraception, myths, and what to expect from a pelvic examination. (Rev: SLJ 5/99; VOYA 8/99) [612]

11544 Dunbar, Robert E. *Homosexuality* (7–10). Series: Issues in Focus. 1995, Enslow LB $20.95 (0-89490-665-8). An objective introduction to homosexuality that contains some interesting first-person accounts. (Rev: BL 12/15/95; SLJ 6/96; VOYA 2/96) [305.9]

11545 Ford, Michael T. *Outspoken: Role Models from the Lesbian and Gay Community* (7–12). 1998, Morrow $16.00 (0-688-14896-4). Six men and five women who represent the gay, lesbian, bisexual, and transgendered community tell about their lives, families, and how they have grown to accept their identity. (Rev: BL 5/1/98; BR 9–10/98; HB 5–6/98; SLJ 6/98; VOYA 8/98) [305.9]

11546 Gowen, L. Kris. *Making Sexual Decisions: The Ultimate Teen Guide* (7–12). Illus. Series: It Happened to Me. 2003, Scarecrow $32.50 (0-8108-4647-0). Puberty, safe sex, birth control, and rape are among the topics raised in this volume that stresses the value of being fully informed about one's options. (Rev: SLJ 11/03) [306.7]

11547 Gravelle, Karen, and Nick Castro. *What's Going on Down There? Answers to Questions Boys Find Hard to Ask* (5–10). 1998, Walker paper $8.95 (0-8027-7540-3). Straightforward information for boys covers such topics as physical changes, sexual intercourse, peer pressure, and pregnancy and birth. (Rev: BL 11/1/98; BR 5–6/99; HB 1–2/99; HBG 3/99; SLJ 12/98) [613]

11548 Gravelle, Karen, and Jennifer Gravelle. *The Period Book: Everything You Don't Want to Ask (But Need to Know)* (6–10). Illus. 1996, Walker $15.95 (0-8027-8420-8); paper $8.95 (0-8027-7478-4). Presented in an appealing format, this chatty discussion of menstruation gives basic information, with cartoon-style illustrations. (Rev: BL 3/15/96; BR 9–10/96; SLJ 3/96; VOYA 6/96) [618]

11549 Gurian, Michael. *Understanding Guys: A Guide for Teenage Girls* (8–10). Illus. Series: Plugged In. 1999, Price Stern Sloan $13.89 (0-8431-

7476-5); paper $4.99 (0-8431-7475-7). A practical, often humorous explanation of what boys go through physically, emotionally, and psychologically during puberty, with advice for girls on how to deal with them. (Rev: BR 9–10/99; SLJ 8/99) [612]

11550 Harris, Robie H. *It's Perfectly Normal: A Book About Changing Bodies, Growing Up, Sex, and Sexual Health* (4–7). 1994, Candlewick $19.99 (1-56402-199-8). A frank discussion with candid illustrations are contained in this discussion of the changes, problems, and choices that puberty brings. (Rev: BCCB 10/94; BL 9/15/94*; SLJ 12/94*) [613]

11551 Hoch, Dean, and Nancy Hoch. *The Sex Education Dictionary for Today's Teens and Pre-Teens* (7–12). Illus. 1990, Landmark paper $12.95 (0-9624209-0-5). A dictionary of 350 words related to sex, sexuality, and reproduction all given clear, concise definitions. (Rev: BL 8/90) [306.7]

11552 Huegel, Kelly. *GLBTQ: The Survival Guide for Queer and Questioning Teens* (7–12). Illus. 2003, Free Spirit paper $15.95 (1-57542-126-7). Quotations from teens are interspersed in the practical, common-sense advice for gay, lesbian, bisexual, transgendered, and questioning teens. (Rev: BL 10/1/03; SLJ 12/03) [300.70]

11553 Hyde, Margaret O., and Elizabeth Forsyth. *Know About Gays and Lesbians* (7–12). 1994, Millbrook LB $23.40 (1-56294-298-0). This overview of homosexuality attacks stereotypes, surveys history, examines current controversies, reviews religious responses, and shows how pervasive homophobia still is. (Rev: BL 3/1/94; SLJ 4/94; VOYA 4/94) [305.9]

11554 Johnson, Eric W. *People, Love, Sex, and Families: Answers to Questions That Preteens Ask* (5–8). Illus. 1985, Walker LB $14.85 (0-8027-6605-6). Based on the results of a survey of 1,000 preteens, this book covers a broad range of topics, from sexual abuse to venereal disease to divorce and incest. (Rev: BL 3/15/86) [306.707]

11555 Jukes, Mavis. *Growing Up: It's a Girl Thing: Straight Talk About First Bras, First Periods and Your Changing Body* (4–8). Illus. 1998, Random LB $16.99 (0-679-99027-5); Knopf paper $10.00 (0-679-89027-0). Essential information about the changes girls experience during puberty, with half the book devoted to what to expect and how to plan for their first period, presented in an easy, big-sister style. (Rev: BL 11/1/98; SLJ 11/98) [612]

11556 Jukes, Mavis. *It's a Girl Thing: How to Stay Healthy, Safe, and in Charge* (5–9). Illus. 1996, Knopf $16.99 (0-679-94325-0); paper $12.00 (0-679-87392-9). This guide to puberty for girls discusses such topics as menstruation, drinking and drugs, body changes, contraceptives, sexually transmitted diseases, and sexual abuse and harassment. (Rev: SLJ 6/96*) [612.6]

11557 Lauersen, Niels H., and Eileen Stukane. *You're in Charge: A Teenage Girl's Guide to Sex and Her Body* (8–12). 1993, Ballantine paper $12.00 (0-449-90464-4). An ob/gyn discusses sexual maturation, including pubertal change, sexually transmitted diseases, orgasm, sexual intimacy, condoms, abortion, menstruation, and more. (Rev: BL 5/1/93) [613.9]

11558 Loulan, JoAnn, and Bonnie Worthen. *Period: A Girl's Guide to Menstruation with a Parent's Guide*. Rev. ed. (5–7). Illus. 2001, Book Peddlers $15.95 (0-916773-97-3); paper $9.99 (0-916773-96-5). This practical guide to menstruation is arranged by such questions as "What do I do when I get my first period?" and "What kind of exercise can I do?" (Rev: BL 2/1/01; HBG 10/01) [612.6]

11559 Madaras, Lynda, and Area Madaras. *The What's Happening to My Body? Book for Boys: A Growing Up Guide for Parents and Sons*. 3rd ed. (4–8). Illus. 2001, Newmarket $22.95 (1-55704-447-3); paper $12.95 (1-55704-443-0). This new edition of the classic guide has been recast to suit today's children and their earlier puberty. (Rev: BL 9/1/01) [613.9]

11560 Madaras, Lynda, and Area Madaras. *The What's Happening to My Body? Book for Girls: A Growing Up Guide for Parents and Daughters*. 3rd ed. (7–12). Illus. 2001, Newmarket $22.95 (1-557044-48-1); paper $12.95 (1-557044-44-9). A thorough introduction for girls to puberty that, in this new edition, includes material on such subjects as pregnancy and AIDS. (Rev: VOYA 6/89) [612]

11561 Mahoney, Ellen Voelckers. *Now You've Got Your Period* (6–9). Illus. 1988, Rosen $12.95 (0-8239-0792-9). In conversational tone, this book describes the process of menstruation and gives tips on how to ease cramps, how to use sanitary protection, and so on. (Rev: BL 7/88; SLJ 8/88; VOYA 10/88) [612]

11562 Marcus, Eric. *What If Someone I Know Is Gay? Answers to Questions About Gay and Lesbian People* (7–12). 2000, Price Stern Sloan LB $13.89 (0-8431-7612-1); paper $4.99 (0-8431-7611-3). The author reflects on his own experiences as a gay man, touching on issues including sexuality, relationships, and discrimination. (Rev: BL 3/1/01; HBG 3/01; SLJ 11/00; VOYA 4/01) [306.76]

11563 Mastoon, Adam. *The Shared Heart* (8–12). Illus. 1997, Morrow $24.50 (0-688-14931-6). Through photographs and personal essays, young gays, lesbians and bisexuals share their memories and the problems of coming out. (Rev: BCCB 3/98; BL 11/15/97; BR 3–4/98; SLJ 2/98*) [305.235]

11564 Mosatche, Harriet S., and Karen Unger. *Too Old for This, Too Young for That! Your Survival Guide for the Middle-School Years* (5–8). Illus. 2000, Free Spirit paper $14.95 (1-57542-067-8). This guide to the early years of puberty contains material on self-esteem, family relationships, friendships, and activities; also included is a lengthy section on bodily changes and such events as the onset of menstruation, erections, and ejaculation. (Rev: BL 7/00; SLJ 9/00) [646.7]

11565 Nardo, Don. *Teen Sexuality* (5–8). Illus. Series: Overview. 1997, Lucent LB $27.45 (1-56006-189-8). This book traces changing attitudes toward sex and looks at what's considered acceptable today. (Rev: BL 3/15/97; BR 11–12/97; SLJ 2/97; VOYA 8/97) [362.29]

11566 O'Grady, Kathleen, and Paula Wansbrough, eds. *Sweet Secrets: Telling Stories of Menstruation* (6–10). 1997, Second Story Pr. paper $9.95 (0-929005-33-3). Following an interesting review of attitudes and rituals related to menstruation in various cultures throughout history, the main body of the book recounts 20 anecdotes about young teens and their first periods, interspersed with boxes providing information on topics including tampons, toxic shock syndrome, and breast examinations. (Rev: VOYA 6/98) [530.8]

11567 Ojeda, Auriana, ed. *Homosexuality* (8–12). Series: Opposing Viewpoints. 2003, Gale LB $33.70 (0-7377-1687-8); paper $22.45 (0-7377-1688-6). The essays in this collection debate such topics as the causes of homosexuality, the possibility of changing sexual orientation, and the extent to which gay relationships should be legalized. (Rev: BL 1/1–15/04) [305.9]

11568 Peacock, Judith. *Birth Control and Protection: Options for Teens* (7–12). Series: Perspectives on Healthy Sexuality. 2000, Capstone LB $22.60 (0-7368-0715-2). Peacock reviews the reasons for using birth control and explains the various options and the pros of cons of each method. Also recommended in this series is *Dating and Sex: Defining and Setting Boundaries*. (Rev: HBG 10/01; SLJ 4/01) [363.9]

11569 Pogany, Susan Browning. *Sex Smart: 501 Reasons to Hold Off on Sex* (8–12). 1998, Fairview paper $14.95 (1-57749-043-6). The author uses quotations from teenagers, "Dear Abby," and other sources to explore emotional issues involved in making sexual choices and to argue for abstinence. (Rev: VOYA 4/99) [613.9]

11570 Pollack, Rachel, and Cheryl Schwartz. *The Journey Out: A Guide for and About Lesbian, Gay, and Bisexual Teens* (7–12). 1995, Viking $14.99 (0-670-85845-5); Penguin paper $6.99 (0-14-037254-7). An approachable discussion with sections on terms commonly used, the varied character of the gay community, and special concerns of bisexuals; offers support and opportunities for activism. (Rev:

BL 12/1/95; BR 9–10/96; SLJ 1/96*; VOYA 4/96) [305.23]

11571 Potash, Marlin S., et al. *Am I Weird or Is This Normal?* (8–12). Illus. 2001, Simon & Schuster paper $13.00 (0-7432-1087-5). A mother and teenage daughter take a question-and-answer look at teen relationships, sex, and other difficult aspects of growing up, with concise and frank information that includes both scientific and slang terms. (Rev: BL 8/01) [305.235]

11572 Roleff, Tamara L., ed. *Sex Education* (7–12). Series: At Issue. 1999, Greenhaven LB $26.20 (0-7377-0009-2); paper $17.45 (0-7377-0008-4). A collection of essays and opinion on issues related to teaching about sex, including contraception, sexual abstinence, safe sex, sexual identity, and families with gay parents. (Rev: BL 5/15/99; BR 9–10/99) [613.9]

11573 Rozakis, Laurie. *Teen Pregnancy: Why Are Kids Having Babies?* (5–8). Illus. Series: Issues of Our Time. 1993, Twenty-First Century LB $22.90 (0-8050-2569-3). A slim, easily read account that explains birth control and deplores the fact that teens do not have access to information about it. (Rev: SLJ 2/94) [612.6]

11574 Rue, Nancy N. *Everything You Need to Know About Getting Your Period* (6–9). Series: Need to Know Library. 1995, Rosen LB $25.25 (0-8239-1870-X). A straightforward discussion of the physiological changes that come with puberty. (Rev: BL 11/1/95; SLJ 1/96) [612.6]

11575 Shaw, Tucker, and Fiona Gibb. *This Book Is About Sex* (8–10). Illus. 2000, Putnam paper $5.99 (0-14-131019-7). A hip presentation on topics including STDs, pregnancy, protection, and more, giving both male and female points of view. (Rev: BL 2/1/01) [613.951]

11576 Silver, Diane. *The New Civil War: The Lesbian and Gay Struggle for Civil Rights* (8–12). Series: The Lesbian and Gay Experience. 1997, Watts LB $24.00 (0-531-11290-X). As gay and lesbian groups are fighting for equality under the law, conservative and religious groups are opposing it. This book gives an unbiased account of both sides of this question. (Rev: BL 9/15/97; SLJ 11/97) [305.9]

11577 Solin, Sabrina, and Paula Elbirt. *The Seventeen Guide to Sex and Your Body* (7–10). 1996, Simon & Schuster $17.00 (0-689-80796-1); paper $8.99 (0-689-80795-3). Using a question-and-answer format, this book by the authors of *Seventeen*'s column "Sex and Body" explores common concerns about sex and puberty. (Rev: BL 10/1/96; SLJ 11/96; VOYA 6/97) [613.9]

11578 Westheimer, Ruth. *Dr. Ruth Talks to Kids: Where You Came From, How Your Body Changes, and What Sex Is All About* (5–9). Illus. 1993,

Macmillan $14.00 (0-02-792532-3). A chatty, frank discussion of a wide range of common preteen and teen concerns including puberty, sex, contraception, birth, and AIDS. (Rev: BCCB 7–8/93; BL 7/93; SLJ 6/93; VOYA 8/93) [306.7]

11579 White, Joe. *Pure Excitement: A Radical Righteous Approach to Sex, Love, and Dating* (7–12). 1996, Focus on the Family paper $10.99 (1-56179-483-X). Taking a conservative approach, this book, written by a minister and using many conversations with teens, proposes that premarital sex is harmful to young adults. (Rev: VOYA 8/97) [613.9]

Sex Problems (Abuse, Harassment, etc.)

11580 Bandon, Alexandra. *Date Rape* (6–9). 1994, Macmillan LB $13.95 (0-382-24755-8). A definition of the controversial subject, with information and profiles of both the victim and the attacker. (Rev: BL 3/1/95; SLJ 3/95) [362.88]

11581 Benedict, Helen. *Safe, Strong, and Streetwise* (8–12). 1987, Little, Brown paper $6.95 (0-87113-100-5). A rape-crisis specialist discusses sexual assault, its prevention and treatment. (Rev: BL 1/1/87; BR 1–2/87; SLJ 5/87; VOYA 2/87) [362.7]

11582 Chaiet, Donna. *Staying Safe at School* (7–12). Series: Get Prepared Library. 1995, Rosen LB $23.95 (0-8239-1864-5). How to stay alert and protect oneself while at school, plus tips for girls on avoiding violent crimes on or near school campuses. (Rev: BL 11/15/95; BR 1–2/96; SLJ 2/96) [613.6]

11583 Chaiet, Donna. *Staying Safe at Work* (7–12). Series: Get Prepared Library. 1995, Rosen LB $23.95 (0-8239-1867-X). How to stay alert and protect oneself at work, with material for girls on how to create their own space and give clear messages to others. (Rev: BL 11/15/95; BR 1–2/96; SLJ 2/96; VOYA 4/96) [613.6]

11584 Chaiet, Donna. *Staying Safe on Public Transportation* (6–12). Series: Get Prepared Library. 1995, Rosen LB $16.95 (0-8239-1866-1). This book for young women traveling alone on buses, trains, or subways stresses the importance of awareness, verbal and physical self-defense, having a plan, and listening to one's instincts. (Rev: BL 11/15/95; BR 1–2/96; SLJ 2/96; VOYA 4/96) [363.1]

11585 Chaiet, Donna. *Staying Safe on the Streets* (7–12). Series: Get Prepared Library. 1995, Rosen LB $16.95 (0-8239-1865-3). Discusses situations young women should avoid outside the home and protection techniques. (Rev: SLJ 1/96) [613.6]

11586 Chaiet, Donna. *Staying Safe While Shopping* (7–12). Series: Get Prepared Library. 1995, Rosen

LB $16.95 (0-8239-1869-6). This book tells girls how to stay alert and protect themselves while shopping. (Rev: BL 11/15/95; BR 1–2/96; SLJ 1/96) [364]

11587 Chaiet, Donna. *Staying Safe While Traveling* (6–12). Series: Get Prepared Library. 1995, Rosen LB $23.95 (0-8239-1868-8). In this book for girls traveling alone, the importance of awareness, how to use verbal and physical self-defense, and listening to one's instincts are stressed and examples are given for handling specific situations. (Rev: BL 11/15/95; BR 1–2/96; SLJ 2/96; VOYA 4/96) [363.1]

11588 Foltz, Linda Lee. *Kids Helping Kids: Break the Silence of Sexual Abuse* (4–9). 2003, Lighthouse Point $21.95 (0-9637966-8-2); paper $14.95 (0-9637966-9-0). Personal stories from young people and adults who suffered abuse as children illustrate the guilt and shame typically experienced and show how to get help. (Rev: SLJ 9/03) [362.7]

11589 Guernsey, JoAnn B. *Sexual Harassment: A Question of Power* (7–12). Series: Frontline. 1995, Lerner LB $19.95 (0-8225-2608-5). The issue of harassment in the workplace, school, and everyday life is discussed. Includes historical background and male perspectives. (Rev: BL 7/95; SLJ 8/95) [305.42]

11590 Landau, Elaine. *Sexual Harassment* (8–12). 1993, Walker LB $15.85 (0-8027-8266-3). Attempts to establish a sense of what constitutes inappropriate behavior, still not agreed upon in the courts or in mainstream America. (Rev: BL 6/1–15/93) [305.42]

11591 Leone, Bruno, ed. *Rape on Campus* (8–12). Series: At Issue. 1995, Greenhaven LB $26.20 (1-56510-296-7); paper $17.45 (1-56510-263-0). This anthology of sources explores the rise in rape cases on campuses and the different definitions of rape. (Rev: BL 3/15/95; SLJ 5/95) [364.1]

11592 McFarland, Rhoda. *Working Together Against Sexual Harassment* (7–12). Series: Library of Social Activism. 1996, Rosen LB $16.95 (0-8239-1775-4). Following a review of the history of sexual harassment (of females) and recent scandals, the book emphasizes how teens can combat sexual harassment by responding politically, from fighting for official policies against it at school to organizing chapters of NOW or other organizations. (Rev: SLJ 4/97; VOYA 6/97) [344.73]

11593 Mufson, Susan, and Rachel Kranz. *Straight Talk About Date Rape* (7–12). Series: Straight Talk. 1993, Facts on File $27.45 (0-8160-2863-X). Using examples and analogies, the authors define date rape, tell how it can be avoided, and give suggestions to help date rape victims. (Rev: BL 9/1/93) [362.88]

11594 Munson, Lulie, and Karen Riskin. *In Their Own Words: A Sexual Abuse Workbook for Teenage Girls* (7–12). 1997, Child Welfare League of America paper $10.95 (0-87868-596-0). This manual (for use in therapy situations) helps girls who have been sexually abused work through their problems and plan for the future. (Rev: VOYA 10/97) [382.88]

11595 Nash, Carol R. *Sexual Harassment: What Teens Should Know* (7–12). Illus. Series: Issues in Focus. 1996, Enslow LB $20.95 (0-89490-735-2). After a general introduction to sexual harassment and its many forms, this account focuses on teens, the ways in which they encounter it, and techniques to fight it. (Rev: BL 7/96; SLJ 10/96; VOYA 8/96) [370.19]

11596 Reinert, Dale R. *Sexual Abuse and Incest* (7–12). Series: Teen Issues. 1997, Enslow LB $17.95 (0-89490-916-9). After a general explanation of what constitutes sexual abuse and incest, this work explains how to identify potential abusive situations, and what to do about them. (Rev: BL 12/1/97; HBG 3/98; SLJ 12/97; VOYA 6/98) [362.76]

11597 Rosen, Marvin. *Dealing with the Effects of Rape and Incest* (6–12). Illus. 2002, Chelsea LB $19.75 (0-7910-6693-2). Teens' personal experiences of sexual abuse draw readers into this straightforward account of the upheavals caused by mistreatment and the various coping strategies recommended for young people. (Rev: BL 10/15/02; SLJ 10/02) [616.85]

11598 Shuker-Haines, Frances. *Everything You Need to Know About Date Rape* (7–12). Illus. 1995, Rosen LB $25.25 (0-8239-2882-9). The author explains how date rape occurs and what precautionary measures can be taken. (Rev: BL 1/15/90; VOYA 4/90) [362.88]

11599 White, Katherine. *Everything You Need to Know About Relationship Violence* (7–12). 2001, Rosen LB $17.95 (0-8239-3398-9). The author offers practical guidance on avoiding dating violence, recognizing risk factors, and assessing the health of a relationship. (Rev: SLJ 12/01) [306.73]

11600 Winkler, Kathleen. *Date Rape* (7–12). Illus. Series: Hot Issues. 1999, Enslow LB $21.95 (0-7660-1198-4). Personal stories and easily read data highlight this treatment of a growing problem. (Rev: BL 9/15/99; HBG 4/00; VOYA 4/01) [362.883]

Human Development and Behavior

General and Miscellaneous

11601 Barron, T. A. *The Hero's Trail: A Guide for Heroic Life* (4–7). Illus. 2002, Putnam $14.99 (0-399-23860-3). This collection of anecdotes about both real and fictional characters aims to define heroism, and explores how one can lead a heroic life. (Rev: BL 10/15/02; HBG 3/03; SLJ 12/02; VOYA 12/02) [170]

11602 Dee, Catherine, ed. *The Girls' Book of Friendship: Cool Quotes, True Stories, Secrets and More* (5–9). 2001, Little, Brown paper $8.95 (0-316-16818-1). A well-organized collection of humorous and affecting entries encompassing material from celebrities and everyday teens. (Rev: SLJ 11/01; VOYA 12/01) [177]

11603 Erlbach, Arlene. *Worth the Risk: True Stories About Risk Takers, Plus How You Can Be One, Too* (5–9). Illus. 1999, Free Spirit paper $12.95 (1-57542-051-1). These are 20 case studies of teenagers who took risks, from defying the dominant cliques in school to entering a burning house to save siblings. (Rev: BL 5/1/99; SLJ 8/99) [158]

11604 Fleischman, Paul, ed. *Cannibal in the Mirror* (5–10). Photos by John Whalen. 2000, Twenty-First Century LB $24.90 (0-7613-0968-3). This thought-provoking book takes 27 quotations that describe barbarous behavior of primitive societies and pairs each with a telling photograph of similar behavior in modern American society. (Rev: BL 4/15/00; HBG 10/00; SLJ 4/00) [150]

11605 Hirsch, Karen D. *Mind Riot: Coming of Age in Comix* (8–12). 1997, Simon & Schuster paper $9.99 (0-689-80622-1). This is an anthology of comic strips dealing with adolescents — their identity, their sexuality, their feelings, their friendships, their families, with thumbnail sketches of the artists. (Rev: BL 6/1–15/97; SLJ 8/97) [741.5]

11606 Peacock, Judith. *Anger Management* (5–8). Illus. Series: Perspectives on Mental Health. 2000, Capstone LB $23.93 (0-7368-0433-1). A discussion of anger, its various types, its causes, its effects on the body and on others, and how and when to control it. (Rev: BL 8/00; HBG 10/00; SLJ 8/00) [152.4]

Psychology and Human Behavior

General and Miscellaneous

11607 Acker, Kerry. *Everything You Need to Know About the Goth Scene* (7–12). Illus. 2000, Rosen LB $17.95 (0-8239-3223-0). An informative and reliable guide to the origins, fashions, preferences, and behavior associated with the "Goth" movement. (Rev: BL 12/1/00; SLJ 3/01) [306]

11608 Allenbaugh, Kay. *Chocolate for a Teen's Dreams: Heartwarming Stories About Making Your Wishes Come True* (8–12). Series: Chocolate. 2003, Fireside paper $12.00 (0-7432-3703-X). A collection of stories by teens and older women about their dreams and desires, and how they came true. (Rev: SLJ 9/03) [305.235]

11609 Carlson, Dale B., and Hannah Carlson. *Where's Your Head? Teenage Psychology* (8–12). Illus. 1998, Bick Publishing House paper $14.95 (1-884158-19-6). This book explores in readable format the basic elements of psychological thought concerning personality, influences on beliefs and behavior, the stages of adolescence, and mental illness. (Rev: VOYA 8/98) [150]

11610 Espeland, Pamela. *Knowing Me, Knowing You: The I-Sight Way to Understand Yourself and Others* (8–12). 2001, Free Spirit paper $13.95 (1-57542-090-2). Combining psychological theories, self-testing, and interesting sidebar features, this is a look at the reasons why some people immediately appeal to us and others don't. (Rev: SLJ 1/02) [155.2]

11611 Gardner, Robert, and Barbara Gardner Conklin. *Health Science Projects About Psychology* (7–12). Illus. 2002, Enslow LB $20.95 (0-7660-1439-8). Interesting activities that illustrate psychological concepts are extended by suggestions for further investigation. (Rev: HBG 10/02; SLJ 7/02) [150]

11612 Musgrave, Susan, ed. *Nerves Out Loud: Critical Moments in the Lives of Seven Teen Girls* (8–12). 2001, Annick $19.95 (1-55037-693-4); paper $9.95 (1-55037-692-6). Seven adult women look back at events and problems that absorbed them as teenagers. (Rev: BL 10/1/01; HBG 3/02; SLJ 10/01; VOYA 2/02) [305.235]

11613 O'Halloran, Barbara Collopy. *Creature Comforts: People and Their Security Objects* (6–12). 2002, Houghton $17.00 (0-618-11864-0). First-person accounts, accompanied by photographs, explain why objects such as "blankies" prove invaluable to both children and adults. (Rev: BL 5/1/02; HBG 10/02; SLJ 3/02) [155.4]

11614 Ojeda, Auriana, ed. *Teens at Risk* (8–12). Illus. Series: Opposing Viewpoints. 2003, Gale LB $26.96 (0-7377-1915-X); paper $17.96 (0-7377-1916-8). Questions explored in this anthology involve the factors that put teens at risk, teenage sex and pregnancy, crime and violence, and substance abuse. (Rev: SLJ 11/03) [306]

11615 Salinger, Adrienne. *In My Room: Teenagers in Their Bedrooms* (8–12). 1995, Chronicle paper $16.95 (0-8118-0796-7). A thought-provoking photoessay that explores the thoughts and private domains — the bedrooms — of 40 teenagers, providing a revealing glimpse of the lives of teenagers in the 1990s. (Rev: VOYA 4/96) [612]

11616 Schreibman, Tamar. *Kissing: The Complete Guide* (7–12). 2000, Simon & Schuster paper $3.99 (0-689-83329-6). A breezy look at the history of kissing, different methods of kissing, and kissing games, with quizzes and amusing first-kiss stories. (Rev: SLJ 5/00) [394]

11617 Wandberg, Robert. *Peer Mediation: Agreeing on Solutions* (6–12). Series: Life Skills. 2001, Capstone LB $23.95 (0-7368-1023-4). The process of peer mediation and its value in solving problems are explained, with examples, self-assessments, and discussion questions. (Rev: HBG 3/02; SLJ 6/02) [658]

Emotions and Emotional Behavior

11618 Alpern, Michele. *Overcoming Feelings of Hatred* (6–12). Series: Focus on Family Matters. 2003, Chelsea $20.75 (0-7910-6953-2). This work explores the social and psychological origins of hatred and show how teens can overcome these feelings, particularly toward other race and ethnicities. (Rev: BL 10/15/02; SLJ 6/03) [616]

11619 Latta, Sara. *Dealing with the Loss of a Loved One* (6–12). Series: Focus on Family Matters. 2002, Chelsea LB $20.75 (0-7910-6955-9). This work discusses the many facets of grief and explains how to deal with the behavioral, emotional, and physical changes that may occur after the death of a loved one. (Rev: BL 1/1–15/03; HBG 3/03) [128]

11620 Muharrar, Aisha. *More than a Label: Why What You Wear and Who You're with Doesn't Define Who You Are* (6–12). Illus. 2002, Free Spirit paper $13.95 (1-57542-110-0). The results of a survey of American youth form the basis of this accessible and lively discussion of the dangers of stereotyping. (Rev: BL 11/1/02; SLJ 12/02; VOYA 12/02) [305.235]

Ethics and Moral Behavior

11621 Canfield, Jack, et al. *Chicken Soup for the Teenage Soul: 101 Stories of Life, Love and Learning* (7–12). 1997, Health Communications paper $12.95 (1-55874-463-0). An inspirational collection of writings, about one-third by teenagers, that discuss the problems of growing up and how others have faced them. (Rev: BL 10/1/97) [158.1]

11622 Canfield, Jack, and Mark V. Hansen. *Chicken Soup for the Teenage Soul II: 101 More Stories of Life, Love and Learning* (7–12). 1998, Health Communications $24.00 (1-55874-615-3); paper $12.95 (1-55874-616-1). A new collection of personal stories from teens that supply inspiration and guidance. (Rev: BL 11/1/98; HBG 3/99) [158.1]

11623 Hurley, Jennifer A., ed. *American Values* (6–12). Series: Opposing Viewpoints. 2000, Greenhaven LB $21.96 (0-7377-0344-X); paper $13.96 (0-7377-0343-1). Conservative and liberal points of view are expressed in this collection of essays that discuss moral relativism, capitalism, religion, violence, pop culture, and character building. (Rev: BL 9/15/00; SLJ 10/00) [304.6]

11624 Kincher, Jonni. *The First Honest Book About Lies* (7–12). 1992, Free Spirit paper $14.95 (0-915793-43-1). Provides tools to extract "real" information from statistics, advertisements, etc., as well as techniques for arguing persuasively. (Rev: BL 3/1/93) [155.9]

11625 Kuklin, Susan. *Speaking Out: Teenagers Take on Sex, Race and Identity* (7–12). 1993, Putnam $8.95 (0-399-22532-3). Students give their views on prejudice, sex, race, and identity. (Rev: BL 8/93; SLJ 7/93) [305.2]

11626 Margulies, Alice. *Compassion* (8–12). Illus. 1990, Rosen LB $15.95 (0-8239-1108-X). A discussion of the different kinds of compassion and how each helps both the individual and society. (Rev: SLJ 6/90) [152.4]

11627 Simpson, Carolyn. *High Performance Through Negotiation* (8–12). Series: Learning-a-Living Library. 1996, Rosen LB $26.50 (0-8239-2206-5). This book discusses negotiation skills and how students can resolve conflicts in a variety of situations. (Rev: BL 9/15/96; BR 1–2/97; SLJ 10/96; VOYA 2/97) [158]

11628 *Teens at Risk* (8–12). Ed. by Laura K. Egendorf and Jennifer A. Hurley. Series: Opposing Viewpoints. 1998, Greenhaven LB $32.45 (1-56510-949-X); paper $21.20 (1-56510-948-1). Questions explored in this anthology involve the factors that put teens at risk, teenage crime and violence, prevention of teenage pregnancy, and the roles of government and the media in teenage difficulties. (Rev: BL 9/15/98) [306]

Etiquette and Manners

11629 Cabot, Meg. *Princess Lessons* (5–7). Series: Princess Diaries. 2003, HarperCollins $12.99 (0-06-052677-7). Princess Mia gives lighthearted tips and often quite practical tips on behaving like a real princess. (Rev: BL 5/15/03; HBG 10/03; VOYA 10/03) [646.7]

11630 Dougherty, Karla. *The Rules to Be Cool: Etiquette and Netiquette* (5–9). Series: Teen Issues. 2001, Enslow LB $17.95 (0-7660-1607-2). Respect and consideration for others are the key elements of Dougherty's rules of behavior, with an emphasis on politeness, kindness, and courtesy, on the Internet as well as at home and at school. (Rev: HBG 3/02; SLJ 10/01) [395]

11631 Hoving, Walter. *Tiffany's Table Manners for Teenagers* (7–12). Illus. 1989, Random $17.00 (0-394-82877-1). A practical guide to good table manners. (Rev: BR 9–10/89; SLJ 6/89) [395]

11632 James, Elizabeth, and Carol Barkin. *Social Smarts: Manners for Today's Kids* (4–7). Illus. 1996, Clarion paper $6.95 (0-395-81312-3). Table manners and responsible, appropriate public behavior are two topics covered. (Rev: BL 9/1/96; SLJ 9/96) [395]

11633 Packer, Alex J. *How Rude! The Teenagers' Guide to Good Manners, Proper Behavior, and Not Grossing People Out* (6–12). Illus. 1997, Free Spirit paper $19.95 (1-57542-024-4). A candid, often humorous guide to good manners for teenagers that stresses common sense and covers situations ranging from inline skating to computer hacking. (Rev: BL 2/1/98; SLJ 2/98; VOYA 6/98) [395.1]

11634 Post, Elizabeth L., and Joan M. Coles. *Emily Post's Teen Etiquette* (7–12). 1995, HarperCollins paper $13.00 (0-06-273337-0). Full of information on good manners and consideration for others. (Rev: BL 10/1/95; VOYA 12/95) [395]

11635 Robert, Henry M. *Robert's Rules of Order* (8–12). 1993, Revell paper $5.99 (0-8007-8610-6). The most authoritative guide to running meetings. [060.4]

11636 Stewart, Marjabelle Young, and Ann Buchwald. *What to Do When and Why* (4–7). 1988, Luce $14.95 (0-88331-105-4). An easily read introduction to the basics of good manners and behavior.

Intelligence and Thinking

11637 Galbraith, Judy, and Jim Delisle. *The Gifted Kids' Survival Guide: A Teen Handbook*. Rev. ed. (7–12). Illus. 1996, Free Spirit paper $15.95 (1-57542-003-1). Topics included in this very useful discussion of gifted children include definitions of giftedness, IQ testing, perfectionism, goal setting, college choices, peers, and suicide among gifted and talented teens. (Rev: SLJ 2/97; VOYA 6/97) [371.95]

11638 Wartik, Nancy, and La Vonne Carlson-Finnerty. *Memory and Learning* (7–12). Series: Encyclopedia of Health. 1993, Chelsea LB $19.95 (0-7910-0022-2). Explores two operations of the brain and explains how they function and sometimes malfunction. (Rev: BL 3/15/93; VOYA 8/93) [153.1]

Personal Guidance

11639 Arredia, Joni. *Sex, Boys, and You: Be Your Own Best Girlfriend* (5–9). Illus. 1998, Perc Publg. paper $15.95 (0-9653203-2-4). A self-help book for younger teen girls with advice on how to accept oneself, when to say "no" to sex, how to assess one's strengths and weaknesses, and how to develop healthy relationships with boys. (Rev: BR 5–6/99; SLJ 10/98) [305.23]

11640 Asgedom, Mawi. *The Code: The Five Secrets of Teen Success* (7–12). 2003, Little, Brown $15.95 (0-316-82633-2); paper $9.99 (0-316-73689-9). Asgedom, a motivational speaker who was a refugee before coming to the United States and later attending Harvard, advises teens on strategies for success. (Rev: SLJ 11/03)

11641 Bachel, Beverly K. *What Do You Really Want? How to Set a Goal and Go for It!* (6–12). Illus. 2001, Free Spirit paper $12.95 (1-57542-085-6). Bachel lays out ways to define and achieve goals, supported by quotations from teens who have tried them and reproducible forms. (Rev: BL 5/15/01; VOYA 8/01) [153.8]

11642 Benson, Peter L., et al. *What Kids Need to Succeed: Proven, Practical Ways to Raise Good Kids* (7–12). 1998, Free Spirit paper $6.95 (1-57542-030-9). This book contains 1,200 ideas for building "assets," such as commitment to learning, positive values, social skills, and positive identity, that have been found to be factors in leading a successful life. (Rev: VOYA 8/99) [305.23]

11643 Benson, Peter L., and Judy Galbraith. *What Teens Need to Succeed: Proven, Practical Ways to Shape Your Own Future* (7–12). Illus. 1998, Free Spirit paper $15.95 (1-57542-027-9). Based on surveys from 350,000 U.S. teens, this book discusses positive "external assets" (families, peers, spiritual support systems, schools) and "internal assets" (honesty, motivation, decision-making skills, resistance skills) that contribute to a successful life. (Rev: SLJ 4/99; VOYA 8/99) [305.23]

11644 Blume, Judy. *Letters to Judy: What Your Kids Wish They Could Tell You* (6–9). 1986, Pocket Books paper $4.50 (0-671-62696-5). This collection of letters and advisory comments covers all the problems encountered by young teens such as menstruation, drugs, popularity, and divorce. (Rev: BL 6/1/86; VOYA 8/86) [305.2]

11645 Bokram, Karen, and Alexis Sinex, eds. *The Girls' Life Guide to Growing Up* (7–12). 2000, Beyond Words paper $11.95 (1-58270-026-5). A compilation of *Girl's Life* advice on topics from friends and family to school, romance, and self-image. (Rev: SLJ 10/00) [646.7]

11646 Bolden, Tonya, ed. *33 Things Every Girl Should Know: Stories, Songs, Poems and Smart Talk by 33 Extraordinary Women* (6–12). 1998, Crown paper $13.00 (0-517-70936-8). A collection of highly readable pieces by well-known and successful women on the difficult transition from childhood to adulthood. (Rev: BL 5/15/98; BR 11–12/98; HBG 9/98; SLJ 5/98) [810.8092827]

11647 Bridgers, Jay. *Everything You Need to Know About Having an Addictive Personality* (7–12). Series: Need to Know Library. 1998, Rosen LB $25.25 (0-8239-2777-6). The author examines the social, psychological, and biochemical aspects of an "addictive personality," explains why some people are more susceptible to addiction than others, and offers sound advice on how teens can cope with addiction. (Rev: SLJ 1/99) [157]

11648 Camron, Roxanne. *60 Clues About Guys: A Guide to Feelings, Flirting, and Falling in Like* (6–10). Series: 60 Clues About. 2002, Lunchbox paper $8.95 (0-9678285-5-4). For girls, this is a how-to manual for coping with relationships with the opposite sex, with a personal dating diary at the end. (Rev: SLJ 7/02)

11649 *Camy Baker's Body Electric: 30 Cool Rules for a Brand-New You* (5–7). Series: Camy Baker. 1999, Bantam paper $3.99 (0-553-48658-6). This is a practical guide to surviving the problems of early adolescence. Also use *Camy Baker's It Must Be Love: 15 Cool Rules for Choosing a Better Boyfriend* (1999). (Rev: SLJ 6/99) [362]

11650 Canfield, Jack, et al., eds. *Chicken Soup for the Christian Teenage Soul: Stories of Faith, Love, Inspiration and Hope* (6–12). 2003, Health Communications paper $12.95 (0-7573-0095-2). Stories, poems, and cartoons of particular relevance to teens are grouped in thematic chapters. (Rev: BL 10/1/03) [242]

11651 Carlson, Dale B., and Hannah Carlson. *Girls Are Equal Too: How to Survive — For Teenage Girls* (6–9). Illus. 1998, Bick Publishing House paper $14.95 (1-884158-18-8). This work tells girls that it is okay to be smart, successful, a leader, and feel good. (Rev: VOYA 10/98) [305.23]

11652 Carter-Scott, Cherie. *If High School Is a Game, Here's How to Break the Rules: A Cutting Edge Guide to Becoming Yourself* (7–12). 2001, Delacorte $12.95 (0-385-32796-X). Topics covered in this guide to teen behavior include substance use and abuse, sexuality, body decorations, and changing family relationships. (Rev: BL 2/15/01; HBG 10/01; SLJ 3/01; VOYA 6/01) [373.238]

11653 Choron, Sandra, and Harry Choron. *The Book of Lists for Teens* (7–12). 2002, Houghton paper $12.00 (0-618-17907-0). More than 300 lists cover a wide range of topics of interest to teens, such as music videos, sports, eating disorders, substance abuse, and bullying. (Rev: SLJ 1/03; VOYA 4/03) [031.02]

11654 *CityKids Speak on Relationships* (7–12). 1995, Random paper $5.99 (0-679-86553-5). Quick bits on everything from meeting people and falling in love to sexual behavior and harassment. (Rev: BL 5/1/95) [302]

11655 Clark, Sondra, and Silvana Clark. *You've Got What It Takes! Sondra's Tips for Making Your Dreams Come True* (4–7). 2002, Revell paper $8.99 (0-8007-5836-6). Twelve-year-old Sondra, a spokesperson for Childcare International, gives practical tips on achieving goals. (Rev: SLJ 3/03) [158.1]

11656 Cohen-Posey, Kate. *How to Handle Bullies, Teasers and Other Meanies: A Book That Takes the Nuisance out of Name Calling and Other Nonsense* (4–7). 1995, Rainbow paper $8.95 (1-56825-029-0). A practical book that offers useful suggestions on how to handle bullies. (Rev: BCCB 12/95; BL 11/15/95) [646.7]

11657 Cordes, Helen. *Girl Power in the Classroom: A Book About Girls, Their Fears, and Their Future* (5–8). Illus. 2000, Lerner LB $30.35 (0-8225-2693-X). This book of personal guidance for girls describes how to conquer fears and cope with difficult situations at school. (Rev: BL 5/15/00; HBG 10/00; SLJ 5/00) [373.1822]

11658 Cordes, Helen. *Girl Power in the Mirror: A Book About Girls, Their Bodies, and Themselves* (5–8). Illus. 2000, Lerner LB $30.35 (0-8225-2691-3). This book for girls explains proper attitudes about appearance and gives coping strategies concerning pressures about one's looks. (Rev: BL 5/15/00; HBG 10/00; SLJ 5/00) [306.4]

11659 Corriveau, Danielle, ed. *Trail Mix: Stories of Youth Overcoming Adversity* (7–12). Illus. 2001, Corvo Communications $14.95 (0-9702366-0-3). Fourteen teens tell inspiring first-person stories about hard times and the value of spending time in an outdoor program. (Rev: BL 12/1/01; SLJ 1/02) [158.1]

11660 Daldry, Jeremy. *The Teenage Guy's Survival Guide: The Real Deal on Girls, Growing Up, and Other Guy Stuff* (6–9). 1999, Little, Brown paper $8.99 (0-316-17824-1). From pimples to pornography, this guide book for boys is humorous, frank, and truthful about such subjects as dating, masturbation, drugs, mood swings, and homosexuality. (Rev: BL 5/15/99; SLJ 7/99; VOYA 10/99) [305.235]

11661 Dee, Catherine, ed. *The Girls' Book of Wisdom: Empowering, Inspirational Quotes from Over 400 Fabulous Females* (5–8). 1999, Little, Brown paper $8.95 (0-316-17956-6). A collection of quotations from more than 400 famous women grouped by such subjects as "Friends," "Happiness," and "Leadership." (Rev: SLJ 12/99; VOYA 4/00) [305.23]

11662 Dee, Catherine. *The Girls' Guide to Life: How to Take Charge of the Issues That Affect You* (5–8). Illus. 1997, Little, Brown paper $15.99 (0-316-17952-3). Concerns including self-esteem, political awareness, cultural stereotypes, and sexual harassment are introduced through first-person narratives, poetry, and advice. (Rev: BCCB 7–8/97; BL 7/97; BR 3–4/98; HB 7–8/97, 11–12/97; VOYA 8/97) [305.42]

11663 Dentemaro, Christine, and Rachel Kranz. *Straight Talk About Student Life* (6–10). Series: Straight Talk. 1993, Facts on File $27.45 (0-8160-2735-8). This book explores problems that students are likely to experience, including communication with teachers and other students, parental pressures, homework, and developing a healthy social life. (Rev: BL 9/1/93) [373.18]

11664 Devillers, Julia. *GirlWise: How to Be Confident, Capable, Cool, and in Control* (8–12). 2002, Prima paper $12.95 (0-7615-6363-6). Topics covered in this accessible volume of advice from experts range from fashion and diet to car repair doing laundry. (Rev: SLJ 12/02) [646.7]

11665 Drill, Esther, et al. *Deal with It! A Whole New Approach to Your Body, Brain and Life as a Gurl* (8–12). Illus. 1999, Pocket paper $15.00 (0-671-04157-6). Much of the flavor of the popular Gurl.com site is duplicated in this eye-catching book full of frank information about sex, adolescent development and behavior, and succeeding in life. (Rev: BL 10/1/99) [305.235]

11666 Erlbach, Arlene. *The Middle School Survival Guide* (5–7). 2003, Walker $16.95 (0-8027-8852-1); paper $8.95 (0-8027-7657-4). The author offers tips on a wide variety of topics of interest to this age group (homework, drugs, sex, and so forth), interspersed with advice from students themselves. (Rev: BL 9/15/03; SLJ 9/03) [373.18]

11667 Espeland, Pamela. *Life Lists for Teens: Tips, Steps, Hints, and How-tos for Growing Up, Getting Along, Learning, and Having Fun* (8–12). 2003, Free Spirit paper $11.95 (1-57542-125-9). Lists of suggestions, tips, and resources cover all topics of interest to teens — health, school, homework, safety, bullying, pregnancy, abuse, and so forth. (Rev: LMC 11–12/03; SLJ 5/03; VOYA 6/03) [646.7]

11668 Fox, Annie. *Can You Relate? Real-World Advice for Teens on Guys, Girls, Growing Up, and Getting Along* (6–12). 2000, Free Spirit paper $15.95 (1-57542-066-X). This guidance book tells teens how to form relationships with family, peers, and girl or boy friends with material on how to understand oneself. (Rev: BL 4/15/00; SLJ 7/00) [305.235.]

11669 Gordon, Sol. *The Teenage Survival Book* (7–12). 1981, Times Books paper $20.00 (0-8129-0972-0). This book discusses the important concerns and worries of adolescents and gives sound practical advice. [155.5]

11670 Grapes, Bryan J., ed. *Interracial Relationships* (8–12). Series: At Issue. 1999, Greenhaven LB $21.96 (0-7377-0152-2); paper $13.96 (0-7377-0154-4). From a variety of perspectives and different kinds of sources, this book explores the social implications of interracial relationships, including marriage. (Rev: BL 12/15/99; SLJ 7/00) [306.73]

11671 Greenberg, Judith E. *A Girl's Guide to Growing Up: Making the Right Choices* (5–8). Illus. 2000, Watts LB $23.00 (0-531-11592-5). Lots of personal stories are quoted in this guidance book for preteen and teenage girls dealing with such subjects as school, risky behaviors, dating, sex, self-esteem, eating disorders, and cliques. (Rev: BL 2/15/01; SLJ 4/01; VOYA 6/01) [305.23]

11672 Gurian, Michael. *From Boys to Men: All About Adolescence and You* (5–7). Series: Plugged In. 1999, Price Stern Sloan paper $4.99 (0-8431-7483-8). Using a conversational tone, the author covers preteen emotional and physical changes and discusses topics including friendship, social and sexual relationships, peer pressure, and keeping healthy as they relate to boys. (Rev: SLJ 7/99) [605.23]

11673 Harlan, Judith. *Girl Talk: Staying Strong, Feeling Good, Sticking Together* (6–10). Illus. 1977, Walker $15.95 (0-8027-8640-5); paper $8.95 (0-8027-7524-1). A breezy, lighthearted guide to approaching everyday problems faced by adolescent girls, with practical tips on how to solve them. (Rev: BL 12/1/97; VOYA 2/98) [305.23]

11674 Harper, Suzanne, ed. *Hands On! 33 More Things Every Girl Should Know* (6–12). Illus. 2001, Crown LB $14.99 (0-517-80099-3); paper $12.95 (0-517-80098-5). A variety of people, including authors and a video DJ, give teens advice about health, boys, school, and projects. (Rev: BL 2/1/01; HBG 10/01; SLJ 3/01; VOYA 4/01) [158.1]

11675 Harris-Johnson, Debrah. *The African-American Teenagers' Guide to Personal Growth, Health, Safety, Sex and Survival: Living and Learning in the 21st Century* (6–12). 2000, Amber paper $19.95 (0-9655064-4-4). This guide for young African Americans growing up in America today covers such topics as family structure, friendships, sexual orientation, work, and spirituality. (Rev: BL 2/15/00; VOYA 6/02) [646.7.]

11676 Johnson, Kevin. *Could Someone Wake Me Up Before I Drool on the Desk? Conquering School and Finding Friends Who Count* (6–9). 1995, Bethany House paper $7.99 (1-55661-416-0). Between Bible verses, the author supplies homey, often humorous observations and advice for about 45 different problems and concerns facing teenagers. (Rev: BL 2/15/96; SLJ 1/96) [242]

11677 Johnson, Kevin. *Does Anybody Know What Planet My Parents Are From?* (6–9). 1996, Bethany House paper $7.99 (1-55661-415-2). Using a religious framework and a breezy style, the author offers young teens advice on how to get along at home and at school. (Rev: BL 10/1/96; VOYA 2/97) [248.8]

11678 Johnston, Andrea. *Girls Speak Out: Finding Your True Self* (6–9). 1997, Scholastic paper $17.95 (0-590-89795-0). Based on a self-esteem and consciousness-raising workshop in which young women are encouraged to speak out and express their true feelings. (Rev: BR 11–12/97; SLJ 2/97) [158]

11679 Johnston, Marianne. *Let's Talk About Being Shy* (4–8). Illus. Series: Let's Talk. 1996, Rosen LB $17.25 (0-8239-2304-5). The causes and possible cures of shyness are covered in this straightforward discussion. Also use *Let's Talk About Being Afraid* (1996). (Rev: BL 3/15/97) [155.4]

11680 Jones, Carolyn. *Every Girl Tells a Story: A Celebration of Girls Speaking Their Minds* (6–8). Illus. 2002, Simon & Schuster $21.95 (0-689-84872-2). Eighty-five American girls between the ages of 12 and 18 share information about their lives and their aspirations in this visually appealing volume produced in collaboration with the Girl Scouts of the USA. (Rev: BL 3/1/02; HBG 10/02; SLJ 4/02; VOYA 8/02) [305.4]

11681 Karnes, Frances A., and Suzanne M. Bean. *Girls and Young Women Inventing: Twenty True Stories About Inventors Plus How You Can Be One Yourself* (6–8). 1995, Free Spirit paper $12.95 (0-915793-89-X). The story of Jennifer Donabar and her invention of the electric clock is just one of the examples given in this survey of 20 young female inventors and their ingenuity, perseverance, imagination, and hard work. (Rev: BL 2/1/96; SLJ 12/95; VOYA 2/96) [920]

11682 Keltner, Nancy, ed. *If You Print This, Please Don't Use My Name* (7–12). Illus. 1992, Terra Nova Pr. paper $8.95 (0-944176-03-8). Letters from a California advice column for teens on topics ranging from sexuality to school. (Rev: BL 1/1/92; SLJ 7/92) [305.23]

11683 Kirberger, Kimberly. *On Relationships: A Book for Teenagers* (7–12). Series: Teen Love. 1999, Health Communications paper $12.95 (1-55874-734-6). Letters, stories, and poems tackle problems that arise in romantic relationships. (Rev: BL 10/15/99; SLJ 1/00) [306.7]

11684 Kirberger, Kimberly, and Colin Mortensen. *On Friendship: A Book for Teenagers* (6–10). Series: Teen Love. 2000, Health Communications paper $12.95 (1-55874-815-6). This comforting overview of the meaning of friendship features writings by teenagers. (Rev: BL 1/1–15/01; SLJ 4/01) [302.3]

11685 Kreiner, Anna. *Creating Your Own Support System* (7–10). Series: Need to Know Library. 1996, Rosen LB $25.25 (0-8239-2215-4). An easy-to-read account that teaches how to create a support system of friends, neighbors, relatives, clergy members, and teachers, if support is not available at home. (Rev: SLJ 1/97) [305.23]

11686 Landau, Elaine. *Interracial Dating and Marriage* (7–12). 1993, Messner LB $13.98 (0-671-75258-8). Narratives by 10 young adults and five adults relate experiences with and reactions to interracial relationships. (Rev: BL 11/1/93) [306.73]

11687 *Let's Talk About Me! A Girl's Personal, Private, and Portable Instruction Book for Life* (6–10). Illus. 1997, Archway paper $12.00 (0-671-01521-4). A self-help book that discusses problems girls experience growing up, best for use with individuals because of its many fill-in-the-blank quizzes and spaces for diary entries. (Rev: VOYA 2/98) [305.23]

11688 Lewis, Barbara A. *What Do You Stand For? A Kid's Guide to Building Character* (6–9). 1997, Free Spirit paper $19.95 (1-57542-029-5). This book explores the topic of character building through self-assessment, recommended readings, and activities that explore one's attitudes and reactions to real-life situations. (Rev: BR 11–12/98; SLJ 1/00; VOYA 8/98) [305.23]

11689 Lindsay, Jeanne W. *Caring, Commitment and Change: How to Build a Relationship That Lasts* (7–12). Series: Teenage Couples. 1995, Morning Glory $15.95 (0-930934-92-X); paper $9.95 (0-930934-93-8). A look at the personal issues involved in marriage. (Rev: BL 4/15/95; SLJ 3/95) [646.7]

11690 Locker, Sari. *Sari Says: The Real Dirt on Everything from Sex to School* (8–12). 2001, HarperCollins paper $11.95 (0-06-447306-6). Teen People online columnist Sari gives frank and friendly advice on everything from braces to sex. (Rev: SLJ 2/02; VOYA 4/02) [305.235]

11691 Lound, Karen. *Girl Power in the Family: A Book About Girls, Their Rights, and Their Voice* (5–10). Series: Girl Power. 2000, Lerner LB $30.35 (0-8225-2692-1). A book that explores the problems of growing up female today with material on gender roles, biases, and relationships. (Rev: HBG 10/00; SLJ 6/00) [303.6]

11692 McCoy, Kathy, and Charles Wibbelsman. *Growing and Changing: A Handbook for Preteens* (6–8). Illus. 1987, Putnam paper $14.95 (0-399-51280-2). A guide to the physical, social, and emotional changes that occur during early adolescence. (Rev: BL 3/1/87; SLJ 4/87) [649]

11693 McCoy, Kathy, and Charles Wibbelsman. *Life Happens* (7–12). 1996, Berkley paper $12.95 (0-399-51987-4). In a concise, practical way, this book covers such teenage crisis-producing situations as death in the family, stress, alcoholism, teen pregnancy, homosexuality, and the breakup of relationships. (Rev: BL 2/1/96) [616.98]

11694 McCoy, Kathy, and Charles Wibbelsman. *The New Teenage Body Book*. Rev. ed. (7–12). Illus. 1992, Putnam paper $15.95 (0-399-51725-1). This revised edition provides information and advice concerning the use of drugs, alcohol, and cigarettes; how to handle peer pressure; contraceptive methods; and abortion. (Rev: BL 6/15/92; SLJ 5/92) [613]

11695 McCune, Bunny, and Deb Traunstein. *Girls to Women: Sharing Our Stories* (7–10). Illus. 1998, Celestial Arts paper $14.95 (0-89087-881-1). Arranged under thematic chapters that deal with self-esteem, friendships, menstruation, sexuality, and mother–daughter relations, this collection of essays, stories, and poems explore various aspects of being young and female. (Rev: SLJ 4/99) [305.23]

11696 Moehn, Heather. *Everything You Need to Know About Cliques* (5–8). Series: Need to Know Library. 2001, Rosen LB $25.25 (0-8239-3326-1). Moehn uses first-person narratives to introduce such topics as making friends, peer pressure, bullies, insecurity, and popularity, with a look at how cliques continue after high school. (Rev: SLJ 12/01) [158.25]

11697 Monson-Burton, Marianne, comp. *Girls Know Best 2: Tips On Life and Fun Stuff to Do!* (5–8). Series: Girl Power. 1998, Beyond Words paper $8.95 (1-885223-84-6). Girls ages 10 to 16 give hundreds of tips, bits of advice, and projects concerning adolescent problems both serious and trivial. (Rev: SLJ 1/99) [155]

11698 Morgenstern, Julie, and Jessi Morgenstern-Colon. *Organizing from the Inside Out for Teens: The Foolproof System for Organizing Your Room, Your Time, and Your Life* (7–12). Illus. 2002, Holt paper $15.00 (0-8050-6470-2). Strategies for managing the time, space, and responsibilities of typical teens are presented in this practical manual. (Rev: BL 1/1–15/03) [646.7]

11699 Morgenstern, Mindy. *The Real Rules for Girls* (8–12). Illus. 2000, Girl Pr. $14.95 (0-9659754-5-2). Advice on life, love, friends, and more, is presented in an attractive, conversational way. (Rev: SLJ 3/00; VOYA 4/00)

11700 Musgrave, Susan, ed. *You Be Me: Friendship in the Lives of Teen Girls* (7–12). 2002, Annick $18.95 (1-55037-739-6); paper $7.95 (1-55037-738-8). Stories of girls' experiences show the sometimes difficult realities of teenage friendships. (Rev: BL 12/15/02; HBG 3/03; SLJ 1/03; VOYA 12/02) [305.235]

11701 Noel, Carol. *Get It? Got It? Good! A Guide for Teenagers* (7–12). Illus. 1996, Serious Business paper $7.95 (0-9649479-0-0). A teenage self-help guide that discusses such topics as self-esteem, sex, health, relations with others, goals, and violence. (Rev: BL 6/1–15/96) [361.8]

11702 Nuwer, Hank. *High School Hazing: When Rites Become Wrongs* (8–12). Illus. 2000, Watts LB $25.00 (0-531-11682-4). After a discussion on the rationale behind hazing rituals, this account describes many that have resulted in unnecessary humiliation, physical harm, and even death. (Rev: BL 4/1/00) [373.18.]

11703 Packard, Gwen K. *Coping When a Parent Goes Back to Work* (8–12). Series: Coping. 1995, Rosen LB $25.25 (0-8239-1698-7). Gives children whose parents return to work tips on adapting to the new situation. Includes real-life examples. (Rev: BL 7/95) [306.874]

11704 Parker, Julie. *High Performance Through Leadership* (8–12). Series: Learning-a-Living Library. 1996, Rosen LB $26.50 (0-8239-2205-7). This book discusses the ability to lead and teach others and shows students how they can take the initiative in problem solving and decision making. (Rev: BL 9/15/96; BR 1–2/97; SLJ 12/96) [158]

11705 Rimm, Sylvia. *See Jane Win for Girls: A Smart Girl's Guide to Success* (5–9). Illus. 2003, Free Spirit paper $13.95 (1-57542-122-4). Rimm offers practical advice on social and academic achievement and general life skills, with quizzes, activities, and success stories. (Rev: LMC 10/03; SLJ 6/03) [305.235]

11706 Robinson, Sharon. *Jackie's Nine: Jackie Robinson's Values to Live By* (5–8). Illus. 2001, Scholastic paper $15.95 (0-439-23764-5). A collection of inspirational writings, selected by baseball legend Jackie Robinson's daughter and organized under headings including "Courage" and "Determination," that include material by and about such well-known individuals as Christopher Reeve and Oprah Winfrey. (Rev: BL 7/01; HBG 10/01; SLJ 6/01; VOYA 8/01) [158]

11707 Roehm, Michelle, comp. *Girls Know Best: Advice for Girls from Girls on Just About Everything!* (5–9). 1997, Beyond Words paper $8.95 (1-885223-63-3). In 26 topically arranged chapters, girls ranging in age from 7 to 16 give advice on such matters as life's embarrassments, difficult parents, volunteerism, boys, depression, divorce, backyard camping, and saving the environment. (Rev: SLJ 12/97) [305.23]

11708 Sanders, Pete, and Steve Myers. *It's My Life* (5–9). Illus. Series: Life Education. 1997, Watts paper $19.00 (0-531-14429-1). This book of practical advice focuses on the emotional changes that accompany the onset of puberty and adolescence, including relationships with families and friends, lifestyle choices, peer pressure, drugs, and making decisions. (Rev: BCCB 3/98; HBG 3/98; SLJ 1/98) [305.23]

11709 Santamaria, Peggy. *High Performance Through Self-Management* (8–12). Series: Learning-a-Living Library. 1996, Rosen LB $26.50 (0-8239-2208-1). This volume shows students how to work with others and teaches them to identify, discuss, and resolve problems as a group. (Rev: BL 9/15/96; BR 1–2/97; SLJ 8/96) [640]

11710 Schleifer, Jay. *The Dangers of Hazing* (7–12). Series: Need to Know Library. 1996, Rosen LB $25.25 (0-8239-2217-0). The phenomenon of hazing in high schools and colleges is discussed, with material on how to avoid it, its dangers, and how to report incidents. (Rev: SLJ 1/97) [305.23]

11711 Schneider, Meg. *Popularity Has Its Ups and Downs* (6–8). 1992, Messner paper $5.95 (0-671-72849-0). Common-sense information is presented about popularity and why it may not be what it seems, along with a discussion of self-confidence and friendship. (Rev: BL 11/15/92) [158]

11712 Schwager, Tina, and Michele Schuerger. *Gutsy Girls: Young Women Who Dare* (7–12). Illus. 1999, Free Spirit paper $14.95 (1-57542-059-7). The first part of this book profiles 25 "gutsy" individuals who have tackled a variety of challenges; the second part suggests ways to motivate yourself to achieve more. (Rev: SLJ 11/99; VOYA 2/00) [155.5]

11713 Schwager, Tina, and Michele Schuerger. *The Right Moves: A Girl's Guide to Getting Fit and Feeling Good* (6–12). 1998, Free Spirit paper $15.95 (1-57542-035-X). Topics including self-esteem, diet, and exercise are covered in this upbeat guide for girls that promotes a positive, healthy lifestyle. (Rev: BL 1/1–15/99; BR 5–6/99; SLJ 1/99*; VOYA 8/99) [613.7]

11714 Shaw, Tucker. *"What's That Smell?" (Oh, It's Me): 50 Mortifying Situations and How to Deal* (7–12). Illus. 2003, Penguin paper $7.99 (0-14-250011-9). With a smart, sarcastic tone, this book deals with problems including odors, bodily functions, awkward situations, and legal concerns. (Rev: BL 2/15/03; SLJ 4/03) [646.7]

11715 Taylor, Julie. *The Girls' Guide to Friends* (7–12). 2002, Three Rivers Press paper $12.00 (0-609-80857-5). A lighthearted look at getting and keeping friends, with quizzes and other entertaining features. (Rev: BL 12/15/02) [158.2]

11716 Wesson, Carolyn McLenahan. *Teen Troubles* (7–12). 1988, Walker $17.95 (0-8027-1011-5); paper $11.95 (0-8027-7310-9). A candid, sometimes humorous self-help book on teenage problems and how to face them. (Rev: VOYA 12/88) [155.5]

11717 Weston, Carol. *For Girls Only: Wise Words, Good Advice* (4–8). 1998, Avon paper $5.99 (0-380-79538-8). Arranged by broad topics — friendship, love, and family, for example — this is a collection of quotations from people ranging from Aesop and Socrates to Oprah Winfrey and Madonna. (Rev: SLJ 7/98; VOYA 8/98) [305.23]

11718 Weston, Carol. *For Teens Only: Quotes, Notes, and Advice You Can Use* (6–12). 2002, HarperCollins paper $8.99 (0-06-000214-X). More than 500 quotations introduce advice and inspiration for all areas of teenage life. (Rev: BL 12/1/02; SLJ 2/03; VOYA 2/03) [646.7]

11719 Weston, Carol. *Private and Personal: Questions and Answers for Girls Only* (5–7). 2000, HarperCollins paper $10.99 (0-380-81025-5). Using categories such as family, friendship, boyfriends, and growing up, this book consists of letters requesting advice and the author's responses to these letters. (Rev: BL 5/1/00; SLJ 7/00) [158]

11720 White, Lee, and Mary Ditson. *The Teenage Human Body Operator's Manual* (6–10). Illus. 1999, Northwest Media paper $9.95 (1-892194-01-5). Using an appealing layout and cartoon illustrations, this is an overview of teenagers' physical and psychological needs, touching on hygiene, nutrition, disease, pregnancy and birth control, and mental health. (Rev: SLJ 11/98) [305.23]

11721 Williams, Terrie. *Stay Strong: Simple Life Lessons for Teens* (6–10). 2001, Scholastic $15.95 (0-439-12971-0). Williams offers advice on topics of interest to teens — ethical behavior, manners, money, and relationships — with success stories and quotations from celebrities. (Rev: BL 5/15/01; HBG 10/01; SLJ 6/01; VOYA 6/01) [305.235]

11722 Wirths, Claudine G., and Mary Bowman-Kruhm. *Coping with Confrontations and Encounters with the Police* (7–12). Series: Coping. 1997, Rosen LB $25.25 (0-8239-2431-9). This book gives teens essential and realistic information that will help them deal successfully with police encounters and minimize potential risks. (Rev: SLJ 4/98; VOYA 2/98) [364.3]

11723 Wolfelt, Alan D. *Healing Your Grieving Heart for Teens: 100 Practical Ideas* (6–12). 2001, Companion Pr. paper $11.95 (1-879651-23-8). The author, a teacher and grief counselor, offers 100 practical tips on accepting and dealing with grief and provides tasks that will help teens identify their needs. (Rev: BL 3/15/01; SLJ 9/01; VOYA 8/01)

11724 *Yikes! A Smart Girl's Guide to Surviving Tricky, Sticky, Icky Situations* (4–8). Series: American Girl Library. 2002, Pleasant paper $8.95 (1-58485-530-4). Advice on everything from dealing with teachers and friends to coping with embarrassing situations and dangerous incidents. (Rev: SLJ 12/02) [305.23]

Social Groups

Family and Family Problems

11725 Alpern, Michele. *Let's Talk: Sharing Our Thoughts and Feelings During Times of Crisis* (6–12). Series: Focus on Family Matters. 2003, Chelsea $20.75 (0-7910-6954-0). This account examines reactions that accompany times of crisis, such as anxiety and depression, and shows how teens can share their feelings with parents and friends. (Rev: BL 10/15/02) [306.9]

11726 Armitage, Ronda. *Family Violence* (6–10). Series: Talking Points. 1999, Raintree Steck-Vaughn LB $18.98 (0-7398-1371-4). This brief but balanced account explores family violence, its causes, types, and effects. (Rev: BL 12/15/99; HBG 9/00) [362.82]

11727 Block, Joel D., and Susan S. Bartell. *Stepliving for Teens: Getting Along with Stepparents, Parents, and Siblings* (7–12). Series: Plugged In. 2001, Price Stern Sloan LB $13.89 (0-8431-7569-9); paper $4.99 (0-8431-7568-0). This helpful and practical guide to coping with new family members, written by two psychologists, includes advice on communicating effectively. (Rev: BCCB 7–8/01; BR 11–12/01; SLJ 8/01) [306.8]

11728 Blue, Rose. *Staying Out of Trouble in a Troubled Family* (7–10). 1998, Twenty-First Century LB $24.90 (0-7613-0365-0). Using eight case studies, this book features family problems that will be familiar to teens, analyses by professionals, and avenues for help. (Rev: BL 2/1/99; HBG 3/99; SLJ 6/99) [362.7]

11729 Bode, Janet. *For Better, For Worse: A Guide to Surviving Divorce for Preteens and Their Families* (5–8). Illus. 2001, Simon & Schuster $16.00 (0-689-81945-5). Using extensive interviews with preteens, this is a practical guide to handling divorce. Half of the book is for preteens, the other half for parents. (Rev: BCCB 2/01; BL 1/1–15/01; HBG 10/01; SLJ 2/01) [306.89]

11730 Bode, Janet. *Truce: Ending the Sibling War* (8–12). 1991, Watts LB $23.00 (0-531-10996-8). Case studies and interviews with teens, followed by professional analyses and potential solutions. (Rev: BL 3/15/91; SLJ 6/91) [155.44]

11731 Bollick, Nancy O'Keefe. *How to Survive Your Parents' Divorce* (7–12). Series: The Changing Family. 1994, Watts paper $24.00 (0-531-11054-0). Interviews with teens who have lived through the divorce of their parents, with analysis of their feelings and behaviors. (Rev: BL 1/1/95; SLJ 3/95; VOYA 4/95) [306.89]

11732 Brondino, Jeanne, et al. *Raising Each Other* (7–12). Illus. 1988, Hunter House paper $8.95 (0-89793-044-4). This book, written and illustrated by a high school class, is about parent–teen relationships, problems, and solutions. (Rev: SLJ 1/89; VOYA 4/89) [306.1]

11733 Charlish, Anne. *Divorce* (5–10). Series: Talking Points. 1999, Raintree Steck-Vaughn LB $27.12 (0-8172-5310-6). An overview of the causes of divorce, the legal aspects, and the difficult adjustments that must be made. (Rev: BL 8/99; BR 9–10/99) [306.89]

11734 Cooper, Kay. *Where Did You Get Those Eyes? A Guide to Discovering Your Family History* (5–7). 1988, Walker LB $14.85 (0-8027-6803-2). A helpful guide for researching the family tree. (Rev: BCCB 11/88; BL 1/15/89; SLJ 2/89)

11735 Currie, Stephen. *Adoption* (5–8). Illus. Series: Overview. 1997, Lucent LB $27.45 (1-56006-183-9). A well-illustrated account of the history of adoption and present-day practices, procedures, and problems. (Rev: BL 5/15/97; BR 11–12/97; SLJ 4/97) [362.7]

11736 Davies, Nancy M. *Foster Care* (6–12). 1994, Watts LB $25.00 (0-531-11081-8). Details foster-care laws and operational procedures and explores the varied feelings of children in foster homes, with suggestions for possible alternatives. (Rev: BL 8/94; SLJ 7/94; VOYA 10/94) [362.7]

11737 Douglas, Ann. *The Family Tree Detective: Cracking the Case of Your Family's Story* (4–8). Illus. 1999, Owl paper $9.95 (1-895688-89-2). In 16 compact chapters, this book covers the basics of genealogical research — gathering information, using appropriate organizations, forms for making a family tree, and recording family facts. (Rev: SLJ 6/99) [929]

11738 Dudevszky, Szabinka. *Close-Up* (6–8). Trans. by Wanda Boeke. 1999, Front Street $15.95 (1-886910-40-5). The stories of 15 teens from the Netherlands who left their homes and lived in foster homes, reform schools, alone, or with friends. (Rev: HBG 4/00; SLJ 9/99; VOYA 12/99) [306]

11739 DuPrau, Jeanne. *Adoption: The Facts, Feelings, and Issues of a Double Heritage* (7–12). 1990, Messner LB $12.95 (0-671-69328-X); paper $5.95 (0-671-69329-8). A book that deals primarily with the conflicts and emotional problems related to adoption and how to get help. (Rev: BL 3/15/90; SLJ 7/90; VOYA 6/90) [362.7]

11740 Flaming, Allen, and Kate Scowen, eds. *My Crazy Life: How I Survived My Family* (8–12). 2002, Annick paper $9.95 (1-55037-732-9). Ten teen narratives describe how each managed to deal with family problems such as abuse, addiction, AIDS, divorce, and homosexuality. (Rev: BL 9/1/02; HBG 10/02; SLJ 7/02) [306.87]

11741 Gardner, Richard. *The Boys and Girls Book About Stepfamilies* (6–9). 1985, Creative Therapeutics paper $6.50 (0-933812-13-2). Written from a youngster's view, this is a frank discussion of the problems that can exist in stepfamilies. [306.8]

11742 Gardner, Richard A. *Boys and Girls Book About Divorce* (5–8). Illus. 1992, Bantam paper $6.99 (0-553-27619-0). A self-help book written for adolescents trying to cope with parental marriage problems. [306.8]

11743 Gellman, Marc. *"Always Wear Clean Underwear!" and Other Ways Parents Say "I Love You"* (4–7). 1997, Morrow $14.95 (0-688-14492-6). Some kids think that the expressions featured in this book are parental nagging, but the message really is that parents care. (Rev: BL 10/1/97; HBG 3/98; SLJ 11/97) [306.874]

11744 Gerdes, Louise, ed. *Battered Women* (7–12). Series: Contemporary Issues Companion. 1998, Greenhaven LB $32.45 (1-56510-897-3). Personal narratives of battered women are used in this anthol-

ogy that investigates patterns of domestic violence and examines legal and other measures that can be used to protect women. (Rev: BL 3/15/99; BR 9–10/99) [362.82]

11745 Goldentyer, Debra. *Child Abuse* (4–8). Series: Preteen Pressures. 1998, Raintree Steck-Vaughn LB $25.69 (0-8172-5032-8). This work describes the types, causes, and effects of child abuse and supplies material on how to change an abusive situation. (Rev: BL 5/15/98; HBG 10/98) [362.7]

11746 Goldentyer, Debra. *Divorce* (4–8). Series: Preteen Pressures. 1998, Raintree Steck-Vaughn LB $25.69 (0-8172-5030-1). This work discusses the reasons for divorce, the legal aspects, the effect on children, remarriage, and relationships with new family members. (Rev: BL 5/15/98; HBG 10/98; SLJ 6/98) [306.8]

11747 Grapes, Bryan J., ed. *Child Abuse* (6–12). Series: Current Controversies. 2001, Greenhaven LB $22.96 (0-7377-0679-1); paper $14.96 (0-7377-0678-3). This collection of essays discusses the extent of child abuse, the underlying factors (substance abuse, poverty, childhood experience, and so forth) that are prevalent in abuse cases, and efforts to end the abuse and to rehabilitate the victims. (Rev: BL 9/1/01; SLJ 11/01) [362.76]

11748 Gravelle, Karen, and Susan Fischer. *Where Are My Birth Parents? A Guide for Teenage Adoptees* (7–12). 1993, Walker LB $15.85 (0-8027-8258-2). Includes firsthand experiences of young people who searched for their birth families with varied success. (Rev: BL 9/1/93; SLJ 7/93; VOYA 10/93) [362.7]

11749 Greenberg, Keith E. *Family Abuse: Why Do People Hurt Each Other?* (6–9). Illus. Series: Issues of Our Time. 1994, Twenty-First Century LB $22.90 (0-8050-3183-9). The causes and forms of family violence and abuse are traced, with coverage of their effects and how they can be prevented or contained. (Rev: BL 6/1–15/94; SLJ 9/94) [362.82]

11750 Greenberg, Keith E. *Runaways* (6–10). 1995, Lerner LB $19.93 (0-8225-2557-7). Greenberg uses the personal approach, focusing on the lives of two runaways, to dispel the idea that runaways are "bad" kids. (Rev: BL 10/15/95; SLJ 12/95) [362.7]

11751 Greenberg, Keith E. *Zack's Story: Growing Up with Same-Sex Parents* (5–7). Illus. Series: Meeting the Challenge. 1996, Lerner LB $25.55 (0-8225-2581-X). A true account of 11-year-old Zack, who is growing up with his lesbian mother and her lover, whom he has grown to regard as a second mother. (Rev: BL 10/15/96; SLJ 3/97) [306]

11752 Harnack, Andrew. *Adoption* (7–12). Series: Opposing Viewpoints. 1995, Greenhaven LB $26.20 (1-56510-213-4); paper $21.20 (1-56510-212-6). Presents various perspectives on the hot-button issues related to adoption, with provocative articles from well-known advocates. (Rev: BL 10/15/95; VOYA 6/96) [362.7]

11753 Hong, Maria. *Family Abuse: A National Epidemic* (8–12). Illus. Series: Issues in Focus. 1997, Enslow LB $20.95 (0-89490-720-4). This book takes a long, thorough look at this national epidemic that includes spousal and child abuse as well as children terrorizing a family and abuse of elderly parents. (Rev: BL 12/1/97; SLJ 12/97; VOYA 6/98) [362.82]

11754 Hurley, Jennifer A., ed. *Child Abuse* (8–12). Series: Opposing Viewpoints. 1998, Greenhaven LB $32.45 (1-56510-935-X). Questions explored in this anthology of opinions include the causes of child abuse, false accusations, how the legal system should deal with child molesters, and how child abuse can be reduced. (Rev: BL 9/15/98) [362.7]

11755 Hyde, Margaret O. *Know About Abuse* (7–12). Series: Know About. 1992, Walker LB $14.85 (0-8027-8177-2). Provides facts on child abuse, reasons, symptoms, examples, and solutions, covering a wide range of abuse, from obvious to subtle. (Rev: BL 11/1/92; SLJ 9/92) [362.7]

11756 Isler, Claudia. *Caught in the Middle: A Teen Guide to Custody* (5–8). Series: The Divorce Resource. 2000, Rosen LB $26.50 (0-8239-3109-9). This book about divorce uses many actual case histories to explore such questions as what happens to the children when parents divorce and whether grandparents get visitation rights. (Rev: SLJ 6/00) [306.8]

11757 Kim, Henny H. *Child Abuse* (6–12). Illus. Series: Opposing Viewpoints Digests. 2000, Greenhaven LB $21.96 (1-56510-867-1); paper $13.96 (1-56510-866-3). Various points of views are reported on in this book that discusses the nature of child abuse, its causes, and ways it can be reduced. (Rev: BL 7/00) [362.76]

11758 Kinstlinger-Bruhn, Charlotte. *Everything You Need to Know About Breaking the Cycle of Domestic Violence* (6–10). Series: Need to Know Library. 1997, Rosen LB $25.25 (0-8239-2434-3). This book discusses physical, emotional, and sexual abuse, focusing on dating relationships and parental violence against children, and provides information on warning signs of an abusive relationship, how to seek help, and self-protection. (Rev: SLJ 4/98) [364.3]

11759 Koh, Frances M. *Adopted from Asia: How It Feels to Grow Up in America* (5–8). 1993, East-West $16.95 (0-9606090-6-7). The author has gathered stories, impressions, and opinions from 11 young people who were born in Korea and adopted by Caucasian Americans. (Rev: BL 2/15/94) [306.874]

11760 Kosof, Anna. *Battered Women: Living with the Enemy* (7–12). 1995, Watts LB $25.00 (0-531-

11203-9). Attempts to answer the fundamental question "Why don't you just leave?" and discusses the development of abusive relationships. (Rev: BL 4/15/95; SLJ 3/95) [362.82]

11761 Krementz, Jill. *How It Feels to Be Adopted* (5–8). Illus. 1988, Knopf paper $15.00 (0-394-75853-6). Interviews with 19 young people, ages 8 to 16, on how it feels to be adopted. [362.7]

11762 Krementz, Jill. *How It Feels When Parents Divorce* (4–8). Illus. 1988, Knopf paper $15.00 (0-394-75855-2). Boys and girls, ages 8 to 16, share their experiences with divorced parents. [306.8]

11763 Krohn, Katherine. *Everything You Need to Know About Birth Order* (5–9). Series: Need to Know Library. 2000, Rosen LB $18.95 (0-8239-3228-1). An interesting book that looks at a number of theories about how birth order affects people. (Rev: SLJ 12/00) [306.85]

11764 Krohn, Katherine. *You and Your Parents' Divorce* (5–8). Series: Family Matters. 2001, Rosen LB $23.95 (0-8239-3354-7). Krohn writes about the practicalities and emotional problems of divorce in a style suitable for reluctant readers. (Rev: SLJ 8/01) [155.44]

11765 La Valle, John. *Coping When a Parent Is in Jail* (8–12). Series: Coping. 1995, Rosen LB $18.95 (0-8239-1967-6). Discusses the effects of having a parent in jail on a child and tries to give an idea of what the parent's life in prison is like. (Rev: BL 7/95) [362.7]

11766 Leibowitz, Julie. *Finding Your Place: A Teen Guide to Life in a Blended Family* (5–8). 2000, Rosen LB $26.50 (0-8239-3114-5). This book explores possible problems and solutions for members of blended families. (Rev: SLJ 6/00) [645.7]

11767 LeShan, Eda. *When Grownups Drive You Crazy* (4–7). 1988, Macmillan paper $14.00 (0-02-756340-5). A book that tries to bridge the gap of misunderstanding between children and their parents. (Rev: BL 4/15/88; HB 7–8/88; SLJ 6–7/88) [306.874]

11768 Levine, Beth. *Divorce: Young People Caught in the Middle* (7–12). 1995, Enslow LB $20.95 (0-89490-633-X). A straightforward, commonsense manual for teens dealing with divorce. (Rev: BL 3/15/95; SLJ 6/95) [306.89]

11769 Lindsay, Jeanne W. *Coping with Reality: Dealing with Money, In-Laws, Babies and Other Details of Daily Life* (7–12). Series: Teenage Couples. 1995, Morning Glory $15.95 (0-930934-87-3); paper $9.95 (0-930934-86-5). Counsel on the day-to-day aspects of being a part of a couple. (Rev: BL 4/15/95; SLJ 3/95) [306.81]

11770 Lloyd, J. D., ed. *Family Violence* (8–12). Series: Current Controversies. 2000, Greenhaven LB $22.96 (0-7377-0452-7); paper $14.96 (0-7377-

0451-9). The 19 selections in this anthology cover various types of family violence mainly against spouses and children but also directed toward the elderly and gays and lesbians. (Rev: BL 12/1/00) [362.82]

11771 McCue, Margi L. *Domestic Violence* (7–12). Series: Contemporary World Issues. 1995, ABC-CLIO LB $39.50 (0-87436-762-X). This book concentrates on spousal abuse, reactions to the problem, important events, laws and legislation, statistics, and interviews with survivors of violence. (Rev: BR 9–10/96; SLJ 5/96) [362.82]

11772 MacGregor, Cynthia. *The Divorce Helpbook for Kids* (4–7). 2001, Impact Publishers paper $12.95 (1-886230-39-0). In this candid, honest book, a divorced mother gives advice to children about how to survive their parent's divorce. (Rev: BL 2/1/02; SLJ 3/02) [306.89]

11773 Mufson, Susan, and Rachel Kranz. *Straight Talk About Child Abuse* (7–12). Series: Straight Talk. 1991, Facts on File $27.45 (0-8160-2376-X). Beginning with a general discussion of child abuse, this book describes the common signs of physical, emotional, and sexual abuse, gives some case studies, and offers some solutions. (Rev: BL 4/1/91; SLJ 3/91) [362.7]

11774 Packer, Alex J. *Bringing Up Parents: The Teenager's Handbook* (8–12). Illus. 1993, Free Spirit paper $15.95 (0-915793-48-2). Discusses in detail the art of coping with parents: building trust, diffusing family power struggles, waging effective verbal battles, developing listening skills, and expressing feelings nonaggressively. (Rev: BL 5/1/93*; VOYA 8/93) [306.874]

11775 Rench, Janice E. *Family Violence: How to Recognize and Survive It* (6–8). 1992, Lerner LB $19.93 (0-8225-0047-7). This book speaks directly to children, with explanations of what constitutes different kinds of abuse, who is at fault, what motivates abusers, and what to do if violence occurs. (Rev: BL 11/1/92; SLJ 9/92) [362.82]

11776 Rofes, Eric, ed. *The Kids' Book of Divorce: By, for and About Kids* (6–10). 1982, Random paper $10.00 (0-394-71018-5). Twenty youngsters from ages 11 to 14 who are children of divorce were asked to state their reactions and feelings. [306.8]

11777 Roleff, Tamara L., and Mary E. Williams, eds. *Marriage and Divorce* (8–12). Series: Current Controversies. 1997, Greenhaven LB $32.45 (1-56510-568-0); paper $21.20 (1-56510-567-2). An anthology of 32 articles presenting diverse viewpoints on premarital cohabitation, the effect of divorce on children, child custody, and same-sex marriage. (Rev: SLJ 10/97) [306.8]

11778 Rosenberg, Maxine B. *Living with a Single Parent* (4–7). 1992, Macmillan $14.95 (0-02-777915-7). In interview format, this topic is presented through the opinions of youngsters from eight to 13. (Rev: BCCB 2/93; BL 11/15/92; SLJ 12/92) [306.85]

11779 Rue, Nancy N. *Coping with an Illiterate Parent* (7–12). Series: Coping. 1990, Rosen LB $25.25 (0-8239-1070-9). The causes, problems, and treatment of illiteracy as seen from a teenager's point of view. (Rev: BL 3/1/90; SLJ 10/90) [306]

11780 Ryan, Elizabeth A. *Straight Talk About Parents* (7–12). 1989, Facts on File $27.45 (0-8160-1526-0). A self-help manual to help teens sort out their feelings about parents. (Rev: BL 8/89; BR 11–12/89; SLJ 9/89; VOYA 2/90) [306.8]

11781 Sadler, A. E., ed. *Family Violence* (7–12). Series: Current Controversies. 1996, Greenhaven LB $26.20 (1-56510-371-8); paper $16.20 (1-56510-370-X). An anthology of original sources that explores the prevalence of family violence, its victims and perpetrators, and how this violence can be reduced. (Rev: BL 6/1–15/96; SLJ 4/96) [362.82]

11782 St. Pierre, Stephanie. *Everything You Need to Know When a Parent Is in Jail* (7–12). Illus. Series: Everything You Need to Know. 1994, Rosen $17.95 (0-8239-1526-3). Using many real-life examples, this book gives advice to youngsters who suffer both emotional and financial crises after a parent is sent to prison. (Rev: BL 4/15/94) [362.7]

11783 St. Pierre, Stephanie. *Everything You Need to Know When a Parent Is Out of Work* (6–12). Series: Need to Know Library. 1991, Rosen $12.95 (0-8239-1217-5). Explains how parents can lose their jobs and the effects unemployment can have on a parent's behavior, family routines, and relationships. (Rev: BL 10/1/91) [331.137]

11784 Sanders, Pete, and Steve Myers. *Divorce and Separation* (4–8). Illus. Series: What Do You Know About. 1997, Millbrook LB $23.90 (0-7613-0574-2). An introduction to separation and divorce, with an emphasis on tips to help youngsters adjust and cope. (Rev: SLJ 10/97) [306.8]

11785 Schwartz, Perry. *Carolyn's Story: A Book About an Adopted Girl* (5–7). Illus. Series: Meeting the Challenge. 1996, Lerner LB $25.55 (0-8225-2580-1). Using fictional case histories, various aspects of adoption are explored. (Rev: BL 10/15/96; SLJ 4/97) [362.7]

11786 Shires-Sneddon, Pamela. *Brothers and Sisters: Born to Bicker?* (6–10). Series: Teen Issues. 1997, Enslow LB $20.95 (0-89490-914-2). This book explores a variety of sibling relationships, how social pressures affect them, and the damaging impact of drugs, alcohol, divorce, death, and abuse. (Rev: BL 4/15/97; BR 9–10/97; VOYA 10/97) [306.875]

11787 Shultz, Margaret A. *Teens with Single Parents: Why Me?* (6–12). Series: Teen Issues. 1997, Enslow LB $20.95 (0-89490-913-4). Using interviews with teens as a focus, this book examines the problems of living with a single parent and makes some suggestions for coping strategies. (Rev: BL 7/97; BR 11–12/97; SLJ 10/97) [306.5]

11788 Simpson, Carolyn. *Everything You Need to Know About Living with a Grandparent or Other Relatives* (8–12). 1995, Rosen LB $25.25 (0-8239-1872-6). This book explores the various situations that may cause teenagers to move in with grandparents, how to adjust, ways to maintain privacy, and the different emotions involved on both sides. (Rev: BR 9–10/96; VOYA 2/96) [306]

11789 Smook, Rachel Gaillard. *Stepfamilies: How a New Family Works* (6–9). Illus. 2001, Enslow LB $17.95 (0-7660-1666-8). Teens relate their experiences in becoming part of a new family, and the author shows offers tips on adapting to new family situations. (Rev: BL 1/1–15/02; HBG 7/01) [306.874]

11790 Stewart, Gail B. *Teens and Divorce* (6–12). Series: Overview: Teen Issues. 2000, Lucent LB $18.96 (1-56006-656-3). This account concentrates on the effects of divorce on teenagers and coping with such emotions as anger, grief, guilt, and worries about the future. (Rev: BL 6/1–15/00; HBG 9/00) [306.89]

11791 Swisher, Karin L., ed. *Domestic Violence* (8–12). Series: At Issue. 1996, Greenhaven LB $18.70 (1-56510-381-5); paper $17.45 (1-56510-380-7). An anthology of different viewpoints involving the incidence and seriousness of spousal abuse by both men and women. (Rev: BL 1/1–15/96) [362.82]

11792 Swisher, Karin L., ed. *Single-Parent Families* (8–12). Series: At Issue. 1997, Greenhaven LB $26.20 (1-56510-544-3); paper $17.45 (1-56510-543-5). An anthology that presents different viewpoints about the problems and rewards of single-parenting. (Rev: BL 1/1–15/97; SLJ 7/97) [306.85]

11793 Taylor, Paul, and Diane Taylor. *Coping with a Dysfunctional Family* (7–12). Series: Coping. 1990, Rosen $22.95 (0-8239-1180-2). Through case studies, this account explores family problems that stem from such conditions as abuse, drugs, and neglect. (Rev: BL 11/1/90) [362.82]

11794 Wagner, Heather Lehr. *The Blending of Foster and Adopted Children into the Family* (6–12). Series: Focus on Family Matters. 2002, Chelsea $20.75 (0-7910-6694-0). Various family structures and situations are described, with material on how to accept, nurture, and embrace these new family constructs. (Rev: BL 10/15/02; HBG 3/03; SLJ 12/02) [606.8]

11795 Wagner, Heather Lehr. *Understanding and Coping with Divorce* (6–12). Series: Focus on Family Matters. 2002, Chelsea $20.75 (0-7910-6691-6). The causes and effects of divorce are discussed, with emphasis on how teens can get through the difficult time when parents divorce. (Rev: BL 10/15/02; HBG 3/03; SLJ 12/02) [306.8]

11796 Weiss, Ann E. *Adoptions Today: Questions and Controversy* (7–12). Illus. 2001, Twenty-First Century LB $24.90 (0-7613-1914-X). This comprehensive and informative overview covers such topics as international adoptions, adoption by unconventional couples, open adoption, and privacy. (Rev: BL 12/15/01; HBG 3/02; VOYA 12/01) [362.73]

11797 Williams, Mary E., ed. *The Family* (8–12). Series: Opposing Viewpoints. 1997, Greenhaven paper $21.20 (1-56510-668-7). An anthology of articles presenting different points of view on the status of the family, divorce, work-related topics, adoption, and the changing values in society that affect the family structure. (Rev: BL 10/15/97; SLJ 12/97) [306.8]

11798 Wolfman, Ira. *Climbing Your Family Tree: Online and Off-Line Genealogy for Kids*. Rev. ed. (5–9). 2002, Workman paper $13.95 (0-7611-2539-6). A wide-ranging look at genealogy and the ways of tracing family names through document research, interviews, and the World Wide Web. (Rev: SLJ 2/03; VOYA 10/03) [929]

11799 Wolfman, Ira. *Do People Grow on Family Trees? Genealogy for Kids and Other Beginners* (5–8). 1991, Workman paper $9.95 (0-89480-348-4). The purposes of genealogy are discussed and information is given on how to trace family history. (Rev: SLJ 1/92) [929]

Youth Groups

11800 Moore, David L. *Dark Sky, Dark Land: Stories of the Hmong Boy Scouts of Troop 100* (7–10). Illus. 1989, Tessera paper $14.95 (0-9623029-0-2). A collection of stories of hardship and bravery behind Boy Scout Troop 100 in Minneapolis composed of young refugees from war-torn Laos. (Rev: BL 9/15/90) [977.6]

758

Physical and Applied Sciences

General and Miscellaneous

11801 Aaseng, Nathan. *Yearbooks in Science: 1930–1939* (5–8). Illus. Series: Yearbooks in Science. 1995, Twenty-First Century LB $22.90 (0-8050-3433-1). An overview of the accomplishments in science in the 1930s arranged by such divisions as physics and chemistry. (Rev: BL 12/1/95; SLJ 1/96) [609]

11802 Aaseng, Nathan. *Yearbooks in Science: 1940–1949* (5–8). Illus. Series: Yearbooks in Science. 1995, Twenty-First Century LB $22.90 (0-8050-3434-X). An important decade in scientific discovery is chronicled, with emphasis on the impact of these advances on society. (Rev: BL 1/1–15/96; SLJ 5/96) [609]

11803 Beres, Samantha. *101 Things Every Kid Should Know About Science* (4–7). Illus. 1998, Lowell House $14.95 (1-56565-956-2); paper $9.95 (1-56565-916-3). This information-packed book supplies basic scientific facts organized under headings such as chemistry, physics, biology, and geography. (Rev: BL 10/15/98; SLJ 12/98) [500]

11804 Bridgman, Roger. *1000 Inventions and Discoveries* (5–9). Illus. 2002, DK paper $24.99 (0-7894-8826-4). A heavily illustrated overview of scientific discoveries, arranged chronologically with a timeline of concurrent historical and cultural events. (Rev: SLJ 3/03) [609]

11805 Bruno, Leonard C. *Science and Technology Breakthroughs: From the Wheel to the World Wide Web* (5–8). 1997, Gale LB $158.40 (0-7876-1927-2). This expanded version contains more than 1,200 paragraph-long entries in 12 chronologically arranged chapters: agriculture and everyday life; astronomy; biology; chemistry; communications; computers; earth sciences; energy, power systems, and weaponry; mathematics; medicine; physics; and transportation. (Rev: BL 3/1/98; BR 5–6/98; SLJ 5/98) [509]

11806 Bruno, Leonard C. *Science and Technology Firsts* (6–12). 1997, Gale $95.00 (0-7876-0256-6). More than 4,000 entries chronicle famous "firsts," arranged by branches of science and technology such as agriculture, astronomy, biology, chemistry, communications, and computers. (Rev: BL 8/97; BR 5–6/97; SLJ 5/97) [500]

11807 Carlson, Dale. *In and Out of Your Mind: Teen Science: Human Bites* (8–12). 2002, Bick paper $14.95 (1-884158-27-7). Teens with a curious, contemplative nature will find food for thought in this look at the wonders of science, humankind, and the universe that touches on topics including evolution, environmental concerns, and medicine. (Rev: SLJ 9/02) [500]

11808 Crump, Donald J., ed. *On the Brink of Tomorrow: Frontiers of Science* (7–9). Illus. 1982, National Geographic $12.95 (0-87044-414-X). With many color illustrations, this account covers recent advances in such areas as physics, astronomy, and medicine. [500]

11809 *The DK Science Encyclopedia*. Rev. ed. (4–8). 1998, DK paper $39.99 (0-7894-2190-9). Using one- or two-page articles and a profusion of illustrations, this topically arranged, slightly updated version of the 1993 edition gives an overview of the field of science, emphasizing its interconnectedness with technology, under such headings as weather, ecology, and reactions. (Rev: BL 12/1/98; SLJ 2/99; VOYA 4/99) [500]

11810 Dolan, Graham. *The Greenwich Guide to Time and the Millennium* (4–7). 1999, Heinemann $16.95 (1-57572-802-8). Covers such subjects as time zones, calendars, centuries, and longitude. (Rev: SLJ 9/99) [529]

11811 Duffy, Trent. *The Clock* (3–9). Series: Turning Points. 2000, Simon & Schuster $17.95 (0-689-82814-4). After a general introduction to the concept of time, this visually interesting volume tells how time has been measured with a special focus on clocks and watches and a foldout on how a clock works. (Rev: BCCB 5/00; HBG 10/00; SLJ 5/00) [529]

11812 Francis, Raymond L. *The Illustrated Almanac of Science, Technology, and Invention: Day by Day Facts, Figures, and the Fanciful* (6–12). Illus. 1997, Plenum $28.95 (0-306-45633-8). For each day of the year, this almanac cites scientific events that occurred on that date, birth dates of famous scientists, discoveries, interesting technological achievements, or just quirky scientific happenings that made worldwide or even only local headlines. (Rev: BL 12/1/97; SLJ 5/98) [509]

11813 Gutfreund, Geraldine M. *Yearbooks in Science: 1970–1979* (5–8). Illus. Series: Yearbooks in Science. 1995, Twenty-First Century LB $22.90 (0-8050-3437-4). A decade of new scientific concepts and inventions is discussed, with profiles of the scientists behind them. (Rev: BL 1/1–15/96; SLJ 5/96) [609]

11814 *Inside Out: The Best of National Geographic Diagrams and Cutaways* (6–12). Illus. 1998, National Geographic $25.00 (0-7922-7371-0). A collection of 60 illustrations from the magazine's past 75 years, with drawings, cross sections, and cutaways of such subjects as a prairie dog town, Chernobyl's ruined core, and a beluga whale's sound-producing mechanism. (Rev: BL 10/15/98; SLJ 10/98) [686.2]

11815 Jespersen, James, and Jane Fitz-Randolph. *Mummies, Dinosaurs, Moon Rocks: How We Know How Old Things Are* (6–8). Illus. 1996, Simon & Schuster $16.00 (0-689-31848-0). An investigation of the various ways that scientists are able to determine the age of natural and man-made materials. (Rev: BL 10/1/96; SLJ 9/96) [930.1]

11816 Kramer, Stephen. *Hidden Worlds: Looking Through a Scientist's Microscope* (4–7). Illus. Series: Scientists in the Field. 2001, Houghton $16.00 (0-618-05546-0). Striking photographs, mostly taken with electron microscopes by scientist Dennis Kunkel, serve to illustrate this explanation of how scientists use microscopes in their work. (Rev: BL 8/01; HB 1–2/02; HBG 3/02; SLJ 9/01*) [570]

11817 McGowen, Tom. *The Beginnings of Science* (5–8). Illus. 1998, Twenty-First Century LB $26.90 (0-7613-3016-X). Beginning with primitive people and their use of magic, fire, counting, writing, and astronomy, this book traces the history of science up to the 16th century. (Rev: BL 12/1/98; HBG 3/99) [509]

11818 McGowen, Tom. *Yearbooks in Science: 1900–1919* (5–8). Illus. Series: Yearbooks in Science. 1995, Twenty-First Century LB $22.90 (0-8050-3431-5). An overview of human achievements in science and technology during the first 20 years of the 20th century, how they helped humanity, and the men and women involved. (Rev: BL 12/1/95; SLJ 1/96) [609]

11819 McGowen, Tom. *Yearbooks in Science: 1960–1969* (5–8). Illus. Series: Yearbooks in Science. 1996, Twenty-First Century LB $22.90 (0-8050-3436-6). Developments in the history of science and technology during the 1960s are covered in an exciting step-by-step approach. (Rev: BL 1/1–15/96; SLJ 5/96) [609]

11820 Martin, Paul D. *Science: It's Changing Your World* (5–8). Illus. 1985, National Geographic LB $12.50 (0-87044-521-9). An overview of the science field today, crediting computers and lasers with the vast growth of scientific information. (Rev: BL 9/15/85; SLJ 10/85) [500]

11821 Masoff, Joy. *Oh, Yuck! The Encyclopedia of Everything Nasty* (4–8). 2001, Workman paper $14.95 (0-7611-0771-1). This unsavory, fact-filled look at smells, noises, creepy-crawlies, toilets, and other fascinating topics even includes some suitably gross experiments. (Rev: SLJ 5/01) [031.02]

11822 Newton, David E. *Yearbooks in Science: 1920–1929* (5–8). Illus. Series: Yearbooks in Science. 1995, Twenty-First Century LB $22.90 (0-8050-3432-3). The history of scientific advances in the 1920s, with chapters on various fields that explain the breakthroughs, how they helped humanity, and the scientists involved. (Rev: BL 12/1/95; SLJ 1/96) [609]

11823 Robinson, Richard. *Science Magic in the Bedroom: Amazing Tricks with Ordinary Stuff* (4–7). Series: Science Magic. 2002, Simon & Schuster paper $4.99 (0-689-84335-6). Robinson presents tricks that fool the sight, hearing, and touch and explains the underlying science and physiology. (Rev: SLJ 7/02) [507.8]

11824 Schwartz, David M. *Q Is for Quark: A Science Alphabet Book* (4–9). 2001, Tricycle Pr. $15.95 (1-58246-021-3). An entertaining and informative alphabet book from atom to Zzzzzzzz that doesn't hesitate to tackle difficult topics. (Rev: HBG 3/02; SLJ 11/01) [500]

11825 Silverstein, Herma. *Yearbooks in Science: 1990 and Beyond* (5–8). Illus. Series: Yearbooks in Science. 1995, Twenty-First Century LB $22.90 (0-8050-3439-0). The final volume in this series not only traces recent developments in science and technology but also presents the challenges of the future. (Rev: BL 1/1–15/96) [609]

11826 Spangenburg, Raymond. *The History of Science from 1895 to 1994* (7–12). 1994, Facts on File $25.00 (0-8160-2742-0). Surveys scientific progress, discussing atomic energy, relativity, space exploration, genetics, and the achievements of various scientists spanning 100 years. (Rev: BL 9/1/94; VOYA 10/94) [509]

11827 Spangenburg, Raymond, and Diane Moser. *Science and Invention* (6–12). Illus. Series: American Historic Places. 1997, Facts on File $25.00 (0-8160-3402-8). Illustrated profiles of eight sites around the country connected with great scientists and inventions, including the homes of Joseph Priestly, Luther Burbank, George Washington Carver, and Rachel Carson as well as Thomas Edison's lab, the Lick Observatory, and the Wright Brothers National Monument. (Rev: BL 12/1/97; BR 5–6/98) [609.73]

11828 Stein, Sara Bonnett. *The Science Book* (4–8). 1980, Workman paper $9.95 (0-89480-120-1). A whole-earth approach to strange and fascinating science facts.

11829 Swanson, Diane. *Nibbling on Einstein's Brain* (5–8). 2001, Firefly $24.95 (1-55037-687-X); paper $14.95 (1-55037-686-1). Swanson looks at "bad" science and examines the difference between sound

scientific theory and hype, teaching kids how to ask the right questions when analyzing advertisers' claims. (Rev: BL 2/15/02; HBG 3/02; SLJ 11/01) [507.2]

11830 *Ultimate Visual Dictionary of Science* (6–10). Illus. 1998, DK paper $30.00 (0-7894-3512-8). Though not in dictionary form (as the title suggests), this is a heavily illustrated introduction that presents basic information about physics, chemistry, anatomy, medical science, ecology, earth science, astronomy, electronics, mathematics, and computers. (Rev: BL 12/1/98; SLJ 11/98; VOYA 4/99) [500]

11831 Wollard, Kathy. *How Come?* (5–9). 1993, Workman paper $12.95 (1-56305-324-1). Provides answers to some common and not-so-common questions about ordinary things. (Rev: BL 5/1/94) [500]

11832 Wollard, Kathy. *How Come Planet Earth?* (4–7). 1999, Workman paper $12.95 (0-7611-1239-1). This book contains 125 science questions asked by children involving subjects such as warts, dust, cholesterol, and volcanoes. (Rev: SLJ 5/00) [500]

Experiments and Projects

11833 Bochinski, Julianne Blair. *The Complete Handbook of Science Fair Projects* (7–12). 1996, Wiley $32.50 (0-471-12378-1); paper $14.95 (0-471-12377-3). This revision of the 1991 edition contains 50 experiments (10 of them new) plus material on the international rules for science fairs. (Rev: BL 2/1/96; BR 5–6/96; SLJ 4/96) [507.9]

11834 Brown, Bob. *More Science for You: 112 Illustrated Experiments* (6–8). Illus. 1988, TAB paper $7.95 (0-8306-3125-9). A collection of simple experiments involving such topics as heat, sound, weight, and tricks. (Rev: VOYA 4/89) [507]

11835 Brown, Robert J. *333 Science Tricks and Experiments* (7–12). Illus. 1984, McGraw-Hill $15.95 (0-8306-0825-7). Basic scientific principles are demonstrated in experiments and projects. (Rev: BL 4/1/89) [507]

11836 Carrow, Robert. *Put a Fan in Your Hat! Inventions, Contraptions, and Gadgets Kids Can Build* (5–8). 1997, McGraw-Hill paper $14.95 (0-07-011658-X). Interesting projects include making a natural battery, building a motor, and creating a hat with a cooling fan. (Rev: BL 4/15/97; SLJ 5/97) [507]

11837 Cobb, Vicki. *Science Experiments You Can Eat* (5–7). 1994, HarperCollins LB $15.89 (0-060-23551-9). Experiments illustrating principles of chemistry and physics use edible ingredients. Also use *More Science Experiments You Can Eat* (1979). [507]

11838 Cobb, Vicki. *The Secret Life of Cosmetics: A Science Experiment Book* (6–8). Illus. 1985, Harper-Collins $14.89 (0-397-32122-8). An examination of the history and composition of cosmetics and a number of experiments to perform using these materials. (Rev: BL 3/15/86; SLJ 1/86) [668]

11839 Cobb, Vicki. *The Secret Life of Hardware: A Science Experiment Book* (7–9). Illus. 1982, Harper-Collins LB $13.89 (0-397-32000-0). A book of science activities and experiments that involve a hammer, saw, soaps, paints, and other commonly found items. [670]

11840 Cobb, Vicki, and Kathy Darling. *Bet You Can't! Science Impossibilities to Fool You* (5–8). 1983, Avon paper $4.95 (0-380-54502-0). Sixty different tricks and experiments involving such scientific subjects as fluids and energy. Also use *Bet You Can! Science Possibilities to Fool You* (1983).

11841 Cobb, Vicki, and Kathy Darling. *You Gotta Try This! Absolutely Irresistible Science* (4–8). Illus. 1999, Morrow $15.99 (0-688-15740-8). An easy, enjoyable book of 50 experiments, that gives clear directions, lists of materials, and an explanation of the concepts involved. Some require adult assistance. (Rev: BCCB 5/99; BL 8/99; HBG 4/00; SLJ 8/99) [507]

11842 Dashefsky, H. Steven. *Zoology: 49 Science Fair Projects* (8–12). 1994, TAB paper $11.95 (0-07-015683-2). A step-by-step description of interesting science fair projects from various branches of science. (Rev: BL 1/15/95; SLJ 3/95) [591]

11843 Duensing, Edward. *Talking to Fireflies, Shrinking the Moon: Nature Activities for All Ages* (5–9). Illus. 1997, Fulcrum paper $15.95 (1-55591-310-5). More than 40 nature activities are included in this volume, including how to hypnotize a frog, weave a daisy chain, and whistle for woodchucks. (Rev: VOYA 10/97) [507]

11844 Gardner, Robert. *Kitchen Chemistry: Science Experiments to Do at Home* (4–8). Illus. 1989, Silver Burdett paper $4.95 (0-671-67576-1). These entertaining and instructive experiments can be performed in the kitchen with everyday equipment and supplies. [542]

11845 Gardner, Robert. *Projects in Space Science* (4–8). Illus. 1988, Silver Burdett paper $5.95 (0-671-65993-6). Science projects involving space travel and astronomy. (Rev: BL 1/15/89; SLJ 2/89) [500.2]

11846 Gardner, Robert. *Science Projects About Kitchen Chemistry* (6–9). Series: Science Projects. 1999, Enslow LB $20.95 (0-89490-953-3). A book of clearly outlined experiments that range widely in difficulty and revolve around the kitchen and its contents. (Rev: SLJ 7/99) [507]

11847 Gardner, Robert. *Science Projects About Solids, Liquids, and Gases* (6–12). Series: Science Projects. 2000, Enslow LB $19.95 (0-7660-1168-2). The three states of matter are explored through a series of experiments and projects using material and objects found around the house. (Rev: BL 8/00; HBG 3/01; VOYA 2/01) [507]

11848 Gardner, Robert. *Science Projects About Sound* (6–12). Series: Science Projects. 2000, Enslow LB $19.95 (0-7660-1166-6). The experiments contained in the innovative project book explore the properties of sound and how it travels. (Rev: BL 8/00; HBG 3/01) [507]

11849 Gardner, Robert. *Science Projects About the Physics of Sports* (6–9). Illus. Series: Science Projects. 2000, Enslow LB $19.95 (0-7660-1167-4). Projects and experiments look at the scientific concepts involved in speed, force and motion, gravity, friction, and collisions. (Rev: HBG 9/00; SLJ 7/00) [530]

11850 Gardner, Robert. *Science Projects About the Science Behind Magic* (6–12). Series: Science Projects. 2000, Enslow LB $19.95 (0-7660-1164-X). Several science projects are outlined the explain the scientific principles behind some magic tricks. (Rev: BL 5/15/00; HBG 9/00; SLJ 7/00) [507]

11851 Haduch, Bill. *Science Fair Success Secrets: How to Win Prizes, Have Fun, and Think Like a Scientist* (5–8). 2002, Dutton paper $10.99 (0-525-46534-0). A handy and appealing introduction to how to conduct a science experiment, with examples of award-winning projects, a list of ideas, and metric conversion tables. (Rev: BL 12/1/02; SLJ 3/03) [507]

11852 Hauser, Jill F. *Gizmos and Gadgets: Creating Science Contraptions That Work (and Knowing Why)* (4–7). Series: Kids Can! 1999, Williamson paper $12.95 (1-885593-26-0). Outlines the construction of all sorts of gadgets from objects found in kitchen and garage closets and relates each to such scientific topics as motion, energy, balancing, and gravity. (Rev: SLJ 1/00) [745]

11853 Herbert, Don. *Mr. Wizard's Experiments for Young Scientists* (5–8). 1991, Doubleday paper $10.95 (0-385-26585-9). Directions for 13 science experiments that can be done easily with equipment found in the home. [507.8]

11854 Herbert, Don. *Mr. Wizard's Supermarket Science* (4–7). 1980, Random paper $10.99 (0-394-83800-9). More than 100 projects using supermarket items test offer room for creativity and learning. [507]

11855 Hussey, Lois J., and Catherine Pessino. *Collecting for the City Naturalist* (7–9). Illus. 1975, HarperCollins $12.95 (0-690-00317-X). Science activities that can be carried out in an urban environment, such as collecting spider webs, are outlined. [500.7]

11856 Iritz, Maxine Haren. *Blue-Ribbon Science Fair Projects* (7–12). 1991, McGraw Hill paper $9.95 (0-07-157629-0). A variety of science fair projects for the novice are presented, with charts, graphs, photographs, and a chapter on choosing a topic. (Rev: BL 9/15/91) [507.8]

11857 Iritz, Maxine Haren. *Science Fair: Developing a Successful and Fun Project* (8–12). Illus. 1987, TAB $16.95 (0-8306-0936-9); paper $9.95 (0-8306-2936-X). A thorough step-by-step introduction to doing a science project. (Rev: BL 4/15/88) [507]

11858 Kramer, Alan. *How to Make a Chemical Volcano and Other Mysterious Experiments* (4–7). 1991, Watts paper $6.95 (0-531-15610-9). Thirty experiments for "detectives of chemistry" by a 13-year-old student. (Rev: BCCB 2/90; BL 12/15/89; SLJ 3/90) [532]

11859 Krieger, Melanie Jacobs. *How to Excel in Science Competitions*. Rev. ed. (6–10). Series: Science Fair Success. 1999, Enslow LB $19.95 (0-7660-1292-1). Students will find detailed guidance on choosing and conducting a science project, stories of winning projects, and profiles of successful students. (Rev: HBG 4/00; SLJ 4/00) [507.8]

11860 Markle, Sandra. *Exploring Autumn: A Season of Science Activities, Puzzlers, and Games* (4–7). Illus. Series: Exploring Seasons. 1991, Avon paper $3.50 (0-380-71910-X). Science, history, myth, quizzes, and more combined in this book on seasonal activities in the classroom and home. (Rev: BL 1/1/91; SLJ 1/92) [574.5]

11861 Markle, Sandra. *Science to the Rescue* (4–7). Illus. 1994, Atheneum $15.95 (0-689-31783-2). Explains the scientific method and shows how science has found solutions to many problems. (Rev: BL 3/15/94; SLJ 4/94) [507.8]

11862 Nye, Bill. *Bill Nye the Science Guy's Big Blast of Science* (5–8). Illus. 1993, Addison-Wesley paper $16.00 (0-201-60864-2). Matter, heat, light, electricity, magnetism, weather, and space are among the topics introduced in this quick and entertaining tour of the world of science. (Rev: BL 2/15/94) [507.8]

11863 Rainis, Kenneth G. *Exploring with a Magnifying Glass* (7–12). 1991, Watts LB $25.00 (0-531-12508-4). An introduction to how magnification works and a series of projects exploring photographs, plants, minerals, fabrics, and more. (Rev: BL 1/15/92; SLJ 4/92) [507.8]

11864 Rhatigan, Joe, and Heather Smith. *Sure-To-Win Science Fair Projects* (6–10). Illus. 2001, Sterling $21.95 (1-57990-238-3). Readers will find plenty of science fair ideas complete with planning checklists and other tools. (Rev: BL 12/1/01; SLJ 11/01*) [507]

11865 Richards, Roy. *101 Science Tricks: Fun Experiments with Everyday Materials* (4–8). 1992, Sterling $16.95 (0-8069-8388-4). Interesting, easy-to-do science and math activities emphasize the underlying principles. (Rev: BL 2/1/92; SLJ 1/92) [507.8]

11866 Rybolt, Thomas R., and Leah M. Rybolt. *Science Fair Success with Scents, Aromas, and Smells* (5–8). Series: Science Fair Success. 2002, Enslow LB $20.95 (0-7660-1625-0). Several science fair projects using the sense of smell are presented with clear instructions and easy-to-find materials. (Rev: BL 5/15/02; HBG 10/02; SLJ 11/02) [507]

11867 *Science Fairs: Ideas and Activities* (4–8). 1998, World Book $15.00 (0-7166-4498-3). Using many diagrams and logical step-by-step explanations, this work offers science projects in such areas as space, earth science, geology, botany, and machines. (Rev: SLJ 1/99) [507]

11868 Smith, Norman F. *How to Do Successful Science Projects*. Rev. ed. (5–8). Illus. 1990, Messner paper $5.95 (0-671-70686-1). This guide gives many fine tips and concentrates on the applications of the scientific method. (Rev: BL 7/90) [507.8]

11869 Sobey, Ed. *Wrapper Rockets and Trombone Straws: Science at Every Meal* (4–7). Illus. 1996, McGraw-Hill paper $14.95 (0-07-021745-9). Using simple items found in restaurants such as glasses, straws, and napkins, a number of simple tricks and experiments are introduced. (Rev: BL 3/1/97; SLJ 6/97) [500]

11870 Tocci, Salvatore. *Science Fair Success in the Hardware Store* (5–8). Series: Science Fair Success. 2000, Enslow LB $20.95 (0-7660-1287-5). A group of science fair projects that use materials and objects found in a hardware store, with clear explanations of the scientific principles behind each project. (Rev: BL 4/15/00; HBG 10/00) [507]

11871 Tocci, Salvatore. *Science Fair Success Using Supermarket Products* (5–8). Series: Science Fair Success. 2000, Enslow LB $20.95 (0-7660-1288-3). Using common items found in a supermarket, this work outlines a number of excellent science projects that demonstrate important scientific principles. (Rev: BL 4/15/00; HBG 10/00; SLJ 4/00) [507]

11872 Tocci, Salvatore. *Using Household Products* (5–8). Series: Science Fair Success. 2002, Enslow LB $20.95 (0-7660-1626-9). This useful volume outlines a number of science fair projects that can be done using materials found around the house. (Rev: BL 4/15/02; HBG 10/02) [509]

11873 UNESCO. *700 Science Experiments for Everyone* (5–8). Illus. 1964, Doubleday $19.95 (0-385-05275-8). An excellent collection of experi-

ments, noted for its number of entries and breadth of coverage.

11874 VanCleave, Janice. *Janice VanCleave's A+ Projects in Chemistry: Winning Experiments for Science Fairs and Extra Credit* (6–10). 1993, Wiley $32.50 (0-471-58631-5); paper $12.95 (0-471-58630-7). Thirty experiments that investigate such topics as calories, acids, and electrolytes, among others. (Rev: BL 12/1/95; SLJ 4/94) [930]

11875 VanCleave, Janice. *Janice VanCleave's Biology for Every Kid: 101 Easy Experiments That Really Work* (4–7). Illus. 1989, Wiley paper $12.95 (0-471-50381-9). This book outlines simple experiments that use readily available equipment and supplies. (Rev: BL 2/15/90) [574]

11876 VanCleave, Janice. *Janice VanCleave's Guide to More of the Best Science Fair Projects* (4–8). 2000, Wiley paper $14.95 (0-471-32627-5). After general information about the scientific method, research, and presentation, this book outlines about 50 projects in the areas of astronomy, biology, earth science, engineering, physical science, and mathematics. (Rev: SLJ 5/00) [509]

11877 VanCleave, Janice. *Janice VanCleave's 203 Icy, Freezing, Frosty, Cool and Wild Experiments* (4–7). 1999, Wiley paper $12.95 (0-471-25223-9). An excellent book filled with easily performed experiments in such areas as biology, chemistry, earth science, and physics. (Rev: SLJ 4/00) [507.8]

11878 Vecchione, Glen. *100 Award-Winning Science Fair Projects* (6–8). Illus. 2001, Sterling $21.95 (0-8069-4261-4). Varied ideas for unusual science fair projects are organized by theme and include step-by-step instructions and a list of the materials needed. (Rev: BL 12/15/01; HBG 3/02; SLJ 10/01; VOYA 12/01) [507]

11879 Vecchione, Glen. *100 First Prize Make It Yourself Science Fair Projects* (4–8). Illus. 1998, Sterling $19.95 (0-8069-0703-7). The projects outlined in this good resource for project ideas range from the simple to complex and cover a wide range of branches of science. (Rev: SLJ 4/99) [507]

11880 Voth, Danna. *Kidsource: Science Fair Handbook* (5–8). Illus. 1998, Lowell House paper $9.95 (1-56565-514-1). This source provides excellent advice on selecting, preparing, and presenting science projects, with material on choosing workable topics, equipment needed, safety, measuring devices, and record keeping. (Rev: BL 2/15/99; SLJ 5/99) [507]

11881 Young, Jay. *The Art of Science* (5–8). Illus. 1999, Candlewick $27.99 (0-7636-0754-1). This interactive book contains removable pieces that demonstrate scientific phenomena, including a magnetic pendulum and wave sculpture. (Rev: BL 12/15/99; SLJ 4/00) [507]

Astronomy and Space Science

General and Miscellaneous

11882 Bortz, Fred. *Collision Course! Cosmic Impacts and Life on Earth* (4–7). Illus. 2001, Millbrook LB $25.90 (0-7613-1403-2). A straightforward discussion of an intriguing subject that includes material on past collisions and on detecting and perhaps deflecting future "near Earth objects." (Rev: BL 5/1/01; HBG 10/01; SLJ 5/01) [523.44]

11883 Campbell, Ann-Jeanette. *The New York Public Library: Amazing Space: A Book of Answers for Kids* (5–8). Illus. 1997, Wiley paper $12.95 (0-471-14498-3). This question-and-answer book introduces space exploration, the solar system, individual planets, galaxies, and related phenomena. (Rev: SLJ 7/97) [523]

11884 Cole, Michael D. *Hubble Space Telescope: Exploring the Universe* (4–7). Illus. Series: Countdown to Space. 1999, Enslow LB $18.95 (0-7660-1120-8). This close-up look at the Hubble space telescope covers its parts, uses, problems, and photographs that the telescope has sent back to earth. (Rev: BL 2/1/99; HBG 10/99) [522]

11885 Couper, Heather, and Nigel Henbest. *The Space Atlas* (5–8). 1992, Harcourt $19.00 (0-15-200598-6). An oversize book that gives a guided tour of the solar system and outer space through maps, paintings, photographs, and charts. (Rev: SLJ 5/92) [523]

11886 Dickinson, Terence. *NightWatch: A Practical Guide to Viewing the Universe*. Rev. ed. (6–12). Illus. 1998, Firefly $45.00 (1-55209-300-X); paper $29.95 (1 55209 302 6). Exciting text and charts tables, and full-color photographs make this an excellent handbook for amateur astronomers, with information on the sky, heavenly bodies, kinds of equipment, and how to photograph the universe. (Rev: SLJ 2/99) [523]

11887 Jackson, Ellen. *Looking for Life in the Universe: The Search for Extraterrestrial Intelligence* (4–7). 2002, Houghton $16.00 (0-618-12894-8). Jackson examines the possibility of life elsewhere and profiles Dr. Jill Tarter, a research astrophysicist, as she searches for traces of an extraterrestrial signal. (Rev: BL 12/1/02; HB 1–2/03; HBG 3/03; SLJ 12/02*; VOYA 4/03) [576.8]

11888 Kerrod, Robin. *Starwatch: A Month-by-Month Guide to the Night Sky* (5–8). Illus. 2003, Barron's $18.95 (0-7641-5666-7). An appealing introduction to astronomy with illustrations that make it easy to identify stellar objects from both northern and southern hemispheres. (Rev: BL 12/1/03) [523]

11889 Maynard, Christopher. *The Young Scientist Book of Stars and Planets* (4–7). Illus. 1978, EDC LB $14.95 (0-88110-313-6); paper $6.95 (0-86020-094-9). Attractive illustrations and plentiful experiments and projects add to this book's appeal.

11890 Menzel, Donald H., and Jay M. Pasachoff. *A Field Guide to the Stars and Planets*. 2nd ed. (7–12). Illus. 1999, Houghton $9.00 (0-395-93432-X). Photographs, sky maps, charts, and timetables are features of this volume in the Peterson Field Guide series. [523]

11891 Miller, Ron. *Extrasolar Planets* (7–12). Illus. Series: Worlds Beyond. 2002, Millbrook LB $25.90 (0-7613-2354-6). A handsome and accessible overview of the planets in our solar system and elsewhere in the universe that includes historical information, biographies of scientists, basic concepts, and many attention-grabbing illustrations. (Rev: BL 2/15/02; HBG 10/02; SLJ 3/02) [523]

11892 Mitton, Simon, and Jacqueline Mitton. *Astronomy* (5–8). Illus. Series: Young Oxford Books. 1996, Oxford LB $30.00 (0-19-521168-5). A well-written, lavishly illustrated introduction to astronomy, with large fact boxes to add depth and asides. (Rev: BL 3/15/96; SLJ 6/96) [520]

11893 Moche, Dinah L. *Astronomy Today: Planets, Stars, Space Exploration* (5–8). 1982, Random paper $12.99 (0-394-84423-8). A history of astronomy and survey of space exploration. (Rev: HBG 3/00) [523]

11894 Moeschl, Richard. *Exploring the Sky: 100 Projects for Beginning Astronomers* (5–8). Illus. 1992, Chicago Review paper $16.95 (1-55652-160-X). Many ideas for experiments and observations in an information-packed book. (Rev: BL 5/1/89)

11895 Moore, Patrick. *The New Atlas of the Universe* (7–12). Illus. 1984, Crown $12.99 (0-517-55500-X). A detailed series of maps that introduce our solar system and the universe beyond. [523]

11896 Oleksy, Walter. *Mapping the Skies* (5–7). Series: Watts Library: Geography. 2002, Watts LB $24.00 (0-531-12031-7); paper $8.95 (0-531-16635-X). From the ancient Greeks and Romans through Galileo to astronomers today, this is a history of how the stars, planets, and space have been mapped. (Rev: BL 10/15/02) [520]

11897 Rasmussen, Richard Michael. *Mysteries of Space* (6–10). Series: Great Mysteries. 1994, Greenhaven LB $22.45 (1-56510-097-2). This introduction to astronomy explores some of the great unanswered questions about the universe. (Rev: BL 4/15/94) [520]

11898 Ronan, Colin A. *The Skywatcher's Handbook* (8–12). Illus. 1989, Crown paper $16.00 (0-517-57326-1). An excellent handbook that describes and explains a wide range of phenomena that occur in both the day and night skies. (Rev: BR 3–4/90; VOYA 2/90) [523]

11899 *Seeing Stars: The McDonald Observatory and Its Astronomers* (6–10). 1997, Sunbelt Media $16.95 (1-57168-117-5). This is a history of the famous observatory operated by the University of Texas in Austin, with material on the equipment used and the day-to-day operation. (Rev: HBG 9/98; SLJ 5/98) [523]

11900 Spangenburg, Ray, and Kit Moser. *The Hubble Space Telescope* (5–9). Illus. Series: Out of This World. 2002, Watts LB $33.50 (0-531-11894-0); paper $14.95 (0-531-15565-X). A look at the telescope itself, its development and launch, the subsequent problems, and the information it has provided to scientists. (Rev: SLJ 12/02) [522]

11901 Steele, Philip. *Astronomy* (4–8). Illus. Series: Pocket Facts. 1991, Macmillan LB $11.95 (0-89686-586-X). A concise introduction to astronomy, complemented by color photographs and drawings. (Rev: BL 3/15/92) [520]

11902 Stott, Carole, and Clint Twist. *1001 Facts About Space* (7–12). Illus. Series: Backpack Books. 2002, DK paper $8.95 (0-7894-8450-1). A handy-sized overview full of illustrations that presents useful facts about the universe, galaxies, stars, solar system, and planets as well as pulsars, space history, and stellar classification. (Rev: BL 3/15/02) [590]

11903 Vogt, Gregory L. *Deep Space Astronomy* (5–8). Illus. 1999, Twenty-First Century LB $25.90 (0-7613-1369-9). This look beyond our own star system covers such topics as the development of space-based detectors, information-gathering techniques, and recent discoveries. (Rev: BL 1/1–15/00; HBG 3/00; SLJ 2/00) [520]

11904 Wills, Susan, and Steven Wills. *Astronomy: Looking at the Stars* (5–8). Illus. Series: Innovators. 2001, Oliver $21.95 (1-881508-76-5). A good starting point for research into astronomy, with profiles of individuals including Ptolemy, Copernicus, Galileo, and Newton. (Rev: HBG 10/02; SLJ 2/02) [520.922]

Astronautics and Space Exploration

11905 Angliss, Sarah. *Cosmic Journeys: A Beginner's Guide to Space and Time Travel* (5–7). Series: Future Files. 1998, Millbrook LB $23.90 (0-7613-0620-X). This book explores such topics as traveling to other solar systems, time travel, black holes, and parallel universes. (Rev: HBG 10/98; SLJ 10/98) [629.4]

11906 Asimov, Isaac, and Frank White. *Think About Space: Where Have We Been and Where Are We Going?* (7–10). Illus. 1989, Walker LB $14.85 (0-8027-6766-4); paper $5.95 (0-8027-6767-2). A history of space exploration and a discussion of possible future developments. (Rev: BL 10/1/89; BR 5–6/90; SLJ 11/89) [500.5]

11907 Bredeson, Carmen. *The Challenger Disaster: Tragic Space Flight* (4–8). Series: American Disasters. 1999, Enslow LB $18.95 (0-7660-1222-0). An account of the 1986 tragedy. (Rev: BL 10/15/99; HBG 3/00) [629.5]

11908 Bredeson, Carmen. *John Glenn Returns to Orbit: Life on the Space Shuttle* (4–7). Series: Countdown to Space. 2000, Enslow LB $18.95 (0-7660-1304-9). This is the story of John Glenn, now a famous politician, his return to space, and the different conditions he encountered. (Rev: BL 8/00; HBG 10/00) [629.4]

11909 Bredeson, Carmen. *NASA Planetary Spacecraft: Galileo, Magellan, Pathfinder, and Voyager* (4–7). Series: Countdown to Space. 2000, Enslow LB $18.95 (0-7660-1303-0). This gives a good rundown on the NASA spacecraft used to explore planets, their individual missions, and their findings. (Rev: BL 9/15/00; HBG 10/01) [629.4]

11910 Briggs, Carole S. *Women in Space* (4–7). Series: A&E Biography. 1999, Lerner LB $25.26 (0-8225-4937-9). Includes profiles of astronauts including Sally Ride, Mae Jemison, Shannon Lucid, Eileen Collins, and two of their Russian counterparts. (Rev: SLJ 5/99) [629.45]

11911 Clay, Rebecca. *Space Travel and Exploration* (4–8). Illus. Series: Secrets of Space. 1995, Twenty-First Century LB $23.90 (0-8050-4474-4). A history of modern space exploration, covering manned flights, space stations, space probes, and telescopes. (Rev: BL 7/97; SLJ 1/98) [629.5]

11912 Cole, Michael D. *Astronauts: Training for Space* (4–7). Illus. Series: Countdown to Space. 1999, Enslow LB $18.95 (0-7660-1116-X). Focusing mainly on Sally Ride, this account describes the rigorous training of NASA astronauts. (Rev: BL 2/1/99; HBG 10/99) [629.45]

11913 Cole, Michael D. *Galileo Spacecraft: Mission to Jupiter* (4–7). Series: Countdown to Space. 1999, Enslow LB $18.95 (0-7660-1119-4). *Galileo*'s journey to Jupiter is described with details of the preparations for the flight and its findings. Photographs, a glossary, and Web sites round out the coverage. (Rev: BL 2/15/99; HBG 10/99; SLJ 5/99) [629.45]

11914 Cole, Michael D. *Moon Base: First Colony on Space* (4–7). Series: Countdown to Space. 1999, Enslow LB $18.95 (0-7660-1118-6). A futuristic look at what a space colony on the moon might look like and the problems involved in creating it. (Rev: BL 2/15/99; HBG 10/99; SLJ 5/99) [629.45]

11915 Cole, Michael D. *NASA Space Vehicles: Capsules, Shuttles, and Space Stations* (4–7). Series: Countdown to Space. 2000, Enslow LB $18.95 (0-7660-1308-1). Gives a rundown on these specialized vehicles plus a description of space stations and how they operate, with full-color photographs and clear, readable text. (Rev: BL 5/15/00; HBG 10/00; SLJ 12/00) [629.4]

11916 Cole, Michael D. *Space Emergency: Astronauts in Danger* (4–8). Illus. Series: Countdown to Space. 2000, Enslow LB $18.95 (0-7660-1307-3). An explosion on the command module of *Apollo 13* and a faulty landing bag on *Friendship 7* are two of the emergencies described in this book on crises in space exploration. (Rev: BL 2/1/00; HBG 10/00; SLJ 12/00) [629.45]

11917 Cole, Michael D. *Space Launch Disaster: When Liftoff Goes Wrong* (4–7). Series: Countdown to Space. 2000, Enslow LB $18.95 (0-7660-1309-X). This is a rundown of problems that can occur during the liftoff of space vehicles, with examples of actual disasters, many caught on camera. (Rev: BL 3/15/00; HBG 10/00; SLJ 8/00) [629]

11918 Dolan, Terrance. *Probing Deep Space* (6–9). Series: World Explorers. 1993, Chelsea LB $21.95 (0-7910-1326-X). A chronicle of how we have learned about outer space and the challenges that remain. (Rev: BL 10/1/93; VOYA 2/94) [520]

11919 Dyson, Marianne J. *Home on the Moon: Living on a Space Frontier* (5–8). Illus. 2003, National Geographic $18.95 (0-7922-7193-9). Dyson, a former NASA mission controller, discusses the resources available on the moon, explores the possibilities of building facilities there, and suggests activities. (Rev: BL 7/03; HBG 10/03; SLJ 9/03) [919.91]

11920 Dyson, Marianne J. *Space Station Science: Life in Free Fall* (4–7). Illus. 1999, Scholastic paper $16.95 (0-590-05889-4). Written by a former member of a NASA control team, this work explores living and working in space including details on a space station bathroom. (Rev: BL 11/15/99; HBG 10/00; SLJ 12/99) [629.45]

11921 Engelbert, Phillis. *Astronomy and Space: From the Big Bang to the Big Crunch* (4–8). Illus. 1997, Gale LB $232.00 (0-7876-0942-0). Some 300 alphabetically arranged entries consider space exploration, the laws and features of the universe, the history of astronomy, important astronauts, famous observatories, and the greenhouse effect. (Rev: BL 5/1/97; BR 5–6/97; SLJ 5/97) [523]

11922 English, June A., and Thomas D. Jones. *Mission: Earth: Voyage to the Home Planet* (4–7). Illus. 1996, Scholastic paper $16.95 (0-590-48571-7). The space program is introduced, with special coverage of the flights of the shuttle *Endeavor* in 1994 and its environmental studies. (Rev: BL 10/15/96; SLJ 10/96) [550]

11923 Fallen, Anne-Catherine. *USA from Space* (4–7). Illus. 1997, Firefly LB $19.95 (1-55209-159-7); paper $7.95 (1-55209-157-0). Excellent satellite pictures of parts of the earth are contained in this book, which also explains the value of satellite imagery in tracking pollution, population, and natural disasters. (Rev: BL 3/1/98; SLJ 12/97) [917.3]

11924 Farbman, Melinda, and Frye Gaillard. *Spacechimp: NASA's Ape in Space* (4–7). Series: Countdown to Space. 2000, Enslow LB $18.95 (0-7660-1478-9). The story of how animals in general have helped the space program and how one chimp's voyage into space contributed to progress. (Rev: BL 8/00; HBG 10/00) [629.4]

11925 Gaffney, Timothy R. *Secret Spy Satellites: America's Eyes in Space* (4–7). Series: Countdown to Space. 2000, Enslow LB $18.95 (0-7660-1402-9). With sharp illustrations and a strong narrative, this book describes U.S. spy satellites, their purposes, and findings. (Rev: BL 9/15/00; HBG 10/01) [629.4]

11926 Harris, Alan, and Paul Weissman. *The Great Voyager Adventure: A Guided Tour Through the Solar System* (4–8). Illus. 1990, Simon & Schuster paper $16.95 (0-671-72538-6). Two scientists introduce the missions, paths, and discoveries of the Voyager spacecraft. (Rev: BL 2/1/91; SLJ 2/91) [523.4]

11927 Hasday, Judy L. *The Apollo 13 Mission* (6–9). Series: Overcoming Adversity. 2000, Chelsea LB $19.95 (0-7910-5310-5). This straightforward account of the difficulties encountered on this moon mission includes black-and-white photographs, a brief history of the space program, and the transcript of an interview with Apollo 13's flight director. (Rev: HBG 10/01; SLJ 1/01) [629.45]

11928 Kennedy, Gregory. *The First Men in Space* (5–7). Illus. Series: World Explorers. 1991, Chelsea LB $21.95 (0-7910-1324-3). This book covers the early years and accomplishments of both Soviet and American space programs. (Rev: SLJ 8/91) [629.44]

11929 Kennedy, Gregory P. *Apollo to the Moon* (6–9). Series: World Explorers. 1992, Chelsea LB $21.95 (0-7910-1322-7). A chronicle of the Apollo moon landing expedition and descriptions of the astronauts involved. (Rev: BL 9/1/92; SLJ 7/92) [629.45]

11930 Kettelkamp, Larry. *ETs and UFOs: Are They Real?* (5–8). Illus. 1996, Morrow $16.00 (0-688-12868-8). Kettelkamp explores the evidence supporting extraterrestrial beings and unidentified flying objects. (Rev: BL 12/15/96; SLJ 1/97) [001.9]

11931 Kettelkamp, Larry. *Living in Space* (5–7). Illus. 1993, Morrow $14.00 (0-688-10018-X). Tells how astronauts live in space and discusses plans for space exploration in the future. (Rev: BL 10/1/93; SLJ 9/93) [629.4]

11932 Kupperberg, Paul. *Spy Satellites* (4–8). Illus. Series: Library of Satellites. 2003, Rosen LB $26.50 (0-8239-3854-9). The author discusses the history of U.S. spy satellites and how the country has used the information they have gleaned. (Rev: BL 5/15/03) [327.1273]

11933 Landau, Elaine. *Space Disasters* (5–7). Illus. Series: Watts Library. 1999, Watts LB $24.00 (0-531-20345-X); paper $8.95 (0-531-16431-4). This work covers four space disasters *Apollo 1, Soyuz 1, Apollo 13,* and the *Challenger.* (Rev: BL 2/1/00; SLJ 2/00) [363.12]

11934 Lieurance, Suzanne. *The Space Shuttle Challenger Disaster in American History* (6–10). Series: In American History. 2001, Enslow LB $20.95 (0-7660-1419-3). The story of the tragic destruction of the Challenger space shuttle in January, 1986, that killed seven astronauts including teacher Christa McAuliffe. (Rev: BL 8/1/01; HBG 10/01; SLJ 9/01) [629]

11935 McCormick, Anita Louise. *Space Exploration* (6–8). Series: Overview. 1994, Lucent LB $27.45 (1-56006-149-9). A review of accomplishments in space exploration and an examination of questions about the future, including what the goals should be and who should decide. (Rev: BL 7/94) [919.9]

11936 McKay, David W., and Bruce G. Smith. *Space Science Projects for Young Scientists* (7–12). Illus. 1986, Watts paper $24.00 (0-531-10244-0). A series of clearly explained projects that involve possible space environments and forces such as gravity. (Rev: BL 12/15/86; BR 1–2/87; SLJ 12/86) [500.5]

11937 Markle, Sandra. *Pioneering Space* (5–8). 1992, Atheneum LB $14.95 (0-689-31748-4). A look at space travel and how people may succeed in living in space. (Rev: BL 9/1/92; SLJ 2/93) [629.4]

11938 Marsh, Carole. *Unidentified Flying Objects and Extraterrestrial Life* (5–8). Series: Secrets of Space. 1996, Twenty-First Century LB $25.90 (0-8050-4472-8). This book touches on a wide range of topics associated with UFOs, including a history of famous sightings, but the emphasis is on major SETI (Search for Extra Terrestrial Intelligence) projects undertaken to detect alien radio signals. The author concludes that there is no definitive proof of the existence of intelligent life outside Earth. (Rev: BL 12/1/96; SLJ 12/96) [001.9]

11939 Maurer, Richard. *Junk in Space* (4–8). Illus. 1989, Simon & Schuster paper $5.95 (0-671-67767-5). Discussing the various kinds of space garbage orbiting earth. (Rev: BL 11/15/89) [363]

11940 Nardo, Don. *Flying Saucers* (6–9). Illus. Series: Opposing Viewpoints Great Mysteries. 1996, Greenhaven LB $27.45 (1-56510-351-3). The pros and cons concerning flying saucers are detailed in this "Opposing Viewpoints" title. (Rev: BL 4/15/96) [001.9]

11941 Netzley, Patricia D. *Alien Abductions* (7–10). Series: Mystery Library. 2001, Lucent LB $19.96 (1-56006-767-5). This is a serious examination of claims concerning abductions by aliens with reference to cases that have been reported. (Rev: BL 9/15/01; SLJ 2/01) [001.9]

11942 Pogue, William R. *How Do You Go to the Bathroom in Space?* (7–12). 1991, Tor paper $7.99 (0-8125-1728-8). In a question-and-answer format, the author, who spent 84 days in space, discusses the practical aspects of space travel. (Rev: VOYA 12/85) [629.47]

11943 Ride, Sally, and Susan Okie. *To Space and Back* (8–12). Illus. 1986, Lothrop $19.99 (0-688-06159-1); paper $13.95 (0-688-09112-1). A photojourney that begins four hours before launch and ends after landing. (Rev: BL 11/86; BR 11–12/86; SLJ 11/86; VOYA 12/86) [629]

11944 Riva, Peter, and Barbara Hitchcock, comps. *Sightseeing: A Space Panorama* (8–12). Illus. 1985, Knopf $24.95 (0-394-54243-6). A spectacular view of space as pictured in 84 captioned photographs from NASA's archives. (Rev: SLJ 5/86) [629.4]

11945 Scott, Elaine. *Adventure in Space: The Flight to Fix the Hubble* (4–7). Illus. 1995, Hyperion LB $17.49 (0-7868-2031-4). A behind-the-scenes look at NASA and the mission to repair the Hubble telescope in 1993. (Rev: BL 7/95*; SLJ 4/95*) [522]

11946 Sherman, Josepha. *Deep Space Observation Satellites* (4–8). Illus. Series: Library of Satellites. 2003, Rosen LB $26.50 (0-8239-3852-2). The author discusses the history of U.S. observation satellites and how the country has benefited from their discoveries. (Rev: BL 5/15/03) [522]

11947 Spangenburg, Ray, and Kit Moser. *Life on Other Worlds* (5–9). Illus. Series: Out of This World. 2002, Watts LB $33.50 (0-531-11895-9); paper $14.95 (0-531-15566-8). The possibilities of extraterrestrial life and the efforts to intercept any communications are discussed in this narrative, along with the origins of the solar system and the composition of the planet Mars. (Rev: SLJ 12/02) [001.9]

11948 Spangenburg, Ray, and Kit Moser. *Onboard the Space Shuttle* (5–9). Illus. Series: Out of This World. 2002, Watts LB $33.50 (0-531-11896-7); paper $14.95 (0-531-15568-4). The problems of living and working in space are presented, plus the history of the shuttle program, information on individual astronauts, statistics, and lots of photographs. (Rev: SLJ 9/02) [629.441]

11949 Spangenburg, Raymond, and Diane Moser. *Opening the Space Frontier* (8–12). Illus. 1989, Facts on File $22.95 (0-8160-1848-0). A history of space exploration from the fiction of Jules Verne to the realities of today. (Rev: BR 5–6/90; SLJ 4/90; VOYA 4/90) [500.5]

11950 Steele, Philip. *Space Travel* (4–8). Illus. Series: Pocket Facts. 1991, Macmillan LB $11.95 (0-89686-585-1). An introduction to space exploration, packed with basic facts and color illustrations. (Rev: BL 3/15/92) [629.4]

11951 Stott, Carole. *Space Exploration* (4–8). Series: Eyewitness Books. 1997, Knopf $20.99 (0-679-98563-8). An overview of the history of space exploration, including the various missions and their findings. (Rev: BL 11/15/97; HBG 3/98; SLJ 1/98) [523]

11952 Sullivan, George. *The Day We Walked on the Moon: A Photo History of Space Exploration* (5–8). Illus. 1990, Scholastic paper $4.95 (0-685-58532-8). The history of U.S. space exploration, showing the accomplishments of both the United States and the Soviet Union. (Rev: BL 9/1/90; SLJ 2/91) [629.4]

11953 Taylor, Robert. *Life Aboard the Space Shuttle* (6–10). Series: The Way People Live. 2002, Gale LB $27.45 (1-59018-154-9). How the astronauts live in a space shuttle and their daily chores are covered in this account that uses many primary and secondary quotations. (Rev: BL 7/02) [629.4]

11954 Vogt, Gregory L. *Apollo Moonwalks: The Amazing Lunar Missions* (4–7). Series: Countdown to Space. 2000, Enslow LB $18.95 (0-7660-1306-5). This account focuses on the moonwalks during the *Apollo 11* expedition and details what was found. (Rev: BL 8/00; HBG 10/00) [629.4]

11955 Vogt, Gregory L. *Disasters in Space Exploration* (5–8). Illus. 2001, Millbrook LB $25.90 (0-7613-1920-4). Accidents and failures that have marred the success rates of the American and Soviet space programs are covered in interesting detail with many photographs. (Rev: BL 10/1/01; HBG 3/02; SLJ 8/01*) [363.12]

11956 Vogt, Gregory L. *Spacewalks: The Ultimate Adventures in Orbit* (4–7). Series: Countdown to Space. 2000, Enslow LB $18.95 (0-7660-1305-7). This gives a history of spacewalks, tells who were the pioneers, and explains their purpose. (Rev: BL 8/00; HBG 10/00) [629.4]

11957 Wunsch, Susi Trautmann. *The Adventures of Sojourner: The Mission to Mars that Thrilled the World* (5–9). 1998, Mikaya LB $22.95 (0-9650493-5-3); paper $9.95 (0-9650493-6-1). This book describes the construction of the *Sojourner* rover and its performance on Mars after landing on July 4, 1997. (Rev: SLJ 2/99*) [629.5]

Comets, Meteors, and Asteroids

11958 Asimov, Isaac. *How Did We Find Out About Comets?* (5–7). Illus. 1975, Walker LB $10.85 (0-8027-6204-2). An introduction to comets and our knowledge and attitudes about them since ancient times. [523.6]

11959 Kraske, Robert. *Asteroids: Invaders from Space* (5–7). Illus. 1995, Simon & Schuster $15.00 (0-689-31860-X). A history of these cosmic wanderers, their formation, and the results, positive and negative, when they collide with earth. (Rev: BCCB 11/95; BL 7/95; SLJ 9/95) [523.4]

Earth and the Moon

11960 Alessandrello, Anna. *The Earth: Origins and Evolution* (4–8). Illus. Series: Beginnings — Origins and Evolution. 1995, Raintree Steck-Vaughn LB $24.26 (0-8114-3331-5). An oversize book with lavish illustrations that discusses the theories concerning the formation of the earth, its structure and composition, and ways in which it is changing. (Rev: BL 4/15/95; SLJ 6/95) [550]

11961 Caes, Charles J. *How Do We Know the Age of the Earth* (6–9). Illus. Series: Great Scientific Questions and the Scientists Who Answered Them. 2001, Rosen LB $19.95 (0-8239-3381-4). An absorbing account of efforts through the ages to establish the age of the our planet. (Rev: SLJ 12/01; VOYA 8/02) [551.7]

11962 Dixon, Dougal, and John Adams. *The Future Is Wild: A Natural History of the Future* (6–10). Illus. 2003, Firefly $35.00 (1-55297-724-2); paper $24.95 (1-55297-723-4). Scientists speculate on the future evolution of our planet, envisioning the decline of mankind and the appearance of new species, which are shown in full-color, computer-generated images with detailed habitat. (Rev: SLJ 6/03; VOYA 4/03) [576.8]

11963 Erickson, Jon. *Exploring Earth from Space* (8–12). Illus. 1989, TAB paper $15.95 (0-8306-3242-5). Beginning with the history of space exploration, this account also covers how we on Earth profit from the use of space. (Rev: BR 1–2/90) [500.5]

11964 Gallant, Roy A. *Earth's Place in Space* (5–8). Series: The Story of Science. 1999, Benchmark LB $28.50 (0-7614-0963-7). Using a chronological approach, this account traces our knowledge of the earth and its place in the solar system and space. (Rev: BL 2/15/00; HBG 3/00; SLJ 2/00) [525]

11965 Gallant, Roy A., and Christopher J. Schuberth. *Earth: The Making of a Planet* (7–10). Illus. 1998, Marshall Cavendish $14.95 (0-7614-5012-2). Beginning with the big bang, this book describes the creation of Earth, with material on landforms, seas, the moon, rocks and minerals, and the ocean floor, and speculates about Earth's future. (Rev: BL 7/98; BR 11–12/98; HBG 9/98; SLJ 7/98) [550]

11966 Gardner, Robert. *Science Project Ideas About the Moon* (4–7). Illus. Series: Science Project Ideas. 1997, Enslow LB $19.95 (0-89490-844-8). After giving basic information about the moon, this book outlines projects involving ways of observing the moon and how to make models to show its movements. (Rev: BL 12/1/97; HBG 3/98) [523.3]

11967 Miller, Ron. *Earth and the Moon* (5–7). Illus. Series: Worlds Beyond. 2003, Twenty-First Century LB $25.90 (0-7613-2358-9). NASA photographs and computer-generated images are used throughout this account of the origin, composition, and evolution the Earth and its moon. (Rev: HBG 10/03; SLJ 8/03) [525]

11968 Patent, Dorothy Hinshaw. *Shaping the Earth* (4–7). Illus. 2000, Clarion $18.00 (0-395-85691-4). The evolution of the earth is traced in this compelling book that describes how the surface has changed and continues to change, with coverage of plate tectonics, ice ages, natural disasters, and descriptions of its natural wonders. (Rev: BL 3/15/00; HBG 10/00; SLJ 4/00) [550]

Stars

11969 Cobb, Allan. *How Do We Know How Stars Shine?* (6–9). Illus. Series: Great Scientific Questions and the Scientists Who Answered Them. 2001, Rosen LB $19.95 (0-8239-3380-6). Cobb traces man's growing knowledge of the stars from the ancient astronomers through recent discoveries, showing how each new fact builds upon the ones that came before. (Rev: BL 10/15/01; SLJ 12/01) [523.8]

11970 Croswell, Ken. *See the Stars* (4–8). Illus. 2000, Boyds Mills $16.95 (1-56397-757-5). Twelve constellations are introduced in double-page spreads, with material on where and when to look for them. (Rev: BL 11/1/00; HBG 3/01; SLJ 10/00) [523]

11971 Gallant, Roy A. *The Life Stories of Stars* (6–10). Series: The Story of Science. 2000, Marshall Cavendish LB $28.50 (0-7614-1152-6). This is a colorful introduction to stars, how they are formed, and how they die. (Rev: BL 12/15/00; HBG 10/01; SLJ 2/01) [523.8]

11972 Gustafson, John. *Stars, Clusters and Galaxies* (5–8). Illus. Series: Young Stargazer's Guide to the Galaxy. 1993, Simon & Schuster LB $18.95 (0-671-72536-X); paper $6.95 (0-671-72537-8). Introduces stars, binary stars, star clusters, nebulae, and galaxies, and provides tips for viewing the night sky through binoculars and telescopes. (Rev: BL 7/93; SLJ 6/93; VOYA 10/93) [523.8]

11973 Pearce, Q. L. *The Stargazer's Guide to the Galaxy* (4–8). 1991, Tor paper $6.99 (0-812-59423-1). In this introduction to star gazing in the Northern Hemisphere, material covered includes a look at the night sky in each of the four seasons. (Rev: SLJ 12/91) [523]

11974 Rey, H. A. *Find the Constellations* (5–7). Illus. 1976, Houghton LB $20.00 (0-395-24509-5); paper $9.95 (0-395-24418-8). Through clear text and illustrations, the reader is helped to recognize stars and constellations in the northern United States. Also use *The Stars: A New Way to See Them* (1973).

11975 Sasaki, Chris. *The Constellations: Stars and Stories* (6–12). Illus. 2003, Sterling $24.95 (0-8069-7635-7). Observing constellations offers an opportunity to connect science and history, and this book provides tips for finding constellations and seeing the patterns that connect to their names. (Rev: BL 2/15/03; HBG 10/03; SLJ 7/03; VOYA 10/03) [523.8]

11976 VanCleave, Janice. *Janice VanCleave's Constellations for Every Kid: Easy Activities That Make Learning Science Fun* (8–12). Illus. 1997, Wiley $32.50 (0-471-15981-6); paper $12.95 (0-471-15979-4). An excellent guide to the heavens, with each chapter presenting a different constellation with concise facts, new concepts, simple activities, and solutions to problems. (Rev: BL 12/1/97; HBG 3/98; SLJ 10/97) [523.8]

Sun and the Solar System

11977 Bortolotti, Dan. *Exploring Saturn* (4–8). Illus. 2003, Firefly $19.95 (1-55297-766-8); paper $9.95 (1-55297-765-X). This highly visual volume with readable text presents facts about Saturn, explains how and when we acquired this knowledge, and looks at the Cassini-Huygens mission, scheduled to reach the planet in 2004. (Rev: BL 12/1/03) [523.46]

11978 Dickinson, Terence. *Other Worlds: A Beginner's Guide to Planets and Moons* (4–8). Illus. 1995, Firefly paper $9.95 (1-895565-70-7). An entertaining, well-illustrated introduction to the solar system, the planets, important moons, comets, brown dwarfs, and the search for evidence of other planetary systems. (Rev: BL 11/15/95; SLJ 1/96) [523.4]

11979 Fradin, Dennis B. *The Planet Hunters: The Search for Other Worlds* (5–8). Illus. 1997, Simon & Schuster $19.95 (0-689-81323-6). This well-researched book traces the search for other worlds from the time of early civilization and the discovery of each of the planets, including the difficulty scientists had convincing the world that the Earth is also a planet. (Rev: BL 12/1/97*; BR 3–4/98; HBG 3/98; SLJ 1/98) [523.4]

11980 Gallant, Roy A. *When the Sun Dies* (6–10). 1998, Marshall Cavendish $14.95 (0-7614-5036-X). After discussing the history and structure of the solar system, the author gives a blow-by-blow account of our sun's last 9 billion years and his projections for its likely ending about a billion years from now. (Rev: SLJ 1/99; VOYA 6/99) [523.2]

11981 Gustafson, John. *Planets, Moons and Meteors: The Young Stargazer's Guide to the Galaxy* (4–8). Illus. 1992, Simon & Schuster LB $12.95 (0-671-72534-3); paper $6.95 (0-671-72535-1). This guidebook tells how and when to observe the solar system and provides basic information about the planets. (Rev: BL 11/1/92) [523]

11982 Landau, Elaine. *Jupiter* (5–7). Series: Watts Library. 1999, Watts LB $24.00 (0-531-20387-5). This is an update of the fine earlier book, with material on the Ulysses and Galileo probes. (Rev: SLJ 2/00) [523.4]

11983 Landau, Elaine. *Mars* (5–7). Series: Watts Library. 1999, Watts LB $24.00 (0-531-20388-3). This updated version of an earlier title is a fine introduction to the planet Mars with new material on the *Pathfinder* landing that launched little *Sojourner* in 1993. (Rev: SLJ 2/00) [523.4]

11984 Miller, Ron. *Jupiter* (5–8). Series: Worlds Beyond. 2002, Millbrook LB $25.90 (0-7613-2356-2). An excellent oversize volume that explores the largest of the planets with amazing full-page color illustrations and a detailed text. Also use *Venus* (2002). (Rev: BL 8/02; HBG 3/03; SLJ 8/02) [523.4]

11985 Miller, Ron. *Mercury and Pluto* (5–8). Series: Worlds Beyond. 2003, Millbrook LB $25.90 (0-7613-2361-9). Information on these planets and their discoveries is presented clearly, with helpful illustrations. Also use *Saturn* (2003). (Rev: BL 11/15/03; SLJ 12/03) [523.4]

11986 Miller, Ron. *Saturn* (5–8). Series: Worlds Beyond. 2003, Millbrook LB $25.90 (0-7613-2360-0). A colorful volume that describes the discovery of the solar system and supplies details about the planet Saturn and its many rings. (Rev: BL 11/15/03; SLJ 12/03) [523.4]

11987 Miller, Ron. *The Sun* (5–8). Illus. Series: Worlds Beyond. 2002, Millbrook LB $25.90 (0-7613-2355-4). Miller explores the nature and structure of the sun and the importance of solar energy. (Rev: BL 4/1/02; HBG 10/02; SLJ 5/02) [523.7]

11988 Miller, Ron. *Uranus and Neptune* (5–7). Illus. Series: Worlds Beyond. 2003, Twenty-First Century LB $25.90 (0-7613-2357-0). NASA photographs and computer-generated images are used throughout this account of the discovery and exploration of these two planets and what we know about their origin, composition, and evolution. (Rev: HBG 10/03; SLJ 8/03) [523.47]

11989 Ride, Sally, and Tam O'Shaughnessy. *Exploring Our Solar System* (4–8). Illus. 2003, Crown $19.95 (0-375-81204-0). This enthralling look at each of the planets includes excellent images and charts. (Rev: BL 12/1/03; HB 1–2/04) [523.2]

11990 Simon, Seymour. *Neptune* (4–8). Illus. 1991, Morrow $17.89 (0-688-09632-8). The voyage of *Voyager II* as it swept past Neptune provided scientists with more information on this planet than they had ever had. (Rev: BCCB 4/91; BL 2/15/91; HB 5–6/91; SLJ 4/91) [523.4]

11991 Spangenburg, Ray, and Kit Moser. *A Look at Saturn* (6–8). Illus. Series: Out of This World. 2001, Watts LB $32.00 (0-531-11770-7); paper $14.95 (0-531-16564-7). A detailed examination of Saturn's composition, rings, and moons, with discussion of puzzles that remain, color photographs, timeline, and biographical information on key scientists. Also use *A Look at Venus* (2001). (Rev: SLJ 5/02) [523.46]

11992 Spangenburg, Raymond, and Diane Moser. *Exploring the Reaches of the Solar System* (6–10). Illus. 1990, Facts on File $22.95 (0-8160-1850-2). This is a fine summary of what the space probes have told us about the solar system. For historical information use *Opening the Space Frontier* (1989). (Rev: BL 4/15/90; SLJ 12/90) [639]

11993 Tabak, John. *A Look at Neptune* (6–8). Illus. Series: Out of This World. 2003, Watts LB $33.50 (0-531-12267-0); paper $14.95 (0-531-15584-6). Tabak describes the discovery of the planet, the current state of our knowledge about it, and the information we gained from the Voyager 2 expedition and the Hubble telescope. Also use *A Look at Pluto* (2003). (Rev: SLJ 9/03) [523.48]

11994 Wilsdon, Christina. *The Solar System: An A–Z Guide* (4–7). 2000, Watts LB $32.00 (0-531-11710-3). An alphabetically arranged book that covers many aspect of the solar system including planets, space probes and missions, famous personalities, and such phenomena as greenhouse effect and solar wind. (Rev: SLJ 7/00) [523.4]

Universe

11995 Couper, Heather, and Nigel Henbest. *Big Bang* (5–8). Illus. 1997, DK paper $16.95 (0-7894-1484-8). This work explains, in double-page spreads, the Big Bang theory and its implications for the future. (Rev: BL 6/1–15/97; SLJ 8/97) [523.1]

11996 Miotto, Enrico. *The Universe: Origins and Evolution* (5–8). Series: Beginnings. 1995, Raintree Steck-Vaughn LB $24.26 (0-8114-3334-X). This basic outline of the history of the universe begins with the Big Bang theory and finishes with the "Big Crunch" that may end time. (Rev: BL 4/15/95) [523.1]

11997 Reed, George. *Eyes on the Universe* (6–10). Series: The Story of Science. 2000, Marshall Cavendish LB $19.95 (0-7614-1154-2). A clear, attractively-presented introduction to the universe and its components. (Rev: BL 12/15/00; HBG 10/01) [523]

11998 Ruiz, Andres L. *The Origin of the Universe* (4–9). Series: Sequences of Earth and Space. 1997, Sterling $12.95 (0-8069-9744-3). In simple, concise language, this work discusses various theories concerning the origin of the universe, including the Big Bang theory. (Rev: BL 12/15/97) [523]

Biological Sciences

General and Miscellaneous

11999 Bottone, Frank G., Jr. *The Science of Life: Projects and Principles for Beginning Biologists* (5–8). Illus. 2001, Chicago Review paper $14.95 (1-55652-382-3). Twenty-five projects introduce readers to the basics of biology and the rigors of scientific research. (Rev: SLJ 11/01) [570.78]

12000 Brooks, Bruce. *The Red Wasteland* (6–10). 1995, Holt $15.95 (0-8050-4495-7). A fine anthology of essays, stories, poems, and book excerpts by some of the best nature writers, who raise themes and questions about crucial issues related to the environment. (Rev: BL 8/98; BR 1–2/99; HBG 3/99; SLJ 6/98; VOYA 8/98) [808]

12001 Castner, James L. *Layers of Life* (6–12). Illus. Series: Deep in the Amazon. 2001, Marshall Cavendish LB $18.95 (0-7614-1130-5). This volume explores the biodiversity found in each "layer" of the Amazonian rainforest, with color photographs. Also use *Partners and Rivals*, *River Life*, and *Surviving in the Rain Forest* (all 2001). (Rev: BL 12/15/01; HBG 3/02) [577.34]

12002 *DK Nature Encyclopedia* (5–8). 1998, DK paper $29.99 (0-7894-3411-3). A browsable reference book that covers topics including classification of living things, ecology, the origins and evolution of life, specific animal and plant groups, and the inner workings of plants and animals, all in a series of beautifully illustrated double-page spreads. (Rev: BL 12/1/98; SLJ 2/99) [574]

12003 Doris, Ellen. *Woods, Ponds, and Fields* (4–7). Illus. Series: Real Kids Real Science. 1994, Thames & Hudson $16.95 (0-500-19006-2). A book that gives background essays as well as step-by-step directions for nature study projects in all seasons. (Rev: BL 9/1/94) [508]

12004 Emory, Jerry. *Dirty, Rotten, Dead? A Worm's-eye View of Death, Decomposition . . . and Life* (5–8). Illus. 1996, Harcourt paper $15.00 (0-15-200695-8). Along with a number of experiments and ecological projects, this book discusses death and recycling in nature, including such topics as the parts of the human body that become waste (e.g. hair, nails, skin), digestion and human excretion, processing of sewage, water pollution, diseases of the immune system, and contemporary mortician practices. (Rev: SLJ 8/96) [628.4]

12005 Gallant, Roy A. *The Wonders of Biodiversity* (5–8). Illus. Series: The Story of Science. 2002, Benchmark $19.95 (0-7614-1427-4). Gallant discusses the importance of biodiversity, the plight of species that are affected by loss of habitat and other environmental factors, and species interdependence. (Rev: HBG 3/03; SLJ 2/03) [578]

12006 Gifford, Clive, and Jerry Cadle. *The Kingfisher Young People's Book of Living Worlds* (5–7). Illus. Series: Kingfisher Young People's Book Of. 2002, Kingfisher $21.95 (0-7534-5390-8). Habitats and ecosystems are covered in an attractive, fact-filled format that looks at man's impact on nature. (Rev: HBG 3/03; SLJ 12/02) [577]

12007 Maynard, Caitlin, and Thane Maynard. *Rain Forests and Reefs: A Kid's-Eye View of the Tropics* (4–8). Illus. 1996, Watts LB $24.00 (0-531-11281-0). The flora and fauna of rain forests and coral reefs in Belize are described in text and stunning photographs. (Rev: BL 2/15/97; SLJ 3/97*) [574.5]

12008 Parker, Steve. *Survival and Change* (4–7). Series: Life Processes. 2001, Heinemann LB $21.36 (1-57572-340-9). Parker considers how organisms evolve and looks at how species behave under threat and the origin of new species in this concise book with diagrams, charts, and color photographs. (Rev: HBG 10/01; SLJ 7/01) [578.4]

12009 Patent, Dorothy Hinshaw. *Biodiversity* (6–10). Illus. 1996, Clarion $18.00 (0-395-68704-7). This book discusses broad topics such as habitats, ecosystems, and important species to show connections in nature. (Rev: BL 12/1/96; SLJ 12/96*) [333.95]

12010 Quinlan, Susan E. *The Case of the Monkeys That Fell from the Trees: And Other Mysteries in Tropical Nature* (5–8). Illus. 2003, Boyds Mills $15.95 (1-56397-902-0). Quinlan introduces plant and animal mysteries in South and Central American tropical forests and shows how scientists approached solving them. (Rev: BL 3/1/03; HBG 10/03; SLJ 3/03; VOYA 10/03) [508.313]

12011 Raham, R. Gary. *Dinosaurs in the Garden: An Evolutionary Guide to Backyard Biology* (6–10). Illus. 1988, Plexus $22.95 (0-937548-10-3). The author uses common creatures to explain how they fit into the scheme of nature and overall patterns of evolution. (Rev: BL 12/1/88) [575]

12012 Silverstein, Alvin, et al. *Food Chains* (6–9). Series: Science Concepts. 1998, Twenty-First Century LB $26.90 (0-7613-3002-X). A clearly written account that explains the concept of food chains, with background information and many examples, and reviews the most current information. (Rev: HBG 3/99; SLJ 1/99) [574.5]

12013 Silverstein, Alvin, et al. *Symbiosis* (5–9). Series: Science Concepts. 1998, Twenty-First Century LB $26.90 (0-7613-3001-1). The concept of cooperation in nature for mutual benefit is explored, with explanations of various forms of symbiotic partnerships including the relationships humans have with animals, plants, fungi, and microorganisms. (Rev: HBG 3/99; SLJ 2/99) [574.5]

12014 Squire, Ann. *101 Questions and Answers About Backyard Wildlife* (5–8). Illus. 1996, Walker LB $16.85 (0-8027-8458-5). Using a question-and-answer format, this work provides fascinating information about common insects, birds, mammals, and reptiles. (Rev: SLJ 1/97; VOYA 8/97) [574]

12015 VanCleave, Janice. *Janice VanCleave's A+ Projects in Biology: Winning Experiments for Science Fairs and Extra Credit* (6–10). 1993, Wiley paper $12.95 (0-471-58628-5). Offers a variety of experiments in botany, zoology, and the human body. (Rev: BL 1/15/94; SLJ 11/93) [574]

12016 Wallace, Holly. *Classification* (4–7). Series: Life Processes. 2001, Heinemann LB $21.36 (1-57572-337-9). A concise look at the system that we use for classifying plants and animals, with diagrams, charts, and color photographs. Also use *Adaptation* and *Cells and Systems* (both 2001). (Rev: HBG 10/01; SLJ 7/01) [570]

Botany

General and Miscellaneous

12017 Arnold, Katya, and Sam Swope. *Katya's Book of Mushrooms* (5–8). Illus. 1997, Holt $16.95 (0-8050-4136-2). A field manual on edible and poisonous mushrooms, how to find and identify them, and the folklore surrounding them. (Rev: BL 4/1/97; SLJ 4/97) [589.2]

12018 Bonnet, Robert L., and G. Daniel Keen. *Botany: 49 Science Fair Projects* (6–10). Illus. 1989, TAB $16.95 (0-8306-9277-0). Well-explained projects involving such phenomena as photosynthesis, hydroponics, fungi, and germination. (Rev: BL 1/15/90; BR 1–2/90; VOYA 2/90) [581]

12019 Greenaway, Theresa. *The Plant Kingdom* (5–8). Illus. 1999, Raintree Steck-Vaughn LB $27.12 (0-8172-5886-8). Using diagrams, sidebars, and color photographs, this account introduces the basics of plant classification while also covering such topics as photosynthesis and plant reproduction. (Rev: BL 2/1/00) [580]

12020 Lincoff, Gary. *The Audubon Society Field Guide to North American Mushrooms* (7–12). Illus. 1981, Knopf $19.95 (0-394-51992-2). More than 700 species are introduced and pictured in color photographs. [589.2]

12021 Pascoe, Elaine. *Slime, Molds, and Fungus* (4–7). Series: Nature Close-Up. 1998, Blackbirch LB $27.44 (1-56711-182-3). Stunning photographs, good background information, and a number of interesting projects help introduce the world of fungi. (Rev: BL 9/15/98; HBG 3/99; SLJ 3/99) [589.2]

12022 Patent, Dorothy Hinshaw. *Plants on the Trail with Lewis and Clark.* (5–8). Photos by William Muñoz. 2003, Clarion $18.00 (0-618-06776-0). This introduction to the trees and plants seen by Lewis and Clark also discusses Lewis's training as a botanist and his contributions to the field. (Rev: BL 3/1/03; HBG 10/03; SLJ 5/03) [581.978]

12023 Ross, Bill. *Straight from the Bear's Mouth: The Story of Photosynthesis* (6–9). 1995, Atheneum $16.00 (0-689-31726-3). Young people at a science camp are asked to develop hypotheses and test them, in the process gaining knowledge about chemistry, physics, and botany. (Rev: BL 12/1/95; SLJ 12/95) [581.1]

12024 Silverstein, Alvin, et al. *Photosynthesis* (5–9). Series: Science Concepts. 1998, Twenty-First Century LB $26.90 (0-7613-3000-3). Photosynthesis is explained, with a history of the discoveries about the process and material on related issues including acid rain and the greenhouse effect. (Rev: HBG 3/99; SLJ 2/99) [581.1]

12025 Souza, D. M. *What Is a Fungus?* (4–7). Series: Watts Library. 2002, Watts LB $24.00 (0-531-11979-3); paper $8.95 (0-531-16223-0). In readable and appealing text, Souza explains what a fungus is and how it lives, eats, and reproduces. (Rev: SLJ 8/02) [579.5]

12026 Tesar, Jenny. *Fungi* (5–7). Illus. Series: Our Living World. 1994, Blackbirch LB $27.44 (1-56711-044-4). A volume that explains what a fungus is, how the various types reproduce and grow, their unique characteristics, and how they fit into food webs and chains. (Rev: BL 12/1/94) [589.2]

Foods, Farms, and Ranches

GENERAL AND MISCELLANEOUS

12027 Artley, Bob. *Once Upon a Farm* (4–9). 2000, Pelican $21.95 (1-56554-753-5). Fine watercolors accompany a readable look at the seasons as experienced by the author while growing up on a farm in Iowa. (Rev: SLJ 12/00) [630]

12028 Bial, Raymond. *The Farms* (4–7). Photos by author. Illus. Series: Building America. 2001, Benchmark LB $25.64 (0-7614-1332-4). An interesting, beautifully illustrated look at the ways in which farms developed in America, with information on their structure and significance to the country as a whole. Also use *The Mills* (2001). (Rev: HBG 3/02; SLJ 2/02*) [630]

12029 Bial, Raymond. *Portrait of a Farm Family* (4–7). Illus. 1995, Houghton $17.00 (0-395-69936-3). A behind-the-scenes look at a dairy farm in Illinois that gives details on day-to-day operations and problems. (Rev: BCCB 10/95; BL 9/1/95*; HB 11–12/95; SLJ 12/95) [338.1]

12030 Bramwell, Martyn. *Food Watch* (5–7). Illus. Series: Protecting Our Planet. 2001, DK paper $16.95 (0-7894-7765-3). Bramwell explains the agricultural problems we face, the different production techniques, and the kinds of professionals who work in this field. (Rev: BL 8/01; HBG 3/02) [641.7]

12031 Busenberg, Bonnie. *Vanilla, Chocolate and Strawberry: The Story of Your Favorite Flavors* (6–9). Illus. Series: Discovery! 1994, Lerner LB $23.93 (0-8225-1573-3). With the generous use of maps, diagrams, and photographs, this is the breezy overview of three popular flavors, how they are produced, and how they are used. (Rev: BL 6/1–15/94) [664.5]

12032 Chandler, Gary, and Kevin Graham. *Natural Foods and Products* (4–8). Illus. Series: Making a Better World. 1996, Twenty-First Century LB $25.90 (0-8050-4623-2). This work discusses genetically engineered foods, safe eco-friendly methods of growing crops, and companies that engage in safe practices. (Rev: BL 12/15/96; SLJ 1/97) [333.76]

12033 Damerow, Gail. *Your Chickens: A Kid's Guide to Raising and Showing* (4–7). Illus. 1993, Storey paper $14.95 (0-88266-823-4). A straightforward, practical guide on raising prize-winning chickens that is both thorough and filled with information. (Rev: BL 5/15/94; SLJ 1/94) [636.5]

12034 Damerow, Gail. *Your Goats: A Kid's Guide to Raising and Showing* (4–7). Illus. 1993, Storey paper $14.95 (0-88266-825-0). This is a complete guide to raising, breeding, and showing goats, with many useful tips and helpful illustrations. (Rev: BL 5/15/94; SLJ 1/94) [636.3]

12035 Dunn-Georgiou, Elisha. *Everything You Need to Know About Organic Foods* (6–10). Illus. Series: Need to Know Library. 2002, Rosen LB $23.95 (0-8239-3551-5). An examination of the techniques that produce organic foods and the benefits of eating foods that are free of certain additives. (Rev: BL 5/1/02; SLJ 6/02) [641.3]

12036 Goldberg, Jake. *The Disappearing American Farm* (8–12). Illus. 1996, Watts LB $24.00 (0-531-11261-6). After a brief history of farming and the economic aspects of U.S. farm policy, the author discusses the impact of technology and agricultural research on the farm industry, government intervention, and a number of other difficult issues facing farmers and the nation today. (Rev: BL 6/1–15/96; BR 11–12/96; SLJ 6/96; VOYA 10/96) [338.1]

12037 Goldberg, Jake. *Food: The Struggle to Sustain the Human Community* (8–12). Illus. 1999, Watts LB $26.00 (0-531-11411-2). This illustrated volume covers humans' use of food since the beginning of time—including its distribution, production, and politics. (Rev: BL 11/15/99) [641.3]

12038 Halley, Ned. *Farm* (4–9). Illus. Series: Eyewitness Books. 1996, Knopf $20.99 (0-679-98078-4). A behind-the-scenes look at a farm, explaining with many illustrations its inner workings and the problems and rewards involved in managing one. (Rev: BL 6/1–15/96; SLJ 7/96) [630]

12039 Hayhurst, Chris. *Everything You Need to Know About Food Additives* (6–10). Illus. Series: Need to Know Library. 2002, Rosen LB $23.95 (0-8239-3548-5). An examination of the kinds of additives used in foods, their benefits and disadvantages, and the alternatives available to people seeking a healthier diet. (Rev: BL 5/1/02) [664]

12040 Hughes, Meredith S. *Flavor Foods: Spices and Herbs* (5–8). Series: Plants We Eat. 2000, Lerner LB $26.60 (0-8225-2835-5). This book explains how roots, leaves, flowers, seeds, fruit, and bark of some plants are transformed in the seasonings that flavor so many dishes. (Rev: BL 7/00; HBG 10/00) [633.8]

12041 Hughes, Meredith S. *Glorious Grasses: The Grains* (5–8). Series: Plants We Eat. 1999, Lerner LB $26.60 (0-8225-2831-2). A description of the history, cultivation, processing, and dietary importance of wheat, rice, corn, millet, barley, oats, and rye, plus recipes and activities. (Rev: BL 7/99; HBG 10/99; SLJ 8/99) [633.1]

12042 Hughes, Meredith S. *Tall and Tasty: Fruit Trees* (5–8). Series: Plants We Eat. 2000, Lerner LB $31.95 (0-8225-2837-1). This book explores the world of apples, peaches, mangoes, and other fruits that grow on trees and explains each one's life cycle, and how the fruit has migrated during its history. (Rev: BL 4/15/00; HBG 10/00) [641.3]

12043 Hughes, Meredith S. *Yes, We Have Bananas: Fruits from Shrubs and Vines* (5–8). Series: Plants We Eat. 1999, Lerner LB $26.60 (0-8225-2836-3). A fascinating introduction to bananas, pineapples, grapes, berries, and melons with material on how and where they grow, their cultivation and marketing, plus fun recipes and activities. (Rev: BL 11/15/99; HBG 3/00; SLJ 3/00) [641]

12044 Johnson, Sylvia A. *Apple Trees* (5–8). 1983, Lerner LB $31.95 (0-8225-1479-6). The story of the apple tree and seed and fruit formation.

12045 Johnson, Sylvia A. *Potatoes, Tomatoes, Corn, and Beans: How the Foods in America Changed the World* (6–10). Illus. 1997, Simon & Schuster $16.95 (0-689-80141-6). The story of common foods that originated in America is told in this blend of history, botany, culinary arts, and geography. (Rev: BL 4/15/97; BR 11–12/97; SLJ 5/97; VOYA 12/97) [641.6]

12046 Jones, Carol. *Cheese* (4–7). Illus. Series: From Farm to You. 2002, Chelsea $17.95 (0-7910-7005-0). This is an absorbing account of the techniques used in manufacturing cheese and the history of cheese, with an overview of the many varieties and a map of cheese eating around the world. Also use *Pasta and Noodles* (2002). (Rev: BL 11/1/02; HBG 3/03) [641.3]

12047 Lasky, Kathryn. *Sugaring Time* (4–7). Illus. 1998, Center for Applied Research paper $4.95 (0-87628-350-4). Through photographs and text, the process of maple sugar production in New England is described.

12048 Maestro, Betsy. *How Do Apples Grow?* (5–8). Series: Let's-Read-and-Find-Out. 1992, Harper-Collins LB $16.89 (0-06-020056-1). The development of the apple from bud to fruit. (Rev: BL 12/15/91; HB 1–2/92; SLJ 2/92) [582]

12049 Marshall, Elizabeth L. *High-Tech Harvest: A Look at Genetically Engineered Foods* (6–9). 1999, Watts LB $20.00 (0-531-11434-1). A thorough discussion of gene manipulation and its results when applied to food production, such as cloning Dolly the sheep and producing the Flavr Savr tomato. (Rev: BL 5/15/99; SLJ 7/99) [641.3]

12050 Meltzer, Milton. *Food* (4–8). Illus. 1998, Millbrook LB $24.90 (0-7613-0354-5). A fascinating history of food and how it affects our lives. (Rev: BL 1/1–15/99; HBG 3/99; SLJ 1/99) [641.3]

12051 Morgan, Sally. *Superfoods: Genetic Modification of Foods* (5–8). Series: Science at the Edge. 2002, Heinemann LB $27.86 (1-58810-702-7). A look at the history and genetic alteration of foods, with discussion of the controversy this has created. (Rev: BL 10/15/02; HBG 3/03; SLJ 4/03) [174.957]

12052 Olney, Ross R. *The Farm Combine* (4–8). Illus. 1984, Walker LB $10.85 (0-8027-6568-8). The development of the reaper and thrasher is discussed, with information on today's combine harvester.

12053 Paladino, Catherine. *One Good Apple; Growing Our Food for the Sake of the Earth* (4–8). 1999, Houghton $15.00 (0-395-85009-6). This photoessay describes the range and effects of the use of pesticides in this country, the government's response, and alternatives offered by organic farming, Community Supported Agriculture, and seed-saving organizations. (Rev: BCCB 7–8/99; BL 4/1/99; HBG 9/99; SLJ 4/99) [630]

12054 Patent, Dorothy Hinshaw. *The Vanishing Feast: How Dwindling Genetic Diversity Threatens the World's Food Supply* (6–10). 1994, Harcourt $17.95 (0-15-292867-7). Explains the importance of maintaining plant and animal diversity and describes experiments with genetic engineering and factory farming. (Rev: BL 10/1/94; SLJ 12/94; VOYA 4/95) [338.1]

12055 Tesar, Jenny. *Food and Water: Threats, Shortages and Solutions* (5–9). Series: Our Fragile Planet. 1992, Facts on File LB $21.95 (0-8160-2495-2). A discussion of the world's water and food supplies, threats to them, and possible solutions. (Rev: BL 6/1/92) [333.91]

12056 Wardlaw, Lee. *Bubblemania* (4–8). 1997, Simon & Schuster paper $4.99 (0-689-81719-3). A thorough history of chewing gum, including descriptions of how gum is made, marketed, and distributed. (Rev: BL 10/1/97; SLJ 1/98) [641.3]

12057 Wardlaw, Lee. *We All Scream for Ice Cream: The Scoop on America's Favorite Dessert* (4–7). 2000, HarperTrophy paper $4.95 (0-380-80250-3). A history of this frozen dessert from ancient times to the present with a concentration on modern times and such variations as Eskimo pies and the Good Humor business. (Rev: SLJ 11/00) [637]

12058 Zubrowski, Bernie. *Soda Science: Designing and Testing Soft Drinks* (5–8). Illus. 1997, Morrow LB $14.89 (0-688-13917-5). More than 50 experiments explore the properties of soft drinks and give directions for producing and bottling one's own product. (Rev: BL 8/97; SLJ 10/97) [641.8]

VEGETABLES

12059 Hughes, Meredith S. *Cool as a Cucumber, Hot as a Pepper* (5–8). Series: Foods We Eat. 1999, Lerner LB $26.60 (0-8225-2832-0). This lively book on vegetables gives botanical information, details on growing and harvesting, the history of many of these plants, and a number of mouth-watering recipes. (Rev: BL 7/99; HBG 10/99; SLJ 8/99) [635]

12060 Hughes, Meredith S. *Spill the Beans and Pass the Peanuts: Legumes* (5–8). Series: Plants We Eat. 1999, Lerner LB $31.95 (0-8225-2834-7). Peas and beans are two of the legumes introduced in this book that explains, in an entertaining way, their origins, how they grow, their appearance, and nutritional value, plus giving the occasional recipe or activity. (Rev: BL 10/15/99; HBG 3/00; SLJ 12/99) [641.6]

12061 Hughes, Meredith S. *Stinky and Stringy* (5–8). Series: Plants We Eat. 1999, Lerner LB $31.95 (0-8225-2833-9). Stem and bulb vegetables onions and garlic are introduced with interesting historical information, details about their cultivation, harvesting and marketing, and a few tempting recipes. (Rev: BL 7/99; HBG 10/99; SLJ 8/99) [635]

12062 Hughes, Meredith S., and E. Thomas Hughes. *Buried Treasure: Roots and Tubers* (4–7). Series: Plants We Eat. 1998, Lerner LB $26.60 (0-8225-2830-4). Covering such vegetables as potatoes, sweet potatoes, carrots, turnips, beets, and radishes, this account describes the origin, history, cultivation, and importance of each. (Rev: HBG 3/99; SLJ 4/99) [635]

Forestry and Trees

12063 Brockman, C. Frank. *Trees of North America* (7–12). Illus. 1998, Demco $22.10 (0-606-12005-X). This handy guide identifies 594 different trees that grow north of Mexico. [582.16]

12064 Burnie, David. *Tree* (4–8). Illus. 1988, Knopf $20.99 (0-394-99617-8). Short, lushly illustrated chapters introduce such topics as bark, leaves, cones, and tree diseases. (Rev: BL 12/1/88; SLJ 12/88) [582.1600222]

12065 Cassie, Brian. *National Audubon Society First Field Guide: Trees* (4–8). 1999, Scholastic $17.95 (0-590-05472-4); paper $8.95 (0-590-05490-2). After a general, illustrated introduction to the characteristics and types of North American trees, this field guide then categorizes the trees according to the shape of their leaves. (Rev: BL 3/15/99; SLJ 7/99) [582.16]

12066 Gallant, Roy A. *Earth's Vanishing Forests* (6–10). 1991, Macmillan LB $15.95 (0-02-735774-0). A carefully researched examination of the reasons for the destruction of the planet's forests and the implications of their loss. (Rev: BL 10/1/91; SLJ 5/92) [333.75]

12067 Gardner, Robert, and David Webster. *Science Project Ideas About Trees* (5–8). Illus. Series: Science Project Ideas. 1997, Enslow LB $19.95 (0-89490-846-4). The parts of trees and their functions are described, with activities involving leaves, seeds, flowers, roots, and twigs. (Rev: BL 12/1/97; BR 5–6/98; HBG 3/98; SLJ 2/98) [582.16]

12068 Jorgensen, Lisa. *Grand Trees of America: Our State and Champion Trees* (4–7). Illus. 1992, Roberts paper $8.95 (1-879373-15-7). This book describes the official tree of each state and introduces the National Register of Big Trees. (Rev: BL 2/15/93) [582.16]

12069 Kittinger, Jo S. *Dead Log Alive!* (4–7). Illus. Series: A First Book. 1996, Watts LB $23.00 (0-531-20237-2). A description of the animals, insects, birds, and fungi that live in or on dead trees. (Rev: SLJ 5/97) [586.16]

12070 Little, Elbert L. *The Audubon Society Field Guide to North American Trees: Eastern Region* (7–12). Illus. 1980, Knopf $19.95 (0-394-50760-6). This volume describes through text and pictures of leaves, needles, and so on, the trees found east of the Rocky Mountains. [582.16]

12071 Little, Elbert L. *The Audubon Society Field Guide to North American Trees: Western Region* (7–12). Illus. 1980, Knopf $19.95 (0-394-50761-4). Trees west of the Rockies are identified and pictured in photographs and drawings. [582.16]

12072 Martin, Patricia A. Fink. *Woods and Forests* (8–12). Illus. Series: Exploring Ecosystems. 2000, Watts LB $24.00 (0-531-11697-2). Practical projects appear throughout the text, allowing readers to explore the concepts presented. (Rev: SLJ 6/00) [577.3]

12073 Pascoe, Elaine. *Leaves and Trees* (4–7). Series: Nature Close-Up. 2001, Blackbirch LB $27.44 (1-56711-474-1). Easy projects and a simple text are used to introduce the nature of trees and leaves and the living processes involved. (Rev: BL 9/15/01; HBG 3/02) [582.16]

12074 Patent, Dorothy Hinshaw. *Fire: Friend or Foe* (4–8). 1998, Clarion $16.00 (0-395-73081-3). Using a concise text and excellent photographs, the author describes the causes of forest fires, their effect on the land, and the equipment and practices used by firefighters, and discusses the growing belief that fire is part of the natural cycle of renewal and scientific evidence refuting the concept that fire is deadly to all wildlife. (Rev: BL 11/15/98; HB 1–2/99; HBG 3/99; SLJ 12/98) [577.2]

12075 Petrides, George A. *A Field Guide to Trees and Shrubs* (7–12). Illus. 1973, Houghton paper $19.00 (0-395-35370-X). A total of 646 varieties found in northern United States and southern Canada are described and illustrated. [582.1]

12076 Tesar, Jenny. *Shrinking Forests* (5–8). Illus. Series: Our Fragile Earth. 1991, Facts on File $21.95 (0-8160-2492-8). A worldwide survey of the decline of forests. (Rev: SLJ 1/92) [582.16]

12077 Zim, Herbert S., and Alexander C. Martin. *Trees* (5–8). Illus. 1991, Western paper $21.27 (0-307-64056-6). A small, handy volume packed with information and color illustrations that help identify our most important trees. [582.16]

Plants and Flowers

12078 Burnie, David. *Plant* (5–9). Illus. 1989, Knopf $20.99 (0-394-92252-2). Extraordinary photographs and clear text are used to introduce the plant world. (Rev: BL 10/15/89) [581]

12079 Busch, Phyllis B. *Wildflowers and the Stories Behind Their Names* (7–9). Illus. 1977, Macmillan $10.00 (0-684-14820-X). In this compact volume, 60 wildflowers are identified and pictured. [582.13]

12080 Dowden, Anne O. *The Clover and the Bee: A Book of Pollination* (5–8). Illus. 1990, HarperCollins LB $17.89 (0-690-04679-0). A beautifully illustrated book with much information on plant pollination. (Rev: BCCB 6/90; BL 5/15/90; SLJ 7/90*; VOYA 6/90) [647]

12081 Dowden, Anne O. *From Flower to Fruit* (6–9). Illus. 1984, HarperCollins $14.95 (0-690-04402-X). A description of seeds, how they are scattered, and how fruit is produced. [582]

12082 Dowden, Anne O. *Poisons in Our Path: Plants That Harm and Heal* (4–7). Illus. 1994, HarperCollins LB $17.89 (0-06-020862-7). An examination of the properties, appearance, and habitats of many plants that have been important in the past or present in medicine or magic. (Rev: BCCB 4/94; BL 7/94; HB 7–8/94; SLJ 6/94) [581.6]

12083 Garassino, Alessandro. *Plants: Origins and Evolution* (4–8). Illus. Series: Beginnings — Origins and Evolution. 1995, Raintree Steck-Vaughn LB $24.26 (0-8114-3332-3). This treatment of plant evolution includes good factual data and discussion of several important concepts. (Rev: BL 4/15/95) [581.3]

12084 Gardner, Robert. *Science Projects About Plants* (5–8). Illus. Series: Science Projects. 1999, Enslow LB $20.95 (0-89490-952-5). This book contains a series of fascinating experiments and projects involving seeds, leaves, roots, stems, flowers, and whole plants. (Rev: BL 2/15/99; BR 5–6/99; SLJ 5/99) [580]

12085 Hood, Susan, and National Audubon Society, eds. *Wildflowers* (5–8). Illus. 1998, Scholastic paper $17.95 (0-590-05464-3). Fifty common wildflowers are pictured and described, along with information on what equipment to use and what to look for to observe and study wildflowers (leaves, blooms, habitat, height, range). (Rev: BL 8/98; SLJ 8/98) [583]

12086 Johnson, Sylvia A. *Morning Glories* (4–7). Illus. 1985, Lerner LB $22.60 (0-8225-1462-1). Color photographs display the stages of this plant's development. (Rev: BCCB 3/86; BL 4/15/86; SLJ 4/86)

12087 Johnson, Sylvia A. *Roses Red, Violets Blue: Why Flowers Have Colors* (5–8). Illus. 1991, Lerner LB $23.93 (0-8225-1594-6). An examination of the role of color in the life of plants and its function in reproduction and communication. (Rev: BCCB 12/91; BL 12/1/91; SLJ 1/92*) [582.13]

12088 Lerner, Carol. *Cactus* (4–7). Illus. 1992, Morrow LB $14.89 (0-688-09637-9). After explaining the parts of the cactus and how it can exist in near-waterless environments, this account describes different species. (Rev: BCCB 10/92; HB 1–2/93; SLJ 12/92) [635.7]

12089 Nielsen, Nancy J. *Carnivorous Plants* (4–8). Illus. 1992, Watts paper $6.95 (0-531-15644-3). A look, with the help of color photographs, at flesh-eating plants, such as the Venus's-flytrap. (Rev: BL 6/1/92; SLJ 7/92) [581.5]

12090 Niering, William A., and Nancy C. Olmstead. *The Audubon Society Field Guide to North American Wildflowers: Eastern Region* (7–12). Illus. 1979, Knopf $19.00 (0-394-50432-1). From the Rockies to the Atlantic this guide identifies, describes, and pictures the most common wildflowers. [582.13]

12091 Overbeck, Cynthia. *Carnivorous Plants* (4–8). 1982, Lerner LB $31.95 (0-8225-1470-2). A survey of these plants and how they evolved. [581.5]

12092 Reading, Susan. *Plants of the Tropics* (4–8). Illus. Series: Plant Life. 1991, Facts on File $15.95 (0-8160-2423-5). A tour of a rain forest, with descriptions of plants, their means of survival, and their relationships with animals. (Rev: BL 6/15/91; SLJ 8/91) [581]

12093 Silverstein, Alvin, et al. *Plants* (7–10). Series: Kingdoms of Life. 1996, Twenty-First Century LB $25.90 (0-8050-3519-2). The classification system of plants is explained, from simple plants through ferns and on to flowering plants. (Rev: BL 6/1–15/96; SLJ 7/96) [581]

12094 Souza, D. M. *Freaky Flowers* (4–7). Series: Watts Library. 2002, Watts LB $24.00 (0-531-11981-5). Flowering plants are the main focus in this discussion of basic botany, the ways in which flowers attract pollinators, and the environmental dangers plants are facing. (Rev: SLJ 7/02) [582]

12095 Spellenberg, Richard. *The Audubon Society Field Guide to North American Wildflowers: Western Region* (7–12). Illus. 1979, Knopf $19.00 (0-394-50431-3). A guide to more than 600 wildflowers found from California to Alaska. [582.13]

12096 Winner, Cherie. *The Sunflower Family* (4–7). Illus. 1996, Carolrhoda LB $23.93 (1-57505-007-2); paper $7.95 (1-57505-029-3). Growth patterns, structures, and reproduction are topics covered in this account of the sunflower family, including thistles, daisies, and asters. (Rev: BL 10/1/96; SLJ 10/96) [583]

Seeds

12097 Burns, Diane L. *Berries, Nuts and Seeds* (4–7). 1996, NorthWord paper $7.95 (1-55971-573-1). Each page in this guide is devoted to a description of a single berry, nut, or seed. (Rev: BL 2/15/97) [582.13]

12098 Pascoe, Elaine. *Seeds and Seedlings* (4–7). Illus. Series: Nature Close-Up. 1996, Blackbirch LB $27.44 (1-56711-178-5). The growth cycle of seeds is explained, with many projects on how to plant and raise seedlings. (Rev: BL 12/1/96; SLJ 3/97) [582]

Zoology

General and Miscellaneous

12099 Aaseng, Nathan. *Invertebrates* (5–8). Illus. 1993, Watts LB $22.00 (0-531-12550-5). Describes the varieties of life forms without backbones, including insects, and how they have diversified through the ages. (Rev: BL 3/15/94; SLJ 3/94) [592]

12100 Aaseng, Nathan. *Nature's Poisonous Creatures* (5–9). Series: Scientific American Sourcebooks. 1997, Twenty-First Century LB $28.90 (0-8050-4690-9). After a general introduction to animal poisons, why they are produced, and their composition, this book devotes separate chapters to such venom-bearing vertebrates and invertebrates as sea wasps, blue-ringed octopi, African killer bees, and marine toads. (Rev: BL 2/1/98; SLJ 8/98) [591.6]

12101 Barrow, Lloyd H. *Science Fair Projects Investigating Earthworms* (5–8). Series: Science Fair Success. 2000, Enslow LB $20.95 (0-7660-1291-3). This book contains a fascinating number of experiments involving earthworms, with very explicit directions and explanations of the scientific principles behind each project. (Rev: BL 4/15/00; HBG 10/00) [595.1]

12102 Breidahl, Harry. *Extremophiles: Life in Extreme Environments* (6–8). Series: Life in Strange Places. 2001, Chelsea LB $16.95 (0-7910-6617-7). In addition to describing the organisms that thrive in environments such as Antarctica and deserts, this volume includes information on a working microbiologist and provides many photographs. (Rev: HBG 3/02; SLJ 1/02)

12103 Browning, Bel. *Animal Welfare* (5–8). Illus. Series: Face the Facts. 2003, Raintree Steck-Vaughn LB $28.56 (0-7398-6430-0). Hot issues in animal protection such as whaling, intensive farming, and zoos are discussed, and practical responses from young people are suggested. (Rev: BL 11/15/03; HBG 10/03) [364.1]

12104 Cobb, Allan B. *Super Science Projects About Animals and Their Habitats* (4–8). Series: Psyched for Science. 2000, Rosen LB $23.95 (0-8239-3175-7). Six hand-on activities are introduced to help children observe animals and to study their adjustments to climate, habitat, and food. (Rev: SLJ 9/00) [591]

12105 Dashefsky, H. Steven. *Zoology: High School Science Fair Experiments* (7–12). 1995, TAB paper $12.95 (0-07-015687-5). Twenty zoology experiments are presented in the categories of people-related, biocides, animal lives, and animals and the environment. (Rev: BL 6/1–15/95) [591]

12106 Day, Nancy. *Animal Experimentation: Cruelty or Science?* Rev. ed. (7–9). Series: Issues in Focus. 2000, Enslow LB $19.95 (0-7660-1244-1). A balanced discussion of animal rights and of experiments that use animals, presenting alternatives to the practice. (Rev: HBG 3/01; SLJ 1/01) [179]

12107 Doris, Ellen. *Meet the Arthropods* (4–7). 1996, Thames & Hudson $16.95 (0-500-19010-0). Such arthropods as the horseshoe crab, potato beetle, and praying mantis are introduced with photographs and activities. (Rev: BL 10/15/96) [595.2]

12108 Fridell, Ron. *Amphibians in Danger: A Worldwide Warning* (7–12). Illus. 1999, Watts LB $23.00 (0-531-11737-5). A wealth of knowledge and lore is presented in this book about the history, place, and role of frogs, toads, and salamanders, along with material on their alarming current death rate and how scientists devise and conduct research. (Rev: BL 6/1–15/99; SLJ 8/99) [597.8]

12109 Halfmann, Janet. *Life in a Garden* (5–7). Photos by David Liebman. 2000, Creative Co. LB $22.60 (1-58341-072-4). This book explores such life forms found in a garden as fungi, beetles, slugs, snails, and aphids. (Rev: SLJ 8/00) [635]

12110 Hecht, Jeff. *Vanishing Life: The Mystery of Mass Extinctions* (7–12). 1993, Scribners LB $15.95 (0-684-19331-0). A study of mass extinctions throughout history and an examination of how geological evidence supports or discredits current theories. (Rev: BL 1/15/94; SLJ 2/94; VOYA 2/94) [575]

12111 Hiller, Ilo. *Introducing Mammals to Young Naturalists* (5–9). Illus. 1990, Texas A & M Univ. Pr. $9.00 (0-89096-427-0). An introduction to a number of mammals, from the common squirrel to the exotic armadillo. (Rev: BL 7/90) [599]

12112 Hodgkins, Fran. *Animals Among Us: Living with Suburban Wildlife* (5–8). Illus. 2000, Linnet LB $19.50 (0-208-02478-6). This book discusses the behavior and lifestyles of animals such as deer, coyotes, bears, skunks, and bats that live in suburbs, close to their original haunts. (Rev: BL 6/1–15/00; HB 7–8/00; HBG 10/00; SLJ 9/00; VOYA 12/00) [591.7]

12113 Johnson, Sylvia A. *Silkworms* (4–7). Illus. 1982, Lerner paper $9.55 (0-8225-9557-5). The life cycle of the silkworm, told in text and striking color pictures. [595.78]

12114 Kneidel, Sally. *Slugs, Bugs, and Salamanders: Discovering Animals in Your Garden* (5–7). 1997, Fulcrum paper $16.95 (1-55591-313-X). As well as introducing backyard insects and other small creatures, this account gives a number of tips on growing healthy flowers and vegetables. (Rev: SLJ 10/97) [595.7]

12115 Lauber, Patricia. *Fur, Feathers, and Flippers: How Animals Live Where They Do* (4–8). Illus. 1994, Scholastic paper $4.95 (0-590-45072-7). Using various habitats such as the grasslands of East Africa as examples, this photoessay describes how animals have adapted to their different environments. (Rev: BL 12/1/94*; SLJ 12/94) [591.5]

12116 Nardi, James B. *The World Beneath Our Feet: A Guide to Life in the Soil* (8–12). Illus. 2003, Oxford LB $35.00 (0-19-513990-9). Creatures that live in the soil (microbes, vertebrates, and invertebrates), soil ecology, and environmental problems such as erosion are the focus of this detailed, well-illustrated study. (Rev: HBG 10/03; SLJ 10/03; VOYA 10/03)

12117 Palazzo, Tony. *The Biggest and the Littlest Animals* (4–7). 1973, Lion LB $13.95 (0-87460-225-4). Many ways of comparing animals, including size and mobility, are explored.

12118 Pascoe, Elaine. *Earthworms* (4–7). Illus. Series: Nature Close-Up. 1996, Blackbirch LB $27.44 (1-56711-177-7). An account of the anatomy of earthworms and how they live, as well as how to collect and care for them. (Rev: BL 12/1/96) [595.1]

12119 Pascoe, Elaine. *Snails and Slugs* (4–7). Series: Nature Close-Up. 1998, Blackbirch LB $27.44 (1-56711-181-5). Outstanding photographs, an interesting text, and several easy-to-do projects highlight this introduction to snails and slugs. (Rev: BL 9/15/98; HBG 3/99) [594.3]

12120 Petersen, Christine. *Invertebrates* (6–12). Illus. 2002, Watts $24.00 (0-531-12021-X). Covers the lifestyles and adaptations of crustaceans, echinoderms, insects, jellies, mollusks, sponges, and worms in concise, accessible text. (Rev: BL 10/15/02; LMC 1/03) [592]

12121 Petersen, Christine. *Vertebrates* (6–12). Illus. 2002, Watts $24.00 (0-531-12020-1). Covers the lifestyles and adaptations of amphibians, birds, fish, mammals, and reptiles in concise, accessible text. (Rev: BL 10/15/02) [569]

12122 Presnall, Judith J. *Animals That Glow* (5–7). Illus. Series: First Books. 1993, Watts LB $23.00 (0-531-20071-X). From fireflies to tiny sea creatures, this book covers the amazing phenomenon of bioluminescence. (Rev: BL 5/15/93; SLJ 6/93) [591]

12123 *The Simon and Schuster Encyclopedia of Animals: A Visual Who's Who of the World's Creatures* (7–12). 1998, Simon & Schuster $50.00 (0-684-85237-3). Arranged by broad taxonomic classification, about 2,000 animals are introduced through pictures and information on their appearance, adaptations, habits, and habitats. (Rev: BL 10/15/98; SLJ 2/99) [591]

12124 Stewart, Melissa. *Life Without Light* (5–8). Illus. 1999, Watts LB $23.00 (0-531-11529-1). This book explores the world of nature that exists without sun, including creatures discovered during research on hydrothermal vents, caves, aquifers, and rocks. (Rev: BL 7/99; SLJ 8/99) [577]

12125 Whyman, Kate. *The Animal Kingdom* (5–8). Illus. 1999, Raintree Steck-Vaughn LB $27.12 (0-8172-5885-X). A valuable account that introduces animal classification basics through text, sidebars, diagrams, and many eye-catching color photographs. (Rev: BL 2/1/00) [596]

12126 Woods, Geraldine. *Animal Experimentation and Testing: A Pro/Con Issue* (5–8). Series: Hot Issues. 1999, Enslow LB $21.95 (0-7660-1191-7). The controversial subject of using animals in experiments is discussed with a history of the problem, arguments for and against, and a summary of important actions taken by government and individual groups. (Rev: HBG 3/00; SLJ 3/00) [179.3]

Amphibians and Reptiles

GENERAL AND MISCELLANEOUS

12127 Behler, John L. *National Audubon Society First Field Guide: Reptiles* (4–8). 1999, Scholastic $17.95 (0-590-05467-8); paper $11.95 (0-590-05487-2). This richly illustrated manual discusses common characteristics of North American reptiles, then presents individual species under four groups: crocodiles, turtles, lizards, and snakes. (Rev: BL 3/15/99; SLJ 7/99) [597.9]

12128 Clarke, Barry. *Amphibian* (5–9). Photos. Series: Eyewitness Books. 1993, Knopf $20.99 (0-679-93879-6). Stunning photographs and text introduce the world of amphibians. (Rev: BL 8/93) [597.6]

12129 Crump, Marty. *Amphibians, Reptiles, and Their Conservation* (6–12). Illus. 2002, Linnet LB $25.00 (0-208-02511-1). After describing these animals and giving the pertinent scientific information, the author describes the challenges to their survival and what can be done to save them. (Rev: BL 12/1/02; HBG 3/03; SLJ 1/03; VOYA 6/03) [597.9]

12130 Gibbons, Whit. *Their Blood Runs Cold: Adventures with Reptiles and Amphibians* (7–12). Illus. 1983, Univ. of Alabama Pr. paper $15.95 (0-8173-0133-X). An informal guide, geographically arranged, to snakes, crocodiles, turtles, salamanders, and toads. [597.6]

ALLIGATORS AND CROCODILES

12131 Dow, Lesley. *Alligators and Crocodiles* (5–8). Illus. 1990, Facts on File $17.95 (0-8160-2273-9). This oversize book illustrates various species of alligators and crocodiles. (Rev: BL 11/15/90; SLJ 5/91) [598.98]

12132 Fitzgerald, Patrick J. *Croc and Gator Attacks* (4–7). Series: Animal Attack! 2000, Children's LB $20.00 (0-516-23314-9); paper $6.95 (0-516-23514-1). Aimed at the reluctant reader, this book tells true stories of attacks by crocodiles and alligators and gives information about these species and their differences. (Rev: SLJ 2/01) [597.98]

12133 Jango-Cohen, Judith. *Crocodiles* (5–8). Series: AnimalWays. 2000, Marshall Cavendish LB $28.50 (0-7614-1136-4). This book examines the habitat, range, classification, evolution, anatomy, behavior, and endangered status of the crocodile. (Rev: BL 1/1–15/01; HBG 3/01) [597.98]

FROGS AND TOADS

12134 Greenberg, Dan. *Frogs* (5–8). Series: AnimalWays. 2000, Marshall Cavendish LB $28.50 (0-7614-1138-0). As well as chapters devoted to the amazing variety of frogs, this book discusses their anatomy, habits, and survival skills. (Rev: BL 1/1–15/01; HBG 3/01) [597.8]

12135 Parsons, Harry. *The Nature of Frogs: Amphibians with Attitude* (6–12). Illus. 2001, Douglas & McIntyre $26.95 (1-55054-761-5). Readers will be drawn to the color photographs in this book and then intrigued by the informative text and mentions of these animals' portrayal in stories and legends. (Rev: BL 1/1–15/01; VOYA 8/01) [597.0]

12136 White, William. *All About the Frog* (4–8). Illus. Series: Sterling Color Nature. 1992, Sterling $14.95 (0-8069-8274-8). A brief history of the frog and a discussion of its anatomy, reproduction, food, adaptations, and likely future. (Rev: BL 7/92; SLJ 9/92) [597.8]

SNAKES AND LIZARDS

12137 Barth, Kelly L. *Snakes* (7–10). Series: Endangered Animals and Habitats. 2001, Lucent LB $19.96 (1-56006-696-2). This work focuses on the types of snakes that are threatened with extinction and the efforts employed to save them. (Rev: BL 3/15/01) [597.96]

12138 Behler, Deborah, and John Behler. *Snakes* (5–8). Series: AnimalWays. 2001, Marshall Cavendish LB $28.50 (0-7614-1265-4). Brilliant photographs highlight this fine introduction to snakes, their habitats, behavior, species, evolution, and anatomy. (Rev: BL 3/15/02; HBG 10/02) [597.96]

12139 Cherry, Jim. *Loco for Lizards* (7–12). Illus. 2000, Northland paper $7.95 (0-87358-763-4). This eclectic and entertaining overview of these reptiles provides basic scientific information plus a look at their important role in legends and contemporary culture. (Rev: SLJ 2/01) [597.95]

12140 Gaywood, Martin, and Ian Spellerberg. *Snakes* (6–12). Series: WorldLife Library. 1999, Voyageur paper $16.95 (0-89658-449-6). Facts about snakes and their ability to adapt to their environment are accompanied by discussion of their relationship with humans and eye-catching full-color photographs. (Rev: SLJ 4/00) [597.96]

12141 Greenaway, Theresa. *Snakes* (4–7). Series: The Secret World of . . . 2001, Raintree Steck-Vaughn LB $18.98 (0-7368-3510-6). A look at the world of snakes with material on their structure, habitats, behavior, food, mating habits, and enemies. (Rev: BL 10/15/01) [597.96]

12142 Montgomery, Sy. *The Snake Scientist* (5–8). Series: Scientists in the Field. 1999, Houghton $16.00 (0-395-87169-7). This account captures the excitement of scientific discovery by focusing on a zoologist and young students who are studying the red-sided garter snake in Canada. (Rev: BCCB 4/99; BL 2/15/99; HB 7–8/99; HBG 9/99; SLJ 5/99) [597.96]

12143 Pipe, Jim. *The Giant Book of Snakes and Slithery Creatures* (4–8). Illus. 1998, Millbrook LB $27.90 (0-7613-0804-0). This richly illustrated, oversize volume contains details about snakes, lizards, and amphibians. (Rev: BL 8/98; HBG 9/98; SLJ 12/98) [597.9]

12144 Ricciuti, Edward R. *The Snake Almanac: A Fully Illustrated Natural History of Snakes Worldwide* (7–12). Illus. 2001, Lyons, $29.95 (1-58574-178-7). Packed with facts, this is a comprehensive and detailed guide to snakes — their evolution, characteristics, habitats, and so forth — and to snakes' appearances in legends, snake-human relations, conservation efforts, and snakes as pets. (Rev: SLJ 10/01) [597.96]

12145 Roever, J. M. *Snake Secrets* (6–9). 1979, Walker LB $11.85 (0-8027-6333-2). An in-depth look at snakes, their behavior, and how people react to them. [597.96]

12146 Simon, Seymour. *Poisonous Snakes* (6–9). Illus. 1981, Macmillan $11.95 (0-590-07513-6). An explanation of venom and fangs is given and an introduction to the world's most famous poisonous snakes. [597.9]

TORTOISES AND TURTLES

12147 Hawxhurst, Joan C. *Turtles and Tortoises* (7–10). Series: Endangered Animals and Habitats. 2001, Lucent LB $19.96 (1-56006-731-4). An exploration of the turtles and tortoises that are threatened with extinction, why they are endangered, and methods being used to save them. (Rev: BL 3/15/01) [597.92]

Animal Behavior

GENERAL AND MISCELLANEOUS

12148 Crump, Donald J., ed. *How Animals Behave: A New Look at Wildlife* (5–8). Illus. 1984, National Geographic LB $12.50 (0-87044-505-7). A general, colorful introduction to why and how animals perform such functions as courting, living together, and caring for their young. [591.5]

12149 Crump, Donald J., ed. *Secrets of Animal Survival* (4–8). Illus. 1983, National Geographic LB $12.50 (0-87044-431-X). The survival tactics of animals in five geographical environments are discussed.

12150 Flegg, Jim. *Animal Movement* (4–7). Series: Wild World. 1991, Millbrook LB $17.90 (1-878137-21-2). Various ways animals move and at what speeds are discussed in this well-illustrated book. (Rev: BL 1/1/91; SLJ 2/92) [591.18]

12151 Fredericks, Anthony D. *Animal Sharpshooters* (5–7). Illus. Series: Watts Library: Animals. 1999, Watts LB $24.00 (0-531-11700-6). This book focuses on the strange adaptations some animals have made to protect themselves and to find food. (Rev: BL 12/1/99; SLJ 12/99) [591.47]

12152 Fredericks, Anthony D. *Cannibal Animals: Animals That Eat Their Own Kind* (5–7). Illus. Series: Watts Library: Animals. 1999, Watts LB $24.00 (0-531-11701-4). A book that focuses on such animals as the female praying mantis, sharks, gerbils, and Tyrannosaurus rex, and how they have been accused of cannibalism. (Rev: BL 12/1/99; SLJ 12/99) [591.5]

12153 Gardner, Robert, and David Webster. *Science Project Ideas About Animal Behavior* (4–8). Illus. Series: Science Project Ideas. 1997, Enslow LB $19.95 (0-89490-842-1). A workmanlike compilation of projects involving animal behavior, such as the language of honeybees, with full background information and clear instructions. (Rev: BL 12/15/97; BR 5–6/98; HBG 3/98; SLJ 2/98) [591]

12154 McGrath, Susan. *The Amazing Things Animals Do* (4–7). Illus. 1989, National Geographic $8.95 (0-87044-709-2). Unusual animal behavior is shown in such areas as communication, motion, raising young, and survival. (Rev: SLJ 2/90) [591.5]

12155 Settel, Joanne. *Exploding Ants: Amazing Facts About How Animals Adapt* (4–8). Illus. 1999, Simon & Schuster $16.00 (0-689-81739-8). Lurid details of animal life, such as predatory fireflies, regurgitating birds, and bloodsuckers, are presented in this attention-getting collection of biological facts. (Rev: BCCB 3/99; BL 4/15/99; HBG 10/99; SLJ 4/99) [591.5]

COMMUNICATION

12156 Sayre, April Pulley. *Secrets of Sound: Studying the Calls and Songs of Whales, Elephants, and Birds* (4–7). Illus. 2002, Houghton $16.00 (0-618-01514-0). Fascinating profiles of scientists who study animal sounds serve to introduce readers to a number of scientific concepts. (Rev: BL 12/1/02; HB 9–10/02; HBG 3/03; SLJ 10/02) [559.159]

HOMES

12157 Robinson, W. Wright. *How Mammals Build Their Amazing Homes* (5–8). Series: Animal Architects. 1999, Blackbirch LB $27.44 (1-56711-381-8). After defining what a mammal is, this account shows the homes of animals including beavers, chimpanzees, squirrels, prairie dogs, and moles, and describes how they are constructed. (Rev: HBG 3/00; SLJ 5/00) [591.56]

REPRODUCTION AND BABIES

12158 Seddon, Tony. *Animal Parenting* (5–8). Illus. Series: Nature Watch. 1989, Facts on File $15.95 (0-8160-1654-2). Mating, birth, and parenting are covered, from the primitive to the most complex forms of life. (Rev: SLJ 2/90) [591.56]

TRACKS

12159 Murie, Olaus J. *A Field Guide to Animal Tracks*. 2nd ed. (7–12). Illus. 1996, Houghton paper $8.95 (0-395-58297-6). This important volume in the Peterson Field Guide series first appeared in 1954 and now has become a classic in the area of identifying animal tracks and droppings. [591.5]

Animal Species

GENERAL AND MISCELLANEOUS

12160 Ackerman, Diane. *Bats: Shadows in the Night* (5–8). 1997, Crown $19.99 (0-517-70920-1). The author reports on her bat-watching experiences in the Big Bend National Park in Texas from a unique perspective. (Rev: HBG 3/98; SLJ 10/97*) [599.4]

12161 Alden, Peter. *Peterson First Guide to Mammals of North America* (8–12). Illus. 1988, Houghton paper $5.95 (0-395-91181-8). An uncluttered basic guide to mammal identification with many illustrations and useful background material. (Rev: BL 5/15/87) [599]

12162 Bramwell, Martyn, and Steve Parker. *Mammals: The Small Plant-Eaters* (6–10). Illus. 1989, Facts on File $19.95 (0-8160-1958-4). An introduction to each animal is given in text and outstanding illustrations. (Rev: VOYA 12/89) [559]

12163 Burt, William Henry. *A Field Guide to the Mammals: North America North of Mexico.* 3rd ed. (7–12). Illus. 1976, Houghton $24.95 (0-395-24082-4); paper $16.95 (0-395-24084-0). An identification guide to 380 species of mammals found in North America. [599]

12164 Crump, Donald J., ed. *Amazing Animals of Australia* (6–9). Illus. 1984, National Geographic LB $12.50 (0-87044-520-0). A colorful introduction to such animals as the kangaroo and platypus. (Rev: BL 6/1/85) [591.9]

12165 Fenton, M. Brock. *Just Bats* (7–12). Illus. 1983, Univ. of Toronto Pr. paper $15.95 (0-8020-6464-7). An introduction to this frequently misunderstood and very useful flying rodent. [599.4]

12166 Grassy, John, and Chuck Keene. *National Audubon Society First Field Guide: Mammals* (4–8). Series: Audubon Society First Field Guide. 1998, Scholastic paper $17.95 (0-590-05471-6). An attractive guide to mammals, with maps showing habitats, a picture of each animal, and basic descriptive text. (Rev: SLJ 4/99) [599]

12167 Greenaway, Theresa. *The Secret Life of Bats* (4–7). Series: The Secret World of . . . 2002, Raintree Steck-Vaughn LB $27.12 (0-7398-4982-4). An accessible, attractive volume that begins with little-known facts about bats and continues with information on their structure, habits, food, and habitats. (Rev: BL 8/02) [599.4]

12168 Hare, Tony. *Animal Fact-File: Head-to-Tail Profiles of More Than 90 Mammals* (4–8). 1999, Facts on File $40.00 (0-8160-3921-6); paper $18.95 (0-8160-4016-8). From aardvarks to wombats, this is an alphabetical guide to more than 90 mammals with details including classification, size, coloration, and habits. (Rev: SLJ 9/99; VOYA 6/00) [599]

12169 Jarrow, Gail, and Paul Sherman. *The Naked Mole-Rat Mystery: Scientific Sleuths at Work* (6–8). Illus. Series: Discovery! 1996, Lerner LB $28.75 (0-8225-2853-3). This is a thorough exploration of what we know, and how we found out about, the naked mole-rat, which is a mammal but has a reptilian body temperature and lives in colonies like social insects. (Rev: BL 9/1/96; SLJ 8/96) [599.32]

12170 Jarrow, Gail, and Paul Sherman. *Naked Mole-Rats* (4–7). Illus. Series: Nature Watch. 1996, Carolrhoda LB $28.75 (0-87614-995-6). An informative introduction to the naked mole-rat, a most unusual animal that seems to copy habits from a variety of other species. (Rev: SLJ 10/96) [599.32]

12171 Johnson, Sylvia A. *Bats* (4–7). Illus. 1985, Lerner paper $9.55 (0-8225-9500-1). Characteristics and behavior patterns of this flying mammal. (Rev: BCCB 3/86; BL 4/15/86; SLJ 2/86) [599.4]

12172 MacDonald, David, ed. *The Encyclopedia of Mammals* (7–12). Illus. 1984, Facts on File $80.00 (0-87196-871-1). Almost 200 animal species are compiled in this volume on living mammals, which is illustrated with both photographs and drawings. [599]

12173 North, Sterling. *Rascal: A Memoir of a Better Era* (7–12). Illus. 1963, Dutton $16.99 (0-525-18839-8). Remembrances of growing up in Wisconsin in 1918 and of the joys and problems of owning a pet raccoon. (Rev: BL 9/1/89) [599.74]

12174 Parker, Steve. *Mammal* (5–9). Illus. 1989, Knopf $20.99 (0-394-92258-1). In text and full-color photographs, animal evolution is explained and a variety of mammals are introduced. (Rev: BL 9/15/89; BR 11–12/89) [599]

12175 Pringle, Laurence. *Strange Animals, New to Science* (4–7). Illus. 2002, Marshall Cavendish $16.95 (0-7614-5083-1). The results of scientists' efforts to discover new animal species are presented here, with color photographs and coverage of the reasons behind disappearing habitats. (Rev: BCCB 9/02; BL 7/02; HBG 10/02; SLJ 8/02) [591.68]

12176 Ruff, Sue, and Don E. Wilson. *Bats* (5–8). Series: AnimalWays. 2000, Marshall Cavendish LB $28.50 (0-7614-1137-2). Some of the topics that are covered include anatomy, habits, range, classification, habitats, evolution, and survival skills. (Rev: BL 1/1–15/01; HBG 3/01) [599.4]

12177 Webber, Desiree Morrison. *The Buffalo Train Ride* (4–7). 1999, Eakin $14.95 (1-57168-275-9). This is a history of the American buffalo, how it was hunted to near extinction, and the modern efforts to make sure it survives, with special attention to the work of William Hornaday. (Rev: HBG 3/00; SLJ 3/00) [591.52]

12178 Whitaker, John O., Jr. *The Audubon Society Field Guide to North American Mammals* (7–12). Illus. 1980, Knopf $19.00 (0-394-50762-2). This excellent guide contains almost 200 pages of color photographs. [599]

APE FAMILY

12179 Fleisher, Paul. *Gorillas* (5–8). Illus. Series: AnimalWays. 2000, Marshall Cavendish LB $28.50 (0-7614-1140-2). Color photographs and clear text introduce gorillas, their scientific classification, physical and behavioral characteristics, and relationship to humans. (Rev: BL 1/1–15/01; HBG 3/01) [599.884]

12180 Gilders, Michelle A. *The Nature of Great Apes: Our Next of Kin* (6–12). Illus. 2001, Douglas & McIntyre $24.95 (1-55054-762-3). The clear information in this book is extended by excellent color photographs that will attract readers and report writers. (Rev: BL 1/1–15/01; VOYA 6/01) [599.88]

12181 Goodall, Jane. *The Chimpanzees I Love: Saving Their World and Ours* (5–8). Illus. 2001, Scholastic paper $17.95 (0-439-21310-X). Jane Goodall combines details of her own life researching chimpanzees with fact-filled descriptions of the animals' behavior and a cry for chimpanzee protection. (Rev: BL 12/1/01; HB 1–2/02; HBG 3/02; SLJ 9/01*) [599]

12182 Lasky, Kathryn. *Shadows in the Dawn: The Lemurs of Madagascar* (4–8). Illus. 1997, Harcourt $18.00 (0-15-200258-8); paper $10.00 (0-15-200281-2). An attractive photoessay about the origins and characteristics of the lemurs of Madagascar and the research of Malagasy students working in the field with primatologist Alison Jolly, who has studied the animals for 30 years, making new discoveries and dispelling myths about them. (Rev: BL 4/1/98; HBG 3/99; SLJ 7/98) [599.8]

12183 Levine, Stuart P. *The Orangutan* (7–10). Series: Overview: Endangered Animals and Habitats. 1999, Lucent LB $18.96 (1-56006-560-6). This account introduces the orangutan and its habits with material on why it is endangered and efforts being made to save it. (Rev: BL 12/15/99) [599.8]

12184 Lewin, Ted, and Betsy Lewin. *Gorilla Walk* (4–8). 1999, Lothrop LB $16.89 (0-688-16510-9). A beautifully illustrated book about the Lewins' trip to Uganda to study mountain gorillas. (Rev: BL 8/99; HBG 4/00; SLJ 9/99) [599.8]

12185 Platt, Richard. *Apes and Other Hairy Primates* (4–8). Illus. Series: Secret Worlds. 2001, DK $14.95 (0-7894-8003-4); paper $5.95 (0-7894-8019-0). An engaging introduction to apes and their cousins (including their diet, habitat, and behavior), with photographs and interesting facts. (Rev: BL 10/15/01; HBG 3/02) [599]

12186 Powzyk, Joyce. *In Search of Lemurs: My Days and Nights in a Madagascar Rain Forest* (4–7). Illus. 1998, National Geographic $17.95 (0-

7922-7072-X). The author describes and illustrates her journey into the wilds of Madagascar and the many animals, plants, and birds she encountered, culminating in the elusive lemur. (Rev: BL 9/15/98; HBG 3/99; SLJ 10/98) [599.8]

12187 Redmond, Ian. *Gorilla* (4–8). Illus. Series: Eyewitness Books. 1995, Knopf $20.99 (0-679-97332-X). Good layout, interesting photographs, and fascinating facts introduce the life, personality, and environment of the gorilla in a book that is best for browsing. (Rev: BL 12/15/95; SLJ 1/96) [599.8]

BEARS

12188 Calabro, Marian. *Operation Grizzly Bear* (5–8). Illus. 1989, Macmillan $13.95 (0-02-716241-9). An account by two naturalists on a 12-year study of silvertip bears in Yellowstone Park. (Rev: BL 3/15/90; VOYA 4/90) [599.74]

12189 Fitzgerald, Patrick J. *Bear Attacks* (4–7). Series: Animal Attack! 2000, Children's LB $20.00 (0-516-23312-2); paper $6.95 (0-516-23512-5). Along with reasons why bears attack people and animals, this account describes their habitats, preferred food, and survival techniques. (Rev: SLJ 3/01) [599.7]

12190 Preston-Mafham, Rod. *The Secret Life of Bears* (4–7). Series: The Secret World of . . . 2002, Raintree Steck-Vaughn LB $27.12 (0-7398-4983-2). In this attractive volume readers learn why bears behave as they do, how they feed, communicate, and reproduce, and what dangers face their future. (Rev: BL 8/02) [599.74]

12191 Stefoff, Rebecca. *Bears* (5–8). Series: AnimalWays. 2001, Marshall Cavendish LB $28.50 (0-7614-1268-9). Various species of bears are introduced in text and color photographs with additional material on their location, anatomy, habits, and behavior. (Rev: BL 3/15/02; HBG 10/02) [599.74]

12192 Turbak, Gary. *Grizzly Bears* (6–10). Series: World Life Library. 1997, Voyageur paper $14.95 (0-89658-334-1). High-quality photographs and concise, readable text are used to introduce the grizzly bear's life cycle, origin, habits, anatomy, and future. (Rev: SLJ 10/97) [599.74]

CATS (LIONS, TIGERS, ETC.)

12193 Aaseng, Nathan. *The Cheetah* (7–10). Series: Overview: Endangered Animals and Habitats. 2000, Lucen LB $23.70 (1-56006-680-6). After a description of the cheetah, its habits and environments, there is material on methods employed to save it. (Rev: BL 10/15/2000; HBG 3/01) [599.74]

12194 Aaseng, Nathan. *The Cougar* (7–10). Series: Endangered Animals and Habitats. 2001, Lucent LB $19.96 (1-56006-730-6). This book introduces this large American cat also known as a puma and explains why it is endangered and what efforts are being made to save it. (Rev: BL 3/15/01) [599.73]

12195 Adamson, Joy. *Born Free: A Lioness of Two Worlds* (7–12). 1987, Pantheon $11.95 (0-679-56141-2). First published in 1960, this is an account of a young lioness growing up in captivity in Kenya. [599.74]

12196 Levine, Stuart P. *The Tiger* (7–10). Series: Overview: Endangered Animals and Habitats. 1998, Lucent LB $27.45 (1-56006-465-X). This work describes the habits and habitats of the tiger and current efforts to protect it from extinction. (Rev: BL 10/15/98) [599.74]

12197 Lumpkin, Susan. *Small Cats* (5–8). Series: Great Creatures of the World. 1993, Facts on File $17.95 (0-8160-2848-6). A handsome oversized volume about the smaller wild cats, with many photographs and charts. (Rev: BL 2/15/93) [599.74]

12198 Malaspina, Ann. *The Jaguar* (7–10). Series: Endangered Animals and Habitats. 2001, Lucent LB $19.96 (1-56006-813-2). An introduction to this large cat that is a native to Central and South America, the reasons why it is endangered, and the methods employed to save it. (Rev: BL 3/15/01) [599.74]

12199 Montgomery, Sy. *The Man-Eating Tigers of Sundarbans* (4–7). Illus. 2001, Houghton $16.00 (0-618-07704-9). This oversize volume introduces the savage tigers found in the Sundarbans Tiger Reserve on the border between India and Bangladesh and gives details on their behavior, food, and physical characteristics. (Rev: BCCB 2/01; BL 3/1/01*; HB 3–4/01; HBG 10/01; SLJ 3/01) [599.756]

12200 Schlaepfer, Gloria G. *Cheetahs* (5–8). Series: AnimalWays. 2001, Marshall Cavendish LB $28.50 (0-7614-1266-2). Cheetahs are introduced with material on anatomy, species identification, habitats, behavior, and endangered status. (Rev: BL 3/15/02; HBG 10/02) [599.7]

12201 Schneider, Jost. *Lynx* (4–7). Illus. 1994, Carolrhoda LB $28.75 (0-87614-844-5). The life cycle, habits, and behavior of the lynx are described. (Rev: BL 1/15/95; SLJ 3/95) [599.74]

12202 Silverstein, Alvin, et al. *The Florida Panther* (4–7). Illus. Series: Endangered in America. 1997, Millbrook $24.90 (0-7613-0049-X). Explains why the Florida panther has become endangered, with material on its life cycle and behavior and the efforts being made to save it. (Rev: BL 3/15/97; SLJ 6/97) [599.74]

12203 Thompson, Sharon E. *Built for Speed: The Extraordinary, Enigmatic Cheetah* (5–8). Illus. 1998, Lerner LB $23.93 (0-8225-2854-1). The habits and lifestyle of this endangered animal are introduced with full-color illustrations. (Rev: BL 6/1–15/98; HBG 10/98) [599.75]

COYOTES, FOXES, AND WOLVES

12204 Brandenburg, Jim. *To the Top of the World: Adventures with Arctic Wolves* (5–7). Illus. 1993, Walker LB $17.85 (0-8027-8220-5). Amazing color photographs highlight this account of a photographer's experiences living near a pack of Arctic wolves. (Rev: BCCB 11/93; BL 1/1/94*; SLJ 12/93*) [599.74]

12205 Greenaway, Theresa. *Wolves, Wild Dogs, and Foxes* (4–7). Illus. Series: Secret World Of. 2001, Raintree Steck-Vaughn LB $27.12 (0-7398-3507-6). Report writers will find information here about wolves, wild dogs, and foxes, including their diet, habitat, and behavior, with photographs and interesting facts. (Rev: BL 10/15/01; HBG 3/02; SLJ 1/02) [599.77]

12206 Johnson, Sylvia A., and Alice Aamodt. *Wolf Pack: Tracking Wolves in the Wild* (5–8). Illus. 1985, Lerner paper $11.15 (0-8225-9526-5). Fascinating details of the lives of these animals that travel in packs and share hunting, raising the young, and protection. (Rev: BCCB 12/85; BL 2/1/86; SLJ 1/86) [599.74442]

12207 Murdico, Suzanne J. *Coyote Attacks* (4–7). 2000, Children's LB $20.00 (0-516-23313-0); paper $6.95 (0-516-23513-3). As well as covering the causes of coyote attacks on animals and humans, this account gives basic information on coyotes, their habitat, survival techniques, behavior, and preferred food. (Rev: SLJ 3/01) [599.74]

12208 Patent, Dorothy Hinshaw. *Gray Wolf, Red Wolf* (4–7). 1990, Houghton $16.00 (0-89919-863-5). Two native species of North American wolf are covered. (Rev: BL 12/1/90; HB 1–2/91) [777.74]

12209 Silverstein, Alvin, et al. *The Red Wolf* (4–8). Illus. Series: Endangered Species. 1994, Millbrook LB $24.90 (1-56294-416-9). The story of the red wolf, once thought to have become extinct in the United States, and the recent efforts to reintroduce it in North Carolina. (Rev: BL 4/15/95) [333.95]

12210 Swinburne, Stephen R. *Once a Wolf: How Wildlife Biologists Fought to Bring Back the Gray Wolf* (5–8). Illus. 1999, Houghton $16.00 (0-395-89827-7). This work chronicles the 25-year struggle to reintroduce the gray wolf to Yellowstone Park. (Rev: BCCB 7–8/99; BL 3/1/99; HB 7–8/99; HBG 10/99; SLJ 5/99) [333.95]

DEER FAMILY

12211 Cox, Daniel, and John Ozoga. *Whitetail Country* (8–12). Illus. 1988, Willow Creek Pr. $39.00 (0-932558-43-7). Wonderful photographs complement this account of the life and living habits of the deer. (Rev: BR 3–4/89) [599.73]

ELEPHANTS

12212 Caras, Roger A. *A Most Dangerous Journey: The Life of an African Elephant* (5–8). 1995, Dial $15.99 (0-8037-1880-2). Based on a composite picture of an elephant culled from Caras's observations in Africa, with critical comments about poachers and corrupt officials in search of ivory. (Rev: BL 10/15/95; SLJ 10/95; VOYA 4/96) [599.4]

12213 Levine, Stuart P. *The Elephant* (7–10). Illus. Series: Overview: Endangered Animals and Habitats. 1997, Lucent LB $27.45 (1-56006-522-2). After a general introduction to the elephant and its characteristics, evolution, and habitats, the author describes how it has become endangered and current attempts at conservation. (Rev: BL 5/1/98; HBG 9/98) [599.67]

12214 Lewin, Ted, and Betsy Lewin. *Elephant Quest* (4–9). 2000, HarperCollins $15.95 (0-688-14111-0). This account of the flora and fauna of Botswana's Moremi Reserve also describes the author's search for elephants. (Rev: HB 1–2/01; HBG 3/01; SLJ 9/00) [599.67]

12215 Overbeck, Cynthia. *Elephants* (4–7). Illus. 1981, Lerner LB $22.60 (0-8225-1452-4). Elephants and their life cycle and habitats are discussed in this well-illustrated volume. [599]

12216 Redmond, Ian. *Elephant* (5–9). Photos. Series: Eyewitness Books. 1993, Knopf $19.00 (0-679-83880-5). A description of the elephant using text and pictures, with material on habits, habitats, and the reasons for its current endangered status. (Rev: BL 8/93) [599]

12217 Redmond, Ian. *The Elephant Book: For the Elefriends Campaign* (4–9). 2001, Candlewick $17.99 (0-7636-1634-6). An oversized, attractive presentation of elephant facts with a focus on the animal's complex social life and endangered status. (Rev: BCCB 1/02; HBG 3/02; SLJ 11/01*) [599.61]

12218 Schlaepfer, Gloria G. *Elephants* (5–9). Illus. Series: AnimalWays. 2003, Marshall Cavendish $20.95 (0-7614-1390-1). In addition to material on physical characteristics, behavior, habitats, and threats, Schlaepfer touches on the animal's roles in history, mythology, religion, and literature. (Rev: BL 3/15/03; HBG 3/03) [599.67]

MARSUPIALS

12219 Malaspina, Ann. *The Koala* (7–10). Series: Endangered Animals and Habitats. 2002, Gale LB $27.45 (1-56006-876-0). That story of this animal that is threatened with extinction is told with material on methods currently employed to save it. (Rev: BL 5/15/02; SLJ 6/02) [599.2]

12220 Penny, Malcolm. *The Secret Life of Kangaroos* (4–7). Series: The Secret World of . . . 2002, Raintree Steck-Vaughn LB $27.12 (0-7398-4986-7).

A visually interesting look at the world of the kangaroo with material on behavior, anatomy, reproduction, and how pollution and habitat destruction have affected these animals. (Rev: BL 8/02) [599.2]

PANDAS

12221 Jiguang, Xin, and Markus Kappeler. *The Giant Panda* (5–7). Trans. by Noel Simon. Illus. 1984, China Books paper $9.95 (0-8351-1388-4). China's giant panda is introduced in its natural habitat. (Rev: BL 12/15/86; HB 1–2/87; SLJ 12/86) [599]

12222 Presnall, Judith J. *The Giant Panda* (7–10). Illus. Series: Overview: Endangered Animals and Habitats. 1998, Lucent LB $22.45 (1-56006-522-6). A discussion of the giant panda's evolution, habitats, life span, and breeding habits, how it became endangered, and attempts to conserve this dwindling population. (Rev: BL 5/1/98) [599.789]

Birds

GENERAL AND MISCELLANEOUS

12223 Aziz, Laurel. *Hummingbirds: A Beginner's Guide* (5–8). Illus. 2002, Firefly LB $19.95 (1-55209-487-1); paper $9.95 (1-55209-374-7). This heavily illustrated book offers a great deal of information about hummingbirds, including their bills, metabolism, flight, nesting, and migration. (Rev: BL 6/1–15/02; HBG 10/02) [598.7]

12224 Bailey, Jill, and Steve Parker. *Birds: The Plant- and Seed-Eaters* (5–9). Illus. 1989, Facts on File $19.95 (0-8160-1964-9). Stunning photography and a well-organized text highlight this description of many of our common birds. (Rev: BL 1/15/90; BR 5–6/90) [598.2]

12225 Doris, Ellen. *Ornithology* (4–7). Illus. Series: Real Kids Real Science. 1994, Thames & Hudson $16.95 (0-500-19008-9). An excellent manual on how to study birds in their natural habitats, with accompanying activities for all seasons. (Rev: BL 9/1/94) [598]

12226 Friedman, Judi. *Operation Siberian Crane: The Story Behind the International Effort to Save an Amazing Bird* (4–7). 1992, Macmillan LB $13.95 (0-87518-515-0). Ron Sauey and George Archibald founded the International Crane Foundation and concentrated on the most endangered species. (Rev: BL 1/15/93; SLJ 1/93*) [639.9]

12227 Harris, Joan. *One Wing's Gift: Rescuing Alaska's Wild Birds* (7–12). 2002, Alaska Northwest paper $16.95 (0-88240-560-8). The injured birds that are treated in an Alaskan center are celebrated in beautiful, detailed drawings accompanied by sometimes poignant stories. (Rev: SLJ 10/02) [333.95]

12228 Johnson, Jinny. *Simon and Schuster Children's Guide to Birds* (4–7). Illus. 1996, Simon & Schuster paper $19.95 (0-689-80199-8). After each of the major types of birds is described, one bird from each group is highlighted. (Rev: BL 5/15/96) [676.2]

12229 Kittinger, Jo S. *Birds of North America: East* (5–8). Series: Smithsonian Kids' Field Guides. 2001, DK paper $9.95 (0-7894-7899-4). This guide to the birds found in the eastern United States groups birds by kind and includes photographs, sidebars about special features, and information on calls and migratory patterns. Also use *Birds of North America: West* (2001). (Rev: BL 10/15/01) [598]

12230 Llamas, Andreu. *Birds Conquer the Sky* (4–8). Series: Development of the Earth. 1996, Chelsea LB $17.55 (0-7910-3455-0). A science book that explains the evolution of birds from prehistoric land birds onward and defines their characteristics. (Rev: SLJ 7/96) [598]

12231 Parker, Edward. *Birds* (5–8). Photos by author. Series: Rain Forest. 2003, Raintree Steck-Vaughn LB $27.12 (0-7398-5239-6). Birds that are found in rain forests are the topic of this overview that describes the dangers posed by humans through hunting, pollution, and agriculture. (Rev: HBG 3/03; SLJ 1/03) [598]

12232 Peterson, Roger Tory. *A Field Guide to the Birds.* 4th Rev. ed. (7–12). Illus. 1980, Houghton $30.00 (0-395-74047-X); paper $18.00 (0-395-26619-X). An exhaustive guide to the birds found east of the Rockies. [598]

12233 Stokes, Donald, and Lillian Stokes. *The Bird Feeder Book: An Easy Guide to Attracting, Identifying, and Understanding Your Feeder Birds* (8–12). Illus. 1987, Little, Brown paper $12.95 (0-316-81733-3). A manual that describes, with color photographs, 72 backyard birds, plus tips on how to attract and feed them. (Rev: BL 2/1/88) [598]

12234 Taylor, Kenny. *Puffins* (5–9). Series: World-Life Library. 1999, Voyageur paper $16.95 (0-89658-419-4). Outstanding photographs and conservation awareness are highlights of this introduction to puffins, their characteristics, habitats, and habits. (Rev: BL 8/99) [598.3]

12235 Weidensaul, Scott, and National Audubon Society, eds. *National Audubon Society First Field Guide: Birds* (4–8). Illus. 1998, Scholastic paper $17.95 (0-590-05446-5). After a general introduction to ornithology, this guide describes and pictures several species of birds, including markings, eating, mating and nesting habits, migration, and endangered status. (Rev: BL 8/98; SLJ 10/98) [598]

12236 Zim, Herbert S., and Ira N. Gabrielson. *Birds* (5–8). Illus. 1991, Western paper $21.27 (0-307-64053-1). A guide to the most commonly seen birds, with accompanying illustrations and basic materials. [598]

BEHAVIOR

12237 Johnson, Sylvia A. *Inside an Egg* (5–8). Illus. 1982, Lerner LB $31.95 (0-8225-1472-9); paper $9.55 (0-8225-9522-2). An excellently illustrated account tracing the growth of a chicken in an egg until it is hatched. [598]

12238 Stokes, Donald. *A Guide to the Behavior of Common Birds* (7–12). Illus. 1979, Little, Brown $16.95 (0-316-81722-8); paper $15.00 (0-316-81725-2). The first of three volumes, each of which describes the behavior of 25 different birds. Volume 2 is *A Guide to Bird Behavior: In the Wild and at Your Feeder* (1985); volume 3 is *A Guide to Bird Behavior* (1989). [598]

DUCKS AND GEESE

12239 Kerrod, Robin. *Birds: The Waterbirds* (5–9). Illus. 1989, Facts on File $19.95 (0-8160-1962-2). Ducks and geese are only two of the species described and pictured in this attractive volume. (Rev: BL 1/15/90; BR 5–6/90) [598.29]

EAGLES, HAWKS, AND OTHER BIRDS OF PREY

12240 Arnold, Caroline. *Hawk Highway in the Sky: Watching Raptor Migration* (4–8). 1997, Harcourt $18.00 (0-15-200868-3). This volume describes the HawkWatch International observation site in the Goshute Mountains of Nevada, where scientists and volunteers catch, measure, and trace flight patterns of hawks, eagles, and falcons. (Rev: BL 6/1–15/97; SLJ 6/97) [598.9]

12241 Bailey, Jill. *Birds of Prey* (5–8). Illus. 1988, Facts on File $17.55 (0-8160-1655-0). In brief, lavishly illustrated chapters, various characteristics of birds of prey are explored and the most important types are described. (Rev: SLJ 1/89) [598]

12242 Bailey, Jill. *The Secret Life of Falcons* (4–7). Series: The Secret World of . . . 2002, Raintree Steck-Vaughn LB $27.12 (0-7398-4985-9). This book describes the anatomy and habits of the falcon with material on how they feed, communicate, and reproduce. (Rev: BL 8/02) [598.9]

12243 Barghusen, Joan D. *The Bald Eagle* (7–10). Series: Overview: Endangered Animals and Habitats. 1998, Lucent LB $27.45 (1-56006-254-1). An introduction to the structure, habits, and habitats of the bald eagle and a description of the methods employed to save it. (Rev: BL 10/15/98) [598.9]

12244 Barth, Kelly L. *Birds of Prey* (7–10). Series: Overview: Endangered Animals and Habitats. 1999, Lucent LB $18.96 (1-56006-493-5). A well-illustrated account that introduces various birds of prey, explains why they are endangered, and describes methods used to save them. (Rev: BL 12/15/99; HBG 9/00) [598.9]

12245 Bramwell, Martyn. *Birds: The Aerial Hunters* (5–9). Illus. 1989, Facts on File $19.95 (0-8160-1963-0). Eagles, hawks, and condors are only three of the many predators described and pictured in lavish photographs. (Rev: BL 1/15/90; BR 5–6/90) [598.91]

12246 Collard, Sneed B. *Birds of Prey: A Look at Daytime Raptors* (4–7). Illus. 1999, Watts LB $24.00 (0-531-20363-8). Eagles, hawks, ospreys, falcons, and vultures of North America are introduced with material on the appearance and habits of each. (Rev: BL 10/15/99; HBG 3/00) [598.9]

12247 Grambo, Rebecca L. *Eagles* (5–8). Series: World Life Library. 1999, Voyageur paper $16.95 (0-89658-363-5). This beautifully illustrated book describes the legends and lore surrounding eagles, their physical characteristics, behavior, habitats, and different species. (Rev: BL 8/99) [598.9]

12248 Laubach, Christyna, et al. *Raptor! A Kid's Guide to Birds of Prey* (4–7). Illus. 2002, Storey $21.95 (1-58017-475-2); paper $14.95 (1-58017-445-0). A large-format treasure trove of facts about raptors, with information on individual species, identification, habits, habitat, range maps, and so forth. (Rev: BL 12/1/02; HBG 3/03; SLJ 10/02) [598.9]

12249 Patent, Dorothy Hinshaw. *The Bald Eagle Returns* (4–8). Illus. 2000, Clarion $15.00 (0-395-91416-7). This book not only discusses the successful efforts to save the bald eagle but also gives material on its anatomy, habitats, mating, and behavior. (Rev: BCCB 1/01; BL 10/15/00; HBG 10/01; SLJ 11/00) [598.9]

OWLS

12250 Mowat, Farley. *Owls in the Family* (7–9). 1989, Tundra paper $6.99 (0-7710-6693-7). Two seemingly harmless owls turn a household upside down when they are adopted as pets. [598]

12251 Silverstein, Alvin, et al. *The Spotted Owl* (4–8). Illus. Series: Endangered Species. 1994, Millbrook LB $24.90 (1-56294-415-0). The story of the spotted owl, its endangered status, efforts to protect it, and the conflicts with the timber industry. (Rev: BL 4/15/95) [333.95]

PENGUINS

12252 Johnson, Sylvia A. *Penguins* (4–7). Illus. 1981, Lerner LB $22.60 (0-8225-1453-2). Handsome photographs enliven the text of this introduction to penguins and their habitats. [598]

12253 Lynch, Wayne. *Penguins!* (4–7). Illus. 1999, Firefly LB $19.95 (1-55209-421-9); paper $9.95 (1-55209-424-3). An appealing book that introduces penguins and their various species with coverage of

their evolution, food, life cycle, habits, and habitats. (Rev: BCCB 12/99; BL 9/15/99; HBG 3/00) [598.47]

12254 Webb, Sophie. *My Season with Penguins: An Antarctic Journal* (4–8). 2000, Houghton $15.00 (0-395-92291-7). Journal entries plus effective drawings show the joys and tribulations of a two-month stay in the Antarctic studying penguins and their behavior. (Rev: HB 11–12/00; HBG 3/01; SLJ 12/00) [598]

Environmental Protection and Endangered Species

12255 Barnes, Simon. *Planet Zoo* (4–7). Illus. 2001, Orion $29.95 (1-85881-488-X). An overview of 100 endangered species that conveys information in a conversational manner. (Rev: BL 8/01; SLJ 8/01) [578.68]

12256 Chandler, Gary, and Kevin Graham. *Guardians of Wildlife* (4–8). Illus. Series: Making a Better World. 1996, Twenty-First Century LB $25.90 (0-8050-4626-7). Solutions to overhunting, poaching, and overfishing are explored, as well as new wildlife management techniques. (Rev: BL 12/15/96; SLJ 4/97) [639.9]

12257 De Koster, Katie. *Endangered Species* (8–12). Illus. Series: Opposing Viewpoints. 1998, Greenhaven LB $27.45 (1-56510-747-0); paper $17.45 (1-56510-746-2). In some 30 excerpts from such personalities as Al Gore and Edward O. Wilson, this book presents various points of view on issues related to saving endangered species, including the economics of environment protection, ethical questions, and priorities. (Rev: SLJ 11/98) [591.52]

12258 Few, Roger. *Macmillan Children's Guide to Endangered Animals* (5–8). Illus. 1993, Macmillan LB $17.95 (0-02-734545-9). Using a geographical approach, this account profiles the world's endangered animals in pictures and descriptive text. (Rev: BL 10/1/93; SLJ 12/93) [592.52]

12259 Gardner, Robert. *Science Projects About the Environment and Ecology* (6–9). Series: Science Experiments. 1999, Enslow LB $20.95 (0-89490-951-7). This well-organized, clearly presented book offers a wide range of experiments involving conservation, ecology, and the environment, supplemented by charts, tables, and drawings. (Rev: SLJ 7/99) [363]

12260 Hoff, Mary, and Mary M. Rodgers. *Life on Land* (4–7). Illus. Series: Our Endangered Planet. 1992, Lerner LB $27.15 (0-8225-2507-0). This account covers such topics as the interdependence of all living things, pollution, and necessary food sources. (Rev: BL 1/15/93; SLJ 2/93) [333]

12261 Lessem, Don. *Dinosaurs to Dodos: An Encyclopedia of Extinct Animals* (4–7). Illus. 1999, Scholastic paper $16.95 (0-590-31684-2). Moving through 12 time periods, this book describes each period and how geological changes caused the extinction of certain species and the creation of new ones. (Rev: BL 11/1/99; HBG 3/00; SLJ 11/99) [560]

12262 McClung, Robert M. *Last of the Wild: Vanished and Vanishing Giants of the Animal World* (8–12). Illus. 1997, Shoe String LB $27.50 (0-208-02452-2). Moving from continent to continent, this account gives historical and geographical background material on 60 animal species that have already disappeared or are currently in extreme danger of extinction. (Rev: BL 7/97; HBG 3/98; SLJ 11/97; VOYA 10/97) [591.51]

12263 McClung, Robert M. *Lost Wild America: The Story of Our Extinct and Vanishing Wildlife*. Rev. ed. (5–8). Illus. 1993, Shoe String LB $30.00 (0-208-02359-3). A history of American wildlife management from pioneer days to the present, with information on extinct and endangered species. (Rev: BL 1/1/94; SLJ 2/94*; VOYA 2/94) [591.5]

12264 Mallory, Kenneth. *A Home by the Sea: Protecting Coastal Wildlife* (5–8). Illus. Series: New England Aquarium. 1998, Harcourt $18.00 (0-15-200043-7); paper $9.00 (0-15-201802-6). A description of the many successful efforts to protect coastal wildlife in New Zealand in spite of commercial, residential, and recreational development. (Rev: BL 9/1/98; BR 1–2/99; HBG 3/99; SLJ 9/98) [333.954160993]

12265 Nirgiotis, Nicholas, and Theodore Nigiortis. *No More Dodos: How Zoos Help Endangered Wildlife* (5–8). Illus. 1996, Lerner LB $23.93 (0-8225-2856-8). An introduction to the many organizations that are trying to protect and preserve endangered wildlife worldwide. (Rev: BCCB 2/97; BL 2/15/97; SLJ 2/97) [639.9]

12266 O'Neill, Mary. *Nature in Danger* (4–7). Series: SOS Planet Earth. 1991, Troll paper $5.95 (0-8167-2286-2). Background information and history lead into the problem of animals in danger. (Rev: BL 6/15/91) [333.7]

12267 Penny, Malcolm. *Endangered Species* (5–8). Series: 21st Century Debates. 2002, Raintree Steck-Vaughn LB $27.12 (0-7398-4873-9). Topics covered in this well-illustrated book include a history of conservation, how species become endangered, methods for protection such as captive breeding, and saving habitats. (Rev: BL 6/1–15/02) [591]

12268 Salmansohn, Pete, and Stephen W. Kress. *Saving Birds: Heroes Around the World* (4–7). Illus. 2003, Tilbury $16.95 (0-88448-237-5). Efforts to save endangered bird species are detailed in informative text and arresting, full-color photographs. (Rev: BL 3/15/03; HBG 10/03; SLJ 5/03) [333.95]

12269 Silverstein, Alvin, et al. *Saving Endangered Animals* (6–8). Series: Better Earth. 1993, Enslow LB $20.95 (0-89490-402-7). Practical information about saving threatened animal species and reintro-ducing them into their native environments. (Rev: BL 5/1/93; SLJ 5/93) [333.95]

12270 Simmons, Randy. *Endangered Species* (7–12). Illus. Series: Critical Thinking About Environmental Issues. 2002, Gale $21.96 (0-7377-1266-X). Readers will find a variety of opinions about the necessity of protecting endangered species. (Rev: BL 12/15/02; SLJ 6/03) [333.95]

12271 Tesar, Jenny. *Endangered Habitats* (5–9). Series: Our Fragile Planet. 1992, Facts on File LB $19.95 (0-8160-2493-6). A succinct overview of food chains and ecosystems, and an account of environmental problems, extinction, and endangered species. (Rev: BL 6/1/92; SLJ 9/92) [333.95]

12272 Thomas, Peggy. *Big Cat Conservation* (5–8). Illus. Series: Science of Saving Animals. 2000, Twenty-First Century LB $25.90 (0-7613-3231-6). This book focuses on seven species, including panthers, cheetahs, and tigers, and discusses wildlife conservation programs, challenges, and successes. (Rev: BL 6/1–15/00; HBG 10/00; SLJ 7/00) [333.95]

12273 Thomas, Peggy. *Bird Alert* (5–8). Series: The Science of Saving Animals. 2000, Twenty-First Century LB $25.90 (0-7613-1457-1). This book discusses conservation programs designed to save endangered bird species and tells how youngsters can get involved in saving birds. (Rev: BL 10/15/00; HBG 10/01; SLJ 12/00) [591.52]

12274 Thomas, Peggy. *Marine Mammal Preservation* (5–8). Series: The Science of Saving Animals. 2000, Twenty-First Century LB $25.90 (0-7613-1458-X). Focuses on endangered marine mammals and describes a wide range of conservation programs. (Rev: BL 10/15/00; HBG 10/01; SLJ 1/01) [574.92]

12275 Thomas, Peggy. *Reptile Rescue* (5–8). Illus. Series: Science of Saving Animals. 2000, Twenty-First Century LB $25.90 (0-7613-3232-4). A description of various conservation programs and how they operate in relation to several reptile species, including tortoises, crocodiles, and snakes. (Rev: BL 6/1–15/00; HBG 10/00; SLJ 7/00) [333.95]

12276 Vergoth, Karin, and Christopher Lampton. *Endangered Species*. Rev. ed. (5–7). Illus. 1999, Watts LB $25.00 (0-531-11480-5). A valuable overview of the subject that updates the 1988 edition with good, comprehensive lists of endangered species. (Rev: BL 2/1/00) [578.68]

Insects and Arachnids

GENERAL AND MISCELLANEOUS

12277 Berger, Melvin. *Killer Bugs* (4–8). Illus. 1990, Avon paper $3.50 (0-380-76036-3). This account explores the world of killer bees, fire ants, and other such bugs. (Rev: BL 12/15/90) [595.7]

12278 Dallinger, Jane. *Grasshoppers* (4–7). Illus. 1981, Lerner paper $5.95 (0-8225-9568-0). The life cycle of grasshoppers, well illustrated.

12279 Fleisher, Paul. *Ants* (5–8). Series: Animal-Ways. 2001, Marshall Cavendish LB $28.50 (0-7614-1269-7). This introduction to ants and their habits and habitats also includes fine color images and material on species identification, anatomy, and classification. (Rev: BL 3/15/02; HBG 10/02) [595.79]

12280 Greenaway, Theresa. *Ants* (4–7). Series: The Secret World of . . . 2001, Raintree Steck-Vaughn LB $18.98 (0-7368-3511-4). After presenting interesting and unusual facts about ants, this book examines their structure, homes, behavior, and enemies. (Rev: BL 10/15/01) [595.79]

12281 Jackson, Donna. *The Bug Scientists* (4–7). Illus. Series: Scientists in the Field. 2002, Houghton $16.00 (0-618-10868-8). In addition to describing a variety of professional jobs related to insects, this colorful volume presents excellent information about insects and how they live. (Rev: BCCB 6/02; BL 4/1/02; HB 5–6/02; HBG 10/02; SLJ 4/02) [595.7]

12282 Johnson, Sylvia A. *Beetles* (4–7). Illus. 1982, Lerner LB $22.60 (0-8225-1476-1). Color photography highlights this account that concentrates on the scarab beetle.

12283 Johnson, Sylvia A. *Ladybugs* (5–8). 1983, Lerner LB $22.60 (0-8225-1481-8). A description of the ladybug, its habits, behavior, and uses. [595.7]

12284 Maynard, Chris. *Bugs: A Close-Up View of the Insect World* (4–8). Series: Secret Worlds. 2001, DK $14.99 (0-7894-7969-9); paper $5.99 (0-7894-7970-2). Unusual page layouts and an eight-page reference section are two bonuses of this attractive introduction to insects and their world. (Rev: BL 10/15/01; HBG 3/02) [575.7]

12285 Milne, Lorus, and Margery Milne. *The Audubon Society Field Guide to North American Insects and Spiders* (7–12). Illus. 1980, Knopf $19.95 (0-394-50763-0). An extensive use of color photographs makes this a fine guide for identifying insects. [595.7]

12286 Pascoe, Elaine. *Ants* (4–7). Series: Nature Close-Up. 1998, Blackbirch LB $27.44 (1-56711-183-1). Using outstanding photographs, this book introduces ants and a series of projects designed to teach more about these creatures. (Rev: BL 9/15/98; HBG 3/99; SLJ 3/99) [595.78]

12287 Pascoe, Elaine. *Beetle* (4–7). Series: Nature Close-Up. 2000, Blackbirch LB $27.44 (1-56711-175-0). Outstanding photographs grace this simple introduction to beetles that discusses their anatomy, habits, and food. (Rev: BL 4/15/00; HBG 3/01; SLJ 9/00) [595.76]

12288 Pascoe, Elaine. *Crickets and Grasshoppers* (4–7). Series: Nature Close-Up. 1998, Blackbirch LB $27.44 (1-56711-176-9). Easy projects introduce youngsters to these insects in this book illustrated with color photographs. (Rev: BL 9/15/98; HBG 3/99) [595.7]

12289 Pascoe, Elaine. *Flies* (4–7). Series: Nature Close-Up. 2000, Blackbirch LB $27.44 (1-56711-149-1). This introduction to flies uses stunning photographs and text to describe their body parts, life cycle, and how to observe them; a few focused experiments are also included. (Rev: BL 4/15/00; HBG 3/01; SLJ 9/00) [595.7]

12290 Pipe, Jim. *The Giant Book of Bugs and Creepy Crawlies* (4–8). Illus. 1998, Millbrook LB $27.90 (0-7613-0716-8). Exotic and common insects and spiders are presented in this oversize book with eye-catching pictures and fascinating text. (Rev: BL 8/98) [595.7]

12291 Robertson, Matthew. *Insects and Spiders* (4–8). Illus. Series: Pathfinders. 2000, Reader's Digest $16.99 (1-57584-375-7). This oversize, attractive volume uses double-page spreads to introduce various insects and spiders, their physical characteristics, habits, and habitats. (Rev: BL 9/15/00; HBG 3/01; SLJ 2/01) [595.7]

12292 Robinson, W. Wright. *How Insects Build Their Amazing Homes* (5–8). Series: Animal Architects. 1999, Blackbirch LB $27.44 (1-56711-375-3). After defining what an insect is, this book shows how termites, wasps, ants, and bees construct their houses and nests. (Rev: HBG 3/00; SLJ 5/00) [595.7]

12293 Wangberg, James K. *Do Bees Sneeze? And Other Questions Kids Ask About Insects* (7–10). Illus. 1997, Fulcrum paper $18.95 (1-55591-963-4). Full, interesting answers to over 200 questions about insects on such subjects as physical characteristics, anatomical features, locomotion, behavior, habitat, and human health and safety. (Rev: BL 1/1–15/98; SLJ 4/98) [595.7]

12294 Wilsdon, Christina, and National Audubon Society, eds. *National Audubon Society First Field Guide: Insects* (4–8). Illus. 1998, Scholastic paper $17.95 (0-590-05447-3). Following a general introduction to entomology, specific insects are pictured and information is given on such topics as their eating, mating and social habits, physical structure, habitats, and identification markings. (Rev: BL 8/98; SLJ 10/98) [595]

BUTTERFLIES, MOTHS, AND CATERPILLARS

12295 Lavies, Bianca. *Monarch Butterflies: Mysterious Travelers* (4–7). Illus. 1992, Dutton $15.99 (0-525-44905-1). A secluded forest in Mexico's Sierra Madres is the winter home of these beautiful butterflies that summer in the eastern United States and Canada. (Rev: BL 1/15/93; SLJ 4/93*) [595.78]

12296 Preston-Mafham, Rod. *The Secret Life of Butterflies and Moths* (4–7). Series: The Secret World of . . . 2002, Raintree Steck-Vaughn LB $27.12 (0-7398-4984-0). Beginning with little-known facts about butterflies and moths, this book explores their life cycles, behavior, mating habits, enemies, food, and habitats. (Rev: BL 8/02) [595.78]

12297 Preston-Mafham, Rod, and Ken Preston-Mafham. *Butterflies of the World* (8–12). Illus. 1988, Facts on File $32.95 (0-8160-1601-1). An attractively illustrated book that introduces butterflies and moths and gives facts about their evolution, structure, types, and life cycles. (Rev: BR 3–4/89) [595.78]

12298 Pyle, Robert Michael. *The Audubon Society Field Guide to North American Butterflies* (7–12). Illus. 1981, Knopf $19.95 (0-394-51914-0). An introduction to over 600 species of butterflies in about 1,000 color photographs and text. [595.7]

12299 Whalley, Paul. *Butterfly and Moth* (6–8). Illus. 1988, Knopf $20.99 (0-394-99618-6). Short chapters are used to describe the characteristics of moths and butterflies, the various species, and their life cycles. (Rev: BL 12/1/88; SLJ 12/88) [595.7]

SPIDERS AND SCORPIONS

12300 Dallinger, Jane. *Spiders* (4–7). Illus. 1981, Lerner LB $22.60 (0-8225-1456-7); paper $5.95 (0-8225-9534-6). Excellent color photographs complement the text.

12301 Facklam, Margery. *Spiders and Their Web Sites* (5–8). 2001, Little, Brown $15.95 (0-316-27329-5). This book takes a look at 12 kinds of spiders, with material on webs, lifestyles, and reproduction. (Rev: BL 3/15/01; HB 5–6/01; HBG 10/01; SLJ 8/01) [595.4]

12302 Greenaway, Theresa. *Spiders* (4–7). Series: The Secret World of . . . 2001, Raintree Steck-Vaughn LB $18.98 (0-7368-3509-2). An information-crammed text and attractive illustrations introduce spiders, how and where they live, and their behavior. (Rev: BL 10/15/01) [595.4]

12303 Pringle, Laurence. *Scorpion Man: Exploring the World of Scorpions* (4–7). Illus. 1994, Scribners $15.95 (0-684-19560-7). A profile of the world of scorpions, with material on the life of a man who studied them, Gary Polis. (Rev: BL 1/15/95; SLJ 3/95) [595.4]

Marine and Freshwater Life

GENERAL AND MISCELLANEOUS

12304 Arthur, Alex. *Shell* (4–8). Illus. Series: Eyewitness Books. 1989, Knopf $20.99 (0-394-92256-

5). All kinds of shelled creatures are highlighted, including mollusks, crustaceans, turtles, and tortoises. (Rev: BL 9/15/89; BR 11–12/89; SLJ 8/89) [594]

12305 Boschung, Herbert T., Jr., et al. *The Audubon Society Field Guide to North American Fishes, Whales, and Dolphins* (7–12). Illus. 1983, Knopf $19.00 (0-394-53405-0). About 600 marine and freshwater fish and aquatic mammals are identified and described. [597]

12306 Breidahl, Harry. *Diminutive Drifters: Microscopic Aquatic Life* (6–8). Illus. Series: Life in Strange Places. 2001, Chelsea LB $16.95 (0-7910-6618-5). In addition to describing phytoplankton and the environment in which these organisms thrive, this volume includes information on a working microbiologist and provides many photographs. (Rev: HBG 3/02; SLJ 1/02)

12307 Cerullo, Mary. *The Octopus: Phantom of the Sea* (4–8). Illus. 1997, Dutton $18.99 (0-525-65199-3). The life cycle of this mysterious sea creature is described, with illustrations of its anatomy and of its relatives, such as the squid. (Rev: BCCB 2/97; BL 2/1/97; SLJ 12/97*) [594]

12308 Cerullo, Mary. *Sea Soup: Phytoplankton* (4–7). Illus. 1999, Tilbury $16.95 (0-88448-208-1). An introduction to the microscopic world of tiny plants known as phytoplankton and their contributions to life on this planet. (Rev: BL 3/15/00; SLJ 5/00) [578.77]

12309 Cerullo, Mary M. *Sea Soup: Zooplankton* (4–7). 2001, Tilbury $16.95 (0-88448-219-7). An inviting introduction to the world of tiny drifting animals known as zooplankton, with intriguing photographs. (Rev: BL 7/01; HBG 10/01; SLJ 8/01) [592.1776.]

12310 Goodman, Susan E. *Ultimate Field Trip 3: Wading into Marine Biology* (5–8). Series: Ultimate Field Trip. 1999, Simon & Schuster $17.00 (0-689-81963-3). A description of a field trip by Boston middle school students to the Bay of Fundy, an area of extreme tides, with material on their reactions, the plants and animals that live there, and the tide pools the youngsters explored. (Rev: BL 4/15/99; HBG 9/99; SLJ 6/99) [574.92]

12311 Halfmann, Janet. *Life in the Sea* (5–7). Series: LifeViews. 2000, Creative Co. LB $22.60 (1-58341-074-0). All life in the sea is discussed with a focus on the tiniest — plankton, algae, sea spiders, coral, and worms. (Rev: SLJ 8/00) [591.92]

12312 Johnson, Jinny. *Simon and Schuster Children's Guide to Sea Creatures* (4–7). 1998, Simon & Schuster $19.95 (0-689-81534-4). This book contains broad coverage of the invertebrates, birds, mammals, and fish found in various parts of the oceans and their shores. (Rev: HBG 10/98; SLJ 5/98) [591]

12313 Meinkoth, Norman A. *The Audubon Society Field Guide to North American Seashore Creatures* (7–12). Illus. 1981, Knopf $19.95 (0-394-51993-0). This is a guide to such invertebrates as sponges, corals, urchins, and anemones. [592]

12314 Parker, Steve. *Seashore* (5–9). Illus. 1989, Knopf $20.99 (0-394-92254-9). Text and stunning color photographs are used to supply much information about seashores and the life they support. (Rev: BL 10/15/89) [591.909]

12315 Pascoe, Elaine. *Pill Bugs and Sow Bugs* (4–7). Series: Nature Close-Up. 2001, Blackbirch LB $27.44 (1-56711-473-3). This informative book of facts and easy-to-do projects introduces some small land crustacea found under stones and in other damp places. (Rev: BL 9/15/01; HBG 3/02) [595.3]

12316 Perrine, Doug. *Sharks and Rays of the World* (8–12). Illus. Series: WorldLife Discovery Guides. 2000, Voyageur $29.95 (0-89658-448-8). Scientific information on sharks and rays and their evolution is accompanied by color photographs, stories of shark attacks, and descriptions of diving to watch these animals. (Rev: SLJ 4/00) [597.3]

12317 Rehder, Harold A. *The Audubon Society Field Guide to North American Seashells* (7–12). Illus. 1981, Knopf $19.95 (0-394-51913-2). Seven hundred of the most common seashells from our coasts are pictured in color photographs and described in the text. [594]

12318 Sibbald, Jean H. *Strange Eating Habits of Sea Creatures* (4–8). Illus. 1987, Macmillan LB $13.95 (0-87518-349-2). Eating habits of numerous creatures of the sea are divided into techniques — grazers, gulpers, poisoners, and so on. (Rev: BL 12/1/86; SLJ 2/87)

12319 Treat, Rose. *The Seaweed Book: How to Find and Have Fun with Seaweed* (4–7). Illus. 1995, Star Bright paper $5.95 (1-887724-00-7). The identification, collection, and preservation of various kinds of seaweed. (Rev: BL 2/1/96) [589.45]

CORALS AND JELLYFISH

12320 Buttfield, Helen. *The Secret Life of Fishes: From Angels to Zebras on the Coral Reef* (5–8). 2000, Abrams $19.95 (0-8109-3933-9). As well as introducing the fish found on coral reefs, this handsome book talks about the reef itself and other creatures found there such as the octopus and sea star. (Rev: SLJ 7/00) [574.9]

12321 Cerullo, Mary. *Coral Reef: A City That Never Sleeps* (5–8). Illus. 1996, Dutton $18.99 (0-525-65193-4). Exceptional photographs highlight this account of coral reefs and the life they support. (Rev: BL 3/1/96; SLJ 1/96*) [574.9]

12322 Collard, Sneed B. *Lizard Island: Science and Scientists on Australia's Great Barrier Reef* (5–7).

Illus. 2000, Watts LB $25.00 (0-531-11719-7); paper $12.95 (0-531-16519-1). A lively and absorbing description of the work of scientists studying the forms of life on the Great Barrier Reef. (Rev: BL 2/1/01; SLJ 5/01; VOYA 12/01) [577.7]

12323 Johnson, Rebecca L. *The Great Barrier Reef: A Living Laboratory* (5–8). 1992, Lerner LB $28.75 (0-8225-1596-2). A look at the world's largest coral reef, off the coast of Australia. (Rev: BL 5/15/92; SLJ 7/92) [574.9943]

12324 Siy, Alexandra. *The Great Astrolabe Reef* (5–8). Illus. Series: Circle of Life. 1992, Macmillan $14.95 (0-87518-499-5). Color photographs help to tell the story of this delicate coral ecosystem. (Rev: BL 9/1/92; SLJ 11/92) [574.5]

FISHES

12325 Eschmeyer, William N., and Earl S. Herald. *A Field Guide to Pacific Coast Fishes of North America: Fish the Gulf of Alaska to Baja California* (7–12). Illus. 1983, Houghton $20.00 (0-618-00212-X). In this volume in the Peterson Field Guide series, about 500 fish are described and illustrated. [597]

12326 Filisky, Michael. *Peterson First Guide to Fishes of North America* (7–12). Illus. 1989, Houghton paper $4.95 (0-393-91179-6). This is a concise version of the parent Peterson guide that gives basic material on common fish but with less detail. (Rev: BL 6/1/89) [597]

12327 Hirschmann, Kris. *Rays* (4–7). Illus. 2003, Gale LB $23.70 (0-7377-0988-X). Hirschmann presents basic information about the ray's anatomy, movement, feeding, defense, reproduction, and man's fascination with this fish. (Rev: BL 3/1/03) [597.3]

12328 Parker, Steve. *Fish* (5–9). Illus. 1990, Knopf $20.99 (0-679-90439-5). A general introduction to fish, their physiology, and the main fish groups. (Rev: BL 7/90; SLJ 9/90) [597]

12329 Walker, Sally M. *Fossil Fish Found Alive: Discovering the Coelacanth* (5–8). Illus. 2002, Carolrhoda LB $21.55 (1-57505-536-8). An engaging look at the search for and study of coelacanths, a fish believed to be extinct until 1938. (Rev: BL 3/15/02; HB 1–2/03; HBG 3/03; SLJ 5/02*) [597.3]

12330 Zim, Herbert S., and Hurst H. Shoemaker. *Fishes* (5–8). 1991, Western paper $21.27 (0-307-64059-0). This is a basic guide to both fresh and saltwater species.

SHARKS

12331 Capuzzo, Michael. *Close to Shore: The Terrifying Shark Attacks of 1916* (7–12). Illus. 2003, Crown $16.95 (0-375-82231-3). Photographs and newspaper clippings enhance this true story of a shark's brief and dangerous detour into a New Jersey creek in 1916. (Rev: BL 5/15/03; HBG 10/03; SLJ 4/03) [597.3]

12332 Cerullo, Mary. *The Truth About Great White Sharks* (4–7). Illus. 2000, Chronicle $14.95 (0-8118-2467-5). A fascinating account with excellent underwater photographs that explores such topics about sharks as physical characteristics, behavior, feeding habits, and the difficulty of studying them. (Rev: BL 4/1/00; SLJ 7/00) [597.3]

12333 Coupe, Sheena M. *Sharks* (5–8). Illus. Series: Great Creatures of the World. 1990, Facts on File $17.95 (0-8160-2270-4). An oversized book that contains a well-organized text and many illustrations. (Rev: BL 4/1/90; SLJ 7/90) [597]

12334 Dingerkus, Guido. *The Shark Watchers' Guide* (7–12). Illus. 1989, Messner paper $5.95 (0-671-68815-4). As well as materials on 30 different varieties of sharks this book tells about shark anatomy, habits, and evolution and gives tips on how to handle a shark attack. (Rev: BL 11/15/85; SLJ 12/85) [597]

12335 Grace, Eric S. *Sharks* (5–8). Series: Wildlife Library. 2000, Sierra Club $14.95 (0-87156-926-4). This book explains sharks' evolution, physiology, behavior, and reproduction. (Rev: SLJ 1/01) [597.31]

12336 MacQuitty, Miranda. *Shark* (5–9). Series: Eyewitness Books. 1992, Knopf $20.99 (0-679-91683-0). A guide to the various species of sharks, their habits, and habitats accompanied by excellent photographs. (Rev: BL 11/1/92) [597]

12337 MacQuitty, Miranda. *Sharks and Other Scary Creatures* (4–8). Series: Secret Worlds. 2002, DK $14.95 (0-7894-8533-8); paper $5.99 (0-7894-8534-6). Full-color photographs, interesting page layouts, and plenty of Web sites highlight this book on sharks and other scary creatures. (Rev: BL 8/02; HBG 10/02) [597.31]

12338 Pope, Joyce. *1001 Facts About Sharks* (7–12). Series: Backpack Books. 2002, DK paper $8.95 (0-7894-8449-8). More than 550 illustrations and photographs are used to present basic facts about sharks, their anatomy, habits, and varieties. (Rev: BL 3/15/02) [597]

12339 Reader's Digest, eds. *Sharks: Silent Hunters of the Deep* (8–12). Illus. 1987, Reader's Digest $19.95 (0-86438-014-3). This handsomely illustrated account describes the ways of sharks, gives material on famous encounters, and identifies all 344 species. (Rev: BL 5/15/87; BR 11–12/87; SLJ 1/88; VOYA 8/87) [597]

12340 Sieswerda, Paul L. *Sharks* (5–8). Series: AnimalWays. 2001, Marshall Cavendish LB $28.50 (0-7614-1267-0). Photographs, maps, and text introduce many species of sharks, their behavior, anatomy, and habitats. (Rev: BL 3/15/02; HBG 10/02) [597.31]

WHALES, DOLPHINS, AND OTHER SEA MAMMALS

12341 Darling, Jim. *Gray Whales* (6–12). Series: WorldLife Library. 1999, Voyageur paper $16.95 (0-89658-447-X). Physiology, behavior, habitat, migration, and relations with humans are all discussed in this volume full of full-color photographs. (Rev: SLJ 4/00) [599.5]

12342 Dow, Lesley. *Whales* (5–8). Series: Great Creatures of the World. 1990, Facts on File $17.95 (0-8160-2271-2). A fine introduction to this endangered animal — its species and living habits — with information on legends concerning the whale. (Rev: BL 4/1/90; SLJ 7/90) [599.5]

12343 Greenaway, Theresa. *Whales* (4–7). Illus. Series: Secret World Of. 2001, Raintree Steck-Vaughn LB $27.12 (0-7398-3508-4). A look at whales' diet, habitat, and behavior, with photographs and interesting facts. (Rev: BL 10/15/01; HBG 3/02) [599.5]

12344 Greenberg, Dan. *Whales* (5–9). Illus. Series: AnimalWays. 2003, Marshall Cavendish $20.95 (0-7614-1389-8). In addition to material on physical characteristics, behavior, habitats, and threats, Greenberg touches on the animal's roles in history, mythology, religion, and literature. (Rev: BL 3/15/03; HBG 3/03) [599.5]

12345 Hirschmann, Kris. *Humpback Whales* (4–7). Illus. Series: Creatures of the Sea. 2003, Gale LB $23.70 (0-7377-0984-7). Hirschmann presents basic information about the humpback whale's anatomy, movement, feeding, defense, reproduction, endangered status, and means of communication, with lots of clear photographs. (Rev: BL 3/1/03) [599.5]

12346 Hoyt, Erich. *Meeting the Whales: The Equinox Guide to Giants of the Deep* (5–10). Illus. 1991, Camden House paper $9.95 (0-921820-23-2). This guide to 19 whale species describes their origins and habits. Includes a discussion on whale watching and photography. (Rev: BL 8/91) [599.5]

12347 Kelsey, Elin. *Finding Out About Whales* (4–8). Illus. Series: Science Explorers. 1998, Owl $19.95 (1-895688-79-5); paper $9.95 (1-895688-80-9). This book discusses how information is gathered about whales and introduces five different species: blue, humpback, beluga, gray, and killer. (Rev: BL 3/1/99; SLJ 3/99) [595.5]

12348 Matero, Robert. *The Birth of a Humpback Whale* (5–8). Illus. 1996, Simon & Schuster $16.00 (0-689-31931-2). A narrative with pencil drawings that covers the birth of a humpbacked whale and its journey from Hawaii to Alaska. (Rev: BL 4/1/96; SLJ 6/96) [599.5]

12349 Nuzzolo, Deborah. *Bottlenose Dolphin Training and Interaction* (6–9). Illus. Series: SeaWorld Education. 2003, Sea World paper $7.99 (1-893698-

03-3). An attractive introduction to this dolphin's habitat, physiology, and behavior, and to the ways in which they are trained at Sea World. (Rev: BL 6/1–15/03) [636.]

12350 Papastavrou, Vassili. *Whale* (5–9). Series: Eyewitness Books. 1993, Knopf $20.99 (0-679-93884-2). A heavily illustrated introduction to various kinds of whales, their habits, and where they live. (Rev: BL 10/1/93) [599.5]

12351 Pascoe, Elaine, adapt. *Animal Intelligence: Why Is This Dolphin Smiling?* (5–8). 1997, Blackbirch $17.95 (1-56711-226-9). This book reports on the scientific research on communication between dolphins and humans, with reports on such projects as one by John Lilly to create, via computer, dolphin equivalents of human words. (Rev: HBG 3/98; SLJ 12/97) [599.5]

12352 Price-Groff, Claire. *The Manatee* (7–10). Series: Endangered Animals and Habitats. 1999, Lucent LB $27.45 (1-56006-445-5). This well-illustrated book describes this endangered sea mammal and tells about its habits, habitats, and appearance. (Rev: BL 9/15/99; HBG 4/00) [599.53]

12353 Pringle, Laurence. *Dolphin Man: Exploring the World of Dolphins* (5–9). Illus. 1995, Simon & Schuster $17.00 (0-689-80299-4). A fascinating photoessay about the world of dolphins as explored by marine biologist Randall Wells in a dolphin community in the Sarasota Bay area of Florida. (Rev: BL 1/1–15/96; SLJ 2/96) [599.5]

12354 Read, Andrew. *Porpoises* (5–8). Illus. Series: WorldLife Library. 1999, Voyageur paper $16.95 (0-89658-420-8). With many color illustrations and large print, this book introduces porpoises, their characteristics, behavior, habitats, and how humans study them. (Rev: BL 8/99; VOYA 2/00) [599.53]

12355 Reiter, Chris. *The Blue Whale* (4–7). Series: Endangered and Threatened Animals. 2003, Enslow/MyReportLinks.com LB $19.95 (0-7660-5055-6). Standard information on the blue whale and its endangered status is accompanied by links to Web sites for further research. (Rev: HBG 10/03; SLJ 6/03) [599.5]

12356 Rinard, Judith E. *Amazing Animals of the Sea* (5–8). Illus. 1981, National Geographic LB $12.50 (0-87044-387-9). Whales, dolphins, sea otters, sea lions, seals, manatees, and other marine mammals are described.

12357 Sibbald, Jean H. *The Manatee* (4–7). Illus. 1990, Macmillan LB $13.95 (0-87518-429-4). The life of this gentle sea mammal is examined, along with material on how its survival is threatened by humans. (Rev: BL 6/15/90; SLJ 8/90) [599.5]

12358 Silverstein, Alvin, et al. *The Manatee* (4–7). Illus. Series: Endangered in America. 1995, Millbrook LB $24.90 (1-56294-551-3). A profile of this sea creature, its lifestyle and habits, and how it

became an endangered species. (Rev: BL 10/15/95; SLJ 1/96) [599.5]

Microscopes, Microbiology, and Biotechnology

12359 Bleifeld, Maurice. *Experimenting with a Microscope* (5–9). Illus. 1988, Watts paper $22.50 (0-531-10580-6). The story of the microscope plus many experiments and projects involving its use. (Rev: BL 1/15/89; BR 3–4/89; SLJ 2/89) [578]

12360 Levine, Shar, and Leslie Johnstone. *The Microscope Book* (5–8). Illus. 1997, Sterling $19.95 (0-8069-4898-1); paper $10.95 (0-8069-4899-X). An excellent introduction to microscopes, with material on parts of the microscope, lenses, how to focus and produce slides, and tips on keeping a journal. (Rev: SLJ 7/97) [502]

12361 Nachtigall, Werner. *Exploring with the Microscope: A Book of Discovery and Learning* (7–12). Trans. by Elizabeth Reinersmann. 1995, Sterling $19.95 (0-8069-0866-1). A thorough book about microscopes and their uses, with 100 color slides, diagrams, and black-and-white photographs. (Rev: BL 10/1/95; SLJ 11/95) [578]

12362 Rainis, Kenneth G., and Bruce J. Russell. *Guide to Microlife* (7–12). Illus. 1996, Watts LB $35.00 (0-531-11266-7). A handbook to microscopic animals that describes habitats, the various groups of organisms, and projects. Each entry is accompanied by stunning photographs. (Rev: BL 2/15/97; SLJ 5/97) [576]

12363 Rogers, Kirsteen. *The Usborne Complete Book of the Microscope* (4–8). Illus. 1999, EDC paper $14.95 (0-7460-3106-8). Objects and organisms that can be viewed with a microscope are pictured and described in a series of double-page spreads, along with material on the parts and uses of different kinds of microscopes. (Rev: SLJ 7/99) [535]

12364 Silverstein, Alvin, et al. *Cells* (4–8). Series: Science Concepts. 2002, Millbrook LB $26.90 (0-7613-2254-X). The functions and components of plant and animal cells are discussed along with such topics as cloning, cell fusion, and stem cell research. (Rev: BL 9/15/02; HBG 3/03) [574.87]

12365 Snedden, Robert. *The Benefits of Bacteria* (6–10). Illus. Series: Microlife. 2000, Heinemann LB $22.79 (1-57572-242-9). The beneficial functions of bacteria are discussed in this well-illustrated science book. (Rev: BL 9/15/00; SLJ 12/00) [576]

12366 Snedden, Robert. *Scientists and Discoveries* (6–10). Illus. Series: Microlife. 2000, Heinemann LB $22.79 (1-57572-244-5). This well-written account traces the development of the microscope and describes some of the discoveries that resulted such as vaccination, bacteriology, germ theory, antibiotics, and DNA. (Rev: BL 9/1/00) [579]

12367 Snedden, Robert. *A World of Microorganisms* (6–9). Series: Microlife. 2000, Heinemann LB $22.79 (1-57572-241-0). With clear explanations and many illustrations, this account discusses viruses, bacteria, protists, and fungi as well as the structure of cells and the chemistry of living organisms. (Rev: BL 9/1/00; SLJ 12/00) [579]

12368 Stwertka, Eve, and Albert Stwertka. *Microscope: How to Use It and Enjoy It* (5–9). Illus. 1989, Silver Burdett LB $9.95 (0-671-63705-3); paper $4.95 (0-671-67060-3). A fine introduction that covers such topics as the parts of the microscope, techniques for use, and how to prepare slides. (Rev: BL 3/1/89; BR 9–10/89; SLJ 4/89) [502.8]

Pets

GENERAL AND MISCELLANEOUS

12369 Gerstenfeld, Sheldon L. *The Bird Care Book: All You Need to Know to Keep Your Bird Healthy and Happy*. Rev. ed. (8–12). Illus. 1989, Addison-Wesley paper $17.00 (0-201-09559-9). A basic handbook on the choosing, care, and feeding of both pet and wild birds. (Rev: BL 9/15/89) [636.6]

12370 Hernandez-Divers, Sonia. *Geckos* (4–8). Illus. Series: Keeping Unusual Pets. 2003, Heinemann LB $25.64 (1-40340-282-5). An appealing and informative introduction to geckos that provides much practical guidance on actually keeping one as a pet. Also use *Chinchillas*, *Ferrets*, *Snakes* (all 2002), and *Rats* (2003). (Rev: BL 3/15/03; HBG 10/03; SLJ 4/03) [639.3]

12371 Kent, Deborah. *Animal Helpers for the Disabled* (5–7). Illus. Series: Watts Library: Disability. 2003, Watts LB $24.00 (0-531-12017-1); paper $8.95 (0-531-16663-5). Stories of animal accomplishments draw readers into this account, which covers the history of service animals, the kinds of animals used, and the training they undergo. (Rev: BL 10/15/03; LMC 11–12/03; SLJ 9/03) [636.08]

12372 Simon, Seymour. *Pets in a Jar: Collecting and Caring for Small Wild Animals* (7–10). Illus. 1975, Penguin paper $6.99 (0-14-049186-4). Valuable information is given on caring for such small pets as ants, crickets, crabs, and starfish. [639]

12373 Vriends, Matthew M. *Pigeons* (7–12). Illus. 1988, Barron's paper $7.95 (0-8120-4044-9). A brief but thorough guide to raising pigeons plus material on their behavior and how to breed them. (Rev: BL 2/1/89) [636.5]

CATS

12374 Arnold, Caroline. *Cats: In from the Wild* (4–7). Photos by Richard Hewett. 1993, Carolrhoda

LB $19.93 (0-87614-692-2). Domestic and wild cats are highlighted with comparisons and contrasts. (Rev: BL 8/93) [636.8]

12375 Clutton-Brock, Juliet. *Cat* (5–9). Series: Eyewitness Books. 1991, Knopf $20.99 (0-679-91458-7). An illustrated introduction to the cat family and their habits. (Rev: BL 12/1/91) [599.74]

12376 Gerstenfeld, Sheldon L. *The Cat Care Book: All You Need to Know to Keep Your Cat Healthy and Happy*. Rev. ed. (8–12). Illus. 1989, Addison-Wesley paper $16.00 (0-201-09569-6). Tips on how to choose a cat and detailed information on taking care of cats as pets. (Rev: BL 9/15/89) [636.8]

12377 Mattern, Joanne. *The American Shorthair Cat* (4–7). Illus. Series: Learning About Cats. 2002, Capstone LB $21.26 (0-7368-1300-4). Beautiful photographs of frisky felines are accompanied by data about the physical characteristics and personality, with a glossary, bibliography, and lists of addresses and Web sites. Also use *The Manx Cat* (2002). (Rev: BL 12/1/02; HBG 3/03) [636.8]

12378 Morris, Desmond. *Catwatching* (8–12). 1987, Crown $13.00 (0-517-56518-8); paper $8.95 (0-517-88053-9). Using a question-and-answer approach, the author explores many facets of cat behavior. (Rev: BL 4/1/87) [636.8]

DOGS

12379 American Kennel Club. *The Complete Dog Book*. 19th ed. (7–12). Illus. 1998, Howell Book House $32.95 (0-87605-148-4). The standard manual for dog owners and guide to every AKC-recognized breed. The first edition appeared over 50 years ago. (Rev: BL 6/15/85) [636.7]

12380 Benjamin, Carol Lea. *Dog Training for Kids*. Rev. ed. (5–8). Illus. 1988, Howell Book House $17.95 (0-87605-541-2). A simple guide to dog training that emphasizes the goal of having fun with a dog you are proud of. (Rev: SLJ 4/89) [636.7]

12381 Clutton-Brock, Juliet. *Dog* (4–8). Illus. Series: Eyewitness Books. 1991, Knopf $20.99 (0-679-91459-5). The anatomical features of dogs and their different types and outstanding characteristics are covered in this heavily illustrated book. (Rev: BL 12/1/91) [599.74]

12382 Gerstenfeld, Sheldon L. *The Dog Care Book: All You Need to Know to Keep Your Dog Healthy and Happy*. Rev. ed. (8–12). Illus. 1989, Addison-Wesley paper $17.00 (0-201-09667-6). Tips on selecting a dog plus extensive material on care and feeding. (Rev: BL 9/15/89) [636.7]

12383 Gorrell, Gena K. *Working Like a Dog: The Story of Working Dogs Through History* (4–8). Illus. 2003, Tundra $16.95 (0-88776-589-0). A comprehensive and very appealing look at dogs' services to man throughout history — as hunters and trackers, bomb sniffers, guide dogs, and companions, to name but a few. (Rev: BL 11/1/03; SLJ 12/03) [636.73]

12384 Maggitti, Phil. *Owning the Right Dog* (8–12). 1993, Tetra $29.95 (1-56465-110-X). Provides information on feeding, grooming, breeding, showing, and training, with color illustrations. (Rev: BL 11/1/93) [636.7]

12385 Murphy, Claire Rudolf, and Jane G. Haigh. *Gold Rush Dogs* (6–12). Illus. 2001, Alaska Northwest $16.95 (0-88240-534-9). Nine dogs that played important roles in the Yukon are profiled here with many sidebars that provide background historical detail. (Rev: BL 9/1/01; SLJ 9/01) [636.7]

12386 Paulsen, Gary. *My Life in Dog Years* (5–10). Illus. 1998, Delacorte $15.95 (0-385-32570-3). The famous novelist tells about eight wonderful dogs that he has known and loved over the years. (Rev: BCCB 3/98; BL 1/1–15/98; SLJ 3/98; VOYA 4/98) [636.7]

12387 Paulsen, Gary. *Puppies, Dogs, and Blue Northers: Reflections on Being Raised by a Pack of Sled Dogs* (6–10). Illus. 1996, Harcourt $16.00 (0-15-292881-2). In seven short vignettes, Paulsen describes the life of his lead dog, Cookie, and how she raises her pups to race and pull sleds. (Rev: BR 3–4/97; SLJ 11/96; VOYA 2/97) [636.7]

12388 Presnall, Judith Janda. *Police Dogs* (4–7). Illus. Series: Animals with Jobs. 2002, Gale LB $23.70 (0-7377-0631-7). This well-illustrated account describes the various ways in which dogs are used to fight crime. (Rev: BL 4/1/02) [363.2]

12389 Rosenthal, Lisa. *A Dog's Best Friend: An Activity Book for Kids and Their Dogs* (4–7). 1999, Chicago Review paper $12.95 (1-55652-362-9). This book that gives hints on how to choose a dog and care for a puppy offers 60 projects related to these subjects including crafts, recipes, and games. (Rev: SLJ 1/00) [636.7]

12390 Scalisi, Danny, and Libby Moses. *When Rover Just Won't Do: Over 2000 Suggestions for Naming Your Puppy* (8–12). 1993, Howell Book House $9.95 (0-87605-691-5). This collection of names for dogs includes more than 2,000 ideas, from Fajita to Rocky and Bullwinkle. (Rev: BL 11/1/93) [636.7]

12391 Silverstein, Alvin, et al. *Different Dogs* (4–7). Series: What a Pet! 2000, Twenty-First Century LB $23.90 (0-7613-1371-0). Several different breeds of dogs are introduced in pictures and text plus information on cost, food, housing, and training. (Rev: HBG 10/00; SLJ 5/00) [636.7]

12392 Silverstein, Alvin, and Virginia Silverstein. *Dogs: All About Them* (5–8). Illus. 1986, Lothrop $16.00 (0-688-04805-6). After a history of dogs from the Stone Age on, the authors cover such topics as breeds, uses, and care of dogs. (Rev: BCCB 11/86; BL 3/1/86; SLJ 9/86; VOYA 2/86) [599.74]

FISHES

12393 Emmens, Cliff W. *A Step-by-Step Book About Tropical Fish* (8–12). Illus. 1988, TFH paper $5.95 (0-86622-471-8). A brief, brightly illustrated introduction to various types of tropical fish, their care, and housing. (Rev: BL 1/1/89) [639.34]

12394 Mills, Dick. *Aquarius Fish* (6–12). Illus. 1996, DK paper $5.00 (0-7894-1074-5). A well-illustrated book that covers all aspects of fish as pets, from selecting healthy fish to maintaining a proper habitat and diet. (Rev: VOYA 4/97) [636.6]

HORSES

12395 Budd, Jackie. *Horse and Pony Breeds* (4–8). Series: The Complete Guides to Horses and Ponies. 1998, Gareth Stevens LB $25.26 (0-8368-2046-0). Each type of horse is profiled with action photographs, fact boxes, checklists, and a clear text. (Rev: HBG 10/98; SLJ 7/98) [636.1]

12396 Budd, Jackie. *Horse and Pony Care* (4–8). Series: The Complete Guides to Horses and Ponies. 1998, Gareth Stevens LB $26.60 (0-8368-2047-9). This book discusses such topics related to horse and pony care as feeding, stables, grooming, shoeing, and common ailments. (Rev: HBG 10/98; SLJ 7/98) [636.1]

12397 Budd, Jackie. *Learning to Ride Horses and Ponies* (4–8). Series: The Complete Guides to Horses and Ponies. 1998, Gareth Stevens LB $25.26 (0-8368-2045-2). This book supplies basic information that prospective young riders need to know including gear, types of lessons, and attitudes. (Rev: HBG 10/98; SLJ 7/98) [636.1]

12398 Budiansky, Stephen. *The World According to Horses: How They Run, See, and Think* (4–8). Illus. 2000, Holt $17.95 (0-8050-6054-5). This book explores horses' behavior — such as their sight and thinking powers — and goes on to explain how this knowledge was gained through observation and experiments. (Rev: BCCB 5/00; BL 3/1/00; HB 5–6/00; HBG 10/00; SLJ 7/00; VOYA 6/00) [636.1]

12399 Clutton-Brock, Juliet. *Horse* (5–9). Series: Eyewitness Books. 1992, Knopf $20.99 (0-679-91681-4). An explanation of the origins of the horse, the various breeds, and care and handling procedures. (Rev: BL 6/1/92) [636.1]

12400 Henry, Marguerite. *Album of Horses* (5–8). 1951, Macmillan paper $11.99 (0-689-71709-1). A beautifully illustrated guide to 20 breeds of horses.

12401 Hill, Cherry. *Horse Care for Kids* (4–8). Illus. 2002, Storey $23.95 (1-58017-476-0); paper $16.95 (1-58017-407-8). A very practical guide for young horse lovers and their parents using clear prose and topnotch illustrations to cover everything from selecting a horse and instructor to proper care and equine psychology. (Rev: BL 12/1/02; HBG 3/03; SLJ 1/03) [636.1]

12402 Jurmain, Suzanne. *Once upon a Horse: A History of Horses and How They Shaped Our History* (5–9). Illus. 1989, Lothrop $15.95 (0-688-05550-8). A history of the horse and how it has been domesticated and used by humans. (Rev: BL 12/15/89; BR 3–4/90; SLJ 1/90; VOYA 4/90) [636.1]

12403 Kelley, Brent. *Horse Breeds of the World* (4–8). Series: Horse Library. 2001, Chelsea $19.75 (0-7910-6652-5). In addition to basic facts about nearly 40 types of horses around the world, this account looks briefly at the horse's evolutionary history and related species. (Rev: HBG 3/02; SLJ 3/02) [636.1]

12404 Meltzer, Milton. *Hold Your Horses! A Feedbag Full of Fact and Fable* (4–8). Illus. 1995, HarperCollins LB $16.89 (0-06-024478-X). The place of horses in history is explored in this account that looks at horses' role in art, war, sports, and work. (Rev: BCCB 12/95; BL 11/15/95; SLJ 12/95*) [636.1]

12405 Penny, Malcolm. *The Secret Life of Wild Horses* (4–7). Series: The Secret World of . . . 2002, Raintree Steck-Vaughn LB $27.12 (0-7398-4987-5). A page of little-known facts about wild horses introduces this book that explores the horse's life, habits, mating, behavior, and threats to its future. (Rev: BL 8/02) [636.1]

12406 Presnall, Judith Janda. *Horse Therapists* (4–7). Illus. Series: Animals with Jobs. 2002, Gale LB $23.70 (0-7377-0615-5). Numerous photographs show how horses are used in various therapeutic situations including exercise for people with physical and mental disabilities. (Rev: BL 4/1/02; SLJ 3/02) [636.1]

12407 Ransford, Sandy. *Horse and Pony Care* (4–7). Illus. 2002, Kingfisher $14.95 (0-7534-5439-4). A well-illustrated account that gives clear instructions on such topics as washing and clipping a pony, exercise routines, and caring for pastureland. (Rev: BL 5/1/02; SLJ 7/02) [636.1]

12408 Ryden, Hope. *Wild Horses I Have Known* (4–8). 1999, Clarion $18.00 (0-395-77520-5). This photoessay about the wild mustangs that live around the Wyoming-Montana border details their behavior, social structure, and survival methods. (Rev: BCCB 4/99; BL 4/15/99; HB 3–4/99; HBG 10/99; SLJ 4/99) [636.1]

12409 Silverstein, Alvin, et al. *The Mustang* (4–8). Series: Endangered in America. 1997, Millbrook $24.90 (0-7613-0048-1). Examines the life cycle and behavior of the mustang, the reasons it has become endangered, and the measures being taken to ensure its survival. (Rev: BL 3/15/97; SLJ 6/97) [636.1]

12410 Stefoff, Rebecca. *Horses* (5–8). Illus. Series: AnimalWays. 2000, Marshall Cavendish LB $28.50 (0-7614-1139-9). A well-illustrated account that describes the physical and behavioral characteristics of horses, their place in the classification system, and their relationships with humans. (Rev: BL 1/1–15/01) [599.884]

12411 van der Linde, Laurel. *From Mustangs to Movie Stars: Five True Horse Legends of Our Time* (4–7). Illus. 1995, Millbrook LB $24.40 (1-56294-456-8). Biographies of five famous horses are recounted, from the racer Native Dancer to Cass Olé, who was the star of the film *The Black Stallion*. (Rev: BCCB 12/95; SLJ 12/95) [636.1]

12412 van der Linde, Laurel. *The White Stallions: The Story of the Dancing Horses of Lipizza* (6–8). 1994, Macmillan LB $14.95 (0-02-759055-0). The history of the famous Austrian Lipizzans, including how the horses were protected during World War II. (Rev: BL 5/1/94; SLJ 6/94) [636.1]

12413 *The Visual Dictionary of the Horse* (5–8). Illus. Series: Eyewitness Visual Dictionaries. 1994, DK paper $18.99 (1-56458-504-2). This pictorial study includes information on anatomy, breeds, grooming, racing, jumping, and equipment. (Rev: BCCB 7–8/94; SLJ 7/94) [636]

Zoos, Aquariums, and Animal Care

12414 Ricciuti, Edward R. *A Pelican Swallowed My Head and Other Zoo Stories* (4–8). 2002, Simon & Schuster $17.00 (0-689-82532-3). Anecdotes about a variety of animals and their keepers serve as a framework for information on the Bronx Zoo's innovative approach to designing animal-friendly, environmentally appropriate habitats. (Rev: HBG 3/03; SLJ 10/02) [590.74]

12415 Rinard, Judith E. *Zoos Without Cages* (5–8). Illus. 1981, National Geographic LB $12.50 (0-87044-340-2). A description of the new zoos that strive to reproduce the natural habitat of the enclosed animals. [590.74]

12416 Yancey, Diane. *Zoos* (5–8). Series: Overview. 1995, Lucent LB $27.45 (1-56006-163-4). Discusses the history of zoos, the controversy surrounding them, and species survival plans. (Rev: BL 6/1–15/95; SLJ 3/95) [590]

Chemistry

General and Miscellaneous

12417 Angliss, Sarah. *Gold* (4–8). Series: The Elements. 1999, Marshall Cavendish LB $22.79 (0-7614-0887-8). Easy-to-follow diagrams, fact boxes, and color illustrations accompany an informative text that introduces gold, where it is mined and processed, its properties, value, and uses. (Rev: BL 2/15/00; HBG 10/00) [546]

12418 Beatty, Richard. *Copper* (4–8). Series: The Elements. 2000, Marshall Cavendish LB $22.79 (0-7614-0945-9). This book identifies the element copper, defines its properties and describes its uses in everyday life, especially in electrical cables. (Rev: BL 1/1–15/01; HBG 10/01; SLJ 2/01) [546]

12419 Beatty, Richard. *Phosphorous* (4–8). Series: The Elements. 2000, Marshall Cavendish LB $22.79 (0-7614-0946-7). This book describes this nonmetallic element, lists its properties, tells how it behaves, and discusses such uses as matches and fertilizers. (Rev: BL 1/1–15/01; HBG 10/01; SLJ 2/01) [546]

12420 Beatty, Richard. *Sulfur* (4–8). Series: The Elements. 2000, Marshall Cavendish LB $22.79 (0-7614-0948-3). Introduces this nonmetallic element, its characteristics, various compounds, and uses in everyday life, with color photographs, easy-to-follow diagrams, fact boxes, and a clear text. (Rev: BL 1/1–15/01; HBG 10/01; SLJ 2/01) [546]

12421 Blashfield, Jean F. *Calcium* (6–9). Series: Sparks of Life. 1998, Raintree Steck-Vaughn LB $27.12 (0-8172-5040-9). From seashells to human bone structure, this volume explores the nature of calcium and its importance in the world. (Rev: BL 1/1–15/99) [546]

12422 Blashfield, Jean F. *Carbon* (6–9). Series: Sparks of Life. 1998, Raintree Steck-Vaughn LB $27.12 (0-8172-5041-7). Carbon is a cornerstone of the elements. This book describes its uses and compounds, from the composition of proteins to the plant-based production of starches and sugars. (Rev: BL 1/1–15/99) [546]

12423 Blashfield, Jean F. *Hydrogen* (6–9). Series: Sparks of Life. 1998, Raintree Steck-Vaughn LB $27.12 (0-8172-5038-7). This volume explores the many different forms and uses of hydrogen, from its role as a primary component of water to its role in the hydrocarbons used to fuel the modern world. (Rev: BL 1/1–15/99) [546]

12424 Blashfield, Jean F. *Nitrogen* (6–9). Series: Sparks of Life. 1998, Raintree Steck-Vaughn LB $27.12 (0-8172-5039-5). The properties and value of nitrogen are explored, from its use in explosives to its role in fertilizers. (Rev: BL 1/1–15/99) [546]

12425 Blashfield, Jean F. *Oxygen* (6–9). Series: Sparks of Life. 1998, Raintree Steck-Vaughn LB $27.12 (0-8172-5037-9). An introduction to oxygen, how it was discovered, its reaction with other elements to form compounds and mixtures, and its importance as the "breath of life." (Rev: BL 1/1–15/99) [546]

12426 Blashfield, Jean F. *Sodium* (6–9). Series: Sparks of Life. 1998, Raintree Steck-Vaughn LB $27.12 (0-8172-5042-5). This volume describes the history of sodium, its importance as an element, and its role as an ingredient in table salt, soaps, detergents, explosives, preservatives, and other common and not-so-common items. (Rev: BL 1/1–15/99) [546]

12427 Brandolini, Anita. *Fizz, Bubble and Flash! Element Explorations and Atom Adventures for Hands-On Science Fun!* (4–7). Series: Kids Can! 2003, Williamson paper $12.95 (1-885593-83-X). A friendly narrative and cartoon-style drawing present activities that illustrate basic scientific concepts. (Rev: BL 1/1–15/04; SLJ 11/03) [546]

12428 Cobb, Vicki. *Chemically Active! Experiments You Can Do at Home* (6–9). Illus. 1985, Harper-Collins LB $14.89 (0-397-32080-9). A group of scientific experiments that demonstrate chemical principles and can be performed with common household items. (Rev: BR 9–10/86; SLJ 8/85; VOYA 12/85) [507]

12429 Farndon, John. *Aluminum* (4–8). Series: The Elements. 2000, Marshall Cavendish LB $22.79 (0-7614-0947-5). This silvery, metallic element is introduced, with material on its individual characteristics, how it behaves, and its many uses in everyday life. (Rev: BL 1/1–15/01; HBG 10/01) [546]

12430 Farndon, John. *Calcium* (5–8). 1999, Benchmark LB $22.79 (0-7614-0888-6). An attractive, readable book that explains calcium's atomic structure, where and how it occurs in nature, its reactions, compounds, and uses. (Rev: BL 2/15/00; HBG 10/00; SLJ 6/00) [540]

12431 Farndon, John. *Hydrogen* (5–8). Illus. Series: Elements. 1999, Marshall Cavendish LB $22.79 (0-7614-0886-X). As well as explaining hydrogen's place on the periodic table, this account traces the history of its discovery, its properties, reactive combinations, and uses. (Rev: BL 2/15/00; HBG 10/00; SLJ 6/00) [546]

12432 Farndon, John. *Nitrogen* (5–8). Series: The Elements. 1998, Benchmark LB $22.79 (0-7614-0877-0). An informative science book that introduces nitrogen's properties, reactions, place in the periodic table, and importance in the human body and the environment, and environmental issues relating to nitrogen such as pollution from noxious gases and acid rain. (Rev: HBG 10/99; SLJ 2/99) [540]

12433 Farndon, John. *Oxygen* (5–8). Series: The Elements. 1998, Benchmark LB $22.79 (0-7614-0879-7). Oxygen, its properties, uses, and various chemical combinations are covered in this informative text that also discusses the ozone layer. (Rev: HBG 10/99; SLJ 2/99) [540]

12434 Fitzgerald, Karen. *The Story of Iron* (5–8). Series: First Books: Chemical Elements. 1997, Watts LB $23.00 (0-531-20270-4). This volume outlines the discovery, uses, and chemistry of iron, with explanations of its importance throughout history and the role it plays in our lives today. (Rev: BL 9/1/97; SLJ 10/97) [669]

12435 Fitzgerald, Karen. *The Story of Nitrogen* (5–8). Series: First Books: Chemical Elements. 1997, Watts LB $23.00 (0-531-20248-8). Nitrogen is introduced, with information on its atomic structure, properties, uses, and production. (Rev: BL 9/1/97; SLJ 10/97) [546]

12436 Fitzgerald, Karen. *The Story of Oxygen* (5–8). 1996, Watts LB $22.50 (0-531-20225-9). A discussion of the discovery of oxygen, its role in nature, and its chemistry. (Rev: BL 10/15/96; SLJ 9/96) [546]

12437 Gallant, Roy A. *The Ever-Changing Atom* (5–8). Series: The Story of Science. 1999, Benchmark LB $28.50 (0-7614-0961-0). Using a chronological approach, this book traces how and what we have found out about the atom and its structure. (Rev: BL 2/15/00; HBG 3/00; SLJ 2/00) [539]

12438 Gardner, Robert. *Science Projects About Chemistry* (6–12). Series: Science Projects. 2001, Enslow LB $20.95 (0-89490-531-7). Gardner conveys the fun of learning in this book about the uses of chemistry and science projects involving chemistry. (Rev: BL 3/15/01; HBG 10/01; SLJ 2/95) [540]

12439 Mebane, Robert C., and Thomas R. Rybolt. *Adventures with Atoms and Molecules, Vol. 5: Chemistry Experiments for Young People* (7–10). 1995, Enslow LB $19.95 (0-89490-606-2). A basic user's guide to start young people thinking scientifically, with ideas for science fair projects. (Rev: BL 12/1/95) [540]

12440 O'Daly, Anne. *Sodium* (4–8). Series: The Elements. 2001, Marshall Cavendish LB $22.79 (0-7614-1271-9). Diagrams and full-color illustrations are used to introduce sodium and its characteristics and importance in everyday life. (Rev: BL 3/15/02; HBG 3/02) [546]

12441 Stwertka, Albert. *The World of Atoms and Quarks* (7–12). Series: Scientific American Sourcebooks. 1995, Twenty-First Century LB $28.90 (0-8050-3533-8). Using profiles of important scientists, this work traces humankind's quest for an understanding of matter and its building blocks. (Rev: BL 12/1/95; BR 3–4/96; SLJ 2/96) [539.7]

12442 Thomas, Jens. *Silicon* (4–8). Series: The Elements. 2001, Marshall Cavendish LB $22.79 (0-7614-1274-3). Thomas introduces this important element and its origins, discovery, and many uses. (Rev: BL 3/15/02; HBG 3/02) [546]

12443 Uttley, Colin. *Magnesium* (4–8). Series: The Elements. 1999, Marshall Cavendish LB $22.79 (0-7614-0889-4). This book explores magnesium, a silvery metallic element important in living organisms, and explains its place in the periodic table, as well as its forms, uses, and properties. (Rev: BL 2/15/00; HBG 10/00) [546]

12444 Watt, Susan. *Chlorine* (4–8). Series: The Elements. 2001, Marshall Cavendish LB $22.79 (0-7614-1272-7). Using diagrams, photographs, and a concise text, this book introduces this active, nonmetallic element with material on its composition, characteristics, and many uses — including as a disinfectant and in water purification. (Rev: BL 3/15/02; HBG 3/02) [546]

12445 Watt, Susan. *Lead* (4–8). Series: The Elements. 2001, Marshall Cavendish LB $22.79 (0-7614-1273-5). Explores the history, origins, discovery, characteristics, and uses of this heavy metallic element in everyday life. (Rev: BL 3/15/02; HBG 3/02) [546]

12446 Watt, Susan. *Silver* (4–8). Illus. Series: The Elements. 2002, Benchmark LB $15.95 (0-7614-1464-9). A concise introduction to this element, its history, where it is found and how it is mined, and its many uses. Also in this series is *Potassium* (2002). (Rev: HBG 3/03; LMC 4–5/03; SLJ 4/03) [546]

Geology and Geography

Earth and Geology

12447 Allaby, Michael. *The Environment* (4–7). Series: Inside Look. 2000, Gareth Stevens LB $25.26 (0-8368-2725-2). Topics covered in this brief overview of the natural systems of our planet include the ozone layer, greenhouse effect, plant life and food webs, ecosystems and biomes, the water cycle, soil life, and rivers. (Rev: HBG 10/01; SLJ 3/01) [550]

12448 Campbell, Ann-Jeanette, and Ronald Rood. *The New York Public Library Incredible Earth: A Book of Answers for Kids* (4–7). Illus. 1996, Wiley paper $12.95 (0-471-14497-5). Questions and answers involving science, collected from the reference department of the New York Public Library. (Rev: BL 9/15/96; SLJ 1/97) [550]

12449 Downs, Sandra. *Shaping the Earth: Erosion* (5–8). Series: Exploring Planet Earth. 2000, Twenty-First Century LB $24.90 (0-7613-1414-8). This book explores the force of erosion and how such phenomena as wind, waves, floods, rain, acid rain, freezing, and thawing can change the face of the land. (Rev: HBG 10/00; SLJ 7/00) [551]

12450 Gallant, Roy A. *Dance of the Continents* (5–8). Series: The Story of Science. 1999, Benchmark LB $28.50 (0-7614-0962-9). This book covers geological theory from the ancient Greeks to modern plate tectonics with material on earthquakes, volcanoes, geysers, and other phenomena. (Rev: BL 2/15/00; HBG 3/00; SLJ 3/00) [551]

12451 George, Linda. *Plate Tectonics* (4–9). Illus. 2003, Gale LB $23.70 (0-7377-1405-0). Concise information on the movement of continents, the formation of mountains, and volcanic and earthquake activity is presented with full-color photographs and diagrams. (Rev: SLJ 10/03) [551.1]

12452 Goodman, Billy. *Natural Wonders and Disasters* (4–7). Illus. Series: Planet Earth. 1991, Little, Brown $17.95 (0-316-32016-1). Full-color photographs help to explain the earth's natural wonders as well as such disasters as floods and typhoons. (Rev: BL 12/1/91; SLJ 1/92) [550]

12453 Hehner, Barbara Embury. *Blue Planet* (7–12). Series: Wide World. 1992, Harcourt $17.95 (0-15-200423-8). An examination of the interdependent systems that make up our planet, including plate tectonics, volcanoes, weather, satellites, and the ozone layer. (Rev: BL 11/15/92; SLJ 10/92) [508]

12454 *Inside the Earth* (6–9). Illus. Series: 21st Century Science. 2001, World Almanac LB $29.27 (0-8368-5002-5). An information-packed, highly visual exploration of the composition of the earth. (Rev: SLJ 4/02) [550]

12455 Loeschnig, Louis V. *Simple Earth Science Experiments with Everyday Materials* (6–8). Illus. 1996, Sterling $14.95 (0-8069-0898-X). A well-organized book of activities and demonstrations that explore such subjects as soil, time, earthquakes, glaciers, gravity, and conservation. (Rev: BL 10/15/96) [550]

12456 O'Neill, Catherine. *Natural Wonders of North America* (7–12). Illus. 1984, National Geographic LB $12.50 (0-87044-519-7). Excellent color photographs complement the text and maps that describe such natural wonders as tundra regions, volcanoes, glaciers, and the Badlands of South Dakota. [557]

12457 *Our Planet Today* (6–9). Illus. Series: 21st Century Science. 2001, World Almanac LB $29.27 (0-8368-5003-3). This information-packed, highly visual exploration of our planet looks at physical geography and cartography. (Rev: SLJ 4/02) [551.41]

12458 Redfern, Martin. *The Kingfisher Young People's Book of Planet Earth* (4–8). 1999, Kingfisher

$21.95 (0-7534-5180-8). A useful, enjoyable look at the earth's geology, atmosphere, and weather. (Rev: HBG 10/00; SLJ 2/00) [525]

12459 Silverstein, Alvin, et al. *Plate Tectonics* (5–8). Illus. Series: Science Concepts. 1998, Twenty-First Century LB $26.90 (0-7613-3225-1). An account that includes an introduction to the earth's crust and mantle, an explanation of plate tectonics theory, and information on the prediction of volcanic eruptions and earthquakes. (Rev: BL 2/1/99; HBG 10/99; SLJ 5/99) [555.1]

12460 VanCleave, Janice. *Janice VanCleave's A+ Projects in Earth Science: Winning Experiments for Science Fairs and Extra Credit* (5–10). Illus. 1999, Wiley $32.50 (0-471-17769-5); paper $12.95 (0-471-17770-9). Thirty projects varying in complexity are included in this exploration of topography, minerals, atmospheric composition, the ocean floor, and erosion. (Rev: BL 12/1/98; SLJ 6/99) [550]

Earthquakes and Volcanoes

12461 Archer, Jules. *Earthquake!* (5–7). Illus. Series: Nature's Disasters. 1991, Macmillan LB $16.95 (0-89686-593-2). This colorful account discusses the causes and effects of earthquakes and includes a list of famous quakes of the past. (Rev: BCCB 7–8/91; BL 8/91) [551.2]

12462 Asimov, Isaac. *How Did We Find Out About Volcanoes?* (5–7). 1981, Avon paper $1.95 (0-380-59626-1). An overview of volcanoes, from Pompeii to Mount St. Helens. [550]

12463 Booth, Basil. *Earthquakes and Volcanoes* (5–8). Illus. Series: Repairing the Damage. 1992, Macmillan LB $13.95 (0-02-711735-9). A well-organized photoessay that explains the interrelationship between earthquakes and volcanoes. (Rev: BL 9/15/92; SLJ 10/92) [551.2]

12464 Burleigh, Robert, adapt. *Volcanoes: Journey to the Crater's Edge* (5–9). Photos by Philippe Bourseiller. 2003, Abrams $14.95 (0-8109-4590-8). Volcanoes, lava lakes, ash plumes, and other related phenomena are beautifully illustrated in this over-sized photoessay. (Rev: SLJ 12/03) [550]

12465 Christian, Spencer, and Antonia Felix. *Shake, Rattle and Roll: The World's Most Amazing Natural Forces* (6–10). Series: Spencer Christian's World of Wonders. 1997, Wiley paper $12.95 (0-471-15291-9). This book supplies good information and suitable projects involving earthquakes and volcanoes, with material on topics including plate tectonics, seismic waves, geysers, and hot springs. (Rev: SLJ 6/98) [551.2]

12466 Elting, Mary, et al. *Volcanoes and Earthquakes* (4–7). 1990, Simon & Schuster $9.95 (0-

671-67217-7). Disasters are covered with a you-are-there approach. (Rev: BL 2/1/91) [551.2]

12467 Levy, Matthys, and Mario Salvadori. *Earthquake Games* (5–8). Illus. 1997, Simon & Schuster $16.00 (0-689-81367-8). Games, experiments, and a lucid text answer such questions as what causes earthquakes and volcanoes and what their effects are. (Rev: BL 9/1/97; HBG 3/98; SLJ 12/97) [551.22]

12468 Lindop, Laurie. *Probing Volcanoes* (5–8). Illus. Series: Science on the Edge. 2003, Millbrook LB $26.90 (0-7613-2700-2). A lively introduction to the history of volcanoes and eruptions, the scientists who dare to study volcanoes, and techniques for collecting data and forecasting volcanic activity. (Rev: BL 12/1/03) [551.21]

12469 Sutherland, Lin. *Earthquakes and Volcanoes* (4–8). Illus. Series: Pathfinders. 2000, Reader's Digest $16.99 (1-57584-374-9). An oversize volume that uses double-page spreads to introduce earthquakes and volcanoes along with material on major disasters, their causes, and their effects. (Rev: BL 9/15/00; HBG 3/01) [551.2]

12470 Thomas, Margaret. *Volcano!* (5–7). Illus. Series: Nature's Disasters. 1991, Macmillan LB $12.95 (0-89686-595-9). This book gives solid information about the causes of volcanic eruptions and their effects and includes famous volcanic disasters of the past. (Rev: BL 8/91) [551.2]

12471 VanCleave, Janice. *Janice VanCleave's Volcanoes: Mind-Boggling Experiments You Can Turn into Science Fair Projects* (4–7). Illus. 1994, Wiley paper $10.95 (0-471-30811-0). Twenty experiments that explore the properties of erupting volcanoes using simple materials that can often be found around the house. (Rev: BL 7/94; SLJ 8/94) [551.2]

12472 Van Rose, Susanna. *Volcano and Earthquake* (5–9). Series: Eyewitness Books. 1992, Knopf $20.99 (0-679-91685-7). A basic, well-illustrated book that explains the causes and effects of volcano eruptions and earthquakes. (Rev: BL 11/1/92) [551.2]

12473 Watson, Nancy. *Our Violent Earth* (4–8). Illus. 1982, National Geographic LB $12.50 (0-87044-388-7). A discussion of such phenomena as earthquakes, volcanoes, and floods. [363.3]

Icebergs and Glaciers

12474 Walker, Sally M. *Glaciers: Ice on the Move* (4–7). Illus. 1990, Carolrhoda LB $19.93 (0-87614-373-7). This book explains how glaciers are formed, where they are found, and how they move. (Rev: BCCB 9/90; BL 6/15/90; SLJ 8/90) [551.3]

Physical Geography

General and Miscellaneous

12475 Blaustein, Daniel. *The Everglades and the Gulf Coast* (4–7). 1999, Benchmark LB $27.07 (0-7614-0896-7). In addition to a tour of the wetlands of the southeastern United States, this book describes how the plants and animals there interact and how this changes human life. (Rev: HBG 10/00; SLJ 4/00) [574.5]

12476 Burnie, David. *Shrublands* (5–8). Series: Biomes Atlases. 2003, Raintree Steck-Vaughn LB $31.42 (0-7398-5514-X). This comprehensive overview of shrublands describes the climate, flora and fauna, people, and future of these areas, and includes good maps. (Rev: SLJ 9/03) [577.3]

12477 Gallant, Roy A. *Limestone Caves* (4–7). Series: First Books. 1998, Watts LB $23.00 (0-531-20293-3). Following a general history of caves and their different types, this account focuses on the limestone variety, how they are formed, where they are found, and the creatures that live within them. (Rev: HBG 10/98; SLJ 9/98) [551.4]

12478 George, Jean Craighead. *One Day in the Alpine Tundra* (4–7). 1984, HarperCollins LB $15.89 (0-690-04326-0). An introduction to the geology and ecology of the alpine tundra and an exciting story are woven together. [574.5]

12479 Lisowski, Marylin, and Robert A. Williams. *Wetlands* (7–10). Series: Exploring Ecosystems. 1997, Watts LB $23.00 (0-531-11311-6). Once considered useless places, wetlands are revealed in this book to be areas that provide us with food and water, house a variety of wildlife, act as flood barriers, and provide protection against erosion. (Rev: BL 5/1/97; SLJ 6/97) [574.5]

12480 Lye, Keith. *Coasts* (4–7). Illus. 1989, Silver Burdett LB $12.95 (0-382-09790-4). An explanation of the effects of receding and advancing coastlines. (Rev: BL 5/1/89)

12481 Ricciuti, Edward R. *Chaparral* (5–7). Illus. Series: Biomes of the World. 1996, Benchmark LB $25.64 (0-7614-0137-7). An examination of the climate, vegetation, and life cycles of the chaparral, the biome situated between desert and grassland or forest and grassland, as in western North America from Oregon to Baja California. (Rev: SLJ 7/96) [574.5]

12482 Sauvain, Philip. *Rivers and Valleys* (4–7). Illus. Series: Geography Detectives. 1996, Carolrhoda LB $23.95 (0-87614-996-4). In two-page spreads, rivers and valleys are introduced, with material on geology, flood control, wildlife, and tourism. (Rev: SLJ 3/97) [551.48]

Deserts

12483 MacQuitty, Miranda. *Desert* (5–9). Series: Eyewitness Books. 1994, Knopf $20.99 (0-679-96003-1). A nicely illustrated book on the origins of deserts, where they are found, and their ecology. (Rev: BL 10/15/94) [910]

12484 Patent, Dorothy Hinshaw. *Life in a Desert* (5–8). Series: Ecosystems in Action. 2003, Lerner LB $26.60 (0-8225-2140-7). This account explores the plant and animal life in deserts and how human intervention has changed this ecosystem. (Rev: BL 9/15/03; HBG 10/03) [574.5]

12485 Ruth, Maria Mudd. *The Deserts of the Southwest* (5–8). Series: Ecosystems of North America. 1998, Benchmark LB $27.07 (0-7614-0899-1). After an overview of the deserts of the Southwest and how they were formed, this book introduces desert plants and wildlife, how they interact, adaptations they have made to the desert environment, and the impact of human development. (Rev: BR 5–6/99; HBG 10/99; SLJ 2/99) [591]

12486 Sayre, April Pulley. *Desert* (4–7). Illus. Series: Exploring Earth's Biomes. 1994, Twenty-First Century LB $25.90 (0-8050-2825-0). After a general introduction to deserts, a specific one is explored in brief chapters with excellent illustrations. (Rev: BL 1/1/95*; SLJ 1/95) [574.5]

12487 Steele, Philip. *Deserts* (5–8). Series: Pocket Facts. 1991, Macmillan LB $11.95 (0-89686-588-6). A concise introduction to deserts, featuring easily understand facts and photographs. (Rev: BL 3/15/92) [508.315]

12488 Twist, Clint. *Deserts* (5–8). Series: Ecology Watch. 1991, Dillon LB $13.95 (0-87518-490-1). Traces the evolution of deserts, explains why they are threatened, and offers possible solutions to specific problems. (Rev: BL 3/1/92; SLJ 4/92) [574.5]

Forests and Rain Forests

12489 Aldis, Rodney. *Rainforests* (5–8). Illus. Series: Ecology Watch. 1991, Macmillan LB $13.95 (0-87518-495-2). In an attractive, oversized format, this book discusses how rain forests evolved, why they are threatened, and the plants and animals found in them. (Rev: BL 3/1/92; SLJ 4/92) [574.5]

12490 Chinery, Michael. *Poisoners and Pretenders* (5–8). Series: Secrets of the Rainforests. 2000, Crabtree LB $21.28 (0-7787-0219-7); paper $7.95 (0-7787-0229-4). After a brief description of a rain forest, this book looks at animals found there and their mimicry, camouflage, venom, natural selection, and adaptation to the environment. Also use *Predators and Prey* (2000). (Rev: SLJ 2/01) [574.5]

12491 Collard, Sneed B. *Monteverde: Science and Scientists in a Costa Rican Cloud Forest* (6–9). Illus. 1997, Watts LB $25.00 (0-531-11369-8). A stunning introduction to the amazing tropical cloud forest of Costa Rica, the town of Monteverde founded by Quakers, and the efforts to keep the paradise from disappearing. (Rev: BL 9/1/97; SLJ 9/97) [577.3]

12492 Forsyth, Adrian. *How Monkeys Make Chocolate: Foods and Medicines from the Rainforests* (5–8). Illus. 1995, Firefly $16.95 (1-895688-45-0); paper $9.95 (1-895688-32-9). An account of the interdependence of plants, animals, and humans in the world's rain forests. (Rev: BL 12/1/95; SLJ 1/96) [581.6]

12493 Goodman, Susan E. *Bats, Bugs, and Biodiversity: Adventures in the Amazonian Rain Forest* (4–8). Illus. 1995, Simon & Schuster $16.00 (0-689-31942-6). Some junior high students learn firsthand about the Amazon rain forest and its endangered ecology. (Rev: BL 12/1/97) [508]

12494 Jackson, Tom. *Tropical Forests* (5–8). Series: Biomes Atlases. 2003, Raintree Steck-Vaughn LB $31.42 (0-7398-5250-7). This comprehensive overview of tropical forests describes the climate, flora and fauna, people, and future of these areas, and includes good maps. (Rev: SLJ 9/03) [577.34]

12495 Johnson, Linda Carlson. *Rain Forests: A Pro/Con Issue* (4–8). Series: Hot Issues. 1999, Enslow LB $21.95 (0-7660-1202-6). This book describes the rain forests of the world, how political and economic interests are destroying them, efforts to save them, and the pros and cons of conserving them. (Rev: HBG 10/00; SLJ 4/00) [574.5]

12496 Kallen, Stuart A. *Life in the Amazon Rain Forest* (6–10). Series: The Way People Live. 1999, Lucent LB $27.45 (1-56006-387-4). A description of the Amazon rain forest and of the Yanomami people who live there, their traditions, food, shelter, religion, encounters with Europeans, and the continuous threats to their existence. (Rev: HBG 4/00; SLJ 7/99) [574.5]

12497 Kaplan, Elizabeth. *Taiga* (5–7). Illus. Series: Biomes of the World. 1996, Benchmark LB $25.64 (0-7614-0135-0). This account discusses the climate, animal and plant life, soil, and seasonal changes in the taiga, the extensive forest in the Northern Hemisphere. (Rev: SLJ 7/96) [574.5]

12498 Lasky, Kathryn. *The Most Beautiful Roof in the World: Exploring the Rainforest Canopy* (5–8). 1997, Harcourt $18.00 (0-15-200893-4); paper $9.00 (0-15-200897-7). The canopy of plants and animals found in the rain forest of Belize is explored by the author, a biologist, who also explains the methods scientists use to conduct research in this environment, sometimes under extremely difficult conditions. (Rev: BL 4/1/97; SLJ 4/97) [574.5]

12499 Lewington, Anna. *Atlas of the Rain Forests* (6–12). 1997, Raintree Steck-Vaughn $22.98 (0-8172-4756-4). Enhanced by maps and photographs, this work contains information on the plant and animal life found in rain forests, the cultures of the people who live in them, and how these environments are changed by economic development. (Rev: BL 5/15/97; SLJ 8/97) [574.5]

12500 Lewington, Anna, and Edward Parker. *People of the Rain Forests* (4–7). Series: Wide World. 1998, Raintree Steck-Vaughn $18.98 (0-8172-5061-1). As well as introducing rain forests, this book describes the people who live there, their tribal customs, their homes — including cities — and their everyday lives. (Rev: HBG 3/99; SLJ 1/99) [574.5]

12501 Lyman, Francesca, ed. *Inside the Dzanga-Sangha Rain Forest* (4–7). Illus. 1998, Workman paper $12.95 (0-7611-0870-X). Each page of this book is filled with gorgeous color photographs that introduce the rain forest ecosystem, daily life in it, and its rare plants, animals, and insects. (Rev: BL 12/15/98) [508.674]

12502 MacMillan, Dianne M. *Life in a Deciduous Forest* (5–8). Series: Ecosystems in Action. 2003, Lerner LB $26.60 (0-8225-4684-1). This book explores the ecosystem, its flora and fauna, where trees shed their leaves in autumn. (Rev: BL 9/15/03; HBG 10/03) [574.5]

12503 Montgomery, Sy. *Encantado: Pink Dolphin of the Amazon* (5–8). 2002, Houghton $18.00 (0-618-13103-5). The author describes the flora and fauna of the South American rain forest seen in her unsuccessful journey to locate the encantado, the elusive pink dolphin. (Rev: BL 4/1/02; HB 7–8/02; HBG 10/02; SLJ 5/02*) [599.53]

12504 Morrison, Marion. *The Amazon Rain Forest and Its People* (5–8). Series: People and Places. 1993, Thomson Learning LB $24.26 (1-56847-087-8). After a general history and a description of the region's plants, animals, and people, the author discusses the dangers developers pose to this rain forest. (Rev: BL 11/1/93) [333.75]

12505 Mutel, Cornelia F., and Mary M. Rodgers. *Our Endangered Planet: Tropical Rain Forests* (4–7). Illus. Series: Our Endangered Planet. 1991, Lerner LB $27.15 (0-8225-2503-8); paper $8.95 (0-8225-9629-6). Describes tropical rain forests and the environmental threats they face. (Rev: BL 6/15/91; SLJ 5/91) [333]

12506 Parker, Edward. *People* (5–8). Photos by author. Series: Rain Forest. 2003, Raintree Steck-Vaughn LB $27.12 (0-7398-5242-6). An introduction to the various peoples of the rain forest. (Rev: HBG 3/03; SLJ 1/03) [304.2]

12507 Parker, Edward. *Rain Forest Mammals* (5–9). Illus. Series: Rain Forest. 2002, Raintree Steck-Vaughn LB $27.12 (0-7398-5241-8). Mammals of the rain forest and the importance of preserving their habitat are introduced in close-up color photographs and a catchy layout, with a glossary, bibliography, and list of related organizations. Also use *Rain Forest Reptiles and Amphibians* (2002). (Rev: BL 12/1/02; HBG 3/03) [599]

12508 Rapp, Valerie. *Life in an Old Growth Forest* (5–8). Series: Ecosystems in Action. 2002, Lerner LB $26.60 (0-8225-2135-0). In pictures and text, this book introduces life in an established forest with material on the interdependence of organisms there, and how human intervention has changed this ecosystem. (Rev: BL 12/15/02; HBG 3/03; SLJ 2/03) [574.5]

12509 Sayre, April Pulley. *Taiga* (4–7). Illus. Series: Exploring Earth's Biomes. 1994, Twenty-First Century LB $25.90 (0-8050-2830-7). This book clearly describes the swampy, carnivorous forest and the wildlife found, for example, in northern Canada, where the tundra ends. (Rev: BL 1/15/95; SLJ 2/95) [574.5]

12510 Sayre, April Pulley. *Temperate Deciduous Forest* (4–7). Illus. Series: Exploring Earth's Biomes. 1994, Twenty-First Century LB $25.90 (0-8050-2828-5). Deciduous forests are introduced with material on their composition, uses, and the animal and other plant life found within their community. (Rev: BL 1/1/95*; SLJ 1/95) [574.5]

12511 Sayre, April Pulley. *Tropical Rain Forest* (4–7). Illus. Series: Exploring Earth's Biomes. 1994, Twenty-First Century LB $25.90 (0-8050-2826-9). The structure and contents of rain forests are explored with information on the plants, animals, and people that exist in this habitat. (Rev: BL 1/1/95; SLJ 1/95) [574.5]

12512 Welsbacher, Anne. *Life in a Rainforest* (5–8). Series: Ecosystems in Action. 2003, Lerner LB $26.60 (0-8225-4685-X). This illustrated account covers the plant and animal life in rain forests and explains how human intervention has changed, and often endangered, this ecosystem. (Rev: BL 9/15/03; HBG 10/03) [574.5]

Mountains

12513 Collinson, Alan. *Mountains* (5–8). Series: Ecology Watch. 1992, Dillon LB $13.95 (0-87518-493-6). A discussion of the formation of mountains, how they are gradually being eroded, the flora and fauna of these regions, and the need for preservation. (Rev: BL 11/1/92) [574.5]

12514 Cumming, David. *Mountains* (5–8). Illus. Series: Habitats. 1995, Thomson Learning LB $24.26 (1-56847-388-5). Material covered includes the geology of mountains, their formation, and the life they support, and the effects of industry,

tourism, and transportation. (Rev: BL 2/1/96) [551.4]

12515 Rotter, Charles. *Mountains* (5–8). Illus. Series: Images. 1994, Creative Editions LB $23.95 (0-88682-596-2). How mountains are formed is discussed, with material on how they change and the life they support. (Rev: SLJ 12/94) [551.4]

12516 Steele, Philip. *Mountains* (5–8). Series: Pocket Facts. 1991, Macmillan LB $11.95 (0-89686-587-8). Easy-to-understand facts about mountains, with many photographs. (Rev: BL 3/15/92) [910]

12517 Stronach, Neil. *Mountains* (4–8). Series: Endangered People and Places. 1996, Lerner LB $27.15 (0-8225-2777-4). Geological aspects of mountains are covered, as well as the adjustments people make to live in mountainous regions. (Rev: SLJ 11/96) [333.73]

Ponds, Rivers, and Lakes

12518 Beck, Gregor Gilpin. *Watersheds: A Practical Handbook for Healthy Water* (7–12). Illus. 1999, Firefly $19.95 (1-55037-330-1). This account highlights the importance of water in our lives, with special attention to pollution, flooding, and other environmental problems. (Rev: BL 9/1/99) [333.73]

12519 Cumming, David. *Rivers and Lakes* (5–8). Series: Habitats. 1995, Thomson Learning LB $24.26 (1-56847-389-3). The plant and animal life that is supported by lakes and rivers is introduced, with accompanying information on geology and pollution. (Rev: BL 2/1/96) [551.48]

12520 Ganeri, Anita. *Rivers, Ponds and Lakes* (5–8). Series: Ecology Watch. 1992, Dillon LB $13.95 (0-87518-497-9). A discussion of these water environments and how they are threatened by various forms of pollution. (Rev: BL 11/1/92) [574.5]

12521 Hoff, Mary, and Mary M. Rodgers. *Our Endangered Planet: Rivers and Lakes* (4–7). Illus. Series: Our Endangered Planet. 1991, Lerner LB $22.60 (0-8225-2501-1). The causes and possible cures of water pollution are examined. (Rev: BL 6/15/91; SLJ 5/91) [363.73]

12522 Loewer, Peter. *Pond Water Zoo: An Introduction to Microscopic Life* (5–8). Illus. 1996, Simon & Schuster $16.00 (0-689-31736-0). Various life forms found in a drop of pond water are revealed by microscope. (Rev: BCCB 12/96; BL 9/15/96; SLJ 2/97) [576]

12523 Martin, Patricia A. *Rivers and Streams* (7–12). Illus. 1999, Watts LB $23.00 (0-531-11523-2). This book contains over 30 projects and experiments involving streams, rivers, and the life they support. (Rev: BL 6/1–15/99) [577.6]

12524 Parker, Steve. *Pond and River* (6–8). Illus. 1988, Knopf $20.99 (0-394-99615-1). In 28 short, lavishly illustrated chapters, various aspects of pond and river ecology are explored. (Rev: SLJ 12/88) [551.48]

12525 Rapp, Valerie. *Life in a River* (5–8). Illus. Series: Ecosystems in Action. 2002, Lerner LB $26.60 (0-8225-2136-9). The first title in a new series about ecosystems, this volume uses the example of the Columbia River to explain the concept and the interrelationship of rivers, animals, and humans. (Rev: BL 10/15/02; HBG 3/03; SLJ 1/03; VOYA 2/03) [577.6]

12526 Sayre, April Pulley. *Lake and Pond* (4–7). Illus. Series: Exploring Earth's Biomes. 1996, Twenty-First Century LB $25.90 (0-8050-4089-7). A colorful introduction to lake and pond habitats and the life forms found within them. (Rev: BL 6/1–15/96; SLJ 6/96) [574.05]

12527 Sayre, April Pulley. *River and Stream* (4–7). Illus. Series: Exploring Earth's Biomes. 1996, Twenty-First Century LB $25.90 (0-8050-4088-9). In a clearly written, informative style, this book presents material on rivers and streams, their ecology, and the various creatures and plants living in and around them. (Rev: BL 6/1–15/96; SLJ 6/96) [574.5]

12528 Stewart, Melissa. *Life in a Lake* (5–8). Series: Ecosystems in Action. 2002, Lerner LB $26.60 (0-8225-2138-5). The diversity and interdependence of life in a typical lake are introduced with material on how this ecosystem works and how man's interference has changed the balance of nature. (Rev: BL 12/15/02; HBG 3/03) [551.48]

12529 Walker, Sally M. *Life in an Estuary* (5–8). Series: Ecosystems in Action. 2002, Lerner LB $26.60 (0-8225-2137-7). A look at life at the tidal mouths of rivers and the diversity of life in these areas, its interdependence, the balance of nature, and how human interaction has changed this ecosystem. (Rev: BL 12/15/02; HBG 3/03; SLJ 2/03) [574]

Prairies and Grasslands

12530 Collinson, Alan. *Grasslands* (5–8). Illus. Series: Ecology Watch. 1992, Macmillan $13.95 (0-87518-492-8). The flora and fauna and ecological balance of a grassland environment are introduced. (Rev: BL 11/15/92) [574.5]

12531 Hoare, Ben. *Temperate Grasslands* (5–8). Series: Biomes Atlases. 2003, Raintree Steck-Vaughn LB $31.42 (0-7398-5249-3). This comprehensive overview of grasslands describes the climate, flora and fauna, people, and future of these areas, and includes good maps. (Rev: SLJ 9/03) [577.4]

12532 Martin, Patricia A. Fink. *Prairies, Fields, and Meadows* (8–12). Illus. Series: Exploring Ecosystems. 2003, Scholastic $23.00 (0-531-11859-2). An overview of the geological features and plant and animal life of grasslands, with activities. (Rev: BL 12/1/02) [577.4]

12533 Ormsby, Alison. *The Prairie* (5–8). Series: Ecosystems of North America. 1998, Benchmark LB $27.07 (0-7614-0897-5). A description of the prairie ecosystem and an examination of how the plants and animals in prairies affect one another and their environments. (Rev: BR 5–6/99; HBG 10/99; SLJ 2/99) [551.4]

12534 Patent, Dorothy Hinshaw. *Life in a Grassland* (5–8). Series: Ecosystems in Action. 2002, Lerner LB $26.60 (0-8225-2139-3). Using excellent pictures and a clear text, this volume explores the flora and fauna of different kinds of grasslands, with material on conservation. (Rev: BL 12/15/02; HBG 3/03) [574.5]

12535 Rotter, Charles. *The Prairie* (5–8). Illus. Series: Images. 1994, Creative Editions LB $17.95 (0-88682-598-9). The nature of prairie grasslands is introduced, with material on the animals and plants found there. (Rev: SLJ 12/94) [574.5]

12536 Sayre, April Pulley. *Grassland* (4–7). Illus. Series: Exploring Earth's Biomes. 1994, Twenty-First Century LB $25.90 (0-8050-2827-7). A well-organized, clearly written account that explains what grasslands are and where they exist and the interaction of the creatures who live in this biome. (Rev: BL 1/15/95; SLJ 2/95) [574.5]

Rocks, Minerals, and Soil

12537 Chesterman, Charles W., and Kurt E. Lowe. *The Audubon Society Field Guide to North American Rocks and Minerals* (7–12). Illus. 1978, Knopf $19.95 (0-394-50269-8). A basic guide that includes color illustrations of nearly 800 rocks and minerals. [549]

12538 Downs, Sandra. *Earth's Hidden Treasures* (6–9). Series: Exploring Planet Earth. 1999, Twenty-First Century LB $17.55 (0-7613-1411-3). All about the planet's rocks and minerals and how they have been used by humans. (Rev: HBG 4/00; SLJ 2/00) [549]

12539 Eid, Alain. *1000 Photos of Minerals and Fossils* (5–9). Photos by Michel Viard. 2000, Barron's paper $24.95 (0-7641-5218-1). An oversized, nicely illustrated volume that introduces minerals in their natural and refined states with material on sites, fossils, and jewelry. (Rev: SLJ 10/00) [548]

12540 Friend, Sandra. *Sinkholes* (4–7). Illus. 2002, Pineapple $18.95 (1-56164-258-4). This volume uncovers the geological and ecological causes of sinkholes, holes in the earth's surface that occur naturally, sometimes with devastating consequences. (Rev: BL 8/02; HBG 10/02) [551.44]

12541 Gallant, Roy A. *Rocks* (5–8). Series: Earth Sciences. 2000, Marshall Cavendish LB $22.79 (0-7614-1042-2). Illustrations and full-spread diagrams introduce rocks and minerals and their properties, forms, and uses. (Rev: BL 3/1/01; HBG 3/01; SLJ 3/01) [552.2]

12542 Kallen, Stuart A. *Gems* (4–7). Illus. Series: Wonders of the World. 2003, Gale LB $18.96 (0-7377-1028-4). The formation of precious stones, their mining, and individual stones of note are all covered here. (Rev: BL 5/1/03) [553.8]

12543 Kittinger, Jo S. *A Look at Rocks: From Coal to Kimberlite* (4–7). Illus. Series: First Books. 1997, Watts LB $23.00 (0-531-20310-7). This book describes rocks, rock formations, and such famous rocks as Mount Rushmore, with added material on how and why rocks change. (Rev: BL 12/1/97; HBG 3/98; SLJ 1/98) [552]

12544 Milne, Jean. *The Story of Diamonds* (5–8). 2000, Linnet LB $21.50 (0-208-02476-X). A book that explains where diamonds are found and how they are mined, evaluated, cut, polished, and used as jewels or in industry. (Rev: BL 2/1/00; HBG 10/00; SLJ 6/00; VOYA 4/01) [553.8]

12545 Pough, Frederick H. *A Field Guide to Rocks and Minerals*. 4th ed. (7–12). Illus. 1976, Houghton paper $20.00 (0-395-91096-X). This volume in the Peterson Field Guide series gives photographs and identifying information on 270 rocks and minerals. [549]

12546 Ricciuti, Edward R., and National Audubon Society, eds. *National Audubon Society First Field Guide: Rocks and Minerals* (5–8). Illus. 1998, Scholastic paper $17.95 (0-590-05463-5). A guide to equipment and techniques for observation and general information on geology, followed by an examination of 50 common rocks, their composition, texture, color, and environment. (Rev: BL 8/98; SLJ 8/98) [552]

12547 Staedter, Tracy. *Rocks and Minerals* (4–8). Series: Reader's Digest Pathfinders. 1999, Reader's Digest $16.99 (1-57584-290-4). An outstanding introduction to geology is organized in three sections — "Rocks," "Minerals," and "Collecting Rocks and Minerals" — with "discovery paths" featuring personal accounts, hands-on activities, vocabulary, and facts. (Rev: SLJ 11/99) [552]

12548 VanCleave, Janice. *Janice VanCleave's Rocks and Minerals: Mind-Boggling Experiments You Can Turn Into Science Fair Projects* (6–8). Series: Spectacular Science Projects. 1996, Wiley paper $10.95 (0-471-10269-5). In easy-to-follow steps, a series of experiments and projects are outlined that illustrate the properties and uses of a number of rocks and minerals. (Rev: BL 3/15/96; SLJ 3/96) [552]

12549 Winckler, Suzanne, and Mary M. Rodgers. *Soil* (4–7). Illus. Series: Our Endangered Planet. 1994, Lerner LB $27.15 (0-8225-2508-9). The depletion of our soil resources is the focus of this book, with emphasis on causes and possible solutions. (Rev: BL 5/15/94) [631.4]

Mathematics

General and Miscellaneous

12550 Caron, Lucille, and Philip M. St. Jacques. *Fractions and Decimals* (4–8). Illus. Series: Math Success. 2000, Enslow LB $17.95 (0-7660-1430-4). Many examples accompany explanations of how to add, subtract, multiply, and divide fractions and decimals. Also use *Addition and Subtraction* (2001). (Rev: HBG 3/01; SLJ 7/01) [513.2]

12551 Gardner, Robert. *Science Projects About Methods of Measuring* (6–12). Illus. Series: Science Projects. 2000, Enslow LB $19.95 (0-7660-1169-0). Different kinds of measurements are introduced, their relation to mass, area, volume, and temperature, and interesting suggestions for science projects in each category. (Rev: BL 4/1/00; HBG 9/00) [530.8.]

12552 Haven, Kendall. *Marvels of Math: Fascinating Reads and Awesome Activities* (5–8). Illus. 1998, Teacher Ideas paper $23.50 (1-56308-585-2). This book chronicles 16 turning points in the history of mathematics, including the discovery of zero and the story of the first female to become a professor of mathematics. (Rev: BR 5–6/99; VOYA 4/99) [510]

12553 Hershey, Robert L. *How to Think with Numbers* (7–9). Illus. 1987, Janson paper $7.95 (0-939765-14-4). Elementary mathematical concepts such as percentage and interest are explained through a series of puzzles and problems. [510]

12554 Lieberthal, Edwin M., and Bernadette Lieberthal. *The Complete Book of Fingermath* (7–12). Illus. 1979, McGraw-Hill $21.96 (0-07-037680-8). How hands and fingers can be turned into primitive computers. [513]

12555 Schwartz, David M. *G Is for Googol: A Math Alphabet Book* (6–10). Illus. 1998, Tricycle Pr. $15.95 (1-883672-58-9). A humorous romp through mathematical terms and concepts using an alphabetical approach and cartoon illustrations. (Rev: BL 10/15/98; HBG 3/99; SLJ 11/98) [510]

12556 Vorderman, Carol. *How Math Works* (5–8). Illus. 1996, Reader's Digest $24.00 (0-89577-850-5). A survey of the history of mathematics and the major concepts involved, with a variety of interesting activities. (Rev: BL 11/1/96) [510]

12557 Woods, Mary B., and Michael Woods. *Ancient Computing: From Counting to Calendars* (5–8). Series: Ancient Technologies. 2000, Runestone LB $25.26 (0-8225-2997-1). From the invention of the abacus and sundials to the creation of calculators and computers, this is a history of counting with material on the development of the calendar. (Rev: BL 9/15/00; HBG 3/01; SLJ 1/01) [510]

Algebra, Numbers, and Number Systems

12558 Fisher, Leonard Everett. *Number Art: Thirteen 123's from Around the World* (5–7). 1982, Macmillan paper $16.95 (0-02-735240-4). The development of numbers in various cultures.

Geometry

12559 Hansen-Smith, Bradford. *The Hands-On Marvelous Ball Book* (4–7). Illus. 1995, W. H. Freeman $16.95 (0-7167-6628-0). Directions are given for making a variety of geometric forms using such everyday materials as paper plates and bobby pins. (Rev: BL 10/15/95) [516]

Mathematical Games and Puzzles

12560 Blum, Raymond. *Math Tricks, Puzzles and Games* (4–7). Illus. 1994, Sterling $14.95 (0-8069-0582-4). Kids who like math will particularly enjoy these tricks, mathematical games and puzzles, and calculator riddles. (Rev: BL 11/1/94) [793.7]

12561 Burns, Marilyn. *The I Hate Mathematics! Book* (5–8). 1975, Little, Brown paper $14.99 (0-316-11741-2). A lively collection of puzzles and other mind stretchers that illustrate mathematical concepts.

12562 Burns, Marilyn. *Math for Smarty Pants: Or Who Says Mathematicians Have Little Pig Eyes* (6–9). Illus. 1982, Little, Brown paper $14.99 (0-316-11739-0). A series of games, puzzles, and tricks that use numbers. (Rev: BL 4/15/90) [513]

12563 Gardner, Martin. *Aha! Gotcha: Paradoxes to Puzzle and Delight* (7–12). Illus. 1982, W. H. Freeman paper $12.60 (0-7167-1361-6). A book of puzzles from *Scientific American* that involve mathematics and logic. [793.7]

12564 Gardner, Martin. *Perplexing Puzzles and Tantalizing Teasers* (4–7). 1988, Dover paper $6.95 (0-486-25637-5). An assortment of math problems, visual teasers, and tricky questions to challenge young, alert minds; perky drawings. [793.73]

12565 Hemme, Heinrich. *Math Mind Games* (5–9). 2002, Sterling paper $12.95 (0-8069-7691-8). Challenging text-based puzzles are accompanied by enlightening illustrations and an answer section that is clear and attractive. (Rev: SLJ 9/02) [793.7]

12566 Lobosco, Michael L. *Mental Math Challenges* (5–10). 1999, Sterling $17.95 (1-895569-50-8). The 37 projects in this fascinating collection involve construction of different mathematical applications, models, games, and drawings and are grouped under such headings as "Solitaire Games," "Math in Everyday Life Situations," and "Instant Calculations and Mind Reading." (Rev: SLJ 8/99) [510]

12567 Markle, Sandra. *Discovering Graph Secrets: Experiments, Puzzles, and Games Exploring Graphs* (4–8). 1997, Simon & Schuster $18.00 (0-689-31942-8). An entertaining and informative book that introduces four different graphs and their uses. (Rev: BL 2/15/98; HBG 3/98; SLJ 3/98) [511]

12568 Markle, Sandra. *Measuring Up! Experiments, Puzzles, and Games Exploring Measurement* (4–7). Illus. 1995, Atheneum $17.00 (0-689-31904-5). This book explains through a series of activities how we measure a number of things including temperature, height of trees and flagpoles, weight, and distance. (Rev: SLJ 1/96*) [512]

12569 Salvadori, Mario, and Joseph P. Wright. *Math Games for Middle School: Challenges and Skill-Builders for Students at Every Level* (5–8). Illus. 1998, Chicago Review paper $14.95 (1-55652-288-6). After explaining the concepts involved in such mathematical areas as geometry, arithmetic, graphing, and linear equations, this work presents a series of puzzles for readers to solve. (Rev: BL 11/1/98) [510]

12570 Sharp, Richard M., and Seymour Metzner. *The Sneaky Square and 113 Other Math Activities for Kids* (4–8). Illus. 1990, TAB $15.95 (0-8306-8474-3); paper $8.95 (0-8306-3474-6). Readers are challenged to solve classic as well as new math and logic problems. (Rev: BL 1/1/91) [793.7]

12571 Vecchione, Glen. *Math Challenges: Puzzles, Tricks and Games* (6–10). Illus. 1997, Sterling $14.95 (0-8069-8114-8). A slim volume that contains a number of mathematical puzzles arranged by subject and followed by the solutions. (Rev: SLJ 10/97) [510]

12572 Wise, Bill. *Whodunit Math Puzzles* (5–8). Illus. 2001, Sterling $14.95 (0-8069-5896-0). Cal Q. Leiter tests his wit in a number of pesky puzzles. (Rev: BL 6/1–15/01; HBG 10/01) [793.7]

Meteorology

General and Miscellaneous

12573 Allaby, Michael. *Fog, Smog and Poisoned Rain* (7–12). Series: Dangerous Weather. 2003, Facts on File $35.00 (0-8160-4789-8). Natural sources of pollution such as volcanoes are included in this survey of dangerous weather phenomena. (Rev: SLJ 10/03) [363.739]

12574 Facklam, Margery, and Howard Facklam. *Changes in the Wind: Earth's Shifting Climate* (6–9). Illus. 1986, Harcourt $14.95 (0-15-216115-5). An excellent explanation of what causes climate and how and why it changes. (Rev: BL 8/86; SLJ 12/86) [551.6]

12575 Smith, Trevor. *Earth's Changing Climate* (5–8). Series: Understanding Global Issues. 2003, Smart Apple $19.95 (1-58340-358-2). Topics including global warming are discussed in this well-organized look at the world's climate, how it is gradually changing, and what can be done about it. (Rev: BL 11/15/03; SLJ 12/03) [551.6]

Air

12576 Friend, Sandra. *Earth's Wild Winds* (5–8). Illus. Series: Exploring Planet Earth. 2002, Twenty-First Century LB $24.90 (0-7613-2673-1). Report writers will find good material in this attractively presented coverage of all kinds of winds that also looks at the ways in which humans have attempted to harness wind power. (Rev: HBG 3/03; SLJ 10/02) [551.518]

12577 Gallant, Roy A. *Atmosphere: Sea of Air* (4–8). Illus. Series: Earthworks. 2003, Marshall Cavendish $19.95 (0-7614-1366-9). An intriguing and well-presented look at how changes in the atmosphere affect us — from storms to beautiful rainbows and sunsets — and how we affect the atmosphere. (Rev: BL 3/15/03; HBG 3/03) [551.51]

12578 Gardner, Robert. *Science Project Ideas About Air* (4–7). Series: Science Project Ideas. 1997, Enslow LB $19.95 (0-89490-838-3). The properties of air are explored in a series of experiments and projects with easy-to-follow directions. (Rev: BL 12/15/97; BR 5–6/98; HBG 3/98; SLJ 4/98) [678.5]

12579 Gardner, Robert, and David Webster. *Experiments with Balloons* (4–7). Illus. Series: Getting Started in Science. 1995, Enslow LB $20.95 (0-89490-669-0). More than a dozen experiments explore balloons and the properties of air. (Rev: BL 12/1/95; SLJ 3/96) [507.8]

12580 Hoff, Mary, and Mary M. Rodgers. *Atmosphere* (4–7). Illus. Series: Our Endangered Planet. 1995, Lerner LB $27.15 (0-8225-2509-7). This account describes the atmosphere and current threats including the ozone layer problem. (Rev: BL 8/95; SLJ 12/95) [363.73]

12581 Yount, Lisa, and Mary M. Rodgers. *Our Endangered Planet: Air* (4–7). Illus. Series: Our Endangered Planet. 1995, Lerner LB $27.15 (0-8225-2510-0). The emphasis in this book is on how air pollution has become a major environmental issue and how everyone can take action to improve air quality. (Rev: BL 10/15/95) [363.73]

Storms

12582 Allaby, Michael. *Hurricanes* (7–12). Series: Dangerous Weather. 1997, Facts on File $35.00 (0-8160-3516-4). An exhaustive introduction to hurricanes covering such topics as conditions that can lead to them, why they are common in particular areas, historic hurricanes, their naming and tracking, and how global climate changes will affect them. (Rev: BR 1–2/98; SLJ 4/98) [551.5]

12583 Allaby, Michael. *Tornadoes* (7–12). Series: Dangerous Weather. 1997, Facts on File $35.00 (0-8160-3517-2). This excellent book on tornadoes describes how they begin, their structure, travel patterns, interiors, historic tornadoes, and when and where tornadoes occur. (Rev: BR 1–2/98; SLJ 4/98) [551.55]

12584 Allaby, Michael. *Tornadoes and Other Dramatic Weather Systems* (4–8). Series: Secret Worlds. 2001, DK paper $5.95 (0-7894-7980-X). Unusual page design and attractive illustrations are found in this book on violent weather systems with an emphasis on tornadoes, how they are formed and tracked, and their effects when they strike. (Rev: BL 10/15/01; HBG 3/02) [551.5]

12585 Archer, Jules. *Hurricane!* (5–7). Illus. Series: Nature's Disasters. 1991, Macmillan LB $12.95 (0-89686-597-5). In addition to many real-life examples, this book covers the causes of hurricanes and how we can protect ourselves against them. (Rev: BL 8/91) [551.51]

12586 Archer, Jules. *Tornado!* (5–7). Illus. Series: Nature's Disasters. 1991, Macmillan LB $12.95 (0-89686-594-0). Full-color photographs add to the drama of this weather phenomenon. (Rev: BL 8/91) [551.55]

12587 Bredeson, Carmen. *The Mighty Midwest Flood: Raging Rivers* (4–8). Series: American Disasters. 1999, Enslow LB $18.95 (0-7660-1221-2). This account describes the terrible midwestern flood of 1993 and gives background information on the Mississippi River complex and on the causes of floods. (Rev: BL 10/15/99; HBG 3/00) [363.4]

12588 De Hahn, Tracee. *The Blizzard of 1888* (7–12). Series: Great Disasters: Reforms and Ramifications. 2000, Chelsea $21.95 (0-7910-5787-9). Exciting illustrations and eyewitness account enhance this exploration of the impact of this famous blizzard and of the changes in infrastructure and services that resulted from it. (Rev: BL 4/15/01; HBG 10/01; SLJ 6/01) [974.7]

12589 Gow, Mary. *Johnstown Flood: The Day the Dam Burst* (4–8). Series: American Disasters. 2003, Enslow LB $18.95 (0-7660-2109-2). The story of the terrible Pennsylvania flood of 1889 that resulted in more than 2,000 deaths. (Rev: BL 11/15/03; HBG 10/03) [973.8]

12590 Greenberg, Keith E. *Storm Chaser: Into the Eye of a Hurricane* (4–7). Series: Risky Business. 1997, Blackbirch LD $24.94 (1-56711-161-0). Tells about the people who track the paths of hurricanes and the dangers they often face. (Rev: BL 10/15/97; HBG 3/98; SLJ 12/97) [551.55]

12591 Keller, Ellen. *Floods!* (4–7). Series: Weather Channel. 1999, Simon & Schuster paper $3.99 (0-689-82021-6). Personal accounts are used in an examination of the various causes and types of floods and the damage they cause. (Rev: SLJ 10/99) [363.3]

12592 Lauber, Patricia. *Flood: Wrestling with the Mississippi* (5–8). Illus. 1996, National Geographic $18.95 (0-7922-4141-X). An introduction to floods that focuses on the great Mississippi River flood of 1993. (Rev: BL 10/15/96; SLJ 11/96*) [363.3]

12593 Lauber, Patricia. *Hurricanes: Earth's Mightiest Storms* (4–8). Illus. 1996, Scholastic paper $17.95 (0-590-47406-5). Beginning with an actual hurricane that ravaged Long Island in 1938, this account discusses the causes and effects of these mighty storms and how they are tracked. (Rev: BCCB 10/96; BL 10/1/96; HB 9–10/96; SLJ 9/96*) [363.3]

12594 Lindop, Laurie. *Chasing Tornadoes* (5–8). Illus. Series: Science on the Edge. 2003, Millbrook LB $26.90 (0-7613-2703-7). A lively introduction to tornadoes, the scientists who dare to study them, and techniques for collecting data and forecasting tornado activity. (Rev: BL 12/1/03) [551.55]

12595 Nicolson, Cynthia Pratt. *Hurricane!* (4–8). Illus. Series: Disaster. 2002, Kids Can $14.95 (1-55074-906-4); paper $6.95 (1-55074-970-6). An accessible text and many photographs provide information on hurricane formation and intensity, on the preparations for major hurricanes, and on famous storms of the past. (Rev: HBG 3/03; SLJ 12/02) [551.552]

12596 Rose, Sally. *Tornadoes!* (4–7). Series: Weather Channel. 1999, Simon & Schuster paper $3.99 (0-689-82022-4). The causes of tornado formation are covered plus material on types of tornadoes, wind intensity, tracking and forecasting, and safety precautions. (Rev: SLJ 10/99) [551.5]

12597 Sherrow, Victoria. *Hurricane Andrew: Nature's Rage* (4–8). Series: American Disasters. 1998, Enslow LB $18.95 (0-7660-1057-0). The story of the storm that caused millions of dollars of damage on the Atlantic Coast, told in dramatic text and pictures. (Rev: BL 1/1–15/99; BR 5–6/99; HBG 3/99; VOYA 4/99) [551.5]

12598 Sherrow, Victoria. *Plains Outbreak Tornadoes: Killer Twisters* (4–8). Series: American Disasters. 1998, Enslow LB $18.95 (0-7660-1059-7). The causes and effects of the giant tornadoes that occur in the Midwest, with details of some of the most horrendous. (Rev: BL 1/1–15/99; BR 5–6/99; HBG 3/99) [551.55]

12599 Simon, Seymour. *Tornadoes* (4–8). 1999, Morrow LB $16.89 (0-688-14647-3). Well-organized text discusses the weather conditions that give rise to tornadoes, how they form, where they are most likely to occur, and how scientists predict and track them, supplemented by large, riveting photographs showing meteorologists at work, a variety of tornadoes, and the devastation caused by major tornadoes. (Rev: BCCB 4/99; BL 5/99; HBG 9/99; SLJ 6/99) [551.55]

12600 Wade, Mary Dodson. *Tsunami: Monster Waves* (4–8). Series: American Disasters. 2002, Enslow LB $18.95 (0-7660-1786-9). This book explains in photographs and text how these giant sea swells are created, how they are tracked, and their effects. (Rev: BL 6/1–15/02; HBG 10/02; SLJ 10/02) [551.55]

12601 Walters, John. *Flood!* (5–7). Illus. Series: Nature's Disasters. 1991, Macmillan LB $12.95 (0-89686-596-7). A dramatic account of floods is enhanced by full-color photographs. (Rev: BL 8/91) [551.48]

Water

12602 Branley, Franklyn M. *Down Comes the Rain* (5–8). Series: Let's-Read-and-Find-Out. 1997, HarperCollins LB $17.89 (0-06-025338-X). An introduction to rain and hail as well as the water cycle. (Rev: BL 9/1/97; HBG 3/98; SLJ 10/97) [551.57]

12603 Cossi, Olga. *Water Wars: The Fight to Control and Conserve Nature's Most Precious Resource* (6–12). 1993, Macmillan LB $13.95 (0-02-724595-0). Discusses the sources and uses of fresh water and examines the reasons for drought, water quality problems, and how to conserve water. (Rev: BL 11/1/93; SLJ 2/94; VOYA 4/94) [333.91]

12604 Gallant, Roy A. *Water* (5–8). Series: Earth Sciences. 2000, Marshall Cavendish LB $22.79 (0-7614-1040-6). This work introduces the importance of water on the earth, its three states, and the water cycle. (Rev: BL 3/1/01; HBG 3/01; SLJ 5/01) [551.57]

12605 Gallant, Roy A. *Water: Our Precious Resource* (4–8). Illus. Series: Earthworks. 2003, Marshall Cavendish $19.95 (0-7614-1365-0). A thought-provoking and well-presented overview of the sources of water; the ways in which we use, misuse, and recycle water; and efforts to preserve this vital natural resource. (Rev: BL 3/15/03; HBG 3/03; SLJ 2/03) [553.7]

12606 Gardner, Robert. *Experimenting with Water* (7–12). Series: Venture. 1993, Watts paper $24.00 (0-531-12549-1). The unusual properties of water are described in these simple experiments and "puzzlers" that provide clear explanations of scientific concepts. (Rev: BL 2/15/94; SLJ 4/94) [546]

12607 Morgan, Sally, and Adrian Morgan. *Water* (4–7). Illus. Series: Designs in Science. 1994, Facts on File $23.00 (0-8160-2982-2). The importance and uses of water are described, with information on water storage, filtering, and conservation, plus activities and experiments. (Rev: BL 7/94) [533.7]

12608 Ocko, Stephanie. *Water: Almost Enough for Everyone* (5–10). 1995, Atheneum $16.00 (0-689-31797-2). Ocko traces the interconnectedness of the earth's ecosystems and provides ways people can conserve water and care for the environment. (Rev: BL 6/1–15/95; SLJ 6/95; VOYA 12/95) [363.3]

12609 O'Neill, Mary. *Water Squeeze* (4–7). Series: SOS Planet Earth. 1991, Troll paper $5.95 (0-8167-2081-9). Recent problems, such as a massive die-off of seals, are discussed in this look at the threats to our water supply. (Rev: BL 6/15/91) [363.73]

Weather

12610 Allaby, Michael. *Droughts* (6–12). Illus. Series: Dangerous Weather. 1997, Facts on File $35.00 (0-8160-3519-9). Topics discussed in this comprehensive volume include how droughts are classified, droughts of the past, the Dust Bowl, irrigation, water storage, saving water, and jet streams and storm tracks. (Rev: BL 12/1/97) [551.55]

12611 Arnold, Caroline. *El Niño: Stormy Weather for People and Wildlife* (4–8). Illus. 1998, Clarion $16.00 (0-395-77602-3). A brief overview of El Niño, its causes and history, and how tracking and forecasting are used to make predictions. (Rev: BL 10/1/98; BR 5–6/99; HBG 10/99; SLJ 12/98) [551.6]

12612 Bredeson, Carmen. *El Nino and La Nina: Deadly Weather* (4–8). Series: American Disasters. 2002, Enslow LB $18.95 (0-7660-1551-3). A well-researched account of these two weather phenomena, their effects, and how they can be traced. (Rev: BL 6/1–15/02; HBG 10/02; SLJ 6/02) [551.6]

12613 Cobb, Allan B. *Weather Observation Satellites* (5–9). Series: The Library of Satellites. 2003, Rosen LB $26.50 (0-8239-3856-5). This book shows how the development of satellites from the 1960s on has provided us with clear weather observations and accurate forecasts. (Rev: BL 11/15/03) [551.6]

12614 Dickinson, Terence. *Exploring the Sky by Day: The Equinox Guide to Weather and the Atmosphere* (7–10). Illus. 1988, Camden House paper $9.95 (0-920656-71-4). A book about weather that explores such subjects as types of clouds and kinds of precipitation. (Rev: BL 3/1/89; SLJ 1/89) [551.6]

12615 Elsom, Derek. *Weather Explained: A Beginner's Guide to the Elements* (4–8). Illus. Series:

Your World Explained. 1997, Holt $18.95 (0-8050-4875-8). Basic material on clouds and winds is followed by a discussion of the world's changing climate, the causes and effects of El Niño, and global warming. (Rev: BL 3/1/98; HBG 10/98; SLJ 2/98) [551.5]

12616 Facklam, Howard, and Margery Facklam. *Avalanche!* (5–7). Illus. Series: Nature's Disasters. 1991, Macmillan LB $12.95 (0-89686-598-3). Real-life examples and full-color photographs add to the drama of this weather phenomenon. (Rev: BL 8/91) [551.3]

12617 Gardner, Robert. *Science Project Ideas About Rain* (4–7). Series: Science Project Ideas. 1997, Enslow LB $19.95 (0-89490-843-X). Clear explanations and functional drawings and diagrams for a number of activities that study rain, its causes, and its effects. (Rev: BL 12/15/97; HBG 3/98; SLJ 1/98) [551.55]

12618 Gold, Susan D. *Blame It on El Niño* (5–9). 1999, Raintree Steck-Vaughn LB $28.54 (0-7398-1376-5). Covers El Niño, La Niña, how scientists predict and track them, and the effects of each globally. (Rev: HBG 3/00; SLJ 4/00) [551.6]

12619 Kahl, Jonathan D. *Weather Watch: Forecasting the Weather* (5–8). Series: How's the Weather? 1996, Lerner LB $21.27 (0-8225-2529-1). This work provides basic information on weather systems, maps, and forecasting tools, the history of weather forecasting and keeping weather records, and directions for making a weather station. (Rev: BL 6/1–15/96; SLJ 6/96) [551.6]

12620 Mogil, H. Michael, and Barbara G. Levine. *The Amateur Meteorologist: Explorations and Investigations* (6–10). Illus. Series: Amateur Science. 1993, Watts LB $21.40 (0-531-11045-1). This book shows how to get started in weather observation and forecasting, with projects such as making an anemometer, wind vane, barometer, and rain gauge. (Rev: BL 1/15/94) [551.5]

12621 Ramsey, Dan. *Weather Forecasting: A Young Meteorologist's Guide* (8–12). Illus. 1990, TAB $19.95 (0-8306-8338-0); paper $10.95 (0-8306-3338-3). A detailed and often technical examination of the techniques of weather forecasting with many tables, charts, and diagrams. (Rev: BL 10/15/90) [551.6]

12622 Sayre, April Pulley. *El Nino and La Nina: Weather in the Headlines* (4–8). Illus. 2000, Twenty-First Century LB $25.90 (0-7613-1405-9). An exploration of this complex Pacific Ocean phenomenon that produces unusual weather conditions that affect the entire world. (Rev: BL 9/15/00; HBG 3/01) [551.6]

12623 Silverstein, Alvin, et al. *Weather and Climate* (4–7). Illus. Series: Science Concepts. 1998, Twenty-First Century LB $26.90 (0-7613-3223-5). This book introduces weather by explaining earth's atmosphere, rotation, and different climates with material on air and water movements, cloud formation, and recent climate changes. (Rev: BL 5/1/99; HBG 10/99) [551.5]

12624 Souza, D. M. *Northern Lights* (5–7). Illus. 1994, Carolrhoda LB $23.95 (0-87614-799-6); paper $12.75 (0-87614-629-9). A description of the northern lights and an explanation of what causes them. (Rev: BL 1/15/94) [538]

12625 Stein, Paul. *Forecasting the Climate of the Future* (5–7). Series: The Library of Future Weather and Climate. 2001, Rosen LB $26.50 (0-8239-3413-6). A fascinating, well-organized account that looks at long-range weather predictions and at the use and accuracy of computer models in forecasting future weather patterns, especially with regard to global warming. Also use *Storms of the Future* (2001), which looks at whether global warming might cause stronger storms. (Rev: SLJ 4/02) [551.5]

12626 Stein, Paul. *Ice Ages of the Future* (5–7). Series: The Library of Future Weather and Climate. 2001, Rosen LB $26.50 (0-8239-3415-2). A look at the possibility that the greenhouse effect and other factors could in fact cause a wave of colder rather than warmer air. (Rev: SLJ 11/01) [551.6]

12627 Stonehouse, Bernard. *Snow, Ice and Cold* (5–7). 1993, Macmillan LB $21.00 (0-02-788530-5). This work tells about how cultures and individuals have adjusted to severe cold climates. (Rev: SLJ 7/93) [551.6]

12628 Vogel, Carole Garbuny. *Weather Legends: Native American Lore and the Science of Weather* (4–8). Illus. 2001, Millbrook LB $29.90 (0-7613-1900-X). Native American weather myths are paired with scientific information about actual weather phenomena. (Rev: BL 9/1/01; HBG 3/02; SLJ 10/01) [398.2]

12629 Williams, Terry Tempest, and Ted Major. *The Secret Language of Snow* (4–8). 1984, Pantheon $10.95 (0-394-96574-X). Different words for snow in the Eskimo language are used to explore this phenomenon.

Oceanography

12630 Burleigh, Robert, adapt. *The Sea: Exploring Life on an Ocean Planet* (5–12). Photos by Philip Plisson. 2003, Abrams $14.95 (0-8109-4591-6). The power, economic importance, and fragility of the sea are shown in this oversized photoessay with an ecological emphasis. (Rev: SLJ 12/03)

12631 Cobb, Allan B. *Super Science Projects About Oceans* (4–7). Series: Psyched for Science. 2000, Rosen LB $23.95 (0-8239-3174-9). Although the format is unattractive, this book contains six fine experiments that explore concepts involving the ocean. (Rev: SLJ 7/00) [551.46]

12632 Dudley, William, ed. *Endangered Oceans* (8–12). Series: Opposing Viewpoints. 1999, Greenhaven LB $32.45 (0-7377-0063-7); paper $21.20 (0-7377-0062-9). This anthology of opinions about the spoiling of the oceans debates such topics as the seriousness of the problem, the effectiveness of present practices, international policies, and how to save the whales. (Rev: BL 4/15/99; SLJ 8/99) [574.5]

12633 Heiligman, Deborah. *The Mysterious Ocean Highway: Benjamin Franklin and the Gulf Stream* (4–7). Illus. Series: Turnstone Ocean Pilot. 1999, Raintree Steck-Vaughn $18.98 (0-7398-1226-2). Beginning with Benjamin Franklin's discoveries about the Gulf Stream, this book traces what we know about this ocean current and how it affects our lives. (Rev: BL 10/15/99; HBG 10/00) [551.47]

12634 Lambert, David. *Seas and Oceans* (5–8). Illus. 1988, Silver Burdett LB $12.95 (0-382-09503-0). Covers waves, tides, currents, underwater exploration, and ocean life. (Rev: BL 4/1/88) [551.46]

12635 MacQuitty, Miranda. *Ocean* (4–8). Illus. Series: Eyewitness Books. 1995, Knopf $20.99 (0-

679-97331-1). Two-page spreads with full-color photographs introduce the oceans of the world. (Rev: BL 12/15/95; SLJ 12/95) [551.46]

12636 Robinson, W. Wright. *Incredible Facts About the Ocean: The Land Below, the Life Within*, Vol. 2 (4–8). Illus. 1987, Macmillan LB $13.95 (0-87518-358-1). Maps, diagrams, color photographs, and a glossary add to this detailed explanation. (Rev: BL 11/1/87; SLJ 10/87)

12637 Sayre, April Pulley. *Ocean* (4–7). Illus. Series: Exploring Earth's Biomes. 1996, Twenty-First Century LB $25.90 (0-8050-4084-6). An introduction to the nature and composition of oceans and the animal and plant life that they support. (Rev: BL 10/15/96; SLJ 1/97) [551.46]

12638 Sayre, April Pulley. *Seashore* (4–7). Illus. Series: Exploring Earth's Biomes. 1996, Twenty-First Century LB $25.90 (0-8050-4085-4). The composition of seashores and the life that they support are covered in this nicely illustrated account. (Rev: BL 10/15/96; SLJ 1/97) [574.5]

12639 Simon, Seymour. *How to Be an Ocean Scientist in Your Own Home* (5–8). Illus. 1988, HarperCollins $15.89 (0-397-32292-5). A great deal of information about oceans and life in them is imparted through a series of simple experiments and activities. (Rev: BCCB 11/88; BL 10/1/88) [551.46]

12640 Taylor, Leighton. *The Atlantic Ocean* (4–7). Series: Life in the Sea. 1999, Blackbirch LB $26.19 (1-56711-246-3). In 20 short chapters, this book introduces the Atlantic Ocean and life forms found in it at various levels. (Rev: HBG 3/00; SLJ 2/00) [551.46]

12641 Taylor, Leighton. *The Mediterranean Sea* (4–7). Series: Life in the Sea. 1999, Blackbirch LB $26.19 (1-56711-247-1). This account introduces the Mediterranean Sea, its geography, life forms, uses, and pollution. (Rev: HBG 3/00; SLJ 2/00) [551.46]

12642 Tesar, Jenny. *Threatened Oceans* (5–9). Series: Our Fragile Planet. 1991, Facts on File LB $19.95 (0-8160-2494-4). Basic material for general reading and for research on the oceans' vast resources, their role in land erosion, and marine ecosystems such as coral reefs and shorelines. (Rev: BL 12/1/91; SLJ 1/92) [333.91]

12643 Twist, Clint. *Seas and Oceans* (5–8). Illus. Series: Ecology Watch. 1991, Macmillan LB $13.95 (0-87518-491-X). Ethical issues are discussed in this attractive, oversize volume dealing with problems of the earth's seas and oceans. (Rev: BL 3/1/92) [333.95]

12644 VanCleave, Janice. *Janice VanCleave's Oceans for Every Kid: Easy Activities That Make Learning Science Fun* (5–7). Illus. Series: Science for Every Kid. 1996, Wiley paper $12.95 (0-471-12453-2). This book gives good background information about oceans plus a number of entertaining and instructive projects and activities. (Rev: BL 4/15/96; SLJ 5/96) [551.46]

12645 Zim, Herbert S., and Lester Ingle. *Seashores* (5–8). Illus. 1991, Western $21.27 (0-307-64496-0). This is a guide to animals and plants found along the beaches.

12646 Zubrowski, Bernie. *Making Waves: Finding Out About Rhythmic Motion* (4–8). Illus. Series: Boston Children's Museum Activity Books. 1994, Morrow LB $14.89 (0-688-11787-2). Step-by-step instructions are given for creating a wave machine, plus activities that show waves in various media. (Rev: BL 7/94; SLJ 8/94) [532]

Underwater Exploration and Sea Disasters

12647 Ballard, Robert D. *Exploring the Titanic* (4–8). 1988, Scholastic $15.95 (0-590-41953-6). A compelling description of the undersea search for the ocean liner. (Rev: BCCB 10/88; BL 1/15/89; HB 5–6/89; SLJ 11/88) [363.1]

12648 Cousteau, Jacques, and Frederic Dumas. *The Silent World* (7–12). Illus. 1987, HarperCollins $19.95 (0-06-010890-8). A description of how the aqualung was developed and how it has opened up the exploration of oceans and their sunken treasures. [551.46]

12649 Gaines, Richard. *The Explorers of the Undersea World* (6–9). Illus. Series: World Explorers. 1993, Chelsea LB $19.95 (0-7910-1323-5). A fully illustrated history of underwater exploration, with particular emphasis on the life and work of Cousteau. (Rev: BL 12/15/93; SLJ 2/94) [561.46]

12650 Hackwell, W. John. *Diving to the Past: Recovering Ancient Wrecks* (6–8). Illus. 1988, Macmillan LB $14.95 (0-684-18918-6). An introduction to the many riches contained in sunken ships and the dangers and excitement of salvaging them. (Rev: BL 3/1/88; SLJ 6/88) [930.1]

12651 Lord, Walter. *A Night to Remember* (7–12). 1956, Bantam paper $6.99 (0-553-27827-4). A brilliant re-creation of the maiden and only voyage of the *Titanic*. (Rev: BL 3/15/98) [910.4]

12652 Malam, John. *Titanic: Shipwrecks and Sunken Treasure* (5–9). Illus. 2003, DK $14.99 (0-7894-9704-2); paper $5.99 (0-7894-9225-3). Disasters that befell all types of seagoing vessels, tales of pirates and treasures, survivor stories, and details of salvaging techniques are all covered in this colorful and dramatic volume. (Rev: HBG 10/03; SLJ 9/03) [904]

12653 Platt, Richard. *Shipwreck* (4–9). Series: Eyewitness Books. 1997, Knopf LB $20.99 (0-679-98569-X). An overview of the causes and consequences of the world's most famous maritime disasters. (Rev: BL 12/15/97; BR 1–2/98) [387.2]

12654 Sloan, Frank. *Titanic*. Rev. ed. (5–8). 1998, Raintree Steck-Vaughn $19.98 (0-8172-4091-8). This thorough account of the *Titanic* and its sinking covers the structure of the ship, why it sank, the inquiries that followed, the many attempts to find and explore the wreckage, and movies and plays inspired by it. (Rev: BL 9/1/98; HBG 9/99; SLJ 2/99) [910]

12655 *Sunk! Exploring Underwater Archaeology* (5–8). Series: Buried Worlds. 1994, Lerner LB $28.75 (0-8225-3205-0). Provides a general overview of how archaeologists interpret underwater discoveries to learn about aspects of ancient trade, commerce, and history. (Rev: BL 10/15/94; SLJ 9/94) [930.1]

Physics

General and Miscellaneous

12656 Adams, Richard C., and Peter H. Goodwin. *Physics Projects for Young Scientists*. Rev. ed (7–10). Illus. 2000, Watts LB $25.00 (0-531-11667-0); paper $6.95 (0-531-16461-6). After a general discussion of physics, this book presents clear instructions for number of related science activities and projects. (Rev: BL 6/1–15/00) [530]

12657 Barnett, Lincoln. *The Universe of Dr. Einstein* (8–12). 1980, Amereon $18.95 (0-8488-0146-6). A lucid explanation of Einstein's theory of relativity and how it has changed our ideas of the universe. [530.1]

12658 Bonnet, Bob, and Dan Keen. *Science Fair Projects: Physics* (4–7). Illus. 2000, Sterling $17.95 (0-8069-0707-X). This large-format book presents 47 projects demonstrating concepts in physics and using common materials as equipment. (Rev: BL 2/1/00; SLJ 4/00) [530]

12659 Bortz, Fred. *Techno Matters: The Materials Behind the Marvels* (7–12). Illus. 2001, Twenty-First Century LB $25.90 (0-7613-1469-5). The author, a physicist, uses plentiful illustrations and clear text to explain different types of matter (electro-matter, poly-matter, super-matter, and so forth) and the kinds of materials that have been produced over the years since the Stone Age. (Rev: BL 4/15/01; HBG 10/01; SLJ 10/01) [620.1]

12660 Brackin, A. J. *Clocks: Chronicling Time* (6–10). Series: Encyclopedia of Discovery and Invention. 1991, Lucent LB $52.44 (1-56006-208-8). A history of the measurement of time and how time devices have changed the world. (Rev: BL 4/15/92) [681.1]

12661 DiSpezio, Michael A. *Awesome Experiments in Light and Sound* (5–8). Series: Awesome Experi-

ments. 1999, Sterling $17.95 (0-8069-9823-7). A collection of 73 experiments that deal with such topics as spectra, reflection, and refraction, and vibration, pitch, and resonance. (Rev: SLJ 10/99) [530]

12662 Durant, Penny R. *Bubblemania! Learn the Secrets to Creating Millions of Spectacular Bubbles!* (4–8). 1994, Avon paper $3.99 (0-380-77373-2). Through a series of easy experiments, surface tension, bubble formation, and the uses of bubbles are explained. (Rev: SLJ 7/94) [530]

12663 Evans, Neville. *The Science of Gravity* (5–8). Illus. Series: Science World. 2000, Raintree Steck-Vaughn LB $25.69 (0-7398-1323-4). Explores the force of gravity and how it affects our lives, with additional material on air resistance, mass, and invisible forces. (Rev: BL 9/15/00; HBG 10/00) [531]

12664 Fleisher, Paul. *Liquids and Gases: Principles of Fluid Mechanics* (6–12). Illus. Series: Secrets of the Universe. 2001, Lerner LB $25.26 (0-8225-2988-2). Archimedes's principle, Pascal's law, and Bernoulli's principle are among the topics covered in this volume adapted from an adult title. (Rev: HBG 3/02; SLJ 12/01) [532]

12665 Fleisher, Paul. *Matter and Energy: Principles of Matter and Thermodynamics* (7–12). Illus. Series: Secrets of the Universe. 2001, Lerner LB $25.26 (0-8225-2986-6). The periodic tables and the basic principles of thermodynamics and matter are explained in conversational language with clear diagrams and simple experiments. (Rev: BL 8/01; HBG 3/02; SLJ 1/02) [530.11]

12666 Fleisher, Paul. *Relativity and Quantum Mechanics: Principles of Modern Physics* (6–9). Illus. Series: Secrets of the Universe. 2001, Lerner LB $25.26 (0-8225-2989-0). The basic principles of modern physics are presented in clear text with helpful graphics and explanations of terms and concepts. (Rev: HBG 3/02; SLJ 1/02) [530.11]

12667 Friedhoffer, Robert. *Physics Lab in the Home* (6–9). Illus. Series: Physical Science Labs. 1997, Watts LB $25.00 (0-531-11323-X). Using such common household items as the refrigerator and the toilet, this book explains such concepts in physics as heat transfer and air and water pressure. (Rev: BR 5–6/98; HBG 3/98; SLJ 1/98) [530]

12668 Gardner, Robert. *Experiments with Bubbles* (4–7). Illus. Series: Getting Started in Science. 1995, Enslow LB $20.95 (0-89490-666-6). The properties of bubbles are explored in a series of experiments, each a little more complex than the last. (Rev: BL 12/1/95; SLJ 3/96) [530.4]

12669 Gardner, Robert. *Science Projects About Physics in the Home* (6–9). Series: Science Projects. 1999, Enslow LB $20.95 (0-89490-948-7). Ranging in difficulty from simple to complex, these projects about physics involving ideas from the living room, kitchen, playground, and bathroom are presented in a clear, straightforward way. (Rev: BR 5–6/99; SLJ 5/99) [530]

12670 Gardner, Robert. *Science Projects About the Physics of Toys and Games* (6–12). Series: Science Projects. 2000, Enslow LB $19.95 (0-7660-1165-8). Ordinary toys and games are used to produce a series of projects that are challenging, educational, and fun. (Rev: BL 8/00; HBG 3/01; VOYA 2/01) [507]

12671 Gardner, Robert, and Eric Kemer. *Science Projects About Temperature and Heat* (6–12). Series: Science Projects. 2001, Enslow LB $20.95 (0-89490-534-1). Using clear instructions and detailed drawings, this book outlines a number of activities involving heat and how it is measured. (Rev: BL 3/15/01; HBG 10/01; SLJ 1/95) [536]

12672 Goldstein, Natalie. *How Do We Know the Nature of the Atom* (6–9). Illus. Series: Great Scientific Questions and the Scientists Who Answered Them. 2001, Rosen LB $19.95 (0-8239-3385-7). An absorbing account of efforts through the ages to reveal the secrets of the atom. (Rev: SLJ 12/01) [539.14]

12673 Goodstein, Madeline. *Fish Tank Physics Projects* (5–8). Series: Science Fair Success. 2002, Enslow LB $20.95 (0-7660-1624-2). Using a common fish tank and its contents, various aspects of laws of physics are presented in the form of science fair projects. (Rev: BL 5/15/02; HBG 10/02; SLJ 11/02) [621.9]

12674 Goodstein, Madeline. *Sports Science Projects: The Physics of Balls in Motion* (5–8). Illus. Series: Science Fair Success. 1999, Enslow LB $20.95 (0-7660-1174-7). This book contains 40 projects that use the properties of different sports balls to demon-

strate principles of physics. (Rev: BL 2/15/00; HBG 10/00; SLJ 3/00) [530]

12675 McClafferty, Carla Killough. *The Head Bone's Connected to the Neck Bone: The Weird, Wacky, and Wonderful X-Ray* (6–9). Illus. 2001, Farrar $17.00 (0-374-32908-7). Unusual uses of x-rays — including industrial applications and art appraisal — are included in this entertaining book, along with a look at radiation's better-known function in medicine. (Rev: BL 11/1/01; HBG 3/02; SLJ 12/01; VOYA 2/02) [616.07]

12676 McGrath, Susan. *Fun with Physics* (5–9). Illus. 1986, National Geographic LB $12.50 (0-87044-581-2). An introduction to physics that uses everyday situations as examples and supplies a smattering of experiments. (Rev: SLJ 6/87) [530]

12677 Morgan, Sally, and Adrian Morgan. *Materials* (4–7). Illus. Series: Designs in Science. 1994, Facts on File $23.00 (0-8160-2985-7). Basic properties of matter and materials are explored in a series of experiments using everyday materials. (Rev: BL 7/94) [620.1]

12678 Parker, Barry. *The Mystery of Gravity* (5–8). Illus. Series: The Story of Science. 2002, Benchmark $19.95 (0-7614-1428-2). Parker traces our understanding of gravity from the early Greek philosophers through Einstein and Hubble, with discussion of the Big Bang theory and black holes. (Rev: HBG 3/03; SLJ 2/03) [531]

12679 Stringer, John. *The Science of a Spring* (5–8). Illus. Series: Science World. 2000, Raintree Steck-Vaughn LB $25.69 (0-7398-1322-6). Leaf and coil springs are introduced as well as the balance of forces in physics, the limits of springs, and their uses in such common objects as staplers. (Rev: BL 9/1/00; HBG 10/00; SLJ 8/00) [531]

12680 Tiner, John Hudson. *Gravity* (4–7). Series: Understanding Science. 2002, Smart Apple $24.25 (1-58340-157-1). Through a number of simple projects, colorful illustrations, and a clear text, the fundamentals of gravity are explored. (Rev: BL 3/15/03; HBG 3/03) [531]

Energy and Motion

General and Miscellaneous

12681 Asimov, Isaac. *How Did We Find Out About Solar Power?* (5–8). 1981, Walker LB $12.85 (0-8027-6423-1). An explanation of how man has benefited from solar power from the earliest time until today. [621.47]

12682 Darling, David J. *Between Fire and Ice: The Science of Heat* (4–8). Illus. Series: Experiment! 1992, Macmillan LB $13.95 (0-87518-501-0). After a discussion of the scientific method, characteristics of heat are described and simple experiments are given to demonstrate these properties. (Rev: BL 10/1/92; SLJ 11/92) [536]

12683 DiSpezio, Michael. *Awesome Experiments in Force and Motion* (5–8). Illus. Series: Awesome Experiments. 1999, Sterling $17.95 (0-8069-9821-0). Inertia, buoyancy, surface tension, air pressure, and propulsion are covered in more than 70 well-presented experiments using available materials and supplemented with background material on the concepts involved. (Rev: HBG 10/99; SLJ 7/99) [531]

12684 Doherty, Paul, and Don Rathjen. *The Spinning Blackboard and Other Dynamic Experiments on Force and Motion* (4–8). Illus. Series: Exploratorium Science Snackbook. 1996, Wiley paper $11.95 (0-471-11514-2). The many activities in this well-organized, attractive book reveal important characteristics of force and motion. (Rev: BL 4/15/96; SLJ 6/96) [531]

12685 Gardner, Robert. *Experiments with Motion* (5–8). Series: Getting Started in Science. 1995, Enslow LB $20.95 (0-89490-667-4). Projects using simple equipment illustrate the laws of motion and the ways in which motion differs in various situations. (Rev: BL 2/1/96; SLJ 2/96; VOYA 6/96) [531]

12686 Gardner, Robert. *Science Project Ideas About the Sun* (4–7). Series: Science Project Ideas. 1997, Enslow LB $19.95 (0-89490-845-6). The sun and solar energy are the subjects of this book that illustrates important concepts through a number of interesting projects and experiments. (Rev: BL 12/15/97; HBG 3/98; SLJ 1/98) [697.78]

12687 Gutnik, Martin J., and Natalie B. Gutnik. *Projects That Explore Energy* (5–8). Illus. Series: Investigate! 1994, Millbrook LB $21.40 (1-56294-334-0). A lucid, well-organized series of projects and experiments that explore power, force, and energy sources and resources. (Rev: BL 8/94; SLJ 6/94) [333.79]

12688 Jacobs, Linda. *Letting Off Steam: The Story of Geothermal Energy* (7–12). Illus. 1989, Carolrhoda LB $21.27 (0-87614-300-1). A lucid account that tells about the sources and the use of geothermal energy. (Rev: BL 9/15/89; SLJ 9/89) [333.8]

12689 Morgan, Sally. *Alternative Energy Sources* (7–10). Illus. Series: Science at the Edge. 2002, Heinemann LB $27.86 (1-40340-322-8). A discussion of alternatives to fossil fuels and the respective advantages of wind, solar, geothermal, nuclear, and other sources of energy. (Rev: HBG 3/03; SLJ 1/03) [333.79]

12690 Parker, Edward. *Fuels for the Future* (5–8). 1998, Raintree Steck-Vaughn LB $27.12 (0-8172-4937-0). This work shows how coal, oil, and nuclear power have polluted the environment, and outlines possible alternate energy sources, such as

solar, wind, and geothermal energy. (Rev: BL 7/98; BR 9–10/98; HBG 9/98; VOYA 12/98) [363.7]

12691 Roberts, Jeremy. *How Do We Know the Laws of Motion?* (6–9). Illus. Series: Great Scientific Questions and the Scientists Who Answered Them. 2001, Rosen LB $19.95 (0-8239-3383-0). Roberts traces man's growing understanding of the laws of motion from the ancient Greeks through the discoveries of relativity and the "geometry of space." (Rev: BL 10/15/01) [531.1]

12692 Silverstein, Alvin, et al. *Energy* (4–7). Illus. Series: Science Concepts. 1998, Twenty-First Century LB $26.90 (0-7613-3222-7). Photographs, diagrams, and illustrations help to introduce six types of energy: electrical, magnetic, light, heat, sound, and nuclear. (Rev: BL 5/1/99; HBG 10/99) [621.042]

12693 Snedden, Robert. *Energy Alternatives* (6–10). Illus. Series: Essential Energy. 2001, Heinemann LB $24.22 (1-57572-441-3). Alternatives to fossil fuels are presented in brief but detailed spreads, with discussion of possible future energy solutions. (Rev: BL 1/1–15/02) [333.79]

12694 Woelfle, Gretchen. *The Wind at Work: An Activity Guide to Windmills* (4–8). 1997, Chicago Review paper $14.95 (1-55652-308-4). The history, types, and uses of windmills are covered, with many activities and a discussion of the future of wind power. (Rev: BL 9/1/97; SLJ 10/97*) [621.4]

Nuclear Energy

12695 Brennan, Kristine. *The Chernobyl Nuclear Disaster* (6–8). Series: Great Disasters. 2001, Chelsea LB $21.95 (0-7910-6322-4). The story of the world's worst nuclear disaster, which occurred in 1986, and the resulting reforms and changes. (Rev: BL 6/1–15/02; HBG 10/02) [621.48]

12696 Cole, Michael D. *Three Mile Island: Nuclear Disaster* (4–8). Series: American Disasters. 2002, Enslow LB $18.95 (0-7660-1556-4). An informative, well-researched account of the disaster that affected the development of nuclear power plants in this country. (Rev: BL 6/1–15/02; HBG 10/02; SLJ 6/02) [621.48]

12697 Daley, Michael J. *Nuclear Power: Promise or Peril?* (7–12). Illus. Series: Pro/Con Issues. 1997, Lerner LB $30.35 (0-8225-2611-5). This book examines conflicting opinions about nuclear power, the possibility of nuclear accidents, the demand for energy, and the problems involving storage of nuclear waste. (Rev: BL 11/1/97; SLJ 12/97) [333.792]

12698 DeAngelis, Therese. *Three Mile Island* (6–8). Series: Great Disasters. 2001, Chelsea LB $21.95 (0-7910-5785-2). This account describes the worst nuclear accident to occur in this country and the

820

reforms and improvements it produced. (Rev: BL 6/1–15/02; HBG 10/02) [621.48]

12699 Hampton, Wilborn. *Meltdown: A Race Against Nuclear Disaster at Three Mile Island: A Reporter's Story* (7–12). Illus. 2001, Candlewick $19.99 (0-7636-0715-0). Reporter Hampton gives an exciting account of the disaster at Three Mile Island, with details of the development and dangers of nuclear power. (Rev: BL 1/1–15/02; HB 1–2/02; HBG 3/02; SLJ 11/01*; VOYA 2/02) [363.17]

12700 Higgins, Christopher. *Nuclear Submarine Disasters* (6–8). Series: Great Disasters. 2001, Chelsea LB $21.95 (0-7910-6329-1). After a general introduction to nuclear submarines, this account concentrates on the two American submarines that sank in the 1960s and the Russian submarine that sank in 2000. (Rev: BL 6/1–15/02; HBG 10/02; SLJ 6/02) [623.812]

12701 Kidd, J. S., and Renee A. Kidd. *Quarks and Sparks: The Story of Nuclear Power* (7–12). 1999, Facts on File $25.00 (0-8160-3587-3). A history of the development of nuclear power, with good coverage of the nuclear race during World War II and contemporary uses and problems. (Rev: BL 8/99; VOYA 10/99) [621.48]

12702 O'Neill, Mary. *Power Failure* (4–7). Series: SOS Planet Earth. 1991, Troll paper $4.95 (0-8167-2289-7). The Chernobyl nuclear disaster is just one of the problems discussed in this look at an environmental danger. (Rev: BL 6/15/91) [333.79]

12703 Snedden, Robert. *Nuclear Energy* (6–10). Illus. Series: Essential Energy. 2001, Heinemann LB $24.22 (1-57572-444-8). The process of producing nuclear power is presented in brief but detailed spreads, with discussion of the hazards. (Rev: BL 1/1–15/02) [333.79]

12704 Wilcox, Charlotte. *Powerhouse: Inside a Nuclear Power Plant* (4–8). Illus. 1996, Carolrhoda LB $27.15 (0-87614-945-X); paper $7.95 (0-87614-979-4). A history of nuclear energy is followed by a description of how a power plant operates and the dangers that are present. (Rev: BL 10/1/96; SLJ 9/96) [621.48]

Light, Color, and Laser Science

12705 Asimov, Isaac. *How Did We Find Out About Lasers?* (5–7). 1990, Walker LB $13.85 (0-8027-6936-5). A readable introduction to laser science by the veteran writer. (Rev: BL 8/90; SLJ 11/90) [621.36]

12706 Cobb, Vicki, and Josh Cobb. *Light Action: Amazing Experiments with Optics* (5–8). Illus. 1993, HarperCollins LB $15.89 (0-06-021437-6). Activities involving optics demonstrate shadows, focus,

reflection, and color. (Rev: BL 1/15/94; VOYA 6/94) [535]

12707 Gardner, Robert. *Experiments with Light and Mirrors* (4–7). Illus. 1995, Enslow LB $20.95 (0-89490-668-2). Properties of light are explained and demonstrated using equipment such as mirrors and cardboard. (Rev: BL 2/1/96; SLJ 3/96) [535.2]

12708 Gardner, Robert. *Science Projects About Light* (4–8). Series: Science Projects. 1994, Enslow LB $20.95 (0-89490-529-5). This project book contains a wealth of demonstrations that explain the basic principles of light. (Rev: SLJ 1/95) [535]

12709 Hecht, Jeff. *Optics: Light for a New Age* (5–9). Illus. 1988, Macmillan $15.95 (0-684-18879-1). An overview of optics, including properties of light, optical instruments, and laser technology. (Rev: BL 4/1/88; SLJ 3/88) [535]

12710 Levine, Shar, and Leslie Johnstone. *The Optics Book: Fun Experiments with Light, Vision and Color* (5–8). Illus. 1999, Sterling $21.95 (0-8069-9947-0). This book contains experiments and projects using easily obtained materials demonstrate reflection, refraction, color, polarization, vision, and light rays. (Rev: BL 3/1/99; SLJ 7/99) [535]

12711 Nassau, Kurt. *Experimenting with Color* (7–10). Series: Venture Books: Science Experiments and Projects. 1997, Watts LB $25.00 (0-531-11327-2). The general properties of light, the electromagnetic spectrum, color vision, and electron interactions are explored in this book of 17 easily performed experiments and projects. (Rev: SLJ 10/97; VOYA 6/98) [535]

12712 Wick, Walter. *Walter Wick's Optical Tricks* (4–8). 1998, Scholastic paper $13.95 (0-590-22227-9). A stimulating collection of photographs that present unusual optical illusions, with their secrets revealed in subsequent pages. (Rev: BCCB 10/98; BL 8/98; HB 9–10/98*; HBG 3/99; SLJ 9/98) [152]

12713 Zubrowski, Bernie. *Mirrors: Finding Out About the Properties of Light* (4–7). 1992, Morrow LB $13.89 (0-688-10592-0). In this hands-on approach, games and activities entice the reader to learn more. (Rev: BL 7/92; SLJ 8/92) [535]

Magnetism and Electricity

12714 Bartholomew, Alan. *Electric Mischief* (4–7). Series: Kids Can Do It. 2002, Kids Can $12.95 (1-55074-923-4); paper $5.95 (1-55074-925-0). An activity book that outlines simple, safe experiments with electricity. (Rev: BL 3/15/03; HBG 3/03; SLJ 12/02) [537]

12715 Evans, Neville. *The Science of a Light Bulb* (5–8). Illus. Series: Science World. 2000, Raintree

Steck-Vaughn LB $25.69 (0-7398-1325-0). This work explains how Edison invented the light bulb, describes its parts, and tells how light is produced and how we see it. (Rev: BL 9/15/00; HBG 10/00) [535]

12716 Fleisher, Paul. *Waves: Principles of Light, Electricity, and Magnetism* (6–12). Illus. Series: Secrets of the Universe. 2001, Lerner LB $25.26 (0-8225-2987-4). Optics, electric current, and electromagnetism are among the topics covered in this volume adapted from an adult title. (Rev: HBG 3/02; SLJ 12/01) [539.2]

12717 Gardner, Robert. *Science Projects About Electricity and Magnets* (6–12). Series: Science Projects. 2001, Enslow LB $20.95 (0-89490-530-9). A number of interesting projects about electricity and magnets are presented in a clear text with careful drawings and safety tips. (Rev: BL 3/15/01; HBG 10/01; SLJ 1/95) [537]

12718 Skurzynski, Gloria. *Waves: The Electromagnetic Universe* (4–7). Illus. 1996, National Geographic $16.95 (0-7922-3520-7). Wave theory is explained, with many examples from nature and an explanation of the theory's importance. (Rev: BL 12/1/96; SLJ 11/96*) [539.2]

12719 Stwertka, Albert. *Superconductors: The Irresistible Future* (6–10). Series: Venture. 1991, Watts paper $22.00 (0-531-12526-2). A description of the history, development, and molecular activity of superconducting materials and an explanation of their potential use. (Rev: BL 6/15/91; SLJ 8/91) [621.3]

12720 Tiner, John Hudson. *Magnetism* (4–7). Series: Understanding Science. 2002, Smart Apple LB $24.25 (1-58340-158-X). Using clear explanations, simple projects, and good illustrations, the concept of magnetism is introduced. (Rev: BL 3/15/03; HBG 3/03) [538.4]

12721 Tomecek, Steve. *Simple Attractions: Phantastic Physical Phenomena* (4–7). 1995, W. H. Freeman paper $9.95 (0-7167-6632-9). A collection of experiments related to magnetic attraction and static cling. (Rev: SLJ 3/96) [538]

12722 VanCleave, Janice. *Janice VanCleave's Electricity: Mind-Boggling Experiments You Can Turn into Science Fair Projects* (5–7). Illus. 1994, Wiley paper $10.95 (0-471-31010-7). As well as providing a discussion on the nature of electricity, this book offers 20 informative experiments that move from the very simple to the more complex. (Rev: BL 12/1/94; SLJ 11/94) [537]

12723 Wallace, Joseph. *The Lightbulb* (4–7). Illus. Series: Turning Points. 1999, Simon & Schuster $17.95 (0-689-82816-0). A description of life before the advent of the light bulb introduces a discussion of this invention and its impact on our culture, with biographical information on Thomas Alva Edison. (Rev: BL 10/1/99; HBG 3/00; SLJ 10/99) [621.32]

Nuclear Physics

12724 Cothran, Helen, ed. *Nuclear Security* (6–12). Series: At Issue. 2000, Greenhaven LB $17.96 (0-7377-0478-0); paper $11.96 (0-7377-0477-2). A look at the proliferation of nuclear weapons and the increased danger of accidents that may coincide with the end of the Cold War. (Rev: BL 1/1–15/01) [355.02]

Sound

12725 Morgan, Sally, and Adrian Morgan. *Using Sound* (4–7). Illus. Series: Designs in Science. 1994, Facts on File $23.00 (0-8160-2981-4). The properties of sound and their relation to everyday life are covered in the text and a number of experiments using readily available materials. (Rev: BL 7/94) [534]

12726 Wright, Lynne. *The Science of Noise* (5–8). Illus. Series: Science World. 2000, Raintree Steck-Vaughn LB $25.69 (0-7398-1324-2). This account describes how sound is produced, how it travels, how we hear it, and how it can be changed. (Rev: BL 9/1/00; HBG 10/00; SLJ 8/00) [534]

Technology and Engineering

General Works and Miscellaneous Industries

12727 Aaseng, Nathan. *Twentieth-Century Inventors* (7–10). Series: American Profiles. 1991, Facts on File $25.00 (0-8160-2485-5). Personal profiles of inventors are combined with historical details to explain the events that influenced the development of such items as plastic, rockets, and television. (Rev: BL 11/1/91; SLJ 11/91) [609.2]

12728 Baker, Christopher W. *A New World of Simulators: Training with Technology* (5–8). Illus. 2001, Millbrook LB $23.90 (0-7613-1352-4). An introduction to the uses of simulators and their importance in training workers who operate complex technologies such as those found in airplanes, ships, and nuclear power plants. (Rev: BL 8/01; HBG 3/02; SLJ 8/01) [003]

12729 *CDs, Super Glue, and Salsa Series 2: How Everyday Products Are Made* (5–10). 1996, Gale LB $158.40 (0-7876-0870-X). This two-volume set tells how 30 everyday products are made, including air bags, bungee cords, contact lenses, ketchup, pencils, soda bottles, and umbrellas. (Rev: BR 1–2/97; SLJ 8/97) [6.5.8.5]

12730 Colman, Penny. *Toilets, Bathtubs, Sinks, and Sewers: A History of the Bathroom* (5–8). 1994, Atheneum $16.00 (0-689-31894-4). A fascinating look at sanitation systems and inventions related to personal hygiene from ancient times to the present. (Rev: BCCB 2/95; BL 1/1/95; SLJ 3/95) [643]

12731 Crump, Donald J., ed. *How Things Are Made* (6–9). Illus. 1981, National Geographic LB $12.50 (0-87044-339-9). An inquiry into how such objects as baseballs and light bulbs are made. [670]

12732 Crump, Donald J., ed. *How Things Work* (5–7). Illus. 1984, National Geographic LB $12.50 (0-87044-430-1). A handsome volume that explains the mechanics of a variety of objects from toasters to space shuttles. [600]

12733 Crump, Donald J., ed. *Small Inventions That Make a Big Difference* (6–9). Illus. 1984, National Geographic LB $12.50 (0-87044-503-0). A book on inventions and inventors that covers such common items as the zipper. [608]

12734 Gifford, Clive. *Machines* (5–8). Series: How the Future Began. 2000, Kingfisher $15.95 (0-7534-5188-3). This account traces the history of machines in industry, power production, the military, and everyday life, and projects future developments. (Rev: HBG 3/01; SLJ 9/00) [623.6]

12735 Goldberg, Jan. *Earth Imaging Satellites* (5–9). Series: The Library of Satellites. 2003, Rosen LB $26.50 (0-8239-3853-0). A survey of the various satellites and how their images of the earth's surface measure pollution, locate forest fires, find earthquake faults, and measure the size of polar caps. (Rev: BL 11/15/03) [629.46]

12736 Kassinger, Ruth G. *Iron and Steel: From Thor's Hammer to the Space Shuttle* (5–7). Illus. Series: Material World. 2003, Millbrook LB $25.90 (0-7613-2111-X). The different ways in which humans have used and processed iron and steel through the ages is the focus of this book. (Rev: BL 5/15/03; HBG 10/03) [669]

12737 Levy, Matthys, and Richard Panchyk. *Engineering the City* (6–12). Illus. 2000, Chicago Review $14.95 (1-55652-419-6). There are many curriculum connections in this book that includes information and activities related to electricity, garbage, transportation, and other urban infrastructure issues. (Rev: BL 2/15/01) [624]

12738 Lockie, Mark. *Biometric Technology* (5–8). Series: Science at the Edge. 2002, Heinemann LB $27.86 (1-58810-701-9). Lockie explores the study of biometry and its applications in such areas as voice-speaker identification and facial recognition. (Rev: BL 10/15/02; HBG 3/03) [609]

12739 Macaulay, David, and Neil Ardley. *The New Way Things Work* (6–12). 1998, Houghton $35.00 (0-395-93847-3). With an emphasis on visual cutaways, this revision of a fascinating 1988 introduction to modern machines now includes more material on computers. (Rev: BL 12/1/98; HBG 9/99; SLJ 12/98) [600]

12740 *Machines and Inventions* (5–9). Series: Understanding Science and Nature. 1993, Time-Life Books $17.95 (0-8094-9704-2). Using a question-and-answer format, double-page spreads look at a variety of inventions including the box camera, printing press, and dynamite. (Rev: BL 1/15/94; SLJ 6/94) [621.8]

12741 Parker, Steve. *The Random House Book of How Things Work* (6–12). 1991, Random $19.99 (0-679-90908-7); paper $18.00 (0-679-80908-2). This well-illustrated book shows how everyday appliances and gadgets work. (Rev: BL 5/15/91; SLJ 7/91) [600]

12742 Platt, Richard. *Inventions Explained: A Beginner's Guide to Technological Breakthroughs* (4–8). Illus. Series: Your World Explained. 1997, Holt $18.95 (0-8050-4876-6). An in-depth look at the changing world of technological innovations, covering systems of transportation, energy, medicine, machinery, and computing. (Rev: BL 3/1/98; HBG 10/98; SLJ 2/98) [609]

12743 Platt, Richard. *Stephen Biesty's Incredible Cross-Sections* (4–7). 1992, Knopf $19.95 (0-679-81411-6). Intricately drawn illustrations feature models of vehicles and buildings. (Rev: BL 9/1/92; HBG 3/00) [741.6]

12744 Rubin, Susan G. *Toilets, Toasters, and Telephones: The How and Why of Everyday Objects* (5–8). Illus. 1998, Harcourt $20.00 (0-15-201421-7). In addition to the objects in the title, this book gives details on the invention and design of household items including stoves, vacuum cleaners, bathtubs, and pencils. (Rev: BL 11/1/98; HB 3–4/99; HBG 3/99; SLJ 11/98) [683]

12745 Sandler, Martin W. *Inventors* (5–8). Series: Library of Congress Books. 1996, HarperCollins $24.95 (0-06-024923-4). Concentrating on the late 19th and 20th centuries, the book is divided into sections on inventors, transportation, communication, and entertainment. (Rev: SLJ 2/96) [608]

12746 Skurzynski, Gloria. *Almost the Real Things: Simulation in Your High Tech World* (5–8). 1991, Macmillan LB $16.95 (0-02-778072-4). Skurzynski explains how engineers and scientists simulate

events from weightlessness to complex animation. (Rev: BCCB 10/91; BL 10/15/91; HB 11–12/91; SLJ 10/91) [620]

12747 Smith, Elizabeth Simpson. *Paper* (4–8). Illus. 1984, Walker LB $10.85 (0-8027-6569-6). An exploration of the manufacture and use of paper.

12748 Sobey, Ed. *How to Enter and Win an Invention Contest* (6–12). Illus. 1999, Enslow LB $20.95 (0-7660-1173-9). A book that not only describes how to invent a new product but also tells how to enter it in a local or national competition. (Rev: BL 9/1/99) [607.973]

12749 Taylor, Barbara. *Be an Inventor* (5–9). Illus. 1987, Harcourt $11.95 (0-15-205950-4); paper $7.95 (0-15-205951-2). A discussion of the process of invention and some examples plus coverage of entries in a *Weekly Reader* invention contest. (Rev: BL 12/15/87; SLJ 3/88) [608]

12750 Thimmesh, Catherine. *Girls Think of Everything* (4–7). Illus. 2000, Houghton $16.00 (0-395-93744-2). A fresh, breezy account about women whose inventions include the windshield wiper, chocolate chip cookies, and Glo-paper. (Rev: BCCB 5/00; BL 3/15/00; HB 5–6/00; HBG 10/00; SLJ 4/00) [609.2]

12751 Vare, Ethlie A., and Greg Ptacek. *Women Inventors and Their Discoveries* (6–10). 1993, Oliver LB $19.95 (1-881508-06-4). A review of women who are known in the world of industry and technology for their unusual inventions. (Rev: BL 10/15/93; SLJ 1/94; VOYA 2/94) [609.2]

12752 Wilkinson, Philip, and Jacqueline Dineen. *Art and Technology Through the Ages* (5–8). Illus. Series: Ideas That Changed the World. 1995, Chelsea LB $21.95 (0-7910-2769-4). A survey of the evolution of art and communications, from cave paintings through advanced digital recording and computer graphics. (Rev: BR 5–6/96; SLJ 11/95; VOYA 2/96) [501.4]

Building and Construction

12753 Adkins, Jan. *Bridges: From My Side to Yours* (4–8). Illus. 2002, Millbrook LB $25.90 (0-7613-2510-7). An illustrated and very readable history of bridge building — from the Stone Age to the modern age — with information on materials and techniques used and with detailed sketches. (Rev: BL 7/02; HB 7–8/02; HBG 10/02; SLJ 7/02) [624]

12754 Bial, Raymond. *The Houses* (4–8). Illus. Series: Building America. 2001, Marshall Cavendish LB $25.64 (0-7614-1335-9). A history of different types of housing in the United States that includes excellent photographs and drawings. (Rev: BL 3/1/02; HBG 3/02) [392.3]

12755 Boring, Mel. *Incredible Constructions: And the People Who Built Them* (4–7). Illus. 1985, Walker LB $13.85 (0-8027-6560-2). Hoover Dam, the Statue of Liberty, and other structures are featured in this history of engineering marvels. (Rev: BL 6/1/85; SLJ 8/86) [620]

12756 Darling, David. *Spiderwebs to Skyscrapers: The Science of Structures* (5–8). 1991, Dillon LB $13.95 (0-87518-478-2). Discusses foundations, building materials, and styles of construction, in nature and technology, with experiments and color illustrations. (Rev: BL 6/1/92; SLJ 3/92) [624.1]

12757 Donovan, Sandy. *The Channel Tunnel* (4–7). Series: Great Building Feats. 2003, Lerner LB $27.93 (0-8225-4692-2). Using many black-and-white illustrations, diagrams, and maps, this is the exciting story of the underwater engineering marvel that links England and France. (Rev: BL 11/15/03; HBG 10/03; SLJ 11/03) [624.1]

12758 DuTemple, Lesley A. *The Hoover Dam* (4–7). Series: Great Building Feats. 2003, Lerner LB $27.93 (0-8225-4691-4). This story traces the dam's construction from the planning stages through its technically difficult and dangerous construction and places this impressive structure in historical context. (Rev: BL 11/15/03; HBG 10/03; SLJ 11/03) [627]

12759 DuTemple, Lesley A. *The Panama Canal* (6–9). Series: Great Building Feats. 2002, Lerner LB $27.93 (0-8225-0079-5). An attractive and absorbing overview of this massive and challenging project. (Rev: HBG 10/03; LMC 2/03; SLJ 1/03*) [972.87]

12760 Kent, Peter. *Great Building Stories of the Past* (4–7). Illus. 2002, Oxford $18.95 (0-19-521846-9). Provides information on famous architectural marvels (the Great Pyramid, the Great Wall of China, Beauvais Cathedral, the Panama Canal, and others) and how they were built. (Rev: BL 5/15/02; HBG 10/02; SLJ 10/02) [720]

12761 Kirkwood, Jon. *The Fantastic Cutaway Book of Giant Buildings* (4–7). Illus. 1997, Millbrook paper $9.95 (0-7613-0629-3). Using double-page spreads, outstanding graphics, and many fact boxes, this book features a wide variety of structures including the Statue of Liberty, the pyramids, the Colosseum, churches, operas houses, Grand Central Station, Munich's Olympic stadium, and skyscrapers. (Rev: BL 4/1/98; HBG 10/98) [720]

12762 Korres, Manolis. *The Stones of the Parthenon* (7–12). Trans. by D. Turner. Illus. 2001, Getty paper $14.95 (0-89236-607-9). The construction of the Parthenon is described in text and detailed drawings in this small-format book, which includes notes, a glossary, and a bibliography. (Rev: BL 2/1/01) [622]

12763 Macaulay, David. *Building Big* (7–12). Illus. 2000, Houghton $30.00 (0-395-96331-1). This com-

panion book to a set of videos explains the problems posed by ambitious construction projects such as tunnels, bridges, dams, domes, and skyscrapers. (Rev: BL 12/15/00; HB 1–2/01; HBG 3/01; SLJ 11/00; VOYA 4/01) [720]

12764 Macaulay, David. *Unbuilding* (5–8). 1980, Houghton $18.00 (0-395-29457-6); paper $6.95 (0-395-45360-7). A book that explores the concept of tearing down the Empire State Building.

12765 Macaulay, David. *Underground* (5–10). 1983, Houghton $18.00 (0-395-24739-X); paper $9.95 (0-395-34065-9). An exploration in text and detailed drawings of the intricate network of systems under city streets. [624]

12766 Mann, Elizabeth. *The Brooklyn Bridge* (4–7). Illus. Series: Wonders of the World. 1996, Mikaya $19.95 (0-9650493-0-2). The story of the building of the Brooklyn Bridge is told through the eyes of a family. (Rev: BL 2/1/97; SLJ 6/97*) [624]

12767 Owens, Thomas S. *Football Stadiums* (5–8). Illus. Series: Sports Palaces. 2001, Millbrook LB $25.90 (0-7613-1764-3). Rather than highlighting individual stadiums, this book covers general topics such as their design, replacement, funding, amenities, and history. (Rev: BL 4/1/01; HBG 10/01; SLJ 4/01) [796.332]

12768 Severance, John B. *Skyscrapers: How America Grew Up* (5–9). Illus. 2000, Holiday $18.95 (0-8234-1492-2). Beginning with an explanation of the architectural breakthroughs that made the building of skyscrapers possible, this account traces the construction of these buildings from 1851 to the end of the 20th century. (Rev: BL 6/1–15/00; HB 9–10/00; HBG 10/00; SLJ 7/00; VOYA 4/01) [720]

12769 Wilkinson, Philip. *Building* (4–9). Illus. Series: Eyewitness Books. 1995, Knopf $19.00 (0-679-87256-6). This introduction to structures discusses engineering, building materials, and types of construction. (Rev: BL 8/95; SLJ 8/95) [690]

12770 Woods, Mary B., and Michael Woods. *Ancient Construction: From Tents to Towers* (5–8). Illus. Series: Ancient Technologies. 2000, Runestone LB $25.26 (0-8225-2998-X). From Stonehenge and the Colosseum to the Eiffel Tower and the Golden Gate Bridge, this is a history of building and construction. (Rev: BL 9/15/00; HBG 3/01; SLJ 1/01) [720]

Clothing, Textiles, and Jewelry

12771 Hoobler, Dorothy, and Tom Hoobler. *Vanity Rules: A History of American Fashion and Beauty* (5–8). Illus. 2000, Twenty-First Century LB $28.90 (0-7613-1258-7). From the painted bodies of early Native Americans to today's body piercing, this is a history of the quest for personal beauty in America. (Rev: BL 4/1/00; HBG 10/00; SLJ 5/00) [391]

12772 Lawlor, Laurie. *Where Will This Shoe Take You? A Walk Through the History of Footwear* (5–8). Illus. 1996, Walker LB $18.85 (0-8027-8435-6). This is a history of footwear, from sandals worn by the ancients to the sneakers popular today. (Rev: BCCB 1/97; BL 11/15/96; SLJ 5/97; VOYA 6/97) [391]

12773 MacDonald, Fiona. *Clothing and Jewelry* (5–8). Illus. Series: Discovering World Cultures. 2001, Crabtree paper $8.95 (0-7787-0246-4). Readers will enjoy browsing through this heavily illustrated guide that includes fashion, religious garb, and jewelry from around the world. (Rev: SLJ 5/02) [391]

12774 Miller, Brandon M. *Dressed for the Occasion: What Americans Wore, 1620–1970* (5–8). 1999, Lerner LB $30.35 (0-8225-1738-8). A fascinating look at men's and women's fashions throughout history and how they reflect society's culture and values. (Rev: BCCB 5/99; BL 4/1/99; SLJ 9/99) [391]

12775 Ruby, Jennifer. *Underwear* (7–12). Series: Costumes in Context. 1996, Batsford $24.95 (0-7134-7663-X). This is a thoughtful, information-filled, illustrated history of underwear from 1066 through the 1990s. (Rev: SLJ 1/97) [646]

12776 Smith, Elizabeth Simpson. *Cloth* (5–8). Illus. 1985, Walker LB $10.85 (0-8027-6577-7). The discovery of fiber and how cloth is made. (Rev: BL 8/85; SLJ 11/85) [677.02864]

12777 Tythacott, Louise. *Jewelry* (4–8). Illus. Series: Traditions Around the World. 1995, Thomson Learning LB $24.26 (1-56847-229-3). A history of jewelry, why it is worn, and the variety of materials and designs used. (Rev: SLJ 7/95) [739.27]

12778 Yue, Charlotte, and David Yue. *Shoes: Their History in Words and Pictures* (5–8). Illus. 1997, Houghton $16.00 (0-395-72667-0). An in-depth survey of footwear through the ages with emphasis on Western cultures. (Rev: BL 4/1/97; HB 5–6/97; SLJ 4/97) [391]

Computers, Automation, and the Internet

12779 Ahmad, Nyla. *CyberSurfer: The OWL Internet Guide for Kids* (4–7). Illus. 1996, Firefly $19.95 (1-895688-50-7). Using cartoons, a fast-paced text, and a demonstration disc, the author introduces the Internet, its functions, and important addresses. (Rev: BL 4/1/96; SLJ 9/96) [004.6]

12780 Baker, Christopher W. *Robots Among Us: The Challenges and Promises of Robotics* (5–8). Illus.

Series: New Century Technology. 2002, Millbrook LB $23.90 (0-7613-1969-7). A lavishly illustrated account that describes the science of robotics, current developments, and what might be expected in the future. (Rev: BL 6/1–15/02; HBG 10/02; SLJ 9/02) [629.8]

12781 Baker, Christopher W. *Scientific Visualization: The New Eyes of Science* (5–8). Illus. Series: New Century Technology. 2000, Millbrook LB $23.90 (0-7613-1351-6). This book explores the ways in which computers enable scientists to study the universe and simulate events such as the creation of a black hole. (Rev: BL 4/1/00; HBG 3/01; SLJ 6/00) [507.2]

12782 Billings, Charlene W. *Supercomputers: Shaping the Future* (7–12). Series: Science Sourcebooks. 1995, Facts on File $25.00 (0-8160-3096-0). A history of the silicon revolution — focusing on the megamachines that are the most powerful computers in the world. (Rev: BL 10/15/95; SLJ 4/96; VOYA 4/96) [004.1]

12783 Bortz, Fred. *Mind Tools: The Science of Artificial Intelligence* (7–12). 1992, Watts LB $25.00 (0-531-12515-7). A concise overview of the controversy surrounding the science of artificial intelligence and new computer technologies, with material on the field's pioneers. (Rev: BL 11/1/92) [006.3]

12784 Brooks, Sheldon. *Everything You Need to Know About Romance and the Internet: How to Stay Safe* (6–9). Series: Need to Know Library. 2001, Rosen LB $17.95 (0-8239-3399-7). Newcomers to the Internet will find solid, easily read advice on using chat rooms, email, and online dating services, with warnings about cyberstalkers and about meeting correspondents in person. (Rev: SLJ 9/01; VOYA 2/03) [025.04]

12785 Chorlton, Windsor. *The Invention of the Silicon Chip: A Revolution in Daily Life* (5–8). Series: Point of Impact. 2002, Heinemann LB $25.64 (1-58810-554-7). Chorlton explores computers before and after the invention of the chip, introduces key players in the field, and discusses the impact of this new technology on society. (Rev: SLJ 9/02) [621.3815]

12786 Cothran, Helen, ed. *The Internet* (7–12). Illus. Series: Opposing Viewpoints. 2002, Gale LB $31.20 (0-7377-0780-1); paper $19.95 (0-7377-0779-8). Essays present conflicting opinions on such topics as the value of the Internet as an educational resource, privacy, and the social benefits/disadvantages of the technology. (Rev: SLJ 8/02) [303.48]

12787 Dunn, John M. *The Computer Revolution* (7–10). Series: World History. 2002, Gale LB $27.45 (1-56006-848-5). This account, which quotes many original sources, traces the history of the computer and its effects on our economy and society. (Rev: BL 4/15/02; SLJ 4/02) [004.6]

12788 Fritz, Sandy. *Robotics and Artificial Intelligence* (5–10). Illus. Series: Hot Science. 2003, Smart Apple LB $19.95 (1-58340-364-7). After describing robots' contributions in space, in the workplace, in danger spots, and in medicine, Fritz speculates on the future possibilities. (Rev: BL 12/1/03) [629.8]

12789 Gifford, Clive. *How to Build a Robot* (4–8). Series: How To. 2001, Watts LB $14.50 (0-531-14649-9); paper $4.95 (0-531-13997-2). Robots past, present, and future are presented, with discussion of their suitability for use in high-tech environments and in conditions that make work by humans difficult or dangerous. (Rev: SLJ 6/02) [629.892]

12790 Grady, Sean M. *Virtual Reality: Computers Mimic the Physical World* (7–12). Illus. Series: Science Sourcebooks. 1998, Facts on File $25.00 (0-8160-3605-5). This book provides young readers with a working knowledge of virtual reality, how this technology developed, its uses, drawbacks, and the philosophical questions raised by the manufacture of "reality." (Rev: BL 4/15/98; BR 11–12/98; HBG 3/99; SLJ 7/98) [006]

12791 Graham, Ian. *The Internet: The Impact on Our Lives* (6–10). Illus. Series: 21st Century Debates. 2001, Raintree Steck-Vaughn LB $18.98 (0-7398-3173-9). An absorbing and fact-filled overview of the influence of the Internet on politics and society, with material on issues such as censorship, e-business, and e-crime. (Rev: BR 11–12/01; SLJ 11/01; VOYA 10/01) [303.48]

12792 Graham, Ian. *Internet Revolution* (7–10). Illus. Series: Science at the Edge. 2002, Heinemann LB $27.86 (1-40340-325-2). The author traces the history of the Internet, looks at the ways we use it today, and discusses political and privacy issues. (Rev: HBG 3/03; SLJ 1/03) [004.67]

12793 Graham, Ian. *The World of Computers and Communications* (4–7). Series: Inside Look. 2000, Gareth Stevens LB $25.26 (0-8368-2727-9). As well as computers, computer peripherals, and networking, this overview of electronic communications touches on recordings, radar, and calculators. (Rev: HBG 10/01; SLJ 3/01) [004]

12794 Henderson, Harry. *The Internet* (6–9). Illus. Series: Overview. 1998, Lucent LB $27.45 (1-56006-215-0). A survey of the history of the Net, its uses, its impact on our way of life, and problems and controversies associated with it. (Rev: BL 9/1/98; SLJ 8/98) [004.678]

12795 Henderson, Harry. *Issues in the Information Age* (7–12). Series: Contemporary Issues. 1999, Lucent LB $27.45 (1-56006-365-3). This work examines troubling questions in the new information age involving censorship on the Internet, loss of privacy, parental prerogatives, and human interaction. (Rev: BR 9–10/99; SLJ 7/99) [004.6]

12796 Jefferis, David. *Artificial Intelligence: Robotics and Machine Evolution* (5–7). Series: Megatech. 1999, Crabtree LB $22.60 (0-7787-0046-1); paper $8.95 (0-7787-0056-9). This is a survey of the variety of robotic devices in use at the end of the 20th century, some of the advances that are being made, and a glimpse into the future. (Rev: SLJ 9/99) [004]

12797 Jefferis, David. *Internet: Electronic Global Village* (4–8). Illus. Series: Megatech. 2001, Crabtree LB $22.60 (0-7787-0052-6); paper $8.95 (0-7787-0062-3). An eye-catching look at the development of the Internet and the World Wide Web and their uses in communication and commerce. (Rev: SLJ 6/02) [4.678]

12798 Judson, Karen. *Computer Crime: Phreaks, Spies, and Salami Slicers* (6–10). Illus. Series: Issues in Focus. 2000, Enslow LB $19.95 (0-7660-1243-3). All kinds of cybercrimes are discussed including hacking, viruses, and computer fraud. (Rev: BL 3/15/00; HBG 9/00) [364.16.]

12799 Kalbag, Asha. *Build Your Own Web Site* (4–8). Series: Usborne Computer Guides. 1999, EDC paper $8.95 (0-7460-3293-5). This thorough guide explains how, why, when, and where to create a Web site. (Rev: SLJ 6/99) [004.6]

12800 Knittel, John, and Michael Soto. *Everything You Need to Know About the Dangers of Computer Hacking* (5–8). Illus. 2000, Rosen LB $25.25 (0-8239-3034-3). This book points out the differences between a hacker and a cracker and, through this, discusses beneficial and harmful computer actions and how to avoid the latter. (Rev: BL 4/1/00; SLJ 5/00) [364.16]

12801 Lampton, Christopher. *Home Page: An Introduction to Web Page Design* (4–8). 1997, Watts LB $23.00 (0-531-20255-0). The author explains to youngsters clearly and simply how they can design their own Web pages using offline time. (Rev: BL 7/97; SLJ 2/98) [005.7]

12802 Lampton, Christopher. *The World Wide Web* (4–8). 1997, Watts LB $23.00 (0-531-20262-3). Aspects of the World Wide Web that would be of value and interest to children are covered, with practical suggestions for effective searching. (Rev: BL 7/97; SLJ 2/98) [025.04]

12803 Lawler, Jennifer. *Cyberdanger and Internet Safety: A Hot Issue* (5–10). Series: Hot Issues. 2000, Enslow LB $21.95 (0-7660-1368-5). As well as introducing the Internet, this account explains how people abuse it with hidden identities, threatening or obscene material, loss of privacy, hacking, con tricks, pranks, and hoaxes. (Rev: HBG 3/01; SLJ 1/01; VOYA 4/01) [004.6]

12804 Lindsay, Dave. *Dave's Quick 'n' Easy Web Pages: An Introductory Guide to Creating Web Sites*. 2nd ed. (5–9). 2001, Erin $11.95 (0-9690609-8-X). Young Dave, Webmaster of the popular Redwall site, gives good, basic information on HTML coding and Web page design. (Rev: SLJ 8/01) [005.7]

12805 McCormick, Anita Louise. *The Internet: Surfing the Issues* (5–10). Series: Issues in Focus. 1998, Enslow LB $20.95 (0-89490-956-8). A guide to the history, mechanics, and use of the Internet that also covers such topics as surfing, child pornography, hate groups, and censorship. (Rev: BL 10/1/98; SLJ 12/98) [004]

12806 Macdonald, Joan Vos. *Cybersafety: Surfing Safely Online* (5–7). Illus. Series: Teen Issues. 2001, Enslow LB $17.95 (0-7660-1580-7). Various dangers of venturing online are covered, from viruses and other problems that can infect your computer to activities such as hacking, cyberstalking, and copying software illegally. (Rev: HBG 3/02; SLJ 12/01) [004.6]

12807 Marshall, Elizabeth L. *A Student's Guide to the Internet*. Rev. ed (6–9). 2001, Twenty-First Century LB $23.90 (0-7613-1661-2). This updated edition of a user-friendly guide to accessing the Internet for research and collaborative projects gives plenty of Web sites to explore. (Rev: HBG 10/02; SLJ 1/02; VOYA 2/02) [004.67]

12808 Menhard, Francha Roffe. *Internet Issues: Pirates, Censors, and Cybersquatters* (6–12). Illus. Series: Issues in Focus. 2001, Enslow LB $20.95 (0-7660-1687-0). Menhard's effective overview of problems concerning filtering, copyright, privacy, and piracy uses clear examples, many of which involve young people. (Rev: BL 2/1/02; HBG 10/02; SLJ 2/02) [384.3]

12809 Perry, Robert L. *Build Your Own Website* (4–7). Illus. Series: Watts Library: Computer Science. 2000, Watts LB $24.00 (0-531-11756-1); paper $8.95 (0-531-16469-1). Clear, jargon-free language is used to explain the basics of Web site construction under various conditions and for various purposes. (Rev: BL 10/15/00) [005.7]

12810 Perry, Robert L. *Personal Computer Communications* (4–7). Illus. Series: Watts Library: Computer Science. 2000, Watts LB $24.00 (0-531-11758-8); paper $8.95 (0-531-16483-7). This work covers such topics as modems, networks, satellite and wireless technology, and the future of communications. (Rev: BL 10/15/00) [004.16]

12811 Rothman, Kevin F. *Coping with Dangers on the Internet: Staying Safe On-Line* (7–12). Series: Coping. 2001, Rosen LB $18.95 (0-8239-3201-X). Readers will find practical advice on safe use of the Web sites, e-mail, chat rooms, newsgroups, and so forth, with a useful list of acronyms and emoticons. (Rev: SLJ 8/01) [025.04]

12812 Salzman, Marian, and Robert Pondiscio. *Kids On-Line: 150 Ways for Kids to Surf the Net for Fun and Information* (5–9). 1995, Avon paper $5.99 (0-

380-78231-6). A leap into cyberspace for both adults and youth, with valuable information plus etiquette for Internet users. (Rev: BL 10/15/95) [004.69]

12813 Skurzynski, Gloria. *Robots: Your High-Tech World* (4–7). Illus. 1990, Macmillan LB $16.95 (0-02-782917-0). An overview of robotics and history and an explanation of how robots work. (Rev: BL 11/15/90; HB 1–2/91; SLJ 9/90) [629.8]

12814 Spangenburg, Ray, and Kit Moser. *Savvy Surfing on the Internet: Searching and Evaluating Web Sites* (5–8). Illus. Series: Issues in Focus. 2001, Enslow LB $20.95 (0-7660-1590-4). Readers are encouraged to view much of the information on the Internet with healthy suspicion and are given advice on efficient searching for and assessment of Web sites. (Rev: HBG 3/02; SLJ 12/01) [004.6]

12815 Thro, Ellen. *Robotics: The Marriage of Computers and Machines* (7–12). Series: Science Sourcebooks. 1993, Facts on File $25.00 (0-8160-2628-9). Presents this complicated subject in interesting, understandable terms, covering artificial intelligence and the use of robots underground, in factories, and in space exploration. (Rev: BL 7/93) [629.8]

12816 Trumbauer, Lisa. *Homework Help for Kids on the Net* (4–8). Series: Cool Sites. 2000, Millbrook LB $17.90 (0-7613-1655-8). This useful book lists and describes key sites covering general reference, math, language arts, history, geography, and science. (Rev: HBG 10/00; SLJ 7/00) [004]

12817 Wallace, Mark. *101 Things to Do on the Internet* (4–8). Series: Usborne Computer Guides. 1999, EDC paper $10.95 (0-7460-3294-3). Each of the double-page spreads in this book focuses on a single subject or theme to be explored on the Internet such as space, music, games, movies, or weather. (Rev: HBG 10/99; SLJ 6/99) [004]

12818 Weiss, Ann E. *Virtual Reality: A Door to Cyberspace* (7–12). Illus. 1996, Twenty-First Century LB $26.90 (0-8050-3722-5). This book describes the development of virtual reality and its accomplishments, applications, and uses, as well as the ethical issues surrounding its development. (Rev: BL 5/15/96*; SLJ 7/96; VOYA 10/96) [006]

12819 Whyborny, Sheila. *Virtual Reality* (5–9). Series: Science on the Edge. 2003, Gale LB $20.95 (1-56711-789-9). This book examines the use of sophisticated computer technology to create virtual reality and discusses applications in education, engineering, law, medicine, and entertainment. (Rev: BL 10/15/03) [004]

12820 Wickelgren, Ingrid. *Ramblin' Robots: Building a Breed of Mechanical Beasts* (7–12). Illus. 1996, Watts LB $23.00 (0-531-11301-9). An exciting history of the development of robots with details on current developments. (Rev: BL 11/15/96; SLJ 1/97) [629.8]

12821 Williams, Brian. *Computers* (5–8). Illus. Series: Great Inventions. 2001, Heinemann LB $25.64 (1-58810-210-6). A chronological look at computers and their predecessors, from the abacus onward, with diagrams and information on the inventors. (Rev: HBG 3/02; SLJ 2/02) [004]

12822 Winters, Paul A. *Computers and Society* (7–12). Series: Current Controversies. 1997, Greenhaven LB $32.45 (1-56510-564-8); paper $21.20 (1-56510-563-X). The articles in this anthology discuss the impact of computers on society and education, as well as problems involving privacy and censorship. (Rev: BL 7/97; SLJ 12/97) [303.48]

12823 Wolinsky, Art. *Communicating on the Internet* (4–8). Series: The Internet Library. 1999, Enslow LB $17.95 (0-7660-1260-3). This book on how to communicate safely and effectively on the Internet includes material on e-mail problems, computer etiquette, chat rooms, and newsgroups. (Rev: HBG 3/00; SLJ 3/00) [004]

12824 Wolinsky, Art. *Creating and Publishing Web Pages on the Internet* (4–8). Series: The Internet Library. 1999, Enslow LB $17.95 (0-7660-1262-X). Using many example Web pages, this book gives practical advice on how to create an interesting, well-organized, safe Web page with links to sites for further information. (Rev: HBG 10/00; SLJ 3/00) [004]

12825 Wolinsky, Art. *The History of the Internet and the World Wide Web* (5–9). Illus. Series: Internet Library. 1999, Enslow LB $17.95 (0-7660-1261-1). This volume explains how the Internet evolved during the Cold War and how it transfers and distributes information. (Rev: BL 12/15/99; HBG 3/00; SLJ 1/00; VOYA 2/00) [004.67]

12826 Wolinsky, Art. *Internet Power Research Using the Big6 Approach* (4–8). Illus. Series: The Internet Library. 2002, Enslow LB $17.95 (0-7660-2094-0). Readers accompany young researchers as they conduct searches using the Big6 method. (Rev: HBG 3/03; SLJ 12/02) [025.04]

12827 Wolinsky, Art. *Locating and Evaluating Information on the Internet* (5–9). Illus. 1999, Enslow LB $17.95 (0-7660-1259-X). As well as directions on how to complete successful searches on the Internet, this work tells how to determine the usefulness and credibility of Web pages. (Rev: BL 12/15/99; HBG 3/00; SLJ 1/00; VOYA 2/00) [025.04]

12828 Wolinsky, Art. *Safe Surfing on the Internet* (4–8). Illus. 2003, Enslow LB $17.95 (0-7660-2030-1). Wolinsky presents information on safe use of the Internet and topics including proper use of language, copyright, privacy, and plagiarism. (Rev: HBG 10/03; LMC 8–9/03; SLJ 7/03) [004.67]

12829 Wright, David. *Computers* (5–8). Series: Inventors and Inventions. 1995, Benchmark LB $25.64 (0-7614-0064-8). A look at the development of the computer, with brief profiles of important people in its history and an examination of the uses of computers in the world today. (Rev: SLJ 6/96) [004]

Electronics

12830 Bridgman, Roger. *Electronics* (4–8). Illus. Series: Eyewitness Science. 1993, DK LB $15.95 (1-56458-325-4). The field of electronics is introduced through full-color graphics, 3-D models, and detailed captions that explain important experiments, equipment, and concepts. (Rev: BL 11/15/93; SLJ 12/93) [621.38]

12831 Traister, John E., and Robert J. Traister. *Encyclopedic Dictionary of Electronic Terms* (7–12). Illus. 1984, Prentice Hall $18.95 (0-13-276981-6). All of the basic terms in electronics are explained, usually in fairly simple terms. [621.381]

Telecommunications

12832 Byers, Ann. *Communications Satellites* (5–9). Series: The Library of Satellites. 2003, Rosen LB $26.50 (0-8239-3851-4). From the first important communications satellites launched in 1962, this account traces the growth of this technology and its possible future developments. (Rev: BL 11/15/03) [001.51]

12833 Fisher, Trevor. *Communications* (7–9). Illus. 1985, Batsford $19.95 (0-7134-4631-5). This is a clear history of communication from the development of language to today's sophisticated telecommunications networks. (Rev: SLJ 2/86) [302.2]

12834 Gardner, Robert. *Communication* (6–9). Illus. Series: Yesterday's Science, Today's Technology. 1994, Twenty-First Century LB $25.90 (0-8050-2854-4). Today's electronic methods of communication are introduced with about 20 activities that would make good science fair projects. (Rev: BL 3/15/95) [303.48]

12835 Gearhart, Sarah. *The Telephone* (4–7). Illus. Series: Turning Points. 1999, Simon & Schuster $17.95 (0-689-82815-2). This book describes long-distance communications before the telephone, gives a biography of Alexander Graham Bell, and explains how the telephone was invented. (Rev: BL 10/1/99; HBG 3/00; SLJ 10/99) [384.6]

12836 Hegedus, Alannah, and Kaitlin Rainey. *Bleeps and Blips to Rocket Ships: Great Inventions in Com-*

munications (5–9). 2001, Tundra paper $17.95 (0-88776-452-5). This is a fact-packed and appealing look at the field of communications, with information on history and inventors and inventions as well as suggested activities. (Rev: SLJ 8/01) [609.71]

12837 Streissguth, Thomas. *Communications: Sending the Message* (5–8). Series: Innovators. 1997, Oliver LB $21.95 (1-881508-41-2). A compact, easy-to-understand history of communication from earliest times, through Gutenberg, Edison, and Marconi, to the present "information highway." (Rev: BR 3–4/98; SLJ 2/98) [001.51]

12838 Webb, Marcus. *Telephones: Words over Wires* (6–10). Series: Encyclopedia of Discovery and Invention. 1992, Lucent LB $52.44 (1-56006-219-3). Covers the history of the telephone — including fax machines, communication satellites, and deregulation of the telephone industry — and looks to the future and the potential impact of such technologies as fiber optics. (Rev: BL 12/15/92) [621]

12839 Wilson, Anthony. *Communications* (4–7). Illus. Series: How the Future Began. 1999, Kingfisher $15.95 (0-7534-5179-4). An engaging look at the past, present, and future of communications technologies. (Rev: BL 11/15/99; HBG 3/00) [621.382]

12840 Winters, Paul A., ed. *The Information Revolution* (8–12). Series: Opposing Viewpoints. 1998, Greenhaven LB $32.45 (1-56510-801-9); paper $28.75 (1-56510-800-0). This anthology of essays explores issues raised by the advances in telecommunication technology via the telephone, television, and computer, and discusses the impact of these advances on society and education. (Rev: BL 6/1–15/98) [384]

Television, Motion Pictures, Radio, and Recording

12841 Dowd, Ned. *That's a Wrap: How Movies Are Made* (5–7). Illus. 1991, Silver Burdett paper $4.95 (0-382-24376-5). A behind-the-scenes look at the process of making a movie. (Rev: BCCB 1/92; BL 1/1/92) [791.43]

12842 Gottfried, Ted. *The American Media* (7–12). Illus. Series: Impact. 1997, Watts LB $24.00 (0-531-11315-9). This book provides a look at the history and present-day conditions of the U.S. media — the personalities, major events, the First Amendment and other important issues, and current trends. (Rev: BL 9/1/97; SLJ 6/97) [302.23]

12843 Hamilton, Jake. *Special Effects: In Film and Television* (4–8). Illus. 1998, DK $17.95 (0-7849-2813-X). This is an intriguing glimpse at special effects in film and television, using double-page spreads that each focus on a different aspect of production, such as storyboards, makeup, and stunts. (Rev: BCCB 9/98; BL 8/98; VOYA 10/98) [791.43]

12844 Lewis, Roland. *101 Essential Tips: Video* (6–12). 1995, DK paper $3.95 (0-7894-0183-5). This small-format book gives sound advice on using camcorders for video production and touches on equipment, techniques, composition, lighting, editing, and audio. (Rev: VOYA 6/96) [621]

12845 O'Brien, Lisa. *Lights, Camera, Action! Making Movies and TV from the Inside Out* (4–8). Illus. 1998, Greey dePencier Bks. $19.95 (1-895688-75-2); paper $12.95 (1-895688-76-0). Using a fictitious situation involving two teens who are cast in a movie, this book takes the reader behind the scenes, discusses auditions and the importance of agents, covers acting basics, and describes how movies are filmed and distributed. (Rev: BL 6/1–15/98; SLJ 7/98) [791]

12846 Oleksy, Walter. *Entertainment* (6–12). Series: Information Revolution. 1996, Facts on File $25.00 (0-8160-3077-4). An exploration of the revolutionary changes in the entertainment industry, including satellite TV broadcasting, digital wide-screen TV, laser disk players, interactive CD-ROMs, and computer movies. (Rev: BL 2/15/96; SLJ 4/96; VOYA 10/96) [621]

12847 Petley, Julian. *The Media: The Impact on Our Lives* (6–10). Series: 21st Century Debates. 2001, Raintree Steck-Vaughn LB $18.98 (0-7398-3175-5). An absorbing and fact-filled overview of the various forms of media — from newspapers, radio and TV, and film to commercial advertising — and their influence on politics and society. (Rev: SLJ 11/01) [302.23]

12848 Scott, Elaine. *Movie Magic: Behind the Scenes with Special Effects* (4–7). Illus. 1995, Morrow $16.00 (0-688-12477-1). The techniques used to produce special effects in movies are explained, with special material on the use of computers. (Rev: BL 2/15/96) [791.43]

12849 *Special Effects* (5–10). 1998, DK paper $17.95 (0-7894-2813-X). Using double-page spreads illustrated with many movie stills, this is a dazzling look at how special effects are produced in movies. (Rev: BCCB 9/98; HBG 9/98; SLJ 6/98) [791.43]

12850 Torr, James D., ed. *Violence in Film and Television* (6–12). Series: Examining Pop Culture. 2002, Gale $31.20 (0-7377-0865-4); paper $19.95 (0-7377-0864-6). This collection of essays examines the evolution of violence in television, movies, and video games. (Rev: BL 4/1/02; SLJ 3/02) [303.6]

Transportation

General and Miscellaneous

12851 Bial, Raymond. *The Canals* (4–8). Illus. Series: Building America. 2001, Marshall Cavendish LB $25.64 (0-7614-1336-7). This history of the U.S. canal system and how it works includes excellent photographs and illustrations that help to explain the technical aspects of canals. (Rev: BL 3/1/02; HBG 3/02; SLJ 2/02*) [386]

12852 DuTemple, Lesley A. *New York Subways* (4–7). Illus. Series: Great Building Feats. 2003, Lerner LB $27.93 (0-8225-0378-6). DuTemple presents the history of the subway system with details of its difficult construction, continuing financial problems, and the damage caused in the destruction of the World Trade Center. (Rev: BL 1/1–15/03; HBG 10/03) [388.4]

12853 Hamilton, John. *Transportation: A Pictorial History of the Past One Thousand Years* (4–7). Illus. Series: The Millennium. 2000, ABDO LB $25.65 (1-57765-361-0). A history of 1,000 years of transportation that includes animals, ships, trains, bicycles, motorcycles, cars, airplanes, and spacecraft. (Rev: BL 7/00; HBG 10/00; SLJ 10/00) [388.21]

12854 Spangenburg, Raymond, and Diane Moser. *The Story of America's Bridges* (5–9). Series: Connecting a Continent. 1991, Facts on File LB $18.95 (0-8160-2259-3). History, descriptions of key technological innovations, and short stories are used to present a picture of the country's bridges. (Rev: BL 11/15/91) [624]

12855 Spangenburg, Raymond, and Diane Moser. *The Story of America's Tunnels* (5–9). Series: Connecting a Continent. 1992, Facts on File LB $19.00 (0-8160-2258-5). The story of how the nation's great tunnels were built and the role they play in transportation. (Rev: BL 2/15/93) [624]

12856 Vandewarker, Paul. *The Big Dig: Reshaping an American City* (5–8). Illus. 2001, Little, Brown $17.95 (0-316-60598-0). This is a fascinating and informative account of Boston's massive effort to overhaul its transportation infrastructure. (Rev: BL 10/1/01; HB 1–2/02; HBG 3/02; SLJ 12/01) [624]

12857 Wilkinson, Philip, and Jacqueline Dineen. *Transportation* (5–8). Illus. 1995, Chelsea LB $21.95 (0-7910-2768-6). An informative, simple overview of inventions and changes that created the modern transportation systems of today. (Rev: BR 5–6/96; VOYA 2/96) [629]

Airplanes, Aeronautics, and Ballooning

12858 Aaseng, Nathan. *Breaking the Sound Barrier* (6–9). 1992, Messner paper $7.95 (0-671-74213-2).

The events that led to the breaking of the sound barrier by Chuck Yeager in 1947, including the efforts of early pilots to achieve greater air speed. (Rev: BL 11/15/92) [626.132]

12859 Berliner, Don. *Aviation: Reaching for the Sky* (5–8). Illus. Series: Innovators. 1997, Oliver LB $21.95 (1-881508-33-1). A thorough history of aviation, beginning with early hot-air balloons and dirigibles and continuing through the Wright Brothers and Sikorsky's helicopter to supersonic jets. (Rev: BL 5/1/97; BR 9–10/97; SLJ 7/97) [629.133]

12860 Carson, Mary Kay. *The Wright Brothers for Kids: How They Invented the Airplane: 21 Activities Exploring the Science and History of Flight* (4–8). 2003, Chicago Review paper $14.95 (1-55652-477-3). After an account of the achievements of the Wrights and other early airplane enthusiasts, 21 activities allow readers to investigate some of the basic principles and to learn about equipment and means of communication. (Rev: SLJ 6/03) [629.13]

12861 Cole, Michael D. *TWA Flight 800: Explosion in Midair* (4–8). Series: American Disasters. 1999, Enslow LB $18.95 (0-7660-1217-4). A dramatic account of the air tragedy. (Rev: BL 1/1–15/99; HBG 10/99) [629.136]

12862 DeAngelis, Gina. *The Hindenburg* (6–8). Series: Great Disasters: Reforms and Ramifications. 2000, Chelsea LB $19.95 (0-7910-5272-9). A description of the Hindenburg disaster precedes discussion of how this tragedy has influenced safety regulations. (Rev: HBG 3/01; SLJ 1/01) [363.12]

12863 Friedrich, Belinda. *The Explosion of TWA Flight 800* (8–10). Series: Great Disasters: Reforms and Ramifications. 2001, Chelsea LB $21.95 (0-7910-6325-9). An account of this tragedy over Long Island in 1996, detailing the recovery efforts, the investigation, and the many theories about the cause of the disaster. (Rev: BR 5–6/02; HBG 10/02; SLJ 5/02) [363.12]

12864 Gaffney, Timothy R. *Air Safety: Preventing Future Disasters* (7–12). Illus. Series: Issues in Focus. 1999, Enslow LB $19.95 (0-7660-1108-9). Efforts being made to improve air safety are covered, with information on recent disasters, on why planes crash, and on how the causes of accidents are determined. (Rev: HBG 4/00; SLJ 2/00) [363.12]

12865 Gaffney, Timothy R. *Hurricane Hunters* (4–7). Series: Aircraft. 2001, Enslow LB $18.95 (0-7660-1569-6). Information on the planes that investigate hurricanes is accompanied by quotations from the pilots and scientists who fly in them. (Rev: HBG 3/02; SLJ 2/02) [551.55]

12866 Hansen, Ole Steen. *Amazing Flights: The Golden Age* (4–7). Illus. Series: The Story of Flight. 2003, Crabtree LB $23.92 (0-7787-1202-8); paper $8.95 (0-7787-1218-4). Double-page spreads present text, feature sidebars, color photographs, and paintings on the people and events of flying after World War I — air races, barnstormers, Lindbergh, and more. (Rev: BL 10/15/03) [629.13]

12867 Hansen, Ole Steen. *Commercial Aviation* (4–7). Series: The Story of Flight. 2003, Crabtree $23.93 (0-7787-1205-2). The history and development of airlines and other forms of commercial aviation are discussed with coverage of present-day problems. (Rev: BL 10/15/03) [629.13]

12868 Hansen, Ole Steen. *Modern Military Aircraft* (4–7). Illus. Series: The Story of Flight. 2003, Crabtree LB $23.92 (0-7787-1204-4); paper $8.95 (0-7787-1220-6). A highly visual overview of military aircraft since World War II, with a spotter's guide. (Rev: BL 10/15/03) [623.]

12869 Hart, Philip S. *Flying Free: America's First Black Aviators* (5–9). 1992, Lerner LB $22.60 (0-8225-1598-9). The contributions of African Americans who succeeded against great odds to become aerial performers, combat pilots, and aviation instructors. (Rev: BL 10/15/92; SLJ 1/93) [629.13]

12870 Haskins, Jim. *Black Eagles: African Americans in Aviation* (5–8). Illus. 1995, Scholastic paper $14.95 (0-590-45912-0). This account traces the contributions made to aviation history by African Americans from before World War I to the astronaut Mae Jemison. (Rev: BL 2/15/95; SLJ 4/95) [629]

12871 Hewish, Mark. *The Young Scientist Book of Jets* (4–7). Illus. 1978, EDC paper $6.95 (0-86020-051-5). An attractive, semi-comic-book format is used to cover basic material.

12872 Iversen, Eve. *Animal Aviators: Masters of Flight* (4–7). Illus. 2001, Watts LB $25.00 (0-531-11749-9). An intriguing account that looks at animals' ability to fly and glide and at human attempts to duplicate this talent. (Rev: BL 7/01) [573.7]

12873 Landau, Elaine. *Air Crashes* (4–7). Series: Watts Library. 1999, Watts LB $24.00 (0-531-20346-8). With photographs on almost every page, this book re-creates such air disasters as the Hindenburg, the 1960 Christmas crash, United Airlines Flight 232, and TWA Flight 800. (Rev: SLJ 2/00) [629.136]

12874 Maynard, Chris. *Aircraft* (5–8). Illus. Series: Need for Speed. 1999, Lerner LB $23.93 (0-8225-2485-6); paper $12.75 (0-8225-9855-8). Using double-page spreads, this work introduces high-speed aircraft. (Rev: BL 1/1–15/00; HBG 3/00; SLJ 2/00) [629.133]

12875 Millspaugh, Ben. *Aviation and Space Science Projects* (5–8). Illus. 1992, TAB paper $9.95 (0-8306-2156-3). The principles of flight are explored in 19 projects that vary in difficulty and complexity. (Rev: BL 1/15/92; SLJ 6/92) [629.1]

12876 Parker, Steve. *What's Inside Airplanes?* (4–8). Illus. Series: What's Inside? 1995, Bedrick LB $17.95 (0-87226-394-0). Elaborate illustrations show various types of airplanes and describe their parts, including pistons, propellers, fuel tanks, and landing gear. (Rev: SLJ 12/95) [629.133]

12877 Rinard, Judith E. *Book of Flight* (4–8). Illus. 2001, Firefly $24.95 (1-55209-619-X); paper $14.95 (1-55209-599-1). Significant moments in man's quest for flight each cover a two-page spread in this book based on the Smithsonian's Air and Space Museum collection. (Rev: BL 11/1/01; HBG 3/02; SLJ 12/01; VOYA 2/02) [629.1309]

12878 Santella, Andrew. *Air Force One* (4–7). Illus. 2003, Millbrook LB $24.90 (0-7613-2617-0). An overview of the aircraft that have transported United States presidents, with an inside look at today's Air Force One. (Rev: BL 2/15/03; HBG 10/03; SLJ 8/03) [387.7]

12879 Sherrow, Victoria. *The Hindenburg Disaster: Doomed Airship* (4–8). Series: American Disasters. 2002, Enslow LB $18.95 (0-7660-1554-8). Excellent illustrations and a clear text are used to tell the story of the destruction of the mighty German dirigible. (Rev: BL 6/1–15/02; HBG 10/02; SLJ 6/02) [629.133]

12880 Sullivan, George. *Modern Fighter Planes* (7–12). Series: Military Aircraft. 1991, Facts on File LB $19.95 (0-8160-2352-2). The stories of 11 fighter planes conceived and tested between 1960 and 1990, with black-and-white photographs and a glossary. (Rev: BL 1/15/92; SLJ 3/92) [358.4]

12881 Tessendorf, K. C. *Barnstormers and Daredevils* (5–8). Illus. 1988, Macmillan LB $14.95 (0-689-31346-2). The fascinating story of fearless pioneers of flight including Lindbergh and Wiley Post. (Rev: BCCB 4/88; BL 9/15/88; BR 1–2/89; SLJ 10/88) [797.5]

12882 Tessendorf, K. C. *Wings Around the World: The American World Flight of 1924* (4–8). Illus. 1991, Macmillan LB $14.95 (0-689-31550-3). The thrilling story of the four teams that were involved in the first around-the-world flight in 1924. (Rev: BL 1/15/92; SLJ 11/91) [629.132]

12883 Wilkey, Michael. *They Never Gave Up: Adventures in Early Airation* (5–8). Illus. 1998, Orca paper $9.95 (1-55143-077-0). This history of early aviation in North America emphasizes Canadian pioneers, their fortitude, setbacks, and lasting contributions. (Rev: SLJ 9/98) [629.133]

Automobiles and Trucks

12884 Italia, Bob. *Great Auto Makers and Their Cars* (6–10). Illus. Series: Profiles. 1993, Oliver LB $19.95 (1-881508-08-0). This is a history of automobiles with coverage of famous cars and biographies of famous engineers and automakers. (Rev: BL 10/15/93; SLJ 11/93) [629.2]

12885 Johnstone, Mike. *Monster Trucks* (5–8). Series: Need for Speed. 2002, Lerner LB $28.75 (0-8225-0388-3). In stunning action-filled text and pictures, this book highlights huge trucks that weigh thousands of pounds and stand more than 10 feet high. (Rev: BL 8/02; HBG 10/02; SLJ 7/02) [629.225]

12886 McKenna, A. T. *Corvette* (5–7). Series: Ultimate Car. 2000, ABDO LB $24.21 (1-57765-127-8). This introduction to this famous sports car includes material on its design, construction, and records it has broken. Similar material appears in companion books *Ferrari, Jaguar, Lamborghini, Mustang,* and *Porsche* (all 2000). (Rev: BL 3/1/01; HBG 10/01) [629]

12887 Raby, Philip. *Racing Cars* (5–8). Series: Need for Speed. 1999, Lerner LB $23.93 (0-8225-2487-2). Using an attention-getting format with plenty of color, action photographs, and sidebars, this book covers such topics as Le Mans, dragsters, the Camel T, dune buggies, and carting. (Rev: BL 1/1–15/00; HBG 3/00; SLJ 2/00) [623.8]

12888 Schleifer, Jay. *Corvette: America's Sports Car* (6–10). Series: Cool Classics. 1992, Macmillan LB $13.95 (0-89686-697-1). Presents information on styling, engine development, suspension and braking advances, and other technical matters, with color photographs of various Corvette models. Also use *Ferrari, Mustang,* and *Porsche* (all 1992). (Rev: BL 10/15/92) [629.222]

12889 Simonds, Christopher. *The Model T Ford* (5–7). Illus. Series: Turning Points. 1991, Silver Burdett LB $17.95 (0-382-24122-3); paper $11.00 (0-382-24117-7). The invention and development of the Model T and its impact on America. (Rev: BL 1/15/92) [629.222]

12890 Whitman, Sylvia. *Get Up and Go! The History of American Road Travel* (5–8). Illus. 1996, Lerner LB $30.35 (0-8225-1735-3). From primitive pathways to modern superhighways, this is a history of American roads and the vehicles that traveled them. (Rev: BL 10/15/96; SLJ 10/96; VOYA 2/97) [388.1]

Railroads

12891 Barter, James. *Building the Transcontinental Railroad* (7–10). Series: World History. 2002, Gale LB $27.45 (1-56006-880-9). Using many quotations from primary and secondary sources, this book gives a fine overview of the triumphs and tragedies associated with building the first railroad across the United States. (Rev: BL 4/15/02; SLJ 5/02) [365]

12892 Blumberg, Rhoda. *Full Steam Ahead: The Race to Build a Transcontinental Railroad* (6–12). Illus. 1996, National Geographic $18.95 (0-7922-

2715-8). A realistic account that includes stories of the corruption, greed, exploitation, sacrifice, and heroism that went into the building of the first transcontinental railroad. (Rev: BL 6/1–15/96*; SLJ 8/96*) [365]

12893 Cefrey, Holly. *High Speed Trains* (4–7). Illus. Series: Built for Speed. 2001, Children's LB $20.00 (0-516-23157-X); paper $6.95 (0-516-23260-6). Train fans will enjoy this attractive overview of high-speed rail in various countries, with information on history, design, and future trends. (Rev: BL 12/1/01) [385]

12894 Coiley, John. *Train* (5–9). Series: Eyewitness Books. 1992, Knopf $20.99 (0-679-91684-9). A history of trains, their parts, and their importance, supplemented by lavish illustrations. (Rev: BL 11/1/92) [625.1]

12895 Houghton, Gillian. *The Transcontinental Railroad: A Primary Source History of America's First Coast-to-Coast Railroad* (4–8). Series: Primary Sources in American History. 2003, Rosen LB $29.25 (0-8239-3684-8). Timelines and reproductions of period photographs and relevant items add to the narrative in this introduction to the planning and construction of the railroad in the mid-19th century. (Rev: SLJ 5/03) [385]

12896 Johnstone, Michael. *Look Inside Cross-Sections: Trains* (4–8). Illus. Series: Look Inside Cross-Sections. 1995, DK paper $6.95 (0-7894-0319-6). Cross-sectional drawings with descriptive text are given for 10 past and present locomotives. (Rev: BL 9/15/95) [625.1]

12897 Laughlin, Rosemary. *The Great Iron Link: The Building of the Central Pacific Railroad* (6–9). Illus. 1996, Morgan Reynolds LB $21.95 (1-883846-14-5). An interesting history of the Central Pacific Railroad that focuses on the five men who were responsible for its inception. (Rev: BL 10/15/96; BR 5–6/97; SLJ 4/97) [385]

12898 Levinson, Nancy S. *She's Been Working on the Railroad* (5–8). Illus. 1997, Dutton $16.99 (0-525-67545-0). A history of women's roles as railway workers, including the famous Harvey Girls of the late 1800s. (Rev: BL 9/15/97; HBG 3/98; SLJ 12/97; VOYA 12/97) [331.4]

12899 McNeese, Tim. *America's First Railroads* (4–8). Series: Americans on the Move. 1993, Macmillan LB $11.95 (0-89686-729-3). A history of early railroads and their impact on U.S. history. (Rev: SLJ 8/93) [385]

12900 Maynard, Chris. *High-Speed Trains* (5–8). Series: Need for Speed. 2002, Lerner LB $28.75 (0-8225-0387-5). This action-packed book looks at fast trains from around the world, propelled by steam, oil, magnets, and electricity. (Rev: BL 8/02; HBG 10/02) [625.1]

833

12901 Murphy, Jim. *Across America on an Emigrant Train* (6–12). 1993, Clarion $18.00 (0-395-63390-7). A cross-country train trip by Robert Louis Stevenson in 1879 is the backdrop for information on the history of railroads. (Rev: BCCB 1/94; BL 12/1/93*; SLJ 12/93*) [625.2]

12902 Spangenburg, Raymond, and Diane Moser. *The Story of America's Railroads* (5–9). Series: Connecting a Continent. 1991, Facts on File LB $18.95 (0-8160-2257-7). This history of the railways incorporates stories, biographies, timelines, and charts to show their influence on the development of the nation. (Rev: BL 11/15/91) [625]

12903 Streissguth, Thomas. *The Transcontinental Railroad* (6–8). Illus. Series: Building History. 1999, Lucent LB $18.96 (1-56006-564-8). Complete with a timeline, photographs, sidebars, and maps, this is a realistic account of the building of the transcontinental railroad. (Rev: BL 1/1–15/00; HBG 9/00) [385.]

12904 Warburton, Lois. *Railroads: Bridging the Continents* (6–10). Series: Encyclopedia of Discovery and Invention. 1991, Lucent LB $52.44 (1-56006-216-9). The history of the nation's railroads. (Rev: BL 4/15/92) [385]

12905 Weitzman, David. *Superpower: The Making of a Steam Locomotive* (6–9). Illus. 1987, Godine $35.00 (0-87923-671-X). A step-by-step guide to the parts of a locomotive and how they are assembled. (Rev: SLJ 1/88) [625.2]

12906 Wormser, Richard. *The Iron Horse: How Railroads Changed America* (6–9). 1993, Walker LB $19.85 (0-8027-8222-1). The economic and social impact of the railroad between 1830 and 1900, from the robber barons to the Gold Rush and massive influx of immigrants. (Rev: BL 12/15/93; SLJ 1/94; VOYA 4/94) [385]

12907 Yancey, Diane. *Camels for Uncle Sam* (4–7). Illus. 1995, Hendrick-Long $16.95 (0-937460-91-5). The story of the experiment that involved importing camels to the Southwest in the 1850s to help in railroad construction. (Rev: BL 9/15/95) [357]

Ships and Boats

12908 Adams, Simon. *Titanic* (3–8). Illus. 1999, DK paper $15.99 (0-7894-4724-X). All about the doomed ship, from its construction to its destruction, attractively presented with diagrams, photographs, illustrations, and other graphic elements. (Rev: BL 11/15/99; HBG 4/00) [910]

12909 Ballard, Robert D., and Rick Archbold. *Ghost Liners* (5–9). Illus. 1998, Little, Brown $19.95 (0-316-08020-9). The discoverer of the *Titanic* describes this adventure and discusses other ship disasters including the *Lusitania* and the *Andrea Doria*. (Rev: BL 8/98; HBG 3/99; SLJ 9/98) [363]

12910 Bornhoft, Simon. *High Speed Boats* (5–8). Series: Need for Speed. 1999, Lerner LB $23.93 (0-8225-2488-0). Using a jazzy, attention-getting format with action photographs, sidebars with statistics and interesting facts, and different type sizes, this book covers present and future speedboats. (Rev: BL 1/1–15/00; HBG 3/00) [629.222]

12911 Delgado, James P. *Wrecks of American Warships* (5–7). Series: Shipwrecks. 2000, Watts LB $24.00 (0-531-20376-X). This book describes how underwater archaeologists have discovered and explored such warships as the *Constitution, Philadelphia, Alabama,* and *Arizona.* (Rev: BL 10/15/00) [623.8]

12912 Graham, Ian. *Boats, Ships, Submarines and Other Floating Machinery* (4–7). Illus. Series: How Things Work. 1993, Kingfisher paper $8.95 (1-85697-867-2). This book explains such scientific principles as wind power and buoyancy and how they apply to a wide range of crafts, including hydrofoils and hovercrafts. (Rev: BL 6/1–15/93; SLJ 5/93) [623.8]

12913 Kentley, Eric. *Boat* (5–9). Series: Eyewitness Books. 1992, Knopf $20.99 (0-679-91678-4). A richly illustrated history of boats and their planning, design, construction, and operation. (Rev: BL 6/1/92) [623.8]

12914 Kently, Eric. *The Story of the Titanic* (4–8). 2001, DK paper $17.99 (0-7894-7943-5). Details of life aboard ship, double-page spreads, cutaways and cross-sections, facts and trivia, and a well-designed layout are just a few of the features of this beautifully designed large-format book. (Rev: BL 12/15/01; HBG 3/02; SLJ 12/01) [363.1]

12915 Landau, Elaine. *Maritime Disasters* (5–7). Illus. Series: Watts Library. 1999, Watts LB $24.00 (0-531-20344-1); paper $8.95 (0-531-16427-6). This book discusses four major maritime disasters: the *Titanic, Lusitania, Morro Castle,* and *Andrea Doria.* (Rev: BL 2/1/00; SLJ 2/00) [910.4]

12916 Macaulay, David. *Ship* (5–8). 1993, Houghton $19.95 (0-395-52439-3). A fictional caravel is featured in this exploration of historical seagoing vessels and the work of underwater archaeologists. (Rev: BCCB 11/93; BL 10/15/93*; SLJ 11/93) [387.2]

12917 McNeese, Tim. *Clippers and Whaling Ships* (4–8). Series: Americans on the Move. 1993, Macmillan LB $11.95 (0-89686-735-8). Early American shipping and commerce are discussed. Also use *West by Steamboat* (1993). (Rev: SLJ 8/93) [623.8]

12918 Philbrick, Nathaniel. *Revenge of the Whale: The True Story of the Whaleship Essex* (6–10). Illus. 2002, Putnam $16.99 (0-399-23795-X). This abridged version of *In the Heart of the Sea* (Viking, 2000) relates for a younger audience the amazing story of the sperm whale that sank a ship in 1820 and the survival of a handful of crewmen. (Rev: BCCB 11/02; HB 1–2/03*; HBG 3/03; SLJ 9/02*) [910]

12919 Wilkinson, Phillip. *Ships* (4–7). Illus. 2000, Kingfisher $16.95 (0-7534-5280-4). Straightforward text and handsome illustrations cover maritime history from the earliest sailing ships and discuss piracy, the slave trade, and superstitions about the sea. (Rev: BL 2/1/01; HBG 10/01; SLJ 1/01) [623.8]

Weapons, Submarines, and the Armed Forces

12920 Aaseng, Nathan. *The Marine Corps in Action* (4–8). Series: U.S. Military Branches and Careers. 2001, Enslow LB $20.95 (0-7660-1637-4). An attractive introduction to all aspects of the Marine Corps that looks at the future of this military branch and the number of women and minorities included. (Rev: HBG 3/02; SLJ 4/02) [359.9]

12921 Adams, Simon. *Castles and Forts* (5–8). Illus. Series: Kingfisher Knowledge. 2003, Kingfisher $11.95 (0-7534-5620-6). From Norman mottes to Masada to the Great Wall of China, this is an illustrated exploration of castles, forts, and fortifications, their construction, and their purpose. (Rev: SLJ 12/03) [355.7]

12922 Cohen, Daniel. *The Manhattan Project* (7–12). 1999, Millbrook LB $24.90 (0-7613-0359-6). This account captures the spies, intrigue, politics, secrecy, and science that became part of the story of the first atomic bomb. (Rev: BL 7/99; SLJ 9/99) [355.8]

12923 Day, Malcolm. *The World of Castles and Forts* (5–8). 1997, Bedrick $19.95 (0-87226-278-2). A world history of fortification, from ancient walled cities to the modern Maginot Line and nuclear bastions. (Rev: BL 3/1/97; SLJ 2/97) [355.7]

12924 Dudley, William, ed. *Biological Warfare* (8–12). Series: Opposing Viewpoints. 2003, Gale LB $33.70 (0-7377-1671-1); paper $22.45 (0-7377-1672-X). A collection of essays that explore the seriousness of the threat of biological warfare from terrorists using germs as weapons and how the United States and the world should respond. (Rev: BL 1/1–15/04) [356]

12925 Ferrell, Nancy Warren. *The U.S. Air Force* (1–8). Illus. 1990, Lerner LB $23.93 (0-8225-1433-8). This book includes information on how to enlist, the ranking system in the Air Force, and today's use of modern technology. (Rev: BL 5/15/91) [358.4]

12926 Gay, Kathlyn. *Silent Death: The Threat of Biological and Chemical Warfare* (6–12). Illus. 2001, Twenty-First Century LB $24.90 (0-7613-1401-6). Gay presents a thorough and balanced assessment of the threat presented by biological and chemical weapons, compiled before the Iraq war. (Rev: BL 4/1/01; HBG 10/01; SLJ 4/01) [358]

12927 Gonen, Rivka. *Charge! Weapons and Warfare in Ancient Times* (5–8). Illus. 1993, Lerner LB $23.93 (0-8225-3201-8). A look at the development of weapons from sticks and stones to battering rams. (Rev: BCCB 12/93; BL 2/1/94; SLJ 2/94) [355.8]

12928 Grady, Sean M. *Explosives: Devices of Controlled Destruction* (6–10). Series: Encyclopedia of Discovery and Invention. 1995, Lucent LB $52.44 (1-56006-250-9). A history of explosives and their use in war and peace through the ages. (Rev: BL 4/15/95) [662]

12929 Hamilton, John. *Armed Forces* (4–7). Illus. Series: War on Terrorism. 2002, ABDO LB $25.65 (1-57765-674-1). An introduction to the U.S. military and the roles these services play in protecting the country, with color photographs, a glossary, and list of Web sites. (Rev: BL 8/02; HBG 10/02) [355]

12930 Hamilton, John. *Weapons of War* (4–7). Illus. Series: War on Terrorism. 2002, ABDO LB $25.65 (1-57765-673-3). This account describes the weapons currently available to U.S. military personnel, including fighter planes, bombers, helicopters, bombs, missiles, and ships. (Rev: BL 5/1/02; HBG 10/02) [623.4]

12931 Hamilton, John. *Weapons of War: A Pictorial History of the Past One Thousand Years* (4–7). Illus. Series: The Millennium. 2000, ABDO LB $25.65 (1-57765-362-9). In a short space, this book traces 1,000 years of weapons including small weaponry, ships, firearms, military airplanes, tanks, missiles, and bombs. (Rev: BL 7/00; HBG 10/00; SLJ 10/00) [623.4]

12932 Holmes, Richard. *Battle* (5–8). Series: Eyewitness Books. 1995, Knopf $20.99 (0-679-97333-8). Full-captioned photographs and drawings are used in this introduction to warfare from ancient days to World War I, with descriptions of infantry, artillery, supply and transport, reconnaissance, and so forth. (Rev: BL 12/15/95; SLJ 1/96) [355]

12933 Hurley, Jennifer A., ed. *Weapons of Mass Destruction* (8–12). Series: Opposing Viewpoints. 1999, Greenhaven LB $32.45 (0-7377-0059-9); paper $21.20 (0-7377-0058-0). This collection of writings explores the possibility of a terrorist attack using weapons of mass destruction, domestic and foreign policies concerning these weapons, and ways to defend the country against such attacks. (Rev: BL 4/15/99) [355.02]

12934 Kennedy, Robert C. *Life as a Paratrooper* (4–7). Series: On Duty. 2000, Children's LB $20.00

(0-516-23344-0). An easily read account that describes the work, responsibilities, and opportunities of a paratrooper. Also use *Life as an Air Force Fighter Pilot* (2000). (Rev: BL 3/1/01) [358.4]

12935 Kennedy, Robert C. *Life in the Army Special Forces* (4–7). Series: On Duty. 2000, Children's LB $20.00 (0-516-23350-5). The work, responsibilities, and career possibilities of members of this special army unit are described in this well-illustrated book. (Rev: BL 3/1/01; SLJ 3/01) [335]

12936 Kennedy, Robert C. *Life in the Marines* (4–7). Series: On Duty. 2000, Children's LB $20.00 (0-516-23348-3). This branch of the military is examined with material on the special training and responsibilities involved. (Rev: BL 3/1/01) [359.6]

12937 Kennedy, Robert C. *Life with the Navy Seals* (4–7). Series: On Duty. 2000, Children's LB $20.00 (0-516-23351-3). A look at this special branch of the U.S. Navy with material on its responsibilities, training, and career opportunities. (Rev: BL 3/1/01) [359]

12938 Landau, Elaine. *The New Nuclear Reality* (6–12). Illus. 2000, Twenty-First Century LB $22.90 (0-7613-1555-1). This account chronicles the post-war growth of countries that have nuclear arms including Russia, North Korea, Pakistan, and India. (Rev: BL 7/00; HBG 9/00; SLJ 9/00) [327.1]

12939 Levine, Herbert M. *Chemical and Biological Weapons in Our Times* (8–12). Illus. 2000, Watts LB $25.00 (0-531-11852-5). Levine looks at weapons of mass destruction, and in particular the sarin attack on the Japanese subway, providing a historical perspective to more recent events. (Rev: BL 1/1–15/01) [358]

12940 Meltzer, Milton. *Weapons and Warfare: From the Stone Age to the Space Age* (5–9). Illus. 1996, HarperCollins LB $17.89 (0-06-024876-9). This work describes the evolution of weapons from clubs to the H-bomb, including how these weapons have been used and misused through the ages. (Rev: BCCB 2/97; BL 12/1/96; SLJ 1/97) [355.02]

12941 Pelta, Kathy. *The U.S. Navy* (5–7). Illus. 1990, Lerner LB $23.93 (0-8225-1435-4). A look at the history and present status and activities of the U.S. Navy. (Rev: BL 12/1/90) [359]

12942 Rice, Earl. *Weapons of War* (6–12). Series: American War Library: The Vietnam War. 2001, Lucent LB $19.96 (1-56006-719-5). The weapons used during the Vietnam War are highlighted in archival photographs and a text that uses many first-hand accounts. (Rev: BL 3/15/01) [959.704]

12943 Richie, Jason. *Weapons: Designing the Tools of War* (5–10). Illus. 2000, Oliver LB $21.95 (1-881508-60-9). Using separate chapters for different

categories of weapons — for example, submarines, battleships, and tanks — this is a history of the development of weaponry from 300 B.C. to today. (Rev: BL 5/1/00; HBG 10/00; SLJ 8/00) [623]

12944 Robertshaw, Andrew. *A Soldier's Life: A Visual History of Soldiers Through the Ages* (4–8). 1997, Lodestar $16.99 (0-525-67550-7). Describes a soldier's uniform, equipment, and weapons through the ages, beginning with a Roman soldier in A.D. 50. (Rev: BCCB 6/97; BL 6/1–15/97; SLJ 6/97) [355.02]

12945 Rowan, N. R. *Women in the Marines: The Boot Camp Challenge* (4–8). Illus. Series: Armed Services. 1994, Lerner LB $23.93 (0-8225-1430-3). Covers the harrowing basic training that women face in the Marines. (Rev: BCCB 4/94; BL 2/15/94; SLJ 4/94) [359.9]

12946 Sherrow, Victoria. *The Making of the Atom Bomb* (7–10). Series: World History. 2000, Lucent LB $18.96 (1-56006-585-0). A review of the development of the bomb, the decision to use the first one, and continuing work on these weapons. (Rev: BL 6/1–15/00; HBG 9/00; SLJ 9/00) [940.54]

12947 Speakman, Jay. *Weapons of War* (6–12). Series: American War Library: The Persian Gulf War. 2000, Lucent LB $19.96 (1-56006-640-0). This heavily illustrated book covers the weapons that were used during the Persian Gulf War of 1991. (Rev: BL 3/1/01) [956.7]

12948 Streissguth, Tom. *Nuclear Weapons: More Countries, More Threats* (6–12). Series: Issues in Focus. 2000, Enslow LB $20.96 (0-7660-1248-4). An overview of nuclear weapons, who controls the technology to produce them, and the efforts to control this threat to human survival. (Rev: BL 9/15/00; HBG 3/01) [355.02]

12949 Warner, J. F. *The U.S. Marine Corps* (4–8). Illus. Series: Armed Services. 1991, Lerner LB $22.95 (0-8225-1432-X). From how to enlist to a discussion of the new technology, this is a well-organized introduction to the U.S. Marine Corps. (Rev: BL 2/1/92; SLJ 2/92) [359.6]

12950 Wolny, Philip. *Weapons Satellites* (5–9). Series: The Library of Satellites. 2003, Rosen LB $26.50 (0-8239-3855-7). This account explores the growing technology of weapon satellites that are capable of knocking out enemies' satellites, and launching attacks from outer space. (Rev: BL 11/15/03) [629.46]

12951 Woods, Mary B., and Michael Woods. *Ancient Warfare: From Clubs to Catapults* (5–8). Series: Ancient Technologies. 2000, Runestone LB $25.26 (0-8225-2999-8). The weaponry of ancient civilizations including Greece and China. (Rev: BCCB 12/00; BL 9/15/00; HBG 3/01; SLJ 1/01) [623]

Recreation and Sports

Crafts, Hobbies, and Pastimes

General and Miscellaneous

12952 Adkins, Jan. *String: Tying It Up, Tying It Down* (5–8). Illus. 1992, Macmillan LB $13.95 (0-684-18875-9). With a text that reads like a novel, this book instructs and entertains readers in the art of knot tying. (Rev: BL 4/15/92; SLJ 6/92) [677]

12953 Albregts, Lisa, and Elizabeth Cape. *Best Friends: Tons of Crazy, Cool Things to Do with Your Girlfriends* (4–8). Illus. 1998, Chicago Review paper $12.95 (1-55652-326-2). Arranged by seasons, this activity book contains crafts, games, dances, snacks, and skits to amuse girls when they get together. (Rev: BL 3/1/99; SLJ 1/99) [796.083]

12954 Birdseye, Tom. *A Kids' Guide to Building Forts* (5–8). 1993, Harbinger paper $11.95 (0-943173-69-8). A guide to the building of 19 kinds of forts, from the very simple to the more complex, some of which can be turned into clubhouses. (Rev: SLJ 9/93) [745.5]

12955 Bonnell, Jennifer. *D. I. Y. Girl: The Real Girl's Guide to Making Everything from Lip Gloss to Lamps* (7–12). 2003, Penguin paper $12.99 (0-14-250048-8). Cool crafts — gifts, clothes, and decorations — are introduced in a friendly, conversational text with clear instructions and lists of supplies. (Rev: BL 7/03; SLJ 7/03) [745.5]

12956 Brownrigg, Sheri. *Hearts and Crafts* (4–8). Illus. 1995, Tricycle Pr. paper $9.95 (1-883672-28-7). Clear instructions show how to complete a variety of Valentine's Day projects, including making necklaces and candles. (Rev: BL 3/1/96; SLJ 3/96) [745.5]

12957 Cook, Nick. *Roller Coasters, or, I Had So Much Fun, I Almost Puked* (4–7). Illus. 1998, Carolrhoda LB $27.15 (1-57505-071-4). This intriguing book describes the excitement of a roller-coaster ride and discusses the history, types, construction, and safety features of various roller coasters. (Rev: BCCB 6/98; BL 4/15/98; HBG 10/98) [791]

12958 Deshpande, Chris. *Festival Crafts* (4–7). Illus. Series: World Wide Crafts. 1994, Gareth Stevens LB $23.93 (0-8368-1153-4). Thirteen craft projects that relate to such multicultural festivals as Mardi Gras and Mexico's All Souls Day. (Rev: BL 3/1/95; SLJ 1/95) [745.5]

12959 Drake, Jane, and Ann Love. *The Kids Summer Handbook* (4–7). 1994, Ticknor $15.95 (0-395-68711-X). A guide to all sorts of outdoor crafts and activities, with several involving whittling, weaving, and knotting. (Rev: BL 4/1/94; SLJ 6/94) [790.1]

12960 Goodman, Michael. *Model Railroading* (5–8). Illus. Series: Hobby Guides. 1993, Crestwood LB $12.95 (0-89686-620-3). As well as describing the basics of model railroading as a hobby, this account discusses clubs, displays, and organizations. (Rev: SLJ 2/94) [625.1]

12961 Goodman, Michael. *Radio Control Models* (5–8). Illus. Series: Hobby Guides. 1993, Crestwood LB $12.95 (0-89686-622-X). Gives practical advice on getting started in this fascinating hobby, with good background information on radio control models plus coverage of equipment, competitions, and organizations. (Rev: SLJ 2/94) [621]

12962 Hendry, Linda. *Making Gift Boxes* (4–8). Series: Kids Can! 1999, Kids Can paper $5.95 (1-55074-503-4). The 14 boxes included in this fine craft book with clear instructions include a photo box, a garden box to grow seeds, a box for storing CDs, and a treasure box with false compartments. (Rev: SLJ 12/99) [745]

12963 Jennings, Lynette. *Have Fun with Your Room: 28 Cool Projects for Teens* (6–10). 2001, Simon & Schuster paper $12.00 (0-689-82585-4). The author offers a number of affordable ways to decorate bedrooms, with suggestions for walls, windows, headboards, bulletin boards, and so forth. (Rev: SLJ 11/01)

12964 Johnson, Ginger. *Make Your Own Christmas Ornaments* (6–9). Illus. 2002, Williamson paper $8.95 (1-885593-79-1). A collection of 25 ornaments with clear instructions and photographs of finished products. (Rev: BL 12/15/02; SLJ 10/02) [745.5]

12965 Kerina, Jane. *African Crafts* (5–8). 1970, Lion LB $13.95 (0-87460-084-7). Many projects arranged geographically by the region in Africa where they originated.

12966 Levine, Shar, and Michael Ouchi. *The Ultimate Balloon Book* (5–8). Illus. 2001, Sterling paper $9.95 (0-8069-2959-6). A guide to balloon creations that progresses from the simple (dachshunds) to the advanced. (Rev: BL 8/01; SLJ 10/01) [745.594]

12967 McGraw, Sheila. *Gifts Kids Can Make* (4–8). Photos by Sheila McGraw and Joy von Tiedemann. 1994, Firefly paper $9.95 (1-895565-35-9). A craft book that gives directions for making 14 simple gifts, such as a cotton sock doll and a hobby horse, using easily obtainable materials. (Rev: SLJ 12/94) [745]

12968 MacLeod, Elizabeth. *Gifts to Make and Eat* (4–7). Series: Kids Can Do It. 2001, Kids Can $12.95 (1-55074-956-0); paper $5.95 (1-55074-958-7). Kids learn through step-by-step instructions how to make an array of edible and craft gifts. (Rev: BL 11/1/01; HBG 3/02; SLJ 2/02) [641.5]

12969 Martin, Laura C. *Nature's Art Box: From T-Shirts to Twig Baskets, 65 Cool Projects for Crafty Kids to Make with Natural Materials You Can Find Anywhere* (4–8). 2003, Storey $23.95 (1-58017-503-1); paper $16.95 (1-58017-490-6). These projects use natural materials such as twigs, moss, gourds, stones, shells, flowers, and leaves to make articles including wreaths, necklaces, and a chess set. (Rev: HBG 10/03; SLJ 8/03*) [745.5]

12970 Merrill, Yvonne Y. *Hands-On America: Art Activities About Vikings, Woodland Indians and Early Colonists*, Vol. 1 (4–7). Illus. Series: Hands-On America. 2001, Kits paper $20.00 (0-9643177-6-1). Varied and relatively easy activities focusing on early America will entertain at the same time as enhancing students' knowledge of historical events and concepts. (Rev: SLJ 3/02) [745.5]

12971 Merrill, Yvonne Y. *Hands-On Latin America: Art Activities for All Ages* (4–8). Illus. Series: Hands-On. 1998, Kits paper $20.00 (0-9643177-1-0). A collection of 30 interesting, affordable arts and crafts projects inspired by the ancient cultures of Latin America. (Rev: BL 9/1/98; SLJ 8/98) [980.07]

12972 Monaghan, Kathleen, and Hermon Joyner. *You Can Weave! Projects for Young Weavers* (4–7).

Illus. 2001, Sterling $19.95 (0-87192-493-5). Step-by-step instructions and photographs guide young crafters through weaving projects of varying complexity. (Rev: BL 11/1/01) [746.41]

12973 Olson, Beverly, and Judy Lazzara. *Country Flower Drying* (8–12). 1988, Sterling paper $9.95 (0-8069-6746-3). A concise manual on raising and drying flowers plus tips on creating arrangements and other uses of dried flowers. (Rev: BR 11–12/88) [745.92]

12974 Powell, Michelle. *Mosaics* (4–7). Series: Step-by-Step. 2001, Heinemann LB $24.22 (1-57572-332-8). A number of fascinating projects creating mosaics are described with step-by-step instructions and many colorful illustrations. (Rev: BL 8/1/01; HBG 10/01; SLJ 10/01) [745]

12975 Purdy, Susan. *Christmas Gifts for You to Make* (7–9). 1976, HarperCollins LB $12.89 (0-397-31695-X). Instructions on how to make a wide variety of gifts including puppets, note pads, and aprons. [745.5]

12976 Rhodes, Vicki. *Pumpkin Decorating* (4–8). 1997, Sterling $10.95 (0-8069-9574-2). Clear directions and full-color photographs demonstrate more than 80 designs for pumpkins. (Rev: SLJ 12/97) [745.5]

12977 Schwarz, Renée. *Funky Junk* (4–7). Series: Kids Can Do It. 2002, Kids Can $12.95 (1-55337-387-1); paper $5.95 (1-55337-388-X). Using easily found materials, this craft book supplies details on how to make unusual conversation pieces. (Rev: BL 3/15/03; HBG 10/03; SLJ 4/03) [745.5]

12978 Simons, Robin. *Recyclopedia: Games, Science Equipment and Crafts from Recycled Materials* (5–8). 1976, Houghton paper $13.95 (0-395-59641-6). Clear directions complemented by good illustrations characterize this book of interesting projects using waste materials.

12979 Taylor, Maureen. *Through the Eyes of Your Ancestors: A Step-by-Step Guide to Uncovering Your Family's History* (5–9). Illus. 1999, Houghton $17.00 (0-395-86980-3); paper $8.95 (0-395-86982-X). Budding researchers learn how to investigate family history, from conducting interviews to visiting genealogical libraries. (Rev: BCCB 5/99; BL 3/1/99; HB 5–6/99; HBG 10/99; SLJ 5/99) [929.1]

12980 Temko, Florence. *Traditional Crafts from China* (5–7). Illus. Series: Culture Crafts. 2001, Lerner LB $23.93 (0-8225-2939-4). After a few words about crafts in general, this volume carefully outlines a number of projects relating to Chinese culture, including instructions for picture scrolls and tanagrams. (Rev: BL 2/15/01; HBG 10/01; SLJ 4/01) [745]

12981 Temko, Florence. *Traditional Crafts from the Caribbean* (5–7). Illus. Series: Culture Crafts. 2001,

Lerner LB $23.93 (0-8225-2937-8). Step-by-step instructions with clear diagrams are given for a number of craft projects relating to Caribbean culture including yarn dolls, Puerto Rican masks, and metal cutouts. (Rev: BL 2/15/01; HBG 10/01; SLJ 4/01) [745]

12982 Van Steenwyk, Elizabeth. *Let's Go to the Beach: A History of Sun and Fun by the Sea* (6–9). 2001, Holt $18.95 (0-8050-6235-1). This fascinating exploration of beach-going over the centuries looks at everything from social changes and fashion to sand castle competitions, surfing, music, and beach food. (Rev: BL 5/1/01; HBG 10/01; SLJ 8/01) [797]

12983 White, Linda. *Haunting on a Halloween* (5–7). 2002, Gibbs Smith paper $9.95 (1-58685-112-8). Everything young party planners need to host a Halloween get-together, with instructions for crafts, food, decorations, and costumes. (Rev: BL 9/15/02) [745.594]

American Historical Crafts

12984 Beard, D. C. *The American Boys' Handy Book: What to Do and How to Do It* (5–7). Illus. 1983, Godine paper $12.95 (0-87923-449-0). A facsimile edition of a manual first published in 1882. [790.194]

12985 Caney, Steven. *Steven Caney's Kids' America* (4–7). Illus. 1978, Workman paper $14.95 (0-911104-80-1). Activities that focus on getting children to rediscover parts of America's past.

12986 Greenwood, Barbara. *Pioneer Crafts* (4–8). Illus. 1997, Kids Can paper $4.95 (1-55074-359-7). This guide gives directions for 17 projects such as candle making, soap carving, and basket weaving. (Rev: BL 9/15/97; SLJ 9/97) [745.5]

12987 Merrill, Yvonne Y. *Hands-On Rocky Mountains: Art Activities About Anasazi, American Indians, Settlers, Trappers, and Cowboys* (4–8). Illus. 1996, Kits paper $16.95 (0-9643177-2-9). Historical groups from the Rocky Mountain region — early people, American Indians, trappers, settlers, and cowboys — are introduced and, for each, a series of craft projects is outlined. (Rev: BL 1/1–15/97; SLJ 4/97) [745.5]

12988 Tull, Mary, et al. *North America* (4–7). Series: Artisans Around the World. 1999, Raintree Steck-Vaughn LB $27.12 (0-7398-0117-1). North American folk art is surveyed, from peoples including the Haida of western Canada, New Mexico's Pueblos, the Pennsylvanian German Americans, and African Americans. (Rev: BL 10/15/99; HBG 3/00) [970]

Clay Modeling and Ceramics

12989 Dean, Irene Semanchuk. *Polymer Clay: 30 Terrific Projects to Roll, Mold and Squish* (5–8). Illus. Series: Kids' Crafts. 2003, Sterling $19.95 (1-57990-350-9). Step-by-step instructions are provided for a variety of decorative objects to make from polymer clay. (Rev: SLJ 9/03) [731.4]

12990 Kenny, John B. *The Complete Book of Pottery Making*. 2nd ed. (7–12). Illus. 1976, Chilton paper $29.95 (0-8019-5933-0). Easily followed instructions with many photographs outline the steps in making pottery. [738.1]

12991 Nicholson, Libby, and Yvonne Lau. *Creating with Fimo* (6–10). Illus. Series: Kids Can Crafts. 1999, Kids Can $16.99 (1-55074-310-4); paper $6.99 (1-55074-274-4). Using the nontoxic clay called Fimo (available in crafts stores) and the step-by-step instructions in this book, readers can complete 25 projects suitable for experienced crafters, such as making necklaces, earrings, and pins. (Rev: SLJ 5/99) [738]

12992 Rowe, Christine. *The Children's Book of Pottery* (4–7). Illus. 1989, Trafalgar $24.95 (0-7134-5995-6). A good British import about pottery making. (Rev: BL 12/1/89) [738.1]

Cooking

12993 Albyn, Carole Lisa, and Lois S. Webb. *The Multicultural Cookbook for Students* (6–9). 1993, Oryx paper $30.95 (0-89774-735-6). Provides 337 recipes from 122 countries, arranged geographically. (Rev: BL 2/15/94; SLJ 10/93) [641.59]

12994 Amari, Suad. *Cooking the Lebanese Way*. Rev. ed. (5–10). Series: Easy Menu Ethnic Cookbooks. 2003, Lerner LB $25.26 (0-8225-4116-5). Revised to include low-fat and vegetarian foods, this introduction to Lebanese cooking contains about 40 recipes, clearly explained and well-illustrated. (Rev: BL 9/15/02; HBG 3/03) [641.5]

12995 Andreev, Tania. *Food in Russia* (6–9). Illus. 1989, Rourke LB $26.60 (0-86625-343-2). Both an introduction to Russia and a survey of foods and typical recipes. (Rev: SLJ 12/89) [641.5]

12996 Bacon, Josephine. *Cooking the Israeli Way*. Rev. ed. (5–10). Series: Easy Menu Ethnic Cookbooks. 2002, Lerner LB $25.26 (0-8225-4112-2). After a general introduction to Israel, this book discusses cooking terms and ingredients, and then gives a series of tantalizing recipes with clear instructions. (Rev: BL 7/02; HBG 10/02) [641]

12997 Bisignano, Alphonse. *Cooking the Italian Way*. Rev. ed. (5–10). Series: Easy Menu Ethnic Cookbooks. 2001, Lerner $25.26 (0-8225-4113-0); paper $12.75 (0-8225-4161-0). A revised edition that now includes vegetarian and low-fat recipes as well as an expanded introductory section on the country, the people, and the culture. (Rev: HBG 3/02; SLJ 9/01) [641]

12998 Chung, Okwha, and Judy Monroe. *Cooking the Korean Way*. Rev. ed. (5–10). Illus. Series: Easy Menu Ethnic Cookbooks. 2003, Lerner LB $25.26 (0-8225-4115-7). Tempting recipes and a brief look at where they come from. (Rev: BL 8/88; SLJ 9/88) [641.59519]

12999 Cornell, Kari. *Holiday Cooking Around the World*. Rev. ed. (5–10). Illus. Series: Easy Menu Ethnic Cookbooks. 2002, Lerner LB $25.26 (0-8225-4128-9); paper $7.95 (0-8225-4159-9). Beginning cooks will appreciate the clear instructions and varied options in this appealing book that includes cultural and social information. (Rev: BL 1/1–15/02; HBG 10/02; SLJ 5/02) [641.5]

13000 Coronado, Rosa. *Cooking the Mexican Way*. Rev. ed. (5–10). Series: Easy Menu Ethnic Cookbooks. 2002, Lerner LB $25.26 (0-8225-4117-3). Recipes organized by type of meal are preceded by a section that covers the geography, culture, and festivals and by information on equipment, ingredients, and eating customs. Other titles in this series include *Cooking the East African Way* and *Cooking the Spanish Way* (both 2001). (Rev: HBG 3/02; SLJ 2/02) [641]

13001 Cotler, Amy. *The Secret Garden Cookbook: Recipes Inspired by Frances Hodgson Burnett's The Secret Garden* (4–8). Illus. 1999, HarperCollins $17.95 (0-06-027740-8). A collection of 42 recipes that reflect the locales and characters of Burnett's classic tale, accompanied by fascinating bits of culinary and social history, and quotations from poems, various Victorian personages, and *The Secret Garden*. (Rev: HBG 10/99; SLJ 7/99) [641]

13002 Coyle, Rena. *My First Cookbook* (4–7). Illus. 1985, Workman paper $10.95 (0-89480-846-X). Fifty recipes, including pancakes, salads, and tacos, with an emphasis on safety. (Rev: BL 4/15/86; SLJ 4/86) [641.5123]

13003 D'Amico, Joan, and Karen Eich Drummond. *The Science Chef Travels Around the World: Fun Food Experiments and Recipes for Kids* (4–8). Illus. 1996, Wiley paper $12.95 (0-471-11779-X). An entertaining combination of simple science experiments and international cooking, with recipes from 14 countries and activities that demonstrate scientific principles of various cooking and baking processes. (Rev: BL 2/1/96; SLJ 3/96) [641.5]

13004 Dosier, Susan. *Civil War Cooking: The Union* (6–10). 2000, Blue Earth Books $22.60 (0-7368-0351-3). Recipes accompany information on the foods eaten at the time, with full-color photographs and reproductions. (Rev: BL 8/00; HBG 9/00; SLJ 9/00) [641.5973]

13005 Duden, Jane. *Vegetarianism for Teens* (4–7). Illus. Series: Nutrition and Fitness. 2001, Capstone LB $23.93 (0-7368-0712-8). An overview of vegetarian diets that includes a checklist and tips on coping with people who discount the appeal of a meatless life. (Rev: BL 7/01; HBG 10/01; SLJ 7/01) [613.2]

13006 Erdosh, George. *The African-American Kitchen: Food for Body and Soul* (6–9). Illus. Series: Library of African-American Arts and Culture. 1999, Rosen LB $31.95 (0-8239-1850-5). A survey of dishes associated with African Americans, with recipes and cooking tips. (Rev: BR 9–10/99; SLJ 8/99; VOYA 8/99) [641]

13007 Gaspari, Claudia. *Food in Italy* (6–9). Illus. 1989, Rourke LB $26.60 (0-86625-342-4). This account introduces Italy and its food and gives some recipes. (Rev: SLJ 12/89) [641.5]

13008 Gillies, Judi, and Jennifer Glossop. *The Jumbo Vegetarian Cookbook* (4–8). Illus. 2002, Kids Can paper $14.95 (1-55074-977-3). An introduction to the vegetarian lifestyle, including nutrition and recipes. (Rev: BCCB 7–8/02; BL 3/1/02; SLJ 7/02) [641.5]

13009 Gillies, Judi, and Jennifer Glossop. *The Kids Can Press Jumbo Cookbook* (5–8). Illus. 2000, Kids Can paper $14.95 (1-55074-621-9). After a few cooking tips, this book provides recipes that range from the simple (scrambled eggs) to the difficult (crepes and carrot cake). (Rev: BL 5/1/00; SLJ 6/00) [641.8]

13010 Gioffre, Rosalba. *The Young Chef's French Cookbook* (4–7). Series: I'm the Chef! 2001, Crabtree LB $22.60 (0-7787-0282-0); paper $8.95 (0-7787-0296-0). This oversize book uses double-page spreads to present 15 appetizing French recipes along with good background material, clear directions, and excellent illustrations. (Rev: BL 10/15/01) [641]

13011 Gioffre, Rosalba. *The Young Chef's Italian Cookbook* (4–7). Series: I'm the Chef! 2001, Crabtree LB $22.60 (0-7787-0279-0); paper $8.95 (0-7787-0293-6). Along with good background material, clear instructions are presented for 15 Italian dishes in this well-illustrated, oversize book. (Rev: BL 10/15/01; SLJ 11/01) [641]

13012 Gomez, Paolo. *Food in Mexico* (6–9). Illus. 1989, Rourke LB $26.60 (0-86625-341-6). As well as some typical recipes, this account introduces Mexico and its types of food. (Rev: SLJ 12/89) [641.5]

13013 Greenwald, Michelle. *The Magical Melting Pot: The All-Family Cookbook That Celebrates*

America's Diversity (7–12). Illus. 2003, Cherry Pr. $29.95 (0-9717565-0-3). Chefs from ethnic restaurants around the country contribute favorite recipes and cultural explanations. (Rev: SLJ 11/03)

13014 Gunderson, Mary. *Pioneer Farm Cooking* (6–10). 2000, Blue Earth Books $22.60 (0-7368-0356-4). Recipes accompany information on the foods eaten at the time, with full-color photographs and reproductions. (Rev: HBG 9/00; SLJ 9/00) [394.1]

13015 Hargittai, Magdolna. *Cooking the Hungarian Way*. Rev. ed. (5–10). Series: Easy Menu Ethnic Cookbooks. 2002, Lerner LB $25.26 (0-8225-4132-7). After an introduction to Hungary and its cuisine, there are about 40 clearly presented recipes from appetizers through desserts. (Rev: BL 9/15/02; HBG 3/03) [641.5]

13016 Harrison, Supenn, and Judy Monroe. *Cooking the Thai Way*. Rev. ed. (5–10). Series: Easy Menu Ethnic Cookbooks. 2002, Lerner LB $25.26 (0-8225-4124-6); paper $7.95 (0-8225-0608-4). The country of Thailand is introduced followed by general information on its foods and several easy-to-follow recipes. (Rev: BL 9/15/02) [641.5]

13017 Hill, Barbara W. *Cooking the English Way*. Rev. ed. (5–10). Series: Easy Menu Ethnic Cookbooks. 2002, Lerner LB $25.26 (0-8225-4105-X). The land and people of England are briefly introduced followed by material on their favorite dishes and easy-to-follow recipes. (Rev: BL 9/15/02) [641.5]

13018 Kaufman, Cheryl Davidson. *Cooking the Caribbean Way*. Rev. ed. (5–10). Illus. Series: Easy Menu Ethnic Cookbooks. 1988, Lerner LB $25.26 (0-8225-4103-3). A variety of dishes featuring the spices and fresh fruits that come from these islands. (Rev: BL 8/88; SLJ 9/88) [641.59729]

13019 Kaur, Sharon. *Food in India* (6–9). Illus. 1989, Rourke LB $26.60 (0-86625-339-4). This illustrated book gives recipes, and introduces the foods and dining customs of India. (Rev: SLJ 12/89) [641.5]

13020 Lagasse, Emeril. *Emeril's There's a Chef in My Soup: Recipes for the Kid in Everyone* (5–8). Illus. 2002, HarperCollins $22.99 (0-688-17706-9). The famed TV chef presents a series of simple recipes for main dishes, pasta, desserts, breakfast and lunch items, and salads. (Rev: BL 5/1/02; HBG 10/02) [641.5]

13021 Lee, Frances. *The Young Chef's Chinese Cookbook* (4–7). Illus. Series: I'm the Chef! 2001, Crabtree LB $22.60 (0-7787-0280-4); paper $8.95 (0-7787-0294-4). Fifteen child-friendly recipes for Chinese dishes are presented with step by step directions and photographs. Also use *The Young Chef's Mexican Cookbook* (2001). (Rev: BL 10/15/01; SLJ 11/01) [641.5951]

13022 Locricchio, Matthew. *The Cooking of China* (7–12). Series: Superchef. 2002, Marshall Cavendish LB $19.95 (0-7614-1214-X). After a general introduction to cooking principles, this book gives a region-by-region overview of the cuisine of China followed by a variety of authentic recipes. (Rev: BL 3/15/03; HBG 3/03; SLJ 2/03) [641]

13023 Locricchio, Matthew. *The Cooking of France* (7–12). Illus. Series: Super Chef. 2002, Marshall Cavendish $19.95 (0-7614-1216-6). Recipes are accompanied by details on technique and equipment and by information about the country's traditions and festivals. Also use *The Cooking of Mexico* (2002). (Rev: BL 12/15/02; HBG 3/03; SLJ 2/03) [641.5944]

13024 Locricchio, Matthew. *The Cooking of Italy* (7–12). Series: Superchef. 2002, Marshall Cavendish LB $19.95 (0-7614-1215-8). The different regional cuisines of Italy are described and a number of traditional recipes clearly outlined and colorfully illustrated. (Rev: BL 3/15/03; HBG 3/03; SLJ 4/03) [641]

13025 Madavan, Vijay. *Cooking the Indian Way* (5–8). Illus. 1985, Lerner LB $19.93 (0-8225-0911-3). Cultural information is detailed plus both vegetarian and nonvegetarian recipes. (Rev: SLJ 9/85) [641.5954]

13026 Monroe, Lucy. *Creepy Cuisine: Revolting Recipes that Look Disgusting But Taste Divine* (4–7). 1993, Random paper $5.99 (0-679-84402-3). Recipes that bear such revolting names as Pus Pockets and Worms au Gratin actually contain directions for preparing delicious food, plus all sorts of cooking techniques and tips. (Rev: BCCB 10/93; SLJ 12/93) [641]

13027 Montgomery, Bertha Vining, and Constance Nabwire. *Cooking the West African Way*. Rev. ed. (5–10). Series: Easy Menu Ethnic Cookbooks. 2002, Lerner LB $25.26 (0-8225-4163-7). An appealing introduction to West African cuisine, with information on the land, people, and culture, and several low-fat and vegetarian recipes. (Rev: HBG 10/02; SLJ 5/02) [641.5966]

13028 Munsen, Sylvia. *Cooking the Norwegian Way*. Rev. ed. (5–10). Series: Easy Menu Ethnic Cookbooks. 2002, Lerner LB $25.26 (0-8225-4118-1). A revised edition of an earlier publication that gives information on the country and culture in addition to a selection of typical recipes. (Rev: BL 7/02; SLJ 9/02) [641.59]

13029 Nguyen, Chi, and Judy Monroe. *Cooking the Vietnamese Way* (5–10). Illus. Series: Easy Menu Ethnic Cookbooks. 1985, Lerner LB $25.26 (0-8225-4125-4). The authors introduce the land and people of Vietnam before giving recipes for regional dishes. (Rev: BL 9/15/85; SLJ 9/85) [641]

13030 Osseo-Asare, Fran. *A Good Soup Attracts Chairs: A First African Cookbook for American Kids* (5–9). 1993, Pelican $18.95 (0-88289-816-7). A basic cookbook for youngsters that explores African cooking past and present and gives more than 35 recipes. (Rev: BL 10/15/93; SLJ 8/93) [641.5966]

13031 Parnell, Helga. *Cooking the German Way*. Rev. ed. (5–10). Illus. Series: Easy Menu Ethnic Cookbooks. 1988, Lerner LB $25.26 (0-8225-4107-6). Includes such treats as Black Forest Torte and Apple Cake. (Rev: BL 8/88) [641.5943]

13032 Parnell, Helga. *Cooking the South American Way*. Rev. ed. (5–10). Series: Easy Menu Ethnic Cookbooks. 2002, Lerner LB $25.26 (0-8225-4121-1). The continent of South America is introduced followed by about 40 clearly presented recipes from several different countries. (Rev: BL 9/15/02; HBG 3/03) [641.5]

13033 Plotkin, Gregory, and Rita Plotkin. *Cooking the Russian Way*. Rev. ed. (5–10). Illus. Series: Easy Menu Ethnic Cookbooks. 2002, Lerner LB $25.26 (0-8225-4120-3). Included along with history and information are such recipes as Russian honey spice cake. (Rev: BL 10/15/86) [641.5947]

13034 Raab, Evelyn. *Clueless in the Kitchen: A Cookbook for Teens and Other Beginners* (8–12). Illus. 1998, Firefly paper $12.95 (1-55209-224-0). Cooking and kitchen basics are explained and recipes for good traditional dishes are given in this beginner's cookbook, with an emphasis on fresh ingredients and a section of suggested menus designed for particular guests or occasions. (Rev: BL 7/98; BR 9–10/98; SLJ 9/98) [641.5]

13035 Ralph, Judy, and Ray Gompf. *The Peanut Butter Cookbook for Kids* (5–7). Illus. 1995, Hyperion LB $15.49 (0-7868-2110-8); paper $10.95 (0-7868-1028-9). An amazing collection of recipes involving peanut butter, including soups, snacks, and main dishes. (Rev: BL 10/1/95; SLJ 9/95) [641.6]

13036 Rombauer, Irma S., and Marion Rombauer Becker. *Joy of Cooking* (7–12). Illus. 1997, Dutton $18.00 (0-452-27923-2); NAL paper $16.00 (0-452-27915-1). First published in 1931, this has through several editions become one of the standard basic American cookbooks. [641.5]

13037 Shaw, Maura D., and Synda Altschuler Byrne. *Foods from Mother Earth* (6–10). 1994, Shawangunk Pr. paper $9.95 (1-885482-02-7). A vegetarian cookbook in which most of the recipes can be prepared in three or four easy steps. (Rev: BL 1/15/95; SLJ 2/95) [641.5]

13038 Tan, Jennifer. *Food in China* (6–9). Illus. 1989, Rourke LB $21.27 (0-86625-338-6). Recipes are given plus general information on China, its food, and its people's eating habits. (Rev: SLJ 12/89) [641.5]

13039 Townsend, Sue, and Caroline Young. *Indonesia* (5–8). Illus. Series: A World of Recipes. 2003, Heinemann LB $27.07 (1-4034-0976-5). After a discussion of Indonesian food and ingredients, clear directions, with illustrations, are given for recipes that are graded by ease of preparation. Also use *Russia* and *Vietnam* (both 2003). (Rev: SLJ 9/03)

13040 Vezza, Diane S. *Passport on a Plate: A Round-the-World Cookbook for Children* (6–8). Illus. 1997, Simon & Schuster $21.95 (0-689-80155-6). One hundred recipes are given in this cookbook from 12 areas including Africa, Japan, Italy, Mexico, India, and Russia. (Rev: BL 11/1/97; HBG 3/98; SLJ 10/97) [641.59]

13041 Villios, Lynne W. *Cooking the Greek Way*. Rev, ed. (5–10). Illus. Series: Easy Menu Ethnic Cookbooks. 2003, Lerner LB $25.26 (0-8225-4131-9). The young cook is introduced to the cuisine of Greece, with a chapter covering utensils and ingredient needs and a glossary of basic cooking terms. Recipes are varied and easy to prepare. [641]

13042 Waldee, Lynne Marie. *Cooking the French Way* (5–10). Illus. 2002, Lerner LB $24.26 (0-8225-4106-8). A nicely illustrated introduction to French recipes including breads and sauces. [641.5944]

13043 Walker, Barbara M. *The Little House Cookbook* (5–7). 1979, HarperCollins paper $9.99 (0-06-446090-8). Frontier food, such as green pumpkin pie from the Little House books, served up in tasty, easily used recipes.

13044 Warner, Margaret Brink, and Ruth Ann Hayward. *What's Cooking? Favorite Recipes from Around the World* (5–8). Illus. 1981, Little, Brown $16.95 (0-316-35252-7). A collection of recipes from more than 30 countries contibuted by American teenagers who also supply information on their ethnic origins. [641.5]

13045 Warshaw, Hallie. *The Sleepover Cookbook* (4–8). Photos by Julie Brown. 2000, Sterling $19.95 (0-8069-4497-8). Easy-to-prepare goodies for all kinds of sleepovers are outlined with color photographs on each spread. (Rev: HBG 10/00; SLJ 7/00) [641]

13046 Webb, Lois S. *Holidays of the World Cookbook for Students* (5–8). 1995, Oryx paper $30.95 (0-89774-884-0). This excellent cookbook contains 388 recipes that represent holidays in 136 countries, including many from various regions of the United States. (Rev: SLJ 1/96) [641]

13047 Weston, Reiko. *Cooking the Japanese Way*. Rev. ed. (5–8). Illus. Series: Easy Menu Ethnic Cookbooks. 2002, Lerner LB $25.26 (0-8225-4114-9). Directions for preparing traditional foods are given along with lists of terms, ingredients, and utensils. [641.5952]

13048 Whitman, Sylvia. *What's Cooking? The History of American Food* (7–10). Illus. 2001, Lerner LB $22.60 (0-8225-1732-9). An absorbing account of how American nutrition and tastes have changed over the years, with discussion of methods of food preparation and preservation, the impact of outside forces such as transportation and war, the use of pesticides, and the advent of fast food. (Rev: BCCB 7–8/01; BL 8/01; HBG 10/01; SLJ 7/01; VOYA 8/01) [394.1]

13049 Yu, Ling. *Cooking the Chinese Way.* Rev. ed. (5–10). Illus. Series: Easy Menu Ethnic Cookbooks. 1982, Lerner LB $25.26 (0-8225-4104-1). From appetizers to desserts, with attractive illustrations. [641.5]

13050 Zalben, Jane Breskin. *Beni's Family Cookbook: For the Jewish Holidays* (4–8). Illus. 1996, Holt $21.00 (0-8050-3735-7). An entertaining collection of recipes arranged around the Jewish calendar. (Rev: BL 9/15/96; SLJ 2/97) [641.5]

13051 Zalben, Jane Breskin. *To Every Season: A Family Holiday Cookbook* (4–8). Illus. 1999, Simon & Schuster $19.95 (0-689-81797-5). Arranged by the name of the holiday (from New Year's Day to Kwanzaa), this book explains the importance of each holiday and supplies a total of 69 recipes for the 16 American holidays highlighted. (Rev: BL 12/1/99; HBG 3/00; SLJ 2/00) [641.5]

13052 Zamojska-Hutchins, Danuta. *Cooking the Polish Way.* Rev. ed. (5–10). Illus. Series: Easy Menu Ethnic Cookbooks. 2002, Lerner LB $25.26 (0-8225-4119-X). Simple Polish recipes include traditional dishes such as pierogi. Glossary of terms, plus listing of utensils and ingredients used. [641.5]

13053 Zanzarella, Marianne. *The Good Housekeeping Illustrated Children's Cookbook* (5–8). Illus. 1997, Morrow $17.95 (0-688-13375-4). A visually appealing cookbook containing a number of excellent recipes, some of which require adult supervision. (Rev: BL 12/15/97; HBG 3/98; SLJ 1/98) [641.5]

Costume and Jewelry Making, Dress, and Fashion

13054 Aveline, Erick, and Joyce Chargueraud. *Temporary Tattoos* (6–12). Illus. 2001, Firefly LB $19.95 (1-55209-609-2); paper $9.95 (1-55209-601-7). A book of body art designs that provides plenty of practical tips and guidance on the use of cosmetics. (Rev: BL 11/15/01; HBG 3/02; SLJ 11/01; VOYA 4/02) [391.65]

13055 Baker, Diane. *Jazzy Jewelry. Power Beads, Crystals, Chokers, and Illusion and Tattoo Styles* (5–9). 2001, Williamson paper $12.95 (1-885593-47-3). Jewelry projects for bead lovers include chokers, headbands, and bobby pins, all presented with black-and-white line drawings and guidance on color choice, clasps and knots, and proper storage. (Rev: SLJ 7/01) [745.594]

13056 Baker, Diane. *Make Your Own Hairwear: Beaded Barrettes, Clips, Dangles and Headbands* (4–8). 2001, Williamson paper $8.95 (1-885593-63-5). Easy instructions guide readers through the steps of making hair accessories using beads, shells, rhinestones, and other materials. (Rev: SLJ 4/02) [745.58]

13057 Busch, Marlies. *Friendship Bands: Braiding, Weaving, Knotting* (6–12). Illus. 1997, Sterling paper $7.95 (0-8069-0309-0). A collection of projects to create bracelets, necklaces, decorations, and hair wraps using basic braiding, knotting, and weaving techniques, plus more complicated projects, all with clear, easy-to-follow instructions. (Rev: BL 5/15/98) [746.4222]

13058 Carnegy, Vicky. *Fashions of a Decade: The 1980s* (7–12). 1990, Facts on File $25.00 (0-8160-2471-5). This elegantly illustrated volume traces styles and trends in fashion for this decade, linking them to social and political developments. There are volumes in this set for each decade from the 1920s to the 1990s. (Rev: BL 2/15/91; SLJ 5/91) [391]

13059 Cummings, Richard. *101 Costumes for All Ages, All Occasions* (5–9). Illus. 1987, Plays paper $12.95 (0-8238-0286-8). A variety of easily made costumes are described from Frankenstein and Captain Hook to Cleopatra and even a tube of toothpaste. (Rev: BL 1/1/88; BR 3–4/88) [792.026]

13060 Feldman, Elane. *Fashions of a Decade: The 1990s* (7–12). Series: Fashions of a Decade. 1992, Facts on File $25.00 (0-8160-2472-3). This is the last of the eight-volume set that traces fashion trends and styles decade by decade from the 1920s through the 1990s. (Rev: BL 12/15/92) [391]

13061 Gayle, Katie. *Snappy Jazzy Jewelry* (4–7). Illus. 1996, Sterling $14.95 (0-8069-3854-4). Making necklaces and earrings are two of the craft projects described, with many helpful photographs. (Rev: BL 5/15/96; SLJ 6/96) [745.594]

13062 Leuzzi, Linda. *A Matter of Style: Women in the Fashion Industry* (7–12). Illus. Series: Women Then — Women Now. 1996, Watts LB $25.00 (0-531-11303-5). The important part women have played in the fashion industry in such roles as designers, patternmakers, merchandisers, buyers, and models. (Rev: BL 3/15/97; SLJ 2/97) [338.4]

13063 Litherland, Janet, and Sue McAnally. *Broadway Costumes on a Budget: Big Time Ideas for Amateur Producers* (7–12). Illus. 1996, Meriwether paper $15.95 (1-56608-021-5). Information about period costumes is given in this helpful manual with instructions for making costumes for nearly 100 Broadway plays and musicals. (Rev: BL 12/1/96) [792.6]

13064 MacLeod-Brudenell, Iain. *Costume Crafts* (4–7). Illus. Series: World Wide Crafts. 1994, Gareth Stevens LB $22.60 (0-8368-1152-6). Multicultural projects involving dress and body decoration are featured in this easily followed craft book. (Rev: BL 3/1/95; SLJ 1/95) [745.5]

13065 Rowland-Warne, L. *Costume* (5–10). Series: Eyewitness Books. 1992, Knopf $19.00 (0-679-81680-1). This is a history of dress and fashion with brief, clever text and excellent illustrations. (Rev: BL 8/92; SLJ 2/93) [391]

13066 Sadler, Judy Ann. *Beading: Bracelets, Earrings, Necklaces and More* (4–8). Illus. Series: Kids Can! 1998, Kids Can paper $5.95 (1-55074-338-4). Using photographs and simple instructions, directions are given for making a simple beading loom and creating necklaces and bracelets. (Rev: BL 5/15/98) [745.594]

13067 Sensier, Danielle. *Costumes* (5–7). Illus. Series: Traditions Around the World. 1994, Thomson Learning LB $24.26 (1-56847-227-7). The rituals and uses involved in costumes are introduced, as well as a general discussion of clothing in various regions and cultures. (Rev: BL 2/1/95; SLJ 3/95) [391]

13068 Wilcox, R. Turner. *The Dictionary of Costume* (7–12). Illus. 1969, Macmillan $60.00 (0-684-15150-2). First published in 1969, this book describes in words and drawings more than 3,000 articles of clothing. [391]

Dolls and Other Toys

13069 McClary, Andrew. *Toys with Nine Lives: A Social History of American Toys* (6–12). Illus. 1997, Linnet LB $35.00 (0-208-02386-0). After a general history of toys and how they have changed in format and manufacture through the centuries, this account gives details on eight kinds of toys, including building blocks, dolls, and marbles. (Rev: BL 2/15/97; BR 9–10/97; SLJ 1/98; VOYA 8/97) [790.1]

13070 Sadler, Judy Ann. *Beanbag Buddies and Other Stuffed Toys* (4–7). Series: Kids Can! 1999, Kids Can paper $5.95 (1-55074-590-5). Using clear directions and many step-by-step illustrations, this book offers many ideas on how to create a variety of stuffed toys. (Rev: SLJ 10/99) [745]

Drawing and Painting

13071 Ames, Lee J. *Draw Fifty Cats* (4–7). Illus. 1986, Doubleday paper $8.95 (0-385-24640-4). Step-by-step ways of drawing different breeds and poses of cats. Also use *Draw Fifty Holiday Decorations* (1987). (Rev: BL 11/15/86) [743.69752]

13072 Arnosky, Jim. *Sketching Outdoors in Spring* (6–8). Illus. 1987, Morrow $12.95 (0-688-06284-9). A beautifully illustrated book on how to draw items such as trees, spring flowers, and some animals. There are companion volumes that cover the other seasons — *Autumn, Summer,* and *Winter* (all 1985). (Rev: BL 5/87; BR 9–10/87; SLJ 5/87) [741]

13073 Balchin, Judy. *Creative Lettering* (4–7). Series: Step-by-Step. 2001, Heinemann LB $24.22 (1-57572-331-X). Using easy-to-find materials, this craft book gives clear directions for several fascinating lettering projects. (Rev: BL 8/1/01; HBG 10/01) [745.6]

13074 Balchin, Judy. *Decorative Painting* (4–7). Series: Step-by-Step. 2001, Heinemann LB $24.22 (1-57572-330-1). With easy-to-follow directions and illustrations that describe each step, this colorful book contains a number of simple projects that decorate with paints. (Rev: BL 8/1/01; HBG 10/01; SLJ 10/01) [745]

13075 Baron, Nancy. *Getting Started in Calligraphy* (5–8). 1979, Sterling paper $13.95 (0-8069-8840-1). This well-organized text shows how to draw letters with beauty and grace. [745.6]

13076 Bohl, Al. *Guide to Cartooning* (6–12). Illus. 1997, Pelican paper $13.95 (1-56554-177-4). Though actually a textbook, this work is a splendid guide to the history of cartooning as well as a practical guide to all the basics. (Rev: BL 9/15/97) [741.5]

13077 Butterfield, Moira. *Fun with Paint* (4–8). Illus. Series: Creative Crafts. 1994, Random paper $6.99 (0-679-83942-3). This simple introduction to painting covers various media and a number of creative projects, including making your own paints. (Rev: SLJ 3/94) [745]

13078 DuBosque, Doug. *Draw! Grassland Animals: A Step-by-Step Guide* (4–7). 1996, Peel paper $8.99 (0-939217-25-2). A step-by-step description of how to draw 31 animals from grasslands around the world. (Rev: SLJ 9/96) [741]

13079 DuBosque, Doug. *Draw Insects* (4–8). 1997, Peel paper $8.99 (0-939217-28-7). A carefully constructed drawing book that gives simple directions for drawing more than 80 insects, including millipedes, ticks, and spiders. (Rev: SLJ 6/98) [741.2]

13080 DuBosque, Doug. *Draw 3-D: A Step-by-Step Guide to Perspective Drawing* (4–9). 1999, Peel paper $8.99 (0-939217-14-7). Using easy-to-follow sketches, the author introduces the techniques of 3-D drawing, beginning with basic concepts involving depth and progressing to more difficult areas such as multiple vanishing points. (Rev: SLJ 5/99; VOYA 8/99) [741.2]

13081 DuBosque, Doug. *Learn to Draw Now!* (5–8). Series: Learn to Draw. 1991, Peel paper $8.99 (0-939217-16-3). A simple, easily followed manual on how to draw that contains many interesting practice exercises. (Rev: SLJ 8/91) [743]

13082 Foster, Patience. *Guide to Drawing* (5–8). Illus. 1981, Usborne Hayes LB $14.95 (0-88110-025-0); paper $6.95 (0-86020-540-1). This book covers such topics as color, media, and perspective while dealing with a large number of subjects. Also use *Guide to Painting* (1981). [741]

13083 Gordon, Louise. *How to Draw the Human Figure: An Anatomical Approach* (7–10). Illus. 1979, Penguin paper $18.00 (0-14-046477-8). This is both a short course on anatomy and a fine manual on how to draw the human body. [743]

13084 Harris, David. *The Art of Calligraphy: A Practical Guide to the Skills and Techniques* (7–12). Illus. 1995, DK paper $25.00 (1-56458-849-1). After a brief history of the development of Western writing, this beautifully illustrated book shows how to produce intricate lettering and fanciful human figures. (Rev: BR 3–4/96; SLJ 9/95; VOYA 2/96) [741]

13085 Hart, Christopher. *Drawing on the Funny Side of the Brain* (7–12). Illus. 1998, Watson-Guptill paper $19.95 (0-8230-1381-2). This book describes how to create single and multipanel comic strips, with tips on joke writing, pacing, framing, color, and dialogue. (Rev: BL 7/98) [741.5]

13086 Hart, Christopher. *Kids Draw Anime* (4–8). Illus. 2002, Watson-Guptill paper $10.95 (0-8230-2690-6). Instructions on how to draw anime (Japanese cartoons) characters, with many colorful examples. (Rev: BL 2/1/03; SLJ 11/02) [741.5]

13087 Hart, Christopher. *Manga Mania: How to Draw Japanese Comics* (5–9). Illus. 2001, Watson-Guptill paper $19.95 (0-8230-3035-0). Hart looks at the techniques for drawing typical Japanese comic characters and animals, providing examples of published manga along with an introduction to the various genres of manga and an interview with a manga publisher. (Rev: BL 7/01; SLJ 7/01) [741.5]

13088 Hart, Christopher. *Mecha Mania: How to Draw the Battling Robots, Cool Spaceships, and Military Vehicles of Japanese Comics* (4–8). Illus. 2002, Watson-Guptill paper $19.95 (0-8230-3056-3). Instructions on how to draw the high-tech, scary, fanciful machines and weapons that fill the pages of Japanese comic books. (Rev: BL 2/1/03; SLJ 4/03) [741.5]

13089 Janson, Klaus. *The DC Comics Guide to Penciling Comics* (7–12). Illus. 2002, Watson-Guptill paper $19.95 (0-8230-1028-7). This practical guide for budding comics creators also contains lots of material for comics fans. (Rev: BL 5/1/02) [741.5]

13090 Lewis, Amanda. *Lettering: Make Your Own Cards, Signs, Gifts and More* (4–8). Illus. 1997, Kids Can paper $5.95 (1-55074-232-9). This book describes calligraphy and gothic lettering techniques, covering such topics as typefaces, displays, types of pens to purchase, how to determine pen size, and how to use pens, as well as explaining how to make letterhead stationery and newsletters on the computer. (Rev: BL 10/15/97; SLJ 1/98) [745.6]

13091 Mayne, Don. *Drawing Horses (That Look Real)* (4–8). Series: Quick Starts for Kids! 2002, Williamson paper $7.95 (1-885593-74-0). Cartoon-like instructions take young artists step by step through using basic shapes to draw horses and to show movement and character. (Rev: SLJ 4/03) [743.6]

13092 Pellowski, Michael M. *The Art of Making Comic Books* (4–8). Illus. 1995, Lerner LB $25.55 (0-8225-2304-3). A history of comic books, plus drawing techniques and advice on how to become a comic book artist. (Rev: BCCB 2/96; BL 1/1–15/96; SLJ 1/96) [741.5]

13093 Reinagle, Damon J. *Draw! Medieval Fantasies* (4–8). Illus. 1995, Peel paper $8.99 (0-939217-30-9). A how-to drawing book that gives simple instructions on creating such medieval subjects as dragons and castles. (Rev: BL 1/1–15/96; SLJ 3/96) [743]

13094 Reinagle, Damon J. *Draw Sports Figures* (4–8). Illus. 1997, Peel paper $8.99 (0-939217-32-5). In six chapters arranged by sport or sports category, the author gives easy-to-follow instructions on how to draw action figures. (Rev: SLJ 6/98) [742]

13095 Tallarico, Tony. *Drawing and Cartooning All-Star Sports: A Step by Step Guide for the Aspiring Sports Artist* (4–7). Illus. 1998, Putnam paper $9.95 (0-399-52417-7). Using simple shapes such as circles and squares, this how-to book gives directions for drawing all sorts of athletes, including football, baseball, and basketball players. (Rev: BL 12/15/98) [743]

13096 Wallace, Mary. *I Can Make Art* (4–8). Series: I Can Make. 1997, Firefly $17.95 (1-895688-64-7); paper $6.95 (1-895688-65-5). Art and crafts are combined in these 12 projects involving such techniques as watercolor, still life, chalk drawing, print making, and collage. (Rev: SLJ 12/97) [741.2]

Gardening

13097 Rosen, Michael J., ed. *Down to Earth* (5–8). Illus. 1998, Harcourt $18.00 (0-15-201341-5). In this collection of stories, recipes, and projects, 41 children's authors and illustrators explore the world of gardening. (Rev: BCCB 7–8/98; BL 4/1/98; HBG 10/98; SLJ 4/98) [635]

13098 Winckler, Suzanne. *Planting the Seed: A Guide to Gardening* (6–10). Illus. 2002, Lerner LB $25.26 (0-8225-0081-7); paper $7.95 (0-8225-0471-5). This slim volume offers a wide range of gardening guidance, with material on organic gardening, the use of native plants, community gardens, and Native American traditions. (Rev: BL 5/1/02; HBG 10/02; SLJ 8/02) [635]

Magic Tricks and Optical Illusions

13099 Baker, James W. *Illusions Illustrated: A Professional Magic Show for Young Performers* (5–8). 1994, Lerner paper $6.95 (0-8225-9512-5). Directions on how to put on a magic show with 10 different tricks.

13100 Churchill, E. Richard. *Optical Illusion Tricks and Toys* (6–10). Illus. 1989, Sterling $12.95 (0-8069-6868-0). A collection of more than 60 optical illusions and tricks that are both fun to perform and instructive in the principles of optics. (Rev: BL 7/89; SLJ 10/89) [152.1]

13101 Cobb, Vicki. *Magic . . . Naturally! Science Entertainments and Amusements* (7–9). Illus. 1976, HarperCollins $12.95 (0-397-31631-3). Thirty magic acts are described, each involving a scientific principle. [507]

13102 Colbert, David. *The Magical Worlds of Harry Potter: A Treasury of Myths, Legends, and Fascinating Facts* (5–9). Illus. 2001, Lumina $14.95 (0-9708442-0-4). Information on more than 50 topics in Harry's universe — such as alchemy, Grindylows, and Voldemort — arranged in alphabetical order. (Rev: SLJ 2/02) [823]

13103 Doherty, Paul, et al. *The Cheshire Cat and Other Eye-Popping Experiments on How We See the World* (4–8). Illus. 1995, Wiley paper $10.95 (0-471-11516-9). Based on exhibits at the Exploratorium in San Francisco, this attractive volume outlines activities and experiments that explore optics and vision. (Rev: BL 1/1–15/96; SLJ 1/96) [152.14]

13104 Friedhoffer, Robert. *Magic and Perception: The Art and Science of Fooling the Senses* (5–7). Illus. 1996, Watts LB $25.00 (0-531-11254-3). Simple directions for magic tricks that involve altering perceptions. (Rev: BL 7/96; SLJ 9/96) [793.8]

13105 Hay, Henry. *The Amateur Magician's Handbook*. 4th ed. (7–12). 1982, NAL paper $5.99 (0-451-15502-5). Tricks for magicians of all ages, at various levels of difficulty. [793.8]

13106 Jones, Richard. *That's Magic! 40 Foolproof Tricks to Delight, Amaze and Entertain* (5–8). Illus.

2001, New Holland $19.95 (1-85974-668-3). Simple instructions and photographs teach the beginning magician a few tricks. (Rev: BL 1/1–15/02; SLJ 1/02) [793.8]

13107 Kronzek, Allan Zola, and Elizabeth Kronzek. *The Sorcerer's Companion: A Guide to the Magical World of Harry Potter* (4–9). Illus. 2001, Broadway paper $15.95 (0-7679-0847-3). Young readers may be amazed to learn how much of Harry's magic is standard fare when they read the references here to magical items and concepts in literature, legend, mythology, and religion. (Rev: SLJ 12/01; VOYA 2/02) [823]

13108 Tarr, Bill. *Now You See It, Now You Don't! Lessons in Sleight of Hand* (7–9). Illus. 1976, Random paper $19.95 (0-394-72202-7). More than 100 easy tricks to mystify one's friends. Each is graded by level of difficulty. [793.8]

13109 Wenzel, Angela. *Do You See What I See? The Art of Illusion* (5–8). Trans. from German by Rosie Jackson. 2001, Prestel $14.95 (3-7913-2488-8). Tricks with perspective and color, coded messages, and hidden images are all presented in this attractive volume that makes for excellent browsing. (Rev: HBG 3/02; SLJ 2/02) [152]

Masks and Mask Making

13110 Earl, Amanda, and Danielle Sensier. *Masks* (5–7). Illus. Series: Traditions Around the World. 1994, Thomson Learning LB $24.26 (1-56847-226-9). This multicultural introduction to masks discusses their origins and uses in religion, festivals, and the theater. (Rev: BL 2/1/95; SLJ 3/95) [391.43]

Model Making

13111 Harris, Jack C. *Plastic Model Kits* (5–8). Illus. Series: Hobby Guides. 1993, Crestwood LB $12.95 (0-89686-623-8). The hobby of making plastic models from kits is introduced, with good background information for both the novice and the expert. (Rev: SLJ 2/94) [745]

Paper Crafts

13112 Balchin, Judy. *Papier Mâché* (4–7). Illus. Series: Step-by-Step. 2000, Heinemann LB $24.22 (1-57572-328-X). Combines easy-to-follow projects with information on how papier-mâché has been used over the centuries, including applications in construction and furniture. (Rev: BL 10/15/00; HBG 10/01; SLJ 12/00) [745.54]

13113 Borja, Robert, and Corinne Borja. *Making Chinese Papercuts* (4–7). 1980, Whitman LB $14.95 (0-8075-4948-7). A clear explanation of an ancient art with many examples and photographs.

13114 Boursin, Didier. *Origami Paper Airplanes* (6–8). Illus. 2001, Firefly $19.95 (1-55209-626-2); paper $9.95 (1-55209-616-5). Paper airplane devotees will love the origami models offered here, which are categorized by difficulty of construction. Also use *Origami Paper Animals* (2001). (Rev: BCCB 12/01; BL 1/1–15/02; HBG 3/02; SLJ 12/01) [745.592]

13115 Diehn, Gwen. *Making Books That Fly, Fold, Wrap, Hide, Pop Up, Twist, and Turn: Books for Kids to Make* (4–8). Illus. 1998, Lark $19.95 (1-57990-023-2). Clear directions, diagrams, and many photographs guide youngsters in 18 projects to produce folded, wrapped, and pop-up books. (Rev: BL 7/98; SLJ 8/98) [736.98]

13116 Grummer, Arnold E. *Paper by Kids* (5–7). Illus. 1990, Macmillan $12.95 (0-87518-191-0). A clear, well-organized guide to papermaking.

13117 Irvine, Joan. *How to Make Super Pop-Ups* (4–7). Illus. 1992, Morrow $14.00 (0-688-10690-0); paper $6.95 (0-688-11521-7). Lots of ideas and directions for making three-dimensional paper constructions with moving parts. (Rev: BL 1/15/93) [745]

13118 Kelly, Emery J. *Paper Airplanes: Models to Build and Fly* (4–8). Illus. 1997, Lerner LB $23.93 (0-8225-2401-5). This is a practical manual on making and flying paper airplanes, with good coverage of the principles of aerodynamics. (Rev: BL 12/1/97; HBG 3/98; SLJ 2/98) [745.592]

13119 Nguyen, Duy. *Creepy Crawly Animal Origami* (4–8). Illus. 2003, Sterling $19.95 (0-8069-9012-0). These challenging folded paper designs for 13 animals do require scissors and in some cases glue. (Rev: SLJ 9/03) [736]

13120 Nguyen, Duy. *Fantasy Origami* (6–9). Illus. 2002, Sterling $19.95 (0-8069-8007-9). These 16 origami designs, which are not for beginners, do call for the use of scissors and glue. (Rev: BL 1/1–15/02; SLJ 6/02) [736]

13121 Powell, Michelle. *Printing* (4–7). Illus. Series: Step-by-Step. 2000, Heinemann LB $24.22 (1-57572-329-8). Various easy-to-follow printing projects are presented along with material on printing methods from ancient Egypt onward. (Rev: BL 10/15/00; HBG 10/01) [761]

13122 Schmidt, Norman. *Fabulous Paper Gliders* (6–12). 1998, Tamos Books $19.95 (1-895569-21-4). A history of glider development and the basic principles of aerodynamics are given along with patterns and step-by-step instructions for 16 gliders, all but one based on actual craft. (Rev: BL 5/15/98; SLJ 6/98) [745.592]

13123 Schmidt, Norman. *Incredible Paper Flying Machines* (5–8). Illus. 2001, Sterling $19.95 (1-895569-37-0). Young model builders with some experience will enjoy these intricate models of historical aircraft that are glued and laminated. (Rev: HBG 10/02; SLJ 2/02) [745.592]

13124 Stevens, Clive. *Paperfolding* (4–7). Series: Step-by-Step. 2001, Heinemann LB $24.22 (1-57572-333-6). Easy-to-find materials are used in a number of exciting paper folding projects, each of which is described in clear, detailed directions with step-by-step illustrations. (Rev: BL 8/1/01; HBG 10/01; SLJ 10/01) [745.5]

13125 Tuyen, P. D. *Wild Origami: Amazing Animals You Can Make* (5–8). 1996, Sterling paper $12.95 (0-8069-1380-0). Clear diagrams illustrate how to fold paper to create 18 creatures, from an ant to a dinosaur, with single sheets of origami paper. (Rev: SLJ 12/96) [745.5]

13126 Watson, David. *Papermaking* (4–7). Series: Step-by-Step. 2000, Heinemann LB $24.22 (1-57572-327-1). This book shows how you can use old paper to make new paper and create a number of wonderful art objects following simple step-by-step directions. (Rev: BL 10/15/00; HBG 10/01) [745.5]

Photography, Video, and Film Making

13127 Czech, Kenneth P. *Snapshot: America Discovers the Camera* (6–9). Illus. 1996, Carolrhoda LB $30.35 (0-8225-1736-1). An account of the camera's long history in America and its influence on our culture. (Rev: BL 2/15/97; SLJ 12/96; VOYA 4/97) [770]

13128 Friedman, Debra. *Picture This: Fun Photography and Crafts* (4–7). Series: Kids Can Do It. 2003, Kids Can $12.95 (1-55337-046-5); paper $5.95 (1-55337-047-3). An easy-to-follow project book that combines photographs and crafts. (Rev: BL 3/15/03; HBG 10/03; SLJ 4/03) [770]

13129 Johnson, Neil. *National Geographic Photography Guide for Kids* (4–7). Illus. 2001, National Geographic $18.95 (0-7922-6371-5). A comprehensive and easily understood introduction to cameras, lenses, and films, with tips from *National Geographic* photographers. (Rev: HBG 3/02; SLJ 9/01*; VOYA 12/01) [770]

13130 Morgan, Terri, and Shmuel Thaler. *Photography: Take Your Best Shot* (5–8). Illus. Series: Media Workshop. 1991, Lerner LB $21.27 (0-8225-2302-

7). A comprehensive and well-put-together guide to photography that covers cameras, film, developing, composition, lighting, and special effects, as well as discussing career opportunities. (Rev: BL 10/1/91; SLJ 11/91) [771]

13131 Price, Susanna, and Tim Stephens. *Click! Fun with Photography* (4–8). 1997, Sterling $14.95 (0-8069-9541-6). A fine introduction to photography that covers both beginning and advanced subjects, including the operation of various cameras, exposure, lighting, different types of photography, and filters. (Rev: SLJ 8/97) [771]

13132 Varriale, Jim. *Take a Look Around: Photography Activities for Young People* (5–8). Illus. 1999, Millbrook LB $24.90 (0-7613-1265-X). Photographs taken by children in a summer camp photography class illustrate the importance of such elements as light and camera angles, framing, creating mood, and photographing action. (Rev: BL 3/15/00; HBG 3/00; SLJ 12/99; VOYA 2/00) [770]

13133 Wallace, Joseph. *The Camera* (4–7). Series: Turning Points. 2000, Simon & Schuster $17.95 (0-689-82813-6). This is a basic history of photography — with a focus on the development of the camera and its impact on our lives. (Rev: BL 8/00; HBG 3/01; SLJ 1/01) [778.59]

Sewing and Other Needle Crafts

13134 Bial, Raymond. *With Needle and Thread: A Book About Quilts* (4–7). Illus. 1996, Houghton $16.00 (0-395-73568-8). An attractive introduction to quilts, their history, how they are made, and the people who sew them. (Rev: BCCB 2/96; BL 3/1/96; SLJ 6/96) [746.46]

13135 Falick, Melanie. *Kids Knitting* (4–7). Illus. 1998, Workman $17.95 (1-885183-76-3). Exceptionally clear pictures and text are used to present the basics of knitting for girls and boys, with instructions for such projects as backpacks, hats, scarves, and sweaters. (Rev: BL 4/1/98; SLJ 7/98) [746.43]

13136 Kinsler, Gwen Blakley, and Jackie Young. *Crocheting* (4–7). Series: Kids Can Do It. 2003, Kids Can $12.95 (1-55337-176-3); paper $5.95 (1-55337-177-1). A simple introduction to crocheting with many easily followed diagrams and clear directions. (Rev: BL 3/15/03; HBG 10/03; SLJ 4/03) [745.5]

13137 Sadler, Judy Ann. *Corking* (4–8). Illus. Series: Kids Can! 1998, Kids Can paper $5.95 (1-55074-265-5). Provides directions for a handmade knitting device that is used to create knit tubes or corks popular in toys and headbands. (Rev: BL 5/15/98) [746.4]

13138 Sadler, Judy Ann. *Making Fleece Crafts* (4–7). 2000, Kids Can $12.95 (1-55074-847-5); paper $5.95 (1-55074-739-8). Fifteen colorful and inviting projects using fleece including mittens, a scarf, and a jester's hat. (Rev: BL 9/15/00; SLJ 9/00) [745]

13139 Storms, Biz. *All-American Quilts* (4–7). Series: Kids Can Do It. 2003, Kids Can $12.95 (1-55337-539-6); paper $6.95 (1-55337-539-4). Instructions are provided for making quilts with American themes — eagles, flags, and so forth. (Rev: BL 12/15/03) [746.46]

13140 Storms, Biz. *Quilting* (4–7). Series: Kids Can Do It. 2001, Kids Can $12.95 (1-55074-967-6); paper $5.95 (1-55074-805-X). Easy-to-follow, step-by-step instructions take kids through quilting projects of varying difficulty. (Rev: BL 11/1/01; HBG 3/02; SLJ 2/02) [746.46]

13141 Willing, Karen Bates, and Julie Bates Dock. *Fabric Fun for Kids: Step-by-Step Projects for Children (and Their Grown-ups)* (4–9). 1997, Now & Then LB $17.95 (0-9641820-4-1); paper $12.95 (0-9641820-5-X). From simple sewing projects to more complex quilting work, this book gives good step-by-step instructions, provides a rundown on necessary sewing tools and materials, and discusses methods for putting designs on fabrics. (Rev: SLJ 4/98) [746.46]

13142 Wilson, Sule Greg C. *African American Quilting: The Warmth of Tradition* (4–7). Illus. Series: Library of African American Arts and Culture. 1999, Rosen LB $31.95 (0-8239-1854-8). This book traces African influences on textile patterns and techniques particularly as they have been applied to quilting by African Americans. (Rev: BL 2/15/00; SLJ 9/99) [746.46]

Stamp, Coin, and Other Types of Collecting

13143 Dyson, Cindy. *Rare and Interesting Stamps* (5–8). Series: Costume, Tradition, and Culture: Reflecting on the Past. 1998, Chelsea $19.75 (0-7910-5171-4). The stories behind 25 rare and unusual stamps start with Britain's first one-penny stamp, which bore a portrait of Queen Victoria. (Rev: BL 3/15/99; HBG 10/99) [769.56]

13144 Mackay, James. *The Guinness Book of Stamps, Facts and Feats* (7–12). Illus. 1989, Guinness $34.95 (0-85112-351-1). All sorts of curiosities about postage stamps such as the most valuable, the largest, and so on. (Rev: BL 4/15/89) [769.56]

13145 Owens, Thomas S. *Collecting Baseball Cards: 21st Century Edition*. Rev. ed. (4–8). 2001, Millbrook LB $26.90 (0-7613-1708-2). An entertaining introduction to collecting baseball cards, with information on the history of the industry, on how to determine the condition of cards, and how to use the Internet to buy and sell. (Rev: HBG 10/01; SLJ 7/01) [796]

13146 Owens, Thomas S. *Collecting Comic Books: A Young Person's Guide* (5–8). 1995, Millbrook LB $26.90 (1-56294-580-7). A beginner's guide to comic book collecting, with sections on kinds of collections, sources, and organizations. (Rev: BL 2/1/96; SLJ 1/96) [741.5]

13147 Owens, Thomas S. *Collecting Stock Car Racing Memorabilia* (4–8). Illus. 2001, Millbrook LB $26.90 (0-7613-1853-4). NASCAR fans in particular will appreciate this practical and detailed guide to collecting, which includes extensive lists of useful addresses. (Rev: BL 12/15/01; HBG 3/02; SLJ 11/01) [796.72]

13148 Pellant, Chris. *Collecting Gems and Minerals: Hold the Treasures of the Earth in the Palm of Your Hand* (5–8). Illus. 1998, Sterling $14.95 (0-8069-9760-5). After explaining how gems and minerals are formed, this book discusses necessary equipment for the hunter, where to look, how to identify specimens, and how to organize one's collection. (Rev: BL 6/1–15/98; SLJ 8/98) [553.8]

13149 *Postal Service Guide to U.S. Stamps* (7–12). Illus. 1988, U.S. Postal Service $5.00 (0-9604756-8-0). A well-illustrated history of U.S. postage stamps. [769.56]

13150 *Scott Standard Postage Stamp Catalogue: Countries of the World* (7–12). 1997, Scott paper $35.00 (0-89487-231-1). This is the most comprehensive stamp catalog in print. Volume 1 deals with stamps from the English-speaking world; the other three volumes cover alphabetically the other countries of the world. [769.56]

Woodworking and Carpentry

13151 Walker, Lester. *Housebuilding for Children* (4–7). Illus. 1977, Overlook paper $16.95 (0-87951-332-2). The construction of six different kinds of houses, including a tree house, is clearly described in text and pictures.

Jokes, Puzzles, Riddles, and Word Games

13152 Burns, Marilyn. *The Book of Think (or How to Solve a Problem Twice Your Size)* (5–7). 1976, Little, Brown paper $14.99 (0-316-11743-9). A stimulating collection of puzzles to make children think; informally and entertainingly presented.

13153 de Vicq de Cumptich, Roberto. *Bembo's Zoo* (4–8). Illus. 2000, Holt $19.95 (0-8050-6382-X). A mature alphabet book that that jumbles letters to create a picture of each animal from A to Z. (Rev: BCCB 5/00; BL 6/1–15/00; HB 5–6/00; HBG 10/00; SLJ 5/00) [793.73]

13154 Gardner, Martin. *Mind-Boggling Word Puzzles* (4–8). Illus. 2001, Sterling $14.95 (0-8069-7186-X). Entertaining word games, many illustrated, will challenge students in 4th through 8th grades. (Rev: BL 9/1/01; HBG 3/02) [793.73]

13155 Lewis, J. Patrick. *Riddle-icious* (4–8). Illus. 1996, Knopf $15.00 (0-679-84011-7). A collection of 28 delightful poem-riddles that are bound to please. (Rev: BL 6/1–15/96; SLJ 6/96) [818]

13156 Rosenbloom, Joseph. *Biggest Riddle Book in the World* (6–9). Illus. 1977, Sterling paper $6.95 (0-8069-8884-3). Very clever riddles collected by a children's librarian. [808.7]

13157 Rosenbloom, Joseph. *Dr. Knock-Knock's Official Knock-Knock Dictionary* (6–9). Illus. 1977, Sterling paper $4.95 (0-8069-8936-X). This very humorous collection includes more than 500 knock-knock jokes. [808.7]

13158 Rosenbloom, Joseph. *The Gigantic Joke Book* (6–9). 1978, Sterling paper $6.95 (0-8069-7514-8). A large collection of jokes that span time from King Arthur to the space age. Also use *Funniest Joke Book Ever* (1986). [808.7]

13159 Schwartz, Alvin, comp. *Tomfoolery: Trickery and Foolery with Words* (6–9). Illus. 1973, HarperCollins $12.95 (0-397-31466-3). A collection of jokes and riddles from folklore and from children. [398]

13160 Schwartz, Alvin, comp. *Witcracks: Jokes and Jests from American Folklore* (6–9). Illus. 1973, HarperCollins LB $14.89 (0-397-31475-2). Tall tales, jokes, riddles, and humorous stories are included in this collection from our past. [398]

13161 Townsend, Charles Barry. *The Curious Book of Mind-Boggling Teasers, Tricks, Puzzles and Games* (4–12). Illus. 2003, Sterling paper $12.95 (1-4027-0214-0). Classic puzzles, games, and brain teasers are illustrated with Victorian-style drawings and helpful diagrams; solutions are at the back of the book. (Rev: SLJ 11/03)

Mysteries, Curiosities, and Controversial Subjects

13162 Aaseng, Nathan. *The Bermuda Triangle* (7–10). Series: Mystery Library. 2001, Lucent LB $19.96 (1-56006-769-1). Using a variety of sources, this book explores the past and present of this controversial phenomenon. (Rev: BL 9/15/01) [001.9]

13163 Aaseng, Nathan. *Science Versus Pseudo-science* (7–12). 1994, Watts paper $24.00 (0-531-11182-2). Aaseng explains the difference between true scientific theory and pseudoscience, discussing ESP, near-death experiences, creation science, and cold fusion. (Rev: BL 8/94; SLJ 9/94) [001.7]

13164 Allen, Eugenie. *The Best Ever Kids' Book of Lists* (4–8). Illus. 1991, Avon paper $2.95 (0-380-76357-5). Brief lists of the biggest, smallest, strangest, ugliest, etc., with humorous drawings. (Rev: BL 12/15/91) [031.02]

13165 Ash, Russell. *The Top 10 of Everything 2002* (4–9). 2001, DK $26.95 (0-7894-8042-5); paper $17.95 (0-7894-8043-3). A useful and attractive source of facts on a wide range of topics. (Rev: SLJ 1/02) [031.02]

13166 Aslan, Madalyn. *What's Your Sign? A Cosmic Guide for Young Astrologers* (5–9). 2002, Grosset $12.99 (0-448-42693-5). A lively, spiral-bound guide to the 12 signs of the zodiac and the personality traits they represent, with information on the underlying mythology and lists of famous people born under each sign. (Rev: SLJ 9/02) [133.5]

13167 Ballinger, Erich. *Monster Manual: A Complete Guide to Your Favorite Creatures* (5–8). 1994, Lerner LB $19.93 (0-8225-0722-6). An A-to-Z survey of the great monsters of the world from mythology, literature, and the media. (Rev: BL 12/1/94; SLJ 3/95) [001.9]

13168 Blackwood, Gary L. *Extraordinary Events and Oddball Occurrences* (4–7). Illus. Series: Secrets of the Unexplained. 1999, Marshall Cavendish LB $28.50 (0-7614-0748-0). A book that cov-ers such unusual occurrences as strange things falling from the sky, teleportation, and unexplained appearances and disappearances. (Rev: BL 3/1/00; HBG 10/00) [001.9]

13169 Blackwood, Gary L. *Long-Ago Lives* (4–7). Illus. Series: Secrets of the Unexplained. 1999, Marshall Cavendish LB $19.95 (0-7614-0747-2). A look at the subject of reincarnation. (Rev: BL 3/1/00; HBG 10/00) [133.9]

13170 Buller, Laura. *Myths and Monsters: From Dragons to Werewolves* (5–9). Illus. 2003, DK $14.99 (0-7894-9703-4); paper $5.99 (0-7894-9226-1). This colorful volume includes information and images of a variety of land and sea creatures — some legendary, others new inventions and still others hoaxes — with discussion of the origins of beings including Medusa, Dracula, and Anansi. (Rev: HBG 10/03; SLJ 9/03) [398.24]

13171 Campbell, Peter A. *Alien Encounters* (5–7). Illus. 2000, Millbrook LB $23.90 (0-7613-1402-4). An overview of eight supposed encounters between humans and aliens. (Rev: BL 7/00; HBG 10/00; SLJ 4/00) [001.9]

13172 Cohen, Daniel. *Ghosts of the Deep* (5–7). 1993, Putnam $14.95 (0-399-22435-1). A collection of ghost stories involving sailors and pirates who met untimely ends. (Rev: BL 11/15/93; SLJ 3/94) [133.1]

13173 Cohen, Daniel. *Prophets of Doom: The Millennium Edition* (6–8). 1999, Millbrook LB $24.90 (0-7613-1317-6). An updated edition of the 1992 volume on individuals and groups who have predicted the end of the world, with additions including David Koresh of the Heaven's Gate cult and Shoko Ashara, the cultist who released nerve gas into a Tokyo subway. (Rev: BL 5/15/99; SLJ 6/99) [133.3]

13174 Cohen, Daniel. *The World's Most Famous Ghosts* (6–8). 1989, Pocket paper $2.99 (0-671-69145-7). A report in 10 short chapters of better-known incidents accredited to ghosts.

13175 Cohen, Daniel. *Young Ghosts* (5–8). 1994, Dutton $13.99 (0-525-65154-3). "True" accounts of ghost children, such as Rosalie, who is summoned in seances by her mother. Also includes tales of ghosts that appear to children. (Rev: BL 9/1/94; SLJ 10/94) [133.1]

13176 Crisp, Tony. *Super Minds: People with Amazing Mind Power* (4–7). 1999, Element Books paper $4.95 (1-901881-03-2). A survey of near-death experiences, feral children's case histories, and instances of strange mental powers. (Rev: SLJ 5/99) [001.9]

13177 Deem, James M. *How to Find a Ghost* (5–8). Illus. 1990, Avon paper $3.25 (0-380-70829-9). An attempt to explain how to have a supernatural experience. (Rev: BCCB 11/88; BL 11/1/88; SLJ 11/88) [133.1]

13178 Dugan, Ellen. *Elements of Witchcraft: Natural Magick for Teens* (8–12). 2003, Llewellyn paper $14.94 (1-7387-0393-1). A practicing witch introduces teens to the basics of witchcraft, with tips on proper casting of spells and a discussion of ethical concerns. (Rev: BL 6/1–15/03) [133.4]

13179 Duncan, Lois, and William Rool. *Psychic Connections: A Journey into the Mysterious World of Psi* (6–10). 1995, Delacorte paper $12.95 (0-385-32072-8). After her daughter's murder, Duncan used psychics to learn more about it. Here she joins Psychical Research Foundation project director Rool in a comprehensive look at psychic phenomena. (Rev: BL 6/1–15/95; SLJ 5/95) [133]

13180 Elfman, Eric. *Almanac of Alien Encounters* (6–10). 2001, Random LB $11.99 (0-679-97288-9); paper $4.99 (0-679-87288-4). UFO sightings from the earliest times to the 21st century are the topic of this balanced and thorough survey of encounters worldwide. (Rev: HBG 10/01; SLJ 9/01) [001.942]

13181 Garden, Nancy. *Devils and Demons* (7–9). 1976, HarperCollins $11.95 (0-397-31666-6). An international survey of the weird demons in which various cultures and peoples believe. [133]

13182 Harvey, Michael. *The End of the World* (6–10). Series: Great Mysteries: Opposing Viewpoints. 1992, Greenhaven LB $22.45 (0-89908-096-0). A review of many of the dire predictions that foretold the end of the world. (Rev: BL 1/15/93) [001.9]

13183 Hepplewhite, Peter, and Neil Tonge. *Alien Encounters* (5–8). Series: The Unexplained. 1998, Sterling $14.95 (0-8069-3869-2). This book is filled with reports of strange and unexplained events, such as encounters with aliens and UFOs. Also use *Hauntings: The World of Spirits and Ghosts, Myste-*

rious Places, and *The Uncanny* (all 1998). (Rev: HBG 3/99; SLJ 10/98) [001.9]

13184 Hill, Douglas. *Witches and Magic-Makers* (6–8). 1997, Knopf $20.99 (0-679-98544-1). This book introduces magical charms, talismans, and amulets from around the world, with a brief look at the history of witches and practitioners of magic, witches of fiction and film, and witch-hunting activities. (Rev: SLJ 8/97) [133.4]

13185 Huang, Chungliang Al. *The Chinese Book of Animal Powers* (5–7). Illus. 1999, HarperCollins LB $16.89 (0-06-027729-7). The 12 animals of the Chinese zodiac are introduced in double-page spreads, and the characteristics and powers of each are outlined. (Rev: BCCB 12/99; BL 1/1–15/00; HBG 3/00) [133.5]

13186 Hubbard-Brown, Janet. *The Curse of the Hope Diamond* (4–7). Illus. 1991, Avon paper $2.99 (0-380-76222-6). A mystery style is used to introduce historical information about this jewel and the bad luck it seems to carry. (Rev: BL 12/15/91) [736.23]

13187 Innes, Brian. *The Bermuda Triangle* (4–7). Illus. Series: Unsolved Mysteries. 1999, Raintree Steck-Vaughn LB $30.40 (0-8172-5485-4). The author explores many theories that have been proposed to explain disappearances off the southeast coast of the U.S. (Rev: BL 5/15/99; HBG 10/99) [001.94]

13188 Innes, Brian. *The Cosmic Joker* (4–7). Illus. Series: Unsolved Mysteries. 1999, Raintree Steck-Vaughn LB $25.69 (0-8172-5487-0). This book introduces Charles Fort, the Cosmic Joker, and the many strange facts and coincidences he has uncovered. (Rev: BL 5/15/99; HBG 10/99; SLJ 9/99) [001.94]

13189 Innes, Brian. *Giant Humanlike Beasts* (4–7). Series: Unsolved Mysteries. 1999, Raintree Steck-Vaughn LB $30.40 (0-8172-5484-6). This account explores stories about the Abominable Snowman, or yeti, and other sightings of primitive creatures, while questioning the possibility of living links with Neanderthals. (Rev: BL 5/15/99; HBG 10/99; SLJ 9/99) [001.9]

13190 Innes, Brian. *Millennium Prophecies* (5–8). Illus. 1999, Raintree Steck-Vaughn LB $30.40 (0-8172-5486-2). All sorts of prophecies relating to the calendar and the millennium are explored in this attractive volume. (Rev: BL 5/15/99; HBG 10/99; SLJ 9/99; VOYA 10/99) [001.7]

13191 Innes, Brian. *Mysterious Healing* (5–8). Illus. Series: Unsolved Mysteries. 1999, Raintree Steck-Vaughn LB $25.69 (0-8172-5489-7). Hands-on healing, acupuncture, iridology, and auras are some of the subjects discussed in this volume. (Rev: BL 5/15/99; HBG 10/99; SLJ 9/99; VOYA 10/99) [001.7]

13192 Jenkins, Martin. *Vampires* (6–8). Series: Informania. 1998, Candlewick $15.99 (0-7636-0315-5). Following a graphic-novel version of Bram Stoker's *Dracula,* there are sections on all sorts of animal bloodsuckers, like leeches and various parasitic insects (with photographs); a "history of bloodsucking," especially in Eastern and Central European tradition; a survey of vampire films and TV shows; and a tongue-in-cheek "Vampire Hunter's Survival Guide." (Rev: HBG 3/99; SLJ 2/99) [133.4]

13193 Kallen, Stuart A. *Witches* (7–10). Illus. Series: Mystery Library. 2000, Lucent LB $18.96 (1-56006-688-1). A history of witchcraft precedes discussion of the beliefs and rituals of today's Wiccans. (Rev: BL 9/1/00; HBG 3/01; SLJ 9/00) [133.4]

13194 Kemp, Gillian. *Tea Leaves, Herbs, and Flowers: Fortune-Telling the Gypsy Way* (5–9). Series: Elements of the Extraordinary. 1998, Element Books paper $5.95 (1-901881-92-X). A look at the art of reading tea leaves and the lore and language of flowers. (Rev: SLJ 1/99) [133.3]

13195 Knight, David C. *Best True Ghost Stories of the 20th Century* (5–8). Illus. 1984, Simon & Schuster paper $5.95 (0-671-66557-X). Twenty tales of apparitions and poltergeists.

13196 Krull, Kathleen. *They Saw the Future: Oracles, Psychics, Scientists, Great Thinkers, and Pretty Good Guessers* (5–9). Illus. 1999, Simon & Schuster $19.99 (0-689-81295-7). This chronological survey of people who professed to see into the future includes the Oracle at Delphi, Nostradamus, Jules Verne, Leonardo da Vinci, and Jeane Dixon. (Rev: BCCB 6/99; BL 6/1–15/99; HB 5–6/99; HBG 10/99; SLJ 7/99; VOYA 12/99) [133.3]

13197 Krull, Kathleen. *What Really Happened in Roswell? Just the Facts (Plus the Rumors) About UFOs and Aliens* (4–7). 2003, HarperCollins LB $16.89 (0-688-17249-0); paper $4.25 (0-688-17248-2). Humorous drawings illustrate the story of the crash of a mysterious object in New Mexico in 1947 and the accusations of a government cover-up. (Rev: HBG 10/03; SLJ 10/03) [001.942]

13198 McHargue, Georgess. *Meet the Werewolf* (6–9). 1976, HarperCollins $11.95 (0-397-31662-3). A factual account that explores the evidence concerning the existence of werewolves. Also use *Meet the Witches* (1984). [133.4]

13199 Maynard, Christopher. *Informania: Ghosts* (4–8). Illus. Series: Informania. 1999, Candlewick $15.99 (0-7636-0758-4). This book about ghosts includes coverage of sightings around the world, items needed to be a ghost hunter, and a chart of typical haunting sights. (Rev: HBG 3/00; SLJ 12/99; VOYA 2/00) [133.1]

13200 Myers, Janet Nuzum. *Strange Stuff: True Stories of Odd Places and Things* (5–8). Illus. 1999, Linnet LB $19.50 (0-208-02405-0). A collection of curiosities — items about zombies, quicksand, scorpions, poisonous snakes, black holes, Bigfoot, mermaids, voodoo, the Bermuda Triangle, and feral children raised by wolves. (Rev: HBG 3/00; SLJ 7/99; VOYA 2/00) [001.9]

13201 Netzley, Patricia. *Alien Abductions* (6–9). Series: Opposing Viewpoints Great Mysteries. 1996, Greenhaven LB $27.45 (1-56510-352-1). A balanced examination of claims of kidnappings by creatures from outer space. (Rev: BL 4/15/96; SLJ 6/96) [001.9]

13202 Netzley, Patricia D. *ESP* (7–10). Series: Mystery Library. 2001, Lucent LB $19.96 (1-56006-770-5). A serious look at the phenomenon known as extrasensory perception, incorporating the latest research on the subject. (Rev: BL 9/15/01; SLJ 5/01) [133]

13203 Netzley, Patricia D. *Haunted Houses* (7–10). Illus. Series: Mystery Library. 2000, Lucent LB $18.96 (1-56006-685-7). A balanced account that examines specific cases of hauntings and discusses such topics as ghosts, poltergeists, seances, and mediums. (Rev: BL 9/1/00; HBG 3/01; SLJ 9/00) [133.1]

13204 Netzley, Patricia D. *Unicorns* (6–10). Illus. Series: The Mystery Library. 2000, Lucent LB $19.96 (1-56006-687-3). The unicorn's role in myth and legend is the focus of this interesting, well-illustrated volume. (Rev: SLJ 7/01) [398]

13205 O'Connell, Margaret F. *The Magic Cauldron: Witchcraft for Good and Evil* (7–9). 1976, Phillips $38.95 (0-87599-187-4). In this history of witchcraft, the reader learns that witches can be agents of both good and evil. [133]

13206 Olmstead, Kathleen. *The Girls' Guide to Tarot* (6–12). 2002, Sterling paper $12.95 (0-8069-8072-9). An introduction to tarot card reading, including the meanings of the cards and how to interpret them, with illustrations. (Rev: BL 11/15/02; SLJ 8/02) [133]

13207 O'Neill, Catherine. *Amazing Mysteries of the World* (7–12). Illus. 1983, National Geographic LB $12.50 (0-87044-502-2). UFOs, Bigfoot, and Easter Island are only three of the many mysteries explored. [001.9]

13208 Powell, Jillian. *Body Decoration* (4–8). Illus. Series: Traditions Around the World. 1995, Thomson Learning LB $24.26 (1-56847-276-5). An interesting book that explains the uses of body decoration in history and discusses tattooing, face painting, and body piercing. (Rev: SLJ 7/95) [617]

13209 Reid, Lori. *Hand Reading: Discover Your Future* (5–9). Illus. Series: Elements of the Extraordinary. 1998, Element Books paper $5.95 (1-901881-82-2). Palmistry is explained in detail, including the meaning of the shape of the hand and nails and of each line and curve, and how hand gestures can reveal clues to personalities. (Rev: SLJ 1/99) [133.6]

13210 Roberts, Nancy. *Southern Ghosts* (6–9). Illus. 1979, Sandlapper paper $7.95 (0-87844-075-5). Thirteen ghostly tales from the South are retold with photographs of their locales. [133]

13211 Roberts, Russell. *Vampires* (7–10). Series: Mystery Library. 2001, Lucent LB $19.96 (1-56006-835-3). A research-oriented account that explores the origins of the legends and stories involving vampires. (Rev: BL 9/15/01) [001.9]

13212 Roleff, Tamara L., ed. *Black Magic and Witches* (5–8). Series: Fact or Fiction? 2003, Gale LB $27.45 (0-7377-1318-6); paper $18.70 (0-7377-1319-4). A good starting point for debate over witchcraft, with essays for and against witches, magic, and Harry Potter, and some history of persecution of witches. (Rev: SLJ 3/03) [133.43]

13213 Savage, Candace. *Wizards: An Amazing Journey Through the Last Great Age of Magic* (5–8). Illus. 2003, Greystone $17.95 (1-55054-943-X). An appealing, oversize book full of information on witchcraft and wizardry in the late 17th century, when science and sorcery were not far apart. (Rev: BL 6/1–15/03; VOYA 8/03) [133]

13214 Skal, David J. *V is for Vampire: The A–Z Guide to Everything Undead* (8–12). 1996, NAL paper $15.95 (0-452-27173-8). This compendium of information about vampires examines the myths and beliefs surrounding them, the stories behind wooden stakes, zombies, and Dracula lore, and includes lists of vampire movies and novels. (Rev: BL 10/1/95; VOYA 2/97) [001.7]

13215 Stein, Wendy. *Witches* (6–9). Series: Great Mysteries: Opposing Viewpoints. 1995, Greenhaven LB $17.96 (1-56510-240-1). A discussion of the real nature of witches. (Rev: BL 4/15/95; SLJ 3/95) [133.4]

13216 Tambini, Michael. *Future* (4–9). Series: Eyewitness. 1998, Knopf $20.99 (0-679-99317-7). The world of the future is explored in this oversize, richly illustrated book. (Rev: BL 8/98; HBG 3/99) [133.3]

13217 Tonge, Neil. *Unexplained: Mysterious Places* (5–8). Illus. Series: The Unexplained. 1998, Sterling $14.95 (0-8069-3863-3). Stonehenge and Easter Island are two of the unusual places described, followed by theories about their existence, ranging from scientific to the supernatural. (Rev: HBG 3/99; SLJ 10/98; VOYA 10/98) [001.9]

13218 Unruh, J. Timothy. *Impossible Objects: Amazing Optical Illusions to Confound and Astound* (6–8). Illus. 2001, Sterling $17.95 (0-8069-4996-1). This excursion into a world that defies perspective will attract budding artists and psychologists. (Rev: HBG 3/02; SLJ 10/01) [152.14]

13219 Varasdi, J. Allen. *Myth Information* (8–12). 1989, Ballantine paper $5.99 (0-345-35985-2). A fascinating collection of facts that challenge some popular beliefs such as the belief that the American buffalo is really a bison. (Rev: BL 11/1/89) [001.9]

13220 Williams, Mary E., ed. *Paranormal Phenomena* (7–12). Illus. Series: Opposing Viewpoints. 2003, Gale LB $21.96 (0-7377-1238-4); paper $14.96 (0-7377-1237-6). Near-death experiences, eternal life, ghosts, reincarnation, psychic ability, UFOs, and extraterrestrial life are among the subjects explored from all sides in this compilation of essays. (Rev: SLJ 7/03) [133]

13221 Windham, Kathryn Tucker. *Jeffrey Introduces 13 More Southern Ghosts* (7–10). 1978, Univ. of Alabama Pr. paper $13.95 (0-8173-0381-2). A total of 13 ghosts tell their weird stories. [133]

13222 Winters, Paul A. *Paranormal Phenomena* (8–12). Illus. Series: Opposing Viewpoints. 1997, Greenhaven LB $26.20 (1-56510-558-3). This collection of articles explores such controversial topics as UFOs, life after death, and ESP. (Rev: BL 7/97; BR 1–2/98; SLJ 9/97; VOYA 12/97) [133]

13223 Wyly, Michael J. *Dragons* (7–10). Series: Mystery Library. 2002, Gale LB $27.45 (1-56006-972-4). Numerous illustrations and a clear text are used to explore the phenomenon of dragons, how belief in them began, and why it has persisted to the present. (Rev: BL 7/02) [001.9]

Sports and Games

General and Miscellaneous

13224 Aaseng, Nathan. *The Locker Room Mirror: How Sports Reflect Society* (7–10). 1993, Walker LB $15.85 (0-8027-8218-3). Aaseng argues that problems in professional sports today — cheating, drug abuse, violence, commercialization, discrimination — are reflections of society at large. (Rev: BL 6/1–15/93; SLJ 5/93) [306.4]

13225 Alexander, Kyle. *Pro Wrestling's Most Punishing Finishing Moves* (4–7). Series: Pro Wrestling Legends. 2000, Chelsea $19.75 (0-7910-5833-6). This book describes the most effective finishing moves in the sport of wrestling and fighters who use them. (Rev: BL 3/1/01; HBG 3/01) [796.8]

13226 Alexander, Kyle. *The Women of Pro Wrestling* (4–7). Illus. Series: Pro Wrestling Legends. 2000, Chelsea $19.75 (0-7910-5839-5); paper $8.95 (0-7910-5840-9). After introducing several famous women pro wrestlers, this account describes women's roles in this sport in and out of the ring. (Rev: BL 10/15/00; HBG 3/01) [796.812]

13227 Alter, Judith. *Rodeos: The Greatest Show on Dirt* (4–7). Illus. Series: First Books. 1996, Watts LB $22.00 (0-531-20245-3). Includes a history of rodeos, standard events, rules, legendary performers, and women in rodeos. (Rev: SLJ 3/97) [791.8]

13228 *A Basic Guide to Bobsledding* (6–12). Series: Olympic Guides. 2002, Gareth Stevens LB $22.60 (0-8368-3101-2). Under the editorship of the U.S. Olympic Committee, this is a well illustrated guide to the sport of bobsledding, the equipment used, and important techniques. (Rev: BL 6/1–15/02; HBG 10/02) [796.9]

13229 Berlow, Lawrence H. *Sports Ethics* (7–12). Series: Contemporary World Issues. 1995, ABC-CLIO LB $39.50 (0-87436-769-7). A general intro-

duction to the subject is followed by discussion of questions concerning children in sports, college athletics, the Olympics, racism, women, drug abuse, and media relations. (Rev: BL 8/95; SLJ 1/96) [796]

13230 Bizley, Kirk. *Inline Skating* (4–7). Series: Radical Sports. 1999, Heinemann LB $24.22 (1-57572-942-3). As well as a history of inline skating, this book tells how to get started and gives information on equipment, techniques, terms, and safety. (Rev: SLJ 4/00) [796]

13231 Chambers, Veronica. *Double Dutch: A Celebration of Jump Rope, Rhyme, and Sisterhood* (4–8). Illus. 2002, Hyperion $18.99 (0-7868-0512-9). An exuberant look at this brand of rope jumping, including its history and rhymes, with exciting photographs. (Rev: BCCB 10/02; BL 10/15/02; HBG 3/03; SLJ 12/02*) [796.2]

13232 Chester, Jonathan. *The Young Adventurer's Guide to Everest: From Avalanche to Zopkio* (5–8). Illus. 2002, Tricycle Pr. $15.95 (1-58246-069-8). A book about Mount Everest and those who have climbed it, in an alphabetical format with photographs. (Rev: BL 5/15/02; HBG 10/02; SLJ 4/02) [796.52]

13233 Ching, Jacqueline. *Adventure Racing* (7–10). Series: Ultra Sports. 2002, Rosen LB $26.50 (0-8239-3555-8). This is a fine introduction to this new, outdoor, multidiscipline sport that involves biking, paddling, and climbing plus survival skills and outdoor savvy. (Rev: BL 9/1/02) [796.5]

13234 Coleman, Lori. *Beginning Strength Training* (4–7). Photos by Jimmy Clarke. Series: Beginning Sports. 1998, Lerner LB $27.15 (0-8225-3511-4). This abridged version of *Jeff Savage's Fundamental Strength Training* is a beginner's book on body development. (Rev: HBG 10/99; SLJ 2/99) [796]

13235 Cook, Nick. *Downhill In-Line Skating* (5–8). Series: Extreme Sports. 2000, Capstone LB $21.26

(0-7368-0482-X). Downhill inline skating is introduced with material on its history, equipment, skills, and competitions. (Rev: HBG 10/00; SLJ 8/00) [796]

13236 Corbett, Doris, and John Cheffers, eds. *Unique Games and Sports Around the World: A Reference Guide* (4–9). Illus. 2001, Greenwood $67.95 (0-313-29778-9). More than 300 games and sports are organized by continent and then by country, with details of the number of players, equipment, rules, and so forth, and indications of whether this is a suitable game for the classroom or playground. (Rev: SLJ 8/01) [790.1]

13237 Crisfield, Deborah. *Winning Volleyball for Girls* (5–7). Illus. 1995, Facts on File $24.95 (0-8160-3033-2). An excellent introduction to volleyball that gives girls information on rules, strategies, and techniques. (Rev: BCCB 3/96; BL 9/1/95) [796.32]

13238 Crossingham, John. *Cheerleading in Action* (4–7). Series: Sports in Action. 2003, Crabtree LB $15.96 (0-7787-0333-9); paper $6.26 (0-7787-0353-3). This is a colorful, attractive introduction to cheerleading, the cheers, costumes, duties, and its importance in sports. (Rev: BL 11/15/03) [791]

13239 Crossingham, John. *In-Line Skating in Action* (4–7). Series: Sports in Action. 2002, Crabtree LB $21.28 (0-7787-0328-2); paper $6.95 (0-7737-0348-7). A fine introduction to this fast-growing sport with easy-to-follow descriptions of moves and techniques. (Rev: BL 1/1–15/03; SLJ 10/03) [796.9]

13240 Crossingham, John. *Lacrosse in Action* (4–7). Series: Sports in Action. 2002, Crabtree LB $21.28 (0-7787-0329-0); paper $6.95 (0-7737-0349-5). A clear, concise introduction to lacrosse that discusses techniques, equipment, rules, and safety precautions. (Rev: BL 1/1–15/03) [796.34]

13241 Crossingham, John. *Wrestling in Action* (4–7). Series: Sports in Action. 2003, Crabtree LB $15.96 (0-7787-0336-3); paper $6.26 (0-7787-0356-8). This introduction to wrestling describes basic moves, skills, and rules. (Rev: BL 11/15/03) [796.8]

13242 Currie, Stephen. *Issues in Sports* (7–12). Illus. Series: Contemporary Issues. 1997, Lucent LB $27.45 (1-56006-477-3). Issues in sports that are discussed include the use of steroids and other performance-enhancing drugs, drug testing, the commercialization of sports, sky-rocketing salaries, and athletes as role models. (Rev: BL 5/1/98) [306.4830973]

13243 Curtis, Bruce, and Jay Morelli. *Beginning Golf* (5–8). Illus. 2000, Sterling $19.95 (0-8069-4970-8). Beginning with an overview of golf, equipment, swing, full-play, and short game, and moving on to more complex topics, this fully illustrated volume is a fine introduction to golf. (Rev: BL 9/1/00; SLJ 1/01) [796.352]

13244 Dolan, Ellen M. *Susan Butcher and the Iditarod Trail* (5–7). Illus. 1993, Walker LB $15.85 (0-8027-8212-4). This book gives the history of the Iditarod sled dog race and tells the story of Susan Butcher, who first entered the race in 1978. (Rev: BL 4/1/93; SLJ 4/93) [798.8]

13245 Egendorf, Laura K., ed. *Sports and Athletes* (7–12). Illus. Series: Opposing Viewpoints. 1999, Greenhaven LB $32.45 (0-7377-0057-2); paper $21.20 (0-7377-0056-4). The 30 essays in this critical anthology cover children in sports, college athletics reform, racial discrimination, gender inequality, and drugs. (Rev: BL 9/15/99) [796]

13246 Feinberg, Jeremy R. *Reading the Sports Page: A Guide to Understanding Sports Statistics* (7–10). 1992, Macmillan LB $21.00 (0-02-734420-7). Explains how to read baseball, basketball, football, hockey, and tennis statistics in newspaper sports pages. (Rev: BL 1/15/93; SLJ 1/93) [796]

13247 Flowers, Sarah. *Sports in America* (5–8). Illus. Series: Overview. 1996, Lucent LB $27.45 (1-56006-178-2). An exploration of current controversies in the sports world such sa commercialism, huge salaries, endorsements, racism, sexism, steroids, and the conflict between education and sports in colleges. (Rev: BL 9/1/96) [306.5]

13248 Gay, Kathlyn. *They Don't Wash Their Socks! Sports Superstitions* (6–9). Illus. 1990, Walker LB $14.85 (0-8027-6917-9). A compendium of myths and superstitions that helps explain some of the unusual behavior of players and coaches. (Rev: VOYA 8/90) [796]

13249 Gedatus, Gus. *In-Line Skating for Fitness* (4–7). Series: Nutrition and Fitness. 2001, Capstone LB $23.93 (0-7368-0707-1). Inline skating is introduced with an emphasis on fitness benefits and the necessity of a healthy diet. (Rev: BL 9/15/01; HBG 10/01) [796]

13250 Gedatus, Gus. *Weight Training* (4–7). Illus. Series: Nutrition and Fitness. 2001, Capstone LB $23.95 (0-7368-0708-X). Weight training equipment, proper form, and sample workouts are presented, as well as advice on diet and supplements. (Rev: BL 7/01; HBG 10/01) [613.7]

13251 Gryski, Camilla. *Cat's Cradle, Owl's Eyes: A Book of String Games* (4–7). 1984, Morrow LB $15.93 (0-688-03940-5); paper $6.95 (0-688-03941-3). Explanations of 21 string figures, plus variations. [793.9]

13252 Gryski, Camilla. *Many Stars and More String Games* (4–8). 1985, Morrow paper $7.95 (0-688-05792-6). Figures taken from a range of cultures to be mastered by agile fingers. (Rev: BL 12/15/85; SLJ 1/86) [793.9]

13253 Gryski, Camilla. *Super String Games* (6–8). Illus. 1988, Morrow paper $6.95 (0-688-07684-X). Directions for 26 string games from around the world are given in text and diagrams. (Rev: BL 3/1/88; BR 5–6/88; SLJ 6/88) [793]

13254 Hall, Godfrey. *Games* (5–7). Illus. Series: Traditions Around the World. 1995, Thomson Learning LB $24.26 (1-56847-345-1). An oversize book that covers, in text and large color pictures, various games played in different regions around the world. (Rev: BL 6/1–15/95; SLJ 9/95) [790.1]

13255 Hammond, Tim. *Sports* (4–8). Illus. 1988, Knopf $20.99 (0-394-99616-X). A look at two dozen different sports, including equipment, history, and rules. (Rev: BCCB 11/88; BL 12/1/88; SLJ 12/88) [796]

13256 Hanmer, Trudy J. *The Hunting Debate* (6–9). Illus. Series: Issues in Focus. 1999, Enslow LB $19.95 (0-7660-1110-0). The author discusses various forms of hunting and the motives and methods behind each, with pro and con arguments by animal rights and gun control advocates. (Rev: BL 2/15/00; HBG 9/00; SLJ 6/00) [179.]

13257 Harris, Jack C. *Adventure Gaming* (5–8). Illus. Series: Hobby Guides. 1993, Crestwood $13.95 (0-89686-621-1). Clear, easy-to-read information is given, with coverage of all kinds of adventure games, including war and role-playing games and those that deal with magic and sorcery. (Rev: SLJ 2/94) [793.92]

13258 Hastings, Penny. *Sports for Her: A Reference Guide for Teenage Girls* (7–12). Illus. 1999, Greenwood $45.00 (0-313-30551-X). The basics of many individual sports are covered, with tips on playing sports in general for the young female athlete. (Rev: SLJ 7/00; VOYA 6/00) [796]

13259 Hayhurst, Chris. *Wakeboarding! Throw a Tantrum* (4–8). Series: Extreme Sports. 2000, Rosen LB $26.50 (0-8239-3008-4). This new water sport is described with material on the equipment needed and the necessary safety precautions. (Rev: BL 6/1–15/00; SLJ 8/00) [797.1]

13260 Howes, Chris. *Caving* (4–8). Series: Radical Sports. 2003, Heinemann LB $25.64 (1-58810-626-8). Technique, safety, gear, and other vital aspects are covered in this introduction to the sport. (Rev: BL 2/15/03; HBG 3/03) [796.52]

13261 Hu, Evaleen. *A Big Ticket: Sports and Commercialism* (4–7). Illus. 1998, Lerner LB $28.75 (0-8225-3305-7). This well-organized book explains the connections between sports and the media, including broadcast rights, endorsement contracts, pop culture, and the impact of television. (Rev: BL 7/98; HBG 10/98) [338.4]

13262 Hull, Mary. *The Composite Guide to Golf* (5–7). Series: Composite Guide. 1998, Chelsea LB $18.65 (0-7910-4726-1). An introduction to the game of golf and its history, along with highlights of the game's pioneers and current stars including Tiger Woods. (Rev: HBG 10/98; SLJ 9/98) [796.352]

13263 Hunter, Matt. *Pro Wrestling's Greatest Tag Teams* (4–7). Series: Pro Wrestling Legends. 2000, Chelsea $20.75 (0-7910-5835-2). This title covers such tag teams as the Road Warriors, the Midnight Express, the Nasty Boys, Public Enemy, and Harlem Heat. (Rev: BL 10/15/00; HBG 3/01) [796.8]

13264 Hunter, Matt. *Ric Flair: The Story of the Wrestler They Call "The Natural Boy"* (4–7). Series: Pro Wrestling Legends. 2000, Chelsea $19.75 (0-7910-5825-5). The story of the wrestler who has been at the top of his sport for most of the last three decades. (Rev: BL 10/15/00; HBG 3/01) [796.8]

13265 Janicot, Didier, and Gilbert Pouillart. *Judo Techniques and Tactics* (4–7). Trans. from French by Yana Melnikova. 2000, Sterling $19.95 (0-8069-1970-1). An informative manual that gives material on self-defense techniques and training tips for each level of judo from yellow up to black belt. (Rev: SLJ 3/01) [796.8]

13266 Judson, Karen. *Sports and Money: It's a Sell-out!* (7–12). Series: Issues in Focus. 1995, Enslow LB $20.95 (0-89490-622-4). A straightforward presentation that uses first-person accounts concerning the financial side of being in the sports business. (Rev: BL 11/15/95; SLJ 6/96) [796.0619]

13267 Kalman, Bobbie, and Sarah Dann. *Bowling in Action* (4–7). Series: Sports in Action. 2003, Crabtree LB $15.96 (0-7787-0335-5); paper $6.26 (0-7787-0355-X). This well-illustrated introduction to bowling includes material on equipment, techniques, rules, and bowling alleys. (Rev: BL 11/15/03) [794.6]

13268 Kaminker, Laura. *In-Line Skating! Get Aggressive* (5–8). Series: Extreme Sports. 1999, Rosen LB $26.50 (0-8239-3012-2). This book provides information for both beginning and advanced inline skaters and covers topics including equipment, history, techniques, and safety tips. (Rev: SLJ 4/00) [796]

13269 Kent, Deborah. *Athletes with Disabilities* (5–7). Illus. Series: Watts Library: Disability. 2003, Watts LB $24.00 (0-531-12019-8); paper $8.95 (0-531-16664-3). Achievements of disabled athletes are accompanied by the history of such events as the Special Olympics and by information on new games, equipment, and techniques that widen horizons. (Rev: BL 10/15/03; SLJ 9/03) [371.]

13270 Krause, Peter. *Fundamental Golf* (5–8). Photos by Andy King. Series: Fundamental Sports. 1995, Lerner LB $27.15 (0-8225-3454-1). A clear introduction to golf that covers history, equipment, swings, rules, and courses. (Rev: SLJ 9/95) [796.352]

13271 Luby, Thia. *Yoga for Teens: How to Improve Your Fitness, Confidence, Appearance, and Health — and Have Fun Doing It* (6–12). 2000, Clear Light

$14.95 (1-57416-032-X). The benefits of yoga, particularly in the teen years, are presented with eye-catching photographs and clear instructions for achieving the poses. (Rev: SLJ 5/00) [613.7]

13272 Macy, Sue. *Winning Ways: A Photohistory of American Women in Sports* (7–10). Illus. 1996, Holt $16.95 (0-8050-4147-8). Beginning with the 1880s bicycle craze, this book vividly chronicles the history of women's sports in America. (Rev: BL 6/1–15/96*; SLJ 8/96*; VOYA 10/96) [796]

13273 Macy, Sue, and Jane Gottesman, eds. *Play like a Girl: A Celebration of Women in Sports* (5–9). 1999, Holt $16.95 (0-8050-6071-5). A tribute to women in sports, using material culled from books, photograph archives, newspapers, and magazines. (Rev: BCCB 10/99; BL 7/99; HBG 10/00; SLJ 9/99; VOYA 12/99) [796]

13274 Manley, Claudia B. *Competitive Volleyball for Girls* (4–7). Illus. Series: Sportsgirl. 2001, Rosen LB $26.50 (0-8239-3404-7). An introduction to the rules of volleyball, the training necessary, and the special opportunities for girls, with material on nutrition and the dangers of overtraining. (Rev: SLJ 3/02) [796.325]

13275 Marchon-Arnaud, Catherine. *A Gallery of Games* (5–7). Series: Young Artisan. 1994, Ticknor $12.95 (0-395-68379-3). Historical information, clear directions, and rules of each game are supplied, but young novices might find some of these projects difficult. (Rev: BL 4/1/94; SLJ 3/94) [745]

13276 Margolis, Jeffrey A. *Violence in Sports* (6–12). Illus. 1999, Enslow LB $20.95 (0-89490-961-4). Using extensive documentation and numerous recent incidents, the author traces the decline in sportsmanship and the effect that violence is having on sports. (Rev: BL 9/1/99; HBG 4/00) [796]

13277 Mason, Paul. *Skiing* (4–8). Illus. 2003, Heinemann LB $25.64 (1-58810-628-4). Technique, safety, gear, and profiles of famous skiers are all covered in this introduction to the sport. (Rev: BL 2/15/03; HBG 3/03) [796.93]

13278 Miller, Thomas. *Taking Time Out: Recreation and Play* (5–8). Illus. Series: Our Human Family. 1995, Blackbirch LB $31.19 (1-56711-128-9). Divided into five broad geographic areas, this account describes how people enjoy themselves at play in various cultures. (Rev: SLJ 1/96) [794]

13279 Nace, Don. *Bowling for Beginners: Simple Steps to Strikes and Spares* (6–12). Photos by Bruce Curtis. 2001, Sterling $19.95 (0-8069-4968-6). Equipment, technique, scoring, competition play, and etiquette are all discussed here, with excellent diagrams and color photographs. (Rev: BL 6/1–15/01; SLJ 7/01) [794.6]

13280 Netzley, Patricia D. *Life of an Everest Expedition* (6–10). Series: The Way People Live. 2001, Lucent LB $19.96 (1-56006-792-6). Using primary source material and black-and-white photographs, this work explores the planning and execution of a climb up Everest. (Rev: BL 6/1–15/01) [796.5]

13281 Nicholson, Lois. *The Composite Guide to Lacrosse* (4–8). Series: The Composite Guide. 1998, Chelsea LB $18.65 (0-7910-4719-9). A fine guide to lacrosse, giving its history, how it is played today, and portraits of the game's greatest players. (Rev: HBG 3/99; SLJ 12/98) [796.34]

13282 Paulsen, Gary. *Woodsong* (7–12). Illus. 1990, Bradbury $17.00 (0-02-770221-9). Paulsen describes his experiences with sleds and dogs and his entry into the grueling Iditarod Sled Dog Race in Alaska. (Rev: BL 8/90; SLJ 10/90) [796.5]

13283 Payan, Gregory. *Essential Snowmobiling for Teens* (5–9). Series: Outdoor Life. 2000, Children's LB $20.00 (0-516-23358-0); paper $6.95 (0-516-23558-3). The invention of the snowmobile is covered plus material on license requirements, trail permits, equipment, clothing, safety, driving techniques, and maintenance. (Rev: SLJ 2/01) [796.94]

13284 Perry, Phyllis J. *Soaring* (4–7). Illus. Series: First Books. 1997, Watts LB $22.00 (0-531-20258-5). Covers the history of gliders, scientific principles — lift, thrust, and drag — and the sport of soaring and the equipment needed for it. (Rev: BL 7/97) [797.5]

13285 Peters, Craig. *Chants, Cheers, and Jumps* (5–8). Illus. Series: Let's Go Team. 2003, Mason Crest $19.95 (1-59084-535-8). Readers will learn the difference between cheers and chants and how to do various jumps. Also use *Competitive Cheerleading* (2003). (Rev: BL 10/15/03; SLJ 9/03) [791.6]

13286 Peters, Craig. *Cheerleading Stars* (5–8). Series: Let's Go Team. 2003, Mason Crest LB $19.95 (1-59084-533-1). This book highlights the careers and accomplishments of a select group of star cheerleaders. (Rev: BL 10/15/03) [791]

13287 Peters, Craig. *Techniques of Dance for Cheerleading* (5–8). Series: Let's Go Team. 2003, Mason Crest LB $19.95 (1-59084-531-5). The importance of stretching and safety measures are emphasized in this volume that discusses choreography and the similarities and differences between cheerleading and dancing. (Rev: SLJ 9/03) [791.6]

13288 Roberts, Jeremy. *Rock and Ice Climbing! Top the Tower* (4–8). Illus. Series: Extreme Sports. 2000, Rosen LB $26.50 (0-8239-3009-2). This book on climbing covers the dangers, different climbing styles, equipment, techniques, and venues, and profiles some young climbers. (Rev: BL 3/15/00; SLJ 8/00) [796.52]

13289 Roberts, Robin. *Sports for Life: How Athletes Have More Fun* (5–8). Illus. Series: Get in the Game. 2000, Millbrook LB $23.90 (0-7613-1407-5). This account, mainly for girls, explains how to enjoy sports through applying discipline, patience, cooperation, health, and the sheer fun of competition. (Rev: BL 1/1–15/01; HBG 3/01) [796]

13290 Roberts, Robin. *Which Sport Is Right for You?* (5–8). Series: Get in the Game! 2001, Millbrook LB $23.90 (0-7613-2117-9). Written with girls in mind, this short book explores how to choose a sport that is right for one's capabilities and interests. (Rev: BL 9/15/01; HBG 3/02; SLJ 1/02) [796]

13291 Ross, Dan. *Pro Wrestling's Greatest Wars* (4–7). Illus. Series: Pro Wrestling Legends. 2000, Chelsea $19.75 (0-7910-5837-9); paper $8.95 (0-7910-5838-7). Some of the great feuds in wrestling history, such as Harlem Heat vs. the Nasty Boys, are described in this fast read. (Rev: BL 10/15/00; HBG 3/01) [796.812]

13292 Ross, Dan. *The Story of the Wrestler They Call "The Rock"* (4–7). Series: Pro Wrestling Legends. 2000, Chelsea $19.75 (0-7910-5831-X). This is the story of the third-generation wrestler known as "The Rock." (Rev: BL 10/15/00; HBG 3/01) [796.8]

13293 Rowe, Julian. *Recreation* (4–7). Illus. Series: Science Encounters. 1997, Rigby paper $25.55 (1-57572-092-2). Shows how science is used in theme park rides, backpacking and camping equipment, computer games, television, scuba diving, and hang gliding. (Rev: SLJ 10/97) [796]

13294 Rowe, Julian. *Sports* (4–7). Illus. Series: Science Encounters. 1997, Rigby paper $25.55 (1-57572-089-2). Shows how science is used in such sports-related topics as the design of equipment, protective clothing, and sports medicine. (Rev: SLJ 10/97) [796]

13295 Ryan, Pat. *Rock Climbing* (4–7). Illus. Series: World of Sports. 2000, Smart Apple LB $16.95 (1-887068-57-0). In addition to covering the origins and evolution of rock climbing, this book discusses the basics of the sport, equipment, and star athletes. (Rev: BL 9/15/00) [796.52]

13296 Savage, Jeff. *A Sure Thing? Sports and Gambling* (7–12). Series: Sports Issues. 1996, Lerner LB $28.75 (0-8225-3303-0). After a brief history of gambling, this book looks at the many forms of gambling available today, from church bingo games to horse racing to Las Vegas casinos, with a focus on the connection between gambling and sports and emphasis on the dangers of gambling addiction. (Rev: BL 7/97; HBG 3/98; SLJ 11/97) [796]

13297 Savage, Jeff. *Top 10 Sports Bloopers and Who Made Them* (4–7). Illus. Series: Sports Top 10. 2000, Enslow LB $18.95 (0-7660-1271-9). This collection of 10 famous sports mistakes also gives good background information on the perpetrators and the causes of the errors. (Rev: BL 9/15/00; HBG 10/00; SLJ 10/00) [796]

13298 Scheppler, Bill. *The Ironman Triathlon* (7–10). Illus. 2002, Rosen LB $26.50 (0-8239-3556-6). Scheppler provides tips on training body and mind for the challenge of these races that combine running, swimming, and biking. (Rev: BL 9/1/02; VOYA 8/02) [796.42]

13299 Schwartz, Ellen. *I Love Yoga: A Guide for Kids and Teens* (5–12). 2003, Tundra paper $9.95 (0-88776-598-X). Illustrated instructions for 18 basic poses are accompanied by breathing and relaxation exercises, discussion of the benefits of yoga, and a description of the different types of yoga practiced around the world. (Rev: SLJ 12/03; VOYA 10/03) [613.7]

13300 Shahan, Sherry. *Dashing Through the Snow: The Story of the Jr. Iditarod* (4–7). Illus. 1997, Millbrook $24.90 (0-7613-0208-5); paper $9.95 (0-7613-0143-7). All aspects of the 150-mile Junior Iditarod are touched upon in this account, including how these young mushers communicate with their dogs. (Rev: BL 3/1/97; SLJ 4/97) [798]

13301 Sheely, Robert, and Louis Bourgeois. *Sports Lab: How Science Has Changed Sports* (4–7). Illus. Series: Science Lab. 1994, Silver Moon $14.95 (1-881889-49-1). Traces the effect on sports of applying findings from such branches of science as aerodynamics, psychology, and medicine. (Rev: SLJ 9/94) [617.1]

13302 Sherrow, Victoria. *Encyclopedia of Women and Sports* (7–12). 1996, ABC-CLIO LB $75.00 (0-87436-826-X). This alphabetically arranged book on women's involvement in sports from ancient Greece to modern times covers athletes, sports, organizations, and social issues such as discrimination, steroid use, pregnancy, and eating disorders. (Rev: BL 9/1/97; BR 9–10/97; SLJ 8/97) [796]

13303 Silas, Elizabeth, and Diane Goodney. *Yoga* (4–8). Illus. Series: Life Balance. 2003, Watts LB $19.50 (0-531-12258-1); paper $6.95 (0-531-15577-3). Information on the spiritual and philosophical aspects of yoga follows chapters on basic yoga moves. (Rev: BL 10/15/03) [613.]

13304 Skreslet, Laurie, and Elizabeth MacLeod. *To the Top of Everest* (5–9). Illus. 2001, Kids Can $16.95 (1-55074-721-5). Skreslet relates his lifelong ambition to climb Everest and his actual experiences doing so, with many facts about the mountain and the dangers involved and stunning photographs of his adventure. (Rev: BCCB 10/01; BL 9/15/01; HBG 3/02; SLJ 9/01*) [796.52]

13305 Smith, Graham. *Karting* (4–8). Series: Radical Sports. 2002, Heinemann LB $25.64 (1-58810-624-1). The sport of karting is introduced with discussion of equipment selection, basic skills, fitness and training, and safety. (Rev: BL 2/15/03; HBG 3/03) [796.7]

13306 Steiner, Andy. *Girl Power on the Playing Field: A Book About Girls, Their Goals, and Their Struggles* (5–10). Series: Girl Power. 2000, Lerner LB $30.35 (0-8225-2690-5). This book explains women's roles in sports with good personal guidance for young girls on participation and goals. (Rev: HBG 10/00; SLJ 6/00) [796]

13307 Steiner, Andy. *A Sporting Chance: Sports and Gender* (4–8). Series: Sports Issues. 1995, Lerner LB $28.75 (0-8225-3300-6). An overview of the hurdles that female athletes have had to overcome and the persistent inequality between men and women in sports at all levels, from Little League to the pros. (Rev: BL 1/1–15/96; SLJ 1/96) [796]

13308 Sullivan, George. *Any Number Can Play: The Numbers Athletes Wear* (4–8). Illus. 2000, Millbrook LB $23.90 (0-7613-1557-8). A fascinating glimpse at players' devotion to their assigned numbers, along with information on retired and banned numbers and who uses the number 13. (Rev: BL 12/15/00; HBG 3/01; SLJ 2/01; VOYA 2/01) [796]

13309 Sullivan, George. *Don't Step on the Foul Line: Sports Superstitions* (4–8). Illus. 2000, Millbrook LB $23.90 (0-7613-1558-6). This is an intriguing look at superstitions, customs, and traditions associated with many different sports. (Rev: BL 12/15/00; HBG 3/01; SLJ 2/01; VOYA 2/01) [796.357]

13310 Takeda, Pete. *Climb! Your Guide to Bouldering, Sport Climbing, Trad Climbing, Ice Climbing, Alpinism, and More* (4–9). Illus. Series: Extreme Sports. 2002, National Geographic paper $8.95 (0-7922-6744-3). An attractive guide to climbing of all types — sport, wall, ice, alpine, and so forth — and to the equipment, techniques, and dangers. (Rev: SLJ 1/03) [796.5223]

13311 Teitelbaum, Michael. *Great Moments in Women's Sports* (4–7). Series: Sports Greats. 2002, World Almanac LB $29.26 (0-8368-5349-0). A timeline running from 1904 to 2001 provides a backdrop for information on athletes who participated in the Olympic Games and achieved other significant milestones. (Rev: SLJ 3/03) [796.082]

13312 U.S. Olympic Committee. *A Basic Guide to Decathlon* (4–8). Series: Olympic Guides. 2001, Gareth Stevens LB $22.60 (0-8368-2796-1). This is an attractive introduction to the sport of decathlon, with information about equipment, training, and famous athletes. (Rev: HBG 10/01; SLJ 7/01) [796.42]

13313 Uschan, Michael V. *Golf* (4–8). Series: History of Sports. 2001, Lucent LB $27.45 (1-56006-744-6). An absorbing exploration of the history of golf, with information on etiquette, famous players, tours, and famous courses, with many photographs and reproductions. (Rev: SLJ 7/01) [796.352]

13314 Valliant, Doris. *Going to College* (5–8). Series: Let's Go Team. 2003, Mason Crest LB $19.95 (1-59084-541-2). This well-illustrated, breezy account describes the function of cheerleading in college sports activities. (Rev: BL 10/15/03) [791]

13315 Valliant, Doris. *The History of Cheerleading* (5–8). Series: Let's Go Team. 2003, Mason Crest LB $19.95 (1-59084-534-X). Using many illustrations, this slim volume describes the history and function of cheerleading at various levels in this country. (Rev: BL 10/15/03) [791]

13316 Venables, Stephen. *To the Top: The Story of Everest* (6–12). 2003, Candlewick $17.99 (0-7636-2115-3). The mountain itself gets equal treatment in this engaging book that looks at the important aspects of geology, meteorology, politics, and culture as well as the expeditions that have taken place and the role of the Sherpas in making them possible. (Rev: BCCB 6/03; HBG 10/03; SLJ 7/03*)

13317 Weiss, Stefanie Iris. *Everything You Need to Know About Yoga: An Introduction for Teens* (7–12). Series: Need to Know Library. 1999, Rosen LB $17.95 (0-8239-2959-0). Yoga's ability to improve mental, spiritual, and physical health is the main focus of this volume. (Rev: SLJ 5/00) [613.7]

13318 Willard, Keith. *Ballooning* (4–7). Illus. Series: World of Sports. 2000, Smart Apple LB $16.95 (1-887068-51-1). This brief introduction to ballooning mentions star balloonists, different kinds of ballooning, the origins of this sport, and how one becomes proficient at it. (Rev: BL 9/15/00) [797.5]

13319 Willker, Joshua D. G. *Everything You Need to Know About the Dangers of Sports Gambling* (5–10). Illus. Series: Need to Know Library. 2000, Rosen LB $25.25 (0-8239-3229-X). This brief, well-written book surveys the world of gambling on sports, its legal and illegal aspects, and how it has ruined the careers of many fine athletes. (Rev: BL 1/1–15/01) [796]

13320 Woolum, Janet. *Outstanding Women Athletes: Who They Are and How They Influenced Sports in America* (6–12). Illus. 1998, Oryx $65.95 (1-57356-120-7). This update of the 1992 edition on women in sports captures many of the recent advances that women have made, adds 26 new biographies and a new chapter on outstanding teams, and includes a sport-by-sport annotated bibliography and statistics. (Rev: BL 9/1/98; SLJ 11/98; VOYA 12/98) [796]

13321 Young, Perry D. *Lesbians and Gays and Sports* (8–12). Series: Issues in Lesbian and Gay Life. 1995, Chelsea $24.95 (0-7910-2611-6); paper $12.95 (0-7910-2951-4). Looks at homosexuals in sports, with biographies of Kopay, Tilden, King, and Navratilova. (Rev: BL 6/1–15/95) [796]

13322 Zeigler, Heidi. *Hang Gliding* (4–8). Series: X-treme Outdoors. 2003, Children's LB $20.00 (0-

516-24320-9); paper $6.95 (0-516-24382-9). Dramatic color photographs accompany easily read information on the history of the sport, equipment needed, and major events. Also in this series is *Skysurfing* (2003). (Rev: BL 9/15/03; LMC 8–9/03; SLJ 7/03) [797]

Automobile Racing

13323 Benson, Michael. *Crashes and Collisions* (5–8). Series: Race Car Legends. 1997, Chelsea $18.65 (0-7910-4435-1). Multi-car pileups in car racing and the people who have survived them are the focus of this exciting volume. (Rev: HBG 3/98; SLJ 2/98) [629.228]

13324 Johnstone, Mike. *NASCAR* (5–8). Series: Need for Speed. 2002, Lerner LB $28.75 (0-8225-0389-1). A look at the fast-growing sport of NASCAR auto racing, with detailed descriptions of the drivers, their cars, and the circuits. (Rev: BL 8/02; HBG 10/02; SLJ 7/02) [796.7]

13325 Parr, Danny. *Lowriders* (4–7). Illus. Series: Wild Rides! 2001, Capstone LB $21.26 (0-7368-0928-7). This volume on "lowrider" cars discusses the types of vehicles that are popular, the history of this trend, and the competitions that are held. (Rev: BL 10/15/01; HBG 3/02) [628.28]

13326 Pitt, Matthew. *Drag Racer* (4–7). Illus. Series: Built for Speed. 2001, Children's LB $20.00 (0-516-23159-6); paper $6.95 (0-516-23262-2). The cars, the driving techniques, the race regulations, and other information important to this activity are all covered in this attractive book. (Rev: BL 12/1/01) [796.72]

13327 Savage, Jeff. *Drag Racing* (4–8). Series: Action Events. 1996, Crestwood LB $14.95 (0-89686-890-7); paper $4.95 (0-382-39293-0). The thrill of drag racing is conveyed through many action photographs and a simple text. (Rev: SLJ 2/97) [796.7]

Baseball

13328 Aylesworth, Thomas G. *The Kids' World Almanac of Baseball* (4–8). Illus. 1996, World Almanac $8.95 (0-88687-787-3). An entertaining compendium of baseball facts. (Rev: BL 6/1/90) [796.357]

13329 *A Basic Guide to Softball* (6–12). Illus. Series: Olympic Guides. 2001, Gareth Stevens LB $22.60 (0-8368-2798-8). This is the U.S. Olympic Committee's guide to the sport that was added to the Games in Atlanta in 1996, with information on the history

of the game, rules, and some how-to advice. (Rev: BL 5/1/01; HBG 10/01) [796.357]

13330 Brundage, Buz. *Be a Better Hitter: Baseball Basics* (5–9). Illus. 2000, Sterling $17.95 (0-8069-2461-6). Covers baseball hitting techniques including grip, stance, bunting, swing, contact, and follow-through. (Rev: BL 6/1–15/00; SLJ 9/00) [796.357]

13331 Collins, Ace, and John Hillman. *Blackball Superstars: Legendary Players of the Negro Baseball Leagues* (6–9). 1999, Avisson LB $19.95 (1-888105-38-0). This book profiles 12 stars of the Negro Baseball Leagues, including Satchel Paige and Josh Gibson, all of whom are now in the National Baseball Hall of Fame. (Rev: SLJ 8/99) [796.357]

13332 Eisenhammer, Fred, and Jim Binkley. *Baseball's Most Memorable Trades: Superstars Swapped, All-Stars Copped and Megadeals That Flopped* (8–12). 1997, McFarland paper $28.50 (0-7864-0198-2). The causes and effects of the top 25 baseball trades since the turn of the 20th century are covered. (Rev: VOYA 10/97) [796.323]

13333 Forker, Dom. *Baseball Brain Teasers* (7–12). 1986, Sterling paper $6.95 (0-8069-6284-4). A baseball trivia book in which baseball situations are described and questions are asked about them. (Rev: BR 11–12/86; SLJ 12/86) [796.357]

13334 Fremon, David K. *The Negro Baseball Leagues* (7–12). Series: American Events. 1994, Silver Burdett paper $7.95 (0-382-24730-2). A history of baseball from the segregated Negro Baseball Leagues' point of view. (Rev: BL 3/15/95) [796.357]

13335 Fuerst, Jeffrey B. *The Kids' Baseball Workout: A Fun Way to Get in Shape and Improve Your Game* (5–8). 2002, Millbrook LB $24.90 (0-7613-2307-4). This book offers exercises, stretches, and skills that will help young baseball players improve their game. (Rev: BL 9/1/02; HBG 10/02; SLJ 7/02) [796.357]

13336 Galt, Margot F. *Up to the Plate: The All-American Girls Professional Baseball League* (6–9). Series: Sports Legacy. 1995, Lerner LB $31.95 (0-8225-3326-X). This history of the All-American Girls Professional Baseball League includes interviews with the players and their reactions to the movie *A League of Their Own*. (Rev: BL 7/95; SLJ 6/95) [796.357]

13337 Gardner, Robert, and Dennis Shortelle. *The Forgotten Players: The Story of Black Baseball in America* (5–8). Illus. 1993, Walker LB $13.85 (0-8027-8249-3). A discussion of the challenges that faced the players of the Negro Leagues. (Rev: BL 2/15/93; SLJ 4/93) [769.357]

13338 Gay, Douglas, and Kathlyn Gay. *The Not-So-Minor Leagues* (5–8). Illus. 1996, Millbrook LB $23.40 (1-56294-921-7). The history, importance, and present status of the minor leagues in baseball. (Rev: BL 5/15/96; BR 11–12/96; SLJ 6/96) [796.357]

13339 Gilbert, Thomas. *Damn Yankees: Casey, Yogi, Whitey, and the Mick* (6–9). Series: The American Game. 1997, Watts paper $24.00 (0-531-11338-8). An exciting, partisan account of the New York Yankees under Casey Stengel, with material on Yankee greats Babe Ruth, Lou Gehrig, and Joe DiMaggio, and the stars between 1949 and 1964 — Mickey Mantle, Whitey Ford, Yogi Berra, and Roger Maris. The author recounts each season, weaving in the rivalry with the then Brooklyn Dodgers and New York Giants and the dramatic story of Jackie Robinson. (Rev: BR 5–6/98; SLJ 12/97; VOYA 4/98) [796.357]

13340 Gilbert, Thomas. *The Soaring Twenties: Babe Ruth and the Home-Run Decade* (7–12). Series: The American Game. 1996, Watts LB $24.00 (0-531-11279-9). This book describes an era of spectacular sports stars and business tycoons who "owned" the newly evolving major leagues, widespread graft and game-fixing, beginning with the Black Sox gambling scandal, and the recovery of the game under Babe Ruth and other great players of the 1920s. Coverage is also given to race problems and the Negro Leagues. (Rev: SLJ 1/97) [796.357]

13341 Hanmer, Trudy J. *The All-American Girls Professional Baseball League* (6–9). Illus. Series: American Events. 1994, New Discovery LB $14.95 (0-02-742595-9). As well as discussing the AAGPBL, this account describes women in baseball prior to the league and recent attempts to play at all levels from Little League to the majors. (Rev: BL 3/15/95; SLJ 3/95; VOYA 5/95) [796.357]

13342 Kellogg, David. *True Stories of Baseball's Hall of Famers* (4–8). Illus. 2000, Bluewood $8.95 (0-912517-41-7). Using a chronological approach, this book profiles 60 Hall of Famers and tells why each is there. (Rev: BL 10/15/00; VOYA 8/01) [796.357]

13343 Kisseloff, Jeff. *Who Is Baseball's Greatest Hitter?* (5–8). Illus. 2000, Holt $15.95 (0-8050-6013-8). The author introduces a number of strong candidates for the title of baseball's greatest hitter. (Rev: BL 5/1/00; HBG 10/00; SLJ 7/00; VOYA 6/00) [796.357]

13344 Kisseloff, Jeff. *Who Is Baseball's Greatest Pitcher?* (5–7). Illus. 2003, Cricket $15.95 (0-8126-2685-0). The author presents profiles of 33 pitchers, with relevant statistics, and challenges the reader to choose the best and justify this decision. (Rev: BL 7/03; HBG 10/03; SLJ 5/03) [796.359]

13345 Krasner, Steven. *Play Ball Like the Pros: Tips for Kids from 20 Big League Stars* (5–9). Illus. 2002, Peachtree paper $12.95 (1-56145-261-0). Each chapter features a professional player talking about the position he plays and giving tips to the young athlete. (Rev: BL 5/1/02; SLJ 6/02; VOYA 10/03) [796.357]

13346 Kreutzer, Peter, and Ted Kerley. *Little League's Official How-to-Play Baseball Handbook* (4–8). Illus. 1990, Doubleday paper $11.95 (0-385-24700-1). This guidebook covers all the basics of baseball and supplies strategies for playing various positions. (Rev: BL 5/15/90) [796.357]

13347 Layden, Joe. *The Great American Baseball Strike* (5–8). Series: Headliners. 1995, Millbrook LB $25.90 (1-56294-930-6). A discussion of the issues that led to the 1995 baseball strike, with a review of the history of professional baseball and of the stormy relationship between the owners and players. (Rev: BL 11/15/95; SLJ 1/96) [796.357]

13348 Light, Jonathan F. *The Cultural Encyclopedia of Baseball* (7–12). 1997, McFarland LB $75.00 (0-7864-0311-X). This book contains entries on a broad range of baseball topics, such as alcoholism in baseball, baseball in different countries, and the dumbest players, as well as the standard information including famous players, managers, perfect games and no-hitters, statistics, ballparks, and important games. (Rev: BL 9/1/97; SLJ 2/98) [796.357]

13349 Mackin, Bob. *Record-Breaking Baseball Trivia* (5–8). 2000, Douglas & McIntyre $6.95 (1-55054-757-7). Questions, answers, and quizzes cover topics including baseball history, team play, World Series facts, and trivia from the plate and mound. (Rev: BL 9/15/00) [796.357]

13350 McKissack, Patricia, and Fredrick McKissack. *Black Diamond: The Story of the Negro Baseball Leagues* (6–10). Illus. 1994, Scholastic paper $14.95 (0-590-45809-4). A history of African Americans in baseball and the Negro Baseball Leagues, until Jackie Robinson's entry into the major leagues. (Rev: BL 4/94; VOYA 10/94) [796.357]

13351 Macy, Sue. *A Whole New Ball Game: The Story of the All-American Girls Professional Baseball League* (5–8). Illus. 1993, Holt $14.95 (0-8050-1942-1). A fascinating look at the All-American Girls Professional Baseball League that functioned from 1945 to 1954. (Rev: BL 3/15/93; SLJ 5/93*; VOYA 12/93) [796.357]

13352 Margolies, Jacob. *The Negro Leagues: The Story of Black Baseball* (7–12). Series: African American Experience. 1993, Watts paper $24.00 (0-531-11130-X). The history of African American baseball from the 1880s through the birth of the Negro Leagues in the 1920s and their demise in the 1950s. (Rev: BL 2/15/94; VOYA 6/94) [793.357]

13353 Nitz, Kristin Wolden. *Softball* (5–9). Series: Play-by-Play. 2000, Lerner paper $7.95 (0-8225-9875-2). Good basic information about softball is given including history, rules, equipment, and positions. (Rev: SLJ 9/00) [796.357]

13354 Preller, James. *McGwire and Sosa: A Season to Remember* (4–7). Illus. 1998, Simon & Schuster paper $5.99 (0-689-82871-3). An oversize paperback that traces the baseball season that brought Sosa and McGwire to the nation's attention and made them sports heroes. (Rev: BL 1/1–15/99) [796.357]

13355 Ritter, Lawrence. *The Story of Baseball* (6–12). 1999, Morrow $16.95 (0-688-16264-9). This history of baseball from its origins to the McGwire-Sosa race for the record book in 1998 also contains material on elements of the game such as pitching and fielding. (Rev: BL 4/1/99; HBG 10/99; SLJ 4/99; VOYA 10/99) [796.357]

13356 Skipper, John C. *Umpires: Classic Baseball Stories from the Men Who Made the Calls* (8–12). 1997, McFarland paper $24.95 (0-7864-0364-0). Great, memorable moments in the careers of 19 umpires. (Rev: VOYA 12/97) [796.323]

13357 Smyth, Ian. *The Young Baseball Player* (4–7). Illus. 1998, DK paper $15.99 (0-7894-2825-3). A good beginner's guide to baseball that explains, through illustrations and text, the fundamentals of baseball, the roles of each position, basic skills, and a little of the sport's history. (Rev: BL 6/1–15/98; HBG 10/98; SLJ 6/98) [796.357]

13358 Stewart, John. *The Baseball Clinic: Skills and Drills for Better Baseball: A Handbook for Players and Coaches* (6–10). 1999, Burford paper $12.95 (1-58080-073-4). Written by a major league scout, this book contains useful tips for young baseball players in the areas of pitching, fielding, hitting, base running, and catching. (Rev: SLJ 7/99) [796.357]

13359 Stewart, Mark. *Baseball: A History of the National Pastime* (7–10). Series: Watts History of Sports. 1998, Watts LB $33.50 (0-531-11455-4). A solid overview of the history of baseball, with good coverage of off-the-field aspects including labor-management conflicts and the influence of free agency. (Rev: HBG 9/98; SLJ 7/98) [796.357]

13360 Stewart, Wayne. *Baseball Bafflers* (4–7). Illus. 2000, Sterling paper $6.95 (0-8069-6561-4). Using anecdotes, quotations, and statistics, this book describes some of baseball's most unusual plays and strategies. (Rev: BL 2/1/00) [796.357]

13361 Sullivan, George. *Baseball's Boneheads, Bad Boys, and Just Plain Crazy Guys,* (5–8). 2003, Millbrook LB $23.90 (0-7613-2321-X); paper $8.95 (0-7613-1928-X). An amusing collection of anecdotes that show the humor, superstitions, and general nuttiness of baseball players. (Rev: BL 7/03; HBG 10/03; SLJ 11/03) [790.357]

13362 Sullivan, George. *Glovemen: Twenty-Seven of Baseball's Greatest* (4–7). Illus. 1996, Simon & Schuster $18.00 (0-689-31991-6). A look at the role of defensemen in baseball, with profiles of 27 of the greatest. (Rev: BL 5/15/96; SLJ 8/96) [796.357]

13363 Young, Robert. *A Personal Tour of Camden Yards* (4–7). Series: How It Was. 1999, Lerner LB $30.35 (0-8225-3578-5). Designed to remind fans of famous old ballparks, this book visits Camden Yards, home of the Baltimore Orioles. The reader inspects the field, visits the old warehouse, and views the game from a skybox. (Rev: BL 6/1–15/99; HBG 10/99) [796.357]

Basketball

13364 Anderson, Dave. *The Story of Basketball* (4–8). Illus. 1997, Morrow $16.00 (0-688-14316-4). An updated introduction to basketball history, rules, players, and teams. (Rev: BL 1/1–15/98; HBG 3/98; SLJ 10/97) [796.32]

13365 Bird, Larry. *Bird on Basketball: How-to Strategies from the Great Celtics Champion.* Rev. ed. (8–12). Illus. 1988, Addison-Wesley paper $16.00 (0-201-14209-0). The basketball star associated with the Boston Celtics gives advice to young players on basics. [796.32]

13366 Burgan, Michael. *Great Moments in Basketball* (4–7). Series: Sports Greats. 2002, World Almanac LB $29.26 (0-8368-5345-8). Great basketball achievements of the years from 1962 to 2002 are detailed here, with a timeline that starts in 1891 and comments from coaches and players. (Rev: SLJ 3/03) [796.3230973]

13367 Dunning, Mark. *Basketball* (4–8). Series: Flowmotion. 2003, Sterling paper $9.95 (0-8069-9372-3). Through a series of stop-action photographs, the sport of basketball is introduced in a logical step-by-step sequence. (Rev: BL 10/15/03) [796.323]

13368 Glenn, Mike. *Lessons in Success from the NBA's Top Players* (5–7). Illus. 1998, Visions 3000 paper $14.95 (0-9649795-5-1). This noted sportsman tells about his career in the NBA while introducing each of the NBA teams and its strengths. (Rev: BL 7/98) [796.323]

13369 Grabowski, John F. *The Boston Celtics* (7–9). Series: Sports Greats. 2003, Gale LB $21.96 (1-56006-936-8). The story of the Boston basketball team, its history, accomplishments, and important individual players. (Rev: BL 3/15/03) [796.323]

13370 Grabowski, John F. *The Chicago Bulls* (7–9). Series: Sports Greats. 2002, Gale LB $21.96 (1-56006-937-6). After a chapter on the general history of this famous basketball team, there are individual chapters on famous team members past and present. (Rev: BL 9/1/02) [796.323]

13371 Grabowski, John F. *The Los Angeles Lakers* (7–9). Illus. Series: Sports Greats. 2001, Gale LB $27.45 (1-56006-942-2). A look at the history, victories, and players of the California basketball team. (Rev: BL 4/1/02) [796.323]

13372 Jeremiah, Maryalyce. *Basketball: The Woman's Game* (7–12). Illus. 1983, Athletic Inst. paper $5.95 (0-87670-069-5). The fundamentals of basketball as seen through the specific needs of female players. [796.32]

13373 Lace, William W. *The Houston Rockets Basketball Team* (5–8). Series: Sports Greats. 1997, Enslow LB $18.95 (0-89490-792-1). A profile of the Houston Rockets, with sketches of the key players. (Rev: BL 10/15/97; HBG 3/98) [796.323]

13374 Lannin, Joanne. *A History of Basketball for Girls and Women: From Bloomers to the Big Leagues* (5–9). Illus. Series: Sports Legacy. 2000, Lerner LB $31.95 (0-8225-3331-6); paper $15.95 (0-8225-9863-9). From the creation of basketball in 1891 to today, this account describes women's roles. (Rev: BL 1/1–15/01; HBG 3/01; SLJ 2/01; VOYA 4/01) [796.323]

13375 Lieberman-Cline, Nancy, and Robin Roberts. *Basketball for Women* (7–12). Illus. 1995, Human Kinetics paper $18.95 (0-87322-610-0). After a brief history of women's basketball, Lieberman-Cline, who has played in college, Olympics, and professional women's basketball, discusses the commitment required of a serious basketball player, how to formulate a plan for skill development, the recruitment process, and other concerns, and devotes seven chapters to more than 100 drill exercises. (Rev: VOYA 6/96) [796.323]

13376 McKissack, Fredrick. *Black Hoops: African-Americans in Basketball* (6–10). 1999, Scholastic paper $15.95 (0-590-48712-4). This work gives a concise history of basketball from the early days to the present, documenting the contributions of black players and teams and placing the development of the sport in a social and historic context. The final chapter presents an overview of African American women's participation in basketball. (Rev: BL 2/15/99; BR 9–10/99; HBG 9/99; SLJ 3/99; VOYA 10/99) [796.32308996073]

13377 Morris, Greggory. *Basketball Basics* (7–9). Illus. 1976, TreeHouse $6.95 (0-13-072256-1). A fine book for the beginner that explains basic moves, shots, and skills. [796.32]

13378 Owens, Thomas S. *Basketball Arenas* (5–8). Illus. Series: Sports Palaces. 2002, Millbrook LB $25.90 (0-7613-1766-X). Lots of basketball lore and history are included in a visit to the Boston Garden, Chicago Stadium, and the old Madison Square Garden. (Rev: BL 6/1–15/02; HBG 10/02) [796.323]

13379 Owens, Thomas S. *The Chicago Bulls Basketball Team* (5–8). Illus. Series: Sports Greats. 1997, Enslow LB $18.95 (0-89490-793-X). A history of the Chicago Bulls, with emphasis on the stars who

have made the team famous. (Rev: BL 10/15/97; HBG 3/98) [796.323]

13380 Pietrusza, David. *The Phoenix Suns Basketball Team* (5–8). Series: Sports Greats. 1997, Enslow LB $18.95 (0-89490-795-6). An introduction to the Phoenix Suns, their great games, and their star players. (Rev: BL 10/15/97; HBG 3/98) [796.323]

13381 Ponti, James. *WNBA: Stars of Women's Basketball* (5–8). 1999, Pocket Books paper $4.99 (0-671-03275-5). An introduction to women's professional basketball teams with profiles of key individual players. (Rev: SLJ 8/99) [796.323]

13382 Preller, James. *NBA Game Day: An Inside Look a the NBA* (4–8). Illus. 1997, Scholastic paper $10.95 (0-590-76742-9). A photo-collage of a day in the life of the NBA, from morning workout to cleanup after the game, with pictures of prominent players at work and play. (Rev: BL 1/1–15/98; HBG 3/98; VOYA 8/98) [796.323]

13383 Rogers, Glenn. *The San Antonio Spurs Basketball Team* (5–8). Series: Sports Greats. 1997, Enslow LB $18.95 (0-89490-797-2). Profiles of important players and stories behind important games are included in this introduction to the San Antonio Spurs. (Rev: BL 10/15/97; HBG 3/98) [796.323]

13384 Rutledge, Rachel. *The Best of the Best in Basketball* (4–7). Illus. Series: Women in Sports. 1998, Millbrook LB $24.90 (0-7613-1301-X). After a history of basketball, this account highlights women's role and covers today's most important female players. (Rev: BL 2/15/99; HBG 10/99; SLJ 3/99) [796.323]

13385 Steen, Sandra, and Susan Steen. *Take It to the Hoop: 100 Years of Women's Basketball* (6–8). Illus. 2003, Millbrook LB $25.90 (0-7613-2470-4). A comprehensive overview of women's basketball, from the first public game in the late 19th century. (Rev: BL 5/1/03; HBG 10/03; SLJ 9/03) [796.323]

13386 Stewart, Mark. *Basketball: A History of Hoops* (6–10). Series: Watts History of Sports. 1999, Watts LB $33.50 (0-531-11492-9). A chronological history of basketball that gives alternating treatment to college and pro games and includes how basketball has been influenced by off-the-court financial and social pressures. (Rev: HBG 9/99; SLJ 8/99) [796.323]

13387 Vancil, Mark. *NBA Basketball Offense Basics* (4–8). Illus. 1996, Sterling $16.95 (0-8069-4892-2). Action photographs and lively text demonstrate such techniques as dribbling, passing, and shooting. (Rev: BL 9/1/96) [796.332]

13388 Weatherspoon, Teresa, et al. *Teresa Weatherspoon's Basketball for Girls* (6–10). 1999, Wiley paper $14.95 (0-471-31784-5). This manual, by the famous basketball star and Olympic gold medalist, gives wonderful, practical information about playing the game and becoming a healthy, happy athlete. (Rev: BL 7/99; SLJ 8/99) [796.323]

13389 Wilker, Josh. *The Harlem Globetrotters* (5–10). Series: African American Achievers. 1996, Chelsea LB $21.95 (0-7910-2585-3); paper $8.95 (0-7910-2586-1). This is a chronologically arranged history of the Harlem Globetrotters, the basketball team that has been entertaining crowds since 1927. (Rev: SLJ 3/97) [796.357]

Bicycling, Motorcycling, etc.

13390 Bach, Julie. *Bicycling* (4–7). Illus. Series: World of Sports. 2000, Smart Apple LB $16.95 (1-887068-53-8). A brief introduction to bicycling that gives material on the origins and evolution of the sport, equipment, and techniques, plus coverage of the sport's star athletes. (Rev: BL 9/15/00) [796.6]

13391 Bizley, Kirk. *Mountain Biking* (4–7). Series: Radical Sports. 1999, Heinemann LB $24.22 (1-57572-944-X). Color photographs and a simple text introduce mountain biking, its history, equipment, skills, and safety concerns. (Rev: SLJ 5/00) [796.6]

13392 Brimner, Larry. *Mountain Biking* (5–7). Illus. 1997, Watts LB $22.00 (0-531-20243-7). An attractive book that includes information on the history of mountain bikes, their construction, and how to choose, use, and maintain one. (Rev: BL 9/1/97; SLJ 8/97) [796.6]

13393 Cole, Steve. *Kids' Easy Bike Care: Tune-Ups, Tools and Quick Fixes* (5–9). Series: Quick Starts for Kids! 2003, Williamson paper $8.95 (1-885593-86-4). A detailed and accessible guide to the parts of a bicycle and their maintenance, bicycle safety, and preparing an emergency kit, with cartoon illustrations. (Rev: SLJ 12/03) [629.28]

13394 Cotter, Allison. *Cycling* (6–12). Illus. Series: History of Sports. 2002, Gale LB $27.45 (1-59018-071-2). From the invention of the bicycle to today's high-tech mountain and other specialist bikes, Cotter traces cycling's growth and looks at competitive and recreational aspects of the sport. (Rev: BL 9/1/02) [796.6]

13395 Crossingham, John. *Cycling in Action* (4–7). Series: Sports in Action. 2002, Crabtree LB $21.28 (0-7787-0118-2); paper $5.95 (0-7787-0124-7). Photographs and drawings illustrate important concepts in this introduction to the sport of cycling that covers equipment and technique. (Rev: BL 9/1/02) [796.4]

13396 Crowther, Nicky. *The Ultimate Mountain Bike Book: The Definitive Illustrated Guide to Bikes, Components, Techniques, Thrills and Trails.* Rev. ed. (7–12). 2002, Firefly paper $24.95 (1-55297-

653-X). Beginning and advanced riders will all find material of interest in this revised practical guide full of appealing photographs. (Rev: SLJ 1/03; VOYA 12/02) [796.6]

13397 Deady, Kathleen W. *BMX Bikes* (4–7). Illus. Series: Wild Rides! 2001, Capstone LB $21.26 (0-7368-0925-2). Bicycle motocross fans will enjoy the color photographs and concise text that explains the equipment and skills needed for BMX (bicycle motocross) racing. (Rev: BL 10/15/01; HBG 3/02) [629.22]

13398 Dick, Scott. *BMX* (4–8). Series: Radical Sports. 2002, Heinemann LB $25.64 (1-58810-623-3). This introduction to bicycle motocross gives material on equipment, skills, training, and safety. (Rev: BL 2/15/03; HBG 3/03) [796.6]

13399 Freeman, Gary. *Motocross* (4–8). Series: Radical Sports. 2002, Heinemann LB $25.64 (1-58810-627-6). The sport of cross-country racing on motorcycles is introduced, with an emphasis on safety and skill development. (Rev: BL 2/15/03; HBG 3/03) [796.7]

13400 Gedatus, Gus. *Bicycling for Fitness* (4–7). Series: Nutrition and Fitness. 2001, Capstone LB $23.93 (0-7368-0705-5). This book explains the benefits of bicycling in promoting good health and outlines a fitness plan, nutrition program, and delicious recipes. (Rev: BL 9/15/01; HBG 10/01) [796.6]

13401 Hautzig, David. *Pedal Power: How a Mountain Bike Is Made* (4–8). 1996, Lodestar $15.99 (0-525-67508-6). A fascinating account of the birth of the mountain bike and the processes, materials, and machinery involved in their manufacture, with pointers on how to choose and maintain one. (Rev: BL 4/15/96; SLJ 4/96) [629.227]

13402 Hayhurst, Chris. *Bicycle Stunt Riding!* (4–8). Series: Extreme Sports. 2000, Rosen LB $26.50 (0-8239-3011-4). In this book, readers will learn about stunts like the vert and mega spin as well as finding out about the bikes and the safety equipment needed to start this sport. (Rev: BL 6/1–15/00) [629]

13403 Hayhurst, Chris. *Mountain Biking: Get on the Trail* (4–8). Illus. Series: Extreme Sports. 2000, Rosen LB $26.50 (0-8239-3013-0). Stressing safety throughout, this book covers topics including the history of mountain biking, why mountain bikes are different than others, and riding techniques. (Rev: BL 3/15/00; SLJ 8/00) [796.6]

13404 King, Andy. *Fundamental Mountain Biking* (5–9). Series: Fundamental Sports. 1996, Lerner LB $27.15 (0-8225-3459-2). This introduction to mountain biking discusses its history, equipment, maneuvers, competitions, tricks, safety reminders, and repair tips. (Rev: SLJ 2/97) [796.64]

13405 Molzahn, Arlene Bourgeois. *Extreme Mountain Biking* (5–8). Series: Extreme Sports. 2000,

Capstone LB $21.26 (0-7368-0483-8). This introduction to mountain biking includes material on its history, equipment, safety concerns, skills, and competitions. (Rev: HBG 10/00; SLJ 8/00; VOYA 10/01) [796.6]

13406 Pinchuk, Amy. *The Best Book of Bikes* (4–7). Illus. 2003, Maple Tree $21.95 (1-894379-43-8); paper $12.95 (1-894379-44-6). Diagrams, color photographs, and fascinating facts add to the appeal of the maintenance advice, racing strategies, and stunts provided. (Rev: BCCB 9/03; SLJ 9/03) [629.227]

13407 Raby, Philip, and Simon Nix. *Motorbikes* (5–8). Illus. Series: Need for Speed. 1999, Lerner LB $23.93 (0-8225-2486-4); paper $12.75 (0-8225-9854-X). A variety of motorbikes are introduced including dirt, motorcross, and land speed bikes. (Rev: BL 1/1–15/00; HBG 3/00; SLJ 2/00) [629.227]

13408 Turner, Chérie. *Marathon Cycling* (7–10). Series: Ultra Sports. 2002, Rosen LB $26.50 (0-8239-3553-1). Long-distance cycling competitions are described with material on tips and tricks, safety, gear, and racing events. (Rev: BL 9/1/02; SLJ 9/02) [796.6]

Boxing and Wrestling

13409 Bacho, Peter. *Boxing in Black and White* (7–12). Illus. 1999, Holt $18.95 (0-8050-5779-X). Beginning with a 1926 Filipino boxing champion and ending with Muhammad Ali, this is an interesting study of race relations and the sport of boxing. (Rev: BL 11/1/99; HBG 4/00) [796.83]

13410 Greenberg, Keith Elliot. *Pro Wrestling: From Carnivals to Cable TV* (6–12). Illus. 2000, Lerner LB $26.60 (0-8225-3332-4); paper $9.95 (0-8225-9864-7). With both historical and current information, this will please fans of professional wrestling and offer material for reports. (Rev: BL 2/15/01; HBG 3/01; SLJ 2/01; VOYA 2/01) [796.812]

13411 Jarman, Tom, and Reid Hanley. *Wrestling for Beginners* (7–12). Illus. 1983, Contemporary paper $12.95 (0-8092-5656-8). From a history of wrestling, this book moves on to skills, strategies, moves, and holds. [796.8]

Camping, Hiking, Backpacking, and Mountaineering

13412 Drake, Jane, and Ann Love. *The Kids Campfire Book* (4–8). Illus. 1998, Kids Can paper $9.95 (1-55074-539-5). This manual describes how to select a location, build safe campfires, and later

douse them, suggests fireside activities, including some science demonstrations, and offers safe cooking tips. (Rev: BL 3/15/98; HBG 9/98; SLJ 4/98) [796.54]

13413 Hooks, Kristine. *Essential Hiking for Teens* (5–9). Series: Outdoor Life. 2000, Children's LB $20.00 (0-516-23357-2); paper $6.95 (0-516-23357-5). This book on hiking covers such topics as clothing, equipment, safety, first aid, trails, planning, and calculating hiking time. (Rev: SLJ 2/01) [796.54]

13414 McManus, Patrick F. *Kid Camping from Aaaaiii! to Zip* (5–7). 1979, Avon paper $3.99 (0-380-71311-X). A practical camping guide presented in an amusing way.

Chess, Checkers, and Other Board and Card Games

13415 Basman, Michael. *Chess for Kids* (4–8). Illus. 2001, DK paper $12.99 (0-7894-6540-X). A guide to the game of chess that includes everything from the basic moves and important strategies to information on the game's origins and the roles the game has played in arenas ranging from literature to history. (Rev: BL 7/01; HBG 10/01) [794.1]

13416 Keene, Raymond. *The Simon & Schuster Pocket Book of Chess* (6–8). Illus. 1989, Simon & Schuster paper $9.99 (0-671-67924-4). An introduction to this game and its moves is given through text, diagrams, and attractive photographs. (Rev: BL 6/1/89; BR 11–12/90; VOYA 12/89) [794.1]

13417 Kidder, Harvey. *The Kids' Book of Chess* (4–8). 1990, Workman paper $15.95 (0-89480-767-6). Using their origins in the Middle Ages as a focus, this book explains the role of each chess piece and the basics of the game. (Rev: SLJ 2/91) [794.1]

13418 Nottingham, Ted, and Bob Wade. *Winning Chess: Piece by Piece* (4–8). Illus. 1999, Sterling $17.95 (0-8069-9955-1). This book is for chess players who already know the basics and are ready to improve their techniques. (Rev: BL 11/15/99) [794.1]

13419 Pike, Robert. *Play Winning Checkers: Official American Mensa Game Book* (8–12). 1999, Sterling paper $7.95 (0-8069-3794-7). After a history of the game, this book starts with the basics of checkers and continues through complex strategies. (Rev: SLJ 9/99) [794.2]

13420 Sheinwold, Alfred. *101 Best Family Card Games* (5–12). Illus. 1993, Sterling paper $5.95 (0-8069-8635-2). A book filled with games enjoyed by many age groups. (Rev: BL 2/15/93) [795.4]

Fishing and Hunting

13421 Bailey, John. *Fishing* (5–8). Illus. 2001, DK paper $9.95 (0-7894-7389-5). An appealing introduction to fish and fishing, with details of equipment, technique, and proper respect for the environment. (Rev: BL 6/1–15/01; HBG 10/01) [799.1]

13422 Paulsen, Gary. *Father Water, Mother Woods: Essays on Fishing and Hunting in the North Woods* (6–12). 1994, Delacorte $16.95 (0-385-32053-1). Essays reflecting the author's deep love for the wilderness describe his adventures hunting, fishing, canoeing, and camping. (Rev: BL 7/94; SLJ 8/94; VOYA 10/94) [799]

13423 Schmidt, Gerald D. *Let's Go Fishing: A Book for Beginners* (4–7). 1990, Roberts Rinehart paper $11.95 (0-911797-84-X). This practical guide to freshwater fishing includes material on tackle and kinds of fish. (Rev: BL 3/1/91; SLJ 5/91) [799.1]

Football

13424 Buckley, James, Jr. *America's Greatest Game: The Real Story of Football and the NFL* (4–7). Illus. 1998, Hyperion $16.95 (0-7868-0433-5). A lavishly illustrated introduction to football and its history, with special material on the NFL and key players of yesterday and today. (Rev: BL 11/15/98; SLJ 2/99) [796.332]

13425 Devaney, John. *Winners of the Heisman Trophy*. Rev. ed. (5–8). Illus. 1990, Walker LB $15.85 (0-8027-6907-1). A history of the award is given, with profiles of 15 past winners. (Rev: SLJ 6/90) [796.332]

13426 DiLorenzo, J. J. *The Miami Dolphins Football Team* (5–8). Series: Sports Greats. 1997, Enslow LB $18.95 (0-89490-796-4). A history of the Miami Dolphins that focuses on their brightest stars and best moments on the field. (Rev: BL 10/15/97; HBG 3/98) [796.48]

13427 Grabowski, John F. *The Dallas Cowboys* (7–9). Illus. Series: Sports Greats. 2001, Gale LB $27.45 (1-56006-939-2). The story of the NFL football team and the road it traveled to multiple Super Bowl victories. (Rev: BL 4/1/02) [796.332]

13428 Lace, William W. *The Dallas Cowboys Football Team* (5–8). Illus. Series: Sports Greats. 1997, Enslow LB $18.95 (0-89490-791-3). Opening with the Dallas championship in 1973, this book traces the history of the team, with plenty of sports action. (Rev: BL 10/15/97; HBG 3/98) [796.48]

Golf

13429 Anderson, Dave. *The Story of Golf* (4–8). 1998, Morrow $16.00 (0-688-15796-3). A history of golf that highlights the careers of some of its great stars, plus material on the lure of the game, golf architecture, and caddies. (Rev: BL 5/15/98; HB 9–10/98; HBG 10/98; SLJ 7/98) [796.352]

Gymnastics

13430 Kalman, Bobbie, and John Crossingham. *Gymnastics in Action* (4–7). Series: Sports in Action. 2002, Crabtree LB $21.28 (0-7787-0330-4); paper $6.95 (0-7737-0350-9). Various branches of gymnastics are introduced in text and pictures with coverage of techniques, equipment, and basic movements. (Rev: BL 1/1–15/03) [796.44]

Hockey

13431 Adelson, Bruce. *Hat Trick Trivia: Secrets, Statistics, and Little-Known Facts About Hockey* (4–7). Illus. 1998, Lerner LB $23.93 (0-8225-3315-5). History, statistics, and trivia are combined in this lively discussion of hockey and its players. (Rev: BL 1/1–15/99) [796.962]

13432 *A Basic Guide to Ice Hockey* (6–12). Series: Olympic Guides. 2002, Gareth Stevens LB $22.60 (0-8368-3103-9). The rules, regulations, and fundamentals of ice hockey are covered in this basic introduction edited by the U.S. Olympic Committee. (Rev: BL 6/1–15/02; HBG 10/02) [796.962]

13433 Foley, Mike. *Fundamental Hockey* (4–8). Series: Fundamental Sports. 1996, Lerner LB $27.15 (0-8225-3456-8). The basics of ice hockey are introduced, accompanied by a brief history of the sport and an explanation of what the various players do. (Rev: SLJ 3/96) [796.962]

13434 Hubbard, Kevin, and Stan Fischler. *Hockey America: The Ice Game's Past Growth and Bright Future in the U.S.* (8–12). 1998, NTC paper $24.95 (1-57028-196-3). This work traces the history of ice hockey in this country, introduces some key players, and speculates about the sport's future. (Rev: VOYA 10/98) [796.962]

13435 Jensen, Julie, adapt. *Beginning Hockey* (4–8). Photos by Andy King. Series: Beginning Sports. 1996, Lerner LB $27.15 (0-8225-3506-8). An introduction to hockey, its history, and the techniques and skills used by the players. (Rev: SLJ 3/96) [796.964]

13436 McFarlane, Brian. *Real Stories from the Rink* (5–8). 2002, Tundra paper $14.95 (0-88776-604-8). Entertaining true stories give insight into ice hockey's history, rules, and players. (Rev: BL 2/15/03; SLJ 4/03) [796.962]

13437 Sullivan, George. *All About Hockey* (5–8). 1998, Putnam $15.99 (0-399-23172-6); paper $9.99 (0-399-23173-0). An efficient general introduction to hockey, with a brief history, coverage of basic rules and skills and defensive and offensive strategies, an examination of professional, Olympic, and World Cup hockey, and profiles of players who have had a major impact on the sport. (Rev: BL 3/1/99; SLJ 3/99) [796.962]

13438 Thomas, Keltie. *How Hockey Works* (4–7). Illus. 2002, Maple Tree $19.95 (1-894379-35-7); paper $9.95 (1-894379-36-5). A volume focusing on the game of ice hockey that presents everything from important skills and equipment to common superstitions, with an appealing layout. (Rev: BL 9/1/02; SLJ 4/03) [796.962]

13439 Wilson, Stacy. *The Hockey Book for Girls* (4–7). Illus. 2000, Kids Can $12.95 (1-55074-860-2); paper $6.95 (1-55074-719-3). This book, by the former captain of Canada's women's Olympic hockey team, introduces ice hockey's rules, positions, strategies, and training and includes interviews with star players. (Rev: BL 3/1/01; HBG 3/01; SLJ 12/00) [796.962]

Horse Racing and Horsemanship

13440 *A Basic Guide to Equestrian* (4–8). Illus. 2001, Gareth Stevens LB $22.60 (0-8368-2797-X). An informative guide to Olympic equestrian competitions, edited by the U.S. Olympic Committee and including material on choosing and looking after a horse and learning to ride. (Rev: HBG 10/01; SLJ 7/01) [798.2]

13441 Binder, Sibylle Luise, and Gefion Wolf. *Riding for Beginners* (5–10). Trans. from German by Elisabeth E. Reinersmann. 1999, Sterling $21.95 (0-8069-6205-4). A straightforward text, beautiful color photographs and illustrations, and an attractive layout present the English and Western styles of riding and give tips for the novice. (Rev: SLJ 8/99) [798.4]

13442 Bolt, Betty. *Jumping* (4–8). Series: Horse Library. 2001, Chelsea $19.75 (0-7910-6657-6). Show jumping, eventing, and steeplechase riding are all covered in detail here. Also use *Western Riding*. (Rev: HBG 3/02; SLJ 3/02) [798.4]

13443 Davis, Caroline. *The Young Equestrian* (5–8). Illus. 2000, Firefly $29.95 (1-55209-495-2); paper $19.95 (1-55209-484-7). With a generous use of

color photographs, this account devotes chapters to riding aids and techniques, choosing schools and proper equipment, buying and caring for a horse, and competitions. (Rev: BL 2/15/01; SLJ 2/01; VOYA 2/01) [798.2]

13444 Haas, Jessie. *Safe Horse, Safe Rider: A Young Rider's Guide to Responsible Horsekeeping* (4–7). Illus. 1994, Storey paper $16.95 (0-88266-700-9). This guide to horsemanship stresses safety and covers such topics as understanding horse behavior. (Rev: BL 1/1/95) [636.1]

13445 Kirksmith, Tommie. *Ride Western Style: A Guide for Young Riders* (4–8). Illus. 1991, Howell Book House $16.95 (0-87605-895-0). Background information and step-by-step instructions for young people interested in learning to ride Western style. (Rev: BL 4/1/92; SLJ 7/92) [798.2]

Ice Skating

13446 *A Basic Guide to Figure Skating* (6–12). Series: Olympic Guides. 2002, Gareth Stevens LB $22.60 (0-8368-3102-0). This guide, compiled under the editorship of the U.S. Olympic Committee, is a basic guide to figure skating and its techniques, equipment, and competitions. (Rev: BL 6/1–15/02; HBG 10/02) [796.91]

13447 *A Basic Guide to Speed Skating* (6–12). Series: Olympic Guides. 2002, Gareth Stevens LB $22.60 (0-8368-3105-5). This easy-to-read guide gives the step-by-step fundamentals of speed skating, more advanced tips, and photographs of speed-skating stars of today. (Rev: BL 6/1–15/02; HBG 10/02) [796.91]

13448 Boo, Michael. *The Story of Figure Skating* (5–8). 1998, Morrow $16.95 (0-688-15820-X); paper $7.95 (0-688-15821-8). Beginning with skates made of bone and walrus teeth, this account traces the history of ice skating with decade-by-decade coverage from 1950 to the 1998 Olympics. (Rev: BL 11/1/98; HBG 3/99; SLJ 12/98; VOYA 4/99) [796.91]

13449 Foeste, Aaron. *Ice Skating Basics* (6–10). 1999, Sterling $17.95 (0-8069-9517-3). An excellent, well-illustrated introduction to ice skating that enthusiastically describes maneuvers, types of skates, their care and fit, and appropriate clothing. (Rev: SLJ 2/99) [796.91]

13450 Gutman, Dan. *Ice Skating: From Axels to Zambonis* (5–8). Illus. 1995, Viking $14.99 (0-670-86013-1). A complete guide to ice skating that includes a history, information on techniques, biographies, a chronology, and a list of champions. (Rev: BL 10/1/95; SLJ 12/95; VOYA 4/95) [796.91]

13451 Wilkes, Debbi. *The Figure Skating Book: A Young Person's Guide to Figure Skating* (4–8). Illus. 2000, Firefly LB $19.95 (1-55209-444-8); paper $12.95 (1-55209-445-6). The author, an Olympic silver medalist, gives practical advice on figure skating from buying skates to simple and complicated skating techniques. (Rev: BL 7/00; SLJ 4/00) [796.9]

In-Line Skating

13452 Werner, Doug. *In-Line Skater's Start-Up: A Beginner's Guide to In-Line Skating and Roller Hockey* (6–12). 1995, Tracks paper $9.95 (1-884654-04-5). Using many black-and-white photographs, this book is both a guide to inline skating basics for beginners and an introduction to the growing sport of roller hockey. (Rev: BL 2/1/96) [796.2]

Martial Arts

13453 Atwood, Jane. *Capoeira: A Martial Art and a Cultural Tradition* (5–8). Series: The Library of African American Arts and Culture. 1999, Rosen LB $19.95 (0-8239-1859-9). Capoeira, a unique martial art developed by African slaves in Brazil, is described, along with its history and preparations for its debut in the 2004 Olympic games. (Rev: BR 9–10/99; SLJ 8/99) [796.8]

13454 Konzak, Burt. *Samurai Spirit: Ancient Wisdom for Modern Life* (6–12). 2002, Tundra paper $8.95 (0-88776-611-0). Martial arts are the focus of this combination of traditional tales, historical and cultural information, and advice from the author, a teacher of martial arts. (Rev: SLJ 6/03) [813]

13455 Metil, Luana, and Jace Townsend. *The Story of Karate: From Buddhism to Bruce Lee* (6–9). 1995, Lerner LB $31.95 (0-8225-3325-1). A history of this martial art from its origins in the Far East to its present-day popularity. (Rev: BL 7/95) [796.8]

13456 Queen, J. Allen. *Learn Karate* (4–8). 1999, Sterling $17.95 (0-8069-8136-9). An excellent manual that covers the basics of karate — kicks, blocks, and stances — as well as stretches, meditation, safety, equipment, and sparring. (Rev: SLJ 5/99) [796.8]

13457 Tegner, Bruce. *Bruce Tegner's Complete Book of Jujitsu* (7–12). Illus. 1978, Thor paper $14.00 (0-87407-027-9). A master in the martial arts introduces this ancient Japanese form of self-defense and gives basic information on stances and routines. [796.8]

13458 Tegner, Bruce. *Bruce Tegner's Complete Book of Self-Defense* (7–12). Illus. 1975, Thor paper $14.00 (0-87407-030-9). A basic primer on ways to defend oneself including hand blows and restraints. [796.8]

13459 Tegner, Bruce. *Karate: Beginner to Black Belt* (7–12). Illus. 1982, Thor paper $14.00 (0-87407-040-6). Techniques for both the novice and the experienced practitioner are explained in this account that stresses safety and fitness. [796.8]

13460 Tegner, Bruce, and Alice McGrath. *Self-Defense and Assault Prevention for Girls and Women* (7–12). Illus. 1977, Thor paper $10.00 (0-87407-026-0). Various defensive and offensive techniques are introduced in situations where they would be appropriate. [796.8]

13461 Yates, Keith D., and Bryan Robbins. *Tae Kwon Do for Kids* (4–8). 1999, Sterling paper $5.95 (0-8069-1761-X). A step-by-step manual that introduces and describes Tae Kwon Do, a Korean form of self-defense, with material on stances, blocks, exercises, and important pressure points. (Rev: SLJ 6/99) [796.8]

Olympic Games

13462 Anderson, Dave. *The Story of the Olympics*. Rev. ed. (4–9). 2000, HarperCollins $15.95 (0-688-16734-9). This book on the Olympics is divided into two parts: the first gives historical highlights, the second profiles famous personalities and their trials and tribulations. (Rev: HBG 10/00; SLJ 6/00) [796.48]

13463 Bachrach, Susan D. *The Nazi Olympics: Berlin 1936* (6–12). Illus. 2000, Little, Brown $21.95 (0-316-07086-6); paper $14.95 (0-316-07087-4). This is a complete history of the 1936 games, with background material on the Nazi movement in Germany and the growing oppression of Jews. (Rev: BL 2/15/00; HBG 9/00; SLJ 6/00) [796.48.]

13464 Fischer, David. *The Encyclopedia of the Summer Olympics* (4–8). Illus. Series: Watts Reference. 2003, Watts LB $36.00 (0-531-11886-X). Events from archery to wrestling are organized in alphabetical order, with historical information from the first games to the forthcoming 2004 games, profiles of athletes, lists of gold medal winners, information on rules and equipment, and fast facts. (Rev: SLJ 12/03) [796.4]

13465 Glubok, Shirley, and Alfred Tamarin. *Olympic Games in Ancient Greece* (6–9). 1976, HarperCollins LB $16.89 (0-06-022048-1). History and legend are combined in this account of the first Olympics. (Rev: BL 2/15/88) [796.4]

13466 Greenspan, Bud. *Frozen in Time: The Greatest Moments at the Winter Olympics* (7–12). 1997, General Publishing Group $24.95 (1-57544-027-X). The stories of nearly 60 stars of the Winter Olympics are told in two- or three-page accounts, many of them involving personal triumph and courage. (Rev: VOYA 6/98) [796.98]

13467 Kristy, Davida. *Coubertin's Olympics: How the Games Began* (5–8). 1995, Lerner LB $31.95 (0-8225-3327-8). How the Olympic games began and information about Baron Pierre de Coubertin, their founder. (Rev: BL 8/95; SLJ 11/95) [338.4]

13468 *Olympism: A Basic Guide to the History, Ideals, and Sports of the Olympic Movement* (4–8). Illus. Series: Olympic Guides. 2001, Gareth Stevens LB $22.60 (0-8368-2800-3). This is an attractive and authoritative overview of the Olympics' history and of the games' importance, edited by the U.S. Olympic Committee. (Rev: HBG 10/01; SLJ 7/01) [796.48]

13469 Oxlade, Chris, and David Ballheimer. *Olympics* (4–8). Illus. Series: Eyewitness Books. 1999, Knopf LB $20.99 (0-375-90222-8). Double-page spreads cover the ancient games, the rebirth of the modern Olympics, and the events of the winter and summer games plus material on equipment and past stars. (Rev: SLJ 12/99) [796.48]

13470 Ross, Stewart. *The Original Olympics* (4–7). Illus. Series: Ancient Greece. 2000, Bedrick $18.95 (0-87226-596-X). Using a fictional narrative involving a day at the Olympic Games, this attractive book gives details on the types of events, the history of the games, and the roles of athletes in Greek life. (Rev: BL 1/1–15/01; HBG 10/00; SLJ 8/00) [796.48]

13471 Sandelson, Robert. *Ice Sports* (4–8). Illus. Series: Olympic Sports. 1992, Macmillan LB $13.95 (0-89686-667-X). Discusses Winter Olympic events including bobsledding and ice hockey. (Rev: SLJ 4/92) [796.91]

13472 Wukovits, John. *The Encyclopedia of the Winter Olympics* (5–8). Illus. 2001, Watts LB $36.00 (0-531-11885-1). A fact-filled but lively volume with quotations from athletes, action highlights, and coverage of political controversies. (Rev: SLJ 11/01) [796.48]

Running and Jogging

13473 Hayhurst, Chris. *Ultra Marathon Running* (7–10). Series: Ultra Sports. 2002, Rosen LB $26.50 (0-8239-3557-4). This work looks at different long running races, the athletes that engage in this sport, and the mind-boggling distances they run. (Rev: BL 9/1/02; SLJ 9/02) [796.4]

13474 Hughes, Morgan. *Track and Field: The Jumps: Instructional Guide to Track and Field* (4–8). Series: Compete Like a Champion. 2001, Rourke LB $27.93 (1-57103-290-8). This book includes material on the long jump, the triple jump, the high jump, and the pole vault, along with training tips. Also use in the same series *Track and Field: Middle and Long Distance Runs* and *Track and Field: The Sprints* (both 2001). (Rev: SLJ 3/01) [796.42]

13475 Manley, Claudia B. *Competitive Track and Field for Girls* (4–7). Illus. Series: Sportsgirl. 2001, Rosen LB $26.50 (0-8239-3408-X). An introduction to the rules of track and field competitions, the training necessary, and the special opportunities for girls, with material on nutrition and the dangers of overtraining. (Rev: SLJ 3/02) [796.42]

Sailing, Boating, and Canoeing

13476 Anderson, Scott. *Distant Fires* (8–12). Illus. 1990, Pfeifer-Hamilton paper $14.95 (0-938586-33-5). A journal of a 1,700-mile canoe trip from Minnesota to Canada's Hudson Bay. (Rev: BL 1/15/91; SLJ 4/91) [797.122]

13477 Revell, Phil. *Kayaking* (4–7). Series: Radical Sports. 1999, Heinemann LB $24.22 (1-57572-943-1). A history of kayaks and kayaking is followed by material on basic skills, equipment, safety concerns, and competitions. (Rev: SLJ 5/00) [797.1]

Skateboarding

13478 Andrejtschitsch, Jan, et al. *Action Skateboarding* (6–12). 1993, Sterling $16.95 (0-8069-8500-3). A handbook that provides a history of skateboarding, reviews equipment, and defines styles and terrains, with tips on tricks and maneuvers. (Rev: BL 6/1–15/93; SLJ 7/93) [795.2]

13479 Burke, L. M. *Skateboarding! Surf the Pavement* (5–8). Series: Extreme Sports. 1999, Rosen LB $26.50 (0-8239-3014-9). This book supplies information for beginning and advanced skateboarders with coverage of history, techniques, equipment, and safety considerations. (Rev: SLJ 4/00) [796]

13480 Crossingham, John. *Skateboarding in Action* (4–7). Series: Sports in Action. 2002, Crabtree LB $21.28 (0-7787-0117-4); paper $5.95 (0-7787-0123-9). A well-illustrated introduction to skateboarding with good material on equipment and injury prevention. (Rev: BL 9/1/02; SLJ 11/02) [795.2]

13481 Freimuth, Jeri. *Extreme Skateboarding Moves* (4–7). Illus. Series: Behind the Moves. 2001, Capstone LB $21.26 (0-7368-0783-7). Skateboard slang is just one appealing part of this account of proper equipment and technique, with safety tips and some tricks. (Rev: BL 6/1–15/01; HBG 10/01; SLJ 9/01) [796.22]

13482 Horsley, Andy. *Skateboarding* (4–7). Illus. Series: To the Limit. 2001, Raintree Steck-Vaughn LB $25.69 (0-7398-3163-1). A brief history of skateboarding is included here along with material on equipment, moves, and some advice on turning pro. (Rev: BL 6/1–15/01) [796.22]

13483 Loizos, Constance. *Skateboard! Your Guide to Street, Vert, Downhill, and More* (4–9). Illus. Series: Extreme Sports. 2002, National Geographic paper $8.95 (0-7922-8229-9). An attractive guide to skateboarding equipment, technique, rules, etiquette, jargon, and safety. (Rev: SLJ 1/03) [796.22]

13484 Powell, Ben. *Skateboarding* (4–8). Illus. Series: Flowmotion. 2003, Sterling paper $9.95 (0-8069-9374-X). Clear instructions accompanied by photographs explain techniques and moves, with safety tips and a glossary. (Rev: BL 10/15/03) [796.2]

13485 Werner, Doug. *Skateboarder's Start-Up: A Beginner's Guide to Skateboarding* (4–8). 2000, Tracks paper $11.95 (1-884654-13-4). Using a question-and-answer format, this introduction to skateboarding covers such subjects as equipment, history, and basic skating and technical tricks. (Rev: SLJ 12/00) [795.2]

Skiing and Snowboarding

13486 *A Basic Guide to Skiing and Snowboarding* (6–12). Series: Olympic Guides. 2002, Gareth Stevens LB $22.60 (0-8368-3104-7). In this guide edited by the U.S. Olympic Committee, the sports of skiing and snowboarding are introduced with material on techniques, competitions, and equipment. (Rev: BL 6/1–15/02; HBG 10/02) [796.9]

13487 Brown, Gillian C. P. *Snowboarding* (5–8). Illus. Series: X-treme Outdoors. 2003, Children's LB $20.00 (0-516-24322-5); paper $6.95 (0-516-24383-7). Equipment, technique, competition, and safety are covered here, as well as a history of this sport. (Rev: BL 4/15/03; SLJ 10/03) [796.9]

13488 Crossingham, John. *Snowboarding in Action* (4–7). Series: Sports in Action. 2002, Crabtree LB $21.28 (0-7787-0119-0); paper $5.95 (0-7787-0125-5). Aspiring snowboarders will find much of interest here, including basic techniques. (Rev: BL 9/1/02; SLJ 11/02) [796.9]

13409 Fraser, Andy. *Snowboarding* (4–7). Series: Radical Sports. 1999, Heinemann LB $24.22 (1-57572-946-6). This book covers the history of snowboarding, the equipment and clothing needed,

techniques, terms, and how to get started. (Rev: SLJ 4/00) [796.9]

13490 Haycock, Kate. *Skiing* (4–8). Illus. Series: Olympic Sports. 1992, Macmillan LB $13.95 (0-89686-669-6). The Winter Olympic events in skiing are discussed. (Rev: SLJ 4/92) [796.93]

13491 Hayhurst, Chris. *Snowboarding! Shred the Powder* (5–8). Series: Extreme Sports. 1999, Rosen LB $26.50 (0-8239-3010-6). The book supplies both beginning and advanced information on this sport, including material on history, equipment, techniques, and safety considerations. (Rev: SLJ 4/00; VOYA 6/00) [796.9]

13492 Herran, Joe, and Ron Thomas. *Snowboarding* (5–8). Illus. Series: Action Sports. 2003, Chelsea LB $18.95 (0-7910-7003-4). Basic information on this sport's gear and performance is accompanied by biographical details about snowboarding champions. (Rev: BL 4/15/03; HBG 10/03) [796.9]

13493 Jensen, Julie, adapt. *Beginning Snowboarding* (4–8). Series: Beginning Sports. 1996, Lerner LB $27.15 (0-8225-3507-6). An introduction to snowboarding, with material on equipment, basic maneuvers, types of competition, and advanced stunts. (Rev: SLJ 3/96) [796.9]

13494 Kleh, Cindy. *Snowboarding Skills: The Back-to-Basics Essentials for All Levels* (7–12). Illus. 2002, Annick paper $16.95 (1-55297-626-2). Tips from an expert, with photographs and a glossary, make this a hip title for enthusiasts. (Rev: BL 12/15/02; SLJ 1/03) [796.9]

13495 Lurie, John. *Fundamental Snowboarding* (4–8). Series: Fundamental Sports. 1996, Lerner LB $27.15 (0-8225-3457-6). With eye-catching photographs, the equipment and principles of snowboarding are covered, with material on basic and advanced maneuvers, skills, and stunts. (Rev: SLJ 3/96) [796.9]

13496 Stiefer, Sandy. *Marathon Skiing* (7–10). Series: Ultra Sports. 2002, Rosen LB $26.50 (0-8239-3554-X). This work describes the sport of marathon skiing — cross-country skiing pushed to its limits. (Rev: BL 9/1/02) [796.95]

Soccer

13497 Blackall, Bernie. *Soccer* (4–8). Series: Top Sport. 1999, Heinemann LB $21.36 (1-57572-840-0). This introduction to soccer covers history, equipment, rules, skills, and a few male and female stars. (Rev: SLJ 12/99) [796.334]

13498 Buxton, Ted. *Soccer Skills: For Young Players* (6–12). Illus. 2000, Firefly paper $14.95 (1-55209-329-8). A practical guide to training and technique that will be useful for beginners and advanced players. (Rev: SLJ 10/00; VOYA 12/00)

13499 Coleman, Lori. *Soccer* (5–9). Series: Play-by-Play. 2000, Lerner paper $7.95 (0-8225-9876-0). A fine introduction to the rules, equipment, and tactics of soccer with historical coverage through 1999. (Rev: SLJ 9/00) [796.334]

13500 Gifford, Clive. *Soccer: The Ultimate Guide to the Beautiful Game* (5–8). Illus. 2002, Kingfisher $18.95 (0-7534-5416-5). An attractive and comprehensive guide that covers history, rules, and tactics, with an emphasis on European teams and players. (Rev: BL 7/02; SLJ 7/02) [796.334]

13501 Herbst, Dan. *Sports Illustrated Soccer: The Complete Player* (7–12). Illus. 1988, Sports Illustrated for Kids paper $9.95 (1-56800-038-3). Basic and advanced skills are explained plus a variety of game strategies. [796.334]

13502 Mackin, Bob. *Soccer the Winning Way: Play Like the Pros* (4–7). Illus. 2002, Douglas & McIntyre paper $10.95 (1-55054-825-5). A guide to mastering crucial soccer skills, with photographs and words of wisdom from the pros. (Rev: BL 5/15/02) [796]

13503 Miller, Marla. *All-American Girls: The U.S. Women's National Soccer Team* (4–8). 1999, Pocket Books paper $4.99 (0-671-03599-1). A portrait of members of the U.S. Women's National Soccer Team, with advice for aspiring players. (Rev: SLJ 8/99; VOYA 8/99) [796.334]

13504 Owens, Thomas S., and Diana Star Helmer. *Soccer* (5–8). Series: Game Plan. 2000, Twenty-First Century LB $26.90 (0-7613-1400-8). This introduction to soccer covers the different positions, game strategy, and memorable games and players of the past. (Rev: HBG 10/00; SLJ 7/00) [796.334]

13505 Scott, Nina S. *The Thinking Kids Guide to Successful Soccer* (5–8). 1998, Millbrook LB $21.90 (0-7613-0324-3). An insider's look at strategies for kids playing soccer, including topics not frequently addressed such as dealing with inexperienced coaches, unfair calls from referees, not getting enough playing time, and pressures of competition. The author encourages kids to have a good time and not to worry about making mistakes. (Rev: BL 5/15/99; HBG 9/99; SLJ 4/99) [796..334]

13506 Sherman, Josepha. *Competitive Soccer for Girls* (4–7). Series: Sportsgirl. 2001, Rosen LB $26.50 (0-8239-3405-5). An introduction to the rules of soccer, the training necessary, and the special opportunities for girls, with material on nutrition and the dangers of overtraining. (Rev: SLJ 3/02) [796.334]

13507 Stewart, Mark. *Soccer: An Intimate History of the World's Most Popular Game* (7–10). Series: Watts History of Sports. 1998, Watts LB $33.50 (0-

531-11456-2). With clear text and photographs, this book traces the history of soccer in the United States, with interesting material on memorable games, famous players, related off-the-field developments, and a discussion of why soccer is not as popular as other sports in the United States. (Rev: HBG 9/98; SLJ 7/98) [796.334]

13508 Sullivan, George. *All About Soccer* (4–8). Illus. 2001, Putnam $15.99 (0-399-23481-0). Observers and players alike will find much of interest in this comprehensive look at the internationally popular game. (Rev: BL 6/1–15/01; HBG 10/01; SLJ 5/01) [796.334]

13509 Woog, Dan. *The Ultimate Soccer Almanac* (6–12). Illus. 1998, Lowell House $12.95 (1-56565-951-1); paper $8.95 (1-56565-891-4). A review of the history of soccer, important players and teams, and rules of the game and how to play it. (Rev: BL 7/98) [796.334]

13510 Wukovits, John. *The Composite Guide to Soccer* (4–8). 1998, Chelsea LB $18.65 (0-7910-4718-0). A basic guide to the history, rules, positions, and playing techniques of this sport, with material on its European popularity. (Rev: HBG 3/99; SLJ 12/98; VOYA 6/99) [796.334]

Surfing, Water Skiing, and Other Water Sports

13511 Barker, Amanda. *Windsurfing* (4–7). Series: Radical Sports. 1999, Heinemann LB $24.22 (1-57572-948-2). After a history of windsurfing, this book describes equipment, safety tips, and basic skills. (Rev: SLJ 5/00) [797.2]

13512 Crossingham, John, and Niki Walker. *Swimming in Action* (4–7). Series: Sports in Action. 2002, Crabtree LB $21.28 (0-7787-0331-2); paper $6.95 (0-7737-0351-7). Color photographs and many diagrams are used with a clear text to describe swimming basics, with tips on various strokes and safety. (Rev: BL 1/1–15/03; SLJ 10/03) [977.2]

13513 Manley, Claudia B. *Ultra Swimming* (7–10). Illus. Series: Ultra Sports. 2002, Rosen LB $26.50 (0-8239-3558-2). An introduction to the history of this demanding new sport that gives tips on improving performance, maintaining safety, and training both body and mind for the challenges. (Rev: BL 9/1/02) [797.2]

13514 Vander Hook, Sue. *Scuba Diving* (4–7). Illus. Series: World of Sports. 2000, Smart Apple LB $16.95 (1-887068-59-7). After a section on star scuba divers, this account describes the origins and evolution of the sport, its equipment, hazards, and techniques. (Rev: BL 9/15/00) [797.2]

13515 Voeller, Edward. *Extreme Surfing* (5–8). Series: Surfing. 2000, Capstone LB $21.26 (0-7368-0485-4). An introduction to surfing that contains material on equipment, history, skills, safety considerations, and competitions. (Rev: HBG 10/00; SLJ 8/00) [797]

13516 Werner, Doug. *Surfer's Start-Up: A Beginner's Guide to Surfing.* 2nd ed. (7–12). 1999, Tracks paper $11.95 (1-884654-12-6). A new edition of this standard instructional guide that covers basic instruction, surfing gear, safety, etiquette, and history. (Rev: SLJ 9/99) [797]

Tennis and Other Racquet Games

13517 Blackall, Bernie. *Tennis* (4–8). Series: Top Sport. 1999, Heinemann $21.36 (1-57572-842-7). Double-page spreads present topics including the history of tennis, its equipment and rules, and important skills, plus a rundown on famous stars of the sport. (Rev: SLJ 12/99) [796.342]

13518 Crossingham, John. *Tennis in Action* (4–7). Series: Sports in Action. 2002, Crabtree LB $21.28 (0-7787-0116-6); paper $5.95 (0-7787-0122-0). A fine introduction to tennis told through a concise text with easy-to-follow descriptions and material on equipment, rules, and techniques. (Rev: BL 9/1/02; SLJ 11/02) [796.342]

13519 Kaiman, Bobbie, and Sarah Dann. *Badminton in Action* (4–7). Series: Sports in Action. 2003, Crabtree LB $15.96 (0-7787-0334-7); paper $6.26 (0-7787-0354-1). This basic introduction to badminton includes material on racquets, courts, rules, and strategies. (Rev: BL 11/15/03) [796.34]

13520 Muskat, Carrie. *The Composite Guide to Tennis* (5–7). Series: Composite Guide. 1998, Chelsea LB $18.65 (0-7910-4728-8). Past and present tennis stars are mentioned along with a general introduction to the game. (Rev: HBG 10/98; SLJ 9/98) [796.342]

13521 Rutledge, Rachel. *The Best of the Best in Tennis* (4–7). Illus. 1998, Millbrook LB $24.90 (0-7613-1303-6). Using a lively text and many color photographs, this work gives a history of women in tennis and a rundown of today's most important female players. (Rev: BL 2/15/99; HBG 10/99; SLJ 3/99) [796.342]

13522 Sherrow, Victoria. *Tennis* (6–12). Series: History of Sports. 2003, Gale LB $21.96 (1-56006-959-7). The origins and evolution of the game are followed by information on recreational and competitive tennis and on outstanding players. (Rev: SLJ 9/03) [796.342]

Volleyball

13523 Sherrow, Victoria. *Volleyball* (6–12). Illus. Series: History of Sports. 2002, Gale LB $27.45 (1-56006-961-9). From the invention of volleyball as a second-class version of basketball to today's prominence around the world, Sherrow traces volleyball's growth and looks at competitive and recreational aspects of the sport. (Rev: BL 9/1/02) [796.325]

Author Index

Authors are arranged alphabetically by last name. Authors' and joint authors' names are followed by book titles — which are also arranged alphabetically — and the text entry number. Book titles may refer to those that appear as a main entry or as an internal entry mentioned in the text. Fiction titles are indicated by (F) following the entry number.

Aamodt, Alice (jt. author). *Wolf Pack*, 12206
Aaron, Chester. *Lackawanna*, 1(F)
Out of Sight, Out of Mind, 2(F)
Aaseng, Nathan. *African-American Athletes*, 6523
American Dinosaur Hunters, 7251
Athletes, 6524
Barry Sanders, 6712
The Bermuda Triangle, 13162
Black Inventors, 6263
Breaking the Sound Barrier, 12858
Business Builders in Computers, 6264
Business Builders in Fast Food, 6265
Business Builders in Oil, 6266
Carl Lewis, 6758
The Cheetah, 12193
Cherokee Nation v. Georgia, 8749
Construction, 6267
The Cougar, 12194
The Crash of 1929, 9275
David Robinson, 6669
The Impeachment of President Clinton, 9805
Invertebrates, 12099
John Stockton, 6675
Jose Canseco, 6592
The Locker Room Mirror, 13224
The Marine Corps in Action, 12920
Michael Jordan, 6649
Multiple Sclerosis, 11030
Nature's Poisonous Creatures, 12100
Navajo Code Talkers, 7635
The O. J. Simpson Trial, 9847
Paris, 7636
The Peace Seekers, 6792
Science Versus Pseudoscience, 13163
The Space Race, 7823
Teens and Drunk Driving, 10383
Top 10 Basketball Scoring Small Forwards, 6525

Treacherous Traitors, 10384
True Champions, 6526
Twentieth-Century Inventors, 12727
The White House, 9454
Wildshots, 10746
Women Olympic Champions, 6527
Yearbooks in Science: 1930–1939, 11801
Yearbooks in Science: 1940–1949, 11802
You Are the Corporate Executive, 10597
You Are the Explorer, 7230
You Are the General, 9933
You Are the General II, 7352
You Are the Juror, 9848
You Are the President, 9806
You Are the President II, 9807
You Are the Senator, 9825
You Are the Supreme Court Justice, 9849
Aaseng, Rolfe E. *Augsburg Story Bible*, 9685
Abbink, Emily. *Missions of the Monterey Bay Area*, 9514
Abeel, Samantha. *What Once Was White*, 11376
Abelove, Joan. *Go and Come Back*, 1832(F)
Saying It Out Loud, 398(F)
Able, Deborah. *Hate Groups*, 10251
Abraham-Podietz, Eva (jt. author). *Ten Thousand Children*, 7700
Abrahams, Roger D. *African Folktales*, 4694
Abramovitz, Melissa. *Leukemia*, 11031
Abrams, Liesa. *Chronic Fatigue Syndrome*, 11032
Acker, Kerry. *Everything You Need to Know About the Goth Scene*, 11607
Ackerman, Diane. *Bats*, 12160

Ackerman, Ned. *Spirit Horse*, 2762(F)
Ackroyd, Peter. *The Beginning*, 7293
Adair, Gene. *Alfred Hitchcock*, 5595
Thomas Alva Edison, 6382
Adams, Colleen. *Women's Suffrage*, 9942
Adams, Cynthia. *The Mysterious Case of Sir Arthur Conan Doyle*, 5362
Adams, Faith. *Nicaragua*, 8502
Adams, John (jt. author). *The Future Is Wild*, 11962
Adams, Richard. *Watership Down*, 1893(F)
Adams, Richard C. *Physics Projects for Young Scientists*, 12656
Adams, Simon. *Castles and Forts*, 12921
Code Breakers, 4943
Titanic, 12908
World War I, 7615
World War II, 7637
Adams, W. Royce. *Me and Jay*, 3(F)
Adamson, Joy. *Born Free*, 12195
Adare, Sierra. *Mohawk*, 10215
Adeeb, Bonnetta (jt. author). *Nigeria*, 7972
Adeeb, Hassan. *Nigeria*, 7972
Adeleke, Tunde. *Songhay*, 7973
Adelson, Bruce. *Hat Trick Trivia*, 13431
Adkins, Jan. *Bridges*, 12753
String, 12952
Adler, C. S. *Always and Forever Friends*, 399(F)
Daddy's Climbing Tree, 1298(F)
Ghost Brother, 735(F)
Good-bye Pink Pig, 1894(F)
Help, Pink Pig! 1895(F)
Her Blue Straw Hat, 736(F)
The Lump in the Middle, 737(F)
The Magic of the Glits, 400(F)
More Than a Horse, 234(F)
The No Place Cat, 738(F)

Aslan, Madalyn. *What's Your Sign?* 13166

Aspinwall, Margaret (jt. author). *Alexander Calder and His Magical Mobiles*, 5185

Atinsky, Steve. *Tyler on Prime Time*, 407(F)

Atkin, S. Beth. *Voices from the Fields*, 10608

Atkins, Catherine. *Alt Ed*, 1164(F)

Atkins, Sinclair. *From Stone Age to Conquest*, 8245

Atlema, Martha. *A Time to Choose*, 3301(F)

Atwater-Rhodes, Amelia. *Demon in My View*, 3433(F)
Hawksong, 1917(F)
In the Forests of the Night, 3434(F)
Midnight Predator, 1918(F)
Shattered Mirror, 1919(F)

Atwood, Jane. *Capoeira*, 13453

Auch, Mary Jane. *Ashes of Roses*, 3140(F)
Frozen Summer, 2897(F)
Journey to Nowhere, 2898(F)
The Road to Home, 2899(F)
Seven Long Years Until College, 1311(F)

Audryszewski, Tricia. *The Reform Party*, 9918

Auerbach, Susan. *Queen Elizabeth II*, 6915

Auerbacher, Inge. *I Am a Star*, 7648

Augarde, Steve. *The Various*, 1920(F)

Augustin, Byron. *Bolivia*, 8584
Qatar, 8436
United Arab Emirates, 8435

Augustin, Rebecca A. (jt. author). *Qatar*, 8436

Augustyn, Frank. *Footnotes*, 7180

Avakian, Monique. *A Historical Album of Massachusetts*, 9462
A Historical Album of New York, 9463
Reformers, 6793

Aveline, Erick. *Temporary Tattoos*, 13054

Averill, Esther. *King Philip*, 6238

Avi. *The Barn*, 3029(F)
Beyond the Western Sea, 2900(F), 2901(F)
Blue Heron, 1312(F)
Bright Shadow, 1921(F)
Captain Grey, 18(F)
The Christmas Rat, 19(F)
City of Light, City of Dark, 2456(F)
Crispin, 2516(F)
Devil's Race, 3435(F)
Don't You Know There's a War On? 3302(F)
The Fighting Ground, 2850(F)
The Man Who Was Poe, 1922(F)
Night Journeys, 2795(F)
Nothing but the Truth, 1313(F)
Perloo the Bold, 1923(F)
A Place Called Ugly, 1314(F)

Punch with Judy, 3600(F)
Romeo and Juliet, 3601(F)
S.O.R. Losers, 4256(F)
Something Upstairs, 3436(F)
Sometimes I Think I Hear My Name, 747(F)
The True Confessions of Charlotte Doyle, 2902(F)
What Do Fish Have to Do with Anything? 1315(F)
Who Was That Masked Man, Anyway? 3303(F)
Windcatcher, 20(F)
Wolf Rider, 3759(F)

Avi-Yonah, Michael. *Dig This! How Archaeologists Uncover Our Past*, 7319
Piece by Piece! Mosaics of the Ancient World, 7391

Avila, Alfred. *Mexican Ghost Tales of the Southwest*, 4806

Avraham, Regina. *The Downside of Drugs*, 10896
Substance Abuse, 10897

Axelrod, Alan. *Songs of the Wild West*, 7165

Axelrod, Toby. *Hans and Sophie Scholl*, 6962
In the Camps, 7649
Rescuers Defying the Nazis, 7650
Working Together Against Teen Suicide, 11378

Axelrod-Contrada, Joan. *The Lizzie Borden "Axe Murder" Trial*, 9232
Women Who Led Nations, 6794

Ayazi-Hashjin, Sherry. *Rap and Hip Hop*, 7131

Ayer, Eleanor. *Adolf Hitler*, 6932
The Anasazi, 8754
Berlin, 7651
Colorado, 9438
A Firestorm Unleashed, 7652
From the Ashes, 7824
Germany, 8225
Homeless Children, 10474
In the Ghettos, 7653
Inferno, 7654
Margaret Bourke-White, 5178
Parallel Journeys, 7655
Ruth Bader Ginsburg, 6097
Teen Smoking, 10898

Aykroyd, Clarissa. *Exploration of the California Coast*, 8868

Aylesworth, Thomas G. *Eastern Great Lakes*, 9407
The Kids' World Almanac of Baseball, 13328

Aylesworth, Virginia L. (jt. author). *Eastern Great Lakes*, 9407

Ayo, Yvonne. *Africa*, 7861

Ayodo, Awuor. *Luo*, 7874

Ayres, Katherine. *Macaroni Boy*, 3228(F)
North by Night, 2903(F)
Silver Dollar Girl, 3030(F)
Stealing South, 2851(F)

Aziz, Laurel. *Hummingbirds*, 12223

Azuonye, Chukwuma. *Dogon*, 7923
Edo, 7975

Babbitt, Natalie. *Goody Hall*, 3760(F)
Kneeknock Rise, 3761(F)
The Search for Delicious, 1924(F)

Bach, Julie. *Bicycling*, 13390

Bachel, Beverly K. *What Do You Really Want? How to Set a Goal and Go for It!* 11641

Bacho, Peter. *Boxing in Black and White*, 13409

Bachrach, Deborah. *The Charge of the Light Brigade*, 7594
The Crimean War, 7595

Bachrach, Susan D. *The Nazi Olympics*, 13463
Tell Them We Remember, 7656

Bacon, Josephine. *Cooking the Israeli Way*, 12996

Bacon, Katharine Jay. *Finn*, 21(F)

Badoe, Adwoa. *The Pot of Wisdom*, 4697

Bagdasarian, Adam. *First French Kiss and Other Traumas*, 1316(F)
Forgotten Fire, 2621(F)

Bagnold, Enid. *National Velvet*, 241(F)

Bahree, Patricia. *Hinduism*, 9611

Bailey, Jill. *Birds*, 12224
Birds of Prey, 12241
The Secret Life of Falcons, 12242

Bailey, John. *Fishing*, 13421

Bailey, LaWanda. *Miss Myrtle Frag, the Grammar Nag*, 4947

Bailey, Ronald H. *The Bloodiest Day*, 9071

Baillie, Allan. *Secrets of Walden Rising*, 22(F)

Baines, John. *The United States*, 8668

Baird, Thomas. *Finding Fever*, 23(F)

Baker, Beth. *Sylvia Earle*, 6379

Baker, Charles (jt. author). *Ancient Egyptians*, 6795

Baker, Christopher W. *A New World of Simulators*, 12728
Robots Among Us, 12780
Scientific Visualization, 12781

Baker, Diane. *Jazzy Jewelry*, 13055
Make Your Own Hairwear, 13056

Baker, E. D. *Dragon's Breath*, 1925(F)
The Frog Princess, 1926(F)

Baker, James W. *Illusions Illustrated*, 13099

Baker, Jennifer. *Most Likely to Deceive*, 1317(F)

Baker, Julie. *Up Molasses Mountain*, 3284(F)

Baker, Patricia. *Fashions of a Decade*, 8669, 9350

Ethridge, Kenneth E. *Toothpick,* 1193(F)

Eulo, Elena Yates. *Mixed-Up Doubles,* 846(F)

Evans, Douglas. *So What Do You Do?* 1426(F)

Evans, J. Edward. *Charles Darwin,* 6369

Evans, Neville. *The Science of a Light Bulb,* 12715
The Science of Gravity, 12663

Evans, Roger. *How to Play Guitar,* 7159

Evarts, Hal G. *Jay-Jay and the Peking Monster,* 3807(F)

Everhart, Nancy. *How to Write a Term Paper,* 10661

Evernden, Margery. *The Experimenters,* 6284

Evernden, Margery (jt. author). *Of Swords and Sorcerers,* 4744

Evslin, Bernard. *The Adventures of Ulysses,* 4855
Anteus, 4856
Cerberus, 4857
The Chimaera, 4858
The Cyclopes, 4859
The Furies, 4860
Heroes and Monsters of Greek Myth, 4864
Heroes, Gods and Monsters of Greek Myths, 4861
Ladon, 4862
Pig's Ploughman, 4835
The Trojan War, 4863

Ewing, Lynne. *Drive-By,* 64(F)
Party Girl, 461(F)

Exquemelin, A. O. *Exquemelin and the Pirates of the Caribbean,* 5051

Eyerly, Jeannette. *Someone to Love Me,* 1427(F)

Faber, Doris. *Calamity Jane,* 6197
Eleanor Roosevelt, 6009
Great Lives, 5722, 5111
Nature and the Environment, 6285

Faber, Harold. *The Discoverers of America,* 8870
John Charles Fremont, 5052
La Salle, 5061
Lewis and Clark, 8871

Faber, Harold (jt. author). *Great Lives,* 5722, 5111
Nature and the Environment, 6285

Facchini, Fiorenzo. *Humans,* 7297

Facklam, Howard. *Avalanche!* 12616

Facklam, Howard (jt. author). *Changes in the Wind,* 12574

Facklam, Margery. *Changes in the Wind,* 12574
Spiders and Their Web Sites, 12301
The Trouble with Mothers, 1428(F)

Facklam, Margery (jt. author). *Avalanche!* 12616

Fagan, Cary (jt. author). *Beyond the Dance,* 5576

Faherty, Sara. *Victims and Victims' Rights,* 9968

Fahnestock, Andrea Henderson (jt. author). *The Day Our World Changed,* 10565

Fairbanks, Stephanie S. *Spotlight,* 4450

Fakih, Kimberly O. *Off the Clock,* 4950

Falcone, L. M. *The Mysterious Mummer,* 3808(F)

Falconer, Kieran. *Peru,* 8598

Falick, Melanie. *Kids Knitting,* 13135

Falkof, Lucille. *George Washington,* 6037
Helen Gurley Brown, 6352
John F. Kennedy, 5971
Lyndon B. Johnson, 5964

Fall, Mitchell. *Careers in Fire Departments' Search and Rescue Unit,* 10790

Fallen, Anne-Catherine. *USA from Space,* 11923

Fama, Elizabeth. *Overboard,* 65(F)

Fandel, Jennifer. *William Shakespeare,* 5442

Faragher, John Mack. *Daniel Boone,* 6063

Farber, Erica. *The Secret in the Stones,* 2055(F)

Farbman, Melinda. *Spacechimp,* 11924

Farish, Leah. *The First Amendment,* 9788
Tinker vs. Des Moines, 9969

Farish, Terry. *Talking in Animal,* 1429(F)

Farjeon, Eleanor. *The Glass Slipper,* 2056(F)

Farley, Carol. *The Case of the Vanishing Villain,* 3809(F)

Farley, Steven. *The Black Stallion's Shadow,* 260(F)

Farley, Steven (jt. author). *The Young Black Stallion,* 262(F)

Farley, Walter. *The Black Stallion,* 261(F)
The Young Black Stallion, 262(F)

Farlow, James O. *Bringing Dinosaur Bones to Life,* 7269

Farman, John. *The Short and Bloody History of Spies,* 10401

Farmer, Nancy. *The Ear, the Eye and the Arm,* 4141(F)
A Girl Named Disaster, 2557(F)
House of the Scorpion, 4142(F)

Farmer, Penelope. *Penelope,* 847(F)

Farndon, John. *Aluminum,* 12429
Calcium, 12430
Hydrogen, 12431
Nitrogen, 12432
Oxygen, 12433

Farnes, Catherine. *Snow,* 1194(F)

Farrell, Jeanette. *Invisible Enemies,* 11069

Farrell, Juliana. *Middle School,* 10628

Farrell, Kate (jt. author). *Talking to the Sun,* 4503

Farrell, Mame. *And Sometimes Why,* 462(F)
Bradley and the Billboard, 4300(F)

Fast, Howard. *The Immigrants,* 2858(F)

Favole, Robert J. *Through the Wormhole,* 2057(F)

Fazio, Wende. *West Virginia,* 9571

Feder, Harriet K. *Death on Sacred Ground,* 3810(F)
Mystery of the Kaifeng Scroll, 3811(F)

Feelings, Tom. *Tommy Traveler in the World of Black History,* 10136

Feiffer, Jules. *The Man in the Ceiling,* 3627(F)

Feik, Luanne (jt. author). *Stars in Your Eyes . . . Feet on the Ground,* 10754

Feinberg, Barbara S. *Abraham Lincoln's Gettysburg Address,* 9098
Black Tuesday, 9289
Constitutional Amendments, 9789
Harry S Truman, 6030
John McCain, 6128
The National Government, 9830
State Governments, 9841

Feinberg, Barbara Silberdick. *The Articles of Confederation,* 9790

Feinberg, Brian. *The Musculoskeletal System,* 11338

Feinberg, Jeremy R. *Reading the Sports Page,* 13246

Feinstein, Edward. *Tough Questions Jews Ask,* 9736

Feinstein, Stephen. *Andrew Jackson,* 5948
John Adams, 5897
John Quincy Adams, 5900
The 1910s, 8686
The 1940s, 8687
The 1960s, 8688
The 1970s, 8689
The 1980s, 9359
The 1990s, 8690

Feinstein, Steve. *Israel in Pictures,* 8422
Turkey in Pictures, 8181

Feldman, Douglas A. *The AIDS Crisis,* 11070

Feldman, Elane. *Fashions of a Decade,* 13060

Feldman, Jane. *I Am a Dancer,* 7184

Feldman, Jane (jt. author). *Jefferson's Children,* 5953

Feldman, Ruth Tenzer. *Don't Whistle In School,* 10629

Felgar, Robert. *Understanding Richard Wright's Black Boy,* 4913

Henderson, Harry. *Career Opportunities in Computers and Cyberspace*, 10825
The Internet, 12794
Issues in the Information Age, 12795
Modern Mathematicians, 6296
Henderson, Heather H. *The Flip Side II*, 4419
Henderson, Kathy. *The Young Writer's Guide to Getting Published*, 10671
Hendler, Herb. *Year by Year in the Rock Era*, 9367
Hendrickson, Ann-Marie. *Nat Turner*, 5885
Hendry, Diana. *Harvey Angell*, 2100(F)
Hendry, Linda. *Making Gift Boxes*, 12962
Heneghan, James. *Flood*, 2101(F)
The Grave, 2102(F)
Torn Away, 98(F)
Wish Me Luck, 3340(F)
Heneghan, James (jt. author). *Waiting for Sarah*, 1233(F)
Henkes, Kevin. *The Birthday Room*, 920(F)
Olive's Ocean, 488(F)
Protecting Marie, 276(F)
Henry, Chad. *DogBreath Victorious*, 3642(F)
Henry, Christopher. *Ben Nighthorse Campbell*, 6073
Forever Free, 10148
Henry, Marguerite. *Album of Horses*, 12400
King of the Wind, 277(F)
Misty of Chincoteague, 278(F)
Mustang, Wild Spirit of the West, 279(F)
Henry, O. *The Gift of the Magi*, 383(F), 384(F)
Henry, Sondra (jt. author). *Israel*, 8434
Henson, Burt. *Furman v. Georgia*, 9881
Hentoff, Nat. *The Day They Came to Arrest the Book*, 1856(F)
Hepplewhite, Peter. *Alien Encounters*, 13183
Herald, Earl S. (jt. author). *A Field Guide to Pacific Coast Fishes of North America*, 12325
Herald, Jacqueline. *Fashions of a Decade*, 9295
Herb, Angela. *Beyond the Mississippi*, 9171
Herbert, Don. *Mr. Wizard's Experiments for Young Scientists*, 11853
Mr. Wizard's Supermarket Science, 11854
Herbert, Janis. *The American Revolution for Kids*, 8984
The Civil War for Kids, 9110
Leonardo da Vinci for Kids, 5203

Herbst, Dan. *Sports Illustrated Soccer*, 13501
Herda, D. J. *The Dred Scott Case*, 9035
Earl Warren, 6172
Environmental America, 9481, 9534, 9575, 9599
Ethnic America, 9482
Furman v. Georgia, 9882
New York Times v. United States, 9883
Roe v. Wade, 9884
Sandra Day O'Connor, 6139
Thurgood Marshall, 6131
United States v. Nixon, 9368
Hermann, Spring. *Geronimo*, 6095
R. C. Gorman, 5223
Hermes, Patricia. *Calling Me Home*, 3068(F)
Fly Away Home, 280(F)
Heads, I Win, 921(F)
I Hate Being Gifted, 489(F)
Sweet By and By, 922(F)
A Time to Listen, 11405
You Shouldn't Have to Say Goodbye, 923(F)
Hernandez, Irene B. *Across the Great River*, 633(F)
The Secret of Two Brothers, 924(F)
Hernandez, Jo Ann Y. *White Bread Competition*, 634(F)
Hernandez-Divers, Sonia. *Geckos*, 12370
Herran, Joe. *Snowboarding*, 13492
Herrera, Juan F. *Laughing Out Loud, I Fly (A Caracajadas Yo Vuelo)*, 4589
Herriot, James. *All Creatures Great and Small*, 6443
Herschler, Mildred Barger. *The Darkest Corner*, 925(F)
Hershey, Robert L. *How to Think with Numbers*, 12553
Herstek, Amy Paulson. *Dorothea Dix*, 5807
Hertenstein, Jane. *Beyond Paradise*, 3341(F)
Heslewood, Juliet. *The History of Western Painting*, 7072
The History of Western Sculpture, 7073
Hess, Debra. *Florida*, 9576
Hesse, Karen. *Aleutian Sparrow*, 3342(F)
Letters from Rifka, 3249(F)
A Light in the Storm, 2984(F)
The Music of Dolphins, 1212(F)
Phoenix Rising, 1857(F)
Stowaway, 99(F)
A Time of Angels, 3250(F)
Witness, 3251(F)
Hesser, Terry S. *Kissing Doorknobs*, 1213(F)
Hestler, Anna. *Wales*, 8263
Yemen, 8455
Hettinga, Donald R. *The Brothers Grimm*, 5375

Heubeck, Nancy (jt. author). *Career Ideas for Kids Who Like Adventure*, 10732
Career Ideas for Kids Who Like Animals and Nature, 10733
Hevly, Nancy. *Preachers and Teachers*, 9172
Hewett, Lorri. *Dancer*, 635(F)
Lives of Our Own, 636(F)
Soulfire, 637(F)
Hewish, Mark. *The Young Scientist Book of Jets*, 12871
Hewson, Martha S. *The Electoral College*, 9929
Heyes, Eileen. *O'Dwyer and Grady Starring in Tough Act to Follow*, 3832(F)
Tobacco, USA, 10936
Heynen, Jim. *Being Youngest*, 1500(F)
Hiaasen, Carl. *Hoot*, 1858(F)
Hickman, Janet. *Jericho*, 926(F)
Susannah, 3069(F)
Hicks, Betty. *Animal House and Iz*, 927(F)
Higdon, Elizabeth. *Joan Miró*, 5253
Higgins, Christopher. *Nuclear Submarine Disasters*, 12700
High, Linda O. *Hound Heaven*, 281(F)
Maizie, 928(F)
The Summer of the Great Divide, 1501(F)
Hightower, Paul. *Galileo*, 6419
Highwater, Jamake. *Anpao*, 4790
Legend Days, 2780(F)
Rama, 2103(F)
Hildebrant, Ziporah. *Marina Silva*, 6991
Hilgartner, Beth. *A Murder for Her Majesty*, 100(F)
Hill, Anne E. *Broadcasting and Journalism*, 5122
Denzel Washington, 5694
Ekaterina Gordeeva, 6724
Jennifer Lopez, 5620
Sandra Bullock, 5530
Ten American Movie Directors, 5123
Hill, Barbara W. *Cooking the English Way*, 13017
Hill, Cherry. *Horse Care for Kids*, 12401
Hill, Christine M. *Langston Hughes*, 5385
Ten Hispanic American Authors, 5124
Ten Terrific Authors for Teens, 5125
Hill, David. *Take It Easy*, 101(F)
Time Out, 1502(F)
Hill, Donna. *Shipwreck Season*, 2921(F)
Hill, Douglas. *Witches and Magic-Makers*, 13184
Hill, Mary. *Creepy Classics*, 3487(F)

Hill, Pamela S. *Ghost Horses*, 3070(F)

A Voice from the Border, 2985(F)

Hill, Pamela Smith. *The Last Grail Keeper*, 2104(F)

Hill, Susan. *The Christmas Collection*, 490(F)

Hill, William. *The Magic Bicycle*, 4173(F)

The Vampire Hunters, 3833(F)

Hiller, Ilo. *Introducing Mammals to Young Naturalists*, 12111

Hillerman, Tony. *The Boy Who Made Dragonfly*, 4791

Hillman, John (jt. author). *Blackball Superstars*, 13331

Hills, C. A. R. *The Second World War*, 7722

Hillstrom, Kevin. *Vietnam War*, 7837

Hillstrom, Laurie Collier (jt. author). *Vietnam War*, 7837

Hilton, Suzanne. *Miners, Merchants, and Maids*, 9173

The World of Young George Washington, 6038

The World of Young Herbert Hoover, 5944

Hilts, Len. *Timmy O'Dowd and the Big Ditch*, 2922(F)

Hinds, Kathryn. *The Ancient Romans*, 7512

The Castle, 7562

The Celts of Northern Europe, 7366

The Church, 7563

The City, 7564

The Countryside, 7565

Venice and Its Merchant Empire, 8300

Hinds, Maurene J. *Focus on Body Image*, 11270

Hinds, Uton (jt. author). *The Jacob Ladder*, 918(F)

Hine, Darlene Clark. *The Path to Equality*, 10149

Hinkle, Donald Henry. *Ronald Reagan*, 6005

Hinman, Bonnie. *Faith Hill*, 5592

Tony Blair, 6886

Hinton, Kerry. *Cool Careers Without College for Music Lovers*, 10753

Hinton, S. E. *The Outsiders*, 102(F)

Rumble Fish, 103(F)

Taming the Star Runner, 929(F)

Tex, 104(F)

That Was Then, This Is Now, 105(F)

Hintz, Martin. *Farewell, John Barleycorn*, 9296

Hawaii, 9535

Iowa, 9422

Israel, 8425

Louisiana, 9577

Minnesota, 9423

Missouri, 9424

The Netherlands, 8306

North Carolina, 9578

North Dakota, 9425

Hintz, Stephen (jt. author). *Israel*, 8425

North Carolina, 9578

Hipperson, Carol Edgemon. *The Belly Gunner*, 7723

Hipple, Ted. *Writers for Young Adults*, 5126

Hirsch, Karen D. *Mind Riot*, 11605

Hirsch, Odo. *Bartlett and the Ice Voyage*, 4663(F)

Hirsch, Robin. *FEG*, 4497

Hirschfeld, Robert. *Goalkeeper in Charge*, 4304(F)

Hirschfeld, Arlene. *Artists and Craftspeople*, 5127

Kick Butts! A Kid's Action Guide to a Tobacco-Free America, 10937

Rising Voices, 10217

Hirschfelder, Arlene B. *Photo Odyssey*, 9174

Hirschmann, Kris. *Humpback Whales*, 12345

Rays, 12327

Hirst, Mike. *Freedom of Belief*, 9995

The History of Emigration from Scotland, 8264

Hitchcock, Barbara (jt. author). *Sightseeing*, 11944

Hite, Sid. *Answer My Prayer*, 2105(F)

Cecil in Space, 4039(F)

The Distance of Hope, 2106(F)

Dither Farm, 2107(F)

A Hole in the World, 1503(F)

The Journal of Rufus Rowe, 2986(F)

Stick and Whittle, 3071(F)

Those Darn Dithers, 3643(F)

Hjelmeland, Andy. *Legalized Gambling*, 10273

Prisons, 10416

Ho, Minfong. *The Clay Marble*, 2588(F)

Gathering the Dew, 2589(F)

Rice Without Rain, 1859(F)

Hoare, Ben. *Temperate Grasslands*, 12531

Hoban, Russell. *The Mouse and His Child*, 2108(F)

The Trokeville Way, 2109(F)

Hoban, Sarah. *Daily Life in Ancient and Modern Paris*, 8214

Hobbs, Valerie. *Carolina Crow Girl*, 930(F)

Charlie's Run, 931(F)

Sonny's War, 3421(F)

Stefan's Story, 1860(F)

Tender, 932(F)

Hobbs, Will. *Beardance*, 282(F)

Bearstone, 638(F)

The Big Wander, 106(F)

Down the Yukon, 107(F)

Far North, 108(F)

Ghost Canoe, 109(F)

Jackie's Wild Seattle, 110(F)

Jason's Gold, 111(F)

Kokopelli's Flute, 2110(F)

The Maze, 112(F)

River Thunder, 113(F)

Wild Man Island, 114(F)

Hoch, Dean. *The Sex Education Dictionary for Today's Teens and Pre-Teens*, 11551

Hoch, Nancy (jt. author). *The Sex Education Dictionary for Today's Teens and Pre-Teens*, 11551

Hodge, Merle. *For the Life of Laetitia*, 639(F)

Hodge, Susie. *Ancient Greek Art*, 7474

Ancient Roman Art, 7513

Claude Monet, 5254

Hodges, Margaret. *Gulliver in Lilliput*, 2111(F)

Hauntings, 3488

Of Swords and Sorcerers, 4744

Hodgkins, Fran. *Animals Among Us*, 12112

Hoekstra, Molly. *Upstream*, 1214(F)

Hoeye, Michael. *The Sands of Time*, 2112(F)

Time Stops for No Mouse, 2113(F)

Hoff, Mark. *Gloria Steinem*, 5867

Hoff, Mary. *Atmosphere*, 12580

Life on Land, 12260

Our Endangered Planet, 10353, 12521

Hoffius, Stephen. *Winners and Losers*, 4305(F)

Hoffman, Alice. *Aquamarine*, 2114(F)

Green Angel, 933(F)

Indigo, 2115(F)

Hoffman, Mary. *Stravaganza*, 2116(F), 2117(F)

Hoffman, Nancy. *Eleanor Roosevelt and the Arthurdale Experiment*, 9297

South Carolina, 9579

Hoffman, Nina Kiriki. *A Stir of Bones*, 3489(F)

Hoh, Diane. *Titanic, the Long Night*, 4040(F)

Hohm, Charles F. *Population*, 10374

Hoig, Stan. *Night of the Cruel Moon*, 8801

People of the Sacred Arrows, 10218

Holbrook, Sara. *Walking on the Boundaries of Change*, 4590

Holch, Gregory. *The Things with Wings*, 2118(F)

Holcomb, Jerry Kimble. *The Chinquapin Tree*, 934(F)

Holden, Henry M. *American Women of Flight*, 4998

The Persian Gulf War, 7838

Holdsclaw, Chamique. *Chamique Holdsclaw*, 6643

Holeman, Linda. *Mercy's Birds*, 1504(F)

The Pirate's Son, 2682(F)
Roman Myths, 4874
The Silver Treasure, 4667
The Stones Are Hatching, 2236(F)
Stop the Train! 3092(F)
McCauslin, Mark. *Homelessness*, 10492
MccGwire, Scarlett. *Surveillance*, 10283
McClafferty, Carla Killough. *The Head Bone's Connected to the Neck Bone*, 12675
McClain, Margaret S. *Bellboy*, 3093(F)
McClary, Andrew. *Toys with Nine Lives*, 13069
McClellan, Marilyn. *Organ and Tissue Transplants*, 11026
McCloud, Bill. *What Should We Tell Our Children About Vietnam?* 9402
McCloud, Scott. *The New Adventures of Abraham Lincoln*, 2466(F)
McClung, Robert M. *Last of the Wild*, 12262
Lost Wild America, 12263
Young George Washington and the French and Indian War, 6039
McClure, Judy. *Healers and Researchers*, 6308
McConnell, Malcolm (jt. author). *Born to Fly*, 6236
McCord, David. *All Day Long*, 4513(F)
McCormack, Shaun. *Cool Papa Bell*, 6588
McCormick, Anita Louise. *The Industrial Revolution in American History*, 8717
The Internet, 12805
Native Americans and the Reservation in American History, 8825
The Pony Express in American History, 9182
Space Exploration, 11935
The Vietnam Antiwar Movement, 9403
McCormick, Patricia. *Cut*, 1234(F)
McCoy, Kathy. *Growing and Changing*, 11692
Life Happens, 11693
The New Teenage Body Book, 11694
McCracken, Kristin. *James Van Der Beek*, 5692
McCuan, Walter R. (jt. author). *21st Century Earth*, 10536
McCue, Margi L. *Domestic Violence*, 11771
MacCullough, Carolyn. *Falling Through Darkness*, 526(F)
McCullough, Frances. *Love Is Like a Lion's Tooth*, 4514
McCullough, L. E. *Plays of America from American Folklore for Young Actors*, 4462

McCullough, Sally (jt. author). *Discipline from Birth to Three*, 11514
McCune, Bunny. *Girls to Women*, 11695
McCusker, Paul. *Arin's Judgment*, 2237(F)
McCutcheon, Marc. *The Beast in You!* 7303
McDaniel, Lurlene. *Angel of Hope*, 2565(F)
Angel of Mercy, 2566(F)
Angels Watching Over Me, 4050(F)
Baby Alicia Is Dying, 1866(F)
Don't Die, My Love, 4051(F)
The Girl Death Left Behind, 1598(F)
How Do I Love Thee? Three Stories, 1235(F)
I'll Be Seeing You, 1599(F)
Saving Jessica, 1236(F)
Starry, Starry Night, 1600(F)
Telling Christina Goodbye, 1601(F)
To Live Again, 1237(F)
Too Young to Die, 1238(F)
McDaniel, Melissa. *Arizona*, 9447
Ernest Hemingway, 5381
Spike Lee, 5615
McDaniels, Pellom. *So, You Want to Be a Pro?* 10760
MacDonald, Amy. *No More Nice*, 3671(F)
MacDonald, Andy. *Dropping in with Andy Mac*, 6773
McDonald, Brix. *Riding on the Wind*, 3094(F)
MacDonald, Caroline. *Hostilities*, 3504(F)
Speaking to Miranda, 1602(F)
McDonald, Collin. *The Chilling Hour*, 3505(F)
MacDonald, David. *The Encyclopedia of Mammals*, 12172
MacDonald, Fiona. *Albert Einstein*, 6389
Ancient African Town, 8002
Clothing and Jewelry, 12773
Edwin Hubble, 6446
How Would You Survive as an Aztec? 8549
Inca Town, 8611
The Stone Age News, 7335
Winston Churchill, 6901
Women in Ancient Greece, 7477
Women in Ancient Rome, 7517
Women in Medieval Times, 7575
Women in 19th-Century America, 8718
Women in 19th-Century Europe, 7601
The World in the Time of Albert Einstein, 6390
The World in the Time of Charlemagne, 7576
MacDonald, George. *At the Back of the North Wind*, 2238(F)

The Princess and the Goblin, 4748(F)
MacDonald, James D. (jt. author). *Groogleman*, 4139(F)
The Knight's Wyrd, 2040(F)
McDonald, Janet. *Chill Wind*, 1867(F)
Spellbound, 992(F)
Twists and Turns, 527(F)
Macdonald, Joan Vos. *Cybersafety*, 12806
McDonald, Joyce. *Shades of Simon Gray*, 3506(F)
Swallowing Stones, 1603(F)
McDonald, Laughlin. *The Rights of Racial Minorities*, 10015
MacDonald, Margaret Read. *Peace Tales*, 4668
McDonald, Megan. *All the Stars in the Sky*, 3095(F)
The Sisters Club, 3672(F)
MacDonald, Patricia A. *Pablo Picasso*, 5271
Macdonald, Robert. *Islands of the Pacific Rim and Their People*, 8167
McDowall, David. *The Spanish Armada*, 8386
Mace, Nancy. *In the Company of Men*, 7015
McElfresh, Lynn E. *Can You Feel the Thunder?* 1604(F)
McFann, Jane. *Deathtrap and Dinosaur*, 3673(F)
Maybe by Then I'll Understand, 4052(F)
McFarland, Rhoda. *Working Together Against Sexual Harassment*, 11592
McFarlane, Brian. *Real Stories from the Rink*, 13436
The Youngest Goalie, 6723
McFarlane, Marilyn. *Sacred Myths*, 9656
McGaffey, Leta. *Honduras*, 8516
McGarrahan, Sean (jt. author). *Epilepsy*, 11079
McGibbon, Robin. *New Kids on the Block*, 5635
McGill, Alice. *In the Hollow of Your Hand*, 7170
Miles' Song, 2933(F)
McGill, Allyson. *The Swedish Americans*, 10236
McGinley, Jerry. *Joaquin Strikes Back*, 4316(F)
McGinty, Alice B. *Software Designer*, 10827
McGirr, Nancy (jt. author). *Out of the Dump*, 8505
McGlothlin, Bruce. *High Performance Through Understanding Systems*, 10696
McGough, Roger. *The Kingfisher Book of Funny Poems*, 4515
McGowan, Christopher. *T-Rex to Go*, 7280

Wood, Beverly. *Dog Star*, 2430(F)

Wood, Chris (jt. author). *Dog Star*, 2430(F)

Wood, Dan (jt. author). *Jesse Jackson*, 5826

Wood, Elaine (jt. author). *The Brain and Nervous System*, 11320
The Digestive System, 11335
The Immune System, 11299

Wood, Frances M. *Daughter of Madrugada*, 2959(F)

Wood, Geraldine. *Science of the Early Americas*, 8482

Wood, June R. *The Man Who Loved Clowns*, 1809(F)
A Share of Freedom, 1155(F)
Turtle on a Fence Post, 1810(F)
When Pigs Fly, 1156(F)

Wood, Nancy. *Sacred Fire*, 8862

Wood, Peter H. *Strange New Land*, 8954

Wood, Richard. *Diana*, 6910

Wood, Tim. *The Incas*, 8640
The Renaissance, 7593

Woodbury, Mary. *Brad's Universe*, 1157(F)

Woodford, Chris. *Criminal Investigation*, 10467

Woodford, Susan. *The Parthenon*, 7500

Woodruff, Elvira. *Orphan of Ellis Island*, 2431(F)

Woodruff, Joan L. *The Shiloh Renewal*, 1296(F)

Woods, Brenda. *The Red Rose Box*, 3291(F)

Woods, Geraldine. *Animal Experimentation and Testing*, 12126
Heroin, 11022
The Navajo, 8863
Science in Ancient Egypt, 7468

Woods, Geraldine (jt. author). *Bill Cosby*, 5547

Woods, Harold. *Bill Cosby*, 5547

Woods, Mary (jt. author). *Ancient Agriculture*, 7409
Ancient Machines from Wedges to Waterwheels, 7410

Woods, Mary B. *Ancient Communication*, 4942
Ancient Computing, 12557
Ancient Construction, 12770
Ancient Warfare, 12951

Woods, Mary B. (jt. author). *Ancient Medicine*, 7411
Ancient Transportation, 7412

Woods, Michael. *Ancient Agriculture*, 7409
Ancient Machines from Wedges to Waterwheels, 7410
Ancient Medicine, 7411
Ancient Transportation, 7412

Woods, Michael (jt. author). *Ancient Communication*, 4942
Ancient Computing, 12557
Ancient Construction, 12770
Ancient Warfare, 12951

Woods, Ron. *The Hero*, 1811(F)

Woods, Samuel G. *Everything You Need to Know About Sexually Transmitted Disease*, 11201

Woodson, Jacqueline. *The Dear One*, 724(F)
From the Notebooks of Melanin Sun May, 725(F)
The House You Pass on the Way, 1812(F)
Hush, 1158(F)
If You Come Softly, 4087(F)
Lena, 1159(F)
Maizon at Blue Hill, 726(F)
Miracle's Boys, 1160(F)
A Way out of No Way, 10167

Woodson, Marion. *My Brother's Keeper*, 3993(F)

Woodward, Walter M. *Sam Houston*, 6108

Woog, Adam. *The Beatles*, 5519
Bill Gates, 6428, 6429
Fidel Castro, 6982
Gangsters, 5789
The History of Rock and Roll, 7152
Magicians and Illusionists, 5168
Marilyn Monroe, 5630
New York, 8955
The 1900's, 9268
Rock and Roll Legends, 5169
Roosevelt and the New Deal, 9316
Suicide, 11455
A Sweatshop During the Industrial Revolution, 7607

Woog, Dan. *The Ultimate Soccer Almanac*, 13509

Wooldridge, Frosty. *Strike Three!* 4351(F)

Wooldridge, Susan Goldsmith. *Poemcrazy*, 10689

Woolf, Alex. *Osama Bin Laden*, 6843

Woolum, Janet. *Outstanding Women Athletes*, 13320

Wooten, Sara McIntosh. *Billy Graham*, 6209
Margaret Bourke-White, 5182
Oprah Winfrey, 5699

Wormser, Richard. *American Childhoods*, 8745
American Islam, 9729
Growing Up in the Great Depression, 9317
Hoboes, 8746
The Iron Horse, 12906
Juveniles in Trouble, 10468
The Rise and Fall of Jim Crow, 10062
To the Young Filmmaker, 10779

Woronoff, Kristen. *American Inaugurals*, 9824

Worth, Richard. *Children, Violence, and Murder*, 10469
Cinqué of the Amistad and the Slave Trade, 10063
Gail Devers, 6754
The Insanity Defense, 9916

Pizarro and the Conquest of the Incan Empire in World History, 8641
Ponce de Leon and the Age of Spanish Exploration in World History, 5086
Poverty, 10504
Robert Mugabe of Zimbabwe, 6834
The Spanish Inquisition in World History, 8395
Stanley and Livingstone and the Exploration of Africa in World History, 7872
Westward Expansion and Manifest Destiny, 9229
Women in Combat, 9939

Worthen, Bonnie (jt. author). *Period*, 11558

Worthen, Tom. *Broken Hearts . . . Healing*, 4551

Wrede, Patricia C. *Book of Enchantments*, 2432(F)
Searching for Dragons, 2433(F)
Talking to Dragons, 2434(F)

Wren, Laura Lee. *Garth Brooks*, 5529
Pirates and Privateers of the High Seas, 5010

Wright, Betty R. *The Dollhouse Murders*, 3994(F)
A Ghost in the House, 3588(F)
The Summer of Mrs. MacGregor, 1813(F)

Wright, Betty Ren. *Crandalls' Castle*, 3589(F)

Wright, Cynthia. *Everything You Need to Know About Dealing with Stalking*, 10470

Wright, David. *Computers*, 12829

Wright, David K. *Arthur Ashe*, 6742
Burma, 8149
John Lennon, 5618
Paul Robeson, 5661
Vietnam, 8150
War in Vietnam, 7856

Wright, Joseph P. (jt. author). *Math Games for Middle School*, 12569

Wright, Lynne. *The Science of Noise*, 12726

Wright, Rachel. *Paris 1789*, 8224

Wright, Randall. *A Hundred Days from Home*, 1814(F)

Wright, Richard. *Rite of Passage*, 727(F)

Wroble, Lisa A. *The New Deal and the Great Depression in American History*, 9318

Wu, Dana Ying-Hul. *The Chinese-American Experience*, 10188

Wu, Priscilla. *The Abacus Contest*, 2615(F)

Wukovits, John. *Anne Frank*, 6926
Annie Oakley, 5639
The Composite Guide to Soccer, 13510
The Encyclopedia of the Winter Olympics, 13472
Jim Carrey, 5535

Title Index

This index contains both main entry and internal titles cited in the entries. References are to entry numbers, not page numbers. All fiction titles are indicated by (F), following the entry number.

Subject/Grade Level Index

All entries are listed by subject and then according to grade level suitability (see the key at the foot of pages for grade level designations). Subjects are arranged alphabetically and subject heads may be subdivided into nonfiction (e.g., "Trucks") and fiction (e.g. "Trucks — Fiction"). References to entries are by entry number, not page number.

A

Aaron, Hank
IJ: 6583 JS: 6582

Abandoned children — Fiction
IJ: 1000 J: 816 JS: 1019, 1760

Abbott, Jim
IJ: 6584–85

Abdul, Paula
IJ: 5505

Abdul-Jabbar, Kareem
IJ: 6623

Abelard and Heloise — Fiction
JS: 2542

Abernathy, Ralph
JS: 5790

Abolitionists
See also Slavery
JS: 9866, 9946, 10035, 10045, 10153

Abolitionists — Biography
IJ: 5810, 5818, 5827, 5876–77
JS: 5799, 5809, 5811, 9058

Abolitionists — Fiction
IJ: 2934 J: 2906

Abominable snowman
See also Yeti
IJ: 13189

Aborigines (Australia)
IJ: 8157, 8170, 8174

Aborigines (Australia) — Art
IJ: 7093

Aborigines (Australia) — Fiction
J: 3785

Aborigines (Australia) — Folklore
,JS: 4730

Abortion
JS: 9884, 9910–11, 11493–95, 11515

Abortion — Fiction
J: 3941 JS: 1434, 1570, 1829

Academic guidance
JS: 10691

Accidents
IJ: 11219, 11532

Accidents — Fiction
IJ: 788 J: 181, 1297, 3198 JS: 146, 1452, 3800

Acid rain
See also Ecology and environment — Problems
IJ: 10355

Acne
JS: 11272

Acoma Indians — Fiction
J: 2222

Acropolis (Greece)
IJ: 7498

Acting
IJ: 4431, 7214, 7219 J: 4419
JS: 4423, 4426, 4455, 7223, 7227

Acting — Biography
IJ: 5146, 5506, 5515, 5530–31, 5535, 5538, 5541, 5544, 5551–52, 5555–56, 5585, 5588, 5606, 5609, 5620, 5624, 5631, 5633, 5640–43, 5647, 5653–54, 5661, 5664, 5666, 6191 J: 5113, 5507, 5548, 5578–79, 5628, 5656 JS: 5546, 5549–50, 5554, 5557, 5574, 5577, 5600, 5608, 5629–30, 5634, 5655, 5660, 5670, 5673, 5675–76, 5694

Acting — Careers
J: 10777 JS: 10761

Acting — Fiction
IJ: 407, 1179, 2627, 3490, 3600, 3842
J: 16, 2187 JS: 658, 1781, 5677

Activism
See also Social action
IJ: 10316, 11183 JS: 10544

Activism — Fiction
JS: 587

Adams, Abigail
IJ: 5893–95 J: 5899 JS: 5892, 5896

Adams, Ansel
IJ: 5171 JS: 5170

Adams, John
IJ: 5897 J: 5899 JS: 5898

Adams, John — Fiction
JS: 2877

Adams, John Quincy
IJ: 5900

Adams, Samuel
IJ: 6049–50

Adamson, Joy
JS: 6822

Addams, Jane
IJ: 6176, 6179–80, 9418 JS: 6177–78

Addiction
JS: 10960

Addictions
See also Alcoholism; Drugs and drug abuse; Smoking
IJ: 10856, 10950 J: 10907 JS: 10857, 11084, 11647

Addictive personality
JS: 11647

Addition
IJ: 12550

Adolescence
See also Puberty
IJ: 11538, 11555 J: 11382 JS: 4376, 11609, 11615

Adolescence — Boys
JS: 11549

Adolescence — Comic strips
JS: 11605

Adolescence — Fiction
IJ: 1204 J: 1694, 1851 JS: 1759, 1831

Adolescence — Girls
JS: 1445

6588, 6597, 6599, 6601, 6603, 6612–13, 6622–25, 6636–39, 6642, 6647–50, 6652, 6658, 6662–64, 6666–67, 6669, 6671, 6673, 6677, 6694, 6700–2, 6708, 6711–13, 6715, 6717, 6740, 6749, 6752, 6756, 6758, 6766, 6779, 6987, 6995, 7104, 12869–70 **J:** 5166, 5319, 5365, 5504, 5578, 5590–91, 5632, 5742, 5773, 5836, 5851–52, 5854, 5886, 6168, 6207–8, 6316, 6509, 6528, 6641, 6683, 6739, 6763 **JS:** 5055, 5145, 5244, 5322, 5328, 5334, 5374, 5377–78, 5380, 5385, 5387–88, 5414–16, 5472, 5486–87, 5509, 5516, 5533, 5539, 5543, 5546, 5553, 5565, 5567, 5572–75, 5577, 5589, 5602, 5608, 5614, 5634, 5645, 5660, 5673, 5675–76, 5688, 5694, 5723, 5730–31, 5734, 5749, 5779, 5786–87, 5790, 5795, 5800, 5809, 5811–12, 5814–17, 5820, 5825, 5832, 5834, 5841, 5843, 5848–50, 5853, 5855, 5859, 5874, 5883–84, 5887, 6071, 6115–16, 6131, 6149, 6153, 6226, 6237, 6254, 6263, 6294, 6322, 6327, 6447, 6455, 6523, 6554, 6582, 6596, 6610, 6615, 6643, 6646, 6651, 6681, 6684, 6741, 6744, 6757, 6759, 6764, 6767, 6787, 9281, 10157, 13350

African Americans — Boxing
J: 6688 **JS:** 6682, 6687

African Americans — Business
JS: 6293

African Americans — Children
JS: 10167

African Americans — Civil rights
J: 9970 **JS:** 4991

African Americans — Civil rights — Biography
JS: 5780

African Americans — Cookbooks
J: 13006

African Americans — Crafts
IJ: 13142

African Americans — Dance
JS: 7187

African Americans — Diseases
JS: 11038

African Americans — Explorers
IJ: 4997

African Americans — Fiction
IJ: 156, 210, 399, 406, 410, 418, 430, 466, 497, 509, 528, 601, 614, 616, 618, 621, 629, 640–41, 656, 667, 674–75, 679, 685, 689, 696, 699, 704–5, 726, 734, 766, 849, 892, 908, 910, 925, 1022, 1099, 1117, 1128, 1437, 1646, 1737, 1762, 1890, 2128, 2252, 2426, 2830, 2861–62, 2867, 2920, 2937, 2950, 2952, 2983, 3005, 3038, 3096, 3104, 3145, 3170, 3205–6, 3214, 3268, 3285, 3291, 3436, 3508, 4269, 5831, 6770, 9029, 9709 **J:** 630, 632, 636, 678, 680, 722, 724, 834, 1173, 2896, 2905, 2917, 2933, 2945, 2948, 2963, 2982, 3109, 3169, 3827, 4268, 4313, 6152 **JS:** 396, 458, 527, 582, 592, 595, 597, 602, 609–10, 612, 628, 631, 635, 637, 645, 650, 657,

665, 673, 676–77, 681–82, 686, 714, 725, 727, 838, 850–51, 907, 948, 992, 1041, 1160, 1191, 1221, 1244, 1280, 1654, 1677, 1745, 1796–98, 1841, 1867, 2077, 2582, 2833, 2845, 2881, 2893, 2907, 2931, 2938, 2949, 2968, 3164, 3215, 3271, 3485, 3822, 4041, 4319, 5677

African Americans — Folk songs
IJ: 7170

African Americans — Folklore
IJ: 4809–10, 4812–13

African Americans — History
IJ: 5810, 7151, 7599, 7729, 7769, 8968, 8970, 8983, 9015, 9026–27, 9031, 9036–37, 9042, 9047, 9051, 9079, 9155, 9206, 9213, 9258, 9701, 9990, 10025, 10132, 10136, 10138, 10141–43, 10145–46, 10154, 10159, 10163–64, 10612 **J:** 8971, 9177–78, 9299, 9378, 9998, 10155–56, 10162 **JS:** 4890, 5811, 7220, 8788, 8931, 8954, 9022, 9025, 9053, 9055, 9060–61, 9176, 9221, 9248–49, 9253, 9279, 9356, 9365, 9369, 9485, 9946, 9960, 9975, 10005, 10009, 10014, 10018, 10032, 10035, 10055–56, 10062, 10123, 10127, 10133–35, 10139, 10144, 10147–49, 10151, 10153, 10166, 10233

African Americans — Holidays
IJ: 10130, 10557 **JS:** 10552

African Americans — Inventors
JS: 6294

African Americans — Literature
IJ: 4911

African Americans — Medicine
IJ: 6278

African Americans — Motion pictures
JS: 7212

African Americans — Music
IJ: 7122, 7131, 7147 **J:** 7138
JS: 7129

African Americans — Musicians
JS: 5502, 5512, 5566

African Americans — Newspapers
JS: 4991

African Americans — Personal guidance
JS: 11675

African Americans — Plays
JS: 4459

African Americans — Poetry
IJ: 4586, 4603, 4613, 4628, 5158, 9709
JS: 4523, 4523, 4572, 4582, 4594, 4596, 4601, 4614, 4639

African Americans — Politics
JS: 9366

African Americans — Scientists
IJ: 6338 **JS:** 6327, 6339, 6376

African Americans — Singers
JS: 5510, 5596

African Americans — Songs
IJ: 10164 **J:** 7168

African Americans — Teenagers
JS: 10152

African Americans — Television
JS: 5699, 7212

African Americans — Tennis
JS: 6742

African Americans — Women
IJ: 5772 **J:** 5713, 9943 **JS:** 5878

African Americans — World War II
J: 7720

African Burial Ground (New York City)
JS: 10144

African kingdoms — History
See also specific kingdoms, e.g., Zulu
IJ: 7868 **J:** 7908, 7919, 7983, 7987, 8004, 8022

Africans — Biography
IJ: 7005

Agassi, Andre
IJ: 6737–38

Agikuyu (African people)
JS: 7896

Aging
See also Death; Elderly persons; Euthanasia
JS: 10381

Aging — Fiction
IJ: 1521

Agriculture — History
IJ: 7409 **JS:** 12037

Aida (opera)
IJ: 7124

AIDS
See also HIV (virus)
IJ: 11117, 11120, 11156 **JS:** 11039, 11051, 11063, 11070, 11072–74, 11095, 11100, 11114–15, 11118, 11138, 11151, 11159, 11176, 11184

AIDS — Biography
IJ: 6648 **J:** 6739 **JS:** 6646, 6998

AIDS — Fiction
IJ: 1045 **J:** 1185, 1822 **JS:** 860, 1071, 1866, 2480

Aikman, Troy
IJ: 6689

Air
IJ: 12580–81

Air — Experiments and projects
IJ: 12578–79

Air Force
See Air Force (U.S.)

Air Force — Careers
JS: 10695

Air Force One
JS: 9812

Air Force (U.S.)
IJ: 7729, 12925, 12934

Air Force (U.S.) — Biography
IJ: 6080

IJ = Upper Elementary/Lower Middle School; J = Middle School/Junior High; JS = Junior High/Senior High

Air Force (U.S.) — Fiction
J: 13

Air pollution
See also Ecology and environment —
Problems; Pollution
IJ: 10348, 10356–57, 12580–81
JS: 10351, 12573

Airlines
IJ: 12867

Airplane crashes
IJ: 12861, 12873

Airplane crashes — Fiction
JS: 47

Airplane pilots
IJ: 7666, 9539

Airplane pilots — African American
IJ: 12869–70

Airplane pilots — Biography
IJ: 5005, 5025, 5027, 5046, 5048–49,
5069, 6236, 8661, 12869 **J:** 5012, 5047,
6272 **JS:** 5065–68, 5076

Airplane pilots — Canada
IJ: 12883

Airplane pilots — Careers
IJ: 10715

Airplane pilots — Fiction
IJ: 3415

Airplane pilots — Women
IJ: 5028, 5758, 6256, 7740 **J:** 5012,
7761 **JS:** 4998

**Airplane pilots — Women —
Biography**
IJ: 5026

Airplanes
IJ: 12865, 12867, 12871, 12874, 12876
JS: 9812

Airplanes — Accidents
JS: 12863

Airplanes — Armed forces
JS: 12880

Airplanes — Biography
IJ: 6516, 6519–22 **JS:** 6518

Airplanes — Careers
JS: 10724

Airplanes — Fiction
IJ: 36, 3143 **J:** 3407

Airplanes — History
IJ: 6291, 7625, 12859–60, 12878,
12881–83 **J:** 12858 **JS:** 5045, 5064,
6517

Airplanes — Safety
JS: 12864

Airplanes (model)
IJ: 13118, 13123

Airships
IJ: 12862

Akamba (African people)
JS: 7920

Al Qaeda — Biography
IJ: 6843 **JS:** 6841

Al-Qaeda (terrorist group)
IJ: 10576

Alabama
IJ: 9581, 9585, 9590

Alabama — Fiction
IJ: 618

Alamo, Battle of the
IJ: 6194, 9041, 9046, 9603 **J:** 9043

Alamo, Battle of the — Fiction
IJ: 2918–19

Alamo (TX)
IJ: 6193, 9017, 9056

Alamo (TX) — Biography
IJ: 6990

Alaska
IJ: 8802, 9525, 9527, 9539, 9549–50,
13244 **J:** 9528, 9541 **JS:** 12227,
13282

Alaska — Fiction
IJ: 28, 75, 81, 107, 161, 187, 193, 221,
309, 2430 **JS:** 114, 149, 1730

Alaska — History
IJ: 9235 **JS:** 5002, 9242

Alaska — Oil spills
See Exxon Valdez oil spill; Oil spills

Alaska Gold Rush
See Gold Rush (Alaska and Yukon)

Alaska Purchase
IJ: 9235 **JS:** 9242

Alateen
J: 11011

Alba, Jessica
IJ: 5506

Albanians — Fiction
IJ: 2687

Alberta (Canada)
IJ: 8501

Albinism
IJ: 11485

Albinos — Fiction
IJ: 1194 **JS:** 1229, 1622

Albright, Madeleine
IJ: 6052 **J:** 6054 **JS:** 6051, 6053

Alcatraz Island
IJ: 9542 **JS:** 9518

Alcatraz Island — Fiction
IJ: 32

Alchemy — Fiction
JS: 2247

Alcohol
IJ: 10910, 10930, 10932, 10942, 10959,
10991 **J:** 10907, 10945, 10981, 10983
JS: 10900, 10909, 10913, 10929,
10933–34, 10948, 10962, 10968, 10980,
11005, 11021

Alcohol — Fiction
IJ: 3230 **JS:** 1862

Alcohol — Health problems
J: 10981

Alcohol — Teenagers
JS: 10951

Alcoholism
See also Drugs and drug abuse
IJ: 10942, 10959 **J:** 10945, 10983,
11011 **JS:** 10893, 10899–900, 10905,
10923, 10933, 10951, 10968, 10998–99,
11005, 11008, 11010

Alcoholism — Biography
IJ: 6261

Alcoholism — Fiction
IJ: 617, 823, 903, 1149, 1155, 1426,
1490 **J:** 724, 1205 **JS:** 662, 754, 861,
1075, 1077, 1433, 1605, 1661, 1697

Alcott, Louisa May
IJ: 5314–16

Aleuts — Fiction
JS: 3342

Alexander, Sally Hobart
JS: 6181

Alexander the Great
IJ: 6881

Alexandria (Egypt)
JS: 7446

Alexandrian Library
IJ: 7506

Algeria
IJ: 7928

Algonquin Indians
IJ: 8846

Algonquin Indians — History
JS: 8806

Ali, Muhammad
J: 6683 **JS:** 6680–82, 6684, 9397

Alien abductions
JS: 11941

Aliens
See Extraterrestrial life; Illegal aliens;
Immigration (U.S.)

**All-American Girls Professional
Baseball League**
IJ: 13351 **J:** 13336, 13341

Allen, Ethan
IJ: 6182

Allen, Richard
IJ: 6183

Allen, Tim
J: 5507

Allergies
IJ: 11102, 11133, 11153 **JS:** 11064,
11110, 11167

Alligators — Fiction
J: 290

Alligators and crocodiles
IJ: 7287, 12131–32, 12132–33

Allowances (money)
IJ: 10849

Almanacs
IJ: 7237

IJ = Upper Elementary/Lower Middle School; J = Middle School/Junior High; JS = Junior High/Senior High

Alomar, Roberto
JS: 6586

Alonso, Alicia
JS: 5508

Alou, Moises
JS: 6587

Alpacas — Fiction
IJ: 1401

Alphabet books
IJ: 4955, 4958, 5193, 11824

Alphabets
J: 4951

Alphabets — History
IJ: 4964, 10687 JS: 4970

Alternative energy
JS: 10318, 12689, 12693

Alternative medicine
J: 11217 JS: 11206, 11227

Aluminum
IJ: 12429

Alvarez, Luis
IJ: 6331

Alzheimer's disease
IJ: 1167, 11082 J: 11035 JS: 11090, 11103, 11199

Alzheimer's disease — Fiction
IJ: 1053, 1794 J: 4044 JS: 124, 1035

Amazing Grace **(hymn)**
IJ: 6234

Amazon (company) — Biography
IJ: 6347

Amazon River
IJ: 4830, 8585, 8625, 12493, 12504 JS: 8591, 12001, 12496

Amazon River — Exploration
J: 8588

Amazon River — Fiction
IJ: 215

Ambulances
IJ: 10527

Amelia Earhart
JS: 5045

America — Discovery and exploration
IJ: 5029, 5031, 7365

America — Pre-Columbian
IJ: 8476

American culture
JS: 10308

American Red Cross
IJ: 6060

American Revolution
See Revolutionary War (U.S.)

American Sign Language
See Sign language

Ameru (African people)
JS: 7918

Amish
IJ: 9696 J: 9714 JS: 9680

Amish — Fiction
IJ: 666, 1585–86 JS: 1340

Amistad **mutiny**
IJ: 9037, 9047 J: 9872 JS: 9062

Amnesia — Fiction
JS: 1321, 3443

Amphetamines
J: 10915

Amphibians
See also specific animal names, e.g., Frogs and toads
IJ: 12128, 12143, 12507 JS: 12108, 12129–30

Amphibians — Evolution
IJ: 7279

Amputations — Fiction
JS: 1285

Amsterdam — History
JS: 7789

Amusement parks — Fiction
IJ: 3936

Anagrams
IJ: 4944

Anasazi Indians
IJ: 8751

Anasazi Indians — History
IJ: 9601 J: 8754

Anatomy
See Human body

Ancient history
IJ: 7319, 7394–95 J: 7397 JS: 6824, 7402, 7494

Ancient history — Wars
JS: 7392

Ancient world — Art
JS: 7084

Anderson, Marian
JS: 5509–10

Andersonville Prison — Fiction
IJ: 3023 JS: 3015

Andreessen, Marc
IJ: 6332

Andretti, Mario
J: 6579

Andrews, Roy Chapman
IJ: 6333–34

Angel dust (drug)
See also Drugs and drug abuse
IJ: 10894 JS: 10921

Angelou, Maya
IJ: 5317–18, 5321 J: 5319 JS: 5320, 5322

Angelou, Maya — Criticism
JS: 4907

Angels
JS: 9667

Angels — Fiction
IJ: 1293

Anger
IJ: 11606

Anger — Fiction
IJ: 1257 J: 148

Anglo Saxons — Fiction
JS: 2548

Angola
IJ: 7949 JS: 7905, 7957, 7967

Anielewicz, Mordechai
IJ: 6882

Animal rescues — Fiction
IJ: 110

Animal rights
JS: 10295

Animal welfare
IJ: 12103

Animals
IJ: 12008, 12014, 12112, 12117, 12124–25, 12166, 12168 JS: 12123

Animals — Ark
IJ: 9615

Animals — Art
IJ: 13078

Animals — Australia
J: 12164

Animals — Babies
IJ: 12158

Animals — Behavior
IJ: 12148–50, 12152–55

Animals — Cannibalism
IJ: 12152

Animals — Care — Careers
IJ: 10713–14, 10716, 10723 J: 10705 JS: 10720

Animals — Care — Volunteerism
JS: 10539

Animals — Circuses
IJ: 7179

Animals — Classification
IJ: 12016, 12125

Animals — Defenses
IJ: 12151

Animals — Experimentation
IJ: 12126 J: 10257, 12106 JS: 10272

Animals — Experiments and projects
IJ: 12104, 12153

Animals — Extinct
JS: 12110

Animals — Fiction
IJ: 29, 255, 270, 292, 321, 501, 1264 J: 326

Animals — Flight
IJ: 12872

Animals — Folklore
IJ: 4676–77, 4786, 4788, 4812 JS: 4798

Animals — Food
IJ: 12151

Animals — Habitats
IJ: 12115, 12507

IJ = Upper Elementary/Lower Middle School; J = Middle School/Junior High; JS = Junior High/Senior High

IJ = Upper Elementary/Lower Middle School; J = Middle School/Junior High; JS = Junior High/Senior High

IJ = Upper Elementary/Lower Middle School; J = Middle School/Junior High; JS = Junior High/Senior High

IJ = Upper Elementary/Lower Middle School; J = Middle School/Junior High; JS = Junior High/Senior High

Autism
IJ: 11435 J: 11398 JS: 11413, 11424, 11434

Autism — Fiction
IJ: 1082

Automation
See also Computers; Robots
JS: 12820

Automobile accidents — Fiction
IJ: 1337 JS: 778, 1254, 1601, 1767

Automobile driving — Fiction
JS: 1385

Automobile racing
IJ: 12887, 13147, 13323–24, 13326–27

Automobile racing — Biography
IJ: 6580–81 J: 6579

Automobile racing — Fiction
JS: 4255

Automobiles
IJ: 12886, 13325 JS: 12888

Automobiles — Biography
IJ: 6409 J: 6408 JS: 6410

Automobiles — Fiction
J: 4088

Automobiles — History
IJ: 12889–90 JS: 12884

Avalanches
IJ: 12616

Avalanches — Fiction
IJ: 2744

Avalon — Fiction
IJ: 2264

Avery, Oswald
IJ: 6337

Avi (author)
IJ: 5326 JS: 5327

Aviation
See also Airplanes
IJ: 12868

Aviation — Fiction
J: 730

Aviation — History
IJ: 12859, 12866

Azerbaijan
IJ: 8310

Aztecs
See also Mexico — History
IJ: 8533, 8543, 8548–49, 8552, 8554, 8561, 8564 JS: 8542, 8551

Aztecs — Crafts
IJ: 8537, 8545

Aztecs — Fiction
JS: 2745

Aztecs — Folklore
IJ: 4692

Aztecs — History
JS: 8534, 8538

Aztecs — Mythology
IJ: 4776 J: 4831

Aztecs — Poetry
JS: 8536, 1066, 1349

B

Babies — Fiction
IJ: 739, 1066, 1349

Baboons — Fiction
JS: 2570

Baby boom (post World War II)
JS: 9373

Baby-sitting
IJ: 10841–44

Baby-sitting — Fiction
IJ: 2429, 3647, 3675, 3929 J: 1591
JS: 1105, 1668, 3481

Babylon 5 (television series)
JS: 4134, 7209

Bacon, Roger — Fiction
IJ: 2540

Bacon's Rebellion — Fiction
IJ: 2816

Bacteria
See also Germs
JS: 12365

Bacteriology — Biography
IJ: 6406 JS: 6405

Badgers — Fiction
IJ: 259, 2149

Badminton
IJ: 13519

Bagpipes — Fiction
IJ: 3805

Baha'i faith
JS: 9638

Bahamas — Fiction
JS: 3897

Bahrain
IJ: 8449 JS: 8458

Bailey, Anne
JS: 6184

Balanchine, George
IJ: 5513

Bald eagles
IJ: 12249 JS: 12243

Baldwin, James
JS: 5328

Balkans
IJ: 8199 J: 8205 JS: 8193

Balkans — Fiction
IJ: 2688

Ball, Charles
IJ: 6185

Ballet
IJ: 7180, 7184–86 JS: 7181

Ballet — Biography
IJ: 5513, 5636, 5646 J: 5560
JS: 5508, 5576

Ballet — Fiction
IJ: 1328, 1681, 1737 JS: 469, 635, 1219, 4065

Ballet — Stories
IJ: 7183

Ballooning
IJ: 13318

Ballooning — Fiction
IJ: 783

Balloons — Experiments and projects
IJ: 12579

Ballroom dancing — Fiction
JS: 3791

Baltimore (MD) — Fiction
IJ: 1384, 3261

Baltimore Orioles (baseball team)
IJ: 13363

Bands (music)
IJ: 7121, 7126 J: 7120

Bands (music) — Fiction
JS: 405

Bangladesh
IJ: 8061, 8065, 8072, 8076, 8084

Banks, Tyra
IJ: 5514

Banks and banking — Biography
IJ: 6510 JS: 6476

Banneker, Benjamin
IJ: 6338 JS: 6339

Bar mitzvah
IJ: 9743

Bar mitzvah — Fiction
IJ: 586 J: 1710

Barbados — Fiction
IJ: 2830

Barkley, Charles
IJ: 6624–25

Barnum, P. T.
IJ: 5703–5 J: 5701 JS: 5702

Barr, Roseanne
IJ: 5515

Barrie, J. M.
IJ: 5329

Barton, Clara
IJ: 6060–61

Baseball
IJ: 13330, 13330, 13335, 13338, 13343–47, 13349, 13353–54, 13357, 13360–63 JS: 13329, 13332–33, 13348, 13355–56, 13358

Baseball — Biography
IJ: 6532–34, 6553, 6568, 6573, 6583–85, 6588–95, 6597–603, 6605–7, 6609, 6611–14, 6616–18, 6621–22, 6700, 13342–44 J: 6541 JS: 6529, 6582, 6586–87, 6596, 6604, 6608, 6610, 6615, 6619–20

Baseball — Fiction
IJ: 423, 600, 830, 945, 1000, 1001, 1604, 1975, 2087, 3539, 3638, 4273–74,

IJ = Upper Elementary/Lower Middle School; J = Middle School/Junior High; JS = Junior High/Senior High

IJ = Upper Elementary/Lower Middle School; J = Middle School/Junior High; JS = Junior High/Senior High

IJ = Upper Elementary/Lower Middle School; J = Middle School/Junior High; JS = Junior High/Senior High

IJ = Upper Elementary/Lower Middle School; J = Middle School/Junior High; JS = Junior High/Senior High

IJ = Upper Elementary/Lower Middle School; J = Middle School/Junior High; JS = Junior High/Senior High

Bullock, Sandra
IJ: 5530

Bullying — Fiction
JS: 1772

Bunche, Ralph
JS: 6071

Burial customs
IJ: 7311, 7418, 7453 JS: 10870

Buried treasure
IJ: 7331, 7360, 9426, 9484 JS: 8255

Buried treasure — Fiction
IJ: 20, 71, 223, 225

Burke, Chris
IJ: 5531

Burma
See Myanmar (Burma)

Burma — Biography
J: 6870–71

Burnett, Frances Hodgson
IJ: 5336

Burns — Fiction
IJ: 1406 J: 1297

Burns, Anthony
JS: 5800

Burr, Aaron
IJ: 6072

Burroughs, Edgar Rice
IJ: 5337

Burroughs, John
IJ: 6353

Bush, George H. W.
JS: 5903–5

Bush, George W.
IJ: 5906–7, 5909–12 JS: 5908, 9818

Bush, Laura Welch
IJ: 5913

Bush pilots — Alaska
IJ: 9539

Business
See also Capitalism; Economics;
Money-making ideas
IJ: 10595–96, 10615 JS: 9921, 10594

Business — Biography
IJ: 6299, 6309, 6332, 6346–47, 6360,
6375, 6377, 6427, 6448–49, 6451, 6495,
6502, 9212 J: 6289, 6307, 6509
JS: 6293, 6313–14, 6354, 6381, 6437,
6501

Business — Careers
JS: 10597

Business — History
J: 9173, 9252

Business — Sports
IJ: 13261

Business management
JS: 10839

Butcher, Susan
IJ: 6771

Butler, Jerry
IJ: 7104

Butterflies and moths
IJ: 12295–96, 12296, 12299
JS: 12297–98

Butterflies and moths — Fiction
IJ: 2118 JS: 296

Byars, Betsy
IJ: 5338–39

Byrd, Admiral Richard Evelyn
IJ: 5019

Byzantine Empire
IJ: 7578

Byzantium — Fiction
IJ: 2517

C

Cabeza de Vaca, Alvar Nunez
IJ: 5020

Cable television
JS: 6506

Cabot, John
IJ: 5021

Cactus
IJ: 12088

Caesar, Augustus
IJ: 6891 J: 6890

Caesar, Julius
IJ: 6894, 7531, 7534 JS: 6892–93,
7522

Caffeine
JS: 10853, 10855

Cahokia Mounds (IL)
IJ: 8787

Cahuilla Indians — Fiction
JS: 2119

Cajun people
IJ: 9564

Cajun people — Fiction
IJ: 2972

Cajun people — Folklore
IJ: 4816

Calamity Jane
IJ: 6197

Calcium
IJ: 12430 J: 12421

Calculation (mathematics)
IJ: 12557

Calder, Alexander
J: 5185

Calendars
See also Time
IJ: 12557

California
IJ: 9515, 9517, 9532, 9545, 9547

California — Biography
IJ: 5095, 6169, 6983

California — Fiction
IJ: 32, 162, 1047, 1734, 3047, 3050,
3059, 3220, 3514 J: 181, 461, 3049,
3107, 3353, 4018, 4080 JS: 144, 288,
1588, 2959, 3093

California — History
IJ: 5093, 8713, 8868, 9514, 9516,
9521–22, 9524, 9529, 9533, 9538, 9540,
9556, 9558, 9560 J: 5094 JS: 7171,
9531

California Gold Rush
See Gold Rush (California)

California Indians
IJ: 8827

California Trail
JS: 9164

Calligraphy
IJ: 13075, 13090 J: 4951 JS: 13084

Calusa Indians — Fiction
IJ: 43

Calvin, John
JS: 6895

Cambodia
IJ: 8115, 8139

Cambodia — Fiction
IJ: 2588 J: 2589

Cambodian Americans
IJ: 10087 JS: 10178

Camcorders
JS: 12844

Camden Yards (Baltimore)
IJ: 13363

Cameras
IJ: 13133

Cameroon
IJ: 7989 JS: 7880, 8008

Campbell, Ben Nighthorse
IJ: 6073

Campfires
IJ: 13412

Camps and camping
IJ: 13412, 13414 JS: 13422

Camps and camping — Fiction
IJ: 69, 120, 152, 224, 291, 510, 531,
1379, 1513, 3172, 3644, 3659, 3702,
3823 J: 1375, 1764, 3697 JS: 35, 478,
976, 1595, 1679, 1752, 3901, 3965,
4067

Canada
IJ: 7384, 8483–86, 8492, 8497–99,
8501 JS: 8480

Canada — Biography
IJ: 6760 JS: 6761

Canada — Fiction
IJ: 57, 335, 617, 723, 1011, 1110, 1954,
2728–29, 2731, 2733–35, 2740–41,
2750, 2753–54, 2758, 3674, 3986, 3993,
4363 J: 27, 153, 166, 170, 1032, 1174,
1301, 3259, 3403 JS: 73, 98, 108, 126,
256, 334, 442, 493, 624, 952, 1124,
1339, 1683, 1884, 2797, 3386, 4014

IJ = Upper Elementary/Lower Middle School; J = Middle School/Junior High; JS = Junior High/Senior High

Canada — History
IJ: 2761, 8489, 8932 J: 8495
JS: 8487, 8494

Canada — Poetry
IJ: 4652

Canada — Scientists
IJ: 6318

Canals
IJ: 8517, 8974, 12851

Canals — Fiction
IJ: 2924

Cancer
IJ: 11101, 11104, 11122, 11204
JS: 11037, 11048, 11071, 11087, 11181

Cancer — Fiction
IJ: 495, 771, 923 J: 1397 JS: 398,
645, 794, 1219, 1231, 1680, 1825,
4050–51

Candlemaking — Fiction
IJ: 2374

Canoes and canoeing
JS: 13476

Canoes and canoeing — Fiction
IJ: 69

Canseco, José
IJ: 6592

**Canyonlands National Park —
Fiction**
JS: 112

Cape Cod — Fiction
IJ: 401 JS: 737

Cape Town
IJ: 7966

Capital punishment
See Death penalty

Capitalism
IJ: 10598

Capoeira (martial art)
IJ: 13453

Capone, Al
IJ: 6198 J: 6199

Captal punishment

Carbon
J: 12422

Card games
IJ: 13420

Card tricks
See Tricks

Careers
See also Vocational guidance; and
specific fields, e.g., Business —
Careers
IJ: 7118, 10698–99, 10708, 10710,
10712–16, 10718, 10721, 10723,
10725–29, 10734, 10737–38, 10741–42,
10746–47, 10749, 10755, 10758–59,
10766, 10768–69, 10773, 10775,
10785–86, 10788–92, 10797, 10801,
10804, 10810–11, 10813–14, 10821,
10834 J: 10702, 10748, 10763–64,
10777, 10793, 10795, 10822
JS: 10622, 10700–1, 10703–4, 10707,

10709, 10711, 10717, 10719–20, 10722,
10724, 10730–33, 10735–36, 10739,
10743–45, 10750–54, 10756, 10761–62,
10765, 10767, 10770–72, 10774, 10776,
10778–84, 10787, 10796, 10798–800,
10802–3, 10805, 10807–9, 10815–17,
10820, 10823–25, 10832, 10836

Careers — Guidance
JS: 10697

Careers — Motion pictures
JS: 7195

Careers — Sports
JS: 10760

Careers — Women
IJ: 10806

Carey, Mariah
IJ: 5532, 5534 JS: 5533

Caribbean Islands
IJ: 8568, 8577 JS: 8565

Caribbean Islands — Cookbooks
IJ: 13018

Caribbean Islands — Crafts
IJ: 12981

Caribbean Islands — Fiction
IJ: 59, 210, 213, 2732, 2738, 2843
JS: 759

Carle, Eric
IJ: 5186

Carnegie, Andrew
JS: 6354

Carnivorous plants
IJ: 12089

Carols
See Christmas — Songs and carols

Carpenters — Biography
IJ: 5210

Carr, Emily
IJ: 5187–88

Carrey, Jim
IJ: 5535

Carroll, Lewis
J: 5340

Cars
See Automobiles

Carson, Rachel
IJ: 6355, 6357–58 J: 6356 JS: 6359

Carter, Jimmy
IJ: 5754, 5914–19 JS: 5920

Carter, Rosalynn
IJ: 5916

Carter, Vince
IJ: 6630

Carthage
IJ: 6929 JS: 7527

Cartier, Jacques
IJ: 8489

Cartoonists
JS: 5295

Cartoons
IJ: 5214, 13086–88, 13092 JS: 7108,
13076, 13085

Cartoons — Biography
IJ: 5216, 5260 J: 5156

Cartoons — Fiction
IJ: 3627

**Carver, George Washington —
Poetry**
JS: 4614

Cary, Elizabeth
JS: 6896

Casals, Pablo
IJ: 5536

Case, Steve
IJ: 6360

Cassatt, Mary
IJ: 5189–90, 5192 J: 5191

Cassidy, Butch
IJ: 6200–1

Castles
See also Middle Ages
IJ: 7035, 7037, 7040, 7048, 7558, 7562,
7573, 7589, 12921, 12923 J: 7569
JS: 7047, 7546, 7561

Castles — Fiction
IJ: 2010, 2149, 2428

Castro, Fidel
IJ: 6980–82 JS: 6979

***The Catcher in the Rye* — Criticism**
JS: 4912, 4919

Caterpillars — Folklore
IJ: 4724

Cathedrals
IJ: 7039, 7041 JS: 7038

Cather, Willa
IJ: 5343 JS: 5341–42

Catholicism — Biography
J: 6941 JS: 6896

Catholicism — History
JS: 7588

Cats
See also Big cats
IJ: 12374–75, 12377, 13071
JS: 12376

Cats — Behavior
JS: 12378

Cats — Fiction
IJ: 321, 2233, 2271 J: 1647 JS: 1483,
1949, 2391

Cats — Poetry
IJ: 4506

Catskill Mountains — Fiction
IJ: 3461 J: 77

Catt, Carrie Chapman
IJ: 5801

Cattle drives
IJ: 9180, 9192

Cattle drives — Fiction
IJ: 177, 3207

IJ = Upper Elementary/Lower Middle School; J = Middle School/Junior High; JS = Junior High/Senior High

IJ = Upper Elementary/Lower Middle School; J = Middle School/Junior High; JS = Junior High/Senior High

IJ = Upper Elementary/Lower Middle School; J = Middle School/Junior High; JS = Junior High/Senior High

Christmas — Poetry
IJ: 4496, 4562 JS: 4494

Christmas — Songs and carols
JS: 7169

Chronic fatigue syndrome
IJ: 11032

Church and state — United States
See also Freedom of religion
J: 9890 JS: 9853, 9878

Churches — History
IJ: 7563

Churchill, Sir Winston
IJ: 6899–902

Cickamauga, Battle of
JS: 9086

Cid, El
IJ: 5023

Cinderella — Fiction
J: 2056

Circulatory system
IJ: 11322, 11324 JS: 11292, 11323

Circuses
IJ: 7178, 7221 JS: 5702, 7218

Circuses — Animals
IJ: 7179

Circuses — Biography
IJ: 5703–5 J: 5701

Circuses — Fiction
IJ: 61, 3173, 3646 J: 2502 JS: 1229, 1911

Cisneros, Sandra
IJ: 5347

Cities and city life
See also names of specific cities, e.g., Boston (MA)
IJ: 503, 10589–90, 12765 J: 10591, 11855

Cities and city life — Fiction
IJ: 968, 1021 JS: 4409

Cities and city life — History
IJ: 8674

Cities and city life — Pollution
IJ: 10312

Citizenship (U.S.)
IJ: 9940

Civil disobedience
JS: 10512

Civil engineering
JS: 12737

Civil liberties
JS: 9984

Civil rights
See also names of civil rights leaders, e.g., King, Martin Luther, Jr.; and specific civil rights, e.g., Human rights; Women's rights
IJ: 5735, 5833, 5835, 5838–40, 5857, 9351, 9371, 9392, 9951–53, 9958, 9966, 9983, 9988, 9990–91, 10000–3, 10026, 10028, 10044, 10048, 10060 J: 9943, 9964, 9970, 9980, 10033, 10037

JS: 5736, 8710, 9353, 9356, 9365, 9387, 9804, 9852, 9859, 9869, 9873, 9902, 9905, 9914, 9948, 9950, 9955–56, 9959, 9963, 9967–69, 9971–73, 9975, 9978, 9985, 9992, 9997, 10004, 10006–9, 10011, 10013, 10015, 10017, 10020, 10029–31, 10034, 10036, 10045, 10050, 10052–55, 10057, 10059, 10061, 10064, 10166, 10506, 10516, 11576

Civil rights — Biography
IJ: 5732, 5739, 5791, 5797, 5813, 5821, 5826, 5830–31, 5842, 5847, 5856, 5858, 5870–71, 5873, 6259, 6793 J: 5836, 5851–52, 5854, 6830 JS: 5780, 5786, 5790, 5793–94, 5805, 5814, 5825, 5832, 5834, 5841, 5843, 5849–50, 5853, 5855, 5859–61, 5867, 5874, 5878, 5891, 6175, 6992, 9955

Civil rights — Fiction
IJ: 616 J: 3283 JS: 673

Civil rights — Students
See also specific groups, e.g., Teenagers — Civil rights

Civil War (U.S.)
See also names of specific battles, e.g., Gettysburg, Battle of; and names of individuals, e.g., Lee, Robert E.
IJ: 5940, 5943, 5982, 6087, 6109, 6119, 6204, 8968, 9050, 9064–70, 9073–74, 9076, 9078–80, 9087, 9089, 9092–95, 9097–98, 9101–2, 9106, 9108, 9112, 9115, 9117, 9122–23, 9126, 9131, 9134–38, 9143, 9145, 10016 J: 9100, 9114, 9118, 9121, 9178 JS: 5184, 5986, 9054, 9071–72, 9075, 9077, 9082–86, 9088, 9091, 9099, 9103–5, 9113, 9116, 9120, 9124–25, 9127, 9132–33, 9140–42, 9146

Civil War (U.S.) — African Americans
IJ: 9107

Civil War (U.S.) — Art
IJ: 9119

Civil War (U.S.) — Battles
JS: 9090

Civil War (U.S.) — Biography
IJ: 5183, 5710, 5718, 5727–28, 6060, 6081–82, 6111–12, 6117, 6120, 6161–62, 6166, 6191 J: 5941, 5985, 6121 JS: 5942, 6083, 6110, 6118

Civil War (U.S.) — Children
IJ: 9144

Civil War (U.S.) — Cookbooks
IJ: 9096 JS: 13004

Civil War (U.S.) — Experiments and projects
IJ: 9110

Civil War (U.S.) — Fiction
IJ: 1962, 2961–62, 2964–66, 2969–72, 2975–76, 2978–79, 2983–88, 2990, 2992–93, 2996–98, 3000–1, 3003, 3005, 3007, 3009–10, 3012–13, 3018, 3020–24 J: 2784, 2948, 2963, 2973, 2981–82, 2994, 3008, 3011, 3019 JS: 381, 2925, 2960, 2967–68, 2974,

2977, 2980, 2989, 2991, 2999, 3002, 3004, 3014–17, 3025

Civil War (U.S.) — Navies
IJ: 9128, 9138

Civil War (U.S.) — Prisons
IJ: 9129

Civil War (U.S.) — Songs
J: 7176

Civil War (U.S.) — Weapons
IJ: 9081

Civil War (U.S.) — Women
IJ: 9130, 9147

Civilization
JS: 10308

Clark, Eugenie
IJ: 6361

Clark, William
JS: 5062

Clay modeling
IJ: 12989 JS: 12991

Cleanliness
See Hygiene

Cleary, Beverly
JS: 5348–49

Clemenceau, Georges
JS: 6903

Clemens, Arabella
J: 5024

Clemente, Roberto
IJ: 6593–95

Cleopatra
IJ: 6826, 7443 JS: 6823–25

Cleopatra — Fiction
IJ: 2513, 2559

Clergy
IJ: 5837

Cleveland, Grover
J: 5921

Climate
See also Weather
IJ: 12575, 12623 J: 12574

Clinton, Bill
IJ: 5923–24, 5926–27, 9352 J: 5922
JS: 5925, 9810

Clinton, Bill — Impeachment
J: 9805

Clinton, Hillary Rodham
IJ: 5928 J: 5929

Cliques — Fiction
IJ: 1715, 1749

Clocks and watches
See also Time
JS: 12660

Clones and cloning
See also Genetics; Genetic engineering
IJ: 11024, 11241, 11247, 11251–52, 11254 J: 11248 JS: 10863, 10865, 11242, 11246, 11253, 11259–61

IJ = Upper Elementary/Lower Middle School; J = Middle School/Junior High; JS = Junior High/Senior High

Clones and cloning — Fiction
IJ: 4180 JS: 4192

Close, Chuck
JS: 5199

Clothing and dress
See also Costumes and costume
making; Dress codes; Fashion
design; Shoes
IJ: 12776

Clothing and dress — Fiction
IJ: 12773

Clothing and dress — History
IJ: 8719, 9277, 9382, 9385–86, 12774,
13065 JS: 8669, 12775, 13058, 13060

Cloud forest (Costa Rica)
J: 12491

Clowns
JS: 7228

Clowns — Fiction
JS: 1519

Clubs — Fiction
JS: 457

CNN (Cable Network News)
JS: 6506

Coaches (sports) — Careers
JS: 10765

Coal and coal mining — Fiction
IJ: 3141, 3162 J: 3284 JS: 3210

Coal and coal mining — History
IJ: 9233

Coast Guard (U.S.) — Careers
IJ: 10734

Cocaine
See also Drugs and drug abuse
IJ: 10984 J: 10916 JS: 10906, 10939

Cochran, Jacqueline
IJ: 5025

Codes
See Cryptograms and cryptography

Codes and ciphers
IJ: 4943 JS: 4940

Cody, Buffalo Bill
IJ: 6203, 7177

Cody, Buffalo Bill — Fiction
IJ: 2783, 3131

Coelacanths
IJ: 12329

Cold (disease)
JS: 11099

Cold War
IJ: 6130, 7828, 7852, 9348, 9390
J: 7823 JS: 7826, 7836, 8339, 9393

Cole, Nat King
IJ: 5147

Cole, Natalie
IJ: 5147

Coleman, Bessie
IJ: 5026–28

Coleridge, Samuel Taylor
JS: 4555

Collections and collecting
IJ: 13145, 13147

**Colleges and universities —
Admissions**
JS: 10624

Colleges and universities — Fiction
JS: 1232, 1368, 1626, 3772

Colombia
IJ: 8592, 8597, 8615

Colombia — Fiction
JS: 2743

Colombia — History
JS: 8589

Colonial period (U.S.)
IJ: 6067, 6213, 8673, 8693, 8883, 8885,
8887, 8889, 8891–94, 8897–99, 8901–9,
8911, 8913–15, 8917–19, 8923–24,
8928, 8930, 8932–33, 8937, 8939,
8941–42, 8945–46, 8950–52, 8955,
9476, 9588, 10138 J: 8934 JS: 5816,
8926, 8935

Colonial period (U.S.) — Biography
IJ: 5099, 5475, 6066, 6089, 6144, 6247,
6257 J: 6090 JS: 5890, 6093

Colonial period (U.S.) — Cookbooks
IJ: 8898

Colonial period (U.S.) — Crafts
IJ: 8947

Colonial period (U.S.) — Fiction
IJ: 2057, 2090, 2799, 2805–11,
2813–19, 2822, 2826, 2829–30, 2844
J: 2795, 2800, 2812, 2821, 2824, 2828,
2837, 2839 JS: 2801, 2803, 2823,
2825, 2831–33, 2836, 2845, 2847, 2877,
2893

Colonial period (U.S.) — History
IJ: 8895–96, 8910 J: 8925
JS: 8953–54

Colonial period (U.S.) — Medicine
IJ: 8744, 8949

Colonial period (U.S.) — Religion
IJ: 8888

Colonial period (U.S.) — Science
IJ: 8920

Colonial period (U.S.) — Speeches
JS: 8992

Color — Experiments and projects
IJ: 12710

Colorado
IJ: 9438, 9440

Colorado — Fiction
IJ: 1401, 3030, 3078, 3762 JS: 1696,
3615, 3877

Colorado — History
IJ: 8752, 8829, 9453

Colorado River
IJ: 8724, 9257, 9448, 12758

Colosseum (Rome)
IJ: 7510, 7519

Coltrane, John
JS: 5542–43

Columbus, Christopher
IJ: 5029, 5031 JS: 5030, 5032

Coma — Fiction
J: 1502

Comanche Indians
IJ: 8758 JS: 8828, 8852

Comanche Indians — Fiction
IJ: 3033 J: 2788 JS: 3098

Comanche Indians — History
IJ: 8833

Comedians — Biography
IJ: 5157, 5515, 5535, 5545, 5547, 5580,
5640–42, 5662, 5674 J: 5133, 5579
JS: 5546, 5577, 5627, 5634, 5689

Comets
IJ: 11958

Comic books
IJ: 2474, 3741, 4982, 10136, 13086–88,
13092 JS: 2458, 4983, 4987, 13089

Comic books — Careers
IJ: 10747

Comic books — Collecting
IJ: 13146

Comic books — Fiction
IJ: 2152 JS: 3793

Comic strips
JS: 11605

Comic strips — Fiction
J: 2456

Coming of age
JS: 10526

Coming of age — Fiction
JS: 1457, 1783

Commena, Anna
IJ: 2517

**Commonwealth of Independent
States**
See also specific states, e.g., Ukraine
IJ: 8338

Communication
IJ: 4942, 12793, 12836–37, 12839
J: 12833 JS: 4953, 10679

Communication — Careers
IJ: 10729

Communication — Computers
IJ: 12810

**Communication — Experiments
and projects**
J: 12834

Communication — History
IJ: 12752 J: 9244

Communication — Satellites
IJ: 12832

Communications — Careers
J: 10822

Communism
IJ: 6130, 10599 JS: 8229, 8323, 9393,
9395, 9850

Communism — Biography
JS: 6965

IJ = Upper Elementary/Lower Middle School; J = Middle School/Junior High; JS = Junior High/Senior High

IJ = Upper Elementary/Lower Middle School; J = Middle School/Junior High; JS = Junior High/Senior High

Cooking
See also Cookbooks
IJ: 11097

Cooking — Africa
IJ: 13030

Cooking — Fiction
JS: 4033

Cooking — History
JS: 13048

Coolidge, Calvin
JS: 5930

Cooper, Cynthia
IJ: 6631

Copernicus
IJ: 6362–63

Copper
IJ: 12418

Copts
JS: 7930

Coral reefs
IJ: 12007, 12320–24

Coretta Scott King Award
IJ: 5830

Corking (knitting)
IJ: 13137

Cormier, Robert — Criticism
JS: 4916

Cornwall (England) — Fiction
IJ: 2679

Corot, Jean Camille
IJ: 5200

Corporations
JS: 9921

Corporations — Executives
JS: 10597

Corporations — Power
JS: 9921

Corrigan, Mairead
IJ: 8252

Cortes, Hernando
JS: 8538, 8551

Corvette (automobile)
JS: 12888

Cosby, Bill
IJ: 5545, 5547 **JS:** 5546

Cosmetics — Biography
IJ: 6508

Cosmetics — Careers
JS: 10717

Cosmetics — History
IJ: 12771

Costa Rica
J: 12491

Costa Rica — Fiction
IJ: 3831

Costumes and costume making
IJ: 13059, 13064, 13067 **JS:** 13063, 13068

Cougars
JS: 12194

Cougars — Fiction
IJ: 1835

Country life — Fiction
J: 558

Country music — Biography
IJ: 5527, 5657–59 **JS:** 5529

Courage — Biography
IJ: 7001

Courage — Fiction
JS: 3950

Courlander, Harold
JS: 5351

Courtroom trials
IJ: 9868, 9897 **J:** 9847, 9862, 9872, 9890, 9895, 9908 **JS:** 9848, 9850–51, 9857, 9866–67, 9869–70, 9873, 9878–79, 9881–85, 9887, 9889, 9894, 9900–2, 9905, 9910–12, 9914, 9969, 9974, 10046, 10510, 10512

Courts (U.S.)
See also Jury system; Supreme Court (U.S.)
J: 9847 **JS:** 9855, 9861, 9889, 9906, 9979

Courts (U.S.) — History
J: 9863

Cowboys
IJ: 9162, 9198, 9205, 9280 **J:** 9200

Cowboys — African Americans
IJ: 9155

Cowboys — Biography
IJ: 5664

Cowboys — Cookbooks
IJ: 9166

Cowboys — Fiction
IJ: 1490, 1580, 3038, 3104, 3124, 3130
JS: 196

Cowboys — History
IJ: 8506, 9189, 9211 **J:** 9220
JS: 9183

Cowboys — Mexico
IJ: 8532

Cowboys — Songs
IJ: 7165

Cowgirls
IJ: 10737 **J:** 9204

Coyotes
IJ: 12207

Crack (drug)
IJ: 10984 **JS:** 10906, 10939

Crafts
See also specific crafts, e.g., Paper crafts
IJ: 7260, 7426, 7476, 7503, 7514, 8143, 8162, 8361, 8366, 8539, 8545, 11852, 12953–54, 12956, 12958–59, 12962, 12965–69, 12971, 12974, 12976–78, 12980–81, 12984–88, 12992, 13059–70, 13073–74, 13113, 13116–17, 13124,

13138, 13140, 13275 **J:** 12964, 12975
JS: 12955, 12963

Crafts — Greece
IJ: 7471

Crafts — Historical
IJ: 8947

Crafts — Rome
IJ: 7509

Crafts — Weaving
IJ: 12972

Cranes (bird)
IJ: 12226

Crazy Horse
IJ: 6075 **JS:** 6076–78

Creation — Mythology
IJ: 9651 **JS:** 4693

Creationism
JS: 7312, 7314

Cree Indians — Art
J: 8822

Crick, Francis
IJ: 6271

Crickets
IJ: 12288

Crime and criminals
IJ: 7355, 9165, 9380, 10384–85, 10388, 10402, 10404, 10411–12, 10416, 10428, 10435, 10448, 10452–53, 10457, 10467
J: 9909, 10260, 10391, 10397, 10417, 10421, 10441, 10451, 10458, 10461
JS: 6288, 9859, 9886, 9889, 9896, 9916, 10386–87, 10389, 10395, 10431–33, 10439, 10444–45, 10447, 10456, 10465, 10468–70, 10938, 10967, 12798

Crime and criminals — Biography
IJ: 6201, 6216, 6218, 6253 **J:** 6199, 6231 **JS:** 6249

Crime and criminals — Fiction
IJ: 1539, 3632 **J:** 17, 782 **JS:** 1103, 4275

Crime laboratories — Experiments and projects
J: 10406

Crimean War
JS: 7594–95

Crimean War — Biography
IJ: 7019

Criminal justice
J: 9858, 10391, 10406, 10417
JS: 9861, 9886, 10433, 10439

Criminals

Croatian Americans — Fiction
IJ: 3243

Crocheting
IJ: 13136

Crocodiles
See Alligators and crocodiles

Cromwell, Oliver
JS: 8271

IJ = Upper Elementary/Lower Middle School; J = Middle School/Junior High; JS = Junior High/Senior High

IJ = Upper Elementary/Lower Middle School; J = Middle School/Junior High; JS = Junior High/Senior High

Deafness and the deaf — Biography
IJ: 6222

Deafness and the deaf — Fiction
IJ: 337, 413 J: 1432 JS: 2530

Dean, James
JS: 5554

Death
IJ: 10873, 10878, 10880, 10883, 10887, 10889, 12004 JS: 4895, 10382, 10868, 10870–71, 10874–76, 10879, 10881, 10885–86, 10888, 10890, 11141, 11200, 11619

Death — Customs
IJ: 7351

Death — Fiction
IJ: 74, 182, 240, 245, 267, 409, 418, 468, 547, 735, 751, 771, 788, 839, 894, 922–23, 955, 966, 1000, 1018, 1039, 1056, 1070, 1080, 1104, 1134, 1138, 1169, 1172, 1228, 1240, 1287, 1293, 1298, 1337, 1342, 1365, 1371, 1470, 1484, 1491, 1532, 1547, 1551, 1571, 1613, 1646, 1704, 1777, 1780, 1810, 2321, 2358, 2366, 2619, 3053, 3068, 3312, 3760, 4258 J: 744, 939, 1096, 1359, 1372, 1429, 1556, 1598, 1629, 1666, 1768, 2032, 2297, 3048, 3408, 3818, 4352 JS: 439, 442, 498, 526, 745, 748, 775, 778, 786, 794, 826, 852, 933, 978, 990, 993, 1015, 1073, 1075, 1102, 1114, 1139, 1183, 1191, 1218–19, 1336, 1341, 1353, 1385, 1403, 1438, 1463, 1483, 1579, 1590, 1601, 1603, 1612, 1669, 1676–77, 1691, 1769, 1791, 1795, 1811, 1814, 1820, 1824–25, 2119, 3486, 3813, 3902, 3917, 4007, 4014, 4051, 4359

Death — Poetry
JS: 4479

Death penalty
See also Capital punishment
IJ: 9877 J: 9908–9, 9915 JS: 9865, 9871, 9874–75, 9881–82, 9892–93, 9907

Death Valley
IJ: 9163

de Aviles, Pedro Menendez
IJ: 8876

Decathlon
IJ: 13312

Decathlon — Biography
IJ: 6762

Declaration of Independence (U.S.)
IJ: 8963, 8978–79

Decomposition
IJ: 12004

de Coronado, Francisco Vasquez
IJ: 8881

Deer
JS: 12211

Deer — Fiction
IJ: 240, 327, 4688 J: 325, 1666
JS: 1992

Degas, Edgar
IJ: 7098 JS: 5211

de Gaulle, Charles
IJ: 6905

De La Cruz, Jessie
JS: 5806

De la Hoya, Oscar
IJ: 6686

De la Renta, Oscar
IJ: 6374

de la Rocque, Marguerite — Fiction
JS: 85

Delaware Indians — Folklore
JS: 4784

Delaware (state)
IJ: 9466, 9506

Delaware (state) — History
IJ: 8921

Democracy
IJ: 7363, 9759–60 JS: 9781

Deng Xiaoping
See Xiaoping, Deng

Denmark
IJ: 8359, 8363

Denmark — Fiction
IJ: 63, 2648, 3329, 3355, 3804 J: 3305
JS: 3352, 3382

Denmark — History
JS: 7744

Dental care
See also Teeth
JS: 11347

Dentistry
J: 11348

Dentistry — History
IJ: 11213

De Passe, Suzanne
IJ: 6375

de Portola, Gaspar
IJ: 6983

Depression, Great
IJ: 8672, 8704, 8708, 8733, 9282, 9284, 9303, 9310, 9312, 9318 J: 9276, 9300, 9313 JS: 9278, 9285, 9287, 9290, 9293–94, 9301–2, 9304–5, 9307, 9309, 9311, 9317, 10149

Depression, Great — Fiction
IJ: 237, 313, 716, 1117, 1150, 1187, 1206, 3228, 3230, 3232, 3234–35, 3237–40, 3248, 3253, 3256, 3261, 3266, 3269, 3272, 3274, 3281–82, 3645 J: 1, 3276, 3278, 3280 JS: 665, 2584, 2751, 3265, 3267, 3270, 3706

Depression, Great — Poetry
JS: 4619

Depression, Great — Speeches
JS: 9291

Depression (mental state)
IJ: 11399, 11411, 11425–26, 11457
J: 11453 JS: 11020, 11196, 11388,

11391, 11407, 11422, 11441, 11448, 11454

Depression (mental state) — Fiction
IJ: 772, 866, 1237, 1406, 1517, 3245
J: 867 JS: 526, 1191, 1233, 1292, 3425

Des Moines — Fiction
IJ: 3668

Desegregation
IJ: 9953

Deserts
IJ: 12483–88

Deserts — Fiction
JS: 1885

Design
See Clothing and dress; Fashion design

Design — 1960s
IJ: 7028

Design — History
IJ: 7029–30

Designer drugs
See also Drugs and drug abuse
JS: 10985

DesJarlait, Patrick
IJ: 5212

Desktop publishing
JS: 4978

de Soto, Hernando
IJ: 5040 JS: 5039

Detectives
IJ: 10385, 10460, 10794

Detectives — Biography
IJ: 6240–41

Detectives — Fiction
JS: 3924

Devers, Gail
JS: 6754

de Zavala, Lorenzo
IJ: 6085

Diabetes
IJ: 11155, 11198 JS: 11116, 11142, 11162, 11169

Diabetes — Fiction
J: 880 JS: 1210

Diamonds
IJ: 12544

Diana, Princess of Wales
IJ: 6906–10

Diaries
See also Journals
IJ: 2689, 9027, 9052, 10644, 10664

Diaries — Fiction
IJ: 253, 402, 507, 892, 966, 1187, 1613, 1773, 2559, 2567, 2594, 2670, 2675, 2766, 2789, 2904, 2986, 3031, 3059, 3087, 3170, 3207, 3225, 3254, 3327, 3377, 3622, 3714 J: 3424, 3710
JS: 1124, 1719, 2955, 3299, 3611, 3613

DiCaprio, Leonardo
IJ: 5555–56 JS: 5557

IJ = Upper Elementary/Lower Middle School; J = Middle School/Junior High; JS = Junior High/Senior High

Drake, Sir Francis
IJ: 5042, 5044 J: 5041 JS: 5043

Drake, Sir Francis — Fiction
IJ: 2630

Drama
See Plays

Drawing and painting
See also Art; Crafts
IJ: 7054, 7057, 13071–72, 13074,
13077–82, 13086–88, 13091, 13093–96
JS: 7107, 13076, 13083, 13089

Drawing and painting — Fiction
IJ: 3316

Dreams and dreaming
IJ: 11309 J: 11319 JS: 11315, 11317

Dreams and dreaming — Fiction
J: 2389 JS: 1515, 2572

Dred Scott Case
IJ: 9026, 9036 JS: 9035

Dress
See Clothing and dress; Fashion
design

Dress codes
JS: 10625

Drew, Charles
JS: 6376

Drinking and driving
See also Alcohol
IJ: 10930 JS: 10383, 10948, 10962

Drinking and driving — Fiction
JS: 1191, 1463

Dropouts
JS: 10692

Drought
IJ: 12608 JS: 12610

Drought — Fiction
JS: 2751, 2756

Drowning — Fiction
JS: 3765

Drug testing
IJ: 10952 JS: 9903, 10977

Drug trade
IJ: 10453 JS: 10992

Drugs and drug abuse
See also specific drugs, e.g., Cocaine
IJ: 10453, 10894, 10908, 10911, 10932,
10940, 10952, 10954, 10956, 10970,
10972–73, 10984, 10994, 10996–97,
11000–2, 11012–13, 11019 J: 10907,
10915–18, 10925–26, 10957, 10979,
10987, 10989, 11644 JS: 10386,
10895–97, 10899, 10901, 10903–6,
10913, 10920–22, 10927–29, 10931,
10938–39, 10943–44, 10947, 10951,
10953, 10955, 10958, 10960, 10963–67,
10969, 10974–77, 10980, 10985–86,
10992–93, 10995, 11003–4, 11006–7,
11009, 11014, 11016, 11020–22

Drugs and drug abuse — Fiction
J: 1301 JS: 104–5, 373, 555, 665, 881,
1182, 1226, 1244, 1412, 1685, 1884

Drugs and drug abuse —
Legalization
JS: 10901, 10920, 10928

Drugs and drug abuse — Sports
IJ: 10924 JS: 10922, 10977

Drunk driving
See Drinking and driving

Du Bois, W. E. B.
IJ: 5813 JS: 5814

Ducks and geese
See Water birds

Ducks and geese — Fiction
IJ: 280 JS: 263

Dunbar, Paul Laurence
J: 5365 JS: 5364

Duncan, Isadora
IJ: 5561

Duncan, Tim
IJ: 6632–35

Dunham, Katherine
IJ: 5562

Dunkerque, Battle of
JS: 263

Dust Bowl
IJ: 9286, 9303, 9312 JS: 9301

Dust Bowl — Fiction
IJ: 3240, 3254, 3266, 3272

Duvalier, François and Jean-Claude
J: 6984

Dvorak, Antonin
JS: 5495

Dwarfism
IJ: 11289

Dylan, Bob
J: 5563 JS: 5564

Dysgraphia
IJ: 5326

Dyslexia
IJ: 11394, 11436, 11452 J: 11393

Dyslexia — Biography
J: 5548, 5579

Dyson, Esther
IJ: 6377–78

E

E-mail — Fiction
JS: 1756

Eagles
See also Birds of prey
IJ: 12240, 12247, 12249 JS: 12243

Eagles — Fiction
J: 42

Earhart, Amelia
IJ: 5046, 5048–50 J: 5047 JS: 5045

Earle, Sylvia
IJ: 6379

Earnhardt, Dale, Jr.
IJ: 6580

Earp, Wyatt
IJ: 6086

Earring making
See Jewelry making

Ears
IJ: 11355

Earth
See also Geology
IJ: 7356, 11960, 11964, 11967–68,
12448, 12458–59 J: 11961, 12457
JS: 11963, 11965, 12453

Earth — Geology
J: 12454

Earth imaging satellites
IJ: 12735

Earth science
IJ: 7257

Earth science — Experiments and
projects
IJ: 12455, 12460 JS: 7235

Earthquakes
IJ: 9551, 12461, 12463, 12466, 12469,
12472–73 JS: 9526, 12465

Earthquakes — Experiments and
projects
IJ: 12467

Earthworms
IJ: 12118

Earthworms — Experiments and
projects
IJ: 12101

East Africa — History
IJ: 7885

East Africa — Kings and queens
IJ: 7885

East Timor
JS: 8168

Easter
See also Holidays
IJ: 9692, 9719

Easter Island
IJ: 8154, 8172

Eastern Europe
IJ: 8188 JS: 8192, 8201

Eastman, George
JS: 6380–81

Eating disorders
See also specific disorders, e.g.,
Bulimia
IJ: 10996, 11040, 11068, 11086, 11152
J: 11053–54 JS: 11044–45, 11052,
11067, 11075, 11078, 11089, 11109,
11125, 11131, 11140, 11144, 11150,
11174, 11178, 11182, 11185, 11190,
11194, 11196, 11295

Eating disorders — Fiction
IJ: 956

Eating disorders — Support groups
JS: 11129

IJ = Upper Elementary/Lower Middle School; J = Middle School/Junior High; JS = Junior High/Senior High

IJ = Upper Elementary/Lower Middle School; J = Middle School/Junior High; JS = Junior High/Senior High

IJ = Upper Elementary/Lower Middle School; J = Middle School/Junior High; JS = Junior High/Senior High

Ethics and ethical behavior
See also Medical ethics; Morals, public; Politics — Ethics
JS: 9920, 11623

Ethiopia
IJ: 7881, 7886, 7891, 7897, 7912
JS: 7894

Ethiopia — Fiction
IJ: 1863, 2562–63

Ethiopia — Folklore
IJ: 4696

Ethiopia — History
J: 7908 **JS:** 7502

Ethnic cleansing
See Genocide

Ethnic groups
See also Immigration (U.S.); and specific ethnic groups, e.g., Irish Americans
IJ: 9482, 10074, 10103 **JS:** 10105, 10114–15, 10119

Ethnic groups — Fiction
IJ: 619, 4385

Ethnic groups — Poetry
IJ: 4470

Ethnic groups (U.S.) — History
JS: 8714

Ethnic problems
See Discrimination; Prejudice; Racism

Ethnography
IJ: 7371

Ethnology — Biography
IJ: 6436

Etiquette
IJ: 11629–30, 11630, 11632, 11636
JS: 11631, 11633–34

Etiquette — Colonial period (U.S.)
IJ: 8952

Etymology
IJ: 4963 **J:** 4952

Euphrates River
IJ: 8405

Eurasia
JS: 8312

Europe
IJ: 7375

Europe — Fiction
IJ: 2725

Europe — History
IJ: 7367

Euthanasia
See also Aging; Death; Elderly persons; Right to die
IJ: 10869, 10884 **JS:** 10874, 10888, 10890–92, 11200

Euthanasia — Fiction
JS: 1284

Evangelists — Fiction
JS: 1059

Evans, Minnie
IJ: 5217

Everglades
IJ: 12475

Everglades — Fiction
IJ: 56, 79, 3952

Evers, Medgar
JS: 9387

Everyday life
See also Teenagers — Everyday life
IJ: 4360

Everyday life — Brazil
IJ: 8590

Everyday life — Fiction
J: 408

Everyday life — Israel
IJ: 8421, 8434

Everyday life — Jordan
IJ: 8460

Everyday life — Middle Ages
IJ: 7579

Evolution
See also Scopes Trial
IJ: 6368, 6457, 7264, 7297–98, 7300, 7302–3, 7313, 7315, 12008, 12174
JS: 7299, 7312, 7314, 9306, 12011

Evolution — Biography
IJ: 6371–72 **J:** 6369

Evolution — Forecasting
IJ: 7310 **JS:** 11962

Ewing, Patrick
IJ: 6636

Excretory system
See also Digestive system
IJ: 11331, 11333

Executions — Fiction
IJ: 2552

Exercise
See also Health care; Physical fitness
IJ: 11282, 11365–66, 11371, 13335
JS: 11368–69, 11372, 11713

Experiments
See as subdivision of other subjects, e.g., Air — Experiments and projects; Biology — Experiments and projects

Exploration — Fiction
IJ: 2794

Explorers
See Adventurers and explorers

Explosives
JS: 12928

Expressionism — Art
IJ: 5128

Expressionism — Biography
IJ: 5102

Exquemelin
IJ: 5051

Extinct animals
IJ: 12261

Extinct species
See also Endangered species; Ecology and environment — Problems
IJ: 12263 **JS:** 12262

Extrasensory perception (ESP)
IJ: 10428 **JS:** 13179, 13202

Extrasensory perception (ESP) — Fiction
IJ: 523, 841, 1896, 2173, 2194, 2255, 2351, 2376 **J:** 2, 1948, 2033, 2715, 3467, 3916, 4104 **JS:** 1579, 3802

Extraterrestrial life
IJ: 11887, 11930, 11947, 13171, 13197
J: 13201 **JS:** 11941, 13222

Extraterrestrial life — Fiction
IJ: 4127, 4150, 4181 **J:** 4096
JS: 4193, 4222, 4233, 4242, 4247

Extreme sports
IJ: 13322

***Exxon Valdez* oil spill**
See also Oil spills
IJ: 9550

Eyes
See also Senses
IJ: 11360 **J:** 11357

F

Fabergé, Carl
JS: 5218

Fables
See also Greece — Mythology
JS: 4850

Faces — Art
IJ: 7061

Facial muscles
IJ: 11342

Fairies — Fiction
IJ: 4675 **JS:** 1960

Fairies — Folklore
IJ: 4689

Fairs — Fiction
IJ: 330

Fairy tales
IJ: 2015, 2460, 2470, 4659, 4663, 4672, 4688, 4738, 4747–48, 4773, 4815
J: 2056 **JS:** 991, 1486, 2244, 2270, 2433–34, 4658, 4733, 4737

Fairy tales — Fiction
IJ: 2390 **J:** 4752 **JS:** 2268, 2293, 4661

Falcons
See also Peregrine falcons
IJ: 12240, 12242

Falcons — Fiction
IJ: 265 **J:** 266

Fame — Fiction
JS: 572

Family abuse
See Family problems

IJ = Upper Elementary/Lower Middle School; J = Middle School/Junior High; JS = Junior High/Senior High

IJ = Upper Elementary/Lower Middle School; J = Middle School/Junior High; JS = Junior High/Senior High

Fleming, Alexander
IJ: 6403–4, 6406–7 JS: 6405

Flies
IJ: 12289

Flight — History
IJ: 12877

Floods
IJ: 12587, 12589, 12591–92, 12601

Floods — Fiction
IJ: 2922

Florence (Italy)
IJ: 7545

Florida
IJ: 9102, 9569, 9574, 9576

Florida — Fiction
IJ: 43, 79, 159, 178, 621, 3264, 3604
J: 325 JS: 319, 1063, 3723

Florida — History
IJ: 8876, 9591

Florida panthers
IJ: 12202

Flowers
IJ: 8677, 12085–87, 12094 J: 12079, 12081

Flowers — Dried
JS: 12973

Flowers for Algernon — **Criticism**
JS: 4909

Fluid mechanics
JS: 12664

Flutes — Fiction
IJ: 1513

Flying — Fiction
IJ: 2192

Flying saucers
J: 11940

Fog
JS: 12573

Folk art — Biography
JS: 5230

Folk art — United States
J: 7111

Folk music
See African Americans — Folk songs; Folk songs; Slavery (U.S.) — Folk songs

Folk singers — Biography
JS: 5500

Folk songs
IJ: 9709 J: 7166, 7175–76

Folk songs — United States
IJ: 7165 JS: 7167, 7174

Folklore
See also specific countries and regions, e.g., Germany — Folklore; and specific topics, e.g., Animals — Folklore
IJ: 4675, 4680, 4682, 4685, 4697–98, 4704, 4722, 4771, 4778, 4792, 4803–4, 4827 J: 4743, 4713, 4721, 4758
JS: 4729, 4779, 4800

Folklore — Africa
J: 4702

Folklore — American — Plays
JS: 4462

Folklore — Anthologies
IJ: 3488, 4655–56, 4660, 4662, 4664–65, 4667–69, 4671, 4673, 4676, 4679, 4684, 4687, 4692, 4700–1, 4709–11, 4714, 4716, 4718, 4726, 4732, 4740, 4745, 4750, 4765, 4772, 4788, 4793, 4810, 4813–14, 4820 J: 4674, 4715, 4725, 4749, 4757, 4766, 4770, 4818, 13159–60 JS: 4657, 4694, 4808

Folklore — Biography
JS: 5351

Folklore — Boys
IJ: 4690

Folklore — Celtic
IJ: 4755

Folklore — Great Britain
IJ: 4739

Folklore — India
IJ: 9648

Folklore — Jewish
IJ: 9651

Folklore — Latin America
IJ: 4824

Folklore — Middle Ages
IJ: 345

Folklore — Plays
IJ: 4425

Folklore — Women
IJ: 4670, 4707

Fon (African people)
IJ: 4705

Food
IJ: 4956, 11097, 11330–31, 12030, 12032, 12041, 12051, 12055, 12061
JS: 11468, 12037

Food — Additives
JS: 12039

Food — Careers
IJ: 10725

Food — Experiments and projects
IJ: 11476

Food — Fiction
IJ: 1924

Food — Genetics
J: 12049 JS: 12054

Food — History
IJ: 7538, 12050 JS: 12045, 13048

Food — Women
IJ: 10725

Food chain
J: 12012

Food poisoning
JS: 11111

Food service — Careers
JS: 10719

Food supply
IJ: 10478, 10485

Football
IJ: 6572, 12767, 13424–26, 13428
J: 13427

Football — Biography
IJ: 6545, 6563–64, 6571–72, 6689–709, 6711–19 J: 6566 JS: 6710

Football — Coaches
J: 6566

Football — Fiction
IJ: 4306, 4312, 4334 J: 1171, 4294, 4352 JS: 552, 654, 4283, 4286, 4290, 4293, 4298–99, 4322

Force (physics) — Experiments and projects
IJ: 12683–84

Ford, Henry
IJ: 6409 J: 6408 JS: 6410

Forensic anthropology
J: 10458

Forensic sciences
IJ: 10404, 10419, 10422, 10460, 10467, 10794 J: 10458, 10471 JS: 10418, 10438, 10450

Forensic sciences — Biography
JS: 6288

Forensic sciences — Experiments and projects
IJ: 10443

Forest fires
IJ: 10785, 12074

Forest fires — Fiction
J: 3236

Forests and forestry
IJ: 10330, 12076, 12489, 12497, 12502, 12508, 12510 JS: 12066, 12072

Forests and forestry — Fiction
J: 1933 JS: 1622

Forgiveness — Fiction
JS: 542

Forrest, Albert
J: 6723

Fort Sumter
JS: 9088

Fortifications
IJ: 12921, 12923

Forts
IJ: 7048, 12923, 12954

Forts — Civil War (U.S.)
IJ: 9080

Fortune, Amos
J: 6207

Fortune telling
IJ: 13194, 13209 JS: 13206

Fortune telling — Fiction
JS: 2105

Fossey, Dian
IJ: 6411 JS: 6412

Fossils
See also Paleontology
IJ: 7257, 7263, 7269–70 **JS:** 7290, 7296

Fossils — Collecting
IJ: 7285

Fossils — Fiction
IJ: 502

Foster care
See also Adoption; Family problems
JS: 11736, 11794

Foster care — Fiction
IJ: 422, 454, 776, 855, 881, 913, 921, 1057, 1078, 1120, 1155, 1509 **J:** 912, 1526, 1716, 2576 **JS:** 610, 1361, 4031

Foster homes — Fiction
IJ: 817, 1011

Fourth of July
See July Fourth

Fox, Vicente
IJ: 6985

Foxes
IJ: 12205

Foxes — Fiction
J: 2259

Foxes — Folklore
IJ: 4826

Fractions
IJ: 12550

France
IJ: 8209–12, 8215, 8217, 8219
JS: 8216, 8222

France — Biography
IJ: 6940 **JS:** 6903

France — Cookbooks
IJ: 13010, 13042

France — Fiction
IJ: 453, 530, 2540, 2631–32, 2647, 2664–65, 2675, 3296, 3368, 3576, 3684 **J:** 128, 1872, 3328 **JS:** 342–43, 1633, 1929, 2526, 3309, 3345

France — History
See also specific topics, e.g., French Revolution
IJ: 6887, 6905, 7581, 7667, 7679, 7713, 7741, 8207, 8221, 8223–24 **JS:** 6952, 7604, 8206, 8218

Francis of Assisi, Saint
IJ: 6916

Francis of Assisi, Saint — Fiction
JS: 2536

Frank, Anne
IJ: 6917, 6919, 6923–24 **JS:** 6918, 6920, 6922, 6925–26, 7705, 7732, 7813

Frank, Anne — Diaries
JS: 6921

Franklin, Aretha
JS: 5572–73

Franklin, Benjamin
IJ: 6088–89, 6091, 6094 **J:** 6090
JS: 6092–93

Franklin, Benjamin — Fiction
IJ: 2090, 3662

Franklin, Rosalind
IJ: 6413

Franklin, Sir John
IJ: 8484

Fraunces, Phoebe
J: 6208

Freckles — Fiction
IJ: 2411

Frederick the Great
JS: 8231

Freedom
IJ: 9995

Freedom of movement
IJ: 9951

Freedom of speech
IJ: 10002, 10517 **JS:** 9944, 10064, 10294

Freedom of the press
J: 9860 **JS:** 9883, 9973, 10064

Freeman, Elizabeth
JS: 5816

Freeman, Morgan
JS: 5574

Fremont, John Charles
IJ: 5052 **J:** 9168 **JS:** 9174

French, Daniel Chester
IJ: 9477

French and Indian War
IJ: 8891, 8932 **J:** 6039, 8927

French and Indian War — Biography
IJ: 6247

French and Indian War — Fiction
IJ: 2798, 2815 **J:** 2820, 2838
JS: 2023, 2797, 2804

French Revolution
IJ: 7372, 8207, 8220

French Revolution — Fiction
JS: 366

Fresno (CA) — Fiction
JS: 1735

Freud, Sigmund
JS: 6414

Friendship
IJ: 11602 **JS:** 11684, 11700, 11715

Friendship — Fiction
IJ: 141, 165, 210, 235, 269, 289, 291, 355, 399–400, 406, 410, 421–24, 428, 437–38, 445, 448–49, 451, 453, 459, 465, 480–81, 485–87, 489, 491, 494–95, 501, 504, 508–9, 511, 516, 525, 528, 531, 534, 538, 541, 545, 547, 551, 554, 565–66, 568, 571, 573, 576, 578, 580–81, 583, 585, 588–89, 599, 618, 621, 625, 700, 790–91, 917, 1026, 1064, 1090, 1093, 1108, 1165, 1175–76, 1245, 1259, 1266, 1287, 1294, 1334, 1362, 1381–82, 1388, 1436, 1470, 1472, 1478, 1482, 1538, 1560, 1563–65, 1568, 1571, 1574, 1582, 1637, 1670, 1698, 1731–32,
1813, 1864, 1912, 2052, 2114, 2619, 2648, 2658, 2754, 2924, 3034, 3152, 3217–19, 3232, 3290, 3333, 3354–55, 3684, 3689, 3702, 3704, 3708, 3724, 3736, 3743, 4038, 4307–8, 4314, 4339, 4342 **J:** 246, 287, 415, 462–63, 515, 532, 632, 648, 984, 986, 1076, 1153, 1208, 1230, 1246, 1248, 1304, 1308, 1373–74, 1409, 1443, 1479, 1526, 1559, 1597, 1674, 1708–10, 1713, 1716, 1725, 1755, 1782, 2973, 3216, 3283, 3339, 3619, 4392 **JS:** 398, 405, 414, 464, 498, 521, 546, 590–91, 626, 745, 754, 889, 924, 1005, 1052, 1182–84, 1193, 1196, 1202, 1219, 1256, 1268, 1286, 1346, 1361, 1386, 1413–14, 1416, 1431, 1440, 1447, 1452, 1461, 1500, 1505, 1518–19, 1522, 1530, 1572, 1614, 1620, 1638, 1641, 1650, 1654, 1679–80, 1720, 1745, 1769, 1779, 1785, 1801–2, 1805, 1870, 2571, 3270, 3423, 3703, 3722, 4287, 4293, 4328, 4344

Friendship — Poetry
IJ: 4509 **JS:** 4512

Fright — Fiction
IJ: 3399

Fritz, Jean
IJ: 5371 **JS:** 5370

Frogs and toads
IJ: 12134, 12136 **JS:** 12108, 12135

Frogs and toads — Fiction
IJ: 2080, 2378

Frogs and toads — Folklore
IJ: 4720

Frontier life (U.S.)
IJ: 3121, 6200, 8815, 8845, 9149, 9152–57, 9159, 9161, 9163, 9165, 9167, 9170, 9187, 9189, 9192–93, 9197, 9206, 9208–9, 9214–15, 9218–19, 9227 **J:** 5742, 9151, 9168–69, 9172–73, 9178–79, 9185, 9188, 9202, 9204, 9220, 9228 **JS:** 8828, 9158, 9164, 9171, 9174–75, 9181–83, 9190, 9195–96, 9201, 9203, 9210, 9216, 9221–24, 9229–30, 9243, 9265

Frontier life (U.S.) — African Americans
J: 9177 **JS:** 9176

Frontier life (U.S.) — Biography
IJ: 5717, 5719, 6062, 6065, 6105, 6197, 6214, 6216, 6218, 6235, 6241, 6253 **J:** 5024, 5782 **JS:** 4996, 5708, 5745, 6063–64, 6190, 9217, 9226

Frontier life (U.S.) — Cookbooks
IJ: 9166 **JS:** 13014

Frontier life (U.S.) — Crafts
IJ: 12986

Frontier life (U.S.) — Fiction
IJ: 1148, 2768, 2774–75, 2777, 2808–9, 2897–98, 2926, 2928, 2957, 2995, 3027–30, 3034, 3038–41, 3045–47, 3051–52, 3054, 3056–58, 3060–61, 3063, 3065, 3068–69, 3071–80, 3082, 3088–92, 3094, 3096, 3099–100, 3103, 3105–6, 3108, 3110–13, 3116, 3118–20, 3122, 3125, 3127–35, 3762, 3895 **J:** 2764, 2821, 2837–38, 3032, 3037,

---

IJ = Upper Elementary/Lower Middle School; J = Middle School/Junior High; JS = Junior High/Senior High

Genetics — Biography
IJ: 6463, 6474 JS: 6462

Genghis Khan
IJ: 8027 JS: 6857, 7592

Genocide
See also Ethnic cleansing
IJ: 9774 JS: 9768, 9771–72, 9779

Geography
IJ: 7233, 7238

Geography — Experiments and projects
IJ: 7231 JS: 7235

Geology
See also Rocks and minerals
IJ: 11960, 11968, 12448–50, 12452, 12458, 12473, 12543, 12547 J: 12538
JS: 12110, 12453, 12456

Geology — Biography
IJ: 6276

Geology — Experiments and projects
IJ: 12455, 12460 JS: 7235

Geometry
IJ: 12559

Georgia Colony
IJ: 8902, 8911

Georgia (former Soviet Republic)
IJ: 8322 JS: 8345

Georgia (state)
IJ: 9567, 9582, 9592

Georgia (state) — Fiction
IJ: 704–5, 1352

Geothermal resources
JS: 12688

German Americans
IJ: 10229, 10243 JS: 10228

German Americans — Fiction
IJ: 3167 JS: 3350

Germany
See also Holocaust
IJ: 8184, 8227–28, 8230, 8235
J: 8225, 8241 JS: 8229

Germany — Biography
J: 7022 JS: 6931

Germany — Cookbooks
IJ: 13031

Germany — Fiction
IJ: 1222, 2015, 2539, 2658, 2722, 3336, 3409 J: 4329 JS: 1074, 2697, 3381

Germany — Folklore
IJ: 4740–41, 4769

Germany — History
IJ: 6932, 7657, 7698, 7750, 7796, 7811, 8232 J: 6935 JS: 6934, 6936, 7655, 7660, 7683, 7701, 7709–10, 7736, 7785, 8226, 8231, 8233, 10228, 13463

Germany, East — Fiction
J: 2639

Germs
See Bacteria

Geronimo
IJ: 6096 J: 6095

Gershwin, George
IJ: 5496–97

Getty, John Paul
JS: 6430

Getty Museum (Los Angeles)
IJ: 9548

Gettysburg, Battle of
IJ: 9070 J: 9114 JS: 9075, 9090, 9103–4, 9139

Gettysburg, Battle of — Fiction
IJ: 2961

Gettysburg Address
IJ: 9098 J: 9121

Ghana
IJ: 7977, 7979–80, 7986, 8617

Ghana — Folklore
IJ: 4697

Ghana — History
J: 8021

Ghana Empire
J: 7987

Ghettos — World War II
See Lodz ghetto

Ghosts
See also Haunted houses
IJ: 71, 96, 735, 2010, 2134, 2194, 3436, 3448, 3453, 3456, 3459, 3484, 3494–95, 3526–27, 3537, 3542, 3587–88, 3865, 13172, 13174–75, 13177, 13183, 13195, 13199 J: 13210 JS: 13203, 13221

Ghosts — Fiction
IJ: 150, 891, 1175, 2179, 3427, 3430, 3437, 3440–41, 3445, 3451, 3454–55, 3461, 3465, 3489–90, 3506, 3508, 3514, 3520, 3536, 3538–39, 3541, 3543, 3555, 3558, 3560–61, 3565, 3570–71, 3582, 3589, 3591, 3709, 4324, 4817 J: 1503, 1758, 2032, 2167, 2335, 3457, 3457, 3499, 3503, 3516, 3523, 3569, 3579, 3594, 3819 JS: 359, 1964, 2077, 2086, 2248, 2329, 2424, 3444, 3447, 3450, 3466, 3478, 3486, 3502, 3509, 3517, 3521, 3528–29, 3559, 3575, 3578, 3580, 3590, 3593, 4412

Ghosts — Folklore
IJ: 3488, 4820 J: 4806, 4821

Ghosts — Poetry
IJ: 4545

Ghosts — Short stories
IJ: 3493

Giacometti, Alberto
IJ: 5222

Giant pandas
See Pandas

Gibson, Althea
JS: 6744

Gibson, Josh
IJ: 6597 JS: 6596

Gideon *v*. Wainright
JS: 9869

Gifted children
JS: 11637

Gifted children — Fiction
IJ: 489

Gilbert and Sullivan — Songs
IJ: 7156

Gillespie, Dizzy
JS: 5575

Ginsburg, Ruth Bader
IJ: 6097

Giotto di Bondine
JS: 7067

Giovanni, Nikki
JS: 5374

Girl Scouts of America
See Scouts and scouting

Girlfriends — Fiction
IJ: 3610

Girls — Fiction
JS: 1506–7, 1801–2, 2098

Girls — Grooming
IJ: 11274 JS: 11265

Giuliani, Rudolph W.
IJ: 6098

Glacier National Park — Fiction
IJ: 3953

Glaciers and icebergs
IJ: 12474

Gladiators (Roman)
IJ: 7518, 7542

Glasses
J: 11357

Glasses — Fiction
JS: 1979

Glassmaking — Biography
IJ: 5229

Glenn, John
IJ: 6099–101, 11908

Glenn, Mike
IJ: 13368

Gliders
IJ: 13284

Global warming
See also Ecology and environment — Problems
IJ: 10329, 10334, 12575, 12625
JS: 10320, 10337, 10339

Globe Theatre (London)
IJ: 4934, 5440 JS: 4925

Globe Theatre (London) — Fiction
IJ: 2626

Globes
See Maps and globes

Goats
IJ: 12034

God
IJ: 9670

God — Fiction
IJ: 560

IJ = Upper Elementary/Lower Middle School; J = Middle School/Junior High; JS = Junior High/Senior High

IJ = Upper Elementary/Lower Middle School; J = Middle School/Junior High; JS = Junior High/Senior High

H

IJ = Upper Elementary/Lower Middle School; J = Middle School/Junior High; JS = Junior High/Senior High

IJ = Upper Elementary/Lower Middle School; J = Middle School/Junior High; JS = Junior High/Senior High

High schools — Handbooks
JS: 10691

Highways
IJ: 12890

Hiking
See also Walking
IJ: 13413

Hill, Faith
IJ: 5592

Hill, Grant
IJ: 6642 J: 6641 JS: 6640

Hill, Lauryn
IJ: 5593

Hillary, Sir Edmund
IJ: 5056–58

Hindenburg, Paul von
JS: 6931

Hindenburg (dirigible)
IJ: 12862, 12879 JS: 4024

Hinduism
IJ: 9648, 9657 J: 9611, 9683
JS: 9659

Hinduism — Holidays
See specific holidays, e.g., Diwali

Hindus — Fiction
IJ: 883

Hines, Gregory
IJ: 5594

Hingis, Martina
JS: 6574

Hinton, S. E.
JS: 4914

Hip-hop — Music
IJ: 7131

Hip-hop — Poetry
JS: 4563

Hippies — Fiction
J: 1567

Hiroshima
IJ: 7724, 7731 JS: 7711, 7755, 7791

Hiroshima — Fiction
IJ: 3413

Hiroshima — History
IJ: 7671

Hispanic Americans
See also specific groups, e.g.,
Mexican Americans
IJ: 5823, 9021, 10191–92, 10202
JS: 10193, 10195–96, 10204

Hispanic Americans — Art
JS: 7105

Hispanic Americans — Biography
IJ: 5023, 5139, 5347, 5423, 5434, 5522,
5568–70, 5609, 5620, 5643, 5663, 5672,
5706, 5760–61, 5804, 5822, 5824, 6085,
6169, 6245, 6374, 6591–92, 6594, 6685,
6780, 7007, 10198 J: 5671 JS: 5124,
5691, 5764, 5777, 5802–3, 5806, 6206,
6312, 6529, 6587, 6620, 6710, 10206

Hispanic Americans — Careers
JS: 10743–45, 10762, 10774, 10778,
10783–84, 10799, 10824

Hispanic Americans — Fiction
IJ: 598, 644, 671, 708, 712, 828, 896,
1734, 3730 J: 608, 669–70, 672, 709,
1326, 2608 JS: 600, 611, 633–34, 664,
720, 924, 1327, 1735, 1778, 1843, 1888,
4012, 4408, 10197

Hispanic Americans — Literature
JS: 10206

Hispanic Americans — Memoirs
JS: 10197

Hispanic Americans — Plays
IJ: 4434, 4467 JS: 4466

Hispanic Americans — Poetry
IJ: 4471, 4473, 4631 JS: 4568, 10197

Hiss, Alger
JS: 9850

Historic sites (U.S.)
IJ: 8722

History
See also under specific countries and
continents, e.g., Africa — History;
and wars and historical eras, e.g.,
Colonial Period (U.S.)
IJ: 7363

History — Ancient
IJ: 7390, 7393, 7396, 7403, 7407,
7409–10, 7415

History — Careers
IJ: 10712

History — Eighteenth century
JS: 8691

History — Methodology
IJ: 7387

History — Twentieth century
IJ: 7614

History — Women
IJ: 6808

Hit-and-run accidents — Fiction
JS: 3896

Hitchcock, Alfred
JS: 5595

Hitler, Adolf
IJ: 6932 J: 6933, 6935 JS: 6934,
6936, 7701, 7736, 8233

Hitler, Adolf — Fiction
IJ: 1852

Hitler Youth
IJ: 7698 JS: 7730

HIV (virus)
IJ: 6647, 11117, 11156 JS: 11051,
11095, 11184

HIV (virus) — Fiction
IJ: 1535

Hmong Americans — Fiction
IJ: 701

Hmong people
IJ: 10093, 10175

Hobbies
IJ: 12952

Hockey
See Ice hockey

Hodgkin's Disease — Biography
JS: 6730

Holdsclaw, Chamique
JS: 6643

Holiday, Billie
JS: 5596

Holidays
See also individual countries, e.g.,
Mexico — Holidays; and specific
holidays, e.g., Christmas
J: 10556 JS: 10545

Holidays — Cookbooks
IJ: 13051

Holidays — Crafts
IJ: 12958 J: 12975

Holidays — Plays
J: 4457

Holidays — Poetry
JS: 4485

Holland
See Netherlands

Holland — Fiction
IJ: 3380

Holliday, Doc
IJ: 6105

Hollywood — Fiction
J: 4045

Holocaust
See also Concentration camps
IJ: 6919, 6923–24, 6932, 6942, 6970,
7025, 7638, 7641, 7646, 7648–49, 7653,
7656, 7687, 7695, 7700, 7704, 7715–16,
7735, 7742, 7745–46, 7759, 7767, 7783,
7804, 7811, 7814 J: 3383, 7737, 7758
JS: 3331, 6936–37, 7640, 7642–44,
7652, 7654–55, 7659–61, 7681–83,
7699, 7702, 7705, 7707–10, 7712, 7714,
7717, 7732, 7738–39, 7743–44, 7747,
7757, 7763, 7776–77, 7782, 7785, 7790,
7792, 7794–95, 7797, 7802, 7813, 7824,
7859, 9772, 10268, 10375

Holocaust — Biography
IJ: 6882, 6917, 6958 J: 6950, 6961,
6973 JS: 6800, 6918, 6920–22,
6925–26, 6960, 6972, 7004, 7020–21

Holocaust — Fiction
IJ: 3306, 3319, 3323–24, 3351, 3358,
3364, 3368, 3380, 3385, 3391,
3399–402, 3404, 3406, 3409, 3541,
3576, 4680, 7650 J: 1230, 3300, 3310,
3359 JS: 1394, 2701, 3315, 3325,
3347, 3349, 3352, 3360–61, 3365, 3372,
3375–76, 3378, 3381, 3389, 3398,
3410–11, 3414, 4009, 7686, 7776

Holocaust — Plays
JS: 4454

Holocaust — Poetry
JS: 7776

IJ = Upper Elementary/Lower Middle School; J = Middle School/Junior High; JS = Junior High/Senior High

IJ = Upper Elementary/Lower Middle School; J = Middle School/Junior High; JS = Junior High/Senior High

Human development and behavior
See also Personal guidance;
Psychology
JS: 11305, 11609

Human Genome Project
JS: 11250

Human rights
See also Civil rights
J: 9982 **JS:** 5756, 9945, 9960, 9976,
10030

Human rights — Biography
IJ: 6793

Human rights — Fiction
IJ: 2564

Humanitarians — Biography
IJ: 6873–74, 6876, 6970

Hummingbirds
IJ: 12223

Humor
IJ: 13361

Humor — Fiction
JS: 3613

Humorous poetry
See Poetry — Humorous

Humorous stories
IJ: 71, 318, 338, 391, 449, 472–73, 513,
877, 1030, 1379, 1423, 2075–76, 2100,
2129, 2383, 2412, 3303, 3598, 3602–4,
3606–7, 3627, 3630, 3632–35, 3637–39,
3644–46, 3650–51, 3654–55, 3657–59,
3661–63, 3665–66, 3668, 3671, 3675,
3682–84, 3689, 3693, 3701, 3707–8,
3714–15, 3718–19, 3725, 3727–28,
3730, 3732, 3734, 3738–39, 3741–45,
4148, 4659 **J:** 3626, 3667, 3680
JS: 1510, 3621, 3687, 3703, 3706, 3712

Humorous stories — Fiction
IJ: 468, 474, 756, 972, 1436, 1568,
1706, 1740, 1908, 1927, 2067, 2074,
2382, 2738, 3197, 3255, 3490, 3600–1,
3605, 3608–9, 3622, 3624, 3636, 3640,
3643, 3647, 3664, 3669, 3672, 3674,
3685–86, 3688, 3690–91, 3694, 3696,
3698, 3704, 3731, 3736, 3747, 3752,
4223, 4225–26, 4312 **J:** 848, 865, 1408,
1555, 1705, 2523, 3177, 3617, 3619–20,
3625, 3652, 3656, 3677, 3692, 3695,
3697, 3710, 3721, 3748–49, 3923, 4352
JS: 393, 789, 1398, 1415, 1474,
1594–95, 1653, 1765, 1827, 3500, 3597,
3615–16, 3623, 3628, 3631, 3641–42,
3648–49, 3653, 3660, 3670, 3673, 3676,
3678–79, 3700, 3705, 3713, 3717, 3720,
3723, 3729, 3733, 3740, 3746, 3750,
4026, 4055

Humpback whales
IJ: 12348

Hundred Years War
IJ: 6939

Hungary
IJ: 6970, 8195

Hungary — Biography
JS: 7024

Hungary — Cookbooks
IJ: 13015

Hungary — Fiction
J: 2711 **JS:** 3315

Hungary — Folklore
IJ: 4750

Hungary — History
JS: 7717

Hunger
See also Poverty
JS: 10476, 10484

Hunter, Clementine
JS: 5230

Hunters and hunting
IJ: 8842 **J:** 13256 **JS:** 13422

Hunters and hunting — Fiction
IJ: 1784 **JS:** 1218

Huron Indians
IJ: 8760

Hurricane Andrew
IJ: 12597

Hurricanes
See also Storms
IJ: 12585, 12590, 12593, 12595, 12597
JS: 12582

Hurricanes — Fiction
IJ: 74, 2915, 3193 **J:** 176 **JS:** 66

Hurston, Zora Neale
IJ: 5390 **JS:** 5391–93

Hussein, Saddam
IJ: 6859, 6861 **JS:** 6860

Hutchinson, Anne
IJ: 6213

Hutu (African people)
IJ: 7916

Hydrogen
IJ: 12431 **J:** 12423

Hygiene
See also Health care
IJ: 11266, 11364 **J:** 11273 **JS:** 10866,
11720

Hyperactivity — Fiction
IJ: 1197, 1199

I

**I Know Why the Caged Bird Sings
— Criticism**
JS: 4907

Ibo (African people)
IJ: 8010

Ice — Poetry
IJ: 4645

Ice Ages
IJ: 7308, 8208 **JS:** 7296

Ice climbing
IJ: 13288

Ice cream
IJ: 12057

Ice hockey
IJ: 13431, 13433, 13435–38, 13471
JS: 13432, 13432, 13434

Ice hockey — Biography
IJ: 6726, 6731–33 **J:** 6569, 6723
JS: 6730

Ice hockey — Fiction
IJ: 4265–67, 4269–71, 4291 **JS:** 4302,
4315

Ice hockey — Goalies
J: 6569

Ice hockey — Women
IJ: 13439

Ice skating
IJ: 13448, 13450–51, 13471
JS: 13446, 13446–47, 13449

Ice skating — Biography
IJ: 6555, 6558, 6722, 6725, 6729, 6735
J: 6724, 6724, 6727, 6727, 6736, 6736
JS: 6728, 6728, 6734

Ice skating — Fiction
J: 1662 **JS:** 431

Icebergs
See Glaciers and icebergs

Iceland
IJ: 8364, 8368, 8378

Iceman (Switzerland)
IJ: 7348

Idaho
IJ: 9441, 9449, 9534

Idaho — Fiction
J: 818, 1589, 3677

Idar, Jovita
IJ: 5824

Iditarod
IJ: 6771, 13244

Iditarod — Fiction
IJ: 161

Iditarod (Junior)
IJ: 13300

Igbo (African people)
JS: 8013

Igloos
IJ: 8666

Iliad (mythology)
IJ: 4872 **J:** 4880

Iliad (mythology) — Adaptations
JS: 4883

Illegal aliens
IJ: 10083 **JS:** 10068, 10079

Illegal aliens — Fiction
IJ: 606 **JS:** 1665, 1843, 1888

Illinois
IJ: 9414, 9433

Illinois — Fiction
IJ: 2990 **JS:** 3175

Illinois — History
IJ: 9059, 9413, 9436

Illiteracy
JS: 11779

IJ = Upper Elementary/Lower Middle School; J = Middle School/Junior High; JS = Junior High/Senior High

Illiteracy — Fiction
IJ: 4273 JS: 456

Illness
See Diseases and illness

Imaginary animals
IJ: 7567

Imaginary animals — Fiction
See also specific real or imaginary
animals, e.g., Bears; Dragons
IJ: 2141, 2144, 2154–55, 3662–63,
3701, 3761, 3859, 4144

Immigration
JS: 10077, 10084, 10091

Immigration — Fiction
JS: 624, 1309, 2901, 3390

Immigration (U.S.)
See also Ethnic groups
IJ: 7357, 8053, 8076, 8113, 8138, 8198,
8242, 8264, 8278, 8294, 8568, 9482,
9502, 10065, 10067, 10070, 10074,
10080, 10083, 10085–86, 10093, 10096,
10100, 10124, 10175, 10192, 10203,
10210, 10222, 10229, 10235–36,
10243–44 J: 8257, 10066, 10081
JS: 7893, 8081, 8426, 8509, 8540,
10068–69, 10071–73, 10076, 10078–79,
10082, 10088–90, 10092, 10097–99,
10101, 10116, 10180, 10183, 10190,
10205, 10214, 10226, 10230–31

Immigration (U.S.) — Fiction
IJ: 615, 2935, 2946, 3042, 3142, 3155,
3162, 3167, 3191, 3209, 3249 J: 719,
2902, 3161, 3194–96, 3201 JS: 89,
633, 691, 974, 2598, 3140, 3357, 4412

Immigration (U.S.) — History
IJ: 9465

Immigration (U.S.) — Illegal
See also Illegal aliens
JS: 10075

Immigration (U.S.) — Jews
IJ: 10208

Immune system
JS: 11065, 11077, 11175, 11212,
11280, 11299

Impeachment
J: 9805 JS: 9814

Imperialism
JS: 7385

Impressionism (art)
IJ: 5128, 7078 J: 7070, 7087
JS: 7102

Improvisation (theater)
JS: 7215

In vitro fertilization
IJ: 11517

Inaugurations
JS: 9824

Incas
IJ: 7322, 7343, 8533, 8535, 8610–11,
8613, 8624, 8633, 8635 J: 8640–41
JS: 7345, 8623

Incas — Fiction
IJ: 2730, 2759

Incest
See also Family problems; Sexual
abuse
JS: 11596–97

Incest — Fiction
J: 1076

Inchon, Invasion of (Korean War)
JS: 7845

Indentured servants — Fiction
JS: 2877

Independence Day (U.S.)
See July Fourth

India
IJ: 6851, 7046, 8063, 8065–67, 8069,
8073, 8075–76, 8078, 8080, 9657,
10222 JS: 8062, 8081

India — Biography
IJ: 6840, 6853, 6873, 6875, 6877
J: 6855 JS: 6850, 6852, 6856

India — Cookbooks
IJ: 13025 J: 13019

India — Fiction
IJ: 312, 372, 1891, 2578, 2594, 2609,
2612 J: 603 JS: 624, 2574, 2610

India — Folklore
IJ: 4714 JS: 4717

India — History
IJ: 6854, 8068, 8079 JS: 8082

India — Poetry
JS: 4559

India — Religion
J: 9683

India — Science
IJ: 8079

Indian (Asian) Americans
IJ: 10222

Indian British — Fiction
JS: 694

Indian Canadians — Fiction
IJ: 883

Indiana
IJ: 9415, 9420

Indiana — Fiction
IJ: 3231

Indians of Central America
IJ: 8524

Indians of Central America — Art
IJ: 7116

**Indians of Central America —
Fiction**
JS: 1839

**Indians of Central America —
History**
IJ: 7370

Indians of North America
See also Native Americans and
specific groups, e.g., Cherokee
Indians
IJ: 3089, 7689, 8533, 8812, 8819, 8829,
8831, 8837–38, 8841, 8846–47, 8849

**Indians of North America —
Anthologies**
IJ: 10217

Indians of North America — Art
IJ: 8817

**Indians of North America —
Biography**
IJ: 5223, 5361, 5819, 6163, 6215,
6229–30, 6238, 6242–43, 6250–51,
6768

**Indians of North America —
Children**
IJ: 8860

Indians of North America — Dances
IJ: 8785

Indians of North America — Fiction
IJ: 79, 162, 604, 690, 882, 1931, 2072,
2763, 2765, 2769, 2778, 2781, 2790,
2810, 2818, 2829, 3073 J: 2784
JS: 1839

**Indians of North America —
Folklore**
IJ: 4785, 4787–88, 4790–91, 4793–94

**Indians of North America —
History**
IJ: 8752, 8833, 8842, 8850, 8857, 8859,
8861, 8906

Indians of South America
IJ: 8634 JS: 8628

**Indians of South America —
Folklore**
IJ: 4825 JS: 4837

Indians of the West Indies — Fiction
IJ: 2732

Indonesia
IJ: 8122, 8132, 8151

Indonesia — Cookbooks
IJ: 13039

Industrial Revolution
IJ: 7607, 9019 J: 7381, 7606, 9252
JS: 7597, 9245

**Industrial Revolution — United
States**
IJ: 8717, 9001

Industry — Biography
JS: 6336, 6430

Industry — History
J: 7606, 9252 JS: 6354

Industry (U.S.) — History
IJ: 9237

Influenza — Fiction
IJ: 3250

Influenza epidemic (1918)
JS: 11036

Information handling
JS: 10642

Information Revolution
JS: 12840

Ingles, Mary Draper
IJ: 6214

IJ = Upper Elementary/Lower Middle School; J = Middle School/Junior High; JS = Junior High/Senior High

Inhalants
IJ: 10970, 10997

Inline skating
IJ: 13230, 13235, 13235, 13239, 13249, 13268 JS: 13452

Inner cities
JS: 10497

Inquisition
JS: 7588

Inquisition — Fiction
IJ: 2540, 2709

Inquisition (Spanish)
IJ: 8388 JS: 8395

Insanity
See Mental disorders

Insanity defense
JS: 9916

Insects
See also names of specific insects, e.g., Butterflies and moths
IJ: 12099, 12114, 12277–78, 12280–84, 12290–92, 12294–96 JS: 12285, 12293

Insects — Drawing and painting
IJ: 13079

Insects — Fiction
IJ: 3859

Insects — Homes
IJ: 12292

Insects — Poisonous
IJ: 12277

Insomnia
JS: 11304

Intel Corporation
JS: 6439

Intelligence
See also Human development and behavior
IJ: 11302 JS: 11637

Intelligence service
JS: 9775

International crime
JS: 9771

International relations
JS: 9769–70, 9778

Internet
IJ: 6344, 12779, 12797, 12799, 12801–3, 12805–6, 12812, 12814, 12817, 12823, 12825–28 J: 12784, 12794, 12807 JS: 12786, 12791–92, 12808, 12811

Internet — Biography
IJ: 6378

Internet — Censorship
JS: 12795

Internet — Fiction
J: 567 JS: 1653

Interpersonal relations
JS: 11610

Interpersonal relations — Fiction
JS: 1592

Interracial children — Fiction
IJ: 1322

Interracial dating
See also Dating (social)
JS: 11670, 11686

Interracial dating — Fiction
JS: 582, 4087

Interracial marriage
JS: 9851, 10110, 11670, 11686

Interracial marriage — Fiction
J: 1812, 2909 JS: 692, 1364

Interventionism (international)
JS: 9780

Inuit
See also Alaska; Arctic; Polar regions
IJ: 8645, 8655, 8662, 8666 J: 8770, 9541 JS: 8657

Inuit — Art
IJ: 8655

Inuit — Fiction
IJ: 81 J: 1007, 3277 JS: 169, 207, 334, 2700

Inuit — Folklore
IJ: 4795, 4804

Inuit — History
IJ: 7321

Inuit — Poetry
IJ: 4647

Inventions
See Inventors and inventions; and specific inventions, e.g., Telephones

Inventors and inventions
See also Scientists; and specific inventions, e.g., Telephones
IJ: 6321, 7379, 9686, 11208, 11681, 11804, 12744–45, 12745, 12749, 12785, 12821 J: 6298, 6341, 12733 JS: 6382, 11827, 12727, 12727, 12739, 12748

Inventors and inventions — African American
IJ: 6321 JS: 6263

Inventors and inventions — Biography
IJ: 5203, 5205, 5207–8, 5775, 6306, 6340, 6342, 6384–85, 6399, 6401, 6409, 6416, 6504, 6516, 6519, 6521 J: 6279, 6386, 6408 JS: 5204, 5206, 5209, 6294, 6322, 6343, 6383, 6410, 6455, 6518

Inventors and inventions — History
IJ: 7317, 12740

Inventors and inventions — Women
IJ: 6268, 11681, 12750 J: 6279 JS: 12751

Invertebrates
See also Animals; Insects; etc.
IJ: 12099 JS: 12116, 12120, 12313

Investments
IJ: 10592, 10606 JS: 10602, 10605

Invisibility — Fiction
JS: 4248

Iowa
IJ: 9408, 9422, 9427

Iowa — Fiction
JS: 1500

Iran
See also Persia
IJ: 8441, 8450, 8452, 8457, 8467 JS: 8442, 8461, 8472

Iran — Biography
IJ: 6867

Iran — Emigration
JS: 10245

Iran — Fiction
JS: 649

Iran-Iraq War
IJ: 7849

Iran-U.S. relations
JS: 8472

Iranian Americans
JS: 10245

Iraq
See also Persian Gulf War
IJ: 8437, 8444, 8453 JS: 7843, 8471

Iraq — Biography
IJ: 6859, 6861 JS: 6860

Iraq — Fiction
J: 2715 JS: 649

Iraq — Folklore
J: 4721

Ireland
IJ: 8250, 8259, 8266, 8272, 8278 JS: 8248

Ireland — Fiction
IJ: 302, 2229, 2290, 2649, 2651, 2654–56, 2706, 3099, 3391 J: 2045, 2645 JS: 1450, 2102, 2257, 2635, 2681, 2718–19, 4405

Ireland — Folklore
IJ: 4743, 4745–46

Ireland — History
IJ: 8242, 8260, 8274 J: 8257 JS: 8246

Ireland — Mythology
JS: 4848

Ireland, Northern
See Northern Ireland
IJ: 8252, 8261, 8277 JS: 8248, 10375

Irish Americans
IJ: 10225, 10249 JS: 3140, 10226, 10231, 10237, 10248

Irish Americans — Fiction
IJ: 2935, 2946, 2953, 3155, 3158, 3256 J: 3196 JS: 2960, 4405

Irish potato famine
J: 8257

Irish Republican Army — Fiction
JS: 98

Iron
IJ: 12434

Iron — History
IJ: 12736

IJ = Upper Elementary/Lower Middle School; J = Middle School/Junior High; JS = Junior High/Senior High

Iroquois Indians
JS: 8854

Iroquois Indians — History
JS: 8806

Irvin, Monte
IJ: 6599

Irving, Washington
IJ: 5394

Ishi
IJ: 6215, 8782

Islam
IJ: 9724, 9728, 10125 **J:** 9721–22
JS: 9723, 9725–27, 9729

Islam — Biography
IJ: 6865 **JS:** 6866

Islam — Fiction
IJ: 2637

Islam — History
IJ: 6869, 8396, 9720

Islands
See also Caribbean Islands; and
specific islands, e.g., Cuba
IJ: 9545

Islands — Fiction
IJ: 135, 162, 223, 1272, 1954, 2640,
2755, 3537, 3844 **J:** 1717 **JS:** 84, 218,
1663

Israel
IJ: 8403, 8421–22, 8424–25, 8429,
8431, 8434 **J:** 8417, 8419, 8430
JS: 8427–28, 8433

Israel — Biography
IJ: 6839, 6863 **JS:** 6820, 6858

Israel — Cookbooks
IJ: 12996

Israel — Fiction
IJ: 1671, 1837, 1864, 3358 **J:** 3300
JS: 977, 2505, 2622, 2685

Israel — History
IJ: 6849, 10213 **JS:** 6858, 8404

Israel-U.S. relations
JS: 8423

Israeli-Arab relations
See also Arab-Israeli relations
IJ: 8418 **JS:** 8420

Israeli-Arab relations — Fiction
JS: 2622

Italian Americans
IJ: 10227 **JS:** 10224, 10239

Italian Americans — Biography
JS: 5356, 6402

Italian Americans — Fiction
IJ: 3103, 3171, 3181, 3191

Italian Americans — Poetry
IJ: 4538

Italy
IJ: 7545, 8296–99, 8302, 8304

Italy — Biography
JS: 6927, 6951

Italy — Cookbooks
IJ: 12997, 13011 **J:** 13007 **JS:** 13024

Italy — Fiction
IJ: 887, 2058, 3371 **J:** 2672 **JS:** 2536

Italy — History
See also Roman Empire
IJ: 7055, 7586, 7672

Ivory Coast
See Cote d'Ivoire
IJ: 7984, 7999, 8019

Iwo Jima, Battle of
IJ: 7674 **JS:** 7697, 9321, 5947–48,
9019, 9039 **JS:** 5949–50

J

Jackson, Andrew
IJ: 5752, 5947–48, 9019, 9039
JS: 5949–50

Jackson, Bo
IJ: 6700–2

Jackson, Janet
IJ: 5601

Jackson, Jesse
IJ: 5826 **JS:** 5825

Jackson, Mahalia
IJ: 5603 **JS:** 5602

Jackson, Michael
IJ: 5604–5

Jackson, Samuel L.
IJ: 5606

Jackson, Stonewall
IJ: 6109, 6111–12 **JS:** 6110

Jackson, William Henry
IJ: 5231

Jacobs, Harriet A.
IJ: 5827

Jacobs, Harriet A. — Fiction
JS: 2931

Jacobs, Lionel and Barron
IJ: 9212

Jacobsen, Ruth
JS: 6937

Jaguars
JS: 12198

Jaguars — Fiction
JS: 2756

Jails — Fiction
IJ: 1706 **J:** 1705

Jamaica
IJ: 8571, 8577

Jamaica — Biography
J: 5626

Jamaica — Fiction
IJ: 918 **JS:** 759

Jamaica — Music
JS: 7143

Jamaica — Poetry
JS: 4646

Jamaican Americans
JS: 10230

James, Jesse
IJ: 6216–18

James I, King of England
JS: 6938

Jamestown Colony
IJ: 8943

Jamestown Colony — Fiction
IJ: 2802, 2819

Jamestown (VA) — Fiction
JS: 2796

Jamestown (VA) — History
IJ: 8890, 8936 **JS:** 8900

Jane Eyre — Criticism
JS: 4904

Japan
IJ: 8088, 8090, 8094, 8099, 8101,
8104–5 **JS:** 8086, 8089, 8093,
8097–98, 8102

Japan — Art
J: 7094

Japan — Biography
IJ: 7017

Japan — Cookbooks
IJ: 13047

Japan — Crafts
IJ: 8092

Japan — Fiction
IJ: 2593, 2602–3, 2605, 2619, 3316
J: 2585, 2590, 2608 **JS:** 1820,
2028–29, 2120, 2586, 2597, 2611

Japan — Folklore
IJ: 4724 **J:** 4715

Japan — History
IJ: 8087, 8095–96, 8100, 8103
JS: 7755, 8091

Japan — Mythology
IJ: 4838

Japan — Religions
J: 9645

Japanese Americans
See also Asian Americans
IJ: 9334, 9341, 9344, 10172–73, 10181
JS: 7822, 9319, 9322, 9327, 9343,
9345, 10189–90

Japanese Americans — Biography
IJ: 5644, 7017 **JS:** 6734

Japanese Americans — Fiction
IJ: 715–16, 718, 3220, 3322, 3387,
4350 **J:** 717 **JS:** 642, 668, 686

Japanese Americans — History
IJ: 9325, 9332 **J:** 9336 **JS:** 9324,
9326, 9328, 9333

Japanese Canadians — Fiction
IJ: 723 **J:** 3403

Jason (mythology)
IJ: 4853

IJ = Upper Elementary/Lower Middle School; J = Middle School/Junior High; JS = Junior High/Senior High

IJ = Upper Elementary/Lower Middle School; J = Middle School/Junior High; JS = Junior High/Senior High

Journals
See also Diaries
IJ: 7007, 10664

Journals — Fiction
IJ: 445, 3137, 3222 **J:** 3277 **JS:** 3160

Joyce, William
IJ: 7113

Joyner-Kersee, Jackie
IJ: 6756 **JS:** 6757

Judaism
See also Jews; Jews — History;
Religion
IJ: 9681, 9733, 9735–36, 9742, 9745,
9747 **J:** 9734, 9741 **JS:** 9739, 9746

Judaism — Fiction
J: 3811 **JS:** 2504

Judges
JS: 9891

Judicial system
JS: 9891

Judo
IJ: 13265

Jujitsu
JS: 13457

Julia, Raul
IJ: 5609

Julius Caesar (play) — Criticism
JS: 4927

July Fourth
IJ: 10548

Juneteenth
See also Holidays
IJ: 10557

Jungles
IJ: 7675

Junior Iditarod
See Iditarod (Junior)

Junipero Serro, Father
J: 5094

Jupiter (planet)
IJ: 11913, 11982, 11984

Jury system
JS: 9848, 9855

Justice
JS: 9859

Justice — Fiction
IJ: 3856

Justice — Folklore
IJ: 4664

Juvenile crime
JS: 10469

Juvenile delinquency
J: 10417 **JS:** 10468

Juvenile delinquency — Fiction
JS: 102–5, 175, 929, 1791–36 **J:** 5232

K

Kahlo, Frida
IJ: 5233–36 **J:** 5232

**Kaiulani, Princess of Hawaii —
Fiction**
IJ: 3225

Kalahari (Africa)
IJ: 7946

Kalispel Indians — Dances
IJ: 8785

Ka'liulani, Princess
IJ: 6880

Kangaroos
IJ: 12220

Kansas
IJ: 9411, 9428

Kansas — Fiction
IJ: 250, 3018 **J:** 3619

Kansas — History
JS: 9063

Karan, Donna
IJ: 6451

Karate
See also Martial arts
IJ: 13456 **J:** 13455 **JS:** 13459

Karate — Fiction
IJ: 4339, 4348

Karts and karting
IJ: 13305

Kayaks and kayaking
IJ: 9527, 13477

Kazakhstan
IJ: 8327 **JS:** 8315

Kehret, Peg
IJ: 5395

Keller, Helen
IJ: 5775, 6220, 6222 **J:** 6221
JS: 6223–24

Kelly, Jim
IJ: 6703

Kennedy, Jacqueline
See Onassis, Jacqueline Kennedy

Kennedy, John F.
IJ: 5751, 5969, 5974–75 **J:** 5971
JS: 5970, 5972–73, 5976–78

Kennedy, John F. — Assassination
IJ: 9364, 9380

Kennedy, John F., Jr.
J: 5979

Kennedy, Robert F.
JS: 5829, 9354

Kennedy family
JS: 5968

Kentucky
IJ: 9562, 9573

Kentucky — Fiction
IJ: 761, 2851, 3245, 3288 **JS:** 3204

Kenya
IJ: 7873–75, 7882, 7890, 7898, 7901,
7906–7, 7914, 7921 **JS:** 7879, 7889,
7892, 7894, 7896, 7918, 7920, 7922

Kenya — Biography
IJ: 7013

Kenya — Folktales
J: 4702

Kepler, Johannes
J: 6452–53

Kerr, M. E.
JS: 10677

Kerr, M. E. — Criticism
JS: 5396

Kherdian, Jeron
IJ: 7010

Kibbutz life — Fiction
JS: 2622, 2685

Kidd, Jason
IJ: 6654–55

Kidnapping
J: 10311

Kidnapping — Fiction
IJ: 23, 31, 52, 90, 95, 1360, 2539, 3197,
3860, 3889, 3929, 3970, 3978 **J:** 740,
897, 2820, 2917, 3753, 3898, 3913,
3972 **JS:** 142, 441, 811, 1020, 1676,
2242, 3769, 3801, 3803, 3822, 3843,
3974, 4232

Kidney diseases
JS: 11124

Kidney failure — Fiction
JS: 1236

King, Coretta Scott
IJ: 5830–31 **JS:** 5832

King, Horace
IJ: 6225

King, Martin Luther, Jr.
See also Martin Luther King Day
IJ: 5833, 5835, 5837–40, 5842, 9371,
9958, 9990, 10003 **J:** 5836 **JS:** 5834,
5841, 5843, 9353, 10004

King, Stephen
JS: 5398–99

King Philip's War
IJ: 6239

King-Smith, Dick
JS: 5397

Kings — Biography
IJ: 6812

Kings — Fiction
IJ: 2555

Kipsigis (African people)
IJ: 7875

Kissing
JS: 11616

Kleckley, Elizabeth
JS: 6226

Klee, Paul
IJ: 5237

IJ = Upper Elementary/Lower Middle School; J = Middle School/Junior High; JS = Junior High/Senior High

Klimt, Gustav
IJ: 5238

Klondike Gold Rush
See Gold Rush (Klondike)

Knights
See also Middle Ages
IJ: 7558, 7580 J: 4760, 5013, 7569
JS: 7551

Knights — Fiction
IJ: 2306, 2308, 2533–35, 4751 J: 2538
JS: 2518

Knights — Folklore
IJ: 4669, 4742, 4744, 4761

Knitting
IJ: 13135, 13137

Knossos (palace)
JS: 7344

Knot tying
IJ: 12952

Koalas
JS: 12219

Kolbe, Saint Maximilian
IJ: 6942

Kolff, Willem
IJ: 6454

Kollek, Teddy
IJ: 6863

Kongo
See Congo

Kongo (African empire)
J: 7992

Kongo (African people)
JS: 7905

Kongo Ndongo (African kingdom)
JS: 8006

Koran — Women
JS: 9666

Korea — Fiction
IJ: 2599–601 JS: 2575, 2611, 3418

Korean Americans
IJ: 11759 JS: 10184

Korean Americans — Fiction
IJ: 337, 594, 651, 706 J: 652
JS: 653–54, 1368

Korean War
IJ: 7611, 7833, 7850–51 JS: 7825,
7830, 7839, 7853, 9399

Korean War — Battles
JS: 7845

Korean War — Biography
JS: 6796

Korean War — Fiction
JS: 3418

Korean War Veterans Memorial
IJ: 9460

Kosovo
IJ: 8187

Kosovo War — Fiction
IJ: 2687

Kossman, Nina
IJ: 6943

Kovic, Ron
JS: 6227

Ku Klux Klan
IJ: 9994

Ku Klux Klan — Fiction
IJ: 640, 925, 3231, 3268 JS: 3251

Kung fu — Fiction
JS: 2495

Kurdish Americans
IJ: 10095

Kurdistan
JS: 8438

Kurds — Fiction
JS: 649

Kuwait
See also Persian Gulf War
IJ: 8446, 8464 JS: 8458

Kwan, Michelle
IJ: 6729 JS: 6728

Kwanzaa
See also Holidays
IJ: 10551, 10559 JS: 10552

Kyrgyzstan
JS: 8315

L

Labor movements
IJ: 10613

Labor movements — Biography
JS: 5828

Labor movements — Fiction
JS: 3210

Labor problems
IJ: 9261 J: 5461 JS: 9241, 10614

Labor problems — Fiction
IJ: 3078 JS: 698

Labor unions
IJ: 10612 JS: 10609

Labor unions — Biography
IJ: 5804 JS: 5778

Labor unions — Fiction
J: 3284

Labor unions — History
IJ: 9261 JS: 10611, 10614

La Brea Tar Pits (CA)
IJ: 7291

Lacrosse
IJ: 13240, 13281

Lacrosse — Fiction
IJ: 4272

LaDuke, Winona
IJ: 5844

Ladybugs
IJ: 12283

Lafayette, Marquis de
IJ: 7011–12

Lake Superior — Fiction
IJ: 3199

Lakes
See also Ponds
IJ: 12519–20, 12526, 12528

Lakes (U.S.)
See Great Lakes; and specific lakes,
e.g., Lake Erie

Lakota Indians
JS: 8853

Lancelot (knight)
IJ: 4767

**Landers, Ann and Abigail Van
Buren**
J: 6228

Landmines
JS: 10279

Landmines — Fiction
IJ: 1868 JS: 1850

Lange, Dorothea
JS: 5239

Language
IJ: 4942, 4948, 4962 JS: 4949

Language — Food
IJ: 4956

La Niña (weather)
IJ: 12612, 12618, 12622

Laos
IJ: 8113

Laotian Americans
IJ: 10093

La Purisima Mission
IJ: 9529, 9560

La Salle, Cavelier de
IJ: 5061

Lascaux caves
IJ: 7307, 8208

Lasers
IJ: 11820

Latchkey children — Fiction
IJ: 777

Latifah, Queen
IJ: 5610–11

Latimer, Lewis
JS: 6455

Latin America
See Caribbean Islands; Central
America; South America; national
and ethnic groups, e.g., Hispanic
Americans; and specific countries,
e.g., Mexico

Latin America — Culture
IJ: 7115

Latin America — Folklore
IJ: 4823–24

Latin Americans
See Hispanic Americans

IJ = Upper Elementary/Lower Middle School; J = Middle School/Junior High; JS = Junior High/Senior High

IJ = Upper Elementary/Lower Middle School; J = Middle School/Junior High; JS = Junior High/Senior High

IJ = Upper Elementary/Lower Middle School; J = Middle School/Junior High; JS = Junior High/Senior High

Loving *v.* Virginia
JS: 9851

Lowry, Lois
IJ: 5406–7

LSD
See also Drugs and drug abuse
J: 10917, 10957

Luba (African people)
JS: 7911

Lucas, George
IJ: 5621–23

Lullabies
See also Songs
IJ: 7170

Lungs
See also Respiratory system
IJ: 11349

Luo (African people)
IJ: 7874

Lupus — Fiction
J: 1224

***Lusitania* (ship)**
IJ: 7629

Luxembourg
IJ: 8308

Lying — Fiction
IJ: 1092

Lyme disease
IJ: 11060, 11164 JS: 11059, 11188

Lymphoma — Fiction
JS: 1219

Lynx
IJ: 12201

Lyon, Mary
IJ: 5845–26 J: 6123 JS: 6127

M

MacArthur, Douglas
IJ: 6124–26 J: 6123 JS: 6127

Macbeth
IJ: 4439

McCaffrey, Anne
JS: 5408

McCain, John
IJ: 6128 JS: 6129

McCarthy, Joseph
IJ: 6130 JS: 9355, 9395

McCarthyism — Fiction
J: 1631

McClintock, Barbara
IJ: 6463–64 JS: 6462

MacCready, Paul B.
IJ: 5069

MacDonald, Andy
JS: 6773

Mace, Nancy
JS: 7015

McGregor, Ewan
IJ: 5624

McGwire, Mark
IJ: 6605, 13354 JS: 6604

Machines and machinery
See also Simple machines
IJ: 12052, 12734, 12734 JS: 12739

Machines and machinery — History
IJ: 7410, 12740

Machu Picchu (Peru)
IJ: 8635

McKinley, William
J: 5993

McNair, Ronald
IJ: 5070

Mad cow disease
IJ: 11148

Madagascar
IJ: 7934, 7953, 12182, 12186
JS: 7944

Madagascar — Animals
IJ: 12186

Maddux, Greg
IJ: 6606–7

Madison, Dolley
IJ: 5994–95

Madison, James
IJ: 5996 J: 5997

Madison, James — Fiction
IJ: 2882

Madonna (singer)
JS: 5625

Mafia — Fiction
IJ: 4047

Magazines
JS: 4976, 10649

Magee, John
IJ: 5409

Magellan, Ferdinand
IJ: 5008, 5071–73 JS: 5074

Magellan, Ferdinand — Fiction
IJ: 2794

Magic and magicians
IJ: 13099, 13102, 13104, 13106–7
J: 13101, 13108 JS: 13105, 13178

Magic and magicians — Biography
IJ: 5598 JS: 5168

Magic and magicians — Experiments and projects
JS: 11850

Magic and magicians — Fiction
IJ: 1906, 1947, 2052, 3639 JS: 2198, 2206, 2247, 3533

Magic and magicians — Folktales
IJ: 4682

Magic tricks
See Magic and magicians

Magnesium
IJ: 12443

Magnetism
IJ: 12720 JS: 12716

Magnetism — Experiments and projects
IJ: 12721 JS: 12717

Magnifying glasses — Experiments and projects
JS: 11863

Magritte, Rene
IJ: 7103

Mah, Adeline Yen
JS: 7016

Maine
IJ: 9471, 9479, 9486

Maine — Fiction
IJ: 132, 402, 516, 981, 1133, 1147, 1444, 2811, 2892, 3213, 3844, 3869–70
J: 942

Makeup
See Cosmetics

Malamutes — Fiction
IJ: 1126

Malawi
IJ: 7900 JS: 7903

Malaysia
IJ: 8130–31, 8134, 8136

Malcolm X
IJ: 5846–47 J: 5851–52 JS: 5848–50, 5859, 9357

Mali
IJ: 7973 JS: 7923, 8008

Mali — Fiction
IJ: 2555

Mali Empire
J: 8022

Malinke (African people)
IJ: 8011

Mallory, George
IJ: 5075

Malone, Annie Turnbo
IJ: 6465

Malone, Karl
IJ: 6567

Malta
IJ: 8185

Mammals
See also specific mammals, e.g., Bears
IJ: 12111, 12166, 12168, 12174
JS: 12161–63, 12172, 12178

Mammals — Extinct
JS: 7296

Mammals — History
IJ: 7316

Mammals — Homes
IJ: 12157

Mammoths
IJ: 7252

Manassas, Battle of
JS: 9099

IJ = Upper Elementary/Lower Middle School; J = Middle School/Junior High; JS = Junior High/Senior High

Mathematics — Experiments and projects
IJ: 12566 JS: 12551

Mathematics — Fiction
IJ: 1206, 3718

Mathematics — History
IJ: 12552

Mathematics — Projects
IJ: 12556

Mathematics — Puzzles
See Mathematical puzzles

Matisse, Henri
IJ: 5247–49

Matter (physics)
IJ: 12677 JS: 12659, 12665

Matter (physics) — Experiments and projects
JS: 11847

Mayan Indians
IJ: 7334, 8504, 8519, 8524, 8533
J: 8523, 10221 JS: 8514, 8526

Mayan Indians — Fiction
IJ: 2737 J: 2746 JS: 1839, 2756

Mayan Indians — Folklore
IJ: 4829

Mayan Indians — Mythology
IJ: 4836 J: 4831

Mayer, Maria Goeppert
JS: 6467

***Mayflower* (ship)**
IJ: 8866

***Mayflower* (ship) — Fiction**
IJ: 2826, 2834 J: 2800

Mbundu (African people)
JS: 7957

Mbuti (African people)
JS: 7904

Mead, Margaret
IJ: 6469–70 JS: 6468

Measles
JS: 11168

Measures and measurement
See also Concept books —
Measurement
IJ: 12568

Measures and measurement — Experiments and projects
JS: 12551

Media — Violence
See Mass media — Violence

Media studies
See Mass media

Medical care
See Health care

Medical ethics
See also Ethics and ethical behavior
IJ: 11228 J: 11240 JS: 11215, 11218

Medical imaging
J: 11221

Medical technology
JS: 11235

Medici, Lorenzo de
JS: 6949

Medicine
See also Alternative medicine;
Diseases and illness; Doctors
IJ: 11024, 11183, 11214, 11226, 11228,
12406 J: 11217 JS: 11027, 11223,
11232, 11235

Medicine — Biography
IJ: 6278, 6280, 6282, 6310, 6454, 6480,
6498, 11229

Medicine — Careers
JS: 10744, 10808

Medicine — Computers
JS: 11225

Medicine — Fiction
IJ: 2630 JS: 2712

Medicine — History
IJ: 7411, 8744, 8949, 11208, 11210,
11220, 11231 J: 8771, 11135, 11234
JS: 8789, 11209, 11216

Medieval times
See Middle Ages

Medieval times — Folklore
IJ: 4761, 4764

Mediterranean Sea
IJ: 7407, 12641

Mediterranean Sea — History
IJ: 7408

Megan's Law
IJ: 10402

Mehndi
JS: 11269, 11276

Meitner, Lise
JS: 6471–72

Mekong River
IJ: 8025

Memoirs
JS: 4364, 11612

Memory
JS: 11638

Menchu, Rigoberta
IJ: 8530

Mendel, Gregor
IJ: 6474 JS: 6473

Mengele, Josef
J: 6950

Mennonites
IJ: 9700

Mennonites — Fiction
J: 3332 JS: 1340

Menominee Indians
IJ: 8792

Menstruation
See also Puberty
IJ: 11558 J: 11537, 11561, 11574,
11644 JS: 11548, 11566

Mental disorders
See also Mental illness, and specific
disorders, e.g., Compulsive
behavior
JS: 11440

Mental handicaps
See also Depression (mental state);
Dyslexia; Epilepsy; Learning
disabilities
IJ: 10861, 11394 JS: 10862

Mental handicaps — Biography
IJ: 6542

Mental handicaps — Fiction
IJ: 34, 1151, 1165, 1177, 1206, 1242,
1260, 1267, 1270, 1294 J: 938, 1174,
1181, 1768 JS: 1295

Mental health
IJ: 11374 JS: 11384, 11406

Mental illness
See also Mental disorders and specific
disorders, e.g., Compulsive
behavior
IJ: 11096, 11392, 11417 J: 11439
JS: 9916, 11380, 11387, 11391, 11406,
11410, 11419, 11431, 11437, 11440,
11445, 11451

Mental illness — Fiction
IJ: 3045, 3852 J: 1208, 1251, 1265,
1271, 2835 JS: 770, 876, 1190, 1221,
1241, 1250, 1252–53, 1263, 1290, 1351,
1638, 3803

Mental problems
See Mental disorders

Mental retardation — Fiction
JS: 3186, 3485

Mercury (planet)
IJ: 11985

Merina (African people)
JS: 7944

Merlin — Fiction
IJ: 2443–44, 2446 J: 1936 JS: 1935

Mermaids and mermen — Fiction
IJ: 2114 JS: 2512

Mermaids and mermen — Folklore
JS: 4691

Mesa Verde National Park
IJ: 8829, 8864

Mesa Verde National Park — Fiction
IJ: 195

Mesopotamia
J: 7449, 7457

Mesopotamia — History
IJ: 7423, 7436

Metals — History
IJ: 12736

Meteorology
See Weather

Meteorology — Experiments and projects
JS: 12620

IJ = Upper Elementary/Lower Middle School; J = Middle School/Junior High; JS = Junior High/Senior High

IJ = Upper Elementary/Lower Middle School; J = Middle School/Junior High; JS = Junior High/Senior High

IJ = Upper Elementary/Lower Middle School; J = Middle School/Junior High; JS = Junior High/Senior High

Morgan, Julia
JS: 5256

Morgan, Sir Henry
JS: 5078

Mormons
J: 9716

Mormons — Fiction
JS: 555

Morocco
IJ: 7925, 7931

Morrison, Jim
J: 5632

Morrison, Toni
JS: 5413–15

Mosaics (crafts)
IJ: 12974

Mosaics (crafts) — History
IJ: 7391

Moscow
JS: 8316, 8325

Moses, Grandma
IJ: 5258 JS: 5257

Moses (Bible)
IJ: 9624 J: 9665

Moses (Bible) — Fiction
IJ: 2497 J: 2498

Mosques
JS: 7043

Moss, Cynthia
IJ: 6477

Moss, Randy
IJ: 6708–9

Mossi (African people)
JS: 7996, 8003

Motherhood
See Parenting; Parents

Motherhood — Poetry
IJ: 4644

Mothers — Fiction
IJ: 548, 771, 1138

Mothers and daughters — Fiction
IJ: 3751 JS: 587

Mothers and daughters — Poetry
JS: 4540

Motion (physics)
J: 12691

Motion (physics) — Experiments and projects
IJ: 12683–85

Motion pictures
See also Animation (motion pictures)
IJ: 5214, 7198, 7204, 12841, 12845, 12848 JS: 7193–95, 7203, 7212, 10165, 12846, 12850

Motion pictures — Biography
IJ: 5121, 5538, 5612, 5615–16, 5621–23, 5663, 5682–84 J: 5215, 5628, 5681 JS: 5123, 5537, 5554, 5595, 5600, 5613–14, 5629–30, 5680, 5689

Motion pictures — Careers
IJ: 5321, 10755 JS: 7203, 10779

Motion pictures — Fiction
IJ: 3255, 3490 J: 1556, 3177, 3652
JS: 3641

Motion pictures — History
IJ: 9339 JS: 7197

Motion pictures — Science fiction
JS: 7205

Motion pictures — Scripts
JS: 7191, 7196

Motion pictures — Special effects
IJ: 12843, 12849

Motocross
IJ: 13399

Motorbikes
IJ: 13407

Motorcycles
IJ: 13399

Mount, William Sidney
IJ: 5259

Mount Everest
IJ: 5058, 13232, 13304 JS: 5082, 13280, 13316

Mount Everest — Biography
IJ: 5057, 5075

Mount Rushmore National Park
JS: 9430

Mount Rushmore (SD)
IJ: 9419

Mount St. Helens — Fiction
IJ: 198

Mountain and rock climbing
IJ: 13232, 13288, 13295, 13304, 13310
JS: 13280, 13316

Mountain and rock climbing — Biography
IJ: 5056–58, 5075 JS: 5082

Mountain and rock climbing — Fiction
J: 220

Mountain bikes
IJ: 13391–92, 13401, 13403–5
JS: 13396

Mountain bikes — Fiction
IJ: 4278

Mountain life — Fiction
JS: 1291

Mountain States (U.S.)
See specific states, e.g., Colorado

Mountaineering
See Mountain and rock climbing

Mountains
IJ: 12513–17

Mourning, Alonzo
IJ: 6659

Mouth
IJ: 11361

Moving — Fiction
IJ: 402, 872, 967, 1070, 1135, 1335, 1389, 1858 J: 558, 984, 1443, 1448
JS: 1063

Mozart, Wolfgang Amadeus
IJ: 5503

Mugabe, Robert
IJ: 6834

Muhammad
See Mohammed

Muir, John
IJ: 6478 JS: 6479

Mullin, Chris
IJ: 6660

Multiculturalism
JS: 10110, 10116, 10121, 10697

Multiculturalism — Fiction
JS: 622

Multimedia — Careers
IJ: 10828

Multiple births
IJ: 11505

Multiple intelligences
IJ: 10623

Multiple sclerosis
IJ: 11085, 11187 JS: 11030

Multiple sclerosis — Fiction
JS: 1262

Mummies
IJ: 7311, 7327, 7329, 7332–33, 7337, 7348, 7350–51, 7377, 7437, 7453–54

Municipal engineering
JS: 12737

Muniz, Frankie
IJ: 5633

Muñoz Marín, Luis
IJ: 6989

Murals — History
IJ: 7049, 7065

Murder — Fiction
IJ: 569, 836 JS: 741, 1049, 1393, 3287, 3559

Murphy, Eddie
JS: 5634

Murray, Joseph E.
IJ: 6480

Murrow, Edward R.
J: 6134

Muscles
IJ: 11336–37, 11342 JS: 11338, 11341

Musculoskeletal system
See also Skeletal system
IJ: 11339, 11343–45 JS: 11338

Museums
IJ: 9846

Museums — Fiction
IJ: 127, 3448

Mushrooms
IJ: 12017, 12021 JS: 12020

IJ = Upper Elementary/Lower Middle School; J = Middle School/Junior High; JS = Junior High/Senior High

Music

See also Christmas — Songs and carols; Composers — Biography; Folk songs; Musical instruments; Opera; Rock music; Songs; specific instruments, e.g., Flutes; and as a subdivision under country names, e.g., Jamaica — Music
IJ: 4627, 5687, 7117, 7123, 7125–26, 7144 **J:** 4922

Music — African American
IJ: 7122

Music — Biography
IJ: 5136, 5144, 5161, 5492–93, 5501, 5511, 5519, 5521–24, 5536, 5586, 5668–69, 6234, 7026 **J:** 5135, 5150, 5166, 5504, 5517 **JS:** 5109, 5116, 5162, 5494–95, 5498–500, 5512, 5516, 5520, 5529, 5553, 5567, 5575, 5617–18, 5700

Music — Careers
IJ: 7118, 10757, 10766 **JS:** 10753, 10756, 10767, 10770, 10774

Music — Experiments and projects
IJ: 7163

Music — Fiction
IJ: 872, 896, 1762, 2577 **J:** 499, 1758 **JS:** 1202, 1465

Music — History
IJ: 5163, 7119 **JS:** 7127, 7143

Music — Poetry
JS: 4508, 4633

Music — Popular
IJ: 7133, 7136

Music videos
IJ: 7118

Musical instruments
See also specific instruments, e.g., Flutes
IJ: 7157, 7160, 7162–64 **JS:** 7158

Musicals
See also Motion pictures — Musicals
IJ: 3366

Muslims
See Islam

Mussolini, Benito
JS: 6951

Mustangs
IJ: 12409

Mutes and mutism — Fiction
IJ: 1201, 3570, 3858

Myanmar (Burma)
IJ: 8141, 8149, 8151

Myers, Walter Dean
JS: 5416–17

Mystery stories
See also Detectives — Fiction
IJ: 32, 53, 96, 100, 122, 188, 197, 225, 406, 451, 1954, 2025, 2100, 2112–13, 2194, 2271, 2742, 2798, 3054, 3200, 3202, 3212, 3221, 3241, 3436, 3451–52, 3510, 3512, 3526, 3536–37, 3542–43, 3553, 3556–57, 3650, 3659, 3726, 3756–58, 3761, 3768, 3771, 3779, 3782, 3787–90, 3794–96, 3804–5, 3824, 3828, 3835, 3837, 3840–41, 3846, 3851, 3856, 3858–59, 3863–65, 3869–70, 3876, 3881, 3883–85, 3890, 3892, 3895, 3909, 3928–30, 3932, 3936, 3946, 3948, 3952, 3956–57, 3961, 3964, 3967, 3975, 3982, 3984, 3986, 3992–94, 3996, 3998–99, 4004, 4240, 4303, 4324, 4395 **J:** 2590, 2668, 3083, 3818, 3857, 3962, 3979, 4000 **JS:** 354, 436, 478, 546, 2634, 3450, 3478, 3773, 3838, 3861, 3903, 3938, 3985, 3987, 3995

Mystery stories — Fiction
IJ: 274, 331, 1091, 1947, 2118, 2679, 2817, 2932, 2992, 2995, 3327, 3524, 3571, 3754–55, 3760, 3762, 3781, 3806, 3808, 3823, 3829, 3832, 3834, 3842, 3849, 3852, 3860, 3868, 3871, 3880, 3886–87, 3891, 3900, 3905, 3915, 3934–35, 3937, 3951, 3953–54, 3966, 3978, 3980–81, 3991, 4001, 4184 **J:** 2187, 2650, 3468, 3518, 3753, 3777, 3780, 3785, 3807, 3811, 3817, 3819, 3827, 3845, 3866, 3888, 3898–99, 3906, 3908, 3913–14, 3916, 3926, 3939, 3941, 3944, 3949, 3958, 3972, 3976–77, 3983, 3990, 4002, 4005 **JS:** 82, 146, 367–69, 396–97, 425–26, 952, 978, 1527, 1615, 1922, 3443, 3522, 3532, 3534, 3578, 3759, 3763–67, 3770, 3772, 3774–76, 3778, 3783–84, 3791–93, 3797–801, 3803, 3810, 3812–15, 3820, 3822, 3825–26, 3830, 3833, 3847–48, 3850, 3853–55, 3867, 3872–75, 3875, 3877, 3879, 3882, 3893–94, 3896–97, 3901–2, 3904, 3907, 3910–12, 3917–22, 3924–25, 3927, 3933, 3942–43, 3945, 3959–60, 3965, 3968–69, 3971, 3988–89, 4048

Mystery stories — Poetry
JS: 4584

Mythology
See also specific mythological beings, e.g., Athena (Greek goddess); as subdivision under other subjects, e.g., Animals — Mythology; and as subdivision of specific countries, e.g., Greece — Mythology
IJ: 4833–34, 4838, 4842–44, 4846–47, 4849, 4869, 4877, 4882, 4889 **J:** 4832, 4840 **JS:** 2098, 4693, 4835, 4839, 4845, 4848, 4850, 4875

Mythology — Anthologies
IJ: 4841, 4854, 4870

Mythology — Classical
J: 4880 **JS:** 2289, 4855, 4861, 4863–64

Mythology — Fiction
IJ: 2030 **JS:** 2509, 2511

Mythology — Greece
See also Mythology — Classical; Greece — Mythology
IJ: 4852, 4866, 4884 **J:** 4865, 4879 **JS:** 2289, 2512, 4871, 4883

Mythology — Mayan Indians
IJ: 4836

Mythology — Poetry
J: 4498

Mythology — Rome
IJ: 4878 **J:** 4888 **JS:** 4886–37

N

Nader, Ralph
JS: 6135–37

Nagasaki
JS: 7711

Naked mole-rats
IJ: 12169–70

Namibia
IJ: 7938, 7951 **JS:** 7933, 7967

Namibia — Fiction
JS: 596

Nantucket (MA) — Fiction
IJ: 2950

Napoleonic Wars
IJ: 8276 **JS:** 7603

Napster — Biography
IJ: 6400

Narcotics
See also Drugs and drug abuse
J: 10926

Narrative poetry
IJ: 4653 **J:** 4654

NASCAR
IJ: 6580, 13324

Nash, Kevin
IJ: 6775

Nast, Thomas
IJ: 5260

Natchez Trace
J: 9202

Natchez Trail — Fiction
IJ: 3027

Nation, Carry A.
IJ: 6233

Nation of Islam
IJ: 10125 **JS:** 10133

Nation of Islam — Biography
JS: 5815

National Association for the Advancement of Colored People (NAACP)
J: 10033

National debt
IJ: 9840

National Football League
IJ: 13424

National Guard (U.S.) — Careers
IJ: 10708

National Institutes of Health (U.S.)
J: 9834

National Law Enforcement Officers Memorial (Washington, DC)
IJ: 9456

IJ = Upper Elementary/Lower Middle School; J = Middle School/Junior High; JS = Junior High/Senior High

IJ = Upper Elementary/Lower Middle School; J = Middle School/Junior High; JS = Junior High/Senior High

New Deal
IJ: 9282, 9297, 9318 J: 9300, 9313
JS: 9287, 9304–5, 9316

New England
See also specific states, e.g.,
Massachusetts
IJ: 9484

New England — Fiction
IJ: 812, 3536 J: 1065, 3190 JS: 1544,
3186

New England — History
IJ: 9469

New Guinea — Fiction
JS: 39

New Hampshire
IJ: 9507

New Hampshire — Fiction
IJ: 2904

New Hampshire — History
IJ: 8886

New Hampshire Colony
IJ: 8904

New Jersey
IJ: 9498, 9508

New Jersey — Fiction
IJ: 1006, 3384, 3604, 3714 J: 3177

New Jersey — History
IJ: 8948 JS: 12331

New Jersey Colony
IJ: 8905

**New Kids on the Block (musical
group)**
IJ: 5635

New Mexico
IJ: 9594–95

New Mexico — Biography
IJ: 5014

New Mexico — Fiction
IJ: 1116, 4805 J: 3097

New Orleans — Fiction
IJ: 2916

New Orleans, Battle of
IJ: 9039

New Stone Age
IJ: 7304

New York City
IJ: 9470, 9490, 9497, 9504, 9511,
10527, 12764, 12852

New York City — Biography
IJ: 6260

New York City — Fiction
IJ: 115, 127, 318, 979, 1421, 1442,
1573, 3174, 3181, 3184, 3242, 3256,
3258, 3344, 4053 J: 669, 672, 747,
1409, 1647, 2298, 3176, 3201, 3276
JS: 609, 676, 682, 1163, 1630, 1711,
3263

New York City — History
IJ: 6257, 10088 JS: 9483, 9493,
10144

New York City — Subway system
JS: 9495

New York State
IJ: 9472, 9479, 9505, 9512 JS: 9489

New York State — Fiction
IJ: 2133–34, 2810, 2887, 2897, 2922,
3461, 3496 J: 862, 2909 JS: 385,
2908, 2955, 3139

New York State — History
IJ: 8955, 9052, 9463

New York State Colony
IJ: 8906

New Zealand
IJ: 8161, 8164, 8175

New Zealand — Conservation
IJ: 12264

New Zealand — Fiction
IJ: 764 JS: 101, 1338, 1602, 2582,
2592, 3814–15

New Zealand — Folklore
JS: 4731

Newbery Award — Anthologies
IJ: 4369

Newfoundland — Fiction
IJ: 34, 88, 118, 1532

Newspapers
IJ: 10644, 10666 JS: 4988

Newspapers — Fiction
IJ: 460, 3618 JS: 1870

Newspapers — History
JS: 4991

Newton, Isaac
IJ: 6481–82, 6484–85 JS: 6483

Newton, John
IJ: 6234

Nez Perce Indians
IJ: 8762 JS: 8769

Nez Perce Indians — Biography
JS: 6074

Nez Perce Indians — Fiction
IJ: 2785

Ngoni (African people)
JS: 7903

Niagara Falls
J: 9475

Niagara River
IJ: 8500

Nicaragua
IJ: 8502, 8511, 8522

Nicaraguan Americans
JS: 10195

Nicotine
See also Smoking; Tobacco industry
JS: 10971

Niger
IJ: 7973, 7991, 8014 JS: 7862

Nigeria
IJ: 7972, 7979, 8000, 8009–10, 8014,
8020 JS: 7974–75, 7988, 8008, 8013

Nigeria — Folklore
IJ: 4704

Nigeria — History
IJ: 8002 J: 7998

Night
See also Nocturnal animals
IJ: 503

Nightingale, Florence
IJ: 7019

Nightmares — Fiction
IJ: 3586 JS: 3812, 3959

Nile River
IJ: 7924, 7926

Nir, Yehuda
JS: 7020

Nitrogen
IJ: 12432, 12435 J: 12424

Nixon, Joan Lowery
IJ: 5420

Nixon, Richard M.
IJ: 5754, 6000, 9394 J: 6001
JS: 5999, 6002, 9362, 9368, 9870

Noah (Bible)
IJ: 9615

Noah's Ark
See Animals — Ark; Noah (Bible)

Nobel, Alfred
IJ: 6953

Nobel Prize
IJ: 6394

Nobel Prize — Biography
IJ: 6953

Nobel Prize winners — Biography
JS: 6281, 6462, 6467

Nobel Prizes
IJ: 6045, 6792, 6874, 6876, 8252, 8530

North America — Crafts
IJ: 12988

North America — Exploration
IJ: 8880, 8882 J: 8475 JS: 5032,
8870

North America — Geography
JS: 12456

North Carolina
IJ: 9578, 9586 J: 1051

North Carolina — Fiction
IJ: 545, 815, 836, 1106, 2923, 3145
JS: 673, 3180

North Carolina — History
IJ: 8950, 9589

North Dakota
IJ: 9425

North Dakota — Fiction
JS: 3233

North Korea
JS: 8137

North Pole
See also Arctic; Polar regions
JS: 8663

IJ = Upper Elementary/Lower Middle School; J = Middle School/Junior High; JS = Junior High/Senior High

North Pole — Exploration
See also Polar regions
J: 5081

Northeast Indians
JS: 8807

Northeast (U.S.)
IJ: 9482

Northeast (U.S.) — Anthologies
IJ: 9503

Northeast (U.S.) — History
IJ: 8896, 9260

Northern Ireland
See Ireland, Northern

Northern Ireland — Fiction
IJ: 3311 **J:** 1419, 1717 **JS:** 98

Northern lights
IJ: 12624

Northwest Indians
JS: 8805

Northwest Passage
IJ: 8484

Northwest (U.S.) — Native Americans
JS: 8755

Norway
IJ: 8355, 8358, 8367

Norway — Cookbooks
IJ: 13028

Norway — Fiction
IJ: 3356 **JS:** 2699

Norwegian Americans — Fiction
JS: 859

Noses
IJ: 11361

Nova Scotia
IJ: 8499

Nova Scotia — Fiction
JS: 861

Nubia (African empire)
J: 7867

Nubia (African empire) — History
JS: 7502

Nuclear accidents
JS: 12699

Nuclear energy
IJ: 12704 **JS:** 12697, 12699, 12701, 12703

Nuclear holocaust — Fiction
JS: 2381

Nuclear medicine
JS: 11223

Nuclear physics
JS: 12441

Nuclear physics — Biography
JS: 6286, 6471–72

Nuclear power plants
IJ: 12702

Nuclear power plants — Accidents
IJ: 12695–96, 12698

Nuclear submarines
IJ: 12700

Nuclear submarines — Accidents
IJ: 12700

Nuclear war — Fiction
IJ: 206 **JS:** 144, 1495, 1855, 1879, 4208

Nuclear waste
IJ: 10329

Nuclear waste — Fiction
IJ: 1857 **JS:** 3867

Nuclear weapons
JS: 7791, 9770, 12724, 12933, 12938, 12948

Numbers
See also Mathematics; Statistics
IJ: 12558

Nunez, Tommy
JS: 6661

Nuns — Biography
IJ: 6877

Nupe (African people)
JS: 7996

Nuremberg trials
JS: 7658, 7773

Nureyev, Rudolf
IJ: 5636

Nursery rhymes
JS: 7108

Nurses
J: 11207

Nurses — Biography
IJ: 7019

Nurses — Fiction
JS: 3425

Nurses — World War II
IJ: 7734

Nursing homes — Fiction
IJ: 1322

Nutrition
IJ: 10860, 11267, 11329, 11331, 11366, 11374, 11462–63, 11474–75, 13249, 13400 **J:** 11472 **JS:** 11367, 11372, 11459, 11468

Nzingha (African queen) — Fiction
IJ: 2567

O

Oakland (CA)
IJ: 9523

Oakley, Annie
IJ: 5637–39

Oakley, Annie — Fiction
IJ: 3179

Oatman, Olive
IJ: 6235

Obesity
See also Weight problems
IJ: 11463 **JS:** 11033

Obesity — Fiction
IJ: 491, 3737 **J:** 1168, 1208, 1540
JS: 1184, 1202, 1595, 2053

O'Brien, Dan
IJ: 6762

Observatories
JS: 11899

Obsessive-compulsive disorder
JS: 11408

Obsessive-compulsive disorder — Fiction
IJ: 1206, 1277 **JS:** 1209, 1213

Occupational guidance
See also Vocational guidance

Occupations and work
See Careers; and specific occupations, e.g., Astronauts — Careers

Ocean liners — Fiction
J: 3866

Oceanography
See also Marine biology; Marine life; Underwater exploration
IJ: 12633–34, 12642 **J:** 12649
JS: 12648

Oceanography — Biography
IJ: 6315

Oceanography — Experiments and projects
IJ: 12631, 12639

Oceans
See also Beaches; Marine animals, etc; Oceanography; Seashores; and specific oceans, e.g., Atlantic Ocean
IJ: 12312, 12630, 12635–37, 12639, 12642–43 **JS:** 12632

Oceans — Experiments and projects
IJ: 12644

Oceans — Fiction
IJ: 200

O'Connor, Sandra Day
IJ: 6140 **JS:** 6139

Octopuses
IJ: 12307

O'Donnell, Rosie
IJ: 5640–42

Odysseus
IJ: 4852, 4884

Odysseus — Fiction
IJ: 2452

Odyssey (mythology)
J: 4880

O'Grady, Scott
IJ: 5079

Ohio
IJ: 9421, 9427, 9434

Ohio — Fiction
IJ: 909 **J:** 3048

IJ = Upper Elementary/Lower Middle School; J = Middle School/Junior High; JS = Junior High/Senior High

IJ = Upper Elementary/Lower Middle School; J = Middle School/Junior High; JS = Junior High/Senior High

IJ = Upper Elementary/Lower Middle School; J = Middle School/Junior High; JS = Junior High/Senior High

Pawnee Indians — Fiction
IJ: 3110–11

Pawtucket Indians — Fiction
JS: 2823

Payne, Lucille M. W.
JS: 6237

PCP (drug)
See also Drugs and drug abuse
JS: 10921, 10976

Peace
See Pacifists and pacifism

Peace — Folklore
IJ: 4668

Peace Corps
IJ: 9764

Peace movement
J: 9941

Peace movement — Women
JS: 9954

Peale, Charles Willson
IJ: 5266–67

Peanut butter
IJ: 13035

Pearl Harbor
IJ: 9335 JS: 7647, 7748, 7772

Pearl Harbor — Fiction
IJ: 3326, 3387 J: 3362

Pearl Harbor — History
IJ: 7639, 7676, 7754, 7806–7, 7818
J: 7690 JS: 9342

Peary, Robert E.
IJ: 5080 J: 5081 JS: 8663

Peas
IJ: 12060

Pedophiles — Fiction
JS: 1756

Peer pressure
JS: 10975

Pele (soccer player)
IJ: 6777

Penacook Indians — Fiction
IJ: 604

Penguins
IJ: 12252–54

Penicillin
JS: 6405

Penmanship — Fiction
IJ: 2914

Pennsylvania
IJ: 9480, 9483, 9500

Pennsylvania — Fiction
IJ: 566, 655, 2871, 3141, 3162, 3494,
9513 J: 2795, 3198 JS: 2801, 3101

Pennsylvania — History
IJ: 8940, 12589

Pennsylvania Colony
IJ: 8907

Penraat, Jaap
IJ: 7804

Perception
J: 11353, 11359

Peregrine falcons
See Falcons

Performing arts — Biography
J: 5152 JS: 5145

Perkins, Frances
JS: 6147

Persia
See Iran

Persia — History
JS: 7507

Persian Gulf War
IJ: 6154, 7834, 7838, 7841, 8446, 9396
JS: 7842–43, 7857, 12947

Persian Gulf War — Biography
JS: 6149, 6159

Persian Gulf War — Fiction
J: 2715

Personal appearance
J: 11270

Personal finance
J: 10846 JS: 10616, 10850

Personal guidance
IJ: 10628, 10634, 11540, 11555–56,
11564, 11649, 11655, 11661, 11666,
11672, 11692, 11696, 11706, 11708,
11711 J: 11644, 11676–77, 11688
JS: 9643, 9663, 10691, 11377, 11390,
11536, 11571, 11584, 11587, 11621–22,
11624, 11627, 11640–43, 11650,
11652–54, 11663–65, 11667–69, 11675,
11682, 11685–86, 11689–90, 11693–94,
11698, 11700–2, 11704, 11709–10,
11714, 11716, 11718, 11720–21

Personal guidance — Boys
J: 11660 JS: 10859

Personal guidance — Fiction
JS: 1324, 1639, 1778

Personal guidance — Girls
IJ: 11639, 11657–58, 11671, 11680,
11691, 11705, 11707, 11717, 11719,
11724 J: 11651, 11678 JS: 11645–46,
11648, 11673–74, 11687, 11695, 11699,
11712–13, 11715

Personal problems
See also Bullies; Child abuse; Death;
Divorce; Moving; Personal
guidance; Sexual abuse; Teenagers
— Problems
IJ: 11696–97 JS: 1761, 1806, 10366,
11618, 11659, 11693

Personal problems — Fiction
IJ: 45, 50, 74, 229, 245, 306, 355, 401,
427, 448, 465, 474, 516, 541, 545, 551,
577, 584, 588, 598, 604, 641, 647, 661,
710–11, 771–72, 801, 814, 842, 863,
870, 882, 894–95, 902, 931, 955, 1008,
1022, 1053, 1066, 1090, 1101, 1104,
1112, 1134, 1172, 1197, 1199, 1206,
1216, 1240, 1277, 1298, 1300, 1307,
1310–11, 1315, 1318–19, 1322–23,
1328, 1335, 1342, 1342–43, 1348–49,
1352, 1356–57, 1365, 1370–71, 1379,
1381–84, 1389, 1399, 1401, 1404, 1406,

1421, 1425, 1437, 1439, 1442, 1451,
1455, 1459, 1466, 1468, 1470, 1473,
1475, 1478, 1482, 1484–85, 1487,
1497–99, 1501, 1509, 1513, 1516–17,
1521, 1532, 1535–36, 1538, 1547, 1549,
1551, 1561, 1564–65, 1569, 1571,
1573–75, 1577, 1582–83, 1585, 1604,
1607–8, 1613, 1628, 1632, 1643, 1646,
1658, 1667, 1690, 1695, 1698–703,
1707, 1714, 1721, 1723, 1728, 1731–32,
1736–38, 1742, 1746, 1757, 1770,
1773–75, 1777, 1780, 1784, 1786, 1794,
1799, 1803–4, 1808, 1810, 1818, 1830,
1894, 2197, 2211, 2524, 2569, 2612,
2651, 2658, 2706, 2730, 2741, 2914,
2979, 3044, 3059, 3119, 3127, 3174,
3231, 3238, 3274, 3282, 3291, 3354,
3543, 3549, 3618, 3622, 3686, 3696,
3892, 4254, 4261, 4267, 4337, 4361,
4385 J: 128, 252, 266, 290, 461, 652,
722, 744, 782, 796, 821, 862, 1143,
1173, 1205, 1212, 1301, 1308, 1314,
1326, 1359, 1372, 1374–75, 1380,
1396–97, 1400, 1407, 1424, 1429, 1448,
1471, 1488, 1508, 1520, 1526, 1533–34,
1537, 1553, 1555, 1559, 1566–67, 1587,
1589, 1598–99, 1619, 1629, 1631, 1649,
1657, 1659, 1672, 1705, 1713, 1725,
1741, 1744, 1754, 1758, 1764, 1771,
1812, 1826, 1845, 1847, 1978, 2363,
3392, 3695, 4268, 4295, 4323 JS: 112,
140, 190, 559, 612, 631, 637, 642, 681,
694, 752, 794, 808–9, 929, 961, 1048,
1074, 1094–95, 1105, 1127, 1162, 1178,
1193, 1196, 1213, 1217, 1225, 1227,
1229, 1232, 1236, 1249, 1252, 1282,
1289, 1295–96, 1303, 1313, 1317, 1324,
1332, 1340–41, 1345–47, 1350, 1355,
1363, 1366–67, 1369, 1377–78,
1385–87, 1390–93, 1398, 1402–3, 1405,
1412–13, 1415, 1417–18, 1420, 1422,
1427, 1430, 1434–35, 1438, 1441, 1446,
1450, 1458, 1461, 1464–65, 1469,
1476–77, 1486, 1489, 1493, 1495–96,
1504, 1511, 1515, 1519, 1522, 1527,
1541–45, 1548, 1552, 1562, 1572, 1576,
1578, 1581, 1584, 1588, 1593–94, 1600,
1603, 1605, 1609–12, 1615–16, 1618,
1620, 1624–26, 1630, 1634–35, 1642,
1644, 1648, 1652–53, 1656, 1661,
1663–64, 1669, 1682, 1685, 1687–89,
1691–93, 1696, 1711, 1718, 1720, 1724,
1735, 1739, 1743, 1745, 1747, 1752,
1756, 1759–60, 1763, 1765, 1767, 1776,
1781, 1787, 1789–93, 1795–98, 1800,
1805, 1820–21, 1823–24, 1827–29,
1831, 1879, 1885, 1963, 1990, 2557,
2571, 2699, 3180, 3183, 3260, 3267,
3292, 3386, 3460, 3486, 3552, 3676,
3679, 3687, 3713, 3723, 3784, 3912,
4019, 4032, 4063, 4074, 4079, 4327–28,
4332, 4347

Personal problems — Poetry
IJ: 4585 JS: 4600

Personality
JS: 11610

Peru
IJ: 8594, 8598, 8604, 8608, 8613, 8619,
8626, 8629

Peru — Fiction
J: 155 JS: 1832

IJ = Upper Elementary/Lower Middle School; J = Middle School/Junior High; JS = Junior High/Senior High

IJ = Upper Elementary/Lower Middle School; J = Middle School/Junior High; JS = Junior High/Senior High

IJ = Upper Elementary/Lower Middle School; J = Middle School/Junior High; JS = Junior High/Senior High

IJ = Upper Elementary/Lower Middle School; J = Middle School/Junior High; JS = Junior High/Senior High

Powell, John Wesley
IJ: 5087, 9257

Powers, Harriet
IJ: 5279

Powhatan Indians
IJ: 8764

Powhatan Indians — Biography
IJ: 6242

Powwows
IJ: 8785, 8812

Prague — Fiction
IJ: 2667

Prairies
See also Grasslands
IJ: 7384, 12533

Prayers
See also Blessings
IJ: 9614–15, 9649, 9652 J: 9671

Predictions
See also Fortune telling; Prophecies
IJ: 13173, 13196 JS: 10532, 13182

Pregnancy
IJ: 11573 JS: 11489, 11499, 11502–3,
11506, 11510, 11516, 11520, 11526

Pregnancy — Fiction
IJ: 903, 1045, 1349, 1574 JS: 779,
1427, 1514, 1570, 1644, 1753

Pregnancy — Teenage
IJ: 11573 JS: 11490

Prehistoric animals
See also Dinosaurs; Mammoths
JS: 7282

Prehistoric art
IJ: 7080

Prehistoric life
See also Paleontology; Stone age
IJ: 7295, 7298, 7302, 7304–5, 7307,
7309, 7316–18, 7325, 7329–30, 7335,
7394, 7400, 8787 J: 7320 JS: 7306,
8478

Prehistoric life — Fiction
IJ: 2483–85, 2487, 2489–90, 3606
J: 2481–82, 3807 JS: 2486, 2488

Prejudice
See also Discrimination; Racism
IJ: 7374, 9961, 10026, 10113, 10256
J: 10260 JS: 10010, 10104, 10107,
10111, 10117, 10119, 10121, 10506

Prejudice — Fiction
IJ: 213, 430, 599, 625, 629, 643, 661,
674, 685, 696, 700, 712, 726, 925, 2563,
3066, 3137, 3146, 3188, 3226, 3268,
3290 J: 2213 JS: 82, 556, 582, 612,
623, 635, 654, 668, 673, 688, 693, 702,
714, 732, 1766, 1865, 1869, 1983, 3163,
3298, 4087

Premenstrual syndrome
JS: 11126

Preserved bodies
IJ: 7377

Presidency (U.S.)
JS: 9813, 9930

Presidents (U.S.)
IJ: 9352, 9815–16, 9819, 9821–22
J: 9118 JS: 5930, 5983, 6036, 9807–9,
9823, 9950

Presidents (U.S.) — Assassinations
J: 5770, 8726

Presidents (U.S.) — Biography
See also individual presidents, e.g.,
Bush, George W.
IJ: 5711, 5750–55, 5768, 5771, 5897,
5900–2, 5906–7, 5909–12, 5914–19,
5923–24, 5926–27, 5932–33, 5935,
5938, 5940, 5943–45, 5947–48, 5952,
5956–57, 5960–62, 5964, 5966, 5969,
5974–75, 5982, 5984, 5990–91, 5996,
6000, 6004–6, 6016, 6018–21, 6023,
6025–27, 6029, 6032–35, 6037–38,
6041, 6045–46, 6048, 8712, 9817, 9820
J: 5712, 5774, 5899, 5921–22, 5931,
5937, 5941, 5953, 5971, 5981, 5985,
5987, 5989, 5993, 5997, 6001, 6024,
6028, 6039 JS: 5898, 5903–5, 5908,
5920, 5925, 5934, 5936, 5942, 5949–50,
5954–55, 5958–59, 5963, 5965, 5967,
5970, 5972–73, 5976–78, 5980, 5988,
5998–99, 6002, 6007, 6017, 6022,
6030–31, 6040, 6042–43, 6047

Presidents (U.S.) — Elections
IJ: 9929 JS: 9818, 9931

Presidents (U.S.) — Fiction
IJ: 2849 JS: 1144

Presidents (U.S.) — History
JS: 9806

Presidents (U.S.) — Impeachment
JS: 9810–11, 9814

Presidents (U.S.) — Scandals
J: 5774

Presidents (U.S.) — Speeches
JS: 9824

**Presidents (U.S.) — Wives —
Biography**
IJ: 5711, 5748, 5893, 5895, 5913, 5916,
5928, 5946, 5992, 5994–95, 6003,
6009–11, 6014–15 J: 5781, 5899, 5929,
6008, 6044 JS: 5762, 5892, 5896,
6012–13

Presley, Elvis
IJ: 5651 J: 5648–49 JS: 5650, 5652

Presley, Elvis — Fiction
JS: 662

Press, freedom of the
See Freedom of the press

Prieto, Jorgé
JS: 6710

Primates
IJ: 12185

**Prime ministers (Great Britain) —
Biography**
IJ: 6900, 6964

**Prime ministers (Zimbabwe) —
Biography**
IJ: 6834

Prince Edward Island — Fiction
J: 1032 JS: 833

Princes — Fiction
IJ: 72, 4748 JS: 553

Princesses
IJ: 11629

Princesses — Biography
IJ: 6799

Princesses — Fiction
IJ: 3614, 4748 J: 3612 JS: 2551,
2723, 3611, 3613, 4661

Printing
See also Books and printing
IJ: 9119 JS: 4978

Printing — Biography
IJ: 6440

Printing — Crafts
IJ: 13121

Printing — History
IJ: 4974

Printz, Michael
IJ: 6244

Prisoners of war — Fiction
IJ: 3023

Prisons
IJ: 10416, 10457 JS: 10394, 10400,
10405, 10413, 10430, 10436, 10439,
10442, 11765, 11782

Prisons — Fiction
IJ: 295 J: 148, 2418 JS: 342, 505,
1041, 1430, 2587, 2663, 2747

Privacy rights
J: 9965, 10283 JS: 9963, 9985

Private schools — Fiction
JS: 1390, 1692, 3799, 3853

Prohibition (U.S.)
JS: 9296, 9799

Prohibition (U.S.) — Biography
IJ: 6233

Prohibition (U.S.) — Fiction
J: 3280 JS: 3270

Prophecies
See also Predictions
IJ: 13190

Prophets (Bible)
JS: 9662

Prostitution — Fiction
JS: 1163, 1665

Protestantism
JS: 9706

Protests and demonstrations
JS: 10531

Proverbs (Bible)
JS: 9621

Prozac
J: 10979

Psychiatrists — Fiction
JS: 3812

Psychic abilities — Fiction
J: 627 JS: 425–26

Psychoanalysis
JS: 6414

IJ = Upper Elementary/Lower Middle School; J = Middle School/Junior High; JS = Junior High/Senior High

Psychology
See also Human development and behavior
JS: 11609, 11611

Puberty
See also Adolescence; Menstruation
IJ: 11538–40, 11550, 11556, 11564, 11578 **J:** 11382

Puberty — Boys
IJ: 11547, 11559 **JS:** 11549

Puberty — Fiction
IJ: 1410

Puberty — Girls
IJ: 11555, 11559 **J:** 11537 **JS:** 11560

Public service — Careers
JS: 10784

Public speaking
IJ: 10678 **JS:** 10655

Public welfare
JS: 10481, 10491

Public welfare — Fiction
JS: 1867

Publishing
See also Book making
IJ: 9119 **JS:** 4976

Publishing — Biography
IJ: 6352 **JS:** 6210

Pueblo Indians
IJ: 8765, 8784, 8819, 8829, 8838, 8864
JS: 4802, 8862

Pueblo Indians — Fiction
IJ: 2792 **JS:** 2793

Pueblo Indians — History
IJ: 8752

Pueblo Indians — Legends
JS: 4801

Puerto Ricans
IJ: 10191

Puerto Ricans — Biography
IJ: 5631, 6593, 6595, 6989, 7007

Puerto Ricans — Fiction
IJ: 671, 3514 **J:** 669–70, 672 **JS:** 611, 1127

Puerto Rico
IJ: 8566, 8572, 8575 **JS:** 8567, 8569

Puerto Rico — Fiction
IJ: 599, 2727

Puerto Rico — History
IJ: 6989, 8579

Puffins
IJ: 12234

Pulaski, Casimir
IJ: 6956

Pulitzer, Joseph
IJ: 6493 **JS:** 6492

Pullman strike (1894)
JS: 10611, 10614

Puma

Pumpkin decorating
IJ: 12976

Punctuation
IJ: 10685

Punic Wars
JS: 7521, 7527

Punishment
JS: 10423

Puppets and marionettes — Fiction
IJ: 2602, 4734 **JS:** 3439

Puritans
IJ: 8892

Puritans — Fiction
JS: 2823, 2831

Putin, Vladimir
IJ: 6957

Puzzles
See also Games; Mathematical puzzles; Word games and puzzles
IJ: 11860, 13152, 13161

Puzzles — Fiction
IJ: 3718

Puzzles — Poetry
IJ: 4537

Pygmies
IJ: 7895

Pygmies — Fiction
IJ: 3152

Pyle, Ernie
IJ: 5433

Pyramids
See also Egypt — History
IJ: 7431, 7438, 7460 **J:** 7339
JS: 7044, 7427

Q

Qatar
IJ: 8436

Qin, Emperor of China — Tomb
IJ: 8047

Quaaludes (drugs)
See also Drugs and drug abuse
JS: 11023

Quadruplets — Fiction
IJ: 842

Quakers
JS: 9717

Quakers — Fiction
IJ: 2964 **J:** 2945

Quapaw Indians — Fiction
JS: 2384

Quebec (province)
JS: 8494

Queens — Biography
IJ: 6813

Quilts and quilting
IJ: 5279, 13134, 13139–42

Quilts and quilting — Fiction
JS: 2836

Quinceanera (coming-of-age ritual)
IJ: 10553

Quinceanera (coming-of-age ritual) — Fiction
J: 608 **JS:** 687

Quinn, Anthony
IJ: 5653

Quintanilla, Guadalupe
IJ: 6245

Quotations
IJ: 4972 **JS:** 11718

Quotations — Anthologies
IJ: 10648, 2196 **JS:** 1893

R

Rabbits — Fiction
IJ: 2158, 2196 **JS:** 1893

Raccoons
JS: 12173

Raccoons — Fiction
IJ: 250, 303

Race relations
IJ: 9990

Race relations — Fiction
JS: 3286

Racial prejudice
JS: 11618

Racially mixed people
JS: 10106

Racing cars
IJ: 12887

Racism
See also Discrimination; Prejudice; Segregation (U.S.)
IJ: 10026, 10103, 10256 **J:** 9299, 9378, 9998, 10102, 10112 **JS:** 7763, 9768, 9886, 9974, 10020, 10104, 10107, 10111, 10114, 10117, 10121–22, 10150, 10571, 11625, 13409

Racism — Fiction
IJ: 291, 406, 410, 497, 618, 639, 726, 733, 767, 969, 1158, 2089, 2558, 2722, 3244, 4314 **J:** 1782 **JS:** 612, 623, 653, 662, 725, 732, 1394, 1856, 2581, 2968, 3004, 3215, 3251, 3262, 3271, 3287

Radiation
See Nuclear energy

Radicalism
JS: 10292

Radio — Careers
JS: 10776

Radio — Fiction
IJ: 3303 **JS:** 553

Radio control models
IJ: 12961

Radioactive materials
See also Nuclear energy
JS: 9770

IJ = Upper Elementary/Lower Middle School; J = Middle School/Junior High; JS = Junior High/Senior High

IJ = Upper Elementary/Lower Middle School; J = Middle School/Junior High; JS = Junior High/Senior High

IJ = Upper Elementary/Lower Middle School; J = Middle School/Junior High; JS = Junior High/Senior High

IJ = Upper Elementary/Lower Middle School; J = Middle School/Junior High; JS = Junior High/Senior High

IJ = Upper Elementary/Lower Middle School; J = Middle School/Junior High; JS = Junior High/Senior High

San Juan (Puerto Rico)
IJ: 8572

Santa Anna, Antonio Lopez de
IJ: 6990

Santa Claus
IJ: 9697

Santa Claus — Fiction
J: 2031

Santa Fe Trail
JS: 9203

Santa Fe Trail — Fiction
IJ: 3055–56, 3073, 3095

Santee Sioux Indians
J: 8774

Saratoga, Battle of
IJ: 8990

Sasquatch — Fiction
IJ: 198

Satanism
JS: 9755

Satellites
IJ: 12735, 12832

Satire
See Humor

Saturn (planet)
IJ: 11977, 11986, 11991

Saudi Arabia
See also Arabia
IJ: 8448, 8451, 8454, 8459 **JS:** 8439

Saudi Arabia — Biography
IJ: 8468

Savings (business)
IJ: 10592

Savion
IJ: 5667

Scandinavia
See Denmark; Finland; Norway;
Sweden; Vikings

Scandinavia — Crafts
IJ: 8361

Scandinavia — History
IJ: 8365

Scandinavia — Mythology
JS: 4839

Scandinavian Americans
JS: 10241

Schindler, Oskar
J: 6961 **JS:** 6960

Schizophrenia
See also Mental illness
JS: 11419

Schizophrenia — Fiction
JS: 1221, 1283

Schliemann, Heinrich
IJ: 7323

Scholarships
JS: 10694

Scholl, Hans and Sophie
JS: 6962

School of American Ballet — Fiction
IJ: 1737

Schools
See also Education
IJ: 10627–28, 10633 **JS:** 9903, 10396,
10635

Schools — Censorship
J: 10514

Schools — Fiction
IJ: 253, 433, 447, 460, 466, 468, 477,
483, 486, 496–97, 512–14, 519, 523,
525, 535–36, 561, 577, 581, 583–84,
589, 629, 641, 647, 689, 721, 726, 758,
830, 1166, 1176, 1200, 1300, 1370,
1399, 1437, 1462, 1473, 1499, 1529,
1531, 1568, 1658, 1670, 1698, 1712,
1715, 1732, 1740, 1749, 1751, 1770,
1775, 2026, 2152, 2182, 2211, 3119,
3222, 3290, 3601, 3603, 3610, 3618,
3637, 3681, 3698, 3709, 3724, 3737,
3745, 3747, 3794, 3915, 3980, 4049,
4061, 4223, 4256, 4264, 4334 **J:** 636,
709, 1396, 1407–8, 1479, 1537, 1555,
1587, 1657, 1741, 1755, 1816, 1847,
1874, 2260, 3535, 3617, 3656, 3699,
3949, 4076, 4078, 4316 **JS:** 83, 217,
435, 446, 456–57, 464, 500, 555–56,
591, 628, 702, 1086, 1239, 1302, 1313,
1317, 1325, 1367, 1377–78, 1385–86,
1390, 1440, 1450, 1456, 1460, 1474,
1489, 1507, 1518, 1525, 1528, 1550,
1558, 1576, 1581, 1616, 1633, 1635,
1644, 1650, 1669, 1678, 1692, 1718,
1726, 1766, 1783, 1817, 1862, 1876,
3660, 3678, 3700, 3722, 3733, 3740,
3773, 3797, 3830, 3847, 3853, 4031,
4060, 4064, 4075, 4283, 4286, 4296,
4299, 4344, 4346, 8216

Schools — History
J: 8925

Schools — Libraries
JS: 10510

Schools — Native Americans
IJ: 8783

Schools — Personal guidance
IJ: 10634

Schools — Poetry
IJ: 4486 **JS:** 4583, 4600, 4638

Schools — Prayer
IJ: 9868 **J:** 9890 **JS:** 9853

Schools — Segregation
JS: 9975, 10038

Schools — Violence
IJ: 10627 **JS:** 10297, 10372,
10425–26, 10437

Schools — Violence — Fiction
JS: 1836, 1881, 1886

Schulke, Flip
JS: 5294

Schultz, Charles M.
JS: 5295

Schumann, Clara
IJ: 5668–69

Schwarzenegger, Arnold
JS: 5670

Schwarzkopf, Norman
JS: 6159

Science
See also branches of science, e.g.,
Physics
IJ: 11802–4, 11809, 11813, 11819–20,
11823–25, 11828, 11831–32, 11861,
12010 **J:** 11808, 13101 **JS:** 11807,
11814, 11827, 11830

Science — Biography
IJ: 6271, 6283, 6308, 6310, 6318, 6324,
6331, 6337–38, 6364, 6367, 6371–73,
6387–89, 6391, 6394, 6403–4, 6407,
6411, 6413, 6417, 6419, 6421, 6423,
6431, 6444, 6446, 6456, 6460, 6464,
6466, 6470, 6474, 6481–82, 6484–85,
6487–88, 6490, 6494, 6497, 6500, 6503,
6507, 6511–12 **J:** 6269, 6295, 6316,
6369, 6390 **JS:** 6277, 6281, 6305,
6312, 6322, 6325–27, 6329–30, 6339,
6365, 6370, 6376, 6396, 6402, 6422,
6441, 6473, 6483, 6486, 6489

Science — Careers
IJ: 10813 **JS:** 10744, 10807–8

Science — Experiments and projects
See also under specific branches of
science, e.g., Electricity —
Experiments and projects
IJ: 11834, 11836–38, 11840–41,
11843–45, 11851–54, 11858, 11861–62,
11865, 11867–73, 11875–81, 11889,
11894, 12658, 12682, 12875 **J:** 11839,
11846, 11849, 11855 **JS:** 11244,
11611, 11833, 11835, 11842, 11847–48,
11850, 11856–57, 11863–64, 12670

Science — History
IJ: 7468, 8035, 8396, 8482, 8920, 8942,
11801, 11805, 11817–18, 11822
JS: 11806, 11812, 11826

Science — Methodology
IJ: 11829

Science — Renaissance
IJ: 7568

Science — Research
J: 12023

Science fairs
JS: 11833, 11859

Science fairs — Fiction
IJ: 482

Science fiction
See also Fantasy; Supernatural
IJ: 972, 2122, 2214, 2396, 3719,
4091–93, 4097–101, 4103, 4106–7,
4112, 4115–16, 4122, 4127–33, 4137,
4139–40, 4143–44, 4148, 4150–51,
4154–60, 4164, 4172–74, 4180–82,
4184–86, 4196–98, 4200–3, 4213,
4215–16, 4218–19, 4221, 4223,
4225–26, 4229, 4237, 4240, 4246,
4252–53 **J:** 3625, 4096, 4104, 4113,
4119–20, 4138, 4152, 4166, 4177, 4183,
4195, 4204–5, 4227–28, 4234, 4244,
4251

Science — Fiction
See also Fantasy; Supernatural
JS: 129

IJ = Upper Elementary/Lower Middle School; J = Middle School/Junior High; JS = Junior High/Senior High

1153

IJ = Upper Elementary/Lower Middle School; J = Middle School/Junior High; JS = Junior High/Senior High

IJ = Upper Elementary/Lower Middle School; J = Middle School/Junior High; JS = Junior High/Senior High

IJ = Upper Elementary/Lower Middle School; J = Middle School/Junior High; JS = Junior High/Senior High

IJ = Upper Elementary/Lower Middle School; J = Middle School/Junior High; JS = Junior High/Senior High

IJ = Upper Elementary/Lower Middle School; J = Middle School/Junior High; JS = Junior High/Senior High

IJ = Upper Elementary/Lower Middle School; J = Middle School/Junior High; JS = Junior High/Senior High

Statistics
JS: 11624

Statue of Liberty
IJ: 12755 J: 9467

Stealing — Fiction
IJ: 777, 1952, 3805, 3837 J: 816, 1534

Steamboats — Biography
IJ: 6252, 6415–16

Steel — History
IJ: 12736

Steinbeck, John
IJ: 5449 JS: 5450–51

Steinem, Gloria
IJ: 5868 J: 5869 JS: 5866–67

Stem cells
IJ: 11230 JS: 11232

Stepbrothers — Fiction
IJ: 893 JS: 1653

Stepchildren
IJ: 11766

Stepchildren — Fiction
IJ: 3484, 4282

Stepfamilies
See also Adoption
J: 11741, 11789 JS: 11727

Stepfamilies — Fiction
IJ: 25, 757, 927, 943, 1016, 1762, 1815
JS: 126, 441, 774, 832, 954, 3014, 3483

Stepfathers — Fiction
IJ: 766, 1068

Stepmothers — Fiction
IJ: 3046

Stepparents
IJ: 11766

Stepparents — Fiction
IJ: 944, 3876 JS: 3938

Stereotype (psychology)
JS: 11620

Steroids
IJ: 10972 J: 10918, 10987 JS: 10958

Stevenson, Robert Louis
IJ: 5452–53 JS: 12901

Stewart, Bridgett
JS: 6254

Stewart, Martha
JS: 6501

Stiles, Jackie
IJ: 6674

Still, Peter
JS: 6255

Still, William
IJ: 9014

Still, William Grant
J: 5504

Stine, R. L.
IJ: 5454

Stinson, Katherine
IJ: 6256

Stock markets
IJ: 10604, 10606 JS: 10605

Stock markets — Crash of 1929
IJ: 9289 J: 9275 JS: 9278, 9285, 10603

Stockton, John
IJ: 6567, 6675

Stoker, Bram
JS: 5455

Stomach
IJ: 11334

Stone Age
See also Prehistoric life
IJ: 7335 JS: 7306

Stonehenge
IJ: 7330 JS: 7338

Stonehenge — Fiction
IJ: 2059

Stores — Fiction
IJ: 2235

Storks — Fiction
IJ: 2640

Storms
See also Weather, and specific types of storms, e.g., Hurricanes
IJ: 9260, 12584

Storms — Fiction
IJ: 70, 214

Storytelling
IJ: 10652, 10657–58, 10669

Storytelling — Fiction
JS: 1760, 2496

Stowe, Harriet Beecher
IJ: 5457 J: 5458 JS: 5456

Strauss, Levi
IJ: 6502

Strawberries
J: 12031

Streams
See Rivers

Stress
IJ: 11402, 11416 J: 11383 JS: 11377, 11428, 11432

Stress (mental state)
IJ: 11444 J: 11396 JS: 11401

String games
IJ: 13251–53

Strokes — Fiction
IJ: 1237

Stuart, Jeb
IJ: 6166

Students — Civil rights
JS: 9902, 9969

Study skills
IJ: 10640–41 J: 10643 JS: 10642, 10672

Stunt flying
IJ: 12881

Stunt people — Careers
IJ: 5038

Stuttering
JS: 10851

Stuttering — Fiction
IJ: 1264 JS: 1911

Stuyvesant, Peter
IJ: 6257

Submarines
IJ: 12912

Subways
IJ: 12765, 12852

Subways — Fiction
IJ: 115 JS: 1640

Sudan
IJ: 7913 JS: 7862, 7894

Sudan — Fiction
IJ: 2564

Sudanese Americans
IJ: 10067

Suez Canal
JS: 8413

Suffrage and suffragists — Biography
See also Women's rights
JS: 5865

Sugihara, Chiune
IJ: 7025

Suicide
See also Physician-assisted suicide; Right to die
IJ: 10887, 11455 J: 9751 JS: 10874, 11378, 11389, 11403, 11405, 11412, 11415, 11430, 11456

Suicide — Fiction
IJ: 1466, 1547, 1721, 1916, 3940
J: 867, 1619 JS: 805, 936, 1118, 1188, 1191, 1195, 1202, 1256, 1281, 1351, 1483, 1787, 3764, 4035

Sukuma (African people)
IJ: 7876

Suleiman the Magnificent
JS: 6963

Sulfur
IJ: 12420

Sullivan, Anne — Plays
JS: 4453

Sumerians — History
IJ: 7451

Summer, Donna
JS: 5686

Sun
IJ: 11987, 12686 J: 11969 JS: 11980

Sun — Folklore
IJ: 4790

Sunflowers
IJ: 12096

Super Bowl — Biography
IJ: 6545

Supercomputers
JS: 12782

IJ = Upper Elementary/Lower Middle School; J = Middle School/Junior High; JS = Junior High/Senior High

Superconductors
JS: 12719

Supernatural
See also Fantasy; Folklore; Mystery stories; and specific supernatural creatures, e.g., Ghosts
IJ: 3501, 3531, 13177 J: 3458, 3554, 13181

Supernatural — Fiction
IJ: 1981, 2325, 3438, 3451–52, 3464, 3473, 3482, 3496, 3505, 3508, 3515, 3520, 3524–25, 3544, 3547–48, 3553, 3555, 3557, 3560, 3563–64, 3566–67, 3572, 3581–82, 3585, 4366, 4679
J: 2331, 3435, 3446, 3449, 3457, 3462, 3468, 3507, 3511, 3516, 3518–19, 3551, 3562, 3569, 3594, 3923 JS: 389, 2086, 2094, 2391, 2468, 2751, 3429, 3434, 3443, 3469–72, 3474–75, 3477, 3479–80, 3485, 3491, 3502, 3504, 3509, 3517, 3521–22, 3529, 3532, 3578, 3583–84, 3590, 3593, 3729, 4380

Supernatural — Folklore
IJ: 4813 J: 4806

Supernatural — Poetry
IJ: 4527

Superstitions
J: 13248

Supply and demand (economics)
IJ: 10595

Supreme Court
JS: 10510

Supreme Court (U.S.)
See also Courts (U.S.)
IJ: 9036, 9904, 9983 JS: 7314, 8844, 9035, 9319, 9368, 9397, 9849, 9856, 9867, 9888, 9898, 9944, 9969, 9973–75, 10052, 10624

Supreme Court (U.S.) — Biography
IJ: 6070, 6097, 6132–33, 6140 J: 6168
JS: 6131, 6139, 6171–72

Supremes (musical group)
IJ: 5687

Surfing
IJ: 13511, 13515 JS: 13516

Surfing — Fiction
IJ: 1804 JS: 4262

Surgery
J: 11211

Surgery — Fiction
IJ: 863, 1216

Surrogate mothers — Fiction
JS: 779

Surrogate parents
JS: 11525

Surtsey (Iceland)
IJ: 8368

Surveillance
J: 10283

Surveillance — International
JS: 9775

Survival
IJ: 8652 JS: 85, 12918

Survival — Fiction
IJ: 28, 45, 65, 81, 86, 111, 117, 158, 167, 172–73, 193, 205–6, 213, 221, 227, 229, 934, 1120, 2398, 2560, 2762, 2767, 2775, 2928, 2996, 3110–11, 3129, 3149
J: 38, 41–42, 77, 153, 166, 170, 181, 305, 308, 350, 1159, 2782 JS: 26, 39, 101, 108, 124, 140, 144, 149, 169, 208, 218, 226, 282, 357, 753, 2570, 4094–95, 4162, 4211, 4243

Suu Kyi, Aung San
J: 6870–71

Suzuki, Ichiro
IJ: 6621

Suzuki, Shinichi
IJ: 7026

Swahili city-states
J: 7919

Swamps
See Wetlands

Swamps — Fiction
IJ: 96

Swan Lake (ballet)
IJ: 7183

Swazi (African people)
JS: 7958

Swaziland
IJ: 7936 JS: 7958

Sweden
See also Scandinavia
IJ: 8356–57, 8360, 8362, 8377

Sweden — Fiction
IJ: 2642

Swedish Americans
IJ: 10236

Swedish Americans — Fiction
J: 3194

Swimming
IJ: 13512 JS: 13513

Swimming — Fiction
J: 1185, 1694 JS: 1841

Swindlers and swindling — Fiction
IJ: 507

Swindles and swindling
J: 10461

Switzerland
IJ: 8234, 8236–37, 8240

Switzerland — Fiction
IJ: 1399 J: 220

Swoopes, Sheryl
IJ: 6676

Symbiosis
IJ: 12013

Symbols
See Signs and symbols

Synesthesia — Fiction
JS: 1243

Syphilis
IJ: 11049

Systems analysis
JS: 10696

T

Table manners
JS: 11631

Tae Kwon Do
IJ: 13461

Tahiti
IJ: 8169

Taiga
IJ: 12497, 12509

Taino Indians — Fiction
IJ: 2072

Taiwan
IJ: 8112, 8116, 8133, 8152

Taiwan — Fiction
IJ: 2615 J: 3259

Taiwanese Americans
See Asian Americans

Taj Mahal
IJ: 7046, 8068

Tajikistan
IJ: 8349 JS: 8315

Tall people
IJ: 11290

Tall people — Fiction
IJ: 755

Tamerlane
JS: 6872

***The Taming of the Shrew* — Criticism**
JS: 4932

Tan, Amy
JS: 5459–60

Tanka
IJ: 4604

Tanks — History
IJ: 7750

Tanzania
IJ: 7873, 7876, 7915, 7921

Tanzania — Fiction
JS: 249

Taoism
J: 9639

Tap dancing
IJ: 7188

Tap dancing — Biography
IJ: 5667

Tap jazz
IJ: 7188

Tarbell, Ida
J: 5461

Tarkenton, Fran
IJ: 6716

IJ = Upper Elementary/Lower Middle School; J = Middle School/Junior High; JS = Junior High/Senior High

IJ = Upper Elementary/Lower Middle School; J = Middle School/Junior High; JS = Junior High/Senior High

IJ = Upper Elementary/Lower Middle School; J = Middle School/Junior High; JS = Junior High/Senior High

IJ = Upper Elementary/Lower Middle School; J = Middle School/Junior High; JS = Junior High/Senior High

TWA Flight 800 (disaster)
IJ: 12861 JS: 12863

Twain, Mark
IJ: 5463–64, 5466, 5468–69 JS: 5465, 5467

Twain, Mark — Fiction
IJ: 2995

Twain, Shania
IJ: 5690

Tweed, William "Boss"
IJ: 6260

Twentieth century
IJ: 7358 JS: 7610

Twentieth century — History
IJ: 7612–13 J: 6390 JS: 7608–9, 8698

Twenty-first century
JS: 10532

Twins
IJ: 11288, 11505

Twins — Fiction
IJ: 80, 817, 1187, 1453, 1700, 1927, 2194, 3515, 4061, 4291 J: 2, 2175, 2909, 4195 JS: 3471, 3843, 4194, 4236

Typhoid fever
IJ: 11147

Typing
JS: 10639, 8036

U

U.S.-China relations
JS: 8036, 8036

U.S.S. Indianapolis
JS: 7762

UFOs
IJ: 11930, 11938, 13171, 13197 JS: 13180, 13222

UFOs — Fiction
IJ: 783

Uganda
IJ: 7877, 12184 JS: 7883, 7894

Uganda — Fiction
JS: 2565–66

Ukraine
IJ: 8311, 8318, 8330, 8350 JS: 8333

Ukraine — Fiction
JS: 2707

Ukrainian Americans
IJ: 10234

Uluru
IJ: 8155

Umpires (baseball)
JS: 13356

Uncles — Fiction
IJ: 947

Underground Railroad
See also African Americans — History; Slavery
IJ: 5879, 5881–82, 9014, 9016, 9031, 9033, 9050–51, 9059 JS: 9028, 9038, 9053

Underground Railroad — Biography
IJ: 5880 JS: 5820

Underground Railroad — Fiction
IJ: 910, 2426, 2851, 2861, 2868, 2873, 2920, 2923, 2930, 2952, 3828 J: 2896, 2905, 2944–45, 2948, 2963, 3579 JS: 2903, 2907–8, 2947, 2949

Underground Railroad — Poetry
JS: 4601

Underwater archaeology
IJ: 7347, 8786

Underwater exploration
See also Oceanography
IJ: 12647, 12650, 12655, 12916 J: 12649 JS: 12648

Underwater exploration — Biography
IJ: 6379

Underwater exploration — Fiction
JS: 66, 349

Underwear — History
JS: 12775

Unemployment
JS: 8746, 10505, 11783

Unemployment — Fiction
IJ: 940

Ungerer, Tomi
JS: 5297

Unicorns
IJ: 2009 JS: 13204

Unicorns — Fiction
JS: 2198–99

Unidentified Flying Objects
See UFOs

United Arab Emirates
IJ: 8435

United Farm Workers
IJ: 10610

United Farm Workers — Biography
IJ: 5822 JS: 5806

United Kingdom
See England; Great Britain; Ireland, Northern; Scotland; Wales

United Kingdom — History
JS: 6967–68

United Nations
IJ: 9767 JS: 9763, 9765–66

United Nations — Biography
JS: 6928

United Nations — Children's rights
IJ: 10041

United States
See also specific regions, states, and cities, e.g., Midwest (U.S.); California; New York City
IJ: 7384, 8727, 8743 JS: 8695

United States — Aerial views
IJ: 11923

United States — Art
JS: 7109

United States — Atlases
JS: 7245

United States — Biography
J: 6054

United States — Cities
IJ: 8674

United States — Civil War
See Civil War (U.S.)

United States — Colonial Period
See Colonial period (U.S.)

United States — Congress
See Congress (U.S.)

United States — Constitution
See Constitution (U.S.)

United States — Crafts
IJ: 12985

United States — Discovery and exploration
IJ: 5020, 5040, 5085, 8867, 8873, 8878–79, 8930

United States — Documents
IJ: 8720

United States — Fiction
See also specific topics, e.g., Frontier life (U.S.) — Fiction
IJ: 2791 J: 878, 1878

United States — Folklore
IJ: 4810–11, 4813–15, 4817, 4819–20 J: 4818, 4821, 13159–60 JS: 4822

United States — Foreign policy
IJ: 8515 JS: 8555, 9769, 9829, 9836

United States — Frontier life
See Frontier life (U.S.)

United States — Geography
IJ: 8668, 8737 JS: 8480

United States — Government
See also Congress (U.S.); Senate (U.S.)
IJ: 9783, 9815, 9830, 9835 J: 9250 JS: 9781, 9797, 9813, 9825, 9917, 9931

United States — Government — Biography
IJ: 6072, 6150 J: 5740 JS: 5829, 6071

United States — Government — Careers
J: 10793

United States — Government — Women
IJ: 5765

IJ = Upper Elementary/Lower Middle School; J = Middle School/Junior High; JS = Junior High/Senior High

United States — History
See also specific periods and events, e.g., Colonial period (U.S.); Civil War (U.S.)
IJ: 8676, 8701, 8707, 8711, 8715, 8720, 8729, 8737, 8740, 8965 **J:** 5722, 9299 **JS:** 5744, 8671, 8682–83, 8691, 8696, 8700, 8705–6, 8710, 8714, 8721, 8728, 8745, 8872, 9807

United States — History — Crafts
IJ: 12970

United States — History — Documents
IJ: 8703

United States — History — Modern
IJ: 9314, 9351, 9375, 9390 **J:** 9378, 9384, 9998 **JS:** 9349, 9360, 9367, 9383, 9395

United States — History — Plays
IJ: 4458

United States — History — Songs
IJ: 7172

United States — Immigration
See Immigration (U.S.)

United States — Literary history
IJ: 4911

United States — Pioneer life
See Frontier life (U.S.); Pioneer life (U.S.)

United States — Poetry
IJ: 4598

United States — Politics
JS: 6030, 9807

United States — Prehistory
IJ: 8800

United States — Presidents
See Presidents (U.S.)

United States — Religion
IJ: 8741

United States — Revolutionary War
See Revolutionary War (U.S.)

United States — States
See States (U.S.)

United States — Wars
See also specific wars, e.g., World War II
IJ: 8685

United States — Women
JS: 8705

United States (1776–1876) — History
See also specific topics, e.g., Civil War (U.S.)
JS: 8716

United States (1789–1860) — History
IJ: 8983, 9167

United States (1789–1861) — Biography
JS: 5799

United States (1789–1861) — Fiction
IJ: 2861, 2904, 2912, 2914, 3053, 3087, 3102 **JS:** 2959

United States (1789–1861) — History
IJ: 7042, 8736, 8967, 9013, 9045, 9052, 9822 **JS:** 9055

United States (1789–1876) — Fiction
IJ: 2940

United States (1789–1961) — History
IJ: 9021

United States (1800–1860) — History
JS: 9044

United States (1815–1861) — Fiction
JS: 2901

United States (1828–1860) — History
IJ: 9019

United States (1865–1914) — History
IJ: 9259 **JS:** 9249

United States (1865–1950) — Fiction
IJ: 699, 3138, 3171, 3206, 3220, 3223, 3229, 3246

United States (1865–1950) — History
IJ: 8675, 8687, 8702, 8704, 8731, 8733–34, 9231, 9266, 9821

United States (1869–1914) — History
See also Reconstruction to World War I (U.S.)
J: 9244

United States (1900s) — History
JS: 9251, 9268

United States (1910s) — History
IJ: 8686 **JS:** 8738

United States (1915–1945) — History
JS: 9308

United States (1920s) — History
IJ: 8686, 9314 **JS:** 8747–48, 9295

United States (1930s) — History
JS: 9292

United States (1940s) — History
IJ: 8739 **JS:** 8669, 8697

United States (1948–1976) — History
IJ: 9371

United States (1950s) — Fiction
JS: 3287

United States (1950s) — History
IJ: 9361, 9375, 9390 **JS:** 9350, 9358, 9376, 9381, 9388

United States (1951–) — History
IJ: 7850, 9347–48, 9363, 9394, 9819

United States (1960s) — Fiction
JS: 3292

United States (1960s) — History
IJ: 8688, 8699, 9361 **J:** 9379 **JS:** 8681, 9349, 9358, 9370, 9374

United States (1970s) — History
IJ: 8689, 8699 **JS:** 9389

United States (1980s) — History
IJ: 9359 **JS:** 9358, 9372, 9391

United States (1990s) — Fiction
JS: 3180

United States (1990s) — History
IJ: 8690 **JS:** 9377

United States Army

United States Coast Guard

United States-Israel relations
See Israel-U.S. relations

United States Marine Corps

United States-Mexico relations
See Mexico-U.S. relations

United States *v.* Nixon
JS: 9870

Universe
IJ: 11996, 11998 **JS:** 11895, 11997

Universities and colleges
See Colleges and universities

Uranus (planet)
IJ: 11988

Urban life
JS: 12737

Uruguay
IJ: 8620 **JS:** 8606

USSR
See Soviet Union

Utah
IJ: 7253, 9443, 9446, 9451

Utah — Fiction
JS: 3423

Ute Indians — Fiction
JS: 282

Utopias
JS: 8735

Uzbekistan
IJ: 8351 **JS:** 8315

V

Vacations — Fiction
JS: 2223

Vaccines
JS: 11212, 11224

Valdez (AK)
J: 9528

Valens, Ritchie
JS: 5691

Valentine's Day
IJ: 10549

Valentine's Day — Crafts
IJ: 12956

IJ = Upper Elementary/Lower Middle School; J = Middle School/Junior High; JS = Junior High/Senior High

IJ = Upper Elementary/Lower Middle School; J = Middle School/Junior High; JS = Junior High/Senior High

IJ = Upper Elementary/Lower Middle School; J = Middle School/Junior High; JS = Junior High/Senior High

IJ = Upper Elementary/Lower Middle School; J = Middle School/Junior High; JS = Junior High/Senior High

IJ = Upper Elementary/Lower Middle School; J = Middle School/Junior High; JS = Junior High/Senior High

IJ = Upper Elementary/Lower Middle School; J = Middle School/Junior High; JS = Junior High/Senior High

X

Y

Z

IJ = Upper Elementary/Lower Middle School; J = Middle School/Junior High; JS = Junior High/Senior High